ENCYCLOPEDIA OF
OCCULTISM & PARAPSYCHOLOGY

ENCYCLOPEDIA OF OCCULTISM & PARAPSYCHOLOGY

A Compendium of Information on the Occult Sciences, Magic, Demonology, Superstitions, Spiritism, Mysticism, Metaphysics, Psychical Science, and Parapsychology, with Biographical and Bibliographical Notes and Comprehensive Indexes

THIRD EDITION

In Two Volumes

VOLUME TWO
M-Z
and indexes

Edited by Leslie A. Shepard

Gale Research Inc. • DETROIT • LONDON

Leslie Shepard, *Editor*

Pamela Dear, *Editorial Coordinator*
Nancy Franklin, *Project Coordinator*

Mary Beth Trimper, *Production Manager*
Evi Seoud, *Assistant Production Manager*

Arthur Chartow, *Art Director*
C.J. Jonik, *Keyliner*

Laura Bryant, *Production Supervisor*
Louise Gagné, *Internal Production Associate*
Yolanda Y. Latham, *Internal Production Assistant*

Special thanks to the staff members of the Indexes and Dictionaries Division of Gale Research Inc. for their proofreading and indexing assistance.

Bibliographical Note

Based on *Encyclopedia of Occultism* by Lewis Spence, London, 1920, and *Encyclopaedia of Psychic Science* by Nandor Fodor, London, 1934, substantially revised by Leslie Shepard and supplemented by new material written by him.

™ This book is printed on acid-free paper that meets the minimum requirements of American National Standard for Information Sciences—Permanence Paper for Printed Library Materials, ANSI Z39.48-1984.

This book is printed on recycled paper that meets Environmental Protection Agency standards.

ISBN 0-8103-4907-8 (Complete set)
ISBN 0-8103-4915-9 (Volume I)
ISBN 0-8103-4916-7 (Volume II)
ISSN 1049-9636

Printed in the United States of America

Published in the United States by Gale Research Inc.
Published simultaneously in the United Kingdom
by Gale Research International Limited
(An affiliated company of Gale Research Inc.)

10 9 8 7 6 5 4 3 2

Contents

Volume I

Volume II

Introduction

This third edition of *Encyclopedia of Occultism and Parapsychology* consolidates twelve years of progressive revision, updating and enlargement to produce the most up-to-date and wide-ranging work in a complex subject area.

Broad Topical and Conceptual Scope

In compiling this work, the term "occult" has been interpreted in its widest sense of "hidden, secret, beyond human understanding" as well as pertaining to magical spells, miracles, and witchcraft. Certain mysteries such as the Loch Ness Monster, Bigfoot, and Unidentified Flying Objects have a valid inclusion, even if they may someday be identified as elusive but objective entities around which legends and mythologies have grown. While some users may criticize such a wide coverage, the editor believes that others will welcome a policy of inclusion rather than omission in dealing with reference material in overlapping areas.

With the rise of parapsychology as a reputable study, some of the narrow categories and viewpoints of the past are beginning to dissolve in the newer atmosphere of interdisciplinary studies. Much that was formerly regarded as "supernatural" may now be explicable in scientific terms, since even the suspension of normal physical laws involves other laws and principles, even if these are at present imperfectly understood. And where theories no longer fit, it is still important to establish the facts of phenomena.

The traditional association of religion and mysticism with miracles suggests that the paranormal is often connected with special states of consciousness, and it has, therefore, been considered relevant to include entries relating to mysticism, altered states of consciousness, and some self-improvement cults that promise unusual material or psychical gains. The extensive cross-referencing in this encyclopedia is intended to assist research in new and old correlations of phenomena and overlapping areas of study.

Evolution of Encyclopedia of Occultism and Parapsychology

The first edition of this encyclopedia was based on a novel concept —the creation of a new work by merging, updating, and adding to two highly esteemed earlier encyclopedias of occultism and psychical science. The two works, Lewis Spence's *Encyclopedia of Occultism* (1920) and Nandor Fodor's *Encyclopaedia of Psychic Science* (1934), though old, were still standard reference sources in many libraries throughout the world when the first edition of *Encyclopedia of Occultism and Parapsychology* was published in 1978.

In the original edition, certain major entries included material identified as being from both Spence and Fodor, in order that their complementary views could be compared. In the second edition, published in 1982, such different viewpoints were integrated into an overall text after careful evaluation. Responsibility for presentation and opinion therefore transferred to the present editor.

Editorial Practices for the Third Edition

During the preparation of this third edition, the editor realized that a number of entries deriving from Fodor and Spence contained hitherto unsuspected errors, notably in the attribution of quotations from other sources and the exact text of the quotations. In the case of books by foreign psychical researchers that had been translated into English, Nandor Fodor may have quoted sometimes from his own interpretation of the foreign version; thus his wording did not always agree with the English translation edition cited as a source. In some instances, passages presented as quotations were actually paraphrases. Although the meaning of the passages in question was clear, they have been corrected.

In essence, every entry from the second edition has been researched again. In this process careful attention has been given to points made by readers and critics. Hundreds of new entries have been added, and updates and modifications have been made to existing entries.

Since this completely new edition is part of a progressive development from the base set, the editor retained all the original subjects deriving from Spence and Fodor. Although tempted to reduce some of the longer, more discursive, material (particularly from Spence), the editor felt it was on balance better to retain the material in the present edition than to eliminate facts and opinions already published. Moreover, such detailed treatment (often lengthy quotations from source works) will have value for researchers.

Format of Entries

The format of this edition follows the same plan as the second edition. In the entry headings dealing with individuals, a query for birth or death date indicates that no record of the date has so far been obtained. A blank for a death date indicates uncertainty whether an individual is living or has died without a death date being ascertainable. In the case of some individuals, notably early Spiritualist mediums, the formula "c." followed by a date indicates the period at which they were known to flourish. In this edition, many birth and death dates have been added to entries, and other dates were revised in light of recent research.

Cross-references are indicated by bold type or the formula "See" or "See also" in the body of an entry, indicating that separate entries exist that can amplify these references. The formula "See also" at the end of an entry identifies significantly related entries that are specially recommended for further study. Wherever possible, topics covered within more general entries are also given a brief entry in their own right that may satisfy immediate inquiry, while some other overlapping entries repeat information rather than involve the reader in further searches.

Wide Range of Bibliographic References Given

In certain controversial areas concerned both with individuals and phenomena, the case for and against has been indicated, with sources noted for further study in depth. Indeed, one of the special features of this work is the wide range of bibliographical reference, a feature that has already been welcomed by researchers. These citations list recent books as well as important out-of-print works and reprints. Wherever possible, recent and available editions are listed, whether hardcover or paperback.

In the bibliographical sections of "Recommended reading," American publication is to be assumed after the publisher name; British or other foreign editions are clearly identified. In the case of some unfamiliar imprints, the place of publication is given, whether American or foreign. In a few cases, the publisher's name of long out-of-print nineteenth-century works is not given since the year of publication is sufficient to trace the work in any good public or specialized library.

Comprehensive Indexing

As with most encyclopedias, the key to locating elusive material is the extensive indexing. The editor has retained the nine special indexes praised by reviewers and users of previous editions.

The comprehensive General Index now lists further cross-references, as well as specialized subindexes of entries dealing with such topics as Alchemy, Astrology, Fairies, Fortean Phenomena, Out-of-the-Body Travel, Parapsychology, Psychical Research, Spiritualism, UFO (Unidentified Flying Objects), Witchcraft, and Yoga.

User Comments Are Welcome

With this new edition, the former basis of such authorities as Lewis Spence and Nandor Fodor has been extended and developed to provide an encyclopedia of occultism and parapsychology to meet modern reference needs. This is the only encyclopedia in these areas which has been regularly supplemented and updated, and careful attention is given to all criticism and suggestions.

The editor would like to thank the many individuals and organizations who took the trouble to send helpful data after publication of the first and second editions. Corrections or additional factual information for future editions can be addressed to: Editor, *Encyclopedia of Occultism and Parapsychology*, Gale Research Inc., 835 Penobscot Building, Detroit, Michigan 48226-4094; or call toll-free 1-800-347-4253.

M

M. A., Oxon.

Pseudonym of the Rev. William Stainton **Moses,** prominent British Spiritualist, author of *Spirit Teachings* (1833) and other books.

Ma Yoga Shakti International Mission

Founded in 1979 by Ma Yogashakti Saraswati, an Indian woman guru who immigrated to the U.S. in 1977. She established ashrams in Ozone Park, New York, and Palm Bay and Deerfield Beach, Florida, and alternates her time between them. She has also organized four ashrams in India: Bombay, Calcutta, Delhi, and Gondia.

She teaches a balanced approach to all yogas—hatha, rajah, bhakti, and karma. Devotional services of *Purnima* are held monthly.

Ma Yogashakti has published several books or commentaries, including: *Chhandogya Upanishad, Prayers and Poems from Mother's Heart, Shree Satya Narayana Vrata Katha, Adhyatma Sandesh,* and *The Invisible Seven Psychic Lotuses,* which the Mission distributes. It also publishes the *Yogashakti Mission Newsletter.* The address of the New York center is: 114-23 Lefferts Boulevard, South Ozone, N.Y. 11420.

Maa-Kheru

According to Egyptologist G. Maspero, the Egyptian name of the true intonation with which the dead must recite those magic incantations which would give them power in Amenti, the Egyptian Hades. (See also **Egypt**)

Mabinogion

A collection of ancient Welsh legends translated into English by Lady Charlotte Guest (1812-1895), and published 1838-49. The title is the plural form of the Welsh *maginogi,* originally indicating stories of a hero's childhood, but is here used in the wider sense of "hero tale." The stories in this collection are from various manuscript sources, originally part of the oral tradition of professional minstrels known as *cyvarwyddon.*

In this collection, the section entitled the *Four Branches of the Mabinogi* derives from a manuscript circa 1060, dealing with pre-Christian myths that have affinities with traditional Irish folklore. *Kilhwch and Olwen* is from a manuscript circa 1100, and is an early Arthurian romance. *The Dream of Rhonabwy* is another Arthurian story, related to the French recension of *Didot Perceval.* The *Lady of the Fountain, Geraint,* and *Peredur* are also Arthurian, circa 1200, colored by Breton and French culture, although Celtic in origin. *The Dream of Maxen,* dating from the twelfth century, is a literary rather than folk tale, the plot resembling the Irish *Dream of Oengus. Taliesin* dates from a sixteenth-century manuscript; it concerns a famous bard of the sixth century, and has affinities with Irish legends.

In addition to the translation by Lady Charlotte Guest, frequently reprinted, there is also a later translation by Gwyn Jones and Thomas Jones (1949). (See also **Wales**)

McConnell, R. A. (1914-   )

Associate research professor actively concerned with parapsychology, who was president of the Parapsychological Association in 1958. Born in Pennsylvania, he studied at Carnegie Institute of Technology (B.S. physics, 1935), University of Pittsburgh (Ph.D. physics, 1947). He worked as a physicist with Gulf Research & Development Co., and with a U.S. Naval aircraft factory between 1937 and 1941 and subsequently went to Massachusetts Institute of Technology Radiation Laboratory where he was a group leader from 1944-46. From 1947-53 he was assistant professor of physics, 1953-59 assistant research professor of biophysics, 1959 onwards associate research professor of biophysics, at University of Pittsburgh. He is a member of the American Physical Society, Biophysical Society, Institute of Radio Engineers, Parapsychological Association.

Dr. McConnell was a founding member, of the **Parapsychological Association,** president 1957-58, 1977-78. From 1964 onwards he was resident professor of physics at University of Pittsburgh.

In addition to his articles in technical journals, Dr. McConnell has written widely on parapsychology. With Dr. Gertrude **Schmeidler** he was co-author of the book *ESP and Personality Patterns* (1958). He contributed chapters to a Ciba Foundation symposium on *Extrasensory Perception* (1956) and a symposium edited by Eileen J. Garrett, *Does Man Survive Death?* He also published *ESP Curriculum Guide* (Simon & Schuster, 1971), prepared for secondary-school and college teachers of psychology, biology and general science who may wish to teach extrasensory perception and related subjects. His many articles on parapsychology include: 'ESP, Fact or Fancy?' (*Scientific Monthly,* vol. 69, 1949), 'Why Throw Dice?' (*Journal of Parapsychology,* vol. 16, 1952), 'Wishing With Dice' (co-author, *Journal of Experimental Psychology,* vol. 50, 1955) 'Psi Phenomena and Methodology' (*American*

Scientist, vol. 45, 1957); (*Journal of Parapsychology*): 'Modern Experiments in Telepathy' (vol. 18, 1954), 'Price in "Science"' (vol. 19, 1955), 'Scaled Measurement in Psi Research' (vol. 22, 1958), 'Continuous Variable Trials' (vol. 22, 1958); (*Journal of Psychology*): 'Nature of the Discontinuity in Schmeidler's ESP-Rorschach Data' (vol. 52, 1961), 'Fantasy Testing for ESP in a Fourth and Fifth Grade Class' (co-author, vol. 52, 1961), (with J. Forwald) 'Psychokinetic Placement: I. A Re-examination of the Forwald-Durham Experiment' (*Journal of Parapsychology 1973,* Scarecrow Press, 1974), 'Parapsychology and the Occult' (*Journal* of the American Society for Psychical Research, vol. 67, 1973).

In addition to his work in the field of parapsychology, Dr. McConnell has also specialized in radar moving target indication, theory of the iconoscope and ultrasonic microwaves.

McDonnell Laboratory for Psychic Research

Psychic research laboratory at Washington University, St. Louis, Missouri, funded by a grant from James S. McDonnell, chairman of the McDonnell Foundation. The director of the laboratory is Dr. Peter R. Philips, who has worked on high energy physics and psychical research.

McDougall, William (1871-1938)

Professor of Psychology at Harvard University, author of *Body and Mind* and *Social Psychology,* president of the **Society for Psychical Research** 1920-21 and of the **American Society for Psychical Research** 1921, member of the Scientific American Committee for the investigation of the mediumship of "Margery" (Mina S. **Crandon**), a keen but reserved investigator who took great care not to commit himself as to the genuine occurrence of the supernormal and agencies of an extra-terrene origin.

Born June 22, 1871 in Lancashire, England, he was educated at Owens College, Manchester, St. Thomas Hospital, London, Cambridge, Oxford and Göttingen Universities. He was a fellow of St. John's College, Cambridge, 1898 (hon. fellow 1938), reader, University College, London, reader in mental philosophy and fellow, Corpus Christi College, Oxford, before becoming a professor at Harvard. In 1900 he married Anne Amelia Hickmore.

Professor McDougall was one of the leading psychologists of his time, and his later interest in psychical research was a dominant influence in the development of modern parapsychology. When head of the Psychology Department at Duke University from 1927-38, he encouraged J. B. **Rhine** in founding the **Parapsychology Laboratory,** from which modern research in laboratory controlled experiments developed. Prof. McDougall published a number of articles on psychical subjects, including: 'The Case of Sally Beauchamp' (*Proceedings* of the Society for Psychical Research, London, vols. 19-20, 1905-07), 'The Need for Psychical Research' (*Harvard Graduate Magazine,* reprinted *ASPR Journal,* vol. 17, 1923), 'Further Observations on the "Margery" Case' (*ASPR Journal,* vol. 19, 1925), 'The Margery Mediumship' (*Psyche,* vol. 26, 1926). He contributed the important article on Hypnotism to the eleventh edition of the *Encyclopaedia Britannica* (1910), as well as articles on Hallucination, Suggestion and Trance (11th-14th editions). His books included: *Social Psychology* (1908); *Pagan Tribes of Borneo* (1911), *Psychology* (1912), *Body and Mind* (1912), *Group Mind* (1920), *Is America Safe for Democracy?* (1921), *Outline of Psychology* (1923), *Ethics and Some Modern World Problems* (1924), *Outline of Abnormal Psychology* (1926), *Janus* (1927), *Character and Conduct of Life* (1927), *Modern Materialism and Emergent Evolution* (1929), *World Chaos-The Responsibility of Science* (1931), *Energies of Men* (1933), *Psycho-Analysis and Social Psychology* (1936), *The Riddle of Life* (1938).

He died November 28, 1938.

Machen, Arthur (Llewellyn) (1863-1947)

British novelist, born March 3, 1863 at Carleon-on-Usk, Wales, who became one of the leading authors of occult fiction, although undeservedly neglected during his lifetime. He was a close friend of Arthur Edward **Waite,** one of Britain's greatest authorities on occult literature.

One of Machen's short stories brought a legend to real life. This was "The Bowmen," first published in the newspaper *The Evening News,* London, September 29, 1914. In the story, British troops, hopelessly outnumbered in the French trenches of World War I, are miraculously rescued by phantom English archers from Agincourt, led by St. George.

A few months after publication, a number of eyewitness accounts of 'The Angels of Mons' began to appear, and Machen was taxed with elaborating a true story. This strange example of nature imitating art is detailed by Machen in his introduction to *The Bowmen and other Legends of the War* (London, 1915). His other books include: *The Great God Pan* (1894), *The House of Souls* (1906), *The Hill of Dreams* (1907), *The Great Return* (1915), *The Terror* (1917). In addition to his powerful stories on occult themes, he also published a number of volumes of essays and translations.

For biographical and bibliographical details, see: *Arthur Machen; a short account of his life and work* by Aidan Reynolds & William Charlton (London, 1963).

He died December 15, 1947 at Beaconsfield, Buckinghamshire. (See also **Angels of Mons**; English Occult **Fiction**)

M'Indoe, John B. (c. 1936)

A prominent Scottish Spiritualist, past president of the **Spiritualists National Union** in Britain, trustee and advisory committee member of Edinburgh Psychic College and Library. He was a great authority on the subject of **spirit photography,** and also reported on the controversial mediumship of Mrs. Helen **Duncan.**

Macionica

Slavonic name for a witch. (See **Slavs**)

McKenzie, James Hewat (1869-1929)

Founder of the **British College of Psychic Science.** He was born in Edinburgh, Scotland, November 11, 1869.

He began the study of psychic facts in 1900, led to this by dissatisfaction with the failure of science or theology to throw any light on human destiny. Years of private study and investigation followed, and in 1915 he gave a series of various lectures in London, Edinburgh and Glasgow.

In 1916, he published *Spirit Intercourse, Its Theory and Practice* and a pamphlet *If a Soldier Die,* which had a wide circulation. In 1917, he toured the U.S. as far as Chicago in search of mediums and again in 1920, spending a good deal of time in California on the latter visit.

In 1920, the British College of Psychic Science was established, and for this venture Mr. McKenzie found the entire initial cost. In 1922, *Psychic Science,* the College quarterly journal, was started on its career. In the same year he and Mrs. Barbara McKenzie, who was associated closely in all his investigations, visited Germany, Austria and Poland and had sittings with many of the best Continental psychics.

In Warsaw, they sat with the materializing medium Franek **Kluski,** and secured plaster casts of materialized hands, which they brought to London, the only ones in England. They also brought Frau Maria **Silbert,** of Graz, Austria, to the College for valuable experimental work, and also a **poltergeist** medium, of whom valuable firsthand reports were made.

Mr. McKenzie had a deep interest in physical mediumship in all its aspects and a profound knowledge of the conditions necessary for good results. On many occasions he was asked to investigate cases of haunting and of disturbances and was able to clear up annoying conditions.

He also made an intensive study of trance mediumship with Mrs. Osborne **Leonard** and Mrs. Eileen **Garrett,** and himself helped to develop the psychic talents of several trance mediums. A strong courageous personality, convinced that only through psychic facts is there any proved knowledge of **survival,** he affirmed this continuously by his writings and lectures for the years in which he acted as honorary president of the College, the first substantial organization in London to become a center for psychic demonstration and instruction.

Mrs. McKenzie, who brought a fine intellect and understanding to the study of psychic phenomena, was honorary secretary of the College until 1929, and then became honorary president for one year, being succeeded by Mrs. Champion **de Crespigny.**

Mr. McKenzie died August 29, 1929 in London. For biographical information, see the book *J. Hewat McKenzie, Pioneer of Psychical Research* by Muriel Hankey (Aquarian Press, U.K., 1963).

Mackenzie, Kenneth R(obert) H(enderson) (1833-1886)

Prominent British occultist who was a Honorary Magus of the **Societas Rosicruciana in Anglia** and a member of the Hermetic Society of the **Golden Dawn.** From 1858-59 he edited four numbers of *Biological Review,* devoted to Spiritualism, homeopathy and electro-dentistry.

He was born on October 31, 1833, in London. During the following year, the family lived in Vienna, where the father, Dr. Rowland H. Mackenzie, was assistant surgeon in the midwifery department of the Imperial Hospital. Dr. Mackenzie and his wife returned to England about 1840, but it is probable that Kenneth was educated abroad. According to William Wynn **Westcott,** he received a Rosicrucian initiation in Austria while living with Count Apponyi as an English tutor. Kenneth had returned to London by 1851, and contributed a series of learned notes to *Notes and Queries.*

It is clear that even as a young man he had an impressive knowledge of German, French, Latin, Greek, and Hebrew, and had a precocious talent for antiquarian studies.

He had ambitions to follow a literary career, and as early as 1852, he translated *Briefe aus Aegypten, Aethiopen 1842-5 . . .* by K. R. Lepsius into English. He also contributed articles on Peking, America, and Scandinavia to the Rev. Theodore Alois Buckley's work *Great Cities of the Ancient World* (1852). In the following year, he assisted Walter Savage Landor in a new edition of *Imaginary Conversations.*

In Janauary 1854, he was elected a Fellow of the **Society of Antiquaries, London.** From 1855-61 he was a member of the Royal Asiatic Society, and from 1864-c.1870 a member of the Anthropological Society.

He was author of the *Royal Masonic Cyclopaedia* (1877), and also planned a work called *The Game of Tarot, Archaeologically and Symbolically Considered* which was announced but not published. In 1861 Mackenzie visited the famous French occultist Éliphas Lévi (Alphonse Louis Constant) in Paris, and recorded vivid personal recollections of the man and his outlook, published in *Rosicrucian,* Journal of the Soc. Ros. in Anglia.

In addition to his *Royal Masonic Cyclopaedia,* his other literary publications included: *Burmah and the Burmese* (1853), (transl.) *Schamyl and Circassia* by F. Wagner (1854), (transl. & ed.) *Fairy Tales* by J. W. Wolf (1855), (transl.) *The Marvellous Adventures . . . of Tyll Owlglass* by T. Eulenspiegel (1859), (transl. & ed.) *The Life of Bismarck* by J. G. L. Hesekiel (1870), *Zythogala; or, Borne by the Sea* (a novel, 1872), *Fundamental Constitutions of Freemasonry* (1877), (transl.) *Bismarck: His Authentic Biography* by G. E. L. von Bismarck-Schoenhausen. He also edited early numbers of a Masonic periodical titled *The Kneph* in 1881.

In addition to his acquaintance with the famous French occultist Éliphas **Lévi,** Mackenzie also studied occultism with Frederick **Hockley** (1808-1885).

In 1870, Mackenzie married Alexandrina Aydon, daughter of a Freemason and became a member of the craft himself in the same year.

On April 21, 1873, Mackenzie read a paper on Éliphas Lévi to the Rosicrucian Society **(Societas Rosicruciana in Anglia),** of which he became a member, and subsequently contributed papers to their journal *The Rosicrucian.* He resigned from the Society in 1875 when occupied with preparation of his *Royal Masonic Cyclopaedia.* In subsequent years, he seems to have lived precariously on a modest income from journalism. Amongst odder pursuits, he developed a system of astrological prediction of horse race winners, and also became involved with the promotion of fringe Masonic orders, such as Sat B'Hai.

He died July 3, 1886, before the formation of the Hermetic Order of the **Golden Dawn,** but was claimed posthumously as an Adept of the Order (together with Éliphas Lévi and Frederick Hockley) by W. W. Westcott, one of the founding Chiefs, presuming a continuity of occult tradition through the Rosicrucian Society. (See also Hermetic Order of the **Golden Dawn;** Frederick **Hockley; Rosicrucians; Societas Rosicruciana in Anglia)**

Mackenzie, William (1877- ?)

British biologist and writer, living in Italy, who played a prominent part in the scientific study of parapsychology. Born March 25, 1877 at Genoa, Italy, he studied at University of Turin (Ph.D. 1900). In 1902 he married Marie Bühler. In 1905 he founded the first Marine Biological Laboratory at the University of Genoa, and from 1912-13 conducted research in Germany on the phenomenon of "thinking animals." During World War I he was a volunteer in the Italian Army; from 1939-45 he lectured on biological philosophy at the University of Geneva, and was consultant on foreign scientific literature to publishers in Florence from 1960 onwards.

He was president of the Second International Congress of Psychical Research, Warsaw, 1923, president of the Italian Society for Parapsyhology 1951-54, honorary president from 1954 onwards. He was president of the Third National Congress of Parapsychology, Univesity of Rome, 1956, honory member of the Institut Métapsychique, Paris, and Institut Francais de Florence.

He edited *Parapsicologia* (quarterly journal of parapsycholgy) from 1955-56. Dr. Mackenzie made a special study of psychobiology (parapsychology in living organisms) and has also investigated psychic animals and mathematical mediumship. He published many articles on parapsychology in *Psiche, Archives de Psycholgie, Proceedings of the Italian Society for the Advancement of Science, Quaderni di Psichiatria, Journal of the American Society for Psychical Research, Revue Métapsychique, Uomini e Idee.* His books included: *Alle Fonti della Vita* (At the Sources of Life, 1912; 1916), *Nuove Rivelazioni della Psiche Animale* (New Revelations of Animal Psyche, 1914), *Significato Bio-Filosofico della Guerra* (The Meaning of War from the Viewpoint of Biological Philosophy, 1915), *Metapsichica Moderna* (Modern Psychical Research, 1923).

Mackey, Albert Gallatin (1807-1881)

American authority on **Freemasonry,** editor of numerous books on the subject, including *Encyclopedia of Freemasonry* (1874).

He was a disciple of Albert Pike (1809-1891), one of the leaders of Masonry in Charleston, U.S.A. falsely charged by "Miss Diana Vaughan," and others with the practice of Satanism and sorcery. The whole campaign proved to be an audacious conspiracy on the part of journalist Gabriel **Jogand-Pagès** to discredit and embarrass both the Catholic Church and Freemasonry.

One of the earliest writers to throw doubt on the revelations of "Diana Vaughan" (as expressed in the writings of "Dr. Bataille") was British occultist and mystic Arthur E. **Waite** in his book *Devil-Worship in France* (1896). (See also Dr. **Bataille; Devil Worship;** Gabriel **Jogand-Pagès;** Diana **Vaughan)**

MacLaine, Shirley (Shirley MacLean Beaty) (1934-)

World-famous actress, dancer, movie star, and writer, whose books on her search for spiritual fulfillment have created widespread popular interest in psychic phenomena, **channeling** of spirit guides, and New Age teachings.

She was born April 24, 1934, in Richmond, Virginia, attending high school in Washington, D.C. She began taking dancing lessons before she was three years old; by the time she was sixteen she was a chorus girl in New York in a City Center revival of "Oklahoma!" Four years later, she was dancing in the chorus of "Pajama Game" and acting as understudy to Carol Haney, the show's leading dancer. When Haney injured her ankle soon after the show's opening, Shirley replaced her in the lead. After enthusiastic reviews, the Hollywood producer Hal B. Wallis signed her for a long-term film contract.

Her first motion picture role was in "The Trouble with Harry," directed by Alfred Hitchcock. Later, her performance in "Irma la douce" earned her the Golden Globe Award, and the third of four Academy Award nonimations.

She has appeared in a number of successful Broadway plays and revues, as well as motion pictures. She won an International Stardom Award from Hollywood Foreign Press Association, 1954; Foreign Press Award for best actress, 1958, 1961, 1963; Silver Bear Award for best actress from International Berlin Film Festival, 1959 for "Ask Any Girl"; best actress award from Venice Film Festival and British Film Academy Award for best actress, both 1960, both for "The Apartment"; Golden Globe Award from Foreign Press Association, 1964, for "Irma la douce"; best actress award from Italian Film Festival, 1964; Star of the Year Award from Theater Owners of America, 1967; best actress award from Berlin Film Festival, 1971, for "Desperate Characters"; two Emmy Awards from Academy of Television Arts and Sciences, including one in 1974 for "If They Could See Me Now"; female musical star award from Las Vegas Entertainment Awards, 1976.

Outside her successful career as actress and movie star, Shirley has a considerable reputation as an outspoken courageous personality in the fields of political and humanitarian activities. She has spoken out on such issues as civil rights, women's rights, and environmental protection. During the American involvement in the Vietnam war, she was a vocal support of George McGovern during his 1972 presidential campaign. In that year, she was the first woman speaker in the history of the National Democratic Club, and spoke out on the dangers of overpopulation.

Her extensive travels have taken her to such remote parts of the world as East Africa, where she lived among the Masai tribe, and the Himalayan kingdom of Bhutan, where she was detained by border guards during a political crisis. When traveling in India, she became sympathetic to the plight of the "gutter babies" and helped to establish an orphanage for them in Calcutta.

Her best-selling autobiography *Don't Fall Off the Mountain* (1970) detailed her experience in Africa, India, the Far East, and Hollywood. It was translated into eight languages.

In 1973, she led a delegation of twelve American women, including filmmaker Claudia Weill, on a six-week tour of the People's Republic of China. With Weill acting as her co director, Shirley produced and wrote the narration for the film "The Other Half of the Sky; A China Memoir," a documentary of the trip, broadcast by Public Broadcasting Service, 1975. Her second autobiographical book *You Can Get There From Here* (1975) discussed her China trip and her involvement with George McGovern's presidential campaign.

In 1976, after a twenty year hiatus as an entertainer, she returned to the theatrical stage in "A Gypsy in my Soul," which attracted rave reviews. By 1983, she had appeared in some thirty-five movies.

Her third autobiographical book *Out on a Limb* (1983) described a spiritual odyssey which developed from her world travels. It is a heady exploration of **New Age** beliefs, including meditation, psychic healing, channeling of spirit guides, reincarnation, UFOs, extraterrestrials, and **out-of-the-body** travel. If at times the book appears naive, it is redeemed by its transparent honesty and sincerity, and a deep desire for a spiritual framework to life. The book became the basis for a five-hour prime-time ABC-TV miniseries.

Her inner search was further chronicled in her book *Dancing in the Light* (1986). In this she stated: "I like to think of *Dancing in the Light* as a celebration of all my 'selves.' It was a fulfilling and satisfying exploration of the promises I made to myself in *Out on a Limb.* In it I look with pleasure, humor and some contentment upon my experiences as a daughter, a mother, a lover, a friend, a seeker of spiritual destiny and a voice calling for peace in the world."

The book cites the psychic J. Z. **Knight,** who channels an entity named "Ramtha," who has since been featured on ABC-TV news programs and has attracted a large following.

Shirly MacLaine's reputation as a talented actress and entertainer, and her best-selling books which describe both an inner and outer journey through life, have had a great influence on the general public and helped to regenerate the New Age Movement.

MacLeod, Fiona

Pseudonym of Scottish writer William **Sharp** (1856-1905), virtually a secondary personality who authored mystical writings on Celtic lore which played a large part in the Scottish Celtic Revival. These works were the product of **automatic writing** by Sharp. (See William **Sharp**)

McMahan, Elizabeth Anne (1924-)

Assistant professor of zoology, also active in the field of parapsychology. Born May 5, 1924 at Mocksville, North Carolina, she studied at Duke University (M.A. 1948), University of Hawaii (Ph.D. 1960). From 1943-48 she was a research assistant, from 1948-54 research fellow at the Parapsychology Laboratory, Duke University, Durham, N.C.; graduate teaching assistant, Zoology Department, Duke University from 1954-56; graduate teaching assistant, entomology from 1956-59, research asistant, entomology from 1959-60, Department of Zoology and Entomology, University of Honolulu; fellow, University of Chicago 1960-61; assistant professor of zoology, University of North Carolina 1961 onwards.

She is a charter member of the Parapsychological Association, member of American Association for the Advancement of Science, Entomological Society of America. In addition to her many articles on entomology, she published a number of papers on parapsychology, based on her own investigations in telepathy, psychokinesis and precognition.

Her contributions to the *Journal of Parapsychology* include: 'PK Experiments With Two-Sided Objects' (vol. 9, 1945), 'An Experiment in Pure Telepathy' (vol. 10, 1946), 'A Second Zagreb-Durham ESP Experiment' (with J. B. **Rhine,** vol. 11, 1947), 'A Review of the Evidence for Dowsing' (vol. 11, 1947), 'Extrasensory Perception of Cards in an Unknown Location' (vol. 12, 1948), 'Report of Further Marchesi Experiments' (with E. K. Bates, vol. 18, 1954).

MacRobert, Russell Galbraith (1890-)

Psychiatrist, neurologist, who took a special interest in parapsychology. Born June 4, 1890 at London, Ontario, Canada, he studied at University of Western Ontario (M.D. 1912) and University of Toronto (M.D. 1916). In 1936 he married Fannie G. Perkinson.

From 1922-41 he was associate neuropsychiatrist, Lenox Hill Hospital, New York, 1941-46 captain,

Medical Corps, USNR; 1946-55 attending physician at Lenox Hill Hospital, 1955 onwards consulting neuropsychiatirst; instructor in clinical neurology New York University, Bellevue Hospital Medical Center, New York. His memberships include: American Medical Association, American Academy of Neurology, American Board of Psychiatry and Neurology, Academy of Religion and Mental Health, American Society for Psychical Research. He is a fellow of the American Psychiatric Association, the American Society of Clinical Hypnosis.

In addition to his many published articles on medical, psychiatric and neurological subjects, he took great interest in clairvoyance and mediumship and was author of the survey 'Current Attitudes of American Neuropsychiatrists towards Parapsychology' (*Journal of Parapsychology,* Nov. 1948), which indicated that nearly forty percent of those questioned were familiar with ESP work.

In the *Journal of Insurance Medicine* he wrote on 'Psychiatry and Intuition' (vol. 4, No. 3, 1949) and 'Hallucinations of the Sane' (vol. 5, No. 3, 1950). His articles in *Tomorrow* magazine included: 'Science Studies Intuition' (May 1950), 'When in Healing "Psychic"?' (Spring 1955), 'Where is Bridey Murphy?' (Spring 1956). He contributed the chapter 'Something Better Than Reincarnation' to the book *Reincarnation* (1956) and preface to R. DeWitt **Miller**'s book *You Do Take It With You* (1956).

Macrocosm, The

The whole universe (Greek *Macros,* long, *Kosmos,* the world) symbolized by a six-pointed star, formed of two triangles, and the sacred symbol of Solomon's seal.

It represents the infinite and the absolute—that is, the most simple and complete abridgment of the science of all simple and complete abridgment of the science of all things.

Paracelsus stated that every magical figure and Kabalistic sign of the pantacles which compel spirits may be reduced to two—the Macrocosm and the **Microcosm** (world in miniature). (See also **Magical Diagrams; Microcosm**)

Macroprosopus, The

One of the four magical elements in the **Kabala,** and probably representing one of the four simple elements—air, water, earth, or fire. Macroprosopus means "creator of the great world."

Macumba

General term for the magical practices of spiritists in Brazil. These include spirit **possession** and both white and black magic. For detailed study see A. J. Langguth, *Macumba* (Harper & Row, 1975). (See also **Spiritism**)

Madre Natura

An old and powerful secret society of Italy, who worshiped and idealized nature. It seems to have been founded by members of the ancient Italian priesthood. It had a tradition that one of the Popes as Cardinal de Medici became a member of the fraternity, and there appears to be some documentary evidence for this claim.

The Society accepted the allegorical interpretation which the Neo-Platonists had placed upon the pagan creeds during the first ages of Christianity.

Maeterlinck, Maurice (1862-1949)

Famous Belgian writer and poet, to whom the Nobel Prize of literature was awarded in 1911, a profound thinker in whom the mystic sense and the spirit of inquiry was fortunately blended.

He was born in Ghent August 29, 1862 and educated at the Collège Sainte-Barbe and the University of Ghent. For a time, he lived in Paris, where he became associated with the symbolist school of French poetry. His first publication was *Serres Chaudes,* a volume of poems in 1889. His play *La Princesse Maleine* in the following year was praised by novelist Octave Mirbeau. Although Maeterlinck had already qualified for a legal profession, he decided to follow a literary life.

From the very beginning of his great literary career, he was attracted by the problems of the inner life. His early plays were dominated by the grim specter of death as the destroyer of life. In his later works his interest in psychical phenomena developed and the fearful mystery gave place to wondrous fascination.

The Unknown Guest, Our Eternity and *The Wrack of the Storm* disclosed a familiarity with all the prevailing ideas on psychical subjects and he showed no doubt whatever as to the genuineness of phenomena. "The question of fraud and imposture are naturally the first that suggest themselves" he wrote, "when we begin the study of these phenomena. But the slightest acquaintance with the life, habits and proceedings of the three or four leading mediums is enough to remove even the faintest shadow of suspicion. Of all the explanations conceivable, the one which attributes everything to imposture and trickery is unquestionably the most extraordinary and the least probable . . . From the moment that one enters upon this study, all suspicions are dispelled without leaving a trace behind them; and we are soon convinced that the key to the riddle is not to be found in imposture . . . Less than fifty years ago most of the hypnotic phenomena which are now scientifically classified were likewise looked upon as fraudulent. It seems that man is loth to admit that there lie within him many more things than he imagined."

He considered survival proved, but was uncertain as to the possibility of communication with the dead. Between the telepathic and spirit hypotheses he could not make a choice in favor of the latter. He admitted that "the survival of the spirit is no more improbable than the prodigious faculties which we are obliged to attribute to the medium if we deny them to the dead; but the existence of the medium, contrary to that of the spirit, is unquestionable, and therefore it is for the spirit, or for those who make use of its name, first to prove that it exists."

He added that in his view there were five imaginable solutions of the great problem: the religious solution, annihilation, survival with our consciousness of today, survival without any sort of consciousness and survival with a modified consciousness.

The religious solution he ruled out definitely because it occupied "a citadel without doors or windows into which human reason does not penetrate." Annihilation he considered unthinkable and impossible. "We are the prisoners of an infinity without outlet, wherein nothing perishes, wherein everything is dispersed but nothing lost." Survival without consciousness of today is inconceivable as the change of death and the casting aside of the body must bring about an enlarged understanding and an expansion of the intellectual horizon. Survival without any consciousness amounted to the same thing as annihilation.

The only solution which appealed to him was survival with a modified consciousness. He argued: since we have been able to acquire our present consciousness why should it be impossible for us to acquire another in which our present consciousness is a mere speck, a negligible quantity: "Let us accustom ourselves to regard death as a form of life which we do not as yet understand; let us learn to look upon it with the same eye that looks upon birth; and soon our minds will be accompanied to the steps of the tomb with the same glad expectation that greets a birth."

Maeterlinck died May 6, 1949. Two of his books dealing with the paranormal were reissued by University Books, Inc. as follows: *The Great Secret* (1969), *The Unknown Guest* (1975).

Magi

Priests of ancient Persia, and cultivators of the wisdom of Zoroaster (or Zarathustra) (possibly 1500 B.C.) They were instituted by Cyrus when he founded the new Persian empire, and are supposed to have been of the Median race.

The German scholar K. W. F. von Schlegel stated in his *Lectures on the Philosophy of History* (2 vols., 1829): "they were not so much a hereditary sacerdotal caste as an order or association, divided into various and successive ranks and grades, such as existed in the mysteries—the grade of apprenticeship—that of mastership—that of perfect mastership."

In short, they were a theosophical college; and either its professors were indifferently "magi," or magicians, and "wise men" or they were distinguished into two classes by those names.

Their name, pronounced "Mogh" by later Persians, and "Magh" by the ancients, signified "Wise," and such was the interpretation of it given by the Greek and Roman writers. Stobæus expressly called the science of the magi, the "service of the gods," so Plato. According to Joseph Ennemoser in his book *The History of Magic* (1847), "Magiusiah, Madschusie," signified the office and knowledge of the priest, who was called "Mag, Magius, Magiusi," and afterwards magi and "Magician." The philosopher J. J. Brucker maintained that the primitive meaning of the word was "fire worshiper," "worship of the light," an erroneous opinion. In modern Persian, the word is "Mog," and "Mogbed" signifies high priest. The high priest of the Parsees at Surat is called "Mobed." Others derive the word from "Megh," "Meh-ab" signifying something which is great and noble, and Zoroaster's disciples were called "Meghestom."

Eusèbe Salverte, author of *Des Sciences Occulte* (1829), stated that these Mobeds were named in the Pehivi dialect "Magoi." They were divided into three classes: Those who abstained from all animal food; those who never ate of the flesh of any tame animals; and those who made no scruple to eat any kind of meat. A belief in the transmigration of the soul was the foundation of this abstinence.

They professed the science of **divination,** and for that purpose met together and consulted in their temples. They professed to make truth the great object of their study, for that alone, they said, can make man like God "whose body resembles light, as his soul or spirit resembles truth."

They condemned all images, and those who said that the gods were male and female; they had neither temples nor altars, but worshiped the sky, as a representative of the Deity, on the tops of mountains; they also sacrificed to the sun, moon, earth, fire, water, and winds, said Herodotus, meaning, no doubt that they adored the heavenly bodies and the elements. This was probably before the time of Zoroaster, when the religion of Persia seems to have resembled that of ancient India. Their hymns in praise of the Most High exceeded (according to Dio Chrysostom) the sublimity of anything in Homer or Hesiod. They exposed their dead bodies to wild beasts.

Schlegel maintained that it was an open question "whether the old Persian doctrine and wisdom or tradition of light did not undergo material alterations in the hand of its Median restorer, Zoroaster, or whether this doctrine was preserved in all its purity by the order of the magi." He then remarked that on them devolved the important trust of the monarch's education, which must necessarily have given them great weight and influence in the state. They were in high credit at the "Persian gates" (the Oriental name given to the capital of the empire, and the abode of the prince) and they took the most active part in all the factions that encompassed the throne, or that were formed in the vicinity of the court.

In Greece, and even in Egypt, the sacerdotal fraternities and associations of initiated, formed by the mysteries, had in general but an indirect, although not unimportant influence on affairs of state, but in the Persian monarchy they acquired a complete political ascendency.

Religion, philosophy, and the sciences were all in their hands, they were the universal physicians who healed the sick in body and in spirit, and, in strict consistency with that character, ministered to the state, which is only the individual in a larger sense. The three grades of the magi alluded to were called the "disciples," the "professed," and the "masters."

They were originally from Bactria, where they governed a little state by laws of their own choice, and by their incorporation in the Persian empire, they greatly promoted the consolidation of the conquests of Cyrus.

Their decline dates from the reign of Darius Hystaspes, about 500 B.C., by whom they were fiercely persecuted. This produced an emigration which extended to Cappadocia on the one hand, and to India on the other, but they were still of so much consideration at a later period as to provoke the jealousy of Alexander the Great.

"Magia Posthuma" (of C. F. de Schertz)

A short treatise on Vampirism published at Olmutz in 1706, and written by Charles Ferdinand de Schertz. Reviewing it, Augustin **Calmet** stated in his *Dissertation sur les apparitions, des anges . . . et sur les revenaus et vampires* (1746, transl. as *The Phantom World,* 2. vols., 1850) that the author related a story of a woman that died in a certain village, after having received all the sacraments, and was buried with the usual ceremonies, in the churchyard. About four days after her death, the inhabitants of the village were affrighted with an uncommon noise and outcry, and saw a spectre, sometimes in the shape of a dog, and sometimes in that of a man, which appeared to great multitudes of people, and put them to excessive pain of squeezing their throats, and pressing their breasts, almost to suffocation. There were several whose bodies he bruised all over, and reduced them to the utmost weakness, so that they grew pale, lean, and disfigured. His fury was sometimes so great as not to spare the very beasts, for cows were frequently found beaten to the earth, half dead; at other times with their tails tied to one another, and their hideous lowings sufficiently expressed the pain they felt. Horses were often found almost wearied to death, foaming with sweat, and out of breath, as if they had been running a long and tiresome race; and these calamities continued for several months.

C. F. de Schertz examined the subject in the capacity of a lawyer and discussed both the matter of fact and the points of law arising from it. He was clearly of the opinion that if the suspected person was really the author of these noises, disturbances, and acts of cruelty, the law would justify the burning of the body, as is practiced in the case of other specters which come again and molest the living.

He related also several stories of apparitions of this sort and listed the mischiefs done by them. One, among others, was of a herdsman of the village of Blow near the town of Kadam in Bohemia, who appeared for a considerable time and called upon several persons, who all died within eight days. At last, the inhabitants of Blow dug up the herdsman's body and fixed it in the ground, with a stake driven through it. The man, even in this condition, laughed at the people that were employed about him, and told them they were very obliging to furnish him with a stick to defend himself from the dogs.

The same night, he extricated himself from the stake, frightened several persons by appearing to them, and occasioned the death of many more than he had hitherto done. He was then delivered into the hands of the hangman, who put him into a cart in order to burn him outside the town. As they went along, the carcass shrieked in the most hideous manner, and threw its arms and legs about as if it had been alive, and upon being again run through with a stake, it gave a loud cry, and a great quantity of fresh, florid blood issued from the wound. At last the body was burnt to ashes, and this execution put a final stop to the specter's appearing and infesting the village.

The same method was practiced in other places where these apparitions were seen, and upon taking them out of the ground, their bodies seemed fresh and florid, their limbs pliant and flexible, without any worms or putrefaction, but not without a great stench.

The author quoted several other writers, who attested what he related concerning these specters, which, he stated, still appeared in the mountains of Silesia and Moravia. They were seen, it seems, both by day and night, and the things which formerly belonged to them were observed to stir and change their place without any person being seen to touch them. And the only remedy in these cases, he claimed, was to cut off the head and burn the body of the persons supposed to appear. (See also **Dracula;** Pierre-Daniel **Huet; Vampire**)

Magic

General term for "magic art," believed to derive from Greek *magein,* the science and religion of the priests of Zoroaster (see **Magi**), or, according to philologist Skeat, from Greek *megas* ("great") thus signifying the great science.

Early History

The earliest traces of magical practice are found in the European caves of the middle Paleolithic Age. These belong to the last interglacial period of the Pleistocene period, which has been named the Aurignacian, after the cave-dwellers of Aurignac, whose skeletons, artifacts and drawings link them with the Bushmen of South Africa.

In the cave of Gargas, near Bagnères de Luchon, occur, in addition to spirited and realistic drawings of animals, numerous imprints of human hands in various stages of mutilation. Some hands had been first smeared with a sticky substance and then pressed on the rock, others had been held in position to be dusted round with red ocher, or black pigment. Most of the imprinted hands have mutilated fingers; in some cases the first and second joints of one or more fingers are wanting; in others the stumps only of all fingers remain.

A close study of the hand imprints makes it evident that they are not to be regarded as those of lepers. There can be little doubt that the joints were removed for a specific purpose, and on this point there is general agreement among anthropologists.

A clue to the mystery is provided by the magical custom among the Bushmen of similarly removing finger joints. G. W. Stow, in his book *The Native Races of South Africa* (1905) referred to this strange form of sacrifice. He once came into contact with a number of Bushmen who "had all lost the first joint of the little finger" which had been removed with a "stone knife" for the purpose of ensuring a safe journey to the spirit world. Another writer told of an old Bushman woman whose little fingers of both hands had been mutilated, three joints in all having been removed. She explained that each joint had been sacrificed to express her sorrow as each one of three daughters died. No doubt, however, there was a deeper meaning in the custom than she cared to confess.

In his *Report on the Northwestern Tribes of the Dominion of Canada* (1889), Franz Boas gave evidence of the custom among these peoples. When frequent deaths resulted from disease, the Canadian Indians used to sacrifice the joints of their little fingers in order (they explained) "to cut off the deaths." Among the Indian Madigas (Telugu pariahs), the **evil eye** was averted by sacrificers who dipped their hands in the blood of goats or sheep and impressed them on either side of a house door. This custom was also known to the Brahmans of India. Impressions of hands were also occasionally seen on the walls of Indian Mohammedan mosques. As among the northwest Canadian tribes, the hand ceremony was most frequently practiced in India when epidemics took a heavy toll of lives. The Bushmen also removed finger joints when stricken with sickness. In Australia, where during initiation ceremonies the young aborigine men had teeth knocked out and bodies scarred, the women of some tribes mutilated the little fingers of daughters in order to influence their future careers.

Apparently the finger chopping customs of Paleolithic times had a magical significance. On some of the paintings in the Aurignacian caves appear symbols which suggest the slaying with spears and cutting up of animals. Enigmatical signs are another feature. Of special interest are the figures of animal-headed demons, some with hands upraised in the Egyptian attitude of adoration, and others apparently dancing like the animal-headed dancing gods of the Bushmen.

In the Marsonlas Paleolithic cave, there are semi-human faces of angry demons with staring eyes and monstrous noses. In the Spanish Cave at Cogul, several figures of women wearing half-length skirts and shoulder shawls, are represented dancing round a nude male. So closely do these females resemble such as usually appear in Bushmen paintings that they might well, but for their location, be credited to this interesting people. Religious dances among the Bushman tribes were associated with marriage, birth and burial ceremonies; they were also performed to exorcise demons in cases of sickness. "Dances are to us what prayers are to you," an elderly Bushman once informed a European.

Whether the cave drawings and wood, bone and ivory carvings of the Magdalenian, or late Paleolithic period at the close of the last ice epoch, are of magical significance is a problem on which there is no general agreement. It is significant to find, however, that several carved ornaments bearing animal figures or enigmatical signs are perforated as if worn as charms. On a piece of horn found at Lorthet, Hautes Pyrénées, are beautiful incised drawings of reindeer and salmon, above which appear mystical symbols. An ape-like demon carved on bone was found at Mas d'Azil. On a reindeer horn from Laugerie Basse, a prostrate man with a tail is creeping up on all fours towards a grazing bison. These are some of the instances which lend color to the view that late Paleolithic art had its origin in magical beliefs and practices—that hunters carved on the handles of weapons and implements, or scratched on cave walls, the images of the animals they desired to capture—sometimes with the secured cooperation of demons, and sometimes with the aid of magical spells.

Coming to historic times, we know that the ancient Egyptians possessed a highly-developed magical system (see **Egypt**), as did the Babylonians (see **Semites**) and other pristine civilizations. Indeed, from these the medieval European system of magic is believed to have evolved. **Greece** and **Rome** also possessed distinct national systems, which in some measure were branches of their religions, and thus, like the Egyptian and Babylonian, were preserves of the priesthood.

Magic in early Europe was, of course, merely an appendage of the various religious systems which obtained throughout that continent, and it was these systems which later generated into **witchcraft.** But upon the foundation of Christianity, the church soon began to regard the practice of magic as foreign to the spirit of its religion. Thus the Thirty-sixth Canon of the Ecumenical Council held at Laodicea in 364 A.D. forbad clerks and priests to become magicians, enchanters, mathematicians or astrologers. It ordered, moreover, that the Church should expel from its bosom those who employed ligatures or phylacteries, because, it said, phylacteries are the prisons of the soul. The Fourth Canon of the Council of Oxia, A.D. 525, prohibited the consultation of sorcerers, augurs, diviners, and divinations made with wood or bread, while the Sixtieth Canon of the Council of Constantinople A.D. 692, excommunicated for a period of six years diviners and those who had recourse to them. The prohibition was repeated by the Council of Rome in 721. The Forty-second Canon of the Council of Tours in 613 was to the effect that the priests should teach to the people the inefficacy of magical practices to restore the health of men or animals, and later Councils practically endorsed the church's earlier views.

Medieval Magic

It does not appear that what may be called "medieval magic" took final and definite shape until about the twelfth century. Modeled upon the systems in vogue among the Byzantines and Moors of Spain, which were evolved from the Alexandrian system (see **Neoplatonism**), what might be called the "oriental" type of magic gained footing in Europe, and quite superseded the earlier and semi-barbarian systems in use among the various countries of that continent, most of which, as has been said, were the relics of older pagan practice and ritual. To these relics clung the witch and the wizard and the professors of lesser magic, whereas among the disciples of the imported system we find the magician (black and white), the necromancer and the sorcerer.

The manner in which the theosophy and the magic of the East was imported was probably twofold. First, there is evidence that it was imported into Europe by persons returning from the Crusades; secondly, we know that in matters of wisdom, Byzantium fell heir to Alexandria, and that from Constantinople magic was disseminated throughout Europe, along with other sciences.

It is not necessary to detail here the history of witchcraft and lesser sorcery, as that is already covered in the article **witchcraft.** It is sufficient to confine ourselves strictly to the history of the higher branches of magic. But it is relevant to remark that Europe appears to have obtained its pneumatology largely from the Orient through Christianity, from Jewish and early Semitic sources, and it is an open question how far eastern demonology colored that of the Catholic Church.

Medieval magic of the higher type has practically no landmarks save a series of great names. Its tenets experienced but little alteration during six centuries. From the eighth to the thirteenth century, there does not appear to have been much persecution of the professors of magic, but after that period the opinions of the church underwent a radical change, and the life of the magus was fraught with considerable danger. However, it is pretty clear that he was not victimized in the same manner as his lesser brethren, the sorcerers and wizards, although we find Paracelsus consistently baited by the medical profession of his day. **Agrippa** was also constantly persecuted, and even mystics like Jakob **Boehme** were imprisoned and ill-used.

It is difficult at this distance of time to estimate the enormous vogue that magic experienced, whether for good or evil during the Middle Ages. Although severely punished if discovered, or if its professors became sufficiently notorious to court persecution, the power it seems to have conferred upon them was eagerly sought by scores of people—the majority of whom were quite unfitted for its practice and clumsily betrayed themselves into the hands of the authorities. In the article **Black Magic,** there is an outline of the history of that lesser magic known as sorcery or "black magic," and the persecutions which overtook those who practiced it.

As already mentioned, the history of higher magic in Europe is a matter of great names, and these are somewhat few. They do not include alchemists, who are strictly speaking not magicians, as their application of arcane laws was particular and not universal, but this is not to say that some alchemists were not also magicians (see also **Alchemy**).

The two great names which stand out in the history of European magic are those of Paracelsus and Agrippa, who formulated the science of medieval magic in its broad outlines. They were also the greatest practical magicians of the Middle Ages, as apart from pure mystics, alchemists and others, and their thaumaturgic and necromantic experiences were probably never surpassed. With them, medieval magic comes to a close and the further history of the science in Europe will be found outlined in the division below entitled "Modern Magic."

Scientific Theories Regarding the Nature of Magic

General agreement as to the proper definition of magic is lacking, as it depends upon the view taken of religious belief. According to Sir James George Frazer, author of *The Golden Bough* (1890), magic and religion are one and the same thing, or are so closely allied as to be almost identical. This may be true of peoples in a primitive condition of society, but can scarcely apply to magic and religion as fully fledged, as for example in medieval times, however fundamental may be their original unity.

The objective theory of magic would regard it as entirely distinct from religion, possessed of certain well-marked attributes, and traceable to mental processes differing from those from which the religious idea springs. Here and there, the two have become fused by the superimposition of religious upon magical practice.

The objective idea of magic, in short, rests on the belief that it is based on magical laws which are supposed to operate with the regularity of those of natural science. The subjective view, on the other hand, is that many practices seemingly magical are in reality religious, and that no rite can be called magical which is not so designated by its celebrant or agent.

It has also been said that religion consists of an appeal to the gods, whereas magic is the attempt to force their compliance. Henri Hubert and Marcel Mauss (*Greatness and Decline of the Celts,* 1934) believed that magic is essentially traditional. Holding that the primitive mind is markedly unoriginal, they satisfied themselves that magic is therefore an art which did not exhibit any frequent changes amongst primitive folk, and was fixed by its laws. Religion, they claimed, was official and organized, magic prohibited and secret. Magical power appeared to them to be determined by the contiguity, similarity and contrast of the object of the act, and the object to be effected.

Sir J. G. Frazer believed all magic to be based on the law of sympathy—that is, the assumption that things act on one another at a distance because of their being secretly linked together by invisible bonds. He divided sympathetic magic into homeopathic magic and contagious magic. The first is imitative or mimetic, and may be practiced by itself, but the latter usually necessitates the application of the imitative principle. Well-known instances of mimetic magic are the forming of wax figures in the likeness of an enemy, which are destroyed in the hope that he will perish. This belief persisted in European **witchcraft** into relatively modern times. Contagious magic may be instanced by the savage anointing the weapon which caused a wound instead of the wound itself, in the belief that the blood on the weapon continues to feel with the blood on the body (see also **Powder of Sympathy**).

L. Marillier divided magic into three classes: the magic of the word or act; the magic of the human being independent of rite or formula, and the magic which demands a human being of special powers and the use of ritual. A. Lehmann believed magic to be a practice of superstition, and founded in illusion.

The fault of all such theories is that they strive after too great an exactness, and that they do not allow sufficiently for the feeling of wonder and awe which is native to the human mind. Indeed they designate this "strained attention." We may grant that the attention of savages to a magical rite is "strained," so strained in some cases that it terrifies them into insanity, and it would seem therefore as if the limits of "attention" were overpassed, and as if it shaded into something very much deeper. Moreover it is just possible that in the future it may be granted that so-called sympathetic magic does not partake of the nature of magic at all, but has greater affinities (owing to its strictly natural and non-supernatural character) with pseudoscience.

Magic is recognized by many primitive peoples as a force rather than an art—something which impinges upon the thought of man from outside. It would appear that many tribes believed in what would seem to be a great reservoir of magical power, the exact nature of which they are not prepared to specify.

Thus amongst certain American-Indian tribes we find a force called *Orenda* or spirit-force. Amongst the ancient Peruvians, everything sacred was *huaca* and possessed of magical power. In Melanesia, we find a force spoken of called *mana,* transmissible and contagious, which may be seen in the form of flames or even heard. The Malays used the word *kramat* to signify the same thing, and the Malagasy the term *hasma.* Some of the tribes around Lake Tanganyika believed in such a force, which they called *ngai,* and Australian tribes had similar terms, such as *churinga* and *boolya.* In Mexico there was a strange creed named *nagualism,* which partook of the same conception—everything *nagual* was magical or possessed an inherent spiritual force of its own.

Theories of the Origin of Magic

Many theories have been advanced regarding the origin of magic—some authorities believing that it commenced with the idea of personal superiority, others through animistic beliefs (see **Animism**), and still others through such ideas as that physical pains for which the savage could not account, were supposed to be inflicted by invisible weapons. This last theory is, of course, in itself, merely animistic.

It does not seem, however, that writers on the subject have given sufficient attention to the great influence exerted on the mind of man by odd or peculiar occurrences. Whilst it would be unreasonable to advance the hypothesis that magic entirely originated from such a source, it may have been a powerful factor in the growth of magical belief. To which, too, animism and taboo contributed their quota. The cult of the dead and their worship might also have become fused with magical practice, and a complete demonology would thus speedily arise.

The Dynamics of Magic

Magical practice is governed by well-marked laws, limited in number. It possesses many classes of practitioner, as, for example, the diviner or augur, whose duties are entirely different from those of the witch-doctor (see **Divination**). Chief among these laws, as has been already hinted, is that of sympathy, which, as has been said, must inevitably be subdivided into the laws of similarity, contiguity and antipathy.

The law of similarity and homeopathy is again divisible into two sections: (1) the assumption that like produces like—an illustration of which is the destruction of a model in the form of an enemy, and (2) the idea that like cures like—for instance, that the stone called the bloodstone can staunch the flow of bleeding.

The law dealing with antipathy rests on the assumption that the application of a certain object or drug expels its contrary.

There remains contiguity, which is based on the concept that whatever has once formed part of an object continues to form part of it. Thus, if a magician can obtain a portion of a person's hair, he can work harm upon that person through the invisible bonds which are supposed to extend between the individual and the hair in the sorcerer's possession. It is commonly believed that if the animal **familiar** of a witch be wounded, that the wound will react in a sympathetic manner on the witch herself (see **Werwolf**). This is called "repercussion."

Another widespread belief is that if the magician procures the name of a person he can gain magical dominion over that person. This, of course, arose from the idea that the name of an individual was identical with himself. The doctrine of the "Incommunicable Name," the hidden name of the god or magician, is well instanced by many legends in Egyptian history, the deity usually taking extraordinary care to keep his name secret, in order that no one might gain over him (see **Egypt**). The spell or incantation is connected with this concept, and with these, in a lesser degree, may be associated magical gesture, which is usually introduced for the purpose of accentuating the spoken word.

Gesture is often symbolic or sympathetic, it is sometimes the reversal of a religious rite, such as marching against the sun, which is known as walking "widdershins." The method of pronouncing rites is, too, one of great importance. Archaic or foreign expressions are usually found in spells ancient and modern, and the tone in which the incantation is spoken, no less than its exactness, is also important (see also **Mantra**). To secure exactness, rhythm was often employed, which had the effect of aiding memory.

The Magician

In early society, the magician, which term includes the **shaman**, medicine-man, piagé, and witch-doctor, may hold his position by hereditary right; by an accident of birth, as being the **seventh son** of a seventh son; to revelation from the gods; or through were mastery of ritual.

In primitive life, we find the shaman a good deal of a medium, for instead of summoning the powers of the air at his bidding, as did the magicians of medieval days, he found it necessary to throw himself into a state of trance and seek them in their own sphere.

The magician is also often regarded as possessed by an animal or supernatural being.

The duties of the priest and magician are often combined in primitive society, but it cannot be too strongly asserted that where a religion has been superseded, the priests of the old cult are, for those who have taken their places, nothing but magicians.

Medieval Definition of Magic

The definitions of magic by the great magicians of medieval and modern times naturally differ greatly from those of anthropologists.

For example, Éliphas **Levi** stated in his *History of Magic* (1913): "Magic, therefore, combines in a single science that which is most certain in philosophy which is eternal and infallible in religion. It reconciles perfectly and incontestably those two terms so opposed on the first view—faith and reason, science and belief, authority and liberty. It furnishes the human mind with an instrument of philosophical and religious certainty were as exact as mathematics, and even accounting for the infallibility of mathematics themselves. . . . There is an incontestable truth; there is an infallible method of knowing that truth; while those who attain this knowledge and adopt it as a rule of life, can endow their life with a sovereign power which can make them masters of all inferior things, all wandering spirits, or, in other words, arbiters and kings of the world."

Paracelsus stated: "The magical is a great hidden wisdom, and reason is a great open folly. No armour shields against magic for it strikes at the inward spirit of life. Of this we may rest assured, that through full and powerful imagination only can we bring the spirit of any man into an image. No conjuration, no rites are needful; circle-making and the scattering of incense are mere humbug and jugglery. The human spirit is so great a thing that no man can express it; eternal and unchangeable as God Himself is the mind of man; and could we rightly comprehend the mind of man, nothing would be impossible to us upon the earth. Through faith the imagination is invigorated and completed, for it really happens that every doubt mars its perfection. Faith must strengthen imagination, for faith establishes the will. Because man did not perfectly believe and imagine, the result is that arts are uncertain when they might be wholly certain."

Agrippa also regarded magic as the true road to communion with God, thus linking it with mysticism.

Later Magic

With the death of Agrippa in 1535, the old school of magicians may be said to have ended. But the traditions of magic were handed on to others who were equally capable of preserving them, or revived by modern sensationalists.

We must carefully discriminate at this juncture between those practitioners of magic whose minds were illuminated by a high mystical ideal, and persons of doubtful occult position, like the Comte de **Saint Germain** and others.

At the beginning of the seventeenth century, there were many great alchemists in practice, who were also devoted to the researches of transcendental magic, which they carefully and successfully concealed under the veil of hermetic experiment.

These included Michael **Maier,** Robert **Fludd,** Cosmopolite, Jean **D'Espagnet,** Samuel Norton (see Thomas **Norton**), Baron de **Beausoleil,** and **J. Van Helmont;** another illustrious name is also that of Eirenaeus **Philalethes** (see also **Alchemy**).

The eighteenth century was rich in occult personalities, as for example the alchemist **Lascaris,** Martinez **de Pasqually,** and Louis de **Saint Martin,** who founded the Martinist school, which was continued by "Papus" (Gerard **Encausse**).

After this magic merged for the moment into **Mesmerism,** and many of the secret magical societies which abounded in Europe about this period practiced **Animal Magnetism** experiments as well as **astrology, Kabalism** and **ceremonial magic.**

Mesmerism powerfully influenced mystic life in the time of its chief protagonist, and the mesmerists of the first era are in direct line with the Martinist and the mystical magicians of the late eighteenth century.

Indeed mysticism and magnetism were one and the same thing, in the persons of some of these occultists (see **Secret Tradition**) the most celebrated of which were Cazotte, Ganneau, Comte, Wronski, Du Potet, Hennequin, Comte d'Ourches, and Baron de Guldenstubbé, and last of the initiates known to us, Éliphas Lévi.

Modern Revivals of Magic

During the 1890s, there was a revival of interest in ritual magic in Europe amongst both intellectuals and sensationalists. This "occult underground" permeated much of the intellectual life and progressive movements in Europe, in contrast to the more popular preoccupation with Spiritualism and Table-turning.

At the sensational level, this interest was characterized by Devil Worship cults, and later by hoaxes of claimed devil worship aimed at discrediting the Catholic Church and Freemasonry (see Gabriel **Jogand-Pagès**).

For an excellent survey of nineteenth-century irrationalism, see *The Flight from Reason* (vol. 1 of *The Age of the Irrational*) by James Webb (1971).

On a more dignified level was the founding of the famous Hermetic Order of the **Golden Dawn**, which numbered amongst its members such individuals as Annie Horniman (sponsor of the Abbey Theatre,

Dublin), Florence Farr (mistress of George Bernard Shaw), Israel Regardie, S. L. MacGregor Mathers, Arthur Machen, Arthur Edward Waite and poet W. B. Yeats.

Another famous G. D. member was the magician Aleister Crowley, who left the order to found his own organization A.·.A.·.. Crowley's book *Magick in Theory and Practice* (1929 etc.) is an interesting analysis of the methods of Magic, although marred by some egocentricity and revelations stemming from psychedelic drugs.

A more sinister aspect of magical belief and practice is the claim that Adolf Hitler was strongly influenced by occultism in the formation of Nazi politics. This aspect of magic is explored in *The Spear of Destiny* by Trevor Ravenscroft (1973) and *Satan and Swastika; The Occult and the Nazi Party* by Francis King (1976).

During the 1930s, there was another popular outbreak of public interest in the occult in Britain and Europe, and a number of significant books on Magic were published. Their influence was limited only by the relatively smaller influence of mass media at that time, and the conservatism of intellectual life. Exceptional individuals like Aleister **Crowley** flourished in the 1920s and 30s, but were deplored by polite society, who regarded such occultists as scandalous misfits.

A second wave of popular occultism flared up again in the 1950s in Britain and the U.S., fueled largely by reprints of key books published during the 1930s (see Felix **Morrow**). This modern interest in Magic, however, had little in common with the outlook and ideals of medieval magicians and followers of the hermetic art, stemming largely from the trendiness of post-war affluence and the desire for sensationalist indulgence.

At the seediest level, the occult explosion led to Witchcraft, Satanism and Black Magic cults. Not surprisingly, much of modern occultism has been influenced by drug taking.

During this period, one long kept secret of occultism became generally discussed—that of the important factor of sexual energy in dynamizing the processes of Magic. Although this factor was well known to the occultists of ancient India under the study of Tantra, it was openly discussed in modern times through the practices and writings of Aleister Crowley.

Although the present-day occult revival has generated many neurotic and exhibitionist magicians, whose magical feats have been greatly overrated, certain talented individuals with some special psychic gifts may well have achieved paranormal feats.

There are still two opinions amongst occultists as to how such feats are achieved. First, that it is the achievement of desired effects in the physical world by the exercise of the operator's will-power, assisted by rituals. Secondly, that the desired effects are achieved by means of spirits, evoked by rituals.

There is some anecdotal evidence that old-fashioned magic does achieve minor miracles, mainly in the field of relatively small personal gains in influencing events such as success in love, business or acquiring power over others, or in causing harm to one's enemies. However, the subject is riddled with fraudulent claims and self-deception. In a modern world, science and technology have triumphed as the highest magic, achieving amazing results which the ancient magicians would have considered incredible.

Conjuring Tricks and Stage Magic

Nowadays the term "magic" normally denotes the performance of conjuring, legerdemain or illusion, although it is interesting to note that even the term "conjuring" was originally used to indicate the evocation of spirits.

It should not be supposed, however, that conjuring tricks are only a modern kind of "magic." There is evidence that tricks have been used by priests thousands of years ago to create an illusion of magical miracles (See also Moving **Statues**). For a brief survey of the conjuring of antiquity see the fascinating and authoritative book *The Illustrated History of Magic* by Milbourne **Christopher** (1975).

The astonishing and skillful illusions of modern stage magicians show that special caution is necessary in evaluating many apparently paranormal feats of magic, and stage magicians have also performed valuable service in exposing fraudulent "psychic" feats, notable in such areas as **slate-writing.**

Because of this, there is a tendency for stage magicians to be occupationally skeptical of all claimed paranormal feats. (See also **Abraham the Jew; Black Magic; Ceremonial Magic; Egypt; Magic Darts; Magical Diagrams; Magical Instruments; Magical Numbers; Magical Union of Cologne; Magical Vestments; Magicians; Medieval Magic**)

Recommended reading:

Agrippa, Henry Cornelius. *The Philosophy of Natural Magic,* London, 1651; University Books, 1974

Barrett, Francis. *The Magus; A Complete System of Occult Philosophy,* London, 1801; University Books, 1967

Bonewits, Philip E. I. *Real Magic,* Coward, McCann & Geoghegan, 1971; Berkley Medallion paperback, 1971

Christopher, Milbourne. *The Illustrated History of Magic,* Thos. Crowell, 1973/Robert Hale, London, 1975 [deals with conjuring and stage magic]

Christopher, Milbourne. *Panorama of Magic,* Dover, New York, 1962 [deals with conjuring and stage magic]

Christian, Paul. *The History & Practice of Magic,* 2 vols., Forge Press, London, 1952

Crow, W B. *A History of Magic, Witchcraft & Occultism,* Aquarian Press, U.K., 1968; Abacus paperback, U.K., 1972

(Crowley, Aleister) The Master Therion. *Magick in Theory and Practice,* Paris, 1929; Castle Books, New York, n.d.; new ed. titled *Magick,* ed. annotated by John Symonds & Kenneth Grant, Routledge & Kegan Paul, London, 1973; Samuel Weiser, 1974

Ennemoser, Joseph. *The History of Magic,* 2 vols., London, 1854; University Books, 1970

Freedland, Nat. *The Occult Explosion,* Putnam/ Michael Joseph, London, 1972
Grant, Kenneth. *The Magical Revival,* Frederick Muller, London, 1972; Samuel Weiser, 1973
King, Francis. *Ritual Magic in England (1887 to the Present Day),* Neville Spearman, London, 1970; Macmillan, New York, 1971
King, Francis. *Sexuality, Magic & Perversion,* Neville Spearman, London, 1971; Citadel Press, 1972
Lévi, Éliphas. *Transcendental Magic,* London, 1896; revised edition Rider & Co., 1923 etc.
Lévi, Éliphas. *The History of Magic,* Rider & Co., London, 1913 etc., David McKay, 1914.
Lévi, Éliphas. (edited A. E. Waite) *The Mysteries of Magic; A digest of the Éliphas Lévi,* London, 1886, 1897; University Books, 1974
Seligmann, Kurt. *The History of Magic,* Pantheon Books, New York, 1948 etc. (also titled *Magic, Supernaturalism & Religion*)
Shah, Sayed Idries. *Oriental Magic,* Rider & Co., London, 1956
Shah, Sayed Idries. *The Secret Lore of Magic; The Books of the Sorcerers,* Frederick Muller, London, 1957
Summers, Montague. *Witchcraft & Black Magic,* Rider & Co., London, 1946; Causeway, 1974
Thompson, C. J. S. *The Mysteries and Secrets of Magic,* London, 1927; Causeway, 1973
Waite, Arthur Edward. *The Book of Ceremonial Magic,* London, 1911; University Books, 1961
Webb, James. *The Flight From Reason* (Volume 1 of *The Age of the Irrational*), Macdonald, London, 1971; (American title *The Occult Underground,* Open Court, Illinois, 1974)
Webb, James. *The Occult Establishment,* Open Court, Illinois, 1975

Magic Circle

An important part of ceremonial magic was the drawing of a magic circle around the magician, to protect him from the malice of evil spirits that he might invoke to perform his will.

Magic circles were used for thousands of years, and often took elaborate forms, requiring the inscribing of magical symbols, such as the Seal of Solomon (a double pentacle). In ancient Hindu folk customs, the bed of a woman in childbirth was encircled by red lead or black pebbles to ward off evil influences.

In medieval magic practice, the circle was usually marked or drawn around the magician with a magic sword or knife. It might be some nine feet in diameter, to allow the movements of the magician in his evocations. Portable forms of magic circles were sometimes drawn on parchment and used as **talismans.** (See also **Magic Square; Necromancy**)

Magic Circle, The (Organization)

British organization of professional and amateur conjuring magicians. It was founded in July 1905 at the famous Pinoli's restaurant in Wardour Street, London (long since vanished), and was originally intended to honor a young professional magician Martin Charpender who had just died.

Some members preferred an impersonal name to "The Martin Charpender Club," but when it was pointed out that the initials "M. C." might also stand for "Magic Circle" the latter name was agreed.

In its early period, the Magic Circle convened at St. George's Hall in Portland Place, where the famous stage magicians Maskelyne and Devant performed their feats. In 1910 the Magic Circle moved to Anderton's Hotel, Fleet Street, where it held meetings and monthly concerts (named "seances"). Individual magicians showed off their latest tricks. There were many changes of address over the years, and in the 1970s the Magic Circle was established in Chenies Mews, London, W.C.1.

In addition to providing a club for professional and amateur magicians, the Circle also gave many charity shows. Members have included doctors of medicine, philosophy and divinity as well as engineers and plumbers and a taxi-driver.

Magic Darts

The Laplanders, at one time said to be great magicians, were supposed to launch lead darts, about a finger-length, against their absent enemies, believing that with such magic darts they were sending grievous pains and maladies. (See also **Magic**)

Magic Square

An arithmetical curiosity formerly believed to have occult significance. A square is divided into smaller squares, each containing a number so arranged that the sum of each row, vertical, horizontal, or diagonal, is the same.

In a variant form, letters are used instead of numbers, the most popular arrangement being the rows:

SATOR
AREPO
TENET
OPERA
ROTAS

A variant form:

SALOM
AREPO
LEMEL
OPERA
MOLAS

is specified in *The Book of the Sacred Magic of Abra-Melin the Mage* as a charm to obtain the love of a maiden.

Other magic squares were composed of numbers or letters in irregular arrangements that were believed to have magical power. Such squares were inscribed on parchment or other materials and worn as **talismans.**

Other talismans were made in circular format, in wax or in metal, and used to invoke spirits. These were sometimes termed "seals." The term **magic circle** more properly indicates the protective circle traced upon the ground by the magician when invoking spirits.

Talismans in the form of magic squares have long been used by Hindus and Moslems for magical purposes, and in religious rituals. (See also **Grimoire; Magical Numbers; Talisman**)

Magical Blend Magazine

New Age style publication that embarks "on a voyage of discovery . . . that will take us out of the past and carry us into the future. . . . it charts a course of magic, and sets sail on an excursion into infinite possibilities." Noted contributors include: John Lilly, Carlos Castaneda, Lynn Andrews, Robert Anton Wilson, Yoko Ono, Jacques Cousteau, Timothy Leary, Jean Houston, Whitley Strieber. Subjects covered include trance channeling, occult systems, visionary art, the possibilities of extraterrestrial communication. Address: Magical Blend, P.O. Box 11303, Dept. F, San Francisco, California 94101.

Magical Diagrams

These were geometrical designs, representing the mysteries of deity and creation, therefore supposed to be of special virtue in rites of evocation and conjuration.

The chief of these were the Triangle, the Double Triangle, forming a six-pointed star and known as the Sign or Seal of Solomon; the Tetragram, a four-pointed star formed by the interlacement of two pillars, and the Pentagram, a five-pointed star.

These signs were traced on paper or parchment, or engraved on metals and glass and consecrated to their various uses by special rites.

The Triangle was based on the idea of trinity as found in all things, in deity, time and creation. The triangle was generally traced on the ground with the magic sword or rod, as in circles of evocation where the triangle was drawn within it and, according to the position of the magician at its point or base, so the spirits were "conjured" (summoned up) from heaven or hell.

The Double Triangle, the Sign of Solomon, symbolic of the Macrocosm, was formed by the interlacement of two triangles, thus its points constituted the perfect number six. The magicians wore it, bound on their brows and breasts during the ceremonies and it was engraved on the silver reservoir of the magic lamp.

The Tetragram was symbolic of the four elements and used in the conjuration of the **elementary spirits**—sylphs of the air, undines of the water, the fire salamanders and gnomes of the earth. In **alchemy** it represented the magical elements, salt, sulphur, mercury and azoth; in mystic philosophy the ideas Spirit, Matter, Motion and Rest; in hieroglyphs the man, eagle, lion and bull.

The Pentagram, the sign of the Microcosm, was held to be the most powerful means of conjuration in any rite. It might represent evil as well as good, for while with one point in the ascendant it was the sign of Christ, with two points in the ascendant it was the sign of Satan. By the use of the pentagram in these positions, the powers of light or darkness were evoked. The pentagram was said to be the star which led the Magi to the manger where the infant Christ was laid.

The preparation and consecration of this sign for use in magical rites was prescribed with great detail. It might be composed of seven metals, the ideal form for its expression, or traced in pure gold upon white marble never before used for any purpose. It might also be drawn with vermilion upon lambskin without a blemish prepared under the auspices of the Sun.

The sign was next consecrated with the four elements, breathed on five times, dried by the smoke of five perfumes (incense, myrrh, aloes, sulfur and camphor). The names of five genii were breathed above it, and then the sign was placed successively at the north, south, east and west and center of the astronomical cross, pronouncing the letters of the sacred tetragram and various Kabalistic names (see **Kabala**).

It was believed to be of great efficacy in terrifying phantoms if engraved upon glass, and the magicians traced it on their doorsteps to prevent evil spirits from entering and the good from departing.

This symbol was used by many secret and occult societies, by the **Rosicrucians,** the **Illuminati,** down to the **Freemasonry** of modern times. Modern occultists translate the meaning of the pentagram as symbolic of the human soul and its relation to God.

The symbol is placed with one point in the ascendant. That point represents the Great Spirit, God. A line drawn from there to the left-hand angle at base is the descent of spirit into matter in its lowest form, whence it ascends to right-hand angle typifying matter in its highest form, the brain of man. From here, a line is drawn, across the figure to left angle representing man's development in intellect, while progress in material civilization, the point of danger from which all nations have fallen into moral corruption, is signified by the descent of the line to right angle at base. But the soul of man being derived from God cannot remain at this point, but must struggle upward, as is symbolized by the line reaching again to the apex, God, whence it issued.

It seems likely that the magical diagrams of Western magicians have descended from the comparable magical designs of Hindu religion known as **Yantra**. (See also **Ceremonial Magic; Magic; Magical Instruments & Accessories; Magical Vestments & Appurtenances**)

Recommended reading:

Barrett, Francis. *The Magus; A Complete System of Occult Philosophy,* London, 1801; University Books, 1967

Thompson, C. J. S. *The Mysteries and Secrets of Magic,* London, 1927; Causeway, 1974

Waite, Arthur Edward. *The Book of Ceremonial Magic,* London, 1911; University Books, 1961

Woodroffe, Sir John. *Sakti and Sakta,* Ganesh & Co., Madras, India, 1918 etc.

Magical Instruments and Accessories

In magical rites these were considered of the utmost importance. Indispensable to the efficacy of the ceremonies were the altar, the chalice, the tripod, the censer; the lamp, rod, sword, and magic fork or trident; the sacred fire and consecrated oils; the incense and the candles.

The altar might be of wood or stone, but if of the latter, then of stone that had never been worked or hewn or even touched by the hammer.

The chalice might be of different metals, symbolic of the object of the rites. Where the purpose was evil, a black chalice was used, as in the black masses of sorcerers and witches. In some talismans, the chalice was engraved as a symbol of the moon.

The tripod and its triangular stand were also made in symbolic metals.

The censer might be of bronze, but preferably of silver.

In the construction of the lamp, gold, silver, brass and iron must be used; iron for the pedestal, brass for the mirror, silver for the reservoir and at the apex a golden triangle. Various symbols were traced upon it, including an androgynous figure about the pedestal, a serpent devouring its own tail (see also **Ouroboros**), and the Sign of Solomon.

The rod must be specially fashioned of certain woods and then consecrated to its magical uses. A perfectly straight branch of almond or hazel was to be chosen. This was cut before the tree blossomed, and cut with a golden sickle in the early dawn. Throughout its length must be run a long needle of magnetized iron; at one end there had to be affixed a triangular prism, to the other, one of black resin, and rings of copper and zinc bound about it. At the new moon, it must be consecrated by a magician who already possessed a consecrated rod.

The secret of the construction and consecration of magical rods was jealously guarded by all magicians and the rod itself was displayed as little as possible, being usually concealed in the flowing sleeve of the magician's robe.

The sword must be wrought of unalloyed steel, with copper handle in the form of a crucifix. Mystical signs were engraved on guard and blade and its consecration took place on a Sunday in full rays of the sun, when the sword was thrust into a sacred fire of cypress and laurel, then moistened with the blood of a snake, polished, and next, together with branches of vervain, swathed in silk. The sword was generally used in the service of **Black Magic.**

The magic fork or trident used in **necromancy** was also fashioned of hazel or almond, cut from the tree at one blow with an unused knife, from whose blade must be fashioned the three prongs. Witches and sorceresses were usually depicted using the trident in their infernal rites.

The fire was lit with charcoal on which were cast branches of trees, symbolic of the end desired. In Black Magic, these generally consisted of cypress, alderwood, broken crucifixes and desecrated hosts.

The oil for anointing was compounded of myrrh, cinnamon, galingale and purest oil of Olive. Unguents were used by sorcerers and witches, who smeared their brows, breasts, and wrists with a mixture composed of human fat and blood of corpses, combined with aconite, belladonna and poisonous fungi, thinking thereby to make themselves invisible.

Incense might be of any odoriferous woods and herbs, such as cedar, rose, citron, aloes, cinnamon, sandal, reduced to a fine powder, together with incense and storax. In Black Magic, alum, sulfur and assafoetida were used as incense.

The candles, belonging solely to practices of Black Magic were molded from human fat and set in candlesticks of ebony carved in the form of a crescent.

Bowls also were used in these ceremonies, fashioned of different metals, their shape symbolic of the heavens. In necromantic rites, skulls of criminals were used, generally to hold the blood of some victim or sacrifice. (See also **Ceremonial Magic; Magic; Magical Diagrams; Magical Vestments & Appurtenances; Witchcraft**)

Recommended reading:

Barrett, Francis. *The Magus; A System of Occult Philosophy,* London, 1801; University Books, 1967

Knight, Gareth. *The Practice of Ritual Magic,* Weiser paperback n.d.

Lévi, Éliphas. *Transcendental Magic,* Rider & Co., London, 1923 etc.

Waite, Arthur Eward. *The Book of Ceremonial Magic,* Rider & Co., London, 1911; University Books, 1973

Magical Numbers

Certain numbers and their combinations were traditionally held to be of magical power, by virtue of their representation of divine and creative mysteries.

The doctrines of Pythagoras (see **Greece**) furnished the basis for much of this belief. According to his theory numbers contained the elements of all things, of the natural and spiritual worlds and of the sciences. The real numerals of the universe were the primaries one to ten and in their combination the reason of all else might be found.

To the Pythagoreans, One represented unity, therefore God; Two was duality, the Devil; Four was sacred and holy, the number on which they swore their most solemn oaths; Five was their symbol of marriage.

They also attributed certain numbers to the gods, planets and elements; one represented the Sun, two the Moon; while five was fire, six the earth, eight the air, and twelve water. (See also **Magic Square**)

Cornelius **Agrippa** in his work *Occult Philosophy* first published in Latin 1531-33, discoursed upon numbers as those characters by whose proportion all things were formed. He enumerated the virtues of numerals as displayed in nature, instancing the herb cinquefoil, which by the power of the number five exorcises devils, allays fever and forms an antidote to poisons. Also the virtue of seven, as in the power of the seventh son to cure king's evil.

One was the origin and common measure of all things. It is indivisible, not to be multiplied. In the universe there is one God; one supreme intelligence in the intellectual world, man; in the sidereal world, one Sun; one potent instrument and agency in the elementary world, the **philosopher's stone;** one chief member in the human world, the heart; and one sovereign prince in the nether world, Lucifer.

Two was the number of marriage, charity and social communion. It was also regarded sometimes as an unclean number; beasts of the field went into the Ark by twos.

Three had a mysterious value as shown in Time's trinity—Past, Present and Future; in that of Space—length, breadth and thickness; in the three heavenly virtues—faith, hope and charity; in the three worlds of man—brain (the intellectual), heart (the celestial), and body (elemental).

Four signifies solidity and foundation. There are four seasons, four elements, four cardinal points, four evangelists.

Five, as it divides ten, the sum of all numbers, is also the number of justice. There are five senses; the **Stigmata**, the wounds of Christ were five; the name of the Deity, the Pentagram, is composed of five letters; it also is a protection against beasts of prey.

Six is the sign of creation, because the world was completed in six days. It is the perfect number, because it alone by addition of its half, its third and its sixth reforms itself. It also represents servitude by reason of the Divine injunction "Six days shalt thou labour."

Seven is a miraculous number, consisting of one, unity, and six, sign of perfection. It represents life because it contains body, consisting of four elements, spirit, flesh, bone and humor (ancient concept of bodily fluids affecting the mind); and soul, made up of three elements, passion, desire and reason. The seventh day was that on which God rested from his work of creation.

Eight represents justice and fullness. Divided, its halves are equal; twice divided, it is still even. In the Beatitude, eight is the number of those mentioned—peace-makers, they who strive after righteousness, the meek, the persecuted, the pure, the merciful, the poor in spirit, and they that mourn.

Nine is the number of the muses and of the moving spheres.

Ten is completeness because one cannot count beyond it except by combinations formed with other numbers. In the ancient mysteries, ten days of initiation were prescribed. In ten is found evident signs of a Divine principle.

Eleven is the number of the commandments, while Twelve is the number of signs in the Zodiac, of the apostles, of the tribes of Israel, of the gates of Jerusalem.

This theory of numbers Agrippa applied to the casting of horoscopes. Divination by numbers was one of the favorite methods employed in the Middle Ages.

In magical rites, numbers played a great part. The instruments, vestments and ornaments must be duplicated. The power of the number three is found in the magic triangle: in the three prongs of the trident and fork, and in the three-fold repetition of names in conjurations. Seven was also of great influence, the seven days of the week each representing the period most suitable for certain evocations and these corresponded to the seven magical works: 1) works of light and riches; 2) works of divination and mystery; 3) works of skill, science and eloquence; 4) works of wrath and chastisement; 5) works of love; 6) works of ambition and intrigue; 7) works of malediction and death. (See also **Kabala; Numerology**)

Recommended reading:

Agrippa, Henry Cornelius. *The Philosophy of Natural Magic,* London, 1651; University Books, 1974

Bosman, Leonard. *The Meaning and Philosophy of Numbers,* Rider & Co., London, 1932

Butler, Christopher. *Number Symbolism,* Routledge, Kegan Paul, U.K., 1970

Redgrove, H. Stanley. *A Mathematical Theory of Spirit,* Rider & Co., London, 1912

Waite, Arthur Edward. *The Holy Kabbalah,* Williams & Norgate, London, 1929; University Books, 1960

Westcott, W. Wynn. *Numbers: Their Occult Power & Mystic Virtues,* Theosophical Publishing Society, London, 1890 etc.

Magical Union of Cologne

A society stated in a manuscript of the **Rosicrucians** (under the pseudonym "Omnis Moriar") at Cologne, Germany, to have been founded in that city in the year 1115.

In the *Rosenkreutzer in seiner blosse* (1786) of F. G. E. Weise it was stated that the initiates wore a triangle as symbolizing power, wisdom and love. The more exalted orders among them were called Mage or Wise Masters, and these held the greater mysteries of the fraternity. They were masters of secret sciences and achieved feats that seemed supernatural. (See also **Rosicrucians**)

Magical Vestments and Appurtenances

These were prescribed needful adjuncts to magical rites. Their color, name, form and substance, symbolic of certain powers and elements, added, it was supposed, greater efficacy to the evocations.

Abraham the Jew, a magician of the Middle Ages, prescribed a tunic of white linen, with upper robe of scarlet and girdle of white silk. A crown or fillet of silk and gold was to be worn on the head and the perfumes cast on the fire might be incense, aloes, storax, cedar, citron or rose.

According to other authorities on the subject, it was advisable to vary color of robe and employ certain jewels and other accessories according to the symbolism of the end desired. Éliphas **Lévi,** a magician of the nineteenth century, gave a detailed description of ritual, from which the following details are taken.

If the rites were those of White Magic and performed on a Sunday, then the vestment should be of purple, the tiara, bracelets and ring of gold, the latter set with chrysolith or ruby. Laurel, heliotrope and sunflowers are the symbolic flowers, while other details include a carpet of lionskins and fans of sparrow-hawk feathers. The appropriate perfumes were incense, saffron, cinnamon and red sandal.

If, however, the ceremonial took place on a Monday, the Day of the Moon, then the robe must be of white embroidered with silver and the tiara of yellow silk emblazoned with silver characters, while the wreaths were to be woven of moonwort and yellow ranunculi. The jewels appropriate to the occasion were pearls, crystals and selenite; the perfumes, camphor, amber, aloes, white sandalwood and seed of cucumber.

In evocations concerning transcendent knowledge, green was the color chosen for the vestment, or it might be green shot with various colors. The chief ornament was a necklace of pearls and hollow glass beads enclosing mercury. Agate was the symbolic jewel; narcissus, lily, herb mercury, fumitory, and marjoram the flowers; whilst the perfumes must be benzoin, mace and storax.

For operations connected with religious and political matters, the magician must don a robe of scarlet and bind on his brow a brass tablet inscribed with various characters. His ring must be studded with an emerald or sapphire, and he must burn for incense, balm, ambergris, grain of paradise and saffron. For garlands and wreaths, oak, poplar, fig and pomegranate leaves should be entwined.

If the ceremonial dealt with amatory affairs, the vestment must be of sky blue, the ornaments of copper, and the crown of violets. The magic ring must be set with a turquoise, while the tiara and clasps were wrought of lapis-lazuli and beryl. Roses, myrtle and olive were the symbolic flowers, and fans must be made of swan feathers.

If vengeance was desired on anyone, then robes must be worn whose color was that of blood, flame or rust, belted with steel, with bracelets and ring of the same metal. The tiara must be bound with gold and the wreaths woven of absinthe and rue.

To bring misfortune and death on a person, the vestment must be black and the neck encircled with lead. The ring must be set with an onyx and the garlands twined of cypress, ash and hellebore; whilst the perfumes to be used were sulfur, scammony, alum and assafoetida.

For purposes of **Black Magic,** a seamless and sleeveless robe of black was donned, while on the head was worn a leaden cap inscribed with the signs of the Moon, Venus and Saturn. The wreaths were of vervain and cypress; and the perfumes burned were aloes, camphor and storax. (See also **Ceremonial Magic; Magic; Magical Diagrams; Magical Instruments & Accessories**)

Recommended reading:

Knight, Gareth. *The Practice of Ritual Magic,* Weiser paperback, n.d.

Lévi, Éliphas. *Transcendental Magic,* Rider & Co., London, 1923 etc.

Waite, Arthur Edward. *The Book of Ceremonial Magic,* Rider & Co., London, 1911; University Books, 1973

Magicians (Illusionists)

Nowadays the term "magician" is used to denote professional illusionists. Such magicians and mediums have been in opposing camps since the earliest days of modern Spiritualism.

The first important challenge of a magician to Spiritualism was issued in 1853 by J. H. Anderson of New York. He offered a thousand dollars to any "poverty-stricken medium" who would come to his hall and attempt to produce **raps** there. The **Fox Sisters** accepted immediately and, accompanied by Judge J. W. **Edmonds** and Dr. Grey, went to the hall. But Anderson backed out and, amid the hisses of the audience, refused them admission to the stage.

Some of the most famous magicians acknowledged having witnesses genuine phenomena.

The clairvoyant powers of Alexis **Didier** stupefied and famous conjurer Robert Houdin. His signed declaration was published by Dr. Edwin Lee in his book *Animal Magnetism* (1866) as follows: "I cannot help stating that the facts above related are scrupulously exact and the more I reflect upon them the more impossible do I find it to class them among the tricks which are the objects of my art."

In a letter to M. de Mirville who introduced him to Alexis Didier, Houdin wrote: "I, therefore, came away from this seance as astonished as anyone can be, and fully convinced that it would be quite impossible for anyone to produce such surprising effects by mere skill."

The stage magician Leon Bosco used to laugh immoderately at the belief that the phenomena of the famous medium D. D. **Home** could be thought imitable by the resources of his art. Canti similarly declared to Prince Napoleon "that he could in no way account for the phenomena he saw on the principles of his profession." He also published a letter expressing the same opinion. (See *Outlines of Investigation Into Spiritualism* by T. Barkas, 1862) Robert Houdin also stated: "I have come away from that seance as astounded as I could be, and persuaded that it is perfectly impossible by chance or adroitness to produce such marvellous effects." (*Experimentalpsychologie und Experimentalmetaphysik* by Carl DuPrel, Leipzig, 1891)

The stage magician Hamilton (Pierre Etienne Chocat), successor of Robert Houdin, in a letter to the **Davenport Brothers,** published in the *Gazette des Etrangers,* September 27, 1865, declared: "Yesterday I had the pleasure of being present at the seance you gave, and came away from it convinced that jealousy alone was the cause of the outcry raised against you. The phenomena produced surpassed my expectations; and your experiments were full of interest for me. I consider it my duty to add that those phenomena are inexplicable, and the more so by such persons as have thought themselves able to guess your supposed secret, and who are, in fact, far indeed from having discovered the truth."

This letter was accompanied by a similar statement from M. Rhys, a manufacturer of conjuring implements who examined the cabinet and instruments of the Davenports and declared that the insinuations cast about them were false and malevolent and, the cabinet being completely isolated, all participation in the manifestations by strangers was absolutely impossible.

Prof. Jacobs wrote on April 10, 1881 to the editor of *Licht, Mehr Licht* about the phenomena which occurred through the Davenport Brothers in Paris: "As a prestidigitator of repute and a sincere spiritualist, I affirm that the medianimic facts, demonstrated by the two brothers were absolutely true, and belonged to the spiritualistic order of things in every respect. Messrs. Robin and Robert Houdin, when attempting to imitate these said facts, never presented to the public anything beyond an infantile and almost grotesque parody of the said phenomena, and it would be only ignorant and obstinate persons who could regard the question seriously as set forth by these gentlemen."

However, one should add that in modern times the Davenports are considered to be illusionists rather than mediums.

Samuel Bellachini, Court Conjurer at Berlin, stated in an authenticated statement given to the medium Henry **Slade:** "I must, for the sake of truth, hereby certify that the phenomenal occurrences with Mr. Slade have been thoroughly examined by me with the minutest observation and investigation of his surroundings, including the table, and that I have not in the smallest degree found anything produced by means of prestidigitative manifestations, or by mechanical apparatus; and that any explanation of the experiments which took place under the circumstances and conditions then obtaining by any reference to prestidigitation is absolutely impossible. It must rest with such men of science as Crookes and Wallace in London, Perty in Berne, Butleroff in St. Petersburg to search for the explanation of this phenomenal power, and to prove its reality."

The great illusionist Harry Kellar witnessed, in January 1882 in Calcutta a levitation of the medium William **Eglinton.** He wrote (*Proceedings* of the Society for Psychical Research, vol. 9, p. 359): "A circle having been formed, I was placed on Mr. Eglinton's left and seized his left hand firmly in my right. Immediately on the extinction of the lights I felt him rise slowly in the air and as I retained firm hold of his hand, I was pulled to my feet, and subsequently compelled to jump on a chair and then on the table, in order to retain my hold of him. That his body did ascend into the air on that occasion with an apparently utter disregard to the law of gravity, there can be no doubt. What most excited my wonder was the fact, for I may speak of it as a fact without qualification, that Mr. Eglinton rose from my side, and, by the hold he had on my right hand, pulled me up after him, my own body appeared for the time being to have been rendered nonsusceptible to gravity."

However, the case of S. J. Davey is especially noteworthy. He was a magician who attended some **slate-writing** seances of Eglinton and was impressed. He made a deep study of the problem and, in agreement with Dr. Richard **Hodgson,** presented himself as a medium and produced all the characteristic phenomena of the seance room to the entire satisfaction of his sitters. An account of his demonstration is published in *Proceedings* of the Society for Psychical Research, vol. 4. His revelation that he did everything by trickery was disbelieved. Even Alfred Russel **Wallace** suggested that Davey was also a good physical medium and could get phenomena supernormally as he exhibited all the characteristic physiological symptoms of trance convulsions as other mediums.

Largely as a consequence of the acute controversy which slate-writing aroused, the Society for Psychical Research asked the conjurer Professor Hoffman (Angelo J. Lewis) to report upon Eglinton's performance in his professional capacity. He concluded in his report, published in August, 1886: "If conjuring were the only explanation of the slate-writing phenomena, I should certainly have expected that their secret would long since have become public property."

The two most tenacious magician opponents of Spiritualism, J. N. Maskelyne and Harry **Houdini,** focused public attention on themselves for many years. They both led crusades against mediums. Maskelyne started by claiming to have unmasked the Davenport Brothers. He admitted that in their effect upon the public mind no alleged manifestations of mediums could be compared with their exhibitions. "Certain it is, England was completely taken aback for a time by the wonders presented by these jugglers." Maskelyne, however, was not too successful in dispelling this wonderment. Dr. George Sexton, the former editor of the *Spiritual Magazine,* publicly explained the tricks of Maskelyne and said: "The two bear about as much resemblance to each other as the productions of the poet Close to the sublime and glorious dramas of the immortal bard of Avon." (*Spirit Mediums and Conjurers,* London, 1873). (John Close was a notoriously bad poet of the nineteenth century who achieved a brief notoriety by bombarding the nobility and gentry with his verses.)

Maskelyne nevertheless did not absolutely disbelieve in the supernatural. In a letter to the *Daily Telegraph* in 1881 he wrote: "It may surprise some of your readers to learn that I am a believer in apparitions. Several similar occurrences to those described by many of your correspondents have taken place in my own family, and in the families of near friends and relations."

In the *Pall Mall Gazette,* April 20, 1885, he acknowledged the phenomenon of **table-turning** as genuine. He declared that Faraday's explanation was insufficient and some psychic or nerve force was responsible for the result. At the same time he asserted that he could imitate any Spiritualistic phenomenon, provided his own apparatus, which in many cases exceeded a ton in weight, was at his disposal.

This very point is the one which marks the main difference between the performances of a stage magician and a medium. The former is always master of ceremonies, whereas the latter has to submit himself to the conditions imposed upon him. It is very likely that mediums could discover many of the sleight-of-hand tricks if they were admitted to the stage. The magicians always have a privileged position. They can watch the performance very closely. In the investigations of the **London Dialectical Society** in 1869, the committee invited the services of the two best prestidigitators of London when their sessions were in progress.

Many later psychical researchers were amateur conjurers (notably Hereward **Carrington,** Harry **Price,** W. W. **Baggally**) who were well acquainted with the tricks of the trade. If the seance room phenomena were simply due to trickery it would be reasonable to expect that many mediums, after an exposure, should turn professional magicians. No such incidents are on record, except perhaps the case of Colchester, an American medium, who was compelled, by the verdict of a jury, to take out a license as a juggler. But Colchester was exposed years before by the Spiritualists themselves (see *Spiritual Magazine,* 1861). In one instance quoted in du Prel's *Experimental psychologie*, a medium named Thorn advertised his seances as "anti-Spiritualistic." But when he met Spiritualists he admitted that the sole purpose of the advertisement was to draw the public.

A conjurer's performance may in fact afford presumptive evidence that the phenomena as produced by the medium are genuine. Admiral Usborne Moore (author of *Glimpses of the Next State,* 1911) saw a conjurer reproduce the phenomena of the **Bangs Sisters** on the stage. The effect was crude at first, afterwards very satisfactory. But the point, as he remarked, was that the conjurer's conditions were as different to the conditions of the seances of the Bangs Sisters on the stage. The effect was crude at first, afterwards very satisfactory. But the point, as he remarked, was that the conjurer's conditions were as different to the conditions of the seances of the Bangs Sisters as a locomotive boiler is different from a teapot. His efforts finally convinced him that he had witnessed genuine spirit manifestations with the Bangs Sisters.

After the Rev. F. W. **Monck** was accused of fraud in 1876, Archdeacon **Colley** offered a thousand pounds to J. N. Maskelyne if he could duplicate Monck's materialization performance. Maskelyne accepted the challenge. His performance was declared unsatisfactory. He sued for the money and lost heavily in prestige when Archdeacon Colley won. When, later, Sir Hiram Maxim, the great inventor, challenged Maskelyne to produce some psychic effect he had seen in America under the same conditions, he refused. The challenge and its result were described by the inventor in a pamphlet: *Maxim versus Maskelyne* (1910).

The descendants of J. N. Maskelyne followed in his footsteps. Capt. Clive Maskelyne issued a challenge in February 1925, when the visit of the medium "Margery" (Mrs. **Crandon**) to England was reported, that he could produce any of the phenomena she had produced in America. The author H. Dennis **Bradley,** in an interview to the *Daily Sketch,* promised a hundred guineas to Capt. Maskelyne if he could duplicate the **Valiantine** phenomena. Capt. Maskelyne at first accepted, but withdrew when he heard what was expected from him.

In 1930, psychical researcher Harry **Price** offered a thousand pounds to any conjurer who could repeat Rudi **Schneider's** phenomena under the same conditions. Nobody came forward, but a skit, under the title "Olga," was produced in imitation of Rudi Schneider's phenomena at the Coliseum Theatre ("Olga" was the claimed spirit **control** of Schneider). Harry Price publicly challenged Noel Maskelyne from the stage of that theater on December 10, 1929, to simulate by trickery one single phenomenon of Rudi Schneider under the identical conditions as imposed by the **National Laboratory of Psychic Research.** He offered Maskelyne £250 if he could show the trick. Maskelyne refused.

Earlier than this occurrence, Will Goldston, one of the greatest professional magicians in Europe, the author of forty works on legerdemain, founder and ex-president of the Magicians' Club of London, declared in the *Sunday Graphic* (December 2, 1929) concerning the same phenomena: "I am convinced that what I saw at the seance was not trickery. No group of my fellow-magicians could have produced those effects under such conditions."

Goldston told the story of his conversion to spiritualism in *Secrets of Famous Illusionists* (London, 1933). Two of his great fellow magicians—Ottokar Fischer, of Vienna, and Harry Rigoletto—accepted psychic phenomena.

In the *Sunday Dispatch* (August 1931), Will Goldston testified to Miss Hazel **Ridley's direct voice** phenomena as follows: "Miss Ridley sat at a table in our midst, and without the use of trumpets or any of the usual paraphernalia spoke in three different voices. No ventriloquist could possibly produce the effect this girl produced, and I say that after a long experience of ventriloquists. First there was a powerful, clear, man's voice, ringing through the room in tones one would have thought no woman's throat could have produced. The next voice, a very quiet one, like that of a child of six or seven years of age, added to my surprise. The third guide also spoke in a woman's or a child's voice, but quite unlike the normal voice of the medium. The seance lasted an hour and three quarters." A year later, he also spoke up in favor of Mrs. Helen **Duncan** and declared that he was not aware of any system of trickery which could achieve the astounding results which he witnessed. However, there is alternative testimony from others that Mrs. Duncan was fraudulent on some occasions.

During the Harry Price-Maskelyne controversy, Goldston also stated that Mr. J. N. Maskelyne and Mr. Nevil Maskelyne, grandfather and father respectively of Noel, were secret believers in Spiritualism. He added that Houdini's exposures were simply part of a great publicity stunt and that he, too, was secretly a believer. On this latter point Harry Price remarked in his book *Rudi Schneider* (1930) that he had a letter from Houdini in which he stated that a spirit extra of Prof. James Hyslop, which he had seen, was a genuine one.

But it is a far cry from the inclination to believe in the supernormal to the possession of such powers and Houdini was the first to ridicule the statement of J. Hewat **Mackenzie** in *Spirit Intercourse* (1916) that it was by psychic means that he freed himself from handcuffs and that his feat of escaping from a small iron tank filled with water was performed by the dematerialization of his body within one and a half minutes and its reintegration after passing through the tank.

Nevertheless, the belief was not so easily given up, although clearly mistaken. It was sustained by A. Campbell Holms in *Facts of Psychic Science* (1925) and Sir Arthur Conan Doyle devoted about sixty pages in *The Edge of the Unknown* (1930) to the claim that Houdini was really a medium masquerading as a conjurer! Whatever the true nature of Houdini's inner belief, his demonstrations during the *Scientific American* investigation of the mediumship of "Margery" did not greatly redound to his prestige (see **Crandon**). The exposures which he advertised throughout the United States were not at all supported by substantial proofs. Privately he made some admissions.

On January 5, 1925, he wrote to Harry Price: "Another strange thing happened: with the aid of the spirit slates I produced a photograph of Mrs. Crandon's brother, Walter, who was killed, and of all the miracles in the world, I ran across the photograph of the boy as he was crushed between the engine and the tender of the train, and which was taken one minute before he died . . . I doubt very much if there are any duplicates about." (*Light,* August 12, 1932).

Houdini was a very clever magician, but according to Conan Doyle, his narrow-mindedness was sufficiently indicated by the fact that he died disbelieving that the phenomena of **hypnotism** were genuine. In *Houdini and Conan Doyle* by Bernard M. L. Ernst and Hereward Carrington, many interesting letters were published on Houdini's strange adventures in psychic realms.

After his death there was a long controversy in the American press about the code word which he left behind to prove his identity if messages were claimed to originate from him. Will Goldston, in *Sensational Tales of Mystery Men,* quoted a letter from Mrs. Houdini with this admission: "I have gotten the message that I have been waiting for from my beloved, how, if not by spiritual aid, I do not know." The medium was Arthur **Ford.** The story of the messages, Mrs. Houdini's statements, and the flood of attacks which followed, is told by Francis R. Fast in *The Houdini Messages.*

Some of Houdini's American colleagues made sweeping concessions. David P. **Abbot,** of the American Society for Psychical Research and E. A. Parsons investigated in 1906 the direct voice phenomena of Mrs. E. Blake. They both became convinced of its genuine nature. Abbott published his experiences in the *Omaha World Herald.* Howard Thurston, who inherited the reputation of Harry Kellar, was a convinced Spiritualist.

The current target of the skepticism of many present-day conjuring magicians is Uri **Geller.** Canadian-born magician James **Randi** ("The Amazing Randi") claims to be able to duplicate Geller's feats of telepathy and metal-bending by trickery and accuses Geller of deception. Randi is a well-known illusionist who has inherited the mantle of Houdini as the arch-enemy of psychic phenomena and psychics, and continues to issue challenges to psychics to prove themselves. Milbourne **Christopher,** another modern illusionist skeptic, is more restrained and scholarly in his books criticizing psychics and the occult.

However, an out and out dismissal of all paranormal events as fraudulent is as unreasonable as an absolute endorsement of all apparent miracles. Sincere Spiritualists themselves have often been foremost in exposing fakes, and it seems more likely that there is a reasonable proportion of genuinely paranormal phenomena as well as much ingenious trickery. (See also Milbourne **Christopher; Fraud;** Uri **Geller; Houdini**)

Recommended reading:

Christopher, Milbourne. *Houdini; The Untold Story,* Thomas Y. Crowell, 1969

Christopher, Milbourne. *ESP, Seers & Psychics,* Thomas Y. Crowell, 1970

Christopher, Milbourne. *The Illustrated History of Magic,* Thomas Y. Crowell, 1973; Robert Hale, London, 1975

Dingwall, E. J. & Harry Price (eds.). *Revelations of a Spirit Medium,* Kegan Paul, London, 1925

Dunninger, Joseph. *Inside the Medium's Cabinet,* David Kemp, New York, 1924

Ernst, Bernard M. L. & Hereward Carrington. *Houdini and Conan Doyle; The Story of a Strange Friendship,* Hutchinson, London, 1933

Fast, Francis R. *The Houdini Messages; the Facts Concerning the Messages Received Through the Mediumship of Arthur Ford,* published by the author, New York, 1929

Goldston, Will. *Secrets of Famous Illusionists,* Long, London, 1933

Houdini, Harry. *A Magician Among the Spirits,* Harper & Brothers, 1924

Proskauer, Julien J. *Spook Crooks,* A. L. Burt, New York & Chicago, 1946; Gryphon Books, Ann Arbor, 1971

Randi, James. *The Truth About Uri Geller,* revised ed., Prometheus Books, Buffalo, New York.

Randi, James. *Flim-Flam! Psychics, ESP, Unicorns & Other Delusions,* Prometheus Books, Buffalo, New York, 1982

Sexton, George. *Spirit Mediums & Conjurers,* London, 1873

Truesdell, J. W. *The Bottom Facts Concerning the Science of Spiritualism,* G. W. Carleton, New York, 1883

Maginot, Adèle (c. 1848)

Early French medium, whose phenomena were carefully recorded and well attested. She was psychic from childhood and had attacks against which "magnetic" treatment was employed by Alphonse **Cahagnet.** He soon found her an excellent clairvoyant, especially for medical purposes. From this she progressed to serve as a channel for spirit communications.

From the summer of 1848, many sittings were held in which visitors were put in touch with their departed relatives. Cahagnet made them sign a statement after the sitting indicating which of the particulars were true and which false. These statements were published in the second volume of Cahagnet's book *Magnétisme Arcanes de la vie future dévoilé* (1848-60).

When Adèle was put into trance, she saw the spirits of the departed, described them and gave an intimate description of their family circumstances.

Baron **du Potet,** a well-known writer on **animal magnetism,** and editor of the *Journal du Magnetisme,* witnessed a striking seance in the company of Prince de Kourakine, who was secretary to the Russian Ambassador. Nevertheless, he was inclined to attribute the result to **thought-transference.**

Adèle Maginot's most extraordinary phenomena, however, did not consist in communications from the dead but in communications from the living, combined with traveling **clairvoyance.** A. M. Lucas came to inquire after his brother-in-law who had disappeared after a quarrel twelve years before. Adèle, in trance, found the man, said that he was alive in a foreign country, busy gathering seeds from small shrubs about three feet high. She asked to be awakened since she was afraid of wild beasts. A. M. Lucas returned a few days afterwards with the mother of the vanished man. Adèle gave a correct description of the man's appearance and of the history of his disappearance. She was asked to speak to the man.

"Get him to tell you the name of the country where you see him," says the record. "He will not answer." "Tell him that his good mother, for whom he had a great affection, is with you, and asks for news of him." "Oh, at the mention of his mother he turned around and said to me 'My mother, I shall not die without seeing her again. Comfort her, and tell her that I always think of her. I am not dead.' " "Why doesn't he write to her?" "He has written to her, but the vessel has no doubt been wrecked—at least he supposes this to be so, since he has received no answer. He tells me that he is in Mexico. He has followed the Emperor, Don Pedro; he has been imprisoned for five years; he has suffered a great deal, and will use every effort to return to France; they will see him again." "Can he name the place in which he is living?" "No, it is very far inland. These countries have no names."

A similar experience was recorded by M. Mirande, the head of the printing office in which the first volume of the *Arcanes* had been printed. His missing brother, whom he believed to be dead, was found by Adèle to be living and a plausible account of his long silence and whereabouts was given.

It must be admitted that in neither of these cases was corroboration forthcoming. But there was one instance (quoted in Cahagnet's third volume) in which, a few weeks after the sitting, the mother received a confirmatory letter from her absent son.

Nevertheless, there is some force in the skeptical argument of Frank **Podmore:** "If Adèle, or any other of Cahagnet's clairvoyants really had possessed the power of conversing with the living at a distance, I cannot doubt that Cahagnet, in the course of his many years' experiments, would have been able to present us with some evidence of such power that was not purely hypothetical. Nothing would be more easy to prove. The fact that no such evidence is forthcoming affords a strong presumption that Adèle did not possess the power, and that the conversations here detailed were purely imaginary, the authentic or plausible details which they contained being filched, it may be, telepathically from the minds of those present."

However, Podmore was one of the most skeptical writers on Spiritualism and the very fact that he did not question the phenomena goes a long way to indicate the extraordinary nature of Adèle Maginot's gift. Podmore stated of Cahagnet's investigations: "In the whole literature of Spiritualism I know of no records of the kind which reach a higher evidential standard, nor any in which the writer's good faith or intelligence are alike so conspicuous."

Magnetic Phenomena

There appear to be connections between psychic and magnetic phenomena, giving a new slant on the old-fashioned term "animal magnetism" for mesmeric and psychic faculty.

The medium Henry **Slade** could influence the movements of a magnetic needle. Prof. **Zöllner** made convincing experiments with a glass-covered compass. Slade could also magnetize steel knitting needles and Prof. Zöllner lifted iron filings and sewing needles with their ends. Mlle. Stanislawa **Tomczvk** could exert a similar influence over the compass.

The British psychical researcher and author Stanley **de Brath** also testified to a case in which a young man deflected the magnetic needle. He was searched for a concealed iron or a magnet but nothing was found.

In modern times, the controversial psychic Uri **Geller** has also demonstrated deflection of a compass needle, while his skeptical critics also claim that he must have a concealed iron or magnet.

Magnetometer

A device invented by the Abbé Fortin (c. 1864), consisting of a piece of paper cut to the shape of a compass needle. It was considered to indicate some kind of electromagnetic force.

It is suspended in a glass cylinder by a silk fiber. If the cylinder is approached by a hand, the paper (over a dial of 360 degrees) will either turn towards the hand or away from it.

Carried out in a more substantial form with a "metallic multiplicator," a condenser and a needle the magnetometer was used for the study of terrestrial magnetism to solve meteorological problems. Since 1904 it was used for **dowsing.** (See also **Biometer of Baraduc; De Tromelin Cylinder; Dowsing; Water-Divining**)

Magonia (Journal)

Quarterly journal concerned with anomalies, such as visions, portents, prodigies and UFOs. The name "Magonia" was given in medieval France to a mysterious land beyond the sky, the origin of all kinds of signs and wonders, but inextricably bound up with the destinies of human beings. Inhabitants of Magonia traveled in aerial ships and were believed to destroy crops and kidnap human beings. The Emperor Charlemagne issued edicts to prohibit the Magonians from troubling the air and provoking storms.

Past issues of the journal *Magonia* have covered such subjects as **glossolalia, ouija boards,** pagan occultism, coincidences, **Spiricom,** earth lights, psychical research, **Bigfoot** and other Fortean topics. Address: John Rimmer, 64 Alric Avenue, New Malden, Surrey, KT3 4JW, England.

Magpie

The chattering of a Magpie was formerly considered a sure omen of evil. Another folk belief was that the croaking of a single magpie round a house signified that one of the inhabitants would soon die. In parts of Britain and Ireland it was believed that evil could be averted by being respectful to a magpie—bowing or doffing one's hat. Irish folk would sometimes say "Good morning, your reverence" on seeing a magpie first thing in the morning.

The magpie figures in folklore of the American Indians and was a clan animal amongst the Hopis.

Maguire, Father Joseph (c.1931-)

Catholic priest popularly known as "The Miracle Man," who specializes in spiritual healing.

He was born in Lowell, Massachusetts; his mother was Irish, from Castlegregory, Co. Kerry. Maguire was a successful business man, owning an electronics sales company which sold missile parts to Cape Kennedy, and also operated a chain of hotels, motels, and restaurants across the U.S. At the age of 38, he left his profitable businesses and became a Catholic priest.

His gift of healing developed slowly over a period of years, commencing the year before his ordination. He has since acquired a reputation for a large number of medically unexplained cures which have resulted from him touching people who were terminally ill.

In 1984, Father Maguire visited Ireland, where he had an enthusiastic reception. More than 2,500 people crowded into the Church of Our Lady Queen of Peace in Merrion Road, Dublin (built to accommodate only 1,800 persons). Parents held out babies for Father Maguire to touch.

After celebrating Mass with eight concelebrants, Father Maguire blessed the congregation and went to pray with the sick. Subsequently a 46-year-old mother, paralyzed for several months with a cancerous tumor, claimed that she regained the use of her left arm and was able to walk again after being virtually immobile. (See also **Healing by Touch**)

Magus

A master magician or adept. The *Magi* or magicians (plural form of *Magus*) were the "wise men" of the ancient Persian priesthood.

The three Magi who brought gifts to the infant Jesus were traditionally named Kaspar, Melchior and Balthasar, and their bones are said to be in Cologne Cathedral, Germany.

The term "Magus" is also used as a high degree in magical societies like the **Golden Dawn.**

"Magus"

A spirit **control** of the Rev. Stainton **Moses,** supposed to be a member of the Mystic Band which delivered occult teaching in his scripts. "Magus" did not disclose his name on earth, but he said that he lived 4,000 years ago and belonged to an ancient African wonder-working brotherhood.

In the nineteenth book of the Moses scripts, a topaz is mentioned as the material counterpart of a spiritual jewel worn by "Magus" which was to be given to Stainton Moses to help him to see visions. The stone, set in a ring, was actually dropped from the air in Stainton Moses' bedroom.

For further information on the various spirit controls of Stainton Moses, see his books *Spirit Teachings* (1883 etc.), *More Spirit Teachings* (1897), *Spirit Identity* (1902).

Maharishi Mahesh Yogi (c. 1918-)

A phenomenally successful modern **Guru** who heads a worldwide Spiritual Regeneration Movement, promoting the technique of "TM" or **Transcendental Meditation.**

He was born Mahesh Brasad Warma, c.1918. Originally a physics graduate of Allahabad University, India, he worked for a time in a factory, then studied spiritual science for some years under Swami Brahmananda Saraswati Shankaracharya of Jyotir Math, a teacher of traditional Hindu transcendentalism. After the death of his teacher in 1953, the Maharishi spent some time trying to develop his own simplified non-religious version of traditional Hindu meditation.

In 1958, he conceived an ambitious plan for "the regeneration of the whole world through meditation." He unveiled his "Science of Creative Intelligence," built around the technique of "Transcendental Meditation." This involved a simple initiation ceremony in which the guru bestowed a *mantra* (sacred Sanskrit prayer) on which the pupil concentrated for a short period each day. In this easy technique, the pupil could supposedly by-pass normal intellectual activity and tap a limitless reservoir of energy and creative intelligence.

The system had limited appeal until 1967, when the Maharishi signed up the pop group The Beatles, creating waves of interest throughout the mass media world in a simple non-religious turn-on without drugs. When the Beatles defected some months later, Transcendental Meditation suffered a temporary setback, but it soon bounced back with the initiation of other showbiz personalities, many of whom made the trip East to the Maharishi's luxury ashram at Rishikesh, in the foothills of the Himalayas. The Student's International Meditation Society founded in Los Angeles, California, in 1966 became an instant success among young people tired of protest movements.

In recent years, the movement has been boosted by a well publicized scientific endorsement of the beneficial results of Transcendental Meditation, now firmly established under the initialism "TM." Organized on successful multinational corporation lines, with vice-chairmen, divisions and subdivisions, graphs and charts, computer printouts, and glossy brochures, the movement has now become a kind of ITT of meditation, embodying a host of initialisms like IMS, SIMS, CHIMS, MIU, SRM, AFSSI and today "TM" is now a registered trademark as widely recognized as TWA.

There is a World Plan to develop the full potential of the individual, to improve governmental achievements, to realize the highest ideal of education, to solve the problems of crime and all behavior that brings unhappiness to the family of man, to maximize the intelligent use of the environment, to bring fulfillment to the economic aspirations of individuals and society, and to achieve the spiritual goals of mankind in this generation."

Through all this runs the basic message that man is not born to suffer and through TM, life can be enjoyed to the full. The Maharishi himself lives simply on a vegetarian diet, but enjoys the corporation life of endless conferences, foreign junkets and chauffeured limousines. The movement's headquarters shifted from India, following income tax problems. However, the Indian medical profession has expressed interest in the benefits claimed by TM technique.

In recent years, the movement unveiled a "Siddhi" program (*siddhis* are special paranormal powers) based on the claims of the ancient Yoga Treatise *The Yoga Sutras of Patanjali*. It is claimed that students of this special course have successfully achieved the paranormal feat of **levitation**.

Photographs of students appear to show them hovering a few feet in the air, but critics (and former students) have stated that the "levitators" merely bounce in the air cross-legged and do not float. This was one of the psychic exercises reported by Madame Alexandra **David-Neel** in her book *With Mystics and Magicians in Tibet* (1931 etc.), and was regarded as a training towards the eventual mastery of levitation. To date, no irrefutable evidence of levitation by the Maharishis students has yet been produced. (See **Guru; Kundalini; Levitation; Meditation; Yoga**)

Mahatma Letters

Communications allegedly from the Mahatmas, Masters or Adepts of the **Theosophical Society** of Madame **Blavatsky** during the nineteenth century. These Mahatmas were said to be Eastern Teachers belonging to an occult brotherhood, living in the trans-Himalayan fastnesses of Tibet. They included Koot Humi Lal Singh (K.H.) and Morya (M.).

Notes signed with the initials of these Masters would be mysteriously precipitated out of the air, or discovered in unexpected places. Recipients of such letters included Col. H. S. **Olcott** and A. P. **Sinnett** (editor of the Anglo-Indian newspaper *The Pioneer*). Sinnett was favorably impressed by such letters as well as other occult phenomena demonstrated by Madame Blavatsky, and played a prominent part in the affairs of the Theosophical Society.

However, the **Society for Psychical Research,** London, sent investigator Richard **Hodgson** to Adyar, the Madras headquarters of the Society to investigate these marvels. He reported the discovery of a shrine with a false back, used with the connivance of Madame Coulomb, an employee of the Society, as a kind of fake letter box for Mahatma letters.

In the controversy that followed, many Theosophists preferred to believe that the confession by Madame Coulomb was part of a plot to discredit Madame Blavatsky. After the death of Madame Blavatsky, further Mahatma letters were produced by Theosophist William Q. **Judge,** supporting his claim to take charge of the Society in opposition to the presidency of Annie **Besant.** Col. Olcott declared these letters to be fraudulent.

There seems little doubt that the original Mahatma letters in Madame Blavatsky's time were strongly influenced by her personality, since the handwriting and language was typical of her, although some Theosophists would claim that this resulted from the Masters using her as a medium of communication, in much the same way that a psychic delivers **automatic writing.**

In a paper by Charles Marshall 'The Mahatma Letters—A Syntactic Investigation Into the Possibility of "Forgery" By Helena Petrovna Blavatsky, a 19th Century Russian Occultist' (*Viewpoint Aquarius* No. 96, October 1980), the author described his attempt to prove by computer analysis that there is a strong dissimilarity between Mme. Blavatsky's language and that of the Masters.

However, the computer program, although extensive, was somewhat arbitrary, being confined to certain prepositions and conjunctions. Moreover the comparison between Mahatma Letters and Mme. Blavatsky's writings in such works as "The Secret Doctrine" ignored the extensive editorial work by others on behalf of Mme. Blavatsky's writings, and her own extensive and unacknowledged plagiarisms from other writers, thus making her claimed style unrepresentative.

A less ambitious, non-computer reading of the Mahatma Letters discloses the unmistakable touch of Mme. Blavatsky herself. The whole question of the psychic powers of Madame Blavatsky remains an unsolved riddle, for it seems probable that, like many psychic mediums, she was capable of both genuine and fraudulent phenomena.

some of the Mahatma Letters are now in the Manuscripts Department of the British Library, London.

For a spirited defense of Madame Blavatsky, see 'J' Accuse; An Examination of the Hodgson Report of 1885' by Dr. Vernon Harrison (*Journal* of the Society for Psychical Research, April, 1986, also obtainable from Theosophical History Centre, 50 Gloucester Place, London, W11 3HJ.

Recommended reading:

Barker, A. T. *The Mahatma Letters to A. P. Sinnett from the Mahatmas M. and K. H.* London, 1924

Hare, H. E. & William L. *Who Wrote the Mahatma Letters?* London, 1936

Jinarajadasa, C. (ed.). *Letters from the Masters of Wisdom,* 2 vols., Theosophical Publishing House, Adyar, India, 1919-25

Jinarajadasa, C. (ed.). *The K. H. Letters to C. W. L.,* Theosophical Publishing House, Adyar, India, 1941.

Jinarajadasa, C. *The Story of the Mahatma Letters,* Theosophical Publishing House, Adyar, India, 1946 (pamphlet)

Maier, Michael (c. 1568-1622)

German alchemist, born at Rensburg in Holstein. He was one of the principal figures in the Rosicrucian Controversy in Germany and the greatest adept of his time. He diligently pursued the study of medicine in his youth and settling at Rostock practiced with such success that the Emperor Rudolph appointed him as his physician, ennobling him later for his services.

Some adepts eventually succeeded in luring him from the practical work he followed so long into the complex and tortuous paths of alchemy. In order to confer with those whom he believed possessed of the transcendent mysteries he traveled all over Germany. The *Biographie Universelle* states that in pursuit of these "ruinous absurdities" he sacrificed his health, fortune and time. On a visit to England he became acquainted with Robert **Fludd,** the Kentish mystic.

In the controversy which convulsed Germany on the appearance of his Rosicrucian Manifestoes, he took a vigorous and enthusiastic share and wrote several works in defense of the mysterious society. He is alleged to have traveled in order to seek for members of the "College of Teutonic Philosophers R.C.," and, failing to find them, formed a brotherhood of his own, based on the form of the *Fama Fraternibus.* There is no adequate authority for this statement, but it is believed that towards the end of his life, he was eventually initiated into the genuine order.

A posthumous pamphlet of Maier's called *Ulysses* was published by one of his personal friends in 1624. There was added to the same volume the substance of two pamphlets already published in German but which, in view of their importance, were now translated into Latin for the benefit of the European literati.

The first pamphlet was entitled *Colloquium Rhodostauroticum trium personarium per Famem et Confessionem quodamodo revelatam de Fraternitate Rosœ Crucis.* The second was an *Echo Colloquii* by Hilarion on behalf of the Rosicrucian Fraternity. From these pamphlets it appears that Maier was admitted as a member of the mystical order.

He became the most profuse writer on alchemy of his time. Most of his works, many of which are adorned with curious plates, are obscure with the exception of his Rosicrucian *Apologies.* (See also **Alchemy; Rosicrucians**)

Maimonides, Rabbi Moses (1135-1204)

A great Spanish-Hebrew philosopher and theologian, author of the *Guide for the Perplexed.* His theories were Aristotelian and rational, but there remained in his viewpoint a touch of mysticism.

He was born March 30, 1135 in Cordova, southern Spain, and educated by Arabic teachers. After the Moorish conquest of Cordova in 1148, Jews left the province, and Maimonides settled in Fez. After five years he moved to Cairo, where he became physician to Saladin and married the sister of Ibn Mali, a royal secretary.

In his famous treatise the *Guide for the Perplexed,* he sought to harmonize Rabbinical and philosophical teachings, but maintained that reason should be supplemented by revelation. His treatise has had a profound influence on his Arabic, Jewish and Christian successors.

It has been suggested that Maimonides was sympathetic to the teachings of Kabala in his late period. Certainly he would have been aware of mystical traditions.

He died December 13, 1204. (See also **Kabala**)

Maison des Spirites

Center founded by Jean **Meyer,** who also assisted the foundation of the **Institut Métapsychique** (concerned with psychical research).

The Maison des Spirites was located at 8 Rue Copernic, Paris and was intended to propagate knowledge of Spiritism. It became the secretariat of the Fédération Spirite Internationale (International Spiritualists' Federation), and hosted the Second International Spiritualist Congress in Paris in 1925. (See also **France**)

Maithuna

Sanskrit term for sexual intercourse in the mystic rites of **Tantric Yoga,** the left-hand path of Hindu magic.

In **Tantra,** sexual energy is supposed to be transformed into mystical energy by *coitus interruptus* with a cooperating female, in distinction to the traditional transformation of **Kundalini** energy into mystical channels by **meditation** and self-purification. It is easy to see that there are special problems arising from the use of women in sexual intercourse for claimed mystical purposes, and such practices are open to abuse. Indeed, such abuses undoubtedly occurred with such Western occultists as Aleister **Crowley** in adapting Tantric practices. (See also **Kundalini; Yoga**)

Maitland, Edward (1824-1897)

Co-founder with Anna Bonus **Kingsford** of Esoteric Christianity and the **Hermetic Society.**

Born October 27, 1824 at Ipswich, England, he graduated at Caius College, Cambridge, 1847. He had intended to become a clergyman, but had many reservations about the Church, and instead spent some years traveling in California and Australia, studying life at first hand.

Upon returning to England, he devoted himself "to developing the intuitional faculty as to find the solution of all problems having their basis in man's spiritual nature."

Through his close friendship with Anna Kingsford, he became an ardent vegetarian and the interpreter of her highly individual mystical Christianity. He collaborated with her on the writing of *The Perfect Way; or, the Finding of Christ* (London, 1882 etc.), and related books.

After her death in 1888, he published her biography: *Anna Kingsford; her life, letters, diary* (London, 1896).

He died in the following year on October 2, 1897.

Mak, A(rie) (1914-)

Dutch school director, who experimented in the field of parapsychology. Born November 23, 1914 at Alkmaar, Netherlands. In 1939 he married N. Jansen.

He was instructor and director at Sneek Technical School, Sneek, Netherlands, from 1939-56, director 1959-60. He is a member of the Amsterdam Parapsychologische Kring, formerly research officer of the Dutch Society for Psychical Research. In 1950 he was winner of the van de Bilt gold medal for the best amateur astronomical observations, and has contributed articles to journals of astronomy.

He also studied telepathy, clairvoyance and psychokinesis and took part in experiments (with Dr. Jan Kappers, A. H. de Jong and F. v. d. Berg) to test clairvoyance quantitatively. He also studied the question of evidence for reincarnation.

Malachite

A precious stone (a variety of topaz) of basic copper carbonate. In folklore it was believed to preserve the cradle of an infant from spells.

Malachy Prophecies

St. Malachy O'More was a medieval bishop who is said to have foretold the succession of 112 Popes from Celestinus II (1143) until the final Pope in the future yet to come. These predictions were in the form of a long series of Latin character mottoes instead of actual names, and there is still scholarly doubt as to whether the prophecies really emanated from St. Malachy. However, other prophecies attributed to him are claimed to have been fulfilled.

He was born Maelmhaedhoc Ua Morgair in Armagh, Ireland, in 1095. His biography was written by a famous contemporary, St. Bernard of Clairvaux. Malachy was the son of a well-known scholar; his mother came from a wealthy family in Bangor, County Down. The father died when the boy was eight years old, and Malachy was subsequently educated by a monk who later became Abbot of Armagh.

Malachy was ordained by St. Celsus, an Irish Benedictine of Glastonbury, then archbishop of Armagh. He became vicar-general to Celsus, then abbot of Bangor and bishop of Connor, succeeding to the archbishopric in 1132. He had a reputation as a firm disciplinarian.

After six years, he resigned in order to make a pilgrimage to Rome. But during the course of his journey, he met St. Bernard at the French abbey of Clairvaux, and was so impressed by him that he requested to be allowed to remain at Clairvaux as an ordinary monk. However, Pope Innocent II refused permission, since he had plans for Malachy to be primate of the combined see of Armagh and Tuam, although in the event this did not come to pass.

Malachy traveled through England, Scotland, and Ireland, even making a second pilgrimage to Rome. On the return journey to Ireland, he died at Clairvaux, which had made such an impression on him.

Malachy had a great reputation as a prophet during his own lifetime. When the son of King David of Scotland was critically ill, Malachy sprinkled him with holy water and predicted that the boy would survive. He did. When one individual tried to prevent the building of an oratory, Malachy correctly foretold his early death. According to St. Bernard, Malachy even predicted the date, place, and circumstances of his own death.

The Papal prophecies seem to be extraordinarily apt. The first one commences with Celestine II (1143) continuing through to modern and future times. The first Pope was indicated by the motto "Ex Castro Tiberis" (from a castle on the Tiber) and Celestine II came from Tuscany, where the Tiber rises, and his family name was Catello. The next Pope was indicated by the motto "Inimicus Expulsus" (the enemy driven out) and it transpired that his family name was Caccianemici, which combines "cacciare" (to drive out) and "nemici" (enemies). The next Pope had the motto "Ex Magnitudine Montis" (from the great mountain); he was born in Montemagno (the great mountain).

It has been suggested by some scholars that the prophecies are sixteenth-century forgeries. However, some of the mottos predicted for later popes have still been surprisingly apt, e.g., "Flos Florum" (flower of flowers) for Pope Paul IV (1963) seems validated by the fact that the Pope had three fleur-de-lys on his armorial bearings.

According to the Malachy prophecies, the line of Popes will end after the successor to Pope John Paul

II. The last Pope will be "Petrus Romanus" (Peter the Roman), and after that Rome will be destroyed and the world will be purified by fire. Some believe that this will be the final days of the Last Judgment, others that there will be a cleansing of the world and the commencement of a new cycle of life.

Recommended reading:

Bander, Peter. *The Prophecies of St. Malachy,* Colin Smythe, Gerrards Cross, U.K., 1969

Dorato, M. *Gli ultimi papi e la fine del mondo nelle grandi profezie,* Rome, 1950

MALAYSIA

Malaysia now includes the mainland of West Malaysia, sharing a land border with Thailand in the north, and East Malaysia, consisting of the states of Sarawak and Sabah (formerly North Borneo). The ethnic grouping of Malaysia includes Chinese and Indian races, but the largest population is of Malays, of Moslem religion and speaking their own Malay language.

Much of the folklore and magical tradition of the Malays concerns "sympathetic magic" (see **Magic**). The traveler Hugh Clifford, writing in the nineteenth century, stated:

"The accredited intermediary between men and spirits is the *Pawang;* the *Pawang* is a functionary of great and traditional importance in a *Malay* village, though in places near towns the office is falling into abeyance. In the inland districts, however, the *Pawang* is still a power, and is regarded as part of the constituted order of Society, without whom no village community would be complete. It must be clearly understood that he had nothing whatever to do with the official Muhammadan religion of the mosque; the village has its regular staff of elders—the *Imam, Khatio,* and *Bilal*—for the mosque service. But the *Pawang* is quite outside this system and belongs to a different and much older order of ideas; he may be regarded as the legitimate representative of the primitive 'medicine-man,' or 'village-sorcerer,' and his very existence in these days is an anomaly, though it does not strike *Malays* as such. . . .

"The *Pawang* is a person of very real significance. In all agricultural operations, such as sowing, reaping, irrigation works, and the clearing of jungle for planting, in fishing at sea, in prospecting for minerals, and in cases of sickness, his assistance is invoked. He is entitled by custom to certain small fees; thus, after a good harvest he is allowed in some villages five *gantangs* of padi, one *gantang* of rice (*beras*), and two *chupaks of emping* (a preparation of rice and cocoa-nut made into a sort of sweetmeat) from each householder."

The *Pawang* used to regulate taboos, and employ a familiar spirit known as *hantu pusaka*—a hereditary demon. He also acted as a medium and divined through trance. To become a magician "You must meet the ghost of a murdered man. Take the midrib of a leaf of the 'ivory' cocoa-nut palm *(pelepah niyor gading),* which is to be laid on the grave, and two midribs, which are intended to represent canoe-paddles, and carry them with the help of a companion to the grave of the murdered man at the time of the full moon (the 15th day of the lunar month) when it falls upon a Tuesday. Then take a cent's worth of incense, with glowing embers in a censer, and carry them to the head-post of the grave of the deceased. Fumigate the grave, going three times round it, and call upon the murdered man by name:

'Hearken, So-and-so,
And assist me;
I am taking (this boat) to the saints of God,
And I desire to ask for a little magic.'

Here take the first midrib, fumigate it, and lay it upon the head of the grave, repeating *'Kur Allah'* ('Cluck, Cluck, God!') seven times. You and your companion must now take up a sitting posture, one at the head and the other at the foot of the grave, facing the grave post, and use the canoe-paddles which you have brought. In a little while the surrounding scenery will change and take upon itself the appearance of the sea, and finally an aged man will appear, to whom you must address the same request as before."

Malay magic may be subdivided into preparatory rites, sacrificial, lustration, divination and possession. Sacrifice took the form of a simple gift, or act of homage to the spirit or deity. Lustration was magico-religious and purificatory, principally taking place after childbirth. It might be performed by fire or water. **Divination** consisted for the most part of the reading of dreams, and was, as elsewhere, drawn from the acts of men or nature. Omens were strongly believed in.

"When a star is seen in apparent proximity to the moon, old people say there will be a wedding shortly. . . .

"The entrance into a house of an animal which does not generally seek to share the abode of man is regarded by the Malays as ominous of misfortune. If a wild bird flies into a house it must be carefully caught and smeared with oil, and must then be released in the open air, a formula being recited in which it is bidden to fly away with all the ill-luck and misfortunes (*sial jambalang*) of the occupier. An iguana, a tortoise, and a snake, are perhaps the most dreaded of these unnatural visitors. They are sprinkled with ashes, if possible to counteract their evil influence.

"A swarm of bees settling near a house is an unlucky omen, and prognosticates misfortune."

So, too, omens were taken either from the flight or cries of certain birds, such as the night-owl, the crow, some kinds of wild doves, and the bird called the "Rice's Husband" (*laki padi*).

Astrology

Divination by astrology was, however, the most common method of forecasting the future. The native practitioners possessed long tables of lucky and unlucky periods and reasons. These were mostly translations from Indian and Arabic sources.

The oldest known of these systems of propitious and unpropitious seasons was known as *Katika Lima,* or the Five Times. Under it the day was divided into five parts, and five days formed a cycle. To each division was given a name as follows: Maswara, Kala, S'ri, Brahma, Bisnu (Vishnu) names of Hindu deities, the last name in the series for the first day being the first in that of the second day, and so on until the five days are exhausted. Each of these had a color, and according to the color first seen or noticed on such and such a day would it be fortunate to ask a boon of a certain god.

Another version of this system, known as the "Five Moments" was similar in origin, but possessed a Mohammedan nomenclature.

Another scheme, *Katika Tujoh,* was based on the seven heavenly bodies, dividing each day into seven parts, each of which was distinguished by the Arabic name for the sun, moon, and principal planets.

The astrology proper of the Malays is purely Arabic in origin, but a system of Hindu invocation was in vogue by which the lunar month was divided into parts called *Rejang,* which resembles the *Nacshatras* or lunar houses of the Hindus. Each division had its symbol, usually an animal. Each day was propitious for something, and the whole system was committed to verse for mnemonic purposes.

Demonology

The demoniac form common to Malaysia was that of the Jinn, with some leaven of the older Hindu spirit. They were one hundred and ninety in number. They were sometimes subdivided into "faithful" and "infidel," and further into the Jinns of the royal musical instruments, of the state, and of the royal weapons. The *Afrit* was also known. Angels also abounded, and were purely of Arabic origin.

Besides these, the principal supernatural beings were as follows: the *Polong,* or familiar; the *Hantu Pemburu,* or specter Huntsman; the *Jadi-jadian,* or wer-tiger; the *Hantu,* or ghost of the murdered; the *Jemalang,* or earth-spirit.

Minor Sorcery

The rites of minor sorcery and **witchcraft,** as well as those of the **shaman,** were widely practiced among the Malays, and were practically identical in character with those in use among other peoples in a similar state of culture.

Recommended reading:

Clifford, Hugh. *In Court and Kampong,* Grant Richards, London, 1897

Clifford, Hugh. *Studies in Brown Humanity,* Grant Richards, London, 1898

Skeat, W. W. *Malay Magic; Being an Introduction to the Folklore & Popular Religion of the Malay Peninsula,* Macmillan, London, 1900

Swettenham, Sir Frank A. *Malay Sketches,* John Lane, London, 1895

Winstedt, R. *The Malays; A Cultural History,* Routledge, London, 1950

Mallebranche (c. 1618)

Seventeenth-century Frenchman haunted by his dead wife. M. Mallebranche was a marker of the game of tennis, living in the Rue Sainte-Geneviéve, Paris, who in 1618 was visited by an apparition of his wife, who had died five years before.

She came to advise him to repent and live a better life, and to pray for her also. Both Mallebranche and his wife (for he had married a second time) heard the voice, but the apparition did not become visible. In 1618 a booklet was published in Paris, entitled: *Histoire nouvelle et remarquable de l'esprit d'une femme qui c'est apparue au Faubourg Saint-Marcel après qu'elle a demeué cinq ans entiers ensevelie; elle a parlé a son mari, lui a commandé de faire prier pour elle, ayant commencé de parler le mardi II Decembre, 1618.*

Malleus Maleficarum

The most authoritative and influential sourcebook for inquisitors, judges and magistrates in the great witchcraft persecutions from the fifteenth century onwards.

The authors were Jakob **Sprenger** and Heinrich **Kramer,** leading inquisitors of the Dominican Order.

The book brought together folklore and speculation about witchcraft and magic, combining it with a fierce and relentless persecution which ensured the deaths of hundreds of unfortunate individuals accused of witchcraft. This work is in three parts. Part I fulminates against the evil of witchcraft, which is characterized as renunciation of the Catholic faith, homage to the Devil and carnal intercourse with demons. Even disbelief in witches was declared a grave heresy. Part II details the specific sorceries of witches. Part III sets forth rules for legal action and conviction of witches.

The antiquary Thomas Wright, in his book *Narratives of Sorcery and Magic* (2 vols., 1851), stated: "In this celebrated work, the doctrine of witchcraft was first reduced to a regular system, and it was the model and groundwork of all that was written on the subject long after the date which saw its first appearance. Its writers enter largely into the much-disputed question of the nature of demons; set forth the causes which lead them to seduce men in this manner; and show why women are most prone to listen to their proposals, by reasons which prove that the inquisitors had but a mean estimate of the softer sex.

"The inquisitors show the most extraordinary skill in explaining all the difficulties which seemed to beset the subject; they even prove to their entire satisfaction that persons who have become witches may easily change themselves into beasts, particularly into wolves and cats; and after the exhibition of such a mass of learning, few would venture any longer to entertain a doubt. They investigate not only the methods employed to effect various kinds of mischief, but also the counter-charms and exorcisms that may be used against them. They likewise tell, from their own experience, the dangers to which the inquisitors were exposed, and exult in the fact that they were a class of men against whom sorcery had no power.

"These writers actually tell us, that the demon had tried to frighten them by day and by night in the forms of apes, dogs, goats, etc.; and that they frequently found large pins stuck in their night-caps, which they doubted not came there by witchcraft. When we hear these inquisitors asserting that the crime of which the witches were accused, deserved a more extreme punishment than all the vilest actions of which humanity is capable, we can understand in some degree the complacency with which they relate how, by their means, forty persons had been burnt in one place, and fifty in another, and a still greater number in a third. From the time of the publication of the *Malleus Maleficarum,* the continental press during two or three generations teemed with publications on the all-absorbing subject of sorcery.

"One of the points on which opinion had differed most was, whether the sorcerers were carried bodily through the air to the place of meeting, or whether it was an imaginary journey, suggested to their minds by the agency of the evil one. The authors of the *Malleus* decide at once in favour of the bodily transmission. One of them was personally acquainted with a priest of the diocese of Frisingen, who declared that he had in his younger days been carried through the air by a demon to a place at a very great distance from the spot whence he had been taken. Another priest, his friend, declared that he had seen him carried away, and that he appeared to him to be borne up on a kind of cloud.

"At Baldshut, on the Rhine, in the diocese of Constance, a witch confessed, that offended at not having been invited to the wedding of an acquaintance, she had caused herself to be carried through the air in open daylight to the top of a neighbouring mountain, and there, having made a hole with her hands and filled it with water, she had, by stirring the water with certain incantations caused a heavy storm to burst forth on the heads of the wedding-party; and there were witnesses at the trial who swore they had seen her carried through the air.

"The inquisitors, however, confess that the witches were sometimes carried away, as they term it, in the spirit; and they give the instance of one woman who was watched by her husband; she appeared as if asleep, and was insensible, but he perceived a kind of cloudy vapour arise out of her mouth, and vanish from the room in which she lay—this after a time returned, and she then awoke, and gave an account of her adventures, as though she had been carried bodily to the assembly. . . .

"The witches of the *Malleus Maleficarum* appear to have been more injurious to horses and cattle than to mankind. A witch at Ravenspurg confessed that she had killed twenty-three horses by sorcery. We are led to wonder most at the ease with which people are brought to bear witness to things utterly beyond the limits of belief. A man of the name of Stauff in the territory of Berne, declared that when pursued by the agents of justice, he escaped by taking the form of a mouse; and persons were found to testify that they had seen him perform this transmutation.

"The latter part of the work of the two inquisitors gives minute directions for the mode in which the prisoners are to be treated, the means to be used to force them to a confession, the degree of evidence required for conviction of those who would not confess, and the whole process of the trials. These show sufficiently that the unfortunate wretch who was once brought before the inquisitors of the holy see on the suspicion of sorcery, however slight might be the grounds of the charge, had very small chance of escaping out of their claws.

"The *Malleus* contains no distinct allusion to the proceedings at the Sabbath. The witches of this period differ little from those who had fallen into the hands of the earlier inquisitors at the Council of Constance. We see plainly how, in most countries, the mysteriously indefinite crime of sorcery had first been seized on to ruin the cause of great political offenders, until the fictitious importance thus given to it brought forward into a prominent position, which they would, perhaps, never otherwise have held, the miserable class who were supposed to be more especially engaged in it. It was the judicial prosecutions and the sanguinary executions which followed, that stamped the character of reality on charges of which it required two or three centuries to convince mankind of the emptiness and vanity.

"One of the chief instruments in fixing the belief in sorcery, and in giving it that terrible hold on society which it exhibited in the following century, was the compilation of Jacob Sprenger and his fellow inquisitor. In this book sorcery was reduced to a system but it was not yet perfect; and we must look forward, some half a century before we find it clothed with all the horrors which cast so much terror into every class of society."

The work went into some thirty editions between 1486 and 1669, and was accepted as authoritative by both Protestant and Catholic witch-hunters. Its narrow-minded superstition and dogmatic legalism undoubtedly resulted in hundreds of cases of cruel tortures and judicial murders.

An English translation was published in London (1928; 1948; 1974) by the controversial British scholar the Rev. Montague **Summers,** who embodied in his writings a truly medieval attitude to witchcraft. With typically perverse judgment, he declared (in his learned introduction to the work) that the *Malleus Maleficarum* "is among the most important, wisest, and weightiest books of the world." (See also **Witchcraft**)

Malphas

According to demonologist Johan **Weyer,** Malphas was grand president of the infernal regions, where he appeared under the shape of a crow. When he appeared in human form he had a very raucous voice. He built impregnable citadels and towers, overthrew the ramparts of his enemies, found good workmen, gave familiar spirits, received sacrifices, and deceived the sacrificers. Forty infernal legions were under his command.

Mamaloi

An Obeah priestess (see **Obeah; West Indian Islands**).

Mana

A term indicating vital or magical force, used widely throughout Polynesia. In his book *The Melanesians; Studies in their Anthropology and Folk-lore* (1891), the Rev. R. H. Codrington stated:

"The word is common, I believe, to the whole Pacific. . . . It is a power or influence, not physical, and in a way supernatural, but it shows itself in physical force, or in any kind of power or excellence which a man possesses. This *Mana* is not fixed in anything, and can be conveyed in almost anything; but spirits, whether disembodied souls or supernatural beings, have it and can impart it. . . . All Melanesian religion consists in getting this *Mana* for oneself, or getting it used for one's benefit.

The techniques of arousing and acquiring *mana* were explored by Max Freedom **Long** (1890-1971) in his study of *Kahuna* magic in Hawaii, and described in his books, notably *The Secret Science Behind Miracles* (1948 etc.). Long established Huna Research Association to conduct research and spread knowledge of *mana* and its basis in *Kahuna* magic.

The concepts of *mana* has been expressed in many cultures under different names. Amongst the Iroquois and Huron Indians, it is known as *Orenda*. In his book *Primitive Man* (vol.I of *A History of Experimental Spiritualism,* 2 vols., 1931), Caesar de Vesme wrote:

"We are in a fair way to recognize that we find (approximately) Mana in the *Brahman* and *Akasha* of the Hindus, the *Living Fire* of Zoroaster, the *Generative Fire* of Heraclitus, the *Ruach* of the Jews, the *Telesma* of Hermest Trismegistus, the *Ignis subtilissimus* of Hippocrates, the *Pneuma* of Gallien, the *Soul of the World* of Plato and Giordano Bruno, the *Mens agitat molem* which Vergil drew from the Pythagorean philosophy, the *Astral light* of the Kabbalists, the *Azoth* of the alchemists, the *Magnale* of Paracelsus, the *Alcahest* of Van Helmont, the pantheistic *Substance* of Apinoza, the *Subtle Matter* of Descartes, the *Animal magnetism* of Mesmer, the *Will* of Schopenhauer, the *Od* of Reichenbach and Du Prel, the *Unconscious* of Hartmann, the *Entelechy* of Driesch, the *Plastic Mediator* of Eliphas Levi, the *Psychode* and *Ectenic Force* of Thury, the *Force X* and the *Cryptesthesia* of Richet, the *Metether* of F. W. H. Myers, the *Spiritus* of Fludd, the *Spiritus subtilissimus* of Newton, the *Spiritus Vitae* of St. Thomas Aquinas, and many more *Spiritus* besides, if it were permissible to touch upon the different theologies." (See also Max Freedom **Long; Od (Odic Force; Odyle); Orgone**)

Mananan

Son of the Irish sea-god Lir, magician and owner of strange possessions. His magical boat "Oceansweeper" steered by the wishes of its occupant, his horse Aonban, able to travel on sea or land, and his sword **Fragarach,** a match for any mail, were brought by Lugh from "The Land of the Living" (i.e., fairyland).

As lord of the sea he was the Irish Charon, and his color-changing cloak would flap gaily as he marched with heavy tread around the camp of the hostile force invading Erin. He is comparable with the Cymric Manawiddan and resembles the Hellenic Proteus.

Mandala

A mystical diagram used in India and Tibet to attract spiritual power or for meditation purposes. The term derives from the Sanskrit word for "circle," although a mandala may embody various geometrical shapes.

The Swiss psychologist C. G. **Jung** regarded the mandala as an archetypal image from the deep unconscious mind, and investigated mandalas created spontaneously by psychological patients. (See also **Yantra)**

Recommended reading:

Tucci, Giuseppe. *The Theory and Practice of the Mandala,* London, 1961

Wilhelm, Richard & C. G. Jung. *The Secret of the Golden Flower; a Chinese Book of Life* (rev. ed.), Harcourt, Brace (1962); Causeway, 1975

Mandragoras

Familiar demons who appear in the figures of little men without beards. The name is also applied to the plant popularly known as mandrake, whose roots resemble human form and were believed to be inhabited by demons.

The sixteenth-century **witchcraft** scholar Martin Del Rio stated that one day a *mandragora,* entering a court at the request of a sorcerer who was being tried for wizardry, was caught by the arms by the judge (who did not believe in the existence of the spirit) to convince himself of its existence, and thrown into the fire, where of course it would escape unharmed.

Mandragoras were thought to be little dolls or figures given to sorcerers by the Devil for the purpose of being consulted by them in time of need, and it would seem as if this conception sprung directly from that of the fetish, which is really a dwelling-place made by a **shaman** or medicine man for the reception of any wandering spirit who chooses to take up his abode therein.

The anonymous author of the popular magic manual *Secrets merveilleux de la magie et cabalistique de Petit Albert* (1772 etc.) stated that on one occasion, whilst travelling in Flanders and passing through the town of Lille, he was invited by one of his friends to accompany him to the house of an old woman who posed as being a great prophetess. This aged person conducted the two friends into a dark cabinet lit only by a single lamp, where they could see upon a table covered with a cloth a kind of little statue or *mandragoras,* seated upon a tripod and having the left hand extended and holding a hank of silk very delicately fashioned, from which was suspended a small piece of iron highly polished.

Placing under this a crystal glass, so that the piece of iron was suspended inside the goblet, the old woman commanded the figure to strike the iron against the glass in such a manner as she wished, saying at the same time to the figure: "I command you, *Mandragoras,* in the name of those to whom you are bound to give obedience, to know if the gentleman present will be happy in the journey which he is about to make. If so, strike three times with the iron upon the goblet."

The iron struck three times as demanded without the old woman having touched any of the apparatus, much to the surprise of the two spectators. The sorceress put several other questions to the *Mandragora,* who struck the glass once or thrice as seemed good to him. But the author claimed that this procedure was an artifice of the old woman, for the piece of iron suspended in the goblet was extremely light and when the old woman wished it to strike against the glass, she held in one of her hands a ring set with a large piece of magnetic stone, the virtue of which drew the iron towards the glass. This sounds very much like the folklore practice of putting a ring on a thread and holding it so that it dangles inside a glass and responds to questions put to it (see **Pendulums**).

The ancients attributed great virtues to the plant *mandragoras* or mandrake, the root of which was often uncannily like a human form, and when plucked from the earth was believed to emit a species of human cry. It was also worn to ward off various diseases.

Because of the supposed danger from the resident demon when plucking the plant, an elaborate procedure was prescribed. The mandrake-gatherer was supposed to starve a dog of food for several days, then tie him with a strong cord to the lower part of the plant. The dog was then thrown pieces of meat and when he leapt forward to seize them he pulled up the mandrake.

Other folklore beliefs included the need for an elaborate prayer ritual before pulling the plant, which should only be gathered at dead of night.

For a detailed study of the role of mandrakes, see *The Mystic Mandrake* by C. J. S. Thompson (1934; University Books, 1968). (See also **Alrunes; Exorcism; Ginseng**)

Mandrake

Plant whose roots often bear an uncanny resemblance to a human form (see **Mandragoras**).

Manen

The priest of the **Katean Secret Society** of the Moluccas.

Mangan, Gordon Lavelle (1924-)

University lecturer in psychology who has made a special study of parapsychology. Born December 5, 1924 in Wellington, New Zealand, he studied at University of New Zealand (M.A. 1945), University of Melbourne, Australia (Ed.B. 1950), University of London, England (Ph.D. 1954). In 1954, he married Mary Wilshin.

After working as a high school teacher, he became a fellow of the Parapsychology Foundation, and research associate Duke University, 1954-56; assistant professor at Department of Psychology, Queen's University, Kingston, Ontario, Canada from 1956-58; lecturer in psychology at Victoria University 1958-61; senior lecturer in Psychology Department at University of Queensland, Australia from 1961 onwards.

He is a member of the American Psychological Association and British Psychological Society. In addition to his many writings on psychology, Dr. Mangan has published a monograph *A Review of the Published Research on the Personality Correlates of ESP* (Parapsychology Foundation, 1958). Other articles on parapsychology include: 'Parapsychology: A Science for Psychical Research?' (*Queen's Quarterly,* Spring 1958), 'How Legitimate Are the Claims for ESP?' (*Australian Journal of Psychology,* Sept. 1959) and contributions to the *Journal of Parapsychology:* 'A PK Experiment with Thirty Dice Released for High and Low Face Targets' (Dec. 1954), 'Evidence of Displacement in a Precognitive Test' (March 1955), (with L. C. Wilbur) 'The Relation of PK Object and Throwing Surface in Placement Tests' (vol. 20, 1956; vol. 21, 1957) 'An ESP Experiment with Dual-Aspect Targets Involving One Trial Day' (Dec. 1957); *(Parapsychological Monographs No. 1.) 'A Review of Published Research on the Relationship of Some Personality Variables to ESP Scoring Level' (1958).*

Mankind Research Foundation

Organization "to combine the efforts of leading researchers and experimenters in the multidisciplinary and interacting fields of human development and humanistic psychology which include research involving the body, mind and those forces and phenomena acting upon the health, education and welfare of mankind. Areas of study include biocommunication, biocybernetics, biophysics, psychophysiology, educational development, cancer research and mind-body developments."

Address: 1315 Apple Avenue, Silver Spring, Maryland 20910.

Manning, Matthew (1955-)

Remarkable young British psychic, whose phenomena include **poltergeist, apports, automatic writing, telepathy, precognition** and psychic art. When only a schoolboy aged eleven, Matthew was the center of extraordinary poltergeist disturbance at the family home in Shelford, Cambridge, England, involving repeated knocking and the movement of scores of small articles. After several weeks, the phenomena subsided but returned about a year later, accompanied by childish scribblings on walls and even high ceilings. Chairs and tables were disturbed and dozens of objects moved around in an extraordinary manner.

The phenomena followed Matthew to boarding school, where heavy beds were moved, and knives, nails, electric light bulbs and other objects sent flying through the air. Showers of pebbles and pools of water manifested, and strange lights appeared on walls.

One day, whilst writing an essay in his study, Matthew found himself involved in automatic writing, which signalled cessation of the poltergeist phenomena. Since then he regularly received hundreds of communications apparently from deceased individuals, some in languages unknown to him, including Italian, German, Greek, Latin, Russian and Arabic.

Following upon the automatic writing, he produced psychic art in the manner of Thomas Bewick, Thomas Rowlandson, Aubrey Beardsley, Paul Keel, Henri Matisse, Picasso and other great names with remarkable fidelity to the styles of these artists. He also discovered an ability to bend spoons in the manner of Uri **Geller** and to record startling demonstrations of some unknown force in himself by means of **Kirlian photography.**

His strange powers were described in his book *The Link* (Colin Smythe, U.K./Holt Rinehart, 1974).

Matthew duplicated the Uri Geller effect of starting inactive clocks and watches, as well as radios, tape recorders, music boxes and even electric lights. He had a premonition of the June 1975 plane crash near Kennedy Airport which killed 121 people, as well as the 1975 subway train disaster at Moorgate Station, England, in which 43 people died.

During a tour in Japan he appeared in a special television program, during which 1,200 callers jammed the studio switchboard with reports of bottles, glasses and other objects which exploded in their homes in the course of the transmission. Faucets turned on automatically, burglar alarms went off, auto engines switched themselves on. Lost articles reappeared, small objects materialized in homes, other objects disappeared, while watches and clocks went haywire. These and other remarkable phenomena are described in Matthew's second book: *In the Mind of Millions* (W. H. Allen, London, 1977). Matthew has also predicted that his own death will occur at an early date.

On August 7, 1977, he took part in an ESP test organized by the British newspaper *Sunday Mirror.* Matthew was stationed in London's Post Office Tower (580 ft. high). Between 6 and 6:15 p.m. he mentally transmitted three images: the color green, the number 123 and the shape of a house. Readers of the *Sunday Mirror* were asked to "tune in" to these images and send their results on a postcard. 575 of the 2,500 readers who cooperated scored the right color; one in 44 got the three-figure number right, about one in 30 identified a house-like shape. There were some 30 interesting "near-misses' in which readers reported the color green, the figure 123 and a shape of a triangle on top of a square, or the color green, the number 132 and a house. Mr. Michael Haslam, deputy honorary secretary of the Institute of Statisticians in London confirmed that the results were significantly higher than chance expectation.

Matthew was also the study of a Canadian documentary movie "A Study of a Psychic" made by the Bruce A. Raymond Co. between 1974 and 1977. President Bruce A. Raymond was formerly Controller of Programs at the Canadian Broadcasting Corporation and one of its chief executives. The movie is an objective record of Matthew's career, including interviews with members of his family, his headmaster and school friends. Extracts were shown on British television on the Brian Inglis "Nationwide" program produced by Granada TV.

In December 1977, Matthew created something of a sensation by stating that henceforth he preferred to be described as a "mentalist" instead of a "psychic." This statement came after three years of worldwide publicity as the western world's most gifted psychic, on the same day that Matthew appeared on the Russell Harty Independent Television talk show in London, which included filmed accounts from three first-hand witnesses of the poltergeist phenomena which surrounded Matthew when a schoolboy.

During the program he demonstrated automatic drawing and attempted telepathy tests. He also stated: "I believe also that a lot of people who are doing debunking in the name of science are merely forming a religion of their own, which I call humanism. . . . They believe there is no more to life than everything they can perceive physically, there is nothing beyond the five senses and that when one dies that is the end. They turn that into a religion. Obviously, what I am doing is to them threatening. That is why they will attack me."

During his 1977 U.S. tour, Matthew had been vigorously criticized by the U.S. magician James **Randi,** a well-known hostile opponent of paranormal phenomena who formerly spent much time in a campaign of denouncing Uri Geller as a "clever magician," whose metal-bending abilities are "merely tricks accomplished by sleight of hand."

Randi is a member of the **Committee for the Scientific Investigation of Claims of the Paranormal** (originally sponsored by the American journal. *The Humanist*) and author of *The Magic of Uri Geller* (Ballantine Books, 1975) in which he accused Geller of "massive fraud."

In September 1977, Randi attacked the British *Sunday Mirror* ESP test in the Post Office Tower, suggesting that Matthew Manning could have sent in "an important fraction of the postcards" himself. This and other implications of trickery were strongly refuted by Matthew, who stated: "The man who talks of 'falsehoods' makes statements himself which can be seen to be totally false by anyone who reads my book" (*In the Minds of Millions*). For reports on this controversy see the British newspaper *Psychic News* (September 10, 1977).

It seems possible that Matthew Manning's disclaimer of the term "psychic" in favor of "mentalist" may have been a defensive tactic in response to aggressive campaigns such as Randi's. The full statement by Matthew, delivered to Peter **Bander,** his former publisher and agent, was a front-page story in Britain's *Cambridge Evening News* (December 3, 1977), also reported in *Psychic News* (December 10, 1977). The statement reads:

"Dear Peter,—Without any disrespect to anything which may have been said or done in the past, I would prefer from now on to be known as a mentalist and not as a psychic, a description I have always resented and never liked.

"As I have no intention of giving interviews during my short stay in England, I would like you to be the first person to know. Perhaps you might also be so good as to pass this on to any pressman or future inquirers.

"Certain events in America, for example, have made me reconsider my position. I feel this is probably the best description to explain them.

"I reiterate that I do not wish to withdraw anything I have said or done in the past, and that I wish to be judged by what I'm doing now rather than by what I have been doing in the last four years.

"I have no intention of explaining this any further at present."

In his first book *The Link* (1974) which went into nineteen editions and was translated into many languages, Matthew had accepted the description "teenage psychic" and had described the first occasion that he "entered into direct communication with spirit entities." It may be that like other sensitive individuals in the history of psychic science and parapsychology, he felt threatened by a hostile debunking attitude going beyond criticism and speculation into the realms of psychic persecution.

Whilst no one would wish to defend uncritical acceptance of all claimed paranormal phenomena, it is equally unreasonable to denounce psychics as frauds without positive evidence, or to hound them with hostile criticism and attempt to trap them by trickery.

Such bullying goes far beyond acceptable standards of public courtesy and creates a negative atmosphere which can have a damaging effect upon the personality and actions of sensitive individuals with rare and little-understood talents. In certain instances it may even result in actual frauds through the creation of a strongly suggestible atmosphere.

In recent years, Matthew has specialized in forms of psychic healing, by touch, by sympathetic contact between individuals, by guided imagery, and mental disciplines.

He has founded the Matthew Manning Centre at 34 Abbeygate Street, Bury St. Edmonds, Suffolk, IP33 ILW, England. He has lectured widely on healing and issued audiotapes on the subject. (See also Psychic **Healing; Healing by Touch**)

Mansfield, J. V. (c. 1870)

Nineteenth-century American medium, advertised as the "spirit postmaster" in the *Banner of Light.* He obtained thousands of letters in sealed envelopes addressed to spirit-friends, read them clairvoyantly and wrote out replies automatically in various languages. German, Spanish, Greek, Arabic, Sanskrit and even Chinese answers were sometimes given.

Many witnesses testified to his powers. His scripts were preserved in evidence. His mediumship is described in Dr. N. B. Wolfe's *Startling Facts in Modern Spiritualism* (1875).

However, in The Report of the **Seybert Commission,** Dr. Furness, the acting chairman, discredited Mansfield's powers on the basis of a clairvoyant sitting and a sealed letter test.

For a detailed account of Mansfield's handling of an ingeniously sealed letter, see the *Spiritual Magazine* (1868, p. 425).

Manson, Charles M. (1934-)

Habitual criminal who achieved notoriety as charismatic leader of an infamous "Family" that indulged in sex orgies and brutal murders. Manson demonstrated that drugs, sex, occultism and crime can be an incredibly dangerous mixture.

As a young man, he was frequently arrested on such charges as car theft, parole violation, stealing checks and credit cards. He spent most of the 1960s in jail, where he learnt to play the guitar and studied hypnotism, psychological conditioning, **Scientology** and occultism, as well as reading avidly on the contemporary outside scene of the Vietnam War, peace rallies, rock and roll and the music of the Beatles. He was also greatly impressed by Robert Heinlein's science-fiction story *Stranger in a Strange Land,* which related how an alien intelligence formed a power base of sex and religion on the earth.

In 1967, Manson was released from jail and wandered around Berkeley, California, as a guitar-toting minstrel, picking up girls and spending time in the Haight-Ashbury section, experiencing the drug scene, occult boom and communal living. In the course of time he collected a kind of tribal family, mostly young girls, and established a hippie-style commune at various locales in the Californian desert, ranging over Death Valley in stolen dune buggies in a freaked-out atmosphere of drugs and sex orgies.

In time, Manson developed paranoid fantasies of a forthcoming Doomsday situation, supposedly revealed to him by an album of rock-music songs by the Beatles, particularly "Helter-Skelter" and "Piggies." Manson and his followers shared a delusion that "Helter-Skelter"symbolized an uprising of blacks, which could be exploited by the Family.

In 1969, under the influence of Manson's fantasies, his Family accepted him as a Satanic Jesus Christ, and indulged an orgy of sadistic murders. Manson, with Patricia Krenwinkle, Susan Atkins and Leslie Van Houten were found guilty of the murders of actress Sharon Tate (pregnant at the time) and four other people at her Bel-Air home in Los Angeles—Voyteck Frykowski, Abigail Folger, Jay Sebring and Steven Parent, as well as Leno La Bianca and his wife Rosemary, also in Los Angeles. Nine weeks after the verdict, the jury voted death sentences for all the accused. The trial, which opened July 21, 1970 had taken 32 weeks. During 1976, a movie reconstructing the trial, titled *Helter-Skelter,* was shown on television programs in the U.S.

On February 18, 1972, the California State Supreme Court abolished the death penalty in the state of California, thus reducing the sentence of condemned persons to life imprisonment, which permits a prisoner to apply for parole in seven years. However, this law does not appear to allow parole in the Manson case.

For a general account of the horrifying story of Manson and his family, see *The Family* by Ed Sanders (E. P. Dutton, 1971; Avon paperback, 1972). For detailed information on the trial of Manson and associates including the aftermath of the trial, with comprehensive data on other murders, see *Helter Skelter* by prosecuting attorney Vincent Bugliosi, with Curt Gentry (Norton, 1972; Bantam paperback, 1975; Penguin Books, 1977). Susan Atkins claims to have become a born-again Christian during imprisonment and has published (with Bob Slosser) *Child of Satan, Child of God* (Logos, 1977; Hodder & Stoughton paperback, 1978).

The violence associated with Manson did not cease with his imprisonment. In September 1984, in Vacaville prison, California, Manson was drenched with paint thinner and set on fire by another convicted killer, who claimed that Manson had threatened him for being a member of a Hare Krishna sect. Manson's head was scorched and most of his hair and beard burnt, but he was in a stable although serious condition.

A group of Manson's songs performed by him, recorded prior to the Tate-La Bianca murders, has been issued by Awareness Records, LP disc 0893-0156. The mediocre quality of these songs only enhances their sinister provenance. Producers that Manson had approached with his recordings received death threats, and it is claimed that Manson also targeted for assassination various famous recording artists whose only "crime" was their success (See also **Cults;** rev. Jim **Jones; Rosemary's Baby; Snapping**)

Mantra (or Mantram)

In Hindu mysticism, a mantra is a speech vibration which has a material effect on mind, emotions, physical body or even on physical processes in nature. The term is derived from the root *man,* "to think," and a mantra is thus an instrument of thought.

In Hindu religion, the material universe is said to be formed from divine vibration, a concept echoed in the Judeo-Christian concepts of divine utterance preceding creation—"And God said, let there be light . . . " (*Genesis* I, 3), "In the beginning was the Word, and the Word was with God, and the Word was God" (*John,* I, 1).

In Hinduism, the verses of the sacred scriptures the *Vedas* are regarded as mantras, because they have been transmitted from a divine source, rather like the Christian concept of the Bible as having power as the Word of God, but Hindus also recognize words and phrases as having special powers as expressions of the hidden forces of nature.

Divine creation becomes manifest in form throughout nature, and the latent reality behind form may be affected by correctly uttering the sounds which represent the ideal reality. These mantras were discovered by ancient sages skilled in the knowledge of the *Mantra Shastra* scripture, and taught to initiates.

The universe is called *Jagat,* "that which moves," because everything exists by a combination of forces and movement, and every movement generates vibration and has a sound which is peculiar to it. These subtle sounds have correspondences in the grosser sounds of speech and music, and so everything in the universe has an exact relationship. Everything has its natural name, the sound produced by the action of the moving forces from which it is constructed, thus anyone who is able to utter the natural name of anything with creative force can bring into being the thing which has that name.

The greatest mantra is the trisyllable A-U-M which precedes and concludes reading from the *Vedas* and is chanted as an individual mantra or magical prayer. The three syllables are associated with the processes of creation, preservation and dissolution and with the three states of consciousness (dreaming, deep sleep and waking).

The scripture *Mandukya Upanishad* describes how the trisyllable AUM is the basis of all the other letters in the Sanskrit language and associated with the universe and the human microcosm (analgous concepts exist in such Kabalistic works as the *Sepher Yesirah*). A mantra may also be associated with a Yantra, or mystical diagram. The whole paraphernalia of Western magic spells is clearly a decadent descent of such ancient Hindu mysticism.

Mantras are usually uttered in rhythmic repetition known as *japa,* often with the aid of a *mala,* the ancient Hindu precursor of the Christian rosary. In Japa Yoga, the power of a mantra is enhanced by the accumulation of repetitions. Although mantras have an automatic action, that action is enhanced by proper concentration and attitude of mind. The spoken mantra is also an aid to the mental mantra, which contains the inner meaning and power.

Popular spiritual mantras common in India include variants of the "Hari Rama, Hari Krishna" formula which has been popularized in the West by the Krishna Consciousness movement (see **International Society for Krishna Consciousness**) and the **Gayatri Mantra,** normally recited by Brahmins which involves meditation on the sun.

Special mantras are connected with the basic states of matter in connection with the *chakras* or subtle centers of the human body. These are known as *bija* mantras. (See also **Chakras; Kabala; Kundalini; Yoga**)

Recommended reading:

Easwaran, Eknath. *The Mantram Handbook,* Routledge & Kegan Paul, London, 1978

Gopalacharlu, S. E. *An Introduction to the Mantra Sastra,* Theosophical Publishing House, Adyar, India (paperback), 1934

Kalisch, Isidor (transl.) *Sepher Yezirah. A Book on Creation,* New York, 1877, reprinted A.M.O.R.C., San Jose, California 1950, etc.

Narayana, Har (transl.). *The Vedic Philosophy; or An Exposition of the Sacred and Mysterious Monosyllable AUM; The Mandukya Upanishad,* Bombay, 1895

Woodroffe, Sir John. *The Garland of Letters (Varnamala); Studies in the Mantra-Shastra,* Ganesh & Co., Madras, India, 1951 etc.

Manu

According to **Theosophy,** a grade in the theosophical hierarchy below the Planetary Logoi or Rulers of the Seven Chains. The charge given to *Manus* is that of forming the different races of humanity and guiding its evolution. Each race has its own *Manu,* who represents the racial type.

This Theosophical concept derives from Hindu mythology of *Manu* (man; thinker), a series of fourteen progenitors of the human race, each creation being destroyed in a Mahayuga (vast cycle of time) involving a deluge.

The *Manu* of the present creation is *Manu Vaivasvata,* who built an ark during a cosmic deluge and afterwards renewed the human race. He is the reputed author of the *Manava Dharma Shastra* or *Laws of Manu,* an ancient Hindu treatise which prescribes human religious and social duties.

Recommended reading:

Das, Ghagavan. *The Science of Social Organisation, or the Laws of Manu in the Light of Atma-Vidya,* 2nd ed., revised & enlarged, 2 vols., Theosophical Publishing House, Adyar, India, 1932

Mapes, James Jay (1806-1866)

Professor of Agricultural Chemistry, member of various learned societies, one of the early American converts to **Spiritualism**

He was born May 29, 1806 in New York City. After leaving school he worked as a chemist's clerk before entering business for himself. In 1827, he married Sophia Furman.

He invented a system of sugar refining in 1831, a machine for manufacturing sugar from cane, and a process for making sugar from West Indian molasses. He also invented a method of tanning hides, as well as improvements in distilling, dyeing, color making, and other industrial innovations. He received an honary degree of A.M. from Williams University in 1840. He was also a colonel in the New York state militia.

His conversion was the result of an investigation started to save his friends from "running to imbecility." Mrs. Cora L. V. Hatch (later **Richmond**) produced for him phenomena which he could not explain. Eventually Prof. Mapes became a believer in Spiritualism.

His wife, a lady of advanced age with no talent for art, developed **automatic drawing and painting** mediumship. She executed in a marvelously rapid manner several thousand watercolor drawings which met with praise. His daughter became a writing medium.

One of the early messages that came through the latter agency purported to emanate from Prof. Mapes' father, asking him to look up an encyclopedia, stored in a packing case 27 years before, and there on page 120 he would find his father's name written which he had never seen.

This was found true. With increasing interest Prof. Mapes investigated Katie Fox (See **Fox Sisters**), the **Davenport Brothers,** with whom he heard the first **direct voice** phenomena, and the manifestations of "John **King.**" He followed every new psychical discovery with keen interest.

He died January, 10, 1866.

Maple, Eric (William) (1915-)

British authority on witchcraft, demonology, the supernatural and folklore. In addition to his books on such subjects, he has also lectured widely and was a consultant on the publication *Man, Myth & Magic* (1967-70).

He has given special attention to the role of the so-called "white witch" in the history of witchcraft persecutions, and has also shown the interrelationship of witchcraft with ghost lore, **Spiritism** and the cult of the dead.

His books include: *The Dark World of Witches* (1962), *The Realm of Ghosts* (1964), *The Domain of Devils* (1966), *Magic, Medicine & Quakery* (1968), *Superstition and the Superstitious* (1971), *The Magic of Perfume* (1973), *Witchcraft—the Story of Man's Quest for Psychic Power* (1973), *Incantations & Words of Power* (1974), *The Ancient Art of Occult Healing* (1974), *Deadly Magic* (1976), *Supernatural England* (1977), *Ghosts: Monsters* (1978), (with Lyn Myring) *Haunted Houses; Ghosts & Spectres* (1979), (with Eliot Humberstone) *Mysterious Powers & Strange Forces* (1979), *The Secret Lore of Plants & Flowers* (1980), *Devils & Demons* (1981), *Old Wives Tales* (1981).

Marabini, Enrico (1923-)

Italian specialist in gynecology and obstetrics, also active in the field of parapsychology. Born November 12, 1923, at Casinalbo, Italy, he studied at Bologna University (M.D. cum laude 1949). In 1950 he married Sofia Cifiello. He is a member of Bologna Center of Parapsychological Studies. In 1948, he was one of the founders of the Centro Studi Parapsicologici (Center for Parapsychological Studies).

Dr. Marabini has taken special interest in clairvoyance, telepathy, psychokinesis and mediumship. He worked with mental and physical mediums for several years in controlled experiments concerned with psychosomatic aspects of paranormal behavior. However, he was unable to validate the authenticity of physical mediumship. He has since studied quantitative testing methods.

Some of his views are embodied in his article 'Una Nuova ESP?' (*Bulletin of the Italian Society for Parapsychology,* Jan.-June 1959). Other articles by Dr. Marabini include: 'La Telapatia' (Telepathy, *Metapsichica,* Nos. 1, 2, 3, 4, 1953), 'Esperienze di Telepatia collectiva eseguite nella Citta' di Bologna' (Experiments in Mass Telepathy in Bologna, *Metapsichica,* No. 1, 1954), 'Proposta di una modifica al test di Stuart per la Chiaroveggenza' (Proposal of a Modification of the Stuart Test for Clairvoyance, *Metapsichica,* No. 3, 1954); in *Parapsicologia di Minerva Medica* 'Esperienze trienneli di lettura della mano con una sensitiva Bolognese: Maria Guardini' (Three Years of Experiments in Hand-reading with the Sensitive Maria Guardini of Bologna, June 1957), 'Sogno paragnosico' (Paragnostic Dreams, June 1957), 'Il Comportamento paranormale in rapporto a stati neuro-endocrini) (Paranormal Behavior in Connection with Neuro-Endocrinological Conditions, Nov. 1957); in *Bulletin of the Italian Society for Parapsychology* 'Il Metodo scientifico in parapsicologia' (Scientific Method in Parapsychology, July-Dec. 1957), 'La Psi e' stata dimonstrata sperimentalmente?' (Has Psi Been Experimentally Demonstrated?, July-Dec. 1959); in *Proceedings* of the Third Congress of the Italian Society for Parapsychology 'Esperienze di psicometria con la sensitiva Luisa Godicini' (Experiments in Psychometry with the Sensitive Luisa Godicini, May 1956); in *Medicina psicosomatics* 'Problemi parapsicologici e psicosomatica' *(Parapsychological Problems and Psychosomatics,* No. 1, vol. 2, 1957).

Maranos

A Jewish secret fraternity which arose in Spain in the fourteenth and fifteenth centuries during the persecution of Jews in that country. Its members met in the greatest secrecy at inns, disguised, and used grips, signs and passwords (see *Freemasons' Magazine,* 1860, III, p. 416).

The term "marranos" (hogs) was used contemptuously at the time to denote Moors and Jews.

Marcellus Empiricus (c. 395 A.D.)

A Gallic-Roman writer born at Bordeaux in the fourth century. He was *magister officiorum* under Theodosius (379-395 A.D.) He wrote a work called *De medicamentis conspiricis physicis ac rationalibus,* a collection of medical recipes, for the most part absurd and worthless, and having more in common with popular superstition than with medical science.

Margaritomancy

Divination by means of pearls. A pearl was covered with a vase and placed near the fire, and the names of suspected persons pronounced. When the name of the guilty one was uttered the pearl was supposed to bound upwards and pierce the bottom of the vase.

"Margery"

Pseudonym of famous medium Mina Stinson **Crandon** (189?-1941).

Margiotta, Domenico (c. 1896)

Presumed author of *Souvenirs d'un Trente-Troisième; Adriano Lemmi chef suprème des francs-maçons* (1896) and *Le Palladisme, culte de Satan-Lucifer dans les triangles maçonniques* (1895), which violently impeached the Grand Master Lemmi of the crimes of Satanism and sorcery. These statements were amply proved to be without foundation.

It transpired that these books were part of the astonishing "Diana **Vaughan**" conspiracy of Gabriel **Jogand-Pagès** ("Leo Taxil"), designed to embarrass the Roman Catholic Church and **Freemasonry.** (see also Gabriel **Jogand-Pagès**)

Marie of Agreda (or Maria de Jesus) (1602-1665)

A Spanish nun, Maria Fernandez Coronel, who founded and was abbess of the Franciscan Recollects at Agreda. She published a work entitled *La mystica ciudad de Dios (The Mystic City of God, a Miracle of the All-powerful, the Abyss of Grace: Divine History of the Life of the Most Holy Virgin Mary, Mother of God, our Queen and Mistress, manifested in these last times by the Holy Virgin to the Sister Marie of Jesus, Abbess of the Convent of the Immaculate Conception of the town of Agreda, and written by that same Sister by order of her Superiors and Confessors).*

This work, which was condemned by the Sorbonne, described many strange and miraculous happenings said to have befallen the Virgin Mary from her birth onwards, including a visit to Heaven in her early years, when she was given a guard of nine hundred angels.

These revelations appear to have been the result of genuine spiritual raptures, but of a confused kind, being full of inaccuracies. Marie herself was said to have lived a pious life.

Marion, Frederick (1892- ?)

Stage name of Josef Kraus, famous European performer of stage telepathy and clairvoyance during the 1930s, who also claimed paranormal powers. Born in Prague, Czechoslovakia, October 15, 1892, he was the son of a business man and grew up in a practical atmosphere.

When he manifested psychometric and clairvoyant talents, his family was annoyed rather than impressed, and prescribed castor oil for an over sensitivity. At school, however, the boy became adept at games of locating hidden objects, and sometimes enlarged this talent by giving detailed descriptions and information relating to the owners of the objects. Towards the end of his school days, he found it expedient to present his psychic abilities in the form of so-called "tricks" at school concerts and other entertainments. He passed his final examination in mathematics, not because he understood the principles involved, but because he had the unusual talent of being able to memorize the test volume of problems and formulae from beginning to end.

After matriculation, he saw a newspaper report about a Viennese performer named Rubini who claimed special powers of finding concealed objects. Stimulated by his student friends, Marion issued a challenge that he could rival Rubini's feats. The story was taken up by a local newspaper, and a committee was appointed from amongst the Prague police and personalities of the city. Marion undertook to find, in a stipulated time, several objects hidden by the committee in different parts of Prague and described in a sealed envelope deposited at police headquarters.

Marion later stated that his spectacular success was due to the fact that he established telepathic communication with the chairman of the committee, and indeed, there seems no other way in which he could have obtained access to the sealed information.

He became an overnight celebrity, and at the age of nineteen was invited to perform at music halls throughout Europe. He was billed as "The Telepathic Phenomenon" or "The Man with Six Senses." In 1913, he appeared in Moscow on the same bill as Fred Karno's "Mumming Birds," a show which included Stan Laurel and a little clown who later became world famous as Charlie Chaplin. In England, Marion was sometimes billed as "The Human Bloodhound," since he had assisted the police in various continental countries to unravel crime mysteries through his telepathic powers.

During World War I, Marion served in the Austrian Army, and while stationed in Albania, tried his hand at water divining. He rapidly became so well known as a talented dowser that the military authorities presented him with a commission as an officer, and sent him to different areas to find water for the troops. He found traveling around the country somewhat arduous, and experimented with what has since become known as "Teleradiesthesia," holding his divining twig *over a large-scale map* instead of visiting the area (see **Radiesthesia**). He was remarkably successful, and this gave him more time to spare, which he spent in giving shows to entertain the troops. After a bullet wound and a bout of malaria, he was sent back to base at Innsbruck in the Tyrol.

After the war, he returned to his music hall demonstrations, and in 1920 met the remarkable stage clairvoyant Erik Jan **Hanussen,** who combined extraordinary talents with blatant trickery. Marion warned Hanussen that his growing preoccupation with black magic would have disastrous consequences, but the warning was not heeded. According to Marion, it was Hanussen who instructed the inner circle of the young Nazi Party in the power of signs and words, and first proposed the **swastika** as the Party symbol. Hanussen was later murdered by Nazi thugs in 1933, after disclosures which were embarrassing to the Party.

In his later years, Marion appeared less frequently at music halls, and confined his talents chiefly to lecture demonstrations and private consultations. In 1934, he visited England and gave impressive demonstrations of his psychic talents.

During a lecture at the Aeolian Hall, New Bond Street, London, he was challenged by Lady Oxford, who stated that his reconstructions of past incidents in the lives of members of his audience were too precise to be genuine, and must have involved confederates. Thereupon Marion correctly reconstructed an incident in the life of Lady Oxford's husband Lord Asquith, in August 1914, which no other person could have possibly known. Lady Oxford was tremendously impressed, and made a public apology, acknowledging that Marion's talent was genuine.

In 1934, Marion submitted to a long series of scientific experiments directed by Prof. S. G. **Soal** at the **National Laboratory of Psychical Research,** London. Soal was skeptical of Marion's ESP, but concluded that Marion had unusual **hyperaesthesia** or unusual acuity of the senses. Soal stated: "My laboratory experiments show that Marion performs his amazing feats by the aid of remarkable powers which are probably possessed by not one man in a million. There can be no question of either collusion or trickery in his public performances, judging from what I have seen him do single-handed in the laboratory. . . . " However, this hardly did justice to Marion's amazing feats outside the laboratory, including **precognition, clairvoyance,** and **telepathy,** which were less susceptible to scientific investigation.

Marion was also tested by noted psychical researcher Harry **Price,** chiefly in locating hidden objects. Price, like Soal, concluded that Marion somehow gathered imperceptible indications from the other individuals present who had seen the objects hidden. But he could not say how minute indications were possible, since Marion had no physical contact with the audience (as in the famous **"muscle reading"** technique by which some stage performers make contact with a spectator and can interpret imperceptible movements of their muscles towards or away from objects). Price even attempted to limit Marion's view to only one member of the audience, the others being screened by curtains. Then the single agent's body was further screened off progressively by a box with adjustable panels, so that at times only a fifth of his body was visible to Marion, and eventually only his feet! Even under such extraordinary conditions, Marion had a high rate of success.

After two years laboratory experiments, Dr. R. H. **Thouless** and Dr. B. P. Wiesner stated: "We can say definitely that we are satisfied that Marion shows paranormal capacities of an unusually high order under strictly controlled experimental conditions."

During World War II, Marion joined ENSA (the British troop entertainment service), and traveled around army camps, demonstrating his ESP talents at troop concerts. On May 23, 1946, he took part in a B.B.C. radio program investigating his psychic abilities, one of the first British radio presentations of a subject not then deemed quite respectable.

For detailed information on the life of Frederick Marion, see his autobiography: *In My Mind's Eye* (Rider, London, n.d., c. 1949). For reports on Marion's laboratory experiments, see *Confessions of a Ghost Hunter* by Harry Price (1936, reprinted Causeway Books, 1974); *Preliminary Studies of a Vaudeville Telepathist* (London Council for Psychical Investigation, Bulletin III, 1937). See also *Proceedings* of the Society for Psychical Research, London, vol. 50, 1949, pp. 80-85.

Mark Probert Memorial Foundation

Center which preserves tape recordings of sessions with Mark Probert, a trance medium of the 1950s. Now titled Inner Circle Kethra E'Da Foundation. The Foundation issues a catalog on request. Address: P.O. Box 11672, Palo Alto, California 94306.

Mark Twain (1835-1910)

Pseudonym of author S.L. **Clemens.** The great humorist and creator of Tom Sawyer and Huckleberry Finn wrote an article on "mental telegraphy" in 1880. This related a personal experience of **telepathy.** He also had a vivid premonitory dream of the death of his brother Henry (see *Mark Twain* by Albert Bigelow Paine, 3 vols., 1912). Twain was an early member of the **Society for Psychical Research,** London, until 1903.

After his death, various posthumous communications and writings were claimed. In 1917, a story *Jap Herron* was published in New York, purporting to come from the discarnate Mark Twain, as received by Emily Grant Hutchings and Lola V. Hays. Mrs. Hutchings, the recorder of the *Patience Worth* material of Mrs. John H. **Curran** of St. Louis, was herself an authoress who greatly admired Mark Twain. She had a keen sense of somewhat similar humor and a strong tinge of melancholy like Mark Twain's. She had strongly wished him to communicate through her. All this furnished an ideal condition for subconscious production.

Professor J. H. Hyslop resolved the problem by interesting cross-reference experiments. The two ladies received the communications through the **ouija board,** the presence of both of them being necessary to operate it. They were brought by Hyslop to Boston. He gave each lady, at separate times, five sittings with the medium "Mrs. Chenoweth" (see Mrs. M. M. **Soule**). But he did not admit them to the seance room until "Mrs. Chenoweth," who knew nothing of them, went into trance, and made them sit behind her where they could not be seen.

Instead of the usual family relatives, Mark Twain purported to communicate with each of them. He used many of the same expressions that came through the ouija board, mentioned incidents in his life to prove his identity, described what he was doing through the ladies, and revealed the password which he gave to Prof. Hyslop in a St. Louis sitting for cross reference with Miss Burton (Miss Ada **Besinnet**).

"The outcome of the experiments," concluded Prof. Hyslop in the *Journal* of the American Society for Psychical Research (July 1917), "is that there is abundant evidence that Mark Twain is behind the work connected with his name, though the student of psychology would probably find abundant evidence that it was colored more or less by the mind through which it came." The conclusion also applied to *Brent Roberts,* another posthumous Mark Twain novel which the two ladies received.

In Prof. Hyslop's *Contact with the Other World* (1919), a long chapter was devoted to other evidential spirit communications from Mark Twain.

Marriott, William S. (c. 1910)

British professional magician and illusionist who investigated and exposed fake mediumship. His stage name was "Dr. Wilmar."

One of Marriott's noted illusions was the production of apparently paranormal paintings, duplicating the claimed psychic phenomena of the Chicago mediums, the **Bangs sisters.** The illusion was presented as "Dr. Wilmar's Spirit Painting," and so impressed a fellow magician P. T. Selbit that he agreed to pay Marriott a weekly royalty for the use of the illusion. However, Marriott himself was not entirely straightforward in claiming rights on the illusion, since he had obtained the secret from David P. Abbott, an amateur magician. When Selbit presented the illusion at the Orpheum Theatre in Omaha in 1911, Abbott saw the show and visited Selbit backstage, when he learned that Selbit had already paid Marriott some $10,000 in royalties!

Marriott performed a valuable role in locating and publicizing a rare catalog of fake medium equipment titled *Gambols with the Ghosts: Mind Reading, Spiritualistic Effects, Mental and Psychical Phenomena and Horoscopy,* issued in 1901 by Ralph E. Sylvestre of Chicago. This catalog was designed for private circulation among fake mediums, on the understanding that it would be returned to Sylvestre when tricks had been selected from it.

The catalog had an introductory note which stated: "Our experience during the past thirty years in supplying mediums and others with the peculiar effects in this line enable us to place before you only those which are practical and of use, nothing that you have to experiment with. . . . We wish you to thoroughly appreciate that, while we do not, for obvious reasons, mention the names of our clients and their work (they being kept in strict confidence, the same as a physician treats his patients), we can furnish you with the explanation and, where necessary, the material for the production of any known public "tests" or "phenomena" not mentioned in this, our latest list. You are aware that our effects are being used by nearly all prominent mediums . . . of the entire world . . . "

This infamous catalog included equipment for fake slate-writing, self-playing guitars, self-rapping tables, materializations, and a "Complete Spiritualistic Seance." Marriott obtained a number of these illusions, and had himself photographed posing with them. Marriott also successfully exposed fake "spirit photographs," obliging that champion of Spiritualism Sir Arthur Conan Doyle to state ruefully "Mr. Marriott has clearly proved one point, which is that a trained conjurer can, under the close inspection of three pairs of critical eyes, put a false image upon a plate. We must unreservedly admit it."

A copy of *Gambols with the Ghosts* was obtained by psychical researcher Harry Price, and is now in the Harry Price Library of Magical Literature at the University of London, England.

Marryat, Florence (1837-1899)

Mrs. Ross-Church, later Mrs. Francis Lean, British authoress, daughter of novelist Frederick Capt. Marryat, acquainted with all the celebrated mediums of the seventies-eighties both in England and America, witness of the famous farewell of "Katie King" to Florence Cook at the seance held by Sir William **Crookes.**

Florence Marryat recorded remarkable experiences in two books: *There is No Death* (1891) and *The Spirit World* (1894), both of them immensely popular, and claimed mediumistic gifts herself, among them the strange power of summoning the spirits of the living.

These two books alone created a sensation and secured hundreds of converts to Spiritualism. But this versatile woman also published some ninety novels, wrote plays and acted in them, and edited a popular magazine. Many of her novels were translated into German, French, Swedish, Flemish and Russian and were also popular in America.

She died in London October 27, 1899. Her book *There Is No Death* has been frequently reprinted in Britain and was reissued by Causeway Books, New York in 1973.

In modern times, doubts have been cast upon the accuracy of the marvelous phenomena reported in this book (See J. A. Hill, ed., *Letters from Sir Oliver Lodge,* 1932, pp. 92-93), but at this distance of time it is difficult to evaluate the testimony of Florence Marryat.

That she was sincere there seems little doubt. An intelligent, hard-working and versatile authoress, she had already published over fifty novels (some of them three-deckers), about a hundred short stories, and numerous essays, poems and recitations, in addition to editing journals, lecturing, and touring as an actress with her own company. With such talents and an established reputation, she risked ridicule by espousing the Spiritualist cause in the last years of her life.

Mars, Louis (1906-)

Professor of psychiatry and former Haitian Ambassador to the U.S. who is also interested in parapsychology. Born September 5, 1906 at Grande-Rivière du Nord, Haiti, he studied at University of Haiti Medical School, Port-au-Prince (M.D. 1927) with postgraduate training in psychiatry at Faculté de Médecine, Paris, 1935, postgraduate study Columbia University, New York, N.Y., 1939-41, 1948. In 1943 he married Madeleine Targète.

He was professor of psychiatry, Medical School, University of Haiti in 1937, professor of psychiatry at Institute of Ethnology, University of Haiti 1946-49, dean of the Medical School from 1947-51, rector of University of Haiti 1957, Haitian Minister of Foreign Affairs from 1958-59, Ambassador to France 1960-61, Ambassador to the U.S. from 1962 onwards, director of Psychiatric Institute of Port-au-Prince.

He is a member of New York Academy of Medicine, Academy of the Rights of Man (Berlin); Holder of Grand' Croix, Ordre National Honneur et Mérite (Haiti); Grand' Croix, Ordre du Cèdre (Lebanon); Grand' Croix, Order of the Star of Africa (Liberia). Dr. Mars is author of *La Crise de Possession dans le Voudou* (The Crisis of Possession in Voodoo, 1955), and contributed an article 'Phenomena of Possession' to *Tomorrow* (Autumn 1954).

Marsh, Maurice Clement (1922-)

South African university lecturer in psychology who has taken special interest in parapsychology. Born March 13, 1922 at Bloemfontein, Union of South Africa, he studied at St. Andrew's School, Bloemfontein, University of South Africa (B.A. 1942, B.A. hons. psychology 1946, U.E.D. 1948), Rhodes University, Grahamstown, South Africa (Ph.D. psychology 1959). In 1950 he married Audrey Rittmann.

He served as a sergeant in South African Air Force, demonstrator in the Psychology Department at Rhodes University, teacher at Training School of African Student Teachers, Healdtown Missionary Institution, South Africa, lecturer in psychology at Rhodes University from 1950-61, lecturer in psychology at University of New England, N.S.W., Australia, from 1962 onwards.

He is a member of the Society for Psychical Research, London. Dr. Marsh's Ph.D. thesis dealt with experimental work in ESP and he is interested in laboratory investigation of psychical phenomena. He was a guest researcher at the Parapsychology Laboratory of Duke University, Durham, North Carolina, from November 1951 to January 1952. He has investigated ESP from the viewpoint of relationship between subjects and agents, and also the psychological aspects of conditions favorable to poltergeist, using psychological testing techniques.

Marshall, Mrs. Mary (1842-1884)

The first British professional medium, through whom Sir William **Crookes** and Dr. Alfred Russel **Wallace** obtained their introduction to the phenomena of Spiritualism.

Her manifestations consisted of **raps, movements** and **levitations** of the table, knotting handkerchiefs under the table-leaf and writing on glass. This latter appears to have been a rudimentary form of **slate-writing** with which, in the later-known form, she also confronted her sitters some time after. The first account of this demonstration was published by Thomas P. Barkas in *Outlines of Ten Years' Investigations into the Phenomena of Modern Spiritualism* (London, 1862).

On a small scale, Mrs. Marshall exhibited most of the phenomena of later mediums. From 1867 she held sittings for direct voice in which "John **King**" manifested. In her first seances she was assisted by her niece and occasionally by her young son. Her husband developed drawing mediumship.

A writer in the journal *All the Year Round* (July 28, 1860), characterized Mrs. Marshall's performance as a "dull and barefaced imposition," but Robert Bell, the celebrated dramatist, writing in the *Cornhill Magazine,* was satisfied that the phenomena were genuine spirit manifestations. (See also **Spiritualism**)

Marsi, The

According to Pliny, these people of ancient Italy were from the earliest times skilled in magical practices and sorceries.

They were able to charm poisonous serpents by means of songs. St. Augustine also wrote: "One would think that these animals understood the language of the Marsi, so obedient are they to their orders; we see them come out of their caverns as soon as the Marsian has spoken." (See also **Psylli**)

Martel, Linda (1956-1961)

Remarkable child spiritual healer, who was herself born crippled. Although she only lived for five years, she became a legend through her ability to heal a wide variety of illnesses through touch or through contact with material which she had touched. One of the most extraordinary aspects of her healing was that it persisted long after her death when only five years old.

Born August 21, 1956 at St. Peter Port, Guernsey, Channel Island, U.K., she suffered from hydrocephalus and spina bifida and her legs were paralyzed. After eleven days she was taken to St. Peter Port Hospital, Guernsey, to await death. Over the next few weeks, her head grew disproportionately large. During this period, her father experienced a strange phenomenon when his room was filled with a glowing light and he heard a sound like wind blowing. Linda did not die, and soon afterwards the Matron at the hospital arranged for her to have fluid drained away from her head by means of a new American treatment for hydrocephalus. The operation was successful and the size of the head reduced. However, Linda remained crippled.

At the age of three, Linda frequently spoke about "my Lady" and about Jesus. The Lady had a blue dress and gold chain and lived in heaven with Jesus and also looked after her. At the age of five, Linda foretold her own death, saying "My Jesus Christ is not coming to see me many more times, but I shall soon be going to see Him. . . . " She died October 20, 1961.

During her brief life, Linda manifested healing gifts, even as early as the age of three. Sometimes she would simply put her finger on a painful point, when a cure would take place. At other times, she healed through handkerchiefs which she had handled. After her death, a sufferer from asthma asked Linda's father whether he could have a piece of her clothing, and the father was persuaded to give him a piece of a dress. The sufferer was healed after contact with the material. After that, there were constant demands for pieces of Linda's clothing, and claimed cures through contact with them included warts, eczema, spinal injury, bone disease and throat cancer.

Because so many pieces of material associated with Linda were used up, her father presented one of her dresses to the Guernsey Museum, in the hope that it might be effective in healing through people simply looking at it, since the material itself was only the intermediary of some unknown force.

Recommended reading:

Martel, Roy. *The Mysterious Power of Linda Martel,* pamphlet. The Toucan Press, Guernsey, C.I., 1973.

Martello, Leo Louis

Contemporary Manhattan witch, hypnotist and graphologist. A self-styled exhibitionist, he has appeared on radio and television programs which he enlivens with a sharp wit.

His *Witch Manifesto* demanded $500 million damages from the Catholic Church and $100 million reparation payment from Salem, Massachusetts.

Calling himself "The Gay Witch," he makes no secret of his homophile predilections. He edits various witchcraft magazines, assisted by a young lady rejoicing in the name of Witch Hazel.

He is director of Witches International Craft Association (WICA), leader of the Witches Liberation Movement. He has published a number of popular books on occult subjects, including: *Your Pen Personality: Handwriting Analysis* (1961), *Weird Ways of Witchcraft* (1969), *Hidden World of Hypnotism* (1969), *Curses in Verses* (1971), *Understanding the Tarot* (1972), *Black Magic, Voodoo, Satanism* (1972), *Witchcraft: The Old Religion* (1974), *How to Prevent Psychic Blackmail* (1975).

Martial Arts

A group of Asian skills, combining mental, physical and spiritual energies for self-defense in weaponless fighting, or the achievement of apparently paranormal feats of strength and control.

The martial arts derive from the Samurai or warrior caste fighting systems of ancient Japan, which were conditioned by **Zen** Buddhism, hence they have a spiritual basis. They are closely related to similar systems in ancient China, and Japanese and Chinese martial arts are widely diffused throughout Asia.

These arts have become more widely known and taught in the U.S. since World War II, when many servicemen encountered them in Asian campaigns, and there are now many schools for specific training throughout the U.S. Another influence was that of the popular Chinese actor Bruce Lee, who popularized the art of *kung-fu* in such films as *Fist of Fury* and *Enter the Dragon.* The popular television movie series *Kung Fu* starring David Carradine also did much to popularize martial arts in the U.S. during the 1970s.

The main martial arts are: *aikido* (a kind of *judo* of graceful movement in which an opponent's force is used against him), *bando* (Burmese boxing and wrestling), *judo* (wrestling with special emphasis on balance and leverage), *jiu-jitsu* (a more comprehensive and aggressive forerunner of *judo*), *karate* (kicking, striking and blocking with arms or legs), *kung-fu* (a group of various styles of fighting and defense), *shaolin* (Chinese shadow boxing), *tae kwon do* (Korean system of kick-punching), *t'ai chi chuan* (originally a self-defense art, now a system of physical exercises to harmonize body and mind).

The various forms of martial arts have, as their basis, the attainment of spiritual enlightenment and peace, from which point remarkable feats of skill and strength in self-defense or attack can be generated.

In the process of training, a subtle vital energy named **ch'i** or *ki* is accumulated, amplified and directed by willpower to specific parts of the body, which develop strength and resilience.

This process is sometimes preceded by a sudden exhalation of breath, often accompanied by a shout or yell. The intake of breath which follows appears to result in hyperventilation of the system, generating vitality which can be directed to hands, feet or other parts of the body.

This process has been widely demonstrated by practitioners of *karate* in apparently paranormal feats such as breaking bricks, tiles and planks of wood with a bare hand. It has been suggested that these feats are related to such psychic phenomena as **Psychokinesis,** the ability to move objects at a distance by mental action.

Recommended reading:

Barclay, Glen. *Mind over Matter: Beyond the Bounds of Nature,* Arthur Barker, London, 1973; Pan paperback, 1975

Ching-nan, Lee & R. Figueroa. *Techniques of Self-Defense,* A. S. Barnes, 1963

Feldenkrais, Moshe. *Higher Judo,* Warne, 1952

Freudenberg, Karl. *Natural Weapons: A Manual of Karate, Judo & Jujitsu Techniques,* A. S. Barnes paperback, 1962

Huard, Pierre & Ming Wong. *Oriental Methods of Mental & Physical Fitness: The Complete Book of Meditation, Kinesitherapy, & Martial Arts in China, India, & Japan,* Funk & Wagnall paperback, 1971

Masters, Robert V. *Complete Book of Karate & Self-Defense,* Sterling, 1974

Medeiros, Earl C. *The Complete History & Philosophy of Kung Fu,* Tuttle, 1975

Nakayama, M. *Dynamic Karate,* Wehman, 1966

Tohei, Koichi. *This is Aikido,* Japan Publications, 1975

Westbrook, A. & O. Ratti, *Aikido & the Dynamic Sphere, Tuttle, 1970*

Martian Language

A language purporting to be that of the inhabitants of the planet Mars, written and spoken by the medium known as Hélène **Smith** (pseudonym of Catherine Elise Muller). Hélène was studied by the celebrated investigator, Theodore **Flournoy,** professor of psychology at Geneva. In 1892 Hélène had joined a Spiritualist circle, where she developed marvelous mediumistic powers.

In 1896, after Professor Flournoy had begun his investigations, Hélène claimed to have been spirited during a trance to the planet Mars, and thereafter described to the circle the manners and customs and appearance of the Martians. She learned their language, which she wrote and spoke with ease and consistency.

Unlike most of the "unknown tongues" automatically produced, the martian language was intelligible, its words were used consistently, and on the whole it had every appearance of a genuine language.

That it was in any way connected with Mars was, of course, out of the question. The descriptions of that planet and its inhabitants were quite impossible. And the language itself bore remarkable resemblance to French, the native tongue of the medium. The grammar and construction of both languages were the same, and even the vowel sounds were identical, so that the source of the Martian language was clearly an extraordinary construction from the medium's unconsciousness. (See also Hélène **Smith;** Speaking and Writing in **Tongues; Xenoglossis**)

Martin, Dorothy R(andolph) (1912-)

Associate professor of psychology with special interest in parapsychology. Born April 19, 1912 at Denver, Colorado, she studied at University of Colorado, Boulder, Colo. (B.A. 1934, M.A. 1936, Ph.D. 1947). She was assistant in psychology from 1934-37, instructor in psychology 1937-48, assistant professor of psychology 1948-58 University of Colorado; visiting associate professor of psychology at University of Kansas 1948-49; associate professor of psychology at University of Colorado from 1958 onwards.

She is a member of the American Psychological Association, Rocky Mountain Psychological Association, Colorado Psychological Association, American Association of University Professors and charter associate of the Parapsychological Association. She contributed various articles to the *Journal of Parapsychology,* including: 'Chance and Extra-Chance Results in Card Matching' (vol. 1, 1937), 'Studies in Extrasensory Perception' (with F. P. Stribic): 'An Analysis of 25,000 Trials' (vol. 2, 1938), 'An Analysis of a Second Series of 25,000 Trials' (vol. 2, 1938), 'A Review of All University of Colorado Experiments' (vol. 4, 1940).

Martin, Saint (of Tours) (c.316-400)

One of the most venerated Christian saints in Europe during the Middle Ages. Most of the luminaries of the Christian Church were credited with working miracles, and indeed the great majority of them maintained that if the people were to be won for Christ, the one sure way was to show them extraordinary marvels.

Even Columba, most engaging of saints, was not averse to practicing deception with a view to making converts, and it has often been suggested, not without considerable reason, that some of these early thaumaturgists brought science to their aid.

Perhaps St. Martin was among those who essayed this practice, and certainly the list of miracles attributed to him is formidable, for he is traditionally credited with considerably over two hundred.

Martin was born about the year 316 at Sabaria, in Pannonia. His parents were heathen, yet he very soon came into contact with Christians and their teaching impressed him greatly. As a young man he entered the army, and it was soon after this step that, while stationed with his regiment at Amiens, he performed his famous act of charity, dividing his cloak with a beggar who was shivering with cold. The night after this generous act he was vouchsafed a vision, Christ appearing to him and giving him his blessing. Thereupon Martin espoused the Christian faith formally, was baptized and renounced soldiering once and for all.

Going to Poitiers, he then made the acquaintance of Hilary, who wished to make him a deacon, but at his own request ordained him to the humbler office of an exorcist. A little later, during a visit to his home, Martin experienced the joy of winning his mother from heathendom to the new faith. However, his open zeal in opposing the Arians raised persecution against him, and for a considerable space he found it advisable to live at the island of Gallinaria, near Genoa, in which quiet retreat he had ample leisure for scientific researches and theological studies.

By the year 365, he was back with Hilary at Poitiers, when he founded the Monasterium Locociagense. In 371, the people of Tours chose him as their bishop, and for some time subsequently he showed great activity in trying to extirpate idolatry in his diocese, and in extending the monastic system.

Nevertheless, he was anything but a fierce proseletyzer, and at Trèves, in 385, he entreated that the lives of the Priscillianist heretics should be spared, while he ever afterwards refused to have anything to do with those bishops who had sanctioned their execution.

Meanwhile, being anxious for a period of quiet study, martin established the monastery of Marmontier les Tours, on the banks of the Loire, and here much of his remaining life was spent, although it was at Candes that his death occurred about the year 400.

Martin left no writings behind him, the *Confessio* with which he is sometimes credited being undoubtedly spurious. His life was written by his ardent disciple, Sulpicius Severus, and it is a curious document, filled with accounts of the miracles and marvels worked by the quondam bishop.

Martin was duly sanctified by the church, and he is commemorated on the 11th of November, but the feast of Martinmas, which occurs on that date, and which of course derives its name from him, is, nevertheless, a survival of an old pagan festival. It inherited certain usages thereof, this accounting for the fact that Martin is regarded as the patron saint of drinking, joviality, and reformed drunkards.

Certain of his miracles and other incidents in his life were figured by numerous painters of note, perhaps the finest picture of him being one by the Flemish master, Hugo van der Goes, which is now in the Municipal Museum at Glasgow.

It should be said that the term "martinet," signifying a severe and punctilious person, is not derived from the saint's name, but from one Jean Martinet, a French soldier who, during the reign of Louis XIV won fame by his ardor in promoting discipline in his regiment.

Martin, Stuart (died 1947)

British Spiritualist and journalist, formerly employed on the *Daily Mirror* newspaper. He was editor of the newspaper *Psychic News* from March 16, 1946 until his death on January 17, 1947.

Martinez, Louis

Prominent Mexican physical medium, supposed to have demonstrated **levitation** and **materialization** phenomena. In 1964 he was investigated by parapsychologist W. G. **Roll,** who found evidence of fraud on the part of one of the sitters.

Martiny, M(arcel) (1897-)

Physician with special interests in parapsychology. Born November 11, 1897 at Nice, France, he studied at Faculté de Médecine, Université de Paris, France (M.D. hons. 1925). In 1921 he married Thérèse Gagey. He worked for the Rockefeller Institute Mission during World War I, at Beaujon Hospital 1925-32, Léopold Bellan Hospital, Paris 1933-40, becoming head of medical staff 1940-45, after which he became a member of the medical staff, Hospital Foch.

From 1949 onwards he was director of the Anthropotechnical Laboratory, Prophylactic Institute, Paris. Other appointments include Secretary-General, Medico-Surgical Society of the Free Hospitals of France 1932, president of National Union of Physicians, Surgeons and Specialists of the Free Hospitals of France 1948, president of Physiopsychology Society 1958, president of Institute Métapsychique 1962; member of Paris Medical Society.

Dr. Martiny was author of various medical works and co-author with Dr. Alexis **Carrel** of *Médecine Officielle at Médecine Hérétique* (Orthodox and Unorthodox Medicine). He also spent many years investigating human bio-types in relation to parapsychological phenomena, parapsychology in relation to psychoanalysis, hypnosis and Pavlov's nervous typology in relation to parapsychology, relationships between neurology, cerebral function and parapsychology, space-time concepts in parapsychology. His articles on such subjects have been published in *Revue Métapsychique*. He also contributed papers to international conferences on parapsychology (Utrecht 1953; St. Paul de Vence 1954).

"Mary Celeste"

The name of a ship found abandoned at sea December 5, 1872, one of the most famous unsolved sea mysteries. Her sails were set, she was sound and seaworthy, with plenty of food and water, but not a soul on board. Some garments were hanging out to dry on a line. In the cabin was a slate with notes for the ship's log, with November 25 as the last date. The crew had left pipes, clothing and even oilskin boots. For some unknown reason the ship had been hurriedly abandoned.

The "Mary Celeste" was brought to Gibraltar by the crew of the British brig "Dei Gratia," who claimed salvage. On March 25, 1873, the Chief Justice awarded £1,700 to the master and crew of the "Dei Gratia" (about one-fifth of the total value).

Since then, the mystery of the "Mary Celeste" (sometimes inaccurately called "Marie Celeste") has been widely discussed and many theories advanced. There have also been various literary hoaxes, notably 'The Marie Celeste, the True Story of the Mystery' (*Strand Magazine,* November 1913) and the book *The Great Mary Celeste Hoax* by Laurence J. Keating (London, 1929).

Several years before the creation of Sherlock Holmes, author Sir Arthur Conan Doyle published 'J. Habakuk Jephson's Statement' in the *Cornhill Magazine* (January 1884), a romantic fictional yarn with an air of verisimilitude. The story was republished in Doyle's volume of short stories *The Captain of the Polestar* (London, 1890).

There is a useful discussion of the mystery in *The Stargazer Talks* by Rupert T. Gould (London, 1944; reissued as *More Oddities & Enigmas* (University Books, 1973). The most complete survey is that of Harold T. Wilkins in his book *Mysteries Solved and Unsolved* (London, 1958; reissued in paperback as *Mysteries,* 1961). For the factual background of the story see *Mary Celeste: The Odyssey of an Abandoned Ship* by Charles Eden Fay (Salem, Peabody Museum, 1942).

Maryland Center for Investigation of Unconventional Phenomena

Founded by Dr. Willard F. McIntyre and Arthur F. Rosen for the purpose of gathering and disseminating information of such phenomena as UFOs, Bigfoot, monsters, etc. The center issued a publication *Believe It.* Apparently no longer active. (See also **Fortean Society; Monsters**)

Marylebone Spiritualist Association, Ltd.

One of the earliest British Spiritualist organizations, founded February, 1872. It grew out of informal meetings at the Progressive Library of James **Burns** (editor of *The Medium and Daybreak* journal). In the early years, the Association hired halls for their meetings, often with some difficulty in view of prejudice against Spiritualism. In fact, the Association had to use the name "The Spiritual Evidence Society" in the beginning.

In 1879, premises were obtained in Marylebone, West London, and some famous mediums attended meetings, including Cecil **Husk,** Frank **Herne** and Charles **Williams.** In 1891, new premises were obtained in High Street, Marylebone, at an address which had formerly been a police court. The opening ceremony was performed by the famous writer Florence **Marryat.** In 1894, the Association was addressed by Emma Hardinge **Britten.**

Over the years, there were further changes of address, but many famous names in Spiritualism became connected with the Association.

Distinguished individuals who addressed meetings included such names as Dr. J. M. **Peebles,** Mrs. Cora L. V. **Richmond,** W. J. **Colville,** Sir Arthur Conan **Doyle** (at one time an honorary vice-president), the Rev. G. Vale **Owen,** and Hannen **Swaffer.**

In the course of time, the expansion of the Association's activities and scope led to its name becoming inapplicable, and by 1960 the title was the Spiritualist Association of Great Britain, now one of the largest organizations of its kind. It is located at 33 Belgrave Square, London, W.l. in spacious premises which include meeting hall, chapel, library, prayer and meditation room, and one floor devoted to spiritual healing. It is estimated that some 150,000 people visit these premises every year. (See also **Spiritualist Association of Great Britain)**

Maskelyne, John Nevil (1839-1917)

Famous British stage magician who was a strong opponent of fraudulent Spiritualism. Born at Cheltenham, Gloucestershire, December 22, 1839, he was the son of a saddlemaker.

As a boy he was fascinated by an entertainer who demonstrated spinning plates and practiced this feat himself. He was apprenticed to a clockmaker and at the age of nineteen made his first piece of conjuring apparatus, a box with a secret panel.

By 1865 he was giving demonstrations of amateur conjuring. After seeing the performance of the famous **Davenport Brothers,** he believed that he had observed trickery, and to prove his case he went into partnership with George Alfred Cooke to build a cabinet similar to that of the Davenports and rival their phenomena.

Maskelyne and Cooke were launched on a career of stage magic and leased the Egyptian Hall in London for their entertainments. By 1905, Maskelyne was in partnership with fellow illusionist David Devant (born David Wighton) at St. George's Hall, Langham Place in West London, where they based many of their presentations of the claimed phenomena of Spiritualism.

In 1906, he was involved in a controversy with Spiritualist sympathizer Archdeacon Thomas **Colley,** who had challenged him to reproduce the phenomena of medium F. W. **Monck** (incidentally exposed in fraud). Maskelyne staged a remarkable illusion, but Colley claimed it fell short of the requirements of his challenge. After a court case, Colley's claim was upheld, perhaps surprisingly in view of opposition to Spiritualism at that time.

Maskelyne's publications included: *The Fraud of Modern "Theosophy" Exposed* (1912), *Modern Spiritualism; A Short Account of its Rise and Progress, with some exposures of so-called spirit media* (n.d.)

Notwithstanding his sweeping denunciations of Spiritualism as fraudulent, Maskelyne did not absolutely disbelieve in the supernatural. (See also **Fraud; Magicians)**

Masleh

The angel whom the Jews believed ruled the Zodiac. According to a rabbinical legend, Masleh was the medium through which the power and influence of the Messiah was transmitted to the sphere of the Zodiac.

Mass of St. Secaire

A form of **Black Mass** originating in the Basque countryside, possibly in medieval times. It was a travesty of a Christian mass and celebrated in a ruined church.

The intention was not to worship the Devil, but to direct currents of malevolent spite against a victim. It may have had its origin in ancient folklore practices. For a description, see H. T. F. Rhodes, *The Satanic Mass* (London, 1954; Arrow paperback 1964).

Masse, François (1891- ?)

Commissaire général, French Navy, with interests in parapsychology. Born May 10, 1891 at Vendome, France, he entered the French Navy and served in World War I and II, retiring as commissaire général 1946. He was Commander, Legion of Honor. In 1925 he married Colette Vignal.

He was a member of the Institut Métapsychique International from 1948 onwards, serving as general secretary, and secretary-treasurer. He collaborated with Rene **Warcollier** in telepathy experiments and contributed articles on parapsychological topics to *Revue Métapsychique*.

Massey, Gerald (1828-1907)

British poet, born May 29, 1828 in Hertfordshire, England. He grew up in abject poverty and had to earn a living by working in a factory at the age of eight. He learnt to read at a penny school. He became a Socialist and edited a radical journal. He also wrote poems, which were favorably noticed by established poets such as Browning and Tennyson. His first wife was Rosina Knowles, a Spiritualist medium.

He based his volume of poetry *A Tale of Eternity* on personal experience of a haunted house. He lost some of his earlier popularity when he was said to have gone over to the Spiritualists. He admitted: "For the truth's sake I ought to explain that the spiritualism to be found in my poetry is no delusive idealism, derived from hereditary belief in a resurrection of the dead. My faith in the future life is founded upon facts in nature and realities of my own personal experience. These facts have been more or less known to me personally during forty years of familiar face-to-face acquaintanceship, therefore my certitude is not premature; they have given me proof palpable that our very own human identity and intelligence do persist after the blind of darkness has been drawn down in death."

At the meeting in London in 1872 which bade farewell to Mrs. Emma Hardinge **Britten** on her departure to Australia, Gerald Massey presided. His address with some additions was later printed under the title *Concerning Spiritualism*.

Massey's genius was unrecognized during his lifetime. In his later years he published four large volumes in which he tried to trace the origin of language, symbols, myths and religions in a similar way to that other bold thinker Godfrey **Higgins** (1772-1833).

This vast compendium, in which he cited Africa as the birthplace of mankind, was ignored or ridiculed until recent times, when archaeological discoveries have validated his main theme. His books have now been reprinted, and may earn a more tolerant evaluation. *A Book of the Beginnings*, 2 vols., first published London, 1881, reissued University Books Inc. 1974; *The Natural Genesis*, 2 vols., first published London, 1883; *Ancient Egypt*, 2 vols., first published London, 1907, reissued Samuel Weiser.

Masters

Occult adepts who are supposed to have reached a superhuman stage but elected to remain on earth and guide seekers after wisdom. The founding and guidance of the **Theosophical Society** of Madame **Blavatsky** was supposed to be due to hidden Masters or Mahatmas living in remote Tibetan fastnesses.

Much of Western occultism derives from romantic concepts of adepts with magical powers, but in Hinduism, mystical awareness of God-realization is considered superior to paranormal feats, and to the Hindu pupil the Master is his guru. The term *Mahatma* is used to indicate a special guru or "great soul," and *Maharishi* or *Maharshi* denotes a great sage of transcendental wisdom. Another Sanskrit term *Paramahansa* (literally "greatest swan") is given to a very exalted mystic.

The five Masters claimed by Madame Blavatsky were: Koot Hoomi Lal Singh (usually signing letters "K.H."), the Master Morya (known as "Master M."), Master Ilarion or Hilarion (a Greek), Djual Khul (or "D.K."), and the Maha Chohan. (See also **Adepts; Golden Dawn; Great White Brotherhood; Guru; Mahatma; Theosophical Society**)

Masters, Robert E. L.

Co-founder with wife Jean **Houston** of the **Foundation for Mind Research**, Manhattan, New York, conducting experiments in the borderline between mental and physical experience. Masters has a background of poetry and sexology and was formerly director of the Visual Imagery Research Project, and the Library of Sex Research.

Both Houston and Masters have experimented with psychedelic drugs and hypnosis, and in their Foundation they have investigated induction of mystical experience and altered states of consciousness.

In collaboration with his wife, Masters is author of: *The Varieties of Psychedelic Experience* (1966), *Mind Games; the Guide to Inner Space* (1972), *Listening to the Body* (1978). He has also published: *Eros and Evil; The Sexual Psychopathology of Witchcraft* (1962), *Forbidden Sexual Behavior and Morality* (1962), *The Homosexual Revolution; A Challenging Exposé of the Social & Political Directions of a Minority Group* (1962). (See also **Foundation for Mind Research; Witches' Cradle**)

Mastiphal

The name given to the prince of demons in an apocryphal book entitled *Little Genesis*, which was quoted by the Greek monk and historian Cedrenus (11the century).

Material for Thought

Journal concerned with Eastern and Western teachings concerned with the inner search for self. Address: Far West Press, 3231 Pierce Street, San Francisco, California 94123.

Materialization

The claimed manifestation of temporary, more or less organized, substances in various degrees of solid form and possessing human physical characteristics of limbs, faces, eyes, heads or full figures, shaped for a temporary existence out of a substance named "**ectoplasm,**" Such materializations are generally believed by Spiritualists and some psychical researchers to be due to spirit agency, although other believe that they might arise from some rare and unknown natural force independent of departed spirits, but arising from a gifted psychic.

Materialization is certainly one of the most controversial of claimed paranormal phenomena and it is unfortunate that in modern times the phenomenon is rare and therefore not easily accessible to improved laboratory techniques of investigation. It must also be admitted that many mediums of the past have been exposed in fraudulent materializations and that trade catalogs of apparatus for such frauds were well known.

As one of the most important of the physical phenomena of spiritualism, materialization suggests connections with the appearance of apparitions and perhaps the tenuous "astral projection" forms of **out-of-the-body** experience. Other possible connections may exist with the **"thoughtforms"** of **psychic photography** and the "spirit figures" of **spirit photography**. If mental images may travel across space in **telepathy**, the claim that images might assume a more solid plastic organization under certain conditions does not appear altogether absurd.

In its earlier stages, materialization was confined to the materializing of heads and hands, or vague luminous streaks of light and, later, figures. In common with much of the physical phenomena of Spiritualism, it had its origin in America, where it was reported at a comparatively early period in the history of the movement.

As early as 1860, seances were held with the Fox Sisters by Robert Dale Owen and others, at which veiled and luminous figures were recognized. One sitter, Mr. Livermore, claimed to see and recognize the spirit of his dead wife during seances with Kate Fox extending over some six years. However, there were no other sitters and the seances were held in the dark.

In England, the medium Frank **Herne** and Charles **Williams** succeeded a few months later in apparently materializing shadowy forms and faces in a dark seance room.

However, it was Florence **Cook**, whose phenomena was so strongly championed by scientist Sir William **Crookes** who produced the most sensational materializations. At the commencement of her Spiritualistic career, she was a pretty young girl of sixteen or seventeen years. She was at that time a private medium, though at the outset she held some materialization seances with Herne.

From her childhood, it was said, she had been attended by a spirit-girl, who stated that her name on earth had been "Annie Morgan," but that her name in the spirit-world was "Katie **King.**" Under the latter name Miss Cook's **control** was destined to become very famous in Spiritualist circles.

Usually the medium was put in a sort of cupboard or cabinet, tied to her chair, and the cords sealed. A short interval would ensue, during which the sitters sang Spiritualist hymns, and at length there would emerge from the cabinet a form clad in flowing white draperies, and difficult to distinguish from an ordinary human being.

On one occasion, a seance was held at Mr. Cook's house, at which several distinguished spiritualists were present. Among the invited guests was Mr. W. Volckman, who thought to test for himself the good faith of the medium and the genuineness of "Katie." After some forty minutes close observance of the materialized spirit, Mr. Volckman concluded that Miss Cook and "Katie" were one and the same, and just as the white-robed figure was about to return to the cabinet he rushed forward and seized her. His indignant fellow-sitters released the "spirit," the light was extinguished, and in the confusion that followed the spirit disappeared. Miss Cook was found a few minutes later bound as when she was placed in the cabinet, the cords unbroken, the seal intact. She wore a black dress, and there was no trace of white draperies in the cabinet.

Sir William Crookes, whose investigations into the phenomena of this medium extended over a period of some years, had better opportunity of examining Katie's claims that Mr. Volckman, and he had left it on record that the spirit form was taller that the medium, had a larger face and longer fingers, and whereas Florence Cook had black hair and a dark complexion, "Katie's" complexion was fair, and her hair a light auburn. Moreover Sir William, enjoying as he did the complete confidence of "Katie," had on more than one occasion the privilege of seeing her and Miss Cook at the same time. However, in modern times strong doubts have been expressed about the genuineness of the spirit form.

But Florence Cook was not the only medium who was controlled by "Katie King," who, with her father, "John King," became in time a most popular spirit with materialization mediums. From that time onwards materialization was extensively practiced both by private and professional mediums, among the number being Mrs. **Showers** and her daughter, Miss Lottie **Fowler**, William **Eglinton** and D. D. **Home**; while in later years materializations were state to have occurred in the presence of Eusapia **Palladino**.

Many sitters claimed to see in such draped figures and veiled faces the form and features of deceased relatives and friends, although frequently there was but the smallest ground for such a claim—parents recognized their daughter by her hair, a man recognized his mother by the sort of cap she wore, and so on.

There is no doubt that fraud entered very largely into materialization seances. Lay figures, muslin draperies, false hair, and similar properties have been found in the possession of mediums; accomplices have been smuggled into the seance-room; lights are frequently turned low or extinguished altogether. Add to this the fact that other spirits besides "Katie" have, on being grasped, resolved themselves into the person of the medium, and it will be seen that skepticism is not altogether unjustified. Then, as already mentioned, the rash and premature recognition of deceased friends in draped forms whose resemblance to the medium is patent to the less-interested observer, has also done much to ruin the case for genuine spirit materialization.

Yet that there is a case we must believe on the assertion of some of the most distinguished of modern investigators, men fully alive to the possibilities of fraud, trained to habits of correct observation.

Psychical Researchers and Materialization

Camille **Flammarion** attributed the materializations he had witnessed in the presence of Eusapia **Palladino** to fluidic emanations from the medium's person, while judging the recognition accorded to them the result of illusion. Other researchers state that the physical organization formed by the spirit was composed of fine particles of matter drawn from the material world.

According to Gustav **Geley** in his book *Clairvoyance and Materialisation* (1927), this " is no longer the marvellous and quasi-miraculous affair described and commented on in early spiritualistic works."

"I shall not waste time" stated Prof. Charles **Richet** in *Thirty Years of Psychical Research* (1923) "in stating the absurdities, almost the impossibilities, from a psychophysiological point of view, of this phenomenon. A living being, or living matter, formed under our eyes, which has its proper warmth, apparently a circulation of blood, and a physiological respiration which has also a kind of psychic personality having a will distinct from the will of the medium, in a word, a new human being! This is surely the climax of marvels! Nevertheless, it is a fact."

He suggested that "materialisation is a mechanical projection; we already know the projection of light, of heat and of electricity; it is not a very long step to think that a projection of mechanical energy may be possible. The remarkable demonstrations of Einstein show how close mechanical or luminous energy are to one another."

"I have also, like Geley, Schrenck Notzing, and Mme. Bisson, been able to see the first lineaments of materialisations as they were formed. A kind of liquid or pasty jelly emerges from the mouth or the breast of Marthe which organises itself by degrees, acquiring the shape of a face or a limb. Under very good conditions of visibility , I have seen this paste spread on my knees, and slowly take form so as to show the rudiment of the radius, the cuvitus, or metacarpal bone whose increasing pressure I could feel on my knee."

The Marthe of Prof. Richet's account was the medium Marthe Béraud, also known as "**Eva C**". Geley related his experiences with her: "I have very frequently seen complete representations of an organ, such as a face, a hand, or a finger. In the more complete cases the materialised organ has all the appearance and biologic functions of a living organ. I have seen admirably modelled fingers, with their nails; I have seen compete hands with bones and joints; I have seen a living head, whose bones I could feel under a thick mass of hair. I have seen wel-formed living and human faces! On many occasions these representations have been formed from beginning to end under my own eyes. . . . The forms have, it will be observed, a certain independence, and this independence is both physiological and anatomical. The materialised organs are not inert, but biologically alive. A well-formed hand, for instance, has the functional capacities of a normal hand. I have several times been intentionally touched by a hand or grasped by its fingers. . . . Well-constituted organic forms having all the appearance of life, are often replaced by incomplete formations. The relief is often wanting and the forms are flat. There are some that are partly flat and partly in relief, I have seen in certain cases, a hand or a face appear flat, and then, under my eyes assume the three dimensions, entirely or partially. The incomplete forms are sometimes smaller than natural size, being occasionally miniatures." (*From the Unconscious to the Conscious*, 1920)

On June 13, 1913, the ectoplasm emerged from the medium's mouth with a materialized finger at the end. M. Bourbon took hold of the finger as it came from Eva's mouth and verified the bone in it. The tulle which covered the medium's head showed no hole.

From Thought-forms to Full Grown Phantoms

Many of the photographs taken of Eva C's materializations suggest the evolution of **thought-forms**. Prof. Daumer contended that ectoplasmic forms were neither bodies nor souls. He offered the name: eidolon (shape). A number of Eva C's phantom forms were such shapes and resembled pictures she had seen, caricatures of presidents Wilson and Pioncaré, and they often had folds as if a paper had been uncreased to be photographed.

Prof. Richet remarked that the supposition of fraud would presume extreme stupidity of Eva's part as she knew that photographs would be taken, moreover that there is no ground to suppose that a materialization must be analogous to a human body and must be three dimensional. "The materialisation of a plaster bust is not easier to understand than that of a lithographic drawing; and the formation of an image is not less extraordinary than that of a living human head."

Professor Daumer's speculation is strangely contrasted by Dr. Glen **Hamilton**'s report (*Psychic Science*, January 1933) on the building and photographing of a three dimensional ectoplasmic ship in the Winnipeg circle. The entities "John King" and "Walter" claimed responsibility for the experiment. Coming through the mediums Mary M. and X, they carried on a dialogue feigning that they were aboard John King's pirate ship and amongst a crew of piratical ruffians. It was hinted that this play-acting had a psychological purpose: the recovery of past memories and the creation of the thought image of a sailing ship. Eventually the ship was built, but owing to some indecision in giving the signal to take a flash photograph, it "came into port badly damaged." Dr. Glen Hamilton remarked:

"No matter how great we may conceive the unknown powers of the human organism to be, we cannot conceive of it giving rise to an objective mass showing purposive mechanistic construction such as that disclosed in the ship teleplasm of June 4th [1903]. We are forced to conclude that the supernormal personalities in this case (by some means as yet unknown to us) so manipulated or otherwise influenced the primary materialising substance after it had left the body of the medium, or was otherwise brought into its objective state, as to cause it to represent the idea which they, the unseen directors, had in view, namely the idea of a sailing ship." (*Psychic Science*, vol. 11, No. 4, Jan. 1933)

Generally the appearance of images instead of forms may have something to do with the quantity of available power. It is suggestive that Geley often observed strange, incomplete forms, imitations or simulacra of organs. "There are *simulacra* of fingers, having the general form but, without warmth, flexibility, or joints; *simulacra* of faces like masks, or as if cut out of paper, tufts of hair adhering to undefined formations, etc.

In explanation Geley expressly stated: "They are the products of a force whose metapsychic output is weak and whose means of execution are weaker still. It does what it can. It rarely succeeds, precisely because its activity, directed outside the normal lines, has no longer the certainty which the normal biologic impulse gives to physiological activity." He compared them to the strange formations called dermoid cysts, in which are found hair, teeth, divers organs, viscera, and even more or less complete fœtal forms. The supernormal physiology, like normal physiology, has its finished products and its abortions, monstrosities and dermoid cysts.

The essential thing is that "the formations materialised in mediumistic seances arise from the same biological process as normal birth. They are neither more nor less miraculous or supernormal; they are equally so. The same ideoplastic miracle makes the hands, the face, the viscera, the tissues, and the entire organism of the foetus at the expense of the maternal body, or the hands, the face, or the entire organs of a materialisation. This singular analogy between normal and so-called supernormal physiology extends even to details; the ectoplasm is linked to the medium by a channel of nourishment, a true umbilical cord, comparable to that which joins the embryo to the maternal body. In certain cases the materialised forms appear in an ovoid of the substance.... I have also seen on several occasions, a hand presented wrapped in a membrane closely resembling the placental membrane. The impression produced, both as to sight and touch, was precisely that of a hand presentation in childbirth, when the amnion is unbroken. Another analogy with childbirth is that of pain. The moans and movements of the entranced medium remind one strangely of a woman in travail."

To the legitimate objection why is one biological process regular and the other exceptional, Geley returned the answer that "normal physiology is the product of organic activity such as evolution has made it. The creative and directive idea normally works in a given sense, that of the evolution of the species, and conforms to the manner of that evolution. Supernormal physiology, on the other hand, is the product of ideoplastic activity directed in a divergent manner by an abnormal effort of the directive idea."

Geley certainly showed a greater understanding of all the complexities of the phenomena than Baron **Schrenck-Notzing** when the latter categorically concluded that "a continuation of the materialisation of organic parts beyond the field of vision of the observers is non-existent." It has been suggested that the Baron's interest in anatomy was instrumental in the immature formations, just as Dr. W. J. **Crawford**'s experiments in engineering training may have contributed to the evolution of cantilever functions. Similarly, the appearances resembling internal organs in "Margery's" mediumship may have had something to do with Dr. **Crandon**'s work as a surgeon.

In a higher degree of development we find that the ectoplasmic shapes tend to conform to the bodily pattern of the medium. "I have seen, with my natural vision," state the Rev. J. B. **Ferguson**, "the arms, bust and, on two occasions, the entire person of Ira E. Davenport duplicated at a distance of from two to five feet where he was seated fast bound to his seat. I have seen, also, a full-formed figure of a person, which was not that of any of the company present. In certain conditions, not yet clearly understood, the hands, arms and clothing of the Brothers Davenport and Mr. Fay are duplicated alike to the sight and the touch. In other cases, hands which are visible and tangible, and which have all the characteristics of living human hands, as well as arms, and entire bodies, are presented, which are not theirs or those of anyone present."

Crookes was satisfied that "Katie King" was independent from the medium Florence Cook. Yet on certain occasions he noted a striking resemblance between phantom and medium. There is a highly curious account in the history of the medium Mme. **d'Esperance** which seems to suggest that a total exchange is within the bounds of possibility. Under the auspices of Alexander **Aksakof** and Matthews Fidler, savants from different parts of Europe were holding a series of sittings with Mme. d'Esperance in Sweden. A crucial test was asked and the medium bravely stated to "Walter," the spirit control, that she would take the responsibility. So wrote Mme. d'Esperance:

"A very uncomfortable feeling pervaded the circle but it afterwards gave place to one of curiosity. My senses became keenly alert, the cobwebby sensation, before described, grew horribly intense, and a peculiar feeling of emptiness, which I had previously had, became so strong that my heart seemed as though swinging loosely in an empty space, and resounding like a bell with each stroke. The air seemed to be full of singing, buzzing sounds that pressed on my ears, but through it I could hear the breathing of the sitters outside the curtains. The movements made in the air seemed to sway me backwards and forwards. A fly alighting on my hand caused a pain like that of a toothache to shoot up my arm. I felt faint, almost dying.

"At last the arranged-for signal was given, that all was ready. The curtains were thrown open, and a materialised form stood fully revealed beside me. The lens of the camera was uncovered, the plate exposed, the magnesium light flashed. Then the curtains fell together. I remember the feeling of relief and thinking: Now I can give way. It is possible that I did faint. I do not know. But I was aroused by the sound of a voice saying in my ear: She is not here, she is gone. It was one of the family who spoke and the terror in the boy's voice roused me effectually. I wanted to reassure him, and asked for water, and wondered at the same time whose voice was it that made the request. It was like my own but seemed to come from the air or from another person. The water was brought and drunk, but though I felt refreshed the act seemed to be performed by that other person who had spoken. Then I was left alone . . .

"Now comes the strangest part of this strange experiment. The photographic plate was carefully developed and a print made, which revealed a most astonishing fact. The materialised form, well in focus, was clad in white, flowing garments. The hair was hanging loosely over the shoulder, which, like the arms, were without covering. The figure might have been that of a stranger, but the features were unmistakably mine. Never has a photograph shown a better likeness. On a chair beside it and a little behind, was a figure clad in my dress, the black bands on the wrist, and the tape round the waist showing themselves clearly and intact, but the face was that of a stranger, who seemed to be regarding the proceedings with great complacency and satisfaction. Needless to say, we looked at this extraordinary photograph with something like petrifaction. We were utterly at a loss to understand its meaning, and no explanation was forthcoming, except a rueful remark from "Walter," who when questioned replied that "Things did get considerably mixed up."

In *Light* (December 19, 1903), L. Gilbertson remarked: "My own theory of the strange head is that the manifesting spirit was driven out of the materialised form by Madame's sub-self, which had gained an abnormal excess of power through the weak condition of her normal organism. Finding itself ousted, the visitor took refuge with Madame's other part, and proceeded to operate on it in the way generally known as "transfiguration." Succeeding in this operation, it is not difficult to believe, as Madame says, that it "seemed to be regarding the proceedings with great complacency and satisfaction."

If the health of the medium is weak or the power, for any other reason, low, materialization usually does not progress beyond the stage of resemblance to the medium. It is a staggering phenomenon in itself and it vindicates Prof. Enrico **Morselli**'s psycho-dynamic theory (*Psycologia e Spiritismo*, 1907) according to which the ectoplasmic substance is the result of a kind of human radioactivity and the directive idea seems to have its origin in the mediums' subconscious mind. But Morselli also adds that the mediums's subconscious mind may establish telepathic communication with the sitter's subconscious mind and may shape the ectoplasmic forms into conformance to their thoughts and desires. Or it may be conceived that the medium transmits her psycho-dynamic forces to the spectator and he, by a sort of catalytic action, objectifies his own emotional complexes.

The second part of the hypothesis is a far-fetched assumption. the first is borne out by many observations. St. Augustine believed that the angels make themselves visible by the agency of elements taken from the air. We know better. Surely the human body plays the paramount part. The influence of the human mind, however, is noticeable up to a certain stage only. The phantom shapes do not keep for long the physiognomy, gestures and voice of the medium and disclose, after the transitory period, an apparent independence. Their body has temperature, blood circulation, exhales carbonic acid and behaves in every way as an unrelated entity.

"I took a flask of baryta water," writes Prof. Richet of his experiments with the materialized "Bien Boa" in the Villa Carmen, "to see if his breath would show carbon dioxide. The experiments succeeded. I did not lose sight of the flask from the moment when I put it into the hands of Bien Boa, who seemed to float in the air on the left of the curtain at a height greater than Marthe could have been if standing up. While he blew into the tube the bubbling could be heard."

According to the American researcher Epes **Sargent**, a spirit has been known to cut its finger with a knife, then borrow a handkerchief to wind around the wound, and at the end of the sitting, to return the handkerchief marked with blood. However, this is surely more consistent with fraud.

The materialized form may be physically more perfect than the medium. Crookes found that the lungs of "Katie King" were sounder at a time when Miss Cook was undergoing medical treatment for bronchitis. "Katie" also proved her distinct individuality by changing the color of her face to chocolate and jet black. She did this repeatedly because she was told that she resembled the medium too much.

The will of the phantom apparently has metamorphic powers over the temporary body.

Epes Sargent wrote in *Proof Palpable of Immortality* (1875) that a feminine spirit who manifested herself at Moravia in the seances of Mrs. Mary **Andrews** was, on one occasion, known to produce in rapid succession, facsimiles of her personal appearance at six different periods of her earth-life, ranging from childhood to old age.

"I think," state William Oxley of a materialized spirit "Lily," "that she did not appear twice in exactly the same form; but I always recognised her and never confused her with other apparitions."

The phantoms of Mrs. Etta Roberts often transformed themselves into the forms of other persons in view of the sitters.

According to the experience of E. A. Brackett (another author of books on Spiritualism), the sitter's will has an influence over the phantom shapes as well. In his seances with Mrs. H. B. **Fay**, he found that by the exercise of his will he could cause the materialized forms to recede. If this is so, it should be expected that the willpower of the medium wields a dominant influence. There is some reason to suppose that ectoplasm has a tendency to return to the medium's body and that the invisible operators have to be constantly on guard against this propensity. As long as the medium is passive the tendency is not difficult to overcome, but as soon as his will is active or a sudden emotion sweeps over him the operators become powerless and the reversal of the creative process speedily sets in.

For the exercise of the medium's willpower or a show of emotion, however, there is but little opportunity, as most of the materialization mediums pass into trance before the phenomena begin. D. D. **Home**, Mme. **d'Esperance**, Kate **Fox**, Mrs. **Hollis**, Mrs. **Andrews**, Mrs. **Mellon, Eglinton**, Mrs. **Thompson**, Miss Florence **Cook** and **Kluski**, in the first stage of their mediumship, have given most of their materialization seances in a conscious state. Their subjective experiences should be instructive.

Interdependence of Phantom and Medium

"I feel," state Mrs. Mellon, "as though I were that form, and yet I know I am not and that I am still seated on my chair. It is a kind of double consciousness—a faraway feeling, hard to define. At one moment I am hot, and the next moment cold. I sometimes have a choking, fainting, sinking sensation when the form is out."

Describing an early materialization seance of Mrs. Thompson, F. W. Thurstan state: "All this while Mrs. T. was in full consciousness, but she kept exclaiming that she felt 'all hollow' and another thing she noticed that whenever 'Clare's' fingers touched anyone she distinctly felt a pricking sensation in her body, very similar to her experiences when she had been placed once on an insulating stool and charged with electricity and persons had touched her to make sparks come from her."

This **community of sensations** between the medium and the phantom has important bearings. The interaction between the two bodies is constant. The blending of the two organisms may be manifest in the lines of paraffin moulds (see **Plastics**). Miss Florence Cook once had a dark stain on a covered part of her body after an ink mark had been made on the face of "Katie," while the medium was shut up in the cabinet.

Mme. d'Esperance, who never touched tobacco, suffered from nicotine poisoning if her sitters smoked during the ectoplasmic process.

W. Reichel, author of *Occult Experiences* (1906), observed that the phantoms of the medium C. W. **Miller** smelled of tobacco and even of food and wine if the medium had liberally partaken of them before the seance. When the materilized child of Florence **Marryat** filled her mouth with sugarplums, she nearly choked the medium. "Mahedi," the Egyptian phantom of medium F. W. **Monck**, discovered a dish of baked apples in the room "I got him to eat some" wrote Archdeacon **Colley**. "Our medium was at this time six or seven feet away from the materialised form and had not chosen to take any of the fruit, averring that he could taste the apple the Egyptian was eating. Wondering how this could be, I, with my right hand, gave our abnormal friend another baked apple to eat, holding this very bit of paper in my left hand outstretched towards the medium, when from his lips fell the chewed skin and core of the apple eaten by 'The Mahedi'—and here it is before me now after all these years in this screwed up bit of paper for any scientist to analyse."

The Archdeacon repeated the same experiments many times "but never could I see the transit from the mouth of the psychic form at my right hand of what was masticated, or swallowed, of wine from a measured glass pouring in exact measure again from the mouth or dropping from the lips of the medium six or seven feet at my left into these carefully kept papers."

In a similar account about Monck in *The spiritualist* (December 4, 1877) the story was told of a materialized spirit who drank water. What he swallowed was instantly ejected from the medium's mouth. No such reaction was observed in the case of the materialized phantom "Zion" (of medium George **Spriggs**), who drank water and ate biscuits in Melbourne. It need hardly be emphasized that stories of phantom forms absorbing food and drink are difficult to accept at face value.

The sensitivity of ectoplasm is well known. It must be handled with caution and protected from light. Dr. Geley observed that the shock of sudden light is proportional to the duration of the light and not to its intensity. The magnesium flash hurts the medium less than the rays of a pocket lamp. If the ectoplasm has solidified, the danger of injuring the medium is less. But it is a danger nevertheless. The medium may suffer agonies if the phantom meets with a misadventure, but the injury may not necessarily react on the corresponding part of his body. A phantom hand may be pierced through with a knife, the medium will shriek with pain, yet his hands may bear no trace of the wound. Dr. F. L. Willis had an experience of this kind in his mediumship.

However, seance room atrocities seldom go beyond the stage of spirit grabbing. It is probably that the danger attending such attempts is somewhat exaggerated and often used as an excuse for fraud. In 1876 and 1877, it was for the first time suggested that the medium and the materialized form are in an unstable equilibrium and that whether the union is effected in the hands of the spirit grabber or inside the cabinet depended on the relative proportion of energy in the two forms at the time of the seizure.

When Florence **Marryat** was conducted into the cabinet by a materialized spirit of Miss **Showers**, she was told: "You see that Rosie is half her usual size and weight. *I* have borrowed the other half from her, which, combined with contributions from the sitters, goes to make up the body in which I show myself to you. If you increase the action of the vital half to such a degree, that, if the two halves did not reunite, you would kill her. You see that I can detach certain particles from her organism for my own use, and when I dematerialise, I restore these particles to her, and she becomes once more her normal size. You only hurry the re-union by violently detaining me, so as to injure her."

In an earlier account given to Mr. Luxmoore by "Katie King," the danger was graphically but less scientifically pictured. On the question "When you disappear, where is it to?" she answered: "Into the medium, giving her back all the vitality which I took from her. When I have got very much from her, if anyone of you were to take her suddenly round the waist and try to carry her you might kill her on the spot; she might suffocate. I can go in and out of her readily, but understand, I am not her—not her double; they talk a deal of rubbish about doubles; I am myself all the time."

The experience of Archdeacon Colley with "Mahedi" appears to conform to the above theories. This phantom was a giant. His physical strength was so enormous that he could lift the Archdeacon from his chair to the level of his shoulders apparently without effort. He reminded the Archdeacon of a mummy of gigantic proportions he once saw in some museum.

On his first visit through the medium F. W. Monck, the "Mahedi" wore a kind of "metal skull cap, with an emblem in front which trembled and quivered and glistened, overhanging the brow. I was allowed to feel it, but there was little resistance to my fingers, and it seemed to melt away like a snowflake under my touch, and to grow apparently solid again the moment after. For once (February 18, 1878) by daylight, it was arranged, as a most dangerous experiment, that I should grasp the white-attired Egyptian and try to keep him from getting back to invisibility through the body of the medium. I was, by an invisible force, levitated, as it seemed instantly some eighteen or twenty feet from my drawing room door right up to where the medium stood, whom, strangely and suddenly, wearing white muslin over his black coat, I found in my arms just as I had held The Mahedi. The materialised form had gone, and the psychic clothing that he evolved with him from the left side of my friend must also have gone the same way with the speed of thought back to invisibility through the medium. But whence its substituted drapers' stuff now on the body of our friend not wearing it an instant before?"

It is difficult to find a corroboration of this experience in the literature of Spiritualism. It has happened far more often that the spirit dissolved in the grabber's hand. Mr. Volckman had this experience with "Katie King." Mostly, however, when the light was switched on, the spirit was found to be identical with the medium. Cases of transfiguration in a state of deep trance may offer an excuse, but generally it is a safe assumption that a successful grabbing of the medium in the spirit's guise, establishes a *prima facie* case for fraud. The question which usually complicates the case is of the drapery which is visible in the dark and may serve for purposes of transfiguration. This drapery has often disappeared when the light was switched on. But often it was found and turned out to be very material and enduring.

In case of full materialization, the weight of the medium's body proportionately decreases (see **Ectoplasm**). In exceptional cases, strange means appear to have been adopted to keep the phantom in sufficient solidity.

Col. H. S. **Olcott**, in his experiments with Elizabeth J. **Compton**, shut the medium up in a small cabinet, passed threads through the bored holes of her ears and fastened them to the back of her chair. When a phantom appeared from the cabinet, Olcott asked it to stand on a weighing platform. Twice it was weighed, the records being 77 and 59 lbs. Olcott then left the phantom outside and went into the cabinet. The medium was gone. Stepping out, he again weighed the apparition. The weight this time was 52 lbs. The spirit then reentered the cabinet from which other spirits emerged. Finally, Olcott went inside with a lamp and found the medium just as he had left her at the beginning of the seance with every thread unbroken and every seal undisturbed. After the return of consciousness she was weighted. Her weight was 121 lbs.

Some Early Explanations

According to the explanation of the controls, the phenomena of materialization are not produced by a single spirit. "John King," in a seance with Cecil Husk, pictured to Florence Marryat the concerted work as follows: "When the controls have collected the matter with which I work—some from everybody in the circle, mostly from the medium's brain—I mould with it a plastic mask, somewhat like warm wax in feel, but transparent as gelatine, into the rough likeness of a face. . . . I therefore place this plastic substance over the spirit features and mould it to them. If the spirit's will have the patience to stand still I can generally make an excellent likeness of what they were in earth life, but most of them are in such haste to manifest that they render my task very difficult. That is why very often a spirit appears to his friends and they cannot recognise any likeness."

The solidity of the materialized form greatly varies. Some mediums only produce vaporous and unsubstantial phantoms. They are called "etherealizations." Apparently, the exertion of force is not dependent on solidity. An instructive instance is told in the book *Spiritualism* by Judge J. W. Edmonds & G. T. Dexter (2 vols., 1853-55): "I felt on one of my arms what seemed to be the grip of an iron hand. I felt distinctly the thumb and fingers, the palm of the hand, and the ball of the thumb, and it held me fast by a power which I struggled to escape from in vain. With my other hand I felt all round where the pressure was, and satisfied myself that it was no earthly hand that was thus holding me fast, nor indeed could it be, for I was as powerless in that grip as a fly would be in the grasp of my hand."

The word "materialization" was first used in 1873 in America in place of "spirit-forms." Hands and arms were seen in the Davenport seances in the earliest days of modern Spiritualism. According to Epes Sargent's *The Scientific Basis of Spiritualism* (1881) "as far back as 1850, a full spirit form would not infrequently appear." D. D. **Home** produced many good manifestations.

Professor J. J. **Mapes** was the first scientist who discoursed on the means by which the semblance of such temporary organisms could be produced in accordance with the kinetic theory of gases, with a minimum employment of actual material particles, provided a sufficiently intense energy of motion were imparted to them.

Complete forms were often seen with Mrs. Mary **Andrews** of Moravia about 1860. Shortly after Kate **Fox** gave proof of the same power in the Livermore seances. Dr. John F. Gray of New York testified: "Mr. Livermore's recitals of the seances in which I participated are faithfully and most accurately stated, leaving not a shade of doubt in my mind as to the truth and accuracy of his accounts of those at which I was not a witness. I saw with him the philosopher Franklin, in a living, tangible, physical form, several times; and, on as many different occasions, I also witnessed the production of lights, odours, and sounds; and also the formation of flowers, cloth-textures, etc., and their disintegration and dispersion."

In America, Mrs. Hardy, Mrs. Maud Lord, Mrs. Jennie Lord Webb, Bastian and Taylor; in England, Mrs. Guppy, Herne and Williams, Florence Cook and Miss Showers were the next materializing mediums. The two extremes were well represented by D. D. Home and Florence Cook. Home's phantoms were mostly transparent. "Katie King" was flesh and blood.

Phantom Eyes and Hands

The evolution from ectoplasmic vapor to full phantoms with all the attributes of life is a fascinating subject. In his book *Mondo dei Misteri*, the journalist Luigi Barzini, who observed the phenomena of Eusapia Pallandino, stated:

"From the curtain of the cabinet now and then slowly advancing towards one or another of those controlling, came Things, black and unformed, which seemed nearly always to withdraw without having touched."

A record published in the *Report on Spiritualism* of the **London Dialectical Society** (1871) narrated the metamorphosis of a psychic light into an eye: "Mr W. Lindsay said there was a large bright eye in the centre of the table, from whence other eyes appeared to emanate and approach and retreat." Eyes, winking humorously were frequently reported in the Boston seances of "Margery" (Mrs. **Crandon**).

F. W. Pawlowski, professor of Aeronautical Engineering at the University of Michigan, wrote on his experiences with Franek **Kluski** in the *Journal* of the American society for Psychical Research (1925, pp. 481-504), "Bright bluish stars appear and begin to move high above the table, near the ceiling. When they approached me at a distance of about sixteen inches I recognised to my great astonishment that they were human eyes looking at me. Within a few seconds such a pair of eyes develops into a complete human head, and with a hand moving a luminous palm illuminating it clearly. The hand will move around the head as if to show itself more clearly to the onlooker, the eyes looking at one intensely and the face smiling most pleasantly. I have seen a number of such heads, sometimes two at a time, moving through the air like drifting toy balloons from one sitter to another. On several occasions the apparitions appeared just behind my back, and I was aware of them from the sound of their breathing, which I could hear distinctly before they were noticed by the sitters opposite to me. When I turned around I found their faces just about a foot from me, either smiling or looking intently at me. Some of these were breathing violently as if after a strenuous run, and in these cases I felt their breath on my face. Once I listened to the heartbeat of an apparition. They conducted themselves as callers at a party. The expression of curiosity in their eyes is most appealing. I have seen a similar look only in the eyes of children at the age of the awakening of their intelligence. On one occasion I saw two of them flying high above our heads in the higher room, illuminating each other with the plaques and performing fancy evolutions. It was really a beautiful sight, something like an aerial ballet."

Sir William **Crookes** testified that the phantom hand "is not always a mere form, but sometimes appears perfectly life-like and graceful, the fingers moving and the flesh apparently as human as that of any in the room. At the wrist, or arm, it becomes hazy and fades off into a luminous cloud." To the touch the hand sometimes appeared icy cold and dead, at other times warm and lifelike. Crookes had seen a luminous cloud hover over a heliotrope, break a sprig off and carry it to a lady; he had seen finger and thumb pick the petals from a flower in

Home's button-hole and lay them in from of several persons sitting near him. Phantom hands playing the keys of an accordion floating in the air were of frequent occurrence.

William **Howitt**, S. Carter **Hall** and Mrs. Hardinge **Britten** once saw in the full light of the day in the drawing room of Mr. Hall, with Home's feet and hands in full view the whole time, twenty pairs of hands form and remain visible for about an hour. They were active and unattached, but otherwise could not be distinguished from ordinary human hands.

"One evening," wrote Dr. John Ashburner of his experiences with the medium Charles **Foster**, "I witnessed the presence of nine hands floating over the dining table." (*Notes and Studies on Animal Magnetism & Spiritualism*, 1867)

Signor G. Damiani testified before the London Dialectical Committee as having seen at a seance of the **Davenport Brothers** in London in 1868 "five pink transparent hands appeared ranged perpendicularly behind the door. Subsequently I placed my hand in the small window of the cabinet, when I felt each of my five digits tightly grasped by a distinct hand; while my own was thus held down, five or six other hands protruded from the hole above my wrist. On withdrawing my hand from the aperture, an arm came out therefrom—an arm of such enormous proportions that had it been composed of flesh and bone, it would, I verily believe, have turned the scale (being weighted) against the whole corporeal substance of the small Davenport."

A silver-colored, self-luminous hand, which began at the elbow and was seen in the process of formation was described in the report of a seance with D. D. Home in the *Hartford Times*, March 18, 1853. The question was spelled out whether the sitters would like to see the hand of a colored person. "In a moment there appeared a rather dull looking, grey hand, somewhat shadowy, and not quite so clearly defined as the first, but it was unmistakably there, and its grey hue could be clearly seen."

Eusapia **Palladino** did not produce compact, full size materializations. She was famous for her "third arm" which issued from her shoulders and receded into it. This arm was often seen independently and well materialized. The "counterpartal arms" of the Rev. Stainton **Moses**, extending generally from the shoulder, straight out, and above the true arms, presented a similar phenomenon. They simply retracted into the medium, or vanished if an attempt was made to grasp them.

Describing "John King's" materialized hand, Professor Charles **Richet** stated: "I held it firmly and counted twenty-nine seconds, during all which time I had leisure to observe both of Eusapia's hands on the table, to ask Mme. Curie if she was sure of her control, to call Courtier's attention, and also to feel, press and identify a real hand through the curtain. After twenty-nine seconds I said: 'I want something more, I want uno anello (a ring) on this hand.' At once the hand made me feel a ring: I said 'adesso uno braceletto' and on the wrist I felt the two ends as of a woman's bracelet that closes by a hinge. I then asked that this hand should melt in mine, but the hand disengaged itself by a strong effort, and I felt nothing further."

Sitting with Eusapia **Palladino**, Professor Bottazzi "four times saw an enormous black fist come out from behind the left curtain, which remained motionless, and advance toward the head of Mme. B."

Dr. Eugene Crowell stated in *The Identity of Primitive Christianity with Modern Spiritualism* (1874): "At Moravia, at one time, I saw an arm projected from the aperture of the cabinet, which with the hand, was fully three and a half feet in length. It remained in view, in free motion, for a time sufficient for all to observe and remark upon it. Its enormous length and size startled all present."

Despite such startling testimonies, the inference that telekinetic effects are produced by materialized hands should not be drawn hastily. Dr. Julien **Ochorowicz** noticed an alternative character about these manifestations. a well-materialized hand when clearly visible is mechanically inactive. Mechanical effects are generally produced by invisible hands. The same holds good for chemical, luminous and acoustic effects.

Phantoms of Fame and Name

The best records of full form materializations have been furnished by "familiar" spirits: "Katie King," who attended Florence Cook for three years; "Yolande," who appeared in Mme. d'Esperance's seances for a similar period; "Estella," who manifested in the Livermore sittings for five years and "Bertha," a niece of E. A. Brackett who appeared to him through different mediums for two years.

The materialized spirits seldom come in numbers and their range of activity is limited. The marvelous stories of C. V. **Miller**'s mediumship, which was powerful enough to make twelve materialized figures appear at once, rest mostly on the testimony of W. Reichel.

Corroboration, by a repetition of the occurrence, is also wanting of the peripatetic ghosts of George **Spriggs** who walked about the house and in the garden, and of the open-air materializations of William **Eglinton**, in which the spirits walked away to a distance of 66 feet from the medium.

"Yolande's" case is unique in a queer respect—her body was so carnally feminine that she was assaulted by a man who took her for a real woman. This resulted in a profound injury, and almost mortal illness, to the medium.

Crookes was the first modern scientist who studied materializations under laboratory conditions. "Katie King" offered him every opportunity for investigation. She even allowed Crookes to enter the cabinet where, armed with a phosphorus lamp, he saw both the medium and "Katie" at the same time.

In D. D. Home's mediumship, Crookes did not see many fully materialized figures. "In the dusk of the evening," he wrote, "during a seance with Mr. Home at my house, the curtains of a window about eight feet from Mr. Home were seen to move. A dark, shadowy, semi-transparent form, like that of a man, was then seen by all present standing near the window, waving the curtain with his hand. As we looked, the form faded away and the curtains ceased to move."

A phantom form, semi-transparent, through which the sitters could be seen all the time, holding an accordion in his hand and playing continuously, was described by Mrs. Crookes as seen in the presence of her husband, the Rev. Stainton Moses, and Sergeant Cox in a Home seance: "As the figure approached I felt an intense cold, getting stronger as it got nearer, and as it was giving me the accordion I could not help screaming. The figure seemed to sink into the floor, to the waist, leaving only the head and shoulders visible, still playing the accordion, which was then about a foot off the floor."

Description of a more solid case was given by Lord **Adare**: "Her form gradually became apparent to us; she moved close to Home and kissed him. She stood beside him against the window intercepting the light as a solid body, and appeared fully as material as Home himself, no one could have told which was the mortal body and which was the spirit. It was too dark, however to distinguish features. I could see that she had her full face turned towards us, and that either her hair was parted in the middle, and flowed down over her shoulders or that she had on what appeared to be a veil."

The next systematic investigation attached itself to the name of Prof. Charles **Richet**. "At the Villa Carmen I saw a fully organised form rise from the floor. At first it was only a white, opague spot like a handkerchief lying on the ground before the curtain, then this handkerchief quickly assumed the form of a human head level with the floor, and a few moments later it rose up in a straight line and became a small man enveloped in a kind of white burnous, who took two or three halting steps in front of the curtain and then sank to the floor and disappeared as if through a trap-door. But there was no trap-door."

The phantom "Bien Boa" possessed all the attributes of life: "It walks, speaks, moves and breathes like a human being. Its body is resistant, and has a certain muscular strength. It is neither a lay figure nor a doll, nor an image reflected by a mirror; it is as a living being; it is as a living man; and there are reasons for resolutely setting aside every other supposition than one or other of these two hypotheses: either that of a phantom having the attributes of life; or that of a living person playing the part of a phantom."

In another note Prof. Richet stated: "At certain moments it was obliged to lean and bend, because of the great height which it had assumed. Then suddenly, his head sank, sank right down to the ground, and disappeared. He did this three times in succession. In trying to compare this phenomenon to something, I can find nothing better than the figure in a jack-in-the-box, which comes out all of a sudden."

Hands that Melted Like Snow

The miracle of the birth of human organs or of complete bodies is two fold as it is followed by an equally mysterious dissolution of the temporary organization. This phenomenon has been observed under very dramatic circumstances. There can be no question of delusion when a spirit hand is tightly held and melts away in the sitter's grasp.

Testimonies of this occurrence are numerous: Frank L. Burr, editor of the *Hartford Times*, in a letter to Mrs. Home, published in *D. D. Home: His Life and Mission* by Mdme D. D. Home (1888), added the following particulars to his account of March 14, 1855 of one of Home's last seances before his departure to England: "Turning this strange hand palm towards me, I pushed my right forefinger entirely through the palm, till it came out an inch or more, visibly, from the back of the hand. In other words, I pushed my finger clean through that mysterious hand. When I withdrew it, the place closed up, much as a piece of putty would close under such circumstances, leaving a visible mark or scar, where the wound was, but not a hole. While I was still looking at it the hand vanished, quick as a lightning flash."

Crookes wrote, also of Home: "I have retained one of these hands in my own, firmly resolved not to let it escape. There was no struggle or effort to get loose, but it gradually seemed to resolve itself into vapour, and faded in that manner from my grasp." He observed that the hands and fingers do not always appear to be solid and lifelike. Sometimes they present the appearance of a nebulous cloud partly condensed into the form of a hand. This is not equally visible to all present. Only when fully formed does it become visible to all present."

H. D. Jencken read in his paper before the London Dialectical Society: "I have once been enabled to submit a spirit hand to pressure. The temperature was, as far as I could judge, the same as that of the room, and the spirit hand felt soft, velvety; dissolving slowly under the greatest amount of pressure to which I could submit it."

"Katie's" wrist was once seized in anger by Mr. G. H. Tapp of Dalston whom "Katie" struck on the chest for a joke she resented. As Tapp described it, the hand "crumpled up in my grasp like a piece of paper, or thin cardboard, my fingers meeting through it."

"John King" was seen by Florence Marryat to "hold a slate so that both hands were visible, and then let one hand dematerialise till it was no larger than a doll's, whilst the other remained the normal size."

Prof. Philippe **Bottazzi** of the University of Naples wrote: "I saw and felt at one and the same time a human hand natural in colour, I felt with mine the fingers and the back of a strong, warm, rough hand. I gripped it and it vanished from my grasp, not becoming smaller, but melting, dematerialising, dissolving."

Col. **Rochas** wrote in the *Annales des Sciences Psychiques* (vol. 18, 1908, p. 280) of a seance in which M. Montorguiel seized a materialized hand and called for a light. The hand melted and "all of us thought we saw a luminous trail from his hand to F.'s body."

Dr. Hereward **Carrington**, one of the keenest fraudhunters among psychical researchers, wrote: "I myself have observed materializations under perfect conditions of control, and have had the temporary hand melt within my own, as I held it firmly clasped. This 'hand' was a perfectly formed, physiological structure, warm, life-like and having all the attributes of a human hand—yet both the medium's hands were securely held by two controllers, and *visible* in the red light. Let me repeat, this hand was *not* pulled away, but somehow melted in my grasp as I held it." (*The Story of Psychic Science*, 1930)

Dramatic Exit of Spirit Visitants

The dissolution of a full phantom is one of the most dramatic of claimed phenomena. "Katie King" agreed to demonstrate it on herself. Florence Marryat gave the following account in her book *There is no Death* (1892): "She [Katie King] took up her station against the drawing room wall, with her arms extended as if she were crucified. Then three gas-burners were turned on to their full extent in a room about sixteen feet square. The effect upon 'Katie King' was marvellous. She looked like herself for the space of a second only, then she began gradually to melt away. I can compare the dematerialisation of her form to nothing but a wax doll melting before a hot fire. First the features became blurred and indistinct; they seemed to run into each other. The eyes sunk in the sockets, the nose disappeared, the frontal bone fell in. Next the limbs appeared to give way under her, and she sank lower and lower on the carpet, like a *crumbling* edifice. At last there was *nothing but her head* left above the ground—then a heap of white drapery only, which disappeared with a whisk, as if a hand had pulled it after her—and we were left staring by the light of three gas burners at the spot on which 'Katie King' had stood."

Sometimes the dissolution is unexpected. The power wanes and the form cannot be held together. In a seance with Mrs. H. B. **Fay**, a deceased sister appeared to Florence Marryat. Suddenly she "appeared to faint. Her eyes closed, her head fell back on my shoulder, and before I had time to realise what was going to happen, she had passed *through* the arm that supported her, and sunk down *through* the floor. The sensation of her weight was still making my arm tingle, but 'Emily' was gone, *clean gone*."

"Honto," the Indian spirit squaw of the **Eddy Brother**, smoked a pipe. The light from the burning tobacco enabled Col. Olcott to see distinctly her copper-colored cheek, the bridge of her nose and the white of her eye. She remained out too long. Darting back she collapsed into a shapeless heap before the curtains, only one hand being distinguishable. In half a minute she appeared again.

The process of dissolution varies. Robert Dale **Owen** stated that he had seen a form fade out from head downwards. William Oxley (author of *Modern Messiahs & Wonder Workers*, 1889) said that he saw "Yolande" melting away from the feet upwards until only the head appeared above the floor, and then this grew less and less until a white spot only remained, which, continuing for a moment or two, disappeared. Her materialization, as a rule, occupied ten to fifteen minutes. Her disappearance took place in two to five minutes while the disappearance of the drapery lasted from one half to two minutes.

At one of Mrs. J. B. **Mellon**'s seances in Sydney, Australia, a form, after walking about, lay down on the platform, stretched out the limbs in the presence of all and each member of the body separately dematerialized.

Most often the figures collapse and disappear through the floor. The phantoms of Virginia Roberts, however, (as Florence Marryat testified) if they were strong enough to leave the cabinet, invariably disappeared by floating upwards through the ceiling. "Their mode of doing this was most graceful. They would first clasp their hands behind their heads, and lean backwards; then their feet were lifted off the ground, and they were borne upward in a recumbent position."

The phantoms of Carlo **Mirabelli**, the South American medium, similarly raised themselves and floated in the air before full dissolution which began from the feet upwards.

When matter apparently passes through matter or when **apports** are brought into the seance room, the process of dematerialization may be identical.

At least, this is strongly suggested by the following account given by Mme. d'Esperance in *Shadow Land* (1897): A lady once brought a brilliantly colored Persian silk scarf, which Yolande regarded with great delight, and immediately draped about her shoulders and waist. This scarf she could not be induced to part with. When she had disappeared and the seance closed a careful search was made, but it was not to be found. The next time she came, the lady asked her what she had done with it. Yolande seemed a little nonplussed at the question, but in an instant she made a few movements with her hands in the air and over her shoulders, and the scarf was there, draped as she had arranged it on the previous evening. . . . She never trusted this scarf out of her hands. When sometimes she herself gradually dissolved into mist under the scrutiny of twenty pairs of eyes, the shawl was left lying on the floor, we would say, 'At last she has forgotten it'; but no, the shawl would itself gradually vanish in the same manner as its wearer and no search which we might afterwards make ever discovered its whereabouts. Yet Yolande assured us fleefully that we failed to see it only because we were blind, for the shawl never left the room. This seemed to amuse her, and she was never tired of mystifying us by making things invisible to our eyes or by introducing into the room flowers which had not been brought by human hands."

The Story of Spirit Drapery

The drapery in which materialized phantoms are enveloped may go some way towards helping us to understand how **apparitions**, observed independent of seance conditions, appear clothed. This was always considered as one of the greatest puzzles of ghost lore. The communications received through mediums did not throw too much light on the subject.

"When the soul leaves the body," states Julia's posthumous letters (see W. T. Stead, *Letters from Julia*, 1897), "it is at the first moment quite unclothed, as at birth. When the thought of nakedness crosses the spirit's mind, there comes the clothing which you need. The idea with us is creative. We think and the thing is. I do not remember putting on any garments."

Caroline D. Larsen, in *My Travels in the Spirit World* (1927) similarly stated: "From every spirit emanates a strong aura, a pseudo-phosphoric light. This aura is completely controlled by the mind. Out of this substance is moulded the vesture of the body."

"On one occasion," stated Sylvan J. **Muldoon** of a conscious projection of his **astral body**, "I noticed the clothing forming itself out of the emanation surrounding my astral body, when only a few feet out of coincidence, and the clothing was exactly like that covering my physical body. On another occasion I awakened and found myself moving along at the intermediate speed. A very dense aura surrounded me—so dense, in fact, that I could scarcely see my own body. It remained so until the phantom came to a stop, when I was dressed in the typical ghost-like garb."

The power to form spirit-clothes may not be technically understood but seems to be indicated by observations in materialization seances. There, indeed, the formation of spirit drapery is in a way preliminary to the building up of the body. It appears to serve the purpose of covering up imperfections or vacant spots in the temporary organism, besides which it protects the ectoplasmic substance from the effects of light, of human gaze and also satisfies the requirements of modesty. Once while "Yolande," (who was often seen together with Mme. d'Esperance outside the cabinet) was talking to a sitter, "the top part of her white drapery fell off and revealed her form. I noticed," writes Oxley, "that the form was imperfect, as the bust was undeveloped and the waist uncontracted which was a test that the form was not a lay figure."

The drapery is usually white in color, sometimes of a dazzling whiteness but may also be of greyish appearance; it is often luminous and so material that it is always the last to disappear when the seance concludes. The reason apparently is that the substance of the drapery, though its texture is different and much finer, is—as pointed out by Prof. Cesare **Lombroso**—withdrawn from the medium's clothes to be molded by the invisible operators in a fashion similar to ectoplasm into all kinds of patterns. The rare instances in which the medium's body entirely vanished, during the process of materialization, point to this conclusion. It appears that it is not the body alone which disappears, but the dress as well.

The medium Franek **Kluski** noticed that the curtains and carpets of his apartment where his astounding materialization phenomena were produced had been seriously worn out in an inexplicable manner. The observation was also made at the **British College of Psychic Science** that the lining of the underarms of a medium's jacket exclusively used for seance purposes and apparently subjected to no rough wear had to be renewed frequently. The wife of medium John Lewis of Wales, who had to repair the garment, said that the wear on this was much harder than on garments worn in his occupation of a coal miner. The coloring matter in the garment is apparently of no consequence as the spirit drapery remains white, even if the original dress was black.

How is this substance extracted? The following graphic descriptions furnish little explanation: In a seance with William **Eglinton** on September 9, 1877, Dr. Nichols saw the materialized form "Joey" make, in the presence of three other persons, "twenty yards of white drapery which certainly never saw a Manchester loom. The matter of which it was formed was visibly gathered from the atmosphere and later melted into invisible air. I have seen at least a hundred yards so manufactured."

Katherine Bates wrote in *Seen and Unseen* (1907): "I stood close over her [the phantom] holding out my own dress, and as she rubbed her hands to and fro a sort of white lace or net came from them, like a foam, and lay upon my gown which I was holding up towards her. I touched this material and held it in my hands. It had substance but was light as gossamer, and quite unlike any stuff I ever saw in a shop."

F. W. Thurstan stated in a record of a seance with Mrs. Thompson in 1897, that when she produced physical phenomena, "a soft, gauzy, scented white drapery was flung over my head and seen by the others on my side of the room."

The spirit niece of E. A. Brackett, in seances with Mrs. H. B. **Fay**, made yards and yards of spirit drapery by rubbing her hands together with bare arms. Once she made a seamless robe on Mr. Brackett and dematerialized it instantaneously.

William Harrison, editor of *The Spiritualist*, stated in an account of a seance with Florence **Cook**: "She [Katie King] threw out about a yard of white fabric, but kept hold of it by the other end, saying: 'Look, this is spirit drapery.' I said 'Drop it into the passage Katie, and let us see it melt away; or let us cut a piece off.' She replied: 'I can't; but look here.' She then drew back her hand,which was above the top of the curtain, and as the spirit drapery touched the curtain, it passed right through, just as if there were no resistance whatever. I think at first there was friction between the two fabrics and they rustled against each other, but that when she said 'Look here' some quality which made the drapery common matter was withdrawn from it, and at once it passed through the common matter of the curtain, without experiencing any resistance."

"Katie King" often allowed her sitters to touch her drapery. sometimes she cut as many as a dozen pieces from the lower part of her skirt and made presents of them to different observers. The holes were immediately made good. Crookes examined the skirt inch by inch and found no hole, no marks or seam of any kind.

These pieces of drapery mostly melted into thin air, however carefully they were guarded, but sometimes they were rendered enduring. But in the latter cases and in instances of careless operation, it happened that the medium's dress suffered. "Katie King" said in explanation that nothing material about her could be made to last without taking away some of the medium's vitality and weakening her.

A specimen of "Katie's" drapery was taken by Miss Douglas to Messrs. Howell and James's cloth and dry goods store, London, with the request to match it. They said that they could not, and that they believed it to be of Chinese manufacture.

At a seance in Christiania with Mme. D'Esperance, a sitter abstracted a piece of drapery which clothed one of the spirit forms. Later Mme. D'Esperance discovered that a large square piece of material was missing from her skirt, partly cut, partly torn. the abstracted piece was found to be of the same shape as the missing part, but several times larger, and white in color, the texture fine and thin as gossamer. In the light of this experience Mme. d'Esperance understood a similar happening in England. "Ninia," the child control, was asked for a piece of her abundant clothing. She complied but unwillingly. After the seance Mme. d'Esperance found a hole in her new dress.

"Katie Brink," the spirit of medium Mrs. E. J. **Compton**, cut a piece of her dress for Col. Richard Cross of Montreal, but on the condition that he would buy a new dress for the medium, for a corresponding hole would appear on her skirt. The cut piece was fine, gossamer like material. The medium's dress black alpaca, and much coarser. The cut piece fitted the hole in the medium's dress.

According to the recollection of Alfred Vout **Peters** (*Light*, April 7, 1931), on two or three occasions the spirit Marie gave a piece of white drapery to the sitters. The next morning Mrs. Corner found that a hole had been cut in the middle of her black skirt. Subsequently "Marie" was able to prevent making a hole in the medium's skirt when cutting off the "ectoplasm." Sometimes this material disappeared the next day, at other times it remained, and it is possible that certain pieces are still in existence.

At the Circle of Light, in Cardiff, Wales, in a sitting with medium George **Spriggs**, a piece of rich crimson silk was cut from a girdle worn by a spirit. It began to fade after a few days, but being taken back into the seance room it was manipulated by one of the spirits and restored at once to its original luster.

The Rev. Stainton **Moses** was once given a piece of spirit drapery sweetened by "spirit musk." He sent it to his friend Mrs. Stanhope Speer. The scent on the letter was fresh and pungent seventeen years afterwards.

Part of the available power seems consumed by the creation of this spirit drapery. Sometimes before its appearance, recourse is made to the portieres of the cabinet, the spirit forms wrapping in themselves before thrusting out a hand or head. In some instances, for economical reasons, the operators have accepted ready-made cloth brought in for them to wear. "John King" was photographed in such borrowed garments. There are stories that for similar reasons wearing apparel may be apported.

This, however, carries speculation to uncertain grounds where fraud may easily flourish and find ready excuse. Mrs. Cook, Florence's mother, is said to have once caught "Katie King" wearing a dress of her daughter. "Katie" confessed that she borrowed it because the power was weak. She gave an undertaking that she would never do this again as the medium might be compromised.

In other cases, yards of muslin and grenadine were apported expressly for draping purposes and left in the seance room. Such accounts must obviously be treated with strong reservations.

Traces of spirit cloth appear to have been found in mediumistic **plastics**. The hand, or face seems often enveloped in drapery before the putty is impressed or a paraffin cast made.

Souvenir Locks of Hair, Materialized Jewels and Flowers

Similarly to pieces of drapery, materialized phantoms often gave locks of hair for souvenirs. "Katie King" did it very often. Once in the cabinet, she cut off a lock of her own hair and a lock of the medium's and gave them both to Florence **Marryat**. One was almost black, soft and silky, the other a coarse golden red. On another occasion she asked Florence Marryat to cut her hair with a pair of scissors as fast as she could. "So I cut off curl after curl, and as fast as they fell to the ground the hair grew again upon her head." The severed hair vanished.

In some instances these souvenirs did not disappear. Crookes in a later communication spoke of a lock of "Katie" as still before him. Similarly the lock which Prof. Charles **Richet** cut from the head of an Egyptian beauty (during the mediumship of Marthe Béraud) remained. Prof. Richet stated: "I have kept this lock, it is very fine, silky and undyed. Microscopical examination shows it to be real hair; and I am informed that a wig of the same would cost a thousand francs. Marthe's hair is very dark and she wears her hair rather short."

It would appear from this that the materialized product was finer in quality than the natural one.

The materialized phantoms apparently often wear ornaments. Admiral Usborne Moore, in his seances with the medium J. B. **Jonson** of Detroit, found these ornaments yielding to the touch. In other instances they were solid.

"Abd-u-lah," the one-armed spirit of William **Eglinton**, appeared bedecked with diamonds, emeralds and rubies. The materialization of precious stones was thus described by Mrs. Nichols in the *Spiritualist* (October 26, 1877): "For some time he moved his hands as if gathering something from the atmosphere, just as when he makes muslin. After some minutes he dropped on the table a massive diamond ring. He said: 'Now you may all take the ring, and you may put it on, and hold it while you count twelve.' Miss M. took it and held it under the gaslight. It was a heavy gold ring with a diamond that appeared much like one worn by a friend of mine worth £1000. Joey said the value of this was 900 guineas. Mr. W. examined it as we had done. He now made, as it seemed, and as he said, from the atmosphere two diamonds, very clear and beautiful, about the size of half a large pea. He gave them into our hands on a piece of paper. We examined them as we had the others. He laid the ring and the diamonds on the table before him, and there next appeared a wonderful cluster of rubies, set with a large ruby about half an inch in diameter in the centre. These we all handled as we had the others. Last there came a cross, about four inches in length, having twenty magnificent diamonds set in it; this we held in our hands, and examined as closely as we liked. He told us that the market value of the gems was £25,000. He remarked: 'I could make Willie the richest man in the world, but it would not be the best thing, and might be the worst.' He now took the jewels in front of him and seemed to dissipate them, as one might melt hailstones in heat until they entirely disappeared."

The Rev. Stainton **Moses** was told by "Magus," one of his controls, that he would deliver him a topaz, the material counterpart of his spiritual jewel which would enable him to see scenes in the spheres on looking into it. The jewel was found in his bedroom. Stainton Moses was much exercised over it. He believed it to be an **apport**, waken without the consent of the owner. He never received any definite information as to its origin. It cannot be traced how long the stone, which was set in a ring, remained in his possession.

Gems and pearls were frequently brought to the circle of Stainton Moses. His theory was that they were made by spirits because he could see them falling before they reached the table while others could not see them until they had fallen, and because an emerald had flaws in it and therefore could not have been cut or be an imitation.

Flower materializations are comparatively more frequent. There was a remarkable instance in Mme. d'Esperance's mediumship. On June 28, 1890 at a seance in St. Petersburg, in the presence of Alexander **Aksakof** and Prof. Boutlerof, a golden lily, seven feet high, appeared in the seance room. It was kept for a week, during which time it was six times photographed. After the week it dissolved and disappeared.

In the record of the Livermore seances with Kate Fox, under date February 22, 1862 is the following statement: "Appearance of flowers. Cloudy. Atmosphere damp. Conditions unfavourable. At the expiration of half an hour a bright light rose to the surface of the table, of the usual cylindrical form, covered with gossamer. Held directly over this was a sprig of roses about six inches in length, containing two half-blown white roses, and a bud with leaves. The flowers, leaves and stem were perfect. They were placed at my nose and smelled as though freshly gathered; but the perfume in this instance was weak and delicate. We took them in our fingers and I carefully examined the stem and flowers. The request was made as before to 'be very careful.' I noticed an adhesive, viscous feeling which was explained as being the result of a damp, impure atmosphere. These flowers were held near and over the light, which seemed to feed and give them substance in the same manner as the hand. By raps we were told to 'Notice and see them dissolve.' The sprig was placed over the light, the flowers dropped, and in less than one minute, melted as though made of wax, their substance seeming to spread as they disappeared. By raps 'See them come again.' A faint light immediately shot across the cylinder, grew into a stem; and in about the same time required for its dissolution, the stem, and the roses had grown into created perfection. This was several times repeated, and was truly wonderful."

F. W. Thurstan made the significant observation with medium Mrs. R. **Thompson** (*Light*, March 15, 1901) that when a pineapple was to be materialized the smell and notion of it was all day in "her head." He believed that ideas of shapes, actions and words that are required to be brought into objectivity as a seance were made by unseen operators to be running in the medium's head often for days beforehand.

In experiments with medium T. **Lynn** at the **British College of Psychic Science**, objects were photographed in the course of materialization. They showed flecks and masses of a luminous material, possessing sting-like roots. These light masses floated over a harp lying upon the table and were visible to all present. A finger-like projection extended from a mass of this luminosity, and extended itself towards the harp as if to play upon it. As the photo plates were developed, a bone ring was seen to depend from the medium's nose, and an object similar to the top of an infant's nursing bottle appeared to hang from his lips by a cord. The medium's features also seemed somewhat altered. At a second sitting, a two-pronged fish-hook, and also a small ring materialized. The photo plates of this materialization showed that some remarkable rounded object proceeded from the region of the medium's solar plexus, which had often appeared in previous photographs, and from this a root, or string, seemed to extend to the object materializing, apparently attached thereto. In this case, the root was twisted in a remarkable manner.

Similar observations were reported by Prof. Karl Blacher of Riga University, with the **apport** medium "BX." (*Zeitschrift für Parapsychologie*, June 1933). In trance, and under control, nails, screws or pieces of iron would be visibly drawn out of his chest, his armpits or arms, as could be clearly observed by means of luminous screens. On one occasion a length of wire over a yard long was drawn from the man's bared chest; at another time Prof. Blacher himself caught hold of an end that was protruding from the same spot and drew forth a long leather strap. At another sitting the medium produced a heavy slab of metal from his chest; and from his left arm a piece of wrought steel weighing over 3 lbs.

There is a curious meeting point between apports and materialization here to which sufficient attention has not been devoted yet. The complexity of the problem is further demonstrated by the story of Lajos **Pap**, the Budapest apport medium (*Light*, July 14, 1933) that previous to his first apport of a frog, for two days he heard continual croaking. It seemed to him to come from his stomach, and he kept on asking people if they heard nothing. Similarly he heard the chirping of apported grasshoppers a long time before their arrival; and, preliminary to the apport of a large packet of needles, he felt pricking sensations over the back of his hand. It is, however, only fair to state that in 1935 Dr. Nandor Fodor detected Lajos Pap in fraud.

Marvels of Materialization

On May 25, 1921, Mme. Bisson observed the materialization on the hand of "**Eva C.**" of a naked female eight inches high, with a beautiful body, long fair hair, brilliantly white skin. It vanished and returned several times and either her hair was differently arranged or her height grew less. The little figure performed various gymnastic exercises and finally stood on Mme. Bisson's extended hand. The materialization of small heads of the size of a walnut in a glass of water was the peculiar feature of Mme. **Ignath**'s mediumship. "Nona," the control, asserted these heads to be plastic **thought-forms**.

Describing a visit to an unnamed materialization medium, Mrs. Gladys Osborne Leonard stated in her book *My Life in Two Worlds* (1931): "My husband was sitting with his feet and knees rather wide apart. His gaze suddenly was diverted from the materialised spirit to a kind of glow near his feet. Looking down he saw a tiny man and woman, between 12 and 18 inches high, standing between his knees. They were holding hands and looking up into my husband's face, as if they were thinking 'What on earth is that?' They seemed to be interested, if not more so, in him, and the details of his appearance, as he was in theirs. He was too astonished to call anybody's attention to the tiny people, who were dressed in bright green, like the pictures of elves and fairies, and who wore little pointed caps. A slight glow surrounded them, or emanated from them, he wasn't sure which, but it was strong enough for him to see their little faces and forms clearly. After a moment or two they disappeared, apparently melting into the floor."

In a sitting with Countess Castelwitch in Lisbon, a communicator who called himself "M. Furtado" (husband of Mme. Furtado who was present), rapped out through the table that he would not allow himself to be photographed because he had forgotten what his face was like. At the next seance he said: "I have no face, but I will make one." The photographic plate revealed a tall phantom clothed in white, having a death head instead of a face.

A similar but more gruesome instance was described in the reports of the **Academia de Esutdo Psychicos Cesar Lombroso** of São Paolo, on the mediumship of Carlo **Mirabelli**. "The third sitting followed immediately while the medium was still in a state of exhaustion. A skull inside the closet began to beat against the doors. They opened and the skull floated into the air. Soon the bones of a skeleton appeared one after another from neck to feet. The medium is in a delirium, beats himself and emits a bad smell like that of a cadaver. The skeleton begins to walk, stumble and walk again. It walks round the room while Dr. de Souza touches it. He feels hard, wet, bones. The others touch it. Then the skeleton disappears slowly until the skull alone remains which finally falls on a table. The medium was bound throughout the performance. It lasted 22 counted minutes in bright sunlight."

Alfred Vout **Peters** claimed to have seen in a seance with Cecil **Husk**, the materialization of a living friend of his who was at the time asleep in his home. Horace **Leaf** reported (*Light*, January 29, 1932) on the undoubted materialization of the head, shoulders and arm of a relative of his living 400 miles away. A conversation was carried on for several minutes on matters thoroughly appropriate, then bidding him goodbye, the head vanished.

Indeed, one is tempted to speculate whether it would not be possible to build up, through a process of dematerialization and materialization, a living organism on altered lines. Perhaps some of the miraculous cures in which organic parts of the body appear to have been restored will find an explanation along such speculative lines.

Of the mysterious "Mahedi" whose characteristics were recorded by Archdeacon **Colley**, some unique feats deserve mentioning. The phantom could not speak English. By signs, the Archdeacon Colley made him understand that he wanted him to write. He looked puzzled at the lead pencil. When he was shown how to use it, he held it as he would hold a stylus and began to write quickly from the right to the left in unknown oriental characters, being "in a most peculiar way under the control of 'Samuel'"—one spirit controlling another spirit—the medium having nothing whatever to do with the matter, he being at the time his own normal fully awake natural self some seventeen feet away at the other end of the room talking to a lady.

Archdeacon Colley had samples of "Samuel's" handwriting, obtained direct, moreover he knew that "Samuel" was in control, "for while the Egyptian, left to himself, could not speak any more than he could write it, yet now, with 'Samuel' in him to operate the vocal organs, he could speak real good idiomatic English—'Samuel' speaking through him. The voice was Samuel's while the lips that moved were The Mahedi's. But 'Samuel' and 'The Mahedi' were both the outcome of the medium and the connection between our normal friend, and materialised friend, and friend in control was, as the telescopic lengthening out of a multiple personality to the power of three very remarkable. It was something like what I had before seen and publicly reported relating to the evolution of a spirit form from another spirit form, which first form, as usual, extruded from the medium, so that (December 7, 1877) there stood in line our normal friend (entranced) and next to him the Egyptian thence derived, and from the Egyptian, in turn, the extruded personality of 'Lily,' all at the same time—the three in a row ranked together yet separate and distinct entities."

After all these marvels, Archdeacon Colley's description of the reabsorption of a phantom into the medium's side in plain view appears to lose its wild improbability. Of a seance held on September 25, 1877, the notes having been made on the same evening, Archdeacon Colley state: "As I brought my sweet companion close up to him, the gossamer filament again came into view; its attenuated and vanishing point being, as before, towards the heart. Greatly wondering, yet keen to observe, did I notice how, by means of this vapoury cord, the psychic figure was sucked back into the body of the medium. For like a waterspout at sea—funnel-shaped or sand column such as I have seen in Egypt—horizontal instead of vertical, the vital power of our medium appeared to absorb and draw in the spirit-form, but at my desire, so gradually that I was enabled quite leisurely thus closely to watch the process. For leaning against, and holding my friend with my left arm at his back and my left ear and cheek at his breast, his heart beating in an alarming way, I saw him receive back the lovely birth of the invisible spheres into his robust corporeal person. And as I gazed on the sweet face of the disintegrating spirit, within three or four inches of its features, I again marked the fair lineaments, eyes, hair and delicate complexion, and kissed the dainty hand as in process of absorption it dissolved and was drawn through the texture and substance of his black coat into our friend's bosom.

The Archdeacon once spoke to a materialized phantom before her extrusion was accomplished and he saw recognition in her eyes and heard her whisper, during the psychic parturition "so glad to see you."

On one occasion, a minister friend of Dr. Monck materialized; by common consent the medium was carefully awakened. "Dazed for a moment, and then most astonished, our aroused friend looked enquiringly at the materialised spirit form, and jumping up from the sofa on which we had placed him he excitedly rushed forward to his one-time fellow-student, shouting 'Why, it is Sam' and then there was handshaking and brotherly greetings between the two. When both friends were about to speak at once there was a momentary impasse and neither seemed able to articulate; the medium's breath appearing to be needed by Samuel when he essayed to speak, while the materialised form was also checked in his utterance when the medium began to speak."

C. V. **Miller**, the San Francisco materialization medium, as a rule did not pass into trance and took the phantoms that issued from the cabinet by the hand and introduced them to his sitters.

His amazing seances were duplicated by Dr. R. H. Moore, of San Diego, California. According to the account of N. Meade Layne, in *Psychic Research* (June, 1931) he was a well-known gentleman past seventy years of age, who did not go into trance and accompanied the forms which issued from behind a curtain within a few steps into the circle.The forms were never fully materialized; as a rule they were invisible below the bust, although the ectoplasmic drapery sometimes trailed nearly to the floor. "At a recent seance one of the forms, while conversing with the person at my side, advanced to within about eighteen inches of my face. Dr. Moore then, after telling us what he was about to do, struck the head of the form lightly with his open hand to show the degree of materialization. The movement and the sound were plainly perceived. He then passed his arm through the form at the solar plexus" (*Psychic Research*, July 1930).

Animal Materializations

There is one additional phenomenon to add to the record of all these miracles—the materialization of forms other than human. There are abundant accounts to show that even this seems to have occurred. We owe the strangest reports in this field to three Polish mediums: **Kluski, Guzyk** and Burgik.

Guzyk apparently materialized dogs and other strange animals, Kluski, a large bird of prey, small beasts, a lion and an apemen. The year 1919 abounded with animal materialization in the Kluski seances. "The bird was photographed, and before the exposure a whirring, like the stretching of a huge bird's wings, could be heard, accompanied by slight blasts of wind, as if a large fan were being used . . . Hirkill (an Afghan) materialised . . . Accompanying him always was a rapacious beast, the size of a very big dog, of a tawny colour, with slender neck, mouth full of large teeth, eyes which glowed in the darkness like a cat's, and which reminded the company of a maneless lion. It was occasionally wild in its behaviour, especially if persons were afraid of it, and neither the human nor the animal apparition was much welcomed by the sitters . . . The lion, as we may call him, liked to lick the sitters with a moist and prickly tongue, and gave forth the odour of a great feline, and even after the seance the sitters, and especially the medium, were impregnated with this acrid scent as if they had made a long stay in a menagerie among wild beasts" (*Psychic Science*, April, 1926).

According to Prof. Pawlowski's account (*Journal of the American Society for Psychical Research*, September 1925), the bird was a hawk or a buzzard. It "flew round, beating his wings against the walls and ceiling, and when he finally settled on the shoulder of the medium he was photographed with a magnesium flash, as the camera was accidently focussed on the medium before, and was ready."

An anthropoidal ape showed itself first in July 1919. Dr. Gustav Geley stated in his book *Clairvoyance and Materialisation* (1927): "This being which we have termed Pithecanthropus has shown itself several times at our seances. One of us, at the seance of November 20, 1920, felt its large shaggy head press hard on his right shoulder and against his cheek. The head was covered with thick, coarse hair. A smell came from it like that of a deer or a wet dog. When one of the sitters put out his hand the pithecanthrope seized it and licked it slowly three times. Its tongue was large and soft. At other times we all felt our legs touched by what seemed to be frolicsome dogs."

According to Col. Norbert Ocholowicz's book on Kluski, "this ape was of such great strength that it could easily move a heavy bookcase filled with books through the room, carry a sofa over the heads of the sitters, or lift the heaviest persons with their chairs into the air to the height of a tall person. Though the ape's behaviour sometimes caused fear, and indicated a low level of intelligence, it was never malignant. Indeed it often expressed goodwill, gentleness and readiness to obey . . . After a long stay a strong animal smell was noticed. It was seen for the last time at the seance of December 26, 1922, in the same form as in 1919 and making the same sounds of smacking and scratching."

Mrs. Hewat **McKenzie**, from whose article the above quotation is taken, also wrote of a small animal, reminding the sitters of the "weasel," so often sensed at Guzyk seances: "It used to run quickly over the table on to the sitters' shoulders, stopping every moment and smelling their hands and faces with a small, cold nose; sometimes, as if frightened, it jumped from the table and rambled through the whole room, turning over small objects, and shuffling papers lying on the table and writing desk. It appeared at six or seven seances, and was last seen in June, 1923."

Of Burgik, Prof. Charles **Richet** wrote in *Thirty Years of Psychical Research* (1923): "In the last seance that I had with him the phenomena were very marked. I held his left hand and M. de Gielski his right. He was quite motionless, and none of the experimenters moved at all. My trouser leg was strongly pulled and a strange, ill-defined form that seemed to have paws like those of a dog or small monkey climbed on my knee. I could feel its weight very light and something like the muzzle of an animal (?) touched my cheek. It was moist and made a grunting noise like a thirsty dog."

Dogs were apparently materialized by Mrs. Etta **Wriedt**. Lieut. Col. E. R. Johnson reported in *Light* (November 11, 1922) of a seance with Mrs. Wriedt: "It was quite common to meet one's departed dogs. I had one of these, a very small terrier, placed on my knees. It remained there for about a minute, and both its weight and form were all recognised. It was not taken away but seemed gradually to evaporate or melt. Two others, a large retriever and a medium-sized terrier, came very often, and all three barked with their direct voices in tones suitable to their sizes and breeds. Other sitters saw, heard and were touched by them. Those three had died in India some thirty years previously."

A dog which the medium W. **Haxby** materialized ran about the room. The appearance and pranks of an unseen but palpable pet dog in a seance with Politi on June 18, 1900 was described by General Ballatore in *Vesillo Spiritista.*. It ran about the room, jumped on the knees of one of the sitters, Major Bennati, and put its paws round its mistress's neck, besides performing several other little tricks it had been taught in life.

The psychic photographer Wyllie had on record the psychic picture of a dog.

The flight of birds was often heard in seances with D. D. **Home** and later with the Marquis Scotto **Centurione**. A tame flying squirrel was materialized by "Honto," the Indian squaw, in the seances of the **Eddy Brothers**. Another Indian girl "brought in a robin perched on her finger, which hopped and chirped as naturally as life." (See H. S. Olcott, *People from the Other World*, 1875)

Two triangular areas of light, with curved angles like butterfly wings, audibly flitting and flapping were noticed in the February 24, 1924, seance of "Margery" (Mrs. **Crandon**). The flying creature, claimed to be "Susie," a tame bat of the control "Walter," performed strange antics. The wings would hover over the roses on the table, pick up one, approach a sitter and hit him over the head with it. "Susie" pulled the hair of the sitters, pecked at their faces, flapped her wings in their eyes. Another large, beetle-like area of light which scrambled about the table with a deal of flapping was called by "Walter" his "Nincompoop." Peculiar motions were also performed by a patch of light, said to be a tame bear, over a curtain pole. Clicking and whizzing it tobogganed down the pole and climbed back again. "Walter" was so fond of poking fun at the expense of the sitters that beyond his assertions that he paraded his actual livestock, nothing definite could be established about these curious animated batches of light.

"Materialisation of both beasts and birds sometimes appeared," wrote Gambier Bolton, in his book *Ghosts in Solid Form* (1914), "during our experiments, the largest and most startling being that of a seal which appeared on one occasion when Field-Marshal Lord Wolseley was present. We suddenly heard a remarkable voice calling out some absurd remarks in loud tones, finishing off with a shrill whistle. 'Why, that must be our old parrot,' said the lady of the house.

'He lived in this room for many years, and would constantly repeat those very words.' A small wild animal from India which had been dead for three years or more, and had never been seen or heard of by the Sensitive, and was known to only one sitter, suddenly ran out from the spot where the Sensitive was sitting, breathing heavily and in a state of deep trance, the little creature uttering exactly the same cry which it had always used as a sign of pleasure during its earth life. It has shown itself altogether on about ten different occasions, staying in the room for more than two minutes at a time, and then disappearing as suddenly as it had arrived upon the scene.

"But on this occasion the lady who had owned it during its life called it to her by its pet name, and then it proceeded to climb slowly up on her lap. Resting there quietly for about half a minute it then attempted to return, but in doing so caught one of its legs in the lace with which the lady's skirt was covered. It struggled violently, and at last got itself free, but not until it had torn the lace for nearly three inches. At the conclusion of the experiment a medical man reported that there were five green-coloured hairs hanging in the torn lace, which had evidently become detached from the little animal's legs during its struggles. The lady at once identified the colour and the texture of the hairs, and this was confirmed by the other sitter--himself a naturalist—who had frequently seen and handled the animal during its earth life. The five hairs were carefully collected, placed in tissue paper, and then shut up in a light-tight and damp-proof box. After a few days they commenced to dwindle in size, and finally disappeared entirely."

The story of a materialized seal was told in detail in *Light* (April 22, 1900) on the basis of Gambier Bolton's account before the **London spiritualist Alliance** in a discussion. It reports as follows: Being well-known as a zoologist connected with the Zoological society, he on one occasion received a note from an auctioneer asking if he would call to see a large seal which had been sent from abroad. "The poor thing is suffering; come round and see what you can do," wrote the seal's temporary owner, and being deeply interested in the welfare of animals of all kinds, Mr. Bolton at once obeyed the mandate. He saw the seal. The poor creature had been harpooned, and was lying in a languishing state in a large basket. He saw at once that it could not live, but wishing to do what he could to prolong its life, he at once despatched it to the Zoological Gardens. Later in the day he called to see how it was faring, and found that it had been put into the seal tank. On visiting the tank the seal rose from the water and gave him a long look, which as he humorously suggested, seemed to indicate that the animal recognized him and entertained some sentiments of gratitude for its treatment.

The seal died that night, and ten days later Mr. Bolton was at a seance at which Frederick **Craddock** was the medium. A number of people of social and scientific repute were present. Suddenly someone called out from the cabinet: "Take this great brute away, it is suffocating me." It was the seal! It came slowly from the cabinet, flopping and dragging itself along after the fashion of seals, which (unlike sea-lions) cannot walk. It stayed close to Mr. Bolton for some moments, and then returned to the cabinet and disappeared. "There is no doubt in my mind," said Mr. Bolton, "that it was the identical seal."

To a question as to the *Modus vivendi* of animal materializations, Gambier Bolton obtained the following answer from the spirit controls:

"Their actions are altogether independent of us. Whilst we are busily engaged in conducting our experiments with human entities who wish to materialise in your midst, the animals get into the room in some way which we do not understand, and which we cannot prevent; obtain, from somewhere, sufficient matter with which to build up temporary bodies; coming just when they choose; roaming about the room just as they please; and disappearing just when it suits them, and not before; and we have no power to prevent this so long as the affection existing between them and their late owners is so strong as it was in the instances which have come under our notice."

In contradiction to this information, Col. Norbert Ocholowicz made it a point that at the **Kluski** seances the animal apparitions were seen to be in charge of human apparitions. The only animal which seemed to be able to act independently of a keeper was the "pithecanthropus." Generally the animal and human apparitions were not active at the same moment. When the animal was fully materialized and active, the keeper was passive and kept in the background, and vice versa.

The testimony of clairvoyants also suggests that when animal apparitions are seen the necessary link is furnished by a friend of the sitter.

The question of animal materializations may have some relevance to stories of the animal **familiars** of witches. At the trial of the Chelmsford witches in 1645, Matthew Hopkins the witch-finder, John Sterne and six others, testified that on the previous night they had sat up in the room where the accused was confined to watch for the appearance of her imps which the accused promised and that they indeed saw them: five or six, entering the room in the shape of cats, dogs and other animals. John Sterne was so convinced of the truth of what he saw that he wrote a pamphlet about his experience. (See also **Witchcraft**)

Modern Views of Materialization

Since most of the accounts of the marvels of materialization belong to the past and such astonishing phenomena do not seem to be reported in modern times, there is a tendency to be highly skeptical about the reality of materialization. There have been many undoubted frauds. One of the most impudent was that of Charles **Eldred**, who always took his "highly magnetized" armchair to seances. In 1906, the chair was examined and it was found that the back was really a box with a lock and key. Inside was found a collapsible dummy, yards of cheese-cloth for "ectoplasm," reaching rods, wigs, false beards, a musical box (for "spirit music"), and even scent (for "spirit perfumes").

Other fraudulent materialization mediums were Harry **Bastian**, Frederick F. **Craddock**, Mrs. J B. **Mellon** (Annie Fairlamb), Francis Ward **Monck** and Charles **Williams**. Although seizure of "materialized spirits" which turn out to be the medium are not conclusive evidence of fraud, since there is at least a possibility that an entranced medium may be controlled by spirits, such events are at least presumptive evidence of fraud.

The vexed question is whether mediums caught out in unconscious or deliberate personation of spirits might also at times produce genuine materialization phenomena. Clearly it would be untenable to suppose that spirits influence mediums to purchase wigs, masks, cheese-cloth and other properties used fraudulently at seances, but there is some evidence which tends to show that genuine mediums do sometimes cheat, to fulfill the strong expectation of sitters for regular remarkable phenomena.

A notable example was the famous medium Eusapia **Palladino**, who produced materialization phenomena under strict conditions with a variety of skilled observers, but was known to take short cuts and cheat if the opportunity offered. The mediumistic character is often shallow and childlike, strongly influenced by the desires and expectations of sitters and perhaps even spirits, rather like a subject under hypnosis.

Another controversial medium was Mrs. Helen **Duncan**, convicted in Edinburgh, Scotland, in 1933 for fraudulent mediumship in which an undervest was used as a "materialized spirit." Many reputable observers believed she also produced genuine phenomena, although psychical researchers like Harry **Price** insisted that his photographs of "ectoplasm" clearly indicated cheese-cloth, rubber gloves and cut-out heads from magazine covers. Price did not discover how these objects evaded search, but theorized that the cheese-cloth was swallowed and regurgitated, other properties perhaps being handled by accomplices.

The great days of materialization mediums like D. D. **Home**, with his phantom hands, or Florence **Cook**, with full-length spirit forms apparently indistinguishable from living human beings, are over. No modern mediums have come forward with comparable phenomena to be tested in the more rigorous atmosphere of present times. Until they do, materialization must remain a controversial phenomenon. But it would be unreasonable to dismiss it as totally fraudulent and the claims of reputable scientists of the past as due to incompetence or collusion.

In his book *The Spiritualists: The Story of Florence Cook and William Crookes* (1962), Trevor H. Hall sought to show that not only was the mediumship of Florence Cook shamelessly fraudulent, but that William Crookes was her active accomplice through infatuation with her. Hall is a noted hostile critic of psychical phenomena and although this book is well documented the evidence remains largely speculative and anecdotal. For a refutation of Hall's charges, see the paper 'Crookes and Cook' (*Journal* of the Society for Psychical Research, vol. 42, 1963). For a general discussion of the competence and character of Crookes, see the excellent introduction by K. M. Goldney to the book *Crookes and the Spirit World* (collected) R. G. Medhurst (1972). It must also be stressed that no evidence of fraud was ever discovered on the part of D. D. Home (also tested by Crookes). (See also Florence **Cook**; Sir William **Crookes**; Helen **Duncan; Ectoplasm; Hands of Spirits**; Einer **Nielsen**)

Recommended reading:

Abbot, David P. *Behind the Scenes with Mediums*, Open Court, Chicago, 1907, 5th revised ed. 1926

Aksakof, A. *A Case of Partial Dematerialization of the Body of a Medium*, Boston, Mass., 1898

Anon. *Confessions of a Medium*, London, 1882

Anon. (ed. Harry Price & E. J. Dingwall *Revelations of a Spirit Medium*, Kegan Paul, London, 1922

Bisson, Juliette A. *Les Phénomènes dits de Matérialisations*, Paris, 1914

Bolton, Gambier. *Ghosts in Solid Form*, London, 1914

Brackett, E. A. *Materialized Apparitions*, Boston, 1886; William Rider, London, n.d.

Carrington, Hereward. *The American Seances with Eusapia Palladino*, Barrett/Helix, New York, 1954

Carrington, Hereward. *The Physical Phenomena of Spiritualism*, 3rd ed., Dodd, Mead, 1920; T. Werner Laurie, London, n.d.

Colley, Archdeacon. *Sermons of Spiritualism*, London, 1907

Crookes, William. *Researches in the Phenomena of Spiritualism*, J. Burns, London, 1874 etc. (frequently reprinted)

Crossley, Alan Ernest. *The Story of Helen Duncan, Materialization Medium*, Stockwell, U.K., 1975

Delanne, Gabriel. *Les Apparitions Materialisées des Vivants et des Morts*, Paris, 1911

Gray, Isa. *From Materialisation to Healing*, Regency Press, London, 1973

Hall, Trevor H. *The Spiritualist; The Story of Florence Cook and William Crookes*, Duckworth London, 1962; Garret/Helix, New York, 1963

Henry, T. Shekleton. *Spookland; A Record of Research & Experiment in the Much Talked of Realm of Mystery*, Chicago, 1902

Geley, Gustav. *Clairvoyance and Materialisation*, George Doran, New York, 1927; Arno Press, 1975

Geley, Gustav. *From the Unconscious to the Conscious*, William Collins, London, 1920

Medhurst, R. G. (coll.). *Crookes and the Spirit World; A Collection of Writings by or Concerning the Work of Sir William Crookes, O.M., F.R.S. in the Field of Psychical Research*, Taplinger/Souvenir Press, London, 1972

"Meduim, A." (A. Lunt). *Mysteries of the Seance*, Boston, 1905

Olcott, Henry S. *People From the Other World*, American Publishing Co., Hartford, Conn., 1875; Tuttle, 1972

Putnam, Allen. *Flashes of Light from the Spirit-Land*, Boston, 1872

Sargent, Epes. *Proof Palpable of Immortality*, Boston, 1876

Schrenck-Notzing, Baron von. *Phenomena of Materialisation*, Kegan Paul, London, 1920; Arno Press, 1975

Viereborne, A. *Life of James Riley*, Werner Co., Akron, Ohio, 1911

Wolfe, N. B. *Startling Facts in Modern Spiritualism*, N. B. Wolfe, Cincinnati, 1874

Mather, Increase (1639-1723) and **Cotton** (1662-1728)

Father and son, two eminent divines of Boston, Massachusetts, notorious for their crusade against persons suspected of witchcraft. (See **America, United States of; Witchcraft**)

Mathers, S(amuel) L(iddell) MacGregor (1854-1918)

Leading British occultist who was one of the founders of the Hermetic Order of the **Golden Dawn**. Born in Hackney, London, January 8, 1854, he lived with his mother at Bournemouth after the early death of his father.

As a boy he was intensely interested in symbolism and mysticism. He claimed a romantic descent from Ian MacGregor of Glenstrae, an ardent Jacobite who was given the title of Comte de Glenstrae by Louis XIV.

Mathers became a Freemason October 4, 1877 and a Master Mason January 30, 1878, soon after his twenty-fourth birthday. His mystical interests led him to become a member of the **Societas Rosicruciana in Anglia** (Rosicrucian Society of England), where he was an associate of Dr. William Wynn **Westcott**, Dr. William Robert **Woodman** and Kenneth **MacKenzie**.

Together with Westcott and Woodman, Mathers became a founder of the Golden Dawn in 1888. Meanwhile he lived in some poverty after the death of his mother in 1885, and spent much time researching occultism at the British Museum Library, London.

He met Anna **Kingsford**, who introduced him to Madame **Blavatsky**, who invited him to collaborate in the formation of the Theosophical Society, but he declined. In 1890 he married Mina Bergson, sister of the French philosopher Henri **Bergson**. Soon afterwards he removed to Paris with his wife.

Mathers and his wife received a small allowance from Annie Horniman (daughter of the founder of the Horniman Museum, London, and a member of the Golden Dawn), so that he might continue his studies on behalf of the G.D. However, disputes developed between Annie Horniman and Mathers on financial issues, and in December 1896 Mathers peremptorily expelled her from the G.D.

Mathers was deceived by the charlatans Mr. & Mrs. **Horos**, who acquired G.D. rituals from him for their own misuse. Other disagreements developed in the G.D. During a dispute between Mathers and the British officials of the G.D., occultist Aleister **Crowley** sided with Mathers and attempted to take over the London premises and documents. The poet W. B. **Yeats**, a noted G.D. member, played a prominent part in the rejection of Crowley.

Eventually Mathers himself was expelled from the G.D. He died November 20, 1918.

His translations of important occult texts included: *The Kabbalah Unveiled* (1907), *The Key of Solomon the King* (1889), *The Book of the Sacred Magic of Abra-Melin the Mage* (1898; reissued Causeway, 1974). For a sympathetic study of Mathers and his circle, see *The Sword of Wisdom; MacGregor Mathers and The Golden Dawn* by Ithell Colquhoun (1975).

The MacGregor Mathers Society was founded in Britain as a dining club for men only, membership by invitation. Address: BM#Spirotos (M.M.S.), London, W.C.1., England.

Mathur, Raghuvansh B(ahadur) (1918-)

Indian educator who has investigated parapsychological subjects. Born September 17, 1918 at Lucknow, India, he studied at University of Lucknow (B.A. 1937), London University, England (B.A. hons. 1940), Cambridge University, England (certificate in education 1942), London University (D.P.A. 1942, Ph.D. 1947).

He was Head of the Department of Education, University of Lucknow from 1953 onwards. In 1957 he was a Whitney-Fullbright visiting professor at Washington. He is a member of the Education Society, Research Society, University of Lucknow. He is interested in clairvoyance, telepathy and psychokinesis, and has investigated ESP in school children.

"Matikon"

A mystical work printed at Frankfurt in 1784, whose theories resemble the doctrines of the Brahmins. The following is an example of its teachings. Before the Fall, Adam was a pure spirit, a celestial being, surrounded by a mystic covering which rendered him incapable of being affected by any poison of nature, or by the power of the elements.

The physical body, therefore, is but a coarse husk in which, having lost his primitive invulnerability, man shelters from the elements. In his condition of perfect glory and perfect happiness Adam was a natural king, ruling all things visible and invisible, and showing forth the power of the Almighty. He also bore "a fiery, two-edged, all-piercing lance"—a living word, which united all powers within itself, and by means of which he could perform all things.

Matter Passing Through Matter

This has been claimed frequently as a seance-room phenomenon. It is involved in the marvel of **apports** and **teleportation** of the human body and its validation under test conditions would help towards the recognition of these greater phenomena.

Unfortunately it has seldom occurred under laboratory conditions that would be satisfying to modern investigators. Prof. Robert **Hare**'s notes of the passing of two small balls of platinum into two hermetically sealed glass tubes have been forgotten. The human element is too strong and in most of the cases on record the body of the medium plays some as yet not clearly understood part in the performance.

It should be first mentioned that interpenetration as such is not generally admitted. D. D. **Home** stoutly denied it and his **controls** declared that fissures or cracks are necessary to permit the passage of a solid body through another.

Sir William **Crookes** stated in 'Notes of an Enquiry into the Phenomena called Spiritual' (*Quarterly Journal of Science*, Jan. 1894): "After several phenomena had occurred, the conversation turned upon some circumstances which seemed only explicable on the assumption that matter had actually passed through a solid substance. Thereupon a message was given by means of the alphabet: 'It [is] impossible for matter to pass through matter, but we will show you what we can do.' We waited in silence.

"Presently a luminous appearance was seen hovering over the bouquet of flowers, and then, in full view of all present, a piece of china-grass 15 inches long, which formed the centre ornament of the bouquet, slowly rose from the other flowers, and then descended to the table in front of the vase between it and Mr. Home. It did not stop on reaching the table, but went straight through it and we all watched it till it had entirely passed through. Immediately on the disappearance of the grass, my wife, who was sitting near Mr. Home, saw a hand come up from under the table between them, holding the piece of grass. It tapped her on the shoulder two or three times with a sound audible to all, then laid the grass on the floor and disappeared. Only two persons saw the hand, but all in the room saw the piece of grass moving about as I have described.

"During the time this was taking place Mr. Home's hands were seen by all to be quietly resting on the table in front of him. The place where the grass disappeared was 18 inches from his hands. The table was a telescope dining table, opening with a screw; there was no leaf in it, and the junction of the two sides formed a narrow crack down the middle.The grass had passed through this chink, which I measured and found to be barely one eighth of an inch wide. The stem of the piece of grass was far too thick to enable me to force it through this crack without injuring it, yet we had all seen it pass through quietly and smoothly; and on examination it did not show the slightest signs of pressure or abrasion."

There is ground to suppose, however, that the statements of D. D. Home's controls were somewhat orthodox. Otherwise it would be necessary to discredit most of the evidence. To mention some: The psychical researcher Camille **Flammarion** described the passing of a book through a curtain in a seance with Eusapia **Palladino** on November 21, 1898. A book was held up by M. Jules Bois before the curtain at about the height of a man, 24 inches from each side of the edge. It was seized by an invisible hand and Mme. Flammarion who observed the rear of the curtain, suddenly saw it coming through, upheld in the air, without hands or arms, for a space of one or two seconds. Then she saw it fall down. She cried out: " Oh, the book, it has just passed through the curtain!"

There is some similarity between this observation of Flammarion and an account of Mrs. Speer (friend of the Rev. Stainton **Moses**) dated October 17, 1874: "Before the meeting Mr. Stainton Moses had taken three rings from his hands and threaded them on to his watch chain; his watch was on one end of the chain and a small pocket barometer on the other; both of these articles he placed in side pockets of his waistcoat, the rings hanging midway on his chain in full sight of the circle. We suddenly saw a pillar of light advance from a corner of the room, stand between me and Dr. S. then pass through the table to Mr. S. M. In a moment the figure flashed back again between us and threw something hard down upon the table. We passed our hands over the table, and found the rings had been removed from the medium's chain without his knowledge."

Mr. F. Fusedale, testifying to the **London Dialectical Society** in 1869, submitted an account of spirit manifestations in his own house and wrote: "The children and my wife would see the things they [the spirits] took (in particular a brooch of my wife's) appear to pass through solid substances, such as the wall or the doors, when they were taken from them; and they would take things out of the children's hands, as if in play, and hide them, and then after a little time return them again."

In a seance with the Italian medium Francesco **Carancini**, a dinner plate, covered with soot and out of the medium's reach, was placed in a padlocked wooden box which was in the hand of one of the sitters.

In experiments with Mrs. M. B. **Thayer**, Robert Cooper found a Japanese silk handkerchief which belonged to one of the sitters and flowers which came from nowhere in the locked box which he brought to the seance and the key of which he retained (*Light*, March 15, 1902).

"During my sixteen years of experiments, investigation into the question of the existence of this psychic force," wrote Gambier Bolton (author *Psychic Force*, 1904), "the apparent penetration of matter by matter had been such a common occurrence at our experimental meetings, that unless this happens to take place in connection with some unusually large and ponderous object that is suddenly brought into our midst, or removed from the place in which we are holding our meetings, I take but very little notice of it."

One of the occasions which he found worthwhile to notice came in a seance with the medium Cecil **Husk**. A light table was placed in the middle of the circle and was securely fastened by heavy baize curtains around the four sides, pinning the bottom of the curtain to the floor boards with drawing pins. The table was first heard rocking and tapping the floor boards and in less than three minutes it had apparently passed through the curtain and was found in its old place, 21 feet distant from the curtain.

After having been accused of fraud, the American medium, Mrs. Etta **Roberts**, in a test seance on September 3, 1891, was enclosed into a wire cage out of which many phantom forms issued. Finally Mrs. Roberts herself stepped out through the padlocked and sealed door without breaking the fastenings. The same feat was witnessed by Dr. Paul Gibier, Director of the Bacteriological Institute of New York with Mrs. Carrie M. Sawyer (Mrs. Salmon) in his own laboratory on three occasions. The trellis of the cage was found to be burning hot by several sitters.

Paranormal Knot-tying

Knots tied in an endless cord was the first phenomenon Professor **Zöllner** witnessed in his experiments with the medium Henry **Slade**. Zöllner made a loop of strong cord by tying the ends together. The ends projected beyond the knot and were sealed down to a piece of paper. In the seance room he hung the loop around his neck until the moment of experiment arrived. Then he took it off, placed the sealed knots on the table, placed his thumbs on each side of the knot and dropped the loop over the edge of the table on his knees. Slade kept his hands in sight and touched Zöllner's hands above the table. A few minutes later four symmetrical single knots were found on the cord.

In his further experiments, separate loops of leather were tied together and two wooden rings, one of oak the other of alder wood, were removed from a sealed loop of catgut and passed around the leg of a table. A snail shell which Prof. Zöllner placed on the table under a larger one dropped with a clatter on the slate held under the table surface. It was so hot that Zöllner nearly let it drop. A coin from a closed box on the table passed on in daylight to the slate underneath the top. Zöllner, placing two sheets of paper prepared with lamp-black between two slates in frames, closed the slates, bound them firmly together and, keeping it on his knees all the time, asked Slade to have an impression made inside the slates. He felt a strong pressure, opened the slates and found the impression of a human foot.

Prof. Zöllner's knot-tying experiment was repeated by Dr. Nichols with the medium William **Eglinton** in the presence of six observers. Dr. Nichols cut four yards of common brown twine from a fresh ball, tied the two ends together with a single knot, then passed each end through a hole in one of his visiting cards, tied another square knot and firmly sealed this knot to the card. Sitting around a small table in daylight, the sealed card upon the center of the table, the loop hanging down upon the floor, a minute later five single knots were found tied upon the string about a foot apart.

Paranormal Release and Movement of Clothing

The release of the medium from strong bonds without disturbing the knots or seals was claimed by the **Davenport Brothers**, although justifiable skepticism surrounds their stage performances. The psychic feat was also claimed by Sir William **Crookes** in his experiments with Mrs. Corner, the former Florence **Cook**.

A kindred demonstration, of which the Davenport Brothers were the greatest exponents, was the removal and donning of coats while the medium's hands were held. In a letter to the London newspaper *Daily News*, Dion Boucicault, the famous English actor and author, spoke of a seance at his house on October 11, 1864, in which, by striking a light, they actually witnessed the coat of Mr. Fay, the fellow-medium of the Davenport Brothers, flying off. "It was seen quitting him, plucked off him upwards. It flew up to the chandelier, where it hung for a moment and then fell to the ground. Mr. Fay was seen meanwhile bound hand and foot as before."

Robert Cooper wrote in his book *Spiritual Experiences* (1867): "The coat of Mr. Fay has, scores of times, been taken from his back in my presence, and Mr Fay at the time might be seen sitting like a statue with his hands securely tied behind him and the knots sealed. I have seen coats of various descriptions, from a large overcoat to a light paletot, put on in the place of his own in a moment of time, his hands remaining securely tied and the seal unbroken. I have known the coat that has been placed on Mr. Fay so small that it could only with difficulty be got off him. I have known a coat that was first placed on Mr. Fay transferred in a moment to the back of Ira Davenport, whose hands, like Mr. Fay's, were tied behind him, and the most curious part of the proceedings was that it was put on inside out. I have also known the waistcoat of Ira Davenport taken from under his coat, all buttoned up, with his watch and guard just as he wore it."

The same feat was witnessed in 1886 in Washington by Alfred Russel **Wallace** in a seance with Pierre L. O. A. **Keeler**.

Prof. Cesar **Lombroso** recorded a similar instance with Eusapia **Palladino**. An overcoat was placed on a chair beyond the reach of the medium whose hands and feet had been continuously controlled. Several objects from an inside pocket of the overcoat had been brought and laid on a phosphorescent cardboard on the table. All at once the medium began to complain of something about her neck and binding her tight. On light being produced it was found that she had the overcoat on, her arms being slopped into it, one in each sleeve.

It is scarcely necessary to stress that accounts of release from bonds and flying clothing must be treated with caution as they are stock feats of stage conjurers.

Ring Experiments and Chair Threading

Ring experiments and chair threading were claimed on many occasions. It would seem fraud-proof if two continuous iron rings were linked. In October, 1872, the *Religio-Philosophical Journal* of Chicago claimed to have witnessed this demonstration. The editor wrote: "We had the pleasure of attending a seance at which Capt. Winslow was the medium. The manifestations were very fine. One remarkable feat is the union of two solid iron rings, leaving them thus interlinked, and yet the metal perfectly sound."

In the majority of cases, however, this plain test was always shirked for the far less convincing demonstration of placing an iron ring on the sitter's arm after the clasping of the hands or for placing the ring which was too small to pass through the hand on the medium's wrist.

The medium Cecil **Husk** wore such a ring until his death. The Society for Psychical Research, London, investigated it and claimed that the ring could be forced off if the medium were chloroformed. The statement of Dr. George Wyld, a physician of Edinburgh, that the ring was specially made to his order and secretly marked by him, and that he held the medium's hand tight while the ring was taken from him in the dark was left unconsidered.

A similar wrought-iron ring was passed on to the ankle of the medium F. F. **Craddock**. It was very tight and caused him great discomfort and actual pain until it was filed off by a friendly blacksmith. Hearing of this occurrence, Gambier Bolton procured two welded iron rings and visiting Craddock, he fastened his hands behind his back with strong tape, then led him to a chair and fastened both arms, above the elbows, to the back of the chair with strong tapes and double knots.

Bolton stated: "Placing the two rings at his feet, I turned to the gas pendant hanging over our heads and lowered it somewhat, and before I had time to turn round again I heard the well-known ring of two pieces of iron being brought into sharp contact with each other, and walking up to him I found both rings on his wrist. To make sure that my eyes were not deceiving me. I pulled them strongly, struck one with the other, and found that they really were on his wrists; and I then carefully examined the tapes and found them not only secure, but so tight that his hands were swollen as a result of the tightness with which I had tied them. I stepped backwards, keeping my eyes on him, when suddenly with a crash both rings fell at my feet. To have withdrawn his hands and arms and replaced them in that time was a physical impossibility. On attempting to untie the tapes I found that I had pulled the knots so tightly that it was only after cutting them with a finely pointed pair of scissors, that I was able to release his hands once more, his wrists being marked for some time with a deep red line as the result."

Dr. L. Th. Chazarain, in his pamphlet *Les preuves scientifique de la survivance de l'âme* (1905) wrote of his experience in meetings organized in Paris by Dr. Puel, director of the *Revue des Sciences Psychiques*: "I took the ring which had been laid on the table and passed it round her right wrist. Immediately afterwards I took hold of the corresponding hand, and waited, holding it firmly between my own. At the end of eight or ten minutes she uttered a cry, like a cry of pain or fright, and at the same instant she woke and the ring was seen on the ground." M. August Reveillac observing the same effect found the fallen ring, when picked up, almost burning hot.

Col. W. A. Danskin in *How and Why I Became a Spiritualist* (1869) described a seance in Baltimore in which a secretly marked iron ring, seven inches smaller than the circumference of the medium's head, was repeatedly placed around the medium's neck. From the *Banner of Light* (January 11, 1868) he reproduced the following testimony, signed by thirty-two names: "We, the undersigned, hereby testify that we have attended the social meetings referred to; and that a solid iron ring, seven inches less in size than the young man's head was actually and unmistakably placed around his neck. There was as the advertisement claims, no possibility of fraud or deception, because the ring was freely submitted to the examination of the audience, both before and while on the neck of the young man."

The medium was a 19-year-old boy. Danskin further wrote: "Once, when only three persons were present—the medium, a friend and myself—we sat together in the dark room. I held the left hand of the medium, my friend held his right hand, our other hands being joined; and while thus sitting, the ring, which I had thrown some distance from us on the floor, suddenly came round my arm. I had never loosened my hold upon the medium, yet that solid iron ring, by an invisible power, was made to clasp my arm."

The medium Charles **Williams** often demonstrated the ring test. A. Smedley described instances with a ring which he secretly marked (*Some Reminiscences, an Account of Startling Spiritual Manifestations*, 1890). An interesting case was the following: Col. Lean (husband of Florence **Marryat**) mentally asked the control "John King" to fetch the half-hoop diamond ring from his wife's finger and place it on his. The ring, wrote Florence Marryat "was worn between my wedding ring and a heavy gold snake ring and I was holding the hand of my neighbor all the time and yet the ring was abstracted from between the other two and transferred to Colonel Lean's finger without my being aware of the circumstance."

In experiments with Frau **Vollhardt** in Berlin, two highly skeptical members of the Medical Society for Psychic Research, holding the hands of the medium at either side, found (after one of the crises of the medium) two unbroken wooden rings about their arms.

Robert Cooper, in a seance with the **Eddy Brothers**, experienced an electric shock at his elbow and found two iron rings on his arm which were held by the medium (reported in *Light*, March 15, 1902).

Count Solovovo Petrovo took a marked ring to a seance with the Russian medium **Sambor** on November 15, 1894. The ring was placed on M. Vassilief's arm when he was holding the medium's hands. (*Rebus*, No. 47, 1894). In seances with the same medium at the Spiritist Club, St. Petersburg, Dr. Pogorelski suddenly felt a blow on his right arm (close to the shoulder) and felt a chair passed on to his right arm. He held Sambor's hands by interlacing the fingers so that "it was impossible for our hands to become separated, even for a hundredth part of a second, without my feeling it." The experiment was repeated with another sitter whose hand was tied to Sambor's by means of a nearly ten yards long linen ribbon on the ends of which seals were placed.

John S. Farmer, Eglinton's biographer, wrote in his *Twixt Two Worlds* (1886) that in June 1879, at Mrs. Gregory's house "in the presence of Mr. Eglinton and a non-professional medium, two chairs were threaded at the same moment of time upon the arms of two sitters, each of whom was then holding the hand of the medium. Mr. Serjeant Cox was holding the hand of Mr. Eglinton and the back of the chair passed through his arm, giving him the sensation of a blow against the elbow when it did so. When a light was struck the chair was seen hanging on Mr. Sergeant Cox's arm and his hand was still grasping that of Mr. Eglinton. An immediate examination of the chair showed that the back of it was in good condition, with none of the woodwork loose or broken."

In *Planchette or the Despair of Science* (1880), Epes **Sargent** quoted many testimonies of similar occurrences with Charles Read of Buffalo and other mediums. Gambier **Bolton** wrote of his experience with Cecil **Husk** as follows: "With Mrs. Cecil Husk, on half a dozen occasions, in my own room and using my own chairs, I have held both hands of another experimenter with my two hands, about fifteen inches from the top of the back of one of the chairs, when with a sudden snap the back of the chair has passed over our wrists and has been seen by twelve to sixteen other observers hanging from our arms, in gas light, my hands never for an instant releasing those of my fellow-experimenters."

Well documented experiments in the claimed demonstration of the passage of matter through matter were carried out in June and July 1932, in the "Margery" circle in Boston (see **Crandon**). The phenomena, as reported by William H. Button in *Journal* of the American Society for Psychical Research (Aug.-Sept., 1932) consisted of the removal of a variety of objects from locked or sealed boxes and the introduction of various objects into such boxes. They were undertaken to confirm some of the results of the **Zöllner** experiments and were quite impressive.

The most astonishing phenomenon of the "Margery" mediumship was the interlocking rings. Sir Oliver **Lodge** had suggested the paranormal linking of two rings made of different woods might provide an irrefutable evidence of psychic force. The rings were duly provided, one of white wood and the other of red mahogany. At a seance with "Margery" in 1932, the rings were interlocked. According to Thomas R. Teitze in his book *Margery* (1973), the Irish poet W. B. **Yeats** was present at this seance. The feat of linking two rings made from different woods was apparently repeated. One set was sent to Sir Oliver Lodge for independent verification, but unfortunately arrived cracked and broken, presumably damaged in the post.

Another set of interlocked rings of different woods was shown to the British Spiritualist journalist Hannen Swaffer when he visited the Crandons in 1934. The rings were photographed and clearly show one of white wood and the other of red mahogany. They passed into the care of William Button, then president of the American Society for Psychical Research and were kept in a sealed glass-covered box. On a return visit to Boston in 1936, Hannen Swaffer asked to see the rings again, but when they were taken out of the box it was found that one of the rings was broken. It is unfortunate that permanent evidence of such paranormal linkage should be frustrated by inexplicable accidents.

In 1979, the **SORRAT** group formed by Prof. John G. **Neilhardt**, attempted to validate such paranormal linkages in an unassailable experiment. Since it could be argued that wooden rings might be cleverly separated along the grain and glued together again, parapsychologist W. E. **Cox** proposed seamless rings made from a single layer of ordinary leather. It would not be possible to cut and rejoin leather without trace of manipulation. In the event, the experiment was successful and film records show the paranormal materializing and dematerializing process. The linkages, however, were not permanent, as the leather rings separated again after a few seconds, a curious echo of the "Margery" experiments.

The high standing of the **SORRAT** parapsychologists, in conjunction with the film records, would seem to argue against any claims of fraud.

For an account of these and related experiments, see *SORRAT: A History of the Neilhardt Psychokinesis Experiments, 1961-1981* by John Thomas Richards (Scarecrow Press, 1982).

For a report on the earlier experiments of Prof. Zöllner, see *Transcendental Physics; An Account of Experimental Investigations from the Scientific Treatises of Johann Carl Friedrich Zöllner transl. Charles C. Massey (W. H. Harrison, London, 1882; Boston, 1888; reprinted Arno Press, 1976). See also* **Apports; Asports; Materialization; Movement; Psychokinesis; Teleportation)**

Maxwell, Dr. Joseph (c. 1933)

Attorney-General at the Court of Appeal at Bordeaux, prominent French psychical investigator. The chance reading of a book on Theosophy gave him the first impulse to study occult mysteries.

He found a remarkable medium in Limoge. The result, however, was unconvincing. But he realised that certain manifestations could only be studied with the assistance of nervous and mental pathology and for six years he studied at the University of Bordeaux for a medical degree.

As a trained investigator he had the rare fortune to find a medium in a friend, M. Meurice, who could produce telekinetic phenomena in good light. He obtained further good results with Mme. Agullana, of Bordeaux, two young mediums of Agen, and others. In 1895, in l'Agnelas, he attended, with Col. **Rochas**, Dariex, Sabatier, Count de Gramont and Watteville, experiments with Eusapia **Palladino**.

He made a deep study of the phenomena of **raps** and in *Les Phénomènes Psychiques*, Paris, 1903 (English translation *Metapsychical Phenomena*, 1905) he affirmed the reality of **telekinesis** in these words: "I am certain that we are in the presence of an unknown force; its manifestations do not seem to obey the same laws as those governing other forces more familiar to us; but I have no doubt they obey some law." He admitted that the force is intelligent but wondered if that intelligence did not come from the experimenters. His theory was that a kind of collective consciousness produced the intellectual results. The book, the result of ten years of research, is a valuable contribution to psychical literature.

His later books also merited interest. They were *La Divination* (1927), *La Magie* (1928), *Les Tarots* (1933).

Maya

A term used in Hinduism to denote the illusory nature of the world or empirical reality.

It is to be distinguished from delusion, since it implies that there is something present, although not what it seems to be.

According to the *Vedas,* the ancient scriptures of India, the divine infinity of Brahman (impersonal absolute) or Brahma (creative God) is real and is present in empirical reality, but veiled by the illusory power of *Maya.* (See also **Vedanta; Yoga**)

Mayavi-rupa

According to Theosophical teachings, based on Hindu religious philosophy, this is the invisible part of the physical body. Its appearance is exactly similar to that of the physical body. (See also **Rupa; Seven Principles; Theosophy**)

Maynard, Mrs. Henrietta Sturdevant (1841-1892)

American inspirational speaker, known as Nettie Colburn before her marriage. She was born in Bolton, Connecticut, in 1841.

President Lincoln had a high opinion of her gift and was, to an appreciable extent, influenced by her trance exhortations in the issue of the anti-slavery proclamation. Mrs. Maynard described her meetings with the President in her book *Was Abraham Lincoln a Spiritualist?* (1891). The book was reissued by Psychic Book Club, London, in 1917, revised edition 1956.

She had visited Washington in the spring of 1862 in order to see her brother, then in the Federal Army hospital.

Mrs. Lincoln, wife of the President, had a sitting with the medium and was enormously impressed. Next day she sent a carriage to bring the medium to see the President.

In a state of trance, the medium delivered a powerful address relating to the forthcoming Emancipation Pronouncement, forcefully urging the President "not to aborte the terms of its issue and not to delay its enforcement as a law beyond the opening of the year; and he was assured that it was to be the crowning event of his administration and his life," even although he was being strongly counseled by certain individuals to defer the matter.

According to reports, the President acknowledged the pressures upon him, and was deeply impressed by the medium's message.

Mrs. Maynard died at White Plains, New York, June 27, 1892. (See also Abraham **Lincoln**)

Mayne, Alan James (1927-)

British researcher and consultant. Born November 29, 1927 at Cambridge, England, he studied at Oxford University, England (B.A. 1949, B.Sc. 1951, M.A. 1953). He was Scientific Officer, United Kingdom Atomic Energy Authority from 1951-56; research statistician and consultant with A. C. Nielsen Co., Oxford, from 1956-59; research fellow with Electronic Computing Laboratory, University of Leeds from 1960-61. He edited *The Scientist Speculates,* an anthology.

He is a member of the Royal Statistical Society, Operational Research Society, British Computer Society, Mathematical Association, British Association for the Advancement of Science, Society for Psychical Research, Institute of Mathematical Statistics, British Society for the Philosophy of Science, Parapsychological Association.

In addition to his articles on mathematical statistics and operational research, he has studied parapsychological phenomena and published contributions in the *Journal of the British Society of Dowsers.* He acted as director of research for the Society of Metaphysicians (Archer's Court, Hastings, Sussex, England), and was president of the **Institute of Parascience** (Spryton, Lifton, Devon, U.K.) on its foundation in 1971.

Mazdaznan

An occult organization founded by Otto Hanisch (1854-1936). The name "Mazdaznan" is supposed to derive from the Persian "Mazda" and "Znan" meaning "Master-Thought," although this might be questioned by Persian scholars.

The cult embodied deep-breathing, physical exercises, vegetarian diet, astrology, phrenology and various occult studies, and claimed descent from Zoroastrianism.

Hanisch was born in Leipzig, Germany. When only a boy, he was supposed to have been taken to a Persian monastery of Math-El-Kharman and taught every major art and science, including occultism. At the age of 25, Hanisch traveled through Russia and eventually came to Los Angeles, California, where he established his cult, using the name Rev. Dr. Otoman Zar-Adusht Ha'nish. A European headquarters was established as a colony called "Aryana" (admitting only white-skinned Aryans) at Herliberg, Lake Zurich.

For an account of this cult, see 'A Strange Adventure in Switzerland' by H. R. Ecroyd (*The Quest,* vol. xxi, No. 1, October 1939).

Mead, G(eorge) R(obert) S(tow) (1863-1933)

Theosophist, scholar and writer on Gnosticism and early Christianity. Born 1863, he was educated at King's School, Rochester, England, and St. John's College, Cambridge (M.A. 1885). In 1899 he married Laura Mary Cooper (died 1924).

In 1884 Mead joined the **Theosophical Society** on coming down from Cambridge. In 1889 he gave up his work as a teacher to be closely concerned with the Theosophical Society and its founder Madame **Blavatsky.** Mead became her private secretary for the last three years of her life, sub-edited her monthly magazine *Lucifer,* which he renamed *The Theosophical Review* on becoming editor. Mead was one of the few associates of Madame Blavatsky to have a realistic view of her complex character. He believed her to be a Bohemian and racy personality as well as a powerful medium, and not simply the charlatan alleged by her critics.

In 1890, Mead was appointed General Secretary of the Theosophical Society, a position he held for eight years. In 1908 he resigned from the Society (in company with some 700 other members) in protest against the scandals concerning C. W. **Leadbeater.**

In March 1909, Mead founded The Quest Society, a group of sincere seekers after spiritual wisdom without any taint of charlatanism. He edited *The Quest* quarterly review from 1909-1930. After the death of his wife, Mead became actively interested in psychic science, and sat with several mediums.

He helped to edit the second edition of Madame Blavatsky's famous work *The Secret Doctrine* in 1890, and his own important contributions to mysticism and early religion include the following books: *Simon Magus* (1892), *Orpheus* (1896), *The Upanishads* (1896), *Fragments of a Faith Forgotten* (1900), *Apollonius of Tyana* (1901), *The Gospels and the Gospel* (1902), *Did Jesus Live 100* B.C.? (1903), *Thrice Greatest Hermes* (1906), *Echoes from the Gnosis* (1907), *The World Mystery* (1908), *Some Mystical Adventures* (1910), *Quests Old and New* (1913), *The Doctrine of the Subtle Body* [deals with early religious traditions relative to **Out-of-the-Body** experience or astral projection] (1919), *Pistis Sophia* (1921), *The Gnostic John the Baptizer* (1924), *The Sacred Dance in Christendom* (1926). Some of his most important books were reissued in modern times by University Books, Inc.

Mead died September 28, 1933.

Meddelande Fran Sallskapet fur Parapsykologis

Publication in Swedish language of Swedish Society for Psychical Research. Address: P.O. Box 7045, Stockholm 10386, Sweden.

Medea

In Greek mythology, an enchantress, daughter of the king of Colchis, who fell in love with Jason when he came to that country. Medea enabled him to slay the sleepless dragon that guarded the golden fleece. She fled from Colchis with Jason who made her his wife, and from whom she exacted a pledge never to love another woman. They were pursued by her father, but she delayed the pursuit by the cruel expedient of cutting her brother Absyrtus to pieces and strewing the limbs in the sea.

Medea accompanied Jason to Greece, where she was looked on as a barbarian, but having conciliated King Peleus who was now a very old man, she induced him to try to regain youth by bathing in a magic cauldron of which she was to prepare the contents. So great was his faith in her powers that the old man unhesitatingly plunged into her cauldron and was boiled alive. Her reason for this frightful act of cruelty was to hasten the succession to the throne of Jason, who in due course would have succeeded Peleus, but now the Greeks would have none of either him or Medea, and he was forced to leave Iolcos.

Growing tired of the formidable enchantress to whom he had bound himself, Jason sought to contract an alliance with Glauce, a young princess. Concealing her real intentions, Medea pretended friendship with the bride-elect and sent her as a wedding present a garment, which as soon as Glauce put it on, caused her to die in the greatest agony.

Eventually Medea parted from Jason. Having murdered her two children by him, she fled from Corinth in her car drawn by dragons to Athens, where she married Argeus, by whom she had a son, Medus. But the discovery of an attempt on the life of Theseus forced her to leave Athens. Accompanied by her son, she returned to Colchis, and restored her father to the throne, of which he had been deprived by his own brother Perses.

A great amount of literature has been written around the character of Medea. Euripides, Ennius, Aeschylus, and later, Thomas Corneille made her the theme of tragedies. The story of Medea is very movingly told by Charles Kingsley in his book *The Heroes* (1856 etc.). (See also **Greece**)

Medhurst, R. G. (died 1971)

British writer on parapsychology, a leading member of the **Society for Psychical Research,** London. Co-author with K. M. **Goldney** of the important article 'William Crookes and the Physical Phenomena of Mediumship' (*Proceedings* of the Society for Psychical Research, vol. 54, pt. 195, March 1964).

Dr. Medhurst's degree in mathematics and his outstanding work in mathematical engineering were of special value in evaluating mathematical aspects of ESP. His paper 'On the Origin of the Prepared Random Numbers Used in the Shackleton Experiments' (*Journal* of the Society for Psychical Research, vol. 46, 1971) argued that the method of constructing quasi-random series was incorrect

Other useful contributions by Dr. Medhurst included such subjects as investigation of the paragnost **Croiset,** Duke University's ESP cards, a project to discover ESP agents and percipients, criticism of the Psychophysical Research unit, as well as various book reviews.

His posthumous publication *Crookes and the Spirit World; A Collection of Writings By or Concerning the Work of Sir William Crookes* was edited by K. M. Goldney and M. R. Barrington (Taplinger, 1972).

Medicine, Occult

"The whole power of the occult physician," according to nineteenth century magus Éliphas Lévi, "is in the conscience of his will, while his whole art consists in exciting the faith of his patient. 'If you have faith,' says the Master, 'all things are possible to him who believes.' The subject must be dominated by expression, tone, gesture; confidence must be inspired by a fatherly manner, and cheerfulness stimulated by seasonable and sprightly talk. Rabelais, who was a greater magician than he seemed, made pantagruelism his special panacea. He compelled his patients to laugh, and all the remedies he administered subsequently succeeded better in consequence . . . . He established a magnetic sympathy between himself and them, by means of which he imparted his own confidence and good humour; he flattered them in his prefaces, termed them his precious, most illustrious patients, and dedicated his books to them. So are we convinced that Gargantua and Pantagruel cured more black humours, more tendencies to madness, more atrabilious whims, at that epoch of religious animosities and civil wars, than the whole Faculty of medicine could boast.

"Occult medicine is essentially sympathetic. Reciprocal affection, or at least real good will, must exist between doctor and patient. Syrups and juleps have very little inherent virtue; they are what they become through the mutual opinion of operator and subject; hence homœpathic medicine dispenses with them and no serious inconvenience follows. Oil and wine, combined with salt or camphor, are sufficient for the healing of all wounds, and for all external frictions or soothing applications. Oil and wine are the chief medicaments of the Gospel tradition. They formed the balm of the Good Samaritan, and in the Apocalypse, when describing the last plagues, the prophet prays the avenging powers to spare these substances, that is, to leave a hope and a remedy for so many wounds. What we term Extreme Unction was the pure and simple practice of the Master's traditional medicine, both for the early Christians and in the mind of the apostle Saint James, who has included the precept in his epistle to the faithful of the whole world. 'Is any man sick among you,' he writes, 'let him call in the priests of the church, and let them pray over him, anointing him with oil in the name of the Lord.'

"This divine therapeutic science was lost gradually, and Extreme Unction came to be regarded as a religious formality, as necessary preparation for death. At the same time, the thaumaturgic virtue of consecrated oil could not be effaced altogether from remembrance by the traditional doctrine, and it is perpetuated in the passage of the catechism which refers to Extreme Unction. Faith and charity were the most signal healing powers among the early Christians. The source of most diseases is in moral disorders; we must begin by healing the soul, and then the cure of the body will follow quickly."

Some of these concepts have been revived in the modern New Age concept of holistic medicine.

Recommended reading:

Hartmann, Franz. *The Life and Teachings of Paracelsus,* George Redway, London, 1887 (reprinted in one volume with *The Prophecies of Paracelsus,* Rudolf Steiner Publications, Blauvelt, N.Y., 1973)

Lévi, Éliphas. *Transcendental Magic,* new rev. ed., William Rider, London, 1923

Paracelsus (transl. Robert Turner). *The Archidoxes of Magic,* London, 1656; 2nd ed., Askin Publishers, New York/Samuel Weiser, 1975.

Medieval Magic

In the belief of the medieval professors of the science of magic, it conferred upon the adept power over **angels,** demons (See **Demonology**), **elementary spirits** and the souls of the dead, the possession of esoteric wisdom, and actual knowledge of the discovery and use of the latent forces and undeveloped energies resident in man. This was supposed to be accomplished by a combination of will and aspiration, which by sheer force germinated an intellectual faculty of psychological perception, enabling the adept to view the wonders of a new world and communicate with its inhabitants.

To accomplish this, the ordinary faculties were almost invariably heightened by artificial means. The grandeur of the magical ritual overwhelmed the neophyte, and quickened his senses. **Ceremonial magic** was a marvelous spur to the latent faculties of man's psychic nature, just as were the rich concomitants of religious mysticism.

In the medieval mind, as in other periods of man's history, it was thought that magic could be employed both for good and evil purposes, its branches being designated "white" and "black," according to whether it was used for benevolent or wicked ends. The term "red" magic was also occasionally employed, as indicating a more exalted type of the art, but the designation is fanciful.

White magic to a great extent concerned itself with the evocation of angelic forces and of the spirits of the elements. The angelology of the Catholic Church was undoubtedly derived from the ancient faith of Israel, which in turn was indebted to Egypt and Babylon, and the Alexandrian system of successive emanations from the one and eternal substance evolved a complex hierarchy of angels, all of whom appear to have been at the bidding of the magician who was in possession of the Incommunicable Name, a concept deriving from that of the "Name of Power" so greatly made use of in Egyptian magic (see **Egypt**).

The letters which composed this name were thought to possess a great measure of occult significance, and a power which in turn appears to have been reflected upon the entire Hebrew alphabet (see **Kabala**), which was thus endowed with mystical meaning, each of the letters representing a vital and creative number. Just as a language is formed from the letters of its alphabet, so from the secret powers which resided in the Hebrew alphabet were evolved magical variations. Comparable concepts existed in esoteric Hinduism (see **AUM**).

From the letter "aleph" to that of "jod" the angelical world was symbolized. From "caf" to "tsed" were represented the several orders of angels who inhabited the various spheres, each of which was under the direction of a particular intelligence. From "tsed" to "thau" is in secret correspondence with the elemental world; so that there were intelligences in correspondence with each of the Hebrew letters—"aleph" with the Haioth-ha-kodesch of the seraphim, the first and supreme angelical rank; "beth" the second letter with the ophanim or angels of the second order; "gimel" with the aralim or angels of the third order, and so on to the tenth letter "jod," which completes the enumeration of the angelical spheres.

The rest of the Hebrew alphabet, however, corresponds to individual principalities and powers—all of whom hold an important place in the mystical universe. Thus "caf," the eleventh letter, is in correspondence with **Metratton** who belongs to the first heaven of the astronomic world. Final "caf," the next letter, corresponds to the intelligences of the secret order whose supreme chief is Raziel, and "lamed" the twelfth letter corresponds to those of the third sphere, that of Saturn, whose lord is Schebtaiel, and so on. These intelligences under their queen, with the sixteenth letter "ain" and "pe," the seventeenth of the Hebrew alphabet, refer to the first of the mystical elements—that of Fire, which is ruled over by the seraphim. Final "pe" corresponds to the air where dwell the sylphs, who are presided over by Ariel. "Tsade" refers to water where dwell the nymphs under their queen Tharsis; "koph" corresponds to earth, the sphere of the gnomes, ruled over by the cherubim. The twentieth letter "resh" applies to the animal kingdom, including man. "Shin" corresponds to the vegetable world. "Tau" the last symbol of the Hebrew alphabet refers to the world of minerals.

There are, besides these, many other species of angels and powers, as will be seen from reference to the entries on **Angels** and **Kabala.** More exalted intelligences were conjured by rites to be found in the ancient book known as the **Key of Solomon the King,** and perhaps the most satisfactory collection of formulae for the invocation of the higher angels is that included in the anonymous *Theosophia Pneumatica,* published at Frankfurt in 1686, which bears a strong family resemblance to the *Treatise on Magic* by Arbatel. The names in this work do not tally with those which have been already given, but as it is admitted by occult students that the names of all unseen beings are really unknown to humanity, this does not seem of such importance as it might at first sight.

It would seem that such spiritual knowledge as the medieval magus was capable of attaining was insufficient to raise him above the intellectual limitations of his time, so that the work in question possesses all the faults of its age and type. But that is not to say that it is possessed of no practical value, and it may be taken as well illustrating the white magic of medieval times. It classifies the names of the angels under the title of "Olympic or Celestial Spirits," who abide in the firmament and constellations: they administer inferior destinies and accomplish and teach whatever is portended by the several stars in which they are insphered. They are powerless to act without a special command from the Almighty.

The stewards of Heaven are seven in number—Arathron, Bethor, Phaleg, Och, Hagith, Ophiel, and Phul. Each of them has a numerous host at his command, and the regions in which they dwell are 196 in all. Arathron appears on Saturday at the first hour, and answers for his territory and its inhabitants, as do the others, each at his own day and hour, and each presides for a period of 490 years. The functions of Bethor began in the fifieth year before the birth of Christ 430. Phagle reigned till A.D. 920; Och till the year 1410; Hagith governed until A.D. 1900. The others follow in succession.

These intelligences are the stewards of all the elements, energizing the firmament and, with their armies, depending from each other in a regular hierarchy. The names of the minor Olympian spirits are interpreted in divers ways, but those alone are powerful which they themselves give, which are adapted to the end for which they have been summoned. Generically, they are called "Astra," and their power is seldom prolonged beyond one hundred and forty years. The heavens and their inhabitants come voluntarily to man and often serve against even the will of man, but how much more if we implore their ministry.

That evil and troublesome spirits also approach men is accomplished by the cunning of the devil, at times by conjuration or attraction, and frequently as a penalty for sins. Therefore he who would abide in familiarity with celestial intelligences should take pains to avoid every serious sin. He should diligently pray for the protection of God to vanquish the impediments and schemes of Diabolus, and God will ordain that the devil himself shall work to the direct profit of the worker in magic.

Subject to Divine Providence, some spirits have power over pestilence and famine; some are destroyers of cities, like those of Sodom and Gomorrah; some are rulers over kingdoms, some guardians of provinces, some of a single person. The spirits are the ministers of the word of God, of the Church and its members, or they serve creatures in material things, sometimes to the salvation of soul and body, or, again, to the ruin of both. But nothing, good or bad, is done without knowledge, order, and administration.

It is unnecessary to follow the angelical host farther here, as it has been outlined elsewhere. Many preparations, however, are described by the author of the *Theosophia Pneumatica* for the successful evocation of these exalted beings. The magus must ponder during his period of initiation on the method of attaining the true knowledge of God, both by night and day. He must know the laws of the cosmos, and the practical secrets which may be gleaned from the study of the visible and invisible creatures of God. He must further know himself, and be able to distinguish between his mortal and immortal parts, and the several spheres to which they belong.

Both in his mortal and immortal natures, he must strive to love God, to adore and to fear him in spirit and in truth. He must sedulously attempt to find out whether he is truly fitted for the practice of magic, and if so, to which branch he should turn his talents, experimenting in all to discover in which he is most naturally gifted. He must hold inviolate such secrets as are communicated to him by spirits, and he must accustom himself to their evocation. He must keep himself, however, from the least suspicion of diabolical magic, which has to do with Satan, and which is the perversion of the theurgic power concealed in the word of God.

When he has fulfilled these conditions, and before he proceeds to the practice of his art, he should devote a prefatory period to deep contemplation on the high business which he has voluntarily taken in hand, and must present himself before God with a pure heart, undefiled mouth and innocent hands. He must bathe frequently and wear clean garments, confess his sins and abstain from wine for the space of three days.

On the eve of operation, he must dine sparely at noon, and sup on bread and water, and on the day he has chosen for the invocation he must seek a retired and uncontaminated spot, entirely free from observation. After offering up prayer, he compels the spirit which he has chosen to appear; that is, he has passed into a condition when it is impossible that the spirit should remain invisible to him.

On the arrival of the angel, the desire of the magus is briefly communicated to him, and his answer is written down. More than three questions should not be asked, and the angel is then dismissed into his special sphere. Besides having converse with angels, the magus had also power over the spirits of the elements. These are described in the entry on **Elementary Spirits** and we are here concerned with the manner of their evocation.

To obtain power over the salamanders, for example, the *Comte de Gabalis* of the Abbé de Villars prescribed the following procedure: "If you would recover empire over the salamanders, purify and exalt the natural fire that is within you. Nothing is required for this purpose but the concentration of the Fire of the World by means of concave mirrors in a globe of glass. In that globe is formed the 'solary' powder, which being of itself purified from the mixture of other elements, and being prepared according to Art becomes in a very short time a sovereign process for the exaltation of the fire that is within you, and transmutes you into an igneous nature."

There is very little information extant to show in what manner the evocation of elementary spirits was undertaken, and no ritual has survived which will acquaint us with the method of communicating with them. In older writers, it is difficult to distinguish between angels and elementary spirits; the lower hierarchies of the elementary spirits were also frequently invoked by the black magician. It is probable that the lesser angels of the older magicians were the sylphs of **Paracelsus,** and the more modern professors of the art.

The nineteenth-century magus Éliphas **Lévi** provided a method for the interrogation and government of elementary spirits, but he did not specify its source, and it was merely fragmentary. It is necessary, he claimed, in order to dominate these intelligences, to undergo the four trials of ancient initiation, and as these are unknown, their room must be supplied by similar tests. To approach the salamanders, therefore, one must expose himself in a burning house. To draw near the sylphs he must cross a precipice on a plank, or ascend a lofty mountain in a storm; and he who would win to the abode of the undines must plunge into a cascade or whirlpool. Thus power being acquired through courage and indomitable energy this fire, earth and water must be consecrated and exorcised.

The air is exorcised by the sufflation of the four cardinal points, the recitation of the prayer of the sylphs, and by the following formula: "The Spirit of God moved upon the water, and breathed into the nostrils of man the breath of life. Be Michael my leader, and be Sabtabiel my servant, in the name and by the virtue of light. Be the power of the word in my breath, and I will govern the spirits of this creature of Air, and by the will of my soul, I will restrain the steeds of the sun, and by the thought of my mind, and by the apple of my right eye. I exorcise thee O creature of Air, by the Petagrammaton, and in the name Tetragrammaton, wherein are steadfast will and well-directed faith. Amen. Sela. So be it."

Water is exorcised by the laying on of hands, by breathing and by speech, and by mixing sacred salt with a little of the ash which is left in an incense pan. The aspergillus is made of branches of vervain, periwinkle, sage, mint, ash, and basil, tied by a thread taken from a virgin's distaff, with a handle of hazelwood which has never borne fruit, and on which the characters of the seven spirits must be graven with the magic awl. The salt and ashes of the incense must be separately consecrated. The prayer of the undines should follow.

Fire is exorcised by casting salt, incense, white resin, camphor and sulphur therein, and by thrice pronouncing the three names of the genii of fire: Michael, Samael, and Anael, and then by reciting the prayer of the salamanders.

The Earth is exorcised by the sprinkling of water, by breathing, and by fire, and the prayer of the gnomes. Their signs are: the hieroglyphs of the Bull for the Gnomes who are commanded with the magic sword; of the Lion for the Salamanders, who are commanded with the forked rod, or *magic* trident; of the Eagle for the Sylphs, who are ruled by the holy pentacles; and finally, of Aquarius for the Undines, who are evoked by the cup of libations. Their respective sovereigns are Gob for the Gnomes, Djin for the Salamanders, Paralda for the Sylphs, and Necksa for the Undines. These names, it will be noticed, are borrowed from folklore.

The "laying" of an elementary spirit is accomplished by its adjuration by air, water, fire, and earth, by breathing, sprinkling, the burning of perfumes, by tracing on the ground the Star of Solomon and the sacred Pentagram, which should be drawn either with ash of consecrated fire or with a reed soaked in various colors, mixed with pure loadstone.

The Conjuration of the Four should then be repeated, the magus holding the pentacle of Solomon in his hand and taking up by turns the sword, rod and cup, this operation being preceded and terminated by the Kabalistic sign of the cross.

In order to subjugate an elementary spirit, the magus must be himself free of their besetting sins, thus a changeful person cannot rule the sylphs, nor a fickle one the undines, an angry man the salamanders, or a covetous one the gnomes. (The fomula for the evocation of spirits is given under **Necromancy.**)

The white magician did not concern himself as a rule with such matters as the raising of demons, animal transformations and the like, his whole desire being the exaltation of his spiritual nature, and the questions put by him to the spirits he evoked were all directed to that end. However, the dividing line between white and black magic is extremely ambiguous and it seems likely that the entities evoked might be deceptive as to their nature. (See also **Ceremonial Magic; Elementary Spirits; Grimoire; Magic**)

Recommended reading:

De Villars, l'Abbe de Montfaucon. *Comte de Gabalis,* Paris, 1670; Old Bourne Press, London, 1913

Lévi, Éliphas. *The History of Magic,* William Rider, London, 1913 etc.

Lévi, Éliphas. *Transcendental Magic,* George Redway, London, 1896 etc.

Mathers, S. L. MacGregor. *The Greater Key of Solomon,* George Redway, London, 1888

Shah, Sayed Idries. *Oriental Magic,* Rider & Co., London, 1956

Shah, Sayed Idries. *The Secret Lore of Magic,* Frederick Muller, London, 1956

Waite, Arthur E. *The Book of Ceremonial Magic,* William Rider, London, 1911 etc.

Waite, Arthur E. *The Holy Kabbalah,* Williams & Norgate, London, 1929; University Books, 1960

Walker, D. P. *Spiritual and Demonic Magic; From Ficino to Camperella,* University of Notre Dame Press paperback, Pennsylvania, 1975

Meditation

A tradition spiritual exercise in both Eastern and Western mystical systems, usually involving asceticism, a static sitting position, a blocking of the mind from normal sensory stimuli, and a concentration upon divine thoughts and/or mystical centers in the human body.

In the Christian tradition, meditation was often enhanced by prolonged fasts and other physical mortification, in order to assert the supremacy of the soul over all physical and sensory demands. Certain well-defined stages of spiritual growth are recorded by saints and mystics, notably the awakening of the soul, contemplation, the dark night of the soul, illumination, spiritual ecstasy.

Eastern meditation traditions also record such stages, but the methods of meditation are more numerous and complex. In general, meditation was taught by a guru only to a properly qualified pupil who had already followed a pathway of *sadhana* or spiritual discipline which ensured purification at all levels. The various **Yoga** systems describe such spiritual disciplines in detail, with special emphasis on moral restraints and ethical observances. Meditation without such preliminary training was considered premature and dangerous.

The most generally known system is that of the sage Patanjali (ca. 200 B.C.) which taught that in order to experience true reality one must transcend the body and mind. In his *Yoga Sutras,* Patanjali outlined a program of physical exercises (to strengthen a meditation posture), breathing techniques (to purify the body), withdrawal of the senses, concentration, meditation, culminating in mystical experience.

In this process, supernormal powers might be manifested, but were to be ignored. The ultimate goal of meditation was spiritual illumination transcending individuality and extending the consciousness beyond time, space and causality, but also interfusing it with the everyday duties and responsibilities of the individual.

Thus it was not necessary for an illuminated individual to renounce the world, and there are stories in Hindu scriptures of kings and princes who did not forsake their mundane tasks after transcendental experience.

It is clear from consideration of the practices of many religions that meditation may be active or passive, depending upon the techniques employed and the degree of purification of the meditator. Fixed concentration upon one mental image, sound or center in the body is a passive mechanical technique which may bring relaxation, a sense of well-being and other mundane achievements, but is not in itself spiritual or transcendental in the traditional sense of the terms. The popular so-called "Transcendental Meditation" technique of **Maharishi Mahesh Yogi** appears to be of this order, hence criticism from the traditionalists.

In active meditation systems, there has to be purification at all levels of the individual—physical, mental, emotional and spiritual, and the mind is exercised creatively before it can transcend its own activity. Those meditators, who have attained stages of higher consciousness or mystical illumination, testify that there is a gradual process of refinement arising from the activity of a mysterious energy which Hindu mystics call **Kundalini,** which modifies the entire organism.

In any case, commonsense and the laws of cause and effect suggest that no mechanical habit of meditation could be expected to transform the consciousness without special efforts in other directions.

However, the expectations and attitudes of the mass media consumer society have now permeated the realms of mysticism, and the inducement of high spiritual awareness by a "simple technique" or a "single gift of money" is very compelling to a generation reared on television commercials and the "instant mysticism" of drug states.

Even the desire for spiritual experience often reflects mundane egoistic attitudes, and the transcending of the mundane individual ego is one of the first stages of traditional meditation systems. (See also **Drugs; Guru; Kundalini; Transcendental Meditation; Yoga**)

Recommended reading:

Augustine of Hippo (ed. Francis J. Sheed). *Confessions of St. Augustine,* Sheed, 1943 etc.

John of Ruysbroeck (transl. P. Synschenk). *Adornment of the Spiritual Marriage,* London, 1916

Gopi Krishna. *Kundalini, the Evolutionary Energy in Man,* London, 1970; Shambala, 1970

Gopi Krishna (ed. Gene Kieffer). *Kundalini for the New Age; Selected Writings,* Bantam Books (paperback), 1988

Gopi Krishna. *The Wonder of the Brain,* F.I.N.D. Research Trust, Canada, 1987 (paperback).

Luk, Charles. *The Secrets of Chinese Meditation,* London, 1964; Rider paperback, 1969

Patanjali (transl. M. N. Dvidedi). *The Yoga-Sutras of Patanjali,* Theosophical Publishing House, Adyar, India, 1890, frequently reprinted

Underhill, Evelyn. *Mysticism; a Study in the Nature and Development of Man's Spiritual Consciousness,* London, 1911, frequently reprinted

Medium

Throughout the history of **Spiritualism,** a special place has been occupied by the medium, as an individual qualified in some special manner to form a link between the dead and the living. Through the medium, the spirits of the departed may communicate with their friends or relatives still on earth, either by making use of the material organism of the medium ("automatic phenomena") or by producing in the physical world certain manifestations which cannot be explained by known physical laws ("physical phenomena").

The essential qualification of a medium is an abnormal sensitiveness, which enables him or her to be readily "controlled" by disembodied spirits. Mediums are sometimes also known as "sensitives" or "psychics," although these terms are normally applicable to psychically gifted individuals who are not controlled by spirits of the dead.

There is some doubt as to whether mediumship is an inherent faculty, or whether it may be acquired, and among some Spiritualists at least, the belief is held that all individuals are mediums, although in varying degrees, and consequently that all are in communication with spirits, from whom proceeds what we call "inspiration." Those who are ordinarily designated "mediums" are but gifted with the common faculty in a higher degree than their fellows.

Mediumship, like all the central doctrines of Spiritualism, dates back to very early times. Demoniac **possession** affords an excellent instance, so also does **witchcraft,** while the *somnambule* of the Mesmerists was comparable with the modern psychic or medium. In its usual application, however, the term medium is used only of those sensitives who belong to the modern Spiritualist movement, which had its origin in America in 1848 (see **Fox Sisters**). In this sense, then, Mrs. Fox and her daughters, the heroines of the **Rochester Rappings,** were the earliest mediums. The phenomena of their seances consisted mainly of knockings, by means of which messages were conveyed from the spirits to the sitters.

Other mediums rapidly sprang up, first in America, and later in Britain and the Continent. Their mediumship was of two kinds—"physical" and "automatic." These phases were to be found either separately or combined in one person, as in the case of the Rev. Stainton **Moses.** Indeed, it was practically impossible to find a **trance** speaker who did not at one time or another practice the physical manifestations, until the time of Mrs. **Piper,** whose phenomena were purely subjective.

The early rappings speedily developed into more elaborate manifestations. For a few years an epidemic of **tableturning** caused widespread excitement, and the motions of the table became a favorite means of communicating with the spirits. The playing of musical instruments without visible agency was a form of manifestation which received the attention of mediums from an early date, as also the bringing into the seance room of "**apports**" of fruit, flowers, perfume, and all manner of portable property. Darkness was found to facilitate the spirit-manifestations, and as there are certain physical processes (such as those in photography) to which darkness is essential, no logical objection could be offered to the dimness of the seance room.

The members of the circle were generally seated round a table, holding each other's hands, and they were often enjoined to sing or talk pending the manifestation of a spirit. All this, although offering grounds of suspicion to the incredulous, was plausibly explained by the Spiritualists.

As time went on, and the demand for physical manifestations increased, these became more daring and more varied. The moving of objects without contact, the **levitation** of heavy furniture and of medium or sitters, the **elongation** of the human body, the **fire ordeal,** were all practiced by the medium D. D. **Home.** At the public performances of the **Davenport Brothers** musical instruments were played and moved about the room, and objects moved without being touched, while the brothers were bound hand and foot in a small cabinet. (However, the Davenport Brothers did not claim to be mediums and may have been simply skilled stage performers.)

The **slate-writing** of "Dr." Henry **Slade** and William **Eglinton** had a considerable vogue. The tying of knots in endless cords, the passage of **matter** through matter were typical physical phenomena of the mediumistic circle.

The crowning achievement, however, was the **materialization** of the spirit-form. Quite early in the history of Spiritualism, hands were materialized, then faces, and finally the complete form of the spirit "**control.**" Thereafter the materialized spirits allowed themselves to be touched, and even held conversations with the sitters. Further proof of the actuality of the spirit "control" was offered by **spirit photography.**

To those for whom Spiritualism was a religion, however, the most important part of the mediumistic performances was the trance-utterances and the like which come under the heading of "automatic," or psychological phenomena (see **Automatic Speaking** and **Automatic Writing**). These dealt largely with the conditions of life on the other side of the grave, although in style they often tended to be verbose and vague. Spirit drawings were sometimes amazingly impressive, at other times nondescript (see **Automatic Drawing and Painting**).

Clairvoyance and **crystal vision** were included in the psychological phenomena, and so also are the pseudo-prophetic utterances of mediums, and the speaking in unknown **tongues.**

According to the Spiritualist hypothesis already referred to, that "all individuals are mediums," it would be necessary to class inspiration, not only the inspiration of genius, but all good or evil impulses as spiritual phenomena, and that in turn suggests that the everyday life of the normal individual is to some extent directed by spirit "controls." And therein lies the responsibility of mediumship, for the medium who desires to be controlled by pure spirits from the higher spheres should live a well-conducted and principled life.

Misuse of the divine gift of mediumship carries with it its own punishment, for the medium becomes the sport of base human spirits and **elementals,** his or her will is sapped, and the whole being degraded. Likewise the medium must be wary of giving up individual personality to the first spirit who comes by for the low and earthbound spirits have least difficulty in communicating with the living, having still more affinity with the things of the earth than with those of the spirit.

Great Mediums of the Past

Of the physical mediums, perhaps the most successful was Daniel Dunglas **Home** (1833-1886), who claimed to be of Scottish birth. He went to America at an early age, and it was there that his mediumistic powers were first developed, although not until he came to Britain in 1855 did he rise to fame.

It is worthy of note that Home was never detected in **fraud** (as were many physical mediums at one time or another) although his demonstrations were similar in kind to those of other mediums. This may be due in part to the fact that he did not act as a professional medium. Again, all who came into contact with him were impressed by his simple manners, and frank and affectionate disposition, so that he possessed the most valuable asset of a medium—the ability to inspire confidence in his sitters.

The **Davenport Brothers,** although widely popular in their time, were of a quite different nature. Their performance consisted of allowing themselves to be securely bound in a cabinet by the sitters, and while thus handicapped producing the usual mediumistic phenomena. The Davenports were claimed to be mere conjurers however, and when the stage magicians Maskelyne and Cook successfully imitated their feats, the Davenports lost credibility.

Slate-writing, which proved one of the most widely-accepted forms of psychic phenomena, had as its principal exponents Henry **Slade** and William **Eglinton.** The best argument which can be advanced against their feats is to be found in the pseudo-seances of S. J. **Davey,** given in the interests of the **Society for Psychical Research,** London. Mr. Davey's slate-writing exhibitions were so much like those of the professional mediums that some Spiritualists refused to believe that he was conjuring, and hailed him as a renegade medium!

Automatic drawing was principally represented by David **Duguid,** a Scottish medium who attained considerable success in that line.

Prominent **trance** speakers and writers were **Duguid,** J. J. **Morse,** Mrs. Hardinge **Britten,** and Mrs. Cora L. V. Tappan-**Richmond.**

One of the best-known and most respected of private mediums was the Rev. Stainton **Moses** (1839-92), a clergyman and schoolmaster, whose normal life was beyond reproach. He produced both automatic and physical manifestations, the former including the writing of a work *Spirit Teachings* (1894) dictated from time to time by his spirit controls, while the latter comprised levitations, lights and apports. His position, character, and education gave to his support of Spiritualism a stability of considerable value.

It is to later mediums, however, that we must look for proof worthy of scientific consideration, and of these the most important were Eusapia **Palladino** and Mrs. **Piper.**

Eusapia Palladino, an Italian medium, was born in 1854, and for a good many years had acted as medium for scientific investigators. In 1892, seances were held at Milan, at which were present Professors Schiaparelli, **Brofferio, Lombroso, Richet,** and others. In 1894 Professor Richet conducted some experiments with Eusapia at his house in the Ile Roubaud, to which he invited Professor **Lodge,** F. W. H. **Myers,** and Dr. **Ochorowicz.**

The phenomena occurring in Eusapia's presence were the ordinary manifestations of the mediumistic seance, but their interest lay in the fact that all the distinguished investigators professed themselves satisfied that the medium, with her hands, head, and feet controlled by the sitters, could not of herself produce the phenomena.

Credible witnesses asserted that Eusapia possessed the ability to project psychic limbs from her person. Professor Lodge and F. W. H. Myers were disposed to look for a new force **(ectenic force)** emanating from the medium.

In 1895, however, some seances with Eusapia were held at the house of F. W. H. Myers at Cambridge, England, where it became apparent that she habitually freed a hand or a foot—in short, habitually resorted to fraud if not properly controlled. Yet even these exposures were not conclusive, for in 1898, after a further series of experiments, Myers and Professors Lodge and Richet once more declared their belief in the genuineness of this medium's phenomena.

Mrs. Leonore E. **Piper,** the Boston medium whose trance utterances and writings contain some of the best evidence forthcoming for the truth of Spiritualism, first fell into a spontaneous trance in 1884, and in the following year was observed by Professor William **James** of Harvard. Thereafter her case was carefully studied by the **Society for Psychical Research,** London.

Her first important **control** was a French physician "Dr. Phinuit," who was probably a fiction, but in 1892 she was controlled by "George Pelham," a young author who had died in February of that year. So complete was her impersonation of Pelham that more than thirty of his friends claimed to recognize him, and so well did he establish his identity by the mention of many private matters known only to himself and a few of his friends, that the hypothesis of spirit-control was almost inevitable.

In 1896, "George Pelham" gave place to "Imperator," "Rector," and other spirits, who had formerly controlled the Rev. Stainton **Moses.** From that time, and especially after 1900, the interest of the sittings declined, and they offered less material for the investigator.

Another automatic medium, Hélène **Smith,** came under the observation of Professor Theodor **Flournoy.** Hélène's trance utterances were spoken in the **"Martian language,"** a variant of the "unknown tongue" of the early ecstatics, and she claimed to be a reincarnation of Marie Antoinette and a Hindu princess.

Healing Mediums

The diagnosis and cure of disease have been extensively practiced by Spiritualist mediums, following in the path of the older sumnambules and magnetic subjects. These latter not only used to trace the progress of diseases, but also to diagnose and to prescribe a mode of treatment.

At the outset it was not prescribed for the diseases of those with whom they were in *rapport,* and likewise the medium, having established *rapport* between his control and the patient, was influenced to prescribe a mode of treatment.

It was not considered proper for the healing medium to accept any remuneration for his services, but later healers usually expected a fee.

It is true that healing mediums, like Christian Scientists, mesmerists, magnetists, and others, effected a considerable proportion of *bona fide* cures, but whether by spirit influence or suggestion is a point on which there is too much diversity of opinion for discussion here (see Psychic **Healing**).

It is claimed for many mediums that they have cured diseases of long standing which were pronounced incurable—heart disease, consumption, cancers, paralysis, and many more.

Some also have been credited with the power to heal instantaneously, as did the **Curé d'Ars** and other miraculous healers. The marvelous potency of the waters at **Lourdes** is considered to be the gift of discarnate beings, having been in the first instance revealed to a child by her spirit **guide,** in the form of a white angel (see **Healing by Faith**).

Spiritualist Views of Mediumship

Of the various theories advanced to explain the mediumistic manifestations, the most important is the Spiritualist explanation, which claims that the phenomena are produced by the spirits of the dead acting on the sensitive organism of the medium. The evidence for such a theory, although some investigators of the highest distinction have found it satisfactory, is nevertheless generally considered to be inconclusive.

Although conscious **fraud** is no longer considered to cover the whole ground, yet plays a definite part in the phenomena of both "physical" and trance mediums, it has been shown that some of the latter frequently collect through private inquiry information about possible sitters, which is later retailed by the "controls." The explanation of some Spiritualists of these lapses into fraud is that they are instigated by the spirits themselves, but this is clearly untenable in the majority of cases. However, it does not seem impossible that a genuine medium might have to resort to fraud during a temporary failure of psychic powers.

Automatism covers a still wider field. That automatic utterances, writing, drawing, etc., may be quite involuntary, and outside the sphere of the medium's normal consciousness, is no longer to be doubted. The psychological phenomena may be met with in small children, and in private mediums whose good faith is beyond question, and the state is recognized as being allied to **hypnotism** and hysteria. Besides automatism and fraud, there are some other factors to be considered.

Some deception may be practiced by sitters as well as by the medium. It has been said that the ability to inspire confidence in sitters is essential to a successful medium, and if at the same time the sitters be predisposed to believe in the paranormal nature of the manifestations, it is easy to imagine a lessening of the attention and observation so necessary to the investigator.

The impossibility of continued observation for even a short period is a fact that can be proved by experiment. Memory defects and proneness to exaggeration are also accountable for many of the claimed marvels of the seance room, and possible **hallucination** must be considered. When the medium is in a trance, with its accompanying hyperaesthesia, unconscious suggestion on the part of the sitters might offer a rational explanation of so-called "clairvoyance."

But when all these factors are removed, the basic reality of mediumship still remains. In the case of Mrs. Piper, for example, the least that can be said for her trance utterances is that they were telepathic, that she gathered information from the minds of her sitters, or through them from other living minds. To many investigators, however, they presented definite proof of spirit communication. To meet such instances, F. W. H. Myers formulated his doctrine of transcendental faculties, crediting the medium with **clairvoyance** and **prevision.** But no really conclusive test has ever been complied with.

Psychical researchers have left sealed letters, whose contents are known only to themselves, instructing that after their deaths the letters be submitted to a medium; but the evidence of posthumous communication of such messages is not totally unassailable. Claimed instances still remain controversial.

Again, in the case of Eusapia **Palladino,** F. W. H. Myers, Sir Oliver Lodge and others have inclined to the belief in a force emanating from the medium by which the physical manifestations are produced. Here also, the evidence cannot be considered conclusive. Skilled and scientific investigators have from time to time been deceived by what has actually proved to be sleight of hand, and in fact the only trustworthy evidence possible would be that of automatic records.

At the same time, the testimony of such distinguished scientists as Professor Charles **Richet,** Sir Oliver **Lodge** and others makes it evident that judgment must not be hastily pronounced on the medium, but rather that an earnest endeavor be made to solve the problems in that connection.

Psychical Researchers and Mediumship

Dr. Joseph **Maxwell** defined a medium as "a person in the presence of whom psychical phenomena can be observed." Dr. Gustav **Geley**'s definition was "one whose constituent elements—mental, dynamic and material—are capable of being momentarily decentralised," an intermediary for communication between the material and spirit world. In view of this definition, F. W. H. **Myers** called the word medium "a barbarous and question-begging term" as many mediumistic communications were nothing but subconscious revelation and suggested the use of the word "automatist."

By others, the word "psychic" was proposed, while Prof. Pierre Janet in *L'Automatisme Psychologique* (1889) termed mediums *les individus suggestibles*—persons controlled by an idea or suggestion either self-originated or coming from without, from an unseen source.

Prof. **Lombroso** maintained that there was a close relationship between the phenomena of mediumship and hysteria. Professor **Richet** voiced a warning in saying: "Unless we assign an unwarrantable extension to this morbid state it does not seem favourable to the phenomena." He believed that "mediums are more or less neuropaths, liable to headaches, insomnia and dyspepsia. The facility with which their consciousness suffers dissociation indicates a certain mental instability and their responsibility while in a state of trance is diminished."

The same opinion was expressed slightly more circumstantially, by psychical researcher Frank **Podmore** as follows: "Physiologically speaking, the medium is a person of unstable nervous equilibrium, in whom the control normally exercised by the higher brain centres is liable, on slight provocation, to be abrogated, leaving the organism, as in dream or somnambulism to the guidance of impulses which in a state of unimpaired consciousness would have been suppressed before they could have resulted in action."

Dr. Joseph **Maxwell** advised caution. He admitted that a certain impressionability—or nervous instability—was a favorable condition for the effervescence of mediumnity. But he stressed that the term "nervous instability" was not meant in an ill sense. His best experiments were made with people who were not in any way hysterical; neurasthenics generally gave no result whatever. Nor did "instability" mean want of equilibrium. Many mediums he had known had extremely well-balanced minds from the mental and nervous point of view. Their nervous system was even superior to the average. It was a state such as appears in nervous hypertension. The mediums, perhaps, were precursors, possessing faculties which are abnormal today, but which might become normal in the future.

"There are four chief types of temperament," wrote Dr. Charles **Lancelin,** "nervous, bilious, lymphatic and sanguine. Of these, the nervous temperament is the best suited for psychic experiments of all kinds; the bilious is the most receptive; the sanguine is liable to hallucinations, both subjective and objective; while the lymphatic is the least suitable of all, from every point of view. Of course, one's temperament is usually a compound of all of these, which are rarely found in their ideal state; but the predominantly nervous temperament is the one best suited for this test."

What Mediumship Is and What It Is Not

Agreement is now nearly general that mediumship is not pathological. It is not a development of certain abnormal states like hysteria. As **Myers** remarked, the confusion which is noticeable on the point is the result of the observation that supernormal phenomena use the same channels for manifestation as the abnormal phenomena. The abnormal phenomena are degenerative, the phenomena of mediumship are developmental, they show the promise of powers as yet unknown whereas the abnormal phenomena (like hysteria or epilepsy) show the degeneration of powers already acquired.

Prof. **Flournoy,** after his exhaustive study of the mediumship of Mlle. Hélène **Smith** came to the same conclusion. He stated: "It is far from being demonstrated that mediumship is a pathological phenomenon. It is abnormal, no doubt, in the sense of being rare, exceptional; but rarity is not morbidity. The few years during which these phenomena have been seriously and scientifically studied have not been enough to allow us to pronounce on their true nature. It is interesting to note that in the countries where these studies have been pushed the furthest, in England and America, the dominant view among the savants who have gone deepest into the matter is not at all unfavourable to mediumship; and that, far from regarding it as a special case of hysteria, they see in it a faculty superior, advantageous and healthy, but that hysteria is a form of degeneracy, a pathological parody, a morbid caricature."

Dr. Guiseppe Venzano, an Italian psychical researcher, was similarly emphatic: "Mediumship only represents a temporary deviation from the normal psychic state, and absolutely excludes the idea of morbidity; it is even proved that the slightest alteration of a pathological nature is sufficient to diminish or arrest the mediumistic powers."

Indeed, as Prof. **Flournoy** discovered, the conditions for the successful exercise of mediumistic powers are the same as for the voluntary exercise of any other power—a state of good health, nervous equilibrium, calm, absence of care, good humor, and sympathetic surroundings.

Outwardly there is no sign to disclose mediumistic powers. Dr. J. Maxwell stated that he observed tiny spots in the iris of the eyes of all mediums he came in contact with. They were generally black round marks, bearing a vague resemblance to a cat's head, a bird's head, cat's paws, etc. Sometimes letters appear to be traced on the iris. He knew a medium in whose left eye the letter "M" was very clearly and distinctly marked. Nevertheless he did not affirm that there was any connection between these iris spots and the mediumistic faculties. His observations, which yet await confirmation, recall medieval assertions about tell-tale spots in the eyes of sorcerers.

In many cases, mediumship can be traced as a hereditary gift. If the heredity is not direct it is to be found in ancestors or collaterals and, according to Dr. **Geley,** it is conditioned by a tendency to decentralization of the constituent psychological factors of the medium.

Mother Shipton, supposed to have been a sixteenth-century clairvoyant and prophet, was said to have been the daughter of a witch, but she may have been entirely a legendary figure. An ancestress of the **Eddy Brothers,** nineteenth-century American mediums, was sentenced to the pyre in Harlem. The **Fox Sisters** had visionary forebears. The great medium D. D. **Home** was a descendant on his mother's side of a Scotch Highland family. The medium Franek **Kluski** inherited his gifts from his father.

In the absence of heredity, physical defects or a serious illness may be the potential cause of mediumistic development. It is (as Conan Doyle put it) as if the bodily weakness causes what may be described as a dislocation of the soul, so that it is more detached and capable of independent action. Eusapia **Palladino** had a peculiar depression of her parietal bone caused by an accident in childhood. Mrs. **Piper**'s mediumship developed after two internal operations, and "Imperator," in an automatic script of the Rev. Stainton **Moses,** said: "The tempering effect of a bodily illness has been in all your life an engine of great power with us." In the case of Mary **Jobson,** Mollie **Fancher,** Lurrency Vennum (The **"Watseka Wonder"**) and Vincent **Turvey,** prolonged physical agony was the price of their psychic gifts.

With regard to the contention that everyone is a potential medium. H. Dennis **Bradley** wrote in his book *The Wisdom of the Gods* (1925): "Mediumship, even in the most advanced and powerful stage extant, is relatively a mere incoherent fluttering towards the knowledge we may gain in the future. In fifty years from now, the few great mediums of today will be relegated to the position of the man who first risked the drop from the first parachute."

This prophecy was too enthusiastic and has not been fulfilled so far, and with the possible exceptions of **metalbending** and **psychic surgery,** there is no new mediumistic manifestation which has not been recorded in ages past in similar, or even more marvelous volume than at present. Nor is it likely that the development of the gift simply depends on willingness to experiment. According to an automatic script of Stainton **Moses:** "the mediumistic peculiarity is one of the spirit solely, and not of body. The gift is perpetuated even after the death of the earth body. Those who on earth have been mediums retain the gift and use it with us. They are the most frequent visitors to your world."

Mediumship is a delicate gift. Its voluntary development requires great care and understanding. According to Barbara McKenzie (*Light,* March 18, 1932), who had many years of unparalleled experience at the **British College of Psychic Science,** the production and ripening of physical gifts "involves a lengthy period of homely, warm, appreciative incubation . . . which is found at its best in a family or in a very intimate home circle, in which a continuity of conditions and a warm personal and even reverent interest is assured."

Even after the attainment of a *settled psychic constitution,* "the transplantation of the medium from the home circle to public work, or to a colder scientific group, is attended with risk to the gift, and by far the best way, when it is possible, is for the scientist to join the home group as Dr. Crawford did and try to stiffen up conditions there. . . . It would seem that the imposition of so-called test conditions, of open discussion, of reports and publication of these, and the mixed mental conditions of sitters holding divers views as against the homogeneity of the home circle, awakens the mentality and egotistic nature of the medium to an excessive degree, and endangers the necessary passivity, with the result that phenomena which had been pure and regular become mixed and irregular."

As great an authority as Sir Oliver **Lodge** stated that the medium should be treated "as a delicate piece of apparatus wherewith we are making an investigation. The medium is an instrument whose ways and idiosyncrasies must be learnt, and to a certain extent humoured, just as one studies and humours the ways of some much less delicate piece of physical apparatus turned out by a skilled instrument maker."

There is a great difference between Oriental and Occidental methods of development. The **Yoga** system is the most conspicuous among the Oriental methods. It is also highly complicated. Dr. Hereward **Carrington**'s *Higher Psychical Development* (1920) presented the system in a simple and lucid way. It must be stressed, however, that the prime aim of Yoga practice is spiritual development, and psychic faculties are regarded as side effects which should be ignored as obstacles to spiritual evolution.

In his book *The Secret of Yoga* (1972), Pandit Gopi Krishna stated: "It has already been explained that *kundalini* is the spiritual as well as the biological base of all the phenomena connected with religion, the occult, and the supernatural. Whenever during the whole course of human history some man or woman exhibited uncanny powers which fell in the province of magic, witchcraft, augury, sorcery or mediumship and furnished conclusive evidence that the manifestations were genuine, in every case without exception, it signified the veiled activity of a slightly awake *kundalini.*" In various books, drawing from his personal experience, the Pandit has shown that the ancient Yoga concept of *kundalini,* as the biological basis of sexual activity, psychic phenomena, and higher consciousness is a valid one. It is significant that Western occultists have linked together sexual energy and paranormal phenomena (see also **Kundalini; Sex Magic**).

For a traditional exposition of Yoga, see the various translations of *The Yoga-Sutras of Patanjali,* a standard text of Yoga philosophy.

Age, Race, Sex and Influence on Health and Mental Powers

Inherited mediumship often appears spontaneously and early in life, like artistic gifts. The five-month-old son of Mrs. Kate Fox-Jencken wrote automatically. **Raps** occurred on his pillow and on the iron railing of his bedstead almost every day. The seven-month-old infant of Mrs. Margaretta Cooper (see LaRoy **Sunderland**) gave communications through raps. Alexander **Aksakof,** in his book *Animisme et Spiritism* (1906), recorded many instances of infantile mediumship. The child Alward moved tables that were too heavy for her normal strength. The nephew of Seymour wrote automatically when nine days old.

In Eugène Bonnemère's *Histoire des Camisara* (1869) and in Louis Figuier's *Histoire du Merveilleux* (4 vols., 1886-89) many cases were quoted of Camisard babies of 14-15 months of age and of infants who preached in French in the purest diction. During the persecution of the Huguenots, these babes were confined to prison in numbers as they fell into ecstasy and the psychic contagion spread to Catholic children as well.

Nationality has no influence. The fact that three Polish mediums of Warsaw specialized in animal materializations simply points to a contagion of ideas, or a spirit of emulation, resulting in a special development.

Sex, however, certainly appears to have a mysterious relationship to mediumship. The percentage of female mediums is greater than males. The mediumship of **"Eva C."** and Willie **Schneider** was accompanied by abnormal sex phenomena.

The age of puberty seems to have a peculiar significance. In old chronicles, pure children were mentioned as the best subjects for **crystal reading. Poltergeist** cases mostly occur in the presence of young girls and boys between the age of twelve to sixteen.

Dr. Hereward **Carrington** read a paper on the sexual aspect of mediumship before the First International Congress for Psychical Research in Copenhagen in 1921 and pointed out the possibility that the sexual energies which are blossoming into maturity within the body may, instead of taking their normal course, be somehow turned into another channel and externalized beyond the limits of the body, producing the manifestations in question. He conjectured: "There may be a definite connection between sex and psychical phenomena; and this seems to be borne out by three or four analogies. First, recent physiological researches as to the activities of the ductless glands and particularly the sex glands which have shown the enormous influence which these glands have upon the physical and even upon the psychic life. Second, the observation made in the cases of Kathleen Goligher and Eva C. which show that the plasma which is materialised, frequently issues from the genitals. Third, the clinical observations of Lombroso, Morselli and others upon Eusapia Palladino, which brought to light many recognised sexual stigmata. Fourth, the teachings and practices of the Yogis of India, who have written at great length upon the connection between sexual energies and the higher, ecstatic states, and of the conversion of the former into the latter, just as we find instances of 'sublimation' in modern Freudian psycho-analysis, and connection between sex and religion, here in the West."

In his book *The Story of Psychic Science* (1930) Dr. Carrington added: "These speculations have, I believe, been amply verified by certain recent investigations, wherein it has been shown that (in the case of a celebrated European medium) the production of a physical phenomenon of exceptional violence has been coincidental with a true orgasm. From many accounts it seems probable that the same was frequently true in the case of Eusapia Palladino, and was doubtless the case with other mediums also." He also pointed out that there is said to be a very close connection between the sexual energies and the mysterious "**Kundalini,**" aroused and brought into activity by **Yoga** practices.

After prolonged exercise of mediumship, intemperance often sets in. The reason seems to be a craving for stimulants following the exhaustion and depletion felt after the seance. Many mediums have been known who succumbed to the craving and died of delirium tremens.

The health of the medium otherwise remains unaffected. Recovery is usually very quick and unless too many sittings produce an excessive drain on the vitality of the medium the results, in many respects, may prove more beneficial than harmful. The spirit guides supply constant medical advice, take care of the medium's health to a greater extent than he or she could, and even prescribe treatment in case of illness.

D. D. **Home** lived much longer with his weak lungs than could have been normally expected, and many mediums have attained an age of over eighty years in spite of frail health.

The withdrawal of mediumship is often evidence of care for the health of the medium. Of course, the lapse may come for entirely different reasons. But recuperative rest was given as an explanation when the "Imperator" group announced on May 24, 1911 that Mrs. **Piper**'s trance mediumship would be temporarily withdrawn. The withdrawal lasted until August 8, 1915.

In the case of the Marquis **Centurione Scotto,** it was similarly announced on November 9, 1927: "He will fall ill if he continues thus. His nerves are shattered. By superior will his mediumistic faculty will be taken from him for a time." On another occasion, his mediumship was suspended to allow him to read, study and acquire more belief in the Spiritistic explanation which the Marquis did not quite accept.

Similar experiences befell the Rev. Stainton **Moses,** who revolted against his spirit guides when they tried to convince him, a Minister of the Anglican Church, that religion is eternal, whereas religious dogmas are but fleeting. His mediumship was temporarily removed. The powerful mediumship of D. D. **Home** also lapsed from time to time. As he suffered from a tubercular diathesis, this appears to have been the reason.

For the communicator, the medium is but a delicate machine. He is often referred to as such, sometimes in amusing terms. "White Hawk," the Red Indian control of the British professional clairvoyant medium Mrs. Kathleen **Barkell,** called her "my coat."

The mediums who are conscious during the production of the phenomena appear to suffer more than those in trance. The extrication of power from their organism seems a veritable trial for nerve and flesh. The phenomena in themselves are often equivalent to putting the body on the rack. This was known from ancient days.

The Neoplatonist philosopher Iamblichus (died c. 330 A.D.) said on *Divination:* "Often at the moment of inspiration, or when the afflatus has subsided, a fiery appearance is seen—the entering or departing power. Those who are skilled in this wisdom, can tell by the character of this glory the rank of the divinity who has seized for the time the reins of the mystic's soul, and guides it as he will. Sometimes the body of the man is violently agitated, sometimes it is rigid and motionless. In some instances sweet music is heard, in others discordant and fearful sounds. The person of the subject has been known to dilate and tower to a superhuman height, in other cases it has been lifted into the air. Frequently not merely the ordinary exercise of reason, but sensation and animal life would appear to have been suspended; and the subject of the afflatus has not felt the application of fire, has been pierced with spits, cut with knives and has not been sensible of pain."

However, the disagreeable result of physical phenomena soon vanishes. A quarter of an hour's rest may be quite sufficient to dispel the effect. Many books have been published by those hostile to Spiritualism in the effort to show that mediumship leads to nervous derangement and insanity. Statistical investigations, however, have proved that the percentage of Spiritualists in mental asylums is very small.

Dr. Eugen Crowell, author of *The Spirit World* (1879), examined the reports of 42 institutions. He found out of a total of 32,313 male patients, 215 were clergymen. The total number of male and female Spiritualists was 45. He estimated that the proportion of insane clergymen is one to every 159 inmates, while the proportion of insane Spiritualists is 1 to every 711.

Curiously enough mediumship, if suppressed, may manifest in symptoms of disease. Dr. C. D. Isenberg of Hamburg wrote of a case in *Light* (April 11, 1931) in which a patient of his suffered from sleeplessness and peculiar spasmodic attacks which generally occurred at night. The spasms seized the whole body; even the tongue was affected, blocking the throat and nearly suffocating her.

When the patient mentioned that in her youth she tried table tilting, the doctor thought of the possibility that the mediumistic energy might block his patient's organism.

A sitting was tried. The lady fell into trance and afterwards slept well for a few days. When the sleeplessness became worse again, the sitting was repeated and the results proved to be so beneficial that the chloral hydrate treatment previously employed was discontinued.

"She also tells us," wrote Camille **Flammarion** of Eusapia **Palladino,** "that when she has been a long time without holding a seance she is in a state of irritation, and feels the need of freeing herself of the psychic fluid which saturates her."

As regards a deleterious influence on the mind, Mrs. Osborne Leonard wrote in her book *My Life in Two Worlds* (1931): "I myself have not found that the development of psychic awareness detracts in any way from other so-called normal studies. I am a more successful gardener than I used to be, I am much better cook; in many quite ordinary but extremely useful directions, I know I have improved; my health and nerves are under better control, therefore they are more to be relied upon than they ever were before I developed what many people think of as an abnormal or extraordinary power."

Dangers and Duration of Mediumship; Educational Benefits

Dangers, nevertheless, do exist but of another kind. According to Hereward **Carrington,** there is a true "terror of the dark" and that there are "principalities and powers" with which, in our ignorance we toy, without knowing or realizing the frightful consequence which may result from this tampering with the unseen world. For that reason, he argued that a few men of well-balanced minds should be created lifelong investigators in this field; they should be looked upon as recognized authorities, "and their work accepted upon these problems just as any other physicist is accepted on a problem in physics."

The Rev. Stainton **Moses** stated: "I do not think it would be reasonable to say that it is wise and well for everyone to become acquainted with mediumship in his own proper person. It would not be honest in me to disguise the fact that he who meddles with this subject does so at his peril. I do not say that peril is anything that should always be avoided. In some cases it is not, but I do say that the development of mediumship is sometimes a very questionable benefit, as in others it is a very decided blessing."

The peril alluded to is the liability to the intrusion and control of undesirable spirits. As Stainton Moses further stated: "In developing mediumship one has to consider a question involving three serious points. Can you get into relation with a spirit who is wise enough and strong enough to protect and good enough for you to trust? If you do not, you are exposed to that recurrent danger which the old occultists used to describe as the struggle with the dweller on the threshold. It is true that everybody who crosses the threshold of this occult knowledge does unquestionably come into a new and strange land in which, if he has no guide, he is apt to lose his way."

The nervous equilibrium of the medium during the seance may be easily disturbed. "During the physical manifestations," wrote Hudson **Tuttle,** "I was in semi-trance, intensely sensitive and impressible. The least word, a jarring question, even when the intention was commendable, grated and rasped. Words convey an imperfect idea of this condition. It can only be compared with that physical state when a nerve is exposed."

Yet as regards the moral responsibility of the medium, Hudson Tuttle was emphatic in saying: "A medium cannot be controlled to do anything against his determined will, and the plea that he is compelled by spirits is no excuse for wrong-doing. The medium, like anyone else, knows right from wrong, and if the controlling spirit urges towards the wrong, yielding is as reprehensible as it would be to the promptings of passion or the appetite."

The duration of mediumship, discounting periodical lapses, is always uncertain. The mediumship of Emanuel **Swedenborg** developed at the age of fifty-five and lasted until his death. Stainton Moses maintained his powers for eleven years only. The daughter of Dr. Segard, a friend of Prof. Charles **Richet,** showed remarkable telekinetic phenomena at the age of twelve for three days. No such experience befell her for a quarter of a century afterwards.

The question of the medium's intelligence seems to have nothing to do with the psychic powers. But it may greatly influence the power of the communicators to convey clear ideas. The most stolid mediums may exhibit an extraordinary intelligence in trance. If their brain is educated the manifestation becomes still more marvelous.

The question naturally arises whether in the long run spirit influence imparts an education to rustic minds. The Rev. J. B. **Ferguson** answered the problem in the affirmative. "Supramundane influence," he recorded, "in the unfolding and education of mind has been a common and most interesting experience since my own attention was called to this subject. In the case of Mr. H. B. Champion we have a very remarkable instance. This gentleman, now distinguished for his comprehensiveness of thought on all subjects connected with mental and moral philosophy, and for unrivalled force and beauty of expression, was, to my personal knowledge, educated entirely under these influences. He was not educated even in ordinary branches, such as the orthography of his native tongue; was never at school but a few months in life. That which was at first the gift of a supramundane power is now his own; and unless his history were known he would be considered, as he often is, as a man of the highest accomplishments."

The Rev. J. B. Ferguson testified similarly regarding George W. Harrison, another medium, educated by the psychic power and concluded: "These gentlemen are today highly educated men. They speak and write our language with great precision and accuracy. They converse with men of the first attainments on all questions that engage cultivated thought. They are sought by men distinguished as professors in various departments of science; and where their history is not known, as it is to myself and to others, they are recognised at once as men of very high order of culture."

Such education undoubtedly depends on the quality of the spiritual influence which a medium attracts. The case of Andrew Jackson **Davis** and of Hudson **Tuttle** bear out the truth of the Rev. J. B. Ferguson's testimony and suggest that "men could matriculate at universities unknown to the physical senses." On the other hand, "John King," the somewhat rustic control of Eusapia **Palladino** could not impart much education to his medium in a lifetime and she was always referred to as an illiterate, uneducated woman.

The force involved in paranormal extension of awareness may not necessarily involve the spirit world. Pandit Gopi Krishna, in his book *The Biological Basis of Religion and Genius* (1972) claimed that the psycho-physical mechanism traditionally aroused under the name of **Kundalini** in Yoga practice, resulted in higher consciousness.

Classification and the Source of Power

The classification of mediums is diverse. In general, they fall into two main groups: physical and mental mediums. The dividing line is not stable, as in the aspect of motor and sensory **automatism,** physical phenomena are always present. Physical mediumship as a rule means that there is no intellectual content behind the phenomena.

The distinction is useful, as the coexistence of intellectual and physical phenomena is indeed rare. These gifts either alternate or develop along lines of specification.

Mrs. **Piper** produced no physical phenomena. Mrs. **Leonard** but very few. **Kluski** was a universal medium. **Home** was mostly famous for his telekinetic manifestations. His trance phenomena were not studied in detail. The skepticism of the age in which he lived impeded the chance of invaluable experiments.

The Rev. Stainton **Moses** was in a somewhat reversed position. His powerful physical manifestations occurred in a small circle of friends. He was not subject to scientific experiments as regards these phenomena, but they were recorded and a still more valuable record, affording wonderful opportunity for study, was left behind in automatic scripts of his trance phenomena.

Very young mediums usually have all the potentialities of mediumship. But once the specification has taken place it has a barring effect. Miss C. E. **Wood** could never obtain **psychic photography.** Mrs. Etta **Wriedt** was unable to become a slate writer. Mrs. William Wilkinson (see **Automatic Drawing and Painting**) could draw and paint automatically, she could play the piano in trance but she could not produce automatic scripts. The organism itself may set certain limits. The controls of Stainton **Moses** produced a variety of peculiar musical sounds, but never more than a single note. They explained that the medium's organism was peculiarly unmusical.

Mediums who receive remuneration for their services are termed professional. In a way Samuel (in the *Bible*) seems to have been the first professional medium since Saul paid him the fourth part of a shekel of silver for the recovery of his father's lost asses through his seership.

In the history of modern Spiritualism, professional mediums were slow to appear on the scene. In America in 1853, the *Spiritual Telegraph* hardly contained advertisements other than those of medieval clairvoyants. In Britain, in the first ten years of Spiritualism, Mrs. Mary **Marshall** was alone in the professional field. Nowadays, the services of mediums and psychics are widely advertised.

As a rule, most mediums require assistance for the production of their phenomena. The sitters of the circle are often drained of power. According to Dr. J. **Maxwell,** Eusapia **Palladino** could quickly discern people from whom she could easily draw the force she needed. "In the course of my first experiments with this medium, I found out this vampirism to my cost. One evening, at the close of a sitting at l'Agnelas, she was raised from the floor and carried on to the table with her chair. I was not seated beside her, but, without releasing her neighbours' hands she caught hold of mine while the phenomena was happening. I had cramp in the stomach—I cannot better define my sensation—and was almost overcome by exhaustion."

Dr. Justinus **Kerner** stated that the Seeress of Prevorst (Frau Frederica **Hauffe**) ate little and confessed that she was nourished by the substance of her visitors, especially of those related to her by the ties of blood, their constitution being more sympathetic with her own. Visitors who passed some minutes near her often noticed upon retiring that they were weakened.

Some mediums draw more of the sitters' vitality than others. These mediums become less exhausted and consequently can sit more often. Mrs. Etta **Wriedt,** the direct voice medium, always left her sitters weak. Vice-Admiral Usborne Moore complained that he hardly could use his legs after a sitting.

In one instance in Mme. **d'Esperance**'s mediumship the draw on the sitter apparently proved fatal. The phantom was grabbed, and an old lady (the mother of the spirit grabber), who apparently contributed most of the **ectoplasm** was so seriously injured that, after much suffering, she died from the consequences. (*Light,* November 21, 1903).

If the sitters of the circle are mediumistic themselves, the phenomena tend to increase in strength. Perhaps the strongest mediumistic circle ever recorded was the family of Jonathan **Koons,** of Ohio. From the seven-month-old infant to the eighteen-year-old Nahum, the eldest of the family, all the children were mediumistic, making, with the parents, a total of ten mediums. The same curious power was manifest in the family of John Tippie, who had a similar spirit house at a distance of two or three miles from that of Koons'. Ten children formed his "spirit battery."

In the years of 1859-60, D. D. **Home** often gave joint seances with the American medium and editor, J. R. M. **Squire.** Later he sometimes sat with Mrs. Jencken (see **Fox Sisters**) and Stainton **Moses.** Frank **Herne** and Charles **Williams** joined partnership in 1871; Miss C. E. **Wood** sat with Miss Fairlamb (Mrs. J. B. **Mellon**).

The spirit photographer William **Hope** usually sat with Mrs. Buxton.

Catherine **Berry** was known as a developing medium. According to a note signed by the editor of *Human Nature,* published in Catherine Berry's *Experiences in Spiritualism* (1876), "after sitting with Mrs. Berry a medium has more power to cause the phenomena at any other circle he may have to attend. Messrs. Herne and Williams have been known to visit this lady for the purpose of getting a supply of power when they had a special seance to give. Mrs. Berry is, therefore, successful in developing mediums, and has conferred the spirit voice manifestation, as well as other gifts, upon several mediums. In a public meeting, a speaker or trance medium is benefited by having Mrs. Berry sitting near him. These facts have not been arrived at hastily, but after years of patient investigation."

Automatic writers have often joined forces. Frederick Bligh **Bond** and the automatists with whom he received the **Glastonbury scripts,** presented a case of dual mediumship. Similarly the "Oscar Wilde" scripts were produced through the mediumship of Mrs. Travers-Smith (Hester **Dowden**) and Mr. V. On the other hand, mediums may antagonize each other and nullify the power. Florence **Cook** always objected on this ground to sitting with her sister Katie, although skeptics of the genuineness of Florence's phenomena could suggest a more mundane reason for Katie's absence.

Harm may come to the medium through the careless disregard of the conditions by the sitters, but sometimes also from the invisible operators. An evil operator may take possession of the medium's body or a well-meaning **control** may commit a mistake, just as an experimenting scientist might.

Several instances of such blunders are recorded in the scripts of Stainton **Moses.** Thus, under the heading April 18, 1874, we read: "Prophet's light and two of Chom's, W. B. C. appeared again and touched my finger, the result being that the skin was broken and the joint swollen up. The pain gradually ceased, but the mark still remains after 48 hours."

Once an apport of a bronze candlestick struck a painful blow on the head of Stainton Moses. On July 26, 1874, urgent excited messages were rapped out, urging the sitters to look at the medium. A light was struck and he was discovered to have fallen down by the bookcase, doubled up in a most awkward position, and in a profound trance. So much power was drawn from his body that his legs could not support him and his hands could not hold anything when consciousness was restored.

Things often happen against the will of the medium, quite frequently against the will of the sitter. Mme. **d'Esperance** said that she always entered the seance room "with a feeling of anxiety mixed with wonder if I should ever come out again. As a rule I always felt that I was placing my life in the hands of the persons about to assist, and that they were even more ignorant of danger than myself."

Stainton Moses was very religious, but often found in his automatic scripts statements expressing atheistic and even Satanic sentiments. In the seances of Eusapia **Palladino,** the spirits often broke the promises of the medium and shattered photographic plates or blocks of paraffin which bore complete imprints.

Mediumship often develops from **Poltergeist** phenomena as a ferocious persecution to make the sensitive a medium against his or her will.

The mentality of the sitters appears to have an influence. "It is of no use to disguise or try to explain away the fact," wrote "Miss X" (Ada **Goodrich-Freer**) in *Essays in Psychical Research* (1899) "that, whatever may be the special mechanism which goes to make a 'sensitive,' the machinery will never work at its best under the observation of those avowedly sceptical or even critical."

On the other hand, "The Davenports and Mr. Fay never fail," stated the Rev. J. B. **Ferguson,** "and their extraordinary powers seem at times even to increase with opposition; and in the degree in which timid or inconsiderate friends tremble for their success, and obstinate opponents seek their defeat, they rise to the occasion and give more powerful and triumphant evidences of truth."

Machine Mediumship

An early idea in the history of mediumship was the possibility of mechanical communication. The first confused thought of communicating with the spirit world through instruments occurred to John Murray **Spear** (see also **New Motor**). He arranged copper and zinc batteries in the form of an armor around the medium and expected phenomenal increase of mediumistic powers through the combination of mineral and vital electricity.

The **Dynamistograph,** the **Vandermeulen Spirit Indicator,** the **Reflectograph** and **Communigraph** represent later developments.

The most recent developments concern the **Electronic Voice Phenomenon** (see also **Raudive Voices**) and **SPIRICOM.**

Animal Mediumship

The unique case of a mediumistic cat was published by Aurelian Faifofer, Professor of Mathematics at Venice. It occurred in the experience of Dr. G. B. **Ermacora** of Padua, but he died without publishing it. The medium employed by him said in trance that Macacco (the cat of the medium's house) would be able to write with its paw by drawing it over a paper blackened with smoke; this would be accomplished during the night in a little room in which the animal slept. The medium advised Dr. Ermacora to make such arrangements that the genuineness of the phenomena could not afterwards be doubted.

Dr. Ermacora made a box of two compartments, one above the other, the lower storey having a zigzag course of five passages. The cat entered through a hole in the first course and could only enter the upper compartment through another hole at the end of the fifth passage. Over this hole, a sheet of smoked paper was fixed, the whole box was fastened by two complicated English padlocks and the spirit was asked through the medium to make the imprisoned cat write the word Vittorio.

The next morning, the box was unlocked and the cat released. On the smoked paper, as if done by a cat's paw, the word "Vitt." was found. The size of the paper did not allow more writing. While the box was examined, Macacco jumped on to a chair and shook one of her forepaws, as though she wanted to write. Dr. Ermacora made about fifteen of these experiments. Before he arrived at a degree of certainty, the cat fell from the roof of a house into the street and was killed.

The **Elberfeld horses** were suspected of mediumistic powers.

Capt. A. H. Trapman, in his book *The Dog; Man's Best Friend* (1929) voiced the strange conclusion that "it is easier for the spirits of the dead to communicate with the dog than with man, even when man is represented by the parents and sisters of the departed one."

Mediumistic Induction

It appears as if, similarly to electricity, mediumistic power can be generated by induction. In religious revivals a psychic contagion is noticeable. The transference of predictive power is frequent.

D. D. **Home** was the most famous medium for imparting his powers to others. Cases are on record in which he levitated others. Once he imparted the power of **elongation** to Miss Bertolacci, and he bestowed immunity to fire (see **Fire Immunity**) in a number of cases on his sitters.

But there was a condition. The sitters had to have faith. "Now if you have sufficient faith let me place this coal in your hand," he said to Miss Douglas on April 3, 1869. Miss Douglas first dreaded the test, then held out her hand. She was not the least burned and said that the red hot coal felt rather cold, like marble. Home took the coal and requested Miss Douglas to touch it; she placed her fingers near it but withdrew them immediately, saying that it burned her.

The spread of modern Spiritualism disclosed the phenomenon of mediumistic induction. Those who sat with the **Fox sisters** sometimes discovered mediumistic abilities in themselves. Mrs. **Benedict** and Mrs. **Tamlin,** the two best early mediums, were developed through the gift of Kate Fox. A writer in the *New Haven Journal* in October, 1850, referred to knockings and other phenomena in seven different families in Bridgeport, forty different families in Rochester, in Auburn, in Syracuse, some two hundred in Ohio, in New Jersey, and places more distant, as well as in Hartford, Springfield, Charlestown, etc.

The most famous early investigators became mediums. Judge John W. **Edmonds,** Prof. Robert **Hare,** and William **Howitt,** all confessed to having received the gift.

It is little known that in his last years the psychical researcher Dr. Richard **Hodgson** was in direct contact with the Imperator group. Sir Arthur Conan **Doyle** developed **automatic writing** and **direct voice** in his family. H. Dennis **Bradley** received the power of direct voice after his sittings with George **Valiantine.** The Marquis **Centurione Scotto** developed through the same instrumentality.

Eusapia **Palladino** could transfer her powers by holding the sitter's hand. She made a stool follow the movements of Dr. Hereward **Carrington**'s hand. Camille **Flammarion** noted: "I hold her legs with my left hand, spread out upon them; M. Sardou holds her left hand, she takes my right wrist in her right hand and says to me 'Strike in the direction of M. Sardou.' I do so three or four times. M. Sardou feels upon his body my blows tallying my gesture, with the difference of about a second between my notion and his sensation." (See also **Apports; Automatic Drawing & Painting; Automatic Speaking; Automatic Writing; Automatism; Communigraph; Control; Dynamistograph; Elberfeld Horses; Electronic Voice Phenomenon; Evidence; Fraud; Guide; Materialization; Psychic; Psychical Research; SPIRICOM; Spiritualism; Trance**)

Recommended reading:

Bayless, Raymond. *Voices From Beyond,* University Books, 1975

Bouissou, Michaël. *The Life of a Sensitive,* Sidgwick & Jackson, London, 1955

[Britten], Emma Hardinge. *Modern American Spiritualism,* London, 1870; University Books, 1970

Britten, Emma Hardinge. *Nineteenth Century Miracles,* London & Manchester, 1883

Carrington, Hereward. *Higher Psychical Development,* Kegan Paul, London, 1920; Dodd, Mead, 1924

Carrington, Hereward. *Your Psychic Powers and How to Develop Them,* American Universities Publishing Co., New York, 1920; Causeway, 1973

Chaney, Robert Galen, *Mediums and the Development of Mediumship,* Psychic Books, Michigan, 1946; Books for Libraries, Freeport, New York, 1972

Christopher, Milbourne. *Mediums, Mystics & the Occult,* Thomas Y. Crowell, 1975

Ellis, D. J. *The Mediumship of the Tape Recorder,* D. J. Ellis, Pulborough, U.K., 1978

Flint, Leslie. *Voices in the Dark; My Life As a Medium,* Macmillan, 1971

Fodor, Nandor. *The Haunted Mind; A Psychoanalyst Looks at the Supernatural,* Helix/Garrett, 1959

Garret, Eileen J. *Adventures in the Supernormal; A Personal Memoir,* Garrett/Helix, 1949 Paperback Library, New York, 1968

Garrett, Eileen J. *My Life As a Search for the Meaning of Mediumship,* Rider & Co., London, 1939; Arno Press, 1975

Gopi Krishna. *The Biological Basis of Religion and Genius,* Harper & Row, 1972

Gopi Krishna. *The Secret of Yoga,* Harper & Row, 1972

Home, D. D. *Incidents in My Life,* London, 1863; University Books, 1973

Leaf, Horace. *Psychology and the Development of Mediumship,* London, 1926

Leonard, Maurice. *Battling Bertha; The Biography of Bertha Harris,* Regency Press, London, 1975

Leonard, Maurice. *Medium; The Biography of Jessie Nason,* Regency Press, London, 1974

Leonard, Gladys Osborne. *My Life in Two Worlds,* Cassell, London, 1931

MacGregor, Helen & Margaret V. Underhill. *The Psychic Faculties & Their Unfoldment,* L.S.A. Publications, paperback, London, 1930

Manning, Matthew. *The Link; Matthew Manning's Own Story of His Extraordinary Psychic Gifts,* Corgi paperback, London, 1975; Holt, Rinehart & Winston, 1975

Northage, Ivy. *The Mechanics of Mediumship,* Spiritualist Association of Great Britain, paperback, London, 1973

Patanjali (transl. M. N. Dvivedi). *The Yoga-Sutras of Patanjali,* Theosophical Publishing House, Adyar, India, 1890 (frequently reprinted)

Piper, Alta. *The Life and Work of Mrs. Piper,* Kegan Paul, London, 1929

Podmore, Frank. *Modern Spiritualism,* 2 vols. London, 1902 (reissued under title *Mediums of the Nineteenth Century,* 2 vols., University Books, 1963)

Price, Harry & E. J. Dingwall. (ed.) *Revelations of a Spirit Medium,* Kegan Paul, London, 1922

Roberts, Estelle. *Fifty Years a Medium,* Corgi paperback, London, Avon Books, 1975

Salter, W. H. *Trance Mediumship; An Introductory Study of Mrs. Piper & Mrs. Leonard,* Society for Psychical Research, London, 1950, revised ed. 1962

Smith, Susy. *Confessions of a Psychic,* Macmillan/Collier-Macmillan, London, 1971

Spraggett, Allen & Wm. V. Rauscher. *Arthur Ford, the Man Who Talked with the Dead,* New American Library, 1973

Stemman, Roy. *Medium Rare; The Psychic Life of Ena Twigg,* Spiritualist Association of Great Britain, paperback, London, 1971

Stokes, Doris (with Linda Dearsley). *Voices in My Ear; The Autobiography of a Medium,* Futura paperback, London, 1980

Tietze, Thomas R. *Margery,* Harper & Row, 1973 [deals with the controversial medium "Margery" (Mrs. Crandon)]

Tubby, Gertrude Ogden. *Psychics and Mediums,* Marshall Jones, Boston, 1935

Turvey, Vincent N. *The Beginnings of Seership,* Stead Publishing House, London, 1911; University Books, 1969

Wallis, E. W. & M. H. *A Guide to Mediumship and Spiritual Unfoldment,* 3 parts, London, 1903

Zymonidas, A. *The Problems of Mediumship,* Kegan Paul, London, 1920

Medium and Daybreak, The (Journal)

Spiritualist weekly, started in 1869 by James **Burns,** originally published under the title *The Medium,* later absorbing *The Daybreak,* a provincial paper, founded in 1867.

For years it had the largest circulation of any weekly on Spiritualism. It was published until 1895, the year of the death of its founder.

Medjugorje

Name of a village in Yugoslavia which has been the site of claimed **apparitions** of the Virgin Mary. The case is a classic one, in which teenage visionaries state that the Virgin has given them "secrets" concerning civilization and religion.

Like the parallel claims of **Garabandal,** the apparitions are of special importance since they are in modern times instead of earlier history, and the visionaries have been photographed and filmed in ecstatic states, and also examined and tested by doctors and scientists. In the case of Medjugorje, the visions continued into 1987.

Another remarkable aspect of these events is that they are reported from a Communist country. Although the Socialism of Yugoslavia is independent of the U.S.S.R. and regarded as more open to the Western world, the state political faith tolerates religion but hardly encourages it. There are additional complications about the Medjugorje apparitions since there have been confrontations not only between church and state, but also between different branches of Christianity.

The intricate story of the apparitions has been superbly presented in a British television documentary titled "The Madonna of Medjugorje," produced by Angela Tilby, in the B.B.C. "Everyman" series in 1986. Books on Medjugorje have also been published in various countries. It is an extraordinary and very moving story.

Background History of Medjugorje

Medjugorje is a small village of some three and a half thousand people in Bosnia-Hercegovina, about 200 kilometers inland from the Adriatic coast. The area is a meetingplace between Serbs and Croats, between Moslem traditions, the Eastern Orthodox Church, the established Catholic Church, and the Franciscans. The region has a complex and troubled history, involving military and religious conflicts.

For four centuries, the region was under Turkish rule, when many Christians were converted to Islam. The Franciscans kept the Catholic faith alive and became identified with the concept of Croatian identity. When the Turks lost power in 1878, Pope Leo 13 appointed non-Franciscans to work in the parish. This was resisted by the laity, and by the Franciscans themselves, who did not wish to lose their status. Conflict of interest between the established Church and the Franciscans on the issues of lay priests has remained latent into modern times.

Another historical problem dates from World War II, when in 1941 a Croatian fascist group was formed with strong Catholic ties. It lasted only a few years, but during that period these Croats were responsible for terrible atrocities against their Serbian neighbors of the Eastern Orthodox faith. Only a short distance from the site of the modern apparitions, hundreds of Serbian women, children, and babies had been thrown to their deaths from the top of a high cliff.

The First Apparitions

The first apparition was reported in 1981. There were six visionaries, all teenage children: four girls, Marija Pavlovic (16), Vicka Ivankovic (16), Mirjana Dragicevic (16), Ivanka Ivankovic (15), and two boys, Ivan Dragicevic (16) and Jakov Colo (10).

On the feast of St. John, June 24, 1981, Ivanka and Marija and Mirjana went for a walk to the hill of Crnica. Ivanka suddenly exclaimed "There's Our Lady!" Mirjana felt unable to look, but Ivanka was convinced that she had seen an apparition of the Virgin Mary. The girls returned home, and a few hours later set out again to help a farmer with his sheep. They left a message for their friends to follow them. The apparition again appeared, and was also seen by some of the other children, who had met up with Ivanka and Mirjana. The apparition was a beautiful smiling mother with child, wearing a starry crown and floating above the ground.

The following day, four of the teenagers returned to the same place, followed by friends, and this time, Jakov Colo and Marija Pavlovic saw the apparition. Similar encounters took place on succeeding days, when the Virgin spoke to the children in excellent Croatian.

She said that she was the Blessed Virgin Mary, sent from God with a gospel message. Asked why the message should come through such ordinary children, she replied that it was precisely because they were ordinary and average, neither the best nor worst, that they had been chosen.

Thereafter, the children assembled on the hill each day to witness the apparition.

When news of the apparition reached the church, the parish priest was temporarily absent. The assistant priest was not impressed and thought that maybe the children were on drugs and hallucinating. But after a few days, as the news spread, thousands of devout followers flocked to the hill, many in tears as they witnessed the children in a state of ecstasy.

When Fr. Jozo Zovko, the parish priest, returned from a retreat, he was astonished to find a chaotic situation, with crowds gathering around the hill. His reaction was one of incredulity that people should seek divine revelation on a hillside when the church itself, with its sacraments, was the proper center for worship.

However, Fr. Zovko gave the children some prayer books and rosaries, and tried to instruct them about the church in more detail. He also gave Mirjana a book about the apparitions of **Lourdes,** from which the children concluded that the current apparitions would cease after July 3rd, as they did at Lourdes.

In fact, they did not. On the following day, the children did not visit the hill, but each one had a vision wherever they happened to be at the time.

By now, there were serious difficulties involving both church and state authorities. According to state laws, gatherings for worship had to be regulated, and the daily assembly on the hill was not authorized by state or church.

News of the apparitions had reached Sarajevo, capital of the republic of Bosnia-Hercegovina, where there was alarm that all this might be a right-wing plot in religious disguise. It was thought that this might indicate a return of Croatian nationalism, with a revival of the old Nazi sympathy.

Official observers merged with the crowds to report back on this dangerous situation. The children were interrogated by police and examined by doctors. The gatherings on the hillside were forbidden.

The Second Stage

On July 1, the eighth day of the apparitions, the parish priest was troubled by both religious and state problems. In the church, he pryaed for divine guidance, while the police went to the hill to arrest the young visionaries. The children fled through the fields and vineyards, followed by the police. There was only one place of sanctuary—the church.

In an answer to prayer, the priest heard a voice saying "Go and protect the children, then I will tell you what to do." He went to the door of the church and found the children pleading to be hidden. He concealed them in a room in the presbytery.

That evening, the apparition came to the children again, but this time in the church itself. Now each evening the congregation gathered to pray in the church and the apparitions appeared as usual to the children. Often in tears, the apparition urged the faithful to confess sins, and do penance, to fast once a week on bread and water.

The parish priest now supported the apparitions, and indeed also shared the vision in church. The local bishop, Pavao Zanic, visited the parish on several occasions, but was constrained by his theological and political responsibilities.

Government observers attending a church congregation reported back that a sermon about the need for personal change was really a disguised criticism of socialism. Fr. Jozo was arrested by the police and accused of slandering the state system. In October, he was tried, and sentenced to three years' imprisonment. He saw the apparition in prison.

The Aftermath of the Apparitions

Meanwhile in March 1983, the Bishop had appointed a theological commission to investigate and form a judgment on the apparitions. The visionaries reported that the Virgin recommended special prayers for the Bishop and his heavy responsibility.

The religious authorities in Rome sent representatives to make their own on-the-spot investigations. The children were given extensive medical and psychological tests. Electroencephalographs probed the ecstatic state of the children during the apparitions, and scientists concluded that they were healthy and sane, and not telling lies. The visionaries focused intently on the same spot during the appearance of the apparition. The ecstatic state was genuine and elevating and certainly not a pathological condition. During this state, the children seemed transported into a higher condition of fulfillment.

Thousands of pilgrims continued to flock to Medjugorje, many seeking inspiration and guidance from the young visionaries. Some typical informal question-and-answer sessions in the open air were recorded by the B.B.C. television team. Because of the large number of pilgrims, priests often took confessions in the open air.

The main focal point for these gatherings was a cross opposite the site of the apparitions, erected in 1933. People claimed that the cross sometimes changed into a column of light or into the form of the Virgin, and some photographs taken of the cross certainly show "extras" of this nature.

A somewhat disturbing claim was that people believed that they were able to look into the sun and see it dancing, a phenomenon that had been reported earlier in conjunction with the apparitions at **Fatima.** Naturally gazing at the sun with the naked eye can produce a number of strange visual effects, but it is a highly dangerous practice.

There are now reports of miraculous healing. The B.B.C. television team recorded an interview with a German lady who was previously unable to walk, but now had no difficulty, and had left her crutches behind.

These large-scale demonstrations of revival of faith were alarming both to state and ecclesiastical authorities. Bishop Pavao Zanic found himself in an increasingly delicate position. He had earlier defended the integrity of the children, and was fully aware that their experience might be as valid as others at Lourdes or Fatima, but was reluctant to sanction organized pilgrimages to the site of the apparitions.

While his Commission worked slowly in its investigations, an old controversy was now inflamed. The Franciscans had been the parish clergy in Medjugorje for many years. In 1980, during a reorganization instigated by the authorities in Rome, the Bishop had attempted to replace two of the Franciscans with secular clergy. The two friars now consulted the visionaries, seeking the opinion of the Virgin, and it was reported that the Virgin told the children that the Bishop should not have suspended the friars.

The Bishop was now critical of the claimed apparitions as hallucinations inflamed by disaffected

Franciscans, and refused to endorse the phenomena or to facilitate pilgrimages.

On the other hand, he did not discourage the pilgrims. Consequently a vast pilgrim and tourist trade has grown up at Medjugorje without state or religious sponsorship. In 1985, there were only two primitive toilet facilities (one male, one female) serving sometimes ten thousands pilgrims in one day. This did not discourage the pilgrims, who have continued to come from all over Europe in their thousands.

Ironically, the Virgin's message had been one of peace and reconciliation. The report of the Bishop's Commission was secret, but it was believed to have concluded that the claims of the visionaries were false. The Bishop himself stated that the apparitions were collective hallucinations, exploited by the Franciscans, and strongly criticized the chaplain at Medjugorje, Fr. Tomislav Vlasic, as "a mystifier and charismatic wizard."

There was a theological deadlock. The visionaries were banned from seeing apparitions in the church, but continued in a study bedroom in the presbytery. Meanwhile, the international fame of Medjugorje won a grudging tolerance from the government, which saw the influx of pilgrims as a vindication of Yugoslavia as an open country.

Part of the price of the spiritual revival at Medjugorje has been the inevitable commercialization of the religious tourist trade. The simple village life has been totally uprooted by thousands of tourists, ice cream and soft drink stands, stalls for the sale of religious souvenirs, and other worldly activities. But villagers still meet in small groups, sometimes at night. Two younger girls claim to have seen visions and received messages.

The original group of six young visionaries claimed that the Virgin had confided ten secrets, including warnings of future world chastisements if people did not return to spiritual life. People were recommended to give up watching television, and return instead to a life of prayer, fasting, and penance. The world had advanced civilization but had lost God. It was prophesied that Russia would come to glorify the name of God. As with apparitions elsewhere, it was said that there would be a visible sign left on the hill. The visions have now ceased so far as the six children are concerned.

Ivanka received her last "secret" from the Virgin in May 1985, and in early 1987 married, when her daily apparitions ceased. Mirjana took up the study of agriculture at the University of Sarajevo. Ivan's apparitions ceased when he was enlisted for a year of military service. Vicka became ill with an inoperable brain tumor. Jakov was still at school in 1986. Marija planned to become a nun. The fascinating film records of the children in states of ecstasy, as well as the EEG tests, remain a permanent record, as do other of the numerous medical and scientific studies.

Psychiatrists, doctors, and scientists concluded that the visionaries were psychologically healthy, without neurosis or hysteria, and that their ecstasies were not a pathological phenomeon. The fasts on bread and water recommended once or twice weekly could merely counteract the excesses of normal diet without risk of starvation. The cures at Medjugorje were reported upon favorably by doctors from the University of Milan.

The apparitions at Medjugorje present many intriguing problems, both for skeptics and believers. Such apparitions now follow a regular pattern within the framework of Catholic theology, just as claims of **UFO** contacts are often consistent with a different pattern of belief.

It could be argued that once such conventions are established, knowledge of them influences other visionaries. In the case of Medjugorje, the parish priest had shown one of the visionaries a book about Lourdes, although it must be remembered that the apparitions had established a regular pattern before such information.

The ecstatic state of the young visionaries was undoubtedly very real, and the audio-visual records shown them to be modest, honest, and touchingly sincere, too simple to be able to fabricate intellectually advanced theological discussions.

If there were occasional contradictory elements in the claimed communications from the Virgin (as in the instance of apparent criticism of the Bishop), it must be remembered that the children were subjected to intense pressures from lay and ecclesiastical authorities, and may also have been misquoted from time to time.

The messages about the need for renewal of religious faith and practice may well be a valid comment on the secularism of our time, although with a sophistication normally beyond the awareness of village children.

But, as with Lourdes, Fatima, Garabandal and other apparitions, the messages are only within the framework of the Catholic faith, and there is no insightful communication for Hindus, Buddhists, or other religions.

Undoubtedly, the apparition of the Virgin appears real to the visionaries, and may have some basic reality as a paranormal event, with special relevance to claims of such secular apparitions as **ghosts, fairies,** or UFO contacts. It may be that such visitations are all part of some elusive reality that takes on a form and context appropriate to the visionaries, particularly in apocalyptic times. (See also **Apparitions; Fatima; Garabandal; Guadalupe; Lourdes**)

Recommended reading:

Kraljevic, Svetozar. *Apparitions of Our Lady of Medjugorje (1981-1983),* Franciscan Herald Press, Chicago, 1984

Laurentin, René & L. Rupcic. *Is the Virgin Mary Appearing at Medjugorje?* Fowler-Wright Books, Leominster, U.K.

Laurentin, René & Henri Joyeux. *Scientific & Medical Studies on the Apparitions at Medjugorje,* Veritas paperback, Republic of Ireland, 1987

O'Carroll, Michael. *Medjugorje; Facts, Documents, Theology,* Veritas paperback, Republic of Ireland, 1986

Meehl, Paul E(verett) (1920-)

Professor of psychology who has written on parapsychology. Born January 3, 1920 at Minneapolis, Minnesota, he studied at University of Minnesota (B.A. summa cum laude 1941, Ph.D. 1945). In 1941 he married Alyce Roworth.

From 1951 onwards he was professor of psychology at University of Minnesota, chairman of psychology department 1951-57, professor of clinical psychology, department of psychiatry at Medical School, University of Minnesota from 1951 onwards. He has also been in practice as a psychotherapist.

He was president of Midwestern Psychological Association in 1955, Winner of Distinguished Contributor Award, American Psychological Association, 1958, editor of Prentice-Hall series of publications on psychology; member of Committe on Psychology and Religion, Lutheran Church, Missouri Synod 1956-57, American Psychological Association, Minnesota Psychological Association, American Society for Psychical Research, American Psychological Association (president from 1961-62).

In addition to his various books and many articles on psychological subjects, he has also published: (with M. J. **Scriven**) 'Compatibility of Science and ESP' (*Science,* 123, 1956), (with H. R. Klann, K. H. Breimeter) *What, Then, Is Man?* (1958).

Meerloo, Joost A(braham) M(aurits) (1903-1976)

Psychiatrist, psychoanalyst and writer on parapsychology. Born March 14, 1903 at The Hague, Netherlands, he was educated at Leyden University (M.D. 1927) and Utrecht University (Ph.D. 1932). In 1948 he married Louisa Betty Duits.

His appointments included: Psychiatric-neurologic consultant, Municipal Hospital, Voorburg and The Hague 1934-42, chief of Psychological Department, Netherlands Army 1943-45, High Commissioner for Welfare in the Netherlands 1945-46, Associate in psychiatry, Columbia University 1948-57, professor, political science, New School for Social Research, New York, N.Y. 1958 onwards, Associate professor of psychiatry, New York School of Psychiatry 1962 onwards.

He was a member of: Royal Society of Medicine, American Psychiatric Association, American Academy of Psychoanalysis, secretary of Schilder Society, honorary member of Tokyo Institute for Psychoanalysis, Albany Society for Psychosomatic Medicine. He was also a member of the American Society for Psychical Research, and corresponding member of the Dutch Society for Psychical Research.

He published over 300 articles on psychology, politics and literature. His writings on parapsychological subjects included: 'Telepathy as a Form of Archaic Communication' (*Psychiatric Quarterly,* vol. 23, 1949), 'Telepathy and Foreknowledge' (*Proceedings, First International Conference on Parapsychology,* Utrecht, 1953), 'The Biology of Time' (*Tomorrow,* Winter 1954), 'Man's Ecstatic Healing' (*Tijdschrift voor Parapsychologie,* vol. 27, 1959). His books included: *Patterns of Panic* (1950), *The Two Faces of Man* (1954), *The Rape of the Mind: The Psychology of Thought Control, Menticide and Brainwashing* (1956), *Dance Craze and the Sacred Dance* (1959), *Suicide and Mass Suicide* (1962), (with Edmund Bergler) *Justice and Injustice* (1963), *Hidden Communion* (1964), *Illness and Cure* (1964), *Transference and Trial Adaptation* (1956), *Unobtrusive Communication* (1965). He died November 17, 1976.

Meher Baba (1894-1969)

Eastern mystic, born Merwin S. Irani in Poona, India. His parents were Parsees, but he was strongly influenced by Sufi mysticism, although educated at a Christian high school.

At the age of nineteen, he contacted Hazrat Babajan, an elderly Moslem woman saint, who kissed his forehead and induced divine consciousness and a state of ecstatic bliss. After that, he devoted his life to religious teaching, usually expressed in a rather erratic fashion, involving journeys with disciples which apparently led nowhere, or in searching out the eccentric and sometimes deranged wandering monks of India.

In 1921 he established an ashram devoted largely to philanthropic work. He had contact with the remarkable Hindu mystic **Sai Baba,** of whom the present-day **Satya Sai Baba** is claimed to be a reincarnation.

In 1925, Meher Baba entered upon a period of silence, conversing or giving lectures with an alphabet board. He often prophesied in this way that he would one day speak the One Word which would bring spiritualization and love to the world, but he died January 31, 1969 without utterance.

However, his prophecy may have been symbolic, like his mysterious life itself, and devotees continue to share the intense affection of a Sufi kind which characterized his mission during his lifetime. He is regarded by many disciples as an *avatar* or descent of divine power. (See also **Sufism**)

Meier, C(arl) A(lfred) (1905-)

Swiss psychotherapist who has written on parapsychology. Born April 19, 1905 at Schaffhausen, Switzerland, he was educated at University of Paris Medical School, University of Venice, and University of Zurich Medical School (M.D.). In 1936 he married Johanna Fritzsche.

He was assistant and director of laboratory research at the Burghölzli Psychiatric Clinic of Zurich University from 1930-36, professor of psychology at Swiss Federal Institute of Technology, Zurich, from 1949 onwards, in private practice in 1948, president of the C. G. Jung Institute, Zurich, from 1948-57, founder (in 1957) of the International Association for Analytical Psychology, general secretary of the International Society for Medical Psychotherapy from 1933-43, vice-president, Swiss Society for Practical Psychology from 1933-48, president, Psychological Club of Zurich from 1945-50.

Dr. Meier was editor of *Studien aus dem C. G. Jung Institute* (1949-57) and *Studien zu C. G. Jung's Psychologie* by Toni Wolff (1959), as well as author of *Jung and Analytical Psychology* (1959) and many articles on psychotherapy, Jungian analysis and other psychological topics. He has special interest in relationships between the unconscious and extrasensory perception.

His articles on parapsychology include: 'Jung's "Meaningful Coincidence" ' (*Tomorrow,* Spring 1954), 'C. G. Jung's Concept of Synchronicity' (*Proceedings, First International Conference of Parapsychological Studies,* 1955), 'Psychological Background of So-Called Spontaneous Phenomena' (*Proceedings, Conference on Spontaneous Phenomena,* 1957), 'Projection, Transference and Subject-Object Relation' (*Proceedings, International Symposium on Psychology and Parapsychology,* 1957).

Meisner (or Mesna), Lorentz (c. 1608)

Early alchemist, whose work is recorded in his tract *Gemma Gemmarum Alchimistarum; oder Erleuterung der Parabolischen und Philosophischen Schrifften Fratris Basilij, der zwölff Schlüssel, von dem Stein der vharalten Weisen, und desselben aufsdrücklichen und warhaften praeparation; Sampt etlichen seinen Particularen,* published Leipzig, 1608. This edition also includes a tract on the **Philosopher's Stone** by Conrad Schülern. (See also **Alchemy**)

Mellon, Mrs. J. B. (Annie Fairlamb) (c. 1930)

British **materialization** medium. Her first supernormal experience was at the age of nine, seeing her brother at sea in danger of drowning. Later physical powers manifested in a violent trembling of hand and arm. This was followed, in the family circle by **automatic writing** with lightning-like speed, by **clairvoyance** and **clairaudience**. With bandaged eyes she would fall into a trance and describe events happening at the time many miles away, events which were subsequently verified.

In 1873, as a young girl, together with Miss C. E. **Wood,** she was employed as an official medium of the Newcastle Spiritual Evidence Society. In 1875, with Miss C. E. Wood, she sat for Prof. Henry **Sidgwick** and F. W. H. **Myers** of the Society for Psychical Research at Cambridge, England. The seances, which were held under the strictest test conditions, produced excellent results but neither Prof. Sidgwick nor F. W. H. Myers chose to announce their observations in public.

In 1877 Alderman T. P. Barkas, of Newcastle, made successful experiments to obtain spirit molds (see **Plastics**). Unknown to Miss Fairlamb, he mixed magenta dye with the paraffin. The molds were found to be tinted with magenta, which proved that they were not smuggled in ready-made.

After a Continental tour, during which German investigators found her lose almost half of her bodily weight during materializations, Miss Fairlamb went to Australia. She married J. B. Mellon, of Sydney, but continued to give sittings at her own home. Dr. Charles W. MacCarthy, at whose residence Mrs. Mellon often sat, became convinced of the reality of the phenomena.

On October 12, 1894, a disastrous exposure took place in Mrs. Mellon's house. T. Shekleton Henry, another medium and pretended friend of Mrs. Mellon, grabbed "Cissie," the materialized spirit and found it to be the medium half undressed. The missing pieces of garment were found in the cabinet.

Mrs. Mellon defended herself by saying that she seemed to shoot into the grabbed form and became absorbed. She was said to have suffered serious injury in consequence of the spirit grabbing, and after her recovery she resolved never to sit in the cabinet again but always before the curtain in full view of the sitters.

The story of the exposure is told by T. Shekleton Henry in *Spookland* (Sydney, 1894), to which an answer was returned by "Psyche" under the title *A Counterblast to Spookland or Glimpses of the Marvellous* (1895).

As late as 1931, Mrs. Mellon was still active as a medium. Mr. H. L. Williams, a retired magistrate from the Punjab, wrote to Harry Price (*Psychic Research,* June, 1931): "As regards her (Mrs. Mellon), Dr. Haworth, a well-known doctor of Port Darwin, has testified before me that at Melbourne, in the presence of leading and professional men, he saw many times a spot of mist on the carpet which rose into a column out of which stepped a completely embodied human being who was recognised . . . " Sir William Windeyer, Chief Judge, and Alfred Deaking, Prime Minister of Australia were, according to the letter, convinced that Mrs. Mellon was genuine.

Melton, J(ohn) Gordon (1942-)

Pastor (United Methodist Church) and the leading historian of the development and variety of religions and cults in the U.S. He was born September 19, 1942 in Birmingham, Alabama, educated Birmingham Southern College (A.B. 1964), Garrett Theological Seminary (M.Div. with distinction 1968), Northwestern University (Ph.D. 1975).

He was ordained United Methodist minister, 1968; field representative Spiritual Frontiers Fellowship, 1970-83; pastor of United Methodist churches in Wyanet, Illinois, 1974-75, and Evanston, 1975-80; director of the Institute for the Study of American Religions, Evanston, 1980 onwards; president of Senior Action Services, Inc., 1978-80; visiting lecturer at University of San Francisco, summer 1971, Garrett-Evangelical Theological Seminary, summer 1981, and Loyola University, Chicago, Illinois, summer 1982; senior research associate Santa Barbara Center for Humanistic Studies. He is a member of the American Academy of Religion, Society for the

Scientific Study of Religion, American Society of Church History. As the leading authority on the many different religions and small religious, psychic/occult organizations in the U.S. and Canada, he has documented their origins, interrelationships, and beliefs, and also lectured widely on religious expression. He has taken a special interest in the problems of religious pluralism in the U.S. and the growth of divergent religions and cults. At the Institute for the Study of American Religions, he has created a unique and comprehensive information center, and his *Encyclopedia of America Religions,* regularly updated, is a major reference work.

His publications include: *The History of the Bowling Green Yoked Charge* (1967), (associate editor & contributor) *Encyclopedia of World Methodism* (1968), *Log Cabins to Steeples* (1974), *A Directory of Religious Bodies in the United States* (1977), *The Encyclopedia of American Religions* (2 vols., 1978; 2nd ed., revised format, 1987), *Magical Religion in the United States* (1979), *Paganism, Magic, and Witchcraft* (1982), (with Karl Pruter) *An Old Catholic Sourcebook* (1982), (with Robert L. Moore) *The Cult Experience* (1982), (contributor) Mark A. Noll & others, *Eerdman's Handbook to Christianity in America* (1983), *Encyclopedic Handbook of Cults* (1984), *Dictionary of Cult and Sect Leaders* (1984), (editor of series) *Bibliographies on Alternative Religions* (1982-), (contributor) Robert Basil, *Not Necessarily the New Age* (1988).

Melusina

The most famous of the fays or fairy creatures of medieval French legend. Being condemned to turn into a serpent from the waist downwards every Saturday, she made her husband, Count Raymond of Lusignan, promise never to come near her on a Saturday. This prohibition finally exciting his curiosity and suspicion, he hid himself and witnessed his wife's transformation.

Melusina was now compelled to quit her mortal husband and destined to wander about as a specter until the day of doom. She became The Banshee of Lusignan.

It is said also that the count immured her in the dungeon of his castle. (See also **Banshee; Fairies; Mermaids & Mermen**)

Melzer, Heinrich (1873- ?)

German **apport** medium of Dresden, successor of Frau Rothe, first seances recorded in *Die Uebersinnliche Welt* in November 1905. These were held in darkness, but the medium allowed himself to be fastened into a sack. Flowers and stones were apported in quantities.

The operators were said to be Oriental entities: "Curadiasamy," a Hindu, who spoke with a foreign accent, "Lissipan," a young Indian Buddhist and "Amakai," a Chinaman. "Quirinus," who claimed to be a Roman Christian of the time of Diocletian and "Abraham Hirschkron," a Jewish merchant from Mahren, were other picturesque **controls.**

By occupation Melzer was a small tobacconist. It is said that at one time he was an actor, which may account for his powers of declamation under control.

He visited the **British College of Psychic Science** in 1923 and in 1926. Owing to a significant development in his mediumship, he was able to sit in good white or red light. In 1923, he was examined before each seance and dressed in a one-piece linen suit, secured at wrist and ankles. The flowers arrived when the medium was in deep trance. He seemed to be able to observe them clairvoyantly before they appeared to the physical sight. Occasionally sitters, who knew nothing of this, spoke of seeing shadows of flowers in the air before they arrived.

Sometimes the medium seized upon the flowers and ate them voraciously, together with stalks and soil, often wounding his mouth by thorns on rose stalks. Returning to normal consciousness he blamed a particular control for the occurrence. The flowers seemed to arrive towards the medium and were not thrown out from him.

These phenomena were very impressive. The same could not be said of the stone **apports.** They were invariably very small. In the sittings of 1926, the doctor in charge slipped his hands at the back of the ears of the medium and discovered two small light colored stones affixed by flesh-colored sticking plaster. The medium's only attempt at excuse was that by that stage his power had gone and that he had been tempted by an undesirable control.

Such an exposure of fraud tends to discredit Melzer's phenomena. However, in his report in *Psychic Science,* (April, 1927) J. Hewat **MacKenzie** remarked: "But there is a difference between stones of a quarter to half an inch in size, and flowers of 18 inches stalk length, with leaves and thorns. Twenty-five anemones—or a dozen roots of lilies of the valley, with soil attached, pure bells and delicate leaves—or violets appearing fresh and fragrant, after two and a half hours sitting—have all been received, when the medium's hands have been seen empty a second before, when no friends of his were in the sittings, and when no opportunity could have presented itself to conceal them that would not have resulted in broken stems and blossoms."

Men in Black

The mysterious and sinister visitors who are supposed to have silenced flying saucer investigator Albert K. **Bender,** described in the book *They Knew Too Much About Flying Saucers* by Gray Barker (1956; 1967).

They have since become part of flying saucer mythology, with claimed visitors to other UFO investigators. Some investigators prefer to believe that they are officials of some C.I.A. type organization, determined to suppress information. (See also **UFO**)

Meng-Koehler, Heinrich Otto (1887-)

Physician, professor of mental hygiene, author and writer on parapsychology. Born July 9, 1887 at

Hohnhurst, Baden, Germany, he studied at University of Heidelberg (M.D. 1912), University of Leipzig, University of Würzburg. In 1929 he married Mathilde Koehler.

He was director of the Institute of Psychoanalysis, Frankfurt, from 1928-33, professor of mental hygiene at University of Basel, Switzerland, 1945-55, professor emeritus from 1956 onwards, and psychoanalyst.

Dr. Meng-Koehler edited and contributed to important works on Mental Hygiene and was author of *Psychohygiene* (Mental Hygiene, 1960). In the field of parapsychology, he took special interest in connections with psychoanalysis. He attended the International Conference on Parapsychological Studies held in Utrecht, Netherlands, in 1953 and the Conference on Unorthodox Healing at St. Paul de Vence, 1954.

His articles on parapsychology included: 'Wunderheilungen' (Miracles of Healing) and 'Parapsychologie, Psychohygiene and Aerztliche Fortbildung' (Parapsychology, Mental Hygiene and Medical Training) published in *Hippokrates,* 1954.

Mental World (in Theosophy)

Formerly known as the Manas Plane. In the Theosophic scheme of things, this is the third lowest of the seven worlds. It is the world of thought into which man passes on the death of the **astral body,** and it is composed of the seven divisions of matter in common with the other worlds. It is observed that the mental world is the world of thought, but it is necessary to realize that it is the world of good thoughts only, for the base thoughts have all been purged away during the soul's stay in the **astral world.**

Depending on these thoughts is the power to perceive the mental world. The perfected individual would be free of the whole of it, but the ordinary individual in past imperfect experience, has gathered only a comparatively small amount of thought and is, therefore, unable to perceive more than a small part of surroundings. It follows from this that although the individual's bliss is inconceivably great, the sphere of action is very limited. This limitation, however, becomes less and less with the individual's abode there after each fresh incarnation.

In the Heaven world-division into which we awake after dying in the astral world, we find vast, unthought-of means of pursuing what has seemed to us good—art, science, philosophy and so forth. Here, all these come to a glorious fruition of which we can have no conception, and at last the time arrives when one casts aside the mental body and awakens in the causal body to the still greater bliss of the higher division of the mental world.

At this stage, one has done with the bodies which form mortal personality, and which form one's home in successive incarnations, and one is now truly whole, a spirit, immortal and unchangeable except for increasing development and evolution. Into this causal body is worked all that one has experienced in the physical, astral and mental bodies, and when one still finds that experience insufficient for one's needs, one descends again into grosser matter in order to learn yet more and more.

These concepts derive from the Hindu religious classification of three bodies or states of being: gross (or physical), subtle and causal (*sthula, sukshma* and *karana shariras*), surrounded by five sheaths (*koshas*): *annamayakosha* (food or physical sheath), *pranamayakosha* (subtle energy sheath), *manamayakosha* (mental sheath), *vijnanamayakosha* (wisdom sheath), *anandamayakosha* (bliss sheath of spiritual unity).

Mentalphysics

A spiritual development system founded in 1927 by British born Edwin John **Dingle.** It was incorporated as a religion in 1936, and embodies belief in the universality of divine manifestation. Membership covers U.S.A., Great Britain, Australia, France, Germany and India, and there is an Institute of Mentalphysics headquarters with buildings designed by architect Frank Lloyd Wright in Los Angeles.

The system of Mentalphysics is based on diet, *pranayama* (yoga breathing techniques), chanting, meditation and development of extrasensory perception. Address: Institute of Mentalphysics, 59700-29 Palms Highway, P.O. Box 640, Yucca Valley, California 92284.

"Mentor"

One of the controls of the Rev. Stainton **Moses,** said to be Algazzali or Ghazali, Professor of Theology at Baghdad in the eleventh century, the greatest representative of the Arabian Philosophical School. His main duty was to manage the phenomena at the seances. He was very successful with lights and scents and brought many **apports.**

In Book XVI of the spirit communications of Stainton Moses there is a story of "Mentor" carving heads on two shells in the dining room while dinner was going on; the sound of the process was heard. (See also William Stainton **Moses**)

Mephis (or Memphitis)

A fabled precious stone which, when bruised to powder and drunk in water, was said to cause insensibility to torture.

Mercury

Also popularly known as quicksilver. A metal which has been known for many centuries, and which has played an important part in the history of **alchemy.** In its refined state it forms a coherent, very mobile liquid. The early alchemists believed that nature formed all metals of mercury, and that it was a living and feminine principle. It went through many processes, and the metal evolved was pure or impure according to the locality of its production.

The mercury of the **Philosopher's Stone** needed to be a purified and revivified form of the ordinary metal. The Arabian alchemist **Geber** stated in his

Summa perfectionis: "Mercury, taken as Nature produces it, is not our material or our physic, but it must be added to." (See also **Alchemy**)

Merlin

A legendary enchanter of Britain who dwelt at the court of King **Arthur.** His origin is obscure, but early legends concerning him agree that he was the offspring of Satan. He was probably an early Celtic god, who in process of time came to be regarded as a great sorcerer.

There appears to have been more than one Merlin, and it is necessary to discriminate between the Merlin of Arthurian romance and Merlin Caledonius, but it is probable that originally the two conceptions sprang from the one idea.

Mermaids and Mermen

Legends of supernatural sea people, human down to the waist but with a fish tail instead of legs, have been told since ancient times. In German folklore, a mermaid was known as "Meerfrau," in Danish "maremind," Irish "murduac" (or "merrow"). In Brittany, the "Morgans" were beautiful sirenlike women, dangerous to men, while in British maritime lore, seeing a mermaid might precede a storm or other disaster. A traditional ballad "The Mermaid" (Child ballad No. 289) tells how a ship's crew saw a mermaid sitting on a rock, combing her hair and holding a mirror. Soon afterwards the ship was wrecked in a raging sea. Traditionally, one can gain power over a mermaid by seizing her cap or belt.

There are many folk tales of marriages between a mermaid and a man, and in Machaire, Ireland, there are individuals who claim descent from such a union. The medieval romance of the fair **Melusine** of the house of Lusignan in France concerns the daughter of a union between a human and a fairy who cursed the daughter Melusine so that she became a serpent from the waist down every Saturday.

Hans Christian Andersen's pathetic story *The Little Mermaid* echoes folk tales in its theme of a mermaid who falls in love with a prince in a passing ship; the mermaid takes on human form in order to gain a human soul and be close to the prince, but although constantly near him cannot speak. When the prince marries a human princess, the mermaid's heart breaks. There is a similar haunting pathos in Matthew Arnold's poem "The Forsaken Merman."

In *Curious Myths of the Middle Ages* (1884; University Books, 1967), folklorist S. Baring-Gould suggested that mermaid and merman stories originated from the half-fish half-human gods and goddesses of early religions. The Chaldean Oannes and the Philistine Dagon are typical deities of this kind, and a representation of Oannes with a human body down to the waist and a fish tail has been found on sculpture at Khorsabad. Such goddesses as Derceto (Atergatis) and Semiramis have been represented in mermaid form. The classic Venus, goddess of love, was born out of the sea-foam, and was propitated by barren couples who desired children. The Mexican Coxcox or Teocipactli was a fish god, as also some Peruvian deities. North American Indians have a legend that they were led from Asia by a man-fish. In classical mythology the Tritons and Sirens are represented as half-fish half-human.

In addition to legends of mythology and folklore, however, there are many claimed accounts of actual mermaids and mermen throughout history. The twelfth-century *Speculum Regale* of Iceland describes a mermaid called the Margygr found near Greenland; "This creature appears like a woman as far down as her waist, with breast and bosom like a woman, long hands, and soft hair, the neck and head in all respects like those of a human being. From the waist downwards, this monster resembles a fish, with scales, tail, and fins. This prodigy is believed to show itself especially before heavy storms."

In 1187, a merman was fished up off the coast of Suffolk in England; it closely resembled a man but was not able to speak. The *Landnama* or Icelandic Doomsday Book tells of a merman caught off the island of Grimsey, and the annals of the country describe such creatures as appearing off the coast in 1305 and 1329.

In 1430 in Holland, there were violent storms which broke the dykes near Edam, West Friesland. Some girls from Edam had to take a boat to milk their cows, and saw a mermaid floundering in shallow muddy water. They brought her home, dressed her in female clothing and taught her to weave and spin and show reverance for a crucifix, but she could never learn to speak.

In 1560, some fishermen near the island of Mandar off the west coast of Ceylon caught no less than seven mermen and mermaids, which were witnessed by several Jesuit fathers and M. Bosquez, physician to the Viceroy of Goa. The physician made a careful examination of the mer-people, dissected them, and pronounced that their internal and external structure resembled that of human beings. There is a well authenticated case of a merman seen near a rock off the coast of Martinique. Several individuals affirmed that they saw it wipe its hands over its face and even blow its nose; their accounts were attested before a notary.

A merman captured in the Baltic in 1531 was sent as a present to Sigismund, King of Poland, and seen by all his court; the creature lived for three days. In 1608, the British navigator Henry Hudson (discoverer of Hudson Bay) reported the discovery of mermaid: "This morning, one of our company looking overboard saw a mermaid; and calling up some of the company to see her, one more came up, and by that time she was come close to the ship's side, looking earnestly at the men. A little after, a sea came and overturned her. From the navel upward, her back and breasts were like a woman's, as they say that saw her; her body as big as one of us, her skin very white and long hair hanging down behind, of colour black. In her going down they saw her tail, which was like the tail of a porpoise, speckled like a mackerel. Their names that saw her were Thomas Hilles and Robert Rayner."

In 1755, Erik Pontoppidan, Bishop of Bergen, published his *New Natural History of Norway* (2 vols.), in which there is an account of a merman observed by three sailors on a ship off the coast of Denmark, near Landscrona; the witnesses made a deposition on oath. In another book, *Poissons, écrevisses et crabes de diverses couleurs et figures extraordinaires, que l'on trouve autour des Isles Moluques* (published in 1717 by Louis Renard, Amsterdam), there is an illustration of a mermaid with the following description: "See-wyf. A monster resembling a Siren, caught near the island of Borné, or Boeren, in the Department of Amboine. It was 59 inches long, and in proportion as an eel. It lived on land, in a vat full of water, during four days seven hours. From time to time it uttered little cries like those of a mouse. It would not eat, though it was offered small fish, shells, crabs, lobsters, &c. After its death, some excrement was discovered in the vat, like the secretion of a cat." Several individuals testified to the truth of this account.

In 1857, two Scottish fishermen made the following declaration, recorded in the *Shipping Gazette:* "We, the undersigned, do declare, that on Thursday last, the 4th June 1857, when on our way to the fishing station, Lochindale, in a boat, and when about four miles S.W. from the village of Port Charlotte, being then about 6 p.m., we distinctly saw an object about six yards distant from us in the shape of a woman, with full breast, dark complexion, comely face, and fine hair hanging in ringlets over the neck and shoulders. It was about the surface of the water to about the middle, gazing at us and shaking its head. The weather being fine, we had a full view of it and that for three or four minutes.—John Williamson, John Cameron."

In spite of these and other circumstantial accounts, the conventional explanation for sightings of mermaids and mermen is usually that they are inaccurate or romantic viewings of a marine mammal called a Dugong (*Halicore*), of the order *Sirenia,* which also includes the Manatee or sea-cow. Such creatures suckle their young at the breast and have a vaguely human appearance. They used to be hunted for their oil, used as a substitute for cod-liver oil, and are now rare.

It is possible that the dugong known as *Rhytina gigas* or "Steller sea-cow," long believed extinct, may survive in the Bering Sea, near the Aleutian Islands. Vitus Bering, after whom the Sea is named, was a Danish navigator who was shipwrecked on the desert island of Avacha (now known as Bering Island) in 1741. His party included a naturalist named George W. Steller, who made copious notes while the party were dying of starvation. Steller observed large herds of *Sirenia* a short distance from the shore.

The creatures were mammals about 25 to 35 feet long and grazed off the kelp like cows on a pasture. They were unafraid of human beings, and it was easy to harpoon them, drag them ashore and eat the flesh, which sustained the party.

The top half of the creature resembled a seal, and the bottom half a dolphin. It had small flippers, and the females had mammary glands like a woman, suckling their young at the breast. Even courtship habits seemed human, as well as other behavior. When one creature was harpooned, the others would gather round it and try to comfort it, and even swim across the rope and try to dislodge the hook.

In 1977, Derek Hutchinson, a British schoolteacher, started planning an expedition to the Aleutian Islands to film the Steller sea-cow from kayaks.

Meanwhile it has to be said that *Sirenia* bear only a very vague resemblance to historic accounts of mermaids, especially those which were brought ashore and kept in captivity before they died. These also have no connection with the stuffed 'mermaids' displayed in showmen's booths in the nineteenth and early twentieth centuries, which were invariably clever fakes assembled by Japanese craftsmen. (See also **Lorelei; Sirens**)

Recommended reading:

Bassett, F. S. *Legends and Traditions of the Sea and of Sailors,* Belford, Clarke & Co., Chicago & New York, 1885

Benwell, Gwen & Arthur Waugh. *Sea Enchantress; The Tale of the Mermaid and Her Kin,* Hutchinson, London, 1961

Hutchins, Jane. *Discovering Mermaids and Monsters,* Shire Publications (booklet), U.K., 1968

Rappoport, Angelo S. *Superstitions of Sailors,* Stanley Paul, London, 1928; Gryphon Books, Ann Arbor, 1971

Merrell-Wolff, Franklin (c. 1887-)

American teacher of a system of higher consciousness deriving from Hindu **Yoga** and related philosophies. Born c. 1887, Dr. Wolff was the son of a Christian clergyman, but felt himself drawn beyond religious orthodoxy. He graduated with Phi Beta Kappa from Stanford University in 1911, majoring in mathematics, with philosophy and psychology as minors. He did graduate work at Stanford and in the Grade School in Philosophy of Harvard.

After teaching mathematics at Stanford, he withdrew from the academic life to seek metaphysical knowledge beyond sense perception and conception. After twenty-four years he attained a state of higher consciousness, described in his books *Pathways Through to Space* (1973; Warner Books, 1976) and *The Philosophy of Consciousness Without an Object* (Julian Press, 1973).

Although then in his late 80s, Dr. Wolff continued to teach students at a community in California, originally designated The Assembly of Man and now known as Friends of the Wisdom Religion, located at the Wolff residence, near Lone Pine, California, U.S. Highway 395, about half way between Reno and Los Angeles. Meetings at which Dr. Wolff's tape-recorded lectures are played take place at the home of Mrs. James A. Briggs, 4648 E. Lafayette Blvd., Phoenix, Arizona 85018. (See also **Kundalini**)

Mesmer, Franz Anton (1733-1815)

Famous Austrian doctor, originator of the technique of **Mesmerism,** forerunner of **hypnotism.** He was born at Weil, near Constance, May 23, 1733. In 1766 he took a degree in medicine at Vienna, the subject of his inaugural thesis being *De planetarum Influxu* (De L'influence des Planettes sur le corps humain). In this, he identified the influence of the planets with magnetism, and developed the idea that stroking diseased bodies with magnets would be curative. On seeing the remarkable cures of J. J. Gassner in Switzerland, he concluded that magnetic force must also reside in the human body, and thereupon dispensed with magnets.

In 1778 he went to Paris where he was very favorably received—by the public, that is, for the medical authorities there, as elsewhere, refused to countenance him. His curative technique was to seat his patients round a large circular vat or *baquet,* in which various substances were mixed. Each patient held one end of an iron rod, the other end of which was in the baquet. In due time the crisis ensued. Violent convulsions, cries, laughter, and various physical symptoms followed, these being in turn superseded by lethargy. Many claimed to have been healed by this method.

In 1784, the government appointed a commission of members of the Faculté de Médecine, the Societé Royale de Médecine, and the Academy of Sciences, the commissioners from the latter body including Benjamin **Franklin,** Bailly, and Lavoisier. The report of the Committee stated, in effect, that there was no such thing as **"animal magnetism,"** and referred the facts of the crisis to the imagination of the patient. This had the effect of quenching to a considerable extent the public interest in Mesmerism, as animal magnetism was called, for the time at least, although it was afterwards to be revived.

Mesmer died at Meersburg, Switzerland, March 5, 1815. (See also **Animal Magnetism; Hypnotism; Mesmerism**)

Mesmerism

A system of healing, founded by Franz Anton **Mesmer** (1733-1815), a German doctor who received his degree at Vienna in 1766 and expounded the main principles of his discovery of **"animal magnetism"** in *De Planetarum Influxu,* his inaugural thesis from which the following statements are extracted:

"There is a mutual influence between the celestial bodies, the earth and animated bodies.

"The means of this influence is a fluid which is universal and so continuous that it cannot suffer void, subtle beyond comparison and susceptible to receive, propagate and communicate every impression of movement.

"This reciprocal action is subject to as yet unknown mechanical laws.

"The result of this action consists of alternating effects which may be considered fluxes and refluxes . . .

"It is by this operation (the most universal in nature) that the active relations are exercised between the heavenly bodies, the earth and its constituent particles . . .

"It particularly manifests itself in the human body with properties analogous to the magnet; there are poles, diverse and opposed, which can be communicated, changed, destroyed and reinforced; the phenomenon of inclination is also observable.

"This property of the animal body which renders it susceptible to the influence of celestial bodies and to the reciprocal action of the environing ones I felt prompted to name, from its analogy to the magnet, animal magnetism. . . .

"It acts from a distance without the intermediary of other bodies.

"Similarly to light it is augmented and reflected by the mirror.

"It is communicated, propagated and augmented by the voice."

By applying magnetic plates to the patient's limbs, Mesmer effected his first cures in 1773. The arousal of public attention was due to a bitter controversy between Mesmer and a Jesuit Father Maximilian Hell, Professor of Astronomy at the University of Vienna, who claimed priority of discovery. Mesmer won.

In 1778, after a bitter public controversy over the cure of a blind girl, Mesmer went to Paris. In a short time he became famous. His first convert was Charles d'Eslon, medical adviser to the Count d'Artois. In September 1780, d'Eslon asked the Faculty of Medicine to investigate the doctrines of Mesmer. The proposal was rejected and d'Eslon was threatened that his name would be struck off the rolls at the end of the year if he did not recant.

In the meantime public enthusiasm grew to such a high pitch that in March 1871, Minister de Maurepas offered Mesmer, on behalf of the King, 20,000 livres (francs) and a further annuity of 10,000 livres if he established a school and divulged the secret of his treatment.

Mesmer refused, but two years later accepted a subscription of 340,000 livres for lectures to pupils. In 1784, the Government charged the Faculté de Médicine and the Societé Royale de Médicine to examine Animal Magnetism. A body of nine commissioners was convened under the presidency of Benjamin Franklin, including Jean Sylvain Bailly and J. K. Lavater; four more commissioners were added from the Royal Society of Medicine. The delegates restricted their activity to the search for evidence of a new physical force which was claimed as the agent of the cure. They had seen the famous *baquet* in operation.

This *baquet* was a large circular tub, filled with bottles, which dipped into the water. The *baquet* was covered. Iron rods projected from the lid through holes therein. The rods were bent and could be applied to any part of their body by the patients who sat in rows. The patients were tied together by a cord which passed round the circle, sometimes they held hands in a chain. There was music. The operator, with an iron rod in his hands, walked around, touched the patients; they fell into convulsions, sweated, vomited, cried—and were cured.

The committees, in their verdict, stated that they found no evidence of a magnetic fluid and the cures might be due to vivid imagination. M. de Jussieu was the only member who dissented. He claimed to have discovered something—animal heat which radiated from the human body and could be directed and intensified by willpower. Later magnetists adopted the theory. It marked the discovery of the human element in animal magnetism.

The next important development is attached to the name of the Marquis de Puységur. He began his cures at Busancy in the same year that animal magnetism was officially turned down. He did not employ the *baquet.* He "magnetized" a tree, fastened cords around and invited the sufferers to tie themselves to it. One of his invalid patients, a young peasant of 23 years of age, Victor by name, fell asleep in the operator's arms. He began to talk. On waking he remembered nothing. This was the discovery of the somnambulic stage.

Puységur and the earlier magnetizers attributed many curious phenomena to the state of *rapport* and they insisted on the theory of a magnetic effluence. Their patients claimed they could see it radiating as a brilliant shaft of light from the operator, from trees and other substances. Some substances could conduct it, others not. Water and milk could retain it and work cures.

Tardy de Montravel discovered the **transposition of senses.** His somnambule not only walked in the town with her eyes fast closed but could see by the pit of the stomach (see also **Eyeless Sight**). J. H. Desire Pétetin, a doctor at Lyons, enlarged upon these observations. He changed the theory of Mesmer to "animal electricity" and cited many experiments to prove that the phenomena were of an electrical nature.

J. P. F. Deleuze objected, insisted on the magnetic fluid theory and pointed out its analogies with nerve-force. He explained the phenomena of the transposition of the senses by the idea that it was the magnetic fluid which conveyed the impressions from without. He offered a similar theory to the explanation of medical diagnoses which the patients gave of others and themselves. Every phenomenon was, however, attributed to physiological causes. **Thought reading** and **clairvoyance** as transcendental faculties were rejected. The phenomena of traveling clairvoyance were yet very rare. Tardy de Montravel was alone in his supposition of a sixth sense as an explanatory theory.

The era of new thought was inaugurated by a nonmedical man, Abbé Faria. In 1813, he ascribed the magnetic phenomena to the power of imagination. General Noizet and Alexandre Bertrand adopted his view. Bertrand's *Traité du Somnambulisme* was published in 1823. It definitely established a new departure. Bertrand denied the existence of the magnetic fluid and pointed out the preternormal sensitivity of the subject to the least suggestion, whether by word, look, gesture or thought. Yet he admitted the supernormal phenomena of trance.

Marvelous stories were agitating the country. Professional clairvoyants arose. They gave medical diagnosis and treatment. Billot discovered most of the phenomena of **Spiritualism.** From Germany and Russia came rumors of a wide recognition of magnetic treatment. The Royal Academy of Medicine could not long ignore the stir.

On December 13, 1825, the proposal of P. Foissac that another investigation should be ordered was, after a bitter struggle, carried. The report of the committee was not submitted until five and a half years later. It stated that the alleged phenomena were genuine and that the existence of **somnambulism** was well authenticated. They found evidence of clairvoyance and successful medical diagnosis in the state of *rapport.* They also established that the will of the operator could produce the magnetic state without the subject's knowledge, even from another room.

In the meantime, developments in Germany proceeded. Animal magnetism ceased to remain a science of healing. Under the influence of Jung-Stilling (see Johann Heinrich **Jung**) it soon developed into a spiritual science. While Gmelin, Wienholt, Fischer, Kluge, Kieser and Weserman observed all the reported properties of the magnetic fluid and insisted on its essential importance, the practice of holding intercourse with the spirits through entranced somnambules soon gained popularity and increasing trust.

In the United States the students of Mesmerism believed they had discovered a new science—**Phreno-Mesmerism.** Dr. J. Rodes **Buchanan,** Dr. R. H. Collyer and the Rev. Laroy **Sunderland** contended for the honor of the first discovery. Dr. J. Rodes Buchanan mapped out an entirely new distribution of the phrenological organs in 1848 and developed the theory of "nerve-aura" as a connecting link between will and consciousness.

The title page of Dr. Collyer's *Psychography, or the Embodiment of Thought* (Philadelphia, 1843), represented two persons looking into a bowl, illustrating, in Dr. Collyer's words, that "when the angle of incidence from my brain was equal to the angle of reflection from her brain she distinctly saw the image of my thought at the point of coincidence."

The Rev. Laroy Sunderland discovered no less than 150 new phrenologic organs by means of mesmeric experiments. Professor J. S. Grime substituted the magnetic fluid with "etherium," the Rev. J. Bovee Dods with "vital electricity."

Andrew Jackson **Davis** was started on his career of seership by Mesmeric experiments for medical purposes. He became the herald of Spiritualism and on the bridge which he built most of the exponents of Phreno-Mesmerism and Mesmerism went over to the believers of the new faith.

In England the beginnings were slow. Not until Dr. John **Elliotson** was converted by Baron **Du Potet**'s visit in 1837 did Mesmerism assume the proportions of a widespread movement. For propaganda it relied on the journal *The Zoist* and the short-lived *Phreno-Magnet.* Three main classes of phenomena were thus distinguished: the physical effluence; phreno-mesmerism; and **community of sensations,** including clairvoyance.

The controversy between official medical science and Mesmerism raged bitterly. The evolution of "Animal Magnetism" into **"Hypnotism"** was due to James **Braid.** But James **Esdaile**'s name also occupies an important place. While Elliotson practically introduced curative magnetism into England, Esdaile proved the reality of Mesmeric trance by performing operations under Mesmeric anaesthesia.

As early as 1841, Braid read an address before the British Association in which he expounded his discovery of hypnotism. He described it as a special condition of the nervous system, characterized by an abnormal exaltation of suggestibility, which can be brought about automatically by the mere fixation of the eyes on bright objects with an inward and upward squint.

In 1843, his address was published under the title *Neurypnology.* This work was followed three years later by his *Power of the Mind Over the Body,* in which he pointed out that the Mesmerists were not on their guard against suggestion and hyperaesthesia. He produced all the characteristic results of Mesmerism without a magnet and claimed that the sensitives could not see flames at the poles of the most powerful magnets until warned to look at them. If warned, they saw flames issuing from any object.

The influence of Dr. Braid's discoveries on the Mesmerists themselves was very slight and strangely enough, official science took little notice. The main attraction of Mesmerism was its therapeutic value. It was the discovery in 1846-47 of the anaesthetic properties of ether and chloroform that deprived Mesmeric trance of its most obvious utility. The conquest by Spiritualism soon began and the leading Mesmerists were absorbed into the ranks of the Spiritualists.

No further advance was registered in England until 1883, when Edmund **Gurney** made his first experiments in hypnotism. He pointed out that in the hypnotic age the formerly numerous cases of *rapport* became extremely rare. He and F. W. H. **Myers** reverted to the earlier theory and declared that hypnotism and Mesmerism appeared to be two different states.

Official recognition was first granted to hypnotism in 1893 by a committee of the British Medical Association which reported to have found the hypnotic state genuine and of value in relieving pain and alleviating functional ailments. Mesmerism remained a controversial subject.

In France, a great revival began in 1875. A. A. Liébeault published his work on hypnotism in 1866. He sided with Bertrand. In 1875 Prof. Charles **Richet** came to the fore. In 1879, Charcot began his work in the Salpetrière. Paris, Bordeaux, Nancy and Toulon became centers of hypnotic activity. The school of Paris, of which Charcot was the chief, adopted and completed the explanation of Braid. Charcot contended that the hypnotic conditions could only be provoked with neuropaths or with hysterical subjects.

The school of Nancy accepted hypnotic sleep but considered suggestion its potent cause. In 1886, in Prof. **Bernheim**'s famous work *Suggestion and its Application to Therapeutics,* he went so far as to declare: "Suggestion is the key of all hypnotic phenomena. There is no such thing as hypnotism, there is only suggestion." The views of Liébeault and Bernheim prevailed almost everywhere over those of Charcot.

But animal magnetism was difficult to kill. Boirac was right in saying that "Animal magnetism is a new America which has been alternately lost and found every twenty or thirty years."

In 1887, Dr. Barety published *Le Magnetisme Animal Etudié sous le nom de' Force Neurique* in which he boldly set out to prove the reality of animal magnetism. Pierre Janet, reviewing Barety's work, admitted that certain phenomena of attraction, anaesthesia, etc., produced on subjects apart from all apparent suggestion, by contact alone or the mere presence of the operators, had often struck him as particularly suggestive of the so-called magnetic chain.

Emil Boirac supported this position. He pointed out that although hypnotism and suggestion exist, it does not follow that animal magnetism has no existence. It may be that the effects attributed to hypnotism and suggestion are caused by a third factor. Experiments with several subjects convinced him of the truth of his theory. "We are not prevented from hoping," he wrote in *Psychic Science* (1918), "that we shall one day succeed in discovering the natural unity of these three orders of phenomena [Mesmerism or animal magnetism, suggestion and Braidic hypnotism] as we begin to discover the natural unity of heat, light and electricity. They too much resemble each other's path not to betray a secret relationship. They are perhaps the effects of one and the same cause, but these effects are assuredly produced under different conditions and according to different laws."

The claim was further supported in 1921 by Dr. Sydney Alrutz, lecturer on psychology at the University of Upsala. He claimed to have proved experimentally the existence of a nervous effluence. Professor Farny, of the Zurich Polytechnicum, showed by electrical tests an emission from the fingers and called it "anthropoflux." His results verified the previous investigations of E. K. Muller, an engineer of Zurich, director of the Salus Institute.

Eventually the phenomena of animal magnetism merged with the developing Spiritualist movement, while hypnotism became established as a valid medical technique.

In 1838, Phineas P. **Quimby** began to practice Mesmerism and later developed from it his own concepts of mental action culminating in the **New Thought** movement from which **Christian Science** established a separate identity. (See also **Animal Magnetism; Community of Sensation; Emanations;**

Hypnotism; Metals (in Animal Magnetism); Mind-Cure; New Thought; Od; Odic Force; Odyle; Phreno-Mesmerism; Somnambulism; Spiritualism Suggestion; Transposition of Senses)

Recommended reading:

Bernheim, H. *Hypnosis & Suggestion in Psychotherapy,* London, 1988; University Books, 1964

Bertrand, A. *Traité du Somnambulisme,* Paris, 1824

Binet, Alfred & Charles Féré. *Animal Magnetism,* Kegan Paul, London, 1887

Braid, James. *Magic, Witchcraft, Animal Magnetism, Hypnotism & Electro-Biology,* John Churchill, London, 1852

Bramwell, J. Milne. *Hypnotism and Treatment by Suggestion,* Cassell, London, 1909

Deleuze, J. P. F. *Practical Instruction in Animal Magnetism,* Samuel R. Wells, New York, 1879

Franklin, Benjamin & others. *Animal Magnetism; Report of Dr. Franklin and Other Commissioners,* H. Perkins, Philadelphia, 1837

Ince, R. B. *Franz Anton Mesmer,* William Rider, pamphlet 1920

Goldsmith, Margaret, *Franz Anton Mesmer; The History of an Idea,* Arthur Barker Ltd., London, 1934

Gregory, William. *Animal Magnetism; or Mesmerism and Its Phenomena,* Nichols & Co., London, 1884

Liébeault, A. A. *Du Sommeil et des Etats Analogues,* Paris, 1886

Mesmer, F. A. (intro. Gilbert Frankau). *Mesmerism by Doctor Mesmer (1779), Being the First Translation of Mesmer's Historic 'Memoire sur la découverte du Magnétism Animal' to Appear in English,* Macdonald, London, 1948

Podmore, Frank. *Mesmerism and Christian Science,* Methuen, London, 1909

Sunderland, LaRoy. *Pathetism; Man Considered in Relation to his Form, Life, Sensation. . . . An Essay Towards a Correct Theory of Mind,* Boston, 1847

Metagnome

Term used by French psychical researchers for a gifted percipient of paranormal knowledge or extrasensory perception. The term avoids the Spiritualist associations of "medium," but is now generally superseded by the term "psychic," indicating an individual with extrasensory perception. (See also **Metagnomy**)

Metagnomy

Term used by French psychical researchers to indicate knowledge acquired through cryptesthesia, i.e., without the use of our five senses.

Although this term was used by French psychical researcher Dr. Eugen **Osty,** it appears to have been originally coined by researcher Emile **Boirac** (1851-1917) in his book *L'Avenir des Sciences Psychiques* (Paris, 1917), and was so ascribed in Dr. Osty's book *Supernormal Faculties in Man* (London, 1923).

The term derives from the Greek words *meta* (after) and *gnomon* (knower) and was used to designate the phenomenon of supernormal cognition, now generally called **"extrasensory perception"** by parapsychologists.

Metagraphology

Term indicating psychometric power on the basis of scripts. It has nothing to do with **graphology** (interpretation of personality traits indicated in handwriting) as the reading of the present, past and the future of the subject is not effected by the study of the writing. The script simply serves as an influence.

The sole justification of the term "metagraphology" is the fact that some graphologists developed their remarkably sensitive powers from the study of scripts. Raphael **Schermann** was the most notable among the metagraphologists. Recently similar powers were discovered in Otto Reimann, of Prague, a bank clerk, born in 1903, who, by simply touching a script, can give a perfect psychometric reading, and also imitate the writing. He was studied by Prof. Fischer, of Prague. (See also **Graphology; Psychometry**)

Metal Bending

One of the very few new directions in claimed psychic phenomena in modern times. It was first publicized by Uri **Geller,** the Israeli psychic from 1976 onwards, when he apparently demonstrated paranormal deformation of metal keys and spoons. When these objects were gently stroked or subjected to passes of his hand without actual contact, they tended to bend and often actually break, allegedly by some unknown force directed by the psychic's mind. The phenomenon became known as "the Geller effect," but is now generally classified by parapsychologists as "Psychokinetic Metal Bending" or "PKMB."

In spite of many demonstrations by Uri Geller and hundreds of laboratory experiments with Geller and other subjects by parapsychologists, the phenomenon remains highly controversial. However, some of the evidence is impressive. Metal samples sealed inside glass tubes appear to have been bent. Some samples have been bent when held by someone other than the psychic, while bends have been shown in alloys which normally break rather than bend when stressed. Videotape records appear to show paranormal bending of samples not held by the psychic concerned, but it must be said that other videotapes taken secretly have revealed fraud by some metal-benders, notably children, who have become known as "mini-Gellers."

The British scientist Prof. John **Taylor** spent three years studying the phenomenon, which he endorsed in his book *Superminds* (1975) but in 1978 he retracted to complete skepticism. However, Dr. John **Hasted,** another British scientist who tested Uri Geller and other claimed metal-benders, has continued to support the reality of PKMB. For a detailed study of his experiments and conclusions, see his book *The Metal Benders* (1981).

The stage magician James **Randi** has demonstrated various methods of apparent metal-bending, and also caused much confusion by planting fake metal-benders in parapsychology laboratory tests, to show that scientists may be deceived.

One of the commonest methods of faking metal-bending in tests with spoons is for the operator to surreptitiously weaken the spoon by prior bending, which can be achieved easily with the aid of a strong belt buckle.

However, such tricks do not seem to cover all the phenomena tested and observed by parapsychologists, and a careful study of the literature is advised before jumping to simplistic conclusions.

Recommended reading:

Hasted, John. *The Metal-Benders,* Routledge & Kegan Paul, London/Boston, Mass., 1981

Panati, Charles (ed.). *The Geller Papers; Scientific Observations on the Paranormal Powers of Uri Geller,* Houghton Mifflin Co., 1976

Randi, James. *The Truth About Uri Geller,* Prometheus Books, Buffalo, N.Y., 1982

Taylor, John. *Superminds; A Scientist Looks at the Paranormal,* Viking Press, N.Y./Macmillan, London, 1975

Taylor, John. *Science and the Supernatural,* Temple Smith, London, 1980

(See also **Movement; Psychic Force; Psychokinesis**)

Metals (in Animal Magnetism)

It was claimed by the magnetists that various metals exercised a characteristic influence on their patients. Physical sensations of heat and cold, numbness, drowsiness, and so on were experienced by the somnambules on contact with metals, or even when metals were secretly introduced into the room. Dr. John **Elliotson,** especially, gave much prominence to the alleged power of metal to transmit the magnetic fluid.

Gold, silver, platinum, and nickel were said to be good conductors, although the magnetism conveyed by the latter was of a highly dangerous character. Copper, tin, pewter, and zinc were bad conductors. Dr. Elliotson found that a magnetized sovereign (British gold coin) would throw into trance his **sensitives,** the **O'Key Sisters,** and that although iron would neutralize the magnetic properties of the sovereign, no other metal would do so.

When Baron Karl von **Reichenbach** propounded his theory of odic force, his sensitives claimed to see a luminous emanation proceed from metals—silver and gold shone white; lead, blue; nickel, red, and so on. Opponents of Reichenbach's theories ascribed such phenomena to **suggestion.** (See also **Od; Odic Force; Odyle; O'Key Sisters;** Baron Karl von **Reichenbach**)

Recommended reading:

Elliotson, John. *Human Physiology,* London, 1840

Reichenbach, Karl von. *Letters on Od and Magnetism,* Hutchinson, London, 1926 (reissued under title *The Odic Force,* University Books, 1968)

Metaphysical Digest (Journal)

Publication of the **Society of Metaphysicians,** Inc., Archers' Court, Stonestile Lane, The Ridge, Hastings, Sussex, England.

Metapsichica (Journal)

Semi-annual publication in Italian language of the Italian Metaphysical Association (Association Italiana Scientifica di Metapsichica). Address: Corso Firenze, N.8, 16136 Genova, Italy.

Metapsychics

The term proposed by Prof. Charles **Richet** in 1905 (when he was elected president of the Society for Psychical Research, London) for phenomena and experiments in psychical research. In his inaugural address he defined metapsychics as "a science dealing with mechanical or psychological phenomena due to forces which seem to be intelligent, or to unknown powers, latent in human intelligence."

He divided it into objective and subjective metapsychics, the first dealing with material, external facts, the second with psychic, internal, nonmaterial facts.

The term was not generally accepted on the Continent. In Germany, the word "parapsychic" was suggested in its stead. This was originally proposed by Emil **Boirac.** Prof. Theodor **Flournoy** suggested that "parapsychics" would be better and Richet's term should be limited to those phenomena which have been definitely proved supernormal in character.

In modern times, all three terms have now been supplanted by **"parapsychology."**

MetaScience Annual

A New Age journal of parapsychology. This is an official publication of the MetaScience Foundation (formerly Occult Studies Foundation), devoted to pursuit of scientific information in the field of parapsychology and related areas, in an academic and professionally responsible manner.

The publication is concerned with a wide range of paranormal topics, including Ufology, Kundalini, the physics of consciousness, psychokinesis, telepathy and Kirlian photography. Address: MetaScience Annual, Box 32, Kingston, Rhode Island 02881.

MetaScience Foundation

Nonprofit organization concerned with the pursuit of scientific information in the field of parapsychology and related areas. Formerly titled the Occult Studies Foundation, the new name reflects reservations about the contemporary connotations of the word "occult."

The Foundation follows an interdisciplinary approach to paranormal phenomena, and endeavors to maintain a high standard of academic and professional responsibility in their investigations. The Foundation publishes **MetaScience Annual** and *Journal of Occult Studies.* Address: MetaScience Foundation, Box 32, Kingston, Rhode Island 02881.

Metempiric

Modern term now increasingly used to denote unexplained phenomena such as UFOs, ghosts, alien creatures, mysterious fires, unusual falls from the sky, etc., usually classified as "Fortean phenomena" after the writer Charles Hoy Fort who pioneered the study of such things. (See also Charles **Fort; Occidental Society of Metempiric Analysis; Society for the Investigation of the Unexplained**)

Metempsychosis (or Transmigration of Souls)

The passing of the soul at death into another body than the one it has vacated. The belief in metempsychosis was very widespread in ancient times, and still survives in Hinduism and Buddhism, as well as in many folktales and superstitions.

The Brahmins and Buddhists believe that the soul may enter another human body, or that of one of the lower animals, or even a plant or tree, according to its deserts in previous incarnation. Thus it is doomed to successive incarnations, until by the transcending of all desires and emotions it merges in the Supreme Being.

Very similar was the idea of Pythagoras and the Greeks, who believed that all material existence was a punishment for sins committed in a former incarnation. Indeed it is probable that Pythagoras (see **Greece**) derived his theory from the Brahminical doctrine.

The ancient Egyptians would also seem to have believed in metempsychosis. Among certain tribes of Africa and American Indians transmigration was also believed. Totemism (see **Fetichism**) may perhaps facilitate a belief in the passing of the soul into the body of an animal.

In Europe also in early times the belief in metempsychosis flourished, and several popular folktales, such as that known in Scotland as "The Milk-white Doo," of which variants are found in many lands, contain references to the souls of the dead entering into beasts, birds, or fishes.

In some places it was thought that witches were at death transformed into hares, and for this reason the people of these localities refused to eat a hare.

The Jewish Kabalists also believed in the doctrine of metempsychosis, and traces of the belief are to be found in the writings of Emanuel **Swedenborg.** (See also **Reincarnation**)

Meteormancy

A branch of **Aeromancy** (**divination** through aerial phenomena such as thunder and lightning), concerned with divination from the appearance and movements of meteors and shooting stars. (See also **Aeromancy; Chaomancy**)

Methetherial

A term coined by F. W. H. **Myers,** meaning: beyond the ether, the transcendental world in which the spirits exist.

Metoposcopy

The art of interpreting character and destiny through the lines in the human forehead (Greek *metopon*). It was developed by the celebrated physician, mathematician and astrologer Jerome **Cardan** (1501-1576).

His work, illustrated by some 800 illustrations of faces, was published in an edition edited by C. M. Laurenderio, titled *Metoposcopia, libris tredecim, et octingentis Faciei humanæ Eiconibus complexa; cui accessis Melampodia de Navis Corporis Tractatus Græce et Latine nunc primum editus* (Lutetiæ Parisorum, 1658).

Although his interpretations were confined to lines in the forehead (coupled with **astrology**), he is thus a forerunner of the Physiognomy of J. K. Lavater (1741-1801).

Metratton

According to Jewish rabbinical legend, Metratton, the angel, is one of the agents by whom God the Father works. He receives the pure and simple essence of the divinity and bestows the gift of life upon all. He dwells in one of the angelic hierarchies.

MEXICO AND CENTRAL AMERICA

Sorcerers and Astrologers

Occult science among the ancient Mexicans may be said to have been in that stage between the primitive simplicities of medicine men and the more sophisticated magical practices of the medieval sorcerer. The sources of information are unfortunately of a most scanty description and are chiefly gleaned from the works of the early missionaries to the country, and from the legends and myths of the people themselves.

Writing upon the sorcerers of Mexico, Bernardino de Sahagun, an early Spanish priest, stated that the *naualli* or magician among the Mexicans was one who enchanted men and sucked the blood of infants during the night. This would seem as if the writer had confused the sorcerer with the **vampire**—a mistake occasionally made by continental writers on magic. He proceeded to say that among the Mexicans, this class was ignorant of nothing which appertained to sorcery, and possessed great craft, that they hired themselves out to people to work evil upon their enemies, and to cause madness and maladies.

"The necromancer," he stated, "is a person who has made pact with a demon, and who is capable of transforming himself into various animal shapes. Such people appear to be tired of life and await death with complaisance. The astrologer practices among the people as a diviner, and has a thorough knowledge of the various signs of the calendar, from which he is able to prognosticate the fortunes of those who employ him. This he accomplishes by weighing the power of one planet against that of another, and thus discovering the resultant applies it to the case in point. These men were called into consultation at births and deaths, as well as upon public occasions, and would dispute with much nicety on their art."

The astrological system of the Mexicans was, like that of their calendar, of the most involved descriptions possible, and no mere summary of it could convey anything but a hazy notion of the system, for which the reader is referred to Lewis **Spence**'s *The Civilisation of Ancient Mexico* (1911), Bernardino de Sahagun's *Historia de la Conquista de Mexico* (1829), and Bulletin 28 of the United States *Bureau of Ethnology.*

In connection with the astrological science of the Aztecs, however, it is worthy of note that the seventh calendric sign was that under which necromancers, sorcerers and evil-doers were usually born. Stated Bernardino de Sahagun: "These work their enchantments in obscurity for four nights running, when they choose a certain evil sign. They then betake themselves in the night to the houses where they desire to work their evil deeds and sorceries. . . . For the rest these sorcerers never know contentment, for all their days they live evilly and know no peace."

The myths of the Mexicans give a good working idea of the status of the enchanter or sorcerer in Aztec society. For example, the Toltec god Quetzalcoatl who, in early times, was regarded as a kind of culture-hero, was bewitched by the god of the incoming and rival race, Tezcatlipoca, who disguised himself as a physician, prescribed for an illness of his enemy's an enchanted draught which made him long for the country of his origin—that is, the home of the rains. From this it appears that potions or philters were in vogue amongst Mexican sorcerers.

In their efforts to rid themselves of the entire Toltec race, the traditional aborigines of Mexico, Tezcatlipoca was pictured as performing upon a magical drum in such a manner as to cause frenzy amongst the Toltecs, who leaped by thousands into a deep ravine hard by their city.

Wonderful stories were told of the feats of the Huaxteca, a people of Maya race, dwelling on the Gulf of Mexico. Sahagun related that they could produce from space a spring with fishes, burn and restore a hut, and dismember and resurrect themselves. The Ocuiltec of the Toluca Valley also possessed a widespread reputation as enchanters and magicians.

Divination and Augury

Although divination was practiced among the Aztecs by means of astrology, there were other and less intricate methods in use. There was in existence a College of Augurs, corresponding in purpose to the Auspices of Ancient Rome, the members of which occupied themselves with observing the flight and listening to the songs of birds, from which they drew their conclusions, and pretended to interpret the speech of all winged creatures.

The *Calmecac,* or training college of the priests, had a department where divination was taught in all its branches. A typical example of augury from birds may be found in the account of the manner in which the Mexicans fixed upon the spot for the foundation of their city.

Halting after years of wandering in the vicinity of the Lake of Tezcuco, they observed a great eagle with wings outspread perched on the stump of a cactus, and holding in its talons a live serpent. Their augurs interpreted this as a good omen as it had been previously announced by an oracle, and upon the spot where the bird had alighted, they drove the first piles upon which they afterwards built the city of Mexico—the legend of the foundation of which is still commemorated in the heraldic arms of modern Mexico.

Dreams and visions also played a great part in Mexican divination, and a special caste of augurs called *Teopixqui,* or *Teotecuhtli* (masters or guardians of divine things) were set apart for the purpose of interpreting dreams and of divining through dreams and visions, which was regarded as the chief route between man and the supernatural.

The senses were even quickened and sharpened by the use of drugs and the ecstatic condition was induced by want of sleep, and pertinacious fixing of the mind upon one subject, the swallowing or inhalation of cerebral intoxicants such as tobacco, the maguey, coca, the snake-plant or *ololiuhqui,* and similar substances.

As among some tribes of the American Indians, it was probably believed that visions came to the prophet or seer pictorially, or that acts were performed before him as in a play. It was also believed that the soul traveled through space and was able to visit those places of which it desired to have knowledge. It is also possible that the seers hypnotized themselves by gazing at certain small highly-polished pieces of sandstone, or that they employed these for the same purpose as crystal-gazers employ the globe. The goddess Tozi was the patron of those who used grains of maize or red beans in divination. (See also **Crystal Gazing; Divination**)

Charms and Amulets

The **amulet** was regarded in Mexico as a personal **fetish.** The Tepitoton, or diminutive household deities of the Mexicans were also fetishistic. It is probable that most of the Mexican amulets were modeled on the various ornaments of the gods. Thus the traveler's staff carved in the shape of a serpent like that of Quetzalcoatl was undoubtedly of this nature, and was even occasionally sacrificed to. The frog was a favorite model for an amulet. As elsewhere, the thunderbolts thrown by the gods were supposed to be flint stones, and were cherished as amulets of much virtue, and as symbols of the fecundating rains.

Vampirism

As mentioned earlier, Bernardino de Sahagun probably confused the Mexican necromancer with the vampire, and it is interesting to note that this folk belief must have originated in America independently of any European connection. But there is also another instance of what would seem something like vampirism in Mexico.

This is found in connection with the *ciupipiltin* or ghosts of women who have died in childbirth. These haunt the crossroads, crying and wailing for the little ones they have left behind them. But as in many other countries, notably in Burma, they are malevolent—their evil tendencies probably being caused by jealousy of the happiness of the living.

Lest they should enter their houses and injure their children, the Mexicans at certain times of the year stopped up every possible hole and crevice. The appearance of these ghosts (Sahagun described them as "goddesses") at crossroads is highly significant, for we know that the burial of criminals at such junctions was merely a survival of a similar disposal of the corpse of the vampire, whose head was cut off and laid at his side, and who was entombed at crossroads for the purpose of confusing him as to his whereabouts. (See also **Vampire**)

The Cult of Nagualism

Both in Mexico and Central America a religio-magical system called Nagualism existed, the purpose of which was to bring occult influence against the whites for their destruction. The rites of this strange cult usually took place in caverns and other deserted localities, and were naturally derived to a large extent from those of the suppressed native religion.

Each worshiper possessed a magical or animal spirit-guide, with which he was endowed early in life. This system certainly flourished as lately as the last quarter of the nineteenth century.

Central America

Information on magic and sorcery amongst the Maya, Kiche, and other Central American peoples is even rarer than that relating to Mexico, and there is little else than local legends as to guide research in these areas.

The great storehouse of Central American legend is the *Popol Vuh,* a study of which was published by Lewis Spence (1908). This fascinating work of mythological history states that some of the elder gods were regarded as magicians, and the hero-twins, Xblanque and Hun-ahpu, whom they sent to earth to rid it of the Titan Vukubcakix, were undoubtedly possessed of magical powers.

As boys they were equipped with magical tools which enabled them to get through an enormous amount of work in a single day, and when they descended into Xibalba (the Kiché Hades) for the purpose of avenging their father and uncle, took full advantage of their magical propensities in combating the inhabitants of that drear abode. Xibalba itself possessed sorcerers, for within its borders were Xulu and Pacaw, who assisted the hero-gods in many of their necromantic practices.

As regards divination, the Maya possessed a caste of augurs, called *Cocomes* or the Listeners, while prophecy appears to have been periodically practiced by their priests.

In the so-called books of *Chilan Balam,* which were native compilations of events occurring in Central America previous to the Spanish Conquest, we find certain prophecies regarding, amongst other things, the coming of the Spaniards.

These appear to have been given forth by a priest who bore the title (not the name) of "Chilan Balam," whose offices were those of divination and astrology but these pronouncements seem to have been colored at a later date by Christian thought, and hardly to be of a genuine aboriginal character.

There are certain astrological formulas in the books, all of which are simply borrowed from European almanacs of the century between 1550 and 1650.

Amulets were in great vogue amongst the Maya, and they had the same fear of the last five days of the year as had the Mexicans, who regarded them as *nemontemi* or unlucky, and did no work of any description upon them. These days the Maya called *uyayayab,* and they considered that a demon entered their towns and villages at the beginning of this period. To avert evil influence they carried an image of him through the village in the hopes that he might afterwards avoid it.

The writer Lewis Spence, who published several books on Mexico and Central America, believed that there was some evidence for the influence of an Atlantean civilization, detailed in his book *Atlantis in America* (1925). (See also **Atlantis**)

Death Day

Ever since the Spanish conquests, the original Indian culture, religion, and superstitions have become inextricably interwoven with Christian beliefs and customs, creating a complex synthesis. With the modern history of war, revolts and revolution extending into the twentieth century, it is not surprising that death has a special place in the symbolism and folklore of the Mexican people.

This is vividly illustrated in the traditional celebration of All Soul's Day on November 2nd, when toys, cakes and candies in the form of skulls are on sale in the streets, with carnival style costumes and plays depicting skeletons.

Although All Soul's Day is an imported Christian feast, it has blended with the Mexican Indian beliefs in which skulls and death goddesses are typical of pre-Columbian art, with the death orientation of the Spanish monastic orders, and the Christian *memento mori* tradition, as well as the memory of wars and revolutions. If the concept of adults and children celebrating death and eating candy skulls seems somewhat distasteful, it must also be remembered that it is not without a certain black humor, an expression of courage and the indomitable desire to live and organize a just society.

The extraordinary profusion of death images was well illustrated by the work of the Mexican printmaker José Guadalupe Posada (1852-1913), famous for his *calaveras* (skeletons) that ate, drank, made merry, rode bicycles and horses, brandished swords and daggers, or were humble workers and revolutionaries.

Something of the extraordinarily complex history and beliefs of Mexico is captured on film by the great Soviet director S. M. Eisenstein in his uncompleted epic *Que Viva Mexico* in 1932. Unfortunately his vast footage remained in limbo, or carved into short films by other hands during Eisenstein's lifetime. Political and ideological complications of the time prevented Eisenstein from completing the film as planned, but a 60-minute version titled *Time in the Sun* was completed by Marie Seton in 1940, and a longer reconstruction by G. Alexandrov (Eisenstein's assistant) and N. Orlov titled *Que Viva Mexico* was completed in the U.S.S.R. in 1979. Both are available on video cassette, but the former was released in Britain on PAL system. The Alexandrov and Orlov film is available on NTSC video from: Ifex Films, 201 West 52 Street, New York, N.Y. 10019. Both versions illustrate the Death Day feast, as well as the history and folklore of Mexico. An earlier short "Death Day" made from Eisenstein's material was released in cinemas in 1934.

Recommended reading:

Berdecio, R. & S. Appelbaum (ed.). *Posada's Popular Mexican Prints,* Dover paperback, 1972

Recinos, Adrián, Delia Goetz & Sylvanus G. Morley (transl. & ed.). *Popul Vuh; The Sacred Book of the Ancient Quiché Maya,* William Hodge, London, 1951

Sahagun, Bernardino de. *Historia de la Conquista de Mexico,* Mexico, 1829

Spence, Lewis. *Atlantis in America,* Ernest Benn, London, 1925; Singing Tree Press, Detroit, 1972

Spence, Lewis. *The Civilisation of Ancient Mexico,* London, 1911

Spence, Lewis. *The Gods of Mexico,* Fisher, Unwin, London, 1913

Spence, Lewis. *The Magic and Mysteries of Mexico,* Rider & Co., London, 1930

Spence, Lewis. *The Myths of Mexico & Peru,* Harrap, London, 1913

Spence, Lewis. *The Popul Vuh; The Mythic & Heroic Sagas of the Kichés of Central America,* David Nutt, London, 1908

Meyer, Gustav (1868-1932)

Famous German occultist and novelist, who wrote under the name Gustav **Meyrink.**

Meyer, Jean (died 1931)

French industrialist, a fervent adherent of the Spiritist doctrines of Allan **Kardec,** founder of the **Maison des Spirites** (8, Rue Copernic, Paris) which aimed, under his personal supervision, at the diffusion of this knowledge.

He was also a founder of the **Institut Métapsychique International,** which pursued psychical research and was recognized as of public utility by the French Government in 1919. He endowed the institution with a portion of his fortune, took a personal interest in its work and presented it, shortly before his death, with an infra-red installation at a cost of 200,000 francs.

The following story indicates the fair-mindedness of Jean Meyer in sponsoring both Spiritualism and scientific research. After the death of Dr. Gustav **Geley,** director of the Institut Métapsychique, M. Meyer desired to appoint Dr. Eugène **Osty** as his successor. Dr. Osty pointed out that the Institut would require complete scientific liberty, and stated "what would you say, if from the laboratory of the Institut there were to issue some day studies of fact which would suggest that the teaching of the Maison des Spirites is in whole or in part illusory interpretation of facts produced exclusively by the innate powers of man as yet unknown?"

With courageous confidence in both Spiritualism and science, M. Meyer replied: "Yes, I accept the risk. I know you for a sincere researcher. That is enough for me."

Meyrink, Gustav (1868-1932)

Pseudonym of German novelist Gustav Meyer, famous for his occult fiction. He was also actively concerned with occult and Theosophical groups in Europe before and during World War I.

Born in Vienna, he was taken by his family to Prague, Czechoslovakia, where his mother's family owned a bank. As a young man, Meyrink worked in the bank, but was attracted to occult teachings. In 1891, he was a member of the Theosophical Lodge of the Blue Star, whose members practiced occult disciplines. Meyrink translated the Tantric work on Hindu mysticism *Nature's Finer Forces* by Rama Prasad.

In 1903, he published his first collection of short stories. Many of his writings have themes of fantasy or occultism, with echoes of E. T. A. Hoffmann, Edgar Allan Poe or Franz Kafka. His best known novel was *Der Golem* (1915; translated by M. Pemberton as *The Golem,* 1928). This is a brilliant and strangely disturbing book concerned with Kabalism and the occult, based on Prague legends of the **Golem,** a mysterious man-monster said to have been created from clay by Rabbi Judah Loew of Prague in the seventeenth century.

The book had added power in relating to the real-life background of Golem legends, since the Prague ghetto had changed little at that time. Indeed, Rabbi Loew's grave may still be seen in the Old Jewish cemetery at Prague. A German silent film *The Golem,* directed and scripted by Paul Wegener, was produced in 1920, adapted very loosely from Meyrink's novel.

Meyrink converted from Protestantism to Buddhism and spent many years in occult investigations, including experiments in alchemy.

He was present at some of the seances of Baron **Schrenck-Notzing** in Munich with the medium **"Eva C."**

Meyrink also practiced Yoga and claimed to have achieved telepathic contact with the famous South Indian holy man Sri **Ramana Maharshi,** guru of Paul **Brunton.**

Meyrink died in December 1932 in Starnberg, Germany. For biographical information see *Gustav Meyrink* by Eduard Frank (Budingen-Gottenbach, 1957). Meyrink's own book *An der Schwelle des Jenseits* (1923) presents some of his own philosophical outlook. (See also **Golem**)

Mezazoth, The

A traditional Jewish schedule which, when fastened on the doorpost, possessed talismanic qualities. It is said in the *Talmud* that whoever has the *mezazoth* fixed on his door, and is provided with certain personal charms, is protected from sin.

Mhorag (or Morag)

A Loch Ness type monster observed and photographed in Loch Morar, West Inverness, Scotland. The loch is 12 miles long, up to 2 miles wide and 1,017 feet deep.

The magazine *Fortean Times* (No. 22, Summer 1977) reproduced a photograph taken by Mrs. Hazel Jackson (of Wakefield, Yorkshire), who stayed at Morar with her husband on a touring holiday. The Jacksons, who are skeptical about monsters, took two photographs of their sheepdog by the side of the loch, and both pictures showed what appeared to be the head of a monster in the loch. Two other photographs reproduced in *Fortean Times* 22 were taken by Miss M. Lindsay of Musselburgh. However, these were also somewhat ambiguous.

A Loch Morar Expedition headed by Adrian Shine has tested underwater surveillance equipment, including a spherical submersible designed by Shine. There are hopes that such equipment may identify the Mhorag monster, since the waters of the loch are crystal clear. (See also **Loch Ness and Morar Project; Loch Ness Monster; Monsters**)

Recommended reading:

Campbell, Elizabeth M. & D. Solomon. *The Search for Morag,* Tom Stacey, London, 1972

Michael

An archangel, the Hebrew name meaning "He who is equal to God." In *Revelation* it is said: "there was war in heaven. Michael and his angels fought against the dragon" and from this it is deduced that Michael was the leader of the celestial hierarchy—as against Lucifer, the head of the disobedient angels.

Michael is mentioned by name four other times in the Scriptures; in *Daniel* as the champion of the Jewish Church against Persia; in *Jude* as the archangel who fought with Satan for the body of Moses; by Gabriel he is called the prince of the Jewish Church; and in the prophecy of Enoch, "Michael. . . . who commands the nations."

His design, according to genealogist Randle Holme, is a banner hanging on a cross, and he is represented as victory with a dart in one hand and a cross on his forehead.

Bishop Horsley and others considered Michael as only another name for the Son of God.

In one of the Jewish rabbinical legends he is the ruler of Mercury, to which sphere he "imparts benignity, motion and intelligence, with elegance and consonance of speech." (See also **Angels**)

Michigan Canadian Bigfoot Information Center

Founded in 1970, covering northern and midwestern U.S. and eastern Canada, to assist persons having a sincere desire for knowledge about the "Sasquatch" or "Bigfoot" (large, hairy, man-like creature reputedly inhabiting various regions of North America), and to obtain a Sasquatch specimen.

The Center conducts overnight vigils in classified areas, receives cooperative assistance from anthropologists, wildlife pathologists, and Department of Natural Resources affiliates. It maintains transcript and tape collection as well as file and indexing system, compiles statistics, maintains research program and data base. Address: 152 W. Sherman, Caro, Michigan 48723. (See also **Bigfoot Information Center; Bigfoot News; Monsters; Sasquatch Investigations of Mid-America**)

Microcosm, The

(Greek *Micros,* small; *Kosmos,* a world) The "little world" of the human being, as distinct from the macrocosm or great world of the universe. The relationship between microcosm and macrocosm has preoccupied philosophers for many centuries, and it was often believed that the macrocosm was symbolized in the microcosm.

According to some occultists, the microcosm was itself symbolized by the Pentagram or Pentacle—a five-pointed star, which represents Man and the summation of the occult forces. It was believed by **Paracelsus** that this sign had a marvelous magical power over spirits, and that all magic figures and Kabalistic signs could be reduced to two—the Microcosm and the **Macrocosm.** (See also **Magical Diagrams; Macrocosm Pentacle**)

Microprosopus, The

One of the four magical elements in the **Kabala,** probably representing one of the four simple elements—air, water, earth, or fire. The word means "creator of the little world." (See also **Kabala; Microcosm**)

Mictlan

The Mexican Hades. (See also **Hell; Mexico and Central America**)

Midday Demons

Ancient peoples frequently made mention of certain demons who became visible especially towards midday to those with whom they had a pact. They appeared in the form of men or of beasts, and let themselves be enclosed in a symbolic character, a figure, a vial, or in the interior of a hollow ring. (See also **Demonology**)

Midiwiwin, The

A secret society or exclusive association of the Ojibway Indians of North America. The myth of the foundation of this society is as follows:

"Michabo, the Creator, looking down to earth saw that the forefathers of the Ojibway were very helpless. . . . Espying a black object floating on the surface of a lake he drew near to it and saw that it was an otter [now one of the sacred animals of the *Midi-*

wiwin]. He instructed it in the mysteries of that caste, and provided it with a sacred rattle, a sacred drum, and tobacco. He built a *Midiwigan,* or Sacred House of Midi, to which he took the otter and confided to it the mysteries of the *Midiwiwin.*"

The society was one of these "medicine" or magical associations so common among the North-American Indians (see **America, U.S. of**). When a candidate was admitted to a grade and prepared to pass on to the next, he gave three feasts, and sang three prayers to the Bear Spirit in order to be permitted to enter that grade.

His progress through the various grades was assisted by several snake-spirits, and at a later stage by the power of certain prayers or invocations—a larger snake appeared and raised its body, thus forming an arch under which the candidate took his way to the higher grade.

When the Indian belonged to the second grade he was supposed to receive supernatural power, to be able to see into the future, to hear what came from far off, to touch friends and foes, however far away they might be, and so on.

In higher grades he could assume the form of any animal. The third grade conferred enhanced power, and it was thought that its members could perform extraordinary exploits, and have power over the entire invisible world. The fourth was still more exalted.

When an Indian was ready to undergo initiation, he erected a wigwam in which he took steambaths for four days, one on each day. On the evening of the day before initiation he visited his teachers in order to obtain from them instructions for the following day. Next morning the priests approached with the candidate at their head, entered the *Midiwigan,* and the proceedings commenced.

The publications of the Bureau of American Ethnology contain several good accounts of the ritual of this society.

Midwest Psychic News

Monthly publication covering psychic events in Chicago and other states. Address: 2517 West 71st Street, Chicago, Illinois 60629.

Miller, Charles Victor (c. 1908)

Remarkable **materialization** medium of San Francisco, born at Nancy, France. By profession he was a dealer in old pictures and Japanese objects of art. Detailed descriptions of his phenomena were given in Willie Reichel's *Occult Experiences* (1906). Reichel claimed to have witnessed many marvels.

For example, Miller did not go into trance as a seance started. He stood outside the cabinet from which a procession of phantoms issued. Miller took them by the hand, asked their names and introduced them to the sitters. Later he went into the cabinet, where he was seen with as many as six white robed figures. They came out one by one, spoke to the sitters and usually dematerialized in front of the cabinet, sinking through the floor.

Of course, in modern times the very substantiality of materialized figures suggest fraud accomplices rather than genuine Spiritualist phenomena. However, the variety of Miller's phenomena and the certainty of witnesses leaves the question unproved either way. On one occasion Reichel's nephew disappeared by floating upwards through the ceiling. Miller was normally under the **control** of the spirits "Betsy" and "Dr. Benton."

The highest number of materialized spirits Reichel claimed to have seen in a seance was twelve. The medium was conscious and kept on talking. The phantoms spoke in various languages and many were recognized by the sitters. Once, in Reichel's own house, a materialized spirit walked out into the hall, a distance of thirty-five feet from the medium.

In the journal *Psychische Studien* (February 1904) Reichel described a seance at which a deceased friend of his materialized eight times, very near to him, at a distance of over three yards from the medium. "He drew near me," wrote Reichel, "like a floating flame, which lowered itself, and in the space of about a minute and a half developed and stood before me quite formed. He held long conversations with me; then, retiring to the curtain, where I followed him, he dematerialised, speaking up to the moment when his head disappeared."

Reichel also witnessed rotating white and blue flames whence voices issued and spoke to him, giving their complete names. In one seance the medium was completely dematerialized and transported to the first floor.

Miller paid two visits to Europe. When he first came in 1906, much criticism was directed against him because he mostly sat with Spiritists (see **Spiritism**) and avoided Col. **Rochas,** with whom he had corresponded, and a circle of scientists who had arranged to test him scientifically.

However, psychical researcher Gabriel **Delanne** concluded that the apparitions were genuine. Gaston Méry, chief editor of the *Libre Parole* and director of the *Echo du Merveilleux* (which was not a Spiritist journal) admitted that it was highly probable that the phenomena which he witnessed were genuine but "until there is fuller information we must be satisfied with not comprehending." The seance took place in Méry's house in a room which Miller did not enter before the proceedings. Moreover, he was completely undressed in the presence of three doctors and donned Méry's own garments.

Dr. Gérard **Encausse** ("Papus") who also attended a seance, stated in *L'Initiation* that his expectation was fully satisfied and that Miller displayed "mediumistic faculties more extraordinary than he had hitherto encountered."

From Paris, Miller went on to Germany and gave many test seances in Munich at private residences. The accounts appear to corroborate Reichel's observations. The materialized form was often seen to develop from luminous globes and clouds which first appeared near the ceiling. If several forms were materialized at the same time they were transparent. It often happened that at the end of the seance Miller was violently thrown out of the cabinet. Yet he suffered no injury.

On his way back to the United States, Miller again visited Paris and gave a few more seances. According to Prof. Charles **Richet,** he would not accept the conditions imposed. Four of his seances were reported in *Annals of Psychic Science* (vol. 4, 1906). Psychical researcher Count Cesar **de Vesme,** who attended the last seance, and objected at not having been given an adequate opportunity to form a well-founded judgment, noted: "A white ball, as of gas, about a quarter of a yard in diameter appeared in the air at the upper extremity of the curtains. Finally it came down, rested on the floor, and in less than a minute, changing into a long shape, was transformed into a draped human form, which subsequently spoke." (*Annals of Psychic Science,* vol. 4, No. 21, 1906) The seance, however, was not sufficient to enable de Vesme to arrive at a very definite opinion as to the genuineness of these manifestations.

In 1908, Miller paid another visit to Paris. On June 25, in the presence of forty persons, a very successful seance was held at the house of Mme. Noeggerath under test conditions. The Committee of Control consisted of Messrs. Benezech, Gaston Méry, Cesar de Vesme and Charles Blech, Secretary of the Societe Theosophique. The medium was disrobed, medically examined and put into black garments which were furnished by the committee and had neither lining nor pockets. The evolution and dissolution of numerous phantom shapes was closely observed.

Cesar de Vesme, however, remained unconvinced. In the *Annals of Psychic Science* (vol. 7, 1908), he complained that in the series of seances which he attended in almost complete darkness Miller never allowed the control of his right hand. Sitting on the left side of the cabinet he could have introduced, with his right hand, a white drapery which he could have manipulated as a small phantom in the course of materialization. He had only been searched in a single seance when forty people were present. There was no telling whether the drapery might not have been passed to him by one of the sitters.

Leon Denis, Baron de Watteville, Charles Blech, de Fremery (director of the *Het Toekomstig Leven,* The Hague), Paul Leymarie (director of the *Reuve Spirite*), M. W. Bormann, (director of *Die Uebersinnliche Welt*) and Dr. Joseph **Maxwell** shared de Vesme's opinion.

Of Miller's public seances no more was heard after this Paris series.

Miller, Ellora Fogle (Mrs. R. DeWitt Miller) (1913-)

Writer in the fields of publicity and psychical research. Born June 8, 1913 at Philadelphia, Pennsylvania, she studied at University of Southern California (M.A. 1945). In 1937 she married R. DeWitt **Miller** (died 1958).

She was a staff member of the publicity department of Young & Rubicam, Hollywood, California, and national editor of *The Baton* (publication of Phi Beta Fraternity) from 1953-56, director of honors, Phi Beta Fraternity, from 1956 onwards, member of Radio and Television Women of Southern California.

With her late husband she collaborated on various books and articles concerned with psychical research. Their books included *Forgotten Mysteries* (1947) and *You Do Take It With You* (1955), and their various articles were published in *Pageant, Tomorrow, Coronet, Popular Science, Popular Mechanics.*

Miller, R(ichard) DeWitt (1910-1958)

Writer on psychical research and parapsychology. Born January 22, 1910 at Los Angeles, California, he was educated at University of Southern California, (B.A. 1933). In 1937 he married Ellora Fogle.

As a freelance writer Mr. Miller contributed many articles to *Coronet, Esquire, Pageant, Popular Mechanics, Popular Science, Tomorrow,* and *Life.*

Many of his writings were concerned with parapsychological topics, and he contributed regular features 'Your Other Life,' 'Forgotten Mysteries' and 'Not of Our Species' to *Coronet* magazine. He often collaborated with his wife. His books include: *The Man Who Lived Forever* (1956), *Forgotten Mysteries* (1947), *Reincarnation* (1956), *You Do Take It With You* (1957). He contributed to the anthology *Beyond the Five Senses* edited by Eileen J. Garrett (1957). He died June 3, 1958.

Millesimo Castle

Located in Italy, province of Savona, property of the Marquis Carlo **Centurione Scotto,** scene of important psychic investigations in 1927-28 and later in the phenomena of **direct voice, apports, levitation** and **materialization.** (See also **Centurione Scotto**)

Mind-Body-Spirit Festival

International festival event coordinating and presenting occult, mystical, psychical, astrological, New Age, human potential and holistic organizations and individuals.

Founded in April 1977 in England by new consciousness entrepreneur Graham **Wilson,** the Festival has since been presented annually in London and the U.S., associated with similar events in British provincial centers, and in São Paulo, Brazil.

The Festival provides an annual stage for contemporary alternative lifestyles in a wide spectrum of mystical, holistic and ecological areas, where traditional philosophies and activities rub shoulders with newer cults.

The Festival includes lectures, demonstrations and workshops as well as exhibits and stands promoting individuals, organizations and publications concerned with psychic phenomena, healing, yoga, astrology, health, physical fitness, dance, UFOs, meditation, organic gardening, mystical arts and crafts and alternative technologies. Address: Mind-

Body-Spirit Festival, New Life Designs Ltd., Arnica House, 170 Campden Hill Road, London, W8 7AS, England.

Mind Cure

A system of healing, distinct from **Mesmerism** and **hypnotism,** first developed in America by Phineas Parkhurst **Quimby** (1802-66), a professional Mesmerist who discovered that his subject, in his clairvoyant diagnosis, simply reproduced the opinion which the patient or Quimby himself had formed of the disease and that his prescriptions could be traced to the same source.

Quimby conceived the idea that disease, if the expectation of the patient is enough to dispel it, is a delusion, an error of the mind. In accordance with this idea he elaborated a new method of mental treatment and began to practice it in Portland, Maine, in 1859.

Quimby did not work out his philosophical ideas into a coherent system. He described it as the "Science of Christ," "Science of Health," and occasionally as "Christian Science."

Pupils were recruited from his patients. The Rev. F. W. Evans, a Methodist minister, was one of the earliest. He published, between 1868-86 a number of books on mental healing, differing on many points from Quimby, and established in late life, a mind-cure sanatorium in Salisbury, Mass. Julius Dresser and his wife also became Quimby's disciples and their son, Horatio W. Dresser, has been acknowledged as the ablest exponent of what came to be called the **"New Thought"** movement.

The most famous patient and pupil turned out to be a woman—Mrs. Mary M. Patterson, later Mary Baker G. Eddy. In her childhood she was delicate, heard voices at the age of eight and spent the greater part of her youth and early womanhood as a confirmed invalid.

In 1862, at the age of 41, she came to Quimby. He restored her to health and this apparent miracle determined her later course of life. Filled with enthusiasm for Quimby, she gave lectures on his doctrines and for some years considered herself as his disciple, even after Quimby's death. At this period she was known as a Spiritualist medium. In trance she received communications from her deceased brother, Albert.

Her first advertisement as a healer was published in the *Banner of Light* in 1868. Soon she began to establish the method of mental healing as her own and in 1875 when she published *Science and Health* a small band of followers grew up around her. She elaborated Quimby's teachings and as a counterpart to distant healing introduced the concept of "malicious animal magnetism," not unlike the superstition of the evil eye and bewitchment of the Middle Ages.

As the years passed, Mrs. Eddy's influence grew and mental healing developed into the religious system **Christian Science** with the following fundamental propositions: 1) God is all in all; 2) God is Good. Good is Mind; 3) God, Spirit, being all, nothing is matter; 4) Life, God, omnipotent good, deny death, evil, sin, disease.

Meanwhile the New Thought movement had developed its own momentum and an international New Thought Alliance adopted a declaration of principles affirming the basis of New Thought as a religious grouping.

Important names in the New Thought movement include Norman Vincent Peale (famous for his book *The Power of Positive Thinking*), Bishop Fulton J. Sheen, and Rabbi Joseph Liebman. Other independent New Thought bodies are The Unity School of Christianity of Charles and Myrtle Fillmore and The United Church of Religious Science of Ernest Holmes.

Other interesting names stemming from Mind Cure and New Thought are those of Prentice **Mulford** (author of the famous White Cross Library) and Ralph Waldo Trine. (See also **Autosuggestion; Christian Science; Mesmerism; New Thought**)

Mind Development and Control Association

Organization founded to develop and promote interest in various facets of paranormal and psychic research, and to foster awareness and understanding of the forces that influence and shape human existence.

The Association sponsors research in the fields of healing and bio-energy, provides monthly correspondence lessons in psychic arts and sciences, and classes in psychic development and ESP skills.

It maintains haunted house investigation group, energy and healing group, and other associated groups. It sponsors the U.S. Psi Squad as a nonprofit project that offers assistance to police and law enforcement departments when consulted in cases such as homicide and missing persons. Publication: *Doorways to the Mind,* monthly magazine. Address: P.O. Box 29396, Sappington, Missouri 63126.

Mind Science Network

Organization concerned with non-traditional religions, holistic healing, psychic development, and related subjects. Publishes the *Mind Science Journal,* a quarterly magazine dealing with these subjects, with calendar of holy days, events, and contacts. Address: Box 1302, Mill Valley, California 94941.

Mines, Haunted

The belief that mines are haunted is an ancient and universal one, probably arising from the many weird sounds and echoes which were heard in them, and the perpetual gloom, stimulating belief in apparitions. Sometimes the haunting specters were gigantic creatures with frightful fiery eyes. Such was the German "Bergmönch, a terrible figure in the garb of a monk, who could, however, appear in ordinary human shape to those towards whom he was well-disposed."

Frequently weird knockings were heard in the mines. In Germany these were attributed to the **Kobolds,** small black beings of a malicious disposition. White hares or rabbits were also seen at times. The continual dangers attending work underground have been productive of many supernatural "warnings," which generally take the form of mysterious voices.

In the Midland Counties of England, the "Seven Whistlers" were well known and their warnings solemnly attended to. A light blue flame settling on a full coal-tub was called "Bluecap," and his work was to move the coal-tub towards the trolley-way. Bluecap did not give his services for nothing. Every fortnight his wages were left in a corner of the mine, and duly appropriated. A more mischievous elf was "Cutty Soames," who would cut the "soams" or traces yoking an assistant putter to the tub.

Basilisks, fearsome monsters whose terrible eyes would strike the miner dead were another source of dread to the worker underground. These, as well as other mysterious foes who dealt fatal blows, may be traced to the dreaded, but by no means ghostly, firedamp or perhaps to underground lizards.

Mines of precious metals were believed to be even more jealously guarded by supernatural beings. Gnomes, the creatures of the earth element, were the special guardians of subterranean treasure, and they were anxious to defend their province.

Mines containing precious stones were equally well looked after. The Indians of Peru declared that evil spirits haunted the emerald mines, while a mine in the neighborhood of Los Esmeraldos was said to be guarded by a frightful dragon. It has also been believed that the poisonous fumes and gases which often destroy the lives of miners were baleful influences radiated by evil spirits.

Other stories of haunted mines are linked to legends of secret underground temples of occultists. (See **Subterranean Crypts and Temples**)

Minnesota Zen Meditation Center

This center stemmed from the 1960s, when a group of individuals in Minneapolis met together to practice *zazen* (**Zen** meditation). They developed an association with the San Francisco Zen Center, and its assistant priest Dainen Katagiri-roshi visited them on several occasions. In 1972, the group invited Katagiri-roshi to become leader of their new Zen Center. He accepted, and the Minnesota Zen Center was formed in January 1973.

Dainen Katagiri-roshi was born in Japan in 1928 and became a Zen monk in 1946. He trained at Eiheji Monastery, the original center of the Soto Shu sect. He came to the U.S. in 1963 to work with the North American Zen Buddhist Church, the Japanese-American Soto group, and had been assigned to their Los Angeles temple. After five months, however, he was sent to San Francisco to assist Shunryu Suzuki-roshi at both the San Francisco temple (Sokoji) and the independent San Francisco Zen Center. While there he assisted in the opening of the Tassajara Zen Mountain Center.

Since coming to Minneapolis, Katagiri-roshi has attracted students from across the Midwest and has accepted invitations to visit various groups interested in Zen. Groups affiliated with the Minnesota Center have been established in Manhattan, Kansas; Iowa City, Iowa; Milwaukee, Wisconsin; and Omaha, Nebraska.

In 1978, the Center purchased 280 acres near Houston, Minnesota, upon which an all-year intensive Zen practice center is being constructed. The center issues a biannual periodical *Udumbara.* The address of the Minnesota Zen Meditation Center is: 3343 East Calhoun Parkway, Minneapolis, Minnesota 55408.

Miñoza, Aurora (1923-)

Assistant professor of psychology who has written on parapsychology. Born January 4, 1923 at Cebu City, Philippines, she studied at University of Michigan (B.S. English 1947, M.A. psychology 1953), University of the Philippines (Ph.D. educational psychology 1957). She was an instructor in English and psychology at Cebu College from 1947-50, instructor in euthenics and psychology from 1950-55, assistant professor in education and psychology, Graduate College of Education, University of the Philippines, from 1957 onwards.

She was president of the Parapsychological Research Society, Philippines, from 1959 onwards, and is a member of the American Psychological Association, and Parapsychological Association. Her master's thesis was *A Study of Extrasensory Perception,* published in abstract by the *Educational Quarterly,* University of the Philippines (vol. 1, No. 1 September 1953).

In 1955 Dr. Miñoza received a U.S. International Cooperation Administration educational scholarship. She attended the first Parapsychology Workshop at Duke University, June 1957. She has special interests in telepathy, clairvoyance and psychokinesis, and has experimented with the effect of thought on plant growth.

Mirabelli, (Carmine) Carlos (1889-1951)

South American physical medium of Italian parentage, born in Botucatu, São Paolo. Such extraordinary accounts of his phenomena have reached England and the U.S. that if they could be proved to the satisfaction of psychical researchers, he would have to be ranked as the greatest medium of all time. Such phenomena included **automatic writing** in more than thirty different languages, **materialization** of persons and objects, **levitation,** impressions of spirit hands, paranormal musical performances and he normally produced phenomena in good light.

The first description of Mirabelli's amazing feats was published in Germany by the *Zeitschrift für Parapsychologie* in August 1929, on the basis of a Brazilian book, *O Medium Mirabelli,* by Amador Bueno.

Fearing a hoax, the German periodical made inquiries first from the Brazilian consul at Munich as to the standing and reputation of the witnesses and supporters of Mirabelli. The answer was positive and the Consul added that fourteen persons of the submitted list were his personal acquaintances to whose veracity he would testify, nor had he the right of questioning the statements of other people on the list, known to him not only as scientists but also as men of character. Thereupon the *Zeitschrift für Parapsychologie* published a summary of the remarkable case.

The summary was further supported by E. J. **Dingwall**'s examination (*Psychic Research,* July 1930) of the original Portuguese documents. It appears that the reality of the Mirabelli phenomena was first acknowledged by psychiatrists. He was committed to an asylum for the insane for observation for nineteen days.

The newspapers took up the case. They wrote of telekinetic **movement,** of **apports,** of a miraculous **teleportation** of the medium from the railroad station of Da Luz to Sao Vincenti, 90 kilometers distance, in two minutes; of his **levitation** in the street two meters high for three minutes; of how he caused a skull to float towards an apothecary; of making an invisible hand turn the leaves of a book in the home of Dr. Alberto Seabra in the presence of many scientists; of making glasses and bottles at a banquet play a military march without human touch; of causing the hat of Antonio Canterello to fly off and float ten meters along a public square; of making and quelling fire by will in the home of Prof. Dr. Alves Lima; of making a cue play billiards without touching it and finally of having the picture of Christ impressed on plaster in the presence of Dr. Caluby, Director of Police.

A conjuring magician imitated some of the phenomena, but this did not lessen the reputation of Mirabelli as a wonder worker. Owing to the heated controversy which grew up around Mirabelli, an arbitration board was instituted for the investigation of the medium, among the members of which were Dr. Ganymed de Sousa, President of the Republic, Brant, of the Institute of Technology and eighteen other men of high position and learning.

After the investigation and the hearing of witnesses, the board established that the majority of the manifestations occurred in daylight, that they occurred spontaneously and in public places, that the manifold intellectual phenomena could not well be based on trickery, that the statements of personalities whose integrity is reputed could not well be doubted.

In 1919, the **Academia de Estudos Psychicos "Cesar Lombroso"** was founded. Mirabelli submitted himself for experiments in **trance** speaking, automatic writing and physical phenomena. The report was published in 1926. It reported 392 sittings in broad daylight or in a room illuminated by powerful electric light, in 349 cases in the rooms of the Academy, attended by 555 people and the summary was as follows:

"The committee carried out with the first group (medical speaking) 189 positive experiments; with the second group (automatic writing) 85 positive and 8 negative; with the third group (physical phenomena) 63 positive and 47 negative experiments. The medium spoke 26 languages including 7 dialects, wrote in 28 languages, among them 3 dead languages, namely Latin, Chaldaic and Hieroglyphics. Of the 63 physical experiments 40 were made in daylight, 23 in bright artificial light."

The automatic writing was inspired by celebrities. Johan Huss impressed Mirabelli to write a treatise of nine pages on the independence of Czechoslovakia in twenty minutes, "Camille **Flammarion**" inspired him to write about inhabited planets, fourteen pages in nineteen minutes in French. "Muri Ka Ksi" delivered five pages in twelve minutes on the Russo-Japanese war in Japanese, "Moses" wrote in Hebrew on slandering, "Harun el Raschid" made him write fifteen pages in Syrian and an untranslatable writing of three pages came in hieroglyphics in thirty-two minutes.

The phenomena of materialization were astounding. The figures were not only complete, and photographed, but medical men made minute examinations which lasted for sometimes as long as fifteen minutes and stated that the newly constituted human beings had perfect anatomical structure. After the examination was completed, one figure began to dissolve from the feet upwards, the bust and arms floating in the air. One of the doctors exclaimed "But this is too much," rushed forward and seized the half of the body. The next moment he uttered a shrill cry and sank unconscious to the ground. On returning to consciousness he only remembered that when he had seized the phantom it had felt as if his fingers were pressing a spongy, flaccid mass of substance. Then he received a shock and lost consciousness.

For thirty-six minutes in broad daylight the materialization of the little daughter of Dr. Souza, who died of influenza, was visible to all the sitters. She appeared in her grave clothes. Her pulse was tested. Father and child were photographed. Then the phantom raised itself and floated in the air. At the third sitting, a skull inside the closet began to beat the doors, came out and slowly grew to a full skeleton (see **Materialization**).

In another sitting Mirabelli announced that he saw the body of Bishop Dr. Jose de Carmago Barros who had lost his life in a shipwreck. "A sweet smell as of roses filled the room. The medium went into trance. A fine mist was seen in the circle. The mist, glowing as if of gold, parted and the bishop materialized, with all the robes and insignia of office. He called his own name. Dr. de Souza stepped to him. He palpated the body, touched his teeth, tested the saliva, listened to the heart-beat, investigated the working of the intestines, nails and eyes, without finding anything amiss. Then the other attending persons convinced themselves of the reality of the apparition. The Bishop smilingly bent over Mirabelli and looked at him silently. Then he slowly dematerialized."

"At the sixth sitting, Mirabelli, tied and sealed, disappeared from the room, and was found in another room still in trance. All seals on doors and windows were found in order, as well as the seals on Mirabelli himself." Once among fourteen investigators his arms dematerialized. On the photograph only a slight shadow is visible.

The British psychical researcher E. J. **Dingwall** ended his review of the documents: "I must confess that, on a lengthy examination of the documents concerning Mirabelli, I find myself totally at a loss to come to any decision whatever on the case. It would be easy to condemn the man as a monstrous fraud and the sitters as equally monstrous fools. But I do not think that such a supposition will help even him who makes it." In reviewing a German translation of a Mirabelli book in 1960, Dr. Dingwall stated that the Mirabelli case "remains another of those unsolved mysteries with which the history of parapsychology abounds."

In the November 1930 issue of *Psychic Research,* Professor Hans **Driesch** threw cold water on all such marvels on the basis of a personal investigation in São Paolo in 1928. He saw no materializations, no transportation, heard only Italian and Esthonian which may have been normally known, but he admitted seeing some remarkable telekinetic phenomena which he could not explain involving the movement of a small vase and the folding of doors in daylight without any visible cause. As to the book *O Medium Mirabelli,* he was unable to find out who had written it, not even an intimate friend of Mirabelli (the overseer of the Town Library of São Paolo) knew it. He wrote: "Might not Mirabelli have written the book—himself?" Of the investigation by the Academia de Estudos Psychicos there was no mention in Prof. Driesch's article.

Mirabelli died April 30, 1951 as the result of a road accident.

For a modern discussion of this remarkable medium see the chapter 'Mirabelli!!' in *The Unknown Power* (British title *The Flying Cow*) by Guy Lyon Playfair (Pocket Book paperback, 1975). Playfair met and interviewed individuals who had known Mirabelli, including living relatives.

Playfair also reviews the negative report of Theodore **Besterman,** who visited Mirabelli in August 1934 and alleged that he had detected fraud on the medium's part, see *Journal* of the society for Psychical Research, Dec. 1935, pp. 141-53)

"Mirabilis Liber"

A collection of predictions concerning the saints and the sibyls, attributed to Saint Césaire (470—542 A.D.). The work appeared in various editions.

It is surprising to find in the edition of 1522 a prophecy of the French Revolution. The expulsion and abolition of the nobility, the violent death of the king and queen, the persecution of the clergy, the suppression of convents, are all mentioned, followed by a further prophecy that the eagle coming from distant lands would reestablish order in France.

Miracles

One objection urged against Spiritualist phenomena is that they represent miracles and that miracles do not happen, therefore the phenomena cannot be genuine. A lively controversy has raged around the subject since the first days when a claim was made for scientific attention to seance room occurrences.

David Hume, the great Scotch philosopher, defined a miracle "as a violation of the laws of nature." Dr. Alfred Russel **Wallace,** in his book *On Miracles and Modern Spiritualism* (1881), objected that we do not know all the laws of nature, therefore we cannot rule out the possibility of an unknown law overcoming the known one. He suggested that a miracle was "any act or event necessarily implying the existence and agency of superhuman intelligences."

According to Hume, no amount of human testimony can prove a miracle. It is perhaps on this basis that in spite of the universal belief in certain supernatural happenings, the pessimistic school of scientists generally refused to investigate their nature and the evidence of their happening. This fact is very curious as the whole history of human progress demonstrates that as Prof. Charles **Richet** stated, "the improbabilities of to-day are the elementary truths of to-morrow."

Sir Isaac Newton had to fight for so long for the recognition of his theory of gravitation that he nearly resolved to publish nothing more and said: "I see that a man must either resolve to put out nothing new, or become a slave to defend it."

Galileo was persecuted and declared "ignorant of his ignorance," the evidence of his telescope was rejected without examination; Galvani was ridiculed and nicknamed "the frog's dancing master;" Harvey, the discoverer of blood circulation, Jenner, the discoverer of preventive vaccination, were "mad;" Benjamin Franklin was laughed at for the idea of the lightning conductor; Young, the proponent of the undulatory theory of light, was scorned; Sir Humphrey Davy thought the idea of lighting London with gas ludicrous; Arago was derided by the French Academy of Sciences when he wanted to discuss the subject of the electric telegraph; learned men produced evidence that Robert Stevenson's railway idea was preposterous; the action of microbes was contested for twenty years. Bouillaud attributed the telephone to ventriloquism. Lavoisier said that stones cannot fall from the sky as there are no stones in the sky, the discovery of the stethoscope, the idea of painless operation in mesmeric coma or the discovery of anaesthetics was extremely "foolish."

As late as 1893, Lord Kelvin wrote in a letter to W. T. **Stead:** "I believe that nearly everything in hypnotism and clairvoyance is imposture and the rest bad observation." Yet he appeared to admit that miracles do exist when he said: "Every action of human free will is a miracle to physical, chemical and mathematical science."

Belief in the reality of miracles has always been one of the cornerstones of religion. In former times it was sufficient to have faith that the divine power which created the universe of matter could also transcend its laws either directly or through the agency of saints.

However, the religious skepticism of the nineteenth century, together with the remarkable advances of science and technology, threw doubt on the reality of all miracles, sacred or secular. Part of the present-day opposition to claims of the paranormal is based on the brilliant achievements of applied scientific laws, reinforcing confidence in the logic of the material world. From this viewpoint, many modern agnostics and atheists deny the possibility of either religious miracles or secular paranormal happenings, claiming that both are the result of malobservation, superstition or fraud.

Meanwhile religious authorities continue to uphold the validity of Biblical miracles as indicating God's omnipotence and intervention in human affairs. Vatican Council I denied that "miracles are impossible." However, some theologians have taken the views that miracles are no longer necessary in modern times as evidence for religious faith. The Roman Catholic Church has long been aware of the necessity for great caution in evaluating apparent miracles in modern times, since it would be foolish to ignore the possibility of misunderstanding or deception. Ever since the claimed miraculous healings associated with pilgrim centers like **Lourdes,** the Church has been careful to insist on satisfactory scientific and medical evidence over a prolonged period of time before a miracle can be accepted.

The most controversial problem, however, remains the distinction between religious and secular miracles. Parapsychologists and Spiritualists may point to the many reported miracles in the Bible as evidence for similar paranormal events in modern times. Church authorities would accept as miraculous only those events which have a clearly established religious purpose, and reject as unproven or false all other claimed paranormal happenings.

Some more orthodox churchmen have even claimed that all psychic phenomena, including that of Spiritualism, is a mere simulacrum of the miraculous and the work of devils or deceptive spirits. Not unnaturally Spiritualists resent such accusations since they too are religious people, and it is unreasonable to claim that the miracles of one religion are genuine and those of all other faiths are false.

Miracles have been reported frequently in Eastern religions, even into modern times, and clearly any attempt to establish a monopoly of miracles by one faith must necessarily cast doubt upon itself as much as on the other faiths condemned as diabolical. Such an extreme position merely echoes medieval intolerance in believing that all other religions except one's own must be false and the work of the devil. Surely there are many different paths to one point?

Nowadays, it is reasonable to suppose that miracles may occasionally occur within the context of any religion and that similar paranormal events may also occur in a secular context. It seems that faith can sometimes be a powerful factor in stimulating paranormal events, particularly in faith healing, and that such faith is often enhanced by group energies. Whether the groups are sincere and enlightened individuals or an ignorant or hysterical crowd may not substantially affect the incidence of the paranormal, although it may have some effect on its quality.

Perhaps the emphasis given to miracles by religions in the past may have been somewhat misplaced, and it is reasonable for the Roman Catholic Church to be cautious about the endorsement of miracles today.

It should be noted that in the **yoga** system of Eastern religion, first place is given to performance of everyday social duties and observation of ethical principles and self-purification in spiritual development. It is claimed that paranormal events may take place in such development but they should be ignored as irrelevant to true spiritual evolution.

The expansion of consciousness from the narrow hopes and fears, mental and emotional limitations of individual existence, into a broader awareness, transcending mental and physical gains and losses, is claimed as the true goal of human endeavor. (See also **Apparitions; Autosuggestion; Bilocation; Christian Science; Fatima; Fire Ordeal; Garabandal; Guadalupe Apparitions;** Psychic **Healing; Healing by Faith; Healing by Touch; Levitation; Lourdes; Medjugorje;** Therese **Neumann;** Padré **Pio; Snake-Handling; Spiritualism; Sitgmata; Yoga**)

Recommended reading:

Ebon, Martin (ed.). *Miracles,* Signet paperback, New American Library, 1981

Hill, J. Arthur. *Spiritualism; Its History, Phenomena & Doctrine,* Cassell, London, 1918

Gopi Krishna. *The Secret of Yoga,* Harper & Row, 1972

LeShan, Lawrence, *The Medium, the Mystic, and the Physicist,* Viking Press, 1974

Réginald-Omez, Fr., O.P. *Psychical Phenomena,* Burns & Oates, London, 1959

Rogo, D. Scott. *Miracles; A Parascientific Inquiry Into Wondrous Phenomena,* Dial Press, New York, 1982

Stemman, Roy. *One Hundred Years of Spiritualism,* Spiritualist Association of Great Britain, London, 1972

Summers, Montague. *The Physical Phenomena of Mysticism,* Rider & Co., London, 1950

Thurston, Herbert, S. J. *The Physical Phenomena of Mysticism,* Burns & Oates, London, 1952; Henry Regnery, Chicago, 1953

West, Donald J. *Eleven Lourdes Miracles,* Duckworth, London, 1957

Mishna, The

A compilation of Jewish oral traditions embodying the religious legal decisions relating to Old Testament laws, gathered together about the end of the second century by a certain Rabbi Judah, grandson of Gamaliel II. Its doctrines are said to be of great antiquity. It forms the framework of the *Talmud.* (See also **Kabala**)

Miss Lucy Westenra Society of the Undead, The

Vampire interest organization. Address: Lewis Sanders, 125 Taylor Street, Jackson, Tennessee 38301.

"Miss X"

Pseudonym of psychical researcher Ada **Goodrich-Freer,** used for her early writings on psychical subjects.

Mitchell, Edgar D. (1930-)

American astronaut with an active interest in parapsychology. Born September 17, 1930 at Hereford, Texas, he was educated at Carnegie Institute of Technology. He entered the U.S. Navy in 1952 and was commissioned a year later. On completing flight training, he was assigned to Patrol Squadron 29 in Okinawa and flew aircraft on carrier duty and Heavy Attack Squadron.

He studied for his doctorate in aeronautics and astronautics at Massachusetts Institute of Technology, and became Chief, Project Management Division, Navy Field Office for Manned Orbiting Laboratory, 1964; later attended Air Force Aerospace Research Pilot School. He was selected by NASA as an astronaut April 1966, and was Lunar Module Pilot of Apollo 14 which landed on the moon February 5, 1971.

His interest in parapsychology dated from 1967, soon after his arrival at the NASA Manned Spacecraft Center in Houston. He was dissatisfied with orthodox theology and began to investigate areas of psychic phenomena and mysticism. In December 1969, Mitchell became friendly with medium Arthur **Ford,** who suggested an interesting ESP test from a man in a rocket to a contact on earth.

Mitchell planned a rocket-to-earth ESP test for the Apollo 14 mission, although Ford died January 4, 1971, twenty-seven days before the mission launch (to which he had been invited as Mitchell's guest). NASA had rejected a telepathy experiment planned by the American Society for Psychical Research in 1970, so Mitchell's test was a private affair in his own rest periods. The tests involved the transmission of symbols associated with a range of chosen numbers.

Eminent parapsychologists J. B. **Rhine** of the **Foundation for Research on the Nature of Man** and K. **Osis** of the American Society for Psychical Research offered cooperation in evaluating the test. In the event, the results of the test were ambiguous, success or failure rating depending upon the evaluation technique used.

After being the sixth man to walk on the moon, Mitchell was a member of the backup crew of further lunar probes. He retired from NASA and the Navy in 1972. His second wife Anita, whom Mitchell married in 1973 after a divorce, shared his interst in parapsychology. In the same year Mitchell founded the **Institute of Noetic Sciences** for the study of human consciousness and mind/body relationships. He supported the efforts of Andrija **Puharich** to test Uri **Geller,** and supervised experiments with Geller at Stanford Research Institute.

Mitchell, T(homas) W(alker) (1869-1944)

British physician, psychologist and active worker in the field of psychical research in Britain. Born January 18, 1869 at Avock, Ross-shire, Scotland, he was educated at Fortrose Academy and University of Edinburgh (M.B., C.M. 1890, M.D. 1906). In 1931 he married Henrietta Violet Kerans. He was president of the British Psycho-Medical Society in 1911, and edited the *British Journal of Medical Psychology* from 1920—35.

He was particularly interested in psychical research in relation to hypnosis and multiple personality. He played a prominent part in the Society for Psychical Research, London, was president in 1921, member of Council from 1909—44, secretary of the medical section from 1911—18. He was author of *The Psychology of Medicine* (1921) and contributed to *Psychology and the Sciences* edited by William **Brown** (1924).

He published a number of contributions in the SPR *Proceedings,* including 'The Appreciation of Time by Somnambules' (1908—09), 'Some Recent Developments in Psychotherapy' (1910), 'The Hypnoidal State of Sidis' (1911), 'Psychotherapy and Psychoanalysis' (1912—13), 'A Study in Hysteria and Multiple Personality' (1912—13), 'Some Types of Multiple Personality' (1912—13), 'Psychology of the Unconscious and Psychoanalysis' (1920), 'The Doris Fischer Case of Multiple Personality' (1921). His paper 'Phenomena of Mediumistic Trance' was read to the British Association for the Advancement of Science, 1927.

Modern Times, The Socialist Community of

A community founded on Long Island, in 1851, which numbered among its members a good many Spiritualists.

It was founded by Josiah Warren, formerly associated with the New Harmony community of Robert Dale Owen. Warren was a remarkably versatile man—orchestral leader, inventor, and master of printing processes.

As distinct from other Utopian socialistic communities of nineteenth-century America, Modern Times was nearer to an anarchist society, with principles of complete toleration and without instituting central government.

It suffered hardship in the general slump of 1857, and ceased to be practicable in the turmoil of the Civil War. Warren died in 1874. (See also **Hopedale Community**)

Moghrebi

Arab sorcerer. (See **Semites**)

Mohanes

Shamans or medicine men of the Indians of the Peruvian Andes. Joseph Skinner referred to them in his *State of Peru* (London 1805):

"These admit an evil being, the inhabitant of the centre of the earth, whom they consider as the author of their misfortunes, and at the mention of whose name they tremble. The most shrewd among them take advantage of this belief, to obtain respect; and represent themselves as his delegates. Under the denomination of *Mohanes,* or *Agoreros,* they are consulted even on the most trivial occasions. They preside over the intrigues of love, the health of the community, and the taking of the field. Whatever repeatedly occurs to defeat their prognostics, falls on themselves; and they are wont to pay their deceptions very dearly. They chew a species of vegetable called *puripiri,* and throw it into the air, accompanying this act by certain recitals and incantations, to injure some, to benefit others, to procure rain, and the inundation of the rivers, or, on the other hand, to occasion settled weather, and a plentiful store of agricultural productions. Any such result having been casually verified on a single occasion, suffices to confirm the Indians in their faith, although they may have been cheated a thousand times. Fully persuaded that they cannot resist the influence of the *puripiri,* as soon as they know that they have been solicited by its means, they fix their eyes on the impassioned object, and discover a thousand amiable traits, either real or fanciful, which indifference had before concealed from their view.

"But the principal power, efficacy, and, it may be said misfortune, of the *Mohanes,* consist in the cure of the sick. Every malady is ascribed to their enchantments, and means are instantly taken to ascertain by whom the mischief may have been wrought. For this purpose the nearest relative takes a quantity of the juice of *floripondium,* and suddenly falls, intoxicated by the violence of the plant. He is placed in a fit posture to prevent suffocation, and on his coming to himself, at the end of three days, the *Mohan* who has the greatest resemblance to the sorcerer he saw in his visions, is to undertake the cure, or if, in the interim, the sick man has perished, it is customary to subject him to the same fate. When not any sorcerer occurs in the visions, the first *Mohan* they encounter has the misfortune to represent his image."

It seems that by practice and tradition, the *Mohanes* acquired a profound knowledge of many plants and poisons, with which they effected surprising cures on the one hand, and did some mischief on the other. They also made use of charms and superstitions.

One method of cure was to place two hammocks close to each other, either in the dwelling, or in the open air. In one of them the patient laid extended, and in the other laid the *Mohan,* or *Agorero.* The latter, in contact with the sick man, began by rocking himself, and then proceeded in falsetto voice to call on the birds, quadrupeds, and fishes to give health to the patient. From time to time he rose on his seat, and made extravagant gestures over the sick man, to whom he applied his powders and herbs, or sucked the wounded or diseased parts. Having been joined by many of the people, the *Agoreros* chanted a short hymn, addressed to the soul of the patient, with this refrain: "Thou must not go, thou must not go." In repeating this he was joined by the people, until at length a terrific clamour was raised, and augmented in proportion as the sick man became still fainter and fainter so that it might reach his ears.

Moleoscopy

A system of interpretation of moles or birthmarks on various parts of the body (usually classed medically as a benign form of *nevus,* and not normally requiring surgery.)

Moles were considered to have special occult significance in ancient times, and their systematic interpretation as indicative of character and destiny was popularized during the sixteenth and seventeenth centuries. The positions of the moles were linked with astrological signs. (See also **Moles** [Birthmarks])

Moles (Animal)

Many superstitions grew up around moles. It was a common error to believe that moles were blind, whereas in fact the eyes are small and often hidden in the animal's hair. As late as Shakepeare's time, moles were popularly believed to be blind, as indicated in the dramatist's play *The Tempest*:

"Pray you tread softly, that the blind mole
may not
Hear a footfall."

Other popular beliefs were that if moles came into a meadow it was a sign of fair weather, that if a mole dug his hole very deep, you could expect a very severe winter, that if a mole threw up earth during a frost, it would disappear in two days.

A gypsy belief was that moles never touched the earth that had been stained with blood. In Britain, farm laborers used to wear the forelegs and a hind leg of a mole in a bag around the neck, to secure immunity from toothache. It was also believed that if you pulled molehills up on St. Sylvester's Day (December 31), the moles would not throw up earth again.

Moles (Birthmarks)

Birthmarks on the human face or body, usually classed medically as a benign form of *nevus.* Many superstitions surround moles, and **Moleoscopy** arose as a system of divination based on the position, character, and astrological connections of these markings.

In folk belief, a mole on the throat was said to be a sign of good luck, but unlucky if located on the left side of the forehead near the hair. A mole on the chin, ear, or neck was said to indicate riches, but on the breast to signify poverty.

Other superstitions concerning the position of moles on the body were as follows: On the feet and hands of a woman, many children; on the right arm and shoulder of a man or woman, great lechery; on the ankles or feet, modesty in men and courage in women; on or about the knees, riches and virtue; on a woman's left knee, many children; on the thighs, great poverty and unhappiness. An old folk rhyme from Nottinghamshire, England, indicated the belief that the position of a mole could affect rank in later life:

"I have a mole above my right eye,
And shall be a lady before I die."

Another curious belief was that hairs growing out of moles were tokens of good luck.

During the great witchcraft manias of the sixteenth and seventeenth centuries, such birthmarks as moles, as well as **warts,** were considered "devil's marks" if they did not bleed when pricked. Professional witch finders like the infamous Matthew **Hopkins** (died 1647) used pricking on suspected witches. Moles, warts, scars, or other birthmarks were pricked with a long pin; if there was no pain or bleeding, the suspect was claimed to be a witch. Special pricking tools like thin daggers were developed, and some enthusiastic witch prickers (who claimed a substantial fee for each convicted witch) even used trick pricking tools with a hollow shaft and retractable blade, to make sure that the suspect would feel no pain and there would be no bleeding. (See also **Moleoscopy; Warts**)

Molybdomancy

A system of **divination** based on the shapes produced by dropping melted lead or tin into water. Interpretations depended upon the psychic ability of the diviner, much as in tea leaf reading or Tasseography.

A related system of divination was **Ceroscopy** (or Ceromancy), in which molten wax was dripped into water and interpreted in a similar way. (See also **Tea Leaves**)

Mompesson, John (c. 1662)

Magistrate at Tedworth, Wiltshire, England in 1661 whose home was disturbed by **poltergeist** phenomena. (See **Drummer of Tedworth**)

Monaciello, The

The *Monaciello* or "Little Monk" was a spirit who seems to have lived exclusively in Naples, Southern Italy. The precise place where he dwelt does not appear to be accurately known, but it is supposed to have been in the remains of abbeys and monasteries.

When the *Monaciello* appeared to mortals, it was always at the dead of night, and then only to those who were in sorest need, who themselves had done all that mortals could do to prevent or alleviate the distress that had befallen them, and after all human aid had failed.

Then it was that the "Monk" appeared, and mutely beckoning them to follow, led them to where treasure was concealed, stipulating no conditions for its expenditure, demanding no promise of repayment, exacting no duty or service in return.

It is not clear whether it was actual treasure that he gave, or whether it merely appeared so to the external senses, to be changed into leaves or stones when the day and the occasion of its requirement had passed. And if actual treasure, how it came in the place of its concealment, and by whom it was deposited there.

In Germany, the wood-spirit "Rubezahl" performed similar acts of beneficence and kindness to poor and deserving persons and the money he gave proved to be, or passed for the current coin of the realm.

In Ireland, the O'Donoghue, who dwelt beneath the waters of an inland lake, and rode over its surface on a steed white as the foam of its waves, was said to distribute treasures that proved genuine to the good, but spurious to the undeserving.

Monad (in Theosophy)

Theosophical term which literally means a unit (Greek *Monas*). The *Monad* is frequently described as a "Divine Spark," and this impression is particularly apt, for it is a part of the **Logos,** the Divine Fire.

The Logos has three aspects—Will, Wisdom, and Activity and, since the *Monad* is part of the Logos, it also has these three aspects. It abides continually in its appropriate world, the monadic, but in order that the divine evolutionary purposes may be carried out, its ray is borne downwards through the various spheres of matter when the outpouring of the third life wave takes place.

It first passes into the Spiritual Sphere by clothing itself with an atom of spiritual matter and thus manifests itself in an atomic body, as a spirit possessing three aspects. When it passes into the next sphere, the Intuitional, it leaves its aspect of Will behind and in the Intuitional Sphere, appears in an Intuitional body as a spirit possessing the aspects of Wisdom and Activity. On passing in turn, from this sphere to the next, the higher Mental, it leaves the aspect of Wisdom behind, and appears in a casual body as a spirit possessing the aspect of activity.

To put this somewhat abstruse doctrine in another form, the *Monad* has, at this stage, manifested itself in three spheres. In the spiritual it has transfused spirit with Will, in the Intuitional it has transfused spirit with Wisdom, and in the higher Mental it has transfused spirit with Activity or Intellect, and it is now a human ego, corresponding approximately to the common term "soul," an ego which, despite all changes, remains the same until eventually the evolutionary purpose is fulfilled and it is received back again into the Logos.

From the higher mental sphere, the *Monad* descends to the lower mental sphere and appears in a mental body as possessing mind, then betakes itself to the astral sphere and appears in the astral body as possessing emotions, and finally to the physical sphere and appears in a physical body as possessing vitality. These three lower bodies, the mental, the astral, and the physical, constitute the human personality which dies at death and is renewed when the *Monad,* in fulfilment of the process of reincarnation, again manifests itself in these bodies. (See also **Evolution of Life; Life Waves; Logos; Sphere; Spirit**)

Monck, Rev. Francis Ward (c. 1878)

British clergyman who started his career as minister of the Baptist Chapel at Earls Barton and gave up his ecclesiastical vocation for professional mediumship.

His adhesion to Spiritualism was first announced in 1873. He claimed great mediumistic powers, toured the British Isles and healed the sick in Ireland. As a result he was called "Dr." Monck by many people, although not a physician.

In London, he convinced Dr. Alfred Russel **Wallace,** the Rev. Stainton **Moses** and Hensleigh Wedgwood (brother-in-law of Darwin) of his genuine psychic gifts by giving a remarkable **materialization** seance in bright daylight. He also excelled in **slate-writing.** An account by Dr. Alfred Russel Wallace of a puzzling slate writing demonstration was certified by Edward T. Bennett, then assistant secretary to the **Society for Psychical Research,** London. He convinced Judge Dailey of America that the dead returned through his body. Monck's reputation was high.

It suffered a severe blow, however, shortly after the trial of Henry **Slade.** At a Huddersfield seance on November 3, 1876, a conjurer named H. B. Lodge suddenly demanded the search of the medium. Monck ran for safety, locked himself into his room upstairs and escaped through the window. As a further evidence of his guilt, a pair of stuffed gloves was found in his room. In the medium's luggage were found "spirit lamps," a "spirit bird," cheesecloth, and reaching rods, as well as some obscene correspondence from women.

Nor was this the first case when Monck was caught in flagrant fraud. Sir William **Barrett** wrote of "a piece of white muslin on a wire frame with a black thread attached being used by the medium to simulate a partially materialised spirit."

The trial which followed the Huddersfield exposure was a great sensation. One of the witnesses was Dr. Alfred Russel Wallace. He deposed that "he had seen Dr. Monck in the trance state, when there appeared a faint white patch on the left side of his coat, which increased in density and spread till it reached his shoulder; then there was a space gradually widening to six feet between it and his body, it became very distinct and had the outline of a woman in flowing white drapery. I was absolutely certain that it could not be produced by any possible trick."

The court found Monck guilty and sentenced him to three months' imprisonment.

The blow was a stunning one. There were, however, friends who did not give up their faith in Monck. There was no greater believer in his powers than Archdeacon Colley, who had reported the most inexplicable and astounding experiences with Monck.

Colley was in India when the Huddersfield incident happened. After his return, he stoutly maintained that a dreadful miscarriage of justice must have taken place. Of a seance held on September 25, 1877, on the basis of notes made the same evening, he published the following account: "Dr. Monck, under control of Samuel, was by the light of the lamp—the writer not being a yard away from him—seen by all to be the living gate for the extrusion of spirit forms from the realm of mind into this world of matter; for standing forth thus plainly before us, the psychic or spirit form was seen to grow out of his left side. First, several faces one after another, of great beauty appeared, and in amazement we saw—and as I was standing close up to the medium, even touching him, I saw most plainly—several times, a perfect face and form of exquisite womanhood partially issue from Dr. Monck, about the region of the heart. Then after several attempts a full formed figure, in a nebulous condition at first, but growing more solid as it issued from the medium, left Dr. Monck, and stood a separate individuality, two or three feet off, bound to him by a slender attachment as of gossamer, which at my request Samuel, the control, severed with the medium's left hand, and there stood embodied a spirit form of unutterable loveliness, robed in attire spirit-spun—a meshy web-work from no mortal loom, of a fleeciness inimitable, and of transfiguration whiteness truly glistening."

Colley was so sure of his own powers of observation that he challenged stage magician J. N. **Maskelyne** and offered him a thousand pounds if he could duplicate Monck's materialization performance. Maskelyne attempted the feat and when Archdeacon Colley declared his performance to be a travesty of what had really taken place in Monck's presence, Maskelyne sued for the money. Mainly on the evidence of Dr. Alfred Russel Wallace, on behalf of Monck, judgment was entered against Maskelyne.

In his materialization seances Monck rarely used a cabinet. He stood in full view of the sitters. Sometimes he was quite conscious. He had two chief controls: "Samuel" and "Mahedi." For a year their individual character was deeply studied by Stainton Moses and Hensleigh Wedgwood who, with two other men interested in psychic research, secured Monck's services with exclusive rights for a modest salary.

Enduring evidence of Monck's phantasmal appearances was obtained by William Oxley in 1876 in Manchester in the form of excellent paraffin molds of hands and feet of the materialized forms (see **Plastics**). Oxley described his psychic experiences in *Modern Messiahs and Wonder Workers* (1889). This disposes of the hallucination theory which psychical researcher Frank **Podmore** put forward in view of Archdeacon Colley's astounding experiences. Paraffin wax cannot be hallucinated. The supposition in itself is difficult that Monck could have played the fool with an intimate friend for many years.

In his lecture before the Church Congress at Weymouth in 1903 Archdeacon Colley said: "Often when I have been sleeping in the same bedroom with him, for the near observation of casual phenomena during the night and, specially, that came through the dark I, on such occasions, would hold my hand over his mouth, and he would now and again be startled into wakefulness not unmixed with fear. For he could see the phantoms which I could not, when I had quietly put out the night-light—for he would not sleep in the dark, which made him apprehensive of phenomena, physically powerful to an extraordinary degree."

The Archdeacon's experiences present a remarkable record in the history of materialization, equalled only by the Brazilian medium Carlos **Mirabelli.** However, Mirabelli was never convincingly exposed in fraud, although on one occasion Theodore Besterman claimed that he had detected some fraudulent manipulation.

Archdeacon Colley claimed to have witnessed astonishing marvels with Monck. He said he saw the birth and dissolution of numbers of full-sized solid forms. He saw a child appear, move about, being kissed by those present and then return to the medium and gradually melt into his body. He seized a materialized form and was flung with great force towards the medium and suddenly found himself clasping him. In 1905, when he published his experiences, he wrote: "I publish these things for the first time, having meditated over them in silence for twenty-eight years, giving my word as clergyman for things which imperil my ecclesiastical position and my future advancement."

One of the most astonishing psychic feats ascribed to Monck was his teleportation from Bristol to Swindon, a distance of 42 miles. This claimed miraculous feat in 1871 was described in the *Spiritualist* (1875, p. 55).

In his later years, Monck concentrated on healing. The closing period of his life was spent in New York.

Monen

A Kabalistic term covering that branch of magic which deals with the reading of the future by the computation of time and observance of the heavenly bodies. It thus includes **astrology.** (See **Kabala**)

Money (in Occult Tradition)

Money which comes from a pact with the devil is of poor quality, and such wealth, like the fairy-money, generally turns to earth, or to lead, toads, or anything else worthless or repulsive.

"A youth," stated St. Gregory of Tours (died 594 A.D.), "received a piece of folded paper from a stranger, who told him that he could get from it as much money as he wished, so long as he did not unfold it. The youth drew many gold pieces from the papers, but at length curiosity overcame him, he unfolded it and discovered within the claws of a cat and a bear, the feet of a toad and other repulsive fragments, while at the same moment his wealth disappeared."

It took an Irishman to outsmart the devil! In his book *Irish Witchcraft & Demonology* (1913; 1973), St. John D. Seymour told the amusing story of Joseph Damer of Tipperary County, who made a bargain with the devil to sell his soul for a top-boot full of gold.

On the appointed day, the devil was ushered into the living room where a top-boot stood in the center of the floor. The devil poured gold into it, but to his surprise, it remained empty. He hastened away for more gold, but the top-boot would not fill, even after repeated efforts. At length, in sheer disgust the devil departed.

It was afterwards found that the shrewd Irishman had taken the sole off the boot and fastened it over a hole in the floor. Underneath was a series of large cellars, where men waited with shovels to remove each shower of gold as it came down!

In popular superstition it is supposed that if a person hears the cuckoo for the first time with money in his pocket, he will have some all the year, while if he greets the new moon for the first time in the same fortunate condition, he will not lack money throughout the month.

Monition

Supernormal warning. In the wider sense of the definition of psychical researcher Prof. Charles **Richet,** it is the revelation of some past or present event by other than the normal senses. The *Proceedings* of the American Society for Psychical Research (1907, p. 487) published a typical instance. Mr. McCready, editor of *The Daily Telegraph,* in church on a Sunday morning, heard a voice calling "Go back to the office." He ran and found a petroleum lamp blazing in his room. It threw out such clouds of smoke that everything was covered with soot.

Monitions may range from trifling events to warnings of death. They occur accidentally and are verifiable as true. All the monitive phenomena lie within the field of nonexperimental **telepathy** and **clairvoyance** and include **apparitions** of the dead and of the living, provided that they are message-bearing. It is characteristic of monitions that they deeply impress the mind of the percipients and permit an accurate remembrance even after the lapse of many years.

They may come in the waking state or in dreams, which sometimes repeat themselves. The borderland between waking and sleeping is usually the most favorable for their reception. They may be visual or auditory—seeing apparitions, or hearing voices, and they often take a symbolical form as, for instance, the idea of death being presented by a coffin, as seen by Lord Beresford in his cabin while steaming between Gibraltar and Marseilles. The coffin contained the body of his father. On arriving at Marseilles he found that his father had died six days before and was buried on the day he saw the vision (see *Proceedings* of the Society for Psychical Research, vol. 5, p. 461).

As regards perception, monitions may be collective yet non-simultaneous and non-identical, or simultaneous and collective. The former is well illustrated by Mrs. Hunter's case, cited by Ernesto **Bozzano** in the *Annals of Psychical Science* (vol. 6, No. 34, 1907, p. 248). Mrs. Hunter saw, in the waking state and in day time, a large coffin on the bed and a tall, stout woman at the foot of the bed looking at it. The governess saw that evening a phantom woman in the same dress in the sitting room where there was nothing visible and cried: "Go away, go away, naughty ugly old woman."

To quote another instance: "During the winter of 1899, Prof. Charles **Richet** was at home while his wife and daughter were at the opera. The professor imagined that the Opera House was on fire. The conviction was so powerful that he wrote on a piece of paper "Feu! Feu!"

About midnight, on the return of his family, he immediately asked them if there had been a fire. They were surprised and said that there was no fire, only a false alarm, and they were very much afraid. At the very time Prof. Richet made his note his sister fancied that the Professor's room was on fire.

In simultaneous and collective monitions, the phantom or symbol is perceived at the same time by several people. (See also **Monitions of Approach; Premonition**)

Monitions of Approach

These are unaccountable ideas of an impending meeting with someone. A man is seen in the street, is believed to be an old friend and the next minute the mistake is perceived, yet soon afterwards the real friend comes into view in flesh and blood. This occurrence is fairly common.

Such monitions often appear in more complicated forms. They may be auditory, when suddenly a voice may be heard, announcing the arrival of someone; they may come in dreams or, in the waking state, they may take the form of actual sight of a phantom of the coming individual.

The Spiritualist contention is that in the latter case, the **double** (or **astral body**) of the coming man was unconsciously projected. In many instances, this may be the right explanation, in some others it does not cover the facts. (See also **Double; Monition; Premonition; Vardøgr)**

Monsters

On the borderland between superstition, occultism and science are the many monsters, human or animal, reported from many parts of the world over the centuries.

The word "monster" is from the Latin *monstrum* and implies a warning or portent. The term includes malformed or misshapen animals or humans as well as creatures of great size. Because of the awe and horror excited by monstrous births, they were traditionally regarded as an omen or a sign of God's wrath with a wicked world. Many street ballads of the sixteenth century moralized about monstrous animals or malformed human beings. Nowadays deformed persons like giants, dwarfs and Siamese twins are studied under the scientific label of "Teratology." Deformed and limbless children are now known to be caused by rare genetic factors or by the use of such drugs as thalidomide in pregnancy.

In modern times, much of the superstitious awe surrounding legendary monsters has passed into the world of fiction, and talented novelists have created such images of doom as the monster of **Frankenstein**, the evil vampire **Dracula**, or the *alter ego* of Dr. Jekyll's Mr. Hyde. Such literary monsters have been given a powerful representation in the realistic medium of horror movies, which have also presented terrifying creatures from swamps, ocean depths and even from other worlds. Such fictional monsters undoubtedly owe their power to the eternal fascination of the clash between good and evil in human affairs and the old theological theme of damnation.

Few stories achieved this metaphysical terror so powerfully as Robert Louis Stevenson's *Dr. Jekyll and Mr. Hyde*, in which the possibilities of evil inherent in all human beings are released from the kindly Dr. Jekyll in the shape of the demonic Mr. Hyde. Stevenson also varied this theme in his short story *Markheim*, where a debauched murderer is confronted by an angelic *alter ego*.

Another aspect of monsters is the eternal attraction and fear of the unknown represented by mysterious creatures reported from isolated places, which have an existence somewhere between myth and natural history. Some may be survivors of ancient species. The main creatures in this category are as follows:

Loch Ness Monster

This is said to inhabit the large area of Loch Ness in Scotland, about 24 miles long and a mile wide, with a depth of from 433-754 feet. Since a monster was reported in ancient Gaelic legends and in a biography of St. Columba circa 565 A.D., it is supposed that there may be a colony of monsters.

Modern interest dates from the 1930s, when a number of witnesses reported sightings. The creature has been photographed repeatedly and even filmed. It appears to be about 45 ft. long, of which 10 ft. is head and neck, 20 ft. the body, and 15 ft. the tail. The head is small and sometimes lifted out of the water on the neck, high above the body. The skin is rough and dark brown in color, and in movement the creature sometimes appears to contort its body into a series of humps. It can move at speeds of around thirteen knots, and in general appearance resembles a prehistoric plesiosaurus.

On April 8, 1976, the monster made the front page of the *New York Times*, which featured records of an underwater camera using a sonar echo technique. Known in Britain affectionately as "Nessie," the creature has been given the formal name of *Nessiteras rhombopteryx* by naturalist Sir Peter Scott in an attempt to secure official protection (see 'Naming the Loch Ness Monster,' *Nature*, Dec. 11, 1975). A British Act of Parliament requires that any rare species of animal qualifying for conservation must have a scientific name.

The Loch Ness monster is not unique, since a similar creature was reported at Lough Muck in Donegal. In other parts of England and Scotland, reported creatures include **Morgawr** in the area of

Falmouth, Cornwall, and **Mhorag** (or Morag) in Loch Morar, West Inverness, Scotland. There are numerous reports of sightings, and some photographs. In 1910, a plesiosaurus type creature was reported in Nahuel Huapi, Patagonia.

Interest in the Loch Ness monster was stimulated by reports of the decomposing body of a sea creature caught by the Japanese trawler "Zuiyo Maru" about 30 miles east of Christchurch, New Zealand, on April 25, 1977. The carcass was about 30 feet long, weighed two tons, and was raised from a depth of approximately 900 feet. For a time, it was suspended above the trawler deck by a crane, but the captain feared that the evil-smelling fluid dripping from the carcass would pollute his catch of whiptail fish and ordered the creature to be dumped overboard. Before this was done, Mr. Michihiko Yano, and official of the Taiyo Fishery Company aboard the vessel took four color photographs and made a sketch of the carcass, after taking measurements. He described the creature as like a snake with a turtle's body and with front and rear flippers and a tail six feet in length. This suggests a creature resembling the plesiosaurus, which flourished from 200 to 100 million years ago.

When Taiyo Fisheries executives heard about the unusual catch, they radioed their trawlers around New Zealand, ordering them to try to recover the carcass, but without success. Japanese journalists named the creature "The New Nessie" after Scotland's famous Loch Ness Monster, and a large Tokyo department store planned to market stuffed dolls of the creature. Prof. Fujior Yasuda of the faculty of fisheries at Tokyo University has examined Mr. Yano's photographs and concluded that the creature was definitely not a species of fish, and Mr. Toshio Shikama, a Yokohama University paleontologist was convinced that the creature was not a fish or a mammoth seal. For reports of this "New Nessie" see London *Daily Telegraph* (July 21, 1977), London *Times* (July 21, 1977) and *Fortean Times* (No. 22, Summer 1977).

Yeti (or Abominable Snowman)

A giant humanoid creature which has long been part of the folklore of the high Himalayan region in Asia. The popular name "Abominable Snowman" derives from the Tibetan term *Metoh-Kangmi* or "Wild Man of the Snows." Other names in the Himalayan regions of Kashmir and Nepal are *Jungli-admi* or *Sogpa*—"Wild Men of the Woods."

There are many stories told by Sherpas of the giant Yeti which carried away human children or even adults. In 1951, such stories suddenly attracted scientific interest with the photograph of a large Yeti footprint taken by mountaineer Eric Shipton on an Everest Reconnaissance Expedition.

But the Abominable Snowman had been reported as early as 1832 by B. H. Hodgson in his article 'On the Mammalia of Nepal' (*Journal of the Asiatic Society of Bengal*, vol. 1).

The first European to see Yeti footprints was Major L. A. Waddell, who found them in the snows of northeastern Sikkim at 17,000 feet in 1889, but believed them to be tracks of the great yellow snow bear (*Ursus isabellinus*). Other reports followed over the years.

In 1925, N. A. Tombazi, a Fellow of the Royal Geographical Society, saw a large humanoid creature walking upright at a distance of 300 yards in Sikkim, and afterwards examined footprints in the snow. In February 1942, Slavomir Rawicz escaped from a Siberian prisoner-of-war camp with six companions and crossed the Himalayas to India. In his book *The Long Walk* (1956), Rawicz claimed that he saw two Yeti-type creatures, eight feet tall, in an area between Bhutan and Sikkim.

In the 1950s, various expeditions to track down the Yeti failed to produce any tangible evidence of its existence, but in 1972 a Sherpa named Da Temba saw a 4′6″ creature, possibly a small Yeti, in Nepal. The cumulative effect of a large number of reports of Yeti sightings from Sherpas reinforces the possibility that there *is* a large humanoid creature in the Himalayas, but the area is a vast one and the creature could be even more elusive than the Loch Ness monster.

Bigfoot

Other creatures of a Yeti type have been reported frequently from different areas of the world, notably isolated regions of the Pacific Northwest. The popular term "Bigfoot" seems to have been a newspaper invention for the creature named "Sasquatch" by the Salish Indians of southwest British Columbia. The Huppa tribe in the Klamath mountains of Northern California use the name *Oh-mah-'ah*, sometimes shorted to *Omah*, while the name *Seeahtiks* is used in Vancouver Island.

It is interesting to note that reports of Yeti-type creatures cover a fairly consistent trail through the remote mountainous regions of Asia across to similar regions in Alaska, Canada and North America, suggesting a rare and elusive species distributed over similar isolated areas. In the Russian areas of Asia, such creatures have been named *Almast, Alma* or *Shezhnyy Chelovek*.

Bigfoot has been frequently reported in Canadian and North American territories from the early nineteenth century onwards. In modern times, construction workers in Northern California claimed to see a large ape-like creature, eight to ten feet tall in Bluff Creek in October 1958. It walked upright and left large footprints, which indicated a creature some 800 pounds weight.

Such creatures were systematically investigated by Dublin-born Peter Byrne, explorer and big-game hunter, who organized a three-year search in 1971. He traveled many thousands of miles between Nepal, Canada and the U.S., interviewing hundreds of individuals and evaluating claimed sightings of Bigfoot. Amongst such investigations is the 16mm color film taken by Roger Patterson, a rancher in Bluff Creek, California, October 7, 1967.

This film shows what appears to be an erect apelike figure at a distance of some 30 feet. Byrne visited Patterson before his death in 1972 and found his story and the film convincing. In 1968, a prankster in Colville, Washington state, tied 16 inch foot-shaped plywood boards to his feet and made tracks in the woods. He sent a photograph to Peter Byrne, who dismissed it as an obvious fake.

Meanwhile a County ordinance in Skamania, Washington, prohibits wanton slaying of ape-creatures, with substantial penalties. For a detailed survey of Bigfoot and Yeti sightings and legends, see the book *Bigfoot* by John Napier (1972). (See also **Jersey Devil**)

Recommended reading:

Baumann, Elwood David. *Bigfoot; America's Abominable Snowman*, Franklin Watts, New York, 1976; Laurel/Dell paperback, 1976

Bord, Janet & Colin. *Alien Animals*, Paul Elek, London, 1980; Stackpole Books, 1981

Byrne, Peter. *The Search for Big Foot; Monster, Myth or Man*, Acropolis Books, Washington, 1975; Pocket Books paperback, 1976

Campbell, Elizabeth M. & D. Solomon. *The Search for Morag*, Tom Stacey, London, 1972

Costello, Peter. *In Search of Lake Monsters*, Garnsteon Press, London/Coward, New York, 1974; Panther paperback, 1975

Dinsdale, Tim. *Loch Ness Monster*, Routledge & Kegan Paul, 1961, revised ed., 1976

Farson, Daniel & Angus Hall. *Mysterious Monsters*, Aldus Books, London, 1978

Florescu, Radu. *In Search of Frankenstein*, New York Graphic Society, 1975

Gould, Rupert T. *The Loch Ness Monster & Others*, Geoffrey Bles, London, Citadel Press, 1976

Gould, Rupert T. *The Case for the Sea-Serpent*, Philip Allan, London, 1930; Singing Tree Press, Detroit, 1969

Halpin, Marjorie & Michael M. Ames (ed.). *Manlike Monsters on Trial; Early Records and Modern Evidence*, University of British Columbia Press, 1980

Heuvelmans, Bernard. *On the Track of Unknown Animals*, revised ed., Hill & Wang, 1965; Paladin Books paperback, 1970

Heuvlmans, Bernard. *In the Wake of the Sea-Serpents*, Rupert Hart-Davis, London, 1968; Hill & Wang, 1968

Mackal, Roy Paul. *The Monster of Loch Ness*, Swallo Press, Chicago/Macdonald, London, 1976

McCloy, James F. & Ray Miller, Jr. *The Jersey Devil*, Middle Atlantic Press, Pennsylvania, 1976

McNally, Raymont T. & Radu Florescu. *In Search of Dracula; A True History of Dracula and Vampire Legends*, New York Graphic Society, 1972; Warner paperback, 1975

Meredith, Dennis L. *Search at Loch Ness; The Expedition of the New York Times & The Academy of Applied Science*, Quadrangle/New York Times Book Co., 1977

Moon, Mary. *Ogopogo; The Okanagan Mystery*, David & Charles, London & Vermont, 1977

Napier, John. *Bigfoot; The Sasquatch & Yeti in Myth and Reality*, Jonathan Cape, London, 1972; Dutton, 1973; Abacus paperback, 1976

Price, Vincent & V.B. Price. *Monsters*, Grosset & Dunlap, 1981

Sanderson, Ivan T. *Abominable Snowman; Legend Comes to Life*, Chilton Co., 1961

Shackley, Myra. *Wildmen; Yeti, Sasquatch & The Neanderthal Enigma*, Thames & Hudson, London, 1983

Thompson, C.J.S. *The Mystery and Lore of Monsters*, London, 1930; University Books, 1968; Citadel Press, 1970

Witchell, Nicholas. *The Loch Ness Story*, London, 1974; revised ed. Penguin Books, 1975

Montgomery, Ruth (Schick)

Contemporary American journalist with special interest in psychic healing, **channeling**, and extrasensory perception. She was born in Sumner, Illinois, educated at Baylor University 1930-35, Purdue University 1934. She married Robert H. Montgomery December 26, 1935.

She was women's editor of *Louisville Herald-Post*, Kentucky; feature writer, *St. Louis Post-Dispatch*, Missouri and *Indianapolis Star*; reporter with *Detroit News, Detroit Times, Waco News-Tribune, Chicago Tribune; New York Daily News*, correspondent in Washington, D.C., 1944-55; special correspondent in Washington for International News Service, 1956-58. Sometime foreign correspondent in Europe, South America, Far East and Middle East from 1946 onwards. She is a member of the National Press Club, Washington Press Club (president 1950-51), member of Board of Governors 1951-54. Awards and honors include Pall Mall Journalism Award 1947; LL.D., Baylor University, 1957, and Ashland College, 1958; Front Page Award, Indianapolis Press Club, 1957; George R. Holmes Journalism Award, 1958; Best Non-Fiction Book of the Year Award, Indiana University, 1966, for *A Gift of Prophecy*.

As a columnist appearing in two hundred newspapers, Ruth Montgomery traveled widely, filing stories from the Orient, the Middle East, Russia, Siberia, Poland, Europe, and South America. She regularly covered presidential press conferences and the national conventions of the Republican and Democratic parties during the 1940s, 1950s and 1960s. In 1945, she was the only woman selected to cover President Roosevelt's funeral.

In 1958, she became interested in psychic phenomena after writing a series of articles on the occult. Although at first skeptical, she continued her research. She met medium Arthur **Ford**, who told her that she had the ability to do automatic writing, and has since been influenced by what she calls "my Guides," discarnate spirits that have assisted her writings on such subjects as psychic healing, reincarnation, Spiritualism, and psychic faculties.

Her publications include: *Once There Was a Nun* (1962), *Mrs. LBJ* (1964), *A Gift of Prophecy; The Phenomenal Jeane Dixon* (1965), *Flowers at the White House* (1966), *A Search for the Truth* (1967), *Here and Hereafter* (1966), *Hail to the Chiefs* (1970), *A World Beyond* (1971), *Born to Heal* (1973), *Companions Along the Way* (1974), *The World Before* (1976), *Strangers Among Us* (1979). Some of her books have been translated into eighteen languages, and have appeared on several national best-seller lists.

Móo, Queen

According to Dr. Augustus le Plongeon, Queen of Yucatan. See his book *Queen Móo and the Egyptian Sphinx* (London, 1896). (See also **Atlantis**)

Moon, Sun Myung (1920-)

A Korean engineer from the village of Kwangjo Sangsa Ri (now in North Korea) who founded a new religious cult of the **Unification Church** (full title Holy Spirit Association for the Unification of World Christianity), based on claimed revelations made personally to him by Jesus Christ.

Moon was born January 6, 1920, as Yong Myung Moon, but changed his name to Sun Myung Moon ("shining sun and moon") after his mystical visions, which commenced at the age of 16. Moon claims that Jesus commissioned him to complete the task of bringing salvation to the earth. According to the Rev. Moon, his revelations took place on numerous occasions over a period of ten years. They were received coldly by the Christian churches in Korea, and the Rev. Moon thereupon moved to North Korea, where he established an underground church in Communist territory. He was arrested and imprisoned in a concentration camp for five years.

He was released in 1950 when a U.N. force liberated the camp, and upon returning to South Korea he founded his Unification Church, later developing branches in Japan, the U.S. and thirty other countries. His followers consider him a new Messiah.

His message derives from his own interpretation of the Bible, establishing a principle of the sanctity of the family. The Rev. Moon's message is also aggressively anti-Communist and centered on right-wing politics. In the 1970s he crusaded in favor of Richard Nixon, stating "You must love Richard Nixon, God has chosen Richard Nixon to be President . . . " Moon's movement derived some of its large financial resources from a South Korean armaments factory, a Titanium plant, and a tea company. He has been accused of political interference and having C.I.A. links in Korea.

His movement has been phenomenally successful with young Americans, whose enthusiasm is oddly reminiscent of the Communist followers whom Moon condemns, and his principle of the sanctity of the family has split up many homes by attracting young converts away from their own families. His critics accuse him of brainwashing. When not traveling on his evangelistic campaigns. Moon has lived regally in a mansion north of New York City.

In 1982, Moon was sentenced to eighteen months imprisonment on charges of income tax evasion. He was released from prison in August 1985, after serving thirteen months. Moon claimed intensified spiritual experiences during his sentence, which appears to have had little effect in subduing the fervor of his followers.

The authoritative scripture of Moon's religious beliefs is his *Divine Principle*, published in English by The Holy Spirit Association for the Unification of World Christianity, New York, 1973.

For critical works on the movement, see Eileen Barker, *The Making of a Moonie* (Basil Blackwell, Oxford, U.K., & New York, 1984), and Robert Boettcher, *Gifts of Deceit; Sun Myung Moon, Tongson Park and the Korean Scandal* (Holt, Rinehart & Winston, 1980).

Moonsign Book

Popular level publication concerned with influence of the moon on plants and health. Includes charts and tables. Address: Llewellyn Publications, P.O. Box 64383, St. Paul, Minnesota 55164.

Mopses, Order of the

A secret association founded in Germany in the eighteenth century, spreading through Holland, Belgium and France. It was popularly believed to be a black magic order, replacing the Satanic goat with a dog as an object of worship. However, it seems clear that it was really a somewhat whimsical crypto-Masonic order, after the papal bull of Pope Clement XII on April 24, 1738, which condemned Freemasonry.

Immediately after their establishment the Mopses became an androgynous order, admitting females to all the offices except that of Grand Master, which was for life, but there was also a Grand Mistress, elected every six months.

The ceremonies were grotesque. The candidate for admission did not knock, but had to scratch at the door, and, being purposely kept waiting, was obliged to bark like a dog. On being admitted into the lodge, he had a collar placed round his neck, to which a chain was attached. He was blindfolded and led nine times round the room, while the Mopses present made as great a din as possible with sticks, swords, chains, shovels, and dismal howlings.

The candidate was then questioned as to his intentions, and having replied that he desired to become a "Mops," was asked by the master whether he was prepared to kiss the most ignoble part of that animal. Of course this raised the candidate's anger, but in spite of his resistance, the model of a dog, made of wax, wood, or some other material, was pushed against his face. Having taken the oath, he had his eyes unbandaged, and was then taught the secret signs, which were all of a ludicrous description.

Morag (or Mhorag)

A Loch Ness type monster observed and photographed in Loch Morar, West Inverness, Scotland. (See also **Mhorag; Monsters**)

Morgan le Fay

Sister of King **Arthur** and wife of King Urien of Gore. Arthur gave into her keeping the scabbard of his sword Excalibur, but she gave it to Sir Accolon whom she loved and had a forged scabbard made. Arthur, however, recovered the real sheath, but was again deceived by her.

Morgan le Fay figured as a Queen of the Land of Faerie and as such appears in French and Italian romance. It was she who, on one occasion, threw Excalibur into a lake.

She usually presented her favorites with a ring and retained them by her side as did Venus in *Tannhaüser.* Her myth is a parallel of that of Eos and Tithonus and is possibly derived from a sun and dawn myth. (See also King **Arthur**)

Morgawr

A Loch Ness type monster observed and photographed in the area of Falmouth, Cornwall, England. On November 17, 1976, Morgawr was sighted by Tony "Doc" Shiels and David Clarke (editor of *Cornish Life* magazine) in the Helford estuary near Falmouth.

A photograph taken by Mr. Clarke was reproduced in *Fortean Times* (No. 22, Summer 1977). Although the camera had unfortunately jammed, resulting in a superimposition of pictures, the general impression is of the head of a creature similar to that photographed by Tony "Doc" Shiels (*Fortean Times* 19) and some Shiels' photographs of the **Loch Ness Monster** May 21, 1977 (best one reproduced in both *Cornish Life* and London *Daily Mirror* for June 9, 1977).

Some doubts have been expressed by Tony Shiels' pictures on the grounds that he is well known in conjuring circles as an exponent of magic simulations of psychic effects. However, he claims to be an avid monster-hunter, and has collected other reports of sightings of Morgawr, as well as publishing his own photographs of the Loch Ness monster.

Two photographs of Morgawr taken by Gerry Bennett of Seworgan, Cornwall, from Mawnan beach on January 31, 1977 were also reproduced in *Fortean Times* 22, together with photographs and reports of **Morag,** another Scottish monster of a Loch Ness type. (See also **Loch Ness Monster; Monsters**)

Morien (or Morienus) (12th century A.D.)

Twelfth-century alchemist. It is commonly supposed that Morien, or Morienus as he is sometimes styled, was born at Rome, and it is also reported that, like Raymond **Lully** and several other early alchemists, he combined evangelical ardor with his scientific tastes. While still a mere boy, and resident in his native city, Morien became acquainted with the writings of Adfar, the Arabian philosopher, and gradually the youth's acquaintance with these developed into tense admiration, the result being that he became filled with the desire to make the personal acquaintance of the author in question.

Accordingly he bade adieu to Rome and set out for Alexandria, this being the home of Adfar, and, on reaching his destination, did not have to wait long before gaining his desired end. The learned Arabian accorded him a hearty welcome, and a little while afterwards the two were living together on very friendly terms, the elder man daily imparting knowledge to the younger, who showed himself a remarkably apt pupil. For some years this state of affairs continued, but at length Adfar died, and thereupon Morien left Alexandria and went to Palestine, found a retreat in the vicinity of Jerusalem, and began to lead a hermit's life there.

Meanwhile the erudition of the deceased Arabian acquired a wide celebrity, and some of his manuscripts chanced to fall into the hands of Kalid, Sultan of Egypt. He was a person of active and enquiring mind, and observing that on the cover of the manuscripts it was stated that the secret of the **philosopher's stone** was written within, he naturally grew doubly inquisitive. He found, however, that he himself could not elucidate the precious documents, and therefore he summoned *illuminati* from far and near to his court at Cairo, offering a large reward to the man who should discover the mystery at issue. Many people presented themselves in consequence, but the majority of them were mere charlatans, and thus the Sultan was duped mercilessly.

Presently news of these doings reached the ears of Morien. It incensed him to think that his old preceptor's wisdom and writings were being made a laughing-stock, so he decided that he must go to Cairo himself, and not only see justice done to Adfar's memory, but also seize what might prove a favorable opportunity of converting Kalid to Christianity.

The Sultan was inclined to be cynical when the hermit arrived, nor would he listen to attacks on the Mahommedan faith, yet he was sufficiently impressed to grant Morien a house wherein to conduct research, and here the alchemist worked for a long time, ultimately perfecting the elixir. However, he did not make any attempt to gain the proferred reward, and instead took his leave without the Sultan's awareness, simply leaving the precious fluid in a vase on which he inscribed the suggestive words: "He who possesses all has no need of others."

But Kalid was at a loss to know how to proceed further, and for a long time he made great efforts to find Morien and bring him again to his court. Years went by, and all search for the vanished alchemist proved vain, but once, when the Sultan was hunting in the neighborhood of Jerusalem, one of his servants chanced to hear of a hermit who was able to create gold.

Convinced that this must be none other than Morien, Kalid straightway sought him out. Once more the two met, and again the alchemist made strenuous efforts to win the other from Mahommedanism. Many discussions took place between the pair, both speaking on behalf of their respective religions, yet Kalid showed no inclination to desert the faith of his fathers. As a result Morien relinquished the quest in despair, but it is said that, on parting with the Sultan, he duly instructed him in the mysteries of the transcendent science.

Nothing is known about Morien's subsequent history, and the likelihood is that the rest of his days were spent quietly at his hermitage. He was credited with sundry alchemistic writings, said to have been translated from Arabic, but the ascription rests on the slenderest evidence. One of these works was entitled *Liber de Distinctione Mercurii Aquarum,* and it is interesting to recall that a manuscript copy of this work belonged to the great chemist Robert Boyle (1627-91), one of the founders of the Royal Society in London, while another is entitled *Liber de Compositione Alchemiæ,* and this is printed in the first volume of *Bibliotheca Chemica Curiosa.*

Better known than either of these, and more likely to be really from Morien's pen, is a third treatise styled *De Re Metallica, Metallorum Transumtatione, et occulta summague Antiquorum Medicine Libellus,* which was repeatedly published, the first edition appearing at Paris 1559. (See also **Alchemy**)

Mormons

A Christian religious sect better known as The Church of the Latter-day Saints. It was founded by Joseph Smith, Jr. (1805-1844) on April 6, 1830 at Fayette, New York. From six original members, the church has now grown to over three million.

While living at Palmyra, N.Y. from 1820-23, Smith had a number of visions which led him to believe that he was chosen by God to restore the true church of Christ, and that all other Christian groups were apostate.

He supported his mission by producing a miraculous scripture called *The Book of Mormon,* claimed to have been revealed to him by an angel named Moroni, who assisted Smith to discover the scripture, inscribed in strange language, on golden plates. These were transcribed by Smith around 1827 by means of magical spectacles named Urim and Thummim, after which the angel took the golden tablets away.

Another work of inspired translation by Smith was the *Book of Abraham,* purchased as a manuscript from a traveling showman in Ohio in 1833. This book, supposed to be written by the Biblical Abraham himself was in hieroglyphics, some of which Smith reproduced. However, James H. Breasted, a leading American Egyptologist, declared that Smith "was absolutely ignorant of the simplest facts of Egyptian writing and civilization."

Critics of the *Book of Mormon* have stated that it was really the work of Solomon Spaulding, a Congregational minister of Monneaut, Ohio, who composed it to support his theories of early Indian origins. Spaulding is supposed to have taken the manuscript to a printer in Pittsburgh, where it was copied by Sidney Rigdon, a Campbellite preacher of Mentor, Ohio, who was an associate of Joseph Smith and an early missionary for his cause.

The Mormon view, however, is that their missionaries called on Rigdon at Mentor, showed him the *Book of Mormon* and converted him to the cause. Whatever the true facts, the work itself quotes heavily from the Authorized Version of the English Bible and is couched in similar style. It purports to tell the story of the true church of Christ on the American continent after migrating from Jerusalem.

The growth of the Mormon sect, its persecution and eventual triumph under Brigham Young, who led 30,000 of the faithful to a permanent settlement in Utah, are part of American history and folklore. The practice of polygamy or plural "spiritual marriage" revealed by Young in 1852 was officially renounced by the church in 1890 and is no longer advocated.

The modern Church of the Latter-day Saints has a very large following and a vigorous campaign of proselytization. One of its admirable but lesser known activities has been the copying of parish registers in Britain and elsewhere which were in danger of being lost through lack of official preservation. They have already compiled 1-1/4 million rolls of microfilm in archives at the Salt Lake City headquarters, Utah. These contain details of millions of people, including their own ancestors, who were born before Joseph Smith founded his Church in 1823. It is a Mormon belief that they will be reunited in the afterlife, and the spirits of the dead should have the opportunity of being baptized into their faith in the afterlife.

The impetus for this important work of preservation is the posthumous baptizing of ancestors. At a multimillion dollar genealogical center in Salt Lake City, some two billion names from 150 countries are stored in a granite vault. These records have assisted identification of more than 250 million dead people for baptism. In 1985 and 1986, the Mormon church was involved in a fantastic series of events that included three bombings, forged documents, and a plot to discredit the Mormon religion. At the heart of these events was a document collector named Mark Hofmann, who forged a number of documents that threw doubt on the true origins of the Mormon religion, and was also responsible for the bombings, which resulted in two deaths. In January 1987, Hofmann entered into a plea bargain arrangement, confessing to the forgeries, fraud and murders, and was sentenced to imprisonment in Utah State Prison.

The key items of forged documents were what has become known as "the Salamander Letter" and the "McLellin Collection." The Salamander Letter, dated October 23, 1830, was purportedly from Martin Harris, one of the original Book of Mormon witnesses, and indicated that Joseph Smith was concerned with money-digging and magic, and that when he went to get the gold plates, a white salamander in the bottom of the hole "transfigured himself" into a "spirit" and struck Harris three times. The tangled story of this and other forged documents, the murders, and the turmoil created amongst Mormon church leaders, is well documented in the publication *Tracking the White Salamander* by Jerald Tanner (Utah Lighthouse Ministry, Salt Lake City, Utah, 3rd ed., 1987) and also in *A Gathering of Saints* by Robert Lindsey (Simon & Shuster, 1989).

Recommended reading:

Arrington, Leonard J. & Davis Bitton. *The Mormon Experience: A History of the Latter-day Saints,* Geo. Allen & Unwin, London & Boston, 1979

Brodie, Fawn M. *No Man Knows My History* (The Life of Joseph Smith, the Mormon Prophet), A. A. Knopf, 1945

Davis, Inez Smith. *The Story of the Church,* Herald, 1948

Gates, Susan Young & Leah Widtroe. *The Life Story of Brigham Young,* Macmillan, 1930

Martin, Walter R. *The Maze of Mormonism,* Zondervan, 1962

Smith, Joseph etc. *The Pearl of Great Price, a selection from the revelations, translations, and narrations of Joseph Smith,* Church of Jesus Christ Latter-day Saints, 1921

Morphogenetic Fields

Term normally used somewhat loosely to indicate the mysterious factors which influence the development of form and characteristics in nature.

A special theory of the action of morphogenetic fields was proposed in 1981 by Rupert Sheldrake in his book *A New Science of Life; The Hypothesis of Formative Causation* (Blond & Briggs, London). This theory also has relevance to such parapsychological phenomena as **clairvoyance, telepathy,** and **reincarnation.** (See also **Formative Causation;** Rupert **Sheldrake**)

Morris, Mrs. L(ouis) A(nne) Meurig (1899- ?)

British inspirational medium through whom an entity who chose the name "Power" delivered high religious and philosophical teaching from the platform before large audiences. In modern times, this would be termed "channeling." Some signs of Mrs. Morris' psychic gifts were noticeable at an early age but they were stifled by an orthodox education.

However, she began to develop rapidly after a first seance with a **direct voice** medium in Newton Abbot in 1922. Within six weeks she went under **control.** "Sunshine," the spirit of a child spoke through her, and "Sister Magdalene," the spirit of a French nun assumed charge as principal trance control. The prediction came through that Mrs. Morris would be trained for the delivery of high teaching by a spirit called "Power." This duly occurred.

Under the control of "Power," the medium's soprano voice changed to a ringing baritone, her mannerisms became masculine and priestly and the teachings disclosed an erudition and deep philosophy which was far above the intellectual capacities of the medium.

In 1929, Laurence Cowen, well known author and playwright came in contact with Mrs. Morris. "Power" convinced him of the truth of survival and filled him with missionary spirit. Hitherto an agnostic Cowen became a convert to Spiritualism, associated himself with Mrs. Meurig Morris and arranged a long series of Sunday meetings in the Fortune Theatre in London for the general public. Wide publicity accompanied the sermons for some time in the Press. Public attention was further aroused by provincial tours which Laurence Cowen arranged at great personal sacrifice.

The rise of Mrs. Morris into the forefront of inspired orators was marked by two publicly attested supernormal occurrences.

An attempt was made by the Columbia Gramophone Company to make a phonograph record of "Power's" voice. According to the publicly rendered account of C. W. Nixon (of the Columbia Gramophone Company), at the very commencement of the experiment an incident occurred which by all the rules should have spoiled the first side of the record.

Mr. Ernest **Oaten,** president of the International Federation of Spiritualists, was in the chair, and, being unaware that the start was to be made without the appearance of the usual red light, he whispered loudly to Mrs. Morris as she stood up: "Wait for the signal." These words were picked up by the microphone and heard by the engineers in the recording room after the apparatus had been started, and it was believed they must be on the record. Later, when the second side of the record was to be made, there was confusion in starting, and towards the end, as if to make technical failure a certainty, Mrs. Morris turned and walked several paces away from the microphone.

A week before the record was ready for reproduction, Cowen rang up Nixon and told him that "Power" had asserted that notwithstanding the technical mistakes the record would be a success, that Mr. Oaten's whispered words would not be reproduced and that the timing and volume of the voice would not be spoiled by the later accidents.

This statement was so extraordinary and appeared to be so preposterous in view of technical expectations, that Nixon had it taken down word by word, and sent it in a sealed envelope to Ernest Oaten in Manchester with the request that he would keep it unopened until the record was ready, and the truth or otherwise of the prediction could be tested. The record was played in the Fortune Theatre on April 25, 1931. It was found perfect. The letter was opened and read. The prediction was true in every detail.

The second strange incident occurred in the studios of the British Movietone Company where a talking film was made of "Power's" oratory. Seventy people saw the microphones high in the air, held up by new half-inch ropes. The rope suddenly snapped (it was found cut as with a sharp knife) and a terrific crash startled all present. Within half an inch of Mrs. Morris' face, the microphone swept across the space and went swaying to and fro. A foreman rushed up and dragged the rope aside to keep it out of sight of the camera. The cameraman never stopped filming. Nor did Mrs. Morris falter. In spite of the obvious danger to her life she never stirred and went on undisturbed with her trance speech.

According to expert opinion the voice registering must have been a failure. Yet it was found that the accident had not the least influence. The record was perfect. According to "Power's" later revelation, everything was planned. The ropes were supernormally severed so as to prove, by the medium's demeanor, that she was indeed in trance (which a newspaper questioned) as no human being could have consciously exhibited such self-possession as she did when the accident occurred.

Sir Oliver Lodge, in his book *Past Years* (1931), referred to Mrs. Meurig Morris in the following terms: "When the medium's own vocal organs are obviously being used—as in most cases of trance utterances—the proof of supernormality rests mainly on the substance of what is being said; but, occasionally the manner is surprising. I have spoken above of a characteristically cultured mode of expression, when a scholar is speaking, not easily imitated by an uncultured person; but, in addition to that a loud male voice may emanate from a female larynx and may occasionally attain oratorical proportions. Moreover, the orator may deal with great themes in a style which we cannot associate with the fragile little woman who has gone into trance and is now under control. This is a phenomenon which undoubtedly calls attention to the existence of something supernormal, and can be appealed to as testifying to the reality and activity of a spiritual world. It is, indeed, being used for purposes of such demonstration, and seems well calculated to attract more and more attention from serious and religious people; who would be discouraged and offended by the trivial and barely intelligible abnormalities associated with what are called physical (or physiological) phenomena and would not be encouraged by what is called clairvoyance."

In April 1932, Mrs. Meurig Morris sued the *Daily Mail* for a poster reading "Trance Medium Found Out," and also for statements made in the article to which the poster referred. The action lasted for eleven days. The summary of Justice McCardie was dramatically interrupted by a sudden entrancement of Mrs. Morris and an address of "Power" to the Judge. The jury found for the defendants on the plea of fair comment but added that no allegations of fraud or dishonesty against Mrs. Morris had been proved, and on this judgment was given for the *Daily Mail.*

Mrs. Morris' appeal, after a hearing of four days before Lord Justices Scrutton, Lawrence and Greer, was dismissed. The House of Lords, to which the case was afterwards carried, agreed with the Court of Appeal.

Morris, Robert L. (1942-)

Parapsychologist who has published articles and edited reprint programs. Born in Canonsburg, Pennsylvania, he studied at University of Pittsburgh (B.S. 1963) and at Duke University, North Carolina (doctorate in biological psychology). After two years of postdoctoral work in Duke Medical Center, he became research coordinator for the Psychical Research Foundation, Durham, N.C.

He served on the Council of the American Society for the Advancement of Science 1971-73; the Board of the American Society for Psychical Research 1979-83 (Secretary, 1980-82); the Board of the Gardner Murphy Research Institute 1971-83 (Secretary, 1971-74); the Board of the Parapsychological Association for many years (AAAS Representative, 1971-77; President, 1974, 1985; Vice-President, 1976, 1984; Secretary, 1977 and Treasurer, 1975); the Board of the Society for Scientific Exploration 1985-86 (Vice-President, 1985).

He has taught parapsychology as well as other areas of psychology at University of California, Santa Barbara; University of California, Irvine; University of Southern California; John F. Kennedy University (Orinda, California), and Syracuse University (New York). He has been an active parapsychology researcher at both the Foundation for Research on the Nature of Man and the Psychical Research Foundation, and has over a hundred professional conference presentations and publications in the area of parapsychology.

He joined the Society for Psychical Research, London, in 1985, and was co-opted to Council in 1986. He has been Koestler Professor of Parapsychology at the University of Edinburgh, Scotland, since 1985.

He edited the Arno Press reprint program 'Perspectives in Psychical Research.' His papers include: 'The Measurement of PK (Psychokinesis) by Electric Clock' (in *Parapsychology from Duke to FRNM* by J. G. Rhine and associates, 1965), 'Some New Techniques in Animal Psi Research' (*Journal of Parapsychology,* vol. 31, Dec. 1967), 'Obtaining Non-Random Entry Points: A Complex Psi Process' (in *Parapsychology Today,* ed. J. B. Rhine & R. Brier, 1968), 'PK on a Bio-Electrical System' (in *Parapsychology Today,* 1968), 'The Psychobiology of Psi' (in *Psychic Exploration* by E. D. Mitchell *et al.* 1974), 'Biology and Psychical Research' (in *Parapsychology: Its Relation to Physics, Biology Psychology, and Psychiatry* ed. G. R. Schmeidler, 1976). Dr. Morris was also a joint editor of *Research in Parapsychology 1972* ed. W. G. Roll, R. L. Morris & J. D. Morris, 1973; *Research in Parapsychology 1973* ed. W. G. Roll, R. L. Morris & J. D. Morris, 1974; *Research in Parapyschology 1974* ed. J. D. Morris, W. G. Roll & R. L. Morris, 1975; *Research in Parapsychology 1975* ed. J. D. Morris, W. G. Roll & R. L. Morris, 1976. This series is published by Scarecrow Press Inc., Metuchen, N.J.

His main research interests include: biological aspects of psi and ANPSI; anomalous interactions between people and equipment; psychic development techniques; the psychology of conjuring, mentalism, and deception.

Morris Pratt Institute Association

The first permanent institution of learning established under the auspices of Spiritualism. It was founded in 1901 in Whitewater, Wisconsin, by Morris Pratt, an American Spiritualist who attributed the fortune which he accumulated to wise spirit guidance. He was told by his Red Indian Guide of certain mineral deposits, unknown to any white man. In a few months he had made over $200,000.

Out of gratitude he established a school to be conducted under the aegis of Spiritualism and deeded the building and land to seven well-known Spiritualists as trustees. Originally the Morris Pratt Institute, its membership now includes individuals interested in supporting and promoting the work of the National Spiritualist Association of Churches. Address: 11811 Watertown Plank Road, Milwaukee, Wisconsin 53226.

Morrow, Felix (1906-1988)

American publisher who virtually created the modern occult boom in the 1960s through his publishing house University Books, Inc. and associated Mystic Arts Book Society.

Born June 3, 1906 in New York City with Hasidic Jewish roots, he grew up in a non-religious atmosphere and became drawn to Marxism and Freudian teaching. He became a graduate student in philosophy at Columbia University from 1929-31, researching the history of religions. As editor of the theoretical monthly magazine *Fourth International,* he wrote a thoughtful article on Marxism and religion.

From 1931-46, he devoted himself to the revolutionary socialist movement and was author of an important study: *Revolution & Counter-revolution in Spain* (1938; 2nd. enl. ed. 1974).

In 1946, he entered the field of publishing as executive vice president of Schocken Books, New York, and became attracted to the writings of Franz Kafka, Martin Buber and Gershom Scholen, and through them to renewed interest in his Hasidic grandfather. From 1948-70, he became immersed in Freudian psychoanalytic training and publishing. At the same time, however, his association with Mel Arnold at Beacon Press, and later with University of Notre Dame Press made him responsive to mysticism, although a socialist at heart. This dichotomy created many personal conflicts for him, although eventually broadening his humanist outlook.

As executive vice president of British Book Center Inc., he took on American rights of *Flying Saucers Have Landed* by Desmond Leslie & George Adamski (first published Britain, 1953), and this led him to research earlier literature in psychic and occult subjects.

In 1954, he incorporated University Books, Inc. in New York, publishing important out-of-print books on occultism, mysticism, psychical research and comparative religion. These included such key works as A. E. Waite's books on the Tarot and Ceremonial Magic, Lewis Spence's *Encyclopedia of Occultism,* Montague Summers' books on Witchcraft and Vampirism, William James' *Varieties of Religious Experience,* R. M. Bucke's *Cosmic Consciousness,* F. W. H. Myers' *Human Personality and its Survival of Bodily Death,* scholarly works by Charles Guignebert on the origins of Christianity, D. T. Suzuki's books on Zen Buddhism, Nandor Fodor's *Encyclopedia of Psychical Research,* G. R. S. Mead's books on Gnosticism, Alexandra David-Neel's *Magic and Mystery in Tibet,* and scores of similar books which initiated the themes of the modern occult revival and provided basic source reference.

Each book carried a new introduction, evaluating the work in a modern context and often supplying original biographical research on the author. Some of these introductions were written by Morrow under the pseudonym 'John C. Wilson;' others were written by such authorities as E. J. Dingwall, Kenneth Rexroth and Leslie Shepard.

University Books, Inc. also published original works as the occult revival threw up names like Timothy **Leary** and new causes like the psychedelic revolution. In addition to publishing, the company marketed chosen titles each month through the Mystic Arts Book Society. A major event of that period was his association with Willem Nyland, in distributing the books of Gurdjieff through the Mystic Arts Book Society. Morrow became a disciple of Nyland and had a great respect for the Gurdjieff work.

After fifteen years of creative and stimulating publishing in the fields of occultism and mysticism, Morrow relinquished the business to Lyle Stuart, Inc., which continued the University Books imprint side by side with its own Citadel Press imprint, moving from New York to Secaucus, New Jersey.

In 1973, Morrow began publishing an occult series for Causeway Books, an imprint of A. & W. Publishers, Inc., New York. Some of the new introductions were written by Morrow under the pseudonym "Charles Sen."

The significant influence of Morrow's publishing work was recognized by the National Endowment for the Humanities and the Rockefeller Foundation, which initiated an oral history recording project on the advanced literary-intellectual life of New York City between 1925 and 1975. Tape recordings have been made of Morrow and other individuals for eventual deposit in the Oral History division of the Columbia libraries.

In recent years, Morrow extended his psychological studies from Freudianism to Maslow's Humanist Psychology and the Holistic Depth Psychology of Ira Progoff. He was in charge of publishing projects in these areas for Dialogue House Library (80 East 11 Street, New York, N.Y. 10003) prior to resuming independent publishing again with the books of Mantok and Maneewan Chia under the imprint Healing Tao Books, in New York.

In his later years he was a regular visitor to the library of the Parapsychology Foundation in New York, where he found excellent facilities for research.

He died suddenly on May 28, 1988, in New York.

Morse, J. J. (1848-1919)

One of the most distinguished trance speakers of the nineteenth century, named as "the Bishop of Spiritualism" by journalist W. T. **Stead.**

Morse was left an orphan at the age of ten, had very little education and served as pot-boy in a public house before his mediumship was discovered. He was described by Sergeant E. W. **Cox** in his book *What Am I?* (2 vols., 1873-74) in the following words: "I have heard an uneducated barman, when in a state of trance, maintain a dialogue with a party of philosophers on Reason and Foreknowledge, Will and Fate, and hold his own against them. I have put him the most difficult questions in psychology, and received answers always thoughtful, often full of wisdom, and invariably conveyed in choice and eloquent language. Nevertheless, in a quarter of an hour afterwards, when released from the trance, he was unable to answer the simplest query on a philosophical subject, and was at a loss for sufficient language in which to express a commonplace idea."

James **Burns,** the well-known Spiritualistic editor and publisher, took an interest in Morse and employed him as an assistant in his printing and publishing office. "Tien Sien Tie," the Chinese philosopher, who said that he lived on earth in the reign of the Emperor Kea-Tsing, gave his first addresses through J. J. Morse in Burns' offices in 1869. Of the other spirits associated with Morse's mediumship the best known was "The Strolling Player," who supplied the humor and lighter elements in the discourses, which were models of literary grace. Many proofs of spirit identity came through, some of which were years after tabulated and republished by Edward T. Bennett.

Morse's physical mediumship was a powerful one. He could demonstrate the fire test and the phenomenon of **elongation.** He visited Australia and New Zealand, edited *The Banner of Light* in Boston in 1904, and from 1906 for many years *The Two Worlds* of Manchester. *The Spiritual Review* (1901-1902) was his own foundation. His mediumship and general propaganda activity was an important factor in the spread and growth of British Spiritualism.

His daughter, Florence, who was clairvoyant from childhood, also developed the faculty of inspirational speaking. She travelled extensively, visiting America, Australia, New Zealand and South Africa. She was almost fully conscious in the course of her inspirational addresses.

Morse published an autobiographical work: *Leaves From My Life; A Narrative of Personal Experiences in the Career of a Servant of the Spirits* (1877).

Morselli, Enrico (1852-1929)

Professor of Psychiatry at Genoa University from 1889 (previously at the University of Turin), a bitter skeptic of psychic phenomena until Eusapia **Palladino** completely convinced him of their reality in thirty sittings.

His book *Psicologia e Spiritismo,* published in two volumes in Turin in 1908 was described by Prof. Cesar **Lombroso** as "a model of erudition."

In 1907 in the *Annals of Psychic Science* (Vol. 5, 1907, p. 322) Morselli wrote: "The question of Spiritism has been discussed for over fifty years; and although no one can at present foresee when it will be settled, all are now agreed in assigning to it great importance among the problems left as a legacy by the nineteenth century to the twentieth. . . .

"If for many years academic science has depreciated the whole category of facts which Spiritism has, for good or ill, rightly or wrongly, absorbed and assimilated, to form the elements of its doctrinal system, so much the worse for science! And worse still for the scientists who have remained deaf and blind before all the affirmations, not of credulous sectarians, but of serious and worthy observers such as Crookes, Lodge and Richet. I am not ashamed to say that I myself, as far as my modest power went, have contributed to this obstinate scepticism, up to the day on which I was enabled to break the chains in which my absolutist preconceptions had bound my judgment."

His psycho-dynamic theory of **materialization** phenomena is a compromise between psychological orthodoxy and the spirit theory. It forms an important chapter in research history.

An earlier book, concerned with paranormal phenomena was published by Morselli under the title: *Il magnetismo animale; la fascinazione e gli stati ipnotici* (1886). Other books included: *I fenomei telepatici e le allucinazioni veridiche* (1897), *Psicologia e "Spiritismo"* (1908)

Morya, Master

One of the mysterious **Mahatmas** or Masters of the **Theosophical Society** of Madame **Blavatsky.** Morya is often simply referred to as "M." (See also **Adepts; Great White Brotherhood; Mahatma Letters; Masters**)

Moses, Rev. William Stainton (1839-1892)

Medium and religious teacher who became one of the most prominent British Spiritualists. He was born November 5, 1839 at Donnington, Lincolnshire. His father was headmaster of the Grammar School of Donnington. In 1852, the family moved to Bedford to give young *Moses* the advantage of an education at Bedford College. In his schooldays he occasionally walked in his sleep, and on one occasion in this state he went down to the sitting room and wrote an essay on a subject which had worried him on the previous evening, and then returned to bed without waking. It was the best essay of the class. No other incidents of a psychic nature of his early years were recorded.

He gained a scholarship at Exeter College, Oxford. Owing to a breakdown in his health he interrupted his studies, traveled for some time and spent six months in a monastery on Mount Athos. When he recovered his health he returned to Oxford, took his degree of M.A. and was ordained as a minister of the Church of England by Bishop Wilberforce. He began his ministry at Kirk Maughold, near Ramsey, in the Isle of Man, at the age of 24.

He gained the esteem and love of his parishioners. On the occasion of an outbreak of smallpox he helped to nurse and bury a man whose malady was so violent that it was very difficult to find anybody to approach him.

His literary activity for *Punch* and the *Saturday Review* began at this time. After four years, he exchanged his curacy with that of St. George's, Douglas, Isle of Man. In 1869 he fell seriously ill. He called in for medical aid Dr. Stanhope Templeman Speer. As a convalescent he spent some time in his house. This was the beginning of a lifelong friendship.

In 1870, he took a curacy in Dorsetshire. Illness again interfered with his parish work and he was obliged to abandon it. For seven years he was the tutor of Dr. Speer's son. In 1871, he was offered a mastership in University College School, London. This office he filled until 1889, when failing health made him resign. He lived for three more years, suffered greatly from gout, influenza and nervous prostration. He died September 5, 1892.

The period of his life between 1872 and 1881 was marked by an inflow of transcendental powers and a consequent religious revolution which completely demolished his narrow orthodoxy and dogmatism. He distrusted Spiritualism and considered all its phenomena spurious. Of Lord **Adare**'s book on D. D. **Home** he said that it was the dreariest twaddle he ever came across. Robert Dale **Owen**'s *Debatable Land* (1870) made a deeper impression.

On Mrs. Speer's persuasion, he agreed to have a closer look into the matter and attended his first seance with Miss Lottie **Fowler** on April 2, 1872. After much nonsense he received a striking description of the spirit presence of a friend who had died in the North of England. Charles **Williams** was the next medium he went to see. A seance with D. D. **Home** and sittings in many private circles followed. Within about six months, Stainton Moses became convinced of the existence of discarnate spirits and of their power to communicate. Soon he showed signs of great psychic powers himself. In 1872, five months after his introduction to Spiritualism, he had his first experience of **levitation.** The physical phenomena continued with gradually lessening frequency until 1881.

They were of extremely varied nature. The power was often so enormous that it kept the room in constant vibration. Sergeant E. W. **Cox** described in his book *What am I?* (2 vols., 1873-74) the swaying and rocking in daylight of an old-fashioned, six-feet-wide and nine-feet-long mahogany table which required the strength of two strong men to be moved an inch. The presence of Stainton Moses was responsible for the table's extraordinary behavior. When Cox and Stainton Moses held their hands over the table, it lifted first on one then on the other side.

When Stainton Moses was levitated for the third time, he was thrown on to the table, and from that position on to an adjacent sofa. In spite of the considerable distance and the magnitude of the force he was in no way hurt.

Objects left in Stainton Moses' bedroom were often found arranged in the shape of a cross.

Apports were frequent phenomena. They were usually objects from a different part of the house, invariably small, coming mysteriously through closed doors or walls and thrown upon the table from a direction mostly over Stainton Moses' head. Sometimes their origin was unknown. Ivory crosses, corals, pearls, precious stones, the latter expressly for Stainton Moses, were also brought from unknown sources.

Psychic lights of greatly varying shapes and intensity were frequently observed. They were most striking when the medium was in trance. They were not always equally seen by all the sitters, never lit up their surroundings and could pass through solid objects, for instance, rise from the floor through the table top.

Scents were produced in abundance, the most common being musk, verbena, new mown hay, and one unfamiliar odor, which was told to be spirit scent. Sometimes breezes heavy with perfumes swept around the circle.

Without any musical instruments in the room, a great variety of musical sounds contributed to the entertainment of the sitters. There were many instances of **direct writing,** demonstration of **matter passing through matter,** of **direct voice** and of **materializations** which, however, did not progress beyond luminous hands or columns of light vaguely suggesting human forms.

The habitual circle of Stainton Moses was very small. Dr. and Mrs. Stanhope Speer and frequently Mr. F. W. Percival were generally the only witnesses of the phenomena. Sergeant Cox, W. H. Harrison, Dr. Thompson, Mrs. Garratt, Miss Birkett and Sir William **Crookes** were occasional sitters. As a rule, the invisible communicators strongly resented the introduction of strangers. The physical phenomena in themselves were of secondary importance. They were produced in evidence of the supernormal power of the communicators to convince Moses and the sitters of their claims.

"That they were not produced fraudulently by Dr. Speer or other sitters," wrote F. W. H. **Myers** in *Proceedings* of the Society for Psychical Research (vol. 9, pt. 25), "I regard as proved both by moral considerations and by the fact that they were constantly reported as occurring when Mr. Moses was alone. That Mr. Moses should have himself fraudulently produced them I regard as both morally and physically incredible. That he should have prepared and produced them in a state of trance I regard both as physically incredible and also as entirely inconsistent with the tenor both of his own reports and those of his friends. I therefore regard the reported phenomena as having actually occurred in a genuinely supernormal manner."

The character and integrity of William Stainton Moses was so high that Andrew Lang was forced to warn the advocates of fraud that "the choice is between a moral and physical miracle." Frank **Podmore** was almost the only critic who preferred to believe in a moral miracle rather than in a physical one.

Podmore suggested that the psychic lights at the seances could have been produced by bottles of phosphorised oil, and quoted a report by Stainton Moses himself in *Proceedings* of the S.P.R. (vol. 11, p. 45) stating: "Suddenly there arose from below me, apparently under the table, or near the floor, right under my nose, a cloud of luminous smoke, just like phosphorous . . . " It seems most improbable that the medium would write such a report if guilty of fraud, and even Podmore himself concluded: "That Stainton Moses, being apparently of sane mind, should deliberately have entered upon a course of systematic and cunningly concerted trickery, for the mere pleasure of mystifying a small circle of friends, or in the hope of any petty personal advantage, such, for instance, as might be found in the enhanced social importance attaching to a position midway between prestidigator and prophet—this is scarcely credible."

The famous automatic scripts of Stainton Moses are known from his books *Spirit Teachings* (1883) and *Spirit Identity* (1879) and from full seance accounts which he commenced to publish in *Light* in 1892. The scripts began in 1872 and lasted until 1883, gradually dying out from 1877. They filled twenty-four notebooks. Except the third which was lost later, they were preserved by the **London Spiritualist Alliance** where both the originals and typed copies were accessible to students. They are completed by four books of records of physical phenomena and three books of retrospect and summary. In his will Moses entrusted the manuscripts to two friends—C. C. Massey and Alaric A. Watts. They handed them to F. W. H. Myers who published an exhaustive analysis in *Proceedings* of the S.P.R. (vols. 9 & 11).

The automatic messages were almost wholly written by Stainton Moses' own hand while he was in a normal waking state. They are interspersed with a few words of direct writing. The tone of the spirits towards him is habitually courteous and respectful. But occasionally they have some criticism which pierces to the quick. This explains why he was unwilling to allow the inspection of his books during his lifetime. Indeed, there are indications that there may have been a still more private book into which very intimate messages were entered. This book must have been destroyed.

The scripts are in the form of a dialogue. The identity of the communicators was not revealed by Moses in his lifetime. Neither did Myers disclose it. They were made public in a later book *The "Controls" of Stainton Moses* by A. W. Trethewy, B.A. Considering the illustrious biblical and historical names which the communicators bore, Stainton Moses' reluctance was wise. He would have met with scorn. Moreover, for a long time, he himself was skeptical, indeed, at first shocked and was often reproved for suspicion and want of faith in the scripts.

He was the charge of an organized band of forty-nine spirits. Their leader called himself "Imperator." For some time he manifested through an amanuensis only, later wrote himself, signing his name with a cross. He spoke directly for the first time on December 19, 1892, but appeared to Moses' clairvoyant vision at an early stage. He claimed to have influenced the medium's career during the whole of his lifetime and said that in turn he was directed by "Preceptor" in the background. "Preceptor" himself communed with "Jesus."

The identity of the communicators was only gradually disclosed and Stainton Moses was much exercised as to whether the personalities of the band were symbolical or real. They asserted that a missionary effort to uplift the human race was being made in the spirit realms and as Stainton Moses had the rarest mediumistic gifts and his personality furnished extraordinary opportunity he was selected as the channel of these communications. Like "Imperator" and "Preceptor" every member of the Band had an assumed name at first. The Biblical characters included the following names, as revealed later: "Malachias" (Imperator), "Elijah" (Preceptor), "Haggai" (The Prophet), "Daniel" (Vates), "Ezekiel," "St. John the Baptist" (Theologus). The ancient philosophers and sages numbered fourteen. They were: "Solon," "Plato," "Aristotle," "Seneca," "Athenodorus" (Doctor), "Hippolytus" (Rector), "Plotinus" (Prudens), "Alexander Achillini" (Philosophus), "Algazzali or Ghazali" (Mentor), "Kabbila," "Chom," "Said," "Roophal," "Magus."

It was not until Book XIV of the communications was written that Stainton Moses became satisfied of the identity of his controls. In his introduction to *Spirit Teachings* he wrote: "The name of God was always written in capitals, and slowly and, as it seemed, reverentially. The subject matter was always of a pure and elevated character, much of it being of personal application, intended for my own guidance and direction. I may say that throughout the whole of these written communications, extending in unbroken continuity to the year 1880, there is no flippant message, no attempt at jest, no vulgarity or incongruity, no false or misleading statement, so far as I know or could discover; nothing incompatible with the avowed object, again and again repeated, of instruction, enlightenment and guidance by spirits fitted for the task. Judged as I should wish to be judged myself, they were what they pretended to be. Their words were words of sincerity and of sober, serious purpose."

Later, when the phenomena lost strength he was again assailed by doubts and showed hesitation. It is obviously impossible to prove the identity of ancient spirits. "Imperator's" answer to this objection was that statements incapable of proof should be accepted as true on the ground that others which could be tested had been verified. For such evidential purposes many modern spirits were admitted for communication. In several cases satisfactory proofs of identity were obtained. "Imperator's" statement was therefore logical. It should also be noted that each of the communicators had his distinctive way of announcing his presence. If, in the case of modern spirits, the handwriting did not agree with the characters employed while on earth, in direct scripts the communication showed the same features as the one which was automatically received.

As to the contents of the communications, Stainton Moses was well aware of the possible role which his own mind might play. He wrote: "It is an interesting subject for speculation whether my own thoughts entered into the subject matter of the communications. I took extraordinary pains to prevent any such admixture. At first the writing was slow, and it was necessary for me to follow it with my eye, but even then the thoughts were not my thoughts. Very soon the messages assumed a character of which I had no doubt whatever that the thought was opposed to my own. But I cultivated the power of occupying my mind with other things during the time that the writing was going on, and was able to read an abstruse book and follow out a line of close reasoning while the message was written with unbroken regularity. Messages so written extended over many pages, and in their course there is no correction, no fault in composition and often a sustained vigour and beauty of style."

These precautions do not exclude the free working possibility of the subconscious mind. This possibility is borne out by posthumous messages claimed as emanating from Stainton Moses and fairly well establishing his identity, according to which he made mistakes in the scripts on certain points.

The life and activity of Stainton Moses left a deep impression on Spiritualism. He took a leading part in several organizations. From 1884 until his death he was president of the **London Spiritualist Alliance.**

The phenomena reported in his mediumship served as a partial inducement for the founding of the **Society for Psychical Research.** He was on its foundation council.

Later, owing to the treatment which the medium William **Eglinton** received, he resigned his membership and censured the Society for its unduly critical attitude.

He edited *Light,* contributed many articles on Spiritualism to *Human Nature* and other periodicals and published, under the pen name of "M. A. Oxon" the following books: *Spirit Identity* (1879); *Psychography, or a Treatise on the Objective Forms of Psychic or Spiritual Phenomena* (1878, reprinted 1952 under the title *Direct Spirit Writing*), *Higher Aspects of Spiritualism* (1880), *Spirit Teachings* (1883).

Moss, Thelma

Contemporary psychologist and parapsychologist, medical psychologist at the University of California, Los Angeles. Her special interests include **telepathy,** radiation, **Kirlian Photography,** energy fields, skin vision (see **Eyeless Sight**).

She visited the USSR to investigate Kirlian photography and has experimented in the field with a modified high-energy photography system.

Moss-Woman, The

According to German folklore, one of the Moss or Wood *Folk,* who dwelt in the forests of Southern Germany. Their stature was small and their form strange and uncouth, bearing a strong resemblance to certain trees which they flourished and decayed.

They were a simple, timid, and inoffensive race, and had little intercourse with mankind, approaching only at rare intervals the lonely cabin of the woodman or forester to borrow some article of domestic use, or to beg a little of the food which the good wife was preparing for the family meal. They would also, for similar purposes, appear to laborers in the fields which lay on the outskirts of the forests. A loan or gift to the Moss-people was always repaid manifold.

But the most highly-prized and eagerly-coveted of all mortal gifts was a draught from the maternal breast to their own little ones, for this they held to be a sovereign remedy for all the ills to which their natures were subject. Yet it was only in the extremity of danger that they could so overcome their natural diffidence and timidity as to ask this boon—for they knew that mortal mothers turned from such nurslings with disgust and fear.

It would appear that the Moss or Wood *folk* also lived in some parts of Scandinavia. Thus it was believed that in the churchyard of Store Hedding, in Zealand, there were the remains of an oak wood which were trees by day and warriors by night.

Mothman

Winged humanoid creature reported in West Virginia from November 1966 to December 1967, along with strange lights, apparitions of **men in black,** and other occult phenomena, supposedly connected with **UFOs.** These phenomena culminated on December 15, 1967, with the collapse of the Silver Bridge across the Ohio River at Point Pleasant.

The name "Mothman" was the inspiration of a newspaper editor, deriving from the Batman comic book hero, then the subject of a popular television series.

In his book *The Mothman Prophecies; An Investigation Into the Mysterious American Visits of the Infamous Feathery Garuda* (1975), author John A. **Keel** suggested that these and other occult appearances might be the work of evil entities. The term "garuda" derives from ancient Hindu mythology, where Garuda is king of the birds, half-man, half-bird, the vehicle of the god Vishnu. In the religious epic the *Ramayana,* Jatayu is the son of Vishnu's Garuda, and dies fighting against the demon Ravana in an attempt to prevent the abduction of the princess Sita.

In February 1976, three school teachers in Texas reported sightings of a "Big Bird," discussed in *Grey Barker's Newsletter* (No. 7, March 1977). An earlier issue of the Newsletter (No. 5, March 1976) had reported a more bizarre claimed abductee experience with "Vegetable Man," pictured as a triffid-style animated tree.

UFO authority Jacques Vallee compared Mothman and similar apparitions to **Springheeled Jack,** the legendary creature of early nineteenth-century

Britain, who attacked travelers and terrified women with his giant leaps and diabolical appearance. Mothman was said to chase motorists and to frighten women. Witnesses stated that he was large, gray in color, without feathers, and with eyes that glowed red. It has been suggested that Mothman is a UFO phenomenon. (See also **Springheeled Jack**)

Recommended reading:

Haining, Peter. *The Legend and Bizarre Crimes of Springheeled Jack,* Frederick Muller, London, 1977

Keel, John A. *The Mothman Prophecies; An Investigation Into the Mysterious American Visits of the Infamous Feathery Garuda,* Saturday Review Press/Dutton, 1975; New American Library, 1976 (British title *Visitors From Space; The Astonishing True Story of the Mothman Prophecies,* Panther paperback, St. Albans, U.K., 1976)

Mott, George Edward (1935-)

Naval officer who has also experimented in the field of parapsychology. Born December 3, 1935 at Virginia Beach, Virginia, he studied at Duke University, Durham, North Carolina (B.S. electrical engineering 1958). In 1958 he married Priscilla Weedon. He was a Lieutenant in the U.S. Navy from 1958 onwards. He is a member of the American Institute of Electrical Engineers, and an associate member of the Parapsychological Association.

At Duke Unversity he assisted W. C. **Stewart** and J. E. Jenkins in developing and testing devices to investigate extrasensory perception, reported in *Journal of Parapsychology* (March 1959) in the article 'Three New ESP Test Machines and Some Preliminary Results' by W. C. Stewart.

Mountain Cove Community, The

A Spiritualist community founded in Mountain Cove, Fayette Co., Virginia, in the autumn of 1851, under the leadership of the Rev. James Scott and the Rev. Thomas Lake **Harris.** Both were mediums who had settled in Auburn in the previous year, and had obtained a considerable following.

While Harris was absent in New York the command to form a community at Mountain Cove was given through the mediumship of Scott, and about a hundred persons accompanied him to Virginia.

The members were obliged to deliver up all their possessions, again at the command of the spirits. Dissensions arose and pecuniary difficulties were experienced, and only the advent of T. L. Harris in the summer of 1852 saved the community from dissolution.

However, the dissensions and difficulties remained, and early in 1853 the community finally broke up. (See also **Apostolic Circle;** Rev. Thomas Lake **Harris**)

Mountain Path, The (Magazine)

Quarterly magazine founded in January 1964, dealing with the life and teachings of Sri **Ramani Maharshi** (1879-1950), celebrated Hindu saint credited with many miracles. Publication address: Sri Ramanasramam, Tiruvannamalai, South India.

Movement (Paranormal)

Paranormal movement has been given various terms—with contact, which is insufficient to explain it (parakinesis), movement without obvious perceptible or normal contact (telekinesis), the most frequent seance room phenomenon. The latter, in its apparent simplicity, is one of the widest import, since behind the displacement of objects and various other mechanical effects an invisible intelligent entity is believed to manifest, performing complicated operations and exercising a directive influence over mysteriously generated and frequently tremendous forces. The generally accepted modern term for paranormal movement is **"psychokinesis"** or "PK." This term could also include the recently claimed phenomenon of paranormal **metal-bending.**

Shaking of the House

Molecular vibrations appear to characterize the phenomenon in its initial stage when the seance table, under the hand of the sitters, begins to tremble, shake, jerk as signs of animation. This vibratory motion is not always restricted to the table. It may spread over the whole room.

P. P. Alexander, in *Spiritualism: A Narrative with a Discussion* (1871) wrote of a seance with the medium D. D. **Home** in Edinburgh: "The first hint or foreshine we had of the phenomena came in the form of certain tremors which began to pervade the apartment. These were of a somewhat peculiar kind; and they gradually increased till they became of considerable violence. Not only did the floor tremble, but the chair of each person, as distinct from it, was felt to rock and—as we Scots say—dirl under him."

In a similar record, Lord Adare, author of *Experiences in Spiritualism with D. D. Home* (1870; 1924), stated: "We soon felt violent vibration of the floor, chairs and table—so violent that the glass pendants of the chandelier struck together, and the windows and doors shook and rattled in their frames not only in our room but also in the next."

The *Journal* of George Fox, the Quaker preacher, disclosed this note: "At Mansfield, where was a great meeting, I was moved to pray, and the Lord's power was so great that the house seemed to be shaken. When I had done, some of the professors said, it was now as in the days of the Apostles, when the house was shaken where they were."

The **levitation** of John Lacy (*Warnings of the Eternal Spirit,* part 2, 1707) made the chamber shake.

The Rev. Maurice Davies in the *Daily Telegraph* and Dr. Gully in the *Morning Star,* described the trembling of the floor during Home's levitation as an effect reminding one of an earthquake.

Felicia Scatcherd wrote of a seance with Mrs. Etta **Wriedt** in *Light* (August 3, 1912): "We all felt the floor, walls and windows vibrating. I have twice experienced earthquake shocks in the Ionian Islands. The sensation was similar."

The Wesley family (see **Epworth Phenomena**), during physical manifestations, heard vast rumblings and clattering of doors and shutters.

In the case of Mary **Jobson,** "a rumbling noise was heard like thunder, the tenants downstairs thought that the house was coming down."

An excess of power held the room in which the Rev. Stainton **Moses** sat in seance in constant vibration.

"On several occasions," wrote Gambier Bolton in *Psychic Force* (1904), "when sitting in my own room with Mr. Cecil Husk, the whole place, floor, walls, and ceiling, have commenced to tremble and vibrate strongly, table and chairs all responding, and glass, china and pictures swaying to and fro, some of the lighter articles eventually falling over; the motion being similar to that experienced when the screw of a steamer, during a gale of wind, and owing to the pitching of the vessel, comes nearly or quite to the surface of the water, and 'races'; or like the tremble of the earthquake which, as I know by experience, when once felt is never forgotten again. So decided was this tremble and vibration that several of the experimenters present not only stated that it made them feel very ill, but their appearance proved to anyone used to ocean travel, that this was not an exaggeration."

Movement of Objects

However, the average telekinetic phenomenon is on a smaller scale. A seance curtain sways and bulges out, a table moves, slides or rotates, weights are lifted, small objects stir, jump into the air and drop slowly or heavily. According to reports, such objects do not follow straight lines but move in curves, as if under the influence of an intelligent mechanical force. Their speed is sometimes alarming. They may come within an inch of one's face. Then they suddenly stop. There is no fumbling, no exploration, no accidental collision. If one puts out his hand in the dark for the reception of an object it neatly drops into his palm.

The sitters may change seats or posture, yet the objects will seek them out perfectly. The invisible manipulator which is behind the phenomena seems to have cat's eyes. A table may incline at a considerable angle, yet the objects may remain unmoved on the leaf or they may glide up the slope.

A switch may be thrown, gas or electricity turned off, the flame of a candle depressed, cords and handkerchiefs knotted, bonds untied. There is every evidence of the operation of invisible hands. Their presence is often felt in touches and quite frequently they are said to be seen in operation.

Lord **Adare** saw, in a seance with D. D. **Home,** a hand stretch over the jet of gas. At the same moment eight jets of gas went out in the house.

Psychical researcher Hereward **Carrington** wrote of the Naples seances with Eusapia **Palladino:** "In one of our seances, a white hand appeared, remained visible to all, and untied both Eusapia's hands and one of her feet.

"Once a gentleman seated to the left of Eusapia had his cigar case extracted from his pocket, placed on the table in full view of all of us, opened, a cigar extracted, and placed between his teeth."

Sir William **Crookes** in his *Researches in the Phenomena of Spiritualism* (1874) gave a good description of the average type of telekinetic phenomena: "The instances in which heavy bodies, such as tables, chairs, sofas, etc., have been moved, when the medium was not touching them are very numerous. I will briefly mention a few of the most striking. My own chair has been twisted partly around, whilst my feet were off the floor. A chair was seen by all present to move slowly up to the table from a far corner, when all were watching it; on another occasion an armchair moved to where we were sitting, and then moved slowly back again (a distance of about three feet) at my request. On three successive evenings, a small table moved slowly across the room, under conditions which I had specially prearranged, so as to answer any objection which might be raised to the evidence. I have had several repetitions of the experiment considered by the Committee of the Dialectical Society to be conclusive, viz., the movement of a heavy table in full light, the chairs turned with their backs to the table, about a foot off, and each person kneeling on his chair, with hands resting over the backs of the chairs, but not touching the table. On one occasion this took place when I was moving about so as to see how everyone was placed."

Dr. J. **Ochorowitz** recorded some very curious telekinetic phenomena in his experiments with Mlle. Stanislawa **Tomczyk.** In good light, before a commission composed of physicians, physiologists and engineers, the medium placed her hands at a small distance on either side of an object.

Between her extended fingers, the object would rise into the air and float without apparent support. In fact, the support appeared to be a thread-like, non-material line of force of which Dr. Ochorowitz stated: "I have felt this thread in my hand, on my face, on my hair. When the medium separates her hands the thread gets thinner and disappears; it gives the same sensation as a spider's web. If it is cut with scissors its continuity is immediately restored. It seems to be formed of points; it can be photographed and it is then seen to be much thinner than an ordinary thread. It starts from the fingers. Needless to remark that the hands of the medium were very carefully examined before every experiment."

When these photographs were projected enlarged upon a screen, the psychic structure became visible. There were swellings and nodes along it, like the waves in a vibrating cord. A whole number of filaments surrounded, like a net, a ball which Mlle. Tomczyk lifted.

With Eusapia **Palladino,** a marked synchronism was noticed between her movements and that of the objects. She could attract and remove pieces of furniture, cause them to rise in the air or drop to the floor by a corresponding motion of her hands. However, this was an exceptional phenomenon at her seances. Usually mediums cannot account for the movement of objects, as they do not know in advance what is going to happen.

In **poltergeist** cases and in cases of **apparitions,** spontaneous telekinetic phenomena have been witnessed. Dr. J. **Maxwell** obtained good phenomena with non-professional mediums in public restaurants in daylight. Miss Cleio made pictures swing out on the wall in the rooms of the Hellenic Society for Psychical Research in full light before dozens of invited guests.

Difficult Operations

The effect of these telekinetic manifestations is often a very complicated one. Pistols were fired in the dark seances of the **Davenport Brothers** against a minute mark which was always hit with marvellous precision. The same phenomenon was witnessed earlier in the loghouse of Jonathan **Koons,** under the control of "John King."

In the presence of the Davenport Brothers, a billiard room at Milwaukee was darkened. After a few moments the balls were heard to roll and click against each other, as if propelled by expert players. The cues moved, the game appeared to be regularly played, and it was marked and counted. However, the Davenports did not claim to be Spiritualist mediums, and are now generally regarded as clever stage performers.

There are several instances on record in which typewriters were faultlessly operated in a dark seance room. In the seances of the **Bangs Sisters,** the typewriter was held in the hands of the sitters above the table and was heard operating in rapid motion. The operators also inserted the paper, addressed the envelopes and sealed them. The *Posthumous Memoirs* of Madame **Blavatsky** (ed. G. W. N. Yost, 1896) is claimed to have been produced by this technical means. The machine, according to J. M. Wade's introduction, wrote nine sheets per hour.

Of a sitting with Franek **Kluski** on November 23, 1919, the Polish Society for Psychical Research recorded: "The typewriter on the table, fully illuminated by the red light, began to write. The sitters remarked that it wrote very quickly, the keys being depressed as if by a skilful typist. There was no one near the machine. The persons holding Mr. Kluski's hands noticed that they twitched during the writing."

In Prof. Tullio Castellani's record of a sitting on July 6, 1927, in **Millesimo Castle,** there is a description of the following artistic exhibition: "After a little while we heard in perfect rhythm with the music, a dance of two drumsticks upon the floor. Then the rhythm of the drumsticks was heard in the air. On being questioned Cristo d'Angelo described it as the dance of a celebrated American negro upon the ground and in the air. The same phenomena occurred later in the presence of Bozzano, and has been described by him. I think, however, it is useful to emphasize so that the reader may form some idea of how these phenomena took place, and the effect which this dance produced on me also, habituated though I am to spiritistic phenomenology. The dance took place upon the rug but the resonance was like that of wooden drumsticks which were dancing in the void. There was observable all the weight of a normal man dancing with vigour. Thus in the dark, by only the slight spectral light of the phosphorescence from the trumpet, one is reminded of a *danse macabre.*"

Many are the mediums in whose presence musical instruments were played by invisible hands (see **Music**). Other forms of artistic expression through telekinetic movements are on record in independent painting and drawing (see **Direct Drawing and Painting**). In Volume XVI of the automatic scripts of the Rev. Stainton **Moses,** there is a description of the carving of two cameo heads by "Mentor" and "Magus." "Magus" produced his own likeness. "Mentor's" artistic efforts are thus narrated under the date August 27, 1875: "A long message was rapped out by Catherine. She said they had brought a shell and were going to cut a cameo. A light was struck, then Dr. and Mrs. S. saw a shell in the middle of the table. Then Mentor came and Imperator. After he left light was called for and in the centre of the table was a cameo and a quantity of debris of shell. Noises had been heard as of picking, and I saw a hand. The shell is more clearly cut than the first, and shows a head laurel-crowned. It is polished inside and shows plain marks of the graving tool."

According to a letter from the unpublished correspondence of Stainton Moses (see *Light,* May 3rd, 1902), "Owasso," one of Henry **Slade**'s controls, extracted, without actual pain, a bad tooth of his suffering medium. A reader of *Light* related in the following issue a similar incident, in the presence of several witnesses, in the history of the medium Miss **Wood.**

The Question of Scientific Verification

Levitation of a table in the full blaze of sunshine was witnessed by Prof. Charles **Richet** in front of his Chateau de Carqueiranne with the medium Eusapia **Palladino.** Dr. J. **Ochorowitz,** with Mlle. **Tomczyk,** saw a garden chair raised in full light.

An ancient instance of table levitation was described in Samuel Brent's *Judischer agestreifter Schlangen Balg,* Œtlingen, (1610) and in Zalman Zebi's reply *Judischer Theriak* (Affenhauser, 1615). Zebi admitted the levitation but he argued that it was not due to magic as "beautiful hymns are sung during the production of the phenomena and no devil is able to approach us when we think of the Lord."

Count Gasparin, Baron **Guldenstubbe,** Prof. Marc **Thury,** Prof. Robert **Hare** and Prof. James J. **Mapes** were the first investigators of table turning. Prof. Hare devised special scientific instruments. Sir William **Crookes** repeated his experiments and improved upon them.

Experiments with an electric bell in a locked and sealed box were successfully carried out with the mediumship of William **Eglinton** by the research committee of the **British National Association of Spiritualists** in January 1878. The bell sounded twice and the armature was depressed with so much force that a spring was strained and an electromagnet disarranged.

Prof. **Zöllner**'s famous knot-tying experiments on an **endless cord** were successfully repeated with Eglinton by Dr. Nichols in his own house.

The fraud-proof trick table of Harry **Price** was lifted by "Margery" (Mrs. **Crandon**) in London. The telekinetoscope and the shadow apparatus of the same researcher established the genuine powers of **"Stella C."** in the **National Laboratory of Psychical Research.**

"Margery" also rivalled Prof. Zöllner's experiments by demonstrating the paranormal linking of two rings made of different woods (see **Matter Passing Through Matter**).

The first demand which the **Scientific American** Committee submitted to "Walter," "Margery's" control, at the time of this well-known investigation was to produce movements inside a closed and sealed space. For this purpose, first a sealed glass jar with a brass hook projecting down into the bottle was used and "Walter" was set the task of opening the snap of the hook and hanging upon it the wooden, brass or cord rings also enclosed into the jar. Two days later the cord ring was found on the hook. A day after its examination by Prof. Comstock, the ring was found off.

Another experiment with fine scales under a celluloid cover produced very satisfactory results. With one of the pans weighted, the other empty, "Walter" held the scales in balance and sent up the weighted pan. This dynamic feat was achieved in good visibility.

Similar results were achieved with a bell box, being physically operated first by the depression of a key or throwing a switch, and later (the instrument being revised), by the depression of the contact boards. Held in the lap of Dr. **Prince,** Research Officer of the **American Society for Psychic Research,** the instrument was operated in daylight. For details of all these experiments with Mrs. Crandon, see *"Margery" the Medium* by J. Malcolm Bird (1925).

The voice-cut-out-machine of Dr. Richardson apparently established the independence of "Walter's" voice (see *Journal* of the American Society for Psychical Research, vol. 19, No. 12, 1925). Modern psychical research laboratories may boast of a number of other instruments which detect or prevent the slightest movement in the seance room and afford opportunities for observation under strict scientific conditions.

Display of Strength

Occasionally the power which accumulates for telekinetic phenomena is so much that astounding feats of strength are exhibited.

At Warsaw, in Dr. Ochorowitz's experiments, a dynamometer marked a force three times as great as Eusapia **Palladino**'s and in excess of that of the strongest man present.

In the mediumship of Mme. **d'Esperance** it was recorded by herself as an interesting incident that in Breslau in the house of Professor Friese, the strongest man in Silesia, a veritable Hercules, vainly tried to prevent the movements of the table.

"A violent crack was suddenly heard," recorded Prof. **Zöllner,** "as in the discharging of a large battery of Leyden jars. On turning, with some alarm, in the direction of the sound, the before-mentioned screen fell apart in two pieces. The wooden screws, half an inch thick, were torn from above and below, without any visible contact of Slade with the screen. The parts broken were at least five feet removed from Slade, who had his back to the screen; but even if he had intended to tear it down by a cleverly devised sideward motion, it would have been necessary to fasten it on the opposite side.

Prof. Zöllner estimated that the strength of two horses was necessary to achieve this effect. He mentioned that one of his colleagues seriously suggested that the medium Henry **Slade** carried dynamite about him, concealed it in the furniture in a clever fashion and exploded it with a match.

In a sitting with Countess **Castelwitch** in Lisbon, which Prof. Feijao attended, a small table, strengthened with sheet-iron was rent into 200 pieces. The fragments were found piled up in a corner of the room.

It was said in the record of a seance with Eusapia Palladino under the supervision of Prof. P. Foà, Dr. A. Herdlitzka, Dr. C. Foà and Dr. A. Aggazotti: "Dr. Arullani asked that the hand behind the curtain should grasp his. The medium replied in her own voice: 'First I am going to break the table, then I will give you a grasp of the hand.' This declaration was followed by three fresh, complete levitations of the table, which fell back heavily on the floor. All those who were on the left of the medium could observe, by a very good red light, the various movements of the table. The table bent down and passed behind the curtain, followed by one of us (Dr. C. Foà) who saw it turn over and rest on one of its two short sides, whilst one of the legs came off violently as if under the action of some force pressing upon it. At this moment the table came violently out of the cabinet, and continued to break up under the eyes of everyone present. At first its different parts were torn off, then the boards themselves went to pieces. Two legs, which still remained united by a thin slip of wood, floated above us and placed themselves on the seance table."

The astronomer Porro reported from his seance with Eusapia Palladino in 1891: "Next a formidable blow, like the stroke of the fist of an athlete is struck in the middle of the table. The blows are now redoubled and are so terrific that it seems as if they would split the table. A single one of these fist blows, planted in the back, would suffice to break the vertebral column."

The Rev. Stainton **Moses** recorded in one instance sledgehammer blows and stated: "The noise was distinctly audible in the room below and gave one the idea that the table would be broken to pieces. In vain we withdrew from the table, hoping to diminish the power. The heavy blows increased in intensity, and the whole room shook with their force."

From the Livermore seance notes with Kate **Fox,** February 15, 1862: "I asked for a manifestation of power; and we at once received the following message: 'Listen, and hear it come through the air; hands off the table.' Immediately a terrific metallic shock was produced, as though a heavy chain in a bag swung by a strong man had been struck with his whole power upon the table, jarring the whole house. This was repeated three times, with decreasing force."

In slate-writing experiments with Henry Slade, the slates were often pulverized. Paul Gibier reported in *Le Spiritisme* (Paris, 1887): "At ten different trials the slate held by Slade under the table was broken into several pieces. These slates were framed in very hard wood. We endeavoured to break them in the same way by striking them against the table, but never succeeded even in cracking them."

Writing of a visit to a Shaker village with the mediums Miss King and H. B. Champion, the Rev. J. B. **Ferguson** said of the latter: "Although a man of most delicate physical organisation, he was, to my knowledge, without food for ten days, and during that time seemed to possess the strength of three men, when under direct spiritual influence; but when not he was as feeble as an infant, and needed all the care I had promised.

Lifting of Heavy Tables and Pianos

There has been a frequent display of great force in the paranormal lifting of heavy tables or pianos.

Sir William **Crookes** saw on five separate occasions a heavy dining table rise between a few inches and one and a half feet off the floor under special circumstances which rendered trickery impossible (see R. G. Medhurst, K. M. Goldney, M. R. Barrington, *Crookes and The Spirit World,* 1972, p. 115).

D. D. **Home** testified before the committee of the **London Dialectical Society:** "I have seen a table lifted into the air with eight men standing on it, when there were only two or three other persons in the room. I have seen the window open and shut at a distance of seven or eight feet, and curtains drawn aside and, in some cases, objects carried over our heads. In the house of Mr. and Mrs. S. C. Hall a table went up so high in the air that we could not touch it."

At a supper party in the house of Henry Dunphy of the *Morning Post,* at which thirty persons, including Miss Florence **Cook,** participated, the heavy dining table, with everything upon it, rose, in full light, bodily into the air, until the feet of the table were level with the knees of those sitting round it; the dishes, plates and glasses swaying about in a perilous manner, without, however, coming to any permanent harm." (See *Psychic Force* by Gambier Bolton, 1904)

Robert Dale **Owen** claimed to have seen in Paris in broad daylight in the dining room of a French nobleman, the dinner table seating seven persons, with fruit and wine on it, rise and settle down, while all the guests stood around without touching it.

Florence **Marryat** writes in her book *There is No Death* (1891 etc.) that after her first seance with Florence Cook the whole dinner table around which perhaps thirty people were sitting, with everything upon it, rose bodily in the air, to a level with their knees, and the dishes and glasses swayed about in a perilous manner, without, however, coming to any permanent harm.

In another seance, with Katie **Cook,** a piano was carried over the heads of the sitters. One of the ladies became nervous, broke the chain of hands, whereupon the piano dropped on the floor, the two carved legs were broken off and the sounding board smashed in.

The levitation of two pianos, in the presence of an eleven-year-old child, was described as early as 1855 in Prof. Marc Thury's *Des Tables Tournantes.* The phenomenon of a levitated piano was witnessed by President Abraham **Lincoln** in Mrs. Laurie's house in 1862.

Mr. Jencken, the husband of Kate **Fox,** said in a paper read before the **London Dialectical Society:** "As regards the lifting of heavy bodies, I can myself testify I have seen the semi-grand at my house raised horizontally eighteen inches off the ground and kept suspended in space two or three minutes."

The Master of Lindsay, before the same body, said: "I was next to him [D. D. Home]. I had one hand on his chair and the other on the piano, and while he played both his chair and the piano rose about three inches and then settled down again."

Dr. John Ashburner, author of *Notes & Studies in the Philosophy of Animal Magnetism and Spiritualism* (1867), recorded the following personal experience: "Mr. Foster, who is possessed of a fine voice, was accompanying himself while he sang. Both feet were on the pedals, when the pianoforte rose into the air and was gracefully swung in the air from side to side for at least five or six minutes. During this time the castors were about at the height of a foot from the carpet."

"As Mr. Home and myself were entering the drawing room lighted with gas," wrote Sergeant E. W. **Cox** in *What am I?* (2 vols., 1873-74), "a very heavy armchair that was standing by the fire, thirteen feet from us, was flung from its place through the whole length of the room and fell at our feet. No other person was in the room and we were crossing the threshold of the door."

Mr. Arthur Lévy wrote in a report on Eusapia **Palladino,** November 16, 1898: "Just as if she was defying some monster, she turns, with inflamed looks, toward an enormous divan, which thereupon marches up to us. She looks at it with a Satanic smile. Finally she blows upon the divan, which goes immediately back to its place." (See Camille Flammarion, *Mysterious Psychic Forces,* 1907)

Vanishing Objects

In phenomena of **apports,** human transportation (see **Teleportation**) and frequently in the phenomenon of **matter passing through matter** there is an intermediate stage in which the objects in question or the human body apparently disappears. Sometimes nothing further than disappearance and subsequent reappearance is accomplished. Whether this is done by a great increase in the vibratory rate of the objects handled or by **dematerialization** is a matter of speculation. Instances to demonstrate the claimed phenomenon are in abundance.

A small table from underneath a larger one disappeared in a seance of Prof. **Zöllner** with the medium Henry **Slade.** They searched the room without result. Five minutes later it was discovered floating in the air upside down. It dropped and struck Zöllner on the head. The vanishing and reappearance of a book was similarly observed. It struck Zöllner on the ear in its descent. (See J. C. F. Zöllner, *Transcendental Physics,* 1882)

The records of the Rev. Stainton **Moses** dated November 27, 1892 stated: "As Dr. S. and I were pacing up and down the room a whole shower of Grimauve lozenges (the remainder of the packet out of which the cross had been made on Friday last) was violently thrown on to my head, whence they spread over the floor round about where we were standing. There were thirteen or fourteen of them, and that number, together with the nine used in making the cross, would just about make up the two ounce packet which I had. I had looked in every conceivable place for these lozenges (which were missing after the cross was made) but could find them nowhere."

"Lily," the guide of Katie **Cook,** asked Florence **Marryat** whether she could take away her fur coat which the authoress put on her shoulders. She was given permission under the stipulation that she returned it when Florence Marryat would have to go home. "Lily" asked for the gas to be turned up. The fur coat was no more in the room. During the later course of the seance, the coat was flung, apparently from the ceiling, and fell right over the owner's head. Apparently the coat had gone through an ordeal for, although it was quite new, now all the fur was coming out and an army of moths could not have damaged it more than "Lily's" trick.

Mrs. Osborne **Leonard,** in her book *My Life in Two Worlds* (1931) told of a **control** "Joey," a famous clown in earth life, who as a proof of his power made things belonging to her husband disappear in daylight in the house and reappear days later in exactly the same place. "Yolande," Mme. **d'Esperance**'s control, often performed similar feats.

In the presence of Eleonore **Zügun,** objects vanished for an indeterminate period. Her patron the Countess Wassilko-Serecki coined the vivid phrase "holes in the world" to describe the effect. (See 'Some Account of the Poltergeist Phenomena of Eleonore Zügun' by Harry Price, *Journal* of the American Society for Psychical Research, August 1926)

The disappearance usually involves no injury. In experiments with the medium T. **Lynn** at the **British College of Psychic Science,** watches frequently vanished from sight without showing harm or stoppage on their reappearance (see *Psychic Science,* vol. 8, No. 2, July 1929). With the Austrian medium Frau **Silbert** it was noticed that she seemed to know intuitively a few minutes beforehand what articles would appear, as if the "cloud of invisibility" which surrounded the objects had been of ectoplasmic nature.

The objects which vanish are not necessarily solids. The invisible operators seem to have the same power over liquids. Lord **Adare** recorded that brandy was invisibly withdrawn from a glass which the medium D. D. **Home** held above his head. When Lord Adare held his hands above the glass the liquor fell over and through his fingers into the glass, dropping from the air above him. Home explained that the spirit making the experiment was obliged to form a material substance to retain the fluid.

Dr. Eugene Crowell, author of *The Identity of Primitive Christianity with Modern Spiritualism* (2 vols., 1875-79) took a small vial filled with pure water to a seance with the medium Henry **Slade** to have it "magnetized." He wrote: "We were seated in a well-lighted room, the rays of the sun falling upon the floor, and no one present but us. Twice the medium said he saw a spirit hand grasping the vial, and I supposed the spirits were magnetising it and kept my eyes directing towards it, but I saw nothing, when suddenly at the same instance we both saw a flash of light apparently proceeding from the vial and the latter disappeared. I immediately arose and inspected every part of the room which from the beginning had been closed, under the table, chairs and sofa, but the vial was not found. Then resuming my seat and questions, in about fifteen minutes, while the two hands of the medium were clasping mine upon the table, I felt something fall into my lap, and looking down I observed the vial rolling off my knees on to the floor. Upon my taking it up we both remarked that the water had acquired a slightly purple tinge, but otherwise its appearance was unchanged."

Max George Albert Bruckner described in the July 1, 1931 issue of the *Zeitschrift für Metapsychische Forschung,* a sitting with Frau Maria **Silbert** in which a bottle filled with water and sealed, was transferred from the top of the table under it. On examination it was found that the water had completely disappeared. The seal and the cord remained intact. Not a drop of water was visible on the floor.

Vice-Admiral Usborne Moore noticed that the ink in his bottle disappeared in a seance with the **Bangs Sisters** (see his book *Glimpses of the Next State,* 1911).

Theories of Explanation

Since the first days of modern Spiritualism, speculation has been rife as to the mechanical agency by which movement without contact takes place. **Animal magnetism** was first thought to furnish the clue. Many theories were formulated. All of them were more or less similar to the "odylo-mesmeric" theory (deriving from the **"Od"** of Baron K. von **Reichenbach**) of E. C. Rogers (*Philosophy of Mysterious Agents, Human and Mundane,* 1853). His definition of a medium was "a person in whom the conscious and personal control of the higher brain centres was for the moment in abeyance leaving the organism open to be acted upon by the universal cosmic forces."

J. Bovee Dods (*Spirit Manifestations,* 1854) possibly came very near the truth in his explanation of rapping as "an electro-magnetic discharge from the fingers and toes of the medium." As regards table-tilting he stated that "the millions of pores in the table are filled with electro-magnetism from human brains, which is inconceivably lighter than the gas that inflates the balloon."

However, the agency of human magnetism or electricity was quickly disproved when no instrument could detect the slightest trace and neither the smallest iron filing nor the tiniest pith ball was attracted by the charged table.

Confederacy, chance, **fraud, hallucination,** or a composite of these suppositions fails to meet all reported data. The other extreme that spirits were responsible for the movement explained little. It was a comparatively early claim that the contribution of the spirits was, at the most, a directive influence and that in some mysterious way the bodily organism of the medium played a dominant role.

The spirits themselves described physical mediums to Allan **Kardec** in the following words: "These persons draw from themselves the fluid necessary to the production of the phenomena and can act without the help of foreign spirits. Thus they are not mediums in the sense attached to this word; but a spirit can assist them and profit by their natural disposition."

The "fluid" of this early age has been replaced by the **"ectoplasm"** of psychical research. The claimed existence of this substance facilitates the idea of a bridge between **telekinesis** and ordinary mechanics. W. J. **Crawford**'s cantilever theory represented the most important attempt in this direction.

It essentially claimed that out of ectoplasmic emanations psychic rods, so strong as to become semi-metallic, are formed, that this extrusion acts as a cantilever, and the phenomena are produced by an intelligent manipulation on the part of unseen operators of these rods.

The contention that structures may exist which are invisible, impalpable, yet rigid is a mechanical paradox. Rigidity means the power of resisting deformation under stress. It presupposes a force opposing the effort of deformation. This force apparently is not applied from any direction with which we are acquainted.

Is it not possible, asked psychical researcher W. Whateley **Carington,** that it is applied from the fourth dimension? We do not know. Crawford was strong in facts, but his theories were few. He found that if the object to be levitated was heavy, the psychic structure beside the medium's body, found support on the floor. He made many exact measurements. He discovered that the objects were usually gripped in a manner resembling suction. He proved the presence of the psychic rods by their pressure on a spring balance and measured their reaction on the medium's body with scales. He photographed psychic structures. He noticed that if an object was lifted or glued to the floor, the medium's body showed a nearly equivalent increase or decrease in weight. The difference was distributed among the sitters. (See W. J. Crawford, *Psychic Structures in The Goligher Circle,* 1921)

Crawford's experiments were confirmed by others. Dr. Karl Grüber, Professor of Zoology in the Polytechnic School of Munich, reported experiments with the medium Willy **Schneider** in 1922: "A rigid body seemed to emanate from the right hip of the medium. At about three quarters of a yard from the floor it traversed the gauze partition, enlarging some of its interstices, and moved objects 80 to 100 centimetres distant from the medium. It seems that the medium has to make a certain effort to cause this fluidic member to traverse the screen. By using luminous bracelets we have verified that during the levitation of a small table a dark stump like that of a member could be distinguished, that it rose up under the table, raised it, and replaced it on the floor and showed itself afresh underneath it."

The advantage of the cantilever theory is its simplicity. For that very reason it only explains an initial stage of telekinetic phenomena. Movements without contact in haunted houses, in **poltergeist** cases and the **levitation** of the human body, apparently demand a different theory.

Prof. Charles **Richet** was probably right in saying that telekinetic phenomena constitute the first stage of materialization which may be called mechanization. When phantom hands or whole bodies are formed, the presence of a separate dynamic organism is suggested. It is created at the expense of the medium and the sitters. By calculation Dr. J. **Ochorowitz** found that the dynamometric energy which the circle loses corresponds to the average power of a man.

If the theory of a separate dynamic organism is accepted, we can fit in experiences like Lord **Adare**'s: "Home . . . told me to go into the next room and place outside the window a certain vase of flowers. I did so, putting the vase outside the ledge and shutting the window. Home opened the window of the room in which we were sitting. The flowers were carried through the air from the window of the next room in at our open window. We could all hear the rustling, and see the curtains moved by the spirit standing there, who was bringing in the flowers; Lindsay saw the spirit distinctly."

Many psychical researchers refused to go thus far. They did not like to narrow down the medium's physical participation in the occurrences. Prof. Theodor **Flournoy** (in *From India to the Planet Mars,* 1900) put forward the following theory: "It may be conceived that, as the atom and the molecule are the centre of a more or less radiating influence of extension, so the organised individual, isolated cell, or colony of cells, is originally in possession of a sphere of action, where it concentrates at times its efforts more especially on one point, and again on another, *ad libitum.* Through repetition, habit, selection, heredity and other principles loved by biologists, certain more constant lines of force would be differentiated in this homogeneous, primordial sphere, and little by little could give birth to motor organs. For example: our four members of flesh and blood, sweeping the space around us, would be but a more economic expedient invented by nature, a machine wrought in the course of better adapted evolution, to obtain at the least expense the same useful effects as this vague, primitive spherical power. Thus supplanted or transformed, these powers would thereafter manifest themselves, only very exceptionally, in certain states, or with abnormal individuals, as an atavic reapparition of a mode of acting long ago fallen into disuse, because it is really very imperfect and necessitates, without any advantage, an expenditure of vital energy far greater than the ordinary use of arms and limbs. Unless it is the Cosmic power itself, the amoral and stupid 'demiurge,' the Unconsciousness of M. Hartman, which comes directly into play upon contact with a deranged nervous system and realises its disordered dreams without passing through the regular channels of muscular movements."

Edmund E. Fournier d'Albe, author of several books on psychical phenomena, wondered if the living principle of the cells which die could not in some way still be attached to us. If so, we would be actually living half in this world and half in the next. Could not then telekinesis be explained by a resumed embodiment or materialized activity of the disembodied epidermal cell principles?

Prof. Cesar **Lombroso** wrote "I see nothing inadmissible in the fact that, with hysterical and hypnotic subjects the excitation of certain centres which become active in proportion as all other centres become paralysed, may cause a transposition of psychical forces, and thus also bring about a transformation into luminous force or into motor force. It is thus conceivable how the force of a medium, which I may nominate as cortical or cerebral, might, for instance, raise a table or pull someone's beard, or strike or caress him, phenomena which frequently occur under these circumstances."

Dr. J. **Maxwell** verified a correlation between the intensity of the muscular effort and the abnormal movement. The movement sometimes may be provoked by shaking the hand about at a certain distance above the table. Rubbing the feet on the floor, rubbing the hands, the back, the arms, in fact any quick or slightly violent movement appears to liberate this force. The breath appears to exercise a great influence as though, in blowing on the object, the sitters emitted a quantity of energy.

Dr. Maxwell had the impression that, within certain limits, the quantity of force liberated varied in direct proportion with the number of experimenters. His observations were thus summed up: "There is a close and positive connection between the movements effectuated by the medium and the sitters, and the displacement of articles of experimentation; there is a relation between these displacements and the muscular contractions of the experimenters; a probable relation, whose precise nature he is unable to state, exists between the will of the experimenters and paranormal movements." (See J. Maxwell, *Metapsychical Phenomena,* 1905)

Exteriorization of motricity was postulated in the case of Eusapia **Palladino** by Prof. Enrico **Morselli,** Prof. Theodor Flournoy, Dr. Gustav Geley and Dr. H. **Carrington.** Essentially the same theory was put forward in 1875 by Francis Gerry Fairfield in *Ten Years With Spiritual Mediums,* suggesting a nerve aura which surrounds every organic structure, capable of receiving sensory impressions, acting as a force and assuming any desired shape. The nerve aura, however, involves more than **ectoplasm.** It suggests the presence of a third factor, a nervous force to which both the medium and the sitters contribute.

During the levitation of a table in the "Margery" seances on June 23, 1923, the sitters felt cold, tingling sensations in their forearms. Dr. Crandon at the same time observed faint, aurora-like emanations from the region of "Margery's" fingers. It may be yet discovered that the tremendous force which occasionally operates through the ectoplasmic structures is of purely nervous origin.

F. W. H. Myers **suggested,** as a correlative to telepathic effect, a "telergic action," by which he meant the excitation of the motor and sensory centers of the medium by an external mind. He said that in the case of **possession,** the external intelligence may directly act upon the body and liberate energies of which we have as yet no knowledge. This theory goes far, as the external mind appears to dwell in the spiritual world, although it is of frequent observation that the sitters' thoughts exercise a certain influence upon the phenomena.

M. Barzini, journalist of *Corriere della Sera,* wrote about his seances with Eusapia Palladino (in Genoa, 1906-07): "It was obvious that our conversations were listened to, so as to yield a suggestion in the execution of the strange performance. If we spoke of levitation the table would rise up. If we began to discuss luminous phenomena instantly a light would appear upon the medium's knees."

As soon as we switch to the spiritual world in search of the ultimate agency, we have to consider what Baron L. de P. **Hellenbach** wrote in his *Birth and Death as a Change of Form of Perception* (1886): "I am convinced," he stated, "that the unseen world has first to learn how to act, so as to make themselves accessible to our senses somewhat in the same way that we have to learn how to swim in water, or communicate with the deaf and dumb."

Experimentation seemed plainly apparent in the "Margery" seances. "Walter" suggested, in explanation of complicated operations with scientific instruments, that he made a psychic double of all our apparatus, working directly on this, and that, automatically or otherwise the results were duplicated on the material prototype. He was always insistent that things be left undisturbed in the seance room as much as possible. He occasionally objected even to cleaning and airing, saying that he had a lot of superphysical apparatus there which gets disturbed if the room is invaded. If his wishes were respected, better phenomena were invariably produced. In view of doubts surrounding much of the "Margery" phenomena, this may seem purely fanciful.

In the weighing scale experiments of the *Scientific American* Committee with "Margery," the photograph of a curious, semi-transparent cylinder was obtained (with flashlight and a quartz lens), looking as if made of glass or celluloid. Seven of twelve exposed plates showed this cylinder. It was five or six inches long and three or a little less in diameter. It stood on its base. When it was photographed on the scale, the pan that carried it was up; when it was photographed upon the platform of the scale, the pans balanced. The deduction was that the cylinder acted as a sort of suction pump to keep the lighter pan up. "Walter" said that if the cylinders had been taken under long exposure they would have looked as though filled with cotton wool.

But even if we admit the possibility that instruments on the other side have to be devised to achieve certain effects, we have not yet come nearer to the understanding of the actual physical operation. The cantilever theory may be but one of the many possible mechanical solutions. There are observations to prove that threads, finer than a spider's, may (somewhat in the manner of cobwebs) connect the medium with the objects of the room.

Mme. **d'Esperance** often complained of a feeling of cobwebs on her face. "Margery" and many of her sitters had the same experience. Ectoplasmic threads may be the instruments of telekinetic action in **poltergeist** cases. With Mlle. **Tomczyk,** Dr. **Ochorowitz** photographed a balance which was supernormally depressed by fine hair-like threads. The method must have been similar when Eusapia **Palladino** genuinely performed the same feat. In fact the thread was seen as (in a seance at the house of Cavalier Peretti in Genoa in 1903) it made a glass of water dance. Slowly and cautiously, Cavalier Peretti drew the thick, white thread to himself. It resisted, then it snapped and disappeared with a nervous shock to the medium.

Ernesto **Bozzano** observed such threads twenty times in the same year; Mme. **Bisson** detected them with the medium "**Eva C.,**" Dr. Jorgen Bull, of Oslo, found them instrumental in an invisible state in producing direct writing on wax tablets in the presence of Mme. Lujza Linczegh **Ignath.**

In some of the excellent photographs obtained by Dr. Glen **Hamilton** with "Mary M.," of Winnipeg, slight threads can be seen reaching up to a bell fixed high above the curtain which was rung occasionally. A similar attachment of threads to apported objects was observed in the photographs taken by Major Mowbray with the medium T. **Lynn.**

The guide of Frau Ideler explicitly stated, in the experiments conducted by Prof. Blacher of the University of Riga (*Zeitschrift für Parapsychologie*, October 1931), that she spun threads to accomplish telekinetic movement. In red light and later in blue light these attachments were observable and the medium seemed to pull the threads from the inner side of her hand with her fingertips. The threads seemed to be of a doughy, elastic substance at first thick, then pulled fine, and felt soft and dry. Even while being handled they diminished perceptibly. A piece was secured and subjected at once to microscopic examination in an adjoining room. An enlargement of the microscopic photo showed that it was composed not of one strand but of many fine but not organized threads. In its chemical composition the structure was not that of the known textile fabrics. Curiously, fire had no power over these threads. They made the flame withdraw. But they were conductors of electricity. The unusual nature and action of such psychic threads makes it necessary to be cautious in hastily assuming fraud with ordinary threads.

The thread-connection with the medium being verified, it is easy to understand that the medium subconsciously may feel, and could indicate in advance, what objects are going to be moved. Dr. Osty established this with the medium Rudi **Schneider** at the Institut Métapsychique. The experience was also well-known to sitters with Frau Maria **Silbert.**

Modern Experiments in Psychokinesis

The bulk of the past observation and theory relating to paranormal movement belongs to a period when physical mediums with unusual phenomena appeared more frequently than in modern times. Consideration of such phenomena is influenced by the fact that much of the evidence is purely anecdotal or belonging to a period of psychical research less skeptical than in modern times.

In the modern period of parapsychology, movement of objects without contact is now studied experimentally under the general term "Psychokinesis" or "PK." The first important experimental studies of this kind were inaugurated by Dr. J. B. **Rhine** in 1934 after he had encountered a gambler who claimed that he would influence the fall of dice by willpower.

Rhine, who had been involved in investigation of the controversial "Margery" mediumship, was anxious to find some type of phenomena that could be studied under control conditions in a laboratory, thus avoiding the endless arguments about fraud and malobservation involved with spontaneous phenomena. Dice fall experiments could be scientifically controlled and were repeatable and also subject to statistical assessment. Rhine and his associates duly set up classic experiments at Duke University, North Carolina, where subjects attempted to influence the fall of dice by willpower.

Over the years, other parapsychologists verified the successful scores of Rhine and others. Eventually one of Rhine's associates, W. E. Cox, introduced interesting variations such as "Placement PK," in which subjects attempted to influence movement of various objects in a target direction.

Another interesting departure in scientific PK tests is the introduction of the "Minilab," a glass tank containing various small objects as targets for PK. The Minilab can be sealed and locked, and is monitored by cine camera or video camera which is activated by a switching apparatus connected to the objects, thus, object movement is automatically recorded.

The Minilab has been used by the parapsychologist J. D. Isaacs who has investigated the phenomenon of paranormal metal-bending, introduced by the Israeli psychic Uri **Geller,** whose feats in bending spoons and keys became a worldwide focus, stimulating imitators and new experiments, as well as providing accusations of fraud. (See 'Psychokinetic metal-bending' *Psi News,* Bulletin of the Parapsychological Association, vol. 4, No. 1.)

Most of Geller's phenomena were produced under casual conditions which did not preclude trickery, although he was later tested under laboratory conditions (see *The Geller Papers,* edited Charles Panati, 1976). However, critics like stage magician James **Randi** deny the possibility of paranormal metal-bending and have questioned the validity of the laboratory tests.

To demonstrate the fallibility of scientific investigations, Randi introduced two fake metal-bending subjects into a test group.

However, the use of the Minilab promises a more acceptable form of evidence for the verification of paranormal metal-bending and other forms of psychokinesis. (See also W. J. **Crawford; Ectoplasm; Exteriorization of Motricity; Goligher Circle;** Nina **Kulagina; Levitation; Metal-bending; Psychic Force; Psychokinesis; Sorrat**)

Recommended reading:

Adare, Viscount (later Earl of Dunraven). *Experiences in Spiritualism with Mr. D. D. Home,* privately printed, 1870; Society for Psychical Research, London, 1924

Bird, J. Malcolm. *"Margery" the Medium,* Small, Maynard & Co., Boston/John Hamilton, London, 1925

Bolton, Gambier. *Psychic Force; An Experimental Investigation,* London, 1904

Carrington, Hereward. *Eusapia Palladino and Her Phenomena,* B. E. Dodge, New York/T. Werner Laurie, London, 1909

Crawford, W. J. *Experiments in Psychical Science,* John M. Watkins, London, 1919

Crawford, W. J. *The Psychic Structures at the Goligher Circle,* John M. Watkins, London, 1921

Crawford, W. J. *The Reality of Psychic Phenomena,* John M. Watkins, London, 1916

Crowell, Eugene. *The Identity of Primitive Christianity and Modern Spiritualism,* New York, 1874

D'Esperance, E. *Shadow Land or Light From the Other Side,* George Redway, London, 1897

Flammarion, Camille. *Mysterious Psychic Forces,* Small, Maynard, Boston/T. Fisher Unwin, London, 1907

Forwald, Haakon. *Mind, Matter, and Gravitation: A Theoretical and Experimental Study,* Parapsychology Foundation, New York, 1970

Hasted, John. *The Metal-Benders,* Routledge & Kegan Paul, London & Boston, 1981

Holms, A. Campbell. *The Facts of Psychic Science and Philosophy Collated and Discussed,* Kegan Paul, London, 1925; University Books, 1969

Leonard, Gladys Osborne. *My Life in Two Worlds,* Cassell, London, 1931

(London Dialectical Society). *Report on Spiritualism of the Committee of the London Dialectical Society,* Longmans, Green, London, 1871

Marryat, Florence. *There Is No Death,* London, 1891 etc.; Causeway Books, 1973

Maxwell, J. *Metapsychical Phenomena,* Duckworth & Co., London, 1905

Medhurst, R. G. (coll.) & K. M. Goldney. *Crookes and the Spirit World; A Collection of Writings by or Concerning the Work of Sir William Crookes, O.M., F.R.S., in the Field of Psychical Research,* Taplinger, 1972; Souvenir Press, London, 1972

Panati, Charles (ed.). *The Geller Papers; Scientific Observations on the Paranormal Powers of Uri Geller,* Houghton Mifflin, 1976

Rhine, Louisa E. *Mind Over Matter; Psychokinesis,* Macmillan, 1970

Rogers, E. C. *Philosophy of Mysterious Agents, Human and Mundane,* Boston, 1853

Zöllner, J. C. F. *Transcendental Physics: An Account of Experimental Investigations,* W. H. Harrison, London, 1882

Moyes, Winifred (died 1957)

The medium of the spirit **guide** "Zodiac" for the spreading of whose teachings *The Greater World* paper and The **Greater World Christian Spiritualist League** were founded in 1931.

"Zodiac" first manifested at Miss Moyes's home circle in 1921. He claimed to have been a teacher at the Temple in the time of Jesus. His earth name was not disclosed but he said he was the scribe who asked Jesus which was the first commandment and to whom Jesus said: "Thou art not far from the Kingdom of God" (Mark xii, 28-34).

Miss Moyes's trance addresses were characterized by singular clarity and lofty wisdom. Although Miss Moyes died in 1957, the work of the League continues in spreading the teachings of "Zodiac."

Mr. Jacobs of Simla (See **Jacobs, Mr.**)

MUFOB (Metempirical UFO Bulletin)

Quarterly journal concerned with reports and sightings of UFOs and Fortean type mysteries. Edited by John Rimmer, 11 Beverley Road, New Malden, Surrey, England KT3 4AW.

MUFON

Initialism for Mutual UFO Network, investigating UFO phenomena and holding conferences on the subject. Founded in 1969, it became one of the most active UFO membership organizations, claiming 1,000 investigators spread over various parts of the world.

MUFON holds an annual symposium and publishes *Skylook,* a monthly bulletin. The director for investigations is Raymond Fowler, author of *UFOs, Interplanetary Visitors* (Exposition, 1974). Address: 103 Oldtowne Road, Seguin, Texas 78155.

Mufon UFO Journal

Monthly bulletin concerned with UFO sightings, published by MUFON (Mutual UFO Network), 103 Oldtowne Road, Seguin, Texas 78155.

Muktanada, Swami (1908-1982)

A charismatic Hindu guru who is a unique exponent of Siddha Yoga, the pathway of spiritual development associated with psychic powers. Born May 16, 1908 at Dharmasthala, South India, he took his Master's degree from Jabalpur University in 1964, and became a lecturer in Hindi at W. M. Ruia College, India.

In February 1966, he first met Swami Nityananda of Ganeshpuri, who became his guru. Swami Nityananda had the rare power of *shaktipat,* the imparting of spiritual force through touch, arousing the **Kundalini** energy which is latent in the human organism at the base of the spine. Through initiation by his guru, Muktananda experienced the arousal of kundalini and its manifestation in various chakras or psychic centers of the body, accompanied by strange visions and enhanced consciousness.

He described his remarkable experiences in his book *Guru* (Harper & Row, 1971), which corroborates comparable experiences of Pandit **Gopi Krishna,** a Kashmir mystic who also aroused Kundalini.

Muktananda became spiritual head of Shree Gurudev Ashram at Ganeshpuri, near Bombay, and attracted followers from all over India. He taught a traditional Hindu mystical doctrine of *sadhana* or spiritual discipline, enhanced by his strange ability to awaken spiritual force in others through *shaktipat.*

He first visited the U.S. in 1970, and four years later made a triumphal tour in California, where he gave an address to a convention of some 500 psychologists and psychotherapists in San Diego. Charles Garfield, clinical psychologist at the University of California, described Muktananda as "a highly developed being."

American ashrams were established in New York, Chicago, Los Angeles, Dallas and Piedmont. Muktananda also made successful visits to Britain. Known affectionately as "Baba" to his devotees, he is also given the courtesy title "Paramahansa," indicating the highest type of Hindu holy man.

Unfortunately after his death in October 1982, there have been serious allegations by former disciples claiming illicit sexual activities on the part of the guru, who had claimed to be completely celibate (see *Cult Awareness Network News,* Citizens Freedom Foundation, April-May, 1984).

Mulchuyse, S.

Dr. Mulchuyse is co-author with Prof. F. A. Heyne of the book *Vorderingen en Problemen van de Parapsychologie* (Progress and Problems in Parapsychology, 1950).

Muldoon, Sylvan J(oseph) (c. 1903-1971)

Pioneer American investigator of **Astral Projection (Out-of-the-Body** traveling). His first experience was at the age of twelve, stimulated by a visit with his mother to a Spiritualist Camp at Clinton, Iowa.

After going to sleep, he apparently awoke to discover himself outside his physical body, looking down at it, and connected by a kind of elastic cord or cable. He thought at first that he had died, and prowled through the house trying to awaken members of his family, but was eventually drawn back into his physical body. This was the first of hundreds of other projections.

In 1927, Mr. Muldoon read some books on occult and psychical science by the famous researcher Hereward **Carrington,** in which Carrington had stated that the book *Le Fantôme des Vivants* by Charles Lancelin covered practically all that was known on the subject of astral projection. Mr. Muldoon wrote to Carrington, challenging this statement and saying that he could write a whole book on things that Lancelin did not know.

As a result, Carrington invited Muldoon to collaborate on the book *The Projection of the Astral Body,* first published 1929, followed by *The Case for Astral Projection* (1936) and *The Phenomena of Astral Projection* (1951). These books have become classic works of their kind on this obscure subject. Two other books by Muldoon are: *Sensational Psychical Experiences* (1941) and *Famous Psychic Stories* (1942).

During much of his life, Muldoon suffered from ill health, and it is thought that this may have facilitated his frequent separation from the physical body in astral projections. In the latter part of his life, his general health improved, but his ability in astral projection correspondingly decreased and he devoted less time to the subject. (See also **Out-of-the-Body Travel**)

Mulford, Prentice (1834-1891)

American journalist and philosopher, a very individual blend of New Thought writer and mystic. He was born at Sag Harbour, Long Island, April 5, 1834 and followed a rambling life. He served as a seaman, ship's cook and whalerman, before becoming a gold prospector. He attempted to run a mining, prospecting and teaching school, then turned to journalism.

From 1863 to 1866, he wrote for the *Democrat,* San Francisco, then *The Golden Era* (a leading literary paper) and the *Dramatic Chronicle.* In 1868 he spent a few months as editor of The Stockton Gazette, a Democratic journal.

In 1872, he persuaded a group of San Francisco business men to sponsor him for a lecture tour, promoting California in England, a project which lasted for two years. Afterwards he worked on the New York *Graphic,* conducting a news column "History of a Day" and in 1878 acted as Paris correspondent for the *San Francisco Bulletin.*

After six years, he retired to the wilderness of New Jersey, where he built a small shanty and commenced writing his famous White Cross Library series of philosophical and occult essays. These covered a wide range of occult, mystical and practical topics, involving a science of thought, and the nature and application of individual powers.

The titles of some of these essays give a good idea of the range of subjects: 'God in the Trees,' 'The

God in Yourself,' 'The Doctor Within,' 'Mental Medicine,' 'Faith: or, Being Led of the Spirit,' 'The Material Mind versus the Spiritual Mind,' 'Healthy and Unhealthy Spirit Communion,' 'You Travel When You Sleep,' 'Prayer in All Ages,' 'The Law of Success,' 'The Slavery of Fear,' 'Some Laws of Health and Beauty,' 'Self-Teaching; or, The Art of Learning How to Learn.'

The first of these essays appeared in May 1886, published in Boston, Massachusetts. One of these White Cross Library series of special interest is 'Prentice Mulford's Story,' a vigorous autobiographical study to about 1872. The White Cross Library essays have been a great source of insight and inspiration to a large readership and still make stimulating reading.

On May 27, 1891, Mulford set out in a small boat, apparently for a vacation cruise, but died on board during his sleep, while anchored off Long Island the same evening. (See also **Mind Cure; New Thought**)

Müller, Fräulein Auguste (c. 1817)

German somnambulist of Carlsruhe, the first sensitive in the age of **animal magnetism** who claimed contact with spirits.

Her trance history was carefully recorded by Dr. Meier in his *Höchst Merkwürdige Geschichte der Magnetisch Hellsehenden Auguste Müller* (Stuttgart, 1818). She was controlled by the spirit of her dead mother and gave frequent exhibitions of a remarkable traveling clairvoyant faculty.

She gave correct medical diagnoses of herself and others and claimed to discern in trance both the thoughts and the character of others. She could also project herself (see **Out-of-the-Body**) and appeared in the night in the bedroom of her friend Catherine, as she promised her.

Muller, Karl E(ugen) (1893-)

Electrical engineer who took a great interest in parapsychology. Born July 14, 1893 at New Orleans, Lousiana, he studied at the Technical University of Switzerland (B.E.E., D.Sc. Tech.). He was a measurement engineer at Swiss Electrotechnical Association in 1918, test engineer with Oerlikon Engineering Co., Zürich in 1919, laboratory director, Mexican Light & Power Co., Mexico City from 1920-25, member of engineering staff of Oerlikon, Zürich from 1925-27 and 1930-34, engineering consultant 1934-40, director of publicity at Oerlikon 1940 until retirement in 1958.

He was president of the International Spiritualist Federation from 1958 onwards, research officer of the International Spiritualist Federation from 1957 onwards; member of Swiss Electrotechnical Association, Society for Psychical Research, London, American Society for Psychical Research, Swiss Society for Parapsychology.

In addition to his many articles in technical journals Dr. Müller published contributions on parapsychology, and also experimented with infra-red photography in the investigation of physical mediumship. His publications relating to parapsychology include: 'Proofs for Reincarnation' (paper delivered before ISF Congress, London, 1960, published in *Psychic News,* (Oct.-Nov. 1960), 'Aspects of Astral Projection' (introduction to book *Excursions to the Spirit World* by F. C. Sculthorp, London, 1962), 'Spiritualist Doctrine' (*Tomorrow,* Autumn 1960). He also published articles in *Yours Fraternally, Chimes* and other magazines. Some of his articles were translated into Swedish, Danish and German.

Mullin, Albert Alkins (1933-)

Mathematician who has studied the relationship between parapsychology and cybernetics. Born August 25, 1933 at Lynn, Massachusetts, he studied at Syracuse University (B.E.E. 1955) and Massachusetts Institute of Technology (M.S. electrical engineering 1957). In 1955 he married Lorraine M. Agacinski.

He was a teaching assistant at Massachusetts Institute of Technology from 1955-57, research assistant at University of Illinois from 1957 onwards. He is a charter associate of the Parapsychological Association, member of American Institute of Electrical Engineers, Institute of Radio Engineers, American Mathematics Society, American Rocket Society. In addition to his technical papers concerned with engineering and mathematics, he contributed the article 'Some Apologies by a Cyberneticist' to the *Journal of Parapsychology* (vol. 23, No. 4, 1959).

Mullins, John (1838-1894)

One of the most famous British water diviners. He was born at Colerne, near Chippenham, Wiltshire on November 12, 1838 in a family of eleven children. His father was a stone mason and John followed the same trade.

At the age of 21, while employed by Sir John Ould to build a house in Gloucestershire, a dowser (water diviner) was employed to locate a water supply. Various people present tried their hand with the rod, including Sir John's daughter, who was frightened when the rod suddenly turned over violently. An abundant water supply was found at the spot.

Sir John was most impressed and later on asked all the workmen on his estate, about one hundred and fifty men, to try divining with a rod. When John Mullins tried in his turn, the rod moved so violently that it snapped in two. Thereafter Mullins was considered a dowser, although continuing his trade as a mason. At his first attempt to locate a water source for Sir John, he located a spring yielding 200 gallons per hour. After that, Mullins was much in demand as a water diviner.

He married in 1859 and continued his trade as a mason, but from 1882 onwards he devoted the last twelve years of his life to dowsing and well-sinking. Such was his confidence in his talent that he made no charge for the expensive work of well-sinking if a good supply of water was not found. In fact, he was immensely successful, locating over five thousand sources of water.

After his death in May 1894, his business was carried on by his sons, one of whom was a dowser, although not so successful as his father.

The firm of John Mullins & Sons was one of the most famous businesses of its kind, claiming royal patronage. A book by John Mullins, *The Divining Rod and Its Results in Discovery of Springs,* published in 1880, went into several editions. (See also **Divining Rod; Dowsing; Pendulum; Radiesthesia**)

Mumbo-Jumbo

A term used to denote an object of senseless veneration, or a meaningless ceremony designed to overpower impressionable people. It has often been applied in a pejorative sense to occult spells.

It dates back to the early eighteenth century, when it was reported as an image used by the Mundingoe tribe in Gambia, Africa, to keep their womenfolk in subjection. If the men had a dispute with the women, the Mumbo-Jumbo image was brought to adjudicate. This image was eight or nine feet high, made from the bark of trees, with straw on the head, and dressed in a long frock coat. A man of the tribe would be hidden under the coat, and would always give a judgment in favor of the men. The women would usually run away when he was brought to them, but he would have power to make them come forward or sing and dance at his pleasure.

A secret society amongst the men maintained the tradition of the Mumbo-Jumbo, and its members were sworn to secrecy. No boy under sixteen was allowed to join.

Mumler, William H. (died 1884)

The first spirit photographer, living in Boston, Massachusetts. He was head engraver of the jewellery firm Bigelow, Kennard & Co., of Boston.

One day, in a friend's studio, he tried to take a photograph of himself by focusing the camera on an empty chair and springing into position on the chair after uncapping the lens. When developing the plate he discovered an extraneous figure, a young, transparent girl sitting in the chair, fading away into a dim mist in the lower parts. He recognized in this his cousin who had died twelve years before.

The experiment was repeated and he became satisfied that the extra faces appearing on his plates were of supernormal origin. The news of Mumler's discovery began to spread and he was besieged with so many requests for sittings that he gave up his position and became a professional spirit-photographer.

Among the first to investigate Mumler's powers was Andrew Jackson **Davis,** then editor of the *Herald of Progress* in New York. He first sent a professional photographer to test Mumler and on his favorable report conducted an investigation himself. He was satisfied that the new psychic manifestation was genuine.

It apparently did not matter whether Mumler worked in his own studio or in that of others, whether he used his own chemicals or not. Photographers came and went, one searching inquiry followed another. Black of Boston, inventor of the nitrate of silver bath, was anxious to establish whether a true spirit photograph was possible. He first sent Horace Weston, a fellow photographer, to Mumler, then came himself, made the most scrupulous examination, developed the plate himself and to his utter amazement found another form on it besides his own, a man leaning on his shoulder.

Mumler's reputation was established, he became in vogue and did tremendous business. His most famous picture was a photograph of the widowed Mrs. Abraham Lincoln, on which appeared a spirit portrait of her late husband.

The first scandal, however, was not long in coming. It was discovered that he obtained from time to time the spirit portraits of men who were very much alive. Apologists claimed that the pictures must be genuine since they had been recognized by relatives and that the processes of production had been properly supervised to obviate trickery. It was thought that the living individuals might be doubles of the "spirits." Mumler himself could not explain the result, but eventually even Spiritualists accused him of trickery and such a hue and cry was raised that in 1868 he transferred his headquarters to New York.

He prospered here for a while until he was arrested by the order of the Mayor of New York on an accusation of fraud raised by a newspaperman. The journalist, Mr. P. V. Hickey, of the *World,* approached Mumler for a spirit photograph, giving a false name, hoping to get a good story for his newspaper. At the trial professional photographers and independent citizens testified for Mumler and he was acquitted.

His further career was full of vicissitudes. He died in poverty. The story of his life is told in his book *Personal Experiences of William H. Mumler in Spirit Photography* (1875). Examples of his spirit photos are to be found in Aksakof's *Animisme et Spiritisme* and in James Coates's *Photographing the Invisible. (See also* **Psychic Photography;** Ted **Serios; Spirit Photography; Thoughtography**)

Mundle, Clement Williams Kennedy (1916-1989)

Professor of philosophy who was actively involved in the study of parapsychology. Born August 10, 1916 in Fife, Scotland, he studied at the University of St. Andrews (M.A. 1939). From 1940-45 he was a Royal Air Force officer, Technical Branch. He took his B.A. in 1947 at Oxford University, and from 1948-50 was holder of a Shaw Philosophical fellowship at Edinburgh University. In 1946 he married Sheila MacGregor Falconer.

He was Head of Philosophy Department, University College of St. Andrews, Dundee, Scotland from 1947-55, Head of Philosophy Department, University College of North Wales, Bangor from 1955 onwards. His memberships include International Conference of Parapsychological Studies, Utrecht, Netherlands (1953), International Conference on

Philosophy and Parapsychology, St. Paul de Vence, France (1954), charter member of Parapsychological Association.

Professor Mundle assisted in the ESP investigations reported by S. G. **Soal** and H. T. Bowden in their book *The Mind Readers* (1959). His own articles on parapsychology include: 'Is Psychical Research Relevant to Philosophy?' (*Proceedings, Aristotelian Society,* Supplemental vol. 24, 1950), 'Professor Rhine's Views on Psychokinesis' (*Mind,* July 1950), 'The Experimental Evidence for Precognition and Psychokinesis' (Society for Psychical Research, *Proceedings,* July 1950), 'Selectivity in Extrasensory Perception' (*SPR Journal,* March 1951), 'Some Philosophical Perspectives for Parapsychology' (*Journal of Parapsychology,* Dec. 1952). He also contributed the chapter 'Broad's Views about Time' in the book *The Philosophy of C. D. Broad* (1959), and the article 'Philosophical Implications of ESP Phenomena' in *Encyclopedia of Philosophy,* ed. P. Edwards, (1967)

Prof. Mundle was president of the Society for Psychical Research, London, 1971-74.

He died July 27, 1989.

Munnings, Frederick T(ansley) (c. 1928)

British fake medium, an ex-burglar whose claims to **direct voice** mediumship were dismissed by author and writer on psychic phenomena H. Dennis **Bradley,** who held several experimental sittings in his home.

Bradley stated that the sittings were entirely valueless and, in February 1926 a public warning against Munnnings was issued in the press by Sir Arthur Conan **Doyle,** Dr. Abraham Wallace, R. H. Saunders and H. D. Bradley.

For publication of the warning, Munnings brought an action for libel against the *Daily Sketch* and the *Sunday Herald* in 1928. However, he did not face the issue before the court and judgment was entered for the defendants.

Thereupon Munnings sold his "Confessions" to *The People* newspaper. It appeared in installments for several weeks, written by journalist Sydney A. Moseley, branding Munnings' whole psychic career as fraudulent. The understanding between Moseley and Munnings, however, was not perfect and in an interview to the *International Psychic Gazette,* Munnings entered a mild protest against his own sensational disclosures.

Psychical researcher Harry **Price** was instrumental in the exposure of Munnings, who claimed to produce the independent voices of "Julius Caesar," "Dan Leno" (famous nineteenth-century comedian), "Dr. Crippen" (a murderer), and "King Henry VIII." Price had invented a Voice Control Recorder and after testing Munnings, proved that all the voices were those of Munnings.

Murphy, Gardner (1895-1979)

Distinguished psychologist and pioneer figure in psychical research and parapsychology. Born July 8, 1895 at Chillicothe, Ohio, he studied at Yale University (B.A. 1916), Harvard University (M.A. 1917) and Columbia University (Ph.D.1923). In 1926 he married Lois Barclay.

He was a lecturer in psychology at Columbia University from 1921-25, instructor, assistant professor from 1925-29; professor, chairman of the Department of Psychology, City College of New York from 1940-52, director of research at Menninger Foundation, Topeka, Kansas from 1952 onwards. He is a member of the American Psychological Association (president in 1944), American Association for the Advancement of Science.

Dr. Murphy was a member of the Society for Psychical Research, London, as early as 1917, and his graduate work at Harvard as Richard Hodgson Fellow concerned psychical research. He served as vice-president of the American Society for Psychical Research from 1940-62, after which he was elected president. He initiated the first telepathic experiments through "wireless" (radio) in Chicago and Newark.

Dr. Murphy's many books on psychology and parapsychology included: *Historical Introduction to Modern Psychology* (first published 1925, still a standard college text in modern editions), *Personality* (1947), *In the Minds of Men* (1953), *Human Potentialities* (1958), (with Robert Ballou) *William James and Psychical Research* (1960), *The Challenge of Psychical Research* (1961). Some of his important contributions to the ASPR *Journal* include: 'Concentration versus Relaxation in Relation to Telepathy' (Jan. 1943), 'Psychical Phenomena and Human Needs' (Oct. 1943), 'Removal of Impediments to the Paranormal' (Jan.1944), 'An Outline of Survival Evidence' (Jan, 1945), 'Difficulties Confronting the Survival Hypothesis' (April 1945), 'An Approach to Precognition' (Jan. 1948), 'Needed: Instruments for Differentiating Between Telepathy and Clairvoyance' (April, 1948), 'Psychical Research and Personality' (Jan. 1950), 'The Natural, the Mystical and the Paranormal' (Oct. 1952), 'Triumphs and Defeats in the Study of Mediumship' (Oct. 1957), 'Progress in Parapsychology" (Jan. 1959)

Dr. Murphy became open-minded about paranormal phenomena as a result of his personal experiences with unorthodox healing. In 1927 he suffered from near-blindness and persistent influenza. His sight was restored by Dr. Frank Marlow of Syracuse who taught him eye muscle exercises, and Dr. William H. Hay prescribed diet and exercise which overcame his semi-invalid condition.

He visualized ESP as "an extended self, an archipelago of mankind," and was quoted as saying "One of the main questions of psychic research is whether we can give up our precious folklore and intuition above vast regions of the unknown without throwing out the useful data."

Dr. Murphy died in George Washington University Hospital, Washington, D.C., March 20, 1979. He was a great psychologist and historian of psychology, as well as a distinguished parapsychologist.

He was survived by his wife Lois (Barclay) Murphy, who collaborated with him on some of his psychical researches.

In 1960, some of Dr. Murphy's former psychology students prepared a *Festschrift for Gardner Murphy,* ed. John G. Peatman & Eugene L. Hartley, published to honor his 65th birthday. Parapsychologist Prof. Gertrude **Schmeidler,** another former student, also published a tribute to Dr. Murphy in an article 'Some Lines About Gardner Murphy, the Psychologist's Parapsychologist' (*Parapsychology Review,* July-August, 1976). There is an obituary of Dr. Murphy in the May-June 1979 issue of *Parapsychology Review.*

Murphy-Lydy, Mrs. Mary (c.1870- ?)

American **materialization** and **trumpet** medium, who practiced for many years in Chesterfield Camp, Indiana. Her chief controls were "Dr. Green" and "Sunflower." She was engaged for a year by the Indiana Psychic Research Society at Indianapolis, toured the United States and attained prominence in 1931 in England by platform demonstration of direct voice.

Impressive accounts of her phenomena were published in the press, but British author and writer on psychic phenomena H. Dennis Bradley considered her performances highly suspicious. In his book . . . *And After* (1931) he described sittings with the medium whom he roundly condemned as "deliberately fraudulent." He also stigmatized her public appearances, stating "There was no semblance whatever of spirituality during the medium's proceedings. The effect produced was merely the boredom of a material and dreary exhibition." The main charge was that in a private sitting the author actually heard the medium speak into the trumpet.

Murray, (George) Gilbert (Aime) (1866-1957)

Regius Professor of Greek at Oxford University, born January 2, 1866, president of the Society for Psychical Research, London, 1915-16. He is a famous figure in psychical research for his experiments in **thought-transference** with Mrs. **Sidgwick** (*Proceedings* of the Society for Psychical Research, vol. 34, 1924), which he considered "perhaps the most important ever brought to the notice of the society."

In an interview for the *Sunday Express* in the summer of 1929, he declared that he discovered his thought-reading faculty by accident. Playing guessing games with his children, one person going out of the room, the others deciding the subject he was to guess and writing it down he found, to his surprise, that in some intangible way an impression would be conveyed to him and he would actually know what the children were thinking.

On the insistence of his wife, he commenced experimenting with grown-ups and though by temperament and training he was intensely skeptical, in the interest of truth he admitted before the public that he was able to read thoughts.

He believed with psychologist William **James** that there exists the "stream of consciousness, with a vivid centre and dim edges." In moments of inattentiveness, subconscious impressions register themselves and afterwards form a sort of dim **memory.** This may account for certain phases of clairvoyance. But William James' "dim edges" idea should be further extended. Prof. Murray suspected that around our perceptions is a fringe of still more delicate sensing apparatus. The "feelers" of this apparatus are constantly registering contacts with their surroundings, but the impressions are too weak to enter the field of normal consciousness. This fringe of consciousness is the key to **telepathy.** Prof. Murray did not believe in communication with the dead.

He published a number of books concerned with Greek traditions in literature and poetry. He related his experiences in telepathy to the meaning of the original Greek term "sympathy" as "the sharing of a feeling of 'co-sensitivity.' "

He died at Oxford, England, May 20, 1957.

Murray, Margaret A(lice) (1863-1963)

British archaeologist whose writings on **Witchcraft** played a prominent part in the modern witchcraft revival. Born in Calcutta, India, July 13, 1863, she entered University College, London, 1894; Fellow of University College, London, D.Lit., F.S.A. (Scot.), F.R.A.I. She was junior lecturer on Egyptology in 1899, University Extension Lecturer at Oxford University in 1910, London University in 1911. She retired from her Assistant Professorship in Egyptology at University College in 1935, and excavated sites in Egypt from 1902-04, Malta from 1921-24, Hertfordshire, England in 1925, Minorca from 1930-31, Petra in 1937, Tell Ajjul, South Palestine in 1938.

She was a member of the Society of Visiting Scientists, and President of the Folklore Society, London, from 1953-55. She published a number of valuable works on archaeology, but is better remembered for her controversial books on witchcraft.

In *The Witch Cult in Western Europe* (1921), she explained witchcraft as a pre-Christian religion in its own right, rather than a heretical deviation from established Christianity. The book had a great influence on Gerald B. **Gardner** (1884-1964), pioneer of the modern witchcraft revival. Dr. Murray contributed an introduction to his book *Witchcraft Today* (1954). She also wrote two other books on witchcraft: *The God of the Witches* (1933) and *The Divine King in England* (1954).

She died November 13, 1963, soon after her hundredth birthday. For biographical information, see her autobiography *My First Hundred Years* (London, 1963).

Muscle Reading

According to Prof. James H. **Hyslop,** "the interpretation by the operator of unconscious muscular movements in the subject experimented on."

As no paranormal perception is involved in the interpretation, psychical research is not specifically concerned in muscle reading, although the special sensitivities involved may have some relevance to the mechanisms of paranormal cognition.

The subject is well treated in George Miller Beard's monograph. *The Study of Trance, Muscle Reading and Allied Nervous Phenomena* (New York, 1882). The *Proceedings* of the Society for Psychical Research, London, contain two studies on the subject: 'Note on Muscle Reading' by the Rev.E. H. Sugden (vol. 1, pt. 4, 1882-83) and 'Experiments in Muscle Reading and Thought-Transference' by Max Dessoir (vol. 4, pt. 10, 1886-87).

Musès, C(harles) A(rthur) (1919-)

Mathematician, physicist, cyberneticist, philosopher, who has worked in the field of parapsychology. Born April 28, 1919 in New Jersey, he studied at City College, New York (B.Sc.), Columbia University (A.M., Ph.D. philosophy). From 1941-43 he was a chemist at Gar-Baker Laboratories Inc.; from 1944-54 consultant; from 1954-59 editor-in-chief of Falcon's Wing Press, Colorado (concerned with philosophical and occult books); from 1960-62 research director of Barth Foundation; from 1963-69 research contributor in mathematics and morphology in Switzerland and California; edited *Journal for the Study of Consciousness.* He is a member of New York Academy of Science, Royal Astronomical Society, Canada.

He worked with the late Dr. Norbert Wiener, pioneer of Cybernetics, whose posthumously published lectures he edited. In the field of mathematics, Musès discovered root and logarithm operations for hyper-numbers following the square root of minus one. In the field of anthropology, he has studied the Maya people, the Lacadones of Chiapas, Mexico, and symbolic systems in India. He edited *Journal of Psychoenergetic Systems* and held editorial positions with *Kybernetes, International Journal of Bio-Medical Computing, Impact of Science on Society* (UNESCO). He also edited *Proceedings of the First International Symposium on Biosimulation* (Locarno, 1960), *Aspects of the Theory of Artificial Intelligence* (New York, 1962). He became director of research for the Center for Research on Mathematics and Morphology, Santa Barbara, California.

At Falcon's Wing Press, he introduced publication of Count Stefan Colonna Walewsky's *A System of Caucasion Yoga* (1955), a facsimile of a fascinating occult manuscript of a Gurdjieff type compiled in the 1920s. Musès own books include: *Illumination of Jacob Boehme; the work of Dionysius Andreas Freher* (1951), *An Evaluation of Relativity Theory after a Half-Century* (1953), *East-West Fire; Schopenhauer's Optimism and the Lankavatara Sutra; An Excursion toward the Common Ground between Oriental and Western Religion* (1955), (ed.) *Prismatic Voices; An International Anthology of Distinctive New Poets* (1958), (ed.) *Esoteric Teachings of the Tibetan Tantra* (1961; 1981), (ed. with A. M. Young) *Consciousness and Reality; the Human Pivot Point* (1972).

In the field of parapsychology, Musès has made important contributions to the study of the nature, alterations and potentials of consciousness, to which he gives the name **Noetics.**

His articles include: (in *Journal for the Study of Consciousness)* 'Hypernumber and Metadimension Theory; Unusual States of Consciousness' (vol. 1, 1968), 'The Limits of Consciousness' (vol. 1, 1968), 'The Noetic Relevance of Psychoactive Molecules' (vol. 2, 1969), 'Altering States of Consciousness by Mathematics' (vol.3, 1970), 'The Emerging Image of Man and "Tain't Necessarily So' " (vol. 4, 1971). Other papers include 'Trance-inducing Techniques in Ancient Egypt' (in *Consciousness and Reality,* ed. C. Musès and A. M. Young, 'Communication of Consciousness Necessitates the Vacuum as Transducer' *(Proceedings of First International Conference on Psychotronics, Prague, 1973),* 'The Psi Dimension in Sciences' *(UNESCO's Impact of Science on Society,* 1974), 'Aspects of Some Crucial Problems in Biological and Medical Cybernetics' (in *Progress in Bio-Cybernetics,* vol. II, ed. N. Wiener & J. P. Schade, 1975), 'Psychotronic Quantum Theory; A Proposal for Understanding Mass/Space/Time/Consciousness Transductions in Terms of a Radically Extended Quantum Theory' (*Proceedings of International Association for Psychotronic Research,* 1975), 'The Politics of Psi; Acculturation & Hypnosis' (in *Extrasensory Ecology; Parapsychology and Anthropology* by Joseph K. Long, 1977).

Museum of Magic and Witchcraft

Founded in 1950 by witchcraft revivalist Gerald B. **Gardner** (1884-1964) at the Witches Mill, Castletown, Isle of Man, Great Britain. It contained witchcraft relics, as well as reconstructed scenes of occult rituals and instruments.

After Gardner's death, the Museum passed to Scottish witch Monique Wilson (witch name "Lady Olwyn").

Later the collection was sold to Ripley International, who created a Museum of Witchcraft and Magic at Fisherman's Wharf, San Francisco, California, and another at Gatlinburg, Tennessee. (See also Cecil H. **Williamson)**

Mushrooms

The narcotic and hallucinogenic properties of certain mushrooms have been known since ancient times. Certain mushrooms were even regarded as sacred and their use prohibited to ordinary people. In modern times, serious medical and scientific interest in hallucinogenic mushrooms dates from the pioneer work *Phantastica; Narcotic and Stimulating Drugs* by Louis Lewin (London, 1931). In this important book, Lewin discussed the use of fly agaric, and incidentally identified the peyotl plant (which he named *anholonium Lewinii)* and the substance mescaline obtained from it.

Over two decades later, the New York banker R. Gordon Wasson with his wife Valentina published their classic study *Mushrooms Russia and History* (Pantheon, 1957). This important work launched a new science of ethno-mycology, i.e., the study of the role played by wild mushrooms in various human cultures throughout history.

The Wassons had undertaken field trips into Mexico during 1955 to study at first hand the sacred mushroom ceremonies of the Indian people. Their record album *Mushroom Ceremony of the Mazatec Indians of Mexico* (Folkways Records, New York, 1957) was the first documented recording of its kind. The Wassons have also given special attention to fly agaric *(A. muscaria)* in history, and in his book *Soma, Divine Mushroom of Immortality* (1968; 1971) Wasson speculated that it was the source of the nectar named *soma* in the ancient Vedic literature of India.

Although some modern writers on psychedelics support this suggestion, it is not soundly based (see **Soma).**

The studies of the Wassons reinforced the suggestions in Aldous Huxley's book *The Doors of Perception* (1954), and intensified interest in psychedelic drugs and their hallucinogenic properties.

Unfortunately it was from popularization of such serious works that the psychedelic revolution and the wide-spread sickness of modern drug-addition developed.

It is not easy for sophisticated civilizations to recapture the cultural value and beliefs of primitive peoples who used hallucinogenic substances in religious rituals, and the over-intellectualized synthetic models of rituals mocked up by such experimenters as Timothy **Leary** and Richard **Alpert** lacked emotional and cultural integrity. On a lower level still are the reckless seekers of drug experience as an escape from social responsibility, and the sordid underworld of hard drugs and dope pushing which has grown up around them. (See also John M. **Allegro;) Drugs; Hallucinogens; Soma)**

Music (Paranormal)

There are various different types of paranormal music, ranging from inspired performances by mediums or compositions dictated by "spirit musicians," to music which is heard without any apparent earthly source. Perhaps this latter form of paranormal music is the most impressive. There are two distinct types of its occurrence.

During the persecution of the Huguenots in France, the hearing of music from invisible sources became a wide-spread phenomenon. The *Pastoral Letter* of Pierre Jurieu (1689) referred to dozens of instances with names. The sound of trumpets, as if an army were going to charge, and the singing of psalms, a composition of many voices, and a number of musical instruments were heard day and night at many places.

After the church in Orthez was razed to the ground, there was hardly a house in Orthez in which people did not hear the music, ordinarily between eight and nine at night. The Parliament of Pau and the Intendant of Bearn forbade men to go and hear these psalms under a forfeiture of 2,000-5,000 crowns. The scale of the phenomenon was too vast to be attributed to **hallucination.** It was experienced throughout the Cevennes. It was largely under the effect of this supernormal phenomenon that Cavalier, Roland and Marion rose against Louis XIV.

Beriah G. Evans, in his account of the Welsh Religious Revival, wrote in the *Daily News* (February 9, 1905): "From all parts of the country come reports of mysterious music descending from above, and always in districts where the Revival fire burns brightly."

In the second type of paranormal music, there are several cases cited in the *Phantasms of the Living* by E. Gurney, F. W. H. Myers & F. Podmore (1886), in which music was heard around the deathbed. After the death of Mr. L. (p. 446), three persons in the death chamber heard for several seconds three female voices singing softly, like the sounds of an Æolian harp. Eliza W. could distinguish the words: "The strife is o'er, the battle done." Mrs. L. who was also present did not hear anything.

Before Mrs. Sewell's little girl died (vol. 2, p. 221) "sounds like the music of an Æolian harp" were heard from a cupboard in the room. "The sounds increased until the room was full of melody, when it seemed slowly to pass down the stairs and ceased. The servant in the kitchen, two storeys below, heard the sounds." The sounds were similarly heard for the next two days by several people, except the child, who was passionately fond of music. She died when the music was heard for the third time.

Following the death of her 21-year-old daughter, Mrs. Yates heard the sweetest spiritual music, "such as mortals never sang" (vol. 2, p. 223).

Music was heard around the sick bed of John Britton, a deaf-mute (*Journal* of the Society for Psychical Research, vol. 4, p. 181) who was dangerously ill with rheumatic fever. His face was lighted up and when he had recovered sufficiently to use his hands he explained that he heard "beautiful music."

In the case of an old Puritan, narrated in *John Bunyan's Works,* "when his soul departed from him the music seemed to withdraw, and to go further and further off from the house, and so it went until the sound was quite gone out of hearing."

The British *Daily Chronicle* reported on May 4, 1905, the case of a dying woman of the Salvation Army, "For three or four nights mysterious and sweet music was heard in her room at frequent intervals by relatives and friends, lasting on each occasion about a quarter of an hour. At times the music appeared to proceed from a distance, and then would gradually grow in strength while the young woman lay unconscious."

There are cases in which the experience may have been subjective. According to a story told by Count de la Resie in the *Gazette de France* of 1855, Urham's *chef d'oeuvre Audition* was supernormally produced. In a narrow glade in the Bois de Boulogne, he heard a sound in the air. Urham beheld a light without form and precision and heard an air and the accompaniment with the accords of an Æolian harp. He fell into a kind of ecstasy and distinctly heard a voice which said to him: "Dear Urham, write down what I have sung." He hurried home and noted down the air with the greatest facility.

In the famous **Versailles Adventure** of C. A. E. Moberley and E. J. Jourdain, two English ladies were apparently transported to the Trianon of 1789, during which experience they heard period music, which has since been transcribed.

On a more hearsay level, folklore abounds with stories of mortals who heard the enchanting music of fairies.

Music Through Mediums Without Instruments

As a mediumistic manifestation of the production of music without instruments is rare, the apparent telekinetic playing of instruments fairly frequent. The sitters of D. D. **Home** and the Rev. Stainton **Moses** were often delighted by music from an invisible source.

D. D. Home wrote in *Incidents In My Life* (1863): "On going to Boston my power returned, and with it the most impressive manifestation of music without any earthly instrument. At night, when I was asleep my room would be filled as it were with sounds of harmony, and these gradually grew louder till persons in other parts of the house could hear them distinctly; if by any chance I was awakened, the music would instantly cease."

In the second volume of his biography, Home quoted the following well-attested experience at Easter Eve 1866, in the home of S. C.Hall: "First we had simple, sweet, soft music for some minutes; then it became intensely sad; then the tramp, tramp as of a body of men marching mingled with the music, and I exclaimed 'The March to Calvary.' Then three times the tap-tapping sound of a hammer on a nail (like two metals meeting). A crash, and a burst of wailing which seemed to fill the room, followed; then there came a burst of glorious triumphal music, more grand than any of us had ever listened to, and we exclaimed 'The Resurrection.' It thrilled all our hearts."

To Lord Adare, who published *Experiences in Spiritualism with Mr. D. D. Home* (1870; 1924), we owe many interesting records of the same phenomenon. "We had not been in bed more than three minutes," he wrote of an experience in Norwood, London, "when both Home and myself simultaneously heard the music: it sounded like a harmonium; sometimes, as if played loudly at a great distance, at other times as if very gently, close by."

On another occasion "the music became louder and louder, until I distinctly heard the words: 'Hallelujah! Praise the Lord God Almighty!' It was no imagination on my part." The music was the same as at Norwood.

The aerial musical sounds sometimes resembled drops of water. According to Home, they were produced by the same method as **raps.**

Dr. James H. Gully, in whose house at Malvern, Home was a guest, wrote: "Ears never listened to anything more sweet and solemn than these voices and instruments; we heard organ, harp and trumpet, also two voices." (*Spiritualist,* vol. 3, p. 124)

In the presence of the Rev. Stainton **Moses,** "drum, harp, fairy bells, trupmet, lyre, tambourine and flapping of wings" were heard (*Proceedings* of the Society for Psychical Research, vol. 11, p. 54). No such instruments were in the room. They were also heard in the open. Mrs. Speer stated (*Light,* January 28, 1893): "September 19, before meeting this evening we heard the fairy bells playing in different parts of the garden, where we were walking; at times they sounded far off seemingly playing at the top of some high elm trees, music and stars mingling together, then they would approach nearer to us, evidently following us into the seance room which opened on to the lawn. After we were seated the music still lingered with us, playing in the corner of the room and over the table, round which we were seated. They played scales and chords by request, with the greatest rapidity and copied notes Dr. Speer made with his voice. After Moses was in trance the music became louder and sounded like brilliant playing on the piano! There was no instrument in the room."

There were similar observations, previous to D. D. Home and Moses, in the case of Mary **Jobson,** a psychic invasion taking place during a spell of mysterious illness. There are experiences in Dorothy Kerin's *The Living Touch* (1919), and there are modern cases on record as well.

Taps "as on a bell so pure as to bear no vibration, in the most exquisite tones, quite beyond description" were produced by "Walter" in the "Margery" seances (see **Crandon)** without any visible instrument. Notes were struck on a "psychic piano," the English Call to Arms was rendered on a "psychic bugle," sounding at a distance and in an open space, the British Reveille was played, an invisible mouth organ and the striking of a "celestial clock" were heard, the latter's character different from any clock known to be in the house or in the neighborhood. (See J. Malcolm Bird, *"Margery" the Medium,* 1925)

Music Telekinetically Produced

According to E. W. Capron in *Modern Spiritualism; Its Facts and Fanaticisms* (1885), "Mrs. Tamlin was, so far as I have been able to learn, the first medium through whom the guitar or other musical instrument was played, without visible contact, so as to give recognisable tunes. In her presence it was played with all the exactness of an experienced musician, although she is not acquainted with music, or herself able to play on any instrument. The tones varied from loud and vigorous to the most refined touches of the strings that could be imagined."

The playing of a locked piano in a seance with James Sangster was reported in the *Age of Progress* (March, 1857).

In the presence of Annie and Jennie **Lord,** of Maine, both unable to play upon any instrument, a double bass violincello, guitar, drums, accordion, tambourine, bells and various small instruments were played "with the most astonishing skill and power" wrote Emma Hardinge in *Modern American Spiritualism* (1870; 1970), "sometimes singly, at others all together, and not unfrequently the strange concert would conclude by placing the young medium, seated in her invalid chair, silently and in a single instant in the centre of the table, piling up all the instruments around her."

In D. D. Homes's mediumship, musical feats of **telekinesis** were particularly well attested. Sir William **Crookes** witnessed it under fraud-proof conditions. The quality of the music was mostly fine. William **Howitt** had an experience to the contrary. He is quoted in a letter in D. D. Home's *Incidents In My Life* (1863): "A few evenings afterwards, a lady desiring that the "Last Rose of Summer" might be played by a spirit on the accordion, the wish was complied with, but in so wretched a style that the company begged that it might be discontinued. This was done, but soon after, evidently by another spirit, the accordion was carried and suspended over the lady's head, and there, without any visible support or action on the instrument, the air was played through most admirably, in the view and hearing of all."

Lord Adare noted this peculiarity: "The last few notes were drawn out so fine as to be scarcely audible—the last note dying away so gradually that I could not tell when it ceased. I do not think it possible for any human hand to produce a note in that way."

At another time: "Then there were sounds like echoes, so fine as to be scarcely audible."

Robert Bell wrote in the *Cornhill Magazine* (August, 1860), under the title *Stranger than Fiction:* "The air was wild and full of strange transitions, with a wail of the most pathetic sweetness running through it. The execution was no less remarkable, for its delicacy than its powers. When the notes swelled in some of the bold passages, the sound rolled through the room with an astounding reverberation; then gently subsiding, sank into a strain of divine tenderness."

The experience was the same when Bell held the accordion in his own hand, with full light upon it; during the loud and vehement passages it became so difficult to hold, in consequence of the extraordinary power with which it was played from below, that he was obliged to grasp the top with both hands."

In a letter to the *Morning Star* (October 1860), Dr. Gully stated: "I have heard Blagrove repeated; but it is no libel on that master of the instrument to say that he never did produce such exquisite distant and echo notes as those which delighted our ears."

Alfred Russel **Wallace** wrote in his own book *My Life* (1902) of his first seance in the company of Sir William **Crookes** with D. D. Home: "As I was the only one of the company who had not witnessed any of the remarkable phenomena that occurred in his presence, I was invited to go under the table while an accordion was playing, held in Home's hand, his other hand being on the table. The room was well lighted and I distinctly saw Home's hand holding the instrument which moved up and down and played a tune without any visible cause. He then said "Now I will take away my hand," which he did; but the instrument went on playing, and I saw a detached hand holding it while Home's two hands were seen above the table by all present."

There were other mediums who apparently performed similar feats of telekinetic music, Henry **Slade** and the Rev. F. W. **Monck** amongst them. Of Eusapia **Palladino,** Hereward **Carrington** wrote, in *The Story of Psychic Science* (1930):

"One of the most remarkable manifestations, however, was the playing of the mandolin, on at least two occasions. The instrument sounded in the cabinet first of all—distinct twangings of the strings being heard, in response to pickings of Eusapia's fingers on the hand of one of her controllers. The mandolin then floated out of the cabinet, on to the seance table, *where, in full view of all, nothing touching it, it continued to play for nearly a minute*—first one string and then another being played upon. Eusapia was at the time in deep trance, and was found to be cataleptic a few moments later. Her hands were gripping the hands of her controllers so tightly that each finger had to be opened in turn, by the aid of passes and suggestion."

H. Dennis **Bradley** wrote in . . . *And After* (1931) "I have had instruments of an orchestra placed in the centre of my own study, with luminous paint covering them so that every movement could be seen instantly, and these instruments have been played by unseen forces in perfect harmony. Whilst operatic selections were being played upon the gramophone, they have been supernormally conducted with a luminous baton in a majestic manner."

Musicians Who Were Mediums

There were also musical mediums who achieved fame, although often without proper musical training or unable to play in a conscious state. Amongst these, Jesse F. G **Shepard** was the most astonishing.

Well-known classical composers were said to play through George **Aubert,** a non-professional medium who was investigated at the Institut Geñéral Psychologique in Paris.

At the International Psychical Congress in 1900, Professor Charles **Richet** introduced Pepito **Ariola,** a three-and-a-half-years-old Spanish child, who played classical pieces.

Blind Tom, a Negro child of South Georgia, almost an idiot, played the piano impressively with both hands, using the black and the white keys, when four years of age. When five years old, he composed his *Rainstorm* and said it was what the rain, wind and thunder had said to him. He could play two tunes on the piano at the same time, one with each hand, while he sang a song in a different air. Each tune was set to a different key as dictated by the audience.

In 1903, the famous palmist "Cheiro" (Count Louis **Hamon)** introduced to London M. de Boyon, a French musical medium to whose extraordinary gift Victorien **Sardou,** M. Massenet, M. Emile Waldteufel, M. Felicien Champsaur and actress Mme. Sarah Bernhardt testified. M. de Boyon had no memory of what he played. He employed a unique fingering and he could not play the same piece twice.

The most remarkable musical medium of recent times is Rosemary **Brown,** a British housewife who performs musical compositions on the piano, claimed to originate from such dead composers as Beethoven, Mozart, Liszt and Chopin. Miss Brown has not had proper musical training, but these psychic compositions have been endorsed by established musicians.

Paranormal Aspects of Music

Because of its powerful influence directly on emotions, music often achieves remarkable effects on the human organism and even on animals. Music therapy is now a recognized treatment for mentally handicapped children.

Ancient legends tell of the paranormal effects of music. Orpheus of ancient Greece charmed wild animals and even trees by his music, and the modal system of the Greeks was said to influence powerfully the social and emotional attitudes of listeners. Naik Gopal, a musician of ancient India, was said to have caused flames to burst forth by his performance of *Dipak Raga* (associated with heat), even when the musician stood in water.

The musical system of India has always emphasized the powerful effects of musical vibration. Different *ragas* (scale patterns) are regarded as specific for certain times of the day or seasons of the year, and their microtonal intervals and grace notes involve vibrations which are unknown to the well-tempered scale of Western nations. *Ragas,* properly performed, are said to evoke beautiful forms or have paranormal effects.

In Hinduism, the first manifestation of creation was said to be that of subtle sound vibration, giving rise to the forms of the material world. Each sound produced a form, and combinations of sound created complicated shapes. This is also the basis of Mantra Yoga, from which developed the system of Western magical spells. The creative power of sound is also echoed in the Judeo-Christian scripture in the formulation "In the beginning was the Word, and the Word was with God, and the Word was God."

Legendary traditions may have some basis in fact. The great Indian scientist Sir Jagadis Chunder **Bose** devised sensitive apparatus to demonstrate subtle plant reactions, many of which resembled nervous responses in animal or human life. Prof. T. C. N. Singh and Miss Stells Ponniah of Annamalai University, India, showed by their experiments that musical sounds excite growth in plants (see **Plants, Psychic Aspects).** Western scientists have demonstrated that ultrasonic sounds beyond human hearing can destroy bacteria, guide ships in the dark and weld together materials.

In recent years, the Hindu musician Swami **Nadabrahmananda Saraswati** has demonstrated an ancient **yoga** of music, involving the arousal of **Kundalini** energy through the psychic power of music vibrations. In a Western context, psychic aspects of music were claimed by the singing teacher Alfred **Wolfsohn.**

In contrast, the aggressiveness and violence of much of modern popular rock music seems to have had a negative and sinister influence on a younger generation, recalling the fears of the ancient Greeks that certain musical modes would have a harmful social effect. It will be remembered that rock music was associated with diabolical themes by Charles **Manson,** culminating in sex orgies, crime and brutal murders. Other rock music has been associated with drug addiction and violence in an overall decadence. (See also Pepito **Ariola;** Rosemary **Brown;** Charles **Manson; Mantra; Nada; Plants; Rock Music;** Jesse F. G. **Shepard; Vibrations)**

Recommended reading

Brown, Rosemary. *Immortals At My Elbow,* Bachman & Turner, London, 1974 (U.S. title *Immortals By My Side,* Henry Regnery, Chicago, 1975)

Crookes, William. *Researches in the Phenomena of Spiritualism,* J. Burns, London, 1974 etc. (frequently reprinted)

Danielou, Alain. *The Ragas of Northern Indian Music,* Barrie & Rockliff, London, 1968

Gurney, Edmund. *The Power of Sound,* Smith, Elder, London, 1880; Basic Books, New York, 1966

Parrott, Ian. *The Music of 'An Adventure'* (paperback), Regency Press, London, 1966

Podolsky, Edward. *Music Therapy,* Philosophical Library, New York, 1954

Rogo, D. Scott. *Nad; A Study of Some Unusual "Other-World" Experiences,* 2 vols., University Books, 1970-72

Scott, Cyril. *Music; Its Secret Influence Throughout the Ages,* 6th enlarged edition, Rider & Co., London, 1956

Sivananda, Swami. *Music As Yoga,* Yoga-Vedanta Forest University, Sivananda Nagar, India, 1956

Musso, J(uan) Ricardo (1917-)

Business consultant, author, editor, professor of parapsychology. Born June 9, 1917 at Buenos Aires, Argentina, he studied at the School of Economic Sciences, Buenos Aires University (Doctor of Economic Sciences 1944). In 1940 he married Elvira Germana Canales. He was professor of parapsychology and psychostatistics at the School of Philosophy, Letters and Educational Sciences, National Littoral University, Rosario Argentina from 1959 onwards, lecturer on parapsychology at National University of the South, Bahia Blanca, Argentina in 1957 and Argentine Institute of Parapsychology, Buenos Aires from 1956-58.

He was president of the Argentine Institute of Parapsychology from 1956 onwards, and a member of the College of Economic Science Graduates, Society for Psychical Research, London, consultant to Parapsychology Foundation, director of Biblioteca de Parapsicología (Parapsychology Publications), director and editor of *Revista de Parapsicología* (Parapsychology Review).

He tested ESP by statistical methods and is author of *En los Límites de la Psicología; Desde el Espiritismo hasta la Parapsicología* (On the Frontiers of Psychology: From Spiritualism to Parapsychology, 1954) and various pamphlets on parapsychology issued by the Argentine Institute of Parapsychology.

His articles in *Revista de Parapsicología* include: 'Las Etapas del Proceso de ESP' (The Stages of the ESP Process, No. 3, 1955), 'La Posesion Espirita: Cuestión Cerrada?' (Spirit Possession: A Closed Question?, No. 4, 1955), 'Insulto pero Opertunidad: Replica a Price' (Insult but Opportunity: A Reply to Price, Nos. 1 & 2, 1956), 'Experimentos con Mediums de Trance' (Experiments with Trance Mediums, No. 3, 1956), and in the *International Review of Parapsychology:* 'Il Movimiento Parapsicologico in Argentina' (The Parapsychology Movement in Argentina, 1956), in *Revista de Educación* (Argentine Ministry of Education): 'La Percepcion Extrasensorial' (Extra-sensory Perception, Jan. 1957), in *Journal of Parapsychology* (with M. Granero) 'An ESP Drawing Experiment with a High-Scoring Subject' (vol. 37, 1973).

In 1971, he attended the Twentieth International Conference of the Parapsychology Foundation, held at Le Piol, St. Paul de Vence, France.

Myers, A(rthur) T(homas) (1851-1894)

Brother of F. W. H. **Myers** and a founding member of the Society for Psychical Research, London, serving on the Society's Council from 1888 91. He used his medical knowledge to investigate cases of alleged paranormal healing and also made a special study of hypnotism.

He was largely responsible for forming the Edmund Gurney Library of books and pamphlets on hypnotism and related subjects. He also participated in the experiments of the French neurologist Pierre Janet in telepathic hypnotism, as well as some of the SPR sittings with the American medium Mrs. Leonore **Piper.**

In addition to his contributions to medical journals and notes in the SPR *Journal*, he also published the following articles in the SPR *Proceedings:* 'Report on a Alleged Physical Phenomenon' (vol. 3, part 9, 1885), 'Mind-Cure, Faith-Cure, and the Miracles of Lourdes' (with F. W. S. Myers, vol 9, part 24, 1893). He died in London, England, January 10, 1894.

Myers, Frederic William Henry (1843-1901)

A leading mind in psychical research, founder of a cosmic philosophy which may yet revolutionize scientific thought, a profound scholar, a poet of distinction and a brilliant psychologist.

He was born February 6, 1843, at Keswick, Cumberland, England, educated at Trinity College, Cambridge. In 1880 he married Eveleen Tennant.

For thirty years he filled the post of an inspector of schools at Cambridge. Here his resolve to pursue psychical investigation was born in 1869 after a starlight walk and talk with Prof. Henry **Sidgwick.**

His starting point was that if a spiritual world ever manifested to man, it must manifest now, and that, in consequence, a serious investigation must end by discovering some unmistakable signs of it. For "if all attempts to verify scientifically the intervention of another world should be definitely proved futile, this would be a terrible blow, a mortal blow, to all our hopes of another life, as well as of traditional religion" for "it would thenceforth be very difficult for men to be persuaded, in our age of clear thinking, that what is now found to be illusion and trickery was in the past thought to be truth and revelation."

He had in mind the same methods of deliberate, dispassionate and exact inquiry which built up our actual knowledge of the visible world. It was in this spirit that the Society for Psychical Research, London, of which he was a fellow-founder came to be established in 1882. He devoted all his energies to its work and concentrated with a deep grasp of science on the psychological side.

Of the sixteen volumes of the Society's *Proceedings* published while he lived, there are few without an important contribution from his pen.

In *Phantasms of the Living*, a collaboration with Edmund **Gurney** and Frank **Podmore,** the system of classification was entirely his idea. The words "telepathy," "supernormal," "veridical" and many others less in use were coined by him. He played a large part in organizing the International Congress of Psychology and acted as secretary to the one held in London in 1892.

In the Society for Psychical Research he filled the post of honorary secretary. In 1900, he was elected to the presidential chair, a post which only distinguished scientists had previously filled.

To periodicals such as the *Fortnightly Review, the Nineteenth Century,* he contributed many articles. They were collected and published, in 1893, under the title *Science and a Future, Life,* and *Other Essays.*

His chief work, *Human Personality and its Survival of Bodily Death,* was posthumously published in 1903. The University of Madras adopted it as a textbook for its courses on lectures on psychology at the faculty of philosophy and letters. It is an exposition of the potential powers of the subliminal self, which he pictured as the real ego, a vast psychic organism of which the ordinary consciousness is but an accidental fraction, the life of the soul, not bound up with the life of the body, of which the so-called supernormal faculties are the ordinary channels of perception.

It is a theory of tremendous implications. It challenged the Spiritualist position that all, or most, of the supernormal phenomena were due to the spirits of the dead. Myers contended that by far the largest proportion was due to the action of the still embodied spirit of the agent or of the percipient himself.

The theory brought order into a chaotic mass of psychical phenomena. On the other hand, it greatly enhanced the probability of **survival** after death. As the powers which he claimed for the subliminal self did not degenerate during the course of evolution and served no purpose in this life they were obviously destined for a future existence. Why, for instance, should the subconscious so carefully preserve all thoughts and memories if there will be no use for them?

Professor William **James** suggested that the problems of the subliminal mind should be called "the problem of Myers." "Whatever the judgment of the future may be on Mr. Myers' speculation," he stated, "the credit will always remain to them of being the first attempt in any language to consider the phenomena of hallucination, automatism, double personality, and mediumship as connected parts of one whole subject."

"If future discoveries confirm his thesis of the intervention of the discarnate, in the web and the woof of our mental and physical world," wrote Prof. Theodor **Flournoy,** "then his name will be inscribed in the golden book of the initiated, and, joined to those of Copernicus and Darwin, he will complete the triad of geniuses who have the most profoundly revoluntionised scienfific thought, in the order, Cosmological, Biological and Psychological."

The same author, a profound psychologist himself, considered Myers "one of the most remarkable personalities of our time in the realm of mental science." Dr. Leaf compared him to Ruskin and considered him in some respects his peer. According to Prof. Charles **Richet** "if Myers were not a mystic, he had all the faith of a mystic and the ardour of an apostle, in conjunction with the sagacity and precision of a *savant*".

"I never knew a man so hopeful concerning his ultimate destiny," wrote Sir Oliver Lodge in memoriam. "He once asked me whether I would barter—if it were possible—my unknown destiny, whatever it might be, for as many aeons of unmitigated and wise terrestrial happiness as might last till the secular fading of the sun, and then an end. He would not."

Myers was so convinced of survival that his friends often heard him say: "I am counting the days until the holidays."

In *Human Personality and Its Survival of Bodily Death,* physical phenomena received but little consideration. Myers believed in the occurrence of telekinetic phenomena (see **Telekinesis),** but in spite of the experiments of Sir William **Crookes** and his own, their genuine occurrence, from the viewpoint of the public, did not appear to him sufficiently believable to justify their discussion in his book. Nevertheless, in dealing with **possession** he suggested an ingenious explanation, i.e., that the possessing spirit may use the organism more skillfully than its owner and may emit some energy which can visibly move ponderable objects not actually in contact with the flesh. Of his own investigations between 1872-76 he said that they were "tiresome and distasteful enough."

On May 9, 1874, in the company of Edmund Gurney, he made the acquaintance of the Rev. Stainton **Moses.** The acquaintance led to friendship. When Stainton Moses died on September 5, 1982, his notebooks were handed to Myers for study.

His articles in *Proceedings* of the Society for Psychical Research (vols. 9 & 11) contained the best accounts of this remarkable mediumship, but his conclusions were not only based on personal experiences with Moses. When he had some startling ones with Miss C. E. **Wood** and Miss Annie Fairlamb (Mrs. J. B. **Mellon)** in 1878 he kept strangely silent. Alfred Russel **Wallace** saw his notes on the seances held under the auspices of the Society for Psychical Research with the two mediums at Cambridge in Prof. Henry **Sidgwick's** rooms. The notes stated that the wrists of the mediums were securely tied with tapes and the ends were tacked down to the floor and sealed. Many **materialization** forms came out of the cabinet, both adults and children. The seals were found untampered. The color of the tape and sealing wax was varied at each seance, the medium put into a hammock which was connected with pulleys to a weighing machine; nevertheless the phenomena occurred as before without the least suspicious cause.

In 1894, on the Ile Roubaud, he was the guest of Professor Richet and participated with Professor Lodge and Dr. Julien **Ochorowitz** in the experiments conducted with Eusapia **Palladino.** He could not refrain from expressing an opinion and admitted that the phenomena were genuine. The Cambridge exposure shook his belief and he then wrote: "I had no doubt that systematic trickery had been used from the first to last, and that there was no adequate ground for attributing any of the phenomena occurring at these sittings to a supernormal cause."

Later, however, he participated in another series of sittings with **Palladino** in Paris and at the solemn adjuration of Prof. Richet he declared himself convinced that both **telekinesis** and **ectoplasm** were genuine phenomena. He also sat with Mr. Thomas **Everitt,** Mme. **d'Esperance,** and David **Duguid.**

He had the stange experience of seeing objective pictures in a crystal ball (see **crystal gazing)** and he investigated the haunted Ballechin House in Perthshire, Scotland. As a result, he published two papers in *Proceedings of the* S.P.R. 'On Alleged Movements of Objects without Contact, occurring not in the Presence of a Paid Medium' (vol 7, pts. 19, 20, 1891-92).

Still, he was not enthusiastic for physical phenomena. It was owing to his discouragement that Mrs. R. **Thompson** ceased to sit for physical demonstrations and developed chiefly as a trance medium for the S.P.R. Myers had his reward. A communication received through Mrs. Thompson finally confirmed his belief in survival. Before the International Psychological Congress in 1900 he read a paper on his experiences.

Attention to some remarkable omissions in Myers' great work was called by James Robertson in an address printed in *Light* (May 30, 1903). He objected that Andrew Jackson **Davis** was passed by with only a single remark and stated that "a clear, unbiased examination of the life and writings of this extraordinary man would have given him more than all he has gathered together in these long drawn out statements as to disintegration of personality, hypnotism, trance, possession, etc."

Myers died January 17, 1901 in Rome, Italy, After his death, a flood of claimed communications from his spirit came from many mediums. The most important ones were those received through Mrs. **Piper,** Mrs. **Verrall** and Mrs. Holland (Alice K. **Fleming).** As regards the latter, Frank **Podmore** and Miss Alice **Johnson** agreed that the "Myers" **control** was a subconscious creation of the medium. The views there expressed were alien to the mentality of the living Myers.

Mrs. Verrall apparently obtained the contents of a sealed letter which Myers had written in 1891 and left in the care of Sir Oliver **Lodge** for such a test. However, when the letter was opened in 1904 the contents were found to be entirely different.

In 1907, Mrs. **Sidgwick** obtained good identity proofs through Mrs. Piper. On her behalf, Mrs. Verrall asked some questions to which she did not know that answer and received correct replies as regards the contents of the last conversation that had taken place between Mrs. Sidgwick and Myers.

Many other impressive indications of his surviving self were found in **cross-correspondences,** especially during Mrs. Piper's second visit to England in 1906-07. The whole system of cross-correspondences appears to have been elaborated by him and the wealth of classical knowledge displayed in the connected fragments given by several mediums, raises a strong presumption that they emanated from Myers' mind.

The most striking evidence of this nature was obtained after Mrs. Piper's return to America by Mr. G. B. Dorr in 1908. Frank Podmore considered it "perhaps the strongest evidence yet obtained for the identity of any communicator."

In *The Road to Immortality* (1932) which was automatically produced by Miss Geraldine **Cummins,** a stupendous vista was apparently opened up by F. W. H. Myers of the soul's progression through the after-death states. As regards the authorship of the book, Sir Oliver Lodge received independent testimony through Mrs. Leonard from "Myers" of his communications through Miss Cummins. Sir Oliver Lodge saw no reason to dissent from the view that the remarkable accounts of the fourth, fifth, sixth and seventh state "are the kind of ideas which F. W. H. Myers may by this time [1932] have been able to form."

Myers, John

Prominent British medium who demonstrated psychic healing and spirit photography. Originally a London dentist, he visited a psychical research society in 1931 and was given a psychic warning about his automobile by a medium. The warning disclosed a defect.

Becoming interested in psychic phenomena, Myers visited the Stead Bureau (see **Julia's Bureau**) founded by W. T. **Stead.** He met the medium Mrs. A. E. **Deane,** who practiced **psychic photography** and tried the phenomena for himself, with successful results. He also discovered a mediumistic talent.

In his seances, he would enter into semi-trance while standing, being controlled by "Blackfoot," a Red Indian. From clairvoyant impressions, he would describe the presence of spirit forms and, quite frequently, the extra which would appear on a photographic plate.

He was challenged by the Marquess of Donegall. In the presence of the art editor of the *Sunday Dispatch,* journalist Hannen **Swaffer** and stage magician Will Goldston, Lord Donegall filled Myers' camera, which he examined, with his own marked plates, took six pictures in bright light while Myers simply stood by, and developed them himself.

Two of the plates showed extras which neither Lord Donegall nor the art editor could explain *(Sunday Dispatch,* October 9, 1932). The following week, however, as a result of a further sitting, Lord Donegall accused Myers of substitution of plates and claimed gross trickery. The accusation left part of his previous admissions unaffected.

In the 1930s, Myers was consulted by Laurence Parish, a New York businessman, who was greatly impressed by the psychic photography demonstrated by Myers. Myers was also instrumental in the psychic healing of Parish's sciatica and restoring normal eyesight after years of defective vision. After these miraculous cures, Parish invited Myers to join his company in New York. Myers accepted and eventually became vice-president of the company.

His life story is told in the book *He Walks in Two Worlds; The Story of John Myers, Psychic Photographer, Healer and Philanthropist* by Maurice Barbanell (London, 1964)

Myomancy

A method of divination by rats or mice, supposed to be alluded to in the *Bible (Isaiah* lxvi., 17). Their peculiar cries, or some marked devastation committed by them, was taken for a prognostic of evil. Æilan related that Fabius Maximus resigned the dictatorship in consequence of a warning from these creatures, and Cassius Flaminius (according to Varro) retired from the command of the cavalry for no greater reason.

Herodotus stated that the army of Sennacherib when he invaded Egypt was infested by mice in the night, and their quivers and bows gnawed in pieces; in the morning, therefore, being without arms, they fled in confusion, and many of them were slain.

Such a foreboding of evil could not very well be questioned, or its consequences averted, by the commander, but very different was the case when one of Cato's soldiers told him in fright that the rats had gnawed one of his shoes. Cato replied that the prodigy would have been much greater if the shoe had gnawed a rat!

Horapollo, in his curious work on the Hieroglyphics of Egypt, described the rat as a symbol of destruction, and that the Hebrew name of this animal is from a root which signifies to separate, divide, or judge. It has been remarked by one of the commentators on Horapollo that the mouse has a finely discriminating taste.

An Egyptian MS. in the Bibliothèque Royale at Paris contains the representation of a soul going to judgment, in which one of the figures is depicted with the head of a rat and the well-known wig. It is understood that the Libian rats and the mouse of Scripture are the same as the Arabian *jerboa,* which is characterized by a long tail, bushy at the end, and short fore-legs.

The mice and emerods of gold (I. *Samuel* v., 6, 7) were essentially charms having a precise symbolic meaning.

Mysteria Mystica Aeterna

A lodge of the occult society O.T.O. (Ordo Templi Orientis) licensed to Rudolf **Steiner** (1861-1925) in 1906, some years before fully developing his own interpretations of mysticism, culminating in his concept of Anthroposophy ('man-wisdom'). See also **Anthroposophical Society; Mysteria Mystica Maxima; O.T.O.**

Mysteria Mystica Maxima

Name given to the British lodge of the occult society **O.T.O.** (Ordo Templi Orientis) when Theodor **Reuss,** head of the German order, proposed that Aleister **Crowley** should start a British section. (See also **Mysteria Mystica Aeterna; O.T.O.**)

Mysteries

From the Greek word *muein,* to shut the mouth, and *mustes* an initiate: a term for what is secret or concealed in a religious context. Although certain mysteries were probably part of the initiatory ceremony of the priests of ancient Egypt, we are ignorant of their exact nature, and the term is usually used in connection with certain semi-religious cermonies held by various cults in ancient Greece.

The mysteries were secret cults, to which only certain initiated people were admitted after a period of preliminary preparation. After this initial period of purification came the mystic communication or exhortation, then the revelation to the neophyte of certain holy things, the crowning with the garlands, and lastly the communion with the deity. But the mysteries appear to have circled round the semi-dramatic representation or mystery-play of the life of a deity.

It has often been advanced as a likely theory to account for the prevalence of these mystic cults in Greece, that they were of pre-Hellenic origin, and that the Pelasgic aboriginal people of the country strove to conceal their religions from the eyes of their conquerors. But against this has to be weighed the evidence that for the most part the higher offices of these cults were in the hands of aristocrats, who, it may be reasonably inferred, had but little to do with the inferior strata of the population which represented the Pelasgic peoples.

Again, the divinities worshiped in the mysteries possess for the most part Greek names and many of them are certainly gods evolved upon Hellenic soil at a comparatively late period. We find a number of them associated with the realm of the dead. The earth-god or goddess is in most countries often allied with the powers of darkness. It is from the underworld that grain arises, and therefore it is not surprising to find that Demeter, Ge, and Aglauros, are identified with the underworld. But there were also the mysteries of Artemis, of Hecate, and the Cherites,—some of which may be regarded as forms of the great earth-mother.

The worships of Dionysus, Trophonious, and Zagreus were also of a mysterious nature. The Eleusinian and Orphic mysteries are undoubtedly those of most importance to the occult student, and from the results of archaeology (such as vase-painting) it is possible to glean some general idea of the trend of these. That is not to say that the heart of the mystery is revealed by any such illustrations, but that these supplemented by what the Christian fathers were able to glean regarding these mystic cults, giving useful hints for further investigations.

Eleusis

The mysteries of Eleusis had for their primal adoration Demeter, Kore or Persephone (the mother and the daughter) whose myth is too well-known to require repetition here. Pluto, the third figure in the drama, is so unimportant as to be relegated to the background.

Other "nameless" divinities appear to have been associated with these, under the name of "the gods" and "the goddesses," but the theory that those are supposed to descend from an aboriginal period, when gods were nameless, seems absurd. The nameless god seems of little value and mythological science surely suggests that such nameless gods are merely those whose higher names are hidden and unspoken.

In Egypt, for example, the concept of the Concealed Name was extremely common. The "name of power" of a god, if discovered, bestowed on the discoverer sway over that deity, and we must therefore dismiss the idea of the nameless divinities of Eleusis as not in accordance with mythological fact. A more probable view is that which would make these gods later titles of the married pair Pluto and Kore, but this, in view of the facts just stated, is also unlikely.

Dionysus is also a figure of some importance in the Eleusinian mystery, and it has been thought that Orphic influence brought about his presence in the cult, but traces of Orphic doctrine have not been discovered in what is known of the mysteries.

A more baffling personality in the great ritual drama is that of Iacchus, who appears to be none other than Dionysus under another name. But Dionysus (or Iacchus) does not appear to be a primary figure of the mystery.

In early Greek legends there are allusions to the sacred character of the Eleusinian mysteries. From the fifth century, their organization was in the hands of the Arthenian city, the royal ruler of which undertook the general management, along with a committee of supervision. The rites took place at the city of Eleusis, and were celebratd by a hereditary priesthood, the Eumolpedie. They alone (or rather their high priest) could penetrate into the innermost holy of holies, but there were also priestesses and female attendants on the goddesses.

The celebration of the mysteries, so far as can be gleaned, was somewhat as follows: in the month of September, the Eleusinian Holy Things were taken from the sacred city to Athens and placed in the Eleusinion. These probably consisted to some extent of small statues of the goddesses. Three days afterwards, the catechumens assembled to hearken to the exhortation of one of the priests, in which those who were for any reason unworthy of initiation were solemnly warned to depart. All must be Greeks or Romans above a certain age, and women and even slaves were admitted, but foreigners and criminals might not partake.

The candidates were questioned as to their purification, and especially as regards the food which they had eaten during that period. After this assembly, they went to the sea-shore and bathed in the sea, being sprinkled afterwards with the blood of pigs. A sacrifice was offered up, and several days afterwards the Eleusinian procession commenced its journey along the sacred way, its central figure being a statue of Iacchus. Many shrines were visited on the way to Eleusis, where, upon their arrival, they celebrated a midnight orgy.

It is difficult to know what occurred in the inner circle, but there appear to have been two grades in the celebration, and we know that a year elapsed before a person who had achieved one grade became fit for election to the higher. Regarding the actual ritual in the hall of mystery, a great deal of controversy has taken place, but it is certain that a dramatic representation was the central point of interest, the chief characters in which were probably Demeter and Kore, and that the myth of the lost daughter and the sorrowing mother was enacted before a highly-impressed audience. It has been stated that the birth of Iacchus was announced during the ceremony, but this has not been handed down on good authority. Of scenic display, there was probably little or none, as excavation has proved that there was not room for it, and we find nothing regarding scenery in the accounts presented in many inscriptions; but the apparel of the actors was probably most magnificent, heightened by the Rembrandtesque effect of gloom and torchlight.

But certain sacred symbols were also displayed before the eyes of the elect. These appear to have been small idols of the goddesses, of great antiquity and sanctity. We know that the original symbols of deity are jealously guarded by many primitive priesthoods. For example, the Uapes of Brazil kept careful watch over the symbols of Jurupari, their god, and these were shown only to the initiated. Any woman who cast eyes on them was instantly poisoned.

It was also stated by Hippolytus that the ancients were shown a cut corn stalk, the symbol of Demeter and Kore. This, however, can hardly be trusted any more than the theory that the Eleusinians worshiped the actual corn as a clan totem. Corn as a totem is not unknown elsewhere, as for example in Peru, where the *cconopa* or godlings of the maize fields were probably originally totemic, and we know that amongst primitive people totemism often caried in its train the concept of the full-fledged mystery.

But if the Eleusinian corn was a totem, it was certainly the only corn totem known to Greece, and corn totems are rare. The totem was usually initiated with the hunting condition of peoples. When they arrived at the agricultural stage we generally find that a fresh pantheon has slowly evolved, in which full-fledged gods took the place of the old totemic deities. The corn appears as a living thing. It is growth, and within it resides a spirit. Therefore the deity which is evolved from this concept is more likely to be of animistic than of totemistic origin.

The neophyte was then made one with the deity, by partaking of holy food or drink. It will be recalled that when Persephone reached the dark shores of Hades she partook of the food of the dead—thus rendering it impossible for her to return. Once the human soul eats or drinks in Hades, it may not return to earth. This belief is universal, and it is highly probable that it was symbolized in the Eleusinian mysteries.

There was nothing, however, particularly secret about this sacrament, as it is painted on many vases which have been brought to light. A great deal of the ritual undoubtedly partook of the character of agricultural magic, a type of sympathetic sorcery. Among primitives, the medicine-man sprinkles water over the soil to incite the rain spirit to do likewise. It is not long ago since, in the Isle of Mull, Scotland, a long carved stone in a certain churchyard was filled with water, until the depressions upon it overflowed, to symbolize a well-watered country. All sorts of imitative rites took place on similar occasions, most of which will be familiar to students of folklore.

It has been thought that the token of the growing corn may have served as an emblem of human resurrection, and the fact that most persons approached the Eleusinian mysteries for the purpose of ensuring themselves a happy immortality would go far to prove this.

M. Foucart ingeniously put forward the theory that the object of the Eleusinian mysteries was much the same as that of the Egyptian *Book of the Dead,* i.e., to provide the initiates with elaborate rules for avoiding the dangers of the underworld, and to instruct them in the necessary magical formulae. But it does not appear that any such purpose was attained in the mysteries, and we know of no magic formulae recited in connection with them. Friendship with the Holy Mother and Daughter was, to the Eleusinian votary, the chief assurance of immortality.

A great many offshoots of the Eleusinian cult were established in several parts of Greece:

Dionysiac

The most important cult next to the Eleusinian was the Orphic, which probably arose in Phrygia, and which came to be associated with the name of Dionysus, originally a god of vegetation, who was of course also a divinity of the nether world. In this case, it was also desired to enter into communion with him so that immortality might be assured. His celebrations were marked by orgies of a bacchic description, in which it was thought that the neophyte partook for the moment of the character and the power of the deity himself.

The rites of the cult of Dionysus were on a much lower grade than those of Eleusis, and partook more of the barbarian element, and the devouring of an animal victim was supposed to symbolize the incarnation, death and resurrection of the divinity. Later the Dionysiac mysteries became purified, but always retained something of their earlier hysteric character. The cult possessed a fairly wide propaganda, and does not appear to have been regarded by the sages of its time with great friendliness.

The golden tablets relating to the Orphic mystery found in tombs in Greece, Crete and Italy, contain fragments of a sacred hymn. As early as the third century B.C. it was buried with the dead as an **amulet** to protect him from the dangers of the underworld, and the fragments bear upon them incantations of a magical character.

Attis and Cybele

These mysteries arrived at a later period on Hellenic soil. Passionate and violent in the extreme, they yet gained considerable sway in a more degenerate age, and communion with the deity was usually attained by bathing in blood in the *taurobolium* or by the letting of blood.

These Phrygian mysteries were full of the conception of the rebirth of the god Attis, who was also of an agrarian character; and in brief it may be said of these mystic cults as a whole that they were primarily barbarian agricultural rites to some extent intellectualized.

Mithraic Mysteries

The Mithraic cult was of Persian origin, Mithra, a personification of Light being worshiped in that country some five hundred years before the Christian era. Carried into Asia Minor by small colonies of **magi,** it was largely influenced by the religions with which it was brought into contact.

Chaldean **astrology** contributed much of the occult traditions surrounding the creed of the Sun-god, while to a certain extent it became hellenized when the **Magi** strove to bring the more barbaric portion of their dogma and its usages into harmony with the Hellenic ideal. To the art of Greece also it owed that ideal representation of Mithra Tauroctonous which formed the central object in the temples of the cult. The wide geographical area it traversed and the immense influence thus exercised was, however, due to the Romans.

According to Plutarch, the rites originally reached Rome, through the agency of Cilician privates conquered and taken there by Pompey. Another source, doubtless, was through the large number of Asiatic slaves employed in Roman households. Again the Roman soldiery must have carried the Mithraic cult to Rome as they certainly were the means of its diffusion, as far north as the mountains of Scotland, and southwards to the borders of the Sahara Desert.

Mithraism may be said to have been the only living religion which Christianity found a need to combat. It was strong enough to exert a formative influence on certain Christian doctrines, such as those relative to the end of the world and the powers of hell.

Mithra was essentially the divinity of beneficence. He was the genius of celestial light, endowing the earth with all its benefits. As in his character of the Sun he puts darkness to flight, so by a natural transition he came to represent ethically truth and integrity, the sun of goodness which conquers the night of evil. To him was ascribed the character of Mediator betwixt God and man. His creed promised a resurrection to a future life of happiness and felicity.

Briefly the story of Mithra is as follows. He owed his life to no mortal mother. Mithra sprang to being in the gloom of a cavern from the heart of a rock, seen by none but humble shepherds. He grew in strength and courage, excelling all, and used his powers to rid the world of evil.

Of all his deeds of prowess, however, the one which became the central motive of his cult was the slaying of a bull, itself possessed of divine potentialities, by which Mithra dowered the earth with fruitfulness and miraculous crops.

From the spinal cord of the bull sprang the wheat of man's daily bread, from its blood the vine, source of the sacred drink of the Mysteries, and from its seed all the different species of useful animals. After this beneficent deed, Mithra ruled in the heavens, yet still keeping watch and ward over human beings, granting the petitions asked in his name. Those who followed him, who were initiated into his mysteries, passed under his divine protection, especially after death when he would rescue their souls from the powers of darkness which sought to seize upon the dead. And yet again Mithra would come when the earth was failing in her life-sustaining powers, and again he would slay a divine bull and give to all abundant life and happiness.

The mysteries and rites inspired the votaries with awe while giving to their hearts hope of a future life, transcending that which they had known. The temples, mithræums as they were called, were either built underground or were caves and grottoes in the depths of dark forests, symbolizing the birthplace of their god.

Among his worshipers were slaves and soldiery, high officials and dignitaries, all mingling fraternally in a religion which called them Brethren.

The rites were of magical significance. In order to bring their lives into closer communion with the divinity of Mithra, the neophytes must pass through seven degrees of initiation successively assuming the names of Raven, Occult, Soldier, Lion, Persian, Runner of the Sun and Father.

Each of these grades carried with them symbolic garments and masks, donned by the celebrants. The masks represented birds and animals and would seem to indicate the existence of belief in the doctrine of metempsychosis, or perhaps they were a remnant of totemic belief. An almost ascetic habit of life was demanded, including prolonged fasting and purification.

The oath of silence regarding the rites was taken, and before entering the higher grades a ceremony called the Sacrament was held where consecrated bread and wine were partaken of. Dramatic trials of strength, faith and endurance were gone through by all, a stoical attitude and unflinching moral courage being demanded as sign of fitness in the participant.

The drinking of the sacred wine, and the baptism of blood were supposed to bring to the initiate not only material benefit but wisdom. They gave power to combat evil, the power to attain to an immortality such as that of their god. An order of priests was connected with this cult, which faithfully carried on the occult tradition and usages, such as that of initiation, the rites of which were arduous, the tending of a perpetual fire on the altars, prayers to the Sun at dawn, noon and evening. There were sacrifices and libations, musical rites including long psalmodics and mystic chants.

The days of the week were each sacred to a planet, the day of the Sun being held especially holy. There were seasonal festivals, the birth of the Sun being solemnized on the 25th of December, and the equinoxes were days of rejoicing, while the initiations were held preferably in the spring, in March or April.

It is believed that in the earliest days of the cult, some of the rites were of a savage and barbaric character, especially the sacrificial element, but these, as indicated, were changed and ennobled as the beneficence of Mithra took precedence over his warlike prowess.

The Mithraic brotherhoods took temporal interests as well as spiritual ones under their care and were in fact highly organized communities, including trustees, councils, senates, attorneys and patrons, people of high status and wealth. The fact of belonging to such a body gave to the initiate, be he of noble birth or but a slave, a sense of brotherhood and comradeship which was doubtless a powerful reason for the ascendancy with the Mithraic cult gained over the Roman army, whose members, dispersed to the ends of the earth in lonely solitudes amid wild and barbaric races, would find in this feeling of fraternity, this sharing in the worship and ritual of the Sun-god, an infinite comfort and solace.

Recommended reading

Angus, Samuel. *The Mystery Religions and Christianity,* John Murray, London 1928; Dover, 1975

Cumont, F. V. M. *Mysteries of Mithra,* Kegan Paul, London/Open Court, Chicago, 1910; Dover, n.d.

Harrison, Jane E. *Prolegmena to the Study of Greek Religion,* Cambridge University Press, U.K., 1922; Arno Press, 1976

Mylonas, George E. *Eleusis and the Eleusian Mysteries,* Princeton University Press (paperback), 1961

Nilsson, Martin P. *The Dionysian Mysteries of the Hellenistic and Roman Age,* C. W. K.Gleerup, Lund, Sweden, 1957; Arno Press, 1976

Ouvaroff, M. *Essay on the Mysteries of Eleusis,* Rodwell & Martin, London, 1817

Wright, Dudley. *The Eleusinian Mysteries & Rites,* Theosophical Publishing House, London/"The Square & Compass," Denver, Colorado, n.d.

Mystical Night (of the Sufis)

It was believed by the **Sufis** that to attain to the coveted state of mystical contemplation, it was necessary to close the gateway of the physical senses, so that the inner or spiritual senses might operate more freely.

This injuction was sometimes taken literally, as by the Brahmin Yogis, who carefully closed eyes, ears, nose and mouth, in order to attain to visionary ecstasy.

The Mystical Night was thus a shutting out of all external sense-impressions, of hope, fear, consciousness of self, and every human emotion, so that the interior light might be more clearly perceived. (See also **Meditation; Sufism; Yoga**)

Mysticism

The attempt of man to attain to the ultimate reality of things and experience communion with the Highest. Mysticism maintains the possibility of a relationship with God, not by means of revelation or the ordinary religious channels, but by introspection, and **meditation** in conjunction with a purified life, culminating in the awareness that the individual partakes of the divine nature.

Mysticism has been identified with pantheism by some authorities, but it differs from pantheism in that its motive is spiritual. But mysticism is greatly more speculative than ordinary religion and instead of commencing its flights of thought from the human side, starts from the divine nature rather than the human.

The name mysticism cannot be applied to any particular system. Whereas religion teaches submission of the will and the ethical harmonies of life, mysticism strains after the realization of a union with the divine source itself. The mystic desires to be as close to God as possible, if not indeed part of the Divine Essence itself, whereas the ordinary devotee of most religious systems merely desires to walk in God's way and obey His will.

Historical Survey

Mysticism may be said to have originated in the East, where it probably evolved from kindred philosophic concepts. The unreality of material things is taught by most Asiatic religions, especially by Hinduism and Buddhism, and the sense of the worth of human ego in these is small (see **India**). The **Sufis** of Persia may be said to be a link between the more austere Indian mystics and those of Europe.

Sufism first arose in the ninth century among the Persian Moslems, probably as a protest against the severe monotheism of their religion, but in all likelihood more ancient springs contributed to its revival. In the Persia of Hafiz and Saadi, pantheism abounded, and their magnificent poetry is read by Moslems as having a deep mystical significance, although for the most part it deals with the intoxication of love. It is certain that many of them exhibit the fervor of souls searching for communion with the highest.

The rise of Alexandrian **Neoplatonism** was the signal for the introduction of mysticism to a waiting Europe, and as this stage of mysticism has been fully reviewed in another entry on the subject, there is no necessity to follow it here. It may be mentioned, however, that Neoplatonism made a definite mark upon early Chistianity, and we find it mirrored in many of the patristic writings of the sixteenth century.

It was Erigena who, in the ninth century, transmitted to Europe the so-called writings of Dionysius the Areopagite, thus giving rise to both the scholasticism and mysticism of the Middle Ages. Erigena based his own system upon that of Dionysius. This was the so-called "negative theology" which placed God above all categories and designated Him as Nothing, or The Incomprehensible Essence from which the world of primordial causes is eternally created. This creation is the Work of Son of God, in Whom all substantial things exist; but God is the beginning and end of everything. On this system Christian mysticism may be said to have been founded with little variation.

With Erigena, reason and authority were identical, and in this he agrees with all speculative mystics, whereas scholasticism is characterized by the acceptance by reason of a given matter which is presupposed even when it cannot be understood. It seemed to Erigena that in the scholastic system, religious truth was external to the mind, while the opposite view was fundamental to mysticism.

That is not to say that mysticism according to Erigena is a mere subordination of reason to faith. Mysticism indeed places every confidence in human reason, and it is essential that it should have the unity of the human mind with the divine as its main tenet, but it accepts nothing from without, and it posits the higher faculty of reason over the realization of absolute truth.

Medieval mysticism may be said to have originated from a reaction of practical religion against dialectics in which the true spirit of Christianity was then enshrined. Thus St. Bernard opposed the dry scholasticism of Abelard. His mysticism was profoundly practical, and dealt chiefly with the means by which human beings may attain the knowledge of God. This is to be accomplished through contemplation and withdrawal from the world.

Thus asceticism is the soul of medieval mysticism, but St. Bernard mistakenly averred regarding self-love that it is proper to love ourselves for God's sake, or because God loved us, thus merging self-love in love for God. We must, so to speak, love ourselves in God, in Whom we ultimately lose ourselves. In this, St. Bernard is almost Buddhistic, and indeed his mysticism is of the universal type.

Perhaps Hugh of St. Victor, a contemporary of St. Bernard's, did more to develop the tenets of mysticism, and his monastery of Augustinians near Paris became, under his influence, a great center of mysticism. One of his apologists, Richard of St. Victor, declared that the objects of mystic contemplation are partly above reason, and partly, as regards intuition, contrary to reason.

The protagonists of this theory, all of whom issued from the same monastery, were known as the Victorines, who put a stout fight against the dialecticians and schoolmen. Bonaventura, who died in 1274, was a disciple of this school, and a believer in the faculty of mystic intuition.

In the twelfth and thirteenth centuries, the worldliness of the church aroused much opposition amongst laymen, and its cold formalism created a reaction towards a more spiritual regime. Many sects arose such as the **Waldenses,** the Cathari (see **Gnosticism)** and the Beguines, all of which strove to infuse into their teachings a warmer enthusiasm than that which burned in the heart of the church of their time.

In Germany, mysticism made great strides, and Machthild of Magdeburg, and Elizabeth of Thuringia, were, if not the originators of mysticism in Germany, perhaps the earliest supporters of it. Joachim of Flores and Amalric of Bena wrote strongly in favor of the reformed church, and their writings are drenched with mystical terms, derived for the most part from Erigena.

Joachim mapped out the duration of the world into three ages, that of the Father, that of the Son, and that of the Spirit—the first of which was to commence with the year 1260, and to be inaugurated by the general adoption of the life monastic and contemplative.

A sect called The New Spirit, or the Free Spirit, became widespread through northern France, Switzerland and Germany; and these did much to infuse the spirit of mysticism throughout the German land.

It is with Meister Eckhart, who died in 1327, that we get the juncture of mysticism with scholastic theology. Of his doctrine it has been said: "The ground of your being lies in God. Reduce yourself to that simplicity, that root, and you are in God. There is no longer any distinction between your spirit and the divine—you have escaped personality and finite limitation. Your particular, creature self, as a something separate and dependent on God is gone. So also, obviously, your creaturely will. Henceforth, therefore, what seems an inclination of yours is in fact the divine good pleasure. You are free from law. You are above means. The very will to do the will of God is resolved into that will itself. This is the Apathy the Negation, the Poverty, he commends.

"With Eckhart personally this self-reduction and deification is connected with a rigorous asceticism and exemplary moral excellence. Yet it is easy to see that it may be a merely intellectual process, consisting in a man's thinking that he is thinking himself away from his personality. He declares the appearance of the Son necessary to enable us to realize our sonship; and yet his language implies that this realization is the perpetual incarnation of that Son—does, as it were, constitute him. Christians are accordingly not less the sons of God by grace than is Christ by nature. Believe yourself divine, and the Son is brought forth in you. The Saviour and the saved are dissolved together in the blank absolute substance."

With the advent of the Black Death, a great spirit of remorse swept over Europe in the fourteenth century, and a vast revival of piety took place. This resulted in the foundation in Germany of a society of Friends of God, whose chief object was to strengthen each other in intercourse with the Creator.

Perhaps the most distinguished of these were Tauler, and Nicolas of Basle, and the society numbered many inmates of the cloister, as well as wealthy men of commerce and others. **Ruysbroeck,** the great Flemish mystic, was connected with them, but his mysticism is perhaps more intensely practical than that of any other visionary. It is the machinery by which the union with God is to be effected which most attracts him. In Ruysbroeck's lifetime, a mystical society arose in Holland called the Brethren of Common Lot, who founded an establishment at which Groot dispensed the principles of mysticism to Radewyn and Thomas à Kempis.

The attitude of mysticism at the period of the Reformation is peculiar. We find a mystical propaganda pretending to be sent forth by a body of **Rosicrucians** denouncing Roman Catholicism in the fiercest terms, and we also observe the spirit of mysticism strongly within those bodies which resisted the coldness and formalism of the Roman Church of that time.

On the other hand, however, we find the principles of Luther strongly opposed by some of the most notable mystics of his time. But the Reformation passed, mysticism went on its way, divided, it is true, so far as the outward theological principles of its votaries were concerned, but strongly united in it general principles.

It is with Nicolas of Kusa, who died in 1464, that mysticism triumphs over scholasticism. Nicolas was the protagonist of super-knowledge, or that higher ignorance which is the knowledge of the intellect in contra-distinction to the mere knowledge of the understanding. His doctrines colored those of Giordano Bruno and his theosophy certainly preceded that of **Paracelsus.**

The next great name in mysticism is that of **Boehme,** who once and for all systematized German philosophy.

The Roman Church produced many mystics of note in the sixteenth and seventeenth centuries, notably Francis of Sales, Mme. Guyon and Molinos,—the last two of which were the protagonists of Quietism, which set forth the theory that there should be no pleasure in the practice of mysticism, and that God did not exist for the enjoyment of man. Perhaps the greatest students of Boehme were William **Law** (1686-1761) and Saint **Martin** (1743-1803).

The Universality of Mystical Experience

It is clear from the statements of mystics that they are not limited to any given religion or theology. When Meister Eckhart stated "If I am to know God directly, I must become completely He, and He I: so that this He and this I become and are one I," he comes to the same point as the Adwaita Vedanta doctrine of Hinduism, where the *jiva* (individual soul) merges with Brahma the creator before absorption in Brahman, the non-personal divine ground.

The apparent differences between Hindu mysticism and Christian mysticism are nominal. Although Christian theology postulates the divine in the form of God as Father, Son and Holy Spirit, such distinctions vanish in the actual mystical experience. Similarly popular Hinduism postulates hundreds of different gods and goddesses, but these are merely legal fictions to the Indian mystic, melting away in the totality of higher consciousness.

Because mind and emotion are transcended in the higher reaches of mysticism, they are merely ways of reaching a reality which lies beyond them, a totality of consciousness without object, beyond the normal human limitations of individual body, ego, personality or hopes and fears.

Like Christianity, Hindu Vedanta (inquiry into ultimate reality), has different schools of theology, ranging from *Advaita* (Monism or Non-dualism, claiming that All is One and only the Divine Ultimate has actual existence, all else being illusory) to degrees of *Dvaita* or Dualism (claiming that there is One Ultimate Divine Principle of God but that the soul is a separate principle with independent existence). Such schools are not really contradictory, but rather different degrees of interpretation of one reality on the way to an actual mystical experience in which intellectual distinctions vanish.

The Way of the Mystic

In both Eastern and Western mysticism, withdrawal from the everyday life of a householder is recognized as an aid to mystical progress, thus both have monastic establishments at which one follows a life of prayer and meditation. In the initial stages, self-purification is facilitated by dedicated service to others, prior to the more secluded life of the contemplative.

Mystics have sometimes been accused of escapism, in retreating from the responsibilities of everyday life into a private world, and indeed, the descriptions of the ecstasies of spiritual awareness often sound rather like a selfish indulgence, oblivious to the problems of the outside world.

It is clear that the ideal mystic partakes fully of the duties and social responsibility of life after spiritual enlightenment, since mystical experience should give deeper meaning to the numinous reality behind the everday mundane world. For most individuals, however, a period of retreat from everyday life is helpful in disengaging oneself from the fears, desires and egoism of mundane existence.

Hinduism places great stress on *dharma,* the duties and responsibilities of the individual, which take priority over any desire for transcendentalism. During this period one would observe the everyday religious rites and rituals related to the gods and goddesses of an individual's life. Later, however, when one had fulfilled one's responsibilities, married, begat a family and provided for them, the realization that everything connected with the material world and physical life was transient would grow steadily, culminating in a hunger for knowledge of what is eternal.

At such a time, one might seek a qualified *guru* or spiritual preceptor and follow an ascetic life, discarding all material possessions, egoism and hopes and fears in the quest for a higher spiritual awareness not subject to birth and death, change or decay.

Various pathways of *yoga* facilitated that quest, involving self-purification, service to others and refinement of perception based upon physical health and its spiritual counterpart.

The modern Western preoccupation with pop *gurus* ignores the traditional emphasis given to ethical restraints and moral observance as essential preliminary to all spiritual training.

The Hindu emphasis on the duties and responsibilities of a householder taking priority over the quest for mystical enlightenment, have something in common with Judaism, which does not seek to separate mystical experience from everyday life. Judism is essentially pragmatic in its approach to the spiritual life and requires that mystical experience be interfused with daily life and religious observance.

The Jewish mystic typified in the period of eighteenth to nineteenth century Hasidism, was a pious rabbi, living a life of prayer, study and meditation within his community and sharing everyday social life and responsibility. In this respect he resembled the Eastern *guru,* around whom a group of pupils would gather for spiritual teaching and experience. The necessity for individual religious experience seems to have been ignored in the rules and regulations and formal worship of modern religions, and clearly the charismatic revival movements seek to restore that essential experiential aspect.

The Mechanisms of Mysticism

It is clear that the concept of self-purification in mystical progress involves psycho-physical mechanisms. Fasting, asceticism, mortification and intense meditation have profound effects on the individual nervous system and other aspects of the body and mind. Very little discussion on this important area appeared in Western literature until Aldous Huxley published *The Doors of Perception* (1954) and *Heaven & Hell* (1956). These two books have had a profound effect on contemporary life.

The starting point for Huxley's speculations about the psycho-physical mechanisms of mystical experience was his own experiment in taking the psychedelic drug mescalin, and it is unfortunate that this particular stimulus has overshadowed the wider implications of his discussion.

A simplistic interpretation of Huxley's speculations led to the psychedelic revolution of the 1960s, spearheaded by Timothy **Leary** and Richard **Alpert,** based on the conviction that merely taking a chemical substance resulted in a spiritual experience comparable with that of the great mystics of history. This was a concept that Huxley himself deplored in his later years.

It is now obvious that the chemical ecstasy and visions produced by psychedelic drugs are qualitatively different from transcendentalism experienced by the mystic who has devoted many years to self-purification of mind, emotions and spiritual perception, and that unless there is such a purification of the individual, any psychedelic experience lacks integrity. The search for chemical ecstasy unfortunately led to the worldwide modern problems of hard drug addiction, criminal rackets, violence and wasted lives.

The modern mass-media society, geared to consumer products, television commercials and lifestyles (as distinct from living itself), is unfortunately susceptible to such simplistic instant recipes for mysticism, to be purchased with no more difficulty than the latest color television set or automobile. Most of the pop *gurus* of the West, with their thousands of adulating devotees, present a spurious mysticism which is merchandized like any detergent or aspirin. The slow patient processes of self-purification and social responsibility are ignored.

A similar over-simplification of Eastern teachings was the popularization of **Zen** Buddhism for the American campus, in which it seemed that merely reading a book of Zen *koans* (spiritual conundrums) by Dr. Suzuki or Christmas Humphreys was all that was needed to gain instant *satori* or spiritual enlightenment. In fact, as Dr. Suzuki himself did not disguise, more was required than a simple intellectual exercise.

The traditional Zen student might spend months or years working hard in the mundane tasks of the Zen monastery, and it was against this background of hard work in the physical field that the intellectual gymnastics of the sound of one hand clapping or the chicken in the bottle were pondered. A student would be fully stretched to the limit on the physical and mental plane so that the resolution of a paradox would be on a higher plane of transcendental enlightenment.

It is now clear that the gradual transformation of the personality on all levels—physical, mental, emotional and spiritual—involves specific psychophysical concomitants. Some of these may be accessible to scientific inspection. It may also be possible to evaluate various degrees of transcendental experience, ranging from emotional euphoria to progressively profound areas of higher consciousness.

The modern Hindu mystic Pandit **Gopi Krishna,** who experienced a dramatic development of higher consciousness following a period of intense yoga discipline and meditation, has published his experiences and the profound perceptions accompanying them in a series of books, and has attracted the attention of scientists in investigating the phenomenon.

The Pandit revived the ancient Hindu concept of **Kundalini** in a scientific context, and suggested a biological aspect of religious experience and the inspiration of geniuses. *Kundalini* is a static force located at the base of the human spine, which is activated dynamically in the processes of procreation, but which may also be aroused in mystical centers in the body (associated with the plexi of the sympathetic nervous system), resulting in activity in a higher center in the head, traditionally associated with meditation, and a consequent enlargement of consciousness beyond the individual mental and emotional limits.

It is interesting to notice that symbolic representation of this schema are found in most great religions of the world which describe an Edenic garden, a tree of knowledge with the divine fruit, and the serpent which tempts to sexual activity. These can be taken as symbols of the twin currents of sex and mysticism in the human body.

Paranormal Side Effects

Most religions have reported miraculous phenomena associated with the path of mysticism, including visions, disembodied voices, levitation and gifts of healing. Christian saints have their miracles and the *yogis* have their occult powers. It would seem that with the transcendence of normal mental and emotional life, there is an area of transcendence of normal physical law.

However, the mystic is warned not to be snared by such phenomena, since it will activate egoism and pride, common faults of the beginner on the spiritual path.

It remains to be seen whether there is a *modus vivendi* for mysticism, in which the undoubted benefits of some paranormal side effects such as miraculous healing might manifest freely without hindering spiritual development. Clearly there are also theological problems involved in the eternal play of good and evil, of creation, destruction and balance, which are characteristic of the physical world and its laws. (See also **Drugs; Gnosticism; Guru; Hasidim; Kundalini; Meditation; Vedanta; Waldenes; Yoga)**

Recommended reading

"AE" (George W. Russell). *The Candle of Vision,* Macmillan, London, 1919; University Books, 1965

Augustine, St. (transl. Edward Pusey) *Confessions,* Dent, London/Dutton, 1954

Blakney, Raymond B. *Meister Eckhart; A Modern Translation,* Harper, 1941

Brinton, Howard H. *The Mystic Will; Based on a Study of the Philosophy of Jacob Boehme,* Macmillan, 1930

Buber, Martin. *Tales of the Hasidim; The Early Masters,* Thames & Hudson, London, 1956; Schocken paperback, 1961

Bucke, Richard M. *Cosmic Consciousness; A Study in the Evolution of the Human Mind,* 1901; University Books, 1961 etc. (frequently reprinted)

Cheney, Sheldon. *Men Who Have Walked with God,* Alfred A. Knopf, 1968; Dell paperback, 1974

Ferguson, John. *An Illustrated Encyclopaedia of Mysticism and The Mystery Religions,* Thames & Hudson (paperback), London, 1976

Gall, Edward. *Mysticism Throughout the Ages,* Rider & Co., London, 1934

Gopi Krishna. *The Biological Basis of Religion and Genius,* Harper & Row, 1972

Gopi Krishna. *Higher Consciousness; The Evolutionary Thrust of Kundalini,* Julian Press, 1974

Huxley, Aldous. *The Doors of Perception,* Chatto & Windus, London, 1954 etc.

Huxley, Aldous. *Heaven & Hell,* Chatto & Windus, London, 1956

James, William. *The Varieties of Religious Experience,* London, 1902; University Books, 1963

Lawrence, Brother. *The Practice of the Presence of God,* London, 1691; New York, 1895 etc. (frequently reprinted)

Maeterlinck, Maurice. *Ruysbroeck and the Mystics,* London, 1908

Patanjali (transl. M. N. Dvivedi). *The Yoga-Sutras of Patanjali.* Theosophical Publishing House, Adyar, India (paperback), 1890; 1947 etc.

Purohect Swami, Shri. (transl.) *The Geeta, The Gospel of the Lord Shri Krishna [Bhagavad Gita]* Faber, London, 1935 etc.

Swedenborg, Emmanuel. *Divine Love & Wisdom,* Swedenborg Foundation, n.d.

Underhill, Evelyn. *The Mystic Way; A Psychological Study in Christian Origins,* London & New York, 1913

Underhill, Evelyn. *Mysticism; A Study in the Nature & Development of Man's Spiritual Consciousness,* Methuen, London/Dutton, 1911 etc. (frequently reprinted)

Waite, Arthur E. *Lamps of Western Mysticism,* Kegan Paul, London/Alfred A. Knopf, 1923; Multimedia, Blauvelt, N.Y., 1973

Waite, Arthur E. *Studies in Mysticism,* Hodder & Stoughton, London, 1906

Younghusband, Francis. *Modern Mystic* John Murray, London, 1935; University Books 1970

Zaehner, R. C. *Mysticism, Sacred & Profane,* Oxford paperback, 1957

N

Nacht, Sacha (1901-   )

Physician and psychoanalyst who has been concerned with relationships between psychology and parapsychology. Born September 23, 1901 at Bacau, Rumania, he studied at the Faculté de Médecine de Paris, France, and was director of the Institut de Psychanalyse de Paris from 1952 onwards. He is author of *La Psychanalyse d'aujourd'hui* (1956, American ed. 1959).

Nada

A Sanskrit term used in Hindu musical theory to denote subtle aspects of musical sound. There are two kinds of *Nada: Anahata* is the mystical essence of sound, *Ahata* is the conscious realization of musical sound by human beings. *Anahata* is heard by yogis in **meditation** and related to different *chakras* or psychic centers in the human body.

Nada Upasana is the yoga of music, which brings God-realization through pure forms of music and meditation. (See also **Music; Swami Nadabrahmananda Saraswati; Vibrations;** Alfred **Wolfsohn)**

Recommended reading

Rogo, D. Scott *Nada; a study of some unusal "other world" experiences*, 2 vols., University Books, 1970-72

Sivananda, Swami. *Music as Yoga,* Rishikesh, India, 1956

Nadabrahmananda Saraswati, Swami (1896-   )

A Hindu musician who has developed a yoga of music, involving the arousal of **Kundalini** energy through the psychic power of sound vibrations. Born May 5, 1896 in Mysore, India, he studied music under Shri Sadasiva Bua, and Ustad Alladiya Khan of Dolahpur, eventually becoming a disciple of Tata Bua of Benares. He spent fifteen years in perfecting his skills.

He not only plays various instruments like Swara Mandala (Indian zither) and tabla (drums) with fantastic skill, but is also a master of the intricate graces of Thaan or vocal exercises. During his vocal performances he directs the sound vibration to any part of his body, and can send out vibrations through his ears and the top of his head when his mouth is covered.

In his performances on the tabla (Indian drums), he suspends respiration for nearly half an hour in a state of trance, playing the most intricate and complex rhythms without movement of his eyes or head.

He can also use sound vibrations for psychic **healing.** He is a devotee of the late Sri Swami Sivananda, and has taught music to many students at the Sivananda Ashram (Divine Life Society), Rishikesh, Himalayas, North India (See also **Nada)**

Naddeo, Alighiero (1930-   )

Italian professor of statistics who has conducted investigations in parapsychology. Born August 18, 1930 at Rome, Italy, he studied at University of Rome (LL.B. 1952, B.S. statistics 1953). In 1960 he married Maria Teresa Patriarca.

He was lecturer in statistics from 1954-58, assistant professor econometrics and methodological statistics from 1958-61 at University of Rome, professor of statistics at University of Trieste from 1961 onwards. He is author (with M. Boldrini) of *Le statistiche empirische e la teoria dei campioni* (Empirical Statistical Studies on the Sample Theory, 1950). In his investigation of ESP ability with 500 students he concluded that the correct results were higher than random expectation.

Napellus

A plant with narcotic properties, with which J. B. Van Helmont (1577-1644) experimented. He stated that, having on one occasion roughly prepared the root, he tasted it with his tongue, and in a very short time found that the center of thought and intellect was situated in the pit of his stomach.

An unusual clarity and distinctness of thought rendered the experience a pleasant one, and he sought on future occasions to repeat it by the same means, but without success. After about two hours he felt a slight dizziness and thereupon thought in the normal fashion with his brain. But throughout the strange experience he claimed that he was conscious that his soul still remained in the brain as a governing power.

The plant with which Van Helmont experimented was *Aconitum napellus* or monkshood, a species of aconite, which is poisonous. (See also **Drugs;** Seeing with the **Stomach)**

Naphology

Term coined by Ufologists to denote a field of study which examines a wide range of reported phenomena and events for which there is no acceptable scientific explanation, such as astrology, Ufology, and occultism generally. A more popular term for apparently inexplicable events is "Fortean Phenomena," deriving from the researches and books of Charles **Fort** (1874-1932), who first classified reports of unexplained phenomena.

Napper (or Napier), Richard (1559-1634)

British astrologer and doctor of medicine of Great Linford, Buckinghamshire, who, according to William **Lilly** (1602-1681), "outwent Forman in physic and holiness of life, cured the falling-sickness perfectly by constellated rings, and some diseases by amulets."

Napper was a pupil of astrologer Simon Forman (1552-1611). He was probably of the stock of the Scottish Napiers although his family had been settled in England since the time of Henry VIII.

Nash, Carroll B(lue) (1914-)

Professor of biology and director of the Parapsychology laboratory at St. Joseph's College, Philadelphia, Pa. since 1956. Born January 29, 1914 at Louisville, Kentucy, he studied at George Washington University, Washington, D.C. (B.S. 1934) and Universtiy of Maryland (M.S. 1937, Ph.D 1939). In 1941 he married Catherine Stifler.

He was instrutor in zoology at University of Arizona from 1939-41, associate professor of biology at Pennsylvania Military College, Chester from 1941-44, assistant professor of biology at American University, Washington, D.C. from 1944-45, chairman of biology department at Washington College, Chestertown, Maryland from 1945-48, professor of biology at St. Joseph's College from 1948 onwards, chairman of biology department at St. Joseph's College. He is a member of the American Association for the Advancement of Science.

Dr. Nash was a founding member of the **Parapsychological Association,** president in 1963. He was director of the Parapsychology Laboratory at Duke University, North Carolina in 1956 and received the William McDougall Award in 1960.

His special interests include precognition, PK, and personality variable in Psi. Dr. Nash was consultant and adviser for a television production "ESP" in 1958, and has taught college-level courses in parapsychology at St. Joseph's College. His articles on parapsychology published in the *Journal of Parapsychology* include: 'PK Tests of a Large Population' (8, 1944), (with A. Richards), 'Comparison of Two Distances in PK Tests' (11, 1947), 'A Comparison of Combined and Single Target Symbols' (20, 1956), 'Correlation Between ESP and Religious Value' (22, 1958), (with M. G. Durkin) 'Terminal Salience with Multiple Digit Targets' (23, 1959), 'Can Precognition Occur Diametrically?' (27, 1963), 'Note on Precognition of the Percipient's Calls as an Hypothesis to Telepathy' (39, 1975), 'Can Precognition Occur Diametrically?' (24, 1960), 'Effect of Subject-Experimenter Attitudes on Clairvoyance Scores' (24, 1960), (with C. S. Nash) 'Effect of Target Selection, Field Dependence and Body Concept on ESP Performances' (32, 1968); in *Journal of the American Society for Psychical Research:* 'Psychokinesis Reconsidered' (45, 1951), 'An Exploratory Analysis for Displacement in PK' (50, 1956), (with C. S. Nash) 'Checking Success and the Relationship of Personality Traits to ESP' (52, 1958), 'The Chesebrough-Pond's ESP Television Contest' (53, 1959), 'Retest of High Scoring Subjects in the Chesebrough-Pond's ESP Television Contest' (57, 1963); (with C. S. Nash) 'Negative Correlations Between The Scores of Subjects in Two Contemporaneous ESP Experiments' (56, 1962), 'Relation Between ESP Scoring and Minnesota Multiphasic Personality Inventory' (60, 1960), (with C. S. Nash), 'Relations Between ESP Scoring Level and The Personality Traits of The Guilford-Zimmerman Temparament Survey' (61, 1967), 'Comparison of ESP Run-Score Averages of Groups Liked and Disliked by the Experimenter' (62, 1968); in *Science:* 'Psi and Probability Theory' (120, 1954), in the *International Journal of Parapsychology:* 'The Unorthodox Science of Parapsychology' (1, 1959); in *Journal* of The Society for Psychical Research: 'The PK Mechanism' (38, 1955), (with E. D. Dean) 'Coincident Plethysmograph Results Under Controlled Conditions' (44, 1967).

Nash, Catherine S(tifler) (Mrs. Carroll B. Nash) (1919-)

Assistant professor of biology, and charter associate of the Parapsychological Association. Born August 31, 1919 at Woodbrook, Maryland, she studied at Goucher College, Baltimore, Maryland (B.A. 1939) and Ohio State University (M.S. 1950). In 1941 she married Carroll B. **Nash.**

She was a lecturer in biology at Temple University, Philadelphia, Pa. from 1942-43, instructor in biology at Pennsylvania Military College, Chester, Pa. from 1943-44, instructor in biology at American University, Washington, D.C. from 1944-45, instructor in biology at Washington College, Chestertown, Maryland from 1945-58, assistant professor of biology at St. Joseph's College, Philadelphia from 1948 onwards.

She has taken particular interest in telepathy and clairvoyance, and her published articles include: 'Checking Success and the Relationship of Personality Traits to ESP' (*Journal of the American Society for Psychical Research,* vol. 52, 1958), 'Experiments in Plant Growth' (*International Journal of Parapsychology,* Autumn 1959), 'Report on the Second Annual Convention of the Parapsychological Association' *Newsletter, Parapsychology Foundation,* Sept.-Oct. 1959), 'A Test of Adding Extrasensorially Perceived Digits' (*Journal of Parapsychology* 23, 1959). (For papers in collaboration with her husband, see Carroll B. **Nash)**

NASO International Astrological Directory

Publication listing local, national, and international astrology societies, organizations, periodicals and practitioners. Address: National Astrological Society, 205 3rd Avenue #2A, New York, N.Y. 10003.

Nastrond

The "Strand of the Dead"—The Scandinavian and Icelandic Hell, said to be of an icy temperature. It lies in the lowest depths of Niflheim; it is a "dark abode far from the sun;" its gates face "the cutting north;" "its walls are formed of wreathed snakes, and their venom is ever falling like rain."

It is surrounded by dark and poisonous streams, and Nidhog, the great dragon, who dwells beneath the central root of Ygdrassil, torments and gnaws the dead. Here it is that Loki is chained to a splintered rock, where the venom of the snake Skada falls on him unceasingly, and it was believed that his shuddering was the cause of earthquakes.

Nastrond is featured in the *Voluspa,* a poem in the Icelandic *Poetic Edda.* (See also **Hell)**

Nat

An evil spirit. (See **Burma)**

National Astrological Society

Non-profit organization founded in 1968 to promote high standards of practice and instruction in astrology, to facilitate communications among astrologers through meetings and publications and to foster cooperation among persons and organizations concerned with astrology. NASO holds an annual conference in cities throughout North America, acts as an educational institution, maintains a library, and facilitates access to IBM computing for members with high level projects.

Voting membership is open to professional or qualified astrologers, non-voting membership for associates. The Society publishes **NASO Journal.** Address: 205 3rd Avenue, New York, N.Y. 10003.

Apparently now inactive.

National Colored Spiritualist Association of the United States of America

Established April 21, 1925 at 206 West 136 Street, New York, N.Y., president Rev. John R. White, vice-president Rev. Sarah Harrington. No longer active.

National Directory of Psychic Counselors

Comprehensive directory listing astrologers, healers, card and palm readers, hypnotherapists, graphologists, trance mediums, etc., in the U.S., giving names, addresses, and telephone numbers. Also lists metaphysical organizations, publishers, resources, and psychic products (tapes, books, courses). Published by Carma Press, Box 12633, St. Paul, Minnesota 55112.

National Enquirer (Newspaper)

Popular nationally distributed newspaper which gives special attention to psychical phenomena and the paranormal, often being the first to report new aspects or developments. Although presentation is popular, reports are usually comprehensive. Reports on **UFO** sightings are often published. Published weekly from: 600 S.E. Coast Avenue, Lantana, Florida 33462.

National Federation of Spiritual Healers

British organization founded in 1955 "to establish a national body which would co-ordinate, protect and advance the work of spiritual healing." Its fourfold purpose is "To speak for the concept of spiritual healing in the councils of this country [Britain] and internationally; to participate in developments promoted by the Federation or elsewhere related to increasing knowledge and understanding of the healing gift; to provide opportunities for its members to develop their full healing potential; to ensure that the public who seek healing receive a proper service and corrrect advice."

The Federation registers as Healer Members those for whom authenticated evidence of spiritual healing has been obtained and accepted by the Membership Panel of the NFSH. "Spiritual healing" is understood to be the healing of the sick in body, mind, and spirit by means of the laying-on of hands or by either prayer or meditation, whether or not in the actual presence of the patient.

The Federation operates a national healer referral service to put members of the public seeking spiritual healing in touch with approved Healer Members of the Federation.

Since 1965 (under an agreement with more than 1,500 National Health Service Hospitals), NFSH Healer Members may attend to those patients in hospitals who request the services of a healer. An important development took place in 1977, when the General Medical Council in England agreed to allow doctors to recommend spiritual healing to their patients.

Address: National Federation of Spiritual Healers, Old Manor Farm Studio, Church Street, Sunbury-on-Thames, Middlesex, TW16 6RG, England. (See also **Healing by Touch)**

National Investigations Committee on Aerial Phenomena (NICAP)

Founded in 1956 for persons interested in aerial phenomena, particularly unidentified flying objects (UFOs). Its panel of advisers includes scientists, engineers, aviation experts, clergymen, retired military officers, and professors.

It exists to gather, analyze, evaluate and disseminate reliable information on aerial phenomena and promotes scientific investigation, carried out in the field by technically oriented subcommittees.

It provides bibliographic and source materials to students, exchange data to scientific societies and indivdual scientists, and semitechnical reports to scientists, Congress and the press. It maintains a large library on aerial phenomena, aviation, astronomy, and a collection of magazine articles, newspaper clippings, letters and other documents.

It publishes *The U.F.O. Investigator* monthly and *UFO Evidence, UFO Wave of 1947, Strange Effects from UFOs.* Address: Center for UFO studies 2457 W. Peterson Avenue, Chicago, Illinois 60659.

National Investigations Committee on UFOs (NICUFO)

Non-profit organization founded in 1967 to investigate "the truth surrounding UFOs and associated phenomena." It probes UFO reports and relates its findings to governmental agencies and the general public via press, radio, television, and newsletters.

It organizes conventions, lectures, seminars and various activities related to Unidentified Flying Objects, with special interest in claimed contracts with UFO occupants. Publishes *Confidential Space-Link* Newsletter. Address: 14617 Victory Boulevard, Suite 4, Van Nuys, California 91411. (See also UFO)

National Laboratory of Psychical Research

Established by psychical researcher Harry Price in 1925 at 13 Roland Gardens, London, S.W.7, "to investigate in a dispassionate manner and by purely scientific means every phase of psychic or alleged psychic phenomena." The honorary president was The Lord Sands, K.C., LL.D., acting president H. G. Bois, honorary director Harry Price.

Publications included: *British Journal of Psychical Research,* bi-monthly, discontinued in 1929, *Proceedings of the National Laboratory of Psychical Research,* Vol. I., discontinued in 1929; *Bulletins of the National Laboratory of Psychical Research:* I. *Regurgitation and the Duncan Mediumship,* by Harry Price, 1932, II. *Fraudulent Mediums,* an essay by Prof. D.S. Fraser-Harris, repr. from *Science Progress,* Jan., 1932, III. *The Identification of the "Walter" Prints,* by E. E. Dudley, 1933, IV. *An Account of Some Further Experiments with Rudi Schneider,* by Harry Price, 1933, V. *Rudi Schneider; the Vienna Experiments of Prof. Meyer and Przibram,* 1933.

One of the most valuable issues of the NLPR *Proceedings* was vol. 1, pt. 2 (April 1929), comprising *Short-Title Catalogue of Works on Psychical Research, Spiritualism, Magic, Psychology, Legerdemain and Other Methods of Deception, Charlatanism, Witchcraft and Technical Works for the Scientific Investigation of Alleged Abnormal Phenomena from circa 1450 A.D. to 1929 A.D.* compiled by Harry Price. This Catalog (supplemented by Bulletin I (1935) listed the splendid collection formed by Price himself. The collection is now in The Harry Price Collection, University College, London.

The Laboratory is no longer in existence.

National New Age Yellow Pages

Directory listing holistic practitioners, astrologers, psychics, social justice organizations, mail-order businesses, intended as a national networking tool. Address: The Light Connection, P.O. Box 5491, Fullerton, California 92635.

National Psychic Science Association

A group of lecturers, healers, preachers and ministers, founded 1929, "to promote the religion of Spiritualism, psychic science and morality and demonstrate the phenomena of the continuity of life through spirit communication and psychic healing through prayer." Address: c/o Rev. Marion Odom, 17 Baird Place, Whippany, New Jersey 07981.

National Psychological Institute, Inc.

Founded for scientific research in normal and abnormal psychology and spirit **obsession** and the complex problem "What becomes of the dead?" by Dr. Carl A. **Wickland,** headquarters Los Angeles, California.

No longer active.

National Spiritual Alliance of the United States of America

Founded in 1913 as an organization of individuals who believe that "intercommunication between the denizens of different worlds is scientifically established."

It promotes studies of Spiritualism, prescribes qualifications of ministers, method of examination and ceremony by which they are set apart, also qualifications of associated ministers, licentiates, healers, mediums, missionaries and other official workers, and issues certificates. Present membership over 3,200. Address: 239 Washington Street, Keene, New Hampshire 03431.

National Spiritualist (Magazine)

Monthly magazine published by the National Spiritualist Association of Churches, Cassadaga, Florida. Editorial and subscription address: P.O. Box 30172, Indianapolis, Indiana 46230.

Another magazine of the same name was published by the **Spiritualists National Union** in England.

National Spiritualist Association of Churches

Founded in 1893; current membership over 5,000, comprising nine state groups. It is an association of 178 churches, 12 camps and 5 societies "to teach and proclaim the science, philosophy and religion of modern Spiritualism; to protest against every attempt to compel mankind to worship God in any particular or prescribed manner; to advocate and promote spiritual healing and to protect and encourage spiritual teachers and mediums in all laudable efforts in giving evidence or proof to mankind of a continued intercourse and relationship between the living and the so-called dead."

It maintains a library of books published for and against Spiritualism since 1948, and publishes the **National Spiritualist** monthly magazine. Address: P.O. Box 128, Cassadaga, Florida 32706.

Natsaw

Burmese wizards. (See **Burma**)

Nature Spirits or Elementals

According to **Theosophy,** nature spirits have bodies composed of the finer kinds of matter. There are countless hosts of them, divided into seven classes, which, allowing for two unmanifested forms, belong to the ether, air, fire, water, and earth—the last four being called by some **Kabalists,** sylphs, salamanders, undines, and gnomes respectively. At the head of each class is a *deva* or inferior god.

Nature spirits are said to work in unsuspected ways, sometimes lending their aid to human beings in the form of certain faculties, while those in the **astral world** are engaged in the creation of form out of the matter which the outpouring of the **Logos** has quickened, hence they form minerals, flowers, and other aspects of nature.

These nature spirits of the astral worlds of course have bodies of astral matter, and they frequently form mischievous or other impulses, change the appearance of these bodies.

They are just beyond the limits of normal human vision, but many sensitives of more acute vision can see them, while the action of drugs is also believed to make them visible. (See also **Elementary Spirits; Fairies**)

Nayler, James (c. 1617-1660)

An English religious fanatic of the seventeenth century, born in the diocese of York. He served for a time in the army, then joined the Quakers where his discourses gained for him a reputation for sanctity. His followers hailed him as a Messiah and he entered Bristol in 1656, mounted on a horse led by a man and a woman, while others ran behind chanting "Holy, holy, holy, is the god of Sabaoth."

He was arrested, charged with blasphemy and punished by having his tongue pierced with a hot iron, and his forehead marked with the letter "B" (blasphemer). This done, he was forced to ride into Bristol in disgrace, his face turned towards the horse's tail.

After two years in prison, Nayler was released sobered and penitent. His return to Quaker preaching was sanctioned by George Fox and Nayler preached with George Whitehead. After a period of ill health, Nayler died in October 1660.

Nazca "Spaceport"

A mysterious area of desert markings on the plains of Nazca, Peru, about 250 miles southeast of Lima between the towns of Nazca and Palpa.

This barren plateau covering 200 square miles has over 13,000 lines, 100 spirals, trapezoids and triangles, and about 800 large animal drawings, etched in the desert through removal of surface stones with lighter colored soil underneath. Many of the lines extend for miles, radiating from centers like star shapes. It is estimated that the markings were made between 400 B.C. and 900 A.D. and their construction may have occupied several centuries.

It has been suggested that these markings were the work of ancient spacemen who landed on the plain and marked out an airfield for their spacecraft. This theory has been propagated by Erick**von Däniken,** author of the book *Chariots of the Gods* (1970) which posed the question "Was God an Astronaut?"

In a later book *Gods From Outer Space* (1973), von Däniken stated: "At some time in the past, unknown intelligences landed on the uninhabited plain near the present-day town of Nazca and built an improvized airfield for their spacecraft which were to operate in the vicinity of the earth." In his article 'Von Däniken's Golden Gods' (*The Zetetic,* Vol. II, No. I, 1977), Ronald D. Story examines this theory and points out a number of weaknesses in von Däniken's reasoning.

First of all, there should be no need for a runway several miles long for a space vehicle capable of vertical landing (only modern air liners need a long runway). Secondly, many of the lines run right into hills, ridges and the sides of mountains. Thirdly, the markings are on soft, sandy soil, unsuitable for any heavy vehicle to land on. Maria Reiche, an expert on Nazca, has commented: "I'm afraid the spacemen would have gotten stuck."

Story cited Professor Kosok of Long Island University, who first mapped and photographed the mysterious markings from the air in June 1941 and discovered apparent alignment with solstices and equinoxes. Perhaps the markings were "the largest astronomy book in the world." Similar astronomical ground markings have been interpreted in Glastonbury, England (see **Glastonbury Zodiac**).

Whilst the ideal viewing position for such markings as Nazca is from a point about 600 feet above the plain, it does not necessarily follow that they were actually designed for viewing from the air. They could be interpreted as a giant image of astronomical mysteries, in which construction and traversing of competed markings might be in the nature of a religious ritual. Most magical ceremonies involve physical traversing of geometrical forms inscribed on the ground.

An ingenious theory cited by Story is that of the International Explorers Society of Florida, who suggested that the "chariots of the gods" sailing over Nazca might have been ancient smoke balloons piloted by early Peruvians. This theory is impressively presented by IES member Jim Woodman in his book *NAZCA: Journey to the Sun* (1977). Woodman has discovered that the thousands of ancient gravesites around Nazca contain finely woven textiles (suitable for balloon fabric), braided rope and ceramic pottery. One clay pot has a picture suggesting a hot-air balloon with tie ropes.

It is not generally known that manned balloon flights were recorded in Brazil as early as 1709, when Bartolomeu de Gusmao made his first flight on August 8.

Jim Woodman has actually tested his theory in collaboration with balloonist Julian Nott. They constructed a balloon using the same materials as those available to the ancient Nazcans. The envelope used cotton fabric similar to that in the gravesites; the basket for pilot and co-pilot was woven from native fibers.

On November 28, 1975, Woodman and Nott actually flew their balloon (named *Condor I*) over the Nazca plains.

However, this impressive demonstration hardly settles the mystery of Nazca, since it is not plausible that the Nazcans would have spent centuries constructing these markings for the benefit of occasional balloonists to view from the air.

Validation of the theory would require evidence of a religious and cultural milieu in which such balloonists maintained an elitist status for hundreds of years, and it is hardly likely that such balloons would have vanished without a trace. (See also **Chariots of the Gods:** Erich **von Däniken**)

Ndembo (or Kita)

A former African secret society which had widespread ramifications on the lower Congo, and especially in the districts lying to the south of that river. Initiation was made through the *ganga* or chief, who instructed the neophyte at a given signal suddenly to lie down as if dead. A shroud was spread over him, and he was carried off to an enclosure outside the village called *vela,* and pronounced to have died a *Ndembo.*

Perhaps twenty, thirty, or even fifty candidates "died" at the one time. It was then assumed that persons "dying" in this manner decayed until only a single bone remained, and this the *ganga* took charge of. The process varied from three months to as many years, and the *ganga* was supposed by art magic to bring every one of the dead back to life within that period.

On a festival day of the *Ndembo,* the members marched through the village in a grand procession amidst universal joy, carrying with them the persons who were supposed to have died. The neophytes who were supposed to have perished comported themselves as if in reality they had come from another world. They took new names, pretended that everything in the terrestrial sphere was new to them, turned a deaf ear to their parents and relatives, and even affected not to know how to eat. They further desired to have everything they set eyes on, and if it was not granted to them immediately, they might fall upon the unhappy owner and beat and even kill him without any consequence to themselves. It was assumed that they were mere children in the affairs of the terrestrial sphere, and therefore knew no better.

Those who went through this rite were called *Nganga,* or the "knowing ones," while the neophytes were designated *Vanga.* During their occupation of the *vela* they learned an esoteric language, which they constantly employed. Perhaps the best picture of their cult was given by ethnologist Adolf Bastian (1826-1905) who stated:—

"The Great Nkissi (who here replaces the fetish) lives in the interior of the woodlands where nobody can see him. When he dies the Nganga carefully collect his bones in order to bring them back to life, and nourish them that they may again put on flesh and blood. But it is not well to speak about it. In the Ambamba country everybody must have died once, and when the Nganga (replacing the fetish-priest) shakes his calabash against a village, those men and youths whose hour is come fall into a state of lifeless torpor, from which they generally rise up in three days.

"But the man whom the Nkissi loves he carries off to the bush and often buries him for a series of years. When he again awakens to life, he begins to eat and drink as before, but his mind is gone, and the Nganga must himself educate him and instruct him in every movement, like the smallest child. At first that can only be done with the rod, but the senses gradually return, so that you can speak with him, and when his education is finished the Nganga takes him back to his parents. These would seldom recognize him but for the positive assurance of the Nganga, who at the same time reminds them of earlier occurrences. Whoever has not yet undergone the experience in Ambamba is universally despised, and is not allowed to join in the dances."

This account in curiously reminiscent of the Haitian tradition of **Zombies.**

Near-Death Experience Project

Project devoted to collecting written, audio and video interviews with individuals who have had near-death experiences or related mystical experience. Also provides public education and workshops connected with Near-Death Experiences. Address: Prof. Howard Mickel, Director: Near-Death Experience Project, Wichita State University, Wichita, Kansas 67208. (See also **Death; Near-Death Experiences)**

Near-Death Experiences

Individuals who have suffered apparent death, then have been restored to life, often report experiences which seem to have a bearing on the questions of survival and the existence of the soul. Such experiences have been studied in modern times under the category of "near-death experiences."

Common to most of such experiences is the powerful sensation of rushing through a long dark tunnel with a bright light at the end. This light brings an ecstatic feeling of joy, peace, and freedom from the body. Often the tunnel experiences is preceded by dual awareness in which some higher reality is interfused with perception of the physical environment surrounding the body, which may be perceived from a detached viewpoint, in which the self can look down on its own body, as in **out-of-the-body** experiences.

Psychologists have studied near-death experiences side by side by out-of-body experiences, and found tunnel experiences common to both. Another common experience is that intense overwhelming effect such experiences have upon the subject, whether awakened from an out-of-the-body experience or "called back to life" after a near-death experience. Many individuals find that such experiences are a powerful vindication of the belief in a soul as a separate entity from the body in which it lives and develops throughout life, but which survives the death of the physical body. Often these are life-changing experiences.

Various materialistic theories have been offered to account for NDEs and OBEs in terms of hallucinations. For example, the tunnel sensations might be a reliving of the powerful experience of passing through the birth canal, since the baby usually emerges head first. Another psychological explanation the behavior of cells in the visual cortex which the brain is hyperactive through lack of oxygen. For a thoughtful examination of psychological theories, see the article 'Down the Tunnel' by Dr. Susan Blackmore (British & Irish Skeptic, vol.III, No.3, May/June 1989). Dr. Blackmore has studied OBEs as a psychological phenomenon, but unlike most psychologists who theorize about such experiences, she has actually had an OBE herself. She rightly draws attention to the fact that skeptical explanations of NDEs and OBEs which ignore the intense insightful and spiritual aspects of such experiences are inadequate. (See also **Astral Projection; Death; Double; Out-of-the-Body Travel; Survival**)

Recommended reading:

Blackmore, Susan J. *Beyond the Body,* Heinemann, London, 1982

Crookall, Robert. *Out-of-the-Body Experiences: A Fourth Analysis,* University Books, 1970

Crookall, Robert. *The Techniques of Astral Projection; Denouement After Fifty Years,* Aquarian Press, U.K., 1964

Gallup, George, Jr. with William Proctor. *Adventures in Immortality,* McGraw-Hill, 1982; Souvenir Press, London, 1983

Kübler-Ross, Elisabeth. *On Death and Dying,* MacMillan, 1969

Moody, Raymond. *Life After Life,* Bantam (paperback), 1975

Ring, Kenneth. *Life at Death: A Scientific Investigation of the Near-Death Experience.* William Morrow, 1980

Necromancy

Divination by means of the spirits of the dead, from the Greek *nekros*, dead, and *manteia*, divination. It is through its Italian form *nigromancia* that it came to be known as the "Black Art." With the Greeks it originally signified the descent into Hades in order to consult the dead rather than summoning the dead into the mortal sphere again.

The art is of almost universal usage. Considerable difference of opinion exists among modern adepts as to the exact methods to be properly pursued in the necromantic art, and it must be borne in mind that necromancy, which in the Middle Ages was called "sorcery," shades into modern Spiritualist practice. There is no doubt, however, that necromancy has long been regarded as the touch-stone of occultism, for if, after careful preparation the adept can carry through to a successful issue, the raising of the soul from the other world, he has proved the success of his art. The occult sages of the past have left full details as to how the process should be attempted.

In the case of a compact existing between the sorcerer and the devil, of course, no ceremony is necessary, as the **familiar** is ever at hand to do the bidding of his masters. This, however, is never the case with the true sorcerer, who preserves his independence and trusts to his profound knowledge of the art and his powers of command. His object therefore is to "constrain" some spirit to appear before him, and to guard himself from the danger of provoking such beings.

The magician, it must be understood, normally has an assistant, and every article and procedure must conform to rules well known in the black art. In the first place, the magician and his assistant must locate a suitable venue for their procedures, which may be either in a subterranean vault, hung round with black, and lighted by a magical torch, or else in the center of some thick wood or desert, or upon some extensive unfrequented plain, where several roads meet, or amidst the ruins of ancient castles, abbeys, and monasteries, or amongst the rocks on the sea shore, in some private detached churchyard, or any other solemn, melancholy place between the hours of twelve and one in the night, either when the moon shines very bright, or else when the elements are disturbed with storms of thunder, lightning, wind, and rain, for in these places, times, and seasons, it is contended that spirits can manifest themselves to mortal eyes with less difficulty and continue visible with the least pain in this elemental external world.

When the proper time and place is fixed on, a magic circle is to be formed, within which the master and his associate are carefully to retire. The dimensions of the circle are as follow: a piece of ground is usually chosen, nine feet square, at the full extent of which parallel lines are drawn one within the other, having sundry crosses and triangles described between them, close to which is formed the first or outer circle, then, about half-a-foot within the same, a second circle is described, and within that another square correspondent to the first, the center of which is the seat of spot where the master and associate are to be placed.

According to one authority: "The vacancies formed by the various lines and angles of the figure are filled up with the holy names of God, having crosses and triangles described between them. The reason assigned by magicians and others for the institution and use of circles, is, that so much ground being blessed and consecrated by such holy words and ceremonies as they make use of in forming it, hath a secret force to expel all evil spirits from the bounds thereof, and, being sprinkled with pure sanctified water, the ground is purified from all uncleanness; besides, the holy names of God being written over every part of it, its force becomes so powerful that no evil spirit hath ability to break through it, or to get at the magician or his companion, by reason of the antipathy in nature they bear to these sacred names. And the reason given for the triangles is, that if the spirit be not easily brought to speak the truth, they may by the exorcist be conjured to enter the same, where, by virtue of the names of the essence and divinity of God, they can speak nothing but what is true and right. The circle, therefore, according to this account of it, is the principal fort and shield of the magician, from which he is not, at the peril of his life, to depart, till he has completely dismissed the spirit, particularly if he be of a fiery or infernal nature. Instances are recorded of many who perished by this means; particularly 'Chiancungi,' the famous Egyptian fortune-teller, who was so famous in England in the 17th century. He undertook for a wager, to raise up the spirit 'Bokim,' and having described the circle, he seated his sister Napula by him as his associate. After frequently repeating the forms of exorcism, and calling upon the spirit to appear, and nothing as yet answering his demand, they grew impatient of the business, and quitted the circle, but it cost them their lives; for they were instantaneously seized and crushed to death by that infernal spirit, who happened not to be sufficiently constrained till that moment, to manifest himself to human eyes."

The magic circle is consecrated by special rituals. The proper attire or "pontificalibus" of a magician, is an ephod made of fine white linen, over that a priestly robe of black bombazine, reaching to the ground, with the two seals of the earth drawn correctly upon virgin parchment, and affixed to the breast of his outer vestment. Round his waist is tied a broad consecrated girdle, with the names "Ya, Ya,—Aie, Aaie,—Elibra,—Elchim,—Sadai,—Pah Adonai,—tuo robore,—Cinctus sum." Upon the magician's shoes must be written "Tetragrammaton," with crosses round about; upon his head a high-crowned cap of sable silk, and in his hand a Holy Bible, printed or written in pure Hebrew.

Thus attired, and standing within the charmed circle, the magician repeats the awful form of exorcism, and presently, the infernal spirits make strange and frightful noises, howlings, tremblings, flashes, and most dreadful shrieks and yells before they become visible. Their first appearance is generally in the form of fierce and terrible lions or tigers, vomiting forth fire, and roaring hideously about the circle, during which time the exorcist must not suffer any tremor of dismay, for, in that event the spirits would gain the ascendancy, and the consequences may endanger his life. On the contrary, he must summon up firm resolution and continue repeating all the forms of constriction and confinement, until the spirits are drawn nearer to the influence of the triangle, when their forms will change to appearances less ferocious and frightful, and become more submissive and tractable.

When the forms of conjuration have in this manner been sufficiently repeated, the spirits forsake their bestial shapes and enter into human form, appearing like naked men of gentle countenance and behavior, yet the magician must remain warily on his guard so that they do not deceive him by such mild gestures, for they are exceedingly fraudulent and deceitful in their dealings with those who constrain them to appear without compact, having nothing in view but to suborn his mind, or accomplish his destruction.

With great care also the spirit must be discharged after the ceremony is finished and he has answered all the demands made upon him. The magician must wait patiently until he has passed through all the terrible forms which announce his coming, and only when the last shriek has died away and every trace of fire and brimstone has disappeared, may he leave the circle and depart home safety.

If the ghost of a deceased person is to be raised, the grave must be resorted to at midnight, and a different form of conjuration is necessary. Still another is the infernal sacrament for "any corpse that hath hanged, drowned, or otherwise made away with itself," and in this will at last arise, and standing upright, answer with a faint and hollow voice the questions that are put to it.

The occultist Éliphas **Lévi** stated in his book *Transcendental Magic* (1896) that "evocations should always have a motive and a becoming end, otherwise they are works of darkness and folly, dangerous of health and reason." The permissible motive of an evocation may be either love or intelligence. Evocations of love require less apparatus and are in every respect easier.

According to Lévi, the procedure is as follows: "We must collect in the first place, carefully the memorials of him (or her) whom we desire to behold, the articles he used, and on which his impression remains; we must also prepare an apartment in which the person lived, or otherwise one of a similar kind, and place his portrait veiled in white therein, surrounded with his favourite flowers, which must be renewed daily. A fixed date must then be chosen, being that of the person's birth or one was that especially fortunate for his and our own affection, one of which we may believe that his soul, however blessed elsewhere, cannot lose the remembrance. This must be the day of the evocation, and we must prepare for it during the space of two weeks.

"Throughout the period we must refrain from extending to anyone the same proofs of affection which we have the right to expect from the dead; we must observe strict chastity, live in retreat, and take only one modest and light collation daily. Every evening at the same hour we must shut ourselves in the chamber consecrated to the memory of the lamented person, using only one small light, such as that of a funeral lamp or taper. This light should be placed behind us, the portrait should be uncovered and we should remain before it for an hour, in silence; finally, we should fumigate the apartment with a little good incense, and go out backwards.

"On the morning of the day fixed for the evocation, we should adorn ourselves as if for a festival, not salute anyone first, make but a single repast of bread, wine, and roots, or fruits. The cloth should be white, two covers should be laid, and one portion of the broken bread should be set aside; a little wine should also be placed in the glass of the person we design to invoke. The meal must be eaten alone in the chamber of evocations, and in presence of the veiled portrait; it must be all cleared away at the end, except the glass belonging to the dead person, and his portion of bread, which must be placed before the portrait. In the evening, at the hour for the regular visit, we must repair in silence to the chamber, light a clear fire of cypress-wood, and cast incense seven times thereon, pronouncing the name of the person whom we desire to behold. The lamp must then be extinguished, and the fire permitted to die out.

"On this day the portrait must not be unveiled. When the flame dies down, put more incense on the ashes, and invoke God according to the forms of the religion to which the dead person belonged, and according to the ideas which he himself possessed of God.

"While making this prayer we must identify ourselves with the evoked person, speak as he spoke, believe in sense as he believed. Then, after a silence of fifteen minutes, we must speak to him as if he were present, with affection and with faith, praying him to appear before us. Renew this prayer mentally, covering the face with both hands; then call him thrice with a loud voice; remain kneeling, the eyes closed or covered, for some minutes; then call again thrice upon him in a sweet and affectionate tone, and slowly open the eyes. Should nothing result, the same experiment must be renewed in the following year, and if necessary a third time, when it is certain that the desired apparition will be obtained, and the longer it has been delayed the more realistic and striking it will be.

"Evocations of knowledge and intelligence are performed with more solemn ceremonies. If concerned with a celebrated personage, we must meditate for twenty-one days upon his life and writings, form an idea of his appearance, converse with him mentally, and imagine his answers. We must carry his portrait, or at least his name, about us; follow a vegetable diet for twenty-one days, and a severe fast during the last seven.

"We must next construct the magical oratory . . . [This oratory must be invariably darkened]. If, however, the proposed operation is to take place during the daytime, we may leave a narrow aperture on the side where the sun will shine at the hour of the evocation, place a triangular prism facing the opening, and a crystal globe, filled with water, before the prism. If the experiment has been arranged for the night, the magic lamp must be so situated that its single ray shall upon the altar smoke. The purpose of the preparations is to furnish the Magic Agent with elements of corporeal appearance, and to ease as much as possible the tension of imagination, which could not be exalted without danger into the absolute illusion of dream. For the rest, it will be easily understood that a beam of sunlight, or the ray of a lamp, coloured variously, and falling upon curling and irregular smoke, can in no way create a perfect image. The chafing-dish containing the sacred fire should be in the centre of the oratory, and the altar of perfumes hard by. The operator must turn towards the East to pray, and the West to invoke; he must be either alone or assisted by two persons preserving the strictest silence; he must wear the magical vestments, which we have described in the seventh chapter, and must be crowned with vervain and gold. He should bathe before the operation, and all his under garments must be of the most intact and scrupulous cleanliness.

"The ceremony should begin with a prayer suited to the genius of the spirit about to be invoked and one which would be approved by himself if he still lived. For example, it would be impossible to evoke Voltaire by reciting prayers in the style of St. Bridget. For the great men of antiquity, we may see the hymns of Cleanthes or Orpheus, with the adjuration terminating the Golden Verses of Pythagoras. In our own evocation of Apollonius, we used the Magical Philosophy of Patricius for the Ritual, containing the doctrines of Zoroaster and the writings of Hermes Trismegistus. We recited the Nuctemeron of Apollonius in Greek with a loud voice and added the following conjuration: 'Vouchsafe to be present, O Father of All, and thou Thrice Mighty Hermes, Conductor of the Dead. Asclepius son of Hephaistus, Patron of the Healing Art; and thou Osiris, Lord of strength and vigour, do thou thyself be present too. Arnebascenis, Patron of Philosophy, and yet again Asclepius, son of Imuthe, who presidest over poetry. Apollonius, Apollonius, Apollonius, Thou teachest the Magic of Zoroaster, son of Oromasdes; and this is the worship of the Gods.'

"For the evocation of spirits belonging to religions issued from Judaism, the following Kabalistic invocation of Solomon should be used, either in Hebrew, or in any other tongue with which the spirit in question is known to have been familiar: 'Powers of the Kingdom, be ye under my left foot and in my right hand! Glory and Eternity, take me by the two shoulders, and direct me in the paths of victory! Mercy and Justice, be ye the equilibrium and splendour of my life! Intelligence and Wisdom, crown me! Spirits of *Malchuth,* lead me betwixt the two pillars upon which rests the whole edifice of the temple! Angels of *Netsah* and *Hod,* strengthen me upon the cubic stone of *Jesod! O Gedulael! O Geburael! O Tiphereth! Binael,* be thou my love! *Ruach Hochmael,* be thou my light! Be that which thou art and thou shalt be, *O Ketheriel!* Tschim, assist me in the name of *Saddai!* Cherubim, be my strength in the name of *Adonai!* Beni-Elohim, be my brethren in the name of the Son, and by the power of *Zebaoth!* Eloim, do battle for me in the name of *Tetragrammation!* Melachim, protect me in the name of *Jod He Vau He!* Seraphim, cleanse my love in the name of *Eloi* and Schechinah! Aralim, act! Ophanim, revolve and shine! Hajoth a Kadosh, cry, speak, roar, bellow! Kadosh, Kadosh, Kadosh, *Saddai, Adonai, Jotchavah, Eieazereie:* Hallelu-Jah, Hallelu-jah, Hallelu-jah. Amen.'

"It should be remembered above all, in conjurations, that the names of Satan, Beelzebub, Adramelek, and others do not designate spiritual unities, but legions of impure spirits. 'Our name is legion, for we are many,' says the spirit of darkness in the Gospel. Number constitutes the law, and progress takes place inversely in hell as the domain of anarchy. That is to say, the most advanced in Satanic development, and consequently the most degraded, are the least intelligent and feeblest.

"Thus, a fatal law drives demons downward when they wish and believe themselves to be ascending. So also those who term themselves chiefs are the most impotent and despised of all. As to the horde of perverse spirits, they tremble before an unknown, invisible, incomprehensible, capricious, implacable chief, who never explains his laws, whose arm is ever stretched out to strike those who fail to understand him. They give this phantom the names of Baal, Jupiter, and even others more venerable, which cannot, without profanation, be pronounced in hell. But this Phantom is only the shadow and remnant of God disfigured by their wilful perversity, and persisting in imagination like a visitation of justice and a remorse of truth.

"When the evoked spirit of light manifests with dejected or irritated countenance, we must offer him a moral sacrifice, that is, be inwardly disposed to renounce whatever offends him; and before leaving the oratory, we must dismiss him, saying: 'May peace be with thee! I have not wished to trouble thee; do thou torment me not. I shall labour to improve myself as to anything that vexes thee. I pray, and will still pray, with thee and for thee. Pray thou also both with and for me, and return to thy great slumber, expecting that day when we shall wake together. Silence and adieu!"

Paul Christian, in his *Historie de le magie* (Paris, 1871; 1952) stated that the place chosen for the evocation is not an unimportant point. The most auspicious is undoubtedly that room which contains the last traces of the lamented person. If it be impossible to fulfil this condition, we must go in search of some isolated rural retreat which corresponds in orientation and aspect, as well as measurement, with the mortuary chamber.

The window must be blocked with boards of olive wood, hermetically joined, so that no exterior light may penetrate. The ceiling, the four interior walls, and the floor must be draped with tapestry of emerald green silk, which the operator must himself secure with copper nails, invoking no assistance from strange hands, because, from this moment, he alone may enter into this spot set apart from all, the arcane Oratory of the Magus. The furniture which belonged to the deceased, his favourite possessions and trinkets, the things on which his final glance may be supposed to have rested—all these must be assiduously collected and arranged in the order which they occupied at the time of his death. If none of these souvenirs can be obtained, a faithful likeness of the departed being must at least be procured, it must be full length, and must be depicted in the dress and colours which he wore during the last period of his life. This portrait must be set up on the eastern wall by means of copper fasteners, must be covered with a veil of white silk, and must be surmounted with a crown of those flowers which were most loved by the deceased.

Before this portrait there must be erected an altar of white marble, supported by four columns which must terminate in bull's feet. A five-pointed star must be emblazoned on the slab of the altar, and must be composed of pure copper plates. The place in the center of the star, between the plates, must be large enough to receive the pedestal of a cup-shaped copper chafing-dish, containing dissected fragments of laurel wood and alder. By the side of the chafing-dish must be placed a censer full of incense. The skin of a white and spotless ram must be stretched beneath the altar, and on it must be emblazoned another pentagram drawn with parallel lines of azure blue, golden yellow, emerald green, and purple red.

A copper tripod must be erected in the middle of the Oratory; it must be perfectly triangular in form, it must be surmounted by another and similar chafing-dish, which must likewise contain quantity of dried olive wood.

A high candelabrum of copper must be placed by the wall on the southern side, and must contain a single taper of purest white wax, which must alone illuminate the mystery of the evocation.

The white color of the altar, of the ram's skin, and of the veil, is consecrated to Gabriel, the planetary archangel of the moon, and the Genius of mysteries; the green of the copper and the tapestries is dedicated to the Genius of Venus.

The altar and tripod must both be encompassed by a magnetized iron chain, and by three garlands composed of the foliage and blossoms of the myrtle, the olive, and the rose.

Finally, facing the portrait, and on the eastern side, there must be a canopy, also draped with emerald silk, and supported by two triangular columns of olive wood, plated with purest copper. On the North and South sides, between each of these columns and the wall, the tapestry must fall in long folds to the ground, forming a kind of tabernacle, which must be open on the eastern side. At the foot of each column there must be a sphinx of white marble, with a cavity in the top of the head to receive spices for burning. It is beneath this canopy that the apparitions will manifest, and it should be remembered that the Magus must turn to the east for prayer, and to the west for evocation.

Before entering this little sanctuary, devoted to the religion of remembrance, the operator must be clothed in a vestment of azure, fastened by clasps of copper, enriched with a single emerald. He must wear upon his head a tiara surrounded by a floriated circle of twelve emeralds, and a crown of violets. On his breast must be a copper ring containing a turquoise. His feet must be covered with shoes of azure silk, and he must be provided with a fan of swan's feathers to dissipate, if needful, the smoke of the perfumes.

The Oratory and all its objects must be consecrated on a Friday, during the hours which are set apart to the Genius of Venus. This consecration is performed by burning violets and roses in a fire of olive wood. A shaft must be provided in the Oratory for the passage of the smoke, but care must be taken to prevent the admission of light through this channel.

When these preparations are finished, the operator must impose on himself a retreat of one-and-twenty days, beginning on the anniversary of the death of the beloved being. During this period he must refrain from conferring on any one the least of those marks of affection which he was accustomed to bestow on the departed; he must be absolutely chaste, alike in deed and thought; he must take daily but one repast, consisting of bread; wine, roots, and fruits. These three conditions are indispensable to success in evocation, and their accomplishment requires complete isolation.

Every day, shortly before midnight, the Magus must assume his consecrated dress. On the stroke of the mystic hour, he must enter the Oratory, bearing a lighted candle in his right hand, and in the other an hour-glass. The candle must be fixed in the candelabra, and the hourglass on the altar to register the flight of time. The operator must then proceed to replenish the garland and the floral crown. Then he shall unveil the portrait, and erect it immovable in front of the altar, being thus with his face to the East, he shall softly go over in his mind the cherished recollections he possesses of the beloved and departed being.

When the upper reservoir of the hour-glass is empty the time of contemplation will be over. By the flame of the taper the operator must then kindle the laurel wood and alder in the chafing-dish which stands on the altar; then, taking a pinch of incense from the censer, let him cast it thrice upon the fire, repeating the following words:—'Glory be to the Father of life universal in the splendor of the infinite altitude, and peace in the twilight of the immeasurable depths of all Spirits of good will!'

Then he shall cover the portrait, and taking up his candle in his hand, shall depart from the Oratory, walking backward at a slow pace as far as the threshold. The same ceremony must be fulfilled at the same hour during every day of the retreat, and at each visit the crown which is above the portrait, and the garlands of the altar and tripod must be carefully renewed. The withered leaves and flowers must be burnt each evening in a room the Oratory.

When the twenty-first day has arrived, the Magus must do his best to have no communication with any one, but if this be impossible, he must not be the first to speak, and he must postpone all business till the morrow. On the stroke of noon, he must arrange a small circular table in the Oratory, and cover it with a new napkin of unblemished whiteness. It must be garnished with two copper chalices, an entire loaf, and a crystal flagon of the purest wine. The bread must be broken and not cut, and the wine emptied in equal portions into the two cups. Half of this mystic communion, which must be his sole nourishment on this supreme day, shall be offered by the operator to the dead, and by the light of the one taper he must eat his own share, standing before the veiled portrait. Then he shall retire as before, walking backward as far as the threshold, and leaving the ghost's share of the bread and wine upon the table.

When the solemn hour of the evening has at length arrived the Magus shall carry into the Oratory some well-dried cypress wood, which he shall set alight on the altar and the tripod. Three pinches of incense shall be cast on the altar flame in honour of the Supreme Potency which manifests itself by Ever Active Intelligence and by Absolute Wisdom. When the wood of the two chafing-dishes has been reduced to embers, he must renew the triple offering of incense on the altar, and must cast some seven times on the fire in the tripod; at each evaporation of the consecrated perfume he must repeat the previous doxology, and then turning to the East, he must call upon God by the prayer of that religion which was professed by the person whom he desires to evoke.

When the prayers are over he must reverse his position and with his face to the West, must enkindle the chafing-dishes on the head of each sphinx, and when the cypress is fully ablaze he must heap over it well-dried violets and roses. Then let him extinguish the candle which illuminates the Oratory, and falling on his knees before the canopy, between the two columns, let him mentally address the beloved person with a plenitude of faith and affection. Let him solemnly entreat it to appear and renew this interior adjuration seven times, under the auspices of the seven providential Genii, endeavoring during the whole of the time to exalt his soul above the natural weakness of humanity.

Finally, the operator, with closed eyes, and with hands covering his face, must call the invoked person in a loud but gentle voice, pronouncing three times all the names which he bore.

Some moments after the third appeal, he must extend his arms in the form of a cross, and lifting up his eyes, he will behold the beloved being, in a recognizable manner, in front of him. That is to say, he will perceive that ethereal substance separated from the perishable terrestrial body the fluidic envelope of the soul, which Kabalistic initiates have termed the *Perispirit.* This substance preserves the human form but is emancipated from human infirmities, and is energised by the special characteristics whereby the imperishable individuality of our essence is manifested. Evoked and Evoker can then inter-communicate intelligibly by a mutual and mysterious thought-transmission.

The departed soul will give counsel to the operator; it will occasionally reveal secrets which may be beneficial to those whom it loved on earth, but it will answer no question which has reference to the desires of the flesh; it will discover no buried treasures, nor will it unveil the secrets of a third person; it is silent on the mysteries of the superior existence to which it has now attained. In certain cases, it will, however, declare itself either happy or in punishment. If it be the latter, it will ask for the prayer of the Magus, or for some religious observance, which we must unfailingly fulfil. Lastly, it will indicate the time when the evocation may be renewed.

When it has disappeared, the operator must turn to the East, rekindle the fire on the altar, and make a final offering of incense. Then he must detach the crown and the garlands, take up his candle, and retire with his face to the West till he is out of the Oratory. His last duty is to burn the final remains of the flowers and leaves. Their ashes, united to those which have been collected during the time of retreat, must be mixed with myrtle seed, and secretly buried in a field at a depth which will secure it from disturbance of the ploughshare.

The last two examples are, of course, those of "white" necromancy. The evocation procedure followed by primitive tribes is totally different. Among certain Australian tribes the necromants were called "Birraark." It is said that a Birraark was supposed to be initiated by the "mrarts" (ghosts) when they met him wandering in the bush. It was from the ghosts that he obtained replies to questions concerning events passing at a distance, or yet to happen, which might be of interest or moment to his tribe.

An account of a spiritual seance in the bush is given in a discussion of the Kamilaroi and Kurnai peoples: "The fires were let down; the Birraark uttered the cry 'Coo-ee' at intervals. At length a distant reply was heard, and shortly afterwards the sound as of persons jumping on the ground in succession. A voice was then heard in the gloom asking in a strange intonation 'What is wanted?' At the termination of the seance, the spirit voice said, 'We are going.' Finally, the Birraark was found in the top of an almost inaccessible tree, apparently asleep." (See also **New Zealand**)

In Japan, ghosts were traditionally raised in various ways. One mode was to "put into an andon [a paper lantern in a frame] a hundred rushlights, and repeat an incantation of a hundred lines. One of these rushlights is taken out at the end of each line, and the would-be-ghost-seer then goes out in the dark with one light still burning, and blows it out, when the ghost ought to appear. Girls who have lost their lovers by death often try that sorcery."

The mode of procedure as practiced in Scotland was thus. The haunted room was made ready. He, "who was to do the daring deed, about nightfall entered the room, bearing with him a table, a chair, a candle, a compass, a crucifix if one could be got, and a Bible. With the compass he cast a circle on the middle of the floor, large enough to hold the chair and the table. He placed within the circle the chair and the table, and on the table he laid the Bible and the crucifix beside the lighted candle. If he had not a crucifix, then he drew the figure of a cross on the floor within the circle. When all this was done, he rested himself on the chair, opened the Bible, and waited for the coming of the spirit. Exactly at midnight the spirit came. Sometimes the door opened slowly, and there glided in noiselessly a lady sheeted in white, with a face of woe and told her story to the man on his asking her in the name of God what she wanted. What she wanted was done in the morning, and the spirit rested ever after. Sometimes the spirit rose from the floor, and sometimes came forth from the wall. One there was who burst into the room with a strong bound, danced wildly round the circle, and flourished a long whip round the man's head, but never dared to step within the circle. During a pause in his frantic dance he was asked, in God's name, what he wanted. He ceased his dance and told his wishes. His wishes were carried out, and the spirit was in peace."

In Sir N. W. Wraxall's *Memoirs of the Courts of Berlin, Dresden, Warsaw, and Vienna* (2 vols., 1799), there is an account of the raising of the ghost of the Chevalier de Saxe. Reports had been circulated that at his palace at Dresden there was secreted a large sum of money, and it was urged that if his spirit could be compelled to appear, interesting secrets might be extorted from him. Curiosity, combined with avarice, accordingly prompted his principal heir, Prince Charles to try the experiment, and, on the appointed night, Schrepfer was the operator, in raising the apparition. He commenced his proceedings by retiring into the corner of the gallery, where, kneeling down with many mysterious ceremonies, he invoked the spirit to appear. At length a loud clatter was heard at all the windows on the outside, resembling more the effect produced by a number of wet fingers drawn over the edge of glasses than anything else to which it could well be compared. This sound announced the arrival of the good spirits, and was shortly followed by a yell of a frightful and unusual nature, which indicated the presence of malignant spirits. Schrepfer continued his invocations, when "the door suddenly opened with violence, and something that resembled a black ball or globe rolled into the room. It was enveloped in smoke or cloud, in the midst of which appeared a human face, like the countenance of the Chevalier de Saxe, from which issued a loud and angry voice, exclaiming in German, 'Carl, was wollte du mit mich?' " (Charles, what would thou do with me?). By reiterated exorcisms Schrepfer finally dismissed the apparition, and the terrified spectators dispersed fully convinced of his magical powers.

Since the rituals of magical evocation date back to the ancient East, it is not surprising to find that European rituals have parallels in Arabia, Persia, India, China, Tibet and Japan. In the modern occult revival, such rituals have been revived and popularized, side by side with European traditions and revivals and various hybrid forms have evolved. (See also **Ceremonial Magic; Magic; Magical Diagrams: Magical Instruments and Accessories**)

Recommended reading:

Christian, Paul. *The History and Practice of Magic,* Forge Press, London, 2 vols., 1952

Lévi, Éliphas. *The History of Magic,* William Rider & Co., London, 1913 etc.

Lévi, Éliphas. *Transcendental Magic; Its Doctrine and Ritual,* George Redway, London, 1896 etc.

Shah, Sayed Idries Shah. *Oriental Magic,* Rider & Co., London, 1956

Shah, Sayed Idries Shah. *The Secret Lore of Magic; Books of the Sorcerers,* Frederick Muller, London, 1957

Smedley, Edward, W. C. Taylor, Henry Thompson & Elihu Rich. *The Occult Sciences,* Richard Griffin, London & Glasgow, 1855

Waite, Arthur E. *The Book of Ceremonial Magic,* William Rider & Son, London, 1911; University Books, New York, 1961; (under title *The Book of Black Magic and Ceremonial Magic*) Causeway Books, 1973

Necronomicon, The

A fabled **grimoire** or textbook of black magic for evoking demons, supposedly compiled by the "mad Arab Abdul Alhazred" in fact, an invention of H. P. **Lovecraft,** writer of supernatural and fantasy fiction. The name "Abdul Alhazred" was adopted playfully by Lovecraft around the age of five, after reading an edition of *The Arabian Nights,* and was used in later life in Lovecraft's fiction. It may also contain a reference to the name "Hazard," an old Rhode Island family.

In 1936, Lovecraft wrote a pseudo-scholarly essay titled *A History of the Necronomicon,* which claimed that its original tittle was *Al Azif,* deriving from the word used by Arabs to designate the nocturnal sound of insects resembling the howling of demons. There followed an account of various editions of the *Necronomicon* from A.D. 730 onwards.

Lovecraft had claimed that there was a copy of the work in the library of Miskatonic University, in Arkham (a city invented by him in his fiction).

Lovecraft's essay was published in leaflet form by Wilson H. Shepherd, Alabama, 1938, and has since been reprinted. The *Necronomicon* was cited in various stories by Lovecraft, and gradually acquired a spurious life of its own.

Someone inserted an index card for the book in the files of Yale Library. A New York bookseller could not resist inserting an entry for a Latin edition in one of his sale catalogs.

Eventually a group of writers and researchers headed by occult scholar Colin **Wilson** solemnly presented *The Necronomicon: The Book of Dead Names* as a newly discovered lost masterpiece of occult literature.

In an introduction to this publication, Wilson suggested that Lovecraft's invention may have had some substance in fact, perhaps revealed through Lovecraft's subconscious mind. Wilson told a story as fabulous as that of the origin of the **Golden Dawn** cipher manuscript, concerning a Dr. Stanislaus Hinterstoisser, president of the Salzburg Institute for the Study of Magic and Occult Phenomena, who claimed that Lovecraft's father was an Egyptian Freemason, that he had seen a copy of *The Necronomicon* in Boston, U.S. (where Lovecraft senior had worked), which was a section of a book by Alkindi (died A.D. 850) known as *The Book of the Essence of the Soul.*

Science-fiction writer L. Sprague de Camp (who published an excellent biography of Lovecraft in 1975) is said to have acquired an Arabic manuscript from Baghdad titled *Al Azif.* The British occultist Robert Turner, after researching in the British Museum Library, claimed that the Alkindi work was known to the famous magician John **Dee** (1527-1608) who had a copy in cipher manuscript. This book, known as *Liber Logaeth,* was recently examined by computer analysis, and so *The Necronomicon: The Book of Dead Names* has now been published, edited by George Hay, introduced by Colin Wilson, researched by Robert Turner and David Langford (Neville Spearman, U.K., 1978; Corgi paperback, 1980).

No doubt other recensions of *The Necronomicon* will be discovered in the course of time. Meanwhile, librarians need no longer be embarrassed by requests for this elusive work.

Neihardt, John G(neisenau) (1881-1973)

Eminent American poet and author, who also founded a remarkable organization for parapsychological research known as SORRAT (Society for Research on Rapport and Telekinesis).

Neihardt was born January 8, 1881 near Sharpsburg, Illinois, son of a farmer. He was educated at Nebraska Normal College (now Nebraska State Teachers College at Wayne), obtaining a diploma in science 1897.

From 1901-07 he lived among Omaha Indians, later among the Sioux.

From 1911-20 he was literary editor of the *Minneapolis Journal.* In 1923, he was appointed professor of poetry at University of Nebraska, Lincoln. From 1926-38 he was literary editor of the *St. Louis Post-Dispatch.* From 1943-46 he worked for the U.S. Department of Interior, Bureau of Indian Affairs, Washington, D.C.; director of information at Chicago office from 1943-46, field representative, 1946-48. From 1949-65, he was lecturer in English and poet-in-residence at university of Missouri-Columbia; Honnold Lecturer, Knox College, 1939, also lecturer at other colleges and universities.

His many books included: *The Divine Enchantment* (1900), *The Lonesome Trail* (1907), *The River and I* (1910, 1927), *The Quest* (1916), *The Song of Three Friends* (1919), *The Splendid Wayfaring* (1920), *The*

Song of the Indian Wars (1925, 1928), *Poetic Values—Their Reality and Our Need of Them* (1925), *Collected Poems* (1926), *Indian Tales and Others* (1926), *Black Elk Speaks* (1932), *The Song of the Messiah* (1935), *All Is But a Beginning* (autobiography, 1972).

He was honored by the Poetry Society of America Prize for best volume of verse in 1919, named poet laureate of Nebraska by an act of the legislature 1921. He was awarded the Gold Scroll Medal of Honor of National Poetry Center in 1936, Writers Foundation award for poetry, 1964, LL.D., Creighton University 1928, Litt.D., University of Nebraska 1917, University of Missouri 1947, Midland Lutheran College 1972. He was elected to Nebraska State Hall of Fame in 1974.

A bronze bust of Neihardt was placed in the rotunda of the Nebraska capital by an act of the state legislature in 1961 and there is another monument in the city park, Wayne, Nebraska. The Garden Club of Bancroft, Nebraska acquired the cottage in which he lived and wrote as a museum of Neihardt memorabilia, and there is a special Neihardt Memorial Collection at the University of Missouri.

Neihardt was friendly with Dr. Joseph B. **Rhine,** famous parapsychologist and director of the **Foundation for Research on the Nature of Man.** Neihardt's experience with Omaha and Sioux Indians probably influenced his philosophical views expressed in what has been called "Pragmatic Mysticism," involving the heightened awareness of prayer and meditation being applied to everyday life. In 1908, he married Mona Martensen who had earlier spent some time as companion to a Spiritualist and who was convinced that psychic experience could not be dismissed. Apparently she had considerable mediumistic talents herself.

From the 1920s onwards, Neihardt spent some time investigating psychic phenomena at first hand. He was also well aware of paranormal experiences amongst the Sioux Indians.

In 1926, he met Caspar Yost, a journalist who had investigated the famous phenomena of Mrs. Pearl **Curren,** through whom the **"Patience Worth"** scripts were produced. Neihardt himself made an in-depth study of the phenomena.

In 1960, with Dr. John T. Richards and other associates, Neihardt formed the Society for Research on Rapport and Telekinesis (see **SORRAT**) in order to develop investigation of psi faculties under conditions which would be favorable. Some remarkable effects of psychokinesis were obtained. The story of the group has been recorded in SORRAT: *A History of the Neihardt Psychokinesis Experiments,* 1961-1981 by John Thomas Richards, published Scarecrow Press, 1982. Neihardt died November 3, 1973. (See also **Movement; Psychokinesis; SORRAT**)

Neil-Smith, the Rev. Christopher

Vicar of a London, England church, and a leading British exorcist. He was ordained in 1944 and became aware of a healing power, which he has since used for dealing with possessed individuals.

He performed his first exorcism in 1949, and has since performed more than 500 exorcisms a year. By 1974, he had performed some 2,200 exorcisms, one of which was filmed for television.

He has appeared on radio and television programs in the U.S., Canada, Italy, Belgium, Switzerland, Germany and Africa, as well as Britain. He described his experiences and beliefs in his book *The Exorcist and the Possessed; the Truth about Exorcism* (Cornwall, U.K., 1974)

Nengraphy

Japanese term for the psychic photography (or "Thoughtography") of the young Japanese psychic Masuaki **Kiyota.** The Japan Nengraphy Association, headed by Tsutomu Miyauchi, investigates such phenomena. Address, Awiji-cho 2-25, Kannda, Chioda, Tokyo. (See also T. **Fukurai; Japan; Psychic Photography;** Ted **Serios; Thoughtforms; Thoughtography**)

Neoplatonism

A mystical philosophical system initiated by Plotinus of Alexandria, 233 A.D., which combined the philosophy of ancient Greece with later spiritual cravings. Although to some extent founded on the teaching of Plato, it was undoubtedly sophisticated by a deep mysticism, which in all probability emanated from the traditions of the land in which it originated. To a great extent it colored the thought of medieval mysticism and magic.

Plotinus, its founder, commenced the study of philosophy in Alexandria at the age of twenty-eight. He early experienced an earnest desire to reach the truth concerning existence, and to that end made a deep study of the dialogues of Plato and the metaphysics of Aristotle. He practiced the most severe austerities, and attempted to live what he called the "angelic" life, or the life of the disembodied in the body.

He was greatly drawn to **Apollonius of Tyana** by reading his *Life* by Philostratus, and gave credence to many of the marvels recorded therein. The union of philosopher and priest in the character of Apollonius fired the imagination of Plotinus, and in his Pythagorean teachings the young student discovered the elements of both Orientalism and Platonism, for both Pythagoras and Plato strove to escape the sensuous, and to realize in contemplative abstraction that tranquility superior to desire and passion which made men approach the gods, although in the hands of the later Pythagoreans and Platonists, the principles of the Hellenic masters degenerated into a species of theurgic freemasonry. Many of the Pythagoreans had joined the various Orphic associations, and indeed became little more than itinerant vendors of charms.

It is probable that at Alexandria Plotinus heard from Orientals the principles of eastern theosophy, which he did not find in Plato. But everywhere he found a growing indifference to religion as known to the more ancient Greeks and Egyptians. By this time, the pantheons of Greece, Rome and Egypt, had become fused in the worship of Serapis, and this fusion had been forwarded by the works of Plutarch, Apuleius, and Lucian.

The position of philosophy at this time was by no means a strong one. In fact, speculation had given place to ethical teaching, and philosophy was regarded more as a branch of literature, or an elegant recreation. Plotinus persuaded himself that philosophy and religion should be one, that speculation should be a search after God. It was at this time that he first heard of Ammonius Saccas, who shortly before had been a porter in the streets of Alexandria, and who lectured upon the possibilities of reconciling Plato and Aristotle.

"Skepticism," stated Ammonius, "was death." He recommended men to travel back across the past, and out of the whole bygone world of thought to construct a system greater than any of its parts. This teaching formed an epoch in the life of Plotinus, who was convinced that Platonism, exalted into a species of illuminism and drawing to itself like a magnet all the scattered truth of the bygone ages, could alone preserve mankind from skepticism. He occupied himself only with the most abstract questions concerning knowledge and being.

"Truth," according to Plotinus, "is not the agreement of our comprehension of an external object with the object itself, but rather, the agreement of the mind with itself. For the philosopher the objects we contemplate, and that which contemplates are identical; both are thought." All truth is then easy. Reduce the soul to its most perfect simplicity, and we find it is capable of exploration into the infinite; indeed it becomes one with the infinite. This is the condition of ecstasy, and to accomplish it, a stoical austerity and asceticism was necessary.

The Neoplatonists were thus ascetics and enthusiasts. Plato was neither. According to Plotinus, the mystic contemplates the divine perfection in himself; all worldly things and logical distinctions vanish during the period of ecstasy. This, of course, is Oriental rather than Platonic, and is reminiscent of the stages of **Yoga** meditation.

Plotinus regarded the individual existence as phenomenal and transitory, and subordinated reason to ecstasy where the Absolute is in question. It is only at the end of his chain of reasoning that he introduced the supernatural. He is first a rationalist, afterwards a mystic, and only a mystic when he finds that he cannot employ the machinery of reason. The following letter of Plotinus, written about 260 A.D., well embodies his ideas on these heads:

"*Plotinus to Flaccus.*—I applaud your devotion to philosophy; I rejoice to hear that your soul has set sail, like the returning Ulysses, for its native land—that glorious, that only real country—the world of unseen truth. To follow philosophy, the senator Rogatianus, one of the noblest of my disciples, gave up the other day all but the whole of his patrimony, set free his slaves, and surrendered all the honours of his station.

"Tidings have reached us that Valerian has been defeated and is now in the hands of Sapor. The threats of Franks and Allemanni, of Goths and Persians, are alike terrible by turns to our degenerate Rome. In days like these, crowded with incessant calamities, the inducements to a life of contemplation are more than ever strong. Even my quiet existence seems now to grow somewhat sensible of the advance of years. Age alone I am unable to debar from my retirement. I am weary already of this prison-house, the body, and calmly await the day when the divine nature within me shall be set free from matter.

"The Egyptian priests used to tell me that a single touch with the wing of their holy bird could charm the crocodile into torpor; it is not thus speedily, my dear friend, that the pinions of your soul will have power to still the untamed body. The creature will yield only to watchful, strenuous constancy of habit. Purify your soul from all undue hope and fear about earthly things, mortify the body, deny self,—affections as well as appetites, and the inner eye will begin to exercise its clear and solemn vision.

"You ask me to tell you how we know, and what is our criterion of certainty. To write is always irksome to me. But for the continual solicitations of Porphyry, I should not have left a line to survive me. For your own sake, and for your father's, my reluctance shall be overcome.

"External objects present us only with appearances. Concerning them, therefore, we may be said to possess opinion rather than knowledge. The distinctions in the actual world of appearance are of import only to ordinary and practical men. Our question lies within the ideal reality which exists behind appearance. How does the mind perceive these ideas? Are they without us, and is the reason, like sensation, occupied with objects external to itself? What certainty could we then have, what assurance that our perception was infallible? The object perceived would be a something different from the mind perceiving it. We should have then an image instead of reality. It would be monstrous to believe for a moment that the mind was unable to perceive ideal truth exactly as it is, and that we had not certainty and real knowledge concerning the world of intelligence. It follows, therefore, that this religion of truth is not to be investigated as a thing external to us, and so only imperfectly known. It is *within* us. Here the objects we contemplate and that which contemplates are identical,—both are thought. The subject cannot surely *know* an object different from itself. The world of ideas lies within our intelligence. Truth, therefore, is not the agreement of our apprehension of an external object with the object itself. It is the agreement of the mind with itself. Consciousness, therefore, is the sole basis of certainty. The mind is its own witness. Reason sees in itself that which is above itself as its source; and again, that which is below itself as still itself once more.

"Knowledge has three degrees—Opinion, Science, Illumination. The means or instrument of the first is sense; of the second, dialectic; of the third, intuition. To the last I subordinate reason. It is absolute knowledge founded on the identity of the mind knowing with the object known.

"There is a raying out of all orders of existence, an external emanation from the ineffable One [*prudos*]. There is again a returning impulse, drawing all upwards and inwards towards the centre from whence all came [epistrophe]. Love, as Plato in the *Banquet* beautifully says, is the child of Poverty and Plenty. In the amorous quest of the soul after the Good, lies the painful sense of gall and deprivation. But that Love is blessing, is salvation, is our guardian genius; without it the centrifugal law would overpower us, and sweep our souls out far from their source toward the cold extremities of the Material and the Manifold. The wise man recognises the idea of the Good within him. This he develops by withdrawal into the Holy Place of his own soul. He who does not understand how the soul contains the Beautiful within itself, seeks to realize beauty without, by laborious production. His aim should rather be to concentrate and simplify, and so to expand his being; instead of going out into the Manifold, to forsake it for the One, and so to float upwards towards the divine fount of being whose stream flows within him.

"You ask, how can we know the Infinite? I answer, not by reason. It is the office of reason to distinguish and define. The Infinite, therefore, cannot be ranked among its objects. You can only apprehend the Infinite by a faculty superior to reason, by entering into a state in which you are your finite self no longer, in which the Divine Essence is communicated to you. This is Ecstasy. It is the liberation of your mind from its infinite consciousness. Like only can apprehend like; when you thus cease to be finite, you become one with the Infinite. In the reduction of your soul to its simplest self (aplosis), its divine essence, you realize this Union, this Identity [enosin].

"But this sublime condition is not of permanent duration. It is only now and then that we can enjoy this elevation (mercifully made possible for us) above the limits of the body and the world. I myself have realized it but three times as yet, and Porphyry hitherto not once. All that tends to purify and elevate the mind will assist you in this attainment, and facilitate the approach and the recurrence of these happy intervals. There are, then, different roads by which this end may be reached. The love of beauty which exalts the poet; that devotion to the One and that ascent of science which makes the ambition of the philosopher; and that love and those prayers by which some devout and ardent soul tends in its moral purity towards perfection. These are the great highways conducting to that height above the actual and the particular where we stand in the immediate presence of the Infinite, who shines out as from the deeps of the soul."

Plotinus appears to have been greatly indebted to Numenius for some of the ideas peculiar to his system. Numenius attempted to harmonize Pythagoras and Plato, to elucidate and confirm the opinions of both by the religious dogmas of the Egyptians, the **Magi** and the Brahmans, and he believed that Plato was indebted to the Hebrew as well as to the Egyptian theology for much of his wisdom. Like Plotinus he was puzzled that the immutable One could find it possible to crate the Manifold without self-degradation, and he therefore posited a Being whom he calls the Demi-urge, or Artificer, who merely carried out the will of God in constructing the universe.

Expressed in summary, the mysticism of Plotinus is as follows: One cannot know God in any partial or finite manner. To know Him truly we must escape from the finite, from all that is earthly, from the very gifts of God to God Himself, and know Him in the infinite way by receiving, or being received into Him directly. To accomplish this, and to attain this identity, we must withdraw into our inmost selves, into our own essence, which alone is susceptible of blending with the Divine Essence. Hence the inmost is the highest, and as with all systems of mysticism introversion is ascension, and God is found within.

Porphyry entered the school of Plotinus when it had become an institution of some standing. At first he strongly opposed the teachings of his master, but soon became his most devoted scholar. He directed a fierce assault on Christianity, and at the same time launched strictures at Paganism, but both forces were too strong for him. The attempt of the school to combine religion and philosophy robbed the first of its only power, and the last of its only principle. Religion in the hands of the Neoplatonists lost all sanctity and authoritativeness, and philosophy all scientific precision, and the attempt to philosophize superstition ended in mere absurdity. But they succeeded in one thing, and that was in making philosophy superstitious—no very difficult task.

Porphyry modified the doctrine of Plotinus regarding ecstasy, by stating that in that condition the mind does not lose its consciousness of personality. He called it a dream in which the soul, dead to the world, rises to a species of divine activity, to an elevation above reason, action and liberty. He believed in a certain order of evil genii, who took pleasure in hunting wild beasts, and others of whom hunted souls that had escaped from the fetters of the body, so that to escape them, the soul must once more take refuge in the flesh. Porphyry's theosophical conceptions, based on those of Plotinus, were strongly and ably traversed by the theurgic mysteries of Iamblichus, to whom the priest was a prophet full of deity. Criticizing Porphyry, Iamblichus stated:

"Often, at the moment of inspiration, or when the afflatus has subsided, a fiery Appearance is seen—the entering or departing Power. Those who are skilled in this wisdom can tell by the character of this glory the rank of divinity who has seized for the time the reins of the mystic's soul, and guides it as he will. Sometimes the body of the man subject to this influence is violently agitated, sometimes it is rigid and motionless. In some instances sweet music is heard, in others, discordant and fearful sounds. The person of the subject has been known to dilate and tower to a superhuman height; in other cases, it has been lifted up into the air. Frequently, not merely the ordinary exercise of reason, but sensation and animal life would appear to have been suspended, and the subject of the afflatus has not felt the application of fire, has been pierced with spits, cut with knives, and been sensible of no pain. Yea, often, the more the body and the mind have been alike enfeebled by vigil and by fasts, the more ignorant or mentally imbecile a youth may be who is brought under this influence, the more freely and unmixedly will the divine power be made manifest. So clearly are these wonders the work, not of human skill or wisdom, but of supernatural agency! Characteristics such as these I have mentioned, are the marks of the true inspiration.

"Now, there are, O Agathocles, four great orders of spiritual existence,—Gods, Dæmons, Heroes or Demi-gods, and Souls. You will naturally be desirous to learn how the apparition of a God or a Dæmon is distinguished from those of Angels, Principalities, or Souls. Know, then, that their appearance to man corresponds to their nature, and that they always manifest themselves to those who invoke them in a manner consonant with their rank in the hierarchy of spiritual natures. The appearances of Gods are uniform, those of Dæmons various. The Gods shine with a benign aspect. When a God manifests himself, he frequently appears to hide sun or moon, and seems as he descends too vast for earth to contain. Archangels are at once awful and mild; Angels yet more gracious; Dæmons terrible. Below the four leading classes I have mentioned are placed the malignant Daemons, the Anti-gods."

Each spiritual order has gifts of its own to bestow on the initiated who evoke them. The Gods confer health of body, power and purity of mind, and, in short, elevate and restore our natures to their proper principles. Angels and archangels have at their command only subordinate bestowments. Dæmons, however, are hostile to the aspirant, afflict both body and mind, and hinder our escape from the sensuous. Principalities, who govern the sublunary elements, confer temporal advantages. Those of a lower rank, who preside over matter, often display their bounty in material gifts. Souls that are pure are, like Angels, salutary in their influence. Their appearance encourages the soul in its upward efforts. Heroes stimulate to great actions. All those powers depend, in a descending chain, each species on that immediately above it. Good Dæmons are seen surrounded by the emblems of blessing, Dæmons who execute judgment appear with the instruments of punishment.

"There is nothing unworthy of belief in what you have been told concerning the sacred sleep, and divination by dreams. I explain in thus:

"The soul has a twofold life, a lower and a higher. In sleep that soul is freed from the constraint of the body, and enters, as one emancipated, on its divine life of intelligence. Then, as the noble faculty which beholds the objects that truly are—the objects in the world of intelligence—stirs within, and awakens to its power, who can be surprised that the mind, which contains in itself the principles of all that happens, should, in this its state of liberation, discern the future in those antecedent principles which will make that future what it is to be? The nobler part of the soul is thus united by abstraction to higher natures, and becomes a participation in the wisdom and foreknowledge of the Gods.

"Recorded examples of this are numerous and well-authenticated; instances occur, too, every day. Numbers of sick, by sleeping in the temple of Æsculapius, have had their cure revealed to them in dreams vouchsafed by the god. Would not Alexander's army have perished but for a dream in which Dionysius pointed out the means of safety? Was not the siege of Aphutis raised through a dream sent by Jupiter Ammon to Lysander? The night-time of the body is the day-time of the soul."

We thus see how in the process of time the principles on which the system of Plotinus rested were surrendered little by little, while **divination** and evocation were practiced with increasing frequency. Plotinus had declared the possibility of the absolute identification of the divine with human nature—the broadest possible basis for mysticism. Porphyry took up narrower ground and contended that in the union which takes place in ecstasy, we still retain consciousness of personality. Iamblichus diminished the real principle of mysticism still farther in theory, and denied that man has a faculty, eternally active and in accessible, to passion: so that the intellectual ambition so lofty in Plotinus subsided among the followers of Iamblichus into magical practice.

Proclus was the last of the Greek Neoplatonists. He elaborated the Trinity of Plotinus into a succession of impalpable triads, and surpassed Iamblichus in his devotion to the practice of theurgy. With him, theurgy was the art which gave human beings the magical passwords that carry them through barrier after barrier, dividing species from species of the upper existences, till at the summit of the hierarchy he arrives at the highest.

Above all being is God, the Non-Being, who is apprehended only by negation. When we are raised out of our weakness and on a level with God, it seems as though reason were silenced for then we are above reason. In short we become intoxicated with God.

Proclus was an adept in the ritual of invocations among every people in the world, and a great magical figure. With the advance of Byzantinism, he represented the old world of Greek thought, and even those who wrote against him as a heathen show the influence he exercised on their doctrines. Thus Dionysius attempted to accommodate the philosophy of Proclus to Christianity, and greatly admired his asceticism.

The theology of the Neoplatonists was always in the first instance a mere matter of logic. They associated Universals with Causes. The highest became with them merely the most comprehensive.

As has been said, Neoplatonism exercised great power among the scholiasts and magicians of the Middle Ages. In fact all that medievalism knew of Plato was through the medium of the Neoplatonists. In Germany in the fourteenth century it became a vivifying principle, for although its doctrine of emanation was abandoned, its allegorical explanation, its exaltation of the spirit above the letter was retained, and Platonism and mysticism together created a party in the church—the sworn foes of scholasticism and mere lifeless orthodoxy. (See also **Divination; Greece; Meditation; Yoga**)

Recommended reading:

Brehier, Emile. *The Philosophy of Plotinus,* University of Chicago Press, 1958

Mead, G. R. S. *Essay Written as a Preface to a New Edition of T. Taylor's "Select Works of Plotinus,"* Theosophical Publishing Society, London, 1895

Rist, J. M. *Plotinus; the Road to Reality,* Cambridge University Press, U.K., 1967

Turnbull, Grace (ed.) *The Essence of Plotinus,* Greenwood Press, 1934

"Nessie"

Popular affectionate name for the Monster of Loch Ness, Scotland. In an article in *Nature* titled 'Naming the Loch Ness Monster,' naturalist Sir Peter Scott and Robert Rines bestowed the scientific name *Nessiteras rhombopteryx.*

They felt obliged to do this following modern photographic evidence suggesting the reality of the Monster, because a British Act of Parliament (1975) requires a scientific name for any rare species of animal qualifying for conservation. Unfortunately some newspapers gleefully pointed out that this scientific name may be converted to the anagram "Monster Hoax by Sir Peter." (For fuller information on "Nessie" see **Loch Ness Monster; Monsters**).

Nessletter (Newsletter)

Newsletter concerned with reports and news of monsters, especially the Loch Ness Monster. Published by Ness Information Service, Huntshieldford, St. Johns Chapel, Bishop Aukland, Co. Durham DL13 1RQ, England. (See also **Loch Ness Monster**)

Nester, Marian L(ow) (Mrs. J. E. Nester) (1910-)

Researcher in parapsychology. Born June 8, 1910 at Jamaica Plain, Massachusetts, she studied at Smith College (B.A. 1932) and Boston University (M.Ed. 1940). In 1951 she married J. E. Nester.

She was a teacher from 1933-44, staff member of United Service Organization, Travelers Aid Society from 1944-46, worked in publishing from 1946-51, freelance editor, secretary and researcher from 1951 on, research assistant at Parapsychology Foundation 1958-62. She is an associate member of the Parapsychological Association.

Mrs. Nester worked on experiments at the Parapsychology Foundation connected with survival and mediumship, and assisted in a survey of death-bed hallucinations. Her articles include: 'New Methods of Parapsychology' *(Tomorrow,* vol. 9, No.4, 1961) and a review of Rene Sudre's book *Parapsychology (International Journal of Parapsychology,* vol.3, No.1 1961).

Networking

A characteristic **New Age** development of data sharing which has particular relevance to contemporary occultism, holistic health, alternative medicine, ecology, and spiritual growth movements.

Networking of one kind or another has been practiced for many decades by means of directories, yearbooks, encyclopedias, specialized magazines, and groups, but with the development of modern computer resources, the facilities for accumulating, storing, and disseminating data on a wide scale have been greatly accelerated.

The concept of rapid access to topical information has special value in relation to New Age Beliefs and practices, since so many groups and centers flourish for a while, change name or address, or disappear, sometimes giving rise to splinter movements.

Encyclopedias, like the present one, which attempt a comprehensive overview of the field, sometimes find difficulty in listing the whereabouts and current status of organizations, publications, or cults, hence the need for inter-edition supplements.

Many networking guides are presented in magazine format for distribution at occult and holistic health shops: some have related publications in different countries through international networking. Many such publications have diaries of forthcoming events, exhibitions, and lectures.

Other networking publications are in more traditional directory format, regularly updated.

Networking makes is possible to accumulate and disseminate New Age information in a variety of formats and at local, state, or city levels. Typical networking publications in magazine format include *New Age Media Resource Directory, Circle Network News, Free Spirit, Resources for Personal and Social Transformation,* PhenomeNews, (each published quarterly), and *Whole Life Times* (published every six weeks).

The Whole Life World Fair Expo, organized annually by the *Whole Life Times,* publishes a catalog that includes networking information on related events, individuals, and publications. The comparable British annual Festival for **Mind-Body-Spirit** has a special Networking feature, inviting the public to "play the Networking Game," i.e., join a Network to exchange information with other people, to keep track of meetings and contacts, to benefit from the use of computers for exchange of information.

The Networking Game charges a small fee and provides guidance notes, a personal networking diary, a networking badge, personal address labels, and information on contacts in one's local area, as well as information on such facilities as Net Workshops, Playshops, a Networking Market for goods and services, and a computer conferencing network for "screen-to-screen" meetings. The address of the Networking Game is: Sabine Kurjo, 21A Goldhurst Terrace, London, NW6 3HD, England.

On more traditional lines, such publications as *The New Times Network* directory, *The New Consciousness Sourcebook,* and the *Whole Again Resource Guide,* all provide regularly updated information on such New Age subjects as spiritual growth, psychic development, and holistic health, in directory format.

The scope of Networking is a vast one, embracing a wide range of subjects and with global scope. For some indication of this unique modern innovation, see *The Networking Book; People Connecting with People* by Jessica Lipnack & Jeffrey Stamps (Methuen, New York/Routledge & Kegan Paul, U.K., 1986). In a Foreword, R. Buckminster Fuller states: "The new human *networks* emergence represents the natural evolutionary expansion into the just completed, thirty-years-in-its-building, world-embracing, physical communications network. The new reorienting of human 'networking' constitutes the heart and mind pumped flow of life and intellect into the world arteries."

Another enthusiastic advocate of Networking is Dr. Robert Muller, former Assistant Director-General of the United Nations, who has stated: "A new world lies just under the crust of today's wrong values and society. Networking by all sensitive souls of this planet will greatly help its birth. I pray for the flowering of networks all over the world." (See also **New Age**)

Neuburg, Victor (Benjamin) (1883-1940)

Poet, editor and associate of occultist Aleister **Crowley.** Born May 6, 1883 in Islington, London, England, he was educated at the City of London School, southwest London, and at Trinity College, Cambridge. An early Freethinker, his first poems were published in the *Agnostic Journal* and *Freethinker.* In 1892 he married Kathleen Rose Goddard.

Around 1906 at Cambridge, Neuburg came in contact with Crowley, also a poet, who had read some of Neuburg's pieces in the *Agnostic Journal.* Crowley initiated Neuburg into his secret society the **A.·. A.·.** giving him the name "Frater Omnia Vincam." He also initiated Neuburg into homosexuality, to enhance their joint occult powers through sex-magic.

In 1909, Crowley took Neuburg to Algiers, and they set off into the North African desert, where they performed occult rituals. Afterwards, with characteristic callousness, Crowley appears to have abandoned Neuburg in the desert. Neuburg fortunately survived.

In 1913, Crowley and Neuburg again joined forces in a homosexual ritual magic operation known as "The Paris Working." Neuburg appears to have broken with Crowley some time in 1914, before Crowley left for the U.S. on a magickal tour. Neuburg was ritually cursed by Crowley and suffered a nervous breakdown.

From 1916-19 he served in the Army in World War I. Thereafter he avoided Crowley and spent most of his time at Vine Cottage, Steyning, Sussex, where he operated a hand-printing press. Many of his poems were issued under the imprint "Vine Press."

In addition to works published under his own name, he used a number of pseudonyms: Alfricobas, Benjie, M. Broyle, Richard Byrde, Christopher Crayne, Lawrence Edwardes, Arthur French, Paul Pentreath, Nicholas Pyne, Harold Stevens, Shirley Tarn, Rold White. His books included: *The Green Garland* (1908), *The Triumph of Pan* (1910), *Lillygay, an Anthology of Anonymous Poems* (1920), *Swift Wings, Songs in Sussex* (1921), *Songs of the Groves* (1921), *Larkspur, a Lyric Garland* (1922).

In 1933, Neuburg edited a section called the Poet's Corner in the British newspaper the *Sunday Referee.* This encouraged new talent by awarding weekly prizes.

A group of talented young writers and poets grew up around Neuburg. He showed his excellent taste and judgment by an award to a then unknown poet named Dylan Thomas. As a result of Neuburg's enthusiasm, the publisher of the *Sunday Referee* sponsored the first book of poems by Dylan Thomas, titled *18 Poems.* The first publication is now a much prized collector's item.

Neuburg died May 30, 1940.

Although a minor poet, his work has a magical lyric quality. Known affectionately as "Vickybird," he was a generous and warmhearted friend of other writers, but his natural mystical inclinations were ruthlessly exploited by Aleister Crowley. There is an account of Neuburg in Arthur Calder-Marshall's *The Magic of My Youth* (1951), and a sympathetic biography *The Magical Dilemma of Victor Neuburg* was published by Jean Overton **Fuller** (1965). See also the booklet *Vickybird; A Memoir by his son* by Victor E. Neuburg (The Polytechnic of North London, Holloway Road, London, N7 8DB, England. 1983).

Neumann, Thérèse (1898-1962)

Bavarian peasant girl of Konnersreuth, whose **stigmata,** vision of the Passion of Christ and other supernormal phenomena aroused world-wide attention. Born April 8, 1898, she was educated to a religious mentality and aspired to become a missionary sister. Constitutionally she appeared robust.

In March, 1918, while she aided in putting out a fire which broke out in a neighboring house by passing buckets of water up the roof, she was stricken by a violent pain in the lumbar regions and collapsed. In the hospital of Waldsassen she was seized with terrible cramp, became blind, from time to time deaf, and paralyzed, first in both legs, then in the right and left cheek. She spent miserable years at the home of her parents in constant suffering and religious meditation.

On April 29, 1923, the beatification day of St. Thérèse, she suddenly recovered her sight. On May 3, 1923 an ulcer between the toes of her left foot which might have necessitated amputation, was unaccountably healed, after she put three rose leaves from the tomb of St. Thérèse in the bandage.

On May 17, 1925, the canonization day of St. Thérèse de Lisieux, she saw a light and heard a voice which comforted and assured her that she would be able to sit up and walk. She sat up immediately and afterwards could walk about the room with the help of a stick and a supporting arm. On September 30 she dispensed with this support and went to the church alone.

In December she was seized with violent intestinal pains. An urgent operation for appendicitis was recommended. She had a vision of St. Thérèse and heard a voice which told her to go to Church and thank God. During the night the pus found a natural outlet and she was cured.

The stigmata appeared during Lent in 1926. An abscess developed in her ear, causing violent headaches. She saw in a vision Jesus in the Garden of Olives and felt a sudden stinging pain in the left side. A wound formed which bled abundantly. It was followed by stigmatic wounds in the hands and legs. There was no pus, no inflammation, but there was a fresh flow of blood every Friday. She also shed tears of blood and became, by Friday, almost blind.

With an awe-inspiring dramatic vividness she lived through the whole tragedy of the crucifixion and in ancient Aramaic (which famous linguists established as such); she reproduced what was claimed to be the words of Christ and the vile swearing of the crowd as she clairaudiently heard them in archaic language. Her pronunciation was always phonetic and many believed it that she was in communication with someone who was a spectator of the Passion.

At Christmas in 1922, an abscess developed in Thérèse Neumann's throat and neck. From this date until Christmas 1926, she abstained from solid food. She took a little liquid, three or four spoonfuls of coffee, tea or fruit juice. After Christmas 1926, she only took a drop of water every morning to swallow the sacred host. From September 1927 until November 1928, she abstained even from this drop of water. Nevertheless she retained her normal weight. But four Roman Catholic sisters declared on oath that during the Friday ecstasies Thérèse lost four pounds of weight which she regained by the following Thursday without taking nourishment in any form.

On August 15, 1927, Thérèse had a vision of the death, burial and ascension of Mary. She visualized Mary's tomb as at Jerusalem, and not at Ephesus as usually assumed.

In the Socialist and Communist press of Germany, Russia and Austria many libellous statements and quasiexposures were published about Thérèse Neumann. Whenever they were followed by suits for libel the editors were found guilty and sentenced to imprisonment and fine.

Thérèse Neumann was something of an embarrassment to the Nazis during World War II, and the authorities made difficulties for visitors to Konnersreuth. After the war, hundreds of thousands of American and other servicemen queued to visit Neumann. She often gave accurate information on distant events through **out-of-the-body** travel, and appears to have traveled astrally to the death chamber of Pope Pius XII.

Although pilgrims presented many gifts to her, she would not use these for her own comfort, and before her death September 18, 1962, she had contributed to the Church a training seminary for priests, as well as a convent.

During her lifetime over 133 books or papers were written about her including: R. W. Hynek, *Konnersreuth: A Medical and Psychological Study of the Case of Teresa Neumann* (1932); Frederick von Lama, *Thérèsa Neumann, une stigmatisée de nos jours* (1928); K. Fahsel, *Konnersreuth: le mystrère des stigmatisés* (1933); J. Danemarie, *The Mystery of Stigmata from Catherine Emmerich to Theresa Neumann* (1934). Recommended English works include: Hilda Graef, *The Case of Thérèse Neumann* (Mercier, Irish Republic, 1952), Paul Siwek, *The Riddle of Konnersreuth* (Browne & Nolan, Irish Republic, 1954), Johannes Steiner, *Thérèse Neumann; a portrait based on authentic accounts, journals, and documents* (Alba, 1967). (See also Catherine **Emmerich;** Padre **Pio; Stigmata**)

Neurypnology

James **Braid's** first term for **hypnotism.**

New Age

A general term for the modern culture complex of organic farming, macrobiotics, environmentalism, alternative energy systems, unorthodox healing, meditation, spiritual development, higher consciousness, experimental communes, **channeling,** crystal power, astrology, and popular occultism. A related term is "holistic," implying wholeness, embracing New Age subjects, whole grain foods, and an ambience of youth opposition to the modern consumer society and materialism.

Two of the most influential personalities in the New Age complex are Marilyn Ferguson (with her book *The Aquarian Conspiracy*) and actress Shirley MacLaine, with her own books and public statements. In many ways, these two personalities symbolize two extremes of the New Age movement—Ferguson's Aquarian Conspiracy representing a sophisticated intellectual and discriminating approach, and MacLaine encouraging the more popular and uncritical aspects (such as channeling).

Of course, there is nothing essentially new about most New Age interests. Sensible vegetarian foods, organic gardening, whole grain bread, yoga, meditation, etc., were all pioneered by older people decades back, but their modern revival owes much to the trendiness of the mass media society and the commercial exploitation of the generation gap—even in the name of revolt against consumerism and materialism. Discriminating older people who were aware of the value of such things long ago will be glad to see them revived, but will regret them being bracketed with uncritical occultism and cultishness. It is unfortunate that irrational or antisocial beliefs and activities should be thrown together in the same New Age melting pot as intelligent ideas about diet, farming, and ecology.

In the New Age complex, many earlier minority interests have been recycled. The craze for "channeling" is only a colorful revival of what used to be called "trance addresses" by spirit guides. The old convention of hidden Masters of Wisdom in Theosophist and occult groups has reappeared in the form of extraterrestrial intelligences on distant planets, manifesting occasionally from flying saucers to favored contactees. Many of the new religious cults are only a trendy rehash of Judeo-Christian traditions, while the Eastern gurus have been sending their missionaries to the U.S. and Europe ever since Swami Vivekananda came to the World Parliament of Religions in Chicago in 1893. The "Transcendental Meditation" and "siddha courses" of **Maharishi Mahesh Yogi** are only a brand-naming and corporation style marketing of part of the traditional teachings of the Hindu sage Patanjali, circa 200 B.C.

Much of present-day interest in and susceptibility to New Age topics may stem from the ambiguous role of religion in an age of scientific materialism. Modern science and technology have achieved miracles of imaginative development through integrity of principles. At a time when we can successfully build the incredibly complex structure of a giant airliner or put men on the moon, the traditional religions have lost their ability to inspire noble ideals, becoming instead banal, pretentious, or politicized into liberation theology, or trivialised into fundamentalism. Irrational and often dangerously antisocial cults have multiplied.

Skeptics, rationalists, and atheists have rightly pointed to the dangers of a society increasingly permeated by irrational beliefs and fanaticisms, but have undervalued the importance of the mystical impulse in human beings. The spiritual insights and inspiration of religious experience, the guidance of scriptures, the poetic symbolism of mythology, provide meaning and purpose in life, and when they are missing, life often degenerates into sordid power games of greed or politics, cruelty, and perverse decadence.

The hunger for religious experience promoted the psychedelic revolution of the 1960s, which promised instant spiritual revelation through the use of soft drugs like mescalin and marijuana. Predictably higher consciousness could not be bought and sold like consumer durables, and the result was drug addiction and dropouts instead of spiritual realization, culminating in the modern anti-social plague of hard drug addiction endemic throughout the world, with pushers, a criminal underworld and an international cartel of Mafia style syndicates that now dictates the economies of Third World countries.

There is no instant path to higher consciousness. Only the patient refinement of individual life through those ethics once taught by the world's great religions—kindness, non-violence, truthfulness, study, meditation, intellectual integrity, and absence of greed, lust and anger, can bring about a real expansion of consciousness. In a secular setting, the agnostic and humanist may also enhance consciousness and social cooperation through such ethics, and the marvelous vistas disclosed by scientific knowledge and cosmology, evoking wonder at the immensity and laws of the cosmos. In this respect, the physicist and the astronomer may be nearer to the secret of life than the fundamentalist religious zealot.

Obviously many of the New Age novelties like crystal power, creative visualization, past-life regression, channeled sermons, exotic cults and communes, etc., are unlikely to achieve much more than the substitution of life styles for actual living. However, much of the New Age complex may be individually and socially valuable if approached with intellectual integrity, and there are hopeful signs that the best of New Age awareness may become part of a general positive movement in modern society and culture rather than an eccentric counterculture.

Meanwhile, the New Age has familiarized a generation with topics and terms formerly of esoteric significance, as well as a whole set of new attitudes. A useful guide to this semantic revolution is *The New Age Dictionary* edited by Alex Jack (Kanthaka Press, Brookline, Mass., 1976). Publications devoted to New Age topics include: *East West Journal* (Box 6769, Syracuse, N.Y. 13217), *Brain/Mind Bulletin* (Box 42211, Los Angeles, California 90042), *New Age Journal* (Box 853, Farmingdale, N.Y. 11735), *Body Mind & Spirit* Magazine (Box 701, Providence, Rhode Island 02901), *Magical Blend* (Box 11303, San Francisco, California 94101), *New Frontiers Newsletter* (Fellowship Farm, Route 1, Oregon, Wisconsin 53575) *New Realities* (4000 Albemarle Street, Washington, D.C. 20016) (See also **Aquarian Conspiracy; Channeling; Crystal Healing; Findhorn; Lindisfarne;** Shirley **MacLaine;** William Irwin **Thompson**)

Recommended reading:

Anderson, Walter Truett. *The Upstart Spring; Esalen & the American Awakening,* Addison-Wesley (paperback), 1983

Basil, Robert (ed.). *Not Necessarily the New Age,* Prometheus, 1988

(Editors of *Body, Mind & Spirit* Magazine). *The New Age Catalogue; Access to Information and Sources,* Dolphin paperback (Doubleday), 1988

Ferguson, Marilyn. *The Aquarian Conspiracy; Personal & Social Transformation in Our Time,* St. Martin's Press, 1980

Schultz, Ted. *The Fringes of Reason; A Whole Earth Catalog,* Harmony Books paperback (Crown Publishers), 1989

Wilson, Robert Anton. *The New Inquisition; Irrational Rationalism and the Citadel of Science,* Falcon Press, Las Vegas, 1986

New Age Journal

Journal of New Age topics, concerned mainly with achievement, commitment, health, creative living, and holistic nutrition. It includes a calendar of a wide range of New Age seminars, lectures, training courses, and symposia. Address: P.O. Box 853, Farmingdale, N.Y. 11735. (See also **New Age**)

New Age Media Resource Directory

Quarterly networking publication concerned with **New Age** information, listing books, publishers, audio tapes, periodicals, film and video productions, educational, therapy and spiritual centers, concerned with psychic studies, Eastern religion and yoga, macrobiotics, holistic health, and related topics. Address: Box 419, New York, N.Y. 10002.

New Age World Religious and Scientific Research Foundation

Formerly Inner Sense Scientist Association, this organization was founded in 1976, with a membership of persons interested in **"New Age"** religious and scientific culture, including inventors, authors, lecturers, students, and scientists.

The purpose of the Foundation is to bring forth the highest and best of religious and scientific understanding to mankind, to serve as a balance between religion and science. It maintains a 15,000-volume library and a speakers bureau, sponsors correspondence course in New Age World Esoteric Wisdom Teachings. Publication: *New Age World Polaris Newsletter.* Address: 62091 Valley View Circle, Joshua Tree, California 92252

New Atlantean Journal

Quarterly publication of New Atlantean Research Society, dealing with research and discussion on Atlantis, UFO sightings and earth changes. Address: P.O. Box 3747, St. Petersburg, Florida 33710.

New Atlantean Research Society

Nonprofit organization that investigates all relevant aspects of the unknown, unexplained, and unexplored. The Society publishes a quarterly *New Atlantean Journal.* Address: P.O. Box 3747, St. Petersburg, Florida 33710.

New Celtic Review, The (Journal)

Quarterly publication of the British based GSO Society for the Preservation of Celtic Lore, Monuments & Antiquities.

The journal is hand illuminated and includes details of festivals, mail order books, cards (of the ancient Celtic Ogham Tree Alphabet), and publications, as well as events throughout Celtic regions and countries. Address: BM Oak Grove, London, WC1N 3XX, U.K.

New Church, The

Religious organization devoted to the teachings of Swedish mystic Emanuel **Swedenborg** (1688-1772). The New Church embodies the writings of Swedenborg which were originally known as the Church of the New Jerusalem.

Followers of Swedenborg believe that the Second Coming of Christ took place in 1757 in the form of the revelation of Swedenborg's esoteric interpretation of the scriptures, as a fulfilment of John's vision of the New Jerusalem coming down out of heaven from God, with the declaration "Behold, I make all things new."

Salvation is regarded as deliverance from sinning itself, and hell a free choice on the part of those who prefer an evil life. Jesus is worshiped directly as Creator, Redeemer, the Word and the Revelation.

Swedenborg's teachings had some influence in America through Jonathan Chapman, known as "Johnny Appleseed," a Swedenborgian who wandered through nineteenth-century settlements planting apple trees and leaving Swedenborg literature at log cabins.

Some of Swedenborg's concepts passed into early American spiritual and occult cults. Andrew Jackson **Davis** (1826-1910), an American Spiritualist, claimed that Swedenborg was one of three spirits who revealed the secrets of the universe to him in 1844.

The New Church has more than forty churches in Britain, administered by a General Conference. For further information, consult The New Church Enquiry Centre, 20 Bloomsbury Way, London, WC1A 2TH. (See also **Swedenborg Society**)

New Consciousness Sourcebook

New format for the *Spiritual Community Guide* (No. 5) in its tenth year of publication.

The range of subject matter in this useful directory is now wider. In addition to listings of organizations concerned with spiritual growth, it now covers such New Age subjects as nutrition, holistic health, healing, therapies, Kundalini, bodywork, life-styles, meditation, in addition to listings of bookstores, publications, occult supplies, records, and tapes. Address: Spiritual Community Publications/NAM, Box 1067, Berkeley, California 94701.

New Dimensions (England)

Quarterly publication dealing with Qabalah and magical teachings in the tradition of the Golden Dawn and Dion Fortune. Address: 8 Acron Avenue, Braintree, Essex, England.

New Dimensions (Florida)

Occasional newsletter of the Florida Society for Psychical Research, Inc., dealing with Society activities and psychic topics. Address: Florida Society for Psychical Research, Inc., 2837 First Avenue North, St. Petersburg, Florida 33713.

New Dimensions Radio Network

Nationally syndicated radio network concerned with New Age speakers on a wide range of New Age topics, offering program guide and audio tapes of broadcasts. Address: P.O. Box 410510, San Francisco, California 94141.

New England Journal of Parapsychology

Quarterly journal which publishes papers from undergraduates of a college course in parapsychology. Address: Franklin Pierce College, Rindge, New Hampshire 03461.

New Existence of Man upon the Earth (Journal)

British journal founded in 1854 by socialist reformer Robert **Owen** (1771-1858), the only journal of the period concerned with **Spiritualism.** The issues included an early report on automatic writing by a child of four years, who wrote in Latin. The journal ceased publication after the death of Owen.

New Frontiers Center Newsletter

Publication with news and views from parapsychologist Walter **Uphoff** and associates. Address: New Frontiers Center, Fellowship Farm, Route 1, Oregon, Wisconsin 53575.

New Humanity (Journal)

British publication founded in February 1975 as "the world's first politicospiritual journal." Its purpose is "to create Peace on Earth, the alleviation of suffering, and the promotion of well-being among mankind. We are neither Left nor Right but Uplifted Forward. We work for Peace, Non-Confrontation, Unity in Diversity, Mental Liberation and Harmony with the God-head."

Articles cover a wide range of mystical topics relating to the improvement of humanity through new consciousness awareness. Issued six times annually. Address: 51A York Mansions, Prince of Wales Drive, London, S.W.11, England.

New Horizons (Journal)

Semi-annual journal of New Horizons Research Foundation, Canada. Contains articles on researches of the Toronto Psychical Society and other parapsychological work. Edited by Dr. A. R. G. Owen, a mathematician at the University of Toronto, who was one of the group of experimenters who created the experimental ghost **"Philip."** Address: New Horizons Research Foundation, P.O. Box 427, Station F, Toronto, Ontario, Canada M4Y 2L8.

New Horizons Newsletter

Monthly publication devoted to spiritual movements, alternate energies and related New Age subjects. Address: 1 Palomar Arcade, #124, Santa Cruz, California 95060.

New Isis Lodge

A sister-lodge of the secret occult organization **O.T.O.** (Ordo Templi Orientalis), which grew out of the Brotherhood of Light at the end of the nineteenth century.

The O.T.O. was organized with ten degrees of initiation by Dr. Karl Kellner, an Austrian occultist in 1895. Its most precious secret was that of **sex magic,** the techniques of utilizing the energies of sex for occult purposes.

After the death of Kellner in 1905, the head of the O.T.O. was Theodore Reuss, who was also a member of the German Secret Service, and had spied upon the Socialist League in England. Reuss concluded from reading publications of occultist Aleister **Crowley** that Crowley had discovered the secret of sex-magic, and in 1912 he invited Crowley to head a British branch of the O.T.O.

When Crowley died in 1947, Karl Germer became head of the O.T.O. and about 1951 granted a charter to Kenneth **Grant,** a Crowley enthusiast in Britain.

In 1955, Grant set up the New Isis Lodge of the O.T.O. with eleven rituals. The "New" was a pun on "Nu" (or "Nuit"), a term borrowed from Egyptian mythology, symbolizing absolute consciousness, associated with the Crowley concept of the Scarlet Woman, whose formula was "love under will." "New-Isis" or "Nu-Isis" therefore symbolized the heavenly and earthly goddess. (See also Aleister **Crowley; Golden Dawn;** Kenneth **Grant**)

New Motor, The

A strange machine constructed in 1854 by Spiritualist medium John Murray **Spear** in association with another medium Charles Hammond, at the instigation of the "Association of Electricizers," one of the bands of spirits by whom he was controlled.

The Motor was to derive its motive power from the magnetic store of nature, and was therefore to be as independent of artificial sources of energy as was the human body. The machine was hailed as the "Physical Saviour of the race," the "New Messiah," and Mrs. Alonzo Newton, wife of one of Spear's collaborators, in obedience to a vision, went to High Rock, Lynn, Massachusetts, where the New Motor was located and for two hours suffered "birth-pangs," whereby she judged that the essence of her spiritual being was imparted to the machine.

At the end of that time it was claimed that pulsations were apparent in the Motor. Mrs. Newton continued to act as nurse to the contraption for several weeks, but the only observed movements seemed to be a slight oscillation of some of the metal balls which adorned it. One disappointed Spiritualist complained that the New Motor could not even turn a coffee mill.

Andrew Jackson **Davis** visited the New Motor at High Rock and expressed the belief that the design was the work of spirits of a mechanical turn of mind, but was of no practical value.

The New Motor was finally smashed by a mob at Randolph, New York, where it had been taken. In all it cost its builder some two thousand dollars.

In common fairness to the Spiritualists it must be said that Spear was widely recognized as a kind and honest man who had championed many liberal reforms. His earlier experience of spirit messages was remarkable, resulting in a healing ministry. It seems that he was deceived by misleading communications from "the Association of Electricizers" (which claimed to include the spirit of Benjamin Franklin).

It is possible that the New Motor fiasco may have suggested a line of research to John Worrell **Keely** (1837-1898), who claimed the discovery of a new motive force in his invention of the Keely Motor. This force was said to be "vibratory etheric force" or cosmic energy. After the death of Keely, evidence of fraud was revealed.

From time to time, Spiritualists have constructed various apparatus to facilitate communication with the spirit world, sometimes basing their constructions on spirit messages.

Amongst modern inventors who were more successful than Spear were those comprising the group known as the **Ashkir-Jobson Trianion,** c. 1930, who built various apparatus which seemed to work. The psychotherapist Wilhelm **Reich** also claimed the discovery of a cosmic motor force in "Orgone energy." (See also **Communication; Communigraph;** John E. W. **Keeley; Orgone;** Wilhelm **Reich;** J. M. **Spear**)

New Realities Magazine

A continuation under new title of *Psychic* Magazine. Vol. 1, No. 1, of *New Realities* appeared in 1977, dedicated to a broader scope of "developments in the emergent areas of human possibilities that affect our everyday lives."

In addition to psychic phenomena and parapsychology, *New Realities* deals with "holistic health" (total approach to human well-being on physical, mental, emotional and spiritual levels), changing consciousness, different life styles in the modern world and mysticism of both East and West.

As from the January/February 1987 issue, *New Realities* was transferred to Heldref Publications, publisher Neal Vahle. James Bolen continued to serve on the Editorial Board, together with a group of other consulting editors. Address: New Realities, Heldref Publications, 4000 Albemarle Street, NW, Washington, D.C. 20016.

New Thought

A relatively modern religious movement which, in some of its tenets resembles faith-healing. Unlike the separate development of **Christian Science,** however, it does not affect entirely to dispense with all material medical aids such as drugs, the setting of broken bones, and so on. Nor does it give the whole credit for cures to the imagination of the patient, as in **hypnotism.** But striking a point midway between the two, it gives considerable prominence to the mind in the healing process, while not altogether despising the doctor.

Mind is considered as highly refined matter and therefore the "mind" cure is, in a measure, a material cure. It is clear that the part of the New Thought which deals with bodily healing had its roots in the **Animal Magnetism** and **Mesmerism** of bygone times. So much have they in common that it is needless to trace mental healing as such further back than Dr. Phineas Parkhurst **Quimby** (1802-1866), the first to make use of the terms "mental-healing" and "Christian Science."

Dr. Quimby was the son of a New Hampshire blacksmith, and was himself apprenticed to a clock-maker, having had but little education. At the age of thirty-six he attended a lecture on Mesmerism, and thereafter practiced for himself. With the aid of a clairvoyant youth he cured diseases, and so successful was his treatment that he soon adopted magnetic healing as a profession.

At length, however, he got a glimpse of the true reason for his success—the expectation of the patient. The diagnoses of his clairvoyant he attributed to the latter's telepathic reading of the patient's own thoughts, and he judged that the treatment prescribed depended for its efficacy on the confidence it inspired rather than on its intrinsic merits.

From this point he gradually evolved his doctrine that disease was a mere delusion, a traditional error that had fixed itself in men's minds, which it behoved them to be rid of as soon as might be. The way to cure disease, therefore, was to destroy the error on which it rested.

Besides Christian Science, Quimby called his doctrine the Science of Health, or the Science of Health and Happiness. He had many disciples, among whom were Mrs. Mary Baker G. **Eddy,** the founder of the Christian Science Church. Others whose influence was felt more in the direction of the New Thought movement were the Rev. W. F. Evans and Mr. and Mrs. Julius Dresser, whose son, Horatio W. Dresser, remained one of the ablest exponents of the New Thought.

As has been said, the method of healing practiced by this school is not considered to be entirely immaterial. It is no longer believed that a fluid emanates from the fingertips of the operator, or that he radiates a luminous odic force (see **Od**), but Mr. Dresser himself stated that the communication was of a vibratory character, made up of ethereal undulations directed and concentrated by the thought of the healer. The power was equally efficacious at a distance and could be used without the patient's knowledge or even against his will.

This belief in action at a distance became a problem for the New Thinker, who feared the ascendancy of an evil influence much as the superstitious of the Middle Ages feared bewitchment. But there is a spiritual aspect of the New Thought as well as a physical one. The health of the soul is as fully considered as the health of the body. Spiritual sanity, then, is to be procured by lifting oneself to a higher plane of existence, by shutting out the things of the earth and living "in tune with the infinite." We must realize our own identity with the Infinite Spirit and open our lives to the Divine inflow.

Ralph Waldo Trine, himself a New Thinker, stated in an expressive metaphor, "To recognize our own divinity and our intimate relation to the Universal, is to attach the belt of our machinery to the powerhouse of the Universe." In short, we must have sufficient self-confidence to cast our fears aside and rise unfettered into the Infinite.

Other influential individuals in the New Thought movement include Emmet Fox (who developed his own interpretation of Christianity), Charles and Myrtle Fillmore, Ernest Holmes, Prentice **Mulford,** Thomas Troward (famous for his *Edinburgh Lectures on Mental Science*), Frederick Bailes (director of the Science of Mind Church), the Rev. David Thompson, Norman Vincent Peale (author of *The Power of Positive Thinking*), Bishop Fulton J. Sheen, Rabbi Joseph Liebman, Lewis Dunnington and Gleen Clark.

In modern times, New Thought exists both as a religious movement of organized and independent churches, and as a secular principle expounded by independent authors. The organized church groupings are: United Churches of Religious Science, Unity Churches, Divine Science Churches, International Churches of Religious Science, Independent New Thought Churches.

An international New Thought Alliance has affirmed a declaration of New Thought principles as follows:

"We affirm the inseparable oneness of God and man, the realization of which comes through spiritual intuition, the implications of which are that man can reproduce the Divine perfection in his body, emotions, and in all his external affairs.

"We affirm the freedom of each person in matters of belief.

"We affirm the Good to be supreme, universal, and eternal.

"We affirm that the Kingdom of Heaven is within us, that we are one with the Father, that we should love one another, and return good for evil.

"We affirm that we should heal the sick through prayer, and that we should endeavor to manifest perfection even as our Father in Heaven is perfect.

"We affirm our belief in God as the Universal Wisdom, Love, Life, Truth, Power, Peace, Beauty, and Joy, in whom we live, move, and have our being."

"We affirm that man's mental states are carried forward into manifestation and become his experience through the Creative Law of Cause and Effect.

"We affirm that the Divine Nature expressing Itself through man manifests Itself as health, supply, wisdom, love, life, truth, power, peace, beauty, and joy.

"We affirm that man is an invisible spiritual dweller within a human body, continuing and unfolding as a spiritual being beyond the change called physical death.

"We affirm that the universe is the body of God, spiritual in essence, governed by God through laws which are spiritual in reality even when material in appearance." (See also **Christian Science;** Mary M. B. **Eddy;** Psychic **Healing; Healing by Faith; Mind Cure;** Prentice **Mulford;** Phineas P. **Quimby**)

Recommended reading:

Beebe, Tom. *Who's Who in New Thought,* CSA Press, Lakemount, Georgia, 1977

Braden, Charles S. *Spirits in Rebellion,* Southern Methodist University Press, Dallas, 1963

Collier, Robert. *The Secret of the Ages,* Collier Publications, Tarrytown, N.Y., 1954 etc.

Dresser, Horatio W. (ed.). *The Quimby Manuscripts,* Julian Press, 1961

Dresser, Horatio W. *The Spirit of New Thought,* Thomas Y. Crowell, 1917

Fillmore, Charles & Cora Fillmore. *Twelve Powers of Man,* Unity School of Christianity, Missouri, 1943

Fillmore, Myrtle. *How to Let God Help You,* Unity School of Christianity, Missouri, 1956

Fox, Emmet. *Power Through Constructive Thinking,* Harper & Bros., 1946; Harper & Row, 1940 etc.

Goldsmith, Joel S. *The Art of Spiritual Healing,* Harper & Bros., 1959

Holmes, Ernest S. *Complete Course of Lessons in the Science of Mind and Spirit,* Dodd, Mead, 1926 etc.

Judah, J. Stillson. *The History and Philosophy of the Metaphysical Movements in America,* Westminister Press, Philadelphia, 1967

Larson, Christian D. *The Creative Power of Mind,* privately printed, Los Angeles, 1930

Meyer, Donald. *The Positive Thinkers,* Doubleday, 1965

Mulford, Prentice. *Your Forces and How to Use Them,* White Cross Library, F. J. Needham, New York, 1888-92

Murphy, Joseph. *The Miracles of Your Mind,* Willing Publishing Co., San Gabriel, California, 1953 etc.

Peale, Norman Vincent. *The Power of Positive Thinking,* Prentice-Hall, 1952 etc.; Fawcett paperback, 1976

Podmore, Frank. *Mesmerism and Christian Science,* Methuen, London, 1909

Trine, Ralph Waldo. *In Tune With the Infinite,* Thomas Y. Crowell, 1897 etc.; Dodd, Mead, 1921; Bobbs Merrill paperback, 1970

Troward, Thomas. *The Edinburg Lectures on Mental Science,* London, 1904; Dodd, Mead, 1904

Troward, Thomas. *The Hidden Power and Other Papers on Mental Science,* Dodd, Mead, 1917, 1958

Wilbur, Sybil. *The Life of Mary Baker Eddy,* The Christian Science Publishing Co., 1907

New Thought Magazine

Quarterly journal concerned with **New Thought** and religion; includes directory of affiliated organizations. Address: New Thought Alliance, 6922 Hollywood Boulevard, Los Angeles, California 90028.

New Times Network (Directory)

A "Directory of Groups and Centres for Personal Growth," compiled by Robert Adams. It includes sections on Health and Healing, Growth and Human

Potential, Holistic Education, Spiritual Traditions, New Age Communities, Networks, Associations, Information Centres. Published by Routledge & Kegan Paul, 39 Store Street, London, WC1E 7DD, England, and 9 Park Street, Boston, Massachusetts 02108.

New Ways of Consciousness Foundation

Founded by Alan Vaughan, a former editor of *Psychic* magazine, to develop consciousness technology and encourage consciousness research. The Foundation was opened in June 1979 and contains a library on consciousness research. Address: 3188 Washington Street, San Francisco, California 94115.

New York Circle

The first experimental Spiritualist organization in America. It was an exclusive body in the initial stages, later broadening its membership.

The principal medium was Edward P. **Fowler,** who had sat with Kate and Margaretta **Fox.** Mr. Fowler provided premises for the use of the group. Early members included John W. Edmonds, Dr. J. B. Gray, Charles Partridge, Dr. & Mrs. Warner, Dr. and Mrs. R. T. Hallock, Robert T. Shannon, W. J. Baner, Dr. Hull, Miss Fowler, Professor Bush, Rev. S. B. Britain and Almon Roff.

At one sitting of the circle, the medium Henry Gordon demonstrated the feat of floating in the air, in the presence of many unimpeachable witnesses.

At the initiative of the Circle, the New York Conference was established in November 1851, providing a focal point for the growing Spiritualist movement. (See also **Spiritualism**)

NEW ZEALAND

Maori Superstitions

"Spirits of the dead" played a very prominent part in Maori tradition. The priests or "Tohungas" were unmistakably mediums in the modern sense of the term. Sometimes they were born with their gift, sometimes they were devoted to the priestly office by their parents and acquired their power after the fashion of Eastern ecstatics, by prayer, fasting and contemplation.

That good prophets existed amongst the Maoris has been abundantly proved. During the time when Great Britain busied herself in colonizing New Zealand, her officials frequently wrote home that the Maori would never be conquered wholly. Information of the parties sent out to attack them, the very color of the boats and the hour when they would arrive, the number of the enemy, and all particulars essential to their safety were invariably communicated to the tribes beforehand by their Tohungas, or prophets.

The best natural prophets and seers amongst the Maoris were of the female sex, and although the missionaries tried to account for the marvelous powers they exhibited above all for the sound of the spirit voice, which was a common phase in their communion with the dead—on the hypothesis that the women who practiced "the arts of sorcery," were ventriloquists, this attempted explanation rarely covered the ground of the intelligence received.

In his book *Old New Zealand* (1863), F. E. Maning cited an interesting case of Tohungaism. A certain young chief had been appointed Registrar of births and deaths, when he suddenly came to a violent end. The book of registries was lost, and much inconvenience ensued. The man's relatives notified their intention of invoking his spirit, and invited General Cummings to be present at the ceremony, an invitation which he accepted.

"The appointed time came. Fires were lit. The Tohunga repaired to the darkest corner of the room. All was silent, save the sobbing of the sisters of the deceased warrior-chief. There were thirty of us, sitting on the rush-strewn floor, the door shut and the fire now burning down to embers. Suddenly there came a voice out from the partial darkness, 'Salutation, salutation to my family, to my tribe, to you, pakeha, my friend!' Our feelings were taken by storm. The oldest sister screamed, and rushed with extended arms in the direction from whence the voice came. Her brother, seizing, restrained her by main force. Others exclaimed, 'Is it you? Is it you? Truly it is you! aue! aue!' and fell quite insensible upon the floor. The older women and some of the aged men were not moved in the slightest degree, though believing it to be the spirit of the chief.

"Whilst reflecting upon the novelty of the scene, the 'darkness visible' and the deep interest manifest, the spirit spoke again, 'Speak to me my family; speak to me, my tribe: speak to me, the pakeha!' At last the silence gave way, and the brother spoke: 'How is it with you? Is it well with you in that country?' The answer came, though not in the voice of the Tohunga-medium, but in strange sepulchral sounds: 'It is well with me; my place is a good place. I have seen our friends; they are all with me!' A woman from another part of the room now anxiously cried out, 'Have you seen my sister?' 'Yes, I have seen her; she is happy in our beautiful country.' 'Tell her my love so great for her will never cease.' 'Yes, I will bear the message.' Here the native woman burst into tears, and my own bosom swelled in sympathy.

"The spirit speaking again, giving directions about property and keepsakes, I thought I would more thoroughly test the genuineness of all this: and I said, 'We cannot find your book with the registered names; where have you concealed it?' The answer came instantly, 'I concealed it between the tahuhu of my house, and the thatch; straight over you, as you go in at the door.' The brother rushed out to see. All was silence. In five minutes he came hurriedly back, with the book in his hand! It astonished me.

"It was now late, and the spirit suddenly said, 'Farewell my family, farewell, my tribe; I go.' Those present breathed an impressive farewell, when the spirit cried out again, from high in the air, 'Farewell!'

"This, though seemingly tragical, is in every respect literally true. But what is that? ventriloquism, the devil, or what! . . . "

Mrs. Emma Hardinge **Britten** stated in her book *Nineteenth Century Miracles* (1883): "The author has herself had several proofs of the Mediumistic power possessed by these 'savages' but as her experiences may be deemed of too personal a character, we shall select our examples from other sources. One of these is furnished by a Mr. Marsden, a person who was well-known in the early days of New Zealand's colonial history, as a miner, who grew rich 'through spiritual communications.' Mr. Marsden was a gentleman who had spent much time amongst the Maoris, and who still keeps a residence in 'the King country,' that is—the district of which they hold control.

"Mr. Marsden informed the author, that his success as a gold miner, was entirely due to a communication he had received through a native woman who claimed to have the power of bringing *down* spirits—the Maoris, be it remembered, always insisting that the spirits *descend* through the air to earth to visit mortals.

"Mr. Marsden had long been prospecting unsuccessfully in the gold regions. He had a friend in partnership with him, to whom he was much attached, but who had been accidentally killed by a fall from a cliff.

"The Spirit of this man came unsolicited, on an occasion when Mr. Marsden was consulting a native seeress, for the purpose of endeavouring to trace out what had become of a valuable watch which he had lost.

"The voice of the Spirit was the first heard in the air, apparently above the roof of the hut in which they sat, calling Mr. Marsden by his familiar name of 'Mars.' Greatly startled by these sounds, several times repeated, at the Medium's command, he remained perfectly still until the voice of his friend speaking in his well-remembered Scotch accent sounded close to his ear, whilst a column of grey misty substance reared itself by his side. This apparition was plainly visible in the subdued light of the hut, to which there was only one open entrance, but no window. Though he was much startled by what he saw and heard, Mr. Marsden had presence of mind enough to gently *put his hand through the misty column* which remained intact, as if its substance offered no resistance to the touch. Being admonished by an earnest whisper from the Maori woman, who had fallen on her knees before the apparition, to keep still, he obeyed, when a voice—seemingly from an immense distance off—yet speaking unmistakably in his friend's Scotch accents, advised him to let the watch alone—for it was irreparably gone—but to go to the stream on the banks of which they had last had a meal together; trace it up for six miles and a half, and then, by following its course amidst the forest, he would come to a *pile* which would make him rich, if he chose to remain so.

"Whilst he was waiting and listening breathlessly to hear more, Mr. Marsden was startled by a slight detonation at his side. Turning his head he observed that the column of mist was gone, and in its place, a quick flash, like the reflection of a candle, was all that he beheld. Here the seance ended, and the astonished miner left the hut, convinced that he had heard the Spirit of his friend talking with him. He added, that he followed the directions given implicitly, and came to a mass of surface gold lying on the stones at the bottom of the brook in the depth of the forest. This he gathered up, and though he prospected for several days in and about that spot, he never found another particle of this precious metal. That which he had secured he added, with a deep sigh, was indeed enough to have made him independent for life, had it not soon been squandered in fruitless speculations."

"Many degrees of superstition exist among the Maoris," state a writer in the *Pall Mall Gazette,* "In the recesses of the Urewera country for example, diablerie has lost little of its early potency; the *tohunga* there remains a power in the land. Among the more enlightened natives a precautionary policy is generally followed; it is always wiser and safer, they say, to avoid conflict with the two mysterious powers *tapu* and *makuta.* Tapu is the less dangerous of the two; a house, an individual, or an article may be rendered tapu, or sacred, and if the tapu be disregarded harm will befall someone. But makuta is a powerful evil spell cast for the deliberate purpose of accomplishing harm, generally to bring about death. The *tohunga* is understood to be in alliance with the spirits of the dead. The Maori dreads death, and he fears the dead. Places of burial are seldom approached during the day, never at night. The spirits of the dead are believed to linger sometimes near places of burial. Without going to experts in Maori lore, who have many and varied theories to set forth, a preferable course is to discover what the average Maori of to-day thinks and believes respecting the strange powers and influences he deems are at work in the world around him.

"A Maori of this type—who can read and write, is under forty years of age, and fairly intelligent—was drawn into a lengthy conversation with the writer. He believed, magistrates notwithstanding, that *tohungas,* somehow, had far more power than ordinary men. He did not think they got that power from the 'tiapo' (the devil?); they just were able to make themselves masters of men and many things in the world. There are many degrees of Tohungaism. An ordinary man or woman was powerless against a *tohunga,* but one *tohunga* could overcome another. The speaker knew of an instance of one *tohunga* driving the tohunga power entirely out of a weaker rival. It was a fairly recent east coast occurrence. Three Maoris had accidentally permitted their pigs to trespass into the *tohunga's* potato paddock, and much damage and loss was the result. The *tohunga* was one of the dangerous type, and being very wroth, he *makutued* the three men, all of whom promptly died. Nobody was brave enough to charge the *tohunga* with causing the death of the men; they were all afraid of this terrible *makuta.* At length another *to hunga* was heard of, one of very great power. This oracle was consulted, and he agreed to deal effectively with *tohunga* number one, and punish him for killing the owner of the pigs. So, following his instructions, the first-mentioned individual was seized, and much against his will, was conveyed to the home of the greater magician. Many Maoris, it should be known, stand in awe of hot water, they will not handle it, even for purposes connected with cooking or cleaning. Into a large tub of hot water the minor *tohunga* struggling frantically, was placed, then he was given a page torn from a Bible, which he was ordered to chew and swallow. The hot water treatment, combined with the small portion of the white man's sacred volume, did the expected work; the man was no longer a *tohunga,* and fretting over his lost powers, he soon afterwards died."

Spiritualism in New Zealand

Amongst the earliest investigators in Dunedin was Mr. John Logan. Before he had become publicly identified with the cause of Spiritualism, an association had been formed, the members of which steadily pursued their investigations in private circles and semi-private gatherings.

One of the most marked events in connection with the early development of Spiritualism in Dunedin, however, was the arraignment and church trial of Mr. Logan, the circumstances of which may be briefly summed up as follows.

This gentleman, although holding a high position in the first Presbyterian church of the city, had attended circles and witnessed Spiritualistic phenomena and it was currently reported that one of his own near relatives was a very remarkable medium.

On March 19, 1873, Mr. Logan was summoned to appear before a Church Convocation, to be held for the purpose of trying his case, and if necessary, dealing with his "delinquency." Mr. Logan was in the event deprived of his church membership.

In many of the principal towns besides Dunedin, circles held at first in mere idle curiosity, produced their usual fruit of mediumistic power, and this again was extended into associative action, and organization into local societies. For over a year, the Spiritualists and Liberalists of Dunedin secured the services of Charles Bright as their lecturer. This gentleman had once been attached to the editorial staff of the *Melbourne Argus,* and had obtained a good reputation as a capable writer, and liberal thinker.

Mr. Bright's lectures in Dunedin were highly appreciated, and by their scholarly style and attractive manner, served to band together the liberal element in the city.

In Auckland, the principal town of the North Island, the same good service was rendered to the cause of religious thought by the addresses of the Rev. Mr. Edgar, a clergyman whose Spiritualist doctrines had tended to sever him from sectarian organizations, and draw around him, the Spiritualists of the town.

Besides the good work effected by these gentlemen, the occasional visits of well-known personalities like the Rev. J. M. Peebles, and J. Tyerman, and the effect of the many private circles held in every portion of the islands, tended to promote a general, although quiet, diffusion of spiritual thought and doctrine, throughout New Zealand.

In 1879, a lecture tour by Mrs. Emma Hardinge Britten gave a powerful impetus to public interest and discussion concerning Spiritualism and its doctrines.

By 1930, the Spiritualist Church of New Zealand in Wellington had branches throughout New Zealand. One of the most prominent mediums was Miss Pearl **Judd,** who demonstrated direct voice phenomena in full light.

Psychical Research

One prominent New Zealand personality in the field of psychical research was the entomologist R. J. Tillyard, who in 1926 became vice-president of the **National Laboratory of Psychical Research** in England.

At the present time, there is an Auckland Psychical Research Society (P.O. Box 5894, Wellesley Street) and a Churches' Fellowship for Psychical and Spiritual Studies, as well as a Federation of Spiritual Healers. There is also a UFO Research Group at Auckland University.

Newbold, William Romaine (1865-1926)

Educator, psychologist and investigator in the field of psychic science. Born November 20, 1865 at Wilmington, Delaware, he studied at University of Pennsylvania (B.A. 1887, Ph.D. 1891), graduate study at University of Berlin 1891-92, and University of Pennsylvania (Hon. LL.D. 1921). In 1896 he married Ethel Kent Sprague Packard. He was a member of the faculty of the University of Pennsylvania for thirty-seven years, and was Adam Seybert Professor of Intellectual and Moral Philosophy from 1907-26.

He was an authority on European politics, archaeology, genealogy, Oriental languages and Greek philosophy. He became famous for his achievement in deciphering a medieval manuscript which he showed to be the work of Roger Bacon, and for his translation of Semitic scrawls on the walls of the Roman catacombs.

He was a member of the American Philosophical Association, the American Philosophical Society, the American Psychological Association, the Society for Psychical Research, London, and the American Society for Psychical Research. He was deeply interested in psychical research and contributed a number of important articles on the subject to the *Journal* and *Proceedings* of the ASPR and the SPR.

He died September 26, 1926 at Philadelphia, Pennsylvania.

Newbrough, Dr. John Ballou (1828-1891)

New York dentist, clairvoyant and clairaudient from childhood, automatic writer and painter.

He was born June 3, 1828, near Springfield, Ohio, son of a school teacher. John was educated in the local schoolhouse, and from the age of sixteen taught himself. He went on to attend Cincinnati Medical college, and practiced both medicine and dentistry.

He migrated to California in 1849 and was fortunate in becoming a gold miner. Several years later, he married Rachel, the sister of his partner John Turnbull. They moved to New York, where Newbrough resumed his dental and medical practice. He also became associated with the Spiritualist movement, becoming a trustee of the New York Spiritualist Association. Eventually his Spiritualist interests led to disagreements with his wife, and some years later they were divorced.

Meanwhile, he was anxious to improve contact with higher spiritual guidance than the commonplace messages of other Spiritualists. He own psychic gifts were remarkable. He could paint in total darkness with both hands at once. It was claimed that closing his eyes he could read printed pages of any book in any library, that he could bring back recollections of astral travels (see **astral projection**) and that under control he could lift enormous weights, even a ton, without apparent effort.

He is chiefly remembered in Spiritualism for **OAHSPE,** *A Kosmon Bible in the Words of Jehovah and his Angel Ambassadors,* first published in 1882 in New York. It is a new Bible purporting to come from the higher heavens, and "to have been directed and looked over by God, the creator's chief representative in the heavens of this earth." In a letter dated January 21, 1883, Dr. Newbrough wrote to the editor of the *Banner of Light.*

"I was crying for the light of Heaven. I did not desire communication for friends or relatives or information about early things; I wished to learn something about the spirit world; what the angels did, how they travelled, and the general plan of the universe. . . . I was directed to get a typewriter which writes by keys, like a piano. This I did and I applied myself industriously to learn it, but with only indifferent success. For two years more the angels propounded to me questions relative to heaven and earth, which no mortal could answer very intelligently. . . .

"One morning the light struck both hands on the back, and they went for the typewriter for some fifteen minutes very vigorously. I was told not to read what was printed, and I have worked myself into such a religious fear of losing this new power that I obeyed reverently. The next morning, also before sunrise the same power came and wrote (or printed rather) again. Again I laid the matter away very religiously, saying little about it to anybody. One morning I accidentally (seemed accidental to me) looked out of the window and beheld the line of light that rested on my hands extending heavenward like a telegraph wire towards the sky. Over my head were three pairs of hands, fully materialised; behind me stood another angel with her hands on my shoulders. My looking did not disturb the scene, my hands kept right on printing . . . printing. For fifty weeks this continued, every morning, half an hour or so before sunrise, and then it ceased, and I was told to read and publish the book *Oahspe*. The peculiar drawings in Oahspe were made with pencil in the same way."

A group formed around Newbrough's revelations, and in 1883 they gave themselves the name "Faithists of the Seed of Abraham" (a term used in *Oahspe*). They moved to Las Cruces, New Mexico, and established a community to implement the *Oahspe* injunction to care for foundlings and orphans.

Newbrough married again, choosing a companion from the community. By 1891, a residential home had been completed, housing some fifty children, but in the following year an outbreak of influenza devastated the area, and Newbrough himself was struck down, dying that year. For a time, his associate Andrew M. Howland continued the community, but it soon disintegrated.

However, Newbrough's followers continued under the name "The Essenes of Kosmon" and are still active today. *Oahspe* is kept in print through the Universal Faithists of Kosmon (Box 664, Salt Lake City, Utah 84110), and a journal, *The Faithist Journal,* is published at: 2324 Suffock Avenue, Kingman, Arizona 86401.

Newcomb, Simon (1835-1909)

Astronomer, mathematician, first president (1885-86) of the American Society for Psychical Research. Born March 12, 1835 at Wallace, Nova Scotia, he studied at Lawrence Scientific School (B.S. 1858), Harvard University. In 1863 he married Mary Caroline Hassler.

He was professor of mathematics, U.S. Navy in 1861, assigned to the U.S. Naval Observatory 1897; Director of the American Nautical Almanac 1877-97, professor of mathematics and astronomy at Johns Hopkins University from 1884-94.

A world famous astronomer and mathematician, Dr. Newcomb's researches made possible the construction of accurate lunar tables. In spite of his interest in psychical research, he remained something of a skeptic. His viewpoint is explained in his *Reminiscences of an Astronomer* (1903). He died July 11, 1909.

News, The (Journal)

A British journal devoted to "Fortean data," i.e., strange phenomena, curiosities, prodigies, portents, coincidences and mysteries in the spirit of the late Charles **Fort,** who first correlated and studied such things. Vol. 1, No. 1, of *The News* was published November 1973.

From No. 16 (June 1976) onwards, the title was change to *Fortean Times.* Published by Robert J. M. Rickard, Fortean Times, 96 Mansfield Road, London NW3 2HX, England (See also **INFO**)

Newsletter of the Parapsychology Foundation

Former publication of the **Parapsychology Foundation** (then located at 29 West 57 Street, New York,

N.Y. 10019) which appeared as a bimonthly, giving news in the field of parapsychology and psychical research with world coverage, from vol. 1 (1956) through vol. 16 (1969), when it was subsumed in **Parapsychology Review.** Back issues of the Newsletter available from the Parapsychology Foundation. Current address: 288 East 71st Street, New York, N.Y. 10021.

Newspaper Tests

Ingenious experiments devised by seance-room communicators to exclude **telepathy** as an explanation. The Rev. C. Drayton **Thomas** in *Some Recent Evidence for Survival* (1922) published many remarkable instances as recorded in sittings with the medium Mrs. Osborne **Leonard.**

The method of communicators was to give in the afternoon names and dates that were to be published in certain columns of next day's *The Times* newspaper, or, if so requested, in coming issues of magazines. The information so obtained was immediately posted to the **Society for Psychical Research,** London. The results when verified were so much more striking since neither the editor nor the compositor in the offices of *The Times* could tell at the hour when the communication was made what text would occupy the column mentioned in the next edition.

The following tests were given on February 13, 1920:

The first page of the paper, in column two and near the top the name of a minister with whom your father was friendly at Leek. (Perks was found, a name which verified from an old diary.)

Lower in this column, say one quarter down, appears his name, your own, your mother's and that of an aunt; all four within the space of two inches. (John and Charles were correctly found, then came the name Emile Souret which presumably suggested Emily and Sarah, his aunt and mother.)

Near these the word "Grange." (It was not found.)

In column one, not quite half-way down, is a name which is your mother's maiden name or one very like it. (The maiden name was *Dore,* the name found *Dorothea.*)

Somewhat above that is named a place where your mother passed some years of her girlhood. (Hants. Correct. Shirley, where she spent her girlhood, being in Hampshire, for which "Hants." is the recognized abbreviation.)

Close to the foregoing is a name, which suggests an action one might make with the body in jumping. (Cummock, a bad pun: come knock.)

Towards the bottom of the column is named a place where you went to school. (Lincolnshire. Correct.)

There is a word close by which looks to your father like Cheadle. (Not found.)

Higher in column one, say two-thirds down, is a name suggesting ammunition. (Found the ecclesiastical title Canon.)

Between that and the teacher's name is a place-name, French, looking like three words hyphened into one. (Braine-le-Chateau.)

About the middle of this page, the middle both down and across, is a mistake in print; it cannot be right. Some wrong letters inserted or something left out, some kind of mistake just there. (The word "page" printed imperfectly: "Paae.")

Out of the items in this test, two entirely failed, the others forecast at 3 p.m. the day previous to the publication of the paper were correct. At 6 p.m. a copy of this test was posted to the Society for Psychical Research. Inquiries at *The Times* revealed the fact that in some cases the particular notices referred to might have already been set up in type at the time of the sitting, in other cases they were probably not set up and in any case their ultimate position on the page could not be normally known until late in the afternoon.

By the spirit of his father the following explanation was furnished to the Rev. C. Drayton Thomas: "These tests have been devised by others in a more advanced sphere than mine, and I have caught their ideas. I am not yet aware exactly how one obtains these tests, and have wondered whether the higher guides exert some influence whereby a suitable advertisement comes into position on the convenient date. I am able to sense what appears to me to be sheets and slips of paper with names and various information upon them. I notice suitable items and, afterwards, visualise a duplicate of the page with these items falling into their places. At first I was unable to do this. It seems to me that it is an ability which throws some light upon foretelling, a visualising of what is to be, but based upon that which already is. Sometimes I see further detail upon visualising which I had not sensed from the letters. I think there is an etheric foreshadowing of things about to be done. It would probably be impossible to get anything very far ahead, but only within a certain number of hours, and I cannot say how many. I scarcely think it would be possible to get a test for the day after the morrow, or, even if possible, that it could result in more than a jumble of the morrow's with a few of the day following. I think they should impress people more than book tests. It becomes clear that telepathy cannot explain; you find in the paper that for which you seek, but given in a form which you did not expect and about which you could, in the nature of the case, have known nothing. Two sets of memory are combined to produce them, my memories of long ago, and my memory of what I found this morning about preparations for the Press." (See also **Book Tests; Chair Test; Prediction; Prevision**)

Newton, Dr. J. R. (1810-1883)

American healing medium. He began his healing career in 1855 and is said to have cured thousands of sufferers from a variety of ailments. However, he cured only a few of the many who came to him.

He claimed to be aided by Christ and other spirits. He usually healed in large halls or other areas with space to move about in and used to handle patients, often giving a sufferer a push and telling him he was cured, which he usually was.

He gave most of his healing free. Many of his cures were reliably recorded both in the United States and in England, which he visited the first time in 1870.

The publication *The Spiritualist* (June 15, 1870) listed 105 cases of persons cured or benefited by Dr. Newton on that visit, while the *Spiritual Magazine* (July 1970) cited full particulars of many cures.

Nganga

Members of the **Ndembo** secret society of the Lower Congo. *Nganga*—literally "the knowing ones"—was a term applied to those who had passed certain curious rites to distinguish them from the *Vanga* or uninitiated. (See also **Ndembo**)

NICAP

Initialism for **National Investigations Committee on Aerial Phenomena,** founded in the U.S. in 1956 to investigate unidentified flying objects (see also **UFO**).

Nichusch

Cabalistic term for prophetic indication, in accordance with the view that all events and natural happenings have a secret connection, and interact upon one another.

It was believed that practically everything could become an object of soothsaying—the flight of birds, movement of clouds, cries of animals, events happening to man, and so on.

Man himself might become *Nichusch* by saying that if such and such a thing took place it would be a good or a bad omen. (See also **Divination; Kabala**)

"Nick" or "Old Nick"

A well-known British nickname for the Devil, comparable with the American "Mr. Splitfoot" or "Old Scratch."

It seems probable that his name is derived from the Dutch *Nikken,* the devil, which again comes from the Anglo-Saxon *nœc-an,* to slay, deriving from the theological view that the devil was "a murderer from the beginning."

In northern countries there is a river spirit named "Neck," "Nikke," or "Nokke," of the same nature as the water Kelpie and the Merman or Triton. (See also **"Old Scratch"; "Splitfoot"**)

Nicol, Betty (Elizabeth) Humphrey (Mrs. J. Fraser Nicol) (1917-)

Psychologist and parapsychologist. Born June 7, 1917 at Indianapolis, Indiana, she studied at Earlham College, Richmond, Indiana (B.A. philosophy 1940), and Duke University, Durham, North Carolina (Ph.D. psychology 1946). She was visiting research fellow (psychology) at Radcliffe College, Cambridge, Massachusetts from 1957-58. In 1955 she married parapsychologist J. Fraser **Nicol.**

Mrs. Nicol collaborated in parapsychology experiments with her husband, with J. B. **Rhine,** J. G. **Pratt,** E. A. **McMahan.** She also undertook a detailed analysis of published precognition cases in order to ascertain optimal psychological and physical conditions for spontaneous precognition. This project was sponsored by a grant from the Parapsychology Foundation. She has contributed articles to the *Journal of Parapsychology* and is author of the publication *Handbook of Tests in Parapsychology* (1948).

Nicol, J(ohn) Fraser (died 1989)

Contemporary parapsychologist. Born in Edinburgh, Scotland, he was educated at Heriot's School, Edinburgh and Heriot-Watt College, Edinburgh University. In 1955 he married Betty M. Humphrey.

He was a researcher member of the Society for psychical research, London from 1934-51, research associate at Parapsychology Laboratory, Duke University, Durham, North Carolina from 1951-52, research grantee, Parapsychology Foundation from 1954 onwards, research associate of American Society for Psychical Research from 1960-63. Member of American Statistical Association, corresponding member of the Society for Psychical Research, London (council member from 1948-57).

Mr. Nicol's researches and experiments have included telepathy, psychokinesis, precognition with falling dice, paranormal cognition in relation to personality factors, spontaneous psychical phenomena, paranormal communication. He has also collaborated with his wife on various experiments and reports. His articles in the *Proceedings* of the Society for Psychical Research include: 'Some Experiments in Willed Dice-Throwing' (with W. W. **Carington**) and 'In Memoriam: Whately Carington' (vol. 48, 1947), in the SPR *Journal:* 'The Fox Sisters and the Development of Spiritualism' (vol. 34, 1948), 'Randomness: The Background and Some New Investigations' (vol. 38, 1955), in the ASPR *Journal:* 'The Exploration of ESP and Human Personality' (with Betty Humphrey, vol. 47, 1953), 'The Feeling of Success in ESP' (with Betty Nicol, vol. 52, 1968), in *International Journal of Parapsychology:* 'The Statistical Controversy in Quantitative Research' (vol. 1, 1959), 'Apparent Spontaneous Precognition' (vol. 3, 1961), in *Tomorrow:* 'Buried Alive—Saved by Telepathy' (with Betty Nicol, vol. 5, 1957), 'Keeping Up with the Joneses' (vol. 8, 1960). He contributed a paper on 'Some Difficulties in the Way of Scientific Recognition of Extrasensory Perception' to the book *Ciba Symposium on Extrasensory Perception* (1956) and collaborated with Betty Nicol on the report 'Experimental Uses of Chemical Compounds' published in

Proceedings of Two Conferences on Parapsychology and Pharmacology (1961).

He contributed a paper on 'The Founders of the Society for Psychical Research' to *Proceeding* of the S.P.R. (vol. 55, 1972), and the paper 'Historical Background to Part IV (Parapsychology 8 Physical Systems) in *Handbook of Parapsychology* ed. Benjamin B. Wolman (1977).

For an important survey of his life and work, see 'J. Fraser Nicol: An Appreciation of His Dedication to Psychical Research' by Mostyn Gilbert (*Journal* of the Society for Psychical Research, vol. 56, No. 818, January 1990).

Nicolai, Christoph Friedrich (1733-1811)

German critic, novelist and bookseller of Berlin, who was of special interest from the occult point of view because of his peculiar experiences which he described in his account read before the Royal Society of Berlin. The case is one of the most celebrated in the annals of psychology. His own account is as follows:

"In the first two months of the year 1791," he stated, "I was much affected in my mind by several incidents of a very disagreeable nature; and on the 24th of February a circumstance occurred which irritated me extremely. At ten o'clock in the forenoon my wife and another person came to console me; I was in a violent perturbation of mind, owing to a series of incidents which had altogether wounded my moral feelings, and from which I saw no possibility of relief, when suddenly I observed at the distance of ten paces from me a figure—the figure of a deceased person. I pointed at it, and asked my wife whether she did not see it. She saw nothing, but being much alarmed, endeavoured to compose me, and sent for the physician. The figure remained some seven or eight minutes, and at length I became a little more calm, and as I was extremely exhausted, I soon afterwards fell into a troubled kind of slumber, which lasted for half an hour. The vision was ascribed to the great agitation of mind in which I had been, and it was supposed I should have nothing more to apprehend from that cause, but the violent affection had put my nerves into some unnatural state. From this arose further consequences, which require a more detailed description.

"In the afternoon, a little after four o'clock, the figure which I had seen in the morning again appeared. I was alone when this happened, a circumstance which, as may be easily conceived, could not be very agreeable. I went therefore to the apartment of my wife, to whom I related it. But thither also the figure pursued me. Sometimes it was present, sometimes it vanished, but it was always the same standing figure. A little after six o'clock several stalking figures also appeared, but they had no connection with the standing figure. I can assign no other cause for this apparition than that, though much more composed in my mind, I had not been able so soon entirely to forget the cause of such deep and distressing vexation, and had reflected on the consequences of it, in order, if possible, to avoid them; and that this happened three hours after dinner, at the time when digestion just begins.

"At length I became more composed with respect to the disagreeable incident which had given rise to the first apparition, but though I had used very excellent medicines and found myself in other respects perfectly well, yet the apparitions did not diminish, but on the contrary rather increased in number, and were transformed in the most extraordinary manner.

"The figure of the deceased person never appeared to me after the first dreadful day, but several other figures showed themselves afterwards very distinctly, sometimes such as I knew, mostly, however, of persons I did not know, and amongst those known to me, were the semblance of both living and deceased persons, but mostly the former, and I made the observation, that acquaintance with whom I daily conversed never appeared to me as phantasms; it was always such as were at a distance.

"It is also to be noted, that these figures appeared to me at all times, and under the most different circumstances, equally distinct and clear. Whether I was alone, or in company, by broad daylight equally as in the night-time, in my own as well as in my neighbour's house; yet when I was at another person's house, they were less frequent, and when I walked the public street they very seldom appeared. When I shut my eyes, sometimes the figures disappeared, sometimes they remained even after I had closed them. If they vanished in the former case, on opening my eyes again, nearly the same figures appeared which I had seen before.

"I sometimes conversed with my physician and my wife concerning the phantasms which at the time hovered around me; for in general the forms appeared oftener in motion than at rest. They did not always continue present—they frequently left me altogether, and again appeared for a short or longer space of time, singly or more at once; but, in general, several appeared together. For the most part I saw human figures of both sexes. They commonly passed to and fro as if they had no connection with each other, like people at a fair where all is bustle. Sometimes they appeared to have business with one another. Once or twice I saw amongst them persons on horseback, and dogs and birds; these figures all appeared to me in their natural size, as distinctly as if they had existed in real life, with the several tints on the uncovered parts of the body, and with all the different kinds and colours of clothes. But I think, however, that the colours were somewhat *paler* than they are in nature.

"None of the figures had any distinguishing characteristic, they were neither terrible, ludicrous, nor repulsive; most of them were ordinary in their appearance—some were even agreeable.

"On the whole, the longer I continued in this state, the more did the number of the phantasms increase, and the apparitions became more frequent. About four weeks afterwards I began to hear them speak. Sometimes the phantasms spoke with one another, but for the most part they addressed themselves to me, these speeches were in general short, and never contained anything disagreeable. Intelligent and respected friends often appeared to me, who endeavoured to console me in my grief, which still left deep traces on my mind. This speaking I heard most frequently when I was alone; though I sometimes heard it in company, intermixed with the conversation of real persons; frequently in single phrases only, but sometimes even in connected discourse.

"Though at this time I enjoyed rather a good state of health both in body and mind, and had become so very familiar with these phantasms, that at last they did not excite the least disagreeable emotion, but on the contrary afforded me frequent subjects for amusement and mirth, yet as the disorder sensibly increase, and the figures appeared to me for whole days together, and even during the night, if I happened to awake, I had recourse to several medicines."

Nicolai then recounted how the apparitions vanished upon blood being let.

"This was performed on the 20th of April, at eleven o'clock in the forenoon. I was alone with the surgeon, but during the operation the room swarmed with human forms of every description, which crowded fast one on another. This continued till half-past four o'clock, exactly the time when the digestion commences. I then observed that the figures began to move more slowly; soon afterwards the colours became gradually paler; every seven minutes they lost more and more of their intensity, without any alteration in the distinct figure of the apparitions. At about half-past six o'clock, all the figures were entirely white, and moved very little, yet the forms appeared perfectly distinct. By degrees they became visibly less plain, without decreasing in number, as had often formerly been the case. The figures did not move off, neither did they vanish, which also had usually happened on other occasions. In this instance they dissolved immediately into air; of some even whole pieces remained for a length of time, which also by degrees were lost to the eye. At about eight o'clock there did not remain a vestige of any of them, and I have never since experienced any appearance of the same kind. Twice or thrice since that time I have felt a propensity, if I may be allowed to express myself, or a sensation as if I saw something which in a moment again was gone. I was even surprised by this sensation whilst writing the present account, having, in order to render it more accurate, perused the papers of 1791, and recalled to my memory all the circumstances of that time. So little are we sometimes, even in the greatest composure of mind, masters of our imagination."

Nicolai was a greatly respected writer who became the organizer and leader of the Enlightenment, together with G. E. Lessing and Moses Mendelssohn. He died January 1, 1811.

His true story 'An Account of the Apparition of Several Phantoms' was published in the periodical *The German Museum* (London, 1800).

Nicoll, (Henry) Maurice (Dunlap) (1884-1953)

Prominent British physician and psychologist who became a leading exponent of the teachings of G. I. **Gurdjieff** and P. D. **Ouspensky.**

Born 1884, he was educated at Aldenham School and Caius College, Cambridge University, going on to study medicine at St. Bartholomew's Hospital, London, and in Vienna, Berlin, Paris and Zurch (B.A., M.B., B.C. Cambridge, M.R.C.S. London). He was Medical Officer to Empire Hospital for Injuries to the Nervous System; lecturer in medical psychology at Birmingham University, England; member of the British Psycho Medical Society. He became a member of the editorial staff of *Journal of Neurology and Psychopathy.* In World War I he served in Gallipoli in 1915, Mesopotamia in 1916.

His publications included: *Dream Psychology* (1917; 1920), *The New Man; an Interpretation of Some Parables and Miracles of Christ* (1950; 1951); *Living Time* (1952), *Psychological Commentaries on the Teaching of G. I. Gurdjieff & P. D. Ouspensky* (5 vols., 1954-1966); *The Mark (On the Symbolism of Various Passages from the Bible)* (1954).

He died August 30, 1953.

Nictalopes

Name given to human beings who can see in the dark. They are extremely rare. Dr. Tentin of Paris reported in 1874 the case of Marie Verdun, a girl of eighteen: "Although her eyes do not present any special morbid character she is forced to keep her eyelids closed during the day, and to cover her head with a thick veil. On the other hand, when the shutters of the room are hermetically fastened, she reads and writes perfectly in the deepest darkness."

Auguste Müller, the Stuttgart somnambulist, saw perfectly well and recognized all persons and objects in the greatest darkness.

In view of the remarkable precision with which objects move in the darkness of the seance room, it was suggested that some mediums might be nictalopes. As, however, the same precision has been observed when the medium goes into trance, the theory as a normal explanation seems untenable. (See also **Eyeless Sight**)

Nielsen, Einer (died 1965)

Remarkable Danish materialization medium, experiments with whom were recorded by Baron **Schrenck-Notzing** in his book *Physikalische Phaenomene des Mediumismus* (1920).

In 1922 in Christiania, Oslo, Nielsen was pronounced a fraud but he had completely reinstated himself in 1924 in Reykjavik, in sittings for the Psychical Research Society of Iceland. The report of the novelist Einar H. Kvaran, endorsed by scientists and other people of high standing, is a remarkable record of the materialization of forms, sometimes two appearing simultaneously near the medium while he himself was within view. Levitations and other telekinetic phenomena were seen in abundance (see **Levitation; Movement**).

However, several years later in Copenhagen, he could not regain the lost confidence of serious researchers. He was again accused of fraud by Johs. Carstensen, the leader of his circle, and a convinced Spiritualist. After his exposure in a pamphlet the medium went to court, but lost his case in April, 1932.

An English Translation (by Mrs. Helmi Krohn) of Nielsen's autobiography was published under the title *Solid Proofs of Survival* (Psychic Book Club, London, 1950).

He died Feburary 26, 1965.

Nielsen, Winnifred Moon (1917-)

Assistant professor of psychology who experimented in the field of parapsychology. Born August 16, 1917 at Key West, Florida, she studied at University of Florida (B.A. 1958, Ph.D. 1962). In 1937 she married Major Kenneth Cooper Smith (died 1943); her second marriage was in 1944 to William Andrew Nielsen (died 1953).

She was a research fellow at the Parapsychology Laboratory, Duke University, Durham, North Carolina from 1954-56, thereafter assistant professor of psychology at Mary Washington College, University of Virginia. She is a charter associate of the Parapsychological Association. Mrs. Nielsen has investigated relationships between Psi and personality. She published reports on her researches in the *Journal of Parapsychology;* these include 'An Exploratory Study in Precognition' (March 1956), 'Mental States Associated with Precognition' (June 1956).

Nielsson, Harald (died 1928)

Professor of Theology in the University of Iceland, who became convinced by experiences with the medium Indridi **Indridason,** that modern Spiritualism was identical with primitive Christianity. Three lectures in which he affirmed this faith were published in a small book: *Mes Expériences en Spiritualisme Experimentale.* Professor Nielsson died in 1928.

Nif

An Egyptian symbol in the form of a ship's sail widely spread, symbolizing breath. (See also **Egypt**)

Niflheim

The region of everlasting cold, mist, and darkness, in Teutonic mythology. It is situated north of Midgard (middle earth—the present human abode), across the river Gjol. It was into this region that the god Odin banished the goddess Hel to rule over the worlds of the dead. The lowest depths are named **Nastrond**—"Strand of the Dead."

Nightmare

Possibly deriving from the Old English *night* and *mara,* a specter, indicating a terrifying dream. It is said to be caused by a disorder of the digestive functions during sleep, inducing the temporary belief that some animal or demon is sitting on the chest. Among primitive people it was thought that the affection proceeded from the attentions of an evil spirit.

Johann Georg Keysler, in his very curious work *Antiquitates selectae Septentrionales et Celticae* (1720), collected many interesting particulars concerning the nightmare. *Nachtmar,* he stated, is from *Mair,* an old woman, because the specter which appears to press upon the breast and impede the action of the lungs is generally in that form. The English and Dutch words coincide with the German. The French *cochemar* is *Mulier incumbens* or *Incuba.* The Swedes use *Mara* alone, according to the *Historia de omnibus Gothorum Sueonumque Regibus* of J. Magnus (1554), where he stated that Valender, the son of Suercher, succeeded to the throne of his father, who was suffocated by a demon in his sleep, of that kind which by the scribes is called *Mara.*

Others, "we suppose Germans," continued Keysler, "call it *Hanon Tramp.*" The French peasantry called it *Dianus* which is a corruption either of Diana or of *Dœzmonium Meridianum* for it seems there is a belief which Keysler thought might not improbably be derived from a false interpretation of an expression in the 91st Psalm ("the destruction that wasteth at noon-day") that persons are most exposed to such attacks at that time and therefore women in childbed are then never left alone.

But though the *Dœzmonium Meridianum* is often used for the Ephialtes, nevertheless it is more correctly any sudden and violent attack which deprives the patient of his senses.

In some parts of Germany, the name given to this disorder is *den alp,* or *das Alp-dructen,* either from the "mass" which appears to press on the sufferer or from *Alp* or *Alf* (elf). In Franconia it is *die Drud* or *das Druddructen,* from the Druid or Weird Women, and there is a belief that it may not only be chased away, but be made to appear on the morrow in a human shape, and lend something required of it by the following charm:

Druid to-morrow
So will I borrow.

These Druids, it seems, were not only in the habit of riding men, but also horses, and in order to keep them out of the stables, the salutary *pentalpha* (which bears the name of *Druden-fuss,* Druid's foot) should be written on the stable doors, in consecrated chalk, on the night of St. Walburgh. It should also be mentioned that the English familiar appellation "Trot" is traced to "Druid," "a decrepit old woman such as the Sagas might be," and the same might perhaps be said of a Scottish Saint, Triduana or Tredwin.

In the *Glossarium Suiogothicum* of Johann Ihre (1769), a somewhat different account of the *Mara* is given. Here again, we find the "witch-riding" of horses, against which a stone **amulet** was suggested by the antiquarian John Aubrey, similar to one described below.

Among the incantations by which the *nightmare* may be chased away, Reginald Scot recorded the following in his *Discovery of Witchcraft* (1584 etc.)

St. George, St. George, our lady's knight,
He walked by day so did he by night:
Until such times as he her found,
He her beat and he her bound,
Until her troth to him plight,
He would not come to her that night.

"Item," continued this author, "hand a stone over the afflicted person's bed, which stone hath naturally such a hole in it, as wherein a string may be put through it, and so be hanged over the diseased or bewitched party, be it man, woman, or horse."

Readers of the above lines may be reminded of the similar charm which Shakespeare put into the mouth of Edgar as Mad Tom in *King Lear:*

Saint Withold footed thrice the Wold;
He met the night-mare and her ninefold
Bid her alight,
And her troth plight
And aroint thee, witch, aroint thee.

Another charm of earlier date occurs in Chaucer's *Miller's Tale.* When the simple Carpenter discovers the crafty Nicholas in his feigned abstraction, he thinks he may perhaps be hag-ridden, and addresses him thus:

I crouch the from Elves and fro wikid wightes
And there with the night-spell he seide arightes,
On four halvis of the house about,
And on the dreshfold of the dore without,
'Jesus Christ, and Seint Benedight,
Blesse this house from evrey wikid wight,
Fro the night's mare, the witc paternoster,
Where wennist thou Seint Peter's sister.

A later author has pointed to some other formularies, and has noticed that Asmodeus was the fiend of most evil repute on these occasions. In the *Otia Imperiala* of Gervase of Tilbury, some other protecting charms are said to exist.

To turn to the medical history of the **Incubus, Pliny** recommended two remedies for this complaint, one of which was the herbal remedy wild peony seed. Another, which it would not be easy to discover in any modern pharmacopœia, was a decoction in wine and oil of the tongue, eyes, liver, and bowels of a dragon, wherewith, after it has been left to cool all night in the open air, the patient should be anointed every morning and evening.

Dr. Bond, a physician, who stated that he himself was much afflicted with the nightmare, published an *Essay on the Incubus* in 1753. At the time at which he wrote, medical attention appears to have been very little called to the disease, and some of the opinions hazarded were sufficiently wild and inconclusive. Thus, a certain Dr. Willis said it was owing to some incongruous matter which is mixed with the nervous fluid in the cerebellum (*de Anima Brutorum*), while Bellini thought it imaginary and to be attributed to the idea of some demon which existed in the mind the day before.

Both of these writers might have known better if they would have turned to Fuchsius (with whom Dr. Bond appeared to be equally acquainted), who in his work *de Curandi Ratione,* published as early as 1548, had an excellent chapter (I, 31) on the causes, symptoms, and cure of nightmare, in which he attributed it to repletion and indigestion, and recommends the customary discipline.

Much of Gothic literature has been ascribed to dreams and nightmares. Horace Walpole's famous story *The Castle of Otranto* (1764) derived from a dream in which Walpole saw upon the uppermost banister of a great staircase a vision of a gigantic hand in armor.

In 1816, Mary Shelley had a gruesome and vivid nightmare which was the basis for her story *Frankenstein.*

Nearly seventy years later, novelist Robert Louis Stevenson had a nightmare that inspired his famous story *The Strange Case of Dr. Jekyll and Mr. Hyde,* which he completed in only three days.

Bram **Stoker's** immortal creation of *Dracula* (1897) was claimed to be the result of a nightmare after a supper of dressed crab, although clearly many of the elements in the story had been germinating in the author's mind much earlier. Many horror stories have also inspired nightmares. (See also **Fiction,** Occult English; **Incubus; Succubus**)

Nirmala Devi Srivastava (1923-)

Modern Hindu mystic, wife of a U.N. diplomat. She was born March 21, 1923, in Chindawara, a small hill station near Nagpur, India. Although born into a Christian family, she has embraced the concept of the basic truth of all religions in a universal teaching, based on ancient Hindu concepts of **Kundalini,** a latent power in the human organism, and an evolutionary force in nature. Kundalini operates as a psycho-physical force in human beings, as the dynamic of sexual activity and also, when properly aroused, as the mechanism of higher consciousness and God-realization.

Kundalini yoga is concerned with the opening of *chakras* or psychic centers in the body, culminating in an energy flow to the highest center in the head, resulting in expansion of consciousness and mystical awareness.

On May 5, 1970, Nirmala Devi experienced the awakening of the *sahasrara chakra* (the highest center) through Kundalini arousal, and perceived a vision of her ability to communicate this arousal to other individuals. She began teaching other people techniques named Sahaja Yoga (inborn technique) in order to transform their lives.

A center was established in New Delhi, India, and also centers came into being in Britain, Australia,

France, Switzerland, Hong Kong, Canada, and the U.S. Known to her followers as "Mataji," Nirmala Devi travels to centers abroad, keeping contact in different countries. A bi-monthly magazine, *Nirmala Yoga,* is published from: 43, Banglow Road, Delhi 110007, India. For an interesting account of meetings with Mataji and her followers, see *The Shortest Journey* by Philippa Pullar (Hamish Hamilton, London, 1981).

For addresses of Sahaja Yoga Centers: Nirmala Palace, 99 Nightingale Lane, Clapham South, Balham, London, S.W.12, England; 12416 Reva Street, Cerritos, California 90701. (See also Pandit **Gopi Krishna; Kundalini**)

Nixon, Queenie (c.1918-1989)

British transfiguration medium. Her psychic gifts manifested in childhood, when she grew up in the care of two aunts, both Spiritualist mediums.

She spend thirty-five years as a medium, traveling widely in Canada, France, Germany, Spain, Egypt, Sweden, Iceland, Australia, and the U.S. In addition to trance communications through her spirit guide "Paul," she manifested the rare phenomenon of transfiguration, when her features would take on the appearance of deceased persons speaking through her.

These transfiguration demonstrations would sometimes last as long as three hours, with various personalities manifesting. In 1967, infra-red photographs captured a record of such appearances, including what appeared to be ectoplasmic clouds around her face (see also **Ectoplasm.**)

Two newspapers who accused the medium of fraud did not interview her or even attend her seances.

Queenie Nixon died at the age of 71, following several heart attacks. (See also **Transfiguration**)

Noetics

Term used by scientific writer Charles A. **Musés** and others to denote the science of consciousness and its alterations.

In his paper 'The Politics of Psi: Acculturation and Hypnosis' (included in *Extrasensory Ecology* edited Joseph K. Long, Scarecrow Press, 1977), Musés stated 'Noetics is concerned with the nature, alterations and potentials of consciousness, and especially human consciousness.'

However, this parapsychological use of "Noetic" is distinct from its existing use as a synonym for "Noachian," meaning pertaining to Noah and his period.

An early use of the word "Noetic" in relation to states of consciousness was the article 'Psychic and Noetic Action' by occultist Madame H. P. **Blavatsky** (1831-1891), originally published in the journal *Lucifer* during the last years of her life.

In this article, Madame Blavatsky equated "noetic" with *manasic* (deriving from *manas,* a Sanskrit term for mind) and compares materialistic psychological views of her time with ancient Hindu religious teachings and occultism.

She concluded that there is a higher noetic character of the Mind-Principle than individual ego, a "Spiritual-Dynamical" force relating to divine consciousness, as distinct from mechanistic psychological dogmas or passive psychicism. This interesting article was reprinted in *Studies in Occultism* by Helena Petrovna Blavatsky (Dennis Wheatley Library of the Occult, London, 1974). (See also **Institute of Noetic Sciences;** Edgar D. **Mitchell**)

Nolan, Finbarr (1952-)

Contemporary Irish healer who is the **seventh son** of a seventh son, and thus, according to folk tradition, destined to heal by touch. He was born October 2, 1952, at Loch Gowna, Co. Cavan, Republic of Ireland. His mother stated "I knew . . . God would give him the power to heal." There were requests for healing when Finbarr was only three months old, but his mother insisted that healing wait until the boy was two years old. At that time, a man brought along his five-year-old child suffering from ringworm. Finbarr's mother circled the spots with holy water, making the sign of the cross in the middle, then placed the two-year-old Finbarr's hand on each spot in turn, while Mrs. Nolan prayed for healing and asked her son to repeat the prayers after her. She claims that the ringworm was cured after two visits.

However, Finbarr did not immediately undertake regular healing, although at the age of nine he touched the paralyzed hand of a local hotel proprietor and the hand became normal in three days time. The father of this man was confined to a wheelchair with severe arthritis, but the day after Finbarr touched him he was able to use his hand, and a month later he had recovered sufficiently to resume his job as a butcher.

At the age of sixteen, while still attending school, Finbarr was asked to go to Donegal to cure an aunt. She notified the local newspaper, with the result that the young Finbarr arrived to find a crowd of three hundred people and a television film crew. For several weeks afterwards, some five thousand people a day came to his home for healing, and he touched them in groups of fourteen or fifteen at a time in the kitchen of the house. After that Finbarr decided to leave school and devote himself full time to healing.

His reputation as a healer spread rapidly, and visitors came from Australia, Europe, India, and the U.S. for treatment. Since Co. Cavan is located near the border with Northern Ireland, the political unrest and disorders began to discourage visitors, so Finbarr moved with his parents and brothers to a house in the suburbs of Dublin. Here the large number of visitors seeking healing soon made it difficult for the family to live a normal life in an average-sized house, so Finbarr hired halls and hotel rooms for regular clinics.

In the early period, Finbarr had been influenced by his mother's religious outlook and used holy water, making the sign of the cross when touching each patient, but eventually he discarded such specifically Catholic tradition. As he said: "It deterred a lot of Protestants and I have nearly as many Protestant patients at my clinic as I do Catholic." Moreover he came to believe that his healing power had nothing to do with religion, and rejected the term "faith healer." He stated: "People should understand my healing has nothing to do with faith; I believe my power is a gift . . . I've proved that faith is not needed by curing animals and babies." Indeed, he became well known for treating injured race horses, and one horse he treated won nine races afterwards.

His healing power appears to be in his right hand, and he therefore places it on each part of a patient's body that is afflicted. He lays his hand on the patient for several seconds and does not himself feel anything unusual happening, although patients often state that they feel a sensation of heat. His healing technique was monitored at a Belfast hospital, and it was found that during healing sessions there were changes in his respiration, pulse rate, and the electrical potential of his skin.

Like other seventh son healers, he has found that three visits are usually necessary. Patients sometimes feel worse after the first healing session, usually a sign that some changes have commenced. Healing is usually consolidated at the second and third visit.

Most patients pay a small voluntary contribution for healing, but some wealthier individuals have been very generous. An elderly lady in New York suffering from rheumatoid arthritis paid Finbarr's 6,000-mile journey and an additional check for several thousand dollars. Finbarr has also flown to Washington to treat a young Vietnamese war soldier. Finbarr has held clinics in London as well as the U.S. and is credited with some remarkable cures.

An interesting experiment with Finbarr was carried out by Dr. Robert E. Willner, Diplomate of Board of Family Practice, in his office in Florida. Dr. Willner selected ten patients on the basis of severity of their disease and failure to respond to multiple attempts at medical therapy. Finbarr was introduced to them as "Dr. Finn, a medical student from the medical school in Dublin, Ireland." His function was ostensibly to confirm Dr. Willner's observations and provide independent evaluation of each patient's disease process. The ten patients were involved with the experiment for three visits a week over a period of two weeks. Under these conditions, Finbarr's touching appeared part of normal medical examination, and suggestion or placebo effect was eliminated, as no therapy was indicated.

Dr. Willner reported as follows: "Four of the ten patients were completely unaffected by the examinations; five patients showed definite response of a positive nature and the improvement was thought to be of significant nature, in some cases 60% to 100% improvement. Two of these cases were extremely difficult and showed dramatic results . . . It is also extremely important to note that all of these patients have been under the care of extremely fine specialists in the fields to which their diseases were related. Except for the increased attention that the patients were getting, I am not aware of any other positive influencing factor on the progress of the disease in any of them. One would expect that a patient in this setting would continue with their symptomatology in the hope that they would be chosen for the continuation of the experiment because their symptoms persisted . . . The patients were not charged for their visits. Therefore, monetary incentive was absent."

Finbarr is an amiable and eminently normal individual, with none of the mystique of professional gurus. He does not think about anything in particular during the laying on of hands and exudes a friendly matter-of-fact atmosphere. His relaxations include Gaelic football, golf, and water skiing. His address is: 11 Foxfield Road, Raheny, Dublin 5, Republic of Ireland. (See also Danny **Gallagher;** Psychic **Healing; Healing by Faith; King's Evil; Seventh Son**)

North American UFO Federation

Founded in 1983, with the object of uniting UFO organizations in an effort to study and resolve the UFO phenomenon, to develop a standard manual, reporting form, and vocabulary for investigation and reporting UFO sightings, to inform the general public through educational materials and speakers, to provide a forum for discussion. The Federation maintains a library and plans to develop and maintain a computer file of UFO reports and to establish a speakers bureau. Address: 325 Langton Avenue, Los Altos, California 94022.

North Door

A possible remnant of pagan beliefs in some old Christian churches in Europe is a bricked-up doorway on the north side. There is a tradition that witches used to enter on the north, which is connected with superstitions of the Devil.

Norton, Thomas (died c. 1477)

The exact date of this alchemist's birth is wrapped in mystery, while comparatively little is recorded about his life in general. But at least it is known that he was born in Bristol, England, towards the end of the fourteenth century, and that, in the year 1436 he was elected to represent that town in Parliament. This suggests that he was an upright and highly-esteemed person, and the conjecture is strengthened by the fact that Edward IV made him a member of his privy council and employed him repeatedly as an ambassador.

At an early age Norton showed curiosity concerning **alchemy,** demonstrating his predilection by attempting to make the personal acquaintance of George **Ripley,** sometime Canon of Bridlington, who was reputedly a man of extraordinary learning, author of numerous alchemical works.

For many months Norton sought this person in vain, but at length the Canon, yielding to the other's importunity, wrote to him in the following manner: "I shall not longer delay; the time is come; you shall receive this grace. Your honest desire and approved virtue, your love of truth, wisdom and long perseverance, shall accomplish your sorrowful desires. It is necessary that, as soon as convenient, we speak together face to face, lest I should by writing betray my trust. I will make you my heir and brother in this art, as I am setting out to travel in foreign countries. Give thanks to God, Who next to His spiritual servants, honours the sons of this sacred science."

After receiving this very friendly and encouraging letter, Norton hurried straightway to Ripley's presence, and thereafter for upwards of a month the two were constantly together, the elder man taught the novice many things, while he even promised that, if he showed himself an apt and worthy pupil, he would impart to him the secret of the **philosopher's stone.** And in due course this promise was fulfilled, yet it is reported that Norton's own alchemical researches met with various disappointments.

On one occasion, for instance, when he had almost perfected a certain tincture, his servant absconded with the crucible containing the precious fluid; while at a later time, when the alchemist was at work on the same experiment and thought he was just about to reach the goal, his entire paraphernalia was stolen by a Mayoress of Bristol. And this defeat must have been doubly galling to the unfortunate philosopher, for soon afterwards the Mayoress became very wealthy, presumably as a result of her theft.

Norton himself does not appear to have reaped pecuniary benefit at any time from his erudition, but to have been a comparatively poor man throughout the whole of his life. This is a little surprising, for his *Ordinall of Alchimy* was a popular work in the Middle Ages, and was repeatedly published. The original edition was anonymous, but the writer's identity has been determined because the initial syllables in the first six lines of the seventh chapter compose the following couplet:

Tomas Norton of Briseto
A parfet master ye maie him trowe.

Norton died circa 1477, and his predilections descended to one of his grandsons. This was Samuel Norton, who was born in 1548, studied science at St. John's College, Cambridge, and afterwards became a Justice of the Peace and Sheriff of Somersetshire. He died about 1604, and in 1630 a collection of his alchemistic tracts was published at Frankfort. (See also **Alchemy;** George **Ripley**)

Nostradamian, The

Monthly journal which analyzes the predictions of **Nostradamus** (1503-1566), discussing prophecies fulfilled and interpreting those which have not yet come to pass. Address: Nostradamus Research, P.O. Box 6463, Lincoln, Nebraska 68506.

Nostradamus (Michael de Nostradame) (1503-1566)

French physician, counselor and astrologer to the kings Henry II and Charles IX, renowned for his predictions both of events of his day and of the distant future.

In 1555, and in later years, he published ten "centuries," each containing 100 quatrains (with the exception of the 7th, containing 42 only). The prediction of the death of Henri II was fulfilled in his own lifetime. "En champ bellique par singulier duelle" (In a field of combat in single fight) is a fitting description of his accidental death in 1559 at the hands of Montgomery.

Nostradamus foresaw the decline of the Church as a result of the advance in astronomy and gave the date as 1607 (Lippershey invented his telescope in 1608); he prophesied the prosecution of the astronomers, the seizure of their books and the coming of rationalism for "there would not be an end to the eye." The "commun advenement," the reign of the people is another event in which he foresaw disaster for the Church and named correctly the year of 1792. The details of the French revolution and of the Napoleonic period are almost overwhelming.

But the decipherment of all this requires scholarly erudition. The knowledge of the future was dangerous, so Nostradamus veiled his meaning in a medley of languages, using French, Spanish, Portuguese, Italian, Latin, Greek and Hebrew words, making anagrams and syllable permutations.

He succeeded so well that the Church did not put his book on the Index until 1781. Nostradamus was a Roman Catholic and no enemy to the Church. In fact he predicted the coming of a purified faith in the faraway future when "le corps sans âme plus n'estre en sacrifice" (the death of the body will no more be considered a sacrifice) and "Jour de la mort mis en nativité" (the day of death will become another birthday). This might even apply to Spiritualism.

Other forecasts apply closely to the Great War (see **Prediction**), some others to years to come. Their meaning, however, can only be grasped in the light of fulfillment. Hundreds of quatrains still await convincing explanation. The following (IX.20) illustrates the difficulties of interpretation:

De nuict viendra par la forest de Reines
Deux pars, vaultorte, Herne la pierre blanche
Le moyne noir en gris dedans Varennes:
Esleu Cap. cause tempeste, feu, sang, tranche.

"Forest" stands for the Latin "fores," door, "pars" for "part" (in old French, husband or wife), "vaultorte" is a composite of "vaulx" (valley) and "de torte" (tortuous), "Herne" is an anagram for "reine" (Queen), "moyne" is Greek for "seul," "noir" another anagram for "roi(n)," "esleu" means "elu" (elected), "Cap." Capet, "tranche" knife.

The meaning is: Two married people, the King alone, dressed in grey, and the Queen, the white precious stone, will leave one night through the "door" of the Queen, take a tortuous road, enter into Varennes. The election of Capet will cause storm, fire, bloodshed, decapitation.

her hair had become white (Prudhomme: *Revolutions de Paris,* VIIIe. Semèstre, No. 102, p. 544) their escape was furtive through the "door" of the Queen (*Op. Cit.* VII, p. 57), the road was altered by Louis XVI, to lead from Verdun into Varennes. The absolute monarchy had been changed in 1791 into an elective one.

In modern times, some commentators have claimed that there are quatrains that foretold World War II, the part played by Mussolini and Hitler and even the name "Hister," which can be taken either as an equivalent of the long "s" instead of "t," or a typical Nostradamian pun on "the upstart from the Danube." Ironically, Hitler himself became interested in Nostradamus and faked prophecies were circulated predicting the victory of Hitler, as part of psychological warfare. The allies also employed fake predictions.

Nostradamus appeared to predict the end of the world around the year 2,000, but in this he may have been echoeing millenial speculations of his time rather than relying on visions.

Skeptics maintain that the quatrains of Nostradamus are so involved and symbolical that they may be twisted to prove anything after the event. Moreover, since they do not follow a consistent time sequence, the sudden jumps between quatrains are misleading.

In spite of these criticisms, some of the prophecies are so remarkably clear that they seem beyond coincidence or wishful thinking. Bearing in mind the necessity for Nostradamus to protect himself by using deliberately involved symbolism and hidden meanings, it is difficult to avoid the conclusion that he did in fact have a rare gift of prophetic vision.

Nostradamus died in the night on July 1, 1566. He had accurately foreseen his death in minute details:

De retour d'ambassade, don de Roy Mis au lieu,
Plus n'en fera, sera allé à Dieu,
Parens plus proches, amis, freres du sang,
Trouve tout mort près du lict et du banc.
(Présage CXLI)

("On return from the embassy, the King's gift safely put away, he will do no more, for he will have gone to God. By his near relations, friends and brothers he will be found dead near the bed and the bench")

He had, in fact, gone to Arles as representative of the town of Salon and had been given a gift of money by the King. The bench was one which he used to help hoist his body into bed, and he was found by the bench in the morning.

The only comparable prophet, capable of a broad sweep over a vast area of the future, with its events and individuals, seems to have been the Hindu sage Bhrigu, who is said to have had a vision of the births of all souls in every country, and compiled a vast astrological treatise, in which every name and destiny is said to be recorded (see **Bhrigu-Samhita).** (See also **Prediction; Second Sight**)

Recommended reading:

Cheetham, Erika. *The Prophecies of Nostradamus,* Putnam, 1972; Neville Spearman, London, 1973; Corgi paperback, 1975

Du Vignois, Elisée. *Notre histoire racontée à l'avance par Nostradamus,* Paris, 1910

Howe, Ellic. *Urania's Children; The Strange World of the Astrologers,* William Kimber, London, 1967 (revised and condensed edition: *Astrology and Psychological Warfare During World War II,* London, 1972; U.S. title *Astrology; A Recent History Including the Untold Story of Its Role in World War II,* Walker & Co., New York, 1968)

Laver, James. *Nostradamus, or the Future Foretold,* Collins, London, 1942; Penguin Books, U.K., 1952; George Mann, London, 1973

Le Pelletier, Anatole. *Les Oracles de Michel de Nostredame,* 2 vols., Paris, 1867

Le Vert, Liberte E. (ed.). *The Prophecies & Enigmas of Nostradamus,* Firebell Books, Glen Rock, N.J., 1979

Prieditis, Arthur A. *Fate of the Nations,* Neville Spearman, London/Llewellyn Publications, St. Paul, Minnesota, 1973

Torné-Chiavigny, H. *L'Histoire prédite et jugée par Nostradamus,* 3 vols., Bordeaux, 1860-62

Voldben, A. *After Nostradamus,* Neville Spearman, London, 1973; Citadel, 1974, Mayflower paperback, 1975

Ward, Charles A. *Oracles of Nostradamus,* London, 1891; Modern Library, New York, 1942

(For a bibliography of the twenty-five oldest editions of Nostradamus until 1689, compiled by Carl Graf von Klinckowstroem, see *Zeitschrift für Bücherfreude,* March, 1913)

Noualli

Aztec magicians (see **Mexico and Central America).**

Nous Letter (Journal)

Semi-annual journal of **Noetics,** science of states of consciousness. (This publication also incorporates *Astrologica,* formerly a separate journal.) Address: 1817 De La Vina Street, Santa Barbara, California 93101.

Nuan

In ancient Irish romance, the last of the sorceress-daughters of Conaran. Having put **Finn Mac Cummal** under taboo to send his men in single combat against her as long as she wished, she was slain by Goll Mac Morna, her sister's slayer.

Numerology

A popular interpretive and prediction system deriving from the mystic values ascribed to numbers. In Jewish mysticism, **Gematria** was the association of numbers with Hebrew letters, discovering hidden meanings in words by systematically converting them into numbers.

Modern numerology was popularized by the palmist and fortune-teller **"Cheiro"** (Count Louis Hamon), who developed a system of what he called "fadic" numbers. These were arrived at by adding together all the digits in the subject's birth date, giving a number of destiny to which special planetary and other significance was attached.

In general, numerology systems assign numerical values to letters of one's name or birthplace. These are added together to ascertain a basic number, which has a special symbolic interpretation, much as astrological types are traditionally assigned particular characteristics of helpful and harmful influences. Sometimes lucky or unlucky numbers are related to the twenty-two symbols of the Major Arcana of the **Tarot** pack.

Recommended reading:

Bosman, Leonard. *The Meaning and Philosophy of Numbers,* Rider, London, 1974 (originally published 1932)

Cheiro (Count Louis Hamon). *The Book of Numbers,* London, n.d. (1926) etc.; revised under title *Cheiro's Book of Numbers,* Barrie & Jenkins, London, 1978

Coates, Austin. *Numerology,* Muller, London, 1974; Mayflower paperback, 1978

Kozminsky, Isidore. *Numbers, Their Meaning and Magic,* London, 1912

Moore, Gerun. *Numbers Will Tell,* Barker, London/ Grossett & Dunlap, 1973; 1977

Sepharial (W. G. Old). *The Kabala of Numbers,* 2 vols., London, 1913; MacKay, 1928; Borgo Press, California, 1980

Stein, Sandra Kovacs. *Instant Numerology; Charting Your Road Map to the Future,* Harper & Row, 1979

Westcott, W. W. *Numbers: Their Occult Power and Mystic Virtue,* London, 1890 etc.

Numeromancy

Alternative term for **Numerology,** or **divination** by the letter and word values ascribed to numbers. Other synonyms are Arithmancy or Arithomancy. (See also **Gematria; Kabala**)

O

"Oahspe"

A "New Bible" revealed to Dr. John Ballou **Newbrough** (1828-1891), a New York medium, manifested through automatic writing on the newly invented typewriter in 1881.

Newbrough spent ten years in self-purification so that he could become inspired by a higher power each day just before dawn. The result was *Oahspe, The Kosmon Bible in the words of Jehovah and his angel ambassador.* It took fifty weeks to complete, working half an hour each morning. The Kosmon Church was founded to practice the teachings of *Oahspe,* but this has since become known as Universal Brotherhood of Faithists. Address: c/o Universal Faithists of Kosmon, Box 664, Salt Lake City, Utah 84110. (See also John B. **Newbrough**)

Oak-Apples

An oak-apple is a spongy, brightly colored gall found on the leaf bud of oak trees; it is globular in shape. In folklore, oak-apples could be used in **divination.** To discover whether a child was bewitched, three oak apples were dropped into a basin of water under the child's cradle, at the same time preserving the strictest silence. If the oak-apples floated, the child was not fascinated, but if they sank, the child was believed to be bewitched.

Oak Tree

Much folklore belief surrounds the oak tree. From time immemorial it has held a high place as a sacred tree. The Druids worshiped the oak and performed many of their rites under the shadow of its branches.

When St. Augustine preached Christianity to the ancient Britons, he stood under an oak tree. The ancient Hebrews evidently held the oak as a sacred tree. There is a tradition that Abraham received his heavenly visitors under an oak. Rebekah's nurse was buried under an oak, called afterwards the oak of weeping. Jacob buried the idols of Shechem under an oak. It was under the oak of Ophra that Gideon saw the angel sitting, who gave him instructions as to what he was to do to free Israel.

When Joshua and Israel made a covenent to serve God, a great stone was set up in evidence under an oak that was by the sanctuary of the Lord. The prophet sent to prophesy against Jeroboam was found at Bethel sitting under an oak. Saul and his sons were buried under an oak, and, according to Isaiah, idols were made of oak wood. Abimelech was made king by the oak that was in Shechem.

During the eighteenth century the oak was believed to have influence in curing diseases. It was believed that toothache could be cured by boring with a nail the tooth or gum until blood came, and then driving the nail into an oak tree. Another folk belief was that a child with rupture could be cured by splitting an oak branch, and passing the child through the opening backwards three times; if the splits grew together afterwards, the child would be cured.

It was widely believed that carrying acorns brought long life and good luck, since the oak tree itself is used as a symbol of strength and endurance.

Oaten, Ernest W(alter) (c. 1937)

Prominent British Spiritualist, former president of the International Federation of Spiritualists, and president of **Spiritualists National Union** from 1915 onwards.

He edited the journal *Two Worlds* from 1919-36. He was also an excellent medium and believed that his leading articles were inspired by the spirit of Mrs. Emma Hardinge **Britten.**

Oaten studied every phase of psychical phenomena and was a clear forceful lecturer. He did valuable work as chairman of the Parliamentary Committee of the Spiritualists National Union in pressing for reform of the archaic British law relating to mediumship (see **Fortune Telling Act**).

OBE (or OOBE or OOB)

Initialism for **Out-of-the-Body** experience, also known as **Astral Projection,** Etheric Projection or Ecsomatic Experience.

Obeah

West Indian witchcraft. The term is believed to derive from an Ashanti word *Obayifo* for a wizard or witch, although some writer claims that it refers to Obi, a West African snake god, and was known to be used in 1764.

M. G. Lewis (1775-1818), author of the sensational Gothic novel *Ambrosio; or the Monk* (1795), spent some time in Jamaica, where his father owned large estates, and reported cases of Obeah. In his posthumously published *Journal of a West India Proprietor* (1834), he wrote an entry on January 12, 1816, describing how ten months earlier "a negro of very suspicious manners and appearance" was arrested, "and on examination there was found upon him a bag containing a great variety of strange materials for incantations; such as thunder-stones, cat's ears, the feet of various animals, human hair, fish bones, the teeth of alligators, etc.: he was conveyed to Montego Bay; and no sooner was it understood that this old African was in prison, than depositions were poured in from all quarters from negroes who deposed to having seen him exercise his magical arts, and, in particular, to his having sold such and such slaves medicines and charms to deliver them from their enemies; being, in plain English, nothing else than rank poisons. He was convicted of Obeah upon the most indubitable evidence. The good old practice of burning had fallen into disrepute; so he was sentenced to be transported, and was shipped off the island, to the great satisfaction of persons of all colours—white, black, and yellow."

On February 25, 1818, Lewis gave a detailed account of a Negro named Adam who, he claimed, "has long been the terror of my whole estate. He was accused of being an Obeah man, and persons notorious for the practice of Obeah had been found concealed from justice in his house, who were afterwards convicted and transported. He was strongly suspected of having poisoned more than twelve negroes." Adam was convicted of Obeah and transported. Jamaican legislation of 1760 enacted that "any Negro or other Slave who shall pretend to any Supernatural Power and be detected in making use of any materials relating to the practice of Obeah or Witchcraft in order to delude or impose upon the Minds of others shall upon Conviction thereof before two Magistrates and three Freeholders suffer Death or Transportation." (See also **Voodoo; West Indian Islands**)

Recommended reading:

Bell, Hesketh J. *Obeah; Witchcraft in the West Indies*, Sampson, Low & Co., London, 1889

Emerick, Abraham J. *Obeah and Duppyism in Jamaica*, (privately printed), Woodstock, 1915

Williams, Joseph J. *Voodoos and Obeahs; Phases of West Indian Witchcraft*, Dial Press, New York, 1933

Obercit, Jacques Hermann (1725-1798)

Swiss mystic and alchemist. Born December 2, 1725 in Arbon, Switzerland, Jacques Obercit was the son of a scientist keenly interested in Hermetic philosophy, and no doubt the boy's own taste developed the more speedily on account of the parental predilection.

Very soon, Jacques became determined to discover the **philosopher's stone,** hoping thereby to resuscitate the fortunes of his family, which were at a low ebb, presumably because the elder Obercit had expended large sums on his alchemistic pursuits. The young man worked strenuously to gain his ends, maintaining all along that whoever would triumph in this endeavor must not depend on scientific skill alone but rather on constant communion with God.

Notwithstanding this pious theory, he soon found himself under the ban of the civic authorities, who came to his laboratory, and forced him to forego further experiments, declaring that these constituted a danger to public health and safety. At least they gave this as their reason, but the likelihood is that, in their ignorance, they were unsympathetic to all scientific researches.

Obercit was bitterly incensed and appears to have left his native place and to have lived for some time thereafter with a certain Lavater, a brother of the noted physiognomist of that name. At a later date, Obercit renounced the civilized world altogether and took up his abode in the lofty fastnesses of the Alps.

However, he did not live the solitary life of a hermit, since according to his own account, he took as bride an angel shepherdess named Theantis, with whom he dwelt peacefully during a number of subsequent years. Whether children were born of this union between the terrestrial and the ethereal is not recorded, and the alchemist's account of the affair reads like a romance, as also did two books which he published: *Les Promenades de Gamaliel, juif Philosophe,* and *La Connexion Originaire des Esprits et des Corps, d'après les Principes de Newton* (Augsburg, 1776). His other writings included *Disquisitio de Universali Methodo Medendi* (1767). *Défense du Mysticisme et de la Vie Solitaire* (1775).

Obercit was undoubtedly a picturesque character, and it is matter for regret that so little is known about his life. He died at Weimar February 2, 1798. (See also **Alchemy; Philosopher's Stone**)

Oberion

One of three spirits (the others were "Andrea Malchus" and "Inchubus") said to have been raised up by the parson of Lesingham and Sir John of Leiston in Norfolk, England, c. 1528. (See **England**)

Object Reading

Modern term for **Psychometry,** in which the operator may form impressions of events relating to an object associated with those events, usually by holding the object in the hand.

Objective Phenomena

Term used by psychical researchers, together with "subjective phenomena" as an alternative classification to "physical" and "mental" phenomena. (See also **Psychical Research; Spiritualism**)

Obsession and Possession

Obsession, from Latin *obsessionem—obsidere,* to besiege, is a form of insanity caused, according to traditional belief, by the persistent attack of an evil spirit from outside the individual, this being the opposite of possession, control by an evil spirit from within. Both meanings, however, involve the usurpation of the individuality and control of the body by a foreign and discarnate entity.

Historical Background

This belief may be found in the earliest records of human history, and in the magical rites and formulæ of ancient religions, used as charms against and **exorcism** of these invading influences. Ancient Indian, Greek and Roman literature teem with in stances. The Bible also furnishes many, from the case of Saul ("troubled with an evil spirit" only to be dispossessed by the music of David's harping) to the miracles of Jesus Christ who cast out legions of possessing spirits.

Plato in his *Republic* not only spoke of demons of various grades, but mentioned a method of treating and providing for those obsessed by them. Sophocles and Euripides described the possessed, and mention of the subject is also to be found in Herodotus, Plutarch, Horace, and many others of the classics.

Terrible and appalling episodes in the Middle Ages are to be traced to the unquestioned belief in the possibility of possession and obsession by the Devil and his legions. All madness was believed to be caused by this and was, indeed, the visible manifestation of the Evil One, only to be exorcised by charms, averted by the observance of sacred rites, or later, to be burned and destroyed bodily for the good of the tortured soul within. The rites of Black Magic, in all ages and places, deliberately evoked this possession by the Devil and his demons for the communication and benefit of the infallible knowledge it was believed they conferred and its consequent power and control of man and his destinies.

Modern science with its patient and laborious researches into human psychology, has shown the human mind to be an incomparably delicate instrument, peculiarly at the mercy of the perceptions of the senses and their multitudinous impressions on the brain, its balance so easily shaken by a shock, a drug, a momentary excitement, oftener by prolonged and intense concentration upon single groups of ideas. It is to be noted that in the hallucinatory epidemics of all ages and countries there is to be found this unvarying characteristic: they are connected with some dominant cause, train of thought or religious sentiment prevalent at the time.

In the Middle Ages, when there flourished an intense belief in the positive apparitions of angels, saints and devils, the people's imagination was dominated and rendered intensely dramatic thereby.

The transmigration of the human soul into animals was another popular belief and to this again can be traced the terrible superstition of **Lycanthropy** which possessed large numbers of people in France and Germany in the fourteenth and sixteenth centuries. The mania of **Flagellation** took its rise at Perouse in the thirteenth century, caused by the panic attendant upon an outbreak of plague. These people maintained that there was no remission of sins without flagellation. This they preached with fanatical fervor and bands of them, gathering adherents everywhere, roamed through city and country, clad in scanty clothing on which were depicted skeletons and with frenzied movements publicly lashed themselves. It was to these exhibitions, the name of the "Dance of Death" was first applied.

The Dancing mania, accompanied by aberration of mind and maniacal distortions of the body was very prevalent in Germany in the fourteenth century, and in the sixteenth century in Italy where it was termed "Tarantism" and as a variant in source, was ascribed to the bite of the Tarantula spider. The music and songs employed for the cure are still preserved.

Edmund Parish in his book *Hallucinations and Illusions* (1897) made the following observations on this subject: "If not reckoned as true chorea, the epidemic of dancing which raged in Germany and the Netherlands in the Middle Ages comes under this head. Appearing in Aix it spread in a few months to Liège, Utrecht and the neighbouring towns, visited Metz, Cologne and Strasburg (1418) and after lingering into the sixteenth century gradually died out. This malady consisted in convulsions, contortions accompanying the dancing, hallucinations and so forth. The attack could be checked by bandaging the abdomen as well as by kicks and blows on that part of the body. Music had a great influence on the dancers, and for this reason it was played in the streets in order that the attacks might by this means reach a crisis and disappear the sooner. Quite trifling circumstances could bring on these seizures, the sight of pointed shoes for instance, and of the colour red which the dancers held in horror. In order to prevent such outbreaks the wearing of pointed shoes was forbidden by the authorites. During their dance many of the afflicted thought they waded in blood, or saw heavenly visions."

The same author remarked on other instances: "To this category also belongs the history of demoniacal possession. The belief of being possessed by spirits, frequently met with in isolated cases, appeared at certain periods in epidemic form. Such an epidemic broke out in Brandenburg, and in Holland and Italy in the sixteenth century, especially in the convents. In 1350-60 it attacked the convent of St. Brigitta, in Xanthen, a convent near Cologne, and others. The nuns declared that they were visited by the Devil, and had carnal conversation with him. These and other 'possessed' wretches were sometimes thrown into dungeons, sometimes burnt. The convent of the Ursulines at Aix was the scene of such a drama (1609-11) where two possessed nuns, tormented by all kinds of apparitions, accused a priest of witchcraft on which charge he was burnt to death [see Urbain **Grandier**]. The famous case of the nuns of **Loudun** (1632-39) led to a like tragic conclusion, as well as the Louvier case (1642) in which the two chief victims found their end in lifelong imprisonment and the stake."

Religious Possession

The widespread belief in and fear of magic and **witchcraft** operating on superstitious minds produced the most extraordinary hallucinations. Certain levels of religious ecstasy partake of the same character, the difference being that they involve posession by and contact with so-called good spirits. The sacred books of all nations teem with instances of this and profane history can also furnish examples. The many familiar cases of ecstatic visions and revelations in the Old Testament may be cited, as well as those found in the legends of saints andmartyrs, where they either appear as revelations from heaven or temptations of the Devil.

In the latter case, the eminent sexologist R. Von Krafft-Ebing, pointed out the close connection of religious ecstasy with sexual disturbances. That this ecstatic condition was sought and induced, the following passage amply indicates: "Among Eastern and primitive peoples such as Hindoos, American Indians, natives of Greenland, Kamtschatka and Yucatan, fetish-worshipping Negroes, and Polynesians, the ecstatic state accompanied with hallucinations is frequently observed, sometimes arising spontaneously, but more often artifically induced. It was known also among the nations of antiquity. The means most often employed to induce this state are beating of magic drums and blowing of trumpets, howlings and hour-long prayers, dancing, flagellation, convulsive movements and contortions, asceticism, fasting and sexual abstinence. Recourse is also had to narcotics to bring about the desired result. Thus the flyagaric is used in Western Siberia, in San Domingo the herb coca, tobacco by some tribes of American Indians, and in the East opium and hashish. The ancient Egyptians had their intoxicating drinks, and receipts for witch's salves and philtres have come down to us from medieval times."

In many countries this condition of possession was induced for religious and prophetic purposes, also for mere fortune-telling. The extent to which this belief in obsession and possession persisted in recent times was testified by Edward Tylor in *Primitive Culture* (2 vols., 1871): "It is not too much to assert that the doctrine of demoniacal possession is kept up, substantially the same theory to account for substantially the same facts, by half the human race, who thus stand as consistent representatives of their forefathers back in primitive antiquity."

Such beliefs persisted in the development of Spiritualism. The obsessional theory was also used to account for forms of insanity and crime. The following passage taken from the publication *Diakka and their Victims* by the seer Andrew Jackson **Davis** (1873) indicates this recent belief: "The country of the diakka is where the morally deficient and the affectionately unclean enter upon a strange probabion. . . . They are continually victimizing sensitive persons still in the flesh making sport of them and having a jolly laugh at the expense of really honest and sincere people. They [these demon-like spirits] teach that they would be elevated and made happy if only they could partake of whiskey and tobacco, or gratify their burning free-love propensities. . . . Being unprincipled intellectualities their play is nothing but pastime amusement at the expense of those beneath their influence." These creatures were also said to be of a malignant and bloodthirsty nature, inciting the beings they possessed to murder, often of a terrible character.

Signs of Demoniac Possession

Philipp Melanchthon (1497-1560) in one of his letters, stated that though there may occasionally be some natural causes for a frenzy or mania, it is also quite certain that devils enter certain persons and there cause torment and fury with or without natural causes, just as one sees at times maladies cured with remedies which are not natural. Moreover, such spectacles were in the nature of wonders and forecasts of things to come. Twelve years before, a woman of Saxony who could neither read nor write, being controlled by a devil, spoke after the torment was over, words in Greek and Latin to the effect that there would be great distress among the people.

The following have been cited in the past as possible signs of possession:

> Imagining oneself possessed; leading an evil life; living alone; chronic ailments, unusual symptoms, a deep sleep, the vomiting of strange things; blaspheming and frequent reference to the Devil; making a compact with the Devil; being controlled by spirits; having a face that inspires horror and fear; being tired of living and the giving up of hope; being enraged and violent in action; making the cries and noises of a beast.

A much more detailed review of objective and subjective indications is found in the authoritative work *Possession Demoniacal & Other* by T. K. Oesterreich (1930; 1966).

In an account of the possession of the nuns of **Loudon** in the seventeenth century, we find the questions put to the University of Montpellier by Santerre, priest and founder of the bishopric and diocese of Nimes touching on the signs and the judicial answers of this university.

Q.—Whether the bending and moving of the body, the head at times, touching the soles of the feet, with other contortions and strange positions are good signs of possession?

A.—Mimics and acrobats make such strange movements, bending and twisting themselves in so many ways that one must conclude that there is no sort of position which men and women cannot take up, after long practice and application, even being able, with the ease of experience, to extend and spread out abnormally the legs and other parts of the body, by the extension of the nerves, muscles and tendon—such performances are not without the bounds of nature.

Q.—Whether the rapidity of the movement of the head backwards and forwards, touching the chest and the back, is an infallible sign of possession?

A.—This movement is so natural that nothing need be added to what has been said about the movements of the other parts of the body.

Q.—Whether the sudden swelling of the tongue, the throat and the face, and the sudden changing of color, are sure signs of possession?

A.—The swelling and disturbance of the chest through interruption are the efforts of breathing or inspiration—the normal actions of respiration—and possession cannot be inferred from them. The swelling of the throat may proceed from the retention of the breath and that of the other parts from the melancholic vapors which are often observed wandering through all parts of the body. Hence it follows that this sign of possession is inadmissible.

Q.—Whether a feeling, stupidly heedless, or the lack of feeling, to the point of being pricked or pinched without complaining or moving and not even changing color are certain signs of possession?

A.—The young Lacedemonian who allowed himself to be bitten by a fox which he had stolen without seeming to feel it, and those who flog themselves, even to death, before the altar of Diana, without turning a hair, they all show that, with resolution, pin-pricks can be endured without complaining. Moreover, it is certain that in the human body, small areas of skin are met with in some persons, which are insensitive, although the neighboring parts may be quite sensitive, a condition which occurs the more frequently after some previous illness. Such a condition has, therefore, no bearing on possession.

Q.—Whether the total lack of bodily movement which, at the command of the exorciser, occurs in those supposedly possessed during, and in the middle of, their most violent actions, is an undeniable sign of a true diabolic possession?

A.—The movements of the parts of the body being voluntary it is natural for well-disposed persons to move themselves or not at will, so that such a cessation of movement, if there is not entire lack of feeling, is not sufficient ground from which to infer a diabolic possession.

Q.—Whether the yelping or noise like that of a dog, which comes from the chest rather than from the throat, is a mark of possession?

A.—Human skill adapts itself so easily to the counterfeiting of all kinds of expressions, that persons are met with every day who can give perfectly the expressions, cries and songs of all sorts of animals, and that with a practically imperceptible movement of the lips. Again, many are to be found who form their words in the stomach and they would seem to come from some other object rather than from the one who forms them. Such persons are called ventriloquists. However, such a condition is natural, as Pasquier shows, in Chap. 38 of his *Researches,* with one Constantin, a jester, as an example.

Q.—Whether keeping the gaze fixed on some object without moving the eye, is a good sign of possession?

A.—The movement of the eye is voluntary, like that of the other parts of the body, and it is natural to move it or keep it still—there is therefore, nothing of note in this.

Q.—Whether the answers, given in French, to questions put in Latin, to those supposedly possessed, are a mark of possession?

A.—We assert that to understand and speak languages which one has not learnt is certainly supernatural, and would lead to the supposition that it occurred through the ministrations of the Devil or from some other cause beyond; but merely to answer some questions suggests nothing more than long practice, or that one of the number is in league with them and able to contribute to such answers making it appear a fallacy to say that the devils hear the questions put to them in Latin and answer in French and in the tongue natural to the one who is to pass for the demoniac. It follows from this that such a result does not infer the occupation by a demon, more especially if the questions are of few words and not involved.

Q.—Whether the vomiting of such things as one has swallowed is a sign of possession?

A.—Delrio, Bodin, and other authors say that by witchcraft, sorcerers sometimes manage to vomit nails, pins, and other strange things, by the work of the devil, who is able to do the same for the truly possessed. But to vomit things one has swallowed is natural, there being people with weak stomachs who keep down for several hours what they have swallowed and then return it as they have taken it; also the lientery returns food through the bowel as it has been taken by the mouth.

Q.—Whether pricks with a lancet, in different parts of the body, without the drawing of blood, are a good sign of possession?

A.—This is realted to the composition of the melancholic temperament, in which the blood is so thick that it cannot issue from such small wounds and it is because of this that many when pricked by the surgeon's lancet, even in their very veins, do not bleed a drop, as is shown by experience. There is thus nothing extraordinary here.

Recorded Instances of Possession

The sixteenth-century writer Jean Boulaese told how twenty-six devils came out of the body of the possessed Nicoli of Laon: "At two o'clock in the afternoon, the said Nicoli, being possessed of the Devil, was brought to the said church, where the said de Motta proceeded as before with the exorcism. In spite of all entreaty the said Beelzebub told them in a loud voice that he would not come out. Returning to their entreaties after dinner, the said de Motta asked him how many had come out, and he answered, 'twenty-six.' 'You and your followers,' then said de Motta, 'must now come out like the others.' 'No,' he replied, 'I will not come out here, but if you like to take me to Saint Restitute, we will come out there. It is sufficient for you that twenty-six are out.' Then the said de Motta asked for a convincing sign of how they had come out. For witness he told them to look in the garden of the treasury over the front gate, for they had taken and carried away three tufts (i.e., branches) from a green maypole (a small fir) and three slates from above the church of Liesse, made into a cross, as others in France commonly, all of which was found true as shown by the Abbot of Saint-Vincent, M. de Velles, Master Robert de May, canon of the Church Notre-Dame of Laon, and others."

The same author gave an account of the contortions of the demoniac of Laon: "As often as the reverend father swung the sacred host before her eyes, saying, 'Begone, enemy of God,' so did she toss from side to side, twisting her face towards her feet, and making horrible noises. Her feet were reversed, with the toes in the position of the heel, and despite the restraining power of eight of the men, she stiffened herself and threw herself into the air a height of six feet, the stature of a man, so that the attendants, sometimes even carried with her into the air, perspired at their work. And although they bore down with all their might, still could they not restrain her, and torn away from the restraining hands, she freed herself without any appearance of being at all ruffled.

"The people, seeing and hearing such a horrible sight, one so monstrous, hideous and terrifying cried out, 'Jesus, have mercy on us!' Some hid themselves, not daring to look; others, recognising the wild cruelty of such excessive and incredible torment, wept bitterly, reiterating piteously, 'Jesus, have mercy on us!' The reverend father then gave permission to those who wished to touch and handle the patient, disfigured, bent, and deformed, and with the rigidity of death. Chief among these were the would-be reformers, such men as Francois Santerre, Christofle, Pasquot, Gratian de la Roche, Masquette, Jean du Glas, and others well-known for their tendencies towards reform, all vigorous men. They all endeavored, but in vain, to straighten her limbs, and bring them to a normal position, and to open her eyes and mouth—it was futile. Further, so stiff and rigid was she, that the limbs would have broken rather than give, as also the nose and ears. And then, as she said afterwards, she was possessed, declaring that she was enduring incredible pain. That is, by the soul torment, the devil makes the body become stone or marble."

Jean Le Breton (in *Recveil de pièces sur les possessions des religieoses de Louviers,* Rouen, 1879) stated the following concerning those possessed in Louviers:

"The fourth fact is that many times a day they show transports of rage and fury, during which they call themselves demons, without, however, offending anyone or even hurting the fingers of the priests, which were put into their mouths at the height of their fury.

"The fifth is that during these furies they show strange convulsions and contortions, bending themselves back, among other things, in the form of a circle, without the use of the hands, and in such a way that their bodies are supported as much on the forehead as on the feet. The rest of the body is unsupported and remains so for a long time—the position being repeated seven or eight times. After such feats as this and many others, kept up sometimes for four hours, chiefly during the exorcism and during the warmest parts of the dog days, they are found on coming to, to be as normal, as fresh and with a pulse as even as if nothing had happened to them.

"The sixth is that some of them faint away at will during the exorcism and this condition occurs at a time when the face is the most suffused with blood and the pulse is the strongest. They come to of themselves and the recovery is more remarkable than the swooning—it begins as a movement of the toe, then of the foot and in their order, of the leg, thigh, abdomen, chest and throat, the movement of the last three being one of wide dilation.

The face, meanwhile is apparently devoid of expression, which finally returns with grimaces and shoutings, the spiritual element returning at the same time with its former disturbing contortions."

Doctor Ese gave the following particulars of the case of Sister Mary, of the Convent at Louviers:

"The last was Sister Mary of St. Esprit, supposedly possessed by Dagon, a large woman, slender-waisted, and of good complexion, with no evidence of illness. She came into the refectory. . . . head erect and eyes wandering from side to side, singing, dancing and skipping. Still moving about and touching lightly those around her, she spoke with an elegance of language expressive of the good feeling and good nature which were his (using the person of the devil). All this was done with movements and carriage alike haughty, following it up with a violence of blasphemy, then a reference to his dear little friend Magdalen, his darling and his favourite mistress. And then, without springing or using effort of any kind, she projected herself into a pane of glass and hanging on to a central bar of iron passed bodily through it, but on making an exit from the other side the command was given in Latin, 'est in nomine Jesu rediret non per aliam sed per eadem viam.' After some discussion and a definite refusal to return she, however, returned by the same route, whereupon the doctors examined her pulse and tongue, all of which she endured while laughing and discussing other things. They found no disturbance such as they had expected, nor any sign of the violence of her actions and words, her coming to being accompanied with some trivial remarks. The company then retired."

Another writer on those possessed in Louviers gave the following astonishing statement:

"Placed in the middle of the nave of this chapel was a vase of some kind of marble, some two feet in diameter and a little under a foot deep, with sides about three fingers' breadth in thickness. So heavy was it that three of the most robust persons would have had difficulty in raising it while on the ground, yet this girl, to all appearances of very low vitality, came into the chapel and grasping the vase merely by the ends of her fingers, raised it from the pedestal on which it was placed, turned it upside down and threw it on to the ground with as much ease as if it had been a piece of cardboard or paper. Such great strength in one so weak astonished all those present. Moreover, the girl, appearing wild and possessed, ran hither and thither with movements so abrupt and violent that it was difficult to stop her. One of the clerics present, having caught her by the arm, was surprised to find that it did not prevent the rest of her body from turning over and over as if the arm were fixed to the shoulder merely by a spring. This wholy unnatural performance was carried out some seven or eight times and that with an ease and speed difficult to imagine."

The *Relation des Ursulines possedées d'Auxonne* (c. 1660) contains the following:

"M. de Chalons was no sooner at the altar (at midnight) than from the garden of the monastery and around the house was heard a confused noise, accompanied by unknown voices and some whistling; at times loud cries with strange and indistinct sounds as from a crowd, all of which was rather terrifying among the shadows of the night. At the same time stones were thrown from different places against the windows of the choir where they were celebrating holy mass and this despite the fact that these windows were a good distance from the walls which enclosed the monastery which made it improbable that they came from without. The glass was broken in one place but the stone did not fall into the choir. This noise was heard by several persons, inside and out. The sentinel in the citadel on that side of the town took alarm at it as he said the next day, and at the altar the bishop of Chalons could not but feel a suspicion that something extraordinary was going on in the house and that demons or sorcerers were making some attempts at that moment which he repelled from where he was by secret imprecations and inward exorcisms.

"The Franciscan nuns of the same town heard the noise and were terrified by it. They thought that the monastery shook beneath them and in this confusion and fear they were compelled to have recourse to prayer.

"At the same time voices were heard in the garden, weak and moaning and as if asking for help. It was nearly an hour after midnight and very dark and stormy. Two clerics were sent out to see what was the matter and found Marguerite Constance and Denise Lamy in the monastery garden, the former up a tree and the latter seated at the foot of the stairway into the choir. They were at liberty and in the full possession of their senses, yet appeared distracted, especially the latter, and very weak and pale, though with blood on her face; she was terrified and had difficulty in composing herself. The other had blood on her face also though she was not wounded. The doors of the house were tightly closed and the walls of the garden were some ten or twelve feet high.

"In the afternoon of the same day the bishop of Chalons, with the intention of exorcising Denise Lamy, sent for her and when she was not found, he inwardly commanded her to come to him in the chapel of St. Anne where he was. It was striking to see the prompt obedience of the demon to this command, formulated merely in the mind, for in about a quarter of an hour a violent knocking was heard at the door of the chapel, as if by one hard pressed. On opening the door this girl entered the chapel abruptly, leaping and bounding, her face changed greatly and with high colour and sparkling eyes. So bold and violent was she that it was difficult to restrain her, nor would she allow the putting on of the stole which she seized and threw violently into the air despite the efforts of four or five clerics who did their best to stop her, so that finally it was proposed to bind her, but this was deemed too difficult in the condition in which she was.

"On another occasion, at the height of her frenzy. . . . the demon was ordered to stop the pulse in one of her arms, and it was immediately done, with less resistance and pain than before. Immediate response was also made to the further order to make it return. The command being given to make the girl insensible to pain, she avowed that she was so, boldly offering her arm to be pierced and burnt as wished. The exorcist, fortified by his earlier experience, took a sufficiently long needle and drove it, full length, into the nail and flesh, at which she laughed aloud, saying that she felt nothing at all. Accordingly as he was ordered, blood was allowed to flow or not, and she herself took the needle and stuck it into different parts of her arm and hand. Further, one of the company took a pin and, having drawn out the skin a little above the wrist, passed it through and through so that the two ends were only visible, the rest of the pin being buried in the arm. Unless the order was given for some no blood issued, nor was there the least sign of feeling or pain."

The same account gave, as proofs of the possession of the Auxonne nuns, the following:

"Violent agitation of the body only conceivable to those who have seen it. Beating of the head with all their might against the pavement or walls, done so often and so hard that it causes one to shudder on seeing it and yet they show no sign of pain, nor is there any blood, wound or contusion.

"The condition of the body in a position of extreme violence, where they support themselves on their knees with the head turned round and inclined towards the ground for a foot or so, which makes it appear as if broken. Their power of bearing, for hours together without moving, the head being lowered behind below the level of the waist; their power of breathing in this condition; the unruffled expression of the face which never alters during these disturbances; the evenness of the pulse; their coolness during these movements; the tranquil state they are in when they suddenly return and the lack of any quickening in the respirations; the turning back of the head, even to the ground, with marvellous rapidity. Sometimes the movement to and fro is done thirty or forty times running, the girl on her knees and with her arms crossed in front; at other times, in the same position with the head turned about, the body is wound around into a sort of semicircle, with results apparently incompatible with nature.

"Fearful convulsions, affecting all the limbs and accompanied with shouts and cries. Sometimes fear at the sight of certain phantoms and spectres by which they say the are menaced, causes such a change in their facial expression that those present are terrified; at other times there is a flood of tears beyond control and accompanied by groans and piercing cries. Again, the widely-opened mouth, eyes wild and showing nothing but the white, the pupil being turned up under cover of the lids—the whole returning to the normal at the mere command of the exorcist in conjunction with the sign of the cross.

"They have often been seen creeping and crawling on the ground without any help from the hands or feet; the back of the head or the forehead may be touching the soles of the feet. Some lie on the ground, touching it with the pit of the stomach only, the rest of the body, head, feet and arms, being in the air for some length of time. Sometimes, bent back so that the top of the head and the soles of the feet touch the ground, the rest of the body being supported in the air like a table, they walk in this position without help from the hands. It is quite common for them, while on their knees to kiss the ground, with the face twisted to the back so that the top of the head touches the soles of the feet. In this position and with the arms crossed on the chest they make the sign of the cross on the pavement with their tongues.

"A marked difference is to be noticed between their condition when free and uncontrolled and that which they show when controlled and in the heat of their frenzy. By reason of their sex and delicate constitutions as much as from illness they may be weak, but when the demon enters them and the authority of the church compels them to appear they may become at times so violent that all the power of four or five men may be unable to stop them. Even their faces become so distorted and changed that they are no longer recognisable. What is more astonishing is that after these violent transports, lasting sometimes three or four hours; after efforts which would make the strongest feel like resting for several days; after continous shrieking and heart-breaking cries; when they become normal again—a momentary proceeding—they are unwearied and quiet, and the mind is as tranquil, the face as composed, the breathing as easy and the pulse as little changed as if they had not stirred out of a chair.

"It may be said, however, that among all the signs of possession which these girls have shown, one of the most surprising, and at the same time the most common, is the understanding of the thought and inward commands which are used every day by exorcists and priests, without there being any outward manifestation either by word or other sign. To be appreciated by them it is merely necessary to address them inwardly or mentally, a fact which has been verified by so many of the experiences during the stay of the bishop of Chalons and by any of the clergy, who wished to investigate, that one cannot reasonably doubt such particulars and many others, the details of which cannot be given here."

A number of archbishops or bishops and doctors in the Sorbonne made the following notification with regard to the condition at Auxonne.

"That among these differently-placed girls there are seculars, novices, postulants and professed nuns; some are young, others old; some from the town, others not; some of high estate, others of lesser parentage; some rich, others poor and of low degree. That it is ten years or more since the trouble began in this monastery; that it is remarkable that a reign of deceit was able for so long to preserve the secret among girls in such numbers and of conditions and interests so varied. That after research and a stricter enquiry, the said Bishop of Chalons has found nobody, either in the monastery or in the town, who could speak other than well of the innocence and integrity, alike of the girls and of the clergy who worked with him in the exorcisms, and, for himself, he finds them with the bearing of persons of uprightness and worth—evidence which he gives in the interest of truth and justice.

"Added to the above is the certificate of Morel, doctor and present at everything, who asserts that all these things exceed the bounds of nature and can only occur as the work of a demon; in short, we consider that all the extraordinary findings with these girls are beyond the powers of human nature and can only be instigated by a demon possessing and controlling their bodies."

Simon Goulart in *Histoires admirables et mémorables de nostre temps* (2 vols., 1610) culled many stories of demoniacs from Johan **Weyer,** including the following:

"Antoine Benivenius in the eighth chapter of the *Livre des causes cachées des maladies* tells of having seen a girl of sixteen years whose hands contracted curiously whenever she was taken with a pain in the abdomen. With a cry of terror her abdomen would swell up so much that she had the appearance of being eight months pregnant—later the swelling went down and, not being able to lie still, she tossed about all over the bed, sometimes putting her feet above her head as if trying a somersault. This she kept up throughout the throes of her illness and until it had gone down by degrees. When asked what had happened to her, she denied any remembrance of it. But on seeking the causes of this affection we were of opinion that it arose from a choking of the womb and from the rising of malignant vapours affecting adversely the heart and brain. We were at length forced to relieve her with drugs but these were of no avail and becoming more violent and congested she at last began to throw up long iron nails all bent, brass needles stuck into wax, and bound up with hair and a part of her breakfast—a mass so large that a man would have had difficulty in swallowing it all. I was afraid, after seeing several of these vomitings, that she was possessed by an evil spirit, who deluded those present while he removed these things and afterwards we heard predictions and other things given which were entirely beyond human comprehension.

"Meiner Clath, a nobleman living in the castle of Boutenbrouch in the duchy of Juliers, had a valet named William who for fourteen years had had the torments of a possession by the devil, and when, at the instigation of the devil, he began to get ill, he asked for the curé of St. Gerard as confessor. . . . who came to carry out his little part. . . . but failed entirely. Seeing him with a swollen throat and discoloured face and with the fear of his suffocating, Judith, wife of Clath and an upright woman, will all in the house, began to pray to God. Immediately there issued from William's mouth, among other odds and ends, the whole of the front part of the trousers of a shepherd, stones, some whole and other broken, small bundles of thread, a peruke such as women are accustomed to use, needles, a piece of the serge jacket of a little boy, and a peacock's feather which William had pulled from the bird's tail eight days before he became ill. Being asked the cause of his trouble he said that he had met a woman near Camphuse who had blown in his face and that his illness was the result of that and nothing else. Some time after he had recovered he contradicted what he had said and confessed that he had been instructed by the devil to say what he had. He added that all those curious things had not been in his stomach but had been put into his throat by the devil despite the fact that he was seen to vomit them. Satan decieves by illusions. The thought comes at times to kill oneself or to run away. One day, having got into a hog-shed and protected more carefully than usual he remained with his eyes so firmly closed that it was impossible to open them. At last Gertrude, the eldest daughter of Clath, eleven years old, came along and advised him to pray to God for the return of his sight, but he asked her to pray and the fact of her praying, to the great surprise of both, opened his eyes. The devil exhorted him often not to listen to his mistress or anyone else who bowed the head at the name of God, who could not help him as he had died once, a fact which was openly preached.

"He had once attempted rudely to touch a kitchenmaid and she had reproved him by name, when he answered in a voice of rage that his name was not William but Beelzebub, at which the mistress asked—'Do you think we fear you? He Whom we serve is infinitely more powerful than you are.' Clath then read the eleventh chapter of St. Luke where mention is made of the casting out of the dumb devil by the power of the Saviour and also of Beelzebub, prince of devils. Finally William began to rest and slept until morning like a man in a swoon, then taking some broth and feeling much relieved he was sent home to his parents, after having thanked his master and mistress and asked God to reward them for the trouble they had been caused by his affliction. He married afterwards and had children, but was never again tormented by the devil.

"On the 18th March, 1566, there occurred a memorable case in Amsterdam, Holland, on which the Chancellor of Gueldres, M. Adrian Nicolas, made a public speech, from which is the following: 'Two months or so ago thirty children of this town began to be strangely disturbed, as if frenzied or mad. At intervals they threw themselves on the ground and for half an hour or an hour at the most this torment lasted. Recovering, they remembered nothing, but thought they had had a sleep and the doctors, sorcerers, and exorcists were all equally unable to do any good. During the exorcism the children vomited a number of pins and needles, finger-stalls for sewing, bits of cloth, and of broken jugs and glass, hair and other things. The children didn't always recover from this but had recurrent attacks of it—the unusualness of such a condition causing great astonishment.'

Jean Languis, a learned doctor, gave the following examples in the first book of his *Epitres,* as having happened in 1539 in Fugenstall, a village in the bishopric of Eysteten and sworn to by a large number of witnesses:

"Ulric Neusesser, a ploughman in this village, was greatly troubled by a pain in the side. On an incision begin made into the skin by a surgeon an iron nail was removed, but this did not relieve the pain, rather did it increase so that, becoming desperate, the poor man finally committed suicide. Before burying him two surgeons opened his stomach, in front of a number of persons, and in it found some long round pieces of wood, four steel knives, some sharp and pointed, other notched like a saw, two iron rods each nine inches long and a large tuft of hair. One wondered how and by wht means this mass of old iron could be collected together into the space of his stomach. There is no doubt that it was the work of the devil who is capable of anything which will maintain a dread of him.

"Antoine Lucquet, knight of the order of the Fleece, of high repute throughout Flanders, and privy counsellor of Brabant, had married in Bruges, and his wife, soon after the nuptials, began to show the torments of an evil spirit, so much so that at times, even in company, she was suddenly taken up and dragged through rooms and thrown from one corner to another, despite the efforts of those around to restrain and hold her. She was little conscious of her bodily welfare while in this frenzy and it was the general opinion that her condition had been induced by a former lover of her young and light-hearted husband. Meanwhile she became pregnant without a cessation in the evil torment and the time of her delivery being at hand the only woman present was sent for the midwife but instead, she came in and herself acted as midwife which disturbed the invalid so much that she fainted. She found, on recovering, that she had been delivered, yet to the astonishment of both there was no sign of a child. The next day on wakening up she found a child in swaddling clothes in the bed and she nursed it a couple of times. Falling asleep shortly afterwards the child was taken from her side and was never seen again. It was reported that notes with the hall-mark of magic had been found inside the door."

Simon Goulart gave an account from Johan Weyer, of the multitude of terrible convulsions suffered by the nuns of the convent of Kentorp near Hammone: "Just before and during the attack their breath was fœtid and sometimes continued so for hours. While affected they did not lose their power of sound judgment nor of hearing and recognising those around them, despite the fact that owing to the spasm of the tongue and respiratory organs they could not speak during the attack. All were not equally affected but as soon as one was affected the others, though in different rooms, were immediately affected also. A soothsayer, who was sent for, said they had been poisoned by the cook, Else Kamense, and the devil taking advantage of the occasion increased their torment, making them bite and strike each other and throw each other down. After Else and her mother had been burnt some of the inhabitants of Hammone began to be tormented by an evil spirit. The minister of the Church took five of them home to warn them and strengthen them against the machinations of the enemy. They laughed at him and mentioned certain women of the place whom they would like to visit on their goats, which were to carry them there. Immediately one straddled a stool calling out that he was off, while another, squatting down, doubled himself up and rolled towards the door of the room which opened suddenly and through which he went falling to the bottom of the steps without hurting himself."

"The nuns of the Convent of Nazareth at Cologne [according to the same writer] were affected much the same as those of Kentorp. After being troubled for a long time and in various ways by the devil they were more terribly affected in 1564 when they would lieout on the ground with clothing disordered, as if for the companionship of man. During this their eyes would be closed and they would open them later with shame and feeling that they had endured some deep injury. A young girl of fourteen named Gertrude who had been shut up in this convent was subject to this misfortune. She had often been troubled by wild apparitions in bed as witness her mocking laughter, although she tried in vain to overcome it. A companion slept near her specially to protect her from the apparition but the poor girl was terrified at the noise from Gertrude's bed, the devil finally controlling the latter and putting her through a variety of contortions . . . The beginning of all this trouble was in the acquaintance picked up with one or two of the nuns on a neighbouring tennis court by some dissolute young man who kept up their amours over the walls.

"The torments suffered by the nuns in Wertet in the county of Horne are also wonderful. The beginning is traced to a poor woman who borrowed from the nuns during Lent some three pounds of salt and returned double the amount before Easter. From that they began to find in their dormitory small white balls like sugarplums, and salt to the taste, which they did not eat, nor did they know whence they came. Shortly after they heard a moaning as of a sick man, then warnings to rise and go to the help of a sick sister, which they would do but would find nothing. Sometimes in endeavouring to use a chamber it would be pulled away suddenly with a consequent soiling of the bed. At times they were pulled out by the feet, dragged some length, and tickled so much on the soles of the feet that they nearly died with laughter. Pieces of flesh were pulled out of some, while others had their legs, arms and heads twisted about. Thus tormented some would throw up a large quantity of black fluid, although for six weeks previously they had taken nothing but the juice of horseradish without bread. The fluid was so bitter and so sharp that it blistered their mouths and one could evolve nothing which would give them an appetite for anything else. Some were raised into the air to the height of a man and was suddenly thrown to the ground again. When some thirty of their females visited this convent to congratule those who seemed relieved and practically cured, some of them immediately fell backwards from the table they were at, losing the power of speech and of recognising anyone, while others were stretched out as if dead with arms and legs turned around. One of them was raised into the air against the restraining efforts of those present and then brought again to the ground so forcibly that she seemed dead. She rose, however, as if from a deep sleep and left the convent uninjured. Some moved about on the fronts of their legs as if lacking feet and as if dragged in a loose sack from behind. Others even climbed trees like cats and came down as easily. The Abbess told Margaret, Countess of Bure, that she cried aloud when pinched in the leg; it was as severe as if a piece had been pulled out, and that she was carried to bed at once and the place became black and blue, but she finally recovered. This derangement of the nuns was an open secret for three years but has been kept dark since.

"What we have just said applies equally to the early case of the Bridget nuns in their convent near Xanthus. Now, they gambol or bleat like sheep or make horrible noises. Sometimes they were pushed from their seats in church where their veils would be fastened above their heads. At other times their throats would be so stopped up that they could swallow no food, and this affliction lasted for ten years in some of them. It was said that the cause of all this was a young nun whose parents had refused to allow her to marry the young man she loved. Further that the devil in the form of this young man had come to her at the height of her passion and had advised her to return to the convent which she did at once and when there she became frenzied and her actions were strange and terrible. The trouble spread like the plague through the other nuns, and the first one abandoned herself to her warder and had two children. Thus does Satan both within and without the convent, carry out his hateful schemes.

"Cardan relates that a ploughman. . . . often threw up glass, nails and hair and, on recovering, felt within a large quantity of broken glass which made a noise like that from a sackful of broken glass. The noise he said troubled him greatly and for some eighteen nights towards seven o'clock, although he had not observed the time and although he had felt cured for some eighteen years, he had felt blows in his heart to the number of hours which were to strike. All this he bore not without great agony."

"I have often seen," stated Goulart, "a demoniac named George, who for thirty years on and off was tormented by an evil spirit and often I have seen her swell up, and become so heavy that eight strong men could not raise her from the ground. Then, exhorted and encouraged in the name of God and the hand of some good man extended to her, she would rise to her feet and return home, bent and groaning. She did harm to no one whether by day or night while in this condition, and she lived with a relative who had a number of children so used to her ways that when they saw her twisting her arms, striking her hands and her body swelling up in this strange way, they would gather in some part of the house and commend her to God and their prayers were never in vain. Finding her one day in another house of the village in which she lived I exhorted her to patience. . . . She began to roar in a strange way and with a marvellous quickness shot out her left hand at me and enclosed in it my two hands, holding me as firmly as if I had been bound with stout cords. I tried, but in vain, to free myself, although I am of average strength. She interfered with me in no other way nor did she touch me with her right hand. I was held as long as it has taken to tell the incident and then she let me go suddenly, begging my pardon, and I commended her to God, and led her quietly home. . . . Some days before her death being much tormented she went to bed with a low fever. The fury of the evil one was then so much curtailed that the patient, wonderfully strengthened inwardly, continued to praise God who had been so merciful to her in her affliction and comforting all who visited her. . . . I may add that Satan was overcome, and that she died peacefully, calling on her Saviour."

According to Goulart, "there was, in the village of Leuensteet and duchy of Brunswick, a young girl of twenty years, Margaret Achels, who lived with her sister. Wishing to clean some shoes one day in June she took a knife some six inches long and sat down in a corner of the room for she was still weak from a fever of long standing, whereupon an old woman entered and inquired how she was and whether she still had the fever and then left without further words. After the shoes were cleaned she let the knife fall in her lap but subsequently could not find it despite a diligent search. The girl was frightened and still more so when she found a black dog under the table. She drove it out, hoping to find the knife, but the dog got angry, showed its teeth and growlingly made its way into the street and fled.

"The girl at once seemed to feel something indefinable which passed down her back like a chill and fainting suddenly she remained so for three days when she began to breathe better and to take a little food. When carefully questioned as to the cause of her illness she said that the knife which had fallen into her lap had entered her left side and that there she felt pain. Although her parents contradicted her, attributing her condition to a melancholic disposition, her long abstinence and other things, she did not cease to complain, to cry and to keep a continuous watch, so much so that her mind became deranged and sometimes for two days at a time she would take nothing even when kindly entreated to do so, so that sometimes force had to be used. Her attacks were more severe at times than others and her rest was broken by the continous pains which beset her, being forced as she was to hold herself doubled over a stick.

"What increased her pain and lessened the chance of relief was her firm belief that the knife was buried in her body and the stubborn contradiction of the others who said it was impossible and thought it nothing but a phantom of the mind, since they saw nothing which would give them ground for believing her unless it were her continual complaints and tears. These were kept up for some months and until there appeared on her left side between the two false ribs a tumour as large as an egg which fluctuated in size with the changes in her own girth. Then the girl said to them: 'Up to the present you haven't wanted to believe that the knife was in my side, but you will soon see now that it is.'

"On the 30th June, that is after almost thirteen months of the trouble, the ulcer which developed on her side poured out so much material that the swelling began to go down and the point of the knife showed and the girl wanted to pull it out but her parents prevented her and sent for the surgeon of Duke Henry who was at the Castle of Walfbutel. This surgeon arrived on the 4th July and begged the curate to comfort, instruct and encourage the girl, and to take particular note of her answers since she was regarded as a demoniac. She agreed to be attended by the surgeon, not without the idea that a quick death would follow. The latter, seeing the point of the knife projecting, grasped it with his intruments and found that it was just like the other in the sheath and very much worn about the middle of the blade. The ulcer was finally cured."

Goulart, quoting Melanchthon, stated that "there was a girl in the marquisate of Brandebourg who pulled some hairs off the clothing of some person and that these hairs were at once changed into coins of the realm which the girl chewed with a horrible cracking of the teeth. Some of these coins are kept still by persons who snatched them away from the girl and found them real. From time to time this girl was much tormented but after some months got quite well and has remained so since. Prayers, but nothing more, are often offered up for her."

The same author also stated: "I have heard that there was in Italy a demented woman who when controlled by a devil and asked by Lazare Bonami for the best verse of Virgil, answered at once:

'Discite Justitiam Moniti et non temnere divos.' 'That,' she added, 'is the best and most-deserving verse that Virgil ever wrote; begone and don't come back here again to try me.'

Louise Maillat, a young demoniac who lived in 1598, lost the use of her limbs and was found to be possessed by five demons who called themselves, "wolf," "cat," "dog," "beauty" and "a griffin." At first, two of these demons came out from her mouth in the form of balls the size of the fist, the first firered, the second, which was the cat, quite black; the others left her with less violence. On leaving her they all made a few turns round the hearth and disappeared. Frances Secretain was known to have made this girl swallow these devils in a crust of bread the colour of manure."

Modern Views of Obsession in Psychical Research

Obsession in psychiatry means that the mind of the patient is dominated by fixed ideas to which an abnormal mental condition corresponds. In traditional belief, obsession is an invasion of the living by a discarnate entity, tending to a complete displacement of normal personality for purposes of selfish gratification which is more or less permanent. The difference between mediumship and obsession is not in principle but in purpose, in duration and in effect.

Mediumship, or to be more precise, trance possession, does not interfere with the ordinary course of life, does not bring about a demoralizing dissociation or disintegration; it shows consideration for the medium and its length is limited. After a certain time it ceases automatically and the medium's normal self, held in voluntary abeyance for the time being, resumes its sway.

Obsession is always abnormal, it is an accompaniment of a shock, organic lesion, or, in cases of psychics, of low morale and weakening will power, induced by an unstable character and debility of-health. Once the existence of spirits is admitted, the possibility of obsession cannot be disregarded. Perhaps, a lesser assumption is just as sufficient to point out the possibility.

"If we believe in telepathy," wrote Dr. James H. **Hyslop** in *Contact with the Other World* (1919), "we believe in a process whichmakes possible the invasion of a personlity by someone at a distance." "It is not at all likely," he stated, "that sane and intelligent spirits are the only ones to exert influence from a transcendental world. If they can act on the living there is no reason why others cannot do so as well. The process in either case would be the same; we should have to possess adequate proof that nature puts more restrictions upon ignorance and evil in the next life than in this in order to establish the certainty that mischievous personalities do not or cannot perform nefarious deeds. The objection that such a doctrine makes the world seem evil applies equally to this situation in the present life."

How are we to distinguish obession from multiple **personality?** It was explained to Hyslop by the "**Imperator**" group of controls of the Rev. Stainton **Moses** that even for the spirits it is sometimes difficult to state how far the subconscious self of the patient is acting under influence and suggestion from spirits or as a secondary personality. Nevertheless Hyslop found a highly satisfactory method to find out the truth in **cross reference.** He wrote: "I take the patient to a psychic under conditions that exclude from the psychic all normal knowledge of the situation and see what happens. If the same phenomena that occur in the patient are repeated through the medium; if I am able to establish the identity of the personalities affecting the patient; or if I can obtain indubitably supernormal information connecting the patient with the statements made through the psychic, I have reason to regard the mental phenomena observed in the patient as of external origin. In a number of cases, persons whose condition would ordinarily be described as due to hysteria, dual, or multiple personality dementia precox, paranoia, or some other form of mental disturbance, showed unmistakable indications of invasion by foreign and discarnate agencies."

This method was a revolutionary innovation. To reach the conviction of the reality of obsession which preceded it, a long time was necessary. "Before accepting such a doctrine," stated Hyslop in *Life After Death* (1918), "I fought against it for ten years after I was convinced that survivial after death was proved. But several cases forced upon me the consideration of the question. The chief interest in such cases is their revolutionary effect in the field of medicine. . . . It is high time for the medical world to wake up and learn something.

Prof. William **James,** shortly before his death, surrendered to the same belief. He wrote: "The refusal of modern enlightenment to treat obsession as a hypothesis to be spoken of as even possible, in spite of the massive human tradition based on concrete experience in its favor, has always seemed to me a curious example of the power of fashion in things scientific. That the demon theory (not necessarily a devil theory) will have its innings again is to my mind absolutely certain. One has to be 'scientific' indeed to be blind and ignorant enough not to suspect any such possibility."

It was the report of the Thompson-Gifford case in *Proceedings* of the American Society for Psychical Research (vol. 3, part 8, 1909) which overcame his resistance to the idea of obsession. The short history of this famous case is as follows: Mr. F. L. Thompson, a Brooklyn goldsmith, was seized in 1905 with an irresistible impulse to sketch and paint. The style was plainly that of Robert Swain Gifford. This well-known American artist had died six months previously but this fact was unknown to Thompson who hardly knew him and, except for a slight taste for sketching in his early years, never shown artistic talents.

He had visions of scenes of the neighborhood of Gifford's country house and often had the hallucination that he was Gifford himself. He saw a notice of an exhibition of Gifford's paintings. He went in and heard a voice whisper: "You see what I have done. Can you take up and finish my work?" The desire to paint became stronger. Soon it was so overpowering that he was unable to follow his former occupation.

He grew afraid that he was losing his sanity. Two physicians diagnosed the case as paranoia. One of them, without offering to cure it, expressed a desire to watch the progress of the malady. Thompson came to Prof. Hyslop for advice, who took him to three different mediums. They all sensed the influence of Gifford, described his character and life and confirmed the vague possiblity which Dr. Hyslop wished to investigate that the case was not the result of mental disorder. As soon as the case was proved as spirit obsession, treatment was comparatively simple. Gifford was reasoned with and persuaded to desist.

Spirit Obsession and Personality Displacement

The importance of such treatment on the assumption of spirit obsession is apparent. An obsessing spirit, if driven out by strengthened willpower of the victim or by psychotherapeutic means, will seek and find another subject, but if it is convinced of the error of its ways the danger is eliminated.

A systematic practice of curing obsession through such means was taken up by Dr. and Mrs. Carl **Wickland** in their Psychopathic Institute of Chicago.

The patient was brought to Mrs. Wickland. She went into trance. Her controls influenced the obsessing spirit to step into Mrs. Wickland's body. If the obsessor was unwilling it was forced to do so by means known to the controls. Dr. Wickland then began to parley with the spirit, explained the position and usually ended in convincing the invader that it did a great wrong to its spiritual evolution by strengthening ties to the earth. The invader usually promised to depart and the patient became normal.

Later Dr. Wickland moved to California and founded the National Psychological Institute for the treatment of obsession. His experiences were narrated in his book *Thirty Years Among the Dead* (1924).

Similar work was done in The Temple of Light in Kansas City in 1910. Dr. Hyslop was so much impressed with the importance of this cure that he established a foundation in his will for the work. The headquarters of the James J. Hyslop Foundation for the Treatment of Obsession were in New York; Dr. Titus **Bull** was its director.

The obsessors are mostly earthbound spirits. They do not necessarily mean harm. All they wish is to enjoy earthly existence once again. But some of them may commit acts of revenge or do other harm, owing to their ignorance. And if an evil personality gets into control, the obsessed individual may be driven to criminal, insane acts.

Just as the trance control will become perfect by practice, the obsessor will feel more at home in the victim's organism after repeated possession and will settle as permanently as possible. Certain historic records suggest that obsession may attain an epidemic character. The case of the Ursuline Nuns of Loudon in 1632-34 has already been cited. Several of the nuns of the convent, including the Mother Superior, were seized with violent convulsions, symptoms of catelepsy and demoniac possession. Blasphemies and obscenities were pouring forth from their mouths, confessed to come from the devil. The curé, Urbain **Grandier,** was accused of rave immoralities, preceding the outbreak. The devils indicated him as the author of their troubles. He was burnt alive in April, 1634.

Obsessions by evil spirits were of frequent occurrence in the congregation of the Rev. Edward **Irving** in 1831. The bystanders rebuked the evil spirits and bade them to come forth. In one such case, recorded by Robert Baxter in his pamphlet *A Narrative of Facts* . . . (1833), the possessed man when released by the "tongue" fell upon the ground crying for mercy, and lay there foaming and struggling like a bound demoniac.

In February 1874, Franklin B. Evans was executed in Concord, New Hampshire, for the murder of a twelve-year-old child. In his confession made just before his execution he said that "for some days before the murder I seemed to be attended continually by one who seemed to bear a human form, urging me on to the deed. At length it became fixed in my mind to take her life."

Hudson Tuttle, in his book *The Arcana of Spiritualism* (1871 etc) described a suicidal obsession as follows: "While sitting in a circle at the home of the vererable Dr. Underhill, I was for the time in an almost unconscious state, and recognised the presence of several Indian spirits. The roar of the Cayahoga River over the rapids could be heard in the still evening air, and to my sensitive ear was very distinct. Suddenly I was seized with a desire to rush away to the rapids, and throw myself into the river started up someone caught hold of me, and aroused me out of the impressible state I was in, so that I gained control of myself. Had the state been more profound, and had I once started, the end might have been different. The desire remained all the evening."

Sometimes the obsession serves beneficial ends. An excellent instance is the "**Watseka Wonder,**" the case of Lurancy Vennum. Her malicious obsessors were forced out by the spirit of Mary Roff who departed from earth life eighteen years previously in the same city. Mary Roff lived in Lurancy Vennum's body, but in the house of her own parents for sixteen weeks and satisfied everybody of her identitiy. Her long inhabitation somehow made the body safe from malicious invasions and when she finally yielded it's control to the returning ego of Lurancy Vennum, the girl's health was mentally and physically reestablished.

In the famous Beauchamp case (see **Personality**), "Sally," one of the four chief personalities, marked as B.III showed evidence of obsession. The case was never treated as such. "Sally," however, claimed to be a spirit, wrote automatically, had a will of her own by which she could hypnotize the other personalities, was always conscious and had no perception of time. She was the connecting link between the memories of the other personalities and was a mischievous entity.

She would go out in the country in the last car and leave the first self to walk home. She would put into a box spiders, toads or other animals to frighten the first self when she opened it, and she waged formal war on the fourth personality. An electric shock, like in the Wickland cases, had the effect of bringing about her eclipse but this fact was not sufficiently noted by Dr. Morton **Prince.**

In the Doris Fischer case investigated by Dr. Walter F. **Prince** (see **Personality**), "Margaret," one of her five personalities, appeared to be a similarly mischievous entity. She would steal so that Doris would be blamed for the theft. She would hide her books at school so that she could not study her lessons. She would scratch the body of the real Doris until it bled, then go out and leave the normal personality to suffer the pain. She would eat the candy that Doris bought for herself. She would jump into a dirty river with clothes on that Doris should suffer from the filth which stuck to her.

But she did not claim to be a spirit; she did not write automatically and showed no ignorance of time. It was with difficulty that her history was traced. Dr. Walter F. Prince succeeded in treating Doris Fischer sufficiently by suggestion to bring her from California to Boston. Dr. Hyslop took her to

Mrs. Chenoweth (Minnie M. **Soule**). Dr. Hodgson came through when Mrs. Chenoweth went into trance and comparied the case to that of Sally Beauchamp, remarking that it was "as important as any that Morton Prince ever had." He knew the Beauchamp case from personal experience. He also communicated that a little Indian was connected with the case.

Soon afterwards, Doris developed **automatic writing** through the **planchette.** A little Indian personality manifested and gave her name as "Minnehaha" or Laughing Water. Later Mrs. Chenoweth's control, "Starlight," found Minnehaha and in trying to give her name said: " I see like a waterfall, just like water falling over and whether it is Water Fall or—something like that." Then she remarked: "She laughs after she shows me the water." Still later "Minnehaha " herself communicated and confessed a number of pranks that she played upon the girl.

As a result of his twenty years' study of obsession at the head of the James Hyslop Institue, Dr. Titus Bull published in 1932 some startling conclusions. He stated:

"An obsessing personality is not composed of the soul, mind and will of one disembodied being, but is, in reality, a composite personality made up of many beings. The pivot obsessor, or the one who first impinges upon the sensorium of the mortal, is generally one with litle resistance to the suggestions of others. He or she, therefore, becomes and easy prey to those who desire to approach a mortal in this way.

" . . . Some people, moreover, may be born with tendencies which make it easier for them to become victims of mental alterations later in life . . . . There is an influence which can be exerted upon the minds of mortals by ideas embodied in thoughts from their departed ancestors. In other words, some departed ancestors, whenever possible, attempt to mould the lives of those incarnated who are akin. . . . There is a type of mortal whose mind is easily influenced by the stronger minds of the family group. . . . The more clannish the family group, the more likely is this to be true on both sides of the veil. It is, however, not to be considered as spirit obsession in the true sense. . . . The intervention of shock, however, or anything that could upset the nerve balance of a member of such family group, would place him in actual danger of becoming a victim of true spirit obsession. . . . The primary obsessor, in this case, would likely be one who claimed the right by ties of blood, who had no desire to do anything but to keep the mortal in line with family ideals."

According to Dr. Bull, obsessors "have three major points of impingement; namely, the base of the brain, the region of the solar plexus and at the-center governing the reproductive organs. As there are three major points of impingement, it may be assumed that there can be three composite groups, each starting with a pivot entity. What satisfaction is to be gained this way includes the whole gamut of human emotions."

The pivot entities "upon which the mound of entity obsession is built" act as automatic channels for the others. Many of them were victims of obsession through their passing. Others may become obsessors "through the machinations or wiles of others." Not understanding what has happened to them they may be readily influenced to turn to obsession.

Another important point is "the possibility of obsessions passing on to the body of mortal pangs which were part of their own physical life." They retained in their memory the possibility of producing pain and as often they are unable to inhibit the production of it in the obsessed body, it must be beyond their control. "Therefore," stated Dr. Bull, "it is a fair assumption to say that often the migratory pains of the living are caused by the memory pangs of the dead." The prime reason of why the production of pain should be beyond control is "the domination of another and more crafty entity who is using the pain-producer for his own purpose. . . . "

Objections to the Concept of Spirit Obsession

Much of the evidence for spirit obsession is subjective, based on the observations and feelings of investigators, many of whom have been reputable individuals. However, so far no really conclusive evidence has been found which will resolve this question definitively.

It should not be overlooked that the subconscious mind has the ability to weave convincing fantasies of personality, while novelists have created imaginary characters who now seem to have a reality of their own. Some cases of apparent secondary or multiple personality seem to be a dramatization of the subject's unconscious emotional desires and fears. Children often pretend to be different personalities, while even the effect of a powerful movie portrayal often awakens both conscious and unconscious imitation of personality traits amongst impressionable viewers.

For a time, it was thought that the technique of hypnotic regression, in which a subject's memory is progressively explored into the past and then into apparent former lives, might offer reliable evidence of the continuity of personality from one life to another. However, although there are some impressive case histories, the evidence so far is not conclusive.

It may well be discovered that there is no one simple explanation for or against the concept of spirit obsessions, that certain cases may be genuinely spirit obsession, others subconscious personation.

The concept of spirit possession is still very much alive in various African and West Indian areas, epecially amongst Voodoo cults.

Exorcism

The pagan and Christian belief in demonic obsession and posession brought about complex rituals of exorcism, designed to drive out the diabolical entities. Although such rituals had virtually fallen into disuse in Christian countries during the more pragmatic materialist philosophy of the twentieth century, they were revived on a startling scale with the occult boom of the 1960s, which generated a widespread public obsession with claimed demonic possession, factual and fictional. The theme permeated popular books and movies, and led to a revival of forgotten rituals of exorcism. It should be noted that the belief in demonic possession seems to generate hundreds of apparent cases. (See also Arnall **Bloxham; Titus Bull; Exorcism; Personality; Personation, Reincarnation; Rescue Circles; Voodoo; Watseka Wonder;** Carl August **Wickland**)

Recommended reading:

Ebon, Martin (ed.). *Exorcism; Fact Not Fiction,* Signet paperback, 1974

Holzer, Hans. *Possessed!,* Fawcett paperbck, 1973

Huxley, Aldous. *The Devils of Loudon,* Chatto & Windus, London, 1952; Harper & Row paperback, 1971

Hyslop, James H. *Contact with the Other World; The Latest Evidence as to Communication with the Dead,* Century Co., New York, 1919

Nicola, John T. *Diabolical Possession and Exorcism,* Tan Books, Rockford, Illinois, 1974

Oesterreich, T. K. *Possession, Demoniacal & Other,* Kegan Paul, London/R. R. Smith, New York, 1930; University Books, 1966 (variant title *Possession and Exorcism,* Causeway Books, 1974) Pettiward, Cynthia. *The Case for Possession,* Colin Smythe, U.K., 1975

Sargant, William. *The Mind Possessed; A Physiology of Possession, Mysticism & Faith Healing,* Heinemann, London, 1973; J.B. Lippincott, 1974

Shepard, Leslie. *How to Protect Yourself Against Black Magic & Witchcraft,* Citadel, 1978

Walker, Sheila S. *Ceremonial Spirit Possession in Africa and Afro-Americana,* E. J. Brill, Leiden, Netherlands/Humanities Press, New York, 1972

Wickland, Carl A. (et al.) *Thirty Years Among the Dead,* National Psychological Institute, Los Angeles, 1924

Occidental Society of Metempiric Analysis

Founded in 1977, to investigate all types of metempiric phenomena (unexplained occurrences ignored or discounted by scientists) such as sightings of UFOs, space aliens, ghosts, and "Bigfoot."

The Society maintains a speakers bureau, museum, and charitable program, and compiles statistics. It maintains a library of 1,500 volumes on metempirical, occult, and UFO topics. Publication: *Beacon,* semiannual. Address: 32055 Highway 24E, Simla, Colorado 80835.

Occult

General term (derived from Latin *occultus, occulere,* to hide) to denote that which is hidden, mysterious, known only to the initiated, imperceptible by normal senses, thus embracing all the pseudosciences of **magic** belief and practice, such as **alchemy, astrology, demonology, ghosts, miracles, poltergeists, prediction** of the future, psychic powers, spells, **Spiritism,** sympathetic magic, etc.

The term is also used to include abnormal or rare phenomena such as reported monsters unknown to contemporary science or paranormal events, all of which might some day become part of normally accepted knowledge, much as so many natural phenomena thought by primitive peoples to be magical.

There is also a specialized scientific use of the term "occult" in astronomy, denoting the hiding or obscuring from view of one heavenly body (as the moon or a planet) by another.

"Occult" is properly used as an adjective, roughly synonymous with "magic," but in common usage it is also employed as a noun, thus "the occult" implies the body of occult belief or practice.

In ancient times, it was believed that apparent deviations from natural law involved mysterious and miraculous "supernatural" or occult laws, deriving from gods, invisible entities or the souls of the dead. The rituals of magic were designed to evoke entities and spirits to ward off misfortune or perform actions in defiance of natural law, such as obtaining knowledge of distant or future events, causing injury or death of one's enemies, or securing sudden wealth (usually in the form of gold). Most primitive peoples had witch-doctors or shamans who claimed such specialized ability to work magic.

Modern **Spiritualism** is basically a revival of ancient belief in the claimed evidence for the continued existence of personality after death and the evolution of the individual soul to perfection. The Spiritism inaugurated by Allan **Kardec** is a form of Spiritualism with emphasis on reincarnation. Both Spiritualism and Spiritism are essentially religious movements, endorsing the miracles cited in the Bible and citing continuing paranormal phenomena as evidence of survival.

Much of primitive occultism was an aspect of religion, deriving from the mystery, wonder and fearfulness of the world in which human beings found themselves. At other times in history, the occult was clearly a degenerate form of earlier belief and practice of the higher religions. Thus, the magic spells and rituals of the Middle Ages are a decadent descent from the more refined religious beliefs and practices of Eastern religions, which were in turn a higher form of primitive beliefs.

Much of the aims and objects of ritual magic and **witchcraft** rituals appear tawdry, egocentric, selfish, immature and power-seeking, lacking in more civilized ethics of self-purification, service to the community, and desire for truth and knowledge. The occult often promises short cuts to wealth, success and power in this life, but has nothing inspiring to contribute on the hereafter.

Opinion of the validity of the occult and the meaning of claimed paranormal phenomena must depend upon one's philosophical or religious viewpoint. From the early nineteenth century onwards, the successes of science and technology in achieving apparent miracles developed a materialistic view of life and its laws, encouraging agnosticism and atheism. It became fashionable (with much justification) to ridicule simplistic literal belief in Biblical teachings, such as the probably allegorical story of creation in *Genesis* and point to the abuse of power by religious authorities in the establishment of the

Christian church and the suppression of heresies, and the blood-thirsty power games of religious wars (which are still unfortunately present). At the same time, it is impossible to deny the validity of the ethical teachings of Christianity, which are shared by all great religions and even the ethical teachings of rationalists.

In modern times, Christianity has tended to play down the question of miraculous phenomena, although there is persuasive evidence that it still occasionally occurs. The Creator of the world and the universe must surely be assumed to have power to suspend created laws. However, certain theological problems are involved in the concept of such intervention, notably the side effects of causation, and their apparently indiscriminate action.

Clearly suspension of natural law in one area will tend to create side effects in adjacent areas, while favoring one individual, however devout or worthy, might involve problems for another individual.

Again, although the empirical evidence for miraculous healing is quite impressive, it is by no means clear why some sufferers should be healed and others never have access to healers. Why are certain noble individuals doomed to suffer disease and pain while immoral and vicious individuals die comfortably in their beds? It would seem that religious explanations for miracles are at present simplistic and inadequate, indicating the need for more complex investigation.

Belief has always appeared to be a powerful creative factor in occult practice, and it is not impossible that even initial fraud could sometimes be a stimulating factor in producing paranormal phenomena by "priming the pump," so to speak. Ancient religions sometimes used mechanical contrivances to simulate divine power, rather like religious conjuring tricks.

The power of prayer may be more closely connected with a creative power of mind rather than validating the actual nature of the gods. Prayers to Eastern or Western deities appear equally to produce results, while spirit entities also appear to perform magical feats. The mental state of the petitioner may be the dominant factor.

Allied with belief is the willpower of the operator in magical practice, which again has some relevance to the mystical concept of concentration and meditation being preliminaries to the manifestations of paranormal phenomena.

At a secular level, psychical researchers and parapsychologists have attempted to bring scientific method into the investigation of claims of the paranormal, removing the subject from a religious context. This is in many ways a welcome development for scientific knowledge, but sometimes tends to bypass the possible religious dimension and ignore the broader aspects of the meaning and purpose of life and the interpretation of natural phenomena. The clinical atmosphere of a parapsychology laboratory, with its scientific controls, specialized jargon and mathematical evaluation removes the paranormal from a natural setting.

By comparison, the sincere Spiritualist views paranormal phenomena in a context of personal knowledge and meaning, and if the evidence of survival of loved ones and hopes of spiritual evolution are not scientifically verifiable, the evidence nevertheless carries its own verisimilitude in a way which is not accessible to objective scrutiny.

The experience of happiness or being in love, or recognizing the individual personality of a friend or relative are all areas which science may comment upon but cannot share.

Of course, simple-minded people are often imposed upon by cheats, but that is surely a case for more general education and clear thinking rather than delegation to "experts." Clearly a fully developed emotional, intellectual and spiritual framework for all phenomena, whether normal or paranormal, is the ultimate desirable context for evaluation.

The senses and the mind are mirrors of reality, but the experience of waking consciousness in the brief span of one's life limits the totality of contact with ultimate reality. Bishop George Berkley (1685-1753) questioned the actual existence of matter outside the idealism of the human mind, explaining the more or less uniformity of shared sensory and mental experience as due to a divine idea which regulated human impressions.

In this he echoed ancient Eastern religions, which also stressed that the reality picture of minds is not the ultimate criterion. Time, space and causation are only limiting adjuncts of human experience, and the minimum data for any valid philosophical scheme are surely the contents of all minds, past, present and future, and all interrelationships in the cosmos. In the absence of this, any individual human mind or sensory impression is a defective instrument, often additionally flawed by immature development or emotional problems.

Eastern religions have proposed a "cosmic consciousness" to which a purified human consciousness may have access and share, and this experience has also been claimed by Western mystics. It would seem that there are various levels of higher consciousness, and that the experience of extended consciousness is sometimes accompanied by paranormal phenomena. Does the experience involve an occasional release of energy that momentarily deforms the mental picture of empirical reality? On a more mundane level, various advocates of New Thought techniques have claimed that intense mental concentration brings about paranormal effects such as healing or obtaining desired aims.

It may be that the empirical reality of waking consciousness is no more substantial than a dream. A dream seems real so long as one is dreaming, but upon awakening, time, space and causation have a different and more extended quality. But even waking life is conditioned by perceptual limitations imposed by the experience of matter and natural law, and it may well be that consciousness itself ultimately has infinite dimensions that transcend the matter and natural law in which it occurs.

Clearly, psychical researchers, parapsychologists, occultists, witches, and gurus of both Eastern and Western religions will act within their own terms of reference, and it may well be that their discoveries and teachings will eventually form part of a more complex and inspiring view of life than the mere question of whether or not occult phenomena are a valid part of life. Like so many other aspects of life, the results of investigation are conditioned by the attitudes of the investigators. (See also **Ceremonial Magic; Consciousness; Evidence; Fraud; Magic; Meditation; Miracles; Mysticism; Parapsychology; Psychical Research; Spiritualism; Witchcraft; Yoga**)

Recommended reading:

Bucke, Richard M. *Cosmic Consciousness; A Study in the Evolution of the Human Mind,* Innes & Sons, Philadelphia, 1901; E. P. Dutton, 1946 etc.; University Books, 1961

Crow, W. B. *A History of Magic, Witchcraft & Occultism,* Aquarian Press, U.K., 1968; Abacus paperback, 1972

Freedland, Nat. *The Occult Explosion,* Putnam/ Michael Joseph, London, 1972

Godwin, John. *Occult America,* Doubleday, 1972

Gopi Krishna. *The Biological Basis of Religion and Genius,* Harper & Row, 1972

Gratton-Guinness, Ivor. *Psychical Research; A Guide to Its History, Principles & Practices,* Aquarian Press, U.K. (paperback), 1982

Grant, Kenneth. *The Magical Revival,* Frederick Muller, London, 1972

James, William. *The Varieties of Religious Experience,* London, 1902; University Books, 1963

Rhine, J. B. & associates. *Parapsychology From Duke to FRNM,* Parapsychological Press, Durham, N.C. (paperback), 1965

Thomas, Keith. *Religion and the Decline of Magic,* Charles Scribner's Sons, 1971

Underhill, Evelyn. *Mysticism; A Study in the Nature and Development of Man's Spiritual Consciousness,* Metheun & Co., London, 1911 etc.

Waite, Arthur E. *The Book of Ceremonial Magic,* William Rider & Son, London, 1911; University Books, 1961; Causeway Books, 1973

Wilson, Colin. *The Occult,* Hodder & Stoughton, London/Random House, 1971; Vintage Books, New York, 1973; Mayflower paperback, U.K., 1973

Occult Americana (Magazine)

Bi-monthly magazine with articles, interviews and other material relating to occultism and psi phenomena. Address: P.O. Box 667, Painesville, Ohio 44077.

Apparently no longer active.

Occult Observer (Magazine)

British journal first published May 1949 by Michael **Houghton,** London. Houghton was a well-known occultist, proprietor of the **Atlantis Book Shop.** The journal contained much useful information, but ceased publication after completion of one volume.

Occult Review, The

British monthly journal founded in 1877, devoted to the investigation and discussion of paranormal phenomena.

In September 1933 its title was changed briefly to *The London Forum.*

From January 1936 to Christmas 1948, it resumed the title *Occult Review,* but in 1949 it changed again to *Rider's Review,* after which it ceased publication.

It was undoubtedly one of the finest British journals of the occult ever published, and contained many notable contributions from authorities in the field.

The high standard of this periodical was due to the intelligent and broadminded approach of the original editor, the Hon. Ralph **Shirley.** He ceased editing when the publications changed hands with the sale of William Rider publications to Hutchinson, but his high standards and good judgment were continued for a time by Harry J. Scrutton.

Occult Studies Foundation

Former name of **MetaScience Foundation,** Rhode Island.

Occultism

The doctrine, theories, principles of the pseudosciences of **magic,** including **alchemy, demonology, ghosts, miracles, poltergeists, prediction,** psychic powers, **spells, Spiritism,** sympathetic magic, etc. The term "the occult" is often used synonymously with "occultism." (See **Occult**)

Ochorowicz, Julien (1850-1917)

Lecturer in psychology at the University of Lemberg, co-director from 1907 of the Institut Général Psychologique of Paris, distinguished psychical researcher. He was born in Radzyn, Poland, February 23, 1850 and educated at the University of Warsaw.

The famous medium Eusapia **Palladino** was his guest from November 1893 until January 1894 in Warsaw. His conclusions did not favor the spirit hypothesis and he expressed his conviction that the phenomena were due to a "fluidic action" and were performed at the expense of the medium's own powers and those of the persons present. The hypothesis that for the greater part of the phenomena a "fluidic double" can, under certain conditions, detach itself and act independently of the body of the medium, appeared to him to be necessary.

After the exposure of the medium's cheating in seances in Cambridge, England, he came to the defense of Eusapia and offered very plausible reasons for her constant attempt to free her hand. He condemned the method employed at Cambridge as a blundering one.

The mediumship of Mlle. **Tomczyk** was discovered by Dr. Ochorowitz. His experiments with her were very important. He achieved conspicuous success in **psychic photography,** having photographed an etheric hand on the film rolled together and enclosed in a bottle. Mlle. Tomczyk was also successful in raising and suspending small objects in the air without contact with her hands. In 1911, Dr. Ochorowitz was awarded a prize of 1,000 francs by the Comité d'Etude de Photographie Transcendental for his experiments. A similar prize was awarded to him by the Academie des Sciences de Paris.

He was an honorary member of the Society for Psychical Research, London, the American Society for Psychical Research, and other societies in Hungary and Germany. He was author of over a hundred books, papers and articles on psychology, philosophy and psychical research.

His books included: *Mental suggestion* (1891), *Mediumistic Phenomena* (1913), *Psychology and Medicine* (1916), *Psychology, Pedagogics and Ethics* (1917). His articles in the journal *Annales des Science Psychiques* include: 'La question de la fraude dans les expériences médiumniques' (The Question of Fraud in Mediumistic Experiments, 1896), 'Un nouveau phénomne médiumnique' (A New Mediumistic Phenomenon, 1909).

He died in Warsaw, Poland, May 1, 1917.

Oculomancy

A somewhat obscure system of identifying a thief by the turning of his eyes when associated with certain ceremonies.

Od (Odic Force or Odyle)

The term first used by Baron Karl von **Reichenbach** to denote the subtle effluence which he claimed emanated from every substance in the universe, particularly from the stars and planets, and from crystals, magnets and the human body.

The term "Od" was derived from *Odin,* the Norse deity, indicating a power that permeated the whole of nature. The name "Od" was retained by Dr. John Ashburner (1816-1878) in his translation of Reichenbach's writings, but another translator, Prof. William Gregory (1803-1858) substituted "Odyle," probably hoping it would sound more scientific than "Od."

Od or Odyle was perceptible to sensitives, in whom it produced vague feelings of heat or cold, according to the substance from which it radiated. A sufficiently sensitive person might perceive the odic light, a clear flame of definite color, issuing from the human fingertips, the poles of the magnet, various metals, crystals and chemicals, and hovering like a luminous cloud over new-made graves.

The colors varied with each substance; thus silver and gold had a white flame; cobalt, a blue; copper and iron, a red.

The English Mesmerists speedily applied Reichenbach's methods to their own sensitives, with results that surpassed their expectations. These observations were confirmed by experiments with persons in perfect health. Prof. D. Endlicher of Vienna saw on the poles of an electromagnet flames forty inches high, unsteady, exhibiting a rich play of colors, and ending in a luminous smoke, which rose to the ceiling and illuminated it. The experiments were controlled by Dr. William Gregory, who was Professor of Chemistry in the University of Edinburgh and Dr. Ashburner in England.

According to the sources from which the energy proceeded, Reichenbach employed the following nomenclature: Crystallod, electrod, photod, thermod, etc. He claimed that this peculiar force also existed in the rays of the sun and the moon, in animal and human bodies, that it could be conducted to distances yet unascertained by all solid and liquid bodies, that bodies may be charged with od, or od may be transferred from one body to another. This transference was apparently affected by contact. But mere proximity, without contact, was sufficient to produce the charge, although in a feebler degree. The mouth, the hands, the forehead and the occiput were the main parts of the body in which the od force manifested.

Reichenbach claimed that the odic tension varied during the day; it diminished with hunger, increased after a meal and also diminished at sunset. He insisted that the odic flame was a material something, that it could be affected by breath or a current of air and that it exhibited a suggestive likeness to the aurora borealis.

The thoroughness of Reichenbach's experiments, and the apparent soundness of his scientific methods, made a deep impression on the public mind. The objections of James Braid, who at this time advanced his theory of suggestion, were ignored by the protagonists of od. In after years, when Spiritualism had established itself in America, there remained a group of "rational" defenders of the movement, who attributed the phenomena of Spiritualism as well as those of **poltergeist** to the action of odylic force. **Table-turning** and rapping were also referred to this emanation by many who laughed to scorn Faraday's theory of unconscious muscular action.

Others again, such as Mr. Guppy, regarded the so-called "spirit" intelligences producing the manifestations as being compounded of odic vapors emanating from the medium, and probably connected with an all-pervading thought-atmosphere—an idea sufficiently like the "cosmic fluid" of the early magnetists.

Reichenbach's Odic Force clearly had possible relevance to psychical research, and in 1883 the Society for Psychical Research, London, formed a committee to report on "Reichenbach Phenomena." The committee's first report was published in the Society's *Proceedings* (vol. 1, part 3, 1883) and contributions on the subject also appeared from time to time in the **S.P.R.** *Proceedings* and *Journal.*

Reichenbach's experiments with Od made interesting comparison with the phenomenon of the human **Aura** reported by Dr. Walter J. **Kilner,** Oscar Bagnall and others, and also with the researches of

Dr. Wilhelm **Reich** and his concept of "Orgone energy." (See also **Aura; Emanations; Orgone;** Baron von **Reichenbach**)

Recommended reading:

Bagnall, Oscar. *The Origin and Properties of the Human Aura,* University Books, 1970

Kilner, Walter J. *The Human Aura,* University Books, 1965

Reich, Wilhelm. *The Discovery of the Orgone* (2 vols.), New York, 1942, 1948

Reichenbach, Karl von (transl. John Ashburner). *Physico-Physiological Researches on the Dynamics of Magnetism, Heat, Light, Crystallization, and Chemism, in their relations to Vital Force,* London, 1851 (an alternative translation by William Gregory was issued under the title *Researches on Magnetism, Electricity, Heat, Light, Crystallization and Chemical Attraction, in their relations to the Vital Force,* London, 1850; University Books, 1974)

Reichenbach, Karl von (transl. F. D. O'Byrne). *Letters on Od and Magnetism,* London, 1926 (reissued as *The Odic Force; Letters on Od and Magnetism,* University Books, 1968)

O'Donnell, Elliott (1872-1965)

Author of popular books on occult subjects. Born in England, he claimed descent from Irish chieftains of ancient times, including Niall of the Nine Hostages (the King Arthur of Irish folklore) and Red Hugh, who fought the English in the sixteenth century. O'Donnell was educated at Clifton College, Bristol, England, and Queen's Service Academy, Dublin, Ireland.

He had a psychic experience at the age of five, in a house where he saw a nude elemental figure covered with spots. As a young man, he was half strangled by a mysterious phantom in Dublin.

In later life he became a ghost hunter, but first he traveled in America, working on a range in Oregon and becoming a policeman in the Chicago Railway Strike of 1894. Returning to England, he worked as a schoolmaster and trained for the theater. He served in the British army in World War I, later acted on stage and in movies.

His first book, written in his spare time, was a psychic thriller titled *For Statan's Sake* (1905). From this point onwards, he became a writer. He wrote several popular novels but specialized in what were claimed as true stories of ghosts and hauntings. These were immensely popular, but his flamboyant style and amazing stories suggest that he embroidered fact with a romantic flair for fiction.

As an authority on the supernatural, he achieved fame as a ghost hunter. He lectured and broadcast on the subject in Britain and the U.S. and also appeared on television. In addition to his books he wrote scores of articles and stories for national newspapers and magazines. He claimed "I have investigated, sometimes alone, and sometimes with other people and the press, many cases of reputed hauntings. I believe in ghosts but am not a spiritualist."

The O'Donnells were reputed to have a **Banshee**—the wailing ghost that heralds a death, and O'Donnell wrote the first book devoted entirely to the subject. It is not known whether his own passing evoked this eerie phantom, but he lived to the ripe old age of ninety-three years. He died May 6, 1965.

He achieved the distinction of an entry in the prestigious British publication *Who's Who,* in which he listed his hobbies "investigating queer cases, inventing queer games, and frightening crooks with the Law." The latter pastime seems a piece of whimsical romanticism, since there are no reports of any criminals being scared by him.

He published over fifty books, including the following typical titles: *For Satan's Sake* (1905), *Unknown Depths* (1906), *Some Haunted Houses* (1908), *Haunted Houses of London* (1909), *Reminiscences of Mrs. E. M. Ward* (1910), *The Meaning of Dreams* (1911), *Byways of Ghostland* (1911), *Scottish Ghost Stories* (1912), *Werewolves* (1912), *The Sorcery Club* (1912), *Animal Ghosts* (1913), *Ghostly Phenomena* (1913), *Haunted Highways and Byways* (1914), *The Irish Abroad* (1915), *Twenty Years' Experience as a Ghost Hunter* (1916), *The Haunted Man* (1917), *Spiritualism Explained* (1917), *Fortunes* (1918), *Haunted Places in England* (1919), *Menace of Spiritualism* (1920), *More Haunted Houses of London* (1920), *The Banshee* (1926), *Ghosts, Helpful and Harmful* (1926), *Strange Disappearances* (1927; reprinted University Books, 1972), *Strange Sea Mysteries* (1927), *Confessions of a Ghost Hunter* (1928), *Fatal Kisses* (1929), *Famous Curses* (1929), *Great Thames Mysteries* (1929), *Rooms of Mystery* (1931), *Ghosts of London* (1932), *The Devil in the Pulpit* (1932), *Family Ghosts* (1934), *Strange Cults & Secret Societies of Modern London* (1934), *Spookerisms; Twenty-five Weird Happenings* (1936), *Haunted Churches* (1939), *Dead Riders* (1953), *Phantoms of the Night* (1956), *Haunted Waters* (1957), *Trees of Ghostly Dread* (1958).

Odor of Sanctity

Perfume said to be exhaled by Christian saints, even after death. The idea that sin has a disagreeable odor and holiness a sweet perfume occurs in Romance literature and reflects folk beliefs of medieval times.

In Malory's *Morte d'Arthur* (c. 1469, translated as *History of Prince Arthur*), the death of the wicked Sir Corsabrin is described as follows: "Then they smote off the head of sir Corsabrin, and therewithal came a stench out of the body, when the soul departed." And in contrast, the death of the noble Sir Launcelot is described thus: "When sir Bors and his fellows came to sir Launcelot's bed, they found him stark dead, and the sweetest savour about him that ever they did smell."

St. Benedicta (c. 1643) claimed that angels had perfumes as various as those of flowers; Benedicta herself was supposed to exhale the sweet perfume of the love of God.

The body of St. Clare (A.D. 660), abbot of Ferriol, exhaled a sweet odor after death, which pervaded St. Blandina's church.

When St. Hubert of Britanny (A.D. 714) died, the whole province was said to be filled with sweet perfume.

St. Casimir, Patron of Poland, died in 1483, and when his body was exhumed one hundred and twenty years later, it exhaled a sweet smell. (See also **Perfumes**)

Oenomancy

An ancient system of **divination** based on interpretations of the patterns made by wine that had been poured out as an offering to gods.

Oesterreich, Traugott Konstantin (1880-1949)

German professor of philosophy, an authority on religious philosophy and one of the first modern scientists in Germany to declare publicly his belief in psychic phenomena.

He taught philosophy at Tübingen University in 1910 and was appointed Professor in 1922. He somehow survived in Nazi Germany, in spite of his Jewish wife and his anti-militarist views, although he was dismissed from his post in 1933, reinstated in 1945 and again forced into retirement on reduced pension soon afterwards. He died in 1949.

He was originally skeptical of psychic phenomena, and in the fourth volume of Friedrich Ueberweg's *Geschichte der Philosophie* (Berlin, 1916) he referred to Baron **Schrenck-Notzing,** pioneer of investigations into **materialization** phenomena, as the dupe of tricksters. In private correspondence with Oesterreich, Schrenck-Notzing protested at this sweeping charge, and submitted his entire literary and photographic material on **Eva C.,** the famous medium. Oesterreich became interested, investigated the mediumship of Frau Maria **Silbert** and Willi **Schneider** and became convinced of the reality of such phenomena.

In 1921, he published two books: *Grundbegriffe de Parapsychologie* and *Der Okkultismus im modernen Weltbield;* the latter book testified to materializations and **telekinesis** as facts. He also revised his earlier views in a new edition of Ueberweg's *Geschichte der Philosophie* published in 1923. His book *Weltbilder der Gegenwart* contained further important contributions to psychic science. As an active and thorough psychical researcher, Professor Oesterreich also published a number of scientific papers and monographs published a number of scientific papers and monographs supporting psychic science.

His classic work, however, was undoubtedly his careful study of psychic possession (see **Obsession and Possession**), translated into English by D. Ibberson from the German publication of 1921 as *Possession: Demoniacal and other among primitive races, in antiquity, the Middle Ages, and modern times.* This is an immensely detailed study of possession and multiple **personality** from earliest times onwards and must be regarded as the standard work on the subject.

For many years it failed to secure other than a highly specialized readership, but following the 1966 reprint by University Books, New York, it attracted the attention of William Peter Blatty, who derived much of the background material for his sensational book *The Exorcist* (1971) from it. After the equally sensational movie of the book, there was a new wave of interest in demonic possession and exorcism, and Oesterreich's book was again reprinted by various publishers, sometimes under variant titles *Possession and Exorcism* and *Possession and Obsession.*

For biographical information on Oesterreich, see the book *Traugott Konstantin Oesterreich—Lebenswerk und Lebensschicksal* (1954) published by his widow Dr. Maria Oesterreich.

Recommended reading:

Oesterreich, T. K. *Occultism of the Present Day,* London, 1922

Oesterreich, T. K. *Occultism and Modern Science,* McBride, 1923

Oesterreich, T. K. *Possession: Demoniacal and Other . . .* (transl. from German *Die Bessessenheit*), University Books, 1966

Official UFO

Magazine published nine times per year, giving articles, photographs, charts and other information relating to extraterrestrial phenomena. Address: Countrywide Publications, 257 Park Avenue South, New York, N.Y. 10010.

Ohio Sky Watcher

Quarterly publication of Ohio UFO Investigators League, Inc. Includes news and discussion of UFO sightings and other mysteries such as monsters, Bermuda Triangle. Address: 5852 East River Road, Fairfield, Ohio 45014.

Ointment, Witches'

It was believed in medieval times that the wonders performed by witches such as changing themselves into animals, or being transported through the air, were wrought by anointing themselves with a potent salve.

As ointments have been used in Oriental countries as a means of inducing visions, it is possible that something of the kind may account for the hallucinations which the witches seem to have experienced.

Francis Bacon (1561-1626) stated: "The *ointment,* that witches use, is reported to made of the *fat* of *children,* digged out of their *graves;* of the *juices* of *smallage, wolfebane,* and *cinque foil,* mingled with the *meal* of fine *wheat:* but I suppose that the soporiferous medicines are likest to do it, which are *hen-bane, hemlock, mandrake, moonshade, tobacco, opium, saffron, poplar leaves,* etc."

Other recipes which have been handed down as flying ointments for witches include the following:

1) Parsley, water of aconite, poplar leaves and soot

2) Water parsnip, sweet flag, cinquefoil, bat's blood, deadly nightshade and oil

3) Baby's fat, juice of water parsnip, aconite, cinquefoil, deadly nightshade and soot.

It should be noted that such poisonous drugs as aconite, hemlock and belladonna, absorbed through the skin, would probably cause mental confusion, dizziness, irregular heart action and shortness of breath. These effects might give the sensation of flying through the air, although witchcraft authorities during the great witch hunts have claimed that witches did actually travel in the air. (See also **Drugs; Transvection; Witchcraft**)

Ojai Foundation

The original plan of Annie **Besant** in 1927 to set up a Utopian colony in Oaji, California (see **Order of the Star in the East**) is now in process of being revived at Ojai under the direction of Dr. Joan Halifax.

The new Foundation is situated on 40 acres of former semi-wilderness land in the Upper Ojai Valley, some eighty miles from Los Angeles. The Foundation offers retreats with well-known healers, scientists, artists, and others from various traditions and disciplines.

Programs have included such individuals as John and Toni Lilly, Jean Houston, Peter Caddy, and R. D. Laing. Address: P.O. Box 1620, Ojai, California 93023.

O'Key Sisters, Jane & Elizabeth (c. 1838)

Two somnambules or hypnotized subjects of Dr. John **Elliotson,** early British experimenter in **Animal Magnetism.**

The two girls were put into trance by passes on the part of Dr. Elliotson and two different states induced: a condition of coma with insensibility and lack of consciousness, and ecstatic delirium in which they spoke, sometimes making clairvoyant predictions and were also subject to the operator's suggestions. In the ecstatic condition, sometimes lasting for days, one of the girls claimed to be able to see with the back of her hand.

After many successful demonstrations, Dr. Elliotson one day met with a complete failure, which excited his opponents to accusations of imposture on the part of the girls, Dr. Elliotson being stigmatized as a weak and credulous man. Eventually he was obliged to resign his position as physician at University College Hospital, London.

However, Dr. Elliotson persisted with his experiments and published his conclusions in an appendix to his *Human Physiology* (London, 1840), in which he detailed his further experiments with the O'Key sisters.

Oki, Masahiro (1921-)

Idiosyncratic teacher-healer-philosopher, originator of a very individual system of **Yoga.** Oki was born in Korea in 1921, and brought up in a strictly religious environment. His early education familiarized him with martial arts and Zen. He was influenced by the politician Ottama Daisojo, who played an important part in the history of Burma. Oki asked him about such great individuals as Buddha, Christ, and Mohammed and their spiritual eminence. Daisojo explained that all three practiced something called yoga, which he would understand through later experience. At the time Oki was only eight years old.

As a young man, he studied at a military academy, and also took a brief course in medicine before becoming a soldier. He became a spy for the Korean government in 1939, after Japan had seized areas on the China coast, and Nazi Germany had invaded Poland. Oki's task was to enter parts of southern Asia and cooperate with Islamic independence movements. As a cover for this, he went to Tibet to train as a lama. At that time, this was a purely utilitarian move without religious significance.

His religious experience was later stimulated when he was arrested on an assignment in Iran and thrown in jail, with a leg chain and an iron ball. He shared a cell with an older man who, although facing a death sentence, was always serene and peaceful. Oki himself was scared that he would be executed, so he became a pupil of the older man, learning from his chanting, meditation, and religious observances that gave him serenity. Later, both men were freed when a raiding party liberated the jail. Oki's first teacher turned out to be Hoseini-shi, father of Ayatollah Khomeini, spiritual leader of Islam in Iran.

After the war was over, Oki concentrated on earning a living. He ran a medical clinic, and also operated a profitable smuggling business between Japan, Korea, and Taiwan. Becoming dissatisfied with material success, he joined a Japanese peace movement, but soon found that all people did was talk. He decided to become a **Zen** monk.

He divorced his wife, built six orphanages, and gave away his money, becoming a monk at a Zen monastery. After some time he grew restless in the monastery and concluded that he should do something more practical than simply purifying himself.

UNESCO officials employed him to work for peace in India and Pakistan, where he lectured, practiced medicine, and taught practical skills in housing and food production. He stayed at the ashram of Mahatma Gandhi in India, where the concept of yoga in relation to practical life matured in Oki's experience.

During 1960, he worked as a researcher for a Japanese newspaper, traveling Europe and the U.S. and lecturing on Zen Buddhism to religious groups. In 1962, the Buddhist Society of America invited him to teach yoga in the U.S. He also taught in Brazil before returning to Japan, where he founded the International Oki Yoga Institute in Mishima in 1967. He has since authored a number of books on healing, mastered thirty-two **martial arts** and taught them to students from all walks of life, and has given private lectures to the Japanese royal family.

He has been criticized for violence in his teaching sessions, since he strikes students with a stick in the old Zen tradition. It is also alleged that he is a hard drinker. However, his success with students and his uncompromisingly individualistic attitude to teaching and living rank him as a kind of Japanese Gurdjieff. For a useful article on Oki and his system, see 'Behind the Scenes of Oki Yoga' (*East West Journal*, vol. 15, No. 9, September 1985). (See also **Oki Yoga**)

Oki Yoga

The highly individual system of Japanese teacher-healer-philosopher Masahiro Oki. Oki Yoga is a unique blend of traditional Indian **hatha yoga** with **Zen** meditation, dancing, physical games, **martial arts,** and chanting. The training method emphasizes balance between opposites: tension and relaxation, heat and cold, stillness and movement.

The headquarters of the Oki system is The International Oki Yoga Institute in Mishima, Japan; there is another full-time center in Shimoda, on the Izu peninsula. There are over 250 centers throughout Japan, and others in North and South America, Europe, and Australia.

Oki's system of *shusei taiso* or corrective exercise through yoga postures stemmed from his detailed observations of the sleeping postures of students. He claims that during sleep people take postures that attempt to correct their physical imbalance. (See also Masahiro **Oki**)

Olcott, Henry Steel (1832-1907)

Joint founder with Madame **Blavatsky** of the **Theosophical Society.**

Olcott was born August 1, 1832 at Orange, New Jersey, where his father had a farm. At the age of twenty-six, Olcott was associate agricultural editor of the New York *Tribune* and traveled abroad to study European farming methods. In 1860, he married Mary E. Morgan and they had three sons. They later divorced. Olcott served in the Civil War and afterwards became a special commissioner with the rank of Colonel. In 1866, he was admitted to the New York bar. In 1878 he was commissioned by the president to report on trade relations between the U.S. and India.

His first contact with psychical phenomena was established in 1874. The *New York Daily Graphic* had assigned him to investigate the phenomena of the **Eddy Brothers** in Vermont. He spent ten weeks at the Chittenden farm and came away convinced of the genuineness of the phenomena which he witnessed. The fifteen articles in which he summarized his experiences started him on the career of a psychical investigator.

His next opportunity was afforded by the Holmes scandal, when the **materialization** mediums Mr. and Mrs. Nelson **Holmes** were accused of fraud. Olcott sifted all the records, collected new affidavits and came to the conclusion that as the evidence of fraudulent mediumship was very conflicting, the mediums should be tested regardless of the past. After making his tests, he affirmed his belief in their genuine powers.

His book *People from the Other World* (1875) into which the Eddy articles were incorporated, contained an account of his experiences with the medium Mrs. Elizabeth **Compton,** whose history presents a strange case of apparent entire dematerialization. The book was made the subject of scathing criticism in D. D. **Home's** *Lights and Shadows of Spiritualism* (1877). It was denounced as "the most worthless and dishonest" book. The bias of D. D. Home against the author, however, was strongly apparent.

As a result of the Eddy and Holmes investigation, Col. Olcott was soon acknowledged as a competent psychical researcher. When the professors of the Imperial University of St. Petersburg decided, by the wish of the Grand Duke Constantine of Russia, to make a scientific investigation of Spiritualism, Olcott and Mme. Blavatsky were asked to select the best American medium they could recommend. Their choice fell on Henry **Slade.**

The association between Col. Olcott and Mme. Blavatsky sprang out of their meeting at the Chittenden farm. Mme. Blavatsky had strong leanings towards Spiritualism and went to the Vermont farm to satisfy her curiosity. For some time she wrote articles on psychic subjects, but she broke with the Spiritualist movement soon after her larger conception, the Theosophical Society, came into being.

It was founded in December 1875. Col. Olcott was elected as chairman and he threw himself with unbounded energy and zeal into the task of founding and organizing the society all over the world. It is a great credit to his organizing genius that the society became firmly established in New York and that it withstood later the emotional earthquake of the Blavatsky exposure by the Society for Psychical Research (see Mme. H. P. **Blavatsky**).

Nobody witnessed more apparent Theosophic marvels accomplished through the agency of Mme. Blavatsky than Olcott. In those early days, Mme. Blavatsky professed to have been controlled by the spirit "John King." She first specialized in precipitated writing, independent drawing and supernormal duplication of letters and other things (among them a $1,000 banknote in the presence of Olcott and the Hon. J. L. Sullivan). The Olcott's great regret, the duplicate had mysteriously dissolved in the drawer.

In justice, it should be remarked that Col. Olcott was convinced that Mme. Blavatsky could produce such illusions by hypnotic suggestion. Apparently the Colonel was a good subject, for Mme. Blavatsky once disappeared from his presence in a closed room and appeared again a short time afterwards from nowhere. The admission of this miracle vitiates Col. Olcott's observations and records, and makes it at once intelligible that he could have testified in good faith to the appearance of **Mahatmas** and to the souvenirs they left behind.

In 1878, Col. Olcott sailed with Mme. Blavatsky for Bombay. On the way, they stopped in London for a short period. A. P. **Sinnett** in his book *The Early Days of Theosophy in Europe* (1922) suggested that the manners of Mme. Blavatsky and Col. Olcott were liable to cause offense in polite society and that the beginning of the unfriendly attitude of the **Society for Psychical Research** was to be traced to a meeting of that body at which Col. Olcott made a speech in his worst style.

The great Blavatsky exposure in 1895 left Col. Olcott's honor unimpugned. According to Dr. Richard **Hodgson,** who compiled the famous S.P.R. Report, Olcott's statements were unreliable either owing to peculiar lapses of memory or to extreme deficiency in the faculty of observation. Hodgson could not place the slightest value upon Olcott's evidence. But he stated definitely also: "Some readers may be inclined to think that Col. Olcott must himself have taken an active and deliberate part in the fraud, and been a partner with Mme. Blavatsky in the conspiracy. Such, I must emphatically state, is not my own opinion." On the other hand V. Solovyoff in *A Modern Priestess of Isis* (1895) called Olcott a "liar and a knave in spite of his stupidity."

The accusation is unjust, although it must be admitted that there are many Theosophic marvels in the Indian history of Theosophy which, on the basis of Dr. Hodgson's findings, make the hypothesis of collusion on the part of the Colonel very plausible.

One of the most problematic of such instances is the story of the William **Eglinton** letter which, from the boat "Vega," was claimed to be "astrally" conveyed first to Bombay, then with superimposed script of Mme. Blavatsky carried to Calcutta, where it was precipitated from the ceiling in Mrs. Gordon's home whilst Col. Olcott pointed to the apparition of two Brothers outside the window.

According to Mrs. Gordon's testimony, Col. Olcott told her that the night before he had an intimation from his Chohan (teacher that K. H. (a Mahatma) had been to the "Vega" and had seen Eglinton.

If then the delivery of this letter was fraudulent (and it has been convincingly claimed by experts that the K. H. letters were written by Mme. Blavatsky), the only excuse for Col. Olcott lies in the supposition that Mme. Blavatsky made him dream, by her powers of suggestion, what she wanted—a supposition which, in view of Mme. Blavatsky's record, is not entirely preposterous. It should be remembered that Hodgson stated "writing about him [Olcott] from America to a Hindu in Bombay, she characterised him as a 'psychologised baby', saying that the Yankees thought themselves very smart and that Colonel Olcott thought he was particularly smart, even for a Yankee, but that he would have to get up much earlier in the morning to be as smart as she was." The revelation of this cruel flippancy by a woman he had loyally supported caused the Colonel to contemplate suicide momentarily.

One of Olcott's greatest achievements was undoubtedly his public espousal of Buddhism, which popularized this religion in Western countries. His *Buddhist Catechism* stemmed from his conversion to Buddhism, publicly affirmed in Ceylon in 1880. First issued in 1881, the book was widely used as a textbook by Western Buddhists, and editions have remained in print every since.

Olcott died February 17, 1907 at Adyar, India. For biographical information on Olcott, together with valuable sidelights on the early history of the Theosophical movement, see Olcott's *Old Diary Leaves,* 4 vols. first published Theosophical Publishing House, 1895-1910, frequently reprinted. His book *People From the Other World* (1875) was reissued by Charles E. Tuttle, 1971. (See also Mme. H. P. **Blavatsky; **Richard **Hodgson; Mahatma Letters; Theosophical Society**)

Old, Walter G(orn) (1864-1929)

British author of works on astrology. Originally named Walter Richard Old, he wrote under the name Walter Gorn Old and the pseudonym "Sepharial." He was born March 20, 1864 at Harndsworth, Birmingham, England and educated at King Edward's School, Birmingham.

At an early age he studied books on **Kabala** and **astrology.** He became friendly with astrologer Alan **Leo** (1860-1917). Old studied a variety of subjects, including medical dispensing, Orientalism and ancient languages, but without a successful career until he eventually found his feet in professional astrology and authorship.

He moved to London in 1889 and joined the Theosophical Society, where he became a member of the Inner Group around Madame **Blavatsky.** He also introduced Alan Leo to Theosophy.

Old had special psychic talent in **astral projection (out-of-the-body** traveling). He left the Society after the death of Madame Blavatsky.

He developed a system of astrological prediction for the stock market, and predicted futures in basic commodities. His most profitable income was from astrological horseracing systems.

He died December 23, 1929, a year before the popularity of newspaper astrology columns, at which he would doubtless have been highly successful. He contributed a number of articles to the *Occult Review.* His books included: *What Is Theosophy?* (1891), *Book of the Crystal and the Seer* (1897), *Prognostic Astronomy* (1901), *Book of the Simple Way of Laotze* (1904), *A Manual of Occultism* (1910; 1920; 1979), *Second Sight* (1911), *The Kabala of Numbers* (2 vols., 1913; new enl. ed. 1928; 1980), *The Book of Charms and Talismans* (n.d., c. 1923; 1928; 1974).

Old Hat Used for Raising the Devil

A popular mode of raising the devil in former times was to make a circle, place an old hat in the center, and repeat the Lord's Prayer backwards. This was really a caricature of magical incantation.

"Old Moore"

Pseudonym assumed by a succession of British astrologers for more than three centuries. The original Dr. Francis Moore, physician, was born in 1657 and published his *Vox Stellarum* almanac in 1701.

The title was still being used in the nineteenth century. A later "Old Moore" was Henry Andrews, whose editions of *Vox Stellarum* reached half a million circulation. *Vox Stellarum* had become *Old Moore's Almanack* by the twentieth century, and in the 1960s "Old Moore" was Edward W. Whitman, secretary of the Federation of British Astrologers.

There is a "Genuine Old Moore" ("Beware of Spurious Editions") credited to John Arigho which at one time featured a portrait of one Theophilus Moore, said to have lived c. 1764. The Irish Old Moores contain an interesting regular feature of word games, conducted by "Lady Di."

Until recently, there were four rival Old Moores in Britain, issued by Roberts, Blakemore, Walker and Foulsham, all claiming "Original Editions." Today Foulsham States that their own original Old Moore ("Beware of Imitations") dates back to a copyright of 1697. Their predictions are now calculated by a team of four astrologers.

A comparable American publication is the *Old Farmer's Almanac,* whose Robert B. Thomas rivals Old Moore in claiming centuries of continuous publication. It maintains the tradition of quaint wit established by Benjamin Franklin's *Poor Richard's Almanac,* which started in 1732. (See also **Astrology; "Zadkiel"**)

Recommended reading:

Capp, Bernard. *Astrology & the Popular Press; English Almanacs 1500-1800,* Faber & Faber, London & Boston, 1979

Howe, Ellic. *Urania's Children; The Strange World of the Astrologers,* William Kimber, London, 1967; (revised *Astrology and Psychological Warfare During World War II,* & condensed ed. Rider, 1972) (Part I deals with the historical background of British astrology)

Old Religion, The

Folklore term for witchcraft as paganism displaced by Christianity. (See also **Witchcraft**)

"Old Scratch"

One of the appellations given to the Devil. It is supposed to have been derived from *Skrati,* an old Teutonic faun or Satyr, half-man and half-goat, and possessed of horns. (See also **"Nick"; "Splitfoot"**)

Om (or AUM)

A Sanskrit word of special sanctity in the Hindu religion. It is pronounced at the beginning and end of every lesson in the *Vedas* (ancient scriptures), and is also the introductory word of the *Puranas* (religious works embodying legends and mythology). It is stated in the *Katha-Upanishad:* "Whoever knows this syllable obtains whatever he wishes."

Various accounts are given of its origin; one that it is the term of assent used by the gods, and probably an old contracted form of the Sanskrit word *evam* meaning "thus."

The *Manu-Sangita* (Laws of Manu), a religious work of social laws, states that the word was formed by Brahma himself, who extracted the letters *a-u-m* from the *Vedas,* one from each, and they thus explain its mysterious power and sanctity.

Om is also the name given by the Hindus to the spiritual sun, as opposed to *Surya,* the natural sun. (See also **AUM**)

Omarr, Sydney

One of the most successful modern astrologers in the U.S. Born in Philadelphia, he served with the Air Force in the Pacific during World War II. After predicting the death of President Roosevelt, the Armed Forces Radio assigned him to a horoscope show; he thus became the first official astrologer in U.S. Army history.

After the war, he wrote many articles on astrology and appeared in radio shows. He was also a CBS radio news editor in Los Angeles. His astrology columns appeared in some 225 newspapers, and at the height of his success he moved to Hollywood. His many books on astrology include: *Astrology; Its Role in Your Life* (1963), *My World of Astrology* (1965), *Sydney Omarr's Astrological Guide to Sex and Love* (1971), *Dream-Scope* (1973), *The Thought Dial Way to a Healthy & Successful Life* (1973), *Sydney Omarr's Astrological Guide* (1974).

Omega New Age Directory

Monthly publication giving news of psychic and New Age resources in the Southwest area; includes articles and information on regional groups. Address: The Order of Omega, 6418 S. 39th Avenue, Phoenix, Arizona 85041.

Omen

A sign or portent of some future event, occurring either as a result of some form of divination, or as an unusual or supernatural event which foreshadows some great development or catastrophe. (See Paranormal **Signs**)

Omez, Réginald, O.P. (Order of Dominicans) (1895-   )

Dominican priest who has studied parapsychological subjects. Born October 12, 1895 at Tourcoing (Nord), France, he studied at Le Saulchoir, Université Francaise des Dominicains (D. Theol. 1922) and Dominican University, Rome, Italy (Ph.D. 1924).

He was professor of the International Dominican University, Rome, from 1922-40, French and international chaplain of Catholic Writers and Journalists from 1942 onwards, member of French Association for Metapsychical Studies, Society of Friends of the Institut Métapsychique International, Academy of Social Education and Mutual Aid.

In addition to his many articles and books on religious subjects, he has published: *Le Subconscient* (The Subconscious Mind), vol. 1 *Sciences Psychiques et Morale Catholique* (Psychic Sciences and Catholic Morality, 1949), vol. 2 *Metapsychique et Mervelleux religieux* (Metapsychics and the Religious Supernatural, 1950), vol. 3 *Le Subconscient destructeur ou serviteur du Moi?* (The Subconscious: Destroyer or Servant of the Ego?, 1951), vol. 4 *Présence de nos morts* (Our Dead Are With Us, 1952), vol. 5 *Subconscient et Liberté* (The Subconscious and Freedom, 1953), *Etudes sur le subconscient* (Studies of the Subconscious, 1954), *Peut-on communiquer avec les morts?* (Can We Communicate with the Dead? 1955, also translated into German and Portuguese), *Supranormal ou surnaturel?* (Supernormal or Supernatural? 1956, Spanish ed. 1958 English translation titled *Psychical Phenomena* 1959), *Religione E. Scienze Metapsichiche* (Religion and the Metaphysical Sciences, 1957), *Psychical Phenomena* (U.S. ed. 1958), Médecine et Merveilleux (Medicine and the Supernatural, 1956), *Le Gouvernement Divin: Coopération des hommes et des esprits* (God's Rule: Cooperation of Men and Spirits, 1959), *Le monde des ressuscités* (The World After Resurrection, 1961), *Jeunesse eternelle* (Everlasting Youth, 1962), *L'Occultisme devant la science* (Occultism and Science, 1963). He has published articles in a number of journals, including: *Revue Métapsychique, Schweizer Rundschau, Présences, La Tour Saint Jacques, Tomorrow, International Journal of Parapsychology.*

Omphalomancy

A system of **divination** by the navel of newborn first children, to ascertain future conceptions by the mother. Indications were obtained from the number of markings or bands of the navel.

Oneiromancy

Special term for **divination** by **dreams**, probably the oldest of the divinatory systems. Written records exist of dream interpretation in a papyrus of c. 1250 B.C.

Prophetic dreams also figure frequently in Biblical history.

In modern times, psychologists and psychoanalysts have claimed that dreams contain various elements, including symbolic hopes and fears, sexual anxieties and recollections of past events, as well as possible precognitive images.

A notable attempt to isolate claimed precognitive factors in dreams was made by J. W. **Dunne** (1875-1949) in his book *An Experiment With Time* (1927).

Onimancy (or Onycomancy)

An elaborate ritual of **divination** said to be based on the observation of the angel Uriel. Upon the nails of the right hand or the palm of the hand of an unpolluted boy or a young virgin is put some oil of olives, or what is better, oil of walnuts mingled with tallow or blacking. If money or things hidden in the earth be sought, the face of the child must be turned towards the east. If crime be inquired into, or the knowledge of a person out of affection, towards the south; for robbery towards the west, and for murder towards the south.

Then the child must repeat the seventy-two verses of the Psalms, which the Hebrew Kabalists (see **Kabala**) collected for the Urim and Thummim. These are found in the third book of Johann Rechlin on the Kabalistical art (De arte cabalistica, 1517) and in a treatise *De verbo mirifoco* (c. 1480). In each of these verses occurs the venerable name of four letters, and the three lettered name of the seventy-two angels, which are referred to the sacred name **Shemhamphorash,** which was hidden in the folds of the lining of the tippet of the high priest. When the curious student has done all this, he is assured that he will "see wonders."

Other authorities give the name Onycomancy to the interpretation of the spots on the human nails. (See also **Divination; Onychomancy**)

Onion

The onion was regarded as a symbol of the universe by the ancient Egyptians, and many curious beliefs were associated with it. It was believed that it attracted and absorbed infectious matters, and was thus usually hung up in rooms to prevent maladies. This belief in the absorptive virtue of the onion is prevalent even in modern times.

"When a youth," stated British folklorist James Napier, "I remember the following story being told, and implicitly believed by all. There was once a certain king or nobleman who was in want of a physician, and two celebrated doctors applied. As both could not obtain the situation, they agreed among themselves that the one was to try to poison the other, and he who succeeded in overcoming the poison would thus be left free to fill the situation. They drew lots as to who should first take the poison. The first dose given was a stewed toad, but the party who took it immediately applied a poultice of peeled onions over his stomach, and thus abstracted all the poison of the toad. Two days after, the other doctor was given the onions to eat. He ate them, and died. It was generally believed that the poultice of peeled onions laid on the stomach, or underneath the armpits, would cure anyone who had taken poison."

Onomancy (or Onomamancy)

Divination by names, satirically said to be nearer to divination by a donkey, and more properly termed Onomamancy or Onomatomancy. The notion that an analogy existed between men's names and their fortunes is supposed to have originated with the Pythagoreans; it provided some speculations to Plato and was the source of some witticism by Ausonius, which may amuse the classical scholar to collate from his epigrams.

Two leading rules in the science of Onomancy were first, that an even number of vowels in a man's name signifies something amiss in his left side; an uneven number a similar affection on the right. Between the two, perfect sanity was little to be expected. Secondly, of two competitors, that one would prove successful when the numeral letters in whose name when summed up exceeded the amount of those in the name of his rival; and this was one of the reasons which enabled Achilles to triumph over Hector.

The Gothic King Theodotus was said, on the authority of Cælius Rhodiginus, to have practiced a peculiar species of Onomancy on the recommendation of a Jew. The diviner advised the prince, when on the eve of a war with Rome, to shut up thirty hogs in three different sties, having previously given some of them Roman and others Gothic names. On an appointed day, when the sties were opened, all the Romans were found alive, but with half their bristles fallen off; all the Goths, on the other hand, were dead. From this the onomantist predicted that the Gothic army would be utterly destroyed by the Romans, who, at the same time, would lose half their own force.

The system recalls the rationale of Jewish **gematria,** which assigns numerical values to the letters of names. (See also **Divination**)

Onychomancy

Divination by the fingernails. It was practiced by watching the reflection of the sun in the nails of a boy, and judging the future by the shape of the figures which showed themselves on their surface. (See also **Divination; Onimancy**)

Onyx

A precious stone whose properties were believed to resemble those of Jasper, besides increasing saliva in boys, and bringing terrible shapes to the dreamer. If applied to the eye it was said to act as if it were alive, by creeping about and removing anything noxious.

The onyx was further believed to create strife, to cause melancholy and to cure epilepsy.

According to the authorized text of the Bible, an onyx was the eleventh stone in the breastplate of the High Priest, but it is more probable that this stone was a **beryl.**

Oom the Omnipotent

Title given to Pierre **Bernard,** pioneer of Hatha Yoga study in the U.S. and founder of the New York Sanskrit College in 1909.

Oomancy

A system of **divination** by the outer and inner forms of eggs. One method was to break an egg into a glass of water and interpret the shapes assumed by the white. (See also **Ooscopy**)

Ooscopy and Oomantia

Two methods of divination by eggs. An example under the former name was related by the Roman historian Suetonius (c. 98-138 A.D.), who stated that Livia, when she was anxious to know whether she should be the mother of a boy or girl, kept an egg in her bosom at the proper temperature, until a chick with a beautiful cockscomb came forth.

The name Oomantia denoted a method of divining the signs or characters appearing in eggs. The custom of pasche or paste eggs, which are stained with various colors and given away at Easter is well known, and was described at considerable length by John Brand in *Observations on Popular Antiquities* (2 vols., London, 1813 etc.). The custom was most religiously observed in Russia, where it is derived from the Greek Church. Gilded or colored eggs were mutually exchanged both by men and women, who kissed one another, and if any coolness existed previously became good friends again on these occasions.

The egg is one of the most ancient and beautiful symbols of new birth, and has been applied to natural philosophy as well as the spiritual creation of man. (See also **Oomancy**)

Opal

Beautiful gemstone of quartz or silica, highly praised by **Pliny** (c. 23-79 A.D.), who wrote: "For in them you shall see the living fire of the ruby, the glorious purple of the amethyst, the green sea of the emerald, all glittering together in an incredible mixture of light."

In ancient times many legends grew up around its claimed virtues. It was believed to recreate the heart, preserve from contagion in the air, and dispel sadness. It was also good for weak eyes. The name *poederos,* applied to the opal, is understood to indicate the beautiful complexion of youth.

The superstition that opals were unlucky seems to have been popularized by Sir Walter Scott's novel *Anne of Geirstein* (1829), in which the opal worn by Baroness Hermione of Arnheim has a drop of holy water fall upon it, whereupon a brilliant spark shot out of the gem and it lost its luster.

Open Deck

Term used by parapsychologists in card guessing tests, where each symbol in the pack is chosen at random, as distinct from a Closed Deck, where each symbol occurs a set number of times.

Open Letter (Newsletter)

Bi-monthly publication of the **Findhorn Community,** Scotland, a famous **"New Age"** spiritual center. Address: Findhorn Publications, The Park, Findhorn Bay, Forres, Moray, Scotland.

Open Mind, The (Newsletter)

Bimonthly newsletter edited by parapsychologist Dr. Charles T. **Tart.** "The open mind, by contrast [with the closed mind], is curious about all sorts of things, appreciates living in a marvelous and mysterious universe and constantly seeks increased self-knowledge." Address: Psychological Processes, Inc., P.O. Box 371, El Cerrito, California 94530.

Open Mind Magazine

Publication by a group of Australian experimenters in the **"Christos Experience,"** which involves a technique culminating in the experience of traveling by mind to other places, identities, and time periods. The technique is described in the book *Worlds Within: Probing the Christos Experience* (1976; 1978) by G. M. Glaskin. The Open Mind group can be contacted for further information on the experience. Address: Open Mind Publications, c/o Post Office, Mahogany Creek, Western Australia 6072.

"Ophiel"

Pseudonym of Edward C. Peach, modern popular writer on occultism. In 1961, after receiving a claims settlement of $1,000 for an accident, he spent the money publishing his own manuscript *The Art and Practice of Astral Projection,* using a Hong Kong printer. The book hit the market at the peak of the occult revival and sold so well that Llewellyn Publications were happy to take it over for their Gnostic Institute imprint.

Since then, "Ophiel" has published several successful occult books for them. Now in his sixties, he lives in an apartment in Hollywood, California, which he claims to have obtained by the method detailed in his book *The Art of Getting Material Things by Creative Visualization* (1966). His other books include: *Art and Practice of the Occult* (1968), *Art and Practice of Clairvoyance* (1969), *The Oracle of Fortuna* (1971), *Art and Practice of Talismanic Magic* (1973), *Art and Practice of Cabala Magic* (1976), *Art and Practice of the Occult* (n.d.).

Ophiomancy

A system of **divination** based on the color and movements of serpents.

Ophites

This Gnostic sect seems to have dated from the second century. A full system of initiation was in vogue among the members, and they possessed symbols to represent purity, life, spirit and fire. The whole appears to have been a compound of the mysteries of the Egyptian goddess Isis, concepts of Oriental mythology, and Christian doctrine.

According to the theologian Origen (c. 185-c. 254 A.D.), they were founded by a man named Euphrates, but it seems more likely that this was a symbolic reference to the water of life in *John* (iv, 10). The sect was believed to have given special prominence to serpents in their rituals. (See also **Gnostics**)

Oracles

Shrines where a god was believed to speak to human beings through the mouths of priests or priestesses. The concept of the god becoming vocal in this manner was by no means confined to ancient Greece or Egypt.

Probably most primitive gods of the fetish class (see **Fetichism**) were consulted as oracles, and from **animism** this was transmitted later to gods of the most advanced type. In early times, the great question was whether people would have food on the next day and perhaps the first oracle was the spirit which directed the hungry primitive in hunting and fishing expeditions.

The Esquimaux used to consult spirits for this purpose, and their wizards were as familiar with the art of giving ambiguous replies to their anxious clients as were the well-informed keepers of the oracles of Greece. As advancement proceeded, the direction of the gods was obtained in all the affairs of private and public life.

The Oracle of Delphi at Greece

When Jupiter was once desirous to ascertain the central point of the earth, he dispatched two eagles, or two crows, as they were named by Strabo. The messengers took flight in opposite courses, from sunrise and sunset, and they met at Delphi, which place was thenceforward dignified with the title "The navel of the earth" and "umbilicus" being represented in white marble within its celebrated temple.

Delphi thus became a place of great distinction, but it was not yet oracular until the fumes which issued from a neighboring cave were first discovered by a shepherd named Coretas. His attention was forcibly attracted to a spot around which whenever his goats were browsing they gambolled and bleated more than usual.

Whether these fumes arose in consequence of an earthquake, or whether they were generated by demoniacal art is not recorded; but the latter hypothesis was suggested by one commentator. Anyway, the story goes that Coretas, on approaching the spot, was seized with ecstacy and uttered words which were deemed inspired. It was not long before the danger arising in consequence of the excitement of curiosity among the neighbors, the deadly stupefaction often produced among those who inhaled the fumes without proper caution, and the inclination which it aroused in some to plunge themselves into the depths of the cavern below, occasioned the fissure to be covered by a sort of table, having a hole in the center and called a tripod, so that those who wished to try the experiment could resort there in safety.

Eventually a young girl of unsophisticated manners became the chosen medium of the responses, now deemed oracular and called "Pythian," as proceeding from Apollo, the slayer of Python, to whom Delphi was consecrated. A sylvan bower of laurel branches was erected over the spot, and at length the marble temple and the priesthood of Delphi arose where the Pythoness, seated on her throne, could be charged with the divine "afflatus," and was thus rendered the vehicle of Apollo's dictation.

As the oracle became more celebrated, its prophetic machinery was constructed of more costly materials. The tripod was then formed of gold but the lid, which was placed in its hollow rim in order to afford the Pythoness a more secure seat, continued to be made of brass. She prepared herself by drinking out of a sacred fountain (Castalia) adjoining the crypt, the waters of which were reserved for her only (and in which she bathed her hair) and by chewing a laurel leaf and circling her brows with a laurel crown.

The person who made inquiry from the oracle, first offered a victim, and then having written his question in a notebook, handed it to the Pythoness before she ascended the tripod, and he also, as well as the priestess, wore a laurel crown. In early times the oracle spoke only in one month of the year named "Byssus," in which it originated, and at first only on the seventh day of that month, which was esteemed the birthday of Apollo and was called "Polypthonus."

Virginity was at first an indispensable requisite in the Pythoness, on account (as Diodorus relates) of the purity of that state and its relation to Diana; moreover, because virgins were thought better adapted than others of their sex to keep oracular mysteries secret and inviolate. But after an untoward accident had occurred to one of these consecrated damsels, the guardians of the temple (in order, as they imagined, to prevent its repetition for the future) permitted no one to fulfil the duties of the office until she had attained the mature age of fifty. They still indulged her, however, with the use of a maiden's habit. The response was always delivered in Greek.

The Oracle of Dodona

Another celebrated oracle, that of Jupiter, was at Dodona in Epirus (from which Jupiter derived the name of Dodonus). It was situated at the foot of Mount Tomarus, in a wood of oaks, and there the answers were given by an old woman under the name of Pelias.

"Pelias" means dove in the Attic dialect, from which the fable arose that the doves prophesied in the groves of Dodona.

According to the historian Herodotus (c. 484-425 B.C.), this legend contains the following incident, which gave rise to the oracle.

Two priestesses of Egyptian Thebes were carried away by Phœnician merchants; one of them was conveyed to Libya, where she founded the oracle of Jupiter Ammon, the other to Greece. The latter one remained in the Dodonian wood, which was much frequented on account of the acorns. There she had a temple built at the foot of an oak in honor of Jupiter, whose priestess she had been in Thebes, and here afterwards a regular oracle was founded. Herodotus added that this priestess was called a dove, because her language could not be understood.

The Dodonic and African oracles were certainly connected, and herodotus distinctly stated that the manner of prophecy in Dodona was the same as that in Egyptian Thebes. Diana was worshiped in Dodona in conjunction with Zeus, and a female figure was associated with Amun in the Libyan Ammonium. Besides this, the dove was the bird of Aphrodite, the Diana of Zeus, or the Mosaic divine love which saved mankind from complete destruction. According to other authors, there was a wondrous intoxicating spring at Dodona, and in later times more material means were employed to produce the prophetic spirit.

Several copper bowls and bells were placed upon a column with the statue of a boy beside them. When the wind moved a rod or scourge having three bones attached to chains, this struck upon the metallic bowls and bells, the sound of which was heard by the applicants. These Dodonian tones gave rise to a proverb: *æs Dodonæum*—an unceasing babbler.

The oracle at Dodona was dedicated to the Pelasgian Zeus, who was worshiped here at the same time as the almighty ruler of the world, and as the friendly associate of mankind. In the course of the theogonic process, Diana was associated with him as his wife, mother of Aphrodite. The servants of Zeus were Selles, the priests of Diana, the so-called Peliades. According to Homer, the Selles inhabited the sanctum at Dodona, sleeping upon the earth, and with naked unwashed feet. They served the Pelasgian Zeus. It is probable that they slept upon the earth on the hides of newly-sacrificed animals, to receive prophetic dreams, as was customary at other places, Calchos and Oropus amongst many others.

As regards the oracular divination of Dodona, it was partly natural, from the excitement of the mind, partly artificial. Of the latter we may mention three modes—the ancient oak of Zeus, with its prophetic doves, the miraculous spring, and the celebrated Dodonian bowls of brass.

The far-spreading speaking tree, the "incredible wonder," as Æschylus calls it, was an oak, a lofty beautiful tree, with evergreen leaves and sweet edible acorns, which according to the belief of the Greeks and Romans, were the first sustenance of mankind. The Pelasgi regarded this tree as the tree of life. In this tree the god was supposed to reside, and the rustling of its leaves and the voices of birds showed his presence. When the questioners entered, the oak rustled and the Peliades said, "Thus speaks Zeus." Incense was burned beneath it, which may be compared to the alter of Abraham under the oak Ogyges, which had stood there since the world's creation. According to the legend, sacred doves continually inhabited the tree, like the Marsoor oracle at Tiora Mattiene, where a sacred hawk foretells futurity from the top of a wooden pillar.

At the foot of the oak, a cold spring gushed as it were from its roots, and from its murmur the inspired priestesses prophesied.

Of this miraculous fountain, it is related that when lighted torches were thrust into it they were extinguished, and that extinguished torches were relit; it also rose and fell at various seasons. Ernst von Lasaulx in *Das pelasgische Orakel d. Zeus zu Dodona* (1841) stated: "That extinction and rekindling has, perhaps, the mystical signification that the usual sober life of the senses must be extinguished, that the prophetic spirit dormant in the soul may be aroused. The torch of human existence must expire, that a divine one may be lighted; the human must die that the divine may be born; the destruction of individuality is the awakening of God in the soul, or, as the mystics say, the setting of sense is the rising of truth."

The extinguishing of a burning light suggests that the spring contained carbonic acid gas, which possesses stupifying and deadly properties, like all exhalations arising especially from minerals. The regular rising and sinking of the water is a frequent phenomenon, and has been observed from the earliest ages.

It appears that predictions were drawn from the tones of the Dodonian brass bowls, as well as from the rustling of the sacred oak and the murmuring of the sacred well.

The Dodonian columns, with that which stood upon them, appears to express the following: The medium-sized brazen bowl was a hemisphere, and symbolized heaven; the boy-like male statue was a figure of the Demiurgos, or constructor of the universe; the bell-like notes were a symbol of the harmony of the universe and music of the spheres. That the Demiurgos was represented as a boy is quite in the spirit of Egypto-Pelasgian theology as it reigned in Samothrace. The miraculous bell told all who came to Dodona to question the god that they were on holy ground, must inquire with pure hearts, and be silent when the god replied. It is easily imagined that these tones, independent and uninfluenced by human will, must have made a deep impression upon the minds of pilgrims. Those who questioned the god were also obliged to take a purificatory bath in the temple, similar to that by which the Delphian Pythia prepared herself for prophecy.

Besides this artificial soothsaying from signs, natural divination by the prophetic movements of the mind was practiced. Where there are prophesying priestesses, there must also be ecstatic ones, similar to those in the magnetic state. Sophocles called the Dodonean priestesses divinely inspired. Plato (Phædrus) stated, more decidedly, that the prophetess at Delphi and the priestesses at Dodona had done much good in sacred madness, in private and public affairs, to their country, but in their senses little or nothing.

We may infer from this that the Delphian Pythia as well as the Dodonian priestesses did not give their oracles in the state of common waking consciousness but in real ecstasy, to which the frequent incense (and drink) offerings would assist. Aristides stated still more clearly than the others, that the priestesses at Dodona neither knew (before being seized upon by the spirit) what would be said, nor remembered afterwards when their natural consciousness returned, what they had uttered, so that all others, rather than they, knew it.

The Oracle of Jupiter Trophonius

Trophonius, according to Pausanias (c. 470 B.C.), was the most skillful architect of his day. Concerning the origin of his oracle there are many opinions. Some say he was swallowed up by an earthquake in the cave, which afterwards became prophetic; others, that after having completed the Adytum of Apollo at Delphi (a very marvelous specimen of his workmanship, he declined asking any specific pay, but modestly requested the god to grant him whatever was the greatest benefit a man could receive—and in three days afterwards he was found dead.

This oracle was discovered after two years of scarcity in its neighborhood, when the Pythoness ordered the starving population who applied to her, to consult Trophonius in Lebadæa. The deputation sent for that purpose could not discover any trace of such an oracle until Saon, the oldest among them, obtained the desired information by following the flight of a swarm of bees.

The responses were given by the genius of Trophonius to the inquirer, who was compelled to descend into a cave, of the nature of which Pausanias left a very lively representation. The votary resided for a certain number of days in a sanctuary of good fortune, in which he underwent customary lustrations, abstained from hot baths, but dipped in the river Hercyna, and was plentifully supplied with meat from the victims which he sacrificed.

Many, indeed, were the sacred personages whom he was bound to propitiate with blood; among them were Trophonius himself and his sons, Apollo, Saturn, Jupiter, Vasileus, Juno Henioche, and Ceres Europa, who is affirmed to have been the nurse of Trophonius. From an inspection of the entrails, a soothsayer pronounced whether Trophonius was in fit humor for consultation. None of the "extra," however favorable they might have been, were of the slightest avail unless a ram, immolated to Agamedes at the mouth of the cave on the very night of the descent, proved auspicious. When that propitious signal had been given, the priests led the inquirer to the river Hercyna, where he was anointed and washed by two Lebadæan youths, thirteen years of age, named "Hermai."

He was then carried farther to the two springheads of the stream, and there he drank first of Lethe, in order that he might forget all past events and present his mind to the oracle as a "tabula rasa" (cleaned tablet); and secondly of Mnemosyne, that he might firmly retain remembrance of every occurrence which was about to happen within the cave. An image, reputed to be the workmanship of Dædalus, was then exhibited to him, and so great was its sanctity, that no other eyes but those of a person about to undertake the adventure of the cave were ever permitted to behold it.

Next he was clad in a linen robe, girt with ribbons, and shod with sandals peculiar to the country. The entrance to the oracle was a very narrow aperture in a grove on the summit of a mountain, protected by a marble parapet about two cubits in height, and by brazen spikes above it. The upper part of the cave was artificial, like an oven, but no steps were cut in the rock, and the descent was made by a ladder brought to the spot on each occasion.

On approaching the mouth of the adytum itself, the adventurer lay flat, and holding in each hand some honeyed cakes, first inserted his feet into the aperture, then drew his knees and the remainder of his body after them, till he was caught by some hidden force and carried downward as if by a whirlpool.

The responses were given sometimes by a vision, sometimes by words, and a forcible exit was then made through the original entrance, and in like manner feet foremost. There was only a single instance on record of any person who had descended failing to return and that one deserved his fate, for his object was to discover treasure, not to consult the oracle.

Immediately on issuing from the cavern, the inquirer was placed on a seat called that of Mnemosyne, not far from the entrance, and there the priests demanded a relation of everything which he had seen and heard; he was then carried once again to the sanctuary of good fortune, where he remained for some time overpowered by terror and lost in forgetfulness. By degrees, his former powers of intellect returned, and, in contradiction to the received opinion, he recovered the power of smiling.

The antiquary Dr. Edward D. Clarke (1769-1822) during his visit to Lebadæa found everything belonging to the hieron of Trophonius in its original state, excepting that the narrow entrance to the adytum was choked with rubbish. The Turkish governor was afraid of a popular commotion if he gave permission for cleansing this aperture. Mr. J. M. Cripps (who accompanied Dr. Clarke) however, introduced the whole length of his body into the cavity, and by thrusting a long pole before him found it utterly stopped. In modern times, the waters of Lethe and Mnemosyne supplied the washer-women of Lebadæa.

The Oracles of Delos and Branchus

The oracle of "Delos," notwithstanding its high reputation, had few peculiarities. Its virtue was derived from the nativity of Apollo and Diana in that island. At Dindyma, or Didyma, near Miletus, Apollo presided over the oracle of the "Branchidæ," so called from either one of his sons or of his favorites Branchus of Thessaly, whom he instructed in soothsaying while alive and canonized after death.

The responses were given by a priestess who bathed and fasted for three days before consultation, and then sat upon an axle or bar, with a charming-rod in her hand, and inhaling the steam from a hot spring.

Offerings and ceremonies were necessary to render the inspiration effectual, including baths, fasting, and solitude, and Iamblichus (c. 330 A.D.) censured those who despised them.

The Oracle of the Clarian Apollo at Colophon

Of the oracle of Apollo at Colophon, Iamblichus related that it prophesied by drinking of water: "It is known that a subterranean spring exists there, from which the prophet drinks; after he has done so, and has performed many consecrations and sacred customs on certain nights, he predicts the future; but he is invisible to all who are present. That this water can induce prophecy is clear, but how it happens, no one knows, says the proverb.

It might appear that the divine spirit pervades this water, but it is not so. God is in all things, and is reflected in this spring, thereby giving it the prophetic power. This inspiration of the water is not of an entirely divine nature, for it only prepares us and purifies the light of the soul, so that we are fit to receive the divine spirit. There the divine presence is of such a nature that it punishes every one who is capable of receiving the god. The soothsayer uses this spirit like a work-tool over which he has no control. After the moment of prediction he does not always remember that which has passed; often he can scarcely collect his faculties. Long before the water-drinking, the soothsayer must abstain day and night from food, and observe religious customs, which are impossible to ordinary people, by which means he is made capable of receiving the god. It is only in this manner that he is able to hold the mirror of his soul to the radiance of free inspiration."

The Oracle of Amphiaraus

Another very celebrated oracle was that of Amphiaraus, who distinguished himself so much in the Theban war.

He was venerated at Oropus, in Bœotia, as a seer. This oracle was consulted more in sickness than on any other occasion. The applicants had here, also, to lie upon the skin of a sacrificed ram, and during sleep had the remedies of their diseases revealed to them.

Not only were sacrifices and lustrations performed here, but the priests also prescribed other preparations by which the minds of the sleepers were to be enlightened. They had to fast one day, and refrain from wine for three.

Amphilochus, as son of Amphiaraus, had a similar oracle at Mallos, in Cilicia, which Pausanias called the most trustworthy and credible of the age. Plutarch spoke of the oracles of Amphilochus and Mopsus as being in a very flourishing state, and Lucian mentioned that all those who wished to question the oracle had to lay down two oboles (small silver coins).

Egyptian Oracles

The oracles of ancient Egypt were as numerous as those of Greece. It must have been due to foreign influence that the oracle, that played so important a part in the Greek world at this time, was also thoroughly established on the banks of the Nile.

Herodotus knew of no fewer than seven gods in Egypt who spoke by oracles. Of these, the most reliable were considered to give an intimation of their intentions by means of remarkable events. These were carefully observed by the Egyptians, who wrote down what followed upon these prodigies.

They also considered that the fate of a person was fixed by the day of his birth, for every day belonged to a special god. The oracle of Jupiter Ammon at the oasis of that name and the same deity at Thebes existed from the twentieth to the twenty-second Dynasty. He was consulted not only concerning the fate of empires but upon such trifling matters as the identification of a thief. In all serious matters, however, it was sought to ascertain his views. Those about to make their wills sought his oracle, and judgments were ratified by his word.

According to the inscriptions, intercourse between king and god was arranged as follows: "The King presented himself before the god and preferred a direct question, so framed as to admit of an answer by simple yes or no; in reply the god nodded an affirmative, or shook his head in negation. This has suggested the idea that the oracles were worked by manipulating statues of divinities mechanically set in motion by the priests. But as yet no such statues have been found in the Valley of the Nile, and contrivances of this kind could have had no other object than to deceive the people, a supposition apparently excluded in this case by the fact that it was customary for the king to visit the god alone and in secret. Probably the king presented himself on such occasions before the sacred animal in which the god was incarnate, believing that the divine will would be manifested by its movements." (See also Moving **Statues**)

The Apis bull also possessed oracles. Bes, too, god of pleasure or of the senses, had an oracle at Abydos.

American Oracles

Among the American races, the oracle was frequently encountered. All the principal gods of aboriginal America universally acted as oracles. With the ancient inhabitants of Peru, the *huillcas* partook of the nature of oracles. Many of these were serpents, trees, and rivers, the noises made by which appeared to the primitive Peruvians (as, indeed, primitive folk all over the world) to be of the quality of articulate speech. Both the Huillcamayu and the Apurimac rivers at Cuzco were *huillca oracles* of this kind, as their names, "Huillcariver" and "Great Speaker," denote. These oracles often set the mandate of the Inca himself at defiance, occasionally supporting popular opinion against his policy.

The Peruvian Indians of the Andes mountain range within recent generations continued to adhere to the superstitions they had inherited from their fathers. A rare and interesting account of these says that they "admit an evil being, the inhabitant of the centre of the earth, whom they consider as the author of their misfortunes, and at the mention of whose name they tremble. The most shrewd among them take advantage of this belief to obtain respect, and represent themselves as his delegates. Under the denomination of *mohanes*, or *agoreros*, they are consulted even on the most trivial occasions. They preside over the intrigues of love, the health of the community, and the taking of the field. Whatever repeatedly occurs to defeat their prognostics, falls on themselves; and they are wont to pay for their deceptions very dearly. They chew a species of vegetable called *piripiri*, and throw it into the air, accompanying this act by certain recitals and incantations, to injure some, to benefit others, to procure rain and the inundation of rivers, or, on the other hand, to occasion settled weather, and a plentiful store of agricultural productions. Any such result, having been casually verified on a single occasion, suffices to confirm the Indians in their faith, although they may have been cheated a thousand times."

There is an instance on record of how the *huillca* could refuse on occasion to recognize even royalty itself. Manco, the Inca who had been given the kingly power by Pizarro, offered a sacrifice to one of these oracular shrines. The oracle refused to recognize him, through the medium of its guardian priest, stating that Manco was not the rightful Inca. Manco therefore caused the oracle, which was in the shape of a rock, to be thrown down, whereupon its guardian spirit emerged in the form of a parrot and flew away. It is possible that the bird thus liberated had been taught by the priests to answer to the questions of those who came to consult the shrine. But upon Manco commanding that the parrot should be pursued, it sought another rock, which opened to receive it, and the spirit of the *huillca* was transferred to this new abode.

Like the greater idols of Mexico, most of the principal *huacas* of Peru seem to have been also oracles. The guardians of the great speaking *huacas* appear to have exercised in virtue of their office an independent influence which was sometimes sufficiently powerful to resist the Apu-Ccapac-Inca himself. It was perhaps natural that they should be the exponents of the popular feeling which supported them, rather than of the policy of the sovereign chiefs, whose interest it was to suppress them. There was even a tradition that the Huillac-umu, a venerable *huillac* whom the rest acknowledged as their head, had in old times possessed jurisdiction over the supreme war chiefs.

Many Indian tribes employed fetishes (See **Fetichism**) as oracles, and among the ancient Mexicans practically all the great gods were oracular. (See also **Greece**)

Recommended reading:

Bouché-Leclercq, A. *Histoire de la divination dans l'antiquité*, Paris, 1879

Dempsey, T. *The Delphic Oracles,* Oxford, U.K., 1918

Halliday, W. R. *Greek Divination,* Macmillan, London, 1913

Parke, Herbert W. *Greek Oracles,* Hutchinson, London, 1967

Parke, Herbert W. *Oracles of Zeus,* Blackwell, Oxford, U.K., 1967

Parke, H. W. & D. E. W. Wormell. *The Delphic Oracles,* Blackwell, Oxford, U.K., 1956

Oram, Arthur T(albot) (1916-)

British accountant and statistician who conducted research on card guessing. Born June 27, 1916 at Devizes, Wiltshire, England. In 1947 he married Reith Eleanor Bettine Williams.

He served in the Civil Service and industry, and has been a council member of the Society for Psychical Research, London. His work on the 'displacement effect' in card guessing was reported in *Nature* (vol. 157, 1946). He also published 'An Experiment with Random Numbers' (*Journal* of the Society for Psychical Research, vol. 37, 1954; vol. 38, 1955).

Orbas

The name given by the French to a species of metallic electrum. According to **Pliny,** a vessel of this substance has a certain magical property; when it is filled with liquor it discovers poison by showing semicircles like rainbows, while the fluid sparkles and hisses as if on the fire. The occult qualities of electrum are of a tell-tale nature.

Orchis, Root of

In ancient times, Root of the *Satyrios Orchis* of the orchid family was believed to be a sure remedy against enchantment.

Order of Bards, Ovates & Druids

A British Druid Order which claims to continue the traditions of the ancient Bardic and Druid Order. The outer grade is concerned with the arts and also studies in history and archaelogy, with outdoor ceremonies. The initiatory order undertakes mystical studies.

Public ceremonies are arranged at ancient sites at times based on the solstices of summer and winter, and the equinoxes of March and September. Address: The Secretary, 42 Gledstanes Road, London, W14 9HU, England.

Order of Elect Cohens

An occult Masonic group founded by Martinees de Pasqually (1710?-74) in Bordeaux, France. The French title "des Élus Cohens" with the French plural is corrupt Hebrew, and the order was also known as the Rite of Elect Priests.

It appears to have had a Sovereign Tribunal at Paris in 1767 with Pasqually at its head. After the death of Pasqually in Port-au-Prince September 20, 1774, the Order continued to exist, probably until the advent of the French Revolution.

Other individuals connected with the Order were Louis Claude de **Saint-Martin** ("The Unknown Philosopher") and "Papus" (Gérard **Encausse**).

Order of New Templars

German occult sect organized between 1894 and 1907 by Austrian occultist Jörg **Lanz von Liebenfels** (1874-1954) at Burg Werfenstein near the river Danube. Temples were also founded at Marienkamp, near Ulm and at Rügen.

The Order used the swastika symbol and claimed divine support for Hitler style race theories. White-robed members held mysterious "Grail" ceremonies. In his journal *Ostara*, von Liebenfels published racist propaganda.

The Order of New Templars went underground after the German invasion of Austria in 1938, but there is little doubt that its fascist ideas directly or indirectly influenced Adolf Hitler and the Nazi party.

Order of the Cubic Stone

A secret order in the **Golden Dawn** tradition, founded in Britain in the 1930s by Theodore Howard and two young technicians, David Edwards and Robert Turner.

The Order teaches a system of "Enochian Magic" and claims to "train the student in our approach to Ceremonial Magic in order that he may use this medium to obtain knowledge and to reach his goal." The Order publishes a magazine *The Monolith*. Address: The Wardens, Order of the Cubic Stone, P.O. Box 40, Wolverhampton, West Midlands, WV2 3PH, England.

Order of the Sacred Word

A breakaway order of the magical society Aurum Solis founded in 1897. The O.S.W. developed separately in 1957, but was reunited with the main Society in 1971. (See also **Aurum Solis**)

Order of the Silver Star

The A.·.A.·. (Argenteum Astrum), a secret order founded by occultist Aleister **Crowley.**

Order of the Star

Modern revival of the earlier **Order of the Star in the East,** which had been formed to promote J. **Krishnamurti** as the expected Great World Teacher.

At its peak, the old Order had over 45,000 members, including politicians, judges, religious leaders, medical practitioners, artists, authors, and ordinary men and women from all walks of life. It was suspended in 1929 after Krishnamurti had publicly rejected the role of Great World Teacher, but continued to teach in a less exalted capacity. He maintained that people should seek the truth within themselves rather than rely upon the authority of external teachers, and he inspired thousands of individuals in their search for spiritual realization.

The present Order of the Star was founded by a group who claimed that a Spiritual Hierarchy had decided to reactivate the Order in preparation for the second coming of Christ.

The Order worked "to establish a peripheral group on the outskirts of the major ashram under the sponsorship of the Master K. H., to initiate an active unit of service in the world, to raise the banner laid down temporarily by the old Order of the Star and to hold it aloft once again and to offer groups and individuals shelter under it."

The Order has published *Star Bulletin* since 1982, the *Embers from the Fire* (1983) containing teaching on esoteric wisdom. Address: 57 Warescot Road, Brentwood, Essex, CM15 9HH, England.

Order of the Star in the East

Organization promoting the teachings of the young Jiddu **Krishnamurti** as a World Teacher. The Order was developed by Annie **Besant** in July 1911 as an international movement, extending the scope of the Order of the Rising Sun (founded seven months earlier).

The new Order was established rapidly throughout the Theosophical movement, with national representatives and organizing secretaries in countries with active branches of the **Theosophical Society.** Ajunior Order of the Servants of the Star was established for members under twenty-one years of age.

Enthusiasm for the coming of a great World Teacher swept through the Theosophical movement, although there were also some dissensions. Many of the German lodges seceded from Adyar headquarters in Madras, India, and formed a breakaway order named the **Anthroposophical Society** under Rudolf **Steiner.** However, other German lodges remained loyal and even increased their membership.

More virulent attacks were made by the Indian newspaper *The Hindu,* which revived the scandal of the Hodgson Report of the Society for Psychical Research, with its allegations of fraudulent phenomena by Madame **Blavatsky** and the sex scandals involving Charles W. **Leadbeater** and young boys in 1906. In retrospect, it appears that Leadbeater, possibly a paedophile, was not guilty of actual sexual impropriety, but may have advised the practice of masturbation, perhaps for occult purposes rather than relief of sexual tensions. Such advice, for whatever purpose, would have been considered grossly indecent at the time, although endorsed by later sexologists as an alternative to premarital sex.

In spite of hostile attacks, the OSE flourished. In 1911, the young Krishnamurti was openly claimed to be "the chosen Vehicle of the Lord Maitreya-Bodhisattva-Christ."

In October 1912, J. Narayniah, the father of Krishnamurti, and his brother, Nityananda, started legal proceedings against the guardianship of the two boys by Annie Besant, claiming that through the influence of C. W. Leadbeater, she was unfit to have custody. The case was heard two years later in Madras, when the judge concluded that charges of sexual immorality against Leadbeater in relation to Krishnamurti were unfounded, but the Leadbeater was not a suitable person to associate with the development of children, and that Mrs. Besant should no longer have custody, and the boys were to become wards of the court.

After an Appeal Court upheld this decision, Mrs. Besant appealed to the Privy Council in England, and in May 1914, the original judgment was reversed.

Meanwhile Katherine **Tingley** of the California branch of the Theosophical Society and the Universal Brotherhood had also attacked Leadbeater, Mrs. Besant, and the OSE, declaring that "Krishnamurti is a fine chap who has been hypnotized by Mrs. Annie Besant, and is really an unwilling follower."

In 1912, the Adyar lodge formed a school and community named "Krotona" ("the place of promise") in the Hollywood Hills on similar comprehensive lines to those of the Point Loma community of Katherine Tingley. Krotona included a temple, vegetarian cafeteria, metaphysical library, and experimental center. It was here that disciples invented "stereometry," a three-dimensional geometric alphabet, involving a structure weighing three tons and using a million pieces of redwood. It was inspected by Dr. Robert Millikan and Albert Einstein, but they failed to grasp its significance.

In 1920, the community moved to Ojai Valley, and it was here that Mrs. Annie Besant brought Krishnamurti for grooming as the great World Teacher. The Order of the Star in the East had been founded "out of the rapidly growing expectation of the near coming of a great spiritual Teacher, which is visible in many parts of the world today. In all the great faiths at the present time, and in practically every race, there are people who are looking for such a Teacher; and this hope is being expressed quite naturally, in each case, in the terms appropriate to the religion and the locality in which it has sprung up. It is the object of the Order of the Star in the East, so far as is possible, to gather up and unify this common expectation, wherever and in whatever form it may exist, and to link it into a single great movement of preparation for the Great One whom the age awaits."

On January 23, 1927, Mrs. Besant announced that the World Master was here, and a new Utopian colony would be set up in Ojai, California. Subscriptions were invited for a $200,000 Happy Valley Foundation at Ojai, covering 465 acres and comprising temples, an art center, places for worship and meditation, and even a playground for Greek games.

During his world lecture tours, Krishnamurti made a favorable impression as a quiet young man with a pleasing manner, without affection, who could even play a game of golf. However in June 1927, he gave a speech which disturbed believers in the Vehicle of the Great Teacher, suggesting that **Masters** and other gurus were superfluous, that there was a more direct way to truth within every individual. Meanwhile the objects of the OSE were now revised and simplified as follows:

"1. To draw together all those who believe in the presence in the world of the World Teacher.

"2. To work for Him in all ways for His realization of His ideal for humanity.

"The Order has no dogmas, no creeds or systems of belief. Its inspiration is the Teacher, its purpose to embody His universal life."

On June 28, 1927, the name of the Order was changed to the simpler form the Order of the Star, implying that the World Teacher had now arrived, but on August 1, Krishnamurti gave an address on "Who brings the truth?"

In this, he specifically stated that the Masters had no objective existence, that they were mental images shaped by belief and imagination. He stated: "What you are troubling about is whether there is such a person as the World Teacher who has manifested Himself in the body of a certain person, Krishnamurti," but that the truth must be sought inside each individual rather than rely upon some external authority such as himself.

In effect, he renounced the role of World Teacher as defined by Mrs. Besant and C. W. Leadbeater. The following day, at the Star Camp at Ommen. The Netherlands, Krishnamurti reiterated his new message. The Order of the Star was formally suspended in 1929.

However, Krishnamurti continued to teach in a more humble capacity than that of the Great World Teacher, and inspired audiences all over the world to a quest of self-discovery of spiritual truth.

From time to time, however, the Messianic concept of a World Teacher, embodying the personality of Lord Maitreya and Jesus Christ, has continued to exert a fascination on individuals and groups concerned with esoteric studies. Announcements of an imminent coming of the World Teacher continue to be made, although so far without expectation being realized.

In 1982, the Order of the Star was revived in something like its earlier form by a group in Britain. (See also Annie **Besant;** Benjamin **Creme;** J. **Krishnamurti;** Charles W. **Leadbeater; Ojai Foundation; Order of the Star**)

Ordo Rosae Rubeae et Aureae Crucis (Order of Rose of Ruby and Cross of Gold)

The Second Order of the Hermetic Order of the **Golden Dawn,** usually known by the initials R. R. et A. C. It was formed in 1892 by S. L. M. Macgregor **Mathers,** with W. W. **Westcott** as Chief Adept.

It was kept secret from ordinary members of the G.D. and accessible only to those who qualified as 5°=6° Adeptus Minor grade. The R. R. et A. C. gave instructions in ritual magic. The poet W. B. **Yeats** was initiated into the 5°=6° grade January 20-21, 1893. During later controversies in the G.D. in 1901, Yeats privately published a pamphlet titled *Is the R. R. et A. C. to Remain a Magical Order?*

Ordre Kabbalistique de la Rosecroix

A French Rosicrucian order founded by Joséphin Péladan (1858-1918) and the Marquis Stanislas de Guaita (1860-98). The occultist Gérard **Encausse** (known as "Papus") was a member on the Supreme Council.

Orenda

A magical force. (See **America, United States of**)

Oresme, Nicole (c.1320-1382)

Bishop of Lisieux, France, in 1378, who published works on theology, politics, economics, mathematics, and physical science. His book *Livre de Divinacions* is important for its expression of orthodox theological thought on various aspects of medieval occultism. The book is titled after the *De Divinatione* of Cicero and sets out the arguments for and against belief in the occult, listing common frauds and deceptions in divination, and distinguishes between **astrology** and astronomy. Oresme accepted the reality of **alchemy,** and ascribed much occult success to the operation of demons.

Oresme was born c.1320, probably in Normandy, entered the College of Navarre in Paris in 1348, and Archdeacon of Bayeux, he accepted the Deanship of Rouen but retained his university office until obliged to relinquish it by a decision of the Parliament of Paris. In 1378, after his translation of the works of Aristotle into French, he was given the bishopric of Lisieux. He died in 1382.

His *Livre de Divinacions* was originally written in Latin, subsequently in French. In the absence of an English translation, there was little scholarly discussion of the work until relatively modern times. In 1934, Prof. Lynn Thorndike devoted three chapters in volume 3 of his monumental *History of Magic and Experimental Science* to a detailed study of Oresme's work.

For a complete scholarly study of Oresme and his work, see *Nicole Oresme and the Astrologers; A Study of His "Livre de Divinacions"* by G. W. Coopland, University Press of Liverpool, U.K., 1952. The book includes Latin, French, and English text of Oresme's *Livre.* (See also **Astrology**)

Orgone

Primordial cosmic energy, claimed to be discovered by Wilhelm Reich between 1936 and 1940. It is supposed to be universally present and demonstrable visually (a blueness in the atmosphere), thermically, electrosopically and by means of a Geiger-Müller counter; manifest in living organisms as biological energy.

Reich invented an "orgone energy accumulator," a device which was claimed to concentrate orgone energy in a kind of box constructed from metallic material covered by organic material. Reich found a significant temperature difference between the inside and outside of the accumulator, and believed that the accumulated energy had a therapeutic effect on individuals.

He made a number of experiments using the accumulator on cancer patients, and reported substantial improvement in the health of patients. He authorized widespread use of the accumulator for therapeutic purposes provided that it was used in conjunction with reputable medical advice. As a result, he was the subject of court action instituted by the F.D.A. in the States, equating the accumulator with worthless crank cures.

As Reich was a reputable physician and psychotherapist and had never sought to make money out of the accumulator, he rejected these charges and denied the right of federal inspectors to arbitrate in matters of natural science. Eventually he was imprisoned for contempt of court, his apparatus destroyed and his books burned. He died in prison (see Wilhelm **Reich**).

Nowadays the notion of a static device accumulating some form of energy does not seem extravagant, and all over the world people have experimented with pyramid forms which are claimed to have this effect and even to sharpen old razor blades (see *The Secret Power of Pyramids* by Bill Schul & Ed Pettit, Fawcett, 1975).

Reich's claimed discovery of a motor force in orgone energy may be compared with other mysterious motors (see entries under John Ernest Worrell **Keely,** and John Murray **Spear**). Another related motor (but somewhat flimsy) is described in the august columns of the British medical journal *The Lancet* (July 30, 1921): 'An Instrument Which is Set in Motion by Vision or by Proximity of the Human Body' by Charles Russ.

Orgone energy concepts also resemble earlier ideas of **"Od,"** investigated by Baron von **Reichenbach** in the nineteenth century, as well as occult concepts of vital force. The biological manifestation of orgone energy in the human organism as described by Reich is strongly reminiscent of the **Kundalini** energy of Hindu **yoga** science.

For an account of the construction of an orgone accumulator, see: *The Cancer Biopathy* (vol. 2 of *The Discovery of the Orgone*) by Wilhelm Reich, Orgone Institute Press, or the booklet *The Orgone Energy Accumulator* published by Orgone Institute Press. Some valuable observations on Orgone energy were published in the mimeographed journal *Orgonomic Functionalism* edited by Paul & Jean Ritter, published between 1954 and 1963 from Nottingham, England, and in *Energy and Character; the Journal of Bioenergetic Research* published from 1970 onwards by David Boadella (an associate of Paul Ritter) from: Abbotsbury, Dorset, England. The official American Association for Medical Orgonomy has published *Orgonomic Medicine* from June 1955 onwards (Orgonomic Publications Inc., 515 East 88 Street, New York, N.Y. 10028). (See also **Kundalini; Od; Psychic Force;** Wilhelm **Reich; Reichenbach**)

Ornithomancy

The ancient Greek term for augury, the method of **divination** by the flight or the song of birds, which, with the Romans, became a part of their national religion, and had a distinct priesthood. (See also **Almoganeses; Birds**)

Orton

A mysterious spirit alluded to by the historian Jean Froissart (1338-c.1410) as the **familiar** of the Lord of Corasse, near Orthes. A clerk whom his lordship had wronged set this spirit the task of tormenting his superior, but by fair words the Lord of Corasse won him over to himself so that Orton became his familiar. Nightly Orton would shake his pillow and waken him to tell him the news of the world. Froissart wrote of their connection:

"So Orton continued to serve the Lord of Corasse for a long time. I do not know whether he had more than one master, but, every week, at night, twice or thrice, he visited his master, and related to him the events which had happened in the different countries he had traversed, and the lord of Corasse wrote of them to the Count of Foix, who took a great pleasure in them, for he was the man in all the world who most willingly heard news of strange countries.

"Now it happened that the Lord of Corasse, as on other nights, was lying in his bed in his chamber by the side of his wife, who had become accustomed to listen to Orton without any alarm. Orton came, and drew away the lord's pillow, for he was fast asleep, and his lord awoke, and cried, 'Who is this?' He answered, 'It is I, Orton.' 'And whence comest thou?' 'I come from Prague, in Bohemia.' 'And how far from hence is this Prague, in Bohemia?' 'Why,' said he, 'about sixty days' journey.' 'And thou hast come so quickly?' 'Faith, I go as quickly as the wind, or even swifter.' 'And thou hast wings?' 'Faith, none.' 'How then canst thou fly so quickly?' Orton replied—'It does not concern thee to know.' 'Nay,' said he, 'I shall be very glad to know what fashion and form thou art of,' Orton answered, 'It does not concern thee to know; it is sufficient that I come hither, and bring thee sure and certain news.' 'By G—, Orton,' exclaimed the lord of Corasse, 'I should love thee better if I had seen thee.' 'Since you have so keen a desire to see me,' said Orton 'the first thing thou shalt see and encounter tomorrow morning, when you rise from your bed, shall be—I.' 'That is enough,' said the Lord of Corasse. 'Go, therefore; I give thee leave for the night.'

"When the morrow came, the Lord of Corasse began to rise, but the lady was so affrighted that she fell sick and could not get up that morning, and she said to her lord, who did not wish her to keep her bed, 'See if thou seest Orton. By my faith, I neither wish, if it please God, to see nor encounter him.' 'But I do,' said the Lord of Corasse. He leapt all nimbly from his bed, and seated himself upon the edge, and waited there to see Orton, but saw nothing. Then he went to the windows and threw them upon that he might see more clearly about the room, but he saw nothing, so that he could say, 'This is Orton.' The day passed, the night returned.

"When the Lord of Corasse was in his bed asleep, Orton came, and began speaking in his wonted manner. 'Go, go,' said his master, 'thou art a fibber: thou didst promise to show me to-day who thou wert, and thou hast not done so.' 'Nay,' said he, 'but I did.' 'Thou didst not.' 'And didst thou not see anything,' inquired Orton, 'when thou didst leap out of bed?' The Lord of Corasse thought a little while, and said—'Yes, while sitting on my bed, and thinking of thee, I saw two long straws upon the pavement, which turned towards each other and played about.' 'And that was I,' cried Orton, 'I had assumed that form.' Said the Lord of Corasse: 'It does not content me: I pray thee change thyself into some other form, so that I may see and know thee.' Orton replied: 'You will act so that you will lose me.' 'Not so,' said the Lord of Corasse: 'When I have once seen you, I shall not want to see you ever again.' 'Then,' said Orton, 'you shall see me tomorrow; and remember that the first thing you shall see upon leaving your chamber, will be I.' 'Be it so,' replied the Lord of Corasse. 'Begone with you, therefore, now. I give thee leave, for I wish to sleep.'

"Orton departed. When the morrow came, and at the third hour, the Lord of Corasse was up and attired in his usual fashion, he went forth from his chamber into a gallery that looked upon the castle-court. He cast therein his glances, and the first thing he saw was the largest sow he had ever seen; but she was so thin she seemed nothing but skin and bones, and she had great and long teats, pendant and quite attenuated, and a long and inflamed snout.

"The Sire de Corasse marvelled very much at this sow, and looked at her in anger, and exclaimed to his people, 'Go quickly, bring the dogs hither, and see that this Sow be well hunted.' The varlets ran nimbly, threw open the place where the dogs lay, and set them at the sow. The sow heaved a loud cry, and looked up at the Lord of Corasse, who supported himself upon a pillar buttress in front of his chamber. She was seen no more afterwards, for she vanished, nor did any one note what became of her. The Sire de Corasse returned into his chamber pensively, and bethought himself of Orton, and said, 'I think that I have seen my familiar; I repent me that I set my dogs upon him, for I doubt if I shall ever behold him again, since he has several times told me that as soon as I should provoke him I should lose him, and he would return no more.' He spoke truly; never again did Orton return to the Lord of Corasse, and the knight died in the following year."

Ortt, Felix (1866-1959)

Dutch engineer who developed a philosophy of "pneumatic-energetic monism," proposing that spirit revealed itself under the dual aspect of energy and entelechy. He wrote widely on parapsychological subjects, including a theory of temperature drop in relation to psychical phenomena, and a "Philosophy of Occultism and Spiritualism," dealing with concepts of substantiality and causality.

Osborn, Arthur W(alter) (1891-)

British author of books on the paranormal, higher consciousness, and mysticism. He was born March 10, 1891, in London, England, educated privately. In 1936 he married Margaret Horgan (died 1971). From 1913-14, he represented a British firm in Dutch East Indies; 1920-54, executive of British firm in Australia, writer. During World War I he served in the British Army, Royal Field Artillery, receiving Military Cross, and being mentioned in dispatches twice. He became a member of the Society for Psychical Research, London, but made his home in Australia. He traveled widely in the U.S., Canada, Europe, Southeast Asia, and India.

His publications included: *Occultism, Christian Science & Healing* (1926), *The Superphysical; A Review of the Evidence for Continued Existence, Reincarnation, and Mystical States of Consciousness* (1937; 1974), *The Expansion of Awareness; One Man's Search for Meaning in Living* (1955; 1961), *The Axis and the Rim; The Quest for Reality in a Modern Setting* (1963; 1967), *The Future Is Now; The Significance of Precognition* (1961),*The Meaning of Personal Existence in the Light of Paranormal Phenomena; The Doctrine of Reincarnation & Mystical States of Consciousness* (1966; 1967), *The Expansion of Awareness* (1967), *The Cosmic Womb; An Interpretation of Man's Relationship to the Infinite* (1969), *What Am I Living For?* (1974). He also contributed articles to various journals.

Osborn, Edward Collet (1909-1957)

British publicist and parapsychologist. Born November 4, 1909 at Irvingdean, Sussex, England, he studied at Giggleswick School, Yorkshire. In 1938 he married Pauline Rhoda Whishaw.

He was a council member of the Society for Psychical Research, London from 1947-57 and edited the SPR *Journal* from 1947-57 and the *Proceedings* from 1951-57. For some years he worked with the publishing company of Benn, and from 1932 onwards with the Royal Institute of International Affairs.

He played an important part in research and organization at the Society for Psychical Research and contributed articles to the *Journal,* including 'The Woman in Brown, an Investigation of an Apparition' (1939), 'An Experiment in the Electro-Encephalography of Mediumistic Trance' (with C. C. Evans, 1952).

He died March 27, 1957 in London.

Oscilloclast

An apparatus invented by unconventional healer Dr. Albert **Abrams** (1863-1924), pioneer of **Radionics.** For a detailed description of the apparatus see *The Abrams Treatment in Practice; an Investigation* by G. Laughton Scott (London, n.d., c. 1925). (See also **Black Box)**

Osis, Karlis (1917-)

Distinguished modern parapsychologist who has investigated extrasensory perception, spontaneous psi phenomena and mediumship. Born December 26, 1917 at Riga, Latvia, he studied at University of Munich (Ph.D. psychology 1950). In 1951 he married Klara Zale. He became a U.S. citizen in 1959.

He was research associate at the Parapsychology Laboratory, Duke University, Durham, North Carolina from 1951-57, director of research at Parapsychology Foundation, New York, N.Y. from 1957-62, director of research at American Society for Psychical Research 1962, council member of the Parapsychological Association (president 1961-62), member of the American Psychological Association.

Dr. Osis's doctorate from the psychology department of University of Munich was for a thesis that reviewed all previous work on the theoretical basis of ESP. Since then he devoted a lifetime to research and study of parapsychology.

In his period at Duke University from 1951-57 he worked with J. B. **Rhine,** and explored the relationship between ESP and psychokinesis, precognition, and psi between men and animals. He investigated the well-publicized poltergeist phenomena at Seaford, Long Island, N.Y. in 1958, although he concluded that the facts did not support a paranormal explanation. His report was published in the *Newsletter* of the Parapsychology Foundation (March-April 1958).

One of his important studies concerned the effect of distance on ESP. He recently conducted an extensive study on the relationship between meditation and ESP. His contributions to the *Journal of Parapsychology* include: 'A Test of the Occurrence of Psi Effect Between Man and Cat' (vol. 16, No. 4, 1952), 'A Test of ESP in Cats' (with Esther Bond **Foster,** vol. 17, No. 3, 1953), 'A Test of the Relationship Between ESP and PK' (vol. 17, No. 4, 1953), 'Precognition Over Time Intervals of One to Thirty Days' (vol. 19, No. 2, 1955), 'ESP Tests at Long and Short Distances' (vol. 20, No. 2, 1956), 'ESP Over a Distance of 7,500 Miles' (with D. C. **Pienaar,** vol. 20, No. 4, 1956), 'Transient States & ESP (vol. 32, 1968); *Journal* of American Society for Psychical Research: 'The Effect of Experimenter Differences & Subjects' Belief Level Upon ESP Scores' (vol. 58, 1964), (with J. Fahler) 'Checking for Awareness of Hits in a Precognition Experiment with Hypnotized Subjects' (vol. 60, 1966), (with E. Bokert) 'ESP and Changed States of Consciousness Induced by Meditation' (vol. 65, 1971), (with M. E. Turner, Jr. & M. L. Carlson) 'ESP Over Distance; Research on the ESP Channel' (vol. 65, 1971); *ASPR Newsletter:* 'Out-of-the-Body Research at the ASPR (No. 22, 1974), 'What Did The Dying See?' (No. 24, 1975). He also contributed to the symposium 'The Future of the Poltergeist' (*Proceedings of the Parapsychological Association*, vol. 7, 1970).

Dr. Osis is also author of *Deathbed Observations by Physicians and Nurses* (published Parapsychology Foundation, 1961), (with Erlendur **Haraldsson**) *At the Hour of Death* (1977), *Man Among His Peers* (1977).

Osmond, Humphrey (Fortescue) (1917-)

Psychiatrist who has made special contributions to the study of psychedelics and parapsychology. Born July 1, 1917 at Milford, Surrey, England, he studied at the Royal College of Physicians and Surgeons, Canada (certificate in psychiatry 1952), Guy's Hospital, London, England (M.R.C.S., L.R.C.P. 1942) and St. George's Hospital, London from 1949-51 (diploma in psychological medicine 1949). In 1947 he married Amy Edith Roffey.

He was a surgeon lieutenant in the Royal Navy from 1942-47, specialist in neuropsychiatry, command psychiatrist at Military Hospital, Malta from 1945-57. In 1948 he was in the Neurology Department, Guy's Hospital, London, was first assistant in Department of Psychological Medicine at St. George's Hospital, London, from 1949-51; clinical director (1951-53), physician superintendent and director of research (1953-61) at Saskatchewan Hospital, Weyburn, Canada; director of the Bureau of Research in Neurology and Psychiatry for the State of New Jersey thereafter.

His memberships include British Medical Association, Canadian Medical Association, Royal Medico-Psychological Association, Canadian Psychiatric Association (editorial staff at Canadian Psychiatric Association *Journal*), Group for Advancement of Psychiatry, Collegium International, Neuro-Psychopharmacology, Saskatchewan Psychiatric Association (president in 1958).

Dr. Osmond has taken special interest in psychedelics, the study of mental activities and states of consciousness in relation to drugs or pharmacological substances. He contributed a paper on 'Analogues of Mediumship and their Bearing on Parapsychology' at the Conference on Parapsychology and Psychedelics held in New York in 1958. He was also co-chairman with Dr. Emilio **Servadio** at the Conference on Parapsychology and Pharmacology held in 1959 at St. Paul de Vence, France. His articles on parapsychology include 'A Call for Imaginative Theory' (*International Journal of Parapsychology*, Autumn 1959) and (with Dr. Robert **Sommer**) 'Studies in Precognition' (International Journal of Parapsychology' (Summer, 1960). He has given special attention to imagery in relation to mediumship and telepathy. With Dr. Abram **Hoffer** he was co-author of *The Chemical Basis of Clinical Psychiatry* (1960), *How to Live with Schizophrenia* (1966, 1974); *The Hallucinogens* (1967); *New Help for Alcoholics* (1968). He was editor (with Bernard Aaronson) of *Psychedelics: The Uses and Implications of Hallucinogenic Drugs* (1970). His other publications include: (with H. Yaker & F. Cheek) *The Future of Time; Man's Temporal Environment* (1971), (with Miriam Sieyler) *Models of Madness, Models of Medicine* (1974), *Predicting the Past* (1981).

Osmont, Anne (1872-1953)

Clairvoyant, author and lecturer. Born August 2, 1872 at Toulouse, France. Miss Osmont published articles on psychic subjects in *Initiation et Science* and *Psychic* magazine (a French journal).

Her books included: *Le Mouvement Symboliste* (The Symbolist Movement), *L'Art d'etre Heureuse* (The Art of Being Happy), *Le Rythme Créateur de forces et de formes* (The Creative Rhythm of Forces and Forms), *Les Plantes médicinales et magiques* (Medical and Magic Plants), *Clartés sur l'occultisme* (Light on Occultism). Her book *Envoutements et exorcisms à travers le ages* (Sorcery and Exorcism Through the Ages) was published posthumously in 1954.

She died in Paris May 13, 1953.

Ossowiecki, Stephan (1877-1944)

Polish engineer, one of the most remarkable and scientifically tested clairvoyants.

He inherited his psychic gifts from his mother's side, and could read thoughts from early childhood. In the Engineering Institute at Petrograd, where he studied, he astounded his professors by answering questions enclosed in an envelope without opening it. He could see colored **auras** of surrounding people, heard raps and could move objects telekinetically. When he practiced **telekinesis** his clairvoyant powers diminished. At the age of thirty-five he lost his telekinetic powers and his gift of reading sealed papers developed remarkably.

With human subjects he showed even more penetration. Most of the persons he met had no secrets from him. He knew their most intimate thoughts, and read their past, present and future as in an open book. On several occasions, mostly involuntarily, but once by an effort of will, he externalized i.e., projected his likeness over a distance. His friends to whom he manifested himself received the impression that he was near in flesh and blood.

His powers were nearer to **psychometry** than **clairvoyance.** He never read the sealed letters word by word. He perceived the ideas. Typewritten or printed texts failed to bring his powers into play. They had to be written by a living person. Nevertheless if the writing was in a strange language which he did not know, he could not disclose the contents but could tell all the circumstances connected with the writer and the writing.

He gave remarkable evidence of clairvoyance to Professor Charles **Richet,** Dr. Gustave **Geley** and many other scientists in reading sealed letters, the contents of which in many cases were unknown to the experimenters. To Geley, he read the contents of a letter as follows: "I am in a zoological garden; a fight is going on, a large animal, an elephant. Is he not in the water? I see his trunk as he swims. I see blood."

Geley said: "Good, but that is not all."

Ossowiecki: "Wait, is he not wounded in his trunk?"

Geley: "Very good. There was a fight."

Ossowiecki: "Yes, with a crocodile."

The sentence which Geley wrote was "An elephant bathing in the Ganges was attacked by a crocodile who bit off his trunk."

At the time of the International Psychical Research Congress in Warsaw in 1923, Ossowiecki was asked to read the contents of a note sent by the **Society for Psychical Research** and carefully sealed by Dr. E. J. **Dingwall** in an envelope after having been wrapped in several folds of paper of various colors.

The note contained the sketch of a flag, a bottle and, in a corner, the data of August 22, 1923.

Ossowiecki reproduced correctly the flag and the bottle, and wrote the numerals of the date, although not in correct order. The seal being broken, Ossowiecki was warmly acclaimed by the Congress. The psychical researcher Baron **Schrenck-Notzing** cried: "Thank you, thank you, in the name of science."

For an account of this remarkable experiment see 'Une sensationelle expérience de M. Stephan Ossowiecki au Congrès de Varsovie' by Gustave Geley (*Revue Métapsychique,* Paris, September-October 1923). Additional reference to Ossowiecki's powers will be found in Geley's book *Materialisation and Clairvoyance* (London, 1927). See also *Collected Papers on the Paranormal* by Theodore Besterman (New York, 1968).

Osty, Dr. Eugèn (1874-1938)

French physician, director of the **Institut Métapsychique Internationale.** He was born May 16, 1874. He trained for a medical career and was physician at Jouet sur l'Aubor's from 1901-24.

In 1910 he set out to investigate psychical phenomena and summed up his researches three years later in *Lucidity and Intuition* (1913).

He admitted that the acquisition of knowledge through paranormal means was possible. His subsequent researches were embodied in *Supernormal Faculties in Man* (1923). He neither affirmed nor denied survival, inclining to find the source of after-death communication in a "crypto-psychism" which lingers after bodily death.

As the successor of Dr. Gustave **Geley** at the head of the Institut Métapsychique he had unequalled opportunities for investigation and by painstaking care and strictly scientific methods considerably advanced the cause of psychical research. Geley considered him "the first living authority on lucidity as applied to a human being, both under its practical and its theoretical aspect. His book *Supernormal Faculties in Man* (La Connaissance Supranormale) [1923] is truly epochal in the study of subjective metapsychics."

In 1931 and 1932, with the collaboration of his son, Marcel Osty, he employed, for the first time in mediumistic research, infra-red and ultra-violet rays in the study of physical and physiological phenomena of Rudi **Schneider,** the results of which were published in *Les Pouvoirs inconnus de l'esprit sur la matiere* (1932) and formed another important contribution to psychical research.

Dr. Osty died August 20, 1938.

Otani, Soji (1924-)

Japanese psychologist who has conducted research in parapsychology. Born December 8, 1924 in Chiba Prefecture, Honshu, Japan, he studied at University of Tokyo (B.A. 1949). In 1958 he married Yoko Okamoto.

He was a research fellow at the National Institute of Education, Tokyo from 1951-52, instructor at Chiba University, Chiba-shi from 1952-56; lecturer in psychology from 1956-60, assistant professor from 1960 onwards at Defense Academy Yokosuka-shi. He is a charter associate of the Parapsychological Association, and councilor at Japan Psychic Science Association, Tokyo.

Prof. Otani investigated relationships between mental and physiological conditions and ESP scoring. His articles in the *Journal of Psychical Research and Spiritualism* include: 'A Survey of Public Opinion on Psychical Phenomena' (1951), 'The Method of ESP Card Testing' (1951), 'The Aim of Parapsychology' (1955), and in *Journal of Parapsychology:* 'Relations of Mental Set and Change of Skin Resistance to ESP Scores' (vol.19, 1955), and in *Journal of the Department of Liberal Arts* (Defense Academy): 'Studies on the Influence of Mental and Physiological Conditions Upon ESP Function' (1959).

In 1979, a group headed by Prof. Otani studied the remarkable phenomena of the Japanese psychic Masuaki Kiyota in **Metal-bending** and Nengraphy (psychic photography).

O.T.O.

Initialism of the *Ordo Templi Orientis* or Order of Templars of the East, an occult society founded in Germany at the beginning of the twentieth century. One of the leaders was Karl Kellner from Vienna, who had toured in the East and met various yogis and fakirs. He learned about the sexual magic of **Tantric Yoga** and together with other associates (including Heinrich Klein and Franz **Hartmann**) launched the O.T.O., combining Eastern sex-magic with Masonic rituals.

The title of the order was a romantic reference to the sex practices which were the downfall of the original Templars in the fourteenth century, and also intended to suggest that the order had descended from the Knights Templars. Glorification of the Templar idol **Baphomet** was a feature of the O.T.O. ceremonies.

Kellner died in 1905, and his place was taken by Theodor **Reuss,** once a Socialist and associate of Eleonor Marx, but expelled from the British Socialist League because he was a spy for the German Secret Service.

British occultist Aleister **Crowley** had independently discovered the secret of sex magic and made guarded references to it in his writings. Reuss noticed these and visited Crowley in London, suggesting that he join the O.T.O. and be head of a British order. Accordingly Crowley visited Berlin and was initiated, returning as "Supreme and Holy King of Ireland, Iona, and all the Britains there are in the Sanctuary of the Gnosis." He also decided to call himself "Baphomet," in addition to his many other self-bestowed titles (which included "Beast 666").

For a time, Rudolf **Steiner** was also a member of the O.T.O., but he left to found his own society of **Anthroposophy,** with broader and more humanitarian aims than the occultism of the O.T.O.

The O.T.O. seems to have been inactive in Germany during the Nazi regime, but was kept alive elsewhere by Crowley and his associates. After the death of Crowley in 1947, Karl Germer claimed to be head of the order.

In 1955, Kenneth **Grant** set up the **New Isis Lodge** of the O.T.O. in Britain and is now the present head.

Ouija Board

Apparatus for psychic **communication.** The name derives from the French *oui* and the German *Ja* 'yes' and the apparatus consists of a wooden tripod on rollers which, under the hand of the medium, moves over a polished board and spells out messages by pointing out letters with its apex.

As an invention it is very ancient. It was in use in the days of Pythagoras, about 540 B.C. According to a French historical account of the philosopher's life, his sect held frequent seances or circles at which "a mystic table, moving on wheels, moved towards signs, which the philosopher and his pupil, Philolaus, interpreted to the audience as being revelations supposedly from the unseen world."

An improvement of the original ouija board is the finger-like pointer at the narrow end, and a simplification is the replacement of the wooden board by a piece of alphabetical cardboard. If the pointer and the roll at the apex is replaced by a pencil thrust through a bored hole so as to form the third leg, the ouija board is transformed into a **planchette.**

Mrs. Hester **Dowden,** one of the best English automatists, found the ouija board very efficient. "The words come through so quickly that it is almost impossible to read them, and it requires an experienced shorthand writer to take them down when the traveller moves at its maximum speed."

She also believed that the cooperation of two automatists leads to the best results. Three seemed to create confusion. She and her fellow-sitter mostly worked blindfolded. The communications were recorded in silence by a friend. She found these blindfold sittings very exhausting. But they had the great advantage of barring any subconscious guidance of the indicator.

As a rule the ouija board as a method of communication is slow and laborious. But it frequently works with those who fail to get automatic writing with a pencil. (See also **Automatic Writing; Communication; Planchette**)

"Oupnekhat, The"

According to Lewis **Spence** in *An Encyclopaedia of Occultism* (1920), the *Oupnekhat* or *Oupnekhata* (Book of the Secret) is a work written in Persian which gives the following instructions for the production of visions. "To produce the wise Maschqgui (vision), we must sit on a four-cornered base, namely the heels, and then close the gates of the body. The ears by the thumbs; the eyes by the forefingers; the nose by the middle; the lips by the four other fingers. The lamp within the body will then be preserved from wind and movement, and the whole body will be full of light. Like the tortoise, man must withdraw every sense within himself; the heart must be guarded, and then Brahma will enter into him, like fire and lightning. In the great fire in the cavity of the heart a small flame will be lit up, and in its center is Atma (the soul); and he who destroys all worldly desires and wisdom will be like a hawk which has broken through the meshes of the net, and will have become one with the great being." Thus will he become Brahma-Atma (divine spirit), and will perceive by a light that far exceeds that of the sun. "Who, therefore, enters this path by Brahma must deny the world and its pleasures; must only cover his nakedness, and staff in hand collect enough, but no more, alms to maintain life. The lesser ones only do this; the greater throw aside pitcher and staff, and do not even read the *Oupnekhata.*"

This book is clearly a somewhat garbled recension of one of the Hindu *Upanishads.* This is probably from a nineteenth century German translation titled

Das Oupnekhat; die aus den Veden zusammengefasste Lebre von dem Brahm (Dresden, 1882) in turn deriving from an earlier Latin edition of 1801.

There is no single *Upanishad* "Book of Secrets." All the *Upanishads* contain the esoteric wisdom of Hindu metaphysics (deriving from the *Vedas*) and comparable forms of meditation to that prescribed above are also found in various Hindu *Yoga* treatises and also in the *Bhagavad-Gita,* a popular Hindu scripture derived from the *Mahabharata* religious epic. (See also **Meditation; Vedanta; Yoga**)

Ouroboros (or Uroboros)

Ancient Greek alchemical symbol of a serpent eating his tail. The mystical work *The Chrysopoeia of Kleopatra* has a drawing of the Serpent Ouroboros eating his tail, with the text "One is All."

Another emblem illustrates the symbols of gold, silver, and mercury enclosed in two concentric circles with the text "One is the serpent which has its poison according to two compositions" and "One is All and through it is All and by it is All and if you have not All, All is Nothing."

The symbol of Ouroboros can also be interpreted as the unity of sacrificer and sacrificed, relating to the symbolism of the mystical life.

The symbol dates back to Mesolithic (Azilian) culture and has appeared in the symbolism of many races. The Gnostic text *Pistis Sophia* describes the disc of the sun as a great dragon with his tail in his mouth. The fourth-century writer Horopollon stated that the Egyptians represented the universe as a serpent devouring its own tail, a symbol of eternity and immortality, an image also found on Gnostic gems.

The alchemists conceived that the tail-eating dragon was the guardian of mystical treasure, symbolized by the sun, and it was the task of mystical alchemy to destroy or dissolve this guardian as a stage towards knowledge of this treasure.

It also seems possible that the familiar Chinese Yin-Yang symbol may be related to the tail-devouring serpent—here the masculine-feminine principles throughout nature are held in balance.

The Worm Ouroboros (published 1922) is the title of a well-known fantasy adventure story by E. R. Eddison (1882-1945). See also **Alchemy**)

Oursler, Will (William Charles) (1913-)

Author who is concerned with certain areas of parapsychology. Born July 12, 1913 at Baltimore, Maryland, he studied at Harvard College (B.A. cum laude 1937). In 1939 he married Adelaide Burr.

He was formerly a police reporter, magazine editor, and war correspondent accredited to U.S. Army and U.S. Navy in World War II. Memberships include: Overseas Press Club, Dutch Treat Club, The Players, P.E.N., Harvard Club of New York, Baker Street Irregulars. His books include: (with the late Fulton Oursler) *Father Flanagan of Boys Town* (1949), (with Lawrence Dwight Smith) *Narcotics; America's Peril* (1952), *The Boy Scout Story* (1955), *The Healing Power of Faith* (1957), *The Road to Faith* (1960), *Family Story* (1963), *The Atheist* (1965), *Marijuana; The Facts and the Truth* (1968), *Religion; Out or Way Out?* (1968). He has published a number of articles dealing with human problems and religious faith in such magazines as *Collier's, Reader's Digest, True, American Weekly, Photoplay.*

Ousby, W(illiam) J(oseph) (1904-)

British authority on hypnosis, who also studied yoga and African witchcraft at first hand. Born in Liverpool, England, he became a journalist. He later set up as an industrial psychological consultant and studied hypnosis.

He lectured and taught self-hypnosis in Britain, Australia and New Zealand. He spent several years in Africa, where he studied the methods of witch doctors. In India he trained in hatha yoga and investigated fire walking and trance conditions.

He later practiced as a specialist in hypnosis and self-hypnosis in Harley Street, London. His writings include: *A Complete Course of Auto-Hypnosis—Self Hypnotism and Auto-Suggestion* (London & Durban, 1950), *Methods of Inducing and Using Hypnosis* (London, 1951), *The Theory and Practice of Hypnotism* (London, 1967).

Ouspensky, P(eter) D(emianovitch) (1878-1947)

A prominent follower of mystic and occultist G. I. **Gurdjieff** (1877?-1949) and an interpreter of his system. Born in Russia, he was the son of an army officer whose wife was a painter, and the artistic and military characteristics of both parents played a large part in the personality of Ouspensky. He became a student of mathematics at Moscow University, then went on to become a successful journalist.

In 1907 he became aware of Theosophical literature and became interested in the possibility of a synthesis of religion, mysticism and science. In 1909 he published *The Fourth Dimension,* dealing with abstract mathematical concepts. He went on to publish a book on Yoga, then followed his major philosophical work *Tertium Organum; the third canon of thought; a key to the enigmas of the world* (English translation London, 1923). It was a remarkable synthesis of concepts of time, space, relativity, Theosophy, cosmic consciousness, and Eastern and Western philosophy. The Latin title of the book implied a complete reorganization of thought under a Third Canon.

From 1913 onwards, Ouspensky traveled in the East, searching for the miraculous, and upon his return gave a series of lectures on his experiences. In 1915 he met Sophia Grigorievna Maximenko (who later became his wife) and the mystic G. I. Gurdjieff (who became his guru).

Although Gurdjieff had already discovered many of the occult truths for which Ouspensky had searched, his approach was in sharp contrast to Ouspensky's more formal mathematical mind. Ouspensky became an enthusiastic disciple and interpreter of Gurdjieff's system until 1924, when he decided to follow his own pathway, although still impressed by his teacher. He lectured and conducted study groups in England and the U.S. on the work of Gurdjieff until his death in 1947.

His later works, published posthumously include: *A New Model of the Universe* (London, 1948), *In Search of the Miraculous* (London, 1950), *The Strange Life of Ivan Osokin* (English translation of *Kinemadrama*, London, 1948).

For an eyewitness account of Ouspensky's lectures, see Chapter VIII of *God Is My Adventure* by Rom Landau (London, 1935); the book also includes reminiscences of meetings with Gurdjieff.

Out-of-the Body Travel

The belief that individuals can leave their physical bodies during sleep or trance and travel to distant places in an etheric or astral counterpart is a very ancient one. It was an important part of early religious teaching that men and women are essentially spiritual beings, incarnated for divine purpose and shedding the body at death, surviving in an after-life or a new incarnation.

Hindu teachings recognize three bodies—physical, subtle and causal. The causal body builds up the characteristics of one's next reincarnation by the desires and fears in present life, but the subtle body may sometimes leave the physical body during lifetime and reenter it after traveling in the physical world.

The ancient Hindus were well aware of the phenomenon of out-of-the-body traveling, which features in such scriptures as the *Yoga-Vashishta-Maharamayana* of Valmiki. Ancient Egyptian teachings also represented the soul as having the ability to hover outside the physical body in the *Ka* or subtle body.

But it was not until comparatively modern times that any detailed study of experiments in out-of-the-body traveling was published. This was the series of articles in the British journal *The Occult Review* from 1920 onwards by "Oliver Fox" (pseudonym of Hugh G. **Callaway**), later author of the pioneer book *Astral Projection* (1939). Meanwhile an American experimenter Sylvan **J. Muldoon** in collaboration with Hereward **Carrington** published *The Projection of the Astral Body* (1929).

Both Callaway and Muldoon gave detailed first-hand accounts of consciously controlled and involuntary journeys outside the body. Sometimes these involved appearances to other individuals or the obtaining of information which could not have been ascertained by other means. Such accounts were thus highly evidential.

Certain techniques were described by both Callaway and Muldoon for facilitating the release of the astral or etheric body from the physical body. These included visualizing such mental images as flying, or being in an elevator traveling upwards, just before going to sleep. Some involuntary releases occurred as a result of regaining waking consciousness while still in a dream condition. This was often stimulated by some apparent incongruity in the dream, such as dreaming of one's own room but noticing that the wallpaper had the wrong pattern, so that one thought "I must be dreaming!" but continuing in the dream state with waking consciousness (see **Lucid Dreaming**). Such awareness sometimes resulted in normal consciousness apparently *outside* the physical body, and being able to look down at it.

Many individuals who have experienced astral projection describe themselves as joined to the physical body as an infinitely extensible connection, rather like a psychic umbilical cord. This would snatch the astral body back to the physical body if disturbed by fear.

Some cases of astral projection have been reported as a result of anesthetics or even a sudden shock.

In spite of the great importance of out-of-the-body experiences, both as a parapsychological phenomenon and for its relevance to the question of survival after death, it did not receive the attention it deserved until recently, when the British scientist Dr. Robert **Crookall** published a number of books in which he cataloged and analyzed hundreds of cases of astral projection from individuals in all walks of life. It seems that the phenomenon is much more widespread than generally supposed, but some people are sensitive about discussing such experiences. Moreover the majority of cases are of involuntary projection and consciously controlled projection under laboratory conditions is rare.

Dr. Crookall distinguished between the physical body of everyday life, a "vehicle of vitality", and a "Soul Body," connected by an extensible cord. Movement from one body to another is reported as often accompanied by strange sounds and sensations—a "click" in the head, a "blackout" or a "journey down a long tunnel." The projector often sees his own physical body lying on the bed and sometimes the semi-physical vehicle of vitality is observed by other people. Dr. Crookall also cited instances of the strange condition of consciousness in which one sees a "double" of oneself (see also **Double** and **Vardøgr**).

Sometimes the transition from the physical body appears to be assisted by "deliverers" or spirit helpers, or even obstructed by "hinderers."

Again, whilst much astral travel is in the world of everyday life, one sometimes moves in regions of other-worldly beauty or depression, characterized by Dr. Crookall as "Paradise condition" (the finer aura of earth) or "Hades condition" (a kind of purgatorial area). Here one sometimes encounters friends and relatives who died, or even angelic or demonic beings. Return to the physical body is often accompanied by violent loud "repercussion" effects.

Projection may be preceded by a cataleptic condition of the body in which there are **Hypnogogic** illusions. Because of the close association of dreaming and hallucinatory images, many people have dismissed claimed out-of-the-body experiences as illusory or merely dreams, but considerable evidence for the reality of astral projection has been collated by Dr. Crookall and other investigators.

One of the most remarkable controlled experiments in astral projection was that undertaken in 1934 by the talented medium Eileen J. **Garrett,** when a test was set up between observers Dr. Mühl in New York and Dr. D. Svenson in Reykjavik, Iceland. Mrs. Garrett projected her astral double from New York to Iceland and acquired test information afterwards verified as correct. The case is described in her book *My Life as a Search for the Meaning of Mediumship* (1939), although at the time the experimenters were not named, in order to protect their anonymity, and "Newfoundland" was substituted for Reykjavik.

Modern parapsychologists have now given special attention to the phenomenon of out-of-the-body experience, now termed "OBE" or "OOBE." A number of special terms were devised by Celia Green, director of the Institute of Psychophysical Research, Oxford, England, in a scientific study of approximately 400 individuals claiming out-of-the-body experiences.

The general term "ecsomatic" was applied where objects of perception appeared organized in such a way that the observer seemed to observe from a point of view not coincident with the physical body. "Parasomatic" was defined as an ecsomatic experience in which the percipient was associated with a seemingly spatial entity with which he felt himself to be in the same kind of relationship as, in the normal state, with his physical body. "Asomatic" denoted an ecsomatic state in which the subject was temporarily unaware of being associated with any body or spatial entity at all.

The project was discussed fully in Celia Green's book *Out-of-the-Body Experiences* (Oxford, U.K., 1968).

An American investigator who has given special attention to OBE is Dr. Charles T. **Tart** of the University of California at Davis. In 1969 he conducted a number of experiments under control conditions in which the subject was required to read a five-digit number placed on a shelf about five feet above the head. Electrodes were attached to the subject's head and EEG records made, to ensure that the subject did not move physically from the bed. In one of four tests, the subject correctly read the number.

Other experiments have been conducted at the American Society for Psychical Research in New York and the Psychical Research Foundation, Durham, North Carolina. At the ASPR Dr. Karlis **Osis** used a special target box designed to eliminate ordinary ESP. Subjects were invited to "fly-in" astrally and read the target. Over a hundred volunteers participated in the test.

Although Dr. Osis reported that the overall results were not significant, some of the subjects were tested further under laboratory conditions. For a progress report on the experiments see ASPR *Newsletter* (Summer 1974).

At the Psychical Research Foundation, brain wave recordings were taken from OBE subjects, with special attention given to detection of the subject at the target location. There is a suggestion that some subjects may have been able to manifest PK effects while projecting. PK effects had been reported earlier in the experiments of Sylvan J. Muldoon, in the book *The Projection of the Astral Body* (1929).

In 1956, Dr. Hornell **Hart** made a survey of reported apparitions of the dead, which he compared with apparitions of living persons when having OOB experiences. He conclude that "the projected personality carries full memories and purposes."

As with other laboratory experiments in parapsychology, OBE tests lack the incentive or intrinsic interest of involuntary experiences, and acceptable evidence is correspondingly reduced. Many laboratory experimenters regard OOB experiences as a form of traveling clairvoyance. It remains to be seen whether scientists can devise techniques which can validate objectively the important phenomenon of OOB experience.

Meanwhile in the many cases of involuntary projection, the experience itself often has a profound effect on the outlook of the subject, since it seems to give firsthand subjective evidence for the existence of a soul that survives the death of the physical body. Those who attempt to explain away the phenomenon as "hallucination" or "dreaming" are clearly expressing an opinion without evidence, since they would need to have had such an experience themselves in order to evaluate it.

Some psychologists are confident that out-of-the-body experiences can be explained as a hallucinatory mental phenomenon. The British parapsychologist Susan J. **Blackmore** has given special attention to the phenomenon in attempting to discover a psychological explanation. Her book *Beyond the Body* (1981) proposes that the experience is an altered state of consciousness, characterized by vivid imagery, in which the subject's cognitive system is disturbed, losing input control, and replacing normal reality construct with one drawing upon memory.

The experiments and theories of Dr. Blackmore have special interest to parapsychologists because, unlike so many investigators of claimed out-of-the-body phenomena, she has actually had such experience herself. However, her attempts to explain this as a psychological phenomenon, although persuasive, are far from conclusive, and remain speculative. (See also **Astral World; Double; Etheric Double; Ka; Lucid Dreaming**)

Recommended reading:

Battersby, H. F. Prevost. *Man Outside Himself,* London, 1942; University Books, 1969

Black, David. *Ekstasy; Out-of-the-body Experiences,* Bobbs-Merrill, 1975

Blackmore, Susan J. *Beyond The Body; An Investigation of Out-of-the-Body Experiences,* Heinemann, London, 1981

Crookall, Robert. *The Study and Practice of Astral Projection,* London, 1960; University Books, 1966

Crookall, Robert. *Out-of-the-Body Experiences,* University Books, 1970

Crookall, Robert. *Case-Book of Astral Projection, 545-746,* University Books, 1972

Crookall, Robert. *Ecstasy; The Release of the Soul from the Body,* Darshand International, Moradabad, India, 1975

Fox, Oliver. *Astral Projection,* London, 1939; University Books, 1963

Green, Celia E. *Out-of-the-Body Experiences,* Oxford, U.K., 1968

Greenhouse, Herbert B. *Astral Journey; Evidence for Out-of-the-Body Experiences from Socrates to the ESP Laboratory,* Doubleday, 1975

King, Francis. *Astral Projection, Ritual Magic and Alchemy; Being Hitherto Unpublished Golden Dawn Material,* Neville Spearman, London, 1971

Mead, G. R. S. *The Doctrine of the Subtle Body in Western Tradition,* London, 1919

Monroe, Robert A. *Journeys Out of the Body* (introduction by Charles T. Tart), Doubleday, 1971; London, 1972; Corgi, 1974

Muldoon, Sylvan J. & Hereward Carrington. *The Projection of the Astral Body,* London, 1929

Muldoon, Sylvan J. & Hereward Carrington. *The Phenomena of Astral Projection,* London, 1951

Shirley, Ralph. *The Mystery of the Human Double,* London, (1938); University Books (1965)

Smith, Susy. *The Enigma of Out-of-body-Travel,* Garrett/Helix, 1968; Signet, 1968

Turvey, Vincent N. *The Beginnings of Seership,* London, 1911; University Books, 1969

Wilkins, Hubert & Harold Sherman. *Thoughts Through Space,* Frederick Muller, London, 1971 (U.S. edition gives authors as Sherman, Harold & Hubert Wilkins, published Fawcett paperback, 1973)

Yram [pseudonym of Marcel L. Forham]. *Practical Astral Projection* (translated from the French 'Le Medecin de l'Ame'), London (1935); Weiser (c. 1966)

Owen, Alan Robert George (1919-)

British university lecturer who has investigated parapsychology. Born July 4, 1919 at Bristol, England, he studied at Cambridge University (B.A. 1940, M.A. 1945, Ph.D. 1948). In 1952 he married Iris May Pepper.

He was a research fellow at Trinity College, Cambridge from 1948-52, university lecturer in genetics at Cambridge from 1950 onwards, fellow and lecturer in mathematics, Trinity College, Cambridge from 1962 onwards, later removing to Canada with his wife, becoming professor of genetics, and also director of The New Horizons Research Foundation in Toronto. He is a member of the Genetical Society, the Society for Psychical Research and the Biometric Society.

He is the author of a number of scientific papers, and has also taken an interest in **telepathy** and **poltergeist** phenomena. He has contributed a number of papers to the *Journal* and *Proceedings* of the Society for Psychical Research. He studied poltergeist cases in collaboration with Trevor H. **Hall,** and conducted a comprehensive card-guessing test with forty subjects.

He investigated the phenomena of famous British psychic Matthew **Manning** as early as 1966, when he first met Matthew and his family. After Dr. Owen moved to Canada with his wife, he corresponded with Matthew, and in 1974 invited him (then 18 years old) to Toronto, to be studied at a seminar on psychokinesis attended by a number of scientists from various countries.

During this visit, Matthew successfully tried the metal-bending phenomenon popularized by Uri **Geller,** although he did not later continue with his activity, believing it to be pointless. However, some valuable observations were made during the experiments, in which electroencephalograph recordings revealed significant movements toward theta and delta frequencies just before Matthew bent metal objects.

Articles by Dr. Owen published in *New Horizons* include: (with J. P. Rindge & W. Cook) 'An Investigation of Psychic Photography with the Beilleux Family' (Vol. 1, 1972), (with J. Whitton) Proceedings of the First Canadian Conference on Psychokinesis' (vol. 1, 1975).

Books by Dr. Owen include: *Can We Explain the Poltergeist?* (1964), *Hysteria, Hypnosis, and Healing* (1971). (See also Irish M. **Owen**)

Owen, Iris M.

Psychical researcher, formerly a registered nurse in England, volunteer in social work, wife of parapsychologist A. R. G. **Owen.** In Britain, she was a member of the governing board of schools, and chairperson of governors of an approved school for delinquent boys.

She became interested and personally involved in poltergeist phenomena over some twenty years. On removing to Canada with her husband, she became secretary of the Toronto Society for Psychical Research, and also assisted her husband's work at the New Horizons Research Foundation, Toronto.

She was one of the group participating with the remarkable "Philip" experiment, recorded in the book which she co-authored with Margared Sparrow: *Conjuring Up Philip; An adventure in Psychokinesis* (1976). (See also Alan Robert George **Owen; "Philip"**)

Owen, Rev. George Vale (1869-1931)

An outstanding British religious teacher of Spiritualism. He was born June 26, 1869 in Birmingham, England, and was educated at the Midland Institute and Queen's College there. After curacies at Seaforth, Fairfield and Liverpool, he became vicar of Orford, new Warrington. Here he created a new church and worked for twenty years.

After some psychic experiences he developed **automatic writing,** and received, from high spirits, an account of life after death and philosophical teachings. Lord Northcliffe published them in his newspaper the *Weekly Dispatch.* The result was persecution from the Church superiors of the Rev. Vale Owen, whereupon he resigned. After a lecturing tour in America and in England he became pastor of a Spiritualist congregation in London.

His most notable book is *Life Beyond the Veil* which comprises five volumes. Other works included: *Facts and the Future Life* (1922), *On Tour in U.S.A.* (1924), *Paul and Albert* (1925), *The Kingdom of God* (1925), *Problems Which Perplex* (1928), *Body, Soul and Spirit*

(1928), *Jesus the Christ* (1929), *How Spirits Communicate* (n.d.), *What happens After Death* (n.d.), *The Priesthood of the Laity* (n.d.), and, in collaboration with H. A. Dallas, *The Nurseries of Heaven* (1920). His key books were frequently reprinted.

He died March 8, 1931.

A Voice from Heaven (1932) received automatically by clairvoyant Frederick H. **Haines,** contains messages which purported to emanate from the surviving ego of Vale Owen.

Owen, Robert (1771-1858)

Famous British socialist and humanitarian. He was born May 14, 1771 at Newtown, Montgomeryshire. He had some success in the cotton mill industry and in 1800 established a new kind of society based on his cotton mills at New Lanark.

Many years after his socialist experiments and writings, he embraced Spiritualism in his 83rd year after several sittings with Mrs. Maria B. **Hayden,** the first American medium who visited England.

In 1853, in his journal, the *Rational Quarterly Review,* Owen published a formal profession of his new faith and of the grounds on which it rested. In the same year he issued as a separate pamphlet a manifesto, *The Future of the Human Race; or great, glorious and peaceful Revolution, to be effected through the agency of departed spirits of good and superior men and women.* The periodical instalments of his *New Existence of Man Upon Earth* (1854-55) were, for some time, the only English publications dealing with Spiritualism.

Owen established a community at New Lanark, news of which induced the settlers of the Harmony Society in Indiana to sell land to Owen, who purchased Harmony with its mills, factories, houses and land when the Harmonists moved to Pennsylvania. Owen came to the U.S. in December 1824 and established the community of New Harmony, based on socialist principles.

The experiment seems to have been ahead of its time and through mismanagement did not succeed, although Owen's ideals were commendable. For an account of New Harmony see *Strange Cults & Utopius of 19th Century America* by J. H. Noyes (Dover, 1966; former title *History of American Socialisms,* 1870).

On May 14, 1856 at The First Meeting of the Congress of the Reformers of the World, detailed plans, based on spiritually-inspired architectural conceptions, were submitted through Owen's agency for building Homes of Harmony.

Nevertheless, he cannot be ranked as a typical Spiritualist. Communication with the Beyond for him was but another means for the advancement of mankind for which he labored. But it is curious to note that Andrew Jackson Davis, who saw him when lecturing in America in 1846, should have written in November 1847, some months before the advent of the Rochester knockings that according to a message which he received from the spiritual spheres, Robert Owen was destined to hold "open intercourse" with the higher world. Some of the communications which apparently fulfil this prophecy were printed in Owen's autobiography *The Life of Robert Owen* (2 pts., London, 1857-58). Another biography of the same title was published by F. A. Packard (Philadelphia, 1866).

Owen died at Newtown November 17, 1858. (See also Robert Dale **Owen**)

Owen, Robert Dale (1801-1877)

Son of the British socialist Robert Owen. He was born November 9, 1801 in Glasgow, Scotland and educated in Switzerland. He eventually emigrated to America, where he hoped to find more scope for his reforming zeal. He lived for several years in his father's socialistic community New Harmony in Indiana, and served in the Indiana legislature and in Congress.

He introduced the bill organizing the Smithsonian Institution and in 1846 became one of its regents and chairman of its Building Committee. He was a member of the Constitutional Convention in Indiana in 1850. W. Hepworth Dixon calls him, in one of his volumes, "the Privy Councillor of America."

In 1853 Owen was appointed Chargé d'Affaires at Naples and Minister in 1855. He remained there until 1858.

Of his father's attachment to Spiritualism, he heard with pain and regret. But experiences with the famous medium D. D. **Home** during his stay in Naples started him on a career of psychic investigation. He vowed not to rest until he proved **survival** a certainty or delusion.

In the event, he found overwhelming evidence in favor of survival. His book *Footfalls on the Boundaries of Another World* was published in 1860, *The Debatable Land Between this World and the Next* in 1871. Both books attracted wide attention and popularity and were influential in the Spiritualist movement. To Robert Dale Owen Spiritualism became the most profound of all revelations. Until the end of his life he continued to write and speak boldly on the subject. His last book was *Threading My Way; Twenty-Seven Years of Autobiography* (1874)

He had the trials and disappointments in its championship, for example, the scandal surrounding the controversial accusation of cheating on the part of the mediums Mr. and Mrs. Nelson **Holmes** in 1874 almost broke his spirit, but he never went back on the proclamation of its truth.

He died June 17, 1877. (See also Robert **Owen**)

Owen, Ted (1920-)

Psychic who claims contact with Space Intelligences from flying saucers. Unlike most other contactees, he does not claim to have taken a ride on a saucer, but merely uses his brain as a kind of radio set for telepathic messages, which he passes on to anyone interested. The ultimate purpose of the Space Intelligences is that Owens will act as a kind of ambassador for them to world governments.

As a psychic, Owens has a considerable reputation, claiming to control weather, predict events, and heal the sick. He has an IQ of 150, and is a member of Mensa, a well known organization of individuals with high mental test scores. (See also **Space Intelligence; UFO**)

Ozanne, Charles E(ugene) (1865-1961)

History and philosophy teacher, who devoted many years to research in parapsychology after retirement from teaching. Born April 14, 1865 in Cleveland, Ohio, he studied at Western Reserve University, Cleveland (B.A. 1889), Yale University (B.S.T. 1892), Harvard University (M.A. 1895).

He was a history instructor at Harvard and Radcliffe colleges from 1896-97, history and civics teacher at Central High School, Cleveland between 1869 and 1935, instructor in philosophy at Fenn College, Cleveland from 1935-36.

Mr. Ozanne provided financial support for research in parapsychology at Duke University, Durham, North Carolina, and after 1951 moved to Durham so that he could be more closely connected with research at the Parapsychology Laboratory.

In 1961 he took a leading part in setting up the **Psychical Research Foundation, Inc.** at Durham, N.C., an independent research organization concerned with mental, spiritual or personality characteristics and survival after death. The director of the Foundation is W. G. **Roll.**

Mr. Ozanne's own writings include 'Significance of "Non-Evidential" Material in Psychical Research' (*Hibbert Journal,* Oct. 1913), 'A Layman Looks at Psychical Research' (*Journal* of the American Society for Psychical Research, April 1942).

He died April 5, 1961, at Durham, North Carolina.

P

Pack, John L(ee) (1927-   )

Research physicist who has experimented in the field of parapsychology. Born June 7, 1927, at Silver City, New Mexico, he studied at University of New Mexico (B.S. physics 1950, M.S. physics 1952). In 1950 he married Dorothy Mae Tracy.

He has been a research engineer at Westinghouse Research Laboratories, Pittsburgh, Pennsylvania from 1952 onwards. Memberships include: American Institute of Physics, American Physical Society, Institute of Radio Engineers, charter associate of Parapsychological Association.

In addition to his work in physics, Mr. Pack has tested a number of subjects under hypnosis for enhanced extrasensory ability as compared with normal state. He believes that hypnosis may enable subjects to develop ESP.

Page Research Library Newsletter

Publication giving news on apparitions, mysteries and general Fortean phenomena. In 1979, this was merged with *Ohio Sky Watcher* and now appears as *UFO Ohio Newsletter.* Published by **UFO Information Network,** Box 5012, Rome, Ohio 44085.

Pagenstecher, Gustav (1855-1942)

German physician who conducted important experiments in **psychometry.** Born in Germany in 1855, he studied at Leipzig University (M.D.). He practiced medicine in Mexico for some forty years.

One day he treated his patient Mrs. Maria Reyes **Zierold** for insomnia by using hypnosis, and was astonished to discover that she claimed to see beyond closed doors of her room and could describe accurately individuals and events outside the range of normal vision.

With the permission of his patient, Dr. Pagenstecher conducted further experiments to test this paranormal perception, and found that when her normal physical senses were blocked by hypnotic sensation, Mrs. Zierold nevertheless reported sensations of vision, smell, taste, hearing or feelings from objects held by her. These sensations enabled Mrs. Zierold to report information connected with the history or associations of the objects held by her.

In 1919 Dr. Pagenstecher reported on these experiments to a medical society in Mexico City, who appointed a committee to study this psychometric ability. The committee gave Mrs. Zierold pumice stones to hold while in trance, and she accurately reported information concerning the stones, their origin and other details. The committee reported favorably on Dr. Pagenstecher's view that the phenomena appeared genuinely paranormal.

Dr. Pagenstecher reported the facts to the **American Society for Psychical Research** in an article 'A Notable Psychometrist' (*ASPR Journal* vol. 14, 1920), and in 1921 Dr. Walter Franklin **Prince** visited Mexico to observe Pagenstecher's experiments and to conduct his own. Prince too endorsed the phenomena, which he reported in 'Psychometrical Experiments with Señora Maria Reyes de Z.' (*ASPR Journal* vol. 16, Jan. 1922) and a more detailed article under the same title in *ASPR Proceedings* (vol. 15, 1921).

Dr. Pagenstecher also contributed a further article 'Past Events Seership' (*ASPR Proceedings* vol. 16, Jan. 1922) and published a book *Die Geheimnisse der Psychometrie oder Hellsehen in die Vergangenheit* (Secrets of Psychometry or Clairvoyance into the Past, 1928).

Dr. Pagenstecher died December 26, 1942, in Mexico City. (See also **Psychometry;** Maria Reyes **Zierold**)

Paigoels, The

According to Nathaniel E. Kindersley in his book *Specimens of Hindoo Literature* (1794), these were devils of Hindustan mythology. Some of the Hindus believed that the *paigoels* were originally created devils; others that they were put out of heaven because of their great sin, and of all worlds that the earth was the only one with which they are allowed intercourse.

Some of these devils had individual names, and were the tempters of men to special sins,—others again enter into the bodies of men and took possession of them. It was also believed that the souls of wicked men went to join the number of the *paigoels.*

Palingenesy

A term employed by the philosophers of the seventeenth century to denote the "resurrection of plants," and the method of achieving their astral appearance after destruction.

In very early times, philosophers were inclined to doubt if **apparitions** might not be accounted for on natural principles, without supposing that a belief in them was either referable to **hallucinations,** to human imagination, or to impositions that might have been practiced.

The Roman poet philosopher Lucretius (c. 98-55 B.C.) attacked the popular notion of ghosts by maintaining that they were not spirits returned from the mansions of the dead, but nothing more than thin films, pellicles, or membranes, cast off from the surface of all bodies like the exuviæ or sloughs of reptiles.

An opinion by no means dissimilar to that of the Epicureans was revived in Europe about the middle of the seventeenth century. It had its origin in Palingenesy, or the "resurrection of plants," a grand secret known to Sir Kenelm Digby, Athanasius Kircher, Abbé de Vallemont and others. These philosophers performed the operation of Palingenesy in the following manner.

They took a plant, bruised it, burnt it, collected its ashes, and, in the process of calcination, extracted from it a salt. This salt they then put into a glass vial, and mixed with it some peculiar substance, which they have not disclosed.

When the compound was formed, it was pulverulent, and possessed a bluish color. The powder was next submitted to a gentle heat, when its particles being instantly put into motion, there then gradually arose (it was claimed), as from the midst of the ashes, a stem, leaves and flowers; in other words, an apparition of the plant which had been submitted to combustion.

But as soon as the heat was taken away, the form of the plant which had been thus sublimed, was precipitated to the bottom of the vessel. Heat was then reapplied and the vegetable phoenix was resuscitated; it was withdrawn, and the form once more became latent among the ashes.

This notable experiment was said to have been performed before the Royal Society of England, and to have satisfactorily proved to this learned body that the presence of heat gave a sort of life to the vegetable apparition, and that the absence of caloric caused its death.

The poet Abraham Cowley was quite delighted with the story of the experiment of the rose and its ashes, and in conceiving that he had detected the same phenomenon in letters written with the juice of lemons, which were revived on the application of heat, he celebrated the mystic power of caloric in the following manner:

"Strange power of heat, thou yet dost show,
Like winter earth, naked, or cloth'd with snow,
But as the quick'ning sun approaching near,
The plants arise up by degrees,
A sudden paint adorns the trees,
And all kind nature's characters appear.

So nothing yet in thee is seen,
But when a genial heat warms thee within,
A new-born wood of various lines there grows;
Here buds an A, and there a B,
Here sprouts a V, and there a T,
And all the flourishing letters stand in rows."

The rationale of this famous experiment made on the ashes of roses was attempted by Kircher. He supposed that the seminal virtue of every known substance and even its substantial form resided in its salt. This salt was concealed in the ashes of the rose. Heat put it in motion. The particles of the salt were quickly sublimed, and being moved about in the vial like a vortex, at length arranged themselves in the same general form they had possessed from nature.

It was evident, then, from the claimed result of this experiment, that there was a tendency in the particles of the salt to observe the same order of position which they had in the living plant. Thus, for instance, each saline corpuscle, which in its prior state had held a place in the stem of the rose-slip, sympathetically fixed itself in a corresponding position when sublimed in the chemist's vial. Other particles were subject to a similar law, and accordingly, by a disposing affinity, resumed their proper position, either in the stalk, the leaves, or the flowers, and thus, at length, the entire apparition of a plant was generated.

The next object of these philosophers was to apply their doctrine to the explanation of the popular belief in ghosts. As the experimenters claimed that it was proved that the substantial form of each body resided in a sort of volatile salt, it was perfectly evident in what manner superstitious notions must have arisen about ghosts haunting churchyards. When a dead body had been committed to the earth, the salts of it, during the heating process of fermentation, were exhaled. The saline particles then each resumed the same relative situation they had held in the living body, and thus a complete human form was induced, calculated to excite superstitious fear in the minds of all but Palingenesists.

It is thus evident that Palingenesy was similar to the early claims of Lucretius involving a chemical explanation of the discovery of filmy substances which he had observed to arise from all bodies.

Yet, in order to prove that apparitions might be really explained on this principle, a crucial experiment was necessary. This deficiency was soon supplied.

Three alchemists had obtained a quantity of earth-mould from St. Innocent's Church in Paris, supposing that this matter might contain the true **philosopher's stone.** They subjected it to a distillatory process. Suddenly they perceived (it was claimed) the forms of men produced, in their vials which immediately cause them to desist from their labors. This was brought to the attention of the Institute of Paris (under the protection of Louis XIV) and this learned body took up the business with much seriousness. The result of their own investigations appeared in the *Miscellania Curiosa.* Dr. James F. Ferrier, in a volume of the *Manchester Philosophical Transactions,* made an abstract of one of these French documents, as follows:

"A malefactor was executed, of whose body a grave physician got possession for the purpose of dissection. After disposing of the other parts of the body, he ordered his assistant to pulverize part of the cranium, which was a remedy at that time admitted in dispensatories. The powder was left in a paper on the table of the museum, where the assistant slept. About midnight he was awakened by a noise in the room, which obliged him to rise immediately. The noise continued about the table, without any visible agent; and at length he traced it to the powder, in the midst of which he now beheld, to his unspeakable dismay, a small head with open eyes staring at him; presently two branches appeared, which formed into arms and hands; then the ribs became visible, which were soon clothed with muscles and integuments; next the lower extremities sprouted out, and when they appeared perfect, the puppet (for his size was small) reared himself on his feet; instantly his clothes came upon him, and he appeared in the very cloak he wore at his execution. The affrighted spectator, who stood hitherto mumbling his prayers with great application, now thought of nothing but making his escape from the revived ruffian; but this was impossible, for the apparition planted himself in the way, and, after divers fierce looks and threatening gestures, opened the door and went out. No doubt the powder was missing next day."

But older analogous results are on record, suggesting that the blood was the chief part of the human frame in which those saline particles resided, the arrangements of which gave rise to the popular notion of ghosts. John Webster, in his book *The Displaying of Supposed Witchcraft* (1677), related an experiment, given on the authority of Robert **Fludd,** in which this conclusion was drawn.

"A certain chymical operator, by name La Pierre, near that place in Paris called Le Temple, received blood from the hands of a certain bishop to operate upon. Which he setting to work upon the Saturday, did continue it for a week with divers degrees of fire. But about midnight, the Friday following, this artificer, lying in a chamber next to his laboratory, betwixt sleeping and waking, heard a horrible noise, like unto the lowing of kine, or the roaring of a lion; and continuing quiet, after the ceasing of the sound in the laboratory, the moon being at the full, and, by shining enlightening the chamber suddenly, betwixt himself and the window he saw a thick little cloud, condensed into an oval form, which, after, by little and little, did seem completely to put on the shape of a man, and making another and a sharp clamour, did suddenly vanish. And not only some noble persons in the next chambers, but also the host with his wife, lying in a lower room of the house, and also the neighbours dwelling in the opposite side of the street, did distinctly hear as well the bellowing as the voice; and some of them were awaked with the vehemency thereof.

"But the artificer said, that in this he found solace, because the bishop, of whom he had it, did admonish him, that if any of them from whom the blood was extracted should die, in the time of its putrefaction, his spirit was wont often to appear to the sight of the artificer, with perturbation. Also forthwith, upon Saturday following, he took the retort from the furnace, and broke it with the light stroke of a little key, and there, in the remaining blood, found the perfect representation of an human head, agreeable in face, eyes, nostrils, mouth, and hairs, that were somewhat thin, and of a golden colour."

Regarding this narrative Webster added: "There were many ocular witnesses, as the noble person, Lord of Bourdalone, the chief secretary to the Duke of Guise; and he [Fludd] had this relation from the Lord of Menanton, living in that house at the same time from a certain doctor of physic, from the owner of the house, and many others."

Apart from such credulous statements, it is hardly necessary to stress that the claimed results of early experiments in Palingenesy have not been validated by modern science, but there have been curious echoes of the subject in borderland researches.

Dr. Charles W. Littlefield, a physician of Seattle, Washington, published a book titled *"M. M. M."—Man, Minerals and Masters* (De Vorss, 1937) in which he described his experiments "To show by demonstration and illustration that thoughts are things, and that their power may be expressed through certain mineral compounds" occurring in organic nature. Dr. Littlefield claims that the crystallization of solutions of organic salts could be modified by mental energy, and stated that he had produced microscopic animal or human-like forms in this way.

The work of another experimenter was reminiscent of the seventeenth-century Royal Society claim of the restoration of the form of a plant which had been destroyed. In the 1920s, a British biological chemist named Morley-Martin claimed that the forms of fishes, plants and animals continued to exist in miniature in ancient azoic rocks. Morley-Martin experimented by taking fragments of such rock and submitting it to a temperature of 2-3,000 degrees Fahrenheit in an electric oven. From the ashes he isolated what he named "primordial protoplasm" which became transformed into crystalloids by Canada balsam. In the course of time, the crystalloids condensed and gave birth to numerous organisms which were miniature creatures, even having life and movement.

These little-known and bizarre experiments were described by Maurice **Maeterlinck** in his book *La Grande Porte* (Paris, 1939), and the work of both Littlefield and Morley-Martin was described in the booklet *The Morley-Martin Experiments* (BSRA booklets No. 1, 1948) issued by the Borderland Sciences Research Associates of San Diego, California.

In these experiments, Palingenesy merges with the old theory of "Spontaneous Generation" which was considered to have been solved by Louis Pasteur's experiments on micro-organisms, although Prof. P. J. A. Béchamp in France and H. Charlton Bastian in Britain claimed that Pasteur's work did not cover all the facts (see also **Homunculus; Paracelsus**).

Of possible relevance to the Palingenesy experiments were the "osmotic growths" produced by Dr. Stéphane Leduc of Nantes. These were formed from crystal solutions and not only presented the cellular structure of living matter, but also reproduced such functions as absorption of food, metabolism and the excretion of waste products. These beautiful growths are described in Leduc's book *The Mechanism of Life* (1914). (See also **Apparitions**)

Palladino, Eusapia (1854-1918)

(Signora Raphael Delgaiz by marriage) the first physical medium who stood in the crossfire of collective scientific investigation for more than twenty years all over Europe and in America. It was in large measure due to this strange woman that the reality of physical phenomena and the psychological complex of fraud was, at the close of the last and in the first decade of the present century, vividly brought home to an array of brilliant minds.

She was born at Minervo-Murge, near Bari, Italy, on January 21, 1854. Her birth cost her mother's life. Her father was assassinated by brigands in 1866. As a little girl she heard **raps** on the furniture against which she was leaning; she saw eyes glaring at her in the darkness and was frequently frightened in the night when invisible hands stripped off her bedclothes.

When she became orphaned, a family of the upper bourgeoisie received her in Naples as a nursemaid. They soon detected that she was not an ordinary girl, but her real discovery and mediumistic education was due to Signor Damiani, a noted Italian psychic investigator. His wife, an English lady, went to a seance in London. "John King" manifested and spoke about a powerful medium in Naples who was his reincarnated daughter. He gave her address, street and number.

Damiani went to the house and found Eusapia Palladino of whom he had never heard before. This was in 1872. The development of Eusapia Palladino's powers progressed at a rapid rate. In the first five or six years she devoted herself mainly to phenomena of **movements** without contact. Then came the famous spectral appearances, the phantom limbs so often noticed to issue from her body and **materialization** of full but incomplete figures.

Her **control** "John King" communicated through raps and in trance spoke in Italian alone. Eusapia Palladino was always impressed what phenomenon was going to take place and could warn the sitters. She suffered extremely during the process and exhibited a very remarkable synchronism between her gestures and the movement without contact. If she glared defiantly at a table it began to move towards her, if she warned it off it backed away. A forcible motion of her head was accompanied by raps and upward movements of her hand would cause the table to lift in the air.

Another peculiarity of her seances was that any particular phenomenon had to be wished for and incessantly asked. Strong desire on the part of the sitters present usually brought about the occurrence.

The first scientist who boldly proclaimed the reality of her extraordinary phenomena was Dr. Ercole **Chiaia.** His opportunity to invite public attention to Eusapia Palladino came when Prof. Cesare **Lombroso** published an article on "The Influence of Civilisation upon Genius" and in it concluded: "Twenty or thirty years are enough to make the whole world admire a discovery which was treated as madness at the moment when it was made. Even at the present day academic bodies laugh at hypnotism and homœopathy. Who knows whether my friends and I, who laugh at Spiritualism, are not in error, just as hypnotised persons are?"

On August 9, 1888 Chiaia addressed an open letter to Lombroso and challenged him to observe a special case, saying: "The case I allude to is that of an invalid woman who belongs to the humblest class of society. She is nearly thirty years old and very ignorant; her appearance is neither fascinating nor endowed with the power which modern criminologists call irresistible; but when she wishes, be it by day or by night, she can divert a curious group for an hour or so with the most surprising phenomena. Either bound to a seat, or firmly held by the hands of the curious, she attracts to her the articles of furniture which surround her, lifts them up, holds them suspended in the air like Mahomet's coffin, and makes them come down again with undulatory movements, as if they were obeying her will. She increases their height or lessens it according to her pleasure. She raps or taps upon the walls, the ceiling, the floor, with fine rhythm and cadence. In response to the requests of the spectators something like flashes of electricity shoot forth from her body, and envelop her or enwrap the spectators of these marvellous scenes. She draws upon cards that you hold out, everything that you want—figures, signatures, numbers, sentences—by just stretching out her hand towards the indicated place.

"If you place in the corner of the room a vessel containing a layer of soft clay, you find after some moments the imprint in it of a small or a large hand, the image of a face (front view or profile) from which a plaster cast can be taken. In this way portraits of a face at different angles have been preserved, and those who desire so to do can thus make serious and important studies.

"This woman rises in the air, no matter what bands tie her down. She seems to lie upon the empty air, as on a couch, contrary to all the laws of gravity; she plays on musical instruments—organs, bells, tambourines—as if they had been touched by her hands or moved by the breath of invisible gnomes. This woman at times can increase her stature by more than four inches.

"She is like an India rubber doll, like an automaton of a new kind; she takes strange forms. How many legs and arms has she? We do not know. While her limbs are being held by incredulous spectators, we see other limbs coming into view, without her knowing where they come from. Her shoes are too small to fit these witch-feet of hers, and this particular circumstance gives rise to the suspicion of the intervention of mysterious power."

It was not until two years later that Lombroso found time enough to visit Naples for a sitting. His first report stated: "Eusapia's feet and hands were held by Professor Tamburini and by Lombroso. A handbell placed on a small table more than a yard distant from Eusapia sounded in the air above the heads of the sitters and then descended on the table, thence going two yards to a bed. While the bell was ringing we struck a match and saw the bell up in the air."

A detailed account of his observations and reflections appeared in the *Annales des Sciences Psychiques* in 1892. Lombroso admitted the reality of the phenomena and, on the basis of the analogy of the **transposition of the senses** observed in hypnotic cases, suggested a transformation of the powers of the medium as an explanation. He continued his researches for many years and ended in the acceptance of the spirit theory.

In his book *After Death—What?* (1909) he gave the following character sketch of his medium: "Her culture is that of a villager of the lower order. She frequently fails in good sense and in common sense, but has a subtlety and intuition of the intellect in sharp contrast with her lack of cultivation, and which make her, in spite of that, judge and appreciate at their true worth the men of genius whom she meets, without being influenced in her judgments by prestige or the false stamp that wealth and authority set upon people.

"She is ingenuous to the extent of allowing herself to be imposed on and mystified by an intriguer, and, on the other hand, sometimes exhibits, both before and during her trance states, a slyness that in some cases goes as far as deception. . . .

"She possesses a most keen visual memory, to the extent of remembering five to ten mental texts presented to her during three seconds. She has the ability to recall very vividly, especially with her eyes shut, the outlines of persons, and with a power of vision so precise as to be able to delineate their characteristic traits.

"But she is not without morbid characteristics, which sometimes extend to hysterical insanity. She passes rapidly from joy to grief, has strange phobias (for example the fear of staining her hands), is extremely impressionable and subject to dreams in spite of her mature age. Not rarely she has hallucinations, frequently sees her own ghost. As a child she believed two eyes glared at her from behind trees and hedges. When she is in anger, especially when her reputation as a medium is insulted, she is so violent and impulsive as actually to fly at her adversaries and beat them.

"These tendencies are offset in her by a singular kindness of heart which leads her to lavish her gains upon the poor and upon infants in order to relieve their misfortunes, and which impels her to feel foundless pity for the old and weak. . . . The same goodness of heart drives her to protect animals that are being maltreated, by sharply rebuking their cruel oppressors."

It is interesting to add here the description of Arthur Levy in his report on a seance held in the house of Camille **Flammarion** in 1898: "Two things arrest the attention when you look at her. First, her large eyes, filled with strange fire, sparkle in their orbits, or again, seem filled with swift gleams of phosphorescent fire, sometimes bluish, sometimes golden. If I did not fear that the metaphor was too easy when it concerns a Neapolitan woman, I should say that her eyes appear like the glowing lava fires of Vesuvius, seen from a distance in a dark night. The other peculiarity is a mouth with strange contours. We do not know whether it expresses amusement, suffering or scorn."

Lombroso made a thorough psychological study of Eusapia. He wrote: "Many are the crafty tricks she plays, both in the state of trance (unconsciously) and out of it—for example, freeing one of her two hands, held by the controllers, for the sake of moving objects near her; making touches; slowly lifting the legs of the table by means of one of her knees and one of her feet, and feigning to adjust her hair and then slyly pulling out one hair and putting it over the little balance tray of a letter-weigher in order to lower it. She was seen by Faifofer, before her seances, furtively gathering flowers in a garden, that she might feign them to be 'apports' by availing herself of the shrouding dark of the room."

Similar observations were made by Prof. Enrico **Morselli** and later investigators. Her penchant to cheat caused Eusapia no end of trouble in her later years.

The sittings in Naples which started Lombroso on his career as a psychical researcher were followed by an investigation in Milan in 1892. Prof. Schiaparelli, Director of the Observatory of Milan, Prof. Gerosa, Dr. G. B. **Ermacora,** Alexander **Aksakof,** Baron Carl **du Prel** and Prof. Charles **Richet** were among the members of the Milan Commission. Part of the report, based on a series of seventeen sittings, said: "It is impossible to count the number of times that a hand appeared and was touched by one of us. Suffice it to say that doubt was no longer possible. It was indeed a living human hand which we saw and touched, while at the same time the bust and the arms of the medium remained visible, and her hands were held by those on either side of her."

At the end of the report the conviction was expressed: "1) That in the circumstances given, none of the phenomena obtained in more or less intense light could have been produced by the aid of any artifice whatever.

2) That the same opinion may be affirmed in a large measure with regard to the phenomena obtained in complete darkness. For some of them we can well admit, strictly speaking, the possibility of imitating them by means of some adroit artifice on the part of the medium; nevertheless, according to what we have said, it is evident that this hypothesis would be not only improbable, but even useless in the present case, since even admitting it, the assembly of facts clearly proved would not be invalidated by it."

In the following year, a series of seances took place in Naples under direction of Prof. Wagner of the University of St. Petersburg, next in Rome in 1893-94 under the direction of M. de Semiradski, interrupted by a visit to Warsaw where Dr. Julien Ochorowitz made many important experiments. He worked out the hypothesis of a "fluidic double" which, under certain conditions, detaches itself and acts independently of the body of the medium. In 1894 at the house of Prof. Richet on the Ile Roubaud, Sir Oliver **Lodge** and F. W. H. **Myers** had their first opportunity to witness genuine physical phenomena of an unusual order. Lodge reported to the **Society for Psychical Research** that as regards the fact of movement without contact there was no further room in his mind for doubt.

Dr. Richard **Hodgson,** who was then resident in Boston, criticized the report and pointed out that the precautions described did not exclude trickery. He suggested explanations for various phenomena on the theory that Eusapia could get a hand or foot free. Lodge, Myers and Richet each replied. Richet pointed out that he attended fifteen seances with Eusapia in Milan and Rome and held forty at Carqueiranne and in the Ile Roubaud over a period of three months under his own supervision. He finished by saying: "It appears to me that after three months' practice and meditation one can arrive at the certainty of holding well a human hand."

As an outcome of the critical reception of this report Eusapia was invited to England. In August and September 1895, at the house of Myers in Cambridge, twenty sittings were held. Dr. Hodgson came from Boston to be present and J. N. **Maskelyne,** the professional conjurer, was also invited. The sitters' attitude was not so much to prevent fraud as to detect it. Dr. Hodgson intentionally left Eusapia's hand free. She was given every opportunity to cheat and she availed herself of this generosity.

In communicating the findings of the Cambridge investigation to the Society for Psychical Research, Myers, who on the Ile Roubaud was convinced of having witnessed supernormal phenomena, stated: "I cannot doubt that we observed much conscious and deliberate fraud, of a kind which must have needed long practice to bring it to its present level of skill. Nor can I find any excuse for her fraud (assuming that such excuse would be valid) in the attitude of mind of the persons, several of them distinguished in the world of science, who assisted in this inquiry. Their attitude was a fair and open one; in all cases they showed patience, and in several cases the impression first made on their minds was distinctly favourable. With growing experience, however, and careful observation of the precise conditions permitted or refused to us, the existence of some fraud became clear; and fraud was attempted when the tests were as good as we were allowed to make them, quite as indisputably as on the few occasions when our holding was intentionally left inadequate in order to trace more exactly the *modus operandi.* Moreover, the fraud occurred both in the medium's waking state and during her real or alleged trance. I do not think there is adequate reason to suppose that any of the phenomena at Cambridge were genuine."

In the very month of the exposure a new series of experiments was made at l'Agnelas, in the residence of Col. **Rochas,** president of the Polytechnic School, Dr. Dariex, editor of the *Annales des Sciences Psychiques,* Count de Gramont, Dr. J. **Maxwell,** Prof. Sabatier and Baron de Watteville participated. They all attested that the phenomena produced were genuine. On the result of the observations Col. Rochas built up his theory of "Externalisation of motricity."

The Cambridge report was not well received by psychical researchers.

Sir Oliver Lodge only attended two of the sittings and declared that he failed to see any resemblance between the phenomena there produced and those witnessed on the Ile Roubaud. He stated that his belief in what he there observed remained unshaken.

Dr. Ochorowitz remarked that Eusapia frequently released her hand for no other reason than to touch her head which was in pain at the moment of the manifestations. It was a natural reflex movement and a fixed habit. Immediately before the mediumistic doubling of her personality, her hand was affected with hyperaesthesia and consequently, the pressure of the hand of another made her ill, especially in the dorsal quarter. The medium acted by autosuggestion and the order to go as far as an indicated point was given by her brain simultaneously to the dynamic hand and the corporeal hand, since in the normal state they form only one. It sometimes happened that the dynamic hand remained in place, while her own hand went in the indicated direction.

Dr. Ochorowitz concluded that "not only was *conscious* fraud not proved on Eusapia at Cambridge, but not the slightest effort was made to do so. *Unconscious* fraud was proved in much larger proportion than in all the preceding experiments. This negative result is vindicated by a blundering method little in accordance with the nature of the phenomena."

"I cannot help thinking," wrote Dr. J. Maxwell in his book *Metapsychical Phenomena* (1905), "that the Cambridge experimenters were either ill-guided, or ill-favoured, for I have obtained raps with Eusapia Palladino in full light, I have obtained them with many other mediums, and it is a minimum phenomenon which they could have and ought to have obtained, had they experimented in a proper manner."

"The Italian medium, Eusapia Palladino," wrote Miss Goodrich Freer in her book *Essays in Psychical Research* (1899), "may have been a fraud of the deepest dye for anything I know to the contrary, but she never had a fair chance in England. Even her cheating seems to have been badly done. The atmosphere was inimical; the poor thing was paralysed."

It appears plainly from the *Journal* of the Society for Psychical Research that the dynamic hands of which Ochorowitz spoke created a strong presumption against Eusapia. The paper said: "It is hardly necessary to remark that the continuity of the spirit limbs with the body of the medium is, *prima facie,* a circumstance strongly suggestive of fraud."

The reality of these phantom limbs was later sufficiently proved. Also the fact that Eusapia would resort to fraud whenever allowed to had gained a wider recognition. Camille Flammarion threw an interesting light on the problem in saying: "She is frequently ill on the following day, sometimes even on the second day following, and is incapable of taking any nourishment without immediately vomiting. One can readily conceive, then, that when she is able to perform certain wonders without any expenditure of force and merely by a more or less skillful piece of deception, she prefers the second procedure to the first. It does not exhaust her at all, and may even amuse her. Let me remark, in the next place, that, during these experiments, she is generally in a half-awake condition which is somewhat similar to the hypnotic or somnambulistic sleep. Her fixed idea is to produce phenomena; and she produces them, no matter how."

On December 1, 1898, a seance was arranged in Prof. Richet's library in Paris for the purpose of assisting Eusapia to regain her reputation. The seance took place in good light, her wrists and ankles were held by the sitters and before each experience she warned the sitters what she was going to do in order that they might establish the phenomenon to the best of their faculties and observation. She did not cease to admonish Myers to pay the closest attention and to remember exactly afterwards what had happened. "Under these conditions," wrote Prof. Theodore **Flournoy,** "I saw phenomena which I then believed, and still believe, to be certainly inexplicable by any known laws of physics and physiology."

When Myers was solemnly adjured by Prof. Richet to state his view, he avowed his renewed belief in the supernormal character of Eusapia's mediumship. Many other distinguished converts were made as the years passed. Prof. Lombroso finally adopted the spirit hypothesis and Flammarion became firmly convinced of the reality of Eusapia's phenomena.

In 1901, Genoa was the scene of important experiments in the presence of Enrico Morselli, Professor of Psychology at the University of Genoa and the astronomer Porro, director of the observatories of Genoa, Turin and later La Plata in the Argentine. Much instrumental investigation was carried on by Doctors Herdlitzka, Charles Foà and Aggazotti, assistants of Professor Mosso, the distinguished physiologist, in Turin and by Prof. Philippe **Bottazzi,** Director of the Physiological Institute at the University of Naples, with the assistance of six other professors.

The Institut Général Psychologique of Paris carried on extensive experiments in 43 sittings from 1905-07. M. and Mme. Curie were among the investigators. Fraud and genuine phenomena were observed in a strange mixture. The report drawn up by Jules Courtier admitted that movements seem to be produced by simple contact with the medium's hands, or even without contact, that such movements were registered by automatic recording instruments which rules out the hypothesis of collective hallucination and that molecular vibrations in external objects at a distance can be positively asserted. They explained the fraud by suggesting that Eusapia was growing old and that she was strongly tempted not to disappoint her clients when genuine power failed. On the whole the phenomena were much less striking and abundant as the years passed. They theorized that Eusapia influenced the ether in some way. On one or two occasions she succeeded in discharging an electroscope without anybody being able to find out how it was done.

In consequence of this report and under the effect of a growing number of testimonies to the genuine powers of Eusapia, the Council of the Society for Psychical Research reconsidered its attitude and delegated in 1908 a committee of three very capable and skeptical investigators; Mr. W. W. **Baggally,** a practical conjurer, Dr. Hereward **Carrington,** an amateur conjurer, whose book *The Physical Phenomena of Spiritualism* (1907) is a reliable authority on fraudulent performances, and the Hon. Everard **Feilding,** who also brought many a fraudulent medium to grief. They held eleven sittings in November and December in a room of a member of the committee at the Hotel Victoria in Naples.

At the end, they admitted that the phenomena were genuine and inexplicable by fraud. Their report was published as Part 59 of the *Proceedings* of the Society for Psychical Research, and even Frank **Podmore,** the most hardened skeptic of the time, felt compelled to say: "Here, for the first time perhaps in the history of modern spiritualism, we seem to find the issue put fairly and squarely before us. It is difficult for any man who reads the Committee's report to dismiss the whole business as mere vulgar cheating." Nevertheless, Podmore tried his best.

It is sufficient, however, against any outside criticism to quote the opinion of the Hon. Everard Feilding as expressed after the sixth seance: "For the first time I have absolute conviction that our observation is not mistaken. I realise as an appreciable fact in life that, from an empty curtain, I have seen hands and heads come forth, and that behind the empty curtain I have been seized by living fingers, the existence and position of the nails of which were perceptible. I have seen this extraordinary woman, sitting outside the curtain, held hand and foot, visible to myself, by my colleagues, immobile, except for the occasional straining of a limb while some entity within the curtain has over and over again pressed my hand in a position clearly beyond her reach. I refuse to entertain the possibility of a doubt that it could be anything else, and, remembering my own belief of a very short time ago. I shall not be able to complain, though I shall unquestionably be annoyed when I find that to be the case."

By this verdict, the standing of Eusapia Palladino was enormously enhanced, and not without reason. Prof. Richet wrote "There have perhaps never been so many different, sceptical and scrupulous investigators into the work of any medium or more minute investigations. During twenty years, from 1888 to 1908, she submitted, at the hands of the most skilled European and American experimentalists, to tests of the most rigorous and decisive kind, and during all this time men of science, resolved not to be deceived, have verified that even very large and massive objects were displaced without contact."

In discussing materializations he added: "More than thirty very sceptical scientific men were convinced, after long testing, that there proceeded from her body material forms having the appearances of life."

The most extraordinary seance recorded with Eusapia was probably the one described in full detail by Prof. Morselli in *Psicologia e 'Spiritismo'* (Turin, 1908, vol. 2, pp. 214-237). The seance was held in Genoa on March 1, 1902. Besides Morselli, Ernesto Bozzano, Dr. Venzano and six other persons were present. The cabinet was examined by Morselli. He himself tied the medium to a camp bed in a manner defying attempts at liberation. In fairly good light six phantoms presented themselves in succession in front of the cabinet, the last one being a woman with a baby in her arms. Each time after the phantom retired, Morselli rushed into the cabinet and found the medium tied as he left her. No doubt was left in Morselli's mind of the genuineness of the phenomena, yet strangely his materialistic attitude remained unshaken.

Still one final blow was in store for Eusapia. Owing to the success of the Naples sittings, the story of which was ably told in Hereward Carrington's *Eusapia Palladino and her Phenomena* (1909), she was invited in 1909 to visit America. She landed in New York on November 10, 1909, and left on June 18, 1910.

Her first twenty seances were comparatively good ones. In the later sittings at Columbia University and at the house of Prof. Lord she was caught in the use of her old trickery. The Press made a tremendous sensation of the exposure. The authenticity of the published account, however, was questioned by Carrington. It said that at a sitting held on December 18, a young man crept under the cover of darkness into the cabinet and during the movement of a small table, while Prof. Munsterberg was controlling the left foot of Eusapia, the young man grabbed a human foot, unshod, by the instep. It proved to be Eusapia's foot pulled out of the shoe. Later she was watched from a concealed window in the cabinet and from a bureau provided with a secret peephole. She was seen to achieve the desired effect by gradual substitution, making one foot do duty for two as regards the control of her limbs, and acting freely with the liberated foot.

It had not been emphasized that Eusapia, at this stage, was so apprehensive of her investigators that she did not allow herself to go into trance for fear that an injury might be done to her. The psychological attitude of her sitters was reflected by the following statement of Eusapia to a newspaper man: "Some people are at the table who expect tricks—in fact they want them. I am in a trance. Nothing happens. They get impatient. They think of the tricks—nothing but tricks. They put their minds on the tricks and I automatically respond. But it is not often. They merely will me to do them. That is all."

Carrington contended that far from having been exposed in America, as the public imagined, Eusapia presented a large number of striking phenomena which have never been explained and that only a certain number of her classical and customary tricks were detected, which every investigator of this medium's phenomena had known to exist and had warned other investigators against for the past twenty years. No new form of trickery was discovered and against the old and well-known methods Carrington warned the sitters in a circular letter in advance. This is why the American exposure did not influence the European investigators in the least.

When her power was strong, the phenomena began almost at once. When it was weak, long waiting was necessary. It was on such occasions that she was tempted to cheat. She did this so often that, as Carrington stated: "practically every scientific committee detected her in attempted fraud, but every one of these committees emerged from their investigations quite convinced of the reality of these phenomena, except the Cambridge and American investigation which ended in exposure."

Nevertheless, Eusapia did not depart from America without making one interesting convert. Howard Thurston, the famous stage magician, declared: "I witnessed in person the table levitations of Madame Eusapia Palladino . . . and am thoroughly convinced that the phenomena I saw were not due to fraud and were not performed by the aid of her feet, knees, or hands."

He also offered to give a thousand dollars to a charitable institution if it could be proved that Eusapia could not levitate a table without trickery.

Writing of the Naples and of the American investigation, Carrington summed up his views in his book *The Story of Psychic Science* (1930): "To sum up the effects of these seances upon my own mind, I may say that, after seeing nearly forty of her seances, there remains not a shadow of doubt in my mind as to the reality of the vast majority of this phenomena occurring in Eusapia Palladino's presence . . . I can but record the fact that further study of this medium has convinced me more than ever that our Naples experiments and deductions were correct, that we were not deceived, but that we did, in very truth, see praeternormal manifestations of a remarkable character. I am as assured of the reality of Eusapia Palladino's phenomena as I am of any other fact in life; and they are, to my mind, just as well established."

Mme. Paole Carrara, the daughter of Prof. Lombroso, published a biography of Eusapia in 1907.

A comprehensive bibliography of Eusapia is to be found in Prof. Morselli's *Psicologia e spiritismo,* (Turin, 1908). See also *Journal* of the S.P.R. vols., 6, 7, 14, 15; *Proceedings* of the S.P.R., vols. 18, 23, 25.

Recommended reading:

Barzini, Luigi. *Nel mondo dei Misteri con Eusapia Palladino,* Milan, 1907

Bottazi, F. *Nelle regioni inesplorate della Biologia Umana,* Rome 1907

Carrington, Hereward. *The American Seances with Eusapia Palladino,* Garrett/Helix, New York, 1954
Carrington, Hereward. *Eusapia Palladino and Her Phenomena,* B. W. Dodge, New York, 1909; T. Werner Laurie, London, 1910
Dingwall, Eric J. *Very Peculiar People; Portrait Studies in the Queer, the Abnormal and the Uncanny,* Rider, London, 1950; University Books, 1962
Feilding, Everard. *Sittings with Eusapia Palladino & Other Studies,* University Books, 1963
Flammarion, Cesar. *After Death—What?,* T. Fisher Unwin, London, 1909
Ochorowicz, Julien. *La Questione della frode negli Experimenti coll' Eusapia Palladino,* Milan, 1896
Podmore, Frank. *The Newer Spiritualism,* Henry Holt, 1911
Podmore, Frank. *Studies in Psychical Research,* Putnam, 1897
Rochas, A. de. *L'Extériorisation de la Motricité,* Paris, 1906

Palladium, Order of

Said to have been a Masonic order, also entitled the Sovereign-Council of Wisdom, founded in Paris on May 20, 1737. It initiated women under the name of "Companions of Penelope." As proof of its existence, Jean Marie Ragon, the Masonic antiquary, published its ritual.

Palmer, Raymond A. (1910-1977)

Entrepreneur publisher of occult and science-fiction magazines, who first published the series of stories in *Amazing Stories* known as the **Shaver Mystery.** He was born August 1, 1910 in Wisconsin. His childhood was marked by various accidents, some very serious.

At the age of 28, Palmer became editor of *Amazing Stories* which had just been bought by the Ziff-David Company. Palmer had sold his first science-fiction story in 1930, and three years later had founded the Jules Verne Prize Club.

He transformed *Amazing Stories* by his colorful editing, drawing upon old and new science-fiction writers and even writing much of the magazine himself under various pseudonyms. He is said to have boosted circulation from 25,000 to over 185,000, although there were waves of protests from readers at the Shaver Mystery, and Palmer's successor Howard Browne killed the series when he took over *Amazing Stories* in 1949.

During his editorship of *Amazing* and *Fantastic Adventures,* Palmer published a number of his own stories under such pseudonyms as G. H. Irwin, Frank Patton, and A. R. Steber.

Palmer also launched **Fate** Magazine, a pocket-size pulp specializing in occultism. The first issue in Spring 1948 contained an article by Kenneth Arnold ('I *Did* See the Flying Disks') which launched the flying saucer craze in the U.S. Palmer followed up with his own book on saucers, written in collaboration with Arnold.

In 1955, Curtis **Fuller** bought out *Fate* magazine and with his wife Mary published and edited it until early 1989 when it was relinquished to Llewelyn Publications.

With his unique flair for popular fantasy, Palmer started his own publication business from a dairy farm in Amherst, Wisconsin. In his magazines *Flying Saucers* and *Search* he generated a new mythology about saucers coming from holes in the polar ice caps.

He died August 15, 1977, after suffering several strokes.

Palmistry

The claimed science of divination by means of lines and marks on the human hand. It is said to have been practiced in very early times by the Brahmins of India, and to have been known to Aristotle, who discovered a treatise on the subject written in letters of gold, which he presented to Alexander the Great, and which was afterwards translated into Latin by Hispanus. There is also extant a work on the subject by Melampus of Alexandria, and Hippocrates, Galen, and several Arabian commentators have also dealt with it.

In the Middle Ages the science was represented by Hartlieb (c. 1448), Cocles (c. 1054), and Fludd, Indigane, Rothmann, and many others wrote on "cheiromancy," as the subject was then known. D'Arpentigny, Desbarolles, Carus and others kept the subject alive in the earlier half of the nineteenth century, since when a very large number of treatises upon it have been written. Since 1860, or thereabouts, palmistry has become very much more popular than ever before and is practiced nearly all over the habitable globe.

Palmistry is subdivided into three lesser arts—cheirognomy, cheirosophy and cheiromancy. The first is the art of recognizing the type of intelligence from the form of the hands; the second is the study of the comparative value of manual formations; the third is the art of divination from the form of the hand and fingers, and the lines and markings thereon.

The palmist first of all studies the shape and general formation of the hand as a whole, afterwards regarding its parts and details, the lines and markings being considered later. From cheirognomy and cheirosophy, the general disposition and tendencies are ascertained, and future events are foretold from the reading of the lines and markings.

There are several types of hands: the elementary or large-palmed type; the necessary, with spatulated fingers; the artistic, with conical-shaped fingers; the useful, the fingers of which are square-shaped; the knotted or philosophical; the pointed, or psychic; the mixed, in which the types are blended.

The principal lines are: those which separate the hand from the forearm at the wrist, and which are known as the rascettes, or the lines of health, wealth and happiness. The line of life stretches from the center of the palm around the base of the thumb almost to the wrist, and is joined for a considerable part of its course by the line of the head. The line of the heart runs across two-thirds of the palm, above the head line; and the line of fate between it and the line of the head nearly at right angles extending towards the wrist. The line of fortune runs from the base of the third finger towards the wrist parallel to the line of fate. If the lines are deep, firm and of narrow width the significance is good—excepting that a strong line of health shows constitutional weakness.

At the base of the fingers, beginning with the first, lie the mounts of Jupiter, Saturn, Apollo, and Mercury; at the base of the thumb the mount of Venus; opposite to it, that of Luna. If well-proportioned they show certain virtues, but if exaggerated they indicate the vices which correspond to these. The first displays religion, reasonable ambition, or pride and superstition; the second wisdom and prudence, or ignorance and failure; the third when large makes for success and intelligence, when small for meanness or love of obscurity; the fourth desire for knowledge and industry, or disinterestedness and laziness. The Lunar mount indicates sensitiveness, imagination, morality or otherwise, and self-will; the mount of Venus, charity and affection, or if exaggerated viciousness.

The phalanges of the fingers are also indicative of certain faculties. For example, the first and second of the thumb, according to their length, indicate the value of the logical faculty and of the will; those of the index finger in their order—materialism, law, and order; of the middle finger—humanity, system, intelligence; of the third finger—truth, economy, energy; of the little finger goodness, prudence, reflectiveness.

There are nearly a hundred other marks and signs, by which certain qualities, influences or events are believed to be recognized. The length of the line of life indicates the length of existence of its owner. If it is short in both hands, the life will be a short one; if broken in one hand and weak in the other, a serious illness is denoted. If broken in both hands, it means death. If it is much chained it means delicacy. If it has a second or sister line, it shows great vitality. A black spot on the line shows illness at the time marked. A cross indicates some fatality. The line of life coming out far into the palm is a sign of long life.

The line of the head, if long and well-colored, denotes intelligence and power. If descending to the mount of the Moon it shows that the head is much influenced by the imagination. Islands on the line denote mental troubles. The head line forked at the end indicates subtlety and a facility for seeing all sides of the question. A double line of the head is an indication of good fortune.

The line of the heart should branch towards the mount of Jupiter. If it should pass over the mount of Jupiter to the edge of the hand and travel round the index finger, it is called "Solomon's ring" and indicates ideality and romance; it is also a sign of occult power. Points or dots in this line may show illness if black, and if white love affairs, while islands on the heart line indicate disease. If the line of fate or Saturn rises from the Lunar mount and ascends towards the line of the heart, it is a sign of a rich marriage. If it extends into the third phalange of Saturn's finger it shows the sinister influence of that planet. A double line of fate is ominous.

There are also numerous other lesser lines and marks which the hand contains, which are detailed in a number of books on the subject.

There are many practitioners of palmistry, some having their own special interpretations. A few of these works are on scientific lines, but others are merely empirical, and their forecasts of events to come are on a par with newspaper **astrology** columns.

One of the most world famous palmists was **"Cheiro"** ("Count" Louis Hamon) (1866-1936), who was patronized by royalty and all the great and famous of his time. His books on palmistry have been frequently reprinted and are still highly regarded, but he seemed to have some additional psychic faculty other than the systems elaborated in his books, since his predictions were said to be uncannily accurate.

Recommended reading:

Abayakoon, Cyrus D. F. *Astro-Palmistry; Signs and Seals of the Hand,* ASI Publishers, New York, 1975

Anderson, Mary. *Palmistry—Your Destiny In Your Hands,* Aquarian Press, U.K., 1973

Bashir, Mir. *Your Past, Your Present, and Your Future Through the Art of Hand Analysis,* Doubleday, 1974

Benham, W. G. *Laws of Scientific Hand Reading,* new ed., Putnam, 1928

Broekman, Marcel. *The Complete Encyclopaedia of Practical Palmistry,* Prentice-Hall, 1972; Mayflower paperback, U.K., 1975

Cheiro. *Cheiro's Guide to the Hand,* Barrie & Jenkins, London, 1948; Corgi paperback, London, 1975

Cheiro. *Cheiro's Language of the Hand; A Complete Practical Work on the Science of Cheirognomy and Cheiromancy,* 28th ed., H. Jenkins, London, 1949; Corgi paperback, London, 1975

Cheiro. *Cheiro's Memoirs; The Reminiscences of a Society Palmist,* William Rider, London, 1912

Desbarolles, A. *Les Mysteres de la Main,* Paris, 1860

Hipskind, Judith. *Palmistry; The Whole View,* Llewellyn Publications, 1977

Jaquin, Noel. *The Hand of Man; A Practical Treatise of the Science of Hand Reading,* Faber & Faber, London, 1933

Jaquin, Noel. *Man's Revealing Hand,* Routledge, London, 1934

Saint-Germain, Comte C. de (pseud.). *The Practice of Palmistry for Professional Purposes,* 2 vols., 1897-98; one volume ed., Newcastle, Hollywood, California, 1973

Steinbach, Marten. *Medical Palmistry; Health & Character in the Hand,* University Books, 1975; New American Library, 1976

Wilson, Joyce. *The Complete Book of Palmistry,* Bantam paperback, 1971

Wolff, Charlotte. *The Human Hand,* Methuen, London, 1942

Pansini Brothers (c. 1904)

Italian mediumistic children, chiefly known for their mysterious bodily **transportations.** In 1901, their father, Signor Mauro Pansini, a building contractor, went to live in an old house close to the town hall at Ruvo, in Apulia. A few days later **poltergeist** phenomena broke out in the house, articles began to be thrown about, crockery to break, etc.

One evening Alfredo Pansini, then seven years of age, fell into trance and began to speak and recite in French, Latin and Greek. These manifestations continued until he was sent to a seminary where he was entirely free from them.

When he returned home in 1904 at ten years of age, a new series of phenomena commenced in which, besides Alfredo, his 8-year-old brother, Paolo, was also concerned. In a few minutes they were bodily transported to places ten to fifteen miles distant (see also **Teleportation**).

The phenomena created great bewilderment. The parents appealed to the Bishop of Bitonto to deliver the children from the obsession of which they were supposed to be the victims. While their mother was talking to the bishop both the boys mysteriously disappeared from the room.

Alfredo Pansini could answer mental questions by **automatic writing.** The spirit speaking through him explained that he achieved the transportation by dematerializing their bodies. No observer could explain the phenomena. Italian scientists who looked into the matter put forward the theory of "ambulatory automatism," moving about in a secondary state and forgetting it when returning to the normal state. This, however, does not explain how the boys could run nine miles in half an hour without anybody perceiving them on the road.

Details of the case are to be found in Joseph Lapponi's *Hypnotism and Spiritism* (1906).

Pansophic Institute

Educational organization founded in 1973, sponsored by the School of Universal Wisdom, functioning through its clerical body, the Church of Universal Light.

The Institute is intended to serve as "a voice for the perennial philosophy or ageless wisdom leading to liberation and enlightenment in the New Age. It unites Eastern and Western forms of gnosis (spiritual wisdom) and theurgy (techniques of enlightenment) in the light of modern science." It provides an educational program consisting of courses in meditation, esoteric cosmology, divinations, spiritual healing, superhealth and longevity, ability, thanatology and empowerment where intellectual learning for its own sake is discouraged in favor of learning "that assists one to become enlightened for the sake of all things." It offers courses for ministership in four types of theurgy and theurgic cosmology, and in child education, creativity and world responsibility.

Address: P.O. Box 2422, Reno, Nevada 89505.

Pantomnesia

Term used by Prof. Charles **Richet** to denote "regression of memory, the imagination that a thing experienced has been seen before." Richet also stated: "I propose *pantomnesia* to indicate that no vestige of our intellectual past is entirely effaced. Probably we are all pantomnesic. In weighing metapsychic facts it should be taken for granted that we do not absolutely forget anything that has once impressed our senses."

Pap, Lajos (1883- ?)

Budapest non-professional medium for **apports** and telekinetic (see **Telekinesis**) phenomena, a carpenter by trade. His powers first manifested in 1922 in a casual sitting for table movement and were developed by Major Cornelius Seefehlner, Dr. John Toronyi and later by Dr. Elmer Chengery Pap (not a relative), a retired Chief Chemist to the Government, president of the Budapest Metapsychic Society.

For some years Lajos Pap gave joint sittings with Tibor Molnar, another Hungarian medium. "Rabbi Isaac," his **control,** first communicated through table rapping, then through **trance** speaking.

Dr. Chengery Pap gradually developed scientific control, not only searching the medium and dressing him in a special seance robe but also providing special garments for his immediate controls and searching every sitter. The medium wore luminous stripes, the sitters tied luminous straps on their ankles and wrists. Instead of red light a 100 watt green lamp was used which, on demand, the control permitted to be switched on during the proceedings for repeated examination.

Under such conditions, telekinetic movements of luminous baskets and strange white and colored lights and the arrival of hundreds of living and inanimate objects were observed.

The majority of the apports were living beetles, butterflies, caterpillars, frogs, lizards, birds, mice, fish, squirrels, but also liquids, perfumes, flowers and other objects.

In *Proceedings* of the Society for Psychical Research (vol. 38), Theodore **Besterman** describes a sitting with Lajos Pap at Dr. John Toronyi's flat on November 18, 1928. He witnessed telekinetic phenomena and the apport of three stones. However, Besterman's verdict was fraud, and his general attitude was made the subject of a strongly worded protest addressed by Pap's advocates to the Society for Psychical Research.

For an amusing account of the phenomena of Lajos Pap and probable explanation of the rationale of fraud, see, the chapter 'Apports of a Carpenter' in *The Haunted Mind* by Nandor Fodor (Helix Press,

1959). Fodor also indulged some shrewd speculations about the psychology of fraud.

Papaloi

An Obeah priest. (See **West Indian Islands**)

Papus

Pseudonym of occultist Dr. Gérard **Encausse** (1865-1916).

Para Committee

Popular term for the **Committee for the Scientific Investigation of Claims of the Paranormal,** established April 30, 1976 at a meeting of the American Humanist Association in Buffalo, New York.

Parabola (Journal)

Journal of the Society for the Study of Myth & Tradition, concerned with exploring the inner being through myth and its manifestations. Published quarterly, address: 150 Fifth Avenue, New York, N.Y. 10011

Parabrahman (or Para Brahm)

Term used in Hindu religious philosophy to denote the supreme absolute transcendental reality. Brahman is the non-personal divine beyond manifestation as gods and goddesses, as distinct from Brahma, the form as divine creator of the universe. Comparable concepts exist in the mysticism of **Kabala.**

Paracelsus (1493-1541)

One of the most striking and picturesque figures in the history of medicine, alchemy and occultism, full name Aurœlus Philippus Theophrastus Paracelsus Bombast von Hohenheim, this illustrious physician and exponent of the hermetic philosophy has gone down to fame under the name of Paracelsus.

He was born November 10, 1493 at Einsideln, near Zurich, Switzerland. His father, the natural son of a prince, himself practiced the "art of medicine," and desired that his only son should follow the same profession. To the fulfillment of that desire was directed the early training of Paracelsus, a training which fostered his imaginative rather than his practical tendencies, and which first cast his mind into the alchemical mould.

It did not take him long to discover that the medical traditions of the time were but empty husks from which all substance had long since dried away. "I considered with myself," he stated, "that if there were no teacher of medicine in the world, how would I set about to learn the art? No otherwise than in the great open book of nature, written with the finger of God."

Having freed himself from the constraining bonds of an outworn medical orthodoxy whose chief resources were bleeding, purging and emetics, he set about evolving a new system to replace the old, and in order that he might study the book of nature to better advantage he traveled extensively between 1513 and 1524, visiting almost every part of the known world, studying metallurgy, chemistry, and medicine, and even consorting with vagabonds of every description.

He was brought before the Cham of Tartary, conversed with the magicians of Egypt and Arabia, and is said to have even reached India. At length his protracted wanderings came to a close, and in 1524 he settled in Basle, then a favorite resort of scholars and physicians, where he was appointed to fill the chair of medicine at the University.

Never had Basle witnessed a more brilliant, erratic professor. His inflated language, his eccentric behavior, the splendor of his conceptions flashing through a fog of obscurity, at once attracted and repelled, and gained for him friends and enemies. His antipathy to the Galenic school became ever more pronounced, and the crisis came when he publicly burned the works of Galen and Avicenna in a brazen vase into which he had cast nitre and sulphur. By such a proceeding he incurred the hatred of his more conservative brethren, and cut himself off for ever from the established school of medicine.

He continued his triumphant career, however, until a conflict with the magistrates brought it to an abrupt close. He was forced to flee from Basle, and thereafter wandered from place to place, gaining a living as best he might.

An element of mystery surrounds the manner of his death, which took place September 24, 1541. Some say that he was poisoned at the instigation of the medical faculty, others that he was thrown down a steep incline.

But interesting as were the events of his life, it is to his work that most attention is due. Not only was he the founder of the modern science of medicine, the magnetic theory of **Mesmer,** the "astral" theory of modern **Spiritualism,** the philosophy of Descartes were all foreshadowed in the fantastic, yet not always illogical, teaching of Paracelsus.

He revived the "microcosmic" theory of ancient Greece, and sought to prove the human body analogous to the Solar System, by establishing a connection between the seven organs of the body and the seven planets. He preached the doctrines of the efficacy of willpower and the imagination in such words as these: "It is possible that my spirit, without the help of my body, and through an ardent will alone, and without a sword, can stab and wound others. It is also possible that I can bring the spirit of my adversary into an image and then fold him up or lame him at my pleasure." "Resolute imagination is the beginning of all magical operations." "Because men do not perfectly believe and imagine, the result is, that arts are uncertain when they might be wholly certain." He was thus a forerunner of **New Thought** teachings.

The first principle of his doctrine was the extraction of the quintessence, or philosophic mercury, from every material body. He believed that if the quintessence were drawn from each animal, plant, and mineral, the combined result would equal the universal spirit, or "astral body" in human beings, and that a draught of the extract would renew youth.

He came at length to the conclusion that "astral bodies" exercised a mutual influence on each other, and declared that he himself had communicated with the dead, and with living persons at a considerable distance. He was the first to connect this influence with that of the magnet, and to use the word "magnetism" with its modern application. It was on this foundation that Mesmer built his theory of magnetic influence.

While Paracelsus busied himself with such problems, however, he did not neglect the study and practice of medicine. Indeed, astrology and the magnet entered largely into his treatment. When he was sought by a patient, his first care was to consult the planets, where the disease had its origin, and if the patient were a woman he took it for granted that the cause of her malady lay in the moon.

His anticipation of the philosophy of Descartes consisted in his theory that by bringing the various elements of the human body into harmony with the elements of nature—fire, light, earth, etc.—old age and death might be indefinitely postponed.

His experiment in the extraction of its essential spirit from the poppy resulted in the production of laudanum, which he prescribed freely in form of "three black pills."

The recipes which he gives for the **Philosopher's Stone,** the **Elixir of Life,** and various universal remedies, are exceedingly obscure. He was deservedly celebrated as the first physician to use opium and mercury, and to recognize the value of sulphur.

He applied himself also to the solution of a problem which exercised the minds of scientific men in the nineteenth and twentieth centuries—whether it was possible to produce life from inorganic matter. Paracelsus asserted that it was, and left on record a quaint recipe for a **homunculus,** or artificial man. By a peculiar treatment of certain "spagyric substances" (which he unfortunately omitted to specify) he declared that he could produce a perfect human child in miniature.

Speculations such as these, medical, alchemical and philosophical, were scattered so profusely throughout his teaching that one concludes that here was a master-mind, a genius, who was a charlatan only incidentally, by reason of training and temperament. Let it be remembered that he lived in an age when practically all scholars and physicians used to impose on popular ignorance, and it should be emphasized that Paracelsus displayed, under all his arrogant exterior, a curious singleness of purpose, and a real desire to penetrate the mysteries of science.

He left on record the principal points of the philosophy on which he founded his researches in his *Archidoxa Medicinæ.* It contains the leading rules of the art of healing, as he practiced and preached them. "I had resolved," he stated, "to give ten books to the *'Archidoxa,'* but I have reserved the tenth in my head. It is a treasure which men are not worthy to possess, and shall only be given to the world when they shall have abjured Aristotle, Avicenna, and Galen, and promised a perfect submission to Paracelsus." The world did not recant, but Paracelsus relented, and at the entreaty of his disciples published this tenth book, the key to the nine others, but a key which might pass for a lock, and for a lock which it is difficult to pick. It is entitled the *Tenth Book of the Arch-Doctrines;* or, *On the Secret Mysteries of Nature.* A brief summary of it is as follows:

Paracelsus begins by supposing, and ends by establishing, that there is a universal spirit infused into the veins of man, forming within us a species of invisible body, of which our visible body, which it directs and governs at its will, is but the wrapping or casket. This universal spirit is not simple—not more simple, for instance, than the number 100, which is a collection of units. Where, then, are the spiritual units of which our complex spirit is composed? Scattered in plants and minerals, but principally in metals. There exists in these inferior productions of the earth a host of sub-spirits which sum themselves up in us, as the universe does in God. So the science of the philosopher has simply to unite them to the body, to disengage them from the grosser matter which clogs and confines them, to separate the pure from the impure.

To separate the pure from the impure is, in other words, to seize upon the soul of the heterogeneous bodies, to evolve their "predestined element," "the seminal essence of beings," "the first being, or quintessence."

To understand this latter word "quintessence," it is necessary to postulate that every body, whatever it may be, is composed of four elements, and that the essence compounded of these elements forms a fifth, which is the soul of the mixed bodies, or, in other words, its "mercury." "I have shown," stated Paracelsus, "in my book of 'Elements,' that the quintessence is the same thing as mercury. There is in mercury whatever wise men seek." That is, not the mercury of modern chemists, but a philosophical "mercury" of which every body has its own. "There are as many mercuries as there are things. The mercury of a vegetable, a mineral, or an animal of the same kind, although strongly resembling each other, does not precisely resemble another mercury, and it is for this reason that vegetables, minerals, and animals of the same species are not exactly alike. . . . The true mercury of philosophers is the radical humidity of each body, and its veritable semen, or essence."

Paracelsus now sought for a plant worthy of holding in the vegetable kingdom the same rank as gold in the metallic—a plant whose "predestined element" should unite in itself the virtues of nearly all the vegetable essences. Although this was not easy to distinguish, he claimed to recognize at a glance (we know not by what signs) the supremacy of excellence in the *melissa,* and first decreed to it that pharmaceutical crown which at a later period the Carmelites ought to have consecrated. How he obtained this new specific was described by one of his biographers:

"He took some balm-mint in flower, which he had taken care to collect before the rising of the sun. He pounded it in a mortar, reduced it to an impalpable dust, poured it into a long-necked vial which he sealed hermetically, and placed it to digest (or settle) for forty hours in a heap of horse-dung. This time expired, he opened the vial, and found there a matter which he reduced into a fluid by pressing it, separating it from its impurities by exposure to the slow heat of a *bain-marie* (a vessel of hot water in which other vessels are heated). The grosser parts sunk to the bottom, and he drew off the liqueur which floated on the top, filtering it through some cotton. This liqueur having been poured into a bottle he added to it the fixed salt, which he had drawn from the same plant when dried. There remained nothing more but to extract from this liqueur the first life or being of the plant. For this purpose Paracelsus mixed the liqueur with so much 'water of salt' (understand by this the mercurial element or radical humidity of the salt), put it in a matrass, exposed it for six weeks to the sun, and finally, at the expiration of this term, discovered a last residuum which was decidedly, according to him, the first life or supreme essence of the plant. But at all events, it is certain that what he found in his matrass was the genie or spirit he required; and with the surplus, if there were any, we need not concern ourselves."

Those who may wish to know what this *genie* was like, are informed that it as exactly resembled, as two drops of water, the spirit of aromatic wine known to-day as *absinthe suisse.* It was a liquid green as emerald—green, the bright color of hope and spring-time. Unfortunately is failed as a specific in the conditions indispensable for an elixir of immortality; but it was a preparation more than half-celestial, which almost rendered old age impossible.

By means and manipulations as subtle and ingenious as those which he employed upon the melissa, Paracelsus did not draw, but learned to extract, the "predestined element" of plants which ranked much higher in the vegetable aristocracy,—the "first life" of the gilly-flower, the cinnamon, the myrrh, the scammony, the celandine. All these supreme essences, which, according to the 5th book of *Archidoxa,* unite with a mass of "magisteries" as precious as they are rude, are the base of so many specifics, equally reparative and regenerative. This depends upon the relationship which exists between the temperament of a privileged plant and the temperament of the individual who asks of it his rejuvenescence.

However brilliant were the results of his discoveries, those he obtained or those he thought he might obtain, they were for Paracelsus but the a b c of Magic. To the eyes of so consummate an alchemist, vegetable life was not important; it was the mineral—the metallic life—which was significant. Paracelsus believed that it was in his power to seize the first life-principle of the moon, the sun, Mars, or Saturn; that is, of silver, gold, iron, or lead. It was equally facile for him to grasp the life of the precious stones, the bitumens, the sulphurs, and even that of animals.

Paracelsus set forth several methods of obtaining this great arcanum. Here is the shortest and most simple as recorded by Incola Francus:—

"Take some mercury, or at least the element of mercury, separating the pure from the impure, and afterwards pounding it to perfect whiteness. Then you shall sublimate it with sal-ammoniac, and this so many times as may be necessary to resolve it into a fluid. Calcine it, coagulate it, and again dissolve it, and let it strain in a pelican [a vessel used for distillation] during a philosophic month, until it thickens and assumes the form of a hard substance. Thereafter this form of stone is incombustible, and nothing can change or alter it; the metallic bodies which it penetrates become fixed and incombustible, for this material is incombustible, and changes the imperfect metals into metal perfect. Although I have given the process in few words, the thing itself demands a long toil, and many difficult circumstances, which I have expressly omitted, not to weary the reader, who ought to be very diligent and intelligent if he wishes to arrive at the accomplishment of this great work."

Paracelsus himself described in his *Archidoxa* his own recipe for the completion of it, and profited by the occasion to criticize his fellow-workers.

"I omit," he wrote, "what I have said in different places on the theory of the stone; I will say only that this *arcanum* does not consist in the blast [*rouille*] or flowers of antimony. It must be sought in the mercury of antimony, which, when it is carried to perfection, is nothing else than the *heaven* of metals; for even as the heaven gives life to plants and minerals, so does the pure quintessence of antimony vitrify everything. This is why the Deluge was not able to deprive any substance of its virtue or properties, for the heaven being the life of all beings, there is nothing superior to it which can modify or destroy it.

"Take the antimony, purge it of its arsenical impurities in an iron vessel until the coagulated mercury of the antimony appears quite white, and is distinguishable by the star which appears in the superficies of the regulus, or semi-metal. But although this regulus, which is the element of mercury, has in itself a veritable hidden life, nevertheless these things are in virtue, and not actually.

"Therefore, if you wish to reduce the power to action, you must disengage the life which is concealed in it by a living fire like to itself, or with a metallic vinegar. To discover this fire many philosophers have proceeded differently, but agreeing to the foundations of the art, have arrived at the desired end. For some with great labour have drawn forth the quintessence of the thickened mercury of the regulus of antimony, and by this means have reduced to action the mercury of the antimony: others have considered that there was a uniform quintessence in the other minerals, as for example in the fixed sulphur of the vitriol, or the stone of the magnet, and having extracted the quintessence, have afterwards matured and exalted their *heaven* with it, and reduced it to action. Their process is good, and has had its result. Meanwhile this fire—this corporeal life—which they seek with toil, is found much more easily and in much greater perfection in the ordinary mercury, which appears through its perpetual fluidity—a proof that it possesses a very powerful fire and a celestial life similar to that which lies hidden in the regulus of the antimony. Therefore, he who would wish to exalt our *metallic heaven,* starred, to its greatest completeness, and to reduce into action its potential virtues, he must first extract from ordinary mercury its corporeal life, which is a celestial fire; that is to say the quintessence of quicksilver, or, in other words, the metallic vinegar, that has resulted from its dissolution in the water which originally produced it, and which is its own mother; that is to say, he must dissolve it in the arcanum of the salt I have described, and mingle it with the 'stomach of Anthion,' which is the spirit of vinegar, and in this menstruum melt and filter and consistent mercury of the antimony, strain it in the said liquor, and finally reduce it into crystals of a yellowish green, of which we have spoken in our manual."

As regards the **Philosopher's Stone,** he gave the following formula:—

"Take the electric mineral not yet mature [antimony], put it in its sphere, in the fire with the iron, to remove its ordures and other superfluities, and purge it as much as you can, following the rules of chymistry, so that it may not suffer by the aforesaid impurities. Make, in a word, the regulus with the mark. This done, cause it to dissolve in the 'stomach of the ostrich' (vitriol), which springs from the earth and is fortified in its virtue by the 'sharpness of the eagle' (the metallic vinegar or essence of mercury). As soon as the essence is perfected, and when after its dissolution it has taken the colour of the herb called *calendule,* do not forget to reduce it into a spiritual luminous essence, which resembles amber. After this, add to it of the 'spread eagle' one half the weight of the election before its preparation, and frequently distil the 'stomach of the ostrich' into the matter, and thus the election will become much more spiritualized. When the 'stomach of the ostrich' is weakened by the labour of digestion, we must strengthen it and frequently distil it. Finally, when it has lost all its impurity, add as much tartarized quintessence as will rest upon your fingers, until it throws off its impurity and rises with it. Repeat this process until the preparation becomes white, and this will suffice; for you shall see yourself as gradually it rises in the form of the 'exalted eagle,' and with little trouble converts itself in its form (like sublimated mercury); and that is what we are seeking.

"I tell you in truth that there is no greater remedy in medicine than that which lies in this election, and that there is nothing like it in the whole world. But not to digress from my purpose, and not to leave this work imperfect, observe the manner in which you ought to operate."

"The election then being destroyed, as I have said, to arrive at the desired end (which is, to make of it a universal medicine for human as well as metallic bodies), take your election, rendered light and volatile by the method above described.

"Take of it as much as you would wish to reduce it to its perfection, and put it in a philosophical egg of glass, and seal it very tightly, that nothing of it may respire; put it into an athanor until of itself it resolves into a liquid, in such a manner that in the middle of this sea there may appear a small island, which daily diminishes, and finally, all shall be changed to a colour black as ink. This colour is the raven, or bird which flies at night without wings, and which, through the celestial dew, that rising continually falls back by a constant circulation, changes into what is called 'the head of the raven,' and afterwards resolves into 'the tail of the peacock,' then it assumes the hue of the 'tail of a peacock,' and afterwards the colour of the 'feathers of a swan'; finally acquiring an extreme redness, which marks its fiery nature, and in virtue of which it expels all kinds of impurities, and strengthens feeble members. This preparation, according to all philosophers, is made in a single vessel, over a single furnace, with an equal and continual fire, and this medicine, which is more than celestial, cures all kinds of infirmities, as well in human as metallic bodies; wherefore no one can understand or attain such an arcanum without the help of God: for its virtue is ineffable and divine."

Recommended reading:

Hartmann, Franz. *The Life of Philippus Theophrastus Bombast of Hohenheim known by the name of Paracelsus and of the Substance of his Teachings,* G. Redway, London, 1887; reissued with *The Prophecies of Paracelsus; Occult Symbols and Magic Figures* in one volume by Rudolf Steiner Publications, Blauvelt, New York, 1973 (paperback)

Stillman, John M. *Theophrastus Bombast von Hohenheim called Paracelsus; his Personality and Influence as Physician, Chemist and Reformer,* Open Court, Chicago, 1920

Waite, Arthur E. (ed.). *The Hermetic and Alchemical Writings of Aureolus Philippus Theophrastus Bombast, of Hohenheim, called Paracelsus the Great,* 2 vols., James Elliott, London, 1894; University Books, 1967

Paradise

Derived from old Persian (Zeud) *pairedaëza,* an enclosure, a walled-in place; Old Persian *pairi,* around, *dig,* to mould, form, shape (hence to form a wall of earth).

Paradise has been sought for or located in many regions of the earth. In Tartary, Armenia, India, and China: on the banks of the Euphrates and of the Ganges; in Mesopotamia, Syria, Persia, Arabia, Palestine, and Ethiopia, and near the mountains of Libanus and Anti-libanus. Perhaps the most noteworthy tradition is that which fixes its situation in the Island of Ceylon (now known as Shri Lanka) the "Serendib" of the ancient Persians, and the "Taprobane" of the Greek geographers.

"It is from the summit of Hamalleel or Adam's Peak," stated Robert Percival in his book *An Account of the Island of Ceylon* (1803), "that Adam took his last view of Paradise before he quitted it never to return. The spot on which his feet stood at the moment is still supposed to be found in an impression on the summit of the mountain, resembling the print of a man's foot, but more than double the ordinary size. After taking this farewell view, the father of mankind is said to have gone over to the continent of Judea, which was at that time joined to the island, but no sooner had he passed Adam's Bridge than the sea closed behind him, and cut off all hopes of return. This tradition, from whatever source it was derived, seems to be interwoven with the earliest notions of religion entertained by the Cingalese; and it is difficult to conceive that it could have been engrafted on them without forming an original part. I have frequently had the curiosity to converse with black men of different castes concerning this tradition of Adam. All of them, with every appearance of belief, assured me that it was really true, and in support of it produced a variety of testimonies, old sayings, and prophecies, which have for ages been current among them. The origin of these traditions I do not pretend to trace; but their connection with Scripture history is very evident, and they afford a new instance how universally the opinions with respect to the origin of man coincide." We are further informed by this writer that a large chair fixed in a rock near the summit of the mountain is said to be the workmanship of Adam. "It has the appearance of having been placed there at a very distant period, but who really placed it there, or for what purpose, it is impossible for any European to discover."

However, this apparently oversize footprint is venerated equally by Buddhists, and Hindus, who ascribe it respectively to Gautama Buddha, or the god Siva.

Paradise is a word of Persian origin, adopted by the Greeks, and literally denotes an inclosure or park planted with fruit-trees, and abounding with various animals. Eden is not termed Paradise in *Genesis,* but simply a garden planted eastwards in the country or district so called, and it is this apparently indefinite locality which has caused so many conjectures as to its exact site.

Some place it in Judea, where is now the sea of Galilee; others in Armenia, near Mount Ararat, and others in Syria, towards the sources of the Orontes, the Chrysorrhoas, and Barrady. Some think that by Eden is meant the whole earth, which was of surprising beauty and fertility before the Fall, and it is curious that a notion prevailed to a great extent among the various nations that the Old World was under a curse, and that the earth became very barren.

Some Eastern philosophies implied that nature is contaminated, and that the earth labors under some defilement—a sentiment which might result from obscure traditions connected with the first human pair. The historian Josephus gravely stated that the Sacred Garden was watered by one river which ran round the whole earth, and was divided into four parts, but he appeared to think Paradise was merely a figurative or allegorical locality. Some of the peoples of Hindustan had traditions of a place resembling Paradise on the banks of the River Ganges; but their accounts were completely blended with mythology and legends respecting the Deluge and the second peopling of the world.

One writer who had diligently studied the Indian Puranas (religious and mythological works) for many years, opened a new source of information, and placed Eden on the Imaus Mountains of India. "It appears from Scripture," he stated, "that Adam and Eve lived in the countries to the eastward of Eden; for at the eastern entrance of it God placed the angel with the flaming sword. This is also confirmed by the Puranics, who place the progenitor of mankind on the mountainous regions between Cabul and the Ganges, on the banks of which, in the hills, they show a place where he resorted occasionally for religious purposes. It is frequented by pilgrims. At the entrance of the passes leading to the place where I suppose was the Garden of Eden, and to the eastward of it, the Hindoos have placed a destroying angel, who appears, and it is generally represented with a cherub; I mean Garudha, or the Eagle, upon whom Vishnu and Jupiter are represented riding. Garudha is represented generally like an eagle, but in his compound character somewhat like a cherub. He is represented like a young man, with the countenance, wings, and talons of the eagle. In Scripture the Deity is represented riding upon a cherub, and flying upon the wings of the wind. Garudha is called Vahan [literally the Vehicle] of Vishnu or Jupiter, and he thus answers to the cherub of Scripture; for many commentators derive this word from the obsolete root c'harab, in the Chaldean language, a word implicitly synonymous with the Sanscrit Vahan."

It is interesting to note that the Puranas considered the northwest part of India, about Kashmir, as the site of Paradise, and the original abode of the first human pair, and that there, at the offering of a sacrifice Daksha was murdered by his jealous brother, who was in consequence doomed to become a fugitive on the earth.

In the fabled Mount Meru of Hindu mythology, on the other hand, there is also a descriptive representation of the Mosaical Garden of Eden. Meru is a conical mountain, the exact locality of which is not fixed, but as the Hindu geographers considered the earth as a flat table and the sacred mountain of Meru rising in the middle, it became at length their decided conviction that Meru was the North Pole, from their notion that the North Pole was the highest part of the world. So firmly we are told, was this tradition believed, that although some Hindu writers admitted that Mount Meru must be situated in the central part of Asia, yet rather than relinquish their notion of and predilection for the North Pole as the real locality of Paradise, they actually forced the sun out of the ecliptic and placed the Pole on the elevated plains of Lesser Bokhara. However, the Hindu description of this Paradise seems to be analagous to the Mosaic account.

The summit of Meru is considered as a circular plain of vast extent, surrounded by a belt of hills—a celestial earth, the abode of immortals, and is designated Ida-Vratta, or the Circle of Ida. It is of four different colors towards the cardinal points, and is believed to be supported by four enormous buttresses of gold, silver, copper and iron. Yet doubts exist as to its real appearance, some alleging that its form is that of a square based pyramid, others maintaining that its shape is conical; others that it resembles an inverted cone, while others thought that instead of a circular belt of mountains, Meru terminated in three lofty peaks.

The Saivas asserted that a vast river rose from the head of the deity Siva, and the Vaishna view was that it sprang from beneath the feet of Vishnu, and, after passing through the circle of the moon, fell upon the summit of Meru and divided itself into four streams, flowing towards the four cardinal points.

Others believed that the four rivers of the sacred mountain sprang from the roots of Jambri, a tree of immense size which, they said, conveyed the most extensive and profound knowledge, and accomplished the most desirable of human aspirations. This recalls the Mosaic account of the Tree of Knowledge, which stood in the middle of the Garden, and of the river which went out of Eden to water it, dividing itself into four branches or streams of other rivers.

The river thus rising in Meru was said to flow in four opposite directions to the four cardinal points and was supposed to issue from four rocks, carved in the shape of many different animals, one of which was a cow. This was said to be the origin of the sacred River Ganges. Some Hindus, however, believed that this river first flowed round the sacred city of Brahma, and then discharged itself into a lake called Mansarovara, from which it issued through the rocky heads of four animals to the different divisions of the globe. The cow's head, from which issued the Ganges, they placed towards the south; and towards the north is the tiger, or lion's head. The horse's head is on the west, and on the east is that of the elephant.

The traditions of Kashmir represent that country as the original site of Paradise, and the abode of the first human pair, while the Buddhists of Tibet held opinions respecting the mountain Meru similar to those of the Hindus. They located the sacred Garden, however, at the foot of the mountain, near the source of the Ganges, but the four holy rivers were made to issue through the heads of the same animals, which were believed to be the guardians of the divisions of the world. The tree of knowledge, or of life, they designated Zambri, which, they said, was a celestial tree bearing immortal fruit, and flourished near four vast rocks, from which issued the several rivers which water the world.

The Moslems inhabiting adjacent countries adopted the popular belief that Paradise was situated in Kashmir, adding that when the first man was driven from it, he and his wife wandered separately for some time. They met at a place called Bahlaka, or Balk, so called because they mutually embraced each other after a long absence. Two gigantic statues, which they said were yet to be seen between Bahlaka and Bamiyan, represented Adam and Eve, and a third of smaller dimensions was that of their son Seish or Seth, whose tomb, or its site, was pointed out near Bahlaka.

Some writers seriously maintained that Paradise was under the North Pole, arguing upon an idea of the ancient Babylonians and Egyptians, that the ecliptic or solar way was originally at right angles to the Equator, and so passed directly over the North Pole. The opinion generally entertained by some Moslems that it was in one of the seven heavens was not stranger than the preceding supposition. One commentator summed up extravagant theories respecting the locality of Paradise. "Some place it as follows: In the third heaven, others in the fourth, some within the orbit of the moon, others in the moon itself, some in the middle regions of the air, or beyond the earth's attraction, some on the earth, others under the earth, and others within the earth."

Before leaving the East, it may be observed that Oriental people generally reckoned four sites of Paradise in Asia: the first Ceylon, already mentioned; the second in Chaldea; the third in a district of Persia, watered by a river called the Nilab; and the fourth about Damascus in Syria, and near the springs of the Jordan. This last supposed site was not peculiar to Oriental writers, as it was also maintained by some Europeans, especially Heidegger, Le Clerc, and Hardouin. The following are the traditions once believed by inhabitants of the city of Damascus—a city which the Emperor Julian the Apostate styled "the Eye of all the East," the most sacred and most magnificent Damascus.

"I understand," stated M. de Lamartine, "that Arabian traditions represent this city and its neighbourhood to form the site of the lost Paradise, and certainly I should think that no place upon earth was better calculated to answer one's ideas of Eden. The vast and fruitful plain, with the seven branches of the blue stream which irrigate it—the majestic framework of the mountains—the glittering lakes which reflect the heaven upon the earth—its geographical situation between the two seas—the perfection of the climate—every thing indicates that Damascus has at least been one of the first towns that were built by the children of men—one of the natural halts of fugitive humanity in primeval times. It is, in fact, one of those sites pointed out by the hand of God for a city—a site predestined to sustain a capital like Constantinople."

According to Oriental tradition, Damascus stood on the site of the Sacred Garden, and outside the city was the most beautiful meadow divided by the river Barrady, of the red earth of which Adam is alleged to have been formed. This field was designated Ager Damascenus by the Latins, and nearly in the center of it a pillar formerly stood, intended to mark the precise spot where the Creator breathed into the first man the breath of life. The modern conflicts in Lebanon and Syria have a melancholy irony beside such noble traditions.

Other traditions which existed among ancient nations of the Garden of Eden doubtless originated those curious and magnificent gardens designed and planted by Eastern princes, such as the Golden Garden of Aristobulus, King of the Jews, which was consecrated by Pompey to Jupiter Capitolinus. Nor is mythology deficient in similar legends. We have the Gardens of Jupiter, of Alcinous, and of the Fortunate Islands, but especially of the Hesperides, in which not only the primeval Paradise, but traditions of the Tree of Knowledge of good and evil, and of the original promise made to the woman, are prominently conspicuous. The Garden of the Hesperides produced golden fruit, guarded by a dangerous serpent—that this fierce reptile encircled with its folds a mysterious tree—and that Hercules procured the fruit by encountering and killing the serpent.

The story of the constellation, as related by Eratosthenes, is applicable to the Garden of Eden, and the primeval history of mankind. "This serpent," said that ancient writer, alluding to the constellation, "is the same as that which guarded the golden apples, and was slain by Hercules. For, when the gods offered presents to Juno on her nuptials with Jupiter, the Earth also brought golden apples. Juno, admiring their beauty, commanded them to be planted in the garden of the gods; but finding that they were continually plucked by the daughter of Atlas, she appointed a vast serpent to guard them. Hercules overcame and slew the monster. Hence, in this constellation the serpent is depicted rearing its head aloft, while Hercules, placed above it with one knee bent, tramples with his foot upon its head, and brandishes a club in his right hand."

The Greeks placed the Garden of the Hesperides close to Mount Atlas, and then removed it far into the regions of Western Africa, yet all knowledge of its Asiatic site was not erased from the classical mythologists, for Apollodorus states that certain writers situated it not in the Libyan Atlas, but in the Atlas of the Hyperboreans; and he added that the serpent had the faculty of uttering articulate sounds.

Our ancestors believed that the world was originally a Paradise, and its first inhabitants more than human, whose dwelling was a magnificent hall, glittering with fine gold, where love, and joy, and friendship presided. The most insignificant of their utensils were made of gold, and hence the appellation of the Golden Age. But this happiness was soon overthrown by certain women from the country of the giants, to whose seductions the first mortals yielded, and their innocence and integrity were lost for ever. The transgression of Eve was the obvious prototype of the fatal curiosity of Pandora, and the arrival of women from the country of the giants, and their intercourse with a distinct and purer line of mortals, strongly recalls the marriages of the sons of Seth with the daughters of Cain, which were the principal causes of the universal depravity of the Antediluvians.

The legends of Hindustan also supply accounts of the happiness of Paradise in the Golden Age of classic mythology. "There can arise little doubt," stated Thomas Maurice, author of *Indian Antiquities* (1793-1800) "that by the Satya age, or Age of Perfection, the Brahmins obviously allude to the state of perfection and happiness enjoyed by man in Paradise. It is impossible to explain what the Indian writers assert concerning the universal purity of manners, and the luxurious and unbounded plenty prevailing in that primitive era, without this supposition. Justice, truth, philanthrophy, were then practised among all the orders and classes of mankind. There was then no extortion, no circumvention, no fraud, used in the dealings one with another. Perpetual oblations smoked on the altars of the Deity; every tongue uttered praises, and every heart glowed with gratitude to the Supreme Creator. The gods, in token of their approbation of the conduct of mortals, condescended frequently to become incarnate, and to hold personal intercourse with the yet undepraved race, to instruct them in arts and sciences; to unveil their own sublime functions and pure nature; and to make them acquainted with the economy of those celestial regions into which they were to be immediately translated, when the period of their terrestial probation expired."

For a discussion of early legends about Paradise, see the chapter 'The Terrestrial Paradise' in *Curious Myths of the Middle Ages* by S. Baring-Gould (1872; University Books, 1967). See also the chapter 'The Creation and Fall of Man' in *Bible Myths and Their Parallels in Other Religions* by T. W. Doane (1884 etc.; University Books, 1971).

Paragnost

Term coined by Dutch parapsychologist Professor W. H. C. **Tenhaeff** in 1932, to indicate an individual gifted with psi or psychic faculties. The term derives from the Greek *para* (beyond) and *gnosis* (knowledge), i.e., paranormal knowledge.

Parakinesis

Term used by psychical researcher Dr. Joseph **Maxwell** to denote movement of objects with contact which, however, is insufficient to explain the extent of the movement. (See also **Movement; Psychokinesis; Telekinesis**)

Paranormal & Psychic Australian
(Magazine)

Quarterly Australian magazine devoted to psychic phenomena and unexplained mysteries; includes news and book reviews. Address: P.O. Box 19, Spit Junction, New South Wales 2088, Australia.

Paraphysical Laboratory

A research unit organized by some members of the Society for Psychical Research (London) to specialize in study of the physical aspects of **psi** phenomena. The laboratory publishes an *International Journal of Paraphysics.* Address: Paraphysical Laboratory, Summerhayes Hotel, 12 Cambridge Road, Bournemouth, Dorset BH2 6AQ, England.

Parapsychic Phenomena

A term used by psychical researcher Emile **Boirac** (1851-1917) for "all phenomena produced in living beings or as a result of their action, which do not seem capable of being entirely explained by already known natural laws and forces." According to Boirac, the term "psychical" is not satisfactory because it is synonymous with "mental." The prefix "para" denotes that it relates to exceptional, abnormal paradoxical phenomena. The term found some acceptance in Germany during the establishment of psychical research.

The term "parapsychic" now appears to have been coined by psychologist Max Dessoir (1867-1947) in Germany in 1889, before its use by Emile Boirac in his book *La Psychologie Inconnue; Introduction et contribution à l'étude expérimentale des sciences psychiques* (Paris, 1908; English translation *Psychic Science; An Introduction and Contribution to the Experimental Study of Psychical Phenomena,* London, 1918).

Dessoir used the term "parapsychic" and also "parapsychology" in his communication 'Die Parapsychologie, Eine Entgegnung auf den Artikel "Der Prophet" ' [by Ludwig Brunn] published in June 1889 issue of the periodical *Sphinx* (pp. 341-44). An English translation 'Parapsychology, A Response to the Article "The Prophet" ' was published in *Journal* of the Society for Psychical Research (vol. 53, No. 802, January 1986) as an addendum to the paper 'The Origin of the Word "Parapsychology" ' by Michael A. Thalbourne & Robert D. Rosenbaum.

Parapsychika (Journal)

Bimonthly journal (in German language) of the Swiss Parapsychological Society (Parapsychologische Arbeitsgruppe Base 1); includes papers on theoretical and experimental aspects of parapsychology. Address: K. Berber, Leonhardsgraben 2, CH-4057, Basel, Switzerland.

Parapsychological Association

Formed in 1957 as the professional society of parapsychology "to advance parapsychology as a science, to disseminate knowledge of the field, and to integrate the findings with those of other branches of science." It holds an annual convention, reported in its *Proceedings,* now published annually as *Research in Parapsychology.*

In 1969 the Association was affiliated with the American Association for the Advancement of Science.

Council members have included Rex G. **Stanford,** John **Beloff,** Charles **Honorton,** J. G. **Pratt,** Helmut **Schmidt,** Montague **Ullman,** Robert **Van de Castle.** The work of the Association is reported in *Journal of Parapsychology* and *Journal* of the American Society for Psychical Research. Address: Box 12236, Research Triangle Park, North Carolina 27709.

Parapsychological Journal of South Africa

Annual publication of South African Society for Psychical Research; includes lectures given to the Society. Address: P.O. Box 23154, Joubert Park, Johannesburg 2044, South Africa.

Parapsychological Research Society (Turkey)

Turkish organization concerned with parapsychological research. Address: c/o Mr. Selman Gerceksever, Sakizzülü Sokak, No. 21 Kat: 1 Bahariye, Kadiköy, Istanbul, Turkey.

Parapsychology

The term "parapsychology" appears to have been coined in Germany in or before 1889 by psychologist Max Dessoir (1867-1947). The term is the subject of a communication 'Die Parapsychologie. Eine Entgegnung auf den Artikel "Der Prophet" ' by Dessoir in the June 1889 issue of the periodical *Sphinx* (pp. 341-44). An English translation 'Parapsychology. A Response to the Article "The Prophet" ' [by Ludwig Brunn] was published in *Journal* of the Society for Psychical Research (vol. 53, No. 802, January 1986) as an addendum to the paper 'The Origin of the Word "Parapsychology" ' by Michael A. Thalbourne & Robert D. Rosenbaum.

Dessoir's use of the term "parapsychology," as also the term "parapsychic," predates the later work of Emile **Boirac** (1851-1917), who used the term "Parapsychology" and also "parapsychical" in his book *La Psychologie Inconnue; Introduction et contribution à l'étude expérimentale des sciences psychiques* (Paris, 1908; English translation *Psychic Science; An Introduction and Contribution to the Experimental Study of Psychical Phenomena,* London, 1918).

The term "parapsychology" was later used by Dr. J. B. **Rhine** (1895-1980). See also the note 'Max Dessoir and the Origin of the Word "Parapsychology" ' in *Journal* of the Society for Psychical Research (vol. 54, No. 806, January 1987).

"Parapsychology" is now generally used to indicate the scientific study of the paranormal in preference to earlier terms like "Psychical Science." The term "paraphysical" is now preferred to "paranormal," indicating phenomena beside or beyond normally understood cause and effect.

Such phenomena are also generally indicated by the greek letter *Psi,* embracing unusual mental phenomena such as **telepathy, clairvoyance, precognition,** and unusual physical phenomena such as **psychokinesis** (movement of objects without contact). "Psychokinesis" suggests the action of the human mind in causing such movement at a distance in preference to the earlier term "Telekinesis." "PK" is the convenient abbreviation for psychokinesis.

Much of the transition from the Psychical Science of the 1900s to the Parapsychology of the last few decades has been largely a semantic revolution, riddled with initialisms like ESP and PK as well as statistical analysis of laboratory tests, giving an air of respectability to what was formerly regarded as a very dubious affair of phenomena associated with mediums and **Spiritualism.**

In the process of making psychical phenomena safe for science, and therefore deserving of grants and sponsorship, the emphasis shifted initially to laboratory tests with card-guessing and dice-rolling, where experiments could be evaluated statistically.

The pioneers of Parapsychology were Professor William **McDougall** and Professor J. B. **Rhine** (with his wife Dr. Louisa E. **Rhine**). In 1927, McDougall and the Rhines began research on mediumship, survival and telepathy in the Department of Psychology at Duke University, Durham, North Carolina. It was Rhine who popularized the terms "parapsychology," "extrasensory perception" and "psi," and his attempts in the 1930s to find a statistical validation of ESP made Parapsychology a legitimate area for scientific research.

He established the now familiar outlines of laboratory method with card-guessing and dice-rolling experiments. Card-guessing had already been used in scientific tests by psychical researchers in Britain, but Rhine popularized the use of the Zener pack, devised by psychologist Dr. Zener. This consisted of 25 cards bearing simple symbols in groups of five of a kind: star, circle, square, cross and waves. This pack simplified the mathematical calculations involved in evaluating chance factors in guessing.

One of Rhine's principal subjects was a student Hubert E. Pearce, assisted by J. Gaither **Pratt** who later became a prominent parapsychologist himself. In a significant set of seventy-four runs which Rhine named the Pearce-Pratt Series, the odds against the successful guesses being merely chance were estimated as 1 in 10,000,000,000,000,000,000,000. Many variants in experimental setup were developed in card-guessing, and the results were often significantly above chance expectation.

The Psychokinetic experiments developed after a casual visitor to Duke boasted that he could will dice to fall so that he could get the numbers he needed to win. Experimental techniques were devised in which subjects threw dice for the face of their choice, and the results were analyzed mathematically. The results over several years indicated strong evidence for the reality of PK, and such findings were later confirmed by experimenters elsewhere, using a variety of experimental techniques. Various methods were developed to ensure that PK tests with dice were not influenced by mechanical factors (weight of dice, etc.) or unconscious skills in throwing. Apparatus was designed which threw dice automatically.

Some special terms that have developed in the study of PK are: PK-MT (psychokinetic effect on moving targets such as dice); PK-LT (influence on living matter, such as growth in plants, healing, influencing animals); PK-ST (influence on static targets). Another initialism that grew up in evaluating PK was "QD," which indicated the division of record sheets into four equal quarters. Study of quarter divisions showed a consistent pattern of fall-off in scoring results as between upper left and lower right quarters of the record sheet, with the other two quarters bridging the gap in success fall-off. It became clear that this fall-off in success during the course of a series of tests was a characteristic feature of PK, suggesting the operation of some unknown mental process which affected the continuity of PK achievement.

In 1934, Rhine published his first book *Extrasensory Perception,* which caused something of a furor in scientific and academic circles, and for a time it was fashionable to attack his preliminary findings favoring ESP. There was still much opposition to parapsychology as a study even at Duke University, where Rhine was obliged to open a separate Parapsychology Laboratory and seek outside sponsorship for research. However, the persistent patient work of Rhine, his associates and other parapsychologists over decades eventually established the validity of Parapsychology as a proper scientific study.

The story of that period is documented in a book by Rhine and others: *Extrasensory perception after sixty years; a critical appraisal of the research in extrasensory perception* (1940). This not only gives a detailed account of the ESP research at Duke University from 1927 through 1940, but also presents the early period of psychical research which preceded it from 1882 to 1927.

It should be remembered that since the establishment of the **Society for Psychical Research** in Britain in 1882, much valuable scientific investigation of ESP and related phenomena took place under the name of "psychical research," even continuing under that name in modern times. From 1921 on, an important series of card tests was conducted by G. N. M. **Tyrrell** in Britain. The British experimenter W. Whately **Carington** did important tests on telepathy and PK and also developed a stimulating "association theory" of telepathy. Other British experimenters include G. W. **Fisk** and Dr. Donald J. **West** working on PK scoring, Dr. S. G. **Soal** and Mrs. K. M. **Goldney.**

In the U.S., notable ESP pioneers included Dr. Gardner **Murphy** and Dr. Gertrude R. **Schmeidler.** Dr. Murphy joined the Society for Psychical Research, London, as early as 1917, and did graduate work in the field as Richard Hodgson Fellow from 1922 to 1925; he was also vice-president of the **American Society for Psychical Research** from 1940-62, becoming president afterwards.

From 1937 onwards, Rhine began publication of the *Journal of Parapsychology,* devoted to original publication of experimental results and other research findings in extra-sensory perception and psychokinesis.

In 1951, Mrs. Eileen J. **Garrett,** a notable Irish-born psychic who had been tested by Rhine in the early days at Duke, established the **Parapsychology Foundation,** New York, concerned with a wide range of parapsychological subjects, and sponsoring research projects. From 1953 on, it published a bimonthly *Newsletter of the Parapsychology Foundation,* superseded in 1970 by the bimonthly journal *Parapsychology Review.* Between 1959 and 1968 the Foundation also published a valuable *International Journal of Parapsychology.*

The Parapsychology Foundation played an important part in encouraging parapsychological research in universities and amongst scholars with established scientific reputations.

During the 1950s and 60s the scope of parapsychology expanded to include the range of subjects formerly covered under the term "psychical research," including Spiritualism, evidence for survival after death, clairvoyance, hauntings, poltergeist, out-of-the-body traveling, reincarnation, psychical healing and magical practices amongst primitive peoples. But by now, such investigations were conducted by learned professors in an atmosphere of academic tolerance.

In the 1960s, scientific studies in such areas coincided with the occult revival on a popular level, creating a general climate of belief in the paranormal at both critical and uncritical levels. Perhaps the most significant sign of the arrival of Parapsychology as a proper scientific study was the acceptance of the Parapsychological Association into membership of the American Association for the Advancement of Science in December 1969, after three previous rejections. This improved scientific status of parapsychology owed much to the patient laboratory work on ESP by Rhine and others since the 1930s. However, from time to time, attempts to discredit parapsychology as a scientific subject are still made by ultra skeptics. Credibility for such attacks is often furnished by revaluations of former well established parapsychological experiments.

For example, the experiments in telepathy carried out by Dr. S. G. Soal with the percipient Basil Shackleton from 1941-43 had been regarded as highly evidential for many years, but in 1971, serious doubts were raised about the experiments and Soal's handling of them. An article by R. G. Medhurst in the *Journal* of the Society for Psychical Research (vol. 46, 1971) on 'The Origin of the Prepared Random Numbers used in the Shackleton Experiments' questioned the method of constructing quasi-random series in the tests. This implied inaccuracy (or worse) in Soal's methods. As early as 1960, Mrs. Gretl Albert, an agent at some of the sittings, had alleged that she had seen Dr. Soal "altering the figures" several times on the score sheets.

A further article by C. Scott, P. Haskell, et al., 'The Soal-Goldney Experiments with Basil Shackleton: A Discussion' (*Proceedings* of the S.P.R., vol. 56, 1974) reinforced criticism of Soal's methods. After various parapsychologists defended Soal, Scott and Haskell published a further critical article 'Fraud in the Shackleton Experiments; A Reply to Critics' (*Journal* of the S.P.R., vol. 48, 1975). Soal himself did not respond to criticisms, and died in 1975. Three years later, a detailed and highly technical paper by Betty Markwick, 'The Soal-Goldney Experiments with Basil Shackleton; New Evidence of Data Manipulation' (*Proceedings* of the S.P.R., vol. 56, 1978) presented an overwhelming case for conscious or unconscious manipulation of data by Soal, based on computer analysis of his records. Not all parapsychologists agree that Soal was deliberately fraudulent, but the validity of his telepathy experiments with Basil Shackleton has been shown to be inadmissible.

A more recent controversy has grown up around the **ganzfeld** psi experiments of Carl Sargent at the University of Cambridge, England. An article 'A Report of a Visit to Carl Sargent's Laboratory' by Susan **Blackmore** (*Journal* of the S.P.R., vol. 54, 1987) cast serious doubt on the methods and validity of Dr. Sargent's experiments. A defense of Sargent against the implication of fraud, 'Cheating, Psi, and the Appliance of Science; A Reply to Blackmore' by Trevor Harley & Gerald Matthews, was published in the same issue of the *Journal.*

It would be foolish to conclude that such controversies prove that parapsychology is unscientific. On the contrary, they indicate a high standard of self-criticism and vigilance, and an insistence on the necessity for rigorous scientific method.

The field of parapsychology is now almost limitless, with as much attention to spontaneous phenomena and the talents of gifted sensitives as to patient and perhaps rather dull laboratory experiments. The leading countries of the world now have parapsychological organizations and participate in international conferences at which scientists and academics present their researches and theories.

ESP has moved far beyond simple card-guessing into measurements of blood pressure changes during concentration on guessing, and long-distance ESP experiments between scientists in Switzerland and a scuba diver 35 feet beneath the surface of the Caribbean.

Notable new directions in parapsychology include the investigation of altered states of consciousness (including alpha-related states and dream experiences), experiments in paranormal healing of animals, and the work of Prof. Ian **Stevenson** in investigation of the evidence for **reincarnation.**

In Britain the work of Prof. John **Taylor** in testing the paranormal feats of Uri **Geller** may open up exciting possibilities for understanding of the rationale of mind over matter.

Privately sponsored bodies like the **Institute of Noetic Sciences,** founded by former astronaut Edgar D. **Mitchell** have extended study of the paranormal from traditional psychic phenomena to areas of human consciousness such as mysticism.

Nowadays, the opposition to parapsychology comes less from the scientific world than the professional conjuring magicians like the scholarly Milbourne **Christopher,** or the flamboyant James **Randi,** who now replaces the late Harry **Houdini** as the arch-skeptic of paranormal phenomena.

There is, of course, also a danger that the uncritical mass acceptance of occultism and witchcraft will generate a backlash of antagonism, with accusations of fraud, claimed exposures of psychics, etc. But popular interest in occultism has made astrology, clairvoyance, witchcraft and other paranormal phenomena a functional part of everyday life, whereas the scientific investigator is trapped into the role of observer and cannot make the paranormal an integral part of his personal life.

Moreover paranormal faculties are elusive, ambiguous and erratic, lacking the possibility of rapid practical application, unlike the amazing advances in such scientific areas as, for example, micro-chips and thin film technology.

The special problems of parapsychology are those of acceptable scientific evidence, and repeatability of experimental findings. Since much claimed paranormal phenomena appears to be spontaneous, or stimulated by personal factors, scientific validation is difficult. Parapsychologists are now taking account of emotional factors, and psychological motivations and incentives in relation to paranormal faculty.

It had to be admitted that more than half a century after the early experiments at Duke University, there is, as yet, no generally accepted scientific validation of paranormal faculty. Equally there is no unassailable scientific evidence that paranormal faculty does *not* exist. The evidence is often ambiguous, or requiring special mathematical techniques of evaluation beyond the capacity of the man and woman in the street committed to uncritical **New Age** beliefs in **crystal healing** and **channeling.**

In contrast, the earlier history of psychical research, with its emphasis on startling mediumistic physical phenomena, studied by scientists like Sir William Crookes, Prof. Charles Richet, Prof. Cesar Lombroso and others, seemed more solidly evidential in its time, even if somewhat disparaged by modern critics.

Inevitably progress in parapsychology is slow and unsensational, involving meticulous attention to details, and an application of highest standards of the scientific method responsible for the great technological triumphs of modern materialism.

Thousands of complex technical and statistical experiments in parapsychology do not lend themselves to commercial development or a new way of life. So far, even experiments in the use of known psi faculty in espionage or other warfare applications in both the U.S. and U.S.S.R. have shown less promise than conventional methods and weaponry and there seems little prospect that psychics will offer the devastating capabilities of an H Bomb. Even so, there is nothing essentially life affirmative about such applications, however remote.

It is the separation of parapsychology from life which makes laboratory experiments often tedious, lacking in warmth or incentive, whereas the uncritical believer, whether Spiritualist, Christian Scientist or member of a witchcraft or Voodoo cult may generate a powerful emotional drive which produces sensational phenomena or exalted states of consciousness.

A single experience of paranormal healing, **out-of-body travel,** prophetic dreaming, seeing an apparition or receiving personal evidence of the survival of a loved relative, will naturally have more meaning to the man and woman in the street than hundreds of technical papers by parapsychologists, or the authoritarian fulminations of arch skeptics of the paranormal.

It may eventually become necessary for certain areas of parapsychology to sacrifice some of their objectivity and discover a philosophical or religious basis for the validation of the paranormal as a functional part of everyday life as it was in primitive societies.

For valuable overviews of the history of parapsychology, see 'What is Parapsychology?' by Joseph H. Rush in *Foundations of Parapsychology* by Hoyt L. Edge, Robert L. Morris, Joseph H. Rush & John Palmer (1986), and 'History of Experimental Studies' by J. B. Rhine in *Handbook of Parapsychology* edited Benjamin B. Wolman et al. (1977; 1986). (See also **Psychical Research**)

Recommended reading:

Beloff, John (ed.) *New Directions in Parapsychology,* London, 1974; Scarecrow, 1975

Blackmore, Susan. *Adventures of a Parapsychologist,* Prometheus Books, Buffalo, N.Y., 1986

Edge, Hoyt L., Robert L. Morris, John Palmer, Joseph H. Rush. *Foundations of Parapsychology; Exploring the Boundaries of Human Capability,* Routledge & Kegan Paul, London & Boston, 1986

Grattan-Guinness, Ivor. *Psychical Research; A Guide to its History, Principles and Practices, in Celebration of 100 Years of the Society for Psychical Research,* Aquarian Press (paperback), U.K., 1982

Hansel, C. E. M. *ESP and Parapsychology; A Critical Re-Evaluation,* Prometheus Books, Buffalo, N.Y., 1980

Haynes, Renée. *The Society for Psychical Research 1882-1982, a History,* Macdonald & Co., London, 1982

Rhine, J. B. *Extrasensory Perception,* Boston Society for Psychic Research, 1934; revised edition Branden, 1964

Rhine, J. B. *The Reach of the Mind,* Sloane, 1947; Morrow, 1971

Rhine, J. B. & others. *Extrasensory perception after sixty years; a critical appraisal of the research in extrasensory perception,* Holt, 1940; Branden, 1966

Rhine, J. B. & others. *Parapsychology Today,* Citadel, 1968

Rhine, J. B. (ed.) *Progress in Parapsychology,* Parapsychology Press, 1971

Richet, Charles. *Thirty Years of Psychical Research,* W. Collins Sons, London, 1923; Arno Press, 1975

Soal, S. G. & F. Bateman. *Modern Experiments in Telepathy,* Yale University Press, 1954

Sudre, René. *Parapsychology,* Citadel, 1960 [covers much of the European work]

Murphy, Gardner & Laura A. Dale. *Challenge of Psychical Research; a primer of Psychical Research,* Harper & Row, 1961

Pratt, J. Gaither. *ESP Research Today; a study of developments in Parapsychology since 1960,* Scarecrow, 1963

Price, Harry. *Fifty Years of Psychical Research; A Critical Survey,* Longmans Green, London, 1939; Arno Press, 1975

Thalbourne, Michael A. *A Glossary of Terms Used in Parapsychology,* Heinemann, London, 1982

Thouless, Robert H. *Experimental Psychical Research,* London, 1963; Gannon, Santa Fe, 1969

Pratt, J. Gaither. *Parapsychology; an insider's view of ESP,* Doubleday, 1964; Dutton, 1966

Rao, K. Ramakrishna. *Experimental Parapsychology: a review and interpretation, with a comprehensive bibliography,* Thomas, 1966

Schmeidler, Gertrude R. *Extrasensory Perception,* Atherton, New York, 1969

Vasiliev, L. L. *Experiments in Mental Suggestion,* Institute for the Study of Mental Images, Church Crookham, U.K., reissued under title *Experiments* in *Distance Influence,* Dutton/Wildwood House, London, 1976

Vasiliev, L. L. *Studies in Mental Telepathy,* CCM Information Corp., New York, 1971 (photocopy publication)

White, Rhea A. & Laura A. Dale. *Parapsychology: Sources of Information,* Scarecrow, 1973 [updated by regular lists from the Parapsychology Foundation, New York]

White, Rhea A. *Surveys in Parapsychology,* Scarecrow, 1976 [updated by regular lists from the Parapsychology Foundation, New York]

Wolman, Benjamin B. et al., *Handbook of Parapsychology,* Van Nostrand Reinhold, 1977; McFarland & Co., Jefferson, N.C. & London, 1986

Parapsychology (Newsletter)

Quarterly journal in Chinese language, published in Taiwan. Address: Society for Parapsychological Studies, 6 Lane 4, Huang Puh Village 7, Genshan, Taiwan.

Parapsychology Abstracts International

An extremely valuable publication commenced in 1983, edited by Rhea W. **White.** This semiannual journal contains about 250 abstracts of varying length, covering both current and historical material. Some 100 parapsychology journals are covered, as well as material in major nonparapsychological journals and books.

The first issue in 1983 was retrospective in scope, abstracting material from the *Journal of Parapsychology* from 1937 to 1960. PAI is well indexed under authors and subjects. This is particularly helpful, since much of the material abstracted was not indexed in detail in original publications. Address: Parapsychology Sources of Information Center, 2 Plane Tree Lane, Dix Hills, New York 11746.

Parapsychology Association of Riverside

Organization sponsoring lectures and study groups on parapsychology and acting as a center for information. Issues a monthly newsletter *PARINFO.* Address: 6370 Magnolia Avenue, #219, Riverside, California 92506.

Parapsychology Bulletin

Former publication of Parapsychology Press (Box 6847, College Station, Durham, North Carolina 27708), to bring together parapsychologists through the medium of their scientific publications.

The Bulletin continued the former **FRNM Bulletin** after Autumn 1969 as New Series No. 15 (1970) through No. 20 (1971). The Old Series *Parapsychology Bulletin* appeared from No. 1 (1946) through No. 72 (1965) before publication of *FRNM Bulletin* from Summer 1965 to Autumn 1969 (Nos. 1-14). The main functions of *Parapsychology Bulletin* have now been taken over by a section of News and Comments in the *Journal of Parapsychology.* Back issues of *Parapsychology Bulletin* are available from Foundation for Research on the Nature of Man (Box 6847, College Station, Durham, N.C. 27708) or from University Microfilms, Ann Arbor, Michigan 48106.

Parapsychology Foundation

Founded in 1951 as a nonprofit educational organization to support impartial scientific inquiry into the total nature and working of the mind and to make available the results of such inquiry.

The Foundation stems from the work of Mrs. Eileen J. **Garrett,** the first president. The Foundation has provided grants for research in parapsychology, and maintained an active program of publications, including monographs, books and journals. It holds international conferences which are reported in the Foundation's *Parapsychology Review* (issued bimonthly).

The Foundation also maintains the Eileen J. Garrett Library which provides valuable reference to students and researchers in the field of parapsychology. Address: 228 East 71 Street, New York, N.Y. 10021.

Parapsychology Laboratory (Netherlands)

Dutch Institute founded by W. H. C. **Tenhaeff** in 1933 (formerly known as the Parapsychology Institute of the State University of Utrecht). The Institute is supported by state funds, conducts experimental programs, and publishes books, periodicals and reports on parapsychological research. It publishes the *European Journal of Parapsychology.* Address: Parapsychology Laboratory, University of Utrecht, Sorbonnelaan 16, 3584 CA Utrecht, The Netherlands.

Parapsychology Now (Journal)

Quarterly journal of parapsychology; includes book reviews, news of parapsychological events in Midwest. Address: 324 Touhy Street, Park Ridge, Illinois 60068.

Parapsychology Research Group, Inc.

Nonprofit organization founded 1962 in Palo Alto, California, to conduct investigations into psychic research. The president was Russell **Targ,** now with **Stanford Research Institute.** Targ has collaborated with Harold E. **Puthoff** on parapsychological researches involving psychics Uri **Geller** and Ingo **Swann.**

Parapsychology Review (Journal)

Published bimonthly from 1970 onwards, to give news of individuals and organizations associated with parapsychology, information on courses, lectures, grants, book reviews, obituaries. Publisher: Parapsychology Foundation, 228 East 71 Street, New York, N.Y. 10021.

Parapsychology Sources of Information Center

Also known as "Psi Center," established by parapsychologist Rhea A. **White** in 1983, providing valuable and comprehensive reference resources for parapsychologists and the public.

The Center has a computerized database of the periodical literature of parapsychology, and has entered thousands of items into *PsiLine,* which provides computer searches on-line covering dissertations, chapters from books, psi-related publications. This service uses the Textbank software, and can be contacted at the Center by calling (516) 271-1243 weekdays between 9 a.m. and 3 p.m., or by mail.

In addition, the Center publishes *Parapsychology Abstracts International,* providing brief summaries of periodical literature from English, Spanish, Dutch, Portuguese, Italian, German, French, Polish, Japanese, and Russian researchers. Other important publications of the Center include bibliographies on specific paranormal topics, and reading lists for students from grades 4 to 12, or the general public, or specialists. The address of the Center is: 2 Plane Tree Lane, Dix Hills, New York 11746.

Parapsychology; The Indian Journal of Parapsychological Research

Indian journal (text in English) published quarterly by: University of Rajasthan, Department of Parapsychology, Jaipur (Rajasthan), India.

Parascience Proceedings

Publication of the **Institute of Parascience,** England; includes research papers and reports of conferences on psi subjects. Address: Institute of Parascience, Spryton, Lifton, Devon PL16 OAY, England.

Parascience Research Journal

Quarterly journal of **Institute of Parascience,** England, dealing with theoretical and experimental research into **ESP, PK, out-of-the-body** experience and related subjects. Address: Parascience Centre, Sprytown, Devon PL16 OAY, England.

Paraskeva, Saint

A saint of the Russian Calendar, whose feast day is August 3. On that day, pilgrims from all parts of Russia used to congregate in St. Petersburg for the purpose of casting out devils. A newspaper report of the proceedings as they occurred in 1913 is as follows:

"Another St. Paraskeva's day has come and gone. The usual fanatical scenes have been enacted in the suburbs of St. Petersburg, and the ecclesiastical authorities have not protested, nor have the police intervened. Special trains have again been run to enable thousands of the lower classes to witness a spectacle, the toleration of which will only be appreciated by those acquainted with the writings of M. Pobiedonostzeff, the late Procurator of the Holy Synod.

"The Church of St. Paraskeva is situated in a factory district of the city. On the exterior side of one of the walls is an image of the Saint, to whom is attributed the power of driving out devils and curing epileptics, neurotics, and others by miraculous intervention. At the same time, the day is made a popular holiday, with games and amusements of the all sorts, booths, and lotteries, refreshment stalls and drinking bars.

"The newspapers publish detailed accounts of this year's proceedings without comment, and it is perhaps significant that the *Novoe Vremya,* a pillar of orthodoxy, ignores them altogether. Nor is this surprising when one reads of women clad in a single undergarment with bare arms being hoisted up by stalwart peasants to the level of the image in order to kiss it, and then having impure water and unclarified oil forced down their throats.

"The treatment of the first sick woman is typical of the rest. One young peasant lifted her in the air, two others held her arms fully extended, while a fourth seized her loosened hair, and, dragging her head from side to side and up and down, shouted 'Kiss, kiss St. Paraskeva!' The woman's garment was soon in tatters. She began groaning. One of the men exclaimed: 'Get out! Satan! Say where thou art lodged!' The woman's head was pulled back by the hair, her mouth was forced open, and mud-coloured water (said to be holy water) was poured into it. She spat the water out, and was heard to moan, 'Oh, they are drowning me!'

"The young man exultantly exclaimed, 'So we've got you, devil, have we? Leave her at once or we will drown you!' He continued pouring water into the victim's mouth, and after that unclarified oil. Her lips were held closed, so that she was obliged to swallow it. The unfortunate woman was again raised and her face pressed against the image. 'Kiss it! kiss it!' she was commanded, and she obeyed. She was asked who was the cause of her being 'possessed.' 'Anna,' was the whispered reply. Who was Anna? What was her village? In which cottage did she live? A regular inquisition.

"The physical and mental sufferings of the first victim lasted about an hour, at the end of which she was handed over to her relatives, after a cross had been given to her, as it was found that she did not own one. According to accounts published by the papers *Retch* and *Molva,* many other women were treated in the same fashion, the exercises lasting a whole day and night. The men 'pilgrims' would seem to have been less severely handled. It is explained that the idea of unclothing the woman is that there should be no knot, bow, or fastening where the devil and his coadjutors could find a lodgment. And one is left with the picture of scores of women crawling around the church on their knees, invoking the aid of the Almighty for the future of His pardon for sins committed in the past."

The treatment of the "possessed" is analogous to that employed by many primitive peoples for the casting out of devils, and notably among the Chams of **Cambodia** who used to force the possessed to eat garbage in order to disgust the fiend they harbored. (See also **Obsession**)

PARINFO

Monthly newsletter of the Parapsychology Association of Riverside. Address: 6370 Magnolia Avenue, #219, Riverside, California 92506.

Parish, W. T. (1873-1946)

Pioneer British spiritual healer, whose profession commenced in 1929 after a surgeon warned that his wife would die from inoperable cancer within six months.

A Spiritualist friend suggested psychic healing, and during a Spiritualist seance, a spirit guide informed Parish that he was a natural healer and would cure his own wife. Parish did in fact effect a cure within nine months, after which he practiced as a healer.

Over seventeen years he received more than 500,000 letters of thanks from grateful patients, many of whom had been declared incurable by doctors. He became popularly known as "Parish the Healer." He died in January 1946.

For biographical information see *Parish the Healer* by Maurice Barbanell (Psychic Book Club, London, 1938).

Parkes, F. M. (c. 1872)

British spirit photographer, who, in association with M. Reeves, the proprietor of a dining room, obtained recognized spirit extras after three months experiments in 1872, the year in which Frederick A. **Hudson** obtained the first such pictures in England. Without the presence of Reeves or his own wife, Parkes could not get a full form and clearly defined pictures, only white patches and cloudy appearances.

In accordance with spirit directions he set it as a condition to have the plates in his possession in the dark room prior to their being placed in the camera for purposes of magnetization. To avert suspicion he had an inspection hole cut in the dark room through which the sitters could see the plate through its entire process.

Dr. Sexton wrote enthusiastically of Parkes' powers in the *Christian Spiritualist.* The Rev. Stainton **Moses** gave the following interesting description in *Human Nature:* "A considerable number of the earlier pictures taken by Messrs. Parkes and Reeves were allegorical. One of the earliest, taken in April, 1872, shows Mr. Reeves' father holding up a cross above his head and displaying an open book on which is written "Holy Bible." Another shows a cloud of light covering two-thirds of the pictures, and made up of the strangest medley of heads and arms, and flashes of light, with a distinct cross in the centre. Another, in which Mr. and Mrs. Everitt were the sitters, taken June 8, 1872, is a symbolical picture of a very curious nature. Mr. Everitt's head is surrounded with a fillet on which 'Truth' is inscribed, while three pencils of light dart up from it. There are at least two figures in the picture which blot out Mrs. Everitt altogether.

"In a later photograph, in which Mr. Burns is the sitter, is a giant hand of which the thumb is half the length of the sitter's body. It is just as if a luminous hand had been projected or flashed on the plate without any regard to focus. Another very startling picture is one which shows on a dark background a huge luminous crucifix. Then we have angels with orthodox wings hovering over some sitters. One is a very striking model: the face of great beauty and of pure classical design. The figure floats with extended arm over the sitter, and below it, almost on the ground, appear nine faces, and, strangest of all, close by the sitter's head, a large eye, with beams of light proceeding from it. The eye is larger than the head of the sitter, and the whole picture presents a most curious appearance. Some show mere faces; some heads; some, again, whole bodies floating in the air; and some partially formed bodies projected on the plate, apparently at haphazard." (See also **Spirit Photography**)

Paroptic Vision

Term coined by French author Jules **Romains** (Louis Farigoule) for the ability to see without the use of the eyes. (See **Eyeless Sight**)

Parsons, Denys (1914-)

British administrator, documentary film director, for some years joint honorary secretary of the Society for Psychical Research London. Born March 12, 1914, in London, England, he was educated at Eton, and London University (M.Sc., A.R.I.C.). In 1962 he married Frances Burke. He was a research chemist from 1939-45, director of scientific, medical and industrial films from 1945-52, manager of Applied Physics Group, National Research Development

Corporation from 1952-73; head of press and public relations, British Library, London, 1973-80.

He has published a number of humorous books and guides, and edited *The Directory of Tunes and Musical Themes* (1975). Mr. Parsons has taken special interest in research relating to quantitative evaluation of extrasensory perception. His articles on parapsychology include: (in *Proceedings* of the Society for Psychical Research) 'Experiments on PK with Inclined Plane and Rotating Cage' (vol. 47, 1945), 'Attempts to Detect Clairvoyance and Telepathy with a Mechanical Device' (vol. 48, 1946) 'On the Need for Caution in Assessing Mediumistic Material' (vol. 48, 1949); (in *Journal* of the Society for Psychical Research) 'Cloud Busting: A Claim Investigated' (vol. 38, Dec. 1956), 'A Nonexistent Building Located' (vol. 41, July 1962).

Pascal, Guillermo B. (1906-)

Uruguayan instructor in parapsychology. Born June 6, 1906, at Montevideo, Uruguay. In 1943 he married Romana E. Scaglia. He is a member of the Brazilian Academy of Social and Political Sciences, Argentine College for Psychic Studies, Buenos Aires, International Institute for Scientific Research, Paris. Mr. Pascal was president of the Parapsychology Society of Montevideo from 1952 onwards, and is instructor in parapsychology at the Institute of Advanced Studies, Montevideo.

He also taught parapsychology at the University of San Salvador, El Salvador. He took special interest in telepathy, clairvoyance, precognition and mediumship.

Paterson, T(homas) T(homson) (1909-)

Scottish professor of industrial administration who took special interest in parapsychology. Born September 29, 1909, at Buckhaven, Fife, Scotland, he studied at University of Edinburgh (B.S. chemistry, mathematics 1930; B.S. geology, zoology, anatomy 1932), Cambridge University (M.A. anthropology 1938, Ph.D. anthropology 1940). In 1938 he married Elna Johanna Hygen.

He was a staff member of the Medical Research Council, Scotland, from 1948-51, senator lecturer in industrial relations, Glasgow University from 1951-62, professor of industrial administration from 1962 onwards at Royal College of Science and Technology, Glasgow. He is a fellow of Trinity College, Cambridge, fellow of Royal Society of Edinburgh, chairman of Symposium on Methodology of Research at Conference on Parapsychology and Psychedelics held November 1958 in New York. He is author of many papers and books on anthropology, geology, psychology, administration and sociology.

In the field of parapsychology he took a special interest in telepathy and clairvoyance in relation to psychedelics.

Path, The

A term which represents an important Theosophical teaching, and is used in different senses to denote not only the Path itself but also the Probationary Path along which an individual must journey before he can enter on the Path proper.

Impelled by profound longing for the highest, for service of God and fellow humans, the individual first begins the journey and must devote himself or herself wholeheartedly to this service. At the entrance on the Probationary Path, one becomes the *chela* or disciple of one of the Masters or Perfected beings who have all finished the great journey, and one must devote oneself to the acquiring of four qualifications, which are (1) knowledge of what only is real; (2) rejection of what is unreal; (3) the six mental attributes of control over thought, control over outward action, tolerance, endurance, faith and balance, these attributes though all necessary in some degree, not being necessary in perfect degree; and (4) the desire to be one with God.

During the period of efforts to acquire these qualifications, the *chela* advances in many ways, for the Master imparts wise counsel, teaching by meditation how to attain divine heights unthought of by ordinary human beings; the *chela* constantly works for the betterment of others, usually in the hours of sleep, and striving thus and in similar directions, becomes fitted for the first initiation at the entrance to the Path proper, but it may be mentioned that the *chela* has the opportunity either during probation or afterwards to forego the heavenly life which is due and so to allow the world to benefit by the powers which he or she has gained, and which in ordinary course, would be utilized in the heavenly life. In this case, the *chela* remains in the **astral world,** from whence he makes frequent returns to the physical world.

Of initiations, there are four, each at the beginning of a new stage on the Path, manifesting the knowledge of that stage. On the first stage there are three obstacles or, as they are commonly termed, fetters, which must be cast aside and these are the illusion of self which must be realized to be only an illusion; doubt which must be cleared away by knowledge; and superstition which must be cleared away by the discovery of what in truth is real.

This stage traversed, the second initiation follows, and after this comes the consciousness that earthly life will now be short, that only once again will physical death be experienced, and the disciple begins more and more to function in the mental body.

After the third initiation, the disciple has two other fetters to unloose—desire and aversion, and now knowledge becomes keen and piercing and the disciple can gaze deep into the heart of things.

After the fourth initiation, the disciple enters on the last stage and is finally freed of what fetters remain—the desire for life whether bodily or not, and the sense of individual difference from fellow human beings. The disciple has now reached the end of the journey, and is no longer trammelled with sin or with anything that can hinder from entering the state of supreme bliss where he or she is reunited with the divine consciousness.

This scheme of spiritual realization is based on Hindu mysticism. (See also **Guru; Masters; Theosophical Society; Theosophy; Yoga**)

Pathetism

Term used to denote **Mesmerism** or **Animal Magnetism** by La Roy Sunderland (1804-1885), an early American experimenter, a contemporary of James Braid.

In his book *Pathetism* (1843), Sunderland wrote: "I use this term to signify, not only the AGENCY by which one person by manipulation, is enabled to produce *emotion, feeling, passion,* or any physical or mental effects, in the system of another but also that SUSCEPTIBILITY of *emotion* or *feeling,* of any kind, from manipulation, in the subject operated upon, by the use of which these effects are produced; as also the *laws* by which this agency is governed. I mean it as a substitute for the terms heretofore in use, in connection with this subject, and I respectfully submit it to all concerned, whether this be not a far better term for the *thing signified,* than either Magnetism or Mesmerism."

In those early days, most magnetists had their own favorite term, such as "etherology" (J. Stanley Grimes), "neurology" (Joseph Rodes Buchanan), "electrobiology" (John Bovee Dods) or "electropsychology" (Dr. Fiske), but eventually the term "hypnotism" devised by James Braid became generally adopted. (See also **Hypnotism**)

Pathways (Directory) (Britain)

Concise British listing of **New Age** and psi events, organizations, periodicals and meetings in England, published quarterly. Address: 16 Great Ormond Street, London, WC1N 3RB, England.

Pathways (Journal) (Maryland)

Quarterly publication of "ideas concerning personal and social transformation." Includes directory of services and events, book reviews. Address: Yes Educational Society, P.O. Box 5719, Takoma Park, Maryland 20912.

Pathways (Journal) (Missouri)

Quarterly publication edited by B. C. Jaegers, head of the State Licensed Psychic Detective Bureau. Address: Aries, Inc., P.O. Box 24571, Creve Coeur, Missouri 63141.

"Patience Worth"

A spirit entity, communicating from 1913 onwards through Mrs. John H. Curran, of St. Louis, Missouri, first through the **ouija board,** then through automatic speech, dictating, in a late medieval English, prose and poetry with extreme rapidity on a wide range of subjects.

The literary merit of the books was remarkable. The following volumes were published: *The Sorry Tale, Hope True-Blood, Light from Beyond, The Pot Upon the Wheel. Telka,* a poem of 60-70,000 words, is unique in its Anglo-Saxon purity, and was considered by psychical researcher Dr. Walter F. **Prince** superior to analogous works.

"Patience Worth" claimed to have lived in Dorsetshire, England, in the seventeenth century, and to have been killed in America by the Indians. Some of her statements as to her home and environment were verified.

The most notable books on the case are: Dr. Walter Franklin Prince, *The Case of Patience Worth* (1927) and Casper S. Yost, *Patience Worth; a Psychic Mystery* (1916). Yost was a newspaperman, editor of the St. Louis *Globe-Democrat,* who took a great personal interest in the Patience Worth phenomenon, and edited publication of the texts.

Dr. Prince's conclusion was: "Either our concept of what we call the subconscious mind must be radically altered so as to include potencies of which we hitherto have had no knowledge, or else some cause operating through, but not originating in, the subconsciousness of Mrs. Curran must be acknowledged."

Prof. Allison, of Manitoba University, said of the case in a personal study that "it must be regarded as the outstanding phenomenon of the age." Dr. Usher, professor of history in Washington University, considered *The Sorry Tale,* a composition of 350,000 words, "the greatest story penned of the life and times of Christ since the Gospels were finished." On occasions Patience Worth demonstrated before professors.

For ten months, from March 1918 onwards, a monthly called *Patience Worth's Magazine* was published to provide an outlet for her prolific literary activity.

For a valuable summary of the Patience Worth case, see the chapter 'Patience Worth' in *Extrasensory Powers* by Alfred Douglas, The Overlook Press, New York, 1977. (See also **Automatic Writing;** Mrs. John Howard **Curran**)

Recommended reading:

Litvag, Irving. *Singer in the Shadows; The Strange Story of Patience Worth,* Macmillan, 1972; Popular Library, New York, 1973

Prince, Walter Franklin. *The Case of Patience Worth; A Critical Study of Certain Unusual Phenomena,* Boston Society for Psychic Research, 1927; University Books, 1964

"Worth, Patience." *The Pot Upon the Wheel,* Patience Worth Publishing Co., New York, 1916; Dorset Press, Missouri, 1921

"Worth, Patience." *The Sorry Tale,* Henry Holt, 1917

"Worth, Patience." *Hope Trueblood,* Henry Holt, 1918

Yost, Casper S. *Patience Worth; A Psychic Mystery,* Henry Holt, 1916; Skeffington, London, 1919

Paton, Mrs. (c. 1878)

Nonprofessional **apport** medium of Melbourne, Australia, who flourished 1872-78. Records of sit tings with her are described in W. C. D. Denovan's *Evidences of Spiritualism* (1882). She accepted no fees for her seances.

The apports were distinguished by identification of the place where the objects came from. It often happened that things were brought from her own house over a distance of two miles.

Occasionally the objects were very heavy or difficult to handle like a glass of wine. A stone from the seashore was found to weigh 14 lbs. It came with a mass of seaweed with shrimp-like creatures among it. Of the apported household objects a soup plate with twenty eggs on it was one of the most notable ones.

Mrs. Paton was not usually entranced during her apport phenomena, but often markedly convulsed. She worked under strict test conditions, being searched before a seance and completed enveloped in a large mosquito-net bag, which was tied and sealed. The apports arrived on a table in the dark, but on some occasions, even in bright light.

One of the most astonishing apports occurred at the house of Miss Finlason, a resident of Castlemaine. During the seance, Mrs. Paton mentioned to one of the sitters that before leaving her home, two miles away, she had made a cup of tea, but forgotten to drink it. The cup of tea and saucer appeared as an apport on the table.

At another seance on April 6, 1874, an iron wheel weighing sixteen and a half lbs. fell with a crash on the table, brought from the yard outside.

Patterson, Mrs. S. E. (c. 1884)

American slate-writing medium, the first subject of the experiments of the **Seybert Commission** in 1884. In two sittings, no results were obtained.

A slate given in charge of the medium was returned six months later without any writing inside. Dr. Furness gave her a second slate. At the end of a fortnight, the announcement was made that the slate pencil inside had disappeared as it was not heard rattling. This was taken as a sign of success, as in Mrs. Patterson's case the completion of the writing was not indicated by **raps,** but by the sudden appearance of the slate fragment on the top of the slates.

When, however, the committee opened the slates, no writing was seen inside. On the other hand, according to the report, the wooden frames bore tell-tale marks of a knife which was inserted to force an aperture for the slate pencil. (See also **Slate-Writing**)

Pauwels, Louis (1920-)

Co-author with Jacques **Bergier** of the sensational bestselling work *Le Matin des Magiciens* (France, 1960), translated under the variant titles *The Dawn of Magic* (London, 1963) and *The Morning of the Magicians* (1971).

The book had a significant influence on the occult revival in Europe and elsewhere, containing revelations of the part played by occultism in the career of Hitler and the establishment of Nazi philosophy.

For a more scholarly but equally startling treatment of the same theme, see *The Spear of Destiny* by Trevor Ravenscroft (G. P. Putnam's Sons, 1973).

Pauwels and Bergier have also collaborated on *Der Planet der unmöglichen Möglichkeiten* (Germany, 1968), translated into English as *Impossible Possibilities* (London, 1974).

Pauwels was born in Paris, 1920, and worked in journalism and French television. As a student he was fascinated by the romance of alchemy. His collaborator Bergier was born 1912, and qualified as a chemical engineer during World War II. Pauwels was an active member of the French resistance movement. In recent years he became chief editor of *Figaro* Magazine.

Pearls

Various occult properties were ascribed to pearls. Amongst the early Greeks and Romans, the wearing of gems as an **amulet** or **talisman,** was much in vogue. For this purpose pearls were often made into crowns.

In *The Occult Sciences* by E. Smedley, W. C. Taylor, H. Thompson and E. Rich (1855), it is stated that: "Pope Adrian, anxious to secure all the virtues in his favour, wore an amulet composed of a sunbaked toad, arsenic, tormentil, pearl, coral, hyacinth, smarag, and tragacanth."

It was popularly believed that to dream of pearls meant many tears. The occult virtues of pearls were said to be brought forth by being boiled in meat, when they healed the quartan ague. When bruised and taken with milk, they were believed to be good for ulcers, and to clear the voice. They were also said to comfort the heart and render their possessor chaste.

The mysterious Mr. **Jacob** ("Jacob of Simla") (c. 1850-1921) described himself as a "Healer of Pearls," able to restore color to a "sick" pearl.

Pederson-Krag, Geraldine Huanayra (Mrs. George Pederson-Krag) (1901-)

Psychoanalytic psychiatrist with interests in parapsychology. Born July 23, 1901, in Schenectady, New York. She is a member of the Royal College of Surgeons, licentiate of Royal College of Physicians, London. In 1931 she married George Pederson-Krag.

She was assistant surgeon and house physician at Westminster Hospital, London, England, in 1928 in practice in New York, N.Y., in 1931, in industrial medicine 1931-37, intern at New York Psychiatric Hospital from 1937-38, executive director at New Rochelle (N.Y.) Guidance Center from 1941-45, consultant of Community Service Society (Queens, N.Y. office) from 1955-59, consultant at Mid-Nassau

Community Center 1958-60, director of Huntington Township Mental Health Clinic from 1960 onwards.

Dr. Pederson-Krag is author of *Personality Factors in Work and Employment* and various articles in *Psychoanalytic Quarterly,* including 'Telepathy and Repression' (vol. 16, 1947). She took a special interest in telepathy and clairvoyance.

Peebles, J(ames) M(artin) (1822-1922)

Prominent American Spiritualist, author and lecturer. He was born March 23, 1822, in a log cabin at Whittingham, Vermont, his ancestors being of Scottish stock. In a lifespan of nearly a century, he either witnessed or took part in some of the greatest events in American history.

He studied at Oxford Academy, New York, graduating Ph.D., LL.D. and practiced as a physician. He was also ordained as a minister and preached in regular parishes in Kellogsville, Elmira, New York and Baltimore. After preaching a sermon in Kellogsville, he was invited by one of his parishioners to attend a seance in Auburn, where he first heard spirit rapping. Soon afterwards he heard a trance lecture delivered by an uneducated boy; the subject was chosen by Peebles: "The Philosophical Influence of the Nations of Antiquity Upon the Civilization and Sciences of modern Europe and America."

As Dr. Peebles described the event: "The boy at once stepped forward and commenced, and for one hour and three-quarters one continual stream of history and philosophy fell from his lips." When Dr. Peebles preached on "The Spiritual Gifts" in his own church, the deacons and congregation protested, as a result of which Dr. Peebles resigned in disgust to follow a secular career and continue his investigation of Spiritualism. He wrote and lectured for more than eighty years, mainly in the cause of Spiritualism.

He was one of the earliest temperance workers and was an Emancipation advocate together with John Brown and William Lloyd Garrison. He knew many of the foremost men of his time, some of them as intimate friends. These included Ralph Waldo Emerson, Thomas Carlyle, Victor Hugo, Walt Whitman, John Bright, Theodore Parker, Henry Ward Beecher and Gerald Massey.

At Cleveland, Ohio, he met the **Davenport Brothers,** and in 1866 became western editor of the Spiritualist journal *Banner of Light.* His brilliant editorials greatly extended circulation. He became editor-in-chief of *The Spiritual Universe,* a journal devoted to Freethought and Spiritualism. He subsequently became editor-in-chief of *The American Spiritualist,* published in Cleveland.

In addition to his medical, editorial and other newspaper contributions, he also published many books and pamphlets on Spiritualism, including: *The Practical of Spiritualism; Biographical Sketch of Abraham James; Historic description of his oil-well discoveries . . . through spirit direction* (1868), *Seers of the Ages* (1869), *Spiritualism Defined and Defended* (1874), *Around the World: or, Travels in Polynesia, China, India, Arabia, Egypt, Syria* (1875), *The Conflict Between Darwinianism and Spiritualism* (1876), *Buddhism and Christianity face to face; or, An Oral Discussion* (1878), *Immortality, and Our Employments Hereafter* (1880), *Spiritual Harmonies, or Spiritual Teachings, Songs and Hymns* (1880), *Celebration of the Fiftieth Anniversary of Modern Spiritualism at Its Birthplace* (1898), *What is Spiritualism, Who are These Spiritualists, and What Has Spiritualism Done for the World?* (1903), *Reincarnation; or, The Doctrine of the "Soul's" Successive Embodiments* (1904), *The Demonism of the Ages, Spirit Obsessions So Common in Spiritism, Oriental and Occidental Occultism* (1904), *Vaccination a Curse and a Menace to Personal Liberty* (1905), *The Spirit's Pathway Traced; Did it Pre-exist and Does It Reincarnate Again Into Mortal Life?* (1906), *Spirit Mates, Their Origin and Destiny, Sex-Life, Marriage, Divorce* (1909), *Five Journeys Around the World: or, Travels in the Pacific Islands, New Zealand, Australia, Ceylon, India, Egypt and Other Oriental Countries* (1910), *Christianity, Churchianity or Spiritualism—Which?* (1913).

Dr. Peebles was a keen fighter for truth as he saw it, and traveled five times round the world, visiting and working in most of the civilized countries and some uncivilized ones. Long after the age of ninety, he stood straight as an arrow, his height being six feet and his physical proportions impressive. A biographer described him as "a magnificent specimen of physical and mental manhood."

He died February 15, 1922, at Los Angeles, California.

Pegomancy

A branch of **Hydromancy** (**divination** by water), also associated with Crystalomancy (**crystal gazing** or scrying). Interpretations were made by dropping stones in sacred pools or springs and observing their movements. (See also **Lecanomancy**)

"Pelham, George"

Pseudonym of "George Pellew," **control** of the famous medium Mrs. Leonore E. **Piper** (1859-1950). In earthly life Pellew was a lawyer by education but a writer by preference, who often argued with his friend Dr. Hodgson, that the idea of survival was not only improbable but inconceivable.

Hodgson claimed that if not probable it was at least conceivable. Pellew promised that if he died first he would return and "make things lively." In February 1892, when he was 32 years old, he was killed in New York by a fall.

On March 22, he made his first appearance in Mrs. Piper's automatic script and from 1892-1898 he talked with one hundred and thirty persons of which thirty had previously known him. He addressed each of them in the tone and manner which he used in his lifetime.

From 1892 until 1897 he shared control with "Phinuit." With the appearance of the "Imperator" group "Phinuit" disappeared and "Pellew's" communications became rare. He said that he was advancing and getting farther away each time. Finally he disappeared altogether. He was originally referred to in seance reports as "Pelham" or "G.P." to protect anonymity. (See also Richard **Hodgson; "Imperator"; "Phinuit"**; Mrs. Leonore E. **Piper**)

Pellet Reading (or Billet Reading)

At one time a popular Spiritualist phenomenon. Sitters at a seance were each requested to write the name of a deceased friend on a slip of paper and either fold the slips into billets or more tightly screwed up into pellets, sometimes sealed in envelopes. The medium would hold each billet or pellet (often to the forehead) and give a message relating to the deceased individual on the slip of paper. The American medium Charles H. **Foster** specialized in this type of clairvoyance.

Variants of this performance are common with stage magicians and the very nature of the procedure suggests a conjuring trick. The psychical researcher Harry **Price** described in his book *Confessions of a Ghost Hunter* (1936, reprinted Causeway Books, 1974) how he bought the secret of the trick from a man from Oshkosh, Wisconsin.

Pencovic, Francis Heindswater

Founder of the **Foundation of the World** cult in California in 1949, under the pseudonym "Krishna Venta." He was dynamited by dissident disciples on December 10, 1958.

Pendulums

Small pendulums are used in **Dowsing, Radiesthesia** and related **divination** systems instead of **divining-rods.**

Questions can be put, to which the clockwise or anticlockwise rotation of the pendulum gives an answer, rather like the **raps** in Spiritualist seances.

In earlier forms of pendulum divination, a wedding ring was suspended on a silk thread. Today, practitioners of radiesthesia obtain a number of subtle indications from the nature of the oscillations of the pendulum, which is used for water divining, discovery of metals, indications of health and medical remedies, and even discovery of missing persons. (See also **Dowsing, Radiesthesia**)

Recommended reading:

De France, Henry. *The Elements of Dowsing,* G. Bell, London, 1971

Hitching, Francis. *Pendulum; The Psi Connection,* Fontana paperback, London, 1977

Letbridge, T. C. *The Power of the Pendulum,* Routledge & Kegan Paul, London & Boston, 1976

Nielsen, Greg & J. Polansky. *Pendulum Power; A Mystery You Can See, a Power You Can Feel,* Destiny Books, New York, 1977; Excalibur, U.K., 1981

Wethered, V. D. *A Radiesthetic Approach to Health and Homeopathy, or Health and the Pendulum,* British Society of Dowsers, London, 1950

Penelhum, Terence Michael (1929-)

Associate professor of philosophy who has also studied in the field of parapsychology. Born April 26, 1929, at Bradford-on-Avon, England, he was educated at University of Edinburgh (M.A. hons., philosophy 1950) and Oxford University, England (B. Phil. 1952). In 1950 he married Edith Andrews.

He was lecturer, assistant professor, associate professor of philosophy at University of Alberta, Edmonton, Canada, from 1953-63, head of the Department of Philosophy, University of Alberta, Calgary. He is a member of Pacific Division of American Philosophical Association, Canadian Philosophical Association. He has published a number of articles on philosophy.

In the field of parapsychology he has studied the question of personal identity with reference to the possibility of a purely psychical entity. He is also interested in theories of survival. Questions of identity and survival are discussed in his book *Survival and Disembodied Existence* (1970).

Pentacle (or Pantacle or Pentagram)

Five-pointed star formed from five straight lines, used in magical rituals. When a single point projects upwards, with two points on the base projecting downwards, the symbol is said to invoke good influences, but when reversed attracts evil.

The Pentacle has been used in Christian symbolism, where the five points stand for the wounds of the crucified Christ.

In ancient Greece, the pentacle was used by the Pythagoreans to symbolize perfection. In folklore, the sign has been traced on windows and doors in order to repel witches.

In ritual magic, the pentacle has played an important part in evoking or repelling spirits, and was usually associated with holy or unholy names of power and inscribed or engraved with great care and concentration. A six-pointed version or hexagram is often known as "The Seal of Solomon." (See also **Magical Diagrams**)

Pentecost Miracles (with D. D. Home)

Viscount Adare, in his book *Experiences in Spiritualism with Mr. D. D. Home* (1870), claimed to have witnessed a modern duplication of Pentecost miracles as follows: "We now had a series of very curious manifestations. Lindsay and Charlie [Charles Wynne] saw tongues or jets of flame proceeding from Home's head. We then all distinctly heard, as it were, a bird flying round the room whistling and chirping, but saw nothing, except Lindsay, who perceived an indistinct form resembling a bird. Then came a sound as of a great wind rushing through the room, we also felt the wind strongly; the moaning rushing sound was the most weird thing I ever heard. Home then got up, being in trance, and spoke something in a language that none of us understood; it may have been nonsense, but it sounded like a sentence in a foreign tongue. Lindsay thought he recognized some words of Russian. He then quoted the text about the different gifts of the spirit, and gave us a translation in English of what he had said in the unknown tongue. He told us that Charlie had that day been discussing the miracles that took place at Pentecost, and that the spirit made the sound of the wind; of the bird descending; of the unknown tongue, and interpretation thereof, and the tongues of fire to show that the same phenomenon could occur again."

(See also Daniel Dunglas **Home; Luminous Phenomena; Sounds; Winds; Xenoglossis**)

Pentecostalism

A modern revival of the Christian phenomenon of "speaking with tongues," characteristic of some West Indian Christian cults. Pentecostalism became widespread in the U.S. at the beginning of the twentieth century through the intense emotional fervor associated with revivalist meetings in Los Angeles and elsewhere as a sign of spiritual baptism.

Pentecostal churches were established, and until recently the phenomenon was regarded as primarily Protestant and associated with backwoods "holy rollers," but in the last decade, Pentecostalism has spread through Catholic churches as a result of the "Catholic Pentecostal Movement," since renamed "Charismatic Revival."

The new term denotes *charisma* or "gifts of the spirit" which includes emotional fervor, joy and even spiritual healing, as well as speaking with tongues.

The phenomena of "tongues" or speaking in unknown or pseudo languages is also known in a nonreligious context, where it is termed Glossolalia or **Xenoglossis.**

No really detailed study has yet been made of its rationale, but it seems likely that deep emotional feelings may be liberated through the medium of unintelligible syllables which by-pass the inhibitions normally associated with language and intellectual concepts.

Babies and young children tend to express emotion freely in "nonsense" sounds while popular vocalists have sometimes found emotional fluency when they are "sent" by "scat singing," using nonlanguage sound (for example, the singer Janis Joplin).

For details of the Charismatic Renewal, see *Catholic Pentecostals* by Kevin & Dorothy Ranaghan (Paulist Press, 1969) and *Tongues of Men and Angels* by William J. Samarin (Macmillan, 1972).

Peoples Temple

Cult founded by Rev. Jim **Jones** from 1971 onwards in San Francisco, Los Angeles, and eventually organized as an agricultural commune in Guyana.

On November 18, 1978, cult members murdered Congressman Leo J. Ryan and newsmen Gregory Robinson, Robert Brown and Don Harris as they were leaving the airstrip near Jonestown, Guyana after conducting an investigation into complaints made by cult members. In late afternoon the same day, the Peoples Temple cult and its founder in Guyana ended their lives in an incredible mass suicide of over 900 men, women and children.

The cult had started off on the basis of evangelical Christianity, enhanced by claimed faith healing, but was later diverted to a somewhat naive kind of Marxist socialism. Towards the end of the period in Guyana, Jones contacted Soviet officials about the possibility of moving the cult to Cuba or the Soviet Union. Survivors of the death ritual claimed that funds from the cult were to be transferred to the Soviet Union. Jones had also made the Russian language a compulsory study for cult members.

For a detailed account of the cult and its founder, see two books published shortly after the tragedy: *The Suicide Cult; The Inside Story of the Peoples Temple Sect & the Massacre in Guyana* by M. Kilduff & Ron Javers (Bantam Books, 1978) and *Guyana Massacre: The Eyewitness Account* by Charles A. Krause, L. M. Stern & R. Harwood (The Washington Post/Pan Books, 1979). (See also **Communes; Cults;** Rev. Jim **Jones**)

Pepper, Mrs. May S. (1868- ?)

Pastor of the First Spiritualist Church of Brooklyn, whose remarkable powers of **clairvoyance** were a subject of lively discussion in the American press for a considerable time. She was born in Mansfield, Massachusetts, in May 1868. When only sixteen years old, she became controlled by the spirit "Bright Eyes," after the death of her mother.

She demonstrated her mediumistic talent at public meetings but was ostracized by members of the public who claimed that her phenomena were from "the evil one." Her father offered to take her back home if she would admit that her mediumship was not genuine, but with considerable courage she renounced his wealth and security, and trusted to her own gifts. She became one of the leading American mediums and president of the Rhode Island State Spiritualist Association.

Her congregation placed letters, addressed inside, to deceased friends and put them in a plain envelope on a small table. After a prayer and short sermon, Mrs. Pepper took a letter and returned a correct answer to the question if it was put in a spirit of serious inquiry, or declared it to be an attempt to mislead her.

It also happened that she asked the spirit she clairvoyantly saw to look for the letter addressed to him. Before all eyes, the pile of letters moved and one of them was taken as though by an invisible hand and was thrown on the floor.

Prof. J. H. **Hyslop,** Prof. William **James,** Dr. J. D. Quackenbos and many distinguished theologians were convinced of Mrs. Pepper's supernormal faculties.

Percipient

General term in parapsychology to denote an individual taking part in a test of **extrasensory** perception. In the case of a subject who is involved in an experiment to receive impressions from an **agent** or sender of information, the term "percipient" is usually used.

Perelandra

Title of a science fiction story by C. S. Lewis (published 1943), denoting Venus, planet of perfection. The book deals with the play between the forces of good and evil, and the need to resolve this conflict with harmonious balance.

The name Perelandra has now been given to a remarkable garden established by Machaelle Small Wright and Clarence Wright, covering some twenty-two acres near Jeffersonton, Virginia. The garden is the showpiece of the Center for nature Research established by the Wrights, and seeks to harmonize the forces of nature in a joint creative process between the Wrights, nature spirits (or **fairies**) and *devas* (divine intelligences). The remarkable success of Perelandra has naturally been compared to the experimental community at **Findhorn,** Scotland, U.K., which has also claimed unusual gardening success in cooperation between human beings and nature spirits. In fact, books on the Findhorn Community stimulated the Wrights to experiment with Perelandra.

Machaelle Wright believes that *devas* are the architects of growth in nature, and that if they are contacted through meditation they will facilitate harmonious growth, communicating instructions for seed choice and planting, arrangement of intervening space, and other data. Wright distinguishes between *devas* and nature spirits. The latter are "more dense in vibration" and closer to the earth, whereas the *devas* guide the overall development of plant forms.

Perelandra is laid out with a central garden of eighteen concentric circles, the innermost circle being a herb ring with a large quartz crystal (see also **Crystal Healing**) in the center. The garden does not use chemical or organic repellents of any description, but produces unusually attractive flowers and vegetables without pest problems.

In an informative article 'The Magic of Perelandra' (*East-West* Magazine, August 1986), writer P. M. H. Atwater describes a visit to Perelandra in the summer of 1985. At that time, this area of Virginia had been officially declared a drought disaster, but the vegetables and roses of Perelandra flourished without added moisture. Various neighbors who did not share the Wrights' belief in nature spirits nevertheless commented that the garden always looked great and produced good food. One remarked "It's not normal."

Perelandra has now flourished for some twelve years and is open annually for day-long tours and occasional workshops with visitors. Wright has authored two books on her methods: *Behaving As If the God in All Life Mattered* (1983) and *The Perelandra Garden Workbook* (1987).

Wright has refreshingly original concepts of a harmonious balance between insects, weather, climate, soil, etc. in nature. She is quoted as saying: "What I am finding that works best is a garden which constantly changes, that is free to breathe and grow on its own without set rules. An organic garden will selectively repel some life but an energy garden repels nothing and includes everything. It took me a long time to learn that. . . . once animals and insects realize they don't have to fight for their lives, that they are free to live and grow, their aggression subsides and they regulate themselves! I had a rabbit living in the herb ring for several years. It never did any damage. I've had turtles, skunks, and all manner of animals living in the garden without difficulty. My few Japanese beetles, for instance, stick to the same flower and leave the others alone now that they are no longer threatened with extinction." Wright leaves ten percent of all produce for animal or insect consumption, and certain sections of land are also left unmowed for their benefit.

The address of Perelandra is: Box 136, Jeffersonton, Virginia 22724. (See also **Findhorn Foundation**)

"Perfect Sermon"

A Hermetic Book. (See **Hermes Trismegistus; Hermetica**)

Perfumes

Modern medicine has observed that in certain illnesses the skin gives out a scent of violets, pineapple, musk, etc. According to Dr. Duma, these phenomena are due to the presence of butyric ether in the system.

Whatever the explanation may be, the observation helps to understand the perfumes produced by mediums, and makes the phrase "the **odor of sanctity**" appear in a new light. Christian saints are said to exhale a sweet perfume which increases at death and may remain for weeks, months or even years afterwards. When the body of St. Casimir, Patron of Poland, was exhumed in 1603, one hundred and twenty years after his death, it was found entire and it exhaled a sweet smell. St. Cajetan emitted the scent of orange blossoms, St. Francis that of musk. Other saints stated to give forth fragrance include St. Clare of Ferriol (660 A.D.), St. Hermann of Brittany (714 A.D.) and St. Patrick (461 A.D.).

Some Hindu yogis are credited with the ability of creating perfumes by miraculous means. In his famous book *Bengal Lancer* (1930), F. Yeats-Brown described his encounter with a Mahatma named Babu Bisudhanan Dhan at Puri, Calcutta. With nothing more than a magnifying-glass and a piece of cotton-wool, the Mahatma conjured perfumes out of the air by focussing light on the cotton-wool through the glass. Each scent was waved away with the hand, to be succeeded by the next request. He produced in quick succession the scent of violets, musk, sandalwood, opium, heliotrope, flowering bamboo, nicotine plant, jasmine and even cow-dung. A later book, *Naked Ascetic* by Victor Dane (1933), described a Tantric yogi in Bhawanipore who produced on request the smell of violets on Dane's handkerchief without it leaving Dane's hand; the perfume lasted for twelve hours.

In view of experiences with modern mediums, there is no reason to doubt the possible truth of such phenomena. It is highly probable that an unknown physiological process is behind the mystery. In the records of the Rev. Stainton **Moses,** we find highly instructive experiences. The scents, at the closing of a seance, were often found to be issuing out of his head. The more they were wiped away, the stronger and more plentiful they became.

The most common scents were musk, verbena, new-mown hay and one unfamiliar odor which was said to be "spirit scent." During the seance it usually came down in showers. On Dr. Speer's request a good tablespoonful was once poured into a glass.

Stainton Moses was fully aware that his organism played an important part in the production of scents. He wrote on July 4, 1874: "While in the garden, before we began to sit, I was conscious of scent all round me, especially on my hair. When I rubbed my hair my hand was scented strongly. I tried the experiment many times. When the peppermint came I was conscious of its presence first near my head, and it seemed, as it were, to be evolved out of the hair. I have before noticed the same thing, but not so markedly on this occasion."

He suspected that the process was remedial, as the effusion of scent from his scalp was most marked when he was suffering pain. He believed that scents were employed to harmonize conditions. Music or singing were never asked for to facilitate the phenomena, and opposing conditions were overcome by odors of a subtle and delicate perfume and waves of cool, scented air.

To quote from his own account: "If a new sitter is present, he or she is sensed, and so initiated. The chair which the stranger occupies is surrounded by luminous haze, from which issues the perfume; and very frequently wet scent, more or less pungent, according to conditions, is sprinkled from the ceiling at the same time. If a new intelligence is to communicate, or special honour to be paid to a chief, the room is pervaded by perfume which grows stronger as the spirit enters. This scenting of the room in which we are about to meet will sometimes commence many hours before we begin. There is a subtle odour in it which is perpetually being changed. Sometimes the aroma of a flower from the garden is drawn out, intensified, and insinuated throughout the house. Sometimes the odour is like nothing of this earth's production, ethereal, delicate, and infinitely delightful. Sandal-wood used to be a favourite, and rose, verbena, and odours of other flowers have been plentifully used.

"I find it difficult to convey any idea of the subtle odours that have been diffused throughout the room, or of the permanence of the scent. It is usually the first manifestation and the last. The perfume is sprinkled in showers from the ceiling, and borne in waves of cool air round the circle, especially when the atmosphere is close and the air oppressive. Its presence in a particular place is shown to me by the luminous haze which accompanies it. I can trace its progress round the circle by the light . . . and can frequently say to a certain sitter: 'You will smell the scent directly. I see the luminous form going to you.' My vision has always been confirmed by the exclamations of delight which follow.

"When we first observed this manifestation, it was attended by a great peculiarity. The odour was circumscribed in space, confined to a belt or band, beyond which it did not penetrate. It surrounded the circle to a few feet, and outside of that belt was not perceptible; or it was drawn across the room as a cordon, so that it was possible to walk into it and out of it again—the presence and absence of the odour and the temperature of the air which accompanied it being most marked. Judge Edmonds (in his book on Spiritualism) especially notes the presence of an odour which was not diffused through the room. He describes the sensation as being like a flower presented to the nostrils at intervals. I should rather describe what I observed as a scented zone or belt, perfectly defined and not more than a few feet in breadth. Within it the temperature was cool and the scent strong, outside of it the air was decidedly warmer, and no trace of the perfume was perceptible. It was no question of fancy. The scent was too strong for that. And the edges of the belt were quite clearly marked, so that it was impossible, instantaneously, to pass from the warm air of the room to the cool perfumed air of this zone.

"I have known the same phenomenon to occur in the open air. I have been walking with a friend, for instance, and we have walked into air laden with scent, and through it again into the natural atmosphere . . . I have even known cases where wet scent has been produced and showered down in the open air. On one special occasion, in the Isle of Wight, my attention was attracted by the patter of some fine spray on a lady's [Mrs. Speer's] silk dress, as we were walking along a road. One side of the dress was plentifully besprinkled with fine spray, which gave forth a delicious odour, very clearly perceptible for some distance round.

"During a seance the scent is either carried, as it seems, round the circle, and is then accompanied by cool air, or it is sprinkled down from the ceiling of the room in liquid form. In the clairvoyant state I am able to see and describe the process before the scent is sprinkled, and can warn a special sitter not to look upwards. For, on certain occasions, when conditions are not favourable, the scent is pungent and most painful if it gets into my eye, and it has caused no more pain than water would. On the contrary, I have seen the effect caused on another [Mrs. Speer] by a similar occurrence. The pain caused was excruciating, the inflammation was most severe, and the effects did not pass off for 24 hours or more. In fact, whatever the liquid was, it caused severe conjunctivitis.

"This variety in the pungency and potency of perfume I attribute to variety in the attendant circumstances. The illness of one of the sitters will cause the scent to become coarse and pungent. Harmonious conditions, physical and mental, are signalised by the presence of delicate subtle odours which are infinitely charming. I have said that sometimes the odour of flowers, either in the house or garden, will be intensified. A vase of fresh flowers put on the table causes the natural perfume in this way. We used frequently to gather fresh flowers, and watch the process. Flowers which had a very slight smell when gathered would, by degrees, throw off such a perfume as to fill the room and strike anyone who came into it most forcibly. In this case the natural odour of the flower was intensified and the bloom received no harm. At other times, however, some liquid was apparently put upon the blossom, and an odour, not its own given to it. In that case it invariably withered and died very rapidly. I have frequently had flowers in my buttonhole scented in this way.

"Great quantities of dry musk have been from time to time thrown about in the house where our circle meets. On a late occasion it fell in very considerable quantities over a writing-desk at which a lady was sitting in the act of writing letters. It was midday, and no one was near at the time, yet the particles of musk were so numerous as to pervade the whole contents of the desk. They were placed, for no throwing would have produced such a result, at the very bottom of the desk, and between the papers which it contained. The odour was most pronounced; and the particles, when gathered together, made up a considerable packet. Some time after this when at a seance, I saw something which looked like luminous dust on the table. No odour was perceptible, but in my clairvoyant state I saw a heap of luminous particles which appeared to be extremely brilliant. I described it, and putting out my hand I found that there was really a heap on the table. I inquired what it was and musk was rapped out. We demurred, for no odour was perceptible, but the statement was reiterated. After the seance we gathered up the dust, which looked like musk, but had no smell whatsoever. The next morning, however, the odour was powerful enough; and the powder still exists, and is indubitably a very good powdered musk. By what imaginable process can that phenomenon have been accomplished?

"One of the astonishing points . . . is the quantity of liquid that is produced. The table is covered with innumerable stains; and if they be removed, another seance will renew them. The spray appears to fall everywhere, for the very fire-irons bear traces of its presence; and I am quite sure that the housemaid's opinion of the manifestation would not be complimentary to the invisible operators."

The scents were not always welcome. In his note of July 4, 1874, Stainton Moses referred to a pungent odor of peppermint which was very unpleasant. Dr. Speer described this happening more outspokenly: "The other evening a newcomer slipped in, and stank us out of the room by throwing down from the ceiling a large quantity of Sp. Pulegii. Everything that it touched was impregnated for 24 hours. The dining-room cloth and my own nether habiliments had to be exposed to view in the back garden; and on the following morning our dining-room floor and passage had to be freely fumigated with pastilles. That spirit has not been invited to join us again."

The experience suggests that the stench observed in some curious cases of haunting belongs into this category of facts. Dr. Justinus **Kerner** recorded the case of Frau Eslinger who, in 1835, in the prison of Weinberg, was visited and talked to by a ghost which emitted an intolerable stench, felt by many others, too.

The sickening stench of a charnel house was reported in a haunted house near London (*Daily Chronicle*, April 15, 1908). On examination it transpired that an imbecile was left unburied some time previously in the house until advanced putrefaction had occurred.

Florence **Marryat** wrote about the phantom "Lenore" of Miss Mary **Showers:** "On one occasion . . . there was a charnel house smell about her, as if she had been buried a few weeks and dug up again. . . . One evening at Mrs. Gregory's . . . I nearly fainted from the smell. It resembled nothing but that of a putrid corpse, and when she returned to the cabinet, I was compelled to leave the room and retch from the nausea it had caused me."

The medium Carlos **Mirabelli** of São Paolo once materialized a skeleton. A bad smell as that of a cadaver was emitted from his body (see **Materialization**).

The withdrawal of the scents of flowers of which Stainton Moses wrote was the only physical phenomenon known in Mrs. **Piper's** mediumship. "Mrs. Piper's fingers," wrote Dr. **Hodgson,** "moved near the flower, as if withdrawing something from it; and in a few hours it had withered."

Lord **Adare** had witnessed the famous medium D. D. **Home** extending his hand towards the flowers on a small table, the fingers pointing towards them. "His hand remained there for few seconds, and was then brought round, and with a motion like sprinkling, cast the perfume of the flowers towards each of us in turn; the perfume was so strong that there could be no mistake about it. This was done twice."

Once, when a quantity of eau de Cologne had been thrown from the ceiling, Home said "we should have the odour changed four times and in effect a totally different scent was blown over us four times on a palpable strong current of air." Handling a hot burning ember, his fingers smelt "of a sweet scent which he threw off from his fingers at us across the table. . . . " "He held his hand—the fingers being extended downwards—about nine inches above a vase of flowers. 'You will see,' he said, 'that I can withdraw the moisture and scent from the flowers.' He came over to me and rubbed my hands, imparting the odour of the flowers to them; his fingers were quite moist as with dew; he also flipped the moisture, and with it the scent from his fingers to each person. . . . "

"Home then made some very curious experiments with flowers; he separated the scent into two portions—one odour smelling exactly like earth; the other being very sweet."

Essences were also similarly withdrawn, "I am going to take the strength from the brandy—and he began to make passes over the glass and flipping his fingers, sending a strong smell of spirit through the room; in about five minutes he had made the brandy as weak as very weak brandy and water, it scarcely tasted at all of spirit; both Lindsay and I tasted it, at the moment, and also some time after the seance was over."

"He withdrew the acid flavour from a half a lemon, freshly cut and tasted. He held it up above his head; a yellowish light came over it, and when offered to taste again the lemon was found most disagreeable, the flavour was like magnesia or washing soda. He then restored the acid. Holding it up, a rose coloured flame came over it. After a little while, he offered it and it was found all right" (see *Experiences in Spiritualism with D. D. Home* by Viscount Adare [1870]).

The psychical researcher Dr. Joseph **Maxwell** found the luminous phenomena of the medium Eusapia **Palladino** at the sittings of Choisy not very convincing because a strong aroma of phosphorus permeated the room. Later, however, he found this odor characteristic and discovered that it was more like the odor of ozone than that of phosphorus. It was like the odor perceptible in the vicinity of frictional electrical machines when in activity.

It is curious to note that this smell often disturbed clairvoyants during their visions. **Swedonborg** was one of the first to record his annoyance over it. In the **poltergeist** disturbance at Tedworth in 1661 (see **Drummer of Tedworth**) the manifestations were sometimes accompanied by "a bloomy noisome smell" as of sulphur.

There are early records of paranormal scents in the correspondence of Dr. G. P. **Billot** with J. P. F. Deleuze in 1839. Billot stated that superior intelligences presented themselves through his somnambules, presided at seances, and manifested themselves by the delicious odors which they diffused around them. The ambrosia of the mythologists, the odor of sanctity of the Church were discovered to be realities.

In the seances of the medium David **Duguid,** perfumes were administered to one sitter at a time, the recipient feeling the cooling odors gently blown over his face. The manifestation was not confined to the seance room. Sometimes it was experienced in the open air.

Among later mediums in whose seances the phenomenon was often recorded the Marquis **Centurione Scotto** and Mrs. **Crandon** ("Margery") stand foremost. (See also **Odor of Sanctity**)

Perispirit

The term applied by Spiritist Allan **Kardec** to denote the spirit body.

Pernety, Antoine Joseph (1716-1801)

Author of the *Dictionnaire Mytho-Hermetique* (1787) and *Les Fables Egyptiennes et Grecques* (1758). According to Pernety, the Golden Fleece in the Jason-Medea legend is symbolical. The labors of Jason represent human strivings towards perfection.

Perovsky-Petrovo-Solovovo, Count (died 1954)

Distinguished Russian-born psychical researcher. He was born Michael Solovioy, succeeding to the title of Count, and generally known as "Count Solovovo" amongst members of the Society for Psychical research, London. He joined the Society in 1890 at a time when the Society had commenced the collection of cases for the important Census of Hallucinations (published in vol. 10 of the Society's *Proceedings*), and he contributed Russian cases to this project.

He investigated the Russian medium **Sambor** (died 1902), and in 1910 cooperated with Everard Feilding and W. Marriott in sittings with the famous medium Eusapia Palladino in Naples. He reported on these sittings in *Proceedings* of the S.P.R. (vol. 25, pp. 57-69). He took a special interest in the question of whether competent researchers, qualified to detect fraud, might still be influenced by illusions induced by seance room conditions. He also contributed to the S.P.R. *Proceedings* and *Journal* on such topics as Extrasensory Perception, and the medium D. D. **Home.** He also reviewed for the *Journal* continental journals devoted to psychical research. He was honorary secretary for Russia for the Society for many years. In view of his eminent services, the Society conferred honorary membership upon him.

In 1936, he recame resident in London, and in his later years acquired British citizenship.

Perriman, Mrs. A. E. (Florence) (died 1936)

Voice medium tested by Dr. Nandor **Fodor,** who was not favorably impressed at the time. Mrs. Perriman's seance at Victoria Hall, London, is described in Fodor's book *The Haunted Mind* (1959); see also report in *Psychic News* May 4, 1936.

Florence Perriman was often known by her married name of Mrs. A. E. Perriman. She spent many years of her life as a society clairvoyant, using the professional name Madame Faustina. She was consulted by famous stars of stage and screen, including Esme Percy, Ivor Novello, Viola Tree, Isabel Jeans and Gladys Cooper.

Mrs. Perriman's reminiscences were published in her book *Secrets of a Famous Clairvoyante* (London, 1936). She died in the same year. She is also referred to in her husband's book: *Broadcasting From Beyond* by A. E. Perriman (London, 1952).

Perry, Michael C(harles) (1933-)

British clergyman who has been concerned with para-psychology. Born June 5, 1933, at Ashby-de-la-Zouch, Leicestershire, England, he studied at Trinity

College, Cambridge University, England (first class hons. in natural sciences and theology). He obtained his B.A. in 1955, M.A. 1959, was ordained as a priest of the Church of England in 1959.

In 1963 he married Margaret Adshead. In the same year, he was appointed chief assistant for publishing at the Society for the Promotion of Christian Knowledge, London. From 1970 onwards, he became archdeacon of Durham and canon residentiary, Durham Cathedral, England; Selwyn Lecturer, St. John's College, Auckland, New Zealand, 1976; Marshall Memorial Lecturer, Trinity College, Melbourne, 1976; Beard Memorial Lecturer, College of Psychic Studies, London, 1977; lecturer in U.S., New Zealand, Singapore, and on British television programs; Secretary to Archbishops, Commission on Christian Doctrine, 1967-70.

He has been a student associate and member of the Society for Psychical Research, London from 1951 onwards, and a member of the Churches' Fellowship for Psychical and Spiritual Studies. He is particularly interested in the relationship between parapsychology and Christianity. His articles include: 'A New View of the Resurrection' (*Tomorrow,* Summer 1954), 'Parapsychology in Apologetics' (*Church Quarterly Review* Jan. 1959). His publications include: *The Eastern Enigma* (1959), *The Pattern of Matins & Evensong* (1961), *Meet the Prayer Book* (1963), (ed.) *Crisis for Confirmation* (1967), (with Dewi Morgan) *Declaring the Faith; The Printed Word* (1969), *Sharing in One Bread* (1973; 1980), *The Resurrection of Man* (1975), *The Paradox of Worship* (1977), *A Handbook of Parish Worship* (1977), (with Phyllis Carter) *A Handbook of Parish Finance* (1981).

He edited the series 'Mowbray's Library of Theology,' and has contributed articles and reviews to Theology and psychic studies journals, including *Theology, Spiritual Frontiers, Parapsychological Review.* He was co-editor of *Christian Parapsychologist* from 1977-78, editor 1978 onwards. He was assistant editor of report of Lambeth Conference of Anglican Bishops, 1968, senior editor, 1978.

Personality

Term which has three aspects: (1) the sum of the characteristics which make up physical and mental being, including appearance, manners, habits, tastes and moral character, (2) the characteristics that distinguish one person from another (this is equivalent to individuality), (3) the capacity for having mental states, i.e., possessing a stream of consciousness (according to psychical researcher J. H. **Hyslop**).

For psychical researchers, this last definition is of primary importance. The question of survival cannot be decided until the continuance of personality as a stream of consciousness is moved. A stream of consciousness is proof of the presence of a personality.

The identity of this personality, however, is inseparably bound up with the faculty of remembrance. With a complete loss of memory a new personality will develop. If the former memory returns the new personality will disappear. It may be resuscitated by another attack of amnesia or under hypnosis, when it will act as an independent personality and tell its story.

The case of Anselm Bourne, investigated by Professor William **James** and Dr. Richard **Hodgson** in 1890, is a good illustration. Bourne suddenly lost his memory in 1887 in Providence, Rhode Island, and eight weeks after awoke in Norristown, Pennsylvania, as a small shopkeeper. He knew nothing of Mr. Albert John Brown, the name under which he lived, neither of the shop nor of the business. In hypnosis the secondary personality came forward and his movements were satisfactorily traced from the moment of his disappearance.

This was a plainly degenerative case. Anselm Bourne suffered from a post-epileptic condition. He had fits of depression from childhood and in later life presented symptoms suggestive of epilepsy. Such degenerative instances are very numerous. A totally different group is presented by cases in which the secondary state is an improvement on the primary one.

The case of Dr. Azam's patient, "Felida X" is a good example (see *Human Personality and its Survival of Bodily Death* by F. W. H. Myers, 1903, vol. 1, p. 333). She was born at Bordeaux, France, in 1843, exhibited symptoms of hysteria towards the age of thirteen, felt pains in her forehead and fell into a profound sleep from which she awoke in a secondary condition.

Whereas in the primary case she was of melancholy disposition, constantly thought of her maladies and suffered acute pains in various parts of her body, in the secondary state she appeared like an entirely different person, smiling and gay and feeling no pains.

Such changes at first occurred every five or six days; they were very marked with a better, more complete development of her faculties. The memory in the secondary state was continuous. This state was her "raison" while the other was always her "crise." This secondary personality became ever more frequent and, relapses of short duration disregarded, slowly suppressed her "état bête."

The various stages of hypnotic sleep to each of which a distinct train of memory may pertain, present the phenomenon of multiple personality in a simplified form. These personalities are of a shallow type. They are incomplete, transient and seldom able to carry on. In rare instances, however, they exhibit a general superiority. The case of Mrs. Anna Cora Mowatt, recorded by Epes Sargent in *The Scientific Basis of Spiritualism* (1881) is an example.

There is a case on record when the hypnotic personality actually suppressed the normal one. Marceline R., the patient of Dr. Jules Janet, was the subject of this curious medical experiment which saved untold miseries for an ailing girl who was doomed to die and made her happy. (See F. W. H. Myers, *Human Personality,* 1903, vol. 1, pp. 331-33).

An interesting series of changes of personality was observed by Col. **Rochas** in his experiments in regression of memory. By longitudinal passes he not only made the subjects trace back their past lives and assume the corresponding change in personality, but also took them back beyond birth into a former reincarnation which involved the manifestation of an entirely different and persistent personality. Since then, there have been various attempts to validate theories of reincarnation by hypnotic regression. Amongst important recent experiments were those of Arnall **Bloxham.**

A well-developed secondary personality is often followed by the appearance of other personalities. As many as eleven personalities were recorded in the case of "Mary Barnes" (see *Journal* of the Society for Psychical Research, vol. 11, p. 231, vol. 12, p. 208). They may come and go, like lodgers in a tenement house. The best investigated case of multiple personality was discussed by Dr. Morton **Prince** in *Dissociation of a Personality* (1906). It was the story of Miss Beauchamp who, under emotional shocks, developed four personalities. They were antithetic to the ordinary one. They not only differed markedly in health, in memories and knowledge of their own life, but they were formally at war with each other. The third personality, "Sally," was the most interesting. She had all the appearance of an invading, outside entity. She wrote her autobiography which claimed conscious but suppressed existence for her right back to Miss Beauchamp's infancy. She had a will of her own, could hypnotize the other personalities, had no notion of time and exhibited complete tactile anaesthesia. She said persistently that she was a spirit. Dr. Prince attempted with hypnotic suggestion to weld the four personalities into one. "Sally" was bitterly resistant. After a long struggle and much reasoning, however, she agreed to be "squeezed" out of existence, and Mrs. Beauchamp was restored to one personality commanding the memories of her former selves with the exception of "Sally."

The case of "Sally" suggests that a new personality may be an obsessing one, and not a cleavage of the medium's self. In the remarkable case of Doris Fischer, five personalities had to be dealt with by her investigator, Dr. Walter F. **Prince.** They were called "Real Doris," "Margaret," "Sleeping Margaret," "Sick Doris" and "Sleeping Doris." "Real Doris" hardly had more than five minutes' conscious existence a day. The alternating personalities were veritably chasing after each other for years. By admirable perseverance, Dr. Prince finally effected a cure. When it was practically complete Prof. J. H. **Hyslop** came on the scene and by taking the girl to the medium Mrs. Chenoweth (Mrs M. M. **Soule**), he discovered, after several trance sittings, that "Margaret" appeared to be an obsessing entity (see **Obsession**).

In the October 1931 issue of the British medical journal *The Lancet,* a case of eight distinct personalities was recorded by Dr. Robert M. Riggall, clinical psychologist to the West End Hospital of Nervous Diseases, London. The personalities were 1) "Mabel," the patient herself, good, patient, moral and economical, without many faults, but usually unhappy, 2) "Miss Dignity," who considered it her duty to do all in her power to hurt "Mabel," 3) "Biddy," bright, cheerful, laughing and helpful, 4) 5) and 6) "Hope," "Faith" and "Dame Trot," harmless, appearing seldom, 7) "Miss Take," so named because she did not know when she first appeared what her name was, and added that she was just a mistake, 8) Another unnamed personality with an evil expression. "Miss Dignity" went so far in her hostility to write a letter to "Mabel," urging her to commit suicide and saying that she enclosed a packet of poison.

Slight causes, such as hunger, fatigue, impure air, light fever, are sometimes sufficient to produce a transient perturbation of personality of the most violent kind. The novelist Robert Louis Stevenson, if ill or feverish, always felt possessed in part of his mind by another personality. According to Frank **Podmore,** an over-indulgence in daydreams is probably the first indication of a tendency to isolated and unregulated psychic activity which, in its more extreme form, may develop into a fixed idea or an obsession.

Prof. Theodore **Flournoy** wrote: "As a crystal splits under the blow of a hammer when struck according to certain definite lines of cleavage, in the same way the human personality under the shock of excessive emotions is sometimes broken along the lines of least resistance or the great structural lines of his temperament. A cleavage is produced between the opposite selves—whose harmonious equilibrium would constitute the normal condition—seriousness and gaiety; optimistic tendencies and pessimistic; goodness and egoism; instincts of prudery and lasciviousness; the taste for solitude and the love of Nature, and the attractions of civilisation, etc. The differences, in which the spiritists see a striking proof of an absolute distinction between the spirits and their so-called instruments, awaken, on the contrary, in the mind of the psychologist the irresistible suspicion that these pretended spirits can be nothing but the products of the subconsciousness of the medium himself."

According to F. W. H. **Myers,** the first symptom of disintegration of personality is an *idée fixe,* the persistence of an uncontrolled and unmodifiable group of thoughts or emotions, which, from their brooding isolation, from the very fact of deficient interchange with the general current of thought, become alien and intrusive, so that some special idea or image presses into consciousness with undue and painful infrequency.

In the second stage, there is a confluence of these *idées fixes* overrunning the whole personality, often accompanied by something of a somnambulic change. This is the birth of the secondary personality from emotionally selected elements of the primary personality. It may attain a morbid intensity and it may lead to so-called demoniacal possession. In other cases, an arbitrary development of a scrap of personality is responsible for the dissociation, its commonest mode of origin is from some access of sleep-walking, which, instead of merging into sleep again, repeats and consolidates itself, until it acquires a chain of memories of its own, alternating with the primary chain.

Sleep walkers may disclose a secondary personality as the acts in repeated spontaneous **somnambulism** form a chain of memory. Considering the wide power and tenacious memory of the subconscious, Myers suggested that the conscious personality should be regarded as a privileged case of personality, a special phase, easiest to study because it is accessible. Its powers of perception he similarly considered a special case of the subliminal faculties.

Myers believed that many phantasmal appearances may be explained by a peculiar dissociation of personality which he called "psychorrhagic diathesis." He thought that certain men may be born with an ability to dissociate elements of their personality which may affect certain parts of space and change it into a phantasmogenetic center in which then they appear to the percipients.

According to Gustave **Geley** in *From the Unconscious to the Conscious* (1920), the root and original cause of multiple personality is the setting aside of the central direction of the self. This is brought about by a defect in the assimilation of the mental elements by the self. Without this defect of assimilative power there may be decentralization but no personality worthy of the name will appear. But mediumistic personalities are in a distinct class. He thinks it probable that "there is in mediumship an action of intelligent entities, distinct from the medium."

An interesting recent investigation of a professional medium by monitoring electrical brain activity revealed three separate EEG brain wave patterns of the medium and her two controls. See J. Solfvin, W. G. Roll & E. F. Kelly, 'A Psychophysical Study of Mediumistic Communications' (*Research in Parapsychology 1976* ed. J. D. Morris, W. G. Roll & R. L. Morris, Scarecrow Press, 1977).

Another important paper is 'A Case of Multiple Personality illustrating the transition from Role-Playing,' by M. H. Congdon, J. Hain & I. Stevenson (*Journal of Nervous & Mental Disease,* vol. 132, 1961).

The question of secondary personalities is a complex one and there is no single explanation applicable to all cases. Some cases appear to concern possession by spirit entities, others possibly indicating **reincarnation.** Many cases appear to be a matter of abnormal psychology, in which artificial personalities are created from repressed desires or anxieties, much as a novelist creates fictional characters.

Much obscurity surrounds the development of normal personality in individuals, associated with a given sex, name, age and experience. Character traits often change during the course of time. Many apparently normal individuals sometimes present different personalities in public to those in private matters.

The maintenance of a recognizable personality depends very much on accumulated experiences and memories, and the reassurance of a familiar body and sensory perception. If one grants the possibility of survival after death, the sudden removal of memories, sensory associations and bodily presence must be a traumatic experience for many worldly individuals, and the confusing or vague messages relating to identity received at many Spiritualist seances could be explained on this basis. Even the triviality of many communications seems explicable, since the departed spirit might place great value on such trivialities as reassurance of a continuity of personality.

In everyday life, individuals often find their personality under pressure from environmental changes and from contact with other individuals, who may be dominating or persuasive. Every period also has its artificial influences to which personality is supposed to conform.

How real are our personalities? Fantasy plays a great part in the maintenance of personality, nourished by the myriad fictions of novels, movies and television plays. The personality of women in particular has been shaped by fashion and role exemplars which have had powerful influence in the modern mass media society. And talented actors and actresses have shown that it is possible to change roles night after night in a physical and psychological masquerade that becomes an intensely shared experience with an audience.

The larger implications of personality involve philosophies and religions. The imperfections and contradictions of earthly personality constitute unfinished chapters in the fascinating story of life, and it is reasonable to postulate sequels in an afterlife involving progressive evolution of personality. (See also Arnall **Bloxham; Identity; Obsession & Possession; Personation; "Philip"; Reincarnation;** Lt. Col. d'Aiglun **Rochas; Trance Personalities; Transfiguration**)

Recommended reading:

Blythe, Henry. *The Three Lives of Naomi Henry,* Frederick Muller, London, 1956

Bernstein, Morey. *The Search for Bridey Murphy,* Doubleday, 1956

Flournoy, Theodor. *From India to the Planet Mars,* Harper, 1900; University Books, 1963

Geley, Gustave. *From the Unconscious to the Conscious,* William Collins, London, 1920

Iverson, Jeffrey. *More Lives Than One?,* Souvenir Press, London, 1976; Pan paperback, London, 1967

Mitchell, T. W. *Medical Psychology and Psychical Research,* Methuen, London, 1922

Myers, F. W. H. *Human Personality and Its Survival of Bodily Death,* 2 vols., Longmans, Green, London, 1903; Longmans, New York, 1954

Oesterreich, T. K. *Possession; Demoniacal & Other, Among Primitive Races, in Antiquity, the Middle Ages, and Modern Times,* London, New York, 1930; University Books, 1966

Prince, Morton. *The Dissociation of a Personality,* Longmans, 1906

Stevens, E. W. *The Watseka Wonder* (pamphlet), Religio-Philosophical Journal, Chicago, 1879

Stevenson, Ian. *Twenty Cases Suggestive of Reincarnation,* American Society for Psychical Research, 1966

Thigpen, C. H. & H. Cleckley. *The Three Faces of Eve,* McGraw Hill, 1957

Personation

The portrayal of alien personalities by a temporary assumption of their bodily and mental characteristics. It is a frequent psychical phenomenon and differs from **trance** possession in that it does not necessarily involve a loss of consciousness and personal identity.

It is an impressive indication of the communicator's identity. It is an indication rather than proof, as experiments in **hypnotism** suggest the need for careful consideration in attributing the phenomena of personation to an outside intelligence. Under the effect of suggestion, the subconscious displays surprising histrionic abilities. The hypnotized subject is not only capable of successfully imitating any suggested personality, but may even sometimes take on animal similitudes. Prof. Charles **Richet** hypnotized a friend and suggested that he was a parrot. Richet asked him: "Why do you look preoccupied?" He answered: "How can I eat the seed in my cage?"

Richet compared the phenomenon of personation to crystallization from a saturated solution. Remembrances and emotions concentrate upon the personality invented like crystals form round a center.

Frank **Podmore,** in *Modern Spiritualism* (2 vols., 1902), quoted a curious instance of personation verging on possession in which the subject of personation was alive.

It appeared that Miss A. B. had a passionate love affair with a young man, C. D., and continued to cherish the belief, even after the young man's abrupt discontinuance of the acquaintance that he was still profoundly attached to her. "A few weeks after the breach she felt one evening a curious feeling in the throat, as of choking, the prelude probably, under ordinary circumstances to an attack of hysteria. This feeling was succeeded by involuntary movements of the hands and a fit of long-continued and apparently causeless sobbing. Then, in the presence of a member of her family she became, in her own belief, possessed by the spirit of C. D., personating his words and gestures and speaking in his character. After this date she continually held conversation, as she believes, with C. D.'s spirit; 'he' sometimes speaking aloud through her mouth, sometimes conversing with her in the inner voice. Occasionally 'he' wrote messages through her hand, and I have the testimony of a member of her family that the writing so produced resembled that of C. D. Occasionally also, A. B. had visions in which she claimed to see C. D. and what he was doing at the moment. At other times she professed to hear him speaking or to understand by some inner sympathy his feelings and his thoughts." Podmore believed the phenomena to be the dream of a hysterical girl.

Had C. D. been dead, the case, as an after-death communication, would have seemed very strong.

An excellent account of personation experiences was rendered by Mr. Charles Hill-Tout, principal of Buckland College, Vancouver, Canada, in *Proceedings* of the Society for Psychical Research (vol. 11, pp. 309-16). On one occasion, during a seance, he was oppressed by a feeling of coldness and loneliness, as of a recently disembodied spirit. His wretchedness and misery were terrible, and he was only kept from falling to the floor by some of the other sitters. At this point one of the sitters "made the remark, which I remember to have overheard 'It is father controlling him,' and I then seemed to realise who I was and whom I was seeking. I began to be distressed in my lungs, and should have fallen if they had not held me by the hands and let me back gently upon the floor. As my head sunk back upon the carpet I experienced dreadful distress in my lungs and could not breathe. I made signs to them to put something under my head. They immediately put the sofa cushion under me, but this was not sufficient—I was not raised high enough yet to breathe easily—and they then added a pillow. I have the most distinct recollection of a sigh of relief I now gave as I sank back like a sick, weak person upon the cool pillow. I was in a measure still conscious of my actions, though not of my surroundings, and I have a clear memory of seeing myself in the character of my dying father lying in the bed and in the room in which he died. It was a most curious sensation. I saw his shrunken hands and face and lived again through his dying moments; only now I was both myself—in some distinct sort of way—and my father, with his feelings and appearance."

The flaw, from the viewpoint of theory of an extraneous influence, is that Mr. Hill-Tout personated his own father with whose circumstances of death he must have been familiar. But many mediums reenact the death-bed scenes people they have never heard of and furnish, in the process, evidential details. This was a feature of the mediumship of Mrs. Newell of Lancashire, England. As a rule such reenactments were accompanied with great suffering. The medium experienced the symptoms of illness and the agonies of the dying. The degree of verisimilitude was sometimes alarming.

The American medium Mrs. J. H. **Conant** was recorded once to have shown the signs of hydrophobia; she foamed at the mouth and snapped at the sitters. The man whom she personated had died from the bite of a mad dog.

Psychometrists also exhibit this curious phenomenon. The object which they hold as a clue may establish a community of sensation with both men and beasts (see **Psychometry**). Mrs. Denton, in describing her impressions from a fragment of mastodon teeth felt herself to be in the body of the monster, although of course she could not very well personate it.

Personation of a dying animal, through telepathic impact, was illustrated by the vivid dream of the novelist H. Rider **Haggard** on the night when his dog Bob was struck and killed by a train (see **Telepathy**).

If the assumption of the bodily characteristics of the departed is effected by the adaptation of **ecto-**

plasm, as in **materialization** seances, the case is known as **transfiguration.** (See also **Personality; Trance Personalities; Transfiguration**)

Perty, Dr. Maximilian (c. 1861)

Professor at the University of Berne, author of *Die Mystischen Erscheinungen der menschlichen Natur* (Leipzig, 1861) which accounted for the supernormal manifestations of mediums by the assumption that they get into communion with planetary spirits by an unconscious exercise of occult powers latent in their organism.

Pessomancy (or Psephomancy)

A system of **divination** using pebbles or beans marked with symbols and colors relating to health, communications, success, travel, etc. The stones were either thrown out after shuffling in a bag, or drawn out at random. (See also **Aleuromancy; Astragalomancy; Belomancy; Sortilege**)

Peter of Abano (Petrus de Abano) (1250-1318)

Famous medieval philosopher, mathematician, and astrologer who also wrote treatises on magic. He was born in Abano, near Padua and became a learned scholar. He traveled widely, visiting France, Sardina and Constantinople. He met the famous traveler Marco Polo, from whom he obtained information on Asia.

He practiced medicine in Paris with so great success that he soon became very rich, but his wealth and attainments were annulled by the accusation of sorcery which was brought against him.

He was said to receive instruction in the seven liberal arts from seven spirits which he kept in crystal vessels. Other rumors claimed that he had the curious and useful faculty of causing the money he spent to return to his own purse.

His downfall was brought about by an act of revenge for which he was called to account by the Inquisition. A neighbor of his had been possessed of a spring of excellent water in his garden, from which he allowed Peter to drink at will. For some reason or another, the permission was withdrawn, and it was claimed that with the assistance of the Devil, Peter caused the water to leave the garden and flow uselessly in some distant street.

The unfortunate physician died before his trial was finished, but so bitter were the inquisitors against him that they ordered his bones to be dug up and burned. This public indignity to his memory was averted by some of his friends, who, hearing of the vindictive sentence, secretly removed the remains from the burying-ground where they lay. The inquisitors thereupon satisfied their animosity by burning him in effigy.

Peter had a considerable literary output. He translated the astrological work *Nativities* by Abraham Aben Ezra, and wrote books on physiognomy, geomancy, prophecy and the practice of occult magic.

Peters, Alfred Vout (1867- ?)

Veteran British clairvoyant and trance medium, who was still active in the Spiritualist movement during his sixties. When only a child he was conscious of the presence of other ghostly children, and remarked to his mother, "I suppose they are God's angels who come and play with me after you leave me?" He often had dreams that came true, and saw visions and heard voices.

His mediumship began in 1895 when he attended a seance at his sister-in-law's house. Three years later he acted regularly as a medium controlled by a guide named "Moonstone."

The mediumship of Peters figures in Sir Oliver **Lodge's** book *Raymond, or Life & Death* (1916), which largely concerned seances with Alfred Vout Peters and Mrs. Gladys Osborne Leonard.

In 1899, Peters held a seance in London in which he had the strange experience of being controlled by a living person. There were two ladies at the sitting and a third, a well-known medium acted as the **control** of Peters from Paris. Evidential messages were given.

Peters was conspicuously successful in demonstrating psychometry in connection with the box of religious enthusiast Joanna **Southcott** at the National Laboratory of Psychical Research in 1927, before the box was officially opened by psychical researcher Harry **Price.**

Phantasmagoria

Term generally used for a shifting series of imaginary or fantastic images as seen in a dream or fevered imagination.

The term appears to have derived from a magic lantern entertainment presented in 1802 by the Frenchman M. Philipstal. Variants of the term have been used to describe appearance of phantoms, as in the collection of stories by Jean Baptiste Eyries, *Fantasmagoriana, or Collection of the Histories of Apparitions, Spectres, Ghosts, etc.* (1812).

This was the volume which Lord Byron read aloud to Percy Shelley, Mary Wollstonecraft (later Mary Shelley), Claire Clairmont and J. W. Polidori on the night of June 16, 1816, which stimulated the suggestion that they should each write a ghost story, culminating in Mary Shelley's *Frankenstein,* first published 1818. (See also **Frankenstein**)

Phelps, The Rev. Dr. Eliakim (c. 1860)

Presbyterian Minister and early mesmeric healer of Stratford, Connecticut, whose house was the scene of alarming **poltergeist** disturbances from March 10, 1850, for a period of eight months.

The documents on the phenomena consist mostly of letters written to the *New Haven Journal* during the progress of the events. Additional testimony from neighbors was collected and published by

C. W. Elliott in his book *Mysteries or Glimpses of the Supernatural* (1852).

Besides annoyance and moral damage, the poltergeists did a lot of financial harm by breakage. The phenomena started with mysterious displacement of objects when the family was absent in church. After their return, inanimate things began to stir and fly about and curious, stuffed effigies were discovered in empty rooms.

The following letter in the *New Haven Journal* described them thus; "While the house of Dr. Phelps was undergoing a rigid examination from cellar to attic, one of the chambers were mysteriously fitted up with eleven figures of angelic beauty, gracefully and imposingly arranged, so as to have the appearance of life. They were all female figures but one, and most of them in attitudes of devotion, with Bibles before them, and pointing to different passages with the apparent design of making the Scriptures sanction and confirm the strange things that were going on. . . .

"Some of the figures were kneeling beside the beds, and some bending their faces to the floor in attitudes of deep humility. In the center of the group was a dwarf, most grotesquely arrayed; and above was a figure so suspended as to seem flying through the air. These manifestations occurred sometimes when the room was locked, and sometimes when it was known that no person had been there. Measures were taken to have a special scrutiny in regard to every person who entered the room that day, and it is known with the most perfect certainty that many of these figures were constructed when there were no persons in the room, and no visible power by which they could have been produced. The *tout ensemble* was most beautiful and picturesque, and had a grace and ease and speaking effect that seemed the attributes of a higher creation."

The effigies were constructed from clothing and other materials in the house, stuffed with pillows to represent human figures.

The *New Haven Journal* correspondence reported that on another occasion, Dr. Phelps was writing in his room alone. For a moment he turned away, and resuming his seat he found the sheet of paper which was quite clean before, now covered with strange-looking writing, the ink still wet. This was the beginning of the spirit correspondences which mostly came in hieroglyphs.

Jocular messages on scraps of paper fluttered down from the ceiling. Other communications were scrawled on walls inside and outside the house. In one case, mysterious symbols were inscribed on a large turnip.

The spirit of a Frenchman named D—s, who claimed to have been a clerk in the lawyer's firm which prepared Mrs. Phelps' settlement, rapped out through the alphabet that he cheated Mrs. Phelps and that he was now in hell. Dr. Phelps investigated the matter and found evidence of fraud, but not sufficiently clear to justify prosecution.

Dr. Phelps never could find out how the phenomena were produced. "I witnessed them," he said, "hundreds and hundreds of times, and I know that in hundreds of instances they took place when there was no visible power by which the motion could have been produced."

The family had four children, two girls, Harry, a stepson of eleven, and another son of six years of age. It was Harry to whom the phenomena mostly seemed to attach themselves. In one case his bed was set on fire. When he was sent to school in Philadelphia he was pursued there, his books were destroyed, his clothes torn and there was such an uproar in the school that he had to be brought home. One of the girls also had some invisible share in the disturbances. When both Harry and she were away, peace reigned in the house.

Andrew Jackson **Davis,** the Poughkeepsie Seer, paid a visit to the house. His explanation was that the raps were produced by discharges of vital electricity from Harry's organism. Indeed he attributed an actual share in the phenomena to Harry, in saying: "Young Harry frequently failed to discriminate during certain moments of mental agitation between the sounds and effects which he himself made and those sounds which were produced by spiritual presence." Davis also offered lofty spiritual interpretations of the symbolic communications.

Not even unconscious fraud is sufficient, however, to explain many of the phenomena, the vanishing and reappearance of objects, their strange ballistics and human behavior.

For a detailed report of the Stratford disturbances, see *Modern Spiritualism, its Facts and Fanaticisms* by E. W. Capron (1855; 1976). (See also **Ashtabula Poltergeist; Cock Lane Ghost; Drummer of Tedworth; Enfield Poltergeist; Epworth Phenomena; Poltergeist**)

PhenomeNews (Periodical)

Quarterly publication concerned with **New Age** topics, including **astrology,** holistic health, diet, Eastern religions, psychic subjects. Includes listings of groups, ongoing events, calendar of lectures, workshops, and meetings. Address: PhenomeNews, 2821 N. Woodward, Royal Oak, Michigan 48072.

Philadelphia Experiment, The

Title of a book by Charles **Berlitz** & William Moore (1979; 1980) which investigated the story that a top secret U.S. Navy experiment in 1943 succeeded in rendering the destroyer *Eldridge* and its crew temporarily invisible and teleported it from its berth in Philadelphia to Norfolk, Virginia. The name "The Philadelphia Experiment" had earlier been used by various writers to denote the classic electrical experiments of Benjamin Franklin using a kite and brass key during a thunderstorm.

The incredible story of the Philadelphia Experiment stems largely from a mysterious Carlos Allende (aka Carl M. Allen), said to have served as a deck hand on the S.S. *Andrew Furuseth* in 1943 and to have witnessed the experiment that rendered the *Eldridge* invisible. Correspondence with Allende was cited by Morris K. Jessup (1900-1959), author of *The Case for the UFO* (1955), after an annotated copy of Jessup's book arrived at the U.S. Office of Naval Research, the annotations relating to UFOs and the Philadelphia Experiment.

Allende was interviewed by L. J. Lorenzen, director of the **Aerial Phenomena Research Organization** (APRO) in 1969, and allegedly stated that his annotations on Jessup's book, cited in the November 1967 issue of *Saga* magazine and later in a Brad Steiger book *The Allende Letters, New UFO Breakthrough* (1968), and even the letters themselves were a hoax "to *encourage* ONR Research and to discourage Professor [sic] Morris K. Jessup from going further with investigations possibly leading to actual research. *Then* I feared invisibility and force-field research. I don't *now.*" Allende was later interviewed by William Moore. It seems that Allende's confession may have stemmed from an expectation of financial gain from the publications concerned with his annotations and letters. However, his confession was later repudiated.

A facsimile edition of Jessup's book, containing the annotations, was published by Gray **Barker,** noted UFO mystery publisher, through his Saucerian Press, 1973. Jessup himself committed suicide at the age of fifty-nine, following a period of deep depression. Some UFO enthusiasts have tried to make a mystery of the suicide.

The book by Charles Berlitz and William Moore reads like an exciting detective story. Amongst intriguing facts, it reveals that Albert Einstein was employed as a scientific consultant to the U.S. Navy from May 31, 1943 to June 30, 1944. However, the suggestion that Einstein and Bertram Russell might have been involved in the Philadelphia Experiment remains highly speculative, and many other individuals cited in the book (notably a mysterious "Dr. Rinehart") remain elusive or suspect. The connection with fringe UFO individuals is not an encouraging ambience.

On July 23, 1976, the Department of the Navy, Office of Information, Washington, D.C., stated in a letter regarding the Philadelphia Experiment (reproduced in full in Berlitz & Moore's book): "ONR [Office of Naval Research] has never conducted any investigations on invisibility, either in 1943 or at any other time. . . . In view of present scientific knowledge, our scientists do not believe that such an experiment could be possible except in the realm of science fiction. A scientific discovery of such import, if it had in fact occurred, could hardly remain secret for such a long time." (See also **Invisibility; Teleportation**)

Philalethes (or **Philaletha**), **Eirenæus** (c. 1660)

The life of this alchemist is wrapped in mystery although a considerable mass of writing stands to his credit. The name is, of course, a pseudonym, and, although some have tried hard to identify the writer who bore it with Thomas Vaughan, brother of Harry Vaughan, the "Silurist" poet, this is an error (see Eugenius **Philalethes**).

Others have striven to identify him with George Starkey, the quack doctor and author of *Liquor Alchahest,* but Starkey died of the plague in London in 1665, whereas it is known that Eirenæus was living for some years after that date.

He appears, also, to have been on intimate terms with Robert Boyle and, although this points to his having spent a considerable time in England, it is certain on the other hand that he emigrated to America. Starkey was born in the Bermudas, and practiced his spurious medical crafts in the English settlements in America, where, according to his contemporary biographers, he met Eirenæus Philalethes.

This meeting may have given rise to the identification at issue, while it is probably Starkey to whom Eirenæus referred when, in a preface to one of his books, he told of certain of his writings falling "into the hands of one who, I conceive, will never return them," for in 1654 Starkey issued a volume with the title, *The Marrow of Alchemy by Eirenæus Philoponus Philalethes.*

It is to prefaces by Philalethes that we must chiefly look for any information about him, while in the thirteenth chapter of his *Introitus Apertus ad Occlusum Regis Palatium* (Amsterdam, 1667) he made a few autobiographical statements which illuminate his character and career.

"For we are like Cain, driven from the pleasant society we formerly had," he wrote, and this suggests that he was persecuted on account of his alchemistic predilections, while elsewhere he heaped scorn on most of the hermetic philosophers of his day. Elsewhere, again, he vituperated the popular worship of money-getting.

"I disdain, loathe, and detest the idolizing of silver and gold," he declared, "by which the pomps and vanities of the world are celebrated. Ah! filthy, evil, ah! vain nothingness." That is vigorously written, and indeed nearly everything from the pen of *Philalethes,* whether in Latin or in English, proclaims him a writer of some care, skill and taste, while his scholarship was also considerable, and it is interesting to find that, in his preface to *Ripley Revived* (London, 1678), he gave some account of the authors to whom he felt himself chiefly indebted.

"For my own part," he stated, "I have cause to honour Bernard Trévisan, who is very ingenious, especially in the letter to Thomas of Boulogne, when I seriously confess I received the main light in the hidden secret. I do not remember that ever I learnt anything from Raymond Lully. . . . I know of none like Ripley, though Flamel be eminent."

Lenglet du Fresnoy, in his *Histoire de la Philosophie Hermétique* (1742), referred to numerous unpublished manuscripts by Eirenæus Philalethes, but nothing is known about these today.

Works ascribed to this alchemist include: *The Marrow of Alchemy* (1654), *Introitus apertus ad occlusum Regis Palatium* (1667), *Tractatus tres: (i) Metallorum Metamorphosis; (ii) Brevis Manuductio ad Rubinum Coelestem; (iii) Fons Chymicæ Veritatis* (1678; 1694), *Ripley Reviv'd; or an Exposition upon Sir George Ripley's Hermetico-Poetical Works,* 5 parts (1677-78), *Enarratio methodica trium Gebri medicinarum* (1678). (See also **Alchemy;** Eugenius **Philalethes)**

Philalethes, Eugenius (1622-1666)

Pseudonym of alchemist Thomas Vaughan, brother of Henry Vaughan, the "Silurist" poet. Eugenius Philalethes has often been confused with Eirenæus Philalethes (or Philaletha), another alchemist. The scholarly writer Arthur E. **Waite** made this error in his book *The Real History of the Rosicrucians* (1887) but corrected it in his new edition of the *Lives of Alchemystical Philosophers* (1888) and his edition of *The Magical Writings of Thomas Vaughan* (1888). (See also **Alchemy;** Eirenæus **Philalethes;** Thomas **Vaughan)**

"Philip"

An experimental ghost created by members of the Toronto Society for Psychical Research, Canada, who wanted to test the connections between living individuals and paranormal phenomena.

In the past, many psychical researchers have pointed out that the entities manifesting at seances may be artificial personalities created by the unconscious attitudes and mentation of the sitters. Many "spirit guides" and "spirits" have been self-evidently synthetic and illusory entities, although acceptance of them as real personalities often favorably influences paranormal phenomena.

In September 1972, the Toronto experimenters began meditating on "Philip," a deliberately created ghost with history, characteristics and even appearance consciously worked out by the group. The eight members of the group comprised Iris M. Owen (former nurse, and wife of mathematician A. R. G. **Owen**), Margaret Sparrow (former chairman of MENSA in Canada, an organization of individuals with high IQs), Andy H. (housewife), Lorne H. (industrial designer, husband of Andy H.), Al P. (heating engineer), Bernice M. (accountant), Dorothy O'D. (housewife and book-keeper), Sidney K. (sociology student); Dr. A. R. G. Owen or Dr. Joel Whitton (psychologist) attended meetings as observer.

After nearly a year without significant results, the group changed their method of sitting to conform with that of a traditional nineteenth-century Spiritualist seance, seated round a table and singing or talking to enhance the atmosphere. This approach embodied the suggestions of British psychologist Kenneth Batcheldor, who claimed that skepticism inhibited paranormal phenomena but that the conventional form of seance tended to dispel skepticism and provide an atmosphere in which paranormal phenomena seemed natural.

Within only a few weeks, the group elicited raps from the table and communications from "Philip" on conventional yes-no lines, answering questions by raps and tilting the table.

On one occasion this phenomenon was successfully demonstrated before a live audience of fifty individuals for a videotaped TV show. In addition, there have been rare instances of noises from various parts of the room, a light blinking, and an apparent levitation of the table.

The experimenters believe that their work may throw light on some of the phenomena of poltergeist, haunting and Spiritualism. The story of the "Philip" experiments is described in *Conjuring up Philip* by Iris M. Owen & Margaret Sparrow (Harper & Row, 1976). (See also **Identity; Personality)**

Philips, James B. (1907-1987)

British businessman who played a prominent part in the practical affairs of the Society for Psychical Research, London. He was born December 20, 1907, and traveled widely during his lifetime. At different periods he was in business in New Zealand, Nigeria, and South Africa.

He joined the Society for Psychical Research in 1970 and was coopted to the Council in June 1973, soon afterwards being appointed deputy treasurer. His wide experience of practical business affairs was of great value to the Society. In May 1975, he was honorary secretary and treasurer. Two years later he resigned as honorary secretary, but continued as treasurer for a further year. He retired in 1978, when he was elected an honorary associate, subsequently returning to service on the executive committee for a further short period.

He died in London on August 7, 1987.

Phillimore, Mercy (died 1975)

Pioneer British journalist and organizer in the field of Spiritualism and psychical research. She became a member of the staff of the **London Spiritualist Alliance** (later renamed **College of Psychic Studies)** in 1913. She stayed with the organization for thirty-nine years, retiring in 1952.

As secretary, she came in contact with such leading mediums of her time as Eileen **Garrett,** as well as many well-known personalities concerned with psychic science of occultism, such as A. E. **Waite,** W. B. **Yeats,** Stanley **De Brath,** Sir Arthur Conan **Doyle,** Sir Oliver **Lodge** and Paul **Brunton.**

She contributed a number of articles to the British journal *Light* and gave many lectures. She was a tireless worker in the cause of Spiritualism and played a significant but unobtrusive part in the modern history of the movement. She was associated with Dr. Nandor **Fodor** in Britain, and after his death published a tribute to him in the journal *Light* (Autumn, 1964).

Philosopher's Stone

A legendary substance which enabled adepts in **alchemy** to compass the transmutation of metals. It was believed by the alchemists that one definite substance was essential to the success of the transmutation of metals. By the application or admixture of this substance, all metals might be transmuted into gold or silver. It was often designated the "Powder of Projection."

Zosimus, who lived at the commencement of the fifth century, was one of the first who alluded to it. He said that the stone was a powder or liquor formed of diverse metals, infusioned under a favorable constellation.

The Philosopher's Stone was supposed to contain the secret not only of transmutation, but of health and life, for through its agency could be distilled the **Elixir of Life.** It was the touchstone of existence.

The author of a *Treatise on Philosophical and Hermetic Chemistry* published in Paris in 1725 stated: "Modern philosophers have extracted from the interior of mercury a fiery spirit, mineral, vegetable and multiplicative, in a humid concavity in which is found the primitive mercury or the universal quintessence. In the midst of this spirit resides the spiritual fluid. . . .

"This is the mercury of the philosophers, which is not solid like a metal, nor soft like quicksilver, but between the two. They have retained for a long time this secret, which is the commencement, the middle, and the end of their work. It is necessary then to proceed first to purge the mercury with salt and with ordinary salad vinegar, to sublime it with vitriol and saltpetre, to dissolve it in aquafortis, to sublime it again, to calcine it and fix it, to put away part of it in salad oil, to distill this liquor for the purpose of separating the spiritual water, air, and fire, to fix the mercurial body in the spiritual water or to distill the spirit of liquid mercury found in it, to putrefy all, and then to raise and exalt the spirit with non-odorous white sulphur—that is to say, sal-ammoniac—to dissolve the sal-ammoniac in the spirit of liquid mercury which when distilled becomes the liquor known as the Vinegar of the Sages, to make it pass from gold to antimony three times and afterwards to reduce it by heat, lastly to steep this warm gold in very harsh vinegar and allow it to putrefy. On the surface of the vinegar it will raise itself in the form of fiery earth of the colour of oriental pearls. This is the first operation in the grand work.

"For the second operation, take in the name of God one part of gold and two parts of the spiritual water, charged with the sal-ammoniac, mix this noble confection in a vase of crystal of the shape of an egg: warm over a soft but continuous fire, and the fiery water will dissolve little by little the gold; this forms a liquor which is called by the sages 'chaos' containing the elementary qualities—cold, dryness, heat and humidity. Allow this composition to putrefy until it becomes black; this blackness is known as the 'crow's head' and the 'darkness of the sages,' and makes known to the artist that he is on the right track. It was also known as the 'black earth.' It must be boiled once more in a vase as white as snow; this stage of the work is called the 'swan,' and from it arises the white liquor, which is divided into two parts—one white for the manufacture of silver, the other red for the manufacture of gold. Now you have accomplished the work, and you possess the Philosopher's Stone.

"In these diverse operations, one finds many by-products; among these is the 'green lion' which is called also 'azoph,' and which draws gold from the more ignoble elements; the 'red lion' which converts the metal into gold; the 'head of the crow,' called also the 'black veil of the ship of Theseus,' which appearing forty days before the end of the operation predicts its success; the white powder which transmutes the white metals to fine silver; the red elixir with which gold is made; the white elixir which also makes silver, and which procures long life—it is also called the 'white daughter of the philosophers.' "

In the lives of the various alchemists, we find many notices of the Powder of Projection in connection with those adepts who were supposed to have arrived at the solution of the grand arcanum. Thus in the story of Alexander **Seton,** a Scotsman who came from Port Seton, near Edinburgh, it is stated that on his various travels on the continent he employed in his alchemical experiments a blackish powder, the application of which turned any metal given him into gold.

Numerous instances are on record of Seton's projections, the majority of which were verified with great thoroughness. On one occasion, while in Holland, he went with some friends from the house at which he was residing to undertake an alchemical experiment at another house near by. One the way there, a quantity of ordinary zinc was purchased, and this Seton succeeded in projecting into pure gold by the application of his powder!

A similar phenomenon was undertaken by him at Cologne and elsewhere throughout Germany, and even the most extreme torture could not wring from him the secret of the quintessence he possessed.

His pupil or assistant, Sendivogius, made great efforts to obtain the secret from him before he died, but all to no purpose. However, out of gratitude Seton bequeathed him what remained of his marvelous powder, which was employed by his Polish successor with the same results as had been achieved in his own case.

The wretched Sendivogius fared badly, however, when the powder at last came to an end. He had used it chiefly in liquid form, and into this he had dipped silver coins which immediately had become the purest gold. Indeed it is on record that one coin, of which he had only immersed the half, remained for many years as a signal instance of the claims of alchemy in a museum or collection in South Germany. The half of this doubloon was gold, while the undipped portion had remained silver, but the notice concerning it is scarcely of a satisfactory nature.

When the powder gave out, Sendivogius was driven to the desperate expedient of gilding coins, which, it was reported, he had hitherto transmuted by legitimate means, and this very naturally brought upon him the wrath of those who had trusted him. (See **Seton**)

There are so many convincing accounts of successful alchemical operations with the Philosopher's Stone that it is tempting to believe that some alchemists may indeed have mastered this great secret. However, the subject is surrounded with so much mystery and symbolism that leads one to suppose that the great transformations claimed were really spiritual rather than practical alchemy. The close association of ideas of the Philosopher's Stone with the Elixir of Life reinforces this view.

The idea of the Philosopher's Stone is an ancient one, and could have arisen from an Eastern talismanic legend. Yet even in Egyptian alchemy, which seems one of the oldest, the idea of a black powder (the detritus or oxide of all metals mingled) is found.

The ancient Chinese believed that gold was immortal and that when absorbed in the human body could bestow immortality, thus we find here ideas of the mystical value of gold together with the concept of the Elixir of Life.

The art of Chinese alchemists can be traced back to circa 100-150 B.C., long before alchemy was practiced in the West. Gold was regarded as a medicine for long life, and there is a story that the great Wei Po-Yang (c. 100-150 A.D.) succeeded in manufacturing the gold medicine and he and his pupil Yu, together with the wise man's dog, thereby became immortal.

The idea of the Philosopher's Stone as wish-fulfilling is found in ancient Indian religious tradition, where this magical stone was named "Chintamani" and cited in scriptures. Similar ideas were found in Buddhism.

The antiquary Rev. S. Baring-Gould suggested that such legends derived from the life-giving properties of the sun, which was such a prominent symbol in so many alchemical works. He reviewed such concepts in an entertaining chapter on 'The Philosopher's Stone' in his book *Curiosities of Olden Times* (1895). (See also **Alchemy; Anonymous Adept; Elixir of Life**)

Recommended reading:

Bacon, Roger. *Mirror of Alchemy.* London, 1597; Globe Bookshop, Los Angeles, 1975

Chkashige, Masumi. *Oriental Alchemy,* Weiser, New York, 1936

Eliade, Mircea. *The Forge and the Crucible; The Origins and Structures of Alchemy,* Harper & Row, 1956

Jung, C. G. *Alchemical Studies* (vol. 13 of *Collected Works*), Princeton University Press, 1967

Redgrove, H. Stanley. *Alchemy; Ancient & Modern,* William Rider, London, 1911; University Books, 1969

Regardie, Israel. *The Philosopher's Stone,* Llewellyn Publications, St. Paul, Minnesota, 1958

Waite, Arthur E. (ed.). *The Hermetic and Alchemical Writings of Paracelsus,* 2 vols., James Elliott, London, 1894; University Books, 1967

Waite, Arthur E. *Alchemists Through the Ages,* Rudolf Steiner Publications, Blauvelt, New York, 1970

Philosophical Research Society

Founded in 1934 "to investigate the essential teachings of scientific, spiritual, and cultural leaders and further clarify and integrate man's body of knowledge, to apply this knowledge to the present needs of mankind by means of modern skills and the cooperation of outstanding experts, to make available these vital concepts to the public through lectures, publications and other medium to increase public awareness of the usefulness of these ideas and ideals in solving the personal and collective problems of modern man."

Founded by Manley P. Hall, the Society maintains a research library of over 50,000 volumes, and a collection of art and rare books, conducts program of lectures, seminars and special events, sponsors research projects, publishes a Journal. The society has also published over 130 books and brochures, produces audiocassettes. Address: 3910 Los Feliz Boulevard, Los Angeles, California 90027.

Philosophical Research Society Journal

Quarterly journal on occult and Eastern topics, edited by Manley Palmer **Hall.** Address. 3910 Los Feliz Boulevard, Los Angeles, California 90027.

"Philosophus"

One of the spirit **controls** of the Rev. Stainton **Moses,** said to have been Alexander Achillini, who succeeded Francatiano in the chair of philosophy at Padua in 1506. The name of Francatiano could not be verified.

"Phinuit"

A picturesque spirit entity, the earliest permanent **control** of the medium Mrs. Leonore E. **Piper.** "Phinuit" succeeded the *soi-disant* spirit of Sebastian Bach, said that he was French, a physician in Metz, but never furnished convincing proof of identity. His statements about himself were hazy and contradictory. Consequently he was not much trusted.

Prof. N. S. Shaler, in a letter to Prof. William James, summed up his opinion on "Phinuit's" first year of manifestation in 1894: "Whatever the medium is, I am convinced that this influence is a preposterous scoundrel."

Attempts to verify the statements of "Phinuit" resulted in failure. The archives of Metz were searched. No trace was found of him. He could not even speak French. When an explanation was asked, he declared that he forgot his maternal tongue. Later, on closer questioning, he disclosed uncertainty whether he was born at Metz or Marseilles, and finally concluded that his name was not "Phinuit," but "Jean Alaen Scliville," and that he never had any connection with Dr. Cocke, from whom his personality appeared to have been borrowed by Mrs. Piper.

Dr. Richard **Hodgson** regarded the existence of "Phinuit" as an open question. To F. W. H. **Myers,** it seemed clear that the name "Phinuit" was the result of suggestion at the earliest seances. Other psychical researchers thought it most probable that "Phinuit" was nothing more than a secondary **personality** of Mrs. Piper.

According to "Imperator's" statements, however, "Phinuit" was an earthbound spirit who had become confused and bewildered in his first attempts at **communication,** and had lost his consciousness of personal identity.

The "Gurney" control also bore out "Phinuit's" claim to an independent existence. He said to Sir Oliver **Lodge** in 1889: "Dr. Phinuit is a peculiar type of man . . . he is eccentric and quaint, but good-hearted . . . a shrewd doctor, he knows his own business thoroughly."

"Phinuit's" regime was exclusive from 1884-1892. From that date on he shared control with "George **Pelham.**" In 1897 the "Imperator" group took Mrs. Piper in charge and "Phinuit" was entirely suppressed.

For accounts of the mediumship of Mrs. Piper, see *Proceedings* of the Society for Psychical Research (vol. 6, pt. 17), and the books *Mrs. Piper and the Society for Psychical Research* by M. Sage (1904), *The Life and Work of Mrs. Piper* by Alta C. Piper (1929). (See also Richard **Hodgson; "Imperator"**; "George **Pelham";** Mrs. Leonore E. **Piper**)

Phoenix: New Directions in the Study of Man (Journal)

Semiannual scholarly publication concerned with the advancement of scientific and philosophical study of paranormal phenomena. Includes book reviews and correspondence. Address: Phoenix Associates, 880 Lathrop Drive, Stanford, California 94305.

Phoenix, William (c. 1927)

Direct voice medium of Glasgow, Scotland. Sir Arthur Conan **Doyle** had a number of sittings with him and thought highly of his powers. However, Phoenix was later believed to be partly fraudulent.

In *Proceedings* of the Society for Psychical Research (vol. 40, pp. 419-427), Lord Charles Hope published an account of some sittings in Glasgow and in London to which he invited Prof. Neville **Whymant.**

In the first sitting, the voice of an Indian attempted to speak in a variety of Persian.

In the second sitting a good conversation of real import was being worked up in Italian but the power failed too soon. Modern Greek was heard. The Persian voice was a little more explicit than on the previous occasion. A Chinese voice, that of a scribe or commentator apparently, also spoke. Something was told in Japanese.

To quote Lord Charles Hope: "Although the Glasgow sittings had not resulted in any communication of the order of importance of Dr. Whymant's experience in New York they had apparently established a strong case for the speaking of languages unknown to the medium."

Thereupon Phoenix was invited to London. In September and October 1927, he gave six sittings. In the first sitting, Chinese and Japanese voices spoke to Gonoské Komai. But "I cannot truthfully say" remarked Dr. Whymant "that I gathered anything at all from this voice. It was over-anxious to tell me something and probably the keenness of its desire prevented its being understood. Other voices struggled for expression without achieving more than whispering and trumpet taps. Then came a voice speaking a queer idiom; it sounded almost like a jargon of some kind and I called out that it sounded like Indo-Chinese border dialect, later giving the impression that it might have been badly spoken Yunnanese. The voice gave bugle calls of a military nature easily recognized and several people suggested that it might have been a soldier."

Of another voice Dr. Whymant stated: "It seemed to me that the voice was that of a Straits Chinese who had lived in Singapore."

Lord Charles Hope stated: "I had become convinced that at any rate on most occasions the medium left his chair before voices spoke to the sitters. I had sat next to the medium on several occasions and had distinctly heard sounds like a creaking boot. After the sitting at which I had heard these sounds I noticed that one of the medium's boots creaked as he walked. The sounds were similar."

In a following sitting, Lord Charles Hope obtained proof that the medium left his chair. Phoenix protested that he was under control. Lord Charles Hope suggested that he should turn out his pockets to prove that he had no appliance with which to produce the psychic lights which appeared at each sitting. Phoenix refused the suggestion. Lord Charles Hope concluded: "Reluctantly I had come to the conclusion that Phoenix was at least in part a fraud."

Phone-Voyance

A kind of psychic television, named as a special form of **clairvoyance,** by talented British psychic Vincent N. **Turvey** in 1905. It implies four things: Psychic vision, physical contact, the wires and instruments of a telephone company and simultaneity of clairvoyance with physical contact.

The phenomenon is superior to physical television, as Turvey often described things which the listener at the other end of the telephone wire did not know, as for instance what his daughter was doing in the room above him, what a man behind his back was reading in a book.

Turvey not only saw things which actually were there, but also things habitually worn by his listener, although they may not have been on the listener at the particular time. Similarly, he could see spirits in the room of his listener. Once he described the picture of a young lady known to the listener, but miles away, and told him that she was not dead and yet not actually in the room.

Turvey possessed the faculty intermittently from 1905-08. He found that it was a great strain on the brain and that too frequent use would lead to very serious injury.

In most cases he seemed to see "through a halo, or aura, of bright heliotrope, or pale violet-coloured fire, the flashes or sparks of which do not appear to cover *all* the window, so to speak, but to leave the centre clear and colourless, and in that centre appears the person or object that is seen. Another extraordinary thing is that occasionally a part of my mentality seems to ooze out of me, and to run along the line for a little distance, say a yard or two; and as 'I' [his spirit] go, so little pieces of the copper wire which lay together, A-B, seem to turn over to B-A, i.e., reverse their position as if on a hinge. These pieces appear to be about four inches in length. At other times phone-voyance seems to be very like mental body-traveling, because 'I' appears to be in the room at the one end of the line, and by a sort of living cord to communicate with 'ME' [his body] at the other end, and to make 'ME' speak about that which 'I' see."

The famous editor and spiritualist W. T. **Stead** in his preface to Turvey's *Beginnings of Seership* (1911; 1969) quoted the case of a professional music hall performer who trained the faculty of "phone-voyance" to such perfection that it could be exercised at will under the most adverse conditions.

The experiments were carried out by a committee of investigators between the stage of the Alhambra Theater in London and the office of the *Daily Mirror.* Articles presented at random to Mr. Zomah (A. T. Giddings) by members of the committee in the Alhambra were immediately seen and described by his wife who was at the other end of the telephone in the newspaper office.

Of course this demonstration may have been simply long-distance telepathy or even clever stage "thought reading" but according to Stead (to judge from the reports that were published), Mrs. Zomah actually saw the article which was held in her husband's hand at the other end of the telephone wire.

However, whatever the nature of this demonstration, it does not affect the undoubted psychic talents displayed by Mr. Turvey. For fuller information, see his book *The Beginnings of Seership,* reissued in 1969 by University Books, Inc. (See also Vincent N. **Turvey**)

Phouka (or Puca)

The nightmare horse of Irish folklore, a supernatural animal spirit. The Phouka would lure his victims to mount him, then take them for a wild ride and throw them off. The Phouka was also believed to be able to take the form of an ass, a bull or a goat, and it is possible that the word *Puca* is related to Puck, another mischievous fairy figure. (See also **Kelpie**)

Phreno-Magnet and Mirror of Nature, The (Journal)

British journal devoted to **Phrenology** in relation to **animal magnetism.** Founded in London 1843, edited by S. T. Hall. No longer published.

Phreno-Mesmerism (or Phreno-Magnetism or Phrenopathy)

An application of the principles of **Mesmerism** to the pseudo-science of **phrenology.** Mesmerism (or **Animal Magnetism**) and phrenology had for some time been regarded by the English Mesmerists as related sciences when it was discovered that a somnambule whose phrenological "bumps" were touched by the fingers of the operator would respond to the stimulus by exhibiting every symptom of the mental trait corresponding to the organ touched.

Thus signs of joy, grief, destructiveness, combativeness, and friendship might be exhibited in rapid succession by the entranced patient.

Among those who claimed to have discovered the new science were Dr. Collyer, a pupil of Dr. John **Elliotson,** and the Rev. LaRoy **Sunderland,** although the former afterwards repudiated it. As time went on, enterprising phreno-mesmerists discovered many new cerebral organs, as many as a hundred and fifty being found beside those already mapped out by Spurzheim and Gall.

Among its supporters phreno-mesmerism numbered the distinguished hypnotist James Braid (see **Hypnotism**), who expressed himself fully satisfied of its reality. He recorded a number of cases in which the patient correctly indicated by his actions the organs touched, although demonstrably ignorant of phrenological principles, and inaccessible to outside information.

Braid himself offered by a very halting and inadequate physiological explanation, and since he may be supposed to have been fully alive to the factors of suggestion and hyperaesthesia, it would seem advisable to admit the possibility of mental **suggestion,** or **telepathy,** by means of which the expectation of the operator, reproducing itself in the mind of the patient, would give rise to the corresponding reactions. (See also **Animal Magnetism; Hypnotism; Mesmerism; Phrenology; Phreno-Magnet** (Journal); **Suggestion**)

Phrenology

A pseudoscience claiming that character and personality can be ascertained by the shape and size of various areas or "bumps" on the skull, resulting from developments of the brain centers. It derives from the traditional belief that character traits were reflected in physical appearances, and was associated with Physiognomy, the study of outward aspects of the individual.

Phrenology was first systematically studied by Franz Joseph Gall (1758-1828) at the end of the nineteenth century. He made observations on hundreds of heads and skulls, and in 1796 lectured in Vienna on the anatomy of the brain and the elements of phrenology. His pupil J. K. Spurzheim continued his work in England and America, where Phrenology vied with Mesmerism and Spiritualism as a popular study during the nineteenth century.

At first, Gall and Spurzheim encountered some opposition from churchmen because their system appeared to imply that personality characteristics were inbuilt in cranial structures instead of being subject to modification by leading a good life.

Gall was an accredited physician with a detailed knowledge of the brain and nervous system, but phrenology soon became popularized and practiced by non-medical individuals and even fairground charlatans. However, it was also the province of many original thinkers of the day, and provided a common forum with **Mesmerism** and **Spiritualism.**

Essentially, phrenology defined more than thirty areas of the skull related to such instincts as amativeness, philogeniture, habitativeness, affection, combativeness, destructiveness, alimentiveness, secretiveness, acquisitiveness, constructiveness, and such moral faculties as self-esteem, approbativeness, circumspection, benevolence, veneration, firmness, conscientiousness, hope, admiration, idealism, cheerfulness, imitativeness.

The size and development of these areas implied strong or weak aspects of these instincts and faculties. The areas were measured by calipers and marked off on a chart, so that a complete character reading could be made.

Early exponents of **animal magnetism** (a precursor of **hypnotism,** but allied with psychic faculties) developed a new psuedoscience named "Phrenomagnetism" or **"Phreno-Mesmerism."** Operators claimed that when any phrenological area of the subject was touched during a trance, the subject acted out the particular faculty associated with that area. Thus, when the operator touched the bump of "combativeness," the entranced subject would exhibit belligerent behavior.

It has to be admitted that the empirical findings of such pioneers as Gall and Spurzheim were astonishingly accurate, but it is possible that the successes of later followers depended as much on intuition as precise measurement, and it may be that many accurate character readings owed more to extrasensory perception than the truths of phrenology. Of course, suggestion must have also played a large part.

Although now generally regarded as discredited, phrenology flourished side by side with Mesmerism and Spiritualism during the nineteenth century. Many noted scientists of the day were sympathetic, and supporters also included such literary figures as Walt Whitman and Edgar Allan Poe.

The British Phrenological Society, founded in 1886 by Lorenzo J. Fowler continued in existence until as recently as 1967, and the modern occult revival has also seen renewed interest in phrenology.

Recommended reading:

Chambers, Howard V. *Phrenology,* Sherbourne paperback, 1968

Davies, John D. *Phrenology: Fad and Science: A Nineteenth Century American Crusade,* Archon, 1955; Shoe String, 1971

De Giustino, David. *Conquest of Mind; Phrenology and Victorian Social Thought,* Croom Helm, London/ Rowman & Littlefield, 1975

Gall, Franz J. *On the Functions of the Brain and of each of its parts: with observations on the possibility of determining the instincts, propensities and talents, or the moral and intellectual dispositions of men and animals, by the configuration of the brain and head,* (6 vols.), Boston, 1835

Stern, Madeleine B. *Heads and Headlines; The Phrenological Fowlers,* University of Oklahoma, 1971

Wells, Samuel R. *How to Read Character: A New Illustrated Handbook of Phrenology and Physiognomy,* Samuel R. Wells, New York, 1871; C. E. Tuttle paperback, 1971

Phrygian Cap

Hargrave Jennings, in his book *The Rosicrucians, Their Rites and Mysteries* (1870 etc.) stated that the Phrygian Cap, the classic cap of the god Mithra, sacrificial Cap, and miter all derive from one common ancestor. The Mithraic or Phrygian Cap is the origin of the priestly miter in all faiths.

It was worn by the priest in sacrifice. When worn by a male, it had its crest, comb, or point, set jutting forward; when worn by a female, it bore the same prominent part of the cap in reverse, or on the nape of the neck, as in the instance of the Amazon's helmet, displayed in all old sculptures, or that of Pallas-Athene, as exhibited in figures of Minerva.

According to Jennings, the peak, pic, or point, of caps or hats (the term "cocked hat" is a case in point) all refer to the same idea. This point had a sanctifying meaning afterwards attributed to it, when it was called the christa, crista, or crest, which signifies a triumphal top, or tuft. The "Grenadier Cap," and the loose black Hussar Cap, derive remotely from the same sacred, Mithraic, or emblematical bonnet, or high pyramidal cap. In this instance, it changes to black, because it is devoted to the illustration of the "fireworkers" (grenadiers) who, among modern military, succeeded the Vulcanists, Cyclopes, classic "smiths," or servants of Vulcan (or Mulciber), the artful worker among the metals in the fire, or amidst the forces of nature.

This idea will be found by a reference to the high cap among the Persians, or fire-worshipers, and to the black cap among the Bohemians, and in the East. Travelers in Eastern lands may remember that the tops of the minarets reminded them of the high-pointed black caps of the Persians.

The Phrygian Cap is a most recondite antiquarian form. The symbol comes from the highest antiquity. It is displayed on the head of the figure sacrificing in the celebrated sculpture called the "Mithraic Sacrifice" (or the Mythical Sacrifice) in the British Museum, London. This loose cap, with the point protruding, gives the original form from which all helmets or defensive headpieces, whether Greek or barbarian, derive.

As a Phrygian Cap, or Symbolizing Cap, it is always sanguine in its color. It then stands as the "Cap of Liberty," a revolutionary form; also, in another way, it is even a civic or incorporated badge. It is always masculine in its meaning. It marks the "needle" of the obelisk, the crown or tip of the phallus, whether "human" or representative. It appears to have its origin in the rite of circumcision.

The real meaning of the "bonnet rouge" or cap of liberty has been involved from time immemorial in deep obscurity, notwithstanding that it has always been regarded as the most important hieroglyph or figure. It signifies the supernatural simultaneous "sacrifice" and "triumph." It has descended from the time of Abraham, and it is supposed to be an emblem of the strange mythic rite of the "circumcisio preputii."

The loose Phrygian "bonnet conique," another form of the cap of liberty, may be accepted as figuring or standing for that detached integument or husk, separated from a certain point or knob, which has various names in different languages, and which supplies the central idea of this sacrificial rite—the spoil or refuse of which (absurd and unpleasant as it may seem) is borne aloft at once as a "trophy" and as the "cap of liberty."

It is now a magic sign, and becomes a **talisman** of supposedly inexpressible power—from what particular dark reason it may be difficult to say. The whole is a sign of "initiation," and of baptism of a peculiar kind.

The Phrygian Cap, ever after this first inauguration, has stood as the sign of the "Enlightened." The heroic figures in most Gnostic Gems have caps of this kind. The sacrificer in the sculptured group of the "Mithraic Sacrifice," among the marbles in the British Museum, has a Phrygian Cap on his head, whilst in the act of striking the bull with the poniard—meaning the office of the immolating priest. The "bonnet conique" is the miter of the Doge of Venice.

Cinteotl, a Mexican god of sacrifice, wears such a cap made from the thigh-skin of an immolated virgin. This head-dress is shaped like a cock's comb.

Besides the "bonnet rouge," the Pope's miter and other miters or conical head-coverings derive their name from the terms "Mithradic," or "Mithraic," the origin of the whole class of names is Mittra, or Mithra. The cap of the grenadier, the shape of which is alike all over Europe, is related to the Tartar lambskin caps, which are dyed black, and it is black also from its associations with Vulcan and the "fire-worshippers" or Smiths. The Scotch Glengarry cap also seems, upon examination, to be a "cocked" Phrygian. All the black conical caps, and the meaning of this strange symbol, came from the East. The loose black fur cap derives from the Tartars.

The "Cap of Liberty" ("bonnet rouge"), the Crista or Crest (Male), and the Female (Amazon) helmet, all express the same idea; in the instance of the female crest, the knob is, however, depressed.

Recommended reading:

Cumont, Franz. *The Mysteries of Mithra,* Open Court, Chicago, 1903; Dover paperback, n.d.

Jennings, Hargrave. *The Rosicrucians; Their Rites and Mysteries,* 3rd ed., greatly enlarged, 2 vols., J. Nimmo, London, 1887

Vermaseren, M. J. *Mithras, The Secret God,* Chatto & Windus, London, 1963

Wynne-Tyson, Esmé. *Mithras, the Fellow in the Cap,* Rider & Co., London, 1968

Phyllorhodomancy

Divination by rose-leaves. The ancient Greeks clapped a rose-leaf on the hand and judged from the resulting sound the success or otherwise of their desires.

Physical World

Theosophical concept (formerly known as the Sthula Plane), the lowest of the seven worlds, the world in which ordinary man moves and is conscious under normal conditions.

It is the limit of the ego's descent into matter, and the matter which composes the appropriate physical body, is the densest of any of these worlds. Physical matter has the seven divisions of solid, liquid, gas, ether, super-ether, sub-atom and atom, in common with the matter of the other worlds.

Beside the physical body, familiar to ordinary vision, there is a finer body, the **etheric double,** which plays a very important part in collecting vitality from the sun for the use of the denser physical body (see **Chakras**). At death, the physical body and the etheric double are cast aside and slowly resolved into their components.

These concepts derive from traditional Hindu mysticism. (See also **Theosophy; Worlds, Planes or Spheres**)

Pickering, Edward Charles (1846-1919)

Astronomer, and founding member of the American Society for the Psychical Research. Born July 19, 1846, in Boston, Massachusetts, he studied at Lawrence Scientific School of Harvard University (B.S. 1865, M.A. hons. 1880). In 1874 he married Lizzie Wadsworth Sparks.

He became a famous astronomer, taught mathematics and physics at Lawrence from 1865-67, was professor of physics at Massachusetts Institute of Technology from 1868-77. In 1877 he was appointed director of the Harvard Observatory and held this position for 42 years.

In the course of his distinguished career as an astronomer, Dr. Pickering devised methods of measuring the magnitudes of stars and supervised cataloguing of some 80,000 stars. He also established the Harvard Observatory auxiliary station at Arequipa, Peru, in 1891.

In the field of parapsychology, Dr. Pickering was vice-president of the **American Society for Psychical Research** from 1885-88 and served on the Society's Committee on Thought Transference. He also participated in the statistical analysis of experiments in telepathy using cards, dice and numbers. In collaboration with Professor J. M. Peirce he reported these experiments in *Proceedings* of the ASPR in the article 'Discussion of Returns in Response to Circular No. 4' (vol. 1, No. 1, July 1885). He contributed other articles to the ASPR *Proceedings.*

He died February 3, 1919, at Cambridge, Massachusetts.

Pico della Mirandola, Giovanni (1463-1494)

Italian astrologer and Kabalist born February 24, 1463. His family played a prominent part in a number of the civil wars which convulsed medieval Italy, while they owned extensive lands in the neighborhood of Modena, the most valuable of their possessions being a castle bearing their own name of Mirandola. It was here that Giovanni was born.

He appears to have been a versatile student, never showing any fondness for playing children's games but devoting himself to study from the very outset. According to tradition, before he was out of his teens he had mastered jurisprudence and mathematics, had studied philosophy and theology, and had even dabbled in occult sciences.

A boy of this kind naturally felt small inclination to remain at home, and so it is not surprising to find that Giovanni soon left his brothers to look after the family estates, and proceeded to various universities in Italy and France. While in the latter country, his interest in astrology and related subjects deepened, thanks partly to his making a close study of the works of Raymond **Lully,** and in 1486 Giovanni went to Rome, where he delivered a series of lectures on various branches of science.

While thus engaged, his erudition won high praise from some of his hearers, but certain members of the clergy suspected him of heresy, reported his doings to the Inquisition, and even sought to have him excommunicated. The pope, however, was rather averse to quarrelling with a member of so powerful a family at the Mirandolas, and accordingly he waived violent measures, instead appointing a body of Churchmen to argue with the scientist.

A lengthy altercation ensued, and throughout it the jury displayed the most consummate ignorance, it being recorded, indeeds that some of them imagined that "Kabal" was a man, who had written against Christianity, and that the Kabalists were the disciples of this hypothetic person.

Giovanni must have been deeply chagrined by this stupidity on the part of his opponents and deplored having to argue with people so utterly vain; yet he published a defence (under the title *Apologia*) of the ideas and theories promulgated in his lectures and in 1493 the pope, Alexander VI, brought the affair to a conclusion by granting the offender absolution.

Thereupon Mirandola went to live at Florence, and stayed there until his death in 1494, occasionally experimenting with **alchemy,** but chiefly busy with further kabalistic studies.

Apart from the *Apologia Pici Mirandoli* cited above, Giovanni was author of several books of a theological nature, the most important of these being his *Conclusiones Philosophicæ, cabalisticæ et theologicæ,* published in 1486, and his *Disputationes adversus Astrologiam Divinaticum,* issued in 1495. His works appear to have been keenly admired by such of his contemporaries as were not averse to speculative thought, and it is interesting to find that a collected edition of his writings was printed at Bologna in 1496, and another at Venice two years later.

He died November 17, 1494, in Florence. (See also **Alchemy; Astrology; Kabala**)

Piddington, J(ohn) G(eorge) (1869-1952)

President of the Society for Psychical Research, London from 1924-25, secretary from 1899-1907, treasurer from 1917-21, member of SPR Council from 1899-1932.

Born J. G. Smith in 1869, he took his mother's family name in order to avoid confusion with other leading members of the SPR. Mr. Piddington joined the Society for Psychical Research in 1890 and subsequently devoted the rest of his life to the cause of psychical research.

He helped to create the SPR research endowment fund in 1902, which enabled the Society to have a full-time paid research officer. In 1905, Mr. Piddington visited the U.S. and assisted the organization of the American branch of the SPR as an independent society.

In the field of psychical research, he played an important part in interpreting the scripts of the "SPR group" of automatic writers concerned with **cross correspondence,** involving Mrs. Henry **Sidgwick,** G. W. **Balfour,** Sir Oliver **Lodge** and Alice **Johnson.** There were over three thousand of these scripts, which became fully meaningful when correctly juxtaposed, indicating a common origin from purposeful intelligences. These cross correspondences have been cited as evidence of survival.

Mr. Piddington contributed a number of articles to the SPR *Proceedings,* including: 'A Series of Concordant Automatisms' (vol. 22, part 57, 1908), 'Supplementary Notes on "A Series of Concordant Automatisms"' (vol. 24, part 60, 1910), 'Note on Mrs. Piper's Hodgson-Control in England' (with Mrs. Henry Sidgwick, vol. 23, part 58, 1909), 'Further Experiments with Mrs. Piper in 1908' (with Mrs. Henry Sidgwick and Mrs. A. W. Verrall, vol. 24, part 60, 1910), 'A Hitherto Unsuspected Answer to the Horace Ode Question' (vol. 26, part 65, 1913), 'Cross Correspondences of a Gallic Type' (vol. 29, part 72, 1916), 'Fresh Light on the "One-Horse

Dawn" Experiment' vol. 30, part 76, 1918), 'A Reply to Sir Oliver Lodge's Note' (vol. 30, part 77, 1918), 'Forecasts in Scripts Concerning the War' (vol. 33, part 87, 1923), 'Presidential Address' (vol. 34, part 89, 1924), 'One Crowded Hour of Glorious Life' (vol. 34, part 100, 1926-28), 'A Reply to Mr. Hall' (vol. 36, part 102, 1926-28), 'The Master Builder' (vol. 36, part 102, 1926-28).

Mr. Piddington died April 1952.

Piddington, Sydney and Lesley (c. 1949)

A husband-wife team who gave one of the most famous stage **telepathy** acts of modern times. Sydney Piddington was born in Australia in 1921. During World War II he served in an artillery regiment in Singapore. After the fall of Singapore he was imprisoned for four years in the dreaded Changi Camp, together with Russell Braddon and Ronald Searle. Some of the hardships of that period are related by Russell Braddon in his book *The Naked Island* (1952) and illustrated in the drawings of Ronald Searle.

As a relief from the harsh treatment, forced labor, malnutrition and disease, the camp prisoners staged theatrical entertainments. An article by Dr. J. B. **Rhine** on parapsychology in a stray copy of *Digest* magazine stimulated Piddington and Braddon to experiment with telepathy, and they devised an act which became a notable feature of the prison camp entertainments.

After his release from the camp, Piddington returned to Australia where he met and married radio actress Lesley Pope in 1946. The couple worked up a telepathy act based on Sydney's experience in Changi jail, and the Piddingtons became a successful show on 2UE in Sydney and 3K2 in Melbourne, followed by live stage shows.

In 1949 the couple went to England, where they appeared over eight weeks on B.B.C. radio programs, which were a sensational success. The Piddingtons became a household word almost overnight. In one remarkable program, twenty million listeners waited with bated breath while Lesley Piddington, sequestered in the Tower of London, correctly stated the difficult test sentence "Be abandoned as the electricians said that they would have no current" relayed by Sydney telepathically from a B.B.C. studio in Piccadilly, several miles away. The line had been chosen independently of the Piddingtons, and only revealed to Sydney when he was asked to concentrate upon it in the studio.

Throughout the B.B.C. shows, the tests were rigorously controlled, and if there *was* a code (as so many theorists suggested) it would have to have been independent of aural and visual signals and operate at a distance. The possibility of concealed electronic devices (in a period long before micro transistor techniques) was also ruled out by searching of the Piddingtons.

One by one each ingenious "explanation" of trickery was eliminated under conditions which precluded codes and confederates. Everyone had his pet theories about how it might be done, and part of the success of the shows was the challenge issued to the public by the Piddingtons: "You are the judge."

However, some psychical researchers (including Dr. S. G. **Soal**) objected to the shows, presumably on the ground that telepathy should be restricted to laboratory investigation. None the less, the Piddingtons made telepathy a talking-point throughout Britain, and years later there has been no revelation of trickery. It is just possible that it might have been telepathy after all. For a discussion of their act, see *Journal* of the Society for Psychical Research (vol. 35, pp. 83-85, 116-19, 187, 244-45, 316-18; vol. 42, p. 250).

Recommended reading:

Braddon, Russell. *The Piddingtons,* T. Werner Laurie, London, 1950

Pienaar, Domenick Cuthbert (1926-1978)

South African personnel officer who has taken an active interest in parapsychology. Born August 2, 1926, at Krugersdorp, Transvaal, South Africa, he studied at University of Potchefstroom (B.S. 1950) and University of South Africa (B.S. hons. psychology 1956).

He was a technical assistant in the uranium plant at Daggafontein Mines, Springs, Transvaal from 1952-53, industrial chemist at Mulfulira Mines, Northern Rhodesia, from 1953-57, assistant personnel officer at Daggafontein Mines, Springs, Transvaal, in 1957, vocational guidance officer at Department of Labour, Johannesburg, from 1958-61, personnel study section of South African Coal, Oil and Gas Corporation from 1961 onwards.

In 1971, he was awarded Ph.D. by the University of South Africa for his thesis 'Studies in ESP; an Investigation of Distortion in ESP Phenomena.' This study was aided by a grant from the **Parapsychology Foundation** and used clock-cards as targets in testing for ESP. He has tested ESP ability in abnormal personalities, using Zener Cards.

With Dr. Karlis **Osis** he was co-author of the article 'ESP Over Seventy-Five Hundred Miles' (*Journal of Parapsychology,* vol. 20, No. 4, 1956).

Dr. Pienaar has also studied factors in the relationship between percipient and agent and distinguished three main factors: "sheep-goat," "friends-strangers" differences, and other agent-centered or percipient-centered factors.

He was associated with the South African Society for Psychical Research and the South African Parapsychology Institute for more than twelve years. He was a council member of the Society, served as secretary, and was president for seven years.

Piérart, Z. J. (died 1878)

Founder of the rival school to the **Spiritism** of Allan **Kardec** in France. He was a Spiritualist and did not accept the doctrine of compulsory reincarnation. At one time, he was professor at the College of Maubeuge and afterwards secretary to Baron **du Potet.**

The Spiritualists that grouped around him were never very numerous, in view of the great popularity of Spiritualism.

In 1858, Prof. Piérart founded the Spiritualist journal *La Revue Spirtualiste* which was in lively controversy with Kardec's journal *La Revue Spirite.* Eventually Kardec's journal was sufficiently successful to displace *La Revue Spiritualiste,* which was discontinued. It was carried on from 1870 under the title *Concile de la Libre Pensée,* but in 1873 it was suppressed after pressure from clerical authorities.

Pike, Albert (1809-1891)

Prominent American Freemason, Grand Commander of the Ancient and Accepted Scottish Rite in its Southern Jurisdiction, generally regarded as "a master-genius of Masonry."

He spent some of his younger years in Mexico before settling in Arkansas, where he followed the legal profession and also journalism. He was on the Southern side in the War of Independence. His election as Grand Commander was in 1859. He died April 2, 1891.

In 1892 he was falsely charged with Satanic practices in **Freemasonry** in the scurrilous book *Le Diable au XIXe Siècle* by Dr. Bataille, which featured the revelations of "Diana Vaughan." The book was later proved to be part of an audacious conspiracy by journalist Gabriel **Jogand-Pagès** to discredit and embarrass both the Catholic Church and Freemasonry. (See also Dr. **Bataille; Devil Worship;** Gabriel **Jogand-Pagès;** Diana **Vaughan**)

Pike, James A(lbert) (1913-1969)

Former Episcopalian Bishop of California, whose bestselling book *The Other Side* (Doubleday, 1968) was a powerful argument for psychic phenomena and communication with the dead.

Born February 14, 1913 in Oklahoma City, Oklahoma, he was educated at University of California, Los Angeles (1932-33), University of Southern California (A.B. 1934, LL.B. 1936), Yale University (J.S.D. 1938). In 1942 he married Esther Yanovsky. He studied at Virginia Theological Seminary from 1945-46, General Theological Seminary from 1936-47. Union Theological Seminary (B.D. magna cum laude 1951).

He was raised as a Roman Catholic and attended the Catholic University of America, Law School, Washington, D.C. as a lecturer in civil procedure from 1939-42, but was ordained a priest of the Episcopal Church in 1944. He was curate of St. John's Church, Washington, D.C. from 1944-46, chaplain at Vassar College from 1947-49, chaplain and head of department of religion at Columbia University, New York, N.Y. from 1942-52, adjunct professor of religion and law from 1952-58, dean of Cathedral of St. John the Divine, New York, N.Y. from 1952-58, bishop coadjutor at Diocese of California, San Francisco in 1958, bishop from 1958-66.

He resigned as bishop in 1966 to become theologian in residence at Center for Democratic Institutions, Santa Barbara, California. He was a member of the bar of U.S. Supreme Court and California State bar, Tucker Fellow at Dartmouth College, lecturer and preacher at universities and seminaries, with a weekly television network program on ABC-TV from 1957-60.

Bishop Pike was already established as an author long before his book *The Other Side.* His other publications include: *The Faith of the Church* (1951), *Beyond Anxiety* (1953), *If You Marry Outside Your Faith* (1954; 1962), (with John M. Krumm) *Roadblocks to Faith* (1954), (with John W. Pyle) *The Church, Politics and Society* (1953), *Doing the Truth* (1958; 1965), (with Howard A. Johnson) *Man in the Middle* (1956), (ed. & contrib.) *Modern Canterbury Pilgrims* (1956; 1959), *A New Look at Preaching* (1961), *Our Christmas Challenge* (1961), *Beyond the Law* (1963), *A Time for Christian Candor* (1964), *Teen-agers and Sex* (1965), *What Is This Treasure* (1966), *You and the New Morality* (1967). He also contributed to numerous magazines, including *Look, Life, Reader's Digest, Coronet.*

Bishop Pike's son Jim had committed suicide at the age of twenty, after experimenting with LSD. In a 1967 television program, the famous American medium Arthur **Ford** communicated a message to Bishop Pike apparently from his son Jim. The message, in the full glare of the television lights, was highly evidential, and Bishop Pike publicly affirmed his belief in the reality of psychic phenomena in his book *The Other Side.* The Bishop also received messages through mediums Ena **Twigg** and George Daisley.

Soon afterwards, Bishop Pike himself died when lost in the Israeli desert in 1969, but three days before the discovery of his body a communication came through medium Ena Twigg stating what had occurred and where the body would be found.

Pilgrim's Guide to Planet Earth: A New Age Traveler's Handbook & Spiritual Directory

A comprehensive directory of shrines, temples, churches, monasteries, holy places, spiritual and New Age teachings, covering fifty countries. It gives useful advice to pilgrims on the customs and facilities of both Eastern and Western countries, and also lists schools, publications, communes, food stores, vegetarian and macrobiotic restaurants. Published by: Spiritual Community Publications, P.O. Box 1080, San Rafael, California 94902. British address: Wildwood House Ltd., Gloucester Mansions, Cambridge Circus, London, W.C.2, England.

Pincott, Hugh (1941-)

British chemist and psychical researcher. Born October 11, 1941 at Swansea, Wales, he was educated at Pontardawe Grammar School and the Universities of St. Andrews and Dundee. He obtained the first Ph.D. from Dundee University on its foundation in 1967, and later became a Chartered Chemist. He was employed for nearly twenty-four years by the British Petroleum group of companies, and occupied several commercial positions of increasing seniority, eventually becoming Assistant Coordinator of B.P.'s chemicals operation in the Western Hemisphere. Following a rationalization of company interest in 1984, Dr. Pincott left B.P. and established his own organization, **Specialist Knowledge Services** (SKS), which undertakes marketing consultancy and specialist bookselling.

Dr. Pincott joined the **Society for Psychical Research** in 1971, was appointed a member of its Council in 1974, and its Honorary Secretary and Treasurer in 1976. He was one of the founder-members of the **Association for the Scientific Study of Anomalous Phenomena** (ASSAP) in 1981 and acted as External Affairs Officer for two years. Since 1983 he has been the Association's honorary General Secretary.

Among his wide research activities are mental mediumship, paranormal metal bending, and, more particularly, regressive hypnosis to alleged previous lives. In his spare time he pursues interest in transport studies and viticulture (vine-growing). See also **Association for the Scientific Study of Anomalous Phenomena; Specialist Knowledge Services**)

Pinto

The Grand Master of Malta, who was assisted in alchemical experiments by **Cagliostro.**

Pio, Padre (da Pietralcini) (1887-1968)

Italian friar of the Capuchin monastery of San Rotundo, near Foggia, with reputed powers of **clairvoyance** and **precognition,** who also demonstrated **Stigmata** (wounds of Christ) from 1915 onwards.

Born Francesco Forgione, he lived a simple life and was a sympathetic personality who did not seek public notice. His phenomena were not endorsed by the Holy Office, but were widely accepted by the public. (See also Therese **Neuman; Stigmata**)

Pioneer of Progress, The (Newspaper)

British Spiritualist weekly, published in London from January 1874 until November of the same year.

Piper, Mrs. Leonora E(velina Simonds) (1859-1950)

Trance medium of Boston, the foremost in the history of psychical research, to whom was due the conversion of Sir Oliver **Lodge,** Dr. Richard **Hodgson,** Prof. James **Hyslop** and many other intellects to a belief in **survival and communication** with the dead. She was born June 27, 1859, in Nashua, New Hampshire.

When eight years old, playing in the garden, she suddenly felt a sharp blow on her right ear, accompanied by a prolonged sibilant sound. This gradually resolved itself into the letter S. which was then followed by the words "Aunt Sara, not dead, but with you still." The child was terrified.

Her mother made a note of the day and the time. Several days later it was found that Aunt Sara had died at the very hour on the very day. A few weeks later the child cried out at night that she could not sleep because of "the bright light in the room and all the faces in it," and because of the bed that "won't stop rocking." Discounting occasional experiences of this kind, her childhood was normal.

At twenty-two years of age she married William Piper of Boston. Soon after this she went to consult Dr. J. R. Cocke, a blind professional clairvoyant who was attracting considerable attention by his medical diagnoses and cures. She fell into a short trance.

At the second visit to the clairvoyant's circle, held for effecting cures and developing latent mediumship, when Dr. Cocke put his hand on her head, she saw in front of her "a flood of light in which many strange faces appeared." In trance she rose from her chair, walked to a table in the center of the room, picked up a pencil and paper, wrote rapidly for a few minutes, and handing the written paper to a member of the circle she returned to her seat.

The particular member was Judge Frost, of Cambridge, a noted jurist; the message, the most remarkable he ever received, came from his dead son.

The report of Judge Frost's experience spread and Mrs. Piper was soon besieged for sittings. She was not at all pleased by this sudden notoriety and apart from members of her family and intimate friends she refused to see anyone. However, when Mrs. Gibbins, the mother-in-law of Professor William **James** applied for a sitting (after hearing strange stories through servant gossip), for some inexplicable reason her request was granted.

Her own, and subsequently her daughter's experience, the marvelous stories which they brought back induced Prof. James to visit the medium in order to explain away reputed psychic talents. But his impression of supernormal powers on the part of the medium was so strong that he not only continued sittings, but for the next eighteen months virtually controlled all seance arrangements.

Referring mainly to this first period of his experiences, he wrote in 1890 in *Proceedings* of the Society for Psychical Research (vol. 6, pt. 17): "And I repeat again what I said before, that, taking everything that I know of Mrs. Piper into account, the result is to make me feel as absolutely certain as I am of any personal fact in the world that she knows things in her trances which she cannot possibly have heard in her waking state, and that the definite philosophy of her trances is yet to be found."

Prof. James also made the famous statement: "If you wish to upset the law that all crows are black . . . it is enough if you prove that one crow is white. My white crow is Mrs. Piper."

When Prof. James began his experiments, a claimed French doctor, **"Phinuit,"** was in exclusive

control of the sittings from the other side. He appeared to have been inherited from Dr. Cocke. He was known there as "Finne" or "Finnett." His manifestation was not immediate. The first control of Mrs. Piper was an Indian girl of the strange name "Chlorine." "Commodore Vanderbilt," "Longfellow," "Lorette Penchini," "J. Sebastian Bach" and "Mrs. Siddons," the actress, were next encountered with as communicators.

"Phinuit" had a deep gruff voice in striking contrast with the voice of the medium. His exclusive regime lasted from 1884-1892 when "George **Pelham,**" (a friend of Dr. Hodgson) who died in an accident, appeared and manifested in **automatic writing.** The trance speaking was left for "Dr. Phinuit" and the control, speaking and writing, was often simultaneous.

In 1897 the **"Imperator"** group took charge of the seance proceedings. "Phinuit" disappeared and "Pelham" became relegated to the role of a minor communicator. While "Phinuit" had much difficulty in keeping back other would-be communicators, the advent of the "Imperator" group of controls made the communications freer from interruptions and from the admixture of apparently foreign elements. They excluded "inferior" intelligences (whom they spoke of as "earth-bound" spirits) from the use of the light.

Under the new regime, the communications assumed a dignity and loftiness of expression, as well as a quasi-religious character, which they had heretofore entirely lacked. Moreover, the passing in and out of the trance state which in the earlier stages had been attended with a certain amount of difficulty and discomfort, now, under the new conditions, became quiet and peaceful.

Prof. James called special attention to the point that the "Imperator" group of controls not only exhibited characteristic personalities, but they could divine the most secret thoughts of the sitters. As a lasting influence of this regime in later years, Mrs. Piper showed remarkable development as spiritual adviser in her waking state. "It is almost," wrote Alta L. Piper in 1929, "as if, since the trance state has been less and less resorted to, the cloak of 'Rector' has fallen upon Mrs. Piper herself, and the good that she has been able to do along these lines, during the past nine or ten years, is almost unbelievable."

Mrs. Piper did not exhibit physical phenomena, except for one single strange manifestation: she could withdraw the scent from flowers and make them wither in a short time. To establish *rapport* with her spirit communicators, she utilized psychometric influences (see **Psychometry**), usually asking for an object which was about the person of the departed. Professor James succeeded in hypnotizing her and found the conditions of the hypnotic and medium-trance entirely different. He found no signs of thought-transference either in the hypnotic condition or immediately after it.

Of the earliest trances there is no contemporary record. When, owing to other duties, Prof. James relinquished direct control of the Piper seances he wrote to various members of the Society for Psychical Research of the puzzling and remarkable facts of the mediumship. It was as a result of these representations that Dr. Richard **Hodgson** arrived in the U.S. for the express purpose of continuing the investigation on behalf of the **Society for Psychical Research,** London.

With his advent there began the most famous period of Mrs. Piper's mediumship. Dr. Hodgson was the keenest fraud-hunter, the most pronounced skeptic and he took every precaution to bar the possibility of deception. For some time Dr. Hodgson engaged the services of a detective to follow Mrs. Piper and watch possible attempts to obtain information by normal means. On the first three days of the week, when sittings were given, Dr. Hodgson forbade her to see a morning newspaper. He arranged the sittings without communicating the name of the sitter to Mrs. Piper. The sitters were in most cases unknown to her and were introduced under the pseudonym "Smith." The sittings were often improvized for the benefit of chance callers, of whose very existence Mrs. Piper could not have been aware.

She was usually weakest precisely where the pseudo-medium is most successful. She was vague about dates, preferred to give Christian names to surnames and mostly concentrated on the description of diseases, personal idiosyncrasies and character of the sitters. She fished out significant and trivial details from their past of which a fradulent medium could least have got hold of. On the other hand, she often failed to answer test questions. The spirit of "Hannah Wild" manifesting through her could not describe the contents of the sealed letter which she wrote before her death, and the names which the Rev. Stainton **Moses** gave as the names of his earthly guides were in each case incorrect.

The hypothesis of fraud was discussed in every aspect by Dr. Hodgson, Prof. James, Prof. **Newbold** (of Pennsylvania University), Dr. Walter **Leaf** and Sir Oliver **Lodge.** In 1898 Professor James wrote in the *Psychological Review:* "Dr. Hodgson considers that the hypothesis of fraud cannot be seriously maintained. I agree with him absolutely. The medium has been under observation, much of the time under close observation, as to most of the conditions of her life, by a large number of persons, eager, many of them to pounce upon any suspicious circumstance for (nearly) fifteen years. During that time not only has there not been one single suspicious circumstance remarked, but not one suggestion has ever been made from any quarter which might tend positively to explain how the medium, living the apparent life she leads, could possibly collect information about so many sitters by natural means. The scientist who is confident of 'fraud' here must remember that in science as much as in common life a hypothesis must receive some positive specification and determination before it can be profitably discussed, and a fraud which is no assigned kind of fraud, but simply 'fraud' at large, fraud in *abstracto,* can hardly be regarded as a specially scientific explanation of concrete facts."

He added, at a later period: "Practically I should be willing now to stake as much money on Mrs. Piper's honesty as on that of anyone I know, and I am quite satisfied to leave my reputation for widsom or folly, so far as human nature is concerned, to stand or fall by this declaration."

Between 1888-89, Prof. James **Hyslop** joined the investigation. On the first two or three occasions he took the extraordinary precaution of putting on a mask before he got out of the cab, removing it only after Mrs. Piper was entranced, and resumed it before she awoke. Twelve sittings were sufficient to convince him of the untenability of the secondary **personality** hypothesis. He declared, without hesitation, that "I prefer to believe that I have been talking to my dead relatives in person; it is simpler." His first report was published in *Proceedings* of the Society for Psychical Research (vol. 16, pt. 41) and concluded: "I give my adhesion to the theory that there is a future life and persistence of personal identity."

With unabated zeal, Dr. Hodgson was seeking for still more stringent precautions and experiments and conceived the idea of removing Mrs. Piper from her normal surroundings and placing her in a foreign country among strangers. This is how Mrs. Piper's first visit to England came about. She arrived in November 1889. She was met at the station by Prof. (Sir Oliver) Lodge and escorted next day to Cambridge by F. W. H. **Myers,** at whose house she stayed.

"I am convinced," stated Myers, "that she brought with her a very slender knowledge of English affairs and English people. The servant who attended on her and on her two children was chosen by myself, and was a young woman from a country village, whom I had full reason to believe to be trustworthy and also quite ignorant of my own or my friend's affairs. For the most part I had myself not determined upon the persons whom I would invite to sit with her. I chose these sitters in great measure by chance; several of them were not residents of Cambridge; and except in one or two cases where anonymity would have been hard to preserve, I brought them to her under false names—sometimes introducing them only when the trance had already begun."

Mrs. Piper gave, under the supervision of Myers, Lodge and Dr. Walter Leaf, eighty-eight sittings between November 1889 and February 1890. Wherever she stayed in England, her movements were planned and arranged for her and even when shopping she was accompanied by some member of the Society for Psychical Research. Lodge even exceeded Myers in caution. Prior to Mrs. Piper's stay in Liverpool, Lodge's wife engaged an entire new staff of servants. Lodge safely locked away the family Bible and, throughout the duration of her stay, all of Mrs. Piper's correspondence passed through the hands of Lodge who had permission to read it in almost every instance.

In his first sitting, his father, "Uncle William," "Aunt Ann" and a child of his who died very young, were described. There were some flaws in the descriptions which were later rectified. Many personal and intimate details of their lives were given. In subsequent sittings the names of the dead relatives were communicated in full, and supernormal knowledge of the history of the whole family was generally exhibited. Sir Oliver Lodge's report was published in 1890 with an introduction by F. W. H. Myers, who concluded:

1. That many of the facts given could not have been learnt even by a skilled detective.

2. That to learn others of them, although possible, would have needed an expenditure of money as well as of time which it seems impossible to suppose that Mrs. Piper could have met.

3. That her conduct has never given any ground whatever for supposing her capable of fraud or trickery. Few persons have been so long and so carefully observed, and she has left on all observers the impression of thorough uprightness, candor and honesty. The second part of the report was contributed by Dr. Walter Leaf. A letter from Prof. William James was appended in conclusion.

Sir Oliver Lodge enumerated thirty-eight cases in which information not within the conscious knowledge of the sitter, was given. In only five instances did the sitter acknowledge that the facts were at one time known to him. Considering the extraordinary familiarity of "Phinuit" with the boyhood days of two of his uncles, Lodge was curious how much of this knowledge might be obtained by normal means. He sent a professional inquiry agent to the scene for the purpose of making full and exhaustive inquiries. "Mrs. Piper," reported the agent, "has certainly beat me. My inquiries in modern Barking yield less information than she gave. Yet the most skilful agent could have done no more than secure the assistance of the local record keepers and the oldest inhabitants living."

In his summary, Lodge stated: "By introducing anonymous strangers and by catechising her myself in various ways, I have satisfied myself that much of the information she possesses in the trance state is not acquired by ordinary common-place methods, but that she has some unusual means of acquiring information. The facts on which she discourses are usually within the knowledge of some person present, though they are often entirely out of his conscious thought at the time. Occasionally facts have been narrated which have only been verified afterwards, and which are in good faith asserted never to have been known; meaning thereby that they have left no trace on the conscious memory of any person present or in the neighborhood and that it is highly improbable that they were ever known to such persons. She is also in the trance state able to diagnose diseases and to specify the owners or late owners of portable property, under circumstances which preclude the application of ordinary methods."

Further he stated: "That there is more than can be explained by any amount of either conscious or unconscious fraud—that the phenomenon is a genuine one, however it is to be explained—I now regard as absolutely certain; and I make the following two statements with the utmost confidence:

1. That Mrs. Piper's attitude is not one of deception.

2. No conceivable deception on the part of Mrs. Piper can explain the facts."

After Mrs. Piper's return to the U.S., Dr. Hodgson took charge again. His first report was published in 1892 in vol. 8, pt. 21 of the S.P.R. *Proceedings.* In an excess of caution he refused to consider, on the available evidence, the acceptance of the spirit hypothesis as justified. Yet his inner self was wavering. He was torn with doubts. But not for long. In 1892 a notable evolution was witnessed in the Piper phenomena in the quality of trance communications by the development of automatic writing and by the advent of "Pelham" as control.

Hodgson's second report, which appeared in the S.P.R. *Proceedings*, vol. 13, pt. 33 in 1897, ended with the adoption of the spirit hypothesis. His statement was very firm: "I cannot profess to have any doubt but that the 'chief communicators' . . . are veritably the personalities that they claim to be; that they have survived the change we call death, and that they have directly communicated with us whom we call living through Mrs. Piper's entranced organism. Having tried the hypothesis of telepathy from the living for several years, and the 'spirit' hypothesis also for several years, I have no hesitation in affirming with the most absolute assurance that the 'spirit' hypothesis is justified by its fruits and the other hypothesis is not."

It is interesting to quote here the following note from Alta L. Piper's biography of her mother: "During the latter years of his investigation I more than once heard Dr. Hodgson say, ruefully, that his *amour propre* had never quite recovered from the shock it received when he found himself forced to accept unreservedly the genuineness of the so-called "Piper phenomena."

A third report which Dr. Hodgson intended to publish was cut short by his unexpected death in 1905. Mr. J. G. **Piddington** came over from England and a committee was formed to dispose of the material on hand. The reports were filled with intimate and personal data concerning the sitters. They trusted Dr. Hodgson but would not trust anybody else. Finally, against a valiant fight of Prof. Hyslop, all these reports were returned to the original sitters and the valuable material was lost. Mrs. Piper remained under the jurisdiction of the S.P.R., and the sittings were continued under the charge of Professor Hyslop.

In 1906, Mrs. Piper made a second visit to England. It was mainly devoted to elucidating the mystery of **cross-correspondences.** Several famous investigators (such as Myers, Gurney, Hodgson) had since died and communications of an intricate nature were purported to emanate from their surviving spirits. Seventy-four sittings were held with Mrs. Piper. Many others were with Mrs. **Verrall** and Mrs. Holland (Alice K. **Fleming**). The result was summed up and analyzed by Mr. Piddington. According to his findings, the coincidences of thought and expression in the various messages were too numerous and too detailed to be accounted for by chance.

In 1909, Prof. James published his report on the Hodgson communications in the English and American S.P.R. *Proceedings* jointly. He felt the presence of an external will, but could not commit himself (see **Hodgson**). On the Myers, Gurney and Isaac Thompson communications in the same number of *Proceedings,* Sir Oliver Lodge wrote: "On the whole they [the messages] tend to render certain the existence of some outside intelligence or control, distinct from the consciousness, and, so far as I can judge, from the subconsciousness also, of Mrs. Piper or other mediums. And they tend to render probable the working hypothesis, on which I choose to proceed, that the version of the nature of the intelligences which they themselves present and favour is something like the truth. In other words, I feel that we are in the secondary or tertiary touch—at least occasionally—with some stratum of the surviving personality of the individuals who are represented as sending messages."

In only one instance were aspersions cast, in public, on Mrs. Piper's character and phenomena, and this happened simply as an advertising stunt. On October 20, 1901, the *New York Herald* published a statement of Mrs. Piper, advertised as a "confession," in which she was quoted to say that she intended to give up the work she had been doing for the S.P.R., as fourteen years' work was not enough to clear up the subject and summed up her own views as follows: "The theory of telepathy strongly appeals to me as the most plausible and genuinely scientific solution of the problem . . . I do not believe that spirits of the dead have spoken through me when I have been in the trance state . . . It may be that they have, but I do not affirm it."

According to the inquiries made by the editor of *Light,* Mrs. Piper forbade the publication of the article as soon as she learnt that they had advertised it with the word "confession" above it. She received a telegram from the *New York Herald* assuring her that the word was used for advertising only and would not appear in the article. On October 25, 1901, Mrs. Piper stated in *The Boston Advertiser:* "I did not make any such statement as that published in the *New York Herald* to the effect that spirits of the departed do not control me . . . My opinion is today as it was eighteen years ago. Spirits of the departed may have controlled me and they may not. I confess that I do not know. I have not changed . . . I make no change in my relations."

As Sir Oliver Lodge pointed out, her honesty was not in question and the *New York Herald* spoke of her throughout in laudatory terms, "since little value would be attached to her opinion in favour of the spiritistic hypothesis, it cannot fairly be urged that her opinion on the other side would weigh with us.

Mrs. Piper in fact . . . is not in a more favourable, but even in a less favourable position for forming an opinion than those who sit with her, since she does not afterwards remember what passes while she is in trance."

The management of Mrs. Piper's work during 1908-09 was a grave mistake, stated Mrs. Piper's biographer. Instead of being carried on along systematic and evidential lines, it was devoted largely to private and personal sittings of which inadequate or no records were kept. The sitters also undertook to make certain physical tests and experiments of an unwarrantably harsh character. According to Alta L. Piper this had an important share in the temporary withdrawal of power.

In October 1909, Mrs. Piper made her third visit to England. Prostrated by a heavy cold, she was not able to give her first two or three sittings before late spring and early summer of 1910. These sittings were supervised by Sir Oliver Lodge. The return from the trance state was very difficult. Both the sitters and the controls were disturbed by the conditions and at a sitting on May 24, 1911, a coming suspension of mediumship was announced. The last sitting was held on July 3. After the appearance of a new control, "Mme. Guyon," the sitting was closed by "Imperator." In the years that followed, communications by automatic writing remained intermittent but the trance state did not make its appearance until 1915 when the famous "Faunus" message, relating to the forthcoming death of Sir Oliver Lodge's son Raymond, was given.

Between 1914 and 1924 no regular work was done by Mrs. Piper. The failing health of her mother to whom she was very devoted, made increasing demands upon her time and strength. Further, no suitable supervisor for her work was found. In October, 1924, Dr. Gardner **Murphy** conducted a series of sittings, at the end of which the S.P.R. agreed that Mrs. Piper should sit with the Boston S.P.R. during the season of 1926-27. She complied.

Mrs. Piper's work in the cause of psychical research was of tremendous importance. For several decades her powers were tested to a degree which no other medium had approximated. Psychical research owes an enormous debt to her generous and sustained cooperation, often under difficult circumstances. Her phenomena converted many educated and skeptical individuals to the belief in **survival.** She was a key figure in the story of enlightened psychical research, and goes down to history as the single "white crow" of Prof. James.

It is now clear that the probable correct forename for Mrs. Piper is "Leonora," rather than "Leonore" as frequently stated. For background information, see the valuable article 'Leonor*a* or Leonor*e*? A Note on Mrs. Piper's First Name' by James G. Matlock (*Journal* of the American Society for Psychical Research, vol.82, No.3, July 1988).

Recommended reading:

Piper, Alta L. *The Life and Work of Mrs. Piper,* Kegan Paul, London, 1929

Robbins, Anne Manning. *Both Sides of the Veil; A Personal Experience,* Sherman & French, Boston, 1909

Sage, M. *Mrs. Piper and the Society for Psychical Research,* London, 1903

Salter, W. H. *Trance Mediumship: An Introductory Study of Mrs. Piper and Mrs. Leonard,* Society of Psychical Research, London, 1950 (booklet)

PK

Initialism for **Psychokinesis,** the ability to move objects at a distance by mental power. (See also **Movement**)

PKMB

Initialism for Psychokinetic Metal-bending, the claimed paranormal bending or deformation of metal objects such as spoons and keys by psi action. (See **Metal Bending; Movement; Psychokinesis**)

Plaat, Frau Lotte (Mme. von Strahl) (c. 1930)

Dutch psychometrist whom, for some time, the German police regularly employed to trace malefactors. She was under the observation of Dr. Paul Sünner, Dr. Gustave Pagenstechner, Dr. Harms, Prof. Ludwig Jahn, Prof. Kasnacich, and other scientific men who recorded brilliant results with her. For details, see *Die psychometrische Begabung der Frau Lotte Plaat* edited by Paul Sünner (Leipzig, 1929).

In 1930, important experiments took place at the **National Laboratory of Psychical Research** in London at the conclusion of which Frau Lotte Plaat left for the U.S., where further experimental work was carried on. (See also **Psychometry**)

Placement Test

Term used by parapsychologists to indicate a test for **psychokinesis** in which the subject attempts to make objects land in a given area.

Planchette

A simple instrument designed for the purpose of communication with spirits. It consists of a thin heart-shaped piece of wood, mounted on two small wheel-castors and carrying a pencil, point downwards, for the third support. The hand is placed on the wood and the pencil writes automatically, or presumably by spirit control operating through the psychic force of the medium.

In 1853, a well-known French Spiritualist, M. Planchette, invented this instrument to which he gave his name. For some fifteen years it was exclusively by French Spiritualists. Then in the year 1868, a firm of American toy makers took up the idea and flooded the shops of booksellers with great numbers of planchettes. They became a popular mania, and the instrument sold in thousands there and in Great Britain. It was used largely as a toy and any results obtained that might be arresting and seemingly inexplicable were explained by **Animal Magnetism** or ascribed to the power of subconscious thought.

Amongst Spiritualists it has been used for spirit communication. **Automatic writing** has often been developed by use of the planchette, some mediums publishing books which, they claimed, were written wholly by their spirit-controls through the use of planchettes.

An early attempt to explain the phenomenon was put forward by Samuel **Guppy** in his book *Mary Jane; or Spiritualism Chemically Explained* published under the modest pseudonym "A Child at School" in 1863. He stated that the human body is a condensation of gases, which constantly exude from the skin in invisible vapor—otherwise electricity; that the fingers coming in contact with the planchette transmit to it an "odic force" (see **Od**), and thus set it in motion. He went on to say that some people have phosphorous in excess in their system and the vapor "thus exuded forms a positively living, thinking, acting body, capable of directing a pencil."

There are variations on the planchette form such as the dial-planchette which consists of a foundation of thick cardboard nine inches square on the face of which the alphabet is printed and also the numerals one to ten. There are the words "Yes," "No," "Goodbye" and "Don't know." These letters, words, and numerals are printed on the outer edge of a circle, the diameter of which is about seven inches. In the center of this circle, and firmly affixed to the cardboard, is a block of wood three inches square.

The upper surface of this block has a circular channel in it and in this run balls. Over the balls is placed a circular piece of hard wood, five inches in diameter, and attached to the outer edge of this a pointer. The upper piece of wood is attached to the lower by an ordinary screw, upon which the upper plate revolves when used for communication.

Another form is the **Ouija** board, on which, in a convenient order, the letters of the alphabet are printed and over which a pointer easily moves under the direction of the hand of the person or persons acting as medium. It is stated that a form of this "mystic toy" was in use in the days of Pythagoras, about 540 B.C.

In a French history of Pythagoras, the author describing his celebrated school of philosophy, asserted that the brotherhood held frequent seances or circles at which a mystic table, moving on wheels, moved towards signs inscribed on the surface of a stone slab on which the moving-table worked.

The author stated that probably Pythagoras, in his travels among the Eastern nations, observed some such apparatus in use amongst them and adapted his idea from them.

Another trace of some such "communicating mechanism" is found in the legend told by the Scandinavian Blomsturvalla how the people of Jomsvikingia in the twelfth century had a high priest, one Völsunga, whose predictions were renowned for their accuracy throughout the length and breadth of the land. He had in his possession a little ivory doll that drew with "a pointed instrument" on parchment or "other substance," certain signs to which the priest had the key. The communications were prophetic utterances, and it is said in every case came true.

The writer who recounted this legend thought it probable that the priest had procured the doll in China. In the National Museum at Stockholm there is a doll of this description which is worked by mechanism, and when wound up walks round and round in circles and occasionally uses its right arm to make curious signs with a pointed instrument like a stylo which is held in the hand. It origin and use have been connected with the legend recounted above.

In modern times, the planchette and ouija board are devices to assist automatic writing. The advantage of such instruments is that they may be used by more than one individual during a sitting, as distinct from automatic writing when only the operator handles the pen or pencil. The planchette is really a more convenient indicator than the old party game in which several individuals place a finger on an upturned glass surrounded by letters of the alphabet, the glass moving apparently of its own volition to touch letters in succession, spelling out words and messages.

A drawback of the glass technique is that the individuals involved have full view of each letter as it is touched by the glass, enhancing conscious and subconscious expectation or desire in the formation of comprehensible words and messages from the letters.

The content of such messages may suggest either communications from spirit entities or unconscious mental processes on the part of the individuals concerned. Sometimes artificial entities appear to be created from the combined energies and the messages, although often startling and apparently authentic, may be deceptive or even delusive.

It is generally assumed that the actual movement of the planchette is due to unconscious muscular effort on the part of the operator or operators using the instrument, but as in table-turning and the rods of water-diviners, it is by no means certain that this explanation covers all the facts.

Clearly the actual contact between fingers and instrument can communicate subtle muscular exertion, but the conversion of this exertion to the complex movements involving in writing intelligible messages is difficult to explain. Even granting the operation of unconscious muscular effort, it is not clear how this is adapted to constructing messages which are often not visible to the operator.

Again, the planchette may sometimes move at remarkable speeds, far in advance of the normal intellectual mode or reflex muscular actions of the operator. The same phenomenon also occurs in automatic writing.

There are also many reported cases of **direct writing,** in which there was no contact between the operator and the writing.

There may be grounds for supposing that some kind of psychic force may be generated in addition to, or perhaps as a side effect of the nervous energy involved in muscular movement. In the case of water-diviners, the movement of their rods or other devices is sometimes out of all proportion to conscious or unconscious muscular exertion on the operator's part.

In table-turning, it has been suggested that there may be an accumulation of psychic energy in the material of the table, and that wood or other organic materials may favor such accumulation. Further experiments are needed to resolve such questions.

Meanwhile it should be stressed that the results of the use of the planchette and similar devices often reflect the intellectual and emotional status of the operator or operators involved, and it is unwise to experiment in the frivolous atmosphere of party games. Suggestible individuals may become obsessive about the messages obtained.

Some very lucid messages have been obtained through the planchette, often indicative of spirit entities. Other messages clearly embody conscious and unconscious mental processes of the sitters and are often nonsensical and mischievous. (See also **Direct Writing; Divining-Rod; Dowsing; Ouija Board; Psychic Force; Table-turning**)

Recommended reading:

"A Child at School." *Mary Jane; or Spiritualism Chemically Explained,* John King & Co., London, 1863

Ellis Ida. *Planchette and Automatic Writing,* Blackpool, U.K., 1904

Hyslop, James H. *Contact With the Other World,* Century Co., 1919

Mühl, Anita M. *Automatic Writing; An Approach to the Unconscious,* Steinkopff, 1930, Helix Press, New York, 1964

Sargent, Epes. *Planchette, or the Despair of Science,* Boston, 1869

Truthseeker, A. *The Planchette Mystery; Being a Candid Inquiry Into the Nature, Origin, Import, and Tendencies of Modern Signs and Wonders,* Samuel R. Wells, New York, 1870

Planetary Logos

According to the Theosophical scheme of creation, the Planetary Logos or Ruler of Seven Chains is one of the grades in the hierarchy which assists in the work of creation and guidance.

It is the supreme Logos who initiates this work, but in it he is helped by the "seven." They receive from him the inspiration and straightway each in his own Planetary Chain carries on the work, directed by him no doubt, yet in an individual fashion, through all the successive stages which go to compose a scheme of Evolution. (See also **Logos; Planetary Spirits; Theosophy**)

Planetary Spirits

In the Theosophical scheme of creation, the number of these spirits is seven. They are emanations from the Absolute, and are the agents by which the Absolute effects all changes in the Universe. (See also **Logos; Planetary Logos; Theosophy**)

Planetary Travels

Claimed travels to other planets by mediums in trance form a romantic chapter in Spiritualist communications. Descriptions through inner vision or spirit enlightenment of conditions and life on the planets were first given by Emanuel **Swedenborg.**

He said that the people of Mars were the best in the whole planetary system. Physiognomy, with them, was an expression of thought. They judged each other by it. They were God-fearing and the Lord sometimes appeared among them.

Of the inhabitants of Venus Swedenborg said: "They are of two kinds; some are gentle and benevolent others wild, cruel and of gigantic stature. The latter rob and plunder, and live by this means; the former have so great a degree of gentleness and kindness that they are always beloved by the good; thus they often see the Lord appear in their own form on their earth.

"The inhabitants of the Moon are small, like children of six or seven years old; at the same time they have the strength of men like ourselves. Their voices roll like thunder, and the sound proceeds from the belly, because the moon is in quite a different atmosphere from the other planets."

Planetary exploration in the form of what appeared to be traveling **clairvoyance** was first recorded with Fraulein Romer, a German somnambule who at the age of 15, in November 1813, was seized with convulsive attacks and developed mediumship.

Dr. C. Romer described, in his book *Ausführliche historische Darstellung einer höchst merkwürdigen Somnambule* (Stuttgart, 1821), how the spirits of dead relatives but more often the spirit of a living companion, Louise, led the medium to the moon. She described its flora, fauna and inhabitants, and the spirits of the dead who spend there their first stage of existence in their progress to higher spheres. Dr. Romer claimed that the descriptions accorded with those the subjects of J. **Ennemoser**'s experiments.

The note of infantility which was struck in these first descriptions was successfully preserved in later adventures. Andrew Jackson **Davis** followed in the footsteps of Swedenborg. Victorien **Sardou** drew automatic sketches of houses and scenes on the planet Jupiter. Auguste Henri **Jacob** (the Zouave), executed drawings of strange fruits and flowers which he said grew on the planet Venus.

Thomas Lake **Harris,** in *Celestial Arcana,* described the inhabitants on other planets of the solar system and also of some of the more remote fixed stars. He told of conversations he held with them. He further peopled space with aromal worlds which are generally associated with some material worlds, or suns, but do not form any part of them.

The rambling mind of loose statements and disclosures was also exemplified by a remarkable revelation in the huge subconscious romance of Mlle. Hélène Smith, Prof. Th. **Flournoy** in *From India to the Planet Mars* (1900), traced the birth of the Martian Cycle to chance remarks and the desire ex pressed by Prof. Lemaitre to know something of the mysterious planet.

On November 25, 1884 "From the beginning . . . Mlle. Smith perceived, in the distance and at a great height, a bright light. Then she felt a tremor which almost caused her heart to cease beating, after which it seemed to her as though her head were empty and as if she were no longer in the body. She found herself in a dense fog, which changed successively from blue to a vivid rose color, to gray, and then to black. She is floating, she says, and the table, supporting itself on one leg, seemed to express a very curious floating movement. Then she sees a star growing larger, always larger, and becomes finally 'as large as our house.'

"Hélène feels that she is ascending; then the table gives, by raps: 'Lemaitre, that which you have so long desired!' Mlle. Smith, who had been ill at ease, finds herself feeling better, she distinguishes three enormous globes, one of them very beautiful. 'On what am I walking?' she asks. And the table replies: 'On a world—Mars.' Hélène then began a description of all strange things which presented themselves to her view, and caused her as much surprise as amusement. Carriages without horses or wheels, emitting sparks as they glided by; houses with fountains on the roof; a cradle having for curtains an angel made of iron with outstretched wings, etc. What seemed less strange were people exactly like the inhabitants of our earth, save that both sexes wore the same costume, formed of trousers, very ample, and a long blouse, drawn tight about the waist and decorated with various designs. The child in the cradle was exactly like our children, according to the sketch which Hélène made from memory after the seance. . . . "

"We are struck by two points," stated Prof. Flournoy in his analysis, "the complete identity of the Martian world, taken in its chief points, with the world in which we live, and its puerile originality in a host of minor details. . . . One would say that it was the work of a young scholar to whom had been given the task of trying to invent a world as different as possible from ours, but real and who had conscientiously applied himself to it loosening the reins of his childish fancy in regard to a multitude of minor points in the limits of what appeared admissible according to his short and narrow experience. All the traits that I discover in the author of the Martian romance can be summed up in a single phrase, its profoundly infantile character."

Greater appreciation was shown by Prof. Flournoy for the Martian language, which was not only revealed but also translated into French. He admitted that it bore the stamp of a natural language. "I will add that in speaking fluently and somewhat quickly, as Hélène sometimes does in somnambulism, it has an acoustic quality altogether its own due to the predominance of certain sounds, and has a peculiar intonation difficult to describe."

On a closer investigation, however, it became clear that the inventor of the language had never known any other idiom than French and that the Martian phonetics was an incomplete reproduction of French phonetics. Yet it had features of its own, as a subliminal creation it was nothing short of marvelous (see **Xenoglossis**).

Owing to the critical remarks of Prof. Flournoy, the subliminal romancer apparently resolved to eliminate the defects of the Martian revelations. An attempt was made to depict life in an undetermined planet still farther away than Mars, seventeen days after the suggestion, and strange visions were seen by the medium of a grotesque world, the language of which singularly differed from the Martian, the tallest people of which were three feet high, with heads twice as broad as high, living in low, long cabins without windows or doors but with a tunnel about ten feet long running from it into the earth.

The language was absolutely new, with a very peculiar rhythm and with a construction totally different from French. But Prof. Flournoy saw no reason to change his opinion as to the earthly origin of both the Ultra-Martian and the Uranian language and writing. Of the still later Lunarian phase he obtained no firsthand material.

In August 1895, Hélène Smith found a rival in America. The medium Mrs. **Smead** made several revelations of the planets Mars and Jupiter, and after an incubation period of five years, burst forth in detailed descriptions which, however, according to Flournoy, presented "the same character of puerility and naive imagination as those of Mlle Smith."

Fraudulent mediums also seized upon the thrilling subject. Isaac K. Funk, in his book *The Widow's Mite* (1904), wrote of a medium who impersonated "a lady eight feet tall from the planet Mars" by the use of a wire bust with rubber over it, and a false face. This was so arranged that it fitted snugly upon the shoulders of the medium and was inflated with air when in use. When not in use it could be made into a small package and easily concealed.

The number of mediums who, from time to time, have given descriptions of Martian life, is very great. Eva Harrison's *Wireless Messages from Other Worlds* (London, 1916) even introduced planetary visitors from the constellation Orion. Perhaps it is worth while to mention one prophetic communication of "Dr. Barnett," the control of the medium George **Valiantine,** who predicted that the Martians would get through to us before we get through to them. And that in fact, they were trying to communicate now.

The recent Martian romance of Dr. Mansfield Robinson should also be mentioned. Through a Mrs. James, the author obtained a Martian alphabet, claimed a Martian trance control "Oumaruru," for himself and poured forth a number of Martian revelations based on trance excursions to the red planet.

Many of the claimed spiritual revelations of life on other planets betray their terrestrial origins by everything being bigger and better than on earth, or by the naive literary expedient of superior naming, i.e., having a more exalted name for the planetary version of familiar terrestrial things. This is demonstrated in an extraordinary pamphlet titled *A Description of the Planet Neptune; or, A Message From the Spirit World* by Japssa Seniel, Spiritual, from the Planet Naculo or Neptune (London, c. 1872), from which the following quotations are typical:

"We have horses, which we call nemilis, but they stand nearly as high again as yours, and are very far superior to any that I have seen on this globe. We have a great variety of peculiar animals called denfan; they resemble your dogs; they are quite harmless, but very useful. . . . In the city of Zinting, which is distant from Vanatha about 80,000 miles, is a carnil or match factory, which employs 30,000 hands. These matches are made of wax, and can only be lighted by dipping them in water. . . .

"Now, we will return to Vanatha, and I will describe a grand piece of workmanship—namely a bridge of metal, which is in length about 59 miles. It passes over two rivers, each seven miles in width, also over corn fields, grazing pastures, and railways; it supporters are black marble pillars. The metal is composed of iron, steel, copper, gold, and silver; but we have another kind of metal we call accelity verua, which far exceeds all the rest in strength and durability. The cross supporters of this magnificent bridge are made of this durable material; they are nine feet in diameter.

"The immense bridge is only for foot passengers; its width is about 2000 feet; it has 2000 lamps of large dimensions—namely, nine feet in diameter; they are circular in form, and are lighted with gas. This bridge took 300 years to construct it, at a cost of £300,000,000 sterling; it employed about 40,000,000 workmen. It was laid out by a seraph; it is paved with pantine pardia, which is more durable than any other material we have. It is neither stone nor iron, yet it is harder than the diamond or sapphire. The pavement is all cut in stars; the balustrade is about twelve feet high, and all this stupendous bridge is covered with lemena or glass. There is on this bridge 500 drinking fountains, and about 200 filestres or water closets; these are placed over the rivers. There is about 300 approaches to this bridge, which are ascended by 300 steps, with landings and windings, and seats to recline on. In the ascent to the top, there are small houses built in the centre of this bridge, where the inhabitants can take tea or coffee, or what you call luncheon or meals. . . . "

Such revelations seems laughable in an age of space exploration and it might be thought that space intelligences could no longer claim inhabitants on the inhospitable planet Venus with a temperature exceeding 900 degrees Fahrenheit.

However, Venusian spaceships are still reported, as well as contactee experiences with Venusian spacemen exploring the more hospitable backwoods of planet earth. The **Aetherius Society,** which boasts a large worldwide membership, regularly receives messages from the planet Venus, where it is claimed that the Master Jesus is alive and well. (See also George **Adamski; Aetherius Society; Martian Language;** Hélène **Smith; UFO**)

Recommended reading:

Adamski, George & Desmond Leslie. *Flying Saucers Have Landed,* T. Werner Laurie, London, 1953 etc.

Flournoy, Theodore. *From India to the Planet Mars,* Harper & Bros., 1900; University Books, 1963

Harris, Thomas Lake. *Arcana of Christianity; Celestial Sense of the Divine Word,* 2 vols., New York, 1858

Lunan, Duncan. *Interstellar Contact; Communication with Other Intelligences in the Universe,* Henry Regnery Co., Chicago, 1975 (British title: *Man and the Stars,* Souvenir Press, London, 1974)

Swedenborg, Emanuel. *Earths in Our Solar System Which Are Called Planets, and Earths in the Starry Heaven, Their Inhabitants, and the Spirits and Angels There,* Swedenborg Society, London, 1860 etc.

Plants, Psychic Aspects of

In recent years, there has been great public interest in the behavior and psychic aspects of plant life. There is evidence to suggest that plants may react to music and human emotions, diagnose disease and act as lie detectors.

Plant life has always fascinated mankind. Plants have provided food, medicine and even hallucinogenic substances.

Ancient legends have told of the power of sound to influence plants. In Hindu mythology, the enchanting flute music of Shri Krishna made flowers bloom, and it is also said of the great musician Tansen, in the days of the Moghul emperor Akbar, that he could cause the flowers to blossom by singing a particular musical *raga* or mode. Tamil literature describes how sugarcane grows in response to the musical sounds of beetles, wasps and bees.

Scientific interest in the special sensitivities of plants dates from the experiments of Charles Darwin, who attempted to stimulate *Mimosa pudica* by playing a bassoon in close proximity, hoping to bring about movements of the pinnae. There was no measurable response, and twenty years later in 1877 the German plant physiologist Wilhelm Pfeffer reported in his book *Physiology of Plants* (translated into English 1900) another unsuccessful experiment in which he had hoped to stimulate the stamens of *Cynararae* by sound.

In 1903, the great Indian scientist Jagadis Chunder **Bose** reported in *Philosophical Transactions* of the Royal Society, Britain, his own experiments with plants from which he concluded that "all characteristics of the responses exhibited by the animal tissues, were also found in those of the plant." Bose devised sensitive apparatus to demonstrate plant reactions, many of which resembled nervous response in animal or human life, and even measured the electrical forces released in the death-spasms of vegetables. In 1917, he was knighted for his valuable services to science.

The American scientist George Crile also conducted experiments to measure the vital response of plant life.

Following Bose, Professor T. C. N. Singh at Annamalai University, India, continued experiments on plants from 1950 onwards, and reported that plants respond measurably to music, dance and prayer. After publication of his papers, experiments were also conducted on similar lines in Canada and the U.S.

From 1966 onwards, Cleve **Backster,** a former interrogator for the C.I.A. and one of America's leading polygraph specialists, conducted experiments in plant ESP, using polygraph techniques. His experiments supported the idea that plants are sensitive to human thoughts. Procedures and results were reported in the *International Journal of Parapsychology* (vol. 10, 1968). The researches of Backster were funded by a grant from the Mary Reynolds Babcock Foundation.

Following publication of Backster's conclusions, many of his findings have been independently confirmed by other experimenters, notably research chemist Marcel Vogel, who claimed that plants and human beings share a common energy field and may affect each other in a manner which can be recorded by instruments. He recorded the claimed ability of a girl named Debbie Sapp (surely a pseudonym?) to "enter the consciousness of a plant."

Other experimenters have shown that plants may be used to trigger electric relays and open doors, stimulated by emotional suggestions from human operators. Today, many owners of garden plots and window boxes now take it for granted that their plant life may be favorably affected by human feelings and talk regularly to their plants.

Recommended reading:

Bolton, Brett L. *The Secret Powers of Plants,* (Medallion) Berkley paperback, Abacus paperback, London, 1974

Bose, J. C. *Plant Autographs and Their Revelations,* Longmans Green, London, 1927

Crile, George. *The Phenomena of Life; A Radio-Electric Interpretation,* London, 1936

Loehr, Rev. Franklin. *The Power of Prayer on Plants,* Signet paperback, 1969

Tompkins, Peter & Christopher Bird. *The Secret Life of Plants,* Harper & Row, 1973; Avon paperback 1974

Whitman, John. *The Psychic Power of Plants,* Signet paperback, Star paperback, W. H. Allen, 1974

Plastics (Spirit Markings)

Paranormally obtained plastics may be divided into two groups; imprints and molds. The first may be produced in any soft, yielding substance or on smoked or chemically treated surfaces; for the second, melted paraffin wax is employed.

Paranormal Imprints

Prof. **Zöllner,** in his experiments with the medium Henry **Slade,** placed a dish filled to the brim with flour under the table with the intention and hope that the spirit hand which took hold of him might leave an impression in the flour, which indeed appeared to happen. The impression which Baron **Hellenbach** testified to have seen was that of a much larger hand than Slade's or any other individual present, while all their hands were without a trace of flour. Prof. Zöllner also obtained the imprint of a foot on two sheets of paper covered with lamp black between two closed slates.

The imprint of a hand with four fingers, the imprint of the two feet of a bird and of a materialized butterfly were obtained in the Valiantine-Bradley sittings in 1925 in England (see George **Valiantine**). Charles Sykes, the great British sculptor, was at a loss to give a normal explanation, Noel Jaquin, a fingerprint expert, was greatly puzzled.

In 1931, however, the same experts claimed to have caught Valiantine in gross fraud. They smeared printing ink in secret on the modeling wax, stripped Valiantine after the seance and found a large stain on his left elbow with the lines of which the imprint corresponded. Other imprints were found identical with those of his toes.

Four different kinds of imprints of the same thumb were given by "Walter," the **control** of "Margery (Mrs. Mina S. **Crandon**), on August 9, 1931. One was a normal negative, the second mirror-negative, the third positive, the fourth mirror-positive. Humanly, only negative imprints can be made. The rest were claimed as extra dimensional.

"Walter" also gave his imprint on an enlarged scale, suggesting a giant's thumb and in October 1930 an independent imprint came through under strictly controlled conditions, from Judge Charles Stanton Hill, a member of "Margery's" circle, who had died on September 2, 1930. According to Captain Fife, the Boston fingerprint expert, the prints (three in number) resembled exactly a print made during his lifetime of Mr. Hill's right thumb. Another right thumbprint came in July, 1931, and was also verified as that of Judge Hill.

"Walter's" ingenuity in devising these experiments seemed inexhaustible. Mr. Button, president of the American Society for Psychical Research, got a "Walter" print within a soundproof, padlocked box on marked plasticine. In July 1931, and later in November, "Walter" produced thumbprints which he declared explicitly to be those of Sir Oliver **Lodge,** taken from "the etheric body" brought from three thousand miles away. The prints were found identical with Sir Oliver's prints.

On March 9, 1932, "Walter" made a print "of an infant not yet born, but expected in a certain family." It was an imprint of a baby's foot. "Walter" even gave the names "Mary Jane" and "Mary and Jane." However, family reasons made it impossible to obtain verification and soon after this, an unexpected development put all of "Walter's" personal prints into a dubious light, some were found to be identical with those of Mr. "Kerwin," an early member of the Margery circle.

Eusapia **Palladino** produced hand and face imprints in putty and clay. They bore her own characteristics, although she was held hand and foot at a distance from the tray while the impression was made. Numerous such plastics were obtained by the psychical researchers **Lombroso, Morselli, Chiaia** and **de Fontenay.** Palladino panted, groaned and writhed during the process.

Camille **Flammarion** was a witness of the phenomenon at Monfort-l'Amaury in 1897. He found it one of the most astonishing and incredible feats of Eusapia. The resemblance of the spirit head to Eusapia was undeniable. Yet she could not have imprinted her face in the putty. Besides having been controlled, Mme. Z. Blech kissed her upon both cheeks to find out whether her face has not the odor of putty. The putty was on the other end of the table on a large and heavy tray and was invisibly transported and placed in the hands of M. Blech.

Dr. Julien **Ochorowitz** wrote of his study of this curious phase of Eusapia's mediumship at Rome: "The imprint of this face was obtained in darkness, yet at a moment when I held two hands of Eusapia, while my arms were entirely around her. Or, rather, it was she who clung to me in such a way that I had accurate knowledge of the position of all her limbs. Her head rested against mine even with violence. At the moment of the production of the phenomena a convulsive trembling shook her whole body, and the pressure of her head on my temples was so intense that it hurt me."

At another time, "the medium was in a very good light: we were separated from her by a distance of from six to ten feet, and we perceived distinctly all the details. All of a sudden Eusapia stretched her hand out abruptly toward the clay, then sank down uttering a groan. We rushed precipitately towards the table and saw, side by side, with the imprint of the head, a new imprint, very marked, of a hand which had been thus produced under the very light of the lamp, and which resembled the hand of Eusapia."

Dr. Ercole **Chiaia** of Naples wrote: "I have imprints in boxes of clay weighing anywhere between 55 and 65 lbs. I mention the weight in order to let you see the impossibility of lifting and transporting with one hand so heavy a tray, even upon the supposition that Eusapia might, unknown to us, free one of her hands. In almost every case, in fact, this tray, placed upon a chair three feet behind the medium, was brought forward and placed very gently upon the table about which we were seated."

A curious feature of these imprints was that traces of texture were clearly visible in the outlines. This peculiarity agrees with the findings of Dr. W. J. **Crawford** in his Belfast experiments with Kathleen Goligher; the impression of psychic rods in soft clay nearly always showed marking identical with the fabric of the medium's stockings.

Haunting **apparitions** occasionally leave footprints behind. Capt. A. W. Monckton, F.R.G.S., saw them forming in brilliant illumination in the sand, as described in his book *Some Experiences of a New Guinea Resident Magistrate* (1921).

A weird true story of the "Devil's hoof-marks" was told in Commander Rupert T. Gould's *Oddities; A Book of Unexplained Facts* (1928; 1965). During the early morning of February 8, 1855, a series of strange imprints were found between Totnes-Topsham-Exmouth, a stretch of more than one hundred miles of the Devonshire Coast, England. They were seen by thousands of people everywhere—on the roofs of high buildings, outside the doors of dwelling houses, inside barns, on tops of haystacks. An apparently paranormal feature of the imprints was that they led into barns where the snow had drifted but had not returned, and apparently passing through the solid wall, continued on the other side of the obstruction. They were hoofmarks and formed a single track, exactly 8½ inches between each impression, their size was four by four and three quarter inches and they could not be identified. The mystery was never cleared up. People in the rural district were afraid to go out after dusk for months.

The fiery imprints which (according to ancient chronicles) apparitions sometimes leave behind, also seem to belong to this class (see **Touches**).

Paranormal Molds

In normal wax molding, technical process of the production of paraffin wax casts is as follows: a bucket of hot and cold water are placed side by side. The hot water will melt the paraffin. If one dips a hand in and withdraws it, a thin shell of the liquid will settle and congeal on it. If the hand is dipped alternately into the hot paraffin and into the cold water the shell will thicken. When the hand is freed, a wax glove is left behind. These gloves are very fragile. They must be filled with plaster of Paris for purposes of preservation. If then the paraffin wax is melted off, the plaster discloses the fine texture of the skin. The hand which has been freed from the paraffin shell must be washed in soap and water before another experiment, or else the second shell will stick to the fingernails. Altogether, it takes about twenty minutes to deliver a finished shell. It stands to reason that the fingers of the hand must be held fairly straight, otherwise they will break the shell in the withdrawal. For the same reason no full cast, up to the wrist, can be obtained.

Now the peculiarity of the molds obtained by psychical researchers in seances with gifted mediums is that they defy normal production. Fingers are bent, hands are joined, wrists show and the mold in fine and delicate, whereas those obtained from living hands are thick and solid.

Their production is remarkably quick. With the medium **Kluski** it did not take more than three minutes. "Walter," in the "Margery" seances, took his time because he claimed to enjoy the experiment, but he dispensed with the cold water entirely. The impression which the process and the molds leave in the mind is clearly as if the hands had evaporated, dematerialized and left the tell-tale casts behind.

The first paraffin wax casts were obtained by Prof. William **Denton** in 1875 in Boston with the medium Mary M. **Hardy.** Mrs. Hardy produced the paraffin wax gloves in public halls. As means of control, the dish of paraffin was weighed before the mold appeared and after. The difference corresponded to the weight of the mold. In later years, another test was devised, locking up the liquid paraffin wax and cold water in a wire cage. After Prof. Denton, Epes **Sargent** made exhaustive investigation of the curious powers of this medium.

In England, William Oxley produced the first psychic molds in 1876 with Mme. **d'Esperance** and later with Mrs. **Firman** and the Rev. F. W. **Monck.** Similar success was claimed with the **Davenport Brothers,** William **Eglinton** and Miss **Fairlamb** at about the same period. T. P. Barkas of Newcastle, England, had the ingenious idea of mixing magenta dye in the paraffin wax when making experiments with Miss Fairlamb in 1876. Upon examination, the gloves clearly showed the traces of the dye, proving thereby that they were not smuggled into the seance room ready-made.

Dr. Carter Blake, Mr. Desmond G. Fitzgerald and Mr. S. Tel published an attestation in *The Spiritualist* that on April 28, 1876, in London, they obtained a mold in paraffin wax, reproducing exactly the right foot of William Eglinton which had been kept in view the whole time by those present. On another occasion the mold furnished proof of spirit return. Owing to a slight characteristic deformity, Dr. Nichols identified the cast of a child hand which he obtained with William Eglinton.

"Bertie," a control of Dr. **Monck,** gave casts of his two hands. They were identical with those obtained through Mrs. Firman.

The psychical researcher Alexander **Aksakof** observed that the plaster casts show a blend between the organism of the medium and the organizing force which produces the materialization. He noted that Oxley made similar observations and quoted his letter: "It is a curious fact that one always recognises in the casts the distinctive token of youth or age. This shows that the materialised limbs, whilst they preserve their juvenile form, evince peculiarities which betray the age of the medium. If you examine the veins of the hand you will find in them characteristic indications which indisputably are associated with the organism of the medium."

The Kluski wax gloves which were exhibited at the Institut Métapsychique in Paris, were obtained under stringent test conditions. Their thickness is less than a sixteenth of an inch, they show a tightness of the wrist and curiously bent position of the finger. Charles Gabrielli, one of the best artistic molders of Paris, gave a certificate that they could not be normally produced. The escapologist **Houdini** and Sir Arthur Keith thought they knew better. But they failed when they tried to imitate them.

In answer to the suggestion that the wax gloves may have been prepared from inflated rubber gloves Gustav **Geley** produced some casts in this way for comparison. They were also put on view. In fact, they are only caricatures of hands. The charge that the gloves may have been made previous to the seance could not be sustained as Geley secretly mixed cholesterin, a coloring substance, into the paraffin wax. The gloves, under chemical tests, show traces of this substance. Besides, in Warsaw, Poland, Geley actually saw the hands dipping into the paraffin. "They were luminous, bearing points of light at the fingertips. They passed slowly before our eyes, dipped into the wax, moved in it for a few seconds, came out, still luminous, and deposited the glove against the hand of one of us."

Strangely enough in one of the seances, when he was controlled, Kluski was discovered to have had direct supernormal contact with wax. His hand was smeared with it after the light was turned up. Once, as he himself stated to the British researcher Hewat **McKenzie,** he found pieces of congealed wax on his skin in the region of the abdomen.

A curious variety of plastics is the working of linen into the semblance of human features by psychic means. We find a well-detailed instance in the Stratford phenomena in Dr. Eliakim **Phelps** of the appearance of eleven figures of "angelic beauty." Occasionally similar phenomena have been reported as a manifestation in haunted houses, cushions assuming the shape of human forms.

There are also artistic efforts which fall under the heading of plastics, i.e., the precipitated **direct paintings** in which the paint appears in relief to give three-dimensional effects. Many such pictures are known.

It is interesting to note that in one of the pastel pictures of John **Alleyne** (Capt. John Bartlett), the medium of the **Glastonbury scripts** (revealing lost chapels), a fine detail is visible in the representation of the Gothic stonework of the interior of the choir, the normal rendering of which with chalk would be extremely difficult.

Another noteworthy artistic effort in plastics was the bas-relief which "Prof. Nell," the control of Frau Maria **Silbert,** produced of his head on a plasticine plaque.

The varieties of plastic demonstrations are numerous. Mrs. Albert Blanchard, of Vermont, an American medium who died in Minnesota, about 1873, produced plastics by the deposit of sediment under water in a china dish. The facts were quoted by F. Bligh **Bond** in *Psychic Research* (October 1930) as obtained from Dr. Horace Newhart, of Minneapolis, who had copies of the photographs taken. The system practiced by Mrs. Blanchard was to take a shallow china dish, into which a small amount of fine material, such as clay, was placed with sufficient water to cover it. She stirred the sediment with her fingers, and then let it settle. When the water evaporated, it was found that the clay had assumed the outlines of a human face or head in low relief.

Summing up, it would seem that there is good presumptive evidence for the reality of plastics phenomena in the case of Franek Kluski and also Eusapia Palladino. The phenomena claimed for the "Margery" (Mrs. Crandon) seances are remarkable, but such controversy surrounds this medium and especially the claimed imprints in dental wax of "Walter" (later found to be identical with those of Dr. "Kerwin," who had attended some of the seances) that the suspicions of fraud cannot be dismissed. Other cases cited above are not as evidential as those of Kluski and Palladino.

It is unfortunate that in modern times there is a shortage of materialization mediums of the caliber of Kluski and Palladino and it has not been possible to make scientific tests of claimed plastic imprints or molds. (See also Franek **Kluski; Materialization;** Eusapia **Palladino; Touches**)

Playfair, Guy Lyon (1935-)

Writer and investigator concerned with anomalous and paranormal phenomena. Born April 5, 1935, in Quetta, India, he was educated at Pembroke College, Cambridge University (B.A. hons. 1959). From 1961-75, he was a free-lance writer and photographer in Brazil; U.S. Agency for International Development, Information Office, Rio de Janeiro, Brazil, writer, 1967-71. He is a member of the Society for Psychical Research, Society of Authors, College of Psychic Studies.

Although regarded as a writer on "occultism," he stresses that his interest is in "border areas of human experience and in anomalous phenomena of all kinds . . . I am not concerned with the 'supernatural' but with unexplored areas of nature that are by definition natural."

His books include: *The Unknown Power* (1975, British title *The Flying Cow), The Indefinite Boundary* (1977), (with Scott Hill) *The Cycles of Heaven* (1978), *This House is Haunted; The True Story of a Poltergeist* (1980). He was also a contributor to the series *The Unexplained* (1980 etc.).

Pliny the Elder (Galius Plinius Secundus) (c. A.D. 23-79)

Roman historian who studied at firsthand the eruption of Vesuvius August 24, A.D. 79, and was one of the earliest writers to record that animals behaved in an unusual way prior to earthquakes.

Many of his writings are no longer extant, but his great surviving work is *Naturalis Historia,* which he described as "learned and full of matter, and as varied as nature herself." It consists of thirty-seven books, covering a mathematical and physical description of the world, geography, ethnography, anthropology, human physiology, zoology, botany, agriculture, horticulture, materia medica, mineralogy, painting, modelling and sculpture.

Although Pliny was skeptical about magic and astrology, he described many of the occult beliefs of his time. (See also **Earthquake Prediction**)

PMIR

Initialism for **Psi-Mediated Instrumental Response,** an experimental concept developed by parapsychologist Rex. G. **Stanford.**

Pneumatographers

Term used to denote **direct writing** mediums.

Podmore, Frank (1856-1910)

One of the ablest British opponents of Spiritualism, well-known psychical investigator, and distinguished author. He was born February 5, 1856, at Elstree, Hertfordshire, and educated at Elstree Hill School and Haileybury College, leaving in 1874 with a classical scholarship to Pembroke College, Oxford University, England. In 1879, he became a higher division clerk in the secretary's department of the Post Office.

His personal experiences in paranormal matters date from his academic studies at Oxford University. He rapidly became a convert to survival and communication with the dead. Between 1875-76, he was a frequent contributor to *Human Nature* on Spiritualist subjects. His belief in the reality of Spiritualism arose from his experiences with the medium Henry **Slade** in 1876. But in 1880, in his address to the **British National Association of Spiritualists,** he was already wavering and could hardly be called a Spiritualist any longer.

His tendency impulsively to accept the evidence on the positive side never left him, but doubts always assailed him on reflection. From being a believer he gradually developed to a very skeptical critic whose caution was excessive and, coupled with exceptional scientific and literary gifts, acted as a brake in the early years of the **Society for Psychical Research,** London.

He was elected to the Council of the S.P.R. in the first year and served for an unbroken period of twenty-seven years. For eight or nine years he held, jointly with F. W. H. **Myers,** the office of honorary secretary. He was a collaborator with Myers and Gurney in the book *Phantasms of the Living* (2 vols., 1903). His own comprehensive work *Modern Spiritualism* (2 vols., 1902) often erred on the side of extreme doubt but is a standard work nevertheless. It recorded his personal experiences faithfully.

He admitted that he was profoundly impressed by Henry Slade and puzzled by David **Duguid** until, many years later, he hit upon the possibility of fraud; that he remained unaffected by the demonstration of Miss C. E. **Wood** and proved that he had reason to reject the Morell **Theobald** case, which he probed with Frank S. Hughes, another member of the S.P.R.

His *à priori* assumption was that all physical phenomena were due to fraud. He exhibited an impressive confidence in his ability to see more from the descriptions of the experiments of others than the experimenters themselves were ever able to infer. He was ready to devote time to a hypothesis as fantastic as that put forward by Mr. E. B. Tylor in *Nature* (February 29, 1872) that the mediums D. D. **Home** and Mrs. **Guppy** were werwolves, when he found that a modified form of this hypothesis would seem to be the only alternative to believing in the manifestation of a new physical force.

Carried away by intense skepticism he treated the Rev. W. Stainton **Moses** in a defamatory manner. In answer, a severe repudiation came from the pen of Ernésto **Bozzano** in the *Annals of Psychical Science* (February 1905). Bozzano pointed out that Podmore's method was founded almost constantly on the system, by no means scientific, of selecting for his own proof those single incidents or episodes which fitted in more or less completely with the theories proposed by him, while passing over in silence everything that did not harmonize, or appear to be in flagrant contradiction, with the same theories. Nevertheless, Bozzano held that "we cannot refuse Mr. Podmore the extenuating circumstances of comparative good faith."

There are redemptory features in Podmore's immoderate skepticism. Sometimes he was carried away by generosity. He suggested, for instance, a wonderful apology for **apport** mediums caught cheating—the "post-hypnotic promise," and stated that we have experimental evidence that an action undertaken by the trance consciousness may be fulfilled at the appointed time during waking hours without the knowledge of the waking agent.

His final conclusion was also fairly generous: "Whether the belief in the intercourse with spirits is well-founded or not, it is certain that no critic has yet succeeded in demonstrating the inadequacy of the evidence upon which the spiritualists rely."

The evidence which kept accumulating rapidly in favor of the spirit hypothesis did not affect his preconceived theories. There was some wavering noticeable in his book *The Naturalisation of the Supernatural,* but in *The Newer Spiritualism,* published posthumously in 1910, he stated: "So far as the evidence at present goes, clairvoyance and precognition are mere chimeras, and telepathy may be no more than a vestigial faculty, to remind us, like the prehensile powers of the newly-born infant, of a time when man was in the making."

On the other hand, dealing with the phenomena of trance, he admitted: "I should, perhaps, state at the outset, as emphatically as possible that it seems to me incredible that fraud should be the sole explanation of the revelations made in trance and automatic writing. No one . . . will believe that any imaginable exercise of fraudulent ingenuity, supplemented by whatever opportuneness of coincidence and laxness on the part of the investigators, could conceivably explain the whole of these communications."

Frank Podmore resigned his position as a Post Office civil servant in 1906 after twenty-five years in order to devote himself fully to literary activities. His death on August 14, 1910, was accidental, due to drowning in a pond in the Malvern Hills.

His books included: *Apparitions and Thought Transference* (1892), *Studies in Psychical Research,* (1897), *Modern Spiritualism* 2 vols., 1902; reissued under title *Mediums of the Nineteen Century,* (1963), *Biography of Robert Owen* (1906), *The Naturalisation of the Supernatural* (1908), *Mesmerism and Christian Science* (1909), *Telepathic Hallucination; the New View of Ghosts* (1909), *The Newer Spiritualism* (1910).

Pohl, Hans Ludwig (1929-)

Patent engineer who also investigated parapsychology. Born April 16, 1929 at Krefeld, Germany, he was educated at Bad Godesberg and Staatliche Ingeniurschule, Essen. In 1951 he married Helga Melsheimer.

He was an engineer at the Institute of Research, Deutsche Edelstahlwerke, Krefeld from 1952-57, patent engineer, Deutsche Edelstahlwerke from 1957 onwards. He took great interest in **psychokinesis,** and contributed the paper 'Investigation of the PK-Effect' (*Journal of Parapsychology,* vol. 24, No. 3, Sept. 1930).

"Poimandres" (or "Poemander")

One of the mystical works known as **Hermetica,** ascribed to **Hermes Trismegistus.**

POLAND

There was considerable interest in psychical phenomena in Poland before World War II. The Metapsychical Society had been founded in Crakow in the 1920s and had around a hundred members, including eminent authors and lecturers.

The honorary chairman of the Society was the famous medium Stefan **Ossowiecki,** born in Moscow of Polish parents in 1877. He manifested remarkable faculties of telepathy, clairvoyance, psychokinesis and projection of the astral body (**Out-of-the-Body** Travel).

He was investigated by such eminent researchers as Prof. Charles **Richet,** Dr. Gustave **Geley** and Baron **Schrenck-Notzing.** Ossowiecki's psychic abilities were also investigated by the Polish Society for Psychical Research. Ossowiecki was murdered by the Nazis in the final days of World War II.

Another active organization of the 1930s was the Psycho-Physical Society in Warsaw. Its president, Prof. P. de Szmulro, edited the journal *Zagadnienia Metapsychiczne.*

At a much earlier date, Poland was the home of the great psychical researcher Dr. Julien **Ochorowicz** (1850-1917), who investigated the phenomena of the famous medium Eusapia **Palladino** in Warsaw in 1892-94, in conjunction with M. Matazewski. Ochorowicz testified to the **levitation** of Palladino. He also experimented with the medium Stanislawa **Tomczyk.**

Little information has emerged from Poland on the subject of contemporary parapsychological work, but it is known that this continues.

Related researches on radiesthesia, hypnosis and clairvoyance are presently taking place by the Bio-Electronic Section of the Copernicus Society of Naturalists, whose president is Dr. Franciszek Chmielewski. The main topics of the section's activity include investigation of electric phenomena in living organisms, higher nerve activity in connection with parapsychological phenomena and hypnosis, the influence on living organisms of cosmic and earth radiation. The address of the Society is: Palace of Culture and Education, Warsaw, Poland.

Psychotronika is a biennial proceedings of papers presented at a symposium of the Society of Radiesthesists held every other year in Poland. Publication commenced in 1983. Address: Towarzystwo Psychotroniczne w Warszawie, ul Noakowskiego 10 m 54, 00-666 Warszawa.

The Polish monthly journal *Trzecie Oko* (Third Eye) is published by Stowarzyszenie Radiestetow, ul Noakowskiego 10 m 54, Warzawa.

Politi, Auguste (1855- ?)

Italian physical medium, a watchmaker by trade. His mediumship was developed by the psychical researcher Captain Enrico de Albertis, and was not subject to rigid scientific examination until a later date.

A series of experiments took place in 1902 in Paris in which Col. **Rochas,** Taton, Lemerle, Baclé, **de Fontenay,** de Albertis and Dr. Dariex took part. Several successful photographs were taken of table **levitations.** The medium's eyes were bandaged to save him from nervous shock. In 1904, he was studied at Rome by a group under the direction of Prof. Milesi.

In the Paris seances, a very heavy piano, which two men could scarcely lift by one of its sides, was several times raised and dropped back noisily. A table of 39 lbs. was lifted so high that it passed over the sitters' head, went through the opening of the curtain, with only seven inches free for the passing, and dropped with a tremendous clatter upside down upon the floor of the cabinet. Luminous phenomena were also obtained.

In the fifth seance, two luminous crosses, about four inches in height, appeared. The sitters were touched by an enormous hairy hand and phantoms were seen. All this while, the medium sat in a big sack which was fastened at the neck and at the wrists and the feet.

In 1908, Politi gave more than seventy seances in Milan at the Societe d'Etudes Psychiques.

Polong

A Malay **familiar.** (See **Malaysia**)

Poltergeist

The name given to paranormally caused outbreaks of rappings, inexplicable noises, and similar disturbances, which from time to time have mystified men of science as well as the general public. The term poltergeist (i.e., *Polter Geist,* rattling ghost) is sufficiently indicative of the character of these beings, whose manifestations are, at the best, puerile and purposeless tricks, and not infrequently display an openly mischievous and destructive tendency. Such disturbances take place in the presence of certain, mostly unsuspecting sensitive persons. The appearance is as if, parallel to haunted houses, there existed haunted people.

Poltergeists rarely cause serious physical injury, but effect much damage by breaking fragile objects and by occasionally setting fire to pieces of furniture or clothing. The phenomena often cease in the presence of strangers. The presence of some others appears to increase the violence of the manifestation.

The display of force may be very great. A person may be pulled out of bed, or levitated. The persecution of the victim of the disturbances is often very cruel and does not stop by leaving the house. There is no control over the phenomena. In rare cases argument and kindness helps. The intelligence which is behind the manifestation mostly aims at mischief, but sometimes it is malicious and becomes a danger to the life and safety of the afflicted person.

Whereas the ordinary psychic manifestations require darkness, poltergeists act in daylight. Curiously, however, the movement of the objects is usually taking place at a moment when nobody looks. A strange feature of movements seen is the frequently reported claim that objects rose or fell through the air *slowly.* Otherwise objects are often seen in flight but seldom beginning to move. It has been suggested that the gaze of the human eye has a checking effect.

To explain the crashing noises, without physical source, such as the sounds of breaking crockery afterwards found intact, Adolphe d'Assier put forward an extraordinary theory in his book *Posthumous Humanity* (1887). He suggested that inanimate objects also possess a double, a phantasmal image and that it is this duplicate which is flung by the poltergeist.

He stated that the sum of motion that a moving body possesses is found by multiplying the mass of the moving body by its velocity and that its live force at the moment of fall is equal to half the bulk by the square of velocity. Accordingly it is possible to obtain any mechanical effect by giving to the projectile a sufficient velocity provided the bulk of the projectile is greater than zero. However, he could not answer the question how the almost infinite projectile force which the theory implicates is generated.

The psychical researcher Ernesto **Bozzano** collected statistics on haunting and found that out of 532 cases, 374 were ghostly manifestations and 158 were poltergeists.

Historical Poltergeists

The poltergeist is by no means indigenous to any one country, nor any particular period. Andrew **Lang** cited several cases belonging to the Middle Ages, and one at least which dates as far back as 856 B.C. In both savage and civilized countries this peculiar form of haunting is well known, and it is a curious fact that the phenomena are almost identical in every case.

The disturbances are usually observed to be particularly active in the neighborhood of one person, generally a child or a young woman, or perhaps an epileptic or hysterical subject. According to the theory advanced by Spiritualists, this center of the disturbances is a natural medium, through whom the spirits desire to communicate with the world of living beings. In earlier times, such a person was regarded as a witch, or the victim of a witch or an evil spirit, whichever supposition was best fitted to the circumstances. The poltergeist has been regarded as a development from witchcraft, and the direct fore runner of modern Spiritualism, or a link between the two.

Amongst the earliest poltergeist cases reliably recorded were those of the **Drummer of Tedworth** (1661) and the **Epworth Phenomena** (1716). In both of these instances, the manifestations witnessed were of the usual order. The spirits, if spirits they were, sought to attract attention by familiar childish tricks, and communicated by means of the same cumbrous process of knocking.

The circumstances of the Drummer of Tedworth are as follow. In 1661, a vagrant drummer was, at the instance of Mr. Mompesson of Tedworth, taken before a Justice of the Peace and deprived of his drum, which instrument finally found a resting-place in the house of Mr. Mompesson, during that gentleman's absence from home.

Immediately violent disturbances broke out in the house. Loud knockings and thumpings were heard, and the beating of an invisible drum. Articles flew recklessly about the rooms, and the bedsteads (particularly those in which the younger children lay) were violently shaken. After a time, the drummer was sentenced to transportation, when the manifestations abruptly ceased, but a recurrence of the outbreak synchronized with his return.

Contemporary opinion put the case down to witchcraft on the part of the drummer, but Frank **Podmore** and other modern psychical researchers inclined to the belief that "two little modest girls in the bed" had more to do with the mysterious knockings and scratchings of the poltergeist.

In the famous Epworth case, where the phenomena was well attested by the whole family of the Rev. Samuel Wesley (father of John Wesley), and described in numerous contemporary letters, the disturbances comprised all the manifestations of **levitations,** loud and terrifying noises, and rappings, together with apparitions of rabbits, badgers, and so on.

Frank Podmore was of the opinion that Hetty, one of the daughters, was in some way implicated in the affair. She alone did not give an account of the manifestations, although she had promised to do so. The poltergeist showed a decided partiality for her company—a circumstance which, although not unobserved, did not seem to have held any special significance for her family.

A later case in which a charge of witchcraft was involved was the Cideville case, described by Andrew Lang in his book *Cock Lane and Common Sense* (1894) under the heading, "A Modern Trial for Witchcraft." In 1849, the Curé of Cideville, Seine Inférieure, France, was summoned to court by a shepherd named Thorel, who alleged that the Curé had denounced him for sorcery. In his defense, the Curé stated that Thorel himself had confessed to having produced by means of sorcery certain mysterious manifestations which had disturbed the inmates of the Abbey.

During the trial it transpired that the Curé, when visiting a sick parishioner, had driven from the bedside a man of notorious character, with an evil reputation for sorcery, who was about to treat the patient. The sorcerer retired, vowing vengeance on the Curé, and was shortly afterwards sent to prison.

Later when two little boys, pupils of the Curé, were at an auction, they were approached by Thorel, who was known as a disciple of the sorcerer. He placed his hand on the head of one of the children, and muttered some strange words. When the boys returned to the Abbey the poltergeist performances commenced. Violent blows on the walls seemed about to demolish them, one of the children complained that he was followed by a man's shadow, and other witnesses declared that they had seen a grey hand and wreaths of smoke. Some of those who visited the Abbey were able to hold a conversation with the spirits by means of knocking. It was agreed that sharp-pointed irons should be driven into the walls, and on this being done, smoke and flames were seen to issue from the incisions.

At last, Thorel sought the Curé and confessed that the disturbances were the work of his master, the sorcerer. The plaintiff was non-suited, and the judge, in summing up, said that the cause of the "extraordinary facts" of this case "remained unknown." In February, 1851, the boys were removed from the Abbey, and the disturbances ceased.

Of those instances where a Spiritualist explanation has been offered, perhaps the most outstanding is the well-known English case of the **Cock Lane Ghost.** In 1761-62, raps and scratches were heard in a house in Cock Lane, London, generally occurring near the bed of the little daughter of the house, Elizabeth Parsons. Very soon the manifestations became so pronounced that people from all parts of the city were crowding to witness them.

A code of raps was agreed upon, through which it was ascertained that the spirit was that of a lady named "Fanny," who declared that she had been poisoned by her deceased sister's husband, with whom she had lodged in the Cock Lane house some two years previously, and expressed a wish that he might be hanged. It seems quite a common thing for the poltergeist to reveal a crime, real or imaginary (more often the latter), which is entirely in keeping with the character of the spirit. In the Cock Lane affair, the manifestations followed the girl when she was removed to another house, and she trembled strongly, even in her sleep, on the approach of the ghost.

The case has strong resemblances to the **Rochester rappings** in Hydesville, New York, which launched modern Spiritualism in 1848.

In Germany Dr. Justinus **Kerner** recorded a case in his book *The Seeress of Prevorst* (1845) as occurring in 1806-07 in the Castle of **Slawensik,** Silesia, Councillor Hahn and a young officer named Charles Kern, being the witnesses.

In Italy, the newspaper *La Stampa* of Turin recorded on November 19, 1900, extraordinary occurrences in a wine and spirit shop at No. 6, Via Bava. Prof. Cesare **Lombroso** investigated the case and wrote: "I went into the cellar, at first in complete darkness, and heard a noise of broken glasses and bottles rolled at my feet. The bottles were ranged in six compartments one above another. In the middle was a rough table on which I had six lighted candles placed, supposing that the spirit phenomena would cease in the bright light. But, on the contrary, I saw three empty bottles, standing on the ground, roll as though pushed by a finger, and break near the table. To obviate any possible trick, I felt and carefully examined by the light of a candle all the full bottles which were on the racks, and assured myself that there was no cord or string which could explain their movements. After a few minutes first two, then four, then two other bottles on the second and third racks detached themselves and fell to the ground, not suddenly but as though carried by someone; and after their descent, rather than fall, six of them broke on the wet floor, already soaked with wine; only two remained whole. Then at the moment of leaving the cellar, just as I was going out, I heard another bottle break."

At Ancona, Italy, in 1903, jets of liquid were produced in the house of Signor Marracino, a public prosecutor in the presence of his young daughter. During the night, hats were filled with water; during the day, water was thrown on the beds. The walls were examined by engineers who discovered nothing unusual. Milk, wine and coffee were spilt on the floors. In a locked buffet, objects were displaced. The case was discussed by Prof. Richet in his book *Thirty Years of Psychical Research* (1923, p. 587).

The *Tribuna* of Rome reported on March 5, 1905, from Tessano, a small village in Calabria, the persecution of Innocenza Bruno, an old woman, and a young girl, Maria Fiore, her niece, by inanimate objects. They were exposed wherever they went, to a shower of diverse objects, they had even been several times struck with a fist. Persons present heard the noise of the blows but saw nothing. The persecution was chiefly directed against the old woman.

"A great quantity of water began to fall from the ceiling on to her bed and even on her person, following her about all over the house. When this rain ceased, her dress began to burn without her feeling any sensation of burning. Her bed, her clothes (although packed away in a trunk) and a quantity of hay in the loft, caught fire also." Innocenza Bruno was eighty years old, Maria Fiore sixteen.

In America, the best-known disturbances occurred in the house of the Rev. Eliakim **Phelps** at Stratford, Connecticut, in 1850. Twelve-year-old Harry Phelps appeared to be the chief victim of the persecution. He was put in a water cistern, and suspended from a tree but Mrs. Phelps, too, was often pinched and pricked, and once, from a vacant room, a bottle of ink was thrown at her white dress as she was about to start on an excursion.

Few cases can vie in gruesomeness with the story of the Ashtabula poltergeist in 1851 in Ohio. The victim was a young widow, H., a medical student. To quote: "One night H. and her room mate, alarmed by the most frightful sounds, beheld standing by their bedside the specter of the corpse that they had been dissecting, all reeking and ghastly as they had left it on the table, save that one of the arms was folded across the breast—a change which was actually found to have taken place when the remains were examined. On another night H.'s brother, at her entreaty, came to the side of the bed where H. and her friend lay, and saw by the moonlight a human skull dancing up and down over their heads." (See Emma Hardinge, *Modern American Spiritualism,* 1870)

The phenomena known as "The Great Amherst Mystery" (after the book of that title by Walter Hubbell, 1888) occurred between 1878-79 at Amherst, Nova Scotia, in the Teed family. They centered around Esther Cox, a sister of Mrs. Teed.

A cardboard box, moving beneath the bed of its own accord, was the first manifestation. The next night, Esther Cox had a frightful experience. Her body began to swell and puffed out to an abnormal size. Soon after, a terrific noise, "like a peal of thunder" woke everyone in the house.

The bedclothes flew off Esther's bed, night after night; an invisible hand cut words into the plaster of the wall, while everyone heard the noise of writing: "Esther Cox, you are mine to kill." Cold water placed on the middle of the kitchen table bubbled and hissed like boiling water, yet its temperature remained unaffected; a voice announced that the house would be set on fire and for many days lighted matches were seen to fall from the ceiling on the bed.

The spirit communicated by raps, said that he was an evil spirit bent on mischief and would torment Esther until she died, and things generally became so bad that Esther was compelled to leave. In the house of a friend, Mr. White, for a month everything was quiet. One day, while she was scrubbing the hall floor, the brush suddenly disappeared from under her hand. A few moments later, it fell from the ceiling narrowly escaping her head.

The spirit was heard to walk about the house, banged the doors, made attempts to fire the house, stabbed Esther in the back with a knife, piled up seven chairs in the parlor on top of each other and pulling out one near the bottom allowed them to fall with a terrific crash. The terrible persecution lasted for nearly a year.

Walter Hubbell, the actor, was a personal witness. In 1907, the psychical researcher Hereward **Carrington** interviewed some of the surviving witnesses at Amherst. The testimonies he gathered confirmed Hubbell's narrative.

The Staus Poltergeist

One case which presented the most formidable array of evidence was that of the Joller family in Switzerland. In 1860-62, serious disturbances broke out in Staus, in the home of M. Joller, a prominent lawyer, and a man of excellent character. Knocks were first heard by a servant-maid, who also averred that she was haunted by strange grey shapes, and the sound of sobbing. In the autumn of 1861, she was dismissed and another maid engaged.

For a time there was peace, but in the summer of 1862 the disturbances commenced with redoubled vigor. The wife and seven children of M. Joller heard and saw many terrifying sights and sounds, but M. Joller himself remained skeptical. At length, however, even he was convinced that neither trickery nor imagination would suffice as an explanation of the phenomena.

Meanwhile the manifestations became more and more outrageous, and continued in full view of the thousands of persons who were attracted by curiosity to the house, including the Land-Captain Zelger, the Director of Police Jaun, the President of the Court of Justice, and other prominent people, some of whom suggested that a commission be appointed to examine the house thoroughly.

Three of the heads of police were deputed to conduct the inquiry. They demanded the withdrawal of M. Joller and his family, and remained in the house for six days without witnessing anything abnormal, and drew up a report to this effect. Directly the Joller family entered the house, however, the interruptions were renewed. M. Joller became the butt of ridicule to all, even his political and personal friends, and was finally compelled to quit his ancestral home.

This is undoubtedly one of the most striking cases of poltergeist haunting on record. Here, as in almost every instance, there are children evidently and intimately bound up with the manifestations.

The existence of children in this case, as in others, suggests that they acted as mediums for the poltergeist. Frank Podmore assumed that all poltergeist visitations were traceable to the cunning tricks of "naughty little girls." He suggested that with the "medium" under careful control it is more than probable that the poltergeist will turn shy, and refuse to perform his traditional functions.

There is much to be said for this theory. The medium of the Spiritualist seance is frequently credited with the loftiest utterances, and the production of literary, musical, and artistic compositions. The poltergeist indulges in such futilities as the breaking of crockery, the throwing about of furniture, and the materialization of coal and carrots in the drawing room. Why, if they are mature spirits, as they purport to be, should they practice such feats of mystification as would seem to be impelled either by the foolish vanity of a child, or the cunning impulses of a deranged mind?

Then there is often a curious hesitancy on the part of the medium, as in the case of Hetty Wesley in the Epworth case, a trembling on the approach of the phenomena, and a tendency to such physical disturbances as epileptic and other fits. And sometimes the poltergeist confesses, as did the maid-servant Ann at Stockwell, to having manipulated the disturbing occurrences with the aid of wires and horsehair.

But in such a case as that of the Joller family, the theory of "naughty little girls" is childishly inadequate. It is all but impossible to believe that children could produce the manifestations in full view of hundreds of people. It is still more difficult to understand how children and ignorant persons, with presumably no knowledge of previous instances, could fix upon exactly the same phenomena which has been produced by the poltergeists of every age and country.

And in the Joller case, there is the evidence of many spectators that the most violent disturbances were witnessed when the whole family were assembled outside the house and thus not in a position to assist the manifestations, which included the throwing open of all windows, doors, cupboards and drawers, the materialization of a "thin grey cloud," noises and apparitions. In short, it must be admitted that there is an element of mystery which calls for elucidation, and which the most scientific and critical minds have hitherto failed to make clear. (See also **Staus Poltergeist**).

Poltergeist Fires

The most alarming poltergeist manifestation is the lighting of fires as they often result in serious material damage and in bodily burns. Aksakof described several such instances in his book *Animisme et Spiritisme* (1906). One of these occurred in 1870 at the country house of M. Shcnapoff, near Orenburg, Russia, and became widely known, being investigated on the spot by various skeptics. It seems that Mrs. Shcnapoff was the medium in this case, since when the phenomena were in progress, she felt a peculiar weakness, as if psychic energy was withdrawn from her. When she was sent away from the house, the phenomena ceased. On one occasion a bluish phosphorescent spark was seen flying through the air bursting into flames a cotton dress in Mrs. Shcnapoff's bedroom. Another time the dress took fire on her own body. In extinguishing it her husband was badly burned, yet Mrs. Shcnapoff suffered no injury.

Sporadically, events were claimed to have occurred which would justify the wide belief of the Russians in the "domovoy," the goblin who performs various domestic offices during the night and watches over the sleep of the household.

The Morell **Theobald** case is the most interesting. Here the poltergeist obligingly lit the kitchen fires.

An even more domesticated poltergeist was recorded by Dr. J. A. Gridley in his book *Astounding Facts from the Spirit World* (1854). He wrote that in his early seances poltergeist-like confusion reigned, and on one occasion the breakfast table was laid by spirit agency!

Stone Throwing

One violent, destructive and hostile poltergeist manifestation is that of stone throwing.

There is a chronicle in the *Annales Fuldenses* of disturbances about 858 A.D. in the little town of Bingen on the Rhine where the Romans fought the Gauls. Stones were thrown about by a malignant spirit, or so it was thought, and they struck the walls of simple dwellings as if with a hammer.

The Rev. Joseph **Glanvill** recorded the witch trial of Mary London in his book *Sadducismus Triumphatus* (1681 etc.). She was a hysterical servant girl who, in

At the Roman Catholic Abbey of Prunois-sous-Ablis in France, poltergeist disturbances broke out in 1835. A great many stones were thrown at the window of the Presbytery by no visible agency, and struck the window panes in showers, without, however, breaking any (see Emma Hardinge Britten, *Nineteenth Century Miracles,* 1883, p. 80).

La Gazette des Tribuneaux, the official organ of the French police, published on February 2, 1849, an extraordinary account of a stone-throwing case. The phenomenon continued every night for three weeks around a house in a wood and coal yard in the neighborhood of the Rue de Grès. A hail of projectiles reduced the woodwork of the doors and windows to splinters.

"Whence came these projectiles, which are paving stones, fragments of the demolished walls near, and ashlar stones entire, which from their weight, and the distance they are hurled, are clearly from no mortal hand? This is just what, up to this moment, it has been impossible to discover. . . . The projectiles have continued to rain down with great noise on the house, launched forth at a great height above the heads of those who have placed themselves in observation on the roof of the small surrounding houses, and seeming to come from a great distance, reaching their aim with a precision as it were mathematical, and without deviating from the parabolic evidently designed for them." This communique mentioned analogous unexplained instances such as the rain of pieces of small money in the Rue de Montesquieu, and the ringing of bells in a house in the Rue de Malte.

Prof. Charles **Richet** quoted the testimony of Constable Mousset of a stone-throwing case in 1867 at Absie, France, in an unoccupied house, stressing the following points:

1. The stones fell without doing any harm;
2. A glass lamp was knocked from the table to the floor by a large stone without being broke;
3. The stones fell in all directions and were only seen when they rolled on the ground;
4. The stones continued to be heaped up in the room even when someone was standing at the chimney piece to observe and there was not the smallest hole in the walls or the windows. (See Charles Richet, *Thirty Years of Psychical Research,* 1923, p. 585)

One of the most remarkable stone-throwing cases is that told by Mr. W. G. Grottendieck, as occurring in the jungle of Sumatra, (see *Journal* of the Society for Psychical Research, vol. 12, pp. 258-66). There was no small boy or girl present, only a servant, the latter asleep. To quote: "At about one o'clock at night I half awoke, hearing something fall near my head outside the mosquito curtain on the floor. After a couple of minutes I completely awoke and turned my head half round to see what was falling on the floor. They were black stones from 1/8 to 3/4 of an inch long. I got out of the curtain and turned up the kerosene lamp, that was standing on the floor at the foot of the bed. I saw then that the stones were falling through the roof in a parabolic line. They fell on the floor close to my headpillow. I went out and awoke the boy (a Malay-Pelambang coolie) who was sleeping on the floor in the next room. I told him to go outside and examine the jungle up to a certain distance. He did so whilst I lighted up the jungle a little by means of a small 'ever ready' electric lantern. At the same time that my boy was outside the stones did not stop falling. My boy came in again, and I told him to search the kitchen to see if anybody could be there. He went to the kitchen and I went inside the room again to watch the stones falling down. I knelt down near the head of my bed and tried to catch the stones while they were falling through the air towards me, but I could never catch them; it seemed to me that they changed direction in the air as soon as I tried to get hold of them. I could not catch any of them before they fell on the floor. Then I climbed up the partition wall between my room and the boy's and examined the roof just above it from which the stones were flying. They came right through the 'kadjang' but there were no holes in the kadjang. When I tried to catch them there at the very spot of coming out, I also failed. . . . "

In answer to questions, Grottendieck added that he heard the stones fall behind him while the boy was standing in front of him, that "the stones were hotter than could be explained by their having been kept in the hand or pocket for some time . . . they fell rather slowly . . . it seemed to me that they were hovering through the air; they described a parabolic curve and then came down with a bang on the floor. The sound they made in falling down on the floor was also abnormal because, considering their slow motion, the bang was much too loud. . . . "

Bishop Weston of Zanzibar wrote in the *Daily Express* in the spring of 1923 of a little hut, built of kneaded clay, in which he saw "large pieces of earth violently plucked from the walls and thrown into the air. As will be easily understood, I went to the place absolutely sceptical on the matter, and I demanded that everyone should leave the hut, which I then had surrounded by a cordon of guards. In spite of this, large pieces of earth continued to be violently detached from the walls and projected against the ceiling. Several of these pieces were even thrown outside the door; one of them hit me on the head. I then went back to the house and began the exorcism, pronouncing the ritual prayers. The manifestations ceased at once. The house has now been repaired, and no disturbing phenomena have reoccurred."

A stone-throwing poltergeist in a dugout at Cheriton, near Folkestone, was studied in 1917 by Sir William **Barrett.** The stones often struck without hurting and on one or two occasions they seemed to hover in the air. A boy was found to be the indirect cause of the disturbance. (*Journal* of the Society for Psychical Research, vol. 18 April-May, 1918)

There are other cases in which the stones apparently arrive with great force through the window, yet the window pane is not broken, as if the stones had been apported and precipitated inside. In other cases the stones pass through an original crack in cases the stones pass through an original crack in the window pane, again in others they may shatter the frame and doors.

Sometimes the throwing of the stones lasts for days, as if sufficient psychic energy were stored up somewhere in or around the house for the physical effects.

The target-shooting ability of the stone-throwing spirits is a near miracle in itself. The stones may come from a distance with great force and strike an object out of the hand without hurting the holder. They may strike a man without hurt, yet they may shatter objects ruthlessly.

There is little doubt as to the objectivity of these stones. Their origin, however, is not always traced. Col. H. S. **Olcott,** in a footnote to Adolphe d'Assier's *Posthumous Humanity* (1887), quoted a narrative by Vijia Raghava Charla who, with others, tested the "pisachas" (evil spirits), by writing their names upon bits of brick, etc., and flinging them out into the enclosure, and closing the house door. In due course the same marked projectiles would drop as if from space.

Writing of a stone throwing case in a hut near Bandong, Java, which took place in 1837, Dr. Gerstaecker stated (*Die Gartenlaube,* 1871): "A mountain stream flowed about fifty yards away, almost under the house. Some ingenious person suggested that some stones be marked with a cross and other signs and be thrown into the torrent. This was done, with surprising results. Several of these stones fell back into the room dripping with water, sometimes in less than a minute after they had reached the bed of the stream."

The deadly aim of the missiles admits the speculation that it may not be the laws of physics alone which prescribe their course. The impression is of something like temporary consciousness associated with the flight of every single missile as if they were intelligent blows, or as if a strong will power were setting an unalterable course from the point of departure.

Modern Poltergeists

In the early period of the Society for Psychical Research, London, opinions about poltergeist phenomena tended to be dominated by the skeptical theories of Frank Podmore, but a valuable and more open-minded review of the subject was presented by Sir William Barrett in his paper 'Poltergeists, Old and New' (*Proceedings* of the S.P.R., vol. 25, pt. 64, August 1911). Amongst other reported cases, Barrett had investigated one at Derrygonnelly, in Ireland. He found that the phenomena were intelligent. Four times he got answers to numbers which he mentally asked.

In 1926, a carefully investigated poltergeist persecution was presented by Eleonore **Zügun,** a Romanian peasant girl, who was brought by psychical researcher Harry **Price** to London, and studied at the **National Laboratory of Psychical Research** for more than three weeks. The girl exhibited remarkable stigmatic phenomena (see **Stigmata**). Poltergeists stuck pins and needles into her body. Objects were wandering about the room when she was in it. No fraud was detected (See 'Same Account of the Poltergeist Phenomena of Eleonore Zügun' by Harry Price (*Journal* of the American Society for Psychical Research, August 1926).

In *Psychic Research* (March, 1930), a long account was published by Harry Price and Miss H. Kohn (a lecturer in languages at Deccan College, Poona, India) of the poltergeist persecution of an Indian boy Damodar Ketkar and his elder brother Ramkrishna Bapat at Poona. Miss Kohn kept records of the occurrences. Damodar Ketkar whom her family adopted, spent the years between 1923 and April 1928 with them, untroubled by paranormal happenings. The earliest manifestations occurred through his older brother. Objects moved about around him, mischief was enacted and once he felt himself transported (see **Transportation**). The disturbances assumed a powerful and violent character in April 1928, about the smaller boy. He was levitated, stones were thrown about him and there was an intense display of animosity and destructive activity. Harry Price desired to make arrangements for the boy's visit to England, but with a nearer approach to the age of maturity the fury of the manifestations abated.

Three significant cases were reported from Nova Scotia. The Great Amherst Mystery, already mentioned, the Antigonish Case, investigated by Dr. Walter Franklin **Prince** (see *Journal* of the American Society for Psychical Research, vol. 16, p. 722) and the spurious Windsor Case, investigated by Dr. Hereward **Carrington.**

The Windsor Poltergeist involved not just a haunted house, but a haunted town! It transpired that many of the inhabitants of Windsor had conspired together to play a prank on an old judge, to mock his belief in Spiritualism. Carrington's account of the hoax was published in his book *Personal Experiences in Spiritualism* (1918, pp. 112-24). The irony of the story is that the victim of this plot refused to accept Carrington's explanation and insisted that the manifestations were genuine!

One of the most interesting things about poltergeist phenomena is that in modern times, when there is a marked decline in the physical phenomena of mediumship, poltergeists continue to be reported, and many have been accessible to parapsychologists with modern monitoring equipment.

In Germany, the Institut für Grenzgebiete der Psychologie (Institute for Border Areas of Psychology) under the direction of Dr. Hans **Bender** has made a special study of poltergeist and over the last three decades, the Institute has studied over thirty-five cases. Of these, the Rosenheim Case, 1967-68, attracted wide attention.

This involved inexplicable events in the office of a lawyer in Rosenheim, Bavaria. Electric lamp bulbs exploded, neon tubes continually went out, fuses blew, photostatic copying machines were interfered with, telephones rang or conversations were cut off unaccountably, fuses blew and sharp bangs were reported. The focus of these events seemed to be Miss

Annemarie Sch., a nineteen-year-old employee. The disturbances ceased when she left the office, although further events took place in the new office to which she moved.

A thorough investigation of the case involved monitoring and recording equipment, interrogation of witnesses and careful checks to rule out the possibility of normal causes of the phenomena. There was a great deal of media coverage, and the final results of investigation were covered by West German television. In the late stages of investigation, the psychokinetic phenomena intensified, with drawers coming out of cabinets, documents being displaced and paintings swinging on walls. The investigators concluded that the phenomena defied explanation by normal theoretical physics, that they seemed to result from non-periodic short duration forces, that the movement of objects seemed to be intelligently controlled by forces that evaded identification.

In Britain, the case of the **Enfield Poltergeist** attracted wide attention during 1977. This took place in an ordinary house in the North London suburb of Enfield, centering around the Hodgson family—divorcee Mrs. Peggy Hodgson and her four children. Over 2,000 uncanny events were reported, including inexplicable movements of objects, often flying through the air, levitation and transportation of one of the children, as well as the usual noisy knockings. The case was investigated by members of the Society for Psychical Research, and author Guy Lyon Playfair who published a book on the phenomena.

In the U.S., parapsychologist William G. **Roll** of the **Foundation for Research on the Nature of Man** has taken a special interest in poltergeist cases since his first investigation of the Seaford Poltergeist of Long Island in 1958, when disturbances took place in the family of Mr. and Mrs. James Herrmann and their two children. Bottles were uncapped and the contents spilled, and toys were broken, in addition to the usual noises and movement of objects. W. G. Roll discusses this case and others which he has investigated in his book *The Poltergeist* (1976), which also contains a review of the parapsychological aspects of the subject, with hints for future investigation.

There is, as yet, no simple answer to the strange phenomenon of poltergeist. The old concept of noisy spirits is no longer favored, although the observation that disturbances center around adolescent children or young adults as a focus appears to hold good. The disturbances seem to be purposive, even if the events are random, and appear to correspond to outbursts of bottled-up emotion. There may be connections between other phenomena involving **psychokinesis** (**movement** of objects without contact) or recently observed events such as paranormal **metal-bending.**

One confusing aspect of poltergeist phenomena is that when children are involved, they are sometimes found to be faking some effects, even if there is no doubt that other events are clearly paranormal. This parallels the discovery that some Spiritualist mediums who seem to have produced genuinely paranormal phenomena have also been found cheating. There is clearly a danger that the detection of isolated faked events may prejudice skeptical investigators into believing that individual cases (or the whole subject of poltergeist) is fraudulent. As with study of the paranormal in general, simplistic views for or against do not do justice to the complexity of the real situation.

For a valuable review of modern poltergeist phenomena, see the paper 'Modern Poltergeist Research—A Plea for an Unprejudiced Approach' by Dr. Hans Bender in *New Directions in Parapsychology* edited by John Beloff (1974). (See also **Ashtabula Poltergeist; Cock Lane Ghost; Drummer of Tedworth; Emanations; Enfield Poltergeist; Epworth Phenomena; Fox Sisters; Haunted Houses; Metal-Bending; Movement; Obsession and Possession;** Rev. Eliakim **Phelps; Psychic Force; Staus Poltergeist**)

Recommended reading

Bell, Charles Bailey. *A Mysterious Spirit.* With Miller, Harriet Parks. *Bell Witch of Tennessee.* Reissue in one volume by C. Elder, Nashville, Tennessee, 1972 (originally published 1934 and 1930 respectively)

Beloff, John (ed.). *New Directions in Parapsychology,* Paul Elek (Scientific Books) Ltd., London, 1974; Scarecrow Press, Metuchen, New Jersey, 1975

Carrington, Hereward & Nandor Fodor. *Haunted People; Story of the Poltergeist Down the Centuries,* Dutton, 1951 (British title *The Story of the Poltergeist Down the Centuries,* Rider & Co., London, 1953)

Dingwall, E. U., K. M. Goldney & Trevor H. Hall. *The Haunting of Borley Rectory,* Duckworth, London, 1955

Fodor, Nandor. *On the Trail of the Poltergeist,* Citadel, 1958; Arco Publications, London, 1959

Lang, Andrew. *Cock Lane and Common-Sense,* Longmans Green, London, 1896

Owen, A. R. G. *Can We Explain the Poltergeist?,* Garrett/Helix, 1964

Playfair, Guy Lyon. *This House is Haunted; An Investigation of the Enfield Poltergeist,* Souvenir, London, 1980

Roll, William G. *The Poltergeist,* Scarecrow Press, Metuchen, New Jersey, 1976

Sitwell, Sacheverell. *Poltergeist,* Faber & Faber, London, 1940

Thurston, Herbert. *Ghosts and Poltergeists,* Henry Regnery, Chicago, 1954

POLYNESIA

The name Polynesia means "region of many islands" and comprises a group of central Pacific islands, including Hawaiian, Ellice, Rotuma, Uved, Tokelau, Samoa, Tonga, Nive, Cook, Easter Islands and New Zealand, and the original inhabitants. Many traditions were also shared with Melanesians of the central and western Pacific islands. Throughout the islands customs, beliefs and life styles have changed radically in the last few decades.

Traditional Magic & Sorcery

Magic in Polynesia used to be the preserve of the priestly and upper classes, although lesser sorcery was practiced by individuals not of these castes. There was a prevailing belief in what was known as *mana,* or supernatural power in certain individuals. The method of using this power was twofold. One of these was practiced by a society known as the *Iniat,* where certain rites were carried out which are supposed to bring calamity upon the enemies of the tribe.

The ability to exercise magic was known as *agagara,* and the magician or wizard was *tena agagura.* If the wizard desired to cast magic upon another man, he usually tried to secure something that the person had touched with his mouth, and to guard against this, the natives were careful to destroy all food refuse that they did not consume, and they carefully gathered up even a single drop of blood when they received a cut or scratch, and burnt it or threw it into the sea, so that the wizard might not obtain it.

The wizard having obtained something belonging to the person whom he wished to injure, buried it in a deep hole, together with leaves of poisonous plants and sharp-pointed pieces of bamboo, accompanying the action by suitable incantations. If he chanced to be a member of the *Iniat* society, he would place on the top of this package one of the sacred stones, as they believed that so long as the stone was pressing down the article which had been buried in the hole, the man to whom it belonged would remain sick.

Because of this, immediately a man fell sick he set inquiries on foot as to who had bewitched him, and there was usually someone who did not deny it. If the victim did not succeed in having the spell removed he would almost certainly succumb, but if he succeeded in having it taken away, he began to recover almost immediately, and the strange thing was that he evinced no enmity towards the person or persons who "bewitched" him—indeed it was taken as a matter of course, and he quietly waited until the time when he could return the compliment.

These practices applied mostly to New Britain, now in the Papua New Guinea grouping, but its system of magic was practically the same as that known in Fiji as *vakadraunikau,* concerning which very little is known. In his book *Melanesians and Polynesians* (1910) the Rev. Dr. George Brown, the pioneer missionary and explorer, gave an interesting account of the magical systems of these people, in which he incorporated several informative letters from brother missionaries, which are well worth quotation. For example, the Rev. W. E. Bromilow stated that at Dobu in southeastern New Guinea:

"*Werabana* (evil spirits) are those which inhabit dark places, and wander in the night, and gave witches their power to smite all round. *Barau* is the wizardry of men, who look with angry eyes out of dark places, and throw small stones, first spitting on them, at men, women, and even children, thus causing death. A tree falls, it is a witch who caused it to do so, though the tree may be quite rotten, or a gust of wind may break it off. A man meets with an accident, it is the *werabana.* He is getting better through the influence of the medicine-man, but has a relapse; this is the *barau* at work, as we have ascertained from the terrified shouts of our workmen, as some sleeper has called out in a horrid dream. These medicine-men, too, have great power, and no wonder, when one of our girls gets a little dust in her eye, and the doctor takes a big stone out of it; and when a chief has a pain in the chest, and *to obaoba* takes therefrom a two-inch nail.

"The people here will have it that all evil spirits are female. *Werabana* is the great word, but the term is applied to witches as well, who are called the *vesses* of the *werabana,* but more often the single word is used. I have the names of spirits inhabiting the glens and forests, but they are all women or enter into women, giving them terrible powers. Whenever any one is sick, it is the *werabana* who has caused the illness, and any old woman who happened to be at enmity with the sick person is set down as the cause. A child died the other day, and the friends were quite angry because the witches had not heeded the words of the *lotu,* i.e., the Christian religion *Taparoro,* and given up smiting the little ones. 'These are times of peace,' said they, 'why should the child die then?' We, of course, took the opportunity and tried to teach them that sickness caused death without the influence of poor old women.

"Sorcerers are *barau,* men whose powers are more terrible than those of all the witches. I was talking to a *to obaoba*—medicine-man—the other day, and I asked him why his taking a stone out of a man's chest did not cure him. 'Oh,' said he, 'he must have been smitten by a *barau.*' A very logical statement this. Cases the *to obaoba* cannot cure are under the fell stroke of the *barau,* from which there is no escape, except by the sorcerer's own incantations.

"The Fijian sorcery of *drau-ni-kau* appears here in another form called *sumana* or rubbish. The sorcerer obtains possession of a small portion of his victim's hair, or skin, or food left after a meal, and carefully wraps it up in a parcel, which he sends off to as great a distance as is possible. In the meantime he very cunningly causes a report of the *sumana* to be made known to the man whom he wishes to kill, and the poor fellow is put into a great fright and dies."

The Rev. S. B. Fellows gave the following account of the beliefs of the people of Kiriwina (Trobiand Islands group):

"The sorcerers, who are very numerous, are credited with the power of creating the wind and rain, of making the gardens to be either fruitful or barren, and of causing sickness which leads to death. Their methods of operation are legion. The great chief, who is also the principal sorcerer, claims the sole right to secure a bountiful harvest every year. This function is considered of transcendent importance by the people.

"Our big chief, Bulitara, was asking me one day if I had these occult powers. When I told him that I made no such claim, he said, 'Who makes the wind and the rain and the harvest in your land?' I answered, 'God.' 'Ah,' said he, 'that's it. God does this work for your people, and I do it for our people.

God and I are equal.' He delivered this dictum very quietly, and with the air of a man who had given a most satisfactory explanation.

"But the one great dread that darkens the life of every native is the fear of the *bogau,* the sorcerer who has the power to cause sickness and death, who, in the darkness of the night, steals to the house of his unsuspecting victim, and places near the doorstep a few leaves from a certain tree, containing the mystic power which he, by his evil arts, has imparted to them. The doomed man, on going out of his house next morning, unwittingly steps over the fatal leaves and is at once stricken down by a mortal sickness. Internal disease of every kind is set down to this agency. Bulitara told me the mode of his witchcraft. He boils his decoctions, containing numerous ingredients, in a special cooking-pot on a small fire, in the secret recesses of his own house, at the dead of night; and while the pot is boiling he speaks into it an incantation known only to a few persons. The bunch of leaves dipped in this is at once ready for use. Passing through the villages the other day, I came across a woman, apparently middle-aged, who was evidently suffering from a wasting disease, she was so thin and worn. I asked if she had any pain, and her friends said 'No.' Then they explained that some *bogau* was sucking her blood. I said, 'How does he do it?' 'Oh,' they said, 'that is known only to herself. He manages to get her blood which makes him strong, while she gets weaker every day, and if he goes on much longer she will die.'

"Deformities at birth, and being born dumb or blind, are attributed to the evil influence of disembodied spirits, who inhabit a lower region called *Tuma.* Once a year the spirits of the ancestors visit their native village in a body after the harvest is gathered. At this time the men perform special dances, the people openly display their valuables, spread out on platforms, and great feasts are made for the spirits. On a certain night, when the moon named *Namarama* is at the full, all the people—men, women and children—join in raising a great shout, and so drive the spirits back to *Tuma.*

"A peculiar custom prevails of wearing, as charms, various parts of the body of a deceased relative. On her breast, suspended by a piece of string round her neck, a widow wears her late husband's lower jaw, the full set of teeth looking ghastly and grim. The small bones of the arms and legs are taken out soon after death, and formed into spoons, which are used to put lime into the mouth when eating betel-nut. Only this week a chief died in a village three miles from us, and a leg and an arm, for the above purpose, were brought to our village by some relatives as their portion of their dead friend.

"An evidence of the passionate nature of this people is seen in the comparatively frequent attempts at suicide. Their method is to climb into the top branches of a high tree, and, after tying the ankles together, to throw themselves down. During the last twelve months two attempts near our home were successful, and several others were prevented. In some cases the causes were trivial. One young man allowed his anger to master him because his wife had smoked a small piece of tobacco belonging to him; he fell from the tree across a piece of root, which was above ground and broke his neck. A woman, middle-aged and childless, who had become jealous, climbed into a tree near her house, and calling out 'Good-bye' to her brother in the village, instantly threw herself down. Falling on her head she died in a few hours; the thick skin on the scalp was cut, but so far as I could see the skull was not broken."

Some of the minor magical traditions of Polynesia are worthy of note. Natives of the Duke of York group believed that by persistently calling upon a man whom they wished to get hold of, he would by their call be drawn to them, even from a great distance. The natives would not eat or drink when at sea. In New Guinea and Fiji the custom prevailed of cutting off a finger joint in token of mourning for a near relative, as did the bushmen of South Africa (See **Magic**). They firmly believed in **mermaids,** tailed men and dwarfs, and regarding these they were most positive in their assertions. The natives of the Duke of York group in fact declared to a missionary that they had caught a mermaid, who had married a stated certain native, and that the pair had several of a family; "but unfortunately," stated the relater of this story, "I could never get to see them."

Like many other races, the Polynesians used to work themselves into a great state of terror whenever an eclipse took place, and during the phenomenon they beat drums, shouted and invoked their gods.

In Samoa, magic was not practiced to such an extent as in other Melanesian groups, the sorcerer was much more sophisticated. Instead of asking merely for any trifling object connected with the person he desired to bewitch, he demanded property, such as valuable mats and other things of use to him.

His method of working magic was to get into communication with his god, who entered the sorcerer's body, which became violently contorted and convulsed. The assembled natives would then hear a voice speaking from behind a screen, probably a ventriloquial effort, which asserted the presence of the god invoked.

Sickness was generally believed to be caused by the anger of some god, who could thus be concealed by the priest or wizard and duly placated. The "god" invariably required some present of substantial value, such as a piece of land, a canoe, or other property, and if the priest happened to know of a particularly valuable object belonging to the person who supposed himself bewitched, he stipulated that it should be given up to him. This caste of priests was known as *taula-aitu,* and also acted as medicine-men.

Lost Secrets of Polynesian Magic

In 1917, Max Freedom **Long** was a teacher in Hawaii and became fascinated by the idea of discovering the lost secrets of the *kahuna* magician priests. Long obtained valuable information on the fire-walk ceremony from Dr. William Tufts Brigham, who had taken part in a fire-walk forty years earlier. Dr. Brigham had also investigated the ancient *kahuna* practice of charging wooden sticks with some vital energy, the sticks being used in combat and giving opponents some kind of electric shock that rendered them unconscious.

It was difficult for Long to obtain precise information on *kahuna* magic, since the laws of Hawaii had outlawed the practice of sorcery and witchcraft, but Long continued to investigate the subject even after leaving Hawaii in the 1930s. He found valuable clues in the Hawaiian language, describing *kahuna* magic and the use of *mana* or vital force.

Eventually Long believed that he had rediscovered the secrets of Polynesian magic, and the concepts of a high, low and middle self or *aka* body through which *mana* was generated and applied for magical purposes. He collated this system with the Western phenomena of psychical research and published his findings in his book *The Secret Science Behind Miracles* (1948 etc.). Soon afterwards, Long founded **Huna Research Associates** for research and experiment in Polynesian magic, now continued by the **Order of Huna International.**

Long's theories of *huna* and *mana* make interesting comparison with the researches of Baron von **Reichenbach** into a vital force which he named "Od" and parallels can also be found in the nineteenth-century concepts of "Animal Magnetism."

In 1952, George Sandwith, a British exponent of **radiesthesia** (dowsing with **pendulums**) who was familiar with the work of Max Freedom Long, visited the South Sea Islands of Fiji, Tonga and Samoa, and made his own investigation of magical practices.

In Fiji, he investigated fire-walking (see **Fire Immunity**) at firsthand and discussed with local priests the concept of *mana* or vital energy involved. He also studied the *atua* or ancient phallic stones of Fiji, regarded as shrines of ancestral spirits, and their activation for magical purposes. He tested the magical charge of these stones by radiesthesia, using a pendulum.

He also had firsthand experience of the way in which *mana* is used for magical purposes, and suffered a magical attack from a local chief.

These experiences were described in the pamphlet *Research in Fiji, Tonga & Samoa,* by George & Helen Sandwith (The Omega Press, Reigate, Surrey, England, 1954), based on a lecture given to the Medical Society for the Study of Radiesthesia in 1953.

Polytrix

According to ancient belief, this was an inauspicious stone, which caused the hair to fall off the head of anyone who had it about his person. It is not clear whether this was a real or fabulous stone.

Pontica

According to ancient belief, this was a blue stone with red stars, or drops and lines like blood. It compelled the devil to answer questions, and also put him to flight.

Poortman, J(ohannes) J(acobus) (1896- ?)

Professor of metaphysics who wrote on parapsychology. Born April 26, 1896 at Rotterdam, Netherlands, he was educated at universities of Gröningen, Hamburg, Paris (Sorbonne), Geneva and Vienna. He was research fellow in philosophy at Harvard University from 1935-36, Ph.D. University of Amsterdam 1954. In 1941 he married Anna W. D. Smelt.

He was co-editor of *Tijdschrift voor Parapsychologie* from 1937-38, head of the Library of the Theosophical Society (Netherlands Section), Amsterdam from 1938-59, secretary of Division of Philosophy, *Winkler Prins Encyclopedia* from 1944-51, lecturer in metaphysics at Leyden University from 1945-53, secretary of Netherlands Theosophical Research Center from 1954 onwards, special professor for metaphysics in the spirit of theosophy at Leyden University from 1958 onwards.

He was a charter member of the Netherlands Society for Psychical Research from 1932-38, treasurer from 1934-38, charter member of the Parapsychological Association, member of Maatschappij der Nederlandse Letterkunde, provincial Utrechts Genootschap, Genootschap voor Wetenschappelijke Philosophie, Korrespondierendes Mitglied Oesterreichische Gesellschaft für Psychische Forschung. He took a special interest in the relationships between philosophy and parapsychology.

He published a number of articles on parapsychology, including: 'Psychophysical Parallelism or Interactionism?' (*Journal* of the American Society for Psychical Research, 1937), 'Mysterious Words' (*Tijdschrift voor Parapsychologie,* 1939, 1940), 'Henri Bergson and Parapsychology' (*Tijdschrift voor Parapsychologie,* 1941), 'The Feeling of Being Stared At' (*Journal* of the Society for Psychical Research, London, 1959). His books included: *Occult Motives in Literature* (1937), *Drei Vorträge über Philosophie und Parapsychologie* (1939), *Variaties op een en meer Themata* (Collected Essays on Philosophy, Parapsychology and Theosophy, 1947), *De Grondparadox* (1961).

Pope, Dorothy Hampson (Mrs. Edward H. Pope) (1905-)

Parapsychologist, for many years editor of *Journal of Parapsychology* published by the *Foundation for Research on the Nature of Man.* Born December 28, 1905, at Providence, Rhode Island, she studied at Brown University, Providence (B.A. 1927), was a graduate student at Duke University, Durham, North Carolina from 1939-41. In 1941 she married Edward H. Pope.

She was a staff member of the Parapsychology Laboratory at Duke University from 1938-59, managing editor of *Journal of Parapsychology* from 1942 onwards, managing editor of *Parapsychology Bulletin* from 1946-58. She is a charter member of the Parapsychological Association (treasurer 1963). Her articles include 'Five Years of the Journal of Parapsychology' (with J. G. **Pratt,** *Journal of Parapsychology,* March 1942), 'The ESP Controversy' (with J. G. Pratt, *Journal of Parapsychology,* Sept. 1942), 'The Search for ESP in Animals' (*Tomorrow,* Summer 1953).

She relinquished editing of the *Journal of Parapsychology* at the end of 1963, but became an editorial consultant.

Poppy Seeds

Divination by smoke was sometimes practiced by magicians. A few jasmine or poppy seeds were flung upon burning coals, for this purpose; if the smoke rose lightly and ascended, straight into the heavens, it augured well; but if it hung about it was regarded as a bad omen. In parts of Europe, a pregnant woman would place poppy seeds on a window sill if she wanted a boy; sugar if she wanted a girl.

Popular Astrology (Magazine)

Monthly magazine which includes astrological forecasts for the year, universal zodiac and day to day guides. Address: P.O. Box 3728, Marion, Ohio 43302.

Portent

An extraordinary event or object which foreshadows some ominous or marvellous future event. (See Paranormal **Signs**)

Possession (in Spiritualism)

In Spiritualism, possession is a developed form of motor **automatism** in which the personality of the automatist is substituted by another, as a rule by a discarnate spirit. The possessing personality aims to establish **communication** with this world through the organism of the entranced medium, by writing or speech.

The incipient stage of possession is **personation,** during which the medium's own personality is still in the body but is assuming the characteristics of someone departed.

The next stage is partial possession, the excitation of the medium's motor or sensory centers by a discarnate agent either through the subconscious self or in some direct way. F. W. H. **Myers** suggested the word "telergic" as a correlative to telepathic for such action.

Full possession postulates the vacation of the organism by the medium to allow the entrance of another spirit. Alternating personalities offer the first suggestion of the possibility of possession. An arbitrary personality may possess the organism of the hypnotic subject at the hypnotizer's suggestion.

Traveling **clairvoyance** in dream points to the wandering of the spirit while the body is asleep (see **Astral Projection**).

Cases of religious **ecstasy** in which an excursion is made into the spiritual world furnish another instance of the temporary separation of body and soul. Once we admit the possibility of the soul leaving the body, we have to admit the possibility of another spirit entering it.

Whether possession has actually taken place or whether it is a secondary personality which speaks through the organism, is a question of evidence. The evidence should be furnished by the nature and contents of the communications. The testimony of the medium is not available. As a rule he or she does not remember what has happened.

Emanuel **Swedenborg** remembered his excursions into the spiritual world but in his case there was no possession. The subjects of Alphonse **Cahagnet** described heavenly visions in trance but there was not enough evidence to rule out the possibility that even when evidential communications from discarnate spirits were forthcoming they were not controlled by the subconscious self alone.

The famous medium Mrs. **Piper** never remembered her visions of the spiritual world and, the fragmentary utterances during her passing from **trance** to the waking life disregarded, she was the tool, for writing and utterances of alien entities.

If no new knowledge is shown in the trance state, there is no reason to ascribe the communication to an external intelligence. The character of the communicator alone does not furnish convincing proof. Secondary personalities are often hostile and antagonistic to the primary one. The cleavage might not be intellectual alone but also moral, therefore the difference between the normal self of the medium and the communicator does not necessarily clinch the case for possession.

Paranormal knowledge which the medium could not have acquired is an indispensible condition to prove the presence of an external spirit. Incoherence in the communicator does not militate against possession. It is rather in favor of it. If the spirit of the medium vacates the body, his brain will be left behind in a dreamlike state. To control such a brain and to make it obey the will of the communicator may not only be an enervating process, but full of pitfalls and possibilities of confusion.

Taken as a phenomenon, possession presents one of the central mysteries of human life. It involves seeing a mind use a brain.

Possession is always temporary and implies a surrender of his or her organism on the part of the medium. If possession takes place against the will of the medium and endures in the waking state, we witness the phenomenon of **obsession.**

The possibility of an instrumental test of possession was first suggested by W. Whately **Carington.** He advised the use of a galvanometer which measured the emotional reactions of the medium to a certain set of questions. The different controls, if they are different personalities, should exhibit different emotional reactions to the same questions. It was by such tests that the independence of the controls of the medium Eileen **Garrett** was established at the Johns Hopkins University and at the New York Psychical Institute in 1933.

Is it possible that a materialized spirit should be possessed by another? Archdeacon **Colley** claimed to have observed such a case in the mediumship of F. W. **Monck.** "Samuel," the guide of the medium, controlled the body of an Egyptian phantom, "the Mahedi," spoke through him in his own voice and wrote in English in his own characters (there were samples of direct writing available for comparison) in good idiomatic English of which the Mahedi himself could not utter a word. However, much dubiety surrounds the phenomena of Monck.

For a discussion of the unwilling possession of sensitive individuals by malicious spirits or demons, see **Obsession and Possession.**

(See also **Control; Exorcism; Obsession and Possession; Personality; Trance Personalities**)

Postel, Guillaume (1510-1581)

A sixteenth-century visionary born in the diocese of Avranches, France. He was so precocious that at fourteen years of age he was made master of a school.

It is said that he was in the habit of reading the most profound works of Jewish rabbis, and the vivacity of his imagination threw him into constant troubles, from which he had the greatest difficulty in extricating himself. He believed that he had been called by God to reunite all men under one law, either by reason or the sword. The pope and the king of France were to be the civil and religious heads of his new republic.

He was made Almoner to a hospital at Venice, where he came under the influence of a woman called Mère Jeanne, who had visions which had turned her head. Because of his heterodox preachings, Postel was denounced as a heretic, but latterly was regarded as merely mad.

After having travelled somewhat extensively in the East, and having written several works in which he dealt with the visions of his coadjustor, he retired to the priory of St. Martin-des-Champs at Paris, where he died penitent.

Posthumous Letters

Many investigators of psychic science, members of the **Society for Psychic Research** and others, have left sealed letters, whose contents are known only to the writer. On the death of the writer, and before the letter shall have been opened, an attempt is made by a medium to reveal the contents.

By this means it is hoped to prove the actuality or otherwise of claimed spirit communication, for since only the writer knows what the letter contains, it is presumed that on his death this knowledge can only be communicated through his discarnate spirit. This hypothesis overlooks the fact that the information might be telepathically acquired during the writer's lifetime by a still living person, and so conveyed to the medium. As yet, however, hypotheses are premature, for few attempts of the kind have met with striking success.

Controversy surrounds cases of secret or coded messages known only to the deceased and a relative who seeks confirmation of survival from a medium, but not recorded in a sealed and safely deposited letter.

In the case of the great escapologist Houdini, a code message was apparently confirmed to his widow by the medium Arthur Ford. However, the genuineness of this story has been alternately confirmed, denied and confirmed again (see Harry **Houdini**). (See also **Survival**)

Poughkeepsie Seer, The

Name given to Andrew Jackson **Davis** (1862-1910), prophet of a new revelation delivered in trance addresses and apparently influenced by Emanuel **Swedenborg.**

Powder of Projection

A powder which was claimed to assist the alchemist in the transmutation of base metal into pure gold. (See Alexander **Seton**)

Powder of Sympathy

An occult remedy which, by its application to the weapon which had caused a wound, was supposed to cure the hurt. This method was in vogue during the reigns of James I and Charles I, and its chief exponent was a gentleman named Sir Kenelm Digby.

An abstract of his theory, contained in an address given before an assembly of nobles and learned men at Montpellier in France, is described in T. J. Pettigrew's book *On Superstitions connected with the History and Practice of Medicine and Surgery* (1844). The following is the recipe for the powder: "Take Roman vitriol six or eight ounces, beat it very small in a mortar, sift it through a fine sieve when the sun enters Leo; keep it in the heat of the sun by day, and dry by night."

This art has been treated by some authors with belief, and by others with unbelieving wit. One writer commented: "If the superstitious person be wounded by any chance, he applies the salve, not to the wound, but, what is more effectual to the weapon by which he received it."

Sir Kenelm Digby's theory was published by him under the title *A late Discourse . . . by Sir Kenelm Digby, Kt. & c. Touching the Cure of Wounds by the Powder of Sympathy* (London, 1658), but Sir Francis Bacon had also written on the subject a few years earlier in his book *Sylva Sylvarum: or, a Natural History* (1627 etc.), in which he quoted a more bizarre recipe for the powder:

"It is constantly Received, and Avouched, that the Anounting of the Weapon, that maketh the Wound wil heale the Wound it selfe. In this Experiment, upon the Relation of Men of Credit, (though my selfe, as yet, am not fully inclined to beleeve it,) you shal note the Points following; First, the Ointment . . . is made of Divers ingredients; whereof the Strangest and Hardest to come by, are the Mosse upon the Skull of a dead Man, Unburied; And the Fats of a Boare, and a Beare, killed in the Art of Generation. These Two last I could easily suspect to be prescribed as a Starting Hole; That if the Experiment proved not, it mought be pretended, that the Beasts were not killed in due Time . . . "

Of course the belief in sympathetic magic is a very ancient one, going back to primitive times (see **Magic**).

Recommended reading:

Redgrove, H. Stanley. *Bygone Beliefs; Being a Series of Excursions in the Byways of Thought,* Rider, London, 1920 (reissued under title *Magic & Mysticism: Studies in Bygone Beliefs,* University Books, 1971) [contains chapter on 'The Powder of Sympathy']

Powell, Ellis T(homas) (1869-1922)

Prominent British barrister, journalist, and Spiritualist. He gave evidence in the American Marconi case.

He was born in Ludlow, Shropshire, and educated at Ludlow Grammar School. He served an apprenticeship to a draper in Ludlow, then came to London, where he became a journalist on the *Financial News,* eventually becoming editor. He mastered several languages, including Hebrew, Greek, and Latin. In his spare time, he studied law and became a barrister. He was a Fellow of the Royal Historical and Royal Economic Societies, fellow of the Institute of Journalists and Royal Colonial Institute (member of Council). He lectured at the London School of Economics and Political Science (University of London).

His publications included: *The Essentials of Self-Government* (1909), *The Mechanism of the City* (1910), *The Evolution of the Money Market* (1915), *The Psychic Element of the New Testament* (n.d.), *The Practical Affairs of Life* (1918).

He became an ardent supporter of the Spiritualist movement, traveling throughout Britain and lecturing on psychic subjects. He was a member of the **British College of Psychic Science,** and was for many years a council member of the **London Spiritualist Alliance.** He was a frequent contributor to the Spiritualist journal *Light.*

As a barrister, he brought a searching legal mind to the problem of what he termed the "barbaric legislation" against mediums, campaigning to amend the Witchcraft Act of George II, still used against mediums during the twentieth century. He died June 1, 1922.

As a good friend of Sir Arthur Conan **Doyle,** his name figured in the famous seance conducted by Doyle and his wife for **Houdini.** In 1922, when the Doyles were in Atlantic City, they met Houdini on the sea front. Lady Jean Doyle (Doyle's second wife) offered to give Houdini an **automatic writing** seance. This took place at the Ambassador Hotel, where they were staying.

Lady Doyle produced automatic writing purporting to come from Houdini's dead mother. At the end of an emotional message, Houdini took up the pencil and was impelled to write one word on the pad—the name "Powell." This convinced Doyle that Houdini was really a medium, since his friend Ellis Powell had died only a few days earlier.

In the event, Houdini later stated that the message claimed to be from his mother was not evidential, since she would have been unable to communicate in fluent English, moreover he himself had been thinking of Frederick Eugene Powell, a fellow stage magician.

Powell, Evan (1881- ?)

Nonprofessional British physical medium, of Paignton, South Devon, originally a coal miner, later a small tradesman in Wales.

Powell usually sat securely tied to his chair before a cabinet with drawn curtains. His chief control was "Black Hawk," an American Indian. **Movements** of objects, psychic lights (see **Luminous Phenomena**) and **direct voice** phenomena were witnessed at his seances. He gave many successful sittings at the **British College of Psychic Science.**

"Black Hawk" claimed that a book has been published about him in America. A friend of Powell commissioned a book agent to locate it and, when found, presented it to the medium. The title was: *Life of Ma-Ka-Tai-Me-She-Kia-Kiak or Black Hawk, dictated by himself* (Boston, 1834). For twenty years "Black Hawk" had also maintained that there was a memorial of himself in Illinois. This was subsequently proved to be true.

For a discussion of Powell's mediumship, see *Revue Métapsychique* (1924, p. 326) and *Journal* of the Society for Psychical Research (vol. 41, p. 161).

Powell, Kenneth F(rancis) (1923-)

Engineer who has investigated parapsychology. Born March 4, 1923, at Boston, Massachusetts, he studied at University of Pittsburgh (B.S. 1949, M.A. 1951). In 1948 he married Melrose L. Evans.

He was physics instructor 1949, mathematics lecturer 1950 at University of Pittsburgh, analytical engineer at Babcock & Wilcox from 1951-55, manager of data processing, applied science and systems at International Business Machines, Pittsburgh from 1955-61, manager, education development, data processing at IBM, Poughkeepsie, New York from 1961. He is a member of the American Nuclear Society, Institute of Radio Engineers, Operations Research Society of America, Parapsychological Association.

He has taken a special interest in **psychokinesis.** His papers include 'Interpretation and Engineering Computations' (Western Joint Computer Conference, 1955), (with R. A. **McConnell** and Ruth J.

Snowden) 'Wishing With Dice' (*Journal of Experimental Psychology*, vol. 50, 1955).

Powell, W. H. (c. 1879)

Slate-writing medium of Philadelphia with whom Epes **Sargent** had remarkable experiments in Boston on June 21, 1879. Under the blaze of the chandelier, "without touching the surface of the slate, he made motions over it with his forefinger in the air, as if making a drawing, and then writing something. I reversed the slate, and there on the under surface, was a neat drawing of a flower, and under it in clear, bold letters, the word 'Winona.' "

Powell was tested by a committee which included chemists and physicians in 1879 in Philadelphia. The committee reported that Powell's slate-writing was "one of those peculiar psychological manifestations that we cannot account for."

PPCC Bulletin

Formerly *Eden Bulletin.* Edited by Jerome **Eden,** for Planetary Professional Citizens Committee, established as an international organization concerned with UFOs and the **Orgone** Energy concepts of Dr. Wilhelm **Reich.** PPCC believes that UFOs are connected with the development of global deserts. Address: P.O. Box 34, Careywood, Idaho 83309.

Prana

According to Hindu **Yoga** teachings, a subtle vitality contained in the air, which is modified by the human body to govern essential functions. In **Hatha Yoga** training, this vitality is enhanced by special Yoga exercises known as *Pranayama.*

By a combination of Hatha Yoga exercises and Pranayama techniques, a latent force called **Kundalini** is aroused in the body. Kundalini normally supplies energy for sexual activity, but when fully aroused can be conducted up the human spine to a subtle center in the head, resulting in higher consciousness or transcendental states.

Recommended reading:

Kuvalayananda, Swami. *Pranayama,* Popular Prakashan, Bombay, India, 1966 etc.

Prasad, Rama. *The Science of Breath and the Philosophy of the Tattvas,* 3rd revised ed., Theosophical Publishing Society, London, New York & Madras, 1897

Prasad, Kali (1901-)

Indian professor of psychology who has investigated parapsychology. Born 1901, at Sitapur, India, he studied at Allahabad University (Ph.D.). He was professor and head of the Department of Philosophy and Psychology of Lucknow University from 1944 onwards, research director of India International Center, New Delhi, Fulbright Visiting Professor at Massachusetts Institute of Technology from 1954-56, chairman of Social Welfare Evaluation Committee of Uttar Pradesh state, India, member of Uttar Pradesh University Grants Committee, Indian Science Congress (Psychology Section), Indian Philosophical Congress.

Dr. Prasad was author of the book *The Psychology of Meaning* (1949), and also responsible for the section on 'Communal Tensions' in the UNESCO *Report on India* (1952), also included in the book *In the Minds of Men* (1953) by Gardner **Murphy.** Dr. Prasad had special interest in telepathy and psychokinesis, and was involved in various research projects funded by grants from the Parapsychology Foundation. These projects concerned experiments in ESP, and the influence of interpersonal relations between subject and experimenter on ESP results.

Pratt, J(oseph) G(aither) (1910-1979)

One of the pioneers of parapsychology, for many years chief assistant to Dr. J. B. **Rhine** at Duke University, Durham, North Carolina. Born August 31, 1910, at Winston-Salem, North Carolina, he studied at Duke University (B.A. 1931, M.A. 1933, Ph.D. 1936). In 1936 he married Nellie Ruth Pratt.

He was research associate, assistant director at the Parapsychology Laboratory, Duke University from 1937-41, U.S. Navy Personnel Research, Washington, D.C. from 1942-46, President of the Parapsychological Association in 1960, council member from 1959-62, member of the American Psychological Association, Southern Society for Philosophy and Psychology, American Association for the Advancement of Science, member of editorial staff of *Journal of Parapsychology.*

He took a special interest in quantitative experiments in extrasensory perception, and his early investigations at Duke University included the famous Pearce-Pratt series (with Hubert E. Pearce Jr.) and the Pratt-Woodruff series (with J. L. **Woodruff**.)

In addition to his many articles on psychology and biology in scholarly journals, Dr. Pratt also published many important contributions to parapsychology, including (in *Journal of Parapsychology*) 'Size of Stimulus Symbols in Extrasensory Perception' (with J. L. Woodruff, vol. 3, 1939), 'Appraising Verbal Test Material in Parapsychology' (with W. R. Birge, vol. 12, 1948), 'The Homing Problem in Pigeons' (vol. 17, 1953), 'A Review of the Pearce-Pratt Distance Series of ESP Tests' (with J. B. Rhine, vol. 18, 1954), and (in *Ciba Foundation Symposium on Extrasensory Perception,* 1956) 'Testing for an ESP Factor in Pigeon Homing.' His books on parapsychology include: *Handbook for Testing Extrasensory Perception* (with C. E. Stuart, 1937), *Extrasensory Perception After Sixty Years* (with J. B. Rhine and others, 1940), *Parapsychology: Frontier Science of the Mind* (with J. B. Rhine, 1957), *ESP Research Today: A Study of Developments in Parapsychology Since 1960* (1973).

After 1965, Dr. Pratt became associated with the Division of Parapsychology, Department of Psychiatry of the University of Virginia, established by Dr. Ian **Stevenson.**

Amongst Dr. Pratt's outstanding achievements in the field of parapsychology was his investigation of the card-guessing subject Pavel Stepanek in Prague, Czechoslovakia. Stepanek had been discovered by parapsychologist Dr. Milan Ryzl in 1961. Pratt and Ryzl collaborated on experiments with Stepanek in Prague and Charlottesville, Virginia for several years, reported in Pratt's monograph 'A Decade of Research with a Selected Subject' (*Proceedings* of American Society for Psychical Research, Sept. 30, 1973).

During his many years as a parapsychologist, Dr. Pratt traveled in Europe, India, South Africa and the Soviet Union. He had hoped to study the talented Russian PK subject Nina **Kulagina,** but did not obtain permission, although he witnessed her phenomena informally in a hotel. He collaborated with H. J. Keil, Benson Herbert and Montague **Ullman** on a monograph about Kulagina, published in *Proceedings* of the Society for Psychical Research, January 1976. Dr. Pratt's last book (in collaboration with novelist Naomi Hintze) was *The Psychic Realm* (Random House, 1975).

He died November 3, 1979 at his home near Charlottesville, Virginia.

Pratyahara

One of the advanced stages of **Yoga** practice. In the system of the Indian sage Patanjali (c. 200 B.C.), the following stages are prescribed: *yama* and *niyama* (ethical restraints and moral observances), *asanas* (the physical positions of **Hatha Yoga**), *pranayama* (breathing exercises), *pratyahara* (sense withdrawal), *dharana* (concentration), dhyana (meditation), culminating in various degrees of samadhi (superconsciousness).

Pratyahara involves withdrawing sensory perception from external objects in order to concentrate on single-minded contemplation as a preliminary phase of meditation proper. (See also **Asanas; Meditation; Prana; Yoga**)

Prayer

Prayer is believed to act in two ways: as a powerful autosuggestion and as a means to secure higher spiritual assistance.

The belief that God intervenes to grant fervent prayers has long been a central aspect of Christian theology, although in modern times more emphasis is laid on submission to divine will than desire for special favors. Faith remains an essential component of successful prayer.

Samuel Jackson, in his biographical sketch of Jung-Stilling (J. Heinrich **Jung**), recorded that he attained the means of his education by a succession of miracles in answer to fervent prayer. J. K. Lavater's life abounded in similar incidents. Augustus Franke of Halle erected a vast orphan asylum and yearly fed and educated thousands of waifs by the power of prayer.

The Rev. Christopher Blumhardt (1805-1880) of Württemberg, Germany, was not only famous for his prayer cures but for his benefactions, the means of which were always procured by answer to prayer. Hundreds of persons reported to have been compelled by a power they could not resist to send presents of clothes or food to the Rev. Blumhardt.

The **Curé d'Ars,** Jean Baptiste Vianney (1786-1859), furnishes a similar example of an extraordinary life of faith. He built tree chapels, and established a "Providence" for destitute children and another home for friendless women. Constant prayer was the source of his beneficence. When food, fuel or money was wanted, he prayed for it and it surely came.

George Muller of Bristol, as related in his *The Life of Trust, being a Narrative of Some of the Lord's Dealings with George Muller* (2 pts., 1837-41), depended on prayer for half a century for his own maintenance and that of his charitable institutions. He never asked anyone, or allowed anyone to be asked, directly or indirectly, for a penny. No subscriptions or collections were ever made. Hundreds of times there was no food in his house, yet he never took a loaf or any other article on credit even for a day. During the thirty years which his narrative covers, neither he nor the hundreds of children dependent upon him for their daily food were ever without a regular meal. Secret prayer was his only resource. The donors always described sudden and uncontrollable impulses to send him a definite sum at a certain date, the exact amount he was in want of.

F. W. Myers stated in *Human Personality and its Survival of Bodily Death* (2 vols., 1903) that the points "that are actually proved by the recorded appearances, intimations, and messages of the departing and the departed" include the fact "that between the spiritual and material worlds an avenue of communication does exist—that which we call the despatch and receipt of telepathic messages, or the utterance and the answer of prayer and supplication."

It is clear that there is no simple explanation of the question of prayer, either spiritual or secular. Since ancient times, billions of prayers have been addressed to thousands of different deities. Some of these prayers appear to have been answered, others ignored.

As with the related question of paranormal **healing,** there are important theological problems for the simplistic view that the prayer of faith is granted by a loving deity. All actions in the physical world are interconnected by complex cause and effect, and the granting of one ordinary petition cannot avoid affecting other events, sometimes for the better, sometimes for worse.

Again, it is not always clear why some prayers should appear to be answered and others ignored. If there is any simple efficacy to devout and heartfelt prayers to a deity, why did the inconceivably monstrous horrors of the Nazi persecutions and prison camps fail to be averted?

On the other hand, it certainly appears that on a smaller personal scale, prayer with faith and confidence has produced the desired results in both a religious and secular setting. With the development of the **New Thought** movement in the nineteenth century there has been a growing emphasis on the power of mental activity in bringing desired events to fruition. One wing of New Thought has retained a Christian prayerful context, while a secular wing has simply emphasized the creative powers of the mind in achieving fulfillment of desires.

It seems possible that there are factors in prayer which are applicable to both religious and secular frames of thought, that faith and confidence enhance psychic factors at present not clearly identified. Even such mundane attempts to influence events as the willing of the fall of dice in parapsychological research may hold clues for the mechanisms of prayer.

Again, it is interesting to note that in such ancient religions as Hinduism, the gods were said to be unable to avoid granting requests when the petitioner had practiced intense austerities. This suggests that spiritual disciplines may bring about psycho-physical changes in the petitioner that influence events.

Secondary aspects of traditional prayer that may also have relevance are the ritualistic forms of prayers, and the need for constant repetition which, like **autosuggestion,** may enhance subconscious powers.

Ultimately, however, divine will takes priority over the mundane desires of petitioners, and in mystical Hinduism the highest wisdom is said to be transcendental awareness that is beyond desires and fears in the mundane world and that accepts favorable or unfavorable destiny with equinamity, much as the petitioner in the Christian tradition concludes "Thy will be done." (See also **Autosuggestion; Christian Science;** Psychic **Dentistry; Healing by Faith;** Psychic **Healing; Mantra; Mind Cure; New Thought**)

Recommended reading:

Bounds, E. M. *Power Through Prayer,* London, 1912; Moody Press, Evanston, Illinois, 1979

Brown, William A. *The Life of Prayer in a World of Science,* Hodder & Stoughton, London, 1927

Carrol, F. *The Prayer of the Early Christians,* Burns & Oates, London, 1930

Fillmore, Charles & Cora. *Teach Us to Pray,* Seabury Press, New York, 1976

Greene, Barbara & W. Gollancz. *God of a Hundred Names,* Gollancz, London, 1962

Humbard, Rex. *Prayer With Power,* Baker Books, Grand Rapids, Michigan, n.d.

James, William. *The Varieties of Religious Experience,* London, 1902; University Books, 1963

Loehr, Franklin. *The Power of Prayer on Plants,* Doubleday, 1959

Patton, William P. *Prayer and Its Answers,* New York, 1885

Petuchowski, Jacob J. (ed.). *Understanding Jewish Prayer,* Ktav Publications, New York, 1972

Stanton, Horace. *Telepathy of the Celestial World,* New York, 1913

Steiner, Rudolf. *The Lord's Prayer,* Anthroposophic Press, London & New York, n.d.

Sherman, Harold. *How to Use the Power of Prayer,* C. & R. Anthony, New York, 1959

Theresa, St. *The Interior Castle,* Baker, London, 1921

Yatiswarananda, Swami. *Universal Prayers* (in San skrit & English), Vedanta Press, Hollywood, California, 6th ed., 1963

"Preceptor"

Pseudonym of one of the spirit **controls** of the Rev. W. Stainton **Moses,** later revealed to be Elijah. "Imperator" (another control) frequently referred to him as his "Great Master" and director of the movement for the uplift of humanity through the teachings they delivered under the leadership of Jesus.

His first signed communication was given on May 27, 1876. He was seen clairvoyantly by Stainton Moses and was said in the communications to be a link between Moses and Malachi in the chain of spirit influence which extended from Melchizedek to Jesus.

Precipitation of Matter

One of the phenomena of Spiritualism which least admits of a rational explanation is that known as the "passing of solids through solids." The statement of the hypothetical fourth dimension of space is an attempt at a solution of the problem, as also is the theory of "precipitation of matter."

The latter suggests that before one solid body passes through another it is resolved into its component atoms, to be precipitated in its original form when the passage is accomplished.

Camille **Flammarion** found a parallel to the process in the passage of a piece of ice (a solid) through a napkin. The ice passes through the napkin in the form of water, and may afterwards be re-frozen.

This is matter passing through matter, a solid passing through a solid, after it has undergone a change of condition. And it is only carrying out Flammarion's inference to suggest that it is something analogous to this process which occurs in all cases of solids passing through solids. (See also **Matter passing through matter; Teleportation;** J. C. F. **Zöllner**)

Recommended reading:

Zöllner, J. C. F. *Transcendental Physics,* W. H. Harrison, London, 1882

Precognition

Paranormal knowledge of impending events. (See also **Prediction; Premonition; Prophecy; Retrocognition**)

Prediction

Prediction of future events is a most perplexing puzzle of psychical science. That it is a fact, there is ample evidence.

Dr. Eugène **Osty** wrote in his important book, *Supernormal Faculties in Man* (1923): "Twelve years of personal experimentation with a large number of metagnomic percipients and on a considerable number of persons have given me complete certitude that there are human beings who can predict the eventuation of the life of another. Of this I have the same degree of certainty as of the existence of what we call the earth, the sun, the stars, minerals, plants and animals."

The mathematician and astronomer P. S. Laplace said that the future depends absolutely on the present, and he who would know the whole of the present would know also the whole of the future. We are no wiser for this statement.

In an attempt to be practical, Dr. Hereward **Carrington** offered the analogy of a rapidly moving train from which we perceive ever-changing scenes. They existed before we came to them but we were unable to see them.

The analogy is not perfect. The astounding feature about prediction is the occasional minuteness of detail. The scenes which we witness from the train did exist before we perceived them but only as a frame in which life itself was constantly changing. In prediction, we meet with a fixation of this changing element, the foresight of incidents which neither on the basis of probabilities nor on the higher knowledge of character and abilities, are likely to occur, as they are of accidental nature like missing a train, tripping in the street, etc.

A most curious case of prediction, involving such incidents of small significance was recorded by the medium Mrs. **Verrall** on December 11, 1911, in the following automatic script: "Nothing should be neglected, the most trifling facts may be useful; be trustful. . . . The cold was intense and a single candle gave poor light. He was lying on the sofa or on a bed, and was reading Marmontel by the light of a single candle. . . . The book was lent him, it did not belong to him."

On December 17, the message was supplemented by the following details: "The name Marmontel is correct. . . . A French book, I think his memoirs. The name Passy may help him to remember Passy or Fleury. The book was bound in two volumes, the binding was old, and the book was lent him. The name Marmontel is not on the cover."

On March 1, Mrs. Verrall was told by a friend, Mr. Marsh, that he read the memoirs of Marmontel on a bitterly cold night in Paris on February 20 by the light of a candle. Once he was in bed, another time he reclined on two chairs. He borrowed the book, it had three volumes, and on February 21, he had read the chapter in which the finding of a picture, painted at Passy, is described by Marmontel, the discovery being associated with Mr. Fleury.

Predictions of this nature may be brought within understanding if we suppose that the future may not be the result of our own actions and thoughts alone but also of planning by higher intelligences, for the very purposes of test, in the spirit realms. Free will is in no way influenced by the supposition that from time to time we may be impressed to certain actions.

The majority of cases are not of this nature. The case of a famous young Italian savant which Prof. **Lombroso** related could not be the result of test and planning. According to his account, Dr. C. predicted, on February 4, 1894, the burning of the Como exhibition (which actually took place on July 6) with such firm assurance that his family sold all their shares in the Milan Fire Insurance Company. At the time of the prediction, even the building of the main edifice had not progressed very far. Dr. C. was a most neurotic man, with not a few marks of degeneracy and grave hereditary defects.

The Shadow of the Future

If, as it is said, future events forecast their shadows, we ought to find predictions for most great events. There are some proofs for the correctness of the assumption.

The great pestilence of 1665, and the great fire of London following the plague in 1666, were predicted. In a book published in 1661, George Fox (the younger) said that the Lord has spoken to him: "The people are too many, the people are too many, I will thin them, an overflowing scourge shall come upon the land." Further he stated: "And the spirit of the Lord signifieth unto me that the time draweth nigh and the decree of the Lord is firm and not to be altered."

This prophecy was reiterated in 1664 (May 29) by Captain Bishop, of Bristol: "To the King and both Houses of Parliament, thus saith the Lord: Meddle not with my people because of their conscience to Me, for if ye do I will send my plagues upon you, and you shall know that I am the Lord. Written in obedience to the Lord by his servant, George Bishop." William Bayley was also seized with inspirational ecstasy and warned the King and the Parliament against the religious persecution: ". . . the plagues will pursue you to destruction, if you proceed in this work . . . The Lord hath spoken it."

In the Great Fire of London, over 13,000 homes and 89 churches were burnt down. George Fox, in his *Journal,* told of his own vision and that of Thomas Ibbott, of Huntingdonshire. Ibbott came to London two days before the fire, alighted off his horse with clothes loose, as one distracted, and ran towards Whitehall in such posture as many inhabitants were forced to flee from the fire, and foretold his vision which he had before, that the City would be laid waste by fire.

Thomas Briggs, the prophet preacher, passing through London some years before the fire, cried out in Cheapside that unless the city repented as Nineveh did, God would destroy it. Humphrey Smith foresaw the great fire in 1660: "there was none that sought to stop the foundations the city stood on, and all the tall buildings fell, and few were left in her . . . and thus she became a desolation, and the vision remained in me as a thing secretly shewed me of the Lord."

Archbishop Usher, Lord Primate of Ireland, in a sermon preached in Dublin in 1601, foretold the Irish Rebellion to the day, 40 years before it came to pass.

In 1625, the German prophet Englebrecht foresaw the French Revolution, the fall of the Ecclesiastical, Political and Family State all over Europe. Still earlier, in 1555, **Nostradamus** gave the date of the

French Revolution as 1789 and foretold the execution of the King and Queen, the new Calendar and the persecution of the Church.

A high degree of predictive power was noticed during the French revival among the Huguenots after the edict of Nantes was revoked and religious persecution began. Thousands of Protestants received the gift of prophecy. Cavalier, Roland, and Marion, their leaders, often foretold the fortunes of war in their ecstasies. Marion and Lacy prophesied eighty years in advance the division of France among the Catholics, the revolution, its spread over the continent and the division between the great Catholic monarchies who would be engaged in exterminating each other instead of slaughtering Protestants, as later happened in the revolutionary wars with France, Spain, Italy, Austria and others.

The French ex-Jesuit Beauregard, preaching before the Court on May 20, 1789, was suddenly seized with a fit of frenzy and pronounced these words: "Yes! Thy temples, O Lord, shall be destroyed. Thy worship abolished. Thy name blasphemed. But what do I hear, Great God! To the holy strains which beneath sacred roofs arose in Thy praise shall succeed profane and licentious songs; the infamous rites of Venus shall usurp the place of worship of the Most High! And she herself sit on the throne of the Holy of Holies, to receive the incense of her new adorers." The prophecy was accomplished in Nôtre Dame, Mme. Maillard personifying the Goddess. The same scene was repeated in the Church of St. Sulpice.

The gift of prophecy is often noted in religious revivals and is apt to spread to other members of the community. They remind one of the times of the Bible. To quote a single startling prophecy, Moses predicted centuries before the occurrence that a fierce nation, swift as the eagle flies, should be brought against the Jews from the end of the earth.

The American Civil War has many prophets. The first pronouncement was made by J. D. Stiles, of Weymouth, Massachusetts, in 1854. As the prediction neared fulfilment, it developed in points of detail and precision through the seership of others. Stiles' prediction was published in book form long before its verification, also giving the final result, the victory of the abolitionists and emancipation of the slaves.

In 1860, in the legislative hall of Alabama, Mrs. Hardinge **Britten** became entranced, saw long lines of regiments, military music, the tramp of vast bodies of infantry with a joyous rhythm, then wild agonizing shrieks and heartrending groans. "Woe, woe to thee, Alabama," she declaimed, like the prophets of old, and foretold all the desolation and fearful suffering that indeed befell Alabama, the most active Southern state in the defence of slavery during the war between North and South. The prophecy was taken down by a press reporter and testified to by six persons present.

A gypsy prophesied to Josephine, while a child in Martinique, that she would become Empress of France. Josephine was so convinced that the dream would come true that during the revolution, while she was in jail and threatened by the jailor that her turn would soon come for the guillotine, she told her shrieking fellow-prisoners that she would not die but would live to be Queen of France.

Daniel Offord, a nine-year-old-boy, predicted the 1853 cholera epidemic two months before it struck England. Dr. Dixon wrote in the *Yorkshire Spiritual Telegraph* (vol. 3, 1856) "Daniel said on August 30, 1853, the cholera would be here in two months; all were to take a half-teaspoonful of carbon every day. Exactly two months to a day the official notification appeared."

The assassination of President Lincoln was predicted by the great medium D. D. **Home** at Dieppe in 1863. He was asked by a Russian to look into a crystal. He saw a crowd and in it a man who was assassinated and in the act of falling from his chair. He said "That is Lincoln, and within the year it will take place." The time was not quite accurate.

Andrew Jackson **Davis,** in his book *Penetralia* (1856), predicted the coming of the automobile and the typewriter. He wrote: "Look out about these days for carriages and traveling saloons on country roads—without horses, without steam, without any visible motive power—moving with greater speed and far more safety than at present. Carriages will be moved by a strange and beautiful and simple admixture of aqueous and atmospheric gases—so easily condensed, so simply ignited, and so imparted by a machine somewhat resembling fire engines as to be entirely concealed and manageable between the forward wheels. These vehicles will prevent many embarrassments now experienced by persons living in thinly populated territories. The first requisite for these land-locomotives will be good roads, upon which, with your engine, without your horses, you may travel with great rapidity. These carriages seem to be of uncomplicated construction."

About the typewriter he wrote: "I am almost moved to invent an automatic psychographer—that is, an artificial soul-writer. It may be constructed something like a piano, one brace or scale of keys to represent the elementary sounds; another and lower tier to represent a combination, and still another for a rapid re-combination so that a person, instead of playing a piece of music may touch off a sermon or a poem."

The assassination of the King and Queen of Serbia took place on June 10, 1903. As the journalist William **Stead** related in the *Review of Reviews* (June 20, 1903), he handed, on March 20, to Mrs. Burchell, the Yorkshire Seeress, an envelope containing the signature of the King of Serbia. She said, "This belongs to Royalty." Then she became very excited and exclaimed: "I see the interior of the Palace, I can see the King and his Queen; now I see a number of men, they are murdering the King. The Queen prays for mercy; I cannot see whether the Queen has been killed, but the King is dead. It is terrible, terrible!" Mrs. Brenchley, another sensitive, corroborated what Mrs. Burchell said with further particulars.

On the same subject, a curious message was received by **raps** at a seance the day previous to the murder in Paris in the presence of the psychical researcher Prof. Charles **Richet.** The message commenced was: "Bancalamo," to which Prof. Richet exclaimed: "Oh, it is Latin, calamo." The message continued: "Banca la mort guette famille." The rest of the message was incoherent. When the news of the assassination of Queen Draga reached Paris, Prof. Richet learned for the first time that Draga's father was named Panka. The message came at 10:30 p.m., exactly the time at which the assassins left the Hotel de la Couronne de Serbie to exterminate the Royal family. Prof. Richet estimated the mathematical probability of chance to be 1 to 500,000, which makes it probable that the message was not accidental.

The Prophets of World War I

Did the first world war have prophets? The question must be answered in the affirmative.

The first amazing prediction was printed by Nostradamus at Lyons in 1555. He spoke of its cruelty and terror, that it would be carried on by land, in the sea and in the air. The airplane especially puzzled him: "a flock of ravens high in the air, and throwing fire from the sky on the cities and on the soldiers below." He named the King of Bulgaria: "fair haired Ferdinand," foretold his fortunes of war and downfall. He foresaw the collapse of the Turkish Empire, independence of Hungary, Bohemia and Poland, the enlargement of Rumania and the formation of Jugoslavia.

Dr. Tardieu put on record in 1914 the following prophecy of Leon Sonrel, a scientist of the Juisy observatory uttered in 1868 of the war in 1914: "Wait, now, wait . . . years pass. It is a vast war. What bloodshed! God? What bloodshed! Oh, France, oh, my country, thou art saved! Thou art on the Rhine!"

Sir Arthur Conan **Doyle** received the following prediction in February 1914, through the well-known Australian medium, Mrs. Foster Turner, before an audience of nearly a thousand people: "Now, although there is not at present a whisper of a great European war at hand, yet I want to warn you that before this year, 1914, has run its course, Europe will be deluged in blood. Great Britain, our beloved nation, will be drawn into the most awful war the world has ever known. Germany will be the great antagonist, and will draw other nations in her train. Austria will totter to its ruin. Kings and kingdoms will fall. Millions of precious lives will be slaughtered, but Britain will finally triumph and emerge victorious."

La Vie Nouvelle of Beauvais published in March 1914, the predictions of a simple peasant girl, communicated by the Abbé J. A. Petit, of an impending war in which France was going to be invaded, saying among other things: "But France is not alone. The violation of neutral territory has displeased other powers who unite with the French, for it is clear that this violation has been made to take possession of that land and to have a direct passage to the French frontier."

The *Revue Métapsychique* printed in December 1925, the prediction of Sophie, a young Greek woman, hypnotized by Dr. Antoniou of Athens on June 6, 1914. She gave many details, such as the neutrality of Italy at the beginning, her subsequent alliance with the Entente and the role of Greece. The prophecy, except for three errors out of twenty-one predictions, proved to be true.

In Major W. Tudor Pole's book *Private Dowding,* published anonymously in London in 1917, the following communication from the Beyond was registered: "So far as I am allowed to see, peace will be re-established during 1919, and world-federations will come into being during the following seven years. Although actual fighting may end in 1918, it will take many years to bring poise and peace into actual and permanent being."

The predictions of the Great War were analyzed by Mr. J. G. **Piddington** in *Proceedings,* of the Society for Psychical Research (vol. 33) under the title 'Forecasts in Scripts Concerning the War.' F. C. S. Schiller dwelt on the same subject in the *Journal* of the S.P.R. (vol. 17, June 1916) under the title 'War Prophecies.' Among predictive books on the subject, Ralph **Shirley's** *Prophecies and Omens of the Great War* (1914), Herbert Thurston's *The War and the Prophets* (1915), and Leon Denis' *Le Monde Invisible et la Guerre* (1919) deserve special mention.

Hypnotic and Dream Predictions

Prediction has sometimes occurred under hypnosis. In his book *Manuel Pratique de Magnétisme Animal* (1845), Dr. Alphonse Teste related that a lady patient in trance foretold that on Tuesday at three something would frighten her and cause her a fall and miscarriage. On the Tuesday at her house he hypnotized her, when she repeated the prediction. She was kept in sight, every precaution was taken, but the shock ensued. She saw a rat, fell, and the result followed as foreseen.

Many visions of the future are imparted in prophetic dreams. John Williams three times dreamed of the shooting of Perceval, Chancellor of the Exchequer, ten days before it really happened on May 11, 1812 (see **Dreams**).

The murder of Terris, the English actor, on the evening of December 16, 1897, was seen in a dream the night before by Countess Toutschkoff and Mr. Lane in an accurate scene. Witnesses testified to the truth of the story as told before the murder.

Camille **Flammarion** wrote on the subject in *L'Inconnu; The Unknown* (1900): "I do not hesitate to affirm at the outset that the occurrence of dreams foretelling future events with accuracy must be accepted as certain. Nor can the realisation of this kind of dream be explained by the fortuitous coincidences which we call chance." Later he stated: "My mother dreamed that she received a letter from my father in which she read the following sentence: 'I am the bearer of sad news; little Henry has just died in convulsions, with hardly any previous illness.' A week after, a letter from my father contained this very phrase. My poor sister had just lost her youngest child."

However true many predictions turn out to be, one is well advised not to receive them with implicit credence. A far larger percentage of predictions prove untrue, and psychical research owes serious loss, at least in two instances, to trust in this incomprehensible gift.

F. W. H. **Myers** was seriously ill with heart disease when he told Sir Lawrence J. Jones that he had four hundred and fourteen days to live. "Yes," he said, "my death had been definitely predicted to me for a day in February, 1902. I have made all my arrangements on this basis. I have divided up the work that still remains to do on my book [*Human Personality*] into twelve parts, and I am going to do one part each month. I shall then finish the book and have a few weeks before my time comes."

He died within a month and the book was not finished. His experiments with Mrs. Thompson, which contained most of the evidence on which he based his belief in survival, were never written out.

Richard **Hodgson** was similarly misled by predictions through Mrs. **Piper,** with the result that his third report on this important mediumship never saw the light.

There are other instances on record in which death was predicted and the forecast was not fulfilled. Eugène **Osty** had been often told of his own death within a certain period. He survived the prediction.

Hodgson received a message through Mrs. Piper that Prof. **Sidgwick** would soon (within months) die of heart failure. In fact, he lived for six more years and did not die of heart failure. (See also **Central Premonitions Registry; Precognition; Premonitions; Prevision; Prophecy; Retrocognition**)

Recommended reading:

Brier, Robert. *Precognition and the Philosophy of Science; An Essay on Backward Causation,* Humanities Press, New York, 1973

Cheetham, Erika. *The Prophecies of Nostradamus,* Neville Spearman, London, 1973; Corgi paperback, 1975

Cheiro. *Cheiro's World Predictions,* London Publishing Co., London, 1928

Criswell, Jeron. *Criswell's Forbidden Predictions; Based on Nostradamus and the Tarot,* Droke House/Hallux, Atlanta, 1972

Davison, Ronald C. *The Technique of Prediction; The New Complete System of Secondary Directing,* L. N. Fowler, London, 1971

De Louise, Joseph & Tom Valentine. *Psychic Mission,* Henry Regnery, Chicago, 1971

De Sabata, Mario. *He Sees the Future,* Award paperback, New York, 1971

Dixon, Jeane. *The Life and Prophecies,* Morrow, 1969; Frederick Muller, London, 1971; Sphere paperback, London, 1973

Delfano, M. (pseud. of P. Flammonde). *Living Prophets,* Dell paperback, 1972

Ellis, Keith. *Prediction and Prophecy,* Wayland, London, 1973

Grey, E. Howard. *Visions, Previsions and Miracles in Modern Times,* L. N. Fowler, London, 1915

Laver, James. *Nostradamus; or, the Future Foretold,* Collins, London, 1942; Penguin paperback, 1952; George Mann, U.K., 1973

Lyttleton, Edith. *Some Cases of Prediction,* G. Bell, London, 1937

Logan, Daniel. *The Anatomy of Prophecy,* Prentice-Hall, 1975

MacKenzie, Andrew. *The Riddle of the Future; A Modern Study of Precognition,* Barker, London, 1974; Taplinger, 1975

Russell, Eric. *The History of Astrology and Prediction,* Drake, New York, 1973; New English Library, London, 1974

Saltmarsh, H. F. *Foreknowledge,* G. Bell, London, 1938; Arno Press, 1975

Shirley, Ralph. *Prophecies and Omens of the Great War,* Rider, London, 1914

Timbs, John. *Predictions Realized in Modern Times,* C. Lockwood, London, 1880; Gryphon Books, Ann Arbor, 1971

Vaughan, Alan. *Patterns of Prophecy,* Hawthorn Books, 1973; Turnstone, London, 1974

Wallechinsk, David & Irving Wallace. *The Peoples' Almanac Presents the Book of Predictions,* Bantam paperback, 1981

Prediction (Magazine)

Long established (founded 1936) popular British magazine dealing with astrology and the occult. Features articles on Tarot, Palmistry, Graphology, Yoga and related subjects, astrological forecasts, editorial news, book reviews. Address: Link House, Dingwall Avenue, Croydon, CR9 4TA, England.

Pre-Existence

The question of pre-existence is believed to be bound up with the religious issue of **reincarnation** but Sir Oliver **Lodge** had an independent view. In *Phantom Walls* (1929) he wrote: "When the question of pre-existence arises I should say that the individual as we know him is a fresh apparition, a new individualisation of something preexisting. . . . We can imagine that, every now and then, an opportunity arises for spirit to enter into relation with matter, and to become gradually an individual, and develop a character and personality which will persist; so that there is almost a kind of 'choice' whether we enter into life or what sort of life we enter into. In that sense we may be said—with apparent absurdity, but possibly with some kind of truth—to select our parentage; and thus may some facts of heredity be accounted for." (See also **Reincarnation**)

Premonition

A paranormal impression of warning of a future event. Premonitions may range from vague feelings of disquiet, suggestive or impending disaster, to actual **hallucinations,** whether visual or auditory. **Dreams** are frequent vehicles of premonitions, either direct or symbolical, and there are many instances of veridical dreams.

In such cases it is hard to say whether the warning may have come from an external intelligent source (as Spiritualists believe) or whether the portended catastrophe may have resulted, in part, at least, from **autosuggestion.**

The latter is plainly the explanation of another form of premonition, i.e., the predictions made by patients in hypnotic or mediumistic trance with regard to their maladies. A "magnetized" subject who prophesied that his malady would reach a crisis on a certain date several weeks ahead, probably himself attended subconsciously to the fulfilling of his prophecy. Might not the same thing happen in "veridical" dreams and hallucinations?

We know that a subject obeying a post-hypnotic suggestion will weave his action quite naturally into the surrounding circumstances, though the very moment of its performance may have been fixed months before. That the dreamer and hallucinated subject also might suggest and fulfill their premonitions, either directly or by telepathic communication of the suggestion to another agent, does not seem very far-fetched or improbable.

Then there is, of course, the question of coincidence. A certain proportion of verified premonitions could be the result of coincidence. Possibly, also, such impressions, whether they remain vague forebodings or are embodied in dreams or otherwise, must at times be subconscious inferences drawn from an actual, if obscure, perception of existing facts. As such, indeed, they are not to be lightly treated. Yet very frequently premonitions prove to be entirely groundless, even the most impressive ones, where the warning is emphasized by a ghostly visitant.

According to psychical researcher Prof. Charles **Richet,** the premonitions should have two fundamental conditions:

1. The fact announced must be absolutely independent of the person to whom the premonition has come.

2. The announcement must be such that it cannot be ascribed to chance or sagacity.

Richet did not employ the term "presentiment." He rules out personal premonitions. Subconscious perception or suggestion might come into play if sickness or death were announced. He alluded to a curious medical fact for illustration. A photograph taken of a person suffering from a slight attack of fever may show signs of a rash or eruption on the face which is quite invisible to ordinary sight. The photograph "foresees" the sickness. Richet accepted, however, personal premonitions ("auto-premonitions," to use his term) in cases when accidental death figured in the paranormal perception.

The terrifying dream of Earl Hartington is a good illustration of pseudo-premonitions. In good health, he saw in his dream a skeleton which looked like him; it raised the coverlet of his bedclothes and slipped between him and his wife. He died fifteen days later.

True premonition is instanced by the dream of Armand Carrell in which he saw his mother clad in mourning and heard her say: "I weep for you my son." On the following day Armand Carrell wrote for the *National* newspaper the famous article as a consequence of which, in a duel with Emile de Girardin, he was killed.

True premonitions where the subconscious is ruled out may be received under hypnosis, in trance, or accidentally in the dream or waking state. The Seeress of Prevorst (see Frau Frederica **Hauffe**), saw in hypnotic sleep a spirit who was anxious to speak of his daughter as misfortune was threatening her. A few weeks later, the girl was nearly killed by a tile which fell on her head.

The son of Dr. Alfred Russel **Wallace** was told by a clairvoyant that "there will be an explosion in your laboratory in February or March and someone will be injured." The explosion took place on March 9. One of the students was seriously injured.

It would be more appropriate to call this an instance of **prediction.** When the event foreseen is not precisely outlined or is too insubstantial to prompt a prophetic utterance, "premonition" is the more appropriate term. For vague future events of a personal nature, "presentiment" should be employed.

If the percipient is positive that the event in question is about to happen, we may use the term "precognition." If the knowledge takes visual form, "prevision" is more appropriate. When predictions involving the fate of larger units, countries, or nations are made, "prophecy" is the more appropriate term. Premonition may be conceived of as the lowest degree of prophecy. The events which it concerns are often trifling occurrences. But whether the premonition comes in the waking state or sleep, the impression is usually deep and lasting. The recipient is apt to write it down or narrate it and thus enable later verification.

The **Society for Psychical Research,** in its early days, collected 668 cases of premonitions of death; 252 more were added in 1922. Camille **Flammarion** collected 1,824 cases. From time to time, dozens were registered in English, German, French and Italian psychical periodicals. E. **Bozzano** collected 260 cases in his *Des Phénomènes Premonitoires.* Count Cesar Baudi **de Vesme** analyzed, with great erudition, the play of premonition in games of chance (*Le Merveilleux dans les jeux de hasard,* Paris, 1930). An earlier work of William MacKenzie (*Metapsichica moderna,* Rome, 1923) related some astonishing experiments in the same field with mediumistic intervention.

But as Prof. Charles **Richet** pointed out in *L'Avenir et la Premonition* (1931), with reference to Dr. **Ochorowicz's** experiment (*Annales des Sciences Psychiques,* 1909 10), the telekinetic explanation in the stopping of the roulette ball at the announced number should, in the case of mediumistic premonitions, also be drawn into consideration.

The following cases give an illustration of the general nature of premonitions:

Two days before his daughter fell ill, Field-Marshal Lord S. dreamed that he urged her to read the *Life of Charles James Fox.* She replied: "Oh, I do not need to read it; it is the end," and showed the last page on which 'The End' was written in large black characters." (*Proceedings* of the Society for Psychical Research, vol. 11, p. 442).

Charles Dickens dreamt of a lady in a red shawl, who said: "I am Miss Napier." He did not know who this woman was. Some hours later, he was visited by two ladies and a girl in a red shawl was introduced as Miss Napier. (*Proceedings* of the American Society for Psychical Research, vol. 14, 1920).

Sir Oliver **Lodge** quoted the account of an English minister who dreamed of a terrible storm and of a globular lightning which entered the dining room and destroyed the chimneys of the roof opposite. Under the impression of the dream, although it was bright sunshine, he directed his wife to prepare lunch at an earlier hour. Events happened just as in the dream. Soon a storm broke out, a fiery globe struck through the dining room and demolished the chimneys of the neighboring roof.

Field-Marshal Earl Roberts (1832-1914), in his autobiography *Forty-one Years in India* (1897), related his experiences when commanding: "My intention, when I left Kabul, was to ride as far as the Kyber Pass, but suddenly a presentiment which I have never been able to explain to myself, made me retrace my steps and hurry back to Kabul, a presentiment of coming trouble which I can only characterise as instinctive. The feeling was justified when, about half way between Butkhak and Kabul I was met by Sir Donald Stewart and my Chief of Staff, who brought me the astounding news of the total defeat by Ayub Khan of Brigadier General Burrow's brigade at Maiwand and of Lieutenant-General Primrose, with the remainder of his force, being besieged at Kandahar."

President Abraham **Lincoln** had strange presentiments of his coming end. John Forster, in his *Life of Dickens* (3 vols., 1872), quoted a letter of the novelist, written to him, dated February 4, 1868. Charles Summer had told Dickens that on the day of Lincoln's assassination an extraordinary change was noticeable in him. Lincoln said: "Gentlemen, something extraordinary will happen, and that very soon." Later he spoke of a dream which came to him for the third time and said: "I am on a deep, broad, rolling river; I am in a boat, and I am falling in! I am falling in!" Six weeks before his assassination he saw a great concourse of mourners in the White House in a dream. The mourners surrounded a coffin in which he saw his own body.

Presidents Garfield, McKinley and Nelson also had premonitions of their coming violent ends. William T. **Stead,** the journalist, had a presentiment that he would not die normally. He thought he would be kicked to death by a mob. Instead, he went down in the "Titanic" in 1912. But strangely enough, in 1892 he had written a fictional story about a ship called the "Majestic," which received a psychic message from a survivor of another ship which had struck an iceberg in the Atlantic. The novelist Emile Zola always dreaded asphyxiation by gas. It was the cause of his death.

A method of experimental premonitions was described by Prof. Richet in *L'Avenir et la Premonition* (1931) and *La Grande Ésperance* (1933). To quote from the latter (p. 198):

"Thirty six pieces of paper, each containing a number written in pencil. They are carefully folded, all alike. Armand, a painter of my friends, the brother of Brigitta, indicates the number which Brigitta is going to draw. There are errors, certainly. Armand is not always correct, but the result is far superior to the probability. There are periods of error and periods of astonishing lucidity. At my formal recommendation Armand only makes one experiment per day which gives the probability of 1/36. Well, during a certain week, in six draws, his predictions was five times correct. This is about 1/30,000,000."

We have no satisfactory explanation of premonitions. Possibly Prof. Richet was right when he stated: "If we knew the totality of things in the present we should know the totality of things to come. Our ignorance of the future is the result of our ignorance of the present."

According to novelist Maurice **Maeterlinck,** the phenomenon of premonitions is far less exceptional than generally thought. He believed in "human foreknowledge." He observed that the great catastrophes usually claim fewer victims than the probabilities of each case would allow. He found that generally some strange chance keeps away a number of people who otherwise would be there and perish. They are warned by a mysterious, unfailing instinct.

The conclusion, drawn by Prof. Richet from the reality of premonitions, that the future is determined, seems obvious but not necessarily the right one. The basis of premonitions need not be the supposition of an Eternal Present. If time is an illusion of earthly existence, our unknown powers may occasionally place us outside time and give us a glimpse of the accomplished future. Premonition, in that sense, would in no way interfere with free agency, for what the seer sees would always be the result of free choice and not a preordained course.

In each case, premonition announces a future state which cannot be altered. If, therefore, the announcement did not come to pass, we do not have true premonition. The forecast might have been based on the potential instead of the accomplished future. In everyday life we often make such forecasts. With psychic perceptions they might be made with far greater accuracy, yet they will not be infallible. The trouble is that there is no telling whether a certain announcement has been made on the potential or accomplished future, except, perhaps, an announcement of distant events with minute and humanly unforeseeable detail.

Several bureaux now exist for the registration of premonitions, so that they may be properly validated:

Central Premonitions Registry, Box 482 Times Square Station, New York, NY 10036

The Southern California SPR, via Carolyn Jones, 4325 East Broadway, Long Beach, California 90803

Toronto Society for Psychical Research, 10 North Sherbourne Street, Toronto 5, Ontario, Canada

(See also **Central Premonitions Registry; Precognition; Prediction; Prophecy; Retrocognition**)

Recommended reading:

Barker, J. C. *Scared to Death; An Examination of Fear, Its Causes and Effects,* Muller, London, 1958; Dell paperback, 1969

Brier, Robert. *Precognition and the Philosophy of Science; An Essay on Backward Causation,* Humanities Press, New York, 1973

Dunne, J. W. *An Experiment With Time,* Macmillan, London, 1927; Hillary, New York, 1958

Greenhouse, Herbert B. *Premonitions; A Leap Into the Future,* Turnstone Press, London, 1972; Warner paperback, 1973; Pan paperback, London, 1975

Jaffé, Aniela. *Apparitions and Precognition; A Study From the Point of View of C. G. Jung's Analytical Psychology,* University Books, 1963

MacKenzie, Andrew. *The Riddle of the Future; A Modern Study of Precognition,* Barker, London, 1974; Taplinger, 1975

Osborn, Arthur W. *The Future Is Now; The Significance of Precognition,* University Books, 1962

Saltmarsh, H. F. *Foreknowledge,* G. Bell, London, 1938

Prenestine Lots, The

Also known as *Sortes Prenestinæ.* A method of **divination** by lots, in vogue in Italy in early times. The letters of the alphabet were placed in an urn which was shaken, and the letters then turned out on the floor; the words thus formed were received as omens. In the East, a similar method of divination was also common. (See also **Divination**)

Presentiment

Personal premonition of vague events still in the future. (See **Premonition**)

Preta

Hindu term for the soul of a departed. After death the soul was said to inhabit a subtle body of the size of a man's thumb and remain in the keeping of Yama, judge of the dead. Punishment or reward arises for the *Preta,* depending upon the actions of the individual's life, and may involve many rebirths.

Eventually through faith and enlightenment, the soul is translated to the heaven of the *Pitris* (the Manes or progenitors of the human race).

Prevision

Foreknowledge of the future acquired in a visual form. Such visions are mostly spontaneous.But there are means of experimentally inducingthem through **crystal gazing** and other forms of **divination.**

The experiments of Col. **Rochas** stand in a class by themselves. He plunged his hypnotic subjects by longitudinal passes back into past phases of their life and brought them back to transversal passes. If these passes were continued beyond the present age the subject went into the future. Unfortunately the subjects passed out of the sphere of Col. Rochas' observation and the future could not be verified. Modern experiments of this kind are known as "hypnotic regression." (See Arnall **Bloxham**)

Examination of the circumstances of such cases suggests that they are often simply subjective fancies.

Those who contend that prevision is primarily an attribute of life in the spiritual world may quote in support the interesting story of Florence Marryat in her book *There is No Death* (1892) of an instance in which her own spirit was summoned by friends, sitting in a circle, while she was fast asleep in her home. Her spirit begged to be sent back with the words: "There is a great danger hanging over my children, I must go back to my children." The day after the seance, her brother-in-law accidentally discharged a rifle in the midst of her seven children, the ball passing through the wall within two inches of her eldest daughter's head.

The mechanism of prevision was described in an interesting way in Vincent Turvey's *The Beginnings of Seership* (1911): "At certain times I see a sort of film or ribbon continually moving as does an endless belt in a cinematograph film. This film is in colour of a very, very pale pinky-heliotrope, and it seems to vibrate with very great velocity. Upon it are numerous little pictures, some of which appear to be engraved on the film itself, whilst others are like pale blue photographs stuck on the film. The former I have found to refer to past events, the latter to those about to happen. The locality of the event is judged by the scenery and the climatic heat. I have to estimate dates by the clearness of the pictures. I foresee more unpleasant than pleasant things. I believe the reason to be that evil, being nearer to matter than to spirit, is more ponderous in the ether than its opposite, and is therefore sensed more easily by a Seer. I not only see, but feel, the density of evil."

Prevision was both sentimentally and physically painful to Mr. Turvey. If the event foreseen was a murder or an accident in which pain would be felt by the victim, he actually felt the pain. When he described a revolver mystery which eventually happened, he felt as if shot through the head and when he foresaw a robbery in which the watchman was stunned by a blow he felt it delivered on his own head. (See also **Crystal Gazing; Prediction**)

Recommended reading:

Besterman, Theodore. *Crystal Gazing; A Study in the History, Distribution, Theory and Practice of Scrying,* William Rider, London, 1924; University Books, 1965

Grey, E. Howard. *Visions, Previsions and Miracles in Modern Times,* L. N. Fowler, London, 1915

Turvey, Vincent N. *The Beginnings of Seership,* Stead's Publishing House, London, 1911; University Books, 1969

Price, E(lias) Alan (1918-)

Physician and radiologist who has also been concerned with parapsychology. Born April 15, 1918 at

Dolhinow, Poland, he studied at University of Witwatersrand, South Africa (M.B., Ch.B) and at London University College Hospital, England (D.M.R.D. diagnostic radiology 1953). In 1951 he married Ellen Katzenstein.

He served in the Israeli Army from 1948-49, was resident house physician from 1949-51, consultant radiologist from 1954-58 at Johannesburg General Hospital, Johannesburg, South Africa, in private medical practice at Johannesburg from 1958 onwards.

He is a member of the Society for Psychical Research, London, founder-member in 1955 of the South African Society for Psychical Research (vice-president 1956-57, president 1958, executive member from 1959 onwards). In addition to his articles on radiology and medical subjects, Dr. Price is co-author with Dr. Marius **Valkhoff** and Dr. J. H. Van Der Merwe of *Parapsychology and Modern Science* (1958, South African Society for Psychical Research).

He has also studied the diagnoses of a successful practitioner of medical radiesthesia.

Price, George R(obert) (1922-)

Writer on chemistry and biology, who has also published articles critical of the findings of parapsychology. Born October 16, 1922 at Scarsdale, New York, he studied at Harvard University and at University of Chicago (B.S. 1943, Ph.D. chemistry 1946). In 1947 he married Julia Edith Madigan (divorced 1955).

He was engaged in chemical research at Manhattan Project, University of Chicago from 1944-46, was instructor in chemistry at Harvard, consultant to Argonne National Laboratory 1946-48, member of technical staff of Bell Telephone Laboratories from 1948-50, research associate in medicine at University of Minnesota from 1950-57, writer from 1957 onwards. He is a fellow of the American Association for the Advancement of Science and member of the Association for Computing Machinery.

In August 1955, Dr. Price started a controversy by publishing an article in *Science* magazine (Journal of the American Association for the Advancement of Science) which criticized the findings of parapsychologists as "dependent on clerical and statistical errors and unintentional use of sensory clues" and claimed that "all extra-chance results not so explicable are dependent on deliberate fraud or mildly abnormal mental conditions."

This article was widely quoted by newspapers and journals. It suggested various fraudulent methods which might be used to show such results as those claimed by parapsychologists like Dr. J. B. **Rhine** and Dr. S. B. **Soal,** and stated that their claims were not acceptable as proof of ESP. Dr. Rhine and Dr. Soal replied to these criticisms in the *Newsletter of the Parapsychology Foundation* (October 1955) which also published a further statement from Dr. Price. The controversy over Soal's experiments continued after his death in 1975, and there is now a strong case for believing that Soal consciously or unconsciously manipulated his date (see 'The Soal-Goldney Experiments with Basil Shackleton; New Evidence of Data Manipulation' by Betty Markwick, *Proceedings* of the Society for Psychical Research, vol. 56, 1978).

The skeptical attitude of Dr. Price has some importance in the history of the development of parapsychology, since it represented a backlash of orthodox scientists of the time, particularly by members of the American Association for the Advancement of Science, a body which for sometime persistently refused to permit affiliation by the **Parapsychological Association.**

On the positive side, skeptical and hostile criticisms stimulated parapsychologists to develop methods of testing extrasensory perception which could not be faulted by scientists. The most significant indication of the acceptability of Parapsychology as a proper scientific study was the acceptance of the Parapsychological Society into membership of the American Association for the Advancement of Science in December 1969. Dr. Price's articles in *Science* magazine were 'Science and the Supernatural' (August 26, 1955) and 'Where Is the Definitive Experiment?' (January 6, 1956).

Price, Harry (1881-1948)

Prominent British psychical researcher, pioneer of scientific investigation of psychical phenomena, founder and honorary director of the National Laboratory of Psychical Research, London, former foreign research officer of the American Society for Psychical Research. He represented British psychical research at the International Psychic Exhibition held at Copenhagen in 1925.

In a lifetime of research into the abnormal and uncanny, he also became chairman of the National Film Library of the British Film Institute, honorary curator of numismatics at Ripon Museum, and Fellow of the Numismatic Society. He took a prominent part in achaeological excavations in Greenwich Park and discovered a prehistoric cave in Shropshire. He assisted the early flying experiments of José Weiss, a year before the historic flight of the Wright Brothers at Kitty Hawk. He was also a well-known amateur conjurer, a member of the Magic Circle, and was elected to the Society of American Magicians, and from 1921 onwards was honorary librarian of the exclusive Magician's Club.

He was born January 17, 1881, educated at London and Shropshire. His interest in conjuring dated from his boyhood, when he watched the medicine show of "The Great Sequah" at a fairground, a performance complete with quack remedies, tooth drawing and magical tricks. His fascination with conjuring magic was of great value in his later investigation of claimed mediumship. At the age of fifteen, he conducted his first scientific investigation of poltergeist phenomena, staying until midnight in a reputed haunted house with photographic apparatus and flash powder.

As a psychical researcher, he made significant contributions with his investigations of Stella C., Eleonore Zügun and Rudi Schneider. He was a tireless publicist for the cause of psychical research, and his most newsworthy activity was his expedition to the Hartz Mountains, Germany, during the Goethe centenary of 1932, to test a fifteenth-century white magic ritual said to change a goat into a "fair youth of surpassing beauty."

Seventy-three pressmen, forty-two photographers, and a film cameraman all assembled to record this sensational story. Not surprisingly, the goat was not metamorphosed, but magic and psychical phenomena became a talking point all over the world.

Price also attracted great attention by his investigation of Borley Rectory, Essex, "The Most Haunted House in England," and his connection (with R. S. **Lambert**) with the weird story of the **Talking Mongoose** of the Isle of Man.

Price published many books and pamphlets, including: *Coins of Kent and Kentish Tokens* (1902), *Shropshire Tokens and Mints* (1902), *Cold Light on Spiritualistic Phenomena* (1922), *Stella C.; An Account of Some Original Experiments in Psychical Research* (1925), *Short-Title Catalogue of Works on Psychical Research, Spiritualism, Magic, etc.* (1929), *Rudi Schneider; A Scientific Examination of His Mediumship* (1930), *Regurgitation and the Duncan Mediumship* (1931), *An Account of Some Further Experiments with Rudi Schneider* (1933), *Leaves From a Psychist's Case-Book* (1933), *Confessions of a Ghost-Hunter* (1936; 1974), *A Report on Two Experimental Fire-Walks* (1936), (with R. S. Lambert) *The Haunting of Cashen's Gap* (1936), *Fifty Years of Psychical Research* (1939), *The Most Haunted House in England; Ten Years' Investigation of Borley Rectory* (1940), *Search for Truth; My Life for Psychical Research* (1942), *Poltergeist Over England* (1945), *The End of Borley Rectory* (1946).

He also made an early talking picture "Psychical Research" in 1935, contributed an article on 'Faith and Fire-Walking' to the *Encyclopedia Britannica,* 1936, and collaborated on a film script of the Borley hauntings with novelist Upton Sinclair.

Price died March 29, 1948. His collection of some 20,000 volumes of works on psychical research, magic, and related subjects, passed to the University of London as the Harry Price Library of Magical Literature.

After his death, Price was accused by fellow psychical researchers of helping out or faking some of the Borley Rectory phenomena. For details, see the article 'The Haunting of Borley Rectory; A Critical Survey of the Evidence' by E. J. Dingwall, K. M. Goldney & Trevor H. Hall (*Proceedings* of the Society for Psychical Research, vol. 51, pp. i-xiv, 1-181) also *Journal* of the S.P.R. vol. 38, pp. 200, 229, vol. 39, Suppl. 21, ii, vol. 38, pp. 249-64, vol. 39, pp. 304-05, vol. 42, pp. 370-73, 420-22.

There are two biographies of Price.

Harry Price; The Biography of a Ghost Hunter by Paul Tabori (1950), his executor, presents a sympathetic and comprehensive picture of Price's life and activities.

Search for Harry Price by Trevor H. Hall (1978) is relentlessly critical of every aspect of Price and his activities, presenting him as a poseur, fraud and dishonest investigator. It is cleverly done, with a wealth of research and background detail, and it will be remembered that Trevor H. Hall also attempted to demolish the character of Sir William **Crookes** in his equally carefully researched book *The Spiritualists* (1962).

The case seems overstated. No doubt Price was vain, given to boasting and exaggeration, possessive about his work and sometimes deceptive. These are common human failings, and should not detract from a fair evaluation of the pioneer work of Price in psychical research.

In Paul Tabori's biography of Price, Mrs. Lucie Meeker, Price's secretary for five years, wrote of his courage, indefatigable capacity for work and his generosity. Tabori stated that his death was a great loss to psychical research, and that he was a most loyal friend.

Recommended reading:

Hall, Trevor H. *Search for Harry Price,* Duckworth, London/Southwest Book Services, Texas, 1978

Price, Harry. *Confessions of a Ghost-Hunter,* Putnam, London, 1936; Causeway Books, 1974

Price, Harry. *Fifty Years of Psychical Research,* Longmans, London, 1939; Arno Press, 1975

Price, Harry. *Leaves From a Psychist's Case-Book,* Gollancz, London, 1933

Price, Harry. *Search for Truth; My Life for Psychical Research,* Collins, London, 1942

Price, Harry & E. J. Dingwall (eds.). *Revelations of a Spirit Medium,* Kegan Paul, London & New York, 1922

Tabori, Paul. *Harry Price; The Biography of a Ghost-Hunter,* Athenænum Press, London, 1930

Price, Henry Habberley (1899-1984)

Emeritus professor of logic who also became a prominent figure in the field of parapsychology. Born May 17, 1899 at Neath, South Wales, Britain, he was educated at Winchester College and New College, Oxford (M.A., B.S. Oxford, Hon. D.Litt. Dublin, Hon. D.C.L., St. Andrews). He was a fellow of Magdalen College, Oxford from 1922-24, fellow of Trinity College, Oxford from 1924-35, Wykeham Professor of Logic, University of Oxford, fellow of New College, Oxford, from 1935-59, subsequently emeritus fellow of New College, Gifford Lecturer at Aberdeen University from 1959-60, Visiting professor at Princeton University, N.J. in 1948, University of California at Los Angeles 1962.

He was president of the Society for Psychical Research, London from 1939-41, subsequently a council member, charter member of the Parapsychological Association, member of the Aristotelian Society, Mind Association. His books included: *Perception* (1932), *Hume's Theory of the External World* (1940), *Thinking and Experience* (1953).

In the field of parapsychology, he published articles on such subjects as telepathy, apparitions, mediumship and survival. His contributions to the SPR *Proceedings* included: 'Haunting and the "Psychic

Ether" Hypothesis' (vol.45, 1939), 'Survival and the Idea of Another World' (vol.50, Jan. 1953), in the journal *Philosophy:* 'Some Philosophical Questions About Telepathy and Clairvoyance' (October 1940), in the *Hibbert Journal:* 'Psychical Research and Human Personality' (January 1949), in *Newsletter of the Parapsychology Foundation:* 'The Divisible Mind' (Jan.-Feb. 1955), in *Light:* 'Disbelief in the problem of Survival' (vol.79, 1959).

His books included: *Perception* (1932; 1973), *Hume's Theory of the External World* (1940), *Thinking and Experience* (1953), *Belief* (Gifford Lectures, 1969), *Essays in the Philosophy of Religion* (1972).

He also delivered a lecture 'Some Philosophical Implications of Paranormal Cognition' at the International Conference on Philosophy and Parapsychology, St. Paul de Vence, France in 1954.

He died in Oxford, England, November 26, 1984, at the age of 85.

Price-Mars, Jean (1875-1969)

Haitian educator and diplomat who also studied parapsychology. Born October 15, 1875 at Grande-Rivière du Nord, Haiti, he studied at University of Dakar, French West Africa (Hon. LL.D.). In 1930 he married Clara Perez.

Dr. Price-Mars was a professor and rector of the University of Haiti, and a member of the Haitian Senate. Since 1900 he served in the Haitian diplomatic service in Germany, the U.S., France, the Dominican Republic, the U.N., and as Minister of Foreign Affairs. He published various books on the folklore, history, culture and ethnology of Haiti.

He took a special interest in parapsychology in relation to Vodun (voodoo). His article 'Africa in the Americas' was published in *Tomorrow* (Autumn 1954).

Prince, Morton (1854-1929)

Physician, neurologist, psychologist who was also concerned with areas of parapsychology. Born December 21, 1854 at Boston, Massachusetts, he studied at Boston Latin School, Harvard (B.A. 1875), Harvard Medical School (M.D. 1879) and also in Vienna, Strasbourg, Paris and Nancy. In 1885 he married Fanny Lithgow Payson.

He was particularly interested in the work of Jean Charcot and Pierre Janet in hysteria and hypnosis. He was a physician for diseases of the nervous system at Boston Dispensary from 1882-86 and Boston City Hospital from 1885-1913, instructor in neurology at Harvard Medical School from 1895-98, professor of neurology at Tufts Medical School from 1902-12, subsequently professor emeritus; associate professor, abnormal and dynamic psychology at Harvard University from 1926-28.

He was founder and editor from 1906-29 of the *Journal of Abnormal Psychology,* president in 1911 of the American Psychological Association (serving as president on both societies), member of the American Society for Psychical Research. As a leading neurologist, Dr. Prince delivered lectures at universities in the U.S. and Britain. His books include: *The Nature of Mind and Human Automatism* (1885), *The Unconscious* (1913), *The Psychology of the Kaiser* (1915), *Clinical and Experimental Studies in Personality* (1929).

His book on *The Dissociation of a Personality* (1906) dealt with the famous case of "Sally Beauchamp" and is considered a basic work in the field of abnormal psychology, with an important bearing on the parapsychological phenomenon of secondary and multiple personality. In addition to his many articles on medical and psychological subjects, Dr. Prince also contributed to the *Proceedings* of the Society for Psychical Research, London: 'A Contribution to the Study of Hysteria' (vol.14, 1899), 'The Development and Genealogy of the Misses Beauchamp' (vol.15, 1900-01).

Recommended reading:

Taylor, W. S. *Morton Prince and Abnormal Psychology,* 1928

Prince, Walter Franklin (1863-1934)

Prominent American psychical researcher, research officer of the **American Society for Psychical Research** from 1920-24, founder and research officer of the **Boston Society for Psychical Research** 1931-32, president of the **Society for Psychical Research,** London, 1930-31.

He was born in Detroit, Maine, April 22, 1863 and attended the Maine Wesleyan Seminary, graduating in 1881. He went on to Yale, where he received the degrees of B.A. (1896) and Ph.D (1899), and to Drew Theological Seminary (B.D., 1896). In 1885, he married Lelia Madora Colman (died 1925).

He became pastor of Methodist Episcopal Churches in Maine and Connecticut, then of Protestant Episcopal Churches in Brooklyn, Pittsburgh and San Bernardino, California.

Through his church social work he was led to study abnormal psychology. From 1916-17, he was director of psychotherapeutics at St. Mark's Episcopal Church, New York City, afterwards becoming assistant to Dr. James Hervey **Hyslop,** founder of the American Society for Psychical Research. His books included: *The Psychic in the House* (1926), *The Case of Patience Worth* (1927), (with Lydia W. Allison) *Leonard and Soule Experiments* (1929), *The Enchanted Foundary; A Survey to Negative Reactions to Claims of Psychic Phenomena* (1930). He also published important papers on 'The Doris Case of Multiple Personality,' 'Psychometric Experiments with Senora Maria Reyes De Z.,' 'Survey of American Slate-writing Mediumship,' 'Past Events Seership; A Study in Psychometry,' 'Experiments with Physical Mediums in Europe,' 'Human Experiences; A Report on the Results of a Questionnaire Sent to 10,000 Persons Listed in *Who's Who in America.*'

He was responsible for a remarkable cure in the multiple personality case of Doris Fischer, and conducted important investigations of the cases of **"Patience Worth"** and the Antigonish poltergeist.

In eighteen years of research with the American Society for Psychical Research and the Society for Psychical Research, London, Dr. Prince investigated many different kinds of paranormal phenomena in hundreds of cases, but in spite of his doubts about certain phenomena, he eventually concluded that a case for the reality of telepathy and clairvoyance has been "absolutely and scientifically proved." In addition, he was inclined to belief in survival of personality after death and considered the evidence "very promising."

He was a delegate to the First International Congress on Psychical Research, Copenhagen, in 1921, and the Third International Congress in Paris, 1927.

For biographical information see 'Walter Franklin Prince' by Also J. Smith (*Tomorrow,* Summer 1955). He died August 7, 1934.

Private UFO Investigations (Group)

Organization concerned with UFO reports and international sightings. Issues a quarterly publication *The UFO Examiner.* Address: Route 1, Hazelton, Iowa 50641.

Probe—The Unknown (Magazine)

Bi-monthly publication which includes articles on psychic phenomena, Astrology, Tarot and ESP generally, with readers forum and book reviews. Address: 1845 W. Empire Street, Burbank, California 91504.

Probe (Woonsocket) (Magazine)

Quarterly magazine concerned with controversial phenomena. Published by Joseph L. Ferriere, 132 Fifth Avenue, Woonsocket, Rhode Island 02895.

Probing the Unexplained (Newsletter)

Newsletter of the International Association for Investigation of the Unexplained; includes articles and news concerning UFOs and other mysteries, book reviews, local events. Address: P.O. Box 441, Edmond, Oklahoma 73034.

Proceedings (of Psychical Research Societies)

Official publications of the societies for psychical research. The first in the field was the *Proceedings* of the **Society for Psychical Research,** London, the second the *Proceedings* of the old **American Society for Psychical Research** (1885-89), the third the *Proceedings* of the independent A.S.P.R. (1907-27) and the fourth the *Proceedings* of the **National Laboratory of Psychical Research.** The **Boston Society for Psychical Research** issued books and Bulletins, but no Proceedings.

Proceedings of the first four psychical research societies cited above, and the reconstituted American Society for Psychical Research from 1907 onwards, are the subject of separate entries.

Proceedings of the American Society for Psychical Research

The first two decades of the A.S.P.R. were important years in the history of psychical research in the U.S. and were reflected in the published *Proceedings* listed below.

Vol. 1, 1907

Part 1. History of the American Institute for Scientific Research. Introduction by James H. Hyslop. Address by Dr. R. Heber Newton: The Dogmatism of Science. Some Facts in Mesmerism, by Dr. Weston D. Bailey. Prospectus of the American Institute. Letter on Animal Magnetism, by William L. Stone. An Examination of M. Aksakof's Case of Partial Dematerialisation of a Medium's Body, by Hereward Carrington. Parallelism and Materialism, by James H. Hyslop.

Part 2. A case of Clairvoyance, by Prof. William James. A Record of Experiences, by G. A. T. The McCaffrey Case, by James Hyslop. A Case of Alleged Movement of Physical Objects Without Contact, by James H. Hyslop and Hereward Carrington.

Part 3. Preliminary Report of the Trance Phenomena of Mrs. Smead, by James H. Hyslop.

Vol. 2, 1908

Part 4. Lily Dale: A Report of a Two Weeks' Investigation into Alleged Spiritualistic Phenomena, Witnessed at Lily Dale, New York, by Hereward Carrington.

Part 5. Report on the Case of Miss Edith Wright, by the Rev. Willis M. Cleveland. Clairvoyant Diagnosis, and other Experiments, by James H. Hyslop. Experiments with the Planchette by Egbert L. Monson. A Record of Experiences in Planchette Writing, by Charles Morris. A Record of Experiments, by Helen Lambert.

Part 6. A Further Record of Experiments by Helen Lambert. A Record of Dreams and other Coincidental Experiences, by Marie F. Shipley. A Record of Experiences, by G. A. T.

Vol. 3, 1909

Part 7. A Case of Veridical Hallucinations, by James H. Hyslop. Report on Mrs. Piper's Hodgson Control, by William James.

Part 8. Observations on the Mediumistic Records in the Thompson Case, by J. H. Hyslop. The Subconscious in the Light of Dream Imagery and Imaginative Expression, by Hartley B. Alexander.

Vol. 4, 1910

Part 9. A Record and Discussion of Mediumistic Experiments, by J. H. Hyslop.

Vol. 5, 1911

Part 10. A Case of Hysteria, by Dr. W. H. Hamilton, Dr. J. S. Smyth, and J. H. Hyslop.

Part 11. Experiments and Experiences in Telepathy, by Miss Miles, Miss Ramsden and Miss Statkowski.

Vol. 6, 1912

Part 12. A Record of Experiments, by J. H. Hyslop.

Vol. 7, 1913

Part 13. The Subconscious and its Function, by J. H. Hyslop.

Part 14. A Case of Poltergeist, by J. H. Hyslop.

Part 15. A Case of Medical Control, by J. H. Hyslop. The Case of Mrs. Blake, by Dr. L. V. Guthrie, David P. Abbot, J. H. Hyslop and Mr. and Mrs. Clawson.

Vol. 8, 1914

Part 16. Experiments with Mrs. Caton, by Henry A. Burr. Telepathic Experiments, by J. H. Hyslop.

Part 17. Investigation with a Trumpet Medium, by John E. Coover. F. W. H. Myers, Swedenborg and Buddha, by A. J. Edmunds. An Analysis and Discussion of 225 Personal Dreams, by George Hall Hyslop. An Analysis of Some Personal Dreams, by John Watson. Note on Philosophies and Revelations from the Spiritual World.

Part 18. On Some Experiments with the Ouija Board and Blindfolded Sitters, by Sir William F. Barrett. Some Unusual Phenomena of Photography, by J. H. Hyslop. Recent Experiments in Hypnotic Practice, by Sidney Silkinson. Experiment in Non-Evidential Phenomena, by J. H. Hyslop.

Vol. 9, 1915

Part 19. The Doris Case of Multiple Personality, by Dr. W. F. Prince.

Vol. 10, 1916

Part 20. The Doris Case of Multiple Personality, II, by Dr. W. F. Prince.

Vol. 11, 1917

Part 21. The Doris Case of Multiple Personality, III, by J. H. Hyslop. The Patison Case, by J. H. Hyslop.

Vol. 12, 1918

Part 22. The Smead Case, by J. H. Hyslop.

Vol. 13, 1919-20

Part 23. Chance Coincidence and Guessing in a Mediumistic Experiment, by J. H. Hyslop. A Critical Study of The Great Amherst Mystery, by Dr. W. F. Prince. A Case of Pictographic Phenomena, by J. H. Hyslop. Rolf of Mannheim—A Great Psychological Problem, by W. MacKenzie.

Part 24. The Harrison Case, by Prescott F. Hall. A Case of Incipient Possession, by J. H. Hyslop. Supplementary Report on the Keeler-Lee Photographs, by W. F. Prince. A Note on the Mannheim Dog Case, by Gertrude Ogden Tubby.

Vol. 14, 1920

Part 25. Cross-Reference Experiments for Mark Twain, by J. H. Hyslop. Miscellaneous Incidents Experienced or Collected and Reported, by Mrs. Kezia E. Alexander. Experiences Centering in the Young Family, by Oscar E. Young and others. Experiences in a House, by Mrs. Elizabeth G. Wood.

Vol. 15, 1921

Part 26. The Chenoweth-Drew Automatic Scripts, by J. H. Hyslop. Psychometrical Experiments with Senora Maria Reyes de Z., by Walter F. Prince. A Survey of American Slate Writing Mediumship, by W. F. Prince.

Vol. 16, 1922-23

Part 27. Past Events Seership, by Gustave Pagenstecher, M.D.

Vol. 17, 1923

Part 28. The Mother of Doris, by W. F. Prince. Heinrich Meyer Case, by W. F. Prince. The Charleburg Record, by Nellie M. Smith.

Vol. 18, 1924

Part 29. Five Sittings with Mrs. Sanders, by W. F. Prince. Studies in Psychometry, by W. F. Prince.

Vol. 19, 1925

Part 30. A Further Record of Mediumistic Experiments, by J. H. Hyslop.

Vols. 20-21, 1926-27

Part 31. The Margery Mediumship, Vol. 1, edited by J. M. Bird. The Margery Mediumship, Vol. 2, edited by J. M. Bird.

After 1927 the regular publication of the *Proceedings* was discontinued to give a larger scope to the *Journal.* (See also **Proceedings of the Old American Society for Psychical Research**)

Proceedings of the College of Universal Wisdom

Publication edited by George W. **Van Tassell** (died 1978), author of *I Rode in a Flying Saucer* (1952) and organizer of **Giant Rock Space Convention,** held annually at Giant Rock Airport, near Yucca Valley, California. Van Tassell claimed to have visits from inhabitants of UFOs and to contact them telepathically. Claimed messages from **UFO** entities were published in the *Proceedings.* No longer issued.

Proceedings of the Institute of Psychophysical Research

Irregular publication in book form of researches undertaken by the Institute into paranormal phenomena. Vol. I is titled *Lucid Dreams* by Celia (E.) **Green** (London, 1968); Vol. II is titled *Out-of-the-Body Experiences* by Celia (E.) Green (London, 1968). Address: Institute of Psychophysical Research, 118 Banbury Road, Oxford, OX2 6JN, England.

Proceedings of the National Laboratory of Psychical Research

The **National Laboratory of Psychical Research** was founded by psychical researcher Harry **Price** for scientific investigation of phenomena. The *Proceedings* published from 1927-29 contain valuable material.

Part 1, January 1927. *A Report on the Telekinetic and other phenomena witnessed through Eleonore Zügun.*

Part 2, April 1929. *Short-Title Catalogue of Works on Psychical Research, Spiritualism, Magic, Psychology, Legerdemain and Other Methods of Deception, Charlatanism, Witchcraft and Technical Works for the Scientific Investi-*

gation of Alleged Abnormal Phenomena from circa 1450 a.d. to 1919 a.d.

In 1934, the National Laboratory of Psychical Research was taken over by the University of London Council for Psychical Research, London, and published various issues of a *Bulletin* concerned with psychical research. *Bulletin I* issued in 1935 was a *Supplement* to the *Short-Title Catalogue.*

The National Laboratory of Psychical Research also issued a *Bulletin* of psychical investigations.

Proceedings of the Old American Society for Psychical Research

The American Society for Psychical Research was originally formed in 1885 as an independent organization until 1889, when it became a branch of the British Society for Psychical Research, under the leadership of Dr. Richard **Hodgson.** When Dr. Hodgson died in 1905, the branch was dissolved, and after a year of preparation, the present American Society for Psychical Research was formed under the leadership of Dr. James H. **Hyslop.** The main *Proceedings* of the original A.S.P.R. from 1885-89 continued the following studies:

First Report of the Committee on Thought-Transference

The Number Habit, Reports of Committees on Hypnotism, Mediumistic Phenomena, Thought transference, etc.

Experiments in Thought-Transferences

The Reality of Reichenbach's Flames

On the Supernatural Among the Omaha Tribe of Indians by Alice C. Fletcher, Criticism of Phantoms of the Living by C. S. Pierce; Reply by Edmund Gurney

Deductions Suggested by the Study of Hypnotic Phenomena by C. B. Cory

Reaction Time in the Hypnotic Trance by Prof. W. James

Some Experiments in Thought-Transference by Mr. and Mrs. John F. Brown

Report of the Committee on Phantasms and Presentiments by Prof. J. Royce

On Some Objections to the Theory of Telepathy by Dr. Richard Hodgson

Notes on Automatic Writing by Prof. William James

Notes on Two Recently Reported Cases of Pathological and Other Pseudo-Presentiments by Prof. J. Royce (See also **Proceedings of the American Society for Psychical Research**)

Proceedings of the Parapsychological Association

Annual publication from 1966 onwards "to provide a published record of the annual convention of the Parapsychological Association." This scholarly journal was edited by W. G. **Roll,** R. L. Morris and J. D. Morris, Nos. 1-7 inclusive published by the Parapsychological Association, c/o Psychical Research Foundation, Duke Station, Durham, North Carolina 27706, thereafter by Scarecrow Press Inc., Metuchen, New Jersey, as an annual volume of abstracts and papers under the running title *Research in Parapsychology.*

The current address of the Parapsychological Association is: P.O. Box 12236, Research Triangle Park, North Carolina 27709.

Proceedings of the Psychological Society of Great Britain

A volume, published in London in 1880 with reports of the papers and discussions in Sergeant **Cox**'s Society for 1875-79. The Society expired by 1880 and no further papers were published.

Contents include:

E. W. Cox, 'The Province of Psychology'
'On some of the Phenomena of Sleep and Dreams'
'Some more Phenomena of Sleep and Dream'
George Harris, 'The Psychology of Memory'
E. W. Cox, 'The Duality of the Mind'
'Sessional Address'
Professor Tyndall's article on 'Materialism and its Opponents' in the *Fortnightly Review*
George Harris, 'Caligraphy considered as affording an Exhibition of Character'
E. W. Cox, 'Matter and Spirit'
'The Psychology of Memory and Recollection'
'The Progress and Prospects of Psychology'
Charles Bray, 'Cerebral Psychology'
'Natural Law'
E. W. Cox, 'Has Man a Soul?'
James Croll, 'Psychology Proved by Physical Science'
E. W. Cox, 'The Claims of Psychology to a Place in the Circle of the Sciences'
'The Psychology of Hamlet'
'Protoplasm and Psychology'

There is a copy of this volume in the library of the Society for Psychical Research, London.

Proceedings of the Society for Psychical Research

The Society was founded in 1882 and has published *Proceedings* since then. The *Journal* was first published from 1883 onwards and until 1949 was available only to members of the Society.

The *Proceedings* for the first half century of the Society's existence offer a comprehensive view of psychical research over that period and the main contents are detailed below for their historic interest.

A *Combined Index* to the *Journal* and the *Proceedings* is issued by the Society.

Vol. 1, 1882-83

Part 1. Objects of the Society. First Presidential Address, by Prof. H. Sidgwick. First Report of the Committee on Thought-Reading. Note on Thought-Reading, by Prof. Balfour Stewart. Note on Thought-Reading, by Rev. A. M. Creery. Appendix to the Report on Thought-Reading, by Prof. W. F. Barrett.

Part 2. Second Presidential Address, by Prof. H. Sidgwick. Second Report of the Committee on Thought-Transference. Preliminary Report of the "Reichenbach" Committee. First Report of the Committee on "Haunted Houses." First Report of the Literary Committee.

Part 3. Third Report of the Committee on Thought-Transference. First Report of the Committee on Mesmerism. First Report of the "Reichenbach" Committee. On Some Phenomena Associated with Abnormal Conditions of Mind, by Prof. W. F. Barrett.

Part 4. Third Presidential Address, by Prof. H. Sidgwick. Second Report of the Committee on Mesmerism. Record of Experiments in Thought-Transference at Liverpool, by Malcolm Guthrie, J. P., and James Birchall. Note on Muscle-Reading, by the Rev. E. H. Sugden.

Vol. 2, 1884

Part 5. Fourth Report of the Committee on Thought-Transference. Third Report of the Committee on Mesmerism. An Account of some Experiments in Thought-Transference, by Malcolm Guthrie, J. P. Second Report of the Literary Committee. The Stages of Hypnotism, by Edmund Gurney. Report on Wells Sunk at Locking, Somerset, to Test the Alleged Power of the Divining Rod, by Prof. W. J. Sollas. The Divining Rod, by Edward R. Pease.

Part 6. A Theory of Apparitions. Second Report of the Committee on Haunted Houses, etc. Fourth Presidential Address, by Prof. H. Sidgwick. An Account of some Experiments in Thought-Transference, by Prof. Oliver J. Lodge, D.Sc. An Account of some Experiments in Mesmerism, by Edmund Gurney.

Part 7. On a Telepathic Explanation of some so-called Spiritualistic Phenomena, by F. W. H. Myers. M. Richet's Recent Researches in Thought-Transference. The Problems of Hypnotism, by Edmund Gurney.

Vol. 3, 1885

Part 8. Automatic Writing, by F. W. H. Myers. First Presidential Address, by Prof. Balfour Stewart, F.R.S. Notes on the Evidence, collected by the Society, for Phantasms of the Dead, by Mrs. H. Sidgwick. Hallucinations, by Edmund Gurney. The Calculus of Probabilities applied to Psychical Research, I., by F. Y. Edgeworth.

Part 9. Report on Phenomena connected with Theosophy, by Richard Hodgson, Mrs. H. Sidgwick and others. Some Higher Aspects of Mesmerism, by E. Gurney and F. W. H. Myers. Further Report on the Experiments in Thought-Transference at Liverpool, by Malcolm Guthrie, J. P. Local Anaesthesia induced in the Normal State by Mesmeric Passes. Report on an Alleged Physical Phenomenon.

Vol. 4, 1886-87

Part 10. Human Personality in the Light of Hypnotic Suggestion, by F. W. H. Myers. On Some Physical Phenomena, commonly called Spiritualistic, witnessed by the Author, by Prof. W. F. Barrett. Results of a Personal Investigation into the "Physical Phenomena" of Spiritualism, by Mrs. H. Sidgwick. The Possibilities of Mal-Observation in relation to Evidence for the Phenomena of Spiritualism, by C. C. Massey; with discussion by Prof. Sidgwick. Experiments in Muscle-Reading and Thought-Transference, by Max Dessoir. On Telepathic Hypnotism and its relation to other forms of Hypnotic Suggestion, by F. W. H. Myers. The Calculus of Probabilities applied to Psychical Research, II., by F. Y. Edgeworth.

Part 11. Automatic Writing, by F. W. H. Myers. Second Presidential Address, by Prof. Balfour Stewart, F.R.S. Peculiarities of Certain Posthypnotic States, by Edmund Gurney. Experiments in Thought-Transference, by Anton Schmoll. Accounts of some so-called "Spiritualistic" Seances, by Prof. H. Carvill Lewis, M.A., F.G.S., and others. The Possibilities of Mal-Observation and Lapse of Memory from a Practical Point of View, by Richard Hodgson and S. J. Davey. Multiplex Personality, by F. W. H. Myers. Stages of Hypnotic Memory, by Edmund Gurney. Note on Certain Reported Cases of Hypnotic Hyperaesthesia, by F. W. H. Myers. Reviews of Books.

Vol. 5, 1888-89

Part 12. Recent Experiments in Hypnotism, by Edmund Gurney. Reletion de Diverses Expériences sur la Transmission Mentale, la Lucidité et Autres Phénomènes non Explicables par les Données Scientifiques Actuelles, par M. Charles Richet. Experiments in Thought-Transference, by A. Schmoll and J. E. Mabire. Hypnotism, and Telepathy, by Edmund Gurney. Report of the Seybert Commission reviewed by F. W. H. Myers.

Part 13. Fifth Presidential Address, by Prof. H. Sidgwick. The Connection of Hypnotism with the Subjective Phenomena of Spiritualism. On the Evidence for Premonitions, by Mrs. H. Sidgwick. Experiments in Thought-Transference, by Max Dessoir. The Work of Edmund Gurney in Experimental Psychology, by F. W. H. Myers. French Experiments on Strata of Personality, by F. W. H. Myers.

Part 14. Sixth Presidential Address, by Prof. H. Sidgwick. On Apparitions Occurring soon after Death, by the late Edmund Gurney, completed by F. W. H. Myers. Recent Experiments in Crystal Vision. The Daemon of Socrates, by F. W. H. Myers. On a Series of Experiments at Pesaro, by H. Babington Smith. Dr. Albert Moll's "Hypnotism," by Max Dessoir.

Vol. 6, 1889-90

Part 15. Addresses by the President, Prof. Sidgwick, on The Canons of Evidence in Psychical Research and on The Census of Hallucinations. On Recognised Apparitions Occurring more than a Year after Death, by F. W. H. Myers. Further Experiments in Hypnotic Lucidity or Clairvoyance, by Prof. Charles Richet. Duplex Personality, by Thomas Barkworth. Notes on Seances with D. D. Home, by William Crookes, F.R.S. Experiments in Thought-Transference, by Professor and Mrs. H. Sidgwick and Mr. G. A. Smith. Reviews of Books, etc.

Part 16. Phantasms of the Dead: Another Point of View, by F. Podmore. A Defence of Phantasms of the Dead, by F. W. H. Myers. A Record of Telepathic and Other Experiences, by "Miss X." Experimental Comparison between Chance and Thought-Transference in Correspondence of Diagrams, by Lieut.-Col. G. Le M. Taylor. Observations on Clairvoyance, etc., by Drs. Dufay and Azam.

Part 17. A Second Address by the President, Prof. Sidgwick, on the Census of Hallucinations. A Record of Observations of Certain Phenomena of Trance (Mrs. Piper), by F. W. H. Myers; Prof. O. J. Lodge, F.R.S.; Walter Leaf, Ltt.D.; and Prof. William James. Review of A. Aksakof's *Animismus und Spiritismus*, by F. W. H. Myers.

Vol. 7, 1891-92

Part 18. Experimental Studies in Thought-Transference, by Baron von Schrenck-Notzing, M.D. Some Recent Experiments in Automatic Writing, by Thomas Barkworth. On the Evidence for Clairvoyance, by Mrs. H. Sidgwick. Apparitions of the Virgin in Dordogne, by Leon Marillier. Prof. William James' "Principles of Psychology," by F. W. H. Myers.

Part 19. On Alleged Movements of Objects, without Contact, occurring not in the Presence of a Paid Medium, Part I., by F. W. H. Myers. Experiments in Clairvoyance, by Dr. Alfred Backman. A Case of Double Consciousness (Ansel Bourne), by Richard Hodgson. On Spirit Photographs, by Mrs. Henry Sidgwick.

Part 20. The Subliminal Consciousness. Chap I., General Characteristics of Subliminal Messages. Chap. II., The Mechanism of Suggestion, by F. W. H. Myers. Note on a Visit to Kalmar, by F. W. H. Myers. Some Recent Thought-Transference Experiments, by Prof. Oliver J. Lodge, F.R.S. On the Alleged Movements of Objects, without Contact, occurring not in the Presence of a Paid Medium, Part II., by F. W. H. Myers.

Vol. 8, 1892

Part 21. A Record of Observations of Certain Phenomena of Trance (Mrs. Piper), by Richard Hodgson, LL.D.

Part 22. On Indications of continued Terrene Knowledge on the Part of Phantasms of the Dead, by F. W. H. Myers. Mr. Davey's Imitations by Conjuring of Phenomena sometimes attributed to Spirit Agency, by Richard Hodgson, LL.D. Record of a Haunted House, by "Miss R. C. Morton." The Subliminal Consciousness. Chap. III., The Mechanism of Suggestion. Chap. IV., Hypermnesic Dreams, by F. W. H. Myers.

Part 23. De l'Appreciation du Temps par les Somnambules, par M. J. Delboeuf. Some Experiments in Thought-Transference, by Dr. A. Blair Thaw. The Subliminal Consciousness. Chap. V., Sensory Automatism and Induced Hallucinations, by F. W. H. Myers. Experiments in Thought-Transference, by Mrs. H. Sidgwick and Miss Alice Johnson.

Vol. 9, 1893-94

Part 24. The Subliminal Consciousness. Chap. VI., The Mechanism of Hysteria. Chap. VII., Motor Automatism, by F. W. H. Myers. The Defence of the Theosophists, by Richard Hodgson, LL.D. Mind-Cure, Faith-Cure, and the Miracles of Lourdes, by A. T. Myers, M.D., F.R.C.P., and F. W. H. Myers. Reviews of Books.

Part 25. Partial Anaesthesia, by Prof. William Ramsay, F.R.S. The Experiences of W. Stainton Moses, I., by F. W. H. Myers. Indian Magic and the Testimony of Conjurers, by Richard Hodgson, LL.D.

Vol. 10, 1894

Part 26. Presidential Address by the Right Hon. Arthur J. Balfour, M.P., F.R.S. On the Difficulty of making Crucial Experiments as to the Source of the Intelligence Manifested in Trance-Speech, Automatic Writing, etc., by Prof. Oliver J. Lodge, F.R.S. Report on the Census of Hallucinations, by Prof. Sidgwick's Committee.

Vol. 11, 1895

Part 27. Experiments in Thought-Transference, by Henry G. Rawson. Dipsomania and Hypnotism, by J. Gordon Dill, M.A., M.D. The Experiences of W. Stainton Moses, II., by F. W. H. Myers. On the Apparent Sources of Subliminal Messages, by "Miss X." Reviews of Books, including: Mr. W. Leaf's "Modern Priestess of Isis" and Mr. E. Garrett's "Isis very much Unveiled," by Frank Podmore, and Herr Edmund Parish's "Trugwahrnehmung," by Miss Alice Johnson.

Part 28. Some Experiments on the Supernormal Acquisition of Knowledge, by Mrs. A. W. Verrall. The Voices of Jeanne d'Arc, by Andrew Lang. Resolute Credulity, by F. W. H. Myers. Telepathic Dreams Experimentally Induced, by Dr. C. B. Ermacora. Some Psychical Phenomena bearing upon the question of Spirit Control, by Charles Hill-Tout. Subliminal Self or Unconscious Cerebration? Discussion by A. H. Pierce and F. Podmore.

Part 29. The subliminal Self: The Relation of Supernormal Phenomena to Time; Chap. VIII., Retrocognition. Chap. IX., Precognition, by F. W. H. Myers.

Vol. 12, 1896-97

Part 30. Presidential Address, by Professor William James. Sub-conscious Reasoning, by Wm. Romaine Newbold. Suggestion without Hypnotism, by C. M. Barrows. Poltergeists, by Frank Podmore. A Case of Information Supernormally Acquired, by Miss Alice Johnson. James Braid: his Work and Writings, by Dr. J. Milne Bramwell. Glossary of Terms used in Psychical Research, by F. W. H. Myers.

Part 31. Personally Observed Hypnotic Phenomena, by Dr. J. Milne Bramwell. What is Hypnotism? by Dr. J. Milne Bramwell. Some Experiments in Crystal Vision, by Prof. James H. Hyslop. A Case of Psychic Automatism, including "Speaking with Tongues," by "Albert Le Baron. Involuntary Whispering considered in relation to Experiments in Thought-Transference, by Prof. Henry Sidgwick. Reviews of Books, etc.

Appendix to Part 31. Presidential Address by William Crookes, F.R.S.

Supplementary Appendix to Part 31. Supplementary Catalogue of the Edmund Gurney Library. Officers and Council and List of Members and Associates for 1897.

Vol. 13, 1897-98

Part 32. On the So-Called Divining Rod, Book I., By Prof. W. F. Barrett.

Part 33. A Further Record of Observations of Certain Phenomena of Trance (Mrs. Piper), by Richard Hodgson, LL.D. Reviews of Books, including Herr Edmund Parish's "Zur Kritik des Telepathischen Beweismaterials," by Mrs. H. Sidgwick.

Vol. 14, 1898-99

Part 34. A Further Record of Observations of Certain Phenomena of Trance (Mrs. Piper), by Prof. Wm. Romaine Newbold, Discussion of the Trance-Phenomena of Mrs. Piper, by Frank Podmore. A Contribution to Study of Hysteria and Hypnosis, by Morton Prince, M.D. Addresses on Hypnotism delivered at the British Medical Association, by Dr. J. Milne Bramwell, F. W. H. Myers and others. Reviews of Books, including: Some Cases Recorded in the "Annales des Sciences Psychiques," by J. G. Smith.

Part 35. On the Conditions of Certainty, by Prof. Ch. Richet. Coincidences, by Alice Johnson. The Forms of Apparitions in West Africa, by Mary H. Kingsley. Dr. Morton Prince's "Experimental Study of Visions," by F. W. H. Myers. Extract from J. E. de Mirville's "Des Esprits et de leurs Manifestations Fluidiques" (Experiments with Alexis Didier). Review of Books, including: Judge Dailey's "Mollie Fancher; the Brooklyn Enigma," by Prof. W. Romaine Newbold.

Vol. 15, 1900-1901

Part 36. The Fire Walk, by Andrew Lang. Discussions of the Trance-Phenomena of Mrs. Piper, by Mrs. Henry Sidgwick and Andrew Lang. On Some Philosophic Assumptions in the Investigation of the Problem of a Future Life, by F. C. S. Schiller. Reviews of Books, etc.

Part 37. Presidential Address, by F. W. H. Myers.

Part 38. On the So-called Divining Rod. Book II., by Prof. W. F. Barrett, F.R.S. Pseudo-Possession, by F. W. H. Myers. Reviews of Books, etc.

Part 39. In Memory of Henry Sidgwick (with portrait), by F. W. H. Myers.

Part 40. The Misses Beauchamp: a Preliminary Report of a Case of Multiple Personality, by Dr. Morton Prince.

Vol. 16, 1901

Part 41. A Further Record of Observations of Certain Trance Phenomena (Mrs. Piper), by Professor James Hervey Hyslop, Ph.D.

Vol. 17, 1901-1903

Part 42. In Memory of F. W. H. Myers (with portrait), by Sir Oliver Lodge, D.Sc., F.R.S., Professor William James, Professor Charles Richet, Frank Podmore and Walter Leaf, Litt.D.

Part 43. Presidential Address, by Sir Oliver Lodge, F.R.S.

Part 44. Introduction to the Reports of Sittings with Mrs. Thompson, by Sir Oliver Lodge, F.R.S. On the Trance Phenomena of Mrs. Thompson, by the late F. W. H. Myers. Account of Sittings with Mrs. Thompson, by Dr. F. van Eeden. A Record of Two Sittings with Mrs. Thompson, by "J. O. Wilson" and J. G. Piddington. Report on Six Sittings with Mrs. Thompson, by Richard Hodgson, LL.D. Note on a Possibly Automatic Incident observed in the case of Mrs. Thompson, by Alice Johnson. Notes on the Trance Phenomena of Mrs. Thompson, by Mrs. A. W. Verrall. Supplement.--Reviews: Professor Flournoy's "Nouvelles Observations sur un Cas de Somnambulisme avec Glossolalie," by F. C. S. Schiller. Prof. Jastrow's "Fact and Fable in Psychology," by F. N. Hales. Dr. A. Binet's "La Suggestibilité," by Dr. F. van Eeden. Dr. Osgood Mason's "Hypnotism and Suggestion in Therapeutics, Education and Reform," by the Hon. E. Fielding. M. Sage's "Madame Piper et la Société Anglo-Américaine pour les Recherches Psychiques," by Mrs. A. W. Verrall. Mr. Andrew Lang's "Magic and Religion," by E. N. Bennett.

Part 45. Some Experiments in Hypnotism, by "Edward Greenwood." Malay Spiritualism, by Walter Skeat. The Poltergeist, Historically Considered, by Andrew Lang. Remarks on Mr. Lang's Paper, by Frank Podmore. Further Remarks, by Andrew Lang. Discussion of the Trance Phenomena of Mrs. Piper, by Hereward Carrington. Remarks on Mr. Carrington's Paper, by Professor J. H. Hyslop. On Professor Hyslop's Report on his Sittings with Mrs. Piper, by Frank Podmore. Supplement.—Reviews: Mr. F. Podmore's "Modern Spiritualism; a History and a Criticism," by Alice Johnson. Professor W. James's "The Varieties of Religious Experience," by F. C. S. Schiller. M. Maurice Maeterlinck's "Le Temple Enseveli," by J. G. Piddington. M. Ch. de Coynart's "Une Sorcière au XVIII Siècle," by J. G. Piddington.

Vol. 18, 1903-1904

Part 46. Presidential Address, by Sir Oliver Lodge, F.R.S. Supplement.—Reviews: Mr. F. W. H. Myers's "Human Personality and its Survival of Bodily Death," by Professor William James, Sir Oliver Lodge, F.R.S., Professor Th. Flournoy and Walter Leaf, Litt.D. "The Nineteenth Century" and Mr. Frederic Myers, by Andrew Lang. Reply to Mr. Podmore's Criticism, by Professor James H. Hyslop.

Part 47. On the types of Phenomena displayed in Mrs. Thompson's Trance, by J. G. Piddington. On Certain Unusual Psychological Phenomena, by John Honeyman, R.S.A.

Part 48. Presidential Address, by Professor W. F. Barrett, F.R.S.

Part 49. A Case of Multiple Personality, by Albert Wilson, M.D. The Answers to the American Branch's Questionnaire regarding Human Sentiment as to a Future Life, by F. C. S. Schiller. The Poltergeist at Cideville, by Andrew Lang. Supplement—The History of a Haunted House, by Dr. J. Grasset (*Trans.*) Reviews: Dr. J. Milne Bramwell's "Hypnotism: its History, Practice and Theory," by Walter Leaf, Litt. D. Dr. J. Maxwell's "Les Phénomènes Psychiques," by the Hon. Everard Feilding.

Mr. F. C. S. Schiller's "Humanism: Philosophical Essays," by F. N. Hales. Officers and Council for 1904, and List of Members and Associates. Index to Vol. 18.

Vol. 19, 1905-1907

Part 50. La Métapsychique, par Professeur Charles Richet. Report on Various Spiritualistic Phenomena, by Lieut.-Colonel G. L. Le M. Taylor. The Light thrown on Psychological Processes by the Action of Drugs, by Ernest Dunbar.

Part 51. Psychological Aspects of the Welsh Revival, 1904-5, by the Rev. A. T. Fryer. Xénoglossie: l'Ecriture Automatique en Langues Entrangères, par Professeur Charles Richet. Discussion of Professor Richet's Case of Automatic Writing in a Language unknown to the Writer, by Sir Oliver Lodge, Mrs. A. W. Verrall, the Hon. Everard Feilding and Alice Johnson. Supplement--Dr. Henry Head's "Goulstonian Lectures for 1901," by J. G. Piddington. Reviews: Mr. F. W. H. Myers's "Fragments of Prose and Poetry," by Walter Leaf, Litt.D. Drs. Boris Sidis and S. P. Goodhart's "Multiple Personality," by W. M'Dougall.

Part 52. Richard Hodgson: In Memoriam (with Portrait), by Mrs. Henry Sidgwick, J. G. Piddington and M. A. de Wolfe Howe. Presidential Address, by the Right Hon. Gerald W. Balfour. Supplement—Mr. Petrovo-Solovovo on Spiritism, by Walter Leaf, Litt.D. The Case of Sally Beauchamp, by W. M'Dougall, M.Sc., M.B. Reviews: "Henry Sidgwick: A Memoir, by A. S. and E. M. S.," by Frank Podmore. Professor J. H. Hyslop's "Borderland of Psychical Research," "Enigmas of Psychical Research" and "Science and a Future Life," by Hereward Carrington. Professor Jastrow's "The Subconscious," by Frank Podmore.

Appendix for Part 52. Officers and Council for 1907, and List of Members and Associates. Index to Vol. 19.

Vol. 20, 1906

Part 53. On a Series of Automatic Writings, by Mrs. A. W. Verrall. Part I., General Description of the Script; Part II., Verifiable Matter contained in the Script.

Vol. 21, 1907-1909

Part 54. The Appreciation of Time by Somnambules, by T. W. Mitchell, M.D. Experiments in Thought-Transference, by Clarissa Miles and Hermione Ramsden. Report on some Recent Sittings for Physical Phenomena in America, by Alice Johnson. Supplement—Vis-Knut, by Walter Leaf, Litt. D. Reviews: Dr. C. Lloyd Tuckey's "Treatment by Hypnotism and Suggestion," by Frank Podmore. Dr. August Forel's "Hypnotism or Suggestion and Psychotherapy," by C. Lloyd Tuckey, M.D. Dr. T. S. Clouston's "The Hygiene of Mind," by C. Lloyd Tuckey, M.D. Miss Mary Hamilton's "Incubation," by the Rev. M. A. Bayfield.

Part 55. On the Automatic Writing of Mrs. Holland, by Alice Johnson. Supplement.—Review: Mr. Hereward Carrington's "Physical Phenomena of Spiritualism," by Count Perovsky-Petrovo-Solovovo.

Part 56. The Alleged Miraculous Hailstones of Remiremont, by M. Sage. The Hallucination Theory as applied to Certain Cases of Physical Phenomena, by Count Perovsky-Petrovo-Solovovo. The Education of the Sitter, by Alice Johnson. Note on Miss Johnson's Paper, by Count Perovsky-Petrovo-Solovovo. Supplement.—Reviews: Professor Morselli's "Psicologia e 'Spiritismo.' Impressioni e note critiche sui fenomeni medianici di Eusapia Palladino," by Mrs. Henry Sidgwick. Mr. F. Podmore's "Naturalisation of the Supernatural," by Count Perovsky-Petrovo-Solovovo. Officers and Council for 1909, and List of Members and Associates. Index to Vol. 21.

Vol. 22, 1908

Part 57. Presidential Address, by Mrs. Henry Sidgwick. A Series of Concordant Automatisms, by J. G. Piddington. An incident in Mrs. Piper's Trance: being an attempt to elicit from Myers evidence of acquaintance with a circumstance in the life of Frederic Myers, by Mrs. Henry Sidgwick.

Vol. 23, 1909

Part 58. Report on Mrs. Piper's Hodgson-Control, by Professor William James. Note on Mrs. Piper's Hodgson-Control in England in 1906-7, by H. Sidgwick and J. G. Piddington. Report on Some Trance Communications received chiefly through Mrs. Piper, by Sir Oliver Lodge. Psychical Research and Survival after Bodily Death, by Professor A. C. Pigou.

Part 59. Introductory Note to the "Report on Sittings with Eusapia Palladino." Report on a Series of Sittings with Eusapia Palladino, by the Hon. Everard Fielding, W. W. Baggally, and Hereward Carrington. Supplement.—M. Courtier's Report on the Experiments with Eusapia Palladino at the Paris Institut Général Psychologique, by Count Perovsky-Petrovo-Solovovo. Index to Vol. 23.

Vol. 24, 1910

Part 60. Supplementary Notes on the First Report on Mrs. Holland's Script, by Alice Johnson. Supplementary Notes on "A Series of Concordant Automatisms," by J. G. Piddington. Further Experiments with Mrs. Piper in 1908, by Mrs. Henry Sidgwick, Mrs. A. W. Verrall, and J. G. Piddington. Second Report on Mrs. Holland's Script, by Alice Johnson. A New Group of Experimenters, by Mrs. A. W. Verrall. Sequel to the "Sesame and Lilies" Incident, by Alice Johnson. Postscript to the Lethe Incident, by J. G. Piddington.

Part 61. Presidential Address, by H. Arthur Smith. Report on the Junot sittings with Mrs. Piper, by Helen de G. Verrall. Supplement—Some Recent Developments in Psychotherapy, by T. W. Mitchell, M.D. Review: Mr. Frank Podmore's "Mesmerism and Christian Science," by T. W. Mitchell, M.D. Appendix to Part LXI.—Officers and Council for 1910, and List of Members and Associates. Index to Vol. 24.

Vol. 25, 1911

Part 62. Commemorative Address: William James and Frank Podmore, by H. Arthur Smith. Frank Podmore and Psychical Research, by Mrs. Henry Sidgwick. In Memory of William James, by W.

M'Dougal. William James as Philosopher, by Professor J. H. Muirhead. Professor Pigou on Cross-Correspondences, by the Right Hon. Gerald W. Balfour. Report on a Further Series of Sittings with Eusapia Palladino at Naples: I. General Report, by the Hon. Everard Feilding and W. Marriott. II. Statement by Count Perovsky-Petrovo-Solovovo. III. Detailed Account of the Table-lifting Incident. IV. Comments on the above, by Alice Johnson. V. Note on the Report, by W. W. Baggally. Supplement.—Reviews: Mr. F. Podmore's "The Newer Spiritualism," by the Rev. M. A. Bayfield. Open Letter to Dr. Stanley Hall from Andrew Lang. Dr. Tanner's "Studies in Spiritism," by Mrs. Henry Sidgwick. "The One-Horse Dawn": Additional Note on an Experiment described in *Proc.* Vol. 20, by Mrs. A. W. Verrall.

Part 63. Evidence of Classical Scholarship and of Cross Correspondence in some New Automatic Writings, by Sir Oliver Lodge. Notes on Mrs. Willett's Scripts of February, 1910, by Mrs. A. W. Verrall. Third Report on Mrs. Holland's Script, by Alice Johnson. Note on the Cross-Correspondence "Cup," by Mrs. A. W. Verrall. Miss Verrall's Script of March 16, 1908: a Correction and an Addition, by Mrs. A. W. Verrall. The Hypnoidal State of Sidis, by T. W. Mitchell, M.D. Supplement.—Reviews: "An Adventure." Professor Robinson Ellis's "The Tenth Declamation of (Pseudo-) Quintilian," by F. C. S. Schiller, D.Sc.

Part 64. Presidential Address, by Andrew Lang. Poltergeists, Old and New, by Professor W. F. Barrett, F.R.S. Les Phénomènes Physiques du Spiritisme: Quelques Difficultés. Par le Comte Perovsky-Petrovo-Solovovo. On the *a Priori* Argument against Physical Phenomena, by Sir Oliver Lodge. A Case of Emergence of a Latent Memory under Hypnosis, by G. Lowes Dickinson. Supplement.—Review: Professor Flournoy's "Esprits et Médiums," by the Rev. M. A. Bayfield. Appendix to Part LXIV.—Officers and Council for 1911, and List of Members and Associates. Index to Vol. 25.

Vol. 26, 1913

Part 65. Presidential Address, by the Right Rev. Bishop W. Boyd Carpenter, D.D. A Month's Record of Automatisms, by Mrs. A. W. Verrall. Correspondences Croisées, by Joseph Maxwell, M.D. The Latin Message Experiment, by Mrs. Anna Hude. A Hitherto Unsuspected Answer to the Horace Ode Question, by J. G. Piddington. Some Observations on Mr. Piddington's Paper, by the Right Hon. G. W. Balfour. A Reply to Mr. Balfour's Observations, by J. G. Piddington. Two Tennysonian Quotations in Mrs. Verrall's Scripts, by J. G. Piddington. Supplement.—Review: N. Vaschide's "Les Hallucinations Télépathiques" by Mrs. Henry Sidgwick.

Part 66. (Special Medical Part.) Some Types of Multiple Personality, by T. W. Mitchell, M.D. A Study of Hysteria and Multiple Personality, with Report of a Case, by T. W. Mitchell, M.D. A Note on the Unconscious in Psycho-Analysis, by Professor Sigm. Freud, M.D., LL.D. (Vienna). The Theory of the Subconscious, by Boris Sidis, M.A., Ph.D., M.D. Supplement.—Reviews: Mr. M'Dougall's "Body and Mind, a History and a Defence of Animism," by the Right Hon. Gerald W. Balfour. Prof. Dr. E. Bleuler's "Die Psychanalyse Freuds," by V. J. Woolley, M.D. Dr. Edwin Ash's "Faith and Suggestion," by C. Lloyd Tuckey, M.D. The Liverpool Psycho-Therapeutic Clinic, by A. Betts Taplin, L.R.C.P.

Part 67. A Reply to Dr. Joseph Maxwell's Paper on "Cross-Correspondences and the Experimental Method," by Mrs. Henry Sidgwick; with Appendices by Mrs. A. W. Verrall, Alice Johnson and J. G. Piddington. Andrew Lang and Psychical Research, by the Rev. M. A. Bayfield. A Study of Dreams, by Dr. Frederik van Eeden. Presidential Address, by Professor Henri Bergson. Officers and Council for 1913, and List of Members and Associates. Index to Vol. 26.

Vol. 27, 1915

Part 68. A Reconstruction of some "Concordant Automatisms," by Alice Johnson. Presidential Address, by Professor Henri Bergson; translated by H. Wildon Carr, D. Litt. Supplement.—Review: Mr. Hereward Carrington's "Personal Experiences in Spiritualism," by Count Perovsky-Petrovo-Solovovo. Thought-Transference—Experimental, by John E. Coover, Ph.D.

Part 69. Philosophy, Science, and Psychical Research: a Presidential Address, by F. C. S. Schiller, D.Sc. Some Recent Scripts affording Evidence of Personal Survival, by the Right Hon. Gerald W. Balfour. Note on the Same Scripts, by the Rev. M. A. Bayfield. A Further Study of the Mac Scripts, by Helen de G. Verrall. Experiments in Thought-Transference, by Clarissa Miles and Hermione Ramsden. To Clear the Air, by the Rev. M. A. Bayfield. The History of Marthe Béraud ("Eva C"), by Helen de G. Verrall. Special Medical Supplement.—Recent Experience in Hypnotic Practice, by Sidney Wilkinson, M.R.C.S., L.R.C.P. Some Auto-Suggested Visions as Illustrating Dream-Formation, by V. J. Woolley, M.D. Pseudo-Physical Phenomena in the Case of Mr. Grünbaum, by Alice Johnson. Review: Professor S. Freud's "Psychopathology of Everyday Life" (Translated by Dr. A. A. Brill), by Constance E. Long, M.D.

Part 70. Some Recent Experiments in Thought-Transference, by Helen de G. Verrall. A Discussion of the Willett Scripts. I., by Hereward Carrington. II., by Ivor Lloyd Tuckett, M.D. III., by the Rev. M. A. Bayfield. Review: Dr. Morton Prince's "The Unconscious, The Fundamentals of Human Personality, Normal and Abnormal," by F. C. S. Schiller, D.Sc. Officers and Council for 1915, and List of Members and Associates. Index to Vol. 27.

Vol. 28, 1915

Part 71. A Contribution to the Study of the Psychology of Mrs. Piper's Trance Phenomena, by Mrs. Henry Sidgwick. Index to Vol. 28.

Vol. 29, 1916-1918

Part 72. Cross-Correspondence of a Gallic Type, by J. G. Piddington. Presidential Address, by Professor Gilbert Murray. Report on a Series of Experiments in "Guessing," by Mrs. A. W. Verrall. Recent Evidence about Prevision and Survival, by Sir Oliver Lodge. Obituary Notice: Mrs. A. W. Verrall. Supplement.—Reviews: Mr. Henry Holt's "On the Cosmic Relations," by Professor W. Romaine Newbold. Professor Boris Sidis's "The Foundations of Normal and Abnormal Psychology," by F. C. S. Schiller, D.Sc. Professor C. G. Jung's "Collected Papers on Analytical Psychology" (Translated by Constance E. Long, M.D.), by T. W. Mitchell, M.D.

Part 73. The Ear of Dionysius: Further Scripts affording Evidence of Personal Survival, by the Right Hon. Gerald W. Balfour.

Part 74. On the Development of Different Types of Evidence for Survival in the Work of the Society, by Mrs. Henry Sidgwick. The Ear of Dionysius: A Discussion of the Evidence, by Miss F. Melian Stawell, The Ear of Dionysius: A Reply, by the Right Hon. G. W. Balfour. Presidential Address: The Theory of Survival in the Light of its Context, by L. P. Jacks, LL.D. Some Experiments with a New Automatist, by Mrs. W. H. Salter. Some Recent Cases of Premonition and Telepathy, by the Rev. M. A. Bayfield. Supplement—In Memoriam: Mrs. A. W. Verrall. Reviews: Proceedings of the American Society for Psychical Research, "The Doris Fischer Case of Multiple Personality," by F. C. S. Schiller, D.Sc. Sir Oliver Lodge's "Raymond," by Mrs. Henry Sidgwick.

Appendix to Part 74. Officers and Council for 1917, and List of Members and Associates. Index to Vol. 29.

Vol. 30, 1918-1919

Part 75. (Special Medical Part). The Psychoanalytical Use of Subliminal Material, by Constance E. Long, M.D. Dream-Analysis, by Miss Alice Johnson. Psychology of the Unconscious and Psychoanalysis, by T. W. Mitchell, M.D.

Part 76. Fresh Light on the "One-Horse Dawn" Experiment, by J. G. Piddington. Evidence of Supernormal Communications through Motor Automatism, by Sir William Barrett, F.R.S. Note on Telepathy and Telergy, by Sir William Barrett, F.R.S. Review of Experiments in Psychical Research, being the "Leland Stanford Junior University's Psychical Research Monograph, No. 1," by F. C. S. Schiller, D.Sc.

Part 77. Presidential Address, by the Rt. Hon. Lord Rayleigh. Note on Mr. Piddington's Paper, called "Fresh Light on the One-Horse Dawn Experiment," by Sir Oliver Lodge. A Reply to Sir Oliver Lodge's Note, by J. G. Piddington. "The Reality of Psychic Phenomena," by W. Whately Smith.

Part 78. On a Series of Sittings with Mrs. Osborne Leonard, by Miss Radclyffe-Hall and (Una) Lady Troubridge.

Appendix to Part 78. Officers and Council for 1920, and List of Members and Associates. Index to Vol. 30.

Vol. 31, 1920-1921

Part 79. In Memory of Lord Rayleigh, O.M., F.R.S., by Sir Oliver Lodge, F.R.S. In Memory of Sir William Crookes, O.M., F.R.S., by Sir William Barrett, F.R.S. The Doris Fischer Case of Multiple Personality, by T. W. Mitchell, M.D. The Psychological Foundations of Belief in Spirits, by C. G. Jung, M.D., LL.D. Supplement.—Review: Dr. Ernest Jones's "Papers on Psycho-Analysis," by T. W. Mitchell, M.D. Note on "A Record of Observations of Certain Phenomena of Trance" (*Proc.* S.P.R., Vol. 6), by Sir Oliver Lodge, F.R.S.

Part 80. Presidential Address, by William McDougall, F.R.S., M.B. Report on a Series of Cases of Apparent Thought-Transference without Conscious Agency, by Hubert Wales. Supplement.—Reviews: Dr. Troland's "A Technique for the Experimental Study of Telepathy and other Alleged Clairvoyant Processes," by F. C. S. Schiller, D.Sc. Professor Sigmund Freud's "Totem and Taboo. Resemblances between the Psychic Lives and Savages and Neurotics," by J. C. Flügel. Lieut. E. H. Jones's "The Road to En-dor," by W. H. Salter.

Part 81. An Examination of Book-Tests obtained in Sittings with Mrs. Leonard, by Mrs. Henry Sidgwick. A Suggested New Method of Research, by W. Whately Smith.

Appendix to Part 81. Officers and Council for 1921, and List of Members and Associates. Index to Vol. 31.

Vol. 32, 1921-1922

Part 82. A Further Report on Sittings with Mrs. Leonard, by Mrs. W. H. Salter. Supplement—Reviews: Dr. A. v. Schrenck-Notzing's "Physikalische Phaemonene des Mediumismus," by F. C. S. Schiller, D.Sc. Dr. Max Dessoir's "Vom Jenseits der Seele," by F. C. S. Schiller, D.Sc. Dr. W. J. Crawford's "The Psychic Structures at the Goligher Circle," by E. J. Dingwall.

Part 83. Problems of Hypnotism: An Experimental Investigation, by Dr. Sydney Alrutz. The Phenomena of Stigmatization, by the Rev. Herbert Thurston. S.J.

Part 84. Report on a Series of Sittings with Eva C. The *Modus Operandi* in So-Called Mediumistic Trance, by (Una) Lady Troubridge. Supplement—Review: Dr. William Brown's "Psychology and Psychotherapy"; Dr. Constance E. Long's "Collected Papers on the Psychology of Phantasy"; Mr. A. G. Tansley's "The New Psychology and Its Relation to Life," by T. W. Mitchell, M.D.

Vol. 33, 1923

Part 85. Presidential Address, by T. W. Mitchell, M.D.

Part 86. Phantasms of the Living. *An Examination and Analysis of Cases of Telepathy between Living Persons printed in the "Journal" of the Society since the publication of the book "Phantasms of the Living,"* by Gurney,Myers and Podmore, in 1886, by Mrs. Henry Sidgwick. Supplement—Reviews: Dr. T. W. Mitchell's "The Psychology of Medicine," by J. C. Flügel. Prof. Sigm. Freud's "Introductory Lectures on Psycho-Analysis" (Authorised English Translation), by J. C. Flügel. Prof. T. K. Oesterreich's "Die Besessenheit," by F. C. S. Schiller, D.Sc. Dr. Rudolf Tischner's "Einführung in den Okkultismus und Spiritismus," by F. C. S. Schiller, D.Sc. Dr. Rudolf Tischner's "Ueber Telepathie und Hellsehen, experimentell-theoretische Untersuchungen," by F. C. S. Schiller, D.Sc.

Part 87. Forecasts in Scripts Concerning the War, by J. G. Piddington. On the Element of Chance in Book Tests.

Part 88. An Experimental Study of the Appreciation of Time by Somnambules, by Sydney E. Hooper, M.A. Concerning the Possibility of Deception in Sittings with Eva C., by Dr. Freiherr von Schrenck-Notzing. Supplement.—Review: Dr. T. W. Mitchell's "Medical Psychology and Psychical Research," by Dr. F. C. S. Schiller.

Appendix to Part 88. Officers and Council for 1923, and List of Members and Associates. Index to Vol. 33.

Vol. 34, 1924

Part 89. Frontispiece: M. Camille Flammarion. Presidential Address, By Camille Flammarion. On Hindrances and Complications in Telepathic Communication, by Mrs. Henry Sidgwick. Supplement.—Review: Prof. Charles Richet's "Traité de Metapsychique" (Eng. Trans. "Thirty Years of Psychical Research"), Review and Critique, by Sir Oliver Lodge.

Part 90. For and Against Survival.—The Difficulty of Survival from the Scientific Point of View, by Prof. Charles Richet. The Possibility of Survival from the Scientific Point of View, by Sir Oliver Lodge.

Part 91. Presidential Address, by J. G. Piddington. Elucidation of Two Points in the "One-Horse Dawn Scripts"—I. The Herb Moly, by W. H. Salter. II. The Precocious Olive, by J. G. Piddington. The Mechanism of the So-Called Mediumistic Trance, by Dr. Sydney Alrutz. A Method of Scoring Coincidences in Tests with Playing Cards, by R. A. Fisher, M.A. Supplement.—Reviews: "The 'Oscar Wilde' Script," by Mrs. Henry Sidgwick. Dr. F. C. S. Schiller's "Problems of Belief," by G. Lowes Dickinson. Sir Oliver Lodge's "Making of Man," by W. Whately Smith.

Part 92. In Memoriam—Gustave Geley (1868-1924), by Sir Oliver Lodge, F.R.S. Report on Further Experiments in Thought-Transference carried out by Professor Gilbert Murray, LL.D., Litt.D., by Mrs. Henry Sidgwick. Some Reminiscences of Fifty Years' Psychical Research, by Sir William Barrett, F.R.S. Some Further Consideration of the *Modus Operandi* in Mediumistic Trance, by (Una) Lady Troubridge. Supplement.—The Life of Crookes, by Sir Oliver Lodge F.R.S. Telekinetic and Teleplastic Mediumship, by E. J. Dingwall. Review: Dr. Osty's "Supernormal Faculties in Man," by Dr. F. C. S. Schiller. Appendix II. to Mrs. Sidgwick's Paper.

Appendix to Part 92. Officers and Council for 1925, and List of Members and Associates. Index to Vol. 34.

Vol. 35, 1925

Part 93. Experiences in Spiritualism with D. D. Home, by the Earl of Dunraven; with an Introduction by Sir Oliver Lodge, F.R.S.

Part 94. An Introductory Study of Hypnagogic Phenomena, by F. E. Leaning.

Part 95. In Memory of Sir William F. Barrett, F.R.S. In Memory of Monsieur Camille Flammarion. Des Conditions de la Certitude, by Professor Charles Richet. Mrs. Piper and the Imperator Band of Controls, by A. W. Trethewy. Supplement.—Reviews: Dr. Carl Bruck's "Experimentelle Telepathic." Dr. C. Schröder's "Grundversuche auf dem Gebiete der psychischen Grenzwissenschaften."

Part 96. A Report on Some Communications received through Mrs. Blanche Cooper, by S. G. Soal, M.A., B.Sc. Index to Vol. 35.

Vol. 36, 1926-1928

Part 97. A Report on a Series of Sittings with Mr. Willy Schneider, by E. J. Dingwall. Luminous and other Phenomena observed with the Medium Janusz Fronczek, by V. J. Woolley and E. J. Dingwall. An Account of a Series of Sittings with Mr. George Valiantine, by V. G. Woolley.

Part 98. A Report on a Series of Sittings with the Medium Margery, by E. J. Dingwall. Supplement.—Reviews: Mrs. Hudson Hoagland's "Report on Sittings with Margery."

Part 99. Presidential Address: Psychical Research and Established Science, by Dr. Hans Driesch. A Report on Some Recent Sittings with Mrs. Leonard, by Mrs. W. H. Salter. Supplement.—Review: "Der Okkultismus in Urkunden," Vol. I and II.

Part 100. "One Crowded Hour of Glorious Life," by J. G. Piddington. Supplement.—Reviews: Dr. William McDougall's "An Outline of Abnormal Psychology." "Proceedings of the Boston Society for Psychic Research." Die Physikalischen Phänomene des Grossen Medium."

Part 101. The Psychology of Plotinus, and its Interest to the Student of Psychical Research, by G. W. Lambert. Supplement: Concerning Mr. Feilding's Review of Mr. Hudson Hoagland's "Report on Sittings with Margery." Review: Professor Sigmund Freud's—"Collected Papers."

Part 102. Report of a Demonstration of Experiments on Hypnotism by Mr. Gustaf Wallenius, by F. H. G. Van Loon and R. H. Thouless. "One Crowded Hour of Glorious Life," by A. F. Hall. A Reply to Mr. Hall, by J. G. Piddington. The Master Builder, by J. G. Piddington. Supplement.—Review: Sir Arthur Conan Doyle's "History of Spiritualism."

Part 103. Statement by Mrs. Crandon (Margery). Case of the Will of Mr. James L. Chaffin. An Experiment in Pseudo-Scripts, by W. H. Salter. More Thoughts on Trance Phenomena, by Rev. W. S. Irving. Supplement.—Review: Dr. Walter Franklin Prince's "The Case of Patience Worth."

Appendix to Part 103. Officers and Council for 1928, and List of Members and Associates. Index to Vol. 36.

Vol. 37, 1927

Part 104. Library Catalogue.

Vol. 38, 1928-1929

Part 105. The Broadcasting Experiment in Mass Telepathy, by V. J. Woolley. Supplement.—Review:

Miss Nea Walker's "The Bridge: A Case for Survival."

Part 106. Presidential Address, by Sir Lawrence J. Jones, Bart.

Part 107. The *Modus Operandi* of Trance-Communication, According to Descriptions received through Mrs. Osborne Leonard, by C. Drayton Thomas. Review: Dr. T. W. Mitchell's "Problems in Psychopathology," by Prof. W. McDougall.

Part 108. Library Catalogue. (Supplement 1927-1928.)

Part 109. Evocation of the Dead and Kindred Phenomena among the Natives of Madagascar, by Theodore Besterman. Evidence for Clairvoyance in Card-Guessing: A Report on Some Recent Experiments, by Ina Jephson. Supplement—Review: M. Leroy's "La Levitation."

Part 110. Some Automatic Scripts Purporting to be Inspired by Margaret Veley, Poet and Novelist (1843-1887). Part I by W. H. Salter; Part II. by Mrs. V. Some Reincarnationist Automatic Script, by J. Arthur Hill. Supplement—Reviews: A Case of Apparent Obsession: And its Treatment on the Assumption that the Obsessing Entities are to be taken at their Face Values. The Margery-Cross-Correspondences.

Part 111. Report of a Four Months' Tour of Psychical Investigation, by Theodore Besterman. On the Asserted Difficulty of the Spiritualistic Hypothesis from a Scientific Point of View, by Sir Oliver Lodge.

Appendix to Part 111. Officers and Council for 1929 and List of Members and Associates. Index to Vol. 38.

Vol. 39, 1930-31

Part 112. The Tony Burman Case, by Nea Walker. Report on the Investigation of Some Sittings with Mrs. Warren Elliott, by H. F. Saltmarsh. Supplement: A reply to M. Sudre's Article "An Experiment in Guessing," by Ina Jephson. The Statistical Method in Psychical Research, by R. A. Fisher, Sc.D., F.R.S.

Part 113. Library Catalogue (Supplement 1928-29).

Part 114. Some Thoughts on D. D. Home, by Count Perovsky-Petrovo-Solovovo. A Method of Estimating the Supernormal Content of Mediumistic Communications, by H. F. Saltmarsh and S. G. Soal.

Part 115. Presidential Address, By Dr. Walter Franklin Prince.

Part 116. Arthur James, Earl of Balfour (Portrait). Some Incidents occurring at Sittings with Mrs. Leonard which may throw light on their *Modus Operandi,* by Mrs. W. H. Salter. Thoughts on Mrs. Saltmarsh's Report on a Series of sittings, by the Rev. W. S. Irving. Review: Upton Sinclair's "Mental Radio."

Part 117. The visit of M. Pascal Forthuny to the Society in 1929, by V. J. Woolley. The Margery Mediumship and the London Sittings of December, 1929, by V. J. Woolley and E. Brackenbury. Review: Henry Monnier's "Etude médicale de quelques guérisons survenues à Lourdes."

Part 118. Report of a Series of Experiments in Clairvoyance conducted at a distance under approximately Fraud-proof Conditions, by Ina Jephson, S. G. Soal and Theodore Besterman. Review: W. F. Prince's "The Enchanted Boundary."

Part 119. Officers and Council for 1931. List of Members and Associates. Index to Vol. 39.

Vol. 40, 1931-1932

Part 120. Library Catalogue (Supplement 1929-30).

Part 121. Further Inquiries into the Element of Chance in Book-tests, by Theodore Besterman. Review: *Transactions of the Fourth International Congress for Psychical Research.*

Part 122. Is Proof of Survival Possible? I. Is Proof of Survival Possible? By H. F. Saltmarsh. II. On the difficulty of proving Individual Survival, by Sir Oliver Lodge. III. Reply to Sir Oliver Lodge, by H. F. Saltmarsh. Evidential Extracts from Sittings with Mrs. Leonard, by the Rev. W. S. Irving and Theodore Besterman. Review: Oliver Leroy's "Les hommes salamandres. Recherches et réflexions sur l'incombustibilité du corps humain."

Part 123. Experiments in Supernormal Perception at a Distance, by S. G. Soal.

Part 124. The psychology of Testimony in relation to Paraphysical Phenomena; Report of an Experiment by Theodore Besterman.

Part 125. The History of George Valiantine, by Mrs. W. H. Salter. Appendix—Report on Some Sittings with Valiantine and Phoenix in 1927, by Lord Charles Hope. The Mediumship of Rudi Schneider, by Theodore Besterman. Index to Vol. 40.

Vol. 41, 1932-33

Part 126. The Society for Psychical Research, by Mrs. Henry Sidgwick. Appendix—Classified List of the Contents of the Society's *Proceedings* and *Journal.*

Part 127. The Past and the Future. Presidential Address by Sir Oliver Lodge. Psychology and Psychical Research, by Dr. William Brown.

Part 128. On a Method of Silhouette Photography by Infra-Red Rays for Use in Mediumistic Investigation, by Lord Rayleigh, F.R.S. A Behaviourist Experiment in Clairvoyance, by Ina Jephson. Review: Boston Society for Psychic Research, Bulletin XVIII.

Part 129. Report of an Investigation into Spirit-Photography, by Fred Barlow and Major W. Rampling-Rose.

Part 130. A Consideration of a series of proxy Sittings. By the Rev. C. Drayton Thomas. Report of an Inquiry into Precognitive Dreams. By Theodore Besterman. Visions and Apparitions Collectively and Reciprocally Perceived. By Hornell Hart and Ella B. Hart. Review: Josef Deutsch, *Konnersreuth.* By Count Perovsky-Petrovo Solovovo.

Part 131. Report of Sittings with Rudi Schneider, by Lord Charles Hope.

Part 132. Presidential Address. By the Hon. Mrs. Alfred Lyttleton, G.B.E. An Experiment in 'Clairvoyance' with M. Stefan Ossowiecki, By Theodore Besterman. Officers and Council for 1933. List of Members and Associates. Index to Vol. 41.

Process, The

A cult also known as **Church of the Final Judgment,** founded in London, England by ex-Scientologist Robert Moor aka Robert Moor Sylvester de Grimstone and his wife Mary Anne.

The term "process," borrowed from **Scientology,** indicated a kind of conditioning supposed to liberate devotees from destruction in a forthcoming Doomsday. The processing included a trendy mixture of I Ching, awareness games, tarot, Kabala and Satan-Christ philosophy. De Grimstone cultivated a Rasputin-like appearance and became known in the movement as "The Oracle" or "God" and his wife as "The Goddess."

In May 1974, there was a major schism in the movement when the ruling body, known picturesquely as "The Council of Masters," disagreed with de Grimstone on basic tenets, notably the unity of Christ and Satan, as a result of which the name "The Process Church of the Final Judgment" was changed to "The Foundation Church of the Millennium," and the message watered down to a more conventional but trendy apocalypticism. Meanwhile de Grimstone led his own splinter Process group.

Procter & Gamble Logo

The familiar logo of Procter & Gamble for decades was a simple and harmless design of thirteen stars enclosed in a circle, with a man-in-the-moon.

Astonishingly this quite ordinary logo gave rise to persistent rumors that the company was run by Satan sympathizers and that the logo expressed allegiance to the devil!

It is not clear how such as fantastic and irrational interpretation first arose, but in 1982 the company was obliged to take legal measures to defend themselves. Procter & Gamble filed two libel suits in July 1982, one against a WXIA Television weatherman, another against a Tennessee couple, for spreading such rumors.

On April 24, 1985, Procter & Gamble withdrew when all three individuals publicly apologized, but Procter & Gamble withdrew the logo from use.

Professional Psychics United

Organization founded in 1977 by professional psychics with the object of helping police in crime solving.

It provides psychic rescue team to assist in locating missing persons, offers educational programs on the nature of extrasensory perception, and conducts teaching seminars.

It maintains biographical archives and library of 203 volumes, sponsors psychic fairs. It bestows awards, maintains speakers bureau, offers placement service, conducts research programs. Address: c/o Edward S. Peters, 1839 S. Elmwood, Berwyn, Illinois 60402.

Progoff, Ira (1921-)

Consulting psychologist who has investigated areas of parapsychology. Born August 2, 1921 at New York, N.Y., he studied at New School for Social Research, New York (Ph.D. 1951). In 1951 he married Rose Goldwin. He was a Bollingen fellow from 1952-58, lecturer at the Jung Institute, Zürich in 1953, lecturer at New School for Social Research from 1957-58, director of Institute for Research in Depth Psychology, Drew University, Madison, New Jersey from 1959 onwards.

He is a member of the American Psychological Association, the Parapsychological Association, American Ontological Analytical Association, member of advisory board of Institute for Religion in an Age of Science, member of the board of editors of *Journal of Humanistic Psychology.*

Dr. Progoff has taken a special interest in mediumship, psychedelics, religious and creative experience, personality growth and psychic sensitivity, image-making at depth-psychological levels. His articles in the *International Journal of Parapsychology* include: 'Parapsychology in Modern Thinking' (vol. 1, No. 1, Summer 1959), 'Transformation of Jewish Mysticism' (vol. 2, No. 2, Autumn 1960). His books include: *Jung's Psychology and Its Social Meaning* (1953, 1955), *Death and Rebirth of Psychology* (1956), *Depth Psychology and Modern Man* (1959). He also edited *The Cloud of Unknowing* (1957) and *The Symbolic and the Real* (1963).

Dr. Progoff developed a system of Process Meditation, characterized by an "Intensive Journal" method of individual progress. He organized Life Context Workshops and published the *National Intensive Journal* at Dialogue House, 80 East 11 Street, New York, N.Y. 10003. His meditation system was the subject of his book *The Practice of Process Meditation* (1980).

Progressive Library & Spiritual Institution

Established by pioneer British Spiritualist James **Burns** in 1863. The organization included a lending library of several thousand volumes on Spiritualism and related subjects, with a reading room and rooms for seances or experiments relating to Spiritualism.

In addition, the Institution included a publishing department to assist and promote literature connected with Spiritualism. These included an edition of the writings of prominent American Spiritualist Judge Edmonds, and the important *Report on Spiritualism of the London Dialectical Society* (1872). The Institution became an influential meeting place for Spiritualists in London.

Progressive Thinker, The (Newspaper)

American Spiritualist weekly, founded by J. R. Francis in 1899, editor and publisher M. E. Cadwallader. Address: 106 S. Loomis Street, Chicago, Illinois. No longer published.

Project Starlight International

Founded in 1964, to gather and disseminate a broad range of instrumented **UFO** hard data to the scientific community. The Project utilizes magnetometers, a gravimeter, spectrometer, radar, laser-telescope-video system, and other electronic and optical systems for recording physical effects, optical images, and location of UFOs.

The Project conducts in-depth analyses of motion-picture films of UFOs obtained by PSI staff members, along with magnetometric, spectrographic, and other new hard data recorded during UFO events. It maintains a specially equipped mobile laboratory unit. Address: P.O. Box 599, College Park, Maryland 20740.

Project VISIT—Vehicle Internal Systems Investigative Team

Founded in 1976 with a membership of researchers, including engineers, scientists, analysts, and investigators, interested in **UFOs.**

The Project exists to conduct research in order to determine whether or not there is a correlation of engineering systems among UFO cases, to identify and evaluate such systems and determine the mode of operation of UFOs, and to share research findings with government agencies, public corporations, and the general public.

The Project maintains archives containing 10,000 clippings, reports, and reviews on current UFO cases, and also compiles statistics. It sponsored the 1980 Mutual UFO Network. It has also published study and monographs. Address: P.O. Box 890327, Houston, Texas 77289.

Prophecy

In an early state of society, the prophet and **shaman** were probably one and the same, as is still the case among primitive peoples. It is difficult to say whether the position of the prophet was more truly religious or magical. He was usually a priest, but the ability to look into the future and read its portents is not necessarily a religious attribute.

In many instances prophecy is merely utterances in the ecstatic condition. We know that the pythonesses attached to the oracles of ancient **Greece** uttered prophetic words under the influences of natural gases or drugs, and when the medicine-men of primitive tribes attempt to peer into the future, they usually attain a condition of ecstasy by taking some drug, the action of which is well known to them. But this was not always the case; the shaman often summoned a spirit to his aid to discover what portents and truths lie in the future; but this cannot be called prophecy.

Neither is **divination** prophecy in the true sense of the term, as artificial aids are employed, and it is merely by the appearance of certain objects that the augur can pretend to predict future events. We often find prophecy disassociated from the ecstatic condition, as for example among the prophets of ancient Israel, who occupied themselves in great measure with the calm statement of future political events, the priests of the Maya Indians of Central America, known as *Chilan Balam,* at stated intervals in the year made certain statements regarding the period which lay immediately before them.

Is prophecy then to be regarded as a direct utterance of the deity, taking a human being as mouthpiece, or the statement of one who seeks inspiration from the fountain of wisdom? Technically, both are true of prophecy, for we find it stated in scripture that when the deity desired to communicate with human beings He chose certain persons as mouthpieces. Again individuals (often the same as those chosen by God) applied to the deity for inspiration in critical moments. Prophecy then may be the utterances of God by the medium of the practically unconscious shaman or seer, or the inspired utterance of that person after inspiration has been sought from the deity.

In ancient Assyria the prophetic class were called *nabu,* meaning "to call" or "announce"—a name probably adopted from that of the god Na-bi-u, the speaker or proclaimer of destiny, the tablets of which he inscribed.

Among the ancient Hebrews the prophet was called *nabhia,* a borrowed title probably adopted from the Canaanites. That is not to say, however, that the Hebrew *nabhiim* were indebted to the surrounding peoples for their prophetic system, which appears to have been of a much loftier type than that of the Canaanite peoples.

Prophets appear to have swarmed in Palestine in biblical times, and we are told that four hundred prophets of Baal sat at Jezebel's table. The fact that they were prophets of this deity would almost go to prove that they were also priests. We find that the most celebrated prophets of Israel belonged to the northern portion of that country, which was more subject to the influence of the Canaanites.

Later, distinct prophetic societies were formed, the chief reason for whose existence appears to have been the preservation of nationality, and this class appears to have absorbed the older castes of seers and magicians, and to some extent to have taken over their offices.

Some of the later prophets—Micah, for example—appear to have regarded some of these lesser seers as mere diviners, who were in reality not unlike the prophets of Baal. With Amos may be said to have commenced a new school of prophecy—the canonical prophets, who were also authors and historians, and who disclaimed all connection with mere professional prophets.

The general idea in Hebrew Palestine was that Yahveh, or God, was in the closest possible touch with the prophets, and that he would do nothing without revealing it to them. The greatest importance was given to their utterances, which more than once determined the fate of the nation. Indeed no people lent so close an ear to the utterance of their prophetic class as did the Jews of old times.

In ancient Greece, the prophetic class were generally found attached to the oracles, and in Rome were represented by the augurs. In **Egypt,** the priests of Ra at Memphis acted as prophets as, perhaps, did those of Hekt.

Among the ancient Celts and Teutons, prophecy was frequent, the prophetic agent usually placing him or herself in the ecstatic condition. The Druids were famous practitioners of the prophetic art, and some of their utterances may be still extant in the so-called "Prophecies of Merlin."

In **America,** as has been stated, prophetic utterance took practically the same forms as in Europe and Asia. Captain Jonathan Carver, an early traveler in North America, cited a peculiar instance where the seers of a certain tribe stated that a famine would be ended by assistance being sent from another tribe at a certain hour on the following day. At the very moment mentioned by them, a canoe rounded a headland, bringing news of relief.

A strange story was told in the *Atlantic Monthly* many years ago by a traveler among the Plains tribes, who stated that an Indian medicine-man had prophesied the coming of himself and his companions to his tribe two days before their arrival among them. (See also **Divination; Prediction**)

Recommended reading:

Cheetham, Erika. *The Prophecies of Nostradamus,* Neville Spearman, London, 1973; Corgi paperback, 1975

Ellis, Keith. *Prediction and Prophecy,* Wayland, London, 1973

Garrison, Omar V. *Encyclopedia of Prophecy,* Citadel paperback, 1979

Rowley, Harold H. *Prophecy and Religion in Ancient China and Israel,* Harper, c. 1956; Allenson-Breckinridge, Geneva, Alabama, n.d.

Timms, Moira. *Prophecies and Predictions; Everyone's Guide to the Coming Changes,* Unity Press, Santa Cruz, California, 1981

Vaughan, Alan. *Patterns of Prophecy,* Hawthorn Books, 1973; Turnstone, London, 1974

"Prophet, The"

A **control** of the medium Rev. W. Stainton **Moses,** said to have been Haggai, a contemporary of Malachi, brought in by "Imperator" as an assistant with Vates (Daniel), another contemporary. He signed communications several times jointly with "Imperator" but never gave independent teaching. (See W. Stainton **Moses**)

Prosperos, The

A group stemming from the philosophy of G. I. **Gurdjieff** founded in 1956 by Thane **Walker,** a charismatic student of Gurdjieff, and Phez Kahlil. The Prosperos were chartered in Florida, but have moved around the country, and now have some 3,000 members in California.

The Prosperos believe in One Mind, and claim that reality can be experienced only from its perspective by removing the distortions of the senses and memory that hide the true self. This is generally in accord with traditional mystical teaching, but whereas the way of the fakir is through willpower, the yogi through intellect and the monk through emotions, the "Fourth Way" is available to individuals within world experience.

The Prosperos believe that God is pure consciousness, and use five processes to achieve identification of the individual with the One Consciousness: 1) Statement of Being (the facts of reality); 2) Uncovering the Lie or Error (the claims of the senses); 3) Argument (resting of claims); 4) Summing up the Results; 5) Establishing the Absolute.

Lectures and classes are conducted on such topics as "Translation," "Releasing the Hidden Splendor," and there is also an inner circle named with High Watch, for those who complete three classes of development.

The name "Prosperos" derives from the magician Prospero in Shakespeare's play *The Tempest.* Through his magical powers, Prospero can interpret, project, rationalize and imagine life as he wishes, but on his island he is interconnected with Caliban the monster (who parallels the unconscious mind), and Ariel (the intuitive agent who aids Prospero when called upon).

Proxy Sitting

A consultation with a medium in which the individual uses a substitute or "proxy," in order to avoid possible telepathic communication or other indications from the sitter.

Pruden, Mrs. Laura A. (died 1939)

Slate-writing medium of Cincinnati, widow of a judge, who practiced mediumship for well over half a century. She did not go into trance.

Dr. Hereward **Carrington** sat with her on October 27, 1925. In his book, *The Story of Psychic Science* (1930), he gave a highly interesting account of his experiences. After describing the result of his preliminary examination of the table and the slates, he stated that, at the medium's request, he wrote two questions on slips of paper, one addressed to Dr. Richard **Hodgson,** and the other to his own father. He folded them up and placed one upon the floor under the seance table, the other on a small table to his right where it remained visible throughout the sitting, until used.

Mrs. Pruden, sitting on a very low rocking chair, thrust the pair of slates, a small piece of slate pencil between them, through the slit on the tablecloth, with her right hand under the table. Her left hand rested in her lap and remained visible throughout the seance.

Carrington continued: "The first pair of slates remained under the table for about half an hour, when they were removed and a brief message was found written upon one of the inner surfaces, signed "R. Hodgson," and answering my question, written upon the first slip. These slates were then put to one side. I was then requested to remove the first slip from under the seance table and place the second one there. This I did. The second pair of slates was then examined and held under the table in the same manner as the first pair. At the end of about half an hour these were removed and a general message from my 'father' was found upon them, answering the question written upon the second slip. The slips and slates I took with me, and now have them in my possession."

Carrington further stated: "It is my opinion that, on any theory whatever, Mrs. Pruden's slate-writing is a very remarkable performance. The table and slates were certainly free from any previous preparation. She certainly could not have seen the written questions before they were placed on the floor under the seance table. She certainly keeps up an animated conversation with her sitter throughout the sitting. Her left hand is always visible and her body appears to be practically stationary throughout. At no time does she stoop to pick up anything from the floor."

Dr. Carrington advanced a theory as a hypothetical explanation of the feat, but he himself admitted that his observations tended to support the genuine character of the manifestation.

A series of articles which gave a favorable impression of Mrs. Pruden's powers was published in the *Journal* of the American Society for Psychical Research (1926-27). The British psychical researcher Harry **Price,** in his report of seances held with Mrs. Pruden in London in 1925, withheld favorable pronouncement, as he found fault with Mrs. Pruden's conditions. See also *Journal* of the Society for Psychical Research (vol. 23, pp. 76, 97, 139; vol. 24, p. 128). She died March 10, 1939, aged 86 years. (See also **Slate-writing**)

"Prudens"

One of the spirit **controls** of the Rev. W. Stainton Moses, said to be Plotinus. He contributed the Platonic tone of thought in the spirit teachings. At an early stage he was appointed one of Stainton Moses' guardians and was left in charge of him during the absence of the controls "Imperator" and "Doctor." (See also W. Stainton **Moses**)

Psi

Greek letter used by parapsychologists to indicate psychic or paranormal phenomena such as extrasensory perception (ESP) or psychokinesis (PK). (See also **Parapsychology**)

PSI Center

Full name: Parapsychology Sources of Information Center. Organized as "a clearinghouse for information, research findings, theories, organizations, publications, and persons involved in parapsychology and its interface with psychology, psychiatry, physics, religion, medicine, mysticism, philosophy, and education."

The Center currently publishes a semi-annual journal **Parapsychology Abstracts International** (PAI), which covers English-language abstracts of the contents of all parapsychology journals, some of which commenced publication in the nineteenth century, to date.

The Center is also organizing PsiLine, a computerized database expected to be fully operable about 1990, to contain bibliographical citations, abstracts, and subjector descriptors for all important books in parapsychology and the major English-language journals from earliest times to date. It is also planned to contain the same information as in PAI, as well as English abstracts of many foreign-language parapsychological journals, articles on parapsychology in monographs, non-parapsychological journals and magazines, proceedings, dissertations and chapters. PsiLine will also include coverage of parapsychological newsletters (with selective abstracts).

A thesaurus of parapsychological terms and a searcher's manual is also planned.

The Center also compiles and publishes a series called "PSI Center Bibliographies," each updated as new sources are noted.

The Center was established by noted parapsychologist Rhea A. White in 1983. Address: PSI Center, 2 Plane Tree Lane, Dix Hills, New York 11746. (See **Parapsychology Sources of Information Center**)

Psi-Conducive

Term used by parapsychologists to indicate environmental or personal factors in the test situation which are favorable for the occurrence of **psi**. This is the opposite of **Psi-Inhibiting.**

Psi-Forum (Journal)

Dutch-language journal published in Belgium by De Werkgroep Parapsychologie. It ceased publication after vol. 3, 1986.

Psi-Hitting

Term used by parapsychologists to indicate a situation in a test of **extrasensory** perception when the subject's rate of scoring is above chance. This is the opposite to **Psi-Missing.**

Psi-Inhibiting

Term used by parapsychologists to indicate environmental or personal facts in the test situation which inhibit the occurrence of **psi.** This is the opposite of **Psi-Conducive.**

PsiLine

Computer service providing on-line reference materials on parapsychology, covering dissertations, chapters from books, psi-related publications. This is only one of the valuable services of the Parapsychology Sources of Information Center (Psi Center) established by parapsychologist Rhea A. **White** in

1983. *PsiLine* can be contacted at the Center by calling (516) 271-1243 weekdays between 9 a.m. and 3 p.m., or by mail. The address of the Center is: 2 Plane Tree Lane, Dix Hills, New York 11746. (See also **Parapsychology Sources of Information Center**)

Psi Magazine

Bimonthly published by Bartonian Metaphysical Society, P.O. Box 4022, Station East, Ottawa, Ontario, Canada (formerly titled *Metaphysical Society Newsletter*).

Psi-Mediated Instrumental Response

An experimental concept developed by parapsychologist Rex. G. **Stanford.** This proposes a model for spontaneous psi events where individuals may unconsciously obtain extrasensory knowledge of events relevant to their personal needs and use this knowledge to modify their behavior in a way which will be instrumental in satisfying those needs.

Dr. Stanford and other parapsychologists have published various papers on experimental researches relating to the PMIR model, notably: 'Unconscious Psi-mediated Instrumental Response and its Relation to Conscious ESP Performance' by Rex G. Stanford & Gary Thompson (*Research in Parapsychology 1973* ed. W. G. Roll, R. L. Morris & J. D. Morris, 1974), 'Associative Mediation in Psi-mediated Instrumental Response (PMIR)' by Rex G. Stanford & Angela Stio (*Research in Parapsychology 1975* ed. J. D. Morris, W. G. Roll & R. L. Morris, 1976), 'Psychokinesis as a Psi-mediated Instrumental Response' by Rex G. Stanford, R. Zennhausern, A. Taylor & M. Dwyer (*Journal* of the American Society for Psychical Research, vol. 69, 1975), 'Psi-mediated Helping Behavior; Experimental Paradigm & Initial Results' by Rex G. Stanford & Peter Rust (*Research in Parapsychology 1976* ed. J. D. Morris, W. G. Roll & R. L. Morris, 1977), 'Cognitive Mode and Extrasensory Function in a Timing-Based PMIR Task' by Rex G. Stanford & Angelo Castello (*Research in Parapsychology 1976,* 1977).

Psi-Missing

Term used by parapsychologists to indicate a situation in a test of **extrasensory perception** when the subject's rate of scoring is below chance. This is the opposite of **Psi-Hitting.**

Psi Network

Recently formed organization "to promote a broader understanding and acceptance of psychic phenomena through lectures, discussions and experiments." Psi Network shares information with members and also with the general field of parapsychology research. Address: Psi Network, P.O. Box 998, Carpinteria, California 93013.

Psi News

Quarterly bulletin of the **Parapsychological Association,** an international society for professional parapsychologists and psychical researchers. This publication features up-to-date news on scientific and educational activities in the field of parapsychology and includes reviews of new books and correspondence from readers. Address: Box 12236, Research Triangle Park, North Carolina 27709.

Psi Patterns (Journal)

Monthly publication of Midwestern Institute of Parapsychology. Includes articles on parapsychology and information on local psi events. Address: P.O. Box 262, Masŏn City, Iowa 50401.

Psi Research (Journal)

International publication circulating in various countries, including Soviet controlled territories, dealing with psi research. *Psi Research* is edited by Larissa Vilenskaya. Address: Foundation for Human Sciences, 484B Washington Street, #317, Monterey, California 93940.

Psi Science Institute of Japan

Organization concerned with parapsychological research in Japan. Its *Journal,* first published in 1977, is now issued quarterly. It is in Japanese language, but includes English abstracts. Address: Psi Science Institute of Japan, Puti-Kozu, 17-12 Komi-Ochiai l-Chome, Shinjuki-ku, Tokyo 161, Japan. (See also **Japan**)

Psi-Trailing

A term used to indicate a form of **Anpsi** or **psi** faculty in animals, in which a pet may trace its owner in a distant location it has not previously visited. (See also **Animals**)

Psionics

A term coined by science-fiction editor John W. Campbell, Jr. to denote a combination of **Radionics** and psi phenomena. His editorial 'The Science of Psionics" published in his magazine *Astounding Science Fiction* (February 1956) discussed "psychic electronic machines."

One such machine was invented by Thomas G. Hieronymus (U.S. Patent No. 2,482,773) and resembles the **Black Box** of Radionics. Campbell described the machine in his article 'Psionic Machine-Type One' (*Astounding Science Fiction,* June 1956).

Psyche

(1) Greek term for soul; (2) German Spiritualist monthly founded in 1894, replaced (following the union in 1900 of the three largest Spiritualist societies of Berlin) by a joint organ, the *Spiritistiche Rundschau,* of which Prof. Karl Obertimpfler became the editor; (3) English monthly magazine devoted to the philosophy and phenomena of life, running for some years from 1899; (4) English quar-

terly journal which succeeded W. Whately **Carington's** *Psychic Research Quarterly* in 1921 as a journal of general and applied psychology. It was edited by C. K. Ogden, London.

Psychenautics

Term coined by Robert E. L. **Masters** and Jean **Houston** to denote the combination of mechanical and hypnotic techniques by means of which they have probed psi faculty in their **Foundation for Mind Research** in Manhattan, New York.

Psychic

(1) Denoting, as an adjective, the paranormal character of certain phenomena, (2) meaning, as a noun, a sensitive individual, one susceptible to psychic influences.

A psychic is not necessarily a medium, unless he is sufficiently sensitive to be controlled by disembodied spirits. The term psychic includes the somnambule, the magnetic or mesmeric subject, anyone who is in any degree sensitive.

According to one view, all individuals are in some measure susceptible to spiritual influences, and to that extent deserve the name of psychic.

Camille Flammarion was the first to use the word as a French term in France, Sergeant E. W. **Cox** was the first to suggest it in England.

The term is generally used in the U.S. in preference to "medium."

Psychic Body

A Spiritualist term loosely applied to an impalpable body which clothes the soul on the "great dissolution of death" or to the soul itself.

Sergeant E. W. **Cox** in his book *Mechanism of Man* (2 vols., 1876) declared that the soul (quite distinct from mind, or intelligence, which is only a function of the brain) is composed of attentuated matter, and has the same form as the physical body, which it permeates in every part.

From the soul, radiates the psychic force, by means of which all the wonders of Spiritualism are performed. Through its agency, human beings become endowed with telekinetic and clairvoyant powers, and with its aid they can affect such natural forces as gravitation. When free of the body, the soul can travel at a lightning speed, nor is it hindered by such material objects as stone walls or closed doors.

The psychic body is also regarded as an intermediary between the physical body and the soul, a sort of envelope, more material than the soul itself, which encloses it at death. It is this envelope, the psychic body or *nervengeist,* which becomes visible at a materialization by attracting to itself other and still more material particles.

In time the psychic body decays just as did the physical, and leaves the soul free.

During trance, the soul leaves the body, but the vital functions are continued by the psychic body. (See also **Astral Body: Etheric Double**)

Psychic Detective Bureau

State licensed organization, also known as U.S. Psi Squad, headed by Beverly C. Jaegers, who also edits a quarterly publication *Pathways,* containing articles, reports on activities, reviews and comments.

The organization brings together "persons interested in utilizing mind skills such as psi to combat crime as a public service, to work with and for law enforcement officials in solving mysteries, to learn mind development to a higher, more useful stage." Address: Psychic Detective Bureau, U.S. Psi Squad, P.O. Box 29396, Sappington, Missouri 63126.

Psychic Directory, The

First issue, in 1984, of a comprehensive guide to practicing psychics in Britain, with listing of Spiritualist churches, associations, societies, festivals and bookshops. Edited by Howard Rodway, published Futura paperbacks, Macdonald & Co. (Publishers) Ltd., Maxwell House, 74 Worship Street, London, EC2A 2EN, England.

Psychic Esperanto League (Palka Esperantista Ligo)

Founded in Britain by Alexander W. Thomson, F.B.E.A. in August 1934, with members in eleven countries.

The work of the League was carried on mainly by correspondence, and its aim was to bring about psychic awareness in various parts of the world untouched by other means because of the language barrier. The League appears to have ceased operation after World War II.

Psychic Evidence Society, The

Founded in London, England 1931 for inquiry into the actuality and meaning of psychical phenomena for clergymen throughout Great Britain. Founder and general secretary was John Engledow. No longer in existence. (See also **Churches' Fellowship for Psychical and Spiritual Studies**)

Psychic Eye Directory, The

Annual listing of psychics, healers, dowsers, lecturers, etc. published by the Parapsychology League of Toledo. Address: 521 Mulberry Street, Toledo, Ohio 43604.

Psychic Force

It was claimed by inquirers into Spiritualism at an early stage that the human organism is in some mysterious way bound up with seance room phenomena. A psychic force seemed to operate beyond the periphery of the body, with no physical contact.

The researches of Baron von **Reichenbach** suggested the term "Odic force" (see **Od**) to Dr. E. C. Rogers of Boston in 1852, Professor Mahan, also in

America, and Count A. **de Gasparin** in France accepted it as such.

Professor Marc **Thury** called it "ectenic force." Professor Mayo of the Royal College of Surgeons, London, postulated on "exo-neural action of the brain."

Sergeant E. W. **Cox** recommended the term "Psychic force" and this euphemism is now in general use.

In a letter to Sir William **Crookes,** Sergeant Cox wrote in 1871: "I noticed that the force was exhibited in tremulous pulsations, and not in the form of steady, continuous pressure, the indicator rising and falling incessantly throughout the experiment. The fact seems to me of great significance as tending to confirm the opinion that assigns its source to the nerve organisation, and it goes far to establish Dr. Richardson's important discovery of a nerve atmosphere of various intensity enveloping the human structure. . . . To avoid the appearance of any foregone conclusion, I would recommend the adoption for it of some appropriate name, and I venture to suggest that the force be termed Psychic Force; the persons to whom it is manifested in extraordinary power Psychics; and the science relating to it Psychism as being a branch of psychology."

"The theory of Psychic Force," he wrote at a late period, "is in itself merely the recognition of the fact that under certain conditions, as yet but imperfectly ascertained, and within limited, but as yet undefined, distance from the bodies of certain persons having a special nerve organisation, a Force operates by which, without muscular contact or connection, action at a distance is caused, and visible motions and audible sounds are produced in solid substances."

The speculation of the existence of a nervous atmosphere to which Sergeant Cox alluded was expounded, by Dr. Benjamin W. Richardson, in the *Medical Times,* on May 6, 1871. As it came from a medical source, Crookes welcomed it; it agreed with his observations.

"I think I perceive," wrote Crookes in his contribution 'Some Further Experiments on Psychic Force' (*Quarterly Journal of Science,* October 1, 1871), "what it is that this psychic force uses up for its development. In employing the terms *vital force,* or *nervous energy,* I am aware that I am employing words which convey very different significations to many investigators; but after witnessing the painful state of nervous and bodily prostration in which some of these experiments have left Mr. Home [The medium D. D. **Home**]—after seeing him lying in an almost fainting condition on the floor, pale and speechless—I could scarcely doubt that the evolution of psychic force is accompanied by a corresponding drain on vital force."

"Certain peculiar sensations accompany the emission of this nervous force," wrote Dr. Joseph **Maxwell,** in *Metapsychical Phenomena* (1905), "and with custom the passage of the energy expanded in a seance can be felt, just as the interruption of the flow can be discerned."

Maxwell was inclined to discern four principal sensations in connection with the generation of the force:

1) The sensation of cool breezes, generally over the hands.

2) The sensation of a slight tingling in the palm of the hand, and at the tips of the fingers, near the mounts.

3) The sensation of a sort of current through the body.

4) The sensation of a spider's web in contact with the hands and face, and other parts of the body—notably the back and the loins. ". . . If the sensation of the 'passage of the current' may be feeble, it is not so with its abrupt interruption. . . . It may even cause a sensation of sudden indisposition, if the interruption coincide with the phenomenon in course of production. . . . The sensation of the breaking of the current is distinctly felt; and it is this which makes me think, that the feeble impression of the passage of the current is not altogether imaginary.

The medium Mrs. Gladys Osborne **Leonard,** in her book *My Life in Two Worlds* (1931), wrote of a visit to a materializing medium: "He [the **control**] instructed the sitter who sat at the extreme end of the left side of the horse-shoe, to release her left hand and throw it out towards him. She did so, and we could all see a stream of pale grey matter, like fog or steam from a kettle, oozing from her fingers. It was shaped like rods, about a foot long and an inch thick. The medium reached out his hands carefully towards the end of the rods, and seemed to try and coax the grey material to come farther away from the sitter, towards himself. The rods thinned slightly, as he induced them to extend, and after a couple of minutes the French control said, speaking through the medium again 'No, not strong enough, link hands up, and close in the power again.' "

"I cannot help wondering," wrote psychical researcher Harry **Price** in *Rudi Schneider; A Scientific Examination of his Mediumship* (1930) "whether there is really anything in the curious stroking movements which Rudi (or Olga) makes during the height of the trance and when she is leaving us. She 'gathers power' she says, by drawing his hands down my body and legs, or those of the second controller's. She 'releases' it at the end of the seance by similar movements, but in a reverse direction."

On the basis of his observations in the **Goligher Circle,** Dr. W. J. **Crawford** elaborated a precise theory: "Operators are acting on the brains of the sitters and thence on their nervous systems. Small particles, it may even be molecules, are driven off the nervous system, out through the bodies of the sitters at wrists, hands, fingers, or elsewhere. These small particles, now free, have a considerable amount of latent energy inherent in them, an energy which can react on any human nervous system with which they come into contact. This stream of energised particles flows round the circle, probably partly on the periphery of their bodies. The stream, by gradual augmentation from the sitters, reaches the medium at a high degree of 'tension,' energises her, receives increment from her, traverses the circle again, and so on. Finally, when the 'tension' is sufficiently great, the circulating process ceases, and the energised particles collect on or are attached to the nervous system of the medium, who has henceforth a reservoir from which to draw. The operators having now a good supply of the right kind of energy at their disposal, viz., nerve energy can act upon the body of the medium, who is so constituted that gross matter from her body can, by means of the nervous tension applied to it, be actually temporarily detached from its usual position and projected into the seance room." (*The Reality of Psychic Phenomena*, 1916, p. 243.)

The control "Walter," in the "Margery" sittings, (see Mina S. **Crandon**) always stated that he used the brain of the sitters. His assertion was no novelty. The control of the great medium D. D. **Home** indicated the same source of power at an early period. The observations of the neurologist, Dr. Charles Féré afford interesting speculations. He noticed that excitation of almost any kind tended to increase dynamometrical power. The average squeezing power, exhibited by educated students, was greater than that of robust laboring men.

It is a tempting inference that it is not so much the developed muscle as the active brain which renders a sudden concentration of muscular power possible. The seat of psychic force should then be looked for in the brain, and better and stronger phenomena should be obtained if the reasoning is quite correct, with intelligent and learned people than with mentally undeveloped ones.

Dr. J. Maxwell observed in his seances with the medium Eusapia **Palladino** that there was a marked loss in dynamometric force not only on the part of the medium, but also on the part of the sitters at the end of the seance. Sometimes the loss amounted to six kilos on the right side and fourteen on the left.

Dr. W. J. Crawford put both his sitters and his medium on the scale and found that the loss of weight of the sitters was, at the end of the seance, greater than that of the medium. The sitters lost, on an average, 5-10 ounces and were more exhausted than the medium.

Admiral Usborne Moore complained of a drain on his vitality after his direct voice seances with medium Mrs. Etta **Wriedt.**

One of the reasons why Lord **Adare** retired from his researches with D. D. Home was that the seances physically exhausted him.

Cromwell **Varley,** who assisted Crookes in his experiments with the medium Florence **Cook,** always felt depleted, while Crookes himself remained unaffected.

Prof. J. H. **Hyslop** had to go to bed for two days after his first sitting with the medium Mrs. **Piper.** Dr. Richard **Hodgson** was markedly affected.

Col. **Rochas** said, in describing the case of levitation with Eusapia Palladino in his home: "We ought to add that one of the persons who was quite close to the table [Dr. Maxwell; see **Mediums**] almost completely fainted away, not from emotion, but through weakness, saying that he felt drained of his strength as the result of Eusapia's efforts."

The method of the liberation of this vital force, the circumstances regulating the quantity of the supply, its use by the invisible operators of the seance room, its relation to **ectoplasm,** is little known. The force is subject to an ebb and flow. In some cases fasting or seclusion increase it, in some others a hearty meal. Psychological factors also enter to a great extent.

In a calm, harmonious atmosphere it is more liberally generated. The operators speak of lines of force, of a vibratory synchronization. They often ask the sitters to change places and the results of such combination is frequently surprising. Dr. Féré stated that "all our sensations are accompanied by a development of potential energy which passes into a kinetic state and externalises itself in motor manifestations."

This suggests why a skeptic whom the phenomena of the seance room leave cold and suspicious cannot witness strong manifestations. In the absence of sensations, he may not contribute to the psychic power in the same proportion as other sitters do. He may even have an effect of negative force.

Certain bodies and materials such as tables, linen, wood, dresses, etc., appear to conduct the force. Perhaps this is why women's dresses so frequently bulge out and approach the table during a seance. It also appears that some of the nervous force or fluid settles in the seance room or in the objects in use. According to the statements of controls, once the seance room has become charged the manifestations are easier to produce at the next opportunity. Controls often protest against the use of the seance room for other purposes. Again, in other instances, for reasons of their own, they may not care to preserve the remains of the force.

Mrs. Stanhope Speer, in an account given to F. H. **Myers,** described nocturnal disturbances in her house after a seance with the Rev. W. Stainton **Moses.** "The servants heard so much pounding in the seance room that they felt frightened and went to bed as quickly as possible. We were told afterwards that so much power had been generated that the spirits had to make the noise to get rid of it." She also described a similar circumstance which occurred to her and Dr. Speer. Their bedroom door was violently shaken after they went to bed and they were afterwards told that a spirit had been attracted by the spiritual light over the house, and had used up power that had been left by shaking the doors.

P. P. Alexander, in his book *Spiritualism; A Narrative with a Discussion* (1871) gave the evidence of a scientific friend and his wife in whose veracity he implicitly believed, that physical phenomena transpired after D. D. Home had left their house. Chairs moved slowly across the carpet and set themselves beside his own. Dr. Down's wife was a witness to this astonishing phenomenon.

In the early mediumship of Mrs. **Guppy,** (then Agnes Nichols), powerful phenomena were witnessed in the empty seance room afterwards. Displacement of furniture was recorded in the adjoining rooms. Robert Cooper stated in his book *Spiritual Experiences, Including Seven Months with The Brothers Davenport* (1867): "I have occasionally heard the furniture in the room where we had been holding a seance, in motion after retiring to bed . . . On leaving a room in which I had been with Ira Davenport for the purpose of talking with the spirits in a chair followed me into the passage, myself being the last to leave."

When a medium-visitor of Col. **Rochas** was shown into the room where the seance-suit of medium Auguste **Politi** was lying folded up and where, unknown to her, the investigations with Politi were going on, she became almost immediately controlled by an adverse and highly disagreeable influence. Col. Rochas took up part of the suit and gave it to the medium. The effect was instantaneous, the controlling influence becoming violent and furious, and was thought to be the spirit of a deceased monk who sometimes got hold of Politi and damaged the conditions as much as he could.

In one of Dr. W. J. **Crawford**'s photographs, a vaporous substance seems to connect the medium Kathleen Goligher with the various sitters. Whether it was ectoplasmic emanation or a nervous fluid he did not attempt to answer.

Prof. Curie was preoccupied with the idea of devising an instrument which could register and direct the liberated psychic power. His death cut short his experiments. (See also **Ectenic Force; Emanations; Movement; Psychokinesis**)

Psychic Guide Magazine

Quarterly publication devoted to "improving and understanding body, mind and spirit." It covers a wide range of New Age topics, including healing, psychics, astrology, yoga, tarot, health and diet, and features a guide to people, places, and services. It also has a comprehensive Book Shop mail order service.

After issue of Vol. 6, No. 4 (September-October 1987), the magazine changed its title to *Body, Mind & Spirit Magazine,* first issue November/December 1987. Address: Box 701, Providence, Rhode Island 02901.

Psychic Magazine

Bimonthly magazine which presents topical aspects of parapsychology, psychic phenomena and related subjects, with interviews, feature articles, book lists and other material. Published from 1969 onwards, it has a high standard of popular presentation without the sensationalism or vulgarity of so many other magazines dealing with the occult.

After Vol. 7, No. 6, *Psychic* Magazine changed its title to *New Realities,* indicating a broadening area of interest which included "developments in the emergent areas of human possibilities that affect our everyday lives" in addition to psychic phenomena and new psychic research. This wider view embraces "holistic health" (total approach to human well- being on all levels), aspects of consciousness, Eastern and Western mysticism, new life styles and parapsychology. Back numbers of some (but not all) issues of *Psychic* Magazine are available from: Library of Past Issues, *Psychic* Magazine, P.O. Box 26289, San Francisco, California 94126. *New Realities* is published from the same address. (See also **New Realities** Magazine)

Psychic Museum

Founded by veteran Spiritualist Sir Arthur Conan **Doyle,** in 1925 at 2, Victoria Street, London, S.W., containing an interesting collection of apports, automatic scripts, automatic and direct sketches and paintings, paraffin molds, photographs and other psychic objects.

Unfortunately this Museum was dispersed at a later date and some of the collection appears to have been lost or destroyed.

Some archives of the **British College of Psychic Science** were also dispersed, but items from the Institute for Psychic Research (of which Dr. Nandor **Fodor** was Research Officer) were absorbed by the **Society for Psychical Research,** London. The Harry **Price** archives are still kept at University of London, Senate House, Malet Street, London, W.C.I., England.

There are probably many psychic collections in existence in other parts of the world. T. W. Stanford, a Melbourne millionaire, collected all the **apports** of the controversial medium Charles **Bailey** and donated them to the Psychical Research Department of Leland Stanford University, California.

In Budapest (I. Mészáros u.2.) Dr. Chengery Pap established a museum of the objects apported through the mediumship of Lajos **Pap.** There was an *Other World Museum* in Rome, Lungo-Tevere Prati 12, founded by Father V. Jouet, containing many rare objects and documents bearing upon different manifestations of the departed.

In Virginia, the **Association for Research and Enlightenment** has preserved for study 15,000 transcripts of the psychic readings of Edgar **Cayce.**

The most recent psychic museum is the **Britten Memorial Museum** on the grounds of the **Arthur Findlay College** (of the **Spiritualists National Union**) in Essex, England.

Psychic News (Newspaper)

The oldest Spiritualist weekly newspaper in Britain, founded in 1932. For many years it was edited with total dedication by Maurice **Barbanell.** After his passing in 1981, the new editor was Tony Ortzen.

Psychic News has always been the preeminent source for news, discussion and controversy on Spiritualism in Britain. It also maintains a bookshop for books and magazines connected with Spiritualism and psychical research.

In November 1989, the proprietors Psychic Press Ltd. acquired the long established **Atlantis Book Shop,** 49a Museum Street, London, WC1A 1LY, and removed their own book shop to these premises, with an augmented stock of new secondhand books on the paranormal, Spiritualism, occult studies, and New Age topics.

The office of the newspaper *Psychic News* removed to: 2 Tavistock Chambers, Bloomsbury Way, London, WC1A 2SE, England.

Psychic Observer & Chimes (Magazine)

Long established American journal of spiritual science and related psychic topics, absorbing *Chimes,* formerly published separately. Address: ESPress, Inc., Box 8606, Washington, D.C. 20011. Back issues were available on microfilm.

This publication was discontinued with the last issue, July/October, 1981.

Psychic Photography

Numerous experiments have been conducted to register on sensitive plates or film **emanations** of the human body, a phenomenon on the borderline of the normal and paranormal and to prove the existence of "N" Rays (see **Emanations**), digital effluvium, ectoplasmic flow, **aura, astral body** and thought waves. On rarer occasions, phantoms were photographed in haunted houses or, without light, in the darkness of the seance room; the objectivity of clairvoyant visions was claimed and even pictures in the crystal ball were said to have been caught by the camera.

The majority of psychic photographs in the early period of psychical research consist of flashlight records of psychic structures, psychic lights, materialized figures, and of claimed spirit forms or representations invisible to the eye but obtained in daylight by so-called spirit photographers.

No group shows so many facets of mystery as this last one. **Spirit photography** was accidentally discovered by William **Mumler,** an American engraver, in 1861. To obtain the picture of a dead relative on an exposed plate is a strange experience in itself, but still more mysterious occurrences were witnessed and, paradoxical as it may sound, nothing caused greater bewilderment than the first spirit photograph which turned out to be the portrait of a living man. Those who suspected fraud from the first believed they had clinched their case. But no hue and cry stopped the fact from recurring.

Master Harrod, of N. Bridgwater, Massachusetts, accompanied by his father, went to visit Mumler. Some months previously he had been controlled in **trance** and a spirit told him that if he went to Mumler's studio, three spirits would show themselves, representing Europe, Africa and America. After Mumler developed the plate which he had exposed, the face of a European, a Negro and an Indian confronted the sitter.

"It then occurred to me," wrote Mumler of a later sitting, "to take his picture while entranced, to see if I could get the controlling power; and to that end I asked if there was any spirit present would he please entrance the medium. In a few moments he threw his head back, apparently in a deep trance. I then adjusted the focus and exposed the plate, and took the picture as represented. The spirit seen here is undoubtedly his double as it is unmistakably a true likeness of himself."

Another American spirit photographer named Evans, was taking pictures in 1875 in the studio of Mr. A. C. Maxwell in New York. While he was busy with a customer named Mr. Demarest, Mr. Maxwell was sitting asleep by the stove, some ten feet in the rear of where the camera stood. When the plate was developed Mr. Maxwell's face and full figure was discovered beside the sitter. The resemblance was unmistakable.

The success of the American medium photographers in taking pictures of the dead and of the living was quickly duplicated in England. Frederick A. **Hudson,** the first British spirit photographer, appeared on the scene in 1872. On one occasion, he claimed to have photographed the double of Frank **Herne** while the medium was in trance. His contemporaries, John **Beattie** and Thomas **Slater** were satisfied with psychic markings or with features of the dead, while the American mediums F. M. **Parkes** and M. **Reeves** obtained curious symbolic pictures on their plates. In France, Ēdouard **Buguet** was becoming famous for spirit photography. In a letter dated December 10, 1874, published in *Human Nature,* Comte de Bullet testified to having obtained on a photographic plate in Paris the double of his sister who lived in Baltimore. Writing to the Rev. W. Stainton **Moses,** he stated:

"On New Year's Day I went to Buguet and said mentally: 'You read my thoughts, my dear sister, and it would be a grand New Year's gift for me if you would come to me with all your children.' When the operation was done she appeared on the plate with her three daughters. I sat a second time, and she came with her two boys, making in all her five children—all perfect likenesses. . . . On the plate with her daughters she appears holding a card on which is written: 'Your desire is realised, receive the felicitations of my children,' signed with her name. Here I would observe that M. Buguet did not know whether she had any children, nor how many, nor how they were divided—three girls and two boys."

At another sitting with Buguet, the image of Comte de Bullet's sister appeared with her mother standing beside her. This was the fulfillment of a written promise on a previous plate by the sister to bring her mother. From a comparison of time, it appeared likely that the ladies were asleep at the time the photograph was taken. Encouraged by these marvelous occurrences, Stainton Moses made arrangements that he would appear in spirit in Buguet's studio in Paris on January 31, 1875 while his body remained in London. On the first plate there was a faint image of Stainton Moses, on the second, a perfect likeness. Writing in *The Spiritualist* (vol. 6, 1875, p. 119) Stainton Moses stated:

"There is no doubt whatever as to the fact that the spirit of a person whose body was lying asleep in London was photographed by M. Buguet in Paris. And there is no doubt that this is not a solitary instance. Nor do the communications which I have received respecting it from those who have never deceived me yet, leave any room for doubt that the spirit was actually present in the studio, and that the picture is not one of some image made up by the invisibles as is sometimes the case."

When Buguet eventually received a term of imprisonment on his own confession of fraud, there was much controversy about psychic photography, even although Buguet subsequently retracted his confession. But interest in spirit photography was successfully sustained in Britain by Richard **Boursnell** and David **Duguid** until the advent of William **Hope** and Mrs. Emma **Deane.**

Boursnell was brought to the attention of the public by William T. **Stead.** In an article in *The Fortnightly Review* on 'How I Know the Dead Return,' he told the story of the spirit photograph of Piet Botha, the first Boer commandant killed at the siege of Kimberley. Boursnell described the presence of the spirit before the exposure of the plate and gave his name. Stead knew several Bothas, but none of the name of Piet. He kept the matter to himself. After the South African War, he sent the photograph to General Botha. It was instantly recognized as a striking likeness of Pietrus Johannes Botha, a relative.

The stage magician J. N. Maskelyne wrote in *The Magic Mirror* ridiculing the case, and pointed out that Botha was killed on October 24, 1899. Four days later, the news arrived in England and on October 28 his portrait was published in the *Daily Graphic.* According to Stead, however, this portrait bore not the least resemblance to the Piet Botha of the Boursnell picture, which was not a reproduction from the *Daily Graphic.*

Boursnell and Duguid presented strange new problems in evaluating the validity of claimed psychic photography.

Mr. F. C. Barnes, a business man of Brisbane, Australia, visited Richard Boursnell in London in 1908. Boursnell was then old, did not like to oblige his guest but with much difficulty he was persuaded. During the sitting he said: "There is a spirit of a beautiful lady here, who seems in a very bright light, and suffered greatly on earth." "I concluded," wrote F. C. Barnes, "that it was my wife, and on receipt of the proofs was greatly disappointed to find it was not. I asked those present if they could recognise it. 'No,' said a lady, 'but it looks like royalty.' "

Then Mr. Barnes suddenly remembered that in 1908 a friend lent him a book *The Martyrdom of an Empress,* which made a deep impression on his mind and which contained a portrait in the frontispiece. He obtained a copy of the book for comparison. "The most surprising thing to myself, and which opens a large subject as to reflected thought-forms, is the absolute identity of the spirit photograph with the one in the book, even the cross worn there."

J. W. **Brodie-Innes,** an Edinburgh solicitor and occultist, called on the Scottish medium David **Duguid** and obtained a remarkable spirit photograph of a Cyprian priestess, of whom the impression was given to the medium that she was dedicated to the Temple of Venus in Cyprus. It was afterwards discovered by Mme. Isabelle de Steiger that the photograph was a copy of a German picture "Night" in the possession of Mr. Brodie-Innes.

It was always known that spirit photographs could be produced in many ways by fraudulent means. Experts state that there are over two hundred ways of producing "extras" by normal means. To mention one—bisulphate of quinine is invisible to the eye, but a skull painted on the forehead with this substance would appear afterwards on the photographic plate. In 1908, the London *Daily Mail* decided to look into the matter and appointed a committee for the investigation of spirit photography. It consisted of six members: R. Child Bailey, F. J. Mortimer, E. Sanger-Shepherd, three skeptics and three believers: A. P. Sinnett, E. R. Serocold Skeels and Robert King. The result of the inquiry was negative, owing, in the view of the latter three members, to the unfortunate and impractical attitude adopted by those who had no previous knowledge of the subject.

In the meantime many claims of paranormal photography were put forward in America. Jay J. Hartman of Cincinnati obtained a certificate in 1876, signed by six professional photographers and other prominent people of his city, as a result of a public investigation, that his pictures could not be normally produced.

The **Seybert Commission** planned to investigate spirit photography but it could not come to terms with the photographer W. M. **Keeler.**

Frank Foster of Grand Rapids, Michigan, used to take sitter's portrait in the ordinary way and use the camera as a dark chamber afterwards for obtaining the spirit extra. According to Judge Monck's testimony, quoted in James Coates' *Photographing the Invisible* (1911): "I first sat for my picture and then went to the camera, and he placed his fingers on the same and I placed my fingers on his hand. He was in a quiver till a shock came, and he said: 'That is sufficient.' " The case was weak, however, as the developed pictures were not handed to the Judge until a few days later and he recognized none of the spirit extras.

Alexander Martin of Denver, Colorado, produced groups of children and baby faces on his plates. They appeared in veritable clouds, often obliterating the faces of the sitters, or in column-like formation like a tree. A personal investigation by Dr. J. H. **Hyslop** (*Journal* of the American Society for Psychical Research, vol. 14, 1920), however, was inconclusive.

The most convincing demonstrations were made by Edward **Wyllie** in California, and later in England, around 1900. His powers were singular and showed a blending between **psychometry** and spirit photography, as he often found it possible to obtain a psychic extra by having an article of the departed sent to him and exposed to the camera. His extras were not restricted to human faces.

Once he obtained the portrait of a large dog which was recognized by his sitter. In a sitting in Manchester England, on March 22, 1910, the extra of a boy appeared on his plate beside the picture of Mr. A. W. Orr, who was for many years president of the Manchester Psychic Research Society. James **Coates** discovered that the boy was a child of a friend of his. He did not then know whether the boy had passed over, but found out in due time that he was very much alive. Wyllie, the medium, was unacquainted with his existence, never saw him and could not explain the occurrence.

"There are well-authenticated cases," wrote Coates on the problem (in *Photographing the Invisible*) "where the living subject could not be photographed. This has occurred with hypnotised subjects. Indeed, I have recently had the facts presented to me by Mr. Bailey, of Birmingham, where he failed to photograph Dr. Hooper when the latter was in a semi-trance state. The testimony in this case was most conclusive."

One of the most striking spirit photographs was produced by William Walker—the first man to obtain psychic extras in colors—in the **Crewe Circle** of William T. **Stead** on May 6, 1912, twenty-two days after the latter's death in the "Titanic."

Walker had visited Stead in September 1911, to show him his album of psychic photographs. Stead desired that Walker should "keep him posted" in regard to future success. He did not get in touch with him afterwards and when the tragedy of the "Titanic" became known, Walker's wife told him: "You promised to keep Mr. Stead posted, but now it is too late." Walker replied: "Possibly he will comprehend why I did not write to him and send him copies as I promised but he will perhaps try to keep me posted." On May 6, 1912, Walker sat in Crewe for psychic photography. Strict test conditions were imposed. A very clear photograph of W. T. Stead was obtained, surrounded by a white nebulous mass with a circular inscription: "Dear Mr. Walker, I will try to keep you posted, W. T. Stead." The message was in Stead's handwriting which Miss Harper, Stead's secretary, found undoubtedly genuine.

The case introduces the problem of "psychographs" or psychical text printing on sensitive plates. One of its most curious instances as it occurred in Hope's mediumship is recorded in detail, with illustrations, in Prof. Henslow's book *The Proofs of the Truths of Spiritualism* (1919). To a member of the Crewe Circle, the spirit offered to produce a Greek text on a chosen plate. The fifth plate was chosen and the packet was held unopened in the sitters' hands. The result was found, as indicated: a passage from St. Luke's Gospel as contained in a unique book, given by Cyril Lucar, of Constantinople, to Charles I and preserved in the British Museum. Comparison revealed that the psychograph was not a facsimile but a copy, inexact in the formation of the letters. The manuscript in the British Museum was inaccessible to near approach as the glass case was railed around.

To the question how all these miracles are done no satisfactory answer can be returned. Charges of trickery are often based on surmise and not on evidence. The **Society for the Study of Supernormal Pictures,** which was largely composed of skeptical professional photographers, reported after hundreds of experiments (1919-1923) that they had received supernormal results but they have been unable to trace the *modus operandi.*

What seems certain is that the *modus operandi* varies. The first thing which should be made clear is that the appearance of a portrait on the exposed plate is in itself no proof that a spirit was actually present. The portrait may not be more than an image to convey the message of continued existence. It may be the duplicate of an existing portrait or it may be one which was never taken, or it may be of people who have never been photographed. To furnish proof that the picture is meant as a representation only, the invisible operators sometimes show the departed in various periods of earth life.

So far everything is plain. But complications arise when evidence is furnished that the image is not independent of the subconscious influence of the sitter. The Society for the Study of Supernormal Pictures had a case on record where the psychic picture of the deceased son of a sitter was found to be an exact but reversed duplicate of a photograph the sitter was wearing tucked away in her blouse in a locket. Even the rim of the locket could be seen.

A number of similar experiences have been recorded from time to time. From the Spiritualist viewpoint, such pictures may be the result of planning and devising of ways by spirits to demonstrate multifarious power. But the acceptance of such views is a grave commitment in spite of presumptive evidence that the power which produces these results is indeed remarkable. Of course, some pictures might be due to accidental double-exposure, or particularly with reversed images) to deliberate fraud.

The lens and the camera appear to be of little importance. The spirit photographer William **Hope** obtained psychic pictures on unexposed plates if he held them in a carrier. M. J. Vearncombe, of Bridgwater, England, impressed plates in sealed packets. In a similar manner, Madge Donohoe produced a bewildering variety of **"skotographs."** The "radiographs" of Dr. Julien **Ochorowicz** and the "chemicographs" of Guillaume **de Fontenay** all mean the same thing—pictures produced without a camera.

If several cameras are simultaneously focused, it often happens that only one registers the picture. As in nine cases out of ten the psychic extras are the same way up as the sitter, it is legitimate to infer that the plate is only impressed after it has been put into the dark slide.

So little is known of the actual process that it would be too dangerous to generalize. There are many cases in which something extraneous appears to be presented to the camera—a materialized form, a simulacrum built on a psychic screen, or a text written in patches of **ectoplasm.** Again, the suggestion is often strong, as if a psychic transparency were used to print a photograph, a painting or quotation. Identical markings have been found on spirit photographs from different parts of the world.

As a rule, the spirit photographs are more animated and life-like than the original photographs. They differ in expression and are often accompanied by writing, sometimes very minute, or reversed, resembling mirror writing and often exhibiting the identical character which the departed used in this life.

The draperies in which they are clothed remind one of the tradition of the "white sheeted ghost." A roll or arch of white substance appears over many psychic faces. It seems to form part of the process of building up an image; it may represent an enclosed space within which psychic forces are generated. A series of slides which Sir Arthur Conan **Doyle** took with William Hope gave a glimpse of this process. The first photograph shows a sort of cocoon of thinly-veined, filmy material, tenuous as a soap bubble, nothing within. The second shows a face inside the cocoon and an opening down the center. The opening becomes larger and finally the face looks out with the cocoon festooned back and forming an arch over the face, and a hanging veil on either side of it.

Dr. Gustav **Geley** experimented with Stanley **de Brath** in paranormal photography. Shortly before Geley was killed in an airplane accident, he intended to come to England to continue his studies. Stanley de Brath went to the sitting alone and on the fourth plate of a packet specially marked and kept in his possession, he obtained a perfect portrait of Dr. Geley.

On the evening of the following day, in response to an inquiry through a medium, he received the following explanation: "He was at last calmed and put to sleep; his guide and helpers made the model and brought it. Conditions were so loving and desirous to help that the way was clear." It should be noted that this was a distinct statement that the picture was made from a model.

Similarly a message from "Julia," the guiding spirit of W. T. **Stead,** stated that the spirits prepare a mold which they impress upon the photographic plate. If they have a good mold, they don't take the trouble to make another an/d reproduce "copies" with it whenever they are wanted. But this statement was contradicted in the book *The Blue Island* (1922) by the discarnate W. T. Stead, according to whom it is either the idea of a face in the **control's** mind, or the impression of the actual faces passed through a sheet of **ectoplasm** which gives the appearance of masks to many spirit photographs.

The "extras" seldom show relationship with the sitter. They are most often strange faces. Frequently the spirit **guide** of the medium appears on the plate. His or her picture is usually clearer and more perfect. The origin of the unknown faces is uncertain. Sometimes they are said to be spirit entities *en rapport* with the place in question as it was reasonable to suppose in a curious period of Edward **Wyllie's** mediumship. They may be "trespassers" nearer to the earth than the desired communicator or they may be produced by the strong emotional impressions left by a previous sitter.

The state of the medium's health and the atmospheric conditions appear to play an important part, also to some extent the mental atmosphere. In the case of William **Hope** the average was one psychic image on every seven exposed plates. Hope preferred to use the plates the sitters brought.

Mrs. Ada E. **Deane,** an elderly working woman, on the other hand, insisted, for some time in her psychic career, on having them sent to her in advance for the purpose of "magnetizing" them. However, she produced psychic pictures on plates which were substituted for the "magnetized" ones without her knowledge.

The "extras" of the British medium John **Myers** were remarkably clear and well-defined, which was considered a reason for further suspicion when he was accused of fraud.

The spirit photographer often foretells success. He may be a clairvoyant and see and describe spirit faces, as Richard Boursnell and John Myers did, so that their identity could be compared afterwards. Or he may simply see lights about the sitter, which is always considered a good sign. Laxity of mind on the part of the sitter is helpful. Tenseness, anxiety or antagonism makes success very doubtful. Some sitters, for reasons unknown, have an antagonistic influence. If Miss C. E. **Wood,** the **materialization** medium, sat for psychic photography, the collodion was always found scraped off the plate.

The actinic action of the spirit forms is peculiar. The "extras" may appear at the moment the developing fluid touches them, while the figures of the sitters develop much later. With some mediums, the exposure is unusually long. Mrs. Deane sometimes took fifteen minutes to half an hour. Hope took less, Myers took about seven minutes. No photographer has yet explained why such over-exposed plates do not burn up.

Nor does the mystery stop there. The plates may show the background and the "extra," but not a trace of the sitter. Sometimes even the background will be invisible or the background will show through the body of the sitter which had been rendered transparent. The "extra" may have a different tone and color from the normal picture. In freakish cases, it appears as positive or, in still more extraordinary instances, the sitter's picture is positive and the psychic "extra" negative.

In an experience of W. T. Stead, a stereoscopic and an ordinary camera were simultaneously exposed. The stereoscopic camera showed a spirit form and the sitter in exact relationship; the ordinary camera only showed the sitter.

J. Trail Taylor, then editor of the *British Journal of Photography,* experimenting with David **Duguid** in 1892, obtained "extras" which were not in stereoscopic relationship and showed no relief when viewed through a stereoscope. He concluded that the picture was not formed through the lens at all but was impressed within the camera.

It is unfortunate that the whole subject of psychic photography, whether "spirit photographs," or the scripts of "skotographs" and "psychographs," is riddled with fraud. William Mumler was prosecuted in 1868, Édouard Buguet prosecuted and imprisoned in 1876, Richard Boursnell was exposed, so too was Edward Wyllie and William Hope. The two brothers C. and G. R. Falconer were fined for fraudulent spirit photography in South Africa. Charges of fraud were leveled at Mrs. A. E. Deane and John **Myers.** This is not conclusive evidence that all spirit photography is fraudulent, but it is difficult to accept that genuine phenomena and fraud may be intermingled, since faked photographs involve deliberate planning and technical processes. In some cases, trick cameras have been used.

The psychical researcher Harry **Price** examined such a trick camera which had been specially constructed for the spirit photographer Frederick A. **Hudson,** who was responsible for fifty-four of the photographs in *Chronicles of Spirit Photography* by Georgina Houghton (1882). The trick camera contained a special mechanism for imprinting a previously prepared "spirit extra" on a photographic plate.

There is a very shrewd chapter on 'Secrets of "Spirit" Photography' in Harry Price's book *Confessions of a Ghost Hunter* (1936; 1974). Technical developments in photographic method and apparatus since Price's time have made fake spirit photography even easier to achieve.

Another crushing blow for claimed paranormal photography was the revelation in 1983 that the photographs of the **Cottingley fairies** taken between 1917 and 1920 were fakes after all. These photographs were the subject of Sir Arthur Conan Doyle's book *The Coming of the Fairies* (1922, 1928) and had been believed genuine for over sixty years.

Many competent individuals had believed that the photographs might be "thoughtforms" impressed on photographic plates rather than actual fairies, since there is reasonable evidence that mental images are sometimes produced in this way.

In 1921 Dr. Tomobichi **Fukurai** of the Imperial University of Tokyo in Japan had published a book of his experiments titled *Clairvoyance and Thoughtography.* Although Dr. Fukurai had been obliged to resign his university post through his interest in psychic subjects, the question of "thoughtography" was later revived through experiments with a seventeen-year-old boy Masuaki Kiyota who claimed unusual faculties in "thoughtography" (now known in Japan as **"Nengraphy"**) and mental-bending.

In the U.S., some remarkable experiments were undertaken by parapsychologist Dr. Jule **Eisenbud** in 1964 with Ted **Serios,** who claimed the ability to project photographic images on to camera film by staring into the camera lens, using a Polaroid camera. Dr. Eisenbud's book *The World of Ted Serios* (1966) offers persuasive evidence that such images were paranormal.

For a skeptical view on psychic photography, see the chapter 'Ted Serios—Thought Photographer' in Milbourne Christopher's book *Mediums, Mystics & the Occult* (1975).

Another modern development in paranormal photography is the innovation of Kirlian photography of an aura surrounding human beings, animals and plants. For many years, the human aura has been considered a psychic phenomenon, visible to gifted sensitives. In the nineteenth century, the subject was investigated by the scientist Karl von Reichenbach, and later by the British physician Walter J. Kilner (1847-1920), who devised a method of making the aura visible through spectacle screens or goggles impregnated with the chemical dicyanin.

In 1958, Semyon Davidovich and his wife Khrisanova Kirlian described a photographic technique of converting the non-electrical properties of an object into electrical properties recorded on photographic film. Such experiments would appear to validate the objective reality of the human aura (see **Kirlian Aura**). (See also **Aura; Ectoplasm;** Tomobichi **Fukurai; Materialization; Nengraphy;** Ted **Serios; Skotograph; Society for the Study of Supernormal Photography; Spirit Photography; Thoughtforms; Thoughtography**)

Recommended reading:

Coates, James. *Photographing the Invisible; Practical Studies in Supernormal Photography, Script, and Other Allied Phenomena,* L. N. Fowler, London, 1911; Arno Press, 1973

Crawford, W. J. *The Psychic Structures in the Goligher Circle,* John M. Watkins, London, 1921

De Fontenay, Guillaume. *La Photographie de l'Étude des Phénomès* Psychiques, Paris, 1912

Doyle, Arthur Conan. *The Case for Spirit Photography,* Hutchinson, London, 1922; George H. Doran, New York, 1923

Eisenbud, Jule. *The World of Ted Serios; "Thoughtographic" Studies of an Extraordinary Mind,* William Morrow, 1967

Foveau de Courmelles, F. V. *La Photographie Transcendentale,* Paris, n.d.

Fukurai, T. *Clairvoyance & Thoughtography,* Rider & Co., London, 1931; Arno Press, 1975

Girod, Fernand. *Pour Photographier les Rayons Humaines,* Paris, 1912

Glendinning, Andrew. *The Veil Lifted; Modern Developments of Spirit Photography,* Whittaker & Co., London, 1894

Houghton, Miss [Georgiana]. *Chronicles of the Photographs of Spiritual Beings and Phenomena Invisible to the Material Eye,* E. W. Allen, London, 1882

Imoda, Enrico. *Fotografie de Fantasmi,* Turin, Italy, 1912

Krippner, Stanley & Daniel Rubin. *Galaxies of Life; The Human Aura in Acupuncture and Kirlian Photographies,* Gordon & Breach, 1973 (reissued *The Kirlian Aura; Photographing the Galaxies of Life,* Anchor paperback, 1974)

Lancelin, Charles. *L'Âme Humaine; Etudes Expérimentales de Psycho-Physiologie,* Paris, 1921

Montandon, Raoul. *La Photographie Transcendentale,* Paris & Geneva, 1936

Mumler, William H. *Personal Experiences of William H. Mumler in Spirit Photography,* Boston, 1875

Patrick, C. V. *The Case Against Spirit Photography,* Kegan Paul, London, 1921

Patterson, Tom. *100 Years of Spirit Photography,* Regency Press, London, 1965

Permutt, Cyril. *Beyond the Spectrum; A Survey of Supernormal Photography,* Patrick Stephens, Cambridge, U.K., 1983

Price, Harry. *Confessions of a Ghost Hunter,* London/Putnam, 1936; Causeway Books, 1974

Rochas d'Aiglun, A. *L'Extériorisation de la Motricité; Recueil d'Experiences,* Paris, 1896

Schrenck-Notzing, Baron von. *Phenomena of Materialisation,* Kegan Paul, London, 1923; Arno Press, 1975

Stead, Estelle W. *Faces of the Living Dead,* London, 1925

Wilmot, T. S. *Twenty Photographs of the Risen Dead,* Midland Educational Co., Birmingham, U.K., 1894

Psychic Register International

Annual directory listing psychics in Great Britain, Canada and the U.S. Address: Ornion Press, P.O. Box 1816T, Erie, Pennsylvania 16507.

Psychic Research (Journal)

The Journal of the **American Society for Psychical Research** published under this title between 1928-1932, edited by Frederick Bligh **Bond.**

Now known as *Journal* of the American Society for Psychical Research, published by the Society at 5 West 73 Street, New York, N.Y. 10023.

Psychic Research Quarterly

British journal issued in 1920, edited by W. Whately **Carington.** The title was changed to *Psyche* in 1921, and the scope was enlarged to deal with psychology.

Psychic Science

A system of data to demonstrate the existence of spirits independent of the human body, and to validate their ability to communicate with humanity. According to J. Hewat **McKenzie**'s summary in his book *Spirit Intercourse,* (1916), the following claims fall within the scope of Psychic Science:

1) That at the death of the body, a human being continues to function as a conscious being.

2) That he or she functions after death in a refined spirit-body or soul, which has substance and weight, and which can be seen and photographed.

3) That this soul existed within the physical body during life, and is organic, having brain, nerves, blood-vessels, heart, etc.

4) That the soul can communicate in various ways with persons on earth both before and after death.

5) That the world in which the soul dwells after the death of the body lies immediately around the physical earth.

6) That a man or woman while alive may leave the physical body, and by use of the soul, may explore spheres of refined physical states, commonly called the spirit world.

The foundation of various British societies or colleges of Psychic Science stems from such claims. (See also **British College of Psychic Science; College of Psychic Studies**)

Psychic Science (Journal)

Quarterly journal of the **British College of Psychic Science,** London, issued from April 1922 onwards. The first volume was titled *Quarterly Transactions of the British College of Psychic Science.* After January 1923, the title was simplified to *Psychic Science* with the issue of April 1923 onwards.

After 1945, this publication was superseded by *Light,* as the journal of the **College of Psychic Studies** published from 16 Queensberry Place, South Kensington, London, SW7 2EB England. (See also **Light**)

Psychic Science International Special Interest Group

Founded in 1976 from among members and associates of Mensa (persons who have established by score in a standard intelligence test that their intelligence is higher than that of 98 percent of the population). PSISIG is concerned with interest in and conducting of scientific research in the psychic sciences and arts such as theories of existence and reality, states of mind, human **auras, clairvoyance,** mental and thought projection, **telepathy, dowsing, psychometry, healing** and defense, multiple personalities and possession, psychokinesis, survival after death, discarnate entities, and extraterrestrial life. It disseminates research findings, applies research and education for the benefit of humanity in mental health, reduction of superstition and fraud, safety, and enhancement of human relations.

It provides educational programs to promote awareness and capabilities in the psychic sciences and arts, offers grants, scholarships, and other aids to persons or organizations studying psychic sciences. It operates a speakers bureau, provides members for surveys by responsible, noncommercial organizations, compiles statistics. It plans to develop a facility for housing the group's activities, including a school, laboratories, and libraries. It maintains data bases, biographical archives, and lending library of 200 volumes. Divisions of PSISIG include: Anti-Crime Team; Auras; Dowsing; Healing; Out-of-Body Experiences; Premonitions; Psychometry; Survival. Publications: *PSI-M* Newsletter/Journal (ten per year), *Yearbook,* also the *Handbook/Mindbook,* and special research reports. Address: 7514 Belleplain Drive, Dayton, Ohio 45424.

Psychic Surgery

A special branch of psychic **healing** which involves varying techniques. Some psychic surgeons believe that the spirit of a dead doctor influences them, and they mime operations while in a trance condition. Other healers appear to perform real operations, making an incision with bare hands, removing pathological matter, and causing an instantaneous healing of the incision.

Typical of the first type is British healer George Chapman, who claimed to be controlled by the dead surgeon "Dr. Lang." Chapman diagnosed while in trance and simply laid his hands on the patient or made movements indicative of a phantom operation.

The second group of psychic surgeons includes individuals like Tony **Agpaoa** and others in the Philippines, and José **Arigó** in Brazil. Agpaoa used no anesthetic or scalpel, yet appeared to make an incision in which there was some flow of blood. He inserted his hands in the body and either removed pathological tissue with his hands or cut it away with unsterilized scissors. He then moved his hand over the incision, which closed instantaneously, leaving no scar.

Operations conducted by Agpaoa and similar psychic surgeons in the Philippines have been photographed and even filmed, and appear highly evidential. However, there is a strong possibility that some "operations" of this kind by certain healers and perhaps even at times by Agpaoa have been fakes. It is suggested that if a small quantity of blood and a piece of animal tissue is palmed, the flesh "operated" on can be pinched and made to appear as if an incision has been made. The cure that follows would then be a matter of strong suggestion rather than actual surgery, although it could be a cure none the less.

However, the issue is not so simple. Dr. Andrija **Puharich,** himself a physician, visited José Argió in Brazil and was the subject of a psychic operation for a small lipoma on the elbow. Arigó, who claimed to be controlled by the spirit "Dr. Fritz," made an incision with a pocket knife without anesthetic or sterilization and removed the tumor. A small incision scar was left, which healed within four days. The operation was filmed, and it was clear that the tumor had been removed.

Some of the psychic surgeons in the Philippines have apparently removed not only pathological tissue but also such things as eggshells, coffee grounds and even a crayfish. Author Tom Valentine, who conducted on-the-spot researches in the Philippines, believes that such phenomena are related to **apports** in Spiritualism and that healers like Agpaoa materialize and dematerialize matter. They might also be shamanistic tricks to enhance auto suggestion.

Skeptics like magicians James **Randi** and Milbourne **Christopher** dismiss psychic surgery as clever conjuring and the healers as frauds. But, as with Spiritualist and related paranormal phenomena, it is possible that the healers and a large proportion of their phenomena are genuine, but that trickery may sometimes be resorted to when natural powers fail, or that trickery results in healing of suggestible subjects.

Thousands of invalids and merely curious travelers visit the Philippines every year to seek the psychic surgeons. Many of these return home disillusioned. Often sick visitors are pestered by touts the moment they arrive at Manila airport. They may be taken by taxi to an alleged healer, only to discover that he is a fraud after he has relieved them of thousands of dollars. Even if they are told that they will be driven to some famous and successful healer, they may actually arrive at the surgery of some complete nonentity without any healing skill, and have no way of knowing who they are entrusting themselves to. In one or two cases, perhaps, the faith of the patient may achieve some cure, even at the hands of a fake.

Such cautions are emphasized in a book by Gert Chesi titled *Faith Healers in the Philippines* (1981, translated from *Geistheiler auf den Philippinen*). The author is an Austrian writer and journalist who has also worked with the Australian Broadcasting Corporation. He had previously studied **Voodoo** in Africa. His superbly illustrated book on Philippine healers describes his detailed investigations of scores of healers over a period of nearly a year.

He discovered genuine as well as fake healers, and concluded that the dividing line is often a confusing one, since although the blood and the objects apparently removed from a patient's body may be unrelated to genuine surgery, they may still be part of a mysterious shamanistic healing process.

Uneducated healers often achieve more impressive results than those with some medical knowledge, and such primitive healers appear to remove objects from a diseased body which are clearly unrelated to any genuine illness, such as coins, leaves, nails, plastic objects, or even garbage.

Chesi suggests that such objects, as well as the blood, may be the products of the healer's imagination, becoming solidified as **materializations** or **apports.**

Many healers believe that patients will not believe in the healer's power unless they see an apparent incision with plenty of blood, and a tangible object removed from the body. Although this can be achieved by sleight of hand (and probably often is), it may also be part of a paranormal process of materialization and dematerialization. Other Philippine healers regard such bloody operations as unnecessary and practice "magnetic healing."

Chesi's book is one of the most important contributions to a controversial subject, and should be required reading for anyone contemplating a visit to Philippine healers. The author includes a useful list of forty known Philippine healers with their current addresses.

Recommended reading:

Chesi, Gert. *Faith Healers in the Philippines,* Perlinger Verlag, Austria 1981

Christopher, Milbourne. *Mediums, Mystics & the Occult,* Thomas Y. Crowell, 1975

Fuller, John G. *Arigó. Surgeon of the Rusty Knife,* Thomas Y. Crowell, 1974
Sherman, Harold. *Wonder Healers of the Philippines,* DeVorss, 1967
Valentine, Tom. *Psychic Surgery,* Henry Regnery, 1973

Psychic Telephone

An instrument invented by F. R. Melton of Nottingham, England, consisting of a box inside of which was a rubber bag connected with a pair of earphones from a radio set. The idea was that if a medium inflated the bag with his or her breath and then sealed it, the bag would take place of the medium and direct voices would be heard through the earphones in his absence.

The psychical researcher Harry **Price** subjected the instrument to a thorough test in the **National Laboratory for Psychical Research,** London. It did not work.

Psychic Yellow Pages, The

1977 listing of psi practitioners and organizations in Northern California. Includes psychics, astrologers, holistic centers, palmists, tarot readers. Address: P.O. Box 998, Saratoga, California 95070.

Apparently no longer issued.

Psychical Research

Scientific inquiry into the facts and causes of unexplained paranormal and mediumistic phenomena. Its first concern is to establish the occurrence of the claimed facts.

If they are not due to fraud, observational error, the laws of chance, i.e., if they are found to occur, the next stage of the inquiry is to establish the reason of their occurrence, whether known natural laws are sufficient to explain them or whether there is reason to suppose the action of unknown force.

The nature of such unknown force, the mode of its manifestation, has to be experimentally investigated. If it is not a blind force but operated by intelligence it has to be examined whether this intelligence is mundane. Not until every other explanation and test fails can the claim of a paranormal source be accepted.

The Historical Background

The term "psychical research" covers all scientific investigation into the obscure phenomena traditionally connected with the so-called "supernatural," undertaken with a view to their elucidation. Certain of these phenomena are known all over the world, and have remained practically unaltered almost since prehistoric times.

Such are the phenomena of **levitation,** and **fire ordeal, crystal-gazing, thought-reading** and **apparitions,** and whenever these were met with there was seldom lacking the critical inquiry of some researcher, not carried away on the tide of popular credulity, but reserving some judgment for the impartial investigation of the manifestations.

Thus John Gaule, in his *Select Cases of Conscience Touching Witches and Witchcraft* (London, 1646), stated: "But the more prodigious or stupendous [of the feats mentioned in the witches' confessions] are effected meerly by the devill; the witch all the while either in a rapt ecstasie, a charmed sleepe, or a melancholy dreame; and the witches' imagination, phantasie, common sense, only deluded with what is now done, or pretended." And a few other writers of the same period arrived at a similar conclusion.

The result of many of these medieval records was to confirm the genuineness some of the phenomena witnessed, but here and there, even in those days, there were skeptics who refused to see in them any supernatural significance.

Poltergeist disturbances came in for a large share of attention and investigation, to which, indeed, they seemed to lend themselves. The case of the **Drummer of Tedworth** was examined by Joseph Glanvill, and the results set forth in his *Saducisimus Triumphatus,* published in 1668. The **Epworth phenomena,** which occurred in the house of John Wesley's father, called forth many comments, as did also the **Cock Lane Ghost,** the Stockwell Poltergeist and many others.

Those who investigated Animal **Magnetism** and **Mesmerism** may, in a manner, be considered psychical researchers, since these forerunners of **Hypnotism** were the fruits of prolonged investigation into the phenomena, which indubitably existed in connection with the **trance** state. Moreover many of the investigators were scientists or physicians. If their speculations were wild and their inquiries failed to elicit the truth of the matter, it was only natural, at that stage of scientific progress, that this should be so.

And here and there, even in the writings of **Paracelsus** and **Mesmer,** we find that they had glimpses of scientific truths which were in advance of their age, foreshadowings of scientific discoveries which were to prove the triumph of future generations. Paracelsus, for example, stated in his writings: "By the magic power of the will, a person on this side of the ocean may make a person on the other side hear what is said on this side. . . . The ethereal body of a man may know what another man thinks at a distance of 100 miles and more."

This reads uncommonly like an anticipation of **telepathy,** which has since attained to such remarkable prominence although it is not now generally attributed to "the ethereal body of a man." Such things as these would seem to entitle many of the Mesmerists and the older mystics to the designation of "psychical researchers."

As knowledge increased and systematized methods came into use, such inquiries became ever more searching and more fruitful in definite results.

The introduction of modern Spiritualism in 1848 undoubtedly gave a remarkable impetus to psychical research. The movement was so widespread, its effects so apparent, that it was inevitable that scientists should be drawn into an examination of the alleged phenomena.

Thus we find engaged in the investigation of Spiritualism such individuals as William Carpenter, Michael **Faraday** and Augustus **De Morgan,** and on the Continent, Count **de Gasparin,** Prof. Marc **Thury** and Prof. J. C. F. **Zöllner.** One of the most important of individual investigators was undoubtedly Sir William **Crookes,** who worked independently for some time before the founding of the Society for Psychical Research.

However, although much good work was done by independent students of "psychic science," as it came to be called, the **London Dialectical Society** was established in 1867, and a resolution was carried two years later "to investigate the phenomena alleged to be Spiritual Manifestations, and to report thereon." The Committee included many distinguished individuals. A report was published in 1871.

In 1875 Sergeant **Cox,** also concerned with the London Dialectical Society, founded the **Psychological Society** of Great Britain for similar investigations. A volume of *Proceedings* of the Society's work was published in 1878. The Rev. W. Stainton **Moses,** C. C. Massey and Walter H. Coffin were among the members. When Sergeant Cox died in 1879 the society came to an end.

From 1878 onwards, the **British National Association of Spiritualists,** London (founded in 1873), appointed a research council which carried on significant research work with well-known mediums of the day under strict test conditions. Early in 1882, conferences were held at the Association's rooms presided over by Prof. William F. **Barrett,** which resulted in the formation of the **Society for Psychical Research.**

The Society was founded in the same year.

The Establishment of Psychical Research

The Society for Psychical Research was founded largely by a group of scientists and philosophers connected with Trinity College, Cambridge. The Society was formed "to examine without prejudice or prepossession and in a scientific spirit those faculties of man, real or supposed, which appear to be inexplicable in terms of any generally recognized hypothesis."

The following passage from the Society's original prospectus, quoted by Frank **Podmore** in his book *The Naturalisation of the Supernatural* (1908) indicated with sufficient clearness its aim and proposed methods.

"It has been widely felt that the present is an opportune time for making an organised and systematic attempt to investigate that large group of debatable phenomena designated by such terms as mesmeric, psychical, and spiritualistic.

"From the recorded testimony of many competent witnesses, past and present, including observations recently made by scientific men of eminence in various countries, there appears to be, amid much delusion and deception, an important body of remarkable phenomena, which are *prima facie* inexplicable on any generally recognised hypothesis, and which, if incontestably established, would be of the highest possible value.

"The task of examining such residual phenomena has often been undertaken by individual effort, but never hitherto by a scientific society organised on a sufficiently broad basis."

The first president of the Society was Professor Henry **Sidgwick,** and among later presidents were Professor Balfour **Stewart,** Professor William **James,** Sir William **Crookes,** The Earl of **Balfour,** Professor Charles **Richet** and Sir Oliver **Lodge,** while prominent among the original members were Frank **Podmore,** F. W. H. **Myers,** Edmund **Gurney,** Professor W. F. **Barrett,** Rev. W. Stainton **Moses** and Mrs. **Sidgwick.** Lord **Rayleigh** and Andrew **Lang** were also early members of the Society.

Good work was done in America in connection with the Society by Dr. Richard **Hodgson** and Professor J. H. **Hyslop.**

On the continent Cesar **Lombroso,** J. Maxwell, Camille **Flammarion,** and Professor **Richet**—all men of the highest standing in their respective branches of science—conducted exhaustive researches into the phenomena of Spiritualism, chiefly in connection with the Italian medium Eusapia **Palladino.**

At first, the members of the Society for Psychical Research found it convenient to work in concert, but as they became more conversant with the broad outlines of the subject, it was judged necessary for certain sections or individuals to specialize in various branches. The original plan, sketched roughly in 1882, grouped the phenomena under five different heads, each of which was placed under the direction of a separate Committee:

1) An examination of the nature and extent of any influence which may be exerted by one mind upon another, apart from any generally recognized mode of perception. (Hon. Secretary of Committee, Professor W. F. Barrett.)

2) The study of hypnotism, and the forms of so-called mesmeric trance, with its alleged insensibility to pain; clairvoyance, and other allied phenomena. (Hon. Secretary of Committee, Dr. G. Wyld.)

3) A critical revision of Reichenbach's researches with certain organisations called "sensitive," and an inquiry whether such organisations possess any power of perception beyond a highly-exalted sensibility of the recognised sensory organs. (Hon. Secretary of Committee, Walter H. Coffin.)

4) A careful investigation of any reports, resting on strong testimony, regarding apparitions at the moment of death, or otherwise, or regarding disturbances in houses reputed to be haunted. (Hon. Secretary of Committee, Hensleigh Wedgwood.)

5) An inquiry into the various physical phenomena commonly called Spiritualistic; with an attempt to discover their causes and general laws. (Hon. Secretary, Dr. C. Lockhart Robertson.)

Besides these, there was a Committee appointed to consider the literature of the subject, having as its honorary secretaries Edmund Gurney and Frederic W. H. Myers, who, with Frank Podmore, collected a number of historic instances.

Of the various heads, however, the first is now generally considered the most important, and is certainly that which has yielded the best results to investigators. In the case of hypnotism, it is largely through the exertions of psychical researchers that it has been admitted to the sphere of legitimate physiology, whereas it was formerly classed among doubtful phenomena, even at the time the Society was founded.

The examination of Baron **Reichenbach's** claims to having discovered a new psychic fluid or force (**Od** or Odyle) which issued like flame from the points of a magnet or the human fingertips, was at length abandoned, nothing having been found to verify his conclusions which, however, previous to this had been largely accepted.

The investigations in connection with apparitions and haunted houses, and with the Spiritualist phenomena, continued for many years, although on the whole no definite conclusion was arrived at.

Although the members of the Society undertook to carry out their investigations in an entirely unbiased spirit, and some members who had joined the Society originally as avowed Spiritualists soon dropped out, yet after prolonged and exhaustive research the opinion of the various investigators often showed marked divergence. So far from being pledged to accept a spirit, or any other hypothesis, it was expressly stated in a note appended to the prospectus that "Membership of this Society does not imply the acceptance of any particular explanation of the phenomena investigated, nor any belief as to the operation, in the physical world, of forces other than those recognised by Physical Science."

Nevertheless F. W. H. Myers and Sir Oliver Lodge, to take two notable instances, found the evidence sufficient to convince them of the operation in the physical world of disembodied intelligences, who manifest themselves through the organism of the "medium" or "sensitive."

Frank Podmore, on the other hand, was the exponent of a telepathic theory. Any phase of the "manifestations" which was not explicable by means of such known physiological facts as suggestion and hyperesthesia, the so-called "subconscious whispering," exaltation of memory and automatism, or the unfamiliar but presumably natural telepathy, must, according to him, fall under the grave suspicion of fraud.

His theory of poltergeists, for example, by which he regards these uncanny disturbances as being the work of naughty children, did not admit the intervention of a mischievous disembodied spirit. In coincident hallucination, again, he considered telepathy a suitable explanation, as well as in all cases of "personation" by the medium. His view—one that was shared by Andrew Lang and others—was that if telepathy were once established the spirit hypothesis would not only be unnecessary, but impossible of proof.

The most important of telepathic experiments were those conducted by Professor and Mrs. Sidgwick in 1889-91. The percipients were hypnotized by G. A. Smith, who also acted as agent, and the matter to be transmitted consisted at first of numbers and later of mental pictures. The agent and percipient were generally separated by a screen, or were sometimes in different rooms, although the results in the latter case were perceptibly less satisfactory. On the whole, however, the percentage of correct guesses was far above that which the doctrine of chance warranted, and the experiments did much to encourage a belief that some hitherto unknown mode of communication existed.

At a later date, the trance communication of Mrs. **Piper** would seem to point to some such theory, although F. W. H. Myers, Dr. Hodgson and Dr. Hyslop, who conducted a very profound investigation into those communications, were inclined to believe that the spirits of the dead were the agencies in this case.

Telepathy cannot yet be considered, as scientifically proved. At the best it is merely a surmise, which, if it could be established, might provide a natural explanation for much of the so-called occult phenomena. Even its most ardent protagonists admit that its action is extremely uncertain and experiment correspondingly difficult.

Nevertheless, each year sees an increasing body of scientific and popular opinion favorable to the theory, so that we may hope that the surmised mode of communication may at last be within a reasonable distance of becoming an acknowledged fact.

The machinery of telepathy is generally supposed to be in the form of ethereal vibrations, or "brain waves," acting in accordance with natural laws, although Gerald Balfour and others inclined to an entirely metamorphosed theory, urging, e.g., that the action does not conform to the law of inverse squares.

The subject of **hallucinations,** coincidental or otherwise, has also been largely investigated over the years, and has been found to be closely connected with the question of telepathy. **Apparitions** were in former times regarded as the "doubled" or "ethereal bodies" of the persons they represented, but they are not now considered to be otherwise than subjective.

Nevertheless the study of "coincidental hallucinations," i.e., hallucinatory apparitions which coincide with the death of the person represented, or with some other crises in his or her life—raises the question as to whether the agent may not produce such an hallucination in the mind of the percipient by the exercise of telepathic influence, which may be judged to be more powerful during an emotional crisis.

Now hallucinations have been shown to be fairly common among sane people, about one person in ten having experienced one or more. But the chances that such an hallucination should coincide with the death of the person it represents are about, 1 in 19,000; that is, if no other factor than chance determines their ratio.

With a view to ascertaining whether coincidental hallucinations did actually bear a higher proportion to the total number of hallucinations than chance would justify, the Society for Psychical Research took a census in 1889 and the three or four years immediately following (see **Census of Hallucinations**).

Professor Sidgwick and a committee of members of the Society conducted the investigations and printed forms were distributed among 410 accredited agents of the Society, including, besides its own members, many medical men and others belonging to the professional classes, all of whom gave their services without fee in the interests of science.

In all some 17,000 persons were questioned, and negative as well as affirmative answers were sent in just as they were received, the agents being specially instructed to make no discrimination between the various replies. Out of 8,372 men, 655 claimed to have had an hallucination, and 1,029 out of 8,628 women—9.9 percent of the total. When ample allowance had been made for defects of memory with regard to early hallucinations by multiplying the 322 recognized and definite cases by 4, it was found that 62 coincided with a death; but, again making allowances, this number was reduced to 30.

Thus we find 1 coincidental hallucination in 43 where, there being no causal connection we should expect 1 in 19,000. Clearly, then, if these figures be accepted, there must be some causal connection between the death and the apparition, whether it be a Spiritualist or telepathic theory that may be used. Although it be true that memory plays strange tricks, yet it is difficult to understand how persons of education and standing could write down and attest minutes and dated records of events that never happened.

Apart from telepathy, which, because it postulates the working of a hitherto unknown natural law, takes premier place, perhaps the most interesting field of research is that of **automatism.** Trance writings and utterances have been known since the earliest times, when they were attributed to demoniac possession, or, sometimes, angelic possession.

By means of **planchette, ouija,** and such contrivances many people are able to write automatically and divulge information which they themselves were unaware of possessing.

But here again, the phenomena are purely subjective, and are the result of cerebral dissociation, such as may be induced in hypnosis. In this state, exaltation of the memory may occur, and thus account for such phenomena as the speaking in foreign **tongues** with which the agent is but ill-acquainted. Or, conceivably, cerebral dissociation may produce a sensitiveness to telepathic influences, as would seem apparent in the case of the medium Mrs. Leonore E. **Piper,** whose automatic productions in writing and speaking have supplied investigators with plentiful material, and have done more, perhaps, than anything else to stimulate an interest in so-called Spiritualist phenomena.

In connection with the "physical" phenomema—probably no less the result of automatism than the "subjective," although in a different direction—the Italian medium Eusapia **Palladino** was carefully studied by many eminent investigators, both in Great Britain and on the Continent, with the result that Camille **Flammarion**, Professor **Richet**, Sir Oliver **Lodge** (to mention only a few) satisfied themselves with regard to the genuineness of some of her phenomena.

On the whole, even if psychical research has not succeeded in scientifically validating such matters as the immortality of the soul or the possibility of communication between the living and the dead, it has done good work in widening the field of psychology and therapeutics and in gaining admission for that doctrine of suggestion which since the time of Bertrand (see **Hypnotism**) and **Braid** was not openly received and acknowledged by the medical profession.

Many of the obscure phenomena attending Mesmerism, animal magnetism, witchcraft, poltergeists, and kindred subjects have been brought into line with modern scientific knowledge. Much has been accomplished in over a century since the Society for Psychical Research was founded, and probably in time to come it will accomplish still more, both in conducting experiments and investigations in connection with psychic phenomena, and in educating the public in the use of scientific methods and habits of thought in their dealings with the "supernatural."

In the U.S., the **American Society for Psychical Research,** founded in 1885, and the **Boston Society for Psychical Research,** founded in 1925, were representative bodies of similar standing.

The American S.P.R. had been founded on the initiative of Sir. William F. **Barrett** with the active cooperation of Dr. Richard **Hodgson.** Many distinguished scientists were involved and the general attitude was at first somewhat skeptical towards psychical phenomena.

The first period of the old American Society for Psychical Research was from 1885 to 1889, after which it was absorbed with the Society for Psychical Research, London. In 1907, the American branch was formally reconstituted as "Section B" of the American Institute for Scientific Research, "Section A" being devoted to abnormal psychology. The title of American Society for Psychical Research was readopted in 1922.

From this period onwards, the Society owed much to the dedicated work of Prof. James H. **Hyslop.** Early support for the Society's work was forthcoming from grants from the American universities at Stanford, Harvard and Clark.

After the death of Hyslop in 1920, the work of the Society was carried on by his assistant Walter Franklin **Prince,** who became director of research and edited the Society's publications. In 1921, Prof. William **McDougall,** a noted psychologist, became president. He was succeeded the following year by Frederick Edwards, a clergyman.

During the 1920s there were policy dissensions within the Society, sparked off by the American tour of Spiritualist Sir Arthur Conan **Doyle** and the controversial investigations of the medium "Margery" (Mrs. Mina S. **Crandon**). In 1925, Prince, McDougall and Gardner **Murphy** led a group which split off into the Boston Society for Psychical Research, which existed until the death of Prince in 1934. Meanwhile the A.S.P.R. continued to be preoccupied with the problem of the "Margery" mediumship.

From 1930 onwards, there was a new phase in American psychical research, spearheaded by Dr. J. B. **Rhine,** whose experimental work at Duke University had been encouraged by McDougall. This work involved using ordinary college students as subjects instead of mediums, with an emphasis on statistical and scientific method in evaluating experiments.

Rhine's report *Extra-sensory Perception* (1934) described 85,724 card-guessing trials and aroused much controversy, but in 1938 the American Psychological Association upheld Rhine's testing procedures and his statistical method. The American Institute of Mathematical Statistics stated: "If the Rhine investigations is to be fairly attacked, it must be on other than mathematical grounds."

It was through the work of Rhine that the terms "parapsychology," "extrasensory perception" and "psychokinesis" became widespread. The *Journal of Parapsychology* was first published in 1937, and the Parapsychological Association was founded in 1957.

The work of Rhine and his associates established parapsychology as a reputable field for scientific study. In the last few decades there has been a movement away from the purely card-guessing and similar studies to a broader field of research, embracing all the phenomena formerly associated with Spiritualist mediums and shamans, and the spontaneous phenomena of **poltergeists** and **out-of-the-body** travel. Newer developments of psychokinesis investigation now include the metal-bending phenomena first popularized by psychic **Uri Geller.**

European developments in psychical research and parapsychology and their precursors are dealt with under the headings France, Germany, Italy.

The societies for psychical research and individual investigators have built up an impressive edifice of facts. Many of the first skeptical investigators, like Sir Oliver Lodge, Professor William Barrett, F. W. H. Myers and Professor Hyslop, became firm believers in demonstrated survival. Many others remained hesitative, like Edmund Gurney, Prof. William James, Prof. Hans Driesch, Prof. E. C. S. Schiller, Prof. William MacDougall, Mrs. Henry Sidgwick, Camille Flammarion, Professor Richet, Dr. Gustave Geley, Hereward Carrington, Dr. Walter Franklin Prince, J. Malcolm Bird and Harry Price but very few could preserve the extreme skepticism which Frank Podmore evidenced. As a working theory the spirit hypothesis is now accepted by many psychical researchers.

If the opposition of orthodox science is not yet yielding the reason is probably to be found in the observation of Stanley **de Brath:** "History shows that even in the case of normal and verifiable physical facts involving a departure from habitual modes of thought, a period of two generations usually elapses between the first verification and the general acceptance." (See also **Parapsychology; Proceedings of the American Society for Psychical Research; Proceedings of the Old American Society for Psychical Research; Proceedings of the National Laboratory of Psychical Research; Proceedings of the Society for Psychical Research**)

Recommended reading:

Carrington, Hereward. *The Story of Psychic Science,* Rider, London, 1930

Coover, J. E. *Experiments in Psychical Research at Leland Stanford Junior University,* Stanford University, California, 1917; Arno Press, 1975

Crookes, William. *Researches in the Phenomena of Spiritualism,* J. Burns, London, 1874

Douglas, Alfred. *Extra-sensory Powers; A Century of Psychical Research,* Overlook Press, Woodstock, New York, 1977

Driesch, Hans. *Psychical Research; The Science of the Supernormal,* G. Bell, London, 1933; Arno Press, 1975

Edge, Hoyt L., Robert L. Morris, John Palmer & Joseph H. Rush. *Foundations of Parapsychology; Exploring the Boundaries of Human Capability,* Routledge & Kegan Paul, 1986 [contains valuable historical perspective of psychical Research and Parapsychology]

Gauld, Alan. *The Founders of Psychical Research,* Routledge & Kegan Paul, London, 1968

Grattan-Guinness, Ivor (ed.). *Psychical Research; A Guide to Its History, Principles & Practices, in Celebration of 100 Years of the Society for Psychical Research,* Aquarian Press (paperback), U.K., 1982

Haynes, Renée. *The Society for Psychical Research 1882-1982; A History,* Macdonald & Co., London, 1982

Hyslop, James H. *Enigmas of Psychical Research,* Putnam, 1906

(London Dialectical Society). *Report on Spiritualism of the Committee of the London Dialectical Society,* Longmans, Green, Reader & Dyer, London, 1971

Maxwell, Joseph. *Metapsychical Phenomena,* Duckworth, London, 1905

Podmore, Frank. *Studies in Psychical Research,* Putnam, 1897; Arno Press, 1975

Price, Harry. *Fifty Years of Psychical Research; A Critical Study,* Longmans, Green, London, 1939; Arno Press, 1975

Richet, Charles. *Thirty Years of Psychical Research,* Collins, London/Macmillan, New York, 1923

Rhine, J. B. *Extra-sensory Perception,* Boston Society for Psychical Research, 1934; revised ed. Branden (paperback), Boston, 1964

Rhine, J. B. & others. *Extrasensory Perception After Sixty Years,* Holt, 1940; Branden, Boston, 1966

Rhine, J. B. (ed.). *Progress in Parapsychology,* Parapsychology Press, Durham, North Carolina, 1971

Rhine, J. B. & Robert Briwer (eds.). *Parapsychology Today,* Citadel, 1968

Thouless, Robert H. *From Anecdote to Experiment in Psychical Research,* Routledge & Kegan Paul, London, 1972
Tyrrell, G. N. M. *Science and Psychical Phenomena,* Harper, 1938; Arno Press, 1975
White, Rhea A. & Laura A. Dale. *Parapsychology; Sources of Information,* Scarecrow Press, 1973

Psychical Research Foundation

Established in 1960 by Charles E. **Ozanne** to investigate phenomena relating to the survival of human personality after death.

It serves as a scientific and educational research center to investigate the possibilities of continuation of consciousness after death of the physical body. Its research program includes study of sensitives, haunting and poltergeist phenomena, as well as out-of-the-body travel. The Foundation conducts undergraduate tutorials in parapsychology, and sponsors "visiting research assistantships." News of its activities are published in its quarterly bulletin *Theta.*

Address: P.O. Box 217, Carrollton, Georgia 30117.

Psychics & Mystics Fayre

An offshoot of the **Mind-Body-Spirit Festivals** in Britain by Graham **Wilson,** comprising smaller exhibitions held regularly at different London and provincial centers, feature practitioners and groups concerned with **yoga, Tarot, astrology, clairvoyance,** health and healing, arts and crafts, Ufology. Address: New Life Designs Ltd., Arnica House, 170 Campden Hill Road, London, W8 7AS, England.

Psychische Studien (Journal)

Journal of psychical studies, founded by Alexander **Aksakof** in 1874 in Leipzig, Germany, running since 1925 under the title *Zeitschrift für Parapsychologie.* It ceased publication in 1934.

Psycho-Therapeutic Society, The

Founded in London, England, on April 1, 1901, for the advocacy of health reform, medical hypnotism, suggestive therapeutics, curative human radiations, and general drugless healing. The first president was George **Spriggs,** whose services as healing medium were gratuitously at the disposal of patients for years.

No longer active.

Psychode

Term used by psychical researcher Prof. Marc **Thury** for **ectoplasm.**

Psychoenergetic (Journal)

Quarterly British publication edited by American parapsychologist Dr. Stanley S. **Krippner,** includes discussions on psi phenomena by distinguished writers and parapsychologists. Address: Gordon & Breach, 41 William IV Street, London, W.C.2. England.

Psychograph

Paranormal script obtained by spirit photographers on a sensitive plate. (See also **Psychic Photography; Skotograph**)

Psychography

Term used by British medium the Rev. W. Stainton **Moses** (1839-1892) to denote all forms of **direct writing** by spirit entities.

Psychokinesis

The ability to move objects at a distance by some as yet unidentified mental power. The term has now largely displaced "Telekinesis" formerly used by psychical researchers, and Spiritualists.

The term "psychokinesis" or "PK" was adopted by psychologist J. B. **Rhine** and his associates at the Psychology Department, Duke University, Durham, North Carolina from 1934 onwards in relation to experiments with influencing the fall of dice by mental concentration.

Special terms have developed during the study of PK, such as: "PK-MT" (psychokinetic effect on moving targets, such as dice), "PK-LT" (influence on living target, such as plants, healing, influencing of animals), "PK-ST" (influence on static targets). A "PK Placement Test" denotes a PK-MT experiment in which the subject attempts to influence falling objects to land in a designated area. (See also **Movement**)

Psychological Society, The

The Psychological Society came into being in Britain in April 1875, having as its founder and president Sergeant E. W. **Cox** and numbering among its members the Rev. William Stainton **Moses,** Walter H. Coffin, and C. C. Massey.

The avowed aim of the Society, as set forth in the president's inaugural address, was the elucidation of those Spiritualist and other problems now grouped under the term "psychical research," and to which the Society somewhat loosely attached the designation of "psychology."

To this end they proposed to collect and consider the available material bearing on psychic phenomena, but in reality they accomplished little of any practical value, as may be seen from their published *Proceedings* (1875-79), published London, 1880. The president himself had not the necessary scientific qualifications for investigation of such phenomena. In November 1879, on the death of its president, the Society came to an end.

But although the Psychological Society regarded psychic phenomena from a more or less popular standpoint, and conducted its investigations in a somewhat superficial manner, nevertheless it contained the germ of scientific inquiry into the domain of psychic science which, a few years later, with the founding of the **Society for Psychical Research,** was to raise the study to a level where it became worthy of the attention of philosophers and scientists.

Hitherto those who were satisfied of the genuineness of Spiritualist marvels had been content, for the most part, to accept the explanation of spirit intervention, but the Psychological Society was the crystalization of a small body of "rationalist" opinion which had existed since the days of **Mesmer.**

Sergeant Cox, in his book *The Mechanism of Man* (2 vols., 1876-79) stated that "spirit" was refined matter, or molecular matter split into its constituent atoms, which thus become imperceptible to our physical organism; a view which was possibly shared by some members of the Psychological Society. (See also **London Dialectical Society; Psychical Research**)

Psychology

The science of mental processes and consciousness in relation to sensory experience and physical life.

To the extent that psychology is concerned with individual human experience, it has connections with philosophy and metaphysics.

Psychical research is a different branch of inquiry, inasmuch as it is mainly concerned with the demonstration and investigation of paranormal faculties and the concept of the soul, with the question of survival after bodily death as a legitimate inference.

According to the criterion of Prof. Charles **Richet**: everything that the human intelligence can do, even when it is most profound and penetrating is psychological. Everything of which such intelligence is incapable belongs to metapsychics.

The crux of the matter is that the greatest difficulty is experienced in drawing the line between what the human intelligence can and what it cannot do, as many paranormal faculties appear to originate in the subconscious mind and manifest along the same channels as the phenomena of abnormal psychology.

That an abnormal bodily condition may facilitate the function of a paranormal faculty without being the reason and cause of it, as psychologists would contend, is well illustrated by an example mentioned by Hereward **Carrington** in *The Story of Psychic Science* (1930) concerning a girl acquaintance of his who fell into Lake Minnetonka, sank three times and was rescued unconscious.

A severe illness complicated with pneumonia followed her misadventure. During her convalescence she became clairvoyant and could tell what letters were in the mailbox in the morning and often their approximate contents. When she was completely restored her clairvoyant faculty disappeared.

Neither pneumonia nor near-drowning can be supposed the cause of such clairvoyance. Similarly it is reasonable to infer that in the clairvoyance of hysteric subjects, the abnormal bodily condition is simply a coincident phenomenon but not the cause and explanation. An abnormal condition may open up a channel of function for paranormal faculties. If the abnormal condition becomes permanent, mediumship may develop in organisms which constitutionally were not adapted for paranormal manifestations.

The study of abnormal psychology may also have relevance to the emotional and temperamental problems of some mediums, particularly those who are disposed to fraudulent tricks, even if gifted with some genuine psychic faculties.

The preferred modern term "parapsychology" for psychical research seem felicitous insofar as much paranormal faculty seems "beside" or "beyond" psychology, but requiring awareness of the findings of psychology for adequate understanding and study. Some of the great psychical researchers, like Prof. William James, came to their psychical studies from a background of psychology. (See also **Parapsychology; Psychical Research**)

Recommended reading:

Beloff, John. *The Existence of Mind,* MacGibbon, London, 1962; Citadel, 1965

Brown, William. *Science and Personality,* Yale University Press, 1929; McGrath, College Park, Maryland, 1972

Burt, Cyril. *Psychology and Psychical Research,* Society for Psychical Research, London, 1968

Ehrenwald, Jan. *Telepathy and Medical Psychology,* W. W. Norton, 1948

Eysenck, H. J. *Sense and Nonsense in Psychology,* Penguin paperback, London, 1957

Hudson, Thomas J. *The Law of Psychic Phenomena; A Working Hypothesis for the Systematic Study of the Vast Potential of Man's Mind,* McClurg, G. P. Putnam's Sons, 1894 etc.; Hudson-Cohan, Chicago, 1970; Weiser, New York, 1972

LeShan, Lawrence. *The Medium, The Mystic, and the Physicist; Towards a General Theory of the Paranormal,* Viking Press/Turnstone Books, London, 1974

McCreery, Charles. *Science, Philosophy, and ESP.* Faber & Faber, London, 1967; Archon Books, Hamden, Conn., 1968

Mitchell, T. W. *Medical Psychology and Psychical Research,* Methuen, London, 1922

Myers, F. W. H. *Human Personality and Its Survival of Bodily Death,* 2 vols., Longmans, Green, London, 1903; Longmans, Green, New York, 1954; one vol. abridged ed., University Books, 1961

Osty, Eugene. *Supernormal Faculties in Man,* Methuen, London, 1923

Rhine, J. B. & Robert Brier. *Parapsychology Today,* Citadel, 1968

Rosenthal, Robert. *Experimenter Effects in Behavioral Research,* Appleton-Century-Crofts, New York, 1966

Schmeidler, Gertrude R. *ESP in Relation to Rorschach Test Evaluation,* Parapsychology Foundation (paperback), New York, 1960

Wolman, Benjamin B. (ed.) *Handbook of Parapsychology,* Van Nostrand Reinhold, 1977; McFarland & Co., 1986

Psychomancy

Divination by spirits or the art of evoking the dead. (See also **Ceremonial Magic; Necromancy**)

Psychometry

A term used to denote the faculty, supposed to be common among mediums, of becoming aware of the characters, surroundings, or events connected with persons by holding in the hand small objects, such as a watch or ring, which they have had in their possession.

The famous medium Mrs. Hester **Dowden** described psychometry as "a psychic power possessed by certain individuals which enables them to divine the history of, or events connected with, a material object with which they come in close contact."

No doubt such a faculty has been manifest from ancient times, but it was first named and discussed in modern history by the American scientist J. Rodes **Buchanan** in 1842. The term derives from the Greek *psyche* (soul) and *metron* (measure) and signifies "soul-measuring," or measurement by the human soul.

Dr. Buchanan's theory was based on the belief that everything that has ever existed, every object, scene, event, that has occurred since the beginning of the world, has left on the ether or astral light a trace of its being, indelible while the world endures, and not only on the ether, but likewise on more palpable objects such as trees and stones. Sounds and perfumes also leave impressions on their surroundings.

Just as a photograph may be taken on a film or plate and remain invisible until it has been developed, so may those psychometric "photographs" remain impalpable until the developing process has been applied. And that which is to bring them to light is the psychic faculty and mind of the medium. One authority, Professor William **Denton,** declared that he found this psychic faculty in one man in every ten, and four women in ten.

The exercise of this faculty is claimed to be coupled with a **community of sensation** of varying intensity. The psychometric effect of medicines in the experiments of Dr. Buchanan was similar to their ordinary action. When an emetic was handed to a subject, he could only avoid vomitting by suspending the experiment. Dr. Buchanan's earliest experiments, with his own students, showed that some of them were able to distinguish different metals merely by holding them in their hands. Later he found that some among them could diagnose a patient's disease simply by holding his hand.

Many persons of his acquaintance, on pressing a letter against their forehead, could tell the character and surroundings of the writer, the circumstances under which the letter was written and other particulars. Many mediums who have since practiced psychometry have become famous in their line. As has been said, the method to hold in the hand or place against the forehead some small object, such as a fragment of clothing, a letter, or a watch, when the appropriate visions are seen or sensations experienced.

Psychometrists may be entranced, but are generally in a condition scarcely varying from the normal. The psychometric pictures, presumably somehow imprinted on the article to be psychometrized, have been likened to pictures carried in the memory, seemingly faded, yet ready to start into vividness when the right spring is touched. It is tempting to suppose that the rehearsal of bygone tragedies so frequently witnessed in haunted houses is really a psychometric picture which at the original occurrence impressed itself on the room. The same may be said of the sounds and perfumes which haunt certain houses. (See **Apparitions**)

The psychological effect of the experimental objects appears to be very strong. When Mrs. Cridge, Prof. Denton's subject, examined a piece of lava from the Kilauea volcano she was seized with terror and the feeling did not pass off for more than an hour.

On examining the fragment of a mastodon tooth, Mrs. Denton said: "My impression is that it is a part of some monstrous animal, probably part of a tooth. I feel like a perfect monster, with heavy legs, unwieldy head, and very large body. I go down to a shallow stream to drink. I can hardly speak, my jaws are so heavy. I feel like getting down on all fours. What a noise comes through the wood! I have an impulse to answer it. My ears are very large and leathery, and I can almost fancy they flap my face as I move my head. There are some older ones than I. It seems, too, so out of keeping to be talking with these heavy jaws. They are dark brown, as if they had been completely tanned. There is one old fellow, with large tusks, that looks very tough. I see several young ones; in fact, there is a whole herd."

From a fragment of meteorite, she derived these impressions: "It carries my eyes right up. I see an appearance of misty light. I seem to go miles and miles very quickly, up and up. Streams of light come from the right, a great way off. . . . Light shining at a vast distance."

Some influences prostrate the psychic and cause illness. Some are too antagonistic to be interfered with and the medium will refuse to handle the object. Some psychometrists are so sensitive that if an object belonging to a deceased person is handed to them they will take on the personal appearance and mannerism of the owner and may suffer from his or her ailments.

Eugene Crowell, in *The Identity of Primitive Christianity and Modern Spiritualism* (2 vols., 1875-79) wrote of a sentry box in Paris in which the sentry on duty committed suicide by hanging. Another soldier was assigned to the same duty, and within three weeks thereafter took his life by similar means. Still another succeeded to the post, and in a short time this third sentry was met a similar fate. These events being reported to the Emperor Louis Napoleon, he ordered the sentry box to be removed and destroyed.

There are many instances on record in which the bodies of dead men have been traced through psychometric influence. Attempts have been made to employ it in criminology with varying results.

In his book *Thirty Years of Psychical Research* (1923), Prof. Charles **Richet** quoted the experience of Dr. Dufay with a non-professional somnambulist called Marie. He handed her something in several folds of paper. She said that the paper contained something that had killed a man. A rope? No. A necktie—she then continued. This was a prisoner who had hanged himself because he had committed a murder. He killed his victim with a gouet (a woodman's hatchet). Marie indicated the spot where the gouet was thrown on the ground. All was as she said. The gouet was searched for and found in the place indicated.

Most of the psychometrists give their readings in normal state. A few are hypnotized. Señora Maria Reyes de Z. of Mexico with whom Dr. **Pagenstecher** (*Proceedings* of the American Society for Psychical Research, vol. 16) and Dr. Walter Franklin **Prince** (*Proceedings* of the A.S.P.R., vol. 18) conducted a series of successful experiments, belongs to the latter class. From a shell picked up on the beach of Vera Cruz she gave the following reading:

"I am under water and feel a great weight pressing upon my body. I am surrounded by fishes of all kinds, colors, shapes and sizes. I see white and pink coral. I also see different kinds of plants, some of them with large leaves. The water has a dark green, transparent colour. I am among the creatures but they do not seem to notice my presence, as they are not afraid of me in spite of touching me as they pass by."

Many psychometrists assert that they are simply instruments and that spirits do the reading. Positive proof to this effect was claimed in the book *Spirit-Psychometry* by D. J. d'Aute **Hooper** (1914).

Trance mediums often ask for objects belonging to the dead to establish contact. It was a habit with Mrs. Leonore **Piper.** But other psychics, like Pascal **Forthuny,** repudiated spirit intervention and considered psychometry a personal gift, a sensitivity to the influence of which objects are possessed. This influence, or emanation, was likened by Dr. Waldemar Wasielawski to the rhabdic force which apparently bends the rod of the dowser or water-witcher (see **Dowsing**).

It appears that very slight contact will suffice to impart such personal influence. William T. **Stead** cut pieces of blank paper from the bottom pages of letters of eminent people, just below the signature of each, and sent them to Miss Ross marked "No. 1. Lady," "No. 2. Gentleman." The readings were very successful (see Stead's journal *Borderland,* October 1895).

The psychometric vision sometimes comes in quick flashes of images and requires an effort of will to be slowed down. According to D'Aute Hooper, "it would be impossible to follow up and write the impressions as they pass through my consciousness. It is far too rapid. They are like cinematographic pictures. I seem to fly, and at other times I seem to be the piece of stone, without thinking power but seeing things and happenings around me." (quoted from *Spirit Psychometry*)

The size of the visions may be small or encompass the whole room. There is no definite order in their emergence. The picture is kaleidoscopic, there is an oscillation in periods of time, but the image of more important events seem to have better sway.

The methods are individual. The percipient is passive. The exercise of the faculty requires a relaxed, receptive mind. After the clue is handed over, some psychometrists feel immediately on the spot, others mentally travel there first. Some may tear off a piece of paper from the envelope brought and put it into their mouth. Others are satisfied to handle an object, or hold it wrapped up in their hands.

As a rule, a clue containing an "influence," is indispensable for psychometric readings. But experiments with exceptional psychics led Dr. Buchanan to the conclusion that the clue may be supplanted by an index, for instance, by a name written on a piece of paper. Such cases appear to be very exceptional.

It is usually said that by psychometry a medium cannot get a reading for himself or herself. An incident told some years ago in the journal *Light* is therefore very interesting. Mrs. E. A. Cannock was handed, without her knowing the origin, a broad piece of elastic which was actually her own. She not only gave a character reading of herself, but also made a prediction which proved to be correct.

It is said that the image of engravings is retained by the glass and that by some processes, as by the employment of mercury vapor, this image can be developed. There is a suggestion of some similar effect in the following:

Mrs. Denton entered a car from which the passengers had gone to dinner. She was surprised to see all the seats occupied. "Many of them," she wrote, "were sitting perfectly composed, as if, for them, little interest was attached to this station, while others were already in motion (a kind of compressed motion), as if preparing to leave. I thought this was somewhat strange, and was about turning to find a vacant seat in another car, when a second glance around showed me that the passengers who had appeared so indifferent were really losing their identity, and, in a moment more, were invisible to me. I had had sufficient time to note the personal appearance of several; and taking a seat, I awaited the return of the passengers, thinking it more than probable I might find them the prototypes of the faces and forms I had a moment before so singularly beheld. Nor was I disappointed. A number of those who returned to the cars I recognized as being, in every particular, the counterparts of their late, but transient representatives."

Psychometric impressions may come so spontaneously as to seriously worry the sensitive in the ordinary course of life. The British medium Bessie **Williams** complained of this trouble. The Dutch psychometrist Frau Lotte **Plaat** could not go into the British Museum, London, because she felt that the exhibits were literally shouting their history. By a strong effort of will, however, such impressions can usually be dispelled.

Dr. Buchanan made a suggestion to test direct spirit writing (see **Direct Writing**) by submitting it to psychometric reading. He thought that if the writing was purely the product of the medium, the reading would give the medium's character, if not the character of the spirit author would be described. But he overlooked the complications of the **ectoplasm** from which the spirit hand was formed. If the writing was done by a materialized hand, built out of the bodily substance of the medium, it might bear as little impress of the spirit as a dictated text bears of the dictator.

As already mentioned, haunting is another psychic mystery to the elucidation of which psychometry might be called in. "That the victim of some century old villainy," wrote Sir Arthur Conan **Doyle** in his book *The Edge of the Unknown* (1930), "should still in her ancient garments frequent in person the scene of her former martyrdom, is indeed, hard to believe. It is more credible, little as we understand the details, that some thought-form is used and remains visible at the spot where great mental agony has been endured." But he was not unmindful of the difficulties of such speculation and added: "Why such a thought-form should only come at certain hours, I am compelled to answer that I do not know." For the psychometric impression should always be there and should always be perceived. But the ghost apparently is not. Its ways are strange.

Searching for Explanations

Were the psychometric speculation even partially true, it would explain nothing. "Psychometry" is just a word and not an explanation. Its essential nature, its exercise is a mystery. Stated Stephan **Ossowiecki**, perhaps the foremost psychometrist of modern times:

"I begin by stopping all reasoning, and I throw all my inner power into perception of spiritual sensation. I affirm that this condition is brought about by my unshakable faith in the spiritual unity of all humanity. I then find myself in a new and special state in which I see and hear outside time and space . . . Whether I am reading a sealed letter, or finding a lost object, or psychometrising, the sensations are nearly the same. I seem to lose some energy; my temperature becomes febrile, and the heartbeats unequal. I am confirmed in this supposition because, as soon as I cease from reasoning, something like electricity flows through my extremities for a few seconds. This lasts a moment only, and then lucidity takes possession of me, pictures arise, usually of the past. I see the man who wrote the letter, and I know what he wrote. I see the object at the moment of its loss, with the details of the event; or again, I perceive or feel the history of the thing I am holding in my hands. The vision is misty and needs great tension. Considerable effort is required to perceive some details and conditions of the scenes presented. The lucid state sometimes arises in a few minutes, and sometimes it takes hours of waiting. This largely depends on the surroundings; scepticism, incredulity, or even attention too much concentrated on my person, paralyses quick success in reading or sensation."

Illuminating as this subjective account is, it conveys little about the specific nature of psychometric influence. Dr. Pagenstecher conjectured as follows:

"The associated object which practically witnessed certain events of the past, acting in the way of a tuning fork, automatically starts in our brain the specific vibrations corresponding to the said events; furthermore, the vibrations of our brain once being set in tune with certain parts of the Cosmic Brain already stricken by the same events, call forth sympathetic vibrations between the human brain and the Cosmic Brain, giving birth to thought pictures which reproduce the events in question."

Sir Arthur Conan Doyle, in plainer language, compared psychometric impressions to shadows on a screen. The screen is the ether, "the whole material universe being embedded in and interpenetrated by this subtle material which would not necessarily change its position since it is too fine for wind or any coarser material to influence it."

Doyle himself, although by no means psychic, would always be conscious of a curious effect, almost a darkening of the landscape with a marked sense of heaviness, when he was on an old battlefield. A more familiar example of the same faculty may be suspected in the gloom which gathers over the mind of even an average person upon entering certain houses. Such sensitivity may find expression in more subtle and varied forms. "Is not the emotion felt on looking at an old master [painting] a kind of thought transference from the departed?" asked Sir Oliver **Lodge.** The query cannot be answered conclusively, since the labels attached to psychic phenomena are purely arbitrary. There may be an inclusive explanation, higher than that which Ossowiecki suggested.

"Akashic Records"

Attempts at such a synthesis have been made by Theosophists. In his introduction to W. Scott-Elliot's *The Story of Atlantis & the Last Lemuria* (1904), the first book drawn from the so-called **"Akashic Records,"** A. P. **Sinnett** explained that the pictures of memory are imprinted on some nonphysical medium, they are photographed by Nature on some imperishable page of superphysical matter. They are accessible, but the interior spiritual capacities of ordinary humanity are as yet too imperfectly developed to establish touch.

"But in a flickering fashion," he continued, "we have experience in ordinary life of efforts that are a little more effectual. Thought-transference is a humble example. In that case, 'impressions on the mind' of one person, Nature's memory pictures with which he is in normal relationship, are caught up by someone else who is just able, however unconscious of the method he uses, to range Nature's memory under favourable conditions a little beyond the area with which he himself is in normal relationship. Such a person has begun, however, slightly, to exercise the faculty of astral clairvoyance."

While such highly speculative ideas are beyond the scope of psychical research, the conception of the Akashic Records in its philosophical depths is partly supported by astronomical analogy. Owing to the vastness of interstellar distances it takes hundreds of thousands of years for light, traveling at the enormous rate of 186,000 miles per second, to reach us from distant stars. Anyone who could look at the earth from such a distant star would witness, at the present moment, the primeval past. From varying distances the creation of our world could be seen as a present reality. Theoretically, therefore, astronomy admits the existence of a scenic record of world's history. The conception of this **cosmic picture gallery** and the Akashic Records is similar.

But there is no generally validated method of access to such records in sublimated psychometry. However in G. R. S. Mead's *Did Jesus Live 100* B.C.? (1903), the author stated regarding Akashic research:

". . . it would be as well to have it understood that the method of investigation to which I am referring does not bring into consideration any question of trance, either self-induced, or mesmerically or hypnotically effected. As far as I can judge, my colleagues are to all outward seeming in quite their normal state. They go through no outward ceremonies, or internal ones for that matter, nor even any outward preparation but that of assuming a comfortable position; moreover, they not only describe, as each normally has the power of description, what is passing before their inner vision in precisely the same fashion as one would describe some objective scene, but they are frequently as surprised as their auditors that the scenes or events they are attempting to explain are not at all as they expected to see them, and remark on them as critically, and frequently as sceptically, as those who cannot 'see' for themselves but whose knowledge of the subject from objective study may be greater than theirs.

"Now, although it is true that in the majority of cases I have not been able to check their statements, and doubt whether it will ever be possible to do so, owing to the lack of objective material, nevertheless in a number of instances, few when compared with the mass of statements made, but numerous enough in themselves, I have been able to do so. It can, of course, be argued, as has been done in somewhat similar cases, that all of this is merely the bringing into subjective objectivity the imaginative dramatisation of facts which have been normally heard or read, or even momentarily glanced at, and which have sunk beneath the threshold of consciousness, either of that the seers themselves or of one or other of their auditors, or even some permutation or combination of these. But such an explanation seems somewhat feeble to one who, like myself, has taken down laboriously dictated passages from MSS., described, for instance, as written in archaic Greek uncials—MSS., the contents of which, as far as I am aware, are not known to exist—passages laboriously dictated letter by letter, by a friend whose knowledge of the language extended hardly beyond the alphabet. Occasionally gaps had to be left for certain forms of letters, with which not only my colleague, but also myself, were previously entirely unacquainted; these gaps had to be filled up afterwards, when the matter was transcribed and broken up into words and sentences, which turned out to be in good construable Greek, the original or copy of which, I am as sure as I can be of anything, neither my colleague nor myself have ever seen physically. Moreover I have had dates and information given by these methods which I could only verify afterwards by long and patient research, and which, I am convinced, no one but a widely read scholar of classical antiquity could have come across."

Simultaneous Perception of "Memory Records"

One need not go to occultists for psychic experiences in which there is a clear suggestion of memory records in independent existence of individual powers of cognition. Something of that nature has been perceived by several people simultaneously, thus suggesting some sort of objectivity.

The Battle of Edge Hill (on the borders of Warwickshire and Oxfordshire, England) was fought on October 22, 1624. Two months later a number of shepherds and village people witnessed an aerial reenactment of the battle with all the noises of the guns, the neighing of the horses and the groans of the wounded. The vision lasted for hours, was witnessed by people of reputation for several consecutive days and when rumors of it reached the ears of Charles I, a commission was sent out to investigate. The commission not only reported having seen the vision on two occasions, but actually recognized fallen friends of theirs among the fighters, amongst others Sir Edmund Varney.

A similar ancient instance was recorded by Pausanias (2nd century B.C.) according to whom on the plains of Marathon, four hundred years after the great battle, the neighing of horses, the shouts of the victors, the cries of the vanquished, and all the noise of a well-contested conflict, were frequently to be heard.

Patrick Walker, the Covenanter, is quoted in *Biographia Presbyteriana* (Edinburgh, 1827) as stating that in 1686, about two miles below Lanark, on the water of Clyde "many people gather together for several afternoons, where there were showers of bonnets, hats, guns and swords, which covered the trees and ground, companies of men in arms marching in order, upon the waterside, companies meeting companies . . . and then all falling to the ground and disappearing, and other companies immediately appearing in the same way." But Patrick Walker himself saw nothing unusual occur. About two-thirds of the crowds saw the phenomena, the others saw nothing strange.

"Patrick Walker's account," stated Andrew Lang in his book *Cock Lane and Common Sense* (1896) "is triumphantly honest and is, perhaps, as odd a piece of psychology as any on record, thanks to his escape from the prevalent illusion, which, no doubt, he would gladly have shared."

Under the pseudonyms of "Miss Morrison" and "Miss Lamont," Miss Anne Moberly, daughter of the Bishop of Salisbury and Dr. Eleanor Jourdain, published in 1911 a remarkable book entitled *An Adventure* (see **Versailles Adventure**). According to this book, in 1901 and 1902 they had simultaneous vision, in the grounds of Versailles, of the place as it was in 1789.

Some time after the first publication, testimony was given by people who lived in the neighborhood of Versailles that they had also seen the mysterious appearances, the strange phenomena being only witnessed on the anniversary of the attack on Versailles during the French Revolution.

The most inexplicable feature of the story is that the people of the eighteenth century saw, heard and spoke to the people of the twentieth century, who never doubted at the time that they were in communication with real individuals.

Psychometric Premonitions

Another class of phenomena could be classified as psychometric foreshadowings of the future. The Report on the **"Census of Hallucinations"** (*Proceedings* of the Society for Psychical Research, vol. 10, p. 332) in speaking of a solitary excursion to a lake, stated: "My attention was quite taken up with the extreme beauty of the scene before me. There was not a sound or movement, except the soft ripple of the water on the sand at my feet. Presently I felt a cold chill creep through me, and a curious stiffness of my limbs, as if I could not move, though wishing to do so. I felt frightened, yet chained to the spot, and as if impelled to stare at the water straight in front of me. Gradually a black cloud seemed to rise, and in the midst of it I saw a tall man, in a suit of tweed, jump into the water and sink. In a moment the darkness was gone, and I again became sensible of the heat and sunshine, but I was awed and felt eery. . . . A week afterwards Mr. Espie, a bank clerk (unknown to me) committed suicide by drowning in that very spot. He left a letter for his wife, indicating that he had for some time contemplated death."

Princess Karadja quoted in the *Zeitschrift für Metapsychische Forschung* (March 15, 1931) a story of a personal experience of the late Count Buerger Moerner containing this incident: "Passing through the little garden and glancing in at the window as he approached the house (looking for public refreshment) the Count was horrified to see the body of an old woman hanging from a ceiling beam. He burst into the room with a cry of horror, but once across the threshold was stunned with amazement to find the old woman rising startled from her chair, demanding the reason of his surprising intrusion. No hanging body was to be seen and the old lady herself was not only very much alive, but indignant as well . . . Some days later, being again in that locality, he decided to visit the hut once more, curious to see if by some peculiarity of the window pane he might not have been observing an optical illusion. Nearing the hut through the garden as before, the same terrible sight met his eye. This time, however, the Count stood for some minutes studying the picture, then after some hesitation knocked at the door. No answer, even to repeated knocks, until at length Count Moerner opened the door and entered to find what he saw this time was no vision. The old woman's body was indeed hanging from the beam. She had committed suicide."

Recommended reading:

Buchanan, J. Rodes. *Manual of Psychometry; The Dawn of a New Civilization,* Dudley M. Holman, Boston, 1885

Butler, W. E. *How to Develop Psychometry,* Aquarian Press, U.K./Weiser, New York, 1971

Denton, William & Elizabeth. *Nature's Secrets, or Psychometric Researches,* Houston & Wright, London, 1863

Ellis, Ida. *Thoughts on Psychometry,* Blackpool, U.K., 1899

(Hooper, T. D'Aute). *Spirit-Psychometry and Trance Communications by Unseen Agencies,* Rider, London, 1914

Verner, A. *Practical Psychometry* (pamphlet), Blackpool, U.K., 1903

Psychophone

Term suggested by James **Coates** for **direct voice** communications at seances.

Psychophysical Research Laboratories

Organization devoted to scientific investigation of **psi** phenomena, directed by parapsychologist Charles **Honorton.** Address: 301 College Road East, Princeton, New Jersey 08540.

Psychoplasm

Alternative term for **ectoplasm.**

Psychorrhagic Diathesis

Formidable term used by psychical researcher F. W. H. **Myers** for his theory of phantasmal appearances, a psychic faculty of detaching elements of personality and transforming by them a certain part of space into a phantasmogenetic center. In this center, in a manner not material or optical, the phantasm of the psychorrhagist appears and may become collectively visible. (See also **Apparitions**)

Psychosynthesis Institute

Founded around the work of Dr. Roberto **Assagioli,** psychiatrist, psychotherapist and parapsychologist. Basic concepts in Psychosynthesis include the supraconscious (a higher unconscious, source of meaning and purpose in life), the Self and the will.

Essentially psychosynthesis is a psychological and educational method of harmonizing one's relationship to environment through inner integration and synthesis. This involves a continuing process of expanding self-awareness and higher consciousness, leading from the personal to the transpersonal or universal. The approach varies according to the needs of the individual and the most suitable way of releasing inner guidance, combining the methods of psychology and spiritual disciplines.

The Institute offers theoretical and practical training for professionals and concerned individuals, as well as supporting research on psychosynthesis. Address: High Point Foundation, 647 North Madison Avenue, Pasadena, California 91101; also at Nan Clark Lane, Mill Hill, London, NW7, England.

Psychotronics

A modern term coined recently to extend parapsychology by indicating the relationship of man to the universe, interaction with other physical bodies and matter, and fields of energy, known or unknown.

The First International Conference on psychotronics was held in Prague, Czechoslovakia in 1974. Delegates included professors of physics and psychology, doctors of medicine and psychiatry, parapsychologists. Subjects discussed included Dowsing (water-witching and location of hidden objects), **Radionics, Telepathy, Kirlian Aura, Out-of-the-Body** travel and bio-electric energy fields.

Psylli

A class of persons in ancient Italy who had the power of charming serpents.

This name was given by other writers to the snake-charmers of Africa, and it is said that the serpents twisted round the bodies of these *Psylli* without doing them any injury, although the reptiles did not have their fangs extracted or broken.

In Kahira when a viper entered a house, the charmer was sent for, and he enticed it out by the use of certain words. At other times, music was used, and it is believed that the serpents understood what was said to them by the snake-charmers with complete obedience.

Puharich, Andrija (Henry Karl) (1918-)

Physician, research consultant, parapsychologist. Born February 19, 1918 in Chicago, Illinois of Yugoslavian ancestry, he studied at Northwestern University (B.A. 1942) and Northwestern University Medical School (M.B., M.D. 1946). He served in the Medical Field Service School, U.S. Army, 1953. In 1943 he married Virginia Jackson (died 1959); his second marriage in 1959 was to Huberta Gertrude Hermans. He was an interne from 1946-47, resident, medical research from 1947-48 at Permanente Foundation Hospital, Oaklands, California. In 1948 he set up the Round Table Foundation, Glen Cove, Maine, to study the physico-chemical basis for paranormal phenomena. From 1953-55 he was a captain, M.C., U.S. Army, Chemical Corps, from 1958-59 staff physician, U.S. Army Hospital, Fort Ord, California.

He was subsequently research consultant of Mind Science Foundation, San Antonio, Texas, Belk Research Foundation, New York, N.Y., Consciousness Research Foundation, Metro-Goldwyn-Mayer One Step Beyond Productions, Marco Engineering Company, Los Angeles, California, and various industrial and scientific organizations, director of Medical research, Intelectron Corporation, New York. He is a member of the New York Academy of Sciences, American Medical Association, American Association for the Advancement of Science, San Francisco Mycological Society.

A versatile man, Dr. Puharich invented an orthopedic cast and other corrective devices, holding some fifty patents. But in April 1971 he decided to free himself from foundations and companies and devote himself to parapsychological investigation. This decision was stimulated by his brief contact with the Brazilian psychic surgeon **Arigó,** who died suddenly in an auto accident in 1971.

Dr. Puharich went to Tel Aviv, Israel to meet metal-bending psychic Uri **Geller** and commenced a series of tests of Geller's strange talents.

During these tests Geller apparently manifested psychokinetic ability, and dematerialization of objects which reappeared elsewhere. Under hypnosis, a mysterious voice was heard in the same room as Geller, claiming to be a superior intelligence of an extraterrestrial nature. Similar messages had been conveyed to Puharich by a Hindu scholar and psychic Dr. D. G. Vinod in 1953, and also by Dr. Charles Laughead of Whipple, Arizona three years later.

These messages are described in detail in Puharich's biography of Uri Geller. It must be emphasized that these astonishing communications claiming to originate from superior intelligences in spaceships manifested in the presence of Dr. Puharich and seemed to follow him around from one psychic to another.

Without further information it is difficult to attempt an evaluation of such revelations. Books by Dr. Puharich include: *The Sacred Mushroom: Key to the Door of Eternity* (1959), *Beyond Telepathy* (1962), *Uri: A Journal of the Mystery of Uri Geller* (1974), (with Harold E. Puthoff) *The Iceland Papers* (1979), *Time No Longer* (1980).

Purce, Jill (1947-)

British biophysicist, author, editor, and lecturer on mystical aspects of sound vibration and the human voice.

She was born October 10, 1947, at Newcastle, Staffordshire, educated at Headington School, Oxford and Reading University (1966-70), B.A. Hons.; Chelsea College of Art, London (1970-71); Kings College, London (1971-72). Her special interest in mystical aspects of life began when she studied Fine Arts at Reading University and became fascinated with relationships between form and pattern in nature, and patterns in the development of human consciousness. She was awarded a research fellowship in the biophysics departments at Kings College, and studied the spiral form in science, religion, and art. This became the basis for her book *The Mystic*

Spiral; Journey of the Soul (1974), concerned with the evolution of consciousness in spiritual traditions and in psychology.

She also investigated the effect of sound vibrations on particles and on water, a subject that had been much neglected since the early experiments of E. F. F. Chladni in 1785 and Mrs. Margaret Watts Hughes between 1885-1904.

Jill's first introduction to the effect of sound in matter came from seeing photographs concerning the work of Hans Jenny, a Swiss engineer and doctor who had been influenced by the teachings of Rudolph **Steiner.** Jenny used liquids, pastes, and fine powders to demonstrate that formless matter could be organized into exquisite and precise patterns through sound vibration. In 1885, Mrs. Watts Hughes had studied the patterns formed by lycopodium seeds, sand, and also semi-liquid pastes when vibrated by the human voice. She invented the "Eidophone" instrument to facilitate control and direction of voice vibrations on the medium.

Jill Purce spent a period of study with the eminent composer Karlheinz Stockhausen in Germany. It was at this time that Stockhausen composed his 'Alphabet for Lieges,' illustrating relationships between sound vibration and matter. Afterwards Jill extended her studies with special reference to vibrations of the human voice. She studies Mongolian and Tibetan overtone chanting (producing chords of simultaneous notes octaves apart, with harmonics) in the Himalayas, India, her teacher being the Chantmaster of the Gyutö Tibetan Monastery and Tantric College. She subsequently developed her studies with American Indians and shamans from various traditions.

The investigations not only shed light on ancient traditions and practices concerning the mystic power of sound vibrations, but also showed that the human voice can act as a creative link between body and mind. In her lectures and workshops in various countries, Jill Purce has demonstrated that understanding and liberation of the voice can transform the personality, in both a psychotherapeutic and a spiritual way. She has also shown that such use of the voice may have a positive value for women in childbirth. She has conducted workshops on the healing and meditative effects of sound and voice in London, Switzerland, Norway, France, Sweden, and the U.S.

In addition to this specialized work, she is also general editor of the Thames & Hudson series of books on sacred traditions, art, and imagination. She is married to the biologist Rupert **Sheldrake.** (See also Paranormal **Music; Mantra; Nada;** Alfred **Wolfsohn**)

Purna Yoga (Journal)

Annual publication (supported by donations) of Atmaniketan Ashram, devoted to the teachings of Sir **Aurobindo;** includes news of **Auroville,** the new religious city in India. Address: Atmaniketan Ashram, 1291 Weber Street, Pomona, California 91768.

Purohit Swami, Shri (1882-c. 1936)

Hindu monk, poet and philosopher, who greatly influenced the poet W. B. **Yeats** and (through him) actress Margot Ruddock, close friend of Yeats in his later years.

Born October 12, 1882, at Badnera, near Amraoti in Berar, India (Central Provinces) of a religious and wealthy Brahmin family, his father had renounced a large fortune out of respect for the memory of his own father.

As a boy, Purohit grew up in a devout religious atmosphere and had several encounters with wonder-working Mahatmas.

After attending a local Anglo-vernacular school, he studied at University of Bombay, matriculating in 1898. He went on to the Morris College at Nagpur, where he entered the Arts course. After passing his examination in 1901 he joined the B.A. class and studied philosophy. He failed his examination, but took a position as teacher at Amraoti, eventually receiving his B.A. from Calcutta University in 1903. He went on to Poona and studied at the Deccan College, where he obtained his LL.B. degree.

However, he was more interested in obtaining spiritual experience from yogis and mahatmas than in practicing law. He made several religious pilgrimages. At the request of his parents, he married a sixteen-year-old girl Godu Bai, but after the birth of two daughters and a son, he obtained his wife's permission to renounce the life of householder. He studied under his guru Bhagwan Shri Hamsa, and about 1923 became a renunciate and traveling monk. He practiced severe austerities and made religious pilgrimages throughout India. At the request of his guru, he traveled to Europe in 1930.

In London, he became a close friend of W. B. Yeats, then in his sixties, and strongly influenced his outlook on Hindu philosophy and mysticism. Yeats wrote introductions to the Swami's autobiography *An Indian Monk* (Macmillan, London, 1932) and his translation of his guru's book *The Holy Mountain* (Faber, London, 1934).

In 1935, the Swami published a translation of *Bhagavad-Gita* under the title *The Geeta; The Gospel of the Lord Shri Krishna* (Faber, London), which he dedicated "To my friend William Butler Yeats" on his seventieth birthday. In the same year, the Swami published a translation of the *Mandukya Upanishad,* for which Yeats provided an introduction. Yeats had planned to travel to India to assist the Swami in translating the ten principal Upanishads, but eventually the work was completed by the two friends at Majorca in 1936.

From 1934 onwards, Yeats developed a romantic friendship with the young actress Margot Ruddock, then twenty-seven years old. He introduced her to the Swami, who thereafter became her spiritual adviser and influenced the poems which she wrote. The Swami also composed many religious poems, some of which Margot Ruddock rendered into English.

The Swami featured frequently in the correspondence between Yeats and Margot Ruddock, published as *Ah, Sweet Dancer; W. B. Yeats and Margot Ruddock* edited by Roger McHugh (Macmillan, 1970). Yeats corresponded with the Swami for some years before his own death. The Swami returned to India in 1936 after receiving news of the illness of his guru, who died the same year. The Swami died soon afterwards.

Yeats's letters to the Swami were bought privately by Mr. Claude Driver, director of the Rosenbach Foundation, Philadelphia. Extracts from some letters were quoted in *The Later Phase of the Development of W. B. Yeats* by S. Mokashi-Punekar (Kanatak University, Dharwar, India, 1966).

Yeats's introductions to the Swami's books contain some of the poet's most perceptive writing. The Swami himself also wrote with great lucidity and spiritual insight. His autobiography *An Indian Monk* is a very moving work of great sincerity and spiritual awareness, and his translations of *Aphorisms of Yoga by Bhagwan Shree Patanjali* (Faber, London, 1938), with an introduction by W. B. Yeats, is one of the clearest and most inspiring editions of the famous *Yoga-Sutras of Patanjali* ever published, being enlivened by a perceptive commentary arising from the Swami's personal experiences of Hindu mysticism.

Purrah, The

A former secret society of the Tulka-Susus, an African tribe who used to dwell between the Sierra Leone river and Cape mount. The *Tulka* consisted of five small communities which together formed a kind of republic. Each group had its own chiefs and council, but all were under a controlling-power which was called the *purrah.* Each of the five communities also had its own *purrah,* from which was formed the great or general *purrah,* which held supreme sway over the five bodies.

Before an African could join a district *purrah,* he had to be thirty years of age, and before being received into membership of the great *purrah,* he had to have reached the age of fifty. Thus the oldest members of each district *purrah* were members of the head *purrah.* On desiring admittance to the examination for the district *purrah,* the relations of the candidate had to swear to kill him if he did not stand the test, or if he revealed the mysteries and the secrets of the society. The explorer Leo Frobenius stated: "In each district belonging to a *purrah* there is a sacred grove to which the candidate is conducted, and where he must stay in a place assigned to him, living for several months quite alone in a hut, whither masked persons bring him food. He must neither speak nor leave his appointed place of residence.

"Should he venture into the surrounding forest, he is as good as dead.

"After several months the candidate is admitted to stand his trial, which is said to be terrible. Recourse is had to all the elements in order to gain satisfaction as to his firmness and courage. We are even assured that at these mysteries use is made of fettered lions and leopards, that during the time of the tests and enrolment the sacred groves echo with fearful shrieks, that here great fires are seen at night, that formerly the fire flared up in these mysterious woods in all directions, that every outsider who through curiosity was tempted to stray into the woods was mercilessly sacrificed, that foolish people who would have penetrated into them disappeared and were never heard of again.

"If the candidate stands all the tests, he is admitted to the initiation. But he must first swear to keep all the secrets and without hesitation carry out the decisions of the *purrah* of his community and all the decrees of the great head *purrah.* If a member of the society betrays it or revolts against it, he is condemned to death, and the sentence is often carried out in the bosom of his family. When the criminal least expects it, a disguised, masked and armed warrior appears and says to him:—

" 'The great *purrah* sends thee death!'

"At these words everybody stands back, no one dares to offer the least resistance, and the victim is murdered.

"The Court of each district *purrah* consists of twenty-five members, and from each of these separate courts five persons are chosen, who constitute the great *purrah,* or the High Court of the general association. Hence this also consists of twenty-five persons, who elect the head chief from their own body.

"The special *purrah* of each community investigates the offences committed in its district, sits in judgment on them, and sees that its sentences are carried out. It makes peace between the powerful families, and stops their wranglings.

"The great *purrah* meets only on special occasions, and pronounces judgment on those who betray the mysteries and secrets of the order, or on those who show themselves disobedient to its mandates. But usually it puts an end to the feuds that often break out between two communities belonging to the confederacy. When these begin to fight, after a few months of mutual hostilities, one or other of the parties, when they have inflicted sufficient injury on each other, usually wants peace. The commune repairs secretly to the great *purrah,* and invites it to become the mediator and put an end to the strife.

"Thereupon the great *purrah* meets in a neutral district, and when all are assembled announces to the communes at war that it cannot allow men who should live together as brothers, friends and good neighbours, to wage war, to waste each others' lands, to plunder and burn; that it is time to put an end to these disorders; that the great *purrah* will inquire into the cause of the strife; that it requires that this should cease and decrees that all hostilities be forthwith arrested.

"A main feature of this arrangement is that, as soon as the great *purrah* assembles to put a stop to the feud, and until its decision is given, all the belligerents of the two districts at war are forbidden to shed a drop of blood; this always carries with it the penalty of death. Hence everybody is careful not to infringe this decree, and abstains from all hostilities.

"The session of the High Court lasts one month, during which it collects all necessary information to ascertain which commune caused the provocation and the rupture. At the same time it summons as many of the society's fighting-men as may be required to carry out the decision. When all the necessary particulars are brought in, and everything is duly weighed, it settles the question by condemning the guilty commune to a four days' sack.

"The warriors who have to give effect to this decision are all chosen from the neutral districts; they set out by night from the place where the great *purrah* is assembled. All are disguised, the face being covered with an ugly mask, and armed with lighted torches and daggers. They divide into bands of forty, fifty, or sixty, and all meet unexpectedly before dawn in the district that they have to pillage, proclaiming with fearful shouts the decision of the High Court. On their approach men, women, children and old people, all take to flight, that is, take refuge in their houses, and should anyone be found in the fields, on the highway, or in any other place, he is either killed or carried off and no more is ever heard of him.

"The booty obtained by such plundering is divided into two parts, one of which is given to the injured commune, the other to the great *purrah*, which shares it with the warriors that have executed its decree. This is the reward for their zeal, their obedience and loyalty.

"If one of the families in a commune subject to the *purrah* becomes too powerful and too formidable, the great *purrah* meets, and nearly always condemns it to unexpected sack, which is carried out by night and, as usual, by masked and disguised men. Should the heads of such a dangerous family offer any resistance, they are killed, or carried off, and conveyed to the depths of a sacred and lonely grove where they are tried by the *purrah* for their insubordination; they are seldom heard of again.

"Such, in part, is the constitution of this extraordinary institution. Its existence is known; the display of its power is felt; it is dreaded; yet the veil covering its intentions, decisions and decrees is impenetrable, and not till he is about to be executed does the outlaw know that he has been condemned. The power and reputation of the *purrah* is immense, not only in the homeland, but also in the surrounding districts. It is reported to be in league with the spirits (instead of the devil).

"According to the general belief the number of armed men who are members and at the disposal of the *purrah* exceeds 6,000. Moreover, the rules, the secrets and the mysteries of this society are strictly obeyed and observed by its numerous associated members, who understand and recognise each other by words and signs." (See also **Africa**)

Pursuit (Journal)

Quarterly publication of the **Society for the Investigation of the Unexplained.** Includes reports on Fortean phenomena, i.e., bizarre events, strange anomalies, synchronicities and scientific ambiguities often ignored or explained away, such as unusual falls from the skies, mysterious disappearances and reappearances, stigmata, earthquake and tornado anomalies, invisible assassins, teleportation, unidentified flying objects, levitation, monsters, inexplicable fires and explosions, etc.

The Society for the Investigation of the Unexplained was founded by explorer-author Ivan T. **Sanderson,** following up the earlier researchers of Charles H. Fort. Address: SITU, Box 265, Little Silver, New Jersey 07739. (See also **Doubt; Fortean Society; Fortean Times; INFO; The News**)

Puthoff, Harold E. (1936-)

Contemporary parapsychologist who is also a specialist in quantum physics. He has a Ph.D. from **Stanford Research Institute,** where he worked from 1972 onwards in the field of lasers and initiated research in **Biofeedback** and biofield measurements. He was responsible for developing a tunable Raman laser producing high-power radiation throughout the infrared section of the spectrum. He has supervised research for Ph.D. candidates in electrical engineering and applied physics at Stanford University.

In his parapsychological researches he has collaborated with Russell **Targ** at Stanford. Their joint papers include: 'A Perceptual Channel for Information Transfer over Kilometer Distances; historical perspective and recent research' (*Proceedings, Institute of Electrical and Electronics Engineers,* vol. 64, 1975); (papers presented at annual conventions of the Parapsychological Association) 'ESP Experiments with Uri Geller' (1973), 'PK Experiments with Uri Geller and Ingo Swann' (1973), 'Remote Viewing of Natural Targets' (1974), 'Replication Study on the Remote Viewing of Natural Targets' (1975); 'Information Transmission under Conditions of Sensory Shielding' (*Nature,* (October 1974). Papers from the Parapsychological Association annual conventions were published in: *Research in Parapsychology 1973, Research in Parapsychology 1974* and *Research in Parapsychology 1975* (Scarecrow Press, N.J.). (See also Uri **Geller;** Ingo **Swann**)

Pyramid Guide (Newsletter)

Bi-monthly newsletter of the Life Understanding Foundation, concerned with Pyramid energy and related subjects.

Now superseded by *Univercolian* magazine. Address: P.O. Box 292, Dalton, Massachusetts 01226. (See also **Pyramids & Pyramidology**)

Pyramids and Pyramidology

There has been much speculation by occultists about the pyramid structures of ancient civilizations in Egypt, Peru and Central America. Although usually designed as burial places for royal or exalted personages, some pyramids have no clearly discernible purpose, and the uniqueness of pyramid construction and shape is thought to have some occult significance.

There were some eighty pyramids in Egypt, built under the reign of the Pharaohs from 3,100 to 332 B.C. Egyptian tombs have reflected early religious ideas about the afterlife. In predynastic times, the dead were buried in sand pits of an oval or square shape; in the dynastic era a structure called a *mastaba* was erected over the burial place of kings and nobles. This was made of dried mud bricks, and reproduced the house or palace of the deceased, so that his soul could have a replica of earthly existence.

Eventually stone was used instead of mud bricks, culminated in the Step Pyramid of the Third Dynasty (c. 2686-2181 B.C.). The familiar square-based triangular-sided pyramid is seen at its best in the Great Pyramid of Giza, built in the reign of Cheops (or Khufu) of the Fourth Dynasty, regarded as one of the Seven Wonders of the World. It measures 756 feet square, with a height of 480 feet. It is made of some 2,300,000 blocks of stone, average 2½ tons each. The core is of local stone and the outer facing of limestone, while the granite and limestone blocks are hewn to within 1/100th of an inch. The accuracy of the joints is within 1/5th of an inch.

The pyramid is entered through a shaft on the north side, where a descending corridor leads to an unfinished chamber with a blind passage; an ascending corridor leads to what is called "the Queen's Chamber," containing two dead end shafts, and eventually to the "Grand Gallery," 100 feet long and 30 feet high, and the "King's Chamber," containing an empty sarcophagus. It is thought that it originally contained a mummy, rifled by tomb robbers who surmounted the granite plugs, false passages and other precautions of the pyramid builders.

Occult speculations regarding the Great Pyramid have arisen mainly around its constructions, dimensions and possible use. It is certainly a remarkable engineering feat, and it has been suggested that it could have been achieved only by supernormal techniques, such as levitating the great blocks of stone by mysterious occult force. However, tomb paintings, tool marks on stone, and quarry workings suggest more conventional technology.

Ruins found near the pyramid are thought to have been the barracks for about 4,000 skilled workmen. The heavy work could have been done by conscripted labor, as depicted on other tomb paintings. One such painting depicts about 172 men shifting a sixty-ton statue. The stones were probably moved on sleds and by barges and rafts. Earthen mounds may have surrounded the pyramid in the course of construction, with ramps for elevating the stones.

The Pyramidology cults which ascribe occult significance to the dimensions and measurements of the Great Pyramid date back to the 1830s, after Colonel Howard Vyse blasted a way inside and took measurement. The British mathematician John Taylor and Scottish astronomer Charles Piazza Smyth claimed that the pyramid embodied divine revelations and prophecy, calculated from its measurements, assuming a unit of a "pyramid inch" which was later the Anglo-Saxon inch.

By considering the inch a symbol for a year, the internal structures of the pyramid are calculated to indicate the important dates of the world's past and present history. This involves identifying the pyramid itself with Biblical versions of history, such as the Fundamentalist view that the world was created about 4,004 B.C., duly verified by pyramid measurements, which also showed that the Second Coming of Christ was due in 1881. When this latter "prophecy" was not fulfilled, pyramidologists revised their calculations to show that the end of the world was scheduled for 1953. Since then, further reshufflings of calculations have taken place.

Unfortunately there is still no precise agreement on pyramid measurements, so revised prophecies are inevitable for some time to come. In addition to all this involved numerology, pyramid cults have also claimed that the British are the lineal descendants of the Ten Tribes of Israel.

It was from Smyth's calculations that Charles Taze Russell, founder of the sect of **Jehovah's Witnesses,** based his own prophecy of the Second Coming of Christ, which is supposed to have taken place unobtrusively except to the eye of faith in 1914.

It remains to be added that calculations based on identification of the Empire State Building and the Eiffel Tower with Biblical prophecy would also yield striking prophecies.

Less far fetched is the suggestion that the plan of the Great Pyramid and its internal structures may have embodied a mystical symbolism of the journey of the soul, as described in the Egyptian *Book of the Dead* (Papyrus of Ani). It is also not unlikely that the north-south orientation of the pyramid and the nature of its dimensions reveal astronomical and geometrical knowledge of a high order. It seems clear that the Egyptians were aware of the mathematical radio of *pi.*

Pyramid Energy

In recent years, a new direction has been given to connections between occultism and pyramids by widespread discussion and experiment relating to an unknown energy concentrated in pyramidical structures.

In 1950, at the Scientific and Technical Congress of Radionics and Radiesthesia, held in London, England, Mr. Noel Macbeth claimed that a cardboard model pyramid could mummify organic substances such as an egg, and that this energy was connected with that radiated by the hands of gifted human healers.

In 1928, at Lyons, a 33-year old Frenchman named Georges Gaillard demonstrated the ability to mummify two mutton chops by holding them in his hands for a minute (see also **Emanations**).

The French radiesthetist Antoine Bovis reported that meat, eggs and other organic substances could be mummified by placing them in a cardboard model of the Great Pyramid, which he claimed accumulated the same radiations as the King's chamber of the pyramid. His claims were later investigated by

Karl Drbal, a radio engineer in Czechoslovakia, who applied for a patent for a cardboard pyramid claimed to sharpen razor blades left under it.

Such claims had also been made in Britain during World War II, when there was a shortage of razor blades. Drbal ascribed the phenomenon to a microwave energy which had the effect of electromagnetic dehydration on the blades.

Other researchers have constructed large 6-8 ft. high pyramids which are reported to exercise a beneficial effect on the health of the persons sitting in them. Pyramid tents have been made for meditation purposes. It is possible that there are connections between the energies of **Radiesthesia** or **Dowsing** and perhaps the so-called **Orgone** energy of Dr. Wilhelm **Reich,** whose "Orgone Energy Accumulator" invites comparison with pyramid structures.

An organization named the Institute of Pyramidology was founded in London, England in 1940, and became an international body a year later with the launching of *Pyramidology Magazine,* with special emphasis on "Divine Revelation" and prophecies. Address: 31 Station Road, Harpenden, Herts. AL5 4XB, England.

Pyramid tents and energy generators are marketed by Pyramid Products, P.O. Box 6839, Glendale, California 91205.

Recommended reading:

Davidson, David. *The Great Pyramid: Its Divine Message,* London, 1924 (frequently revised and reprinted)

De Camp, L. Sprague. *The Ancient Engineers,* Doubleday, 1960; Ballantine paperback, 1974

Smyth, Charles Piazzi. *Our Inheritance in the Great Pyramid,* London, 1864 (frequently revised and reprinted)

Stewart, Basil. *The Mystery of the Great Pyramid; traditions concerning it and its connection with the Egyptian Book of the Dead,* London, 1929

Tompkins, Peter. *Secrets of the Great Pyramid,* Harper & Row, 1971

Toth, Max & Greg Nielsen. *Pyramid Power,* Freeway paperback, 1974

Pyromancy

Divination by fire, already alluded to in **Extispicy.** The presage was good when the flame was vigorous and quickly consumed the sacrifice; when it was clear of all smoke, transparent, neither red nor dark in color; when it did not crackle, but burnt silently in a pyramidal form. On the contrary, if it was difficult to kindle, if the wind disturbed it, if it was slow to consume the victim, the presage was evil.

Besides the sacrificial fire, the ancients divined by observing the flames of torches, and even by throwing powdered pitch into a fire; if it caught quickly, the omen was good.

The flame of a torch was good if it formed one point, bad if it divided into two; but three was a better omen than one.

Sickness for the healthy, and death for the sick, was presaged by the bending of the flame, and some frightful disaster by its sudden extinction.

The vestal virgins in the Temple of Minerva at Athens were charged to make particular observations on the light perpetually burning there.

Pyroscopy

A branch of **Pyromancy** (**divination** by fire), based on the burn stains left on a light surface after burning a sheet of paper on it.

Q

Q Directory, The

Annual British directory of Occult, Pagan and New Age Groups, Services and Publications from 1977 onwards. In 1984, the title changed to *Quest List of Esoteric Sources.* Address: BCM SCL Quest, London, WCIN 3XX, England.

Quaesitor (Organization)

This British relative of **Esalen** Institute was recently reorganized and located as Quaesitor II, Top Flat, 17 Hornsey Lane Gardens, London, N6 5NX, England. It is concerned with such subjects as Meditation, Body-Mind relationships.

The word "Quaesitor" means seeker, and the organization's workshops, courses, and sessions "are to explore this longing, to give us insight into how our lives can become more rich and more fulfilling."

Quest List of Esoteric Sources (Directory)

Comprehensive directory of British groups, societies, and courses, publications and suppliers in occult and mystical fields. Compiled and edited by Marian Green. Formerly titled *The Q Directory.* Address: Quest, BCM-S C L Quest, London, WCIN 3XX, England. (See also **Q Directory**)

Quest Society, The

An offshoot of the **Theosophical Society,** founded by scholar G. R. S. **Mead** (1863-1933) who had been secretary to Madame **Blavatsky** and General Secretary of the Theosophical Society. He resigned (in company with some 700 other members) in protest over the scandals concerning C. W. **Leadbeater.**

In March 1909, Mead founded the Quest Society as a group of sincere seekers after spiritual wisdom without any taint of charlatanism. The objects were "to promote investigation and comparative study of religion, philosophy and science on the basis of experience; to encourage the expression of the ideal in beautiful form." From 1909–1930, the Society published a quarterly journal *The Quest* (edited by Mead), with an extremely high standard of contributions.

The Society faded away after the death of Mead in 1933.

Quigley, Joan

Contemporary San Francisco astrologer who claims that her astrological advice had "absolute control" over the movements, and influenced the decisions, of former president Ronald Reagan. Her secret role as an astrological influence at the White House was referred to by Donald Regan, former chief of staff to Ronald Reagan, but more far-reaching claims are made in Quigley's book *What Does Joan Say? My Seven Years as White House Astrologer to Nancy and Ronald Reagan* (1990).

Quigley advised Nancy Reagan from 1981—9, and claims that her astrological advice decided the timing of key political events, including speeches, televised campaign debates, the signing of arms control treaties, and even dates for Ronald Reagan's cancer surgery and the announcement that he would run for a second term. Quigley claims that she stood "guard astrologically over Reagan's travels, that Air Force One would only take off if she reported a favorable alignment of the planets, and that she sometimes also gave the president and his wife political advice.

Quigley states, "I was responsible for timing all press conferences, most speeches, the State of the Union addresses, the take-offs and landing of Air Force One . . . I picked the time of Ronald Reagan's debate with Carter and the two debates with Walter Mondale, all extended trips abroad, as well as the shorter trips and one-day excursions, the announcement that Reagan would run for a second term, and briefings for all the summits except Moscow." Quigley also claims credit for influencing the president's favorable view of the Soviet leader Gorbachev, whose astrological chart indicated a genuine reformer.

The title of Quigley's book derives from the period in late 1986 when the Iran-contra scandal broke. She claims that the president asked "What does Joan say?" and that her advice was to stay in the White House and say nothing, because his stars were bad and she feared another assassination attempt.

Although the revelations of astrological influence on a modern leader's actions and decisions may seem bizarre to a Western people, it is my no means unusual in Eastern countries. Astrology plays a significant part in the life of people in India, and marriages, dates of important meetings, dedication of temples, and other decisions normally involve the services of an astrologer for millions of Indians in all walks of life, including politics. The successes and personal popularity of Reagan's terms in office may have owed something to good astrological advice as much as to political acumen or good luck.

Quimby, Phineas P(arkhurst) (1802-1866)

An early influential exponent of **Mind Cure,** later known as **New Thought.** Born in Lebanon, New Hampshire, he became a clockmaker before becoming interested in **Mesmerism** in 1838. He had great success in treating patients but eventually developed his own system based on mental influence. He practiced in Portland, Maine from 1859 onwards, where he treated some 12,000 individuals during seven years.

One of his patients, Mary Baker Glover Patterson (later Mary Baker **Eddy**) developed her own system based on variations of Quimby's teachings (see **Christian Science**). (See also **Mind Cure; New Thought**)

Quincey P. Morris Dracula Society, The

Vampire interest organization; issues quarterly Newsletter *Transfusion.* Address: Charlott Simson. P.O. Box 381, Ocean Gate, New Jersey 08740.

Quincunx

As astrology term denoting an aspect of planets when they are at a distance of five signs of 150 degrees from each other.

The term was once generally used to denote a disposition of five objects (especially plants or trees) placed so that there is one in each corner of a square or rectangle and the fifth in the center.

The use of the quincunx in various aspects throughout history was exhaustively discussed by the English physician and author Sir Thomas **Browne** (1605-1682) in his book *The Garden of Cyrus* (1658).

Quirinus (or Quirus)

A fabled precious stone, described as "a juggling stone, found in the nest of the hoopoo" (hoopoe bird). If laid on the breast of one sleeping, it "forces him to discover his rogueries." The word "quirinus" is also used to describe the third of the ancient gods (after Jupiter and Mars).

Qvarnstrom, S(ven) Birger (1897- ?)

Swedish teacher and journalist active in the field of parapsychology. Born June 22, 1897, at Vissefjärda, Kalmer län, Sweden, he studied at University of Lund. He was an instructor in languages and political economics at colleges in Hälsingborg, Eskilstuna, Malmö, Orebro, from 1934-39, College for Girls, Norrköping, from 1949-54, Solna College from 1854 onwards.

He contributed to a number of Swedish newspapers as a columnist and literary critic, and as a member of the Swedish Society for Psychical Research spent some years investigating psychic phenomena such as clairvoyance, telekinesis and precognition. He published a book *Parapskologi-Resultat och Perspecktiv* (Parapsychology-Results and Perspectives, 1959; 1960).

R

Radcliffe, Maud Elizabeth Furse (Lady Gorell) (died 1954)

In December 1980, an auction sale at Sotheby's, London, included a batch of over thirty letters to Bessie (Elizabeth) Radcliffe from poet W. B. **Yeats,** revealing that Miss Radcliffe had acted as a Spiritualist medium for **automatic writing** during the occult researches of Yeats.

Miss Radcliffe was introduced to Yeats in the summer of 1913, possibly through Mrs. Eva Fowler, friend of Olivia and Dorothy Shakespear and of Ezra Pound. The mediumship continued for some four years until Yeats married Georgie Hyde-Lees in 1917, after which his wife acted as his medium. Before his marriage, Yeats had initiated Georgie into the Stella Matutina temple of the **Golden Dawn** occult society.

The mediumistic activities of Miss Radcliffe remained secret. In 1922, she married Ronald Gorell Barnes, 3rd Baron Gorell (1884-1963); they had two sons and a daughter. Baron Gorell, C.B.E., O.B.E., had a distinguished military career, was Deputy Director of Staff Duties (Education) at the War Office from 1918-20, was Under-Secretary of State for Air, July 1921-October 1922, president of various societies, editor of *Cornhill Magazine,* 1933-39. He published various volumes of poetry, fact, fiction, and religion.

The correspondence from Yeats at the Sotheby sale revealed that Miss Radcliffe's mediumship had a profound influence on the poet, and in one letter he stated that her script "contained the most important evidence of the most important problem of the world" and in others: "I can never make known to you my profound gratitude. You have changed most things for me and I know not how far that change will go. A year ago your spirits saved me from serious error in a crisis of life." (See also W. B. **Yeats**)

Radha, Swami Sivananda

Well-known woman swami, founder and spiritual leader of **Yasodhara Ashram,** Kootenay Bay, British Columbia, Canada. Swami Radha (formerly Sylvia Hellman) was born in Germany, and demonstrated psychic ability when only a child. However, she eventually trained to become a professional dancer. She was widowed twice during World War II and emigrated to Canada, in an effort to forget the horrors of the Nazi regime.

She felt a strong urge for spiritual fulfillment, and during meditation she had a vision of a Hindu sage. A few days later, while looking at books in a Montreal store, she picked up one volume casually, flipped the pages and saw a photograph of the Hindu sage she had seen in meditation. His name was Swami **Sivananda** Saraswati, a famous yogi with an ashram at Rishikesh, India, in the foothills of the Himalayas.

Mrs. Hellman wrote to Swami Sivananda and received a reply asking her to "come home" to India. With some considerable sacrifices, she finished up her job and traveled to Rishikesh, where she received intensive training in yoga and Eastern philosophy.

In January 1956, she was initiated as a renunciate by Swami Sivananda, and instructed to carry his spiritual message to the West. At that period, women swamis, particularly Westerners, were rare, and the prospect of returning to Canada without income was a daunting one, but with faith in her guru, Swami Radha returned to Canada with only 25 cents, and a society somehow grew up around her to spread yoga teachings of the spiritual life.

The Sivananda Ashram was originally founded at South Burnaby, Vancouver, but later moved to Kootenay Bay, British Columbia. Whilst searching for a possible site in this area, Swami Radha found an ideal setting by the side of a lake, officially listed since 1897 as "Yasodhara." It was a happy omen, since in Hindusim, Yasoda is the foster-mother of Shree Krishna, incarnation of God.

Under the name Yasodhara Ashram, the society now occupies an 83 acre site with lake, forests, and mountains, reminiscent of the foothills of India. Several acres have been cleared, and the ashram premises include residential buildings, a guest lodge, prayer room, print shop, bookstore, office, recording studio, and a Temple of All Faiths. Various workshop programs and courses are given in yoga, and spiritual teachings of East and West. There are no religious limitations, as the aim of the ashram is to integrate the spiritual ideals and practices of all major religions.

As spiritual director, Swami Radha specifically avoids being a cult figure, and there are no pictures of herself or her guru in the prayer rooms. Instead, the basic spiritual light of different religions is emphasized by their traditional symbols. Swami Radha has been responsible for issuing various tape and gramophone recordings, and her teachings may be heard on her Long Play discs *Divine Light Invocation* and *Mantras: Songs of Yoga,* published by Ashram Records, Kootenay Bay, B.C., Canada V0B 1X0.

Swami Radha has lectured widely in Canada, the U.S. and Europe. (See also Swami **Sivananda**)

Radhasoami Satsang

An Indian spiritual movement founded in 1861 by Shiv Dayal Singh (1818-1878) of Agra. Known as "Soamiji Maharaj" by his disciples, he taught three basic principles of religious life: 1) *Satguru,* a term embracing the Absolute Lord and living human Master; 2) *Shabd* or sound current (spoken or written expression, and also inner spiritual sound); 3) *Satsang,* association of devotees seeking spiritual truth.

Although stemming from Sikh religion, Radhasoami is heterodox Sikhism insofar as it recognizes a living human guru (Soamiji Maharaj), whereas orthodox Sikhs believe that the succession of human gurus ended in 1718.

After Soamiji Maharaj passed away, he was succeeded by Rai Salig Ram, and in turn by Pandit Brahma Shankar Misra in 1907. After the passing of Brahma Shankar Misra, the main *satsang* divided under two different gurus: Sri Kamta Prasad Sinha (known as "Param Guru Sarkar Sahib") and Buaji Maharaj, sister of Brahma Shankar Misra. Further divisions occurred by various gurus who conducted *satsangs* in different areas, culminating in the present existence of some thirty different Radhasoami centers in India.

The two principal divisions became the Radhasoami Satsang, Beas, and the **Ruhani Satsang,** both descended from the founder Shiv Dayal Singh through Baba Jaimal Singh, whose satsang was based at Beas, Punjam.

Baba Jaimal Singh passed away in 1903 and was succeeded by his disciple Sawan Singh (1858-1948). Sawan Singh had a profound influence in the spread of teachings relating to *Shabd-Yoga,* the pathway of sacred sound current. On the passing of Sawan Singh, he was succeeded by his grandson Charan Singh, some of those disciples founded individual sects. Amongst these was Kirpal Singh, who established Ruhani Satsang in Delhi.

Western popularizers such as Paul Twitchell (founder of Eckankar) were disciples of Kirpal Singh, later developing his teachings in a new context without proper acknowledgment. Movements which appear to be stemmed from Radhasoami teachings include the Divine Light Mission and the M.S.I.A. (Movement of Spiritual Inner Awareness) of John-Roger Hinkins. For a careful study of these and other influences, see the writings of David Christopher Lane, especially *The New Panths; Shabdism in North America* (American Academy of Religion, Stanford University, 1981), and the Research Series *Understanding Cults & Spiritual Movements* (Del Mar Press, California).

The teaching that a mystical sound current heard in meditation may bring about higher consciousness is central to Radhasoami beliefs, and is also an important part of the meditation techniques of traditional yoga practice.

It is cited in such yoga manuals as the *Hatha-Yoga-Pradipika* of Svatmarama Svamin, and the *Siva Samhita.* It is also related to the special significance attached to the sacred trisyllable AUM in Hindu Vedanta.

The main address of Radhasoami Satsang is: P.O. Dera Baba Jaimal Singh, Via Beas, Dist. Amritsar, India. American address: c/o Roland de Vries, 2922 La Flores, Arlington (Riverside), California 92503. (See also **AUM; Divine Light Mission; Eckankar;** Ruhani Satsang; Paul **Twitchell; Vedanta; Yoga**)

Radiesthesia

A development of the art of **dowsing** (water witching) which extends the use of indicators such as rod and pendulum as used for water finding, to the tracing of missing persons and the diagnosis and treatment of disease. The terms "dowsing" and "radiesthésie" are now virtually synonymous, and "radiesthésie" is generally used throughout France to include all forms of dowsing.

The term *Radiesthésie* was coined in 1930 by the Abbé Bouly, in France, where the use of a pendulum has largely replaced the divining rod. L'Association des Amis de la Radiesthésie was founded in 1930 and the **British Society of Dowsers** in 1933. International Congresses of Radiesthesia are held regularly in Europe.

The dowser or radiesthetist is an individual sensitive to hidden objects or other information, who uses a simple indicator such as a rod or pendulum to amplify this sensitivity. It is still not entirely clear just what kind of radiation is involved, and many investigators believe the individual to be rather like a psychic medium, and certainly some of the special applications of radiesthesia seem nearer to ESP than conventional physics.

The pendulum is usually a small ball attached to a thread on the end of a short stick. It is best to use a nonspun thread or thin nylon, since the twist in a thread may communicate extraneous movement to the pendulum bob. The stick is held just above its connection with the thread and the pendulum bob tends to gyrate or oscillate. The length of the thread can be adjusted by winding it round the stick, so that the pendulum movement is clearly visible. There are characteristic pendulum movements relating to various substances, indicated by the number of gyrations and whether their movement is clockwise or anticlockwise. Like the dowsing rod, the pendulum, also seems to be drawn towards hidden objects.

The pendulum is often used to diagnose disease conditions in the body or indicate remedies. The pendulum is first adjusted over a healthy part of the body. When moved to an unhealthy area its movement changes.

Another use of the pendulum is simply to answer questions put to it, rather in the manner of an **ouija board,** "Yes" usually being indicated by a clockwise gyration and "No" by anticlockwise movement. An even more psychic use of the pendulum is known as

Teleradiesthesia or Superpendulism. Instead of using a pendulum over an actual area in which underground water or minerals are sought, the operator holds the pendulum over a map of the district. It is claimed that there is a subtle link between a locality and its symbolic representation on a map. Some teleradiesthetists have also used a map to trace the movements of a missing person.

Some operators use a hollow pendulum, with inserted sample of the material sought. Others hold something connected with the object of their enquiries in one hand while using the pendulum in the other. Since the indications of a pendulum are subtle, and may also be deflected by conscious or unconscious muscular movements, some preliminary study is recommended before practice. There is a considerable literature on the subject and much evidence for the reality of its phenomena.

In the U.S., the American Society of Dowsers Inc. encourages the practice of various forms of dowsing and gives guidance and information on the subject. Address: Danville, Vermont 05828. In Britain, the British Society of Dowsers is concerned with all aspects of Dowsing and Radiesthesia and published a journal. Address: British Society of Dowsers, Sycamore Cottage, Tamley Lane, Hastingleigh, Ashford, Kent, TN25 5HW, England. (See also **Divining Rod; Dowsing; Ouija Board; Pendulums; Planchette; Table-Turning**)

Recommended reading:

Beasse, Pierre. *A New and Rational Treatise of Dowsing according to the methods of Physical Radiesthesia,* France, 1941

Cameron, Verne. *Map Dowsing,* El Carismo, 1971

Cooper, Irving S. & Willi Kowa. *The Pendulum: Operational Practice & Theory,* Academic Publications, Haywards Heath, U.K., 1978

De France, Henry. *The Elements of Dowsing,* London, 1971

Hitching, Francis. *Pendulum; The Psi Connection,* Fontana paperback, London, 1977

Franklin, T. Bedford. *Radiations,* London, 1949

Nielsen, Greg & Joseph Polansky. *Pendulum Power; A Mystery You Can See, A Power you Can Feel,* Destiny Books, New York, 1977/Excalibur, Wellingborough, U.K., 1981 (paperback)

Wethered, V. D. *A Radiesthetic Approach to Health and Homeopathy, or Health and the Pendulum,* London, 1950

Radiesthésie

(Radiation-perception), the term used in France for divining with pendulums or rod (see **Radiesthesia**).

Radionics

The instrumental detection of vital energy patterns and associated diagnosis and therapy. In radionic theory, all living things radiate an electromagnetic field which has different characteristics in health and disease conditions. Energy patterns are given a numerical value or "rate" usually calibrated on the dials of a diagnostic apparatus called a **Black Box.** The original black box, sometimes called the E.R.A. or Oscilloclast, was the invention of Dr. Albert **Abrams,** a San Francisco physician.

It consisted of several variable rheostats and a thin sheet of rubber mounted over a metal plate. A blood sample from the patient was put into the machine, which was connected with a metal plate placed on the forehead of a healthy person. By tapping on the abdomen of this person, the doctor determined the disease of the patient according to "areas of dullness" in relation to dial readings on the apparatus. This strange procedure brought together the special sensitivities of **Radiesthesia, Dowsing** and medical auscultation. It seems clear, however, that Abrams was not a quack, and various other physicians endorsed his techniques.

After the death of Abrams in 1924, his procedures were developed by Dr. Ruth **Drown** of the U.S. in the 1930s and George **De la Warr** in Britain. De la Warr devised black boxes which dispensed with the auscultation techniques of Abrams, and even an apparatus which produced photographs relating to the condition of the patient whose sample was placed in the machine.

De la Warr claimed that they registered a radiation pattern showing the shape and chemical structure of the radiating body, and given a suitable sample the camera plate would register not only regional tissue but also its pathology.

The De la Warr Laboratories currently design and manufacture radionic instruments as well as diagnosing and treating patients. Address: Raleigh Park, Oxford, England. There is also a Radionic Association in Britain, which trains and represents radionic practitioners. Address: Field House, Peaslake, Guildford, Surrey, England.

Professor William A. Tiller, chairman of the Department of Material Medicine at Stanford University spent a year studying Radionics at the De la Warr Laboratories, and reported at length in his paper 'Radionics, Radiesthesia and Physics' (*Proceedings of the Academy of Paraspsychology & Medicine,* Symposium on the Varieties of Healing Experience, 1971).

An important development in American Radionics studies was the U.S. Radionic Congress held in Indianapolis April 19-20, 1975 at which papers on researches in the field were presented and discussed. Amongst those present was Thomas G. Hieronymus, regarded as the dean of American Radionics researches, whose patented invention of a machine to analyze a new type of radiation in 1949 led to American interest in Radionics under the name "Psionics." John Campbell, Jr., editor of *Astounding Science Fiction,* gave instructions for building a Hieronymus machine in the June 1956 issue of *ASF.*

Recommended reading:

Abrams, Albert. *New Concepts in Diagnosis and Treatment,* Physico-Clinical Co., 1924

Day, Langston & G. De la Warr. *New Worlds Beyond the Atom,* London, 1956

Proceedings of the Scientific and Technical Congress of Radionics and Radiesthesia London May 16-18, 1950, London, n.d.

Raelian Movement

A New Age movement originated in France in 1973 by motor-racing journalist Claude Vorilhon. He claims that when walking in the Claremont-Ferrand region, he saw a UFO land in front of him and a four-feet tall humanoid emerge. The space visitor instructed Vorilhon to change his name to "Rael" ("The Man Who Brings Light") and publish worldwide messages from space.

These state that the human race was created by space aliens using genetic engineering techniques some 25,000 years ago. Rael seeks to collect funds for the construction of an embassy for the space aliens to promote their mission to guide human beings through the present troubled times.

Raffé W(alter) G(eorge) (1888-c. 1950)

British writer, lecturer and designer, who took a special interest in the occult in relation to art and color. He was educated at Halifax Technical College, Leeds College of Art, and the Royal College of Art, South Kensington, England.

He was a Fellow of the Royal Society of Arts, London, Fellow of the Institute of Decorators, Great Britain, member of the Illuminating Engraving Society. He was art director of the Northern Polytechnic, London, 1919-21; principal, Lucknow School of Art, India, 1921-23; lecturer to London County Council, 1925.

His books included *Poems in Black & White* (1922), *Graphic Design* (1927), *Art and Labour* (1927), *The Control of the Mind* (1934). He contributed to many periodicals dealing with arts, crafts, color, psychology of art, occultism. He was a reviewer and contributor to *Occult Review, Theosophical Review, Hindustan Review.*

Ragnarok

A term meaning "rain of dust," derived from an ancient Scandinavian legend of a titanic conflict between gods and giants.

It also became the title of a remarkable book by the Minnesota Irishman Ignatius **Donnelly** (1831-1901), who was a U.S. Congressman and senator.

More than a century before Immanuel **Velikovsky**'s bestselling *Worlds in Collision,* Donnely's *Ragnarok: the Age of Fire and Gravel* (1883) pioneered the provocative concept that a comet passed close to or struck the earth in ancient times, causing cataclysmic changes dimly remembered in mythologies and scripture history.

Donnelly was an original thinker, and although some of his ideas may not stand up to modern scientific scrutiny, the theme of Cometology is now persuasively argued by Velikovsky. Donnelly's *Ragnarok* was reissued by University Books in 1970.

Rahu

According to Hindu mythology, Rahu is a demon who swallows the sun and moon. He is thus the cause of eclipses, and Rahu and Ketu are the ascending and descending nodes in Hindu astronomy.

Raj-Yoga Math and Retreat

A monastic community founded in 1974 by Yogi Father Satchakrananda Bodhisattvaguru on an ecumenical basis, combing both Hindu and Christian traditions and practices.

Satchakrananda started **yoga** practice in 1967 and is said to have experienced the raising of **Kundalini** energy after only two months. He went on to spend a period at a Trappist monastery, attended Kenyon College, and became coordinator of the Northwest Free University, where he taught hatha yoga.

In 1973, he was mystically initiated by the late Swami **Sivananda** (1887-1963), founder of the **Divine Life Society,** Rishikesh, India, and went on to found his own monastic community the following year. In 1977, he was ordained a priest by Archbishop Adrian Spruit of the Church of Antioch, and has since combined teaching of traditional yoga practices with regular celebration of the Mass.

The community is located in the foothills of Mt. Baker overlooking the Nooksuck River near Deming, Washington. In addition to classes for residents, it also offers a mail-order package, based on Satchakrananda's book *Coming and Going; The Mother's Drama* (1975). Address: P.O. Box 547, Deming, Washington 98244.

Rajneesh (Journal)

Bimonthly publication of Shree Rajneesh Ashram, India. It contained lectures by Bhagwan Shree **Rajneesh,** a controversial Hindu guru teaching a controversial modern adaptation of Sufi and Tantric techniques, and included news of meditation centers in different countries. Published in Poona, India, during the period that Shree Rajneesh's mission flourished. (See also Bhagwan Shree **Rajneesh**)

Rajneesh, Bhagwan Shree (1931-)

Controversial Indian guru, popularly known as "Bhagwan" (Lord), who taught a highly individual system of "spiritual sexuality," combining Tantric, Sufi and Zen techniques. From modest beginnings in India, he built up a worldwide following at centers in the U.S., Britain and elsewhere, before his American headquarters collapsed in a horrendous scandal involving attempted murder, poisoning, rape, drug abuse and other criminality on the part of his followers.

He was born Mohan Chandra Rajneesh, on December 11, 1931, in Kutchwara, India, with a Jain religious background. At the age of seven, he attended the Gunj School at Gadwara, where he showed great intelligence. He went on to study at Jabalpur University (B.A. 1955) and University of Saugar (M.A. 1957).

According to those who knew him, he was a fearless child, given to playing pranks, and fascinated by the occult and hypnosis. He was also said to have been obsessed by problems of death and sex. An astrologer had predicted that he might die at the age of twenty-one. In surviving that year, he was said to have achieved total enlightenment.

He read widely, was an independent thinker, and displayed an original approach to traditional Indian concepts, often at odds with authority. In 1968, he became a traveling lecturer on the theme of the importance and sacredness of sex as a step on the path to higher consciousness. He had been greatly impressed with the personality and teachings of Gurdjieff, whose concepts he knew through reading the books of his disciple **Ouspensky.** He attracted a number of followers, becoming established as a kind of Gurdjieff style **guru,** being known as "Acharya [Professor] Rajneesh."

He developed a system of "dynamic (or chaotic) meditation," said to be specially suitable for Western consciousness and physique. This involved fast intensive breathing, intended to break through tensions and related emotional blocks, followed by a cathartic release of emotional energy (rather like the **Subud Latihan**). The Sufi mantra "Hoo" was then shouted intensely, again raising the energy level, with special effects on the sexual centers of the body. This was followed by a period of absolute stillness and silence, during which a form of meditation ensued.

The concept of emotional tensions rooted in different segments of the body recalls the "muscular armoring" postulated by Wilhelm **Reich,** whose therapeutic techniques also involved intensive breathing to achieve catharsis. The relationship between sexual energy and higher consciousness had been charted in ancient Hindu texts on Kundalini energy, but the idea of achieving higher consciousness through unrestrained sexual expression is a heterodox one. Even the techniques of Tantric Yoga (yoga of sex) involve a disciplined sexual activity under exacting conditions.

However, the simplistic technique of unrestrained sexual activity had a great appeal to Western followers who had grown up in the uninhibited freedoms of the modern so-called "sexual revolution."

In 1970, Rajneesh was established with his following in Bombay, when he became known as "Bhagwan" (Lord) to his followers, who regarded him as a spiritually enlightened Master. In 1974, he acquired land for an ashram in Poona, which became his headquarters for several years. Here Western devotees flocked to a guru who promised spiritual enlightenment through sexual freedom.

In spite of his controversial sexual teachings, Rajneesh retained some nominal aspects of Hindu guru-chela (Master-pupil) relationship. Devotees initiated into his cult were required to wear the traditional ocher-colored robe of a renunciate and the rosary necklace, and given a new ashram name. Such things were offensive to traditional Hindus, since a renunciate normally becomes a celibate, and the spectacle of Indian and Western devotees expressing wildly permissive sexual activity while clad in the robes of renunciation seemed a travesty of Hindu religion. Moreover, the guru himself undoubtedly had sexual relations with chosen female devotees.

As a neo-Tantric guru, Rajneesh generated intense affection from his followers, particularly Western devotees, who showered gifts and money on his mission, which flourished. He himself clearly enjoyed his power and influence over the lives of thousands of devotees, who accepted him as a spiritually enlightened Master. In the hothouse atmosphere of uninhibited physical and emotional expression and sexual activity, many devotees experienced overwhelming blissful sensations. Rajneesh would deliver daily lectures on spiritual realization, many of which were later printed. There was much rivalry for the guru's personal attention, particularly from young women devotees anxious to become "mediums" for the guru's energy by experiencing his touch. Only a selected few were allowed to have close contact with him. He was particularly sensitive to scents, since he suffered allergies from perfumes, soaps, etc. "Sniffer" guards were used to weed out undesirable individuals with "fragrances."

There were many complaints from local residents about the activities of the Rajneesh Foundation. Some of the female devotees turned to prostitution in order to make money to stay at the ashram. Other devotees became drug runners, and a number were caught and prosecuted. Drugs were forbidden at the ashram itself, but there were problems of sexually transmitted diseases. After a British devotee had allegedly made advances to an Indian lady outside the ashram, there were attacks on the devotees by enraged local residents. The Indian authorities questioned the charitable status of the ashram, which had reputedly acquired some $80 million in donations in only a few years, and the ashram accountants were accused of not keeping proper receipts and documentation. The State charity commissioners in Bombay ruled against the ashram, which was pursued for some $4 million in unpaid taxes.

In 1981, Rajneesh astonished and bewildered his followers by suddenly leaving the ashram with a handful of key workers who were involved in his secret plans. He traveled to Bombay in one of his Rolls-Royce automobiles and boarded a Pan-Am 747 to America. Arriving at JFK airport, he looked around as he left the plane and stated grandly: "I am the Messiah America has been waiting for."

Within a few days of the guru's departure, the ashram at Poona began to break up. The property and effects were sold off at knockdown rates, and riot police were called in to control the fierce competition for expensive equipment going at bargain prices. Many of the penniless ashram devotees faced great hardships in returning to their homes in their own countries. The Rajneesh Foundation was wound up, and a new corporation, Rajneesh International, was founded in the U.S.

A prominent figure in handling Rajneesh's practical affairs was his disciple Ma Anand Sheela (Sheela Ambalal Patel), who became a key figure in ashram activities since first coming to the guru in 1972. She had found the mansion in Montclair, New Jersey, where the guru and his staff were first established in the U.S. She next set about locating a larger site for a more ambitious American ashram community.

This was the Big Muddy Ranch and lands in eastern Oregon, near the village of Antelope. In July 1981, the 64,000 acre site was purchased for $5.75 million. Over the next two months, some two hundred devotees settled in, building fifty new houses. Rajneesh himself had arrived in August, ostensibly "on a visit," in order to avoid immigration rules. Plans were made to construct an ashram city on two thousand acres of the site, to be named Rajneeshpuram. Large sums of money amounting to some $120 million flowed into the project from sympathizers and Indian assets.

As in India, the local residents fiercely opposed the creation of an ashram city. Sheela and her associates became increasingly dictatorial and ambitious in their plans. In 1984, in an attempt to pack ballot boxes during the Oregon elections, 3,800 homeless people were bussed into the commune. The plan was nothing less than for Rajneeshees to win seats at the Wasco County Court and take over Antelope itself. However, under the establishment clause of the First Amendment, it is unconstitutional for a municipical government to be run by a religious organization. When this scheme failed, the derelicts were dumped out of the ranch without funds, after having their food laced with non-lethal poisons to make them docile. Shortly before polling day, undercover Rajneeshees sprinkled salmonella bacteria over salad bars in large restaurants in the county's largest town, as an experimental technique. It worked. Nobody died, but some seven hundred people became ill.

Federal and local authorities, fearing another Jonestown tragedy, put the National Guard on stand-by. Various law enforcement agencies were investigating the commune's affairs. Over seventy of the ashram devotees were denied visa extensions and were served with notice to leave the country. The guru himself was investigated by U.S. Immigration.

In the final period of Rajneeshpuram, the power games and plots within the commune itself intensified. It transpired that Sheela had installed listening devices at houses in the commune, and even bugged the guru's own bedroom. The ashram had a security force of nearly 150 people and substantial quantities of arms and ammunition.

Even Rajneesh seemed to become disillusioned, and his long time personal bodyguard Hugh Milne has recorded that he found Rajneesh had developed a habit of ingesting nitrous oxide to induce a euphoric trance-like state. Milne stated that during one of these sessions the guru said: "I'm so glad I can fly. Sheela wants to buy me an aeroplane. But I don't need an aeroplane, I am flying already. I'm so glad I don't have to pretend to be enlightened any more." Milne himself later commented: "Me having been with him for ten years because he *was* enlightened, and he was saying 'I don't have to pretend' . . . what am I doing here! If he is not enlightened what am I doing in this hell-hole . . . "

In September 1985, Sheela and some other officials fled from Oregon to Europe, and Rajneesh called news conferences to state that the commune was now "free from a fascist regime," accusing Sheela of maintaining a secret "poison lab" and trying to kill his personal doctor, dentist, and housekeeper. He claimed that she poisoned Jefferson County District Attorney Michael Sullivan, who had suffered a serious undiagnosed illness during a 1983 dispute with Sheela. He confirmed speculation that Sheela had masterminded the 1984 bus-lift of homeless people to pack the Oregon elections, and was responsible for drugging the derelicts' food. He claimed that when one man died, "they just threw his body out of Rancho Rajneesh."

In an interview with a German magazine, Sheela denied these charges and also the accusation that she created a $55 million debt at the commune in a fraud scheme, diverting some of the funds to a Swiss bank account. She countercharged that the commune debts arose from the guru's opulent tastes, which included a collection over 90 Rolls-Royce automobiles and six private planes.

Meanwhile back at the Rajneesh ranch, the guru ordered the burning of 5,000 copies of *The Book of Rajneeshism,* along with many pendants and the red robes formerly worn by Sheela, thus symbolizing repudiation of ideas and projects which were Sheela's and not those of Rajneesh himself.

But grand juries, immigration authorities, and State authorities were building a strong case against Rajneesh for being in the country under false pretenses, lying to the Immigration and Naturalization Service, arranging bogus marriages at the ashram, and contravening the establishment clause of The First Amendment regarding separation of church and state, in seeking to influence county and state elections.

In October 1985, for the second time, Rajneesh suddenly left his flock without warning. A Lear jet took him and a few officials of his movement to an undisclosed destination, but when the jet landed at Charlotte, North Carolina, for refuelling, police had already been alerted. On October 28, he was arrested, together with six followers; with them was $58,000 in cash, 35 jewel-encrusted watches, and a throne. The claim that the party was going to Bermuda for a visit was not believed. Coincidentally on the same day Sheela and two associates were arrested in Germany.

Rajneesh was handcuffed and taken back to Oregon to stand trial, but his progress in and out of jail and across several States was marked by a manner of simple dignity, and became more like a triumphant procession.

The authorities were unable to connect him with crimes on the ranch, but he was found guilty of immigration violation and conspiracy to evade visa regulations. He was fined $400,000, given a suspended prison sentence of ten years, and ordered to leave the U.S. for a minimum of five years. Sheela was returned from Germany on charges of attempted murder, poisoning, and wire-tapping. She was jailed for four and a half years.

After his sentence, Rajneesh left the country for India, staying at a luxury hotel, but leaving after a month with a large unpaid bill. He stayed briefly in Ireland, but was not welcome, and obliged to leave. He became *persona non grata* all over the world. Countries which refused him entry or expelled him after entry include Antigua, Australia, Bermuda, Canada, Costa Rica, England, Fiji, France, Greece, Holland, Ireland, Italy, Jamaica, Mauritius, Seychelles, Spain, Sweden, Switzerland, Uruguay, Venezeula, West Germany. Back at the ranch, a thousand Rajneeshees found themselves abandoned, penniless, with winter coming on. Within a few weeks, the ashram was sold up, and its assets (including eighty-five Rolls-Royces that remained) were liquidated.

For thousands of followers of Rajneesh, who had been promised peace and love in return for total surrender, a golden dream had become a nightmare of the very crime and corruption that they had hoped to escape in the everyday world.

For the detailed story of the rise and fall of the Rajneesh movement, see *Bhagwan; The God That Failed* by Hugh Milne (Caliban Books, 1986; Sphere Books paperback, 1987). Rajneesh himself is author of more than a hundred books in Hindu, and almost as many in English, or translated into Japanese, Dutch, Italian, French, German, Spanish, and Portuguese. These contain transcripts of his ashram discourses.

Rakshasa

An Indian demon. In one of the Indian folktales he appears black as soot, with hair yellow as the lightning, looking like a thunder-cloud. He had made himself a wreath of entrails and he wore a sacrificial cord of hair; he was gnawing the flesh of a man's head and drinking blood out of a skull.

In another story, these *Rakshasas* have formidable tusks, flaming hair, and insatiable hunger. They wander about the forests catching animals and eating them.

Rakshasas feature in the Hindu religious epic of the *Ramayana*. When the monkey god Hanuman goes to the city of Lanka of search of Sita, he sees *rakshasas* of many varied kinds, some disgusting in appearance, others quite beautiful. "Some had long arms and fearful shapes; some were fat, others very lean, some were dwarfs, others exceedingly tall. Some had only one eye and others one ear. Some had monstrous bellies, hanging breasts, projecting teeth and crooked thighs; others were exceedingly beautiful in appearance and clothed in splendor. Some had two legs, some three legs and some four legs. Some had the heads of donkeys, some the heads of horses and some the heads of elephants."

Ram Dass, Baba

Name assumed by Richard **Alpert,** associate of Dr. Timothy **Leary,** after giving up the psychedelic revolution of the 1960s and embracing traditional Hindu mysticism.

Rama, Swami (1925-)

Well-known Indian teacher of **yoga, meditation,** and holistic heath. At an early age he was ordained as a monk by a great sage of the Himalayas, and later journeyed to numerous monasteries and caves, studying with many spiritual masters. Notable teachers he encountered included Mahatma Gandhi, Rabindranath Tagore, Sri **Aurobindo,** and Sri **Ramana Maharshi**.

At a later date, he pursued a formal education at Oxford University, continuing his studies of Western psychology and philosophy in Germany and Holland for three years before coming to the U.S. in 1969.

In the following year, he served as a consultant to the Voluntary Controls Project of the Research Department of the Menninger Foundation at Topeka, Kansas. Under scientific controls, he demonstrated such feats as manipulating his heartbeat at will to 300 beats per minute (effectively stopping the flow of blood) for seventeen seconds, and then rushing off to give a lecture.

The results of such tests had a profound effect on medical interest in body-mind relationships and generated great public interest in yoga techniques.

Swami Rama has consistently sought to establish a clear scientific basis for the practice of yoga and meditation. He has published books and audiotapes for the **Himalayan International Institute of Yoga Science and Philosophy** (Honesdale, Pennsylvania) which he founded in 1971. The Institute has a 422-acre campus in the Pocono Mountains of northeastern Pennsylvania. Branch centers have also been established throughout the U.S. The Swami also continues to teach and write from his centers in India.

He is widely respected in the East, where he held, and later renounced, the office of Shankaracharya, Indian's highest spiritual position. His lifetime of contributing to a reconciliation of scientific and spiritual knowledge brought him the Martin Buber Award for Service to Humanity in 1977.

For biographical background, see *Living with the Himalayan Masters: Spiritual Experiences of Swami Rama* edited by Swami Ajaya (Himalayan Institute, Honesdale, Pa., 1978), and *Swami* by Doug Boyd (Random House, 1976).

Ramacharaka, Yogi (1862-1932)

Pseudonym of American writer and editor William Walker Atkinson. Born December 5, 1862 in

Baltimore, Maryland, he led a commercial life from 1882-94, was admitted to Pennsylvania bar in 1894 and Illinois bar 1903.

He became associate editor of the Chicago magazine *Suggestion* from 1900-05 and edited *Advanced Thought* (Chicago, 1916-19). Thereafter he wrote a number of popular books on New Thought, Mental-Fascination, Self-Healing, Mind-Power and popular occultism.

From about 1903 onwards he began to write books on yoga philosophy using the pseudonym "Yogi Ramacharaka." These were ingenious compilations from other works, but assembled so skillfully that even today "Yogi Ramacharaka" is mistakenly quoted as an authority in India!

His books on yoga and occultism were issued by the Yogi Publication Society, Chicago, and are still reprinted today. Atkinson died in California November 22, 1932.

Ramakrishna, Sri (1836-1886)

One of the most remarkable Hindu mystics of recent history. He was born February 18, 1836 in a village in Bengal, after the divine hero Sri Rama had appeared in a vision to an old Brahmin named Khudiram, saying that he would be reborn as his son.

In due course, the boy was born and named Gadadhar. He grew up to worship the goddess Kali, the great mother, and even when he was obliged to marry, he worshiped his bride, identifying her with Kali. At the age of eighteen, Gadadhar was taken to Calcutta by his brother Ramkumar, whom he assisted as a teacher.

He settled in a temple at Dakshineswar, where he became known as "Ramakrishna," and after a period of intense spiritual discipline had ecstatic visions and trances. He was virtually intoxicated with the bliss of *samadhi* or divine trance, and a number of miracles were credited to him. His chief disciple Swami **Vivekananda** successfully carried the mission of Hindu spiritual wisdom to the U.S. and other Western countries from 1893.

Sri Ramakrishna passed into the *mahasamadhi* (great sleep) of death August 16, 1886. His teachings are now known throughout the world through the establishment of Ramakrishna Vedanta Centers. The Ramakrishna Order is today the largest and most widely known monastic order in India, with colleges, schools, hospitals, relief projects and publishing houses. Publications and information are available from Sri Ramakrishna Math, Mylapore, Madras 4, India, or from U.S. branches: Vedanta Press & Book Shop, 1946 Vedanta Place, Hollywood, California 90028; Vedanta Society, 2323 Vallejo Street, San Francisco, California 94123; Vedanta Society, 34 West 71 Street, New York, N.Y. 10023. (See also **Vedanta**)

Recommended reading:

Isherwood, Christopher. *Ramakrishna and His Disciples*, Simon & Schuster, 1965

Ramana Maharshi, Sri (1879-1950)

Undoubtedly the most important of recent Hindu saints and holy men, whose life and teachings were those of the classic God-realized sage. Born December 30, 1879 in the village of Tiruchuzhi, near Madura, South India, he was the second son of a pleader or solicitor. The boy attended elementary school at Tiruchuzhi and Dindigul, and went on to Scott's Middle School, Madura and the American Mission High School.

As a boy, he was impressed by a casual remark from a visitor that he had come from Arunachalam, a holy place in Tiruvannamalai, and his mind was directed to study of the lives of Tamil saints. At the age of seventeen, he had a strange mystical experience following a period of trance-like condition. He felt that he was going to die, but perceived that only the body could die, the true self being independent. He lost interest in his everyday studies and felt an intense desire to go to Arunachalam.

On August 29, 1896, he renounced his everyday life and set out for Arunachalam, where he spent the rest of his life in a condition of mystical meditation which transformed his understanding. Impervious to physical or mental discomforts, he remained in ecstatic spiritual meditation, at first in complete silence, living under a tree, or in temples, accepting minimum food which he ate mechanically.

In the course of time, the young renunciate attracted the attention of devotees, who found that he was able to answer the most abstruse metaphysical questions with wit and incisive wisdom. Eventually a religious settlement grew up around him, and he was visited by devotees from all over India and even from western countries.

He gave no formal teaching as such, but merely answered questions put to him in such a way that traditional Hindu metaphysical teachings had personal relevance to the questioner.

His constant theme was the discovery of the essential Self present in all beings, summarized in the formulation "Who Am I?"—not the individual body, mind or senses, which are transient, but the ever-enlightened divine consciousness which is the Self of all.

His statements combined metaphysical subtlety and great simplicity, while his gentle and perceptive presence was inspiring to his devotees. Even the local creatures (monkeys, cows, peacocks, birds) were attracted to him as if to a latter-day St. Francis of Assisi. He was also visited by leading Western scholars and seekers, including Paul **Brunton** and W. Y. **Evans-Wentz.**

In his later years, he developed various illnesses and a cancerous tumor on his left elbow, but remained indifferent to intense physical pain. He passed into *mahasamadhi* (death) at 8:47 p.m. April 14, 1950 after assuring devotees of continued presence. He stated "I am not going away. Where could I go? I am here." This implied the omnipresence of the Universal Self.

At the precise moment of death a large star was seen to trail slowly across the sky. It was witnessed by the famous French photographer Henri Cartier-Bresson, who was visiting the ashram.

The ashram is still in existence and has published a number of books dealing with the teachings of Sri Ramana Maharshi. A biography *Ramana Maharshi and the Path of Self-Knowledge* by Arthur Osborne was published London, 1957, reissued Jaico paperbacks, Bombay, 1958. The ashram is located at: Sri Ramananasramam, Tiruvannamalai, South India.

Rampa, T(uesday) Lopsang (1911?-1981)

Pseudonym of British author Cyril Henry Hoskins, whose first book *The Third Eye* (London, 1956; Doubleday, 1957) became a sensational bestseller. It purported to be written by a Tibetan Lama and described a kind of occult leucotomy in which his "third eye" in the center of the forehead was opened surgically, resulting in psychic powers.

The book was well written, but Tibetan critics found many inconsistencies. There is no tradition of surgical opening of the third eye, which is considered a structure in the subtle body, the basis of meditation techniques in various yoga systems.

In a perceptive review in the journal *Tomorrow* (vol. 6, No. 2, Spring 1958) the Tibetan scholar Prof. Chen Chi **Chang** declared the book a literary entertainment, stating: "we have here a work of interesting and highly imaginative fiction—but certainly not . . . a source of authentic information on Buddhist teachings or training."

While this review was being published, an independent inquiry had been undertaken by Clifford Burgess, a Liverpool (England) detective on behalf of a group of Tibetan scholars. Burgess tracked down Hoskins to a village overlooking Dublin Bay in the Irish Republic, and revealed that Hoskins had never been in Tibet or had an operation on his forehead.

Hoskins (born c. 1911) was the son of Joseph Henry Hoskins, a plumber. After leaving school he assisted his father for a time, and when his father died in 1937 he lived with his mother in Nottinghamshire. He worked for a surgical instrument company, then became a clerk with a correspondence school, teaching time and motion studies. About this time he shaved his head, grew a beard and adopted the name of "Dr. Kuan-suo." Later, with his wife Sanya, he moved to Ireland.

After exposure of the literary hoax, Hoskins stated that his own body had been taken over by the spirit of a Tibetan lama. He published a number of other successful books on occultism. None of these had the panache of *The Third Eye,* being mainly a trendy rehash of standard occult and psychic themes.

His follow-up book to *The Third Eye* was *Doctor From Lhasa* (1959) which has some science-fiction style episodes and is generally less plausible. His other books included: *Cave of the Ancients* (1963), *Living With the Lama* (1964), *Wisdom of the Ancients* (1965), *You—Forever* (1965), *The Saffron Robe* (1964), *My Visit to Venus* (1966), *The Rampa Story* (1967), *Beyond the Tenth* (1969), *The Hermit* (1971), *The Thirteenth Candle* (1972), *Candlelight* (1974), *As It Was!* (1976).

He died of heart trouble January 25, 1981, in Calgary, Alberta, Canada.

"Ramtha"

Spirit guide channeled through psychic J. Z. **Knight**, now the focus of a fast-growing, successful, popular movement in the U.S. "Ramtha" is said to be a 35,000-year-old spirit from the lost continent of Lemuria, and his messages, channeled through Ms. Knight, echo themes of the New Age movement. Ramtha stated: "You . . . are the creators of the universe . . . Everything you think is felt into reality." According to Ramtha, Jesus was a good teacher, but the Christian religion "has kept monarchs in power and controlled nations of people and incurred grand wealth . . . the overall purpose, it is for total enslavement and not freedom."

Ramtha's messages are contained in the book *Voyage to the New World* (1986). (See also J. Z. **Knight**)

Randall, Edward Caleb (1860-1935)

American lawyer, author and psychical researcher. He was born at Ripley, New York, July 19, 1860. He was educated at Allegheny College and practiced as a lawyer at Buffalo, New York from 1884 onwards. He became president of Niagara Terminal Corporation, American Super-Power Corporation and South Buffalo Gas Corporation.

He experimented with the **direct voice** medium Mrs. Emily **French** for twenty years, during which period she refused to accept fees or compensation. Randall also carried on Spiritualist work with **"rescue circles."**

His books included: *Life's Progression,* 1906, *Future of Man,* 1908, *The Dead Have Never Died,* 1916, *Frontiers of the After Life,* 1922, *Told In The After Life* 1925, *The Living Dead,* 1927. He also contributed articles to Spiritualist journals. He died at Buffalo July 3, 1935.

Randall, John L(eslie) (1933-)

British school teacher and parapsychologist. Born November 27, in Warwick, England, he studied at Leicester University (graduate certificate in education) and Leicester College of Technology (honors degree in chemistry; minor in biology). University of London (B.Sc. honours). He was a teacher at secondary schools for four years prior to his position as biology master at Leamington College, a grammar school for boys 1962-79; biology teacher King Henry VIII School, Coventry, 1979 onwards; organist and choir master, 1976-80. He is a member of The Society for Psychical Research, London and served on the council from 1978 onwards.

He introduced psi experiments and the study of parapsychology into a General Studies course for sixth form students. He has special interest in the philosophical implications of psi, and biological theories relating to psi.

His papers on parapsychology include: (in *Journal of the Society for Psychical Research*) 'An Attempt to Detect Psi Effects with Protozoa' (vol. 45, June 1970), 'Experiments to Detect a Psi Effect with Small Animals' (vol. 46, March 1971), 'Psi Phenomena and Biological Theory' (vol. 46, 1971; reprinted in the book *Surveys in Parapsychology* by Rhea A. White, 1976), 'Two Psi Experiments with Gerbils' (vol. 46, March 1972). His paper 'Biological Aspects of Psi' was published in the book *New Directions in Parapsychology* ed. J. Beloff (London, 1974; Metuchen, N.J., 1975). His paper 'Psi Phenomena and Biological Theory' was published in *Surveys in Parapsychology* by Rhea A. White (Scarecrow Press, 1976). He has also published an introduction to modern psychical research: *Parapsychology and the Nature of Life* (1975), and *Tests for Extrasensory Perception & Psychokinesis* (1980), *Psychokinesis; A Study of Paranormal Forces Through the Ages* (1982). He was a contributor to *Psychical Research; A Guide to its History, Principles & Practices* (1982).

Randi, James (1928-)

Pseudonym of James Randall Zwinge, brilliant stage magician who has also appointed himself as arch-enemy of psychics and the paranormal. Born in Toronto, Canada, he was exceptionally talented as a child, although he did not have the advantage of college education.

He was passionately interested in conjuring magic, and in adult life he achieved worldwide fame for his skill in legerdemain. He has performed before royalty in Europe and Asia, appeared on national television programs and at college campuses, under the stage name of "The Amazing Randi."

In addition to his own stage magic, Randi has deliberately set out to show that because he can apparently duplicate by trickery the claimed paranormal feats of prominent psychics, they must necessarily be exposed as frauds or fakes.

According to journalist Richard Pyatt in *USA Today* (August 29, 1986), Randi's interest in investigating psychic phenomena started at the age of fifteen. Randi is quoted as stating: "When I was 15 years of age, I had already started out on my career as an amateur magician. When I attended a spiritualist church in Toronto, I saw they were using the same gimmicks that I had been reading about in the catalog and had been learning to do myself. Ministers were apparently speaking with the dead. I saw people in that congregation who really believed that the minister was able to read the contents of sealed envelopes and bring them messages from beyond the grave. I resented that highly, and I tried to expose that. I was arrested for my troubles. So at 15, I ended up in a police station, sitting there for four hours waiting for my father to come and get me out. I guess that was the worst four hours the psychic world ever spent, though they didn't know it until recently."

Like the late **Houdini** (1874-1926), also a brilliant stage magician, he has declared himself the scourge of psychics, and in addition to imitating their feats by means of conjuring, he also issues challenges to psychics to perform paranormal feats under his own exacting conditions and to his satisfaction for a prize of ten thousand dollars. He has also issued wild accusations of fraud, unsupported by firm evidence. One of his major targets has been Uri **Geller,** and he has published a book claiming that Geller's feats are not paranormal: *The Magic of Uri Geller* by the Amazing Randi (Ballantine paperback, 1975).

Randi is also a committee member of the **Committee for the Scientific Investigation of Claims of the Paranormal** and a member of the editorial board of their journal *The Skeptical Inquirer: The Zetetic.* When he is not traveling the world performing and exposing the paranormal as fraud and conjuring, Randi lives in New Jersey in a house full of unusual and remarkable illusions, with doors that open unexpectedly on the side opposite the door knob and clocks that run backwards.

There can be little doubt that Randi performs valuable service in drawing attention to the undoubted fraud that continues to exist in the field of the paranormal, but his often wild and sweeping accusations and campaigns have frequently been criticized by those who do not agree that all psychics are frauds. His book *Flim-Flam! Psychics, ESP, Unicorns and Other Delusions* (Prometheus Books, 1982) typifies his attitudes. It contains much common sense, deserved debunking, shrewd guesswork and flamboyant overstatement.

One of the most brilliantly organized exposures of fraudulent spiritual healing arranged by Randi was that of the Rev. Peter Popoff in San Francisco in 1986.

In his healing crusades, the Rev. Popoff actually called sufferers by name and described their ailments, claiming to receive such information directly from God. Randi had noticed that Popoff had a "hearing aid" inside his ear. There was circumstantial evidence that someone was broadcasting precise information to Popoff; the problem was how to obtain definite evidence that the identification of sufferers was fraudulent.

In a special report 'Exposing the Faith-Healers' by Robert A. Steiner (*The Skeptical Inquirer*, vol.XI, No.1, Fall 1986), full details of Randi's remarkable campaign were revealed. Randi enlisted the aid of trusted individuals from the Bay Area Skeptics group and the Society of American Magicians. Some members of the group took up strategic places in the Civic Auditorium in San Francisco, where the crusade was held. Robert Steiner and Alexander Jason (an electronics expert) established themselves behind the balcony of the auditorium with hidden tape recorders and electronic listening equipment.

Just before the healing service started, Jason succeeded in tuning in to and recording a backstage broadcast from Elizabeth Popoff to her husband, the minister. The message began: "Hello Petey. I love you. I'm talking to you. Can you hear me? If you can't, you're in trouble." Here was firm evidence that the "messages from God" were in fact information relayed to Rev. Popoff by his wife, received through Popoff's "hearing aid." The broadcast continued: "I'm looking up the names right now." This appeared to be a reference to the "prayer cards" which those attending the healing service were asked to fill out, giving names, description of ailments, and other information.

The tape recordings of a claimed healing from a service of the Popoff Crusade a few weeks later in Anaheim, California, on March 16, 1986, provided evidence of a backstage prompting broadcast by Elizabeth Popoff to her husband. She gave the name "Virgil Jorgenson. Virgil. . . . Way back in the back somewhere. Arthritis in knees. He's got a cane . . . He's got arthritis. He's praying for his sister in Sweden, too."

In the auditorium, the Rev. Popoff called out: "Virgil. Is it Jorgenson? Who is Virgil?" A man, apparently in his sixties and limping with a cane, came forward, and Popoff continued: "Are you ready for God to overhaul those knees?" Jorgenson then appeared to walk more easily, and Popoff continued: "Oh, glory to God. I'll tell you, God's going to touch that sister of yours all the way over in Sweden." Popoff then broke Jorgenson's cane, while the sufferer, apparently cured of his arthritis, walked about the auditorium, praising God and the minister Popoff.

This remarkable healing was so impressive that Peter Popoff used the film clip for three consecutive weeks on his television show. Unfortunately for the Popoff Crusade, "Virgil Jorgenson" was Don Henvick, program coordinator for Bay Area Skeptics and president of Assembly #70 of the Society of American Magicians, and does not suffer from arthritis. His disguise as "Virgil Jorgenson" was only one of several appearances that challenged the claimed divine source of Peter Popoff's information and healing. Under the name "Tom Hendrys," Henvick was "healed" of nonexistent alcoholism at the San Francisco Civic Auditorium. In a Detroit healing crusade, Popoff "healed" Henvick of uterine cancer when this master of disguise appeared dressed in woman's garb under the name "Bernice Manicoff," seated in a wheelchair.

The decisive exposure of the electronic source of Popoff's claimed divine messages from God was made by Randi nationwide on a Johnny Carson "Tonight" show on April 22, 1986, when scenes of a claimed healing were shown with a soundtrack of the secret information broadcast identifying the sufferer.

This brilliantly organized and presented exposure shows Randi at his best, in cleverly identifying the techniques of charlatans and organizing irrefutable evidence, presented with maximum showmanship, to alert the public to impudent frauds. It would be wrong, however, to conclude that all spiritual healers and clairvoyants are frauds, using similar hi-tech methods. Many are sincere, giving their services for very modest fees.

On July 14, 1986, Randi was the recipient of a $272,000 award by the MacArthur Foundation of Chicago through his efforts in "alerting the unsuspecting public to hoaxers who, for example, claim to perform miracle cures of cancer, and also to support his exposure of shoddy, pseudo-science through his investigations and public lectures." The MacArthur Fellow Awards are tax-free, no-strings grants to individuals to permit them to continue their work without economic hindrance. (See also **Fraud; Magicians; Metal-Bending**)

Randles, Jenny (Jennifer Christine) (1951-)

British author, journalist, and Ufologist. She was born October 30, 1951, in Bacup, England, and studied chemistry, mathematics, and physics, receiving advanced level General Certificates of Education in these subjects. She went on to post advanced level studies in geography and geology, receiving City and Guilds Certificates with distinctions in audio-visual technology and education.

From 1972-74, she was a teacher at a Cheshire Middle School, from 1977-78, an audio-visual technician in a college of education, servicing teachers. From 1975-77, she was a Research Coordinator on the council of the British UFO Research Association (BUFORA).

After 1978 she became secretary of the Northern UFO Network (NUFON) and the UFO Investigators' Network (UFOIN), concerned with procuring reports on UFO sightings in Britain, and also undertaking administrative and secretarial work for the important British publication *Flying Saucer Review.* She was coauthor with Peter Warrington of *UFOs; A British Viewpoint* (1979).

As a result of many years of study and investigation of the UFO phenomenon, she advised caution in reaching firm conclusions about the subject, and stated that she had found no objective evidence to support the belief that we are visited by extraterrestrials. She suggested that there may be several different answers to the unexplained cases, some of them possibly relating to new types of natural, physical phenomena.

In recent years, she has extended her researches to areas of physical phenomena and the paranormal. In 1983, she wrote and presented a thirty-week series of features on mysterious phenomena for the independent British radio station Radio City.

She has also appeared in, researched, and helped to produce numerous other radio and television programs on British and foreign channels.

During these media appearances, she met many celebrities who provided the inspiration and material of her book *Beyond Explanation?* (1985) This deals with the paranormal experiences of past and present public figures such as John Lennon, Edgar Allan Poe, Susannah York, Kevin Keegan, Donald Sutherland, Arthur Koestler, Winston Churchill, Anthony Hopkins, Lindsay Wagner, Sir Arthur Conan Doyle, and many others.

Randolph, P(ascal) B(everley) (1825-1875)

Author, and founder of Rosicrucian sects in America. Born October 8, 1825 in New York, he became a physician.

He traveled to Europe in 1850, and was initiated into the Rosicrucian Fraternity in Germany. In 1854, he met various occult scholars in Britain and France, and four years later, in Paris, he became Supreme Grand Master in the Rosicrucian movement.

During the American Civil War he recruited black soldiers, and later became a teacher to freed slaves.

He published a number of novels and some books dealing with Spiritualism, including: *The Unveiling* (1860), *Dealings With The Dead* (1861), *Ravalette, Rosicrucian's Story* (1863), *After Death; or, Disembodied Man* (1868) *Seership* (1868), *Love & the Master Passion* (1870), *Eulis, the History of Love* (1874), *The Book of the Triplicate Order* (1875) From 1852-61 he edited *The Leader* (Boston), *The Messenger of Light* (New York) and contributed to *Journal of Progress* and *Spiritual Telegraph.*

He was also a trance medium, manifesting psychic lights and shadowy forms and delivered messages claimed to be from a spirit known as "Philip Lemoine." During his visit to Britain in 1857, he delivered trance addresses at the Charing Cross Spiritual Circle, London, when he was alleged to be inspired by the spirit of the dead scientist Sir Humphry Davy.

In 1858 he founded the Rose Cross Order and the Triple Order in America. In 1903, these and other Rosicrucian type organizations associated with Randolph were subsumed in the Royal Fraternity Association, Inc.

For further background information on Randolph and the American Rosicrucian movement, see *The Rose Cross Order and the Rosicrucians; Their Teachings* by R. Swinburne Clymer, who became leader of the Rosicrucian Fraternity at Quakertown, Pennsylvania. This fraternity was continued by Emerson Clymer, son of R. Swinburne **Clymer.** (See also **Rosicrucians**)

Randolph has a special place in occult history for his identification of the closely guarded secret of **sex magic.**

He died July 29, 1875, in Boston, Massachusetts.

Ransom, Champe (1936-)

Editor in a law book publishing company, and writer on parapsychology. Born in San Diego, California, he became a seaman in the Merchant Marines after leaving high school. He obtained B.A. degree from Lawrence University, majoring in history in 1961; J.D. degree from St. Mary's University School of Law in 1966. He served as legislative counsel to the state legislature in Juneau, Alaska from 1966-70.

During his final year in law school he took an interest in parapsychology and became research assistant at the Division of Parapsychology, University of Virginia from 1970-72. He became editor with Michie Company, law book publishers, Charlottesville, North Carolina.

His paper 'Recent Criticisms of Parapsychology: A Review' was supported by a grant from the **Parapsychology Foundation,** New York, and was first published in *Journal* of the American Society for Psychical Research (vol. 65, July 1971); it was reprinted in *Surveys in Parapsychology* by Rhea A. White (1976). Other papers include 'Recent Criticisms of Parapsychology; A Review' (*Journal* of American Society for Psychical Research, vol. 65, 1971); (with J. G. Pratt) 'Exploratory Observations of the Movement of Static Objects Without the Apparent Use of Known Physical Energies by Nina S. Kulagina' (*Proceedings of the Parapsychological Association* vol. 8, 1971), (with J. G. Pratt) 'Extrasensory Perception or Extraordinary Sensory Perception?' (*Journal* of American Society for Psychical Research vol. 66, 1972).

Rao, K(oneru) Ramakrishna (1932-)

Lecturer in philosophy and parapsychologist. Born October 4, 1932, at Enikepadu, India, he studied at Andhra University, Waltair, India (B.A. hons., philosophy 1953; M.A. hons., psychology 1955; Ph.D. 1962). In 1950 he married Sarojini Devi.

He was a lecturer in the Department of Philosophy at Andhra University from 1953-58, Fulbright scholar in the U.S. from 1958-59, Rockefeller fellow, Department of Philosophy at University of Chicago from 1959-60, chief librarian at Andhra University from 1960-61, thereafter staff member of the Parapsychology Laboratory, Duke University, Durham, North Carolina. He was convener of the Andhra Philosophical Congress 1954, member of the Indian Philosophical Congress, member of the Parapsychology Association (secretary, 1963), hon. editor of *Santhi* (philosophical and religious journal) from 1956-57.

Dr. Rao received a Smith-Mundt Fulbright grant to study at the University of Chicago during 1958-59. Later he was awarded a Rockefeller Fellowship. He was elected president of the **Parapsychological Association,** an international society of parapsychologists, for 1965 and 1978. In 1976 he received a Ph.D. in Philosophy from Andhra University in India, where he is professor of Psychology (on leave). Dr. Rao became director of the **Institute for Parapsychology,** Durham, North Carolina.

In addition to his writings on philosophy and a number of research papers on psychology, he is also author of the following books: *Psi Cognition* (Tagore Publishing House, India, 1957), *Experimental Parapsychology* (1966), *Gandhi and Pragmatism* (Calcutta & Oxford, 1968), *Mystic Awareness* (Mysore, India, 1972), (with P. Sailaja) *Experimental Studies of the Differential Effect in Life Setting* (1972), (with K. S. Murty) *Current Trends in Indian Thought* (New Delhi, 1972).

He became editor of the *Journal of Indian Psychology* and a coeditor of the **Journal of Parapsychology.** His papers on parapsychology include the following: 'A Note on Jung's Conception of Psyche' (*Proceedings of the Indian Philosophical Congress,* 1956), 'Vedanta and the Modus Operandi of Paranormal Cognition'

(Philosophical Quarterly, 1955); in *Journal of Parapsychology:* 'A Consideration of Some Theories in Parapsychology' (March 1961), 'The Preferential Effect in ESP' (vol.26 1962), 'Studies in The Preferential Effect I. Target Preference with tapes of Target Unknown (vol.27, 1963), 'Studies in the Preferential Effect. II. A Language ESP Test Involving Precognition & "Intervention' (vol.27, 1963), 'Studies in the Preferential Effect. III. The Reversal Effect in Psi Preference' (vol.27, 1963), 'Studies in the Preferential Effect. IV. The Role of Key Cards in Preference Response Situations' (vol.28, 1964), 'The Differential Response in Three New Situations' (vol.28, 1964), "ESP and the Manifest Anxiety Scale' (vol.29, 1965), 'The Biodirectionality of Psi' (vol.29, 1965); (with B. K. Kanthamani) 'Personality Characteristics of ESP Subjects. I. Primary Personality Characteristics & ESP' (vol.35, 1971), 'Personality Characteristics of ESP Subjects. II. The Combined Personality Measure (CPM) & ESP (vol.36, 1972), 'Personality Characteristic of ESP Subjects. III. Extraversion & ESP (vol.36, 1972), 'Personality Characteristic of ESP Subjects. IV. Neuroticism & ESP' (vol.37, 1973), 'Personality Characteristics of ESP Subjects. V. Graphic Expansiveness & ESP (vol.37, 1973).

Raphael

In the prophecy of *Enoch* it was said that: "Raphael presides over the spirits of men." In Jewish rabbinical legend of the angelic hierarchies, Raphael was the medium through which the power of Tsebaoth, or the Lord of Hosts, passed into the sphere of the sun, giving motion, heat and brightness to it.

The name "Raphael" was also used by British astrologer Robert Cross Smith (1795-1832) who published *Raphael's Astronomical Ephemeris,* still used for astrological calculations.

Like the other famous astrological pseudonym "Old Moore," the name "Raphael" was assumed by other astrologers.

Raphael II was John Palmer (1807-1837), editor of *Raphael's Sanctuary of the Astral Art* (1834), Raphael III was a Mr. Medhurst, who edited the *Prophetic Messenger* almanac (1837-1847?), Raphael IV was Mr. Wakeley (died 1853) who wrote under the name "Edwin Raphael," Raphael V was Mr. Sparkes (1820-1875) who edited *The Oracle* (May-June 1861). Raphael VI was Robert C. Cross (1850-1923) who acquired the Raphael copyrights, including the ephemeris.

Rapping

Phenomena of knockings or rappings have usually accompanied **poltergeist** disturbances, even before the commencement of the modern Spiritualist movement. Thus they were observed in the case of the **"Drummer of Tedworth,"** the **"Cock Lane Ghost,"** and other disturbances of the kind, and also in the presence of various somnambules, such as the Seeress of Prevorst (see Frau Frederica **Hauffe**).

With the **"Rochester Rappings"**—the famous outbreak at Hydesville in 1848—to which may be directly traced the beginning of modern Spiritualism—the phenomenon took on a new importance, rapidly increasing to an epidemic, remaining throughout the earlier stages of the movement the chief mode of communication with spirits.

Although it was afterwards supplanted to some extent by more elaborate and complicated phenomena, it continued, and still continues, to occupy a place of some importance among the manifestations of the seance-room. It is apparent from descriptions furnished by witnesses that raps varied considerably both in quality and intensity, being sometimes characterized as dull thuds, sometimes as clear sounds like an electric spark, and again as deep, vibrating tones.

It has been shown that raps may be produced by the ankle-joints, knee-joints, shoulders, and other joints, and one man (the Rev. Eli Noyes) claimed to have discovered seventeen different methods.

There are also instances on record where specially constructed "medium" tables were responsible for the manifestations. Besides the Spiritualist explanation and the frankly skeptical one of fraud, there have been other scientific or pseudo-scientific theories advanced, such as electricity, **od** (or odyle), **ectenic force,** or **animal magnetism.**

For a detailed examination of the case for Spiritualist rappings, see **Raps.**

Rapport

A mystical sympathetic or antipathetic connection between two persons. It was formerly believed that for a witch to harm her victims, the latter must first have become in *rapport* with her, either by contact with her person, or by contact with some garment she has worn. A certain Irish witch, Florence Newton (tried in 1661), was accused of establishing *rapport* between herself and those she sought to bewitch by kissing them, whereby she was able to compass their destruction.

In the practice of **animal magnetism,** it was considered that the only invariable and characteristic symptom of the genuine trance was the *rapport* between patient and operator. It consisted of a **community of sensations**—the subject perceiving the sensations of the magnetizer and also divining his thought. In modern times *rapport* denotes the community of sensation between the hypnotizer and his subject.

According to the psychical researcher Julien **Ochorowicz,** *rapport* was solely a "magnetic" condition. He observed that under hypnosis his subject was indifferent to anybody with whom he came in contact but in animal magnetism he had an incontestable preference for the magnetizer. In general, the touch of the magnetizer was agreeable while that of others was painful. This condition is not found in hypnosis.

The term *rapport* is also used in Spiritualism, signifying sympathy between the spirit **control** and the medium or any of the sitters. The control (through the medium) may be placed in *rapport* with anyone who is absent or dead, merely by handling something which has belonged to them (see also **Psychometry**).

It is for a similar reason that in **crystal gazing** the crystal is sometimes held for a few moments prior to the inspection by the person on whose behalf the crystal-gazer is about to examine it.

(See also **Animal Magnetism; Community of Sensation; Hypnotism; Mesmerism; Psychometry**)

Raps

Percussive sounds of varying intensity without visible, known or normal agency, a simple phenomenon of tremendous import. The psychical researcher Prof. Charles **Richet** wrote in *Thirty Years of Psychical Research* (1923): "The reality of these raps is of primary importance, and this phenomenon carries the implication of the whole of metapsychics. If it is established that mechanical vibrations can be produced in matter, at a distance, and without contact, and that these vibrations are intelligent, we have the truly far-reaching fact that there are in the universe human or non-human intelligences that can act directly on matter."

Modern **Spiritualism** began with **raps** at Hydesville, New York in 1848 (see **Fox Sisters**). But the history of this paranormal manifestation reaches back into antiquity and the belief that it was in the house of the Fox family that intelligent contact with the unseen world through such agency was established for the first time is erroneous.

Historical Background

Rudolf of Fulda, a chronicle dating from 858 A.D. spoke of communications with a rapping intelligence. The sixteenth century physician **Paracelsus** called it "pulsatio mortuorum"—an omen of approaching death. The early Church knew of *spiritus percutiens* (rapping spirits). They were conjured away by old Catholic formulae at the benediction of Churches.

Raps were recorded by the theologian Philipp Melancthon in 1520 at Oppenheim, Germany. Montalambert, chaplain to François I, described raps which he heard in Lyon about 1521. According to a manuscript from 1610 at the University of Glasgow, Scotland, Mr. Welsh, a clergyman in Ayr, conversed with spirits by raps and observed movements of objects without contact.

The first detailed account of the phenomenon is in the Rev. Joseph **Glanvill**'s *Saducismus Triumphatus* (1681). It described the disturbances in Magistrate Mompesson's house at Tedworth in 1661 (see **Drummer of Tedworth**). It was discovered that an invisible entity would answer in drumming anything that was beaten or called for. But no further progress was made.

The phenomenon was again noticed at Epworth Vicarage in 1716 by the Wesley family (see **Epworth Phenomena**). In the first quarter of the nineteenth century, Dr. Justinus **Kerner** detected in raps a means of conversation with the spirit visitants of the Seeress of Prevorst (see Frau Frederica **Hauffe**). Then came the historic outbreak at Hydesville, followed two years later by the Stratford disturbances (see Rev. Eliakim **Phelps**), and amid much public acrimony quite a literature grew up around the reality of the strange knocks on the portals of our world.

The theories which has been advanced to explain the phenomenon are of historic interest. The cracking of knee joints, toe joints, the snapping of fingers and the contraction of the respiratory muscles were variously called the scientific solution to the mystery. To strengthen the position of the first attempt at scientific elucidation, Professor S. L. Loomis (1822-1896) published his discovery of the effect of the vibrations of a dam over which water falls. These sounds are transmitted to a distance by the earth and produce sudden alarming knocking sounds in dwellings. (Incidentally, Loomis, a good scientist, reported favorably on the phenomena of the Davenport Brothers, although discounting spiritualist explanations).

It is doubtless true that raps were very often produced by fraudulent means. William Faulkner, a surgeon, testified before the committee of the **London Dialectical Society** in 1869 that he was in the habit of selling trick magnets to produce rapping sounds at Spiritualist seances. The magnets could be concealed about the person, or attached to furniture. By pressing a small brass button, raps could be produced whenever desired.

Methods of fraud were described in Hereward Carrington's book *The Physical Phenomena of Spiritualism* (1907), in *Mysteries of the Seance* by "A Medium" (Ed Lunt) (1905) and in David P. Abbott's *Behind the Scenes with The Mediums* (1907).

It is also true that underneath the scientific theories there was a physiological foundation, as in a way it is the bodily mechanism of the medium which is responsible for the raps. Still it is one of the aberrations of scientific orthodoxy that when the **Seybert Commission** investigated the raps of Margaret Kane-Fox (see **Fox Sisters**) in 1884, the evidence for the genuine nature of the phenomenon was ruled out because one of the members of the committee, when placing his hand on her feet, distinctly felt an unusual pulsation although there was not a particle of motion in it. Nobody seems to have recalled this discovery when the sensational confession of Margaret and Kate Fox reverberated in the Press, and whereas previously the raps were ruled out because of their reaction on the medium's body, it passed unnoticed that the confession and its acceptance, on face value, confirmed the occurrence of the very phenomenon which it attempted to demolish.

Why should spirits knock and rap? According to Andrew **Lang**: "Were we inventing a form for a spirit's manifestation to take, we never should invent that." He frankly admitted that medieval and later tales of rapping have never been satisfactorily accounted for on any theory. His theory of "spectral aphasia" advanced as regards haunting may partially explain; raps may be the easiest signs which a spirit wishing to affect the physical plane, may produce, though he may aim at a different effect.

At present there is a place for raps in medical science. A curious connection was discovered between raps and chorea. In *Psyche* (March 1882), Dr. Purdon reported the case of two soldiers in Guernsey, both of them of neurotic temperament, in whose presence rappings of an unnatural character were heard. Under the administration of iodide of potassium, salicylate of soda and arsenic in full doses, the men improved wonderfully and the rappings became less frequent.

E. Howard Grey, in his book *Visions, Previsions and Miracles in Modern Times* (1915), quoted a similar experience with a member of his own family. The attack commenced during the cutting of a child's permanent teeth, sometimes convulsions occurred in the night, and these generally seized upon the little girl about the same hour. He stated: "We were usually well prepared for these nocturnal troubles by explosive and other auditory sounds, either on the wall or by Drs. Drury and Purdon, indeterminate or derial. Sometimes a tinkling sound as of dropping water would be heard, but none was visible, they occurred when the child was asleep, also in her absence . . . " When she was in bed upstairs, they heard them in a room below; sometimes her mother heard them sounding like little taps on a newspaper she was reading. They did not exhibit intelligence. The last, or departing rap was especially loud. The cure was effected in a few months by the administration of bromide of potassium.

In speaking of the curious "thrilling" of the table in the presence of the great medium D. D. **Home**, Mrs. Augustus de Morgan wrote in *From Matter to Spirit:* (1863): "The last time I witnessed this phenomenon, an acute surgeon present said that this *thrilling*, the genuineness of which was unmistakable, was exactly like what takes place in that affection of the muscles called *subsultus tendinum*. When it ceased the table rose more than two feet from the floor."

In the closing years of the medium Henry **Slade,** loud raps were heard on the bedstead, walls and furniture while he was asleep. Chairs and other furniture moved about. The phenomena occurred even after he sank into senile dementia. The same phenomenon was observed around the death-bed of Margaret Fox (see **Fox Sisters**). The mysterious illness of Mary **Jobson** started with loud rapping sounds. When D. D. Home was ill the same manifestation was continually witnessed.

It is widely believed that abnormal conditions often open up channels for supernormal phenomena. But the larger percentage of such manifestations involves no bodily affliction, and whereas higher phenomena are often accompanied by utter exhaustion on the part of the medium, raps seldom bring about a feeling of significant depletion.

Simple as the phenomenon appears to be, various important accounts reflect an astounding variety of manifestation.

The Varieties of Rapping Experience

Judge J. W. **Edmonds** heard raps on his own person. The Rev. Samuel Watson, a Methodist parson, had similar experiences. "The noise made on my shirt bosom," he wrote, "resembled more the telegraph machine than anything else."

Abby **Warner,** of Massillon, Ohio was prosecuted in 1851 for disturbing the Christmas service in St. Timothy's Church by raps which sounded in her presence.

Considerable excitement was caused in New York in 1871 in the congregation of Henry Ward Beecher. In front of the rostrum at the reporter's table, raps were heard for a succession of Sabbaths, and slow and deliberate motion of the table was witnessed. It kept time with the preacher's words and assented to the reform demands of the Minister with great pushes and traveling to the opposite side as if to say: "That's so, that is the truth." (See Eugene Crowell, *Identity of Primitive Christianity and Modern Spiritualism*, (2 vols., 1875-79, p. 499)

Mrs. Leah Underhill, the eldest of the **Fox sisters,** wrote in her book *The Missing Link in Modern Spiritualism* (1885) that during the funeral of her second husband, Mr. Calvin Brown, raps were heard all over the room while S. B. Brittan delivered the funeral sermon and Judge Edmunds the eulogy.

Robert Dale **Owen** recorded some very curious experiments in raps with Mrs. Underhill in 1861. He heard raps on the seaside in a ledge of rock. "Placing my hands on the same ledge, a few steps from Mrs. Underhill and asking for raps, when this came audibly I felt, simultaneously with each rap, a slight but unmistakably distinct vibration or concussion of the rock." Owen heard raps on board an excursion boat and later in a sailing boat sounding from underneath. He also obtained them in the open air on the ground; "a dull sound, as of blows struck on the earth; then I asked Mrs. Underhill to touch one of the trees with the tips of her fingers and applying my ear to the tree I heard the raps from beneath the bark."

In an account of a seance on February 22, 1860, in which psychic lights were seen, Robert Dale Owen wrote: "While I was looking intently at such a light, about as large as a small fist, it rose and fell, as a hammer would, with which one was striking against the floor. At each stroke a loud rap was heard in connection. It was exactly as if an invisible hand held an illuminated hammer and pounded with it."

As to the objectivity of the raps produced by Kate **Fox**, Sir William **Crookes** said: " . . . it seems only necessary for her to place her hand on any substance for loud thuds to be heard in it, like a triple pulsation, sometimes loud enough to be heard several rooms off. In this manner I have heard them in a living tree—on a sheet of glass—on a stretched iron wire—on a stretched membrane—a tambourine—on the roof of a cab—and on the floor of a theatre. Moreover, actual contact is not always necessary. I have had these sounds proceeding from the floor, walls, &c. when the medium's hands and feet were held—when she was standing on a chair—when she was suspended in a swing from the ceiling—when she was enclosed in a wire cage—and when she had fallen fainting on a sofa. I have heard them on a glass harmonium—I have felt them on my own shoulder and under my own hands. I have heard them on a sheet of paper, held between the fingers by a piece of thread passed through one corner."

The membrane of which Crookes spoke was part of a complicated apparatus. A small piece of graphite was placed on it so as to be thrown upward by the slightest jar. The point of a lever registered in curves the amount of mechanical energy employed in the effect.

As to the sounds, Crookes observed "delicate ticks, as with the point of a pin; a cascade of sharp sounds as from an induction coil in full work; detonations in the air; sharp, metallic taps; a cracking like that heard when a frictional machine is at work; sounds like scratching; the twittering as of a bird, &c."

"We have been present with Kate Fox," wrote J. J. **Morse** in *The Two Worlds* newspaper (vol. 19) "when the raps were heard on a sheet of paper, held between the thumb and forefinger of another person standing beside the medium, the paper visibly shaking from the violence of the raps produced upon its surface."

Lord **Adare**'s father, in experiments with D. D. **Home,** heard raps upon the medium's hand when he placed it upon his head. Raps came on a sheet of paper which they held by the corners. Lord Adare heard raps under his feet and distinctly felt the jar while the raps were taking place. He saw a table leg rap. The spirits by raps joined into their conversation and signified approval in a most emphatic way. Adare was told to understand that by remaining in the earth's atmosphere, spirits get so charged that it is a positive relief to make sounds. Sometimes they cannot help rapping, and cannot control them. They discharge their electricity by a whole volley of taps.

The sounds may be single or combined knockings. "It was the most singular noise," wrote the Rev. W. Stainton **Moses** on December 5, 1873, "that the combined knockings made. The room seemed to be full of intelligences manifesting their presence."

The sounds have distinct individuality. They have characteristics as permanent as the voice, and the communicator is often recognized by his rapping style.

Dr. J. Garth Wilkinson wrote of an inward thrill going through the table and chairs and found the sensation best conveyed by the exclamation of his daughter: "Oh, papa, there is a heart in my chair."

"The departure of the spirits," wrote J. H. Powell in *Spiritualism; Its Facts and Phases* (1864), "was preceded by an indistinguishable number of raps, loud at first, then gradually faint and fainter until, like echoes on a hill, they faded away in the echoing distance."

In volume, the sounds may grow from a tiny tick to a loud crash. But the crashing blows leave no mark, although normally such force would be expected to smash the table. The tonality of the raps differs according to the object upon which they resound. They may resemble the slight noises made by a mouse, a fretsaw, or the scratching of a finger-nail on wood or cloth, and their rhythm is as varied as their tonality.

They often sound like detonations. There are instances in which the impression is borne out by effect. Archdeacon **Colley,** in a **slate-writing** experiment with the medium Francis W. **Monck,** placed his foot on the slate and felt a sensation of throbbing in the enclosed space—a heaving as when the confined steam lifts the lid of a kettle—and in a moment, an explosion took place that scattered the slate in fragments over the carpet, like spray from a fountain.

Such explosions and shatterings of the slate were frequently reported in seances with the medium Henry **Slade**.

According to biographers of Mme. **Blavatsky,** the founder of **Theosophy** was a powerful rapping medium in her teens. She was said to have caused raps inside the spectacles of a skeptical professor with such force that they were sent flying from his nose. In reply to a somewhat frivolous woman who asked what was the best conductor for raps, the table spelt out "gold," and the next moment the lady in question rushed out of the room with her hand clapped on her mouth, as she had felt the raps on the gold in her artificial teeth.

Dr. J. **Maxwell** obtained raps in restaurants and railway refreshment rooms which were loud enough to attract public attention. In his book *Metapsychical Phenomena* (1905), there is the following description of experiences by "Doctor X," with the medium Meurice: "The raps on the open umbrella are extremely curious. We have heard raps on the woodwork and on the silk at one and the same time; it is easy to perceive that the shock actually occurs in the wood—that the molecules of the latter are set in motion. The same thing occurs with the silk, and here observation is even more interesting still; and each rap *looks* like a drop of some invisible liquid falling on the silk from a respectable height. The stretched silk of the umbrella is quickly and slightly but surely dented in; sometimes the force with which the raps are given is such as to shake the umbrella. Nothing is more absorbing than the observation of an apparent conversation—by means of the umbrella—between the medium's personifications. Raps, imitating a burst of laughter in response to the observer's remarks, resound on the silk, like the rapid play of strong but tiny fingers. When raps on the umbrella are forthcoming, M. Meurice either holds the handle of the umbrella, or someone else does, whilst he simply touches the handle very lightly with his open palm. He never touches the silk."

Maxwell's own observations were summed up as follows: "(1) Every muscular movement, even a feeble one, is generally followed by a rap. (2) The intensity of the raps does not strike me as being in proportion with the movement made. (3) The intensity of the raps did not seem to me to vary proportionately according to their distance from the medium."

He often questioned mediums about their sensations when raps were being produced. They all acknowledged a feeling of fatigue, of depletion, after a good seance. This feeling was perceptible even to observers themselves. One of the mediums experienced a feeling like cramp in the epigastric region when the raps were particularly loud.

Mrs. de Morgan wrote in *From Matter to Spirit* (1863) that once, through typtological communication (i.e., through raps), she was informed that raps would come through herself that day. "This was not expected but it was worth trying, and I therefore went into an uncarpeted room barely furnished, and sat down by the table, on which I laid my arm. Very soon loud raps, which I called some of the family to hear, resounded on the table. There seemed to be power enough to rap the number of times desired, but not to indicate letters so as to spell anything. The sounds soon ceased and never returned. As each rap seemed to be shot through my arm it was accompanied by a feeling like a slight blow or shock of electricity and an aching pain extending from the shoulder to the hand, which remained for more than an hour after they had entirely ceased. This experiment seemed to prove that the nerves of the human body were necessary, if not for the production, at least for the propagation of the sounds."

In the experiments of Dr. W. J. **Crawford,** the loudness of the raps varied with weight and massiveness of the psychic "rods." Crawford put the medium on a weighing machine and measured the exact amount of ectoplasm necessary for the increase of rapping strength. He also found that the raps reacted upon the medium's body but that she was not conscious of any stress. The reaction, however, was not always the case.

"As soon as the seance begins," he wrote, "we hear noises, raps, rap, rap on the floor near the medium. They become louder and louder, on the table, on the chairs of the sitters. Sometimes they are like hammerblows, so loud that they can be heard outside, and they shake the floor and the chairs. They can imitate any different sounds, the step of a man, the trot of a horse, the rubbing of a match, or the bouncing of a ball."

Sir William F. **Barrett** who sat in the **Goligher circle** wrote *The Unseen* (1917): "Very soon knocks came and messages were spelt out as one of us repeated the alphabet aloud. Suddenly the knocks increased in violence, and being encouraged, a tremendous bang came which shook the room and resembled the blow of a sledge hammer on an anvil."

In *Proceedings* of the Society for Psychical Research (vol. 17, p. 726), a most extraordinary case of rapping is described. Mrs. Davis received a letter from India with the request to forward it to Mrs. W. She placed the letter on the mantelpiece. Some time after, raps were heard. They seemed to emanate from the neighborhood of the letter. She placed it on another spot. The raps followed the letter. It was learnt afterwards that the letter announced the death of Mrs. W.'s husband.

Prof. J. H. **Hyslop,** in a sitting with a young nonprofessional lady, heard loud raps in a closed piano. He wrote, in *Contact with the Other World* (1919): "After getting raps under her feet I had her stand on a very thick cushion. When she was standing on the cushion, which was at least six or eight inches thick, the raps occurred exactly as before, with the same quality of sound. If made by the joints, the raps would have been muffled when the feet were on the cushion. I then had her stand with a foot on each of my hands, which rested on the cushion, and the raps occurred apparently on the floor with the same quality of sound as when her feet were on the floor. I then tried the steam radiator some distance away, and the rap had a metallic ring, as if on iron. I then tried the piano experiment again . . . The raps were very loud, and made the string ring so that the sound could be heard perhaps a hundred feet away."

Sir William F. Barrett wrote in *On the Threshold of the Unseen* (1917): "On one occasion I asked for the raps to come on a small table near me, which Florrie [the medium] was not touching, they did so; I then placed one of my hands on the upper and the other on the under surface of the table, and in this position I felt the slight jarring made by the raps on the part of the table enclosed between my hands. It made no difference whether Florrie and I were alone in the room, as was often the case, or other observers were called in."

The distance to which the sound of raps carry may be considerable. In Southend, England, on the seashore in bright moonlight, metallic raps produced on the rail in the presence of the Rev. W. Stainton **Moses** and Dr. Speer were audible to both of them when they were seventy yards apart. The raps were apparently made in the space between them.

An interesting non-psychic method of procuring raps was described in *Psychic Research* (February 1930) by Mr. John E. Springer, Attorney-at-law of Palo Alto, California. He wrote: "In one face of a small cardboard box I cut an aperture the size and shape of my ear. When fitted to the ear the box sticks on securely and becomes a sort of sounding board. Upon retiring I affix the box to the ear which is not to rest on the pillow, and I will as strongly as possible that as I fall asleep I shall be awakened by a given series of raps upon the cardboard. It frequently—but not always—happens that when I reach the stage of drowsiness where unconsciousness is about to supervene, loud and clear raps upon the box in the predetermined series bring me back to wakefulness with a start. The raps may be subjective, but it is difficult for one who experiences them to escape from the conviction that they are objective psychic raps."

The medium Eusapia **Palladino** frequently rapped a certain number of times on the table with her fingers. Holding her hands about eighteen inches above the table the faint echoes of the raps were heard in the wood about two seconds later. She produced the same phenomenon with scratching sounds.

In the "Margery" seances (see Mina A. **Crandon**), the first raps were faint but definite, sounding like something soft inside a wooden box. Dr. Crandon listened to them through a stethoscope applied to the table. They were so magnified as to be unlike anything in his experience. Later they developed to such a degree that the **control** "Walter" could render tunes or rhythmical phrases with a marked syncopation upon the cabinet, the table, the arm of "Margery," the hands of the sitters, and even on the limited surface of a ring. Once he rapped out a popular tune unknown in his day and answered in explanation that they (the spirits) go everywhere, to our theaters and other places.

There are some rare cases on record in which raps were produced in the distance. The Seeress of Prevorst (see Frau Frederica **Hauffe**) could cause raps in the houses of others. There were similar testimonies in the mediumship of D. D. **Home.** Cromwell **Varley** stated before the **London Dialectical Society** that he heard raps in his home after his arrival from a seance with D. D. Home. Next morning he received a letter from Home which disclosed that the medium knew of the occurrence.

Countess Panaigai wrote in a letter to *Human Nature* (vol. 11) that in a sitting with Home the name of her deceased child was rapped out and that Home predicted the hearing of raps in her own house. The prediction not only came true, but when a friend called her attention to it she found the little boot of her child (kept in a locked box in a bureau) from which the raps appeared to proceed, imprinted by a perfect star with a letter at each of the six points forming the name "Stella," as the deceased was called. Not even the family of the Countess knew anything of the box and Home, to whom she was an utter stranger, was never in her house.

Interconnection of Psychic Phenomena

According to the hypothesis and presumptive evidence of spirit communication, raps represent the most primitive form of such communication. They may be manifest independently or through the faculties of a psychic individual. They may be obtained collectively through table-tipping or **table-turning,** in which a group sit round a table with their hands resting on it, and the raps indicate a letter of the alphabet, or a simple "yes" or "no" by one rap or two. This is a slow and tedious procedure.

Much more rapid communication is established through such simple devices as the **ouija board** or the **planchette.** Much swifter and more direct is **automatic writing,** in which the communicating entity operates the hand of the psychic.

In the presence of specially gifted mediums, **direct writing** by spirit hands has been reported. More direct still are the messages received vocally through a medium and, in rare instances, **direct voice** independent of the vocal apparatus of the medium.

It is not always clear how far claimed spirit messages are the product of the subconscious mentation of the medium or the sitters, since fictitious entities can be created in seances (see "**Philip**"). Evaluation depends upon the detail and overall paranormal quality of the evidence in individual cases.

It seem possible that the energies involved in the production of raps, especially through table-turning, may be related to the mechanism of the movements of rods and **pendulums** in water-witching and **radiesthesia** (see **Divining-Rod**). (See also **Fox Sisters; Rochester Rappings; Spiritualism; Table-Turning; Typtology**)

Recommended reading:

"A Searcher After Truth." *The Rappers; or, the Mysteries, Fallacies, and Absurdities of Spirit Rapping, Table-Tipping and Entrancement,* Long, New York, 1854

Abbott, David P. *Behind the Scenes With the Mediums,* Open Court, Chicago, 1907

(Anon.). *Rochester Knockings! Discovery and Explanation of the Source of the Phenomena Generally Known as the Rochester Knockings,* Buffalo & New York, 1851

Brownson, Orestes Augustus. *The Spirit-Rapper,* Little, Brown, 1854

Carrington, Hereward. *The Physical Phenomena of Spiritualism,* Small, Boston/T. Werner Laurie, London, 1907

Doyle, Arthur Conan. *The History of Spiritualism,* 2 vols., Cassell, London/Geo. H. Doran, New York, 1926; Arno Press, 1975 (2 vols. in 1)

Jackson, Herbert G., Jr. *The Spirit Rappers,* Doubleday, 1972

Lang, Andrew. *Cock Lane and Common-Sense,* Longmans, Green, London, 1896

Maxwell, J. *Metapsychical Phenomena,* Duckworth, London, 1905

Pearsall, Ronald. *Table-Rappers,* Joseph, London, 1972; St. Martin's Press, New York, 1973

Rasmussen, Mrs. Anna (Melloni) (1898-)

Danish medium for physical and intellectual phenomena. Her mediumship was first manifested at the age of twelve, when a table moved both with and without contact. **Poltergeist** phenomena developed, then died out to give place to true **telekinesis, raps, slate-writing,** automatic writing, **luminous phenomena** and **trance** speech under the control of an entity "Dr. Lasaruz."

In October and November 1921, the mediumship was examined at Fritz Grünewald's laboratory at Berlin. The results were placed before the second International Congress for Psychical Research at Warsaw, Poland, in 1923. The electrical condition of the seance room was a particularly noticeable phenomenon.

In September 1922, Prof. Christian Winther, S.D., of the Polytechnic Academy of Copenhagen, commenced a series of scientific experiments in which Prof. Bondorff, of the Danish Agricultural High School, the Laboratory Director R. Dons, and Dr. A. Marner, a practicing physician also participated. According to Prof. Winther's detailed account in *Psychic*

Research (1928) among 116 seances which he had with the medium not a single one was completely negative.

There appeared a steady outpouring of psychical energy and if a seance was not organized the medium became restless and felt ill. In many cases she gave two, three or even four sittings in a single day.

All the sittings took place in actual daylight or in very strong artificial light. The medium sat quietly in the circle at the table, took her share of the conversation, took refreshments, read a newspaper and had apparently on connection with what was going on. Trance, however, was always a great fatigue, and it was only employed when this was the special subject of study.

Some of the automatic scripts came in English. The spelling was bad, but the medium and her immediate family did not have the slightest knowledge of the language. A unique feature of her mediumship was that raps emanated from her left shoulder and answered questions.

The British psychical researcher Harry **Price** placed his ear against the medium's shoulder and distinctly heard decided thumps from her body (*Psychic Research,* 1928, p. 377).

Rasputin, Grigory Efimovitch
(c. 1871-1916)

Charismatic Russian monk, who became a powerful figure in the court of Csar Nicholas II, before the Romanov dynasty was swept aside by the Russian Revolution of 1917.

The son of a peasant, Rasputin had a reputation for his sexual prowess as a young man. At the age of sixteen, he joined a monastery as a novice. In those days, Russia was experiencing an outbreak of strange religious sects. The Khlysty sect, with whom Rasputin came in contact, was reputed to include sexual orgies and dancing, associated with a crude kind of revivalism. In many ways, this mixture of sex and religion resembled a kind of **Tantric Yoga**.

Rasputin married around 1890, but his first son died when only six months old. The tragedy sent Rasputin to a strange hermit named Makary, and subsequently Rasputin became absorbed in scriptures, prayer and meditation. One day he saw an image of the Virgin in the sky, and Makary told him "God has chosen you for a great achievement. In Order to strengthen your spiritual power, you should go and pray to the Virgin in the convent of Afon."

The convent was at Mount Athos, in Greece, two thousand miles away, but in 1891, Rasputin made the pilgrimage on foot. Later he made a pilgrimage to the Holy Land, traveling across Turkey.

For the next few years he became a wandering *staretz* (lay priest). He was widely believed to possess occult power, which made him both loved and feared. He undoubtedly had gifts of healing and prophecy.

In 1903, he traveled to St. Petersburg, where he met influential churchmen, including the monk Illiodor, who later became a hateful rival. Rasputin's reputation as a prophet and miracle worker spread widely, and he was sought by rich and poor.

In those days, Russian court life and high society were still strongly attracted to the marvels of Spiritualist mediums and table-rapping, and any wonder worker was in great demand. Soon Rasputin came to the attention of the Csar of Russia, becoming an indispensable adviser and healer to the royal family. An uncouth peasant became a court favorite, confidant and genius of an Emperor and Empress.

Surrounded by the madhouse of tyranny, secret police, bomb plots, crippling wars, ruthless suppression of liberty of the Romanov empire, Rasputin towered above the sycophants, bureacratics and plotters, self-absorbed in his own sense of destiny. His manners were those of a fearless peasant. He could be overbearing and insolent, shouting at people, at other times exerting a hypnotic influence in silence. He treated the Csar and Csarina with complete familiarity, and would kiss the four teen-age princesses goodnight at bedtime. It was their nurse that Rasputin seduced, although she regarded his embraces as holy. He was widely reputed to have seduced every eligible woman in Russia from the Tsarina downward.

In 1911, tiring of court life, he undertook another pilgrimage to the Holy Land, and during his absence his enemies intrigued against him. In 1912, he status at court was strengthened by a miracle of healing, after the Tsarevitch had an accident. But his enemies, headed by Prince Yussupov, planned his murder.

The day before, Csar Nicholas requested Rasputin to bless him, and with curious presience, Rasputin said "This time it is for you to bless me." Yussupov invited Rasputin to his palace, and persuaded him to eat poisoned food and drink poisoned wine. The poison was ineffectual. Thereupon the treacherous Yussupov sang gay gypsy songs and played the guitar before leaving the room and returning with a loaded revolver, shooting his victim in the back. Other conspirators rushed in clumsily, accidentally switching off the room light. When the light was switched on again, Rasputin appeared dead, but suddenly the corpse came to life, stood up and pursued his murderer! Another conspirator shot Rasputin again, the body was dragged from the house and battered with a steel press, but Rasputin was still alive when he was pushed through a hole in the ice on the River Neva. And although his wrists had been bound, he had still managed to free his right hand and make the sign of the cross before drowning. He died December 31, 1916.

His strange life and barbaric death seemed to be signals of the incoherent forces pent up in prerevolutionary Russia, and soon afterwards these burst forth in a torrent of death and renewal. (See also **Kundalini; Sex Magic; Tantric Yoga**)

Recommended reading:

Fülop-Miller. René. *Rasputin; The Holy Devil,* Viking Press, 1928

Rasputina, Maria. *My Father,* McClelland/Cassell, London, 1934; University Books, 1970 [Contains *My*

Thoughts and Meditations by Grigory Rasputin]
Vogel-Jorgensen, T. *Rasputin: Prophet, Libertine, Plotter*, T. Fisher Unwin, London, 1917; University Books, 1970
Wilson, Colin. *Rasputin and the Fall of the Romanovs*, Arthur Barker, London, 1964

Rastafarians

A West Indian religious cult which links a black power interpretation of Christianity with the sacramental use of marijuana. The movement developed in the 1930s in Jamaica, following the teachings of Marcus Garvey, founder of the Universal Negro Improvement Association. With the coronation of Ras Tafari Makonnen (later known as Haile Selassie, Emperor of Ethiopia), the Jamaican followers of Garvey interpreted Haile Selassie's official title "King of Kings, Conquering Lion of Judah, Elect of God" to mean that he was a black Messiah, that the blacks, exiled all over the world, were like the ancient Israelites and would be led by the Emperor to an African homeland.

According to this doctrine, the ten lost tribes were exiled into slavery because of their sins and the wickedness of white men, who were their oppressors. Garvey was said to have predicted: "Look to Africa, where a black king shall be crowned, for the day of deliverance is near."

The original Ras Tafari movement comprised various organizations, such as the United Afro-West Indian Federation, United Ethiopian Body, Ethiopian Youth Cosmic Faith, Ethiopian Coptic League, and African Cultural League. Members of these groups lived in shanty town shacks in conditions of poverty and squalor.

The concept that they were really a chosen people, destined to be led to a black power salvation with white men as their inferiors, reinforced their feelings of identity and pride. At their meetings, they smoked *ganja* (marijuana) which they believed to be a "holy herb" sanctioned by the Bible, and also developed a characteristic form of revivalist music, originally based on standard Christian revivalist hymns, modified by lively West Indian rhythms. Male Rastafarians also affected beards, and long hair braided in the manner of African warriors (known as "dreadlocks"), perhaps also echoing the distinctive hair styles of orthodox Jews.

The adulation of Haile Selassie as a living God by Rastafarians may have surprised the Emperor when he visited Jamaica in 1966 and was given a Messianic welcome by thousands of Rastafarians. The Emperor made a land grant of about five hundred acres in the Arushi province of Ethiopia for West Indian migrants, although few Rastafarians were able to afford the cost of transport and settlement.

The Emperor himself was exiled following the successful Italian invasion of Ethiopia in 1935. In the following year, Italy annexed Ethiopia and combined it with Eritrea and Italian Somaliland to form Italian East Africa. Haile Selassie found refuge in Britain, but returned in 1941 when the Ethiopian and British troops liberated the territory—although in recent history, Ethiopia has again been ravaged by war and famine.

The death of Haile Selassie in 1975 did not terminate the Rastafarian movement. By that date, the cult had been spread abroad by emigrating Jamaicans, and is now well established in urban areas of the U.S. and Britain. Even with the establishment of a Marxist military regime in Ethiopia, Rastafarian faith persisted that the Emperor would be resurrected to lead blacks form all over the world to their African homeland.

Opinions differ on the present-day status of Rastafarians. In Jamaica, the movement has become a focus of organized social and political protest, but with extremes of passive nonconformity and violent action. A *Report on the Rastafari Movement in Kingston, Jamaica,* prepared by the University of the West Indies at Kingston, concluded: "The general public believes in a stereotype Ras Tafarian, who wears a beard, avoids work, steals, smokes ganja, and is liable to sudden violence. This type exists, but is a minority. The real danger is that if all Ras Tafarians are treated as if they are like this, more and more will become extremists. What strikes the investigator, on the contrary, is how deeply religious the brethren are."

However, modern expatriate Rastafarianism has lost much of its original fervent religious impulse in the urban ghettoes of the U.S. and Britain. Even a sacramental drug habit is difficult to maintain in an environment of poverty and unemployment. When allied with a nonconformist life-style and a hostility to white people, it frequently becomes a shallow rationalization for street crime and burglary to support a drug trade. Moreover, fake Rastafarians have adopted the appearance of genuine members of the movement in order to conceal profitable drug smuggling and gang violence. It is also difficult to see how genuine Rastafarians can claim a mystical basis for a religion of hallucination.

Meanwhile, however, the music of the movement has flourished internationally in the form known as "reggae," popularized by the Jamaican superstar Bob Marley.

Ratte, Rena J(osephine) (1928-)

Instructor in philosophy who has experimented in the field of parapsychology. Born September 7, 1928 at Waterville, Maine, she studied at University of Maine (B.A. 1951) and Duke University, Durham, North Carolina (M.A. 1958, Ph.D. 1959).

She was a research fellow at the Parapychology Laboratory, Duke University from 1959-60, instructor in philosophy at Lewis and Clark College, Portland, Oregon from 1960 onwards. She is a member of the Parapsychological Association.

She has specialized in the study of **psychokinesis** and experimented in the use of game techniques in PK to ascertain whether the PK effect would be enhanced by a game atmosphere. Her experiments are described in her article (with Frances M. Greene) 'An Exploratory Investigation of PK in a Game Situation' (*Journal of Parapsychology,* 1960), and her article 'Three Exploratory Studies of ESP in a Game Situation' (*Journal of Parapsychology*, vol. 25, 1961).

Raudive, Konstantin (1909-1974)

Latvian psychologist and parapsychologist who spent many years investigating the **Electronic Voice Phenomenon** which has been popularly known as **Raudive Voices.** His surname is pronounced "Rowdee-vay."

Born in Latvia he studied psychology in Switzerland, Germany and England. For some time he was a teacher at the University of Riga, and also edited a Latvian newspaper. He studied psychology under Carl Jung and was also a pupil of the Spanish philosopher Ortega y Gasset.

He left Latvia when the Soviet Army invaded the Baltic and absorbed Latvia in 1945. With his wife Dr. Zenta Maurina he lived for a time in Sweden, later moving to Bad Kroningen, Germany, near the border with Switzerland.

It was during his period in Sweden in 1965 that Dr. Raudive met Friedrich **Jürgenson** who had pioneered the study of paranormal voice recordings. In 1959, Jürgenson tape-recorded a Swedish finch, and on playback heard what appeared to be a human voice in addition to the bird. He thought there must be some fault in the apparatus, but subsequent recordings contained a message which seemed to be recognizably from his dead mother. Jürgenson described his experiments in his book *Rösterna från Rymden* (Voices From Space), published in Sweden in 1964.

From 1965 onwards, Dr. Raudive and his wife devoted themselves to investigating this phenomenon of paranormal voices manifesting on tape recordings, later assisted by Swiss physicist Alex Schneider and various engineers. Other scientists and parapsychologists who investigated the electronic voice phenomenon included Prof. Hans **Bender** of the University of Freiburg, Germany and Dr. Friedebert Karger of the Max Planck Institute in Munich. After 1969, differences of opinion arose between Mr. Jürgenson and Dr. Raudive, and thereafter they conducted their researches independently.

Essentially the electronic voice phenomenon, often known as "Raudive Voices," consists of paranormal voice communications (apparently from dead individuals) manifesting on recordings made on a standard tape recorder (sometimes enhanced by a simple diode circuit). The voices are also apparent on the "white noise" of certain radio bands.

The communications are usually fragmentary and ambiguous, rather like those produced by a **ouija board,** and need considerable amplification. The voices are sometimes in a mixture of different languages, rather like scrambled radio bands, but in many cases they appear to be recognizably from men, women or children known to the experimenters during life time. They comment on the experimenters or convey cryptic messages in a kind of terse disjointed telegram style.

So far no communications appear to indicate high intelligence and most appear relatively trivial, but this does not invalidate their possible paranormal nature. Other theories suggest they may be sounds relayed back to earth from other planets by some unknown natural phenomenon, or a potpourri of ordinary radio communications.

Skeptics think the voices may be imaginary, since listening to amplified electronics static and hum may suggest voices that do not really exist. Another theory is that the voices come from the subconscious of the experimenters, impressed on the tapes like the thought-forms of **Psychic Photography**.

Against such theories and criticisms, a number of highly qualified engineers and scientists have conducted and analyzed thousands of careful experiments which seem to validate the claim that some of these recordings are of paranormal voices, and voice prints of communications purporting to be from the same source show matching patterns. There is *prima facie* evidence that some of the communications may be from dead individuals.

Dr. Raudive's researches included collection and study of over 100,000 recordings. His book in German *Unhörbares Wird Hörbar* (The Inaudible Made Audible) was first published in 1968, then translated into English by Peter **Bander** in an enlarged edition under the title *Breakthrough: An Amazing Experiment in Electronic Communication with the Dead* (U.K., 1971; Taplinger, 1971). The book included a small long-play record containing samples of Raudive's recordings of the voice phenomenon.

In June 1970, Mr. David Ellis, a Cambridge (England) graduate, had been elected to the Perrott-Warrick Studentship which grant aids psychic research, and Mr. Ellis commenced a study of the Raudive Voice phenomenon in October 1970, published by the author in 1978 as *The Mediumship of the Tape Recorded.* His findings were largely skeptical, and he believed that on occasion Raudive may have mistaken fragments of foreign language broadcasts for paranormal voice communications.

However, Ellis was inclined to believe some of the voices might be paranormal, but their faintness and the background noise prevented positive identification. It should be pointed out that Ellis studied only existing recordings from the Raudive archives and did not himself experiment in making recordings.

Dr. Raudive died September 2, 1974, and his widow Dr. Zenta Maurina-Raudive published a tribute to his work: *Konstantin Raudive zum Gedaechtnis* (Maximilian Dietrich Verlag, Germany, 1975). This included contributions from twenty-nine parapsychologists, scientists, theologians and journalists. In spite of the importance of Dr. Raudive's researches, there has been as yet no major breakthrough by other parapsychologists in validating the electronic voice phenomenon. However, a great deal of amateur research has been stimulated by publications of the useful *Handbook of Psi Discoveries* by Sheila Ostrander and Lynn Schroeder (Putnam, 1974; Berkley paperback 1975; Abacus paperback, 1977), which includes a detailed chapter on 'How to Record Voice Phenomena.'

After Dr. Raudive's death, controversy arose on the question of archive storage and availability for study of the Raudive Collection, which the Society for Psychical Research expressed willingness to house.

Raudive Voices

Popular term for the electronic voice phenomenon first discovered by Friedrich **Jürgenson** in 1959. Voices, apparently from dead individuals, are found to be electronically impressed on tape recordings made on standard apparatus (sometimes enhanced by a simple diode circuit). The voices are also apparent on the "white noise" of certain radio bands. The suggestion that they are communications from the dead is based on many thousands of experimental recordings made by Mr. Jürgenson and Dr. Konstantin Raudive, as well as other parapsychologists, including Dr. Hans **Bender**.

Dr. Konstantin **Raudive** (1909-1974), a Latvian psychologist, conducted joint experiments with Mr. Jürgenson between 1964 and 1969 after reading a reference to the paranormal voice phenomenon in a book by Jürgenson. Subsequently the two men had some differences of opinion and conducted their further researches independently.

Dr. Raudive's researches were very extensive and included collection and study of over 100,000 recordings. After the publicity given to his book *Unhörbares Wird Hörbar*, translated into English in an enlarged edition as *Breakthrough: an amazing experiment in Electronic Communication* (Colin Smythe, U.K./Taplingler, 1971), the phenomenon became generally known and discussed as "Raudive Voices."

The book was translated by Peter **Bander,** a British psychologist who subsequently appeared on twenty-seven television and radio programs in connection with "Raudive Voices." His own book *Carry On Talking: How Dead are the Voices?* (Colin Smythe, U.K., 1972) reviews how the Raudive voice phenomenon was investigated in Britain and the Irish Republic, the attitudes of religious authorities, the experiments carried out by the electronic experts, and the various theories to explain the phenomenon.

Professor Bender of Freiburg University suggested that electronic impulses might be transmitted by the subconscious mind and impressed on tapes, rather like **Psychic Photographs.** However, there is some evidence tending to suggest that the communications are mainly from dead individuals.

A later development of Dr. Raudive's researches into paranormal voices were his investigation of a budgerigar named Putzi, owned by Mrs. Editha von Damaros in Germany. In March 1972, Mrs. von Damaros wrote to Dr. Raudive stating that a few weeks after the death of her daughter Barbara at the age of fourteen, her pet budgerigar started giving extraordinary messages suggestive of spirit communications; one of these advised contacting "the Latvian doctor."

Dr. Raudive made a careful investigation of the budgerigar and took a number of recordings. It seemed possible that the bird was being used as an energy field for the direct transmission of paranormal voices.

This investigation has led to some confusion, since the original researches of Mr. Jürgenson into paranormal voices on tape recordings were stimulated by attempts to record bird song. "Bird voices" remain a quite separate phenomenon from "Raudive Voices."

After the death of Dr. Raudive September 2, 1974, his wife Dr. Zenta Maurina-Raudive published a tribute to his work: *Konstantin Raudive zum Gedaechtnis* (Maximilian Dietrich Verlag, Germany, 1975). This book included contributions from twenty-nine parapsychologists, scientists, theologians and journalists. (see also Friedrich **Jürgenson;** Konstantin **Raudive**)

Ray, P(ramode) C(handra) (1916-)

Psychologist who has carried out research in the field of parapsychology. Born January 1, 1916 in East Bengal, India, he studied at University of Calcutta (M.Sc. psychology 1940), graduate work in clinical psychology at Institute of Psychiatry, Maudsley Hospital, London, England. In 1942 he married Nakamallika Das (died 1958); second marriage in 1959 to Sadhana Bose.

He was a laboratory assistant to Anthropological Survey of India, Government of India from 1947-57, assistant psychologist (1957-60), psychologist and officer in charge of Psychology Section, Anthropological Survey of India, Calcutta from 1960 onwards. He is a member of the Indian Science Congress, Indian Psychological Association.

In addition to his studies and papers on psychological subjects, he has carried out a research project on possession amongst the Lodha tribe of Bengal.

Rayleigh, Lord (1842-1919)

John William **Strutt,** one of the last intellectual giants of the Victorian era, world-famous as experimental physicist and discoverer of argon. He was president of the **Society for Psychical Research,** London, in 1919.

He was born November 12, 1842, educated at Trinity College, Cambridge (Senior Wrangler and Smith's Prizeman 1865, Fellow 1866). He was Professor of Experimental Physics, Cambridge, 1879-96; Lord-Lieutenant of Essex, 1892-1901; Professor of Natural Philosophy, Royal Institution, 1887-1905; Officer of Legion of Honour.

He published many scientific papers, and an important book *Theory of Sound* (2 vols., 1894-96).

In 1876 in the discussion of Prof. W. F. **Barrett's** paper on Spiritualism before the British Association for the Advancement of Science, he declared that his own interest in the subject dated from 1874. He was first attracted to it by the investigations of Sir

William **Crookes.** "Although," he stated, "my opportunities have not been so good as those enjoyed by Professor Barrett, I have seen enough to convince me that those are wrong who wish to prevent investigation by casting ridicule on those who may feel inclined to engage in it."

Physical phenomena impressed him more than mental phenomena. He had many sittings with Mrs. Kate Fox-Jencken (see **Fox Sisters**) and Eusapia **Palladino.** He was nonplussed by the result. Yet he never felt sufficiently convinced to declare himself in public. He paid little attention to **automatic writing** and **trance** phenomena. He did not think the evidence for **telepathy** conclusive, but he declared that, given irrefragable evidence, for telepathy between living persons, he would have no difficulty in extending it to telepathy from the dead.

Speaking of Mrs. Kate Fox-Jencken and the famous medium D. D. **Home** in his presidential address before the Society for Psychical Research, London, in 1919 (see **Proceedings** of the S.P.R., vol. 30, pp. 275-290) he said: "I repudiate altogether the idea of hallucination as an explanation. The incidents were almost always unexpected, and our impressions of them agreed."

He died June 30, 1919. (See also John William **Strutt**)

Rays From The Rose Cross (Magazine)

Monthly publication of the **Rosicrucian Fellowship** founded by Max **Heindel** (1865-1919). Address: 2222 Mission Avenue, Oceanside, California 92054.

Reality Change (Magazine)

Quarterly magazine "for people who want to change their lives," discusses the Seth Material channeled through medium Jane **Roberts** (1929-1984). The magazine contains news of Seth conferences and local groups, as well as contributions reporting personal experiences in relation to the Seth teachings. Address: P.O. Box 7786, Austin, Texas 78713-7786. (See also **Austin Seth Center**; Jane **Roberts**)

"Rebazar Tarzs"

Claimed to be the Tibetan lama guide of Paul **Twitchell,** founder of the religious organization **Eckankar** promoting "the ancient science of soul travel," a kind of **Out-of-the-Body** traveling or **astral projection** to other planes.

Rebus (Newspaper)

The first Spiritualist periodical in Russia, founded in 1881, which, owing to the antagonism of the authorities to Spiritualism was professedly devoted to rebuses and charades. It was commenced by Captain (later Admiral) Victor Ivanovitch Pribytkoff, and it was largely financed by Alexander **Aksakof.**

Records and Cassettes; A Selected Guide (Catalog)

Comprehensive mail order catalog issued by the **Yes! Bookshop** founded by Cris Popenoe. It lists records and cassette tapes of New Age music, non-Western music, choral music, instrumental music, spoken tapes on health, healing and meditation, past lives, relaxation, sleep, dreams, visualization, weight control, yoga, and related subjects. It forms a useful companion to the Yes! Bookshop Guide *Inner Development*. Address: Yes! Bookshop, 1035 31st Street N.W., Washington, D.C. 20007.

"Rector"

One of the spirit controls of the Rev. W. Stainton **Moses,** said to have been Hippolytus, pupil of Irenaeus, who was Bishop of Portus, the harbor of Rome opposite to Ostia. He was banished in 235 A.D. when Maximin succeeded Alexander Severus.

"Rector" first manifested on January 4, 1873. His distinctive sign was his heavy tread, which shook the room. His main duty was to act as amanuensis for "Imperator" and the other spirits. After the earlier books, almost all the writing was done by him.

He had the power of reading books paranormally. The experiments which were conducted to test this ability proved highly successful. When the "Imperator" group took control of the seances of the medium Mrs. Leonore E. **Piper,** "Rector" manifested in his old role as amanuensis and spiritual adviser again. (See also Rev. W. Stainton **Moses**)

Red Cap (of Witches)

The witches of Ireland used to put on a magical red cap before flying through the air to their meeting-place. It has been suggested that witches in various countries may have experienced the illusion of traveling through the air after ingesting the "red cap" hallucinatory mushroom *amanita muscaria* (fly-agaric).

Red Man

The demon of the tempests. He was supposed to be furious when the rash voyager intruded on his solitude, and to show his anger in the winds and storms.

The French peasants believed that a mysterious little red man appeared to Napoleon to announce coming military reverses.

Red Pigs

It was formerly believed that Irish witches could turn wisps of straw or hay into red pigs, which they sold at the market. But when the pigs were driven homeward by the buyers, they resumed their original shape on crossing running water.

Reese, Bert (1851-1926)

American-Polish medium with whom remarkable experiments in clairvoyance were conducted by Baron von **Schrenck-Notzing,** Thomas A. Edison, Hereward **Carrington,** and Felix Hollaender.

Reese was said to have manifested extraordinary psychic faculties at the age of six. According to Felix Hollaender (in *Annals of Psychic Science,* September 1913), these so terrified the people of the little town where he was born that they deserted the shop where his father sold miscellaneous goods, and to avoid ruin he had to send his son away to Posen. The people of the country town were filled with horror. They considered the child a wizard and possessed by the devil.

In America, Reese was arrested and condemned for disorderly conduct. Appealing against his sentence he appeared before Judge Rosalsky and proved his powers to him. He asked the Judge to write something on three different pieces of paper, to fold them up and place them in three different pockets, mixing them in such a way that they could not be recognized.

Then Judge Rosalsky took one of the pellets and pressed it against Reese's forehead. He immediately answered: "You have fifteen dollars in the bank mentioned in your question." He continued to read the second paper, it contained the name of Miss O'Connor, a former governess to Judge Rosalsky's children. He also read the third paper, whereupon Judge Rosalsky acquitted him.

Schrenck-Notzing considered him one of the most extraordinary men of the time. Thought reading could not sufficiently account for his performances as the experimenters mostly took care that they themselves should not know which piece of paper contains which question. In certain of his performances, "X-ray clairvoyance" also fell short as an explanation. Psychometric powers must have been displayed when, according to the account of Felix Hollaender, he indicated to a commercial firm the pages on which there was a fraudulent entry. He was given five percent of the amount of the fraud.

However, the great **Houdini** claimed that Reese was fraudulent and that he knew his methods. In a letter to Sir Arthur Conan **Doyle** Houdini wrote: "I have no hesitancy in telling you that I set a snare at the seance I had with Reese, and caught him cold-blooded. He was startled when it was over, as he knew that I had bowled him over. So much so that he claimed I was the only one that had ever detected him." (See *Houdini and Conan Doyle,* by B. M. L. Ernst & Hereward Carrington, 1932.B

Reese was at one time an assistant to Thomas A. Edison, who held seances with him (See *Annales des Sciences Psychiques,* Now. 1913). In his later years, Edison was working on apparatus to communicate with the dead. Reese also had a reputation for **dowsing** and was said to have discovered valuable oil deposits for the Rockefeller company.

Reeves, M. (c. 1877)

London restaurant proprietor who, in association with F. M. **Parkes,** gained renown in 1877 as one of the earliest English spirit photographers. He was said to have contributed a considerable part of the power as without him Parkes could not obtain recognizable spirit "extras" on his photographic plates.

The association broke up with the emigration of Reeves to Canada.

Many of the psychic pictures that appeared on their plates were symbolic. (See also **Psychic Photography; Spirit Photography**)

Reflectograph

An instrument for mechanical communication with spirits, invented by George Jobson and B. K. Kirkby. It consisted of a large typewriter, the key-contacts of which were so sensitive that by merely blowing upon them they could be depressed, closing an electric circuit and making an illuminated letter appear.

The machine, however, was not quite independent of human action. The presence of the medium Mrs. L. E. Singleton was necessary. When she was entranced, a hand appeared out of the cabinet, tapped the keys and spelled out messages which were then flashed in luminous letters on a six-foot indicator. (See also **Ashkir-Jobson Trianion; Communigraph**)

REG (Random Event Generator)

Electronic apparatus which generates random numbers, used as targets in a **psi** test. For details of an REG designed and built by physicist Dr. Helmut **Schmidt,** see the paper 'A PK Test with Electronic Equipment' (*Journal of Parapsychology,* vol. 34, 1970).

A basic form of REG is an electronic coin-tossing machine, generating a series of "heads and tails" outputs. Other REGs have more complex outputs.

Tests with REGs are often conducted in conjunction with computers, so that the timing and running of the experiment can be mechanically controlled and analyzed, thus obviating fraud on the part of the subject, and facilitating evaluation of a long series of runs. (See also **Retro-PK**)

Regang

Malay system of Astrology (see **Malaysia**).

Regardie, (Francis) Israel (1907-1985)

Former member of the famous secret order the **Golden Dawn** and associate of occultist Aleister **Crowley,** and later a psychotherapist on lines deriving from the work of Wilhelm **Reich.** Born in England November 17, 1907, he emigrated to the U.S. at the age of 13, where he has since resided most of his life. Through the writings of Charles Stansfeld **Jones,** he became aware of the occult tradition and was fascinated by the outlook and exploits of Aleister Crowley. From 1928-34, he traveled through Europe as a companion to Cowley.

Although he later parted company with Crowley, he has also defended him from attacks as a monster of depravity and evil, and has spoken of his "real genius and grandeur." In this special pleading he seemed to gloss over Crowley's darker side and his callousness to individuals he ruined, but Regardie's succinct description of Crowley as a kind of "Victorian hippie" hit the right note and has been widely copied.

Regardie's first book on occultism was *The Tree of Life,* (1932), followed by *The Garden of Pomegranates* (1932). The latter book stirred up controversies in Golden Dawn circles, and in 1934 Regardie joined the **Stella Matutina** temple of the Golden Dawn. He believed that the Golden Dawn teachings should be published openly, and when he eventually left the organization he broke his oath of secrecy and published the complete rituals in four volumes as: *The Golden Dawn; an Encyclopedia of Practical Occultism* (1937-40).

It is possible that this wholesale disclosure contributed to the decline of the Stella Matutina, for without any secrets it could hardly continue to function as a secret order. However, these published rituals had only specialist interest until the occult revival of the last two decades, when Regardie's compendium was reprinted in a revised and enlarged edition 1969, reprinted 1971.

Regardie later became a chiropractor, and on the outbreak of World War II served in the U.S. Army, afterwards settling in Southern California, where he practiced psychotherapy. His writings on occultism include the following: *My Rosicrucian Adventure* (1936; 1971), *Middle Pillar* (1945; 1970) *The Romance of Metaphysics* (1946), *The Art of Healing* (1964), *Roll Away The Stone* (1964), *Tree of Life; A Study in Magic* (1969), *The Eye in The Triangle* (1970), *What Is The Qabalah?* (1973), *To Invoke Your Higher Self* (1973), *Twelve Steps to Spiritual Enlightenment* (1975).

In the 1930s, he had practiced in New York City and was associated with the psychoanalyst and authority on the occult Dr. Nandor **Fodor.** Regardie's highly individual linking of the **Golden Dawn** teachings with the work of Wilhelm **Reich** in psychophysical therapy showed a unique perception of connections between mysticism, occultism, and psychotherapy. In his introduction to the second edition of *The Golden Dawn* (Hazel Hills/Llewellyn, 2 vols., 1969), Regardie stated: " . . . Reich has succeeded in building a bridge between the modern psychologies and occultism. . . . What he had to say, and the therapeutic method he developed and called vegetotherapy, have been found of inestimable value in my life, and the two hundred hours of therapy I had years ago comprise an experience that today, in retrospect, I would not be without." Regardie retained his respect for the Golden Dawn teachings, and in 1983 visited New Zealand, where a Stella Matutina lodge had been founded by Dr. R. W. Felkin in 1912 and had continued to exist there.

Regardie died March 10, 1985, at the age of 78, in Sedona, Arizona, where he lived for several years after retirement from practice as a Reichian therapist for some thirty years in Los Angeles.

The forename "Francis" was adopted by Regardie at the suggestion of Winifred Burke (wife of the famous novelist Thomas Burke), who thought that his spiritual direction was reminiscent of St. Francis of Assisi, noted for his faith, humility, and love.

Regurgitation

An explanatory theory of fraudulent **materialization** phenomena which suggests that the white substance issuing from the medium's body which is taken for **ectoplasm** is something which the medium swallowed before the sitting and brought up at the appropriate moment.

The theory was put forward by the **Society for Psychical Research,** London, in the case of **Eva C.** in 1922, when the medium sat in London.

Wide public attention was also aroused by the case of the British medium Mrs. Helen **Duncan,** in which the theory was considered a satisfactory explanation. For details see *Regurgitation and the Duncan Mediumship,* by Harry **Price** (1931). (See also **Ectoplasm; Materialization**)

Reich, Wilhelm (1897-1957)

Austrian psychoanalyst, whose later researches into life energy have analogies with occult and mystical concepts. Born March 24, 1897 in Dobrzcynica, Galicia, son of a farmer, he was tutored at home for entrance to German Gymnasium at Czernowitz (Cernauti) at the age of 14, boarding with a family in Czernowitz and helping on his father's farm during vacations. Reich passed his Abiturium in 1915, joined the Austrian army (officer in 1916) and served on the Italian front.

In 1918, he returned to the study in Vienna, matriculating at the Faculty of Law, University of Vienna, then went on to study on the Faculty of Medicine. He obtained his M.D. in 1922 and after graduate studies in neurology and psychiatry became First Clinical Assistant at Freud's Psychoanalytic Polyclinic in 1922, vice director in 1928. He joined the Austrian Socialist Party in 1924 and hoped to reconcile Freudian and Marxist theories, convinced that much neurosis was caused by poverty, bad housing conditions and other social ills.

In the event, he was to suffer from both orthodox psychoanalysts and doctrinaire Marxists. He joined the Communist Party in 1928 and was a pioneer in advocating health centers, but after a visit to Russia in 1929 he was disappointed with the Russian bureaucracy and bourgeois moralistic attitudes to sexuality.

He was expelled from the Communist Party in 1933 because of his advocacy of sexual politics. Later, the International Psychoanalytic Association excluded him because of his Communist associations.

He moved to Berlin in 1930 and the following year helped establish Verlag für Sexualpolitik (Sexpol-Verlag) for the sexual education of young people. He left Germany to escape the Nazis in 1939, after fearlessly exposing the sham Socialism and perverse character of the Hitler regime.

His insistence on the original Freudian concept of the overriding importance of the sexual urge in human affairs led to a vicious newspaper smear campaign in Scandinavia from 1933-39. Ironically it was the Scandinavians who pioneered the so-called "sexual revolution" in post-war Europe with condoned pornography, blue films and perversity instead of the healthy sexuality advocated by Reich.

He removed to the U.S. and settled in Forest Hills, Long Island, but again moved to Oregon, Maine in the 1940s, where he established the Orgone Institute Research Laboratories. He was once again the subject of smear campaigns from journalists in the McCarthy atmosphere of the 40s and was persecuted by the F.D.A. on charges of arising from a tragi-comic misunderstanding of Reich's theories of cosmic "Orgone" energy in relation to cancer cure.

He developed what he called an "orgone accumulator," a large box-like arrangement of materials supposedly trapping cosmic orgone energy which entered the walls of the device more rapidly than it exited. Reich believed that this energy had a tonic effect on individuals sitting in the accumulator, and that it was particularly beneficial for cancer sufferers.

He supplied this device only to individuals who would use it experimentally under the guidance of a qualified physician. But the F.D.A. proceeded against Reich as if he was a common charlatan peddling a worthless cancer cure.

Reich refused to comply with a court injunction banning the use of his "orgone accumulator" and insisting on the removal of the word "orgone" from all his books, and was eventually sentenced to two years imprisonment for contempt of court. Most of his books (some of which had been burned in Nazi Germany) were seized by the American authorities and burned at the Gansevoort Incinerator, New York, August 23, 1956.

Reich died in the Federal Penitentiary, Lewisburg, Pa. November 3, 1957.

Reich was a tragic example of a brilliant scientist who was always in the wrong place at the wrong time, and whose life work was persistently misunderstood and misapplied even long after his death. There is irony and paradox throughout his story.

An advocate of a stable happy sex life, he failed to achieve it himself. He married Annie Pink in 1921, later lived with Elsa Lindenberg, was separated from Annie Reich in 1933 and married Ilse Ollendorff in 1939.

It is perhaps just to attribute much of the eccentricity of his private life to the social and political pressures under which he suffered. His concept of Orgone energy in the cosmos and the human organism has much in common with **yoga** teachings on **Kundalini** energy and with mysticism, but he condemned both yoga and mysticism as dangerous and misleading. He emphasized his role as a natural scientist, but his later work on **Cloud Busting** comes close to occultism.

His "cloudbuster" was an apparatus composed of hollow tubes connected with running water, pointed at the sky by the operator in a certain manner. Reich believed that he generated a hurricane. He claimed that spacemen were visiting the earth in **flying saucers.**

His vindication of the original concepts of the importance of sexual expression in Freudianism was rejected by psychoanalysts, although they used many of his therapeutic insights. His reconciliation of psychic and somatic aspects of psychoanalysis, long desired by Freud, was regarded with suspicion and mistrust by Freud himself. Reich's teachings on "sexual revolution" as opposed to authoritarian repression, were grossly misinterpreted after his death by cranks, pornographers and hippies on one hand, and a humorless orthodoxy of authoritarian Reichian physicians on the other.

There can be no doubt that new techniques and insights introduced by Reich in psychoanalysis were brilliant innovations in therapy, and may also be profitably compared with certain yoga and occult teachings. Reich's later experiments and theories may seem eccentric and extravagant, but will require patient and tolerant scrutiny for either validation or rejection. (See also **Cloud Busting; Kundalini; Od; Orgone; Yoga**)

Recommended reading:

Reich, Wilhelm. *The Mass Psychology of Fascism,* Orgone Institute Press, 1946

Reich, Wilhelm. *The Function of the Orgasm; Sex-economic problems of biological energy,* Orgone Institute Press, 1942; 1948; reissued Farrar, Straus & Giroux, 1961. Originally issued as vol. 1 *The Discovery of the Orgone*

Reich, Wilhelm. *The Cancer Biopathy,* Orgone Institute Press, 1948 (vol. 2 *The Discovery of the Orgone*)

Reich, Wilhelm. *Character Analysis,* Orgone Institute Press, 1949; reissued in paperback by Farrar, Straus & Giroux, 1961

Orgone Energy Bulletin, April 1951 (deals with "cloud busting" experiments)

Reich, Peter. *A Book of Dreams,* Harper & Row, 1973 by Reich's son

Reich, Ilse Ollendorff, *Wilhelm Reich; a personal biography,* St. Martin's Press, 1969

Reichenbach, Baron Karl von (1788-1869)

Brilliant German scientist of the nineteenth century, preeminent expert on meteorites, highly respected as chemist, technologist and metallurgist, discoverer of Kerosene. He also spent over two decades experimenting with the mysterious force which he named **"Od"** (also know as Odic Force of Odyle in various translations). This claimed force had particular relevance to concepts of the human **aura.**

He was born February 12, 1788 at Württemberg and died at Leipzig January 22, 1869. His life was thus roughly parallel with the British scientist Michael **Faraday** (1791-1867).

Reichenbach was educated at the Gymnasium (High School) in Württemberg and afterwards at the State University of Tübingen, studying natural science, political economy and law. During his student days, Germany was under the military control of France, and at the age of sixteen Reichenbach founded a secret society to set up a German state in the South Sea Islands. However, he was arrested by the Napoleonic police and detained for some months as a political prisoner. After his release he continued his studies and obtained his Ph.D.

He later traveled in France and Germany investigating the construction and operation of ironworks, and in 1815 set up his own plant at Villigen in Baden. He later built a large charcoal furnace at Hausach in Baden. He established a beet-sugar factory, steelworks and blast-furnaces, and devoted much time to experimental researches. He discovered paraffin in 1830 and other coal-tar products such as eupion, creosote, pittacal (pitch) in following years.

Between 1835 and 1860, he published a long series of scientific papers on meteorites. By now, Reichenbach had a brilliant reputation as scientist and industrialist.

Meanwhile his experiments in human sensitivity from 1939 onwards were not well received by other scientists, in fact, he was ruthlessly criticized for them. These experiments involved the demonstration of a mysterious vital force which he named "Od," derived from the Norse deity Odin, indicating a power permeating the whole of nature.

Detection and demonstration of this force depended upon sensitives—specially gifted individuals rather like psychics, although Reichenbach's sensitives were ordinary people from all walks of life. These individuals experienced specific reactions to the proximity of other people—feelings of pleasant coolness and drowsiness or, on the other hand, disagreeable, numbing or exciting feelings. They also manifested a special right-hand left-hand polarity in the human body, which affected their reactions to other people standing or sitting near to their right or left sides, and particularly to sleeping positions with partners. They were also sympathetic to the color blue, and antipathetic to yellow; they had particular food fads, were sensitive to certain metals and unpleasantly affected by mirrors.

In a long series of experiments with some two hundred individuals, Reichenbach established that the sensitive person could see **emanations** from crystals and magnets in total darkness and could detect alternations of electric current. They could also perceive an **aura** surrounding the human body.

Reichenbach studied the various manifestations of this vital force in its relationship to electricity, magnetism and chemistry. He showed that it was connected with the phenomena of water-witching, **Mesmerism** and similar psychic subjects. He demonstrated that the force could move objects without conscious effort, as in the **table-turning** of the Spiritualists.

However, Reichenbach was not a Spiritualist or Mesmerist. His interest was purely scientific, and his hundreds of careful experiments were conducted as precisely as in the other varied subject-areas in which he had become so famous. Unfortunately the unavoidable reliance upon sensitiveness laid him open to accusations of suggestion or Mesmerism, at a time when orthodox scientists were striving to maintain a mechanistic view of life.

Reichenbach's researches were published in Germany in 1850. There were two English translations, one by Dr. John Ashburner in 1851 under the title *Physico-Physiological Researches on the Dynamics of Magnetism, Electricity, Heat, Light, Crystallization, and Chemism, in their relations to Vital Force,* the other by Prof. William Gregory under the title *Researches on Magnetism, Electricity, Heat, Light, Crystallization, and Chemical Attraction, in their relations to the Vital Force* in 1850.

Both translations are good, but Gregory's was the official translation and is generally regarded as the best. Gregory translated Reichenbach's "Od" as "Odyle." perhaps feeling that this term would sound more acceptable to scientists. Gregory also translated Reichenbach's essays *Letters on Od and Magnetism* (1926; 1968) which are a simpler general introduction to Reichenbach's experiments and concepts than his main work.

It is painful to record that Reichenbach's careful experiments were ridiculed by fellow scientists of his time. When he attempted a demonstration in Berlin, a certain Professor Dove set himself to catch Reichenbach out in just the same ruthless manner that poor Mesmer was dogged by the implacable Mr. Ingenhousze, who interfered with his experiments and attempted to antagonize or confuse his subjects. Another comparable case of such dogmatic opposition was that of Oskar Pfungst and the **Elberfeld Horses** in the following century.

In spite of Reichenbach's great reputation in other branches of science, his researches on Odic phenomena and his publications on the subject were ridiculed, attacked and suppressed until his death on January 22, 1869. His great work vanished in obscurity and misrepresentation. A conspiracy of silence prevented its proper revival.

Reichenbach died at the age of eighty and, as Gustav Fechner, another great scientist, commented: "Up to the last days of his life, he grieved at the thought of having to die without obtaining recognition for his system, and such was the tragic fate that actually befell him.

Some years after Reichenbach's death, there was a belated revival of interest by the **Society for Psychical Research** in Britain, who formed a Reichenbach Committee which included Prof. W. F. **Barrett,** Edmund **Gurney** and F. W. H. **Myers.** In this case, it was precisely the possible connection with psychic phenomena that inspired this renewal of interest in a subject pointedly ignored by orthodox science.

The Committee made careful investigations, but was less fortunate than Reichenbach in obtaining suitable sensitives. Only three out of the forty-five individuals tested possessed the sensitivity postulated by Reichenbach but these three provided interesting confirmation of Reichenbach's observations.

In 1908, Dr. Walter J. **Kilner,** who was familiar with the work of Reichenbach, developed a technique for making the human **aura** visible.

More recently, the work of Dr. Wilhelm **Reich** and his theories of "Orgone energy" have much in common with Reichenbach's "Od." Reich was also ridiculed by orthodoxy.

Another possible correlation of Reichenbach's work is the ancient Hindu concept of **Kundalini,** a cosmic energy expressed in the human body in different phases of **prana** or vital currents, and related to sexuality and mystical states.

The concept of vital energy flows in the human body is also found in the ancient Chinese medical practice of **Acupuncture;** which has recently been revived. (See also **Animal Magnetism; Aura; Emanations; Mesmerism; Od; Orgone**)

Recommended reading:

Bagnall, Oscar. *The Origin and Properties of The Human Aura,* London, 1937; revised ed. University Books, 1970

Gopi Krishna. *Kundalini; The Evolutionary Energy in Man,* New Delhi, 1967; London, 1970; Shambala, U.S., 1970

Kilner, Walter J. *The Human Atmosphere,* London, 1911; reissued under title *The Human Aura,* University Books, 1965

Reich, Wilhelm. *The Function of the Orgasm,* Orgone Institute Press, New York, 1948; Farrar, Straus & Giroux, 1973

Reichenbach, Karl von. *Researches on Magnetism, Electricity, Heat, Light, Crystallization and Chemical Attraction in relation to the Vital Force,* University Books, 1974

Reichenbach, Karl von. *The Odic Force; Letters on Od and Magnetism,* University Books, 1968 (originally published under title *Letters on Od and Magnetism,* London, 1926)

Reiki

Japanese term indicating universal life force energy, used in a healing system. This energy is said to flow through the hands of a Reiki therapist.

In the U.S., practice of Reiki healing is regulated by the American-International Reiki Association, P.O. Box 86038-EW, St. Petersburg, Florida 33839. A.I.R.A. published an authoritative book on technique: *The Reiki Factor* by Dr. Barbara Ray; also a reference work *The Official Reiki Handbook.*

Reincarnation

The return to a new corporeal life of souls that have passed over at death. This arises from primitive concept of metempsychosis or transmigration of souls, in which an individual soul might at death, pass into another human body, animal, insect, vegetable life (tree or plant), or even inanimate object (such as a stone). The belief was given a moral purpose in ancient religions, claiming that such transmigration gave a soul the opportunity to expiate past sins and eventually perfect itself in a succession of lives. This is a fundamental belief of such Eastern religions as Hinduism and Buddhism and the belief is an ancient one. Pythagoras claimed that he was Euphorbus in a previous existence. In modern times, reincarnation is also a doctrine of **Theosophy** (deriving from Hinduism) and French **Spiritism.**

The succession of lives in different bodies is regarded as one indivisible life which the experience of each incarnation must use as an opportunity for expiating sins in former lives and perfecting the soul so that further incarnations will not be necessary, and the individual soul can then be absorbed in the divine plan. Until then, the body of one's next life (whether human or animal) is shaped by the actions in the present life. Ultimately, all lives may be seen as illusions of consciousness. Some religious like Hinduism, teach that reincarnation is not always immediate. That some souls may enjoy a period in a heavenly or purgatorial Beyond before rebirth.

The doctrine of transmigration of souls is found in early Greek philosophy, taught by Pythagoras and Plato. In Roman literature, it is found in the writings of Ennius, probably deriving from Greek thought. There is little trace of it in Jewish literature, although it later became part of Kabalistic teaching. Within the early Christian church, it occurs in the Gnostic sects, and later amongst the Manichaeans and **Cathari,** but it was repudiated by orthodox Christian Theologians.

The theory underlying the concept of reincarnation differs from the eschatology of rewards and punishments in Christianity. Each individual soul will eventually attain perfection, although some will take more reincarnations than others, learning by painful experience, in one life after another, the inexorable laws of **Karma**—of cause and effect. All actions involve consequences, some immediately, others delayed, others in future lives. We punish ourselves by our actions, and the very defects and difficulties under which we suffer offer scope for expiation and perfection.

The essential soul is said to be pure and impersonal, part of a universal soul, but overlaid by illusions of individual egoism relating to desires and fears of the body and senses. The classic statements relating to reincarnation are to be found in the Hindu scripture *Bhagavad-Gita,* which stresses: "The soul is never born nor dies, nor does it exist on coming into being. For it is unborn, eternal, and primeval. Even although the body is slain, the soul is not." (II,20).

Theosophical Teachings on Reincarnation

Comparable views are expressed in Theosophy. The various manifestations in the flesh are merely small portions of one whole. The **Monad,** The Divine Spark, or individuality, remains the same throughout the whole course of reincarnation and is truly a denizen of the three higher worlds; the spiritual, the intuitional and the higher mental—but in order to further its growth and the widening of its experience and knowledge, it is necessary that it should descend into the worlds of denser matter, the lower mental, the actual and the physical, and take back with it to the higher worlds what it has learned in these. Since it is impossible to progress far during one manifestation, it must return again and again to the lower worlds.

The laws of progress, the laws which govern reincarnation, are of those evolution and of karma. **Evolution of life** decrees that all shall attain perfection by developing to the utmost their latent powers and qualities, and each manifestation in the lower worlds is but one short journey nearer the goal. Those who realize this law shorten the journey by their own efforts while those who do not realize it and so assist its working, of course lengthen the journey.

Karma decrees that effects good or bad, follow whoever was their cause. Hence, what an individual has done in one manifestation must be benefited by or suffer for in another. It may be impossible that actions should be immediately effective, but each is stored up and sooner or later will bear fruit.

It may be asked how one long life in the lower worlds should not suffice instead of a multitude of manifestations, but this is explicable by the fact that the dense matter, which is the vehicle of these bodies, becomes after a time of progress, incapable of further alteration to suit the developing monad's needs and must accordingly be laid aside for a new body.

After physical death, the individual passes first to the **astral world,** then to the heaven portion of the **mental world,** and in this latter world most time is spent, except when descending into the denser worlds to garner fresh experience and knowledge for further development, in preparation for passage into the still higher sphere.

In the heaven world, these experiences and this knowledge are woven together into the texture of the individual's nature. In those who have not progressed far on the journey of evolution, the manifestations in the lower worlds are comparatively frequent, but with passage of time and development, these manifestations become rarer and more time is spent in the heaven world, until at last, the great process of reincarnation draws to an end, and the pilgrims enter the **Path** which leads to perfection.

Reincarnation and Spiritism

In France, reincarnation was advocated before the time of Allan **Kardec** by several philosophers and mystics—by St. Simon, Prosper Enfantin, St. Martin, Fourier, Pierre Leroux and Jean Reynaud.

From an article by Alexander **Aksakof** in the *London Spiritualist* during 1875, it appears that Allan Kardec adopted the doctrine of reincarnation from spirit communications which were received by the medium Celina Japhet. The mediumship of Celina Japhet was developed by M. Roustan, a Mesmerist, who believed in reincarnation.

If the medium disclosed the doctrine under the effect of the Mesmeriser's belief, it is easy to understand how Kardec and his school could receive ample confirmation through automatists of his tenet that spiritual progress is achieved through a series of incarnations, always in the human race, that successive corporeal existences are the necessary steps to perfection and that the soul retains its individuality and memory after separation from the body.

The influence of the Kardec school was powerful and, by the appeal of its reconciliation with the apparent injustices of life, easily gained the upper hand over the Spiritualist A. T. **Pierart** and his followers, who denied reincarnation and relied on the same kind of evidence as that which the Kardecists produced.

Indeed, Alphonse **Cahagnet,** to whom we owe the earliest careful trance records in France, was the first to whom the communicators emphatically denied reincarnation, but admitted the existence of the soul anterior to its appearance on earth.

Outside France, the doctrine of Allan Kardec was denounced by many Spiritualists. In America, Andrew Jackson **Davis** declared it to be "a magnificent mansion built on sand." But he also believed in preexistence and taught that "all souls existed from the beginning in the divine soul; all individuality which is, has been, or will be, had its pre-existence, has its present existence in creative being."

In England, William **Howitt** was the chief antagonist. He said that the doctrine was pitiable and repellent, and argued that if it were true there must have been millions of spirits who, on entering the other world, have sought in vain their kindred, children and friends.

A very pertinent remark may be quoted from a published letter of the great medium D. D. **Home:** "I have had the pleasure of meeting at least twelve Marie Antoinettes, six or seven Marys of Scotland, a whole host of Louis and other kings, about twenty Great Alexanders, but never a plain John Smith. I, indeed, would like to cage the latter curiosity."

For its psychological import, it is also interesting to note that at the exact time of Allan Kardec's death, D. D. Home, claimed to have received the following communication: "I regret having taught the Spiritist doctrine. Allan Kardec." (See Home's book *Lights and Shadows of Spiritualism,* 1877.)

All this, however, is no argument as reincarnation, if true, may not necessarily be a universal fact. It may not take place at once, and as regards Howitt's objection, it may be claimed that the **double,** in sleep, may establish meetings without recollecting it on awakening. Sir Arthur Conan **Doyle** was probably right in pointing out that as reincarnation for the spirits is a question of their own future, they may not be more enlightened on it than we are on our own future fate.

It may be that reincarnation is optional, it may be that it is punitive. It may be imposed for the purposes of retribution or it may be undertaken for the fulfilment of a mission. The teachings of the spirit **control "Imperator"** through the Rev. W. Stainton **Moses** admitted reincarnation as another chance for souls that had sunk so low as practically to lose identity and in the case of high spirits who descend with a mission.

The opposition to the philosophy of Allan Kardec in England was not universal. He had some followers. Dr. Anna **Kingsford** translated many of his books. She believed herself to be the reincarnation of the Virgin Mary, while her follower Mr. Edward **Maitland** believed that he had been St. John the Divine.

Reincarnation and Spiritualism

In general Spiritualist experience, there is little to support the theory of reincarnation. "John King," the famous control of the medium Eusapia **Palladino,** claimed to have been the father of Eusapia in a previous existence. But "John King" has claimed manifestation through many different mediums at different times.

The experiences of Dr. Carl A. **Wickland** and his wife in **obsession** cases did not bear out the theory. They were told by earthbound spirits, brought into their **rescue circles,** that on passing over they had entered the aura of young children and obsessed them. The children, however, never ceased to struggle against these invaders. In those cases in which the rescue circle of Dr. Wickland enlightened the obsessors of their error, the sanity of the patient quickly returned as the obsessing influence was relieved.

The following borderland case was quoted by Prof. Charles **Richet** from *Les Miracles de la Volonté* (n.d.) by E. Duchatel and R. Warcollier: "A distinguished physician of Palermo, M. Carmelo Samona, well-acquainted with metapsychic science, lost his little daughter, Alexandrina, aged five, in 1910. Mme. Samona was wild with grief. Three days after she saw the child in a dream who said to her: 'I have not left you; I have become tiny like that,' designating some very small object. A fresh pregnancy was the more unlikely in that Mme. Samona had undergone a serious ovarian operation a year previously. On April 10, however, she became aware that she was pregnant. On May 4th it was predicted by Alexandrina, communicating by means of the table, that Mme. Samona would be delivered of twin girls, one of whom would entirely resemble Alexandrina. This came to pass. One of the twins had a mark on the the left eye and another mark on the right ear with a symmetry of the face, precisely like the deceased child."

Among various **automatic writing** scripts, Mr. Frederick Bligh **Bond,** whose famous discovery of Edgar Chapel, Glastonbury Abbey, was described in his book *The Gate of Remembrance* (1918) (see also **Glastonbury Scripts**), noticed reincarnation claims in the communications he received through Miss X. The old monks who communicated asserted that Miss X was one of the early Glastonbury monks and addressed her as "Brother Simon." Neither Miss X nor Mr. Bligh Bond believed in reincarnation when the script came through. The incident was referred to in Bligh Bond's book *The Company of Avalon* (1924).

There was a interesting study by J. Arthur Hill, 'Some Reincarnationist Automatic Scripts,' in *Proceedings* of the Society for Psychical Research (vol. 38), concerning scripts received by Mrs. Cary (pseudonym), a British working woman of about fifty years of age. No attempt was made to verify the historicity of the names and the case was weakened by Mrs. Cary's Theosophical beliefs.

In *The Road to Immortality* by Geraldine Cummins (1932), "F. W. H. **Myers,**" communicating from the other side, admitted reincarnation as an optional choice and as a necessity for "animal men," but not through a series of existences, and ruled out the Theosophical conception of Karma by his fascinating theory of **group-souls.**

The Strange Experiments of Col. Rochas

The feeling of "**dējà vu,**" which is so often quoted as an argument for reincarnation may be explained in a variety of ways. Letourneau's ancestral dreams (see **Dreams**) is perhaps the most far-fetched theory, but inherently it is not more devoid of proof than reincarnation itself. The evidence which the Spiritists advance is mostly weak, wanting in experimental proof.

But Col. **Rochas** believed that he came very near to producing acceptable evidence. He claimed that certain subjects, if put into hypnotic sleep by means of longitudinal passes, could be made to retrace the previous phases of their existence down to their birth and beyond "into the grey" and then into a still earlier state of incarnation. By means of transversal passes the subject was brought back to his normal state by going through the same phases in order of their time. If the transversal passes were continued, the subject, as in his recollection of past lives, was led into the future.

Mlle. Marie Mayo, the daughter of a French engineer, was on of Col. Rochas' subjects. She passed through various stages of hypnotic sleep into the first stage of lethargy, in which she was suggestible for brief moment, into the first state of **somnambulism** in which she was not at all suggestible and retained the memory of what happened in her preceding state and in her waking life; then into the state of **rapport** in which she heard no one else but the hypnotizer.

In this state she began to exteriorize herself, a half phantom formed at the left and a half at the right, the colors red and blue. In a successive state, the phantom halves united, the exteriorization of the astral body became complete but was attached to the body by a fluidic cord. In this state of exteriorization, the **astral body** assumed shapes which accorded with the age in which the subject saw herself in going through the stages of her life.

At the age of eight, she wrote her name in Arabic. At that age she attended a school at Beirut. Beyond that birth she called herself Lina, the daughter of a fisherman in Brittany. She married at the age of twenty, her husband was also a fisherman, his name was Yvon; she did not remember his family name. She had one child who died at the age of two; her husband perished in shipwreck. In a fit of despair she had thrown herself into the sea from the top of a precipice. Her body was eaten by fishes.

All this information was successively elicited. She first passed through the convulsions of drowning and then went back to her life as Lina, through the childbirth to girlhood, infancy, the state of "grey" and then spoke in a previous incarnation as a man, named Charles Mauville, who lived in the time of

Louis XVIII. He was a clerk in a ministerial office in Paris, a bad man, a murderer who died at the age of fifty.

Still further back, she was a lady whose husband was a gentleman attached to the court. Her name was Madeleine de Saint-Marc. Being brought back to the present by transversal passes she successively reached her real age of eighteen and then was pushed, by a continuation of the passes two years into the future. Beyond this she could not go. She saw herself in a strange country with negroes, in a house rather far away from a railway station, the name of which she could not read. Nor could she give any precise information which could be used for identification.

Another subject of Col. Rochas, Juliette Durand, a girl of sixteen, was pushed ahead up to the age of twenty-five, when she died at Nice and then, after a time, become reincarnated in the future as Emile Chaumette in a family of easy circumstances, studied for the ministry and was appointed vicaire at Havre in 1940.

Unfortunately as regards the past, it could never be proved that the personalities enacted by the subject had really lived. They were often very plausible. In some cases, the places and the families spoken of existed, but the individuals could never be traced in parish registers or family documents and the incarnations swarmed with improbabilities.

Were they the result of suggestion? "They certainly do not come from me" stated Col. Rochas, "for I have not only avoided everything that could lead the subject into any determined path, but I have often tried in vain to lead her astray by different suggestions; and the same has been the case with the experimenters who have devoted themselves to this study. . . . Are we to assimilate these phenomena to mere dreams? Certainly not. There is in them a constancy, a regularity, which we do not find in ordinary dreams. . . . And besides, how are we to explain why physical causes, such as longitudinal and transversal passes should have absolutely certain effects on the memory of the subjects between the moments of their birth and that of their present life, and they produce phenomena which do not rest on any basis of fact. I believe that we must compare these manifestations with those which have been studied in the case of Mlle. Hélène Smith, and generally with all those which are provisionally attributed to spirits, and in which we see the true and the false intermingled in a way calculated to drive to despair those who do not reflect upon the darkness in which all observers have to struggle at the beginning of every new science."

In his book *Les Vies Successives* (1911), Col. Rochas told the detailed story of these experiments. (See also Arnall **Bloxham**).

Psychical Researchers and Reincarnation

When Allan Kardec died, Leon **Denis** and Gabriel **Delanne** became the main pillars of the reincarnationist school in France. The general evidence which they relied on was fourfold: (1) infant prodigies, (2) spontaneous recollection of past lives, (3) exploration of memory under hypnosis, (4) the claims announced of coming reincarnation.

They found a powerful supporter in psychical researcher—Dr. Gustav **Geley.** His book, *From the Unconscious to the Conscious* (1920) was described as a veritable Bible for reincarnation by Dr. Innocinzo Calderone, founder and director of the Italian review *Filosofia della Scienza* which made a widespread international inquiry in 1913 on reincarnation.

Geley declared in his answer: "I am a reincarnationist for three reasons: (1) because the doctrine seems to me from the moral point of view fully satisfactory, (2) from the philosophic point of view absolutely rational and (3) from the scientific point of view likely, or—better still—probably true."

Another distinguished representative of French psychical thinking, René **Sudre,** whose outlook was pronouncedly materialistic, ranked himself definitely in the opposite camp. He declared in an article in *Psychic Research* (May 1930): "Even as I can admit the faith in survival from the religious point of view, I should in like measure reject as absurd the doctrine of reincarnation and I well understand how it is that the common-sense of the Anglo-Saxon refuses to bow to this teaching."

Modern Experiments in Hypnotic Regression

In 1954, the subject of reincarnation received new impetus with the serialization of the story of "Bridey Murphy" in the *Denver Post,* followed by Morey Bernstein's bestselling book *The Search for Bridey Murphy* (Doubleday, 1956).

Bernstein was a businessman in Pueblo, Colorado who had hypnotized a housewife "Ruth Simmons" (pseudonym of Mrs. Virginia Tighe). In those sessions, Bernstein probed the early memories of Mrs. Tighe back to childhood and then, as it seemed to an earlier life as "Bridey Murphy," an Irish girl. The book stimulated "Come as you were" social parties, pop songs and a spate of amateur hypnotic sessions.

After all the ballyhoo, the *Chicago American* published a series of articles which effectively disproved the claim that Mrs. Tighe was really Bridey Murphy in a former existence (see Morey **Bernstein**).

Other experimenters in hypnotic regression techniques have produced more convincing results. The British hypnotherapist Arnall **Bloxham** spent over twenty years tape-recording hypnotic subjects whose memories apparently regressed to former incarnations.

Reincarnation and Parapsychology

Renewed popular interest in reincarnation also led to serious researches by parapsychologists, notably Prof. Ian **Stevenson** of the Department of Neurology and Psychiatry, School of Medicine, University of Virginia.

His book *Twenty Cases Suggestive of Reincarnation* was published by the American Society for Psychical Research as the Society's *Proceedings* (vol. 26, September 1966). Cases were studied personally by the author on field trips to Alaska, Brazil, Ceylon, India and Lebanon. It is a model of careful investigation.

(See also Arnall **Bloxham; Evolution of Life;** Joan **Grant**; Allan **Kardec; Logos; Monad;** The **Path; Spiritism;** Ian **Stevenson**)

Recommended reading:

Banerjee, H. N. & W. C. Oursler. *Lives Unlimited; Reincarnation East and West,* Doubleday, 1974

Duncasse, C. J. *A Critical Examination of the Belief in a Life After Death,* Thomas, 1961

Ellwood Gracia Fay. *Psychic Visits to the Past: An Exploration of Retrocognition,* New American Library (paperback), 1971

Guirdham, Arthur. *The Cathars and Reincarnation,* Neville Spearman, London, 1960

Head, Joseph & S. L. Cranston (eds.). *Reincarnation: An East-West Anthology,* Julian Press, 1961; Theosophical Publishing House paperback, 1968

Head, Joseph & S. L. Cranston. *Reincarnation: The Phoenix Fire Mystery, An East-West Dialogue on Death and Rebirth . . . ,* Julian Press/Crown Publishers, 1977

Head, Joseph (ed.). *Reincarnation in World Thought: A Living Study of Reincarnation in All Ages,* Julian Press, 1967

Holzer, Hans. *Born Again; The Truth about Reincarnation,* Doubleday, 1970; Bailey Bros. & Swinfen, London, 1975

Leek, Sybil. *Reincarnation, The Second Chance,* Stein & Day, 1974; Bantam paperback, 1975

Osborn, Arthur. *Superphysical; A Review of the Evidence for Continued Existence, Reincarnation, and Mystical States of Consciousness,* revised ed. Barnes & Noble/Muller, London, 1974

Pierce, Henry W. *Science Looks at ESP,* New American Library paperback, 1970 [includes discussion of reincarnation]

Stevenson, Ian. *Cases of the Reincarnation Type,* Vol. I, *Ten Cases From India,* University Press of Virginia, 1975

Stevenson, Ian. *Cases of the Reincarnation Type, Vol. 2, Ten Cases in Sri Lanka,* University Press of *Virginia,* 1977

Stevenson, Ian. *Cases of the Reincarnation Type, Vol. 3, Twelve Cases in Lebanon and Turkey,* University Press of Virginia, 1980

Stevenson, Ian. *Twenty Cases Suggestive of Reincarnation,* 2nd revised ed., University Press of Virginia, 1974

Story, Francis & Nyanaponika Thera. *Rebirth as Doctrine and Experience,* Buddhist Publication Society, Kandy, Sri Lanka, 1975

Underwood, Peter & Leonard Wilder. *Lives to Remember; A Case Book on Reincarnation.* Robert Hale, London, 1975

Wilson, Ian. *Mind Out of Time? Reincarnation Claims Investigated,* Gollancz, London, 1981 (revised ed. titled *Reincarnation?,* Penguin Books, 1982)

Religio-Philosophical Journal, The

American Spiritualistic weekly founded in 1865, published in Chicago. Its founder and publisher, Stevens J. Jones, was murdered in 1877. His son-in-law, Col. J. C. Bundy assumed charge. Successive editors were M. E. Bundy, B. F. Underwood, T. G. Newan.

The New Series (vols. 34-42) were published in San Francisco. The publication ceased April 22, 1905, and was succeeded by *The Mountain Pine* (1906-1908).

Religious Experience Research Unit

British organization founded in 1969 "to provide a center where ordinary people, religious or not, who have had experiences of feeling themselves upheld or given new strength 'by some kind of power which seems to come from beyond themselves' will contribute their information.

"These reports were studied, using social anthropology and psychology techniques, followed when necessary by interviews in depth." The Unit is also interested in research on telepathy and other parapsychological phenomena. The director of the Unit was Sir Alister **Hardy.**

Since the death of Prof. Sir Alister **Hardy** in 1985, the organization has become the **Alister Hardy Research Centre,** with branches in Britain and the U.S.

REM

Initialism for Rapid Eye Movement, a phenomenon accompanying dreaming (see **Dreams; Dream Laboratory**).

Renier, Noreen

Contemporary professional psychic with ten years' experience as a teacher, investigator, and lecturer. Originally from Massachusetts, Noreen lived in Florida for eighteen years, working in advertising and public relations.

In 1976, she was introduced to meditation and discovered a psychic ability. She submitted her gift to scientific testing and research, working with the **Psychical Research Foundation** in Durham, North Carolina, the Parapsychology Department and Department of Behavioral Medicine and Psychiatry at the University of Virginia in Charlottesville. He experiments in archaeology and anthropology with Dr. David Jones at the University of Central Florida were reported in his book *Visions of Time* (Quest Publications, 1979).

Noreen became a consultant to law enforcement agencies, and claims to have worked on more than a hundred cases. From 1980-82, she reached out to people in three states through a weekly call-in radio program 'In Touch with Noreen.' In 1984, she began work on a book about her experiences, returning to Orlando in 1985 to continue teaching, consultation, and lecturing.

During 1985, John D. Merrell of Beaverton, Oregon, published an article in the Newsletter of the Northwest Skeptics (a group of which Merrell was co-founder) questioning Noreen's background credentials and what he claimed were "fraudulent claims" of psychic ability. Northwest Skeptics is a group dedicated to combating pseudoscience and uncovering false claims of paranormal phenomena, with aims similar to the **Committee for the Scientific Investigation of Claims of the Paranormal.**

The Newsletter was mailed to newspapers, broadcast media, and police departments.

Noreen filed a defamation suit against Merrell, claiming that the Newsletter had damaged her reputation as a practicing psychic. The case was heard in September 1986, when Noreen testified that she lost a least one lecturing job with Oregon State Police trainees because of Merrell's article. The suit claimed that Merrell's statements "held the plaintiff up to public ridicule, humiliation, embarrassment and loss of reputation causing her to suffer loss of self-esteem, mental anguish, humiliation and loss of reputation regarding her occupation."

The jury's verdict was that Merrell knew that at least some of his story was false or written with a reckless disregard for the truth. Noreen was awarded $25,000 damages.

The case was something of a landmark in the present battle between skeptics and psychics. Militant skeptics claim that belief in paranormal phenomena is unscientific and socially irresponsible and must be exposed as pseudoscience or fraud. Some skeptics have performed a useful service in exposing a number of fraudulent claims; others have themselves been irresponsible in prejudging the validity of claims of the paranormal or making wild allegations without firm evidence. Psychics believe that they have a right to their beliefs and activities, and object to being classed indiscriminately as frauds.

Res Bureaux Bulletin

A Canadian Bulletin about Fortean type phenomena, published occasionally by Mr. X, Box 1598, Kingston, Ontario K7L 5C8, Canada. It circulates amongst serious students of unusual and obscure events in exchange for reciprocity on cuttings and articles. (See also **INFO; Fortean Times**)

Reschith Hajalalim

The name of the ministering spirit Jewish rabbinical legend of the angelic hierarchies. To this angel, the pure and simple essence of the divinity, flows through Hajoth Hakakos; he guides the *primum mobile,* and bestows the gift of life on all.

Rescue Circles

Groups formed by Spiritualists for the purpose of "waking up" the dead and freeing them from their earthbound state, based on the idea that earthbound spirits are too gross to be reached by the influence of higher spirits from the other side. They exist closer to the material plane than to the spiritual. In many cases they do not realize that they are dead at all, and live in a state of bewilderment. If they are enlightened on their true condition and if prayers are offered for them, they will progress to a higher existence.

The beginning of rescue circles may be traced to the Shaker communities of America (see **Shakers**). The appearance of a tribe of Indian spirit controls aroused the impression that the Shakers were to teach and proselytize them.

The first such circles were held by the wife of Col. Danskin of Baltimore and other ladies. The best work was performed by a circle in Buffalo between 1875 and 1900, and by by Dr. Carl **Wickland** and his wife.

The mediums in the Buffalo circle were Marcia M. Swain and Leander Fischer (a professor of music). The circle consisted of Daniel E. Bailey and his wife, the mother of the professor and Mrs. Aline M. Eggleston, the stenographer. The identity of the spirit brought to be "woken" was often verified but as the search after such proofs entailed considerable labor and time it was, after a while, given up.

The work of this circle was described in D. E. Bailey's book *Thoughts from the Inner Life* (Boston, 1886). Twelve impressive records of these rescue seances were published in an appendix in Admiral Usborne Moore's book *Glimpses of the Next State* (1911).

Similar mission work was carried on by E. C. **Randall,** also in Buffalo. The medium was Mrs. Emily S. **French.** Randall's book *Frontiers of the After Life* (New York, 1922) described the results.

Dr. Wickland's book *Thirty Years Among the Dead* (Los Angeles, 1924) contains hundreds of interesting records. The work of the Tozer rescue circle in Melbourne is described in Sir Arthur Conan **Doyle**'s book *Wanderings of a Spiritualist* (1921). (See also Titus **Bull;** Carl August **Wickland**)

Research Institute for Supersensonic Healing Energies

Branch of **University of the Trees,** founded by Christopher **Hills** at Boulder Creek, California. RISHE is devoted to practical, applied research in subtle energy therapeutics. This includes such subject areas as **radiesthesia, radionics,** homeopathy, Bach flower remedies, negative ionization, healing with crystals and gemstones. Address: P.O. Box 644, 13151 Pine Street, Boulder Creek, California 95006. (See also **Bach Centre**)

Resurrection

The central claim of Christianity is based on the bodily resurrection of Jesus. Many Spiritualists do not admit the claim in this sense, although they do not question in any way the spiritual resurrection of Jesus. Indeed, F. W. H. **Myers** voiced the conviction that owing to the evidence of psychical research there will be no reasonable man a century hence who will not believe in the resurrection of Jesus.

The term "resurrection" is supplanted by "**survival**" in Spiritualism. It is not the physical but the spiritual body which rises from death and survives. This is not a question of faith but a question of evidence. By proving that **apparitions** do occur, psychical research and Spiritualism may effect a reconciliation between science and religion.

Retro-PK (Retroactive PK)

Term used by parapsychologists for time-displaced **psychokinesis,** indicating an influence exerted on an experiment after it has been run.

The term arises from the experiments of Dr. Helmut **Schmidt** with an electronic random event generator **(REG),** an automatic coin-tossing machine.

Experiments tended to show that if a subject was replayed the output of an REG after the output had been generated, he could still have an effect upon it. For details, see the paper 'PK Effects on Pre-Recorded Targets' by Helmut Schmidt (*Journal of the American Society for Psychical Research*, vol. 70, 1976). (See also **Psychokinesis**)

Retrocognition

Term used in psychical research and parapsychology to indicate a form of extrasensory perception in which the subject obtains knowledge of some event in the past by paranormal cognition. This amounts to a kind of backwards precognition (see **Precognition**).

F. W. H. **Myers** combined retrocognition with his theory of "**psychorrhagic diathesis**" to explain the phenomena of haunting. It was also suggested that apparitions of the dead and visions of the future, owing to a curious inversion of time, may be amenable to retrocognition.

Reuss, Theodor (died 1924)

German occultist who recruited Aleister **Crowley** to the **O.T.O.** (Ordo Templi Orientis). Reuss was a mysterious and many-sided character. He lived in Britain during the 1880s and earned a living as a music-hall singer under the name Charles Theodore. He sang at fund-raising concerts organized by the British Social League (of which he was an executive member) while acting as an undercover agent for the German Secret Service, spying on the Karl Marx family. Eleanor Marx considered him a vulgar and dirty person, and he was expelled from the League when his spying was discovered.

About 1920, Reuss lived in Switzerland where he claimed to be a Grand Master of a Masonic order. He became friendly with Heinrich Tränker, a member of a Rosicrucian society, who had links with other German occult groups such as the **Fraternitas Saturni** and the O.T.O. (then a German secret order). Reuss became head of the O.T.O. after the death of Karl Kellner, and was known as "Brother Merlin."

The most closely guarded secret of the O.T.O. was that of sex-magic, the use of sexual energy for occult purposes. Reuss inferred from the writings of British occultist Aleister Crowley that Crowley had discovered and even written about this secret.

Reuss thereupon visited Crowley in London in 1912 and begged him to conceal the secret, inviting him to enter the O.T.O. and become head of a British branch. The British lodge was duly launched under the name **Mysteria Mystica Maxima.** Reuss resigned from leadership of the O.T.O. in 1922, two years before his death, nominating Crowley as his successor.

In 1916, Reuss had authorized a North American Branch (The Ancient and Mystical Order Rosae Crucis or **AMORC**), headed by H. Spencer **Lewis,** who later abandoned the connection with the O.T.O. and organized a popular mail-order Rosicrucianism. (See also **Golden Dawn; O.T.O.; Rosicrucians; Tantric Yoga**)

Reuter, Florizel von (1893- ?)

Professor and Director of the Master School for Violin at the Vienna State Academy of Music. His mother developed **automatic writing,** receiving messages in seventeen languages, many of them being evidential in character and often coming in mirror writing. In *The Psychic Experiences of a Musician* (1928), Prof. von Reuter gave a full analytical account of these phenomena.

His second book *The Consoling Angel* (1930), narrated the return of a school friend of his mother with over three hundred proofs of identity, all dealing with matters totally unknown to von Reuter and his mother.

Ernesto **Bozzano** considered the book as one of the most evidential publications of recent times.

A third book by Prof. von Reuter, *A Musician's Talks with Unseen Friends* (1931) is a record of automatic scripts received by himself alone, dealing with ethical and philosophical matters, and given (as in the case of the Rev. W. Stainton **Moses**) by a band of communicators.

At a later date Prof. von Reuter and his mother also developed **direct voice** and received **apport** phenomena in their own circle.

Prof. von Reuter lectured on psychic matters all over Germany and the British Isles. He was associated with Baron von **Schrenck-Notzing** in a series of experiments with the mediums the **Schneider** Brothers.

Review of Indian Spiritualism

Indian monthly publication. Address: 39 S.R. das Road, Calcutta 700026, India.

ReVision; The Journal of Consciousness and Change

Semiannual journal devoted to scholarly articles on consciousness and change in modern society. Typical subjects include interdisciplinary studies on Eastern and Western meditation and philosophy, mysticism, religion in contemporary transpersonal experiences, research on higher consciousness.

The journal is published by Heldref Publications (division of the Helen Dwight Reid Educational Foundation) in cooperation with the International Transpersonal Association. The editors include such distinguished individuals as Stanislav Grof, Fritjof Capra, Stanley Krippner, Ralph Metzner, and Dr. Karan Singh. Address: Heldref Publications, 4000 Albemarle Street N.W., Washington, D.C. 20016

Revista de Parapsicologia (Brazil)

Bi-monthly Brazilian publication (in Spanish or Portuguese) of Centro Latino Americano de Parap sicologia. Illustrated articles cover parapsychological phenomena and research. Address: Caixa Postal 11.587, 05.000, Sao Paulo, Brazil (Obtainable in the U.S. from: Parapsicologia, Revista Ideal, P.O. Box 450521, Miami, Florida 33145; Spanish edition obtainable from: Revista de Parapsicologia, Ibiza 50, Madrid, Spain 9.)

Revista de Parapsicologia (Chile)

Annual publication of Laboratorio de Investigaciones Parapsicologicas in Chile. It gives national and internal news in the field of parapsychology, reviews of experiments, books and journals, critical and bibliographical surveys. Address: Centro de Investigationes Parapsicologia J. B. Rhine, Constitution 187, Santiago, Chile.

Revivals

Outbreaks of religious mass enthusiasm, inspired by fervor or persecution. They have often been accompanied by a variety of psychic manifestations, such as **luminous phenomena,** aerial music, gift of **healing,** gift of **tongues** and **prophecy.**

From June 1688, to February 19, 1689, five to six hundred prophets arose in France in Dauphiny and in the Vivarez as a result of the revocation of the Edict of Nantes by Louis XIV and the consequent persecution. Under its effect, eight thousand seers were counted in Languedoc in the first year.

There hardly was a house which did not have inspired orators. Even children prophesied in tongues unknown to them. Heavenly music was heard day and night in the air, tongues of fire were observed and, at least in one case, the ordeal of the pyre was harmlessly undergone by the entranced leader Claris. Cavalier, Roland and Marion, the organizers of the insurgency, were all inspired orators. The army which they assembled chose its own chief by their gifts of the spirit.

The great Irish revival in 1859 and the Welsh revival in 1904 were accompanied by similar phenomena, especially by hearing of unearthly music and seeing unexplainable lights. Similar experiences were recorded in American revivals.

The Rev. John Crapsey, of Brookfield, Tioga County, was quoting the words of Jesus on the cross when "a mighty invisible power seemed suddenly to possess him, and a luminous appearance scintillated upon and around his hand, shining with brilliant effulgence in the eyes of all beholders. Under an impulse which I could not resist, I sprang," stated Mr. Crapsey, "from the desk out upon the middle of the floor into the midst of the congregation; great signs and wonders then ensued and were witnessed by all. Fire and pillars of smoke and luminous light rose up bodily in our midst; men, women and even stammering children were seized, speaking with new tongues, and uttering prophecies. Prayers and exhortations were poured forth in abundance, and many of the congregation broke out into the most marvellous and heavenly singing."

A paper on the psychological aspects of the Welsh Revival of 1904-05 was published by the Rev. A. F. Fryer in *Proceedings* of the Society for Psychical Research (vol. 19, 1905-07). (See also **Convulsionaries of St. Médard; Healing by Faith; Pentecostalism; Snake-Handling; Tremblers of the Cevennes**)

Recommended reading:

Grey, E. Howard. *Visions, Previsions and Miracles in Modern Times,* L. N. Fowler, London, 1915

Kelsey, Morton T. *Tongue Speaking,* Doubleday, 1964

Lewis, Mrs. J. *The Awakening in Wales,* Marshall, London/Revell, New York, 1905

Simson, Eve. *The Faith Healer; Deliverance Evangelism in North America,* Concordia/Pyramid paperback, 1977

Revue Des Études Psychiques

French edition of the *Rivista di Studi Psichici,* founded by Count Cesar Baudi **de Vesme** in 1898, after the death of Dr. G. B. **Ermacora** whom he succeeded in the editorial chair of the Rivista di S.P. In 1905 it was amalgamated with the *Annales des Sciences Psychiques,* which ceased publication in 1924.

Revue Métapsychique

Official organ of the Institut Métapsychique Internationale. It was founded in 1920, with Dr. Eugene **Osty** as editor.

Currently published annually as a French-language journal by The Association Bordelaise d'Études Métapsychiques. It reports parapsychological research and news in France and elsewhere, including book reviews. Address: 1 Place Wagram, Paris 75017, France.

Revue Scientifique et Morale du Spiritisme

Periodical founded by spiritist Gabriel **Delanne,** running from 1894-1923.

Revue Spirite

Monthly journal founded by Allan **Kardec** in 1858, the official journal of French **Spiritism,** published in Paris. After Allan Kardec's death, P. G. Leymarie succeeded to the editorial chair. In the 1920s, it was directed by Jean **Meyer** and edited by Pascal **Forthuny.**

Revue Spiritualiste

Journal representing French **Spiritualism** (as distinct from the more popular school of **Spiritism**) founded by Z. J. Pierart. It was published from 1858 until 1870.

Rhabdic Force

Name given to the force which causes muscular contortions in the hands of sensitives, bending violently a hazel switch which is used as a **divining-rod,** or oscillating a **pendulum.** In Germany Prof. Benedict called it "telluric force." (See also **Dowsing; Rhabdomancy**)

Rhabdomancy

Term for divining by rods. Deriving from Greek words meaning "a rod" and "divination," it was thus alluded to by Sir Thomas Browne (1605-82): "As for the divination or decision from the staff, it is an augurial relic, and the practice thereof is accused by God himself: 'My people ask counsel of their stocks, and their staff declareth unto them.' Of this kind was that practised by Nabuchadonosor in that Caldean miscellany delivered by Ezekiel."

In John Brand's *Observations on Popular Antiquities* (1777; 1813) the following description was cited from a manuscript *Discourse on Witchcraft*, written by Mr. John Bell, 1705; it is derived from Theophylact: "They set up two staffs, and having whispered some verses and incantations, the staffs fell by the operation of demons. Then they considered which way each of them fell, forward or backward, to the right or left hand, and agreeably gave responses, having made use of the fall of their staffs for their signs." This was the Grecian method of Rhabdomancy, and St. Jerome thought it was the same that was alluded to in the above passage of Hosea, and in *Ezekiel* (xxi. 21, 22) where it is rendered "arrows."

Belomancy and Rhabdomancy, in fact, have been confused in these two passages, and it is a question whether in one of the methods, arrows and rods or stones were not used indifferently.

The practice is said to have passed from the Chaldeans and Scythians to the German tribes, who used pieces from the branch of a fruit tree, which they marked with certain characters, and threw at hazard upon a white cloth. Something like this, according to one of the rabbis, was the practice of the Hebrews, only instead of characters, they peeled their rods on one side, and drew the presage from their manner of falling. The Scythians and the Alani used rods of the myrtle and sallow, and as the latter chose "fine straight wands" according to Herodotus, it may be inferred that their method was that of the Hebrews, or some modification of it. (See also **Aaron's Rod; Belomancy; Divining-Rod; Dowsing**)

Rhapsodomancy

Divination by means of opening the works of a poet at hazard and reading the verse which first presents itself oracularly. This is similar to the well-known divination technique of opening a Bible at random and reading the verse on which the finger or other indicator lights as an oracular statement relative to the inquirer's problem. (See also **Bibliomancy**)

Rhasis (or Rhazes) (c. 825-925)

Name given to the famous Arabian physician, chemist and alchemist Abu Bekr Muhammed Ben Zakeriyah er-Rasi. His popular name "Al-Rhasis" (Man of Ray) derives from his birthplace of Ray, near Teheran, on the frontiers of Khorassan. He first studied philosophy, logic, metaphysics, poetry and music, becoming a skilled player on the lute.

At the age of thirty years, he began to study medicine and soon became one of the most famous physicians of his time. He was director of the famous hospital of Bhagdad, and a great many books on medicine, chemistry and philosophy are ascribed to him.

He also wrote treatises on **alchemy** and the transmutation of metals. Some commentators have compared his intellecutal attainments with those of Galileo and Robert Boyle. He had a great reputation for his insistence upon the importance of practical experiment in preference to theories. He was one of the first experimenters to mention borax, orpiment, realgar, and other chemical compounds.

There is a probably apocryphal story that he dedicated an alchemical work to the Emir El Mansur, prince of Khorassan, who rewarded him with a thousand pieces of gold, but desired to witness a transmutation. Rhasis was by now an elderly man and his experiments were unfortunately negative.

El Mansur was enraged, and struck him with a whip, saying "I have rewarded you richly for your trouble, and now I must punish you for your affirmation of lies!" As a result, Rhasis became blind. However, other explanations have been offered for his failing eyesight, including the somewhat ridiculous claim that it resulted from an inordinate appetite for eating beans!

In his studies in chemistry he left some results of real value, notwithstanding the time and trouble he spent in the pursuit of the **philosopher's stone.** Another theory which he held in common with Geber and others was that the planets influenced metallic formation under the earth's surface.

For a brief account of Rhasis, see *Alchemists Through the Ages* by Arthur Edward Waite, Rudolf Steiner Publications, 1970 (a revised edition of the anonymous work attributed to Francis Barrett, *The Lives of the Alchemystical Philosophers,* 1815). (See also **Alchemy**)

Rhine, J(oseph) B(anks) (1895-1980)

One of the pioneers of **parapsychology,** founder (with William **McDougall**) of the Parapsychology Laboratory, Duke University, Durham, North Carolina. Born September 29, 1895 in Juniata County, Pennsylvania, he studied at University of Chicago (B.S. 1922, M.S. 1923, Ph.D. 1925). In 1920 he married Louisa Ella Weckesser, who later shared his researches in the field of parapsychology.

He was a research fellow in plant physiology at Boyce Thompson Institute from 1923-24, instructor in plant physiology at West Virginia University from 1924-26, instructor in philosophy and psychology at Duke University from 1928-29, instructor to professor, psychology, Duke University from 1929-49, director of Parapsychology Laboratory from 1935 onwards. He was a member of the Parapsychological Association, Southern Society for Philosophy and Psychology, American Association for the Advancement of Science, American Society for Psychical Research, Society for Psychical Research, London.

Dr. Rhine's interest in parapsychology grew out of his investigations of mediumship with Dr. Walter Franklin **Prince** at Harvard University in 1926. Rhine went on to Duke University the following year and studied psychic phenomena with Dr. William McDougall, head of the psychology department. It was Rhine's training in plant physiology which gave him the idea that psychic faculties might be tested with scientific disciplines.

With the encouragement of McDougall, Rhine commenced a program for statistical validation of ESP, working in collaboration with colleagues on the psychology faculty, with students as subjects. The emphasis was first on clairvoyance and telepathy, transmitting images from sender to receiver, and the now familiar Zener card pack with its simple symbols of cross, star, circle, square and waves assisted statistical evaluation of tests. Later work included experiments in "**psychokinesis**" using dice to test the ability of the human mind to affect movement of objects at a distance. Psychokinesis or "PK" has since largely displaced the term "telekinesis" formerly used in psychical research.

The publication of Dr. Rhine's monograph *Extra-sensory Perception* by the Boston Society for Psychic Research in 1934 was a key point in the development of parapsychology as a scientific study, and opinion sharply divided on the validity of the work.

There was still some opposition to parapsychology even at Duke University, where Rhine was obliged to open a separate Parapsychology Laboratory and seek outside sponsorship for research. However, the persistent patient work of Rhine, his wife Louisa Rhine and their associates eventually established parapsychology as a proper scientific study.

From 1937 onwards, Rhine began publication of the *Journal of Parapsychology* at Duke. His other publications included: *The Reach of the Mind* (1947), *New World of the Mind* (1953), *Parapsychology, Frontier Science of the Mind* (with J. G. **Pratt,** 1957). With J. G. Pratt, Charles E. Stuart, Burke M. Smith & Joseph A. Greenwood, Rhine documented the story of ESP in: *Extrasensory Perception After Sixty Years; a critical evaluation* (1940; 1960). Two other books bring the story up to date: *Parapsychology Today* by J. B. Rhine & Others (1968), and *Progress in Parapsychology* edited by J. B. Rhine (1971).

Dr. Rhine died February 20, 1980 at the age of 84.

Financial support for the work at the Parapsychology Laboratory at Duke University owed much to the generosity of Mr. Charles E. **Ozanne** who made regular financial gifts to support research. In 1960 he established the **Psychical Research Foundation** at Duke Station, Durham, N.C. as an independent research center to investigate phenomena relating to survival of human personality after death as well as other aspects of parapsychology.

Another generous donor in the field of parapsychology was the late Mr. Chester F. Carlson, inventor of xerography, whose financial support assisted the establishment of the **Foundation for Research on the Nature of Man,** a private institution established in 1962 with Dr. J. B. Rhine as director. Situated at Durham, N.C., this foundation made possible the transition from the Parapsychology Laboratory at Duke University to an independent world center for the study of parapsychology and related fields. The story of this important development is told in *Parapsychology from Duke to FRNM* by J. B. Rhine and associates (Parapsychology Press, 1965).

Rhine, Louisa Ella Weckesser (Mrs. Joseph Banks Rhine) (1891-1983)

Pioneer worker in the field of parapsychology. Born November 9, 1891 at Sanborn, New York, she studied at University of Chicago (B.S. 1919, M.S. 1921, Ph.D. 1923). In 1920 she married Joseph Banks Rhine. She was a staff member of the Parapsychology Laboratory, Duke University, from 1948-62, thereafter research director of the **Institute for Parapsychology,** research branch of the **Foundation for Research on the Nature of Man.** She was a charter member of the Parapsychological Association and co-edited the *Journal of Parapsychology.*

With her husband, Mrs. Rhine played a prominent part in the establishment of parapsychology as a scientific study, and shared his researches in ESP, psi phenomena and psychokinesis.

Her book *Hidden Channels of the Mind* (1961) surveys the field of spontaneous psi experiences. Her articles in the *Journal of Parapsychology* included: 'Placement PK Tests with Three Types of Objects' (vol. 15, No. 2, 1951), 'Conviction and Associated Conditions in Spontaneous Cases (vol. 15, No. 4, 1951), 'Relations of Experiences and Associated Events' (vol. 17, No. 3, 1953), 'Frequency of Types in Spontaneous Precognition' (vol. 18, No. 2, 1954), 'Precognition and Intervention' (vol. 19, No. 1, 1955), 'Relationship of Agent and Percipient in Spontaneous Telepathy' (vol. 20, No. 1, 1956), 'Hallucinatory Psi Experiences' (vols. 20, No. 4, 1956, 21, Nos. 1 & 3, 1957).

Her books included: *ESP in Life and Lab* (1967), *Mind Over Matter* (1970), *Psi: What It It?* (a children's introduction to parapsychology, 1975), *The Invisible Picture* (1980).

She died March 17, 1983 at the age of 91.

In addition to substantial joint contributions to parapsychology, she and her husband also raised four children. Although committed to scientific disciplines in their parapsychology work, both the Rhines shared a humane and religious view of the implications of the subject.

Ricerca Psichica (Journal)

The title which *Luce e Ombra,* the oldest Italian Spiritualist monthly, assumed in 1932.

Richet, Dr. Charles (1850-1935)

Professor of Physiology at the Faculty of Medicine in Paris, honorary president of La Societé Universelle d'Études Psychiques, president of the **Institut Métapsychique Internationale**, president of the **Society for Psychical Research**, London, in 1905, one of the foremost psychical researchers of recent times. He was born August 26, 1850 and educated at the University of Paris. He was winner of the 1913 Nobel Prize in Physiology and Medicine; member of the Académie de Médecine.

He had his first experiences in **lucidity** (paranormal knowledge) in 1872. He confessed that although it had tremendous effect on him, he lacked the requisite intellectual courage to draw conclusions. In 1875, while yet a student, he proved that the hypnotic state was a purely physiological phenomenon which had nothing to do with "magnetic fluids."

"Following my article," he wrote of the result, "many experiments were widely made, and animal magnetism ceased to be an occult science."

A few years later, he published his studies in multiple **personality.** He sat with various mediums, including William **Eglinton** and Mme. **d'Esperance,** and in 1886-87 conducted many experiments in **cryptesthesia** with four subjects—Alice, Claire, Eugenie and Leontine. Some were in hypnotic, some in waking state. They reproduced drawings enclosed in sealed envelopes. As a result of these experiments Richet formulated the theory of cryptesthesia in these words: "In certain persons, at certain times, there exists a faculty of cognition which has no relation to our normal means of knowledge."

He founded with Dr. Dariex the *Annales des Sciences Psychiques* in 1890 and he took part in the investigation of the Milan Commission with the medium Eusapia **Palladino** in 1892. The report admitted the reality of puzzling phenomena, expressing also the conviction that the results obtained in light, and many of those obtained in darkness, could not have been produced by trickery of any kind.

Prof. Richet did not sign the report and in his notes on it in the *Annales des Sciences Psychiques* carefully stated his conclusions as follows: "Absurd and unsatisfactory though they were, it seems to me very difficult to attribute the phenomena produced to deception, conscious or unconscious, or to a series of deceptions. Nevertheless, conclusive and indisputable proof that there was no fraud on Eusapia's part, or illusion on our part, is wanting: we must therefore renew our efforts to obtain such proof."

He became convinced of the reality of **materialization** phenomena by his experiments with the medium Marthe Béraud (see **Eva C.**) at the Villa Carmen, Algiers, in General Noel's house. His report, published in the *Annales des Sciences Psychiques* (April 1906) aroused wide attention He confirmed his experiments in later sittings at the house of Mme. Bisson and at the Institut Métapsychique of which, after the resignation of Prof. Santoliquido, he was elected president.

He made many experiments with the mediums Burgik, **Kluski, Guzyk** and **Ossowiecki,** both in Paris and Warsaw.

His book *Traité de Métapsychique* (1922, translated as *Thirty Years of Psychical Research*, 1923) summed up the experiences of a lifetime. The book was dedicated to Sir William **Crookes** and F. W. H. **Myers.** This was a sign of repentance for his earlier skepticism. He stated in his work: "The idolatry of current ideas was so dominant at that time that no pains were taken either to verify or to refute Crookes' statements. Men were content to ridicule them, and I avow with shame that I was among the wilfully blind. Instead of admiring the heroism of a recognized man of science who dared then, in 1872, to say that there really are phantoms that can be photographed and whose heart beats can be heard, I laughed."

He accepted **cryptesthesia, telekinesis, ectoplasm, materializations** and **premonitions** as abundantly proved. On the other hand, he considered doubtful **apports, levitations,** the phenomena of the **double,** which he had no opportunity to examine thoroughly or experience. He was most emphatic in stating: "The fact that intelligent forces are projected from an organism that can act mechanically, can move objects and make sounds, is a phenomenon as certainly established as any fact in physics."

As if to leave a loophole for more definite proofs on **psychic photography, direct writing, apports,** psychic **music** and **luminous phenomena** he added: "No one would have thought of simulating them if they had never really occurred. I do not hesitate to think them fairly probable, but they are not proven."

His struggle with the problem of **survival** was very interesting. He stated: "I admit that there are some very puzzling cases that tend to make one admit the survival of human personality—the cases of Mrs. Piper's George Pelham, of Raymond Lodge and some others,"

His basis for disbelief in survival was twofold: Firstly, the human mind has mysterious faculties of cognition, secondly these mysterious cognitions have an invincible tendency to group themselves round a new personality. "The doctrine of survival," he explained, "seems to me to involve so many impossibilities, while that of an intensive cryptesthesia is (relatively) so easy to admit that I do not hesitate at all. I go so far as to claim—at the risk of being confounded by some new and unforeseen discovery—that subjective metapsychics will always be radically incapable of proving survival. Even if a new case even more astounding than that of George Pelham were to appear, I should prefer to suppose an extreme perfection of transcendental cognitions giving a great multiplicity of notions grouping themselves round the imaginary centre of a factitious personality, than to suppose that this centre is a real personality—the surviving soul, the will and consciousness of a self that has disappeared, a self which depended on a brain now reduced to dust. . . .

"But except in a few rare cases, the inconsistency between the past and the present mentality is so great that in the immense majority of spiritist experiences it is impossible to admit survival, even as a very tentative hypothesis. I could more easily admit a non-human intelligence, distinct from both medium and discarnate, than the mental survival of the latter."

Treating of the so-called **death** bed meeting cases he stated: "Among all the facts adduced to prove survival, these even seem to me to be the most disquieting."

He did not accept the facts of materialization as proof of survival. "The case of George Pelham, though there was no materialization, is vastly more evidential for survival than all the materializations yet known. I do not even see how decisive proof could be given. Even if (which is not the case) a form identical with that of a deceased person could be photographed I should not understand how an individual two hundred years dead, whose body has become a skeleton, could live again with this vanished body any more than with any other material form."

He called the phenomena of materialization absurd, yet true, and explained: "Spiritualists have blamed me for using this word 'absurd'; and have not been able to understand that to admit the reality of these phenomena was to me an actual pain; but to ask a physiologist, a physicist, or a chemist to admit that a form that has a circulation of blood, warmth, and muscles, that exhales carbonic acid, has weight, speaks, and thinks, can issue from a human body is to ask of him an intellectual effort that is really painful."

In concluding his weighty *Thirty Years of Psychical Research*, he was assailed by doubts: "Truth to tell—and one must be as cautious in denial as in assertion— some facts tend to make us believe strongly in the survival of vanished personalities. Why should mediums, even when they have read no spiritualist books, and are unacquainted with spiritualist doctrines, proceed at once to personify some deceased person or other? Why does the new personality affirm itself so persistently, so energetically, and sometimes with so much verisimilitude? Why does it separate itself so sharply from the personality of the medium? All the words of powerful mediums are pregnant, so to say, with the theory of survival? These are semblances, perhaps, but why should the semblances be there?"

Then, again, as if repenting his doubts, he explained: "Mysterious beings, angels or demons, existences devoid of form, or spirits, which now and then seek to intervene in our lives, who can by means, entirely unknown, mould matter at will, who direct some of our thoughts and participate in some of our destinies, and who, to make themselves known (which they could not otherwise do) assume the bodily and psychological aspect of vanished human personalities—all this is a simple manner of expressing and understanding the greater part of the metapsychic phenomena."

His next book, *Notre Sixième Sens* (1927, translated as *Our Sixth Sense*, 1929), was a courageous attempt to grapple with the problem of **cryptesthesia.** He conceived it physiologically as a new sense which is sensitive to what he called the vibrations of reality (see **Sixth Sense**). It is a sweeping theory which, in its implications, is nearly as far reaching as the spirit theory. If obscure incidents, for the sole reason of having happened, keep on existing in vibrations it is to do violence to the intellect to conceive it as eliminatory of the survival of the soul.

In *La Grande Espérance* (1933), following an important monograph, *L'Avenir et la Premonition* (1931), he himself admitted that this vibratory theory is far from being sufficient for "there are cases in which *á la rigeur* one could suppose the intervention of a foreign intelligence."

These were the cases of veridical hallucinations. Even there he would have preferred to fall back on the vibratory explanation but for the puzzle of collective veridical **hallucinations** in which "one is almost compelled to admit the objective reality of the phantom." That admission did not allow him to doubt that "in cases of simple veridical hallucinations there is an objective reality as well." Pursuing this line of reasoning, he stated: "It appears that in certain cases phantoms are also inhabiting a house. I hesitate to write this down. It is so extraordinary that my pen almost refuses to write but just the same it is true."

Still, after having analyzed the purely psychological phenomena, if the choice was between the spirit hypothesis and a prodigious lucidity he would lean towards the second. For that explained all cases, whereas the former, although it is the better one in a small number of cases, was inadmissible in many others.

The grand hope of humanity lay in psychical research, in that immense incertitude which we feel in face of its extraordinary, truly absurd phenomena. "The more I reflect and weigh in my mind these materializations, hauntings, marvellous lucidity, apports, xenoglossie, apparitions and, above all, premonitions, the more I am persuaded that we know absolutely nothing of the universe which surrounds us. We live in a sort of dream and have not yet understood anything of the agitations and tumults of this dream."

Everything came down to this: "Either the human intelligence is capable of working miracles. I call miracles the phantoms, ectoplasm, lucidity, premonitions. Or assisting in our doings, controlling our thoughts, writing by our hand, or speaking by our voice there are, interblending with our life, mysterious, invisible entities, angels or demons, perhaps the souls of the dead, as the spiritualists are convinced. Death would not be death but the entrance into a new life. In each case we hurl ourselves against monstrous improbabilities (*invraisemblances*), we float in the inhabitual, the miraculous, the prodigious."

Prof. Richet died December 3, 1935.

Richmond, Kenneth Forbes (1882-1945)

Writer and educational psychologist who edited the *Journal* of the Society for Psychical Research, London, from 1939-45. He was also part-time secretary of the SPR from 1944-45. Born August 8, 1882 at Glenarmond, Scotland, he was educated at Glenarmond School. In 1914 he married Zoe Russell.

He published many articles on education, psychology and philosophy. His interest in psychical research was stimulated by the book *Raymond: Or Life After Death* by Sir Oliver **Lodge** (1916), which Richmond reviewed. He became a member of the Society for Psychical Research and investigated the phenomena of mediumship. He made a special study of the medium Mrs. Osborne **Leonard** and her **control** "Feda." In addition to his many articles in newspapers and journals, he also published *Evidence of Identity* (1939), 'Preliminary Studies of the Recorded Leonard Material' (*Proceedings* of the Society for Psychical Research, 1936).

He died November 30, 1945.

Richmond, Mrs. Cora L(inn) V(ictoria) (1840-1923)

The most famous American inspirational speaker and healer, variously known as Cora Scott, Cora Hatch, Mrs. Cora L. V. Tappan and Mrs. Cora L. V. Tappan-Richmond.

In 1851, as a child of eleven, she passed some months in the community of Adin **Ballou** at **Hopedale.** Passing into trance she was controlled by the spirit of young Ballou. Two years later, she appeared on platforms as a public speaker. At the age of sixteen she was famous, had traveled throughout the United States, often lecturing with great elocution before scientists on random-selected subjects.

In 1873, she paid a visit to England where she spent several years. At that time she had delivered some three thousand lectures.

"That the flow of verbiage never fails," wrote the arch-critic Frank **Podmore,** in his book *Modern Spiritualism* (2 vols., 1902), "is a small matter; Mrs. Tappan's trance-utterances surpass those of almost every other automatist in that there is a fairly coherent argument throughout. Two at least of the subjects set to her in 1874 'The Origin of Man' and 'The Comparative Influence of Science and Morality on the Rise and Progress of Nations,' may be presumed to have been little familiar. But the speaker is never at a loss . . . Again, we find none of the literary artifices by which ordinary speakers are wont to give relief—there is no antithesis, no climax, no irony or humour in any form. And the dead level of style reflects a dead level of sentiment; there is no scorn or indignation, no recognition of human effort and pain, no sense of the mystery of things. The style is clear, as jelly is clear; it is the protoplasm of human speech; and it is flavoured throughout with mild, cosmic emotions.

"Frequently at the close of an address Mrs. Tappan would recite an impromptu poem, again on a subject chosen at the moment by the audience. Some of these poems are strikingly melodious, and it is interesting to note how the melody continually overpowers the sense."

In later years, Mrs. Richmond became Pastor of the First Society of Spiritualists in Chicago. Subsequently, she assisted in founding the **National Spiritualist Association of Churches** and became its vice-President and national lecturer, which position she retained until her health gave way. She officiated at the funeral of Mrs. Nettie Colburn Maynard (Henrietta S. **Maynard**), June 30, 1892.

She was equally renowned for her healing power and for her **trance** utterances. Of her excursions into the spirit world in trance she brought back recollections of an absorbing interest. They were told in her book *My Experiments While out of the Body* (1923). As an author she was prolific and popular. *Discourses Through the Mediumship of Mrs. Cora L. V. Tappan*, (London, 1878) is a reprint of her trance addresses. *Soul—Its Nature, Relations and Expressions* (1887) was one of her important books. The story of the main period of her life was told by H. B. Barrett in *The Life and Work of Cora L. V. Richmond* (1895).

She died January 2, 1923.

Richmond, Thomas (c. 1870)

U.S. Senator, a leading man of Chicago, and also a medium. He was author of the book *God Dealing with Slavery* (1870), which told the story of his psychic influence which prevailed upon President Lincoln to abolish slavery. (See also Abraham **Lincoln:** Mrs. Henrietta S. **Maynard**)

Richmond, Zoe Blanche Russell (Mrs. Kenneth F. Richmond) (1888-)

Honorary associate of the Society for Psychical Research, London. Born June 14, 1888 in London, England. In 1914 she married Kenneth Forbes **Richmond**, whom she assisted in investigations of mediumship, in particular the phenomena of Mrs. Osborne **Leonard.**

She joined the Society for Psychical Research in 1922. Subsequently she developed the faculty of **automatic writing** and was herself the subject of SPR experiments. She contributed a number of articles to *Light* (published by the London Spiritualist Alliance), and published *Evidence of Purpose* (1938), in which she reviewed purposive messages through mediums from deceased individuals.

Ridley, Hazel (Hurd) (c. 1900- ?)

American **direct voice** medium of Buffalo, New York. Her psychic development began at the age of eighteen. "Grey Wolf," an Indian **control,** manifested in trance and declared that the medium would develop voices. She did. The voices were of a curious, whispering quality, coming from her larynx alone with no function of her mouth, lips and tongue.

Dr. Wilson G. Bailey, a physician of Camden, New Jersey, wrote in his book *No, Not Dead; They Live* (1923): "I filled her mouth with water and then with salt, and still the voice came through without interruption or impediment and I also punctured her arm when in trance, and though I drew blood she did not feel any pain."

Miss Ridley toured the American continent and paid three visits to England, the first in 1926, the second in 1931, the third in 1932. In the book "... *And After*" (1931), the author H. Dennis **Bradley** caustically condemned her performance as fraudulent rubbish.

Against this stands the testimony of Will Goldston, one of the greatest professional magicians in Europe, that she had genuine powers (see also **Magicians**).

In *Death Unveiled*, Mrs. D. U. Fletcher, wife of a Senator of Florida, described how through Miss Ridley's mediumship a violin was restored to its owner after thirty-seven years.

Rinaldo des Trois-Echelles du Mayne (died c. 1571)

A much-dreaded French sorcerer of the reign of Charles IX, who, at his execution, boasted before the king that he had in France three hundred thousand confederates, whom they could not thus commit to the flames—meaning, perhaps, the demons of the witches **Sabbat.** Trois-Echelles is cited in Jean **Bodin**'s *De la démonomanie des Sorciers* (1580 etc.).

Ringger, Peter (1923-)

Swiss author who has written on parapsychological subjects. Born February 1, 1923 at Zürich, Switzerland, he studied at Zürich University (Ph.D. 1948). In 1950 he married Lili Bonomi.

He was director of the Swiss Society for Parapsychology (Schweizer Parapsychologische Gesellschaft), which he founded in 1951. And edited the journal *Neue Wissenschaft* from 1950 onwards. He published a number of articles in this journal, and is also author of the following books: *Das Problem der Besessenheit* (The Problem of Possession, 1953), *Parapsychologie: Die Wissenschaft des Okkulten* (Parapsychology: The Science of the Occult, 1957), *Das Weltbild der Parapsychologie* (The World View of Parapsychology, 1959).

Rinpoche

An honorific used in Tibetan Buddhism, meaning "precious master." Specifically applied to the incarnate Lama **Tarthang Tulku** by his disciples in the U.S.

Ripley, George (c. 1415-1490)

British alchemist born in Ripley, Yorkshire, in which county his kinsfolk appear to have been powerful and numerous. He entered the Church becoming an Augustinian, and was subsequently appointed Canon of Bridlington in his native Yorkshire, a priory which had been founded in the time of Henry I by Walter de Ghent.

Ripley's sacerdotal office did not prevent him traveling, and he studied physical science and **alchemy** in France, Germany and Italy, even penetrating as far afield as the island of Rhodes, where he is said to have made a large quantity of gold for the knights of St. John of Jerusalem.

Afterwards he went to Rome, where he was dignified by the Pope, the result being that, when he returned to Bridlington, he found his brethren there intensely jealous of him. It was reported, indeed, that he even resigned his position and retired to a priory at Boston, but this story is probably unfounded, the likelihood being that Ripley the alchemist was confused with George Ripley, a Carmelite friar, who lived at Boston in the thirteenth century, and wrote a biography of St. Botolph.

Ripley died in England in 1490, but his fame did not die with him, and in fact his name continued to be familiar for many years after his decease.

He was among the first to popularize the alchemical writings attributed to Raymond **Lully,** which first became known in England about 1445, at which time an interest in alchemy was increasing steadily among English scholars—the more so because the law against multiplying gold had lately been repealed.

Ripley wrote a number of learned treatises himself, notably *Medulla Alchimiœ*, *The Treatise of Mercury* and *The Compound of Alchemie* (first printed 1591), latter work dedicated to King Edward IV.

A collected edition of his writings was issued at Cassel in Germany in 1649, while in 1678, an anonymous English writer published a strange volume in London, *Ripley Revived, or an Exposition upon George Ripley's Hermetico-Poetical Works.*

"Rita"

Pseudonym of British novelist and Spiritualist Mrs. Desmond **Humphreys** (died 1938).

Rita, A. (c. 1878)

British private medium, who sat only with friends in darkness, without passing into **trance,** and kept up a running conversation throughout with **apparitions** who apparently brought their own light.

In 1878, in a seance in Amsterdam, Holland, he was exposed in fraud as an accomplice of the medium Charles **Williams.** Masks, false beard and white muslin were found secreted on him.

Rivers, Olivia Burnett (Mrs. Dorris Wilmer Rivers) (1919-)

Assistant professor of psychology and parapsychologist. Born June 16, 1919 at Booneville, Mississippi, she studied at Blue Mountain College, Miss. (B.A. 1941) and Peabody College, Nashville, Tennessee (M.A. 1942). In 1946 she married Dorris Wilmer Rivers.

She was instructor, assistant professor of psychology, Southwestern Louisiana Institute, Lafayette, La. from 1942-44, assistant professor of psychology at Woman's College, University of North Carolina, Greensboro, N.C. From 1944-47, instructor at Mississippi State University from 1947-49 and from 1952 onwards; staff member of the Parapsychology

Laboratory, Duke University, Durham, N.C. from 1950-51.

Rivista Di Studi Psichici (Journal)

The first Italian psychical research periodical, founded by Dr. G. B. **Ermacora** with Georgio Finzi in January 1895. The journal was carefully and critically conducted on principles analogous to those of the *Proceedings* of the Society for Psychical Research, London, for many years.

After the death of Dr. Ermacora in 1898, Count Cesar Baudi **de Vesme** became its editor, publishing a simultaneous French edition (*Revue des Etudes Psychiques*) until 1905, when the journal was amalgamated with the *Annales des Sciences Psychiques.*

"Robert the Devil"

A popular thirteenth-century romance legend, known in France in both prose and verse forms as *Robert le Diable.* The story was printed in England c.1502 by Wynkyn de Worde (Caxton's assistant) as *Lyfe of Robert the Devyll.*

According to the story, Robert was the son of a Duke and Duchess of Normandy. He was endowed with marvelous physical strength, which he used only to minister to his evil passions. Explaining to him the cause of his wicked impulses, his mother told him that he had been born in answer to prayers addressed to the devil.

He sought religious advice, and was directed by the Pope to a hermit, who ordered him to maintain complete silence, to take his food from the mouths of dogs, to feign madness and to provoke abuse from common people without attempting to retaliate.

He became court fool to the Roman Emperor, and three times delivered the city from Saracen invasions, having, in each case, been prompted to fight by a heavenly message.

The emperor's dumb daughter was given speech in order to identify the savior of the city with the court fool, but he refused his due recompense, as well as her hand in marriage, and went back to the hermit, his former confessor.

Roberts, Estelle (1889-1970)

One of the most remarkable modern British Spiritualists. Born May 10, 1889, she claimed to see a spirit at the age of ten. At school, she constantly heard voices and saw apparitions. Her parents scolded her for having a too vivid imagination. At the age of fifteen, she was employed as a nursemaid, but the visions and voices followed her wherever she went.

She married at the age of seventeen, and later foretold her husband's death. After that she had a hard struggle to support her three children, and took a job as a waitress, working from 7 a.m. until late at night.

One day a neighbor persuaded her to attend a Spiritualist service, where the clairvoyant said: "You are a born medium. You have great work to do in the world." In due course, she became a medium, controlled by the spirit guide "Red Cloud." She manifested **clairvoyance, clairaudience, direct voice, materialization, psychometry,** psychic **healing, trance** oratory, **automatic writing** and production of **apports.**

She even gave a demonstration of Spiritualism in the august surroundings of the House of Commons in Britain. Her autobiography *Fifty Years a Medium* was published London, 1969; Avon, 1972.

Roberts, Jane (1929-)

Modern American psychic who became the medium for communications from an entity named "Seth," claimed to be a minor pope of the fourth century. She was born May 8, 1929.

In 1963, Jane and her husband Robert Butts experimented with an **ouija board** and received the first "Seth" messages. Later, Jane started going into trance, when "Seth" spoke through her, the voice and features of Jane changing character. In her autobiographical work *Adventures in Consciousness; An Introduction to Aspect Psychology* (Prentice-Hall, 1975), Jane gives the background and development of the "Seth" communications and discusses what she calls "Aspect Psychology," based on the concept that human consciousness is mobile.

The "Seth" communications developed in various levels of awareness (Seth I, II, and III). They were tape recorded, and have been transcribed and published in other books, notably *Seth Speaks; The Eternal Validity of the Soul* (1972) and *The Nature of Personal Reality; A Seth Book* (1974). The communications cover a wide range of topics dealing with aspects of personal belief and development, such as mental and physical health, illumination, good and evil, sexuality, art, creativity, spiritual grace, and modern problems.

An early book by Jane titled *How to Develop Your ESP Power* (Fell, New York, 1966) was reissued under the title *The Coming of Seth* (Pocket Books paperback, 1976). It describes the day-to-day emergence of the personality of "Seth" and the experiments involved, with suggestions for experiments which readers can attempt.

Jane subsequently regarded this early book as occasionally naive, reflecting her own inexperience at the time. It has now been supplemented by *The God of Jane; A Psychic Manifesto* (Prentice-Hall, 1981), discussing her early life, psychic experiences, and outlook. Other "Seth" books include: *The "Unknown" Reality* (1977), *The Nature of the Psyche; Its Human Expression* (1979), *The Individual and the Nature of Mass Events* (1981). Some of the "Seth" titles have been reprinted by Bantam in paperback.

She died September 5, 1984, after 504 consecutive days in a hospital at Elmira, New York. She had suffered for a long time from rheumatoid arthritis.

In Jane's posthumously published book *Seth, Dreams and Projection of Consciousness* (Stillpoint Publishing, 1986), her husband Robert Butts stated: "I think that I've had a number of waking and dreaming experiences in which Jane and I have communicated with each other since her physical death. So have others."

Additional books by Jane Roberts include: *The Seth Material* (1970), *The Education of Oversoul Seven* (novel, 1973), *Dialogues of the Soul and Mortal Self in Time* (1975), *Psychic Politics; An Aspect Psychology Book* (1976), *The World View of Paul Cezanne* (1977), *The Afterdeath Journal of an American Philosopher; The World View of William James* (1978), *The Further Education of Oversoul Seven* (novel, 1979), *The Nature of the Psyche; Its Human Expression. A Seth Book* (1979), *Emir's Education in the Proper Use of Magical Powers* (1979), *If We Live Again or, Public Magic and Private Love* (poems, 1982), *Oversoul Seven and the Museum of Time* (novel, 1984), *Dreams, "Evolution," and Value Fulfillment; A Seth Book* (2 vols., 1986).

Books by other writers dealing with Jane Roberts include: *Conversations with Seth. The Story of Jane Roberts's ESP Class* by Susan M. Watkins (2 vols., 1980-81), *Create Your Own Reality; A Seth Workbook* by Nancy Ashley (1984).

The **Austin Seth Center** was formed to spread the ideas of the Seth Material; it publishes the quarterly magazine *Reality Change.* (See also "**Seth**")

Roberts, Mrs. Etta (c. 1891)

American materialization medium. After being accused of fraud she held a remarkable test seance at Onset Grove, Onset Bay, Massachusetts on September 3, 1891, before sixty people. She was enclosed in a wire cage. Not only phantoms appeared, but the medium herself was mysteriously brought out of the cage without disturbing the seals.

Many of the phantoms were seen to build up before the cage, and also to transform into other shapes. The full account of the seance, signed by twelve people present, was published in the *Banner of Light* (September, 1891). There is a brief description of this seance in Dr. Paul **Joire**'s book *Psychical and Supernormal Phenomena* (1916), pp. 469-71.

Robertson, Olivia (1917-)

Irish writer and painter who founded the **Fellowship of Isis,** to revive worship and communication with the feminine principle in deity.

Born in London, she worked as a play leader in Dublin Corporation playgrounds, Eire, from 1941-45. Her book *St. Malachy's Court* (1946) is based on these experiences. Other publications include *Field of the Stranger* (1948, which was a Book Society choice and also published in a Braille edition); *The Golden Eye* (1949); *Miranda Speaks* (1950); *It's an Old Irish Custom* (1954); *Dublin Phoenix* (1957). She has exhibited paintings in Dublin.

She founded the Fellowship of Isis at Clonegal Castle, Enniscorthy, Eire in 1976.

Rocail

According to ancient Oriental legend, Rocail was the younger brother of Seth, the son of Adam. The circumstances of his history were picturesque and unique. A Dive, or giant of Mount Caucasus, finding himself in difficulties, applied for aid to the human race. Rocail offered his services to the giant, and so acceptable did these prove that the Dive made his benefactor his grand vizier.

For a long period Rocail governed the giant's realm with entire success, and reached a position of dignity and honor. However, when he felt himself growing old, he desired to leave behind him a more lasting monument than public respect, so he built a magnificent palace and sepulcher.

The palace he peopled with statues, which, by the power of magic, he made to walk and talk, and act in all ways as though they were living men, as, indeed, all who beheld them judged them to be (see Barthélemy d'Herbelot, *Bibliotheque Oriental,* Paris, 1697).

Rochas, Lt.-Col. Eugene Auguste-Albert D'Aiglun (1837-1914)

Prominent French psychical investigator, famous for his researches in human **emanations, hypnotism, reincarnation** and physical phenomena. He was born May 20, 1837. He served as attaché to the French General Staff during the Franco-Prussian War, retiring with the rank of major. He was Administrator of the École Polytechnique of Paris, but owing to his interest in occult investigations was forced to resign.

He was the first writer to acquaint the French public with the claims of Baron von **Reichenbach.** In his own experiments in the **exteriorization of sensitivity** he was preceded by Dr. Paul **Joire,** but he had unique observations to his credit.

He contributed an important theory to elucidation of the mystery of physical phenomena—the **exteriorization of motricity.** His book of the same title, in which it is expounded, summed up his experiments with the medium Eusapia **Palladino,** who was his guest in his country house at l'Agnelas, near Voiron and sat in the presence of a large committee of scientists.

The interest of Col. Rochas extended to every branch of psychical research. As an investigator he was keen and competent. C. V. **Miller,** the San Francisco materialization medium, came to Europe at his request, although in the event, he did not sit for Col. Rochas. Nor did Rochas succeed in witnessing full materializations with other mediums.

The second visit of Charles **Bailey,** the Australian **apport** medium, was arranged by him. Bailey came to Grenoble in 1910 and, as it turned out was exposed in fraud amid much excitement.

Books by Col. Rochas include: *La Science des Philosophes et l'Art des Thaumaturges dans l'Antiquité* (1882), *Les Forces non définies* (1887), (ed.) *Aphorismen über Sensitivität und Od,* by Karl Reichenbach undertitle *Le Fluide des Magnétiseurs* (1891), *Les Etats Profonds de l'hypnose* (1892), *L'Exteriorisation de la Sensibilité* (1895), *L'Exteriorisation de la motricité* (1896), *Receuil de documents relatifs à la levitation du corps humain* (1897), *Les États Superficiels de l'hypnose* (1898),

Les Effleuves odique; L'Envoutement; Les Frontières de la Science (1902), *Les Sentiments, la Musique et le Geste; Les Vies Successives* (1911), *La Suspension de la Vie* (1913).

Rochester Rappings

The outbreak of **rappings** which occurred in Hydesville, near Rochester, New York, in 1848, and which became popularly known as the "Rochester Rappings," was a peculiar importance, not because of its intrinsic superiority to any other **poltergeist** disturbance, but because it inaugurated the movement of modern **Spiritualism.**

Hydesville is a small village in Arcadia, Wayne County, New York, and there, in 1848, lived John D. Fox, with his wife and two young daughters, Margaretta, aged fifteen, and Kate, aged twelve. Their house was a small wooden structure previously tenanted by Michael Weekman, who afterwards claimed that he had frequently been disturbed by knockings and other strange sounds in the Hydesville house.

Towards the end of March 1848, the Fox family were much disturbed by mysterious rappings, and on the evening of the 31st, they went to bed early, hoping to get some undisturbed sleep. But the rappings broke out even more vigorously than they had done on the previous occasions, and Mrs. Fox, much alarmed and excited when the **raps** manifested signs of intelligence, decided to call in her neighbors to witness the phenomenon.

The neighbors heard the raps as distinctly as did the Fox family themselves. When the sounds had indicated that they were directed by some sort of intelligence, it was no difficult matter to get into communication with the unseen.

Questions were asked by the "sitters" of this informal "seance," and if the answer was in the affirmative, raps were heard, if in the negative, the silence remained unbroken. By this means the knocker indicated that he was a spirit, the spirit of a peddler who had been murdered for his money by a former resident in the house.

The raps also answered correctly other questions put, relating to the ages of those present and other particulars concerning persons who lived in the neighborhood.

In the few days immediately following, hundreds of people made their way to Hydesville to witness the marvel.

Fox's married son, David, who lived about two miles from his father's house, recorded a statement to the effect that the Fox family, following the directions of the raps, which indicated that the peddler was buried in the cellar, had begun to dig therein early in April, but were stopped by water.

Later, however, hair, bones, and teeth were found in the cellar. Vague rumors were afloat that a peddler had visited the village one winter, had been seen in the kitchen of the house afterwards tenanted by the Foxes, and had mysteriously disappeared, without fulfilling his promise to the villagers to return next day. But of real evidence there was not a scrap, whether for the murder or for the existence of the peddler, particulars of whose life were furnished by the raps.

Soon after these happenings, Kate Fox went to Auburn, and Margaretta to Rochester, New York, where her married sister Mrs. Fish (formerly Mrs. Underhill), lived, and at both places outbreaks of rappings occurred.

New mediums sprang up, circles were formed, and soon Spiritualism was fairly started on its career. (See also **Fox Sisters; Poltergeist; Spiritualism**)

Rock Music

The association of diabolical themes with rock music dated from the paranoid interpretations made by Charles **Manson** of numbers performed by The Beatles group in the 1960s, but the general trend to sensationalist themes, and presentations of other groups, allied with drug fantasies, culminated in more directly occult associations.

This trend reached a peak on December 6, 1969, when something like 300,000 young people gathered for a free pop music festival at Altamount Raceway, California, featuring the Rolling Stones group, who specialized in sensational themes. It was to be the great free hedonistic happening to which a modern generation aspired, huddling together in carnival costume or displaying oneself nude, smoking pot and listening to electronically amplified rock.

At the high point of the ceremony, they heard Mick Jagger singing "Homage to the Devil" while Hell's Angels hoodlums, engaged as bodyguards, beat up spectators and clubbed and kicked a man to death with incredible ferocity. After the event, everybody concerned blamed everybody else, but it seems clear that the sensationalist trend of rock music could have dangerous results if tied to occult fantasies.

Many pop stars have moved into a fantasy world of drug addiction, associated with aggressive and hysterical music. The contagious emotional atmosphere of large pop concerts by groups featuring weird sexual themes and over amplified heavy rock music can often be nearer to an orgy than a catharsis. Under some circumstances, it recalls descriptions of medieval **witchcraft** sabbats. (See also **Paranormal Music; Vibrations**)

In spring 1990, New York's Roman Catholic Church campaigned against the evil influence of extremist rock music. In a pulpit address, Cardinal John O'Connor stated that heavy metal music was "pornography in sound" and could invite demonic possession. Many other people have been disquieted by the way in which large-scale capital investment and media manipulation have promoted antisocial and negative emotions through rock music with an ambience of weird sex and drug taking, sometimes linked with Satanic cults.

The infamous Charles **Manson** believed that rock music contained secret subversive messages. Since then, various writers have claimed that some rock groups have deliberately inserted hidden Satanic messages in their lyrics, influencing listeners subliminally.

While such claims are often based on fundamentalist hysteria, there is some support for the claim that certain rock music groups have created an aura of sinister secret influence through such techniques as electronic overdubbing and "backward masking." The latter technique involves phrases and lines in lyrics which have a hidden message when played backwards. For example, an Electric Light Orchestra song is said to contain the backward message: "The music is reversible, but time is not. Turn back, turn back, turn back." Other examples quoted by fundamentalist opponents of rock music may be coincidental or as ludicrously far-fetched as the accusation that a Procter & Gamble logo was a secret expression of Satanism. One writer claimed that Black Oak Arkansas has a song with the backward message "Satan, Satan, He is God, He is God," while a Queen song "Another One Bites the Dust" seems to sound like "decide to smoke marijuana marijuana" in backward play.

Claims of this kind are not always absurd. The persistent accusations of Satanic messages through backward masking could have inspired some heavy metal groups to shock listeners by experimenting with secret messages.

The technique is not a new one, as many movie film editors are familiar with the effects of running sound backwards. As early as 1929, occultist Aleister Crowley also suggested listening to phonograph recordings in reverse. Much of black magic invocation involves reversing words and phrases, thus "God" becomes "Dog" by diabolic inversion. Interestingly enough, Jimmy Page of the Led Zeppelin rock group bought Aleister **Crowley**'s Scottish mansion of Boleskine, on the shores of Loch Ness. The group's song "Stairway to Heaven" is said to contain the message "Here's to my sweet Satan" if "there's still time" is reversed, while their "Houses of the Holy" album is said to contain the words "Satan is really Lord" in reverse.

For an authoritative survey of the belief that rock music contains hidden Satanic messages, see the valuable article "Backward Masking, and Other Backward Thoughts About Music" by Tom McIver. (*The Skeptical Inquirer*, vol. 13, Fall 1988), which also contains a useful bibliography. McIver concludes: "The ironic thing about the anti-backmasking crusade is that much of the music accused of harboring these demonic messages truly is an unhealthy influence on kids. Many of the rock musicians really are degenerate, greedy, contemptuous of authority, spoiled and selfish, and their music may indeed reflect and encourage these attitudes. But whatever bad influence this music may have, it is the result of the words and behavior of real people, not supernatural demons." (See also Charles **Manson; Nad;** Paranormal **Music; Vibrations**)

Recommended reading:

Aranza, Jacob. *Backward Masking Unmasked; Backward Satanic Messages of Rock and Roll Exposed*, Huntington House, Shreveport, 1983

Godwin, Jeff. *The Devil's Disciples; The Truth About Rock*, Chick Publications, Chino, 1985

Scott, Cyril. *Music; Its Secret Influence Throughout the Ages*, Rider, London, new & extended ed., 1950

Tane, David. *The Secret Power of Music; The Transformation of Self and Society Through Musical Energy*, Destiny Books, New York, 1984

Rodhe, Gosta (1912-)

Swedish physician with special interest in psychical research. Born May 11, 1912 at Kristanstad, Sweden, he studied at Caroline Medical School, Stockholm (M.D. 1939). In 1940 he married Helena Blanck.

He was a practicing pediatrician from 1948-53, child psychiatrist and school psychiatrist from 1948-59, chief medical officer of National Board of Education from 1959 onwards. He has been president of the Swedish Society for Psychical Research for many years.

Roerich, Nicholas K(onstantin) (1874-1947)

Versatile Russian born painter, poet, writer, and mystic, founder of the Agni Yoga Society. He was born in St. Petersburg on September 27, 1874, and educated at the University of St. Petersburg, becoming a graduate of the Law School. He studied drawing and painting at the Academy of Fine Arts, St. Petersburg, and in Paris, France. In 1901, he married Helena Ivanov Shaposhnikov, and they had two children. The Roerichs were initially influenced by the Theosophical writings of Madame **Blavatsky,** later by Rudolf **Steiner,** founder of Anthroposophy.

Between 1901-04, Roerich made a pilgrimage through Russia, producing 75 paintings, exhibited at La Purchase Exposition, St. Louis. From 1906-10, he was director of the School for Encouragement of Fine Arts, Russia. He was president of the Museum of Russian Arts, first president of "Mir Iskusstva" and a leader in Moscow Art Theatre Diagilev Ballet.

He came to the U.S. in 1920 under the auspices of the Art Institute of Chicago, and established a number of institutions with the aim of bringing humanity together through education, art, and culture. He traveled extensively and spent much time in Eastern countries, which strongly influenced his philosophy.

He exhibited his paintings in New York in December 1920. In 1921, he showed his work at the Institute of United Arts in New York. He took an active part in the foundation of Cor Ardeus (Flaming Heart) by a group of artists in Chicago, and in September 1922, he was concerned with an international cultural center named Corona Mundi (Crown of the World), promoting cooperation among scientists and cultural workers in different countries.

In 1923, President Calvin Coolidge sent greetings to the Roerich Museum which was inaugurated in New York. Roerich was also concerned with the American-Russian Cultural Association.

In all these activities, he was assisted by his wife Helena, who also published books on Oriental philosophy and the history of Buddhism. She carried on a friendly correspondence with President Franklin D. Roosevelt, and her letters are now housed at the Franklin Delano Roosevelt Library in Hyde Park, New York.

Roerich spent five years in Central Asia as head of an expedition, making 500 paintings. He took a great interest in U.S. agriculture at a time when soil erosion threatened the holdings of American farmers during the thirties. Roerich had established an Institute at Uruswathi, in Kulu, India, and sent specimens of drought-resistant plants collected in Central Asia to botanical research agencies in the U.S. At the suggestion of the U.S. Department of Agriculture he headed an expedition to collect seeds of plants that prevented the destruction of fertile layers of soil. He also headed a further expedition to Japan in May 1934, and later continued these studies in Manchuria.

Although the Roerichs had left Russia after the revolution, they devoted much time to attempting to bring about friendly cultural relations between the U.S.S.R. and the U.S. Their efforts were appreciated by the Soviet authorities, and Georgi Chickerin, a People's Commissar for Foreign Affairs, once described Roerich as "a half-Communist and a half-Buddhist." In one of Helena Roerich's letters to President Roosevelt, she wrote: "The attention of the President must turn to the East. Speaking of the East, he must have in mind also Russia . . . America was since long linked with Asia. . . . Once must accept that the peoples occupying the larger part of Asia are destined to respond to the friendship of America. . . . Russia is the equibalance of America and only with such a construction will the World Peace become a solved problem."

Roerich was accepted internationally at a time when his mysticism and artistic talents ranked equally with his efforts to improve agriculture and to bring about world peace. He was honored by many counties, and awards included: Commander, lst class, Royal Swedish Order of North Star; Grand Cross, Legion of Honor (France); Order of Saint Sava, lst class (Yugoslavia); Commander of Order of Imperial Russians of St. Stanislas, St. Anne and St. Vladimir; medal of city of Bruges, Belgium (for plan of Roerich Pact and Banner of Peace). His Roerich Pact and Banner of Peace was signed by twenty-two Pan-American countries at the White House, Washington, D.C., in 1935.

Among his many artistic activities, he was responsible for a number of works for the Chicago Opera Company, for the Russian Ballet (scenery in "Prince Igor"), for Stanislavsky setting of "Peer Gynt." He wrote libretto, designed scenery and costumes for "Sacre du Printempts" for which Stravinsky composed music. Ten Roerich Halls were established, in Paris, Belgrade, Riga, Benares, Bruges, Allahabad, Zagreb, Buenos Aires, Kyoto, and Praha.

He propagated a system of Agni Yoga—the yoga of fire. Fire symbolizes life, knowledge, feeling and action. Roerich claimed that this yoga dealt with intuition, direct insight, instant understanding. Books dealing with Roerich's concept of Agni Yoga have been published by the Agni Yoga Society, 319 West 107 Street, New York, N.Y. 10025. Roerich's own works included: *Complete Work* (1914), *Adamant* (1924), *The Messenger* (1925), *Paths of Blessing* (1925), *Himalaya* (1926), *Joys of Sikkim* (1928), *Heart of Asia* (1930), *Flame in Chalice* (1930), *Shambhala (1936)*, *Realm of Light* (1931), *Maitreya* (1932), *Fiery Stronghold* (1933), *Sacred Vigil* (1934), *Gates into the Future* (1936), *The Immutable* (1936).

Roerich died December 12, 1947. For detailed information on his teachings and life work, see *Nicholas Roerich* by Garabed Paelian, published Aquarian Education Group (30188 Mulholland Highway, Agoura, California 91301), 1974.

Roessling, Bernhardt Emil (1892-1961)

Teacher who wrote on parapsychology. Born November 27, 1892 in Brussels, Belgium, he studied at Green Cove Spring, Florida, U.S. and Louvain University, Belgium (Doctor of psychology 1914). In 1917 he married Clara Agnes Pinyard.

He was a language teacher at St. Joseph's College, Philadelphia from 1919-23, assistant to agronomy professor at University of Florida from 1924-27, high school teacher at Florida and Georgia public schools from 1929-52.

He was executive secretary of the Florida Society for Psychical Research, vice-president of the Florida Wildlife Federation and a member of the National Education Association. From 1955 onwards Dr. Roessling investigated mental and physical mediumship, and contributed articles on psychical research to *Psychic Observer and Chimes.*

Rofé, (Fevzi) Husein (1922-   )

Author, teacher, orientalist who was active in the field of parapsychology and spiritual development. Born May 3, 1922 in Manchester, England, he studied at University of London. He traveled widely as a lecturer and teacher, particularly in Eastern countries. He became a fellow of the Royal Asiatic Society, London.

He served in the Royal Air Force, 1940-45, becoming sergeant, and received the Africa Star. He was a teacher at the London School of Languages, England, 1945-46; interpreter, British Consulate, Tetuan, Morocco, 1947-49, teacher in government secondary schools, Djokjakarta, Indonesia, 1950-54, Turkish Lycee, Nicosia, Cyprus, 1955-56; language tutor, University of Hong Kong, 1959-65; head of translation service, Asian Development Bank, Manila, Philippines, 197 onwards; occasional translator for U.N. agencies in Europe.

He took special interest in spiritual **healing** and was associated with the **Subud** movement, on which he published two books: *Path of Subud* (1959), *Reflections on Subud* (1961). Other publications included: *Evolution of Islam* (1952), (with T. C. Lai) *Things Chinese* (1971). He also contributed papers on parapsychological topics to *The Voice* (England), *Die Weisse Fahne* (Germany), *La Conciencia* (Argentina), *Ananaikyo* (Japan) and *Tomorrow.*

Rogo, D. Scott (1950-1990)

Parapsychologist, and writer on psychological, scientific and psychic subjects. Born February 1, 1950 in Los Angeles, California, he studied at University of Cincinnati from 1967-68, San Fernando Valley State College (B.A. 1971).

A freelance musician, he became a student of parapsychology, and has written various articles and books on the subject. In 1968-69 he coordinated an experimental course in parapsychology at the University of California, Los Angeles. He is a member of American Society for Psychical Research, Society for Psychical Research (London).

He has contributed to various journals, including *Psychic* (renamed *New Realities*), for whom he became Reviews Editor. His paper 'ESP in the Ganzfield: An Exploration of Parameters' was published in *Research in Parapsychology 1975*, edited J. D. Morris, W. G. Roll & R. L. Morris (1976). His books include: *NAD: a Study of Some Unusual Other-World Experiences* (1970), *NAD Vol. 2: A Psychic Study of "The Music of the Spheres"* (1972), *Methods and Models for Education in Parapsychology* (1973), *The Welcoming Silence* (1973), *An Experience of Phantoms* (1974), *Parapsychology: a Century of Inquiry* (1975), *In Search of the Unknown: the Odyssey of a Psychic Investigator* (1976), *Exploring Psychic Phenomena* (1976), *Parapsychology* (1976), *The Haunted Universe* (1977), *Exploring the Out-of-Body Experience* (1977), *PK; The Psychic Force of the Will* (1977), *Man Does Survive Death* (1977), *Mind Beyond the Body; The Mystery of ESP Projection* (1978), *Haunted Houses Handbook* (1978), *Minds and Motion* (1978), *The Poltergeist Experience* (1979), (with Raymond Bayless) *Phone Calls from the Dead* (1979), *The Poltergeist Experience* (1979), *Miracles: A Parascientific Study into Wondrous Phenomena* (1982), *Leaving the Body: A Practical Guide to Astral Projection* (1983), *Reincarnation* (1985).

"Rohmer, Sax"

Pseudonym of British author Arthur H. (Sarsfield) **Ward,** creator of the celebrated fictional character Dr. Fu-Manchu, and a student of the occult.

Roll, William George, Jr. (1926-   )

Prominent parapsychologist. Born July 3, 1926 in Bremen, Germany, he studied at University of California, Berkeley (B.A. 1949) and Oxford University, England (B.Litt. 1960). In 1950 he married Muriel Gold.

He was Louis K. Anspacher Visting Research Fellow at Duke University, Durham, North Carolina in 1957, research associate at Parapsychology Laboratory, Duke University from 1958-60, director of research project on incorporeal personal agency (concerned with survival) at the Parapsychological Laboratory 1960, member of the editorial staff of *Journal of Parapsychology* from 1958-60, project director of **Psychical Research Foundation** set up by Charles E. **Ozanne** from 1961 onwards.

He was president of the Oxford University Society for Psychical Research, England from 1952-57, member of the founding council of the Parapsychology Association 1957, treasurer (1958), secretary (1959-60), vice-president (1963); member of the Society for Psychical Research, London, American Society for Psychical Research, American Association for Advancement of Science, grantee of Committee for Advanced Studies, Oxford University 1952, grantee of Parapsychology Foundation 1954-56. He attended the First International Conference on Parapsychology at Utrecht, 1953, Conference on Spontaneous Phenomena at Cambridge 1955, Duke Symposium on Incorporeal Personal Agency 1959.

During his period at Oxford University, his researches covered the effects of hypnosis, and the correlation of ESP with personality traits. With the help of the Parapsychology Foundation he was able to establish a laboratory and reading room for psi experiments at Oxford. He has also investigated recurrent spontaneous phenomena. He has published a number of articles in the *Journal of Parapsychology*, the *Journal* of the American Society for Psychical Research, and *Journal* of the SPR, London. Since 1963 he edited *Theta*, quarterly journal for research on the problem of survival after bodily death.

He contributed to *The Highest State of Consciousness* edited by John White (1970). Other books include: *The Poltergeist* (1972: 1976), (edited with J. D. Morris & R. L. Morris) *Research in Parapsychology 1973* (1974), also editions for *1974, 1975, 1976*, sole editor editions for *1977, 1978, 1979*, coeditor (with John Beloff & John McAllister) *1980*, coeditor (with Robert L. Morris & Rhea A. White) *1981, 1982; Theory and Experiment in Psychical Research* (1975), (contributor) *Psychiatry and Mysticism* edited by Stanley R. Dean (1975), (contributor) *Philosophical Dimensions of Parapsychology* edited by Hoyt Edge & James Wheatley (1976), (contributor) *Handbook of Parapsychology* edited by Benjamin B. Wolman (1976).

Romains, Jules (1885-1972)

Famous French author who also first studied the phenomenon of **Eyeless Sight.** Born Louis Farigoule on August 26, 1885 at Saint-Julien, Chapteuil in Velay, Haute-Loire district of France, he grew up in Paris. He was a talented scholar and received his bachelor's degree by 1903.

In that year he also had a sudden mystical experience of universalism, which he embodied in his philosophy of "Unanism," expressed in his book of poems *La Vie Unanime* (1908).

In 1909, he received his degree in philosophy and science, becoming professor of philosophy at the Lycée of Brest. He published some more poems, a play and a novel before World War I shattered his universalist hopes of human society. After the war he devoted much time to travel and writing.

His book on Eyeless Sight is his only scientific work. First published in France as *La Vision extra-rétinienne*, an English translation titled *Eyeless Sight* was published London, 1924. It dealt with his researches in developing the faculty of vision in blind people through some little-known faculty of perception of a kind usually associated with psychics.

The book should have opened up an exciting new direction for further research, but instead it was ridiculed by orthodox scientists and Farigoule refused access to subjects for experiments.

He abandoned his scientific researches, and under the name "Jules Romains" became a universally acclaimed poet, dramatist and novelist. He is best known for his vast series of novels surveying the world scene from the beginning of the twentieth century into modern times, published in English as *Men of Good Will* in 27 volumes (1932-48). Romains died August 14, 1972.

The subject of Eyeless Sight was revived again in 1963 with the Soviet experiments in 'Fingertip Vision' with Rosa **Kuleshova,** and Romains lived to see his own researches taken up again by Dr. Yvonne Duplessis in France. His book *Eyeless Sight* was reissued by Citadel, 1978. (See also **Eyeless Sight;** Seeing with the **Stomach; Transposition of the Senses**)

Rome (Ancient Religion & Magic)

Magical practice was widespread amongst the ancient Romans. Magic was the motive power of their worship, which was largely an organized system of magical rites for communal ends. It was the basis of their mode of thought and outlook upon the world, it entered into every moment and action of their daily life, it affected their laws and customs.

This ingrained tendency, instead of diminishing, developed to an enormous extent, into a great system of superstition, and in the later years led to a frenzy for strange gods, borrowed from various countries. In times of misfortune and disaster, the Romans were always ready to borrow a god if his favors promised more than those of their own deities.

Although there was a strong conservative element in the native character, and the "custom of the elders" was strongly upheld by the priestly fraternity, yet this usually gave way before the will and temper of the people. Thus, as a rock shows its geological history by its differing strata, so the theogony of the Roman gods tells its tale of the race who conceived it. There are prehistoric nature deities, borrowed from indigenous tribes, gods of the Sabines, from whom the young colony stole its wives; gods of the Etruscans, of the Egyptians, Greeks and Persians. The temple of Jupiter on the Capitol contained the altar of a primitive deity, a stone-god, Terminus, the spirit of boundaries. In the temple of Diana of the Grove, a fountain nymph was worshiped. Instances of this kind were numerous.

Belief in Spirits

In addition to the gods, there were spirits to be propitiated. Indeed the objects offered to the Roman for adoration were numberless. Apuleius gave a description of this when he told of a country road where one might meet an altar wreathed with flowers, a cave hung with garlands, an oak tree laden with horns of cattle, a hill marked by fences as sacred, a log rough-hewn into shape, an altar of turf smoking with libations, or a stone anointed with oil.

Every single action of man's daily life had a presiding spirit; so too did commerce and husbandry. There was Ednea concerned with eating, Potina with drinking; there were spirits of departure, of journeying, of approaching and homecoming. In commerce there was Mercurius, the spirit of gain, Pecunia of money; in farming, the spirits of cutting, grinding, sowing and bee-keeping. A deity presided over streets and highways; there was Cloacina, a goddess of the sewers, Mephitis, a spirit of bad smells. Spirits of evil also had to be propitiated by pacificatory rites, such as Robigo, the spirit of mildew. In Rome there was an altar to Fever and Bad Fortune.

From the country came Silvanus, god of farms and woods, and his Fauns and nymphs with Picus, the woodpecker god who had fed the twins Romulus and Remus with berries. All these were possessed of influences, and were approached with peculiar rites. The names of these spirits were inscribed on tablets, *indigitamenta*, which were in the charge of the pontiffs, who thus knew which spirit to evoke according to need. Most of these spirits were animistic in origin.

Rites and Worship

Roman worship consisted of magical rites destined to propitiate the powers controlling human beings, to bring people into touch with them, to renew life and that which supported it, the land with its trees, corn and cattle, to stop that process of degeneration constantly set in motion by evil influences.

Everything connected with worship typified this restoration. The priests, who represented the life of the community, were therefore bound by strict observances from endangering it in any way. Rules as to attire, eating and touch were numerous. Sacrifices were systematized according to the end desired and the deity invoked.

There were rules as to whether the victim must be young or full-grown, male or female; oxen were to be offered to Jupiter and Mars, swine to Juno, to Ceres the corn-goddess and to Silvanus. At one shrine, a cow in calf was sacrificed and the ashes of the unborn young were of special magical efficacy. Even human sacrifice existed within historical times. After the battle of Cannæ, the Romans had sought to divert misfortune by burying two Greeks alive in the cattle-market, while in the time of Julius Cæsar, two men were put to death with sacrificial solemnities by the Pontiff and Flamen of Mars. Again, in the time of Cicero and Horace, boys were killed for magical purposes.

Fire possessed great virtue and was held sacred in the worship of Vesta, in early belief Vesta being the fire itself; it presided over the family hearth; it restored purity and conferred protection.

Blood had the same quality and smeared on the face of the god symbolized and brought about the oneness of the deity with the community. On great occasions the statue of Jupiter was treated thus: the priests of Bellona made incisions in their shoulders and sprinkled the blood upon the image. The face of a triumphant general was painted with vermilion to represent blood.

Kneeling and prostration brought one into direct contact with the earth of the sacred place.

Music was also used as a species of incantation, probably deriving its origin in sound made to drive away evil spirits. Dancing too was of magical efficacy. In Rome there were colleges of dancers for the purposes of religion, youths who danced in solemn measure about the altars, who, in the sacred month of Mars took part in the festivals and sent throughout the city dancing and singing. One authority stated that there were four kinds of "holy solemnity"—sacrifice, sacred banquets, public festivals and games. Theatrical performances also belonged to this category, in one instance being used as a means of diverting a pestilence.

The sacred banquets were often decreed by the Senate as thanksgiving to the gods. Tables were spread with a sumptuous repast in the public places and were first offered to the statues of the deities seated around.

The festivals were numerous, all of a magical and symbolic nature. In the spring there was the *Parilia*, when fires of straw were lighted, through which persons passed to be purified; the *Cerealia*, celebrated with sacrifice and offerings to Ceres, the corn-goddess, and followed by banquets. The *Lupercalia*, the festival of Faunus, was held in February and symbolized the wakening of Spring and growth. Goats were slain as sacrifice and with their blood the *Luperci*, youths clad in skins, smeared their faces. They took thongs of the goat-skin and, laughing wildly, rushed through the city striking the crowd, Roman matrons believing that the blows thus received rendered them prolific.

Juno, the goddess of marriage and childbirth, also had her festival, the *Matronalia*, celebrated by the women of Rome. There were the festivals of the dead, when the door leading to the other world was opened, the stone removed from its entrance in the Comitium, and the shades coming forth were appeased with offerings. On these days, three times in the year, when the gods of gloom were abroad, complete cessation from all work was decreed. No battle could be fought nor ship set sail, neither could a man marry.

To the Sacred Games were taken the statues of the gods in gorgeous procession, chariots of silver, companies of priests, youths singing and dancing. The gods viewed the games reclining on couches.

The chariot races also partook of the nature of rites. After the races, in the Field of Mars, came one of the most important Roman rites, the sacrifice of the October Horse. The right-hand horse of the victorious team was sacrificed to Mars, and the tail of the animal, running with blood, carried to the Altar of the Regia. The blood was stored in the temple of Vesta until the following spring and used in the sacrifice of the festival of Parilia. The sacrifice was essentially magical, all citizens present being looked upon as purified by the blood-sprinkling and lustral bonfire.

The Roman outlook upon life was largely colored by magic. Bodily foes had their counterpart in the unseen world, wandering spirits of the dead, spirits of evil, the anger of innocently offended deities, the menace of the evil eye. Portents and prodigies were everywhere. In the heavens, strange things might be seen. The sun had been known to double, even treble itself, its light turn to blood, or a magical halo to appear round the orb. Thunder and lightning were always fraught with presage. Jove was angered when he opened the heavens and hurled his bolts to earth.

Phantoms, too, hovered amid the clouds, a great fleet of ships had been seen sailing over the marshes. Upon the Campagna, the gods were observed in conflict, and afterwards tracks of the combatants were visible across the plain. Unearthly voices were heard amid the mountains and groves and cries of portent had sounded within the temples.

Blood haunted the Roman imagination. Sometimes it was said to have covered the land as a mantle, the standing corn was dyed with blood, the rivers and fountains flowed with it, while walls and statues were covered with a bloody sweat.

The flight and song of birds might be foretelling the decrees of Fate; unappeased spirits of the dead were known to lurk near and steal away the souls of men and then they too were dead. All these happenings were attributable to the gods and spirits, who, if the portent be one of menace, must be propitiated, if one of good fortune, thanked with offerings.

Down to later times, this deep belief in the occurrence of prodigies persisted. When Otho set out for Italy in 69 A.D., Rome rang with reports of a gigantic phantom rushing forth from the Temple of Juno, of the statue of Julius turning from east to west.

Divination and Augury

Divination was connected with the Roman worship. There was a spot on the Capitol from which the augur, with veiled head, read the auspices in the flight of birds. Augurs also accompanied armies and fleets and read the omens before an engagement was entered upon.

Divination was also practiced by reading the intestines of animals, by dreams, by divine possession, as in the case of the Oracles, when prophecies were uttered. These had been gathered together in the **Sibylline Books** and were consulted as oracles by the State. With the worship of Fortune were connected the *Lots of Praœneste*. The questions put to the goddess were answered by means of oaken lots which a boy drew from a case made of sacred wood. The fortune-tellers also used a narrow-necked urn which, filled with water, only allowed one lot at a time to rise.

Astrologers from Chaldea were also much sought after and were attached to the kingly and noble houses. Familiar things of everyday life were of magical import. Words and Numbers, especially odd ones, were of special significance. The Kalends, Nones and Ides were so arranged as to fall upon odd days. Touch was binding, and so recognized in the law of Rome, as the grasp of a thing sold, from a slave to a turf of distant estate. Knotting and twisting of thread was injurious, so that women must never pass by cornfields twisting their spindles, they must not even be uncovered.

There was a strange sympathy between the trees and mankind, and great honor was paid to the sacred trees of Rome. On the oak tree of Jupiter, the triumphant general hung the shield and arms of his fallen foe, while the hedges about the Temple of Diana at Nemi were covered with votive offerings. The trees also harbored the spirits of the dead, who came forth as dreams to the souls of men. **Pliny** the Elder stated in this matter "Trees have a soul since nothing on earth lives without one. They are the temples of spirits and the simple countryside dedicates still a noble tree to some god. The various kinds of trees are sacred to their protecting spirits: the oak to Jupiter, the laurel to Apollo, olive to Minerva, myrtle to Venus, white poplar to Hercules."

These trees therefore partook of the nature of their presiding spirits and it was desirable to bring about communion with their magical influence, as in the spring, when laurel boughs were hung at the doors of the flamens and pontiffs, and in the temple of Vesta, where they remained hanging until the following year. Trees and their leaves were also possessed of healing and purifying value. Laurel was used for the latter quality as in the Roman triumphs the fasces of the commander, the spears and javelins of legionaries were wreathed with its branches to purify them from the blood of the enemy.

Man himself had a presiding spirit, his genius, each woman her "Juno" and the Saturnalia was really a holiday for this "other self." The Roman kept his birthday in honor of his genius, offering frankincense, cakes and unmixed wine on an altar garlanded with flowers and making solemn prayers for the coming year. City and village had their genii, also bodies of men from the senate to the scullions.

Beliefs About Death

Death was believed to be the life and soul enticed away by revengeful ghosts, hence death would never occur save by such agencies. The dead therefore must be appeased with offerings or else they wandered abroad working evil among the living.

This belief was present in Ovid's lines: "Once upon a time the great feast of the dead was not observed and the manes failed to receive the customary gifts, the fruit, the salt, the corn steeped in unmixed wine, the violets. The injured spirits revenged themselves on the living and the city was encircled with the funeral fires of their victims. The townsfolk heard their grandsires complaining in the quiet hours of the night, and told each other how the unsubstantial troop of monstrous specters rising from their tombs, shrieked along the city streets and up and down the fields." Beans were used in the funeral feasts. They were supposed to harbor the souls of the dead, and the bean-blossom to be inscribed with characters of mourning.

Dreams were considered of great importance by the Romans and many historical instances of prophetic dreams may be found. They were thought to be like birds, the "bronze-colored" hawks; they were also thought to be the souls of human beings visiting others in their sleep or the souls of the dead returning to earth. In Virgil much may be found on this subject. Lucretius tried to find a scientific reason for dreams; Cicero, although writing in a slighting manner of the prevalent belief in these manifestations of sleep, yet recorded dreams of his own, which events proved true.

Sorcery & Witchcraft

Sorcery in all its forms, love-magic and death-magic was rife amongst all classes, besides necromantic practices. There were charms and spells for everything under the sun. The rain-charm of the pontiffs consisting of the throwing of puppets into the Tiber. The charm against thunderbolts was compounded of onions, hair and sprats. The charm against an epidemic required the matrons of Rome to sweep the temple-floors with their hair. There were many more charms, including the simple love-charm strung around the neck of the country maiden.

Witches were prevalent. The poets often chose these sinister figures for their subjects, as when Horace described the ghastly rites of two witches in the cemetery of the Esquiline.

Under the light of the new moon they crawled about looking for poisonous herbs and bones. They called the specters to a banquet consisting of a black lamb torn to pieces with their teeth, and afterwards these phantoms had to answer the questions of the sorceresses.

Witches made images of their victims and prayed to the infernal powers for help; hounds and snakes glided over the ground, the moon turned to blood, and as the images were melted so the lives of the victims ebbed away.

Virgil gave a picture of a sorceress performing love-magic by means of a waxen image of the youth whose love she desired. Lucan, in his *Pharsalia,* treated of Thessaly, notorious in all ages for sorcery and drew a terrific figure of Erichtho, a sorceress of illimitable powers, one whom even the gods obeyed, to whom the forces of earth and heaven were bond-slaves, and Fate awaited her least command.

Both Nero and his mother Agrippina were reported to have had recourse to the infamous arts of sorcery, while in the New Testament may be found testimony as to these practices in Rome.

The attitude of the cultured class towards magic is illustrated by an illuminating passage to be found in the writings of Pliny the Elder. He stated "The art of magic has prevailed in most ages an in most parts of the globe. Let no one wonder that it has wielded very great authority inasmuch as it embraces three other sources of influence. No one doubts that it took its rise in medicine and sought to cloak itself in the garb of a science more profound and holy than the common run. It added to its tempting promises the force of religion, after which the human race is groping, especially at this time. Further it has brought in the arts of astrology and divination. For everyone desires to know what is to come to him and believes that certainty can be gained by consulting the stars. Having in this way taken captive the feelings of man by a triple chain, it has reached such a pitch that it rules over all the world and in the East, governs the King of Kings." (See also **Italy**)

Rose

From early times, the rose has been an emblem of silence. Eros, in Greek mythology, presents a rose to the god of silence, and to this day *sub rosa*, or "under the rose," means the keeping of a secret.

Roses were used in very early times as a potent ingredient in love philters. In Greece it was customary to leave bequests for the maintenance of rose gardens, a custom which as come down to recent times. Rose gardens were common during the Middle Ages. According to Indian mythology, one of the wives of Vishnu was found in a rose.

In Rome it was the custom to bless the rose on a certain Sunday, called Rose Sunday. The custom of blessing the golden rose came into vogue about the eleventh century. The golden rose thus consecrated was given to princes as a mark of the Roman Pontiffs' favor.

In the east, it was believed that the first rose was generated by a tear of the prophet Mohammed, and it was further believed that on a certain day in the year the rose had a heart of gold.

In the west of Scotland, if a white rose bloomed in autumn it was a token of an early marriage. The red rose, it was said, would not bloom over a grave. If a young girl had several lovers, and wished to know which of them would be her husband, she would take a rose leaf for each of her sweethearts, and, naming each leaf after the name of one of her lovers, she would watch them until one after another they sank, and the last to sink would be her future husband.

Rose leaves thrown upon a fire gave good luck. If a rose bush were pruned on St. John's Eve, it would bloom again in the autumn. Superstitions respecting the rose are more numerous in England than in Scotland.

The rose has also been a prominent symbol in occultism, relating to enchantment and sacred mysteries. The rose color has special significance in the **Rosicrucians,** the Brotherhood of the Rosy Cross. The rose has often been used in the symbolism of **alchemy.** Both pagan and Christian religions have considered the rose as a symbol of regeneration and love.

Rose, Ronald K(riss) H(ume) (1920-)

Australian author who has investigated parapsychology and written extensively on the subject. Born March 9, 1920 at Lakemba, New South Wales, Australia, he studied at University of Queensland (B.A. 1953). In 1942 he married Lyndon Margaret Harvey.

He was in the Public Relations Department of New South Wales Railways from 1935-49, was student, research worker from 1950-51, statistician from 1951-52, journalist from 1953-54; research worker from 1955-56, Information Officer of Department of Territories, Commonwealth of Australia from 1957 onwards. He is an associate member of the British Psychological Society.

He has taken special interest in investigating parapsychology amongst primitive peoples in Australia, New Zealand and Samoa. His articles in *Tomorrow* magazine include: 'Australia's Medicine Men' (Spring 1954), 'Crisis Telepathy in Australia' (Winter 1957); in *Journal* of the American Society for Psychical Research: 'Psi and Australian Aborigines' (Jan. 1952); in *Journal of Parapsychology*: 'Some Notes on a Preliminary Experiment with Six Dice' (June 1950), 'Experiments in ESP and PK with Aboriginal Subjects' (Sept. 1952), 'A Second Report on Psi Experiments with Australian Aborigines' (June 1955).

He is also the author of *Living Magic* (U.S. 1956; British ed. 1957) based on his observations of parapsychological phenomena amongst Australian aborigines, *South Seas Magic* (1959), and (with Mrs. Rose) *People in the Sun.* In 1968 Mr. Rose's book *Living Magic* was reissued in paperback under the title *Primitive Psychic Power; the Realities underlying the psychical practices and beliefs of Australian aborigines*, with a foreword by J. B. Rhine (New American Library). Mr. and Mrs. Rose appear to have been the first to conduct ESP and PK tests with these primitive peoples.

"Rosemary's Baby"

The sensational occult novel by Ira Levin, first published by Random House in 1967. Around it grew a terrifying network of diabolical events.

The Paramount movie version was directed by Roman Polanski, starring Mia Farrow, with Satanist Anton **LaVey** playing the part of the Devil and advising him on the production. LaVey called the film "the best paid commercial for Satanism since the Inquisition." It sparked off worldwide fascination with Satanism in the wake of Anton LaVey's proclamation of a new Satanic era.

Polanski's earlier movies had scenes of sadistic cruelty. His 1965 movie *Repulsion* featured a girl with hallucinations who ends up hacking and beating two men to death. Polanski's wife Sharon Tate had earlier played in a film *Eye of the Devil,* for which British "King of the Witches" Alex **Sanders** (an antiseptic British version of LaVey) was hired as technical adviser. Sanders claimed to have initiated Sharon Tate into his witch coven.

On June 5, 1968, ten days before *Rosemary's Baby* was released, Roman and Sharon dined with Robert Kennedy in Malibu; shortly afterwards Kennedy left for the Ambassador Hotel where he was assassinated.

On August 7, 1969, members of Charles **Manson's** Satanist Family brutally stabbed, mutilated and murdered Sharon Tate and her unborn baby, together with four other people at the Polanski residence, Los Angeles.

There is a curious irony in the fact that the new premises of the **American Society for Psychical Research** were housed immediately behind the famous Dakota Apartments in Manhattan, the large Gothic building that was the setting for *Rosemary's Baby.*

Rosen, (Samuel) Paul (c. 1890)

A sovereign Grand Inspector-General of the 33rd degree of the French rite of Masonry, who in 1888 decided that Masonry was diabolical in conception, and to prove his strictures published a work called *Satan et Cie.* The Satanism credited to Freemasonry by Rosen was social anarchy and the destruction of the Catholic religion.

In 1890, he published a further attack titled *L'Ennemie Sociale; histoire documentée des faits et gestes de la Franc-Maçonnerie de 1717 à 1890 en France, en Belgie et en Italie.* He made wild accusations of a "supreme directory" of Freemasonry in Berlin.

Such paranoid conspiracy accusations were common from the eighteenth century onwards, reflecting social unrest and revolutionary plots of the period, usually branding Freemasonry as anti-Catholic, pro-Jewish, subversive or even diabolical.

Rosen's delusions were soon eclipsed by the infamous and sustained hoaxes of Gabriel **Jogand-Pagès,** who, under the name "Léo Taxil" claimed to have exposed Satanism in Freemasonry. This plot was double-edged, since it was also designed to embarrass and compromise the Catholic church.

Rosher, Grace (died 1980)

Noted British automatist of exponent of **Automatic Writing.**

She was an artist who exhibited miniature paintings in the Royal Academy, London. Her psychic talent became manifest after the loss of her fiance Gordon E. Burdick, whom she had known for many years. In June 1956, he was serving in the Canadian Navy, stationed at Vancouver, and intended to come to London to marry Miss Rosher. A week before sailing, he died.

Fifteen months later, Grace Rosher had written a letter concerning an aunt, and was wondering if she had time to write another letter before tea-time when she had a strong urge to keep her hand on the writing pad. The pen began to move without her conscious volition on her part, and she discovered to her astonishment that it had written a letter in the handwriting of her dead fiance. In the course of time, many other such automatic letters followed, stating that this phenomenon would be the means of bringing other people to realize that life continues after death.

Miss Rosher was not a Spiritualist, and sought guidance from the Rev. G. Maurice Elliot, then secretary of the **Churches' Fellowship for Psychic and Spiritual Studies.** Elliot enlisted the aid of handwriting expert F. T. Hilliger who studied the automatic scripts and compared them to the handwriting of Gordon E. Burdick when alive. Although initially skeptical, Hilliger reported that the automatic scripts bore a close resemblance to the genuine writing of Gordon E. Burdick in a large number of different ways, and were so consistent that "the writing reproduced by Grace Rosher was, if it were humanly possible, genuinely inspired by the personality of Gordon E. Burdick."

Grace Rosher subsequently produced many other scripts, including messages from her mother, father and three sisters, and a relative who had died in 1752. On one occasion, she produced a communication claimed to be the famous scientist Sir William Crookes, in handwriting remarkably similar to that of Crookes in his lifetime.

A special characteristic of these automatic scripts was the way in which they were written with a pen lying loosely across the joint of Miss Rosher's index finger, the nib resting on a writing pad. Although she did not hold the pen, it wrote swiftly and intelligently. Skeptical stage magicians have pointed out that it is possible to guide a pen under these circumstances, but it is not clear whether they are suggesting a conscious or even subconscious deception on the part of Miss Rosher. The circumstances of the production of Miss Rosher's automatic scripts are in no way comparable with the deliberate mystification of a professional magician.

Some of the evidence for survival contained in the automatic scripts in the handwriting of Grace Rosher's fiance Gordon E. Burdick is contained in Rosher's book *Beyond the Horizon* (London, 1961). She has also published another book, *The Travellers' Return,* which includes communications believed to be from other deceased individuals.

Grace Rosher died in July 1980.

Rosicrucian Fellowship

Founded in 1907 by Carl Louis van Grashof who used the pseudonym Max **Heindel.** Born in Germany in 1865, he came to America in 1895 and in 1904 was vice-president of a **Theosophical Society** lodge in Los Angeles.

He claimed that during a visit to Europe in 1907 he met a mysterious occult Rosicrucian who took him to a Rose Cross temple on the borders of Germany and Bohemia, where he was initiated. Heindel expounded this Rosicrucian teaching in his book *The Rosicrucian Cosmo-Conception* (1909) and established various Fellowship Centers.

In 1911, the Fellowship was established at Mt. Ecclesia, Oceanside, California to disseminate Rosicrucian philosophy by books, magazines, lectures and correspondence courses. The Oceanside headquarters now cover a vast estate with stucco temples, a healing department and a vegetarian restaurant at El Toro Marine base.

Much of Heindel's teaching seems to derive from the lectures of Anthroposophist Rudolf **Steiner** (1861-1925) which Heindel had attended in Germany during the 1900s, and Steiner may have been Heindel's mysterious Rosicrucian.

Heindel died in 1919, and his widow Augusta Foss Heindel became leader and director of the Fellowship until her own death in 1938. Another prominent official of the Fellowship during this later period was author Manly Palmer **Hall.**

Address: P.O. Box 713, 2222 Mission Avenue, Oceanside, California 92054. (See also **Rays from the Rosy Cross; Rosicrucians**)

Rosicrucians

The idea of a Rosicrucian Brotherhood has probably aroused more interest in the popular mind than that of any other secret society of a kindred nature, but that such a brotherhood ever existed is extremely doubtful. The very name of Rosicrucian seems to have exercised a spell upon people of an imaginative nature for over three centuries, and a great deal of romantic fiction has clustered around the fraternity, such as, for example, Lord Lytton's romance of *Zanoi,* Shelley's novel *St. Irvyne the Rosicrucian,* Harrison Ainworth's *Auriol,* and similar works.

The name Rosicrucian is used by mystics to some extent as the equivalent of **magus,** but in its more specific application it was the title of a member of a suppositious society which arose in the late sixteenth century.

There are several theories regarding the derivation of the name. The most commonly accepted appears to be that it was derived from the appellation of the supposed founder, Christian Rosenkreuze, but as history has been proved to be fabulous, this theory must fall to the ground. The historian Johann von Mosheim gave it as his opinion that the name was formed from the Latin words *ros* (dew) *crux* (a cross), on the assumption that the alchemical dew of the philosophers was the most powerful dissolvent of gold, while the cross was equivalent to light.

It is more probable that the name Rosicrucian is derived from *rosa* (a rose) and *crux* (a cross), and we find that the general symbol of the supposed order was a rose crucified in the center of a cross. In an old Rosicrucian book of the last century, there is a symbol of a red cross-marked heart in the center of an open rose, which the writer Arthur E. **Waite** believed to be a development of the monogram of Martin Luther, which was a cross-crowned heart rising from the center of an open rose.

History of the Brotherhood

Practically nothing definite was known concerning the Rosicrucian Brotherhood before the publication of Waite's work *The Real History of the Rosicrucians* in 1887. Prior to that, a great deal had been written concerning the fraternity, and shortly before Waite produced his well-known book, another had made its appearance under the title of *The Rosicrucians, their Rites and Mysteries* (1870) by Hargrave Jennings.

This book contained many absurdities, through the attitude of the author, who pretended to be the guardianship of occult secrets. It was typical of many writings regarding the fraternity of the Rosy Cross, and as the *Westminster Review* wittily commented in its notice of the volume, it dealt with practically everything under the sun except the Rosicrucians.

Waite's work, however, was the result of arduous personal research, and gathered together all that could be known regarding the Rosicrucians at that time, and his facts were drawn from manuscripts, in some cases discovered by himself, and from skillful analogy. As it is the first significant study on the subject, its findings are outlined below.

The name "Rosicrucian" appears to have been unknown previously to the year 1598. The history of the movement originates in Germany, where in the town of Cassel, in the year 1614, the professors of magic, mysticism, and alchemy, were surprised by the publication of a pamphlet bearing the title *The Fama of the Fraternity of the Meritorious Order of the Rosy Cross Addressed to the Learned in General and the Governors of Europe.*

It purported to be a message from certain anonymous adepts who were deeply concerned for the condition of mankind, and who greatly desired its moral renewal and perfection. It proposed that all men of learning throughout the world should join forces for the establishment of a synthesis of science, through which would be discovered the perfect method for all the arts. The squabblings and quarrellings of the literati of the period were to be forgone, and the antiquated authorities of the elder world to be discredited. It pointed out that a reformation had taken place in religion, that the church had been cleansed, and that a similar new career was now open to science. All this was to be brought about by the assistance of the illuminated Brotherhood, the children of light who had been initiated in the mysteries of the Grand Orient, and would lead the age of perfection.

The fraternity supplied what purported to be an account of its history. The head and front of the movement was one C. R. C. of Teutonic race, a magical hierophant of the highest rank, who in the fifth year of his age had been placed in a convent, where he studied the Humanities. At the age of fifteen, he accompanied one Brother P. A. L. on his travels to the Holy Land, but the brother died at Cyprus, to the great grief of C. R. C., who however resolved to undertake the arduous journey himself.

Arriving at Damascus, he there obtained knowledge of a secret circle of mystics who dwelt in an unknown city of Arabia called Damcar, who were expert in all magical arts. Turning aside from his quest of the Holy Sepulcher, the lad made up his mind to trace these illuminati and sought out certain Arabians, who duly carried him to the city of Damcar. There he arrived at the age of sixteen years, and was graciously welcomed by the magi, who intimated to him that they had long been expecting him, and relating to him several passages in his past life.

They proceeded to initiate him into the mysteries of occult science, and he speedily became acquainted with Arabic, from which tongue he translated the divine book "M" into Latin. After three years of mystic instruction, he departed from the mysterious city for Egypt, whence he sailed to Fez, as the wise men of Damcar had instructed him to do. There he fell in with other masters who taught him how to evoke the elemental spirits.

After a further two years' sojourn at Fez, his period of initiation was over, and he proceeded to Spain to confer with the wisdom of that country, and convince its professors of the errors of their ways.

Unhappily, the scholars of Spain turned their backs upon him with loud laughter, and intimated to him that they had learned the principles and practice of the black art from a much higher authority, namely Satin himself, who had unveiled to them the secrets of **necromancy** within the walls of the University of Salamanca.

With noble indignation, the young man shook the dust of Spain from his feet, and turned his face to other countries only, alas, to find the same treatment within their boundaries. At last he sought his native land of Germany, where he pored over the great truths he had learned in solitude and seclusion, and reduced his universal philosophy to writing. Five years of a hermit's life, however, only served to strengthen him in his opinions, and he could not but feel that the one who had achieved the transmutation of metals (see **Alchemy**) and had manufactured the **elixir of life** was designed for a nobler purpose than rumination in solitude.

Slowly and carefully he began to collect around him assistants who became the nucleus of the Rosicrucian fraternity. When he had gathered four of these persons into the brotherhood, they invented amongst them a magical language, a cipher writing of equal magical potency, and a large dictionary replete with occult wisdom. They erected a House of the Holy Ghost, healed the sick, and initiated further members, and then betook themselves as missionaries to the various countries of Europe to disseminate their wisdom.

In course of time, their founder, C. R. C., breathed his last, and for a hundred and twenty years the secret of his burial place was concealed. The original members also died one by one, and it was not until the third generation of adepts had arisen that the tomb of their illustrious founder was unearthed during the rebuilding of one of their secret dwellings.

The vault in which this tomb was found was illuminated by the sun of the magi, and inscribed with magical characters. The body of the illustrious founder was discovered in perfect preservation, and a number of marvels were discovered buried beside him, which convinced the existing members of the fraternity that it was their duty to make these publicly known to the world.

It was this discovery which immediately inspired the brotherhood to make its existence public in the circular mentioned above, and they invited all worthy persons to apply to them for initiation. They refused, however, to supply their names and addresses, and desired that those who wished for initiation could signify their intention by the publication of printed letters, which they would be certain to notice. In conclusion they assured the public of the circumstance that they were believers in the reformed Church of Christ, and denounced in the most solemn manner all pseudo occultists and alchemists.

This *Fama* created tremendous excitement among the occultists of Europe, and a large number of pamphlets were published criticizing or defending the society and its manifesto, in which it was pointed out there were a number of discrepancies. To begin with, no such city as Damcar existed within the bounds of Arabia. Where, it was asked, was the House of the Holy Ghost, which the Rosicrucians stated had been seen by 100,000 persons and was yet concealed from the world? C. R. C., the founder, as a boy of fifteen must have achieved great occult skill to have astonished the magi of Damcar.

But despite these objections, considerable credit was given to the Rosicrucian publication. After a lapse of a year, appeared the *Confession of the Rosicrucian Fraternity,* addressed to the learned in Europe. This offered initiation by gradual stages to selected applicants, and discovered its ultra-Protestant character by what an old Scots minister used to call a "dig at the Pope," whom it publicly execrated, expressing the hope that his "asinine braying" would finally be put a stop to by tearing him to pieces with nails! This impious comment did not enhance the reputation of Rosicrucians in the Catholic church.

A year later, in 1616, *The Chymical Nuptials of Christian Rosencreutz* was published, purporting to recount incidents in the life of the mysterious founder of the Brotherhood of the Rosy Cross. But the "chymical marriage" makes Christian Rosencreutz an old man when he achieved initiation, and this hardly squares with the original account of his life as given in the *Fama.* By this time, a number of persons had applied for initiation but had received no answer to their applications. As many believed themselves to be alchemical and magical adepts, great irritation arose among the brotherhood, and it was generally considered that the whole business was a hoax. By 1620, the Rosicrucians and their publication had lapsed into absolute obscurity.

Numerous theories have been put forward as to the probable authorship of these manifestoes, and it had been generally considered that the theologian Andreæ produced them as a kind of laborious jest, but this view is open to so many objections that it may be dismissed summarily. Their authorship has also been claimed for Taulerus, Joachim Jünge, and Ægidius Guttmann, but the individual in whose mind originated the Brotherhood of the Rosy Cross remains unknown.

It is, however, unlikely that the manifesto was of the nature of a hoax, because it bears upon its surface the marks of intense earnestness, and the desire for philosophical and spiritual reformation, and it is not unlikely that it sprang from some mystic of the Lutheran school who desired the cooperation of like-minded persons.

Waite believed there was reasonable presumptive evidence to show that some corporate body such as the Rosicrucian Brotherhood did exist, but he stated that the documents which are the basis of this belief also give evidence that the association did not originate as it pretended, and was devoid of the powers which it claimed.

Because of this, the hypothesis of an actual Brotherhood seems improbable. Such documents would probably emanate from one individual, and it is almost impossible to conceive that a body of men professing such aims and objects as the manifesto lays claim to, could possible have lent themselves to such a farrago of absurdity as the history of C. R. C.

A great many writers have credited the Brotherhood with immense antiquity, but as the publisher of the manifesto placed its origin so late as the fifteenth century, there is little necessity to take these theories seriously.

So far as can be gleaned from their publications, the Rosicrucians (or the person in whose imagination they existed) were believers in the doctrines of **Paracelsus.** They believed in alchemy, astrology and occult forces in nature and their credence in these is identical with the doctrines of that great master of occult philosophy and medicine. They were thus essentially modern in their occult beliefs, just as they were modern in their religious ideas.

Waite thought it possible that in Nuremburg, in the year 1598, a Rosicrucian Society was founded by a mystic and alchemist named Simon Studion, under the title of *Militia Crucifera Evangelica,* which held periodical meetings in that city. Its proceedings were reported in an unprinted work of Studion's, and in opinions and objects it was identical with the supposed Rosicrucian Society. "Evidently," stated Waite, "the Rosicrucian Society of 1614 was a transfiguration or development of the sect established by Simon Studion." But there is no good evidence for this statement.

After a lapse of nearly a century, the Rosicrucians reappeared in Germany. In 1710, a certain Sincerus Racatus or Sigmund Richter, published *A Perfect and True Preparation of the Philosophical Stone according to the Secret Methods of the Brotherhood of the Golden and Rosy Cross,* and annexed to this treatise were the rules of the Rosicrucian Society for the initiation of new members. Waite was of the opinion that these rules were equivalent to a proof of the society's existence at the period, and that they help to establish the important fact that it still held its meetings at Nuremburg, where it was originally established by Studion.

In 1785, the publication of *The Secret Symbols of the Rosicrucians of the Sixteenth and Seventeenth Centuries* took place at Altona, showing, in Waite's opinion, that the mysterious Brotherhood still existed, but this was their last manifesto. These things are certainly of the nature of evidence, but they are so scanty that any reasonable and workable hypotheses that such a society ever existed can scarcely be founded upon them. For all we know to the contrary, they may be publications of enthusiastic and slightly unbalanced pseudo-mystics, and nothing definite can be gleaned from their existence.

In 1618, Henrichus Neuhuseus published a Latin pamphlet, which stated that the Rosicrucian adepts had migrated to India, and modern Theosophists believed that they still existed in the table-lands of Tibet. It is this kind of claim which throws doubt on occultism in the eyes of the general public. Without the slightest shadow of proof of any kind, such statements are wildly disseminated, and it has even been alleged that the Rosicrucians developed into a Tibetan Brotherhood, and exchanged Protestant Christianity for esoteric Buddhism!

Waite humorously stated that he was not able to trace the eastern progress of the Brotherhood further than the Isle of Mauritius, where it is related in a curious manuscript that a certain Comte De Chazal initiated Dr. Sigismond **Bacstrom** into the mysteries of the Rose Cross Order in 1794, but we know nothing about the Comte De Chazal or his character, and it is just possible that Dr. Bacstrom might have been one of those persons who in all times and countries have been willing to purchase problematical honors. Bacstrom's manuscripts passed into the hands of Frederick **Hockley** later concerned with a revival Rosicrucian society.

From the *Fama* and *Confessio,* it is possible to glean some definite ideas of the occult conceptions of the Rosicrucians. In these documents is included the doctrine of the **Microcosm,** which considers man as containing the potentialities of the whole universe. This is a distinctly Paracelsian belief. There is also the belief of the doctrine of **Elementary Spirits,** which many people wrongly think originated with the Rosicrucians, but which was probably reintroduced by Paracelsus.

The manifestoes contain the doctrine of the *Signatura Rerum,* which also is of Paracelsian origin. This is the magical writing referred to in the *Fama,* and the mystic characters of that book of nature, which, according to the *Confessio,* stand open for all eyes, but can be read or understood by only the very few. These characters are the seal of God imprinted on the wonderful work of creation, on the heavens and earth, and on all beasts.

It would appear, too, that some form of practical magic was known to the Brotherhood. They were also, according to themselves, alchemists, for they claimed to have achieved the transmutation of metals and the manufacture of the elixir of life.

In England the Rosicrucian idea was taken up by Robert **Fludd,** who wrote a spirited defence of the Brotherhood, by the alchemist Thomas Vaughan (see Eugenius **Philalethes**), who translated the *Fama* and the *Confessio,* and by John Heydon, who furnished a peculiarly quaint and interesting account of the Rosicrucians in *The Wise Man's Crown,* or *The Glory of the Rosie-Cross* (1664), as well as other treatises regarding alchemical skill and medical ability in *El Havareuna,* or *The English Physician's Tutor* (1665), and *A New Method of Rosie Crucian Physick* (1658). In

France, Rosicrucianism was also widely discussed. It has been stated that there was much connection between Rosicrucians and Freemasons.

A pseudo-Rosicrucian Society existed in England before the year 1836, and this was remodeled about the middle of last century under the title "The Rosicrucian Society of England." To join this, it was necessary to be a Mason. The officers of the society consisted of three magi, a master-general for the first and second orders, a deputy master-general, a treasurer, a secretary and seven ancients. The assisting officers numbered a precentor, organists, torch-bearer, herald, and so forth. The society was composed of nine grades or classes.

It published a little quarterly magazine from 1868 to 1879, which in an early number stated that the Society was "calculated to meet the requirements of those worthy masons who wished to study the science and antiquities of the craft, and trace it through its successive developments to the present time; also to cull information from all the records extant from those mysterious societies which had their existence in the dark ages of the world, when might meant right."

These objects were, however, fulfilled in a very perfunctory manner, if the magazine of the association is any criterion of its work. For this publication was filled with occult serial stories, reports of masonic meetings and verse. Waite stated that the most notable circumstance connected with this society was the complete ignorance which seemed to have prevailed among its members generally concerning everything connected with Rosicrucianism. This may have been a rather sweeping judgment.

The prime movers of the association were Robert Wentworth Little, Frederick **Hockley,** Kenneth **Mackenzie** and Hargrave Jennings, and in the year 1872 they seem to have become conscious that their society had not borne out its original intention.

By this time, the Yorkshire College and East of Scotland College at Edinburgh, had been founded. "This harmless association," stated Waite, "deserves a mild sympathy at the hands of the student of occultism. Its character," he continued "could hardly have deceived the most credulous of its postulants. Some of its members wrapped themselves in darkness and mystery, proclaimed themselves Rosicrucians with intent to deceive. These persons found a few—very few—believers and admirers. Others assert that the society is a cloak to something else—the last resource of cornered credulity and exposed imposture. There are similar associations in other parts of Europe, and also in America: e.g., the *Societas Rosicruciana* of Boston."

But in the concluding pages of Waite's book there is the following enigmatic passage: "On the faith of a follower of Honnes, I can promise that nothing shall be held back from these true Sons of the Doctrine, the sincere seekers after light, who are empowered to preach the supreme Arcana of the psychic world with a clean heart and an earnest aim. True Rosicrucians and true alchemical adepts, if there be any in existence at this day, will not resent a new procedure when circumstances have been radically changed."

Waite appealed to those students of occultism who are men of method as well of imagination to assist him in clearing away the dust and rubbish which had accumulated during centuries of oblivion in the silent sanctuaries of the transcendental sciences, that the traditional secrets of nature might shine forth in the darkness of doubt and uncertainty to illuminate the straight and narrow avenues which communicate between the seen and the unseen.

A. E. Waite's *The Real History of the Rosicrucians* was revised and enlarged by the author under the title *The Brotherhood of the Rosy Cross* (1924). This valuable work was reissued by University Books Inc. in 1961. Waite's writings on the Rosicrucians laid the groundwork for serious study of the subject. Since his time, there has been more scholarly work on the subject, but Waite's approach retains special value as that of a practicing mystic as well as historian.

The "Rosicrucian Society of England" referred to was organized in 1865 under the name Societas Rosicruciana in Anglia; a Metropolitan College was founded in London in 1866, and the Soc. Ros. in Scotia about the same time. Other colleges were later formed in the provinces. Kenneth Mackenzie, author of *The Royal Masonic Cyclopaedia* (1877), became Honorary Magus and gave many lectures to the Society.

In 1916, the Supreme Magus was Dr. William Wynn **Westcott,** who later became one of the heads of the Hermetic Order of the **Golden Dawn** occult society, which was strongly influenced by Rosicrucian concepts. S. L. MacGregor **Mathers,** another of the Golden Dawn chiefs, formed a second order known as R.R. et A.C. (Rose of Ruby and Cross of Gold), supposed to be a British branch of a German occult order known as Ordo Roseae Rubeae et Aureae Crucis. The Golden Dawn was regarded as the probationary order of the R.R. et A.C. and the initiation rite dramatized the Rosicrucian legend of Christian Rosenkreutz in his tomb. When executive dissensions arose in The Golden Dawn in 1901, member W. B. Yeats privately published a pamphlet titled *Is the Order of R.R. & A.C. to remain a Magical Order?*

Meanwhile, less esoteric Rosicrucian societies have flourished in the U.S. The Ancient and Mystic Order Rosae Crucis (**AMORC**), founded in 1925 by H. Spencer **Lewis,** sold mystical literature by mail-order.

The **Rosicrucian Fellowship** founded in 1907 in California drew much of its teachings from the ideas of Rudolf **Steiner.** The founder Col. Louis van Grashof, known as Max **Heindel,** had attended Steiner's lectures.

The Rose Cross Order derived from the researches of P. B. **Randolph,** physician, Spiritualist medium and self-styled Professor of Oriental Interior Science, who published a *Rosicrucian Dream Book* in 1871. In 1903, the organization was absorbed by the Royal Fraternity Association Inc., comprising the Order and Temple of the Illuminati, The

Church of Illumination, The Rose Cross Order and Fraternity of the Rosicrucians, The Triple Order and Grand Temple of Eulis, The Imperial Order and Council of the Magi, The Aeth Fire, The Fraternity and Order Sons of Isis and Osiris.

In 1922, P. B. Randolph was succeeded by R. Swinburne **Clymer,** who became Supreme Hierarch of the Rosicrucian Fraternity at Beverly Hall, Quakerstown, Pennsylvania. Clymer laid exclusive claim to the title "Rosicrucian" and registered his organizations with the state of Pennsylvania. There is another Society of Rosicrucians in New York, founded by G. E. S. DeWitow. (See also **A.M.O.R.C.**; Hermetic Order of the **Golden Dawn**; Rosicrucian **Fellowship**; **Societas Rosicruciana in Anglia**; **Society of Rosicrucians in America**).

Recommended reading:

Arnold, Paul. *Histoire des Rose-Crois,* Paris, 1934

Allen, Paul M. *Christian Rosenkreutz Anthology,* Steinerbooks, Blauvelt, New York, 1974

Gardener, F. Leigh, *A Catalogue Raisonne of Works on the Occult Sciences,* Vol. 1, *Rosicrucian Books,* privately printed, 1923

Harper, George Mills, *Yeats's Golden Dawn,* Macmillan, 1974

Howe, Ellic. *The Magicians of The Golden Dawn,* Routledge & Kegan Paul, London, 1972.

Pryse, F. N. (ed.) *The Fame and Confession of the Fraternity of R:C: Commonly of the Rosie Cross . . . by Eugenius Philalethes . . . now reprinted in facsimile together with an Introduction, Notes and a Translation of the letter of Adam Haselmeyer,* Societas Rosicruciana in Anglia, U.K., 1923

Silberer, Herbert. *The Hidden Symbolism of Alchemy and the Occult Arts,* Dover, 1971

Waite, A. E. *The Real History of the Rosicrucians,* George Redway, London, 1887; Steinerbooks, Blauvelt, New York, 1977

Waite, A. E. *The Brotherhood of the Rosy Cross,* William Rider & Son, London, 1924; University Books, 1961

Yates, Frances. *The Rosicrucian Enlightenment,* Routledge & Kegan Paul, London & Boston, 1972; Paladin paperback, U.K. 1975

Rosma, Charles B.

Claimed as the murdered peddler of Hydesville, New York, in 1848, when spirit rappings were heard in the Fox household. (See also **Fox Sisters; Rochester Rappings**)

Rossetti, Dante Gabriel (1828-1882)

English author and painter Gabriel Charles Dante Rossetti, commonly known as Dante Gabriel Rossetti, was born in London, May 12, 1828, his father being an Italian who had settled in England.

While yet a boy, Rossetti manifested esthetic leanings, and accordingly he was sent to study drawing under no less distinguished a preceptor than John Sell Cotman, while shortly afterwards he entered the Royal Academy Schools. In 1848, feeling the need of still further tuition, he commenced working in the studio of Ford Madox Brown, a master who undoubtedly influenced him greatly. While under Brown's tuition, he began to show himself a painter of distinct individuality, while simultaneously he made his first essays in translating Italian literature into English, and became known among his friends as a poet of rare promise.

Meanwhile, however, Rossetti was really more interested in the painting than writing, and soon after finally quitting Brown's studio he brought about a memorable event in the history of English painting by founding the Pre-Raphaelite Brotherhood, a body consisting of seven members, whose central aim was to render precisely and literally every separate object figured in their pictures.

Leaving his father's house in 1849, Rossetti went to live at Chatham Place, Blackfriars Bridge, London, and during the next ten years his activity as a painter was enormous.

The year 1860 was a notable one in his career, as it marked his marriage to Eleanor Siddal. The love between the pair was of an exceptionally passionate order, and from it sprang Rossetti's immortal poetic sonnet sequence called *The House of Life,* published in 1881. However, Mrs. Rossetti died in 1862, and thereupon the poet, terrible cast down by his bereavement, went to live at a house in Chelsea with Swinburne and Meredith.

Here he continued to write fitfully, while in 1871 he completed one of his most famous pictures, *Dante's Dream.* The loss of his wife preyed upon him persistently; he was tortured by insomnia, and in consequence, began to take occasional doses of the drug chloral. Gradually this practice developed into a habit, sapping alike the physical and mental strength of the poet, and although he rallied for a while during a stay in Scotland, where he lived at Penkill Castle in Ayrshire, it soon became evident that his death was imminent unless he gave up his addiction to the drug. But unfortunately he had not the strength of will necessary. He died April 9, 1882 at Birchington, near Margate, and his remains were interred in the cemetery there.

Rossetti had a marked bias for mysticism in various forms. William Bell Scott, in his *Autobiographical Notes* (2 vols., 1892), told how the poet became at one time much enamored of **table-turning.** His temperament was undoubtedly a very religious one, and once towards the close of his life he declared that he had "seen and heard those that died long ago."

Was it, then, a belief in the possibility of communicating with the dead which induced him, on his wife's death to have some of his love poems inclosed in the coffin of the deceased? Whatever the answer to this question, Rossetti's mysticism certainly bore good fruit in his art, his *Rose Mary* being among the most beautiful of English poems introducing the supernatural element.

Nevertheless, it is by his painting rather than by his poetry that Rossetti holds a place as a great mystic, for despite his fondness for precise handling, all his pictures (with the exception of *Found*) are essentially of a mystical nature. They are not concerned with the tangible and visible world, but embody the scenes and incidents beheld in dreams, and do this with a mastery reflected by no other similar works save those of William **Blake.**

Rothe, Frau Anna (1850-1907)

German working woman who, after the death of her daughter's fiancé, about 1892, developed mediumship. She constantly saw the deceased seated on the sofa in his accustomed attitude. She saw visions as a child, too, but now physical phenomena also developed and Frau Rothe soon specialized in **apports** of flowers and fruits in quantity. Her mediumistic career, however, was a stormy one and finally, after a sensational trial, landed her in prison.

Camille **Flammarion** held a seance with Frau Anna Rothe in May 1901, at his own apartment. "During its continuance," he wrote, "bouquets of flowers of all sizes did, in truth, make their appearance, but always from a quarter in the room opposite to that to which our attention was drawn by Frau Rothe and her manager, Max Jentsch."

"Being well-nigh convinced that all was fraud, but not having the time to devote to such sittings, I begged M. Cail to be present, as often as he could, at the meetings which were to be held in different Parisian salons. He gladly consented, and got invited to a seance at the Clément Marot house. Having taken his station a little in the rear of the flower-scattering medium, he saw her adroitly slip one hand beneath her skirt and draw out branches which she tossed into the air."

He also saw her take oranges from her corsage, and ascertained that they were warm.

"The imposture was a glaring one, and he immediately unmasked her, to the great scandal of the assistants, who heaped insults upon him. A final seance had been planned, to be held in my salon on the following Tuesday. But Frau Rothe and her two accomplices took the train at the Eastern Railway station that very morning and we saw them no more."

Professor Richet stated in his book *Thirty Years of Psychical Research* (1923): "The first time that I saw the surprising performances of Anna Roth, The 'Blumen-medium,' I was dazzled; at a second sitting I was perplexed; at the third I was convinced that the thing was a fraud. I asked Anna Roth to allow a more complete control which would have settled the question. She refused."

The fact on which Prof. Richet based his belief in the imposture of Frau Rothe was that he weighed her before the seance and after. The difference was two pounds, exactly the weight of the "apported" flowers. Therefore, he concludes, they must have been secreted about her person.

A serious exposure took place in Germany in 1902, as a result of which Frau Rothe was kept in prison for a year and three weeks before the trial and was afterwards sentenced to eighteen months imprisonment and a fine of 500 marks. Detectives posing as inquirers found 150 flowers and several oranges and apples in a series of bag-like folds in her petticoat.

At the trial, Judge Georges Sulzer, President of the Zurich High Court of Appeal, stated on oath that Frau Rothe put him in communication with the spirits of his wife and father, who gave information unknown to any mortal. He also declared that the medium produced flowers in quantity in a room flooded with light. They came down slowly from above, and he saw four nebulous points on the hand of the medium condense into bonbons.

Altogether forty witnesses, mostly doctors and professors, gave evidence on behalf of the medium. But the presiding judge stated in the sentence: "The Court cannot allow itself to criticize the spiritistic theory, for it must be acknowledged that science, with the generality of men of culture, declares supernatural manifestations to be impossible."

In *Die Zukunft* (April 4, 1903), Maxmilian Harden, perhaps the greatest journalist in Germany at the time, editorially criticized the sentence. He wrote: "Before the conclusion of the testimony one could not but ask: Does this Rothe case, taken as a whole, show the proof-marks of fraud? This question was answered by us in the negative; but the court answered it affirmatively after a short deliberation. The flower medium was condemned to imprisonment for a year and half—a strange transaction, an incomprehensible sentence. The court summons witnesses for the defence—dozens—although the proof-notes show that almost all testify to the same effect. They come, are sworn, and declare almost without exception 'we feel ourselves in no way injured.' The most say 'we are convinced that no false representations were worked off on us by the Rothe woman.' . . . But the sentence has been pronounced on Frau Rothe in the name of justice."

The exposure and the trial was described in *Der Fall Rothe* by Dr. Erich Bohn (Breslau, 1901). (See also **Fraud**)

Roy, William (1911-1977)

Pseudonym of William George Holroyd Plowright, the most notorious fake medium in British Spiritualist history. He boasted that he had earned £50,000 by cheating the bereaved and others who attended his fake seances. He even made money out of publishing his own confessions. His sordid career illustrates the folly of unquestioning trust in mediumship. It is to the credit of the British Spiritualist movement that they first exposed Roy.

Born in Cobham, Surrey, England, Roy was boastful and deceptive even at an early age. He was only seventeen years old when he married Mary Castle, who owned a night club in the sleazy Soho area of London's West End. Mary was the first of many women who were deceived by Roy's glamorous tall tales. He was imprisoned five times on charges of burglary, receiving and falsification of accounts.

During the 1930s, his wife died and Roy married again. He set up in business as a professional psychic medium. Roy used ingenious technical devices for fraudulent mediumship and also employed confederates. He concealed a microphone in the seance room and recorded the conversations of sitters before commencement of a seance.

When people wrote to ask if they could attend his seances, Roy researched at the registry of births, deaths and marriages in order to obtain detailed information about their relatives. When they visited his house for a sitting, they would be asked to leave their bags and coats outside the seance room. These were searched by a confederate for letters, tickets, bills or other scraps of personal information. All the facts concerning sitters were recorded in a detailed card index system, and cleverly worked into Roy's "psychic" messages during seances.

Roy also produced "spirit voices" and **"materialization"** phenomena through use of tape recorders, microphones with confederate, amplifiers, butter muslin and masks. Ironically, it seems that he had some genuine psychic talent, but found fraud much more remunerative.

One of Roy's most shameless con tricks was the exploitation of a widow who attended his seances. Through a female accomplice, Roy obtained detailed information about the widow's dead husband and son, duly relayed to the widow at seances as messages from her loved ones. At the same time, Roy made advances to the widow and claimed that he wanted to marry her as soon as he could obtain a divorce.

During a seance, the widow was given "spirit messages" advising her to offer Roy's wife £15,000 in return for an arranged divorce. In due course, Roy produced a letter apparently from his wife through a firm of solicitors, giving consent for this arrangement. The letter and the firm of solicitors were both bogus, but the widow paid Roy £15,000, which went into his own pocket, and the pair went away on a "honeymoon."

Meanwhile Roy's second wife Dorothy committed suicide. Three weeks after her death, Roy married Mary Rose Halligan, aged 17.

Roy had rich clients and lived in style, with expensive motorcars. He separated from his third wife in 1956, but was not divorced.

Meanwhile in August 1955, his mediumistic trickery was first exposed by veteran Spiritualist Maurice **Barbanell** (editor of *Psychic News*) in an article in the journal *Two Worlds.* Roy's frauds first came to light when he quarreled with his accomplice, who supplied evidence and explained Roy's methods and apparatus.

Roy instituted libel proceedings, but withdrew the action in 1958, undertaking to pay costs. However, he fled the country, and it was not until twelve years later that these costs were finally recouped. Most of the money came from a wealthy widow whom Roy had ensnared.

In 1958, Roy unblushingly published his own confessions in the newspaper *Sunday Pictorial.* But he continued his fraudulent activities as a fake medium, using the name "Bill Silver." At the age or 58, Roy bigamously married Ann Clements, from whom he parted five years later. He died at Hastings, Sussex, suffering from cancer, leaving three children from his various alliances, three widows and a bigamous bride.

Roy's ingenious apparatus for fake mediumship is now in the care of Scotland Yard, in a museum at the Metropolitan Police Detective Training School. After Roy's death, Maurice Barbanell devoted a whole front page of *Psychic News* (August 13, 1977) to the story of Roy's frauds, illustrated by photographs of the apparatus and techniques used for fake meduiumship. It may not be generally recognized that British Spriritualists are usually the first to expose fraudulent mediums in the interest of genuine phenomena, and are not easily imposed upon. (See also **Fraud**)

Royce, Josiah (1855-1916)

Philosopher and a founding member of the **American Society for Psychical Research.** Born November 20, 1855 at Grass Valley, California, he studied at University of California (B.A. 1875), John Hopkins University (Ph.D. 1878), and universities of Leipzig and Göttingen, Germany. In 1880 he married Katharine Head.

From 1878 onwards he was an instructor in English literature and logic at the University of California, in 1882 he was an instructor in philosophy on the Harvard faculty, becoming assistant professor in 1892, and Alford Professor of Religion, Moral Philosophy and Civil Polity in 1914.

Dr. Royce was one of the most prominent modern American philosophers to consider the individual self part of the world mind. His books include: *The Spirit of Modern Philosophy* (1892), *The Conception of Immortality* (1900), *The World and the Individual* (1900), *The Philosophy of Loyalty* (1908), *William James and Other Essays on the Philosophy of Life* (1911), *The Problem of Christianity* (1913).

He was a founding member of the ASPR in 1884 and served as chairman on the Committee on Apparitions and Haunting Houses (vice-president of the committee 1889). The committee's name was changed later to Committee on Phantasms and Presentiments; it classified cases sent in from individuals all over the U.S. Dr. Royce's report appeared in *Proceedings* of the ASPR (vol. 1, No. 3, Dec. 1877; vol. 1, No. 4, March 1889).

He died September 14, 1916, at Cambridge, Massachusetts.

RSPK

Initialism for Recurrent Spontaneous Psychokinesis, a term suggested by parapsychologist W. G. **Roll** to denote **Poltergeist** phenomena.

Rudhyar, Dane (1895-1985)

Astrologer, musician, painter, poet, novelist. Born in Paris, France, May 23, 1895, he lived for many years in California. He studied at the Sorbonne, University of Paris, and at Paris Conservatoire, 1912.

He was married four times, first to Malya Contento, June 9, 1930, then to Eya Fechin, June 27, 1945 (divorced 1954), third wife Gale Tana Whittall, May 27, 1964 (divorced 1976), fourth wife Leyla Rasle, 1977.

He was once secretary to the French sculptor F. A. Rodin, was a lecturer for fifty years in Europe and the U.S., and a well-known composer.

His orchestral works in polytonal style ("Poèmes Ironiques" and "Vision Vegetale") were performed at New York Metropolitan Opera Festival, 1917. He composed scenic music for Hollywood Pilgrimage plays in 1920 and 1922 and wrote numerous orchestral and piano works. His paintings were exhibited at Long Beach University and the Minneapolis University Gallery.

He came to the U.S. in 1916, becoming naturalized in 1926.

In addition to his published music and paintings, he was responsible for many works on **astrology.** His publications included: (under pseudonym Daniel Chenneviere) *Claude Debussy et son oeuvre* (1913); *Rhapsodies* (poems in French, 1919), *Astrology of Personality; A Re-Formulation of Astrological Concepts and Ideals* (1926, 1963, 1970), *The Rebirth of Hindu Music* (1928), *Towards Man* (poems, 1928), *Art as Release of Power* (1928-29, 1930), *White Thunder,* (1938, 1976), *New Mansions for New Men* (1942), *The Pulse of Life; New Dynamics in Astrology* (1943, 1970), *Modern Man's Conflicts; The Creative Challenge of a Global Society* (1948), *Gifts of the Spirit* (1956), *La Roc enflammé; Le renouvellement des grand images de la tradition chrétienne* (1960; English translation *Fire Out of the Stone; A Reinterpretation of the Basic Image of the Christian Tradition,* (1963), *Astrological Study of Psychological Complexes and Emotional Problems* (1966), *The Lunation Cycle; A Key to the Understanding of Personality* (1967), *The Rhythm of Human Fulfillment* (1968), *Of Vibrancy and Peace* (poems, 1968), *Practice of Astrology* (1968), *Birth Patterns for a New Humanity; A Study of Astrology Cycles Structuring the Present World Crisis* (1969), *The Planetarization of Consciousness* (1970, 1977), *Directives for New Life* (1971), *The Astrological Houses* (1972), *Rania; An Epic Narrative* (1973), *Return from No Return; A Paraphysical Novel* (1974), *An Astrological Mandala* (1974), *The Astrology of America's Destiny* (1975), *The Sun Is Also a Star; The Galactic Dimension of Astrology* (1976), *Occult Preparations for a New Age* (1976), *Culture, Crisis and Creativity* (1977), *Astrology and the Modern Psyche* (1977), *Astrological Triptych* (1978), *Beyond Individualism* (1979), *Astrological Insights* (1979), *Astrology of Transformation* (1980).

He died in California, September 13, 1985.

Ruggles, A. D. (c. 1853)

Early American Spiritualist medium, the subject of experiments by Prof. Robert **Hare.** According to testimonies in contemporary periodicals, Ruggles wrote and spoke in foreign languages which he did not understand.

Ruh Ve Madde (Journal)

Monthly journal (in Turkish language) of the Metaphysic Research Society of Turkey, covering Spiritualism, healing, astrology, UFOs and parapsychology. Address: P.O. Box 1157, Istanbul, Turkey.

Ruhani Satsang

A branch of the **Radhasoami** spiritual movement of India, stemming from the guru Sawan Singh (1858-1948), a disciple of Baba Jaimal Singh.

Central to the teaching is the concept of an inner light and inner sound experienced in meditation.

There is an international headquarters at: Kirpal Ashram, 2 Canal Road, Vijay Nagar, Delhi-11009. In the U.S., there is a Sawan Kirpal Meditation Center at: Route l, Box 24, Bowling Green, Virginia 22427. (See also **Radhsaoami Satsang**)

Rumi, Jalal al-Din (died 1273)

A Sufi poet of the thirteenth century A.D. He taught the Sufi doctrine that the chief end of life is to emancipate oneself from human thoughts and wishes, human needs and the outward impressions of the senses, so that one may become a mere mirror for the Deity. So refined an essence does one's mind become that it is as nearly as possible nothing, yet while in this state it can, by a union with the Divine Essence, mysteriously become the All.

In his teachings, Rumi declared that names and words must not be taken for the things they represent:

> "Names thou mayest know; go, seek the truth they name
> Search not the brook, but heaven, for the moon."

Nature figured largely in the imagery of Rumi's poems. He also used the image of the reed-pipe, which figures largely in the symbolism of the Mevlevi order of whirling dervishes, which Rumi founded in Konia (Iconium). (See also **Dervishes; Sufism**)

Runes

An ancient alphabet found in inscriptions on stone in Scandinavian countries. The runic alphabet belongs to the Germanic group of languages, but is related to Greek and Latin alphabets.

Dating from the 3rd century A.D., runic inscriptions have been found in areas between the Black Sea and the Baltic (territories occupied by Goths) as well as throughout Scandinavia.

Runes were inscribed on stone monuments to commemorate events and individuals, and also for magical purposes. They were also used on objects like brooches. Typical of runic inscriptions is the writing on an ancient Danish monument which reads: "Rolf raised this stone, priest and chieftain of the Helnaes dwellers, in memory of his brother's son, Gudmund. The men were drowned at sea. Aveir wrote (the runes)." A Norwegian monument indicates that runes were believed to give magical protection: "This is the secret meaning of the runes; I hid here power-runes, undisturbed by evil witchcraft. In exile shall he die by means of magic art who destroys this monument."

The magical use of runic inscriptions has been revived in modern New Age ideas and activities. Ralph Blum, a Fullbright scholar and Harvard graduate has adapted runes for oracular purposes. His publications *The Book of Runes* (1984) and *Rune Play* (1985) are issued in conjunction with a package of twenty-five runic letters on ceramic counters. These counters are "cast," rather in the manner of a simplified **I Ching** system, to give oracular guidance on personal questions and decisions.

The concept of "casting the runes" also occurs in Western magical practice, where spells are inscribed on a slip of paper in runic letters, to be unobtrusively delivered to and accepted by the victim of the spell. This is brilliantly described in the short story *Casting the Runes* by M. R. James (included in *More Ghost Stories of an Antiquary,* 1911 etc.) in which one character takes a ticket-case belonging to the victim and places the slip of paper with the runic spell on it inside the case. He then hands it to the victim, implying casually that he must have dropped it. The victim recognizes the ticket-case as his own, and gratefully accepts it, so the runes are cast.

Recommended reading:

Blum, Ralph. *The Book of Runes,* St. Martin's Press, 1984

Blum, Ralph. *Rune Play,* St. Martin's Press, 1985

Elliott, R. W. V. *Runes,* revised edition, Manchester University Press, U.K., 1963

Hermannsson, H. *Catalogue of Runic Literature Forming Part of the Icelandic Collection at Cornell University,* Cornell University Press, Ithaca, N.Y., 1918

Willis, Tony. *The Runic Workbook,* Sterling Publishers, New York, 1986

Rupa

In Theosophical teachings, *rupa* denotes form, appearance, or the physical body, the most gross of the seven principles of which personality consists. It is a term originating in Hindu philosophy denoting the subtle essence of form. (See also **Mayavi-Rupa; Seven Principles; Theosophy**)

Rusalki

The lovely river nymph of southern Russian legend seems to have been endowed with the beauty of person and the gentle characteristics of the **Mermaids** of Northern nations. Shy and benevolent, she lived on the small alluvial islands that stud the mighty rivers which drain this extensive and thinly-peopled country, or in the detached coppices that fringe their banks, in bowers woven of flowering reeds and green-willow boughs. Her pastime and occupation were to aid in secret the poor fishermen in their laborious and precarious calling.

Little is known of these beautiful creatures, as if the mystery and secrecy which was inculcated and enforced in all affairs of government in that country had been extended to its fairy faith. Even Thomas Keightley, learned in fairy lore, says little of *Rusalki,* in his book *The Fairy Mythology* (1850), and gives only this brief notice:

"They are of a beautiful form, with long green hair; they swim and balance themselves on the branches of trees, bathe in the lakes and rivers, play on the surface of the water, and wring their locks on the green meads at the water's edge. It is chiefly at Whitsuntide that they appear; and the people then, singing and dancing, weave garlands for them, which they cast into the stream." (See also **Fairies**)

Rush, J(oseph) H(arold) (1911-)

Physicist and science writer who also studied aspects of parapsychology. Born April 17, 1911 at Mount Calm, Texas, he studied at University of Texas (B.A. 1940, M.A. 1941) and Duke University, Durham, North Carolina (Ph.D. 1950). In 1936 he married Juanita Erickson.

He was a radio operator in Dallas, Texas from 1931-38, physics instructor at Texas Technological College from 1941-42, assistant professor of physics and astronomy at Denison University, Granville, Ohio from 1942-44, associate physicist at Clinton Laboratories, Oak Ridge, Tennessee from 1944-46, secretary-treasurer of Federation of American Scientists, Washington, D.C. from 1946-47, research physicist at High Altitude Observatory, Boulder, Colorado from 1949-54, professor of physics at Texas Technological College from 1954-56, physics consultant and science writer from 1956-62, physicist at National Center for Atmospheric Research from 1962 onwards.

He is a charter member of the **Parapsychological Association,** member of American Institute of Physics, Optical Society of America, American Astronomical Society, Federation of American Scientists, American Association for the Advancement of Science. He has published a number of papers on astronomy and physics and is author of *The Dawn of Life* (1958; 1962).

In the field of parapsychology, he has studied the associative aspects of psi phenomena and the functioning of psi with ordinary sensorimotor activities. He has been concerned to discover how techniques and procedures might enhance psi results. His articles in the *Journal of Parapsychology* include: 'Some Considerations as to a Physical Basis of Extrasensory Perception' (1943), 'A Reciprocal Distance GESP Test with Drawings' (1949)

Rushton, W(illiam A(lbert) H(ugh) (1901-1980)

Distinguished British physiologist who also took an active interest in parapsychology, becoming president of the **Society for Psychical Research,** London, from 1969-71.

Born December 8, 1901, he was educated at Gresham's, Bolt; Emmanuel College, Cambridge; University College Hospital, London. He was Stokes Student, Pennsylvania, 1929; Research Fellow, Emmanuel College, 1931; Lecturer in Physiology, Cambridge University, 1935-53, Reader, 1952-65;

Professor of Visual Physiology, Cambridge University, 1966-68; Emeritus Professor, 1977; Distinguished Resident Professor in Psychobiology, Florida State University, Tallahassee, 1967-76; Visiting Professor, University of Sydney, 1973-74; Visiting Fellow, Australian National University, 1973-74.

He achieved many academic awards and distinctions, was an F.R.S., Sc.D., M.R.C.S., L.R.C.P., and Fellow of Trinity College, Cambridge, since 1938.

He contributed to the *Journal of Physiology* and took a special interest in nerve excitation and vision. In the field of psychical research, his expert pshysiological knowledge stimulated inquiry into the possible mechanisms of ESP. He was critical about false assumptions or unscientific thinking in study of the paranormal, but maintained a keen interest in the subject and believed in the reality of some phenomena.

He died June 21, 1980.

Ruskin, John (1819-1900)

Famous British author and critic who owed his belief in survival to Spiritualism. In *Pre-Raphaelitism and the Pre-Raphaelite Brotherhood* by W. Holman Hunt (2 vols., 1913) there occurs the following conversation:

"When we last met," said Holman Hunt to Ruskin, "you declared you had given up all belief in immortality." "I remember well," Ruskin replied, "but what has mainly caused the change in my views is the unanswerable evidence of spiritualism. I know there is much vulgar fraud and stupidity connected with it, but underneath there is, I am sure, enough to convince us that there is personal life independent of the body, but with this once proved, I have no further interest in spiritualism.

Russell, Eric Frank (1905-1978)

Prolific science-fiction writer, who based some of his stories on the ideas and data of Charles **Fort,** and was British representative of the **Fortean Society.** Born January 6, 1905 at Sandhurst, Surrey, England, he spent his early years at military bases abroad before returning to England, where he had a scientific and technical education.

In the 1930s he published science-fiction stories, later serving in the Royal Air Force during World War II. He was active in promoting Fortean ideas at a time when Fort's books were little known in Britain and difficult to obtain. Some of Russell's stories were originally published serially or in science-fiction magazines.

His first major novel *Sinister Barrier* (1943), published serially in 1939, was built around the Fortean theme "I think we're property," suggesting that the inhabitants of earth may be controlled by alien entities. His story *Three to Conquer* (1956) is a science-fiction treatment of the theme of psi powers.

Other Russell books included: *Dreadful Sanctuary* (1953), *Sentinels From Space* (1954), *Deep Space* (1956), *Men, Martians & Machines* (1956), *Wasp* (1958), *The Space Willies* (U.K. title *Next of Kin,* 1959), *Far Stars* (1961), *The Great Explosion* (1962), *With a Strange Device* (1964), *Somewhere a Voice* (1965).

With the decline of the Fortean Society, his enthusiasm waned and during the 1960s he also stopped writing, probably through ill health.

Although never officially dissolved, the work of the Fortean Society was later taken over by **INFO** in the U.S. and **Fortean Times** in Britain, and in recent years the study of Forteana has been revived on a large scale.

Russell died February 28, 1978.

Russell, George W(illiam) (1867-1935)

Irish poet, essayist and mystic, who wrote under the pseudonym "AE." Born April 10, 1867 at Lurgan, County Armagh, Northern Ireland, he was educated at Rathmines School, Dublin. He had a natural talent for painting and attended the Metropolitan School of Art in Dublin, where he met W. B. **Yeats,** who introduced him to **Theosophy.** At that time, Russell earned his living by working as a clerk, while contributing poems and articles to *The Irish Theosophist.*

Theosophical teachings and the literature of Hindu philosophy opened his mind to heightened consciousness of Celtic myth and nature spirits. He painted visionary pictures of the Irish landscape.

He felt a strange impulse to call one of his paintings "The Birth of Aeon," A Gnostic concept, and signed one of his articles "AEON." A proof-reader rendered this as "AE-?" and thereafter Russell used the initials for his poems.

He also wrote many political articles and became organizer for the Irish Agriculture Organization, successfully combining his mystical visions with everyday practical tasks, in the spirit of the ancient Hindu scripture *Bhagavad Gita,* a work which greatly impressed him.

His major mystical book is *The Candle of Vision* (1918; reissued University Books, 1965). His book *Song and Its Fountains* (1932) developed the mystical meditations of *Candle of Vision* and spoke of poetry as "oracles breathed from inner to outer being." His book *The Avatars: A Futurist Fantasy* (1933) indicated his debt to Hindu philosophy. His books of poems included: *Homeward: Songs By the Way* (1894), *The Earth Breath* (1897), *The Divine Vision* (1903), *The Nuts of Knowledge* (1903), *By Still Waters* (1906), *Gods of War* (1915), *Voices of the Stones* (1925), *Midsummer Eve* (1928), *Dark Weeping* (1929), *Enchantment* (1930), *Vale* (1931), *The House of the Titans* (1934).

Russell died July 17, 1935.

RUSSIA

(For early history of occult matters in Russia, see **Slavs;** for recent developments in Russian parapsychology, see **U.S.S.R.**)

Spiritualism was first introduced into Russia by persons who had become interested in the subject whilst abroad through witnessing manifestations of psychic phenomena and acquaintance with the works of Allan **Kardec,** the French exponent of **Spiritism.**

From the first, the new doctrine found its followers chiefly among the members of the professions and the aristocracy, finally including the reigning monarch of that time, Alexander II, with members of his family and entourage as devoted adherents.

Because of the immense influence of such converts, the progress of Spiritualism in Russia was made smoother than might have been expected in a country where the laws of Church and State were then authoritarian and anything unconventional in religious, or intellectual matters was regarded as partaking of a revolutionary character.

Even so, much of the Spiritualist propaganda, manifestations and publications were conducted under various ruses and subterfuges such as the circulation of a paper entitled "The Rebus," professedly devoted to innocent rebuses and charades and only incidentally mentioning Spiritualism, the real object of its being.

Chief amongst the distinguished devotees of the subject was Prince Wittgenstein, aide-de-camp and trusted friend of Alexander II, who not only avowed his beliefs openly but arranged for various mediums to give seances before the Emperor, one of these being the famous medium D. D. **Home.**

So impressed was the Czar that, it is said, from that time onwards he consulted mediums and their prophetic powers as to the advisability or otherwise of any contemplated change or step in his life, doubtless helped or driven to such dependence on mediums by the uncertain conditions under which occupants of the Russian throne seemed to exist.

Another Russian of high position socially and officially was Alexander N. **Aksakof,** who interested himself in Spritualism, arranging seances to which he invited the scientific men of the University, editing a paper *Psychische Studien* (of necessity published abroad), translating the works of Emanuel **Swedenborg** into Russian beside various French, American and English works on the same subject, and thus becoming a leader in the movement.

Later, with his friends Boutlerof and Wagner, professors respectively of chemistry and zoology at the University of St. Petersburg, he specially commenced a series of seances for the investigation of the phenomena in an experimental manner and a scientific committee was formed under the leadership of Professor Mendeleyef, who afterwards issued an adverse report on the matter. This accused the mediums of trickery and their followers of easy credulity and the usual warfare proceeded between the scientific investigators and spiritual enthusiasts.

Aksakof's commission was reported upon unfavorably by M. Mendeleyef, but Aksakof protested against the report.

At the other extreme of the social scale among the peasantry and uneducated classes generally, the grossest superstition existed, a profound belief in supernatural agencies and cases were often reported in the columns of Russian papers of wonderworking, obsession and various miraculous happenings, all ascribed, according to their character, to demoniac or angelic influence, or in districts where the inhabitants were still pagan to local deities and witchcraft.

The final years of the Romanov dynasty were dominated by the strange charismatic figure of the monk **Rasputin,** murdered shortly before the outbreak of the Russian Revolution of 1917. (See also **Rasputin; U.S.S.R.**)

Rutot's Spirit Indicator

Actually the invention of a young man named Vandermeulen, who died in 1930 before his apparatus could be tested properly. It was revived by M. Rutot, a Belgian professor, who claimed that by means of this apparatus he had been able to contact the dead inventor. Other experimenters were unable to confirm such results. For fuller details, see entry **Vandermeulen Spirit Indicator.**

Ruysbroek (or Ruysbrock), Jan van (1293-1381)

Flemish mystic, whose name probably derived from the village of Ruysbroek, near Brussels, where he was born. Even as a child he showed distinct religious inclinations, and before he was out of his teens he had steeped himself in a wealth of mystical literature. Naturally, then, he decided to follow the clerical profession, and in 1317 he was duly ordained. A little later he became vicar of St. Gudule, one of the parishes of Brussels.

During his long term in this capacity he became widely esteemed for his erudition and for his personal piety, while his sermons and even his letters were passed from hand to hand, and perused with great admiration by many of his fellow clerics.

But he was never guilty of courting fame or publicity of any kind, and at the age of sixty he retired to Groenendale, not far from the battlefield of Waterloo, where he founded a monastery. There he lived until his death, devoting himself chiefly to the study of mysticism, yet maintaining those charitable actions befitting a monk.

Ruysbroek was known to his disciples as "the ecstatic teacher." As a thinker he was speculative and broad-minded, and indeed he was one of those who prefigured the Reformation, the result being that although he won the encomiums of many famous theologians in the age immediately succeeding his, an attempt to beatify him was sternly suppressed.

He wrote a great deal, and at Cologne, in 1552, one of his manuscripts found its way into print with the title, *De Naptu svel de Ornatu Nuptiarum Spiritualium,* while subsequently a number of his other works were published, notably *De Vera Contemplatione* and *De Septem Gradivus Amoris* (Hanover, 1848).

The central tenet of his teaching was that "the soul finds God in its own depths." but in contradistinction to many other mystics, he did not teach the fusion of the self in God, holding that at the summit of the ascent towards righteousness the soul still preserves its identity.

Ruysbroek and his teaching gave rise to many voluminous commentaries throughout the Middle Ages, and he has attracted a number of great writers, for example the Abbé Bossuet, and at at a later date Maurice **Maeterlinck.** In 1891 Maeterlinck published *L'Ornemant des Noces Spirituelles, de Ruysbroeck l'admirable,* and an English translation titled *Ruysbroeck and the Mystics* was issued in 1904. For further information, see *Studies in Mystical Religion* by Rufus M. Jones (1909).

Ryzl, Milan (1928-)

Czech biochemist who has experimented in the field of parapsychology. Born May 22, 1928, at Prague, Czechoslovakia, he studied at Charles University, Prague (D.Sc. 1952). In 1951 he married Jirina Soucková.

He became a biochemist at the Institute of Biology of the Czechoslovak Academy of Science, charter associate of the Parapsychological Association, winner of the 1962 McDougall Award for parapsychological research.

He has taken a special interest in paranormal cognition of subjects under hypnosis, and developed a method by which the ESP of such subjects may be brought under voluntary control. He organized a parapsychology study group in Prague.

He later defected from Czechoslovakia and obtained a position as biochemist at San José College, California.

His publications include: 'Training the Psi Faculty by Hypnosis' (*Journal* of Society for Psychical Research, vol. 41, 1962); in *Journal of Parapsychology* (with J. G. Pratt) 'The Focusing of ESP Upon Particular Targets' (vol. 27, 1963), (with J. G. Pratt) 'A Repeated-Calling ESP Test with Sealed Cards' (vol. 27, 1963), (with J. G. Pratt) 'A Further Confirmation of Stabilized ESP Performance in a Selected Subject' (vol. 27, 1963), (with J. Bekoff) 'Loss of Stability of ESP Performance in a High-Scoring Subject' (vol. 29, 1965), (with J. T. Barendregt, P. R. Barkema & J. Kappers) 'An ESP Experiment in Prague' (vol. 29, 1965).

S

Saba

In ancient Irish legend, the wife of **Finn Mac Cummal** and mother of Oisin. In the form of a fawn, she was captured by Finn in the chase, but noticing that his man-hounds would do her no hurt, he gave her shelter in his Dun of Allen.

The next morning he found her transformed into a beautiful woman. She told him than an enchanter had compelled her to assume the shape of a fawn, but that her original form would be restored if she reached Dun Allen. Finn made her his wife, and ceased for a while from battle and the chase.

Hearing one day, however, that the Northmen's warships were in the Bay of Dublin, he mustered his men and went to fight them. He returned victorious, but to find Saba gone. The enchanter, taking advantage of his absence, had appeared to her in the likeness of Finn with his hounds and so lured her from the dun, when she became a fawn again.

Sabbat

A feast day gathering of witches, probably deriving from the Hebrew word for the seventh day of the week. The term "sabbat" first appears in fourteenth-century witch trials, where it denoted an assembly of witches to honor the devil and indulge obscene rites, in mockery of Christian ritual.

In modern revival witchcraft, there are eight Sabbats or major festivals in the year: Candlemas, May eve, Lammas, Halloween, the midsummer and midwinter solstices and spring and autumn equinoxes. These Sabbats are celebrated with food, wine and dancing. When held outdoors, bonfires may be lit.

As distinct from the Sabbat, witchcraft covens also hold a monthly **Esbat** to deal with routine affairs and minor magical operations. (See also **Litanies** of the Sabbat; **Witchcraft**)

Sabbathi

To this angel, in the Jewish rabbinical legend of the celestial hierarchies, is assigned the sphere of Saturn. He receives the divine light of the Holy Spirit, and communicates it to the dwellers in his kingdom.

Sabellicus, Georgius (c. 1490)

A magician who lived about the same time as the legendary necromancer **Faust,** about the end of the fifteenth century. The chief claim of the fame of Sabellicus as a sorcerer rest on his own wide and arrogant advertisement of his skill in **necromancy.**

He styled himself: "The most accomplished Georgius Sabellicus, a second Faustus, the spring and centre of necromantic art, an astrologer, a magician, consummate in chiromancy, and in agromancy, pyromancy and hydromancy inferior to none that ever lived."

However, no proof is forthcoming that he ever substantiated these bombastic claims, or was ever regarded by anyone else as anything but a charlatan.

Sabian Assembly

Founded in Los Angeles, California as "an unincorporated and unorganized free assembly of spiritual citizens" by Marc Edmund **Jones.** The object of the Sabian Assembly was the restoration of the Solar Mysteries,with the occult interpretation of "Solar" as "proving from within."

Jones is a well-known writer and exponent of astrology, and for many years students of the Sabian Assembly requested him to give spontaneous interpretations of charts without study or prior knowledge of them. 500 of these horoscope sessions were tape-recorded and transcribed, and the first volume of *The Marc Edmund Jones 500* was published in 1977 by ASI Publishers Inc., New York.

Sabine, William H(enry) W(aldo) (1903-)

Author, historian and writer on parapsychological subjects. (His surname rhymes with "cab sign"). Born April 2, 1903 in Birkenhead, England, he was educated in private schools and emigrated to the U.S. in 1947. He married artist Ellen Rosina Borcherding in 1937. Before leaving England he taught at schools at Middlesex and London.

In the U.S. he worked as an editor and book dealer from 1947 onwards. He had a number of spontaneous psi experiences, mainly of a precognitive kind, some of which he recorded in his book *Second Sight in Daily Life* (1949).

His paper 'Is There a Case for Retrocognition?' was published in *Journal* of the American Society for Psychic Research (44: 43-64, April 1950) and reprinted in *Surveys in Parapsychology* by Rhea A. White (1976). His other books include: *Suppressed History of General Nathaniel Woodhull* (1954), *New York Diary of Lieutenant Jabez Fitch* (1954), *Historical Memoirs of William Smith: 1763-1783* (1956-71), *Katarina Van*

Buskirk (1957), *A Prophecy Concerning the Swedish Monarchy* (1968), *Murder: 1776 and Washington's Policy of Silence* (1973), *A Letter About Distorted History* (1975).

S.A.F.E. Newsletter

Quarterly publication of the Society for the Application of Free Energy (associated with Mankind Research Foundation), dealing with **Dowsing, Radiesthesia** and pyramid energies. Address: 1640 Kalmia Road, Washington, D.C. 20012.

Saga UFO Report

Journal edited by Martin M. Singer, published ten times a year. Address: Gambi Publications, 333 Johnson Avenue, Brooklyn, New York 11206

Sahu

The Egyptian name for the spiritual or incorruptible body. It is figured in the *Book of the Dead* as a lily springing from the Khat or corruptible body.

Sai Baba (died 1918)

Remarkable Eastern mystic who, like the celebrated spiritual poet **Kabir,** was accepted equally by both Hindus and Moslems. Little is known of his early life. It seems probable that he was born into a Brahmin family in Hyderabad State, and left home at an early age to follow a Moslem fakir, and on the death of his teacher became attached to a Hindu guru whom he called "Venkusa."

However, even these details are uncertain, since there was a profound symbolism attached to all the utterances of Sai Baba. It is known that in 1872 he appeared as a lad of sixteen in the village of Shirdi, in the Ahmadnagar district, Bombay. He first attempted to settle at a small Hindu temple, but was asked to go to a half-ruined mosque nearby.

He made the mud-walled mosque his home, where he kept an oil lamp burning and occasionally smoked a clay pipe. He muttered to himself and performed such strange secret rites as emptying and refilling water pots, regarded by devotees as symbolic gestures relating to divine grace.

His following grew amongst both Hindus and Moslems. His actions and instructions were unconventional and erratic, but often culminated in a great many extraordinary miracles and an outpouring of divine grace.

In 1886, almost as a rehearsal for death, he told a devotee that he was going to Allah, and that his body should be preserved carefully for three days against a possible return. His heart stopped beating, his breathing ceased, and local authorities pronounced him dead.

On the third day he opened his eyes and started breathing again.

He finally died October 15, 1918 and was buried in a Hindu shrine.

Since his death, the miracle-working guru **Satya Sai Baba** is regarded by many devotees as a reincarnation of Sai Baba.

Recommended reading

Osborne, Arthur. *The Incredible Sai Baba,* London, 1958

Pradhan, Rao Bahadur M. W. *Shri Sai Baba of Shirdi; A Glimpse of Indian Spirituality,* R. A. Turkhud, Bandra, India.

St. Clair, David (1932-)

Actor, journalist, writer and lecturer on the occult. Born October 2, 1932 in Newton Falls, Ohio, he was educated at Columbia University and New School for Social Research. He spent five years as a professional actor in summer stock, and did some television work.

In 1956 he went to Mexico and then started to travel by land into Central and South America; he reached Brazil, where he worked full-time for *Time* and *Life* until 1965. Afterwards he became a freelance writer and lecturer. He is a member of Screen Writers Guild, Authors Guild, International Platform Association.

His books include: *The Mighty, Mighty Amazon* (1968), (with C. A. Cabell) *Safari: Pan Am's Guide to Hunting with Gun* (Pan American Airways, 1968), *Drum and Candle* (1971; paperback 1972), *The Psychic World of California* (1972; paperback 1973), *Psychic Healers* (1974), *The Easy Way to County Living* (1975); *Watseka: America's Most Extraordinary Case of Possession & Exorcism* (1977), *David St. Clair's Lessons in Instant ESP* (1978).

He has made expeditions into the Amazon and Mato Grosso jungles, lived with Indians and been initiated into voodoo temples. He states "I've talked to spirits, communicated with and even photographed a ghost, but the living still interest me more than the dead. I believe in the spirit world, in reincarnation, and in spirit intervention in our lives. I've seen too much of it *not* to believe."

Saint Germain, Comte de (c. 1710-c. 1780)

One of the most celebrated mystic adventurers of history. Like **Cagliostro** and others of his kind, little is known concerning his origin, but there is reason to believe that he was a Portuguese Jew. There were, however, hints that he was of royal birth, but these have never been substantiated.

One thing is fairly certain, that he was an accomplished spy, for he resided at many European Courts, spoke and wrote various languages, including Greek, Latin, Sanskit, Arabic, Chinese, French, German, English, Italian, Portuguese and Spanish, and was even sent upon diplomatic missions by Louis XV. He had always abundant funds at his command, and was alluded to by Baron Friedrich Melchior Grimm as the most capable and able man he had ever known. He was a composer of music and a capable performer on the violin.

Saint Germain claimed to have lived for centuries, to have known Solomon, the Queen of Sheba and many other persons of antiquity, but although regarded as a charlatan, the accomplishments upon which he based his reputation were in many ways real and considerable.

Especially was this the case as regards chemistry, a science in which he was certainly an adept, and he claimed to have a secret for removing the flaws from diamonds, and to be able to transmute metals, and was supposed to possess the secret of the **elixir of life.**

He was mentioned by Horace Walpole as being in London about 1743, and as being arrested as a Jacobite spy, but later released.

Walpole wrote: "He is called an Italian, a Spaniard, a Pole, a somebody who married a great fortune in Mexico and ran away with her jewels to Constantinople, a priest, a fiddler, a vast nobleman." The Prince of Wales has had unsatiated curiosity about him, but in vain. However, nothing has been made out against him; he is released, and, what convinces me he is not a gentleman, stays here, and talks of his being taken up as a spy."

Five years after this London experience, Saint Germain attached himself to the court of Louis XV, where he exercised considerable influence over that monarch, and was employed by him upon several secret missions.

He was much sought after and discussed, since Europe was greatly inclined to the pursuit of the occult at that time, and as Saint Germain combined mystical conversation with a pleasing character, and some flippancy, he was extremely popular. But he ruined his chances at the French court by interfering in a dispute between Austria and France, and was forced to remove himself to England.

He resided in London for one or two years, but in 1762 was in St. Petersburg, where he is said to have assisted in the conspiracy which placed Catherine II on the Russian throne. After this he traveled in Germany, where he was reported in the *Memoirs of Cagliostro* to have become the founder of **Freemasonry,** and to have initiated Cagliostro into that rite.

If Cagliostro's account can be credited, Saint Germain set about the business with remarkable splendor and bombast, posing as a "deity," and behaving in a manner calculated to delight pseudo-mystics of the age.

Saint Germain seems to have had a flamboyant character and it was probable that he attracted the Landgrave Charles of Hesse, who set aside a residence for the study of the occult sciences.

Saint Germain died at Schleswig somewhere between the years 1780 and 1785, but the exact date of his death and its circumstances are unknown.

It would be difficult to say whether he really possessed genuine occult power or whether he was merely one of those charlatans in whom his age abounded. A great many really clever and able people of his own time thoroughly believed in him, but we must also remember the credulous nature of the age in which he flourished. It has been said that eighteenth-century Europe was skeptical regarding everything save occultism and its professors, and it would appear to unbiased minds that this circumstance could have no better illustration than the career of the Comte de Saint Germain.

A notable circumstance regarding him was that he possessed a magnificent collection of precious stones, which some considered to be artificial, but which others better able to judge, believed to have been genuine. Thus he presented Louis XV with a diamond worth 10,000 livres.

All sorts of stories were in circulation concerning Saint Germain. One old lady professed to have encountered him at Venice fifty years before, where he posed as a man of sixty, and even his valet was supposed to have discovered the secret of immortality. On one occasion a visitor teased this man, asking if he had been present at the marriage of Cana in Galilee. "You forget, sir," was the reply, "I have only been in the Comte's service a century."

Legend has it that Saint Germain made various appearances after his death. He is said to have appeared to Marie Antoinette and to other individuals during the French Revolution. He was also believed to have been one of the **Rosicrucians,** from whom he obtained his occult knowledge.

The deathless count was also resurrected in modern times by Guy W. **Ballard,** as one of the ascended **Masters** of the **I Am** cult at Mt. Shasta, northern California. Saint Germain also figures in the splinter group Theosophy of Alice **Bailey,** as one of the Masters of the Seventh Ray, and more recently as one of the Ascended Masters of the **Church Universal and Triumphant** of Elizabeth Clare Prophet.

Recommended reading

Lang, Andrew. *Historical Mysteries,* Smith, Elder & Co., London, 1904

Wraxall, Lascelles. *Remarkable Adventurers and Unrevealed Mysteries,* 2 vols., London, 1863

"St. Irvyne; or the Rosicrucian"

A turgid Gothic novel published in 1811 by Percy Bysshe Shelley under the pseudonym "Gentleman of the University of Oxford."

It derives from the genre of Mrs. Ann Radcliffe and Matthew Gregory **Lewis,** and may also have been influenced by William Godwin's novel *St. Leon; A Tale of the Sixteenth Century* (1799). (See also Occult English **Fiction; Rosicrucians; "St. Leon; A Tale of the Sixteenth Century"**)

Saint-Jacques, R. P. de (c.1675)

A monk of the seventeenth century, who published a book entitled *Lumiere aux vivants par l'expérience des morts, ou diverses apparitions des âmes du Purgatoire* (Light to the Living by the Experiences of the Dead, or Divers Apparitions of Souls from Purgatory) published at Lyons in 1675.

St. John's Crystal Gold

A mysterious and possibly symbolical operation, described by alchemist Thomas Vaughan (1622-1666) as follows: "In regard of the Ashes of Vegetables, although their weaker exterior Elements expire by violence of the fire, yet their Earth cannot be destroyed, but is Vitrified. The Fusion and Transparency of this substance is occasioned by the Radicall moysture or Seminal water of the Compound. This water resists the fury of the fire, and cannot possibly be vanquished. 'In hac Aquâ' (saith the learned Severine), 'Rosa latet in Hieme.'

"These two principles are never separated; for Nature proceeds not so far in her Dissolutions. When death hath done her worst, there is a Union between these two, and out of them shall God raise us to the last day, and restore us to a spiritual constitution. I do not conceive there shall be a Resurrection of every Species, but rather their Terrestrial parts, together with the element of water (for 'there shall be no more sea'—*Revelations*), shall be united in one mixture with the Earth, and fixed to a pure Diaphanous substance.

"This is St. John's Crystal Gold, a fundamental of the New Jerusalem—so called, not in respect of Colour, but constitution. Their Spirits, I suppose, shall be reduced to their first Limbus, a sphere of pure, ethereal fire, like rich Eternal Tapestry spread under the throne of God." (See also **Alchemy;** Eugenius **Philalethes**)

St. John's Wort

General term for the plant species *Hypericum.* In classical mythology, the summer solstice was a day dedicated to the sun, and was believed to be a day on which witches held their festivities. St. John's Wort was their symbolical plant, and people used to judge from it whether their future would be lucky or unlucky, and as it grew they read in its progressive character their future lot.

The Christians dedicated this festival period to St. John's Wort or root, and it became a talisman against evil. In one of the old Scottish romantic ballads, a young lady falls in love with a demon, who tells her:

"Gin you wish to be leman mine [my lover]
Lay aside the St. John's Wort and the vervain."

When hung up on St. John's Day, together with a cross over the doors of houses, this plant was supposed to keep out the devil and other evil spirits. To gather the root on St. John's Day morning at sunrise, and retain it in the house, gave luck to the family in their undertakings, especially in those begun on that day.

"St. Leon; A Tale of the Sixteenth Century"

A Gothic novel by William Godwin (1756-1836), first published 1799. It may have been suggested by stories of the mysterious Comte de **Saint Germain** and the curious book *Hermippus Redivivus; or The Sage's Triumph Over Old Age and the Grave* by J. H. Cohausen (1744) (see Signor **Gualdi**).

Godwin used this novel to propagate some of the ideas expressed in his serious work *An Enquiry Concerning Political Justice and its Influence on General Virtue and Happiness* (2 vols., 1793). *St. Leon* sought to show that "boundless wealth, freedom from disease, weakness and death are as nothing in the scale against domestic affection and the charities of private life." (See also Occult English **Fiction;** Signor **Gualdi; "St. Irvyne; or the Rosicrucian"**)

Saint-Martin, Louis Claude de (1743-1803)

French mystic and philosopher, commonly known as "le philosophe inconnu" (The Unknown Philosopher), the pseudonym under which his books were published. The name of Louis de St. Martin is a familiar one, more familiar, perhaps, than that of almost any other French mystic. This is partly due to his having been a voluminous author, and partly to his being virtually the founder of a sect, "the Martinistes" while St. Beuve wrote about him in his *Causeries du Lundi,* and this naturally brought him under wide notice.

Born Jan. 18, 1743, at Amboise, St. Martin came from a family of some wealth and of gentle birth. His mother died while he was a child, but this proved anything but unfortunate for him, since his step-mother besides lavishing a wealth of affection on him, early discerned his rare intellectual gifts, and made every effort to nurture them.

"C'est à elle," St. Martin wrote in manhood, "que je dois peut-être tout mon bonheur, puisque c'est elle que m'a donné les premiers éléments de cette education douce, attentive et pieuse, qui m'a fait aimer de Dieu et des hommes."

The boy was educated at the Collège de Pontlevoy, where he read with interest numerous books of a mystical order, one which impressed him particularly being Jacques Abbadie's *Art de se connaître soi-même* (1692). At first he intended to make law his profession, but he soon decided on a military career instead, and accordingly entered the army.

A little before taking this step he had affiliated himself with the Freemasons and, on his regiment being sent to garrison Bordeaux, he became intimate with certain mystical rites which Martinez **de Pasqually** had lately introduced into the masonic ledge there.

For a while St. Martin was deeply interested in the philosophy of Pasqually who became his teacher. Later he became immersed in the writings of **Swedenborg.** The result of his studies was that he began to feel a great distaste for regimental life, and so, in 1771, he resigned his commission, determining to devote the rest of his life to philosophical speculations.

He now began writing a book *Des Erreurs et de la Vérite, ou les Hommes rappelés au Principe de la Science,* which was published in 1775, at Edinburgh, Scot land, which at this time was becoming a center of literary activity. It is worth recalling that this initial work by St. Martin was brought under the notice of Voltaire, the old cynic observing shrewdly that half a dozen folio volumes might well be devoted to the topic of *erreurs,* but that a page would suffice for the treatment of *vérité!*

The young author's next important step was to pay a visit to England, and thence in 1787 he went to Italy together with Prince Galitzin, with whom he had become friendly. They stayed together for some time at Rome, and then St. Martin left for Strassburg, his intention being to study German there, for he had recently grown interested in the teachings of the mystic Jakob **Boehme** and he was anxious to study the subject thoroughly. Very soon he had achieved this end, and at a later date, indeed, he translated a number of the German mystic's writings into French, but meanwhile returning to France, he found his outlook suddenly changed.

The revolution had broken out in 1789, and a reign of terror set in. No one was safe. St. Martin was arrested at Paris simply on account of being a gentleman by birth, but his affiliation with the Freemasons stood him in good stead in this hour of need, and he was liberated by a decree of the ninth Thermidor. Accordingly he resumed activity with his pen, and in 1792 he issued a new book, *Le Nouvel Homme,* while two years later he was commissioned to go to his native Amboise, inspect the archives and libraries of the monasteries in that region, and draw up occasional reports on the subject.

Shortly afterwards, he was appointed an *élève professeur* at the *Ecole Normale* in Paris, in consequence of which he now made his home in that city. Among others with whom he became acquainted there was Chateaubriand, of whose writing he was an enthusiastic devotee, but who, on his part, appears to have received the mystic with his usual haughty coldness.

St. Martin did not lack a large circle of admirers however, and he continued to work hard, publishing in 1795 one of his most important books, *Lèttres à un Ami, ou Considérations politiques, philosophiques et réligieuses sur la Révolution,* which was succeeded in 1800 by two speculative treatises: *Ecce Homo* and *L'Esprit des Choses.* Then, in 1802, he issued yet another volume, *Ministère de l'Homme Esprit,* but in the following year his labors were brought to an abrupt close, for awhile staying at Annay, not far from Paris, with a friend called Lenoir-Laroche, he succumbed to an apopleptic seizure, and died October 23, 1803.

After his death it was found that he had left a considerable mass of manuscripts, and some of these were issued by his executors in 1807, while in 1862 a collection of his letters appeared.

St. Martin was never married, but he appears to have exercised a most extraordinary fascination over women, and in fact various scandalous stories were told in this connection, some of them implicating various courtly dames of the French nobility of the Empire.

As a philosopher, St. Martin found a host of disciples among his contemporaries, these gradually forming themselves almost into a distinct sect, and, as mentioned earlier, acquiring the name of "Martinistes." What, then, was the teaching of their leader? And what the nature of the tenets promulgated in his voluminous writings?

It is difficult to give an epitome in a limited space, but turning to the author's *l'Homme du Désir* (1790), and again to his *Tableau natural des Rapports qui existent entre Die, et l'Homme et l'Univers* (1782), we find these books fairly representative of all his writing, and their keynote may certainly be defined as consisting in aspiration.

Human beings are divine despite the fall recounted in the Scriptures, dormant within them lies a lofty quality of which we are too often scarcely conscious, and it is incumbent on us to develop this quality, striving thereafter without ceasing, and avoiding meanwhile the snares of materialism.

Such is the salient principle in St. Martin's teaching, a principle which has been endorsed by many modern mystics, notably the Irish poet "AE" (George W. Russell) in his book *The Hero in Man* (1909). In writing in this vein, the French mystic undoubtedly owed a good deal to Swedenborg, while obligations to Boehme are, of course, manifest throughout his later works.

Recommended reading

Matter, A. J. *Saint-Martin, le philosophe inconnu,* Paris, 1862

Waite, A. E. *The Life of Louis Claude de Saint-Martin, The Unknown Philosopher,* Philip Welby, London, 1901

Saintes Maries de la Mer

A small village in the Camargue, France, on the shores of the Mediterranean, where every year, about the 24th and 25th of May, gypsies congregate to celebrate the feast day of their patron saint Sara. (See **Gypsies**)

Salagrama

An Indian stone, credited with possessing magical properties, and worn as an amulet. This stone is black in color, about the size of a billiard ball, and pierced with holes. It is actually an ammonite, and valued according to the number of its spirals and holes.

It is said that it is found in the Gandaki, a river in Nepal, which some believe rises at the foot of Vishnu, and others in the head of Siva. It is kept in a clean cloth, and often washed and perfumed by its fortunate owner.

The water in which it has been dipped is supposed thereby to gain sin-expelling potency, and is therefore drunk and greatly valued. It possesses other occult powers, and is a necessary ingredient of the preparations of those about to die. The departing Hindu holds it in his hand, and believing in its powers has hope for the future, and dies peacefully.

Salamander's Feather

Another name for Asbestos. It is a mineral of an incombustible nature, which resembles flax, being of fine fibrous texture. It was used by pagans in their temples. (See **Asbestos**)

Saleh, Wadih (1910-)

Attorney and parapsychologist. Born October 31, 1910 at Mansura, Egypt, he was educated in Egypt, Lebanon, and University of Lyons in France.

He was a research associate of the Parapsychology Laboratory, Duke University, Durham, North Carolina from 1958-60, charter associate of the Parapsychology Association. He has taken special interest in the question of the psychological conditions favoring psi phenomena.

Saller, K(arl) F(elix) (1902-)

German professor of anthropology and genetics who has also studied parapsychology. Born September 3, 1902 at Kempten, Germany he studied at University of Munich (Ph.D. 1924, M.D. 1926, Ph.D. hon. 1962). In 1930 he married Herta Gross; second marriage to Nina Elsner, 1948.

He was a lecturer in anthropology and anatomy at Universities of Kiel and Göttingen in 1935 and dismissed for opposing Nazi racial doctrines. He was in private medical practice and sanatorium physician at Badenweiler from 1936-39, medical service with the German Army from 1939-45, director of the Robert Bosch Hospital, Stuttgart from 1945-48, professor of anthropology and genetics at University of Munich from 1948 onwards, director of the Institute of Anthropology and Human Genetics at Munich from 1949 onwards.

He was publisher of the journal *Die Heilkunst,* senator at German-European Academy, chairman of Bundesverband Deutscher Ärzte für Naturheilverfahren. In addition to his papers on anthropology for scholarly journals, he contributed the article 'Die Parapsychologie vom Standpunkt des Anthropologen' (Parapsychology from the Anthropologist's point of view, *Die Heilkunst,* vol. 68, No. 7, 1955), and took an interest in the question of parapsychology as related to racial and age differences. He attended the First International Conference of Parapsychological Studies, Utrecht, Netherlands in 1953, and the International Study Group on Unorthodox Healing at St. Paul de Vence, France in 1954.

Sallow

A tree or shrub of the willow kind. Rods of this particular wood were much in use amongst the ancient Scythians and the Alani for purposes of augurial **divination.**

Fine straight wands were chosen, on which certain characters were written, and they were then thrown on a white cloth. From the way in which they fell the magician gained the desired information. (See also **Divination; I Ching**)

Salter, Helen Woollgar de Gaudrion Verrall (Mrs. William Henry Salter) (1883-1959)

Daughter of Mrs. A. W. **Verrall** who also developed the faculty of **automatic writing,** and was a prominent member of the **Society for Psychical Research,** London. She was vice-president 1953-57, member of Council 1921-57, assistant research officer 1910-16, research officer 1916-21, editor of the SPR *Journal* from 1921-29 and *Proceedings* from 1921-46, 1948-54. Born July 4, 1883, in Cambridge, England, she was educated at Newnham College, Cambridge University from 1902-06 (M.A.). In 1915 she married William Henry **Salter.**

Some of her automatic writing scripts form part of the important **"cross-correspondence"** project which involved piecing together a number of scripts from different communicators which were meaningful only as a whole. Mrs. Salter also participated in various telepathy experiments.

She contributed various articles to the SPR *Proceedings,* including: 'Some Experiments with a New Automatist' (1918), 'A Further Report on Sittings with Mrs. Leonard' (1921), 'Some Incidents Which May Throw Light on their Modus Operandi' (1930), 'The History of George Valiantine' (1931); her articles in *Journal* of the American SPR included: 'Some Observations on Scripts of the SPR Group of Automatists' (1951), 'Evidence for Telepathy' (1951). Her Myers Memorial Lecture in 1945 was titled 'Psychical Research: Where Do We Stand?'.

She died April 22, 1959.

Salter, W(illiam) H(enry) (1880-1969)

British barrister who was President of the **Society for Psychical Research,** London from 1947-48 and who worked with famous psychical researchers. Born March 19, 1880, in London, England, he was educated at St. Paul's School, London and Trinity College, Cambridge University (M.A., LL.B.). In 1915 he married Helen Woollgar de Gaudrion Verrall (died 1959).

From 1905-11 he was a barrister, from 1916-21 served with Ministry of Munitions in Britain, awarded M.B.E. in 1918.

Mr. Salter joined the Society for Psychical Research in 1916, and was honorary treasurer from 1920-31, honorary secretary from 1924-48, president 1967-68.

His wife was a well-known automatic writer, and took part in the famous SPR **"cross-correspondence"** tests. Mr. Salter himself became an authority on the subject of **automatic writing,** although also interested in telepathy, apparitions, mediumship and the evidence for survival.

His articles in the SPR *Proceedings* included: 'An Experiment in Pseudo-Scripts' (vol. 36, part 103, 1927), 'Some Automatic Scripts Purported to be Inspired by Margaret Veley' (vol. 38, part 110, 1928-29). His books included: *Ghosts and Apparitions* (1938), *The Society for Psychical Research; An Outline of*

Its History (1948), *Zoar: The Evidence of Psychical Research Concerning Survival* (1961); *Trance Mediumship: An Introductory Study of Mrs. Piper and Mrs. Leonard* (1962).

Saltmarsh, H. F. (1881-1943)

Shipping agent who became a prominent member of the **Society for Psychical Research,** London. He was born in London, July 16, 1881. His business career was interrupted by ill health, and in his early retirement he became interested in Theosophical literature, philosophy and eventually psychical research.

He joined the S.P.R. in 1921 and served on the Council from 1931-43. He organized sittings with the medium Mrs. Warren Elliot, which were reported in the SPR *Proceedings* (vol. 39, parts 112, 114, 1930) and made a special study of **"cross-correspondence"** tests.

He also classified evidences for precognition and survival. His articles in SPR *Proceedings* included: 'Report on the Investigation of Some Sittings with Mrs. Warren Elliott' (vol. 39, part 112, 1930), 'A Method of Estimating the Supernormal Content of Mediumistic Communications' (with S. G. **Soal,** vol. 39, part 114, 1930), 'Is Proof of Survival Possible?' (vol. 40, part 122, 1931-32), 'Report on Cases of Apparent Precognition' (vol. 42, part 134, 1934), 'Some Comments on Mr. Tyrrell's Paper on Individuality' (vol. 44, part 148, 1936-37), 'Ambiguity in the Question of Survival' (vol. 46, part 165, 1941). His books included: *Foreknowledge* (1938), *Evidence of Personal Survival from Cross Correspondences* (1939).

He died February 24,1943.

Sambor, S. F. (died 1902)

A Russian telegraph operator who was discovered to be a powerful medium for **materialization** and **telekinesis.** A series of his sittings between 1896 and 1902 was recorded in the Russian Spiritualist journal *Rebus.* Phantoms materialized from luminous vapor before the sitters, were seen together with the medium, and telekinetic phenomena were produced in abundance.

Many of the experiments were conducted by Count **Perovsky-Petrovo-Solovovo.** However, his belief in the phenomena of Sambor was considerably shaken when he discovered that one of the sitters intentionally released Sambor's hand, which he was supposed to be holding.

This discovery offered a convenient general explanation for the movement of objects although not for the action of a white mandolin (as reported by Mme. Youdenitch in the *Annales des Sciences Psychiques,* vol. 14, 1904, p. 193) which began to play itself in the adjoining room and, visible in the faint light, was seen to come in and settle on the table in the seance room.

Neither could complicity explain the phenomena of materialization from a white column rising from the floor and turning into a human form in good light. Some other phenomena, for instance, the threading of a chair on the medium's or on a sitter's arm while the hands were held in a chain also defied fraudulent explanation.

Such events were observed on several occasions in conditions which, stated Count Solovovo in the *Annales des Sciences Psychique,* "if they do not absolutely eliminate all possibility of error, render it improbable to a degree which almost amounts to absolute certainty." Count Solovovo also heard sounds from a piano after the lid had been locked with a key remaining on the table in the midst of the experimenters.

Sambor died a few months after the seances in 1902.

Sanders, Alex(ander) (1926-)

Self-styled British "King of the Witches," who came into the limelight in the permissive atmosphere of the sixties. Accounts of his life seem vague and fabulous, depending on statements by himself or his biographer June Johns.

Sanders, who claimed to be the most powerful white witch in Europe, was born in Manchester, England and is supposed to have been initiated into hereditary witchcraft by an old grandmother. At the age of nine, he took part in his first full witchcraft ritual and was given permission to copy his grandmother's manuscript **Book of Shadows.**

In due course, Sanders became aware of healing talent and boasted of his occult abilities, staging orgiastic meetings. However, on the death of his sister, he decided to purify himself and abandon the "left-hand path" of magic and he joined a coven of practicing witches. He was not satisfied with the existing rituals, and eventually formed a break-away coven using ceremonies of his own invention.

He met Maxine Morris, a Roman Catholic at the time, who came to respect Sanders' sincerity and kindness, and eventually became High Priestess of his coven and married him according to witchcraft ritual.

Many other covens grew up in Britain deriving from the leadership of Sanders, and in 1965, 1,600 members are said to have appointed him "King of the Witches." In 1967, he moved to London, where he and Maxine gave witchcraft instruction and ceremonials from a basement apartment.

Sanders and Maxine were probably the most publicized witches in Britain, with a glossy antiseptic image of white witchcraft, nature cult and a constant battle with the forces of evil. Sanders appeared on radio and television programs and was regularly written up in Sunday newspapers. An account of how he and a young male assistant once casually created a spiritual baby which eventually invaded Sanders' body reads like the worst of Aleister Crowley's occult fiction, from which it may have derived.

Like **Crowley,** Sanders likes exalted titles and has signed letters "Sir Alexander Sanders." For further information, see the biography by reporter June Johns: *King of the Witches: the World of Alex Sanders* (London, 1969; Pan paperback, 1971).

Sanders, Mrs. Celestine G. (c. 1920)

American **trance** medium of high standing. Reports on her trance phenomena were published by Dr. J. H. **Hyslop** in *Proceedings* of the American Society for Psychical Research (vol. 15, 1921) and by Dr. W. F. **Prince** in *Proceedings* of A.S.P.R. (vol. 18, 1924).

Sanders, Rev. C. B. (1831- ?)

A Presbyterian minister of Alabama, subject to nervous attacks from 1854 to 1876, during which a secondary **personality,** assuming the title of "X + Y = Z," developed and exhibited remarkable powers of **telepathy** and **clairvoyance.**

His story is told in *X + Y = Z; or the Sleeping Preacher of North Alabama* by Rev. G. W. Mitchell (New York, 1876). It appears that the secondary personality had command over the memories of the normal self whereas the primary consciousness remained ignorant of the doings of "X + Y = Z."

There were twelve cases on record in which this mysterious secondary personality could find lost objects, money or jewellery; he could shoot ducks at night which were invisible to his companions and write letters and sermons with his hand completely concealed under the bedcloth. A review of the case was published by Dr. W. F. **Prince** in *Bulletin* XI of the Boston S.P.R.

Sanderson, Ivan T(erence) (1911-1973)

Scottish-born naturalist, traveler, collector and exhibitor of rare animals, radio and television broadcaster, author. In addition to his many books on nature, travel and zoology, Sanderson also had special interest in such mysteries as the Abominable Snowman, UFOs and Fortean phenomena. In 1965 he founded the **Society for the Investigation of the Unexplained.**

Born January 30, 1911 in Edinburgh, Scotland, he was the son of Arthur Buchanan, famous whisky manufacturer who also founded the first game reserve in Kenya, East Africa. Ivan Sanderson was educated at Eton College (1924-27), Trinity College, Cambridge (1930-32), University of London (1933-34), M.A. honors, Cambridge University 1969. He started collecting animals in 1924, and from 1927-29 traveled around the world collecting for the British Museum. From 1932-33 he was leader of Percy Sladen Expedition to Cameron, West Africa for the British Museum, Royal Society of London and other institutions.

From 1933-34 he researched at the University of London, and from 1936-37 collected animals in the West Indies, where he also investigated the problem of human rabies carried by bats. From 1934-40 he made an expedition to Jamaica, British Honduras and Mexico, collecting animals and information for the British Museum and Chicago Museum of Natural History.

He was a member of British Naval Intelligence from 1940-45, rising to the rank of commander. He was information and overseas press analyst for the British Government in New York from 1945-57, after which he took up residence in the U.S., engaging in television and radio work from 1947-58.

From 1961-65 he was senior trade editor and special science editor for Chilton Book Co., Philadelphia, freelance writer and editor from 1965-67, science editor of *Argosy* 1968-70. His first radio show was for the British Broadcasting Corporation in 1930; he also conducted radio and television series in the field of natural science for NBC and other stations in 1948, inaugurated the first commercial color television program for CBS in 1950 and was featured regularly in the Garry Moore program for 1950-58, exhibiting live animals.

In 1959 he made a 60,000 mile trip around the North American continent, studying its phytogeography and basic biotic ecology. As an importer of rare animals, he exhibited them at his private zoo in New Jersey. Unfortunately his unique collection was destroyed by fire in 1953, and a second collection by floods in 1955. Sanderson was a fellow of the Royal Geographical Society, the Zoological Society, London, and the Linnean Society.

In addition to Sanderson's many contributions to such magazines as *Saturday Evening Post, Reader's Digest, American Heritage, Horizon, True, Sports Afield* and *Saga,* he also published the following books (some illustrated by himself): *Animal Treasure* (Book-of-the-Month Club selection, 1937), *Caribbean Treasure* (1939), *Animals Nobody Knows* (1940), *Living Treasure* (1941), (under pseudonym Terence Roberts) *Mystery Schooner* (junior Literary Guild selection, 1941), (ed.) *Animal Tales* (1946), *How to Know the North American Mammals* (1951), *The Silver Mink* (fiction, 1952), *John and Juan in the Jungle* (juvenile fiction, 1953), *Living Mammals of the World* (1955), (under the pseudonym Terence Roberts) *The Status Quo* (fiction, 1956), *Follow the Whale* (1956), *The Monkey Kingdom* (1957), *Abominable Snowmen: Legend Comes to Life* (1961; abridged ed. Pyramid Publications, 1968), *The Continent We Live On* (1961; British ed. titled *The Natural Wonders of North America,* 1962), *The Dynasty of Abu* (1962), *Ivan Sanderson's Book of Great Jungles* (1965), (with editors of *Country Beautiful*) *This Treasured Land* (1966), *Uninvited Visitors; A Biologist Looks at UFO's* (1967), *"Things"* (1967), *More "Things"* (1969), *Invisible Residents: A Disquisition Upon Certain Matters Maritime, and the Possibility of Intelligent Life Under the Waters of This Earth* (1970), *Investigating the Unexplained* (1972), *Green Silence* (1974).

He died February 19, 1973.

His Society for the Investigation of the Unexplained continues his work in collecting data and maintaining a library on such subjects as unusual precipitations of animals, earthquake and tornado anomalies, mysterious explosions, spontaneous combustion, bleeding statues, mysterious cattle mutilations, winged cats, sea monsters, men with tails, abominable snowmen and other strange phenomena.

Sandwich, The Earl of (Edward George Henry Montagu) (1839-1916)

British baron, who, in later years of a life spent in diplomatic service, was prominently before the public in consequence of his claim to be able to cure both organic diseases and functional derangement by prayer and the laying on of hands.

He testified before the clerical and medical committee of inquiry into spiritual, faith and mental healing, over which the Dean of Westminster presided in June 1912, that his power was a Divine gift which he was unable to explain. He never accepted reward for his services.

Accounts of many of his cases, with letters of gratitude, are published in a small book, *My Experiences in Spiritual Healing* (London, 1915). The story of his long and eventful life was told by Steuart Erskine in *Memoirs of Edward, Eighth Earl of Sandwich,* 1839-1916 (London, 1919).

Sangha Newsletter

Quarterly publication supported by donation, devoted to the Tibetan mysticism of **Chogyan Trungpa,** Rinpoche (**Tarthang Tulku**) and other teachers now in the U.S. Address: Vajradhatu, 1111 Pearl Street, Boulder, Colorado 80302.

Santoliquido, Dr. Rocco (1854-c. 1930)

Italian scientist, University professor, Director General of Public Health of Italy, State Councillor, Technical Adviser of the International Red Cross and first president of the **Institut Métapsychique International,** which was founded in 1919 at Paris by Jean **Meyer** on the initiative of Dr. Santoliquido and Dr. Gustave **Geley.**

Dr. Santoliquido's first experience in psychical research had taken place in 1906 in his own home. Messages were rapped out by the table in the presence of his niece, "Louise." He soon became convinced that the information furnished could not have been acquired normally.

One of these messages was: "Instead of criticising my experiments you ought to be working on your report which is not yet finished." Prof. Santoliquido believed that the report had been posted. He found out, however, that owing to the negligence of an employee it was still in his office.

He published a pamphlet on these experiments under the title *Observation d'un cas de mediumnité intellectuel.*

During the war his international hygienic activities obliged him to reside in Paris. He became acquainted with Dr. Geley and took him on as a secretary. They often discussed the problems of psychical research. Dr. Santoliquido found a rich and generous man in Jean Meyer to endow the Institut. He remained its president for ten years and was then elected honorary president.

To provide permanent headquarters for international psychical congresses and research he founded another center in Geneva with a provisional committee consisting of: Prof. Hans Driesch, Dr. Young, Prof. Grandjean and Dr. Osty. This "Centre International de Conferences et de Congres de Recherches Psychiques de Geneve" dissolved after his death.

Sanyojanas

According to Theosophical teachings, these are obstacles which the traveler along the **Path** must surmount. There are ten of them, as follows:

(1) Belief in the Ego as unchangeable.
(2) Lack of faith in higher effort.
(3) Reliance on ritual.
(4) Lust.
(5) Ill-will.
(6) Love of the world.
(7) Egotistic longing for a future life.
(8) Pride.
(9) Self-righteousness.
(10) Nescience.

(See also The **Path; Theosophy**)

Saphy (or Grigris)

Perhaps deriving from the Arabic *safi* ("pure, select, excellent"), saphy were charms or amulets worn by Africans as protection against thunderbolts and diseases, to procure wives, or avert disasters of all kinds.

They are composed of strips of paper on which sentences from the *Koran* are inscribed, sometimes intermixed with Kabalistic signs. These strips are enclosed in silver tubes or silk bags, which are worn near the skin, and often fastened in the dress. Africans of both sexes and various religions were great believers in the occult properties of such talismans. The Scottish explorer Mungo Park (1771-c. 1806) is said to have depended on the making of Saphy or Grigris, as they are sometimes called.

Sapphire

Many legends of occult properties surround this precious stone. Next to the diamond it is the hardest mineral; its true color is blue, but it may also be red, yellow, violet, green or brown.

It was said that the vision seen by Moses and the Law given to him were made out of the stone Sapphire. It was frequently worn by priests and associated with chastity. In the selection of a new Pope, a gold ring set with a sapphire is traditionally placed on the ring-finger of the Cardinal, symbolizing marriage to the Church. Buddhists ascribed sacred magical power to the sapphire and believed that it reconciled mankind to God.

It was said to be a good **amulet** against fear, to promote the flow of good spirits, to prevent ague and gout, and prevent the eyes being affected by smallpox. The sixteenth-century writer Camillo Leonardo claimed: "The sapphire heals sores, and is found to discharge a carbuncle with a single touch."

The occult writer Francis Barrett stated in his book *The Magus* (1801): "A Sapphire, or a stone that is of a deep blue colour, if it be rubbed on a tumour wherein the plague discovers itself, (before the party is too far gone) and if, by and by it be removed from the sick, the absent jewel attracts all the poison, or contagion therefrom."

Sara, St.

Patron saint of gypsies, said to have been a maid to Marie Jacobé and Marie Salomé, two sisters of the Holy Virgin. St. Sara is a local saint at les **Saintes Maries de la Mer** in The Camargue, France.

Sarcognomy

A term coined by Prof. J. Rodes **Buchanan,** pioneer writer on **Psychometry,** to denote a therapeutic science of the relationship between body and brain.

He advanced the idea that the whole body is expressive; that the entire form is an embodiment of character, that each part of the evolving surface not only possesses a physiological characteristic but also psychological powers, that each portion of this cutaneous surface exercises, through the nervous system, a direct action upon some particular part of the brain.

Prof. Buchanan considered that a study of these relationships would have therapeutic value in the treatment of disease.

Sardius (or Sard)

A precious stone which is a variety of cornelian, varying in color from pale yellow to reddish orange. According to ancient tradition, it is an antidote to the onyx. It was believed to prevent unpleasant dreams, to make its possessor wealthy, and sharpen the wit.

Sardou, Victorien (1831-1908)

Famous French dramatist and Academician, who attracted considerable attention in Spiritistic circles in the 1860s with curious automatic drawings, signed "Bernard Palissy, of Jupiter."

He was born September 5, 1831, in Paris. For a short period, he studied medicine, but gave it up in order to devote himself to writing. He was not at first successful, and was seriously ill in great poverty until rescued by Mlle. de Brécourt (whom he later married), who introduced him to Mlle. Déjazet, for whom he wrote successful plays. In due course, many outstanding actors and actresses acted in a long line of successful plays by Sardou. His plays enjoyed long runs in France, England and America. His drama *La Tosca* became the basis of Puccini's opera *Tosca.*

He wrote plays for the great actress Sarah Bernhardt. One controversial play by Sardou in which Bernhardt appeared was titled *Spiritisme.* It had a plot which involved mediumship, and included a discussion by believers in occultism and skeptics.

Sardou himself was a remarkable medium, and produced many intricate automatic drawings. Some of these were supposed to delineate the dwellings of people in Jupiter. He sketched the houses of Mozart, Zoroaster and of Bernard Palissy, who were country neighbors on the immense planet which, at the time, was commonly believed to be inhabited by a superior race of beings.

As to his own opinions, this was made clear in a letter published in *Le Temps* at the date when he was putting on the boards his drama *Spiritisme.* He spoke of himself as an observer, incredulous by nature but who had been obliged to admit, in the long run, that **Spiritism** concerns itself with facts which defy any present scientific explanation.

"Respecting the dwellings of the planet Jupiter," he wrote, "I must ask the good folks who suppose that I am convinced of the real existence of these things whether they are well persuaded that Gulliver (Swift) believed in Lilliput, Campanella in the City of the Sun, and Sir Thomas More in his Utopia."

In another letter, written to Charles Frohman on the same occasion, he spoke with much greater freedom: "Everybody knows that for forty years I have been a wonderful medium myself, and I have had in my own house wonderful manifestations. My piano has played by itself. Flowers have fallen from my ceiling upon a table; and it is I who have brought this about, and they dare not lay at my door calumnies such as true mediums are exposed to, and say of me, as they had the impudence to say of Home, that I am a charlatan."

Sardou was elected to the French Academy in 1878.

He died in Paris November 8, 1908. (See also **Apports; Automatic Drawing & Painting**)

Sargent, Epes (1813-1880)

Well-known American author, editor and psychical investigator. He was born September 27, 1813, at Gloucester, Massachusetts, graduated from Boston Latin School in 1829, and joined the editorial staff of the Boston *Daily Advertiser* and subsequently the *Daily Atlas,* becoming Washington correspondent. His two plays *(The Bride of Genoa* and *Velasco)* were successful. He then moved to New York City, where he worked as a journalist, founding *Sargent's New Monthly Magazine* (Jan.-June 1843). He also published a biography of Henry Clay (1842), and a popular novel *Fleetwood, or the Stain of Birth* (1845).

Returning to Boston, he edited the Boston *Transcript* (1847-1853), and published his own works, including two volumes of verse, the song "A Life on the Ocean Wave," *The Woman Who Dared* (1870), and a number of widely used textbooks for schools.

His attention was drawn to Mesmerism about the year 1837. He studied the subject and soon became convinced of clairvoyance and thought-reading.

When the phenomena at Hydesville broke out he was editing the Boston *Transcript* and did much to direct public attention to the problem.

In 1869 he published anonymously an earnest and comprehensive work under the title *Planchette; or, The Despair of Science.* He followed it with *The Proof Palpable of Immortality* (1875) which is chiefly devoted to his experiences in materialization, and *The Scientific*

Basis of Spiritualism (1880). He wrote extensively on the subject of Spiritualism, and was acknowledged as a capable researcher.

He died in Boston on December 30, 1880.

Sarkar, Probhat Ranjan

Former Indian railway accounts clerk and journalist, later known as Shri Anandamurti. In 1955 he founded the controversial socio-spiritual sect **Ananda Marga.**

He was sentenced to life imprisonment in India in November 1976, after five years in jail, on charges of conspiracy to murder. The case against him rested on statements by his wife and a former sect member.

In August 1978, following the downfall of the Indira Gandhi government, Sarkar was released from prison after the Indian High Court dismissed charges against him. His movement formed branches in many Western countries, including the U.S. and Britain.

Sasquatch

Another name for Bigfoot, the mysterious humanoid creature reported as inhabiting remote areas of North America. (See **Monsters**)

Sasquatch Investigations of Mid-America

Founded in 1976, with a membership interested in the scientific study of the "Sasquatch," also known as "Bigfoot," a large hairy nocturnal creature allegedly sighted in thickly wooded regions throughout the world. Sasquatches are reportedly about eight feet tall, walk upright, and appear to be intelligent and peaceful.

About 1,000 reports of Sasquatch sightings have been documented in the U.S. SIA collects and evaluates data on "Bigfoot" and releases findings to the general public through lectures, publications, and radio and television programs.

It maintains a library of books and magazines pertaining to "Bigfoot." Members investigate and report sightings in their areas. Publication: *Bigfoot News,* annual. Address: P.O. Box 441, Edmond, Oklahoma 73083. (See also **Bigfoot Information Center; Bigfoot News; Michigan Canadian Bigfoot Information Center; Monsters)**

Sat B'Hai

A Masonic type of society supposed to be of Anglo-Indian origin. The name signifies "Seven Feathers," and alludes to the bird *Malacocersis Grisis,* which flies in groups of seven.

The society was introduced into England about the year 1872 by Major J. H. Lawrence Archer. It had seven descending degrees, each of seven disciples, and seven ascending degrees of perfection, Ekata or Unity.

The British authority on the occult A. E. **Waite** believed that the rituals were compiled by Masonic writer John **Yarker** and that occultist Kenneth **MacKenzie** may have been involved and have incorporated some rites into the Order of Light, another Masonic society.

Satanic Bible

The credo of Satanist Anton Szandor **LaVey,** known as "The Black Pope" by many followers. The book embodies the basic principles of LaVey's **Church of Satan,** founded April 1966, and includes basic invocations and conjurations. It was first published by Avon paperbacks, 1969.

Satanism

During the 1980s, a new wave of Satanism swept through America. Like the problem of drug addiction, with which Satanism is often linked, this is not a nationally orchestrated phenomenon of specialized groups, but rather an unorganized outbreak of independent groups and cults who have become familiar with the topic of Satanism from books, radio, and television programs. The most disquieting feature is the extent to which teenagers are involved, either in youth Satanic cults, or as victims for adult child abuse Satanists.

But contemporary Satanism is not confined to youth cults, since individual adults have reportedly committed murders associated with Satanic rituals. Nor is the phenomenon confined to the U.S., since criminal cases involving Satanic beliefs and practices have been reported from Latin America, Canada, Britain, and Europe.

One of the most lurid cases was the sensational discovery in 1989 at the Rancho Santa Elena, near Matamoros, Mexico, of cauldrons filled with animal parts and human organs. The authorities stated that at least thirteen people had been killed by a Satanic cult of drug smugglers, who allegedly performed human sacrifices to win favor with evil spirits. The cult was believed to be linked with a Cuban variety of voodoo named Santeria, widely practiced among Latin American drug-traffickers in the Miami area, where the houses of captured drug pushers were often found littered with gruesome icons and the headless bodies of chickens.

The growth of teenage Satanism is perhaps the most disturbing modern development. In an important article 'Teen satanism evident across the country' in *Cult Awareness Network News* (January 1989), Steve Stanek and Cynthia Kisser stated:

"Teenage involvement with satanism is not orchestrated by a monolithic national organization, nor are all teens exposed to the same experiences and information when they are exposed to satanism. Teens recreate independently—in hundreds of groups large and small across the country—their unique versions of what practicing satanists are supposed to do. Some of this activity preconditions teens for involvement with adult-led groups of a more serious nature. . . .

"Satanism promises to be a continuing popular youth subculture movement into the nineties. . . . Educational programs to help the public evaluate the signs of satanism must be made available. A team approach by law enforcement, mental health professionals, legitimate clergy, school officials, and affected families must be implemented to develop appropriate evaluation and treatment for those teens who need them. Youth who dabble in satanism must be redirected into healthier avenues for social experiences because left unchecked, the end result of dabbling can be death or criminal conviction for the teens involved."

The question of child abuse by adult Satanists is an equally serious problem. Children are lured into Satanic covens and subjected to ritual abuse by devil worshipers. This practice has recently received special attention in Britain, where some twenty horrific cases were reported in 1988 and believed to be only the tip of the iceberg. Reachout Trust, formed to help victims of the criminal occult, stated that child victims who broke free from black magic covens told of being raped, of bestiality, animal and even human sacrifice. "The Cook Report," an investigative television program, telecast in July 1989, was devoted entirely to this growing problem.

To many critics, the growing fascination with occultism and black magic on the part of teenagers, is an inevitable development of the sensationalism associated with extreme forms of rock music such as heavy metal, involving Nazi insignia, Satanic symbols, aggressive and sexually charged lyrics, in a setting of strobe lights, deafening sound volume, and mass audiences. Large-scale capital investment and the promise of a quick short-cut to godlike stardom for performers with limited musical talent assisted by electronic wizardry, has created a mass youth obsession with performances nearer to orgies than entertainment.

Many Fundamentalist Christians have condemned all forms of rock music as diabolical, and have been eager to perceive concealed Satanic messages in otherwise nondescript lyrics (See **Backward masking**). However, not all popular music is Satanic, and it will be remembered that in former times such critics stigmatized Jazz and Negro Blues as "the Devil's music." The goodnatured, inventive, and often hauntingly sad emotional content of such music is now readily recognizable. When rock music transmits emotions of greed, selfishness, aggression, sexual confusion, and sado-masochism in an overheated mass sensationalist setting, it is clearly anitsocial, if not necessarily Satanic. (See also **Black Magic; Church of Satan; Cults, Charles Manson; Paranormal Music; Rock Music; Vibrations**)

Satchidananda, Swami (1914-)

Disciple of the late Swami **Sivananda** of Rishikesh, India from the age of 28 onwards. He was initiated as a renunciate in 1949 and became professor of Raja Yoga and Hatha Yoga at the forest academy of Swami Sivananda (see **Divine Life Society**).

At the suggestion of his guru, he traveled throughout the East setting up branches of the Divine Life Society. In 1966 he undertook a global tour sponsored by artist Peter Max, and established the **Integral Yoga Institute** in New York. This specializes in a combination of various yoga methods which harmonize the personality, resulting in happiness and spiritual awareness.

Saturn-Gnosis

The teachings of the **Fraternitas Saturni** or Brotherhood of Saturn, a German occult group circa 1930 and after World War II. One essential feature of the Gnosis was the sex-magic adjustment of coital positions to match planetary movements. The Fraternitas Saturni was connected with Theodor **Reuss.**

Satya Sai Baba (1926-)

Modern Hindu guru, regarded by many devotees as a reincarnation of **Sai Baba** (died 1918). Born November 23, 1926 in the village of Puttaparthi, South India, he manifested psychic powers at an early age.

At the age of thirteen, he stated "I am Sai Baba," a name hardly known to anyone in his obscure village. He then became a religious teacher and healer, manifesting extraordinary miracles.

He quite frequently materializes small objects out of the air—pictures, statuettes, prayer beads or rings—which he gives to his devotees. A widespread religious movement has grown up around him, and devotees have built schools and medical centers.

His fame has spread far beyond India into African and Western countries. As a charismatic figure, he is regarded by many devotees as a divine *avatar.*

Recommended reading:

Murphet, Howard. *Sai Baba, Man of Miracles,* Transatlantic Arts, Levittown, New York, 1972

Murphet, Howard. *Sai Baba Avatar,* Frederick Muller, London, 1979

Schulman, Arnold. *Baba,* Viking Press, 1971

Saucer and Unexplained Celestial Events Research Society

Founded in 1954 for persons interested in UFOs (unidentified flying objects or "flying saucers"). It sponsored monthly lectures in New York City and speeches to colleges and other institutions throughout the U.S. It also conducted research and maintains a library of several thousand books and periodicals.

It published an occasional Newsletter. This ceased operations for a time, but was revived by Gray **Barker,** who was executive officer, as *Gray Barker's Newsletter.*

The organization was originally based in Clarksburg, West Virginia. Since 1981, it has been renamed **Space and Unexplained Celestial Events Research Society.** Current address: P.O. Box D, Jane Lew, West Virginia 26378. (See also Gray **Barker; UFO**)

SAUCERS

Initialism for Saucers and Unexplained Celestial Events Research Society, conducted by Gray Barker, author of various UFO publications. Since 1981, the organization was renamed **Space and Celestial Events Research Society.** Address: P.O. Box D, Jane Lew, West Virginia 26378.

Savage, Minot Judson (1841-1918)

Unitarian clergyman, author, and an early member of the American Society for Psychical Research. Born June 10, 1841 at Norridgewock, Maine, he studied at Bangor Theological Seminary, graduating 1864. In 1864 he married Ella Augusta Dodge. He was ordained a Congregational minister in the same year, and served churches in California, Massachusetts and Missouri.

In 1873, he joined the Unitarian Church and was pastor of The Third Unitarian Church, Chicago from 1873-74, the Church of the Unity, Boston from 1874-96, the Church of the Messiah (now the Community Church), New York City from 1896-1906.

Mr. Savage frequently pressed for evolutionary theories of Darwin to be understood and accepted by the Church, as tending to strengthen rather than weaken religious faith. His views were expressed in his books: *Christianity, the Science of Mankind* (1873), *The Religion of Evolution* (1876), *The Morals of Evolution* (1880). His books dealing with issues of religion and survival included: *Life Beyond Death* (1899), *Can Telepathy Explain?* (1902), *Immortality* (1906).

He died May 22, 1918 at Boston, Massachusetts.

Sawyer, Mrs. Carrie M. (c. 1901)

American **materialization** medium with whom Dr. Paul **Gibier,** Director of the Bacteriological Institute of New York, conducted experiments in his own laboratory for ten years.

According to his report published in 1901 in the *Annales des Sciences Psychiques*, he enclosed the medium into a large wire cage, the meshes of which were so small that they only admitted his little finger. The cage was darkened and served as a cabinet. After the appearance of several spirit forms Dr. Gibier was asked to receive the medium who required his care.

Stepping before the door of the cage, he was astounded to see the medium fall into his arms through the door, which was locked with intact paper slip fastenings and a stamp over the keyhole. The phenomenon was repeated on three occasions. According to sitters the wire cage felt burning hot at the point of egress. Dr. Gibier could not confirm this observation.

Dr. Gibier intended to take this medium on a three years' tour to England, France and Egypt, but he died through an accident before the project could be realized.

E. A. Brackett, a Boston sculptor, was in a seance at which he was led into the cabinet by a spirit. The medium was not entranced. Taking her left and right arm the three of them walked out of the cabinet in full view of twenty-five sitters. Brackett, in his book *Materialized Apparitions* (1886) wrote of evil influences that were sometimes noticeable in Mrs. Sawyer's seances.

SCANDINAVIA

For the early history of occultism in Scandinavia (see entry on **Teutons**).

Witchcraft

In medieval times, Scandinavian examples of witchcraft were rare, but in 1669 and 1670 a great outbreak of fanaticism against it commenced in Sweden in the district of Elfdale.

The villages of Mohra and Elfdale are situated in the dales of the mountainous districts of the central parts of Sweden. In the first of the years mentioned above, a strange report was circulated that the children of the neighborhood were carried away nightly to a place they called **Blockula,** where they were received by Satan in person. The children themselves, who were responsible for the report, pointed out to them numerous women, who, they said, were witches and carried them there.

The alarm and terror in the district became so great that a report was at last made to King Charles XI, who nominated commissioners, partly clergy and partly laymen, to inquire into the extraordinary circumstances which had been brought under his notice. These commissioners arrived in Mohra and announced their intention of opening proceedings on the 13th of August, 1670.

On the 12th of August, the commissioners met at the parsonage-house, and heard the complaints of the minister and several people of the better class, who told them of the miserable condition they were in, and prayed that by some means or other they might be delivered from calamity. They gravely told the commissioners that by the help of witches, some hundreds of their children had been drawn to Satan, who had been seen to go in a visible shape through the country, and to appear daily to the people. They said that the poorer people had been seduced by him by feasting them with meat and drink.

The commissioners entered upon their duties next day with the utmost diligence, and the result of their misguided zeal formed one of the most remarkable examples of cruel and remorseless persecution that stains the annals of sorcery. No less than threescore and ten inhabitants of the village and district of Mohra, twenty-three of whom made confessions, were condemned and executed. One woman pleaded that she was with child, and the rest denied their guilt, but they were sent to Fahluna, where most of them were afterwards put to death.

Fifteen children were among those who suffered death, and thirty-six more, of different ages between nine and sixteen, were forced to run the gauntlet, and be scourged on the hands at the churchdoor every Sunday for one year. Twenty more, who had been drawn into these practices more unwillingly, and were very young, were condemned to be scourged with rods upon their hands for three successive Sundays at the churchdoor. The number of the children accused was about three hundred.

It appears that the commissioners began by taking the confessions of the children, and then they confronted them with the witches, whom the children accused as their seducers. The latter, to use the words of the authorized report, having "most of them children with them, which they had either seduced or attempted to seduce, some seven years of age, nay, from four to sixteen years," now appeared before the commissioners.

"Some of the children complained lamentably of the misery and mischief they were forced sometimes to suffer of the devil and the witches." Being asked, whether they were sure, that they were at any time carried away by the devil, they all replied in the affirmative. "Hereupon the witches themselves were asked, whether the confessions of those children were true, and admonished to confess the truth, that they might turn away from the devil unto the living God.

"At first, most of them did very stiffly, and without shedding the least tear, deny it, though much against their will and inclination. After this the children were examined every one by themselves, to see whether their confessions did agree or no, and the commissioners found that all of them, except some very little ones, which could not tell all the circumstances, did punctually agree in their confessions of particulars.

"In the meanwhile, the commissioners that were of the clergy examined the witches, but could not bring them to any confession, all continuing steadfast in their denials, till at last some of them burst into tears, and their confession agreed with what the children said; and these expressed their abhorrence of the fact, and begged pardon. Adding that the devil, whom they called Locyta, had stopped the mouths of some of them, so loath was he to part with his prey, and had stopped the ears of others. And being now gone from them, they could no longer conceal it; for they had now perceived his treachery."

The witches asserted that the journey to Blockula was not always made with the same kind of conveyance. They commonly used men, beasts, even spits and posts, according to opportunity. They preferred, however, riding upon goats, and if they had more children with them than the animal could conveniently carry, they elongated its back by means of a spit anointed with their magical ointment.

It was further stated that if the children did at any time name the names of those, either man or woman, that had been with them, and had carried them away, they were again carried by force, either to Blockula or the crossway, and there beaten, insomuch that some of them died of it, "and this some of the witches confessed, and added, that now they were exceedingly troubled and tortured in their minds for it."

One thing was wanting to confirm this circumstance of their confession. The marks of the whip could not be found on the persons of the victims, except on one boy, who had some wounds and holes in his back, that were given him with thorns; but the witches said they would quickly vanish.

The account they gave of Blockula was, that it was situated in a large meadow, like a plain sea, "wherein you can see no end." The house they met at had a great gate painted with many different colors. Through this gate they went into a little meadow distinct from the other, and here they turned their animals to graze. When they had made use of men for their beasts of burden, they set them up against the wall in a state of helpless slumber, and there they remained until needed for the homeward flight. In a very large room of this house, stood a long table, at which the witches sat down, and adjoining this room was another chamber, where there were "lovely and delicate beds."

As soon as they arrived at Blockula, the visitors were required to deny their baptism, and devote themselves body and soul to Satan, whom they promised to serve faithfully. Hereupon the devil cut their fingers, and they wrote their name with blood in his book. He then caused them to be baptized anew, by priests appointed for that purpose.

Upon this the devil gave them a purse, wherein there were filings of clocks, with a big stone tied to it, which they threw into the water, and said, "As these filings of the clock do never return to the clock, from which they were taken, so may my soul never return to heaven!"

Another difficulty arose in verifying this statement, since few of the children had any marks on their fingers to show where they had been cut. But here again the story was helped by a girl who had her finger much hurt, and who declared, that because she would not stretch out her finger, the devil in anger had thus wounded it.

When the ceremonies were completed, the witches sat down at the table, those whom the devil esteemed most being placed nearest to him, but the children were made to stand at the door, where he himself gave them meat and drink. The food with which the visitors to Blockula were regaled consisted of "broth, with coleworts and bacon in it, oatmeal bread spread with butter, milk and cheese." Sometimes they said, it tasted very well, and sometimes very ill.

After meals, they went to dancing, and it was one peculiarity of these northern witches' sabbats that the dance was usually followed by fighting. Those of Elfdale confessed that the devil used to play upon a harp before them. Another peculiarity of these northern witches was, that children resulted from their having intercourse with Satan, and these children, having married together, became the parents of toads and serpents.

The witches of Sweden appear to have been less noxious than those of most other countries, for, whatever they confessed themselves, there seems to have been no real evidence of mischief done by them. They confessed that they were obliged to promise Satan that they would do all kinds of mischief, and that the devil taught them to "milk" in the following manner. They used to stick a knife in the wall, and hang a kind of label on it, which they drew and stroked, and as long as this lasted, the persons they had power over were miserably plagued, and the beasts were milked that way, till sometimes they died of it.

One woman confessed that the devil gave her a wooden knife, with which, going into houses, she had power to kill anything she touched with it. However, there were few that could confess that they had hurt any man or woman.

Being asked whether they had murdered any children, they confessed that they had indeed tormented many, but did not know whether any of them died of these plagues, although they said that the devil had showed them several places where he had power to do mischief.

The minister of Elfdale declared that one night these witches were, to his thinking, on the crown of his head, and that from thence he had a long continued pain of the head. And upon this, one of the witches confessed that the devil had sent her to torment that minister, and that she was ordered to use a nail, and strike it into his head, but his skull was so hard that the nail would not penetrate it, and merely produced that headache. The hard-headed minister said further, that one night he felt a pain as if he were torn with an instrument used for combing flax, and when he awoke, he heard somebody scratching and scraping at the window, but could see nobody, and one of the witches confessed, that she was the person that had thus disturbed him.

The minister of Mohra declared also that one night one of these witches came into his house, and did so violently take him by the throat that he thought he should have been choked, and upon awaking, he saw the person that did it, but could not know her, and that for some weeks he was not able to speak, or perform divine service. An old woman of Elfdale confessed that the devil had helped her to make a nail, which she stuck into a boy's knee, of which stroke the boy remained lame a long time. And she added that before she was burned or executed by the hand of justice, the boy would recover.

Another circumstance confessed by these witches was that the devil gave them a beast, about the shape and size of a cat, which they called a "carrier," and a bird as big as a raven, but white, and these they could send anywhere, and wherever they came, they took away all sorts of victuals, such as butter, cheese, milk, bacon, and all sorts of seeds, and carried them to the witches.

What the bird brought, they kept for themselves, but what the carrier brought they took to Blockula, where the arch-fiend gave them as much of it as he thought good. The carriers, they said, often filled themselves so full that they were forced to disgorge by the way, and what they thus rendered fell to the ground, and was found in several gardens where coleworts grew, and far from the houses of the witches. It was of a yellow color like gold, and was called witches' butter.

Such were the details, as far as they can now be obtained, of this extraordinary delusion, the only one of a similar kind that we know to have occurred in the northern part of Europe during the age of witchcraft.

In other countries, we can generally trace some particular cause which gave rise to great persecutions of this kind, but here, as the story is told, we see none, for it is hardly likely that such a strange series of accusations should have been the mere involuntary creation of a party of little children.

Suspicion is excited by the peculiar part which the two clergymen of Elfdale and Mohra acted in this affair, and perhaps they were not altogether innocent of fabrication. They seem to have been weak superstitious men, and perhaps they had been reading the witchcraft books of the south until they imagined the country around them to be overrun with witches.

The proceedings at Mohra caused so much alarm throughout Sweden that prayers were ordered in all the churches for delivery from the snares of Satan, who was believed to have been let loose in that kingdom.

Suddenly a new edict of the king put a stop to the whole process, and the matter was brought to a close rather mysteriously. It is said that the witch prosecution was increasing so much in intensity that accusations began to be made against people of a higher class in society, and then a complaint was made to the king, and the mania brought to a close.

Perhaps the two clergymen themselves became alarmed, but one thing seems certain, that the moment the commission was revoked and the persecution ceased, no more witches were heard of.

Spiritualism

In 1843, an epidemic of preaching occurred in Southern Sweden, which provided Joseph Ennemoser with material for an interesting passage in his *History of Magic* (2 vols., 1854). The manifestation of this was similar in character to other outbreaks described elsewhere.

A writer in the London *Medium and Daybreak* of 1878 stated: "It is about a year and a half since I changed my abode from Stockholm to this place, and during that period it is wonderful how Spiritualism has gained ground in Sweden. The leading papers, that used in my time to refuse to publish any article on Spiritualism excepting such as ridiculed the doctrine, have of late thrown their columns wide open to the serious discussion of the matter. Many a Spiritualist in secret, has thus been encouraged to give publicity to his opinions without standing any longer in awe of that demon, public ridicule, which intimidates so many of our brethren.

"Several of Allan Kardec's works have been translated into Swedish, among which I may mention his *Evangile selon le Spiritisme* as particularly well-rendered in Swedish by Walter Jochnick. A spiritual Library was opened in Stockholm on the 1st of April last, which will no doubt greatly contribute to the spreading of the blessed doctrine. The visit of Mr. Eglinton to Stockholm was of the greatest benefit to the cause. Let us hope that the stay of Mrs. Esperance in the south of Sweden may have an equally beneficial effect.

"Notwithstanding all this progress of the cause in the neighbouring country, Spiritualism is looked upon here as something akin to madness, but even here there are thin, very thin rays, and very wide apart, struggling to pierce the darkness."

In Norway, Spiritualism as known to modern Europe, did not seem to have become existent until about 1880. A writer in a number of the *Dawn of Light* published in that year stated: "Spiritualism is just commencing to give a sign of its existence here in Norway. The newspapers have begun to attack it as a delusion and the 'expose' of Mrs. C., which recently took place at 38, Great Russell Street, London, has made the round through all the papers in *Scandinavia.* After all, it must sooner or later take root as in all other parts of the world. Mr. Eglinton, the English medium, has done a good work in Stockholm, showing some of the great savants a new world; and a couple of years ago Mr. Slade visited Copenhagen. The works of Mr. Zollner, the great astronomer of Leipzig, have been mentioned in the papers and caused a good deal of sensation.

"Of mediums there are several here, but all, as yet, afraid to speak out. One writes with both hands; a gentleman is developing as a drawing medium. A peasant, who died about five years ago, and lived not far from here, was an excellent healing medium; his name was Knud, and the people had given him the nickname of Vise Knud (the wise Knud); directly when he touched a patient he knew if the same could be cured or not, and often, in severe cases, the pains of the sick person went through his own body. He was also an auditive medium, startling the people many times by telling them what was going to happen in the future; but the poor fellow suffered much from the ignorance and fanaticism around him, and was several times put in prison. I am doing all I can to make people acquainted with our grand cause."

A second and more hopeful letter of 1881, addressed to the editor of the *Revue Spirite,* was as follows:

"My dear Brothers, Here our science advances without noise. An excellent writing medium has been developed among us, one who writes simultaneously with both hands; while we have music in a room where there are no musical instruments; and where there is a piano it plays itself. At Bergen, where I have recently been, I found mediums, who in the dark, made sketches—were dessinateurs—using also both hands. I have seen, also, with pleasure that several men of letters and of science have begun to investigate our science spirite. The pastor Eckhoff, of Bergen, has for the second time preached against Spiritualism, 'this instrument of the devil, this psychographie'; and to give more of eclat to his sermon he has had the goodness to have it printed; so we see that the spirits are working. The suit against the medium, Mme. F., in London, is going the rounds of the papers of Christiania; these journals opening their columns, when occasion offers, to ridicule Spiritualism. We are, however, friends of the truth, but there are scabby sheep among us of a different temperament. From Stockholm they write me that a library of spiritual works has been opened there, and that they are to have a medium from Newcastle, with whom seances are to be held."

In the *London Spiritual Magazine* of May 1885, was a long and interesting paper on Swedish Spiritualism by William **Howitt,** in which he gave quite a notable collection of narratives concerning 'Phenomenal Spiritual Manifestations in Sweden,' most of which were furnished by an eminent and learned Swedish gentleman—Count Piper. Howitt stated that the public had become so thoroughly sated with tales of hauntings, apparitions, prevision, etc., that Count Piper's narrations would present few, if any features of interest, save in justification of one assertion, that Spiritualism was rife in human experience everywhere, even although it might not take the same form as a public movement that it had done in America and England.

As early as 1864, a number of excellent leading articles commending the belief in Spiritual ministry, and the study of such phenomena as would promote communion between the "two worlds," appeared in the columns of the *Afton Blad,* one of the most popular journals circulated in Sweden.

Psychical Research and Parapsychology

Scandinavia has produced some notable psychical researchers, including Prof. Sydney Alrutz (1868-1925) of Uppsala University, Prof. Chr. Winther of Copenhagen, who was president of the Danish Society for Psychical Research (Selskapet for Psykisk Forsking), and experimented with the medium Anna **Rasmussen,** Aage **Slomann** (died 1970), a full-time parapsychologist and president of the Danish Society; in Norway, Prof. Jaeger and Prof. Thorstein **Wereide** (who edited the Oslo *Psykisk Tidsschrift*); in Iceland, Prof. Haraldur **Nielsson** (died 1928), author of books on theological and psychic subjects, Prof. Gudmundur Hannesson, University of Reykjavik, and Prof. Einar Hjorleifsson Kvaran (1859-1938), who founded the Icelandic Society for Psychical Research in 1918.

In 1942, the Swedish Sällskapet för Parapsykologisk Forskning (Society for Parapsychological Research) was founded in Stockholm. Well-known members include Dr. Gösta **Rodhe,** Dr. Rolf Evjegård, Eric Uggla, and Mrs. Eva **Hellström** (who is also clairvoyant). The engineer Haakon **Forwald** (1897-1978) carried out valuable studies in psychokinesis. Other Swedish parapsychologists include Martin Johnson and Nils Olof Jacobson. The Society may be contacted c/o Mrs. Eva Hellström, Bjûrnbo 62, Lidingo 1.

In Norway, there is the Norsk Parapsykologist Selskap, under Prof. Kirsten Pauss (Dahlsgt. 33, ⅕, Oslo 3). The dramatist Wiers **Jensen** (1866-1925) made notable contributions to the study of the "vardøgr" or "projected double" phenomenon, and also edited the journal *Norsk Tiddesskrift for Psykisk Forskning* from 1922-25.

Finland has also been very active in parapsychological research, which has received favorable notice from such scientists as Sven Segerstråle, professor of biology, Sven **Krohn,** professor of Philosophy and former president of Parapsykologinen Tutkimusseura, Prof. Väinö Auer, famous geologist, and Prof. Uuno Saarnio, philosopher and mathematician. The Finnish Society for Psychical Research was established as early as 1907 under the name Sällskapet för Forsking i Finland-Suomen Psyykkinen Tutkimusseura. The psychical researcher Jarl **Fahler** was president for a number of years, and also experimented with ESP and psychokinesis; a later president was Stefan Talqvist. In 1938, the Parapsykologinen Tutkimusseura was established and has been active ever since. In 1965, an Institute of Parapsychology was established in Helsingfors, directed by Jarl Fahler, who is also president of the Society for Hypnosis in Finland. Another parapsychological organization is Tampereen Parapsykologinen Tutkimusseura, in Tammersfors, under the presidency of Gunnar Strömmer.

Scandinavian UFO Information (Organization)

Founded in 1957 to research and disseminate information relating to the UFO phenomenon. It publishes the quarterly *UFO-Nyt* (Danish language), and UFO-VISION (Hearbook of UFO Literature, Danish language), also an occasional Newsletter in English language. Address: P.O. Box 6, DK 2820 Gentofte, Denmark.

Scapulomancy

An ancient branch of **Pyromancy (divination through fire)**, based on the interpretation of the cracks in the shoulder blade of an animal that had been burnt in sacrifice.

Schaefer, Hans (1906-)

Physiologist, director of Department of Physiology, College of Medicine, University of Heidelberg, Germany, who has also written on parapsychology. Born August 13, 1906 in Düsseldorf, Germany, he studied at University of Bonn (M.D. 1931). In 1931 he married Marietta Ditgens.

He was lecturer in physiology at University of Bonn from 1935-40, head of Department of Experimental Physiology at Kerckhoff Foundation, Bad Nauheim in 1940, director of Kerckhoff Institute for Circulation Research, Bad Nauheim in 1941, assistant professor of physiology at Giessen University from 1941-49, professor of physiology at Giessen University from 1949-50, professor of physiology and director of Department of Physiology, College of Medicine, Heidelberg University from 1950 onwards.

He was editor of *Medizin, Theorie and Klinik,* winner of the Adolf Fick Prize in Physiology in 1944, honorary life member of New York Academy of Sciences, member of the German Physiological Society, the Heidelberger Akademie der Wissenschaften, the Leopoldinische Akademie der Naturforscher, Halle.

In addition to his books and papers on electrophysiology, electrocardiography and physiology, his writings on parapsychology include: 'Parapsychologie' (*Arztliche Praxis,* vol. 3, No. 48, 1951), 'Telepathie und Hellshehen' (Telepathy and Clairvoyance, *Die Umschau,* vol. 52, 1952), 'Ist die Existenz Parapsychologischer Phänomene Bewiesen?' (Have Parapsychological Phenomena Been Proved? *Münchner Medizinische Wochenschrift,* vol. 99, 1957).

Schepis, Giovanni (1894-1963)

Italian official who experimented in the field of parapsychology. Born June 3, 1894 at Catania, Italy, he studied at University of Rome. In 1943 he married Terzilla Siroli.

He was a lecturer in statistics at University of Rome from 1936-63, staff member of the Interior Ministry from 1951-63, director of mechanographic center of Department of Elections, Ministry of the Interior, Italy in 1963. He was a Knight Commander, Order of Merit, Republic of Italy, general secretary of Italian section of the Carnegie Foundation for Heroism from 1914 onwards, co-founder in 1937 and general secretary of Società Italiana de Metapsichica, president of Società Italiana de Parapsicologia from 1959-63.

Professor Schepis conducted mass experiments in telepathy using radio and television, and also studied the personality of sensitives and the statistical approach to parapsychological experiments.

In addition to his various papers on statistical and sociological subjects, he also published articles on parapsychology, including: 'La Esplorazione delle Percezioni Extra-Sensoriali col Metodo Statistico' (Exploring Extrasensory Perception by Statistical Methods, *Notiziario di Metapsichica,* March 1949), 'La Statistica e La Metapsichica' (Statistics and Metapsychics, preface to book *Nuove Frontiere della Mente,* 1940), 'La Ricerca Scientifica in Metapsichica' (Scientific Research in Metapsychics, chapter in book *Studi e Ricerche di Metapsichica,* 1942), 'Un Nuovo Campo di Applicazione del Metodo Statistico: Lo Studio dell' effetto detto di ESP' (A New Field for the Application of Statistical Methods: The Study of So-called Extrasensory Perception, *Proceedings,* Società Italiana di Demografia e Statistica, 1947), 'I "Poteri magici" e l'Uomo Normale' ("Magical Powers" and the Normal Man, *Ulisse,* October 1948), 'Questioni di Metodo in Parapsicologia' (Questions of Method in Parapsychology, *Revista de Parapsicologia,* April-June 1955).

He also contributed the following papers: 'Carattere e finalità del Simposio' (Character and Finality of the Symposium) in Acts of the Symposium on Parapsychology held in Rome, November 1960; 'La Parapsicologia in Italia e la scienza ufficiale: Anno Zero' (Parapsychology in Italy and Official Science:

The Year Zero) in *Studies and Problems of Parapsychology* (1961). He died December 1, 1963.

Scherer, Wallace B(rown) (1913-)

Director of Psychological Instrument Company, experimenter in parapsychology. Born January 27, 1913 at Bristol, Tennessee, he studied at Davidson College, North Carolina (B.S. 1940), Duke University, Durham, N.C. (M.A. 1948). In 1943 he married Sara Wideman Denny.

He was associate professor of psychology at Atlantic Christian College, Wilson, N.C. in 1949 and 1951, assistant professor of psychology at Richmond Professional Institute of College of William and Mary, Richmond, Virginia from 1951-53, director and owner of Psychological Instruments Co., Richmond from 1953 onwards.

He is a member of the American Psychological Association, Southeastern Psychological Association, Virginia Academy of Science, Virginia Psychological Association, Richmond Psychological Association.

Dr. Scherer has taken special interest in telepathy, clairvoyance, precognition and psychokinesis. He conducted experiments to ascertain whether spontaneous responses enhanced ESP results, reported in his article 'Spontaneity as a Factor in ESP' (*Journal of Parapsychology,* June 1948).

Schermann, Raphael (1879- ?)

Austrian clairvoyant, mostly known as a graphologist but with powers far transcending character reading from scripts. He was credited with telling the past and future with an uncanny precision, the script apparently performing the same service as the ordinary clue with psychometrists. From the writing Schermann could visualize the writer, from a face he could visualize and reproduce the script. "Psychographology," the term employed by E.S. Bagger, as the title of his book on Schermann, best describes his strange gift.

Schermann was born in Cracow, then part of Austrian Galicia, in 1879. He was self-educated. By the age of 12, he had developed a serious study of the characteristics of handwriting.

He visited the U.S. early in the twentieth century, but soon returned to Europe and settled down in Vienna, where he earned a living as a claims inspector for an insurance company. His privately exhibited talents as a psycho-graphologist soon earned him a considerable reputation, and he was consulted by the police to assist their work, eventually being appointed an official handwriting expert at the Vienna Central Law Court.

During World War I, Schermann served in the Austrian army. He was wounded and invalided out of the forces. In civilian life, he became famous for his unique gifts as a psycho-graphologist, combining the science of graphology with psychic talents.

In 1923, he again visited the U.S., where he delivered lectures and cooperated with the New York police in solving a murder mystery. He then returned to Vienna, where he acted in two silent movies based on some of his most interesting cases. After this, he continued to work as consultant for a group of insurance companies, but spending his spare time on psycho-graphology. He made no charge for his remarkable talents, and took part in many experiments conducted by psychical researchers.

During World War II, he returned to his birthplace in Cracow and was killed during the Nazi occupation of Poland.

Professor Oskar Fischer, of the University of Prague, conducted between 1916 and 1981 a series of experiments in character reading from writing with Raphael Schermann. He summed up his results:

	No. of Experiments	Centesima! Proportions Successes	Doubtful	Failures
Psychological characters described from seen writing	109	70	6	24
Psychological characters from touch and sight of writing	12	58	25	17
Psychological characters described from touch alone	17	53	—	47
From writing in enevelope	28	39	8	53
From telepathy	55	73	3	24
Imitations of writing to dictation without vision	59	63	17	20
Totals	280	65%	8%	27%

The first book on Schermann's powers was published by Max Hayek in 1921 under the title: *Der Schriftdeuter Raffael Schermann.* E. S. Bagger's *Psycho-Graphology* was published in 1924. The same year saw the publication of Prof. Oskar Fischer's voluminous work: *Experimente mit Raffael Schermann. Ein Beitrag zum Problem der Graphologie, Telepathie und des Hellsehens.*

There is a short study of Schermann in Paul Tabori's book *Pioneers of the Unseen,* London, 1972.

Schierling, Charlotte Anna (1911-)

German archivist who conducted research in parapsychology. Born January 10, 1911 at Tiegenhof, West Prussia, she studied at University of Berlin (Ph.D.). She was a staff member of Danzig Library in 1946, undertook evangelical relief work in 1948, becoming archivist with the Federal Board for Employment Service, Frankfurt am Main, West Germany. Memberships include: International Federation of University Women, Association on American Indian Affairs.

Dr. Schierling published a number of books and pamphlets for children and on evangelical subjects. She also studied shamanism in Asia and the U.S. and took special interest in telepathy and the study of poltergeist phenomena. She published an article 'Red Indian Studies' in *Dakota Scout* (1960), and subsequently undertook research in shamanistic practices among American Indians.

Schiller, F(erdinand) C(anning) S(cott) (1864-1937)

Author and philosopher, president of the **Society for Psychical Research,** London in 1914. He was born August 16, 1864, at Ottensen, near Altona, Germany. He was educated at Rugby School, and Balliol College, Oxford University (M.A., D.Sc., LL.D.). In 1935, he married Louise L. Griswold.

He was an instructor in philosophy, Cornell University, 1893-97; assistant tutor, Corpus Christi College, Oxford, 1897; tutor 1903-26, professor of philosophy, University of Southern California, 1929 (emeritus, 1936).

He became an active member of the Society for Psychical Research and was vice president from 1920-28. His earliest contribution to the Society's *Proceedings* was on Automatic Writing experiments (vol. 4, pt. 11, 1887). He later contributed frequent reviews and articles on psychological and philosophical aspects to the *Proceedings,* and the *Journal* of the S.P.R. and other psychic and non-psychic periodicals.

He was author of the articles on progress of Psychical Research in the *Encyclopaedia Britannica* (11th edition, 1920) and of articles on Spiritism and Telepathy in Hasting's *Encyclopedia of Religion and Ethics.*

His books included: *The Riddle of the Sphinx,* (1891), *Humanism* (1903), *Studies in Humanism* (1907), *Tantalus, or the Future of Man* (1924), *Psychology and Logic in Psychology and the Sciences* (1924), *Problems of Belief* (1924).

He died August 6, 1937.

Schlatter, Francis (1855-1895)

Mystic and miracle-worker of the nineteenth century. Born in Alsace 1855, he emigrated to America and traveled the States with head and feet bare, preaching the love of God and peace amongst men. When imprisoned as a vagrant, he continued to preach in jail.

He had an extraordinary gift of healing, and cured many sick individuals by merely placing his hand on their heads. He appeared in San Francisco, California in 1894, traveled through Mexico, crossed the Mohave Desert and spent several weeks at Flagstaff, then wandered amongst the Indian tribes, staying five days with the chief of the Navajos and performing many miracles.

Thousands came to see him in Denver, Colorado, where he once identified a secret murderer. He reputedly healed blindness, deafness, diphtheria, cancer and other diseases with a touch of the hand, and also cured a number of cripples.

He claimed that faith was the cause of his cures, and that even touching was unnecessary. He would sometimes sensitize a piece of material or a handkerchief with healing force. He treated from three to five thousand people a day by standing with outstretched hands blessing them.

Eventually he undertook a forty-day fast, during which he continued to heal the sick. In November 1895 he disappeared from Denver without warning. He left a note at the house of Alderman Fox, where he was a guest, stating "Mr. Fox—my mission is ended, and the Father calls me. I salute you. Francis Schlatter, November 13th." He was never heard of again.

Schmeidler, Gertrude Raffel (Mrs. Robert Schmeidler) (1912-)

Professor of psychology and parapsychologist. Born July 15, 1912 in Long Branch, New Jersey, she studied at Smith College, Northampton, Massachusetts (B.A. magna cum laude, 1932), Clark University, Worcester (M.A. 1933), Radcliffe College, Cambridge, Mass. (Ph.D. 1935). In 1937 she married Robert Schmeidler.

She was statistical assistant at Foundation for Neuro-Endocrine Research from 1932-33, instructor at Monmouth College, Long Branch, N.J. from 1935-37, research associate at Harvard University from 1942-44, research officer at American Society for Psychical Research from 1945-46, psychology department at City College of New York from 1945 onwards, consultant at Barnard College from 1949-55, research at Parapsychology Foundation from 1955-59.

She is a member of the American Psychological Association, Eastern Psychological Association, Society for Psychological Study of Social Issues, American Association for the Advancement of Science, Parapsychological Association (vice-president 1958, 1960; president in 1959).

Dr. Schmeidler has conducted quantitative experiments in telepathy and clairvoyance with hundreds of students and other subjects, in an attempt to evaluate connections between objective interpersonal and personality factors and success or failure in **ESP** experiments. She has also taken an interest in the question of theories of survival after death.

In addition to her many articles on psychology, she has also published a number of articles on parapsychology, including: in *Journal* of the ASPR, 'Separating the Sheep from the Goats' (1945), 'Comparison of ESP Scores with Rorschach Scores by Different Workers' (1949), 'The Spontaneity Factory in Extrasensory Perception' (with A. O. Ross & Gardner Murphy, 1952), 'A Note on the Need for Rigid Testing Conditions' (1955), 'Agent-Percipient Relationships' (1958), 'Are There Two Kinds of Telepathy?' (1961), 'ESP and Tests of Perception' (1962); in *Journal of Parapsychology,* 'Personality Correlates of ESP as Shown by Rorschach Studies' (1949), 'Rorschachs and ESP Scores of Patients Suffering from Cerebral Concussion' (1952), 'Picture-Frustration Ratings and ESP Scores' (1954); and 'Personality Dynamics and Psychical Research' (*Bulletin of the Menninger Clinic,* 1954), 'Evidence for Two Kinds of Telepathy' (*International Journal of Parapsychology,* 1961), 'Note on Precognition With and Without Knowledge of Results' (*Psychological Reports,* 1961). She is co-author with R. A. McConnell of *ESP and Personality Patterns* (1958; 1973), and has also published *Extrasensory Perception* (1969), *ESP in Relation to Rorschach Test Evaluation* (1960), *Parapsychology;*

Its Relation to Physics, Biology, Psychology, and Psychiatry (1976), *Parapsychology and Psychology; Matches and Mismatches* (1988).

Schmidt, Helmut (1928-)

Physicist who has also specialized in parapsychology. Born in Danzig, Germany, February 21, 1928, he was educated at University of Göttingen (M.A. 1953), University of Cologne (Ph.D. physics 1958). From 1954-55 he was assistant professor of physics at University of Cologne, docent, 1960-63; visiting lecturer at University of British Columbia from 1964-65; senior research physicist at Boeing Science Research Laboratory from 1966-69; resident associate, Institute of Parapsychology from 1969-70, director from 1970-73.

He was concurrently National Academy of Science fellow at University of California, Berkeley from 1956-67; NATO exchange professor at Southern Methodist University, 1962. He is a member of the American Physics Society, the Parapsychological Association.

He has conducted research on quantum physics, cosmology and solid state physics. In the field of parapsychology, he has conducted research with electronic random generators and (with E. H. Walker) proposed a Psi Enhancement paradigm in which it is suggested that psi faculty is triggered at the instant of feedback of success in hits. He also worked with Walter J. **Levy** Jr. on possible PK in chickens, cockroaches and rats, but Levy was accused of manipulation in one of his studies concerned with rodent precognition.

Dr. Schmidt's many papers on parapsychology include: 'Clairvoyance Tests with a Machine' (*Journal of Parapsychology,* 1969), 'Precognition of a Quantum Process' (*Journal of Parapsychology,* 1969), 'PK Experiments with Animals as Subjects' (*Journal of Parapsychology,* 1970), 'The Psi Quotients (PQ): An Efficiency Measure for Psi Tests' (*Journal of Parapsychology,* 1970), 'A Quantum Process in Psi Testing' (in *Progress in Parapsychology* ed. J. B. Rhine, 1971), 'A PK Test with Electronic Equipment' (*Journal of Parapsychology,* 1970), 'PK Tests with a High Speed Random Number Generator' (*Journal of Parapsychology,* 1973), 'Comparison of PK Action on Two Different Random Number Generators' (in *Journal of Parapsychology* 1974), 'PK Effect on Random Time Intervals' (*Research in Parapsychology* 1973), 'Psychokinesis' (in *Psychic Exploration: A Challenge for Science* by E. D. Mitchell et al., Putnam, 1974), 'A Concept of a Mathematical Psi Theory' (*Research in Parapsychology* 1974, Scarecrow Press, 1975), 'Observation of Subconscious PK Effects With and Without Time Displacement' (*Research in Parapsychology* 1974), 'PK Experiment with Repeated, Time Displaced Feedback' (*Research in Parapsychology* 1975, Scarecrow Press, 1976), 'Towards a Mathematical Theory of Psi' (*Journal of the American Society for Psychical Research,* 1975), 'PK Effect on Pre-recorded Targets' (*Journal of ASPR,* 1976), 'A Take-Home Test in PK With Pre-Recorded Targets' (*Research in Parapsychology* 1977, Scarecrow Press, 1978), 'A Remark on the "Divergence Problem" ' (*European Journal of Parapsychology,* 1978), 'Use of Stroboscopic Light as Rewarding Feedback in a PK Test with Pre-recorded and Momentarily Generated Random Events' (*Research in Parapsychology* 1978, Scarecrow Press, 1979), (with R. L. Morris & L. Rudolph) 'Channeling Evidence to "Critical" Observers' (*Research in Parapsychology* 1981, Scarecrow Press, 1982), (with L. Pantas), 'Psi Tests with Internally Different Machines' (*Journal of Parapsychology,* 1981).

Schneider Brothers, Willi (1903-1971) and Rudi (1908-1957)

Powerful physical mediums of Braunau, Austria, discovered and tested by Baron **Schrenck-Notzing** under stringent conditions in the presence of a number of scientists. The father of the Schneider Brother was a linotype compositor. Of his six sons, four—Willi, Rudi, Hans and Karl—had psychic power, the latter two only in a slight degree.

The trance personality of Willi was a girl, "Olga," who said that her full name was Olga Lintner, and that she was identical with the notorious Lola Montez (Marie Dolores Eliza Rosanna Gilbert) who died in New York in 1861; she was the mistress of Ludwig I, the old king of Bavaria. Willi's mediumistic development was taken up by Baron Schrenck-Notzing.

Between December 3, 1921, and July 1, 1922, a hundred scientists witnessed Willi's **telekinesis** and **ectoplasm** phenomena under very strict test conditions and declared themselves completely convinced of their reality. The room was searched, the medium was examined by specialists, luminous bracelets and hands were sewn on his tight garment, and luminous pins were affixed so that his slightest movements could be seen by witnesses even in the dark. Besides, Willi sat outside the cabinet, two witnesses held his wrists and a third sat in front of him, holding his hands and keeping his legs between his own. Both medium and experimenters were shut off from the objects to be telekinetically moved by a gauze screen in the form of a cage.

The severity of the control did not prevent the phenomena. The result of these sittings was published in Schrenck-Notzing's *Experimente de Fernbewegung,* in 1924.

In English-speaking countries, the mediumship of the Schneider Brothers began to be talked about after British psychical researcher Harry **Price,** accompanied by Eric J. **Dingwall,** attended, on the Baron's invitation, some sittings in 1922 at Munich. Both Price and Dingwall signed statements that they witnessed genuine phenomena.

Meanwhile Willi aspired to be a dentist. With the concentration on his studies, his mediumship showed signs of weakening. Having left the Baron he went to Vienna where he lived with Dr. E. Holub, the head of a large asylum at Steinhof. He gave a series of sittings. When Dr. Holub died in 1924 the sittings were continued with university professors.

Late in 1924, at the invitation of the **Society for Psychical Research,** Willi Schneider, accompanied by Mrs. Holub, came to London, and from November 12 to December 13 gave twelve sittings on the Society's premises. According to E. J. Dingwall's report in *Proceedings* of the S.P.R. (vol. 36): "The only phenomena clearly observed were telekinetic, and even these were only striking upon a few occasions."

Making every effort to find a normal explanation he stated: "In order to raise an object 2-3 feet distant from him, the medium must have had concealed in his mouth an extensible apparatus workable by the mouth alone and by this means have supported a flat object lying on the table and raise it into the air from below. This feat must have been accomplished without any obvious interference with his breathing or speech; and when completed the rod must have been in some inexplicable manner withdrawn and again concealed in his mouth. We frankly do not believe such a device exists, and therefore are driven to the conclusion that the only reasonable hypothesis which covers the facts is that some supernormal agency produced the results."

The development of Rudi Schneider's powers was also under Baron Schrenck-Notzing's supervision. One night in a seance with Willi, "Olga" said that the power was not strong enough and that she wanted Rudi to assist. As Rudi was only eleven years of age then and was at the moment asleep in bed, the parents objected. "Olga" did not answer.

A few minutes later, however, the door opened and Rudi, in deep trance, entered and joined the circle. After that night, "Olga" permanently attached herself to Rudi and never spoke through Willi again. Her place was taken by "Mina," another female personality.

Rudi's first independent seance was held in November 1919, at Braunau. The **materialization** of a tiny hand was witnessed. A peculiarity of his sittings consisted of frequent intermissions which "Olga" demanded.

In 1923-24, Prof. Dr. Stefan Meyer and Prof. Dr. Karl Przibram, of the Institut für Radiumforschung der Academie der Wissenschaffen, Vienna, detected Rudi evading control. After that they had no reason to believe that any of the phenomena they witnessed were of supernormal character. Actually, however, fraud was more assumed than proved.

Rudi went on with his sittings. Reports of his mediumship appeared in the *Journal* of the American Society for Psychical Research, December 1925 by Prof. Thirring, in January-February 1926, by Harry Price, in March 1926, by Capt. Kogelnik, and May-June 1926, by Prof. Gruber.

In April, 1927, the journal *Psyche* published an article by Warren Jay Vinton which made a detailed and categorical charge of fraud through confederacy. Vinton was introduced at Braunau by Dingwall, attended a total of ten seances and concluded that the phenomena were caused by someone who secretly invaded the seance room.

The article made a stir and provoked strong comment both for and against these claims. Malcolm **Bird,** the research officer of the American Society for Psychical Research, desired to see the position for himself. He arrived at Braunau in October 1927, but owing to presssure of business could only stay for a single seance. His conclusion was that all the essentials of the Dingwall-Vinton theory were verified and all the conditions requisite to its operation were reproduced.

Some time after, Dr. Walter F. **Prince** attended a series of ten sittings with Rudi in Braunau and in Dr. Rudolf Lambert's house at Stuttgart. Phenomena were scarce. In his notes in Bulletin VII of the Boston Society for Psychical Research, published under the title 'Experiments with Physical Mediums in Europe' (1928), he came to the conclusion that the phenomena could not be considered genuine.

"Throughout the thirteen sittings" he wrote, "despite my studied and unremitting complaisance, no phenomena have occurred when I had any part in the control, save curtain movements which were capable of the simplest explanation."

These events somewhat dimmed the luster of Rudi's reputation. Baron Schrenck Notzing desired to settle the matter definitely and arranged an elaborate program of experiments for 1929. They were to be conducted in Herr Krall's laboratory under a completed system of partly electrical, partly tactual control. Early in 1929, however, both Baron Schrench-Notzing and Krall died.

In the same year, Harry Price paid a visit to Munich. On this occasion he made arrangements with Rudi to visit the **National Laboratory for Psychical Research** in London. Karl Amereller, an electrician who employed Rudi, accompanied him to London and installed his electric indicator in the laboratory. This indicator was developed from the electric chair idea of Harry Price.

As developed at the beginning of 1923, it consisted of a number of electric contact-makers, normally kept apart by light springs which corresponded to various parts of the medium's anatomy. The contacts were connected up with a row of colored indicator lights, so that should a person under test move a limb, or rise from the chair, the corresponding light immediately failed.

The plan of this indicator had been submitted to Baron Schrenck-Notzing and perfected by him and Amereller. In its latest phase, it controlled only the four limbs of the medium by four separate electric circuits. In the experiments at the National Laboratory, however, Harry Price decided to control the hands and feet of the sitters in the same way, making six separate circuits and corresponding lights in all.

The first series of seances took place between April 12-22, 1929. The second series lasted from November 14, 1929 to January 20, 1930. Both were eminently successful. As Harry Price stated in his conclusions in his book *Rudi Schneider; A Scientific Investigation of his Mediumship* (1930): "But the fact remains that Rudi has been subjected to the most merciless triple control ever imposed upon a medium in this or any other country and has come through the ordeal with flying colours. The genuineness of the phenomena produced at his London seances has impressed nearly one hundred persons, including scientists, doctors, business men, professional magicians, journalists, etc." The triple control involved: The holding of Rudi's hands and feet by one controller, a second person always having one hand upon the four locked hands of the medium and the controller; the electric indicator; the dressing of the medium in a pyjama jacket to which metallic gloves were sewn, he being invariably searched besides.

The phenomena witnessed were summed up by Harry Price as follows:

". . . cold breezes felt by everyone; an occasional fall in the temperature of the cabinet . . . violent movements of the pair of curtains . . . movements and levitations of the luminous waste paper basket . . . and the coffee table . . . the ringing of the bells and the twanging of the toy zither, even in midair; the emergence from, and withdrawal into, the cabinet of a handkerchief, afterwards found in a far corner, tied into a *tight* knot, the 'touchings' and 'brushings' of the sitters at the wonderful thirteenth, fifteenth, twenty-first and other seances; the intelligent knocking of the table . . . when it was resting against a sitter's leg near the end of the circle farthest from the medium; the tugs-of-war with Olga, and finally the emergence from, and withdrawal into, the cabinet of 'hands,' 'arms,' and 'tubes,' some perfectly formed. . . .

". . . the following scientists have been present at the Rudi experiments: Lord Rayleigh, Prof. A. O. Rankine, Dr. F. C. S. Schiller, Dr. William Brown, Prof. Nils von Hofsten, Prof. A. F. C. Pollard, Mr. C. E. M. Joad, Mr. A. Egerton, Prof. A. M. Low, Dr. Braun, Dr. David Efron, Dr. Eugene Osty and Dr. Jeans."

After the end of the seance on April 15, Harry Price casually remarked to journalist Hannen **Swaffer** that he would give a thousand pounds to any person who could produce the same effects under identical conditions, provided that if the person failed he would pay a like sum to the Laboratory. This was published as a challenge in the *Daily Express* and other papers. "No one appeared," wrote Harry Price, "to want a thousand pounds, and the magical fraternity showed a sudden and strange lack of interest in psychic things. . . . What baffled magicians was the fact that the phenomena occurred inside the cabinet while Rudi was outside, nearly five feet away."

Will Goldston, the famous stage magician, attended some seances and declared that under the same conditions a whole group of prestidigitators could not produce the phenomena which he witnessed.

As regards the personality, "Olga": "After many seances and 'confidential talks' with her," wrote Harry Price, "I am completely at a loss to know whether she is really a figment of Rudi's subconscious mind or actually a discarnate entity." After the end of the experiments, Harry Price handed a certificate to Rudi Schneider, on behalf of the Council of the National Laboratory of Psychical Research, stating that absolutely genuine phenomena have been produced through his mediumship. He added: "If the Laboratory issued a 'gold medal,' or 'diploma' for genuine mediumship under our own scientific conditions, we should have no hesitation in awarding it to Rudi. I know of no other physical medium who could claim it—except perhaps Miss Stella C. . . . If Rudi were to be 'exposed' a hundred times in the future it would not invalidate or affect to the slightest degree our considered judgment that the boy has produced genuine abnormal phenomena while he has been at the National Laboratory of Psychical Research."

The Schneider Brothers did not accept payment for their services. In London, Rudi was only paid as much as he would have earned at his trade as a motor engineer, from which he was taken. At a later date (1932), however, he raised his maintenance fees considerably.

In October and November 1930, Rudi sat at the **Institut Métapsychique** in Paris. According to the report of Dr. Eugene **Osty,** in the fourteenth seance infra-red photography revealed, at a distance from the medium, the existence of an invisible substance, localized in space but rigorously commanded by the psychical organism of the medium. Sound registering and recording instruments signaled the movements of this invisible substance. No screens and meshes of various materials, nor electrically charged plates could intercept it. An increase in red light, a change in the conditions of the room or of the position of the medium, however, always sensibly diminshed the action of the substance.

Under the conditions laid down by Dr. Osty, no fraud seemed possible. He was satisfied as to the reality of telekinetic movements. At the end of ninety sittings, Rudi was presented with a gift of 5,000 francs from the Institut in recognition of the willing manner in which he had submitted to experimentations. For details of the experiments see Dr. Osty's book *Les Pouvoirs inconnus de l'esprit sur la matière* (1932).

In the Spring of 1932, Rudi again sat at the National Laboratory of Psychical Research. Out of twenty-seven seances, eighteen were negative. His powers appeared to be on the wane. Nevertheless Osty's infra-red experiments were successfully duplicated and a number of distinguished scientists were convinced of the reality of the phenomena.

As, however, an automatic photograph taken in the twenty-fifth sitting apparently revealed (as disclosed a year later in Price's report *An Account of Some Further Experiments with Rudi Schneider*) an arm free behind Rudi when both his hands were supposed to be controlled by the sitter in front, Harry Price concluded that "it will be necessary for previous investigators to revise their findings."

Both this conclusion and its basis were subjected to vigorous attack by Prof. Fraser-Harris (*Light,* March 17, 1933). He gave his unqualified testimony to the genuineness of the medium. Several members of the Council of the Laboratory resigned in protest against the report.

Strong exception to Price's methods was also taken by Dr. Osty in an off-print from the *Revue Metapsychique,* April, 1933, (*L'Etrange Conduit de M. Harry Price*). It has also been suggested that Price misinterpreted or deliberately falsified this photograph.

In October-December 1932, Rudi gave twenty-seven sittings in London to Lord Charles Hope's research group. According to the report in *Proceedings* of the Society for Psychical Research (vol. 41, p. 131): "On the whole, the phenomena noted were weaker and less frequent than those reported as having taken place with the same medium elsewhere, but the results obtained go far to support the claims put forward by Dr. Osty in his report." Replying to Harry Price's allegation of trickery, Lord Charles Hope stated in a special section of the report:

"I submit that neither the evidence Mr. Price adduces nor his method of presentation is such as to make his charges count for anything against a medium with Rudi's record. What does emerge damaged from Mr. Price's report is his own reputation as controller, conductor of investigations and critic."

In an addendum, Theodore **Besterman** stated: "Quite apart from other and important considerations, Mr. Price's report appears to me to be in itself quite worthless as an exposure. It can have no effect on Rudi Schneider's standing."

The next development was *Bulletin V* of the National Laboratory of Psychical Research (*Rudi Schneider, the Vienna Experiments of Professors Meyer and Przibram*). This referred to sittings in 1924. The theories of fraud there advanced, however, had been dealt with earlier in Schrenck-Notzing's posthumous *Die Phenomene des Mediums Rudi Schneider* (December 1932) and by Dr. Osty (in his book). The rest of the Bulletin was devoted to answering the criticism which Dr. Osty and others levelled against Harry Price.

Meanwhile, Willi Schneider had retired from mediumship much earlier, after sittings with Baron Schrenck-Notzing. His psychic talents had waned, and he transferred his attention to studying dentistry. He died in 1971. Rudi eventually gave up mediumship, married, and became an automobile mechanic, eventually owning a garage. He died April 28, 1957 at Weyer, Austria.

For a critical view of Price's involvement with Willi and Rudi Schneider, see the chapter 'The Schneider Brothers' in *Search for Harry Price* by Trevor H. Hall (Duckworth, London, 1978). For an excellent examination of the Schneider mediumship and its investigators, see *The Strange Case of Rudi Schneider* by Anita Gregory (Scarecrow Press, 1985).

School of Economic Science

Shadowy British based organization which helped to promote the **Transcendental Meditation** technique of **Maharishi Mahesh Yogi** in Britain in the 1960s.

The School's roots actually stem from the land reform economic theories of Henry George (author of *Progess and Poverty,* 1879) and the mystical theories of G. I. **Gurdjieff** and his disciple P. D. **Ouspensky.** It commenced primarily as a political and economic group, founded by the Scot Andrew MacLaren in Glasgow. It was developed by his son Leon (Leonardo da Vinci), who added the esoteric philosophy of Gurdjieff and later the meditation popularized by Maharishi Mahesh Yogi, in the belief that the practical problems of the world could best be solved by transforming the nature of human beings.

Leon MacLaren was strongly attracted to the teachings of the Mahareshi at the latter's first visit to London in 1960, and in the following year organized the Maharishi's first world assembly in the prestigious Albert Hall, London. In that year a School of Meditation was established by members of the SES. Leon MacLaren made a pilgrimage to India and became convinced of the importance of Hindu-based meditation and philosophy. The connection with the Maharishi appears to have been eventually discarded and the School's own technique put in place.

Leon MacLaren began to devote more time to the SES, giving up his professional work as a barrister. Through the enthusiasm of members, the SES acquired a number of valuable properties throughout the U.K. and with the success of its teachings soon expanded abroad, with branches in European countries and in Ireland, the U.S., Canada, Australia, New Zealand, Greece, Cyprus, Malta, South Africa, Trinidad, and Fiji. The organization was variously styled "School of Philosophy," or "School of Economics and Philosophy." The enormous successful expansion appears to owe much to the systematic method organized by Leon MacLaren and his firm control over the organization's branches.

As with the Gurdjieff tradition itself, secrecy is part of the SES system of development, which incorporates a fairly traditional Hindu-based mysticism in the Vedantic tradition, involving knowledge of Sanscrit, as a transforming structure for creative influence in the world.

The organization has encountered some criticism. Dissidents have charged it with "brainwashing," and some have stigmatized it as an elite hierarchy. A hostile book *Secret Cult* by Peter Hounam & Andrew Hogg (Lion paperback, 1984) branded it as "a strange, eccentric, essentially Eastern cult," but many of the philosophical teachings described appear socially valuable. In the absence of any authoritative defense by the SES and its members, it is difficult to evaluate a movement which is essentially secretive.

School of Universal Philosophy and Healing

British Spiritualist organization founded in 1946 by the medium Mrs. Grace Spearman-Cook, based on the teachings of her spirit guide "Ra-Men-Ra." The purpose of Universal Philosophy is to awaken the soul to its spiritual destiny so that it may participate actively in the working and unfolding of the Cosmos. The School publishes a monthly journal

The Occult Gazette. Address: 6 Phillimore Place, Kensington, London, W.8, England.

Schrenck-Notzing, Baron Albert von (1862-1929)

German pioneer of psychical research, a physician of Munich who specialized in psychiatry which eventually led him into psychical research. He was born May 18, 1862, at Oldenburg, Germany, educated at the University of Munich. He investigated the mysteries of somnambulism while a student, when, in hypnotic experiments, he succeeded in obtaining duplications of **personality.** He soon realised that there was a new realm of science awaiting discovery here.

With a young woman of Munich, Lina M., he made experiments in **thought-transference.** They were described by Baron Carl **du Prel** in his books. Lina M. also presented the curious phenomenon of the **transposition of the senses.**

Magdeleine C., a musical medium, gave Schrenck-Notzing opportunity to study hypnotic alterations of personality. She was a dancer who, in trance, interpreted the feelings and reproduced the actions of various personalities, and played any piece of music mentally suggested by a committee on the stage.

These cases, the study of which was described in Schrenck-Notzing's monograph *Die Traumtanzerin Magdeleine C.* (Stuttgart, 1904) marked the transition between his researches on hypnosis and metapsychics. His medical reputation at the time was high, his outlook materialistic. He resigned from the Gesellschaft für Wiessenschaftliche Psychologie, a Spiritualist society which Carl du Prel founded, established himself as an authority in sexual anomalies and criminal psychopathy, published important essays upon the importance of **suggestion** in medico-legal practice, and wrote many other remarkable books.

By marriage (to Gabrielle Siegle in 1892) he became financially independent, surrendered his medical practice and devoted himself exclusively to research. With the awakening of his interest in metapsychics he founded the Gesellschaft für Metapsychische Forshung and began his study of **telekinesis** and teleplastics (see **Ectoplasm**) which rendered him famous. Up to the time of his death, there was no important medium in Europe with whom he did not conduct personal experiments.

He commenced with Eusapia **Palladino,** at whose seances he was present as early as 1894 in Rome. He followed her all over Europe and invited her twice as his guest to Munich. But he did not declare his belief in the reality of her phenomena until 1914, and only published his Rome and Munich seance records in *Physikalische Phenomena des Mediumismus* in 1920.

For many years he studied the phenomena of materialization of **Eva C.** (Marthe Béraud), at Mme. Bisson's house in Paris and at Munich. His book, *Materialisations-Phenomene* published in Germany in 1914, at the same time with Mme. Bisson's work in France, is amply illustrated with photographs and is one of the most significant contributions to modern psychical literature. The author discusses the phenomena with prudence and judgment and says: "I am of the opinion that the hypothesis of spirits not only fails to explain the least detail of these processes, but in every way it obstructs and shackles serious scientific research." He only arrived at some vague biological theory of teleplasmic phenomena.

The book evoked much public criticism. The pros and cons were summed up by the Baron in book form under the title *Der Kampf um die Materialisations Phenomene* (Battle for the Phenomena of Materialization). The two main works appeared in English translation under the title *Phenomena of Materialisation* (London, 1920, 1923; New York, 1975).

A supplementary volume to the original book was published in 1922. In it the cases of Willi **Schneider, Stanislava P.,** Maria **Silbert** and Einar **Nielsen** were presented. Schrenck-Notzing also sat with Stanislava **Tomczyk,** Franek **Kluski,** Linda **Gazzera,** Lucia **Sordi** and many other mediums. Their cases were reviewed in his book *Physikalische Phenomene des Mediumismus* (1920). He expressed his conclusions as follows:

"The telekinetic and teleplasmic phenomena are not only different degrees of the same animistic process, they depend in the end upon physical manifestations in the subconscious sphere of the medium. The *soi-disant* occult intelligences which manifest and materialise themselves in the seance, never display any higher spiritual faculty than is owned by the medium and the sitters; they are wholly of oneiric type, dream personifications that correspond to detached memories, to beliefs, to all the miscellaneous things that lie dormant in the minds of the participants. It is not on a foundation of extra-corporeal beings that one will find the secret of the psycho-dynamical phenomena of these subjects, but rather through consideration of hitherto unknown transformations of the biopsychical forces of the medium's organism."

When he discovered the mediumistic gifts of the **Schneider** children, he trained Willi Schneider so that the same phenomenon could be repeated under similar conditions at specified times and before varying observers. The conditions of these experiments were very strict and the records considered unimpeachable. An electrical system of control made the phenomena apparently fraud-proof.

The best evidence of this is the statement of a hundred profoundly skeptical, often hostile scientists who witnessed the phenomena in 1922 and declared themselves completely convinced of the reality of telekinesis and ectoplasm. The book, *Experimente der Fernbewegung,* Stugggart, 1924, in which he summed up the story of these researches, is one of the most important works on telekinesis.

In *Der Betrug des Mediums Ladislaus László,* published in the same year in Leipzig, he described his experiences in Budapest with a pseudo-medium. At the conclusion of a series of four sittings he advised Mr. Torday, the sponsor of the medium, of his uncertainties. Soon after László confessed to gross fraud.

When Willi Schneider lost much of his power, the Baron trained his brother, Rudi. He discovered another subject, Karl Weber (Karl Kraus), a young man who produced **levitations** at will and while awake. He reported on him at the Paris Congress.

However, Malcolm **Bird** in *Psychic Research* (July 1930) accused the Baron of "extraordinary improprieties in the way of suppressing unfavorable evidence," and cited as one instance that the Baron completely concealed at the Paris Congress that "Karl Weber" was identical with the notorious Karl Kraus.

In his last years, Baron Schrenck-Notzing devoted much attention to the phenomena of haunting. He left behind a posthumous book: *Gefälschte Wunder: Kraus-László-Schlag* in manuscript. In 1929, his widow published his collected articles: *Gesammelte Aufsätze zur Parapsichologie,* in which 47 pages were devoted to intellectual and more than 300 to experimental physical phenomena.

Another posthumous volume (*Die Phenomene des Mediums Rudi Schneider*) was published in December 1932. As René **Sudre** pointed out in his memorial article in *Psychic Research* (May 1929), the Baron never made any attempt at an inner interpretation of the phenomena he observed. "He lacked the spirit of the philosopher. With him there existed no urgent need for construction; he felt only the urge of accumulating material."

He certainly performed an immense service by his scientific approach and pioneer efforts to establish the reality of the physical phenomena of psychical research.

He died February 12, 1929 at Munich, Germany.

For a useful survey of his life and work, see the chapter 'Baron von Schrenck-Notzing' in *Pioneers of the Unseen* by Paul Tabori (Souvenir Press, London, 1972). (See also **Materialization; Schneider Brothers**)

Schuctzinger, C(aroline) E(va) (1909-)

Associate professor of psychology and German language, who also explored parapsychological subjects. Born February 14, 1909 in Munich, Germany, she was educated at Pädagogisches Institut, Munich (M.Ed. 1945), Incarnate Word College, San Antonio, Texas (B.A. 1951), St. Louis University, St. Louis, Missouri (M.A. 1955).

She was a lecturer at the Pädagogisches Institut, Munich from 1947-49; instructor (1956-57), assistant professor (1957-60), associate professor of psychology, German and philosophy (1960 onwards) at Mercy College, Detroit, Michigan. She is a member of the American Association of University Professors, Medieval Academy of America, Parapsychological Association, Katholischer Akademischer Verband, Germany, American Catholic Philosophical Association, American Catholic Psychological Association, American Association of Teacher of German Language.

She is author of the book *German Controversy on St. Augustine's Illumination Theory* (1960), and has studied such parapsychological subjects as telepathy, clairvoyance, psychokinesis and theories of survival.

Schwartz, Emanual K(ing) (1912-1973)

Psychologist who has written on parapsychology. Born June 11, 1912 in New York, N.Y., he studied at College of the City of New York (B.S.S. 1932; M.S. 1933), New York University (Ph.D. 1937), New School for Social Research, New York (D.S.Sc. 1949). In 1943 he married Reta Shacknove.

He was a practicing psychoanalyst for U.S. Army from 1942-46, associate dean, Postgraduate Center for Psychotherapy, New York from 1947-60, dean and director of training from 1963-73; associate professor, Long Island University from 1951-57; adjunct professor of psychology, New York University, 1960-73; clinical professor of psychology, Adelphi University, Garden City, New York, 1960-73. He was a former president of New York Society for Clinical Psychologists, chairman of Clinical Division, New York State Psychological Association, member of American Psychological Association, Society of Projective Techniques, Mexican Psychoanalytic Association, Academy of Psychotherapists, Council of Psychoanalytic Psychotherapists.

His studies in the field of parapsychology concern personality determinants in psychical experiences, and he has conducted research to ascertain whether hypnosis can facilitate such experiences. His articles in *Journal* of the American Society for Psychical Research included: 'The Study of Spontaneous Psi Experiences' (vol. 43, 1949), 'The Psychodynamics of Spontaneous Psi Experiences' (vol. 46, 1952). His essay on 'Bridey Murphy, A Symptom of Our Times' was included in the book *Beyond the Five Senses* (1957). His publications included: (with Alexander Wolf) *Psychoanalysis in Groups* (1962), (with A. Wolf) *Beyond the Couch* (1970), (with Lewis R. Wolberg) *Group Therapy, An Overview* (1973). He also contributed the column 'Facts, Fancies, and Reflections' to *Human Context,* London.

He died January 22, 1973.

Schweighöfer, Jurgen (1921-)

German psychologist who has written on parapsychology. Born June 22, 1921 at Allenstein, Germany, he studied at University of Mainz (Diplom-psychologe 1951; Ph.D. 1956). In 1947 he married Brigitte John. He served in the Germany Army from 1940-46, was clinical psychologist from 1951-52, school psychologist, vocational guidance officer from 1952 onwards. He is a charter associate of the Parapsychological Association.

Dr. Schweighöfer translated into German the book *Handbook of Tests in Parapsychology* by Betty Humphrey **Nicol,** and his psychology degree thesis was 'Probleme der Aussersinnlichen Wahrnehmung und Telekinese im Lichte der Amerikanischen Forschung' (Problems of Extrasensory Perception and Psychokinesis in the Light of American Researches, 1950). His Ph.D. thesis was 'Auffassungsstörungen bei Kindern aus Gestörten Familien' (Disturbances of Apperception in Children of Defective Families, 1956).

Schweizerische Vereinigung fur Parapsychologie

Semi-annual German-language publication containing information on parapsychological research in Switzerland and elsewhere, reports on conferences and details of courses at Berne University. Address: Industriestrasse 5, 2555 Brugg, Switzerland.

Scientific American (Journal)

In the summer of 1922, this well known New York journal decided to investigate the subject of psychical research. Contributions were invited but as these proved to be rather contradictory, a plan was worked out for first-hand investigation, and the sum of $2,500 promised for the demonstration of an objective psychic phenomenon before a committee of five.

From January 1923, when the offer was published in the *Scientific American,* it was to remain open until December 31, 1924. The committee consisted of William **McDougall,** Professor of Psychology at Harvard, Dr. Daniel Frost Comstock, late of the Massachusetts Institute of Technology, then a retired inventor, Dr. Walter Franklin **Prince,** Principal Research Officer of the American Society of Psychical Research, Hereward **Carrington,** the well-known psychical investigator and author, and **Houdini,** the stage magician and escapologist. For the secretaries duties, J. Malcolm **Bird,** associate editor of the *Scientific American,* was assigned to the committee in the quality of a non-voting member.

The psychics of America were reluctant to appear before the committee, the composition of which was objected to. This objection appears to have been vindicated by later events. In fourteen months, the committee had only three applicants. The verdict in each case was fraud, conscious or otherwise.

The offer of the *Scientific American* was enlarged in April 1924. It comprised the payment of the expenses of any high-class medium who would come forward regardless of the verdict. No response came, but Malcolm Bird succeeded in making arrangements with "Margery," the wife of Dr. L. R. **Crandon** of Boston, to sit for investigation in Boston. In return for the change of scene, necessitated by Dr. Crandon's professional engagements, the doctor waived the *Scientific American*'s offer to pay expenses and himself undertook to pay the expenses of the committee in Boston.

The first seance was held on April 12. The committee witnessed gradual development of interesting phenomena and made very good headway by the introduction of scientific instruments, to the stage of experience where final judgment might have been reached. However, friction, dissension and distrust arose between the members and culminated in unsavory developments.

The original mistake, as it was discovered too late, lay in the inclusion of Houdini among the members. He had established, at that time, a large reputation in the unmasking of fraudulent mediums. He was hopelessly committed against all possibility of genuine psychic phenomena and as, by the progess of the committee, he felt his reputation jeopardized, he soon abandoned all pretence of judicial consideration, assumed a dictatorial attitude and, in his eager search for fraud, did not refrain from suspecting his own colleagues, openly accusing Malcolm Bird with confederacy in producing the mediumistic phenomena.

Houdini obtained no proof whatever which the records of the sittings, also signed by him, would support against "Margery," yet after two sittings in July, against fifty previous sittings of his colleagues, witnessing the liberal occurrence of phenomena under strict test conditions, he was ready to expose her as a fraud, published a scurrilous pamphlet which could have been taken for an exposure of Malcolm Bird as well, and in numerous press interviews and lectures from the stage claimed to have infallibly demonstrated that the rest of the committee was duped.

At this stage, howver, Orson D. Munn, the publisher of the *Scientific American,* stepped in and as the finality of the exposure was in no way acknowledged by the committee itself, Munn prevailed upon Houdini to go back for further sittings in August, in which an attempt was to be made at getting a final verdict. At that stage, Carrington had pronounced the mediumship genuine and withdrew from further sittings. McDougall was otherwise engaged, so Comstock, Houdini and Prince remained on the scene.

Houdini constructed a "fraud-proof" wooden cage for the critical seance, but refused to sit with it in red light, demanded total darkness and categorically denied the request of his colleagues for its examination.

The committee, owing to Houdini's unscrupulous ways of controversy, did not insist. But the suspicion that Houdini was up to tricks was confirmed by a violent clatter after the first few minutes of the seance. The entire top of the cage was found open and Houdini at once stated that anybody sitting in it could throw it open with her shoulders. It appeared, therefore, that the cage served more the purpose of facilitating than preventing fraud.

This incident was followed with clashes between Houdini and "Margery's" spirit **control** "Walter," who demanded to know how much Houdini was getting for stopping phenomena. He advised Comstock to take the bell box out into white light and examine it. Sure enough, a rubber eraser, off the end of a pencil, was found tucked down into the angle between the contact boards, necessitating four times the usual pressure to ring the bell.

At the next seance, when the top of the cage was properly secured, Houdini, on some pretext, put his arm in through the porthole at the last minute. "Walter" thereupon denounced Houdini in the most fearful language that was ever used from the Beyond and accused him of putting a ruler in the cage under the cushion on which Margery's feet rested.

The accusation was proved. A two-feet jointed rule, of the sort used by carpenters, folding into four sections, was found at the designated spot. After this, an ultimatum was delivered to Houdini for handing over the cage to the committee. Houdini refused to comply with it, packed it up and carted it away.

The attitude of the rest of the committee towards the mediumship of "Margery" was also open to criticism. Prince sat ten times, Comstock fifty-six times, McDougall twenty-two times; none of them discovered fraud, yet they refused to agree the phenomena genuine. They were afraid, they disagreed between each other, they questioned the records afterwards and displayed gross negligence in their conduct of the case.

In eighty sittings with "Margery," not a single attempt was made to take her temperature, pulse, respiration, blood-pressure or weight before, during or after the seances. "Walter" several times accused Comstock of unfairness, of not telling the truth.

The climax came with Malcolm Bird's unofficial account of the investigation in the *Scientific American.* In the press reproductions, the distinction between the *Scientific American* and the committee was lost; headlines shrieked across the country that "Margery" was about to win the prize.

Prince insisted that the *Scientific American* articles be stopped until the committee was through with the case, and threatened resignation. Houdini sided with him.

So the articles were discontinued and Malcolm Bird, owing to the charges broadcast against him by Houdini, resigned the position of secretary to the committee.

When the August seances were over and still no verdict was reached, the *Scientific American* insisted on its rights and demanded a statement from the committee or from its individual members. These statements were published in November 1924. Carrington pronounced the mediumship genuine and so proved, Houdini pronounced it fraudulent and so proved. Comstock said he found it interesting and wanted to see more of it. Prince disclaimed to have seen enough. McDougall could not be reached, but later sided with Comstock. After this, Prince and McDougall attended some more seances. Prince witnessed bell ringing in perfect daylight with the bell box in his lap; McDougall had seen it ringing while being carried about the room, yet still they refused to commit themselves. And this was about the end of the investigation of the Committee of the *Scientific American.*

In April 1925, O. D. Munn announced: "The famous Margery case is over so far as the *Scientific American* investigation is concerned."

At the same date, J. Malcolm Bird left the editorial board of the *Scientific American* and became a staff member of the **American Society for Psychical Research,** while Walter Franklin Prince, formerly the Society's research officer and associate editor of its journal, resigned from the Society. The question of the "Margery" mediumship was now transferred from the *Scientific American* fiasco to the A.S.P.R. Bird's first article in the A.S.P.R. *Journal* was a notice of his own book *"Margery" the Medium* (1925).

For the continuing story of the controversial mediumship of "Margery," see Mina Stinson **Crandon.** For a skeptical view of her mediumship, see *Margery* by Thomas R. Tietze (1973).

Scientology

A second stage development of the **Dianetics** system invented by science-fiction writer L. Ron **Hubbard** (1911-1986). Like Dianetics, Scientology offers a kind of lay psychological and philosophical deconditioning to free the "analytic mind" from the confusions of the "reactive mind" caused by "engrams" (painful impressions from past experiences), but it goes beyond Dianetics in proposing engrams stretching back into innumerable previous births.

According to Hubbard's book *The History of Man* (1952), the human body houses two entities—a "genetic entity" (carrying on the evolutionary line), and a "Thetan" or consciousness, rather like an individual soul, which has the capacity to separate from body and mind. In the long evolutionary development from atoms through single-cell creatures, seaweed, jellyfish, clam, etc., the Thetan is trapped by the engrams formed at various stages of embodiment, such as "The Clam," "The Weeper," "Sloth," "Ape," "Caveman," "Piltdown Man," etc. These traps are described by such names as "Jack-in-the-Box" of "The Coffee-Grinder." The earlier Dianetics concept of a "clear" or liberated individual progressed in Scientology to the more difficult state of "MEST-Clear" (MEST = Matter-Energy-Space-Time).

Much of this might be considered as a colorful allegorical description of concepts of **reincarnation** and **transmigration** of souls found in Eastern religions.

During counseling sessions to remove engrams, a device called an "**E-meter**" is often used. This indicates galvanic skin resistance of a subject, drawing attention to areas of reactive tension in response to verbal and other stimuli during the sessions.

No short summary can do justice to the complexity of Scientology concepts and procedures, for which a continuing series of counseling and training fees are charged, and although the movement has nominally relaxed its former attitude of antagonism to critics and recidivists, there is still great sensitivity to criticism which is characterized as religious persecution. Various books critical of the movement, some by former followers, have been withdrawn from sale.

In November 1963, the State of Victoria in Australia instituted an inquiry into Scientology. After hearing evidence from 151 witnesses, it published the Anderson Report in 1965, resulting in the outlawing of teaching, practice and advertising of Scientology within State boundaries. On July 25, 1968, the Health Minister in Britain announced restrictions on the entry of Scientologists to Britain stating that Scientology centers would no longer be recognized as educational establishments.

Meanwhile Scientology had established religious status. In 1952, The Hubbard Association of Scientologists International was incorporated as a "religious fellowship" in Phoenix, Arizona. In the following year, the Church of Scientology was incorporated as a nondenominational church, and in 1954 the Founding Church of Scientology was established in Washington, D.C. On March 12, 1966, Hubbard announced that the British body had also become a church, stating "As all auditors will be ministers, ministers have in many places special privileges including tax and housing allowances."

A pamphlet entitled *The Character of Scientology* states that a Scientology minister is called an auditor, and that he "gives Confessionals and in Scientology the Confessional is called Auditing." This refers to the psychological techniques of investigating and processing the engrams of subjects.

A recent fact sheet issued by the Church of Scientology International states: "Scientology is a religion in the truest sense of the word. It is a study of wisdom, a study of life, a study of man's spiritual destiny. It is knowledge about why people have the problems that they have, about why people sometimes have trouble communicating with others, about the spiritual side of man, and about the things that stop people from using all their abilities. In short, Scientology covers the very basic knowledge about man and about life that is vital for each person to have if he is to be happy and accomplish those things he has set out to do. Scientology improves life in a troubled world."

Since its foundation, the Church of Scientology has grown to 466 Churches of Scientology and Scientology missions in more than 54 countries around the world. In the U.S. there are 48 churches and 83 missions, and a claimed international membership approaching the seven million mark. The Church has launched various social reform groups run by Scientologists, including The Citizens Commission on Human Rights, the Association for Better Living and Education, Narconon (concerned with eradication of drug abuse), Criminon (to rehabilitate prison inmates), and The Way to Happiness Foundation (stemming from Hubbard's booklet on moral codes *The Way to Happiness*, 1980).

Scientology remains a controversial movement, the subject of many legal actions for and against, and a topic of much discussion. Scientology has attracted much hostile criticism, as well as laudatory testimonials from converts who claim psychological and spiritual gains.

The case for Scientology is vigorously presented at any of their many churches and centers, and Hubbard's books *Dianetics: The Modern Science of Mental Healing*, and *The History of Man* are available from the Church of Scientology International, Los Angeles, and from individual churches throughout the world. For critical views, see *Cults of Unreason* by Dr. Christopher Evans (Farrar, Straus & Giroux, 1973; Dell Publishing Co. paperback, 1975), and the two biographies: *L. Ron Hubbard, Messiah or Madman?* by Bent Corydon & L. Ron Hubbard, Jr. (Lyle Stuart, 1987), *Bare-Faced Messiah: The True Story of L. Ron Hubbard* by Russell Miller (Michael Joseph, London/ Penguin Books, 1987). Both biographies suggest that Hubbard was strongly influenced by the ideas of occultist Aleister **Crowley.** For Hubbard's alleged early association with a black magic group, see entry under **Hubbard.**

Sciomancy

A somewhat obscure branch of **divination** concerned with the evocation of astral reflections to ascertain future events.

Scoresby, William (1789-1857)

British Arctic explorer, whaler, physicist, author and clergyman, who was also a pioneer in the study of **Animal Magnetism** (forerunner of **psychic science**).

He was born October 5, 1789, at Cropton, near Whitby. At the age of eleven, he accompanied his father (a master mariner) on a whaling expedition, afterwards resuming his education at a simple country school. Three years later, he was apprenticed to his father on a whaler, making annual voyages to Greenland, and becoming a ship's chief officer in 1806. Later in the same year, he resumed his studies, entering Edinburgh University, Scotland, studing chemistry and natural philosophy.

In 1807, he undertook a voyage to survey and chart the Balta Sound in the Shetland Islands. Afterwards he served with the fleet at Copenhagen. He left the navy a year later, and became acquainted with Sr. Joseph Banks, who introduced him to other scientists of the day. Scoresby made studies of natural phenomena and resumed attendance at Edinburgh University. On September 25, 1811, he married Mary Eliza Lockwood.

From 1813-17, he was at sea again, in charge of whaling vessels. In January 1819, he was elected a fellow of the Royal Society of Edinburgh, and in the following month contributed a paper on variations of the magnetic needle to the Royal Society of London.

In 1819, Scoresby moved with his family to Liverpool, where he superintended the building of the "Baffin," a vessel fitted for the Greenland trade. He made three successful voyages in this vessel, but on returning to Liverpool in 1822, he was grieved to find that his wife had died. He had been greatly attached to her, and her passing stimulated his strong religious convictions. On returning from a voyage in 1823, he entered Queen's College, Cambridge, England, to prepare for the minstry, studying Latin and Greek, but continuing to publish papers on science and exploration in his spare time. He was ordained in 1825, and for two years became curate of Bessingby, near Bridlington Quay.

He became corresponding member of the Institute of France in 1827, chaplain of Mariners Church, Liverpool, 1827-32, incumbent of Bedford

Chapel, Exeter, 1932-39. He was Vicar of Bradford from 1839-47, when he resigned through ill health, having spent six months leave on a voyage to the U.S. in search of a cure.

During earlier visits to Ireland, he had met and fallen in love with Elizabeth Fitzgerald of Corkbegg, and married her in June 1828. She passed away during another tour by Scoresby in Canada and the U.S. in 1848. Scoresby married for a third time in 1849, his third wife being Georgiana Ker. During his later years, Scoresby suffered a good deal from ill health, although he continued to publish valuable works on science and explorations. He died at Torquay on March 21, 1857.

His publications included: *An Account of the Arctic Regions, with a History and Description of the Northern Whale-Fishery* (2 vols., 1820; regarded as the standard work on the subject), *Magnetical Investigations* (2 vols., 1839-52); *The Northern Whale Fishery* (1849); *Zoistic Magnetism* (1849); *Memorials of the Sea; Sabbath in the Arctic Regions (1850); Memorials of the Sea; The Mary Russell* (1850); *The Franklin Expedition* (1850); *Memorials of the Sea; My Father; being records of the adventurous life of W. Scoresby Esq. of Whitby* (1951); *Journal of a Voyage to Australia for magnetical Research* (published posthumously in 1859). Among his stimulating scientific papers for the British Association and the Royal Society were discussions of after-images, titled 'Optical Spectra' and 'Pictorial and Photo-Chromatic Impressions on the Retina of the Human Eye.'

It was during his later years at Torquay that Scoresby became interested in Animal Magnetism (**Mesmerism**), arising from his observations on terrestrial magnetism during his polar voyages. He conducted a number of experiments, having found that he could mesmerize subjects easily. He gave the name "Zoistic Magnetism" to this hypnotic faculty. His third wife was one of his hypnotic subjects.

Scoresby's careful researches into possible clairvoyant faculty resulted in persuasive evidence for **thought transference** or **community of sensaton** between operator and subject. One entranced subject was able to describe accurately food which Scoresby tasted, and also identified sympathetically physical sensations in Scoresby's body. Another subject was immobilized as she sat on a sofa which had been "magnetized" by Scoresby, or was unable to move outside an imaginary circle which Scoresby had traced on the floor. The power of purely imaginary diagrams to imprison hypnotized subjects was often explored by early mesmerists and suggests affinities with the magic circles of occult magicians.

Scoresby's work in the field of Animal Magnetism is of special importance. His book *Zoistic Magnetism* influenced James **Esdaile,** who read it while he was in India. Esdaile claimed to have repeated successfully Scoresby's experiment in "magnetizing" a sofa, using an armchair with knobs which Esdaile had "magnetized." The subject was unable to remove his hands from the chair knobs until Esdaile had made mesmeric passes over him.

For detailed biographical information on Scoresby and his work, see *William Scoresby, Arctic Scientist* by Tom & Cordelia Stamp, Caedmon of Whitby Press, U.K., 1975. (See also **Animal Magnetism**; **Hypnotism**; **Mesmerism**)

SCOTLAND

(For early historical material, see the entry **Celts.**) **Witchcraft** and sorcery appear to have been practiced in the earliest historical and traditional times in Scotland. It is related that during the reign of Natholocus in the second century there dwelt in Iona a witch of great renown, so celebrated for her marvelous power that the king sent one of his captains to consult her regarding the issue of a rebellion then troubling his kingdom.

The witch declared that within a short period the king would be murdered, not by his open enemies but by one of his most favored friends, in whom he had most especial trust. The messenger inquired the assassin's name. "Even by thine own hands as shall be well known within these few dayes," replied the witch.

So troubled was the captain on hearing these words that he abused her bitterly, vowing that he would see her burnt before he would commit such a villainous crime. But after reviewing the matter carefully in his mind, he arrived at the conclusion that if he informed the king of the witch's prophecy, the king might, for the sake of his personal safety, have him put to death, so thereupon he decoyed Natholocus into his private chamber and falling upon him with a dagger slew him outright.

About the year 388, the devil was said to be so enraged at the piety of St. Patrick that he assailed the saint by the whole band of witches in Scotland. The story goes that St. Patrick fled to the river Clyde, embarking in a small boat for Ireland. As witches cannot pursue their victims over running water, they flung a huge rock after the escaping saint, which however fell harmlessly to the ground, and which tradition says now forms Dumbarton Rock.

Undoubtedly the persecution of witches constitutes one of the blackest chapters of history. All classes, Catholic and Protestant alike, pursued the crusade with equal vigor, probably inspired by the passage in *Exodus* (xxii,18) "Thou shalt not suffer a witch to live." While it is most probable that the majority of those who practiced witchcraft and sorcery were of weak mind and enfeebled intellect, yet a large number adopted the supposed art for the purpose of intimidation and extortion from their neighbors.

Witches were believed to have sold themselves body and soul to the devil. The ceremony is said to consist of kneeling before the devil, who placed one hand on her head and the other under her feet, while she dedicated all between to the service of the devil and renounced baptism. The witch was thereafter deemed to be incapable of reformation. No minister of any denomination whatever would intercede or pray for her. On sealing the compact, the devil then proceeded to put his mark upon her.

Writing on the "Witches' Mark," the Rev. Bell, minister of Gladsmuir in 1705 stated: "The witches' mark is sometimes like a blew spot, or a little tale, or reid spots, like fleabiting, sometimes the flesh is sunk in and hollow and this is put in secret places, as among the hair of the head, or eyebrows, within the lips, under the armpits, and even in the most secret parts of the body."

The Rev. Robert Kirk of Aberfoyle (see also **Fairies**) in his *Secret Commonwealth of Elves, Fauns and Fairies* (written in 1691) stated: "A spot that I have seen, as a small mole, horny, and brown colored, throw which mark when a large brass pin was thrust (both in buttock, nose, and rooff of the mouth) till it bowed [bent] and became crooked, the witches, both men and women, nather felt a pain nor did bleed, nor knew the precise time when this was doing to them (their eyes only being covered)."

In many cases the mark was invisible, and as it was considered that no pain accompanied the pricking of it, there arose a body of persons who pretended great skill therein constituted themselves as "witch prickers" and whose office was to discover and find out witches.

The method employed was barbarous in the extreme. Having stripped and bound his victim, the witch pricker proceeded to thrust his needles into every part of the body. When at last the victim, worn out with exhaustion and agony, remained silent, the witch pricker declared that he had discovered the mark.

Another test for detection was trial by water. The suspects were tied hands and great toes together, wrapped in a sheet and flung into a deep pool. In cases where the body floated, the water of baptism was supposed to give up the accused, while those who sank to the bottom were absolved, but no attempt was made at rescue.

When confession was demanded, the most horrible of tortures were resorted to, burning with irons being generally the last torture applied. In some cases a diabolic contrivance called the "witches' bridle" was used. The "bridle" encircled the victim's head while an iron bit was thrust into the mouth from which prongs protruded, piercing the tongue, palate and cheeks. In cases of execution, the victim was usually strangled and thereafter burned at the stake.

Witches were accused of a great variety of crimes. A common offense was to bewitch milch cattle by turning their milk sour, or curtailing the supply, raising storms, stealing children from their graves, and promoting various illnesses. A popular device was to make a waxen image of their victim, thrust pins into it and sear it with hot irons, all of which their victim was supposed to feel and at length succumb. Upon domestic animals they cast an **evil eye,** causing emaciation and refusal to take food until at length death ensued. To those who believed in them and acknowledged their power, witches were supposed to use their powers for good by curing disease and causing prosperity.

Witches had a weekly meeting at which the devil presided, every Saturday commonly called "the witches' Sabbat," their meetings generally being held in desolate places or in ruined churches, to which they rode through the air mounted on broomsticks (see **Transvection**). If the devil was not present on their arrival, they evoked him by beating the earth with a fir stick, and saying "Rise up foul thief."

The witches appeared to see the devil in different guises; to some he appeared as a boy clothed in green, others saw him dressed in white, while to others he appeared mounted on a black horse. After delivering a mock sermon, he held a court at which the witches had to make a full statement of their doings during the week. Those who had not accomplished sufficient evil were beaten with their own broomsticks, while those who had been more successful were rewarded with enchanted bones. The proceedings finished with a dance, the music to which the fiend played on his bagpipes.

The poet Robert Burns in his *Tale of Tam o'Shanter* gave a graphic description of this orgy. There were great annual gatherings at Candlemas, Beltane and Hallow-eve. These were of an international character at which the witch sisterhood of all nations assembled, those who had to cross the sea performing the journey in barges of eggshell, while their aerial journeys were on goblin horses with enchanted bridles.

Laws Against Witchcraft

Witchcraft was first dealt with by law in Scotland when by a statute passed in 1563 in the Parliament of Queen Mary, it was enacted: "That na maner of person nor persons of quhatsumever estaite, degree or condition they be of, take upon hand in onie times hereafter to use onie maner of witchcraft, sorcerie, or necromancie, under the paine of death, alsweil to be execute against the user, abuser, as the seeker of the response of consultation."

The great reformer John Knox was accused by the Catholics of Scotland of being a renowned wizard and having by sorcery raised up saints in the churchyard of St. Andrews, when Satan himself was said to appear and so terrified Knox's secretary that he became insane and died. Knox was also charged that by his magical arts in his old age he persuaded the beautiful young daughter of Lord Ochiltree to marry him. Nicol Burne bitterly denounced Knox for having secured the affections of "ane damosil of nobil blude, and he ane auld decrepit creatur of maist bais degree of onie that could be found in the country."

There were numerous trials for witchcraft in the Justiciary Court in Edinburgh and at the Circuit Courts, while session records preserved from churches all over Scotland also show that numerous cases were dealt with by the local authorities and church officials.

C. Rodgers, in his book *Social Life in Scotland,* (3 vols. 1884-86) stated: "From the year 1479 when the first capital sentence was carried out thirty thousand persons had on the charge of using enchantment been in Great Britain cruelly immolated; of these one fourth belonged to Scotland. No inconsiderable number of those who suffered on the charge of sorcery laid claim to necromantic acts with intents felonious or unworthy."

When James VI of Scotland in the year 1603 was called upon to ascend the throne of Great Britain and Ireland (as James I), his own native kingdom was in rather a curious condition. James himself was a man of considerable learning, intimate with Latin and Theology, yet his book on *Demonology* marks him as distinctly superstitious. Moreover while education and even scholarship were comparatively common at this date in Scotland (more common in fact than they were in contemporary England), the great mass of Scottish people shared abundantly their sovereign's dread of witches and sorcery. The efforts of Knox and his associates had brought about momentous changes in Scottish life, but if the Reformation ejected certain superstitions, it undoubtedly tended to introduce others. For that stern Calvinistic faith which now began to take root in Scotland nourished the idea that sickness and accident were a mark of divine anger, nor did this theory cease to be common in the north till long after King James' day.

It is a pity that the royal author, in the curious treatise mentioned above, volunteered few precise facts concerning the practitioners of magic who said to flourish in Scotland during his reign. But other sources of information claim that these people were very numerous, and whereas in Elizabethan England, it was customary to put a witch to death by the process of hanging, in Jacobean Scotland it was usual to take stronger measures. In fact, the victim was burnt at the stake, and it is interesting to note that on North Berwick Law, in the county of East Lothian, there is a tall stone which, according to local tradition, was formerly used as a site for such burnings.

Yet it would be wrong to suppose that witches and sorcerers, although handled roughly, were regarded with universal hatred, for in seventeenth-century Scotland medicine and magic went hand in hand, and the man suffering from a physical malady (particularly one whose cause he could not understand) very seldom entrusted himself to a professional leech, and much preferred to consult one who claimed healing capacities derived from intercourse with the unseen world.

Witches and wizards, however, were generally also experts in the art of poisoning, and while a good many cures are credited to them, their triumphs in the opposite direction would seem to have been much more numerous.

Thus we find that in July 1702, a certain James Reid of Musselburgh was brought to trial, being charged not merely with achieving miraculous cures, but with contriving the murder of one David Libbertoun, a baker in Edinburgh. This David and his family, it transpired, were sworn enemies of a neighboring household, by the name of Christie, and eventually their feud grew as fierce as that between the Montagues and Capulets. The Christies swore they would bring things to a conclusion, and going to Reid they petitioned his nefarious aid.

His first act was to bewitch nine stones, these to be cast on the fields of the offending baker with a view to destroying his crops, while Reid then proceeded to enchant a piece of raw flesh, and also to make a statuette of wax. The nature of the design is not recorded, but presumably Libbertoun himself was represented. Mrs. Christie was instructed to thrust the meat under her enemy's door, and then to go home and melt the waxwork before her own fire. These instructions she duly obeyed, and a little later the victim breathed his last, but Reid did not escape justice, and after his trial suffered the usual fate of being burnt alive.

A similar sentence was passed in July 1605 on Patrick Lowrie, a native of Halic in Ayrshire, and known there as "Pat the Witch," who was found guilty of foregathering with numerous sorceresses of the neighborhood, and of assisting them in disinterring bodies which they afterwards dismembered. Doubtless "Alloway's auld haunted Kirk," sacred to the memory of Burns, was among those ransacked for corpses by the band, yet if the crime was a gruesome one it was relatively harmless, and assuredly Lowrie's ultimate fate was distinctly a severe one.

On the other hand, Isobel Griersone, a Prestonpans woman who was burnt to death on the Castle Rock, Edinburgh, in March 1607, had a record of poisonings rivalling that of Cellini himself, while it is even recorded that she contrived to put an end to several people simply by cursing them.

Equally sinister were the exploits of another sorceress, Belgis Todd of Longniddry, who was reported to have brought about the death of a man she hated just by enchanting his cat. This picturesque method was scorned by a notorious Perthshire witch Janet Irwing, who about the year 1610 poisoned various members of the family of Erskine of Dun, in the county of Angus. The criminal was eventually detected and suffered the usual fate, while a few years later a long series of tortures, culminating in burning, were inflicted on Margaret Dein (née Barclay), whose accomplishments appear to have been of no commonplace nature.

The wife of John Dein, a burgess of Irvine, this woman conceived a violent aversion for her brother-in-law, Archibald, and on one occasion, when the latter was setting out for France, Margaret hurled imprecations at his ship, vowing none of its crew or passengers would ever return to their native Scotland. Months went by, and no word of Archibald's arrival reached Irvine, while one day a peddler named Stewart came to John Dein's house, and declared that the baneful prophecy had been duly fulfilled.

The municipal authorities now heard of the affair, and arresting Stewart, whom they had long suspected of practicing magic, they commenced to cross-examine him. At first he would tell nothing, but when torture had loosened his tongue he confessed how, along with Margaret Dein, he had made a clay model of the ill-starred barque, and thrown this into the sea on a particularly stormy night. His audience were horrified at the news, but they hastened to lay hands on the sorceress, whereupon they dealt with her as noted above.

No doubt this tale, and many others like it, have blossomed very considerably in the course of being handed down from generation to generation, and no doubt the witches of Jacobean Scotland are credited with triumphs far greater than they really achieved. At the same time, scanning the annals of sorcery, we find that a number of its practitioners firmly maintained, when confronted by a terrible death, that they had been initiated in their craft by the devil himself, or perhaps by a band of **fairies,** and thus, whatever capacities these bygone magicians really had, it is manifest that they possessed in abundance that confidence which is among the secrets of power, and is perhaps the very key to success in any line of action.

It is not surprising that they were dreaded by the simple, illiterate folk of their day, and, musing on these facts, we may feel less amazed at the credulity displayed by an erudite man like James VI, in declaring that all sorcerers "ought to be put to death according to the law of God, the civill and imperiale Law, and municipall Law of all Christian nations."

The last execution of a witch in Scotland took place in Sutherland in 1722. An old woman residing at Loth was charged, amongst other crimes, with having transformed her daughter into a pony, shod by the devil, which caused the girl to turn lame both in hands and feet, a calamity which entailed upon her son. Sentence of death was pronounced by Captain David Ross, the Sheriff-substitute. C. Rodgers related: "The poor creature when led to the stake was unconscious of the stir made on her account, and warming her wrinkled hands at the fire kindled to consume her, said she was thankful for so good a blaze. For his rashness in pronouncing the sentence of death, the Sheriff was emphatically reproved."

The reign of ignorance and superstition was fast drawing to a close.

Witchcraft, if it can be so called nowadays, was dealt with in modern times under laws pertaining to rogues, vagabonds, fortune-tellers, gamesters, and such like characters (see **Fortune-telling**).

Magic and Demonology

Magic of the lower cultus, perhaps the detritus of Druidism, appears to have been common in Scotland until a late period. In the pages of Adamnan, Abbot of Iona (c. 625-704 A.D.), the Druids were regarded by St. Columba and his priest as magicians, and he met their sorcery with a superior celestial magic of his own. Thus does the religion of one race become magic in the eyes of another.

Notices of sorcery in Scotland before the thirteenth century are scanty, if we except the tradition that Macbeth encountered three witches who prophesied his fate to him.

There is no reason to believe that **Thomas the Rhymer** (who was endowed by later superstition with adventures similar to those of Tannhauser) was really other than a minstrel and maker of epigrams, or that Sir Michael **Scott** was other than a scholar and man of letters. Other alleged of sorcery were numerous but obscure, and although often of noble birth as Lady Glamis and Lady Fowlis, were probably mostly ignorant persons.

We get a glimpse of Scottish **demonology** in the later Middle Ages in the rhymed fragment known as "The Cursing of Sir John Rowil," a priest of Corstorphine, near Edinburgh, which dates perhaps from the last quarter of the fifteenth century. It is an invective against certain persons who rifled his poultry-yard, upon whom the priest called down divine vengeance. The demons who were to torment the evildoers were: Garog, Harog, Sym Skynar, Devetinus "the devill that maid the dyce," Firemouth, Cokadame, Tutivillus, Browny, and Syr Garnega, who may be the same as that Girnigo, to whom cross children are often likened by angry mothers of the Scottish working-classes, in such a phrase as "eh, ye're a wee girnigo." The Scottish verb, to "girn" (to pull grotesque faces or grin), may find its origin in the name of a medieval fiend, the last shadow of some Teutonic or Celtic deity of unlovable attributes.

In Sym Skynar, we may have Skyrnir, a Norse giant in whose glove Thor found shelter from an earthquake, and who sadly fooled him and his companions. Skyrnir was, of course, one of the Jotunn or Norse Titans, and probably one of the powers of winter, and he may have received the popular surname of "Sym" in the same manner as we speak of "Jack" Frost.

A great deal has still to be done in unearthing the minor figures of Scottish mythology and demonology, and even the greater ones have not received the attention due to them. For example, in Newhaven, a fishing district near Edinburgh, we find the belief current in a fiend called Brounger, who is described as an old man who levies a toll of fish and oysters upon the local fisherman. If he is not placated with these, he wreaks vengeance on the persons who fail to supply him. He is also described as "a Flint and the son of a Flint," which strongly suggests that, like Thor and many other gods of Asia and America, he was a thunder or weather deity. In fact his name is probably a mere corruption of an ancient Scandinavian word meaning "to strike," which still survives in the Scottish expression to "make a breenge" at one.

With regard to practical magic, a terrifying and picturesque legend tells how Sir Lewis Bellenden, a lord of session, and superior of the Barony of Broughton, near Edinburgh, succeeded by the aid of a sorcerer in raising the devil in the backyard of his own house in the Canongate, somewhere about the end of the sixteenth century. Sir Lewis was a notorious trafficker with witches, with whom his barony of Broughton was overrun. Being desirous of beholding the devil in person, he secured the services of one Richard Graham. The results of the evocation were disastrous to the inquisitive judge, whose nerves were so shattered at the apparition of the Lord of Hades that he fell ill and shortly afterwards expired.

The case of Major Thomas Weir in 1670 is one of the most interesting in the annals of Scottish sorcery. "It is certain," stated Sir Walter Scott, "that no story of witchcraft or necromancy, so many of which occurred near and in Edinburgh, made such a lasting impression on the public mind as that of Major Weir. The remains of the house in which he and his sister lived are still shown at the head of the West Bow, which has a gloomy aspect, well suited for a necromancer. It was, at different times, a brazier's shop and a magazine for lint, and in my younger days was employed for the latter use; but no family would inhabit the haunted walls as a residence; and bold was the urchin from the High School who dared approach the gloomy ruin at the risk of seeing the Major's enchanted staff parading through the old apartments, or hearing the hum of the necromantic wheel, which procured for his sister such a character as a spinner.

"The case of this notorious wizard was remarkable chiefly from his being a man of some condition (the son of a gentleman, and his mother a lady of family in Clydesdale), which was seldom the case with those that fell under similar accusations. It was also remarkable in his case that he had been a Covenanter, and peculiarly attached to that cause. In the years of the Commonwealth this man was trusted and employed by those who were then at the head of affairs, and was in 1649 commander of the City-Guard of Edinburgh, which procured him his title of Major. In this capacity he was understood, as was indeed implied in the duties of that officer at the period, to be very strict in executing severity upon such Royalists as fell under his military charge. It appears that the Major, with a maiden sister who had kept his house, was subject to fits of melancholic lunacy, an infirmity easily reconcilable with the formal pretences which he made to a high show of religious zeal. He was peculiar in his gift of prayer, and, as was the custom of the period, was often called to exercise his talent by the bedside of sick persons, until it came to be observed that, by some association, which it is more easy to conceive than to explain, he could not pray with the same warmth and fluency of expression unless when he had in his hand a stick of peculiar shape and appearance, which he generally walked with. It was noticed, in short, that when this stick was taken from him, his wit and talent appeared to forsake him.

"This Major Weir was seized by the magistrates on a strange whisper that became current respecting vile practices, which he seems to have admitted without either shame or contrition. The disgusting profligacies which he confessed were of such a character that it may be charitably hoped most of them were the fruits of a depraved imagination, though he appears to have been in many respects a wicked and criminal hypocrite. When he had completed his confession, he avowed solemnly that he had not confessed the hundredth part of the crimes which he had committed.

"From this time he would answer no interrogatory, nor would he have recourse to prayer, arguing that, as he had no hope whatever of escaping Satan, there was no need of incensing him by vain efforts at repentance. His witchcraft seems to have been taken for granted on his own confession, as his indictment was chiefly founded on the same document, in which he alleged he had never seen the devil, but any feeling he had of him was in the dark.

"He received sentence of death, which he suffered 12th April, 1670, at the Gallow-hill, between Leith and Edinburgh. He died so stupidly sullen and impenitent as to justify the opinion that he was oppressed with a kind of melancholy frenzy, the consequence perhaps of remorse, but such as urged him not to repent, but to despair. It seems probable that he was burnt alive.

"His sister, with whom he was supposed to have had an incestuous connection, was condemned also to death, leaving a stronger and more explicit testimony of their mutual sins than could be extracted from the Major. She gave, as usual, some account of her connection with the queen of the fairies, and acknowledged the assistance she received from that sovereign in spinning an unusual quantity of yarn. Of her brother she said that one day a friend called upon them at noonday with a fiery chariot, and invited them to visit a friend at Dalkeith, and that while there her brother received information of the event of the battle of Worcester. No one saw the style of their equipage except themselves.

"On the scaffold this woman, determining, as she said, to die with the greatest shame possible was with difficulty prevented from throwing off her clothing before the people, and with scarce less trouble was she flung from the ladder by the executioner. Her last words were in the tone of the sect to which her brother had so long affected to belong: 'Many,' she said, 'weep and lament for a poor old wretch like me; but alas, few are weeping for a broken covenant.' "

The most reasonable view is that this seventy-year-old man, who suddenly confessed to crimes ranging from fornication, incest, sodomy and bestiality to witchcraft, was probably mad, obsessed by a religion of hell-fire and damnation. Undoubtedly his sister was a lunatic. For a discussion of this strange case, see Charles Kirkpatrick Sharpe, *Historical Account of the Belief in Witchcraft in Scotland* (1819, 1884) and Robert Chambers, *Traditions of Edinburgh* (1825 etc.).

Alchemy

James IV was attached to the science of **alchemy.** The poet William Dunbar described the patronage which the king bestowed upon certain adventurers, who had studied the mysteries of alchemy, and were ingenious in making "quintiscence," which should convert other metals into pure gold. In the Treasurer's Accounts there are numerous payments for the "quinta essentia," including wages to the persons employed, utensils of various kinds, coals and wood for the furnaces, and for a variety of other materials such as quicksilver, aqua vitae, litharge, auri, fine tin, burnt silver, alum, salt and eggs, saltpeter, etc. Considerable sums were also paid to several "Potingairs" for stuff of various kinds to the Quinta Essentia.

Thus, on the 3rd of March, 1501, "the king sent to Strivelin (Stirling) four Harry nobles in gold," a sum equal, as it is stated, to nine pounds Scots money "for the leech to multiply." On the 27th of May, 1502, the Treasurer paid to Robert Bartoun, one of the king's mariners, "for certain droggis [drugs] brocht home by him to the French leich, £31 : 4 : 0." On the 11th of February, 1503-04, we find twenty shillings given "to the man suld mak *aurum potabile,* be the king's commands." And on the 13th of October, 1507, the Treasurer paid six pounds for a puncheon of wine to the Abbott of Tungland, to "mak Quinta Essentia."

The credulity and indiscriminate generosity of the Scottish monarch appears to have collected around him a multitude of quacks of all sorts for, besides the Abbot, mention is made of "the leech with the curland hair," of "the lang Dutch doctor," of one Fullertone, who was believed to possess the secret of making precious stones, of a Dr. Ogilvy who labored hard at the transmutation of metals, and many other empirics, whom James not only supported in their experiments, but himself assisted in their laboratory.

The most noted of these adventurers was the person variously styled in the Treasurer's Accounts "the French Leich," "Maister John the French Leich," "Maister John the French Medicinar," and "French Maister John." The real name of this empiric was John Damian, and we learn from Dunbar that he was a native of Lombardy, and had practiced surgery and other arts in France before his arrival in Scotland. His first appearance at the court of James was in the capacity of a French leech, and as he is mentioned among the persons who received "leveray" (livery) in 1501-02, there can be no doubt that he held an appointment as a physician in the royal household.

He soon succeeded in ingratiating himself with the king, and it is probable that it was from him that James absorbed a strong passion for alchemy, as he about this time erected at Stirling a furnace for conducting such experiments, and continued during the rest of his reign to expend considerable sums of money in attempts to discover the **philosopher's stone.**

"Maister John," stated Bishop Lesley, "caused the king believe, that he by multiplying and utheris his inventions sold [should] make fine gold of uther metal, quhilk science he callit the Quintassence, whereupon the king made great cost, but all in vain." There are numerous entries in the Treasurer's Accounts of sums paid for saltpeter, bellows, two great stillatours, brass mortars, coals, and numerous vessels of various shapes, sizes, and denominations, for the use of this foreign adept in his mystical studies.

These, however, were not his sole occupations, for after the mysterious labors of the day were concluded, Master John used to play at cards with the sovereign—a mode by which he probably transferred the contents of the royal exchequer into his own purse, as efficaciously as by his distillations.

We find that on the 4th of March, 1501, nine pounds five shillings were paid "to the king and the French leich to play at cartis." A few months later, on the occasion of a temporary visit which the empiric found it necessary to pay to France, James made him a present of his own horse and two hundred pounds.

Early in the year 1504, the Abbot of Tungland, in Galloway, died, and the king, with a reckless disregard of the dictates of duty, and even of common decency, appointed the unprincipled adventurer to the vacant office. On the 11th March, the Treasurer paid "to Gareoch Parsuivant fourteen shillings to pass to Tungland for the Abbacy to the French Maister John," On the 12th of the same month, "by the king's command," he paid "to Bardus Altovite Lumbard twenty-five pounds for Maister John, the French Mediciner, new maid Abbot of Tungland, whilk he aucht (owed) to the said Bardus," and a few days later on the 17th, there was given "to Maister John the new maid Abbot of Tungland, seven pounds." Three years after, in 1507, July 27, occurs the following entry: "Item, lent, by the king's command to the Abbot of Tungland, and can nocht be gettin fra him £33 : 6 : 8."

An adventure which befell this dexterous impostor afforded great amusement to the Scottish court. On the occasion of an embassy setting out from Stirling to the court of France, he had the audacity to declare that by means of a pair of artificial wings which he had constructed, he would undertake to fly to Paris and arrive long before the ambassadors. "This time," said Bishop Lesley, "there was an Italiane with the king, who was made Abbot of Tungland. This abbot tuke in hand to flie with wings, and to be in France before the said ambassadors; and to that effect he caused make ane pair of wings of feathers, quhilk bein festinitt uponn him he flew off the castle-wall of Stirling; but shortly he fell to the ground and broke his thie-bane; but the wyte [blame] thereof he ascribed to their beand some hen feathers in the wings, quhilk yarnit, and coveted the myddin and not the skies." This incident gave rise to Dunbar's satirical ballad entitled "Of the Fenyeit Friar of Tungland," in which the poet exposed in the most sarcastic strain the pretensions of the luckless adventurer, and related with great humor the result of his attempt to soar into the skies, when he was dragged to the earth by the low-minded propensities of the "hen feathers," which he had inadvertently admitted into the construction of his wings.

The unsuccessful attempt of the abbot, although according to Lesley, it subjected him to the ridicule of the whole kingdom, does not appear to have lost him the king's favor, for the Treasurer's books, from October 1507 to August 1508, repeatedly mention him as having played at dice and cards with his majesty, and on the 8th of September 1508, "Damiane, Abbot of Tungland," obtained the royal permission to pursue his studies abroad during the space of five years.

He must have returned to Scotland, however, before the death of James, since the last notice given to this impostor is quite in character. On the 27th of March 1513, the sum of twenty pounds was paid to him for his journey to the mine in Crawford Moor, where the king had at that time artisans at work searching for gold.

From this reign to that of Mary, no magician or alchemical practitioner of note appears to have existed in Scotland, and in the reign of James VI, too great severity was exhibited against such to permit of them avowing themselves publicly. In James's reign, however, lived the celebrated Alexander **Seton** of Port Seton near Edinburgh, known abroad as "The Cosmopolite," who is said to have succeeded in achieving the transmutation of metals.

Magic and Religion in the Scottish Highlands

Pagan Scotland appears to have been lacking in benevolent deities. Those representatives of the spirit world who were on friendly terms with mankind were either held captive by magic spells, or had some sinister object in view which caused them to act with the most plausible duplicity.

The chief demon or deity (one hesitates which to call her) was a one-eyed Hag who had tusks like a wild boar. She was referred to in folk tales as "the old wife" (Cailleach), "Grey Eyebrows" or "the Yellow Muitearteach," and reputed to be a great worker of spells. Apparently she figured in a lost creation myth, for fragmentary accounts survive of how she fashioned the hills, brought lochs into existence and caused whirlpools by vengeful operations in the sea. Echoes of this boar-like hag survive in folk ballads of "Old Bangum" & "Sir Lionel" (Child No. 18), prefigured in ancient Hindu legends of the god Vishnu as the giant boar Vahara.

The Hag was a lover of darkness, desolations and winter. With her hammer she alternately splintered mountains, prevented the growth of grass or raised storms. Numerous wild animals followed her, including deer, goats, wild boars. When one of her sons was thwarted in his love affairs by her, he transformed her into a mountain boulder "looking over the sea," a form she retained during the summer. She was liberated again on the approach of winter. During the spring months, the Hag drowned fishermen and preyed on the food supply; she also stole children and roasted them in her cave.

Her progeny included a brood of monstrous giants, each with several heads and arms. These were continually operating against mankind, throwing down houses, abducting women and destroying growing crops. Heroes who fought against them required the assistance of a witch who was called the "Wise Woman," from whom they obtained magic wands.

The witch of Scottish folk tales is the "friend of man" and her profession was evidently regarded in ancient times as a highly honorable one. Wizards also enjoyed high repute; they were the witch-doctors, priests and magicians of the Scottish pagans, and it was not until the sixteenth century that legal steps were taken to suppress them in the Highland districts.

There seems to have been no sun-worship or moon-worship in Scotland, neither sun nor moon were individualized in the Gaelic language; these bodies, however, were reputed to exercise a magical influence. The moon especially was a "Magic Tank," from which supplies of power were drawn by those capable of performing requisite ceremonies. This practice has been revived by modern "white" witches in the ritual of "drawing down the moon."

But although there appear to have been no lunar or solar spirits, there were numerous earth and water spirits. The "water wife," like the English "mer wife," (see **Mermaids**), was a greatly dreaded being who greedily devoured victims. She must not be confused with the **Banshee,** that Fate whose chief business it was to foretell disasters, either by washing blood-stained garments or knocking on a certain boulder beside the river, or in the locality where some great tragedy was impending.

The water wife usually confronted a late traveler at a ford. She claimed him as her own, and if he disputed her claim asked what weapons he had to use against her. The unwary one named each in turn, and when he did so, the power to harm her passed away. One story of this character is as follows:

"The wife rose up against the smith who rode his horse, and she said, 'I have you: what have you against me?' 'My sword,' the man answered. 'I have that,' she said, 'what else?' 'My shield,' the man said. 'I have that and you are mine.' 'But,' protested the man, 'I have something else.' 'What is that?' the water wife demanded. To this question the cautious smith answered, 'I have the long, grey, sharp thing at my thigh.' This was his dirk, and not having named it, he was able to make use of it. As he spoke he flung his plaid round the water wife and lifted her up on his horse behind him. Enclosed in the magic circle she was powerless to harm him, and he rode home with her, deaf to her entreaties and promises.

"He took her to his smithy and tied her to the anvil. That night, her brood came to release her. They raised a tempest and tore the roof off the smithy, but the smith defied them. When day dawned they had to retreat. Then he bargained with the water wife, and she consented that if he would release her, neither he nor any of his descendants should ever be drowned in any three rivers he might name. He named three and received her promise, but as she made her escape she reminded him of a fourth river. 'It is mine still,' she added. In that particular river the smith himself ultimately perished."

Ever since, fishermen do not like to name either the fish they desire to procure or those that prey on their catches. Haddocks are "white bellies," salmon "red ones," and the dog-fish "the big black fellow." It is also regarded unlucky to name a minister, or refer to Sunday, in a fishing boat—a fact which suggests that in early Christian times fishermen might be pious churchmen on land but continued to practice paganism when they went to sea, like the Icelandic Norsemen who believed that Christ ruled their island, and Thor the ocean. Fairies must not be named on Fridays or at Hallowe'en, and Beltain (May Day) when charm fires were lit.

Earth worship, or rather the propitiation of earth spirits, was a prominent feature of Scottish paganism. There too magic played a leading role. Compacts were confirmed by swearing over a piece of turf, certain moors or mounds were set apart for ceremonial practices, and these were visited for the performance of child-procuring and other ceremonies which were performed at a standing stone.

In cases of sickness, a divination cake was baked and left at a sacred place: If it disappeared during the night, the patient was supposed to recover, if it remained untouched until the following morning it was believed that the patient would die.

Offerings were constantly made to the earth spirits. In a witch trial recorded in Humbie Kirk Session Register (September 23, 1649) one Agnes Gourlay was accused of having made offerings of milk, saying, "God betuch ws to; they are wnder the yird that have as much need of it as they that are above the yird" ("God preserve us too; they are under the earth that have as much need of it as they that are above the earth").

The milk poured out upon the earth at magical ceremonies was supposed to go to the fairies. "Gruagach" stones survived into relatively modern times in the Highlands. These were flat stones with deep "cup" marks. After a cow was milked, the milker poured into a hole the portion of milk required by the Gruagach, a long-haired spirit who is usually "dressed like a gentleman." If no offering was given to him, the cream would not rise on the milk, or even if it did, the churning would be a failure. There are interesting records in the Presbytery records of Dingwall, Ross-shire, regarding the prevalence of milk pouring and other ceremonies during the seventeenth century.

Among various "abominations" also referred to are those for which Gairloch parish continued to be notorious—"frequent approaches to some ruinous chappels and circulateing them; and that future events in reference especiallie to lyfe and death, in takeing of Journeyes, was exspect to be manifested by a holl [hole] of a round stone quherein [wherein] they tryed the entering of their heade, which [if they] could doe, to witt, be able to put in their heade, they exspect thair returning to that place, and failing they considered it ominous." Objection was also taken by the horrified Presbytery to "their adoring of wells and superstitious monuments and stones," and to the "sacrifice of bulls at a certaine tyme uppon the 25 of August" and to "pouring milk upon hills as oblationes."

The seer was usually wrapped in the skin of a sacrificed bull and left lying all night beside the river. He was visited by supernatural beings in the darkness and obtained answers regarding future events. Another and horrifying way to perform this divination ceremony was to roast a live cat. The cat was turned on a spit until the "Big Cat" (the devil) appeared and either granted the wish of the performer of the ceremony, or foretold what was to take place in answer to a query. In modern times, there are still memories of traditional beliefs regarding witchcraft, fairies, the evil eye, second sight and magical charms to cure or injure.

Individuals, domesticated animals and dwellings were charmed against witchcraft by iron and certain herbs or berries. The evil eye influence was dispelled by drinking "water of silver" from a wooden bowl or ladle. The water was taken from a river or well of high repute, silver placed in it, then a charm repeated, and when it had been passed over a fire, the victim was given it to drink and what remained was sprinkled round the hearth-stone with ceremony which varied in districts.

Curative charms were handed down in families from a male to a female and a female to a male. Blood-stopping charms were regarded with great sanctity and the most persistent folklore collectors were unable to obtain them from those who were reported to be able to use these with effect.

Accounts were given of "blood-stopping" from a distance. Although the possessor of the power usually had a traditional charm, he or she rarely used it without also praying. Some Highland doctors testified in private to the wonderful effects of "blood-stopping" operations. In relatively recent times, a medical officer of Inverness-shire stated in his official report to the County Council that he was watching with interest the operations of "King's Evil Curers" who still enjoyed great repute in the Western Isles. These were usually "**seventh sons.**"

"**Second-sight,**" like the power to cure and stop blood, runs in families. There is scarcely a parish in the Scottish Highlands without its family in which one or more individuals were reputed to have occult powers. Some had visions, either while awake or asleep. Others heard ominous sounds on occasions and were able to understand what they signified. Certain individuals confessed, but with no appreciation of the faculty, that they were sometimes able to foretell that a person was likely to die soon.

Two instances of this kind may be cited. A younger brother caught a chill. When an elder brother visited him, he knew at once that the young man would die soon, and communicated a statement to that effect to a mutual friend. According to medical opinion, the patient, who was not confined to bed, was in no danger, but three months afterwards, he developed serious symptoms and died suddenly. When news of the death was communicated to the elder brother, he had a temporary illness.

The same individual met a gentleman in a friend's house and had a similar experience; he "felt," he could not explain how, that this man was near death. On two occasions within the following week he questioned the gentleman's daughter regarding her father's health and was informed that he was "as usual." The daughter was surprised at the inquiries. Two days after this meeting, the gentleman in question expired suddenly while sitting in his chair.

Again the individual, on hearing of the death, had a brief but distressing illness, with symptoms usually associated with shock. The mother of this man had a similar faculty. On several occasions she saw lights. One day during the Boer War, an officer passing her door bade her goodbye, since he had been ordered to South Africa. She said, "He will either be slain or come back deformed," and turned ill immediately. A few months afterwards the officer was wounded in the lower jaw with a bullet, and returned home with his face much deformed.

The "Second-sight" faculty manifests itself in various ways, as these instances show, and evidence that it is possessed by individuals may occur only once or twice in a lifetime. There are cases, however, in which it is constantly active. Those reputed to have the faculty are most reticent regarding it, and appear to dread it.

At the close of the nineteenth century, "tow-charms" to cure sprains and bruises were sold in a well-known Highland town by a woman who muttered a metrical spell over each magic knot she tied as the afflicted part was treated by her. She had numerous patients among all classes. Bone-setters enjoyed high repute in some localities. In modern memory a public presentation was made to a Ross-shire bone-setter in recognition of his life-long services to the community. His faculty was inherited from his forbears.

Numerous instances may be gleaned in the Highlands of the appearance of the spirits of the living and the dead. The appearance of the spirit of a living person is said to be a sure indication of the approaching death of that individual. It is never seen by a member of the family, but appears to intimate friends. Sometimes it speaks and gives indication of the fate of some other mutual acquaintance.

The Supernatural in Scottish Fiction

Sir Walter Scott frequently introduced supernatural traditions into some of his novels and poems, while writers like Robert Louis Stevenson published powerful stories on occult subjects (see **English Occult Fiction**).

But the great source for magical and supernatural legends was the ancient balladry of Scotland. Many of the 305 ballads classified by Prof. Francis James Child of Harvard University in his great collection, regarded as definitive in its time, echo ancient stories and beliefs from a magical past. Some of these themes also descended from Scandinavian balladry.

For a scholarly presentation of such themes, see F. J. Child's monumental work *The English & Scottish Popular Ballads* (5 vols., 1882-98), recently supplemented by Bertrand Harris Bronson's *The Traditional Tunes of the Child Ballads* (4 vols., 1959-72).

From Folklore to Psychical Research

One of the earliest folklorists was surely the Rev. Robert Kirk, mentioned earlier, whose strange work *The Secret Commonwealth of Elves, Fauns, and Fairies,* written in 1691, reads like an anthropologist's report on a foreign country. The work is precise in its descriptions of fairy life and customs, and it is believed that Kirk himself became a prisoner in fairyland (see **Fairies**). The book was first printed in a limited edition in 1815, in 1893, and again in 1933.

Amongst Scottish folklorists whose researches preserved ancient legends and magical traditions, the most prominent was John Francis Campbell of Islay (1822-1885). From 1860-62, he published his four-volume work *Popular Tales of the West Highlands, Orally Collected.* Campbell's great collection achieved for Scotland what Jacob Grimm had done for the *Household Tales* of Europe.

Another important collector was Alexander Carmichael (1832-1912), who had collaborated with Campbell. Carmichael preserved the ancient Gaelic culture in his collection *Carmina Gadelica, Hymns and Incantations, With Illustrated Notes in Words, Rites, and Customs, Dying and Obsolete, Orally Collected in the Highlands and Islands of Scotland* (2 vols., 1900) and supplementary works.

Another great folklore scholar was Andrew Lang (1844-1912), a versatile genius who published over fifty major works concerned with poetry, book collecting, classical studies, Scottish history, English literature, anthropology, folklore and fairy tales. Lang was a founder-member of the **Society for Psychical Research,** and of the **Folk-Lore Society,** becoming a president of both organizations.

Lang was one of the earliest writers on psychical research to collate modern phenomena with the traditions and beliefs of ancient peoples, and his knowledge in this wide field was encyclopedic.

It was Lang who commented on reports of **crystal-gazing** that it was difficult to understand that so long as such things rested only on tradition, they were a matter of respectable folklore, but whenever contemporary evidence was produced, folklorists dropped the subject hastily!

In 1897, he published *The Book of Dreams and Ghosts,* in which he collated stories from all ages dealing with the whole field of the supernatural, including uncanny dreams, hauntings, bilocation, crystal-gazing, animal ghosts, and poltergeist.

Another important work by Lang was *Cock Lane and Common-Sense* (1894), which reviewed ancient Spiritualism, haunted houses, the famous Cock Lane poltergeist of London in 1762, apparitions, ghosts, hallucinations, second-sight, table-turning, and comparative psychical research.

Recommended reading:

Black, George F. *A Calendar of Cases of Witchcraft in Scotland 1510-1727,* New York Public Library (paperback), 1938

Bliss, Douglas Percy (ed.) *The Devil in Scotland,* Alexander MacLehose, London, 1937

Campbell, John F. *Popular Tales of the West Highlands, Orally Collected,* 4 vols., Edinburgh, Scotland, 1860-62; new edition, Alexander Gardner, London & Paisley, 1890; Singing Tree Press, 1969

Campbell, John L. & Trevor H. Hall. *Strange Things; The Story of Fr Allan McDonald, Ada Goodrich Freer, and the Society for Psychical Research's Enquiry into Highland Second Sight,* Routledge & Kegan Paul, London/Folklore Associates, Pennsylvania, 1968

Carmichael, Alexander. *Carmina Gadelica, Hymns and Incantations,* 2 vols., 1900; 2nd ed., 5 vols., Edinburgh & London, 1928-54

Child, Francis J. *The English & Scottish Popular Ballads,* 5 vols., Boston, 1882-98; 5 vols. in 3, Folklore Press/Pageant Book Co., 1957

Ferguson, John. *Witchcraft Literature of Scotland,* Edinburgh Bibliographical Society Papers, vol. III, 1899

James I. (King). *Daemonologie,* Edinburgh, Scotland, 1597; London, 1603; John Lane, London/Dutton, 1924

Kirk, Robert. *The Secret Commonwealth of Elves, Fauns and Fairies,* Edinburgh, 1815, 1893; Eaneas Mackay, Stirling, Scotland, 1933

Lang, Andrew. *The Book of Dreams and Ghosts,* London, 1897; Causeway Books, 1974

Lang, Andrew. *Cock Lane and Common-Sense,* London, 1894, 1896; AMS, 1970

Macgregor, Alexander. *Highland Superstitions Connected with the Druids, Fairies, Witchcraft, Second-Sight, Hallowe'en, Sacred Wells and Lochs,* Eneas Mackay, Stirling, Scotland, 1922

Mackenzie, Alexander. *The Prophecies of the Brahan Seer,* Eneas Mackay, Stirling, Scotland, 1935 (frequently reprinted)

Maclagan, R. C. *The Evil Eye in the Western Highlands,* David Nutt, London, 1902; E. P. Publishing, U.K., 1972; Norwood, Pennsylvania, 1973

MacLeod, Nicholas A. *Scottish Witchcraft,* James Pike, St. Ives, U.K., 1975

Macrae, Norman (ed.). *Highland Second-Sight; With Prophecies of Conneach Odhar of Petty,* G. Souter, Dingwall, Scotland, 1908; Norwood, Pennsylvania, 1972

Scott, Sir Walter. *Letters on Demonology and Witchcraft,* London, 1830; New York, 1831, 1855

Sinclair, George. *Satan's Invisible World Discovered,* Edinburgh, 1685; Edinburgh, 1865, 1971.

Scott, Christopher S(avile) O'D(onoghue) (1927-)

British sociologist who has experimented in the field of parapsychology. Born August 12, 1927 at Cuckfield, Sussex, England, he studied at Cambridge University (B.A. 1948, M.A. 1952). In 1955 he married Vilma Howard.

He was a psychologist at the British Admiralty, London from 1948-52, statistician at UNESCO, Paris from 1952-55, research officer of The Social Survey at British Central Office of Information, London from 1955-61, regional statistical adviser (Africa), United Nations, Addis Ababa from 1961 onwards. He is a Fellow of the Royal Statistical Society, member of the British Psychological Society, Society of Psychical Research, London, and an SPR Council member from 1957-60.

Mr. Scott experimented in an attempt to find a repeatable technique for the demonstration of extrasensory perception, and reported his finding in the *Journal* of the SPR (December 1959). He has also written on his theoretical study of models for psi in *Proceedings* of the SPR (October 1961).

He examined the work of Dr. Gertrude R. **Schmeidler** on the so-called "sheep-goat" effect on scoring in quantitative psi experiments.

In addition to articles on sociological subjects, Mr. Scott also published the following articles: in the SPR *Journal,* 'G. Spencer Brown and Probability: A Critique' (June 1958), in SPR *Proceedings,* 'Experimental Object-Reading: A Critical Review of the Work of Dr. J. Hettinger' (November 1959), 'Models for Psi' (October 1961). He contributed a review of the book *Probability and Scientific Inference* by G. Spencer Brown (*Journal* of the SPR, vol. 39) and *ESP and Personality Patterns* by McConnell & Schmeidler (*Journal* of the SPR, vol. 40).

Scott, Cyril (Meir) (1879-1970)

Eminent British composer, librettist, poet, Theosophist and author of books on occultism. Born September 27, 1879 at Oxton, Birkenhead (England), he studied music at Frankfort-on-Main, Germany. In 1921 he married novelist Rose Laure (Allatini).

He was only 21 when his *Heroic Suite* was performed at Darmstadt, Germany. He wrote for the piano, on which he also performed capably, as well as composing orchestral pieces, chamber and choral works and violin studies. He composed an opera *The Alchemist,* a ballet and a cantata, songs and ballads.

His poetic works included: *The Celestial Aftermath; The Vales of Unity; The Voice of the Ancient.* Mr. Scott made no secret of his Theosophical and mystical preoccupations, and his book *Music; Its Secret Influence Throughout the Ages* (1933; enlarged ed. 1950) was dedicated to "Master Koot Hoomi Lal Singh and his pupil Nelsa Chaplin." It deals with occult aspects of musical inspiration and its effects on the morals and aesthetics of different periods in history. This was a very original work and few writers have dealt with the subject, which deserves fuller investigation.

His occult and philosophical works included: *The Initiate* (1920;1977), *The Adept of Galilee* (1920), *The Initiate in the New World* (1927; 1977), *The Initiate in the Dark Cycle* (1932; 1977), *The Vision of the Nazarene* (1933), *An Outline of Modern Occultism* (1935), *The Christian Paradox* (1942). Other writings included: *Doctors, Disease & Health* (1938), *Cancer Prevention* (1968), *Victory Over Cancer* (1969), *Health, Diet & Commonsense* (1969). For autobiographical details see his books: *Memoirs, Entitled My Years of Indiscretion* (1924); *Bone of Contention* (1969).

He died December 31, 1970.

Scott, David (1806-1849) and William Bell (1811-1890)

These two brothers displayed unusual talent in the treatment of supernatural themes in art.

David Scott was born October 10 or 12, 1806, in Edinburgh, Scotland, and lived a comparatively uneventful life, his remarkable gifts being largely unrecognized by his contemporaries. His death on March 5, 1849 was hastened in some degree by this persistent neglect.

In modern times, however, connoisseurs have appreciated his paintings, perceiving in his work technical merits far transcending those of Raeburn himself, while people who care for art dealing with the supernatural have perceived that Scott's "Paracelsus" and "Vasco de Gama" are in the forefront of work of this kind.

His beautiful drawings for *The Ancient Mariner* express the very spirit of Coleridge, the arch-mystic, rendering it with a skill unsurpassed in any previous or subsequent illustrations to this poem.

William Bell Scott was also born in Edinburgh, his birth date being September 12, 1811. His career was very different from David's, for he won worldly success from the first, and before his death on November 22, 1890, he had received much acclaim.

Etching some of his brother's works, and painting a host of pictures, he was also a voluminous writer, and his *Autobiographical Notes of the Life of William Bell Scott* (2 vols., published posthumously, 1892) contains some really valuable comments on the mystic symbolism permeating the painting of the Middle Ages, and embodies also a shrewd and interesting account of D. G. Rossetti's essays in **table turning** and other Spiritualist practices. Moreover, William Bell's poems are almost all of a metaphysical order; and although it is extravagant to call him "the Scottish Blake," as many people have done, his mystical verse undoubtedly reflects a certain "meditative beauty," as "Fiona Macleod" (William **Sharp**) once wrote on the subject.

Scott (or Scot), Michael (c.1175-c.1234)

Scottish mathematician, physician, astrologer and reputed magician.

Although Michael Scott's life is shrouded in obscurity, his name is rather a familiar one, various causes having brought this about. In the first place, the poet Dante referred to him in his *Inferno,* speaking of him as one singularly skilled in magical arts, while Scott was also mentioned by Boccaccio, who hailed him as among the greatest masters of **necromancy.** Moreover, Coleridge planned a drama dealing with *Scott,* whom he asserted was a much more interesting personality than Dr. Faustus (see **Faust**), and then there is also a novel about him by Allan Cunningham, while above all, he figures in Sir Walter Scott's *The Lay of the Last Minstrel.*

Sir Walter Scott, no very careful antiquarian, identified the astrologer with one Sir Michael Scott of Balwearie, who, along with Sir David Wemyss of Wemyss, went to bring the Maid of Norway to Scotland in 1290. However, this identification is manifestly wrong, for in a poem by Vincent de Beauvais published so early as 1235, Michael Scott was mentioned as lately deceased.

Of course this does not altogether dispose the idea that he emanated from the family of Balwearie, whose estates were situated near Kirkcaldy, in Fife, and it is almost certain indeed, that he was a man of gentle birth, it being recorded that he studied at Oxford University, where it is improbable he would have attended had his parents not been in comparatively affluent circumstances.

When his Oxford days were over, Scott proceeded to the Sorbonne in Paris, where he acquired the title of *mathematicus,* and from the French capital he wandered on to Bologna, in those days famous as a seat of learning. He did not stay here for long, however, but went on to Palermo, while subsequently he settled for a while at Toledo, for he was anxious to study Arabic, and that town afforded good facilities.

He appears to have been successful with these studies thoroughly mastering the intricacies of the Arabic language, yet there was nothing to induce him to continue in Spain, and accordingly he went to Sicily, where he became attached to the court of Ferdinand II, probably in the capacity of state astrologer. At least, he is so designated in an early manuscript copy (now in the Bodleian Library, Oxford, England) of his book on astronomy, yet it is clear that, at some time or other, Scott had taken holy orders. For in 1223, Pope Honorius III wrote to the Archbishop of Canterbury, urging him to procure an English benefice for Scott, while it appears that in the following year the Archbishopric of Cashel in Ireland was offered to him, and that he declined this on account of his total ignorance of the Irish language.

This refusal to take a post for which he was unsuited reflected great credit on him, and it is clear that he was highly esteemed at the Vatican, for in 1227 Gregory IX, successor of Honorius, made further overtures to the English primate on behalf of Scott. Whether these proved fruitful or not, according to Roger **Bacon,** Scott came to England in 1230, bringing with him the works of Aristotle—at that date virtually unknown in this country—and contriving to give them a certain popularity amongst scholars.

It is reasonable to suppose that Scott, having come to England, also paid a visit to his native Scotland. And, although no documentary evidence is forthcoming to support this theory, local tradition at Melrose contends that the astrologer came to that town in his old age, and that he died there and was buried somewhere in the neighborhood.

Various other places in the Borders likewise claimed this distinction, and Sir Walter Scott stated that, throughout the south of Scotland, "any great work of great labour or antiquity is ascribed either to Auld Michael, Sir William Wallace, or the Devil."

One popular story about Scott maintains that he used to ride through the air on a demon horse, and another that he used to sail the seas on the back of some fabulous animal, while yet a further legend recounts that he went as Scottish envoy to the king of France, and that the first stamp of his black steed's horse rang the bells of Notre Dame, whereupon his most Christian majesty granted the messenger all he desired.

As regards the writings of Scott, he is credited with a translation of Aristotle's *De Animalibus,* but the ascription is not very well founded. However, it is almost certain that he wrote *Quæsto Curiosa de Natura Solis et Lunae,* which is included in the *Theatrum Chemicum,* while he was undoubtedly author of *Mensa Philosophica,* published at Frankfurt in 1602, and also of *Liber Physiognomiæ Magistri Michaelis Scot,* a book which was reprinted nearly twenty times, and was translated into various languages.

Reference has already been madc to a manuscript attributed to Scott in the Bodleian Library and it should be noted that at Corpus Christi College, Oxford, at the Vatican and at the Sorbonne, there are further documents purporting to have been penned by the astrologer himself, to have been written at his dictation, or to have been copied out by scribes soon after the actual author's decease.

Scottish Society for Psychical Research

Organization concerned with the study of parapsychology in Scotland, U.K. Organizes meetings and lectures, issues a regular Newsletter. Address: (c/o) Ms. Daphne Plowman, 131 Stirling Drive, Bishopbriggs, Glasgow, G64 3AX, Scotland, U.K.

Screech Owl

A variety of owl (*Megascops asio*) commonly found in America. The cry of the screech owl at midnight is said to portend evil.

Scriven, Michael John (1928-)

Professor of the logic of science who has written widely on parapsychology. Born March 28, 1928 at Beaulieu, Hampshire, England, he studied at University of Melbourne, Australia (B.A. 1948, math. hons., M.A. Math. & phil. hons. 1950). He took his Ph.D. at Oxford University, 1956. He was a tutor in the mathematics department at University of Melbourne from 1949-50, philosophy instructor at University of Minnesota from 1952-56, assistant professor of philosophy at Swarthmore College from 1956-60, professor of the history and philosophy of science at Indiana University 1960-66, professor of philosophy at University of California, 1966 onwards.

He was founder and former secretary of Melbourne University Society for Psychical Research, former president of Oxford University Society for Psychical Research. His memberships include: Mind Association, Symbolic Logic Association, Parapsychological Association, American Association of University Professors (chapter secretary from 1958-60); consultant to *Journal of Nervous and Mental Diseases, Contemporary Psychology, Philosophy of Science;* winner of *British Journal for the Philosophy of Science* essay award for 'The Origin of the Universe'; co-editor of *Minnesota Studies on the Philosophy of Science* vols. 1 & 2; co-author of *Psychology* (1960).

Prof. Scriven's interests include research in psychokinesis and spontaneous phenomena, and in the theoretical and philosophical implications of parapsychology. His articles include: 'Modern Experiments in Telepathy' (*Philosophical Review,* April 1956), 'New Experimental Designs for Psi Research' (*Journal* of the Society for Psychical Research, June 1956), 'Some Theoretical Possibilities in Psi Research' (*Journal* of the SPR, June 1957), 'Randomness and the Causal Order' (*Analysis,* October 1956), 'Extrasensory Perception' (*American Peoples Encyclopedia,* 1956). He has reviewed books on parapsychology for *Contemporary Psychology.*

His publications include: (with Herbert Feigl, ed.) *Foundations of Science and the Concepts of Psychology and Psychoanalysis* (1956), *Applied Logic* (1964), *Primary Philosophy* (1966), (with W. J. Moore & Eugene P. Wigner, ed.) *Symmetries and Reflections* (1967), *Evaluation* (1974).

Scrying

Divination by gazing into crystals or at shining surfaces. (See **Crystal-Gazing; Divination**)

Sea Phantoms and Superstitions

Sailors in general are often superstitious, as also fishermen, and others who dwell by deep waters. The old songs of the outer Hebrides off the coast of Scotland are full of wizardry, and this figures too in some of the old sea shanties. The novelist Captain Frederick Marryat, (1792-1848) who understood sailors as few others have done, testified repeatedly to their firm belief in the supernatural.

Nor was he the only author who has dealt with this subject. Coleridge also touched on the matter in his poem of the Ancient Mariner, and turning from literature to painting, that exquisite Scottish master David **Scott,** in a memorable canvas now in the seaport town of Leith, Scotland, showed Vasco de Gama and his henchmen gazing thunderstruck at an apparition rising from the waves.

And it is scarcely surprising, after all, that the supernatural should be a preoccupation of sailors, the mere fact that they live in constant danger of sudden death constituting a good reason.

In the duchy of Cornwall, England, so rich in romantic associations of all sorts, quite a number of stories concerning marine specters have been handed down from generation to generation, and are still remembered.

One of these stories relates how, on a winter's evening when a fierce gale was raging round the Cornish headlands, a fisherman chanced to see a ship in distress. The man hastened away at once, calling on some of his fellows to come and aid him in the work of rescuing the perishing. In a few minutes, a rowing boat had been manned, for Cornish fisherfolk are accustomed to go afloat in all weathers and to face the peril of drowning, while very soon the gallant rescuers were almost within earshot of the distressed vessel, and could see her name clearly on the stern. They thought to jump on board, their idea being that if the ship had a skillful pilot acquainted with the dangers of the coast, she might be steered safely into Falmouth harbour, but, just as one of the fishermen stood up in the prow of the boat intending to throw a rope, the great vessel looming before him disappeared from sight altogether.

She could not have sunk, for had that been her fate, some relics would certainly have survived upon the seething foam and billows, so vowing that the devil had conjured up a phantom to induce them to put out to sea, the rowers put their boat about speedily, and pulled for home with might and main. One and all, they were more afraid of the devil's machinations than of the more genuine perils they were encountering.

Another Cornish tradition of fishermen is associated with the village of Sennen Cove. This place is situated at the head of a bay flanked by two mighty capes. Sometimes a band of misty vapor stretches right across the bay, obscuring the villagers' outlook towards the sea beyond, and whenever this occurs, the fisherfolk regard it with awe, believing that it warns them not to put out in their boats. At one time, Sennen Cove numbered among its inhabitants a group of skeptical fishermen who laughed at this superstition. Accordingly, when the warning band of vapor next made its appearance, they sailed off singing gaily. But their boat never returned, their fate remained a mystery, and in the event they had strengthened rather than weakened the belief they had ridiculed.

Scotland has stories of phantom ships. Near Ballachulish, on the west coast of Argyllshire, there is a rocky island on which the Macdonalds of Glencoe used to bury their honored and laurelled dead, and the tradition of the district tells that once, some hundreds of years ago, a skiff bearing a beloved chieftain's corpse to this place of interment foundered before reaching its destination. For the Macdonalds, it was a horrible catastrophe that the father of the clan should be swept from sea to sea, and be denied a resting-place beside his ancestors. Soon it appeared as though the affair had actually been contrived by supernatural agency, for invariably, just before any misfortune overtook the tribe of Macdonald, the wrecked skiff was seen drifting about the sea, its dead oarsman clinging to it, and a coffin floating in its wake. This weird vision appeared only too often, and it was said that on the eve of the massacre of Glencoe, the specter boat bore a crew of ghostly female mourners who sang a loud coronach, their wails reverberating far among the neighboring mountains.

Another Scottish Highland story claims that a large ship, wrecked off the coast of Ross at the time of the first transportation of Celts to Canada, still rises occasionally from the waves which earlier claimed it as their prey, and, after sailing gallantly for a few minutes, suddenly lurches and sinks beneath the ocean. Dwellers by the shores of the Solway tell how a certain craft, which went down there while conveying a happy bridal party towards Stranraer, is frequently seen driving at full speed before the gale, the bride and bridegroom clinging to the rigging as though in terror of immediate death by drowning.

Nor is this the only phantom in the Solway firth, for that proverbially treacherous seaway, around which Sir Walter Scott cast so potent a halo of romance in *Redgauntlet,* witnessed once upon a time the foundering of two Scandinavian pirate vessels, and these are said to rise periodically from the water, the fierce and murderous crew of each calling for the mercy which they themselves never accorded their victims.

Religion has played a prominent part in some stories of specter ships. At Boulogne, France, for example, there is a tradition to the effect that on one occasion, at a remote date in the Middle Ages, the townspeople wanted to build a church, for at this time they were without any public place of worship, but they were anxious to choose a site which God would approve and found it difficult to come to a decision on this head, everyone concerned suggesting a different place.

Finally, in despair, a group of them assembled on the beach, intending to offer up prayer for a solution to the problem. While they were engaged thus they happened to look out to sea, when to their astonishment a vessel was seen sailing towards them, the sacred Virgin herself on board. Standing erect in the bows, she pointed with her hand in a certain direction, and the devout people concluded at once that their petition had been answered, whereupon the mysterious phantom vanished as quickly as it had come.

Another French specter ship, however, used to remain in sight for longer periods, while its appearance invariably struck terror into the hearts of all who beheld it. This was hardly surprising, since the vessel was manned by a crew of demons and great dogs—the perjured souls of men who had been guilty of fearful crimes. Yet the pious knew that in reality they had little to fear, the priests having told them that the repetition of a *paternoster* was adamantine proof against molestations from the hideous vision.

Somewhat similar to this story is one associated with Venice, where one stormy evening about the middle of the fourteenth century, a fisherman was requested to row three saints to a neighboring village on the Adriatic. After rowing for a while, he suddenly stopped and gazed as though petrified, a galley filled with swarthy Saracens having risen beside his boat. The oarsman vowed he would put back with all speed, but his godly passengers told him be of good cheer, and while they sang an *Ave Maria* the ominous galley was submerged by the hungry waves. So the fisherman rowed forward and reached his haven, the three saints rewarding him with a present of a gold ring. That ring figures in the old coat-of-arms of the Venetian Republic.

There are legends of the sea in most countries. In Japan, there are tales of phantom junks. The Chinese used to paint a pair of great eyes on the prow of their craft, so that these would detect any monsters which chanced to be prowling afloat. On the coasts of America, there are traditions of spectral vessels. Kindred stories are known in the Ionian Islands, and the folklore of Shetland embodies a wealth of such tales, while around the serried coast of Denmark, and the windswept fiords of Norway, many a phantom vessel was supposed to hover.

Indeed it was on the North Sea that the most famous of all supernatural ships was said to sail, the ship known to us as "The Flying Dutchman," and to the Germans as "Der Fliegende Holländer."

The story goes that a sailor who had loved a maiden but wronged her, grew weary of the liaison, left his sweetheart to languish, and put forth on the high seas where he committed many flagrant acts of piracy. But he was not to go unpunished, and the fates condemned him to sail wearily and everlastingly from shore to shore, this punishment to be endured till he should contrive to win the staunch affection of a virtuous woman and prove faithful to her.

So the wayfarer's vessel was driven hither and thither, the guilty man longing to tread solid ground once more, but whenever he dared to put in to port, and tried to win the right woman who might be able to save him, the devil drove him on board ship again, and his interminable voyage commenced afresh.

Century after century passed in this way, the ill fated vessel gradually becoming familiar to all who sailed upon the grey North Sea, or dwelt by its shores. The legend did not cease with a more skeptical civilization, for a great artist arose to give a new and more genuine immortality to the story. Richard Wagner evolved from legend a mighty drama, and his powerful music—charged so abundantly with the weirdness, mystery and glamor of the surging ocean—vividly evokes the Dutchman's ship driving before a fearsome gale, the criminal sitting terror-struck and hopeless at his useless helm.

Amongst persistent legends of the sea is the belief in great monsters of the deep. The sea serpent has been reported since earliest times. The Roman historian Pliny the Elder (c.23-79A.D.) described in his *Naturalis Historia* how a Greek squadron on a voyage for Alexander the Great saw a shoal of sea serpents, each thirty feet long, in the Persian Gulf.

Much more terrifying is the great sea serpent two hundred feet long and twenty feet broad cited by Olaus Magnus in his *History of Northern People* in 1555. It would be mistaken to assume that all reports of great sea serpents belong to a fabulous past or represent confused accounts of known sea creatures like whales or giant squids. Sea serpents continued to be reported into modern times, although some accounts would indicate creatures nearer to a plesiosaurus than a serpent. This is understandable, as the prehistoric plesiosaurus has a long neck which might appear like a serpent. One of the most celebrated such creatures is the famed **Loch Ness Monster** of Scotland (see **Monsters**).

More legendary are the ancient accounts of a gigantic sea creature named the Kraken. Bishop Eric Pontoppidan discussed the Kraken in his *Natural History of Norway* (1751) and concluded that it was of the nature of an enormous Polype or Starfish type. It is probable that it was one of the cephalopods popularly known as cuttlefish.

Less ominous are the enchanting stories of **Mermaids,** around whom many strange myths have grown. Nowadays it is generally supposed that mermaid stories grew around the dugong or sea-cow, which superficially resembles a human form. However, there are fascinating earlier accounts of mermaids which are difficult to dismiss out of hand. In an old history of the Netherlands, there is the following charming account of a sea-woman of Harlem in the fifteenth century:

"At that time there was a great tempest at sea, with exceeding high tides, the which did drowne many villages in Friseland and Holland; by which tempest there came a sea-woman swimming in the Zuyderzee betwixt the towns of Campen and Edam, the which passing by the Purmeric, entered into the straight of a broken dyke in the Purmermer, where she remained a long time, and could not find the hole by which she entered, for that the breach had been stopped after that the tempest had ceased.

"Some country women and their servants, who did dayly pass the Pourmery, to milk their kine in the next pastures, did often see this woman swimming on the water, thereof at the first they were much afraid; but in the end being accustomed to see it very often, they viewed it neerer, and at last they resolved to take it if they could. Having discovered it they rowed towards it, and drew it out of the water by force, carrying it in one of their barkes unto the towne of Edam.

"When she had been well washed and cleansed from the sea-moss which was grown about her, she was like unto another woman; she was appareled, and began to accustome herself to ordinary meats like unto any other, yet she sought still means to escape, and to get into the water, but she was straightly guarded.

"They came from farrre to see her. Those of Harlem made great sute to them of Edam to have this woman by reason of the strangenesse thereof. In the end they obtained her, where she did learn to spin, and lived many years (some say fifteen), and for the reverance which she bare unto the signe of the crosse whereunto she had beene accustomed, she was buried in the church-yarde. Many persons worthy of credit have justified in their writings that they had seene her in the said towne of Harlem."

A strange superstition of seafaring life related to the **caul,** a thin membrane found around the head of some new-born babies. A caul was considered a good omen for the child, and also for anyone who acquired a caul, and many seamen considered it was a powerful lucky charm against shipwrecks or death from drowning. There are many allusions to the occult power of the caul by early writers, and in Ben Jonson's play "The Alchemists" (Act i, sc.2), the character Face says to Dapper: "Ye were born with a Cawl o' your head." Belief in the power of the caul persisted even into the late nineteenth century, when advertisements relating to the sale of a caul frequently appeared in British newspapers.

As much as fifteen, twenty or even thirty guineas were asked by sellers. In the *Western Daily News* of Plymouth (February 9, 1867) a notice offered mariners a child's caul for five guineas. The *Times* (May 8, 1848) offered a caul for six guineas and described it as "having been afloat with its last owner forty years, through all the perils of a seaman's life, and the owner died at last in his bed, at the place of his birth."

Great stress was laid in the soundness of the article, thus in the *Times* (February 17, 1813) an advertisement stated, "A child's caul in a *perfect state* for sale."

The notion respecting a child's caul to prevent drowning prevailed in France as well as in England. It was alluded to in a *rondeau* by Claude de Malleville (born 1597).

The superstition respecting the caul is from remote antiquity, and was prevalent in the days of the Roman empire. Ælius Lampridius in his life of Antonine (surnamed Diadumeninus) stated that he was so called from having been brought into the world with a band of membrane round his forehead, in the shape of a diadem, and that he enjoyed a perpetual state of felicity from this circumstance during the whole of his life and reign. Pagan midwives, however, made no scruple of selling the caul, and their best market was the Forum, where they got high prices for it from the lawyers. Many of the councils of the early Christian Church denounced the superstition. St. John Chrysostom frequently inveighed against it in his homilics.

"Il est né coiffé," is a well-known French expression, describing a lucky man, and indicating that he was born with a caul.

It was believed that so long as the child from whom the caul had been taken enjoyed good health, the caul experienced the same, and was dry, flexible, and healthy, but on the caul-born person suffering from any sickness, or decline of health, the membrane also underwent a change, which became daily more apparent, either becoming totally crisp, or regaining its former flexibility, according to whether the person either died or recovered. Often these cauls became hereditary, being handed down from father to son (especially if it was born in the family), and were regarded by their respective owners with as much superstition as if the caul-born person was still living. (See also **Caul; Flying Dutchman; Loch Ness Monster**)

Recommended reading:

Bassett, F. S. *Legends and Traditions of the Sea and Sailors,* Belford, Clarke & Co., Chicago & New York, 1886

Benwell, G. & A. Waugh. *The Sea Enchantress; The Tale of the Mermaid and Her Kin,* Hutchinson, London, 1961

Gibson, John. *Monsters of the Sea; Legendary and Authentic,* T. Nelson & Sons, London, 1887

Gould, Rupert T. *The Case for the Sea-Serpent,* Philip Allan, London, 1930; Singing Tree Press, 1969

Heuvelmans, Bernard. *In the Wake of the Sea-Serpents,* Rupert Hart-Davis, London, 1968

Jones, William. *Credulities Past and Present,* Chatto & Windus, London, 1880; Singing Tree Press, 1967

Rappoport, Angelo. *Superstitions of Sailors,* Stanley Paul, London, 1928; Gryphon Books, Ann Arbor, Michigan, 1971

Seabrook, William (Buehler) (1886-1945)

American traveler and author who explored paranormal phenomena and occultism many years before the contemporary occult revival.

From the 1920s onwards, he lived with a Bedouin tribe in Arabia, witnessed whirling dervish dancing at a monastery in Tripoli, saw Yezidee devil worshipers in Kurdistan, studied voodoo in Haiti for a year, and also investigated black magic in West Africa.

Born February 22, 1886 in Westminster, Maryland, he was educated at Mercersburg Academy, Roanoke College, Salem, Virginia (Ph.B.); Newberry College, South Carolina (M.A.) and University of Geneva.

In 1908 he worked as a reporter on the Augusta *Chronicle,* Georgia, becoming city editor at the age of twenty-two. He went on to become a partner in an advertising agency in Augusta, then enlisted in the French Army in 1915. He was invalidated out after a gas attack at Verdun and awarded a Croix de Guerre. After a period as a farmer in Georgia, he went to New York, where he worked as a reporter on the *New York Times,* then as a writer for King Features Syndicate.

In 1924, he visited Arabia where he lived with a Bedouin tribe, and thereafter devoted himself to traveling and writing.

In 1933, he committed himself to a New York hospital where he was treated for alcoholism; his seven months treatment became the basis of his book *Asylum* (1935). He concluded that he had been running away from himself for twenty-seven years, and thereafter became cured.

In 1912, he married Katherine Pauline Edmondson. After divorce in 1934, he married novelist Marjorie Muir Worthington in 1935. They settled on a farm at Rhinebeck, New York.

He died September 20, 1945, at Rhinebeck.

His books included: *Jungle Ways* (1931), *Air Adventure* (1933), *The White Monk of Timbuctoo* (1934), *Adventures in Arabia* (1937), *These Foreigners* (1938), *Witchcraft: Its Power in the World Today* (1940), *Wizard of the Laboratory,* a biography of Dr. Robert W. Wood (1941), *No Hiding Place,* an autobiography (1942).

Seance

Sitting of a group of individuals for the purpose of obtaining paranormal manifestations or establishing communication with the dead. For success, at least one member of the group should be possessed of mediumistic powers (see **Medium**).

There are many ancient reports of seances, for example the Biblical account of Saul's consultation with the Witch of Endor, but the term is generally used only in connection with modern Spiritualism.

When, in 1848, the **Fox** family at Hydesville called in their neighbors to listen to the mysterious sounds which since become famous as the "**Rochester Rappings,**" the gathering was too informal to be called a seance, although all the necessary elements were present, but within the following two or three years, the concept of spirit communication spread throughout a large part of the eastern states and many Spiritualist **circles** were formed, and the phenomena which was, in the first instance apparently spontaneous, was not deliberately induced.

In the early stages of the movement these seances were conducted by private mediums, who took no fee for their performances, but later, professional mediums arose whose seances were open to the public on the payment of a fee. Both public and private seances continued, and still continue, to be an indispensable feature of Spiritualism.

Other early references to sitting of a seance type are found in the writings of the ancient Greek historian Porphyry (233-c. 304 A.D.) and in the book *A True and Faithful Relation of what passed between Dr. Dee and some Spirits* by the Rev. Meric Casaubon (1659).

Number of Sitters

The sitters need not have psychic powers, although the phenomena are stronger if they have. Their number should be limited and well chosen. As a rule seances are held with a single medium. Another powerful medium introduces another spirit **control** and the ensuing conflict between the controls often confuses the seance. But there are exceptions, too, especially as regards physical phenomena (see **Medium**).

The best average number of sitters is 8-9, but many mediums sit in larger circles. The great medium D. D. **Home,** even at the risk of offending the Empress of France, refused to sit with more than eight individuals. However, the sitters of Indride **Indridason** sometimes approached seventy. Mrs. **Ignath** demonstrated direct writing before a hundred people.

In isolated instances mediums have been known to demonstrate on the stage, although doubts surround the genuineness of such displays. The **Davenport Brothers** demonstrated before as many as a thousand people, but there is no firm evidence that their phenomena was genuinely Spiritualist.

Others who held seances in public halls were: The **Bangs Sisters,** for spirit paintings; Mrs. Suydam, for fire-resistance; Mrs. A. E. **Fay,** Lulu Hurst, Mrs. Annie Abbot, and Miss Richardson for feats of strength; Mrs. Etta **Roberts** and Mrs. Bliss for **materializations;** Mrs. M. M. Hardy for paraffin wax molds (see **Plastics**); William **Eglinton** for **slate-writing** and Mrs. **Murphy-Lydy** for **direct voice.**

Composition and Conditions of the Seance

Ideally the two sexes should be about equally represented. The majority of the sitters should not be too old. Young sitters provide favorable conditions if their attitude is serious and not flippant. Persons of doubtful morality should not be admitted into the circle. Those in ill health, preoccupied or nervous, should withdraw. Skepticism does not prevent success, but the effect of a hostile or suspicious mind is not helpful and may be a hindrance.

The establishment of a favorable environment is an essential condition of experimentation. Excitement or fatigue before the sitting should be avoided. The medium should not take any stimulants. He or she should be comfortable and kept in a genial frame of mind.

Both the medium and the experimenters have an equal share in success or failure. As the psychical researcher Gustave **Geley** aptly remarked: "Mediumistic investigations belong to the class of 'collective experiments,' for the phenomena are the result of subconscious psycho-physiological collaboration between the medium and the experimenters."

"There is much reason to think," wrote Prof. **De Morgan** to Dr. Alfred Russel **Wallace** at an early period, "that the state of mind of the inquirer has something—be it external or internal—to do with the power of the phenomena to manifest themselves. This I take to be one of the phenomena—to be associated with the rest in inquiry into cause. It may be a consequence of action of incredulous feeling on the nervous system of the recipient; or it may be that the volition—say the spirit if you like—finds difficulty in communicating with a repellent organization; or, may be, is offended. Be it which it may, there is the fact."

Strangers should not be introduced frequently into the circle. A series of at least six sittings should be held without modifying the group. New sitters should be admitted one by one at intervals of three or four sittings. No more than two or three sittings should be held a week. The abuse of experimentation may bring about a nervous breakdown in some cases.

Many seances are held in darkness or semi-darkness of the seance room which is believed to favor phenomena. The reason given by Spiritualists is that light often interferes with spirit manifestation. Skeptics retort that it favors fraudulent manipulations. However, darkness is not essential and much remarkable phenomena have been produced in good light.

The order of the sitting appears to be a matter of consequence. The controls often make changes to produce a better combination of psychic currents. After a chain has been formed by holding hands or placing them on the table with fingertips touching, the sitters are requested to engage in general conversation or to sing. It is said that speech or singing creates vibrations which are helpful to the production of the phenomena. For the same purpose, a phonograph or audio tape player can be used.

The Rev. W. Stainton **Moses** believed that the chief merit of music in the seance room was its soothing effect. It harmonized conditions. In his own circle, music was very seldom asked for by the communicators. The harmonizing was effected by means of perfumes and waves of cool scented air.

Nor was singing introduced. Indeed, any noise, even loud conversation, was checked at once and the sitters were told to keep still.

The utility of a general conversation, free and easy chatter, is that it prevents too much concentration on the part of the sitters. Tension, solemnity, eagerness, depression, are obstructive. Even with the great medium D. D. **Home** it often happened that strong attention prevented phenomena. When everybody stopped talking and looked at him, he awoke from the **trance.**

A medium often enters into a trance condition during a seance, although it is also known for a medium to retain normal consciousness throughout.

A natural, easy, relaxed attitude of the sitters is best conducive to phenomena. Fear or terror has an effect of breaking the manifestation. A table, partly levitated, may drop, a phantom may disappear at a scream. During his **levitations,** Home always asked the sitters not to get excited and talk of something else as, until he had risen above the heads of the circle, any movement or excitement on the part of the persons present appeared to have the effect of checking the force at work.

Once in Nice in 1874, he was nearly overtaken by disaster. In trance he buried his face and hands in the flames of the open fireplace. On seeing his head encircled by flames, Count de Komar started from his chair crying "Daniel! Daniel!" Home recoiled brusquely and after some moments he said: "You might have caused great harm to Daniel by your want of faith, and now we can do nothing more."

The medium should be carefully guarded from sudden emotions.

Dr. Frederick L. H. Willis, Professor of the New York Medical College, described his experience with a musical medium in *The Spiritual Magazine* (1867): "Scarcely had the medium struck the first note upon the piano when the tambourine and the bells seemed to leap from the floor and join in unison. Carefully and noiselessly I stole into the room, and for several seconds it was my privilege to witness a rare and wonderful sight. I saw the bells and tambourine in motion. I saw the bells lifted as by invisible hands and chimed, each in its turn, accurately and beautifully with the piano. I saw the tambourine dexterously and scientifically manipulated with no mortal hand near it. But suddenly . . . the medium became aware of my presence . . . instantly everything ceased . . . A wave of mental emotion passed over her mind, which was in itself sufficient to stop the phenomena at once."

In exemplification of the detrimental effect of any strong emotion on phenomena, Mrs. Emma Hardinge **[Britten],** in testifying before the committee of the **London Dialectical Society,** narrated the case of the medium J. B. **Conklin,** who was invited to hold a number of seances in Washington with five or six gentlemen who were desirous not to be known. "The manifestations were very marked and decisive until Mr. Conklin discovered that one of the gentlemen present was no other than President Lincoln, when his anxiety and surprise became so great as entirely to stop the manifestations which were not again renewed till a mutual explanation had restored him to his normal state of mind."

The medium should not be made eager to produce the phenomena. He should not be impressed that it is of decisive importance to have results. Speaking of D. D. Home, the psychical researcher Sir William **Crookes** wrote: "I used to say, let us sit round the fire and have a quiet chat and see if our friends are here and will do anything for us; we won't have any tests or precautions. On these occasions, when only my own family were present, some of the most convincing phenomena took place."

Atmospheric conditions have an important bearing. Dry climates are more favorable than wet ones. A thunderstorm is inimical. Dr. J. **Maxwell** observed that dry cold is helpful and rain and wind are often followed by failure. He found better phenomena when outside conditions favored the production of numerous sparks under the wheels of electric trams.

From 1880, the medium William **Eglinton** kept a careful record of the atmospheric conditions during his seances. He found that of the 170 total failures in 1884-85 the weather was either very wet, damp, or depressing in the majority of instances.

The locality and the furniture of the seance room are also of consequence. A place saturated with historic atmosphere facilitates manifestations. With the Marquis **Centurione Scotto,** much better results were obtained in the medieval **Millesimo Castle** than in Genoa. The psychical researcher Harry **Price** had striking clairvoyant descriptions of the life of St. Agnes in a seance held in the Roman catacombs (*Psychic Research,* 1928, p. 665).

The seance room should be plainly furnished. The table should if possible, be, entirely of wood, the chairs plain and wooden. Carpets, cushions, and heavy drapes should be dispensed with. They appear to absorb the psychic force, whereas a wooden table apparently stores it up. If possible the same room should be used on subsequent occasions and in the interval it should not be disturbed.

The Phenomena of Seances

The advent of manifestations is usually preceded by a current of cold air passing through the hands of the sitters or by a chilling of the atmosphere. Sometimes there are rapping sounds or movements of furniture. In some cases there are moving lights.

If there is a medium in the circle, he or she may breath heavily or groan before becoming entranced. The medium may then speak and deliver messages in the character of a spirit entity, with a marked change of voice. In the case of regular sittings, a spirit **control** may take charge of the proceedings and indicate how best the seance may be conducted, or what departed spirits give messages. With certain powerful mediums, messages may be given in **direct voice,** without using the medium's vocal apparatus.

In the simplest form of seance, communication is through **raps** or audible movements of the table. Questions are asked and the answers given by a single rap for "Yes" or a double-rap for "No," or whatever code of communication is agreed upon by the circle. The **ouija board** and **planchette** are more sophisticated forms of such communication suitable for one to three individuals rather than a full seance sitting. Another mode of communication for a single sitter or small group is **slate-writing,** although considerable doubt may surround the genuineness of this particular method since it is amenable to conjuring frauds.

It is convenient to classify phenomena such as **automatic writing** or speaking by a medium as "psychical," as distinct from the "mental" phenomena of **telepathy.** Such manifestations as raps, **table-turning** and slate-writing are also largely psychical, but also partly "physical." Physical manifestations proper involve more remarkable phenomena, such as **movement** of objects without contact (**telekinesis**), **levitation** of objects or human beings, bringing small objects such as flowers, fruit, jewels, etc., from a distance through closed doors (**apports**), heavy objects or people becoming very light, the manifestation of spirit forms which appear to have independent existence from the medium (**materialization**).

In the case of mediums who regularly manifest materialization phenomena, the medium is usually seated inside a small **cabinet** with a heavy curtain in front and the materialized forms issue from the cabinet. This cabinet is believed to conserve and condense psychic force in the production of spirit forms. Incidentally, not all materializations are of full-length spirit forms. Some are only faces or other partial shapes, in some instances even grotesque forms. Materialization mediums were often securely tied inside the cabinet as a protection against fraud.

Some of the great physical mediums of the past have demonstrated astonishing phenomena, such as handling live coals without injury, or the manifestation of spirit hands that wrote messages in clear daylight instead of the darkness or subdued light of a seance room. The most talented medium was undoubtedly Daniel Dunglas **Home,** who was never detected in fraud. An account of one of his most remarkable seances was given by H. D. Jencken in the journal *Human Nature* (February 1867) as follows:

"Mr. Home had passed into the trance still so often witnessed, rising from his seat, he laid hold of an armchair, which he held at arms' length, and was then lifted about three feet clear of the ground; travelling thus suspended in space, he placed the chair next Lord Adare, and made a circuit round those in the room, being lowered and raised as he passed each of us. One of those present measured the elevation, and passed his leg and arm under Mr. Home's feet. The elevation lasted from four to five minutes. On resuming his seat, Mr. Home addressed Captain Wynne, communicating news to him of which the departed alone could have been cognisant.

"The spirit form that had been seen reclining on the sofa, now stepped up to Mr. Home and mesmerised him; a hand was then seen luminously visible over his head, about 18 inches in a vertical line from his head. The trance state of Mr. Home now assumed a different character; gently rising he spoke a few words to those present, and then opening the door proceeded into the corridor; a voice then said:—He will go out of this window and come in at that window.'

"The only one who heard the voice was the Master of Lindsay, and a cold shudder seized upon him as he contemplated the possibility of this occurring, a feat which the great height of the third floor windows in Ashley Place rendered more than ordinarily perilous. The others present, however, having closely questioned him as to what he had heard, he at first replied, 'I dare not tell you,' when, to the amazement of all, a voice said, 'You must tell; tell directly.'

"The Master then said, 'Yes; yes, terrible to say, he will go out at that window and come in at this; do not be frightened, be quiet.' Mr. Home now reentered the room, and opening the drawing-room window, was pushed out demi-horizontally into space, and carried from one window of the drawing-room to the farthermost window of the adjoining room. This feat being performed at a height of about sixty feet from the ground, naturally caused a shudder in all present. The body of Mr. Home, when it appeared at the window of the adjoining room, was shunted into the room feet foremost—the window being only 18 inches open. As soon as he had recovered his footing he laughed and said, 'I wonder what a policeman would have said had he seen me go round and round like a teetotum!'

"The scene was, however, too terrible—too strange, to elicit a smile; cold beads of perspiration stood on every brow, while a feeling pervaded all as if some great danger had passed; the nerves of those present had been kept in a state of tension that refused to respond to a joke. A change now passed over Mr. Home, one often observable during the trance states, indicative, no doubt, of some other power operating on his system.

"Lord Adare had in the meantime stepped up to the open window in the adjoining room to close it—the cold air, as it came pouring in, chilling the room; when, to his surprise, he only found the window 18 to 24 inches open! This puzzled him, for how could Mr. Home have passed outside through a window only 18 to 24 inches open. Mr. Home, however soon set his doubts at rest; stepping up to Lord Adare he said, 'No, no; I did not close the window; I passed thus into the air outside.' An invisible power then supported Mr. Home all but horizontally in space, and thrust his body into space through the open window, head-foremost, bringing him back again feet foremost into the room, shunted not unlike a shutter into a basement below.

"The circle round the table having re-formed, a cold current of air passed over those present, like the rushing of winds. This repeated itself several times. The cold blast of air, or electric fluid, or call it what you may, was accompanied by a loud whistle like a gust of wind on the mountain top, or through the leaves of the forest in late autumn; the sound was deep, sonorous, and powerful in the extreme, and a shudder kept passing over those present, who all heard and felt it. This rushing sound lasted quite ten minutes, in broken intervals of one or two minutes. All present were much surprised; and the interest became intensified by the unknown tongue in which Mr. Home now conversed. Passing from one language to another in rapid succession, he spoke for ten minutes in unknown languages.

"A spirit form now became distinctly visible; it stood next to the Master of Lindsay, clad, as seen on former occasions, in a long robe with a girdle, the feet scarcely touching the ground, the outline of the face only clear, and the tones of the voice, though sufficiently distinct to be understood, whispered rather than spoken. Other voices were now heard, and large globes of phosphorescent lights passed slowly through the room."

The following extract is taken from an account of a seance held by Professor Cesare **Lombroso** with the famous Italian medium Eusapia **Palladino.**

"After a rather long wait the table began to move, slowly at first,—a matter explained by the scepticism, not to say the positively hostile spirit, of those who were this night in a seance circle for the first time. Then little by little, the movements increased in intensity. M. Lombroso proved the levitation of the table, and estimated at twelve or fifteen pounds the resistance to the pressure which he had to make with his hands in order to overcome that levitation.

"This phenomenon of a heavy body sustained in the air, off its centre of gravity and resisting a pressure of twelve or fifteen pounds, very much surprised and astonished the learned gentleman, who attributed it to the action of an unknown magnetic force.

"At my request, taps and scratchings were heard in the table. This was a new cause for astonishment, and led the gentlemen to themselves call for the putting out of the candles in order to ascertain whether the intensity of the noises would be increased, as had been stated. All remained seated and in contact.

"In a dim light which did not hinder the most careful surveillance, violent blows were first heard at the middle point of the table. Then a bell placed upon a round table, at a distance of a yard to the left of the medium (in such a way that she was placed behind and to the right of M. Lombroso), rose into the air, and went tinkling over the heads of the company, describing a circle around our table where it finally came to rest."

At this seance members of the company also felt themselves pinched and their clothes plucked, and experienced the touchings of invisible hands on their faces and fingers. The accuracy of the account—written by M. Ciolfi—was testified to by Professor Lombroso himself.

Some Problems of Seance Phenomena

It may seem surprising that a group of people sitting together can induce extraordinary phenomena that appear to defy normal physical laws, and it has been urged that suggestion may play a part. It will be recalled that the patients and disciples of Anton **Mesmer** were seated around the *baquet* or "magnetic" tub, connected by cords, and encouraged to sing or had some musical instruments played to create an atmosphere. It is difficult to rule out the possibility of conscious or even subconscious suggestion as a factor, bearing in mind the recent experiments of the Toronto Society for Psychical Research in creating an artificial seance entity named **'Philip,'** which eventually appeared to take on independent existence.

The occurrence of phenomena in itself is no proof of spirit agency, and the criterion must be a qualitative one. Even if a claimed spirit control is manifestly an artificial creation, the information or phenomena established through the seance convention may lead to evidence for survival that can be validated.

The important thing is that the paranormal character of phenomena should be established, that fraud, chance, unconscious muscular action etc., should be excluded and, in the case of mental phenomena, the possibilities of subconscious acting should be examined.

It is helpful to introduce visual and aural recording apparatus to register the objectivity of the manifestations. Experiments have shown that the senses may be deceived in the seance room atmosphere, and that individuals do not always remember accurately things seen or heard.

Nowadays the availability of still and movie cameras with sensitive films, video cameras, and tape recorders greatly simplifies the possibility of accurate records of seances. It is somewhat unfortunate that the perfection of recording apparatus has improved at a time when there are fewer great physical mediums. Had such apparatus been available to early experimenters like Sir William **Crookes,** we might have had permanent records of the extraordinary phenomena claimed for such mediums as D. D. Home and Florence **Cook.**

In conducting the seance, the influence of suggestion should be tested so far as possible. If things do not happen in accordance with the desire of the medium and of the sitters and the phenomena are intelligent, the presence of an extraneous will gains added probability. In seances with Eusapia Palladino, promises which she made were frustrated. The invisible operators broke photographic plates or blocks of paraffin wax with complete paranormal imprints.

It is true that secondary personalities often disclose an antagonistic character. In practice the possibility is not so difficult to deal with. The psychical researcher Ernesto **Bozzano,** in a seance with Palladino, had seen himself confronted with the image of his wife with whom he had been in constant litigation all his life and whose appearance he did not desire in the least. It takes an effort to suppose that such impersonation had been enacted by a secondary personality.

Hypnotic or secondary personalities cannot speak in strange languages which they have never acquired, cannot play instruments which require an unknown technique, nor can they produce the usual phenomena of the seance room. Subconscious impersonation could not reveal the future or things happening at a distance and would tend to concentrate on the appearance of those desired or thought of.

The other extreme of the problem is the claim of spirit impersonation, declared by Spiritualists to explain the frequent assumption of famous characters such as Shakespeare, Benjamin Franklin or even God (as claimed by a spirit entity cited in J. Maxwell's book *Metapsychical Phenomena,* 1905), on the part of the manifesting entities or to elucidate obviously lying messages. This is a delicate and difficult matter in which it is best to consult an experienced psychologist with knowledge of such manifestations.

Some seances of Home, according to the late Earl of Dunraven, were very touching and beautiful. A pure, lofty and religious tone more or less pervaded them. The solemnity which was always manifested at the name of God was remarkable.

The degree of perception among the sitters varies. It often happens at a seance, wrote Dr. Alfred Russel **Wallace** "that some will see distinct light of which they will describe the form, appearance and position, while others see nothing at all. If only one or two persons see the lights, the rest will naturally impute it to their imagination; but there are cases in which only one or two of those present are unable to see them. There also are cases in which all see them, but in very different degrees of distinctness; yet that they see the same object is proved by their all agreeing as to the position and movement of the lights. Again, what some see as merely luminous clouds, others will see as distinct human forms, either partial or entire."

It is said that the phenomena often require careful preparation from the other side. When William **Eglinton** produced materialized forms in the open air in Dr. Nichol's garden, "Dr. Richardson," the guide, declared: "It was an experiment for our own satisfaction; we have been preparing this seance for two days past." He also said that the manifestations required thought, experiment and perseverance on the part of the spirits, and that not merely a few, but myriads were associated to produce them.

The Wider Implications of the Seance

As mentioned earlier, the purposes and aims of a group of people sitting together may influence the result. Not enough research has been done on the mechanics of group phenomena. It is clear that the medium and the sitters usually feel a drain on their energies, manifest in fatigue and weakness afterwards; sometimes there is a demonstrable loss of weight.

We do not at present know how nervous energy is related to psychic force. There are hints in the claimed currents of energy in the human body which may be modified by **acupuncture** techniques, resulting in improvements in health, as also in the comparable concepts of **yoga** and the psycho-physical energy which the ancient yogis called **Kundalini,** expressed alternatively in sexual activity or the transformations of higher consciousness, sometimes with paranormal side effects.

Large groups of people in an atmosphere of emotional fervor may contribute to the spiritual or psychic **healing** of revival meetings. Analogies exist between entertainer and audience at concerts, theaters, rock music freakouts and even traditional religious services in churches.

In all cases, there is a single individual (or small group of individuals) acting as a focal point for the mass vital energies of the group. Entertainer, actor, minister or medium are all involved in vital energy exchanges and transformations.

The nature of such energy transformations is clearly affected by the established convention of the group occasion, and whereas a Spiritualist meeting or a church service may uplift the spirit, an entertainment may give cultural satisfaction, and some seances may merely lift up a table.

It is not clear how a street demonstration accumulates and releases the lowest common denominator of the mob, resulting in stone throwing, window smashing or other anti-social behavior while a revival meeting may result in paranormal healing. A small group of individuals around adolescent age may produce **poltergeist** phenomena; another small group of adults may facilitate messages apparently from departed souls.

Few psychical researchers have followed the lead of Dr. Nandor **Fodor** in investigating sexual aspects of mediumship. The connections between occultism and sexuality have been noted in other entries (see Aleister **Crowley; Sex Magic; Tantric Yoga**). So far, the only comprehensive view which links religious and psychical phenomena with the psycho-physical energies of individuals is the ancient Hindu concept of **Kundalini.**

More research and experimentation is necessary to test such concepts and elucidate the mass-energy equations involved which await the inspiration of some parapsychological Einstein. (See also **Cabinet;** Spiritualist **Circles; Control; Kundalini; Medium; Psychic Force; Spiritualism; Table-turning; Trance; Yoga**)

Recommended reading:

Abbott, David P. *Behind the Scenes With the Mediums,* Open Court, Chicago, 1907 etc.

Bayless, Raymond. *Voices From Beyond,* University Books, 1975

Carrington, Hereward. *The Physical Phenomena of Spiritualism; Fraudulent and Genuine,* Dodd, Mead, 1920

Carrington, Hereward. *The Story of Psychic Science,* Rider & Co., London, 1930

Flammarion, Camille. *Mysterious Psychic Forces,* Small, Maynard/T. Fisher Unwin, London, 1907

Gopi Krishna. *The Awakening of Kundalini,* Dutton (paperback), 1975

Hardinge [Britten], Emma. *Modern American Spiritualism; A Twenty Years' Record of the Communion Between Earth and the World of Spirits,* London, 1869, University Books, 1970

Holms, A. Campbell. *The Facts of Psychic Science,* Kegan Paul, London, 1925; University Books, 1969
Hyslop, James H. *Contact With the Other World,* Century, 1919
Le Bon, Gustave. *The Crowd; A Study of the Popular Mind,* T. Fisher Unwin, London, 1896
Leonard, Gladys Osborne. *My Life in Two Worlds,* Cassell, London, 1931
MacGregor, Helen & Margaret V. Underhill. *The Psychic Faculties & Their Development,* L.S.A. Publications (paperback), London, 1930
Maxwell, J. *Metapsychical Phenomena,* Duckworth, London, 1905
Myers, F. W. H. *Human Personality and Its Survival of Bodily Death,* Longmans, London, 2 vols., 1903, 1954; abridged one vol. ed., University Books, 1961
Owen, Iris M. & Margaret Sparrow. *Conjuring Up Philip,* Harper & Row, 1976
Richards, John Thomas. *SORRAT: A History of the Neihardt Psychokinesis Experiments, 1961-1981,* Scarecrow Press, Metuchen, N.J., 1982
Richmond, Kenneth. *Evidence of Identity,* G. Bell, London, 1939
Society for Psychical Research. *Hints on Sitting With Mediums,* (booklet), London, revised edition, 1965
Stemman, Roy. *Spirits and Spirit Worlds,* Aldus Books, London, 1975; Doubleday, 1976

Search Magazine

Quarterly publication dealing with UFOs and other mysteries, founded by entrepreneur occult publisher Raymond A. **Palmer.** *Search* magazine has now amalgamated with *Flying Saucers* magazine, formerly a separate publication.

Address: Palmer Publications Inc., P.O. Box 296, Amherst, Wisconsin 54406.

Sebottendorf, Rudolf Freiherr von
(1875-1945)

Name assumed by Adam Glauer, founder of the occult political **Thule Society** in pre-war Germany, and the Germanen Order.

Second Sight

Paranormal perception at a distance in time and space. This faculty of foreseeing future events is traditionally supposed to belong to certain individuals in the Scottish Highlands.

The great medium Daniel Dunglas **Home** who claimed descent from a Highland family was supposed to have second sight and described it in the following way:

"A deadly tremor comes over me, and there is a film on my eyes, and I not only see persons, but hear conversations taking place at a distance." While in Paris he saw his brother then in the North Sea. He saw his fingers and toes fall off. Six months afterwards tidings came of his having been found dead on the ice, his fingers and toes having fallen off through the effects of scurvy.

The chief peculiarity of second sight is that the visions are often of a symbolic character.

"The vision of coming events which some of the Highlanders possess," said Mr. F. G. Fraser in a lecture before the Societé Internationale de Philologie, Sciences et Beaux Arts in March 1927, "used to be accompanied, in some cases, by a nerve storm and by a subsequent prostration. It must not be confused with the sight of apparitions, nor does it depend upon artificial aids, such as accompanied by the invocation of the oracles in classic times."

"The foresight of the seers is not always prescience," wrote Dr. Samuel **Johnson** in *A Journey to the Western Islands of Scotland* (1775). "They are impressed with images, of which the event only shows them the meaning." He denied that "to the second sight nothing is presented but phantoms of evil. Good seems to have the same proportion in those visionary scenes as it obtains in real life."

According to some old books (Ranulf **Higden's** *Polychronicon,* 1482 and Robert **Kirk's** *Secret Commonwealth of Elves, Fauns and Fairies,* written in 1691, published 1815 etc.) second sight is communicated by touch. Napier's *Folklore or Superstitious Beliefs in the West of Scotland* (1879) mentions the practice as surviving in the nineteenth century.

The belief in second sight dates back to a very early period in the history of these regions, and is still not altogether extinct.

Apart from the name, which is used in Scotland, second sight itself is not exclusive to the Celts of Scotland, for it is allied to the **clairvoyance,** prophetic vision, soothsaying, and so on, which have existed from time immemorial in practically every part of the world. Yet the second sight has certain distinctive features of its own.

It may, for instance, be either congenital or acquired. In the former case, it generally falls to the **seventh son** of a seventh son, by reason, probably, of the potency of the mystic number seven.

Sometimes a Highlander may find himself suddenly endowed with the mysterious faculty. A person gifted with second sight is said to be "fey." Generally there is no apparent departure from the normal consciousness during the vision, although sometimes a seer may complain of a feeling of disquiet or uneasiness. A vision may be communicated from one person to another, usually by contact, but the secondary vision is dimmer than that of the original seer.

A frequent vision is that of a funeral, indicating that a death will shortly take place in the community. This is an instance of the second sight taking a symbolical turn, and this is its usual form. Occasionally the apparition of the doomed man will be seen—his wraith, or **double**—while he himself is far distant.

Another form frequently taken by the second sight is that of "seeing lights." The lights, too, may indicate death, but they may likewise predict lesser happenings. In one instance, a light was seen by two persons to hover above the "Big House" (the mansion of the laird), then to travel swiftly in the direction of the gamekeeper's cottage, where it remains stationary for a while. Next day the gamekeeper was found dead.

Animals also are said to possess second sight, which is especially frequent among dogs and horses. Two men were travelling from Easdale to Oban on a stormy night. In traversing a short cut through a wood, one of them died from fatigue and exposure. That night more than one horse had to be carefully led past the spot by his driver, who as yet knew nothing of the tragedy.

Indeed, many Highlanders used to believe that the faculty was common to all the lower animals, else why should they whine and bristle when there is nothing visible to human eyes, nothing audible to human ears?

Notwithstanding that the march of civilization has eroded the occult beliefs of the Highlanders, second sight is still believed in, even by those who claim that they are not in the least "superstitious." (See also **Clairvoyance; Crystal Gazing; Premonition; Prediction; Scotland**)

Recommended reading

Campbell, John L. & Trevor H. Hall. *Strange Things; The Story of Fr Allan McDonald, Ada Goodrich Freer, and the Society for Psychical Research's Enquiry into Highland Second Sight,* Routledge & Kegan Paul, London/Folklore Associates, Pennsylvania, 1968

Mackenzie, Alexander. *The Prophecies of the Brahan Seer,* Eneas Mackay, Stirling, Scotland, 1935

Macrae, Norman (ed.). *Highland Second-Sight; With Prophecies of Conneach Odhar of Petty,* G. Souter, Dingwall, Scotland, 1908; Norwood, Pennsylvania, 1972

Napier, James. *Folklore, or Superstitious Beliefs in the West of Scotland, within this Century,* Paisley, Scotland, 1879

Secret Chiefs

Traditionally the hidden superhuman adepts who founded secret orders and mystical societies. However, their very elusiveness often suggests that they might be entities of a mediumistic nature created by the expectations of vivid imaginations of occult and psychic leaders.

There were *Superiores Incogniti* or Secret Chiefs introduced by Baron Hund (1722-76) for his Strikt Observanz Masonic system, while the **Theosophical Society** was formed from the inspiration of Madame **Blavatsky's** mysterious **Mahatmas** Morya and Koot Hoomi, who communicated on sheets of paper in Madame Blavatsky's handwriting.

The Secret Chiefs of the famous **Golden Dawn** occult society were said to be the Unknown Magi who were "Concealed Rulers of the Wisdom of the True Rosicrucian Magic of Light," but in practice seemed to be founders **Westcott, Mathers** and **Woodman.** (See also **Adepts;** Hermetic Order of the **Golden Dawn; Great White Brotherhood; Mahatmas; Masters**)

Secret Fire

Described by Philostratus (c. 170-245 A.D.) in his *Life of Apollonius* as issuing from a basin in a well on the hill **Athanor.**

A blue vapor was said to rise from the well, changing into all the colors of the rainbow. The bottom was strewn with red arsenic; on it was the basin full of fire, and from it rose flame without smell or smoke. Two stone reservoirs were beside it, one containing rain, the other wind. This description is probably a symbolical one.

Secret Tradition

It has long been an article of faith with students of occultism that the secret tenets of the various sciences embraced within it have been preserved to modern times by a series of adepts, who have handed them down from generation to generation in their entirety.

There may be no reason to dismiss this belief, but that the adepts in question existed in one unbroken line, and that they all professed similar principles is somewhat improbable. But one thing seems fairly certain, that proficiency in any one of the occult sciences requires tuition from a master of that branch. All serious writers on the subject are at one on this point.

It is possible that in Neolithic times, societies existed among our barbarian ancestors, similar in character to the **Midiwiwin** of the North-American Indians, the snake-dancers of the Hopi of New Mexico, or the numerous secret societies of aboriginal Australians. This is inferred from the probability that **totemism** existed amongst Neolithic peoples. Hierophantic castes would naturally hand down the tradition of the secret things of the Society from one generation to another.

The early **mysteries** of Egypt, Eleusis, Samothrace, and Cabiri were probably the elaboration of such primitive mysteries. There would appear to have been throughout the ages, what might be called a fusion of occult beliefs, that when the hierophants of one system found themselves in juxtaposition, or even in conflict, with the professors of another, the systems in question appear to have received much from one another.

It has been said that when the ancient mysteries are spoken about, it should be understood that one and the same series of sacred ceremonies is intended, one and the same initiatory processes and revelations, and that what is true of one applies with equal certainty to all the others.

Thus Strabo recorded that the strange orgies in honor of the mystic birth of Jupiter resembled those of Bacchus, Ceres and Cybele, and the Orphic poems identified the orgies of Bacchus with those of Ceres, Rhea, Venus and Isis. Euripides also mentioned that the rites of Cybele were celebrated in Asia Minor in a manner identical with the Grecian mysteries of Dionysius and the Cretan rites of the Cabiri.

The Rev. Geo. Oliver in his book *The History of Initiation* (1829) asserted that the rites of the science which is now received under the name of **Freemasonry** were exercised in the antediluvian world, received by Noah after the Flood, practiced by man at the building of Babel, conveniences for which were undoubtedly contained in that edifice, and at the dispersion spread with every settlement already deteriorated by the gradual innovations of the Cabiric priests, and molded into a form, the great outlines of which are distinctly to be traced in the mysteries of every heathen nation, and exhibit shattered remains of the one true system, whence they were derived.

This theory is, of course, totally mistaken, and although there may have been likenesses between the rites of certain societies, the idea that all sprang from one common source is absurd. One thing, however, is fairly certain. Anthropology permits us to believe that the concepts of human beings, religious and mystical, are practically identical in whatever part of the world people may exist, and there is every possibility that the similarity between early mysteries results in this manner, and that it brought about a strong resemblance between the mystical systems of the older world.

We have satisfactory evidence that the ancient mysteries were receptacles of a great deal of occult wisdom, symbolism, magical or semi-magical rite, and mystical practice in general, and we are assured that when these fell into disuse among the more intellectual classes of the various countries in which they obtained, they were taken up and practiced in secret by the lesser ranks of society, even the lowest ranks, who are in all ages the most conservative, and who cling faithfully to the ancient systems, refusing to partake in the rites of the religions which had ousted them.

The same can be posited of magical practice. The principles of magic are universal, and there can be no reason to doubt that these were handed on throughout the long centuries by hereditary castes of priests, **shamans,** medicine-men, magicians, sorcerers, and witches. But the same evidence does not exist with regard to the higher magic, concerning which much more difficult questions arise. Was this handed on by means of secret societies, occult schools or universities, or from adept to adept?

This magic is not of sorceries of empirics and primitives, but that spiritual magic which, taken in its best sense, shades into **mysticism.** The schools of Salamanca, the mystic colleges of Alexandria, could not impart the great truths of this science to their disciples. Its nature is such that communication by lecture would be worse than useless. It is necessary to suppose then that it was imparted by one adept to another. But it is not likely that it arose at a very early period in human history.

In the early psychological state, human beings would not require it, and we see no reason for belief that its professors came into existence at an earlier period than some three or four thousand years B.C. The undisturbed nature of Egyptian and Babylonian civilization leads to the belief that these countries brought forth a long series of adepts in the higher magic.

We know that Alexandria was heir to the works of these adepts, but it is unlikely that their teachings were publicly disseminated in her public schools. Individuals of high magical standing would, however, be in possession of the occult knowledge of ancient Egypt, and it seems likely that they imparted this to the Greeks of Alexandria. Later Hellenic and Byzantine magical theory is distinctly Egyptian in character, and we know that its esoteric forms were disseminated in Europe at a comparatively early date, and that they placed all other native systems in the background, where they were pursued in the shadow by the aboriginal witch and sorcerer.

We have thus outlined the genealogy of the higher magic from early Egyptian times to the European medieval period.

Regarding **alchemy,** the evidence from analogy is much more sure, and the same may be said as regards **astrology.** These are occult studies in which it is peculiarly necessary to obtain the assistance of an adept if any excellence is to be gained in their practice, and we know that the first originated in Egypt, and the second in ancient Babylon.

We are not aware of the names of those early adepts who carried the sciences forward until the days of Alexandria, but subsequent to that period the identity of practically every alchemical and astrological practitioner of any note is fully known. In the history of no other occult study is the sequence of its professors so clear as is the case in alchemy, and the same might almost be said as regards astrology, whose protagonists, if they have not been so famous, have at least been equally conscientious.

We must pass over in our consideration the manner in which occult science survived, the absurd legends which presume to state how such societies as the Freemasons existed from antediluvian times, and will content ourselves with stating that the probabilities are that in the case of mystical brotherhoods, a long line of these existed from early times, the traditions of which were practically similar. Many persons would be members of several of these, and would import the conceptions of one society into the heart of another, as we know **Rosicrucian** ideas were imported into Masonry (see **Freemasonry**).

In the mystic societies of the Middle Ages there seem to be reflections of the older Egyptian and classical mysteries, and there is nothing absurd in the theory that the spirit and in some instances even the letter of these may have descended to medieval and perhaps to present times.

Such organizations die much harder than any credit is given them for doing. We know, for example, that Freemasonry was transformed at one part of its career, about the middle of the seventeenth century, by an influx of alchemists and astrologers, who crowded out the operative members, and strengthened the mystical position of the brotherhood.

It is therefore surely reasonable to suppose that on the fall or disuse of the ancient mysteries, their disciples, looking eagerly for some methods of saving their cults from entire extinction, would join the ranks of some similar society, or would keep alive the flame in secret.

The fact remains that the occult idea was undoubtedly preserved through the ages, that it was the same in essence amongst the believers in all religions and all mysteries, and that to a great extent its trend was in the one direction, so that the fusion of the older mystical societies and their rebirth as a new brotherhood was by no means an unlikely hypothesis.

In the entry on the **Templars** for example, it is suggested that there is a possibility of that brotherhood having received its tenets from the East, where it sojourned for such a protracted period. It seems very likely from what we learn of its rites that they were oriental in origin, and we know that the occult systems of Europe owed much to the Templars, who, probably, after the fall of their own Order secretly formed others or joined existing societies.

Masons have a hypothesis that through older origins they inherited from the Dionysian artificers, the artisans of Byzantium, and the building brotherhoods of Western Europe. To state this dogmatically as a fact would not be to gain so much credence for their theory as is due to that concerning the dissemination of occult lore by the Templars. However, it is much more feasible in every way than the romantic legend concerning the rise of Freemasonry at the time of the building of the Temple of Solomon.

Secret societies of any description possess a strong attraction for a certain class of mind, or else a merely operative handicraft society, such as was medieval Masonry, would not have been utilized so largely by the mystics of that time. One of the chief reasons that we know so little concerning these brotherhoods in medieval times is that the charge of dabbling in the occult arts was a serious one in the eyes of the law and the church, therefore occultists found it necessary to carry on their practices in secret.

But after the Reformation, a modern spirit took possession of Europe, and the protagonists of the occult sciences came out of their secrecy and practiced in the open light of day. In England, for example, numerous persons avowed themselves alchem- ists; in Germany the "Rosicrucians" sent out a manifesto; in Scotland, Alexander **Seton,** a great master of the hermetic art, flourished.

But it was nearly a century later until further secret societies were formed, such as the Academy of the Ancients and of the Mysteries in 1767, the Knights of the True Light founded in Austria about 1780; the Knights and Brethren of Asia, which appeared in Germany in the same year; the Order of Jerusalem, which originated in America in 1791; the Society of the Universal Aurora established at Paris in 1783.

Besides being masonic, these societies practiced **animal magnetism**, astrology, **Kabalism** and even **ceremonial magic.** Others were political, such as the **Illuminati,** which came to such an inglorious end. But the individual tradition was kept up by an illustrious line of adepts, who were much more instrumental in keeping alive the flame of mysticism than even such societies as those mentioned.

Mesmer, Swedenborg, Saint-Martin, de Pasqually, all labored to that end. We may regard all these as belonging to the school of Christian magicians, distinct from those who practiced the rites of the **grimoires** or Jewish Kabalism. The line may be carried back through Lavater, **Eckartshausen,** and so on to the seventeenth century. These men were mystics besides being practitioners of theurgic magic, and they combined in themselves the knowledge of practically all the occult sciences.

With Anton **Mesmer** began the revival of a science which cannot be altogether regarded as occult, when consideration is given to its modern developments, but which powerfully influenced the mystic life of his time and even later. The Mesmerists of the first era were in direct line with the Martinists and the mystical magicians of the France of the late eighteenth century. Indeed, in the persons of some English mystics such as **Greatrakes,** mysticism and "magnetism" are one and the same thing. But upon **Hypnotism,** to give it its modern name, becoming numbered with the more practical sciences, persons of a mystical cast of mind appear to have deserted it to a great extent.

Hypnotism does not bear the same relation to Mesmerism and animal magnetism as modern chemistry does to alchemy, but the persons who practice it nowadays are as dissimilar to the older professors of the science as is the modern practitioner of chemistry to the medieval alchemist. This is symptomatic of the occult studies, that they despise that knowledge which is "exact" in the common sense of the term, that is to say, pertaining to materialistic science. Their practitioners do not delight in laboring upon a science, the basic laws of which are already known in a quite formal way.

The student of occultism, as a rule, possesses all the attributes of an explorer. The occult studies have from time to time deeply enriched the exact sciences, but these enrichments have been acts of intellectual generosity. It is in effect as if the occultist made a present of them to the scientist, but did not desire to be troubled with their future development in any way. Occultism of the higher sort, therefore, does not to-day possess any great interest in hypnotism, and modern mystics of standing scarcely recognize it as a part of the hidden mysteries.

But there is little doubt that the early Mesmerists formed a link between the adepts of eighteenth-century France and those of modern times.

The discriminating occultists of today, however, draw upon an older inspiration. They recognize that their forerunners of the seventeenth and eighteenth centuries were influenced by older traditions and they feel that these may have had knowledge of records and traditions that are now obscure. The recovery of these is, perhaps, the great question of modern occultism. But apart from this, modern occultism of the highest type strains towards mysticism, and partakes more than ever of its character. It disdains and ignores ceremonial, and exalts spiritual experience.

Of course, there are numerous groups throughout the world for the celebration of magical rites, but such fraternities have existed from time immemorial, and their protagonists cannot be placed on a higher footing than the hallucinated sorcerers of medieval times. (See also **Alchemy; Freemasonry; Gnosticism; Kabala; Mysticism; Neoplatonism; Rosicrucians**)

Recommended reading:

Hall, Manly P. *An Encyclopedic Outline of Masonic, Hermetic, Qabbalistic and Rosicrucian Symbolical Philosophy* (alternative title: *The Secret Teachings of All Ages*), Philosophical Research Society, Los Angeles, 1928; paperback ed., 1978

Hartmann, Franz. *Magic White and Black; or The Science of Finite and Infinite Life*, George Redway, London, 1886; University Books, 1970

Maeterlinck, Maurice. *The Great Secret*, Methuen, London, 1922; University Books, 1969

Shirley, Ralph. *Occultists & Mystics of All Ages*, William Rider, London, 1920; University Books, 1972

Waite, Arthur E. *The Brotherhood of the Rosy Cross*, William Rider, London, 1924; University Books, 1961

Waite, Arthur E. *The Life of Louis Claude de Saint-Martin; The Unknown Philosopher*, Philip Wellby, London, 1901; reprinted under title *The Unknown Philosopher; The Life of Louis Claude de Saint-Martin*, Rudolf Steiner Publications, Blauvelt, N.Y., 1970

Waite, Arthur E. *The Secret Tradition in Alchemy*, Kegan Paul, London, Alfred A. Knopf, 1926

Waite, Arthur E. *The Secret Tradition in Freemasonry*, Rider & Co., London, Dutton, 1937

Yarker, John. *The Arcane Schools; A Review of Their Origin and Antiquity; With a General History of Freemasonry*, William Tait, Belfast, Ireland, 1909

Secret Words

Certain words relating to the Eucharist were said to have been communicated by Christ to Joseph of Arimathea and were committed orally from keeper to keeper of the Holy **Grail.**

In Robert de Borron's metrical romance of *Joseph of Arimathea* (c. 1170-1212), material power is added to their spiritual efficacy and whoever could acquire and retain them, had a mysterious power over all around him, could not suffer by evil judgments, could not suffer deprivation of his own rights, need not fear the result of battle, provided his cause were good.

The words were the secret of the Grail and were either incommunicable in writing or were written only in the Book of the Grail which, de Borron implied, was itself written by Joseph of Arimathea. These words are the chief mystery of the Lesser Holy Grail, as the prose version of de Borron's poem is called.

They were most probably a form of eucharistic consecration, and there is evidence that the Celtic church, following the example of the Eastern Church, used them in addition to the usual consecration as practiced in the Latin Church, which is merely a repetition of the New Testament account of the Lord's Supper. The separate clause they are supposed to have formed is called Epiclesis and consisted of an invocation of the Holy Ghost. (See also **Glastonbury; Holy Grail**)

Recommended reading:

Furnivall, F. J. (ed.). *The History of the Holy Grail . . . from the French prose of Sires R. de Borron*, Early English Text Society, London, 1874 etc. (in parts)

Waite, Arthur E. *The Holy Grail; The Galahad Quest in the Arthurian Literature*, Rider & Co., London, 1933; University Books, 1961

Weston, Jessie L. *The Quest of the Holy Grail*, G. Bell, London, 1913; Frank Cass, London, 1964

Seekers, The

Founded at Queens Gate, South West London in 1926 by C. A. Simpson, formerly a New Zealand electrical engineer, who gave up his profession to establish a healing and spiritual center under the direction of the spirit guide "Dr. Lascelles."

The center was originally named The Guild of Spiritual Healing. Many cures were reported in cases generally classed as incurable. Absent healing treatment was given in a specially consecrated chapel through Harmony Prayer Circles throughout Britain.

In 1933, the Seekers center moved to larger premises at West Malling, Kent, where over 5,000 members were linked in prayer circles. Address: Seekers' Trust, The Close, Addington Park, West Malling, Kent, England.

Seer (or Seeress)

A natural born clairvoyant. (See **Clairvoyance; Second Sight**)

Seer, The (Journal)

Monthly review of occult and psychic sciences, founded 1928, published in Nice, France, later in Carthage, Tunisia. Edited by Dr. Francis Rolt-Wheeler. Contributors included Ernesto **Bozzano,** Lewis **Spence** and Jollivet Castelot. No longer published.

Seik Kasso

Burmese evil spirits inhabiting trees. (See **Burma**)

Seiktha

A Burmese evil spirit. (See **Burma**)

Self-Realization Fellowship

A well-conducted East-West spiritual organization founded in 1920 by Paramahansa **Yogananda,** one of the early **yoga** gurus to leave India to live and teach in the West. The Fellowship teaches the scientific practice of yoga "to attain direct personal experience of God," and seeks to promote harmony between basic Christian and Yoga teachings.

One famous member was Dr. W. Y. **Evans-Wentz,** scholar of Eastern mysticism and author of various books dealing with authoritative Tibetan and Yogic texts.

The Fellowship has forty-four centers in the U.S., nine of which are in California, including a retreat at Encinitas. There are also branches in other countries, the Indian section being known as Yogoda Satsang. The Fellowship publishes a quarterly, *Self-Realization* Magazine. Address for information: 3880 San Rafael Avenue, Los Angeles, California 90065.

Self-Realization Magazine

Quarterly publication dealing with the teachings of Paramahansa **Yogananda** (1893-1952). Published by: Self-Realization Fellowship, 3880 San Rafael Avenue, Los Angeles, California 90065.

Semites, The

This entry on the Semites applies to the more ancient divisions of the race, such as the Babylonians and Assyrians, and the Hebrews in Biblical times. For later Semitic Occultism, see **Arabs** and **Kabala.**

In ancient Babylon and Chaldea, magic was a department of priestly activity, and in Mesopotamia a sect of priests named the *Asipu,* were set apart for the practice of magic, which in their case probably consisted of hypnotism, the casting out of demons, the banning of troublesome spirits and so forth.

The *Baru* were augurs, who consulted the oracles on the future by inspection of the entrails of animals and the flight of birds, "the observation of oil in water, the secret of Anu, Bel, and Ea, the tablet of the gods, the sachet of leather of the oracles of the heavens and earth, the wand of cedar dear to the great gods."

These priests of *Baru* and *Asipu* were clothed investments peculiar to their rank, which they changed frequently during the ceremonies in which they took part. In ancient tablets we find kings making frequent enquiry through these priestly castes, and in a tablet of Sippar, we find treated the installation of a *Baru* to the Sun-Temple, and also Sennachrib seeking through the *Baru* the causes of his father's violent death. The *Asipu* again were exorcists, who removed taboos and laid ghosts. An *Asipu's* functions are set forth in the following incantatory poem:

[The man] of Ea am I,
[The man] of Damkina am I,
The messenger of Marduk am I,
My spell is the spell of Ea,
My incantation is the incantation of Marduk,

The circle of Ea is in my hand,
The tamarisk, the powerful weapon of Anu,
In my hand I hold,
The date-spathe, mighty in decision,
In my hand I hold.

He that stilleth all to rest, that pacifieth all,
By whose incantation everything is at peace,
He is the great Lord Ea,
Stilling all to rest, and pacifying all,
By whose incantation everything is at peace.
When I draw nigh unto the sick man
All shall be assuaged.
I am the magician born of Eridu,
Begotten in Eridu and Subari.
When I draw nigh unto the sick man
May Ea, King of the Deep, safeguard me!

O Ea, King of the Deep, to see. . . .
I, the magician, am thy slave.
March thou on my right hand,
Assist [me] on my left;
Add thy pure spell to mine,
Add thy pure voice to mine,
Vouchsafe (to me) pure words,
Make fortunate the utterances of my mouth,
Ordain that my decisions be happy,
Let me be blessed where'er I tread,
Let the man whom I [now] touch be blessed.
Before me may lucky thoughts be spoken.
After me may a lucky finger be pointed.
Oh that thou wert my guardian genius,
And my guardian spirit!
O God that blesseth, Marduk,
Let me be blessed, where'er my path may be!
Thy power shall god and man proclaim;
This man shall do thy service,
And I too, the magician thy slave."

Unto the house on entering. . . .
Samas is before me,
Sin [is] behind [me],
Nergal [is] at (my) right hand,
Ninib [is] at my left hand;
When I draw near unto the sick man,
When I lay my hand on the head of the sick man,
May a kindly Spirit, a kindly Guardian, stand at my side.

The third caste was the Zammaru, who sang or chanted certain ceremonials.

The lower ranks of sorcery were represented by the *Kassapu* and *Kassaptu,* the wizard and witch, who, as elsewhere, practiced black magic, and who were fiercely combated by the priest-magician caste. In the code of Hammurabi there was a stringent law against the professors of black magic:

"If a man has charged a man with sorcery and has not justified himself, he who is charged with sorcery shall go to the river, he shall plunge into the river, and if the river overcome him, he who accused him shall take to himself his house. If the river makes that man to be innocent, and he be saved, he who accused him shall be put to death. He who plunged into the river shall take to himself the house of him who accused him."

This recalls the water test for a witch in the seventeenth century, that if she sank when thrown in a pond, she was innocent, but if she floated, she was a witch indeed. Another series of tablets dealt with the black magician and the witch who were represented as roaming the streets, entering houses, and prowling through towns, stealing the love of men, and withering the beauty of women.

The exorcist went on to say that he had made an image of the witch and he called upon the fire-god to burn it. He seized the mouth, tongue, eyes, feet, and other members of the witch, and piously prayed that Sin may cast her into an abyss of water and fire, and that her face may grow yellow and green. He feared that the witch was directing a similar sorcery against himself, that she sat making spells against him in the shade of the wall, fashioning images of him. But he sent against her the *haltappan* plant and sesame to undo her spells and force back the words into her mouth. He devoutly trusted that the images she had fashioned would assume her own character, and that her spells might recoil upon herself.

Another tablet expressed the desire that the god of night might smite the witch in her magic, that the three watches of the night might loose her evil sorcery, that her mouth be fat and her tongue salt, that the words of evil that she had spoken might be poured out like tallow, and that the magic she was working be crumbled like salt.

The tablets abound in magical matter and in them we have a record of the actual wizardry in vogue at the time they were written, which runs at least from the seventh century B.C. onwards until the time when the cuneiform inscription ceased to be used.

Chaldean magic was renowned throughout the world, especially for its astrology. The book of *Isaiah* stated. "Let now the astrologers, star-gazers, monthly prognosticators, stand up and save thee from the things that shall come upon thee." In the book of *Daniel,* the magicians were called Chaldeans, and even in modern times occultists have praised Chaldean magi. Strabo and Ælian alluded to their knowledge of astrology, as did Diodorus Siculus, and it is supposed to have been a Chaldean magician Œthanes who introduced his science into Greece, which he entered with Xerxes.

The great library of Assurbanipal, king of Assyria, who died in 626 B.C., affords first-hand knowledge of Assyrian magic. Assurbanipal gathered together numerous volumes from the cities of Babylonia, stored them in his great library at Nineveh, and had them copied and translated. In fact, letters have been discovered from Assurbanipal to some of his officials, giving instructions for the copying of certain incantations. Many **grimoires** too come from Babylonia, written during the later empire, the best known of which are the series entitled *Maklu* (burning), *Utukki limnuti* (evil spirits), *Labartu* (hag-demon) and *Nis kati* (raising of the hand).

There are also available many ceremonial texts which throw considerable light on magical practice. The *Maklu,* for example, contains eight tablets of incantations and spells against wizards and witches—the general idea running through it being to instruct the bewitched person how to manufacture figures of his enemies, and thus destroy them.

The series dealing with the **exorcism** of evil spirits enumerates demons, goblins and ghosts, and consists of at least sixteen tablets. They were for the use of the exorcist in driving out devils from possessed people, and this was to be accomplished by invoking the aid of the gods, so that the demons might be laid under a divine taboo. The demon who possessed the unfortunate victim had to be described in the most minute manner.

The series dealing with the *Labartu* or hag-demon, a kind of female devil who delighted in attacking children, gave directions for making a figure of the *Labartu* and the incantations to be repeated over it. The magician and philosopher appear to have worked together in Assyria, for medical men constantly used incantations to drive out demons, and incantations were often associated with prescriptions. Medical magic indeed appears to have been of much the same sort as we find amongst the American Indians and peoples in a primitive condition of existence.

The doctrine of the "Incommunicable Name" was established among the early Semites, as among the Egyptians, related to secret name of a god which, when discovered, gave the speaker complete power over him by its mere utterance. The knowledge of the name or description of the person or demon against whom the magician directed his charm was also essential to success. Drugs were originally ascribed the power vouchsafed by the gods for the welfare of mankind, and were supposed to aid greatly in exorcism.

In Assyrian sorcery, Ea and Marduk were the most powerful gods, the latter being appealed to as intermediary between human beings and their father, Ea; indeed the legend of Marduk going to his father for advice was commonly repeated in incantations. When working magic against an individual it was necessary to have something belonging to him or her—clippings of hair, or fingernails if possible. The possessed person was usually washed, the principle of cleansing probably underlying this ceremony. An incantation called the Incantation of Eridu was often prescribed, and this must have related to some such cleansing, for Eridu was the Home of Ea, the Sea-god.

A formula for exorcising or washing away a demon named Rabesu stated that the patient was to be sprinkled with clean water twice seven times. Of all water none was so sacred as the Euphrates, and water from it was frequently used for charms and exorcisms.

Fumigation with a censor was also employed by the Assyrians for exorcism, but the possessed person was often guarded from the attack of fiends by placing him in the middle of an enchanted circle of flour, through which it was thought no spirit could break. Wearing the glands from the mouth of a fish was also a charm against possession. In making a magic circle, the sorcerer usually formed seven little winged figures to set before the god Nergal, with a long spell, which stated that he had completed the *usurtu* or magic circle with a sprinkling of lime. The wizard further prayed that the incantation might be performed for his patient by the god. This would seem to be a prototype of the circle in use amongst magicians of medieval times.

R. Campbell Thompson in his book *Semitic Magic* (1908) stated:

"Armed with all these things—the word of power, the acquisition of some part of the enemy, the use of the magic circle and holy water, and the knowledge of the magical properties of substances—the ancient warlock was well fitted for his trade. He was then capable of defying hostile demons or summoning friendly spirits, of driving out disease or casting spells, of making amulets to guard the credulous who came to him. Furthermore, he had a certain stock-in-trade of tricks which were a steady source of revenues. Lovesick youths and maidens always hoped for some result from his philtres or love-charms; at the demand of jealousy, he was ever ready to put hatred between husband and wife; and for such as had not the pluck or skill even to use a dagger on a dark night, his little effigies, pierced with pins, would bring death to a rival. He was at once a physician and wonder-worker for such as would pay him fee."

"Among the more modern Semites magic is greatly in vogue in many forms, some of them quite familiar to Europeans: indeed we find the *Arabian Nights* edited by Lane, a story of old women riding on a broom-stick. Among Mahommedans the wizard is thought to deserve death by reason of the fact that he is an unbeliever. Witches are fairly common in Arabic lore, and we usually find them figuring as sellers of potions and philtres. The European witch is usually supposed to be able to leave her dwelling at night by sprinkling some of the ashes of the hearth on the forehead of her husband, whereby he sleeps soundly till the morning. This is identical with French medieval practice. In Arab folk tales the *moghrebi* is the sorcerer who has converse with demons, and we find many such in the Old and New Testaments, as well as diviners and other practitioners of the occult arts. In the *Sanhedrin,* Rabbi Akiba defines an enchanter as one who calculates the times and hours, and other rabbis state that 'an enchanter is he who grows ill when his bread drops from his mouth, or if he drops the stick that supports him from his hand, or if his son calls after him, or a crow caws in his hearing, or a deer crosses his path, or he sees a serpent at his right hand, or a fox on his left.' "

The Arabs used to believe that magic would not work while he that employs it was asleep. Besides it is possible to over-reach Satan himself, and many Arabic tales exist in which men of wisdom and cunning have succeeded in accomplishing this. The Devil Iblis once sent his son to an assembly of honorable people with a flint stone, and told him to have the flint stone woven. He came in and said, "My father sends his peace, and wishes to have this flint stone woven." A man with a goat-beard said, "Tell your father to have it spun, and then we will weave it."

The son went back, and the Devil was very angry, and told his son never to put forth any suggestion when a goat-bearded man was present, "for he is more devilish than we."

Curiously enough, Rabbi Joshua ben Hananiah made a similar request in a contest against the wise men of Athens, who required him to sew together the fragments of a broken millstone. He asked in reply for a few threads made of the fiber of the stone. The good folk of Mosul, too, always prided themselves on a ready wit against the Devil. Once upon a time, the Devil Iblis came to Mosul and found a man planting onions. They fell to talking, and in their fellowship agreed to divide the produce of the garden. Then, on a day when the onions were ready, the partners went to their vegetable patch and the man said, "Master, wilt thou take as thy half that which is above ground or that which is below?"

Now the Devil saw the good green shoots of the onions sprouting high, and so carried these off as his share, leaving the gardener chuckling over his bargain. But when wheat time came round, and the man was sowing his soil one day, the Devil looked over the ditch and complained that he had made nothing out of the compact. "This time," quoth he, "we will divide differently, and thou shalt take the tops"; and so it fell out.

They visited the tilth together and when the corn was ripe, the fellah reaped the field and took away the ears, leaving the Devil stubbing up the roots. Presently, after he had been digging for a month, he began to find out his error, and went to the man, who was cheerily threshing his portion.

"This is a paltry quibble," said Iblis, "thou hast cozened me this twice." "Nay," said the former, "I gave thee thy desire, and furthermore, thou didst not thresh out thine onion-tops, as I am doing this." So it was a hopeful Devil that went away to beat the dry onion-stalks, but in vain, and he left Mosul sullenly, stalking away in frustrated anger, stopping once in a while to shake his hand against so crafty a town. "Cursed be he, ye tricksters! who can outmatch devilry like yours?"

"In modern times in the East," stated R. C. Thompson, "from Morocco to Mesopotamia, books of magic are by no means rare, and manuscripts in Arabic, Hebrew, Gershuni, and Syriac can frequently be bought, all dealing with some form of magic or popular medicine. In Suakin in the Soudan I was offered a printed book of astrology in Arabic illustrated by the most grotesque and bizarre woodcuts of the signs of the Zodiac, the blocks for which seem to have done duty in other places. Such books existed in manuscript in ancient days, as is vouched for by the story of the Sibylline books or the passage in Acts xix, 19; 'Not a few of them that practised curious arts brought their books together, and burned them in the sight of all.' "

It is curious to find the charm for raising hatred was practically the same among the Semites as is amongst the peoples of Hungary and the Balkan States—that is, through the agency of the egg of a black hen.

We find, too, many minor sorceries the same among the Semites as among European races. To be invisible was another attainment much sought after, and it was thought that if one wore a ring of copper and iron engraved with certain magic signs this result would be secured. The heart of a black cat, dried and steeped in honey was also believed to be effective.

For various instances of potent enchantments, see **Solomon.**

Sympathetic magic was often resorted to by the Arabic witch and wizard, just as it was amongst the ancient Hebrews and Assyrians. The great repertory of Semitic occultism is the **Kabala,** but here the occult has been transmuted into Hebrew **mysticism.** (See also **Arabs; Babylonia; Kabala; Magi**)

Recommended reading

Thompson, C. J. S. *The Mysteries and Secrets of Magic,* Allen Lane, London, 1927; Causeway, 1973

Thompson, R. C. *Devils & Evil Spirits of Babylonia,* 2 vols., Luzac, London, 1903-04

Thompson, R. C. *Semitic Magic,* Luzac, London, 1908

Sensitive

A sensitive or a "psychic" is a person with psychic powers, but without the ability to establish communication with the dead. A sensitive is not a medium, and a medium is not necessarily a sensitive but rather an instrument for spirit communication.

Sensitives may excel in **psychometry, telepathy, clairvoyance** (ordinary and medical), they may foresee the future, find lost objects and give accurate character delineations. Yet they would not claim an external source.

They would have no spirit "**guide**" and there would be no exteriorization of **ectoplasm** or **psychic force** to make manifestations from the Beyond possible.

In the case of mediums who are also sensitives, but with weak psychic powers, they may subconsciously rely on these powers and give confused messages, as the subconscious mind may readily accept the suggestion of acting as a departed spirit. The term "sensitive" was popular in the nineteenth century with the rise of **Spiritualism,** but although used loosely as synonymous with "medium," its major connotation is non-Spiritualist, approximating to the term "psychic."

During the nineteenth century, the great German scientist Baron Karl von **Reichenbach** conducted numerous experiments with sensitives in order to validate his concept of a mysterious vital force in nature which he termed "**Od**" or "Odyle." These individuals, drawn from all walks of life, were selected on the basis of specific sensitive reactions—feelings of pleasant coolness or alternatively disagreeable feelings in relation to other people or to metals, as well as reactions to colors and foods.

Reichenbach published the first detailed study of such sensitives in his book *Der sensitive Mensch und sein Verhalten zum Ode* (2 vols., Stuttgart & Tübingen, 1854-55) [The Sensitive Man and his Relation to Od]. (See also **Medium; Psychic;** Baron Karl von **Reichenbach**)

Sensory Deprivation

The blocking of normal sensory input has been found to result in **hallucinations** and weird fantasies. Partial sensory blocking has been achieved by blindfolding, ear plugging, covering hands and feet and lying on a soft couch.

Other techniques include floating in water at controlled temperature in a soundproof, lightproof chamber. Such experiments may be exhausting and even dangerous, but can throw light on personality disorders and apparent paranormal experiences.

A related technique is the use of the **Witches' Cradle** devised by Robert **Masters** and Jean **Houston** of the **Foundation for Mind Research.**

Recommended reading:

Solomon, P. & others (eds.) *Sensory Deprivation,* Harvard University, 1961

Zubeck, John P. (ed.). *Sensory Deprivation: Fifteen Years of Research,* Appleton-Century-Crofts, 1969

"Sepharial"

Pseudonym of British astrologer and occult author Walter Gorn **Old** (1864-1929).

Serios, Ted

A former Chicago bellhop, with the claimed ability to project photographic images on to camera film by staring into the lens of a Polaroid camera. He sometimes used a piece of rolled cardboard to look into the camera lens at the moment the picture is taken. This "gismo," as he called it, tended to arouse suspicions of fraud, even although there was no evidence that it was a device for trickery. Serios also produced images using a camera without a lens.

A report of the strange talent of Serios by Mrs. Pauline Oehler of the Illinois Society for Psychic Research was published in *Fate* magazine. Curtis **Fuller,** proprietor of *Fate,* sent a copy of the article to parapsychologist Dr. Jule **Eisenbud,** as a result Eisenbud conducted an extensive and careful investigation of the phenomena of Serios in 1964.

The results were published in Eisenbud's book *The World of Ted Serios: "Thoughtographic" Studies of an Extraordinary Mind* (Morrow, 1966). Eisenbud found the phenomena as erratic as Serios himself, but probably genuine.

Amongst some of the extraordinary images produced by Serios with a Polaroid camera were pictures of Mariner IV and also some Russian Vostok rockets.

Many pictures produced by Serios are ambiguous, in soft focus, or too vague to identify, but others seem projections of the consciousness of Serios or his ability to form some visual link with scenes in distant places. (See also Dr. Tomobichi **Fukurai; Psychic Photography; Spirit Photography; Thought-forms**)

Serling, Rod (1924-1975)

Television producer, dramatist, narrator, creator of the famous series "Twilight Zone" dealing with the supernatural; author of screenplays and short stories. Born December 25, 1924 in Syracuse, New York, he studied at Antioch College (B.A. 1950), Emerson College (L.H.D. 1971), Ithaca College, 1972, Alfred University 1972. He married Carolyn Kramer July 31, 1948.

He was a writer for Network radio from 1946-48; television writer from 1948 onwards; his plays were produced on Kraft Theatre, Studio One, U.S. Steel Hour, Playhouse 90, Suspense, Danger. He was writer-producer of "The Twilight Zone," "Rod Serling's Night Gallery," narrator "In Search of Ancient Astronauts." During World War II, he served with the paratroopers A.U.S.

He received an Emmy award for best teleplay writing in 1955, '56, '57, '59-61, '63-64; Sylvania award 1955, 1956; Peabody award 1957; Christopher award 1956, 1971. His publications include: *Patterns* (1957), *Stories From the Twilight Zone* (1960), *More Stories From the Twilight Zone* (1961), *Night Gallery* (1971), *Night Gallery Two* (1972). He died June 28, 1975.

Servadio, Emilio (1904-)

Italian psychoanalyst, author, and co-founder in 1937 of the Italian Society for Psychic Research (now Italian Society for Parapsychology). Born August 14, 1904 at Genoa, Italy, he studied at Genoa University (LL.D. 1926). In 1951 he married Clara Volloscuro.

He was Professor and Fellow at Andhra Research University (Madras College), India in 1938, president of the Psychoanalytic Center of Rome from 1962 onwards, vice-president of Italian Society for Parapsychology from 1955-56, vice-president of Italian Psychoanalytic Society from 1953-55 and 1958-60, charter member of the Parapsychological Association. His memberships include: International Psychoanalytic Association, Italian Association for Psychological Medicine and Psychotherapy, Italian Society of Scientific Psychology; corresponding member of Assn. des Psychanalystes de Belgique, Society for Psychical Research, London; chairman of International Committee for Study of Methods in Parapsychology; subeditor and contributor to *Enciclopedia Italiana* and various scholarly and scientific journals.

Dr. Servadio has taken special interest in psychodynamic and psychoanalytic aspects of ESP. In 1932 he investigated the phenomena of the medium Pasquale **Erto,** and in 1957 the miraculous healers in Lucania, South Italy.

In addition to his numerous articles on psychology and psychoanalysis, he has published the following articles on parapsychology: 'Psychoanalyse and Telepathie' (Psychoanalysis and Telepathy, *Imago,* 1935, No. 4, reprinted in *Psychoanalysis and the Occult* edited by George **Devereux,** 1953), 'La Baguette des sourciers (The Divining Rod, *Revue Francaise de Psychoanalyse,* 1935, No. 3), 'La percezione extra sensoriale' (Extrasensory Perception, *Nuovi Problemi de Metapsichica,* 1950), 'A Presumptively Telepathic-Precognitive Dream During Analysis' (*International Journal of Psycho-Analysis,* 1955, No. 1), 'Le conditionnement transferentiel et contre-transférentiel des événements "psi" au cours de l'analyse' (Transference and Counter-Transference Conditioning of "Psi" Events During Analysis, *Acta Psychotherapeutica,* Suppl. vol. 3, 1955), 'Freud et la Parapsychologie (*Revue Francaise de Psychoanalyse,* 1956, No. 3), 'Transference and Thought-Transference' (*International Journal of Psycho-Analysis,* 1956, No. 4, 5), 'Parapsychologie und Ungläubigkeitsreaktion' (Parapsychology and the Reaction of Disbelief, *Zeitschrift für Parapsychologie und Grenzgebiete der Psychologie,* 1958, H.1), 'The "Normal" and the "Paranormal" Dream' (*International Journal of Parapsychology,* 1962).

He is author of *La Ricerca Psichica* (Psychical Research, 1930; 1946), and contributed to *Proceedings of an International Conference on Methodology in Psi Research: Psi Favorable States of Consciousness* edited by Roberto Cavanna (Parapsychology Foundation, 1970) and *Proceedings of an International Conference: Psi Factors in Creativity* edited by Allan Angoff & Betty Shapin (Parapsychology Foundation, 1970).

Servants of the Light Association

Mystical organization influenced by the work and teachings of occultists Dion Fortune (Violet M. **Firth**) and W. E. **Butler.** S.O.L. offers a safe and comprehensive introduction into Western Mystery Tradition, with elementary and advanced practical teaching and advice in ritual magic. There are public lectures as well as residential weekend courses. The director of Studies is Dolores Ashcroft-Nowicki, author of *First Steps in Ritual, The Shining Paths, Ritual Magic Workbook, Highways of the Mind.*

Address: P.O. Box 215, St. Helier, Jersey, Channel Islands.

Servier, Jean H(enri) (1918-)

Professor of ethnology who has written on parapsychology. Born November 2, 1918 at Constantine, Algeria, he studied at University of Paris (Sorbonne), Licencié ès lettres 1947, diplôme de l'Ecole Nationale des Langues Orientales 1948, docteur ès lettres 1955.

He was a faculty member of Centre National de la Recherche Scientifique from 1949-56, professor of sociology and ethnology at University of Montpellier, France from 1956 onwards; member of Société des Africanistes.

In addition to his studies in ethnology and anthropology, Professor Servier has taken special interest in clairvoyance, mediumship and ethnological aspects of the history of magic. His publications include: 'Geomancy, Clairvoyance and Initiation' (in *La Tour Saint-Jacques,* Sept.-Dec. 1956 and in *Proceedings of Four Conferences of Parapsychology,* 1957), and the books *Les Partes de l'Année* (1963) and *L'Homme et l'Invisible.*

"Seth"

Entity channeled through the mediumship of Jane **Roberts** (1929-1984). Communications date from 1963, when Jane and her husband Robert Butts first experimented with an **ouija board** and received the first "Seth" messages. Later, Jane went into trance, when "Seth" spoke through her, the voice and features of Jane changing character.

The Seth Material comprises a mass of teachings in manuscript and on tape recordings, much of which has been issued in a series of books. The philosophy presented is coherent and continuous, covering teachings on dreams, health, reincarnation, **astral projection,** and the relationship of human beings to their creator. The teachings are lucid, comprehensive, and often profound, dealing with "aspect psychology" (different levels of awareness and grades of reality in relation to mobile consciousness), the nature of the soul, death, and after-death experiences.

In communications titled "The Unknown Reality," "Seth" stated: "The individual self must become aware of far more reality, it must allow its identity to expand to include previously unconscious knowledge. Your species is in a time of change—you are now poised on the threshold from which the race can go many ways. Potentials within the body's mechanisms, not as yet used, can immeasurably enrich the race and bring it to levels of spiritual, psychic, and physical fulfillment. But if some changes are not made, the race will not endure. . . . I am suggesting ways in which the unknown reality can become a known one."

Jane Roberts and her husband Robert Butts published a number of stimulating books dealing with the Seth Material. Introductory works include Jane's books: *The Seth Material* (Prentice-Hall, 1970) and *Seth Speaks* (Prentice-Hall, 1972). (See also **Austin Seth Center; Channeling;** Jane **Roberts**)

Sethos (c. 12th century A.D.)

According to M. A. Del Rio (1561-1608) Sethos was a diviner, who was deprived of his sight by the Emperor Manuel (twelfth century) because of his addiction to magic. It is said that the Emperor Andronicus Comnenus, cousin of Manuel, obtained through Sethos by **hydromancy** an answer to the question of who was to succeed him.

The spirit gave the letters "S I" in reply; and on being asked when, said before the Feast of the exaltation of the Cross. This prediction was fulfilled, for before the date mentioned, Isaac Angelus had thrown Andronicus to be torn in pieces by the mob. It is said that when the devil spells, he spells backwards, so that "S I" may quite fairly be taken to represent Isaac according to the laws of magic.

Setna, Papyrus of

A papyrus of very ancient date, dealing with the personality of Prince Setna Kha-em-ust, son of Rameses II of Egypt, and said to have been discovered by him under the head of a mummy in the Necropolis at Memphis.

The Egyptologist Alfred Wiedemann stated in his book *Popular Literature in Ancient Egypt* (1902): "The first text, which has been known to us since 1867, tells that this prince, being skilled and zealous in the practice of necromancy, was one day exhibiting his acquirements to the learned men of the court, when an old man told him of a magic book containing two spells written by the hand of Thoth himself, the god of wisdom.

"He who repeated the first spell bewitched thereby heaven and earth and the realm of night, the mountains and the depth of the sea; he knew the fowls of the air and every creeping thing; he saw the fishes, for a divine power brought them up out of the depth. He who read the second spell should have power to resume his earthly shape, even though he dwelt in the grave; to see the sun rising in the sky with all the gods and the moon in the form wherein she displays herself.

"Senta inquired where this book was to be found, and learned that it was lying in the tomb of Nefer-ka-Ptah, a son of King Mer-neb-ptah (who is nowhere else named), and that any attempt to take away the book would certainly meet with obstinate resistance. These difficulties did not withhold Setna from the adventure. He entered the tomb of Nefer-ka-Ptah, where he found not only the dead man, but the Ka of his wife Ahuri and their son, though these latter had been buried in Koptos.

"Ahuri told all the trouble that the possession of the book had brought upon her husband and herself, but her tale of woe produced no effect upon the intruder. Setna persisted in his undertaking, and at length, by the help of magic, he gained his end.

"But as in many other tales among many other peoples, success brought no blessing to the man who had disturbed the repose of the dead. Setna fell in love with the daughter of a priest at Memphis, who turned out to be a witch, and took advantage of his intimate connection with her to bring him to ignominy and wretchedness.

"At length the prince recognised and repented of the sacrilege he had committed in carrying off the book, and brought it back to Nefer-ka-Ptah. In the hope of atoning to some extent for his sin he journeyed to Koptos, and finding the graves of the wife and child of Nefer-ka-Ptah, he solemnly restored their mummies to the tomb of the father and husband, carefully closing the tomb he had so sacrilegiously disturbed.

"The second text, edited two years ago by Griffith from a London papyrus, is also genuinely Egyptian in its details. Three magic tales, interwoven one with another, are brought into connection with Saosiri, the supernaturally born son of Setna.

"In the first, Saosiri, who was greatly Setna's superior in the arts of magic, led his father down into the underworld. They penetrated into the judgment-hall of Osiris, where the sights they saw convinced Setna that a glorious future awaited the poor man who should cleave to righteousness, while he who led an evil life on earth, though rich and powerful, must expect a terrible doom. Saosiri next succeeded in saving his father, and with him all Egypt, from great difficulty by reading without breaking the seal a closed letter brought by an Ethiopian magician, whom he thus forced to recognise the superior power of Egypt.

"The last part of the text tells of a powerful magician once dwelling in Ethiopia who modelled in wax a litter with four bearers to whom he gave his life. He sent them to Egypt, and at his command they sought out Pharaoh in his palace, carried him off to Ethiopia, and, after giving him five hundred blows with a cudgel, conveyed him during the same night back to Memphis. Next morning the king displayed the weals on his back to his courtiers, one of whom, Horus by name, was sufficiently skilled in the use of amulets to ward off by their means any immediate repetition of the outrage.

"Horus then set forth to bring from Hermopolis, the allpowerful magic book of the god Thoth, and by its aid he succeeded in treating the Ethiopian king as the Ethiopian sorcerer had treated Pharaoh. The foreign magician then hastened to Egypt to engage in a contest with Horus in magic tricks. His skill was shown to be inferior, and in the end he and his mother received permission to return to Ethiopia under a solemn promise not to set foot on Egyptian territory for a space of fifteen hundred years."

Seton (or **Sethon**), **Alexander** (died c. 1604)

One of the very few alchemists who succeeded in the great experiment of the transmutation of metals. He was said to have taken his name from the village of Seton, in the vicinity of Edinburgh, Scotland, and close to the seashore, so that one may reasonably conclude that the little fishing community of Port Seton is meant, although the antiquary William Camden in his book *Brittania* (1586) stated that Seton was the name of his house.

In the year 1601, the crew of a Dutch vessel had the misfortune to be wrecked on the coast near the dwelling of Seton, and he personally rescued several of them, lodged them in his house, and treated them with great kindness, ultimately sending them back to Holland at his own expense. In the following year, he visited Holland and renewed his acquaintance with at least one of the shipwrecked crew, James Haussen, the pilot, who lived at Arksun.

Haussen, determined on repaying him for the hospitality he had received in Scotland, entertained him for some time in his house, and to him Seton disclosed the information that he was a master of the art of **alchemy,** and proved his words by performing several transmutations. Haussen could not keep this information to himself and confided it to Venderlinden, a physician of Enkhuysen, to whom he showed a piece of gold which he had himself seen transmuted from lead. Venderlinden's grandson, in turn, showed it to the celebrated author, D. G. Morhoff, who wrote a letter concerning it to Langlet du Fresnoy, author of the *Histoire de la Philosophie Hermétique* (3 vols., 1742).

Seton visited Amsterdam and Rotterdam, traveled by sea to Italy, and thence through Switzerland to Germany, accompanied by Wolfgang Dienheim, a professed skeptic of alchemy, whom he convinced of the error of his views at Basle before several of its principal inhabitants. This person described Seton, and from the pen picture he gave of him we can discern a typical Scot of the seventeenth century. "Seton," he said "was short but stout, and highcoloured, with a pointed beard, but despite his corpulence, his expression was spiritual and exalted." "He was," added Dienheim, "a native of Molier, in an island of the ocean." One wonders if Molier is the German's corruption of Lothian.

Several experiments of importance were now demonstrated by Seton. In one of these the celebrated physician Zwinger himself brought the lead which was to be transmuted from his own house. A common crucible was obtained at a goldsmith's, and ordinary sulphur was bought on the road to the house where the experiment was to take place. Seton handled none of these materials and took no part in the operation except to give to those who followed his directions a small packet of powder which transformed the lead into the purest gold of exactly the same weight.

Zwinger appears to have been absolutely convinced of the genuine nature of the experiment, for he wrote an account of it to his friend Dr. Schobinger, which appears in Lonig's *Ephemerides.*

Shortly after this Seton left Basle, and changing his name went to Strasbourg, whence he travelled to Cologne, lodging with Anton Bordemann, who was something of an alchemist himself. In this city, Seton was sufficiently imprudent to exhibit his alchemical skill openly, on one occasion producing six ounces of gold through the application of one grain of his magical powder. The circumstance seems to have made an impression on at least one of the savants of the Cathedral City, for Theobald de Hoghelande in his *Historiæ Aliquot Transmutationis Mettalicæ,* which was published at Cologne in 1604, alluded to it.

Seton then went to Hamburg, whence he traveled south to Munich, where something more important than alchemy engaged his attention, for he eloped with the daughter of a citizen, whom he married. Christian II, the young Elector of Saxony, had heard of Seton's brilliant alchemical successes and invited him to his court, but Seton, reluctant to leave his young wife, sent his friend William Hamilton (probably a brother-Scot) instead, with a supply of the transmuting agent.

In the presence of the whole Court, Hamilton undertook and carried through an experiment with perfect success and the gold then manufactured resisted every known test. This naturally only excited the Elector's desire to see and converse with the magus himself, and a pressing invitation, which amounted to a command, was dispatched to Seton, who thus rendered unable to refuse, came to the electoral court.

He was received there with every mark of honor, but it soon became evident to him that Christian II had only invited him for the purpose of extracting from him the nature of his grand secret, but Seton, as an adept in the mysteries of alchemy, remained true to his high calling, and flatly refused to gratify the Elector's greed.

Promises of preferment and threats were alike indifferent to him, and in the end the Elector, in a passion, ordered him to be imprisoned in a tower, where he was guarded by forty soldiers. There he was subjected to every conceivable species of torture, but all to no purpose. The rack, the fire, and the scourge, failed to extort from him the methods by which he had achieved the grand arcanum. The Elector at last ceased the torture.

At this point, Michael Sendivogius a Moravian chemist who happened to be in Dresden, heard of Seton's terrible experiences and possessed sufficient influence to obtain permission to visit him. Himself a searcher after the **philosopher's stone,** he sympathized deeply with the adept, and proposed to him that he should attempt to effect his rescue. To this Seton agreed, and promised that if he were fortunate enough to escape, he would reward Sendivogius with his secret.

The Moravian traveled back to Cracow, where he resided, sold up his property, and returned to Dresden, where he lodged near Seton's place of confinement, entertaining the soldiers who guarded the alchemist, and judiciously bribing those who were directly concerned in his imprisonment.

At last he judged that the time was ripe to attempt Seton's salvation. He feasted the guards in a manner so liberal that all of them were soon in a condition of drunken carelessness. He then hastened to the tower in which Seton was imprisoned, but found him unable to walk through the severity of his tortures. He therefore supported him to a carriage which stood waiting, and which they reached without being observed. They halted at Seton's house to take up his wife, who had in her possession some of the all-important powder, and whipping up the horses, sped as swiftly as possible to Cracow, which they reached in safety.

When quietly settled in that city, Sendivogius reminded Seton of his promise to assist him in his alchemical projects, but was met with a stern refusal, Seton explaining to him that it was impossible for him as an adept to reveal to his rescuer the terms of such a great mystery. The health of the alchemist was, however, shattered by the dreadful torments through which he had passed, and which he survived only for about two years, and he presented the remains of his magical precipitate to his preserver.

The possession of this powder only made Sendivogius more eager than ever to penetrate the mysteries of the grand arcanum. He married Seton's widow, perhaps with the idea that she was in possession of her late husband's occult knowledge, but if so, he was doomed to disappointment, for she was absolutely ignorant of the matter.

Seton had left behind him, however, a treatise entitled *The New Light of Alchymy,* which Sendivogius laid hands on and published as his own. In its pages he thought he saw a method of increasing the powder, but to his intense disappointment and disgust, he only succeeded in lessening it.

With what remained, however, he posed as a successful projector of the grand mystery, and proceeded with much splendor from court to court in a sort of triumphal procession. In his own country of Moravia, he was imprisoned, but escaped. His powder, however, was rapidly diminishing, but he still continued his experiments. Pierce Borel in his work *Tresor de Recherches et Antiquites Galoises et Françoises* (1655) mentioned that he saw a crown piece which had been partially dipped into a mixture of the powder dissolved in spirits of wine, and that the part steeped in the elixir was of gold, was porous, and was not soldered or otherwise tampered with.

The powder expended, Sendivogius degenerated into a mere charlatan, pretending that he could manufacture gold, and receiving large sums on the strength of being able to do so. He survived until the year 1646 when he died at Parma at the age of eighty-four. Seton's book *The New Light of Alchymy* would appear, from an examination of it, to deny that the philosopher's stone was to be achieved by the successful transmutation of metals. It stated:

"The extraction of the soul out of gold or silver, by what vulgar way of alchymy soever, is but a mere fancy, On the contrary, he which, in a philosophical way, can without any fraud, and colourable deceit, make it that it shall really tinge the basest metal, whether with gain or without gain, with the colour of gold or silver (abiding all requisite tryals whatever), hath the gates of Nature opened to him for the enquiring into further and higher secrets, and with the blessing of God to obtain them." (See also **Alchemy**)

Seven Principles (in Theosophy)

According to Theosophical teachings (derived from esoteric Hinduism), there are seven principles or parts of the human being which reflect cosmic principles. The latter concern the evolution of life from the unmanifest principles through creation.

The seven principles of the human being are: *Atman* (the universal self), *Buddhi* (the intellectual principle), *Manas* (the mental principle), *Kama* (desire), *Prana* (subtle vitality), *Linga-sarira* (astral body), *Sthula-sarira* (gross physical matter).

For convenience, these are sometimes simplified into three principles of the human being: Spirit, Soul, and Body, as in Christianity. These three parts are: first and highest, the Divine Spirit or the Divine Monad, rooted in the Universe, which spirit is linked with the All, being in a mystical sense a ray of the All; second, the intermediate part of Spiritual Monad, which in its higher and lower aspects is the spiritual and human soul; third, the lowest part of the human constitution, the vital-astralphysical part, composed of material or quasi-material lifeatoms. (See also **Evolution of Life; Logos; Monad; Planetary Logos; Rupa; Theosophy**)

For details of relevant concepts, see *The Seven Principles of Man* by Annie **Besant** (1892).

Seven Stewards of Heaven

According to the sixteenth-century magical ritual **Arbatel,** these are the spirits by whom God governs the world. They are known as the Olympian Spirits, and they govern the Olympian spheres, which are composed of one hundred and ninety-six regions.

Their names in the Olympian language are: Aratron, the celestial spirit of Saturn, whose day is Saturday; Bethor, the angel of Jupiter, whose day is Monday; Phaleg, the prince of Mars, whose day is Tuesday; Och, the master of the Sun, whose day is Sunday; Hagith, the sovereign of Venus, whose day is Friday; Ophiel, the spirit of Mercury, who must be invoked on Wednesday; Phul, the administrator of affairs in the Moon, whose day is Monday.

Each of these Seven Celestial Spirits may be invoked by magicians by the aid of ceremonies and preparations.

Seventh-Day Adventism

Heterodox Christian cult stemming from the teachings of William Miller (1782-1849), formerly a Baptist convert, whose simplistic interpretation of scripture led him to assert that Christ would return to earth March 21, 1843. He built up a considerable following, but lost support when the return did not take place, even for a revised calculation of October 22, 1844.

His teachings were later modified by the Millerite Hiram Edson in New York State, who claimed that he had a vision which confirmed that Miller was right about the time of redemption but wrong about the *place,* which should have been the "heavenly sanctuary" and not the earth. Edson's doctrine was further developed by "Father Bates" (former sea captain), Elder James White of the S.D.A. church which had been organized in 1860 and his wife Ellen G. White.

Since those early days, S.D.A. has built up a membership claimed at over two million in the U.S. and abroad. Two of its doctrinal points influenced Charles Taze Russell (1870-1916) in the formation of his evangelical cult of 'Russellites' which became known as **Jehovah's Witnesses** under "Judge" Joseph Rutherford (1916-1942).

These doctrines were those of a "soul-sleep" after death, and of annihilation of the wicked. Other specifically S.D.A. doctrines include the concept of a completion of Christ's atonement which had remained unfinished, and the need to observe the Sabbath on Saturday.

Seventh Son

It has long been believed in Europe and the U.S. that a seventh son is especially lucky or gifted with occult powers, and that the seventh son of a seventh son has healing powers. In Scotland, the seventh daughter of a seventh daughter was said to have the gift of **second sight** (prophetic vision). In Ireland, the saliva of a seventh son was said to have healing properties. However, in Romanian folklore, a seventh child was believed to be fated to become a vampire.

As early as the beginning of the seventeenth century, the *Diary of Walter Yonge 1604-1628* (published by the Camden Society, 1847, edited by G. Roberts) had a skeptical reference to the healing powers of a seventh son: "In January, 1606-7, it is reported from London by credible letters, that a child being the seventh son of his mother, and no woman child born between, healeth deaf, blind, and lame; but the parents of the child are popish, as so many say as are healed by it. The Bishop of London, Doctor Vaughan, caused divers [various people] to be brought to the child as aforesaid, who said a short prayer as [he] imposed his hands upon, as 'tis said he did unto others; but no miracle followeth any, so that it appeareth to be a plain lie invented to win grace to the popish faction."

Thomas Lupton recorded in the second edition of his book *A Thousand Notable Things* (London, 1660), that "It is manifest, by experience, that the seventh male child, by just order (never a girl or wench being born between) doth heal only with touching (through a natural gift) the king's evil [scrofula], which is a special gift of God, given to kings and queens, as daily experience doth witnesse."

In France, there was also a tradition that a seventh son had the power to cure the king's evil. He was called a "Marcou" and branded with a fleur-de-lis. The Marcou breathed on the part affected, or else the patient touched the Marcou's fleur-de-lis.

Robert Chambers, in his *Domestic Annals of Scotland from the Reformation to the Revolution* (2 vols., Edinburgh, 1858) stated (vol. 2) that in February 1682, a certain Hugh McGie "gave in a bill to the Privy Council, representing that, by the practice of other nations, any tradesman having seven sons together, without the intervention of a daughter, is declared free of all public burdens and taxes, and has other encouragements bestowed on him, to enable him to bring up the said children for the use and benefit of the commonwealth; and claiming a similar privilege on the strength of his having that qualification. The Council recommended the magistrates [of Edinburgh] to take Hugh's seven sons into consideration when they laid their 'stents' (trade taxes) upon him."

A tradition in Donegal, Ireland, claimed that the healing powers of a seventh son required a special ceremony at the moment of the infant's birth. The woman who received the child in her arms should place in his hand whatever substance she decided that he should rub with in after-life. This substance could be metal (e.g., a silver coin) or a common substance like salt, or even hair; when the child was old enough, it would rub the substance and the patient would apply it to an afflicted part for healing purposes. There was a similar Irish tradition to the Scottish belief that a seventh son of a seventh son possessed prophetic as well as healing powers.

There was a general belief in Britain that the seventh son of a seventh son was destined to be a physician, having an intuitive knowledge of the art of healing, often curing a patient simply by touching an afflicted part. This belief also extended to the seventh daughter of a seventh daughter. A contributor to *Notes & Queries* (June 12, 1852) observed: "In Saltash Street, Plymouth [England], my friend copied, on the 10th December, 1851, the following inscription on a board, indicating the profession and claims of the inhabitant: 'A. Shepherd, the third seventh daughter, Doctress.'"

The belief in the healing powers of a seventh son of a seventh son has persisted into modern time, and there are currently two Irish healers of this kind: Danny **Gallagher** and Finbarr **Nolan.** Both are "touch healers," although Gallagher additionally "blesses" soil which is to be mixed with water and applied to the afflicted area of the patient; both healers recommend a sequence of two or three visits for maximum healing.

They are credited with remarkable cures. Gallagher is reported as restoring the sight of a woman blind for twenty-two years, and Nolan claims to have healed successfully injured race horses as well as human beings. (See also Danny **Gallagher;** Psychic **Healing; Healing by Faith; King's Evil;** Finbarr **Nolan; Second Sight**)

Sex Magic

The use of sexual energy for occult purposes, derived from a vulgarized tradition of **Tantric Yoga** by Western occultists such as Aleister **Crowley.**

The conversion of sexual energy into spiritual energy, resulting in higher consciousness, has always been a feature of ancient **Yoga** practices of Indian mystics and the energy is considered a divine force, named **Kundalini.**

It is possible that Hindu asceticism influenced early Christianity and helped to form the tradition of sacerdotal celibacy in the priesthood. Celibacy involves the pressurizing and sublimation of sexual energy, resulting in higher spiritual development or even miraculous phenomena.

Suppression of normal sexual outlet may have a beneficial result in a sincere religious context, as in such cults as the **Shakers,** or it may lead to eccentricity or even madness.

Tantric Yoga ritualized sexual intercourse, but involved the assistance of a woman and the withholding of sperm by the yogi through special techniques. Although yogis have considered the male sperm the essential principle in sexual energy, and to be jealously guarded (a teaching which also runs through **alchemy** and Western occultism), it seems possible that the real dynamic of sex magic is the nervous vitality which charges the human organism in both sexual and spiritual exercises. (See also Aleister **Crowley; Kundalini;** Theodor **Reuss; Shakers; Tantra; Tantric Yoga**)

Sexton, Dr. George (c. 1874)

British secularist teacher of the nineteenth century. Robert **Owen** invited his attention to the phenomena of Spiritualism.

After a crusade against its doctrines, personal experiences with the **Davenport Brothers** convinced Sexton of their genuine occurrence. Continuing his experiments he finally ended by accepting Spiritualism and proclaimed its truth in lectures with the same outspokenness with which he formerly fought against it.

He denounced the pretensions of conjurers who claimed to have exposed Spiritualism and, pointing out the difference in condition and effect, he actually performed the sham spiritual manifestations before his audience.

One of his lectures was printed in pamphlet form under the title: *Scientific Materialism Calmly Considered; A Reply to Prof. Tyndall's Belfast Address* (1874).

Sexton became editor of the *Spiritual Magazine* and a member of the **British National Association of Spiritualists.** (See also **Magicians**)

Sextus V, Pope (1521-1590)

One of the Popes accused of sorcery. J. A. de Thou said of him in his *Histoire Universelle* (1734, tome xi): "The Spaniards continued their vengeance against this Pontiff even after his death, and they forgot nothing in their anxiety to blacken his memory by the libels which they flung against him. Sextus, said they, who, by means of the magical art, was for a long time in confederacy with a demon, had made a compact with this enemy of humanity to give himself up to him, on condition he was made Pope, and allowed to reign six years.

"Sextus was raised to the chair of St. Peter, and during the five years he held sway in Rome he distinguished his pontificate by actions surpassing the feeble reach of the human intellect. Finally, at the end of this term, the Pope fell sick, and the devil arriving to keep him to his pact, Sextus inveighed strongly against his bad faith, reproaching him with the fact that the term they had agreed upon was not fulfilled, and that there still remained to him more than a twelve-month.

"But the devil reminded him that at the beginning of his pontificate he had condemned a man who, according to the laws, was too young by a year to suffer death, and that he had nevertheless caused him to be executed, saying that he would give him a year out of his own life; that this year, added to the other five, completed the six years which had been promised to him, and that in consequence he did very wrong to complain.

"Sextus, confused and unable to make any answer, remained mute, and turning himself towards the *ruelle* of his bed, prepared for death in the midst of the terrible mental agitation caused by the remorse of his conscience.

"For the rest," added de Thou, with amiable frankness, "I only mention this trait as a rumor spread by the Spaniards, and I should be very sorry to guarantee its truth."

During the papacy of Sextus, he authorized very large sums to be expended on public works, including completion of the dome of St. Peter's, the loggia of Sextus in the Lateran, and the chapel of the Praesepe in Sta. Maria Maggiore. Sextus was ranked amongst the greatest Popes.

Seybert Commission

A commission for the investigation of Spiritualism, appointed in conformity with the wish of Henry Seybert, a Philadelphia Spiritualist who, in his will, left $60,000 to the University of Pennsylvania to be devoted "to the maintenance of a chair in the said University to be known as the 'Adam Seybert Chair of Moral and Intellectual Philosophy,' upon the condition that the incumbent of the said chair, either individually or in conjunction with a commission of the university faculty will make a thorough and impartial investigation of all systems of morals, religion, or philosophy which assume to represent the truth, and particularly of modern spiritualism."

The commission, which began its investigations in March 1884, was composed as follows: Dr. William Pepper, Dr. Joseph Leidy, Dr. George A. Koenig, Prof. Robert Ellis Thompson, Prof. George S. Fullerton and Dr. Horace Howard Furness; to whom afterwards were added Mr. Coleman Sellers, Dr. James W. White, Dr. Calvin B. Knerr and Dr. S. Weir Mitchell. Dr. Pepper, as Provost of the University was ex-officio chairman, Dr. Furness acting chairman, and Prof. Fullerton as secretary to the committee.

The testator was represented in the committee by Thomas R. Hazard, a personal friend. He was charged by Henry Seybert to prescribe the methods to be pursued in the investigation, designate the mediums to be consulted and reject the attendance of those whose presence might be in conflict with the harmony or good order of the spirit circles.

In May 1887, the committee published a preliminary report with negative conclusions in the whole field of Spiritualist phenomena. No final report was ever published, nor was the investigation continued or reassumed.

The committee first turned its attention to **slate-writing.** Two seances with Mrs. S. E. **Patterson** led to no result. The committee then sent to New York for Henry **Slade,** and promptly caught him in fraud. As no other slate-writing medium was available for test, a mock seance was arranged for the committee by conjuring magician Harry Kellar, in which messages were delivered in French, Spanish, Dutch, Chinese, Japanese, Gujerati and German, without the committee being able to discover the trick.

Spirit **rappings** were next grappled with. Mrs. Margaret Kane-Fox (see **Fox Sisters**), the medium of these experiments, was stood on four glass tumblers, the heels of her shoes resting upon the rear tumblers and the soles upon the first tumblers. After many attempts raps were heard and Mr. Furness remarked to the medium "This is the most wonderful thing of all, Mrs. Kane, I distinctly feel them in your feet. There is not a particle of motion in your foot, but there is an unusual pulsation." After two seances the experiments were abandoned as the medium expressed doubt that in her state of health a third meeting would bring more striking results.

According to the committee, this investigation was not sufficiently extensive to warrant any positive conclusions. The report, however, points out that "sounds of varying intensity may be produced in almost any portion of the human body by voluntary muscular action. To determine the exact location of this muscular activity is at times a matter of delicacy."

An attempt was made to study **spirit photography.** This was frustrated as the committee felt disinclined to accept the high terms of W. M. **Keeler.** He asked three hundred dollars for three seances and the right to demand, if conditions made it necessary, the exclusive use of the dark room and his own instruments. The committee refused and concluded "that in these days of composite photography it is worse than childish to claim a spiritual source for results which can be obtained at any time by any tyro in the art."

The investigation into materialization with Pierre L. O. **Keeler,** into **telekinesis** phenomena with Dr. Rothermel and into **direct voice** with Mrs. Maud **Lord** were declared to have been negative.

The appendix of the report contained Prof. Fullerton's investigation in Europe into the sanity of Prof. **Zöllner's** mind and various experiments of individual committee members with the reading of sealed envelopes. The purpose of Prof. Fullerton's visit to Germany in 1886 was to discredit Prof. Zöllner's experiments with Henry Slade. He interviewed William Wundt, Prof. of Philosophy in the University of Leipzig, Gustave Theodore Fechner, Prof. Emeritus of Physics in the University of Leipzig, W. Schneibner, Prof. of Mathematics in the University of Leipzig, and Wilhelm Weber, Prof. Emeritus of Physics in the University of Goettingen. With the exception of Weber, the learned professors declared that Zöllner's mental condition was not normal.

At the same time Prof. Fullerton established from cross testimonies that Fechner was partly blind, Scheibner was also afflicted with defective vision and not entirely satisfied in his own mind as to the phenomena, Weber was in advanced age and did not recognize the disabilities of his associates. No one had had experiences of this sort before, nor was any one of them acquainted with the ordinary possibilities of deception.

The report of the Seybert Commission was received with indignation by the Spiritualists. Thomas R. Hazard, the only Spiritualist on the committee, declared that he repeatedly protested against the committee's methods, but his protests were disregarded.

In the Philadelphia *North American,* presumably after vain representations with the University authorities, Hazard publicly advised the Trustees to remove Messrs. Fullerton, Thompson and Koenig from the commission for "had the object in view been to belittle and bring into discredit, hatred and general contempt the cause . . . the Trustees could scarcely have selected more suitable instruments for the object intended from all the denizens of Philadelphia than are the gentlemen who constitute a majority of the Seybert Commission." This protest remained similarly unheeded.

The *Preliminary Report of the Commission Appointed by the University of Pennsylvania to Investigate Modern Spiritualism* was published by J. B. Lippincott in 1887. A caustic criticism of the report was published by A. B. Richmond, a member of the Pennsylvania bar in book form. In 1889 it was followed by a second book: *What I Saw at Cassadaga Lake; A Review of the Seybert Commissioners' Report* (1888).

"Spiritualists contend," wrote Frank Podmore in *Modern Spiritualism* (2 vols., 1902), "and not apparently without justification, that the intentions of Mr. Seybert were never fairly carried out, and that the prepossessions of the committee against the subject under investigation are demonstrated by their willingness to leave the inquiry unfinished and to divert the funds entrusted to them to an object which was regarded by the testator as at most of secondary importance."

It may be claimed, however, that the unduly negative approach of the Seybert Commission and the more sympathetic approach of the *Report on Spiritualism* of the committee of the **London Dialectical Society** in 1871 both focused the attention of scientists on claimed psychical phenomena.

Shaddai

According to the mysticism of Kabala, this was one of ten divine names in angelic hierarchy. The *Zohar* speaks of three Supernal Degrees or Divine Hypostases, the first being Kether.

When the world of manifest things was in the condition of Tohu, God revealed himself therein in the hypostasis Shaddai; when it had proceeded to the condition called Bohu, He manifested as the hypostasis Tsabaoth, but when the darkness had disappeared from the face of things He appeared as Elohim. (See also **Kabala; Metratton**)

Shah, (Sayed) Idries (1924-)

Author and translator of important works on occultism and Eastern mysticism. Born June 16, 1924 in Simla, India, he came from an Afghan family of Arabian origin that claims descent through the Prophet Mohammed to the Sasanian Emperors of Persia. He was educated privately, and holds British nationality.

He was proprietor of International Press Agency in 1953, director of studies of Institute for Cultural Research, London from 1966 onwards, literary and film director of Mulla Nasrudin Enterprises. He is a member of the Author's Club and Society of Authors, both in London, England.

He was awarded the Dictionary of International Biography Certificate of Merit for Distinguished Service to Human Thought, and in 1972 was appointed Visiting Professor in Intercultural Studies at the University of Geneva, Switzerland. He is also Prof. Honoris Causa, National University of La Plata, Argentina since 1974.

His writings range over travel, bibliography, literature, philosophy and history, but he is best known for his works on occultism and Sufi mysticism.

His books include: *Oriental Magic* (1956), *Destination Mecca* (1957), *The Secret Lore of Magic* (1957), *Special Problems in the Study of Sufi Ideas* (1966), (transl.) *The Exploits of the Incomparable Mulla Nasrudin* (1966), (transl.) *Tales of the Dervishes* (1967), *Reflections* (1968), *Caravan of Dreams* (1968), (transl.) *Way of the Sufi* (1968), (transl.) *Wisdom of the Idiots* (1969), (transl.) *The Book of the Book* (1969), *The Sufis* (1969), (ed.) *Textos Sufis* (1969), *The Dermis Probe* (1970), *Thinkers of the East* (1971), *The Dermis Probe* (1971; also filmed), *The Magic Monastery* (1972), *Lo que un pajaro deberia Parecer* (1972), (transl.) *The Subtleties of Nasrudin* (1973), (transl.) *The Pleasantries of the Incredible Mulla Nasrudin* (1973), *The Elephant in the Dark* (1974), *World Tales* (1979), *Learning How to Learn; Psychology and Spirituality in the Sufi Way* (1981).

Shakers

A spiritual community established in New Lebanon, New York, near the Massachusetts lines, formally known as the United Society of Believers in Christ's Second Appearing.

It had its origin in England in 1747, when Jane and James Wardley became the first leaders of a Lancashire revivalist sect. They were Quaker tailors influenced by French prophets. Ann Lee, twenty-two year old daughter of a Manchester blacksmith, joined this group of "shaking Quakers" in 1758, and through her strange visionary gifts became leader. She was imprisoned in 1772 for disturbing the Sabbath and preaching a doctrine of celibacy.

In 1774, after visions and inspired revelations, she moved to America with a handful of members of her sect. In New York she was deserted by her husband Abraham Stanley, a blacksmith.

By 1780, the Shaker colony had grown, attracting many settlers. Men and women lived together in celibacy with common ownership of property and characteristic religious songs. One of these songs "Tis The Gift to be Simple," is still widely known. Between 1781 and 1783 Mother Ann and her elders visited thirty-six towns in Massachusetts and Connecticut on a missionary campaign, but Shakers were ridiculed and subjected to every kind of indignity.

However, the community prospered and established an enviable reputation for hard work, excellent furniture making, and community happiness.

From 1837 onwards, the Watervliet Community near Albany, New York, was visited by Spiritualist type manifestations of shaking and jerking, when various Shakers were possessed by Indian spirits and spoke with tongues. These manifestations were not made known until long after the establishment of Spiritualist as a popular movement.

Some Shakers became Spiritualists. One of the most prominent was Elder Frederick W. Evans, who spoke at Spiritualist convention and attended seances, although remaining an active Shaker. He claimed that the Shaker interest in the spirit world derived from the interest of Mother Ann Lee in

Emanuel **Swedenborg,** but as she was illiterate and had left England in 1774, it seems unlikely that there could have been any influence.

It is not generally known that poet Walt Whitman visited the Shaker community at Mt. Lebanon. For an account, see the article 'Walt Whitman's Visit to the Shakers; With Whitman's Notebook Containing his Description and Observations of the Shaker Group at Mt. Lebanon' by Emory Holloway (*The Colophon,* First Issue, Spring 1930).

Mother Ann died in 1784. The eventual decline of Shakerism owed partly to materialistic influences from outside and partly to the inevitable dwindling of a community that outlawed sexual activity.

It seems clear that much of the very genuine joy and creativeness of the Shaker community arose from the intense energy of sexual sublimation. (See also **Kundalini; Sex Magic**)

Recommended reading:

Andrews, Edward Deming. *The People Called Shakers; A Search for the Perfect Society,* Oxford University Press, New York, 1953

[Evans, Frederick W.] *Autobiography of a Shaker,* Mount Lebanon, New York, 1869

Evans, Frederick W. *Shakers and Shakerism,* New York, 1859

Flinn, H. C. *Spiritualism Among the Shakers,* East Canterbury, New Hampshire, 1899

MacLean, John P. *Bibliography of Shaker Literature,* 1905; (Burt Franklin 1971)

Shaman

The magician or "medicine man" of primitive tribes, with powers of healing, prophecy or paranormal phenomena. The term is thought to derive from Tungus *shaman* and Sanskrit *sramana* (ascetic).

As distinct from priests, shamans have no ritualistic knowledge, but operate rather like Spiritualist mediums. The gift of shamanism is inborn, sometimes hereditary, and is communicated from one shaman to another.

Shamanism has been studied amongst the Eskimos, and in Scandinavia, Tibet, China, Japan, Korea, Siberia, Manchuria, Mexico, Yutacan, Guatemala and the North Pacific coast. A shamanistic performance often includes dancing, mediumistic-trance and spirit possession. The role of the shaman (and shamaness) has been revived in the New Age movement with such figures as Lynn Andrews, drawing upon American Indian traditions to become a guide for spiritual transformation. (See also **Siberia**)

Recommended reading:

Andrews, Lynn V. *Star Woman,* Warner Books, 1986

Eliade, Mircea. *Shamanism: Archaic Techniques of Ecstasy,* Princeton University, 1964; London, 1967

Shamballah

Fabulous mystical city of ancient legend, believed to be the site of the Garden of Eden.

Shanti Nilaya

A healing and growth center founded in Escondido, California, in 1978. The name means "final home of peace" and is concerned with the work of physician Dr. Elisabeth **Kübler-Ross,** author of the book *On Death and Dying* (New York, 1970).

An extension of her well-known "Life-Death and Transition" workshops, Shanti Nilaya offers short and long-term therapeutic sessions connected with the experience of death and the question of life after death.

The *Shanti Nilaya Newsletter,* giving news of the work of Dr. Kübler-Ross and Shanti Nilaya centers is published from: General Delivery, Headwaters, Virginia 24442.

Sharp, William (1856-1905)

Scottish poet, biographer and editor, who also achieved fame under the name of "Fiona MacLeod"—not so much a literary pseudonym as virtually a psychic secondary personality.

Sharp was born in Paisley, Scotland, September 12, 1856 and spent his childhood in the Scottish Highlands. He ran away from home three times, on one occasion spending a whole summer in a gypsy encampment. He studied for two years as a student at Glasgow University before becoming an attorney's clerk.

He suffered from ill health and his family sent him on a Pacific cruise. Afterwards he settled in London as a bank clerk, eventually becoming acquainted with literary circles that included B. G. Rossetti and Walter Pater.

Pater encouraged his literary work, which first appeared in the *Pall Mall Gazette,* and in 1885 Sharp became art critic for the *Glasgow Herald.* In the same year he married his first cousin Elizabeth Amelia Sharp, who became companion and co-worker rather than wife. They worked jointly on the anthology *Lyra Celtica* (1896).

Sharp abandoned banking for a journalistic career, becoming editor of *The Pagan Review* in 1892. He traveled throughout Europe and even visited the U.S., where he met Walt Whitman.

Sharp's enthusiasm for the Celtic literary revival brought him into contact with W. B. **Yeats** and the Isis Urania Temple of the famous **Golden Dawn** occult society. Here he was initiated into the Neophyte grade.

This occult connection may have been a stimulus to the development of his *anima* personality of "Fiona MacLeod." Sharp and "Fiona" remained distinctly different identities in literary style and outlook, even involving correspondence with friends as separate personalities for many years.

Sharp himself kept up a correspondence with Yeats and AE (George W. **Russell)** on occult and mystical experiments, while also writing to them on literary, poetical and Celtic matters as Fiona MacLeod.

The identical nature of the two personalities remained a closely guarded secret between Sharp, his wife and one or two personal friends until after Sharp's death. The Fiona letters were in the handwriting of Sharp's sister, but the style and personality were those of a distinct individual. Fiona's letter, poems, and books were quite feminine in outlook, quite unlike the masculine lifestyle and writings of the bearded and mustachioed Sharp.

The Fiona works played a leading part in the Scottish Celtic literary revival and were the product of automatic writing by Sharp, who virtually acknowledged Fiona as a separate personality. She was said to be a distant cousin, and even had a biography in the prestigious British biographical annual *Who's Who*.

Sharp's own publications included the poetry volumes *Human Inheritance* (1882), *Earth's Voices* (1884), *Flower o' the Vine* (1894); biographies *Life of D. G. Rossetts* (1882), *Life of P. B. Shelley* (1887), *Life of Heinrich Heine* (1888), *Life of Robert Browning* (1890), *Life and Letters of Joseph Severen* (1892); novels *Wives in Exile* (1896), *Silence Farm* (1899). He also published two volumes of short stories: *The Gypsy Christ* (1895) and *Ecce Puella* (1896), as well as books of literary criticism: *Progress of Art in the Century* (1902), *Literary Geography* (1904).

The "Fiona MacLeod" books included: *Pharais* (1894), *The Mountain Lovers* (1895), *The Sin-Eater* (1895), *The Washer of the Ford* (1896), *Green Fire* (1896), *The Dominion of Dreams* (1899), *The Divine Adventure* (1900), *Winged Destiny* (1904), *The Immortal Hour* (1908).

Sharp died December 12, 1905, after catching a cold during a visit to a friend in Sicily. His widow died a few years later, leaving two large packets of materials "to be destroyed unexamined." It is believed that these may have contained Golden Dawn documents. (See also Hermetic Order of the **Golden Dawn**)

Shasta, Mount

Many occult legends have grown up around the area of Mount Shasta in Sishiyou County, northern California, supposedly the haunt of the monster Bigfoot, a secret home of lost Lemurians and a **flying saucer** base.

Many of these legends derive from the "I Am" cult founded by Guy W. **Ballard** (1878-1939), who claimed to have encountered spiritual Masters on Mount Shasta and acquired occult knowledge.

Shaver, Richard S(harpe) (1907-1975)

Pennsylvania welder and author, responsible for the series of revelations known as the **"Shaver Mystery"** published by Raymond A. **Palmer** in *Amazing Stories* from 1945-49. Drawing upon "racial memories," Shaver described a race of "deros" or vicious dwarfs living in underground caverns, indulging in sexual orgies and harassing human beings by means of secret rays and telepathy.

Shaver's somewhat crude original manuscript titled *A Warning to Future Man* was extensively worked over by Palmer to emerge in the March 1945 issue of *Amazing Stories* as 'I Remember Lemuria.' At first the series boosted the magazine circulation to a record 185,000, but many earnest readers were clearly paranoid, describing their own knowledge of secret influences from deros who were also apparently responsible for the disaster of Pearl Harbor.

More traditional science-fiction readers were indignant at such stories being presented as factual, and after thousands of protests, Howard Browne, who took over from Palmer, killed the series.

The Shaver legend was revived from time to time in *Other Worlds* and *Fantastic* magazines, and there was also a fanzine *Shaver Mystery Magazine* which appeared for several issues (now collector's items). *I Remember Lemuria* and *The Return of Sathanas* were reissued in book format in 1948.

Shaver Mystery

A celebrated creation of science-fiction publisher Raymond A. **Palmer.** As editor of the pulp magazine *Amazing Stories,* he published in 1945 what were claimed to be factual narratives by Pennsylvania welder Richard S. **Shaver** concerning a mysterious race of malevolent beings living under the earth. These "deros" were said to be responsible for catastrophes such as shipwrecks, fires, wars, airplane crashes and even mental persecution, using secret rays and telepathy.

Palmer edited and developed Shaver's rough drafts, which drew on "racial memories." As these stories got more and more amazing, many readers found it impossible to swallow them as factual, and protested so strongly that the series was killed in 1949 by Howard Browne, who took over from Palmer. Browne described the Shaver material as "the sickest crap I'd run into."

She-Goat

One of the branches of augury in ancient Rome dealt especially with the signs which might be derived from animals, and it was believed that if a she-goat crossed the path of a man who was stepping out of his house it was a good omen, and he might proceed on his way rejoicing and "think upon Caranus."

Sheargold, Richard K(empsell) (1911-1988)

British parapsychologist. Born December 20, 1911 at Caterham, Surrey, England. In 1933 he married Margarita Beretta. He was Departmental Manager at McMichael Radio, Slough, England. He was a member of the Society for Psychical Research, London, with special interest in scientific experiments relating to the question of human survival.

He completed a series of card-guessing tests sponsored by the Society for Psychical Research, with mediums as percipients, in order to investigate the possibility of a relationship between telepathic faculty and the ESP demonstrated by mental mediums.

These experiments were reported in the *Journal* of the Society for Psychical Research (June 1961).

From 1971 onwards, Mr. Sheargold expermented with the **Electronic Voice** phenomenon earlier reported by Friedrick Jürgenson and Dr. Konstantin Raudive (see also **Raudive Voices).**

In September 1973, Mr. Sheargold gave a talk on 'Experiments on the Jürgenson Voice Phenomena' at a symposium organized by The Institute of Parascience (extracts were quoted in the book *The Mediumship of the Tape Recorder* by D. J. Ellis, 1978). Mr. Sheargold published a useful booklet *Hints on Receiving the Voice Phenomenon* (1973).

He died January 25, 1988.

Sheep-Goat Hypothesis

A concept in parapsychology relating to the effect of belief and attitude to success in ESP scoring.

The term derives from the pioneer researches of parapsychologist Gertrude R. **Schmeidler** in 1958. She conducted experiments in which her subjects were divided into two groups—"sheep" and "goats."

The sheep had belief in the possibility of **psi,** whilst the goats were skeptics who rejected the possibility.

It was observed that in individual and group tests, the sheep scored higher in **ESP** trials than the goats, suggesting that belief strongly influenced successful ESP. However, the differences in scoring were relatively small, although statistically significant, and many later experiments have been conducted by other parapsychologists to test the hypothesis, and the term "sheep-goat" has now become a commonplace in para-psychological discussions.

Sheldrake, Rupert (1942-)

British biochemist with specialized experience in plant research, who has proposed a bold new theory of "formative causation," concerned with the origin and growth of form and characteristics in nature. While not denying the inheritance of characteristics through the gene complex, he has suggested a literal view of what has been termed for convenience "morphogenetic fields" as actual structures independent of time and space. Although Sheldrake's field theory applies primarily to organisms, plants, and animals, it also has important relevance to concepts of parapsychological phenomena, such as **telepathy, clairvoyance** and **reincarnation.**

Sheldrake was educated at Clare College, Cambridge University, England, becoming a fellow and director of studies in biochemistry and cell biology. In 1973, he was awarded a Rosenheim Research Fellowship of the Royal Society. Instead of taking a professorship at a university, he decided to study growing plants at first hand, and became a member of the staff of the International Crops Research Institute for the Semi-Arid Tropics in Hyderabad, India, becoming a consultant to the Institute in 1978.

In 1966, Sheldrake had been associated with the Epiphany Philosophers, a group of scientists and philosophers at Cambridge University concerned with exploring interconnections between science, philosophy, and mysticism. This contact stimulated his early ideas on formative causation. Other influences were the theories of Henri **Bergson** and Hans **Driesch.** (See also **Formative Causation)**

Shelta Thari

An esoteric language spoken by the tinkers of Britain and Ireland and possibly a descendant of an "inner" language employed by the ancient Celtic Druids or bards.

It was in 1876 that the first hint of the existence of Shelta Thari reached the ears of that prince of practical philologists Charles Godfrey **Leland.** It seems strange that George Borrow, the first authority on Romany and gypsy lore, had never stumbled upon the language, and that fact may be taken as a strong evidence of the jealousy with which the nomadic classes guarded it.

Leland related how he and Professor E. H. Palmer were wandering on the beach at Aberystwyth in Wales when they met a tramp, who heard them indulging in a conversation in Romany. Leland questioned the man as to how he gained a living, and he replied, "Shelkin gallopas." The words were foreign even to the master of dialect, and he inquired their import. "Why," said the man, "it means selling ferns. That is tinker's language or minklers' thari. I thought as you knew Romany, you might understand it. The right name for the tinkers' language is Shelta."

"It was," said Leland, "with the feelings of Columbus the night before he discovered America that I heard the word Shelta, and I asked the fern-dealer if he could talk it." The man replied "A little," and on the spot the philologist collected a number of words and phrases from the fern-seller which gave him sufficient insight into the language to prove to him that it was absolutely different from Romany.

The Celtic origin of the dialect soon began to suggest itself to Leland, and he attempted to obtain from the man some verse or jingle in it, possible for the purpose of observing its syntactial arrangement. But all he was able to drag from his informant were some rhymes of no philological value, and he found he had soon exhausted the tramp's knowledge.

It was later on in America that Leland nearly terrified a tinker out of his wits by speaking to him in the lost dislect. The man, questioned as to whether he could speak Shelta admitted that he could. He proved to be an Irishman, Owen Macdonald by name, and he furnished Leland with an invaluable list of several hundred words. But Leland could not be sure upon which of the Celtic languages the dialect was based.

Owen Macdonald declared to him that it was a fourth language, which had nothing in common with old Irish, Welsh, or Gaelic, and hazarded the information that it was the idiom of the "Ould Picts," but this appeared to be rather too conjectural for the consumption of the philologist.

Shelta is not a jargon, for it can be spoken grammatically without using English, as in the British form of Romany. Pictish in all probability was not a Celtic language, nor even an Aryan one, however intimately it may have been affected by Celtic speech in the later stages of its existence.

Leland's discovery was greeted in some quarters with inextinguishable laughter. The *Saturday Review* jocosely suggested that he had been conned and that old Irish had been palmed off on him for a mysterious lingo. Leland put this view of the matter before his tinker friend, who replied with grave solemnity, "And what'd I be afther makin' two languages av thim for, if there was but wan av thim?"

Since Leland's time, much has been done to reclaim this mysterious tongue, chiefly through the investigations of John Sampson and professor Kuno Meyer. The basis of these investigations rested on the fact that the tinker caste of Great Britain and Ireland was a separate class—so separate indeed as almost to form a race by itself. For hundreds of years, possibly, this fraternity existed with nearly all its ancient characteristics, and on the general disuse of Celtic speech had conserved it as a secret dialect.

The peculiar thing concerning Shelta is the extent of territory over which it is spoken. That it was known rather extensively in London itself was discovered by Leland, who heard it spoken by two small boys in the Euston Road They were not Gypsies, and Leland found out that one of them spoke the language with great fluency.

Since Leland's discoveries Shelta has been to some extent mapped out into dialects, one of the most important of which is that of Ulster. It would be difficult to explain briefly exactly how long the Ulster dialect of this strange and ancient tongue differed from that in use in other parts of Britain and Ireland. But that it did so is certain.

John Sampson, a worthy successor to Borrow and Leland, and a linguist of repute, published in the *Journal* of the Gypsy Lore Society (new series, vol. 1, 1908), a number of sayings and proverbs which he had collected in Liverpool from two old Irish tinkers—John Barlow and Phil Murray. Sampson stated that these were in the Ulster dialect of Shelta.

Some of these may be quoted to provide the reader with specimens of the language: "Krish gyukera have muni Sheldru" (Old beggars have good Shelta). "Stimera dhi-ilsha, stimera aga dhi-ilsha" (If you're a piper, have your own pipe). "Mislo granhes thaber" (The traveler knows the road). "Thom Blorne mjesh Nip gloch" (Every Protestant isn't an Orangeman). "Nus a dhabjon dhuilsha" (The blessing of God on you). "Misli, gami gra dhi-il" (Be off, and bad luck to you).

There seems to be considerable reason to believe that the tinker (or more properly "tinkler") class of Britain and Ireland sprang from the remnants of its ancient Celtic inhabitants, and differed as completely from the Gypsy or Romany race as one people can well differ from another. This is strongly suggested by the criterion of speech, for Shelta is a Celtic tongue and that Romany is a dialect of Northern Hindustan is not open to doubt.

Those who now speak Romany habitually almost invariably make use of Shelta as well, but that only proves that the two nomadic races, having occupied the same territory for hundreds of years, had gained a knowledge of each other's languages. Who, then, were the original progenitors of the tinkers? Whoever they were, they were a Celtic-speaking race, and probably a nomadic one. Shelta has been referred to as the language of the ancient bards of Ireland, the esoteric tongue of an Irish priesthood.

Leland put forward the hypothesis that the Shelta-speaking tinker is a descendant of a prehistoric guild of bronze-workers. This, he thought, accounted in part for his secretiveness as regards his language. In Italy, to this very day, the tinker class is identified with the itinerant bronze workers. The tinker fraternity of Britain and Ireland existed with perhaps nearly all it ancient characteristics until the advent of railroads. But long before this, it had probably amalgamated to a great extent with the Gypsy population, and the two languages had become common to the two peoples.

This seems to be the only explanation that can be given for the appearance of Shelta, a Celtic language, in the non-Celtic portions of Great Britain. That it originated in Ireland appears to be highly probable, for in no other part of these islands during the later Celtic period was there a state of civilization sufficiently advanced to permit of the existence of a close corporation of metal-workers possessing a secret language. Moreover, the affinities of Shelta appear to be with old Irish more than with any other Celtic dialect.

There is one other theory that presents itself in connection with the origin of Shelta, and that is, that it is the modern descendant of the language of the "Ould Picts" mentioned by Owen Macdonald, Leland's tinker friend.

It has by no means been proved that Pictish was a non-Aryan language, and, despite the labors of Professor Rhys, we are as far off as ever from any definite knowledge concerning the idiom spoken by that mysterious people. But there are great difficulties in the way of accepting the hypothesis of the Pictish origin of Shelta, the chief among them being its obvious Irish origin. There were, it is known, Picts in the North of Ireland, but they were almost certainly a small and primitive colony, and a very unlikely community to form a metal-working confraternity, possessing the luxury of a private dialect.

It still remains for the Celtic student to classify Shelta in a definitive way. It may prove to be "Pictish," strongly influenced by the Gaelic of Ireland and Scotland. A comparison with Basque and the dialect of the Iberian tribes of Morocco might bring affinities to light, and thus establish the theory of its non-Aryan origin, but its strong kinship with Erse seems likely. (See also **Gypsies)**

Recommended reading:

Leland, Charles Godfrey. *The Gypsies,* Houghton, Mifflin, 1882

MacRithie, David. *Shelta; The Cairds' Language* (*Transactions* of Gaelic Society of Inverness, vol. 24, Inverness, Scotland, 1904)

Shemhamphorash

In the *Talmud,* the external term representing the hidden word of power, by whose virtues a new world might be. But it is lost to the human race, although even sounds approximating to it have a magic power, and can give to whoever pronounces them dominion in the spirit world.

Some of the old Rabbis believed that the word of power contains twelve letters, others, forty-two, and yet others seventy-two, but these are the letters of the divine alphabet, which God created from certain luminous points made by the concentration of the primal universal Light. *Shemhamphorash* is, in fact, the *name* of this word.

This ancient Jewish mystical concept is curiously paralleled by the ancient Hindu teachings of the creation of the world through the mystical trisyllable **"AUM,"** said to contain the origin of the alphabet and all sounds. Related to such concepts are the use of certain letters and sounds known as Mantras for magical purposes. (See also **AUM; Kabala; Mantra; Nada; Yoga)**

Shepard, Jesse Francis Grierson (1849-1927)

Mystic, seer, author and musical medium, who performed before famous musicians and royal personages. His musical seances were held both in light and darkness. In darkness his renderings were marvelous. He did not always actually play the piano. The music came sometimes through the shut keyboards. He rendered duets and sang simultaneously in bass and soprano. He also played the organ and sang in cathedrals. He could give trance addresses in English, French, German, Latin, Greek, Chaldean and Arabic on any subject.

His full name was Benjamin Henry Jesse Francis Grierson Shepard. He was of Scottish-Irish descent, brought to the U.S. in his first year. He spent his boyhood on the Illinois prairie. At the age of 13 he became a pageboy to General John C. Frémont and made the acquaintance of both Grant and Sherman.

When in his twenty-first year, he set out for Paris without any funds. Within a short time he became one of the most famous mediums in Europe, demonstrating **psychometry, clairvoyance, prediction** and diagnosis of disease. He also displayed uncanny musical gifts.

Without extensive formal training in music, he gave performances at the piano and claimed to be possessed by the spirits of Mozart, Beethoven, Meyerbeer, Rossini, Sontag, Persiani, Malibran, Lablache, Liszt, Berlioz and Chopin. He performed to the rich, famous and royalty of Europe.

The audience at one concert in Holland in 1894 included H. R. H. the Duchess of Cumberland, the Queen of Hanover, the Reigning Duke of Saxe-Altenburg, and the Queen of Denmark.

In addition to his piano performances, Shepard sometimes sang, in every range of voice from bass to soprano. So incredible were his talents that one man lost his job for publicly stating his belief in them. Henry Kiddle, Superintendent of Schools in New York, was imprudent enough to state that he heard Shepard playing a splendid piano symphony under the control of Mozart, while at the same time delivering a learned philosophical discourse under the influence of Aristotle. Kiddle was forced to resign his position.

In Catherine Berry's *Experiences in Spiritualism* (1876), historical fragments relating to Semiramide were published as recorded after Shepard's trance statements under the control of an Egyptian spirit. In 1889 he published two inspired volumes of which Maurice **Maeterlinck** declared that he knows nothing in literature more admirable or profound.

Prince Adam Wisniewski wrote in an account quoted by *Light* in 1894: "After having secured the most complete obscurity we placed ourselves in a circle around the medium, seated before the piano. Hardly were the first chords struck when we saw lights appearing at every corner of the room . . . The first piece played through Shepard was a fantasie of Thalberg's on the air from "Semiramide." This is unpublished, as is all the music which is played by the spirits through Shepard. The second was a rhapsody for four hands, played by Liszt and Thalberg with astounding fire, a sonority truly grand, and a masterly interpretation. Notwithstanding this extra ordinarily complex technique, the harmony was admirable, and such as no one present had ever know paralleled, even by Liszt himself, whom I personally knew, and in whom passion and delicacy were united. In the circle were musicians who, like me, had heard the greatest pianists of Europe; but we can say that we never heard such truly supernatural execution."

Shepard was also occasionally a **direct voice** medium. During a seance at The Hague, Holland, in 1907, direct voices were heard speaking in Dutch. High officials of the Dutch government who were present also heard voices speaking in Sundanese (a Javanese dialect) and Mandarin Chinese.

In 1907, after his fabulous success in Europe and return visits to America, Shepard broke with his psychic connections and mediumship, and settled in London, where he ceased his musical exhibitions and devoted himself to writing. He changed his name to "Francis Grierson" and made a great reputation through his essays in both English and French. At the age of fifty, he published his book *Modern Mysticism and Other Essays* (1899), followed by *The Celtic Temperament and Other Essays* (1901). The latter work was adopted as a textbook by Japanese universities. Other publications included. *The Valley of Shadows: Recollections of the Lincoln Country, 1858-63* (1909), *Portraits* (1910), *La Vie* and *Les Hommes*

(1911), *The Humour of the Underman* (1911), *The Invisible Alliance* (1913), *Illusions and Realities of the War* (1918), *Abraham Lincoln: The Practical Mystic* (1918).

The quality of his literary work secured him a place in the prestigious Kunitz & Haycraft *Twentieth Century Authors* (1942). Many of Shepard's readers were unaware of his earlier psychic activities until in 1921 he published a Spiritualist pamphet *Psycho-Phone Messages.*

By all accounts, Shepard must have been one of the most brilliant psychics in history, but in spite of his mystical and artistic talents or perhaps because of his dedication to mystic insight rather than material things, he died in utter poverty. As an old man of 78, he died May 29, 1927 from hunger while a case worker from the Los Angeles Assistance League was knocking on his door. She was unaware of his glittering past as a musician or his fame as a writer. He had earlier pawned his last valuable—a watch given to him by the King of England.

Shepard's own account of his psychic talents was published under the title 'How I Became a Musical Medium' in the May 6, 1970 issue of the *Medium.* For other biographical material, see 'The Genius of Francis Grierson' by W. Tonner in *Trend* (March 1914) and the book *King of Paris* by Guy Endore (Pocket Books, 1958).

Sherman, Harold (Morrow) (1898-1987)

Author, broadcaster and lecturer in the field of parapsychology. Born July 13, 1898 at Traverse City, Michigan, he was educated at Traverse City High School and University of Michigan. In 1920 he married Martha Frances Bain. Memberships include Authors League of America, Dramatists Guild. After a period as a freelance writer, he worked with CBS-Radio in New York from 1935-36. He was founder and president of E.S.P. Research Associates Foundation, Little Rock, Arkansas from 1964 onwards.

He conducted experiments in clairvoyance, telepathy, psychokinesis, precognition, mediumship and survival, and lectured on ESP generally. With psychologist Leslie **LeCron** and scientists affiliated with the University of California, L.A., he investigated the question of the method of operation of ESP faculty. He contributed articles to *Mind Digest, Journal of Living, Success Unlimited* and *Tomorrow.*

During a distinguished career as a writer, commencing as a young newspaper reporter in Marion, Indiana, at the age of twenty-two, he authored some sixty books on such subjects as sports, adventure, and short stories, as well as books concerned with extrasensory perception and mental power. He was also interested in the theater and produced plays, and a Hollywood movie "The Adventures of Mark Twain." His book *Your Key to Happiness* (1935) was presented on radio, and he also conducted a radio series on popular philosophy three times a week under the title "The Man Who Helps You to Help Yourself."

His book *Thoughts Through Space* (1942; 1957) was written with explorer Sir Hubert Wilkins and deals with their long-distance telepathy experiments. His other books include: *You Live After Death* (1947; 1956), *Know Your Own Mind* (1952), *TNT—The Power Within You* (with Claude Bristol, 1954), *Adventures in Thinking* (1955), *How to Use the Power of Prayer* (1958), *How to Turn Failure Into Success* (1958), *How to Foresee and Control Your Future* (1973), *How to Make ESP Work for You* (1973), *Your Power to Heal* (1973), *You Can Communicate with the Unseen World* (1974), *Wonder Healers of the Philippines* (1974), *How to Know What to Believe* (1976), *How to Picture What You Want* (1978), *Your Key to Happiness* (1979).

He died August 19, 1987, at the age of 89, at his home on Highway 5 South, Mountain View, Arkansas. One of his final messages to his many friends was: "I expect it will be a great moment when I greet you in the next dimension."

Sherwood, Carlton M(ontgomery) (1895-)

Financial counselor also active in the field of parapsychology. Born April 12, 1895 at Buffalo, New York. In 1926 he married Ann Glover.

He was secretary of YMCA, Buffalo from 1915-17, served in U.S. Army from 1917-19, general secretary of New York State Christian Endeavor Union from 1919-27, executive secretary of Citizens Committee of 100 from 1926-36, extension secretary from 1927-31, general secretary from 1931-34, International Society of Christian Endeavor; editor of *Christian Endeavour World* from 1930-34, secretary of World's Christian Endeavor Union from 1931-34, executive director of Associated Boards for Christian Colleges in China from 1934-36, thereafter president of Pierce, Hedrick & Sherwood, Inc., counselors in institutional financing.

His memberships include: executive council of Foundation for Integrative Education, board of directors of Parapsychology Foundation, board of trustees of American Society for Psychical Research, board of trustees of Wainwright House, board of trustees of Biblical Seminary in New York, Society for Psychical Research, London, American Association of Fund Raising Counsel (president 1945-57), Commission on Religion and Health, National Council of Churches (chairman 1954-57). He was also chairman of the Conference on Parapsychology and Psychedelics, New York, November 1958.

Shiatsu (or Shiatzu)

A Japanese term meaning "finger-pressure," applied to a system of pressure points in the body which govern energy flow, preserving health and rejuvenating the mind. The system is comparable to **Acupuncture**, but dispenses with needles, using finger pressure instead.

In regulating the flow of energy, the goal is to achieve balance, manifested physically, mentally and spiritually. A prominent teacher of Shiatsu in the U.S. is Wataru Ohashi, author of *Do It Yourself Shiatsu*, A.S.I. Publishing Inc., (New York, N.Y. 10016), 1976. There is also a Shiatsu Education Center, 52 West 55 Street, New York, N.Y. 10019.

Shiels, Tony ("Doc")

Well known contemporary conjuring magician who presents conjuring and mentalism in a setting of "psychic power." In his publicity to fellow stage magicians, Shiels gives instructions how "to bend metal in the Geller style . . . to teleport and levitate . . . to become a successful witch . . . to raise ghosts and poltergeists, etc."

However, Shiels also acknowledges the reality of ESP as well as the conjuring and mentalism versions. His book *Entertaining With "ESP"* (David & Charles, U.K., 1974) describes both kinds.

Shiels has also taken several photographs claimed as pictures of the **Loch Ness Monster.**

Ship of the Dead

Similar to the superstitious idea of the death-coach is the belief that at times a phantom ship carries away the souls of men. In the form of a cloud-ship, or wrapped in a driving mist, it sails over mountains and moors, and at sea it sails without hindrance, no matter what wind and tide.

A story is told of a certain pirate, as whose death a spectral ship approached in a cloud. As it sailed over the roof, the house was filled with a sound as of a stormy sea, and when the ship had passed by, the soul of the pirate accompanied it. (See also **Flying Dutchman**)

Shipton, Mother

Legendary British prophetess, supposed to have been born in the reign of King Henry VII and to have predicted the death of Cardinal Wolsey and Lord Percy, as well as other events with absolute accuracy and a clarity quite unlike the other great sage **Nostradamus.**

Mother Shipton was also credited with even more remarkable prescience in the following rhymed couplets:

"Carriages without horses shall go,
And accidents fill the world with woe.
Around the world thoughts shall fly
In the twinkling of an eye.
The world upside down shall be
And gold be found at the root of a tree.
Through hills man shall ride,
And no horse be at his side.
Under water men shall walk,
Shall ride, shall sleep, shall talk.
In the air men shall be seen,
In white, in black, in green;
Iron in the water shall float,
As easily as a wooden boat.
Gold shall be found and shown
In a land that's now not known.
Fire and water shall wonders do,
England shall at last admit a foe.
The world to an end shall come,
In eighteen hundred and eighty one."

These alleged prophecies, in a palpably modern poetical style, occurred in a chapbook pamphlet published in 1862 by the bookseller Charles Hindley, who claimed that they were reprinted from an earlier chapbook by Richard Head titled *The Life and Death of Mother Shipton,* first published in 1684.

The final couplet about the end of the world caused a great deal of panic in country districts of Britain during 1881, people leaving their houses and spending the night in the open fields or praying in churches and chapels.

Meanwhile Hindley had already confessed that these lines were a fabrication in 1873, but of course, by then they had passed into folk tradition, and ordinary country folk did not read learned antiquarian journals. Even in modern times, these spurious prophecies of Hindley, which seem to predict automobiles, steamships, submarines, the telegraph, radio, aircraft, etc., are still often quoted as genuine!

Richard Head's chapbook of 1684 contained undoubtedly imaginary accounts of the birth of Ursula Shipton from a union between her mother Agatha and the Devil in Yorkshire, England.

The prophecies quoted by Head appear to be an embellished version of an earlier pamphlet of 1641 titled *The Prophesie of Mother Shipton, In the Raigne of King Henry the Eighth. Fortelling the death of Cardinall Wolsey, the Lord Percy and others, as also what should happen in insuing times.*

Four years later, the famous astrologer, William **Lilly** published *A Collection of Ancient and Moderne Prophesies* which included what he called "Shipton's Prophecy, after the most exact Copy." This gave twenty prophecies attributed to Mother Shipton, most of which were said to have been fulfilled.

There is no validation that these prophecies were actually made or that Mother Shipton was a real person, but she rapidly became a folk heroine and even the subject of stage comedies. In *The Life of Mother Shipton: A New Comedy* (1660), the heroine and prophetess is named Agatha Shipton, daughter of Solomon Shipton. In a later work titled *Mother Shipton and Nixon's Prophecies* (1797), she is stated to have been born in July 1488 and baptized Ursula Sonthiel. This account added: "Her stature was larger than common, her body crooked, her face frightful; but her understanding extraordinary."

Interestingly enough, early chapbook portraits of Mother Shipton represent her as an ugly woman with the characteristic hooked nose, chin and humped back associated with Mr. Punch in the traditional Punch and Judy puppet show of itinerant showmen. Mr. Punch is believed to have been introduced in Naples, Italy around 1600, but the earliest likeness in Britain seems to be in a book by the puppet showman Robert Powell in 1715.

It is curious that Mr. Punch appears as a male version of Ursula Shipton's portrait in a chapbook of 1663, since the earliest claimed likeness in 1641 was not particularly ugly. Unlike Nostradamus, who was a real person and left posterity genuine prophecies (although veiled in obscure language), Mother Shipton is probably wholly legendary, and many prophecies attributed to her are spurious inventions.

For details of Charles Hindley's confession of having invented Shipton prophecies, see *Notes & Queries*

(4th series, vol. XI, page 355). For information on Hindley himself, see the Foreword by Leslie Shepard to the reprint of Hindley's *Curiosities of Street Literature* (1871) by The Broadsheet King, London, 1966. For a critical discussion of the literature of Mother Shipton, see *Mother Shipton Investigated* by William H. Harrison (published by the author, London, 1881). (See also **Nostradamus)**

Shirley, Ralph (1865-1946)

Leading British pioneer in the publication of occult and mystical literature. The Hon. Ralph Shirley was born at Oxford, England, December 30, 1865, of aristocratic stock, brother of the eleventh Earl Ferrers and a direct descendant of Robert Devereux, Earl of Essex. He was educated at Winchester, and New College, Oxford University.

From 1892-1925 he was director of William Rider & Son, the foremost British publishers of literature dealing with occultism, mysticism, New Thought, astrology, psychical research and related subjects. Rider's authors included Éliphas **Lévi,** Arthur Edward **Waite,** Hereward **Carrington,** Franz **Hartmann** and many others whose names have become legendary in the field.

In 1905, Shirley founded the *Occult Review,* which he edited for twenty-one years. It included contributions from the leading occultists of the time and set a high standard of both popular and scholarly occultism. Shirley also became vice-president of the **International Institute for Psychic Investigation,** for whom he edited Ernesto **Bozzano's** important study *Discarnate Influence in Human Life* (1938).

It was in the pages of the *Occult Review* that Shirley published the important first-hand experiences of Oliver Fox (pseudonym of Hugh G. **Callaway)** on **Astral Projection (Out-of-the-Body** traveling) from April to May 1920. Shirley also published other pioneer writings on the subject, including his own book *The Mystery of the Human Double; the Case for Astral Projection* (1938; reprinted University Books, 1965).

Shirley had a special interest in Astrology and had edited *The Horoscope* (under the pseudonym 'Rollo Ireton'). From 1943-44 he was chairman of the journal *Light,* but suffered from failing health and was obliged to retire.

He died December 29, 1946. His own books include: *The New God, and other essays* (1911), *A Short Life of Abraham Lincoln* (1919), *Occultists and Mystics of All Ages* (1920; 1972), *The Problem of Rebirth* (1936). He also published a pamphlet *The Angel Warriors at Mons* (1915) reviewing the legends that accumulated around Arthur **Machen's** famous short story *The Bowmen.* (See also **Occult Review)**

Shivapuri Baba (Sri Govinananda Bharati) (1826-1963)

Remarkable long-lived Indian mystic, who made a great impression on his biographer J. G. **Bennett,** who met him in 1961 when the sage was already 135 years old. Bennett stated: "He was a true saint who produced an immediate and uplifting effect on everyone who entered his presence." Shivapuri Baba had a profound influence on many individuals during his long life, including Hindus, Buddhists, Moslems, and Christians.

When he was born, Britain was under the reign of George IV, and the future Queen Victoria was only a child of seven. Later in life, Shivapuri Baba visited England and made no less than eighteen visits to Queen Victoria, possibly the first Indian holy man invited to meet the Queen.

Shivapuri Baba was born in a Brahmin family in Kerala. His grandfather, a famous astrologer, announced that the boy would become a great sannyasin (renunciate or wandering monk). The grandfather became his guru until about 1840, when the grandfather became a hermit and retired from the life of a householder.

The boy himself decided to leave a worldly life in 1844, at the age of eighteen. After making a will leaving his rights of succession in his father's property to his sister, he joined his grandfather in the forest of the upper Deccan, near the banks of the river Narbada. The grandfather insisted that after his own death, the boy should meditate until he obtained God-realization, then make a pilgrimage on foot not only through India, but also round the world, and had set aside money for this purpose.

After the death of his grandfather, the young man received initiation as a sannyasin and took the name of Govindananda Bharati. He then retreated to the Narbada forest and spent twenty-five years in absolute seclusion. During this period he was even completely unaware of the Indian Mutiny of 1856. At the age of fifty, he achieved the beatific vision and became aware of the divine as Absolute, beyond name and form, the highest and most difficult stage of God-realization. He then undertook his great pilgrimages.

He visited all the holy places of India, meeting Sri **Ramakrishna** in Calcutta and Sri **Aurobindo** Ghose (then only a young man). The Shivapuri Baba must therefore be considered one of the most influential of Hindu mystics. He went on to travel through Afghanistan and Persia, then made a pilgrimage to Mecca. After this experience of the Moslem shrine, he next traveled to Jerusalem, the holy city of Judaism and Christianity. He went on to Turkey, through the Balkans into Greece and then through Italy to Rome, so that he might better understand the Christian religion.

After visiting most European countries, he was invited to England by Queen Victoria's Indian Secretariat, and had eighteen private visits to Queen Victoria. There is no public record of what the two discussed, but clearly he must have brought a great awareness of the spiritual life of India.

In 1901, after the death of the Queen, Govindananda crossed the Atlantic and visited the U.S., meeting President Theodore Roosevelt. He spent two or three years in the U.S. before walking on to Mexico, where he met Porfirio Diaz, then on through the Andes to Colombia and Peru. After a period in South America, he embarked on a ship for the Pacific Islands, moving through New Zealand and Australia and visiting Japan in 1913. He then followed an ancient pilgrim route into Nepal, then back to India, visiting Benares. He must have traveled more than 25,000 miles, eighty percent on foot.

He now returned to his own home in Kerala as a wandering sannyasin after seventy years. It must have been like Rip Van Winkle's return to his village. Govinananda found no trace of his sister, who had also become a renunciate. He concluded remaining family affairs, then retired to the forests of Nepal. Although he was by now famous as a holy man, equally at ease with the religions of Buddhism, Christianity, and Islam, he insisted on remaining isolated, living in a small wooden hut and seeing only a few genuine seekers. His inner peace and realization were communicated to all who had the privilege of meeting him, and one visitor recalls that even the wild beasts of the forest were on friendly terms. He saw a fully grown leopard enter the hut and sit by the Shivapuri Baba just like a household cat.

J. G. Bennett, who promoted the mission of **Subud,** met the Shivapuri Baba in Easter 1961 and found him, at the age of 135 years, alert, quick, graceful, with a phenomenal memory and an inspiring spiritual presence. One of the most remarkable features of his teaching was the ability to communicate spiritual wisdom in only a few works in the idiom of his questioners. He explained his teaching in three words to Dr. S. Radhakrishnan, famous philosopher and former president of India. Afterwards Dr. Radhakrishnan expounded for fifteen minutes on the theme of these three words.

The Shivapuri Baba spoke excellent English and had met Lord Salisbury and Lord Randolph Churchill. In 1898, the playwright George Bernard Shaw, who was contemptuous of yogis, said to him: "You Indian saints are the most useless of men; you have no respect for time." The Shivapuri Baba replied "It is you who are slaves of time. I live in Eternity."

The Shivapuri Baba died on January 28, 1963. His final message was: "Live Right Life, Worship God. That is all. Nothing more." He took a drink of water then said "Gaya" (I'm gone), laid down on his right side and passed away.

His teaching of Right Living involved duty, morality, and worship. The sole purpose of human life was to find the Ultimate Truth or God, and to this end a certain code of life was required—spiritual, moral, and intellectual order. The Shivapuri Baba's detailed teaching on these matters is recorded in J. G. Bennett's biography (in collaboration with Thakur Lal Manandhar) *Long Pilgrimage; The Life and Teaching of Sri Govinananda Bharati known as the Shivapuri Baba* (Hodder & Stoughton, London, 1965). Many details of the Shivapuri Baba's long life could not be traced, but as he impressed upon Bennett: "It is not my person that matters, but my teaching."

Showers, Mary (c. 1890)

British **materialization** medium, daughter of General C. L. Showers of the Bombay Army. As a child she conversed with invisible people, sat for the first time in the circle of her family in the spring of 1872, produced **raps, movement** without contact, obtained **Poltergeist** manifestations in daylight, **direct writing** and saw spirit forms among which "John **King"** and "Peter" rose into prominence.

In 1874, Miss Showers and her mother came from Teignmouth to London to give seances to representative Spiritualists. The test conditions in these early seances were taken charge of by the spirits. At the beginning of the seance, coils of rope or tape would be placed in the cabinet. At a signal, the curtain of the cabinet was drawn aside and the medium was discovered tightly bound.

The usual materialized spirit form was a girl, "Florence," who was eight inches taller than the medium, could vary her height and was often seen by Mrs. Ross Church (Florence **Marryat)** together with the medium. The story of the experiences of Florence Marryat was described in her book told in *There is No Death* (1892).

Florence Marryat found herself so much in *rapport* with Miss Showers that she wrote: "We could not sit next each other at an ordinary tea or supper table when we had no thought of, or desire to hold a seance, without manifestations occurring in the full light. A hand that did not belong to either of us would make itself apparent under the table-cloth between us—a hand with power to grasp ours—or our feet would be squeezed or kicked beneath the table, or fingers would suddently appear and whisk the food off our plates."

An attempt at exposure of Miss Showers was made on April 2, 1874, at the house of Sergeant **Cox,** When "Florence" appeared between the curtains of the cabinet, Sergeant Cox's daughter, Mrs. Edwards, opened the curtains wider. The spirit resisted; in the struggle the headdress fell off and revealed Miss Showers. Sergeant Cox, however, seemed satisfied that the medium was entranced and had unconsciously impersonated the spirit.

Although Sergeant Cox may have appeared satisfied that the medium was entranced, the episode cast strong doubts upon the genuineness of the phenomena of Miss Showers. Cox himself reinforced such doubts in a letter dated March 8, 1876 to the medium D. D. **Home** (printed in full in Home's *Light and Shadows of Spiritualism,* London, 1877):

"I am satisfied that a large amount of fraud has been and still is practised. Some of it is, doubtless, deliberately planned and executed. But some is, I think, done while the medium is in a state of somnambulism, and therefore unconscious. As all familiar with phenomena of somnambulism are aware, the patient acts to perfection any part suggested to his mind, but wholly without self-perception at the time, or memory afterwards. But such an explanation serves only to acquit the medium of deliberate imposture; it does not affect the fact that the apparent manifestation is not genuine.

"The great field for fraud has been offered by the production and presentation of alleged spirit-forms. All the conditions imposed are as if carefully designed to favour fraud if contemplated, and even to tempt to imposture. The curtain is guarded at either end by some friend. The light is so dim that the features cannot be distinctly seen. A white veil thrown over the body from head to foot is put on and off in a moment, and gives the necessary aspect of spirituality. A white band round head and chin at once conceals the hair, and disguises the face. A considerable interval precedes the appearance—just such as would be necessary for the preparations. A like interval succeeds the retirement of the form before the cabinet is permitted to be opened for inspection. This just enables the ordinary dress to be restored. While the preparation is going on behind the curtain the company are always vehemently exhorted to sing. This would conveniently conceal any sounds of motion in the act of preparation. The spectators are made to promise not to peep behind the curtain, and not grasp the form. They are solemnly told that if they were to seize the spirit they would kill the medium. This is an obvious contrivance to deter the onlookers from doing anything that might cause detection. It is not true. Several spirits have been grasped, and no medium has died of it; although in each case the supposed spirit was found to be the medium. That the detected medium was somewhat disturbed in health after such a public detection and exposure is not at all surprising. Every one of the five mediums who have been actually seized in the act of personating a spirit is now alive and well. There need be no fear for the consequences in putting them to the proof.

"But I have learned how the trick is done. I have seen the description of it given by a medium to another medium who desired instruction. The letter was in her own handwriting, and the whole style of it showed it to be genuine.

"She informs her friend that she comes to the *séance* prepared with a dress that is easily taken off with a little pratice. She says it may be done in two or three minutes. She wears two shifts (probably for warmth). She brings a muslin veil of thin material (she gives its name, which I forget). It is carried *in her drawers*! It can be compressed into a small space, although when spread it covers the whole person. A pocket-handkerchief pinned around the head keeps back the hair. She states that she takes off all her clothes except the two shifts, and is covered by the veil. The gown is spread carefully upon the sofa over the pillows. In this array she comes out. She makes very merry with the spiritualists whom she thus gulls, and her language about them is anything but complimentary.

"This explains the whole business. The question so often asked before was—where the robe could be carried? It could not be contained in the bosom or in a sleeve. Nobody seems to have thought of the drawers.

"But it will be asked how we can explain the fact that some persons have been permitted to go behind the curtain when the form was before it, and have asserted that they saw or felt the medium. I am sorry to say the confession to which I have referred states without reserve that these persons knew that it was a trick, and lent themselves to it. I am, of course, reluctant to adopt such a formidable conclusion, although the so-called 'confession' was a confidential communication from one medium to another medium who had asked to be instructed how the trick was done. I prefer to adopt the more charitable conclusion that they were imposed upon, and that it is easy to find how this was likely to be. The same suspicious precautions against detection were always adopted. The favoured visitor was an assured friend; one who, if detecting trickery, would shrink from proclaiming the cheat. But one was permitted to enter. A light was not allowed. There was nothing but the 'darkness visible' of the lowered gas rays struggling through the curtain. I have noted that no one of them ever was permitted to see the face of the medium. It was always 'wrapped in a shawl.' The hands felt a dress, and imagination did the rest. The revealer of the secret above referred to says that, when she took off her gown to put on the white veil, she spread it upon the sofa or chair with pillows or something under it, and this is what they felt and took for her body!

"The lesson to be learned from all this is, that no phenomena should be accepted as genuine that are not produced under strict test conditions. Investigators should be satisfied with no evidence short of the very best that the circumstances will permit. . . ."

Cox's reference to the means by which "spirit forms" were produced fraudulently in a "communication from one medium to another medium who had asked to be instructed how the trick was done" is thought by Trevor H. **Hall** (in his book *The Spiritualists*, London, 1962) to refer to Florence **Cook** and Mary Showers, who were known to each other and indeed gave a joint performance of fully materialized "spirit forms" at the house of William **Crookes.** It is particularly significant that at the final seance with the phantom "Katie **King**" on May 21, 1874, Crookes himself noted that the face of the medium Florence Cook was covered with a red shawl, ostensibly to protect her from the effects of light, and that this established the separate identity of phantom and medium, seen together.

Although some sitters at the Crookes seances with Florence Cook noted marked similarities between the medium and the phantom "Katie King," Crookes himself was at pains to establish specific differences. If the phenomena of Florence Cook was fraudulent, it is possible that her friend Mary Showers was an occasional accomplice at seances when the differences between medium and "spirit form" were apparent.

Both Trevor H. Hall and E. J. **Dingwall** are satisfied that the circumstantial evidence strongly indicates that Florence Cook's phenomena were fraudulent, and that Mary Showers could have been an accomplice. Their conclusion that such fraud was known to William Crookes and that he connived at it, using the seances as a cover for an affair with Florence Cook is much more speculative, although it is undeniable that Crookes was tremendously impressed and captivated by the beauty of the materialized phantom "Katie King."

The story of the connections between Mary Showers, Florence Cook, and the investigations of Crookes and Cox is a complex one. The best source is Trevor H. Hall's book *The Spiritualists* (1962), his subsequent *Florence Cook & William Crookes: A Footnote to an Enquiry* (booklet published by Tomorrow Publications, London, 1963) and the chapter 'Florence Cook and William Crookes' in his book *New Light on Old Ghosts* (London, 1965), together with *The Critic's Dilemma* by E. J. Dingwall (published by the author, Dewsbury, U.K., 1966).

For a rebuttal of the charge that Crookes was having an illicit love affair with Florence Cook and connived at fraud, see the article 'Crookes and Cook' by Dr. R. H. Thouless (*Journal* of the Society for Psychic Research, vol. 42, 1963). (See also Florence **Cook**; Sir William **Crookes; Materialization**)

Shrine of the Eternal Breath of Tao

Organization founded by Master Ni, Hua Ching, who had studied Taoism as a child in China. He moved to Taiwan after the Chinese Revolution, continuing his studies and becoming a teacher of Taoism and related martial and healing arts. During the 1970s, he moved to the U.S. and began to teach in Los Angeles.

This teaching is of a universal law of subtle energy response. According to Master Ni, everything in the universe is a manifestation of energy in either its grosser or more subtle states. Understanding of developing the proper response to the energies of one's environment will bring harmony to one's life. The practice of Taoist meditation, **martial arts** (kung fu and **t'ai chi ch'uan),** and medical practices (acupuncture and herbs) assist in attaining a balanced relationship to life. The universal law of response is claimed to be the basis of all spiritual practices. This law is explained by Master Ni in his book *The Subtle Universal Law and the Integral Way of Life* (Shrine of the Eternal Breath of Tao, Malibu, California, 1979).

The Shrine is located in Los Angeles, with a second center in Malibu. (See also **Tao; Taoism)**

Shroud of Turin Research Project

Founded in 1978, with a membership of professionals, logistics support personnel, and physical scientists acting as principal investigators in research work being performed on the Shroud of **Turin.**

The purpose of the Project is to determine the physics and chemistry of both the cloth and image in order to verify or refute the authenticity of the Shroud. The Project conducts nondestructive testing and research, and attempts to simulate and analyze various images and stains found on the Shroud through laboratory testings, including chemical analysis, infrared spectroscopy and thermography, optical and ultraviolet reflectance and fluorescent spectroscopy, photography, X-radiography and X-ray fluorescence.

The Project reports findings in the form of technical papers in the scientific press; it seeks to coordinate all activities in the field; reviews research proposals and distributes funding. It maintains several sections dealing with current areas of research; maintains data base and speakers bureau. Publication: *Update,* quarterly. Address: P.O. Box 7, Amston, Connecticut 06231. (See also **Turin Shroud; Sindonology)**

S.I.

Initialism for **Space Intelligence.**

Siberia

Siberia is a vast territory of northern Asia, now part of the Russian Soviet Federative Socialist Republic of the U.S.S.R. It is bounded by the Urals on the west, by Kazakhstan, China and North Korea on the south, by the Pacific on the east and the Arctic on the north.

In former times, primitive tribes of Siberia all more or less practiced the art of sorcery, and this was in the hands of the **shaman** or medicine man. The Samoyeds who were idol-worshipers believed in the existence of an order of invisible spirits which they called *tadebtsois.* These were ever circling through the atmosphere, and were a constant menace to the people, who were anxious to propitiate them.

This could only be effected through the intervention of a *tadibe* or necromancer, who, when his services were requisitioned, attired himself in magical costume of reindeer leather trimmed with red cloth, a mask of red cloth, and a breast-plate of polished metal. He then took a drum of reindeer skin (see also **Lapland**) ornamented with brass rings, and attended by an assistant, walked round in a circle invoking the presence of the spirits, shaking a large rattle all the while.

The noise grew louder, and as the spirits were supposed to draw near the sorcerer, he addressed them, beating his drum more gently, and pausing in his chant to listen to their answers. Gradually he worked himself into a condition of frenzy, beat the drum with great violence, and appeared to be possessed by the supernatural influence, writhing and foaming at the mouth. All at once he stopped, and oracularly pronounced the will of the spirits.

The *Tadibe*'s office was a hereditary one, but if a member of the tribe exhibited special qualifications, he was adopted into the priesthood, and by fasts, vigils, the use of narcotics and stimulants in the same manner as is employed by the North American Indians (see **America**), he came to believe that he was visited by the spirits. He was then adopted as a *Tadibe* with midnight ceremonial, and invested with a magic drum.

A great many of the tricks of the priesthood were merely those of ordinary conjuring, such as the rope trick, but some of the illusions which these men secured were exceedingly striking. With their hands and feet tied together, they sat on a carpet of reindeer skin, and putting out the light, summoned the assistance of the spirits. Peculiar noises heralded their approach, snakes hissed and bears growled, the lights were rekindled, and the *tadibe* seen released from his bonds.

The Samoyeds sacrificed much to the dead, and performed various ceremonies in their honor, but they believed that only the souls of the *tadibes* enjoyed immortality and hovered through the air, demanding constant sacrifice.

Further to the east, inhabiting the more northerly part of Siberia dwelt the Ostiaks, who nominally adopted the rites of the Greek Church, but magic was also common amongst them. Many Ostiaks carried about with them a kind of fetish (see **Fetichism**), which they called *Schaitan.* Whether this name, like the Arabic *Shaitan,* was merely a corruption of that of Satan, it would be difficult to say.

Larger images of this kind were part of the furniture of an Ostiak lodge, but they were attired in seven pearl embroidered garments, and suspended to the neck by a string of silver coins. In a strange sort of dualism they were placed in many of the huts cheek by jowl with the image of the Virgin Mary, and at mealtimes their lips were smeared with the blood of raw game or fish.

It is this people, the Ostiaks, with whom the word "Shaman" originated. These Shamans were merely medicine-men.

The Mongols, who inhabited the more southern parts of the great waste of Siberia, were also ancient practitioners in sorcery, and relied greatly on **divination.** In order to discover what description of weather would be prevalent for any length of time, they employed a stone endowed with magic virtues called *yadeh-tash.* This was suspended over, or laid in a basin of water with sundry ceremonies, and appeared to be the same kind of stone in use among the Turcomans as related by Ibn Mohalhal, an early Arab traveler.

The celebrated fourteenth-century conqueror Tamerlane, in his *Memoirs,* recorded that the Jets resorted to incantations to produce heavy rains which hindered his cavalry from acting against them. A *Yadachi,* or weather-conjuror, was taken prisoner, and after he had been beheaded, the storm ceased. The Mogul conqueror Babur referred to one of his early friends, Khwaja ka Mulai, as conspicuous for his skill in falconry and his knowledge of *Yadageri,* or the science of inducing rain and snow by means of enchantment.

The Russians were much distressed by heavy rains in 1552, when besieging Kazan, and universally ascribed the unfavorable weather to the arts of the Tatar queen, who was an enchantress.

Early in the eighteenth century, the Chinese Emperor Shitsung issued a proclamation against rain-conjuring, addressed to the Eight Banners of Mongolia. "If," indignantly observed the Emperor, "if I, offering prayers in sincerity, have yet cause to fear that it may please heaven to leave *my* prayer unanswered, it is truly intolerable that mere common people wishing for rain should of their own fancy set up altars of earth; and bring together a rabble of Hoshang (Buddhist Bonzes) and Taossi to conjure the spirits to gratify their wishes." (See also **Cloud Busting**)

Many primitive beliefs and practices in Siberia changed in modern times with Soviet development of the area. (See also **U.S.S.R.**; **shaman**)

Sibly, Ebenezer (died 1800)

Famous seventeenth-century astrologer. The son of a mechanic, he is believed to have been born in Bristol, England. He came to London to study surgery, and in 1792 graduated as doctor of medicine at King's College, Aberdeen, Scotland. He settled for a time at Ipswich, but soon returned to London, where his brother Manoah was a Swedenborgian preacher and had a place of worship near Ludgate Hill.

Ebenezer Sibly styled himself an "Astro-philosopher." He claimed to have cast the horoscope of the forger-poet Thomas Chatterton, and to have prognosticated a fatal end, such as "death by poison."

Sibly was sufficiently enterprising to design a small notebook for astrologers, engraved from plates but with blank spaces for recording the position of various planets and recording horoscopes.

Amongst various successful prognostications, Sibly claimed to have foretold the American War of Independence in a symbolic picture in his book *Celestial Science of Astrology* (1776). His other publications included: *A Key to Physic, and the Occult Sciences* (c. 1800), *The Medical Mirror; or a Treatise on the Impregnation of the Human Female* (c. 1800), *Uranoscopia; or the Pure Language of the Stars Unfolded by the Motion of the Seven Erratics* (c. 1780). His *Celestial Science of Astrology* was immensely popular and went into twelve editions. The *New and Complete Illustration of the Celestial Science of Astrology* was in 2 vols., published 1817. (See also **Astrology**)

Sibyl

General term for a prophetess. The original Sibyl was believed to have lived in Asia Minor in the seventh century B.C., but three centuries later various sibyls were claimed in different parts.

Sibylline prophecies in hexameters ascribed to the Sibyl were current in classical Greece and were referred to by Aristophanes and Plato. (See also **Sibylline Books**)

Sibylline Books

The manuscripts which embodied the secrets of human destiny, the work of the Sibyls or prophetesses of the ancient world.

According to the historian Tacitus (c. 55-120 A.D.), these books were first preserved in the Roman Capitol. When it was burnt down, the previous leaves of Fate were preserved, and removed to the temple of Apollo Palatinus. Their after-fate is enshrouded in mystery, but it would seem that the Cumean books existed until 339 A.D., when they were destroyed by the consul Stilikon.

Augustus sent three ambassadors—Paulus Gabinus, Marcus Otacillius, and Lucius Valerius—into Asia, Africa, and Italy, but especially to the Erythraean Sibyl, to collect whatever could be discovered of the Sibylline Oracles, to replace those which had been lost or burnt.

The books were of two kinds; namely, the books of the elder Sibyls, that is, of the earlier Greek and Roman times; and the later, which were much falsified, and disfigured with numerous interpolations. Of the latter, eight books in Greek and Latin are still said to be extant.

Those which are preserved in Rome had been collected from various places, at various times, and contained predictions of future events couched in the most mysterious of symbolic languages.

At first they were permitted only to be read by descendants of Apollo, but later by the priests, until their care was entrusted to certain officials, who only replied to inquiries at the command of the Senate, in cases of extraordinary emergency. They were two at first, and named *duumviri:* these were appointed by Tarquinius Superbus. Two hundred and thirteen years afterwards, ten more were appointed to their guardianship (*decemviri*), and Sulla increased the number to fifteen (*quindecemviri*). (See also **Sibyl**)

Siddhas

According to Hindu mythology, the 88,000 semidivine beings of great holiness dwelling between earth and sun.

Siddhis

The eight occult powers resulting from practice of yoga, according to the system of Patanjali (c. 200 B.C.). These are: *anima* (to become infinitely small at will), *mahima* (large), *laghima* (light), *garima* (heavy), *prapti* (to be able to reach anywhere), *prakamya* (gratification of any wishes), *ishatwa* (power to create), *vashitwa* (power to command).

There are many accounts of Hindu yogis possessing such powers, even in relatively modern times. However, the *siddhis* were regarded as obstacles to spiritual realization as they might distract the seeker from his true goal.

In recent years, the **Transcendental Meditation** movement of **Maharishi Mahesh Yogi** inaugurated a controversial Siddha Course for advanced students and claimed the ability to levitate had been developed. (See also **Levitation**)

Recommended reading:

Dvidedi, M. N. (ed.) *The Yoga-Sutras of Patanjali,* Theosophical Publishing House, 1890 etc.

Siderealist (Journal)

Publication for professional astrologers and students, concerned with sidereal aspects of astrology. Includes charts of public personalities in relation to star patterns. Address: Sidereal Registry and Exchange, 11 Valley Street, Endwell, New York 13760.

Siderite

An old name for the loadstone or magnet. The term has also been variously used to indicate a steel-colored stone (possibly sapphire), a blue-colored quartz, carbonate of iron, and a meteorite containing iron.

Sideromancy

A branch of **Pyromancy** (**divination** by fire), based on interpretation of the flame, smoke, and pattern of straws placed on a red hot piece of iron.

Sidgwick, Henry (1838-1900)

First president of the **Society for Psychical Research,** London, the most influential professor at Cambridge University, who filled the chair of moral philosophy, and once was described as "the most incorrigibly and exasperatingly critical and sceptical mind in England," on whose acceptance of the presidential post of the S. P. R., F. W. H. **Myers** (who pursued investigations with him from 1872) and Edmund **Gurney,** made their cooperation contingent.

Sidgwick was born May 31, 1838, at Skipton, Yorkshire, England, and was educated at Rugby, and Trinity College, Cambridge (fellow, 1859-69). In 1876, he married Eleanor Mildred Balfour.

In his first presidential address to the Society for Psychical Research, on July 17, 1882, Prof. Sidgwick used plain words: "We are all agreed that the present state of things is a scandal to the enlightened age in which we live, that the dispute as to the reality of these marvellous phenomena of which it is quite impossible to exaggerate the scientific importance, if only a tenth part of what has been alleged by generally credible witnesses could be shown to be true—I say it is a scandal that the dispute as to the reality of these phenomena should still be going on, that so many competent witnesses should have declared their belief in them, that so many others should be profoundly interested in having the question determined, and yet the educated world, as a body, should still be simply in an attitude of incredulity."

He declared that he did not expect to produce evidence of a better quality than that of **Crookes, Wallace** and Prof. **de Morgan,** but they wanted a great deal more of it. Speaking on scientific incredulity he concluded: "We have done all that we can when the critic has nothing left to allege except that the investigator is in the trick. But when he has nothing else left he will allege that . . . We must drive the objector into the position of being forced either to admit the phenomena as inexplicable, at least by him, or to accuse the investigators either of lying or cheating or of a blindness or forgetfulness incompatible with any intellectual condition except absolute idiocy."

For eighteen years Prof. Sidgwick claimed an active share in the work of the S.P.R., contributed many important studies to the *Proceedings* and helped the investigations by his personal means. He edited the Society's *Journal* in 1885.

He died without admitting the reality of **telekinesis** or **ectoplasm.** But as early as 1864 he wrote to Mr. Dakyns, a friend: "I (fancy I) have actually heard the raps . . . "and added: "However, I have no kind of evidence to come before a jury. So keep it still till I blaze forth." He never blazed forth.

He had sittings with mediums Frank **Herne** and Henry **Slade,** seances of materialization with Miss **Wood** and Miss **Fairlamb** in his own home at Cambridge under the most stringent test conditions, as testified to by Myers' notes, yet he kept the facts secret throughout his life. Mrs. Sidgwick published an account of those she attended in the S.P.R. *Proceedings* (vol. 4), and admitted that it was exceedingly difficult "but not perhaps impossible" to impute the results to imposture. In justice, however, it should be added that the most astounding and conclusive phenomena, according to Myers, occurred in the absence of both Mrs. and Prof. Sidgwick.

It is more widely known that Prof. Sidgwick was impressed by the phenomena of Eusapia **Palladino,** which he witnessed with Mrs. Sidgwick on the Ile. Roubaud in 1894, as the guest of Prof. Charles **Richet** during the latter part of Eusapia Palladino's stay there when her phenomena were less striking. He took a leading part in the sittings held at Cambridge in 1895, which resulted in her exposure. He had a number of sittings with Mrs. Leonore **Piper** in 1889-90 and retained the keenest interest in her trance phenomena.

Prof. Sidgwik contributed the following articles to SPR *Proceedings:* 'Canons of Evidence in Psychical Research' (1888-90), 'Presidential Addresses' (1882-83, 1883-84, 1888-89, 1889-90), and SPR *Journal:* 'Presidential Address' (1884-85), 'Disinterested Deception' (1893-94). His books included: *Ethics of Conformity and Subscription* (1870), *The Methods of Ethics* (1874), *Principles of Political Economy* (1883), *The Scope and Method of Economic Science* (1885), *Outlines of the History of Ethics for English Readers* (1886), *Elements of Politics* (1891), *Practical Ethics* (1898). For biography, see *Henry Sidgwick: A Memoir* by A. S. & E. M. S., 1906.

He died August 28, 1900. The first communications, purporting to come from Prof. Sidgwick after his death, were obtained through Mrs. R. **Thompson** on January 11, 1901. According to J. G. **Piddington,** who was present, the diction, manner and voice were astonishingly lifelike and he felt that he was indeed speaking with and hearing the voice of the man he had known. The written communications which followed the oral one bear out a striking resemblance to Prof. Sidgwick's handwriting. The first such script was received through Mrs. Thompson in J. G. Piddington's presence. Other messages, of varying evidential value, were received through the hand of Mrs. A. W. **Verrall.**

Sidgwick, Mrs. Henry (Eleanor Mildred Balfour) (1845-1936)

Mrs. Sidgwick (born March 11, 1845), the sister of Premier Balfour, was an equally skeptical and very able investigator of psychical phenomena.

She drew up the report of the Committee on the **Census of Hallucinations,** discussed many psychical problems with great acumen in the S.P.R. *Proceedings* and was elected president of the Society in 1908-09. After her term of office was finished she acted as honorary secretary until 1931. At the Jubilee Celebrations of the Society in 1932, she was appointed as President d'Honneur.

Lord Balfour, who read her paper on the activities of the society from the time of its inception made the important announcement: "I have Mrs. Sidgwick's assurance that she herself holds a firm belief in survival, and in the reality of communication between the living and the dead."

Mrs. Sidgwick reported on the **"book tests"** made with the medium Mrs. Osborne **Leonard.** She also published a number of articles on parapsychological topics, including: (in SPR *Proceedings*) 'Phantasms of the Dead' (1885), 'The Physical Phenomena of Spiritualism' (1886), 'Premonitions' (1888), 'On the Evidence for Clairvoyance' (1891), 'Spirit Photography, A Reply to Mr. A. R. Wallace' (1891), 'Discussion of the Trance Phenomena of Mrs. Piper' (1899), 'Presidential Address' (1908), 'An Examination of Book-Tests Obtained in Sittings with Mrs. Osborne Leonard' (1921), 'Phantasms of the Living' (1923), 'Hindrances and Complications in Telepathic Communication' (1923), 'Report on Further Experiments in Thought-Transference Carried out by Professor Gilbert Murray' (1924), 'History of the SPR' (1932-33).

She assisted E. Gurney, F. W. H. Myers and Frank Podmore in the compilation of their key work *Phantasms of the Living* (2 vols., 1886) and edited an abridged edition in 1918, reissued with additional matter by University Books, 1962. She also contributed the entry on Spiritualism in the 9th edition of the *Encyclopedia Britannica* (1875-89).

She died February 10, 1936.

Sierra, Ralph U(son) (1904-)

Chiropractic doctor who conducted research in parapsychology. Born December 6, 1904 in San Juan, Puerto Rico, he graduated at Atlantic States Chiropractic Institute of New York. He was a physical therapist at Kings County Hospital, Brooklyn, N.Y. from 1935-47, instructor in neurology at Atlantic States Chiropractic Institute from 1947-49, lecturer on healing and natural sciences, author of *Handbook of Neurology* (chiropractic text).

He investigated respiratory and diaphragmatic changes in mediums during manifestation of phenomena.

Sigil

A sign or seal which is the mark of celestial intelligences, employed as a **talisman.**

According to occultists, such signs are like the signatures of gods and other supernatural entities, and the inscribing of such sigils evokes the entity which they symbolize. (See also **Yantra**)

Signs (Paranormal)

Paranormal signs, believed to portend great events, were recorded in history in times of great suffering and persecution. When priests were ejected from their churches, places of worship closed or razed, when religious fervor was barred from its usual expression, it appears as if the very air became charged with **psychic force.** The ecstatic state became epidemic, prophecies were uttered and unusual physical phenomena produced.

The ancient historians Josephus and Tacitus wrote of fearful sights and great signs from heaven before the judgment on Jerusalem. Aerial armies were seen, supernatural voices heard, gates were shutting and opening by themselves. When, three centuries later, Julian the Apostate attempted to rebuild Jerusalem, fiery balls burst forth upon the workmen and took strange shapes. Some resembled crosses and stars, filling the men with terror. This was recorded not only by Julian's own historian but by Jewish and heathen writers as well.

Of the signs and wonders during the persecution of the Huguenots in France, many fairly modern accounts testify.

From the dawn of printing onwards, unnatural events or prodigies of nature became the subject of broadside balladsheets and chapbook pamphlets, the street literature of poor people. Monstrous births and other signs and wonders were made the occasion for moralizing about the sins of the day and predicted divine judgment.

Even in modern times, visions of the Virgin Mary are linked with predicted signs that will demonstrate divine wrath at a sinful world (see **Fatima; Garabandhal**).

Recommended reading:

Eniatos. *Mirabilis Annus; or, The Year of Prodigies & Wonders; Being a Collection of Several Signs That Have Been Seen in the Heavens, in the Earth, and in the Waters, Together with Many Remarkable Accidents and Judgments . . . Within the Space of One Year Last Past,* London, 1661

Grey, E. Howard. *Visions, Previsions and Miracles in Modern Times,* L. N. Fowler, London, 1915

Rollins, Hyder E. (ed.). *The Pack of Autolycus or Strange and Terrible News of Ghosts, Apparitions, Monstrous Births, Showers of Wheat, Judgments of God, and other Prodigious and Fearful Happenings as told in Broadside Ballads of the Years 1624-1693,* Harvard University Press, 1927

Thompson, C. J. S. *The Mystery and Lore of Monsters,* Williams & Norgate, London, 1930; University Books, 1968

Silbert, Frau Maria (died 1936)

Powerful Austrian physical medium of Waltendorf, near Graz, mainly known for **telekinesis, stigmata, apport** and **trance** phenomena. As a child she could predict future events. The physical phenomena developed at the expense of her clairvoyant powers.

Her apports were preceded by remarkable lights resembling lightning strokes. A deceased doctor, calling himself Dr. "Franciscus Nell," was her chief control. One of his curious demonstrations was engraving cigarette cases with his name when they were held under the table. However, such a feat is more reminiscent of conjuring than paranormal phenomena.

Professor Dr. Paul Sünner recorded in *Psychic Science,* (January 1931) some sittings in which, while the medium's hands were visible above the table, the engraving feat was demonstrated five times in succession, additions being scratched on the same cigarette case on his request.

The standing of Frau Silbert on the Continent was high. But except her three visits to the **British College of Psychic Science** in London, she did not have the good fortune to sit with sympathetic British investigators.

Dr. W. F. **Prince,** of the Boston Society for Psychical Research, published a negative report after two sittings in Graz in 1927. Theodore **Besterman,** in an accout of a personal investigation in November 1928 (*Proceedings* of the Society for Psychical Research, vol. 38), admitted some interesting phenomena which he could not explain but nevertheless concluded fraud. But this report was scathingly criticized and denounced by well-known investigators all over the Continent and in England.

During 1925, the British psychical researcher Harry Price was in Graz, and on November 3 he attended a sitting with Maria Silbert. Various objects, including Price's gold cigarette lighter, were placed under the table. The lighter suddenly appeared on top of the table with the word "Well" engraved on it.

Price obtained permission to look under the table to see the movement of the objects. After thirty minutes he saw the medium's right foot outside her shoe with the toes visible where the end of a stocking had been cut off. Price was satisfied that the medium used her toes to handle objects. He did not accuse the medium of fraud because he was hoping to make further investigations later, and also because he learnt that five other individuals who had publicly criticized Maria Silbert had suffered inexplicable misfortunes.

Moreover Price believed that the medium actually possessed paranormal powers, especially in the **raps** which she produced.

Maria Silbert died in September 1936.

Silva, Edivaldo Oliveira (c. 1930-1974)

Brazilian Spiritualist healer specializing in psychic surgery. Born in Vitoria da Conquista, Bahia, he became a school teacher, taxidermist and entomologist.

In his later years he studied medicine and law, hoping thereby to qualify as a doctor so that his spiritual healing would be secured against prosecution for illegal medical practice. Although brought up as a Roman Catholic, he was an unconventional Christian who did not endorse the monopoly of the church authorities, and preferred to believe in Christ in his own way. He did not claim to be a Spiritist, although his healing work was ascribed to spirit controls.

He first discovered his healing abilities in 1962, when he visited a neighbor who had a fit of temporary insanity. Edivaldo went into a trance and was taken over by a spirit personality, becoming very violent. When he recovered normal consciousness, his neighbor had been cured.

Later, Edivaldo visited a Spiritist center where he again went into trance, discovering on his way home that he had performed psychic surgery while in trance. Over the next ten years, he performed psychic healing on some 65,000 individuals.

During his healing sessions, Edivaldo went into a trance-like condition while his spirit controls performed the work. He only learned the details of his healing afterwards from conversations, photographs or tape recordings. His spirit controls included "Dr. Calazans," "Pierre" (a Frenchman), "Dr. Fritz" (a German), as well as an Englishman, a Japanese, an Italian and a Brazilian.

Edivaldo believed that the psychic surgery operated on two planes—plasmic and ectoplasmic. In the former, red globules were actually separated from the plasma; in the latter, the operation was on a subtle body rather than a physical body.

As with other psychic surgeons, he would make instantaneous incisions, which were afterwards apparently paranormally healed.

Edivaldo was investigated by author Guy Lyon **Playfair,** a member of the Brazilian Institute for Psycho-Biophysical Research, who spent two years studying Brazilian healers at first hand. Two operations were performed on Playfair himself, who was also allowed to witness the making of an incision in another patient and allowed to put his own fingers into the hole before the flesh was miraculously reunited.

Edivaldo performed over 10,000 psychic operations during his lifetime. He died in 1974 after being involved in a road accident. For further information, see Playfair's book *The Flying Cow* (U.K., 1975; retitled *The Unknown Power,* Pocket Books, New York, 1975). (See also **Psychic Surgery**)

Silvester II, Pope (died 1003)

Silvester II (Gerbert), a distinguished scholar and statesman, was pope from 999 until 1003. He was one of a number of popes who from the tenth century onwards were regarded as sorcerers. It was said—and the story probably emanated from the Gnostics who had been proscribed by the Church—that Gerbert had evoked a demon who obtained for him the papacy, and who further promised him that he should die only after he had celebrated High Mass in Jerusalem.

One day, so this libelous story goes, while he was saying mass in a church in Rome, he felt suddenly ill, and remembering that he was in the Church of the Holy Cross in Jerusalem, he knew that the demon had played him a trick. Before he died, he confessed to his cardinals his compact with the devil.

However, as Gerbert had been preceptor of two monarchs, and a friend of others, it is more likely that he owed his preference to one of these.

He was one of the most learned men of his day, proficient in mathematics, astronomy, and mechanics. He introduced clocks, and some writers credit him with the invention of arithmetic as we now have it. It is not at all improbable that his scientific pursuits seemed to the ignorant to savor of magic. The technical language employed in his various studies might well have a sinister significance to the ignorant.

The brazen head which the chronicler William of Malmesbury stated as belonging to Silvester, and which answered questions in an oracular manner probably had its origin in a similar misinterpretation of scientific apparatus. It also recalls folk stories of the wonderful brazen head of Roger **Bacon.**

But however that may be, there is no lack of picturesque detail in some of the stories told of Silvester. He was said to have discovered buried treasure by the aid of sorcery, and to have visited a marvelous underground palace, whose riches and splendor vanished at a touch. His very tomb was believed to possess the powers of sorcery, and to shed tears when one of the succeeding popes was about to die.

Simon Magus (c. 67 A.D.)

Founder of the heterodox sect of Simonites; the reputed sorcerer mentioned in the New Testament (*Acts viii*) who was said to have bewitched the people of Samaria, and led them to believe that he was possessed of divine power.

He was born in Samaria or Cyprus and was among the number of Samaritans who, moved by the preaching of Philip, came to him for baptism. Later, when Peter and John laid their hands on the new converts, so that they received the Holy Ghost, Simon offered the disciples money to procure a similar power. But Peter sternly rebuked him for seeking to buy the gift of God with money, and bade him pray that his evil thought might be forgiven, whereupon the already repentant Simon said, "Pray ye to the Lord for me, that none of these things which ye have spoken come upon me."

Though we are not told in detail the sorceries with which Simon was supposed to have bewitched the people of Samaria, certain early ecclesiastical writers have left a record of his doings. They claimed that he could make himself invisible when he pleased, assume the appearance of another person, or of the lower animals, pass unharmed through fire, cause statues to become alive, make furniture move without any visible means of imparting motion, and perform many other miracles.

In explanation of his desire to possess the apostles' power of working miracles, he is said to have affirmed that his sorceries took a great deal of time and trouble to perform, owing to the necessity for a multitude of magical rites and incantations, while the miracles of the apostles were accomplished easily and successfully by the mere utterance of a few words.

The adept from whom Simon was supposed to have learnt the art of magic was Dositheus, who pretended to be the Messiah foretold by the prophets, and who was contemporary with Christ. From this person Simon was said to have acquired a great store of occult erudition, and owned his power chiefly to the hysterical conditions into which he was capable of throwing himself. Through these, he was enabled to make himself look either old or young, returning at will to childhood or old age.

It seems that he had not been initiated into Transcendental Magic, but was merely consumed by a thirst for power over humanity and the mysteries of nature. Repulsed by the apostles, he is said to have undertaken pilgrimages, like them, in which he permitted himself to be worshiped by the mob. He declared that he himself was the manifestation of the Splendor of God, and that Helena, his Greek slave, was its reflection. Thus he imitated Christianity in the reverse sense, affirmed the eternal reign of evil and revolt, and was, in fact, an antichrist.

After a while, according to popular legend, he went to Rome, where he appeared before the Emperor Nero. He is said to have been decapitated by him, but his head restored to his shoulders, and he was instituted by the tyrant as court sorcerer. Legend also states that St. Peter, alarmed at the spread of the doctrine of Simon in Rome, hurried there to combat it, that Nero was made aware of his arrival, and imagining Peter to be a rival sorcerer resolved to bring them together for his amusement.

An account ascribed to St. Clement states that on the arrival of Peter, Simon flew gracefully through a window into the outside air. The apostle made a vehement prayer, whereupon the magician, with a loud cry, crashed to the earth, and broke both his legs. Nero, greatly annoyed, immediatley imprisoned the saint, and it is related that Simon died of his fall.

He had, however, founded a distinct school headed by Merrander, which promised immortality of soul and body to its followers. As late as 1858, there existed in France and America a sect which credited the principles of this magician.

For a sympathetic (and probably realistic) view of Simon Magus as one of the early Gnostics, see *The Gnostics* by Jacques Lacarrière (1977). (See also **Gnosticism**)

Sinclair, Upton (Beall) (1878-1968)

Famous American novelist, fearless champion of many unpopular causes. He was born September 20, 1878, in Baltimore, Maryland, studied at City College of New York. He married three times: (1) Meta H. Fuller, 1900 (divorced 1911), (2) Mary Craig Kimbrough, 1913 (died 1961), (3) Mary Elizabeth Willis, 1961.

Upton Sinclair was Socialist candidate for the U.S. House of Representatives 1906, 1920; for the Senate, 1922; for governorship of the state of California, 1926, 1930. In 1934, he was narrowly defeated as Democratic candidate for the governorship of California.

He published over eighty books, some of which were translated into more than fifty languages. The most well known books included *The Jungle* (1906), *King Coal* (1917), *The Brass Check* (1919), *The Goose Step* (1923), *Oil* (1927), *Between Two Worlds* (1941), *Presidential Agent* (1944), *Presidential Mission* (1947), *O Shepherd Speak* (1947), *My Lifetime in Letters* (1960), *The Autobiography of Upton Sinclair* (1962).

In his book *Mental Radio. Does it Work, and How?* (1930), he detailed his investigations into the phenomena of **telepathy** with his wife, Mary Craig Sinclair. The book, to which Prof. William **McDougall** wrote the introduction in the English, and Prof. Einstein in the German edition, is an important record.

It appears that Mrs. Sinclair was a very good **sensitive** or psychic. She first became aware of her powers after the death of several intimate friends. They were further awakened by her contact with Jan, a Pole, who had studied **Yoga** in India and performed some of the feats of the fakirs. He was, for some time, a guest in the Sinclair home.

Upton Sinclair himself was, for some time, irritated by his wife's gift. In the waking state and in her dreams she could follow her husband and describe his doings. Finally he decided to experiment. The usual method was to make half a dozen drawings of anything that came into his mind. These were folded. Mrs. Sinclair, in a dark room, would take them one by one, place them on her solar plexus and then write or draw her impression.

The curious thing was that sometimes the second drawing was registered on her mind before she finished with the first one. When, for instance, a necktie was drawn she added puffs of smoke at the end of the tie. The next object was a burning match.

Upton Sinclair concluded: "We have something more than telepathy, for no human mind knows what drawings she has taken from that envelope. No human mind but her own even knows that she is trying an experiment. Either there is some superhuman mind or else there is something that comes from the drawings, some way of 'seeing' other than the way we know and use all the time."

Under the title *The Sinclair Experiments Demonstrating Telepathy,* Dr. W. Franklin **Prince** made the book the subject-matter of the sixteenth bulletin of the Boston Society for Psychical Research, dealing also with a great deal of unpublished material and giving an account of a series of control tests with ten different persons.

Sinclair died November 25, 1968. (See also **Telepathy**)

Sindonology

Term given to studies relating to the Holy Shroud of Turin, the most sacred relic of Christendom. Evidence for the reality of the Shroud as the sheet in which Jesus was wrapped after crucifixion has accumulated since 1898, and culminated in the first Sindonological Congress held in Turin 1939, attended by many distinguished scholars (see **Turin Shroud**).

Sinnett, A(lfred) P(ercy) (1840-1921)

British journalist and occultist, who played an important part in the affairs of the **Theosophical So-**

ciety. Born January 18, 1840, in London, his father was a journalist and his mother an authoress who had published numerous books. A. P. Sinnett became a journalist himself at the age of nineteen, working on the staff of the London *Globe.* Later he went to Hong Kong, where he became editor of the *Daily Press.* He returned to England in 1868 and became a leader-writer on the *Standard,* then traveled to India to take up a position as editor of the *Pioneer* in Allahabad in 1871.

He published some articles on Spiritualism and met Mme. **Blavatsky** and Col. **Olcott.** Sinnett and his wife Patience became members of the Theosophical Society. The publicity given to Theosophy in the *Pioneer* assisted membership, but it cost Sinnett his job. He returned to London in 1883. He became friendly with Frederic W. **Myers,** who (with Edmund **Gurney** and Henry **Sidgwick**) had founded the **Society for Psychical Research** a year earlier.

For a period, Sinnett was vice-president of the Theosophical Society, but his independent views made it difficult for him to cooperate fully with other officials, although Sinnett's book *The Occult World* had attracted many individuals to the Society.

During his association with the Society, Sinnett received a number of **Mahatma Letters,** supposedly from the mysterious Masters who had directed the formation of the Society. Sinnett's book *Esoteric Buddhism* was said to have derived from communications from the "Master K. H." on human evolution and cosmogony.

By 1887, Sinnett and his wife formed associations with the occult order the **Golden Dawn,** and in 1896 the poet W. B. **Yeats,** a prominent member of the G.D., wrote that Sinnett was in charge of the order's neophytes.

Sinnett was also friendly with the important occult and mystical writer Arthur Edward **Waite,** and with Mrs. Mary A. **Atwood,** who sent Sinnett her library of alchemical texts.

Sinnett died June 26, 1921, at the ripe age of 81.

His publications included: *Our Policy in China* (1869), *The Occult World* (1881), *Esoteric Buddhism* (1883), *Karma; a novel* (1885), *Incidents in the Life of Madame Blavatsky* (1886), *United; a novel* (2 vols., 1886), *The "Occult World Phenomena," and the Society for Psychical Research* (1886), *The Rationale of Mesmerism* (1892), *The Growth of the Soul; a sequel to "Esoteric Buddhism"* (1896). His *Early Days of Theosophy in Europe* was published posthumously in 1922. His play *Married by Degrees* was produced in London in 1911. *The Mahatma Letters to A. P. Sinnett* (edited A. T. Barker) was published 1924. A. T. Barker also edited *Letters of H. P. Blavatsky to A. P. Sinnett* (1925).

Sirens

The sea nymphs of Greek mythology whose hynotically sweet song lured mariners to their death. The island of the Sirens had a meadow strewn with the bones of victims of these deadly nymphs.

In Homer's *Odyssey,* Odysseus has to steer his vessel past the island, and takes the precaution of having his men stop their ears with wax to avoid hearing the siren song, while he himself is lashed to the vessel's mast. Jason and his band of heroes also had to sail past that island, but Orpheus sang so sweetly that he drowned the song of the sirens, although Butes, one of the Argonauts, leaped from the ship and swam ashore. But after Orpheus' song vanquished the sirens, they sprang into the sea and became rocks.

The sirens, two or three in number, were said to be offspring of Phorcys or Achelous, part women, part birds. Some believed they were unhappy souls of the dead, envious of the living, like the Harpies or Erinyes, hideous hags with bird-like talons, goddesses of the storm winds.

The modern story of the **Lorelei** has something in common with the myths of the Sirens. (See also **Lorelei; Mermaids and Mermen**)

Sirius Mystery, The

Title of a book by Robert K. G. Temple (1976), discussing the extraordinary discovery that a primitive African tribe, the Dogon of Mali in former French Sudan were apparently aware for centuries that the Dog Star Sirius was orbited by a white dwarf neighbor invisible to the naked eye and only recently discovered.

Temple claimed that this knowledge of the Dogon tribe was five thousand years old, being known also to the ancient Egyptians in pre-dynastic times prior to 3200 B.C., and that the Dogon people may have partially descended from them.

Sivananda, Swami (1887-1963)

One of the most remarkable and influential of modern Hindu gurus. He was the first essentially popular teacher of Hindu **Vendata** and **Yoga,** and his **Divine Life Society** achieved an international following. In this sense, he was the forerunner of today's mass media pop Hinduism cults, but with the difference that his own teachings were strictly traditional, although presented in a popular way.

It was his unique personality, combining profound spiritual awareness with the common touch, that secured him an international following, even although he never visited the Western countries. Venerated as a God-realized soul by thousands of devotees, he nevertheless remained accessible to all comers, giving individual spiritual instructions illuminated by a delightful sense of humor.

He laid great stress on the need for practical service to others, as distinct from renunciation, and his ashram at Rishikesh maintained a hospital, eye clinic and pharmacy, as well as a printing press for dissemination of his many books. His deep understanding of human nature secured him a following amongst all classes and types, from scholars, musicians and high Government officials to ordinary men, women and children.

Born Kuppuswami Iyer on September 8, 1877 in Pattamadai, near Tirunelveli, South India, he was a son of Vengu Iyer, a revenue official and a sincere devotee of the god Siva. Kuppuswami was educated in Ettayapuram, attending the Rajah's High School, where he was a good scholar and proficient in athletics. In 1903 he matriculated and went on to the Society for the Propagation of the Gospel College at Tiruchirappalli.

In 1905 he entered the Tanjore Medical Institute as a medical student, but was obliged to leave when the death of his father made it financially impossible to continue at the Institute. He moved back to Tiruchirappalli, where he started a medical journal *Ambrosia* in 1909. Soon he supplemented a small income from the journal by working at a pharmacy in Madras.

In 1913 he decided to take up medical work in Malaya, where he earned a reputation for combining medical work, spiritual observance and selfless service to the poor. By 1920, he was working with three European doctors and managing a hospital. He became a member of the Royal Institute of Public Health, London, member of the Royal Asiatic Society, London, and associate of the Royal Sanitary Institute, London. In addition, he published several books, including: *Household Remedies, Fruits and Health, Diseases and their Tamil Terms, Obstetric Ready Reckoner, Fourteen Lectures on Public Health.*

During his spare time, he studied traditional Yoga and Vedanta, spending much time in **meditation.** In 1923, he became increasingly preoccupied with the desire to realize spiritual truth. He gave up his job and returned to India. He became a religious mendicant, making pilgrimages to Varanasi (Benares), Poona, Nasik, Pandharpur and Hardwar, staying at ashrams.

In Rishikesh, North India, a traditional holy place, he was formally initiated as a Sannyasi or renunciate by Swami Viswananda, an elderly monk, and became Swami Sivananda Saraswati on June 1, 1924.

For some time, he lived at Swargashram by the side of the river Ganges, subjecting himself to intense spiritual disciplines and using his medical knowledge to help the sick. He also made pilgrimages to Kedarnath and Badrinath, holy places high in the Himalayan mountains. He excited great enthusiasm by his popular lectures, inspiring chanting and singing of spiritual verses. In 1933, he was invited to attend the birthday celebration of Swami Ram Tirtha in Lucknow, and subsequently traveled through India inspiring a great spiritual revival.

Returning to Rishikesh, he established an ashram in abandoned cowsheds on the banks of the Ganges in March 1934. With the help of disciples and supporters, the humble premises named *Ananda Kutir* (hut of bliss) grew into a large self-contained community with temple, hospitals, pharmacy, printing press for literature, and even a post office. As the Divine Life Society, the ashram sent its spiritual literature all over the world.

The rapid and successful establishment of the ashram was accelerated by the Swami's dynamic personality and an astonishingly simple financial routine involving the spending of all donations on the day of receipt. Hindu swamis traditionally renounce the accumulation of wealth, so all contributions were immediately applied to practical purposes—feeding the sadhus of the district, maintaining hospital and medical treatment for the poor, leper relief, building huts and developing a printing department for literature.

Traditional teachings of Yoga and Vedanta were propagated in simple language in hundreds of books, pamphlets and magazines issued by the Swami. They were often printed on poor quality paper in quaint English as well as vernacular literature, yet they powerfully influenced thousands of devotees all over the world.

The Sivananda Ashram or Divine Life Society became a kind of Shangri-La in the foothills of the Himalayas, a half unreal world, poised between past and present, between materialism and religion, popular and advanced teaching. Part of its strange power lay in its paradoxical contrasts as a world in miniature, where high Government officals and Maharajahs rubbed shoulders with wandering mendicants, saints and rogues.

Each day, the Swami would receive visitors and resident monks, giving instructions with a few succinct words, a gift or a good-humored joke. In the evening, he would preside over *Satsang* (association of the wise), a kind of religious meeting at which visitors, Indian or Western, would be encouraged to lecture, sing, dance or tell a joke.

Many individuals underwent a sudden uprush of spiritual awareness in this highly charged atmosphere. The Swami was credited with many miracles and his teaching was often manifest obliquely in the collective unconscious of the ashram itself. The key to one's present problem might come from a casual remark from a stranger or the events of the day.

One of the quaint but practical mottoes of the Swami was "D.I.N." (Do It Now!). In the same succinct manner, he condensed all religious teachings of various creeds to the simple formula: "Serve—Love—Give—Purify—Meditate—Realise. Be Good—Do Good—Be Kind—Be Compassionate. Inquire 'Who am I?'—Know the Self, and Be Free!"

Many swamis now well known in the Western world, were disciples of Swami Sivananda or influenced by his teachings. These include Swami **Vishnudevananda** (famous teacher of Hatha Yoga), Swami Venkateshananda, Swami Hridayananda (formerly a woman eye surgeon), Swami **Satchidananda** (founder of Integral Yoga Institute), Swami **Jyotir Maya Nanda,** Swami **Nadabrahmananada** (famous for his application of yoga principles to music), and Swami Sivananda **Radha** (Western founder of **Yasodhara Ashram**).

After the death of Swami Sivananda on July 14, 1963, his successor as president of the ashram was his leading disciple Swami **Chidananda,** the secretarial work continuing in the hands of Swami Krishananda.

There is a record of life at the Sivananda Ashram in the late 1950s: *The Sounds of Yoga-Vedanta; Documentary of Life in an Indian Ashram* (Folkways Records, 33 ⅓ rpm Album 8970). Another recording is: *Sounds of Sivananda Ashram,* vols. 1 & 2 (two C60 cassette tapes), issued by Ashram Records, Box 9, Kootenay Bay, B.C., Canada VOB 1XO.

For additional biographical material see: *From Man to God-Man* by N. Ananthanarayan (New Delhi, 1970).

Sivananda Yoga Vedanta Centers

Founded from 1959 onwards by Swami **Vishnudevananda,** disciple of the late Swami **Sivananda** of Rishikesh, India. Vishnudevananda became a world-famous exponent of the science of **Hatha Yoga,** traveling throughout Western countries demonstrating and lecturing on the relationshp of Yoga to ethical life and peace.

His system derives from the traditional teachings of the Hindu sage Patanjali, involving *yama* and *niyama* (moral restraints and ethical observance), yoga *asanas* (physical exercises), *pranayama* (breathing exercises), *pratyahara* (control of senses), *dharana* (concentration), *dhyana* (meditation), culminating in *samadhi* (superconsciousness). In traditional Hinduism, yoga is not simply a matter of practicing physical exercises, but an all-round ethical and spiritual development.

Swami Vishnudevananda has established yoga centers in twenty-five communities. Headquarters: 8th Avenue, Val Morin, Quebec, Canada.

Sixth Sense

The theory of the existence of a sixth sense as a convenient explanation of paranormal phenomena was first put forward in the era of **animal magnetism** by Tardy de Monravel in his *Essai sur la Théorie du Somnambolisme Magnétique* (1785). He considered the sixth sense as the source and sum of all our partial senses. His contemporaries were of a different opinion and explained **clairvoyance** and **prevision** by the "magnetic fluid."

In modern times, the sixth sense was given prominence as Prof. Charles **Richet**'s comprehensive term for the phenomena of **telepathy, clairvoyance, psychometry, premonitions, predictions, crystal gazing** and phantasmal appearances. They were, in his view, manifestations of a new unknown sense which perceives the vibrations of reality. The conception is largely an attempt to do away with the spirit hypothesis, making its invocation unnecessary.

Richet admitted, however, that the working of this sense is incomprehensible when a *choice* has to be made between vibrations of reality, for instance in the case of a **book test,** when the **sensitive** is called upon to read a certain line on a certain page in a certain book on the shelf which nobody opened.

His main argument in favor of his theory was that the hypothesis of the sixth sense as a new physiological notion contradicted nothing that we learn from physiology, whereas the spirit hypothesis does.

Besides Prof. Richet's book *Notre Sixième Sens* (1928), there is also *The Sixth Sense* by Joseph Sinel, an amateur biologist, published in 1927.

Skotograph

A term (from the Greek "dark-writing"), proposed by Miss Felicia Scatcherd for psychographs, spirit writing on a photographic plate in an unopened packet, and similar effects. Miss Scatcherd was a member of the **Society for Psychical Research,** London and was one of the helpers of W. T. **Stead** in founding **Julia's Bureau.** She was associated with the study of psychic photography. She died in 1927.

Madge Donohoe, widow of Martin H. Donohoe, British war correspondent of the *Daily Chronicle,* was known to produce a bewildering variety of skotographs—landscapes (often peopled), flowers, star contstellations, jewels, birds, dogs, hands, eyes and faces. Her gift was tested by F.W. Warrick, a chemical manufacturer and well-known British psychical researcher. (See also **Psychic Photography**)

Skylook (Bulletin)

Monthly bulletin concerned with UFO sightings, published by **MUFON** (Mutual UFO Network), 103 Oldtowne Road, Seguin, Texas 78155. After issue No. 102 (May 1976) *Skylook* has been supplemented by **MUFON UFO Journal.**

Skynet (Project)

Founded in 1965, by a team of physicists, engineers, scientists, and other individuals interested in **UFO** research

It conducts scientifically oriented research into UFOs in the Los Angeles and southern California area, and also investigates local sightings worldwide.

It engages in statistical studies and operates a tracking system to help identify UFOs, and works with other UFO networks. However, it holds no socioeconomic or philosophical opinions on the sightings. It publishes a listing of UFO sightings. Address: c/o Ann Druffel, 257 Sycamore Glen, Pasadena, California 91105.

Skywatch (Journal)

Quarterly publication of the Manchester Aerial Phenomena Investigation Team in England; includes reports on local **UFO** sightings, information from other areas, letters from readers and editorial comment. Address: 92 Hillcrest Road, Offerton, Stockport, Cheshire SK2 5SE, England.

Apparently no longer active at this address.

Slade, Henry (died 1905)

Controversial American medium, best known for his **slate-writing** phenomena. He was familiar to the American public for fifteen years when the choice fell on him to demonstrate paranormal phenomena in St. Petersburg, Russia, before the investigators of the University.

Mme. **Blavatsky** and Col. **Olcott,** who were asked to find a suitable medium, sat with him for weeks and testified to "messages inside double slates, sometimes tied and sealed together, while they either lay upon the table in full view of all, or were laid upon the heads of members of the committee, or held flat against the under surface of the table-top, or held in a committee man's hand without the medium touching it."

En route to Russia, Slade arrived in England on July 13, 1876. He gave many sittings in London and was examined by both Spiritualists and non-Spiritualists.

Besides slate-writing he produced partial **materialization** and strong **telekinesis** phenomena. The table moved, matter was apparently penetrated by matter (see **Matter passing through matter**), he was levitated, and musical instruments were played by invisible hands. For six weeks all went well, his fame spread and J. Enmore Jones, the editor of *The Spiritual Magazine,* declared that he was taking the place vacated by the great medium D. D. **Home.** *The World* wrote in a long article on August 30, 1876:

"Then came more and violent knockings at the table, a chair at the farthest corner from Dr. Slade was lifted rapidly in the air and hurled to the ground without visible agency. My coat and trousers were plucked violently, and I was pinched and patted, all with great rapidity, and in quarters which it seemed absolutely impossible Dr. Slade could reach. A hand appeared and disappeared fitfully, but with unmistakable reality, close to me; and when the slate was produced with a similar crumb of pencil, once on it when it was held under the table, and once under it when it was placed on the table, messages of various kinds were inscribed rapidly and in different handwritings. One, the longest, was of a religious character, and inculcated the usual religious lessons. Others were in reply to questions in which I pressed hard for a communication on some subject which could be only known to myself."

The article on the seance at which the reporter was alone with Slade and, presumably from the context, in daylight, concluded: "I had not, and have not, a glimmering of an idea how the effects described had been produced, and I came away inexpressibly puzzled and perplexed."

Slade was visited by men of science who were unable to explain what they saw. Lord Rayleigh stated at a meeting of the British Association for the Advancement of Science in September 1876 that he had attended a seance with Slade in the company of a professional conjurer, who admitted that he was completely puzzled.

Slade convinced Alfred Russel **Wallace** of his genuine powers and "finally" solved the doubts of skeptic Frank **Podmore** as to the truth of **Spiritualism.**

Podmore, author of the skeptical work *Modern Spiritualism* (2 vols., 1902), preserved silence in his later writings over this stage of his beliefs, but he frankly admitted that he was profoundly impressed by Slade's performance.

Early in September 1876, at the peak of his fame, Slade was entangled in a serious controversy with accusations of fraud. Professor Ray Lankester, who was outvoted as a member of the Selecting Committee of the British Association for the Advancement of Science when Prof. William F. **Barrett**'s paper on Spiritualism was admitted, intended to strike a deadly blow at this new "superstition" and when Sergeant **Cox** told him of the puzzling slate-writing demonstrations of Slade, he went to Slade with his friend Dr. Donkin determined to unmask the medium at whatever cost.

He paid the usual fee of a pound, and in the second sitting he suddenly seized the slate before the writing was supposed to have taken place. He found a message ready, published his exposure on September 16 in *The Times* and brought an action against the medium for obtaining money under false pretenses.

Over this exposure a fierce controversy ensued. Besides Prof. Lankester the skeptics were represented by Prof. **Sidgwick,** R. H. Hatton, Edmund **Gurney** and W. B. Carpenter. According to Frank Podmore, "the Spiritualists were perhaps justified in not accepting the incident as conclusive. Slade defended himself by asserting that, immediately before the slate was snatched from his hand, he heard the spirit writing, and had said so, but that his words were lost in the confusion which followed. If we grant that Slade's testimony was as good as Prof. Lankester's or Dr. Donkin's it was difficult summarily to dismiss this plea."

The case came up for trial at the Bow Street Police Court, London, on October 1, 1876. Evidence in favor of the genuineness of Slade's mediumship was given by Alfred Russel Wallace, Sergeant Cox, and Dr. George Wyld. Only four witnesses were allowed. The magistrate overruled their evidence, saying that he must base his decision on "inferences to be drawn from the known course of nature," and on the ground of the deposition of Prof. Lankester and Dr. Donkin he sentenced Slade, under the Vagrancy Act, to three months' imprisonment with hard labor.

In the course of the appeal, the conviction was quashed on technical grounds and Slade quickly left for the Continent before Prof. Lankester could obtain a fresh summons. However, Slade wrote from Prague, Czechoslovakia, offering exhaustive private tests to Prof. Lankester if he would let him come. To this he received no answer, nor did Slade come to London again until 1878, and later in 1887 under the assumed name of "Dr. Wilson."

Armed with many testimonies of Spiritualists and other people of distinction against the blot of the conviction, Slade spent interesting months on the Continent in the Hague, in Berlin, and in Denmark. In Berlin, Bellachini, the famous conjurer, testified on oath to his powers.

In St. Petersburg the seances were satisfactory, but owing to the disturbed state of Russia the investigation did not assume the character originally intended. A successful sitting was given to the Grand Duke Constantine in the presence of Aksakof and Prof. Boutlerof. According to an account there had been accidentally two bits of pencil on the slate. When he held it under the table the writing of two pencils was heard at the same time and when he drew out the slate it was found that one pencil had written from left to right, the other from right to left.

Still, it appears that things were not generally successful there. In a letter to Camille Flammarion Schiaparelli writes: "Aksakof, whose authority is very great in similar matters, told me himself that he had detected him in trickery."

In December 1877, the experiments of Prof. Zöllner, which are so well known in psychical literature, commenced in Leipzig. Zöllner hoped to establish his theory of four-dimensional space. Professors Fechner, Scheibner and Weber participated in the investigation. Writing on sealed slates was produced under the strictest test conditions, knots were tied on an endless string, there were remarkable displays of force and the apparent penetration of matter through matter was several times demonstrated.

After this brilliant success, Slade went to Paris and placed himself at the disposal of Camille **Flammarion,** "but I obtained nothing certain," stated Flammarion. He added: "In the cases that did succeed, there was possible substitution of slates. Tired of so much loss of time, I agreed with Admiral Mouchez, director of the observatory of Paris, to confide to Slade a double slate prepared by ourselves, with the precautions which were necessary in order that we should not be entrapped. The two slates were sealed in such a way with paper of the observatory that if he took them apart he could not conceal the fraud. He accepted the conditions of the experiment. I carried the slates to his apartment. They remained under the influence of the medium, in this apartment, not a quarter of an hour, not a half hour or an hour, but ten consecutive days, and when he sent them back to us there was not the least trace of writing inside."

Prof. Charles **Richet** wrote of the same period: "I saw Slade once with Gibier. Slade handed me a slate and put a small fragment of a slate-pencil on it. I held one end and Slade the other, and we put the slate under the table. In a few moments we heard a noise as of writing. There was some writing and the bit of slate pencil was worn. But I give this experiment (my only one of the kind) under all reserves: (1) It was long ago; (2) I cannot find the notes I took; (3) Slade's honesty is open to question, and (4) Experiments with slates lend themselves to trickery."

The next stage of Slade's career was his visit to Australia. His activities there were recorded in a book by James Curtis titled *Rustlings in the Golden City* (Ballard, 1894).

In 1885, he appeared before the **Seybert Commission** in Philadelphia. He was caught in glaring fraud. On one occasion, the sitters distinctly saw his foot before it had time to get back into the slippers, as the instrument of claimed telekinetic phenomena! Once a slate, resting against the leg of the table, was upset by a sitter. It was seen that it had a message on it prepared in advance.

The writing obtained was generally of two kinds. The general messages were very legible and clearly punctuated, but when the communication came in answer to questions it was clumsy, scarcely legible, abrupt and vague. It bore traces of hasty work under difficult conditions, as these impromptu messages could not be prepared in advance.

According to the Seybert Committee's report, Slade declared that Prof. Zöllner watched him closely only during the first three or four sittings, but afterwards let him do as he pleased. This was the starting point of Prof. Fullerton's trip to Germany to interview Prof. Zöllner's surviving colleagues in an attempt to discredit his favorable findings.

The exposure by the Seybert Commission was preceded by J. W. Truesdell's revelations. In *Bottom Facts of Spiritualism* (New York, 1883), he claimed to have caught Slade in cheating and narrates an amusing incident. He had discovered a slate with a prepared message in the seance room. He stealthily added another message of his own: "Henry, look out for this fellow; he is up to snuff—Alcinda." He says that he enjoyed Slade's discomfiture when, at the appropriate moment, the unrehearsed message came to light.

Another highly damaging incident was recorded on February 2, 1886, in the *Boston Herald,* namely an account of the denunciation of Slade as an impostor in Weston, West Virginia. Both Slade and his business manager were arrested but they were afterwards released without prosecution. The manger frankly stated that he himself had seen phantom hands which he could have sworn to be those of Slade had it been possible for him to hold Slade's hands in that position.

It is possible that Slade had little genuine power at this period. He fell victim to the drink habit; his moral standing was far from high, and he sank lower and lower. He died penniless and in mental decrepitude in a Michigan Sanatorium in 1905. (See also **Slate-writing;** J. C. F. **Zöllner**)

Slate-Writing

A form of so-called "direct" spirit writing (see **Direct Writing**), or "autography," which has been one of the popular phenomena of seances. The method is the same in the majority of cases.

The medium and the sitter take their seats at opposite ends of a small table, each grasping a corner of an ordinary school slate, which they thus hold firmly pressed against the underside of the table. A small fragment of slate-pencil is first inclosed between slate and table, for the use of the supposed spirit-writer. Should the seance be successful, a scratching sound, as of someone writing on a slate, is heard at the end of a few moments; three loud raps indicate the conclusion of the message, and on the withdrawal of the slate, it is found to be partly covered with writing—either a general message allegedly from the spirit world, or an answer to some question previously written down by the sitter.

Among the mediums who were most successful in obtaining spirit writing in this manner were Henry **Slade** and William **Eglinton.** The former, an American medium, came to England in 1876, and succeeded in mystifying a number of men of education and of scientific attainments. His critics attributed his success, in part at least, to his frank and engaging manner, which did much to disarm suspicious sitters.

However, before long, Professor Ray Lankester exposed his trickery, though the exposure was regarded by many as inconclusive, and "Dr." Henry Slade was prosecuted. Although sentenced to three months' hard labor, the omission of certain words in the accusation made the conviction of no effect. But Slade found that England had become too hot for him, and speedily left.

Many of the accounts of his seances in different countries are of interest, chiefly because of the discrepancy which exists between those of credulous Spiritualists and those of trained investigators. Dr. Richard **Hodgson,** however, has pointed out that even in the latter class, instances of malobservation were the rule rather than the exception, particularly where sleight of hand played a prominent part.

William Eglinton was worthy successor to Slade as a medium for slate-writing manifestations, and attained an extraordinary popularity, upwards of a hundred people testifying to his mediumistic powers in the Spiritualist journal *Light.*

Speaking of Eglinton's performances, C. C. Massey of the Psychological Society said; "Many, of whom I am one, are of the opinion that the case for these phenomena generally, and for autography, in particular, is already complete."

Eglinton's manifestations were produced in full light, and his seances were seldom without results, so it is hardly surprising that very many persons, ignorant of the lengths to which conjuring can be carried, and over-confident in their own ability to observe correctly, should have seen in slate-writing a phenomenon explicable only by a Spiritualist theory.

But there was definite proof of fraud in several cases. Muslin and a false beard, part of the make-up of a "spirit" had been found in Eglinton's portmanteau, various persons declared that they had seen his messages written on prepared slates previous to the seance, and that he had been concerned in other matters of an equally doubtful character. And although these detections also were disputed, they left in the unbiassed mind little doubt of the fraudulent nature of Eglinton's mediumship.

Other well-known exponents of slate-writing were Fred P. **Evans** of San Francisco and Mrs. Laura **Prudens** of Cincinnati.

Spiritualists themselves admitted that fraud might occasionally be practiced by genuine mediums, owing to the uncertainty of the "power," and the constant expectation of phenomena. Particularly was this so in the case of professional mediums, who felt obliged to produce *some* results, and who had to resort to trickery when other means failed them.

S. J. Davey, an associate of the **Society for Psychical Research,** London, having discovered the tricks of slate-writing, practiced them himself, and was accordingly claimed by certain Spiritualists as a medium as well as a conjurer, notwithstanding his protestations to the contrary! This was undoubtedly a powerful argument against the good faith of slate-writing. If his sitters could mistake these sleight-of-hand tricks (which Mr. Davey practiced with the express purpose of discrediting professional mediums) for genuine spirit manifestations, might they not also be misled by the legerdemain of Slade and Eglinton, and other well-known mediums?

It has been objected that even a skilled conjurer such as Professor Hoffmann (Angelo J. Lewis) professed himself mystified by slate-writing performances, but the answer is fairly obvious, that quite a clever conjurer may be baffled by the performances of a brother expert.

The methods adopted by Mr. Davey were of a simple nature, requiring little or no apparatus. In the case of a long, general message, he would prepare a slate beforehand, and substitute it for the test slate. A shorter message, or a reply to a question, he would write on the reverse side of the slate, with a scrap of pencil fastened in a thimble, and so withdraw the slate that the side written on would be uppermost. There is reason to believe that similar devices were used in other seances for their very simplicity and the absence of all apparatus rendered them particularly difficult of detection. But where the sitters were more credulous, intricate furniture and appliances were used, and the most elaborate preparations made for the seance.

In modern times, slate-writing is a largely discredited phenomenon, partly because it is so open to conjuring fraud, and partly because it has never required anything in the nature of the reverent atmosphere of a Spiritualist seance. The businesslike way in which vague messages or answers to questions are obtained does not suggest either spirit agency or the operation of paranormal faculty. Much more remarkable and evidential communications are obtained through **planchette, ouija board** or **automatic writing.** (See also **Direct Writing;** William **Eglinton;** Henry **Slade**)

Recommended reading:

Abbott, David P. *Behind the Scenes with the Mediums,* Open Court, Chicago/Kegan Paul, London, 1909

Anon. *The Revelations of a Spirit Medium,* Farrington & Co., St. Paul, Minnesota, 1891; reissued edited Harry Price & E. J. Dingwall, Kegan Paul, London, 1922

Farmer, John S. *'Twixt Two Worlds: A Narrative of the Life and Work of William Eglinton,* The Psychological Press, London, 1886

Owen, J. J. *Psychography; Marvelous Manifestations of Psychic Power Given Through the Mediumship of Fred P. Evans,* San Francisco, 1893

Slater, John (1861-1932)

American clairvoyant who, for fifty years, gave remarkable demonstrations of reading sealed letters and giving names, data and specific information of deceased people from the platform.

He traveled all over the U.S. and attracted big audiences. In 1930, he established his right to function as a medium in Detroit, Michigan. A clergyman had him arrested for making predictions, then a statutory offense, but he won the case with costs and continued his work thereafter undisturbed. He later moved to San Francisco.

For biographical information, see his article 'Memories' in *National Spiritualist,* Chicago (September 1926).

Slater, Thomas (c. 1872)

British spirit photographer, the first after the initial success of Frederick A. **Hudson** in England. He was an established optician and amateur photographer in London. After a sitting with Hudson in 1872, he experimented at his own home and, the family being mediumistic, obtained striking success.

By the side of a portrait of his sister two heads appeared on the plate. One of them was unmistakably Lord Brougham, the other, much less distinct, was recognized by Slater as Robert Dale Owen. The curious thing about this picture is that in 1856, when Slater was holding a seance with Lord Brougham and Robert Dale **Owen,** it was predicted by **raps** that the time would come when he would be a spirit photographer. Owen immediately remarked that if dead at the time he would attempt to appear.

That the Slater pictures were genuine was vouched for by Dr. Alfred R. **Wallace.** (See also **Psychic Photography; Spirit Photography; Thoughtography**)

Slavs

The Slavonic races had an extensive demonology, and in some measure their religious pantheon appears to have been in a stage between **animism** and polytheism, that is between god, and spirit-worship. Among them all **witchcraft,** fairy and folklore rested mainly on a belief in certain spirits of nature, which in some measure recalls the pneumatology of **Paracelsus** and the Comte de Gabalis.

"In the *vile,*" stated folklorist Dr. F. S. Krauss, "also known as *Samovile, Samodivi,* and *Vilivrjaci,* we have near relations to the forest and field spirits or the wood and moss folk of Middle Germany, France and Bavaria the "wild people of Hesse, Eifel, Salzburg and the Tyrol, the wood-women and woodmen of Bohemia, the Tyrolese Fanggen, Fanken, Norkel and Happy Ladies, the Roumanish Orken, Euguane, and Dialen, the Danish Ellekoner, the Swedish Skogsnufvaz, and the Russian Ljesje, while in certain respects they have affinity with the Teutonic Valkyries."

They were, however, more like divine beings, constantly watching over and controlling the destinies of men. They were prayed to or exorcised on all occasions. In short their origin was certainly Shamanistic.

Stated Charles Godfrey **Leland:** "We can still find the *vila* as set forth in old ballads, the incarnation of beauty and power, the benevolent friend of sufferers, the geniuses of heroes, the dwellers by rock and river and greenwood tree. But they are implacable in their wrath to all who deceive them, or who break a promise. Nay, they inflict terrible punishment even on those who disturb their rings, or the dances which they make by midsummer moonlight. Hence the proverb applied to any man who suddenly fell ill, 'he stepped on a fairy ring.' "

There were three varieties of witches or spirits among the southern Slavs: the *Zracne vile,* or aerial spirits, evilly disposed to human beings, and inflicting serious injuries upon them, Will-'o-the-wisps, who led people astray by nights, the *Pozemne vile,* companionable spirits who gave sage counsel to mankind, and dwelt in the earth, and the *Podovne vile,* or water sprites, kindly to man on shore, but treacherous to a degree on their own element.

Another water-spirit was the *Likho,* the Slavonic Polyphemus, a dread and terrible monster. The *Leshy* was a wood-demon, *Norka* the frightful Lord of the Lower World, and *Koschei* a kind of ogre whose specialty was the abduction of princesses.

Witchcraft

The witch was very frequently mentioned in Slavonic folktales, especially among the southern Slavs. She was called *vjestica,* (masculine *viestae*) meaning originally "the knowing" or "well-informed one," *Viedma* in Russian. In Dalmatia and elsewhere among the Southern Slavs the witch was called *Krstaca,* "the crossed" in allusion to the idea that she was of the horned race of Hell.

It enraged the witches so much to be called by this word that when they heard that any one had used it, they came to his house by night and tore him into four pieces, which they cast to the four winds of heaven, and drove away all his cattle and stock. Therefore the shrewd farmers of the country called the witch *hmana zena,* or "Common woman."

There were many forms of Slavonic witch, however, and the *vjestica* differed from the *macionica* and the latter from the *Zlokobnica,* or "evil-meeter," one whom it was unlucky to encounter in the morning, or who possessed the **evil eye.**

A Serbian authority stated: "I have often heard from old Hodzas and Kadijas that every female Wallach as soon as she is forty years old, abandons the "God be with us," and becomes a witch (*vjestica*) or at least a *Zlokobnica* or *macionica.* A real witch has the mark of a cross under her nose, a *zlokobnica* has some hairs of a beard, and a *macionica* may be known by a forehead full of dark folds with bloodspots in her face."

In South Slavonian countries on St. George's Day, the peasants adorned the horns of the cattle with garlands to protect them from witches. They attached great importance to a seventh or a twelfth child, who, they believed, were the great protectors of the world against witchcraft (see also **seventh son**).

But these were in great danger on St. John's Eve, for then the witches, having the most power, attacked them with stakes or the stumps of saplings, for which reason the peasantry carefully removed everything of the kind from the ground in the autumn season.

The *Krstnik* or wizards notoriously attracted the *vila* ladies, who in most instances were desirous of becoming their mistresses, just as the womenkind of the salamanders desired to mate with men. (See the

Curiosa of Heinrich Kornmann, 1666.) The man who gained the love of a *vila* was supposed to be extremely lucky.

The *Slavs* believed that on St. George's Day the witches climbed into the steeples of churches with the object of getting the grease from the axle of the bell, which, for some reason, they prized exceedingly. Transformation stories were fairly common too, in Slavonic folklore, which indicates that this was a form of magic employed by the witches of these countries.

The belief in vampires was an outstanding superstition in Slavonic countries, and its connections are fully discussed in the entry **Vampire** (see **Magia Posthuma**). (See also **Russia**)

Slawensik Poltergeist

A curious case of poltergeist in 1806 in the Castle of Slawensik, Upper Silesia. Councillor Hahn, in the service of the Prince of Hohenlohe, was directed to proceed to Slawensik, where he stayed in the castle with his old friend Charles Kern, attended by John, Hahn's servant.

On the third day of their residence, the disturbances commenced with a shower of lime, apparently from the ceiling. This was repeated the next day, accompanied by the sound of heavy blows. Soon afterwards, noises like a drum beating were heard, and a sound as if someone was walking around the room with slippers on and striking a stick on the door.

Soon various small articles in the room were thrown around, including knives, forks, brushes, caps, slippers, padlocks, funnels, snuffers and soap, while lights darted from corner to corner.

The showers of lime and heavy noises continued. Various witnesses were called and confirmed the phenomena.

One day, Kern saw a figure in the mirror staring at him, apparently interposed between himself and the glass. Another evening, Hahn was about to shave when the soap-box, razor, brush and soap flew at him and fell at his feet. When he tried to sleep he was awakened by the heavy noises, and once it seemed as if someone had sprinkled water on him while he lay in bed, although he could find no water.

Hahn now had to make a journey to Breslau, but when he returned he was told that rather than be alone, Kern had asked Hahn's servant John to stay in the room with him.

As Kern lay in his bed, John was talking to him when to his amazement he saw a jug of beer which stood on a table in the room some distance away slowly lift to a height of about three feet and pour the beer into a glass until it was half full. The jug was then gently replaced and the glass lifted and emptied as if by some invisible thirsty specter. John exclaimed in terrified surprise, "Lord Jesus! It swallows!" The glass was quietly replaced.

After some time, the disturbances ceased as suddenly as they had begun. Councillor Hahn wrote a detailed narrative of the events and signed it November 19, 1808.

Many years later the castle was destroyed by lightning, and among the ruins was found the coffinless skeleton of a man, his skull split open and a sword by his side. It was believed that Kern may have been a powerful sensitive.

For details of this strange case, see *The Night Side of Nature, or Ghosts and Ghost Seers* by Catherine Crowe (1848). (See also **Poltergeist**)

Sleep

A state of unconsciousness or partial consciousness in which, according to psychical conception, the human organism is being perpetually replenished with energy from an unseen world.

Hereward **Carrington** wrote in *Your Psychic Powers and How to Develop Them* (1920): "Various theories have been advanced in the past to explain sleep, but no satisfactory theory has even been fully accepted. Thus we have the so-called 'chemical theories,' which endeavour to account for sleep by assuming that certain poisonous substances are formed in the body during waking hours and are eliminated during sleep. Others have suggested that sleep is due to peculiar conditions of the circulations of blood in the brain; still others that the action of certain glands explains sleep; others that muscular relaxation accounts for it, others that the lack of external stimuli is sufficient to induce profound slumber. All these theories have been shown insufficient to explain the facts. We shall never arrive at a satisfactory theory of sleep, doubtless, until we admit the presence of a *vital force* and the existence of an individual *human spirit* which withdraws more or less completely from the body during the hours of sleep, and derives spiritual invigoration and nourishment during its sojourn in the spiritual world."

In the paranormal phenomena observed in dreams and hypnotic state, F. W. H. **Myers** found indications "that the self of sleep is a spirit freed from ordinary material limitations, and this conclusion conforms to the hypothesis that we live in two worlds; the waking personality is adapted to the needs of terrestrial life, the personality of sleep maintains the fundamental connection between the spiritual world and the organism, so as to provide the latter with energy while developing itself by the exercise of its spiritual powers."

According to the theory of Sylvan J. **Muldoon,** pioneer of **Astral Projection,** "the astral body discoincides during sleep for the purpose of recharging and the depth of sleep and the amount of recuperation depend upon the distance between the astral and physical bodies; i.e., the greater the distance of separation, the freer the inflow of cosmic energy, or prana, into it."

Besides fatigue and need for recuperation, the state of sleep may be brought about in a qualified form by psychological factors, as in **hypnotism** and **trance.** (See also **Astral Projection; Dream Body;**

Dreams; Hypnotism; Trance; Out-of-the-Body; Sleeping Preacher; Somnambulism)

Recommended reading:

Angoff, Allan (ed.) *The Psychic Force; Essays in Modern Psychical Research from the International Journal of Parapsychology,* [includes papers on 'Mesmerism and Hypnosis', 'Sleep and Dreaming,' 'Visions and Hallucinations'], Putnam, 1970

Bigelow, J. *The Mystery of Sleep,* Unwin, London/Harper, New York, 1903

Braid, James. *Neurypnology; or, The Rationale of Nervous Sleep,* London, 1843, AMS Press, 1976

Cohen, D. *Sleep & Dreaming: Origins, Nature & Functions,* Pergamon Press, 1981

Dement, William C. *Some Must Watch While Some Must Sleep; Exploring the World of Sleep,* San Francisco Book Co. (paperback), 1976; Norton (paperback), 1978

Crookall, Robert. *During Sleep; The Possibility of "Co-operation" Between the Living and the Dead,* University Books, 1974

Green, Celia E. *Lucid Dreams,* Hamish Hamilton, London, 1968

Jones, Richard M. *The New Psychology of Dreaming,* Grune & Stratton, New York, 1970

Jyotir Maya Nanda, Swami. *Waking, Dream & Sleep Sleep,* Yoga Research Foundation (paperback), Florida, 1974

Muldoon, Sylvan & Hereward Carrington. *The Projection of the Astral Body,* Rider & Co., London, 1929 etc.

Ullman, Montague & Stanley Krippner. *Dream Studies and Telepathy; An Experimental Approach,* Parapsychology Foundation, New York, 1970

Sleeping Preacher, The

Rachel Baker, known as "The Sleeping Preacher," was born at Pelham, Massachusetts, in 1794. When she was nine years old, her parents removed to Marcellus, New York. As a child she had a religious training, her parents being devout people, and she early manifested a strong conviction of sinfulness.

In 1811, she showed symptoms of **somnambulism,** in which she seemed stricken with horror and despondency. But gradually her mind became calmer, and she delivered discourses of singular clarity, marked by a devout and solemn tone. These fits of somnambulism, or trance-speaking, seized her regularly every day, and soon became habitual.

She began and concluded her devotional exercises with prayer, between which came the discourse. Then a state of apparent physical distress supervened, and sobs and groans shook her frame. At length the paroxysm passed, and she subsided into a natural sleep. Change of scene did not affect these exercises, but the administration of opium would interrupt them.

Her trance discourses were afterwards published: *Devotional Somnium; or a Collection of Prayers and Exhortations Uttered by Rachel Baker . . . During her Abstracted and Unconscious State,* New York, 1815; *Remarkable Sermons of Rachel Baker and Pious Ejaculations Delivered During Sleep Taken Down in Shorthand,* London, 1815.

Such trance sermons later became a characteristic phenomenon of the Spiritualist movement. Among famous later trance speakers were Nettie Colburn (**Maynard**), who gave an inspiring trance address to President Abraham **Lincoln,** and Mrs. L. A. Meurig **Morris** in Britain.

Trance addresses of an inspirational or a spiritually guiding nature have been revived under the modern New Age banner as "**Channeling.**"

Sloan, John C. (1870-1951)

British physical medium of Glasgow, Scotland, a packer in a warehouse, later small shopkeeper who accepted no remuneration for his seances and used no **cabinet.**

He was controlled by "White Feather," an American Indian, a genial personality who preferred to be called "Whitey." He spoke both through the medium's vocal organs and direct through a **trumpet.**

To have the medium at the disposal of the **British College of Psychic Science,** Hewat **McKenzie** found employment for Sloan in a London garage and made him accessible to various experimenters. After his return to Glasgow, Sloan cooperated in experiments with J. Arthur **Findlay.**

In 1924, Findlay published a small book on his findings. *An Investigation of Psychic Phenomena,* with a preface by Sir William Barrett. This was followed by a larger volume: *On the Edge of the Etheric* (1931), in which Findlay graded his evidential cases A1 and A2, according to the quality of the evidence.

Examining three of the 180 A1 communications he stated: "An eminent mathematician on calculating the chances of correctly guessing all the facts recorded, answers that to have reached such accuracy, represented the equivalent of 1 to 5,000,000,000,000 in other words the odds were 5,000,000,000,000 to 1 against chance being the explanation."

Slomann, Aage (1891-1970)

Danish chemical engineer who was specially concerned with parapsychology. Born October 25, 1891 at Copenhagen, he graduated as a chemical engineer in 1914 at Technical University of Denmark. In 1925 he married Esther Hebo.

He worked as a chemical engineer in Denmark from 1914-18, in Bordeaux, France from 1919-20, in New York from 1920-31, was factory superintendent at Colgate-Palmolive Co., Copenhagen from 1932-56, member of the company board of directors from 1947-56.

He was a member of the executive committee of the Danish Society for Psychical Research from 1950 onwards, honorary librarian and research officer from 1956 onwards, president from 1961 onwards; member of Society for Psychical Research, Swedish Society for Parapsychological Research, charter associate of the Parapsychological Association.

Mr. Slomann was particularly interested in qualitative research and philosophical aspects of parapsychology, lectured in Denmark, Sweden, Norway and Finland and broadcast over Danish radio.

In 1959, he completed a two-year survey of paranormal phenomena in Denmark. He published many articles on parapsychology in the *Journal* of the American Society for Psychical Research and the *Journal* of the Society for Psychical Research, London, and in *Psykisk Forum* and *Psykisk Information*. He was also author of two books on Japanese games.

"Smagorad"

A mysterious book of magic power in the possession of Arnaud Guillaume in 1393, during the reign of Charles VI of France (see **France**).

Smaragdine Table

Believed to be the earliest statement of the principles of spiritual alchemy, ascribed to Hermes Trismegistus. It was said to have been inscribed on emerald (smaragdine) in Phoenician letters. (See the **Emerald Table of Hermes**)

Smead, Mrs. (c. 1902)

Pseudonym of Mrs. Willis M. Cleaveland, wife of an American preacher, to whom Prof. J. H. **Hyslop**'s attention was invited in December 1901.

Mrs. Smead had occasionally practiced **planchette** writing from her childhood and began systematic experiments in 1895. Records were kept of the communications received and put at the disposal of Prof. Hyslop. He was impressed with both Mrs. and Mrs. Smead as honest, conscientious people. The communicators claimed to be the deceased children of the couple and a deceased brother of Mr. Smead's. Their identity was very plausible.

The curious feature of Mrs. Smead's mediumship began to develop when in August 1895, several references were made to the planet Mars and Jupiter. A short time before, an article by Prof. Lowell was published in the *Atlantic Monthly* on the canals of the planet Mars. It may have had something to do with the new variety of phenomena in which Jupiter played an additional but minor part.

A crude map of Jupiter's surface was given and the planet was said to be the "babies' heaven." At the next sitting, the map of Mars was drawn, the different zones were named in Martian and several communications were given about the inhabitants and the canals.

There followed then an incubation period of five years during which no Martian revelations were granted. In September 1900, the communications returned in a developed state. Men, boats, houses, flowers were drawn, named in Martian and written in hieroglyphic characters. Some of the sketches, such as one of a self-winding double clock, were very ingenious; others, like a Martian airship, were peculiar but unconvincing. A curious coincidence with Mlle. Hélène **Smith**'s Martian drawings appeared in the sketch of an observatory with a tunnel in it.

In general, according to Prof. Theodore **Flournoy**'s review in *Spiritism and Psychology,* "the Martian revelations of Mrs. Smead present the same character of puerility and naive imagination as those of Mlle. Smith." He could only think that the psychological explanation was at basis the same. Prof. Flournoy's book was actually in the house, but it was carefully kept from the medium.

The number of Martian scripts went on increasing when a new **personality,** calling himself "Harrison Clark," abruptly came on the scene and shut out all other communicators. He showed great facility in inverted and mirror writing and gave his autobiography which, however, proved to be spurious. When he was confronted by Prof. Hyslop with the findings of his investigation, he began "a battle of intellectual sparring and defiance which perhaps has hardly its equal in the annals of secondary personality."

For a considerable period, Prof. Hyslop attributed all the communications to a secondary personality, although the communicators gave more plausibility to the spirit explanation than in the case of Mlle. Hélène Smith. In this view Hyslop was confirmed by opinions of the controls of the medium Mrs. Leonore **Piper.** They sent a message to Prof. Hyslop that he should be wary. "The so-called light as seen by us is not a light given from out world at all, but the conditions are hypocritic and fanciful."

Later, however, the mediumship improved, scraps and bits of paranormal information came through, and although at first Prof. Hyslop only classified the case as an intermediate one between Hélène Smith and Mrs. Piper, he later surrendered his hesitations and admitted the existence of genuinely paranormal phenomena beyond question. (See also James Hervey **Hyslop;** Hélène **Smith**)

Smells (Psychic)

Smells, both pleasant and unpleasant have been apparently of psychic origin. **Materializations** in sittings with the medium Franek **Kluski** were associated with strong animal odors.

Psychic perfumes were reported at seances of Carlos **Mirabelli** and Daniel Dunglas **Home.** (See also **Odor of Sanctity; Perfumes**)

Smith, Alson Jesse (1908-1965)

Writer and lecturer on religion and parapsychology. Born August 12, 1908 at Danbury, Connecticut, he studied at Dickinson College, Carlisle, Penn. (B.A. 1930), Garrett Biblical Institute, Evanston, Illinois (B.D. 1933), graduate work at Yale University 1936-37. In 1932 he married Florence E. McLeod.

He was a social worker at Marcy Center Settlement, Chicago in 1933, minister of Methodist Church, Montana from 1933-34, minister of Methodist Church at New York East Conference from 1935-54, serving churches in Waterbury, Meriden and Stamford, Connecticut, Bayport, Brooklyn, New York, author and lecturer from 1954 onwards. He edited *Social Questions Bulletin*, Methodist Federation for Social Action from 1945-49, and received a citation for writing from Dickinson College in 1948.

He published many articles dealing with parapsychology and psychic research. His books include: *Faith to Live by* (1948), *Religion and the New Psychology* (1950), *Psychic Source Book* (1950), *Immortality: The Scientific Evidence* (1954), *Chicago's Left Bank* (1955), *Syndicate City* (1956), *Live All Your Life* (1957), *View of the Spree* (1962), *Primer for the Perplexed* (1962), *Men Against the Mountains* (1965).

He died May 17, 1965.

Smith, Barbara Gosline (Mrs. Raymond R. Smith) (1909-)

Newspaper columnist who studied parapsychological subjects. Born November 4, 1909 in Dallas, Texas, she studied at University of California at Los Angeles (B.A. 1929), University of Southern California (M.A. 1933). In 1934 she married Raymond R. Smith.

She was an elementary school teacher from 1930-35, high school teacher from 1935-45 at Los Angeles Public Schools, instructor at University of Southern California, Scripps College (Claremount, California) from 1945-50, freelance writer, from 1950-60, author of column 'Here and There' (*Athens Daily News,* Greece), 1960. She is a member of Bema Forensic Society. With Dr. Karlis **Osis** she investigated possible relationships between religious backgrounds and ESP amongst elementary school children.

Smith, Hélène (1861-1929)

Pseudonym of Catherine Elise Muller of Geneva, the medium whose case caused much dissension among continental psychologists for many years and was considered as the **Dreyfus** case of science by some.

Had Professor Theodore **Flournoy** not written his brilliant work, *Des Indes à la Planète Mars* (From India to the Planet Mars, 1900), in which he psychoanalysed and disproved most of the paranormal claims of Hélène Smith, she might have been acclaimed as the greatest medium of her time, the first human being to whom the glory was due of having established intelligent communication with Mars and of having revealed the language and writing of the red planet. It must be remembered that this was long before the modern triumphs of interplanetary research and space probes which have revealed the actual nature of the surface of Mars and Venus.

The father of Mlle. Smith, a merchant, was an Hungarian who possessed a remarkable facility for languages; her mother had sporadic visions but showed no mediumistic powers. As a young girl, Hélène Smith was always fond of indulging in daydreams. She used to see highly colored landscapes, a lion of stone with a mutilated head, fanciful objects on pedestals, etc. These visions made her discontented.

She asked her parents on one occasion whether she was really their child or a changeling. When fourteen or fifteen years old, she had seen a bright light thrown against the wall of her room, which then seemed to be filled with strange and unknown things.

She heard of Spiritualism for the first time in the winter of 1891-92. An acquaintance lent her the book *d'Après la Mort* by Leon Denis. It excited her curiosity and led her to a Spiritualist circle. At the second seance which she attended, her hand moved automatically. Soon the table began to move and in April 1892, a spirit communicated through typtology and said that he was Victor Hugo, the guide and protector of Mlle. Hélène Smith. His reign as a **control** lasted undisturbed for about six months. Then another control appeared, "Leopold" who, against the warning of "Victor Hugo," forced the medium into trance and after a struggle lasting for a year completely ousted his predecessor.

At this period Hélène Smith possessed every attribute of a powerful medium. She produced **telekinesis** phenomena, strange **apports,** found lost objects, predicted future events, saw spirit visitors, clairaudiently heard their names and received the explanation of visions which unfolded before her eyes by **raps.**

Prof. Theodore Flournory was admitted to her circle in the winter of 1894-95. The seances which he attended for five years alternated with a series given to Prof. August Lemaitre and to Prof. Cuendet, vice-president of the Geneva Society for Psychic Studies.

"I found the medium in question," wrote Prof. Flournoy in his book *From India to the Planet Mars* (1900), "to be a beautiful woman about thirty years of age, tall, vigorous, of a fresh, healthy complexion, with hair and eyes almost black, of an open and intelligent countenance, which at once invoked sympathy. She evinced nothing of the emaciated or tragic aspect which one habitually ascribes to the sybils of tradition, but wore an air of health, of physical and mental vigour, very pleasant to behold, and which, by the way, is not often encountered in those who are good mediums."

In describing her triple mediumship (visual, auditive and typtological) he admitted: "Speaking for myself alone . . . I was greatly surprised to recognize in scenes which passed before my eyes events which had transpired in my own family prior to my birth. Whence could the medium, whom I had never met before, have derived the knowledge of events belonging to a remote past, of a private nature, and utterly unknown to any living person?"

The professor made good friends with the spirit control "Leopold." The secret of his identity which for a long time he refused to reveal was already known. He claimed to have been Guiseppe Balsamo, alias Cagliostro. With the exception of Prof. Flournoy, everybody believed in his existence as a spirit. Even he admitted that "it would be impossible to imagine a being more independent and more different from Mlle. Smith herself, having a more personal character, and individuality more marked, or a more certain actual existence."

When "Leopold" wrote with the hand of Mlle. Smith she held the pen in a different way, her handwriting differed from her usual calligraphy and showed the style of the last century. The voice of "Leopold" was a deep bass. He had a strong, easily recognizable Italian accent.

But Flournory was firm in his conviction that "there is no reason to suspect the real presence of Joseph Balsamo behind the automatisms of Mlle. Smith." He traced the psychogenesis of "Leopold" to a great fright which Hélène had when ten years old. She was attacked in the street by a big dog. She was terrified but the terror was dispelled by the sudden appearance, as if by a miracle, of a personage clothed in a long brown robe with flowing sleeves and with a white cross on the breast who chased the dog away and disappeared before she had time to thank him.

"Leopold" claimed that this was his first appearance. Whenever some unpleasant sight or a dangerous encounter lay in the way of Hélène, the phantom always rose at a distance of about ten yards, walked or glided in silence at the same rate as she advanced towards him, attracting and fascinating her gaze in such a manner as to prevent her turning her eyes away either to the right or left, until she passed the place of danger.

Prof. Flournoy found some curious analogies between what is known to us of Cagliostro and certain characteristics of "Leopold," but he believed that they accorded well with the subliminal medley. "Leopold" did not know Italian and turned a deaf ear if anyone addressed him in that language. His handwriting showed striking dissimilarities to that known of the real Cagliostro. His answers to questions regarding his terrestrial existence were evasive or vague. He did not furnish a single name, date or precise fact. He was, on the other hand, as archaic in his therapeutics as in his orthography and treated all maladies in an old-fashioned way. He claimed that his sentiments for Mlle. Smith were only the continuation of those of Cagliostro for Marie Antionette.

Marie Antoinette was the first great romance of Mlle. Smith's mediumship. Flournoy called it the "Royal Cycle." It was roughly outlined at seances in the house of Prof. Cuendet in December 1893. The announcement that Hélène was the reincarnation of Marie Antoinette was made by the table on January 30, 1894. In the interval she had for some time believed herself to be the reincarnation of Lorenze Feliciani. When, however, she was told that Lorenze Feliciani only existed in the fantasy of novelist Dumas, she quickly dropped this role.

There was less difference between the autograph of Cagliostro and "Leopold" than between the handwriting of the real Marie Antoinette and the somnambulic one. The role of the queen was acted in a very lifelike manner. Probably the innate tastes of Mlle. Smith for everything that was noble, distinguished and elevated made the task easier. In the surroundings of the queen, the king was conspicuous by his absence. Three personages figured most often. "Cagliostro" ("ce cher sorcier"), "Louis Philippe d'Orleans" and the "Marquis de Mirabeau." They were discovered reincarnated in two sitters: M. Eugene Demole and M. August de Morsier. For the spectators, the royal somnambulism was the most interesting on account of the brilliancy and life of the role and the length of time during which it was sustained. But for lovers of the paranormal it was the least extraordinary.

The Hindu dream in which Prof. Flournoy was cast in the role of Prince Sivrouka Nayaka began on October 16, 1894, eight weeks before his admission to the circle. The Martian romance dated from the same period and was to be attributed, in Flournoy's view, to an involuntary suggestion of Prof. Lemaitre. In the Oriental Cycle, Mlle. Smith was Simandini, the daughter of an Arab sheik in the sixth century, and was courted and married by Prince Sivrouka, lord of the fortress of Tchandraguiri built in the province of Kanara, Hindustani, in 1401. After many years of married life she was burned alive on her husband's funeral pyre.

In enacting the role of the Oriental princess, Mlle. Hélène Smith spoke Hindustani and wrote a few words in good Arabic. She did not speak it. Strangely enough, while recovering in trance the use of Hindustani, which she formerly spoke at the court of Sivrouka, she appeared to have forgotten her mother tongue. Her Hindustani was a mixture of improvised articulations and of veritable Sanskrit words well adapted to the situation. This means that it expressed personal thought and was not merely a series of senseless phrases. Besides Prof. Flournoy, Prof. Seipel, another investigator, also figured in the Oriental romance. He was an Arab slave.

Historians appeared to be singularly ignorant of Kanara, Sivrouka and Simandini. One day, however, Flournoy accidentally came across an old history of India by De Marles printed in Paris in 1828, and found in it a confirmation of the main facts. It was objected that De Marles was a very unreliable historian. The fact was, however, that only two copies of the work existed in Geneva, both covered with dust and it could only have happened by a combination of absolutely exceptional and almost unimaginable circumstances that the work found its way into Hélène's hands.

Prof. Flournoy saw himself forced to admit that the precise historical information given by "Leopold" and the language spoken by "Simandini" defied normal explanation. He said: "The Hindoo romance, in particular, remains for those who have taken part in it a psychological enigma, not yet solved in a satisfactory manner, because it reveals and implies in regard to Hélène, a knowledge relative to the costumes and languages of the Orient, the actual source of which it has up to the present time not been possible to discover."

The Martian romance was the most striking of all. In November 1894, the spirit of the entranced medium was carried to the planet Mars. She described the human, animal and floral life of the planet from night to night and supported her story by writing in

Martian characters and speaking fluently in that language.

The characters were unlike any written characters used on the earth and the language had many characteristics of genuineness. From the translation she furnished in French, Professor Flournoy concluded that the Martian language was a subconscious elaboration.

The vowels and consonant sounds were the same as in French, and the grammar, the inflections and the construction were modeled on French. As a work of art Flournoy considered the subconscious construction of this language infantile, as a feat of memory prodigious. The Martian descriptions he found similarly childish and the landscapes suggested Japanese lacquer and Nankin dishes (see **Xenoglossis** and **Planetary Travels**).

Curiously enough, when the defects were pointed out to the medium by Prof. Flournoy, her subconscious mind appeared to have been impressed and set a new task before itself. Not long afterwards, an Ultra-Martian romance developed and descriptions were given of the life of still another, more distant planet (Uranus), with grotesque inhabitants and a language totally different from the former one, and having apparently no relationship with the known languages of the earth.

The medium and the other investigators of the phenomena did not share Prof. Flournoy's view of the earthly origin of the Martian romance. In articles published in the *Annales des Sciences Psychiques* in March-April and May-June, 1897, the extraterrene origin of Martian language was acknowledged by Prof. Lemaitre. The medium's defense was also taken up in an anonymous volume (*Autour des Indes à la Planète Mars*) published under the auspices of the Societé d'Etudes Psychiques de Genève (1901). On the other hand, V. Henry, Professor of Sanskrit at the Sorbonne, completely vindicated Prof. Flournoy's conclusions in a book *La Language Martien* (1901) and showed how the Martian words, with the exception of a residue of two percent, were derivable from known terrestrial words.

Prof. Flournoy did not stop at the claim that all the controls of the medium were secondary personalities and that the source of the incarnation dreams was to be found in the strong suggestion which the reincarnationist tenets of Allan **Kardec** exercized on the minds of various automatic writers. He also disputed the paranormal character of the other manifestations.

"As to the Supernormal," he stated, "I believe I have actually found a little telekinesis and telepathy. As to lucidity and spiritistic messages, I have only encountered some brilliant reconstructions, which the hypnoid imagination, aided by latent memory, excels in fabricating in the case of mediums."

At a seance in 1899, Hélène had a vision of a village and a landscape which she could not recognize. At the same time, an old man whom she also saw possessed her hand and wrote: "Chaumontet Syndic." Later, further information was divulged. The old man was syndic of Chessenaz in 1839. At another seance these words came: "Burnier, Curé de Chessenaz." Professor Flournoy made inquiries and found out there was a little village named Chessenaz in Haute Savoie, that in 1839 the syndic of the village was Jean Chaumontet, and the curé was named Burnier, furthermore the signatures resembled the authentic signatures of these two people. Nevertheless he dismissed the case, as he found out that Hélène had relations in a neighboring village and had been to visit them.

To the physical phenomena of the mediumship he devoted little attention. He was inclined to admit that a force may radiate from the medium which may be capable of attracting or repelling objects in the neighborhood. How such a force could be employed to levitate a table, play on distant instruments and apport branches of trees, leaves of ivy bearing in legible characters the name of the control, shells filled with sand and still wet from the sea, a China vase full of water containing a rose, Chinese money, etc., he did not even attempt to explain. The physical phenomena did not last long and ceased at an early period.

In 1901, Prof. Flournoy published another extensive study on some further developments in the *Archives de Psychologie (Nouvelles Observations sur un case de Somnambulisme avec Glossolalie)*. He related that owing to the sensation which his previous work created, Hélène Smith was inundated with letters and request for Spiritualist sittings. A rich American lady provided her with a life income. Hélène resigned her position and gave many sittings to her new friends, but Prof. Flournoy and Prof. Lemaitre were not among the invited ones. In the summer of 1900 there came a complete break. Prof. Flournoy was no more accorded facilities for study. The material which he dealt with in his new book hardly covered the period of a year.

He stated that the Martian romance passed into oblivion, but the Martian personalities "Astané" and "Ramier" were retained as guides and interpreters in the exploration of the Ultra-Martian and Uranian worlds. A Lunarian phase also developed at a later period, with descriptions, language and writing. But of this Prof. Flournoy had no firsthand information. The Ultra-Martian romance was accompanied by several painted scenes. The writing was ideographic. Its curious hieroglyphs did not express letters but words. The ideograms showed no resemblance to the objects which they represented.

In this, Prof. Flournoy found another proof of infantile imagination. This essential characteristic was omitted because the medium strove to create something defying all analysis. The Uranian language and writing differed totally from the Ultra-Martian. But, stated Prof. Flournoy, the phonetic and alphabetic system was a copy of the Martian, and the Uranian language differed less from French than French from the languages of the neighboring countries. The origin of the strange notion of Lunarian inhabitants presumably sprung from reading an article in *La Paix Universelle* in which, after flattering allusions to Hélène Smith, mention was made of the claims of certain Yogis of psychic visits to the inhabitants of that side of the moon which is turned away from the earth.

The duration of the astronomic cycle was not long. It was superseded, after a complete break with the Spiritualists, by a religious cycle in which Christ, the Virgin, the apostles and the archangels played the dominant roles. In 1903, a luminous vision filled the room of Hélène Smith. "Christ" appeared and she heard the voice of "Leopold": "You will draw him." Two years later, Hélène began with crayon. This was later changed to oil. On large wooden boards, in a state of trance she executed twelve religious tableaus.

Prof. Lemaitre stated in a study that according to certain mediumistic communications which she had received, Hélène Smith was a reincarnation of "Raphael," or of "Michaelangelo"; the medium herself, however, refused to believe these absurdities.

In May 1913, at the International Congress for Psychical Research at Geneva, eight of her striking pictures were exhibited. In a statement to *Light* (October 11, 1913) she said:

"On the days when I am to paint I am always roused very early—generally between five and six in the morning—by three loud knocks at my bed. I open my eyes and see my bedroom brightly illuminated, and immediately understand that I have to stand up and work. I dress myself by the beautiful iridescent light, and wait a few moments, sitting in my armchair, until the feeling comes that I have to work. It never delays. All at once I stand up and walk to the picture. When about two steps before it I feel a strange sensation, and probably fall asleep at the same moment. I know, later on, that I must have slept because I notice that my fingers are covered with different colours, and I do not remember at all to have used them, though, when a picture is being begun, I am ordered to prepare colours on my palette every evening, and have it near my bed."

Brush was very seldom used in these pictures. She put on the first coating of paint with her three middle fingers in the same way as if pressing an electric bell button. For the second coating, she moved the same fingers very lightly from right to left and back, thus producing a very smooth surface. The outlines were made by the nails, and the sky with the palm of her hand.

This last phase of Hélène Smith's mediumship was exhaustively dealt with by Prof. W. Deonna in his book *De La Planète Mars en Terre Sainte* (1932). As the medium did not again subject herself to scientific investigation, Prof. Deonna's psychoanalytic examination was based on the voluminous correspondence which Hélène Smith left behind and on the painting themselves. The religious cycle was arrested in 1915 in its further progress by the shock which the medium received when her dearest Italian friend died. Her later years were dominated by visions and automatic communications of and from this friend.

Prof. Deonna attached no particular value to the paintings. He stated that their inspiration did not surpass the usual level of religious imagery. The tableaus did not have an elevating effect, indeed a striking mediocrity was often noticeable. But he also admitted certain qualities and said that the paintings were far above what Hélène could produce normally. He looked for an explanation to the regression of infantile memories. He offered no explanation for certain paranormal features.

It was a habit of Hélène Smith to have photographs taken of the successive stages of the pictures. To her utter despair, some of the negatives of the painting "Judas" were spoiled. Her guardian angel appeared and announced a miracle. Two days later, the portrait began to fade out. The beards, the moustache, the tears of Judas and other details gradually disappeared until the painting returned to the stage where it was last successfully photographed. Then an inscription appeared: "God's will, November 18, 1913." The photographs were taken again. The inscription vanished and Hélène Smith finished the picture as before.

She always painted from visions. The eyes appeared first. But Judas was painted into the landscape from the leg upwards. The visions were accompanied by luminous phenomena. They began with a ball of light which expanded and filled the room. This was not a subjective phenomenon. Hélène Smith exposed photographic plates which indeed registered strong luminous effects. But to Prof. Deonna, they had no scientific value as they were only supported by the good faith of the medium.

The extraordinary case of Hélène Smith well illustrates some of the problems for both Spiritualists and psychical researchers. It is clear that there were remarkable physical and mental phenomena, but that there were great difficulties in interpretation. The fact that claimed spirit entities are capable of paranormal prescience and almost miraculous feats does not in itself validate the genuineness of their personality. Spiritualists must often be on their guard against the claims and demands of entities who may prove to be fictitious, deceptive or even mischievous. (See also **Control;** Theodore **Flournoy; Personality; Xenoglossis**)

Recommended reading:

Flournoy, Theodore. *From India to the Planet Mars; A Study of a Case of Somnambulism with Glossolalia* (translation of *Des Indes à la Planête Mars*), Harper, New York & London, 1900; University Books, 1963

Maxwell, J. *Metapsychical Phenomena; Methods and Observations,* Duckworth, London, 1905 [includes valuable Appendix detailing a remarkable case of false spirit personality]

Smith, Helene Veeder Altpeter (Mrs. Charles H. Smith) (1890-)

Active worker in the field of parapsychology. Born July 31, 1890 at Redding, California, she became a school teacher, business college teacher and secretarial worker. In 1925 she married Charles H. Smith.

From 1957 onwards Mrs. Smith was secretary, treasurer and librarian for the California Society for Psychical Study, meeting in Berkeley. Her own special interests included telepathy, clairvoyance and spontaneous psi phenomena.

Smith, Susy (1911-)

Journalist and author of a number of books on psychical subjects and parapsychology. Born June 2, 1911 in Washington, D.C., she was educated at University of Texas and University of Arizona. She was a columnist for *Salt Lake Tribune* and *Desert News*, Salt Lake City, Utah, before becoming a free-lance writer. She also conducted radio programs on shopping information at Daytona Beach, Florida.

She became editor of Sherbourne Press. In addition to her many popular books on parapsychology she also lectured on the subject. She is herself psychic, as related in her book *Confessions of a Psychic* (Macmillan, 1971). Her other books include: *ESP* (1962), *World of the Strange* (1936), *The Mediumship of Mrs. Leonard* (1963), *The Enigma of Out-of-the-Body Travel* (1964), *ESP for the Millions* (1965), *A Supernatural Primer for the Millions* (1965), *Prominent American Ghosts* (1966; 1969), *Haunted Houses for the Millions* (1966), *Stories of the Supernormal* (1967), *Talking Animals* (1967), *Adventures in the Supernormal* (1968), *Out-of-Body Experiences* (1969), *Reincarnation* (1969), *More ESP for the Millions* (1969), *Prominent American Ghosts* (1969), *Ghosts Around the House* (1970; 1971), *Confessions of a Psychic* (1971), *Today's Witches* (c. 1970, 1971), *Susy Smith's Supernatural World* (1971), *Confessions of a Psychic* (1971), *How to Develop Your ESP* (1972), *ESP and You* (1972), *ESP and Hypnosis* (1973), *The Book of James* (dealing with psychologist William James, 1974), *Life is Forever; evidence for survival after death* (1974), *The Conversion of a Psychic* (1978). She edited the one-volume edition of F. W. H. Myers, *Human Personality and Its Survival of Bodily Death* (University Books, 1961). She is a member of the Society for Psychical Research, London; American Society for Psychical Research; Spiritual Frontiers Fellowship; Association for Research and Enlightenment.

Smith, W. W. (1884-1947)

Original name of Walter Whately **Carington,** British psychic researcher. He changed his name in 1933 for family reasons.

Smythies, J(ohn) R(aymond) (1922-)

University lecturer and psychiatrist who has written widely on parapsychology. Born November 30, 1922 at Naini Tal, U.P., India, he studied at Cambridge University, England (M.B.B. Chir, 1945) and University of British Columbia (D.P.M. 1952, London; M.A. 1954, M.D. 1955, Cambridge, M.Sc. 1955). In 1950 he married Vanna Maria Gatormo.

He was a surgeon lieutenant in Royal Volunteer Reserve from 1946-58; psychiatrist at Saskatchewan Hospital, Weyburn, Canada from 1952-53; Nuffield Fellow in Medicine, Cambridge University from 1955-57; scientist at Galesburg State Research Hospital, Galesburg, Illinois from 1957-58; scientist at Worcester Foundation, Shrewsburg, Massachusetts from 1958-59; senior registrar at Maudsley Hospital, London, England, from 1959-61; senior lecturer at Department of Psychological Medicine, University of Edinburgh, consultant psychiatrist at Royal Edinburgh Hospital, Scotland 1961-73; visiting professor, University of Alabama, Birmingham, 1970-73; C. B. Ireland Professor of Psychiatry, 1973 onwards.

He was editor of *International Review of Neurobiology* from 1957 onwards, fellow of Chemical Society, Royal Society of Medicine, consultant to World Health Organization, 1963-68, and Allergan Pharmaceuticals, 1970, member of Society for Psychical Research, London, American Society for Pharmacology and Experimental Therapeutics; attended International Conferences on Philosophy and Parapsychology, Unorthodox Healing, St. Paul de Vence, France, 1954 and Conference on Parapsychology and Psychedelics, New York, 1958.

In addition to his many papers on psychological and psychiatric subjects, Dr. Smythies has special interest in the theoretical basis of ESP and has published various articles on the subject in *Journal* of the Society for Psychical Research, London, and *Tomorrow*. His books include: *Analysis of Perception* (1956), *Science and the ESP* (1967), *Biological Psychiatry* (1968), (with Arthur Koestler, ed.) *Beyond Reductionism; New Perspectives in the Science of Life* (1970), *Brain Mechanism and Behavior* (1970).

Snake-Handling

Snakes have played a prominent part in pagan mythologies and religious ceremonies long before the Judeo-Christian story of the Garden of Eden.

The snake has often been regarded as a fertility symbol. In the Mayan scripture *Popul Vuh,* the plumed serpent assists the creation of life, as also with the Aztec and the Pueblo Indians. Snakes are also featured in the Haitian **Voodoo** cults.

Various American Indian tribes have dances in which live snakes are carried, whilst the Yokut shamans of central California handled rattlesnakes at public ceremonies.

There are, however, present-day Christian Pentecostal churches in southeast Appalachia where members regularly handle deadly snakes and even drink poisons, as part of their religious ceremonies. These practices arise from a quite literal application of the five "signs" in the *Bible* (St. Mark, 16, v. 17 & 18):

"And these signs shall follow them that believe:

"In my name shall they cast out devils; they shall speak with new tongues.

They shall take up serpents; and if they drink any deadly thing, it shall not hurt them; they shall lay hands on the sick, and they shall recover."

Modern **Pentecostalism** has roots in seventeenth-century southern France, after the revocation of the Edict of Nantes, when miraculous events and "speaking in tongues" (Glossolalia or **Xenoglossis**) took place amongst enthusiastic ecstatics, who became known as "the French Prophets." During the nineteenth century, the phenomenon of speaking in tongues became manifest amongst the Holiness Church people in the U.S., later associated with fire baptism.

The modern Appalachian churches stem from the 1906 Pentecostal revival of Los Angeles, when the ministry of Rev. W. J. Seymour spread the phenomenon of speaking in tongues as a sign of the Holy Spirit. However, the Appalachian churches added the additional "signs" of snake-handling and poison drinking. This dates from 1909, when George W. Hensley of Tennessee captured a rattlesnake and brought it out during a church service for snake-handling as a test of religious faith.

After Hensley, Raymond Hays and Thomas Harden founded the Dolley Pond Church of God with Signs Following, in Pine Mountain, Tennessee; it became a mother church of Southern snake-handling. This activity became clandestine in 1947, when state laws were passed to forbid the practice, following the publicity given to deaths from snake bite at church services.

However, the astonishing fact is that scores of sincere devotees of snake-handling have survived the bites of deadly snakes and also the effects of drinking such poisons as strychnine at church ceremonies. Those cases of deaths which have occurred are ascribed to lack of faith. Snake-handling adds a dramatic element to religious faith, and has much in common with the earlier practice of **Fire Ordeal** in non-Christian religions.

Present-day members of the Holiness Church of God in Jesus Name in the southeast are more concerned by the dangers of persecution through punitive laws against snake-handling than from the practice itself. They regard such laws as a breach of their freedom to exercise their religious convictions sincerely in accordance with Holy Scripture.

Estimates place the number of snake-handling church members at about 1,000, located chiefly in Ohio, Indiana, and Appalachia.

Recommended reading:

Carden, Karen W. & R. W. Pelton. *The Persecuted Prophets; the Story of the Frenzied Snake Handlers,* A. S. Barnes, N.J./Thomas Yoseloff, London, 1976

La Barre, Weston. *They Shall Take Up Serpents,* Schocken Books, 1969

Stekert, Ellen. 'The Snake Handling Sect of Harlan County, Kentucky; Its Influences on Folk Tradition' (in *Southern Folklore Quarterly,* vol. 27, Dec. 1963)

Snapping

Term used by Flo Conway and Jim Siegelman in their perceptive book of that title, to describe the contemporary epidemic of sudden personality change that has become a feature of modern religious and self-improvement cults.

The authors claim that mind-altering techniques employed by such cults affect the kind and quality of information supplied to the brain, resulting in a sudden drastic alteration of personality. Such techniques include isolation, lack of sleep, repetition of chants and monotonous music, intimate touching, persistent interrogation and indoctrination, fatigue and even physical duress. These tactics interfere with the ability of the brain to process information in a discriminating manner, and can result in disorientation, impaired awareness, irrationaliity, delusion and even violent and destructive behavior.

Amongst the groups discussed in the book are the Krishna Consciousness people, Unification Church of Rev. **Moon, est,** Divine Light Mission, **Jesus Freaks, Transcendental Meditation, Children of God,** Synanon, the **Manson** Family, **Scientology** and the **Peoples Temple** of Rev. Jim **Jones,** as well as individuals like Patty Hearst and "Son of Sam" (the murderer David Berkowitz). Many of the new cults grew up in the "consciousness explosion" of the sixties and seventies in the search for new religious and social faith, as a reaction against the materialism of the affluent society.

However, the phenomenon of "snapping" is not new. In the past, it has always been experienced as sudden conversion to established religions, characterized by the immediate removal of all doubts, the experience of claimed "ecstasies" and "transcendental experience" and complete personalilty change.

What *is* new is firstly, qualitative aspect of such conversion, and secondly, the way in which it is now produced by mass marketed methods assisted by sophisticated modern psychological techniques known as "brain-washing."

The traditional religious conversion of the past usually involved high standards of social and ethical practice and an integrity of self discovery and reform, resulting in a high quality of new awareness and inspiration. The "snapping" phase represented a resolution on a higher plane of irreconcilables that had been explored to their limits, thus the sudden resolution was nearer to the Zen buddhist *satori.*

In contrast, today's mass media cults rely more upon psychological techniques of manipulation than ethical standards, and often approach prospective converts with an implicit attitude of exploitation. Indeed, some modern religious cults have encouraged blatant lies, insincere gestures of affection and even prostitution in order to attract new recruits.

There is an ego satisfaction in gaining more and more new members, and often psychological and practical rewards from the cult leaders. Moreover the emphasis on proselytizing tends to displace subconscious reservations about the cult beliefs. And because of the absence of discriminating ethical and cultural preliminary training, the claimed euphoria of sudden conversion tends to be of a depressingly mediocre quality, as distinct from the higher spiritual awareness of the best conversions of established religions.

The most significant difference between old and new religious conversion is that the recruits to modern cults are discouraged from thinking for themselves; instead, they are required to sacrifice their own mental and emotional processes to the authority of the cult leader.

Following the horrific mass murders and suicides associated with the Peoples Temple cult in Guyana, there is increasing public disquiet at the absence of legislation to regulate the activities of cults using brainwashing techniques.

It should also be said that the phenomenon of "snapping" is not confined to religious and self-improvement cults, since it is also a well-established aspect of modern political cultism of the new Left and reactionary Right, resulting in the growing menace of urban guerillas, committing inhuman atrocities in the name of "freedom," "justice" and "human rights."

Research on Snapping

Authors Flo Conway and Jim Siegelman were research associates on an extensive University of Oregon study project, investigating more than a hundred aspects of cult activities and effects on members. Typical activities included initial contact, conversion, ritual practices, fund-raising, sexual practices, separation, deprogramming, and aftereffects. The study was a follow-up to the book *Snapping* (1978) by Conway and Siegelmlan, and was part of the Project on Information and Social Change in the University of Oregon Department of Speech. It covered nearly 400 former members of 48 cults in 39 states and four Canadian provinces.

A sampling of preliminary findings which was published in *Science Digest* (January 1982) received a National Mental Health Association Media Award. Siegelman stated: "Among the reported physical effects our study uncovered were abnormal weight gains or loss, sexual dysfunction and, in women, menstrual dysfunction."

Among emotional effects were overwhelming feelings of fear, guilt, anger, humiliation, hostility, anxiety, sleeplessness, depression, violent outbursts, and self-destructive tendencies. Reported mental disturbances included disorientation, confusion, nightmares, hallucinations, delusions, amnesia, "floating" in and out of altered states, and inability of ex members to break images, rhythms, and patterns associated with group practices.

On June 4, 1985, Carl W. Carmichael, director of the University of Oregon Communication Research Center, with Conway and Siegelman, reported that they had uncovered over twenty physical, emotional, and mental symptoms that appeared to be related to extended practice of cult mental techniques and rituals such as chanting, meditation, and "speaking in tongues."

Some of the sects reported on in the study included the **Unification Church,** the Church of **Scientology,** the **International Society for Krishna Consciousness,** the Divine Light Misson and the Way International, as well as many smaller sects in both Eastern tradition and Christian fundamentalism. The study indicated that the effects of "covert techniques" (forms of indoctrination without the individual's awareness or consent) lingered for a long period after members had left the sects. It appeared that many members were unaware of the change they were undergoing while in the sect, but only after leaving and attempting to resume life in the larger society did the troubling symptoms occur. Siegelman stated: "Some of the most dramatic symptoms revealed in our detailed analysis of the study's data bear striking similarity to clinical reports of 'post-traumatic stress disorders' that have been identified among returning Vietnam war veterans and survivors of other traumatic episodes."

When the research began to reveal the extent and duration of reported distress, Conway and Siegelman speculated that because of the basic mental processes engaged by many sect rituals, the apparent cult-related effects might reflect deeper and more fundamental neurophysiological changes. They suggested that such changes might signify a new category of communication-based disorders which they tentatively named "information disease." In order to test their theories, project associates entered the raw data into the unversity's computer and made statistical analyses.

Carmichael stated: "We found 63 significant correlations between ritual time and reported effects. We haven't established causation, but we have found correlation. The strength of Conway and Siegelman's assumptions appears to be confirmed in the number and extent of these correlations."

John Coggins, the chief statistician on the project, explained that the research methods were subjected to rigorous review. He stated: "We examined the design of the questionnaire, the method of distribution, the proportional breakdown of the total sample, and satisfied ourselves that the methods employed were the best available to minimize the possibility of systematic bias."

On the question of deprogramming of ex-cult members, three-quarters of those surveyed had been deprogrammed, but reported a third fewer disorders and recovered from all effects in 30 percent less time than those who were not. Only 10 of the nearly 400 subjects reported any physical injury during deprogramming, and six such cases were self-inflicted. The survey did not find significant evidence to support the frequent charge that deprogramming is a brutal technique. Conway and Siegelman suggested that their statistics seemed to confirm that deprogramming could be a valuable method of treating information disorders, given appropriate circumstances and legal safeguards.

The research associates plan further related studies, including a five-year follow-up on original subjects, and invite subjects to make contact. Address: Project on Information and Social Change, Communication Research Center, University of Oregon, Eugene, Oregon 97403. (See also **Communes; Cult Awareness Network; Cults; Spiritual Counterfeits Project**)

Recommended reading:

Conway, Flo & Jim Siegelman. *Snapping; America's Epidemic of Sudden Personality Change,* J. B. Lippincott, 1978; Delta paperback, 1979

Kilduff, M. & Ron Javers. *The Suicide Cult; The Inside Story of the Peoples Temple Sect and the Massacre in Guyana,* Bantam paperback, 1978

Sargent, William. *Battle for the Mind; A Physiology of Conversion & Brainwashing,* Perennial Library/harper & Row, 1957; 1959
Schein, Edgar H., Inge Scheier & Curtis H. Barker. *Coercive Persuasian,* W. W. Norton, 1961

Sneezing (Superstitions About)

It is said that the custom of blessing one who sneezes originated in Italy in the time of Pope Gregory the Great (c. 540-604) during a pestilence which proved mortal to those who sneezed.

A still older date is given to this custom by some writers, who state that sneezing was fatal from the time of Adam to that of Jacob, when the latter begged that its fatal effects might be removed. On his request being granted, the people gratefully instituted the custom of saluting the sneezer.

In some diseases, sneezing was a bad, in others a good omen. Sneezing to the right was lucky, to the left, unlucky; from noon to midnight good, from night to noon, bad. St. Augustine (died 430) stated that the ancients would return to bed if they sneezed while putting on a shoe.

Snowdon, Ruth J(ohnson) (1896-)

Research associate in biophysics who published articles on parapsychology. Born 1896 in Philadelphia, Pennsylvania, she studied at Vassar College, Poughkeepsie, New York (B.A.).

She was research associate in biophysics at University of Pittsburgh from 1948 onwards, and a charter member of the Parapsychological Association. She was coauthor (with R. A. **MacConnell** and K. F. **Powell**) of the article 'Wishing with Dice' (*Journal of Experimental Psychology,* vol. 50, October 1955).

Soal, S(amuel) G(eorge) (1889-1975)

Mathematician, author, lecturer and an important figure in British parapsychology, president of the **Society for Psychical Research,** London in 1950. Born April 29, 1889 at Kirby Moorside, Yorkshire, England, he studied at London University (B.Sc. first class honors mathematics, 1910, M.A. mathematics 1914, D.Sc. psychology 1945). In 1942 he married Beatrice Anne Potter. He was a lecturer in mathematics at Queen Mary College, University of London from 1911-38, chief instructor in mathematics at Army Officers' School of Education, Oxford from 1918-19, senior lecturer in pure mathematics, Queen Mary College from 1938-54, part-time lecturer at Queen Mary College from 1954-58, examiner at London University from 1960-62.

He was Myers Memorial lecturer in 1947, Perrott Student in Psychical Research, Cambridge from 1948-49. Fulbright Research Scholar in Parapsychology in 1951, examiner for higher degrees in mathematics at London University from 1928-58, member of the Board of Studies in Mathematics, London University from 1938-54, president of Nottingham University Society for Psychical Research 1938, member of the London Mathematical Society.

From 1919 onwards he conducted parapsychological studies, in mediumship (1919-24), automatic writing (1923-28), statistical experiments in telepathy and clairvoyance (1927 onwards). He collaborated in quantitative research with Mrs. K. M. **Goldney,** Frederick **Bateman** and J. G. **Pratt.** He lectured widely on parapsychology in Britain and the U.S. His articles include: 'The Experimental Situation in Psychic Research' (Myers Memorial Lecture, 1947), 'Preliminary Studies of a Vaudeville Telepathists' (*Bulletin of the University of London Council for Psychical Investigation,* 1937); (in SPR *Proceedings:*) 'A Report on Some Communications Received Through Mrs. Blanche Cooper' (vol. 35, December 1925), 'Experiments in Supernormal Perception at a Distance' (part 123, 1932), 'Fresh Light on Card Guessing' (vol. 46, 1940), 'Experiments in Precognitive Telepathy' (with K. M. Goldney, vol. 47, 1943); (in *Journal of Parapsychology:*), 'Agents in Opposition and Conjunction' (with Frederick Bateman, September 1950), 'ESP Performance and Target Sequence' (with J. G. Pratt, September 1951), 'Some Relations Between Call Sequence and ESP Performance' (with J. G. Pratt, September 1952).

His books included: (with F. Bateman) *Modern Experiments in Telepathy* (1954), (with H. T. Bowden) *The Mind Readers* (1959).

In 1960, Dr. C. E. M. **Hansel** criticized the claimed precognitive findings of Dr. Soal in a long series of card guessing experiments to test telepathy, carried out between 1936-39. Originally the series had appeared to be largely a failure, but after a suggestion from W. Whateley **Carington,** Dr. Soal reexamined the records in the light of possible "displacement" of guesses before or after the target, and concluded that there were indeed "positive deviations from chance expectation both on the card before and the card after that shown." Dr. Hansel suggested a number of ways in which there might have been conscious or unconscious falsification of the evidence.

In March 1971, an article in the *Journal* of the Society for Psychical Research by Dr. R. G. **Medhurst** ('On the Origin of the Prepared Random Numbers Used in the Shackleton Experiments') pointed out inaccuracies in the method of constructing quasi-random series in the experiments. By 1974, such criticism had become hostile, with papers by other experimenters suggesting that Dr. Soal had deliberately falsified or manipulated his data.

It was also suggested that experimenters J. G. Pratt and Dr.J. B. Rhine, who had checked Soal's statistical evaluation, had failed to disclose in detail a glaring error in the assessment of probability, using instead the vague term "very significant." There may, of course, have been a number of quite valid reasons for Pratt and Rhine to have failed to be specific. Soal himself ascribed his initial error to an assistant.

Soal died in 1975. Three years later Betty Markwick, a computer expert, published a complex technical paper in which computer analysis indicated that Soal was guilty of fraud. Other researchers have attempted to defend Soal from the charge of conscious deception, although it seems clear that his experiments are no longer valid evidence for ESP.

See the paper 'The Soal-Goldney Experiments with Basil Shackleton; New Evidence of Data Manipulation' by Betty Markwick, with statements by K. M. Goldney and J. G. Pratt (*Proceedings* of the Society for Psychical Research, vol. 56, 1978).

Societas Rosicruciana in America

Alternative name for the **Society of Rosicrucians in America.**

Societas Rosicruciana in Anglia

The Rosicrucian Society of England, organized in 1865 by Robert Wentworth Little (who claimed to have found some old Freemasonry rituals) and Kenneth R. H. **Mackenzie** (who claimed to have received Rosicrucian initiation in Austria). The Metropolitan College was founded in London in 1865 with Little as Supreme Magus, and a Soc. Ros. in Scotia was started soon afterwards, followed by provincial lodges.

Some famous names asociated with the Soc. Ros. in Anglia included Sir Francis Burdett (vice-president), author-occultist-politician Lord Lytton (Grand Patron 1871-73) (see Bulwer **Lytton**). Kenneth Mackenzie became an Honorary Magus. Dr. William Wynn **Westcott** was Supreme Magus in 1916.

The aims of the Society were: "to afford mutual aid and encouragement in working out the great problems of Life, and in discovering the Secrets of Nature; to facilitate the study of the system of Philosophy founded upon the Kabalah and the doctrines of Hermes Trismegistus, which was inculcated by the original Fratres Rosae Crucis, of Germany, A.D.1450; and to investigate the meaning and symbolism of all that now remains of the wisdom, art and literature of the ancient world." In spite of these resounding aims, the Society confined itself mainly to lectures and Freemasonry rituals.

In 1887, Westcott, Mackenzie and Dr. W. R. Woodman were concerned in the formation of the Isis-Urania Temple of the Hermetic Order of the **Golden Dawn,** in which the esoteric Freemasonry of the Soc. Ros. in Anglia was expanded into more complex occultism. (See also **Golden Dawn; Secret Chiefs, Society of Rosicrucians in America**)

Societies of Harmony

Associations formed for the practice of **"animal magnetism"** by the pupils of Franz Anton **Mesmer.** The first *Société de Harmonie* was formed at Paris, and its members seem to have acted in a manner that was anything but harmonious, for after some quarreling among themselves they at length broke their contract with Mesmer, whereby they had promised before being admitted to his lectures, that they would not practice on their own account, or give away the secret of his methods, without his consent.

Other Societies of Harmony soon sprang up, the most important being that of Strasbourg, founded in 1785 by the Marquis Chastenet de Puységur. (See also **Animal Magnetism;** Franz Anton **Mesmer; Mesmerism**)

Society for Interdisciplinary Studies

British organization founded in 1974 to act as a link between specialists in various disciplines who are interested in the theories of Dr. Immanuel **Velikovsky.**

The aim of the Society has been "to bring a rational and objective approach to the study of Velikovsky's theories and encourage the detailed evaluation which is their due in the light of the evidence accumulating in their favour." Meetings for members are held in the U.K. and public seminars and conferences organized at universities. The Society maintains an extensive archive of reviews, reports and other material. International membership covers the U.S., Canada, Australia, Israel, Africa and ten European countries. The Society publishes *S.I.S. Review,* a quarterly journal with original research contributions by scientists and scholars, informed discussion of Velikovsky's work, correspondence, reports of meetings, and book reviews. Address: The Hon. Secretary, Society for Interdisciplinary Studies, 6 Jersey House, Cotton Lane, Manchester 20.

Society for Parapsychological Studies (Taiwan)

Organization for parapsychological investigations; publishes a *Parapsychology* newsletter in Chinese language.

Society for Psychic Research (California)

(Not to be confused with the long established British organization, the Society for Psychical Research.) This is the new name of the former "Southern California Society for Psychical Research." It conducts research into extra-sensory perception, altered states of consciousness and related subjects, and issues a monthly Newsletter to members. Address: 170 S. Beverly Drive, Suite 303, Beverly Hills, California 90212.

No longer active at this address.

Society for Psychical Research

The British body to which the growing acknowledgment of psychical research as the coming science was principally due. Its establishment for organized and systematic psychical research was proposed on June 6, 1882, at a meeting by Sir William F. **Barrett,** and on February 20, 1882, the society came into being. Prof. Henry **Sidgwick,** of Cambridge, was elected President. The first council included Edmund **Gurney,** Prof. Barrett, Prof. Balfour **Stewart,** F. W. H. **Myers,** Richard Hutton as non-Spiritualists, and the Rev. W. Stainton **Moses,** Dawson Rogers, Morell **Theobald,** E. T. **Bennett,** Dr. George Wyld and others as Spiritualists. Mrs. Sidgwick, Frank **Podmore** and Dr. Richard **Hodgson** were among the first to join. The objects of the society were summed upon the following points:

1. An examination of the nature and extent of any influence which may be exerted by one mind upon another, apart from any generally recognized mode of perception.
2. The study of hypnotism and the forms of so-called mesmeric trance, with its alleged insensibility to pain; clairvoyance and other allied phenomena.
3. A critical revision of Reichenbach's researches with certain organizations called sensitive, and an inquiry whether such organizations possess any power of perception beyond a highly exalted sensibility of the recognized sensory organs.
4. A careful investigation of any reports, resting on strong testimony regarding apparitions at the moment of death, or otherwise, or regarding disturbances in houses reputed to be haunted.
5. An inquiry into the various physical phenomena commonly called spiritualistic; with an attempt to discover their causes and general laws.
6. The collection and collation of existing materials bearing on the history of these subjects.

The early activity of the society was devoted to an experimental investigation of **thought-transference.** They established it to their satisfaction as a fact. Equally important to this achievement was the finding of the authors of *Phantasms of the Living* (Gurney, Myers and Podmore) that between death and apparitions a connection existed which was not due to chance alone. The report of the committee on the **"Census of Hallucinations"** came to the same conclusion. It was largely attributable to the S.P.R.'s investigation that **hypnotism** was officially received by the British Medical Association.

Hysteria, haunted houses, Reichenbach's phenomena, the divining rod, multiple personality, automatic writing, and trance-speaking were other subjects taken up in due course.

Very valuable work was done in the study of **cross-correspondence** and in the investigation of the mediumship of Mrs. Lenore **Piper.** The subject of communication with the dead was not included in the original program of the society, but the presumption for evidence became so strong that the S.P.R. was eventually obliged to consider it.

In 1889 the **American Society for Psychical Research** was affiliated. From 1887 until his death in 1905, Dr. Hodgson was in charge and concentrated most of his activity on the mystery of Mrs. Piper's trance communications. This investigation is one of the most memorable events in the whole existence of the Society, for, to the satisfaction of many distinguished psychical researchers, it dealt with the question of **survival** and the possibility of holding intercourse with the departed. Dr. Hodgson himself became converted, to the great jubilation of Spiritualists, for, in the words of E. Dawson Rogers, President of the **London Spiritualist Alliance,** "he was a very Saul persecuting the Christians." Officially, however, the Society reached no conclusions, and in the century of its existence it has made no collective pronouncement on the question of survival, maintaining that the constitution of the Society precludes a collective opinion.

At first the cooperation between the Society for Psychical Research and the Spiritualists was friendly. The line of distinction was that psychical researchers only attempt to establish the veridity of the phenomena whereas Spiritualists not only consider them proved but also attribute them to the action of disembodied spirits. Sympathy, however, soon changed to hostility as in the views of the Spiritualists no amount of testimony was sufficient to make an impression upon the Society for Psychical Research.

Spiritualists objected to the extreme suspicion and the all too frequently voiced charges of fraud by psychical researchers, and said that their standard of evidence, when they wished to prove fraud, was far more elastic than when the genuine occurrence of phenomena was in question.

Early resentment was shown for the treatment of mediums Mrs. Kate Fox-Jencken (see **Fox Sisters**), Henry **Slade** and William **Eglinton** and that this feature of the situation remained constant through a great many years is best evidenced by the statement of Sir Oliver **Lodge** in his book *The Survival of Man,* published in 1909: "It has been called a society for the suppression of facts, for the wholesale imputation of imposture, for the discouragement of the sensitive, and for the repudiation of every revelation of the kind which was said to be pressing itself upon humanity from the regions of light and knowledge."

It cannot be denied that a certain bias against physical phenomena was observable in the Society. The exposure of Mme. **Blavatsky** by Dr. Hodgson in India appears to have prejudiced the Society against this side of psychical research.

Eusapia **Palladino** was branded an impostor in 1895, and it was only after the Society's commitment had been reduced to an amusing anachronism by many years of competent investigation all over Europe that the case was reopened in 1908, and a committee was delegated to sit with her in Naples. The verdict was in favor of Eusapia.

E. T. **Bennett,** who was assistant secretary to the Society for twenty years, published a book in 1904 under the title *Twenty Years of Psychical Research.* It was a review of the work of the Society and stated: "the question of the movement of tables without contact is exactly in the state in which it was left by the Dialectical Society in the year 1869. In all the series of the *Proceedings* there is no light whatever thrown on this simple phenomenon. Some investigation was made as regards direct writing and spirit photography, but to a large extent with negative result."

As far as the official attitude of the Society is concerned the question is in about the same state even now and it would be difficult to find a single physical phenomenon which, in a century research, has been established as an unquestionably genuine fact. This attitude of reserve and the gradual dying out of the first famous group of psychical investigators dimmed the luster of the Society for many years. The Society could have never been accused of being unduly credulous. Prof. William **James** wrote in his book *The Will to Believe and Other Essays* (1902): "In fact, were I asked to point to a scientific journal where hard-headedness and never-sleeping suspicion of sources of error might be seen in their full bloom, I think that I should have to fall back on the Proceedings of the Society for Psychical Research."

The mental reserve served good purpose in the early days but continued skepticism often exposed the Society to charges of having grown obsolete. Brilliant investigators like Dr. Gustave **Geley** scathingly criticized the Society's report on **Eva C.** The Hope Scandal in 1922 (see William **Hope**) reflected on the good reputation of the Society. In public protest against its methods Sir Arthur Conan **Doyle** resigned his membership in 1930. His example (as pointed out in an indictment by H. Dennis **Bradley**) was followed by some other members supporting his views. This indictment was published in March 1931, in the daily press but elicited no public reply on the part of the Society.

In his Jubilee address in June 1932, Sir Oliver **Lodge** remarked that hitherto, in their corporate capacity, they entertained no corporate conviction and reported no progress except to the extent that they might have committed themselves to a corporate belief in telepathy.

"Many of us," he added, "are now similarly convinced of the reality of a spiritual world and of its interaction with this world. I wonder whether it would be premature to say so and thus show that we are not merely working towards some unknown and perhaps unprofitable end, but are really in our opinion making progress. . . . I suggest," he concluded, "that that time has now arrived and that during the next 50 years we might announce this as a verified hypothesis and use it as an explanation of occurrences in which it is evidently an operative factor."

As against criticisms of negative or over-skeptical attitudes, it must be said that the Society has maintained a high standard of investigation and discussion. The middle period of elitism and rejection has long passed and over the last few decades the membership has broadened and the scope of investigations is a wide one.

It would be unrealistic to expect a consensus of opinion in a Society with a very varied membership, or to expect that elusive and often spontaneous phenomena could be suddenly validated scientifically. Like the inspirations of genius, paranormal faculties are relatively rare and difficult to study.

The style of contributions to the Society's *Journal* and *Proceedings* varies from the simple clairity of a down-to-earth investigation to the highly technical project heavily structured with statistical analysis. Members hold a wide variety of viewpoints and there are lively and stimulating controversies. The Society has successfully avoided the uncritical contagion of the "occult explosion" of the 1960s and also the negative backlash of the 1980s. Much useful research and evaluation has come from members of the Society and will continue in years to come.

The presidential chair of the Society has been filled by many brilliant minds as is shown by the following list: Prof. Henry Sidgwick, 1882-84, Prof. Balfour Stewart, 1885-87, Prof. Henry Sidgwick, 1888-92, The Earl of Balfour, 1893, Prof. William James, 1894-95, Sir William Crookes, 1896-99, F. W. H. Myers, 1900, Sir Oliver Lodge, 1901-03, Sir William Barrett, 1904, Prof. Charles Richet, 1905, The Right Hon. G. W. Balfour, 1906-07, Mrs. Henry Sidgwick, 1908-09, H. Arthur Smith, 1910, Andrew Lang, 1911. The Rt. Rev. Bishop W. Boyd Carpenter, 1912, Prof. Henri Bergson, 1913, F. C. S. Schiller, 1914, Prof. Gilbert Murray, 1915-16, L. P. Jacks, 1917-18, Lord Rayleigh, 1919, William M'Dougall, 1920-21, T. W. Mitchell, 1922, Camille Flammarion, 1923, J. G. Piddington, 1924-25, Prof. Dr. Hans Driesch, 1926-27, Sir Lawrence J. Jones, 1928-29, Dr. W. F. Prince, 1930-31, Mrs. Henry Sidgwick (President of Honour) and Sir Oliver Lodge, 1932, Dame Edith Lyttelton, 1933-34, Prof. C. D. Broad, 1935-36, R. J. Strutt (Baron Rayleigh), 1937-38, Henry Habberley Price, 1939-41, Robert H. Thouless, 1942-44, G. N. M. Tyrrell, 1945-46, W. H. Slater, 1947-48, Prof. Gardner Murphy, 1949-50, S. G. Soal, 1950-51, Prof. Gilbert Murray, 1952, Prof. F. J. M. Stratton, 1953-55, G. W. Lambert, 1955-58, Prof. C. D. Broad, 1958-60, H. H. Price, 1960-61, Prof. E. R. Dodds, 1961-63, Prof. D. J. West, 1963-65, Prof. Sir Alister Hardy, 1965-69, Prof. W. A. H. Rushton, 1969-71, Prof. C. W. K. Mundle, 1971-74, Dr. John Beloff, 1974-76, Prof. A. J. Ellison, 1976-79, Dr. J. B. Rhine, 1980, Dr. Louisa E. Rhine, 1980, Prof. A. J. Ellison, 1981-83.

In addition to the *Journal* and *Proceedings,* the Society has published a number of books and pamphlets on a wide range of topics concerned with psychical research, and also tape-recorded cassettes of important lectures.

The address of the Society is: 1 Adam & Eve Mews, Kensington, London, W8 6UQ, England. (See also **American Society for Psychical Research; Proceedings of the American Society for Psychical Research; Proceedings of the National Laboratory of Psychical Research; Proceedings of the Old A.S.P.R.; Proceedings of the Society for Psychical Research**)

Recommended reading:

Grattan-Guinness, Ivor. (ed.) *Psychical Research; A Guide to Its History, Principles & Practices, in Celebration of 100 Years of the Society for Psychical Research,* Aquarian Press, paperback, U.K., 1982

Haynes, Renee. *The Society for Psychical Research 1882-1982; A History,* Macdonald & Co., London, 1982

Thouless, R. H. *Psychical Research Past and Present,* Society for Psychical Research (pamphlet), London, 1952

Society for Research on Parapsychological Phenomena (Germany)

Founded in 1976 in Freiburg, Germany. In March 1980, the Society organized an International Congress of Parapsychology in Freiburg, attended by eminent parapsychologists from a number of different countries.

Society for Scientific Exploration

Society devoted to advancing the study of anomalous phenomena in various areas inside and outside the established science. It publishes a semi-annual *Journal of Scientific Exploration.* Address: Pergamon Journals Inc., Fairview Park, Elmsford, New York 10523.

Society for the Diffusion of Spiritual Knowledge

The first American Spiritualist organization, established in New York on June 10, 1854. It published the *Christian Spiritualist* and engaged mediums to give seances free. Judge J. W. Edmonds and Governor N. P. **Tallmadge** were among its members.

Society for the Investigation of the Unexplained

Founded in 1965 "for the acquisition, investigation and dissemination of information on reports of all tangible items in the fields of chemistry, astronomy, geology, biology and anthropology, that are not readily explained."

It encourages field work and on-the-spot investigation by offering advice, helping to raise funds and arranging contacts for members who are planning field trips and expeditions. Field work and research are reviewed by a panel of twenty scientists.

The Society disseminates information on findings through a quarterly journal, papers and reports. Investigations by Society members include such areas as ancient Egyptian television, ringing rocks, entombed toads and poltergeist manifestations. The Society maintains information files of original material, a map collection and a specialized library. It publishes *Pursuit,* quarterly. Current membership: 1,250. Address: Box 265, Little Silver, New Jersey 07739.

Society for the Study of Supernormal Pictures, The

Established in 1918 in London, England. The first president was Dr. Abraham Wallace, first vice-presidents: W. G. Mitchell, Sir Arthur Conan **Doyle** and H. Blackwell.

The object of the society was to promote the scientific study and investigation of supernormal pictures. Its members consisted largely of professional photographers.

After many hundreds of experiments, the Society reported in May 1920: "The members here present desire to place on record the fact that after many tests and the examination of thousands of pictures, they are unanimously of opinion that results have been obtained supernormally on sensitive photographic plates under reliable test conditions. At present the members do not undertake to explain how the results have been obtained, but they assert that they have undoubtedly been secured under conditions excluding the possibility of fraud."

The Society ceased operation in 1923.

Society of Metaphysicians

British organization devoted to a science of unity between physical and psychical fields, founded by J. J. Williamson, electronic engineer, in 1948. Williamson manifested such psychic abilities as astral projection (**out-of-body** experience) and **clairvoyance** at an early age, and in later life attempted to find a basis for integrating such faculties with normal physical science.

The Society commenced by experimenting in such areas as out-of-body experience, **aura** studies and **dowsing,** more recently in **biofeedback** phenomena.

An early associate of the Society was "Oliver Fox" (Hugh G. **Callaway**), pioneer of astral projection, who prepared a mail-order course on the subject for the Society.

In modern times, the Society concentrates largely on postal courses in conjunction with a mail-order business for books and such psychic appliances as aura goggles for viewing the human aura (as described in the books of Walter J. **Kilner** and Oscar **Bagnall**). Address: Archers Court, Stonestile Lane, The Ridge, Hastings, Sussex, England.

Society of Rosicrucians in America

Founded in 1912, "to promote spiritual, moral, and intellectual development through teachings that correlate religion, science and philosophy." Based on the teachings of Christian Rosenkreutz (1378-1484.) It does not seek to change members' religions, rather encourages members to find the meaning of whatever they have already been taught in religion. It promotes development of spiritual faculties which members "must manifest in a wholesome, natural and sane outlook on life and an ever-increasing usefulness to humanity." The Society offers lectures in Christian mysticism; maintains large library and also study centers; publishes *Mercury* quarterly newsletter. Address: 10 East Chestnut Street, Kingston, New York 12401. (See also **Societas Rosicruciana in Anglia**)

Solar System (in Theosophy)

Theosophists have special doctrines as to the formation of solar systems. They start by postulating the existence of all pervading ether, or, as it is termed in Theosophical occult chemistry **koilon,** an ether which is quite imperceptible to ordinary senses and indeed even to clairvoyants except the most highly-developed. It is, despite its diffusion, of extreme density.

The Deity, intending to create a universe, invests this ether with divine force, whereupon it becomes the constituent of matter in the shape of minute drops or bubbles, and of this the universe with its solar systems is formed. First a mass is aggregated by the appropriate agitation of these drops, and to this mass is imparted a rotatory motion. The mass thus formed, of course, contains the matter from which will be formed all the seven worlds, the existence of which Theosophy teaches, and it may be well here to observe that these worlds are not separate in the manner we usually conceive separate worlds to be, but interpenetrate each other.

The substance in its original form is of the texture of the first world, and in order to create the texture of the second—and lower—world the Deity sets up a vast number of rotatory agitations into each of which is collected forty-nine atoms arranged in a certain way, sufficient of the first atom having been left to form the first world.

This process continues six times, the atoms of the succeeding lower worlds being formed from those of the world immediately higher and each time of a multiple of forty-nine atoms. Gradually, and with the passing of long ages, the aggregation, which contains the atoms of all seven worlds completely intermingled, contracts and becomes more closely knit until it forms a nebula which eventually attains the flat, circular form familiar to students of astronomy.

Towards the center it is much more dense than at the fringes, and in the process of flattening and because of the initial revolving motion, rings are formed encircling the center. From these rings the planets are formed, and after the further passing of ages, it is possible for human life to exist on them.

The various worlds as has been said, penetrate each other substantially within the same bounds, the exceptions being the worlds of finer texture which extend beyond those relatively more dense. The names of the worlds are: the first which has not as yet been experienced by man— the Divine; the second, the Monadic whence come the impulses that form human beings; the third, the Spiritual, the highest world which human beings have as yet been able to experience; the fourth, the Intuitional; the fifth, the Mental; the sixth, the Emotional (Astral) world; and the seventh is the world of matter in the way that matter is familiar to us.

Some other terms for some of these worlds, referred to in other entries, are as follows: *Adi* plane (see **Divine World**), *Anupadaka* plane (see **Monad**), *Atmic* or *Nirvanic* plane (see **Spiritual World**), *Buddhic* plane (see **Intuitional World**). (See also **Astral World; Evolution of Life; Mental World; Theosophy**)

Solomon

The connection of Solomon, son of David, the King of Israel, with magical practice, although it does not possess any Biblical authority, has yet a very considerable body of Oriental tradition behind it. It is supposed, however, that the Jewish Solomon has in many cases been confused with a still older and mythical figure.

There are also Arabic and Persian legends of a prehistoric race who were ruled by seventy-two monarchs of the name of Suleiman, of whom the last reigned one thousand years.

John Yarker, author of *The Arcane Schools* (1909) stated: "It does not seem that these Suleimans who are par excellence the rulers of all Djinn, Afreets and other elemental spirits, bear any relationship to the Israelite King." The name, he said, is found in that of a god of the Babylonians, and the late Dr. Kenealy, the translator of Hafiz, says that the earliest Aryan teachers were named Mohn, Bodles or Solymi, and that Suleiman was an ancient title of royal power, synonymous with "Sultan" or "Pharaoh."

A Persian legend states that in the mountains of **Kaf,** which can only be reached by the magic ring of Solomon, there is a gallery built by the giant Arzeak, where there are statues of a race who were ruled by the Suleiman or wise King of the East. There is a great chair or throne of Solomon hewn out of the solid rock, on the confines of the Afghanistan and India called the Takht-i-Suleiman or throne of Solomon, its ancient Aryan name being Shanker Acharga.

It is to these older Suleimans then, that we must probably look for a connection with the tradition of occultism, and it is not unlikely that the legend relating to Solomon and his temple have been confused with these, and that the protagonists of the antiquity of **Freemasonry,** who date their cult from the building of Solomon's Temple, have intermingled some still older rite or mystery relating to the ancient dynasty of Suleiman with the circumstances of the Masonic activities of the Hebrew monarch.

"God," stated the ancient historian Josephus, "enabled Solomon to learn that skill which expels demons, which is a science useful and sanative to men. He composed such incantations, also, by which distempers are alleviated, and he left behind him the manner of using exorcisms, by which they drive away demons, so that they never return. And this method of cure is of great force unto this day; for I have seen a certain man of my own country, whose name was Eleazar, releasing people that were demoniacal, in the presence of Vespasian and his sons, and his captains, and the whole multitude of his soldiers.

"The manner of the cure was this. He put a ring that had a root of one of these sorts mentioned by Solomon to the nostrils; and when the man fell down immediately, he adjured him to return unto him no more, making still mention of Solomon, and reciting the incantations which he composed. And when Eleazar would persuade and demonstrate to the spectators that he had such a power, he set, a little way off, a cup, or basin full of water, and commanded the demon as he went out of the man, to overturn it, and thereby to let the spectators know that he had left the man."

Some claimed fragments of these magical books of Solomon are mentioned in the Codex Pseudepigraphus of Fabricius, and Josephus himself has described one of the antidemoniacal roots, which appears to refer to legends of the perils involved in gathering the mandrake root (see **Mandragoras**).

The Koran alleges that Solomon had power over the winds, and that he rode on his throne throughout the world during the day, and the wind brought it back every night to Jerusalem. This throne was placed on a carpet of green silk, of a prodigious length and breadth, and sufficient to afford standing room to all Solomon's army, the men on his right hand and the **Jinn** on his left. An army of the most beautiful birds hovered near the throne, forming a kind of canopy over it and the attendants, to screen the king and his soldiers from the sun.

A certain number of evil spirits were also made subject to Solomon, whose business it was to dive for pearls, and perform other work.

It is also stated that the devils, having received permission to tempt Solomon, in which they were not successful, conspired to ruin his character. They wrote several books of magic, and hid them under his throne, and when he died they told the chief men among the Jews that if they wished to ascertain the manner in which Solomon obtained his absolute power over men, Genii, and the winds, they should dig under his throne. They did so and found the books, abounding with the most impious superstitions.

The more learned and enlightened refused to participate in the practices described in those books, but they were willingly adopted by the common people. The Moslems asserted that the Jewish priests published this scandalous story concerning Solomon, which was believed until Mahomet, by God's command, declared him to have been no idolater.

It was further maintained by the Moslems that Solomon brought a thousand horses from Damascus and other cities he conquered, although some say they were left to him by his father David, who seized them from the Amalekites; others claimed that they came out of the Red Sea, and were provided with wings.

The King wished to inspect his horses, and ordered them to be paraded before him. Their symmetry and beauty so much occupied his attention that he gazed on them after sunset, and thus neglected evening prayers until it was too late.

When aware of his omission, he was so greatly concerned at it that he ordered the horses to be killed as an offering to God, keeping a hundred of the best of them. This, we are informed, procured for him an ample recompense, as he received for the loss of his horses dominion over the winds.

The following tradition was narrated by Moslem commentators relative to the building of the temple of Jerusalem. According to them, David laid the foundations of it, and when he died he left it to be finished by Solomon. That prince employed Jinn, and not men, in the work; and this idea might probably relate to what is said in the first Book of *Kings* (vi, 7) that the Temple was "built of stone, made ready before it was brought thither, so that there was neither hammer, no axe, nor any tool of iron, heard in the house while it was building."

The Rabbis noticed a worm which, they claimed, assisted the workmen, the power of which was such as to cause the rocks and stones to separate in chiseled blocks.

While engaged in the erection of the Temple, Solomon found his end approaching, and he prayed that his death might be concealed from the Jinn until the building was finished. His request was granted. He died while in the act of praying, and leaning on his staff, which supported his body in that posture for a whole year, and the Jinn, who supposed him to be still alive, continued their work.

At the expiration of the year the edifice was completed, when a worm which had entered the staff, ate it through, and to the amazement even of the Jinn, the body fell to the ground, and the King was discovered to be dead.

The inhabitants of the valley of Lebanon believed that the celebrated city and temple of Baalbec were erected by the Jinn under Solomon's direction. The object of the erection of Baalbec was variously stated, one tradition affirming that it was intended to be a residence for the Egyptian princess whom Solomon married, and another that it was built for the Queen of Sheba.

From the sixteenth century onwards, occultists have studied the great grimoire known as *The Key of Solomon (Clavicula Salomonis)* to which tradition ascribes an ancient history before it was committed to writing. This book of ceremonial magic has two sections: the *Great Key*, and the *Lemegeton or Lesser Key*. The first is concerned with magic spells, rituals and talismans, the second with the evocation of spirits.

There is also another work known as *The Testament of Solomon*, which was translated into German from an ancient Greek manuscript, a version of which was translated by F. C. Conybeare as *The Key of Truth* from an Armenian text. Manuscripts of the *Testament* have also been reported from Greek monasteries, and the work is extremely rare in any format.

The work claims to be Solomon's own story covering the period between the building of the Temple in Jerusalem and his own fall from grace. It tells the story of a vampire-like Jinn and the magic ring of Solomon, and details the various spirits and the magical means of controlling them. The ring of Solomon is also the subject of stories in the *Arabian Nights*.

Recommended reading:

Conybeare, F. C. (ed.) *The Key of Truth*, London, 1898

Mathers, F. L. MacGregor. (ed.) *The Key of Solomon the King*, G. Redway, London, 1908; Routledge & Kegan Paul, London, 1972

Shah, Sayed Idires. *The Secret Lore of Magic; Books of the Sorcerers*, Frederick Muller, London, 1957

Waite, Arthur E. *The Book of Ceremonial Magic*, William Rider, London, 1911; University Books, 1961; Causeway Books, 1973

Solomon, Mirror of

Popular name given to a "magic mirror" used for **divination.** Various magical signs and devices were attributed to King **Solomon,** deriving from folk legends.

The method of making the Mirror of Solomon is as follows: Take a shining and well-polished plate of fine steel, slightly concave, and with the blood of a white pigeon inscribe at the four corners the names "Jehovah," "Eloym," "Metatron," "Adonay."

Place the mirror in a clean and white cloth, and when you behold a new moon during the first hour after sunset, repeat a prayer that the angel Anaël may command and ordain his companions to act as they are instructed, that is, to assist the operator in divining from the mirror. Then cast upon burning coals a suitable perfume, at the same time uttering a prayer.

Repeat this thrice, then breathe upon the mirror and evoke the angel Anaël. The sign of the cross is then made upon the operator and upon the mirror for forty-five days in succession, at the end of which period Anaël appears in the form of a beautiful child to accomplish the operator's wishes. Sometimes he appears on the fourteenth day, according to the devotion and fervor of the operator. The perfume used in evoking him is saffron.

For another method of constructing a magic mirror which does not involve the sacrifice of a white pigeon, see the appendix to *The Philosophy of Natural Magic* by Henry C. Agrippa (University Books, 1974). (See also **Solomon**)

Solomon Ibn Gabirol (1021-1058)

Spanish-Hebrew poet and mystic philosopher. He was a Neoplatonist, but at the same time subscribed to the mystical doctrine which states that the Deity can only be regarded as a negation of all attributes. This he considered essential to the preservation of Jewish monotheism. (See also **Neoplatonism**)

Solovovo, Count (died 1954)

Prominent Russian-born psychical researcher. See Count **Perovsky-Petrovo-Solovovo.**

Soma

A term found in the hymns of the *Rig-Veda,* one of the four sacred scriptures of ancient India (the others are: *Sama Veda, Yajur Veda, Artharva Veda*) c.1,500 B.C. The essential teachings of the *Vedas* were recast in the form of the *Upanishads,* of which there are 108 principal scriptures and a number of minor ones.

The ninth chapter of the *Rig-Veda* comprises 114 verses in praise of *Soma,* the ambrosia of the gods, the elixir of immortality. It is clear that *Soma* was also an intoxicating drink (possibly the milk-weed *Asclepias acida*) described in the *Yajur Veda* as a dark, sour creeper, without leaves. This drink was offered by the priests as a libation to the gods, much as wine is used sparingly in the sacraments of the Christian religion for symbolic purposes.

In modern times, writers like R. Gordon Wasson (in his book *Soma, Divine Mushroom of Immortality,* 1968; 1971) have speculated that *Soma* was the *amanita muscaria* mushroom with hallucinogenic properties, and that Hindu mysticism arose from intoxication of the priests. This suggestion stemmed from Wasson's researches in Mexico, when he discovered a religious cult based on the use of a hallucinogenic mushroom by the Mazatec Indians.

This *Soma* theory became attractive during the psychedelic revolution of the sixties, and it became fashionable to assume that transcendental revelation had always been stimulated by the use of psychedelic drugs. Another writer, John M. Allegro, even suggested in his book *The Sacred Mushroom and the Cross* (1970) that the crucifixion story of Jesus was a myth, symbolic of the ecstasy of a psychedelic drug cult!

Intoxicating beverages have certainly been known since ancient times in Egypt, India, Greece and Rome. Warnings about intoxication abound in ancient writings, notably in the Bible, in the *Proverbs* of Solomon, in *Isaiah, Jeremiah, Amos* and *Hosea.* In the Christian religion, the apostle Paul complained of drunkenness at the *agape* or love-feasts celebrated in common. Novatian, a Church Father of the third century, spoke of Christians who in the morning, after fasting, began the day by drinking, and poured wine into their still "empty veins," and were drunk before eating.

In India, the *Manava Dharma Shastra* (Ordinances of Manu), a code of religious and civil duties, also prohibited intoxication on the part of Brahmin priests, and incidentally made it clear that the *Soma* drink was from a plant, not a mushroom. This plant is sometimes called the "moon plant," and *Soma* was traditionally associated with the moon.

Yoga treatises on meditation make it clear that the true *Soma* or elixir of life is the union of the twin currents of **Kundalini** energy in the human body, culminating in higher consciousness. *Kundalini* is a latent energy situated at the base of the spine, which is activated in normal life in sexual activity, but which may also be drawn upwards in subtle channels of the spine to a center in the head, illuminating the consciousness with mystical awareness. The goal of Yoga practice is often referred to as the union of the sun and moon, the fiery and cool *Kundalini* currents in the spinal column. At the junction of these currents, the blissful condition is described as "drinking the *Soma* juice," and the energy flow as "*Amaravaruni*" (wine drinking).

The elaborate symbolism and metaphor of Hindu mysticism has often misled commentators into literal interpretations. Common sense dictates that the combination of complex detailed logic and transcendental experience which characterizes the religious philosophy of ancient India could never be the result of drunken orgies or hallucinatory drugs. Throughout history, great prophets and mystics, as well as scientists and geniuses, have been inspired by a higher consciousness that owed nothing to intoxication or hallucinogenic mushrooms.

The twentieth-century discovery of psychedelic drugs and their power temporarily to transform normal consciousness has misled many people into identifying mystical experience with a spurious chemical counterpart. The idea that higher consciousness can be achieved effortlessly by ingesting a drug is peculiarly attractive to the consumerism of the affluent society. It is significant that decades of hard and soft drug addiction on the part of thousands upon thousands of individuals from all walks of life, from street people to scholars and professional psychologists, have not so far produced a single inspiring statement on the philosophy and meaning of life comparable with the wisdom of the prophets and mystics of history.

In both Eastern and Western religious traditions, higher consciousness is achieved through the patient gradual character transformations of spiritual disciplines, in which body, mind and emotions are purified so that there is an integrity of new insights and mystical realizations. A chemical experience emphasizes ego-centered hedonism and does not truly expand the consciousness in its intense sensory and emotional overload of stimuli.

Yet the psychedelic mushroom theory of *Soma* and transcendental consciousness is still being revived in the more scholarly strata of New Age teachings, notwithstanding the tragic consequences of the psychedelic revolution of the sixties.

The journal *ReVision* (vol. 10, No. 4, Spring 1988) is devoted to a revival of Wasson's theories and related apologia for psychedelic drugs in allegedly illuminating inner space. For an effective rebuttal, see the series of three articles by Gene Kieffer, 'ReVision Revisits the Sacred Mushroom,' 'It's Not the Soma that the Brahmans Know!,' 'An Appeal for Common Sense' (*SFF Newsletter,* Spiritual Frontiers Fellowship, Aug.-Oct. 1988).

With regard to *Kundalini,* modern commentators have suggested that it may be identified with the right vagus nerve, and its arousal in the human body with the pathways of the autonomic nervous system, the **chakras** or mystical centers being associated with the main nervous plexi, the center of illumination with the central canal of the spinal cord and the lateral ventricles of the human brain. Such nerve pathways might also be correlated with the network of **acupuncture** paths in the Chinese medical system.

Whether one is dealing with known physiological phenomena or a subtle vitality associated with them, it is apparent that the arousal of *Kundalini* may have a biological basis. This has been emphasized in the books of the late Pandit **Gopi Krishna,** who described the arousal of Kundalini from his own personal experience of this fabled force.

Meanwhile it is clear that the hymns to *Soma* in the *Vedas* are typical of the rich symbolism of Indian religion and philosophy, comparable with the symbolism of the Christian Eucharist, and related to the transcendental awareness associated with the arousal of *Kundalini,* revered as a goddess. (See also **Drugs; Hallucinogens; Gopi Krishna; Kundalini;** R. Gordon **Wasson**)

Recommended reading:

Gopi Krishna. *The Biological Basis of Religion and Genius,* Harper & Row, 1971; Turnstone Press, London, 1973

Gopi Krishna. *The Awakening of Kundalini,* E. P. Dutton paperback, 1973

Iyangar, Yogi Srinivasa. *Hatha-Yoga-Pradipika of Svatmarama Svamin,* Bombay Theosophical Publication Fund, n.d.; Theosophical Publishing House, Adyar, India, 1933 etc.

Rele, Vasant G. *The Mysterious Kundalini; The Physical Basis of the "Kundalini (Hatha) Yoga" in Terms of Western Anatomy and Physiology,* D. B. Taraporevala, Bombay, India, c.1928

Zaehner, R. C. *Mysticism; Sacred & Profane,* Clardenon Press, U.K., 1957; Galaxy Book paperback (O.U.P.), 1961

Somatography

A fringe-medical technique deriving from study of the human **aura,** devised by Welsh healer Bryn Jones. The term derives from the Greek and implies "mapping-out of the soul." Mr. Jones massages the aura of his patients, using a radionic device for diagnosis, designed by an American named Mark Gallot (see **Radionics**).

This therapy of healing through the human aura recalls an earlier technique of Dr. H. **Baraduc,** who used to "clip" a short distance around the face and body of his patient with large copper scissors, to free the etheric body from the physical part of the aura.

Mr. Bryn Jones operates a center for healing known as the company of Somatographers, located in Nottingham Place, London, W.1., England.

Sommer, Robert (1929-)

Research psychologist with special interest in imagery and its relationship to paranormal experience. Born April 26, 1929 in New York, N.Y. he studied at Hobart College, Geneva, N.Y. (B.A. 1950), University of Oklahoma (M.S. 1952), University of Kansas (Ph.D. 1956).

He was research assistant in Menninger Foundation from 1953-56, research fellow at Southeast Louisiana Hospital 1956, research psychologist at Saskatchewan Hospital, Canada from 1957-63, assistant professor, University of Alberta, Edmonton from 1961-63; Department of Psychology, University of California, Davis, California, associate professor, 1963-65, professor of psychology, 1965 onwards.

He is a member of the American Psychological Association, American Sociological Society, Canadian Psychological Association, Society for Psychological Study of Social Issues.

He contributed a paper on parapsychology to *The Psychic Force: Essays in Modern Psychical Research* edited by Allan Angoff (1970). Other publications include: *Expertland* (1963), *The Ecology of Study Areas* (1968), *Personal Space; The Behavioral Basis of Design* (1969). *Design Awareness* (1972), *Tight Spaces* (1974), *Street Art* (1975), *Sidewalk Family* (1975), *The End of Imprisonment* (1976), *The Mind's Eye* (1978), (with Barbara A. Sommer) *A Practical Guide to Behavioral Research* (1980), *Farmers Markets of America* (1980).

Somnambulism

Term derived from Latin *somnus* (sleep) and *ambulare* (to walk). A state of sleep, or half-waking trance, spontaneously or artificially induced, in which subconscious faculties take the place of normal consciousness and direct the body in the performance of erratic (sleep walking) or highly intellectual actions (solving problems).

It often starts as an exaggerated dream and it develops into a kind of secondary personality with a chain of memory of its own. This chain of memory will often be found part of the hypnotic memory. The personality itself, in some cases, seems very wise and exhibits paranormal powers.

The somnambulist may have his or her eyes closed, and ears deaf to auditory impressions or sense impressions, without awakening any gleam of consciousness. This may have some effect in rousing new trains of association and suggesting a new line of action. It is suggested that the sleep-walker may see only a mental picture of what he or she is doing as in a dream instead of objective reality, and certain experimental tests have suggested that this occurs in some cases at least.

The somnambulic state was the discovery of the Marquis Chastenet de Puysègur in 1784 in the context of **Mesmerism** and **"animal magnetism."** He induced it by passes, and finally, by a simple act of will, the Abbé Faria brought it on by shouting, Chevalier de Barbarin by praying, James **Braid** by staring at a bright object, usually his lancet case.

The nineteenth-century physician Alexandre Bertrand assigned somnambulism to four cases: (1) A particular nervous temperament which predisposes individuals otherwise in good health to paroxysm of somnambulism during their ordinary sleep. (2) It is sometimes produced in the course of certain diseases of which it may be considered a symptom of a crisis. (3) It is often seen in the course of the proceedings necessary to bring on the condition known as animal magnetism. (4) It may result as a consequence of a high degree of mental exaltation. Accordingly, he distinguished four kinds of somnambulism: the natural, the symptomatic, the artificial and ecstatic. Hypnotism would fall under the artificial, trance under the ecstatic variety.

Physiologically, somnambulism differs from sleep in that the muscles retain the ordinary tension of the waking life. The eyeballs are usually in an unnatural position, drawn upwards and inwards so that the vision is directed to the top of the forehead. There is an insensibility to pain, taste and smell are paralyzed. The external senses are perfectly sealed. No memory is carried into the waking state.

There are various degrees of somnambulism. Prof. Charles **Richet** spoke of semi-somnambulism, the state in which the medium retains consciousness while automatic manifestations take place. Catalepsy is a deep stage of somnambulism. The fakirs and yogis of India induced it by an effort of will.

The mildest form of somnambulism is typified in the inarticulate murmurings or vague gestures of a dreaming child, while in the most extreme cases where all the senses are active, and the actions apparently as purposive as in the normal waking state, it borders on the condition of spontaneous hypnotism.

Indeed its affinity with hypnosis was early recognized, when the hypnotic subjects of the animal magnetists were designated "somnambules." It is remarkable that somnambulists may walk in dangerous paths with perfect safety, but if they are suddenly awakened they are liable to fall. Spontaneous somnambulism generally indicates some morbid tendency of the nervous system, since as a rule, only in some abnormal state could the dream ideas exercise so exciting an influence on the brain as to rouse to activity centers normally controlling voluntary movements.

Sylvan J. **Muldoon** (with H. Carrington) in *The Projection of the Astral Body* (1929 etc.) wrote of "astral somnambulism," a state of unconscious **astral projection** which, according to Muldoon was far more common than generally supposed. It mostly occurred in the dream state. (see also **Animal Magnetism; Astral Projection; Hypnotism; Mesmerism; Sleep; Sleeping Preacher; Suggestion; Trance**)

Recommended reading:

Belden, L. W. *Somnambulism; The Extraordinary Case of J. C. Rider, the Springfield Somnambulist,* London, 1834

Bertrand, A. *Traité du Somnambulisme,* Paris, 1824

Braid, James. *Neurpnology; Or, the Rationale of Nervous Sleep,* London, 1843; Arno Press, 1975

Cahagnet, L. A. *The Celestial Telegraph; Or, Secrets of the Life to Some Revealed Through Magnetism,* London, 1850; Arno Press, 1976

Colquhoun, J. C. *Report of the Experiments on Animal Magnetism; Made By a Committee of the Medical Section of the French Royal Academy of Sciences . . . 1831,* Edinburgh, 1833; Arno Press, 1975

Esdaile, James. *Natural and Mesmerism Clairvoyance,* London, 1852; Arno Press, 1975

Haddock, Joseph W. *Somnolism and Psycheism; Or, the Science of the Soul and the Phenomena of Nervation as Revealed by Vital Magnetism or Mesmerism,* London, 1851; Arno Press, 1975

Fahnestock, W. B. *Statuvolism; Artificial Somnambulism,* Religio-Philosophical Publishing House, Chicago, 1871

Tuke, W. H. *Sleep-walking and Hypnotism,* Blakiston, Philadelphia, Churchill, London, 1884

Weinhold, Dr. Arnold. *Seven Lectures on Somnambulism,* Edinburgh, Scotland, 1845

Sons Ahman Israel (Organization)

Religious offshoot of the **Mormons.** It was founded in 1981 by Presiding Patriarch David Israel and four other former members of the Church of Jesus Christ of Latter Day Saints. The group believes in the continued visitation of and revelations from angels, and David Israel claims to receive regular revelations in the form of morning and evening oracles.

Besides the Bible and the *Book of Mormon,* a wide variety of materials are accepted as scripture, including ancient apocryphal writings (*Gospel of Thomas, Gospel of Philip, Book of Enoch,* writings from Nag Hammadi) and modern Mormon revelations (*Oracles of Mohonri, The Order of the Sons of Zadok*). The group believes in a secret oral tradition passed from Moses to the Essenes, the Gnostics and eventually to Joseph Smith Jr. That tradition is believed to be preserved in mystical books such as the *Pistis Sophia* and *Sepher Yetzira.*

A twenty-two item statement of "S.A.I. Beliefs" affirms belief in a heavenly hierarchy consisting of a Heavenly Father and Mother, their son Jesus Christ, the Holy Spirit, angels and archangels, and ministers of the flame (just men made perfect). Human beings are the literal offspring of the heavenly Parents and have come into earthly existence to experience the mystery of mortality. Redemption for humans comes only through surrendering their life to Yetshuah the Christ, and subsequently developing a relationship to Him in the holy temple ordinances and ritualistic ceremonies. The Sons Ahman Israel also follow the Old Testament feasts and holy days.

The Sons Ahman Israel is headed by a Presiding Patriarch and Matriarch under whom function (when the organization is at full strength) a First Presidency, twelve Apostles, seven Arch Seventies and twelve Stake Princes. Each stake is headed by twelve High Counselmen, a Quorum of Seventy, and twelve Bishops. The Church endorses the practice of polygamy, but also believes in the perfect equality of the sexes. Women are accepted into the priesthood on an equal basis with men.

The headquarters of the group is in Washington, Utah. A monthly periodical, *The Stone,* is published.

Sorcery

(From Latin *sortiarius,* one who practices **divination** by lots.) The use of supposed supernatural power by the agency of evil spirits called forth by spells by a witch or black magician. (See also **Magic**)

Sordi, Signora Lucia (1871- ?)

Powerful Italian physical medium, a working-class woman controlled by "Remigio," a spirit who specialized in giving remarkable demonstrations, under test conditions, of **matter passing through matter,** producing many-colored psychic lights, **materializations** and very strong **telekinesis** effects.

The clothes of the securely fastened medium were often removed from under a labyrinth of knots while not the slightest ringing was heard from the small bells attached to her garment. Handcuffs and a straitjacket were similarly taken off, and the medium herself was repeatedly placed outside of an enclosure of a more than two yards high strong and padlocked wooden fence.

In 1911, the Societa de Studi Psichici de Milano engaged Signora Lucia's services for test sittings during a period of not less than a year. During this investigation, Baron **Schrenck-Notzing** attended two of the sittings. He discovered no trickery but expressed an opinion in *Psychische Studien* that the results might have been obtained by purely mechanical means.

This opinion stimulated an animated controversy. In December 1911, and the following January, the medium sat for scientists in Rome. An interesting account of an attempted exposure was given by Professor V. Tummolo in *Luce e Ombra.* A sitter, being touched by a solid materialized limb, switched on an electric lamp and produced a dazzling light.

"Then to my sight," wrote Professor Tummolo, "there appeared a sort of transparent shirt, which vanished immediately, instantaneously entering the medium. The latter, who happened to be standing at some distance from the cabinet and not far from the individual responsible for the sudden illumination, fell to the ground like a corpse, and then commenced to wail in an indescribable manner. Every possible attention was hastily rendered her; but she expectorated blood, and felt terrible pains in the region of the heart until the next day—pains which forced her to utter cries which she was unable to repress. . . . In the cabinet, immediately after the event just narrated, the medium's gown was found completely buttoned up, in spite of the fact that she was still bound in the manner previously described—bound, that is to say, in respect to her hands and body, with a network of ribbon."

Professor Tummolo expressed his conviction of the genuineness of Signora Sordi's mediumship. It cannot be stressed too often that sudden lights and grabbing at phenomena on the presumption of fraud are unforgiveable offences at seances and may result in serious injuries to the medium. Where there is strong suspicion of fraud, less reckless and violent methods of exposure are possible.

Sorokin, Pitirim Alexandrovitch (1889-1968)

Emeritus professor of sociology with special interest in the supraconscious, manifestations of genius and creativity. Born January 21, 1889 at Turya, Vologda Province, Russia, he studied at University of St. Petersburg (Master's degrees in criminal law 1916, Ph.D. sociology 1922), Harvard University (LL.M.), University of Mexico (Ph.D. hon.) In 1917 he married Elena Petrovna Baratynskayia.

He was a lecturer at University of St. Petersburg, Psychoneurological Institute, Agricultural Academy from 1914-17, co-founder of Russian Peasant Soviet, member of Council of Russian Republic, secretary to Prime Minister Alexander Kerensky, 1917, professor of criminal law and sociology, University of St. Petersburg from 1918-22, banished by Soviet Government 1922, professor of sociology at University of Minnesota from 1924-30, founder, professor and chairman, Department of Sociology, Harvard University, 1930-43, director of Harvard Research Center in Creative Altruism from 1949 onwards, president of International Society for Comparative Study of Civilizations 1960-63. Memberships included: American Academy of Arts and Sciences, hon. member of Royal Academies of Science and Arts, Belgium and Rumania, hon. member of German, Czech and other national sociological societies.

Dr. Sorokin published thirty books on sociology and history. He contributed an introduction to *The Psychic Source Book* edited by Alson J. **Smith,** which includes an appendix in which Sorokin wrote on the importance of parapsychology.

He died February 19, 1968.

SORRAT

Acronym for Society for Research on Rapport and Telekinesis, a group founded by Prof. John G. **Neihardt.** Meetings were usually held at Neihardt's home at Skyrim Farm, near Columbia, Missouri.

Neihardt's interest in psychic matters stemmed from his close association with Indian Rights movements from 1903 onwards. Neihardt was accepted as a participant in secret medicine-men ceremonies and was actively concerned with the Indian shaman Black Elk, the subject of his book *Black Elk Speaks* (William Morrow, 1932). Neihardt's wife Mona had been associated with a Spiritualist and was mediumistic, and Neihardt investigated the phenomena of various mediums.

The SORRAT group was formed during the mid-1960s. Neihardt discussed the group methods with veteran parapsychologist J. B. **Rhine,** in order to conduct experiments in a congenial atmosphere that would also be fraud-proof.

One technique employed was that of the **"mini-lab"**—a sealed transparent box containing target objects for testing psychokinesis. With the assistance of parapsychologist William Edward **Cox,** an automatic filming method was developed in which a fixed movie camera and lights are trained on a mini-lab, activated by an electrical signal. The **McDonnell Laboratory for Psychical Research** has also supported these techniques.

From 1965 onwards, the SORRAT group developed remarkable phenomena tending to validate **psychokinesis, levitation, apports, apparitions,** and **communication** with entities.

For a detailed report on the group and its achievements, see *SORRAT: A History of the Neihardt Psychokinesis Experiments, 1961-1981* by John Thomas Richards, Scarecrow Press, Metuchen, New Jersey & London, 1982.

Sorrel Leaf

A sorrel leaf was sometimes used to bewitch people, as in the case of the Irish witch mentioned in George Sinclair's *Satan's Invisible World Displayed* (1685 etc.) who gave to a girl a leaf of sorrel which the child put into her mouth. Great torture ensued for the child, such tortures being increased on the approach of the witch.

Sortilege

Divination by lots, one of the most ancient and common superstitions. It was used among Oriental nations to detect a guilty person, as when Saul by this means discovered that Jonathan had disobeyed his command by taking food, and when the sailors by a similar process found Jonah to be the cause of the tempest by which they were overtaken.

The various methods of using the lot have been very numerous, including **Rhabdomancy, Clidomancy,** the Sortes Sagittariæ or **Belomancy,** and the common casting of dice. The following are the more classical methods:

Sortes Thriæcæ, or Thriæn lots, were chiefly used in Greece; they were pebbles or counters distinguished by certain characters which were cast into an urn, and the first that came out was supposed to contain the right direction. This form of divination received its name from the Thriæ, three nymphs supposed to have nursed Apollo, and to have invented this mode of predicting futurity.

Sortes Viales, or street and road lots, were used both in Greece and Rome. The person that was desirous to learn his fortune carried with him a certain number of lots, distinguished by several characters or inscriptions, and walking to and fro in the public ways desired the first boy whom he met to draw, and the inscription on the lot thus drawn was received as an infallible prophecy. Plutarch declared that this form of divination was derived from the Egyptians, by whom the actions and words of boys were carefully observed as containing in them something prophetical.

Another form of the Sortes Viales was exhibited by a boy, but sometimes by a man, who positioned himself in a public place to give responses to all comers. He was provided with a tablet, on which certain predictive verses were written; when consulted, he cast dice on the tablet, and the verses on which they fell were supposed to contain the proper direction. Sometimes instead of tablets they had urns, in which the verses were thrown, written upon slips of parchment. The verse drawn out was received as a sure guide and direction. Tibullus alluded to this custom as follows:

Thrice in the streets the sacred lots she threw,
And thrice the boy a happy omen drew.

This form of divining was often practiced with the Sibylline oracles, and hence was named Sortes Sibyllina.

Sortes Prenestinæ, or the Prenestine lots, were used in Italy. The letters of the alphabet were placed in an urn and shaken; they were then turned out upon the floor, and the words which they accidentally formed were received as omens.

This superstitious use of letters is still known in Eastern countries. The Moslems had a divining table, which they said was invented by the prophet Edris or Enoch. It was divided into a hundred little squares, each of which contained a letter of the Arabic alphabet. The person who consulted it repeated three times the opening chapter of the *Koran,* and the 57th verse of the 6th chapter: "With Him are the keys of the secret things; none knoweth them but Him; He knoweth whatever is on the dry ground, or in the sea: there falleth no leaf but he knoweth it; neither is there a single grain in the dark parts of the earth, nor a green thing, nor a dry thing, but it is written in a perspicuous book."

Having concluded this recitation, he averted his head from the table and placed his finger upon it; he then looked to see upon what letter his finger was placed, wrote that letter; the fifth following it; the fifth following that again; and so on until he came back to the first he had touched. The letters thus collected formed the answer.

Sortes Homericæ and Sortes Virgilianæ, involve divination by opening some poem at hazard, and accepting the passage which first turns up as an answer. This practice probably arose from the esteem which poets had among the ancients, by whom they were reputed divine and inspired persons.

Homer's works among the Greeks had the most credit, but the tragedies of Euripides and other celebrated poems were occasionally used for the same purpose. The Latins chiefly consulted Virgil, and many curious coincidences were related by grave historians, between the prediction and the event; thus, the elevation of Severus to the Empire is supposed to have been foretold by his opening at this verse:

Remember, Roman, with imperial sway
to rule the nations.

It is said that Charles I and Lord Falkland made trial of the Virgilian lots a short time before the commencement of the great Civil War. The former opened at that passage in the fourth book of the Æneid where Dido predicts the violent death of her faithless lover; the latter at the lamentation of Evander over his son in the eleventh book. If the story is true, the coincidences between the responses and events are remarkable.

Sortes Biblicæ was divination by the Bible, which the early Christians used instead of the profane poets. Nicephorus Gregoras recommended the Psalter as the fittest book for the purpose, but Cedrenus stated that the New Testament was more commonly used. St. Augustine denounced this practice in temporal affairs, but declared in one of his letters that he had recourse to it in all cases of spiritual difficulty. Another form of the Biblical lots was to go to a place of worship, and take as an omen the first passage of Scripture read by the minister, or the text from which he preached. This was no uncommon practice even in recent history.

The Moslems consulted the *Koran* in a similar manner, but one of their methods was to deduce their answer from the seventh line of the right-hand page. Others counted how often the letters *kha* and *shin* occurred in the page; if *kha* (the first letter of *kheyr,* "good") predominated, the answer was deemed favorable, but if *shin* (the first letter of *shin* "evil") be more frequent, the inference was that the projects of the inquirer were forbidden or dangerous.

It would be easy to multiply examples of these efforts to obtain guidance from blind chance. They were once so frequent, that it was deemed necessary to denounce them from the pulpit as being clearly forbidden by the divine precept, "Thou shalt not tempt the Lord thy God." (See also **Divination**)

Soul

The term is used in two senses—it indicates the ego and the spirit-body. In ancient writings, an individual was described as a triune being: body, soul and spirit. According to this concept, the soul is just as much an envelope, animated by the spirit, as the physical body is an envelope for the soul. At death the soul withdraws and continues to function in the spiritual world. **Astral body** and soul are almost equivalent terms.

Occult and Oriental teachings, however, speak of five bodies of differing degrees of refinement which will be cast away in time just as the physical body is left behind.

In his book *Man and the Universe* (1908), Sir Oliver **Lodge** defined the soul and ego as "that controlling and guiding principle which is responsible for our personal expression and for the construction of the body, under the restrictions of physical condition and ancestry. In its higher development it includes also feeling and intelligence and will, and is the storehouse of mental experience. The body is its instrument or organ, enabling it to receive and convey physical impressions, and to effect and be effected by matter and energy."

Because such concepts as "soul" and "spirit" (as its animating essence) are not available for scientific scrutiny like the body or the world of matter generally, many scientists have denied their existence as real entities, although retaining as useful the concept of consciousness, with which the ego is associated.

Spiritualists claim that there is evidence for **survival** of consciousness after death, and that there is sufficient individuality in the surviving consciousness to justify the use of the term soul. A good deal of psychical research tends to confirm this position, without necessarily accepting the religious implications of such survival.

In Christian eschatology, the early doctrine of the resurrection of the material body is no longer generally acceptable, but the concept of the immortality of the individual soul is still current. This association of ego with soul is a simplistic one, and raises certain theological problems which do not exist in Eastern metaphysics.

In Eastern religious philosophy, there are clear distinctions between the gross ego of name and form (with individual experience) and the subtle ego which is claimed as a universal substratum of all individual souls. The gross ego, by reason of its limitations of experience and consciousness, is tied to the world of matter, which is transient. This ego is an obstruction to fuller awareness of reality and must be transcended by selfless service and refinement of consciousness. In this process, the individual soul loses its attachment to the transient desires and fears of material life and is eventually subsumed in a divine consciousness. In this progress, the world of matter becomes like an illusion that ceases to have validity when divine reality supervenes, rather as the world of a vivid dream fades away as one awakes.

However, within the framework of worldly concept, the individual soul wins its divine freedom through effort to redeem unethical actions of the past, involving rebirth in different bodies until unethical actions are extinguished through ethical behavior (see **Reincarnation**).

Whether one forms concepts of a struggle to perfect the human soul, or alternatively a release from the illusions of matter, the process remains the same, affected only by the position from which concepts are constructed. The relatively irrational logic of dream experience persists while one is dreaming, but changes in waking consciousness.

The concept of the soul remains unverifiable by normal experimental method, which is based on the limitations of material existence itself, but it is a useful concept insofar as it relates to individual subjective experience, which is often more relevant to ethical goals than laboratory experiments.

For many individuals, the conviction that there is a soul which is independent of (although shaped by) the physical body occurs in **out-of-the-body** traveling **(astral projection).** The experience of being a conscious entity outside one's physical body is an overwhelming one, and has had the impact of religious experience to many individuals. (See also **Astral Projection; Reincarnation; Spirit; Survival; Out-of-the-Body**)

Recommended reading:

Bernard, Theos. *The Philosophical Foundations of India, Rider & Co., 1945*

Broad, C. D. *The Mind and Its Place in Nature,* Kegan Paul, London, 1925

Carrington, Hereward. *Psychic Science and Survival,* Two Worlds Publishing Co., Manchester, U.K./American Psychical Institute, New York, 1939

Carus, Paul. *The Soul of Man,* Open Court, Chicago, 1900

Crookall, Robert. *The Supreme Adventure,* James Clarke & Co., London, 1961; 1975

Crookall, Robert. *Out-of-the-Body Experiences and Survival,* World Fellowship Press, U.K., 1970

Ducasse, C. J. *A Critical Examination of the Belief in a Life After Death,* Charles C. Thomas, Springfield, Illinois, 1961

James, William. *The Varieties of Religious Experience,* Longmans, Green, London, 1903; University Books, 1963

Head, Joseph & S. L. Cranston. *Reincarnation; The Phoenix Fire Mystery,* Julian Press/Crown Publishers, 1977

Myers, F. W. H. *Human Personality and Its Survival of Bodily Death,* 2 vols., Longmans, Green, London, 1903

Purohit Swami, Shri. *The Geeta; The Gospel of the Lord Shri Krishna,* Faber & Faber, London, 1935

Soul Travel

Also known as **ECKANKAR,** a religious organization developed by Sri Paul **Twitchell.** Basically it is his own variety of astral projection (**Out-of-the-Body** travel) to other planes in a framework of Hindu and Sikh mysticism.

Soule, Mrs. Minnie Meserve (died 1936)

Trance medium of the **American Society for Psychical Research,** known in early experiments under the pseudonym "Mrs. Chenoweth."

For many years Prof. J. H. **Hyslop** made interesting tests in cases of **obsession** with her mediumship. She produced excellent trance phenomena, similar to those of Mrs. Leonore **Piper.** Mrs. Soule was controlled by "Imperator" and "Sunbeam," the spirit of a child.

In the publications of the Boston Society for Psychical Research, an interesting record of seances narrates the experiences of Lydia W. **Allison,** with supplementary material by Dr. W. F. Prince under the title *Leonard and Soule Experiments in Psychical Research* (Boston, 1929) while in an earlier work, *Spirit Messages* (Rochester, 1914), dedicated to the medium, Prof. Hiram Corson of Cornell University recorded unique communications received through Mrs. Soule, apparently from Browning, Mrs. Browning, Lord Tennyson, H. W. Longfellow and many other eminent minds.

Mrs. Soule and her phenomena were included in the study *Beyond Normal Cognition* by John F. Thomas, published by the Boston Society for Psychical Research in 1937, reissued by University Microfilms, Ann Arbor, Michigan.

Sounds (in Psychical Research)

Sounds produced in the seance room fall into two main categories: ordinary and psychic. In the first category belong all the natural sounds emitted by the manipulation of certain objects without any visible agency. In the second, the sounds that apparently do not relate to any visible object, both the source and the production of which is unknown.

The noises which accompany the movement of objects, such as lifting of table, shaking of bells, tambourines, etc., are ordinary noises. **Raps, direct voice,** direct music, sounds of invisible instruments, machines, rattle of chains, clashing noise of swords, horse galloping, etc., without having the noise-producing object in the room, are psychic.

Another differentiation may be made according to the intelligence required for the sound production. To bang a table or shake a bell, no intellectual effort is necessary. The phonograph requires certain experience, the playing of an instrument artistic education.

The simplest psychic sounds are the **raps.** Their tonal scale and expressive power is surprising and their strength may increase to formidable blows (see **Movement**).

"At one time," wrote Lord Adare in *Experiences in Spiritualism with D. D. Home* (1870), "Miss Wynne, Home and I heard a very singular rumbling and rolling sort of sound in the air behind us, which was repeated three times."

The sounds in the seances of the Rev. W. Stainton **Moses** showed an extraordinary range. The first sound, as distinct from raps, was heard on March 23, 1873 and resembled the plucking of a string in mid-air. It soon imitated a musical clock which was in the next room.

Two months later, the sound became so loud that the vibration of the table was marked. "The sound would traverse the room and seem to die away in the distance, and suddenly burst forth into great power over the table, which appeared, in some inexplicable way, to be used as a sounding board. The wood of the table vibrated under our hands exactly as it would have done had a violincello been twanged while resting upon it. . . . The sounds were at times deafening and alternated between those made by the very small strings of a harp and such as would be caused by the violent thrumming of a violincello resting on the top of a drum. . . . With them, as with other phenomena, a great variety was caused by good or bad conditions. Just as illness or atmospheric disturbance made the perfumes and drapery coarse and unrefined, so the lyre sounds became harsh, unmusical and wooden. . . . The table was used until at times the musical twang would shade into a sort of musical knock, and finally become an ordinary dull thud upon the table. . . . When things were not all right, the sound would assume a most melancholy wailing character, which was indescribably weird and saddening. It was not unlike the soughing of the wind through trees in the dead of night; a ghost-like dreary sound that few persons would sit long to listen to. That sound was always accompanied by black darkness in the room. . . . No point, indeed, connected with these strange sounds is more remarkable than the intensity of feeling conveyed by them. . . . Anger, sadness, content and mirth, solemnity and eagerness, are conveyed in a way that is quite inexplicable. . . . The wailing sounds above noticed seem at times almost to sob and shriek as if in a burst of sadness. Sometimes to a question put silence will be maintained for a while, and then little hesitating sounds will be made, very slowly and tremulously, as to convey perfectly the idea of uncertainty and doubt. Then again the reply will come clear, sonorous, and immediate as the 'I do' of a witness in the box who has no doubt as to the answer he should give.

"The sounds used always to commence near the circle, and, so to say, radiate from it as a centre into different parts of the room. Of late they have changed, and are usually audible to me before they strike the ear of any other person. How far this may be attributable to clairaudience, a faculty lately developed in me, I cannot say positively. But at any rate, they seem to me to commence by a distant rumble, not unlike the roll of a drum. This gradually draws nearer until it is audible to all, and the old sounds are in our midst.

"Hitherto I only mentioned the stringed musical sounds. . . . But there are other sounds which professedly emanate from the same source and which resemble the sound of a tambourine played over our heads, or, at times, the flapping of a pair of large wings. . . . Still later other sounds, like those made by a small zither, have presented themselves."

Charlton Speer, in an account given to F. W. H. **Myers** described four kinds of musical sounds produced without any instrument in the room. The first was called "fairy bells." These resembled the tones produced by striking musical glasses with a small hammer. No definite tune was ever played, but the bells, on request, would always run up and down a scale in perfect tune. It was difficult to judge where the sounds came from but when Speer applied his ear to the top of the table it seemed to be somehow in the wood. The second was a stringed instrument, akin to a violincello but more powerful and sonorous. It was only heard in single notes and was employed to answer questions. The third sound was an exact imitation of an ordinary handbell. It denoted the presence of a particular spirit. The fourth sound could best be described by imagining the soft tone of a clarionet gradually increasing in intensity, until it rivaled the sound of a trumpet, then by degrees gradually diminishing to the original subdued tone of the clarionet, until it eventually died away in a long drawn-out melancholy wail. In no case were more than single notes, or at best isolated passages produced. The controlling agencies accounted for this with the peculiarly unmusical organization of the medium.

Various sounds were used by some of the **controls** as a special mark of identity. "Grocyn" produced pure sounds like those of a thick harp string, "Chom" made the sound of an old Egyptian harp with four strings. "Said" used a three stringed lyre, "Roophal" a seven-stringed one with a rippling sound, "Kabbila's" sound was like a drum, very deep, a sort of prolonged roll.

It is said in mediumistic communications that the spirits, in their world, can create for themselves from fluidic material the things they wish. It seems that they can produce the sound of anything thus manufactured, although we do not know how.

But in Mrs. Gwendolyn K. Hack's *Modern Psychic Mysteries at Millesimo Castle* (1929), there is the interesting note that the spirit of the young aviator Vittorio Centurione always arrived and departed in his airplane. The coming of the airplane was heard from a distance, it descended into the seance room with the characteristic noise, flew above as if there was no limit of space and finally stopped. On the first occasion when he manifested, the approach of the plane was followed by the sound of falling, hissing and splashing into the water illustrating the very manner by which this aviator perished over Lake Varese.

Dancing performances and duels were executed for the sitters' entertainment at the seances at Millesimo Castle. In the notes of the seance August 12, 1928, we find: "D'Angelo: 'Here, in the midst of you, a little battle between two Romans is going to take place' . . . we heard the sound of two swords hastily withdrawn from their scabbards. They were crossed and glanced off each other in a sinister manner. Then we heard the most formidable blows, given first by one side and then by the other. These blows rained upon metal, echoing upon the shields and helmets of the warriors. We heard rapid footsteps pounding the floor as the combatants fought, now advancing, now retreating. It was quite alarming, and one could not avoid cowering instinctively, when a powerful thrust came too close, for one felt that the next blow might glance off and strike one's head or neck."

Will Goldston wrote an account of a seance with Rudi **Schneider** in the *Sunday Graphic* (December 22, 1929): "Several heavy thuds followed, as though a giant were striking a block of marble with a mallet. The extraordinary thing was that the thuds did not seem to come from the walls, the ceiling or the floor, but from the table. They were powerful thuds, and yet they did not cause any vibration in the room, as such thuds caused by normal means would create." (See also **Music; Raps**)

Southcott, Joanna (1750-1814)

Charismatic British prophetess of the eighteenth and nineteenth centuries who announced that she had a divine pregnancy, but failed to fulfill the event. Although often denounced as a charlatan, it seems clear that she was genuinely misled by Spiritualistic "voices" and **automatic writing.** In spite of her deathbed recantation, she still has followers even today.

She was born in April 1750, one of the daughters of a farmer in the village of Gittisham, East Devon, England. She grew up in a devout religious atmosphere, being obliged to read a chapter of the Bible daily and discuss it with her father. She became a sturdy, self-reliant young woman, pretty, vivacious, and attractive to men.

When she was twenty-one, her father suffered from ill health and she was obliged to take charge of the farm, which she managed admirably for a couple of years until her father recovered. Joanna left the farm and went into domestic service for five years at the house of an upholsterer in Exeter, where she also became skilled in the trade.

Her master, Mr. Wills, was a Methodist, but his wife was incorrigibly unfaithful, having affairs with many men. Joanna was pained by this behavior and considered leaving, but thought that her presence might be a good influence. To her horror, after two years Wills himself confessed that he was in love with her. She threatened to leave unless Wills gave up the idea of sinful love.

For a time, Mrs. Wills mended her ways, but slipped back into adultery with a Methodist preacher named Saunderson, who had been expelled from the movement. Saunderson lodged at the Wills house, and when Joanna saw that she could not change the behavior of Mrs. Wills, she left and went to stay with her brother, and wrote long letters of rebuke to Mrs. Wills.

Saunderson was a strange fanatical character, who terrified people by stories of his miracles wrought by prayer, and who had successfully prayed for the death of a man who had reproved him. It is possible that Saunderson's presence had infected Joanna in a negative way, sowing the seeds of later religious delusions. Meanwhile, Joanna had become a daily maid with a couple named Taylor.

For forty-two years Joanna had lived a normal life, but in 1792, at the time of her menopause, she began to have strange experiences.

These were apocalyptic times. In France, revolutionary mobs had stormed the king's palace, and the houses of noblemen were in flames. Radical propagandists sought to forment revolution in Britain. Tom Paine's *The Rights of Man* had just been published. In the wake of the revivalism of John Wesley, extreme fanatical religious movements were springing up.

A young naval officer named Richard Brothers had become immersed in Bible study and preached powerful sermons on his apocalyptic visions, with warnings of the Day of Doom. He believed that the time had come for the Jews to regain Palestine, that the British were the lost tribe of Israel, that the Second Coming of the Lord was at hand. Brothers was eventually arrested and charged with "maliciously publishing fantastical prophecies with intent to cause disturbances," certified as insane, and sent to a mental asylum, where he stayed for eleven years.

Joanna began to have similar apocalyptic dreams and visions. She was visited by a "Voice" which told her: "The Lord is awakened out of sleep. He will terribly shake the earth." At first, Joanna thought she was being deluded by Satan, but the Voice began to make amazingly accurate prophecies about events, both great and small.

Asked for a sign, the Voice knocked three times on the bedstead—an early precursor of the rappings at nineteenth-century Spiritualist seances (see **Raps**). Then she suddenly found her hand writing messages without conscious guidance. As she stated: "The writing comes extremely fast, much faster than I could keep up by voluntary effort. I have to turn over the pages and guard the lines of writing from running into each other; but, except for this, I need not look at the paper. I can talk on other subjects while writing. The mass of the writings consists in teachings on Religion. Some messages, however, deal with earthly matters." Many of the writings were in simple verse form.

When her prophecies on domestic affairs began to be vindicated, Joanna began to be confident that the Voice was a true guide, and she attempted to interest religious authorities in her messages. A Methodist preacher listened to her, then pronounced "This is from Satan to disturb your peace." She approached the Dissenters, but their minister stated that her revelations were unscriptural. She now turned to the Established Church, and wrote to a preacher named Joseph Pomeroy, vicar of St. Kew in Cornwall, who had himself warned of perilous times to come.

Pomeroy received Joanna in a kindly fashion and said he saw nothing diabolical in the messages, but he told Joanna's mistress, Mrs. Taylor, "She will be out of her mind soon." On a subsequent visit, Joanna spoke to Pomeroy of impending events of an apocalyptical nature, and he said "You have advanced things that make me shudder. It is bordering on blasphemy." At a loss to refute Joanna's sincerity, he suggested that she have her writings examined by a jury of clergymen.

Thereupon Joanna sent Pomeroy a number of prophecies that were fulfilled. She predicted that the Bishop of Exeter, then in good health, would not live till Christmas of that year. He died on December 12. In 1796, Lord Malmesbury went on a peace mission to Paris. Joanna foretold that it would fail, and so it did. At that time it would have seemed unreasonable to believe that the French revolutionary armies would conquer Italy, as predicted by Joanna, but young Bonaparte's success brought this to pass.

Joanna was sincerely convinced that her messages were from God, in accordance with the texts in *Deuteronomy* (xviii, 22): "When a Prophet speaketh in the Name of the Lord, if the thing follow not, nor come to pass, that is the thing which the Lord hath not spoken, but the Prophet hath spoken it presumptiously; thou shalt not be afraid of him" and (18): "I will raise them up a Prophet from among their brethren, like unto thee, and will put my words in his mouth, and he shall speak unto them all that I shall command him."

In 1797, Joanna left the service of the Taylors, and worked for several Exeter tradesmen in upholstering. She was a good worker and her income helped to support her father, who was ill. She also saved some money for her eventual retirement.

All this time her messages continued. These were the last times of the Second Coming. Joanna introduced an early feminist view into her messages, claiming that when the time was right, God used a woman to fulfill divine purpose. She stated: "Is it a new thing for a woman to deliver her people? Did not Esther do it? And Judith? Was it not a woman that nailed Sisera to the ground?" She became convinced that she herself was the destined "woman clothed with the sun" and "the Bride of the Lamb" cited in *Revelations* (xii, 19). In 1794, her Voice had stated: "Now I'll tell thee who thou art, The true and faithful Bride."

She alarmed the kindly Mr. Pomeroy with what seemed to him a blasphemous claim, as well as with more prophecies. She demanded that her messages be considered by a panel of clergymen. She wrote to the Bishop, the Archdeacon and the Chancellor urging them to visit Mr. Pomeroy and test her teaching.

On January 5, 1801 she wrote again to five clergymen, and decided that if they did not prove within seven days that the messages were not divine revelations, they would go no further. After a week she heard nothing, so she took her messages to an Exeter printer, paying him £100 she had saved for her old age.

In February that year, *The Strange Effects of Faith* appeared as a 48-page nine-penny pamphlet, describing how the messages had come to Joanna and how she had sought to get clerical recognition of them. The following month she published a *Second Part.* By now, her life savings were exhausted, so she borrowed from a moneylender to sponsor publication of further parts.

The Rev. T. P. Foley, Fellow of Jesus College, Cambridge, an intelligent educated man and a former follower of the unfortunate fanatic Richard Brothers, saw these modest pamphlets and was immediately impressed with them. He consulted other friends, including the engraver William Sharp (who had also been a follower of Brothers) and they attempted to interest clergymen in forming a jury to consider Joanna's writings.

Afterwards, many of the prophecies and other papers were put in a box fastened with cords and sealed with seven seals. Sharp had charge of this. It was later to become a central point in controversies over Joanna's writings.

When some of Joanna's followers printed her letters, Pomeroy was alarmed to find his name frequently quoted, and in a weak moment threw her papers on the fire. Almost immediately he had a letter from Joanna demanding their return, and thereafter his life was made miserable by scores of letters from Joanna and her followers, denouncing him as a second Johoiakim who burnt the roll of the prophet, and threatening him with divine and diabolical justice.

As Joanna's followers increased, she devised a strange sign of her mission, indicating that true believers endorsed the reclaiming of the world from the Devil. This was her famous "seal."

Years earlier, when working in the shop of Mr. and Mrs. Taylor, she had found a seal with the initials "I. C." and two stars. One day she formed the idea that this was the initials of Jesus Christ ("I" and "J" were then interchangeable as initials), and marked her prophecies with this seal. Now the idea came to her that this also indicated the sealing of people as well as writings, as cited in the Apocalypse: "Hurt not the earth till we have sealed the servants of our God."

She had been given a present of a ream of paper, and she cut this into squares and marked a circle on each square, writing inside: "The Seal of the Lord, the Elect and Precious, Man's Redemption to Inherit the Tree of Life, to be made Heirs of God and Joint Heirs with Jesus Christ." Believers received one of these squares after signing it, and it was folded up like an envelope and marked with the "I. C." seal.

Within a year she had issued several thousand of these "seals." Unfortunately she was accused of selling them and making a rich income out of it, although the seals were actually freely issued by her without any charge. It is possible that middlemen asked money for them, since many people regarded them as lucky charms or passports to heaven.

From time to time, Joanna was genuinely tortured by doubts as to whether her inner voice was a delusion of Satan, and toyed with the idea of giving up her mission and going back to the trade of upholstery. Some of her prophecies had failed. After one depressed period, she published her doubts in a pamphlet titled "A Dispute between the Woman and the Powers of Darkness." It was an honest work by a sincere woman, caught up in a strange mission which she had never sought.

But after eighteen months, with followers in London and the provinces, her mission grew rapidly, and presently she enrolled over eight thousand disciples. She continued to demand that the Bishops examine her claims and prophecies and agreed to abide by their decision, but the Church dignitaries were unwilling to become involved. Two alternative trials had vindicated Joanna, but these had been organized by believers and the affirmation that the prophecies and other writings were of a divine origin was a foregone conclusion.

Her mission continued to grow, in spite of various unfortunate setbacks. One of these was the case of the infamous Mary Bateman, thief and abortionist, who had obtained a seal from Joanna and claimed that her hens were laying eggs with an inscription announcing the coming of Christ. Mary Bateman was executed for the murder of Rebecca Perigo, whom she had unmercifully fleeced for years, selling her charms against evil. For a time this scandalous episode of one of the "sealed followers" caused much embarrassment to the movement.

But Joanna's writings sold well, and many people who had followed the unhappy Richard Brothers now came to join Joanna's mission. In 1812, a legacy from a disciple gave her financial independence. During 1813, her ecstacies increased and she felt surrounded by angels.

She was now 64 years old when her Voice commanded: "Order twelve gowns for thy wedding." She was greatly disconcerted by this, as she had no desire for matrimony, but in early 1814, the Voice stated: "This year in the sixty-fifth year of thy age thou shalt bear a son by the power of the Most High." Back in 1794, she had already declared her conviction that she was the "Bride of the Lamb," but now the full significance of this dawned on her. The Virgin Mary had born a divine son. Joanna's child would have a divine destiny. In *Genesis* (xl, 10) Jacob says that the scepter should not depart from Judah "until Shiloh come." However, it is now widely believed that the Authorized Version of the Bible mistranslated "Shiloh" as a person instead of a town in central Palestine.

This passage has confused many religious sects. Richard Brothers had declared "I am Shiloh," but Joanna believed that this was a misunderstanding and that Shiloh was to arise in the Last Days. In March 1814, she declared her belief that Shiloh was her unborn child. By now she showed every sign of pregnancy, and astonishingly enough this was confirmed by a leading surgeon and no less than twenty other medical practitioners.

The followers received the news of the divine Virgin birth with great joy, and gifts flowed in. A satinwood cradle for the baby was prepared at a cost of £200. A superbly bound Bible was presented, and dozens of christening mugs and pap-spoons. Joanna now recalled her message to Mr. Pomeroy that she was the Bride mentioned in scripture. She concluded that she must make an earthly marriage so that Shiloh had a foster father, as with Joseph and the child Jesus. Accordingly on November 12, she was married in her bedroom to John Smith, steward of the Earl of Darnley.

Joanna expected the divine birth in July, but as late as September nothing had happened. During November, painful doubts began to manifest in Joanna's mind, and once again she began to feel that her Voice had misled her. She called her close friends to her bedside and confessed despairingly, "Now it all appears delusion." She grew weaker and by December 16 the symptoms of pregnancy had vanished. She told her doctor she was gradually dying, and requested that after presumed death her body be kept warm for four days, in case she was only in a trance. She died early in the morning of December 27.

After the four days had elapsed, her own doctor and fourteen other medical practitioners examined the body and found no organic disease beyond a condition of dropsy, which may have enhanced the false pregnancy. It is possible that Joanna suffered a deep depression and no longer wished to live after her final disillusionment on her divine mission.

Just before her death, she had made a will in which she sadly claimed that she had been deceived by the Devil, directing that all the gifts intended for the coming Shiloh should be returned to their donors.

She was buried in Marylebone cemetery, London, on January 2, 1815, and her tombstone, evidently supplied by a believer, predicted great wonders yet to come, but inaccurately stated her age as 60 instead of 64. The tombstone was shattered in a gunpowder explosion at Regent's Park in 1874.

The Successors of Joanna Southcott

Her death and recantation left her thousands of followers in great confusion. A large number refused to believe that her mission had been a delusion. Others formed splinter sects. Amongst these was a group led by George Turner, Herald of Shiloh, who claimed to be Joanna's successor. He explained that Shiloh had been taken from Joanna's womb into Paradise until the appointed time.

His demented "Proclamation of the Final Days" was to be delivered in Palace Yard, London, denouncing "the Treasury, Horse Guards, Carlton House, the Playhouses, Churches and Chapels, the Tower, Somerset House, and other public places. The Angel of the Lord shall sink all by earthquake." His radical manifesto dictated: "The whole United Kingdom is to be divided to the People on the Roll. Those who are not worth a penny now must be lords of the land. No rents must be paid. No postage for letters. No turnpikes. No taxes. Porter a gallon for one halfpenny. Ale the same. The dead must be carried in carts three miles from the city and put into deep pits covered with pigs' flesh."

Confined to a benevolent Quaker asylum for the insane, Turner continued with fantastic directions for his faithful followers. Shiloh's palace must have walls of pure gold adorned with precious stones. "There must be in attendance 70,000 men that play musical instruments and 70,000 singing women. He must have 500,000 servants, and his carriages must be of pure gold." Turner himself was to have 300,000 servants and similar accommodation to that of Shiloh.

In 1820, Turner was declared cured of insanity, and his followers petitioned the Lord Chancellor for his release, granted a few months later. After an extravagant "Marriage Supper," Turner promised that Shiloh would appear in London on October 14, being born as a boy already six years old. When the date passed uneventfully, the faithful took it as merely a divine test of their love. Turner's own "Voice" ordered him to marry, so that Shiloh might have a foster-mother. Accordingly Turner chose a whore as wife, and a new date of April 10, 1821 was pronounced for the birth of Shiloh. When nothing happened, some followers were disillusioned; others followed new fanatics.

Visions came to a woolcomber named John Wroe, another member of the Southcott sect, who came into prominence when he challenged Turner's original prophecy of October 14, 1820 for the birth of Shiloh as a lie. Wroe now took over Turner's sect and his followers proclaimed themselves Christian Israelites.

Wroe dictated new laws for the Final Days. Males must be circumcised, and everyone must eat only kosher meat. Men had to wear dark broad-brimmed hats and special clothing; even the sober dress for women was stipulated in great detail. Men were also to give up shaving and wear beards. Everyone had to give up snuff, tobacco, and spirits. Those who transgressed these laws were severely beaten.

One child died after circumcision and the man performing the operation was charged with manslaughter. He was acquitted after the genuine Jewish committee of the day pressurized the Government, fearing that their own legitimate rite would be prohibited.

Eventually the movement renounced Wroe after persistent debaucheries on his part, but he emigrated to America and Australia, where his mission continued to have followers. In his old age, he became fraudulent and cheated his followers of money, dying in Australia in 1863.

Meanwhile another large group of Southcott believers had followed John Ward, a pauper Irish shoemaker. He had been a disciple of George Turner before his faith in Joanna Southcott was shaken by reading an attack on the New Testament account of Christ by the freethinker Richard Carlile. Eventually he concluded that the scriptures were not history but prophecies, foretelling future events, that the accounts of the birth of Jesus were allegorical. He had visions of Joanna who told him "Thou art Shiloh."

He decided that he himself was the Jesus foretold in the Gospels, since he had been born on Christmas Day and his mother's name was Mary. Even more fantastic was Ward's belief that he was Satan before becoming Christ, and that the Devil was now the Son of God. All the Scriptures indicated himself in a multiplicity of roles. He was Adam, Judah, and Elijah. He claimed "There is no name in Scripture which I may not with propriety apply to myself." Because of the many texts using the name Zion, he chose this for general use, becoming "Zion Ward."

Ward escaped from the workhouse where he had been confined and talked followers into supporting his mission, publishing literature and handbills. He roamed the country preaching a strange mixture of Messianism and Radicalism, attacking landlords, the Government and the established Church. He was a remarkable orator and obtained considerable support for his mission. Eventually his health broke down, and he died of a stroke on March 12, 1837. Faithful followers continued to support him long after his death, and as late as 1921, one supporter published his book *The Shilohites' Bible.* By then, there was no public mission, and a handful of the faithful simply read his books and meditated on his message.

In 1875, the Southcott followers were given a new direction by another prophet, a soldier named James White, whose friends called him "The Stranger." Like Joanna, he was inspired by a mysterious Voice that ordered him to regroup the faithful. He adopted the name "James Jershom Jezreel." "Jershom" was a misspelling of "Gershom," the name of the first child of Moses, "for I have been a stranger in a strange land." "Jezreel" came from *Hosea:* "Then shall the Children of Israel and the children of Judah be gathered together and appoint themselves one Head, for great shall be the day of Jezreel."

White published a book titled *The Flying Roll* (deriving from the book of *Zechariah*) in which he stated his new creed. In *Revelations,* seven angels are given seven trumpets to sound before the Day of Doom. These angels were seven prophets. The first five were Brothers, Joanna, Turner, Shaw (another Southcott successor), and Wroe. White was the sixth angel. One more prophet would arise, then Shiloh would come.

Although Jezreel's mission endorsed the British-Israel theory, he did not require circumcision of Gentiles as John Wroe had done, but the Jezreelites were required to wear long hair looped at the back and pushed under a violet colored cap.

One of Jezreel's important converts was a girl of fifteen named Clarissa Rogers. She too heard a mystical Voice which called on her to preach in America. Her beauty and eloquence converted many Americans, some of whom returned with her to Gillingham, Kent, where Jezreel was now established. The prophet himself married her, and they both toured America in 1880 with six wagons, a large tent and a hundred benches.

They collected enough financial support to enable them to buy a twenty-acre site in Gillingham, where they built a housing estate for their followers, with shops and bakeries so that they could follow a trade.

They ran a successful delivery service in Gillingham and Chatham with their carts selling bread, meat, greengroceries and other provisions. The Jezreel estate also had an International College for boys and girls, with special emphasis on harp-playing and study in Jezreel's writings.

In 1884, after a successful tour in Australia, Jezreel returned with plans for an ambitious Jezreel Temple, cubic in shape, a hundred feet high, a hundred feet wide, and a hundred feet long. It was to house printing presses for Jezreel's message, offices for the trading concerts, and an assembly hall with accommodation for six thousand people. It was to last for a thousand years, and the walls were reinforced with steel girders and cement used instead of mortar. After six months' building, Jezreel died in March 1885.

His wife, who had now adopted the name Esther, continued to develop the movement in a most efficient way, opening Jezreel chapels in many areas and employing hawkers to carry the movement's literature all over the country. There were Jezreel followers in America, Australia, and New Zealand. Esther was accepted as the sixth angel with a trumpet, to be followed by Shiloh. She died in 1888, only three years after her husband. The great Temple remained unfinished.

There were now quarrels and schisms in the movement. One branch followed Michael Keyfor Mills, who organized a Jezreel community in Detroit, Michigan, but it soon broke up. In 1903, Benjamin Purnell, who had been expelled from the Detroit community, founded his own colony, The House of David, in Benton Harbor, Lake Michigan. Things went well for several years, and their orchestra and baseball team became famous.

In 1922, when the community had 900 colonists, Purnell was arrested on a rape charge. The community's affairs were plunged into confusion, and members filed for return of their property and payment for their services. The colony was disbanded. Meanwhile Purnell had escaped and fled to Australia, where he was discovered four years later and brought to trial, but died of tuberculosis a few weeks later. An Australian branch of the House of David continued.

The Panacea Society

The final phase of the Southcott movement commenced in 1907, with four ladies who became skillful propagandists for the movement. They were Alice Seymour, who edited editions of Joanna's books, Rachel Fox, a Quakeress, and her friend Helen Exeter, who received Spiritualistic messages about Joanna's sealed box, and Mabel Barltrop, widow of an Anglican curate, who was a godchild of the poet Coventry Patmore.

Mable Barltrop pestered innumerable clergymen and bishops, demanding that they open Joanna Southcott's box. She joined forces with Mrs. Exeter, whose spirit messages through automatic writing informed her that she would be the mother of Shiloh. Helen Exeter now adopted the name Octavia. She was to be the eighth prophet.

She established a settlement at Bedford, and many supporters of the emerging Suffragette movement joined her. Octavia successfully resolved the problem of the Biblical account of the creation of Adam in 4004 B.C., in spite of scientific evidence of life 200,000 years earlier. Octavia explained that there were two races in ancient times—the Adamic race, who had souls, and anthropoids, who were descendants of apemen and did not have souls. Octavia continued to badger the bishops to open Joanna's box and study the writings and prophecies it contained. For twenty years she propagandized with handbills, posters, and petitions.

In 1918, the Bishop of Lambeth stated that he had the consent of twenty-four bishops to receive the box and open it on March 7 or 8. But Octavia's followers were not satisfied unless all the bishops were prepared to spend a whole week studying the contents. Not surprisingly, Bishop Carpenter could not agree, and the matter was dropped. It was the nearest the famous box ever came to be officially examined as Joanna Southcott had always desired.

By now Octavia was declared the Shiloh by her followers. Shiloh had spent fifty years in heaven then returned to earth on the birth of Octavia. By 1920, Octavia had a team of thirty-six residents at Bedford and a large following through Britain, Australia, and America.

In 1923, the movement took a new direction. One night Octavia tried to swallow a pill, but it slipped away and rolled under a cupboard. Accordingly she took the glass of water and prayed that it would serve the purpose of the pill. When it did, her Voice proclaimed that she had been given a healing power.

Thereafter the community prepared small linen squares "with the breath of prayer." These were to be dipped in water, which was to be drunk or poured on to wounds. The community now adopted the name "The Panacea Society," convinced that they had a universal remedy for all ills. It was enormously successful.

Octavia herself died in 1934, notwithstanding the universal remedy, but her movement continued into modern times. Nowadays the medical remedy is no longer fashionable and might anyway run into grave difficulties with official bodies like the F.D.A., but the panacea of opening the famous box continues. It has become as much a part of popular folklore as the earlier box of Pandora. For decades, quaint notices have continued to appear in British newspapers, stating: "War, disease, crime and banditry will increase until the Bishops open Joanna Southcott's box."

In 1927, an attempt to resolve this persistent problem was undertaken by the British psychical researcher Harry **Price,** who had a great flair for publicity.

The Opening of the Southcott Box

On April 28, 1927, Harry Price arrived at his **National Laboratory of Psychical Research** to be greeted by his secretary with the news "Joanna Southcott's box has arrived!"

According to Price, it had been sent by the employer of two servants who were descendants of Mrs.

Rebecca Morgan (née Pengarth), said to have been the sole companion of Joanna Southcott between 1798 and 1814. The covering letter stated that the Morgans had become custodians of Southcott's box, which had been earlier entrusted to Rebecca, and it was now felt that the National Laboratory of Psychical Research should arrange for a formal opening of the box, since the writer was now moving to the U.S.

This account has been challenged by Trevor H. **Hall** in his book *Search for Harry Price* (1978), who suggested the letter was a forgery by Price in order to obtain publicity for the Southcott Box. It is certainly true that there is no mention of Rebecca Pengarth as a companion to Joanna in histories of the movement, although the box itself appeared to be a genuine Southcott relic, however Price came into possession of it.

It was a strongly-built casket of walnut, stained with age, with a heavy lid with a mother-of-pearl plate bearing the engraved initials "I. S." (i.e. J. S.). The casket was secured by two rusty steel bands, and by strong silk tapes, secured in five places with large black seals bearing a profile of George III.

Price invited eight psychics, a psychologist, and a dowser to inspect the box and give their impressions of its contents. In the event, most of the psychometric impressions proved reasonably accurate.

A few hours later, Price X-rayed the box in his laboratory, and identified the following objects: an old horse pistol (c.1814), a dice box, a fob purse with coins in it, a bone puzzle with rings, some blocks (one with metal clasps), a framed painting or miniature, a pair of earrings, a cameo or engraved pebble.

Price secured much publicity for the box, and sensational stories were published that it might contain a boobytrap bomb intended to kill the bishops! Price wrote to three archbishops and eighty bishops stating his intention to make a formal opening of the box, and asking if they would consent to be present, to honor the wishes of the dead Joanna, and perhaps to end a persistent superstition.

Some replies were noncommittal. The Bishop of Derby hoped that Price could get a quorum for the opening, in order "to lay to rest the Joanna Southcott legend." The Bishop of Lincoln strongly advised opening the box "with or without the presence of bishops." The Bishop of Liverpool wrote: "I join you in hoping that the Southcott myth will be exploded." In contrast, the Bishop of Kensington was unsympathetic, saying that he did not wish to be a party to providing amusement for a public who would like nothing better than to see a company of bishops the victims of a hoax, even if it had been arranged 100 years earlier.

However, the Bishop of Chichester wrote that he would be glad if the Southcott myth could be exploded and would be willing to be present, if in London at the time. The bishop of London replied that he would try to be present. The Bishop of Carlisle replied that he would be present if the Archbishop of Canterbury "should be satisfied as to the propriety of bishops being present at the opening of the box."

The Archbishop of Canterbury replied that his correspondence over Joanna Southcott's box was voluminous and extended over many years. He was not sympathetic to the idea, "partly profane and partly comic," that twenty-four bishops representing the twenty-four elders in *Revelations* should sit around the box. He approved of the box being opened speedily, but thought that immediately it was opened, a rival box would at once be found. Other bishops expressed interest in being present if in London, or if given permission by the Archbishop of Canterbury.

The opening of the box took place before a large audience at the Hoare Memorial Hall, Church House, Westminster, London, on July 11, 1927. In the event, only the Bishop of Grantham turned up, but the Bishop of Crediton was represented by his son, the Rev. Trefusis.

As already mentioned, the psychometric impressions given by the psychics contained many accurate statements. Not surprisingly, the X-rays of the solid objects were also correct. Amongst the fifty-six objects in the box, the pamphlets and books included: *The Surprises of Love, Exemplified in the Romance of a Day . . .* (1765) with annotations, *Rider's British Merlin* (1715), *Calendier de la Cour* (Paris, 1773), Ovid's *Metamorphoses* (1794). There was a paper souvenir "printed on the River Thames, Feb. 3rd, 1814," and a lottery ticket for 1796. Amongst the objects, the fob purse (containing silver and copper coins and tokens), a horse pistol, a miniature case, an ivory dice-cup, a bone puzzle, a woman's embroidered night cap, and a set of brass money weights.

Naturally the loyal Southcottians did not accept that these pathetic souvenirs were the contents of the right box, and the appeals to bishops to attend the opening of the true box continued, although it was by no means clear where this box might be. Certainly one would have expected the real Southcott box to contain voluminous prophecies, correspondence, and religious pamphlets.

The incredible story of Joanna Southcott and her prophecies has continued over nearly two centuries and is still not wholly extinct. It has given rise to eccentric sects and extravagant claims. Yet it is clear that Joanna herself was an honest, sincere peasant woman, genuinely misled by paranormal communications. She herself often doubted whether her "Voice" was a divine guide, but many of her prophecies proved amazingly correct, giving her confidence that she had a true religious mission until the anguished doubts and eventual disillusionment at the end of her troubled life.

Joan of Arc also heard such a spiritual Voice, which guided her to messages from her favorite saints, Margaret and Catherine, and a mission to liberate France. Many mystics like St. Theresa of Avila and St. John of the Cross have been similarly inspired by divine voices. The ancient Greek philosopher Socrates was guided by his inner Voice.

Spiritualists themselves have insisted that spirit communications cannot be taken at face value, however impressive, but must be tested carefully over a period of time, even if they give amazingly accurate predictions or effect paranormal phenomena. Credulous belief in messages through a **planchette** or **ouija board** can be harmful to sanity. The tragic story of Joanna Southcott illustrates vividly the danger of paranormal communications, especially when associated with simplistic fundamentalist interpretations of the Authorized Edition of the Bible. The phenomenon of **automatic writing** is remarkable, but often deceptive rather than veridical.

The literature of Joanna Southcott is voluminous. She herself published some sixty-five books or pamphlets, while her followers and schismatics added a flood of additional turgid communications. Some useful works bearing on the Southcott story are listed below.

Recommended reading:

Balleine, G. R. *Past Finding Out; The Tragic Story of Joanna Southcott and Her Successors,* S.P.C.K., London, 1956

Lane, C. *Life and Bibliography of Joanna Southcott,* London, 1912

Octavia. *Healing for All; The "Joanna Southcott Healing," Panacea Society, London, 1925*

Panacea Society. *Transactions of the Panacea Society with the Archbishops and Bishops of the Church of England with Reference to Joanna Southcott,* Panacea Society, London, 1935

Pullen, Philip. *Index to the Divine and Spiritual Writings of Joanna Southcott,* The Clock House Press, Ashford, Middlesex, U.K., 1921

Reece, Richard. *A Correct Statement of the Circumstances that Attended the Last Illness and Death of Mrs. Southcott,* London, 1815

Southcott, J. *The Divine Writings of Joanna Southcott,* 2 vols., Bolton, U.K., 1931

Southcott, J. *The Book of Wonders, Marvellous and True,* 5 parts, London, 1813-14

Southcott, J. *The Strange Effects of Faith; with Remarkable Prophecies,* 2 parts, Exeter, 1801-02; with three "*Continuations,*" 1802-03

Southcott, J. *Prophecies. A Warning to the Whole World from the Sealed Prophecies of Joanna Southcott,* 2 parts, London, 1803

Xenes. *Joanna Southcott and Her Box,* W. Foulsham & Co., London, 1927

Southern California Society for Psychical Research, Inc.

Founded by the late Marjorie D. Kern in Beverly Hills, California, to promote scientific psychical research and transmit reliable information to the public.

The Society stems from the **American Society for Psychical Research,** founded in 1885 in New York, with which it is affiliated. There is a scientific advisory committee, and many members are physicians, psychiatrists, physicists, psychologists and social workers, although membership is open to the general public.

The Society maintains a library at the Beverly Hills office and issues a monthly newsletter. There are also lectures, study groups and demonstrations on various psychic subjects.

The name of the Society changed to: Society for Psychic Research at 170 S. Beverly Drive, Suite 303, Beverly Hills, California 90212, but is apparently no longer operative at that address.

Space and Unexplained Celestial Events Research Society

New name for **Saucer and Unexplained Celestial Events Research Society,** founded in 1954. Current membership is claimed as 6,000, bringing together persons interested in **UFOs.**

The Society sponsors monthly lectures in New York City and speeches to colleges and other institutions throughout the U.S., conducts research, maintains library of several thousand books and periodicals on the UFO phenomenon. It publishes an occasional Newsletter, participates in an annual convention known as the Congress of Scientific Ufologists. Address: P.O. Box D, Jane Lew, West Virginia 26378. (See also **Saucer and Unexplained Celestial Events Research Society**)

Space Intelligence

Term given to alleged extraterrestrial entities, usually claiming to be inhabitants of Mars, Venus or other planets and related to **flying saucers** or **UFOs**. SIs allegedly communicate telepathically to chosen individuals or through Spiritualist mediums.

The most topical SIs at present include the Master Aetherius (communicating through cult leader George **King**), the Nine Principles, Hoova, Spectra and Rhombus 4D (communicating with Andrija **Puharich,** using various methods including mediumship and paranormal tape recordings). (See also George **Adamski; Aetherius Society;** Guy W. **Ballard**)

SPAIN

Witchcraft

From early times, Spain was regarded as the special abode of superstition, and in the Middle Ages as the home of sorcery and magic, probably because of the immense notoriety given to the discoveries of the Moorish alchemists (see **Moors**). The Inquisition quickly took root in the country, and reaped a rich harvest among Jews, Moriscos, and superstitious Christians.

Alfonso de Spina, a Franciscan of Castille, where the Inquisition was not then established, wrote (about the year 1458 or 1460) a work especially directed against heretics and unbelievers, in which he gave a chapter on those articles of popular belief which were derived from the ancient pagan beliefs of the people. Among these, witches, under the name of *Xurguine (jurgina)* or *bruxe,* held a prominent place.

He stated that in his time these offenders abounded in Dauphiny and Gascony, where they assembled in great numbers by night on a wild tableland, carrying candles with them to worship Satan, who appeared in the form of a boar on a certain rock, popularly known by the name Elboch de Biterne, and that many of them had been taken by the Inquisition of Toulouse and burnt.

From that time we find, in Spanish history, the charge of **witchcraft** and **sorcery** not infrequently brought forward under different forms and circumstances, of which several remarkable examples were given by J. A. Llorente in his *History of the Inquisition of Spain* (1826).

The first auto-da-fé against sorcery appears to have been that of Calahorra in 1507, when thirty women charged before the Inquisition as witches, were burnt. In 1527, a great number of women were accused in Navarre of the practice of sorcery, through the information of two girls, one of eleven, the other only of nine years old, who confessed before the royal council of Navarre that they had been received into the sect of the *jurginas,* and promised on condition of being pardoned, to discover all the women who were implicated in these practices.

The moment the attention of the Inquisition was thus drawn to the crime of sorcery, the prevalence of this superstition in the Basque provinces became notorious, and Charles V, rightly judging that it was to be attributed more to the ignorance of the population of those districts than to any other cause, directed that preachers should be sent to instruct them.

The first treatise in the Spanish language on the subject of sorcery was by a Franciscan monk named Martin de Castanaga, printed under approbation of the Bishop of Calahorra in 1529. About this time, the zeal of the Inquisitors of Saragossa was excited by the appearance of many witches who were said to have come from Navarre, and to have been sent by their sect as missionaries to make disciples of the women of Arragon.

This sudden witch persecution in Spain appears to have had an influence on the fate of the witches of Italy. Pope Adrian IV, who was raised to the papal chair in 1522, was a Spanish bishop, and had held the office of Inquisitor-General in Spain.

In the time of Julius II, who ruled the papal world from 1503 to 1513, a sect of witches and sorcerers had been discovered in Lombardy, who were extremely numerous, and had their Sabbats and all the other activities of the Continental witches. The proceedings against them appear to have been hindered by a dispute between the Inquisitors and the ecclesiastical judges who claimed the jurisdiction in such cases. On July 20, 1523, Pope Adrian issued a bull against the crime of sorcery, placing it in the sole jurisdiction of the Inquisitors. This bull perhaps gave the new impulse to the prosecution of witches in Spain.

Of the cases which followed during more than a century, the most remarkable was that of the auto-da-fé at Logrono on the 7th and 8th of November, 1610, which arose in some measure from the visitation of the French Basque province in the preceding year. The valley of Bastan is situated at the foot of the Pyrenees, on the French Frontier, and at no great distance from Labourd. It was within the jurisdiction of the inquisition established at Logrono in Castille. The mass of the population of this valley were said to have been sorcerers, and they held their meetings or Sabbats at a place called Zugarramurdi.

A woman who was condemned implicated a number of other persons. All the persons arrested on this occasion agreed in their description of the Sabbat, and of the practices of the witches, which in their general features bore a close resemblance to those of the witches of Labourd. The usual place of meeting was known here, as in Labourd, by the popular name of Aquelarre, a Gascon word, signifying the meadow of the goat. Their ordinary meetings were held on the nights of Monday, Wednesday and Friday, every week, but they had grand feasts on the principal holidays of the church, such as Easter, Pentecost, Christmas, etc. All these feasts appear to have been fixed by the Christian teachers at the period of older pagan festivals.

The accounts of their claimed Sabbats were similar to those given of such meetings elsewhere. They danced, sang, took part in orgies, and came into personal contact with Satan.

The auto-da-fé of Logrono, as far as it related to the sect of the sorcerers of Zugarramurdi, caused a great sensation, and brought the subject of witchcraft under the consideration of the Spanish theologians. These were so far more enlightened than the body of their contemporaries in other countries, that they generally leant to the opinion that witchcraft was a mere delusion, and that the details of the confessions of the miserable creatures who were its victims were all creations of the imagination.

They were punished because their belief was a heresy, contrary to the doctrines of the church. Llorente gave the abstract of a treatise on this subject by a Spanish ecclesiastic named Pedro de Valentia, addressed to the Grand Inquisitor in consequence of the trial at Logrono in 1610, and which remained in manuscript among the archives of the Inquisition.

This writer adopted entirely the opinion that the acts confessed by the witches were imaginary; he attributed them partly to the methods in which the examinations were carried on, and to the desire of the ignorant people examined to escape by saying what seemed to please their persecutors, and partly to the effects of the ointments and draughts which they had been taught to use, and which were composed of ingredients that produced sleep, and acted upon the imagination and the mental faculties.

It is strange to reflect that although the heresy-hunting of the Spanish Inquisition resulted in a vast number of heretics being burnt throughout Europe, in Spain itself witchcraft persecutions were relatively more restrained than elsewhere, and there were fewer burnings. Skepticism on the part of the Suprema as to the reality of witchcraft discouraged mass persecutions from 1526 onwards. During the witchcraft panic of 1610 in Navarre, the secular judges had burnt their victims before the Inquisition could act. Subsequently the Suprema restrained punishment for alleged witches and in some cases denounced the charges as a delusion.

Spiritualism

A writer in the *Religio-Philosophical Journal* (flourished 1865-1905) stated: "The language that furnishes the largest number of periodicals devoted to the dissemination of the doctrine and philosophy of modern Spiritualism, is the Spanish. This statement will be somewhat surprising to many of our readers, for we have been accustomed to look upon the Spaniards as non-progressive and conservative in the extreme. Spain, until a few years, has always been intolerant of any religions except the Roman Catholic, and was the latest of European nations to yield to the spirit of religious progress. Protestantism has with the greatest difficulty obtained a foothold in that country within the last few years, but it has been attended with annoying restrictions and persecutions, while its progress has been exceedingly slow and discouraging."

Spiritualism in Spain commenced, as in many other lands, with a series of disturbances, which took place in a family residing in the outskirts of Cadiz. Stone-throwing, bell-ringing, and other **poltergeist** style annoyances were the first means of awakening attention to the subject, and as they occurred at the house of a Spanish gentleman who had just returned from the United States, full of the marvels of the **"Rochester Rappings,"** circles were at once formed, intelligent responses by rappings obtained, and a foothold gained, upon which the edifice of Spiritual progress was founded.

So rapidly did the interest thus awakened spread, that the first promulgators were soon lost sight of, and as early as 1854, a society was formed at Cadiz, which was organized for the sole purpose of publishing the communications received from "the Spirits" during two preceding years.

From 1854 to 1860, Spiritualism spread through the principal towns and villages of Spain in the usual fashion. Circles were held in private families, and an endless number of "societies" were formed and dissolved, according to the exigencies of the time.

One of the first public events of note in connection with Spanish Spiritualism, was of so remarkable a character that it deserves special mention. This was no other than an auto-da-fé, the only difference between the occasion under consideration and the fiery executions of olden times being, that the victims were formerly human beings, whereas in the present instance, they were all the books, pamphlets, and works of a Spiritualist character that could be procured at that period of the movement.

Amongst the pile thus offered up on the altar of religious prejudice were the writings of **Kardec,** Dufau, Grand, and **Guldenstubbe;** some copies of English and American Spiritual papers, and a large collection of tracts issued by the Spiritualists of Spain. This memorable scene occurred on the morning of October 9, 1861, at the Esplanade Barcelona.

Among the well-known residents of Barcelona was a Señor Navarez, whose daughter Rosa had, for many years, been the subject of spasmodic attacks, called by the Catholic clergy "the obsession of demons," by the medical faculty, "an aggravated condition of epilepsy." Within two years after the auto-da-fé, Rosa was pronounced entirely cured by the "magnetic" passes of a gentleman who was the medium of the private circle held in the city.

Shortly after this, Barcelona could boast of its well-approved Spiritualist publications, numerous societies for investigation, and several mediums, who from their exclusive positions in private life, would object to their names being mentioned. A journal published by Señor Alcantara was warmly supported by the Viscount de Torres Solanot, and numbers of other leaders of science and literature in Spain. Through this publication the opponents of Spiritualism were amazed to learn of the immense progress the cause was making, and the number of distinguished persons who assembled nightly in circles to promote investigation.

A circular calling the attention of the Spanish public to the phenomena of Spiritualism was published in 1875 by Viscount Solanot. The authors of this circular met with no response worthy of their fraternal intentions. It might have been difficult to define exactly what they proposed to do or wished others to unite with them in doing, certainly no tangible results could be expected to follow from a very transcendental address. "Our Spanish friends mean well, but is it possible there can be unity enough amongst them to send a delegation to America?" asked a shrewd critic on perusing his grandiloquent circular.

However, the energetic Viscount Solanot again agitated the subject prior to the Paris Exposition of 1878. In the articles written for *El Criterio* on this proposition, the Viscount named amongst those societies of Spiritualists prepared to promote an International representation: La Federation Espirita, of Belgium; The British National Association of Spiritualists, England; La Sociedad Central Espirita, of the Republic of Mexico; and El Central General del Espiritismo. Notice was also taken, with a hope of its ultimate success, of the attempt to form a national association and unite all the discordant elements under the one broad banner of Spiritualism.

Animal Magnetism and Mediums

In Spain as in Italy, a considerable amount of attention was directed towards the unfoldment of mediumistic faculty by means of **Animal Magnetism.** Magnetic Societies abounded in Spain up to early twentieth century, when many elements of internal discord prevailed in the ranks, and succeeded in dissolving the bonds which had united flourishing associations. Amongst the amateur mesmerists of Spain may be mentioned Don Juan Escudero, of Madrid, a gentleman who having witnessed some experiments in "animal magnetism" in California, tried its effect in his own family with success.

Among the numerous circles of groups formed in the different parts of Spain for the study of Spiritualism and its phenomena, was one of long standing at Tarragona called "The Christian Circle." The President of this circle sent the following communication to the *Revue Spirite* of Paris:

"The convict prison here in Tarragona has 800 inmates sentenced to forced labour. By some means, Spiritualistic books have been introduced among the prisoners. The circulation of these books among them has been the means of bringing seventy or eighty of them to be believers in our doctrine. These converts have ceased to regard their miserable position from their old point of view; they no longer entertain schemes of revolt against the authorities. They endure their lot with resignation under the influence of the teaching that this world is but a preliminary stage to another, where, if repentant of the ill they have done, and seeking the good of others, they will be better off than here.

"Not long since one of these men died; at his death he declined the established offices of the prison priest, on the ground that he was a Spiritualist and did not need them. The priest then discovered that Spiritualism was a subject of discussion with many of the prisoners. He made a representation of the matter to his bishop, who made formal complaint of it to the commandant of the prison, and the commandant made an investigation. In the end a particular prisoner was selected for punishment in the form of an additional weight of fetters. This coming to the knowledge of the Spiritualists of Tarragona, Barcelona, and Lerida, they had a meeting upon the subject and delegated one of their number, a man of position, to interview the commandant. The representations which he made, led the commandant to cancel his order as to the additional fetters. The bishop's censure against Spiritualist books placed them under prohibition, which was maintained. It is known, however, that although never found by gaolers, the books are still there."

In April 1881, the editor of the Madrid *El Criterio* stated that "great progress has been made in the cause of Spiritualism; that the hall of meeting of the Spiritual Society is completely full every Thursday evening, and is not now large enough to hold the public who come to the sessions, that Dr. Merschejewski has called the attention of the University of St. Petersburg to a psychometric phenomena of much importance; to wit: A young man deemed from childhood to be an idiot, who will in some seconds solve any mathematical problem, while if a poem be read to him, even of many hundred verses, he will repeat the whole of it without failing in a single word."

In the same issue of *El Criterio* Señor Manuel Lopez wrote on the progress of a society of Spiritualists in Madrid: "We have received a mediumistic work of extraordinary merit, executed by a medium of the Society of Spiritualists of Zaragoza. It consists of a portrait of Isabel the Catholic, made with a pencil, and is a work truly admirable. It is said by intelligent persons who have examined it to be an exact copy of one preserved in the Royal Museum of Painters of this court. Many thanks are tendered to the Zaragozan Society for this highly appreciated present."

It was about the end of the year 1880 that the Spiritualists of Spain sustained another series of attacks from the Church. The first of these was the refusal of the clergy to accord the customary rites of interment to the remains of two ladies, both of irreproachable character, and good standing in society, but both "guilty" of having believed in Spiritualist manifestations.

The second attack by the Church in Spain about this time was the suppression of a well-written Spiritualist paper published at Lerida, entitled *El Buen Sentido.* The Bishop of Lerida had long threatened this step, and warned the editor to beware how he presumed to allow any writings reflecting upon clerical doings to appear in his columns.

As some of the principal contributors were Madame Soler, Mdlle. Sans, Don Murillo, and others equally capable of arraigning the intolerant acts which Church policy seemed determined to push against the Spiritualists, it was scarcely likely that the Bishop's threats would produce much effect. The last article which seemed to inflame the clergy to retaliate was an indignant protest which appeared in the columns of *El Buen Sentido* on the condemnation of a working man to three years' imprisonment, leaving a family of children destitute and all for daring to speak in public against the intolerance of the Church.

In an issue of *El Criterio* dated 1881 was a letter from Don Migueles, in which he gave a somewhat discouraging account of the cause of Spiritualism as it existed at that time in Spain. The editor commented:—"Don Migueles visited many cities to examine into the state of affairs of a spiritual nature, but found many who were only to be enticed by physical phenomena, caring nothing for the esoteric beauties of our faith; many who were convinced that they knew all there was to be known concerning it, and others who were timid fearing the disapproval of neighbours."

In some places, however, excellent mediums were discovered. In Santiago, in Oviedo, in Corunna and Valladolid, an exceptional interest was manifest. Near Santiago, there was a young girl possessed of wonderful faculties. Two bars of magnetized iron held over her horizontally, half a meter distant, were said to be sufficient to suspend her body in the air.

The proceedings of the Spanish Society under the name of the *Sesiones de Controversio,* in the month of April last, are spoken of in *El Criterio* as markedly impressive on account of the lofty sentiments maintained throughout the discussions, by the various speakers:

"In the past month were given also very interesting conferencias by our illustrious brothers, the Sres. Rebolledo and Huelbes. The able engineer and inventor, belonging to the Society of Santiago de Chili and founder of that of Lima, D. R. Caruana y Berard, has just arrived in Madrid. The *Revista Espiritista* of Barcelona mentions the visit which its editor has made to the central societies of Spiritualists of Sabodell and Tarrasa, where a great number of brethren were assembled on the occasion, and which will result in great good to the doctrine."

In 1881, the Barcelona *Lux* gave encouraging accounts of seances held at Cordova, Tarragona, Seville, and many other places. The editor, Madame Soler, also referred to the prohibition to Catholics by an archbishop to have or to read the Spiritualist work of Niram Aliv of the Society of Spiritualists of Tarrasa; of the circle of Santa Cruz of Tenerif; of that of Faith, Hope, and Charity, of Andujar, and of St. Vincent de Bogota.

Psychical Research

In spite of much discouragement, both Spiritualism and psychical research continued in Spain during the present century.

By 1930, Don Manuel Otero of Madrid and Signor Tassi of Perugia were active psychical researchers who had investigated the phenomena of the famous medium Eusapia **Palladino** in Naples in 1899.

The Ferderacion Espirita Española was an active Spiritual group in Sabadel. Periodicals include *Hacia La Iguidad y el Amor* of Barcelona and *Lumen* of Tarrasa. Spain was represented at international congresses of psychical research.

The Civil War and World War II disrupted developments from the 1930s onwards. However, interest in Spiritualism and activities in the field of parapsychology have continued. At the present time, paraphychological research is represented by the Sociedad Española de Parapsicologia (Bedén 15, 1, Madrid-4) and their publication *Psicomunicacion.*

Spare, Austin Osmond (1889-1956)

The supreme artist of the occult, with a terrifying talent for evoking phallic spirits and demons. Born in Snow Hill, London, England, December 31, 1888 or 1889, he was the son of a London policeman. After leaving school at the age of thirteen, he worked in a stained-glass factory during the daytime and studied at Lambeth School of Art during evenings, eventually winning a scholarship to the Royal College of Art, Kensington. One of his drawings was exhibited at the Royal Academy and praised by the famous painter John Singer Sargent.

During Spare's childhood, he was not fond of his mother and became attached instead to a mysterious old lady named Mrs. Paterson, whom he claimed as his second or "witch-mother." She taught him how to visualize and evoke spirit forms and elementals. She is also supposed to have initiated him into a witches' **Sabbat** on another dimension, in which he claimed to have seen a geometrical city of the future.

It was also from the teachings of his witch-mother that Spare developed a grimoire (unpublished during his lifetime) called *The Book of the Living Word of Zos,* embodying a system of magic utterance and symbolism linked by willpower.

Spare had an instinctive understanding of sex-magic, and developed a form of magical masturbation involving an earthenware urn, and believed this was a rediscovery of the ancient Greek secret of *urnings,* and the origin of the legend of **Solomon** and the genii of the brass vessel.

Spare was highly charged sexually, and expressed this energy in his powerful drawings, and magical operations. He was a haunted man and seems to have had weird occult powers, although he spent most of his life in some poverty as a recluse, surrounded by his pet cats.

Very little has so far been published on this strange genius, but there is a chapter dealing with him in Kenneth **Grant's** book *The Magical Revival* (London, 1972).

Spare's own publications included: *The Book of Pleasure (Self-love); the Psychology of Ecstasy* (1913), *The Focus of Life* (1921). His work titled *A Book of Automatic Drawing* was published by Catalpa Press, London, 1972.

He died May 15, 1956, in London, at the age of 67. (See also **Sex Magic**)

Speal Bone (Divination by)

An early form of **divination** used in Scotland. A speal bone, or blade bone of a shoulder of mutton was used, but full details of the method are lacking. A soldier accompanying Lord Loudon on his retreat to Skye foretold the result of the battle of Culloden at the very moment it was decided, claiming to have seen the event by looking through the bone.

Spear, John Murray (c. 1804-1887)

Famous American Universalist preacher, an outstanding figure in the history of early American Spiritualism. He was baptized by John Murray, whose name he bore.

In the early years of his public activity he distinguished himself as an ardent Abolitionist. In 1845, he published a weekly newspaper (with his brother Charles) *The Prisoner's Friend* in Boston, and for many years devoted himself to helping the poor, especially prisoners and their relatives. In one year alone he delivered eighty lectures on criminal reform and against capital punishment, distributing 7,500 books to prisoners and traveling 8,000 miles in the cause.

His attention was first drawn to Spiritualism in 1851. A year later, he developed **automatic writing** and **healing.** Messages came through his hand giving addresses and names of sick people. He visited them and drove the pain out of their bodies by his touch.

Later he began to draw and deliver inspirational discourses. It was asserted that they came from John Murray. Under the title *Messages from the Superior State* they were published in 1852. In the following year he was made the instrument of a spirit band called "The Association of Beneficents," and produced a large work which bore resemblance in scope to the *Divine Revelations* of Andrew Jackson **Davis** (1847).

The first volume of Spear's work was published in 1857 in Boston under the title *The Educator, being Suggestions, theoretical and practical, designed to promote Man-Culture and Integral Reform, with a view of the Ultimate Establishment of a Divine Social State on Earth.* In the spirit world several similar organizations to the Association of Beneficents appear to have existed. One of them, the Association of Electricizers, involved John Murray Spear in one of the strangest adventures in the history of Spiritualism.

As announced in April 1854, in *The New Era,* they instructed him to construct a "new motor" which would be self-generative, drawing upon the great reservoir of the magnetic life in Nature and acting in analogy of the human body as a living organism.

The machine was duly built at High Rock, near Lynn, Massachusetts, of zinc and copper at the cost of $2,000. One of Mrs. Spear's disciples, Mrs. Newton (wife of Alonzo E. Newton, one of Spear's assistants) was appointed, in a vision which she saw, to be "the Mary of the New Dispensation." At High Rock, near the machine, she fell into trance and went through frightful convulsions for a period of two hours, at the end of which there were said to be indications of life in the machine, a movement and pulsation which all present claimed to see. The machine was considered as a new born child, the medium nursed it for weeks and the enthusiastic band announced it as "the Art of Arts, the Science of all Sciences, the New Messiah, God's last Best Gift to Man."

About the birth of this modern **Frankenstein** style creation, and the practices by which the life principle had been infused, reports of a shocking nature had been circulated. Andrew Jackson Davis explained "that by means of a spiritual overshadowing, à la Virgin Mary, the maternal functions were brought into active operation; a few of the usual physiological symptoms followed; the crisis arrived and being in presence of the mechanism, the first living motion was communicated to it." In an anonymous article the husband of the lady proceeded to show that Mrs. **Newton** had been made the subject of a set of most remarkable psychological experiences and prophetic visions at or about the same time as Mr. Spear was engaged in directing the construction of the machinery at High Rock, that the coincidence between their experiences was but later discovered and the crisis reached when the lady visited the machine. She communicated, and subsequently maintained, through certain mediumistic processes, an actual living principle until the machine was pronounced 'a thing of life.' "

When the machine did not work, Andrew Jackson Davis concluded that mechanically minded spirits, deficient in practical knowledge, were conducting experiments at Spear's expense. A few months later in Randolph, where the machine was moved to have the advantage of a lofty electrical position, superstitious villagers destroyed the New Motor in the night.

The destruction of the New Motor had a certain advantage in silencing critics of the machine's failure to work as predicted. Other Spiritualists took the loss philosophically, S. B. Brittan commenting in the *Spiritual Telegraph:* "If the New Motor is to be the physical savior of the race, it will probably rise again."

John Murray Spear also projected plans for the building of a "circular city," or "perfect earthly home." These plans were also inspired by spirits.

"That Mr. Spear," stated Emma Hardinge in *Modern American Spiritualism* (1869), "honestly believed in a spiritual origin for the various missions he undertook, and the remarkable part he played, none who ever have come into personal relations with him can question. The unwavering patience with which he endured reproach and odium of their execution, would attest his sincerity, were other evidence wanting."

On April 15, 1869, Spear made a statement about his introduction to spiritualism at a meeting of The **London Dialectical Society,** England (see *Report on Spiritualism of The Committee of The London Dialectical Society,* 1871).

Since the time of John Murray Spear, other individuals have claimed to have discovered a motor force in nature, (See also John Worrell **Keely;** The **New Motor; Orgone**)

Spear of Destiny

One of the most extraordinary Christian relics, the Spear of Longinus, is said to have been the spear that pierced the side of Christ nearly two thousand years ago. Occult legend states that whoever claims this Spear and understands its occult significance holds the destiny of the world in his hands.

According to Houston Stewart **Chamberlain,** British born propagandist for anti-Semitism and the German philosophy of an Aryan master race, this Spear had been claimed by Constantine the Great, Justinian, Charles Martel, Charlemagne and various German emperors, all men of destiny.

Before World War II, the Spear of Destiny (also known as the Maurice Spear) was exhibited in the Hofburg Museum in Vienna. It attracted the attention of the young Adolf Hitler, who linked it with legends of the Holy Grail and made his own plans to be a man of destiny.

The Spear held a special fascination for Hitler and his associates in the hothouse atmosphere of occultism and evil philosophies which gave rise to the Nazi plan for world domination. In 1935, Heinrich Himmler had a replica of the spear made and kept it in his private room. Three years later, Hitler led his troops into Austria, the first stage of his plan for world conquest. One of his first acts was to remove the Spear of Destiny from the Hofburg Museum.

The Spear was buried beneath the Nuremberg Fortress, where it was discovered on the day that Hitler shot himself in the Berlin bunker on April 30, 1945. It was recovered together with other treasures of the Imperial collection, by the American forces under General Patton, who took a great interest in the Spear.

On January 6, 1946, these treasures were returned to the authorities at Vienna, and the Spear was reinstated in the Hofburg Museum.

For a carefully documented account of the legend of the Spear and its connection with the strange mixture of occultism and evil in the life of Adolf Hitler, see *The Spear of Destiny* by Trevor Ravenscroft (1973).

Ravenscroft drew much of his unique research information from Dr. Walter Johannes Stein (1891-1957) who knew Hitler as a young man and saw Hitler's books concerned with occultism and Grail legends, with copious manuscript notes by Hitler himself indicating the beginnings of his Nazi philosophy. (See Houston Stewart **Chamberlain;** Jörg **Lanz von Liebenfels;** Guido von **List**)

Specialist Knowledge Services

British organization for research, consultancy, and information in the fields of the paranormal, Fortean and anomalous phenomena, Ufology, earth mysteries, occultism. S. K. S. was founded by Dr. Hugh **Pincott,** secretary of ASSAP **Association for the Scientific Study of Anomalous Phenomena).** S. K. S. issues regular lists of available and newly published books on all aspects of the paranormal and parapsychology. Address: Saint Aldheim, 20 Paul Street, Frome, Somerset, BAII IDX, England.

Spectral Flames

Lights seen in cemeteries and around churches, believed to be paranormal. (See **Luminous Phenomena**)

Spectrum—Society for Psychical and Spiritual Studies

Irish society which conducts study of such paranormal phenomena as haunted sites, ESP, psychokinesis, spiritual healing. It provides a healing service for individuals in need, and is available to investigate hauntings. It is also associated with the Irish UFO Organisation. Address: 70 Glasmeen Road, Glasnevin, Dublin 11, Republic of Ireland.

Specularii

The name by which crystal gazers were known in the sixteenth century. (See **Crystal Gazing**)

Speculum

The crystal ball or any shining light-refracting surface which the scryer uses for divination. (See **Crystal Gazing**)

Spells

Spells are incantations, written or spoken formulas of words supposed to be capable of magical effects. The term "spell" derives from the Anglo-Saxon *spel,* a saying or story, hence a form of words; Icelandic, *spjall,* a saying; Gothic, *spill,* a fable.

The conception of spells appears to have arisen from the idea that there is some natural and intimate connection between words and the things signified by them. Thus if one repeats the name of a supernatural being the effect will be analogous to that produced by the being itself. It is assumed that all things are in sympathy, and act and react upon one another, and things that have once been in contact continue to act on each other even after the contact has been removed. That certain secret names of gods, demi-gods, and demons unknown to human beings might be discovered and used against them by the discoverer, was believed in ancient Egypt.

The power of the spoken word was implicitly believed in by all primitive peoples, especially if it emanated from a known practitioner of the art of magic, and if it be in a language or dialect unknown to ordinary people. Thus the magicians of ancient Egypt employed foreign words for their incantations, such as *Tharthar, thamara, thatha, mommon, thanabotha, opranu, brokhrex, abranazukhel,* which occurred at the end of a spell the purpose of which was to bring dreams.

The magicians and sorcerers of the Middle Ages likewise employed gibberish of a similar kind, as did the medicine men of the North American Indians into relatively modern times. The reason for the spell being usually couched in a well-known formula was probably because experience found that seemed to be most efficacious. Thus in ancient Egypt not only were the formulas of spells well fixed, but the exact tone of voice in which they were to be pronounced was specially taught. The power of a spell remained until such time as it was broken by an antidote or exorcism. Therefore it was not a transient thing.

Spells or enchantments can be divided into several classes: (1) Protective spells; (2) The curse or taboo; (3) Spells by which a person, animal or object is to be injured or transformed; (4) Spells to procure some minor end, love-spells, or the curing of persons and cattle, etc.

(1) The protective spell—the commonest form of this was an incantation, usually rhymed, imploring the protection of certain gods, saints, or beneficent beings, who in waking or sleeping hours would guard the speaker from maleficent powers, such as:

"Matthew, Mark, Luke and John, Bless the bed that I lie on."

Of a deeper significance were those spells supposed to be spoken by a dead Egyptian on his journey through Amenti (the kingdom of the dead), by which he warded off the evil beings who would hinder his way, and so the serpent who would bite the dead was addressed thus: "O serpent come not! Geb and Shu stand against thee. Thou hast eaten mice. That is loathsome to the Gods. Thou hast gnawed the bones of a putrid cat."

E. A. W. Budge stated in his book *Egyptian Magic* (1899), "The Book of the Dead says, 'Whoever read eth the spells daily over himself, he is whole upon earth, he escapes from death, and never doth anything evil meet him.' "

We learn how great was the confidence which the deceased placed in his words of power, and also that the sources from which they sprang were the gods of Thoth and Isis. It will be remembered that Thoth is called the "scribe of the gods," the "lord of writing," the "master of papyrus," the "maker of the palette and the ink-jar," the "lord of divine words," i.e., the holy writings or scriptures, and as he was the lord of books and master of the power of speech, he was considered to be the possessor of all knowledge both human and divine.

At the creation of the world, it was he who reduced to words the will of the unseen and unknown creative Power, and who uttered them in such wise that the universe came into being and it was he who proved himself by the exercise of his knowledge to be the protector and the friend of Osiris, and of Isis, and of their son Horus.

From the evidence of the texts we know that it was not by physical might that Thoth helped these three gods, but by giving them words of power and instructing them how to use them. We know that Osiris vanquished his foes, and that he reconstituted his body and became the king of the underworld and god of the dead, but he was only able to do these things by means of the words of power which Thoth had given to him, and which he had taught him to pronounce properly and in a proper tone of voice. It is this belief which made the deceased cry out, "Hail, Thoth, who madest Osiris victorious over his enemies, make thou Ani to be victorious over his enemies in the presence of the great and sovereign princes who are in Tattu, or in any other place."

Without the words of power given to him by Thoth, Osiris would have been powerless under the attacks of his foes, and similarly the dead man, who was always identified with Osiris, would have passed out of existence at his death but for the words of power provided by the writings that were buried with him. In the Judgment Scene it is Thoth who reports to the gods the result of the weighing of the heart in the balance, and who has supplied its owner with the words which he has uttered in his supplications, and whatever can be said in favor of the deceased he says to the gods, and whatever can be done for him he does.

But apart from being the protector and friend of Osiris, Thoth was the refuge to which Isis fled in her trouble. The words of a hymn declare that she knew "how to turn aside evil happening," and that she was "strong of tongue and uttered the words of power which she knew with correct pronunciation, and halted not in her speech, and was perfect both in giving the command, and in saying the word," but this description only proves that she had been instructed by Thoth in the art of uttering words of power with effect, and to him, indeed, she owed more than this. Spells to keep away disease are of this class.

The **amulets** found upon Egyptian mummies, and the inscriptions on Gnostic gems are for the most part, of a protective nature (see **Egypt; Gnostics**). The protective spell may be said to be an amulet in words, and is often found in connection with the amulet, on which it is inscribed.

(2) The curse or taboo—(a) The word of blighting, the damaging word. (b) The word of prohibition or restriction.

(a) The curse is of the nature of a spell, even if it is not in the shape of a definite formula. Thus we have the Highland Scottish curses: "A bad meeting to you." "Bad understanding to you." "A down mouth be yours" which are certainly popular as formulas.

Those who had seen old women, of the type of Madge Wildfire (in Sir Walter Scott's novel *The Heart of Midlothian*) cursing and banning, say their manner is well-calculated to inspire terror. Some years ago, a party of Scottish tinkers quarreled and fought, first among themselves, and then with some Tiree villagers. In the excitement, a tinker wife threw off her cap and allowed her hair to fall over her shoulders in wild disorder. She then bared her knees, and falling on them to the ground in a praying attitude, poured forth a torrent of wishes that struck awe into all who heard her.

She imprecated "Drowning by sea and conflagration by land; may you never see a son to follow your body to the graveyard, or a daughter to mourn your death. I have made my wish before this, and I will make it now, and there was not yet a day I did not see my wish fulfilled."

Curses employed by witches usually invoked a blight upon the person cursed, their flocks, their herds and crops. Barrenness, too, was frequently called down upon women. A person under a curse or spell was believed in the Scottish Highlands "to become powerless over his own volition . . . alive and awake but moves and acts as if asleep." Curses or spells which invoked death were frequently mentioned in works which deal with Medieval magic (see **Summons by the Dying**).

(b) The Taboo, the word of prohibition or restriction. This is typified in the mystic expression "thou shalt not." Thus a number of the Biblical commandments are taboos, and the book of *Leviticus* teems with them. The taboo is the "don't" applied to children—a curb on primitive desire. To break a taboo was to bring dire misfortune upon oneself, and often upon one's family.

(3) Of injuring or transformation of a person, animal or object there are copious examples. These were nearly always affected by a spell of a given formula. Thus no less than twelve chapters of the *Book of the Dead* (chapters 77 to 88) are devoted to providing the deceased with words of power, the recital of which was necessary to enable him to transform himself into various animal and human forms.

The Rev. S. Baring Gould in his *Book of Folklore* (1913) stated that in such cases the consequence of a spell being cast on an individual required him or her to become a beast or a monster with no escape except under conditions difficult of exection or of obtaining. To this category belong a number of so-called fairy tales that are actually folk tales. And these do not all pertain to Aryan peoples, for wherever magical arts are believed to be all-powerful, one of its greatest achievements is the casting of a spell so as to alter completely the appearance of the person on whom it is cast, so that this individual becomes an animal. One need only recall the story in the *Arabian Nights* of the Calenders and the three noble ladies of Baghdad, in which the wicked sisters are transformed into bitches that have to be thrashed every day. Of this class are the stories of "Beauty and the Beast" and "The Frog Prince."

(4) Spells to procure some minor end, love-spells, etc. Love-spells were engraved on metal tables by the Gnostics, and the magicians of the Middle Ages. Instances of these are to be found in *The Book of the Sacred Magic* of **Abraham the Jew.** Spells were often employed to imprison evil spirits.

The later Jews had many extravagant opinions and legends relating to this subject, which appear to have derived in a great measure from the Babylonians. The ancient historian Josephus affirmed that it was generally believed by his countrymen that **Solomon** left behind him many spells, which had the power of terrifying and expelling evil spirits. Some of the old Rabbis also described Solomon as an accomplished magician. It is possible that the belief in the power of spells and incantations became general among the Jews during the captivity, and that the invention of them was attributed to Solomon, as a more creditable personage than the deities of the Assyrians.

Those fictions acquired currency, not only among the Arabs, Persians, and other Mohammedan nations, but, in process of time, also in many Christian communities.

They were first adopted by the Gnostics and similar sects, in whose creed pagan beliefs preponderated over Christianity, and in the dark ages they found their way among Catholics too, principally by means of the Pseudo-gospels and fabulous legends of saints.

An incident in the life of St. Margaret is typical. This holy virgin, having vanquished an evil spirit who assaulted her, demanded his name. "My name," replied the demon, "is Veltis, and I am one of those whom Solomon, by virtue of his spells, confined in a copper caldron at Babylon, but when the Babylonians, in the hope of finding treasures, dug up the caldron and opened it, we all made our escape. Since that time, our efforts have been directed to the destruction of righteous persons, and I have long been striving to turn thee from the course which thou hast embraced." The reader of the *Arabian Nights' Entertainments* will be immediately reminded of the story of the "Fisherman." The Oriental origin of many similar legends, e.g., of St. George of Cappadocia, seems equally clear.

Many of the spells used by Western occultists in ceremonial magic rituals have probably descended from a vulgarization of the religious **mantras** (mystical words of power) and **yantras** (mystical diagrams) of Hindu tradition. (See also **Abraham the Jew; Ceremonial Magic; Magic; Mantra; Solomon; Yantra**)

Recommended reading

Abbott, John. *The Keys of Power; A Study of Indian Ritual and Belief,* Methuen, London, 1932; University Books, 1974

Budge, E. A. Wallis. *Egyptian Magic,* Kegan Paul, London, 1899; 1901; Benjamin Blom, 1971; Peter Smith, Muss., 1972; Dover Books (paperback)

Campbell, J. *Witchcraft & Second Sight in Scottish Highlands and Islands,* Alex, MacLehose, Glasgow, 1902

Cohen, Daniel. *Curses, Hexes & Spells,* Lippincott, 1974

De Pascale, Marc. *The Book of Spells,* Taplinger, 1971

Easwaran, Eknath. *The Mantram Handbook,* Routledge & Kegan Paul (paperback), London, 1978

Grimm, Macob. *Teutonic Mythology,* 4 vols., Bell, London, 1880-88

Heim, Richard (ed.). *Incantamenta Magica Graeca Latina,* Teubner, Leipzic, 1893

Holroyd, Stuart. *Magic, Words, and Numbers,* Aldus Books, London/Doubleday, 1975

Leek, Sybil. *Sybil Leek's Book of Curses,* Prentice-Hall, 1975

MacKenzie, William (ed.). *Gaelic Incantations, Charms & Blessings of the Hebrides,* Inverness, Scotland, 1895

Maple, Eric. *Incantations and Words of Power,* Weiser (paperback), 1974

Morrison, Sarah Lyddon. *The Modern Witch's Spell book,* McKay, 1971

Norris, David & Jacquemine Charrott-Lodwidge. *The Book of Spells,* Lorrimer, London, 1974

Summers, Rev. Montague (ed.). *Malleus Maleficarum,* John Rodker, London, 1928, 1948

Waite, Arthur E. *The Book of Ceremonial Magic,* William Rider, London, 1911; University Books, 1961; Causeway Books, 1973

Woodroffe, Sir John. *The Garland of Letters (Varna mala); Studies in the Mantra-Shastra,* Ganesh & Co., Madras, India, 1951 etc.

Spence, (James) Lewis (Thomas Chalmers) (1874-1955)

Scottish scholar of the occult who took a particular interest in the **Atlantis** theme. Born November 25, 1874 in Forfarshire, Scotland, he was educated privately and at Edinburgh University before following a journalistic career. In 1899 he married Helen Bruce.

From 1899-1906 he was sub-editor of the leading newspaper *The Scotsman,* editor of *The Edinburgh Magazine* from 1904-05, sub-editor of *The British Weekly* from 1906-09. About this time he took to serious study of mythology and folklore, with special reference to Mexico and Central America. He published some important books on the subject, including his own study of *The Popul Vuh,* the sacred book of the ancient Quiché Indians of Maya (1908) and *A Dictionary of Mythology* (1910).

He also published more than forty other valuable works dealing with mythology, folklore and the occult, including the authoritative *Encyclopaedia of Occultism* (1920; reissued Universtiy Books, 1960), the first comprehensive work of its kind.

He contributed articles to *Hibbert Journal, Glasgow Herald* and *The Times.* An ardent Scottish Nationalist, he contested North Midlothian as a candidate in 1929. He also found time to write romantic poetry.

He was a Fellow of the Royal Anthropological Institute of Great Britain and Ireland, vice-president of the Scottish Anthropological and Folklore Society. He received a D.Lit. and in 1951 was awarded a Royal pension for Services to Literature.

He is best known, perhaps, for his significant books on Atlantis: *The Problem of Atlantis* (1924; reissued Causeway under title *Atlantis Discovered,* (1974), *Atlantis in America* (1925), *The History of Atlantis* (1926; reissued University Books, 1968), *Will Europe Follow Atlantis?* (1942), *The Occult Sciences in Atlantis* (1943). He also edited the journal *Atlantis Quarterly* in 1932.

Other books by Spence on occult themes include: *The Magic and Mysteries of Mexico* (1932), *The Problem of Lemuria* (1932), *The Occult Causes of the Present War* (1940), *The Magic Arts in Celtic Britain* (1945), *British Fairy Origins* (1945), *The Fairy Tradition in Britain* (1947), *Second Sight; Its History and Origins* (1951), *Scottish Ghosts and Goblins* (1952).

He died March 3, 1955.

Spheres

Divisions of the spirit world, both in spatial and moral-spiritual sense. All the knowledge which Spiritualists claim on the spheres is based on communications of spirits. The information conflicts at many points, but there is a general agreement as to the number of spheres. They are seven: (1) Hell, (2) Sphere of Desires, (3) Summerland, (4) Mind, (5) Abstract, (6) Meeting of the Sexes, (7) Union of the Sexes.

There is some contradiction as to whether the earth should be considered as the first sphere or whether the next above is the first. It is said that the first sphere is the abode of gross and ignorant spirits. It is gloomy and desolate, replete with sadness and misery.

After a realization of their state and the circumstances that cast them into it, the desire for progress and betterment will transfer the spirits into the second sphere where, in a scenery as natural as that on earth, harmony, love and kindness help to develop the higher qualities of the soul.

The period of the stay in a particular sphere varies individually. The higher spheres cannot be perceived by spirits in the lower ones. Information on the higher spheres is obtained from visitors descending to lower spheres. Owing to a lack of conception, no adequate description can be conveyed to us. It is also said that beyond the spheres are the supernal heavens of boundless extent. These are the ultimate abodes of the glorified and blest.

An interesting exposition of the origin of the spheres was furnished by Hudson **Tuttle** in his book *Arcana of Spiritualism* (1871). According to this, the spirit world is built up from atomic emanations. Exhalations from all substances ascend as mist rises from a sheet of water. The spirit world therefore depends on the earth for its existence and is formed through its refining instrumentality. Without the earth there could not have been corresponding spirit spheres.

They are rather zones than spheres. They are one hundred and twenty degrees wide; that is, they extend sixty degrees on each side of the equator. If we take the sixtieth parallel of latitude each side of the equator and imagine it projected against the blue dome of the sky, we have the boundaries of these zones.

The first zone, or the innermost one, is sixty miles from the earth's surface. The next external one is removed from the first by about the same distance. The third is just outside the moon's orbit, or 265,000 miles from the earth. From the third sphere rise the most sublimated exhalations, which mingle with the emanations of the other planets, and form a vast zone around the entire solar system, including even the unknown planets beyond the vast orbit of Neptune.

The first zone is nearly thirty, the second twenty, the third but two miles in thickness. While the earth is slowly diminishing, the spheres are gradually increasing. The surface of the zones is diversified with changing scenery. Matter, when it aggregates there, is prone to assume the forms in which it existed below. Hence there are all the forms of life there as on earth, except those, such as the lowest plants and animals, which cannot exist surrounded by such superior conditions. The scenery of mountain and plain, river, lake and ocean, of forest and prairie, are like daguerrotypes of the same earth. It is like earth with all its imperfections perfected, and it beauties multiplied a thousandfold.

The first trance reference to spheres seems to have been made by the Seeress of Prevorst (see Frau Frederica **Hauffe**). The second is contained in a letter of Dr. G. **Billot** to J. P. F. **Deleuze** in 1831. Billot wrote: "They taught that God was a grand Spiritual Sun—life on earth a probation—the spheres, different degrees of comprehensive happiness or states of retributive suffering—each appropriate to the good or evil deeds done on earth. They described the ascending changes open to every soul in proportion to his own efforts to improve."

The first exact dimensions were claimed by Dr. J. A. Gridley in his book *Astounding Facts from the Spirit World* (1854). According to his data, the first sphere is 5,000 miles, the sixth 30,000 miles from the earth's surface.

Diagrams of the spheres were first drawn by the Seeress of Prevorst. Nahum Koons in the Koon loghouse was the second to expound its detail in sketches and his information was supplemented by accounts given through the trumpet (see also Jonathan **Koons**).

Prof. Robert **Hare** differed from Gridley and agreed with Hudson Tuttle inasmuch as his communicators put the distance of the nearest sphere as sixty miles from the earth's surface. But his further distances did not tally with the calculations of Hudson Tuttle. He placed the sixth sphere within the area of the moon. He was told that the spheres "are concentric zones, or circles, of exceedingly refined matter, encompassing the earth like belts or girdles. They have atmospheres of peculiar vital air, soft and balmy. Their surfaces are diversified with an immense variety of picturesque landscapes, with lofty mountain ranges, valleys, rivers, lakes, forests, trees and shrubbery, and flowers of every colour and variety, sending forth grateful emanations."

Almost every trance description asserts something different. Dr. Eugene Crowell in *The Identity of Primitive Christianity with Modern Spiritualism* (2 vols., 1875-79), stated that he had received the following figures: The first sphere is within our atmosphere, the second is about 60, the third about 160, the fourth 310, the fifth 460, the sixth 635, the seventh 865 miles from the earth.

Precise information was tendered in J. Hewat **McKenzie's** *Spirit Intercourse* (1916). The "spirit" of Prof. William **James** was quoted as the authority behind the statements. The disagreement is all too apparent. It should be quoted for curiosity:

sences cast off by millions of tons of matter, that they condense into solid substance and float in space like vast continents, by the operation of centripetal and centrifugal attraction and that the passage from one sphere to the other is effected by gradual refinement of the spiritual body under the effect of the spirit.

An impressive conception of after-death states was disclosed in Miss Geraldine **Cummins,** *The Road to Immortality* (1932), a book dictated by the "spirit" of F. W. H. **Myers.** According to a chapter "The Chart of Existence," the journey of the soul takes place through the following stages:

1. The Plane of Matter.
2. Hades or the Intermediate State.
3. The Plane of Illusion.
4. The Plane of Color.
5. The Plane of Flame.
6. The Plane of Light.
7. Out Yonder, Timelessness.

"Between each plane or new chapter in experience there is existence in Hades or in an intermediate state, when the soul reviews his past experiences and makes his choice, deciding whether he will go up or down the ladder of consciousness.

1. The Plane of Matter consists of all experiences in physical form, in matter as known to man. These experiences are not confined to the earth life. There are experiences of a similar character in numerous starry regions. Sometimes the body vibrates faster or slower than the body of man in such starry places. But the term physical expresses its character and nature.

First Sphere or Astral World

	Lower	Middle	Upper
Earth's distance	300 miles	550 miles	750 miles
Degree of light	0 to 30°	30–50°	50–70°
Soil	Rock	Shale	Earth
Atmospherics	Dark and Humid	Dull and moist	Slightly moist
Vegetation	Fungus only	Mosses only	Shrubs and grass
Animals	None	None	Pet animals
Vices	Gross animalism	Secondary vices	Thoughtlessness
Virtues	Dormant	A few active	Progressive desires
Dwellings	Practically non	Similar to earth	Extremely simple

Second Sphere

	Lower	Middle	Upper
Earth's distance	1,000 miles	1,150 miles	1,250 miles
Degree of light	70–80°	80–90°	90–99°
Vegetation	Elementary flowers	Secondary flowers	Superior flowers
Animals	Pet animals and birds	Animals, birds, fish	Animals, birds, fish
Characteristics	Narrowly religious	Ultra religious	Restricted excellence

The third sphere, the Summer Land, is 1,350 miles from the earth, the fourth 2,850, the fifth 5,050, the sixth 9,450, and the seventh 18,250.

The author was told that the sustenance of the body in superphysical states is derived from the atmosphere by inhalation in the ordinary act of breathing, that the material for clothing and houses is manufactured, that there is a union of sexes in a bond of affection, with no offspring, that the animals that live there have previously existed on earth, that the spiritual worlds of each planet unite at the seventh sphere, that the spheres are built of es-

3. The Plane of Illusion is the dream period connected with life passed on the Plane of Matter. (Summerland).

4. The Plane of Colour. Existence in this state is not governed by the senses. It is more directly controlled by mind. It is still an existence in form, and therefore an existence in substance. That substance is a very rarified matter. It might be called an air of

matter. The Plane of Colour is within the terrestrial zone or within the corresponding starry zone wherein the soul previously had experience of a physical existence.

5. The Plane of Pure Flame. In this state the soul becomes aware of the pattern his spirit is weaving in the tapestry of eternity and realises all the emotional life of those souls fed by the same spirit.

6. The Plane of Pure Light. Within its borders the soul obtains an intellectual conception of all the previous existences within its group soul. Further, he realises all emotional life within the body of the world or earth soul.

7. Lastly, the Seventh Plane. The spirit and its various souls are now fused and pass into the Supreme Mind, the Imagination of God, wherein resides the Conception of the Whole, of universe after universe, of all states of existence, of past, present and future, of all that has been and all that shall be. Herein is continuous and complete consciousness, the true reality."

Although there is marked disagreement between different accounts of spirit worlds in the after-life, it will be recalled that this is also characteristic of the eschatology of different Eastern and Western religions.

Nowadays, all attempts to locate geographically such spirit worlds have been negated by space travel, and even the claims of flying saucer cults such as the **Aetherius Society** that there are mystic **Masters** on the planet Venus are no longer tenable, although it might be claimed that spiritaul beings and worlds exist on a different plane than that of matter.

It is surprising that there is no single spirit communication about the after-life that carries complete conviction or any kind of verification, since claimed spirit communications on other matters have sometimes proved surprisingly accurate.

If one grants the validity of spirit communication (as distinct from alternative parapsychological theories), the after-life of consciousness without a physical body is clearly bewildering and it may be that different accounts of a spirit environment would be colored by the mental constructions of individual consciousness.

It is also feasible that mental activity in a spirit world might create any environment it desired, based on earthly experience, rather as a novelist creates an imaginary world of characters and incidents. It will be recalled that the claimed spirit of Raymond, the dead son of Sir Oliver **Lodge,** inhabited a spirit world where it was still possible to drink brandy-and-soda.

It could also be claimed that spirits who have not become purified and refined and remain tied to earthly desires, would be easier to contact, and their communications would be unreliable. Advance spirits would have moved on to more rarified planes of existence.

It is interesting to note that many individuals who have experienced **out-of-the-body** traveling describe astral realms characterized as "Paradise condition" and a purgatorial realm of "Hades condition," as well as encountering there relatives and friends who have passed over and even angelic or diabolical entities.

Individuals who have temporarily experienced physical death but been resuscitated have also described spiritual realms and entities. (See also **Astral Body; Astral World; Death; Evolution of Life; NDE Project; Near-Death Experiences; Out-of-the-Body; Spirit; Survival; Theosophy**)

Spider

Various folklore beliefs surround the spider. In England, spiders were known as "money makers." If found on clothing, they were a sign that money was on the way, provided that the spider was not killed. A similar idea prevailed in Polynesia, where a spider dropping down in front of a person was a sign of a present. An American belief is that killing a spider will bring rain.

In folk medicine, a spider was rolled in butter or molasses and swallowed. As a cure for ague, it was tied up and secured on the left arm. A spider was also traditionally used as an **amulet.** The insect was baked and worn around the neck.

The British antiquary Elias Ashmole stated in his *Memoirs* (1717): "I took early in the morning a good dose of elixir, and hung three spiders around my neck, and they drove my ague away. Deo Gratias!"

Robert Burton (1577-1640) stated: "Being in the country in the vacation time, not many years since, at Lindly in Leicestershire, my father's house, I first observed this amulet of a spider in a nut-shell, wrapped in silk, so applied for an ague by my mother. . . . This I thought most absurd and ridiculous, and I could see no warrant in it. . . . till at length, rambling amongst authors, I found this very medicine in Dioscorides, approved by Matthiolus, repeated by Aldrovandus. . . . I began to have a better opinion of it, and to give more credit to amulets, when I saw it in some parties answer to experience."

Spiegelschrift

Writing written *backwards,* from right to left, so as to be read in a mirror. Automatic writing is frequently done in this way, and it is said that the ability to produce *spiegelschrift* is often found where there is a natural tendency to automatism. (See also **Automatic Writing**)

SPIRICOM

Apparatus invented by research engineer George W. Meek of the **MetaScience Foundation Inc.** as a communication system with the dead. This recent development of an **electronic voice phenomenon** involves a frequency modulation system using supplementary audio tones. In contrast to the previously claimed E.V.P. or **Raudive Voices** system, which obtained very weak voice signals, usually of a few words spoken at higher than normal speeds, the inventor of SPIRICOM and his associates claim to have received many hours of sustained conversation at normal speed from the American scientist Dr. George Jeffries Mueller who died of a heart attack fourteen years earlier.

The first announcement of SPIRICOM was made on April 6, 1982 following eleven years of research and development. The system was not entirely mechanical, since like other electronic devices (see **Black Box**) it required the psychic energies of an operator.

In a release published in the journal *New Realities* (vol. 4, No. 6), George W. Meek described his system of SPIRICOM Mark IV as consisting of three components: a transceiver operating in the 30-130 Mhz range; a special combination of 13 audio frequencies from 21 to 701 cps; and the input of energy from an operator who had certain highly psychic abilities, involving energy apparently outside present knowledge of the electromagnetic system, tentatively called "bioplasmic." The system was developed in conjunction with the MetaScience Foundation Inc. at Franklin, North Carolina.

The inventor and his associates made their preliminary announcement in order to encourage other researchers to develop beyond their basic stage so that communication with the dead by means of electronic apparatus might become perfected as quickly as possible. No patent rights were filed on the equipment, and both printed and audio explanatory materials were published to facilitate the work of other experimenters. For further information contact MetaScience Foundation Inc., P.O. Box 747, Franklin, North Carolina 28734. (See also **Ashkir-Jobson Trianion; Clairaudience; Communigraph; Electronic Voice Phenomenon;** Friedrich **Jürgenson;** Konstantin **Raudive; Raudive Voices; Reflectograph**)

Spirit

Variously defined as the inmost principle, the divine particle, the vital essence, the inherent actuating element in life. It manifests through association with protoplasm and dwells in the **astral body,** also called the **soul** which in turn is the connecting link between the spirit and the physical body.

At death the connection is severed and the spirit will find no ordinary means of manifestation. According to accumulated inferences, the spirits appear to be cognizant of space, although not conditioned by it. The same applies to time. Past, present and future do not exist for the spirit in the earthly sense.

There is no reason to suppose that spirits can play the role of Peeping Toms, keeping watch on the most private actions of the living. But it seems as if they are partly conscious of the thoughts and emotions which are directed towards them from the earth. It looks as if they have occasional glimpses of material facts upon the earth without gleaning them from living minds.

They cannot hold communion with the living if their mental attitude bars the way of their approach. Prof. Robert **Hare** was told by the spirits that there were peculiar elementary principles out of which spiritual bodies were constructed which were analogous to, but not identical with material elements, that the spirits have bodies, with a circulation and respiratory apparatus, that they breathe a gaseous or ethereal matter which is also inspired by men, beasts and fishes.

"The vision that can see through brick walls," stated Prof. William **Denton,** "and distinguish objects miles away, does not belong to the body; it must belong to the spirit. Hundreds of times have I had the evidence that the spirit can smell, hear and see, and has powers of locomotion. As the fin in the unhatched fish indicates the water in which he may one day swim, so these powers in man indicate that mighty realm with the spirit is fitted eternally to enjoy."

"Whether spirits can pass to other globes," wrote Hudson **Tuttle,** "depends on their degree of refinement. While some are very pure and ethereal, others are gross and unrefined. The sensualist, the depraved debauchee, in many instances, are so gross that gravity chains them to the earth's surface as it does man. They are denser than the spirit ether, and hence have weight, and cannot rise from earth. Others, who are more spiritual, can only rise to the first sphere; while others, still more refined, pass at will through the universal ocean of ether, visiting other globes and other solar systems."

All this is speculation, resting on assertions which defy experimental verification for the living. A number of observations, however, bear out the curious state of affairs that our material world is almost as invisible to spirit vision as the spirit world is to our eyes. "Your bodies and the atmosphere that surrounds you," quoted a spirit **control** of the great medium Daniel Dunglus **Home,** "is in many cases as solid and impenetrable to us as granite is to you."

In the experiences of Mrs. Travers Smith (see Hester **Dowden**) with the **ouija** board, the communicator generally only saw the medium. If a particularly sensitive person was there, the traveler moved toward him and he was claimed to have been seen dimly as in a mist. Voices other than the medium's were unheeded. "Peter," one of the controls, when sent to the medium's house to describe the state of a disarranged drawing-room in a test seance, came back very indignant and asked how he could have been given all the trouble when there were no human eyes to see through.

Dr. J. H. **Hyslop** wrote in *Contact with the Other World* (1919): "At one time in my experiments with Mrs. Chenoweth I used a headrest to support her head when she was in trance. Her eyes were buried in the pillow. Once, when the automatic writing was going on and Dr. Hodgson was purporting to communicate, she turned her face over so that her eyes, though closed, were exposed to the light. The communicator, apparently not knowing what had happened, remarked that he could almost see. Supposedly the light penetrating the eyelids had affected the communicator so that he could use the sense-organs."

Hyslop did not consider this incident conclusive. But he found a still better support for Dr. Hare's statement that the spirits used his eyes when the medium could not look at the alphabetical dial: "Since the development of Mrs. Chenoweth's trance into what we may call either a deep state or a further dissociation of the subconscious, I have frequently noticed that I must keep my eyes on the sheet of paper to prevent superposition. If I turn away to reach a new pad or to make notes, superposition is sure to begin; I may prevent it by keeping my eyes on the paper. . . . Apparently my own visual picture of the paper is immediately transferred to the control and he or she can regulate the writing accordingly."

The influence of the spirit world, whenever it finds an inroad into ours, is said to be exerted for the uplift of humanity. High teachings are invariably delivered wherever the veil is truly rent although many claimed spiritual teachings are trite or even misleading.

Sir William F. **Barrett** ventured to speculate: "If we can even alter the varieties of plants and animals by artifical selection, is it unreasonable to suppose that the psychical operation of unseen intelligences may have influenced the course of evolution through the ages? Is it possible that some of the unsolved problems in the doctrine of evolution may have to be shifted from the world of sense and gross matter to the unseen world around us, just as in physics we are gradually shifting our penultimate explanation of perceptible things to the imperceptible ether? The great First Cause must ever lie beyond our ken, but science, which deals with secondary causes, is finding that to many obscure questions the visible world appears to offer no intelligible solution." (*On the Threshold of the Unseen*). (See also **Death; Soul; Spheres; Spirit Hypothesis; Spiritualism; Survival)**

Recommended reading

Crawley, A. E. *The Idea of the Soul,* Macmillan, 1909

De Vesme, Caesar. *A History of Experimental Spiritualism,* 2 vols., Rider & Co., London, 1931

Driesch, Hans. *History and Theory of Vitalism,* Macmillan, 1914

Hackforth, R. (transl.) *Plato's Phaedo,* Cambridge University Press, 1955

Hare, Robert. *Experimental Investigation of the Spirit Manifestations,* New York, 1856

Heysinger, Isaac. *Spirit and Matter Before the Bar of Modern Science,* T. Werner Laurie, London, 1910

Hyslop, J. H. *Contact With the Other World,* Century Co., 1919

King, J. H. *The Supernatural,* 2 vols., London, 1892

Mead, G. R. S. *The Doctrine of the Subtle Body in Western Tradition,* J. M. Watkins, London, 1919

Myers, F. W. H. *Human Personality and Its Survival of Bodily Death,* Longmans, Green, London, & New York 1903; 1954; Arno Press, 1975

Tweedale, Rev. C. L. *Man's Survival After Death,* London, 1909; Dutton, 1918 etc.

Tylor, E. B. *Primitive Culture,* 2 vols., London/Putnam, 1871 etc.

Spirit and Nature (Magazine)

Bi-monthly magazine dealing with the teachings of Paramahansa **Yogananda** and his disciple Swami Kriyananda. Published by: Ananda Cooperative Village, 14618 Tyler Foote Road, Nevada City, California 95959.

Spirit Children

Children who passed over (died) and, according to accounts of mediums in **trance,** are growing to maturity on the other side. Child mediums have often claimed spirit children as their playmates.

Florence Marryat in her book *There is No Death* (1892) wrote of medium Bessie Williams' little girl "Mabel": "I have watched her playing at ball with an invisible child, and have seen the ball thrown, arrested half-way in the air, and then tossed back again as if a living child had been Mab's opponent." According to Marryat, when a still-born baby is lauched upon the other side, she is delivered over to the nearest relative of its parent to be named and brought up.

"The nurse of the little Guldenstubbe," wrote Baron Hellenbach in his book *Birth and Death as a Change of Perception* (1886), "who afterwards became a very celebrated medium, noticed with terror that his playthings moved about by themselves, while the child declared that another child was playing with them."

Spirit Hypothesis

The theory that the intelligence which directs the phenomena of the medium is a disembodied spirit. It is the only simple theory that covers every phase of manifestations. It is also the one which is consistently put forward by the invisible communicators.

Opposed to the spirit hypothesis stands the psychological theory of mediumship and the diabolic theory of Catholic theologians. The psychological theory reduces the phenomena to mental processes inherent in the mediums themselves and their associates.

According to prof. Theodore **Flournoy,** one of its ablest champions, "The state of passivity, the abdication of the normal personality, the relaxation of voluntary control over the muscular movements, and the ideas—this whole psycho-physiological attitude, where the subject is in a state of expectancy of communicating with the deceased—strongly predisposes him to mental dissociation and a sort of infantile regression, a relapse into an inferior phase of psychic evolution, where his imagination naturally begins to imitate the discarnate, utilising the resources of the subconscious, the emotional complexes, latent memories, instinctive tendencies ordinarily suppressed, etc., for the various roles it plays."

The information acquired must be supernormal, that is, not explicable by normal perception; (2) The incidents must be verifiable memories of the deceased persons and so representative of their personal identity; (3) The incidents must be trivial and specific—not easily, if at all, duplicated in the common experience of others.

Prof. William **James,** in his report of the Richard **Hodgson** spirit **control** of Mrs. Leonore **Piper** stated: "I myself can perfectly well imagine spirit agency, and find my mind vacillating about it curiously. When I take the phenomena piecemeal, the notion that Mrs. Piper's subliminal self should keep her sitters apart as expertly as she does, remembering its past dealings with each of them so well, not mixing their communications more, and all the while humbugging them so profusely, is quite compatible with what we know of the dreamlife of the hypnotised subjects . . . But I find that when I ascend from the details to the whole meaning of the phenomenon . . . the notion that such an immense current of experience, complex in so many ways, should spell out absolutely nothing but the word humbug, acquires a character of unlikeness. The notion that so many men and women, in all other respects honest enough, should have this preposterous monkeying self annexed to their personality seems to me so weird that the spirit theory immediately takes on a more probable appearance. The spirits, if spirits there be, must indeed work under incredible complications and falsifications, but at least if they are present some honesty is left in the whole department of the universe which otherwise is run by pure deception. The more I realise the quantitative massiveness of the phenomenon and its complexity, the more incredible it seems to me that in a world all of whose vaster features we are in the habit of considering to be sincere at least, however, brutal, this feature should be wholly constituted on insincerity."

In a chapter on 'The Spiritistic Hypothesis' in his book *My Philosophy* (1933), Sir Oliver **Lodge** stated: "My doctrine involves the primary reality of mind in association with whatever physical mechanism it may find available. Matter constitutes only one of these mechanisms, and indeed only constitutes it in a secondary fashion; and by a study limited to matter alone we shall never get the full reality of existence. I hold that all our actions on matter here and now are conducted through empty space, or rather through the entity which fills space; and that if our activity continues, it must be continued in the same sort of way and through the same sort of etheric mechanism that we already unconsciously utilise now. That in brief terms is the spiritistic hypothesis which I proclaim and work on." (See also **Death; Spirit; Spiritualism; Survival**)

Recommended reading

Beard, Paul. *Survival of Death: For and Against,* Hodder & Stoughton, London, 1966

Broad, C. D. *Personal Identity and Survival,* Society for Psychical Research (pamphlet), London, 1968

Carington, Whately, *The Foundations of Spiritualism,* Dutton, 1920

Hart, Hornell. *The Enigma of Survival; The Case for and Against Survival,* C. C. Thomas, Springfield, Illinois, 1959

Hyslop, James H. *Contact With the Other World; The Latest Evidence as to Communication With the Dead,*Century, 1919.

Jacobson, Nils Olof. *Life Without Death? On Parapsychology, Mysticism and the Question of Survival,* Delacorte Press, 1973; Turnstone Books, London, 1974

Richmond, Kenneth. *Evidence of Identity,* G. Bell, London, 1939

Rogo, D. Scott. *Welcoming Silence; A Study of Psychical Phenomena and Survival of Death,* University Books, 1973

Salter, W. H. *Zoar; or, The Evidence of Psychical Research Concerning Survival,* Sidgwick & Jackson, London, 1961; Arno Press, 1975

Smith, Susy. *Life Is Forever; Evidence for Survival After Death,* Putnam, 1974

Spirit Intervention

The intervention of spirits to find lost wills, other papers, objects of importance, or to track down murderers, has been often recorded.

Boccaccio, in his *Life of Dante,* related that the spectral form of Dante appeared in a dream to his son Jacopo Alighiere, and on the son's inquiry whether he had finished his great poem, the thirteenth canto of which they were unable to find, the spirit took him by the hand and led him to the house and into the room where he had been accustomed to sleep and pointed out a blind window covered by matting. On waking, the missing canto, which had not been seen before, was found in this place.

The philosopher Kant, in his revelations on Emanuel **Swedenborg,** narrated the story of Mme. Marteville, a widow who was asked to pay a debt of her deceased husband. She remembered that the debt was paid but could not find the receipt. During a visit to Swedenborg Mms. Marteville asked the seer if he had known her husband. Swedenborg answered in the negative, because he lived the whole time in London while the deceased was in Stockholm.

Eight days afterwards, the spirit of the dead appeared to the widow in a dream and showed her where she would find a casket of finest workmanship with the receipt and with a magnificent pin adorned with twenty brilliants which was believed also lost. She immediately got out of bed, ran to the place indicated and found the casket and contents.

In the morning, she was hardly awake when Swedenborg was announced. Without having knowledge of her dream Swedenborg told her that during the night he conversed with many spirits, among them with her deceased husband who, however, cut short the conversation by saying that he must visit his wife in order to reveal to her the whereabouts of a paper of the highest importance and of a diamond breast pin she thought lost. Swedenborg called to find out whether the spirit had kept his promise.

The Master of Lindsay (Lord **Adare**) on being questioned before the Committee of the **London Dialectical Society** on July 6, 1869, whether he ever obtained any information which could not have been known to the medium or to any present, told the following story:

"A friend of mine was very anxious to find a will of his grandmother, who had been dead forty years, but could not even find the certificate of her death. I went with him to the Marshall's, and we had a seance; we sat at a table, and soon the raps came; my friend then asked his questions *mentally;* he went over the alphabet himself, or sometimes I did so, not knowing the question. We were told the will had been drawn by a man named William Walker, who lived in Whitechapel; the name of the street, and the number of the house were given. We went to Whitechapel, found the man, and subsequently, through his aid, obtained a copy of the draft; he was quite unknown to us, and had not always lived in the locatlity, for he had once seen better days. The medium could not possibly have known anything about the matter, and even if she had, her knowledge would have been of no avail, as all the questions were mental ones."

Robert Macnish in his book *The Philosophy of Sleep* (1830) narrated the court case of R. of Bowland. He was summoned to pay a sum which his father had already paid. When he was about to pay again, the spirit of his father appeared to him in a dream and informed him that the respective papers were in the hands of M. of Inveresk, near Edinburgh. If he had no recollection of it, he should be reminded of the difference of opinion which he had with the deceased about a Portuguese coin. The reminder was most helpful. With the help of it the old attorney remembered and found the papers.

Gabriel Delanne, in his book *Le Spiritisme devant la Science* (1885), told the story of a spirit communication given to a descendant of Johann Sebastian Bach by the spirit of an Italian musician named Baldasarini who lived at the court of Henry III of France. The communication led to the discovery of a small strip of paper inside a spinet of 1664 with four lines of verse in the handwriting of Henry III. The authenticity of the writing was proved by comparing the strip with manuscripts in the Imperial Library.

The "Widow's Mite" incident was described by Dr. Isaac K. Funk in his book of this title, published in 1904. In February, 1903 he heard of a Brooklyn family where every Wednesday evening sittings took place in the presence of a few invited guests. He secured an invitation. On his third visit, when he was getting reconciled to the notion that the mediumship was a remarkably good case of secondary personality, the **control** "George" asked: "Has anyone here got anything that belonged to Mr. Beecher?"

There was no reply. On his emphatic repetition of the question, Funk replied: "I have in my pocket aletter from the Rev. Dr. Hillis, Mr. Beecher's successor. Is that what you mean?"

The answer was: "No, I am told by a spirit present, John Rakestraw that Mr. Beecher, who is not present, is concerned about an ancient coin, the Widow's Mite. This coin is out of place, and should be returned, and he looks to you, doctor, to return it."

Dr. Funk was greatly surprised and asked: "What do you mean by saying that he looks to me to return it? I have no coin of Mrs. Beecher's." The control then explained that he knew nothing about it, except that he was told that the coin was out of place and has been for a number of years and that Mr. Beecher said that Dr. Funk can find it, and can return it. The control also added that he was impressed that the coin was in a large iron safe in a drawer under a lot of papers.

Dr. Funk then remembered that when they were making the Standard Dictionary, he borrowed from a close friend of Beecher, who died several days before, a valuable ancient coin, known as the Widow's Mite. He asked that the coin was returned. The answer came that it was not.

After Dr. Funk had instituted a search the coin was in fact found in his office in a little drawer in the large iron safe under a lot of papers. In later inquiries through the control Dr. Funk was told that Mr. Beecher was not concerned about the return of the coin. His purpose was to give him a test to prove communication between the two worlds.

Prof. J. H. **Hyslop** in his report on the **direct voice** mediumship of Mrs. Elisabeth Blake of Ohio (*Proceedings* of the American Society for Psychical Research, vol. 7, p. 581) quoted the following case given by Dr. L. V. Guthrie, superintendent of the West Virginia Asylum at Huntington, Mrs. Blake's medical adviser:

"An acquaintance of mine, of prominent family in this end of the State, whose grandfather had been found at the foot of a high bridge with his skull smashed and life extinct, called on Mrs. Blake a few years ago and was not thinking of her grandfather at the time. She was very much surprised to have the spirit of her grandfather tell her that he had not fallen off the bridge while intoxicated, as had been presumed at the time, but that he had been murdered by two men who met him in a buggy and had proceeded to sandbag him, relieve him of his valuables, and throw him over the bridge. The spirit then proceeded to describe minutely the appearance of the two men who had murdered him, and gave such other information that had led to the arrest and conviction of one or both of these individuals."

Spirit Messenger (Journal)

(Full title: "The Spirit Messenger, and The Star of Truth"). Started in Springfield, Massachusetts, in 1849, the chief organ of Andrew Jackson **Davis'** "harmonial philosophy" after the *Univercoelum* journal expired. Rev. R. P. Amber, a Universalist minister and Apollos Munn were joint editors.

Spirit Photography

The production of photographs on which alleged spirit forms are visible. When the plate or film is developed there appears, in addition to the likeness of the sitter, a shape resembling more or less distinctly the human form, which at the moment of exposure was imperceptible to normal vision.

Spiritualists assert that there are photographs of spirits (the spirits of departed friends and relatives of the sitters) and that the presence of a medium is required to facilitate their production. Notwithstanding that on recognition of the supposed spirit by the sitter and others rests the main evidence in favor of spirit photography, the "astral figure" is often very vague and indistinct, with the head and shoulders enveloped in close-clinging draperies.

The practice of spirit photography originated in America in the nineteenth century, and enjoyed a fitful existence to the present day.

It was first introduced in 1862 by William H. **Mumler,** a Boston photographer. Dr. Gardner, of the same city, was photographed by Mumler, and on the plate appeared an image which the sitter identified as his cousin, who had died twelve years before. Dr. Gardner published his experience, and the new spirit photography was at once adopted by Spiritualists, who saw in it a means of proving their beliefs.

In 1863, however, Dr. Gardner discovered that in at least two instances a living model was the subject of Mumler's "spirit" pictures. Although he continued to believe that some of the photographs might be genuine, his exposure of Mumler as fraudulent effectively checked the movement for a time.

After a lapse of six years, Mumler appeared in New York, where the authorities endeavored to prosecute him, but the evidence against him was insufficient to prove fraud, and he was acquitted.

Spirit photography had flourished in America for some ten years before it became known in Britain. Mr. and Mrs. Samuel **Guppy,** the well-known Spiritualist mediums, endeavored without success to produce spirit photographs in private, and at length called in the aid of Frederick A. **Hudson,** a professional photographer. A Photograph of Mr. Guppy now revealed a dim, draped "spirit" form.

Hudson speedily became popular, and his studio was as largely patronized as Mumler's had been. Thomas **Slater**, a London optician, made careful observations of his process without being able to detect any fraud. John **Beattie**, a professional photographer, and something of a skeptic, made the following statement concerning Hudson's performances: "They were not made by double exposure, nor by figures projected in space in any way; they were not the result of mirrors; they were not produced by any machinery in the background, behind it, above it, or below it, nor by any contrivance connected with the bath, the camera, or the camera-slide."

Trail Taylor, editor of the *British Journal of Photography* said that "at no time during the preparation-,exposure, or development of the pictures was Mr. Hudson within ten feet of the camera or dark room.Appearances of an abnormal kind did certainly appear on several plates."

Such testimonies as these from the lips of skilled and disinterested witnesses, would naturally seem to raise spirit photography to the level of a genuine psychic phenomenon. But a careful analysis of the evidence, such as is given by Mrs. Sidwick in her article on Spirit Photography in *Proceedings* of the Society for Psychical Research ('On Spirit Photographs', vol. 7 pt. 19) serve to show how even a trained investigator may be deceived by sleight-of-hand. And it is notable that Mr. Beattie himself afterwards pointed out instances of double exposure in Hudson's productions.

In spite of this, Hudson continued to practice, and various Spiritualist magazines continued to lend him their support, with the exception of the *Spiritualist,* whose editor, himself a practical photographer, had aided John Beattie in the denunciation of spirit photography. Another enthusiastic Spiritualist, Enmore Jones, who at first claimed to recognize a dead daughter in one of the pictured "spirits," afterwards admitted that he had been mistaken.

Those who had pinned their faith to the genuineness of the photographic manifestations were naturally unwilling to relinquish their belief in what they considered a sure proof of the reality of the spirit world, and ingenious explanations were offered to cover the circumstance of the apparent double exposure.

The spirit aura, they said, differed from the natural atmosphere in its refracting power, and it was not to be wondered at that objects were sometimes duplicated. And so Hudson retained a considerable measure of popularity.

Beattie himself afterwards attempted to produce spirit photographs, and succeeded in obtaining vague blotches and flaws on his pictures, some of them bearing a dim resemblance to a human figure. but there is reason to believe that a hired assistant, who provided studio and apparatus, was not entirely above suspicion.

In 1874, the Paris photographer E. **Buguet** crossed over to London where he commenced the practice of spirit photography. Many of his pictures were recognized by his clients, and even when he had been tried by the French Government, and had admitted deception, there were those who refused to regard his confession as spontaneous, and inclined to the opinion that he had been bribed by Jesuits to confess to fraud of which he was innocent!

Other spirit photographers were F. M. **Parkes,** a contemporary of Hudson, and Richard **Boursnell,** who produced spirit pictures in London in later years.

The principal evidence in favor of spirit photography is undoubtedly the recognition of the spirits by their friends and relatives, but the unreliable nature of such a test can be seen when we remember that time and again a single "spirit" has been claimed by several persons as a near relative—the sister of one, the grandfather of another, and so on.

One of the most prominent defenders of the mediumistic photographers was the Rev. W. Stainton **Moses** (who wrote under the pseudonym "M. A. Oxon"), who saw in them the best proof of the reality of Spiritualism.

The same view was shared by Alfred Russel **Wallace,** who said in the *Arena* (January, 1891): "It is that which furnishes, perhaps, the most unassailable demonstration it is possible to obtain of the objective reality of spiritual forms."

Spirit "extras" are not the only paranormal effects claimed in psychic photography. Many photographs have been produced which include "extras" of "spirit writing," some on photographic plates not exposed in a camera (see **Skotograph**).

In modern times, Ted **Serios** of Chicago has produced what appear to be thought pictures of distant scenes on a Polaroid film. The Japanese investigator Dr. T. **Fukurai** used the term "Thoughtography" for paranormal images on photographic materials.

The whole subject of psychic photography, of which spirit photography is a part, is treated more fully, with a list of recommended books on the subject in a separate entry. (See also **Nengraphy; Psychic Photography**)

"Spirit Teachings" (by "M. A. Oxon")

The famous book written by the Rev. W. Stainton **Moses** which recorded the teachings of the "Imperator" group of spirit controls.

Spirit World, The (Periodical)

(1) The first Spiritualist periodical in England, published by W. R. Hayden in May, 1853. Only one number appeared. (2) The title to which "The Spiritual Philosophy" periodical of La Roy **Sunderland** was changed in America in 1851.

Spiritism

A general term for the belief that the spirits or souls of the dead can communicate with the living through a medium or psychically sensitive individual.

Although often regarded as synonymous with **"Spiritualism"** (which usually embodies Spiritism in a Christian religious and philosophical context), the term "Spiritism" is more properly indicative of the particular Spiritualist teachings of Allen **Kardec** (1804-1869) in France, involving a doctrine of **reincarnation.**

Prior to his adoption of Spiritualist beliefs about 1862, Kardec had been an exponent of **animal magnetism** and **phrenology.** He based his new teachings on spirit revelations received through clairvoyants, and so popular were these teachings that they rapidly spread over the Continent.

In Britain, however, Spiritism obtained little hold, its only prominent exponent being Miss Anna **Blackwell,** who endeavored without success to establish the doctrine of reincarnation.

Spiritism and Spiritualism should not be confused, since the adherents of each section were opposed to the tenets of the other, and even in France, where Spiritism obtained the strongest footing, there was a distinct Spiritualist party who were reluctant to accept the doctrine of reincarnation.

The term Spiritist is sometimes also applied to one who seeks only the physical phenomena, and neglects the religious and philosophic aspect of Spiritualism.

Kardec's Spiritism flourished in nineteenth-century France, and is today well established in South America, especially Brazil, where it is estimated that there are now some four million Spiritists. The Spiritism of Kardec discouraged such physical mediumship as materialization in favor of **automatic writing,** believing this to be a more direct and unambiguous contact with departed spirits.

Modern Brazilian Spiritists also make a distinction between ordinary automatic writing (*escrita automotica*) which might involve the medium's own subconscious, and *psicografia* (dictation from a spirit entity).

However, modern South American Spiritism tends to blur formal distinctions between Spiritism and Spiritualism, particularly in Brazil, where all kinds of physical phenomena are manifest, including **psychic surgery.** Brazil has also honored Allan Kardec in three separate postage stamp commemorative issues. (See also **France; Reincarnation; Spiritualism)**

Recommended reading

Kardec, Allan. *The Spirits' Book,* London, 1875 etc. (frequently reprinted)

Kardec, Allan. *Experimental Spiritism; The Mediums' Book,* London, 1876 etc. (frequently reprinted)

Playfair, Guy Lyon. *The Flying Cow; Research Into Paranormal Phenomena in the World's Most Psychic Country* [Brazil], Souvenir Press, London/Dent, Ontario, 1975; paperback edition under title *The Unknown Power,* Pocket Books, 1975; Panther paperback, U.K., 1977

Spirito, Ugo (1896-)

Professor of philosophy who wrote on parapsychology. Born September 9, 1896 at Arezzo, Italy, he studied at University of Rome (LL.B. 1918, Ph.D. 1920).

He was professor of politics and corporate economics at University of Pisa from 1932-34, professor of philosophy and history of philosophy at University of Messina in 1935, professor of theoretical philosophy at University of Genoa in 1935, professor of philosophy (1937-50), professor of theoretical philosophy (1951 onwards) at University of Rome.

Dr. Spirito published a number of books on sociology and philosophy. His books relating to parapsychology include: *Scienza e Filosofia* (Science and Philosophy, 1933; 1950),*La vita come ricerca* (Life as a Search, 1937; 1948), *La Vita come arte* (Life as Art, 1941; 1948), *Il Problematicismo* (Problematicism, 1948), *La vita come amore* (Life as Love, 1953), *Significato del nostro tempo* (Meaning of the Present Age, 1955), *Inizio di una nuova epoca* (Beginning of a New

Epoch, 1961), *Critica della democrazia* (Critique of Democracy, 1963). He attended the First International Conference of Parapsychological Studies In Utrecht, Netherlands in 1953.

Spiritoid

Term used by psychical researcher Emile **Boirac** for messages which originate in the subconscious mind and appear in a dramatic and personalized form. It was also used by Prof. Cesar **Lombroso** and Prof. Theodore **Flournoy.**

Spiritual Advisory Council Newsletter

Bi-monthly publication with information on seminars and groups concerned with psi phenomena. Address: 2965 W. State Road 434, #300, Longwood, Florida 32779.

Spiritual Age, The (Periodical)

Early American Spiritualist periodical. (See also **Spiritualism**)

Spiritual Athenaeum

The headquarters of British Spiritualists in London in 1866. Dr. John **Elliotson** was on the Council. The post of residential secretary was offered to the great medium D. D. **Home.** The real intent behind the foundations's offer was to help Home who was struggling with financial difficulties. When, owing to a change of fortune, he resigned his post, the Institution died a natural death.

Spiritual Clarion, The (Periodical)

One of the first American Spiritualist periodicals, published Auburn, New York. (See also **Spiritualism**)

Spiritual Community Guide

Regularly updated directory type publication with three major sections: Resources for the New Age, Guide to Spiritual and Growth Centers (includes brief descriptions), Community Directory with geographical listing of organizations.

This useful publication has articles and photographs dealing with New Age leaders, publications, booksellers, vegetarian suppliers and restaurants, constituting a complete conspectus of modern New Age and New Consciousness activities.

This useful directory has now been subsumed in *The New Consciousness Sourcebook* with a wider range of subject matter. Address: Spiritual Community Publications/NAM, Box 1067, Berkeley, California 94701.

Spiritual Counterfeits Project

Evangelical Christian group disseminating information exposing alleged false claims and aims of popular religious and pseudo-religious cults. SCP has also taken legal action to inhibit the activities of cults.

In 1985, the S.C.P. was put into bankruptcy as a result of being a third defendant in a libel action brought by Witness Lee, leader of the Local Church based in Anaheim, California, who claimed that he was libeled in a book by Neil Duddy titled *The Peculiar Teachings of Witness Lee and His Local Church,* originally published in German by a Swiss publisher in 1979. The Duddy book updated an English-language edition published in 1977 by the S.C.P. A $12 million award was made against Duddy, living in Denmark, and Schwengeler-Verlag, the Swiss publisher, neither of whom contested the suit since damages cannot be collected abroad.

The S.C.P. was dropped as third defendant after spending over $300,000 in defense, but was obliged to declare bankruptcy. Bill Squires, a cofounder of the S.C.P., was quoted as saying, "I wonder whether this case means that you can't go to press with a book if you don't have as much money to defend yourself as those you're writing about." Although the S.C.P. went out of business, it hoped to resume publishing when it emerged from bankruptcy. Address: P.O. Box 4308, Berkeley, California. (See also **Citizens Freedom Foundation; Cults**)

Spiritual Frontiers Fellowship

Spiritualist organization founded in 1956 "to sponsor, explore and interpret the growing interest in psychic phenomena and mystical experience within the church, wherever these experiences relate to effective prayer, spiritual healing and personal survival."

It maintains a library of 5,000 volumes and publishes a monthly Newsletter. It has a membership of 7,500 and is affiliated with the Academy of Religion and Psychical Research. Address: c/o Elizabeth W. Fenske, Ph.D., 3310 Baring Street, Philadelphia, Pennsylvania 19104.

Spiritual Frontiers Journal

Quarterly journal published by **Spiritual Frontiers Fellowship.** Includes articles on psi research, and the relationship between spiritual sciences and the church. Address: 10819 Winner Road, Independence, Missouri 64052.

Spiritual Gazette

Monthly publication of the **Spiritualist Association of Great Britain,** including reports on psychic phenomena and events of interest to Spiritualists. Address: 33 Belgrave Square, London, S.W.1., England.

Spiritual Herald, The (Journal)

A short-lived British journal of Swedenborgian Spiritualists published in London from February till July, 1856.

Spiritual India and Kundalini (Magazine)

Quarterly journal of international spiritual and scientific progress in the study of **Kundalini,** the mysterious energy in human beings related to sexual activity and higher consciousness.

Published by the Kundalini Research and Publication Trust, New Delhi, this journal centers round the experience and theories of Pandit **Gopi Krishna,** and worldwide authority on the subject of Kundalini, who has attracted the attention of modern scientists, scholars and spiritual teachers. Address: Kundalini, D-291 Sarvodaya Enclave, New Delhi 110017, India.

Presently inactive.

Spiritual Institution

Established by pioneer British Spiritualists James **Burns,** at 15 Southampton Row, London, in conjunction with a Progressive Library dealing with books of Spiritualism. The organization included a lending library of several thousand volumes on Spiritualism and related subjects, with a reading room, and rooms for seances or experiments connected with Spiritualism.

The organization became a center for Spiritualism in London, providing regular programs of developing circles, seances, concerts and other social events, and an influential meeting place for Spiritualists.

No longer in existence.

Spiritual Magazine, The

The British Spiritualist monthly of its period, successor to the *British Spiritual Telegraph.* It was founded by William Wilkinson who jointly edited it with Thomas Shorter, William **Howitt** being the chief contributor. It flourished from 1860-77.

Spiritual Messenger, The (Journal)

British Spiritualist monthly which published a few numbers in London in the winter of 1858-59, edited by W. Carpenter.

Spiritual Notes (Journal)

Monthly official publication of the **British National Association of Spiritualists,** which flourished from 1878-81.

Spiritual Philosopher, The (Periodical)

The first Spiritualist periodical in America, founded by La Roy Sunderland in 1850, as a monthly, then becoming weekly, the title changing to *Spirit World* after the first year.

Spiritual Quarterly Magazine, The

British periodical of Spiritualism, published by the Two Worlds Publishing Company in Manchester from October 1902. It was edited by Will Phillips, and had only a short life.

Spiritual Regeneration Movement of America

Founded in 1959 to teach the philosophy of **Transcendental Meditation** and its technique, as developed by **Maharishi Mahesh Yogi.** It sponsors lectures and conducts studies on the effect of transcendental meditation on the individual. It publishes a semiannual Newsletter. Address: 11428 Santa Monica Boulevard, Los Angeles, California 90025. Apparently now inactive at this address.

Spiritual Review (Journal)

British monthly, founded by J. J. **Morse** in 1900 running until May 1902, when Morse departed from England for an extensive lecture tour to Australia, New Zealand and the United States.

Spiritual Scientist, The (Journal)

American weekly, founded in 1874 in Boston, edited by E. Gerry Brown. No longer published.

Spiritual Telegraph (Periodical)

American Spiritualist weekly, founded by S. B. Brittan and Charles Partridge, published in New York from 1852-60. In 1860 it merged into the *Herald of Progress* which Andrew Jackson **Davis** founded.

Spiritual Times, The (Periodical)

British Spiritualist weekly, published in London from 1864-66, edited by J. H. Powell and W. H. Harrison.

Spiritualism

Spiritualism, according to a definition adopted by the **National Spiritualist Association of the United States of America,** "is the Science, Philosophy and Religion of continuous life, based upon the demonstrated fact of communication, by means of mediumship, with those who live in the Spirit World. Spiritualism is a science because it investigates, analyses and classifies facts and manifestations, demonstrated from the spirit side of life. Spiritualism is a philosophy because it studies the laws of nature both on the seen and unseen sides of life and bases its conclusions upon present observed facts. It accepts statements of observed facts of past ages and conclusions drawn therefrom, when sustained by reason and by results of observed facts of the present day. Spiritualism is a religion because it strives to understand and to comply with the Physical, Mental and Spiritual Laws of Nature which are the laws of God."

According to the British medium the Rev. W. Stainton **Moses,** a Spiritualist is "one who has proven for himself, or has accepted on adequate evidence, the fact that death does not kill the spirit."

There are two basic teachings in Spiritualism: the continuity of personality and the powers of communication after death. Spiritualism teaches that death works no miracle, that it is a new birth into a spiritual body, the counterpart of the physical which is gifted with new powers.

Neither punishment, nor rewards are meted out. Individuality, character, memory undergo no change. The main principle of the new life is the progression of the fittest. The rapidity of progress is in proportion to the mental and moral faculties acquired in earth life. Every spirit is left to discover the truth for himself or herself. Evil passions, sinful life, may chain a spirit to the earth, but the road of endless progress opens up even for these as soon as they discover the light. Higher and higher spiritual **spheres** correspond to the state of progress. The gradation is apparently endless. Communion with the higher intelligences is open but of God they know no more than we do.

Spiritualism and Religion

"Spiritualism" wrote Sir Arthur Conan **Doyle,** "is a religion for those who find themselves outside all religions; while on the contrary it greatly strengthens the faith of those who already possess religious beliefs."

The important aspect of the relationship of Spiritualism to other religious creeds is that it founds the belief in survival upon claimed provable facts instead of ancient traditions and thereby reconciles religion with science. It offers a progressive and evolutionary religion. It does not look "backward to fading tradition, but onward to dawning experience." And there is hope that the intercourse consciously begun may lead through long effort into a direct communion with the higher world.

It restores primitive Christianity and teaches that the angels are with us now as in olden days; it returns a definite answer to the age-old question: "If a man dies shall he live again?", and does away with the terror of death.

Inscriptions in the Catacombs show that the early Christians spoke of the dead as though they were still living. Saint Augustine in his *De cura pro Mortuis* stated: "The spirits of the dead can be sent to the living and can unveil to them the future which they themselves have learned from other spirits or from angels, or by divine revelation."

Spiritualism does not admit unchangeable bliss or eternal damnation. There is no hell with brimstone and flames of fire in the orthodox sense, no devils, no last judgment, no vicarious atonement. Christ was a Great Teacher who descended to set an example. "It is our task to do for Christianity what Jesus did for Judaism," said a message received by the Rev. W. Stainton **Moses** from his teachers in the Beyond.

There is no resurrection of the physical body. The hieracites, a sect which flourished in the fourth century, were described as heretics because they maintained that it was the soul alone which arose again and the resurrection was entirely spiritual.

In that sense and in that sense alone, Spiritualism is a heresy. Yet it was not too bold of F. W. H. Myers to declare in *Human Personality and Its Survival of Bodily Death* (2 vols., 1903): "I predict that, in consequence of the new evidence, all reasonable men, a century hence, will believe the Resurrection of Christ, whereas, in default of the new evidence, no reasonable men, a century hence would have believed it. . . . We have shown that amid much deception and self-deception, fraud and illusion, veritable manifestations do reach us from beyond the grave. The central claim of Christianity is thus confirmed, as never before. If our own friends, men like ourselves, can sometimes return to tell us of love and hope, a mightier Spirit may well have used the eternal laws with a more commanding power."

Spiritualism admits all the truths of morality and religion in all other sects. Its own moral and religious teachings are sane and rational. The good which they achieved both in personal respect and for the progress of humanity is immeasurable. President Abraham **Lincoln** freed the American slaves largely under Spiritualist influence.

In November 1872, the *Religio-Philosophical Journal of Chicago* published the following statement of Elder Evans, the Shaker: "At a public dinner, given by the Emperor of Russia, he confessed with the simplicity of a child what was confirmed by the Empress and other members of their suite, that he was influenced by spirits through the American medium Home, to emancipate the twenty million of serfs; and that the spirits helped and sustained him in the accomplishment of his arduous undertaking." To the inquiry of Dr. Eugene Crowell, Elder Evans confirmed the truth of the statement and said he received it from the mouth of a physician who was a guest at the public dinner referred to.

Gerald **Massey** said in a beautiful tribute: "Spiritualism will make religion infinitely more real, and translate it from the domain of belief to that of life. It has been to me, in common with many others, such a lifting of the mental horizon and a letting in of the heavens—such a transformation of faith into facts—that I can only compare life without it to sailing on board ship with hatches battened down, and being kept prisoner, cribbed, cabined, and confined, living by the light of a candle—dark to the glory overhead, and blind to a thousand possibilities of being—and then suddenly on some starry night allowed to go on deck for the first time to see the stupendous mechanism of the starry heavens all aglow with the glory of God, to feel that vast vision glittering in the eyes, bewilderingly beautiful, and drink in a new life with every breath of its wondrous liberty, which makes you dilate almost large enough in soul to fill the immensity which you see around you."

There are those who maintain that those mediums who hold seances and become the direct mouthpieces of the spirits are only supereminently endowed with a faculty common to all humanity—that all men and woman are mediums in a greater or less degree, and that all inspiration, whether good or bad, comes from the spirits. It is in connection with this idea of the universality of mediumship that the effect of Spiritualism on the morals and daily life of its adherents is most clearly seen. For the spirits are naturally attracted to those mediums whose qualities resemble their own.

Enlightened spirits from the highest spheres seek high-souled and earnest mediums through whom to express themselves, while mediums who use their divine gifts for a base end are sought by the lowest and wickedest human spirits, or by beings termed "elementals," who do not even reach the human standard of goodness.

Indeed, it is claimed that the lower spirits communicate with the living much more readily than do the higher, by reason of a certain gross or material quality which binds them to earth.

The path of the medium is thus beset with many difficulties, and it is essential that he or she should be principled and sincere, an individual of pure life and high ideals, so that the circle of spirit "controls" be select. For not only do the tricky elementals deceive the sitters and the investigators with their lying ways, but they often encourage the medium to fraud, so that he or she secretes false **"apports"** and "materializes" false beards and dirty muslin.

As with the full-fledged medium, so with the normal individual. If one is to insure that the source of inspiration be a high one, one must live in such a way that only the best spirits will control and so one's impulses be for good and the betterment of the human race.

It will thus be seen that Spiritualism is in itself a complete religion, but it also combines well with other religions and creeds. In America, the Spiritualist and the early Socialist elements mingled harmoniously and many of the socialist communities of the nineteenth century were founded by Spiritualists.

Other sects which associated themselves with Spiritualism during the early history of the movement in America were less creditable ones, such as those which advocated Free Love. But the many forms which Spiritualism took in America were the product of the country and the time.

In other lands, the forms were different. In England, for instance where habit and tradition were more happily settled, Spiritualism was regarded as by no means incompatible with Christianity but rather as affording a fuller revelation of the Christian religion, a view which the trance utterances of mediums confirmed.

In France, Allan Kardec's doctrines of **reincarnation** blended with the doctrines of Spiritualism to produce **Spiritism.** Then we have the later example of **Theosophy,** a blending of Spiritualism with Oriental religions. But all these varied forms contain the central creed of Spiritualism—the belief in the continuance of life after the "great dissolution," or death of the body, and in continual progress of the soul, and in the fact of communication between the freed spirit and living human beings.

On the whole, Spiritualists have shown themselves rather tolerant than otherwise to those who were not of their faith. Spiritualism is regarded by its adherents as a religion, or a supplement to an existing religion, imposing certain moral obligations and offering new and far-reaching revelations on the conditions of existence beyond the grave.

The continuity of life after death is, of course, one of its most important tenets, although not a distinctive one; since on it depend most of the world's creeds and religions. But the Spiritualist's ideas concerning the *nature* of the life of the freed soul are characteristic of this creed.

The soul, or spirit, is said to be composed of a sort of attenuated matter, inhabiting the body and resembling it in form. On the death of the body the soul withdraws itself, without however, undergoing any direct change, and for a longer or shorter period remains on the "earth plane." But the keynote of the spirit world is *progress,* so after a time the spirit proceeds to the lowest "discarnate plane," and from that to a higher and a higher, gradually evolving into a purer and nobler type, until at length it reaches the sphere of pure spirit.

The other central belief of Spiritualism is that the so-called "dead" can, and do, communicate with the living, through the agency of mediums, and can produce in the physical world certain phenomena depending for their operation transcending known physical laws.

To the earnest Spiritualist, requiring no further proof of the reality of the creed, the subjective phenomena, as they are called, comprising trance-speaking, automatic writing, clairvoyance, etc., are of greater importance than the more sensational physical manifestations, just as the latter are more in favor with psychical researchers, because of the better opportunities they offer for investigation.

From the trance-speaking of the medium are gathered those particulars of the spirit world which to the outsider present a picture extant of that domain. The spirit life is, in fact, represented as a somewhat attenuated reproduction of earthly life, conducted in a highly rarified atmosphere.

Automatic drawings, purporting to depict spirit scenes, afford a description no less flattering than the written picture, although many such drawings appear imaginative rather than factual.

From their exalted spheres the spirits are said to be cognisant of the doings of their fellow individuals still on earth, and at all times ready to aid and counsel the latter. This they can do mainly through the medium, who is a link between the seen and the unseen, through some quality of paranormal sensitivity.

Phenomena therefore occupies a central place in Spiritualism, and the question of the genuineness of claimed phenomena is of great importance. It is true, of course, that paranormal phenomena is also central to the development of other great religions which have claimed miracles in support of doctrine.

The Spiritualist can rightly point to the fact that the Judaeo-Christian *Holy Bible* is full of miraculous phenomena which are not essentially different from those demonstrated by modern mediums—inspired trance addresses, paranormal healing, apparitions, prophetic statements, as well as physical miracles have been claimed by Spiritualists.

The Phenomena of Spiritualism

These fall into two main groups: physical and mental. Both groups contain a great variety of manifestation. The following phenomena belong to the physical order:

Acoustic phenomena (Percussive sounds as **raps** and blows; noises, voices, **music** on instruments or without).

Apports, disappearance of objects, passing of **matter through matter, transportation** of the human body **(teleporation).**

Automatism in various forms: agitation of the body or limbs, **automatic writing, drawing, painting, slate-writing; direct writing,** drawing and painting.

Biological phenomena, such as influencing the growth of **plants** by vital bodily emanations or by other unknown means.

Chemical phenomena: psychic lights **(luminous phenomena), perfumes,** catalytic action, production of water, **psychic photography.**

Electric phenomena: discharge of electroscopes, phenomena suggesting human radioactivity.

Fire Immunity.

Levitation of the human body.

Magnetic phenomena.

Materialization and dematerialization.

Movement of objects without contact **(telekinesis),** vibratory effects, increase and decrease in weight, spelling out messages by **typtology,** and other complicated operations, as untying of bonds, etc.

Plastics: imprints of fingers, hands, faces, legs, and psychic rods, molds of faces, hands and legs.

Psychic **touches.**

Psycho-physiological phenomena, change of stature: **elongation,** shrinking or puffing out of the human body; **stigmata,** effects of **personation, transfiguration, obsession** and **trance** in general; loss of weight, nervous drain, **ectoplasm, aura** and **emanations.**

Thermodynamic effects: variations of temperature, increase of heat in apported objects or in case of penetration of matter through matter, currents of air, psychic **winds.**

Many of the mental phenomena have a physical background, yet the intellectual operation on the part of the medium gives a definite line of distinction. **Clairvoyance,** in all its variegated forms, **clairaudience, crystal gazing, divination** in general, involving **prediction** with its rudimentary forms as **premonition, monition, monitions of approach, dowsing** as regards the interpretation of the movement of the rod, **healing, possession, personation, obsession** in their intellectual aspects, **psychometry, trance** speaking, other forms of spirit communications, **telepathy** and **xenoglossis** or the gift of tongues constitute the range of mental phenomena.

Unknown mental processes of the medium may furnish the key to much of the mystery. But there are phenomena in which the interplay of an extraneous factor was variously speculated to be the will of someone living, a disembodied human consciousness, or something of non-human origin.

Professor Maximilian **Perty,** of the University of Berne, in his book *Die Mystischen Euscheinungen der menlischlichen Natur,* published in 1861, assumed the existence of planetary spirits with whom the spirit ofthe entranced medium can enter into communion. Dr. Edward von **Hartmann** similarly conjectured that the mind of the seer is in connection with the Absolute and through the Absolute with other individual minds. Many Catholic theologians solved the question in a simplistic way. They were almost dogmatic that the phenomena were inspired by the devil.

Charles Bray, the author of *The Philosophy of Necessity* (revised ed. 1863) theorized that our bodies are continually giving off thought rays just as they give off heat rays. These thought emanations are not lost, "many facts now point to an atmosphere or reservoir of thought, the result of cerebration into which the thought and feeling generated by the brain are continually passing." He supposed that mediums might be in communication with this thought reservoir.

Among later speculations we find "the psychic factor" of Prof. C. D. **Broad,** author of *The Mind and Its Place in Nature* (1925), which he conceives as a kind of mind detritus, able to create a personality, but no more personal than matter, and Dr. Joseph **Maxwell's** "collective consciousness" which is the correlative of Prof. Enrico **Morselli's** "psychodynamic" theory. Last, but with the greatest practical appeal, comes the **spirit hypothesis,** the modern working theory of many well-known psychical researchers, meaning that a human spirit which has survived the change of death is instrumental in causing the manifestations.

Of course, both the Spiritualist belief and alternative explanations by parapsychologists rest on assessment of the validity of the claimed phenomena. Because of this, most modern scientific investigation tends to be removed from the suggestible atmosphere of the seance room and the opportunities for fraud in a religious setting.

It is unfortunately a matter of record that the history of Spiritualism has been riddled with fraud and deception by fake mediums. On this account, many skeptics have dismissed all claimed Spiritualist phenomena as fraud or malobservation. This absolutist view does not do justice to the facts.

Typical of such views is the recent book *The Spiritualists* by Ruth Brandon (1983) which attempts to debunk all claimed paranormal phenomena as either fraudulent or explicable in some natural way. Taking this as her preconceived opinion, it is not difficult for her to apparently validate it by a selective or biased interpretation of a century of psychical research.

The phenomena of the seance room have been manifest throughout history in many of the world's great religions, occurring amongst intelligent and shrewd individuals as much as amongst the credulous. Those who claim that all psychical researchers who have endorsed such phenomena, including many great scientists, were all deceived or even accessories to fraud must also cast doubts upon their own absolutist judgments! Surely they are equally fallible?

A commonsense position does not deny a proportion of fraud and malobservation amongst Spiritualists and also amongst their skeptical critics, but is prepared to accept the probable genuineness of some phenomena as a working hypothesis until disproved or vindicated.

Perhaps the greatest error in reviewing paranormal phenomena is to concentrate only on their physical aspects, ignoring the qualitative aspects. For example, trance mediumship may be inspiring or it may be trite and banal. Paranormal bending of spoons may be genuine or just fraud, but in itself contributes little to the great questions of meaning in human life and endeavor.

If Spiritualists derive faith, courage and wisdom from the claimed phenomena and communications of mediums, that is, in itself, a desirable social and cultural development, as much as in other religions. If, however, acceptance of phenomena makes people narrow-minded and eccentric, that is to be deplored as much as comparable fanaticisms in other religions and cults.

Meanwhile it is important to stress that Spiritualists are usually the first to discover and denounce frauds.

Origins of Spiritualism

Although modern Spiritualism in its present form dates no further back than 1848, it is possible to trace its ancestry in the animistic beliefs of primitive peoples, in the miracles of world religions, and the phenomena associates with **witchcraft, poltergeist, possession** and **Animal Magnetism.** Although at the time, such phenomena were not always associated with the spirits of the dead, the belief that they were caused by demons merely reflected the dogmatic theology of their time.

Many famous outbreaks of an epidemic nature, such as that among the **Tremblers of the Cevennes** and the **Convulsionaries of St. Mèdard,** which to the beholders showed clear indications of demonic possession, had in their symptoms considerable analogy with modern Spiritualism. They were accompanied by spontaneous **trance** or **ecstasy,** utterance of lengthy discourses, and speaking in unknown **tongues,** all of which are phenomena to be found in the seance room.

The fluency of speech, especially of such ignorant peasants, has been equalled, if not surpassed, by the outpourings of the unlearned medium under the influence of a **"control."** In such historical cases, the symptoms were generally referred either to angelic or diabolic possession, and most frequently to the later.

Witches also were supposed to hold converse with the Devil, and many aspects of witchcraft, notably the part played by persecuted young women and children show an obvious relationship to those **poltergeist** disturbances which were the connecting link between early forms of **possession** and modern Spiritualism. Cases in which children of morbid tendencies pretended to be the victims of a witch are to be found in many records of witchcraft.

It was the poltergeist, however, who showed affinity to the "control" of the mediumistic circle. For at least the past few centuries, poltergeist disturbances have occurred from time to time, and the mischievous spirit's favorite modes of manifesting itself have been similar to those adopted by the spirit control of our days.

Both spirits require the agency of a medium for the production of their phenomena, and it is in the immediate presence of the medium that the phenomena generally make their appearance. Both also tend to display personality, if of an infantile nature in the case of poltergeist. Intelligent communication has often developed through raps in poltergeist phenomena.

Partly evolving from these phases of spirit manifestation, and partly running parallel with them, was an extensive movement whose significance, from the Spiritualist point of view, was very considerable. The doctrine of **Animal Magnetism** was said to have originated with **Paracelsus,** and was much in favor with the old alchemists. The actual magnet was not greatly used, but was regarded as a symbol of the magnetic philosophy, which rested on the idea of a force or fluid radiating from the heavenly bodies, human beings, and indeed, from every substance, animate or inanimate, by means of which all things interacted upon one another.

While the mystics were engaged in formulating a magnetic philosophy, there were others, such as the seventeenth-century healer Valentine **Greatrakes,** who cured diseases, claiming such power as a divine gift, and not connecting it with the ideas of the alchemists.

These two phases of "magnetism" united and came to a height in the work of Franz Antoine **Mesmer,** who in 1766 published his *De planetarium influxu,* a treatise on the influence of the planets on the human body.

His ideas were essentially those of the magnetic philosophers, and his cures probably on a level with those of Valentine Greatrakes, but he infused new life into both theory and practice and won for himself the recognition, if not of the learned societies, at least of the general public.

To him is due that application of the "magnetic" system which resulted in the discovery of the induced hypnotic trance, which has a bearing on the phenomena of Spiritualism.

In 1784, a commission was appointed by the French Government to consider magnetism as practiced by Mesmer and his followers but its report only served to cast discredit on the science, and exclude it from scientific discussion. Until the third decade of the nineteenth century, the rationalist explanations of **Mesmerism** concerned themselves entirely with a fluid or force emanating from the person of the operator, and even visible to the eye of a clairvoyant, but in 1823 Alexandre Bertrand, a Paris Physician, published his *Traité du Somnambulisme,* and in 1826 a treatise *Du Magnetisme Animal en France,* in which he established the relationship between ordinary sleep-walking, **somnambulism** associated with disease, and epidemic ecstasy, and advanced the doctrine, now generally accepted, of **suggestion.**

Animal Magnetism was by this time receiving a good deal of attention all over Europe. A second French Commission appointed in 1825 presented in 1831 a report which, although of no great value, contained an unanimous testimony to the actuality of the phenomena.

In Germany, also, magnetism was practiced to a considerable extent, and rationalist explanations found some acceptance. There was a class however, more numerous in Germany than elsewhere, who inclined towards a Spiritualist explanation of Mesmeric phenomena. Indeed, the belief in spirit intercourse had grown up beside magnetism from its earliest conception, in opposition to the theory of a magnetic fluid.

In the earlier phases of "miraculous" healing, the cures were ascribed to the divine gift of the operator, who expelled the evil spirits from the patient. In epidemic cases in religious communities, as well as in individual instances, the spirits were questioned both on personal matters and on abstract theological questions.

A detailed account of the trance utterances of an hypnotic subject was given in 1787 in the journals of the Swedish Exegetical and Philanthropic Society. The society naturally inclined to the doctrines of their countryman Emanuel **Swedenborg,** who was the first to identify the "spirits" with the souls of deceased men and women.

In Germany, Dr. Justinus Kerner experimented with Frederica **Hauffe,** the "Seeress of Prevorst," in whose presence physical manifestations took place, and who described the conditions of the soul after death and the constitution of man—the physical body, the soul, spirit, and *nervengeist,* an ethereal body which clothes the soul after death—theories afterwards elaborated by Spiritualists.

Other German investigators, such as J. H. **Jung** (Jung-Stilling), Dr. C. Römer, and Dr. Heinrich Werner, recorded the phenomenon of **clairvoyance** in their somnambules.

A French Spiritualist, Alphonse **Cahagnet,** produced some of the best evidence which Spiritualism can show, his accounts being as remarkable for their sincerity and good faith as for the intelligence they display.

Animal Magnetism received little attention in England until the third decade of the nineteenth century. Towards the end of the eighteenth century Dr. Bell, Loutherbourg, and others, practiced the science in England, but for about thirty years from 1798 to 1828, it was quite neglected.

In the latter year, Richard Chevinix, an Irishman, gave mesmeric demonstrations. Dr. John **Elliotson,** of University College Hospital, London, practiced Mesmerism with his somnambules, the **O'Key Sisters,** and although he first believed in the magnetic fluid, he afterwards became a Spiritualist.

In 1843, two journals dealing with the subject were founded—the *Zoist* and the *Phreno-magnet.* Most of the English magnetists of the time believed in a physical explanation of the phenomena.

In 1845, Baron von **Reichenbach** published his researches, claiming to demonstrate the existence of an emanation which he called **od** or odyllic force, radiating from every substance. This effluence could be seen by clairvoyants, and had definite colors, and produced a feeling of heat or cold.

Working on individual lines, James **Braid** arrived at the same conclusions as Bertrand had done, and demonstrated the power of suggestion in "magnetic" experiments, but his theories were neglected as Bertrand's had been. By the medical profession, especially, the whole matter was freely ridiculed, and declared to be fraudulent.

There is no doubt that their attitude would have changed—it had, indeed, already begun to do so—but for the wave of Spiritualism that swept over America and Europe, and concentrated on the paranormal mental phenomena associated with the trance condition.

It will thus be seen not only that Animal Magnetism contained the basis of Spiritualistic phenomena, but that in many cases the phenomena were identical with those of Spiritualism in its present stage of development.

Trance-speaking was well-known, physical manifestations, although less frequently met with, were also witnessed, as in the case of Frau Hauffe, and clairvoyance was regarded as a common adjunct of the trance. In later years, as has been seen, the so-called "magnetic" phenomena were largely attributed to the agency of the spirits of the deceased.

For such an obviously paranormal faculty as clairvoyance—by means of which the subject professed himself or herself able to see what was going on at a distance, or to distinguish objects carefully concealed from normal sight—even such men as Bertrand and Braid do not seem to have offered an adequate explanation, nor did they refute the evidence for it; although it was extensively practiced both in France and England. Indeed, there sprang up in these countries a class who specialized in clairvoyance, and still further prepared the way for Spiritualism.

What is generally regarded as the birth of modern Spiritualism took place in America in 1848. In that year an outbreak of rapping occurred in the home of the Fox family, at Hydesville, in Arcadia, Wayne County, N.Y.

However, Spiritualism had already been signaled over ten years earlier. At Mount Lebanon, in 1837, communications were received for seven years in which spirits predicted the spreading of the phenomena all over the world, that there would not be a hamlet or palace which they would not visit. The American seer Andrew Jackson **Davis** prophesied similarly in 1847. The world soon learned of the phenomena at Hydesville, New York, a year later.

From this time onwards, Spiritualism flourished rapidly all over the world. It will be convenient, however, to review its growth and development in individual countries.

Spiritualism in the United States

In March 1848, the Fox household comprised John Fox, his wife, and their two young daughters, Margaretta and Kate, aged fifteen and twelve years respectively, and the house itself was a small wooden erection. One March 31, 1848, Mrs. Fox summoned her neighbors to hear the knockings, which had disturbed the family for a few days past. On being questioned, the raps manifested signs of intelligence, and it was finally elicited that the disturbing influence was the spirit of a peddler, done to death by a former resident of the house at Hydesville for the sake of his money.

It was subsequently claimed that in April of the same year the Foxes, while digging in their cellar at the instigation of the spirits, had discovered therein fragments of hair, teeth, and bones, supposed to be those of a human being.

The neighbors of the Fox family were deeply impressed by the "revelations," and, by way of a test, questioned the spirits on such matters as the ages of their acquaintances, questions which were answered, apparently, with some correctness. Soon afterwards Margaretta Fox visited her married sister, Mrs. Fish, at Rochester, New York, where the knockings broke out as vigorously as they had done at Hydesville. Her sister Catherine visited some friends at Auburn, and here, too, the rappings were heard.

Committee after committee was appointed and forced to confess that the cause of the sounds and the mystery of answers to mental questions was undiscoverable. Those who sat with the Fox sisters soon found that they had similar powers. So the movement spread.

The first experimental organization, The New York Circle, was formed in 1851. By its initiative the New York Conference was established in the same year and the preaching of a new science and faith began to make converts among the notabilities of the day. Governor N. P. Tallmadge, of Wisconsin, William Lloyd Garrison, the abolitionist, Professors Britten, David Wells, Bryant and Bliss of the University of Pennsylvania, Chief Justice Williams, Judge Edmonds, Professor Hare, Professor Mapes, General Bullard, Horace Greeley, Fennimore Cooper and William Cullan Bryant were the distinguished early converts.

According to an estimate in the *Spirit World* there were, in 1851, a hundred mediums in New York and fifty to sixty private circles in Philadelphia. The *North American Review* wrote in April 1855, that the New England Spiritualist Association, which computed the number of Spiritualists in America as nearly two million, did not overstate the facts.

The strangest developments in the early history of American Spiritualism were the **New Motor** movement of John Murray **Spear,** and the **Mountain Cove** settlement of Rev. James Scott and Thomas Lake **Harris.** As time progressed, Spiritualists had a serious struggle against many other movements which claimed justification for Free Love and community of property from spirit communications of mediums.

Soon physical phenomena began to supplement the simple means of spirit communication. **Table-turning** and tilting in part replaced the phenomena of raps. Playing on musical instruments by invisible hands, "direct" spirit writing, bell-ringing, levitation, and **materialization** of spirit hands, were some of the phenomena which were witnessed and vouched for by distinguished sitters.

The **levitation** of the great medium Daniel D. **Home** was recorded at an early stage in his career. **Slate-writing** and playing on musical instruments were also feats practiced by the spirits who frequented the "spirit-room" of Jonathan **Koons** in Dover, Athens County, Ohio.

At Keokuk, in Iowa, in 1854, two mediums spoke in tongues identified on somewhat insufficient data, as "Swiss," Latin, and Indian languages, and henceforth trance-speaking in their native language and in foreign tongues was much practiced by other mediums.

The recognized foreign tongues included Latin and Greek, French, German, Spanish, Italian, Chinese and Gaelic, but generally the trance utterances, when they were not in English, were not recognized definitely as any known language, and frequently the "spirits" themselves interpreted the "tongue."

The latter phenomena were evidently related to the early outpourings of the "possessed" or the articulate but meaningless fluency of ecstatics during a religious epidemic. There were cases, however, where persons in a state of exaltation spoke fluently in a language of which they know but little in their normal state.

Many of the "spirit" writings were signed with the names of great people—particularly Franklin, Swedenborg, Plato, Aristotle, St. John and St. Paul. Trance-lecturing before audiences was also practiced, books of inspirational utterances were published, and poetry and drawings produced in abundance.

These automatic productions had a character of their own—they often were vague, high-sounding, incoherent, and distinctly reminiscent. In cases where they displayed even a fair amount of merit, as in the poems of T. L. Harris, it was pointed out that they were not beyond the capacity of the medium in a normal state. As a rule they had a superficial appearance of intelligence, but on analysis were often found to be devoid of meaning.

Conjointly with the spread of the movement, Spiritualist periodicals sprung up. The *Univercoelum* of 1847 and the *Spirit Messenger* of Springfield, which succeeded it in 1849, were mouthpieces of Andrew Jackson Davis' harmonial philosophy. A similar paper was published by the Rev. James L. Scott, the later founder of the Mountain Cove Community in joint editorship with Thomas Lake Harris in Auburn. It was called *Disclosures from the Interior and Superior Care for Mortals.*

Another paper, *The Spiritual and Moral Instructor,* was edited in the same town by T. S. Hiatt. These organs, to which we may add the *Heat and Light* of Boston, represented a special school of philosophy.

The first Spiritualist periodical was issued on July 1850, by La Roy **Sunderland.** The title, *The Spiritual Philosopher,* was changed a year later to *Spirit World.*

In 1852, the *Shekinah* was started by S. B. Brittan and Charles Partridge on its short career. After eighteen months of existence it was absorbed by Dr. Buchanan's *Journal of Man.*

The first periodical which could boast of permanence was the *Spiritual Telegraph,* born out of a resolution of the New York Conference in 1852. It ran until 1860, when in its turn it was absorbed by Andrew Jackson Davis' *The Herald of Progress.*

In 1854, the Society for the Diffusion of Spiritual Knowledge, the first well-organized body, started the *Christian Spiritualist* (1854-57) and the year 1857 witnessed the appearance of *The Banner of Light* in Boston, which ran into the 1930s. Other early periodicals which should be mentioned were *The Spiritual Clarion,* of Auburn, *The New Eva,* of Boston, *The Light from the Spirit World,* of St. Louis, the *Age of Progress* and *The Sunbeam,* of Buffalo; later ones included the *Religio-Philosophical Journal* of Chicago, the *Western Star* and *The Spiritual Scientist,* of Boston, *The American Spiritualist,* the *New England Spiritualist, The Spiritual Age* and *The Lyceum Banner.*

From the beginning of the movement, those who accepted the actuality of the phenomena ranged themselves into two separate schools, each represented by a considerable body of opinion. The theory of the first was frankly Spiritualistic, the explanation of the second was that of Mesmerism or Animal Magnetism under one name or another, with a flavor of contemporary scientific thought.

These two schools, as we have seen, had their foundation in the early days for Animal Magnetism, when the rationalist ideas of the magnetists were ranged against the theological theories of angelic or diabolic possession.

In America, the suppositious "force" of the rationalists went by such names as "od," "odylic force," "electro-magnetism," and so forth, and to it was attributed not only the subjective phenomena, but the physical manifestations as well. Poltergeist disturbances, occurring from time to time, were ascribed either to spirits or odylic force, as in the case of the **Ashtabula Poltergeist.**

The Rev. Asa Mahan, one of the "rationalists," suggested that a medium could read the thoughts of the sitter by means of odylic force. The protagonists of a magnetic theory attributed trance-speaking to the subject's own intelligence, but after the birth of American Spiritualism in 1848, a Spiritualist interpretation was more commonly accepted.

Notwithstanding these conflicting theories, little was done in the way of scientific investigation, with the exception of the experiments conducted by Dr. Robert Hare, Professor of Chemistry in the University of Pennsylvania, which resulted in Hare becoming converted to Spiritualism. His critics denounced him violently, and he was obliged to resign.

Very few exposures of fraud were made, partly because the majority of the sitters accepted the phenomena with unquestioning faith, and partly because the techniques with which such detection might be made was not forthcoming. The collaboration of skillful, trained, and disinterested investigators, such as have recently applied themselves to the elucidation of parapsychology, was entirely lacking in the those days, and the public was left to form its own conclusions.

Spiritualism ran on democratic lines in America. Mediums were discovered in every class. The tillers of the soil were represented by the family of Jonathan **Koons** in the wilds of Ohio, their loghouse was the scene of ghostly pandemonium. Mrs. Andrews, who initiated full-form materializations and the Eddy Brothers, were later representatives of the same class.

Spiritualism in America was, from the first, intimately bound up with socialism.

Spiritualism was, in fact, the outgrowth of the same original outlook which produced socialistic communities, and occasioned the rise and fall of so many strange religions. Warren Chase, Horace Greeley, T. L. Harris, and other prominent Spiritualists founded such communities, and the "inspirational" writings frequently gave directions for their construction.

It was characteristic of the nation and the time that the general trend of religious and philosophical speculation should run on democratic lines. The rigid standards of thought which obtained in Europe were not recognized in America; everyone thought for himself, often with little educational training on which to base his ideas, and the result was that the vigor of speculation often outran its discretion.

As for the causes which made Spiritualism more popular and more lasting than other doctrines of the time, they were probably to be found in the special conditions which prepared the way for Spiritualism. Clairvoyants had made use of rapping prior to the mediumship of the Fox girls. The induced trance had only recently been brought to the notice of the American people by lecturers, the clergy and others, accustomed to departures from orthodoxy in every direction, who found no difficulty in admitting the intervention of good or evil spirits in human affairs, while for those who refused to accept the spirit hypothesis a satisfactory explanation of the phenomena was found in electricity, electromagnetism, or "odic force."

Meanwhile, American Spiritualism was characterized by a wide range of phenomena and the problem of distinguishing genuine phenomena from fraud.

The **Davenport Brothers,** who traveled far and wide, advertised Spiritualism by inexplicable noisy demonstrations but may have been stage magicians. The medium Henry **Gordon** introduced **levitation** of the human body, D. D. **Home** improved upon the demonstration and produced phantom hands, which dissolved in the grasp of the sitters. Dr. Rodes **Buchanan** discovered **psychometry,** which Prof. William **Denton** corroborated in thrilling experiments. William H. **Mumler** accidentally became the first exponent of **spirit photography.** Mrs. Mary **Hardy** produced the first paraffin wax molds, Mrs. Emma Hardinge **Britten,** Nettie Colburn (Mrs. **Maynard**), and Cora Scott (Mrs. Cora L. V. **Richmond**) represented inspirational speaking, Mrs. **Hollis** and Mrs. J. H. **Conant** trance mediumship in a well developed state, Henry **Slade** slate-writing and Charles **Foster** the art of **pellet reading** and skin writing (**dermography**).

The **Fox sisters,** who gave the first impetus to modern Spiritualism, were soon eclipsed in power and variety of demonstrations by these and other mediums. But they were also the first who had to bear the brunt of the backlash against Spiritualism which was soon to come in.

In the first university examination, Professors Austin Flint, Charles A. Dee. and C. B. Coventry, of Buffalo University, brought on February 17, 1851, the following verdict on the phenomena of the Fox sisters: "It is sufficient to state that the muscles inserted into the upper and inner side of the large bone of the leg (the tibia) near the knee joint, are brought into action so as to move the upper surface of the bone just named, laterally upon the lower surface of the thigh bone (the femur), giving rise, in fact, to a partial lateral dislocation. This is effected by an act of the will, without any obvious movements of the limb, occasioning a loud noise and a return of the bone to its place is attended by a second sound."

The revelation of Mrs. Norman Culver of an alleged confession of the Fox sisters had aggravated their position. But no disclosures and professional verdicts could stem the advance of Spiritualism.

In 1857, the editor of *The Boston Courier* offered $500 for the production of genuine phenomena, provided a committee of Harvard University should be the umpires. On behalf of the Spiritualists, Dr. Gardner accepted the challenge. The committee consisted of Professors Pierce, Agassiz and Horsford, of Harvard University, and Dr. N. B. Gould of the Albany Observatory, the editor of the *Boston Courier* and a few friends of Dr. Gardner. The mediums were Mrs. Brown (Leah Fox), Kate Fox, Mr. J. V. Mansfield, Mrs. Kendrick, George Redman and the Davenport Brothers.

Two days were devoted to the manifestations. They were imperfect and unsatisfactory and the committee returned a negative verdict, promising also a later report of additional investigations which, however, never came forth. Following the failure of the Cambridge investigation, Dr. Gardner extended invitations to the Press to attend seances with the same mediums. Several papers published impressive accounts.

As the years passed by, important records of observations and long experiments were published by E. A. Brackett, Epes **Sargent,** Dr. Wolfe, Allan Putnam and Dr. Eugene Crowell. The early history of Spiritualism by E. W. Capron was supplemented by Emma Hardinge **Britten,** who narrated twenty years of progress. Many organizations and Spiritualist churches worked for the advancement of the cause.

In 1873, the first camp meeting was initiated at Lake Pleasant, Massachusetts. It was quickly followed by others.

The years between 1880 and 1890 witnessed four outstanding events: the report of the **Seybert Commission,** the self-exposure of Margaret and Kate Fox in 1885, the foundation of the **American Society for Psychical Research,** for systematic and organized psychical research, in 1885, with the participation of a group of distinguished scientists, and the discovery of the remarkable mediumship of Mrs. Leonore **Piper.**

The Seybert commission was delegated by the University of Pennsylvania, which received an endowment of $60,000 from the will of Spiritualist Henry Seybert, on the understanding that the commission would investigate the understanding only in a limited sense as, after a preliminary negative report in 1887, which was widely resented, the investigation was discontinued.

The self-exposure of Margaret and Kate Fox did not realize the fond expectations of the anti-Spiritualists as a death-blow, as the motives of the sisters appeared to be sordid and the revelation was followed a year later by full retraction.

The birth of the American Society for Psychical Research was of far-reaching importance. The discovery of Mrs. Piper's powers secured the prestige of psychical research by Prof. William **James.** The keen intellect of Dr. Richard **Hodgson,** his fifteen years of tireless investigation and Prof. J. H. **Hyslop's** erudition laid the scientific foundations for the ultimate charting of an unknown territory. In 1905, the A.S.P.R. was dissolved and reorganized as an independent body. Prof. Hyslop took charge and conducted its work until his death in 1920.

Other keen and able investigators arose. Hereward **Carrington** established his claim to renown and the mantle of Prof. Hyslop was placed on the shoulders of Dr. W. F. **Prince.** The discovery of the mediumship of "Margery" (Mrs. **Crandon**) and the investigation of the *Scientific American* and of Harvard committees created a wide stir.

The **Boston Society for Psychical Research** was founded in 1925 by Dr. W. F. Prince and J. Malcolm **Bird** stepped into his vacated place in New York.

From November 29 to December 11, 1926, the Clark University, Worcester, Massachusetts, which had a lecture endowment for psychical research, held an International Symposium on the subject. Dr. Carl Murchison presided and papers were presented by Sir Oliver **Lodge,** Sir Arthur Conan **Doyle,** Frederick Bligh **Bond,** L. R. G. Crandon, Mary Austin, Margaret Deland, William **McDougal,** Hans **Driesch,** Walter Franklin **Prince,** F. C. S. **Schiller,** John E. **Coover,** Gardner **Murphy,** Joseph Jastrow and Harry **Houdini.** Under the title 'The Case for and Against Psychical Research' the papers were later published in book form.

A Hodgson fellowship was established at Harvard University with $10,000 in 1913, but activities only began in 1917 when a special gift of Mrs. John

Wallace Riddle demanded immediate application. Leonard Thompson Troland was the first Fellow in Psychical Research, Prof. Gardner **Murphy** the second.

In 1923, Leland Stanford University of California was given an endowment of $400,000 for psychical research by a brother of the late Senator Stanford, a convinced Spiritualist. This was in addition to T. W. Stanford's first endowment of $50,000 in 1911 and other generous gifts. The Psychical Research Department, thus established, began its activities in 1912-13. It published in 1920 a ponderous volume: *Experiments in Psychical Research, being The Leland Stanford Junior University's Psychical Research Monograph No. 1,* by John Edgar Coover, Fellow in Psychical Research and Assistant Professor of Psychology.

Part of the book was written by Lillien J. Martin, Professor Emeritus of Psychology. Having given a summary of the past history of the subject, the book outlined original investigations into **thought transference** and the subliminal mind. It did not accept **telepathy** as proven. The extreme critical attitude of the author was best disclosed by this condemnation of pioneer work into telepathy: "The Society on account of its fiascoes and persistent lack of psychological vision is immeasurably farther from its goal than it was in 1886 in its efforts to produce proof of thought transference."

The popular side of American psychical research was well represented by the American Society for Psychical Research, still well established in modern times. The central Spiritualist organization was The **National Spiritualist Association of Churches,** founded in 1893, which still flourishes, with over 8,000 members. Other influential organizations are the **National Spiritual Alliance of the United States of America, Morris Pratt Institute, National Psychic Science Association, International General Assembly of Spiritualists,** and the **Spiritual Frontiers Fellowship.**

In modern times, psychical research into areas associated with Spiritualist phenomena has been supplemented by the development of scientific investigations under the term "Parapsychology," and a number of organizations have been founded. For a summary of the development, scope and outlook of **Psychical Research** and **Parapsychology,** see entries under those headings. See also the section on 'Modern American Occultism & Parapsychology' in the entry on **America, United States of.**

Today Spiritualism still fourishes in the U.S., but it faces some competition from new occult and religious **cults** which sprang up in the occult boom of the 1960s.

Spiritualism in Britain

The transition from **Mesmerism** into Spiritualism was effected in Britain under the impetus of visiting American mediums. The arrival of Mrs. W. R. **Hayden** the first visiting medium from America in 1852, was in a way prepared by the publication in the previous year of Dr. Gregory's book *Animal Magnetism* which contained records of supernormal occurrences, and by the accounts published from time to time in the journal *Zoist* of the Mesmerists. Mrs. Hayden had been brought over by a lecturer on "electro-biology."

Table-turning soon became epidemic in Britain and society invitations, it is said, were extended to five o'clock tea and table-turning. Out of this social contagion, an early controversy arose over Michael Faraday's unconscious muscular action theory and over Dr. Carpenter's supplementary theory of "unconscious cerebration."

Mrs. Hayden herself was treated with derision by the Press, and returned to America in 1853. Yet, besides acting as forerunner for the great medium D. D. **Home,** she registered important conquests: Robert **Owen,** the veteran socialist, Robert **Chambers,** the publisher, Professor **de Morgan,** the famous mathematician, Sir Charles Isham and Dr. John Ashburner mostly owed their conversion to a belief in survival and communication with the dead to her limited powers.

Mrs. Roberts, a second American medium and the later arrival of P. B. **Randolph** and J. R. M. **Squire** left comparatively slight impressions. But this was due to the tremendous difference in power and the consequent effect on the public which the mediumship of D. D. Home elicited.

Without Home, Spiritualism in England would probably have made but little further headway. He was received in the highest society and he, in turn, received the visit of famous people of the day. Some of them (like **Thackeray,** Anthony Trollope, Robert Bell, Lord **Lytton** and Lord Brougham) were deeply impressed but kept quiet for fear of public ridicule. Some figured in Press sensations when they vented their anger for having become associated with Spiritualism before the public (like Sir David **Brewster** and Robert **Browning**), others like William **Howitt,** J. Garth Wilkinson, Lord **Adare,** The Earl of Dunraven, The Master of **Lindsay,** Nassau Senior, Cromwell **Varley** and Alfred Russel **Wallace** braved the scorn of the public.

Home first visited England in 1855 at the age of twenty-three, after acting as a medium in America for some four years. He made a tremendous impression before returning to America in 1856.

In 1859, Thomas Lake **Harris** was deputed by spirits to visit England. A British medium named Mrs. Mary **Marshall** gave professional seances, but less successfully than D. D. Home and the American mediums.

British spiritualists, however, did not seek publicity, but practiced for the most part anonymously. The phenomena at these seances resembled those in America—playing of instruments without visible agency, **materialization** of hands, **table-turning,** and so on, but on a less sensational scale.

It was not so much these physical manifestations which inspired early British Spiritualists so much as automatic writing and speaking, which, although at first rare, soon became a feature of seances.

As early as 1854, the trance utterances of a medium named "Annie" were recorded by a circle of Swedenborgians presided over by Elihu Rich.

In 1860, a new Spiritualist era commenced, and the whole subject came into greater prominence. This was due to the increase in the number of British mediums and the emigration to Britain of many American mediums, including the stage performers the Davenport Brothers, who did not claim to be Spiritualists but were hailed as such.

Kate **Fox** married and settled in England as Mrs. Jencken. It is said that her baby became a writing medium. Thomas Lake **Harris,** Mrs. Emma Hardinge **Britten** and Mrs. Cora L. V. **Richmond** were remembered for inspirational addresses, Charles H. **Foster** for rather dubious **pellet-reading** and skin-writing phenomena (see **Dermography**), the Davenport Brothers for noisy telekinetic demonstrations, Lottie **Fowler** for trance communications and predictions and Henry **Slade** for **state-writing** demonstrations which had a stormy epilogue.

British mediums were rather slow to arise. Mrs. Marshall was, for a long time, the only professional medium. In October 1867, the journal *Human Nature* knew of only one more, W. Wallace. The number of private mediums, however, was considerable. Mrs. Thomas **Everitt** was the most powerful. Dr. Edward **Childs** was another.

William Howitt, William Wilkinson and Mrs. Newton Crossland developed as automatists. Miss Nichols (later Mrs. **Guppy**), presented mysterious **apport** phenomena and the first **materializations** in England. The partnership of Frank **Herne** and Charles **Williams** produced impressive if suspect phenomena.

F. **Hudson** introduced **spirit photography** to London, Slater, Parkes and Reeves, Beattie and Boursnell followed in his footsteps. Marvelous things were reported to occur in the seances of Florence **Cook,** the Rev. W. Stainton Moses, William **Eglinton,** Annie Eva **Fay,** the Rev. F. W. **Monck,** Miss Mary **Showers,** Arthur **Colman,** Mme. **d'Esperance,** Miss C. E. **Wood,** Miss Fairlamb (Mrs. J. B. **Mellon**), Cecil **Husk** and David **Duguid.**

There was plenty to investigate. Mrs. De Morgan, Lord Adare and Alfred Russel Wallace published the first important books. In 1869 the **London Dialectical Society** delegated a committee to investigate and after its favorable report which brought the testimonies of many important people before the public, William **Crookes** stepped to the fore and announced an investigation which, when his tremendous findings were published in 1871, and later in 1874, simply stupefied the contemporary savants.

Sergeant E. W. **Cox** founded in 1875 the **Psychological Society** of Great Britain. The **British National Association of Spiritualists** appointed a research committee in 1878 and the year 1882 witnessed a historic event, the foundation of the **Society for Psychical Research.**

British mediums were slow to arise, the organization of Spiritualism, as a movement, was delayed until comparatively late. The **Charing Cross Spirit Circle** was the first experimental organization. In July 1857, it was superseded by the London Spiritualistic Union, called a year later London Spiritualist Union and in 1865 the Association of Progressive Spiritualists in Great Britain was formed. The Spiritual Athenaeum of 1866 was a temporary institution, established mainly to offer D. D. Home a paid position and the first really representative body was not born until 1873. This was the **British National Association of Spiritualists** renamed in 1882 The Central Association of Spiritualists and again in 1884 The **London Spiritualist Alliance.**

The tardiness in organization was also manifested in the field of Spiritualist periodicals. *The Spirit World,* published by W. R. Hayden during his wife's visit in May 1853 had only one number. Robert Owen's *The New Existence of Man Upon the Earth,* published in 1854 was spiritual but not Spiritualist. In April 1855, the *Yorkshire Spiritual telegraph* was established by D. W. Weatherhead in Keighley, the chief provincial center of British Spiritualism. In 1857 it was renamed to *British Spiritual Telegraph* and expired in 1858-59.

Towards the end of 1860, *The Spiritual Magazine* was founded by William Wilkinson and became the leading organ. It ran until 1875. Thomas Shorter and William Wilkinson were the editors for the greater part of its career and William Howitt the chief contributor.

The Spiritual Times ran from 1864-66. In 1867, James **Burns** founded *Human Nature,* a monthly which ran until 1877 and in 1869 he brought out a weekly, *The Medium,* which absorbed the provincial *Daybreak,* founded in 1867, and was continued under the title *The Medium and Daybreak* until 1895.

In 1869, W. H. Harrison's paper *The Spiritualist Newspaper* entered the field and, under the later abbreviated title *The Spiritualist* held its own until 1881. *The Christian Spiritualist* began its monthly career in 1871. *The Pioneer of Progress* lasted for ten months, appearing weekly from January 1874. In 1878, *Spiritual Notes* was founded and ran until 1881, the year in which *Light* appeared.

Light is the oldest British Spiritualist journal, which has continued publication with various changes of format and sponsorship. It was founded by Dawson Rogers and the Rev. W. Stainton **Moses.** Later editors included E. W. **Wallis** and David **Gow.** It was the official organ of the **London Spiritualist Alliance,** but is now published quarterly by the **College of Psychic Studies,** London.

The *Proceedings* of the Society for Psychical Research and the *Journal* had their inception in 1882, *The Two Worlds* in 1888 at Manchester. The second oldest Spiritualist journal in Britain, *Two Worlds* is now published at The Headquarters Publishing Co. Ltd., 5 Alexandria Road, West Ealing, London W13 ONP.

1892-93 saw the establishment and expiration of Emma Hardinge **Britten's** *Unseen Universe;* W. T. **Stead's** *Borderland* ran from 1893-97, **J. J. Morse's** *The Spiritual Review* from 1900-1902. *The Spiritual*

Quarterly Magazine was started by The Two Worlds Publishing Co. in October, 1902; an English edition of the *Annales des Sciences Psychiques* was published between 1905-10 under the title *Annals of Psychic Science* and closed the list of older editorial ventures.

In addition to *Light* and *Two Worlds,* the most important of surviving Spiritualist journals is *Psychic News,* founded by Maurice Barbanell in 1932, and now published at 2 Tavistock Chambers, Bloomsbury Way, London, WCIA ILY.

The development of Spiritualism in Britain has been closely associated with the work of the **Society for Psychical Research,** although it has often been an uneasy relationship. Indeed, many Spiritualist used to claim that the initials S.P.R. really meant "Suppression of Psychical Research"! It is true that from time to time the skepticism of some members of the Society has often seemed hostile, but the Society has had a wide range of membership and is not tied to corporate opinion on the genuineness or otherwise of claimed phenomena.

The S.P.R. was formed in 1882 to investigate psychic phenomena in a scientific and impartial spirit, free from the bias of preconceived ideas. The first president was Prof. Henry **Sidgwick,** and the Council numbered among its members Edmund **Gurney,** Frank **Podmore,** F. W. H. **Myers,** Prof. W. F. Barrett, the Rev. W. Stainton Moses, Morell **Theobald,** Dr. George Wild and Dawson Rogers, the latter four individuals being Spiritualists. However, avowedly Spiritualist membership of the Society gradually declined in the course of time.

Other notable presidents of the Society were Prof. Balfour **Stewart,** the Rt. Hon. A. J. **Balfour,** Prof. William **James,** Sir William **Crookes,** Sir Oliver **Lodge,** and Prof. W. F. **Barrett,** several of these being among original members of the Society.

The initial scope of the Society was defined by the appointment of six committees: (1) Committee on Thought Transference, (2) Committee on Hypnotism, (3) Committee on Reichenbach Phenomena, (4) Committee on Apparitions, (5) Committee on Physical (Spiritualist) Phenomena, (6) Committee to consider the history and existing literature on the subject. The field of the Society was further enlarge in later years, when a committee headed by Dr. Richard **Hodgson** conducted an inquiry into the claimed phenomena of **Theosophy.**

In order to find alternative explanations for Spiritualist phenomena, members explored psychological theories and studied automatism, hallucinations and thought-transference. Some members were also instrumental in detecting a great deal of fraud in connection with mediumistic performances, particularly in the field of **slate-writing.**

Many individuals had declared slate-writing to be such a simple and straightforward phenomenon that fraud was impossible. Mr. S. T. **Davey,** a member of the Society had attended seances by the well-known medium William **Eglinton** and considered that the phenomenon was fraudulent. He set himself to study the rationale of slate-writing and emulate Eglinton's phenomena by conjuring methods. He then gave a number of pseudo-seances, which were carefully recorded by Dr. Hodgson.

Mr. Davey's techniques were so successful that none of the sitters could detect the fraud, even although they had been assured in advance that it was simply a conjuring trick—indeed some Spiritualist sitters refused to believe that the performances were fraudulent! Since then, slate-writing declined in Spiritualist circles and, like the phenomenon of **spirit photography,** has become largely discredited. This does not, of course, settle the matter once and for all. It is one of the vexed problems of Spiritualism that even the probability of a great deal of fraudulent phenomena does not decisively dispose of the rarer cases of genuine phenomena.

Excellent work was done by the Society in the collection of evidence relating to apparitions of the dead and the living, reported in the monumental *Human Personality and Its Survival of Bodily Death* by F. W. H. Myers (2 vols., 1903) and *Phantasms of the Living* by F. W. H. Myers, Frank Podmore & Edmund Gurney (2 vols., 1886).

A statistical inquiry on a large scale was undertaken by a committee of the Society in 1889 and some 17,000 cases of **apparitions** were collected by the committee and its assistants. The main object in taking such a census was to obtain evidence for the working of **telepathy** in veridical or coincidental apparitions, and in order to make such evidence of scientific value, the utmost care was taken to insure the impartiality and responsible character of all who took part in the inquiry. The result was, that after every precaution had been taken, the apparitions coinciding with a death or other crisis were found greatly to exceed the number which could be ascribed to chance alone.

At the same time there was much to encourage the belief in some "supernormal" agency, especially in the last decade of the nineteenth century. The two mediums whose manifestations led many able men in Britain, in America, and on the Continent, to conclude that the spirits of the dead were concerned in their phenomena were the Italian medium Eusapia **Palladino** and the American Mrs. Leonore **Piper.**

In 1885, Professor William **James,** of Harvard, studied the case of Mrs. Piper, and a few years later Dr. Richard Hodgson of the American Society for Psychical Research also investigated her case, the latter commencing his investigations in an entirely skeptical spirit.

Of all the trance mediums, Mrs. Piper offered the best evidence for a spirit agency. Dr. Hodgson himself declared his belief that the spirits of the dead spoke through the lips of the medium, and among others who held that fraud would not account for the revelations given by Mrs. Piper in the trance state were Professor James, Sir Oliver **Lodge,** F. W. H. Myers and Professor J. H. **Hyslop.**

On the other hand, Frank Podmore, while not admitting any supernormal agency, suggested that telepathy might help to explain the matter, probably aided by skillful observations and carefully-conducted inquiries concerning the affairs of prospective sitters. Mrs. Sidgwick also suggested that probably Mrs. Piper received telepathic communications from the spirits of the dead, which she reproduced in her automatic speaking and writing.

The other medium, Eusapia Palladino, after attracting considerable attention from Professors **Lombroso, Richet, Flammarion,** and others on the Continent, came to Britain in 1895. Several British scientists had already witnessed her powers on the Continent, at the invitation of Professor Charles Richet; these included Sir Oliver Lodge and F. W. H. Myers. Sir Oliver Lodge, at least, expressed himself as satisfied that no known agency was responsible for the remarkable manifestations of Palladino.

The British sittings were held at Cambridge, and as it was proved conclusively that the medium made use of fraud, the majority of the investigators ascribed her "manifestations" entirely to that. Later, however, in 1898, a further series of seances were held at Paris, and so successfully that Richet, Myers, and Sir Oliver Lodge once more declared themselves satisfied of the genuineness of the phenomena. There seems little doubt that this medium produced genuine phenomena, but was inclined to cheat (perhaps unconsciously) if test conditions were relaxed.

Perhaps the most convincing evidence for the working of some paranormal agency, however, was to be found in the famous **cross-correspondence** experiments conducted in the early twentieth century. F. W. H. Myers had suggested before he died that if a spirit **control** were to give the same message to two or more mediums, it would go far to establish the independent existence of such control.

On the death of Professor Sidgwick (in August, 1900) and of F. W. H. Myers (in January, 1901) it was thought that if mediums were controlled by these, some agreement might be looked for in the scripts. The first correspondences were found in the script of Mrs. Thompson and Miss Rawson, the former in London, the latter in the south of France. The Sidgwick control appeared for the first time to these ladies on the same day, January 11, 1901.

On May 8, 1901, the Myers control appeared in the script of Mrs. Thompson and Mrs. Verrall, and later in that of Mrs. Piper and others. So remarkable were the correspondences obtained in some cases where there could not possibly be collusion between the mediums, that it is difficult to believe that some discarnate intelligence was not responsible for some, at least of the scripts (see **Cross-Correspondence**).

Towards the end of 1916 a great sensation was caused with the publication by Sir Oliver Lodge of a memoir on his son, the late Lieutenant Raymond Lodge, who was killed near Ypres in September, 1915. The book titled *Raymond, or Life and Death,* is divided into three parts, the first of which contains a history of the brief life of the subject of the memoir. The second part details numerous records of sittings both in the company of mediums and at the table by Sir Oliver Lodge and members of his family, and it was claimed that in these many evidences of the personal survival of his son were obtained, that the whole trend of the messages was eloquent of his personality and that although if the evidential matter were taken apart for examination, single isolated proofs would not be deemed conclusive, yet when taken in a body it provided evidential material of an important nature.

There was certainly ground for this contention and it must be admitted that proofs of identity are more valuable when experienced by those who were familiar with the subject during his earthly career. But to those who have not had this opportunity the balance of the evidence seems meager and it is notable that in this special case, most of the tests of real value broke down when put into practice. The third part of the book deals with the scientific material relating to the life after death which is reviewed and summarized in a spirit of great fairness, although a natural bias towards belief in immortality is obvious.

Notwithstanding much useful work of this kind by the Society for Psychical Research on the phenomena of Spiritualism, there was frequent antagonism from Spiritualists during the first half-century or so of the Society's existence. The pioneer Spiritualist W. T. **Stead** fulminated against it, and Sir Arthur **Doyle,** after several disputes, resigned his membership as a public protest shortly before his death in 1930. Controversies over the "Margery" mediumship of Mrs. **Crandon** in the U.S. also involved the Society in London.

Meanwhile, however, many independent research organizations had been formed. In 1920, the **British College of Psychic Science** was founded by prominent Spiritualists Mr. and Mrs. Hewat **McKenzie.** It provided a valuable center for information, advice and guidance for consultation of reputable mediums and the investigation of psychical phenomena.

It was McKenzie who assisted in the development of the psychic faculties of the medium Eileen J. **Garrett,** who was to become world famous. Mrs. Garrett was invited to the U.S. by the **American Society for Psychical Research** in 1931, and took parts in parapsychological investigations with William **McDougall** and J. B. **Rhine.** In 1951, she founded the **Parapsychology Foundation** in New York.

Meanwhile the British College of Psychic Science performed useful work for a number of years, finally closing in 1947. Similar work was carried on by the **College of Psychic Science,** London (not to be confused with the B.C.P.S.), which grew from the **London Spiritualist Alliance** in 1955, in turn an outgrowth of the **British National Association of Spiritualists,** founded in 1896.

In 1970, the college of Psychic Science was renamed the **College of Psychic Studies.** It publishes the long-established journal *Light* and maintains an excellent library, organizes lectures and other activities associated with Spiritualism and psychical research.

The **National Laboratory of Psychical Research** was founded by Harry **Price** in 1925 as an independent research body, and conducted valuable investigations with such mediums as Rudi **Schneider,** Eleonore **Zügun, Stella C.,** and Helen **Duncan.** In

1936, the Laboratory, with its splendid library collected by Harry Price, passed to the University of London council for Psychical Investigation. Although laboratory work ceased, the Library remains at the University of London.

Ever since the famous experiments of Sir William **Crookes** with the mediums Daniel Dunglas **Home** and Florence **Cook** between 1871 and 1874 onwards, Spiritualists had hoped that science would validate the phenomena of Spiritualism. In the event, the overall trend of psychical research tended to be skeptical and sometimes hostile, particularly as careful investigation disclosed mediumistic frauds.

The different viewpoints of researchers and Spiritualists were largely irreconcilable, since Spiritualists operated within a framework of religious belief and researchers from a largely agnostic stance. None the less, many members of the Society for Psychical Research of a tolerant and impartial nature have built up some impressive evidence for the reality of **survival** and the **spirit hypotheses.** But for the most part, Spiritualists and psychical researchers have gone their separate ways.

Some interesting Spiritualist organizations did not survive the passage of time. **Julia's Bureau,** associated with W. T. Stead, was absorbed by the W. T. Stead **Borderland Library** in 1914, but closed in 1936. Other ephemeral groups included the Spiritualist community, a Jewish Society for Psychical Research, a Society for the Study of Supernormal Pictures, the Link Association of Home Circles, and the Survival League.

In spite of two World Wars, the British Spiritualist movement as a whole has continued to flourish. The exposure of famous mediums in the past as fraudulent or partially fraudulent proved largely irrelevant to the less publicized activities of nonprofessional mediums in home circles and churches. The larger Spiritualist organizations are now careful to apply the strictest scrutiny to mediums and to regulate their activities through professional organizations. Any unsatisfactory conduct is firmly controlled, frauds exposed and only the highest standards of integrity permitted.

As a result, British Spiritualist mediums and public demonstrators of evidence for survival are the most famous in the world. Such personalities as **Doris Stokes** became international figures on television and radio programs as well as public demonstrations, but remained dedicated to the Spiritualist cause and did not become rich or self-centered. There are now over four hundred Spiritualist churches in Britain.

Many of the Spiritualist organizations founded in the nineteenth century have continued into modern times, and new organizations have also grown up. The **Marylebone Spiritualists Association,** founded in 1872, became the **Spiritualist Association of Great Britain,** claimed as the largest of its kind in the world. it is located at 33 Belgrave Square, London, S.W.1.

The **British Spiritualist Lyceum Union,** founded in 1890, was amalgamated with the **Spiritualists' National Union** in 1948. The S.N.U. itself had been founded in 1891. It is now located at Britten House, Stanstead Hall, Stanstead, Essex, CM24 8UD.

White Eagle Lodge grew from the mediumship of Grace **Cooke.** It was founded in 1936 and includes a publishing trust. It has branches in Edinburgh, Bournemouth, Plymouth, Worthing and Reading, as well as in New Jersey, U.S.A. The headquarters address is: New Lands, Rake, Liss, Hampshire, GU33 7HY.

The **Greater World Christian Spiritualist League** was founded in 1921 around the mediumship of Winifred **Moyes.** It has over a hundred and forty local branches throughout Britain, as well as in a dozen foreign countries. Headquarters address: 3 Landsdowne Road, Holland Park, London, W.11.

Associated with the Spiritualist movement are the healers, represented by talented individuals and organizations. One of the most famous was Harry **Edwards,** who died in 1976. He claimed the assistance of spirit helpers, and established a healing clinic, which is now carried on by Joan and Ray Branch, whom he had designated as his successors. Edwards had published several books on healing, and the magazine *The Spiritual Healer,* which continues publication. The address of the Harry Edwards Spiritual Healing Sanctuary is: Burrows Lea, Shere, Guildford, Surrey, GU5 9QG.

The National Federation of Spiritual Healers is located at: Shortacres, Churchill, Loughton, Essex. There is also a World Healing Crusade at 476 Lytham Road, Blackpool, Lancashire and a Churches' Council for Health and Healing at 8-10 Denman Street, London, W.1.

Throughout the history of Spiritualism in Britain, the established churches have been largely antagonistic. In 1881, Canon Basil Wilberforce was the partisan of Spiritualism before the Church Congress. The reception was hostile and denunciatory.

The General Assembly of the Church of Scotland was three times petitioned, by the Rev. W. A. Reid, to investigate psychic phenomena. On the first occasion, a committee was appointed which reported that psychic phenomena did occur and expressed the opinion that investigation was lawful. Subsequent appeals, however, resulted in no fresh investigation.

Books have been published by Catholics insisting that Spiritualism is the work of evil spirits. In the period of post-war permissiveness, active opposition declined, but even today there are occasional fulminations from dogmatic clergymen that Spiritualism is the work of the devil. The obsession with themes of possession and exorcism during the occult boom of the 1950s and 60s confused many people.

However, enlightened clergymen founded the **Churches' Fellowship of Psychical and Spiritual Studies** in 1953, which investigates paranormal healing, psychic phenomena and mysticism in a sympathetic manner, and publishes a quarterly journal *Christian Parapsychologist.* Address: St. Mary Abchurch, Abchurch Lane, London, EC4N 7BA.

One of the greatest obstacles to Spiritualism was the cruel, old-fashioned legislation under which mediums were persecuted under the archaic Witchcraft laws of 1735 for "pretending to communicate with spirits." Throughout the interwar years, the Witchcraft Act of 1735 and the Vagrancy Act of 1824 were frequently invoked to prosecute mediums. Disguised policewomen, posing as bereaved parents, would approach a medium, begging for some consolatory message. A small sum of money would be proferred as a "love-offering" and if this was accepted the medium was prosecuted and often fined or imprisoned for up to three months (see **Fortune Telling**).

This punitive legislation was repealed in 1951 by the new Fraudulent Mediums Act, which, although not wholly satisfactory, implicitly acknowledged that there might be genuine mediumship.

However, even in the 1980s, the matter is by no means settled. The Spiritualists' National Union recently warned its churches against the possibility of prosecutions under the Vagrancy Act of 1824, which was only partially amended. In 1956, a clairvoyant was fined £75, although six mediums testified to his genuine psychic faculties. The 1824 Vagrancy Act has recently halted plans for a large commercial enterprise to combine fortune telling and computer technology. This has revived fears that mediums are still not adequately protected by law.

Spiritualism in France

As **animal magnetism** was launched on its long and complex career in France, it was to be expected that the meeting ground of trance between **Mesmerism** and Spiritualism should reveal some of the later marvels of Spiritualism at a comparatively early period.

From a correspondence between J. P. F. **Deleuze** and G. **Billot** from the year 1829 on 2 vols., 1838-39, it appears that phantom forms and the phenomena of **apports** were well-known in this early age, although Deleuze frankly admitted that his experience was more limited.

Almost the full range of the phenomena of Spiritualism are to be met with in Baron **Du Potet's** *Journal du Magnétisme,* which records his investigations between 1836-1848. His magnetized subjects excelled in **clairvoyance, trance** speaking, **healing, dermography, levitation, fire immunity, telekinesis, apports, xenoglossy, prophecy, crystal gazing, materializations** and descriptions of scenes in the spirit world. The seances were witnessed by Bertrand, d'Hunin, Séguin and Morin.

The best early seance records come from Alphonse **Cahagnet,** the author of *Arcanes de la vie future dévoilés* 3 vols., (1848-54, Translated as *The Celestial Telegraph,* 2 vols., c. 1850). He received many evidential communications from departed spirits through his somnambule, Adèle Maginot.

Table-turning was introduced into France by Baron **Guldenstubbe** and Comte **d'Ourches** in 1850 and became an epidemic as in England. People—if we are to believe Eugene Bonnemère's statement in the *Siècle*—ceased to ask for each other's health, but asked how the table was. "Thank you, mine turns beautifully, and how goes yours?"—this was the habitual question. Soon other phenomena followed. The famous direct scripts of Baron Guldenstubbe were obtained in 1856.

In the same year Allan **Kardec's** book *Le Livre des Esprits* was published and developments took a radically different route from that in America and England. Allan Kardec founded a school of thought which was dominated by the idea of a series of compulsory reincarnations. This was Spiritism, the opposing school to the Spiritualism which followed the American and English ideas.

Spiritualism was represented in France by Z. J. **Pierart** and *La Revue Spiritualiste,* founded in 1858; Spiritism by the organ of Kardec, *La Revue Spirite,* founded in the same year.

Kardec won and Pierart, after years of bitter controversy, retired into the country. By 1864 there were ten periodicals published in France: three in Paris, the two already mentioned and *l'Avenir,* four in Bordeaux, which, in 1865, became merged into *l'Union Spirite Bordelaise, La Médium Evangélique* of Toulouse, *l'Echo d'Outre Tombe,* of Marseilles, and *La Vérité,* of Lyons. With the exception of *La Revue Spiritualiste* all represented the school of Kardec.

Allan Kardec and his followers discouraged physical phenomena. The stimulus for experimental investigators was largely provided by the visits of D. D. **Home,** the **Davenport Brothers,** Henry **Slade,** William **Eglinton,** Frank **Herne,** Charles **Williams,** Mme. **d'Esperance,** Florence **Cook,** Lottie **Fowler** and other famous mediums.

Dr. J. **Maxwell,** Camille **Flammarion,** Col. **Rochas,** Dr. Paul **Joire,** Prof. Charles **Richet,** Emile **Boirac,** Count Cesar **de Vesme,** Gustav **Geley** and Eugene **Osty** represented psychical research, Gabriel **Delanne** and Leon **Denis** the old school of thought.

Delanne founded the *Revue scientifique et morale du spiritisme.* The first attempt at organized psychical research was La Societé de Psychologie physiologique and *La Revue des Sciences Psychiques,* of which Dr. Puel was the director.

In 1890, the *Annales des Sciences Psychiques* was founded by Prof. Richet and Dr. Dariex. In 1920, it was replaced by *La Revue Métapsychique,* the official organ of the Institut Metapsychique. In 1904 the Institut Général Psychologique was established in Paris under the presidency of Prof. d'Arsonval of the Academy.

The real benefactor of Spiritism and psychical research arrived during the war in the person of Jean **Meyer,** a rich industrialist. He founded La Maison des Spirits for spiritistic propaganda and the Institut Métapsychique for psychical research. In 1918 the Institut was recognized as a public utility. Meyer endowed it with a portion of his fortune. The work which it has carried on in experimentation and in demonstration of supernormal phenomena before invited scientists is of great importance for the future of psychical research. (See also **France**).

Spiritualism in Germany

In Germany, the development of Spiritualism was very slow. I. H. von Fichte believed in the facts of Spiritualism, Gustav Fechner, the founder of psychophysiology admitted personal immortality, while Edward von Hartman, the author of *The Philosophy of the Unconscious* (1869) desired to give the phenomena a definite place in philosophy. Carl Du Prel, author of *The Philosophy of Mysticism* (2 vols., 1889) delved into the subconscious for explanation and founded the first Spiritualist monthly, *The Sphynx.*

Most of the Spiritualist activity was ascribable to a foreigner, Alexander **Aksakof,** Imperial Councillor of Russia, who, owing to the Russian censorship, concentrated his work in Germany.

In 1874, he commenced the publication of *Psychische Studien,* which continued for many years, changing its title in 1926 to *Zeitschrift für Parapsychologie.*

A great impetus was given to Spiritualism by the visit of the well-known medium Henry **Slade** in 1877. The conversion of Prof. **Zöllner** caused a sensation and was the subject of strong language on the part of other scientists. The visits of such mediums as William **Eglinton,** Mme. **d'Esperance,** Annie Fairlamb (Mrs. J. B. **Mellon**) and others kept the interest alive. *Spiritualistische Blaetter* was started in 1883.

Modern psychical research was best represented by Baron **Schrenck Notzing.** His book on the materialization phenomena of **Eva C.,** *Materialisations-Phaenomene* (Phenomena of Materialisation, 1914) aroused heated scientific controversy. With this work and also the investigation of the mediumship of Willi **Schneider** he convinced a hundred well-known scientists of the reality of **telekinesis** phenomena and the claimed Spiritualist phenomena **ectoplasm.** Other important thinkers and researchers included Prof. Hans **Driesch,** Prof. Konstantin **Oesterreich** and Dr. Rudolph **Tischner.**

A Society for Psychical Research and also a Medical Society for Psychical Research were founded in prewar Germany the Deutsche Gesellschaft für wissenschaftliches Okkultismus and the Deutscher Spiritisten Verein. Periodicals included: *Zeitschrift für Parapsychologie, Zeitschrift für Metapsychische Forschung, Zeitschrift für Psychisch Forschung, Zeitschrift für Seelenleben, Psyche und die Ubersinnliche Welt.* (See also **Germany**)

Since World War II, there has been considerable German activity in the field of parapsychological research with the Lehrstühl für Psychologie und Grenzgebiete de Psychologie at Freiburg University, and the independent Institut für Grenzgebiete der Psychologie und Psychohygiene directed by Drittans **Bender.** A new direction to Spiritualist beliefs in survival was stimulated by the experiments in **electronic voice phenomena (Raudive Voices)** of Friedrich **Jürgenson,** who cooperated with the Freiburg Institute.

Spiritualism in Italy

In Italy, the birth of the Spiritualist movement was largely due to French periodicals and developed on the lines of the **Kardec** school.

The visit of the famous medium Daniel Dunglas **Home** in 1855 led to the formation of many societies and to the publication of the first journal on Spiritualism *L'Amore del Vero.* In 1863, La Società Spirituale di Palermo was formed, of which men like Paolo Morelle, Professor of Latin and Philosophy, were members. In the same year the first representative Spiritualist organ, *Annali dello Spiritismo,* was started in Turin by Signor Niceforo Filalete (Prof. Vincenzo Scarpa).

The Magnetic Society of Florence, which had very influential members, began its activity. Baron Seymour Kirkup sent many accounts of activities to the London *Spiritual Magazine.* By 1870, there were over a hundred societies in different parts of Italy. Both Spiritists and Spiritualists were represented.

In 1873, Baron Guitern de Bozzi founded the Pneumatological Psychological Academy at Florence, where the visit of the British medium Mrs. **Guppy** in 1868, extending to a period of almost three years, left a deep impression. However, the academy's existence was short lived.

Soon a period of lively psychic activity ensued. In 1872, Signor Damiani discovered the medium Eusapia **Palladino,** around whom famous scientists gathered for a great many years. Dr. G. B. **Ermacora,** founder and coeditor with Dr. Finzi of the *Rivista di Studi Psichici,* Schiaparelli, **Lombroso, Bozzano, Morselli,** Chiaia, Pictet, Foà, Porro, **Brofferio, Bottazzi, Bianchi** and many other well-known researchers established the reality of psychic phenomena through their indefatigable work. A succession of such powerful mediums as **Politi, Carancini, Zuccarini,** Lucia **Sordi,** and Linda **Gazzera** helped them in their task.

Various organizations were formed, including a Società di Studi Psichici in Rome, a Society for Psychic Studies at Florence. Ernesto **Bozzano,** a leading psychical researcher, presided over the Italian Spiritualists Association, and a very well organized society, Circulo Arnaldo Vassallo, was formed in Genoa. It was named after one of the pioneers of the movement in Italy; Prof. Tullio Castellani was one of its presidents.

The leading Italian Spiritualist organ, the monthly *Luce e Ombra,* changed its title to *La Ricerca Psichica* but has since reverted to the original title. There was a bi-monthly under the title *Mondo Occulto,* published in Naples.

Spiritualism made considerable progress in Italy, in spite of constant opposition from dogmatic Catholics, who stigmatized the movement as diabolical. Progress owed much to the open-minded investigations of psychical research such as Prof. Angelo **Brofferio,** author of *Per lo Spiritismo* (1892), Dr. Ercole **Chiaia,** and Ernesto **Bozzano,** who published a defence of the British medium the Rev. W. Stainton **Moses.** (See also **Italy**)

The Literature of Spiritualism

There is a vast literature of Spiritualism, although many important works from the nineteenth century are long out of print. This literature ranges from mediumistic communications of varying value (including spirit revelations from automatic writing, trance sermons and seances) through personal experiences of investigators and theories of psychical researchers, to histories of Spiritualism and attacks on the subject.

It is by now difficult to evaluate many of the claimed classic phenomena of the past, since different writers have tended to distort or suppress facts to prove or disprove their committed beliefs or disbeliefs. However, if one reads various accounts of the mediumship of the past, it is possible to see where such distortion occurs and to form a personal opinion on the basis of reasonable probability, particularly in the light of phenomena still claimed to occur in modern times.

For example, it is difficult to doubt the reality of the mediumship of Daniel Dunglas **Home** in view of the great number of reliable witnesses who have presented the data fairly from many viewpoints. Claims of fraud which rest upon speculation alone and which have been debated at length do not stand up to fair-minded study. The scientific investigation of Home by Sir William **Crookes** stands up well.

On the other hand, the Crookes investigations with the medium Florence Cook are now under a cloud (see Trevor H. Hall's *The Spiritualists; The Story of Florence Cook and William Crookes,* 1962). It is suggested that Crookes was having an illicit affair with Florence Cook and connived at fraud. Although Trevor Hall's book is painstakingly researched and well presented, some may feel that he acts more like a shrewd prosecuting counsel than a magistrate.

For a brief reasoned refutation, see the introduction by K. M. Goldney to *Crookes and the Spirit World* edited by R. G. Medhurst (1972), as well as discussions in the *Journal* of the Society for Psychical Research (See also entries on **Crookes, Cook,** and Mary **Showers**).

At the same time, the possibility of a full-length materialization of the Phantom "Katie King," responding as if normal flesh-and-blood, seems incredible, and Crookes may well have been deceived, much as Col. H. S. **Olcott** was bemused by the claimed miracles of Madame **Blavatsky.** By now it is very difficult to tell, but it is important to study such subjects in an impartial spirit of inquiry.

Much of the phenomena of Eusapia **Palladino** seems reasonably established, as also the accusations of occasional fraud, possibly a subconsciously motivated attempt to produce expected phenomena in the easy way, or perhaps part of a curious character quirk of a peasant woman in a position to mock credulous savants.

The whole question of fraud is a difficult one. Even when there has been no financial advantage, fraud has often taken place for reasons of vanity. The mediumistic temperament is sometimes marred by vanity, hysteria or other character weakness.

The very act of placing onself constantly at the disposal of alien influences from spirits or sitters in semi-darkened rooms in an atmosphere of desired miracles or hostile skepticism is not conducive to strict rectitude.

There certainly appear to have been cases of mediums producing genuinely inexplicable phenomena intermingled with deliberate cheating. William **Roy,** one well-known modern fraudulent medium, was unable to explain apparently genuine phenomena which occasionally occurred in a career of shameless deception and exclaimed hysterically "How should I know?" However, when there have been exposures which reveal a series of carefully prepared frauds for financial gain, using special apparatus, properties and techniques, there is no good reason to doubt that the phenomena have been deceptive from beginning to end.

In order to understand how easy it is to be imposed upon by skillful conjuring, it is salutary to read books on the subject like John W. Truesdell's *The Bottom Facts Concerning the Science of Spiritualism* (1884), Julien J. Proskauer's *Spook Crooks! Exposing the Secrets of the Prophet-eers Who Conduct Our Wickedest Industry* (1932), Harry Houdini's *A Magician Among the Spirits* (1924) and the anonymous *Revelations of a Spirit Medium* (1891; reissued by Harry Price and Eric J. Dingwall).

The evidence in favor of the reality of much Spiritualist phenomena such as automatic writing, mediumistic communications and clairvoyance has often been strong, confirmed by reputable scientists as well as ordinary people. Since such phenomena constantly occur in modern times, there is no difficulty in studying them at first hand and comparing them with accounts of phenomena from the past.

The view that such phenomena are genuine but diabolical is an extreme one. Those who have studied histories of religious miracles may find if difficult to accept that such things as well-attested **levitation, transfiguration, prophecy** and **bilocation** should be genuine if concerned with saints, but diabolical if related to ordinary mediumship.

For hostile views of this kind, see Herbert Thurston's pamphlet *Modern Spiritualism* (1928). Warnings of mental deterioration through mediumship are typified in Harold Dearden's *Devilish But True; The Doctor Looks at Spiritualism* (1936) and J. Godfrey Raupert's *The Dangers of Spiritualism* (1906) and *The New Black Magic* (1922).

Books which chart the transition from **Mesmerism** and **Animal Magnetism** to Spiritualism are valuable for the information and opinions of the time. Mrs. Emma Hardinge Britten's *Nineteenth Century Miracles* (1884) and *Modern American Spiritualism* (1869) are full of detailed hard-to-find information on the events of the period, but are written from the viewpoint of a firm believer and worker in the field, and sometimes marred by inaccurate quotations. An excellent modern survey is Slater Brown's *The Heyday of Spiritualism* (1970). Alphonse Cahagnet's *The Celestial Telegraph* (2 vols., 1851) and Robert Hare's *Experimental Investigation of the Spirit Manifestations* (1856) are of special period interest.

Autobiographies of mediums are fascinating and well worth studying for their firsthand subjective viewpoint. A classic work of this kind is D. D. Home's *Incidents in My Life* (1863). More recent popular works of this kind are Estelle Roberts' *Fifty Years a Medium* (1969) and Doris Stokes' *Voices in My Ear* (1980).

There are various histories of Spiritualism, but no single satisfactory work. It is advisable to study different histories, bearing in mind the commitment of their writers. Cesar de Vesme's *History if Experimental Spiritualism* (2 vols., 1931) is a comprehensive survey of Spiritualist type phenomena in many countries from primitive times onwards. William Howitt's *The History of the Supernatural* (1863) is useful, if simplistic in tracing the antecedents of Spiritualism in past ages. E. W. Capron's *Modern Spiritualism; Its Facts and Fanaticism, Its Consistencies and Contradictions* (1855) has special interest as a contemporary account.

Sir Arthur Conan Doyle's *History of Spiritualism* (2 vols., 1926) is an important review of the background and history of the movement, but uncritical in its presentation. Frank Podmore's *Modern Spiritualism* (2 vols., 1902) is a skeptical review, but valuable for its detailed information of early mediumship. J. Arthur Hill's *Spiritualism; Its History, Phenomena and Doctrine* (1918) is useful but fragmentary. A. Campbell Holms' *The Facts of Psychic Science and Philosophy* (1925) is a very useful tabulation of the phenomena of Spiritualism but uncritical in treatment.

Hereward Carrington's *The Story of Psychic Science* (1931) is a lucid and impartial survey of the range of Spiritualism and psychical research. In contrast, Joseph McCabe's *Spiritualism; A Popular History from 1847* (1920) is a hostile study from a rationalist viewpoint but well worth reading. Harry Price's *Fifty Years of Psychical Research* (1939) is a carefully researched source work which includes factual material on most aspects of mediumship. Renée Haynes' *The Society for Psychical Research, 1882-1982; A History* is a sympathetic and well-written survey with valuable information on mediums and psychical researchers.

The book list which follows is as comprehensive as possible, including books which are skeptical of Spiritualism as well as those which are favorable, and some which are uncompromisingly hostile. Other writers included attempt an impartial presentation of the case for and against.

Recommended reading:

Barbanell, Maurice. *Spiritualism Today,* Herbert Jenkins, London, 1969

Barrett, Sir William F. *On the Threshold of the Unseen; An Examination of the Phenomena of Spiritualism and of the Evidence for Survival After Death,* Kegan Paul, London/E. P. Dutton, 1917

Bayless, Raymond. *Voices From Beyond,* University Books, 1975

Beard, Paul. *Survival of Death; For and Against,* Psychic Press, London, 1972

Bolton, Gambier. *Ghosts in Solid Form,* Rider, London, 1914

Brandon, Ruth. *The Spiritualists; the Passion for the Occult in the Nineteenth and Twentieth Centuries,* Weidenfeld & Nicolson, London, 1983

Britten, Emma Hardinge. *Nineteenth Century Miracles; or, Spirits and Their Works in Every Country of the Earth,* John Heywood, London & Manchester, 1884; Arno Press, 1976

[Britten] Emma Hardinge. *Modern American Spiritualism; A Twenty Years' Record of the Communion Between Earth and the World of Spirits,* New York, 1870; University Books, 1970

Brofferio, Angelo. *Per Lo Spiritismo,* 3rd ed., Turin, 1903

Cahagnet, Alphonse. *The Celestial Telegraph; or Secrets of LIfe to Come Revealed Through Magnetism,* 2 vols., London, n.d. (c.1850); New York, 1851

Capron, E. W. *Modern Spiritualism; Its Facts and Fanaticisms, Its Consistencies and Contradictions,* Boston, 1855; Arno Press, 1976

Carrington, Hereward. *The Story of Psychic Science,* Rider & Co., London, 1930

Crookall, Robert. *The Supreme Adventure; Analyses of Psychic Communications,* J. Clarke for Churches' Fellowship for Psychical Study, U.K., 1961

De Vesme, Cesar. *History of Experimental Spiritualism,* 2 vols., Rider & Co., London, 1931

Dearden, Harold. *Devilish But True; The Doctor Looks at Spiritualism,* Hutchinson, London, 1936; EP Publishing, U.K./Rowman & Littlefield, 1975

Doyle, Arthur Conan. *The History of Spiritualism,* 2 vols., Cassell & Co., London/George H. Doran, 1926; Arno Press, 1975

Ducasse, C. J. *A Critical Examination of the Belief in a Life After Death,* Charles C. Thomas, Springfield, Illinois, 1961

Edmunds, Simeon. *Spiritualism; A Critical Survey,* Aquarian Press, U.K., 1966

Findlay, Arthur. *On the Edge of the Etheric; or, Survival After Death Scientifically Explained,* Psychic Press, London, 1931; Corgi paperback, London, 1971

Garrett, Eileen J. *My LIfe as a Search for the Meaning of Mediumship,* Oquaga, New York/Rider & Co., London, 1939; Arno Press, 1975

Gauld, Alan. *The Founders of Psychical Research,* Routledge & Kegan Paul, London, 1968; Schocken Books, 1973

Gauld, Alan. *Mediumship and Survival; A Century of Investigations,* Heinemann, London, 1982

Gregory, William. *Animal Magnetism, or Mesmerism and Its Phenomena,* Nichols & Co., London, 2nd revised edition, 1877; 5th ed., 1909; Arno Press, 1975

Hall, Trevor H. *The Spiritualists; The Story of Florence Cook and William Crookes,* Gerald Duckworth, London, 1962; Garrett/Helix, New York, 1963

Hare, Robert. *Experimental Investigation of the Spirit Manifestations,* New York, 1855

Hart, Hornell. *The Enigma of Survival; The Case For and Against an After Life,* Charles C. Thomas, Springfield, Illinois, 1959

Haynes, Renee. *The Society for Psychical Research, 1882-1982; A History,* Macdonald & Co., London, 1982

Hill, J. Arthur. *Spiritualism; Its History, Phenomena and Doctrine,* Cassell & Co., London/George H. Doran, 1918

Holms, A. Campbell. *The Facts of Psychic Science and Philosophy,* Kegan Paul, London, 1925/University Books, 1969

Home, Daniel Dunglas. *Incidents in My Life*, Longmans, Green, London, 1863; University Books, 1972
Holzer, Hans. *Life After Death; The Challenge and the Evidence*, Bobbs-Merrill, 1969; Sidgwick & Jackson, London, 1971
Houdini, Harry. *A Magician Among the Spirits*, Harper & Row, 1924; Arno Press, 1972
Jackson, Herbert G., Jr. *The Spirit Rappers*, Doubleday, 1972
Jacobson, Nils Olof. *Life Without Death?; On Parapsychology, Mysticism and the Question of Survival*, Delacorte Press, 1973; Turnstone Books, London, 1974; Dell paperback, 1974
Kardec, Allan. *Spiritualist Philosophy; The Spirits' Books*, London, 1875 (frequently reprinted)
Kerr, Howard. *Mediums and Spirit-Rappers and Roaring Radicals*, University of Illinois Press, 1972
Lodge, Sir Oliver. *Raymond, or Life and Death; with Examples of The Evidence for Survival of Memory and Affection After Death*, Methven & Co., London, George H. Doran, New York, 1916
McCabe, Joseph. *Spiritualism; A Popular History from 1847*, Fisher Unwin, London, 1920
McHargue, Georgess. *Facts, Frauds, and Phantasms; A Survey of the Spiritualist Movement*, Doubleday, 1972
Marryatt, Florence. *There Is No Death*, London, 1892 etc.; Causeway Books, 1973
Medhurst, R. G. (collected). *Crookes and the Spirit World; A Collection of Writings by or Concerning the Work of Sir William Crookes*, Taplinger, 1972
Meek, George W. & Bertha Harris. *From Seance to Science*, Regency Press, London, 1973
Mulholland, John. *Beware Familiar Spirits*, Scribner's 1938; Arno Press, 1975
Murchison, Carl (ed.). *The Case For and Against Psychical Belief*, Worcester, Massachusetts, 1927; Arno Press, 1975
Myers, F. W. H. *Human Personality and Its Survival of Bodily Death*, 2 vols., Longmans, Green, London, 1903; Arno Press, 1975; abridged one vol. ed., University Books, 1961
Olcott, H. S. *People From the Other World*, American Publishing Co., 1875; Charles W. Tuttle, Vermont, 1972
Osty, Eugene. *Supernormal Faculties in Man*, Methuen, London, 1923
Podmore, Frank. *Modern Spiritualism; A History and a Criticism*, 2 vols., London, 1902 (reissued under title *Mediums of the 19th Century*, University Books, 1963)
Podmore, Frank. *The Newer Spiritualism*, T. Fisher Unwin, London, 1910; Arno Press, 1975
Price, Harry. *Fifty Years of Psychical Research; A Critical Survey*, Longmans, Green, London, 1939; Arno Press, 1975
Price, Harry & E. J. Dingwall (ed.). *Revelations of a Spirit Medium*, Kegan Paul, London/E. P. Dutton, 1922
Proskauer, Julien J. *Spook Crooks! Exposing the Secrets of the Prophet-eers Who Conduct Our Wickedest Industry*, A. L. Burt, New York, 1932; Gryphon Books, Ann Arbor, Michigan, 1971
[*Psychic* Magazine, Editors] *Psychics*/In-depth interviews/, Harper, 1972; Turnstone Press, London, 1973
Richet, Charles. *Thirty Years of Psychical Research*, London & New York, 1923; Arno Press, 1975
Roberts, Estelle. *Fifty Years a Medium*,Corgi Paperback, London, 1969 (enlarged edition of *Forty Years a Medium*, Herbert Jenkins, London, 1959)
Salter, W. H. *Zoar; Or, The Evidence of Psychical Research Concerning Survival*, Sidgwick & Jackson, London, 1961; Arno Press, 1975
Saltmarsh, H. F. *Evidence of Personal Survival from Cross Correspondences*, G. Bell, London, 1938; Arno Press, 1975
Sargent, Epes. *The Scientific Basis of Spiritualism*, Colby & Rich, Boston, 1880
Schrenck-Notzing, Baron von. *Phenomena of Materialisation*, Kegan Paul, London/E. P. Dutton, 1920; Arno Press, 1975
Spicer, Henry. *Sights and Sounds; The Mystery of the Day; Comprising an Entire History of the American "Spirit" Manifestations*, Thomas Bosworth, London, 1853
Stokes, Doris & Linda Dearsley. *Voices In My Ear; The Autobiography of a Medium*, Futura paperback, London, 1980
Stemman, Roy. *One Hundred Years of Spiritualism; The Story of the Spiritualist Association of Great Britain, 1872-1912*, S.A.G.B. (paperback), London, 1972
Stemman, Roy. *Spirits and Spirit Worlds*, Aldus Books, London/Doubleday, 1975
Tabori, Paul. *Companions of the Unseen*, H. A. Humphrey, London, 1968
Tabori, Paul. *Pioneers of the Unseen*, Souvenir Press, London, 1972
Thomas, John F. *Beyond Normal Cognition; An Evaluative and Methodological Study of the Mental Content of Certain Trance Phenomena*, Boston Society for Psychical Research, 1973; Arno Press, 1975
Truesdell, John W. *The Bottom Facts Concerning the Science of Spiritualism*, G. W. Carlton, New York, 1883
Wallace, Alfred Russel. *On Miracles and Modern Spiritualism*, London, 1875; revised and enlarged edition, Arno Press, 1975
Wickland, Carl A. *Thirty Years Among the Dead*, National Psychological Institute, Los Angeles, 1924; Newcastle Publishing Co., Hollywood, California, 1974

Spiritualist, The (Periodical)

(1) Influential British weekly, edited by W. H. Harrison, published in London from 1869 until 1881 (first publishing as *The Spiritualist Newspaper*). It was closely associated with the **British National Association Spiritualists** until 1879; Monthly journal published in New York, edited by C. P. Christenson, from August 1915 to November 1916; (3) British monthly journal of the **Spiritualist Community**, London, founded in 1932.

Spiritualist Association of Great Britain

One of the oldest and largest Spiritualist associations. It grew out of the **Marylebone Spiritualist**

Alliance founded in 1872. The story of the Association's early struggles "to propagate spiritual truths in the Marylebone area of London" has been told in an S.A.G.B. publication *One Hundred Years of Spiritualism,* which also states that Queen Victoria held several seances after the death of the Prince Consort.

Even the term "Spiritualist" led to many difficulties in the early days of the Association, which had to change its name to The Spiritual Evidence Society in order to hire halls. Widespread opposition to Spiritualism was also encouraged by the outdated Witchcraft Act of 1735, which was frequently invoked for police prosecution of mediums.

Four years after the repeal of the Witchcraft Act in 1951, the S.A.G.B. moved to its present large premises in South West London. It now provides lectures, demonstrations of clairvoyance, healing clinics, Sunday services, library, bookstall and other facilities for the study and practice of Spiritualism. It also links together "a commonwealth" of Spiritualist churches throughout Britain.

Membership of the Association is open to interested members of the public, who are put in touch with their local Spiritualist church. Members may also attend psychic development classes or book sittings with approved mediums. The Association publishes a quarterly magazine *The Spiritualist and Spiritual Gazette* monthly. Address: 33 Belgrave Square, London, S.W.1., England.

Spiritualist Community, The

British organization, active in the period between the two world wars in presenting religious and educational aspects of Spiritualism. It was founded by Mrs. St. Clair **Stobart,** known as "the woman on the black horse," who had led one half of the Serbian Army in their retreat during World War I and was an early member of the **British College of Psychic Science,** becoming chairperson of its Advisory Council. Mrs. Stobart published books on Spiritualism.

The Community, under the presidency of well-known Spiritualist Hannen **Swaffer,** conducted religious services, with speakers, clairvoyant and healing services, and organized instruction groups, also publishing a monthly journal *The Spiritualist* from 1932 onwards. The community is no longer active.

Spiritualist Mediums' Alliance, The

American national body in the prewar period, with headquarters in Saginaw, Michigan.

Spiritualist Outlook (Magazine)

Monthly publication of the First United Spiritualist Church; includes poetry, inspirational articles and a directory of affiliated Spiritualist churches. Address: 813 West 165th Place, Gardena, California 90247.

Spiritualistic Dramatic Society, The

British society of the 1930s, located in London, which presented plays with a Spiritualist theme to spread knowledge of Spiritualism through the channels of dramatic art. The Duchess of Hamilton and Brandon, Miss Lind-af-Hageby, Hannen **Swaffer** and Robert McAllen were its patrons.

Spiritualistische Blaetter (Periodical)

Early German Spiritualist periodical of 1883. No longer published.

Spiritualists' National Union

One of the oldest and most influential British Spiritualist organizations. It was founded in July 1890 at the suggestion of Mrs. Emma Hardinge **Britten.** In the beginning, it was known as the Spiritualists' National Federation, bringing together a number of leading Spiritualists in Manchester for an annual conference, with delegates from Spiritualist societies and including individual Spiritualists, to discuss matters of common interest.

In October 1901, the Spiritualists' National Union Ltd. was incorporated under the Companies Acts, taking over the assets, rights and obligations of the Federation in July 1902.

In 1948, the **British Spiritualists' Lyceum Union,** founded in 1890 amalgamated with the S.N.U., transferring its work of spiritual education for children and young people. The S.N.U. formulates policy through a democratically elected Council, and there is a National Executive Committee to implement policies from various individual committees such as the Trust Property, Education and Publications Committee, Exponents and Public Relations, General Purposes, and in particular the **Arthur Findlay College** Committees. The College is a large residential center for students to attend courses on Spiritualist philosophy and religious practice, spiritual healing and other related subjects.

The S.N.U. delegates local matters to fourteen district councils, with executive committees formed by directly elected members in the districts. Nearly five hundred Spiritualist churches are affiliated to the S.N.U., which are autonomous in their management. The Union maintains a register of National Spiritualist Ministers.

Membership of the Union is open to individual Spiritualists as well as churches and other organizations. The primary aims of the Union are to promote the advancement and diffusion of the religion and religious philosophy of Spiritualism as affirmed in the basic Seven Principles:

1. The Fatherhood of God
2. The Brotherhood of Man
3. The Communion of Spirits and the Ministry of Angles
4. The continuous existence of the human soul
5. Personal responsibility
6. Compensation and retribution hereafter for good and evil deeds done on earth
7. Eternal progress open to every human soul

The Union takes a leading part in the International Spiritualist Federation, uniting Spiritualists from other countries. Address for inquiries: The Spiritualists' National Union, Britten House, Stansted Hall, Stansted, Essex, England. (See also **Spiritualism**)

Spirituelles Addressbuch (Directory)

Annual publication in German language giving comprehensive listing of mystical, spiritual, yoga, and New Age organizations all over Germany. Address: PARAM, Verlag Gunther Köch, Kurz Strasse 5, D-2161 Ahlerstedt 1, Germany.

Splitfoot

A facetious name for the Devil (he of the cloven hoof), sometimes expressed as "Old Splitfoot" or "Mr. Splitfoot."

When the **Fox Sisters** first encountered the mysterious **rappings** at Hydesville, Wayne County, New York, which heralded the beginnings of **Spiritualism,** the youngest child Cathie said "Mr. Splitfoot, do as I do" and clapped her hands, when the raps immediately repeated her clapping. At first, Cathie thought somebody was tricking her, since it was the day before April Fools Day. (See also **Fox Sisters**)

Spodomancy

Divination by means of the cinders from sacrificial fires.

Spokesman (Newsletter)

Monthly publication of the Universal Christ Church: includes inspiration messages, advice to readers and directory of churches. Address: 1704 West Venice Boulevard, Los Angeles, California 90006.

Spontaneous Phenomena

Unexpected experiences of **ESP** or **PK** and other paranormal phenomena in everyday life, as distinct from laboratory tests that can be adequately controlled and repeated.

Spotlight, The (Magazine)

Published by the Lyceum section of the **National Spiritualist Association of Churches** and directed towards young people. Includes poetry, stories, cartoon and spiritual lessons, with a directory of Lyceums. Address: P.O. Box 77, Cassadaga, Florida 32706.

Sprengel, Fraulein (c.1888)

The probably mythical Rosicrucian adept and member of the German occult society Die Goldene Dämmerung who is supposed to have given permission to Rosicrucian W. W. **Westcott** to found the British Hermetic Order of the **Golden Dawn.**

Westcott claimed to find the name and address of Fraulein Sprengel on a sheet of paper inserted in the pages of a mysterious cipher manuscript bought from a bookstall in Farringdon Road, London in 1887.

Correspondence exists between Westcott and Sprengel relating to the Golden Dawn, but its authenticity has been questioned, and the cipher manuscript is believed to be an ingenious forgery, which nevertheless launched a remarkable occult society of which many talented and prominent people of the day were members.

For information on the formation and development of the Golden Dawn, see *The Magicians of the Golden Dawn* by Ellic Howe (London, 1972). (See also **Golden Dawn**)

Sprenger, Jakob (1436-1495)

Dominican inquisitor of Cologne, Germany, coauthor with Heinrich **Kramer** of the infamous *Malleus Maleficarum,* the most influential source book of the great witchcraft persecutions in Europe.

Sprenger was born in Basel and became a novice in a Dominican house. He rapidly rose to a responsible position, and in 1468 the General Chapter ordered him to lecture on the Sentences of Peter Lombard at the University of Cologne. He soon became Master of Theology at the university and was elected Prior and Regent of Studies of the Cologne Convent. On June 30, 1480 he was elected Dean of the Faculty of Theology at Cologne University, and a year later became Inquisitor Extraordinary for the provinces of Mainz, Trèves and Cologne, and traveled extensively throughout these provinces. In 1488, he was elected Provincial of the whole German Province.

His miscellaneous writings included: *The Paradoxes of John of Westphalia Refuted* (1479); *The Institution and Approbation of the Confraternity of the Most Holy Rosary, which was first erected at Cologne on 8 September in the year 1475* (1475). This latter work marked his fervent and zealous activities for the Confraternity of the Most Holy Rosary, which brought him much praise amongst leading Dominicans as an apostle of the rosary.

In 1484, Sprenger was associated with Heinrich **Kramer** in the inquisition and trying of alleged witches and sorcerers. In the following year, Kramer prepared a treatise on witchcraft (later incorporated in the *Malleus Maleficarum*) which circulated in manuscript.

Both Sprenger and Kramer collaborated in the production of the *Malleus Maleficarum,* first published 1486, which became the authoritative manual for inquisitors, judges and magistrates dealing with witchcraft cases, and was accepted by Protestants as well as Catholics. The book went into some thirty editions between 1486 and 1669, and was also published in French, Italian and English editions as well as German.

Sprenger died December 6, 1495 at Strasburg, where he was buried. (See also **Malleus Maleficarum**)

Spriggs, George (1850-1912)

Powerful British **materialization** medium. The first records of his phenomena date from 1877-79. Having discovered his psychic gifts he became the non-professional medium of The Circle of Light in Cardiff, Wales.

He had two Indian controls: "Swiftwater" was the first, "Shiwaukee," the second, was "captured" from the medium Mrs. Billings (Mrs. Mary J. **Hollis**), with whom Spriggs sat in London.

The unique feature of the seances of Spriggs was that the phantoms which appeared moved away to a distance from the medium, walked about the house, went out into the garden in evening light (on one occasion three phantoms simultaneously), and sometimes changed in the meanwhile into the form of somebody else. These peripatetic visitants were seen by next-door neighbors as well, and they threatened the host with the police for "dealings with the devil."

In November 1880, Spriggs went to Melbourne, Australia. Similar wonderful phenomena were reported there of spirits who held out a stone weighing 14 pounds at arm's length, drank water, ate biscuits and wrote letters to former sitters.

After six years, the power for materializations lapsed, but other phenomena remained. Spriggs gave **direct voice** sittings and clairvoyant diagnosis of diseases and treatment.

In 1900, he returned to England and from 1903 until 1905, he gave free medical advice in the rooms of the **London Spiritualist Alliance.** The **Psycho-Therapeutic Society** was largely formed through his efforts. For years he diagnosed diseases for the Society without charge.

W. C. D. Denovan's *The Evidences of Spiritualism* (published by Melbourne, 1882) gives a detailed account of Spriggs' mediumistic career.

Springheeled Jack

Legendary nineteenth-century British creature who harassed travelers and terrified women with his giant leaps, vicious behavior, and diabolical appearance. He successfully eluded capture for many years, evading police and the Army, mocking them with his daring leaps and wild eerie laughter.

His appearance was hideous. He was a large man in a black cloak, and when the cloak was thrown aside, blue and white flames shot from his mouth and his eyes appeared like balls of fire. His hands appeared to be clad in metallic claws, with which he slashed at people or tore their clothing. He was able to leap across high walls and hedges with the greatest ease. Sometimes he even knocked or rang at front doors, using his athletic feats for rapid escape after terrifying the occupant of the house. A typical press account in 1838, quoted in the valuable book *The Legend and Bizarre Crimes of Springheeled Jack* by Peter Haining (1977), reads as follows:

"She returned into the house and brought a candle and handed it to the person, who appeared enveloped in a large cloak, and whom she at first really believed to be a policeman. The instant she had done so, however, he threw off his outer garment, and applying the lighted candle to his breast, presented a more hideous and frightful appearance, and vomitted forth a quantity of blue and white flame from his mouth, and his eyes resembled red balls of fire.

"From the hasty glance which her fright enabled her to get at his person, she observed that he wore a large helmet, and his dress, which appeared to fit him very tight, seemed to her to resemble white oilskin. Without uttering a sentence he darted at her, and catching her partly by the dress and the back part of her neck, placed her head under one of his arms, and commenced tearing her gown with his claws, which she was certain were of some metallic substance.

"She screamed out as loud as she could for assistance, and by considerable exertion got away from him and ran towards the house to get in. Her assailant, however, followed her, and caught her on the steps leading to the hall-door, where he again used considerable violence, tore her neck and arms with his claws, as well as a quantity of hair from her head; but she was at length rescued from his grasp by one of her sisters. . . . "

Springheeled Jack terrorized many people in London and the provinces, establishing a reign of terror from 1837 to 1877. In 1880, he was even reported to have appeared in the U.S., in Louisville, Kentucky.

He reappeared in Britain during the twentieth century in 1904, and again in the U.S. in 1944 at Mattoon, Illinois for a month, stupefying women and leaving a strange smell behind. He was also reported in Houston, Texas in June 1953.

Not surprisingly he has been considered a supernatural being by many people, some claiming that he might be an evil entity connected with **UFOs**, such as **Mothman** and the legendary **Men in Black.** No doubt he also had many subsequent imitators. In her book *Stand and Deliver* (1928), historian Elizabeth Villiers commented:

"A thousand tales were afloat and all lost nothing in the telling. Plenty of people definitely swore they had seen him leap right over the roofs of large houses, the cottages and hayricks were as nothing to him, the mail coaches and post chaises and family barouches were taken in his stride. Then, rather unaccountably, public opinion veered from thinking him a new form of highwayman and declared he was an inventor experimenting with a form of flying machine, while others maintained he was not flesh and blood but a haunting spirit."

It is generally believed that the original Springheeled Jack was the eccentric Marquis of Waterford, Henry de la Poer Beresford, who was also Baron Tyrone of Haverfordwest (1811-1859). According to the Rev. Brewer in *The Reader's Handbook* (1899; reprinted Gale Research Co., 1966): "The marquis of Waterford in the early parts of the nineteenth century used to amuse himself by springing on travellers unawares, to terrify them; and from time to time others have followed his silly example. Even so late as 1877-78, an officer in her majesty's service caused much excitement, in the garrisons stationed at Aldershot, Colchester, and elsewhere, by his 'spring-heel' pranks. In Chichester and its neighbourhood the tales told of this adventurer caused quite a little panic, and many nervous people were afraid to venture out after sunset, for fear of being 'sprung' upon. I myself investigated some of the cases reported to me. . . . "

The Marquis of Waterford was certainly known to have been responsible for a number of somewhat sadistic pranks, particularly involving offensive behavior to women. But there is no firm evidence that he devised special boots fitted with steel springs or a phosphorescent mask with provision for emitting flames or smoke (as reported by victims and onlookers).

He was, however, reported as having protuberant eyes and also a peculiar ringing laugh. Moreover, one account by a servant boy of an encounter with the sinister cloaked figure with fiery eyes and claw-like hand spoke of an ornate crest on the cloak, with the initial "W" in gold filigree. The trick of breathing out blue and white flames sounds a more difficult fear than managing the spring-heeled boots, even though "fire-eaters" had performed for centuries, but Springheeled Jack was usually reported as having both arms free.

If the original Springheeled Jack *was* the Marquis of Waterford, he soon outgrew his wild behavior when he met and married the beautiful Louisa Stuart in 1842. The Marquis seems to have been benevolent towards the tenants on his Irish estates, and like many noblemen of the period spent a good deal of time in sport and hunting. He died while hunting when his horse stumbled and threw him, dislocating his neck.

Meanwhile, continued reports of Springheeled Jack generated either through legend or a succession of imitators, and led to him being the central character of plays, "penny-dreadful" comic books, and popular thrillers. As late as 1945, there was a British movie about Springheeled Jack titled *The Curse of the Wraydons,* starring veteran melodrama actor Tod Slaughter.

The suggestion that Springheeled Jack might have been a creature from outer space was argued in an article in *Flying Saucer Review* (May-June, 1961) titled 'The Mystery of Springheel Jack' by J. Vyner. It cited the twentieth-century reports from the U.S.

Even less plausible was an earlier suggestion that Springheel Jack might have been a kangeroo which had escaped from captivity. The many reliable reports of a creature breathing flames, molesting women, and with a eerie ringing laughter seem to indicate characteristics beyond the capacity of a kangeroo. (See also **Mothman**)

Recommended reading:

Haining, Peter. *The Legend and Bizarre Crimes of Springheeled Jack,* Frederick Muller, London, 1977

Keel, John A. *Strange Creatures from Time and Space,* Fawcett, 1970; Neville Spearman, London, 1975

Spunkie, The

A **goblin** similar to the Scottish **Kelpie.** He was popularly believed to be an agent of Satan, and travelers who had lost their way were his special prey.

He attracted his unfortunate victim by means of a light, which looked as if it were a reflection on a window, and was apparently not far away, but as the victim proceeded towards it, it recedes like the rainbow. However, he still followed its gleam until the Spunkie successfully lured him over a precipice or into a morass.

Squinting

It was a popular superstition that a squint was an ill omen. It used to be said that if you met a squint-eyed person, you should spit three times, to avert bad fortune.

The superstition is an old one, and was referred to in the treatise on **Fascination** (*de Fascino*) published in 1589 by Vairus, prior of the Benedictine Convent of Sta. Sophia in Benevento. In this work he stated "Let no servant ever hire himself to a squinting master." (See also **Evil Eye; Fascination**)

Squire, J. R. M. (c.1860)

American medium, editor of the *Banner of Light,* who paid a visit to England in 1859, and was introduced into society under the auspices of the great medium Daniel Dunglas **Home,** with whom he frequently held joint sittings. In the same year, the American Minister presented Squire at Court.

Dr. Lockhart Robertson described in the *Spiritual Magazine* (1860) some extraordinary displays of psychic force in his presence with Squire. A heavy circular table was somersaulted in the air and thrown on the bed when the medium placed his left hand on the surface, the other hand being held and his legs tied to the chair on which he sat. The table was afterwards twice lifted on to the head of Dr. Lockhart Robertson and the medium.

Stafford-Clark, David (1916-)

Distinguished British consultant physician and authority on psychiatry with interests in parapsychology. Born March 17, 1916 in Bromley, Kent, England, he studied at Guy's Hospital, London and University of London, M.R.C.S., L.R.C.P., M.R.C.P., M.D., D.P.M., F.R.C.P. In 1941 he married Dorothy Crossley Oldfield.

He was consultant physician at Department of Psychological Medicine, Guy's Hospital from 1950-74, and to Bethlem Royal and Maudsley Hospitals and Institute of Psychiatry from 1954 onwards; visiting professor at Johns Hopkins University, 1962; visiting lecturer at a number of universities: Oxford, Cambridge London, Harvard, Yale, Stanford, etc.; consultant to Royal College of Music, National Association for Mental Health, Canadian Mental Health Association; consultant-adviser on medical aspects to motion picture companies and radio and television programs. He was a member of the Archbishop of Canterbury's Commission of Divine Healing, and attended the Conferences on Parapsychology and Pharmacology as U.K. delegate in July 1959 at St. Paul de Vence, France.

His publications include: *Psychiatry Today* (1952; 1963), *Mental Health for Red Cross Workers* (1958), *Psychiatry for Students* (1964 etc.), *What Freud Really Said* (1965), *Five Questions in Search of an Answer; Religion and Life* (1970). He has contributed to many other medical and psychiatry works, and also to the *Encyclopedia Britannica.*

Stanford, Rex G(ale) (1938-)

Psychologist and parapsychologist, vice-president of the **Parapsychological Association** 1970-71, president in 1973, served on the Publication Committee of the **American Society for Psychical Research.**

Born in Robstown, Texas, he received his B.A. (1963) and Ph.D. (1967) in psychology from University of Texas at Austin. He was a research associate at **Division of Parapsychology,** Department of Psychiatry, University of Virginia School of Medicine, 1968-75. From 1973 onwards, he was assistant professor of psychology at St. John's University, Jamaica, New York, and he is currently director of Center for Parapsychological Research, Austin, Texas. C.P.R. is a research division of the non-profit corporation Association for the Understanding of Man.

He has special interests in development and experimental testing of models for spontaneous psi, the factors involved in ESP response, and the basic nature of psi events. He took part in the symposium 'Parapsychology (Psi) Processes; Towards a Conceptual Integration' held at the annual convention of the American Psychological Association, Montreal, August 27-31, 1973.

His papers on parapsychology include: 'A Study of the Cause of Low Run-Score Variance' (*Journal of Parapsychology,* vol. 30, 1966), 'Shifts in EEG Alpha Rhythms as Related to Calling Patterns and ESP Run-Score Variance' (*Journal of Parapsychology,* vol. 3, 1969), 'Response Factors in Extrasensory Performance' (*Journal of Communication* vol. 25, Winter 1975); in *Journal* of the American Society for Psychical Research: "Associative Activation of the Unconscious" and "Visualization" As Methods for Influencing the PK Target' (October 1969), 'Extrasensory Effects Upon "Memory"' (vol. 64, April 1970), (with C. A. Lovin) 'EEG Alpha Activity and ESP Performance' (vol. 64, October 1970), 'EEG Alpha Activity and ESP Performance: A Replicative Study' (vol. 65, April 1971), 'Suggestibility and Success at Augury—Divination from "Chance" Outcomes' (vol. 66, 1972), (with I. Stevenson) 'EEG Correlates of Free-Response GESP in an Individual Subject' (vol. 66, October 1972), 'An Experimentally Testable Model for Spontaneous Psi Events. II. Psychokinetic Events' (vol. 68, 1974), (with B. Mayer) 'Relaxation as a Psi-Conductive State: A Replication and Exploration of Parameters' (vol. 68, 1974), (with R. Zenhausern, A. Taylor & M. A. Dwyer) 'Psychokinesis as Psi-Mediated Instrumental Response' (vol. 69, April 1975). The following papers were published in books: 'Cancellation Effects Within the Test Run' (in *Parapsychology Today* ed. J. B. Rhine & R. Brier, 1968), (with J. Palmer) 'EEG Alpha Rhythms and Free-Response ESP Performance' (in *Research in Parapsychology 1973* ed. W. G. Roll, R. L. Morris & J. D. Morris, 1974), 'Concept and Psi' (in *Research in Parapsychology 1973* ed. Roll, Morris & Morris, 1974), 'Clairvoyance' (in *Psychic Exploration* by E. D. Mitchell et al. 1974).

Since 1975, his papers on parapsychology include: (in *Journal* of the American Society for Psychical Research), (with Angelo Stio) 'A Study of Associative Mediation in Psi-Mediated Instrumental Response' (vol. 70, 1976), (with several associates) 'A Study of Motivational Arousal and Self-concept in Psi-mediated Instrumental Response' (vol. 70, 1976), (with Mary Schmitt) 'Free-response ESP During Ganzfeld Stimulation; The Possible Influence of Menstrual Cycle Phase' (vol. 72, 1978), 'Towards Reinterpreting Psi Events' (vol. 72, 1978), 'The Influence of Auditory Ganzfeld Characteristics Upon Free-response ESP Performance' (vol. 73, 1979); (in *Surveys in Parapsychology* ed. Rhea White, 1976), 'Scientific, Ethical and Clinical Problems in the "Training" of Psi Ability'; (in *Research in Parapsychology 1976* ed. W. G. Roll & R. L. Morris, 1977) (with Peter Rust) 'Psi-mediated Helping Behavior; Experimental Paradigm and Initial Results,' (with Angelo Castello) 'Cognitive Mode and Extrasensory Function in a Timing-based PMIR Task'; (with R. Zenhausern & Carlo Esposito) 'The Application of Signal Detection Theory to Clairvoyance and Precognition Tasks'; (in *Research in Parapsychology 1977* ed. J. D. Morris, W. G. Roll & R. L. Morris, 1978) 'Extrasensory Effects Upon Associative Processes in a Directed Free-response Task; An Attempted Replication and Extension'; (in *Handbook of Parapsychology* ed. B. Wolman, 1977) 'Conceptual Frameworks of Contemporary Psi Research', 'Experimental Psychokinesis; A Review from Diverse Perspectives' (with Gail Lafosse) 'Type of Music, Target-Programming Rate, and Performance in a Motor ESP Task' (in *Research in Parapsychology 1979* ed. W. G. Roll, 1980), (with Miguel Roig) 'Toward Understanding the Cognitive Consequences of the Auditory Stimulation Used for Ganzfeld; Two Studies' (in *Research in Parapsychology 1981* ed. W. G. Roll, R. L. Morris & Rhe A. White, 1982), (with Raymond F. Angelini) 'The Role of Noise & the Trait of Absorption in Ganzfeld ESP Performance; The Application of Methods Based Upon Signal Detection Theory' (in *Research in Parapsychology 1983* ed. Rhea A. White & Richard S. Broughton, 1984), (with Raymon F. Angelini & Amy J. Raphael) 'Cognition & Mood During Ganzfeld: The Effects of Extraversion & Noise Versus Silence' (in *Research in Parapsychology 1984* ed. Rhea A. White & Jerry Solfvin, 1985), (with Thomas M. Kottoor 'Disruption of Attention & PK-Task Performance', 'Altered Internal States & Parapsychological Research Retrospect & Prospect' (in *Research in Parapsychology 1985* ed. Debra H.

Weiner & Dean I. Radin, 1986), 'The Out-of-Body Experience as an Imaginal Journey; A Study From the Development Perspective', 'The Ethics of Clinically Relevant Situations Encountered in Research' (in *Research in Parapsychology 1986* ed. Debra H. Weiner & Roger D. Nelson, 1987.

Stanford Research Institute

Non-profit corporation conducting advanced research in physics, electronics, bioengineering and also parapsychology. Originally affiliated with Stanford University, it became an independent organization in 1970.

SRI headquarters occupy a seventy-acre site in Menlo Park, California, a few miles away from Stanford University campus at Palo Alto. Some important parapsychological researches at SRI were conducted by Harold E. **Puthoff** and Russell **Targ** from 1973 onwards, involving laboratory experiments with psychics Uri **Geller** and Ingo **Swann.**

Stanislawa P. (c. 1930)

Polish medium, wife of a Polish officer, and subject of psychical research Baron **Schrenck-Notzing** for important **materialization experiments.**

At the age of eighteen, she saw the phantom of a friend, Sophie M., who died at the exact time. Soon afterwards spontaneous **telekinesis** phenomena developed. Having joined a Spiritualist circle, "Sophie M." materialized through Stanislawa, and became the medium's permanent attendant, occasionally sharing control with "Adalbert" and a young Polish boy.

In 1911, P. Lebiedzinski, a Polish engineer, began a series of experimental seances which lasted intermittently until 1916. His report, published in the *Revue Métapsychique* (1921, No. 4) was favorable.

The experiments of Baron Schrenck-Notzing began in 1913. After a few months, the mediumship lapsed and did not return until 1915. In 1906, when Baron Schrenck-Notzing recommenced his seance observations, he became satisfied that Mme. Stanislawa P. produced flows of **ectoplasm.** The Baron took many striking photographs. As a result of Baron Schrenck-Notzing's findings, Stanislawa P. was generally acknowledged as a powerful medium.

In 1930, her reputation suffered a heavy blow. She appeared at the Institut Métapsychique, shortly after a special automatic registering apparatus for phenomena produced in the dark was installed. She made her own conditions and produced nearly blank seances until assured that no registering apparatus would remain in the room.

Dr. Eugene **Osty** suspected that the abortive phenomena noticed on the second seance were brought about by her secretly freed hand. He decided to catch her *in flagranto delicto.* In the fourth seance, when the movement of the objects placed on the table was heard, a secret flashlight was exploded and three stereoscopic photographs were taken. Both the sudden light and the developed photographs clearly showed that a hand of the medium was free and manipulated the table.

Dr. Osty concluded in the *Revue Métapsychique* (Nov.-Dec. 1930): (1) Stanislawa P. played a comedy of mediumship at the Institute; (2) Her fraud was persevering and perfectly organized; (3) Her procedure consisted in giving the illusion of perfect control while she was capable of disengaging one of her hands from its controls and putting it back without apparently disturbing them; (4) With this procedure it was easy for her to displace objects and show luminous movements, etc. Dr. Osty, however, hastened to add that his findings meant no attempt to judge the phenomena of Mme. Stanislawa P. which were produced elsewhere.

Stapleton, Ruth Carter

Somewhat midway between traditional psychic therapy and revivalist faith healing is the "inner healing" practiced by evangelist Ruth Carter Stapleton, younger sister of former President Jimmy Carter.

Ruth Stapleton is wife of a North Carolina veterinarian and mother of four children. Her career as a healer dates from her own recovery from periods of deep depression. She combined attendance at group therapy sessions with an interdenominational retreat at a North Carolina hotel, and "experienced God as a God of love." Some three months later she attended a second retreat and came in contact with Pentecostalism. She received "Baptism of the Holy Spirit" in a Pentecostal rite, experiencing speaking in **tongues.**

She subsequently developed her own kind of healing technique which might be described as a spiritually based psychotherapy. She combines prayer with a probing of the unhappy memories of the individuals who seek her help. She teaches them to recreate painful past experiences in a "guided daydream" in which the figure of Jesus is introduced to neutralize emotional difficulties by love and forgiveness.

In her book *The Gift of Inner Healing* (World Books, 1976), she described her work over nine years with various denominations. As well as Protestants, she has preached and prayed for Roman Catholics at her spiritual workshops in over seventy U.S. cities, and abroad in Indonesia, Malaysia, Japan and Britain. She rejects the label of "faith healer" since she claims God is the healer, but has also been involved in traditional style faith healing of physical ailments by means of prayer.

In 1977, Ruth Stapleton hit the headlines when she was instrumental in bringing religious conviction to Larry C. Flynt, editor of the notorious *Hustler* magazine. On February 8. 1977, Flynt had been found guilty of engaging in organized crime and pandering to obscenity. CBS News producer Joe Wershba introduced Flint to Stapleton, and after a discussion on religion and sexual repression, Flynt claims a religious conversion was set in motion.

According to his own account, Flynt discovered God at 40,000 feet while on a jet aircraft trip from Denver to Houston. Both Stapleton and Flynt appeared together on a "Today" program on November 23, 1977, when Flynt publicly acknowledged that God had entered his life and that henceforth his magazine would introduce a religious element. *Hustler* would be transformed into a religious magazine, and Flynt's multimillion-dollar empire of sex and smut would be turned into a nonprofit religious foundation. At a Pentecostal congregation in Houston, Flynt stated: "I owe every woman in America an apology."

In the light of Flynt's new life style, it is sad to report that on March 6, 1976 he was shot and seriously wounded by an unknown assailant, soon after testifying in one of his court cases.

Star, Ely

Pseudonym of Eugène Jacob (1847-1942), French astrologer and medical charlatan. He was a member of the Ahathoor (or Athoor) Temple of the **Golden Dawn.** He was prosecuted and sentenced for fraud in 1914.

Statues, Moving

The belief that images of gods, goddesses, and saints might become imbued with divine force and acquire movement is an ancient one, and such miracles have been reported of both Christian and non-Christian images. In modern times, the belief has been revived in Ireland, where a statue of the Virgin Mary at **Ballinspittle,** Co. Cork, has attracted nationwide interest after claims by many witnesses that they had seen it move.

Moving Statues in Ancient History

Many miraculous statues in pagan times were undoubtedly fraudulent, just as there are known cases of moving statue hoaxes in modern times. It is well known that ancient peoples constructed images of the gods and goddesses that appeared to have independent life.

Plato and Aristotle stated that the Greek Daedalus was said to have made statues which not only walked but also needed to be tethered at night, to keep them from walking away! Aristotle described a wooden statue of Venus which moved as a result of quicksilver being poured into its interior. Pliny reported that the architect Timochares had started to use loadstone (magnetized ore) in the construction of the vaulting in the temple of Arsinoê at Alexandria, so that the iron statue in it could be suspended in midair. Such a levitating statue would have been a great wonder if the plan had succeeded. The engineering talent of the ancient Romans was responsible for a complex clock, described by Procopius, which had figures of gods and heroes that moved on the hour.

Lucian related how a certain Alexander caused a statue of Aesculapius to speak by using the gullet of a crane and transmitting a voice through it to the mouth of the statue. In the fourth century, Bishop Theophilus described statues at Alexandria which he broke open and discovered to be hollow; they were placed against a wall in such a position that a priest could slip behind them and speak through the mouth of the god.

Miraculous statues of gods, said to deliver oracles, were believed to be numerous in ancient Egypt. The *Pymander Asclepios* (attributed to Hermes Trismegistus) asserted that the Egyptians "knew how to make gods," i.e., to install deities, angels or demons in statues, with the power to do good or evil. Although such statues have not survived, it seems probable that they were actually animated by priests. The archaeologist Gaston Maspéro (1846-1916) stated (*Journal des Debats,* December 21, 1898):

"There were thus obtained genuine terrestrial gods, exact counterparts of the celestial gods, and, as their ambassadors here below, capable of protecting, punishing and instructing men, of sending them dreams and delivering oracles.

"When these idols were addressed, they replied either by gesture or by voice. They would speak and utter the right verdict on any particular questions. They moved their arms and shook their heads to an invariable rhythm. . . . And as they assuredly did nothing of all this by themselves, someone had to do it for them. Indeed, there were priests in the temples whose business it was to attend to these things. Their functions, being anything but secret, were carried out openly, in the sight and to the knowledge of all. They had their appointed places in ceremonies, in processions and the sacerdotal hierarchy; each individual knew that they were the voice or the hand of the god, and that they pulled the string to set his head wagging at the right moment. Consequently this was not one of those pious frauds which the moderns always suspect in like circumstances; no one was ignorant that the divine consultation was brought about by this purely human agency.

"Things being so, one wonders how not only the people but the kings, nobles, and scribes could have confidence in advice thus proffered. . . . The testimony afforded by monuments compels us to acknowledge that it was taken seriously until paganism died a natural death, and that all who played any part in it did so with the utmost respect. They had been brought up from childhood to believe that divine souls animated the statues, to approach these living statues only in the most respectful dread and awe. . . . Their mental attitude was that of the modern-day priest who ascends the altar. No sooner has he donned the sacerdotal garb and repeated the first few sacramental words than he no longer belongs to himself but to the sacrifice he is about to consummate; he knows that at this voice and gesture the elements will change into precious blood and flesh, and he continues unperturbed the work which he is certain he can accomplish."

Such a reverential attitude to manipulation of statues, if true, offers an alternative theory to hard-and-fast views of either miracle or fraud, and has something in common with claims that some fraud practiced by Spiritualist mediums may only be "priming the pump" for genuine phenomena. Similarly in primitive societies, **shamans** may invoke divine inspiration by initial trickery, acting out a miraculous situation by conjuring tricks as a preliminary to creating the emotional atmosphere in which heightened consciousness and genuine phenomena may arise.

However, there are also many claims in both ancient and modern times that statues have actually moved independently of human artifice. In some cases, rival religions did not deny the miracles but asserted that they were demonic, not divine. In analyzing a passage from Hermes Trismegistus concerned with "statues animated by divine association, which do great things, foretell the future and heal diseases," St. Augustine did not dispute the claims, but commented that "this art of binding genii to statues is an ungodly art . . . Instead of serving men, these would-be gods can do nothing, except as devils" (*Civitas Dei,* book 8, chapters 23, 24). The Synod of Laodicea defined idolatry as "the art of invoking demons and incorporating them in statues."

Moving Statues in Modern History

Throughout history, moving statues tended to be reported at times of great civil, political, or religious crisis, in which a breakdown of morale or the imminence of national disaster seemed beyond human aid, inviting divine intervention.

During 1524, Italy was overrun by French armies and menaced by floods, famine, and plague. At this critical time, when Rome itself seemed threatened, a statue of the Virgin Mary at Brescia was reported to open and close its eyes, and to move its hands, bringing them together and separating them in a gesture of sympathy. Thousands of witnesses attested to the phenomenon, and similar moving statues were reported in other towns. After the crisis, such miracles ceased.

A similar event took place in 1716, when Turkish forces threatened war on Venice. One man claimed that the Virgin Mary had appeared to him in a vision and stated that if enough prayers for souls in purgatory were offered up, the infidels would be defeated. A crowd assembled in front of a statue of the Virgin Mary and declared that the statue opened and closed its eyes to confirm what the visionary had stated. The senate of the city and also the local bishop affirmed their support for the reality of the phenomenon.

Eighty years later, there was an extraordinary outburst of reports of statues of the Virgin Mary opening and closing their eyes or shedding tears, when the French revolutionary forces threatened the Papal States during 1796-97. These miracles were claimed in many churches in Rome and also all over the country. A Papal Commission examined over nine hundred witnesses and reported favorably on the reality of the phenomena. The manifestations subsided when Napoleon Bonaparte entered Ancone and ordered the statue of the Virgin Mary, which had been one of those reported as moving, to be covered up.

In 1870, at Soriano, Calabria, Spain, there were reputed miracles of a statue that appeared to move its hand and arm. In 1919, at Limpias, Santander, Spain, pictures of saints were reported as moving their eyes or dripping blood, some even stepping out of their panels. Hundreds of sworn statements attesting to such miracles were obtained, many from educated and professional persons. Many similar incidents were reported from Spain, at Campocavallo in 1893, and on five separate occasions at Rimini between 1850 and 1905. In the latter cases, the paintings of saints were said to shed tears.

The reports from Limpias were investigated by Prof. A. Encinas of Santander University, who compared notes with the scientist Prof. Jaensch. These and similar cases were ascribed to collective hallucination, specifically arising from the psychological phenomenon of eidetic imagery.

In his book *The Mechanism of Thought, Imagery and Hallucination* (1939), J. Rosett commented: "The reports of mystics and of devotees about pictures and statues which moved and spoke like living persons and performed miracles are . . . not necessarily fraudulent. An understanding of the mechanism of attention and its relation to the state of falling asleep, and of the hallucinations associated with that state, offers a rational explanation of such reports.

According to Prof. E. R. Jaensch in his important study *Eidetic Imagery* (1930): "Topical perceptual (or eidetic) images are phenomena that take up an intermediate position between sensations and images. Like ordinary physiological after-images, they are always *seen* in the literal sense. They have this property of necessity and under all conditions, and share it with sensations. In other respects they can also exhibit the properties of images (*Vorstellungen*). In those cases in which the imagination has little influence, they are merely modified after-images, deviating from the norm in a definite way, and when that influence is nearly, or completely zero, we can look upon them as slightly intensified after-images. In the other limiting case, when the influence of the imagination is at its maximum, they are ideas that, like after-images, are projected outward and literally *seen.*" Eidetic imagery clearly has relevance to the visual faculty of artists, who can "see" their subject on the blank paper or canvas. It may also have relevance to the phenomenon of **Crystal Gazing.** The existence of various explanations of moving statues—deliberate fraud, sacramental or ritualistic manipulation, hallucination through eidetic imagery—does not preclude actual paranormal existence in some cases, indeed it argues for the possibilities of different explanations for different cases rather than one simplistic answer.

It would be wrong to assume that moving statues belong only to earlier history or unsophisticated communities. During 1985, there was an astonishing outburst of cases of statues moving, bleeding, or weeping throughout the Republic of Ireland. Cases were reported from over thirty localities in only a few months of the year. Interestingly enough, no cases were reported from Northern Ireland during this period, although there is a large Catholic population there.

Characteristically, the period was one of great cultural, political, and religious unrest. For decades, Ireland's radio and television media had spread an alien pop culture, allied with the consumerism of postwar industrialization and the economics of the Common Market following membership of the European Economic Community. The EEC farm subsidies had first floated a new affluence, particularly amongst the Irish farmers, but the sudden restriction on such financial aid in the general depression of the late 1970s and early 1980s imposed new hardships. Rapid changes of government had done little to reduce unemployment and a large national debt. The continuing unrest in the North, with its regular toll of bomb outrages and brutal murders had uneasy echoes in the South, intensifying divisiveness on the issue of national unity. With the abolition of censorship of books and films, the old certainties and conservatism of religion had been challenged.

This came to a head in 1983 with the ferment caused by a referendum on amending the Constitution to protect the rights of unborn children. Fierce pro- and anti-abortion lobbies campaigned for support, at a time when hundreds of Irish women traveled to Britain for their abortions. New legislation liberalizing the availability of contraceptives, with the promise of a referendum on the issue of divorce (not permitted by the Constitution), had excited conservative protests that the sanctity of marriage and family life was in danger of being destroyed. However, tragic reports of lonely deaths in unwanted pregnancies, victimization of unmarried mothers, and the heart-breaking legal and social tangles of marriages that could not be dissolved or remarriages that were illegal, all indicated that neither the old religious conservatism or the newer liberalism had come to terms with the problems of modern life. All this came to a head with the reports in 1985 of the protracted judicial inquiry into the extraordinary case of the Kerry Babies, stemming from the discovery of an infant corpse with stab-wounds on the White Strand rocks at Cahirciveen.

It was against this apocalyptic background that the statues of the Virgin Mary throughout the Republic were reported as moving. It began on February 14, when several children in Asdee, Co. Kerry, claimed to have seen a statue of the Madonna and child at the parish church of St. Mary open its eyes and move its hands. An eighty-year-old farmer also stated that he saw the Madonna blink three times. Thousands of people visited the church, but there were no further reports and the excitement died down.

A few weeks later, children at Ballydesmond, Co. Cork, stated that they saw a statue move in the local church, but parents ascribed this to an overactive imagination.

A group of tourists at Courtmacsharry, Co. Cork, claimed to have seen a statue near the town move, but no other movements were reported and the affair died down.

In July, two teenage girls reported seeing movement in a statue of the Virgin Mary in a grotto some 20 feet up on the side of a hill at Ballinspittle, Co. Cork. Soon other people reported seeing the statue change expression or move, and large crowds gathered regularly to watch and recite the rosary. Many people claimed to see the Virgin's eyes or hands move, or the statue to move backwards and forwards or sway from side to side. Thousands of pilgrims visited the shrine, which became a central focus for stories of statues that moved. Pilgrimages and reports of movement of the statue persisted for over three months and only subsided at the end of October, when vandals smashed the hands and face of the statue with an axe and a hammer (see **Ballinspittle**).

Meanwhile throughout August and September, further reports of phenomena associated with the Virgin Mary came from all over the Republic. In Mitchelstown, Co. Cork, children stated that they had seen black blood flowing from a statue of the Virgin Mary, and an apparition of the devil appearing behind the statue. Many pilgrims gathered, and other young people claimed that they saw the statue move. Four teenage girls said that a statue at the local Marian shrine spoke to them and called for peace.

In Dunkitt, Co. Waterford, a statue of the Virgin Mary in a grotto on the main Waterford to Kilkenny road was reported to have been seen to move. Some people claimed that the statue breathed and the hands moved from center to right. A local publican and his wife stated that the statue shimmered. Thousands of pilgrims visited the grotto.

In Waterford city, two young boys stated that a statue of the Virgin Mary, outside the Mercy Convent School moved its eyes, which were full of tears, and spoke of Pope John Paul II being assassinated. Hundreds of people kept vigil around the statue.

At Mooncoin, Co. Waterford, several youths stated that they saw a statue move, and a girl said she saw a tear fall from the right eye of the statue and the left eye open and close. Local people gathered at site for novenas and vigils.

Many statues in Co. Limerick were said to move. In Limerick city, a statue of the Virgin Mary at Garryowen was said by several witnesses to have blood on the hands. Other statues in St. Mary's Park and the Moycross housing estate were reported to move. In Mountcollins, Co. Limerick, crowds assembled at a grotto after some local women and children said they saw the statue move and sway. Other people believed they saw manifestations of the Sacred Heart over the statue and blood coming out of the statue's eyes. Other Co. Limerick locations reported moving statues, including Foyes, Coolard, Cahermoyle, and Mainster.

Two reports came from Co. Wexford, from Camolin, and from Enniscorthy. At Glenbrien in Co. Clare, two local women stated that they saw a statue of the Virgin Mary move. At Cartloe in Co. Clare, pilgrims gathered after two women in a local prayer group claimed that the statue moved. There were also reports of a face resembling Christ which was superimposed on the Virgin's face. Some children stated that they saw the face of Padre **Pio** and one of the Popes on the statue. A woman stated that she saw the face of Christ from the **Turin Shroud** appear. Hundreds of people prayed around the statue.

At Rosecrea, Co. Tipperary, local people claimed that a statue of the Virgin Mary in the grounds of

St. Ann's Convent had moved, although the nuns were skeptical.

At Mount Mellary, Co. Waterford, three children made the astonishing claim that a statue of the Virgin Mary near the Cistercian Abbey had walked down from its pedestal and told them that "God was very angry with the world." Thousands of people gathered around the statue, by then back on its pedestal.

At Monasterevin, Co. Kildare, a statue of the Virgin Mary was said to have been seen to move regularly and also to have had the face of Padre Pio superimposed on it. At Abbeyleix, Co. Laois, a statue in the ground of Knock church was said to have moved. At Stradbally, Co. Laois, bloodstains were said to have been seen on a statue of the Virgin Mary, and there were also reports that the face changed to that of Padre Pio and to the Sacred Heart.

In Co. Carlow, there were reports of moving statues from Killeshin, Spink, and St. Dympna's Hospital. In Carlow itself, a small glass-covered image on Rossmore Hill was said to have moved inside the glass.

In Carrick on Shannon, Co. Leitrim, a young girl stated that she saw the statue of the Virgin Mary in the grounds of convent move. In Carns, Co. Sligo, large crowds attended vigils at a location where four local school girls claimed that they saw a vision of the Virgin Mary. Other people stated that they saw images of the Virgin and of St. Bernardette and a crucifix in the night sky.

In Cork city, three school children claimed to have seen the statue of the Virgin Mary in the Church of the Resurrection, Farranree, move. They said the statue almost toppled over. The mother of one of the children claimed that the Virgin's eyes were red and her cheeks and feet black.

Even in Dublin, there were reports of a moving statue in the grounds of the Oblate church in Inchicore, although local priests dismissed it as "just messing" by local children.

In the scores of cases reported from all over the country, it seems clear that the statues *appeared* to move, rather than physically shifting position. Psychologists pointed out that staring at statues in half light, especially with a glare from an illuminated halo, could result in optical illusions. However, the essential and more elusive aspect of the phenomenon was the religious fervor associated with it, the feelings of spiritual grace experienced by many individuals, including a number of skeptics. This wave of religious renewal, sweeping across a whole country, was in every sense a moving experience. (See also **Apparitions; Ballinspittle; Stigmata**)

Staus Poltergeist

Between 1860-62, the village of Staus, on the shores of Lake Lucerne, Switzerland, was the scene of one of the most remarkable case of poltergeist haunting.

The outbreak occurred in the house of M. Joller, a distinguished lawyer and a member of the Swiss national council, a man, moreover, whose character, both in public and private life, was beyond reproach. The household comprised M. Joller himself, his wife, seven children (four boys and three girls), and a servant-maid.

One night in the autumn of 1860, the maid was disturbed by a loud rapping on her bedstead, which she regarded as a presage of death. M. Joller ascribed the sounds to the girl's imagination, and forbade her to speak about them.

A few weeks later, returning after a short absence, he found his family much alarmed. The knocks had been repeated in the presence of his wife and daughter, and had even manifested signs of intelligence. When, a few days afterwards, they had news of the death of a friend, they imagined that this must have been what the raps portended.

But again in June 1861, the outbreak was renewed. This time one of the boys fainted at the apparition of a white, indistinct figure. Other strange things began to be seen and heard by the children, and a few months later the maid complained that the kitchen was haunted by dim, grey shapes who followed her to her chamber, and sobbed all night in the lumber-room.

In October of the same year, the maid was replaced by another, the rappings ceased, and the disturbances seemed to be at an end. They were renewed, however, and with greatly increased vigor, in August 1862, during the absence on business of M. Joller, his wife, and their eldest son. So great was the annoyance that the children fled from the house into the garden, in spite of their father's threat to punish their credulity.

But at length the poltergeist began to persecute M. Joller himself, pursuing him from room to room with loud knocks, and in spite of all his efforts, he was unable to elucidate the mystery. Things began to be thrown about by invisible hands, locked doors and fastened windows were flung wide, strange music and voices and the humming of spinning-wheels were heard.

In spite of M. Joller's attempts to conceal these happenings, the news spread abroad, and hundreds, even thousands, of persons flocked to witness the phenomena. Finding no rational hypothesis to fit the circumstances, M. Joller begged the Commissary Niederberger to come and investigate, but in the latter's absence, Father Guardian visited the haunted house, blessed it, although without alleviating the disturbances, and suggested that an inquiry be made by men of authority.

M. Joller privately called in several scientific men of his acquaintance, but they also were unable to find a solution, although various theories of electricity, galvanism, and magnetism were advanced.

Other persons of authority, Land-Captain Zelger, the Director of Police Jann, Dr. Christen, the President of the Court of Justice, were present while Commissary Niederberger and Father Guardian made a careful examination of the house, without discovering any cause for the disturbances, which still continued unabated.

At length M. Joller demanded of the police a formal examination, and three of the heads of the police were chosen to investigate. The Joller family were instructed to withdraw, and for six days the police remained in undisturbed possession. At the end of that period, having neither heard nor seen any sign of the poltergeist, they drew up a report to that effect, and took their departure.

Immediately on the Jollers reentering the house, the phenomena began afresh. Ridicule was heaped upon the unfortunate member of council, even by those of his own party, and his house was in such an uproar that he found it impossible to carry on his business. Add to this the unwelcome curiosity of the crowds who flocked to witness the marvels, and it is not surprising that at length, in October 1862, M. Joller left his ancestral home for ever.

In the following spring he succeeded in finding a tenant for the house in Staus, but the poltergeist outbreak was not renewed. These events afford good evidence for the hypothesis of discarnate intelligence operating in poltergeist cases. The Joller case was exceedingly well-attested, not only by the curious crowds who saw the opening and shutting of windows, and so on, but also by men of responsibility, members of the national council, court of justice, and other institutions. (See also **Poltergeist**)

Stead, William T(homas) (1849-1912)

Famous British editor, journalist, publicist, and champion of Spiritualism. He was born July 5, 1849, at Embleton, Northumberland, England, son of a Congregationalist minister. He was first educated by his father, then attended a school in Wakefield.

In 1863, he left school to be apprenticed in a merchant's countinghouse in Newcastle-on-Tyne. At the age of eighteen, he was impressed by the poems of James Russell Lowell, and resolved to dedicate his life to helping other people. Throughout his subsequent career as an editor, he became a fearless campaigner for truth and justice. In 1880, while editing the *Northern Echo* at Darlington, England, he raised his voice in passionate protest against the Bulgarian atrocities. The *Pall Mall Gazette* of London, a pro-Turk paper, unexpectedly changed hands and he was offered the post of assistant editor. Three years later, the full control of the paper passed into his hands.

He founded the *Review of Reviews* in 1890. The first manifestation of his interest in psychic subjects was the publication (as the Christmas Number of the *Review of Reviews*) of his book *Real Ghost Stories* in 1891. Next year it was followed by *More Ghost Stories.*

In 1892, he discovered that he had the gift of receiving communications in **automatic writing.** This was the beginning of important psychic activities. He received striking proofs of survival, through his own hands, from Miss Julia Ames, a journalist acquaintance, editor of *The Woman's Union Signal* of Chicago, who had died shortly before.

On March 14, 1893, in an address to members of the **London Spiritualist Alliance,** Stead made his first public confession of faith, narrating the full details of his own discoveries and early psychic experiences.

It was suggested to him in a communication from "Julia" that he could obtain automatic scripts from living friends as well. "I put my hand," he said, "at the disposal of friends at various degrees of distance, and I found that, although the faculty varied, some friends could write extremely well, imitating at first the style of their own handwriting, sometimes for the first few words until they had more or less established their identity, and then going on to write exactly as they would write an ordinary letter. They would write what they were thinking about—whether they wanted to see me, or where they had been."

In 1893, Stead began publication of *Borderland,* a quarterly psychic magazine running until 1897, in which the "Letters from Julia" which he obtained automatically were published for the first time. They were printed in book form in 1897 under the title *After Death.*

Stead was assisted in the editorial work by Miss X. (Ada Goodrich-Freer, later Mrs. H. Spoer). In her notes on the origin of *Borderland* she stated: "Mr. Stead was as definitely spiritualist as I was definitely an anti-spiritualist. He believed in everybody until they were found out, and often afterwards, and he would seek to introduce into *Borderland* the lucubrations of people at whom as a disciple of Lavater I shuddered."

In the Christmas number of the *Review of Reviews* for 1893, Stead wrote a story entitled 'From the Old World to the New.' It was pure fiction which dwelt on the dangers of icebergs in the Atlantic Ocean. The scene was laid on a ship named the "Majestic" and as Commander the same Capt. Smith was portrayed who twenty-one years later went down with the "Titanic." The narrative pictured the sinking of the liner and depicted the Atlantic Ocean as a grave.

His eldest son, Willie Stead, died in December 1907. The need for consoling the bereaved was poignantly brought home to him. "Julia" never ceased to urge the establishment of a bureau where free communication with the Beyond should serve anxious inquirers.

The Bureau was opened on April 24, 1909, (see **Julia's Bureau**). A small circle of sensitives chosen by "Julia" herself to make a psychic focus of great and increasing power met every morning at ten at Mowbray House, Norfolk Street, London, W.C. Strangers were not admitted to this circle. The sittings were invariably held in broad daylight. As special clairaudient and clairvoyant, Robert **King** was engaged. Whenever he was unable to come, Alfred Vout **Peters** attended.

For applicants, private sittings were given, of which careful records were kept. **Psychometry** was often very successful. In fact, in case of distant inquirers it was invariably resorted to.

In the three years of its existence about 1,300 sittings were given in the Bureau. Its maintenance cost Stead £1,500 a year. Besides Robert King and Vout Peters, Mrs. Wesley Adams and Mr. J. J. Vango were employed as psychics.

As well as "Julia," Stead claimed an influence, calling itself "Catherine II" of Russia, among his communicators. In the *Contemporary Review* for January 1909, under the title 'The Arrival of the Slav,' an article was published under Stead's name. It contained Catherine's *Manifesto to the Slavs,* a singularly prophetic script which was made up of different Catherine messages obtained through his and his secretary's hand.

His review of Sir Oliver **Lodge**'s book *The Survival of Man* (1909) disclosed an interesting experiment. Arriving at a certain stage in writing the review, the idea occurred to him of asking one of Sir Oliver's spirit friends on the other side to write the concluding passage of the review, through two automatists, one of whom had read the book and the other who had not. The automatists were separated by a distance of seventy miles and the second did not know where the script of the first had broken off. They acquitted themselves of the task in a very satisfactory way and Stead's review was accordingly concluded.

As a result of his article 'When the Door Opened' in the *Fortnightly Review,* Stead was challenged by the *Daily Chronicle* on the eve of general elections to obtain Gladstone's views on the political crisis. He consulted "Julia." She deprecated the attempt but did not forbid it. Accordingly, Robert King listened for a clairaudient communication which seemed to come to him as though from a long distance. When it was published there was a great deal of ridicule and public derision. Stead himself did not claim that it emanated from the spirit of Gladstone, but thought that it bore a strong resemblance to the recorded utterances of Gladstone on earth.

There was a sequel to this interview in scripts obtained through a non-professional automatist as letters of further explanation. They were not published at the time. Stead waited for the psychological moment which never came. But in 1911, Admiral Usborne Moore telephoned him and informed him that in a seance with the medium Mrs. Etta **Wriedt** in Detroit, Gladstone purported to speak and asked him whether he remembered the name of the lady in England through whose hand he had given a message. The voice then gave the correct name. As the story of the sequel to the Gladstone interview was only known privately to a few, Stead considered this as a good test of identity.

Stead was constantly at war with the **Society for Psychical Research.** "What are known as psychical research methods," wrote Edith K. Harper in her book *Stead, the Man* (1918), "was abhorrent to him. He held them truly unscientific in the most extended meaning of the word. He said he would rather die in the workhouse than believe that anyone would tell him a deliberate falsehood for the mere purpose of deceiving him."

Speaking against the rigor of the Society in admitting evidence as regards communications from the dead, he drew, before the members of the Cosmos Club in 1909, a graphic, imaginary picture of himself, shipwrecked and drowning in the sea and calling frantically for help. Suppose that instead of throwing me a rope the rescuers would shout back: "'Who are you? What is your name? 'I am Stead! W. T. Stead! I am drowning here in the sea. Throw me the rope. Be quick!' But instead of throwing me the rope they continue to shout back: 'How do we know you are Stead? Where were you born? Tell us the name of your grandmother.'"

It is quite astonishing how often the picture of a sinking ocean liner with its attendant horrors recurred in Stead's writings. His earliest foreboding took the form of a narrative by a survivor in the *Pall Mall Gazette.* It was attended by the following editorial note: "This is exactly what might take place if liners are sent to sea short of boats." Twenty-six years afterwards 1,600 lives were lost on the "Titanic," owing to a shortage of boats, and Stead went down among them.

He was invited to speak at Carnegie Hall, New York, on April 21, 1912, on the subject of the World's Peace. Before his departure on the "Titanic" he wrote to his secretary: "I feel as if something was going to happen, somewhere, or somehow. And that it will be for good . . . "

Prof. George **Henslow**'s book *The Proofs of the Truths of Spiritualism* (1919) stated that Archdeacon **Colley** (who later printed a pamphlet *The Foreordained Wreck of the Titanic*) sent a forecast of the disaster to Mr. Stead and received the answer: "I sincerely hope that none of the misfortunes which you seem to think may happen, will happen; but I will keep your letter and will write to you when I come back."

He intended to bring Mrs. Etta Wriedt, the Detroit **direct voice** medium, to England when he returned. Mrs. Wriedt was waiting for him in New York. The "Titanic" was struck by an iceberg on the night of April 14, 1912. Two nights later, "Dr. Sharp," Mrs. Wriedt's **control,** gave full details of the "Titanic" disaster, assured sitters of the passing of Stead and gave the names of many prominent people who went down with the ship. The following night, three days after his passing, Stead himself communicated. He was weak in articulation at first, but he was understood.

The messages which purported to emanate from Stead through **automatic writing, direct voice, materialization** and **psychic photography** were summed up by James Coates in his book *Has W. T. Stead Returned?* (1913). He concluded that they definitely established his identity.

There is a W. T. Stead Memorial Society in Britain: c/o Victor Jones, "Rosamund," 7A Seagrave Avenue (Hants.), Hayling Island, PO11 9EU, England.

Steen, Douglas (1925-)

Researcher in finance, weather, astropsychology and parapsychology. Born July 22, 1925 at Los Angeles, California, he studied at University of California at Los Angeles (M.A. 1951). In 1956 he married Jo Clark Griffin. He served in the U.S. Navy, was mathematical physicist on guided missiles at

Northrop Air Corp., from 1951-54, freelance researcher from 1954 onwards. He became president of Commetrics, Inc., Oil for Executives, Inc.

He assisted at the Parapsychology Laboratory at Duke University, Durham, N.C. in adapting the playing of four sports to dice-throwing for laboratory research in psychokinesis. He published an article 'Success with Complex Targets in a PK Baseball Game' in *Journal of Parapsychology*, June 1957.

Steiger, Brad (1936-)

Pseudonym of Eugene E. Olson, prolific writer on occult subjects. Born February 19, 1936 in Bode, Iowa, he was educated at Luther College 1953-57, University of Iowa 1963. From 1957-63 he was a high school English teacher in Clinton, Iowa, from 1963-67 teacher of literature and creative writing at Luther College, Decorah, Iowa. From 1970 onwards he had been president of Other Dimensions, Inc., Decorah, Iowa.

He has lectured at colleges and to private groups and conducted syndicated radio program "The Strange World of Brad Steiger." He co-hosted "Threshold" radio interview program. He is a member of the American Society for Psychical Research, Author's Guild.

His books under pseudonym "Brad Steiger" include: *Strange Guests* (1966), *The Unknown* (1966), *ESP: Your Sixth Sense* (1966), (with Chaw Mank) *Valentino* (1966), (with Joan Whritenour) *Flying Saucers Are Hostile* (1967), *The Mass Murderer* (1967), *The Enigma of Reincarnation* (1967), *Real Ghosts, Restless Spirits & Haunted Minds* (1968), (with John Pendragon) *Pendragon: A Clairvoyant's Power of Prophecy* (1968) *Voices from Beyond* (1968), *UFO Breakthrough* (1968), *In My Soul I Am Free* (1968), *Sex and the Supernatural* (1968), *The Mind Travellers* (1968), (with Pendragon) *Cupid and the Stars* (1969), (with Ron Warmoth) *Tarot* (1969), *Sex and Satanism* (1969), (with Dorothy Spence) *Your Mind* (1969), *The Weird, the Wild, and the Wicked* (1969), (with Loring G. Williams) *Other Lives* (1969), (with Warren Smith) *What the Seers Predict in 1971* (1970), (with William Howard) *Handwriting Analysis* (1970), *Aquarian Revelations* (1971), (with Williams) *Minds Through Space and Time* (1971), *Secrets of Kahuna Magic* (1971), *Haunted Lovers* (1971), *The Psychic Feats of Olof Jonsson* (1971), *Strange Encounters with Ghosts* (1972) *Irene Hughes on Psychic Safari* (1972), *Revelation: The Divine Fine* (1973), *Atlantis Rising* (1973), *The Unknown* (1974), *Medicine Power: The American Indian's Revival of His Spiritual Heritage & Its Relevance for Modern Man* (1974), *Mysteries of Time & Space* (1974), *Medicine Talk: A Guide to Walking in Balance & Surviving on the Earth Mother* (1975), (with John White) *Other Worlds, Other Universes; Playing the Reality Game* (1975), *Psychic City: Chicago; Doorway to Another Dimension* (1976), *Project Blue Book* (1976), *Gods of Aquarius, UFOs & the Transformation of Man* (1976), *Worlds Before Our Own* (1978), *The Hypnotist* (1979), *In My Soul I Am Free* (biography of Paul Twitchell, 1978) *Alien Meetings* (1978), *Encounters of the Angelic Kind* (1979), *The Chindi* (1980), *Revelation; The Divine Power* (1981), *Unknown Powers* (1981), (with Francis Steiger) *The Star People* (1981), (with F. Steiger) *The Star People* (1981), (with F. Steiger) *Discover Your Own Past Lives* (1981), *Pendragon; A Clairvoyant's Power of Prophecy* (1982).

In addition, Steiger has been represented in science fiction anthologies, including *The Flying Saucer Reader* and *Ghost, Witches, and Demons.* He has contributed numerous articles and short stories to various magazines, including *Fate, Family Weekly, Saga, Strange* and *Occult.* In 1974 he received the Genie Award for Metaphysical Writer of the Year.

Steiner, Rudolf (1861-1925)

Austrian social philosopher and mystic, founder of the movement known as **Anthroposophy.** Born at Kraljevic, Austro-Hungary (now Yugoslavia) February 27, 1861, he attended village schools. In October 1872 he entered the Realschule (a secondary school) at Wiener-Neustadt, Lower Austria.

He studied philosophy and attended lectures at the Technische Hochschule in Vienna. He became a tutor, edited the works of Goethe and published philosophical studies. In due course he became interested in **Theosophy.** In 1897 he moved to Berlin, where he edited the *Magazin für Literatur.* In 1899 he married Anna Eunicke (died 1911).

For a brief period from 1906 onwards, Steiner was associated with the **O.T.O.** occult order and headed the Mysteria Mystica Aeterna lodge. Eventually his Theosophical interests broadened into a very personal kind of mysticism associated with the **Rosicrucian** tradition, culminated in a movement known as Der Anthroposophische Bund, founded in 1912. Branches of this Anthroposophical movement grew up throughout Germany and later in Britain and elsewhere. One strong influence on Steiner was the actress and Theosophist Marie von Sivers, whom he married in 1914.

The name "Anthroposophy" derives from the Greek *anthropos* (man) and *sophia* (wisdom). Steiner developed theories of color and architecture derived from Goethe, and designed a remarkable wooden building called the Goetheanum, which the Anthroposophical movement built in Dornach, Switzerland, as a headquarters. It was burnt down on New Year's Eve 1922-23, but a replace building was constructed in concrete.

Steiner's Anthroposophical teaching is a remarkable mixture of Rosicrucian, Theosophical, Christian and occult traditions, synthesized in a very individual way. Steiner was a seer, and much of his insight was derived from clairvoyant perception. Many of his teachings were given in the form of lectures, later published in book form by his followers.

The movement has organized a number of schools, which place great emphasis on color, form, rhythm and the life of nature. Such schools are noted for their sensitivity and insight. The Waldorf Institute (23399 Evergreen, Southfield, Michigan 48075) offers studies and teacher training courses in anthroposophy.

Special Anthroposophical schools for retarded children have achieved remarkable results and have a high reputation. The Anthroposophists were also pioneers of bio-dynamic farming, which dispenses with the use of chemical fertilizers.

Steiner died March 30, 1925. His work is carried on by the Anthroposophical Society in various countries. The address of the Anthroposophical Society in America is: RD 2, Ghent, New York 12075. Books on Steiner and anthroposophy are published by Anthroposophic Press, 258 Hungry Hollow Road, Spring Valley, New York 10977. There is a Steiner Book Centre in Canada: 151 Carisbrooke Crescent, North Vancouver, V7N 2S2. In Britain, The Rudolf Steiner Press & Bookshop is at: 38 Museum Street, London, WCI. The Anthroposophical Society in Britain is at: Rudolf Steiner House, 35 Park Road, London, NW1 6XT.

Recommended reading:

Davey, John (ed.). *Work Arising From the Life of Rudolph Steiner,* U.K., 1975

Steiner, Rudolf. *The Story of My Life* (English translation of *Mein Lebensgang*), London & New York, 1928

Steinschneider, Heinrich

Real name of famous clairvoyant and stage performer Erik Jan **Hanussen** (died 1933), who established a great reputation in Germany during the 1920s and 30s.

Stella C. (Mrs. Leslie Deacon) (c.1950)

A London hospital nurse (Stella Cranshaw) whose mediumship was discovered by psychical researcher Harry **Price** in 1923. Price met her by chance when they shared a compartment on a railway journey and during a casual conversation on psychical matters it was apparent that she had unusual psychic gifts.

She gave a series of remarkable sittings in Price's **National Laboratory of Psychical Research** in London. **Telekinesis** phenomena were produced, with the usual changes in temperature, which were very carefully recorded by a self-registering thermometer. On many occasions, the temperature of the seance room was found to have been lowered.

Harry Price read a paper on the subject before the Third International Congress for Psychical Research in Paris. It was entitled: "Some Account of the Thermal Variations as Recorded During the Trance State of the Psychic Stella C." The physical phenomena of **raps, movements** and **levitations** of the table took place under exceptionally stringent conditions.

A trick table which since became famous, as well as many other ingenious pieces of apparatus, were devised by Harry Price. This table was, in fact, a double table, the inner one fitting into a table rim of four legs, the surfaces being quite even. The space under the table was barred by strips of wood connecting the legs of the outer table. The inner table had a shelf nearly as large as the top. This shelf was surrounded on the sides by gauze of a fine mesh so that the only access to the space thus enclosed was through a trap door in the table top which was easy to push open from the inside but very difficult to lift from the outside.

Various musical instruments were placed on the shelf which was thus double protected—by the strips of wood of the outer table and the gauze mesh of the inner table. Nevertheless, the operators of Stella C. found no difficulty in getting within and playing upon the instruments.

Another apparatus, the telekinetoscope, yielded still more interesting results. An electric telegraph key was placed into a brass cup and connected to a red light under a hermetically sealed glass shade. A soap bubble was blown over the cup and covered by a glass shade. It was only through the depression of the telegraph key that the red light could be flashed. The whole apparatus was placed on the shelf inside the double table. The telegraph key was repeatedly depressed. The soap bubble, at the end of the seance, was found unbroken.

A shadow apparatus, consisting of a battery and lamp in a metal box with a Zeiss telephoto lens as a projector and a Wratten ruby filter to project a pencil of light on a luminous screen, was employed to detect the shape of the invisible arms which moved the bell or the trumpet. When the light was switched on, the shadow of the arm was thrown on the screen.

To quote the result of this experiment in the words of Eric J. **Dingwall:** "When the red light was switched on under the table I lay down on the floor and looked through the passage towards the luminous screen. From near the medium's foot, which was invisible, I saw an eggshaped body beginning to crawl towards the centre of the floor under the table. It was white and where the light was reflected it appeared opal. To the end nearest the medium was attached a thin white neck, like a piece of macaroni. It advanced towards the centre, and then rapidly withdrew to the shadow."

Stella Cranshaw married Leslie Deacon in 1928 and thereafter ceased to give sittings. She occupies an important place as a modern non-professional psychic whose unusual faculties were tested under stringent conditions.

For a general account of her phenomena, see the chapter 'Stella: The Gentle Maiden' in *Companions of the Unseen* by Paul Tabori (H. A. Humphrey, London, 1968). For a detailed account of Stella's last sittings in 1926 and 1928, attended by such notable scientists as Prof. Julian Huxley, Prof. E. N. da C. Andrade, and Dr. R. J. Tillyard, see *Stella C. An Account of Some Original Experiments in Psychical Research* edited by James Turner (Souvenir Press, London, 1973).

Stella Matutina (Order of the Morning Star)

A temple of the Hermetic Order of the **Golden Dawn,** deriving from the outer order, after breaking with the G.D. chief S. L. M. **Mathers** in 1900. Its members included Dion **Fortune,** Irsael **Regardie,**

W. B. **Yeats** and "E. Nesbit" (pseudonym of Mrs. Bland, author of some excellent stories for children).

Stendek (Journal)

Spanish-language quarterly publication concerned with Unidentified Flying Objects. Address: Box 282, Barcelona, Spain.

Sterner, Katherine Schmidt (Mrs. Paul Sterner)

Founder and president of the California Parapsychology Foundation; editor of *Parapsychology News-Notes* from 1956 onwards. Born at Steelton, Pennsylvania, she attended Akron University, Juilliard School (N.Y.), Columbia University. San Diego City College. She was a public school teacher at Akron, Ohio from 1940-45.

Stevens, William Oliver (1878-1955)

Author and educator who wrote on parapsychology. Born October 7, 1878 in Rangoon, Burma, he studied at Colby College, Waterville, Maine (B.A. 1899) and Yale University (Ph.D. 1903), Litt.D. 1923 from Colby College. In 1904 he married Claudia Miles.

He was professor of English at U.S. Naval Academy, Annapolis, Maryland, from 1905-24, headmaster of Roger Ascham School, White Plains, N.Y. from 1924-27, headmaster of Cranbrook School, Bloomfield Hills, Michigan from 1927-35, dean of School of Literature and Journalism, Oglethorpe University, Georgia from 1936-37. Member of Century Association, American Society for Psychical Research. Dr. Stevens wrote many books on naval history, travel, biography and other subjects. His books dealing with psychic research include: *Beyond the Sunset* (1944), *Unbidden Guests* (1945), *Mystery of Dreams* (1949), *Psychics and Common Sense* (1953).

He died January 16, 1955.

Stevenson, Ian (1918-)

Physician, professor of psychiatry, parapsychologist. His special area of study has been evidence for survival, and apparent memories of former incarnations. Born October 31, 1918 in Montreal, Quebec, Canada, he studied at McGill University, Montreal (B.S. 1943, M.D.C.M. 1944). In 1947 he married Octavia Reynolds.

He was a fellow, internal medicine at Alton Ochsner Medical Foundation, New Orleans, Louisiana from 1946-47, Commonwealth Fellow in Medicine at Cornell Medical College from 1947-49, assistant professor at Departments of Medicine and Psychiatry (1949-52), associate professor of psychiatry (1952-57) at Louisiana State University School of Medicine, professor of psychiatry, chairman, Department of Neurology and Psychiatry, University of Virginia School of Medicine, Charlottesville, Virginia from 1957 onwards.

He is a member of the American Federation for Clinical Research, American Psychosomatic Society, American Psychiatric Association, Group for Advancement of Psychiatry, American Society for Psychical Research, American Medical Association, Washington Psychoanalytic Society, charter member of Parapsychological Association.

In addition to his papers on psychiatric subjects, Dr. Stevenson has published articles on parapsychology, including: 'A Proposal for Studying Rapport' (*Journal* of American Society for Psychical Research, vol. 53, 1959), 'The Uncomfortable Facts About Extrasensory Perception' (*Harper's,* July 1959, 'An Antagonist's View of Parapsychology. A Review of Professor Hansel's "ESP: A Scientific Evaluation"' (*Journal* of ASPR, vol. 61, July 1967), 'A Review & Analysis of Paranormal Experiences Connected with the Sinking of the Titanic' (*Journal* of ASPR, vol. 54), 'Seven More Paranormal Experiences Associated with the Sinking of the Titanic' (*Journal* of ASPR, vol. 59), 'The Combination Lock Test for Survival' (*Journal* of ASPR, vol. 62), 'Xenoglossy: A Review & Report of a Case' (*Proceedings* of ASPR, vol. 31), (with J. G. Pratt) 'Exploratory Investigations of the Psychic Photography of Ted Serios (*Journal* of ASPR, vol. 62), (with J. G. Pratt) 'Further Investigations of the Psychic Photography of Ted Serios' (*Journal* of ASPR, vol. 63), (with S. Pastricha) 'A Preliminary Report on an Unusual Case of the Reincarnation Type with Xenoglossy' (*Journal* of ASPR, vol. 74), 'The Contribution of Apparitions to the Evidence for Survival' (*Journal* of the ASPR, vol. 76).

His Winning Essay of the Contest in Honor of William James, *The Evidence for Survival from Claimed Memories of Former Incarnations* was published England, 1961. His books include: *Telepathic Impressions: A Review and Report of Thirty-five New Cases* (University Press of Virginia, 1970), *Twenty Cases Suggestive of Reincarnation* 1966, 1980, *Cases of the Reincarnation Type, Vol. 1; Ten Cases in India* (1975), *Cases of the Reincarnation Type, Vol. 2; Ten Cases in Sri Lanka* (1978), *Cases of the Reincarnation Type,* Vol. 3; *Twelve Cases in Lebanon & Turkey* (1980). He contributed the chapter 'Reincarnation: Field Studies and Theoretical Issues' to *Handbook of Parapsychology* ed. Benjamin B. Wolman (1977).

Stewart, Balfour (1828-1887)

Professor of Natural Philosophy in Owens College, Manchester, who received the Rumford Medal of the Royal Society for his discovery of the law of equality between the absorptive and radiative powers of bodies. He occupied the presidential chair of the **Society for Psychical Research,** London, from 1885-87.

Born November 1, 1828 at Edinburgh, Scotland, he was educated in Dundee and the universities of St. Andrews and Edinburgh. He traveled to Australia, where he acquired a reputation as a physicist. After returning to Britain in 1856, he joined the staff of Kew Observatory, becoming a director in 1859. He also made important scientific contributions in mathematics and radiant heat.

He was greatly interested in the phenomena of the medium Daniel Dunglas **Home,** of whom he commented to Sir William **Crookes:** "Mr. Home possesses great electrobiological power by which he influences those present . . . however susceptible the persons in the room to that assumed influence, it will hardly be contended that Mr. Home biologized the recording instrument."

Prof. Stewart was the joint author with Professor Tait of the anonymously published *The Unseen Universe* (1875), a book which created a stir as the first serious scientific attempt to oppose a spiritual view of the universe to the prevailing materialistic one.

He died December 19, 1887.

Stewart, Kenneth Malcolm (1916-)

Professor of anthropology who studied possession and shamanism. Born June 16, 1916 at Tecumseh, Nebraska, he studied at University of California (B.A. 1938, M.A. 1940, Ph.D. 1946). In 1942 he married Marguerite Reed (divorced 1951); second marriage in 1960 to Louise Garland Dyer.

He was assistant professor of anthropology at Fresno State College, California in 1947, professor of anthropology at Arizona State University from 1947 onwards; member of the American Anthropological Association. He has done ethnological field work among the Mohave and the Pagago Indians of the American Southwest. He contributed the article 'Spirit Possession in Native America' to *Southwestern Journal of Anthropology* (vol. 2, No. 3, 1946) and 'Spirit Possession' to *Tomorrow* (Spring, 1956).

Stewart, W(ilber) C(larence) (1936-)

Research assistant and graduate student at Duke University, Durham, N.C. Born July 22, 1936 at Durham, N.C., he studied at Duke University (B.S. electrical engineering 1958, M.S. electrical engineering 1960). He is a member of the American Institute of Electrical Engineers, associate member of the Parapsychological Association.

He experimented with electrical devices for testing extrasensory perception. His article 'Three New ESP Test Machines and Some Preliminary Results' was published in *Journal of Parapsychology* (March 1959).

Sthenometer

The instrument which psychical researcher Dr. Paul **Joire** invented to demonstrate the existence of a nervous force, acting externally to the body.

In the center of a horizontal dial, marked out in 360 degrees, is a light needle or pointer, mostly of straw, balanced by a pivot on a glass support. The device is covered with a glass shade.

When the extended fingers of one's hand are brought at right angles to the pointer, near the shade without touching it, after a few seconds, in the majority of cases, a decided movement of the pointer takes place, it being attracted towards the hand. This movement extends over fifteen, twenty, and sometimes up to forty and fifty degrees.

Certain substances which have been previously held in the hand also produce this movement. Wood, water, linen, cardboard, appear to store up this nervous energy. Tinfoil, iron and cotton produce no effect.

The Society for Psychical Research, London, and some French scientific groups attributed the movement of the needle to the action of radiating heat rather than psychic force. (See also **Biometer of Baradoc; De Tromelin Cylinder; Emanations; Exteriorization of Sensitivity; Magnetometer**)

Stichomancy

Another term for **bibliomancy** (**divination** through random choice of words in a book).

Stigmata

Marks resembling the wounds of the crucified Christ which appear inexplicably upon the limbs and body of certain sensitive individuals, especially Christian mystics.

The most common stigmata are the marks on hands and feet resembling piercing with nails, sometimes accompanied by actual bleeding. Other stigmata include the weals of scourging, wounds on the shoulder and on the side, the livid bruising of the wrists (where Christ was bound with cords) and the marking of the mouth (paralleling the effect of the sponge soaked in vinegar). The most dangerous stigma is the *Ferita* or heart wound, which under normal circumstances might cause death.

There have been some 300 cases of stigmata in two thousand years, many of them women. In spite of some actual or suspected frauds, most of these cases seem genuine, and some individuals bearing stigmata have been canonized or beatified by the Roman Catholic Church. However, present-day Catholic Church authorities do not insist upon belief in stigmatization as a fact or as a mark of holiness.

Some people believe the Apostle St. Paul to have been the first stigmatic. He wrote in an epistle: *Ego enim stigmata Domini Jesus in corpore meo porto.* In the first twelve centuries of the history of the Church his words were taken figuratively. There were ascetics who had wounds attributed to the teeth and claws of the devil on their body, but it was St. Francis of Assisi (died 1226) from whom the history of stigmatic wounds really dates. He was also reported to have manifested the phenomenon of **bilocation.** He carried the marks of stigmata during the final two years of his life. He fasted all through the forty days fast of St. Michael and concentrated his thoughts on the Passion of Christ.

Not only was his flesh torn and bleeding at the five places, but "his hands and feet appeared to be pierced through the middle with nails, the heads of which were in the palm of his hands and the soles of his feet; and the points came out again in the back of the hands and the feet, and were turned back and clinched in such a manner that within the bend formed by the reversal of the points a finger could easily be placed as in a ring, and the heads of the nails were found and black. They were the source of constant pain and of the utmost inconvenience. He could walk no more and became exhausted by the suffering and loss of blood. It hastened his premature decease. . . . After the death of Francis . . . a certain cavalier, named Jeronime, who had much doubted and was incredulous concerning them . . . ventured, in the presence of the brethren and many seculars to move about the nails in the hands and feet."

The Rev. F. Fielding-Ould, in his book *Wonders of the Saints* (1919), conjectured that the nails were of some horny material such as the bodies of the lower animals are able naturally to develop.

La Bienheureuse Lucie de Narni (1476-1544) carried stigmata for seven years from 1496 onwards. Four years after her death, her body was exhumed. It was in a state of perfect preservation and exhaled a sweet scent. The stigmatic wounds on her sides were open and blood flowed from time to time. In 1710 she was again exhumed and the body found still intact.

The stigmatic wounds of Johnanna della Croce, 1524, appeared every Friday and vanished the following Sunday.

St. Veronique Giuliani, born in 1660, received the crown of thorns at the age of thirty-three. On April 5, 1679, the five wounds developed. She was subject to very severe examinations. The reality of the phenomena was established beyond question.

Seventy-five years after the death of St. Francis thirty stigmatic cases were on record, twenty-five among women. Dr. Antoine Imbert-Gourbeyre in his monograph *L'Hypnotisme et la Stigmatisation* (1899) recorded more than 321 cases of which a seventh part occurred among men. This number, however, includes the "compatients" and leaves out many other cases since discovered and all those instances in which the stigmatic wounds were considered the work of the devil.

The "compatients" or participants did not exhibit the physiological signs of stigmatization in the form of wounds. With them it was an inner, psychical experience, noticeable, however, for outsiders as well. For instance, the complexion of Jeanne de Marie-Jesus in the ecstatic state of the Passion became dark and blue, the blood mounted under her nails, bruises appeared on her arms and hands as if left by cruel chains, her forehead and other parts of her body sweated blood. It is difficult to draw a dividing line between the participant and stigmatism, as the former appears to be its incipient stage.

Of the cases enumerated by Dr. Imbert-Gourbeyre, twenty-nine occurred in the nineteenth century. Catherine **Emmerich** (1774-1821) furnished one of the best cases. Count Stolberg, the celebrated naturalist, visited her in 1821. We learn from his description that the nun of Dolmen did not for many a month take other nourishment than water and small portions of an apple, plum or cherry daily. Her trances were prolonged for an incredible period. The thorn wounds on her head opened every Friday morning and later a continuous flow of blood was seen from eight wounds on her hands and feet.

Marie-Dominique Lazzari, Marie-Agnes Steiner, Marie de Moerl (1812-68), Crescenzia Nierklutsch, Victorie Courtier (1811-88), Louise Lateau (1858-83), Marie-Julie Jahenny, Therese **Neumann** (died 1962) and Padre Pio (died 1968) bring the line of famous stigmatists to modern times.

Padre Pio (Francesco Forgione of Pietrelcina) was a Capucin monk in the convent of San Giovanni Rotondo. In 1918, bleeding scars pierced his hands and feet and exuded each day about a glassful of blood and water. Physicians certified the fact. The stigmata of Therese Neumann, of Konnersreuth, developed during Lent in 1926. There was no pus, no inflammation, blood flowed freely every Friday from the wounds and she also shed tears of blood.

In some cases the stigmata appear as simple red marks, in others as blister-like wounds oozing blood and lymph. The flow of blood, according to many testimonies, conformed to the supposed position of a body on the cross.

The stigmata may lie in bed yet the blood will flow up the toes in apparent defiance of gravitation. In the case of Dominique Lazzari, of Tyrol, Lord Shrewsbury testified to this fact. He also referred to the statement of a German physician that the stigmatic could not endure water, was never washed, yet the blood sometimes suddenly disappeared, leaving a clean skin behind with an unsoiled bedcloth. The wounds were often said to be luminous and exhaling scent. They never produced pus, and after death frequently the entire body became exempt from putrefaction.

During the nineteenth century, reputable physicians carefully investigated some twenty-nine reported cases of stigmatization, and were convinced of the honesty of the subjects and the objective reality of the phenomenon.

One difficulty in assessing the strictly Christian spiritual value of stigmatization lies in the fact that some stigmatists have not been especially religious. Moreover similar phenomena have been reported of Moslem ascetics, who appear to have reproduced the wounds received by Mohammed the Prophet in spreading the message of Islam.

Experiments with post-hypnotic suggestion have shown that burns, blisters and similar wounds may be produced on the body as a result of strong **suggestion,** and it is possible that some cases of stigmatization resulted from conscious or unconscious self-hypnosis.

Professor Charcot was the first in its experimental demonstration. The role which auto-suggestion may play in stigmatic or borderland phenomena is well illustrated by the following case, quoted by Hereward Carrington in *Psychic Oddities* (1952) from an original document: "On the afternoon of May 1st, 1916, I was standing in my hall, preparing to go out, when I saw the knob of my front door slowly turn. I stood still, awaiting developments; gradually the door opened, and I saw a man standing there. As he saw me he quickly closed the door and ran down the stairs and out of the front door. (He was, in fact, a burglar, trying to enter my apartment.) The interesting thing about the experience is this: that during the moment he was standing in the door, although he did not actually move, I had the distinct impression that he had run up the hall and grasped me firmly by the arm, and I was for the moment petrified with fear. The next day my arm was black and blue in the exact spot where I thought he had pinched me; and this mark continued for several days until it finally wore off. I told Dr. Carrington about this two days later when he called, and showed him the mark. Louise W. Kops."

The psychical researcher Prof. Charles Richet stated that marks of stigmata "may and do often appear on hysterical persons, bearing predetermined forms and shapes, under the influence either of a strong moral emotion, or of religious delirium. These are facts which have been thoroughly and scientifically established, and they only prove the power of the action of the brain upon the circulatory processes and upon the trophism of the skin."

As a mediumistic phenomenon, it was reported by many experimenters. J. Malcolm **Bird,** in his book *My Psychic Adventures* (1924) stated: "Frau Vollhardt suddenly gave a very realistic shriek of pain and held out her hand for all to see. On the back of her hand was a quantity of red marks, some actually bleeding . . . A handful of forks could not have been held in such a manner as to inflict these wounds, but no single instrument that I ever saw would have done the trick—unless it be a nutmeg grater. The holes were small and round, and quite deep; after ten or fifteen minutes they were still plainly to be seen." (See also Maria **Vollhardt**)

The stigmatization of Eleonore **Zügun** (strange bites and scratches on her arms, neck, etc.) was recorded in the process of invisible production by the camera.

A curious experience, resembling stigmatization, was mentioned by Prof. Richet in a footnote in his book *Thirty Years of Psychical Research* (1923). Count Baschieri placed a handkerchief to his eyes and withdrew it stained with blood, perhaps five grams, undiluted. His eyes had sweated blood. He could not discover any conjunctional ecchymosis.

In the September 1920 issue of the *Zeitschrift für Parapsychologie* Hans Schubert wrote of the tears of blood of Edwig S. during deep emotional states induced by a certain piece of music.

Dermography (skin writing) is a phenomenon of the stigmatic class, but there is an essential difference. The real stigmata last for months, years or throughout a lifetime, whereas skin writing disappears in a few minutes or in a few hours at the most.

A kindred phenomenon to stigmatization is the mark of burn or blood which, in rare cases, the touch of phantom hands leaves behind.

However, there can be no denying the ecstatic spiritual and mystical condition of devout Christians suffering stigmatization. Such individuals usually exhibit wounds (often with bleeding) on Good Friday, sometimes accompanied by a personal identification with the sufferings of Christ during crucifixion.

The phenomenon of stigmatization has been studied closely in modern times in the unusual case of the British subject Ethel Chapman. A victim of multiple sclerosis, Ethel Chapman was paralyzed from the waist down. She was unable to hold things properly in her hands, and hence not physically capable of deception. Ethel was an inmate of the Cheshire Home in Britain, where she was interviewed by geriatrician Dr. Colin Powell, who found no indication of depression, neurosis or psychosis. There was no indication of the condition known as *dermatitis artifacta,* when subjects scratch or otherwise harm themselves for various reasons. Ethel appeared friendly, mentally stable and far from gaining any psychological advantage from stigmata, she found it rather more a burden. Various reliable witnesses testified to seeing wounds on Ethel's hands and feet on Good Friday. In a B.B.C. radio interview in 1973, Ethel gave a vivid description of her first vision and sensations in the following words:

"I remember saying quite plainly 'Oh Lord, please show me in some way you're there.' In the early hours of the morning, I thought it was a dream. I felt myself being drawn on to the Cross. I felt the pain of the nails through my hands and through my feet. I could see the crowds, all jeering and shouting and, of course, it was in a foreign language, I don't know what they were saying. I felt myself all the agony and all the pain that the Lord Himself went through. . . . "

Ethel also claimed that on occasions she had been lifted up in the air and smelled supernatural sweet **perfumes** (see also **Odor of Sanctity**). Although there was no firm evidence of **levitation,** her bedclothes were sometimes disarranged to an extent that might have been unusual in the case of a largely paralyzed individual. However, sensations of floating often occur in subjects with heightened or mystical consciousness, and need not involve an actual physical levitation. In some cases, "astral projection" or **out-of-body** experience may be present, in which a subtle body appears to leave the physical body.

But the reality of the physical manifestation of stigmata cannot be doubted. Reliable witnesses affirmed seeing the fresh blood on the hands of Ethel Chapman on Good Friday, and it will be recalled that Ethel was sufficiently paralyzed to be unable to inflict such wounds herself. Moreover, neither Ethel nor her medical adviser at the Cheshire Home encouraged publicity-seeking or cultism. Ethel herself, like some other stigmatists, seemed to regard the phenomenon as a mark of divine love at a time when she was in great need of such reassurance because of a serious illness that had terminated her career. She also radiated peace and serenity to other individuals who were troubled. Inevitably word spread about Ethel's stigmata and many people wrote to her asking for help or healing. She regularly devoted time to prayers on behalf of the afflicted.

The case of Ethel Chapman is of great interest, firstly because it is a very recent one, and secondly because individuals who were closely concerned with her were able to report on her personal and religious outlook, as well as the physical condition itself. Those skeptics who claim that stigmata is simply a morbid, hysterical or nervous disorder associated with **auto-suggestion** tend to ignore the important questions raised by the personality and religious convictions of the subject.

Where it is clear (as in the case of Ethel Chapman) that one is dealing with a sincere and rational individual trying to come to terms with the problem of religious faith in the light of the mystery of pain or disability, the objective aspects of such phenomena as stigmata take second place to the spiritual issues and their resolution. The rationalistic explanation of stigmata seems to be of interest chiefly for any light it may throw on the *way* that the phenomenon works, but says nothing of the deeper mystery of its function in the spiritual life of the subject.

Stigmata is essentially concerned with the theological issue of the relationship of pain and suffering to faith and grace, both in the individual and the community, and indeed, the mystery of the Crucifixion itself, which is central to Christianity.

Recommended reading:

Carty, Charles M. *The Two Stigmatists: Padre Pio & Therese Neumann,* Veritas, Dublin, 1956

Fielding-Ould, Fielding. *The Wonders of the Saints in the Light of Spiritualism,* John M. Watkins, London, 1919

Siwek, Paul. *The Riddle of Konnersreuth,* Browne & Nolan, Dublin, 1956; concerns Therese Neumann

Summers, Montague. *The Physical Phenomena of Mysticism,* Rider & Co., London, 1950

Thurston, H. *The Physical Phenomena of Mysticism,* London, 1952

Wilson, Ian. *The Bleeding Mind,* Weidenfeld & Nicolson, London, 1988

Stiles, Joseph D. (c. 1858)

American printer who, in the early age of Spiritualism, received through **automatic writing** remarkable prophecies of the impending Civil War.

The story was published under the title *Twelve Messages from John Quincy Adams through Joseph D. Stiles* in 1859 by Josiah Brigham. The author made the acquaintance of Stiles in June, 1854.

The messages were written by Stiles in trance from August 1854 until March 1858. They came in John Quincy Adams' writing and under his signature.

Stiles also produced other remarkable autographs. This prophecy "I thus boldly prophesy the dissolution of the American Confederacy, and the destruction of slavery" was signed "George Washington" with every peculiarity of his (George Washington's) difficult signature.

Stobart, Mrs. St. Clair (Mrs. Stobart Greenhalgh) (died 1954)

Author, playwright, prominent figure in British Spiritualism. She was founder of the Women's Sick and Wounded Convoy Corps during the Balkan War 1912-13, when she served with the Bulgarian Red Cross. During World War I she organized hospitals in Belgium and France for St. John's Ambulance Association, was taken prisoner by the Germans and condemned to be shot as a spy. She survived, and in September 1915 was appointed Commander of Column, First Serbian English Field Hospital.

She lectured for the British Ministry of Information in Canada and Ireland from 1917-18, and was a candidate for Westminister borough at London County Council Election 1913. She was a founder and vice-president of the S.O.S. Society, chairman and leader of the Spiritualist Community, London (concerned with religious and educational aspects of Spiritualism).

She was Life Patron of the **British College of Psychic Science,** and a member of the council of World Congress of Faiths. She was an active lecturer and campaigner for alliance between Spiritualism and Christianity. Her books included: *Ancient Lights* (1923), *Torchbearers of Spiritualism* (1925), *The Either Or of Spiritualism* (1928).

She died December 7, 1954. (See also **Spiritualist Community**)

Stoicheomancy

A method of **divination** which was practiced by opening the works of Homer or Virgil, and reading as an oracular statement the first verse which presented itself. It is regarded as a form of **rhapsodomancy.**

Stoker, Bram [Abraham](1847-1912)

Writer of books on occult themes, creator of the deathless vampire **Dracula.** Born November 8, 1847 in Dublin, Ireland, Stoker was named Abraham after his father, but later preferred the short form "Bram."

He was a sickly child for some years although quite athletic as a young man. Perhaps his brooding childhood first engendered those imaginative horrors that found expression in his great vampire story and other weird thrillers. His mother had told him tales of the **Banshee,** the Irish fairy whose terrifying wails announce death in the family, and also of the great cholera plague which had claimed thousands of victims in an unhappy Ireland ravaged by starvation and foreign occupation.

Stoker studied at Trinity College, Dublin and became a member of the college Philosophical Society, later being elected president. His first essay delivered to the society was titled 'Sensationalism in Fiction and Society.' He was auditor for the Historical Society and also developed a great interest in theater.

At the age of nineteen, he was electrified by a performance of the great actor Henry Irving, whose company he later joined as a manager.

Stoker graduated with honors in Science in 1870, but spent ten uneventful years as an Irish civil servant at Dublin Castle. His first book was the prosaic but useful *The Duties of Clerks of Petty Sessions* (1879). In 1878, he married Florence Balcombe, a beautiful woman who had been friendly with Oscar Wilde.

After a period as part-time drama critic, newspaper editor and barrister at law, he became acting manager for Henry Irving, accompanying him on his British and American tours. Stoker was a hard-working manager and faithful friend to Irving for twenty-seven years until Irving's death in 1905.

His masterpiece *Dracula* was written at odd moments and week-ends during a busy career. It owed its basic character to chance conversation with the intrepid Hungarian explorer Prof. Arminius **Vambéry** (1832-1913), who visited Dublin on a lecture tour.

It seems that Vambéry told Stoker about Transylvanian legends of the blood-thirsty tyrant Vlad Tepes (known as "Dracula" or son of Dracul). Stoker also researched in libraries in Whitby and London and perfected his knowledge of the background of the Transylvanian countryside. Some of the weird atmosphere of his story probably derived from the vampire story *Carmilla,* written by another Dubliner, Sheridan Le Fanu, first published 1871, which Stoker read at the time.

In addition to his immortal *Dracula,* Stoker also published: *The Snake's Pass* (1890), *The Watter's Mou'* [Mouth] (1895), *The Shoulder of Shasta* (1895), *Miss Betty* (1898), *The Mystery of the Sea* (1902), *The Jewel of Seven Stars* (1904), *The Man* (1905), *Personal Reminiscences of Henry Irving* (2 vols., 1906), *The Gates of Life* (1908), *Lady Athlyne* (1908), *Snowbound* (1908), *The Lady of the Shroud* (1909), *Famous Impostors* (1910), *The Liar of the White Worm* (1911). His volume of short stories *Dracula's Guest* was published posthumously in 1937; the title story was originally a chapter in the manuscript of *Dracula,* deleted to shorten the work. He died April 20, 1912.

There are three biographical works on Stoker: Harry Ludlam, *A Biography of Dracula; the Life Story of Bram Stoker* (London, 1962); Daniel Farson, *The Man Who Wrote Dracula; A Biography of Bram Stoker* (London/New York, 1975); Phyllis A. Roth, *Bram Stoker* (Boston, 1982). For a valuable bibliography, see Richard Dalby, *Bram Stoker; A Bibliography of First Editions* (London, 1983).

The memory of Bram Stoker and his association with Gothic literature is kept alive by various societies, notably: The Bram Stoker Society (c/o Albert Power, 227 Rochestown Avenue, Dun Laoghaire, Co. Dublin, Eire); **The Dracula Society** (36 Elliston House, 100 Wellington Street, London, SE10 QQF, England); The Count Dracula Fan Club, 29 Washington Square W., New York, (New York, N.Y. 10011). (See also **Dracula;** Occult English **Fiction;** A. **Vambëry; Vampires**)

Stokes, Doris (1920-1987)

Notable British psychic who has established a world-wide reputation for her **clairaudience.** Born Doris Sutton, January 6, 1920, in Grantham, Lincolnshire, she grew up in great poverty. Her father was gassed in World War I and retired on a small pension; Doris' mother was obliged to take in laundry work to assist the family finances, and Mr. Sutton died while Doris was still in school. Doris left school at the age of 14 and became a nurse. During this period she discovered she had psychic abilities, but did not develop them.

At the age of twenty-four, she married John Stokes, a British Army paratrooper. During World War II, Doris was officially notified that her husband had been killed in action, but her dead father appeared to her and stated that her husband was alive and would return. This duly occurred.

Later, Doris had another vision when her father appeared again to warn her that her baby son would soon die, but Mr. Sutton would take good care of him after death. Although the child was perfectly healthy, he died at the time and date predicted. Subsequently John and Doris attended a local Spiritualist church, where Doris was told that she would become a medium. She was unwilling at first, but gradually found her mediumship developed. It principally took the form of hearing spirit voices.

In her autobiography, *Voices in My Ear* (1980), she described quite frankly the problems and temptations of a young medium. She was often worried about losing continuity with the spirit voices and the members of the audience for whom the messages came.

She was advised by a prominent visiting medium to use one of the "tricks of the trade" by arriving at the meeting early, listening to what people said to each other, then slipping away and writing down conversations and names, to be used later to keep contact between the spirit voices and the audience.

It seemed like cheating, but at her next meeting Doris tried this, and it was successful, until in the middle of a communication which had been helped out in this way she found contact with the spirit voice was suddenly broken. She struggled to continue, but dried up and had to break off. After two more spirit communications, her spirit guide "Ramonov" told her to go back to the original recipient and apologize.

This happened at two meetings, after which Doris determined never again to help out spirit communications in this way, in spite of the fear she felt at losing contact. Ever since, she openly admitted to the audience if she lost contact with the spirit voices and simply tried to reestablish the link. She warned other developing mediums to be brave enough to admit if no messages are coming through. In 1948, her credentials as a bona fide clairaudient were endorsed by the **Spiritualists National Union** in England.

In more than thirty years of successful mediumship, Doris attracted large and enthusiastic audiences, and also appeared on popular radio and television shows in Australia, New Zealand and the U.S. She often dumbfounded skeptical reporters and presenters by the accuracy of her spirit messages.

Her reputation as a "Spiritualist superstar" was phenomenal. On her Australian tour, she packed the massive Sydney Opera House three nights in a row, and a private plane was chartered to take her from city to city. A television soap opera was postponed to make room for her.

Yet this international fame only came in later life. Prior to the mid 1970s, she had lived in modest circumstances in Lancaster, working as a nurse, or giving her mediumistic services to Spiritualist churches for no more than modest traveling expenses by bus or train, sometimes giving private consultation for £1 (two or three dollars).

Her husband John was a paratrooper in World War II, and captured by the enemy. Although Doris was officially informed that John had died of wounds, she received a psychic communication from her dead father that John was alive and would return to her. This came to pass. So also did another spirit prediction that Doris' healthy baby son John Michael would die. After this tragic event, she adopted a little boy named Terry.

After she moved to London, Doris became well known as a remarkable clairaudient medium, but she never ceased to be amazed by her growing fame, and made no show-biz concessions to large audiences. She appeared on stage in an unglamorous frock, sitting in an armchair, addressing her audience in homely language as "love" or "my dear" just like any village grandmother. Courted by celebrities and TV presenters, she would insist "I am still the same old Doris Stokes."

Her fame attracted derisive and often hostile criticism from skeptics, but she met controversy head on and would not be over awed or bullied.

In 1980, she appeared on the Don Lane television show with professional magician James Randi, archenemy of claims of the paranormal, who denounced her (without evidence) as a liar and a fake. He said he had seen her demonstrate in London and she was "no good." However, at the date he claimed he had seen Doris perform in London, she had actually been undergoing surgery in hospital.

Presenter Don Lane became so incensed at Randi's statements that he swore at him and stormed out of the studio. Lane later told a Melbourne journalist "I apologize to my viewers if I have offended them, but not to that man until he can back his statements." When Doris challenged Randi to appear with her and prove her a fake, he declined.

Whilst there have been many criticisms by stage magicians that public clairaudience and clairvoyance is often too vague and trivial, and that psychics can "fish" for information supplied by members of the audience themselves, it must be remembered that if, as claimed, the psychic receives messages for different individuals present, it must be difficult to sort out correct names and other data, rather like trying to operate a large telephone switchboard full of crossed lines.

Moreover much that appears trivial to a bystander may have great significance for the recipient of the message. Many "spirit messages" relate to ordinary people with ordinary interests and outlooks, and often the message of survival and continuing affection from deceased relations or friends is reassuring or even inspiring, especially when validated by information known as genuine by the recipient.

Public performances and television programs have the advantage that they may be recorded and studied, in contrast to private sessions when fake or partly fake psychics may fish for information from a credulous sitter and relay it back as a "spirit message." And it must be said that any unbiased individual who has seen or heard Doris Stokes in public performance cannot doubt her genuine sympathy and sincerity. In the face of this, wild and unsupported accusations of fraud are not only inappropriate; they are also in bad taste, and infringe the elementary courtesy which is due to any human being whose claims or talents are being considered.

In addition to *Voices in My Ear* Doris Stokes authored several other popular books of reminiscences (with Linda Dearsley): *More Voices in My Ear* (1981), *Innocent Voices in My Ear* (1983), *A Host of Voices* (1984), *Whispering Voices* (1985), *Voices of Love* (1986), *Joyful Voices* (1987). Their combined sales exceeded two million copies.

In her last years, her income as an internationally famous medium did not change her simple life style, and she was generous in her donations to charitable projects. She also gave freely of her time in long telephone conversations with the bereaved who sought consolation.

It is sad to report that the woman who gave so much of her life to the consolation of others should have suffered much ill health in her late years, involving operations for removal of her thyroid, part of her liver, and a mastectomy. She died May 8, 1987, two weeks after surgery for removal of a brain tumor.

Stolisomancy

Divination from the manner in which a person dresses himself. In ancient Rome, the emperor Augustus believed that a military revolt was predicted on the morning of its occurrence by the fact that his attendant had buckled his right sandal to his left foot.

Stomach, Seeing with the

A phenomenon frequently observed by the followers of **Mesmer** in their somnambules. The subject, in a cataleptic state closely resembling death, would show no signs of intelligence when questions were directed to his ears, but if the questions were addressed to the pit of the stomach, or sometimes to the fingertips or toes, an answer would be immediately forthcoming.

Several such cases were recorded by Dr. Pététin, of Lyons, France, who in 1808 published his *Electricité Animale,* and by other Mesmerists. Not only hearing, but seeing, tasting and smelling were performed by the stomach, independent of the sensory organs.

Pétéin attributed the phenomenon to "animal electricity" and stated that objects placed on the patient's stomach were not seen when they were wrapped in wax or silk, that is, non-conductors.

The best way to communicate with a patient in the cataleptic state was for the operator to place his hand on the stomach of the subject, and address his question to the fingertips of his own free hand.

This **trance** phenomenon, as well as others, may now be considered as due to suggestion and hyperæsthesia. (See also **Eyeless Sight; Transposition of the Senses**)

Stonehenge

Mysterious prehistoric monument of standing stones, located in Wiltshire, England. The name derives from the Old English *hengen* ("hung up"), referring to the horizontal lintel stones. Over the centuries, legend ascribed Stonehenge to Druidic, Roman and Danish construction, but it is not generally accepted that it dates from Neolithic times, and was probably last in use about 1400 B.C. A number of such megalithic (large stone) monuments exist in Europe (notably the Grand Menhir Brise, Locmariaquer, and the vast site of Carnac, Brittany), and they appear to have sacred astronomical significance, probably related to sun-worship.

The Stonehenge site comprises three stages—an outer circle of local sarsen stones, and two inner circles of Blue Stones from the Prescelly mountains of Wales, 200 kilometers away. The first and third circles are capped with stone lintels, and the whole construction encircled by a ditch, inside the bank of which are fifty-six pits known as the "Aubrey holes," and a cremation-cemetary associated with them.

Isolated outside the stone circles is the Hele Stone, over which the sun rises on Midsummer Day. It is clear that Stonehenge had special astronomical significance, since, in addition to the marking of the summer solstice by the Hele Stone, the center of the great circle indicated the orbits of sun and moon, and holes were positioned for posts to mark these orbits. The whole construction indicates remarkable astronomical and mathematical knowledge on the part of the ancient builders. Like the pyramids of ancient Egypt, Stonehenge and similar monuments also involved considerable engineering skill in mining and transporting the huge stones.

Prior to modern archaeological investigations, Stonehenge was surrounded by confusing legends of origin and use. Radio-carbon dating has now established a date of c.2000 B.C. for the first monument, the second a few centuries later, and the third about the middle of the second millennium B.C. It is possible that the Druids inherited an oral tradition of the significance of Stonehenge and used it for sacred rituals involving sun-worship.

Folklore credits such sites with magical power, and they have been associated with witchcraft rites. In France, young girls would slide down such ancient stones with a bare buttock, in the belief that it would make them fertile.

Early Christian missionaries attempted to absorb or neutralize such occult traditions by building churches inside prehistoric mounds. In medieval times, at the great stone monument at Avebury in southern Britain, there was a ceremony in which a single stone was dislodged and ritually attacked, to symbolize the victory of the Christian Church over the Devil. Most sites, including Stonehenge, have also suffered over the centuries through vandalism.

Stonehenge is now the center of another strange ritual every midsummer. Thousands of hippies, living a nomadic life in battered automobiles (often unlicensed), reminiscent of the American Dust Bowl days, descend on the fields surrounding Stonehenge and set up makeshift camps at midsummer, intending to gain access to Stonehenge to celebrate the summer solstice at the stones. But the site has been fenced off by barbed wire, and the solstice ceremony is restricted to a modern revival Druid organization and no more than 600 ticket-holding visitors. In order to prevent the hippies from overrunning the site, farmers annually barricade tracks and byways with trailers and machinery, while hundreds of police stand by in riot gear.

Each year there is a ritual battle between hippies and police. Missiles, bottles and other objects are thrown, while police with helmets and batons force back the intruders and arrest many of them. After the summer solstice, the hippies are obliged to retreat in their battered vehicles.

Opinions on this annual neo-pagan battle vary. An extreme view from a newspaper columnist fulminated that the hippies were "drunks and junkies and the scum of the earth from which they should be swept and tidied up." However, some local farmers are sympathetic to the hippies and plan to provide them with a festival site each year. Not all the violence comes from the hippie families, many of whom are artistic craftsmen and musicians, dedicated to a neo-pagan life-style.

Clearly the prospect of a confrontation with police appeals to non-hippie hooligans of the kind that start drunken fights in discos and at football games, and they flock to the Stonehenge battle. Some of the hippies may be intoxicated with alcohol and cannabis and become belligerent in the excitement and frustration of what appears to them to be interference with their right to celebrate midsummer at a pagan site. But the majority appear to be gentle people with a nonconformist life-style. (See also **Celts**)

Recommended reading:

Hawkins, Gerald. *Stonehenge Decoded,* Souvenir Press, London, 1966

Hitching, Francis. *Earth Magic,* Picador paperback, London, 1977

Mitchell, J. *Astro-Archaeology,* Thames & Hudson, London, 1977

Newham, C. A. *The Astronomical Significance of Stonehenge,* John Blackburn, U.K., 1972

Thom, Alexander. *Megalithic Sites in Britain,* Oxford University Press, U.K., 1967

Strange Magazine

Quarterly magazine featuring "all aspects of the inexplicable as it appears in science, art, literature, philosophy, technology, magic, religion and everything else we call reality." It gives special attention to Fortean phenomena (see Charles H. **Fort**), and includes book reviews and news. Address: Strange Magazine, P.O. Box 2246, Rockville, Maryland 20852.

"Strange Story, A"

Celebrated occult story by the novelist Bulwer **Lytton** (1803-1873). (See also Occult English **Fiction; Vril**)

Stratton, F(rederick) J(ohn) M(arrian) (1881-1960)

Professor of astrophysics and a notable member of the **Society for Psychical Research**, London. Born October 16, 1881 in Birmingham, England, he studied at Gonville and Caius College, Cambridge University, England (B.A. 1904, M.A. 1908). He served in the first world war, was professor of astrophysics and director of the Solar Physics Observatory, Cambridge University from 1928-47, Royal Corps of Signals from 1940-45, president of Gonville and Caius College 1946-48, deputy scientific advisor to the British Army Council 1948-50, Hon. LL.D., Glasgow University, hon. Ph.D., Copenhagen University, Fellow of the Royal Society 1947.

He was president of the Cambridge Philosophical Society from 1930-31, president of the Royal Astronomical Society from 1933-35, general secretary of International Astronomical Union from 1925-35, secretary of British Association for Advancement of Science from 1930-35, general secretary of International Council of Scientific Unions from 1937-52, correspondence of Académic des Sciences, Paris, charter member of the Parapsychological Association.

Prof. Stratton was a member of the Society for Psychical Research for some sixty years, president from 1953-55, and vice-president from 1955-60. He took a great interest in spontaneous phenomena concerning psi and hauntings, and his reports appear in the *Journal* of the Society for Psychical Research. His presidential address 'Psychical Research—A Lifelong Interest' was published in the Society's *Proceedings* (1953).

He died September 2, 1960.

Strauch, Inge H(enriette) (1932-)

German research associate in psychology; parapsychologist. Born April 4, 1932 in Dresden, Germany, she studied at Freiburg University (M.A. psychology 1956, Ph.D. 1958).

She was research associate at Institut für Grenzgebiete der Psychologie and Psychohygiene, Freiburg from 1956-58, research associate at Department for Border Areas of Psychology, Freiburg University from 1958 onwards. Member of Deutsche Gesellschaft für Psychologie, associate member of the Parapsychological Association, managing editor of *Zeitschrift für Parapsychologie und Grenzgebiete der Psychologie*.

Her paper 'Untersuchungen über verschiedene Stufen der Traumerinnerung' (Investigations into Various Stages of Dream Recall) was Report 22 at the Congress of Deutsche Gesellschaft für Psychologie in 1960. During 1961-62 she undertook a study tour in the U.S. and conducted electroencephalographical research on dreams at Mount Sinai Hospital, and electroencephalographical studies in the neurological basis of psychic phenomena at the Parapsychology Foundation, New York City, and quantitative research at the Parapsychology Laboratory, Duke University, Durham, N.C. Her publications include 'Medical Aspects of "Mental" Healing' (*International Journal of Parapsychology*, vol. 5, 1963), 'Dreams and Psi in the Laboratory' (in R, Cavenna, ed., *Psi Favorable States of Consciousness*, Parapsychology Foundation, 1970).

Strieber, Whitley (1945-)

Author of fantasy/horror stories which have been adapted as successful movies. He has also published a remarkable book *Communion* (1987), in which he describes what appear to have been personal experiences of abduction and examination by strange creatures, who might have been extraterrestrials, interdimensional beings, or even hallucinations. A follow-up book on the same theme is his *Transformation: The Breakthrough* (1988).

Strieber was born June 13, 1945 in San Antonio, Texas. He was educated at University of Texas (B.A., 1968) and London School of Economics and Political Science (certificate, 1968). From 1970 through 1977, he commenced writing novels while working in an advertising company, becoming account supervisor and vice-president. He is a member of Authors Guild, Authors League of America, Writers Guild, Poets and Writers.

The idea for his novel *The Wolfen* (1978), later a successful movie, is said to have arisen from an experience when he encountered a pack of feral dogs while walking through Central Park, New York. His other publications include: *Black Magic* (1982), *The Night Church* (1983), *Wolf of Shadows* (1985-6), (with James W. Kunetka) *The Consequences of the Twentieth Century* (1986). His horror novel *The Hunger* (1981) was filmed in 1983, with Catherine Deneuve, David Bowie and Susan Sarandon playing leading roles.

Strieber has also designed games based on various periods of history, including a game about the late Middle Ages entitled "1480: Age of Exploration," and one covering computer games, participated in archaeological projects in Central America, and been involved with a scientific group attempting to authenticate the **Turin Shroud**.

Strieber's book *Communion* has excited considerable interest and controversy, and Strieber has appeared on various television programs, including the Johnny Carson "Tonight Show" (May 6, 1987). Soon after publication of the book, Strieber received over 500 letters, many claiming similar experiences of claimed contact by extraterrestrials or other creatures. In an article in *International UFO Reporter* (January/February, 1987), published by the J. Allen Hynek **Center for UFO Studies**, Strieber characterized such reports as "visitor experiences," and has tentatively formed a nonprofit organization, the Triad Group, to catalog such reports into a database by professional psychologists, with planned follow-up studies involving mental and physical tests with selected volunteers. (See also **Contactee; "Communion"; UFO**)

Striges

In ancient Greek folklore, women with the power to transform themselves into birds of prey or other sinister animals. They were said to have a demonic taste for blood, and were therefore often confused with the **Lamia,** another Greek blood-sucking monster, or with the **vampire**. They are also analagous with the numerous *rakshasas* or evil demons of Hindu mythology.

Strioporta

Frankish title for a witch. (See also section on 'Early Belief in Sorcery' in entry on **France**.)

Stroboscopes

These are devices that create light pulsations at intervals varying from one flash every few seconds to several flashes per second. They are capable of inducing hallucinatory experiences when seen with half-open or even closed eyes.

They have become a familiar part of the spurious excitement of some dance halls and discotheques. A strobe which claims to synchronize flashes with your individual brain waves is named the Brain Wave Synchronizer, and is marketed by Schneider Instrument Co., Skokie, Illinois.

Stroking Stones and Images

It was related by Cotton **Mather** (1662-1728) that an Irish-American witch produced pain and disease in others by merely wetting her finger with saliva, and stroking small images, or sometimes a long, slender stone.

Stromberg, Gustaf (Benjamin) (1882-1962)

Astronomer, lecturer and author of books on parapsychological subjects. Born December 16, 1882 at Gothenburg, Sweden, he studied at University of Lund, Sweden (Ph.D. 1916). In 1914 he married Helga Sofia Henning.

He was assistant at Stockholm Observatory from 1906-13, astronomer at Mount Wilson Observatory, California from 1917-46, conducted scientific research for the U.S. Navy from 1940-41. He was a member of the Royal Society of Sciences, Sweden.

Dr. Stromberg sought for scientific explanations of psychic phenomena. His books included: *The Soul of the Universe* (1940; 1948, translated into Swedish, Dutch, French), *Det Eviga Sökandet* (The Eternal Quest, 1948), *The Searchers* (1948), *Psychic Phenomena and Modern Science* (1957), *God's Place in Modern Science* (1958). He also contributed articles to *Science of the Mind* and *Tomorrow.*

He died January 30, 1962.

Strutt, Arthur Charles (1878-1973)

Vice-admiral of the British Navy; treasurer of the Society for Psychical Research, London from 1933-58. Born October 2, 1878 at Chelmsford, England, he entered the Navy in 1892, was Master of Fleet in World War I, Director of Navigation, Royal Navy from 1923-25, Commodore of convoys, naval officer in charge of Dartmouth College, World War II. Commander, Order of the British Empire. In 1934 he married Baroness Irene de Brienen.

He died in February, 1973.

Strutt, John William (3rd Baron Rayleigh) (1842-1919)

Physicist who was president of the **Society for Psychical Research,** London in 1919. Born November 12, 1842 at Witham, Essex, England, he was educated at Trinity College Cambridge (Fellow, 1866). In 1871 he married Evelyn Balfour.

He was Cavendish professor of experimental physics at Cambridge University, England from 1879-84, secretary to the Royal Society from 1887-96, professor of natural philosophy, Royal Institution from 1887-1905. He was awarded the Order of Merit in 1902, Nobel Prize for physics in 1904. He was a Fellow of the Royal Society.

Lord Rayleigh was a notable physicist. He became interested in psychical research after reading about the investigations of Sir William **Crookes.** He was present at sittings with Kate **Fox** and Eusapia **Palladino**. His 1919 Presidential Address to the SPR was published in *Proceedings* of the Society for Psychical Research (vol. 30, part 77, 1918-19).

He died June 30, 1919.

Strutt, Robert John (4th Baron Rayleigh) (1875-1947)

Physicist who was president of the **Society for Psychical Research**, London from 1937-38. Born August 28, 1875 at Witham, Essex, England, he was educated at Eton College and Trinity College, Cambridge, England (B.A. 1897, M.A. 1901). In 1905 he married Lady Mary Hilda Clements (died 1919); second marriage in 1920 to Kathleen Alice Cuthbert.

He was a fellow of Trinity College, Cambridge from 1900-06, professor of physics, Imperial College of Science and Technology, Kensington from 1908-19, president of the Royal Institution of Great Britain from 1945 onwards, fellow of the Royal Society, hon. D.Sc. Dublin University 1933, Durham University 1929, hon. LL.D. Edinburgh University 1933.

Like his father, he had an intense interest in psychic research, which gave the subject some standing with fellow scientists. He published one of the first volumes on radioactivity. In addition to his many papers in technical and scientific journals, his articles in *Proceedings* of the Society for Psychical Research included: 'A Method of Silhouette Photography by Infra-Red Rays for Use in Mediumistic Investigation' (vol. 41, part 128, 1932), Presidential Address: 'The Problem of Physical Phenomena in Connection with Psychical Research' (vol. 44, part 152, 1938), 'The Question of Lights Supposed to Have Been Observed near the Poles of a Magnet' (vol. 44, part 153, 1938-39), 'Some Recollections of Henry Sidgwick' (vol. 44, part 156, 1936-39).

He died December 13, 1947.

Stuart, C(harles) E. (1907-1947)

Parapsychologist. Born December 5, 1907 in Pennsylvania, he studied at Duke University, Durham, N.C. (B.A. 1932, Ph.D. 1941). In 1939 he married Wilma Kelly. He was a research associate at the Parapsychology Laboratory, Duke University from 1934-47.

He became interested in the work of J. B. **Rhine** when an undergraduate at Duke, and started ESP tests on himself and friends. He went on to become a research associate in the Parapsychology Laboratory in 1934, and his doctoral thesis dealt with experimental research in ESP. He was on the laboratory staff at Duke for the rest of his life except for two years at Stanford University in 1942-44 as a fellow in psychic research.

He took a special interest in psychological conditions and personality factors in relation to ESP. His papers in the *Journal of Parapsychology* included: 'The Effect of Rate of Movement in Card Matching Tests of Extrasensory Perception' (vol. 2, 1938), 'A Review of Recent Criticisms of ESP Research' (vols. 2, 3, 1939), 'A Classroom ESP Experiment with the Free Response Method' (vol. 9, 1945), 'GESP Experiment with the Free Response Method' (vol. 10, 1946), 'An Interest Inventory Relation to ESP Scores' (vol. 10, 1945). He was co-author with J. G. **Pratt** of *Handbook for Testing Extrasensory Perception,* and with Pratt, Rhine, B. M. Smith & J. A. Greenwood of *Extrasensory Perception After Sixty Years* (1940).

He died March 23, 1947.

Student's International Meditation Society

Founded in 1965 to promote the **Transcendental Meditation** technique taught by **Maharishi Mahesh Yogi**. Based in California, it claimed a membership of several thousand, operating through World Plan centers.

Sturdevant, William D(esmond) (1922-)

Assistant professor of Art who has been active in the field of parapsychology. Born July 3, 1922 at Des Moines, Iowa, he was educated at Drake University, Des Moines (B.S. education 1945, M.S. education 1947). In 1943 he married Dorothy Marie Goode.

He was an art instructor in Ann Arbor public schools, Michigan from 1945-47, New Mexico Western College, Silver City from 1947-48, Minnesota State College at Mankato from 1948-55; art supervisor at Joliet public schools, Joliet, Illinois from 1955-59; assistant professor of art at California Western University, San Diego, Calif. from 1959-61.

He is a member of the Society of American Graphic Artists, Boston Printmakers, charter associate of the Parapsychological Association. A talented artist, Mr. Sturdevant has works in the Permanent Collection of the Boston Museum of Fine Arts, and has exhibited widely. He has also made experimental studies concerning extrasensory color perception, and has published the following monographs: *Fluorescent Color Perception and Graphic Response in the Perceptually Impaired Child* (1957), *Extrasensory Color Perception* (1958).

Subconscious

Mental phenomena dissociated from those directly or introspectively cognized. For orthodox psychology, the subconscious discloses no new functions of the mind; it simply acts without being aware of the stimuli.

Supernormal faculties were ascribed to it by F. W. H. **Myers**. While theories involving such faculties eliminate, in many cases, the appeal to spirits, they also reconcile mental activity with spirit agencies, since the subconscious may be—as Prof. J. H. **Hyslop** pointed out—the very instrument for receiving and transmission of foreign transcendental stimuli to which, on favorable occasions, it becomes sensitive.

The subconscious might thus be an intermediary between a purely physical and a purely spiritual existence. (See also **Consciousness**)

Subjective Phenomena

Subjective, as distinguished from objective, is an alternative classification for mental phenomena which are not capable of objective validation, as in the case of physical phenomena.

Subliminal

A term first used by A. H. Pierce of Harvard University for sensations beneath the threshold of consciousness, too feeble to be individually recognized.

F. W. H. **Myers** extended the meaning to cover all that takes place beneath the consciousness threshold—sensations, thoughts, emotions, which seldom emerge, but which form a consciousness quite as complex and coherent as the supraliminal one, since they demonstrate processes of mentation and exhibit a continuous chain of memory.

Nevertheless, Myers did not consider the subliminal consciousness a separate Self but, together with the supraliminal (normal consciousness) one, a fragment of the larger Self revealed through an organism which cannot afford it full manifestation. In this concept he came close to the Hindu Vedanta concepts of *jiva* (individual soul) as part of *Atman* (collective soul).

Myers attributed most supernormal psychical phenomena to the subliminal self, but not as a complete explanation or exclusion of the **spirit hypothesis.** On the contrary, his inference was that if our incarnate selves may act in **telepathy** in at least apparent independence of the fleshly body, the presumption is strong that other spirits may exist independently of the body and may affect us in a similar manner.

Myers divided the influence of the subliminal on the supraliminal under three main heads: (1) When the subliminal mentation cooperates with and supplements the supraliminal, without changing the apparent phase of personality, we have genius. (2) When subliminal operations change the apparent phase of personality from the state of waking in the direction of trance, we have hypnotism. (3) When the subliminal mentation forces itself up through the supraliminal, without amalgamation, as in crystal vision, automatic writing, etc., we have sensory or motor automatism (See also **Consciousness; Subconscious; Subliminal Self**)

Subliminal Self

A term used in psychical research to denote that part of the personality which is normally beneath the "threshold" *(limen)* separating consciousness from unconsciousness. The phrase owed its popularity largely to F. W. H. **Myers**, who made use of it to explain the psychic phenomena which he had observed.

The view of Myers was that only a fraction of the human personality, or soul, finds adequate expression through the ordinary cerebral processes, because of the fact that the brain and physical organism have not yet reached a very advanced stage of evolution. The soul, in short, is like an iceberg, with a fraction of its bulk above water, but having much the greater part submerged.

The subliminal self, again according to Myers, was in touch with a reservoir of psychical energy, from which it drew forces which influenced the physical organism. Thus the inspiration of genius, the exaltation of the perceptive and intellectual faculties in hypnosis, and such exercises as **automatic writing** and talking and **table-turning,** were referred to great influxes of these psychical forces rather than to any morbid tendencies in the agent.

Indeed, abnormal manifestations were, and still are, regarded by some authorities as foreshadowing a new type in the progress of evolution, whose faculties will transcend those of human beings just as our human faculties transcend those of the lower animals. The soul, thus dependent for a very inadequate expression on a nervous system of limited scope, is at death freed from its limitations and comes into its heritage of full consciousness.

These hypotheses have been pressed into service to explain **telepathy** and communication between the living and the dead, as well as **hallucination,** automatism, and all the phenomena of **hypnotism**. But the two former, even if they could be demonstrated, would require to be explained on other grounds, while the others, whose existence is undisputed, are more generally regarded as resultant from cerebral dissociation—i.e., the temporary dislocation of the connecting links between the various neural systems. (See also **Consciousness; Subconscious; Subliminal**)

Subterranean Cities

A persistent theme in modern popular occultism is the story of underground caverns inhabited by malevolent **Deros**, or subterranean cities inhabited by survivors of **Atlantis** or **Lemuria**, by masters of wisdom or by **flying saucer** pilots and their craft.

Much of this new mythology stems from the publications of the enterprising Raymond A. **Palmer** in *Amazing Stories, Flying Saucers* and *Search* magazines. In 1945, Palmer introduced the readers of *Amazing Stories* to the wild fantasies of Richard B. **Shaver**, with whom Palmer collaborated on producing what was stoutly claimed to be factual "racial memories" of survivors from Atlantis and Lemuria, originally giants but now degenerated into malevolent dwarfs, influencing mankind by secret rays.

Palmer, who also generated the first excitement about flying saucers in his magazine *Fate* in Spring 1948, later went on to suggest that saucers came from an underground world entered through the polar ice caps.

Other sources for subterranean mythology include the writings of Robert Ernest **Dickhoff** and Milinko S. Stevic. In Dickhoff's book *Agharta*, he described a vast network of underground tunnels radiating from Antarctica with openings in the U.S., Brazil, Tibet and Pacific islands. These underground strongholds are inhabited by descendants of Martians, who colonized the earth in prehistory.

Stevic is a Yugoslav-born engineer who lectures about the extensive subterranean cities beneath New York, Tokyo, Leningrad, São Paulo and large areas of the Atlantic Ocean. Survivors of Atlantis reside in this subterranean world, where they have built huge domes of fiberglass. There are millions of inhabitants, who also contribute illegal immigrants to the U.S. There are, apparently, secret entrances to the underground world through a number of churches, including specifically St. John the Divine at 103 Street and Amsterdam in New York. Mr. Stevic also claims that Adolf Hitler did not die, but reached the U.S. through a secret tunnel and now lives quietly in New Jersey.

In Livingston, Montana, Mr. and Mrs. **Hefferlin** also publicize Rainbow City in the Antarctic, founded 2½ million years ago as the focal point of a network of underground tunnels. Head of the large population in Rainbow City are the Ancient Three, descendants of Martians who exercise as favorable an influence on world affairs as Shaver's deros are malevolent. These powerful mystics of Rainbow City won World War II for the Allies by stopping Rommel in Egypt and halting the Japanese in the Pacific.

Ever since the revelations of Guy W. **Ballard**, founder of the **I AM** cult, Mount Shasta in northern California has been the center of legends of a hidden city inhabited by masters of wisdom and mysterious flying boats.

In 1934, writing under the pseudonym Godfré Ray King, Ballard published *Unveiled Mysteries*, in which he allegedly encountered a godlike figure named as "The Master Saint-Germain" in the woods near Mount Shasta. Every since then, Shasta cults have persisted, with stories of underground temples, secret machines and stores of gold dust.

It has to be said that modern mythologies of underground cities owe more to sensationalist media publications than to genuine traditions. There may have been a factual basis to earlier European stories of underground dwarfs and fairies, both in traditions of such peoples as the Pictish races living in remote places, and in the claimed ability of nature spirits to manifest in a variety of forms. But such traditions merged dimly remembered history with mystical allegories of an inspiring character altogether lacking in the banal inventions of modern mythologies.

There seems to be a genuine Tibetan tradition of the underground kingdom of **Agharta**, presided over by the "King of the World," and no doubt the fantasies of such writers as Dickhoff derive from such traditions.

It is also interesting to note that Sri **Ramana Maharshi**, one of the greatest saints of modern India, once told Paul **Brunton** that he had seen visions of caves and cities in the sacred hill of Arunachala, South India, but that these, like the scenes of everyday life, were within the Self rather than an objective reality (see *Talks with Sri Ramana Maharshi*, vol. 1, Sri Ramanasramam, Tiruvannamalai, South India, 1957). (See also **Subterranean Crypts and Temples**)

Subterranean Crypts and Temples

Subterranean resorts, crypts and places of worship, have constantly exercised a deep fascination upon the mind of the human race. The mysteries of the Egyptian and of other peoples were held in underground crypts, possibly for the purposes of rendering these ceremonies still more secret and mysterious to ordinary people, but also, perhaps, because it was essential to the privacy they required. The caves of Elephanta, the Catacombs and similar subterranean edifices are also well-known examples. But there are also several lesser and perhaps more interesting underground meeting places and temples in various parts of the world.

Hargrave Jennings, author of *The Rosicrucians* (1870), quoted Dr. Plot's *History of Staffordshire*, written in the third quarter of the seventeenth century, giving an interesting account of a supposed Rosicrucian crypt in that country, which, however, cannot be found in the work alluded to. However, a shortened version of this story appeared in *The Spectator* (May 15, 1712). It may be imaginary, but is typical of the appeal of such legends.

The story goes that a countryman was employed, at the close of a certain dull summer's day, in digging a trench in a field in a valley, round which the country rose into somber, silent woods, vocal only with the quaint cries of the infrequent magpies. It was some little time after the sun had sunk, and the countryman was just about giving up his labor for the day.

In one or two of the last languid strokes of his pick, the rustic came upon something stony and hard, which struck a spark, clearly visible in the increasing gloom. At this surprise, he resumed his labor, and, curiously enough, found a large, flat stone in the center of the field. This field was far away from any of the farms or "cotes," as they were called, with which the now almost twilight country was sparingly dotted.

In a short time, he cleared the stone free of the grass and weeds which had grown over it; and it proved to be a large, oblong slab, with an immense iron ring fixed at one end in a socket. For half an hour the countryman attempted to move this stone in vain. At last he remembered a coil of rope which he had lying near amongst his tools, and, being an ingenious, inquisitive, inventive man, he made a tackle, by means of which, and by passing the sling round a bent tree in a line with the axis of the stone, he contrived, in the last of the light, and with much expenditure of toil to raise it.

Then, greatly to his surprise, he saw a large, deep, hollow place, buried in the darkness, which, when his eyes grew accustomed to the gloom, he discovered was the top to a stone staircase, seemingly of extraordinary depth, for he saw nothing below. The countryman had not the slightest idea of where this could lead to, but being a man of courage, and most probably urged by his idea that the staircase led to some secret repository where treasure lay buried, he descended the first few steps cautiously, and tried to peer in vain down into the darkness.

Looking up to the fresh air, and seeing the star Venus, the evening star, shining suddenly like a planet, in encouraging, unexpected brilliancy, although the sky had still some sunset light in it, the puzzled man left the upper ground and descended the staircase. Here, at an angle, as near as he could judge, of a hundred feet underground, he came upon a square landing-place, with a niche in the wall, and then he saw a further long staircase, descending at right angles to the first staircase, and still going down into deep, cold, darkness.

The man cast a glance upwards, as if questioning the small segment of light from the upper world which shot down whether he should continue his search, or desist and return. All was absolutely still about him, but he saw no particular reason for fear. So, imagining that he would in some way soon penetrate the mystery, and feeling in the darkness by his hands upon the wall, and by his toes first on each step, he resolutely descended, and deliberately counted two hundred and twenty steps. He felt no difficulty in his breathing, except a certain sort of aromatic smell of distant incense that he thought Egyptian, coming up now and then from below, as if from a subterranean world. "Possibly," he thought, "the world of the mining gnomes, and I am breaking in upon their secrets, which is forbidden for man." The man, although courageous, was superstitious.

But, in spite of occasional qualms of fear, the man went on, and at a much lower angle he met a wall in his face. Making a turn to the right, with great credit to his nerves, the explorer went down again. And now he saw at a vast distance below, at the foot of a deeper staircase of stone, a steady pale light. This was shining up as if from a star, or coming from the center of the earth. Cheered by this light, though absolutely astounded, even frightened, at thus discovering natural or artificial light in the deep bowels of the earth, the man again descended, meeting a thin, humid trail of light, as it seemed, mounting up the center line of the shining moldering old stairs, which apparently had not been pressed by a human foot for very many ages.

He thought now, although it was probably only the wind in some hidden recess, or creeping down some gallery, that he heard a murmur overhead, as if of the uncertain rumble of horses, of heavy wagons, or lumbering hay carts. The next moment, there was total stillness, but the distant light seemed to flicker, as if in answer to the strange sound. Half a dozen times the man paused and turned as if he would remount—almost flee for his life upwards, as he thought, for this might be the secret haunt of robbers, or the dreadful abode of evil spirits. What if, in a few moments, he should come upon desperate ruffians, or be caught by murderers.

He listened eagerly. He now almost bitterly repented his descent. Still the light streamed at a distance, but still there was no sound to interpret the meaning of the light, or to display the character of this mysterious place, in which the man himself was entangled hopelessly.

At last, summoning courage, and recommending himself devoutly to God, he determined to complete his discovery. Above, he had been working in no strange place, the field he knew well, the woods were very familiar to him, and his own hamlet and his family were only a few miles distant. He now hastily, and more in fear than through courage, descended noisily the remainder of the stairs.

The light grew brighter as he approached, until at last, at another turn, he came upon a square chamber built up of large hewn stones. He stopped, silent and awestruck. Here was a flagged pavement and a somewhat lofty roof, gathering up into a center, in the groins of which was a rose, carved exquisitely in some dark stone, or in marble. But imagine the poor man's fright when, making another sudden turn, from between the jambs, and from under the large curve of a Gothic stone portal, light streamed out over him with inexpressible brilliancy, shining over everything, and lighting up the place with brilliant radiance, like an intense golden sunset.

He started back. Then his limbs shook and bent under him as he gazed with terror at the figure of a man, whose face was hidden, as he sat in a studious attitude in a stone chair, reading in a great book, with his elbow resting on a table like a rectangular altar, in the light of a large, ancient iron lamp, suspended by a thick chain to the middle of the roof.

A cry of alarm, which he could not suppress, escaped from the scared discoverer, who involuntarily advanced one pace, beside himself with terror. He was now within the illuminated chamber. As his feet fell on the stone, the figure started bolt upright from his seated position as if in awful astonishment. He erected his hooded head, and showed himself as if in anger about to question the intruder. Doubtful if what he saw were a reality, or whether he was not in some terrific dream, the countryman advanced, without being aware of it, another audacious step.

The hooded man now thrust out a long arm, as if in warning, and in a moment the discoverer perceived that his hand was armed with an iron baton, and that he pointed it as if to forbid further approach. Now, however, to restrain himself, with a cry, and in a passion of fear, took a third fatal step, and as his foot descended on the groaning stone, which seemed to give away for a moment under him, the dreadful man, or image, raised his arm high like a machine, and with his truncheon struck a prodigious blow upon the lamp, shattering it into a thousand pieces, and leaving the place in utter darkness.

This was the end of this terrifying adventure. There was total silence now, far and near. Only a long, low roll of thunder, or a noise similar to thunder, seemed to begin from a distance, and then to move with snatches, as if making turns, and it then rumbled sullenly to sleep as if through unknown, inaccessible passages. What such passages might be, nobody ever found out. We are not told how the terrified countryman made his way back to the familiar world we know.

It was suspected that this hidden place referred in some way to the **Rosicrucians**, and that the mysterious people of that famous order had there concealed some of their scientific secrets. The place in Staffordshire became afterwards famed as the sepulcher of one of the brotherhood, whom, for want of a more distinct recognition or name, the people chose to call "Rosicrucius," in general reference to his order, and from the circumstances of the lamp, and its sudden extinguishment by the figure that started up, it was supposed that some rosicrucian had determined to inform posterity that he had penetrated to the secret of the making of the ever-burning lamps of the ancients, although, at the moment that he displayed this knowledge, he took effectual means that no one should reap any advantage from it.

The Jesuit priests of the early eighteenth century left descriptions of the palace of Mitla in Central America, which leave no doubt that in their time it contained many subterranean chambers and one especially which appeared to have surpassed all others in the dreadful uses to which it was put.

Father Torquemada said of the place: "When some monks of my order, the Franciscan, passed, preaching and shriving through the province of Zapoteca, whose capital city is Tehuantepec, they came to a village which was called Mictlan, that is, underworld (hell). Besides mentioning the large number of people in the village they told of buildings which were prouder and more magnificent than any which they had hitherto seen in New Spain. Among them was the temple of the evil spirit and living rooms for his demoniacal servants, and among other fine things there was a hall with ornamented panels, which were constructed of stone in a variety of arabesques and other very remarkable designs. There were doorways there, each one of which was built of but three stones, two upright at the sides and one across them, in such a manner that, although these doorways were very high and broad, the stone sufficed for their entire construction. They were so thick and broad that we were assured there were few like them. There was another hall in these buildings, or rectangular temples, which was erected entirely on round stone pillars very high and very thick that two grown men could scarcely encircle them with their arms, nor could one of them reach the finger-tips of the other. These pillars were all in one piece and, it was said, the whole shaft of the pillar measured 5 ells from top to bottom, and they were very much like those of the church of Santa Maria Maggiore in Rome, very skillfully made and polished."

Father Burgoa was more explicit with regard to these subterranean chambers. He stated, "There were four chambers above ground and four below. The latter were arranged according to their purpose in such a way that one front chamber served as chapel and sanctuary for the idols, which were placed on a great stone which served as an altar. And for the most important feasts which they celebrated with sacrifices, or at the burial of a king or great lord, the high priest instructed the lesser priests or the subordinate temple officials who served him to prepare the chapel and his vestments and a large quantity of the incense used by them.

"And then he descended with a great retinue, when none of the common people saw him or dared to look in his face, convinced that if they did so they would fall dead to the earth as a punishment for their boldness. And when he entered the chapel they put on him a long white cotton garment made like an alb, and over that a garment shaped like a dalmatic, which was embroidered with pictures of wild beasts and birds; and they put a cap on his head, and on his feet a kind of shoe woven of many-colored feathers.

"And when he had put on these garments he walked with solemn mien and measured step to the altar, bowed low before the idols, renewed the incense, and then in quite unintelligible murmurs [muy entre dientes] he began to converse with these images, these depositories of infernal spirits, and continued in this sort of prayer with hideous grimaces and writhings, uttering inarticulate sounds, which filled all present with fear and terror, till he came out of that diabolical trance and told those standing around the lies and fabrications which the spirit had imparted to him or which he had invented himself.

"When human beings were sacrificed the ceremonies were multiplied, and the assistants of the high priest stretched the victim out upon a large stone, bareing his breast, which they tore open with a great stone knife, while the body writhed in fearful convulsions and they laid the heart bare, ripping it out, and with it the soul, which the devil took, while they carried the heart to the high priest that he might offer it to the idols by holding it to their mouths, among other ceremonies; and the body was thrown into the burial-place of their 'blessed,' as they called them. And if after the sacrifice he felt inclined to detain those who begged any favor he sent them word by the subordinate priests not to leave their houses till their gods were appeased, and he commanded them to do penance meanwhile, to fast and to speak with no woman, so that, until this father of sin had interceded for the absolution of the penitents and had declared the gods appeased they did not dare to cross their threshold.

"The second [underground] chamber was the burial place of these high priests, and third that of the kings of Theozapotlan, whom they brought thither richly dressed in their best attire, feathers, jewels, golden necklaces, and precious stones, placing a shield in their left hand and a javelin in the right, just as they used them in war. And at their burial rites great mourning prevailed; the instruments which were played made mournful sounds; and with loud wailing and continuous sobbing they chanted the life and exploits of their lord until they laid him on the structure which they had prepared for this purpose.

"The last [underground] chamber had a second door at the rear, which led to a dark and gruesome room. This was closed with a stone slab, which occupied the whole entrance. Through this door they threw the bodies of the victims and of the great lords and chieftains who had fallen in battle, and they brought them from the spot where they fell, even when it was very far off, to this burial place; and so great was the barbarous infatuation of these Indians that, in the belief of the happy life which awaited them, many who were oppressed by diseases or hardships begged this infamous priest to accept them as living sacrifices and allow them to enter through that portal and roam about in the dark interior of the mountains, to seek the great feasting places of their forefather. And when anyone obtained this favour the servants of the high priest led him thither with special ceremonies, and after they had allowed him to enter through the small door they rolled the stone before it again and took leave of him, and the unhappy man, wandering in that abyss of darkness, died of hunger and thirst, beginning already in life the pain of his damnation; and on account of this horrible abyss they called this village Liyobaa, The Cavern of Death.

"When later there fell upon these people the light of the Gospel, its servants took much trouble to instruct them to find out whether this error, common to all these nations, still prevailed, and they learned from the stories which had been handed down that all were convinced that this damp cavern extended more than 30 leagues underground, and that its roof was supported by pillars. And there were people, zealous prelates anxious for knowledge, who, in order to convince these ignorant people of their terror, went into this cave accompanied by a large number of people bearing lighted torches and firebrands, and descended several large steps. And they soon came upon many buttresses which formed a kind of street. They had prudently brought a quantity of rope with them to use as a guiding line, that they might not lose themselves in this confusing labyrinth. And the putrefaction and the bad odour and the dampness of the earth were very great and there was also a cold wind which blew out their torches. And after they had gone a short distance, fearing to be overpowered by the stench or to step on poisonous reptiles, of which some had been seen, they resolved to go out again and to completely wall up this back door of hell. The four buildings above ground were the only ones which still remained open, and they had a court and chambers like those underground; and the ruins of these have lasted even to the present day."

The vast subterranean vaults under the temple hill at Jerusalem were probably used as a secret meeting place by the Templars during their occupation of the Holy City, and it was perhaps there that the strange Eastern rites of **Baphomet** which they later affected were first celebrated.

In his book *Recent Discoveries on the Temple Hill* (1884) the Rev. James King stated, "On the occasion of a visit to the Noble Sanctuary, the author had an opportunity of examining the ancient masonry inside the wall at the south-east corner, as well as the vast subterranean vaults popularly known as Solomon's stables. A small doorway, under a little dome at the south-east corner, admits by a flight of steps to a small chamber known as the Mosque of the Cradle of our Lord, from the existence of a hollowed stone which somewhat resembles a cradle, and a tradition that the Virgin Mary remained in this chamber for some time after her purification in the Temple. Passing through the chamber, the spacious vaults, which extend over an acre of ground, are reached. These subterranean substructures consist of one hundred square piers arranged in fifteen rows, each pier being five feet wide and composed of large marginal drafted stones, placed singly over each other. The rows are connected by semi-circular arches, the intercolumniations of which range from ten to twenty-three feet. The floor of these vaults is about forty-feet below the Haram Area, and more than a hundred feet above the great foundation corner-stone. They are called Solomon's Stables by the Franks. But the Moslems call the place, Al Masjed al Kadim, that is, The Old Mosque. These vaults were used as stables by the Frank kings and the Knights Templar, and holes in which rings were fastened can still be traced on some of the piers.

"Since the floor of Solomon's Stables is upwards of a hundred feet above the foundation stone, it seems highly probable that there exists another system of vaults below, for the vast space from the rock upwards is not likely to be filled with solid earth.

"Some allusion seems to be made to these vaults in the writings of Procopius, a Greek historian of the sixth century. He was born at Caesarea, in Palestine, about 500 A.D., and as a young man went to Constantinople, where his eminent talents brought him under the notice of the Emperor Justinian. In 529 A.D. Justinian built a splendid church on the Temple Hill, in honour of the Virgin Mary, and in the writings of Procopius there is a full and detailed account of the edifice. The historian relates that the fourth part of the ground required for the building was wanting towards the south-east; the builders therefore laid their foundations on the sloping ground, and constructed a series of arched vaults, in order to raise the ground to the level of the other parts of the enclosure. This account is eminently descriptive of the subterranean vaults at the south-east portion of the Haram, and, according to Mr. Fergusson, the stone-work of these vaults certainly belongs to the age of Justinian." (See also **Subterranean Cities**)

Subud

A spiritual movement which has grown up around the Indonesian mystic Muhammad **Subuh**, known as "Bapak" or spiritual father. Beginning in Java, it spread to Europe and elsewhere, after winning support from the Gurdjieff disciples at Coombe Springs, England, led by J. G. **Bennett**. Gurdjieff himself had predicted that there would be an Indonesian teacher to bring emotional warmth to his system.

Subud came into the public eye in 1959 when the movement held an International Congress in England. Soon afterwards, the Hungarian actress Eva Bartok was initiated and claimed to be healed from childbirth complications.

Essentially Bapak is a charismatic individual who generates a kind of contagious spiritual energy, reminiscent of the traditional *shaktipat* of such Hindu gurus as Swami **Muktananda**.

The basis of the Subud movement is the **Latihan**, an initiation ceremony for newcomers and a spiritual exercise for those already initiated. A "helper" prepares the initiate for "opening" or receptivity to the descent of spiritual energy. This often causes pronounced convulsions, similar to the "shakes" or "jerks" elicited by backwoods evangelists, or the onset of **Kundalini** energy in traditional Hindu mysticism.

This energy has a purificatory function, and brings intense feelings of peace when there is submission to divine will. Subud is unlike established religions or cults insofar as it has no creed, dogma, rules or regulations, but makes available the experience of the Latihan to initiates. Subud groups meet regularly in each other's homes or in rented halls. The movement does not advertise or proseletize.

There are over seventy U.S. cities with Subud centers, and a telephone call will elicit the time and place of the Latihan. There are also Subud groups in most of the larger cities of Britain. For further information in the U.S., contact; Subud USA, 13701 Bel-Red Road, Suite B, Bellevue, Washington 98005. British address: Subud, 342 Cricklewood Lane, London, NW2 2QH. (See also **Kundalini; Shakers;** Muhammad **Subuh**)

Recommended reading:

Barter, J. P. *Towards Subud,* London, 1967

Bennett, John, G. *Concerning Subud*, University Books, 1959

Rofé, H. *The Path of Subud*, Rider & Co., London, 1959

Van Hien, G. *What is Subud?*, Rider & Co., London, 1963

Subuh, Muhammad (1901-)

Indonesian mystic whose spiritual mission led to the formation of the movement known as **Subud**. Subuh had an initiatory experience in 1925 on his twenty-fourth birthday, when a sphere of light appeared in the night and seemed to enter his head, filling him with vibrating energy and light.

Three years later, this strange energy source stopped abruptly, and Subuh continued his everyday life as a government official and married man, while passing through the equivalent of the Western mystical stage of the "dark night of the soul." On his thirty-second birthday, he had an enlightenment which revealed his spiritual mission and he devoted himself to his work.

The name "Subud" derives from an abbreviation of three words: *Susila* (Morality in line with Divine Will), *Budhi* (enlightenment in man), *Dharma* (attitude of submission and sincerity towards God).

Subud's own name actually means "sunrise," but he is known to his followers as "Bapak," an affectionate Javanese term meaning "father," often applied to a spiritual teacher.

From 1933 onwards, Subud was little known outside Indonesia, but by 1956 it had attracted European interest. When Bapak visited the **Gurdjieff** headquarters of Coombe Springs in Britain, its director J. G. **Bennett** and followers were won over by his emotional and spiritual vibrancy. During his lifetime, Gurdjieff had made mysterious allusions to a forthcoming Indonesian teacher, and it was clear that Bapak was that teacher. (See also **Subud**)

Succubus

A demon who takes the shape of a woman, stealing the vitality of men during sleep. Old Rabbinical writings relate the legend of how Adam was visited during a hundred and thirty years by female demons, and had intercourse with demons, spirits, specters, lemurs, and phantoms.

Another legend relates how under the reign of Roger, king of Sicily, a young man was bathing by moonlight and thought he was someone drowning, and hastened to the rescue. Having drawn from the water a beautiful woman, he became enamored of her, married her, and had by her a child. Afterwards she disappeared mysteriously with her child, which made everyone believe that she was a succubus.

The historian Hector Boece (1465-1536), in his history of Scotland, related that a very handsome young man was pursued by a female demon, who would pass through his closed door, and offer to marry him. He complained to his bishop, who enjoined him to fast, pray, and confess himself, and as a result, the infernal visitor ceased to trouble him.

The witchcraft judge Pierre **de Lancre** (1553-1631) stated that in Egypt, an honest maréchal-ferrant was occupied in forging during the night when there appeared to him a demon under the shape of a beautiful woman. He threw a hot iron in the face of the demon, which at once took to flight.

The succubus, and the comparable demon named **incubus** (which takes the form of a man, to seduce women) were generally believed to appear most frequently during sleep or in a nightmare.

A standard treatise on the subject is *Demoniality or Incubi and Succubi* by Fr. L. M. Sinistari of Ameno, written in Latin and first translated and published by the bibliophile Isidore Liseux, Paris, 1879. A later translation was that of the Rev. Montague Summers (Fortune Press, London, 1927, reprinted B. Blom, New York, 1972). (See also **Incubus**)

Sudre, René (1880-)

Scientific writer and parapsychologist. Born April 19, 1880 at Angoulême, France, he studied at Poitiers Academy (Bachelier ès lettres, sciences) and University of Paris (licencié ès sciences, Sorbonne). In 1915 he married Suzanne Samuel-Rousseau.

He was a scientific commentator for Radiodiffusion Française from 1926-40, writer on psychic research for *Mercure de France* from 1925-28, professor at École des Hautes Etudes Sociales, Paris from 1931-40, scientific writer for *Journal des Débats* from 1935-40, and for the French Ministry of Information and Foreign Ministry from 1945-56, for *Revue des Deux Mondes* from 1949 onwards. Chevalier of the Legion of Honor 1921, officier of Legion of Honor 1932, lauréat of Académie Française 1943, lauréat of Académie des Sciences (for his book *Almanach des Sciences,* 1948-52), secretary of Institut Général Psychologique, corresponding member of National Laboratory of Psychical Research, London University, secretary of French committees for International conferences on psychical research, Copenhagen, 1922 and Warsaw 1923, member of Society for Psychical Research, London.

He experimented in many fields of parapsychology, and spent many years in attempts to show that psi phenomena are a matter for science. He believed that the assumptions of Spiritualism are erroneous. He also considered that all living creatures possess some extrasensory faculty.

His books included: *La Lutte pour la métapsychique* (The Fight for Parapsychology, 1928), *Introduction a la métapsychique humaine* (Introduction to Human Metapsychics, 1929), *Les Nouvelles énigmes de l'univers* (New Enigmas of the Universe, 1943), *Personnages d'au-delà* (People from the Beyond, 1945), *Le Huitième art—Mission de la radio* (The Eighth Art—Mission of Radio, 1946), *Traité de parapsychologie* (1956, English edition titled *Parapsychology*, 1960). He translated into French various books on parapsychology by William James, Sir William Barrett, J. B. Rhine and T. K. Oesterreich, and contributed articles to such journals as *Psychic Research* (1926-31) and *Revue Métapsychique* (1922-26).

Sufism

A mystical movement of Islam. The name derives from the fact that Sufis wore woollen clothing *(Suf)*, as a token of penitence, like the similar tradition of Christian penitents wearing hair shirts.

In medieval times Sufism was characterized by a complex system of striving for spiritual attainment and divine grace. A short version of the spiritual stages involved includes: conversion, abstinence, renunciation, poverty, patience, trust in God, contentment; with spiritual states of meditation, nearness to God, love, fear, hope, longing, intimacy, tranquility, contemplation, certainty. Much of this has analogies with the *yama* and *niyama* of Hindu **Yoga**.

There were four orders of Sufis: the *Qadiriyya*, an orthodox wing emphasizing devotional exercises leading to spiritual experience, *Suhrawardiyya*, less orthodox and with a suggestion of pantheism, the *Shadhiliyya* (wide-spread in Egypt and North Africa) with intense devotion and utter dependence on God, and the *Mevlevi* order founded by the poet Rumi, which developed the special mystical dance of the **Dervishes**.

Sufism has influenced religious movements in India, Java and elsewhere, and played a part in the development of such unorthodox prophets as Baha'u'llah of the **Baha'i** faith and the mystic Meher Baba. The major emphasis in Sufism is intense love for God, expressed in the perfection of the soul.

A Western Sufi organization is the Sufi Order (headed by Pir Vilayat Inayat Khan), whose traditions are said to predate Islam and became incorporated in it. In 1910 the Sufi Order was established in Europe and the U.S. through the lectures of Hazrat Pir-o-Murshid Inayat Khan. The Order stresses that "God is One" and there are no barriers between religions. Address for information: Sufi Order Secretariat, Box 574, Lebanon Springs, New York 12114. There is a British branch of the Sufi Order at: Barton Farm, Pound Lake, Bradford-on-Avon, Wiltshire, England.

A separate group of the Sufi movement is the Sufi Islamia Ruhaniat Society: The Mentorgarten, 10 Precita Avenue, San Francisco, California 94110.

Another group of the Sufi movement, is the Sufi Cultural Center in London, established in 1971. It places great emphasis on the mysticism of music, and encourages the teaching of classical Indian music, with a more modern adjunct of health foods and alternative healing. (See also **Dervishes;** Idries **Shah**)

Recommended reading:

Khan, Pir V. *The Message in Our Time; The Life and Teachings of the Sufi Master, Hazrat Inayat Khan*, Harper & Row, 1979

Shah, Idries. *The Sufis*, W. H. Allen, London, 1964; Dutton paperback, 1971

Shah, Idries. *The Way of the Sufi*, Dutton paperback, 1970

Subhan, John. *Sufism; Its Saints and Shrines,* Weiser paperback, 1973

Williams, L. F. R. (ed.). *Sufi Studies; East & West,* Dutton/Octagon Press, London, 1974

Suggestion

The sensitiveness to suggestion of the entranced subject is the characteristic and invariable accompaniment of the hypnotic state, and is also a distinctive feature of hysteria. Indeed, many scientists give to hypnotism the name "Suggestion."

An abnormal suggestibility implies some measure of cerebral dissociation (see **Hypnotism**). In this state every suggestion advanced by the operator, whether conveyed by word, gesture, or even unconscious glance, operates with abnormal force in the brain of the subject, which becomes relieved from the counter-excitement of other ideas and stimuli.

In the view of Prof. Pierre Janet, all suggestibility implies a departure from perfect sanity, but this, although perhaps true in the strictest sense, is somewhat misleading, since all individuals are more or less amenable to suggestion. In hypnotism and hysteria, however, the normal suggestibility is greatly exaggerated, and the suggestion, meeting with no opposition from the recipient's critical or judicial faculties (because there are no other ideas with which to compare it) becomes, for the time, his dominant idea. The suggestion thus accepted has a powerful effect on both mind and body, hence the value of suggestion in certain complaints is incalculable.

The miracles of healing claimed by Christian Scientists and others, the efficacy of a pilgrimage to **Lourdes**, the feats of healing mediums, all testify to its powerful effect.

Post-hypnotic suggestion is the term applied to a suggestion made while the subject is entranced, but which is to be carried out after awakening. Sometimes an interval of months may elapse between the utterance of a command and its fulfilment, but almost invariably at the stated time or stipulated stimulus, the **suggestion** is obeyed, the recipient usually being unaware of the source of the impulse, not finding adequate logical grounds for the action performed, or perhaps automatically lapsing into the hypnotic state.

Autosuggestion does not proceed from any extraneous source, but arises in one's own mind, either spontaneously or from a misconception of existing circumstances, as in the case of a person who is persuaded to drink colored water under the impression that it is poison, and exhibits every symptom of poisoning. Autosuggestion may arise spontaneously in dreams, the automatic obedience to such suggestion often giving rise to stories of "veridical" dreams.

The outbreaks of religious frenzy or ecstasy which swept Europe in the Middle Ages were examples of the results of mass-suggestion—i.e., suggestion made by a crowd, and much more potent than that made by an individual. Cases of so-called collective **hallucination** may be referred to the same cause.

Psychical researchers have been interested in suggestion, since it involves abnormal conditions of mind and body. It may cause and cure diseases, and bad habits, remove inhibitions, improve deficiencies of character, stimulate the imagination, vivify the senses and heighten intellectual powers.

William James described it as "another name for the power of ideas, so far as they prove efficacious over belief and conduct." According to F. W. H. **Myers**, the power is exercised by the subliminal self. He defined suggestion as "successful appeal to the subliminal self." It is well known that dreams may be influenced by external stimuli applied to the sleeper, such as whispering in the ear, or moving the limbs. In modern times, suggestion is a powerful factor in advertising, particularly in the use of persuasive repetition and "subliminal suggestions" in television commercials.

Frank **Podmore** in his book *The Newer Spiritualism* (1910) selected some curious instances to demonstrate the influence of suggestion on the **automatic writing** in Mrs. Leonore **Piper**'s trances. Her script was difficult to read. At a sitting with Miss Bancroft the Hodgson control wrote: "Don't you remember how I had to laugh at you on that boat about that boat." The last word was wrongly deciphered by the sitter as "hat" and she therefore replied: "Whose hat blew off?" The control wrote: "My hat. Do you not remember the day it blew off?" and then proceeded to connect the incident of the hat blowing off with a fishing party. "But Miss Bancroft," continued Podmore, "can remember nothing definite about a hat, and the whole incident was apparently suggested by her misreading of the word."

Such occurrences may shed some light on how it was that Dr. Stanley Hall in a sitting with Mrs. Piper obtained messages from Bessie Beals, a niece after whom he inquired. But the niece had never existed.

An amusing experiment in mass suggestion was tried by a man in London who, for a wager, stopped in what is now Northumberland Avenue and looking at the stone lion on the top of Northumberland House, attracted the attention of the passersby, and when the crowd was big enough began to mutter that the lion was wagging its tail. Some of the crowd accepted the suggestion, the majority passed by, but many waited for hours in the hope of seeing the remarkable phenomenon.

Collective psychic suggestion at a distance was conjectured by M. J. Delevsky, a French mining engineer, to explain such curious coincidences in scientific progress as the simultaneous discovery around 1830 of the non-Euclidian geometry by the German Gauss, the Russian Lobatchewski and the Hungarian Janos Bolyai, quite apart from the works of Schweikart and de Taurinus (*Revue Métapsychique,* November-December 1930).

The same speculation may apply to some amazing coincidences. According to G. D. McIntyre's note in *Psychic Research* (March 1931), "an unusual coincidence in authorship took place in the old McClure's magazine 20 years ago. Two manuscripts arrived on the same day, one from Maine, and the other from Oregon. Save for two words, the opening paragraphs of about 60 words each were identical. Investigation proved that they were written at exactly the same hour, hundreds of miles apart."

To determine to what extent the willpower of a patient is affected by suggestion, Dr. Gaston Durville constructed an apparatus: the suggestometer. It consisted of an elliptical steel spring, furnished with a dial and pointer. The patient, standing upright, with the arms hanging naturally at the sides, squeezes the spring, whereupon the figure on the dial will show his strength. After five or ten minutes rest, the patient repeats the operation, but this time the suggestion is made to him that his arm has now become heavy, his shoulder and forearm numbed, that his fingers are stiff, and that he is quite incapable of gripping. On reading the dial, it is now found that the figure indicated by the pointer is usually much smaller and sometimes it falls to zero. Dr. Durville instituted a "scale of suggestibility," classifying his subjects in five groups, according to the results obtained. (See also **Autosuggestion; Christian Science; Healing by Faith; Hypnotism; New Thought**)

Sukias

Central American witches. (See **America**, United States of)

Summerland

The land of bliss of spirits, so named by Andrew Jackson **Davis**, similar to the "Plane of Illusion" described by the claimed spirit of F. W. H. **Myers** in the book *The Road to Immortality* by Geraldine Cummins (1932).

Summers, Alphonsus Joseph-Mary Augustus Montague (1880-1948)

Leading British scholar of **witchcraft** and **black magic**, born in the Barton Regis district of Clifton, near Bristol, England on April 10, 1880. The youngest of a family of seven children, his father was a banker and Justice of the Peace. Montague Summers was educated at a private academy, then at Clifton College.

Even at the age of sixteen, he had an intimate knowledge of out-of-the-way areas of English literature; he also delighted in a toy theater, which was the beginning of a lifelong interest in the drama. Although brought up in the Anglican Church, he later transferred his allegiance to the Roman Catholic Church.

In 1899, he commenced studies at Trinity College, Oxford, after which he entered Lichfield Theological College as a candidate for holy orders. He took his B.A. in 1905, M.A. 1906, and spent some time in Italy. In 1908, he was ordained deacon and appointed to a curacy in Bath, then in the Bristol suburb of Bitton. It was here that he was prosecuted, together with another clergyman, on a charge of pederasty, although acquitted. In 1909 he was received into the Roman Catholic church. After a brief period of pastoral work in south-east London, he took up residence at Wonersh, near Guildford.

There is some mystery surrounding his ordination to the priesthood, but it is possible that this took place in Italy. At all events, his title of Reverend was accepted as valid, and he maintained his own private oratory at his various residences.

From 1911-26, he was a teacher at various schools, and also published several books during this period. He became a respected authority on Restoration literature and drama, and the Gothic novelists of the eighteenth and nineteenth centuries. He also became world famous for his writings on **Magic, Demonology, Vampires, Werwolves** and Witches, and accumulated a unique library of thousands of rare and curious volumes in Greek, Latin, Italian, Spanish, French and German, as well as English.

Strange rumors surrounded this plump, pink-faced priestly scholar who admired Oscar Wilde and respected the writings of black magician Aleister **Crowley** although castigating black magic in his own writings and maintaining that witches were rightly burnt. He seems to have been something of a split personality, combining piety, kindness and learning with an unholy fascination with evil, stern morality with secret lust. In his later years he lived and studied at Oxford, and is remembered as a picturesque and somewhat sinister figure in a broad black cloak, with bejewelled hands and a high-pitched feminine voice.

His many important publications included: *The History of Witchcraft & Demonology* (1926; reprinted 1956), *The Geography of Witchcraft* (1927; reprinted 1958), *The Vampire: His Kith and Kin* (1928; reprinted 1960), *The Vampire in Europe* (1929; reprinted 1962), *The Werewolf* (1933; reprinted 1966), *The Restoration Theatre* (1934), *A Bibliography of the Restoration Drama* (1935; 1943), *A Popular History of Witchcraft* (1937; reprinted 1973), *The Gothic Quest; a History of the Gothic Novel* (1938), *A Gothic Bibliography* (1940), *Witchcraft and Black Magic* (1946; 1957; reprinted 1974), *The Physical Phenomena of Mysticism* (1950).

In addition to his many articles and his editions of Restoration drama and miscellaneous works, Summers also edited *Malleus Maleficarum* (1928; reprinted 1974), *Compendium Maleficarum* (1929), *Demonolatry* (1930; reprinted 1974), *The Discoverie of Witchcraft* by R. Scott (1930), *The Supernatural Omnibus, being a collection of stories* (1931; reprinted 1932; 1974), *The Confessions of Madeleine Bavent* (1933), *Victorian Ghost Stories* (1933), *The Grimoire and other supernatural stories* (1936).

For a detailed bibliography see *A Bibliography of the Works of Montague Summers* by Timothy d'Arch Smith (University Books, 1964; revised ed. 1983). For biographical information see: *Montague Summers, a Memoir by Joseph Jerome* (London, 1965). Summers' autobiography *The Galanty Show* was announced for publication in 1948 but not issued at the time. It was eventually published by Cecil Woolf, London, 1980.

Summers died August 10, 1948.

Summit Lighthouse

A religious and philosophical organization founded in 1958 under the guidance of the **Masters** El Morya and Saint Germain, claiming authority from the **Great White Brotherhood**,

"Morya" echoes the **Theosophical Society** Mahatma, while "St. Germain" recalls the **I AM** cult of Guy W. **Ballard**.

The organization is now known as **Church Universal and Triumphant**, although the name "Summit Lighthouse" has been retained for the publishing division.

Literature and cassette tape recordings of lectures by Elizabeth Clare Prophet, leader of the Church Universal and Triumphant are now available from: Summit Lighthouse, P.O. Box A, Malibu, California 90265.

Summons by the Dying

It was formerly maintained by theologians that if anyone who was unjustly accused or persecuted should, with his dying breath summon his oppressor to appear before the supreme tribunal, a miracle would take place, and the person thus summoned would die on the day fixed by his innocent victim.

Thus the Grand Master of the **Templars** cited the Pope and the King of France to appear before God on a certain date not very far ahead, and the story goes on to relate that both died at the appointed time.

François I, Duke of Brittany, hired assassins to murder his brother in 1450. The dying prince summoned his murderer before the highest of all courts, and François shortly expired. Yet another instance was that of Ferdinand IV, of Spain, who was summoned by two nobles whom he had condemned unjustly, and he also responded reluctantly at the end of thirty days.

Many more examples could be quoted to show how firmly rooted was this belief in the power of the dying to avenge their death by supernatural means. Indeed, it would be safe to say that, by an inversion of the usual order of cause and effect, the popular faith in the efficacy of the summons was responsible for such evidence as was forthcoming on its behalf.

Fear, and possibly remorse, acting on the imagination of the guilty person, might well cause him to expire at the stated time, and authenticated accounts of death caused by these agents are not unknown.

This is further borne out by the fact that if the condemned man was guilty—that is, if the judge's conscience was clear—the summons had no effect. Sorcerers, especially, summoned their judges, but in vain.

An old story tells of Gonzalo of Cordova (1453-1515), who sentenced a soldier to death for sorcery. The soldier exclaimed that he was innocent, and summoned Gonzalo to appear before God. "go, then," said the judge, "and hasten the proceedings. My brother who is in heaven, will appear for me." Gonzalo did not die at that time, as he believed he had dealt justly and had no fear of the consequences of the summons.

Sundari, T(irunelveli) A(vudaippan) (1934-)

School psychologist who has also taken an active interest in parapsychology. Born December 25, 1934 at Dindigul, Madras State, India, she studied at Presidency College, Madras (B.A. hons. psychology 1956), Madras University (M.Litt. 1959).

She was a researcher, Department of Psychology, Madras University from 1956-59, psychologist, Juvenile Guidance Bureau, Egnore, Madras from 1959-60, psychologist, Government Girls' Approved School and the Vigilance Home, Madras from 1960 onwards. She is a member of Madras Psychological Society.

Her master's thesis was on 'Experimental Studies in Time Perception,' and she has attempted to train subjects in precognition. She has collected data relating to clairvoyance and telepathy.

Sunderland, La Roy (1804-1885)

Nineteenth-century demonstrator of **animal magnetism** or **hypnotism**, who attempted to popularize his own term of **"pathetism."**

He was born May 18, 1804, in Exeter, Rhode island, and apprenticed to a shoemaker. He became converted to methodism and became a revivalist preacher at the age of eighteen. He had a reputation as an orator of great power and was prominent in the temperance and anti-slavery movement, presiding at the meeting in New York in October 1834 when the first Methodist anti-slavery society was organized. He was a delegate to the first anti-slavery convention at Cincinnati in 1841 and the World Convention in London in 1843.

He was founder and editor of the *Watchman* (1835-42) and also edited the *Magnet* (1842), in which he expounded his beliefs in mesmeric power and suggestion. In 1851, he founded *The Spiritual Philosopher*, the first Spiritualist periodical in America. A year later, the title changed to *The Spirit World*. Although in the first issue he criticized the spirit theory and the evidence adduced on its behalf, he quickly became a believer when his own daughter, Mrs. Margarette Cooper, became a medium.

His enthusiasm cooled somewhat in the following year as a result of a hoax played upon him, and he warned his readers against believing that all the phenomena ascribed to spirit intervention had necessarily an extra-mundane cause, as many might be due to unconscious action on the part of the medium.

He made a special study of animal magnetism and **Mesmerism**, and in 1843 published *Pathetism; With Practical Instructions: Demonstrating the Falsity of the Hitherto Prevalent Assumptions in regard to what has been called "Mesmerism" and "Neurology," and Illustrating those Laws which Induce Somnambulism, Second Sight, Sleep, Dreaming, Trance, and Clairvoyance, with Numerous Facts tending to show the Pathology of Monomania, Insanity, Witchcraft, and Various Other Mental or Nervous Phenomena.*

Sunderland was also an exponent of **Phrenology**, which he combined with pathetism in his demonstrations. Of special interest is the fact that he sometimes exhibited painless tooth extraction with entranced subjects, and on two occasions even the dentist was also hypnotized. Sunderland's ideas were mentioned by James **Braid**, whose term "hypnotism" eventually won general consent.

In 1868, Sunderland's doubts about spirit phenomena returned, and in his book *The Trance and Correlative Phenomena* he proposed pathetism as a sufficient explanation, stating that neither mediums nor spirits have ever been able to show where human actions end and the real spiritual begins in phenomena.

Sunderland's other books included: *Biblical Institutes* (1834), *Appeal on the Subject of Slavery* (1834), *History of the United States* (1834), *History of South America* (1834), *Testimony of God Against Slavery* (1834), *Anti-Slavery Manual* (1837), *Mormonism Exposed* (1842), *Book of Health* (1847), *Pathetism; Statement of its Philosophy, and its Discovery Defended* (1850), *Book of Psychology* (1852), *Theory of Nutrition and Philosophy of Healing Without Medicine* (1853), *The Trance, and How Introduced* (1860).

He died in Quincy, Massachusetts, May 15, 1885.

Super-Extrasensory Perception

Term used by parapsychologists for the hypothesis that some individuals may have unlimited powers of acquiring information from living persons or objects, thus making the conventional Spiritualist explanation of discarnate entities unnecessary. (See also **Extrasensory perception**)

Supernatural

An occurrence in violation of the known laws of nature. Spiritualism contends that the phenomena of the seance room are ruled by as yet unknown laws and rejects the term.

The term "paranormal" is now more generally used. An earlier term "**supernormal**" is sometimes used.

Supernormal

Term substituted in Spiritualism for "**supernatural**." It was coined by F. W. H. **Myers** and was aplied to phenomena which are beyond what usually happens—beyond, that is, in the sense of suggesting unknown physical laws. While supernormal phenomena point to new powers, abnormal phenomena indicate the degeneration of powers already acquired. In modern times, the term "paranormal" is preferred.

Supersensonics

Term devised by New Age teacher Christopher **Hills** to indicate a science of subtle energy therapeutics, involving **radiesthesia, radionics**, homeopathy, Bach flower remedies, and related fields. (See also **Bach Centre**)

Supreme Council of the Independent Associated Spiritualists

Founded in 1925 as a federation of churches and groups of churches concerned with Spiritualism. It participates in research on psychic phenomena, psychic photography and spiritual healing. It is affiliated with Duke Research Foundation. Address: 7230 Fourth Street North, #2304, St. Petersburg, Florida 33702.

Survival

The continued possession of personality after the change called death. It is the fundamental doctrine of Spiritualism and an object of investigation, although in an indirect manner, of psychical research.

The basis of survival is the contention that mind can exist independently of brain, that thought is not the result of changes in the brain, but that these changes (as William **James** suggested in his book *Human Immortality,* 1903) merely coincide with the flow of thought through it, the brain fulfilling the role of an instrument of transmission. **Thought transference** and experiments in **telepathy** furnished the first scientific support of this contention.

The **trance** communications received through the mediumship of Mrs. Leonore **Piper** convinced many famous skeptical investigators that the communicators survived the change of death. Even Mrs. **Sidgwick** admitted in her brilliant but extremely skeptical study of Mrs. Piper's phenomena: "Veridical communications are received, some of which, there is good reason to believe, come from the dead, and therefore imply a genuine communicator in the background." (*Proceedings* of the Society for Psychical Research (vol. 28 December 1915, p. 204)

The arguments for and against survival are mainly centered around the evidential value of such communications. The first and most powerful point of attack is made on the subconscious front. The communicating personality is said to be artificial, a masquerading secondary self, and that the occasional supernormal information lies within the bounds of acquisition of the subconscious mind.

It is also pointed out that many of the communications are erroneous, of a lying nature, uncharacteristic of the dead and easily obtainable by fraudulent means.

The arguments for survival deny the sufficiency of subconscious powers as an explanation, pointing to the distinct personalities of the communicators, their greatly differing abilities to communicate, their recognition of old friends, their behavior, temper, memories and ability to give information outside the mind of everybody present and perhaps of everybody living.

They also point out the inconsistency of the telepathic theory in those frequent cases where mistakes are committed or confusion is evidenced, the selectiveness which it would postulate in fishing out the appropriate information from the subconscious mind of others and the power to weave them into a consistent personality, and that it gradually leads to the supposition of a cosmic mind which is tapped by the telepathist, forming thereby a more far reaching and less justified theory than individual survival. As a direct evidence against telepathy, the results of some astonishing **cross-correspondences, book** (and newspaper) **tests** are quoted. They present a strong case.

Philosophic speculation has often supported the concept of survival. Professors P. G. Tait and Balfour **Stewart** posited in their book, *The Unseen Universe* (1875), that the main realities of the universe are not in matter at all, but in the ether of space. Although the concept of the ether has since been refuted, the enigma of the relationship between matter and consciousness remains, and it is feasible that consciousness continues to survive the death and disintegrating changes of the physical body. This implies that consciousness is a superior system to matter.

According to Sir Oliver **Lodge**, "the marvel is that we are associated with matter at all . . . I used to say that death was an adventure to which we might look forward. So it is; but I believe that really and truly it is earth-life that is the adventure. It is this earth-life that has been the strange and exceptional thing. The wonder is that we ever succeeded in entering a matter body at all. Many fail." (*Phantom Walls*, 1929). In the same book he also considered the possibility of grades of survival, stating: "Now survival only applies to things that really exist. If there is no individuality, then there is nothing to persist. Whether all human beings have sufficient personality to make their individual persistence likely is a question that may be argued. Whether some of the higher animals have acquired a kind of individuality, a character and wealth of affection which seem worthy of continued existence, may also be argued. There may be many grades of personality, and accordingly there may be many grades of survival."

The subjective experience of **out-of-the-body** traveling or **astral projection** is often cited as presumptive evidence that the personality can exist independently of the body. (See also **Death; Identity; Immortality; Out-of-the-Body; Personality; Psychical Research; Spiritualism**)

Recommended reading:

Baird, Alexander T. *One Hundred Cases for Survival After Death*, Bernard Ackerman, New York, 1944

Beard, Paul. *Survival of Death; For and Against,* Hodder & Stoughton, London, 1966
Broad, C. D. *Personal Identity and Survival,* Society for Psychical Research (pamphlet), London, 1968
Crookall, Robert. *Case-Book of Astral Projection,* 545-746, University Books, 1972
Ducasse, C. J. *A Critical Examination of the Belief in a Life After Death,* Charles C. THomas, Springfield, Illinois, 1961
Garrett, Eileen J. (ed.). *Does Man Survive Death?; A Symposium,* Garrett/Helix, New York, 1957
Hart, Hornell. *The Enigma of Survival; The Case For and Against an After Life,* C. C. Thomas, Springfield, Illinois, 1959
Jacobson, Nils Olof. *Life Without Death?; On Parapsychology, Mysticism and the Question of Survival,* Delacorte Press, 1973, Turnstone Books, London/Dell, 1974
Myers, F. W. H. *Human Personality and its Survival of Bodily Death,* 2 vols., Longmans, Green, London, 1903; Arno Press, 1975; abridged one vol. ed., University Books, 1961
Rogo, D. Scott. *Welcoming Silence; A Study of Psychical Phenomena and Survival of Death,* University Books, 1973
Salter, W. H. *Zoar; or, The Evidence of Psychical Research Concerning Survival,* Sidgwick & Jackson, London, 1961
Saltmarsh, H. F. *Evidence of Personal Survival From Cross Correspondences,* G. Bell, London, 1939
Smith, Susy. *Life is Forever; Evidence for Survival After Death,* Putnam, 1974

Survival Joint Research Committee Trust

British organization founded in 1963, "exclusively concerned with survival of human personality after bodily death." In November 1987, the Trust held a one-day E. J. Dingwall Memorial Conference on 'Science and Survival.' Address: 47 Mayfield Road, Hornsey, London, N8 9LL, England. (See also **Survival**)

Survival League, The

British organization founded in London by Mrs. C. A. Dawson Scott in October 1929, to affirm the unity of all religions and spread the knowledge of the scientific demonstrability of **survival** after death. The first chairman was author H. Dennis **Bradley**. The Survival League of America was an affiliated organization.

No longer active.

Survival Magazine

Spiritualist monthly, founded in 1929, incorporating *Immortality and Survival,* official organ of The **Survival League** but independent. No longer published.

Survival Research Foundation

Incorporated 1971 by author and psychical researcher Susy **Smith**. The foundation is engaged in scientific research into the question of human survival after death and in related educational activities.

It launched "Project: Unrecorded Information" based on cipher tests for survival devised by Prof. Robert H. **Thouless** and Frank C. Tribbe and on a lock test devised by Dr. Ian **Stevenson**. This long-term project is to educate the public concerning these tests, to encourage their use, to conduct controlled experiments and obtain multiple replications. A number of successes would provide evidence strongly supportive of the **survival** hypothesis.

The directors of the Foundation include Honorary President Prof. Robert H. **Thouless**, President and Chairman of Board of Directors Arthur S. **Berger** (project director of the **Psychical Research Foundation**), Vice-Chairman and Secretary Joyce Berger (former associate editor of *Theta*), General Counsel and Director Frank C. Tribbe, Director Susy Smith. Address: P.O. Box 8565, Pembroke Pines, Florida 33084 (See also **Survival**)

Swaffer, Hannen (1879-1962)

Journalist, drama critic, author and publicist for Spiritualism. He was born November 1, 1879, in Lindfield, Sussex and educated at Stroud Green Grammar School. The family moved to London and lived next door to neighbors who were wealthy enough to all have bicycles. The young Swaffer found that the neighbor was a journalist, and thereupon determined that this would be his profession. Many years later, that neighbor worked for Swaffer on the *Weekly Dispatch*.

Swaffer joined the *Daily Mail* in 1902 and spent a number of years working under Lord Northcliffe, becoming in succession, news editor, art editor, night editor and assistant editor of the *Daily Mirror*. He originated a gossip column on the *Daily Sketch,* which was soon extensively copied by other newspapers. He also worked on the *Daily Herald* and was drama critic for the *Daily Express*. He was editor of the *Weekly Dispatch*, and later of *The People*.

For many years, "Swaff" was a familiar and eccentric figure in London's Fleet Street, center of the national newspaper offices. He affected somewhat Bohemian costume, as befitted a drama critic, and was popularly known as "The Poet."

He became convinced of **survival** in 1924, through attending direct voice sittings with the medium Mrs. Osborne **Leonard** in the circle of H. Dennis **Bradley**. These sittings were strongly evidential of the survival of Swaffer's old chief Lord Northcliffe, who had died in 1922.

Swaffer published accounts of the seances in *The People,* and created a sensation with his book *Northcliffe's Return* (1924). His other books included: *Behind the Scenes* (1928), *Adventures with Inspiration* (1929), *Hannen Swaffer's Who's Who* (1929), *Studies in Psychology* (1933).

He became an indefatigable propagandist for Spiritualism, and argued that Spiritualism and socialism were two halves of one great whole. He succeeded Sir Arthur Conan **Doyle** as honorary president of the **Spiritualists' National Union** and the **Spiritualist Community**, and was connected with other Spiritualist organizations.

In 1932, Swaffer was one of the three cofounders of the well-known British newspaper *Psychic News*—the other two were his accountant Jack Rubens and friend Maurice **Barbanell** (who became editor for many years).

For biographical information on Swaffer, see *"Swaff"; The Life & Times of* Hannen Swaffer by Tom Driberg (Macdonald, London, 1974).

He died January 16, 1962.

Swain, Mrs. Marcia M. (1819-1900)

Voice medium of a **rescue circle** in Buffalo from 1875-1900 under the direction of Leander Fisher, a music teacher and medium.

Daniel E. Bailey, a wealthy man, took interest in the work and at his death made provision for the support of Mrs. Swain for the rest of her life. She was never a public medium, and did not give seances for money.

D. E. Bailey's book *Thoughts from the Inner Life* (Boston, 1886) dwelt largely on Mrs. Swain's work in the **rescue circle,** the activity of which was devoted to the enlightenment of the dead in making them realize their true condition.

Swaminarayan, Shree (1781-1830)

Famous saint of nineteenth-century India, born as Nilakantha at Capaiya, near Ayodhya. He developed a revised form of the traditional *Vishishadvaita* **Vedanta** of Shree Ramanujan and traveled all over India for thirty years with his disciples, initiating a powerful religious revival which had great impact upon the masses in Gujarat, Saurashtra and Kutch.

The movement eradicated violence, drunkenness and lawlessness on a large scale and attracted favorable notice from the Christian Bishop Heber and the British rulers.

Shree Swaminarayan performed miracles and was accepted by his followers as in incarnation of God and the first of a succession of such incarnations, of which His Holiness Shree Pramukh Swami is the current living representative.

Modern followers of Shree Swaminarayan number hundreds of thousands, and prior to the recent expulsion of Asians from Uganda, this faith was widespread amongst Indian people throughout East Africa. The Swaminarayan faith is one of the most popular traditional Hindu sects in Great Britain amongst Asian immigrants.

Recommended reading:

Dave, H. T. *Life and Philosophy of Shree Swaminarayan,* 1781-1930, Allen & Unwin, London, 1974

Swann, Ingo (1933-)

Prominent American psychic and author. Born September 14, 1933 at Telluride, Colorado, he studied at Westminster College, Salt Lake City, receiving a bachelor's degree in biology 1955. He enlisted in the U.S. Army and served three years in Korea. Afterwards he lived in New York City, where he worked for twelve years at the United Nations Secretariat, painting pictures as a hobby in his free time.

During the 1960s, he became actively interested in **Scientology,** which released a psychic potential which had been partly evident in childhood. Thereafter he took part in a number of laboratory experiments in parapsychology.

In October 1972 he experimented with Cleve **Backster** in attempting to influence plants by mental activity. Later psychokinetic experiments involved successfully influencing temperature recording in a controlled setting devised by parapsychologists Gertrude **Schmeidler** and Larry Lewis at City College, New York. This involved PK effects upon target thermistors (temperature measuring devices) in insulated thermos bottles at a distance of 25 feet from Swann.

For a report, see G. .R. Schmeidler, 'PK Effects Upon Continuously Recorded Temperature' (*Journal* of the American Society for Psychical Research No. 4, Oct. 1973).

Swann also took part in other experiments from 1973 onwards at **Stanford Research Institute,** Menlo Park, California with parapsychologist Harold E. **Puthoff.** One of the most remarkable experiments involved a successful attempt to influence the stable magnetic field inside a quark detector (a complex apparatus designed to detect subatomic particles). The apparatus was completely inaccessible, being encased in aluminum and copper containers with protective shield, buried in five feet of concrete. There could be no possibility of fraudulent physical interference. When Swann mentally visualized the hidden target, significant variations were recorded in sine waves.

This extraordinary PK effect was reported at a Conference on Quantum Physics and Parapsychology (see H. E. Puthoff & Russell Targ, 'Physics, Entrophy, and Psychokinesis' in *Proceedings of the Conference on Quantum Physics and Parapsychology, Geneva, August 26-27, 1974,* Parapsychology Foundation).

Swann was also the subject of experiments in **Out-of-the-Body** travel, or psychic perception at a distance. These took place in 1972 at the American Society for Psychical Research. They involved Swann sitting in a chair and attempting to project his consciousness to a sealed box on a small platform several feet above his head, in which there was a target symbol completely shielded from view. Swann was monitored by electrodes which would have recorded any movement from the chair.

Under these difficult laboratory conditions, Swann nevertheless scored significant success in describing the targets, and in one test he was actually able to state correctly that a light which should have illuminated the target had somehow been inoperative.

There was no normal way of ascertaining this fact from ground level, since the interior of the target box could only be inspected from an overhead position several feet in the air.

In another extraordinary out-of-body experiment conducted by parapsychologists Harold Puthoff and Russell **Targ** at Stanford Research Institute March 11, 1974, Swann "visited" the planets Mercury and Jupiter in a joint "psychic probe" shared by fellow psychic Harold **Sherman.**

Swann is author of *To Kiss Earth Goody-bye* (Hawthorn Books, 1975; Laurel/Dell paperback, 1975), which has a foreword by parapsychologist Gertrude Schmeidler.

In this book Swann describes his early out-of-body experiences in childhood.

Swann, William F(rancis) G(ray) (1884-1962)

Physicist and educator, who wrote on parapsychology. Born August 29, 1884 at Ironbridge, Shropshire, England, he studied at the Royal College of Science, London, University College, King's College, University of London, and City and Guilds of London Institute. In 1909 he married Sara Thompson; his second marriage in 1955 was to Helene Diedrichs.

Dr. Swann was an authority on cosmic radiation and atomic structure, and was head of the Bartol Research Foundation of Franklin Institute, Swarthmore for thirty-two years. He had previously taught at the Royal College of Science, London and at the University of Sheffield.

In 1913 he was head of the physical division of the Department of Terrestrial Magnetism at the Carnegie Institution, Washington, D.C. He taught physics at University of Minnesota, from 1918-23, University of Chicago from 1923-24, Yale University from 1924-27. He was awarded honorary degrees by London University, Yale, Swarthmore and Temple.

In 1960 he was a member of a number of scholarly and scientific societies in Britain and the U.S. He was awarded the Elliott Cresson Medal of the Franklin Institute for research in cosmic radiation. He contributed a number of papers to learned journals. His interest in parapsychology was by way of physics and philosophy, and his articles in this area included: (in *Journal of the Franklin Institute*) 'Is the Universe Planned?' (May, 1953), 'The Known and the Unknown' (May 1955), 'Nature and the Mind of Man' (June 1956), 'Reality, Imagery and Fantasy' (May 1957), 'The Science of Yesterday, Today and Tomorrow' (March 1960).

He died January 29, 1962 at Swarthmore, Pennsylvania.

Swastika

One of the most important and widespread symbols of ancient religion, mysticism and magic is the swastika or *tetraskelion.* Essentially it is a Greek cross with arms of equal length, each with four arms at right angles, either right-handed (regarded as a male symbol implying good fortune) or left-handed (female symbol). The right-handed form is sometimes known as *gammadion,* i.e., formed from joining up four gamma letters.

The swastika is generally regarded as a symbol of the power of the sun, and may have been derived from a circle divided into four by cross lines. A variation of the swastika is the *Triskele* ("three-legged") form, often found on Sicilian coins and used as the emblem of the Isle of Man off the coast of Britain.

The swastika dates back to the Neolithic Age, when it was engraved on stone implements, but it has also been found in many cultures—in ancient Britain, Ireland, Mycenae and Gascony, as well as amongst the Etruscans, Celts, Hindus, Germanic peoples, Central Asians and pre-Columbian Americans. The Buddhists regarded it as a *chakra* or wheel of the Law; the Tibetans called it *Yun-drun* or path of life. The swastika has traveled from Troy and Mycenae down to the 9th century in Ireland, as well as Persia, China, North Africa and Scandinavia.

Some authorities have interpreted the swastika as indicating the deity during the Iron Age, others have associated it with agriculture and compass points and the origin of the universe. No doubt this universally diffused symbol has acquired many secondary associations in addition to its main representation of a sun wheel.

The name "swastika" derives from its long established use in India, where the expression *Su-asti* means "Be well," implying auspiciousness and good fortune. Hindu parents mark the symbol on the breast and forehead of a baby, and a swastika formed of ears of wheat is marked in the birth chamber. Hindu writers often place a red swastika at the beginning and end of manuscripts; the sign is also marked on floors and paths at weddings. There is a Hatha Yoga sitting position known as "Swatikasana" or the auspicious posture, in which the legs are crossed and the feet rest on opposite thighs.

The used of the swastika as a Nazi symbol may have derived from German scholarship in the field of Hindu folklore and religion, distorted by such pseudo-mystical occultists as Guido von **List,** who originated weird theories of Germanic and Nordic folklore as early as the 1870s. According to von List, the swastika was a symbol of a secret band of initiates called the Armanen or "children of the sun," who flourished in ancient times.

It may also have been reputable scholarly discussions of the Indo-European migrations of ancient peoples and cultures that were perverted to antisemitic doctrines of an Aryan master-race. Before World War I, the use of the swastika symbol was popular amongst romantic youth folklore movements like the *Wandervögel.* It was continued by political revolutionaries who had been *Wandervögel* members and by Hitler's National Socialist German Workers' Party in the post-war period.

The Nazi swastika was designed by Dr. Friedrich Krohn, formerly a member of the Germanen Order, a fanatical secret order founded by followers of Guido von List. Krohn's design was adopted around 1920. Ever since, this ancient Hindu sacred symbol of auspiciousness has become inextricably associated with the perverse doctrines, blood lust and sadomasochistic madness of the German Nazis.

Swawm

Burmese Vampires. (See **Burma**)

SWEDEN

Witchcraft

In 1649, Queen Christina had banned witch trials, stating that witchcraft confession of women were due to illusions or disorders of health. However, there was an extraordinary outbreak of witchcraft hysteria between 1669-70 at Mora, in Dalecarlia, resulting in the burning of eighty-five individuals accused of transporting no less than three hundred children by magical flights to a witches sabbat on the island of **Blockula.**

On July 5, 1668, the pastor of Elfdale in Dalecarlia stated that Gertrude Svensen, aged eighteen, had been accused by Eric Ericsen, aged fifteen, of stealing children for the Devil. There followed similar charges. Then in May 1669, King Charles XI appointed a commission to look into the matter and attempt to redeem the accused by prayers rather than punishment or torture. However, the prayers resulted in mass hysteria amongst the three thousand people who had assembled.

The commissioners claimed to have discovered seventy adult witches, who were all burned, together with fifteen children. Fifty-six other children were given lesser sentences and punished by having to run the gauntlet or be lashed with rods.

The witches were said to have carried the children on goats, sticks or the backs of sleeping men, even flying through windows. One writer recorded that "being asked how they could go with their Bodies through Chimneys and broken panes of Glass, they said, that the Devil did first remove all that might hinder them in their flight, and so they had room enough to go." They assembled for their sabbat in a large meadow, where they feasted, danced and performed diabolical rituals.

Commenting on the affair, Bishop Francis Hutchinson stated in his book *An Historical Essay Concerning Witchcraft* (1718): "Is it not plain that the people had frightened their children with so many tales, that they could not sleep without dreaming of the devil, and then made the poor women of the town confess what the children said of them."

Other witchcraft persecutions followed, and between 1674-75, seventy-one individuals were burned or beheaded in three parishes. There was also a witchcraft mania in Stockholm in following years, but when it was discovered that accusations were due to the malice or greed of young informers, Charles XI proscribed witchcraft prosecutions.

Spiritualism and Psychical Research

In the inter-war years, there was general apathy or hostility to Spiritualism, fortune-telling and psychic matters.

On March 14, 1931, a Bill was presented to the Swedish Parliament with the intention of regularizing mediumship and legitimizing psychical research. Unfortunately it did not succeed and Spiritualism was actively discouraged. However, there was a revival of interest in the postwar period. A branch of the **Churches' Fellowship for Psychic and Spiritualist** Studies was organized, c/o Mrs. Eva Lejam, St. Sodergatan 17, Lund.

In the field of parapsychology, there is the long established Sällskapet för Parapsykologisk Forskning in Stockholm, which has carried out valuable experimental work. Dr. Gösta **Rodhe,** the president, has now been succeeded by Dr. Rolf Evjegård. The former secretary Mrs. Eva **Hellström,** well known as a clairvoyant, was succeeded by Eric Uggla.

The Society maintains a good research library, has organized lectures and meetings, and carried out research in psychometry and precognition. The Society can be contacted: c/o Mrs. Eva Hellstrom, Bjurnbo 62, Lidingo 1. Another important experimenter is Haakon **Forwald,** of Ludvika, who has conducted research in psychokinesis.

Swedenborg, Emanuel (1688-1772)

Swedish seer, primarily a scientist, an authority on metallurgy, a mining and military engineer, a learned astronomer, reputed physicist, zoologist, anatomist, financier and political economist, also a profound Biblical student.

He was born January 29, 1688, at Stockholm, Sweden, son of a professor of Theology at Upsala, afterwards Bishop of Scara. Swedenborg graduated at Upsala University in 1710, and traveled in England, Holland, France and Germany, studying natural philosophy. He studied and was influenced by, the work of the most famous mathematicians and physicians—Sir Isaac Newton, Flamsteed, Halley and De Lahire. He made sketches of inventions as varied as a flying machine, a submarine, a rapid-fire gun, an air pump and a fire engine. He wrote many poems in Latin and when, after five years of study he returned to Sweden, he was appointed Assessor of the Royal College of Mines.

Originally known as Swedberg, nobility was bestowed upon him by Queen Ulrica, and he changed his name to Swedenborg.

Sitting in the House of Nobles, his political utterances had great weight, but his tendencies were distinctly democratic. He busied himself privately in scientific gropings for the explanation of the universe, and published at least two works dealing with the origin of things which are of no great account, unless as foreshadowing many scientific facts and ventures of the future.

Thus his theories regarding light, cosmic atoms, geology and physics, were distinctly in advance of histime, and had they been suitably disseminated could not but have influenced scientific Europe.

In 1734 he published his *Prodomus Philosophiœ Ra tiocinantrio de Infinite* which treats of the relation of the finite to the infinite and of the soul to the body. In this work he sought to establish a definite connection between the two as a means of overcoming the difficulty of their relationship. The spiritual and the divine appeared to him as the supreme study of man.

He searched the countries of Europe in quest of the most eminent teachers and the best books dealing with anatomy, for he considered that in that science lay the germ of the knowledge of soul and spirit. Through his anatomical studies he anticipated certain modern views dealing with the functions of the brain, which are most remarkable.

At the height of his scientific career he resigned his office to devote the rest of his life to the spreading of the spiritual enlightenment, for which he believed himself to have been specially selected by God.

He showed signs of psychic power as a child. His ability to cease breathing for a considerable period probably means that he passed into the state of trance. He had gifts of clairvoyance. Kant investigated and found the story authentic that in Gothenburg he observed and reported a fire which was raging in Stockholm, 300 miles away. In his book *Dreams of a Spirit Seer* Kant narrated several paranormal experiences from Swedenborg's early life.

Swedenborg's real illumination and intercourse with the spiritual world in visions and dreams began in April, 1744. In a conscious state he wandered in the spirit world and conversed with its inhabitants as freely as with living men.

He was in a sense, the first Spiritualist. Few who went before him communed with the spirits of departed men. Spirits were considered a different order of beings. The great principle of continuity was not known. It was he who bridged the gulf between life and death. But he could not completely break with theological tradition. He still distinguished between heaven and hell but not in the orthodox sense. Of mediumship, he knew little. Spirits of kings, popes, saints, apostles and biblical personalities were his instructors. Of spirit identity, there are only a dozen evidential cases in his writings.

About the age of fifty-five a profound change overtook the character of Swedenborg. Up to this time he had been a scientist, legislator, and man of affairs, but now his inquiries into the region of spiritual things were to divorce him entirely from practical matters. His introduction into the spiritual world, his illumination, was commenced by dreams and extraordinary visions.

He heard wonderful conversations and felt impelled to found a new church. He said that the eyes of his spirit were so opened that he could see heavens and hells, and converse with angels and spirits, but all his doctrines relating to the New Church

He claimed that God revealed Himself to him and told him that He had chosen him to unveil the spiritual sense of the whole scriptures to man. From that moment, worldly knowledge was eschewed by Swedenborg and he worked for spiritual ends alone. He resigned his several appointments and retired upon half pay. Refreshing his knowledge of the Hebrew language, he commenced his great works on the interpretation of the scriptures.

After the year 1747, he lived in Sweden, Holland and London, and died in London on March 29, Prince's Square, in the parish of St. George's in the East London, but in April 1908 his bones were removed, at the request of the Swedish government for reburial in Stockholm.

There can be no question as to the intrinsic honesty of Swedenborg's mind and character. He was neither presumptuous nor overbearing as regards his doctrines, but gentle and reasonable. A man of few wants, his life was simplicity itself, his food consisting for the most part of bread, milk and coffee. He was in the habit of lying in a trance for days together, and day and night had no distinctions for him. His mighty wrestlings with evil spirits at times so terrified his servants that they would seek refuge in the most distant part of the house. He would converse with benign angels in broad daylight.

His descriptions of the spirit world fall in the main into two classes: experimental writings and dogmatic writings. His accounts of what he saw and felt in the spirit world agree fundamentally with present-day spirit teachings, but his theological writings which led to the establishment of the New Church and Swedenborgianism are not only highly involved, but appear to be arbitrary and, though attributed to spirit instruction, suggest a subconscious elaboration of his preconceived ideas.

So far from attempting to divide or interfere with existing religious systems, Swedenborg was of the opinion that the members of all churches could belong to his New Church in a spiritual sense. His works may be divided into (1) expository volumes, notably *The Apocalypse Revealed, The Apocalypse Explained,* and *Arcana Celestia;* books of spiritual philosophy, such as *Intercourse between the Soul and the Body Divine Providence,* and *Divine Love and Wisdom;* (2) books dealing with the hierarchy of supernatural spheres such as *Heaven and Hell* and *The Last Judgment;* and those which are purely doctrinal, such as *The New Jerusalem, The True Christian Religion,* and *Canons of the New Church.*

Of these works, his *Divine Love and Wisdom* is the volume which most succinctly presents his entire religious system. God he regarded as the Divine Man. Spiritually He consists of infinite love, and corporeally of infinite wisdom. From the divine love, all things draw nourishment. The sun, as we know it, is merely a microcosm of a spiritual sun which emanates from the Creator. This spiritual sun is thethe source of nature; but whereas the first is alive, the second is inanimate.

There is no connection between the two worlds of nature and spirit unless in similarity of construction. Love, wisdom, use; and end, cause and effect, are the three infinite and uncreated degrees of being in God and man respectively. The causes of all things exist in the spiritual sphere and their effects in the natural sphere, and the end of all creation is that man may become the image of his Creator, and of the cosmos as a whole. This is to be effected by a love of the degrees enumerated above.

Man possesses two vessels or receptacles for the containment of God—the Will for divine love, and the Understanding for divine wisdom. Before the Fall, the flow of these virtues into the human spirit was perfect, but through the intervention of the forces of evil, and the sins of man himself, it was much interrupted. Seeking to restore the connection between Himself and man, God came into the world as Man, for if He had ventured on earth in His unveiled splendor, he would have destroyed the hells through which he must proceed to redeem man, and this He did not wish to do, merely to conquer them.

The unity of God is an essential of the Swedenborgian theology, and he thoroughly believed that God did not return to His own place without leaving behind Him a visible representative of Himself in the word of scripture, which is an eternal incarnation, in a threefold sense—natural, spiritual and celestial. Of this Swedenborg was the apostle. Nothing seemed hidden from him; he claimed to be aware of the appearance and conditions of other worlds, good and evil, heaven and hell, and of the planets. "The life of religion," he stated, "is to accomplish good. . . . The kingdom of heaven is a kingdom of uses."

One of the central ideas of his system is known as the Doctrine of Correspondences. Everything visible has belonging to it an appropriate spiritual reality. Regarding this, Robert A. Vaughan, author of *Hours With the Mystics* (1905) stated: "The history of man is an acted parable; the universe, a temple covered with hieroglyphics. Behmen, from the light which flashes on certain exalted moments, imagines that he receives the key to these hidden significances—that he can interpret the *Signatura Rerum.* But he does not see spirits, or talk with angels. According to him, such communications would be less reliable than the intuition he enjoyed. Swedenborg takes opposite ground. 'What I relate,' he would say, 'comes from no such mere inward persuasion. I recount the things I have seen. I do not labour to recall and to express the manifestation made me in some moment of ecstatic exaltation. I write you down a plain statement of journeys and conversations in the spiritual world, which have made the greater part of my daily history for many years together. I take my stand upon experience. I have proceeded by observation and induction as strict as that of any man of science among you. Only it has been given me to enjoy an experience reaching into two worlds—that of spirit, as well as that of matter.'

"According to Swedenborg, all the mythology and the symbolisms of ancient times were so many refracted or fragmentary correspondences—relics of that better day when every outward object suggested to man's mind its appropriate divine truth. Suchdesultory and uncertain links between the seen and the unseen are so many imperfect attempts toward that harmony of the two worlds which he believed himself commissioned to reveal. The happy thoughts of the artist, the imaginative analogies of the poet, are exchanged with Swedenborg for an elaborate system. All the terms and objects in the natural and spiritual worlds are catalogued in pairs.

"This method appears so much formal pedantry. Our fancies will not work to order. The meaning and the life with which we continually inform outward objects—those suggestions from sight and sound, which make almost every man at times a poet—are our own creations, are determined by the mood of the hour, cannot be imposed from without, cannot be arranged like the nomenclature of a science.

"As regards the inner sense of scripture, at all events, Swedenborg introduces some such yoke. In that province, however, it is perhaps as well that those who are not satisfied with the obvious sense should find some restraint for their imagination, some method for their ingenuity, some guidance in a curiosity irresistible to a certain class of minds. If an objector say, 'I do not see why the ass should correspond to scientific truth, and the horse to intellectual truth,' Swedenborg will reply, 'This analogy rests on no fancy of mine, but on actual experience and observation in the spiritual world. I have always seen horses and asses present and circumstanced, when, and according as, those inward qualities were central.'

"But I do not believe that it was the design of Swedenborg rigidly to determine the relationships by which men are continually uniting the seen and unseen worlds. He probably conceived it his mission to disclose to men the divinely-ordered correspondences of scripture, the close relationship of man's several states of being, and to make mankind more fully aware that matter and spirit were associated, not only in the varying analogies of imagination, but by the deeper affinity of eternal law.

"In this way, he sought to impart an impulse rather than to prescribe a scheme. His consistent followers will acknowledge that had he lived to another age, and occupied a different social position, the forms under which the spiritual world presented itself in him would have been different. To a large extent, therefore, his *Memorable Relations* must be regarded as true for him only—for such a character, in such a day, though containing principles independent of personal peculiarity and local colouring. It would have been indeed inconsistent, had the Protestant who (as himself a Reformer) essayed to supply the defects and correct the errors of the Reformation—had he designed to prohibit all advance beyond his own position."

The style of Swedenborg is clear-cut and incisive. He is never overpowered by manifestations from the unseen. Whereas other mystics were seized by fear or joy by these and often became incomprehensible, he is in his element, and when on the very pinnacles of ecstasy can observe the smallest details with a scientific eye.

We know nowadays that a great many of his visions do not square with scientific probabilities. Thus those which detail his journeys among the planets and describe the flora and fauna of Mars, for example, can be totally disproved, as we are aware that such forms of life as he claims to have seen could not possibly exist upon that planet.

So the question arises—did the vast amount of work accomplished by Swedenborg in the first half of his life lead to more or less serious mental derangement? There have been numerous cases of similar injury through similar causes.

But the scientific exactness and clarity of his mind survived to the last. So far as he knew science, he applied it admirably and with minute exactness to his system, but just as the science of Dante raises a smile, so we feel slightly intolerant of Swedenborg's scientific application to things spiritual. He was probably the only mystic with a real scientific training; others had been adepts in chemistry and kindred studies, but no mystic ever experienced such a long and arduous scientific apprenticeship as Swedenborg. It colors the whole of his system.

It would be exceedingly difficult to say whether he was more naturally a mystic or a scientist. In the first part of his life he was not greatly exercised by spiritual affairs and it was only when he had passed the meridian of human days that he seriously began to consider matters supernatural.

The change to the life of a mystic, if not rapid, was certainly not prolonged: what then caused it? One can only suspect that his whole tendency was essentially mystical from the first, and that he was a scientist by force of circumstance rather than because of any other reason. The spiritual was constantly simmering within his brain, but, as the world is ever with us, he found it difficult to throw off the superincumbent mass of affairs, which probably trammelled him for years. At length the fountains of his spirit welled up so fiercely that they could no longer be kept back, and throwing aside his scientific oars, he leaped into the spiritual ocean which afterwards speedily engulfed him.

There is perhaps no analogy to be found to his case in the biography of science. It is difficult to unveil the springs of the man's spirituality, but undoubtedly they existed deep down in him. It has often been said that he was a mere visionary, and not a mystic in the proper sense of the word, but the terms of his philosophy dispose of this contention. Although in many ways this does not square with the generally accepted doctrines of mysticism, it is undoubtedly one of the most striking and pregnant contributions to it. He was the apostle of the divine humanity, and the "Grand Man" is with him the beginning and end of the creative purpose. The originality of his system is marked, and the detail with which he surrounded it provides his followers of the present day with a greater body of teaching than that of probably any other mystical master.

The following extracts from Swedenborg's works will assist in giving some idea of his eschatology and general doctrine:

"The universe is an image of God, and was made for use. Providence is the government of the Lord in heaven and on earth. It extends itself over all things, because there is only one fountain of life, namely, the Lord, whose power supports all that exists.

"The influence of the Lord is according to a plan, and is invisible, as is Providence, by which men are not constrained to believe, and thus to lose their freedom. The influence of the Lord passes over from the spiritual to the natural, and from the inward to the outward. The Lord confers his influence on the good and the bad, but the latter converts the good into evil, and the true into the false; for so is the creature of its will fashioned.

"In order to comprehend the origin and progress of this influence, we must first know that that which proceeds from the Lord is the divine sphere which surrounds us, and fills the spiritual and natural world. All that proceeds from an object, and surrounds and clothes it, is called its sphere.

"As all that is spiritual knows neither time nor space, it therefore follows that the general sphere or the divine one has extended itself from the first moment of creation to the last. This divine emanation, which passed over from the spiritual to the natural, penetrates actively and rapidly through the whole created world, to the last grade of it, where it is yet to be found, and produces and maintains all that is animal, vegetable, and mineral. Man is continually surrounded by a sphere of his favourite propensities; these unite themselves to the natural sphere of his body, so that together they form one. The natural sphere surrounds every body of nature, and all the objects of the three kingdoms. Thus it allies itself to the spiritual world. This is the foundation of sympathy and antipathy, of union and separation, according to which there are amongst spirits presence and absence.

"The angel said to me that the sphere surrounded men more lightly on the back than on the breast, where it was thicker and stronger. This sphere of influence, peculiar to man, operates also in general and in particular around him by means of the will, the understanding, and the practice.

"The sphere proceeding from God, which surrounds man and constitutes his strength, while it thereby operates on his neighbour and on the whole creation, is a sphere of peace and innocence; for the Lord is peace and innocence. Then only is man consequently able to make his influence effectual on his fellow man, when peace and innocence rule in his heart, and he himself is in union with heaven. This spiritual union is connected with the natural by a benevolent man through the touch and the laying on of hands, by which the influence of the inner man is quickened, prepared, and imparted. The body communicates with others which are about it through the body, and the spiritual influence diffuses itself chiefly through the hands, because these are the most outward or *ultimum* of man; and through him, as in the whole of nature, the first is contained in the last, as the cause in the effect. The whole soul and the whole body are contained in the hands as a medium of influence. Thus our Lord healed the sick by laying on of hands, on which account so many were healed by the touch; and thence from the remotest times the consecration of priests and of all holy things was effected by laying on of hand. According to the etymology of the word, hands denote power. Man believes that his thoughts and his will proceed from within him, whereas all this flows into him. If he considered things in their true form, he would ascribe evil to hell, and good to the Lord; he would by the Lord's grace recognise good and evil within himself, and be happy. Pride alone has denied the influence of God, and destroyed the human race."

In his work *Heaven and Hell,* Swedenborg wrote of influence and reciprocities—Correspondences. The action of correspondence is perceptible in a person's countenance. In a countenance that has not learned hypocrisy, all emotions are represented naturally according to their true form, whence the face is called the mirror of the soul. In the same way, what belongs to the understanding is represented in the speech, and what belongs to the will in the movements. Every expression in the face, in the speech, in the movements, is called correspondence. By correspondence, man communicates with heaven, and he can thus communicate with the angels if he possess the science of correspondence by means of thought.

In order that communication may exist between heaven and man, the word in language is composed of nothing but correspondences, for everything in the word is correspondent, the whole and the parts; therefore one can learn secrets, of which one perceives nothing in the literal sense, for in the word, there is, besides the literal meaning, a spiritual meaning—one of the world, the other of heaven.

Swedenborg had his visions and communications with the angels and spirits by means of correspondence in the spiritual sense. "Angels speak from the spiritual world, according to inward thought; from wisdom, their speech flows in a tranquil stream, gently and uninterruptedly—they speak only in vowels, the heavenly angels in A and O, the spiritual ones in E and I, for the vowels give tone to the speech, and by the tone the emotion is expressed; the interruptions, on the other hand, correspond with creations of the mind; therefore we prefer, if the subject is lofty, for instance of heaven or God, even in human speech, the vowels U and O, etc. Man, however, is united with heaven by means of the word, and forms thus the link between heaven and earth, between the divine and the natural. (Some of this has interesting affinity with the ancient Hindu teachings of the science of Mantra).

"But when angels speak spiritually with me from heaven, they speak just as intelligently as the man by my side. But if they turn away from man, he hears nothing more whatever, even if they speak close to his ear. It is also remarkable that several angels can speak to a man; they send down a spirit inclined to man, and he thus hears them united."

In another place he stated: "There are also spirits called natural or corporeal spirits; these have no connection with thought, like the others, but they enter the body, possess all the senses, speak with the mouth, and act with the limbs, for they know not but that everything in that man is their own. These are the spirits by which men are possessed. They were, however, sent by the Lord to hell; whence in our days there are no more such possessed ones in existence."

Swedenborg's further doctrines and visions of Harmonies, that is to say, of heaven with men, and with all objects of nature; of the harmony and correspondence of all thing with each other; of Heaven, of Hell, and of the world of spirits; of the various states of man after death, etc., are very characteristic, important, and powerful. Robert A. Vaughan commented: "His contemplations of the enlightened inward eye refer less to everyday associations and objects of life (although he not unfrequently predicted future occurrences), because his mind was only directed to the highest spiritual subjects, in which indeed he had attained an uncommon degree of inward wakefulness, but is therefore not understood or known, because he described his sights so spiritually and unusually by language.

"His chapter on the immensity of heaven attracts more especially because it contains a conversation of spirits and angels about the planetary system. The planets are naturally inhabited as well as the planet Earth, but the inhabitants differ according to the various individual formation of the planets.

"These visions of the inhabitants of the planets agree most remarkably, and almost without exception with the indications of a clairvoyant whom I treated magnetically. I do not think that she knew Swedenborg; to which, however, I attach little importance. The two seers perceived Mars in quite a different manner. The magnetic seer only found images of fright and horror. Swedenborg, on the other hand, describes them as the best of all spirits of the planetary system. Their gentle, tender, zephyr-like language, is more perfect, purer and richer in thought, and nearer to the language of the angels, than others. These people associate together, and judge each other by the physiognomy, which amongst them is always the expression of the thoughts. They honour the Lord as sole God, who appears sometimes on their earth."

"Of the inhabitants of Venus he says: 'They are of two kinds; some are gentle and benevolent, others wild, cruel and of gigantic stature. The latter rob and plunder, and live by this means; the former have so great a degree of gentleness and kindness that they are always beloved by the good; thus they often see the Lord appear in their own form on their earth.' It is remarkable that this description of Venus agrees so well with the old fable, and with the opinions and experience we have of Venus.

"The inhabitants of the Moon are small, like children of six or seven years old; at the same time they have the strength of men like ourselves. Their voice rolls like thunder, and the sound proceeds from the belly, because the moon is in quite a different atmosphere from the other planets."

Spiritualism owes much to Swedenborg. He was one of the first to maintain that death means no immediate change, that the spirit world is a counterpart of this world below, that it is ruled by laws which ensure definite progress and that our conditions in the Beyond are determined by the life we live here.

Swedenborg Foundation Newsletter

Semi-annual publication supported by donation, carrying information on Swedenborg's writings in various languages, with notes on related activities. Address: 139 East 23rd Street, New York, N.Y. 10010. (See also Emanuel **Swedenborg**)

Swedenborg Society

Founded in London, England in 1810 to translate, print and publish the works of Emanuel **Swedenborg** (1688-1772).

The Society organizes meetings and conferences, and assists the needs of the **New Church** which has grown up around Swedenborg's teachings, by keeping Swedenborg's writings in print.

The Society maintains a reference and lending library, with a reading room, at the London headquarters. Address: 20 Bloomsbury Way, London, WC1A 2TH.

SWITZERLAND

For ancient material, see entry on **Teutons.**

Witchcraft & Demonology

Switzerland was by no means free from the witchcraft manias of Europe, although there are few English-language records on the subject.

About the year 1400, there were secular trials of witches in the Alps region now constituting southern and western Switzerland. During the same period, the Inquisition was persecuting heretics in neighboring valleys. One of the most active secular judges was Peter of Berne (Peter von Freyerz) in Simmenthal.

Jeannette Charles was arrested as a sorceress in Geneva in 1401, and after torture admitted evoking the devil. In Basel in 1407, various women from well-to-do families were prosecuted for alleged sorcery in love affairs. In 1423, at Nieder-Hauenstein, near Basel, an alleged witch was condemned after a peasant testified that she had ridden on a wolf.

In the Valais area in 1428, the Bishop of Sion headed early systematic persecutions involving torture by secular authorities. Some two hundred alleged witches were burned. There were many more tortures and burnings throughout the fifteenth century.

The records of the judge Peter of Berne tell of a witch named Staedelin in Boltingen (Lausanne) who confessed after torture to killing seven unborn babies in one house and preventing births in cattle. Also in Lausanne, certain witches were said to have cooked and eaten their own children, and thirteen children were said to have been devoured by witches in Berne. Witches confessed to killing unbaptized children, afterwards digging up the remains and boiling them, making a transmutation ointment from the flesh.

Jakob **Sprenger** (1436-1495), co-author with Heinrich **Kramer** of the infamous *Malleus Maleficarum,* the source book of the great European witchcraft persecutions, was born in Basel, where he grew up in a Dominican house, but his main work was in Germany, after he was established at the University of Cologne.

Even the influence of the Protestant movement led by Ulrich Zwingli (1484-1531) did not eradicate the witchcraft mania in Switzerland, indeed, some of the Zwinglians were active propagators of the superstition. Typical of such attitudes was the book *Magiologia* by Bartholomäus Anhorn (Basel, 1674) which endorsed the demonology of M. A. Del Rio and others.

The last legally executed witch in Switzerland appears to have been Anna Göldi, who was hanged in the Protestant canton of Glarus in 1782.

Mass Hysteria & Demonic Possession

An extraordinary outbreak of mass hysteria took place in the parish of Morzine, a beautiful valley of the Savoy near Lake Geneva, during 1860. The following account is drawn from reports in the *Cornhill Magazine,* London daily journals, the *Revue Spirite* and an article by William Howitt titled 'The Devils of Morzine.'

Morzine was quite remote, and was seldom visited by tourists before 1860. Being shut in by high mountains, and inhabited by a simple, industrious, and pious peasantry. Morzine might have appeared to a casual visitor the very center of health, peace, and good order.

The first appearance of an abnormal visitation was the conduct of a young girl, who, from being quiet, modest, and well-conducted, suddenly began to exhibit what her distressed family and friends supposed to be the symptoms of insanity. She ran about in the most singular and aimless way, climbed high trees, scaled walls, and was found perched on roofs and cornices, which it seemed impossible for any creature but a squirrel to reach. She soon became wholly intractable, was given to fits of hysteria, violent laughter, passionate weeping, and general aberration from her customary modest behavior.

While her parents were anxiously seeking advice in this dilemma, another and still another of the young girl's ordinary companions were seized with the same malady. In the course of ten days, over fifty females ranging from seven years of age to fifty were reported as having been seized in this way, and were exhibiting symptoms of the most bewildering mental aberration. The crawling, climbing, leaping, wild singing, furious swearing, and frantic behavior of these unfortunates, soon found crowds of imitators.

Before the tidings of this frightful affliction had passed beyond the district in which it originated, several hundreds of women and children, and scores of young men, were writhing under the contagion. The seizures were sudden, like the attacks. They seldom lasted long, yet they never seemed to yield to any form of treatment, whether harsh or kind, medical, religious or persuasive.

The first symptoms of this malady do not seem to have been noted with sufficient attention to justify giving details which could be considered accurate. It was only when the number of the possessed exceeded no less than two thousand persons and the case attracted multitudes of curious inquirers from all parts of the Continent, that the medical men, priests, and journalists of the time, began to keep and publish constant records of the progress of the epidemic.

One of the strangest features of the case, and one which most constantly baffled the faculty, was the appearance of rugged health, and freedom from all physical disease, which distinguished this malady. As a general rule, the victims spoke in hoarse, rough tones unlike their own, used profane language, such as few of them could ever have heard, and imitated the actions of crawling, leaping, climbing animals with ghastly fidelity. Sometimes they would roll their bodies up into balls and distort their limbs beyond the power of the attendant physicians to account for, or disentangle.

Many amongst them were levitated in the air, and in a few instances, the women spoke in strange tongues, manifested high conditions of exaltation, described glorious visions, prophesied, gave clairvoyant descriptions of absent persons and distant places, sang hymns, and preached in strains of sublime inspirations. It must be added that these instances were very rare, and were only noticeable in the earlier stages of the obsession.

It is almost needless to say that the tidings of this horrible obsession attracted multitudes of witnesses, no less than the attention of the learned and philosophic. When the attempts of the medical faculty, the church, and the law, had been tried again and again, and all had utterly failed to modify the ever-increasing horrors of this malady, Louis Napoleon, the French emperor, under whose protectorate Morzine was then governed, yielding to the representations of his advisers, and actually sent out three military companies to Morzine, charged with strict orders to quell the disturbances "on the authority of the Emperor, or by force if necessary."

The result of this high-handed policy was to increase tenfold the violence of the disease, and to augment the number of the afflicted, even amongst many of the soldiers themselves, who sank under the contagion which they were expected to quench.

The next move of the baffled French Government was a spiritual one. An army of priests, headed by a venerable Bishop, much beloved in his diocese, was despatched in the company of exorcists, at the suggestion of the Archbishop of Paris.

Unhappily this second experiment worked no better than the first. Respectable looking groups of well-dressed men, women, and children, would pass into the churches in reverent silence, and with all the appearance of health and piety, but no sooner was the sound of the priest's voice, or the notes of the organ heard, than shrieks, execrations, sobbings, and frenzied cries, resounded from different parts of the assembly. Anxious fathers and husbands were busy in carrying their distracted relatives into the open air, and whether in the church or the home, every attempt of a sacerdotal character, seemed to arouse the mania to heights of fury unknown before.

The time came at length, when the good old Bishop thought of a master stroke to achieve a general victory over the diabolical adversary. He commanded that as many as possible of the afflicted should be gathered together to hear high mass, when he trusted that the solemnity of the occasion would be sufficient to defeat what he evidently believed to be the combined forces of Satan.

According to the description cited by William Howitt in his article on 'The Devils of Morzine,' the assemblage in question, which included at least two thousand of the possessed and a number of spectators, must have far more faithfully illustrated Milton's description of Pandemonium than any mortal scene before enacted. Children and women were leaping over the seats and benches; clambering up the pillars, and shrieking defiance from pinnacles which scarcely admitted of a foothold for a bird.

The Bishop's letter contained one remark which seems to offer a clue to these scenes of horror and madness. He stated: "When in my distress and confusion I accidentally laid my hand on the heads of these unfortunates, I found that the paroxysm instantly subsided, and that however wild and clamorous they may have been before, the parties so touched generally sunk down as it were into a swoon, or deep sleep, and woke up most commonly restored to sanity, and a sense of propriety."

However, the failure of episcopal influence threw the Government back on the help of medical science. Dr. Constans had, since his first visit, published a report, in which he held out hopes of cure if his advice was strictly followed. He was again commissioned to do what he could for Morzine. Armed with the powers of a dictator he returned there, and backed by a fresh detachment of sixty soldiers, a brigade of gendarmes and a fresh cure, he issued despotic decrees, and threatened lunatic asylums and deportation for the convulsed.

He fined any person who accused others of magic, or in any way encouraged the prevalent idea of supernatural evil. He desired the curé to preach sermons against the possibility of demoniacal possession, but this order could not be carried out by even the most obedient priest. The persons affected with fits were dispersed in every direction. Some were sent to asylums and hospitals, and many were simply exiled from Chablais. They were not allowed to revisit except by very special favor.

William Howitt, writing in the *London Spiritual Magazine* stated: "We need not point to the salient facts of our narrative, or discuss the various theories that have been invented to account for them. . . . It is impossible not to see the resemblance of the Morzine epidemic with the demonopathy of the sixteenth century, and the history of the Jansenist and

Cevennes convulsionnaires. . . . Some of the facts we have related were often observed in the state of hypnotism, or nervous sleep, with which physicians are familiar. The hallucinations of which we have given instances are too common to astonish us. But the likeness of this epidemic to others that have been observed does not account for its symptoms." (See also **Convulsionaries of St. Medard**)

Psychical Research & Parapsychology

One of the earliest pioneers of Swiss research into paranormal areas was Prof. Maximilian **Perty,** who published studies on occult phenomena and Spiritualism from 1856 onwards. Although originally skeptical of survival of personality after death, he later became sympathetic to the concept.

One of the most famous psychical researchers was Dr. Theodore **Flournoy** (1854-1920), a psychologist at the University of Geneva, who took part in investigations of the mediumship of Eusapia **Palladino.** Flournoy is best known for his important investigation of the famous case of the medium Hélène **Smith,** as recorded in his book *From India to the Planet Mars; A Study of a Case of Somnambulism with Glossolalia* (1900).

Other important Swiss investigators include: Prof. Marc Thury (1822-1905), Prof. Eugene Bleuler of Zürich, Georg Sulzer (died 1929), Karl E. **Muller** (1893-1969), Mrs. Fanny Hoppe-Moser, who published *Okkultismus—Täuschungen und Tatsachen* (1935) and *Spuk* (1950), Guido Huber (died 1953), who published studies on survival and ESP. Prof. Gebhard **Frei** (1905-1967), who published a useful bibliography on the psychology of the subconscious, Dr. Peter **Ringger,** who founded the first parapsychological society in Switzerland and published works on parapsychology, Friedrich A. Volman, specializing in the literature of hauntings.

The great psychologist C. G. **Jung** also occupies a special position for his interest in reconciling occult studies with the psychology of the subconscious. Between 1899-1900, he experimented with a young medium and submitted a doctoral thesis 'On the Psychology and Pathology of the So-Called Occult.' He later cooperated in experiments in **psychokinesis** and **materialization** phenomena with famous mediums. There were a number of paranormal events in his own experience.

There are two major parapsychological societies. The Schweitzer Parapsychologische Gesellschaft Zürich was founded in 1952, with Dr. Peter Ringger as president. Six years later, his place was taken by Dr. Hans Naegeli-Osjord. The SPG organizes lecture programs in Zürich and maintains a library. It issues the periodical *Parapress.* Address Fraumuensterstr. 8, Zürich.

The Schweizerische Vereinigung für Parapsychologie was founded in Zürich in 1966 and organizes public lectures, discussions and high school courses in psychical subjects. Under the presidency of Dr. Theo Locher, it has conducted investigations into a variety of parapsychological subjects. It publishes a bi-annual *Bulletin für Parapsychologie.* Address: Industriestr. 5, 2555 Brügg b. Biel, Zürich.

Sword of Dyrnwyn

Bi-monthly publication of the Association of Cymmry Wicca, devoted to Welsh pagan traditions; includes articles on UFOs, leys, astrology and other occult subjects. Address: P.O. Box 1514, Smyrna, Georgia 30081.

Sycomancy

Divination by the leaves of the fig tree. Questions or propositions on which one wished to be enlightened were written on these leaves. If the leaf dried quickly after the appeal to the diviner, it was an evil omen, but a good augury if the leaf dried slowly.

Symbolism (Metapsychical)

A term used by psychical researcher Ernesto **Bozzano** in relation to "cases in which, by subconscious or mediumistic methods, an idea is expressed by means of hallucinatory perceptions, or ideographic representations, or forms of language differing from the ideas to be transmitted, but capable of suggesting them indirectly or conventionally. In other words, there is metapsychical symbolism every time an idea is transmitted by means of representations which are not reproductions."

A simple instance from F. W. H. **Myers'** book *Human Personality and Its Survival of Bodily Death* (2 vols., 1903) is as follows: A botanical student passing inattentively in front of the glass door of a restaurant thought that he had seen "Verbascum Thapsus" printed thereon. The real word was "Bouillon"; and that happens to be the trivial name in French for the plant Verbascum Thapsus. The actual optical perception had thus been subliminally transformed.

Symbolism often occurs in occultism, particularly in prophetic dreams, which are sometimes represented in visual or etymological puns.

Sigmund Freud drew attention to such symbolic imagery in his psychoanalytical theory of dreams.

Many psychics find their visions of future events occur in the form of symbolism. Traditional astrological predictions used to be presented in symbolic pictures called "hieroglyphs." (See also **Hieroglyphs; Symbolism in Art**)

Symbolism in Art

"It is in and through symbols," stated Thomas Carlyle, "that man, consciously or unconsciously lives, works, and has his being." These words apply very pertinently to art in all its branches for every one of these represents, in the first place, an attempt to reincarnate something in nature, and this attempt cannot be made save with the assistance of some form of symbolism.

An author uses the arbitrary and sadly restricted symbol of language in order to state his conception of life, the composer employs notes to body forth his impressions and emotions, while the painter needs to be still more symbolical, his art consisting as it does in expressing distance on a flat surface, and in suggesting bulk by the practice known technically as modeling.

The sculptor is also a symbolist, for while he has at his disposal a third dimension not available to the painter, he normally tries to delineate colored things in a monochromatic material. Again, it is impossible for him to convey motion or action as the writer can, and he can only suggest this by molding a figure wherein an ephemeral gesture is perpetrated. Modern art development has also given us the constructions known as mobiles, in which usually nonrepresentational symbolic shapes add the dimension of movement.

Some kind of symbolism, then, is the technical basis of all the arts, yet another kind of symbolic significance, a deeper and more mysterious one transpires in many cases. As Coleridge observed. "An idea in the highest sense of the word, cannot be expressed but by a symbol." From time immemorial, painters and sculptors have realized this, and have tried to crystalize abstract ideas by the aid of certain signs, some of them having quite an obvious meaning, but others being cryptic.

Among the Japanese masters of the Akiyoe school, Fuji-no-Yama was a favorite topic, one which many of them figured scores of times, and to Occidental eyes a picture of this sort is just a picture of a mountain, but to the Japanese it meant something deeper, Fuji being almost sacred to them, and its representation in line and color being a sort of symbol of patriotic devotion.

Then Hokusai, commonly accounted the greatest master of this school, loved to draw a pot-bellied man reclining at his ease against cushions, and this too means little in the East but much in the West, for in reality it is more than a study in voluptuousness—it represents Hotei, the god of peace and plenty. And poor people in Japan would buy a copy of this picture, for those woodcuts which are so priceless now were mostly sold for a few pence originally, and were within the reach of the humblest. And they would hang such a print on the wall, trusting thus to win the favor of the deity it personified.

Other Japanese, more religiously minded, preferred a picture of a curious male figure emanating from a plant, and this symbolized the legend that Buddha arose originally from a lotus. Further, in many Japanese draperies and the like we find a strange decoration not unlike a *fleur-de-lys,* and this was originally a drawing of the foot of Buddha, a drawing which evolved throughout the centuries into the above-named form.

The art of the Hindus is similarly permeated with symbolism, much of it quite incomprehensible to Europeans, while the ancient Greek masters also used symbols, one which occurs repeatedly in their output being the fig-leaf, which represented simply amorousness, and was a direct reference to the story of the fall of man as detailed in the book of *Genesis.*

This same symbol is found occasionally in early Italian works of art and it is in these, really, that we find symbolism at its apogee, for in Italy, more essentially than in any other country, art was long the handmaiden of the Church, and thus early Italian painting and sculpture is replete with emblems referring to the Christian faith.

The frequent allusions in the Old Testament to the hand of God, as the instrument of His sovereign power, naturally inspired pristine artists to symbolize the deity's omnipotence by drawing a hand, sometimes with a cross behind it, sometimes emerging from clouds, while equally common among the primitives was the practice of expressing the name of Christ by the first two letters of His name in Greek, and this emblem evolved into divine and intricate forms.

Another familiar Christian symbol, figuring in numerous sarcophagi and mosaics, is a small picture of a fish, and this refers indirectly to baptism but most directly to Christ, for those who first used this sign observed that the letters forming the word fish in Greek, IXOYE, when separated, supplied the initials for the five words: Jesus Christ, Son of God, Saviour. Christ was also represented sometimes by a picture of a lion, this referring to the phrase in the Scriptures, "The lion of the tribe of Judah."

The Passion was frequently symbolized by a drawing of a pelican, tearing open her breast to feed her young (a popular superstition). Then the Holy Ghost was invariably suggested by a dove, while the phœnix and the peacock were both employed as symbols of the Resurrection.

Nor does the symbolism in the art of Italy end here, for an early artist of that country, painting a picture of a saint, would usually add some sign having reference to an event in the subject's career, or to some particular predilection on his part. Thus, if the saint was famous as a devotee of pilgrimage, a shell was drawn at his feet, or, if doing penance was his particular virtue, a skull was figured on some part of the picture, while finally, if his life culminated in the glory of martyrdom, this was hinted at by a sketch of an axe, a lance or a club.

Mystic symbolism waned in Italy before the eleventh century was over. Some of the anonymous early Florentines had symbolized love by a great, flaring lamp, but with the advent of Titian and Veronese, this sort of thing was discontinued, and amorous scenes were painted in realistic fashion. The great medieval masters of religious art, moreover—men like Ghibert and Raphael, Pintunichio and Michelangelo—scorned to deal in mere emblems, and strove to depict Biblical scenes with an absolute veracity to nature, Ghibert going so far as to try to introduce a species of perspective into bas-relief.

But meanwhile the practice of the fathers of Italian art had been taken up in France and in Spain, and more especially in Germany by Altdorfer and Albrecht Dürer, while in England, too, symbolism of various kinds began to become very manifest in ecclesiastical architecture and craftsmanship.

The beautiful Norman Church, with its square tower, gave place to a Gothic one with a spire, symbol of aspiration, while the woodwork was garnished at places with emblems of the passion—three nails and a hammer, pincers, ladder, sponge, reed and spear. In addition, gargoyles commenced to appear on the outsides of churches, the idea being that, when the building was consecrated, the devils took flight from the interior, and perched themselves on the roof. This species of symbolism did not pass away with the Middle Ages, but was carried on for long afterwards, as also was the "rose window," symbol of the crown of thorns.

The churches' control over art was virtually dead by the end of the fifteenth century, and thenceforth, during fully a hundred years, painting found its chief patrons in various enlightened kings and noblemen. But symbolism was not altogether ousted accordingly, for the new patrons were hardly collectors in the usual sense of the term. They did not buy landscapes to decorate their dwellings (very few *bona fide* landscapes were done before the time of Claude, born in 1600) and it was mainly portraits of themselves and their families which they sought.

So now, in consequence of this, a new form of symbolism became very manifest in painting, the artist being almost invariably charged to introduce his patron's coat-of-arms into some part of the canvas or panel, and, although this practice began to wane with the advent of the seventeenth century, when collecting in the real sense began, painters still continued to deal in emblems of one kind and another.

Even Antoine Watteau (born 1684), painting a portrait of the divine Venetian pastellist Rosalba Carriera, showed her with white roses in her lap. Eventually this rather obvious symbolism was deepened by the engraver Liotard, for beneath his print after Watteau he inscribed the beautiful if sentimental phrase, "La plus belle des fleurs ne dure qu'un matin."

A practice similar to this lingered until the close of the eighteenth century in engraving, the engraver of a portrait usually thinking it necessary to surround his sitter with allegorical accessories. For example, in many prints of La Fontaine we find a scene from one of his fables introduced beneath the subject's visage. A few modern engravers have attempted something analogous, William Strange, for example, engraving a tiny portrait of a soldier in the corner of his familiar plate of Rudyard Kipling, while reverting to painting, many of the great English masters of portraiture saw fit to figure, almost in juxtaposition to the sitter, various items symbolizing his tastes or action.

Raeburn was among the last to do this, several of his pictures of great lawyers being only embellished with bundles of briefs tied up with red tape. Although this form of symbolism has died out, the fact remains that most good portrait painters still choose their *repoussoir* with a view to its aiding them in elucidating more completely the sentiment of the subject in hand. Thus, when painting a picture of a child, an artist will usually employ a high-pitched background, this being in some degree emblematic of youth, while delineating an old man, he will often place him in somber surroundings.

And so we see again, as we saw at the outset, that all art is in a sense symbolical, and that it is through symbols that it "lives, works, and has its being." (See also **Hieroglyphs; Magical Diagrams;** Metapsychical **Symbolism**)

Symmes, John Cleves (1780-1829)

A captain in the U.S. Army in the war of 1812-14, nephew of the jurist of the same name.

He served with distinction at the battle of Niagara and in the sortie form Fort Erie. He later devoted himself to philosophical pursuits. In 1818, he promulgated his theory that the earth is a hollow sphere, habitable within, and open at the poles to admit light, and containing within it six or seven concentric hollow spheres also open at the poles.

In May 1818, he circularized prominent people in various countries with a manifesto of his theories, asking for an expedition to be equipped for exploration at the poles.

He lectured widely and his convert James McBride was responsible for the anonymously published *Symmes' Theory of Concentric Spheres; demonstrating that the Earth is Hollow, Habitable within, and Widely Open about the Poles,* by A Citizen of the United States (1826), this was not favorably received, but later influenced other hollow earth theorists.

In 1820, a pseudonymous book by "Captain Seaborn" titled *Symzonia* described a steamship voyage to the south polar opening, when the ship goes over the rim and enters the continent of "Symzonia," where the inhabitants live in a socialist utopia.

This concept may have influenced Edgar Allan Poe's story *Narrative of Arthur Gordon Pym.*

Symmes died May 28, 1829, at the early age of 49, but his theories were revived by his son Americus Vespucius, who published *The Symmes' Theory of Concentric Spheres* (1878). (See also **Hollow Earth**)

Symonds, John (1914-)

British novelist, writer of children's books and author of important works on occultism. He met Aleister **Crowley** in 1945 and tried to assist publication of his writings in the last two years of Crowley's life.

He became Crowley's literary executor, and author of the standard biography of Crowley: *The Great Beast* (first published London, 1951, frequently reprinted; revised and enlarged edition, 1971).

Symonds also published the biography *Madame Blavatsky: Medium and Magician* (1960).

His book *Light Over Water* (1963) is a novel with a theme of yoga and alchemy. His other books include: *The Magic of Aleister Crowley* (1958), *Thomas Brown and the Angels* (1961). With Kenneth **Grant** he edited *The Confessions of Aleister Crowley* and Crowley's own book *Magick* (1973). Symonds was a member of the editorial board of *Man, Myth, and Magic* (1970).

Sympathy

A mutual attraction or identity of feeling between individuals and also animals, the opposite of the reaction of **antipathy.** The term "sympathy" has a special significance in **Mesmerism** or **Animal Mag-**

netism, where it is used to indicate the rapport between operator and subject, by means of which the operator could influence and control the perceptions of the subject.

It has also been suggested that a condition of sympathy might exist between **agent** and **percipient** in **telepathy,** particularly in the transmission of emotions. (See also **Antipathy; Mesmerism; Od**)

Synchronicity

An a-causal connecting principle, expressing the linkage of events without a cause-and-effect relationship in time. In addition to the normal cause-and-effect connections observed in nature, there appears to be another principle expressed in the simultaneous arrangement or connection of events.

As an illustration of this principle, there seems to be a relationship between astrological positions and events in the life of individual human beings, but the human events are not necessarily *caused* by the position of heavenly bodies, only linked in an a-causal relationship.

There are also many everyday coincidences, such as the way in which a very unusual word comes into one's mind, then one picks up a book and sees just that word stand out on the page, or perhaps a friend comes into the room and speaks that word. Such coincidences are often striking, but do not appear to have any discernible causal or meaningful relationship.

The theory of synchronicity was developed by Prof. C. G. **Jung** and related to certain ESP phenomena. There is a discussion of the principle in the book by C. G. Jung & W. Pauli, *The Interpretation of Nature and the Psyche* (London, 1955).

T

Table-turning (or Table-tipping)

A form of psychic phenomena in which a table rotates, tilts or rises completely off the ground by the mere contact of the fingertips of an individual or group of individuals. In exceptional cases, tables have been known to move or even levitate without direct contact (see **Movement**), but the familiar form of seance in table-turning is that in which the sitters place their fingertips on the table, which moves without conscious exercise of muscular force. By relating the **raps** or tilts of the table to the alphabet it becomes possible to receive intelligent messages.

Historical Background

It is the simplest and oldest form of communication with extraneous intelligences or the subconscious self. In ancient times, tables were used for purposes of divination as "mensa divinatoriae." In fourth-century Rome, Ammianus Marcellinus described a table with a slab, engraved with the letters of the alphabet, above which a ring was held, suspended by a thread; by swinging to certain letters, messages were spelt out. Tertullian (c. 155-c. 222) appears to have been one of the first who knew of table communications with the unseen world.

Table-turning in modern Spiritualism dates from the mid-nineteenth century, and seems to have originated in America soon after the **Rochester Rappings** of 1848 (see **Fox Sisters**). At that time, there was considerable interest in **"Animal Magnetism"** or "Electro-biology," stemming from the **Mesmerism** of Europe.

Mesmerism had established the convention of groups of individuals arranged in a circle and a various named "magnetic fluid" linking them. After the phenomena of **rappings** in the presence of the Fox sisters became widely known, groups gathered around other individuals who possessed the same ability to generate raps.

It was natural to sit around a table, and when it was found that the table itself generated raps, as well as other movements, a convention was established. It spread like an epidemic throughout America and was brought to England by such professional mediums as Mrs. Maria B. **Hayden,** who came to London with a lecturer on "electro-biology" in 1852.

The great advantage of table-turning was that it did not require a paid professional medium. Amateur groups could sit round a table and obtain the intelligent rappings which had first been manifest only to specially talented individuals like the Fox sisters.

In 1852, afternoon social invitations to tea and table-turning were common. Table-turning was even more successful in France, with its tradition of Mesmerism and animal magnetism. One widespread jest was that people no longer asked after each other's health, but asked instead how the table was. "Thank you, mine turns beautifully, and how goes yours?"

It was in France that the rather crude form of communication through table-turning was simplified in 1853 by M. Planchette's invention of the instrument which bears his name. Five years later, an American manufacturer took up the idea and thousands of **planchettes** were sold in America and Britain.

Meanwhile Mesmerists welcomed table-turning as a demonstration of animal magnetism or odic force, while Fundamentalist eccelesiastics denounced it as due to Satanic agency.

Scientists and doctors thought that the new craze would be a danger to mental health, and a committee was formed to find a non-Spiritualist explanation for the phenomenon. They reported in the *Medical Times and Gazette* on June 11, 1853 that the motion of the table was due to unconscious muscular action. A few weeks later the great chemist and physicist Michael **Faraday** reported experiments with simple apparatus to demonstrate that the movements of the table were due to unconscious muscular action of the part of the sitters, who were by implication the automatic authors of the messages purporting to come from the spirit world.

Faraday's apparatus consisted of two thin wooden boards with little glass rollers between, the whole bound together with rubber bands, and so contrived that the slightest lateral pressure on the upper board would cause it to slip a little way over the other. A haystalk or a scrap of paper served to indicate any motion of the upper board over the lower.

The conclusion drawn from these experiments was that when the sitters believed themselves to be pressing downwards, they were really pressing obliquely in the direction they expected the table to rotate. Other investigators also held that the expectation of the operators had a good deal to do with the motions of the table.

James **Braid** pointed out in the appendix to his book *Hypnotic Therapeutics* (1853) that someone generally announced beforehand the direction they expected the table to rotate.

Among the earliest investigators of the phenomenon of table-turning were Count Agenor **De Gasparin** and Prof. Marc **Thury** of Geneva, who held seances and were satisfied that the movements resulted from a force radiating from the operators, to which they gave the name of **"ectenic force."**

The public, on the whole, ignored the conclusions of Faraday and others, preferring the more popular Spiritualist explanation or the pseudo-scientific theories of "electro-biology." Other explanations offered included odic force (see **Od**), galvanism, animal magnetism, and, strangest of all, the rotation of the earth. The Rev. G. Sandby and the Rev. C. H. Townshend claimed to have experienced a feeling of fatigue after a table-turning seance as though they had been hypnotizing someone. They reported a tingling sensation in their fingertips, while Townshend claimed somewhat vaguely that spirit rappings might be caused by a "disengagement of Zoogen from the System." Zoogen remains an unidentified force in nature!

Meanwhile various Evangelical clergymen insisted that table-turning involved Satanic agency. The Rev. N. S. Godfrey, the Rev. E. Gillson and others held seances in which the "spirits" confessed themselves to be either spirits of worthless persons of evil inclination, or devils, both of which confessions caused the reverent gentlemen to denounce the whole practice of table-turning. One of them marked apropos the Faraday experiments, that the phenomena "appear to be whatever the investigator supposes them to be," a saying which aptly characterized his own attitude.

The psychical researcher Camille **Flammarion,** whose exhaustive experiments and scientific attainments gave considerable weight to his opinion, offered an explanation of the various phases of table-turning phenomena. Simple rotation of the table he ascribed to an unconscious impulse given by the operators, and other movements of the table while the fingers of the sitters rested upon it were ascribed to similar causes. The tilting of the table on the side furthest away from the operator was explained by muscular action. But vibrations in the wood of the table, or its **levitation** under the fingers, or, to a still greater extent, its rotation without contact of the operator's hands, he attributed to a force emanating from the body, and, in the latter case, capable of acting at a distance by means of ether-waves.

This force, the result of a cerebral disturbance, was greater than that of the muscles, as is seen by the levitation of tables so weighty that the combined muscular strength of the operators would not suffice to lift them.

To the dictating of messages and other intelligent manifestations he gave an origin in this psychic force, which is perhaps identical with Thury's "ectenic force," or "psychode," (see **Ectoplasm**), and which is obedient to the will and desires, or even, in some cases, the subconscious will of the operator. Flammarion did not consider the **spirit hypothesis** necessary. It is possible, however, some fraud may have crept into the seances investigated by M. Flammarion, as it has done in so many other cases.

There are those among the most profound students of psychical research who find the hypothesis of unconscious muscular action or deliberate fraud a satisfactory explanation of the phenomena.

This greatly oversimplifies the matter, and does not do justice to the intelligent communications obtained through table-turning. Nor does it explain well-attested instances when tables moved independently of human contact. Different experimenters often obtain contradictory results. Some of these questions become clearer if one examines the experiences of those who have experimented with table-turning.

Table-Turning in Action

The usual procedure is to form a circle around the table, place hands lightly, with fingertips touching, on the leaf and, with lowered lights or in complete darkness, wait for the manifestations. If someone with psychic powers is present the table may, after a time, show signs of animation. The first such sign is a quivering motion under the sitters' hands; it keeps on increasing until the table pulsates with a mysterious energy.

It was this phenomenon in his experiences with the medium D. D. **Home** which induced Alexander Dumas to conceive, in a fantastic narrative, the table as an intelligence itself. The conception of a spirit entering furniture became a favorite idea with French authors afterwards.

The wooden surface appears to act as a reservoir of externalized nervous force. The psychical researcher Hereward **Carrington** said of his seances with Eusapia **Palladino** that the table appeared to be somehow alive like the back of a dog.

After the vibratory stage, the table may jerk, tilt, stumble about, and may eventually become entirely levitated. Apparently there is an intelligence behind these movements. If the letters of the alphabet are called over in the dark the table, by tilting, knocking on the floor, or tapping, indicates certain letters which connectedly spell out a message, often purporting to come from someone deceased.

The intelligence which thus manifests has personal characteristics. In repeated sittings it is soon noticed that the skill with which the table is manipulated or the eccentricities of its behavior are indications of the presence of the same entity. The strange, stolid or clumsy behavior of the table immediately denotes that a new visitant is tampering with the contact.

But the table may disclose much more than that. Its motions may express humor, emotion, personality. It may climb up into the sitter's lap as a mark of affection, it may chase others all over the room in a hostile manner. As an additional means of expression, the table may convey queer impressions by creaking. P. P. Alexander noted in his book, *Spiritualism: A Narrative with a Discussion* (1871):

"At a particular stage of the proceedings the table began to make strange undulatory movements, and gave out, as these proceeded, a curious accompaniment of creaking sounds. Mr. Home seemed surprised. 'This is very curious,' he said, 'it is a phenomenon of which I have no experience hitherto.' Presently my friend remarked that—movement and sound together—it reminded him of nothing he could think of except a ship in distress, with its timbers straining in a heavy sea. . . . This conclusion being come to . . . the table proceeded to rap out: 'It is David.' Instantly a lady burst into tears, and cried wildly: 'Oh, that must be my poor, dear brother, David, who was lost at sea some time since.' "

When the table moves under contact there is an obvious possibility for the subconscious mind or a secondary **personality** to convey ideas by unconscious muscular pressure. This is valid both as regards the medium and the sitters. According to F. W. H. **Myers,** "the subliminal self, like the telegraphist begins its effort with full knowledge of the alphabet, but with only weak and rude command over our muscular adjustments. It is therefore *a priori* likely that its easiest mode of communication will be through a repetition of simple movements, so arranged as to correspond to letters of the alphabet."

But Myers was inclined to attribute to the subconscious mind the movement of the table without contact as well. "If a table moves when no one is touching it, this is not obviously more likely to have been effected by my deceased grandfather than by myself. We cannot tell how I could move it; but then we cannot tell how he could move it either."

Certainly, there are experiences which bear out this possibility and show how singularly deceptive the interpretation of phenomena may be. George S. Long, an acquaintance of Dr. Richard **Hodgson,** narrated in *Proceedings* of the Society for Psychical Research (vol. 9, p. 65) a strange experience—with a chair. Through a nonprofessional young lady he received what was said to be the most convincing test of spirit return: "First the chair spelt out my name and showed a disposition to get into my lap; then it spelt out 'George, you ought to know me as I am Jim.' But I didn't, and said so. Then without my looking at the board, it spelt out 'Long Island, Jim Rowe' and 'Don't you remember I used to cary you when you were a little fellow,' or words to that effect. I had to acknowledge the truth of it and also to say that as he was an ignorant man he possibly intended 'Cary' for carry. I must own I was puzzled for the moment. To make sure of his power I asked that he count the pickets in the fence. Somehow he could not agree to this, and even the medium objected. As a last resort I asked how long he had been in the spirit land and the answer came, between thirteen and fourteen years. Now to the sequel. First it occurred to me a day or two later, that while all the incidents given were correct the name should have been given as Roe instead of Rowe. Second I was upon Long Island this summer, and the matter coming to my mind I inquired how long Jim Roe had been dead, and was informed he died last Winter; so when I received this test so convincing to the believers the man was not dead."

Chair or table makes no difference once the available power is sufficient to manifest. The reason why a table should be used for spirit communication is that as a piece of furniture it is generally available, convenient, allows contact around it for a large number of people, its surface acts as a receptacle for the generated force and the space underneath comes very near to a cabinet, especially if it is surrounded by a deep hanging table cloth. In the early days of Spiritualism, they often used a table with a hole in the middle through which materialized hands were thrust.

Eusapia Palladino insisted on a seance table built entirely of wood. She considered soft pinewood the best to absorb vital magnetism. She allowed no metal in the construction of the table.

The color of the table does not matter. Dr. J. **Maxwell** found an advantage in covering it with some white material of light texture. He also insisted that the table should, if possible, be fastened with wooden pegs instead of nails since mediums are sometimes extremely sensitive to metals.

With powerful mediums the movement of the table may occur at any time and disclose a tremendous force in operation. "During any meal with Mrs. Elgie Corner [Florence **Cook**] in one's own house," wrote Gambier Bolton in *Psychic Force* (1904): "and whilst she herself is engaged in eating and drinking—both of her hands being visible all the time—the heavy dining table will commence first to quiver, setting all the glasses shaking, and plates, knives, forks and spoons in motion, and then to rock and sway from side to side, occasionally going so far as to tilt up at one end or at one side; and all the time raps and tappings will be heard in the table and in many different parts of the room. Taking a meal with her in a public restaurant is a somewhat serious matter."

In 1923, in experiments conducted by psychical researcher Harry **Price** with the psychic **Stella C.,** powerful and rhythmical vibrations of tables were obtained, and on one occasion, after violent movements of a table, it suddenly snapped, the top breaking into two pieces, and the legs breaking off (See *Stella C. An Account of Some Original Experiments in Psychical Research* by Harry Price, ed. James Turner, Souvenir Press, London, 1973).

Table-Turning and Dowsing

It is interesting to note that the various theories about the rationale of table-turning parallel those advanced for the phenomena of **dowsing** and **radiesthesia,** where there is meaningful movement of a water-witching rod or a **pendulum** or similar indicator. The actual force moving the indicator is still a matter of controversy.

It is generally assumed that unconscious muscular action or nervous energy plays a significant part, but it is still far from clear how information on underground water, minerals or buried objects is conveyed to the mind, or from the mind to the indicator.

One of the earliest investigators to link the action of table-turning with **divining rods,** or pendulums was the French chemist Michel Eugène Chevreul, in his book *De la baguette divinatoire, du pendule dit explorateur et des tables tournantes, au point de vue de l'histoire, de la critique et de la méthode expérimentale* (1854).

In modern times, table-turning is a laborious method of establishing contact with unseen intelligence. **Planchette** and **ouija board** are more satisfactory and faster, but all such indicators can be deceptive. Messages obtained are often misleading or false. Again, the communications received at circles in general tend to reflect the general level of the sitters, and it is unwise for nervous or hysterical individuals to experiment.

Those who desire to investigate the phenomena of seances are advised to do so in the company of experienced Spiritualists or well-balanced individuals, preferably with some scientific background. (See also **Animal Magnetism; Divining Rod; Dowsing; Ectenic Force; Mesmerism; Movement; Ouija Board; Pendulums; Planchette; Psychic Force; Radiesthesia; Raps**)

Recommended reading:

Anon. *Table Turning and Table Talking Considered in Connection with the Dictates of Reason and Common Sense,* S. Gibbs, Bath, U.K., 1853

Anon. *Table Turning by Animal Magnetism Demonstrated,* London, 1853

Barrett, William & Theodore Besterman. *The Divining-Rod; An Experimental & Psychological Investigation,* Methuen, London, 1926; University Books, 1968

Burr, Chauncey. *Knocks for the Knockings,* Burr Brothers, New York, 1851 [pamphlet]

Capron, E. W. *Modern Spiritualism; Its Facts and Fanaticisms, Its Consistencies and Contradictions,* B. Marsh, Boston, 1855, Arno Press, 1976

Capron, E. W. & H. D. Barron. *Singular Revelations; Explanation and History of the Mysterious Communion with Spirits,* Auburn, New York, 1850 [pamphlet]

Chevreul, M. E. *De la baguette divinatoire, du puendule dit explorateur et des tables tournantes, au point de vue du l'histoire, de la critique et de la méthode expérimentale, Paris, 1854*

Close, Rev. F. *The Tester Tested; or Table Moving, Turning, Talking, Not Diabolical; A Review of the Publications of the Rev. Messrs. Godfrey, Gillson, Vincent, and Dibdin,* London & Cheltenham, 1853

Cowan, Charles. *Thoughts on Satanic Influence, or Modern Spiritualism Considered,* London, 1854

De Gasparin, Comte Agenor. *Des table tournantes, de surnaturel en général, et des esprits,* Paris, 1854

De Mirville, Marquis J. E. *Pneumatologie; Des Esprits et de leurs manifestations fluidique devant la science modern,* Paris, 1853–68

De Szapary, Comte F. G. *Les tables tournantes,* Paris, 1854

Dewey, D. M. *History of the Strange Sounds or Rappings Heard in Rochester and Western New York,* Rochester, 1850

Du Potet de Sennevoy, Baron. *Traité complet de magnétisme animal,* Paris, 1856, etc.

Elliott, Charles W. *Mysteries, or Glimpses of the Supernatural,* Harper, New York, 1852

Godfrey, Rev. Nathaniel S. *Table Turning the Devil's Modern Masterpiece; Being the Result of a Course of Experiments,* Thames Ditton, U.K., 1853

Guldenstubbe, Baron L. de. *Pneumatologie positive et expérimentale; La réalité des Espirits et le phenomene merveilleux de leur écriture directe demontrées,* Paris, 1857

Hartmann, E. von. *Spiritism,* London, n.d. (transl. from German *Der Spiritismus,* 1855)

Hornung, D. *Neue Geheimnisse des Tages durch Geistes Magnetismus,* Leipzig, 1857

Kerner, Justinus. *Die Somnambülen Tische; Zur Geschichte und Erklärungen dieser Erscheinungen,* Stuttgart, 1853

Lang, Andrew. *Cock Lane and Common-Sense,* Longmans, Green, London, 1894; AMS Press, 1970

Mahan, Rev. Asa. *Modern Mysteries Explained and Exposed,* Boston, 1855

Mattison, Rev. Hiram. *Spirit Rapping Unveiled!,* Derby, New York, 1853

Maxwell, J. *Metaphysical Phenomena; Methods and Observations,* Duckworth, London, 1905

Morgan, Rev. R. C. *An Inquriy Into Table Miracles,* Bath & London, 1853 [pamphlet]

Page, Charles G. *Psychomancy; Spirit Rappings and Tippings Exposed,* New York, 1853

Perty, Maximilien. *Die Mystischen Erscheinungen der menschlichen Natur,* Leipzig & Heidelberg, 2nd enlarged ed., 1872

Prichard, John. *A Few Sober Words of Table-talk about the Spirits,* Leamington, U.K., 1853 [pamphlet]

Spicer, Henry. *Facts and Fantasies; A Sequel to "Sights and Sounds,"* London, 1853

Tiffany, Joel. *Spiritualism Explained,* Graham & Ellinwood, New York, 1856

Townsend, Rev. C. H. *Mesmerism Proved True,* London, 1854

Taboo (or Tabu or Tapu)

A Polynesian word meaning "prohibited" and signifying a prohibition enforced by religious or magical power, which has come to be applied to similar usages among primitive peoples all over the world. It also has parallels in the religious codes of sophisticated societies, as in the early Hebrew term *Kherem* ("set apart" or prohibited), and in the highly developed social etiquette of modern society.

Taboo, or prohibition is enforced in the cases of sacred things and unclean things. In the first instance, the *taboo* is placed on the object because of the possession by it of inherent mysterious power. But *taboo* may be imposed by a chief or priest. It aims at the protection of important individuals, the safeguarding of the weak, women, children and slaves from the magical influence of more highly-placed individuals, against danger incurred by handling or coming in contact with corpses, or eating certain foods, and the securing of human beings against the power of supernatural agencies, or the depredations of thieves.

Taboo may also be sanctioned by social use or instinct. The violation of a *taboo* makes the offender himself *taboo,* for it is characteristic of the *taboo* that it is transmissible, but can be thrown off by magical or purificatory ceremonies. It may last for a short period, or be imposed in perpetuity.

It may be said, generally speaking, that the practice of *taboo* was instituted through human instinct for human convenience. This applies of course merely to the most simple type of *taboo.* It is, for example, forbidden to reap or steal the patch of corn dedicated to an agricultural deity, for the simple reason that his wrath would be incurred by so doing.

Similarly it is *taboo* to devour the flesh of the totem animal of the tribe (see **Totemism**), except in special circumstances with the object of achieving communion with him. It is *taboo* to interfere in any manner with the affairs of the **shamans** or medicine men. This again is a type of the imposed *taboo* for the convenience of a certain caste. It is prohibited to marry a woman of the same totem as oneself, as all the members of a totemic band are supposed to be consanguineous, and such a union might incur the wrath of the patron deity.

A very strict *taboo* is put upon the witnessing of certain ritual instruments belonging to some primitive tribes, but this only applies to women and uninitiated men. The reason for such *taboo* would be that it was considered degradation for women to behold sacred implements.

Taboo, if it does not spring directly from the system known as totemism, was strongly influenced by it—that is, many intricate *taboos* arose from the totemic system. There is also the *taboo* of the sorcerer, which in effect is merely a spell placed upon a certain object, which makes it become useless to others.

Taboo, or its remains, is still to be found in strong force even in the most civilized communities, and from its use the feeling of reverence for ancient institutions and those who represent them is undoubtedly derived. (See also **Totemism**)

Recommended reading:

Frazer, Sir J. G. *The Golden Bough* [vol. 3, 'Taboo and the Perils of the Soul'], 12 vols., Macmillan, 1935

Ganzfried, Rabbi Solomon. *Code of Jewish Law (Kitzur Schulchan Aruch),* revised ed., Hebrew Publishing Co., New York, 1927

Mead, Margaret. *Inquiry Into the Question of Cultural Stability in Polynesia.* Columbia University, 1928; AMS Press, 1981

Webster, Hutton. *Taboo: A Sociological Study,* Stanford University Press/Oxford University Press, 1942; Octagon, 1981

Tabori, Paul (1908-1974)

Hungarian-born British novelist, journalist, political writer, scriptwriter and psychical researcher. Some of his books were published under the pseudonyms "Christopher Stevens" and "Paul Tabor."

Born August 5, 1908 in Budapest, Hungary, he was educated at Kaiser Friedrich Wilhelm University (Ph.D. 1930), Pazmany Peter University (Doctor of Economics & Political Science). In 1933 he married Katherine Elizabeth Barlay.

From 1926-31, Tabori was a foreign correspondent of Az Est Newspapers, Hungary; 1932-37 director of Mid-European Literary Service, Hungary; 1937-41 director of World Literary Service, London, England; 1941-42 assistant editor of *World Review,* London; 1942-44 diplomatic correspondent of *Britanova,* London, and film critic of the *Daily Mail,* London; 1943-46 European feature editor of Reuters Ltd., London; 1943-48 contract writer to London Films (Sir Alexander Korda), England; 1951-58 director, Telewriters Ltd.; 1960-62 editorial consultant, George Rainbird Ltd., London; 1964-65 coordinating producer, "A Day of Peace" international television series; 1966 visiting professor, Fairleigh Dickinson University, Rutherford, N.J.; 1967 City College of New York; 1956-57 chairman of Hungarian Relief Fund. He was a member of International P.E.N., chairman, Centre for Writers in Exile, 1954-57; Screenwriters Guild, London (international secretary from 1953 onwards); International Writers Fund (hon. secretary 1962 onwards); International Writer's Guild (director 1964-66).

On the death of psychical researcher Harry **Price** (1881-1948), Tabori was literary executor for Price and a trustee of the Harry Price Library at London University, England. He published a biography: *Harry Price; The Biography of a Ghost Hunter* (Athenaeum Press, London, 1950) as well as other books connected with psychical research: (with Cornelius Tabori) *My Occult Diary* (1951), *Companions of the Unseen* (1968), *Beyond the Senses; a Report on Psychical Research in the Sixties* (1971), (with Peter Underwood) *The Borley Ghosts* (1973), (with P. Raphael) *Crime and the Occult* (1974).

His other publications included: *Real Hungary* (1929), *The Nazi Myth; The Real Face of the Third Reich* (1939), *Sneeze on a Monday* (1942), *A Wreath for Europe* (1942), *The Ragged Guard; A Tale of 1941* (1942), *They Came to London* (1943), *Japanese Jeopardy* (1943), *Pierre of Normandy* (1944), *Lion and the Vulture* (1944), *Two Forests* (1945), *Private Gallery* (1945), *Bricks Upon Dust* (1945), *Peace Correspondent* (1946), *Restless Summer* (1946), *The Leaf of a Lime Tree* (U.S. title *He Never Came Back* (1946), *Sun of My Night* (1947), *Solo* (1948), (with James Eastwood) *1848; The Year of Revolutions* (1948), *Uneasy Giant* (1949), *Taken in Adultery* (1949), *Heritage of Mercy* (1949), *The Talking Tree* (1950), *The Frontier* (1950), *Another David: The Story of Jean Cavalier* (1951), *Salvatore* (1951), *Perdita's End* (1952), *Lighter Than Vanity* (1953), *Natural Science of Stupidity* (1959), *Alexander Korda* (1959), *Appointment in Andraix* (1959), *Twenty Tremendous Years* (1961), *The Art of Folly* (1961), *The Book of the Hand* (1962), *The Green Rain* (1962), *The Pictorial History of Love* (1951), (pseud. Christopher Stevens) *The Big Appetite* (1963), *The Survivors* (1965), *Secret and Forbidden* (1967), *Before the Deluge* (1967), *Invisible Eye* (1967), *Doomsday Brain* (1967), *Humor and Technology of Sex* (1968), *Maria Theresa* (1969), *Devil at Angel Falls* (1969), *A Century of Assassins* (1969), *Cleft* (1969), *The Torture Machine* (1969), *The Plague of Sanity* (1970), *Song of the Scorpions* (1970), *Hungary* (1970), *The Six Loves of Casanova* (1971), (pseud. Peter Stafford) *The Instructor* (1971), *Lily Dale* (1972), (with E. Brigg) *Stand Up and Fight* (1972), *The Anatomy of Exile* (1972), *Hazard Island* (1973), (pseud. Peter Stafford) *The Man Who Loved to Blow Up Trains* (1973), *The Pleasure House* (1974), *U.S.S.R.* (1974), *The Salvation Pedlar* (1975).

He also translated a number of books, and edited: *Hungarian Anthology* (1943), *Private Life of Adolph Hitler* by Eva Braun (1949), *The Pen in Exile; An Anthol-*

ogy of Exiled Writers (1954), *Second Anthology* (1956). He was writer of 32 feature films and over a hundred television films and plays.

He died December 2, 1974.

Tadebtsois

Spirits believed in by the Samoyeds. (See **Siberia**)

Tadibe

The name for a Samoyed magician. (See **Siberia**)

Taetzsch, Robert Leonard (1931-)

Statistician, management engineer and parapsychologist. Born July 6, 1931 at Irvington, New Jersey, he studied at Newark College of Engineering, N.J. (B.S. mechanical engineering 1952, M.S. engineering, cum laude 1959). In 1955 he married Sandra Rhea Zeitlin.

He was a manufacturing engineer at Westinghouse Electric Co. from 1953-55, operations analyst at Railway Express Agency from 1955-56 division statistician at Union Carbide Plastics Co. from 1956 onwards. Memberships include: the Parapsychological Association, American Society for Quality Control, American Statistical Association, American Society for Psychical Research.

His special interest in parapsychology has been the use of statistical techniques in order to control psi phenomena, and the development of systems for transmitting messages by psi processes. He developed a psi communication system based on binary targets and sequential sampling, and experimented with this system in conjunction with an IBM 1620 digital computer.

T'ai Chi Ch'uan

A system of ancient Chinese physical movements, designed to build up subtle energy in the body, resulting in spiritual development.

It was originally a secret taught only to males in certain families, but by the middle of the nineteenth century it was taught publicly in Peking. Its graceful flowing movements are a kind of slow-motion dance, and have been described as "yoga in movement, or more facetiously as "shadow boxing."

There are 37 basic exercises and postures, which are repeated with variations, culminating in some 65 or 108 exercises. During practice, it is important to be concerned with centering the body and with meditation and relaxation. T'ai Chi Ch'uan is sometimes linked with the study of the **I Ching** to enhance the philosophical aspects of the system.

T'ai Chi is widely taught at centers in the U.S. and Britain. A T'ai Chi newsletter is published by Wayfarer Publications, P.O. Box 26156, Los Angeles, California 90026. The Center Newsletter of the Center for Healing and Spiritual Understanding (5 Tavistock Place, London, WCI, England) also deals with T'ai Chi Ch'uan.

Recommended reading:

Cheng, Man-ching. *Tai-Chi,* North Atlantic, Berkeley, 1981 (paperback)

Da Liu. *T'ai Chi Ch'uan and I Ching,* Harper & Row, 1972

Smith, Robert W. *Chinese Boxing,* Kodansha, New York, 1981 (paperback)

Taigheirm

A magical sacrifice of cats to the infernal spirits, formerly practiced in the Highlands and Islands of Scotland. It is believed to have been originally a ceremony of sacrifice to the subterranean gods, imported from more northern lands, which became in Christian times an invocation of infernal spirits.

The word *Taigheirm* signifies either an armory, or the cry of a cat, according to the sense in which it is used.

A description of the ceremony, which must be performed with black cats, is given in George C. Horst's *Deuteroscopie* (1830): "After the cats were dedicated to all the devils, and put into a magico-sympathetic condition by the shameful things done to them, and the agony occasioned them, one of them was at once put upon the spit, and, amid terrific howlings, roasted before a slow fire. The moment that the howls of one tortured cat ceased in death, another was put upon the spit, for a minute of interval must not take place if they would control hell; and this continued for the four entire days and nights. If the exorcist could hold it out still longer, and even till his physical powers were absolutely exhausted, he must do so."

When the horrible rites had been continued for a time, the demons began to appear in the shape of black cats, who mingled their dismal cries with those of the unfortunate sacrifices. At length a cat appeared of larger size and more frightful aspect than the others, and the time had come for the exorcist to make known his demands. Usually he asked for the gift of **second sight,** but other rewards might be asked for and received.

The last *Taigheirm* was said to have been held in Mull about the middle of the seventeenth century. The exorcists were Allan Maclean and his assistant Lachlain Maclean, both of whom received the psychic gift of second sight.

Of this particular ceremony Horst stated: "The infernal spirits appeared, some in the early progress of the sacrifices in the shape of black cats. The first who appeared during the sacrifice, after they had cast a furious glance at the sacrifices, said—Lachlain Oer, that is, 'Injurer of Cats.' Allan, the chief operator, warned Lachlain, whatever he might see or hear, not to waver, but to keep the spit incessantly turning. At length the cat of monstrous size appeared; and after it had set up a horrible howl, said to Lachlain Oer, that if he did not cease before their largest brother came he would never see the face of God.

"Lachlain answered that he would not cease till he had finished his work if all the devils in hell came. At the end of the fourth day, there sat on the end of the beam in the roof of the barn a black cat with fire-flaming eyes, and there was heard a terrific howl quite across the straits of Mull into Mowen."

By this time, the elder of the two men was quite exhausted, and sank down in a swoon, but the younger was sufficiently self-possessed to ask for wealth and prosperity, which both received throughout their lifetime.

Shortly before this, Cameron of Lochiel received at a *Taigheirm* a small silver shoe which, put on the foot of a newborn son of his family, would give courage and fortitude to the child. One boy, however, had at his birth, a foot too large for the shoe, a defect inherited from his mother, who was not a Cameron. His lack of the magically bestowed courage was apparent at the battle of Sheriffmuir, where he fled before the enemy.

"Tales of Terror"

Title of an anonymous collection of Gothic style ballads, usually ascribed wrongly to Matthew Gregory **Lewis.** There are actually two books with this title. The first published in 1799, included three of Lewis' ballads, together with others by Sir Walter Scott and Robert Southey, but does not appear to be compiled by Lewis. The three ballads later appeared in his book *Tales of Wonder* (1801).

A second *Tales of Terror,* published in 1801, is a coarse and grotesque collection and contains parodies of the work of Lewis and others, and does not therefore seem to be compiled by Lewis either. (See also Occult English **Fiction;** Matthew Gregory **Lewis**)

Talisman

An inanimate object which is supposed to possess a supernatural capacity of conferring benefits or powers, in contradistinction to the **amulet,** the purpose of which is to ward off evil.

The talisman was usually a disc of metal or stone engraved with astrological or magical figures. Talismans were common in ancient Egypt and Babylon. The virtues of astrological talismans were as follows.

The astrological figure of Mercury, engraven upon silver, which is the corresponding metal, and according to the prescribed rites, gave success in merchandise; that of Mars gave victory to the soldier; that of Venus, beauty, and so of the rest. All such talismans likewise were more powerful in the hour of their planet's ascendency.

There are three general varieties of these potent charms: 1. The astronomical, having the characters of the heavenly signs or constellations, 2. The magical, with extraordinary figures, superstitious words, or the names of angels, 3. The mixed, engraven with celestial signs and barbarous words.

To these, Thomas D. Fosbrook, in his *Encyclopœdia of Antiquities* (2 vols., 1825; 1840), added two others: 4. The *sigilla planetarum,* composed of Hebrew numeral letters, used by astrologers and fortune-tellers, and 5. Hebrew names and characters.

As an example of the most powerful of the latter, may be mentioned the sacred name of Jehovah. The famous **tephillin** or phylacteries, used in Jewish devotion, and which were bound on the head, the arm, and the hand, may be regarded as talismans, and they were the subject of many traditional ceremonies. There is also the **mezazoth** or schedules for doorposts, and another article of this description mentioned in the following quotation from the *Talmud:* "Whoever had the tephillin bound to his head and arm, and the tsitsith thrown over his garments, and the mezuza fixed on his door-post, is protected from sin."

Writing of talismans in his book *The Occult Sciences* (1891), A. E. Waite stated:

"I. The Talisman of the Sun must be composed of a pure and fine gold, fashioned into a circular plate, and well polished on either side. A serpentine circle, enclosed by a pentagram must be engraved on the obverse side with a diamond-pointed graving tool. The reverse must bear a human head in the centre of the six-pointed star of Solomon, which shall itself be surrounded with the name of the solar intelligence Pi-Rhé, written in the characters of the Magi. This talisman is supposed to insure to its bearer the goodwill of influential persons. It is a preservative against death by heart disease, syncope, aneurism, and epidemic complaints. It must be composed on a Sunday during the passage of the moon through the first ten degrees of Leo, and when that luminary is in a favourable aspect with Saturn and the Sun. The consecration consists in the exposure of the talisman to the smoke of a perfume composed of cinnamon, incense, saffron, and red sandal, burnt with laurel wood, and twigs of dessicated heliotrope, in a new chafing-dish, which must be ground into powder and buried in an isolated spot, after the operation is finished. The talisman must be afterwards encased in a satchel of bright yellow silk, which must be fastened on the breast by an interlaced ribbon of the same material, tied in the form of a cross. In all cases the ceremony should be preceded by the conjuration of the Four, to which the reader has already been referred. The form of consecration, accompanied by sprinkling with holy water, may be rendered in the following manner:—

"In the name of Elohim, and by the spirit of the living waters, be thou unto me as a sign of light and a seal of will.

"Presenting it to the smoke of the perfumes:—By the brazen serpent before which fell the serpents of fire, be thou unto me as a sign of light and a seal of will.

"Breathing seven times upon the talisman:—By the firmament and the spirit of the voice, be thou unto me as a sign of light and a seal of will.

"Lastly, when placing some grains of purified earth or salt upon the pentacle:—In the name of the salt of the earth and by virtue of the life eternal, be thou unto me as a sign of light and a seal of will.

"II. The Talisman of the Moon should be composed of a circular and well-polished plate of the purest silver, being of the dimensions of an ordinary medal. The image of a crescent, enclosed in a pentagram, should be graven on the obverse side. On the reverse side, a chalice must be encircled by the duadic seal of Solomon, encompassed by the letters of the lunar genius Pi-Job. This talisman is considered a protection to travellers, and to sojourners in strange lands. It preserves from death by drowning, by epilepsy, by dropsy, by apoplexy, and madness. The danger of a violent end which is predicted by Saturnian aspects in horoscopes of nativity, may be removed by its means. It should be composed on a Monday, when the moon is passing through the first ten degrees of Capricornus or Virgo, and is also well aspected with Saturn. Its consecration consists in exposure to a perfume composed of white sandal, camphor, aloes, amber, and pulverised seed of cucumber, burnt with dessicated stalks of mugwort, moonwort, and ranunculus, in a new earthen chafing-dish, which must be reduced, after the operation, into powder, and buried in a deserted spot. The talisman must be sewn up in a satchel of white silk, and fixed on the breast by a ribbon of the same colour, interlaced and tied in the form of a cross.

"III. The Talisman of Mars must be composed of a well-polished circular plate of the finest iron, and of the dimensions of an ordinary medal. The symbol of a sword in the centre of a pentagram must be engraved on the obverse side. A lion's head surrounded by a six-pointed star must appear on the reverse face, with the letters of the name Erotosi, the planetary genius of Mars, above the outer angles. This talisman passes as a preservative against all combinations of enemies. It averts the chance of death in brawls and battles, in epidemics and fevers, and by corroding ulcers. It also neutralizes the peril of a violent end as a punishment for crime when it is foretold in the horoscope of the nativity.

"This talisman must be composed on a Tuesday, during the passage of the moon through the ten first degrees of Aries or Sagittarius, and when, moreover, it is favourably aspected with Saturn and Mars. The consecration consists in its exposure to the smoke of a perfume composed of dried absinth and rue, burnt in an earthen vessel which has never been previously used, and which must be broken into powder, and buried in a secluded place, when the operation is completed. Finally, the talisman must be sewn up in a satchel of red silk, and fastened on the breast with ribbons of the same material folded and knotted in the form of a cross.

"IV. The Talisman of Mercury must be formed of a circular plate of fixed quicksilver, or according to another account of an amalgam of silver, mercury, and pewter, of the dimensions of an ordinary medal, well-polished on both sides. A winged caduceus, having two serpents twining about it, must be engraved in the centre of a pentagram on the obverse side. The other must bear a dog's head within the star of Solomon, the latter being surrounded with the name of the planetary genius, Pi-Hermes, written in the alphabet of the Magi. This talisman must be composed on a Wednesday, when the moon is passing through the ten first degrees of Gemini or Scorpio, and is well aspected with Saturn and Mercury. The consecration consists in its exposure to the smoke of a perfume composed of benzoin, macis, and storax, burnt with the dried stalks of the lily, the narcissus, fumitory, and marjolane, placed in a clay chafing-dish which has never been devoted to any other purpose, and which must, after the completion of the task, be reduced to powder and buried in an undisturbed place. The Talisman of Mercury is judged to be a defence in all species of commerce and business industry. Buried under the ground in a house of commerce, it will draw customers and prosperity. It preserves all who wear it from epilepsy and madness. It averts death by murder and poison; it is a safeguard against the schemes of treason; and it procures prophetic dreams when it is worn on the head during sleep. It is fastened on the breast by a ribbon of purple silk folded and tied in the form of a cross, and the talisman is itself enclosed in a satchel of the same material.

"V. The Talisman of Jupiter must be formed of a circular plate of the purest English pewter, having the dimensions of an ordinary medal, and being highly polished on either side. The image of a four-pointed crown in the centre of a pentagram must be engraved on the obverse side. On the other must be the head of an eagle in the centre of the six-pointed star of Solomon, which must be surrounded by the name of the planetary genius Pi-Zéous, written in the arcane alphabet.

"This talisman must be composed on a Thursday, during the passage of the moon through the first ten degrees of Libra, and when it is also in a favourable aspect with Saturn and Jupiter. The consecration consists in its exposure to the smoke of a perfume composed of incense, ambergris, balm, grain of Paradise, saffron, and macis, which is the second coat of the nutmeg. These must be burnt with wood of the oak, poplar, fig tree, and pomegranate, and placed in a new earthen dish, which must be ground into powder, and buried in a quiet spot, at the end of the ceremony. The talisman must be wrapped in a satchel of sky-blue silk, suspended on the breast by a ribbon of the same material, folded and fastened in the form of a cross.

"The Talisman of Jupiter is held to attract to the wearer the benevolence and sympathy of everyone. It averts anxieties, favours honourable enterprises, and augments well-being in proportion to social condition. It is a protection against unforeseen accidents, and the perils of a violent death when it is threatened by Saturn in the horoscope of nativity. It also preserves from death by affections of the liver, by inflammation of the lungs, and by that cruel affection of the spinal marrow, which is termed *tabes dorsalis* in medicine.

"VI. The Talisman of Venus must be formed of a circular plate of purified and well-polished copper. It must be of the ordinary dimensions of a medal, perfectly polished on both its sides. It must bear on the obverse face the letter G inscribed in the alphabet of the Magi, and enclosed in a pentagram. A dove must be engraved on the reverse, in the centre of the six-pointed star, which must be surrounded by the letters which compose the name of the planetary Genius Suroth. This talisman must be composed on a Friday, during the passage of the moon through the first ten degrees of Taurus or Virgo, and when that luminary is well aspected with Saturn and Venus. Its consecration consists in its exposure to the smoke of a perfume composed of violets and roses, burnt with olive wood in a new earthen chafing-dish, which must be ground into powder at the end of the operation and buried in a solitary spot. The talisman must, finally, be sewn up in a satchel of green or rose-coloured silk, which must be fastened on the breast by a band of the same material, folded and tied in the form of a cross.

"The Talisman of Venus is accredited with extraordinary power in cementing the bonds of love and harmony between husbands and wives. It averts from those who wear it the spite and machinations of hatred. It preserves women from the terrible and fatal diseases which are known as cancer. It averts from both men and women all danger of death, to which they may be accidentally or purposely exposed. It counterbalances the unfortunate presages which may appear in the horoscope of the nativity. Its last and most singular quality is its power to change the animosity of an enemy into a love and devotion which will be proof against every temptation, and it rests on the sole condition that such a person should be persuaded to partake of a liquid in which the talisman has been dipped.

"VII. The Talisman of Saturn must be composed of a circular plate of refined and purified lead, being of the dimensions of an ordinary medal, elaborately polished. On the obverse side must be engraven with the diamond-pointed tool which is requisite in all these talismanic operations, the image of a sickle enclosed in a pentagram. The reverse side must bear a bull's head, enclosed in the star of Solomon, and surrounded by the mysterious letters which compose, in the alphabet of the Magi, the name of the planetary Genius Tempha. The person who is intended to wear this talisman must engrave it himself, without witnesses, and without taking any one into his confidence.

"This talisman must be composed on a Saturday when the moon is passing through the first ten degrees of Taurus or Capricorn, and is favourably aspected with Saturn. It must be consecrated by exposure to the smoke of a perfume composed of alum, assa-fœtida, cammonée, and sulphur, which must be burnt with cypress, the wood of the ash tree, and sprays of black hellebore, in a new earthen chafing-dish, which must be reduced into powder at the end of the performance, and buried in a deserted place. The talisman must, finally, be sewn up in a satchel of black silk and fastened on the breast with a ribbon of the same material, folded and tied in the form of a cross. The Talisman of Saturn was affirmed to be a safeguard against death by apoplexy and cancer, decay in the bones, consumption, dropsy, paralysis, and decline; it was also a preservative against the possibility of being entombed in a trance, against the danger of violent death by secret crime, poison, or ambush. If the head of the army in wartime were to bury the Talisman of Saturn in a place which it was feared might fall into the hands of the enemy, the limit assigned by the presence of the talisman could not be overstepped by the opposing host, which would speedily withdraw in discouragement, or in the face of a determined assault." (See also **Amulets; Ceremonial Magic**)

Recommended reading:

Beard, Charles R. *Lucks and Talismans; A Chapter of Popular Superstition,* Sampson, Low, London, 1934; Blom, New York, 1972

Budge, E. A. W. *Amulets and Superstitions,* Oxford University Press, U.K., 1930; reprinted under title *Amulets and Talismans,* University Books, 1961

Lamb, Geoffrey. *Discovering Magic Charms and Talismans,* Shire Publications (paperback), U.K., 1974

Lippman, Deborah & Paul Colin. *Amulets, Charms and Talismans: What They Mean and How to Use Them.* M. Evans & Co., New York, 1974

Lockhart, J. G. *Curses, Lucks and Talismans,* Geoffrey Bles, London, 1938; Singing Tree Press, Detroit, 1971

Pavitt, W. T. & Kate. *The Book of Talismans, Amulets, and Zodiacal Gems,* Rider, London, 1914; Tower Books, Detroit, 1971; Wilshire, North Hollywood, 1972

Regardie, Israel. *How to Make and Use Talismans,* Aquarian Press, London/Weiser, 1972

"Sepharial" (W. G. Old). *The Book of Charms and Talismans,* W. Foulsham, London, 1923; Arco, 1971

Talking Mongoose

A celebrated paranormal phenomenon in the Isle of Man, U.K., investigated by psychical researchers Harry **Price** and R. S. **Lambert** in the 1930s.

Named "Gef," the mongoose manifested to the Irving family, and there is some doubt whether it was a real creature or a **poltergeist** phenomenon. The case is reported in Price & Lambert's book *The Haunting of Cashen's Gap* (London, 1936). (See also **Cashen's Gap**)

Tallmadge, Nathaniel Pitcher (1795-1864)

United States Senator from 1833-34, Governor of Wisconsin from 1844-46, one of the early converts to Spiritualism. His experiences with the **Fox sisters,** recounted in a letter to a friend under the date April 12, 1853, were published in most of the newspapers of the time.

He stated that he had received messages in **direct writing** from the spirit of John Calhoun and also witnessed very strong physical manifestations, notably the **levitation** of a table with himself on top of it.

He soon had experiences in his own household. His thirteen-year-old daughter, who never touched the piano, began to play classical works and popular airs in trance.

In April, 1854, a memorial was presented in the Congress by James Shields, asking for an inquiry into the truth of Spiritualism. Thirteen thousand signatures were attached. At the head of the list was the name of Governor Tallmadge.

Tallmadge contributed an introduction to *The Healing of the Nations* by automatic writing medium Charles **Linton,** published in 1855 by The Society for the Diffusion of Spiritual Knowledge.

Talmud, The

From the Hebrew *lamad,* to learn, the *Talmud* is the name of the great code of Jewish civil and canonical law. It is divided into two portions—the *Mishna* and the *Gemara;* the former constitutes the text and the latter is a commentary and supplement. But besides being the basis of a legal code, it is also a collection of Jewish poetry and legend.

The *Mishna* is a development of the laws contained in the Pentateuch. It is divided into six *sedarim* or orders, each containing a number of tractates, which are again divided into *peraqim* or chapters. The *sedarim* are: (1) *Zeraim,* which deals with agriculture; (2) *Moed,* with festivals and sacrifices; (3) *Nashim,* with the law regarding women; (4) *Nezaqin,* with civil law; (5) *Qodashim,* with the sacrificial law; and (6) *Tohoroth* or *Tah,* with purifications. The *Mishna* is said to have been handed down by Ezra and to be in part the work of Joshua, David or Solomon, and originally communicated orally by the Deity in the time of Moses.

There are two recensions—the *Talmud* of Jerusalem, and the *Talmud* of Babylon, the latter, besides the *sedarim* already mentioned, contains seven additional treatises which are regarded as extra-canonical. The first is supposed to have been finally edited towards the close of the fourth century, and the second by Rabbi Ashi, President of the Academy of Syro in Babylon, somewhere in the fourth century. Although revised from time to time before then, both versions have been greatly affected through the interpolation of traditions, and reinterpretations in the light of rabbinical discussions. The rabbinical decisions in the *Mishna* are entitled *helacoth* and the traditional narratives *haggadah.*

The cosmogony of the *Talmud* assumes that the universe has been developed by means of a series of cataclysms—world after world was destroyed until the Creator made the present earth and saw that it was good. In the wonderful treatise on the subject by E. Deutsch which first appeared in the *Quarterly Review* in 1867, and is reprinted in his *Literary Remains,* the following passage appears:

"The *how* of the creation was not mere matter of speculation. The co-operation of angels, whose existence was warranted by Scripture, and a whole hierarchy of whom had been built up under Persian influences, was distinctly denied. In a discussion about the day of their creation, it is agreed on all hands that there were no angels at first, lest men might say, 'Michael spanned out the firmament on the south, and Gabriel to the north.' There is a distinct foreshadowing of the Gnostic Demiurgos—that antique link between the Divine Spirit and the world of matter—to be found in the *Talmud.* What with Plato were the Ideas, with Philo the Logos, with the Kabalists the 'World of Aziluth,' what the Gnostics called more emphatically the wisdom (sophi), or power (dunamis), and Plotinus the nous, that the Talmudical authors call Metation.

"There is a good deal, in the post-captivity *Talmud,* about the Angels, borrowed from the Persian. The Archangels or Angelic princes are seven in number, and their Hebrew names and functions correspond almost exactly to those of their Persian prototypes. There are also hosts of ministering angels, the Persian *Yazatas,* whose functions, besides that of being messengers, were two-fold—to praise God and to be guardians of man. In their first capacity they are daily created by God's breath out of a stream of fire that rolls its waves under the supernal throne. In their second, two of them accompany every man, and for every new good deed man acquires a new guardian angel, who always watches over his steps. When a righteous man dies, three hosts of angels descend from the celestial battlements to meet him. One says (in the words of Scripture), 'He shall go in peace'; the second takes up the strain and says, 'Who has walked in righteousness'; and the third concludes, 'Let him come in peace and rest upon his bed.' In like manner, when the wicked man passes away, three hosts of wicked angels are ready to escort him, but their address is not couched in any spirit of consolation or encouragement."

The *Talmud* is the supreme repository of Jewish moral and spiritual law, and also enshrines a wealth of historical, geographical, philosophical, and poetical traditions. It is one of the great documents of human history and the central focus of Jewish law.

It has been considered by some authorities that a great many of the traditional tales in the *Talmud* have a magical basis, and that magical secrets are contained in them, but this depends entirely upon the interpretation put upon them, and the subject is one which necessitates close study. An English translation of the Jerusalem *Talmud* was published in 1871, and of the Babylonian *Talmud* (35 vols.), 1935-52. (See also **Kabala**)

Tamlin, Sarah (c.1848)

One of the very early American rapping mediums, soon after the famous **Rochester Rappings** of the **Fox Sisters.** E. W. Capron, author of the book *Modern Spiritualism; Its Facts and Fanaticisms* (1855), visited Mrs. Tamlin and attended one of her seances at which **raps** were heard. A table moved in various directions and "was held down to the floor so that it required the whole strength of a man to move it from its position."

At that time, the phenomenon of raps spread like a contagion. Miss Harriet Bebee, a girl of sixteen, visited Mrs. Tamlin and on returning to her own home twenty miles away, the raps broke out again in her presence.

According to Capron's account, about fifty mediums were soon operating in private circles.

Tanagras, Angelos (1875-)

Admiral in the Greek Navy who took an active interest in parapsychology. Born May 20, 1875 in Athens, Greece, he became founder (1923), president (1923 onwards) of the Hellenic Society for Psychical Research. Admiral Tanagras held various decorations, including Commander, Order of King George, holder of the Golden Cross.

He was a corresponding member of the Society for Psychical Research, London as well as various European psychical research societies. He organized the Fourth International Congress of Psychic Research in Athens during 1930, when he worked closely with Prof. Hans **Driesch** and Sir Oliver **Lodge.**

He also took part in experiments in long distance telepathy, collaborating with Rene **Warcollier** in France and Dr. Gardner **Murphy** in the U.S., as well as experimenters in Italian and British psychic research societies. He studied psychometry in Greece. He contributed various articles on parapsychological subjects to *Revue Métapsychique, Zeitschrift für Parapsychologie, Metapsichica.* He edited and contributed to *Psychic Research,* published by the Hellenic Society for Psychical Research. In addition to his books on Greek history and legend, he published *Destiny and Chance* (1934).

Tannhäuser

A medieval German legend which relates how a minstrel and knight of that name, passing by the Hörselberg, or Hill of Venus, entered therein in answer to a call, and remained there with an enchantress, living an unholy life. After a time, he grew weary of sin, and longing to return to normal living, he forswore the worship of Venus and left her.

He then made a pilgrimage to Rome to ask pardon of the Pope, but when he was told by Urban IV himself that the papal staff would as soon blossom as such a sinner as Tannhäuser be forgiven, he returned to Venus. Three days later, the Pope's staff did actually blossom, and the Pope sent messengers into every country to find the despairing minstrel, but to no purpose. Tannhäuser had disappeared.

The story has a mythological basis which has been overlaid by medieval Christian thought, and the original hero of which has been displaced by a more modern personage, just as the Venus of the existing legend is the mythological Venus only in name. She is really the Lady Holda, a German earth-goddess.

Tannhäuser was a "minnesinger" or love-minstrel of the middle of the thirteenth century. He was very popular among the minnesingers of that time and the restless and intemperate life he led probably marked him out as the hero of such a legend as has been recounted.

He was the author of many ballads of considerable excellence, which were published in the second part of the *Minnesinger* of Friedrich H. von der Hagen (Leipzsig, 1838) and in the sixth volume of Moriz Haupt's *Zeitschrift für deutsches Althertum* (1841 etc.). The most authentic version of this legend is given in J. L. Uhland's *Alte hoch und niederdeutsche Volkslieder* (Stuttgart, 1844-45).

Tantra

A group of religious and occult Hindu scriptures which emphasize the *Shakti* or energy of the deity, which comes from the goddess. The scriptures are usually in the form of a dialogue between the god Siva and his wife Parvati.

In treatises where Siva answers the questions, they are called *Agama,* where Parvati answers it is a *Nigama.*

Tantras are considered encyclopedias of esoteric wisdom, covering creation and destruction of the universe, worship of the gods, spiritual disciplines, rituals, occult powers and meditations. The Tantras are also supposed to be specially relevant to *Kali Yuga,* the present age of devolution.

The preeminent Western scholar of Tantra was Sir John **Woodroffe** (1865-1936) who translated important Tantric scriptures using the pseudonym "Arthur Avalon." (See also **Kundalini; Tantric Yoga**)

Recommended reading:

Avalon, Arthur. *Tantra of the Great Liberation (Mahanirvana Tantra),* Luzac & Co., London, 1913; Dover paperback, 1972

Chakravarti, Chintaharan. *Tantras; Studies on Their Religion and Literature,* Punthi Pustak, Calcutta, India, 1963

Mookerjee, Ajit. *Tantra Art,* Random House, 1971

Mookerjee, Ajit & M. Khanna. *The Tantric Way, Art, Science, Ritual,* New York, Graphic, 1977

Rawson, Philip. *Tantra; The Indian Cult of Ecstasy,* Thames & Hudson, U.K., 1974

Woodroffe, Sir John. *The Serpent Power,* Luzac & Co., London, 1919; Ganesh & Co., Madras, India, 1950 etc.; Dover paperback, 1974

Tantric Yoga

A system of Hindu Yoga which emphasizes the *Shakti* or sexual energy associated with the female principle and usually characterized as **Kundalini.**

Whilst the arousal of this energy is normally the goal of **Hatha Yoga** (concerned with physical exercises) in conjunction with **Rajah Yoga** (concerned with spiritual development), there is a specifically left-hand or occult pathway of Tantric Yoga which involves a taboo-breaking ceremony with a female assistant.

This consists of five things which are normally forbidden to a yogi: *Madya* (wine), *Mansa* (flesh), *Matsya* (fish), *Mudra* (a term implying both parched grain and mystic gesture), *Maithuna* (sexual intercourse). Western occultism derives from vestiges of Tantra, with special emphasis on the use of sexual energy for occult purposes, as exemplified in the somewhat confused sex-magic system of occultist Aleister **Crowley**. (See also **Kundalini; Sex Magic; Tantra; Yoga**)

Recommended reading:

Garrison, Omar. *Tantra—The Yoga of Sex*, Causeway, 1973; Academy Editions, London, 1974

Gopi Krishna. *The Awakening of Kundalini*, Dutton paperback, 1975

Mookerjee, Ajit. *Tantra Asana*, Random House, 1971

Marques-Riviere, J. *Tantrik Yoga*, Rider & Co., London, 1940; Weiser paperback, 1970

Tao

Term used in ancient Chinese religious philosophy, signifying "the Way" or pathway of life. The *Tao* is a unity underlying the opposites and diversity of the phenomenal world. Cosmic energy (*Ching Shen Li*) is manifest in the duality of *Yin* and *Yang*, negative and positive, female and male principles in nature. *Yin* and *Yang* are also energies in the individual human body, and the balancing of these energies is one of the tasks of life. The correct harmony between *Yin* and *Yang* may be achieved through diet, meditation, and a life of truth, simplicity, and tranquillity, identifying with the *Tao* of nature.

Taoism teaches union with the law of the universe through wisdom and detached action. Special techniques of Taoist Yoga arose to normalize and enhance the flow of vital energy in the human body. This yoga was variously named *K'ai Men* (Open Door), *Ho Ping* (Unity) and *Ho Hsieh* (Harmony). *K'ai Men* implies opening the path to the channels of mind, spirit, and body so that they reflect the balance of *Yin* and *Yang* and a harmony with the energy of the cosmos.

Taoist Yoga is basically the same as the **Kundalini** Yoga of India, and it is not clear whether such a parallel system originated by direct influence of traveling mystics or by spontaneous rediscovery of basic truths.

Both Indian and Chinese yogas are concerned with the control of vital energy which is the force behind sexual activity, but which may be diverted into different channels in the body for blissful expansion of consciousness. For centuries, the techniques of Chinese Yoga were little known in the West, since teaching manuals were not translated, and the techniques were transmitted from teacher to pupil. In recent years, however, teachers of Chinese Yoga have established schools in the U.S. and have also published translations of basic Chinese Yoga texts.

Modern teachers of Chinese Yoga include Charles Luk (Lu K'uan Yü), who lives in Hong Kong and has translated various Chinese Buddhist and Yoga texts, and Mantak Chia from Thailand, who studied with Taoist and Buddhist masters and has created a synthesis of their spiritual techniques, in conjunction with classical techniques of T'ai Chi Chuan. Together with his wife Maneewan Chia (born in China), Mantak Chia has been instrumental in establishing Healing Tao Centers in the U.S., teaching basic self-development courses of Taoist Esoteric Yoga.

In distinction to the esoteric concept of the *Tao*, later Taoism, associated with temples and popular worship, became one of the three major religious systems of China, together with Confucianism and Buddhism. (See also **China; Kundalini; Taoism; Yin and Yang; Ouroboros; Yoga**)

Recommended reading:

Chang, Chung-Yuan. *Tao; A New Way of Thinking*, Harper & Row, 1975

Chia, Mantak. *Awaken Healing Energy through the Tao*, Aurora Press, New York, 1983

Chia, Mantak & Michael Winn. *Taoist Secrets of Love; Cultivating Male Sexual Energy*, Aurora Press, New York, 1984

Ch'u Ta-Kao (transl.). *Tao Te Ching*, Allen & Unwin, London/Samuel Weiser, 1937

Lu K'uan Yü. *Taoist Yoga; Alchemy and Immortality*, Rider & Co., London, paperback, 1970

Soo, Chee. *The Chinese Art of K'ai Men*, Gordon & Cremonesi, London & New York, 1977

Suzuki, D. T. & Paul Carus (transl.). *The Canon of Reason and Virtue*, Open Court, La Salle, Illinois, 1913

Taoism

One of the three major religious systems of ancient China, together with Confucianism and Buddhism. Early Taoism derives from the Tao teachings of Lao Tzu, expressed in the book *Tao-te-Ching* (Book of the Right Way). Lao Tzu was said to have been born of poor parents in Tau (Honan) under the Emperor Ting of the Kau dynasty, c.605 B.C. It is believed that he was a philosopher who became disgusted with the world and became a pessimist, later resigning his position in the Record Department and retiring to a monastery, dying c.505 B.C. Most details of his life are legendary. He is said to have met Gautama Buddha and to have been taught by him, and to have held discussions with Confucius. Later developments of Taoism as a popular religion sometimes draw upon Buddhist and Confucian elements.

Lao Tzu's book *Tao-te-Ching* was regarded as a sacred work in North and Central China, but was burned with other writings in 220 B.C., reappearing under the Han dynasty and reinforced by the teachings of *Chuang Tzu*, another Taoist classic, believed to have been the work of a philosopher of the same name.

Taoist was originally an esoteric philosophy, concerned with the unity underlying the opposites and diversity of the phenomenal world. Taoism taught union with the law of the universe through wisdom and detached action. The union of cosmic and individual energies is reminiscent of the Vedanta teachings of India.

Taoism also developed its own yoga techniques, which parallel the ancient Hindu system of **Kundalini** Yoga. These involved control of **ch'i** or vital energy, the force behind sexual activity, which could also be diverted into different channels in the body for blissful expansion of consciousness.

The circulation of this generative force in the body, aided by breathing techniques, corresponds with Indian yoga techniques involving *pranayama* breathing, and the ascent of Kundalini energy through the *chakras* or vital centers of the body. This individual alchemy was variously known as *K'ai Men* (Open Door), *Ho Ping* (Unity), or *Ho Hsieh* (Harmony).

Later developments of Taoism were of an esoteric character. Temples were erected to Lao Tzu, and there were legends of miracles. Rituals were evolved, with sacrifices and auxiliary beliefs which are somewhat at variance with the original austere Taoist doctrine.

The extraordinary parallels between ancient Indian and Chinese Taoism in its various forms and Hinduism (Vedanta and Yoga) do not appear to have been documented by historians. The yoga teachings of China descended from teacher to pupil, and it is only in recent times that basic texts have been translated into English. There are now teachers of Chinese Yoga in Western countries and centers for instruction. There are also many translations with commentaries of the earlier Tao teachings in the *Tao-te-Ching*. (See also **Ch'i; China; Kundalini; Tao; Vedanta; Yoga)**

Recommended reading:

Bynner, Witter (transl.). *The Way of Life According to Lao Tzu*, G. P. Putnam's Sons, 1944

Chang, Chung-Yuan. *Tao; A New Way of Thinking*, Harper & Row, 1975

Hughes, E. R. (ed. & transl.). *Chinese Philosophy in Classical Times*, J. M. Dent, London/E. P. Dutton, 1942 etc.

Lu Kuan Yü. *Taoist Yoga; Alchemy and Immortality*, Rider & Co., London, paperback, 1970

Soo, Chee. *The Chinese Art of K'ai Men*, Gordon & Cremonesi, London & New York, 1977

Watson, Burton (transl.). *Chuang Tzu, Basic Writings*, Columbia University Press, 1964

Targ, Russell (1934-)

Physicist with parapsychological interests. Born April 11, 1934 in Chicago, Illinois he studied at Queens College, New York (B.S. physics 1954), graduate study in physics at Columbia University. In 1958 he married Joan Fischer.

He was an engineer with Sperry Gyroscope Co. from 1956-59, research associate at Polytechnic Institute, Brooklyn, N.Y. 1959, senior physicist (plasma and microwaves) at Technical Research Group, Syosset, Long Island, N.Y. from 1959 onwards.

He entered **Stanford Research Institute** as a senior research physicist in 1972, where he collaborated with Harold E. **Puthoff** on parapsychological research. Their joint papers include: 'A Perceptual Channel for Information Transfer over Kilometer Distances: historical perspective and recent research' (*Proceedings, Institute of Electrical and Electronics Engineers*, vol. 64, 1975); (papers presented at annual conventions of the Parapsychological Association) 'ESP Experiments with Uri Geller' (1973), 'PK Experiments with Uri Geller and Ingo Swann' (1973), 'Remote Viewing of Natural Targets' (1974), 'Replication Study on the Remote Viewing of Natural Targets' (1975); 'Information Transmission under Conditions of Sensory Shielding' (*Nature*, October 1974). Papers from the Parapsychological Association annual conventions were published in: *Research in Parapsychology 1973, Research in Parapsychology 1974* and *Research in Parapsychology 1975* (Scarecrow Press, N.J.).

His publications include: (with Harold E. Puthoff) *Mind-Reach: Scientists Look at Psychic Ability* (1977; 1978. Reporting parapsychological research at Stanford Research Institute, 1972-1976), (with Charles T. Tart & Harold E. Puthoff, eds.) Mind at Large (1979), (with Keith Harary) *The Mind Race; Understanding & Using Psychic Abilities* (1984; 1985).

Targ has also published over twenty-five technical papers concerned with laser research, gas plasma technology and optical communications, and has invented a tunable plasma oscillator operating at microwave frequencies. He is co-founder and president of **Parapsychology Research Group, Inc.**, a non-profit organization founded in Palo Alto, California, to conduct investigations into psychic research. (See also Uri **Geller;** Ingo **Swann**)

Target

Term used by parapsychologists to indicate the object (mental or physical) to which a subject attempts to respond paranormally. A mental target would relate to **extrasensory perception**; a physical target to **psychokinesis.**

Tarot (or Tarots)

French name for a special pack of playing-cards popularly used for the purpose of divination, and still immensely popular with modern fortune-tellers. The derivation of the word *tarot* is still uncertain. *Tarot* cards form part of an ordinary pack in countries of southern Europe and the name *tarocchi* is given to an Italian game.

One suggestion is that these cards were so called because they were *tarotées* on the back, that is, marked with plain or dotted lines crossing diagonally. Some confirmation of this theory is indicated by the German form of the word, a *tarock-karte* being a card checkered on the back. However, this may be simply a confusion between cause and effect.

In its familiar form, the tarot pack consists of a pack of seventy-eight cards, comprising four suits of fourteen cards each (the extra court card in each suit being the Cavalier, Knight or Horseman) and twenty-two symbolical picture-cards as *atouts* or trumps. The four suits, related to the modern hearts, clubs, diamonds and spades, are swords, cups, coins and batons (earlier represented as swords, cups, rings and wands).

Much controversy surrounds the whole question of origins of *tarot* and its relationship to the present-day set of fifty-two playing cards. It is not difficult to see symbolic interpretations of the fifty-two pack in its division of four suits, corresponding to the seasons of the year, fifty-two weeks, and the symbolic rulers of the court cards. Some writers have connected the pack with ancient Eastern origins of the game of chess, with its comparable king, queen and knight. Others have confidently suggested an origin in ancient Egypt as an esoteric book of life. Various writers like A. Court de Gébelin, J. F. Vaillant, and S. L. MacGregor **Mathers** have supported such theories. It has been suggested that the word *tarot* relates to the Hungarian gypsy *tar* (pack of cards), and that ancient esoteric symbolism found its way throughout Europe through gypsy migrations.

The idea that the *tarot* was introduced into Europe by the gypsies appears to have been first suggested by Vaillant, who had lived for many years among the gypsies, who instructed him in their traditional lore. Much of the information thus obtained is incorporated in his books *Les Rômes, histoire vraie des vrais Bohémiens* (1857), *La Bible des Bohémiens* (1860) and *La Clef Magique de la Fiction et du Fait* (1863). Vaillant's theory was endorsed by the French writer "Papus" (Gérard Encausse) in his book *The Tarot of the Bohemians* (1919, translation of *Le Tarot des Bohémiens; Le plus ancien livre du Monde*, 1899), in which he claimed that the *tarot* was the absolute key to occult science.

"The Gypsy pack of cards," he stated, "is a wonderful book according to Court de Gébelin and Vaillant. This pack, under the names of *Tarot*, Thora, Rota, has formed the basis of the synthetic teaching of all the ancient nations successively."

The British legal authority De l'Hoste Ranking, writing in 1908, stated: "I would submit that from internal evidence we may deduce that the *tarots* were introduced by a race speaking an Indian dialect; that the form of the Pope shows they had been long in a country where the orthodox Eastern Church predominated; and the form of head-dress of the king, together with the shape of the eagle on the shield, shows that this was governed by Russian Grand Dukes, who had not yet assumed the Imperial insignia. This seems to me confirmatory of the widespread belief that it is to the Gypsies we are indebted for our knowledge of playing-cards."

As early as 1865, two years after the appearance of Vaillant's last book, E. S. Taylor supported the same hypothesis in his book *The History of Playing Cards.* However, W. H. Willshire, in his book *A Descriptive Catalogue of Playing and Other Cards in the British Museum* (1876), questioned Taylor's conclusion, on the ground that "whether the Zingari [gypsies] be of Egyptian or Indian origin, they did not appear in Europe before 1417, when cards had been known for some time." But this objection is nullified by the fact that the presence of gypsies in Europe is now placed at a date considerably before 1417. There was, for example, a well-established *feudum Acinganorum*, or gypsy barony, in the island of Corfu in the fourteenth century. It is also believed that the gypsies themselves were originally the ancient *chandala* caste of India.

The theory that the gypsies were carriers of the *tarot* tradition does not elucidate the riddle of the origins of the cards. Some writers have ascribed the *tarot* to Hermes Trismegistus under the name of *The Book of Thoth*, or *The Golden Book of Hermes.* Raymond Lully (1235-1315) is said to have based his great work *Ars Generalis sive Magna* on the application of the occult philosophy contained in the *tarot.* The twenty-two emblematic figures of the trumps have also been identified with occult meanings of the letters of the Hebrew alphabet and associated with the mystical *Sepher Yesirah* or *Book of Formation* of Jewish **Kabala.**

The twenty-two symbolic cards are as follows: Juggler or Magician, High Priestess or Female Pope, Empress, Emperor, Hierophant or Pope, Lovers, Chariot, Justice, Hermit, Wheel of Fortune, Strength or Fortitude, Hanged Man, Death, Temperance, Devil, Lightning-struck Tower, Star, Moon, Sun, Last Judgment, Fool, Universe. These symbolic designs, which vary slightly from pack to pack, according to different traditions, are popularly interpreted as follows: Willpower, Science or Knowledge, Action, Realization, Mercy and Beneficence, Trial, Triumph, Justice, Prudence, Fortune, Strength, Sacrifice, Transformation, Combination, Fate, Disruption, Hope, Deception or Error, Earthly Happiness, Renewal, Folly or Expiation. These interpretations also vary according to different authorities. In addition, the other cards in the pack are also considered to have symbolic significance.

There are many different ways of consulting the cards for divination, but they mostly involve laying out the cards after shuffling and interpreting the indications of the major symbolic cards in their relationship to each other.

There are differently designed packs, depending upon different traditions, and there are also newly-designed packs from a modern period. A charming modern pack which is very popular is that designed by Pamela Colman Smith in conjunction with Arthur Edward Waite. A popular tradition pack, said to be excellent for divination, is the Marseilles *tarot.* (See also **Divination**)

Recommended reading:

Butler, Bill. *Dictionary of the Tarot*, Schocken Books, 1975

Douglas, Alfred. *The Tarot; The Origins, Meaning and Uses of the Cards*, Taplinger/Gollancz, London, 1972; Penguin paperback, U.K., 1974

Falconnier, R. *Les lames hermétiques du tarot divinatoire*, Paris, 1896

Gettings, Fred. *The Book of Tarot*, Paul Hamlyn, London, 1973

Huson, Paul. *The Devil's Picture Book; The Compleat Guide to Tarot Cards; Their Origins and Their Usage*, Putnam, 1971; Abacus paperback, London, 1972

Hutton, Alice. *The Cards Can't Lie; Prophetic, Educational & Playing-Cards*, Jupiter Books, London, 1979

Lévi, Eliphas. *La clef des grands mystères*, Paris, 1861

MacGregor Mathers, S. L. *The Tarot; Its Occult Signification, Use in Fortune-Telling and Method of Play*, George Redway, London, 1888, Occult Research Press, n.d.; Gordon Press, New York, 1973

Papus. *The Tarot of the Bohemians; The Most Ancient Book in the World; The Use of Initiates*, 2nd revised ed., William Rider, London, 1919

Thierens, A. E. *The General Book of the Tarot*, Rider & Co., London, D. McKay, Philadelphia, 1928; Newcastle Publishing Co. (paperback), Hollywood, 1975

Waite, A. E. *Pictorial Key to the Tarot*, William Rider, London, 1911; University Books, 1959; Causeway Books, 1973; Rudolf Steiner (paperback), Blauvelt, New York, 1971

Tart, Charles T(heodore) (1937-)

Psychophysiologist and parapsychologist. Born April 29, 1937 at Morrisville, Pennsylvania, he studied at University of North Carolina (B.A., 1960, M.A. 1962, Ph.D. 1963). In 1958 he married Judith Ann Bamberger.

He was research assistant at the Psychophysiology Laboratory, Department of Psychiatry, Duke Hospital, Durham, N.C. from 1958-60, teaching assistant at University of North Carolina from 1960-61, U.S. Public Health Service predoctoral research fellow, Department of Psychiatry, University of North Carolina from 1962-63, lecturer in psychology, Stanford University, California, 1964-65; instructor in psychiatry, University of Virginia, School of Medicine, Charlottesville, 1965-66; assistant professor, University of California, Davis, 1966-69, associate professor, 1969-74, professor of psychology, 1974 onwards; research fellow at Round Table Foundation, Glen Cove, Maine in 1957; vice-president (1956), president (1957) of Massachusetts Institute of Technology Society for Psychic Research. He is a member of the American Society for Psychical Research, Association for the Psychophysiological Study of Sleep, associate member of the Parapsychological Association.

He has taken special interest in extrasensory perception projection, hypnosis in relation to psi phenomena, psychological and psychophysiological correlates of psi, psychometry and "aura" phenomena. He has also investigated altered states of consciousness and out-of-the-body experiences (astral projection). His papers include: 'Card Guessing Tests: Learning Paradigm or Extinction Paradigm?' (ASPR *Journal*, 1966), (with M. Boisen, V. Lopez & R. Maddock) 'Some Studies of Psychokinesis With a Spinning Silver Coin' (SPR *Journal*, September 1972). Other publications include: *An Experimental Attempt to Produce ESP Projection* (Parapsychology Foundation, 1957), (ed.) *Altered States of Consciousness: A Book of Readings* (1968; 1972), *On Being Stoned: A Psychological Study of Marijuana Intoxication* (1971), *Transpersonal Psychologies* (1975), *States of Consciousness* (1975), *The Application of Learning Theory to Extrasensory Perception* (1975), (with P. Lee, D. Galin, R. Ornstein & A. Deikman) *Symposium of Consciousness* (1975), *Learning to Use Extrasensory Perception* (1976), *Psi, Scientific Studies of the Psychic Realm* (1977) (with Harold E. Puthoff & Russell Targ, eds.) *Mind at Large* (1979), *Waking Up: Overcoming the Obstacles to Human Potential* (1986).

Dr. Tart also proposed an instrument for automatic testing of ESP, which was constructed at the University of Virginia and named the "ESPATEACHER." It was set up in the Research Laboratory of the American Society for Psychical Research.

Tarthang Tulku

One of several Tibetan lamas known as a **Tulku** (incarnated being) who brought traditional Tibetan Buddhist teachings to the West. He came to the U.S. in the San Francisco Bay area early in 1969, bringing with him his wife and a collection of rare Tibetan sacred texts.

With the help of a small group of students he soon established the Tibetan Nyingmapa Meditation Center in Berkeley. Nyingmapa is one of four Tibetan Buddhism sects with an ancient tradition. It was founded in the eighth century A.D. by Guru Padmasambhava and Shantirakshita. The literature of Nyingmapa is classified as *Kama* (oral tradition from master to disciple) and *Terma* (secret books originally concealed by Padmasambhava, such as *The Tibetan Book of the Dead.*

Known generally as "Rinpoche" (precious master), Tarthang Tulku teaches the advanced system of Buddhist doctrine known as *Vajrayana.* It embodies some teachings of **Tantra** but is essentially directed at enhancing degrees of understanding and awareness.

Tasseography

A formal term for the more homely branch of fortune-telling of divination by **tea leaves.**

Tattvic Yoga

Term for the ancient Hindu science of breath, as expounded in a book titled *The Science of Breath and the Philosophy of the Tattvas* by Pandit Rama Prasad, published 1897.

The "breath" referred to is the life-giving breath of Brahman, and in it are contained the five elementary principles of nature, corresponding to the five senses of man. These principles are known as *Tattvas*, and from them the body and the physical world is composed.

The knowledge of the *Tattvas* is believed to confer wonderful power, and to this end all undertakings must be commenced at times which are known to be propitious for the movements of the *Tattvas* or vital currents in the body. An important method of yoga practice is given in the book. (See also **Acupuncture; Prana; Yoga**)

Taxil, Leo

Pseudonym of Gabriel Jogand-Pagès, an unscrupulous French journalist of the nineteenth century, who sustained a prolonged occult hoax alleging Devil-worship amongst French Freemasons. (See also Gabriel **Jogand-Pagès,** Diana **Vaughan**)

Taylor, Gordon Rattray (1911-1981)

British author and broadcaster, member of the Society for Psychical Research, London (served on

Council 1976 onwards). He was born in Eastbourne, January 11, 1911, educated at Radley College, and Trinity College, Cambridge University. His first marriage, in 1945, was to Lysbeth Morley Sheaf; second marriage, 1962, to Olga Treherne Anthonisz.

He was a journalist on the *Morning Post*, 1933-36, freelance, 1936-38, leader and feature writing *Daily Express*, 1938-40; B.B.C. monitoring service and European news broadcasts, 1940-44; SHAEF psychological warfare division, 1944-1945; freelance writer, author, broadcaster 1945-50; director of social research organization 1950-54. From 1958-66 he wrote and devised science television programs for B.B.C. (Chief Science Advisor 1963-66). He was the first editor of the widely acclaimed "Horizon" television series. In 1966 he became a full-time author, and was editorial consultant of *Discovery*, 1963-65. He planned the British pavilion display for Turin Fair, 1961, and advised on Triumphs of British Genius Exhibition, 1977. He lectured in the U.S., and was founder and past president of International Science Writers Association.

His publications included: *Economic for the Exasperated* (1947), *Conditions of Happiness* (1949), *Are Workers Human?* (1950), *Sex in History* (1953), *The Angel Makers; A Study in the Psychological Origins of Historical Change 1750-1850 (1958)*, *Eye on Research* (1960), *The Science of Life; A Picture History of Biology* (1963), *The Biological Time Bomb* (1968), *The Doomsday Book* (1970), *Rethink; A Paraprimitive Solution* (1972), *How to Avoid the Future* (1975), *The Salute to British Genius* (1977), *The Great Evolution Mystery* (1983).

He died December, 7, 1981.

Taylor, John (Gerald) (1931-)

Professor of applied mathematics at King's College, London, England, who was the first British scientist to investigate the phenomena of Uri **Geller.**

Born August 18, 1931, at Hayes, Kent, he won his way to Christ's College, Cambridge, U.K. at the age of 16, and at 18 enrolled at Mid-Essex Technical College, where he took his B.Sc. in general science. He completed a three-year mathematics degree course in two years at Cambridge and passed with first class honors. His academic career has included visiting professorships in the U.S. as well as being Professor of Theoretical Physics at the University of Southampton, U.K. in 1969 and his present post as professor of Applied Mathematics at King's College, London.

When Uri Geller visited Britain in 1974, Taylor conducted scientific tests of Geller's feats of metal bending and interference with a Geiger counter. Taylor also experimented with some of the children and adults who manifested paranormal abilities after seeing Uri Geller's appearances on British television programs. Taylor's interest in such phenomena is not only in its scientific validation, but also in investigation of the way in which such phenomena take place and the nature of the forces involved, which he suggests may be some low-frequency electromagnetic effect generated by human beings. Taylor described his investigations in his book *Superminds* (Macmillan, London, 1975). He also published other stimulating books, including *The Shape of Minds to Come* (1971), *New Worlds in Physics* (1974), *Black Holes* (London, 1973), *Special Relativity* (1975), *Science and the Supernatural* (1980), *The Horizons of Knowledge* (1982).

After several years research, during which Prof. Taylor was regarded as endorsing the paranormal metal bending of Uri **Geller,** he since changed his viewpoint and largely retracted his support for Geller's paranormal talents.

Taylor spent three years careful investigation of such phenomena as **Psychokinesis,** metal bending and **Dowsing,** but could not discover any reasonable scientific explanation or validation which satisfied him. In particular, he was concerned to establish whether there is an electromagnetic basis for such phenomena, and after failing to find this he did not believe that there was any other explanation that would suffice. Most of his experiments under laboratory conditions were negative, and this left him in a skeptical position regarding the validity of claimed phenomena.

He published a paper expressing his doubts (in contrast to his endorsement in his book *Superminds*, 1975) in a paper in the journal *Nature* (November 2, 1978) titled 'Can Electromagnetism Account for Extra-sensory Phenomena?'.

He followed this with his book *Science and the Supernatural* in which he expressed complete skepticism about every aspect of the paranormal. In his final chapter he stated: "We have searched for the supernatural and not found it. In the main, only poor experimentation, shoddy theory and human gullibility have been encountered."

This is in complete contrast to his position in 1974, when he affirmed: "The Geller effect—of metal-bending—is clearly not brought about by fraud. It is so exceptional it presents a crucial challenge to modern science and could even destroy the latter if no explanation became available."

Prof. Taylor's new position of complete skepticism seems to stem from his failure to find an electromagnetic explanation for paranormal phenomena. In his new book he stated: "We therefore have to accept that when science faces up to the supernatural, it is a case of 'electromagnetism or bust.' "

This would seem to be a somewhat extreme position, since endorsement of claimed paranormal phenomena should surely rest upon the evidence for its occurrence rather than upon validation of any particular theory of the paranormal. Dr. John **Hasted,** another British scientist who has tested Uri Geller, continues to support the reality of the Geller effect and believes that there is evidence of an electromagnetic field in the phenomenon. (See also Uri **Geller;** John **Hasted; Metal Bending**)

Tea Leaves, Divination by

One of the most popular forms of fortune-telling, depending largely upon psychic intuition. After a cup of tea has been poured, without using a tea strainer, the tea is drunk or poured away. The cup should then be shaken well and any remaining liquid drained off in the saucer.

The diviner now looks at the pattern of tea leaves in the cup and allows the imagination to play around the shapes suggested by them. They might look like a letter, a heart shape, a ring, etc. These shapes are then interpreted intuitively or by means of a fairly standard system of symbolism, such as: snake (enmity or falsehood), spade (good fortune through industry), mountain (journey or hindrance), house (changes, success), etc.

With the popularity of tea bags, divination by tea leaves has declined somewhat, but the bags can be opened and placed in a tea-pot and brewed in the old-fashioned way. The system can also be used for coffee grounds. (See also **Divination**)

This long established popular form of fortune-telling has been given the formal name of "Tasseography."

Recommended reading:

Fontana, Marjorie A. *Cup of Fortune; A Guide to Tea Leaf Reading*, Fantastic (paperback), Wisconsin, 1979

Sheridan, Jo. *Teacup Fortune-telling*, Mayflower (paperback), London, 1978

Tears Painted on Shutters

It was mentioned in Thomas Pennant's book *A Tour in Scotland* (1769 etc.) that in some parts of Scotland it was the custom, on the death of any person of distinction, to paint on the doors and window-shutters white tadpole-like shapes on a black ground. These were intended to represent tears, and were a sign of general mourning.

Techter, David (1932-)

Museum worker who has written widely on parapsychology. Born October 5, 1932 at Morristown, New Jersey, he studied at Yale University (B.S. geology 1954). He was assistant in fossil vertebrates at Chicago Natural History Museum from 1955 onwards. He is a member of Society of Vertebrate Paleontology, American Society for Psychical Research, associate member of Parapsychological Association, organizer, executive secretary of Illinois Society for Psychic Research.

He has conducted tests for extrasensory ability with school children, and written reviews of many books on parapsychological subjects, and published: *A Bibliography and Index of Psychic Research and Related Topics for the Year 1962* (Illinois Society for Psychic Research, 1963), and Supplements for 1963 and 1964.

Teesing, H(ubert) P(aul) H(ans) (1907-)

Dutch professor of German literature, former president of Dutch Society for Psychical Research. Born March 6, 1907 in Amsterdam, Netherlands, he studied at University of Groningen (B.A. 1932, M.A. German philology & literature 1935, Ph.D. 1948). In 1953 he married Marie Polak.

He was a grammar school teacher of German from 1935-52, professor of German literature and theory of literature at University of Utrecht from 1952 onwards. In addition to his writings on literary subjects for scholarly journals, he is author of 'Mystiek en Literatuur' (Mysticism and Literature, *Tijdschrift voor Parapsychologie*, 1959).

Telekinesis

A term denoting the claimed faculty of moving material objects without contact, presumably by **psychic force.**

The movement of objects without contact or with only limited contact—a frequent phenomenon of the seance room, including in its wider sense **rappings, table-tiltings, levitations,** the conveyance of **apports,** practically all material phenomena, with the possible exception of **materialization**—is exceeding difficult of explanation on rational grounds, and the attempt to explain it thus, without the intervention of discarnate spirits, has given rise to the telekinetic theory, which holds that all these varied feats are accomplished by the thoughts of medium and sitters, independent of muscular energy, whether direct or indirect.

How thought can act in this immediate way on inanimate matter is beyond our present state of knowledge. The hard evidence for telekinesis is still very much less than, say, that for **telepathy.**

The telekinetic theory is akin to that offered by the magnetists, who regarded a fluidic or energetic emanation as the cause of movements.

The term is now supplanted by **Psychokinesis** or **PK.** (See also **Movement; Parakinesis; Psychic Force; Psychokinesis**)

Telepathy

Term coined by British psychical researcher F. W. H. **Myers** in 1882, as the outcome of his joint investigation with Edmund **Gurney,** Henry **Sidgwick** and Prof. W. F. **Barrett** into the possibilities of **thought-transference.** It was meant as a name for: "a coincidence between two person's thoughts which requires a causal explanation," and it was defined as "transmission of thought independently of the recognized channels of sense."

The name involved no attempt at explanation, yet it was soon construed as such, and from the comparatively simple fact of experimentally demonstrated thought-transference, a mighty jump was made to the portentous claim that it was an agency of communication between mind and mind, even when consciously no such attempt was thought of, that it was a mysterious link between conscious and subconscious minds, that it was endowed with an intelligence by which incidents either from the memory of the person present or from the memories of distant and unknown persons could be selected, in fact that telepathy was a rival of the **spirit hypothesis.**

This misconception spread so widely that many people conceived it as something distinct from thought-transference and claimed a line of division with the following argument: "In telepathy the transmitter is often unaware that he acts as an agent and the receiver does not consciously prepare himself for the reception. Telepathy cannot be made a subject of experiments, while thought-transference can. Thought-transference is a rudimentary faculty. Telepathy is a well-developed mode of supernormal perception and is usually brought into play by the influence of very strong emotions."

The need of differentiation was acknowledged by the old school of telepathists, too, when they spoke of spontaneous as distinct from experimental telepathy. As hardened a skeptic as Frank **Podmore** believed that "whilst the attempt to correlate the two kinds of phenomena is perhaps legitimate, we can hardly be justified in making the spontaneous phenomena the basis of a theory of telepathy." (*The Newer Spiritualism*, 1910).

Myers pointed out that telepathy as a faculty must absolutely exist in the universe if the universe contains any unembodied intelligences at all. Social life requires a method for the exchange of thought. The belief in telepathy is age-old. Prayer is telepathic communion with higher beings. The basis of sympathy and antipathy may be telepathy. The **monitions of approach** appear to be telepathic messages. The knowledge of victory or disaster which so unexplainably spread in ancient Greece may have been telepathically acquired.

It also seems possible that the claimed ability to impress photographic materials with thought forms may also have relevance to the mechanism of telepathy (see also **Nengraphy; Psychic Photography**).

The Implications of Telepathy

Of the various branches of psychic phenomena there are few which deserve more serious attention than telepathy or thought-transference. The idea of intercommunication between brain and brain, by other means than that of the ordinary sense-channels, is a theory deserving of the most careful consideration, not only in its simple aspect as a claimant for recognition as an important scientific fact, but also because there is practically no department of psychic phenomena on which it has not some bearing.

To take one instance—the so-called "rationalist" view of ghosts used to be simply that supernatural phenomena did not exist, but now a telepathic explanation was offered, more or less tentatively, by an ever-increasing body of intelligent opinion.

There are those who, while admitting the genuineness of psychic phenomena, are yet satisfied that pure psychology provides a field sufficiently wide for their researches, and who are reluctant to extend its boundaries to include an unknown "spirit world" where research becomes a hundredfold more difficult. To such students the theory of telepathy affords an obvious way of escape from that element of the supernatural to which they are opposed, since it is generally agreed that in seeking an explanation of thought-transference it is a physical process which must be looked for.

In the words of Sir William **Crookes**: "It is known that the action of thought is accompanied by certain molecular movements in the brain, and here we have physical vibrations capable from their extreme minuteness of acting direct on individual molecules, while their rapidity approaches that of the internal and external movements of the atoms themselves."

There is therefore nothing to render the theory of thought-vibrations impossible, or even improbable, although the difficulty of proving it has yet to be overcome. We have to contend, however, with the fact that in many cases on record the most vivid impressions have been transmitted from a distance, thus showing that the distinctness of the impression does not necessarily decrease in proportion as the distance becomes greater.

In this case we must either conclude that there are other factors to be taken into account, such as the varying intensity of the impression, and the varying degrees of sensitiveness in the percipient, or we must conclude, as some authorities have done, that telepathic communication goes direct from one mind to another, irrespective of distance, just as thought may travel to the opposite side of the globe with as much ease as it can pass to the next room.

Other authorities claim that the transmission of thought is on a different plane from any physical process, although since the action of thought itself has a physical basis, it is difficult to understand why a supernatural explanation should be thought necessary in the case of telepathy. In the former connection it may be remarked that trivial circumstances can be transmitted to a percipient near at hand, while in many cases only the more intense and violent impressions are received from a distance.

The question whether the telepathic principle is diffusive, and spreads equally in all directions, or whether it can be projected directly toward one individual, is still a vexed one. If it be in the form of ethereal vibrations, it would certainly seem easier to regard it as diffusive. On the other hand, practical experience has shown that in many instances, even when acting from a distance, it affects only one or two individuals.

However, this might be explained naturally enough by the assumption that each transmitter requires a special receiver—i.e., a mind in sympathy with itself. But as yet no explanation is forthcoming, and the most that can be done is to suspend judgment for the present, knowing that only the possibility, or, at most, the likelihood, of such a mode of communication has been proved, and that of its mechanism nothing can be said beyond speculation.

The theory of thought-transference is no new one. Like gravitation, it is a daughter of the hoary science of astrology, but while gravitation is a full-grown fact, universally accepted of science, telepathy, in its scientific aspect, is as yet an infant, and a weakling at that. However, it is not difficult to understand how both should spring from astrology, nor to trace the connection between them.

The wise men of ancient times supposed the stars to radiate an invisible influence which held them together in their course, and which affected men and events on our planet, receiving in their turns some subtle emanation from the earth and its inhabitants.

From this idea, it was but a step to assume that a radiant influence, whether magnetic or otherwise, passed from one human being to another. The doctrine of astral influence was shared by **Paracelsus** and his alchemistic successors until the epoch of Sir Isaac Newton, whose discovery of the rationale of gravitation brought the age of simplistic astrology to a close.

To the conception of "magnetic influence," color was lent by the practices of Anton **Mesmer** and his followers, who ascribed to the "magnetic fluid" the phenomena of **hypnosis.**

The possible analogy between the mysterious and inexplicable force binding worlds together and the subtle influence joining mind with mind in sufficiently obvious, but the difficulty is that while gravitation may be readily demonstrated, and never fails to give certain definite results, experiments in telepathy reveal the phenomena only in the most spasmodic fashion and cannot be depended upon to succeed uniformly even under the most favorable conditions.

Nevertheless such systematized experiments as have been conducted from time to time have more than justified the interest which has been displayed in telepathy. Science, which had so long held aloof from hypnosis, was not desirous of repeating error in a new connection.

In 1882, the **Society for Psychical Research,** London, came into being, numbering among its members some of the most distinguished men in Britain. It had for its object the elucidation of the so-called "supernatural" phenomena which were exciting so much popular interest and curiosity, and foremost among these was the phenomenon of thought-transference.

Viewing their subject in a purely scientific light, trained in handling of evidence, and resolved to pursue truth with open and unbiassed minds, they did much to bring the study of psychic phenomena into a purer and more dignified atmosphere. They recognized the untrustworthiness of human nature in general, and the prevalence of **fraud,** even where no object was to be gained but the gratification of a perverted vanity, and their experiments were conducted under the most rigid conditions, with every precaution taken against conscious or unconscious deception.

Among the most valuable evidence obtained from experimental thought-transference was that gleaned by Professor and Mrs. Henry **Sidgwick** from their experiments at Brighton in 1889-91. In this series the percipients—clerks and shop assistants—were hypnotized. Sometimes they were asked to visualize, on a blank card, an image or picture chosen by the agent. At other times, the agent would choose one of a bundle of cards numbered from 10 to 90, and the percipient was required to state the number on the chosen card, which was done correctly in a surprising number of cases.

Curiously enough, the results varied in proportion as the agent and percipient were near or far apart, and were materially affected by the intervention of a door, or even a curtain between the two, but this was ascribed to a lack of confidence on the part of the percipient, or to such physical causes as fatigue or boredom, rather than to the limited scope of the telepathic principle. On the whole one seems justified in thinking that chance alone would not account for the number of correct replies given by the hypnotized subject.

Towards the end of the nineteenth century, a criticism was levelled at these experiments by F. C. C. **Hansen** and A. Lehmann, of Copenhagen, whose belief it was that the phenomenon known as "involuntary whispering," together with hyperæsthesia on the part of the percipient, would suffice to produce the results obtained by the Sidgwicks (see *Journal* of the Society for Psychical Research, vol. 9, p. 113).

This suggested explanation, while it does not cover the entire ground, has some right to our consideration. If hypnotism reveals so marvelous a refinement of the perceptions, may not some elements of hyperæsthesia linger in the subconscious of the normal individual? If dreams contain in the experience of almost everyone, such curious examples of deduction, may not the mental undercurrent follow in waking moments a process of reasoning of which the higher consciousness knows nothing?

It seems that the "other self," which is never quite so much in the background as we imagine, sees and hears a thousand things of which we are unconscious, and which come to the surface in dreams, it may be long afterwards, and there is no reason to suppose that it might not see and hear indications too slight to be perceived in a grosser sphere of consciousness, and thus account for some cases of "thought-transference."

On the other hand, we have evidences of telepathy acting at a distance where subconscious whispering and hyperæsthesia are obviously out of the question. Although hyperæsthesia may be advanced as a plausible explanation in some—or, indeed, in many—instances of telepathy, it cannot be accepted as a complete explanation unless it covers *all* cases, and that it certainly does not.

So we must look elsewhere for the explanation, although it is not without reluctance that we quit a theory so admirably adapted to known conditions that it scarcely requires a stretching of established physiological laws to make telepathy fit as naturally as wireless telegraphy into the scheme of things.

Unusual Kinds of Telepathy

A good instance of audibly received telepathy is the following (*Proceedings* of the Society for Psychical Research, vol. 1, p. 6): "On September 9, 1848, at the siege of Mooltan, Major-General R____, C. B., then adjutant of his regiment, was severely wounded, and thought himself to be dying, and requested that his ring be taken off and sent to his wife. At the same time she was in Ferozepore (150 miles distant), lying on her bed between sleeping and waking, and distinctly saw her husband being carried off the field, and heard his voice saying 'Take this ring off my finger and send it to my wife.' " The case was fully verified. All the names were known to the Society for Psychical Research.

The journalist and pioneer Spiritualist William T. **Stead** often received **automatic writing** from the living. Thinking of a lady with whom he was in such communication more than once, his hand wrote: "I am very sorry to tell you that I have had a very painful experience of which I am almost ashamed to speak. I left Haslemere at 2:27 p.m. in a second-class carriage, in which there were two ladies and one gentleman. When the train stopped at Godalming, the ladies got out, and I was left alone with the man. After the train started he left his seat and came close to me. I was alarmed, and repelled him. He refused to go away and tried to kiss me. I was furious. We had a struggle. I seized his umbrella and struck him, but it broke, and I was beginning to fear that he would master me, when the train began to slow up before arriving at Guildford Station. He got frightened, let go of me, and before the train reached the platform he jumped out and ran away. I was very much upset. But I have the umbrella."

Stead sent his secretary to the lady with a note that he was very sorry to hear what had happened and added: "Be sure and bring the man's umbrella on Wednesday." She wrote in reply: "I am very sorry you know anything about it. I had made up my mind to tell nobody. I will bring the broken umbrella, but it was my umbrella, not his." The determination of the lady not to tell of the painful evidence apparently indicates that a telepathic message may not only be unconscious, but may directly counteract the desire of the conscious mind.

In many instances of **cross-correspondence,** telepathy between the automatic writers would furnish an alternative to the **spirit hypothesis.** When "Mrs. Holland" (Alice K. **Fleming**) described Mrs. **Verrall**'s surroundings and occupation an interaction between their minds is a consistent theory.

The working of telepathy is apparently demonstrated in certain cases of **suggestion.** Hypnotization has been claimed to be effected at a distance. F. W. H. Myers called it "telepathic hypnotism."

The Wave Theory

In a Presidential Address to the British Association for the Advancement of Science in September 1898, Sir William **Crookes** said: "If telepathy takes place we have two physical facts—the physical change in the brain of A, the suggester, and the analogous change in the brain of B, the recipient of the suggestion. Between these two physical events there must exist a train of physical causes." He further argued that "with every fresh advance in knowledge it is shown that ether vibrations have powers and attributes abundantly equal to any demand—even to the transmission of thought."

He believed that these ether waves were of small amplitude and greater frequency than X-rays, continually passing between human brains and arousing a similar image in the second brain to the first.

Against this theory is the fact that the intensity of waves diminishes with the square of distance and that the telepathic image may not only be very vivid, despite the remoteness of the agent, but that the picture is often modified and symbolical. A dying man may appear in normal state of health, unsuffering.

"Mr. L.," quoted Myers, "dies of heart disease when in the act of lying down undressed in bed. At or about the same time Mr. N. J. S. sees Mr. L. standing beside him with a cheerful air, dressed for walking and with a cane in his hand. One does not see how a system of undulations could have transmuted the physical facts in this way."

In cases of collective reception, an added difficulty is presented. Why should only a few people in a room be sensitive to the waves and other strangers outside the room not at all receptive? Take the case of the crystal gazer. Why should he get a telepathic message at the time of his own choosing, when he happens to look into the crystal? How can the pictures in the crystal be sometimes seen to others if they are only produced in his brain by telepathic impact?

In his book *The Survival of Man* (1909), Sir Oliver **Lodge** was of the opinion that the experimental evidence was not sufficient to substantiate the non-physical nature of thought-transference. Of its reality he had no doubt, and as early as 1903 stated in an interview to the *Pall Mall Magazine*: "What we can take before the Royal Society, and what we can challenge the judgment of the world upon, is Telepathy."

Dr. Hereward **Carrington** suggested that telepathic manifestations may take place through a superconscious mind, that there may be a "mentiferous ether," as some writers have suggested, which carries telepathic waves, and that there is a species of spiritual gravitation uniting life, throughout the universe, as physical gravity binds together all matter.

The wave theory of telepathy remains unproven and largely discarded, although modern Soviet investigators have suggested an electromagnetic theory of telepathy. However, in the 1920s, the Italian researcher Prof. F. Cazzamali of the University of Milan conducted experiments which appeared to show that the human brain emits short waves of high frequency under the stress of emotion. In an insulated all-metal room, he carried out a number of experiments inducing, by means of suggestion, an emotional crisis in his subjects. His very delicate receiving sets placed in the room registered cerebral radiations in the form of waves. They were also recorded on photographic plates. The reports were published in the *Revue Métapsychique*, (August 1925, March, May and July 1927), but it must be said that they have been severely criticized.

Animals and Telepathy

There is evidence which indicates that telepathy is not restricted to human beings. The best case of telepathy from animal to man was furnished by the novelist H. Rider Haggard in the *Journal* of the Society for Psychical Research (October 1904). Mrs. Haggard heard her husband groaning and emitting inarticulate sounds like the moaning of a wounded animal during the night of July 7, 1904. She woke him, whereupon her husband told her his dream. It consisted of two distinct parts.

In the first, the novelist only remembered having experienced a sense of grievous oppression, as though he were in danger of suffocation. But between the moment when he heard his wife's voice and that in which he regained full consciousness, the dream became much more vivid.

He stated: "I saw good old Bob [his dog] lying on his side among brushwood by water. My own personality seemed to me to be arising in some mysterious manner from the body of the dog, who lifted up his head at an unnatural angle against my face. Bob was trying to speak to me, and not being able to make himself understood by sounds, transmitted to my mind in an undefined fashion the knowledge that he was dying."

The sequel to the dream was that Bob was found dead four days after, floating in the river, his skull crushed in, his legs broken. He had been struck by a train on a bridge and thrown into the water. His bloodstained collar was found on the bridge the morning after the dream.

William J. Long, in his book *How Animals Talk* (1922), produced many instances in evidence of a telepathic faculty in animals. He noticed for instance that if a mother wolf cannot head off a cub which rushes away because of the distance which he has already put between himself and her, she simply stops quiet, lifts her head high and looks steadily at the running cub. He will suddenly waver, halt, whirl and speed back to the pack.

The famous case of the **Elberfeld horses** also suggests that telepathy may operate between animals and the human mind. Edmund Selous, in his book *Thought Transference—or What?—in Birds* (1931) recorded many curious observations on the subject from bird life.

Telepathy versus Survival

Obviously telepathy is of tremendous importance. But those who tried to find in it an all-inclusive solution of paranormal manifestations faced very great difficulties. If a telepathic message is followed by motor movements, for instance, the automatic announcement of the death of somebody in writing, the question is, who executes the movements:—the subconscious self or the agent himself who sends the message? Similar uncertainty applies if the reception of a telepathic message is accompanied by telekinetic movements (see **Telekinesis**).

An attempt was made to explain all apparitions as "telepathic **hallucinations**." Frank **Podmore** was the great exponent of this theory. He was the author of a book published in 1894, under the title *Apparitions and Thought Transference*, which dealt with the accumulated evidence for telepathy.

F. W. H. Myers was the first to admit the insufficiency of telepathy as an explanation of **apparitions.** Being forced to concede that collective perception of phantasmal appearances militates for something objective, he worked out a theory of "psychical invasion," the creation of a phantasmogenetic center in the percipient's surroundings (see **Apparitions**).

The theory is a halfway house between telepathy and disembodied spirits, and its real value is that it covers many freakish phantasmal manifestations for which no satisfactory solution has yet been offered.

The problem whether telepathy should not be admitted both from the living and the dead forced itself on the attention with an ever-increasing impetus.

Apparitions of the dying are on the borderland between telepathy with the living and telepathy with the dead. A similar borderland phenomenon which lacks all the conditions for the evidence of telepathy is visions of the dead appearing to the dying.

The strain on the telepathic theory grew with instances which made, on one hand, the acquisition of certain knowledge by telepathic process wildly inprobable but were, on the other hand, easily understood on the basis of the **survival** theory. The question that awaited answer was not only how certain information could have been acquired, but also why should it be associated with definite personalities or be disclosed in a personified form.

In *Proceedings* of the Society for Psychical Research (vol. 35, 1926), S. G. **Soal** reported that in a seance with Mrs. Blanche **Cooper** a voice came through, claimed to be his deceased brother and as a proof of identity told him that a year before in a playhut at home he had buried a lead disc which, if he would dig there now, he would probably find. Mr. Soal satisfied himself that none of the surviving acquaintances of his brother knew of the incident, and dug and found the disc.

Nevertheless, he argued that this might have been a case of telepathic transmission in his brother's earth life, the knowledge having remained latent in his own subconscious mind. If yet another man had figured in the telepathic chain we would have an instance of the so-called telepathy *à trois* which was first advanced by Andrew **Lang** in his discussion of the case of the medium Mrs. **Piper** (*Proceedings* of the Society for Psychical Research, vol. 15, pp. 48-51).

Mr. Hugh J. Browne's book *The Holy Truth* (1876) contained the story of two drowned Australian youths, the author's sons. One of them in a communication through the medium George **Spriggs,** told the detailed story of their fatal pleasure cruise and added that his brother's body had been mutilated of an arm by a great shark. This information could not have been telepathically conveyed by anybody living, except by the shark, yet it was found to be true. The shark was caught two days later, and a man testified to Sir Arthur Conan **Doyle** in Australia that he himself cut the shark open and found an arm, part of a waistcoat and a watch, which identified the dead youth. The watch had stopped at the exact hour indicated by the communicators as that in which they were engulfed by the sea.

There are many cases on record in which missing wills, the whereabouts of which was not known to anyone living, have been found through what alleged to be spirit communication (see **Spirit Intervention**). There are others in which the supposition of the latent information, subconsciously received, must be stretched over ages and successive generations.

Such was the claim of the finding of the Edgar Chapel, Glastonbury Abbey, England, as narrated in Mr. F. Bligh **Bond**'s *The Gate of Remembrance* (1920). The abbey was in ruins, every trace of the Chapel was lost, very little was known as to its location and precise dimensions. Nevertheless, in **automatic writing** a series of communications came through, giving detailed information. When excavations were undertaken in 1908, a year after the receipt of the communications, the chapel was found. For a critical view of this case, however, see 'The Quest of Glastonbury' by G. W. Lambert (*Journal* of the Society for Psychical Research, vol. 43, no. 728, June 1966).

The personal element puts insurmountable obstacles in the way of telepathic explanation in the following case recorded by the psychical researcher Ernesto **Bozzano** in notes on the July 14, 1928 sitting at **Millesimo Castle,** Italy. An unknown voice, in Genoese dialect, addressed Gino Gibelli, one of those present: "I am Stefano's father. You must tell my son that I insist on his giving the message to Maria with which I entrusted him. He has not carried out my request in the slightest degree." Signor Gibelli explained that a month before he had been present in Genoa. The father communicated with the son and charged him with a message to his mother. Very probably the young man had not dared to carry out this request. Gibelli stated that he had completely forgotten this incident, it had nothing to do with him personally nor did it interest him in the slightest degree. He was not thinking of Stefano's father, whom he did not know in life, and was unaware of the fact that the request which the father had made to his son had not been carried out.

The technical side of communication also disproves telepathy as the means of the medium gaining knowledge. Telepathy has no allowance for false or confused information, it does not explain the loss of the idea of time, nor the individual style of the different communicators, i.e., the Biblical manner of "Imperator," his haughtiness, "Pelham's" impatience, etc. (see Mrs. Leonore E. **Piper**).

Names are often inaccurately spelt, giving for instance "Margaret" instead of "Maggie." Telepathy cannot reveal coming events, nor can it explain how children who, if recently dead, ask for their toys and act childishly, behave years after as grown ups, although no such memory is retained in any living mind.

On the telepathic theory, the medium has to be endowed with the potency of omniscience. If such a faculty exists it is apparently not meant for this life as it is latent and only emerges on the rare occasions of mediumistic seances. But if we admit faculties for another life, then the position is immediately simplified. There is no need for the supposition of omniscience if a telepathic message may originate as well from the dead as from the living. Once this admission is made one would well understand the futility of the "brain wave" theory.

A discarnate spirit has no physical brain. The message must come from the spirit and not from the percipient. But if it may come from the spirit as an agent, it may be received by the spirit of the medium as a percipient and transmitted from the spirit to the brain.

The meager results of thought-transference experiments against the tremendous scope of telepathy may be explained by the limitations of the brain as a receiver. These limitations are especially demonstrated in the case of **possession** when clearly an external mind is impressing the medium's brain by direct contact. The lack of adaptation to the ideation of the controlling mind often results in confusion and incoherence in the utterance.

The real insufficiency of the telepathic explanation has been amply demonstrated by hundreds of strange **cross-correspondences** and **book** and newspaper **tests.**

Post-mortem letters, many of which have been preserved by the Society for Psychical Research, and wait for opening until after a communication revealing their contents comes through a medium after the writer's death, show as yet no complete success and it is doubtful whether this evidence will ever be conclusive, in view of the fact that in one instance, the content of the letter was revealed, apparently as a result of telepathic operation, by the medium while the writer was still living. The telepathist may always argue that the contents of the letter were subconsciously transferred into another brain while the writer was preparing it.

The "Hannah Wild" case was a well-known failure. Mrs. Blodgett, the sister of the deceased, obtained communications through Mrs. Piper which purported to come from Hannah Wild. The communicator, however, could not explain the words in a letter which "she" left behind and which no one else understood.

The idea of these post-mortem letters was originated by F. W. H. Myers. As a proof of survival, cross-correspondences are far more conclusive, since the partial messages coming through several mediums are by themselves nonsensical and they can only be explained away by the supposition of a tremendous conspiracy between several subconscious minds for the purposes of deceit.

In the **newspaper tests** recorded by the Rev. C. Drayton **Thomas**, such a subconscious conspiracy theory would have to be stretched to the utmost, as at the time when the contents of a certain column in the next day's paper was indicated, neither the editor nor the compositor could tell what particular text would occupy the column in question.

The Arguments of Prof. Hyslop

The original confusion in the ideas which assigned telepathy a rival importance to the spirit theory was, according to Prof. J. H. **Hyslop**—due to the word "transmission," in the first definition of telepathy. He preferred to define it as "a coincidence excluding normal perception, between the thoughts of two minds." It was the word transmission which gave telepathy the implication that "it is a process exclusively between living people and not permitting the intervention of the dead, if the discarnate exist and can act on the living."

Hyslop's definition permits the employment of the term to describe the action of discarnate as well as incarnate minds. Hyslop was certainly right in saying: "We are not entitled to assume the larger meaning of telepathy to be a fact because we are not sure of its limitations. Here is where we have been negligent of the maxims of scientific methods and the legitimate formation of convictions."

"Mediumistic phenomena," he wrote in his book *Contact with the Other World* (1919), "too often suggest the action of spirits, to be cited as direct evidence for telepathy. The possibility of spirits and the fact that an incident is appropriate to illustrate the personal identity of a deceased person forbids using it as positive evidence for telepathy. One can only insist that one theory is as good as the other to account for the facts."

For selective telepathy, "no evidence has been adduced . . . and I do not see how it would be possible to adduce such evidence. Every extension of the term beyond coincidences between the mental states of two persons is wholly without warrant. The introduction of the assumption that this coincidence is due to a direct transmission from one living mind to another has never been justified, and as there is no known process whatever associated with the coincidences we are permitted to use the term only in a descriptive, not in an explanatory sense.

". . . There is no scientific evidence for any of the following conceptions of it: (1) Telepathy as a process of selecting from the contents of the subconscious of any person in the presence of the percipient; (2) Telepathy as a process of selecting from the contents of the mind of some distant person by the percipient and constructing these acquired facts into a complete simulation of a given personality; (3) Telepathy as a process of selecting memories from any living people to impersonate the dead; (4) Telepathy as implying the transmission of the thoughts of all living people to all others individually, with the selection of the necessary facts for impersonation from the present sitter; (5) Telepathy as involving a direct process between agent and percipient; (6) Telepathy as explanatory in any sense whatever, implying any known cause."

"The failures in experiments to read the present active states of the agent and the inability to verify any thoughts outside those states, in the opinion of science is so finite that its very existence is doubted, while the extended hypothesis requires us to believe in its infinity without evidence."

"As a name for facts, with suspended judgment regarding explanation, it is tolerable, but there can be no doubt that spirits explain certain facts, while telepathy explains nothing. At least as a hypothesis, therefore, the spiritistic theory has the priority and the burden of proof rests upon the telepathic theory."

Dr. Richard **Hodgson** similarly concluded in his second report on the phenomena of Mrs. Piper: "Having tried the hypothesis of telepathy from the living for several years, and the spirit hypothesis also for several years, I have no hesitation in affirming with the most absolute assurance that the spirit hypothesis is justified by its fruits, and the other hypothesis is not."

Telepathy—The Result of Spirit Agency?

Prof. Hyslop was not averse to the possibility that spirits might furnish the explanation of telepathy between the living. He stated that Myers saw this implication at the very outset of the investigations into telepathy. He quoted on this point that in the reported experiments of Miss Miles and Miss Ramsden (*Proceedings* of the Society for Psychical Research, vol. 21, pp. 60-93) in long-distance telepathy, only part of the story was told.

Miss Miles was an all-round psychic, and in her correspondence with Prof. Hyslop she disclosed that she could always tell when her telepathy was successful by the **raps** that she heard. She persisted in thinking of the object which Miss Ramsden was to perceive until she heard raps.

Raps are not telepathic phenomena, and carry an entirely different suggestion. Further, Hyslop stated that in communications through the medium Mrs. **Smead,** the deceased Frank **Podmore** purported to come through and said that telepathy was always a message carried by spirits and that they could do it instantly. Had Mrs. Smead known Podmore, such a contradiction could not have been expected, since Podmore always pressed the theory of telepathy between the living to the exclusion of spirits.

The purported spirit of F. W. H. Myers also made a curious allusion through the medium Mrs. Chenoweth (Mrs. M. M. **Soule**), saying as regards telepathy "it all depended on the carrier." When Hyslop asked for explanation, the answer was that "Telepathy was always a message carried by the spirits."

A still more interesting and elaborate statement is to be found in communications purporting to come from the spirit of Mrs. **Verrall**: "I said yesterday that I would write more about the telepathic theory as I now understand it. I am not sure of the passage of thought through space as I was once, and I had begun to question the method by which thought was transferred to brains before I came here, but you will recall that I had some striking instances of what seemed telepathy tapping a reservoir of thought direct, and the necessity for an intervening spirit was uncalled for; but there were other instances when the message was transposed or translated and the interposition of another mind was unquestionably true. I tried many experiments and I think you must know about them. I will say that I found more people involved in my work than I had known and there seemed more reason to believe that I was operated upon than that I operated, in other words, the automatic writing was less mine than I had supposed."

The dividing line between **clairvoyance** and telepathy is vague. The telepathic message may take the form of visual or auditory sensation. If the content indicates future events, clairvoyance should be suspected at work. Past events may be both telepathic communications and the result of psychometric reading (see **Psychometry**).

A constructive and evidential historic resume of past experiments in telepathy was given by Dr. W. Franklin **Prince** in an appendix to the sixteenth Bulletin of the Boston Society for Psychical Research, published under the title: *The Sinclair Experiments Demonstrating Telepathy* (1932).

Parapsychology and Telepathy

From the 1920s onwards, psychical researchers in Britain and the U.S. began to investigate telepathy through intensive scientifically evaluated experiments. Card-guessing was a favored method, but it was not until the 1930s that Prof. J. B. **Rhine** popularized the **Zener** pack of five simple symbols (star; cross; circle; rectangle; wavy lines) that simplified statistical evaluation of experiments.

In Britain and the U.S., experimenters attempted to obtain significant quantitative tests under laboratory conditions. In the experiments by C. W. Olliver with playing cards over some 20,000 trials, a distinction was made between telepathy (as between agent and percipient) and **clairvoyance** (perception without an agent).

In the modern period of parapsychological research, many aspects of telepathy have been investigated, including such questions as expectation, emotional incentives and dream telepathy, in addition to many quantitative and qualitative experiments. So far it is not possible to summarize such researches into one coherent system which will definitely establish telepathy as a scientific fact, repeatable on demand, although there is reasonable evidence for some telepathy under laboratory conditions.

Certain basic problems remain, such as the disparity in telepathic faculty between different percipients, and the problem of assessing spontaneous telepathy. In the U.S.S.R., there has been considerable interest in telepathy, in view of its possible practical applications, and experimenters have given special attention to methods of intensifying visualization on the part of the agent sending impressions to a percipient. In the U.S. researchers like Andrija **Puharich** have experimented with high speed strobe lights on the closed eyes of subjects, in order to heighten telepathic impressions.

Some of the great variety of telepathy experimentation is indicated in the recommended books below, which cover classic psychical studies as well as recent work in the field. (See also **Parapsychology; Telesthesia; Thought-Reading; Thoughtforms; Thoughtography; Thought-Transference**)

Recommended reading:

Braddon, Russell. *The Piddingtons*, Werner Laurie, London, 1950

Carington, Whately. *Telepathy; An Outline of Its Facts, Theory and Implications*, Methuen, London, 1945; Gordon Press, New York, 1972

Ehrenwald, Jan. *New Dimensions of Deep Analysis; A Study of Telepathy in Interpersonal Relationships*, Grune & Stratton, New York, 1954; Arno Press, 1975

Gurney, Edmund, F. W. H. Myers & F. Podmore. *Phantasms of the Living*, 2 vols., Trubner, London, 1886; Scholars' Facsimiles, Gainesville, Florida, 1970; one volume abridgement, University Books, 1962

Hardy, Alister, R. Harvie & Arthur Koestler. *The Challenge of Chance; Experiments and Speculations*, Hutchinson, London, 1973; Random House, 1974; Vintage Books, New York, 1975

Hyslop, James H. *Contact With the Other World*, Century, 1919

Lang, Andrew. *The Making of Religion*, Longmans, London, 1898

Myers, F. W. H. *Human Personality and Its Survival of Bodily Death*, 2 vols., Longmans, Green, London, 1903; Arno Press, 1975; one volume abridgement, University Books, 1961

Ostrander, Sheila & Lynn Schroeder. *Psychic Discoveries Behind the Iron Curtain*, Prentice-Hall, 1970; Bantam paperback, 1971; retitled *Psi; Psychic Discoveries Behind the Iron Curtain*, Abacus paperback, London, 1973

Parish, Edmund. *Hallucinations and Illusions; A Study of the Fallacies of Perception*, Walter Scott Publishing Co., London & Felling-on-Tyne, 1897

Podmore, Frank. *Apparitions and Thought Transference*, Scott, London/Scribner, 1895

Podmore, Frank. *The Naturalisation of the Supernatural*, Putnam, 1908

Podmore, Frank. *Telepathic Hallucinations; The New View of Ghosts*, Milner, London/Stokes, New York, 1909

Puharich, Andrija. *Beyond Telepathy*, Doubleday, 1952; Anchor Press, New York, 1973; Souvenir Press, London, 1974; Pan Books paperback, London, 1975

Rhine, J. B. *Extrasensory Perception*, Boston Society for Psychical Research, 1934; Branden (paperback), Boston, 1964

Schmeidler, Gertrude R. (ed.). *Extrasensory Perception*, Atherton, New York, 1969

Schwarz, Berthold Eric. *Parent-Child Telepathy; Five Hundred and Five Possible Episodes in a Family; A Study of the Telepathy of Everyday Life*, Garrett Publications, New York, 1971

Sinclair, Upton. *Mental Radio*, published by the author, 1930; 2nd revised ed., C. C. Thomas, Springfield, Illinois, 1962; Macmillan paperback, n.d.

Targ, Russell & Harold Puthoff. *Mind-Reach; Scientists Look at Psychic Ability*, Delacorte, 1977
Tenhaeff, W. H. C. *Telepathy and Clairvoyance*, C. C. Thomas, Springfield, Illinois, 1972
Thomas, N. W. *Thought Transference; A Critical & Historical Review of the Evidence for Telepathy*, De La More Press, London, 1905
Tischner, Rudolf. *Telepathy and Clairvoyance*, Harcourt, Brace, 1925
Tyrrell, G. N. M. *Science and Psychical Phenomena*, Harper, 1938; reissued together with Tyrrell's book *Apparitions* in one volume, University Books, 1961
Ullman, Montague & Stanley Krippner. *Dream Studies and Telepathy; An Experimental Approach*, Parapsychology Foundation (paperback), New York, 1970
Ullman, Montague, Stanley Krippner & Alan Vaughan. *Dream Telepathy*, Macmillan/Turnstone Books, London, 1973; Penguin paperback, 1974
Vasiliev, L. L. *Experiments in Mental Suggestion*, Institute for the Study of Mental Images, U.K., 1963
Vasiliev, L. L. *Studies in Mental Telepathy*, CCM Information Corporation, 1971
Warcollier, René. *Experimental Telepathy*, Boston Society for Psychical Research, 1938; Arno Press, 1975
Warcollier, René. *Mind to Mind*, Creative Age Press, 1948; Macmillan (paperback), 1963
Wilkins, Sir Hubert & Harold M. Sherman. *Thoughts Through Space; A Remarkable Adventure in the Realm of the Mind*, House-Warren, Hollywood, 1951; reissued with authors' names in reverse order, Muller, London, 1971; Fawcett paperback, 1973

Telephone Calls (Paranormal)

The extraordinary claimed phenomenon of telephone calls from the dead was raised by parapsychologists D. Scott **Rogo** and Raymond Bayless in their book *Phone Calls From the Dead* (Prentice-Hall, 1979).

Their researches were stimulated by a report in *Fate* Magazine (September 1976) from Don B. Owens, Toledo, Ohio, concerning his close friend Lee Epps. They had lived in the same neighborhood for years before Lee moved away and their contact became limited to occasional meetings or telephone calls.

On October 26, 1968 at 10:30 p.m., Don's wife Ethel answered a telephone call and immediately recognized the voice as that of Lee. He said: "Sis, tell Don I'm feeling real bad. Never felt this way before. Tell him to get in touch with me the minute he comes in. It's important, Sis." Ethel tried to ring him back but got no answer, neither did Don when he came in.

That evening Don learned that Lee was in a coma in hospital, six blocks from their home and died at 10:30 p.m. It would have been impossible for Lee to have made the call himself in his condition, yet Ethel had immediately recognized his voice.

Although this case was purely anecdotal, without firm supporting evidence, Rogo and Bayless were sufficiently intrigued to follow up the phenomenon of "phone calls from the dead." After collecting a few cases, they wrote an article in the October 1977 issue of *Fate* Magazine titled 'Phone Calls from the Dead?' More cases came to hand, and led to a two-year investigation of the claimed phenomenon.

It proved peculiarly difficult to establish objectively, since the accounts dealt with spontaneous events, usually without the opportunity of rigid factual verification, moreover it was difficult to rule out coincidental hoaxes. However, Rogo and Bayless concluded that such paranormal phone calls actually did occur and might even be more common than supposed.

A satisfactory theory to explain such cases presents difficulties. On the face of things, if one grants that mediumistic communication is possible through a **trumpet** at Spiritualist seances, or even by **direct voice**, the use of a telephone earpiece is hardly more far-fetched, but the prior ringing of the telephone announcing a call is another matter. Is there an actual **PK** manipulation of the telephone apparatus, or are the ringing tone and the voices actually in the subject's mind? Many individuals have experienced the hallucination of "phantom bells" when they think they hear a door bell or a telephone ringing but find no one there.

In some of the cases examined by Rogo and Bayless, it seemed that the call was placed in a normal way through an exchange that caused the phone to ring, and in other cases the phone calls appeared to be placed through long-distance operators. Some subjects reported hearing the familiar "click" at the end of the call as the communicator apparently hung up.

Rogo and Bayless suggested PK-mediated electromagnetic effects and discussed the possible relevance to the related phenomenon of **Raudive Voices (Electronic Voice Phenomenon)**. Their book opens up a fascinating if incredible area of claimed discarnate communication. (See also **Ashkir-Jobson Trianion; Communication (Between Living and Dead); Communigraph; Reflectograph; Raudive Voices; SPIRICOM**)

Teleplasm

An alternative term for **ectoplasm.**

Teleportation

The paranormal transportation of human bodies through closed doors and over a distance is a comparatively rare but fairly well authenticated occurrence. It is a composite phenomenon between **levitation** and **apports**, and according to the testimony of the *Bible* by no means new in human experience. We find in *Ezekiel* xi, 1: "Moreover the spirit lifted me up, and brought me unto the East gate of the Lord's house which looketh eastward."

Elijah, walking with Elisha, was carried away by a whirlwind. Habakkuk was carried from Judea to Babylon to bring food to Daniel in the lion's den, then carried back to Judea through the air.

In the *Acts* of the Apostles, the warders of St. Peter's prison testified: "The prison house we found shut in all safety, and the keepers standing before the doors; but when we opened we found no man within."

St. Philip baptized the Ethiopian: "And when they were come up out of the water, the spirit of the Lord caught away Philip that the eunuch saw him no more . . . But Philip was found at Azotus." The distance between Gaza, the scene of the baptism, and Azotus was thirty miles.

In the history of modern Spiritualism, we meet with the phenomenon at an early age. "From as good testimony as I have of any fact that I can accept without personal knowledge," stated the Rev. J. B.**Ferguson,** of the **Davenport Brothers,** "I believe that these young men have been raised into the air to the ceilings of rooms, and have been transported a distance of miles by the same force and intelligence, or intelligent force, that has for eleven years worked in their presence so many marvels."

In England, accounts of transportation were published in the Spiritualist press between 1871-74 of Mrs. **Guppy,** of Charles **Williams** and Frank **Herne** (*Spiritual Magazine*, July 1871), of Miss Lottie **Fowler** (*The Spiritualist*, March 15, 1872) and of Dr. F. W. **Monck** (*Spiritual Magazine*, 1875), the latter having apparently made an aerial journey from Bristol to Swindon.

Mr. Thomas Blyton wrote in his reminiscences in *Light* (April 11, 1931): "I was present on one occasion at a private home seance at Hackney in London, when without warning or preparation, in total darkness, Mr. Frank Herne was suddenly placed in the midst of the sitters; and after recovering from our surprise and resuming the seance, Mr. Herne's overcoat, hat and umbrella were dropped on the table. John King, speaking in the direct voice, explained that his band of spirit people had found an unexpected opportunity to transport Mr. Herne from where he had been with friends, witnessing a theatrical play that evening; on his appearance at Hackney he was in a semi-conscious condition."

However, grave suspicion surrounds the mediumship of Herne and Williams, the latter being exposed in fraud on two occasions. In 1876, Monck was imprisoned after exposure of fake materialization.

Very little evidential value can be attached to the episode in Catherine Berry's *Experiences in Spiritualism* (1876) according to which, at the studio of Frederick A. **Hudson,** the spirit photographer, between the hours of 2 and 5 p.m., in the presence of Frank Herne and herself "Mr. Williams was seen to descend from the roof of the studio; he fell on the ground very gently. I do not think he was hurt, but sadly frightened. The spirit 'John King' was rather vexed with him for not obeying a summons to come into the studio, and told Mr. Williams that this putting him through the roof bodily was done as a punishment, and he hoped it would teach him not to disobey in the future. We all went immediately to see if there was an opening in the roof, but there was none, and the boards had all the appearance of not having been disturbed."

Mrs. Guppy's transportation is the best corroborated early case. It occurred on June 3, 1871. There were ten witnesses—two mediums (Williams and Herne) and eight sitters. It was a sequel to Herne's previous reported transportation to Mrs. Guppy's house. In answer to a facetiously expressed wish of a sitter, in a moment of time Mrs. Guppy was apparently carried bodily from her home in Highbury (North London) to the house of Williams at 61, Lamb's Conduit Street (West Central London), a distance of over three miles.

The case was the occasion of much facetious comment in the daily Press. *The Echo* printed the only serious report. The story was summed up, on the basis of the sitters' written testimony, by Dr. Abraham Wallace in *Light* (1918, p. 259) as follows: "Neither door nor window could have been opened without the admission of light. After various phenomena usual in dark seances had taken place someone asked Katie King, one of the controls, to bring something. Another member of the circle observed, in a joking sort of way, 'I wish you would bring Mrs. Guppy.' Upon which a third remarked: 'Good gracious, I hope not, she is one of the biggest women in London.' Katie's voice at once said 'I will, I will, I will.' Then John's voice was heard to exclaim, 'Keep still, can't you?' In an instant somebody called out: 'Good God, there is something on my head' simultaneously with a heavy bump on the table and one or two screams. A match was struck, and there was Mrs. Guppy on the table with the whole of the sitters seated round it closely packed together as they sat at the commencement. Mrs. Guppy appeared to be in a trance, and was perfectly motionless. Great fears were entertained that the shock would be injurious to her. She had one arm over her eyes, and was arrayed in a loose morning gown with a pair of bedroom slippers on, and in a more or less décolleté condition. When telling me the story, Mrs. Volkman very naturally said how much she disliked having been brought in such a state into the presence of strangers. There was a pen in one hand, which was down by her side. From the first mention of bringing her to the time she was on the table three minutes did not elapse." It seems that Mrs. Guppy had a pen in one hand and an account book in the other. She had been making up her weekly accounts and had just written the word "onions," the ink still being wet on the page.

After Mrs. Guppy had shaken off the effect of the shock, the seance was continued with her presence. During this part of the seance, her boots, hat and clothes arrived from her home, also a lot of flowers. Both Herne and Williams were levitated and disappeared in turns.

The seance over, Mr. Harrison, editor of *The Spiritualist*, together with three of the sitters, offered to escort Mrs. Guppy to her home. Then their inquiries convinced them that Mrs. Guppy was really sitting in the room with Miss Neyland, her companion, writing her accounts at the time that one of the seance sitters wished her to be brought. Her husband also bore testimony to the fact that his wife, shortly before her disappearance had been up to the billiard room where he was playing with a friend. This visitor corroborated his statement.

Regarding this visit of inquiry, Frank **Podmore** stated in his book *Modern Spiritualism* (1902, vol. 2, p. 259): "They there learnt from Miss Neyland, a friend of Mrs. Guppy's, who had come out as a medium under her auspices, that an hour or two previously she had been sitting with Mrs. Guppy near the fire making up accounts when suddenly looking up she found that her companion had disappeared, leaving a slight haze near the ceiling." The report of this marvelous phenomenon gave rise to repetitions.

In one case, the authenticity of which is difficult to establish, the subject of transportation was a sitter in Mrs. Guppy's house. His name was Henderson. The seance was held on November 2, 1873, with ten sitters. Suddenly it was discovered that Henderson broke the seance chain and disappeared. The doors and windows of the room were locked. About the same moment of his disappearance, he was discovered at a distance of a mile and a half in the backyard of the house of his friend, Mr. Stoke. Nine people noticed his sudden arrival. The night was wet. His boots and clothes were almost dry.

There is one transportation case recorded in the history of William **Eglinton**'s mediumship. It occurred on March 16, 1878, at Mrs. Makdougall Gregory's house. Two other mediums, Arthur **Colman** and J. W. **Fletcher** were present with five sitters. One of the sitters suggested that Colman should be taken through the ceiling. Almost immediately Eglinton disappeared. The noise of a violent bump was heard and Eglinton was found in the room above on the floor in a trance.

Several miraculous cases were put on record in the first years of the present century. The story of one is told in Volume 9 of the *Annals of Psychic Science.* The place was San Jose, Costa Rica, the date between 1907-09, the persons concerned were the children of Señor Buenaventura **Corralès.** The oldest child, Ophelia, was eighteen years old. There were two younger sisters and a brother. Separately and together the children frequently vanished from the seance room, found themselves in the garden and returned to their great delight, in the same mysterious manner. To quote from the account of Dr. Alberto Brenes, Professor at the Law Academy:

"A few minutes passed in absolute silence. Suddenly we heard knocks coming from the pavilion; we turned up the gas and found the children were no longer there. The doors were examined and found to be completely closed. Two persons were deputed to look for the children. When the door of the room was opened they were found standing in a row, talking and laughing at what had taken place.

"They said that they had been brought there, one by one; first little Flora, then Berta, and finally Miguel—their respective ages being seven, twelve and ten years.

"We then asked them how they had been carried and they replied that they had felt a pressure under the arms, then they were lifted up in the air and placed where they were found, but they could not tell us anything more.

"The two investigators then asked the spirits to repeat the translation in the reverse direction; they recommended the children to remain silent where they were, and locking the door, returned to the seance room to give an account of what had happened.

"We resumed the seance after taking the necessary precautions of locking the doors. Then 'Ruiz' came and after recommending all to keep up their spirits, said in a clear and energetic voice: 'Let the children come.' Immediately one of them called out: 'We are here.' The light was turned up and the three children appeared in a line in the same order in which they had been previously found. On this occasion all three had been transported at the same time."

It must be said that considerable suspicion surrounds the mediumship of Ophelia Corralès.

Dr. Joseph Lapponi, medical officer to Popes Leo XVII and Pius X, recorded in his *Hypnotism and Spiritism* (1906) the case of the **Pansini** brothers, Alfred and Paul, ten and eight years old respectively. They experienced mysterious transportation in a half hour from Ruvo to Molfetta. Another time, at 12:30 p.m., they disappeared from Ruvo and at 1 o'clock found themselves on a boat at sea near Barletta, making towards Trinitapoli. Once they disappeared from the square of Ruvo and found themselves, ten minutes later, before the house of their uncle Jerome Maggiore in Trani. Several other mysterious flights took place to Gios, Biseglie, Mariotta and Terlizzi. Once they disappeared in Bishop Berardi's presence while he was discussing these phenomena with their mother. The windows and doors were closed.

In another volume, *Spedizione e Spiriti*, the same author told of the flying brothers of Bari who could transfer themselves over a distance of 45 kilometers in 15 minutes.

Henry Llewellyn had a series of sittings with the medium F. F. G. **Craddock** at Burslem, Staffs. The medium sat in a corner of the room from which a door led into a cellar beneath. The cellar door was completely covered with a curtain tacked round the opening, so that any disturbance there would have been at once detected. The curtains were drawn over the medium.

Some time later, on looking in, the medium was discovered in a cataleptic state suspended horizontally across the top of the curtained corner of the room, with his feet and head just lodged on each end of about two inches of boarding. The curtain was opened so that all present could see the wonderful sight for themselves, and then closed, hoping that the medium would be put safely on the floor again. Hearing no movement for some time the curtain was opened again, when to the consternation of the experimenters it was found that Mr. Craddock was gone, the cellar door, with its curtain, being undisturbed. Shortly afterwards they heard someone moving about in the next room, and when the door of that room was unlocked, the medium walked out of it with his hands still tied behind him. On another occasion Mr. Craddock was found to be missing and was discovered in the bedroom directly over the place in which they were sitting. (See Gambier Bolton; *Psychic Force,* 1904). This case must be treated with reserve, since Craddock was exposed in fraud on several occasions.

A summary of Willi Reichel's experiences with C. V. **Miller,** the Californian materialization medium, as given in *Psychische Studien* (January-February 1906) stated: " 'Betsy,' the principal control of Mr. Miller, called Herr Reichel first into the cabinet in order that he might assure himself of the presence of the medium asleep. He examined all again and considers it impossible that the medium could have quitted the cabinet in a normal way; in front of the curtains were seated the 27 persons who formed the circle on that evening, and the windows looked out on a much frequented street. The weather, moreover, was very windy and wet, and it would have been impossible, he says, to open a window without causing a current of air to be felt at once. After about four minutes "Betsy" told him to go with three other persons to the first floor and Mr. Miller's housekeeper gave them the keys. They found the medium breathing heavily on a chair; they brought him back into the seance room, where he awoke, remembering nothing."

Dr. Franz **Hartmann,** the well-known Theosophist and writer on occultism, employed the term "Magical metathesis." In *Occult Review* (July 1906), he quoted the case of Dr. Z., of Florence, a friend of his, who was transported from Livorns to Florence (100 kilometers) in fifteen minutes and deposited in a closed room with a bump.

Stepping into the realm of occult magic, the book of Harry de Windt, *From Paris to New York by Land* (1904), may be cited for an ancient transportation case in which a medicine man, while he was closely watched, disappeared from a tent and was found in an unconscious condition in a tent half a mile distant.

The medium Miss Ada **Besinnet** was said to have been several times the subject of transportation, but there is no evidential record of the feat. Reporting on the Polish medium Franek **Kluski,** Prof. Pawlovski wrote: "The most extraordinary case related to me by the members of the circle is that of Mr. Kluski having been fetched by the apparitions, or disappearing from the sealed and locked seance room. The astonished sitters found him in a rather distant room of the apartment quietly sleeping on a couch. I report the case upon the responsibility of my friends, whom I have no reason to distrust." (*Psychic Science,* October 1925, p. 214).

Prof. Haraldur **Nielsson** stated in an account of his experiences with Indride **Indridason,** the Icelandic medium: "We have had on several occasions the experience of matter being brought through matter, and one evening the medium herself was taken through the wall into a room which was locked and in darkness. This sounds incredible, but many things occur in the presence of physical mediums which must seem absurd to men who have not themselves investigated them. But they are nevertheless true." (*Light,* November 1, 1919)

In *Psychic Research* (March 1930), an account was published by Harry **Price** and Miss H. Kohn, of the **poltergeist** persecution of an Indian boy, Damodar Ketkar, of Poona, India. According to the notes of Miss Kohn, who was a lecturer in languages at the governmental Deccan College (Bombay University), Poona, the following transportation case occurred in April 1928 during the most violent period of the manifestations: "At 9:45 a.m. on April 23, my sister says in a letter, the elder boy (his brother, Ramkrishna Bapat) 'suddenly materialised in front of me in your doorway like a rubber ball. He looked bright but amazed, and said 'I have just come from Karjat.' He didn't come through any door. My sister describes the posture of the boy as having been most remarkable. When she looked up from her letter-writing she saw him bending forward; both his arms were hanging away from his sides, and the hands hanging limp—his feet were not touching the floor, as she saw a distinct space between his feet and the threshold. It was precisely the posture of a person who has been gripped round the waist and carried, and therefore makes no effort but is gently dropped at his destination."

This account is unique, as in no other case was the actual arrival of the transported individual seen.

Two accounts of transportation are to be found in the amazing case of Carlo **Mirabelli,** the South American medium. On the basis of the original Portuguese documents, psychical researcher E. J. **Dingwall,** in *Psychic Research* (July 1930), mentioned as one of his startling phenomena "the transportation of the medium from the railway station at Luz [São Paolo] to the town of S. Vincente, a distance of some 90 kilometres. The report states that at the time the medium was at the station at Luz in company with a number of people and was intending to travel to Santos. Shortly before the train started he suddenly disappeared to the astonishment of everybody, his presence in S. Vincente being ascertained fifteen minutes later by telephone, it being proved that he was met in the town exactly two minutes after his disappearance. . . . On one occasion when the medium had been secured in his armchair by means of various ligatures he vanished utterly from his position, the doors and windows remaining both locked and firmly secured. Five sitters remained in the seance room whilst the rest went in search of the missing man. He was soon discovered in a side room lying in an easy chair and singing to himself."

A well authenticated case was the transportation of the Marquis **Centurione Scotto,** at Millesimo Castle, on July 29, 1928. The following is a summary of the report of psychical researcher Ernesto **Bozzano**'s, attested by ten participants, as published in *Luce e Ombra* (September-October 1928): During the course of the sitting, the medium Marquis Centurione Scotto exclaimed in a frightened voice: "I can no longer feel my legs!" The gramophone was stopped. An interval of death-like silence followed.The medium was addressed, without answer, then felt for. His place was empty. They turned on the red light. The doors were still securely locked with the key on the inside but the medium had disappeared.

All the rooms of the castle were searched without result. Two and a half hours passed when it occurred to the sitters to ask Mrs. Gwendolyn Kelley Hack to try and get into communication, through automatic writing, with her spirit guide "Imperator." After several attempts in which at first only so much was told that "Do not be anxious, we are watching and guarding" and that the "medium is asleep," correct information came through: "Go to the right, then outside. Wall and Gate. He is lying—hay—hay—on soft place." The communication was signed by the cross of "Imperator."

The place indicated a granary in the stable yard. The great entrance door was locked, the key was not in the lock. They ran back to fetch it and entering found a small door which had been previously overlooked. This door was also locked, the key being in the keyhole on the outside. They opened it with the greatest caution. On a heap of hay and oats, the medium was comfortably lying, immersed in profound sleep. When he first regained consciousness and found himself lying in the stable he feared that he had gone out of his mind and burst into tears.

The authenticity of the phenomenon was unexpectedly confirmed by a message from New York from the spirit **guide** "Bert Everitt," who, when manifesting in one of the sitting with the medium George **Valiantine,** referred to the Millesimo experiments and stated "that he had helped Cristo d'Angelo [the spirit guide] to carry out the phenomenon of the transport of the medium into the granary." This was received a whole month before a report of the case had been published in Italy or elsewhere.

The Marquis himself described his impressions as follows: "At this instant I could not feel my legs any more, having the impression of going into trance. I asked Fabienne for her hand, which I took willingly to reassure myself. After having taken the hand I felt something descending over my brain and my face—and I felt myself light . . . light . . . light . . . but of such lightness . . . I felt myself as if fainting and I . . . Then I recall nothing more. Nothing, nothing."

A celebrated case of levitation that may have involved transportation was the occasion when the famous medium Daniel Dunglas **Home** floated out of the window of a third storey room of a house in Victoria Street, London, and floated into another window (see **Levitation**).

Many cases have been reported in history of the transportation of saints, and sometimes their bilocation (simultaneous appearance in different places over a great distance (see **Double**). (See also **Apports; Asports; Disappearances**)

Recommended reading:

Begg, Paul. *Into Thin Air; People Who Disappear*, David & Charles, London & Vermont, 1979

Fodor, Nandor. *Mind Over Space*, Citadel Press, 1962

Fort, Charles. *The Books of Charles Fort* [collected ed. includes *The Book of the Damned, New Lands, Lo!, Wild Talents; Lo!* cites claimed cases of teleportation], Henry Holt, 1941

Harrison, Michael. *Vanishings*, New English Library (paperback), London, 1981

Telergy

Term used by psychical researcher F. W. H. **Myers** to denote the force or its mode of action which is manifest in **telepathy** and perhaps in other **supernormal** operations.

Telesomatic

Term used by psychical researcher Alexander N. **Aksakof** for **materialization.**

Telesthesia

Perception from a distance through psychic *rapport* with the place or environment. It is less than **clairvoyance** since it is restricted to the perception of material things or conditions.

The word was coined by psychical researcher F. W. H. **Myers** in 1882 to express sensation at a distance after it was found that the communications between distant persons is not a transference of thought alone, but also of emotion, of motor impulses, and of many impressions not easy to define.

Frequent instances were described during World War I. The experience of Mrs. Fussey of Wimbledon on November 4, 1914, was typical. At home she suddenly felt in her arm the sharp sting of a wound. She jumped up and cried. There was no trace of an injury. Mrs. Fussey continued to suffer pain and exclaimed: "Tab [her soldier son] is wounded in the arm. I know it." On the following Monday, confirmation arrived. (See also **Telepathy**)

Telluric

Prof. M. Benedict's term for the **rhabdic force** which presumably moves the **divining-rod.**

Tellurism

A name applied by Dietrich G. Kieser (1779-1862) to **Animal Magnetism.** He was one of the early scientific investigators who supported the reality of the phenomenon and drew attention to its legal aspects.

"Téméraire," Charles (or Charles the Bold) (1433-1477)

Duke of Burgundy in the fifteenth century. According to legend, he disappeared after the battle of Morat on June 22, 1476, when he was defeated. It was said by his chroniclers that he was carried off by the devil, others maintained, however, that he had withdrawn to a remote spot and became a hermit.

However, more sober accounts state that he perished in the battle and that his mutilated body was discovered several days later. Charles was introduced into two novels by Sir Walter Scott—*Quentin Durward* and *Anne of Geirstein*. The latter novel contains an account of the battle of Nancy, before the fatal encounter at Morat.

Temperature Changes

Marked changes of temperature sometimes occur in the seance room, usually a sudden lowering. (See **Winds**)

Templars

The Knights Templars of the Temple of Solomon were a military order, founded by a Burgundian, Hugues de Payns, and Godeffroi de St. Omer, a French Knight, in 1119, for the purpose of protecting pilgrims journeying into the Holy Land. They were soon joined by other knights, and a religious chivalry speedily gathered around this nucleus. Baldwin I, King of Jerusalem, gave them as headquarters a portion of his palace, contiguous to a mosque which tradition asserted was part of the Temple of Solomon, and from this building they took their designation.

One of the purposes of the Society was to convert and render useful knights of evil living, and so many of these entered the order as to bring it under the suspicion of the Church, but there is every reason to believe that its founders were instigated by motives of the deepest piety, and the fact that they lived in a condition near poverty, notwithstanding the numerous rich gifts that were showered upon them, is the best proof of this.

They had properly constituted officials, a Grand Master, knights, chaplains, sergeants, craftsmen, sensechals, marshals, and commanders. The order had its own clergy, exempt from the jurisdiction of diocesan rule, and its chapters were held as a rule in secret.

The dress of the brotherhood was a white mantle with a red cross for unmarried knights, and a black or brown mantle with a red cross for the others. Thediscipline was of the very strictest description and the food and clothing stipulated were rough and not abundant.

By the middle of the twelfth century, the new order had firm footing in nearly all the Latin kingdoms of Christendom. Its power grew apace, and its organization became widespread. It formed, as it were, a nucleus of the Christian effort against the paganism of the east, and its history may be said to be that of the Crusades. Moreover it became a great trading corporation, the greatest commercial agency between the east and west, and as such amassed immense wealth.

On the fall of the Latin kingdom in Palestine, the Templars were forced to withdraw from that country, and although they continued to harass the Saracen power they made but little headway against it, and in reality appear to have undertaken commercial pursuits in preference to those of a more warlike character.

When the Temple was at the high point of its power, its success aroused the envy and avarice of Philip IV of France (1285-1314), who commenced a series of attacks upon it. The election of Pope Clement V, who was devoted to Philip's interests, and denounced the order for heresy and immorality, gave Philip his chance.

For several generations before this time, strange stories had been circulating concerning the secret rites of the Templars which were assisted by the very strict privacy of these meetings, which were usually held at daybreak with closely-guarded doors. It was alleged that the most horrible blasphemies and indecencies took place at these meetings, that the cross was trampled under foot and spat upon, and that an idol named **Baphomet** (*Baphe metios*, baptism of wisdom) was adored, or even the Devil in the shape of a black cat. Other tales told of the roasting of children, and the smearing of the idol with their burning fat, and much other wild rumor nonsense was spread by the credulous and ignorant.

A certain Esquian de Horian pretended to betray the "secret" of the Templars to Philip, and they were denounced to the Inquisition, Jacques de Molay, the Grand Master, who had been called from Cyprus to France, was arrested together with one hundred and forty of his brethren in Paris and thrown into prison. A universal arrest of the Templars throughout France followed. The wretched knights were tortured *en masse*, and as was usually the case, under such compulsion, confessed to the most grotesque crimes. The most damning confession of all was that of the Grand Master himself, who said that he had been guilty of denying Christ and spitting upon the Cross, but repudiated all charges of immorality in indignant terms.

The process dragged on slowly during more than three years, in consequence of the jealousies which arose among those who were more or less interested in its prosecution. The Pope wished to bring it entirely under the jurisdiction of the Church, and to have it decided at Rome. The king, on the other hand, mistrusting the Pope, and resolved on the destruction of the order so that none but himself should reap advantage from it, decided that it should be judged at Paris under his own personal influence.

The prosecution was directed by his ministers Nogaret and Enguerrand de Marigny. The Templars asserted their innocence, and demanded a fair trial, but they found few advocates who would undertake their defence, and they were subjected to hardships and tortures which forced many of them into confessions dictated to them by their persecutors.

During this interval, the Pope's orders were carried into other countries, authorizing the arrest of the Templars, and the seizure of their goods, and everywhere the same charges were brought against them. The same means of imprisonment and torture were used to procure their condemnation, although they were not everywhere subjected to the same severity as in France.

At length, in the spring of 1316, the grand process was opened in Paris, and an immense number of Templars, brought from all parts of the kingdom, underwent a public examination. A long act of accusation was read, some of the heads of which were that the Templars, at their reception into the order, denied Christ (and sometimes they denied expressly all the saints) declaring that he was not God truly but a false prophet, a man who had been punished for his crimes, that they had no hope of salvation through him, that they always, at their initiation into the order, spat upon the cross, and trod it under foot; that they did this especially on Good Friday, that they worshiped a certain cat, which sometimes appeared to them in their congregation, that they did not believe in any of the sacraments of the church, that they took secret oaths which they were bound not to reveal, that the brother who officiated at the reception of a new brother kissed the naked body of the latter, often in a very unbecoming manner, that each different province of the order had its idol, which was a head, having sometimes three faces, and at others only one, or sometimes a human skull, that they worshiped these idols in their chapters and congregations, believing that they had the power of making them rich, and of causing the trees to flourish, and the earth to become fruitful, that they girt themselves with cords, with which these idols had been superstitiously touched, that those who betrayed the secrets of their order, or were disobedient, were thrown into prison, and often put to death, that they held their chapters secretly and by night, and placed a watch to prevent them from any danger of interruption or discovery, and that they believed the Grand Master alone had the power of absolving them from their sins.

The publication of these charges, and the agitation which had been deliberately fomented, created such horror throughout France that the Templars who died during the process were treated as condemned heretics, and burial in consecrated ground was refused to their remains.

When one reads the numerous examinations of the Templars in other countries, as well as in France, it is difficult to avoid feeling that some of these charges had a degree of foundation, although perhaps the circumstances on which they were founded were misunderstood.

A very great number of knights agreed to the general points of the formula of initiation, and it seems possible that they did deny Christ, and that they spat and trod upon the cross. The alleged words of the denial were "Je reney Deu" or "Je reney Jhesu," repeated thrice, but most of those who confessed having gone through this ceremony, declared that they did it with repugnance, and that they spat beside the cross, and not on it. The reception took place in a secret room, with closed doors; the candidate was compelled to take off part or (in rare instances) all of his garments, and then he was kissed on various parts of the body.

One of the knights examined, Guischard de Marzici, said he remembered the reception of Hugh de Marhaud, of the diocese of Lyons, whom he saw taken into a small room, which was closed up so that no one could see or hear what took place within, but that when, after some time, he was let out, he was very pale, and looked as though he were troubled and amazed "Juit valde pallidus et quasi turbatus et stepefactus." In conjunction, however, with these strange ceremonies, there were others that showed a reverence for the Christian church and its ordinances, a profound faith in Christ, and the consciousness that the partaker of them was entering into a holy vow.

The historian Jules Michelet (1798-1874), who carefully investigated the materials relating to the trial of the Templars, suggested an ingenious explanation of these anomalies. He imagined that the form of reception was borrowed from the figurative mysteries and rites of the early church. The candidate for admission into the order, according to this notion, was first presented as a sinner and renegade, in which character, after the example of St. Peter, he denied Christ. This denial was a sort of pantomime, in which the novice expressed his reprobate state by spitting on the cross. The candidate was then stripped of his profane clothing, received through the kiss of the order into a higher state of faith, and re-dressed with the garb of its holiness. Forms like these would be easily misunderstood in the Middle Ages, and their original meaning soon forgotten.

Another charge in the accusation of the Templars seems to have been to a great degree proved by the depositions of witnesses, namely the idol or head which they were said to have worshiped, but the real character of meaning of which it is difficult to explain. Many Templars confessed to having seen this idol, but as they described it differently, it must be supposed that it was not in all cases represented under the same form. Some said it was a frightful head, with long beard and sparkling eyes; others said it was a man's skull; some described it as having three faces; some said it was of wood, and others of metal; one witness described it as a painting (*tabula picta*) representing the image of a man (*imago hominis*), and said that when it was shown to him, he was ordered to "adore Christ his creator."

According to some it was a gilt figure, either of wood or metal, while others described it as painted black and white. According to another deposition, the idol had four feet—two before and two behind; the one belonging to the order at Paris was said to be a silver head, with two faces and a beard. The novices of the order were told always to regard this idol as their savior. Deodatus Jaffet, a knight from the south of France, who had been received at Pedenat, deposed that the person who in his case performed the ceremonies of reception, showed him a head or idol, which appeared to have three faces, and said, "You must adore this as your savior, and the savior of the order of the Temple," and that he was made to worship the idol, saying, "Blessed be he who shall save my soul." Cettus Ragonis, a knight received at Rome in a chamber of the palace of the Lateran, gave a somewhat similar account.

Many other witnesses spoke of having seen these heads, which, however, were perhaps not shown to everybody, for the greatest number of those who spoke on this subject said that they had heard others speak of the head, but that they had never seen it themselves, and many of them declared their disbelief in its existence. A friar minor deposed in England that an English Templar had assured him that in that country the order had four principal idols, one at London in the sacristy of the Temple, another at Bristelham, a third at Brueria (Bruern in Lincolnshire), and a fourth beyond the Humber.

Some of the knights from the south added another circumstance in their confessions relating to this head. A Templar of Florence declared that, in the secret meetings of the chapters, one brother said to the others, showing them the idol, "Adore this head. This head is your God, and your Mahomet." Another, Gauserand de Montpesant, said that the idol was made in the figure of Baffomet (*in figuram Baffometi*), and another, Raymond Rubei, described it as a wooden head, on which was painted the figure of Baphomet, and he added, "that he worshiped it by kissing its feet, and exclaiming, *Yalla*," which he describes as "a word of the Saracens" (*verbum Saracenorum*). This was seized upon by some as a proof that the Templars had secretly embraced Mahometanism, since Baffomet or Baphomet could be a corruption of Mahomet, but it must not be forgotten that the Christians of the West constantly used the word "Mahomet" in the mere signification of an idol, and that it was the desire of those who conducted the prosecution against the Templars to show their intimate intercourse with the Saracens.

Baron von Hammer-Purgstall especially gave a Greek derivation of the word as evidence that Gnosticism was the secret doctrine of the Temple. His important essay *Mysterium Baphometis Revelatum* (The Mystery of Baphomet Revealed) was published in vol. 6 of *Fundgraben des Orients* (Vienna, 1811). The suggestion of Baphomet being related to the rituals of Ophite and Gnostic heresies seems very probable.

The confessions with regard to the mysterious cat were much rarer and more vague. Some Italian knights confessed that they had been present at a secret chapter of twelve knights held at Brindisi, at which a grey cat suddenly appeared amongst them, and that they worshiped it. At Nismes, some Templars declared that they had been present at a chapter at Montpellier, at which the demon appeared to them in the form of a cat, and promised them worldly prosperity; and added, that they saw devils in the shape of women. Gilletus de Encreyo, a Templar of the diocese of Rheims, who disbelieved in the story of the cat, deposed that he had heard say, though he knew not by whom, that in some of their battles beyond sea, a cat had appeared to them. An English knight, who was examined at London, deposed, that in England they did not adore the cat or the idol to his knowledge, but he had heard it positively stated that they worshiped the cat and the idol in parts beyond the sea. English witnesses deposed to other acts of "idolatry."

Such accounts suggest the witchcraft accounts of the appearance of the devil at what were basically pagan rituals. A lady, named Agnes Lovecote, examined in England, stated that she had heard that, at a chapter held in Dineslee (Dynnesley, in Hertfordshire), the devil appeared to the Templars in a monstrous form, having precious stones instead of eyes, which shone so bright that they illuminated the whole chapter; the brethren, in succession, kissed him on the posteriors, and marked there the form of the cross. She was told that one young man, who refused to go through this ceremony, was thrown into a well, and a great stone cast upon him.

Another witness, Robert de Folde, said that he had heard twenty years ago, that in the same place, the devil came to the chapter once a year, and flew away with one of the knights, whom he took as a sort of tribute. Two others deposed that certain Templars confessed to them that at a grand annual assembly in the county of York, the Templars worshiped a calf. All this is mere hearsay, but it shows the popular opinion of the conduct of the order.

A Templar examined in Paris, named Jacques de Treces, who said that he had been informed that at secret chapters held at midnight, a head appeared to the assembled brethren, added, that one of them, "had a private demon, by whose council he was wise and rich."

The sordid aim of King Philippe was successful. He seized the whole treasure of the temple in France and became rich. Those who ventured to speak in defence of the order were browbeaten, and received little attention. Torture was employed to force confessions. Fifty-four Templars who refused to confess were carried to the windmill of St. Antoine, in the suburbs of Paris, and there burnt. Many others, among whom was the Grand Master himself, were subsequently brought to the stake. After having lasted two or three years, the process ended in the condemnation and suppression of the Order, and its estates were given in some countries to the knights of St. John.

It was in France that the persecution was most cruel. In England, the order was suppressed, but no executions took place. Even in Italy, the severity of the judges was not everywhere the same. In Lombardy and Tuscany, the Templars were condemned, while they were acquitted at Ravenna and Bologna. They were also pronounced innocent in Castile, while in Arragon they were reduced by force only because they had attempted to resist by force of arms. Both in Spain and in Portugal they only gave up their own Order to be admitted into others. The Pope was offended at the leniency shown towards Templars in England, Spain, and Germany. The Order of the Temple was finally dissolved and abolished, and its memory branded with disgrace.

Some of the knights were said to have remained together and formed secret societies. The result, however, was much the same everywhere. Convicted of heresy, sorcery, and many other abominations, many of the wretched Templars were punished with death by fire, imprisonment, and their goods escheated to the various crowned heads of Europe, nearly all of whom followed the avaricious example of Philip of France.

Jacques de Molay, the Grand Master, brought out on to a scaffold erected in front of Notre Dame in Paris, and asked to repeat his confession and receive sentence of perpetual imprisonment, flared into sudden anger, recanted all he had said, and protested his innocence. He was burnt, and summoned the Pope and the King with his dying breath, to meet him before the bar of Heaven. Both of these dignatories shortly afterwards died, and it remained in the public mind that the outcome of the Grand Master's summons seemed to have proved his innocence.

There is every reason to believe that there was some foundation for the charges of heresy made against the Templars. Their intimate connection with the East, and the long establishment of the order therein had in all probability rendered their Christianity not quite so pure as that of Western Europe. Numerous treatises have been written for the purpose of proving or disproving the Temple heresy, to show that it followed the doctrines and rites of the Gnostic Ophites of Islam, that "Baphomet" was merely a corruption of "Mahomet," and it has been collated with various other eastern systems.

Hans Prutz, in his book *Geheimlehre und Geheimstatutendes Tempelherren-Ordens* (1879), furthered the view of the rejection of Christianity in favor of a religion based on Gnostic dualism, and at once raised up a host of critics.

But many defenders of the Order followed, and it was proved in numerous instances that the confessions wrung from the Templars were the result of extreme torture. In a number of cases they were acquitted, as in Castile, Aragon, Portugal, and at many German and Italian centers. It has also been shown that the answers of a number of the knights under torture were practically dictated to them. In England, out of eighty Templars examined, only four confessed to the charge of heresy, and of these, two were apostates.

The whole question may perhaps be summed up as follows. The Templars, through long association with the East, may have become more tolerant of paganism, more broadminded in their outlook than their bigoted stay-at-home countrymen. Expressions as regards the worthiness of Saracen nations, among whom the Templars had many friends, would be regarded askance in France, Spain and England, and habits acquired by residence in the East would probably add to the growing body of suspicion regarding the loyalty of the order to Christianity. It is even likely that the Templars introduced into their rites practices which savored of Gnosticism.

It is also probable, as persuasively argued by G. Legman in his valuable book *The Guilt of the Templars* (1966) that the Templars institutionalized homosexuality in their Order. Legman's book includes a reprint of two important essays—"The Templars and the Worship of the Generative Powers" by Thomas Wright, George Witt & Sir James Tennent, and "The Proceedings Against the Knights Templars, *Anno Domini* 1309" by Sir William Dugdale.

No doubt the Templars were also the victims of their own arrogance, their commercial success, which excited the avarice of their enemies, and the superstitious ignorance and hatred of their contemporaries.

It has been asserted frequently that, on the death of Jacques de Molay, a conspiracy was entered into by the surviving Templars which had for its objects the destruction of papacy and the various kingdoms of Europe, and that this tradition was handed on through generations of initiates through such societies as the **Illuminati** and the Freemasons, who in the end brought about the French Revolution and the downfall of the French throne. Such a theory, however enticing to the pseudo-occultist, the defender of the theory that occult tradition has descended to us through a direct line of adepts, cannot be endorsed by firm evidence, and must be dismissed as a mere figment of enthusiasm or imagination. (See also **Baphomet; Temple Church**)

Recommended reading:

Campbell, G. A. *The Knights Templars, Their Rise and Fall,* Duckworth, London/McBride, 1937

Charpentier, John. *L'Ordre des Templiers,* La Colombe, Paris, 1945

Lea, Henry Charles. *A History of the Inquisition of the Middle Ages,* 3 vols., Sampson, Low, London/ Harper & Bros., New York, 1888; Citadel, 1954; Harbor Press, 1955; Russell & Russell, 1958

Lees, B A. *Records of the Templars in England in the Twelfth Century; The Inquest of 1185 with Illustrative Charters and Documents* (vol. 9 of *British Academy Records of the Social & Economic History of England and Wales*), Oxford University Press, U.K., 1935

Legman, G. *The Guilt of the Templars,* Basic Books, New York, 1966

Martin, Edward J. *The Trail of the Templars,* Allen & Unwin, London, 1928

Michelet, Jules. *Le Procès des Templiers,* 2 vols., 1841-51

Parker, Thomas W. *The Knights Templars in England,* University of Arizona Press, 1963

Temple Church (London)

The Church of the Knights **Templars** in London, consisting of two parts, the Round Church and the Choir. The Round Church (transition Norman) was built in 1185. The choir (early English style) was finished in 1240.

Hargrave Jennings in his book *The Rosicrucians, their Rites and Mysteries* (1870), stated that the Temple Church, London presents many mythic figures, which have a Rosicrucian expression. In the spandrels of the arches of the long church, besides the "Beauséant" which is repeated in many places, there are the armorial figures following: "Argent, on a cross gules, the Agnus Dei, or Paschal Lamb, or; Gules the Agnus Dei displaying over the right shoulder the standard of the Temple; or, a banner, triple cloven, bearing a cross gules; Azure, a cross prolonged potent issuant out of the crescent moon argent, horns, upwards, on either side of the cross, a star or."

This latter figure signifies the Virgin Mary, and displays the cross as rising like the pole or mast of a ship (argha) out of the midst of the crescent moon or navis biprora, curved at both ends; "azure, semée of estoiles or."

The staff of the Grand Master of the Templars displayed a curved cross of four splays, or blades, red upon white. The eight-pointed red Buddhist cross was also one of the Templar ensigns.

The Temple arches abound with brandished estoiles, or stars, with wavy or crooked flames. The altar at the east end of the Temple Church has a cross flourie, with lower limb prolonged, or, on a field of estoiles, wavy; to the right is the Decalogue, surmounted by the initials, A.O. (Alpha and Omega), on the left are the monograms of the Saviour, I.C., X.C.; beneath, is the Lord's Prayer.

The whole altar displays feminine colours and emblems, the Temple Church being dedicated to the Virgin Maria. The winged horse, or Pegasus, argent, in a field gules, is the badge of the Templars.

The tombs of the Templars, disposed around the circular church in London, are of that early Norman shape called dos d'ane; their tops are triangular; the ridge-moulding passes through the temples and out of the mouth of a mask at the upper end, and issues out of the horned skull, apparently of some purposely trodden creature. The head at the top is shown in the "honour-point" of the cover of the tomb. There is much hidden meaning in every curve of these Templar tombs. (See also **Baphomet; Templars**)

Tempon-teloris (Ship of the Dead)

Among the Dayaks of Borneo the "Ship of the Dead," the vessel which carried the souls of the departed in search of the hereafter, was generally represented as being of the shape of a bird, the hornbill (*rhinoplax vigil*).

Accompanying the souls on their journey through the fire-sea were all the stores which had been laid out at the trivah or feast of the dead, and all the slaves who had been killed for that purpose. After some vicissitudes in the fiery sea, the Ship of the Dead, with Tempon-telon at the helm, reaches the golden shores of the Blessed.

Some of these beliefs echo the ancient Egyptian burial rites. (See also **Book of the Dead; Egypt**)

Tenaille, Jean (1882-1962)

Engineer who was active in the field of parapsychology. Born April 16, 1882 in Paris, France, he followed various occupations, including ranching in Canada, importing and managing a department store in Paris and was manager of industrial plants near Amiens, France from 1931-39. In 1906 he married Miriama Moracchini.

After World War II he was an acoustical engineer. He was author of *Civilisation occidentale* (Western Civilization, 1957), awarded the Académie Francaise prize for history in 1958. He contributed articles on parapsychology to *Revue Métapsychique*, including 'A propos des sourciers' (Concerning Dowsers, 1932).

He died December 31, 1962.

Tenhaeff, W(ilhelm) H(einrich) C(arl) (1894-1981)

Dutch parapsychologist, for some years director of the Parapsychology Institute of the State University of Utrecht, Netherlands (founded by Tenhaeff), now known as Parapsychological Division of the Psychological Laboratory. Born January 18, 1894 in Rotterdam, Netherlands, he studied at University of Utrecht (Ph.D. psychology, 1933). His doctoral thesis *Paragnosie en einfuhlen* was the first on parapsychology in the Netherlands. In 1926 he married Johanna Jacoba Hemmes.

He was a lecturer on psychology from 1932-53, lecturer on parapsychology from 1933-53, professor of parapsychology and director of Parapsychology Institute, University of Utrecht from 1953 onwards. He was founder (1928), editor (from 1928 onwards) of *Tijdschrift voor Parapsychologie*, the journal of the Dutch Society for Psychical Research, secretary (1929-38), advisor (1945 onwards) of the Dutch Society for Psychical Research, corresponding member of Society for Psychical Research, London from 1936 onwards, member of the Dutch Society of Psychologists, Royal Dutch Society for Literature, Utrecht Provincial Association of Arts and Sciences.

Dr. Tenhaeff was interested in parapsychology from an early age, and conducted investigations and reported on psychometry, clairvoyance, precognition, unorthodox healing, the divining rod, and the structure of personality in sensitives. He lectured in many countries on parapsychological subjects, and published articles in *Tijdschrift voor Parapsychologie, Tomorrow* and other journals. In 1945, he commenced a long and detailed investigation of the clairvoyant Gerard **Croiset.**

His books included: *Beknopte Handleiding der "Psychical Research"* (Short Textbook of Parapsychology, 3 vols., 1926), *Het Spiritisme* (Spiritism, 1936), *Oorlogsvoorspellingen* (Previsions—concerning World War II, 1948), *Parapsychologische Verschijnselen en Beschouwingen* (Parapsychological Phenomena and Speculations, 1949), *Het Wichelroedevraagstuk* (The Divining Rod, 1950), *Magnetiseurs, Somnambules en Gebedsgenezers* (Hypnotists, Somnambulists and Healers, 1951, translated into German 1957), *Inleiding tot de Parapsychologie* (Introduction to Parapsychology, 1952), *Beschouwingen over Het Gebruik van Paranognosten* (The Use of Sensitives for Police and Other Purposes, 1957), *Telepathie en Helderziendheid* (Telepathy and Clairvoyance, 1958, translated into German 1962), *De Voorschouw* (Precognition, 1961), *Telepathy and Clairvoyance* (1965, English translation of *Telepathie en Helderziendheid*).

Dr. Tenhaeff died July 9, 1981, in the Netherlands.

Tephillin

In Hebrew, *tephillin* means "attachments." They were originally prayer thongs worn by Jews at morning prayer—one on the left arm and another on the head. They came to be regarded as **talismans** and were used in many traditional ceremonies. The *Tal-*

mud states: "Whoever has the *tephillin* bound to his head and arm . . . is protected from sin."

Tephramancy

A mode of **divination** in which use is made of the ashes of the fire which had consumed the victims of a sacrifice.

Teraphim, The

These appear to have been ancient **oracles.** The *teraphim* were taken away from Jacob by his daughter, Rachel, and this mention in the *Bible* appears to be the earliest record of "magical" apparatus.

Their form was not known, nor the exact use to which they were put; but from an allusion to them in *Hosea iii,* 4, they were evidently not idols. It has been suggested that they were the same as the "Urim" of Mosaic ritual. At any rate it seems likely that they were used as a means of divination.

Tesla, Nikola (1856-1943)

Scientific genius whose inventions in the field of electrical apparatus stemmed from an extraordinary visionary faculty of a paranormal character. Unlike most innovators in the field of engineering and electricity, his inventions did not require patient experiment and trial-and-error testing of models, but flashed into his mind as working units, complete to the final details of component design and size.

Even as a young student of electrical engineering and physics, at a time when the concept of alternating current was considered a fallacy of the perpetual motion type, he knew that he could solve this problem, and only a few years later the complete detailed vision of an alternating current motor using a rotating magnetic field came to him in a flash while gazing at a sunset.

He was born at midnight July 9-10, 1856, in the village of Similjan in the Austro-Hungarian border area of Lika (now in Yugoslavia). Even as a boy, he was inventive, and at the age of nine constructed a sixteen-bug power motor by harnessing June bugs to a thin wooden wheel. He was educated at an elementary school, then for four years at Lower Realschule, Gospic, Lika, followed by three years at the Higher Realschule, Carlstadt, Crotia, graduating in 1873. He was a student for four years at the Polytechnic School, Gratz, studying mathematics, physics and mechanics, afterwards two years in philosophy studies at University of Prague, Bohemia. He was awarded an honorary M.A., Yale, 1894; LL.D, Columbia University, 1894; D.Sc., Vienna Polytechnic.

He commenced his career as an inventor at Budapest, Hungary, in 1881, where he constructed a telephone repeater, and engaged in various branches of engineering and manufacture.

In 1884, he emigrated to the U.S., later becoming a naturalized citizen. For nearly a year, he worked for Thomas A. Edison, who was impressed by his skill and hard work, but the two men were diametrically opposed in temperament and method. Tesla was a visionary who solved problems in a flash of insight, where Edison relied on patient trial-and-error in practical experiments. Tesla insisted on the superiority of alternating current and its applications, whereas Edison believed it a dead end and championed direct current.

In the event, Tesla was right. He parted company with Edison after being promised $50,000 for improving the design and efficiency of dynamos. When Tesla solved the problem and asked for the money, Edison said he was only joking. Tesla immediately resigned.

His salary at the Edison Company had been modest, and for the next two years he had a difficult time, but in 1887 he was backed to form the Tesla Electric Company in New York. He was now able to construct the alternating current machines which he had visualized earlier.

The Tesla system made it possible to supply electricity economically over distances of hundreds of miles, instead of the short distances of the Edison direct current powerhouses. Tesla's demonstrations made a great impression on another inventor, George Westinghouse of the Westinghouse Electric Company of Pittsburgh. Westinghouse paid Tesla $1 million for rights on his alternating current system comprising some forty patents, with a contractadditionally stipulating a royalty of a dollar per horsepower.

In attempting to span the U.S. with an alternating current system, Westinghouse ran into financial difficulties, and his own backers insisted that he renounce his royalty contract to Tesla, otherwise they would withdraw support. When Westinghouse explained his difficulty to Tesla, the latter recalled how Westinghouse had believed in him, and consequently in a magnanimous gesture Tesla tore up his contract, thereby sacrificing some $12 million in unpaid royalties.

Tesla went on to invent new apparatus involving original principles. He was responsible for many important innovations, notably the system of electricity conversion and distribution by oscillatory dischargers, generators of high frequency current, the Tesla coil or transformer, a system of wireless transmission of intelligence, mechanical oscillators and generators of electrical oscillation, researches and discoveries in radiations, material streams and emanations, and high-potential magnifying transmitting. One of his most spectacular achievements was the harnessing of Niagara Falls. In 1895, the Westinghouse Electric Company had installed a gigantic hydroelectric project, using the Tesla polyphase system of alternating current.

Tesla opened up many important avenues of scientific development, often never properly acknowledged by later historians. His experiments with electromagnetic waves formed the basis of the development of radio. He stated that cosmic rays were responsible for the radioactivity of radium, thorium, and uranium and predicted that other substances would be made radioactive by bombardment. He thus anticipated the basic principles of X-ray apparatus and the electron microscope. In his work with wireless controlled automata he anticipated radio-controlled rocket missiles.

Not surprisingly he had one or two blind spots. He did not accept for many years that atomic fission would produce energy. He misunderstood the mechanism of vision, believing that visual images perceived by the brain were returned to the retina of the eye, and might be amplified or projected. However, there was no mistaking his own extraordinary visionary faculty and the discoveries associated with it. In an article titled 'Making Your Imagination Work For You' (*American Magazine,* April 1921), he wrote:

"During my boyhood I had suffered from a peculiar affliction due to the appearance of images, which were often accompanied by strong flashes of light. . . . Then I began to take mental excursions beyond the small world of my actual knowledge. Day and night, in imagination, I went on journeys—saw new places, cities, countries, and all the time I tried hard to make these imaginary things very sharp and clear in my mind . . .

"This I did constantly until I was seventeen, when my thoughts turned seriously to invention. Then, to my delight, I found I could *visualize* with the greatest facility. I needed no models, drawings, or experiments. I could picture them all in my head. . . .

"Here, in brief, is my own method: After experiencing a desire to invent a particular thing, I may go on for months or years with the idea in the back of my head. Whenever I feel like it, I roam around in my imagination and think about the problem without any deliberate concentration. This is a period of incubation.

"There follows a period of direct effort. I choose carefully the possible solutions of the problem I am considering, and gradually center my mind on a narrowed field of investigation. Now, when I am deliberately thinking of the problem in its specific features, I may begin to feel that I am going to get the solution. And the wonderful thing is, that if I do feel this way, *then I know I have really solved the problem and shall get what I am after.*

"The feeling is as convincing to me as though I already had solved it. I have come to the conclusion that at this stage the actual solution is in my mind *subconsciously,* though it may be a long time before I am aware of it *consciously.*

"Before I put a sketch on paper, the whole idea is worked out mentally. In my mind I change the construction, make improvements, and even operate the device. Without ever having drawn a sketch I can give the measurements of all parts to workmen, and when completed all these parts will fit, just as certainly as though I had made the actual drawings. It is immaterial to me whether I run my machine in my mind or test it in my shop.

"The inventions I have conceived in this way have always worked. In thirty years there has not been a single exception. My first electric motor, the vacuum tube wireless light, my turbine engine and many other devices have all been developed in exactly this way."

Tesla's friend and biographer John J. O'Neill stated that Tesla "was unquestionably an abnormal individual, and of a type that does have what are known as 'psychic experiences.' He was emphatic in his denial that he ever had experiences of that sort; yet he has related incidents that clearly belong in the psychic category." According to O'Neill, Tesla was fearful that admitting psychic experiences might cause him to be misunderstood as supporting **Spiritualism** or theories that something operates in life other than matter and energy.

In his later years, Tesla suffered financial difficulties, and was unable to construct some of his most ambitious inventions. He claimed that he had discovered an inexhaustible source of energy which could be transmitted anywhere in the world without wires or loss of power. He correctly foresaw that at some future time "it will be possible for nations to fight without armies, ships or guns by weapons far more terrible, to the destructive action and range of which there is virtually no limit." Tesla is credited with having discovered a protective radiation principle of the kind popularly termed "death ray."

Tesla became a vegetarian late in life, and developed a number of eccentricities. He had a germ phobia of the Howard Hughes type, and discarded handkerchiefs after using them only once. He required a fresh tablecloth for every meal, and used napkins to grasp the silverware, discarding them immediately after use and getting through a couple of dozen napkins during a main meal. Even in extreme poverty, he insisted on spending money for bird seed to feed the pigeons in New York, and cherished an intense love for one particular white pigeon.

Tesla was undoubtedly a genius. His inventions, often pirated, made other men rich. He was often cheated and exploited, but retained a chivalrous code of personal integrity, with an impulsive if quixotic generosity. He had a keen sense of justice, and it is known that in 1912 he refused the Nobel Prize because it was to be awarded jointly to himself and Thomas A. Edison; instead the award went to the Swedish scientist Gustav Dalen.

As a young man, Tesla had reduced his sleep period to only four hours or less, resulting in an illness with a condition of hypersensitivity. Some of his early inspirations of discovery and invention were associated with an ecstatic condition involving hyperventilation. His concept of reasonance in electrical phenomena reflected his own reasonance with the forces of Nature, whose mighty secrets were often revealed to him. Although he believed himself a scientific materialist, it seems that he may have been a natural mystic.

In an unpublished article titled 'Man's Greatest Achievement' (cited in John J. O'Neill's biographical *Prodigal Genius,* 1968), he wrote: "Long ago he [the human being] recognized that all perceptible matter comes from a primary substance, or tenuity beyond conception, filling all space, the Akasa or luminiferous ether, which is acted upon by the life-giving Prana or creative force, calling into existence, in never ending cycles, all things and phenomena. . ."

This is the language of Theosophy or Hindu metaphysics. Tesla's states of higher consciousness, achieved by intense concentration and a celibate life, bear out the ancient Hindu concepts of cosmic energy in the universe, aroused in the human body under the name of **Kundalini** through **yoga** disciplines and **meditation,** resulting in expanded consciousness and access to an infinity of cosmic intelligence. The nature and function of Kundalini have been graphically described from personal experience by Pandit **Gopi Krishna** in numerous books.

Tesla died in some poverty in New York on January 7, 1943. Soon afterwards, F.B.I. operatives opened the safe in his room and took away papers reputedly containing details of a secret invention of possible value in warfare. As early as 1899, Tesla had claimed to have discovered an "inexhaustible source of power" which could be transmitted all over the world without cables. He foresaw a world with boundless energy that would be able to solve problems of cultivation and industrialization, abolish famine and prevent war. If these claims were true, the secret died with him, but may some time be revived by another natural genius.

Recommended reading:

Gopi Krishna. *The Biological Basis of Religion and Genius,* Harper & Row, 1972; Turnstone Press, London, 1973

O'Neill, John J. *Prodigal Genius; The Life of Nikola Tesla,* Neville Spearman, London, 1968; Granada paperback, London/New York, 1980

Peat, David. *In Search of Nikola Tesla,* Ashgrove Press, Bath, U.K., 1983

Wilson, Colin (ed.). *Men of Mystery,* W. H. Allen, London, 1977 [contains chapter 'Nikola Tesla' by Kit Pedler]

Teutons

The Teutonic or "Germanic" nations, the peoples of High and Low German speech, Dutch, Danes, and Scandinavians, have always displayed a marked leaning towards the study and consideration of the occult. We are, however, concerned here with their attitude towards the occult in more ancient times, and refer the reader to the entry on **Germany** and the other countries alluded to for information upon medieval and modern occultism.

Little can be gleaned from the writings of classical authors upon the subject, and it is not until we approach the Middle Ages and study manuscripts concerning the traditions of an earlier day, and the works of such writers as Snorre Sturluson and Sæmundr (The *Eddas*) Saxo-Grammaticus, and such epics or pseudo-histories as *The Nibelungenlied,* that we find any light thrown upon the dark places of Teutonic magical practice and belief.

From the consideration of such authorities one can arrive at several basic conclusions: (1) That magic with the Teutons was non-hierophantic, and was not the province of the priesthood, as with the Celtic Druids, (2) That women were its chief conservators, (3) That it principally resided in the study and elucidation of the runic script, in the same manner as in early Egypt it was essentially part and parcel of the ability to decipher the hieroglyphic characters.

Passing on from the first conclusion, it seems that all kinds of people dabbled in magical practice, and to a great extent sorcery (for efforts seem to have been confined mostly to black magic) was principally the province of women. This is to be explained, perhaps, by the circumstance that only those who could read the runes—that is, those who could read at all—were able to undertake the study of the occult, and that therefore the unlettered warrior too restless for the repose of study, was barred from all advance in the subject.

Women in all ranks of life seem to have been addicted to the practice of sorcery, from the queen on the throne to the wise-woman or witch dwelling apart from the community. Thus the mother-in-law of Siegfried bewitches him by a draught, and scores of similar instances could be adduced.

At the same time, the general type of ancient Teutonic magic was not very high, it was greatly hampered by human considerations, and much at the mercy of the human element on which it acted, and the very human desires which called it forth. Indeed in many cases it was rendered useless by the mere cunning of the object upon which it was wreaked. It does not seem to have risen very much above the type of sorcery in vogue amongst primitive peoples in modern times. It is surprising, with all these weaknesses, how powerful a hold it contrived to get upon the popular imagination, which was literally drenched with belief in supernatural science.

Runes

In its various forms—German, *rune,* Anglo-Saxon *run,* Icelandic *run*—the word is derived from an old Low German word *raunen* "to cut" or "to carve," and as the runes in more ancient times were invariably carved and not written, it latterly came to designate the characters themselves.

As already stated, comparatively few people were able to decipher them, and the elucidation was left to the curious, the ambitious among the females, and the leisured few in general, these perhaps including priests and lawmen. Consequently we find the power to decipher them an object of mysterious veneration among ordinary people and a belief that the ability to elucidate them meant the possession of magical powers. The possessors of this ability would in no way minimize this ability, so that the belief in their prowess would flourish. Again, it is clear that a certain amount of patience and natural ability were necessary to acquirement of such an intricate script. The tradition that they were connected with sorcery lingered on in some parts of Iceland.

In later times, the word runes came to be applied to all the alphabetical systems employed by the Teutonic peoples before the introduction of Christianity.

Their origin is obscure, some authorities denying that it is Teutonic, and asserting that they are merely a transformation or adaptation of Greek characters, and others that they have a Phœnician or even cuneiform ancestry.

That they are of non-Teutonic origin is highly probable, as may be inferred from their strong resemblance to other scripts, and from the circumstance that it is highly unlikely that they could have been separately evolved by the Teutonic race in the state of comparative barbarism in which they first came into general use.

They have been divided into three systems—English, German, and Scandinavian—but the difference between these is merely local. They were not employed in early times for literary purposes, but the inscriptions only, usually found on stone monuments, weapons, implements, and personal ornaments and furniture. In England, runic inscriptions are found in the north only, where Scandinavian influence was strongest.

The first symbols of the runic alphabet have the powers of the letters *f, ú, th, ó, r, c,* for which reason the order of the runic letters is called not an alphabet but a *futhorc.* The system is symbolic. Thus its first quantity or letter pictures the head and horns of an ox, and is called *feoh* after that animal, the second is called *ur,* after the word for "bull," the third *thoru,* a tree, and others following *os,* a door; *rad,* a saddle; *caen,* a torch, all because of some fancied resemblance to the objects, or, more properly speaking, because they were probably derived or evolved from a purely pictorial system in which the pictures of the animals or objects enumerated above stood for the letters of the alphabet.

Since these runes were cut, some connection may be possible between Anglo-Saxon *secgan,* to say, and Latin *secare,* to cut, especially when we find secret signatures made of old by merely cutting a chip from the bark manuscript. In spelling, for example, the old sense of "spell" was a thin chip or shaving. The Roman historian Tacitus mentioned that in Teutonic **divination,** a rod cut from a fruit-bearing tree was cut into slips, and the slips, having marks on them, were thrown confusedly on a white garment to be taken up with prayer to the gods and interpreted as they were taken. A special use of light cuttings for such fateful cross-readings or "Virgilian lots," may have given to "spells" their particular association with the words of the magician.

Belief in Nature Spirits

Among the lesser figures of mythology, who were believed to enter into direct contact with ancient Teutonic peoples and assist them, or were connected with them in magical practice, were the *duergar* or dwarfs, trolls, undines, nixies and other spirits. Belief in them was distinctly of an animistic character. The dwarfs and trolls inhabited the recesses of the mountains, caves, and the underworld. The nixies and undines dwelt in the lakes, rivers, pools, and inlets of the sea. In general these were friendly to human beings, but objected to more than occasional intercourse with them.

Although not of the class of supernatural being who obey the behests of humans in answer to magical summonses, these, especially the dwarfs, often acted as instructors in art-magic, and many instances of this are to be met with in tales and romances of early Teutonic origin.

The dwarfs were usually assisted by adventitious aids in their practice of magic, such as belts which endowed the wearer with strength (like that worn by the dwarf **Laurin**), shoes of swiftness, analogous to the seven-league boots of folk tale, caps of invisibility, and so forth.

Witchcraft

Witchcraft, with its accompaniment of diabolism, was much more in favor among the northern Teutons than it was in Germany, and this circumstance has been attributed to their proximity to the Finns, a race notorious for its magical propensities.

In Norway, Orkney, and Shetland, the practice of sorcery seems to have been almost exclusively in the hands of women of Finnish race, and there is little doubt that the Finns exercised upon the Teutons of Scandinavia the mythic influence of a conquered race, that is, they took full advantage of the terror inspired in their conquerors by an alien and unfamiliar religion and ritual, which partook largely of the magical.

The principal activities of Teutonic witchcraft were the raising of storms, the selling of pieces of knotted rope (each knot representing a wind), divination and prophecy, acquiring invisibility, and such magical practices as usually accompany a condition of semi-barbarism.

In the North of Scotland, the Teutonic and Celtic magical systems may be said to have met and fused, but not to have clashed, as their many points of resemblance outweighed their differences.

Since the sea was the element of the people, it became the chief element of the witch of the northern Teutons. Thus in the saga of *Frithjof,* the two sea witches Heyde and Ham ride the storm and were sent by Helgi to raise the tempest which would drown Frithjof, and they took the shape of a bear and a storm-eagle. In the saga of *Grettir the Strong,* a witch-wife, Thurid, sends adrift a magic log which came to Grettir's island, and which led to his downfall.

Animal transformation played a considerable part in Teutonic magic and witchcraft. In early Germany the witch (hexe) seems to have been also a **vampire.**

Second Sight

It was, however, in prophecy and divination that the Teutons excelled, and this was more widespread among the more northern branches of the people than the southern. Prophetic utterance was usually induced by ecstasy. But it was not the professional diviner alone who was capable of supernatural vision. Anyone under stress of excitement, and particularly if near death, might become "fey," that is, prophetic, and great attention was invariably paid to utterances made whilst in this condition.

Recommended reading:

Berger, H. A. *Nordische Mythologie,* Zittau & Leipzig, 1834

Bugge, E. S. *The Home of the Eddic Poems,* David Nutt, London, 1899
Elliott, Ralph W. *Runes; An Introduction,* Barnes & Noble, 1971; Greenwood, 1981
Golther, W. *Religion und Mythus der Germanen, Leipzig, 1909*
Grimm, Jacob. *Teutonic Mythology,* 4 vols., G. Bell, London, 1880-1919; Peter Smith, n.d
Kauffmann, D. F. *Northern Mythology,* Dent, London, 1903; Norwood, n.d.
Meyer, E. H. *Germanische Mythologie,* Berlin, 1891
Stephens, George. *The Old-Northern Runic Monuments of Scandinavia & England,* 2 vols., London, 1866-68
Stephens, George. *Prof. S. Bugge's "Studies on Northern Mythology" Shortly Examined,* Williams & Norgate, London, 1883
Wilken, Ernst. *Die Prosaische Edda,* Paderhorn, 1878

Texas Monthly UFO Report

Concerned with the technical aspect of **UFO** investigation for individuals with some scientific background; includes reports on parapsychological research. Published by: Texas Scientific Research Center for UFO Studies, P.O. Box 4639, Waco, Texas 76705.

Thackeray, William Makepeace (1811-1863)

The great novelist was introduced to the phenomena of Spiritualism during a lecture tour in America when he attended a seance with the famous medium D. D. **Home**, and also observed the rapping phenomena of Ann (Leah) Underhill, one of the **Fox Sisters.**

His sympathetic reaction was described in Mrs. A. Leah Underhill's book *The Missing Link in Modern Spiritualism* (1885). This experience and subsequent observations in England with the great medium D. D. **Home** led Thackeray to endorse with warmth the sincerity of the anonymous account (written by Robert Bell) 'Stranger Than Fiction,' which was published in the *Cornhill Magazine,* edited by Thackeray. He was severely criticized for this apparent endorsement of Spiritualism.

However, it seems that his attitude was somewhat ambiguous. In a letter to his friends Mrs. Thomas F. Elliot and Kate Perry, he stated:

"Yes I have seen the Rappers, and the table moving, and heard the Spirits. The moving of tables is undoubted, the noises & knocks (continual raps following the person who has the gift of eliciting them) some natural unexplained phenomenon but the Spirits is of course dire humbug & imposture.They try to guess at something and hit or miss as may be. 1000 misses for one hit—It is a most dreary & foolish superstition. . . . But the physical manifestations are undoubted—Tables moving lifted up & men even lifted off the ground to the ceiling so some are ready to swear—but thought I do not believe in this until I see it: I wouldn't have believed in a table turning 3 weeks ago—and that I have seen and swear to . . . "

Both Thackeray and his friend Charles **Dickens** had the highest regard for Dr. John **Elliotson,** a pioneer of **Mesmerism,** who was later converted to Spiritualism after initial skepticism. Thackeray based his sympathetic character "Dr. Goodenough" in *Pendennis* and *The Newcomes* on Elliotson, and dedicated the former novel to him in appreciation of "his constant watchfulness and skill, his great goodness and kindness."

Recommended reading:

Goldfarb, Russell M. & Clare R. *Spiritualism and Nineteenth-Century Letters,* Associated University Presses, New Jersey & London, 1978
Underhill, A. Leah. *The Missing Link in Modern Spiritualism,* Thomas R. Knox, New York, 1885; Arno Press, 1976

Thanatology

Subject area concerned with aspects of death and dying. Parapsychological researches and medical studies suggest that there are three main components relating to the death experience: 1) sensation of floating out of the body; 2) feelings of peace or wholeness; 3) meeting with someone who has died previously.

Significant studies in the field of Thanatology have been conducted by physician Elisabeth **Kübler-Ross,** author of the book *On Death and Dying* (New York, 1970) and a founder of **Shanti Nilaya,** a healing and growth center in Escondido, California. (See also **Death; International Institute for the Study of Death;** Elisabeth **Kübler-Ross; Near Death Experience**)

Recommended reading:

Kastenbaum, Robert (ed.). *Between Life and Death,* Springer Publishing Co., New York, 1979
Kübler-Ross, Elisabeth. *On Death and Dying,* Macmillan, 1969
Osis, Karlis & Erlendor Haraldsson. *At the Hour of Death,* Avon Books (paperback), 1977

Thau Weza

Burmese wizards, literally "wire-man who works in wire." (See **Burma**)

Thayer, Mrs. M(ary) B(aker) (c.1887)

Well-known professional **apport** and **slate-writing** medium of Boston, chiefly producing flowers and fruits, sometimes live birds. In the *Banner of Light* (May 1875) there is an account of a canary apport in answer to a mental request.

In the report of the **Seybert Commission** a **slate-writing** seance attended by Prof. Fullerton was considered as a failure. There was a description of another seance, at which thirty people were present. The Seybert Commission was represented by Dr. Koenig and Dr. Leidy.

According to the latter's account "sounds were heard of objects dropping on the table, and from time to time matches were lit and exposed, strewn before the company, cut plants and flowers. These were all of the kind sold at this season by the florists, consisting of a pine bough, fronds of ferns, roses, pinks, tulips, lilies, callas and smilax. At one time there fell on the table a heavy body, which proved to be a living terrapin, at another time there appeared a pigeon which flew about the room . . . The proprietor of the house declared that the flowers and the other objects brought to view in the seance were not previously in the room, and their appearance could not be explained unless through spiritual agency."

In a footnote to his translation of Adolphe d'Assier's book *Posthumous Humanity* (1887) Col. H. S. **Olcott** wrote: "While she [Mrs. Thayer] was enclosed in a large bag, sealed closely at her neck, and all possibility of trickery guarded against, I have seen a long table, quite covered with vines, plants and flowers, dropped out of space. I marked a certain leaf of a rare plant in the garden without her knowledge, and the same evening, in response to my mental request, it dropped upon the back of my hand, with which I was at the moment holding the medium's two hands. The above occurred in the dark; but once a tree branch was brought me in full daylight, through her mediumship, in the house of a gentleman whose guest I was."

Theobald, Morell (1828-1908)

British Spiritualist, author of *Spiritualism at Home* (1884) and *Spirit Workers in the Home Circle* (1887), the latter describing a series of curious psychic manifestations in his home that lasted for many years.

His family had psychic gifts. His grandfather and father saw spirits. His own friendship with the author William **Howitt** and family initiated him into writing and mediumship in 1855. The psychic ties were further strengthened by intimacy with Mr. & Mrs. Thomas **Everitt.** The two families held seances together for years. Not surprisingly the loss of three children increased the receptivity of the Theobald family and resulted in **rapping** phenomena which, in the presence of three living children, developed to movements of a heavy dining table and intelligent communications.

The book of Morell Theobald's sister: *Heaven Opened; or Messages for the bereaved from their little ones in Glory* by F.J.T. (1870) contained records of these experiences. The intercourse with the Beyond was, at this period, threefold—the elder boy fell into trance and was controlled by the deceased children and others, Morell Theobald and his wife wrote automatically, Mrs. Everitt produced **direct voice** manifestations for the family.

The strange phenomena of later years were first heralded during a joint excursion with the Everitt family to Cornwall in 1871. To quote from *Spirit Workers in the Home Circle:* "As we sat on woodland slopes we had the curious sensations of rapping beneath the solid earth on which we sat. If we took a basket of sandwiches, that was moved about by our sportive invisible friends. At an inn where we stayed with our hamper of provisions we expected the waiter would be scared, for raps resounded on the window, walls and wainscoated panelling, while our hamper was bodily taken off by invisible hands into one corner of the room and there opened and partly unpacked for us."

In 1882, Mary, a new cook, was discovered to have clairvoyant powers. Whilst Tom, the youngest son, complained that his hair was being pulled by invisible beings, Mary could see and describe the phantom visitors. Because of her gifts the cook was soon advanced to the standing of a trusted friend of the family, and after the maid left, Mary and Nellie Theobald occupied the same bedroom and looked jointly after the household duties.

They soon felt the burdens of drudgery and Morell Theobald found it increasingly difficult to get the breakfast punctually at eight o'clock. At this stage, in November 1883, the spirits intervened. Early morning, the fire was found mysteriously lit in the kitchen, the water was prepared and boiled, the morning milk was brought in, the breakfast table was laid by invisible hands and a hundred other useful household services were performed, all unseen, when nobody was looking.

Morell Theobald employed many tests; he often got up in the middle of the night in an attempt to catch the operators in the act, but he was unsuccessful. There is not a single instance in his book, however, in which the fire lighting, as observed by him, could be called strictly evidential. No suspicion appears to have been conceived against Nellie and Mary, indeed a large part of the evidence for the paranormal is based on their testimony, and perhaps the best objective proof for spirit presence is Morell Theobald's statement that "the cat sitting on Mary's lap has frequently got up and 'swore' in feline dialect with arched back, and sometimes she gets so terrified that she flies to the window and tries to escape." But again it is not clear from the context whether this was witnessed by Morell Theobald himself or whether it was the evidence of Mary.

For some time, Morell Theobald resisted every request of competent psychic investigators to take Mary to their own rooms for investigation, and in this resolve he was strangely strengthened by spirit advice in **direct writing.** This decision was apparently wise, as the limited investigation which Frank **Podmore** and Frank S. Hughes of the Society for Psychical Research were finally allowed to continue in the Theobald home in 1884 threw considerable doubt on many of the marvelous occurrences, especially on the spirit writings which appeared in every conceivable place—on the ceiling, on the walls, on locked drawers and receptacles, on marked papers, and which were in many languages, old French, Latin, Hebrew, Greek and Raratongan among others.

The messages of "Saadi," an ancient Persian poet, and his friend "Wamik" appeared to defy normal explanation. "Saadi" gave an account of his life and wrote poems in English.

The Society for Psychical Research investigators could not witness the actual performance of the various household services and found many circumstances which suggested human origin in the spirit writings. The letters were regularly formed and of normal size when they appeared in places accessible to persons of ordinary stature but became straggling and irregular on higher places as if they had been written with a broomstick to which a pencil was attached. The locked secretaire in which writing was produced was not fraud-proof. A piece of paper could be slipped in through a chink.

The investigators also contended that the small characters in certain pieces of spirit writing which seemed to be beyond human production could have been written by anybody with a sharp pencil and patient practice. They found many crude mistakes in the Latin and Greek scripts and discovered finally that the facts contained in the communications coming from "Saadi" were published in an article "Persian Poetry in the Past" in Part 6 of *Chamber's Repository of Instructive and Amusing Tracts.* It also appeared that "Wamik," who claimed to have been "Saadi's" friend and contemporary poet, was a fictitious entity, the imaginary hero of the poem to which he subscribed his name.

The findings of the two investigators were strongly criticized in *Light* (January, February, March, 1885) to which they were submitted. The editor concluded that the investigation was incomplete and hasty but that fraud could not explain the extraordinarily varied phenomena of the Theobald house.

Indeed, nothing but **hallucination** could replace a paranormal explanation in Morell Theobald's following account: "I was standing by the table alone in the room, and again looked over the table, when there seemed to grow under my sight (I cannot describe it any other way) a sheet of paper folded in half, which on being taken up I found to contain greetings in seven different handwritings. I took it from my plate which had been empty a minute before."

On the other hand, Morell Theobald himself admits that "many of the writings . . . are comparatively feeble compositions" and that he found the source of the most puzzling pieces of direct writing, i.e., the Lord's Prayer as used in the twelfth century and the Rarantongan Script, in his own house in a volume of *Sunday at Home* of 1882, which he gave to Mary as a Christmas present.

Still, owing to the diversified styles of handwriting he refused to seek a normal explanation, even when the scripts were handed out by Mary herself from the cabinet in which she sat to develop materializations. All the time, relying on some mysterious vital economy practiced by the spirits, he accepted for transcendental facts "puddings . . . made and cooked when all the family were sitting together on Sunday evening in seance."

There is no better evidence for deep rooted unshakable faith than Morell Theobald's account of the test undertaken on behalf of the Society for Psychical Research in 1886. He was handed two sealed envelopes by Mr. E. T. Bennett, Assistant Secretary of the Society for Psychical Research, in order to have the hidden contents deciphered by spirit agency. After some weeks, writing was obtained on the outside of the envelopes which proved to be a fairly good counterpart of the inside. Thereupon Theobald was handed a third envelope which was, for some months, in his careful keeping, "no one in the house besides myself and my wife knowing of its existence."

Again the contents were revealed but instead of triumph, a very painful disclosure befell the Theobald family, it being stated by the Society for Psychical Research that all the envelopes were opened and gummed up again. To make matters worse, the handwritings were identical in character with the well-known scripts and this, Morell Theobald, by a strange twist of reasoning, accepted as proofs of abnormal production.

He put it down to the work of mischievous and fraudulent spirits that the tests were spoiled. He said that the family has broken essential condition of trust and thereby has opened the door to such evil influences. This conviction of Morell Theobald was apparently borne out by psychometric reading of the envelopes through a clairvoyant and by many mediumistic communications, one of them having been obtained through the mediumship of William **Eglinton.**

It is a very legitimate inference that the atmosphere of blind faith which pervaded the Theobald family had become a hot-bed of conscious and unconscious deception. This theory is not incompatible with occasional genuine phenomena. From Morell Theobald's book alone, however, it is almost impossible to form an opinion as to what degree genuine mediumship may have played a part in the queer manifestations, the scene of which was laid in his house for so many years.

For a summary of the findings of Frank Podmore and E. T. Hughes, see chapter 5 (vol.2) of Frank Podmore's book *Modern Spiritualism* (2 vols., London, 1902; reissued as *Mediums of the Nineteenth Century,* University Books, 1963). See also 'Alleged "Physical Phenomena," in the Family of Morell Theobald' (*Journal* of the Society for Psychical Research, vol. 2, pp. 28, 31, 81, 82).

"Theologus"

One of the spirit controls of the Rev. W. Stainton **Moses,** said to be St. John the Divine.

Theomancy

The part of the Jewish **Kabala** which deals with the mysteries of divine majesty and seeks the sacred names. He who possesses this science knows the future, commands nature, has full power over angels and demons, and can perform miracles.

The rabbis claimed that it was by this means that Moses performed so many marvels, that Joshua was able to stop the sun, that Elias caused fire to fall from heaven, and raised the dead, that Daniel closed the mouths of the lions and that the three youths were not consumed in the furnace. However, in spite of intense study of the divine names, mystical rabbis no longer perform any of the miracles reported in biblical history.

"Theophilus"

One of the spirit controls of the Rev. W. Stainton **Moses**, said to be St. John the Apostle.

Theosophical History (Journal)

Quarterly journal, launched in January 1985, which reports on the expanding historical study of the Theosophical movement, including individuals and impulses associated with Madame H. P. **Blavatsky,** founder of the **Theosophical Society** in 1875. The journal has an independent stance and is sympathetically neutral to various expressions of Theosophy, and seeks to promote the common historical enterprise by Theosophists and non-Theosophists.

It reprints important material difficult of access, and seeks to aid historical assessment of such pioneers of Theosophy as Alice **Bailey,** Annie **Besant,** W. Q. **Judge, J. Krishnamurti,** C. W. **Leadbeater** and G. R. S. **Mead.** By arrangement with the Society for Psychical Research, London, each issue carries an item from its files on Theosophical phenomena.

Theosophical History is edited by Leslie Price. Address: 46 Evelyn Gardens, London, SW7 3HB, England.

Theosophical Society

Founded in New York in 1875 by Helena Petrovna **Blavatsky** and Henry Steel **Olcott** and their associates. It stemmed from the prevailing interest in **Spiritualism** and occultism, but proposed a deeper philosophical and spiritual basis than the often dubious phenomena of the seance room.

Both Madame Blavatsky and Col. Olcott had been closely concerned with Spiritualist investigations, and had met at the house of the **Eddy Brothers** in Vermont. They were also concerned in the claimed phenomena of the mediums Mr. & Mrs. Nelson **Holmes** of Philadelphia, who were accused of cheating. The Holmes partnership involved the alleged manifestation of the spirits "Katie **King**" and "John **King**," associated with the British medium Florence **Cook**. Madame Blavatsky eventually disowned the Holmes phenomena, but endorsed the reality of the spirit "John King."

In May 1875 Madame Blavatsky and Col. Olcott formed a Miracle Club, as a counterblast to prevailing scientific materialism, but the organization languished. Soon Col. Olcott began to receive messages through Madame Blavatsky from a mysterious "Brotherhood of Luxor," prototypes of the famous **Mahatma letters** of later years. These messages claimed the support of hidden Masters of wisdom in the spreading of truth.

In November 1875, the Theosophical Society was founded with Col. Olcott as president and Madame Blavatsky as corresponding secretary, and a membership of twenty. The term "theosophy" was proposed by Charles Sotheran, a well-known bibliophile and editor of the *American Bibliopolist.* The Preamble to the Society's Bylaws stated:

"The Title of the Theosophical Society explains the objects and desires of its founder: they 'seek to obtain knowledge of the nature and attributes of the Supreme Power, and of the higher spirits *by the aid of physical processes.*' In other words, they hope, that by going deeper than modern science has hitherto done, into the esoteric philosophies of ancient times, they may be enabled to obtain, for themselves and other investigators, proof of the existence of an 'Unseen Universe,' the nature of its inhabitants if such there be, and the laws which govern them and their relations with mankind. Whatever may be the private opinions of its members, the society has no dogmas to enforce, no creed to disseminate. It is formed neither as a Spiritualist schism, nor to serve as the foe or friend of any sectarian or philosophic body. Its only axiom is the omnipotence of truth, its only creed a profession of unqualified devotion to its discovery and propaganda. In considering the qualifications of applicants for membership, it knows neither race, sex, color, country nor creed."

The stated Objects of the Society were "to collect and diffuse a knowledge of the laws which govern the universe." These laws clearly involved phenomena of a miraculous kind, as claimed in the history of occultism, **Rosicrucian** and other secret orders.

This preoccupation with the miraculous, which has also been the popular focal point in the establishment of great world religions, proved to be the strength as well as the weakness of the Society. Over the next two years, there was a shortage of unusual phenomena and the Society seemed doomed to failure, many members dropping out.

Meanwhile Madame Blavatsky was preparing her book *Isis Unveiled,* a remarkable survey of religion and occultism through the ages. This book, together with an amalgamation of the Theosophical Society with the Arya Samaj of Swami Dayananda Saraswati in 1878, stimulated new interest in the Society.

In 1879, Madame Blavatsky and Col. Olcott toured India, establishing new contacts and developing an aura of the Mystic East. India was always traditionally associated with supernormal feats of yogis and the esoteric wisdom of the *Vedas* and *Upanishads.* Although Swami Dayananda proved to be something of a disappointment, being a social reformer rather than a repository of miraculous feats of **yoga,** miracles surrounded Madame Blavatsky over the next few years in India and attracted widespread support for the Theosophical Society.

Col. Olcott's tour of Ceylon and acceptance of Buddhism also broadened the society's attraction as a unifying principle in all religions, although exciting opposition from doctrinaire Christian missionaries.

During 1880-82, there were many letters from the mysterious Mahatmas or Masters of Wisdom governing the development of the Society, which established headquarters at Adyar, Madras.

Although the marvels associated with Madame Blavatsky brought new and important supporters for the Society, they also excited opposition and accusations of fraud, even from Swami Dayananda, who publicly repudiated Madame Blavatsky and her Society in April 1882.

The uneasy mixture of presumed miracles and frauds, associated with noble principles, is also a familiar pattern in the history of Spiritualism itself, where sincere idealists have rubbed shoulders with charlatans. Miracles have proved to be attraction in the formation of various religions and cults, but an embarrassment after establishment. The supply of genuine paranormal phenomena in any given period seems to be limited, not available on demand, often freakish and misleading.

It seems unfortunate that the excellent principles of universal brotherhood (and sisterhood) and the underlying unity of religions, as exemplified by the Society, should have been regarded as requiring a regular supply of miraculous phenomena.

Over the years, the Theosophical Society suffered from various dissensions and schisms. Most notable was the controversy over the so-called **Mahatma Letters,** which Madame Blavatsky claimed were supernormally produced messages from Masters or adepts. Accusations by Christian missionaries in India that these letters were fraudulent began in 1884, and in the same year Dr. Richard **Hodgson** of the **Society for Psychical Research,** Britain, went to the headquarters of the Theosophical Society at Adyar, Madras, to conduct an on-the-spot investigation.

He reported the discovery of a shrine with a false back, used with the connivance of Madame Coulomb, an employee of the Society, as a kind of fake mailbox for Mahatma Letters. However, a confession of fraud by Madame Coulomb was dismissed by loyal members of the Society as part of a plot to discredit Madame Blavatsky and the Society.

An internal controversy arose in the Society over the establishment of an Esoteric Section for the study of arcane doctrines. Meanwhile Madame Blavatsky managed to continue work on her vast occult study *The Secret Doctrine*.

After her death in 1891, disputes arose over the production of further Mahatma Letters produced by the American William Q. **Judge,** supporting his claim to take charge of the Society in opposition to the presidency of Annie **Besant.**

In April 1895, there was a schism in the American lodges, resulting in the establishment of the **Theosophical Society in America** as a separate entity in 1896. E. T. Hargrove declared himself Judge's successor and was elected president of the Theosophical Society in America. Soon afterwards leadership passed to Katherine **Tingley,** who established a Theosophical community at Point Loma, San Diego. However, further dissensions arose, revolving largely around Tingley's preoccupation with social reform as distinct from esotericism.

In 1898, Hargrove withdrew while Tingley established the Universal Brotherhood, absorbing the greater part of the membership of the Theosophical Society in America.

Meanwhile, Annie Besant had succeeded Col. Olcott as leader of the Adyar and European Theosophical Society, following the death of Olcott in 1907. Mrs. Besant was assisted by C. W. **Leadbeater,** who seems to have had considerable psychic abilities.

However, Leadbeater was the center of a scandal in 1906, when he was accused of homosexual practices with young boys. Leadbeater resigned from the Society, but was restored to membership in 1908, resulting in the resignation of the scholar G. R. S. **Mead** and some 700 other members in protest.

With Mrs. Besant, Leadbeater adopted a young Brahmin boy named Jiddu **Krishnamurti,** who they claimed would be a future World Teacher or Messiah. There was much consternation in Theosophical circles when Krishnamurti came of age and publicly renounced his Messianic role in 1929. Curiously enough, however, he later became a spiritual lecturer of remarkable insight and sincerity, teaching all over the world in his own uniquely unobtrusive way.

Another offshoot of Theosophy was the arcane school of Alice **Bailey** (1880-1949), deriving from the Adyar lodge named Krotona, established in the Hollywood Hills in 1912, moving to Ojai in the 1920s. Eventually Mrs. Bailey left Krotona to lead her own movement disseminating her books and correspondence courses of the Arcane School and the School for Esoteric Studies, both based in New York.

In spite of its controversial and schismatic background, the Theosophical Society itself has had a considerable and positive influence on the spiritual and intellectual life of many individuals in India, Europe, and the U.S. Much of the power of the Irish literary renaissance of W. B. **Yeats** and AE (George **Russell**) stems from their association with Theosophy, which also exercised a powerful influence on European occultism.

Perhaps its greatest contribution was during the presidency of Annie Besant, when Theosophy provided the people of India with pride in their own cultural and spiritual heritage and paved the way for the nationalism that resulted in the independence of India. Under the auspices of the Theosophical Society, many important Hindu scriptures were translated and published, and the Library at Adyar contains many rare manuscripts preserved by the Society.

The main Theosophical bodies in modern times are now: The Theosophical Society (with international lodges and headquarters at Adyar, Madras, India, international headquarters at Altadena, California); the United Lodge of Theosophists (headquarters in Los Angeles, California); the Theosophical Society in America (headquarters in

Wheaton, Illinois). British headquarters of the Theosophical Society: 50 Gloucester Place, London, W1H 3HJ, England. (See also Helena Petrovna **Blavatsky: Mahatma Letters; Masters;** Henry Steel **Olcott; Theosophy;** Katherine **Tingley**)

Recommended reading:

Besant, Annie. *The Theosophical Society & H. P. Blavatsky,* London, 1891

(The) Christian Literature Society. *Theosophy Exposed: or, Mrs. Besant and Her Guru: Appeal to Educated Hindus,* SPCK Press, Madras, 1893

Coulomb, Madame E. *Some Account of My Intercourse with Madame Blavatsky from 1872 to 1884,* Elliot Stock, London, 1885

Hare, H. E. & W. L. *Who Wrote the Mahatma Letters?* Williams & Norgate, London, 1936

Hodgson, Richard. 'Personal Investigations, in India, of Theosophical Phenomena' (in Society for Psychical Research, *Proceedings,* vol.3, 1885, part 9; vol. 9, parts 24, 25; *Journal,* vols. 1, 2, 1884-1886)

Kingsland, William. *The Real H. P. Blavatsky,* John M. Watkins, London, 1928

Olcott, H. S. *Old Diary Leaves,* 6 vols., Theosophical Publishing House, Adyar, Madras, India, 1895-1910

Ransom, Josephine. *A Short History of the Theosophical Society,* Theosophical Publishing House, Adyar, Madras, India

Solovyoff, V. S. *A Modern Priestess of Isis,* Longmans, Green, London, 1895

Spinks, F. P. *Theosophists Reunite!* Christopher Publishing House, 1958

Symonds, John. *Madame Blavatsky, Medium & Magician,* London, 1958

The Theosophical Movement 1875-1925: A History and a Survey, E. P. Dutton, 1925

Waterman, Adlai E. *Obituary; The "Hodgson Report" on Madame Blavatsky;1895-1960; Re-examination Discredits the Major Charges Against H. P. Blavatsky,* Theosophical Publishing House, Adyar, Madras, 1963

Williams, Gertrude Marvin. *Priestess of the Occult; Madame Blavatsky,* Alfred A. Knopf, 1946

Theosophical Society in America

Founded in 1886; current membership 6,000. It exists "to form a nucleus of the universal brotherhood of humanity without distinction of race, creed, sex, caste or color; to encourage the study of comparative religion, philosophy, and science; to investigate unexplained laws of nature and the powers latent in man."

It maintains a library of 20,000 volumes, and publishes books through the Theosophical Publishing House, and two magazines: *Theosophist* monthly and *Discovery* (9 issues per year). Address: 1926 North Main Street, Wheaton, Illinois 60187.

Theosophical Society of Agrippa

The famous occultist and alchemist Agrippa (1486-1535) established in Paris and other centers a secret theosophical society, the rites of admission to which were of a peculiar character. The fraternity also possessed signs of recognition.

Agrippa visited London in 1510, and whilst there he established a branch of the order in that city. A letter of Agrippa's friend Blasius Caesar Landulph is extant in which he introduced to Agrippa a native of Nuremberg resident at Lyons, and whom he hoped "may be found worthy to become one of the brotherhood."

Theosophy

Term derived from the Greek *theos* (god) and *sophia* (wisdom), denoting a philosophical-religious system which claims absolute knowledge of the existence and nature of the deity, and is not to be confused with the later system evolved by the founders of the Theosophical Society.

This knowledge or theosophy it is claimed, may be obtained by special individual revelation, or through the operation of some higher faculty. It is the transcendent character of the godhead of theosophical systems which differentiates them from the philosophical systems of the speculative or absolute type, which usually proceed deductively from the idea of God. God is conceived in theosophical systems as the transcendent source of being, from whom human beings, in their natural state are far removed.

Theosophy is practically another name for speculative mysticism. Thus the Kabalistic and Neoplatonic conceptions of the divine emanations are in reality theosophical, as are the mystical systems of **Boehme** and Baader.

Theosophy has also come to signify the tenets and teachings of the founders of the Theosophical Society. This Society was founded in the United States in 1875 by Madame H. P. **Blavatsky,** Col. H. S. **Olcott** and others. Its objects were to establish a nucleus of the Universal Brotherhood of Humanity, to promote the study of comparative religion and philosophy and to investigate the mystic powers of life and matter.

The conception of the Universal Brotherhood was based upon the oriental idea of One Life—that ultimate oneness which underlies all diversity, whether inward or outward. The study of comparative religion had materialized into a definite system of belief, the bounds of which were dogmatically fixed. It was set forth in the Theosophical system that all the great religions of the world originated from one supreme source and that they are merely expressions of a central "Wisdom Religion" vouchsafed to various races of the earth in such a manner as was best suited to time and geographical circumstances.

Underlying these was a secret doctrine or esoteric teaching which it was stated had been the possession for ages of certain Mahatmas or adepts in mysticism and occultism. With these Madame Blavatsky claimed to be in direct communication, and she herself manifested occult phenomena, producing the ringing of astral bells, and so forth.

On several occasions these effects were unmasked as fraudulent, but many people believed that Madame Blavatsky was one of those rare personalities who possessed great natural psychic powers, which at times failing her, she augmented by fraudulent methods.

The evidence for the existence of the "**Great White Brotherhood**" of Mahatmas, the existence of which she asserted, was unfortunately somewhat inconclusive. It rested, for the most part, on the statements of Madame Blavatsky, Col. Olcott, A. P. **Sinnett,** C. W. **Leadbeater,** and other committed Theosophists, who claimed to have seen or communicated with them.

With every desire to do justice to these upholders of the Theosophical argument, it is necessary to point out that it has been amply proved that in occult, or pseudo-occult experiences, the question of self-hallucination enters very largely (see **Witchcraft**), and the ecstatic condition may be answerable for subjective appearances which seem real enough to the visionary.

Again, the written communications of the Mahatmas (see **Mahatma Letters**) give rise to much doubt. One Mahatma employed the American system of spelling, and this was accounted for by the circumstance that his English had been sophisticated by reading American books. A study of these letters leaves little doubt that their style, script and purpose were nearer Madame Blavatsky than Tibetan or Himalayan hermitages.

The revelations of Madame Blavatsky in her books *Isis Unveiled* (2 vols., 1877) and *The Secret Doctrine* (2 vols., 1888-97) are an extraordinary mixture of Buddhistic, Brahministic and Kabalistic matter with a basic theme of religious unity and the persistence of occult and miraculous phenomena throughout history.

The Theosophical Society has numbered within its members many persons of very high ability, whose statement and exegesis of their faith has placed it upon a much higher level and more definite foundation.

The system was constructed in a manner akin to genius, and evolved on most highly intricate lines. It was, to a great extent, pieced together after the death of the original founder of the society, on which event a schism occurred in the Brotherhood through the claims to leadership of William Q. **Judge,** of New York, who died in 1896, and who was followed by Mrs. Katherine **Tingley,** the founder of the great Theosophical community at Point Loma, California.

Col. Olcott became the leader of the remaining part of the original Theosophical Society in America and India, being assisted in his work by Mrs. Annie **Besant,** but a more or less independent organization was founded in England.

A brief outline of the tenets of Theosophy may be stated as follows. It posits belief in its views rather than blind faith, and allows for individual differences of opinion. It professes to be the religion which holds the germs of all others. It has also its aspect as a science—a science of life and of the soul.

The basic teaching is that there are three truths which are absolute, and which cannot be lost, but yet may remain silent for lack of speech: The soul of humanity is immortal and its future is the future of the thing, whose growth and splendor has no limit. The principle which gives life dwells in us and without us, is undying and eternally beneficent, is not heard, or seen, or smelt, but is perceived by the man who desires perception. Each individual is his or her own absolute law-giver, the dispenser of glory or gloom to oneself, decreer of one's life, one's reward, one's punishment.

Although Theosophy posits the existence of an Absolute, it does not pretend to knowledge of its attributes. In the Absolute are innumerable universes, and in each universe countless solar systems. Each solar system is the expression of a being called the *Logos,* the Word of God, or Solar Deity, who permeates it and exists above it and outside it.

Below this Solar Deity are his seven ministers, called Planetary Spirits, whose relation to him is like that of the nerve centers to the brain, so that all his voluntary acts come through him to them (see also **Kabala**). Under them are vast hosts or orders of spiritual beings called *devas,* or angels, who assist in many ways. This world is ruled by a great official who represents the Solar Deity, which is in absolute control of all the evolution that takes place upon this planet. When a new religion is to be founded, this being either comes or sends pupils to institute it.

In the earlier stages of the development of humanity, the great officials of the hierarchy are provided from more highly evolved parts of the system, but whenever human beings can be trained to the necessary level of power and wisdom these offices are held by them. They can only be filled by adepts, who in goodness, power and wisdom are immeasurably greater than ordinary individuals, and have attained the summit of human evolution. These advance until they themselves become of the nature of deities.

There are many degrees and many lines of activity among these, but some of them always remain within touch of the earth and assist in the spiritual evolution of humanity. This body is called the **"Great White Brotherhood."** Its members do not dwell together, but live separately apart from the world and are in constant communication with one another and with their head.

Their knowledge of higher forces is so great that they have no necessity for meeting in the physical world, but each dwells in his own country, and their power remains unsuspected among those who live near them. These adepts are willing to take as apprentices those who have resolved to devote themselves utterly to the service of mankind, and anyone who will may attract their attention by showing worthiness of their notice. Madame Blavatsky was presumed to be such an apprentice. One of these masters said: "In order to succeed the pupil must leave his own world and come into ours."

The formation of a solar system and the cosmogonic operation of the Theosophical conception has been treated in separate entries; as also the various planes on which the personality of an individual dwells in its long journey from earth to the final goal of *Nirvana.* The Theosophical conception of the constitution of the human being is that he or she is in essence a spark of the divine fire belonging to the **Monadic world.** For the purposes of human evolution, this monad manifests itself in lower worlds. Entering the Spiritual World it manifests itself there as the triple spirit, having its three aspects, one of which always remains in the Spiritual Sphere.

The second aspect manifests itself in the Intuitional World, and the third in the Higher Mental World, and these two are collated with intuition and intelligence. These three aspects combined make up the ego which is individual personality during the human stage of evolution. The way or path towards enlightenment and emancipation is known as *karma.*

The human personality is composed of a complex organization consisting of seven principles which are united and interdependent, yet divided into certain groups, each capable of maintaining a kind of personality. Each of these principles is composed of its own form of matter and possesses its own laws of time, space and motion.

The most gross of those, the physical body, is known as *rûpa,* which becomes more and more refined until we reach the universal self *âtmâ,* but the circumstance which determines the individual's powers, tests and advantages, or in short his or her character, is the *karma,* which is the sum of bodily, mental and spiritual growth and is spread over many lives past and future, in short, as one soweth, so must one reap, if in one existence the individual is handicapped by any defect, mental or physical, it may be regarded as the outcome of past delinquencies. This doctrine as with many of the associated terms and concepts, is practically common to both Buddhism and Brahminism, from which Theosophy derives.

Returning to concepts of the constitution of the human being, the ego existing in the Higher Mental World cannot enter the Physical World until it has drawn around itself a veil composed of the matter of these spheres, nor can it think in any but an abstract manner without them—its concrete ideas being due to them. Having assumed the astral and physical bodies, it is born as a human being, and having lived out its earth-life sojourns for a time in the **Astral World,** until it can succeed in throwing off the shackles of the astral body.

When that is achieved the individual finds himself or herself living in the mental body. The stay in this sphere is usually a long one—the strength of the mental constitution depending upon the nature of the thoughts to which one has habituated oneself. But he or she is not yet sufficiently developed to proceed to higher planes, and once more descends into the denser physical sphere to again go through the same round. Although coming from on high into these lower worlds, it is only through that descent that a full recognition of the higher worlds is developed in the individual.

In the Higher Mental World, the permanent vehicle is a causal body, which consists of matter of the first, second and third sub-divisions of that world. As the ego unfolds one's latent possibilities in the course of one's evolution, this matter is greatly brought into action, but it is only in the perfect individual or adept, that it is developed to its fullest extent. In the causal body, none of the possibilities of the grosser bodies can manifest themselves.

The mental body is built up of matter of the four lower sub-divisions of the Mental World, and expresses the individual's concrete thoughts. Its size and shape are determined by those of the causal vehicle.

While on earth the personality wears the physical, mental, and astral bodies all at once. It is the astral which connects one with the Astral World during sleep or trance (see **Astral Plane**). It is easy to see how the doctrine of reincarnation arose from this idea. The ego must travel from existence to existence, physical, astral, mental, until it can transcend the Mental World and enter the higher spheres.

The Theosophical path to the goal of *Nirvana* is practically derived from Buddhistic teaching, but there are also other elements in it—Kabalistic and Greek. The path is the great work whereby the inner nature of the individual is consciously transformed and developed. A radical alternation must be made in the aims and motives of the ordinary mortal. The path is long and difficult, and as has been said extends over many existences. Morality alone is insufficient to the full awakening of the spiritual faculty, without which progress in the path is impossible. Something incomparably higher is necessary.

The physical and spiritual exercises recommended by Theosophy are those formulated in the Hindu philosophical system known as *Raja Yoga.* The most strenuous efforts alone can impel the individual along the path, and thus to mount by the practice of *Vidyâ,* that higher wisdom which awakens the latent faculties and concentrates effort in the direction of union with the Absolute.

The way is described as long and difficult, but as the disciple advances he or she becomes more convinced of ultimate success, by the possession of transcendental faculties which greatly assist in overcoming difficulties. But these must not be sought for their own sake, as to gain knowledge of them for evil purposes is tantamount to the practice of Black Magic.

It is not claimed in this brief outline that the whole of the Theosophical doctrine has been set forth, and the reader who desires further information regarding it is recommended to the many books on the subject which are available. (See also **Theosophical Society; Theosophical Society in America**)

Theta (Journal)

Scholarly journal of parapsychology published quarterly by the **Psychical Research Foundation.** Its title derives from the initial letter of the Greek word, *Thanatos* (death), and its concern is mainly with research on the problem of survival of bodily death. Edited by W. G. **Roll.** Published from 1963 onwards by the Psychical Research Foundation, Inc. Address: Psychical Department, W. Georgia College, Carrolton, Georgia 30118.

Thian-ti-hwii

The Heaven and Earth League, an ancient esoteric society in China, said to have still been in existence in 1674. The candidate before reception had to answer 333 questions. It professed to continue a system of brotherhood derived from ancient customs.

Third Eye

The mystical center behind the forehead between the eyes, which is a focus for Oriental mystical **meditation.** It is known as **yoga** philosophy as the *ajna chakra* or center of command, and its activation or opening through meditation is often the preliminary to activation of other *chakras.*

The suggestion in the popular book *The Third Eye* (1956) by T. Lopsang **Rampa** (pseudonym of Cyril Hoskins) that this *chakra* may be opened by a physical operation is a misunderstanding of the whole scheme of the subtle body and its currents of **Kundalini** energy. No such operation features in Hindu or Tibetan mysticism and it must be regarded as an imaginative fantasy.

Thomas, C(harles) Drayton (1867-1953)

British clergyman who was an active member of the Society for Psychical Research, London for many years. He was a Council member from 1934-53 and one of the first regular sitters with the medium Mrs. Osborne **Leonard,** on whose phenomena he reported in the Society's *Journal* and *Proceedings.* He also undertook so called **Book Tests,** to provide evidence in favor of survival by excluding the possibility of telepathy.

He worked with W. Whately **Carington** in the quantitative study of trance personalities. His articles in the SPR *Proceedings* included: 'The Modus Operandi of Trance-Communication According to Descriptions Received Through Mrs. Osborne Leonard' (vol. 38, part 107, 1928-29), 'A Consideration of a Series of Proxy Sittings' (vol. 41, part 130, 1932-33), 'The Word Association Test with Mrs. Osborne Leonard' (vol. 43, part 141, 1935), 'A Proxy Case Extending Over Eleven Sittings with Mrs. Osborne Leonard' (vol. 43, part 143, 1935), 'A Proxy Experiment of Significant Success' (vol. 45, part 159, 1939), 'The Volume of Byron: A Significant Book Test' (vol. 48, part 175, 1946-49).

His books included: *Some New Evidence for Human Survival* (1922), *Life Beyond Death With Evidence* (1928), *The Mental Phenomena of Spiritualism* (1930), *An Amazing Experiment* (n.d.), *Beyond Life's Sunset* (1931), *From Life to Life* (1946), *In the Dawn Beyond Death* (n.d.), *Precognition and Human Survival* (1948).

Thomas died July 14, 1953.

Thomas, John F(rederick) (1874-1940)

Psychologist and educator who studied parapsychology. Born July 22, 1874 at Parker City, Pennsylvania, he studied at University of Michigan (LL.B. 1898, M.A. 1915), Duke University, Durham, N.C. (Ph.D. 1935). In 1898 he married Ethel Louise Gammon (died 1926).

He was a member of the Michigan Education Association (president in 1940), the National Education Association, Boston Society for Psychic Research, Society for Psychical Research, London.

For most of his life Dr. Thomas was concerned with the Detroit public school system. He had been interested in psychic research for many years, but did not become actively involved until the Boston medium Mrs. Minnie M. **Soule** (also known as "Mrs. Chenoweth") sat for him and produced strong evidence of survival.

Dr. Thomas also sat with Mrs. Osborne **Leonard** and Mrs. Eileen J. **Garrett.** Sittings in 1932 formed the subject of his Ph.D. thesis at Duke: *An Evaluative Study of the Mental Content of Certain Trance Phenomena.* This was also the first doctoral thesis dealing with parapsychology.

He also published: *Case Studies Bearing Upon Survival* (1929), *Beyond Normal Cognition* (1937). The evidence for survival in connection with his wife is also considered in 'The Ethel Thomas Case' by Edmond P. **Gibson** (*Tomorrow,* Summer 1954) and in *Journal* of the American Society for Psychical Research (vol. 40, No. 1, Jan. 1946).

Dr. Thomas died November 21, 1940.

Thomas the Rhymer (c. 1220-c. 1297)

Scottish soothsayer (prophet) of the thirteenth century. It is impossible to name the exact birth date of Thomas the Rhymer, who is well known on account of his figuring in a fine old ballad included in Sir Walter Scott's *Minstrelsy of the Scottish Border.*

Thomas is commonly supposed to have lived at the beginning of the thirteenth century, that period being assigned because the name, "Thomas Rimor de Erceldun," is appended as witness to a deed, whereby one "Petrus de Haga de Bemersyde" agreed to pay half a stone of wax annually to the Abbot of Melrose, and this "Petrus" has been identified with a person of that name known to have been living about 1220.

Erceldoune or Ercildun is simply the old way of spelling Earlston, a village in the extreme west of Berwickshire, near the line demarking that county from Roxburgh.

It would seem that Thomas held estates in this region, for he is mentioned as a landed-proprietor by several early writers, most of whom add that he did not hold his lands from the Crown, but from the Earls of Dunbar. Be that as it may, Thomas probably spent the greater part of his life in and around Earlston, and a ruined tower there, singularly rich in ivy, is still pointed out as having been his home, and bears his name, while in a wall of the village church there is a lichened stone with the inscription:—

"Auld Rhymour's Race
Lies in this Place."

According to local tradition, this stone was removed to its present resting place from one in a much older church, long since demolished.

Nor are these things the only relics of the soothsayer, a lovely valley some miles to the west of Earlston being still known as "Rhymer's Glen." It is interesting to recall that the artist J. M. W. Turner painted a watercolor of this place, and no less interesting to remember that Sir Walter Scott, when buying the lands which eventually constituted his estate of Abbotsford, sought eagerly and at last successfully to acquire the glen in question. Naturally he loved it on account of its associations with the shadowy past, and his biographer J. G. Lockhart stated that many of the novelist's happiest times were spent in this romantic place, and related how the novelist Maria Edgeworth visited it in 1823, that thenceforth Sir Walter used always to speak of a certain boulder in the glen as the "Edgeworth stone," the lady writer whom he admired so keenly having rested here for a space. It seems probable, however, that the glen was so named by Scott himself.

It is thought that Thomas died in 1297, and it is clear that he had achieved a wide fame as a prophet, many references to his skill being found in writers who lived comparatively soon after him. A Harleian manuscript in the British Museum known to have been written before 1320, disclosed the significant phrase, "La Comtesse de Donbar demanda a Thomas de Essedoune quant la guere descoce prendreit fyn," but the lady in question was not a contemporary of the prophet. In Barbour's *Bruce,* composed early in the fourteenth century, we find the poet saying,

"Sekerly
I hop Thomas Prophecy
Off Hersildoune sall weryfyd be."

The historian Andrew of Wyntoun in the *Originale Cronykil of Scotland,* also mentioned Thomas as a redoubtable prophet, while Walter Bower, the continuator of Fordun's *Scoticronicon,* recounted how once Rhymer was asked by the Earl of Dunbar what another day would bring forth, whereupon he foretold the death of the king, Alexander III, and the very next morning news of his majesty's decease was noised abroad.

Blind Harry's poem *Wallace,* written midway through the fifteenth century, likewise contains an allusion to Thomas's prophesying capacities.

Coming to later times, Sir Thomas Gray, Constable of Norham, in his Norman-French *Scalacronica,* compiled during his captivity at Edinburgh Castle in 1555, spoke of the predictions of Merlin, which like those of "Banaster ou de Thomas de Ercildoune . . . furount ditz en figure."

A number of predictions attributed to Thomas the Rhymer are still current, for instance that weird verse which Sir Walter Scott made the motto of his novel *The Bride of Lammermuir,* and also a saying concerning a Border family with which, as we have seen, the soothsayer was at one time associated:

"Betide, betide, whate'er betide,
There'll aye be Haigs at Bemersyde."

It will be observed that these lines are in poetic meter, yet there is really no sure proof that the soothsayer was a poet. It is usually supposed that he acquired the nickname "Rhymer" because he was a popular minstrel in his day, but the fact remains that "Rymour" had long been a comparatively common surname in Berwickshire, and, while it may have originated with Thomas, the assumption has but slight foundation.

Again, the prophet of Earlston has been credited with a poem on the story of Sir Tristram, belonging to the Arthurian cycle of romance, and the Advocate's Library contains a manuscript copy of this, probably written as early as 1300. However, while Sir Walter Scott and other authorities believed in this ascription, it is quite likely that the poem is only a paraphrase from some French troubadour.

For generations, however, the Scottish peasantry continued to be influenced by the sayings attributed to "True Thomas," as they named him, as evidenced by the continuing publication of books and chapbook pamphlets containing his prophecies until well into the nineteenth century. For a detailed study, see *The Romance and Prophecies of Thomas Erceldoune* edited by J. A. H. Murray for the English Text Society, London, 1875.

A beautiful legend credits Thomas with obtaining his prophetic powers after visiting fairyland. The ballad of "Thomas Ryner and the Queen of Elfland" in its various forms is classified as No. 37 of the collection of *English and Scottish Popular Ballads* edited by Francis James Child, published in 5 vols., 1882-98.

Thompson, Rosina (Mrs. Edmond Thompson) (1868- ?)

British trance medium, whose powers were developed at Frederic W. Thurstan's **Delphic Circle** at Hertford Lodge, Battersea, London. In her early sittings in 1897 and 1898 the records of which in *Light* refer to her as Mrs. T., she exhibited powerful physical phenomena, **raps, movements** of objects, psychic lights (see **Luminous phenomena), elongation, direct voice, apports,** scents and **materializations.**

Her physical manifestations were discouraged by F. W. H. **Myers** and she was persuaded to give her services to the Society for Psychical Research as a trance medium from 1898 onwards (*Proceedings* of the S.P.R., vol. 17, 1901-03). Her chief control was her deceased daughter, Nelly, who died in infancy. Another communicator of importance was Mrs. Cartwright, the mistress of the school where Mrs. Thompson was educated.

Her trances were much lighter than those of Mrs. **Piper**'s and occasionally they were scarcely distinguishable from the state of normal wakefulness. Many instances of her paranormal perceptions were recorded in the waking state.

Against Dr. Richard **Hodgson,** who, in six sittings, formed an unfavorable opinion of her powers, it was the skeptical Frank **Podmore** who hurried to Mrs. Thompson's defense and considered Dr. Hodgson's conclusion that Mrs. Thompson was untrustworthy to go beyond the warrant of the facts. Podmore expressed his opinion in plain words: "I should perhaps add that the supernormal source of much of the information given at Mrs. Thompson's seances seems to me to be almost beyond dispute."

The reports of J. G. **Piddington** and Dr. F. **van Eeden** contained many curious accounts. Mrs. A. W. **Verrall** had 22 sittings with Mrs. Thompson. She made statistical calculations and found that out of 238 definite statements referring to things past and present, 33 were false, 64 were unidentified and 141—59 percent—were true. Of these 141 true statements, 51 could not have been ascertained from normal sources.

The results of Dr. van Eeden were very convincing. He came from Holland with an article of clothing that belonged to a young man who first cut his throat and then shot himself. He obtained dramatic communications and spoke in Dutch (of which language Mrs. Thompson was ignorant) with the young suicide.

Mrs. Verrall's general opinion of the controlling personalities was that their characteristics were not very marked, all bore strong resemblance to Mrs. Thompson, the voice was hardly to be distinguished from hers and the words and phrases were such as she herself used in the normal state. Nevertheless she admitted that many personalities bore, for the sitters, the marks of independent individuality.

F. W. H. Myers, whose belief in survival was chiefly founded on experiments with Mrs. Thompson (he and his friends had 217 sittings, about two thirds of which he personally attended) died on January 17, 1901. Mrs. Thompson, at this time, had already suspended sittings altogether. But feeling an impulse to do so, she gave two sittings to Sir Oliver **Lodge.** In both of them, communications characteristic of Myers were forthcoming.

Thompson, William Irwin (1938-   )

Author of books analyzing society in the light of contemporary **New Age** movements: founder of **Lindisfarne Association,** a commune based on a "new planetary culture."

Born July 16, 1938 in Chicago, Illinois, Thompson was educated at Pomona College (B.A. 1962), Cornell University (M.A. 1964, Ph.D. 1966). He was assistant professor of humanities at Massachusetts Institute of Technology, Cambridge from 1965-68, associate professor of humanities at York University, Toronto, Canada from 1968 onwards. He is a member of the American Committee for Irish Studies; Esalen Institute. In addition to his articles in *Tulane Drama Review, Sewanee Review, Antioch Review* and other journals, he has published: *The Imagination of an Insurrection: Dublin, Easter 1916* (1967; 1972), *Reflections at the Edge of History; Speculations on the Transformation of Culture* (1971), *Passages About Earth; An Exploration of the New Planetary Culture* (1974), *Evil and World Order* (1976), *From Nation to Emanation* (1981), *The Time Falling Bodies Take to Light* (1981).

In the latter two books, Thompson explored a new culture emerging in the light of occult, spiritual and new consciousness movements. In *Passages About Earth* he analyzed the alternative cultures of Paolo Soleri, H. G. Wells, Werner Heisenberg, Aurelio Peccei and his Club of Rome, the Integral Yoga of Sri **Aurobindo,** the Institute for World Order and W. Warren Wagar, C. F. von Weizäcker of the Max Planck Institute and the Kundalini yogi Pandit **Gopi Krishna.** The book contains valuable insights into the nature and impact of New Age movements and lifestyles on the established technological nation-states.

Thompson was favorably impressed by the alternative culture of **Findhorn,** a Scottish community established by Peter and Eileen Caddy in 1962 as "a training center for the embodiment of universal consciousness in those who recognize their path is one of world service."

He visited the ruins of Lindisfarne, a monastery on Holy Island off the coast of Northumberland, England, founded by St. Aidan in 635 A.D. Later he founded the Lindisfarne Association in Southampton, New York as an educational community for cultural transformation in a new synthesis.

In Thompson's view, the original Lindisfarne typified a historic clash between esoteric Christianity and ecclesiastical Christianity, between religious experience and religious authority. As with Peter and Eileen Caddy's experiments at Findhorn, Thompson's Lindisfarne has great significance as an attempt to extend intellectual theories by practical community work. In such a setting, occultism and higher consciousness movements are integrated into a truly New Age "planetary culture" rather than a counterculture. (See also **Lindisfarne Association; New Age**)

Thorogood, Brackett K(irkwood) (1881-   )

Engineer and educator who wrote on parapsychological subjects. Born December 21, 1881 at Cambridge, Massachusetts, he was educated at Chauncy Hall School, Lowell Institute, Massachusetts Institute of Technology. In 1909 he married Lilian Whittier Bartlett.

He was director of the Franklin Technical Institute from 1938-57 and a technical and technological consultant from 1922 onwards. He was a member of various professional bodies, winner in 1954 of the Professor Charles Francis Park gold medal for outstanding service to Lowell Institute, consultant to American Society for Psychical Research from 1930-39.

In addition to his many articles on engineering subjects, he published papers on mediumship, and the claimed passing of matter through matter, in the ASPR *Journal.* His article 'The Margery Mediumship' was published in ASPR *Proceedings* (vol. 22, 1933).

Thought-Reading

Thought-transference from the reverse aspect. The agent attempts to picture the contents of the subject's mind, i.e., to "read it," instead of impressing it with his own transmitted ideas.

In early times, when outbursts of ecstatic frenzy were ascribed to demonic possession, ecstatics were often credited with the power to read thoughts and witches were supposed to possess the same faculty. In the religious revivals of the Cevennes, thought-reading was one of the minor but very practical miracles that occurred. It was used for the detection of spies who frequently attended the meetings of the proscribed devotees (see **Tremblers of the Cevennes**).

Robert Baxter, a member of the Irvingite congregation seized with Pentecostal fervor in 1831 (see Rev. Edward **Irving**), recorded that when he was possessed by tongues he could often read the unspoken thoughts of his hearers.

In the fifteen century, **Paracelsus** had observed the phenomenon of thought-reading, and it was also reported by early experimenters in **Animal Magnetism.**

The advent of **Spiritualism** gave thought-reading a new impetus. It was now the spirits who read the thoughts of the sitters and replied to them with raps and turning-turning messages.

Thought-reading may occur through emotional or psychic sympathy or positive perception of the ideas existing in another mind. Musical strings furnish an analogy to the first mode. A note struck on one string will be taken up and echoed by another. In cases of mass panic, the sense of fear is communicated to surrounding people who may be ignorant of the original cause of the terror. However, it is often difficult to differentiate between psychic contagion and the transmission of emotions or ideas by subconsciously perceived signs such as facial expressions and postures.

Sergeant E. W. **Cox,** an early investigator of the phenomena of Spiritualism, wrote: "If the Darwinian theory be true, there must have been a time when man had no articulate speech. For intercommunication with his kind he must have then possessed some other faculty than language. Most probably that was what the intercourse of animals is, and the abnormal cases of thought reading that occur among ourselves may be possibly the survival of a faculty which has now almost vanished, because it has gradually fallen into disuse."

The term "thought-reading" is also popularly used for demonstrations by stage performers who actually use subtle codes for apparent telepathic communication. For a description of stage thought-reading, see the book by Stuart Cumberland (pseudonym of Charles Garner, *Thought-Reader's Thoughts; Being the Impressions and Confessions of Stuart Cumberland* (1888; 1975). It is possible that some tricks of stage performers may be similar to methods employed subconsciously by ordinary individuals who appear to manifest thought-reading or telepathic faculty.

Some performers can "read" subtle muscular movements when holding the hand of a subject and thus discover a hidden object. Another explanation of certain apparent thought-transference is subconscious whispering. (See also **Muscle Reading**; Sydney & Lesley **Piddington; Telepathy; Thought-Transference**; Julius & Mrs. **Zancig**)

Thought-Transference

This claimed faculty was baptized "telepathy" by the **Society for Psychical Research,** London, in 1882, but its discovery was not due to its godfathers. In the fifteenth century, **Paracelsus** wrote: "By the magic power of the will, a person on this side of the ocean may make a person on the other side hear what is said on this side . . . the ethereal body of a man may know what another man thinks at a distance of 100 miles or more." The Swedish seer Emanuel **Swedenborg** (1688-1772) clearly stated that spiritual or sympathetic states of consciousness conquer time and space.

The state of *rapport* discovered by the Mesmerists (see **Mesmerism**) demonstrated transference of thoughts and emotions. The mechanism was sought in a "magnetic fluid." Somnambulic, or hypnotic trance induced from a distance seemed to indicate direct action between mind and mind. The possibility that this condition might have been brought about by conscious or subconscious suggestion was not immediately apparent.

Many experiments in thought transference were recorded in Germany in the beginning years of the nineteenth century. A valuable series was published by Dr. Van Ghert, Secretary of the Royal Mineralogical Society at Jena in the *Archive für den Thierischen Magnetismus* and by H. M. Weserman, Government Assessor and Chief Inspector of Roads at Düsseldorf in his *Der Magnetismus und die allgemeine Weltsprache* (Creveld, 1822).

Professor W. F. **Barrett** read a paper on the subject before the British Association in 1876. Psychical researchers W. F. **Barrett,** Edmund **Gurney** and F. W. H. **Myers** concluded in 1881 in their first report on thought-transference: "The possibility must not be overlooked that further advances along the lines indicated may, and we believe, will, necessitate a modification of that general view of the relation of mind to matter to which modern science has long been gravitating." It must be admitted, however, that these experiments were severely criticized for not excluding fraud (see *Nature,* February 9, 1929).

In an extensive series of experiments in Liverpool, England, in 1883-84, conducted by Mr. Malcolm Guthrie and Mr. James Birchall with Miss Ralph and Miss Edwards, impressions of objects, sensations of taste and pain were successfully transmitted. Sir Oliver **Lodge** participated in some of these experiments and initiated some original ones at a later period.

The experiments of Mrs. Henry Sidgwick and Prof. **Sidgwick** in 1889-90 were classic. In thousands of trials, a high percentage of success was registered in transferring simple images. The increase of distance, however, apparently had a marked effect on the results. According to Frank **Podmore,** only Dr. Gilbert's and Professor Janet's experiments with "Leonie" at Havre in 1885 and 1886 could compare in competence, care and precision to the results with these. In the latter case, the effect aimed at was the induction of hypnotic sleep.

Clarissa Miles and Hermione Ramsden experimented through an intervening distance of 20-300 miles in transferring complex images and obtaining **cross-correspondence** of thought-transference. The results were carefully noted down and in many cases an impressive agreement was found between the impressions of the two parties (see *Journal* of the Society for Psychical Research, vol. 12, pp. 214, 221, 223-32, vol. 13, pp. 50, 52, 243; *Proceedings,* vol. 25, pp. 39-42, 44, 45, 54).

The psychical researcher Prof. C. **Lombroso** found 12 neuropaths in 20 subjects who registered success in thought-transference experiments. In some cases transmission was facilitated by alcoholic drinks or coffee stimulating the nerve centers. He assigned great importance to the hysterical state and expressed the opinion that the disequilibrium, even if transitory, of sensibility in hysterical persons was an essential condition for the production of the phenomena, in that they imply a greater accumulation of nervous energy in certain points of the cortex of the brain, and a diminution in others. He did not, however, exclude the possible influence of other causes and held, in alluding to transmission of thought in the dying, that the greater accumulation of energy in the cortex during the period just before death may be due to ptomaines which become lodged in it.

In reviewing this theory, Dr. Guiseppe Venzano declared (*Annals of Psychic Science,* January 1906) that the causes of the accumulation of greater energy in the centers of intelligence must be manifold and diverse, and that disequilibrium of sensibility does not constitute more than, at the most, one among these many causes. His conclusions were: (1) Mediumship favors the development of the phenomenon of transmission of thought, (2) In mediumistic seances, the thought formulated by the agent may be carried out even by material actions absolutely independent both of the medium and of the experimenters, (3) Under special circumstances, thought may be transmitted to the medium in a seance—even at a considerable distance—from a person outside the seance (telepathy), (4) The unconscious transmission of thought is possible.

In *Proceedings,* of the S.P.R. vol. 29 (part 72, 1918), Mrs. A. W. **Verrall** reviewed 504 previous experiments in thought-transference. *Proceedings,* vol. 34, (part 89), 1924, contained Mrs. Henry Sidgwick's report on further experiments of Prof. Gilbert **Murray,** which she considered "perhaps the most important ever brought to the notice of the Society both on account of their frequently brilliant success and on account of the eminence of the experimenter." The percipient of these experiments was Prof. Murray himself. Out of 236 experiments, he registered twenty-eight successes in eighty-one, thirty-six in 102, fourteen in thirty, six in eighteen and one in five instances.

On February 16, 1927, V. J. Woolley, research officer of the Society for Psychical Research, arranged interesting experiments through radio. He and the agents were in the Society's office, with no means of communication with anyone outside it. Sir Oliver Lodge sat in the broadcasting office at the microphone and directed the radio listeners to record any impressions they were able to form of the objects willed. They were shown three minutes each with an interval of two minutes. The only information given to the listeners was that No. 1 and No. 4 were playing cards of unusual design and No. 2 a picture. It was a Japanese print: a skull with a bird on top, No. 3 was a bunch of three sprays of white lilac, No. 5 Woolley himself wearing a bowler hat and a grotesque mask. The agents remained in the Society's premises through the night without access to a telephone.

The morning mail brought in 24,659 answers. According to Woolley's summary in *Proceedings,* vol. 38 (part 105), the card test gave no evidence of telepathic transmission but the answers disclosed the peculiarity of a strong tendency to choose an ace, especially the ace of spades and that there was a marked preference for odd-numbered cards as against even-numbered ones. Of the third object, five listeners gave a skull as the description of the picture, one adding the interesting detail that it represented a skull in a garden, and a sixth noted a human head. Of these six records, no less than three gave flowers for No. 3. Of the last object of the test, five answers gave the impression of Mr. Woolley, 146 of someone present, 236 of someone dressed up or masquerading, 73 of masks or faces, 202 of hats, and 499 of feeling of amusement.

Woolley, however, believed that these numbers in themselves were of little importance as there is no definite chance of expectation with which to compare them. The number of double successes was very small. "There does seem to be an indication of a supernormal faculty," stated Woolley, "on the part of a few of those who took part, though their successes are swamped by the very large mass of failures on the part of others."

The latter part of the conclusion may be objected to as there is nothing to prove that the sensitivity to telepathic impressions is a faculty latent in all of us.

The first attempt to link thought-transference with radio was staged in Chicago some years previous to the S.P.R. experiment, by Dr. Gardner **Murphy,** at that time Hodgson Fellow at Harvard, the next jointly by him and J. Malcolm **Bird** in Newark. Murphy did not publish a complete record. The Newark tests were reported in the *Scientific American* (June 1924).

Interesting results have been obtained by **cross-correspondence** in thought-transference. The principle is that two people at a stated time think of something, write it down and post it to find out whether their thoughts corresponded.

The conditions as summed up by psychical researcher Prof. Charles **Richet** for successful experiments in transferring drawings or cards were: (1) The agent must be absolutely motionless and have his back turned to the percipient, (2) The choice of the number, the card, or the drawing must be made by pure chance, (3) No result, whether success or failure, should be told to the percipient before the end of the sitting, (4) Not more than twenty trials should be made on any one day, (5) All results, whatever they may be, should be stated in full, (6) The percipient must be unable to see anything, directly or indirectly; it is best that his eyes should be bandaged and his back turned.

It has been found that the success of thought-transmission depended upon the moods and health of the experimenters. It requires concentration on the part of the transmitter and passivity of mind on the part of the recipient. It proved helpful if the agent tried to visualize the picture which he or she wished to convey. It was best to keep an object before the eye and think of it while trying to transmit its image.

Sir Oliver Lodge observed that the transference of drawings was much more distinct when tactual contact was maintained between the agent and the percipient. He discovered as early as 1883 that when two agents are acting, each contributes to the effect and the result is due to both combined. He put down between two agents a double opaque sheet of thick paper with a square drawn on one side and a St. Andrew's cross on the other. Each agent looked on one side without any notion what was on the other. One percipient declared that "the thing won't keep still . . . I seem to see things moving about . . . First I see a thing up there and then one down there." Finally the percipient drew a square and drew a cross inside from corner to corner saying afterwards "I don't know what made me put it inside."

Sir Oliver Lodge also attempted to find out what is really transmitted—the idea, or name of the object or the visual impressions. He found that the transmission of irregular drawings was very difficult and that in some cases the idea or name, and not the visual impression at all, was the thing transferred.

The engineer and psychical researcher René **Warcollier** made an interesting table of the comparative facility in transmission. He found the percentage of color transmission 70 percent, of attitudes 55, drawings 45, objects 38, ideas 37, mental images 10, words and figures 10 percent.

A Russian experimenter, Dr. N. Kotik found that the percentage of successes increased when the agent and percipient were linked by a wire (see *Die Emanation der psycho-physischen Energie* (Wiesbaden, 1908).

The objection of skeptics against the reality of thought-transference is two-fold: chance and natural parallelism of kindred minds. Stage demonstrations of thought-transference are known to be explained by a secret code. Sometimes, however, more subtle sensitivity may be present. The stage performer Mrs. **Zancig,** for instance, was found by Hewat **McKenzie** in experiments at the **British College for Psychic Research** to possess a marked gift of **clairvoyance** to the degree of reading passages in closed books.

It seems possible that the claimed ability to impress photographic materials with Thoughtforms may have revelance to thought-transference.

For recommended reading list, see Entry on Telepathy. (See also **Nengraphy; Telepathy; Thoughtforms; Thought-Reading; Thoughtography**)

Thoughtforms

The existence of Thoughtforms has been claimed by occultists and there is interesting evidence to consider it an important experimental problem in psychical research.

The suggestion of psychical researcher Sir William F. **Barrett** that the operator may so stimulate the mind of the subject that he is able to see the thought-shape in the former's mind, is not very far from what Theosophist A. P. **Sinnett** claimed in his book *The Occult World* (1882): "An adept is able to project into and materialize in the visible world the forms that his imagination has constructed out of inert cosmic matter in the visible world. He does not create anything new, but only utilises and manipulates materials which Nature has in store around him."

Prof. J. H. **Hyslop** in his book *Psychical Research and The Resurrection* (1908) quoted a curious communication from a private source. The communicator, while commenting on the peculiarities of his spiritual life, stated that he "sometimes saw, for instance, a man reading a book, but when he approached to talk with him he found it was only a thought."

Prof. Hyslop, however, did not agree with the thought-form theory and suggested that the instance was a case of veridical, or subjective **hallucination** in the spiritual life.

James T. Fields in a lecture on 'Fiction and its Eminent Authors,' said: "Dickens was at one time so taken possession of by the characters of whom he was writing that they followed him everywhere and would never let him be alone for a moment. He told me that when he was writing *The Old Curiosity Shop* the creatures of his imagination haunted him so that they would neither let him sleep or eat in peace." G. H. Lewes wrote in the *Fortnightly Review:* "Dickens once declared to me that every word said by his characters was distinctly heard by him."

Vincent **Turvey** wrote in his book *The Beginnings of Seership* (1911; 1969) of a discussion that took place between him and a man from Christian Evidence Society on psychic matters. The man insisted that Turvey's psychic gifts were from the devil and prayed that the devils should leave him. "On lying down in the afternoon in order to rest and meditate, I suddenly saw three or four 'devils' in the room—typical orthodox fiends. Men with goats' legs, cloven hoofs, little horns just over their ears, curly hair like a negro's 'wool,' tails and clawlike hands. In colour they were entirely brown, like ordinary brown paper. I candidly profess that I was 'a bit shaken' . . . I pulled myself together and rose into the 'higher state of consciousness.' In this 'state' I was able to see not only their fronts, but also their backs. To my utter astonishment they were all *hollow at the back,* like embossed leather, or the ordinary papier maché mask. Then my guardians caused me to make a sign, say a word, or think a sentence—what I do not know; but directly it was done or said, these forms disintegrated or dissolved and vanished."

Thoughtforms are often perceived in the hypnotic state. Dr. Lindsay Johnson, the celebrated British ophthalmic surgeon, described in the May 21, 1921 issue of *Light* an experiment of Professor Koenig of Berlin, in a Paris hospital at which he assisted. A peasant woman was hypnotized. It was suggested that she see an imaginary picture on a plain sheet of paper. She saw it perfectly. Twenty identical sheets of paper were produced and a picture was suggested for each, and a record was kept of the picture and tiny identification marks added on the back of each sheet. Dr. Johnson added five more sheets, shuffled them and handed them back one after the other to the subject. She described the suggested picture in every case, but saw nothing on Dr. Johnson's sheets.

A Russian investigator, Dr. Naum Kotik made similar experiments in Wiesbaden with a fourteen-year-old girl Sophie, and drew the following inference: "Thought is a radiant energy. This energy has physical and psychic properties. It may be called psychophysical. Originating in the brain, it passes to the extremities of the body. It is transmitted through air with some difficulty, more easily through a metallic conductor and can be fixed on paper." (See Charles Richet, *Thirty Years of Psychical Research* 1923, pp.190-191)

It is interesting to compare Prof. Koenig's and Dr. Kotik's experiments with the experience of the engineer and psychical researcher René **Warcollier.** One evening, partially waking, he saw a large quadrangular corded package in a yellow packing paper on a chair. He inquired what was the package. There was no package on the chair but it had been there some time before as described. If the image of a package can impress a chair it is no more improbable that thoughts may similarly impress a sheet of paper.

Dr. H. **Baraduc** informed the Academie de Médecine in May 1896, that he succeeded in photographing thought. He experimented with many people. The subjects placed their hands on a photographic plate in the dark room and were asked to think intently of the object they wished to impress upon the plate. Many curious markings were obtained, some of them representing the features of persons and the outline of objects.

Dr. Baraduc also contended that thought photography was possible from a distance. He quoted the case of Dr. Istrati who promised M. Hasdeu, a friend of his, to appear on a photographic plate at Bucarest, on August 4, 1893, while he slept in Campana. The distance is 300 kilometers. Dr. Istrati willed, before closing his eyes, that his image should impress the plate with which his friend went to bed. The result was achieved. The plate showed a luminous spot, in the midst of which the profile of a man could be traced.

In 1896, Commandant Darget, of Tours, France, obtained several good thought photographs. His procedure was to gaze attentively at a simple object for a few moments in order to engrave it firmly on the mind, then go into the dark room and (1) place a photographic plate with the glass side against the forehead for a quarter of an hour, mentally picturing the object decided upon and strongly desiring to make an impression on the plate, (2) Place the hand on a plate (or hold the plate in the hand) for a quarter of an hour, operating as before, (3) Put the plate into a developing bath, placing the fingers of one hand on the edge of the plate for ten minutes. There should always be the desire to imprint on the plate the picture of the object which is very strongly thought of. (See Paul Joire, *Psychical and Supernormal Phenomena,* 1916, pp. 374-379, 380-381)

An interesting case was quoted by James Coates from the November 1895 issue of the *Amateur Photographer.* W. Inglis Rogers, the experimenter, gazed for a minute at a postage stamp and then went into the dark room and gazed at a sensitive plate for twenty minutes. When the plate was developed two images of postage stamps were plainly visible.

Dr. T. **Fukurai**, Professor of Kohyassan University, carried out important experiments with Mrs. Ikuko Nagao. If the medium concentrated on Japanese alphabetical symbols they were found printed on photographic plates (see Dr. Fukurai's book *Clairvoyance and Thoughtography,* 1931; 1975).

Dr. Walter F. **Prince** reported in the *Journal* of the American Society for Psychical Research (April 1925) the case of the Japanese artist Mikaye. Microscopic symbols were projected by some capillary action from the tip of his brush filled with fluid pigment. The artist simply held the brush downwards whilst he made a mental image of the intended symbol to a large scale.

In his researches with Mlle. Tomczyk, Dr. Julien **Ochorowicz** was deeply puzzled to find that in several of his radiographs the medium's ring appeared on the finger of her "etheric" hand. This seemed to indicate to him: (1) That there is a kind of link between the organism and the object it wears, (2) That the occult notion that material objects have an astral body is not limited to living bodies. The ring, however, did not always appear on the radiographs. Dr. Ochorowicz tried to find out whether objects frequently worn by the sensitive were more easily produced on the plate than others. He chose a thimble which she rarely used. The medium suggested that he should himself retain the thimble on the finger of his left hand, holding her with his right hand. "Perhaps," she added, "the thimble will pass from your body on to my finger."

The experiment appeared absurd, but he was willing to try it. He took a plate from his box, marked it, and laid it on the medium's knees. She was seated on his right; with his right hand he held up her left hand about sixteen inches above the plate, the thimble being on the middle finger of his left hand, which he kept behind his left knee. A red lamp was burning at a distance of about three feet. After a minute had elapsed, the medium said that she felt a sort of tingling in the direction of her forearm, where their hands met. She exclaimed: "Oh, how strange. Something is being placed on the tip of my finger . . . I do not know if it is the thimble; I feel something keeps pressing the end of my finger."

When the plate was developed, it showed the hand of the medium, and on the middle finger was what he called, jokingly, "the soul of her thimble." Dr. Ochorowicz asked in some bewilderment—was the image a double of the thimble, or was it a photograph of the idea of the thimble?

A close examination of the photograph and comparison with the thimble showed that the two corresponded exactly, the one "was a true copy of the other, precise in details and in dimension."

This exactness supported the idea of a direct impression from some object rather than merely a thought-image. The finger supporting the thimble was the palest of all the fingers, probably, as Dr. Ochorowicz suggests, because the light by which the radiograph was taken, proceeded from it. He inclined to the conclusion that an etheric hand wearing an etheric thimble produced the image, and that mental desire gave the direction to the light which was necessary in order to make the details of the thimble visible on the plate.

When, however, he proceeded to test his conclusion, a strange thing happened. Unknown to the medium, he held in his left hand an Austrian five-crown piece. Presently she exclaimed: "I see behind you a white round object. . .it is the moon." "At the same instant," wrote Dr. Ochorowicz, "I saw a faint but distinct light pass near my left hand, which held the coin; it was not round, nor a flash, it was like a little meteor, like a thin ray, lighting up the space round my hand on the side away from the medium." When the plate was developed it showed an image of a full moon. "The moon floats on the background of a less luminous cloud, and is of a rather different form from that in the preceding experiments."

He considered it evident that this time a photograph of thought was obtained although the experiment rendered probable the existence of a quasi-physical intermediary, since the image represented rather the medium's conception of something which existed outside her mind.

The image of the moon was once obtained previous to the experiment. On the night of September 7, 1911, the medium was much impressed by the superb sight of the starry heavens, and particularly by the full moon, which she looked at for some time with admiration.

On the following day, instead of the little hand, which was desired, a full moon appeared on the plate against a background of white cloud. The cinematograph representations of the eclipse of the moon on April 17, 1912, showed the image of the moon slightly flattened in the direction of the axis of rotation. This characteristic appeared in the radiograph of September 7. The impression was double and it looked as if the cloud had not been duplicated. In that case, the moon alone must have moved. How can we conceive—asked Dr. Ochorowicz—of this apparent movement of a mental image? (See Dr. J. Ochorowicz's book *Mental Suggestion,* 1891; translation of *De la suggestion mentale,* 1887)

Many of the psychic extras obtained by spirit photographers may be the thoughts of the sitters. Hereward **Carrington**'s curious experiences with Mrs. A. E. Deane certainly pointed into this direction (see his account in *Journal* of the American Society for Psychical Research, May, 1925).

The experiments of Frederick Bligh **Bond,** with the same medium, appeared conclusive. He prepared a diagram of four by three squares and made, in one of the twelve squares, a cross of two diagonal lines and drew a small circle over the crossed lines. Having deposited this diagram with the principal of the **British College for Psychic Science** he went to meet Mrs. Deane, drew upon a blackboard a similar diagram and asked for a perfect circle over the center of the two intersecting lines.

The camera was loaded by Carrington and he did the development himself, Mrs. Deane simply placing her hand during the exposures on the camera top.

The first plate showed the diagram alone, the second a sort of localized fog over the square in question, the third a circular spot of intense blackness, exactly over the intersection.

In a second trial, Bond hung upon the wall of the studio a small picture frame and asked that an image, the exact character of which he did not specify, might be recorded on the space within the frame. The idea was to preclude any successful pre-exposure of a plate for the purpose of fraud. He obtained a cloud of small size which on the first two plates was not quite rightly centered, but was well within the center of the third plate.

Mr. Warrick, a manufacturing chemist, repeated the experiments but used no camera, only sheets of paper which he had specially sensitized. By impressing upon Mrs. Deane the exact nature of the image he wanted, and placing the paper beneath Mrs. Deane's hands or feet, he obtained circles, squares, triangles, or more complex images, i.e., a three-legged stool. Bond believed that his part in the success was dependent upon a power of mental visualization which, as a professional architect and designer of geometric forms he had special opportunities to cultivate. (See also Dr. Tomobichi **Fukurai; Nengraphy; Psychic Photography;** Ted **Serios; Spirit Photography; Telepathy; Thoughtography; Thought-Transference**)

Recommended reading:

Besant, Annie & Charles W. Leadbeater. *Thought-Forms: A Record of Clairvoyant Investigations,* Theosophical Publishing House, 1901 (8th ed. abridged, 1971)

Darget, Commandant. *Exposé des différentes methodes pour l'obtention des photographies fluido-magnétiques et spirites,* Paris, 1909

Eisenbud, Jule. *The World of Ted Serios: "Thoughtographic Studies of an Extraordinary Mind,* William Morrow, 1967

Fukurai, T. *Clairvoyance and Thoughtography,* London, 1931; Arno Press, 1975

Kotie, Naum. *Die Emanation der psycho-physichen Energie,* Wiesbaden, 1908

Schatzman, Morton. *The Story of Ruth,* Putnam's, 1980

Thoughtography

Term devised by a Japanese experimenter Dr. T. Fukurai for thought photography, the impressing of mental images on photographic plates. His researches were embodied in his book *Clairvoyance and Thoughtography* (London 1921, reprinted Arno Press, 1975).

Modern Japanese experimenters now use the term "Nengraphy." (See also T. **Fukurai; Nengraphy; Psychic Photography;** Ted **Serios; Spirit Photography; Telepathy; Thought-Transference**)

Thouless, Robert Henry (1894-1984)

Psychologist, parapsychologist, president of the **Society for Psychical Research,** London from 1942-45. Born July 15, 1894 in Norwich, England, he studied at Cambridge University, England (B.A. hons. 1914, M.A. 1919, Ph.D. 1922, D.Sc. 1953). In 1924 he married Priscilla Grafton Gorton.

After serving in World War I he was a lecturer in psychology at Manchester University from 1921-26, lecturer in charge of Department of Psychology, Glasgow University 1926, lecturer in psychology at Department of Education, Cambridge University 1938, reader in education psychology at Cambridge from 1945-1961, fellow of Corpus Christi College, Cambridge from 1921-24 and 1945 onwards; president of Psychology Section of British Association 1937, British Psychological Society 1949, member of council of Society for Psychical Research, editor of British Psychological Society Monograph Supplements from 1955-60.

Prof. Thouless conducted many experiments in card-calling, psychokinesis and other areas of parapsychology. His articles in SPR *Proceedings* include: 'The Present Position of Experimental Research into Telepathy and Related Phenomena' (1942), 'A Test of Survival' (1948), 'Report on an Experiment in Psychokinesis with Dice' (1951); in SPR *Journal*: 'Experimental Precognition and Its Implications' (1950), 'Problems of Design in Parapsychological Experiments' (1955), 'Psychical Research Past and Present' (eleventh Myers Memorial Lecture, SPR, 1952); in *British Journal of Psychology,* 'Experiments in Paranormal Guessing' (1942); in *Proceedings of the Royal Institution of Great Britain,* 'Thought transference and Related Phenomena' (1950).

His books included: *An Introduction to the Psychology of Religion* (1923), *General and Social Psychology* (1925; 1958), *Straight and Crooked Thinking* (1930; U.S. edition titled *How to Think Straight,* 1932), *General and Social Psychology* (1937 etc.), *Straight Thinking in War Time* (1942), *Authority and Freedom* (1954), *Map of Education Research* (1968), *From Anecdote to Experiment in Psychical Research* (1972).

Dr. Thouless died at the age of 90 on September 25, 1984. His initial interest in parapsychology about 1934 was stimulated by contact with the experimental work of Dr. J. B. **Rhine.** After that, parapsychology became a prominent theme for half a century of his life. He published nearly ninety articles and book reviews in the *Journal* and *Proceedings* of the Society for Psychical Research and the American Society for Psychical Research.

In distinction to parapsychologists who disparaged the study of spontaneous phenomena, Dr. Thouless maintained that it had value in structuring experimental methods: "The special function of the study of spontaneous cases is to serve as a guide to the problems to be investigated by experimental methods. . .[The] choice is not between statistics and experiment on the one hand and observation of spontaneous cases on the other. Let us have much more of both. . . . New problems for experimental investigation may be suggested by new observations of spontaneously occurring phenomena." ('The Present Position of Experimental Research into Telepathy and Related Phenomena,' *Proceedings* of the Society for Psychical Research, vol. 47, 1943)

On the question of **survival,** he proposed a cautious optimism, and about 1948 devised a cipher test of survival which he believed was his most significant contribution to parapsychology. The test used a standard method of encipherment with a secret key passage. It consisted of two coded sequences: INXPH CJKGM JIRPR FBCVY WYWES NOECN SCVHE GYRJQ TEBJM TGXAT TWPNH CNYBC FNXPF LFXRV QWQL, and BTYRR OOFLH KCDXK FWPCZ KTADR GFHKA HTYXO ALZUP PYPVF AYMMF SDLR UVUB. The key to the first sequence is a passage of poetry or prose indicated by reference to its title, and the key to the second sequence consists of two words. The key passage necessary to cipher the test might be transmitted posthumously as a proof of survival of consciousness. This method obviated the objection that a claimed posthumous communication might be read by clairvoyance if left in a sealed envelope. The Thouless test did not involve any sealed message and only the correct key would solve the enciphered message. In the event of a claimed posthumous message, percipients were asked to contact the Society for Psychical Research, 1 Adam and Eve Mews, London, W8 6UG, England, so that it might be keyed into the Society's computer program to see if it yielded a correct message.

3HO Foundation

Educational branch of the Sikh religion in the U.S., founded by Shri Singh Bhai Sahib Harbhajan Singh Khalsa Yogiji, popularly known as Yogi Bhajan. "3HO" means "Healthy, Happy, Holy Organization," founded in 1968. The Foundation provides nursery school education, and has an accredited elementary school in Albuquerque, New Mexico, based on Sikh way of life initiated by Guru Nanak, and also provides teacher training courses, lectures, and demonstrations in all types of **Yoga,** with special emphasis on **Kundalini** Yoga.

3HO has also a certified government-funded drug rehabilitation center in Tucson, Arizona, and operates a Kundalini Research Institute to investigate all aspects of the drug rehabilitative and other beneficial aspects of Kundalini Yoga. The organization also offers legal services, operates a free food kitchen, and has created a women's division "for the uplift of the dignity and respect of womanhood." Publications include the Journal *Beads of Truth.* Address: 3HO Foundation, P.O. Box 351149, Los Angeles, California 90035. (See also **Kundalini**)

Thule Society

German occult society founded in Munich in 1918 by Adam Glauer (1875-1945) who styled himself Rudolf, Freiherr von Sebottendorf. This was an anti-Semitic society which had links with Adolf Hitler through the German Workers' Party (later National Socialist German Workers Party).

The activities of the Thule Group were as much political as occult, and their sphere of influence included judges, police chiefs, professors and industrialists.

Dietrich Eckart, a central figure in the Thule Group, also played a prominent part in the committee of the German Workers' Party and became one of the seven founder members of the Nazi Party. When he died in December 1923, he is reported to have said: "Follow Hitler! He will dance, but it is I who have called the tune! I have initiated him into the 'Secret Doctrine,' opened his centers in vision and given him the means to communicate with the Powers. Do not mourn for me: I shall have influenced history more than any other German." (See also **Spear of Destiny**)

Recommended reading:

Howe, Ellic. *Urania's Children; the Strange World of the Astrologers,* London, 1967 (U.S. edition under title *Astrology; A Recent History including the untold story of its role in World War 2,* Walker, 1968)

King, Francis. *Satan and Swastika; the Occult and the Nazi Party,* London (Mayflower paperback), 1976

Ravenscroft, Trevor. *The Spear of Destiny,* London, 1973; G. P. Putnams, 1973; Bantam paperback, 1974

Thurston, Herbert Henry Charles (S. J.) (1856-1939)

Priest, historian and writer on parapsychological subjects. Born November 15, 1856 in London, he was educated at Séminaire St. Malo, France; Mount St. Mary's, Derbyshire, England; Stonyhurst, Lancashire, England; Manresa House, Roehampton; University of London, England. He became a novice in the Society of Jesus in 1874, taught at Beaumont College, Windsor, England from 1880-87, at Wimbledon, London from 1892-94, produced over 700 articles, essays, pamphlets and translations.

He joined the Society for Psychical Research, London in 1919. He was particularly interested in poltergeist phenomena and Spiritualism, although as a priest he could not attend seances in person. He contributed an article 'The Phenomena of Stigmatization' to *Proceedings* of the Society for Psychical Research (vol. 32, part 83, 1922).

His books included: *The Memory of Our Dead* (1915), *The Church and Spiritualism* (1933), *Superstition* (1933), *Beauraing and Other Apparitions* (1934), *Physical Phenomena of Mysticism* (published posthumously 1952), *Ghosts and Poltergeists* (1953), *Surprising Mystics* (1955).

He died November 3, 1939. For biography, see *Father Thurston* by J. Crehan (1952).

Thury, Marc (1822-1905)

Swiss psychical researcher, professor of physics and natural history at the University of Geneva, a pioneer of investigations into **telekinesis** phenomena.

In a small pamphlet, *Les Tables tournantes* (Geneva, 1855) he reviewed Count **de Gasparin**'s experiments and detailed his own observations in a circle of private friends under strict test conditions. He was the first exponent of the theory of **ectoplasm.** He named the substance which he believed to be a link between the soul and body "psychode," and the force which manipulated it "**ectenic force.**" This force, he believed, was subject to the will power of the medium.

De Gasparin repudiated **Spiritism** as absurd and contrary to moral truth; Thury contended that while "the known facts are not as yet sufficient for the demonstration of the spirit theory," yet "the absurdity of the belief in the intervention of spirits has not been scientifically demonstrated." He asserted that there may exist in this world wills other than those of man and the animals, wills capable of acting on matter.

TIBET

Historical Background

Tibet is a country with ancient religious and mystical traditions, around which many occult legends have grown. These were abruptly dispelled in the Chinese Communist invasion in October 1950, when Tibet lost its independent status and was obliged to sign a Sino-Tibetan agreement on May 23, 1951 for "the peaceful liberation of Tibet."

Tibetans had formerly been a separate race with distinctive language, culture and religion, but had an uneasy relationship with China since 1720, when the Manchus entered Tibet to help drive out Mongol invaders and used the situation to become overlords. Over the subsequent period, the acknowledgment of Chinese suzerainty was the price of Tibetan autonomy, and for practical purposes Tibet was an independent state.

The 1950 invasion was justified by the Chinese as necessary in order to destroy inequitable feudalism in Tibet and to bring progress, education and social justice. In practice, this involved suppression of the Buddhist religion, destruction of monasteries and their libraries and humiliation of its priests.

In all fairness, it must be said that these and other reported violations of human rights were largely paralleled by similar excesses in China itself in the early period of the communist revolution and the upheavals of the Cultural Revolution. Since then, however, the age old Buddhist religion of Tibet has been largely suppressed and occult traditions replaced by practical socialism and exploitation of Tibetan resources and territory.

These recent convulsions of history have effectively destroyed the extravagant legends of superhuman Tibetan adepts in inaccessible caves and monasteries, guarding the "secrets of the universe" and exerting a powerful influence on occult movements in the rest of the world. The "Lost Horizon" of occultism has proved as vulnerable to modern military conquest as anywhere else. However, it is impossible to doubt that certain feats of occult magic were at one time well known in Tibet, and that the esoteric meditation systems of Tibetan priests reached a high level of spiritual insight.

Religion and Superstition

The national religion of Buddhism, originating from India, absorbed earlier superstitions and demonology of the Tibetan people. Prior to Buddhism, beliefs were largely animistic, and the rites, ceremonies, charms and incantations, of which Buddha had disapproved, became an integral part of Tibetan Buddhism. Popular religion was strongly influenced by Hindu **Tantra** teachings, although the religion of monasteries was an esoteric Buddhism on a higher plane than popular superstition.

Belief in ghosts, demons and magic coexisted with deep spiritual awareness. The present spiritual leader of Tibet, the fourteenth Dalai Lama, who escaped to India in 1959, is dedicated to keeping alive the spiritual traditions and aspirations to independence of the Tibetan people. Like his predecessors, he is claimed as a living incarnation of the Divine Spirit, and was discovered as such by traditional search and testing.

When a Dalai Lama departs from life, priests traditionally conduct a search for his successor through signs and visions. Selected children are tested by their ability to recognize objects belonging to the former Dalai Lama. After identification, the child is brought to the holy city of Lhasa and initiated as a monk in the monastery of the Potala, which becomes a power center of the Divine Spirit, which issues forth from the Dalai Lama over the whole of Tibet.

The title "Dalai Lama" is from a Mongolian term meaning "Wide Ocean," and is not normally used by Tibetans amongst themselves, who prefer such terms as "Precious Protector" or "Precious Ruler," of *Kundun* (Presence), implying spiritual association. The first Dalai Lama was Tsong Ka-pa, born in Amdo in 1358. His disciples became the Yellow Hat sect, as distinct from the earlier priesthood of the Red Hats.

Although the essential teachings of Buddhism are the same, various sects established different pathways to enlightenment. The Yellow Cap sect *(Ge-lug-pas)* follow a Middle Way Buddhism; the Red Caps *(Ning-ma-pas)* follow the *Adi-Yoga* or path of the Great Perfection, founded by the guru Padma Sambhava in 749 A.D.; the Kargyütpas, or Followers of Successive Order (deriving from the great Tibetan saint Milarepa, died 1135, successor of the revered gurus Marpa, Tilopa, and Naropa) follow the way of *Mahamudra* or Great Symbol. As with the various sects of Hindu religious philosophy, with their many subtle emphases, the general overall philosophy is the same.

In addition to the regular monastic disciplines of complex prayer and meditation rites and regular religious festivals, lamas traveling through Tibet were expected to act as oracles, fortune-tellers and healers for the ordinary people. Prayer wheels with the mystic mantra "Om ma-ni pad-me Hum" (Om, The Jewel in the Lotus) and rosaries were in use all over the country, and groups of prayer-flags fluttered around the villages. In the monasteries, *tankas* (complex symbolic mandala banners) became a focus for mystical meditation.

It is not difficult to understand why Lamaism should be permeated with demonology in view of the vast and terrifying grandeur of the Tibetan environment, in which the forces of nature appear to have the power of supernatural beings. Belief in magic was once universal.

Psychic Sports

For centuries, Tibet had been a forbidden territory to Westerners, and only a handful of Europeans succeeded in penetrating the country, usually in disguise. From 1912 onwards, an intrepid Frenchwoman, Madam Alexandra David-Neel, began a series of travels through Tibet over fourteen years. She acquired the rank of Lama.

An Oriental scholar, Mdme. David-Neel learned Sanskrit and Tibetan, and studied the various forms of Buddhism and Lamaism. She became the first European woman to penetrate to the holy city of Lhasa. Although skeptical regarding the supernatural, she gained firsthand knowledge of Tibetan ghosts and demons, and the paranormal feats of mystics. In her book *With Mystics and Magicians in Tibet* (1931 etc.), she revealed how Tibetan mystics acquired the ability to live naked in zero temperatures by generating a protective body heat (*tumo*), how they learned to float in air and walk on water, how they brought corpses back to life or created thoughtforms that had independent existence.

She described such feats as "psychic sports," acquired by special mind and body training. Amongst such feats was the *lung-gom* training of "inner breathing" and meditation which enabled an individual to travel at high speed for days and nights without stopping, sometimes with the feet hardly touching the ground. Mdme. David-Neel herself witnessed a *lung-gom-pa* or swift traveler. She described the special training necessary for feats of levitation and for thought-reading and telepathy ("sending thoughts on the wind").

She successfully experimented in the creation of a *tulpa* or phantom **thoughtform.** After a period in isolation following the special concentration techniques, she succeeded in creating a phantom monk, who became a guest in her party, seen and accepted by the others. But in the course of time, this phantom form changed from a fat jolly monk, becoming lean, mocking and somewhat malignant, and it was necessary for Mdme. David-Neel to concentrate on special techniques to destroy a phantom that was beginning to take on independent life.

She explained that Tibetans believed that such psychic phenomena were the result of utilizing natural forces by the powers of the mind. Her experiences seem to have been the result of a long and intimate association with Tibet and its peoples in a period when magic and mystery were more common. Subsequent travelers have not reported such remarkable phenomena. Her books are a unique record of a Tibet which has long passed away, and a people whose psychic abilities have been overwhelmed by the harsh materialistic preoccupations of life under the rule of a foreign power.

However, it is too early to predict whether the present upheavals in Tibet will involve a permanent loss of spiritual and psychic identity or whether the painful present difficulties will result in a new maturity through the synthesis of old and new experiences. (See also **Tumo**)

Recommended reading:

Bernard, Theos. *Land of a Thousand Buddhas,* Rider & Co., London, 1952

Bromage, Bernard. *Tibetan Yoga,* Aquarian Press, London, 1952

Chang, Garma C. C. (transl.). *The Hundred Thousand Songs of Milarepa,* 2 vols., University Books, 1962

Chang, Garma C. C. *Teachings of Tibetan Yoga,* University Books, 1963

David-Neel, Alexandra. *My Journey to Lhasa,* William Heinemann, London, 1927

David-Neel, Alexandra. *With Mystics and Magicians in Tibet,* John Lane, London, 1931; U.S. title *Magic & Mystery in Tibet,* Claude H. Kendall, New York, 1932; University Books, 1956

David-Neel, Alexandra & Lama Yongden. *The Secret Oral Teachings in Tibetan Buddhist Sects,* Maha Bodhi Society of India, Calcutta, n.d.

Evans-Wentz, W. Y. *Tibet's Great Yogi Milarepa,* Oxford University Press, London, 1928

Harrer, Heinrich. *Seven Years in Tibet,* Rupert Hart-Davis, London/Dutton, 1953

Harrer, Heinrich. *Return to Tibet,* Weinfeld & Nicholson, London, 1984

Tibet Society. *Tibet and Freedom,* The Tibet Society of the United Kingdom, 1961 [pamphlet]

Waddell, L. Austine. *Tibetan Buddhism; With Its Mystic Cults, Symbolism and Mythology, and in Its Relation to Indian Buddhism,* W. H. Allen, London, 1895; Dover paperback, 1972

"Tibetan, The"

The mysterious Master who inspired Alice **Bailey** (1880-1949). Formerly a member of the **Theosophical Society,** she withdrew in 1923 and established the Arcane School in New York.

Tii

A Polynesian vampire (see **Vampire**).

Tijdschrift voor Parapsychologie

Major Dutch journal of parapsychology, founded and edited by Prof. Dr. W. H. C. **Tenhaeff,** later edited by Dick J. Bierman. Now published quarterly. Address: Postbus 786, NL-35 At Utrecht, The Netherlands.

Tillyard, Dr. R(obin) J(ohn) (1881-1937)

British psychical researcher and biologist, vice president of the **National Laboratory of Psychical Research** in 1926.

He was born in Norwich, England, January 31, 1881, educated at Dover College, and Queen's College, Cambridge University, London (M.A., Sc.D.), D.Sc. (Sydney, Australia), Fellow of the Royal Society.

He was Mathematical and Science Master, Sydney Grammar School, Australia, 1904-13, Fellow in Zoology, Sydney University, 1914-17, lecturer in Zoology, 1917, chief of the Biological Department, Cawthorne Institute, New Zealand, 1920, Chief Entomologist to the Commonwealth of Australia.

He became convinced of survival by his study of the medium "Margery" (Mrs. M. S. **Crandon**) and published his convictions in the August 28, 1928, issue of *Nature.* In a "solus" sitting with "Margery" in Boston, he obtained apparent fingerprints of "Walter," the **control.** In a letter to Sir Oliver Lodge he stated:

"This seance is, for me, the culminating point of all my psychical research; I can now say, if I so desire, *nunc dimittis,* and go on with my own legitimate entomological work." However, there now seems little doubt that this particular phenomenon was fraudulent.

During his association with psychical researcher Harry **Price** at the National Laboratory of Psychical Research, Dr. Tillyard investigated the phenomena of Eleonore **Zügun** and **Stella C.**

In his book *Confessions of a Ghost Hunter* (1936; 1974), Harry Price described a visit to Jeanne Laplace, a French clairvoyant, who gave a remarkable series of correct statements about Dr. Tillyard through simply holding a letter from him (without seeing the letter itself). The impressions included the prediction, later fulfilled, that he would die in a railway accident.

Timaeus of Locri (c. 400 B.C.)

One of the earliest known writers on the doctrines of magic. He was a Pythagorean philosopher born in Locri, Italy and flourished c. 420-380 B.C. He is credited with the work *On the Soul of the Universe,* although some historians believe this may be an abridgement of Plato's dialogue of *Timæus.*

The Timæan theory of God, the Universe, and the World-soul was thus set forth by A. F. Büsching: "God shaped the eternal unformed matter by imparting to it His being. The inseparable united itself with the separable; the unvarying with the variable; and, moreover, in the harmonic conditions of the Pythagorean system. To comprehend all things better, infinite space was imagined as divided into three portions, which are,—the centre, the circumference, and the intermediate space.

"The centre is most distant from the highest God, who inhabits the circumference; the space between the two contains the celestial spheres. When God descended to impart His being, the emanations from Him penetrated the whole of heaven, and filled the same with imperishable bodies. Its power decreased with the distance from the source, and lost itself gradually in our world in minute portions, over which matter was still dominant.

"From this proceeds the continuous change of being and decay below the moon, where the power of matter predominates; from this, also, arise the circular movements of the heaven and the earth, the various rapidities of the stars, and the peculiar motion of the planets. By the union of God with matter, a third being was created. namely, the world-soul, which vitalizes and regulates all things, and occupies the space between the centre and the circumference."

Plato's *Timæus* also tells the legendary story of the lost drowned continent of **Atlantis.**

Time (in Paranormal Perception)

Time is an element of uncertainty in paranormal functions. Yet we know from hypnotic experiments that the subconscious mind has a remarkable faculty in estimating time. Dr. J. Milne Bramwell made classical demonstrations, such as suggesting to Miss A. in hypnotic sleep that at the expiration of 11,470 minutes, whatever might happen, she should make a cross on a piece of paper and note the time. Out of 55 similar experiments, 45 were completely successful (see J. Milne Bramwell, *Hypnotism,* 1903).

One would expect that if a trance communicator were a hypnotic or secondary **personality,** we should find evidence of the same faculty. Its surprising absence speaks strongly for the presence of an extraneous entity. Why discarnate spirits should apparently lose their awareness of time in the earthly sense is not clear. It appears that both their time and space concepts are different from ours. "Pelham," a spirit control of Mrs. Piper, was often asked to go and see what a certain friend was doing at the moment. The account which he gave on his return often contained descriptions which applied to happenings a day after or what he thought a day before.

The psychical researcher S. G. **Soal** received through Mrs. Blanche Cooper communication from Gordon Davis, a friend who, a few months after, turned up alive. He gave, through the medium, a description of his house. The description was incorrect at the time he turned up but perfectly matched his home a year after.

In clairvoyant perceptions, a similar uncertainty is often noticed. The percipients often do not know whether the visions of events which unfold themselves refer to the past or future. There is a good instance in Quaker history. George Fox cried "Woe to the bloody city of Lichfield" as he passed through it, and discovered later this was not a prophecy but a psychometric sensation of the martyrdoms in a past age.

The British investigator J. W. Dunne observed a mixture of past and future elements in dreams, as described his experiments in his book *An Experiment with Time* (1927).

Time Pattern Research Institute

A New York astrological corporation founded May 1967, bringing modern technology to horoscopes. The institute used an IBM 360-30 computer in conjunction with well-known astrologer Katina Theodossiou.

The computer's memory banks held twenty-five million items of basic information. Individual horoscopes ran to ten thousand words, including character analysis and future trends, and the company merchandized hundreds of thousands of horoscopes, using U.S. department stores as outlets. (See also **Astroflash**)

Tingley, Katherine (Augusta Westcott) (1847-1929)

Prominent American Theosophist who founded a Theosophical community at Point Loma, California.

Born July 6, 1847 at Newburyport, Massachusetts, she was educated at public school in Newburyport and under a private instructress. She married three times, her third marriage in 1889 was to Philo B. Tingley.

She took an early interest in social work before becoming active in the fields of **Spiritualism** and **Theosophy.** In 1887, she formed the Society of Mercy (concerned with emergency relief work on New York's East Side). About this time she became known as a Spiritualist medium.

Through her social work she met the Theosophist W. Q. **Judge,** who made a profound impression on her. With the sponsorship of Judge, she became an important figure in the American branch of the **Theosophical Society.**

After the death of Madame **Blavatsky** in 1895, Judge headed the majority of American Theosophists in secession from the Annie **Besant**-Col. **Olcott** group, but himself died in March 1896. Judge's independent **Theosophical Society in America** stated that Judge had nominated a successor, referred to in symbolic language as "The Purple Mother." A month later, E. T. Hargrove, then president of the Theosophical Society in America, confirmed that the Purple Mother was Katherine Tingley.

Soon afterwards, Tingley began a World Crusade for Theosophy, during which she claimed to have encountered a Theosophical Master in Darjeeling. Upon returning to the U.S., she founded the School for the Revival of the Lost Mysteries of Antiquity, at Point Loma, California.

She also founded the Universal Brotherhood organization, and in February 1896 took charge of the Theosophical Society, with which she merged the Universal Brotherhood. Permanent headquarters were established at Point Loma in 1900.

During the Spanish-American War, Katherine Tingley organized the War Relief Corps and established an emergency hospital on Long Island for soldiers wounded in Cuba. In 1899, the International Brotherhood League, a department of the Theosophical Society, undertook relief work in Cuba. Later Tingley visited Cuba and brought a group of children to Point Loma for education, after first being obliged to prove the financial and moral competence of the Society to take charge of the children. She was funded by the U.S. Government to establish hospitals in Cuba, and in 1925 was awarded the Medal of Honor of the German Red Cross. In 1924, she established a summer school for children at Visingsoe, Sweden, and in the following year seven new Theosophical Centers in Europe.

She was editor of *Theosophical Path,* published at Point Loma, as well as other Theosophical magazines in Holland, Germany and Sweden. She founded *The New Way,* a monthly magazine for free distribution to prisoners in penitentiaries and jails. Her publications included: *Theosophy and Some of the Vital Problems of the Day* (1915), *Theosophy, The Path of the Mystic* (1922), *The Wine of Life* (1925), *The Gods Await* (1929), *The Voice of the Soul* (1928).

She died July 11, 1929, in Sweden, following an automobile accident in Germany, and was succeeded at the Point Loma community by Dr. Gottfried de Purucker.

Tiromancy

Divination by means of cheese. It was practiced in various ways but the details do not appear to be recorded.

Tischner, Rudolf (1879-1961)

Ophthalmologist of Munich, who entered the ranks of leading German psychical researchers in 1919 with the publication of his *Über Telepathie und Hellsehen,* one of the groundworks on the subject (translated into English as Telepathy & Clairvoyance, 1925). It was followed in 1920 by a small book on the clairvoyant Ludwig Aub and in 1921 by *Einführung in den Okkultismus and Spiritismus,* and *Monismus und Okkultismus.*

Dr. Tischner was also the author of many small monographs and of a large historic work: *Geschichte der okkultistischen Forschung. Von der Antike bis zur Gegenwart,* 1924, which was published as the second volume to Dr. August F. Ludwig's *Geschichte der Okkultistischen Forschung bis zur Gegenwart . . . Mitte des 19 Jahrhunderts.* It is a comprehensive and careful survey of the whole history of psychic research. He published a study in 1925 under the title *Fernfühlen und Mesmerismus,* dealing with the experiments of Col. Rochas on the exteriorization of sensibility.

By his research, lectures and propaganda work Dr. Tischner did a great deal for the advancement of psychic science in Germany.

His later books included: *Der Okkultimus als Natur und Geisteswissenschaft* (Occultism as a Natural and Philosophical Science, 1926), *Ergebnisse Okkulter Forschung* (Results of Occult Research, 1950), *Geschichte der Parapsychologie* (History of Parapsychology, 1960). Dr. Tischner was amongst the first to use the term "extrasensory perception" before it was adopted by **J. B. Rhine.**

He died April 24, 1961 at Vierhöfen, Germany.

Tissot, James Joseph Jacques (1836-1902)

Well-known French painter of the life of Christ, chiefly remembered in Spiritualism for his mezzotint "Apparition Medianimique," which portrayed his impressions of a materialization seance with the medium William **Eglinton** which he attended in 1885. He saw the apparition of his departed fiancée accompanied by "Ernest," the guide of the medium. The painting was acquired by the **London Spiritualist Alliance.**

TM

Initialism for **Transcendental Meditation,** the popular system taught by **Maharishi Mahesh Yogi.**

Tocquet, Robert (1898-)

Professor of chemistry who published books on parapsychology. Born June 5, 1898 at Saint-Oulph (Aube), France. In 1927 he married Henriette Poulain.

He was chemistry professor at Ecole des Travaux Publics, Paris, professor at Ecole d'Anthropologie de Paris, member of board of directors of Bureau du Syndicate Professionel de la Press Scientifique, Institut Métapsychique International, member of Société Astronomique de France.

In addition to his many books on chemistry and science, he published *Encyclopédie pour la Jeunesse,* a five volume encyclopedia for young people.

His books relating to parapsychology include: *Tout l'Occultisme dévoilé* (Secrets of the Occult Revealed, 1952), *La Médecine se tait* (When Medicine is Silent, 1954), *Les Calculateurs prodiges et leurs secrets* (The Magic of Numbers, 1957), *Phénomènes de mediumnité* (Phenomena of Mediumship), *Les Pouvoirs secrets de l'Homme* (The Secret Powers of Man, 1963). He also contributed articles to *Revue Métapsychique, Pschica,* and *Psychic* magazine.

Today's Astrologer

Monthly Bulletin of the American Federation of Astrologers Inc., available to members of the Federation. The Bulletin contains news of classes, lectures and events connected with Astrology, and articles on various aspects of astrology of a professional standard. Address: American Federation of Astrologers Inc., P. O. Box 22040, Tempe, Arizona 85282.

Token Object

An object associated with the subject, held by the psychic giving a reading. It might be a slip of paper with a name on it, unseen to the psychic, who gives information relative to that named person while holding the paper, as in billet-reading or **pellet reading.** It might alternatively be an object which the psychic holds while giving impressions through **psychometry,** i.e., apparently being sensitive to impressions from that object.

Tomczyk, Stanislawa (Mrs. Everard Feilding) (c. 1920)

Remarkable non-professional Polish medium, the subject of the experiments of Dr. Julien **Ochorowicz** in 1908-09, at Wisla, Poland. Mlle. Tomczyk was regularly hypnotized by Dr. Ochorowicz for therapeutic purposes, when she became controlled by an entity "Little Stasia." She could produce **movement** of objects without contact **(telekinesis),** stop the movement of a clock in a glass case and influence a roulette wheel to the extent that the numbers chosen by the medium turned up more often than justified by chance.

Dr. Ochorowicz concluded that the physical movements were performed by rigid "rays" projecting from the fingers of the medium.

The medium's hands were thoroughly examined and washed before each seance. A small object, such as a ball, cork, matchbox or scissors, was placed before her on a table. The medium then placed her fingers on either side of the object about six to eight inches from it. The object would then usually move and eventually rise in the air, floating between the medium's fingers on each side.

Sometimes investigators claimed to feel a subtle "thread," but it was a psychic line of force, not a material thread. Ochorowicz stated: "I have felt this thread on my hand, on my face, on my hair. When the medium separates her hands the thread gets thinner and disappears; it gives the same sensation as a spider's web. If it is cut with scissors its continuity is immediately restored . . . it is then seen to be much thinner than an ordinary thread." These observations have a strong resemblance to the claimed "odic force" of Baron von **Reichenbach,** which sensitive individuals claimed to see in a darkened room issuing from the fingertips (see **Od**). However, Mlle. Tomczyk's phenomena took place in good light.

"Little Stasia" was a mischievous entity who played many tricks on the medium. She said herself that she was not the spirit of any dead person. The medium considered her, at first, as her **double.** This was Dr. Ochorowicz's opinion, too, until he was shaken in this view by having obtained Little Stasia's photograph, as announced by her, in an empty room, with all light excluded, while the medium in a normal condition was with him in an adjoining room.

Prof. Theodore **Flournoy** witnessed a seance in Paris in 1909. It left him "in no doubt as to the reality of simple telekinesis." However, at a later series of seances at Geneva to which, besides Flournoy, Professors Clarapède, Cellerier, Batelli and Flournoy's son were invited, the expectations of the sitters were not fulfilled.

In 1910, Stanislawa Tomczyk was investigated at the Physical Laboratory in Warsaw by a group of scientists. She produced remarkable physical phenomena under strict test conditions. Baron **Schrenck-Notzing** described the experiments in his *Physikalische Phenomene des Mediumismus,* München, 1920. Prof. Charles **Richet** quoted his own observations in his book *Traité de Métapsychique,* 1922 (translated as *Thirty Years of Psychical Research* 1923).

In 1919, Mlle. Tomczyk married the distinguished British psychical researcher the Hon. F. H. Everard Feilding (1867-1936), and seems to have discontinued seances.

Tomga

Eskimo familiar spirits. (See **Eskimos**)

Tongues, Speaking and Writing in

Speaking and writing in foreign tongues, or in unintelligible outpourings mistaken for such, is a very old form of psychic phenomenon. It was a frequent accompaniment of epidemic ecstasy which was so common in medieval Europe. Thus the Nuns of **Loudon** were declared to have understood and replied to questions put to them in Latin, Greek, Spanish, Turkish, and other even less-known languages. The **Tremblers of the Cevennes** spoke in excellent French, whereas French was to them a foreign language.

Practically every epidemic of the kind was characterized by speaking in tongues, which seemed to be infectious, and spread rapidly through whole communities. In these early cases, the phenomenon was ascribed to the power of supernatural agencies, whether demons or angels, who temporarily controlled the organism of the "possessed" (see **Obsession and Possession**). But analogous instances are to be found in plenty in the annals of modern Spiritualism, where they are regarded as manifestations of the spirits of the deceased through the material organism of the medium.

Comparatively early in the Spiritualist movement there were evidences of speaking and writing in Latin, Greek, French, Swiss, Spanish, and Red Indian languages. Judge J. W. **Edmonds** (1799-1874), the pioneer American Spiritualist, testified to these faculties in his daughter and niece, who spoke Greek, Spanish, Polish, and Italian at various times, as well as Red Indian and other languages.

Some of these cases were well attested. Two professional mediums (J. V. **Mansfield** and A. D. **Ruggles**) are known to have produced **automatic writing** in many languages, including Chinese and Gaelic, but whether or not they had any previous acquaintance with these languages remains a matter of doubt. In later times, speaking in tongues was practiced, notably by the medium Hélène **Smith,** who invented the "Martian language."

On the whole, many so-called foreign tongues were generally no more than a meaningless jumble of articulate sounds, of which the spirits themselves sometimes purported to offer a translation. Where there was good evidence to show that the writings were actually executed in a foreign language, as in the case of the professional mediums mentioned above, there was generally some reason to suppose a former acquaintance with the language, which the exaltation of memory incidental to the trance state might revive. When unknown tongues were written they were seldom found to correspond with any real language.

A notable exception in modern times was the spontaneous dictation of poems in German, French, and Italian by Pandit **Gopi Krishna** (1903-1984), without knowledge of these languages, after achieving a condition of higher consciousness through arousal of **Kundalini.** (see *From The Unseen* (F.I.N.D. Trust, Toronto, 1985).

The whole question of speaking in tongues has been revived recently by the growing **Pentecostalism** of West Indian and American religious groups now related to the Charismatic Revival. (See also Pandit **Gopi Krishna; Kundalini; Xenoglossis**)

Recommended reading:

Bozzano, Ernest. *Polyglot Mediumship (Xenoglossy)*, Rider & Co., London, 1932

Flournoy, Theodore. *From India to the Planet Mars*, Harper & Bros., 1900

Kelsey, Morton T. *Tongue Speaking; An Experiment in Spiritual Experience*, Doubleday, 1968; Waymark Books paperback, 1968; Hodder & Stoughton (paperback), London, 1973

Kildahl, John P. *The Psychology of Speaking in Tongues*, Harper & Row, 1972

Samarin, William J. *The Tongues of Men and Angels*, Macmillan, 1972

Whymant, Neville, *Psychic Adventures in New York*, Morley & Mitchell, London, 1931

Toolemak

Eskimo familiar spirits. (See **Eskimos**)

Totemism

A form of religious and social organization amongst primitive peoples, comprising the association of groups of persons with particular animals or objects.

The term derives from the Ojibway Indians, but their own form of totemism was not typical of the use of the term by anthropologists. A totemic tribe consists of a number of totem groups, each closely related to a totem, which may be an animal or an inanimate object. That totem is specific for that particular group, thus while every member of the tribe has a characteristic totem, it will differ from those of other totem groups within the same tribes in the same area. Plants are used as totems in some parts of the world, and other totems are sometimes only a token part of an animal, i.e., a buffalo tongue instead of a buffalo.

One characteristic of totemism is that members of the group respect the animal or object used as totem, and place a **taboo** on it being destroyed by members of the group, although not interfering with other members of the tribe who are not constrained by such taboos.

A totem implies some kinship between the totem and the members of the group, sometimes a belief in descent from an animal totem. Masks and images may reinforce this association. Amongst Australian aborigines, totemism is related to a belief in the constant reincarnation of the spirits of primary animal forms into human beings.

Although the concept of a totem has sometimes been applied to individuals, the totem is essentially characteristic of groups, and related to social and religious ideas. For a detailed discussion of totemism, see the book *Totemism and Exogamy* by Sir J. G. Frazer (4 vols., 1910). (See also **Fetich; Taboo**)

Touches, Psychic

Tactile sensations represent an allied phenomenon to the paranormal **movement** of objects. They are always intentional, as the movement of objects is characterized by perfect localization. Sitters are seldom touched by accident, however swift the motion may be, and the touch is invariably meant for the one who receives it.

While the objects by which the sitters are touched may be well recognized, in psychic contacts the case is different, as there is no apparent material means for their production. If it is by rods of **ectoplasm** that the touches are produced, they may cause an immense variety of sensations according to the manipulation of this mysterious creative substance. There is no doubt as to the reality of the tactile sensation, since it is often announced in advance and, in case it is affected by psychic lights or luminous structures, and is visible to others.

The effect may be as though coming from a soft object, like a rubber ball or an animal's paw sometimes half solid, from feathers, gloves, fur, powder-puff, cobwebs, flowers, fingers, etc. The touch itself may be sharp, soft, dry, wet, clammy, cold. It may be a tap, a caress, a stroke, a slap, a kick, a prick, a push, a punch, a kiss. The invisible operator may pull or rumple your hair, he may rub your legs and search your pockets. None of your extremities are safe from him. He works with an extreme rapidity and accuracy.

In old ghost stories, psychic touches were full of dramatic elements. Hands of flame were said to have left a fiery mark, an indelible impression behind.

In 1905, in the *Annales des Sciences Psychiques*, psychical researcher Prof. Charles **Richet** translated a Latin chronicle of the year 1656 dealing with the phenomena which occurred around a young girl, called Regina Fischerin of Presbourg, Hungary. The chronicle, which is still part of the records of the Venerable Chapter in the Archbishopric of Pest, narrated the apparitions of Jean Clement, a man of Presbourg, who led an evil life, and contained the following dramatic passages:

"Therefore, fearing that she might be the victim of an illusion, Regina asked of the spirit, if it were truly a spirit, to touch her with its finger. Immediately it touched her right arm and she felt the contact instantly. There appeared immediately a blister, giving her the same sensation of pain as though it had been a burn; moreover, fully to attest the phenomenon, the blister remained upon the skin a long time, and all the servants of the house saw it. Thereafter, desirous to be sure that this was not the work of an evil spirit, Regina demanded as proof that the visitor was a good spirit to make the sign of the cross. 'Here then,' said the phantom 'what you ask!' At once a flaming cross appeared outside the cloak which enveloped the figure, and with this it burned deeply the hand of the young girl, leaving thereon a branded cross which everyone could see.

"But the young woman, seeking still further proof, asked another sign. She showed some letters which the Bishop of Smyrna had sent, letters in which the Bishop had asked a number of questions which Regina could not answer, and asked for information. The spirit answered that it did not know how to read these letters. None the less it said it would try to give her satisfaction; but on taking these letters with the thumb and forefinger and second finger of its hand (the hand evidently being a hand of flame) the three fingers passed through the paper of the letters, as though they had been in contact with a flame.

"A little later this spirit of Jean Clement recalled with remorse a crime which he had committed during his life, declaring that the money which had been secured from this crime was not all spent [this proved afterwards to be true]; that part of it had been used for his subsistence, another part had been otherwise spent, but that some still remained and that this should be restored from the possessions which he had left.

"Regina demanded yet other proofs. Surely the proof of the cross burned on her hand, and on her mantle was sufficiently strong, but it did not suffice for the young woman, who, in order to be absolutely sure that the strange visitant was truly a good spirit, insisted that it should make the same Sign of the Cross on a piece of money. The spirit obeyed, took a coin, threw it on the ground, and snatching a piece of cloth from the girl's hands, threw this upon the coin; then, taking Regina's hand violently in his grasp, scorching her deeply as before, burned thereon through the hand and the linen cloth upon the coin the character of a triple cross. 'Here is a further sign,' said he, and launched forth a flame with so much force that it reached the heart of the young woman, while another jet of flame crossed the entire room and struck the opposite wall. Whereupon Regina fell unconscious.

"Her sister, who was present, saw and heard all that passed, and a few minutes later the servants came in and were able to see with their own eyes the scorch of the flame upon the linen material, and also upon the coin. Thereafter, many other persons visited the place and were permitted not only to see but also to touch the scorch marks on the girl's mantle, on the linen material, and on the coin, and also the letters which had been burned through at three places by the spirit's fiery fingers.

"This affair seems extraordinary to us; firstly because a cross and an exact form of the hand have been marked in every detail; secondly, because this brand of burning did not extend beyond limits of the marks, though, upon linen material, fire has a tendency to spread. Finally, the right hand which was thus branded in on flesh and cloth, was an exact replica of the right hand of Clement, just as though he had been operating by his own dead physical hand. And the proof of this is that, during life, the tip phalange of Clement's forefinger had been amputated by a surgeon for a disease which was then known as 'Worms' and the absence of the finger-tip is clearly indicated upon the branded hand." (This account can also be found in the English edition of *Annals of Psychical Science,* No. 4, April, 1905).

Other ancient chronicles contain many similar accounts. In 1908 and 1910 Mrs. Zingarapoli, a Naples lawyer, published a dozen such cases in *Luce e Ombra.* One was recorded from the seventeenth century and the brands or scorch marks of the hands of fire preserved at the Convent St. Claire at Todi. The exhibits in Father V. Jouet's Other World Museum at Rome comprised photographic records of the marks. In another instance in the eighteenth century, the scene of which was the convent of the Franciscan nuns of Saint Anne at Foligno, in 1853, the spirit left an imprint as if by an iron hand heated red-hot on the door and on the grave being reopened the dead hand was found to fit the scorch marks to perfection.

T. M. Jarvis, in *Accredited Ghost Stories,* a book published in 1823, narrated the story of Lady Beresford. Lord Tyrone, with whom the lady made a death compact, appeared to her after his decease, and on being asked to leave an indelible mark of his presence, the apparition seized Lady Breseford's hand and left a mark of burn on her wrist. Throughout her life Lady Beresford wore a dark ribbon to conceal the mark. After her death Lady Netty Cobb, an intimate friend, took off the ribbon and found the burn.

A burn in the shape of a finger from the touch of a specter was recorded in Dr. Justinus Kerner's book *Eine Erscheinung aus dem Nachtgebiete der Natur* (Stuttgart, 1836).

In William **Howitt's** *History of the Supernatural* (2 vols., 1863), a story was quoted of an apparition which appeared to the grandfather and father of a fellow student of Jung-Stilling (Johann H. **Jung**). It stated in part: "Yet there were circumstances which made the father and son believe that he was far from his purification, for fire streamed from every finger when he became angry at their resistance to his wishes. Still more, when he touched the Bible it smoked, and the marks of his thumb and finger shrivelled up the leather of the binding where he held it, and also the paper where he pointed out the place in the hymn 'From guilt of blood deliver me' was black and singed. The Bible with these marks is preserved in the family, and many creditable persons have seen it and may still see it." Howitt added: "The fiery touch of the spirit which induced the father and son to believe it a bad one, modern spiritualists can testify to belong to many spirits. How often have we seen fire streaming even from the finger of a medium? How often have spirits, before shaking hands with you, desired you, at Mr. Home's, to lay your handkerchief over your hand first? How often have you felt the touch of spirit fingers prick as from the sparks of electricity?"

In the mediumship of the Rev. W. Stainton **Moses** there are two instances of somewhat similar character. According to his note dated April 18, 1874, a psychic light touched his fingers, with the result that the skin was broken up and the joint swollen. Mrs. Speer stated in her account in *Light* that a spirit of low order was responsible for the injury.

In the second instances, W. B., a friend of Stainton Moses figured; he had committed suicide. His portrait appeared on a plate on May 16, 1876, when Moses sat for **spirit photography.** On May 20, in the night, Moses woke up and saw the spirit trying to reach him and struggling with two other spirits. He was inspired with horror and revulsion. The spirit got nearer and stretched out his hand. Moses did not remember any more. In the morning, he found on his forehead an oblong dull red mark in the exact place where his friend wounded himself. The mark was a red discoloration and faded in two or three days.

The psychical researcher Frank **Podmore** quoted a similar case in *Proceedings* of the Society for Psychical Research (vol. 10, p. 204). Miss M. P. slept with her sister and was awakened in the night with a jump with a horrible feeling that there was someone in the room. An icy hand pressed against her face. The next moment her sister cried out and complained of a violent burn on her cheek. "The gas having been turned up higher, we saw on one side of her face, a very vivid red mark, which rapidly took the form of a hand, with fingers open."

The psychical researcher Ernesto **Bozzano** analyzed this and many similar cases in the journal *The Seer* (1931) under the title 'Spirit Hands of Flame,' and drew attention to the fact that the elder sister felt an icy sensation and a minute later, apparently by the same hand, her sister was burned. Bozzano asked whether the opposed sensation felt by the two percipients might not be explained by "a rapid change in the ectoplasmic condensation of the phantom hand resulting from a sudden modification of the vibratory tonality. This vibratory tonality, under certain circumstances, seems to be very much more intense either on living or inanimate matter, and as a result, like fire, it would destroy living animal or vegetable tissue."

In a seance with Heinrich Melzer, the Dresden **apport** medium, as reported in the June 1906 issue of *Die Unbersinnliche Welt,* a plant was apported. The sitter, at the very same instant that he received the plant, felt the sensation of burning on the thumb. When the light was switched on the mark of a burn was clearly seen and a blister formed immediately.

In isolated instances, the marks of burning were replaced by marks of blood.

Emma Hardinge [**Britten**] in her book *Modern American Spiritualism* (1870), vouched for the following occurrences in the family of a well-known merchant of San Francisco in a seance with the eldest daughter, a handsome girl of eighteen, about whom very scandalous reports were rife among the neighbors:

"Instantly, and while every eye was fixed upon her, she sank back in her chair in a swoon and there, in the broad glare of the sunlight, appeared on her face, which the moment before was perfectly white and colorless, a large patch of wet, reeking blood, one of her cheeks being marked exactly as if struck with a bloody hand. On approaching the swooning figure, a second patch appeared on the other cheek; and as she stretched out her hand as if to ward off an invisible foe, another wet and reeking stain instantaneously became manifest on its palm.

"The ladies present procured a washbowl and removed the stains from the young woman's face and hand; but though they replaced her in the chair, restored her to consciousness and never for one moment lost sight of her, nor suffered a single movement to escape them, this terrible phenomena was repeated five times in less than an hour."

The house in which this occurred was haunted, and the scene of frightful disturbances at night. The younger children always insisted that these frightful marks were made "by a Spanish girl" who followed their sister about. She had her throat cut. Another apparition who helped to make the marks was their mother whom they represented as reproaching her daughter with an infamous life. The quality of the fluid was several times analyzed and always found to be human blood. The phenomena lasted for many months. Finally the police interfered and the circles were terminated.

It might be argued that some cases of burns and bleeding might be ascribed to autosuggestion (see **Hypnotism** and **Stigmata**).

Tower of London

Ancient British fortress on the east side of the city of London, England, scene of many executions, once used for imprisonment of high-ranking traitors. With its grim history, it is not surprising that various ghosts are associated with it.

The jewel-room of the Tower of London is reported to be haunted, and in 1860, there was published in *Notes and Queries* by Edmund Lenthal Swifte, Keeper of the Crown Jewels, an account of a spectral appearance witnessed by himself in the Tower. He stated that in October 1817, he was at supper with his wife, her sister, and his little boy, in the sitting room of the jewel house. To quote his own words:

"I had offered a glass of wine and water to my wife when, on putting it to her lips, she exclaimed, 'Good God! what is that?' I looked up and saw a cylindrical figure like a glass tube, seemingly about the thickness of my arm, and hovering between the ceiling and the table; its contents appeared to be dense fluid, white and pale azure. This lasted about two minutes, when it began to move before my sister-in-law; then, following the oblong side of the table, before my son and myself, passing behind my wife, it paused for a moment over her right shoulder. Instantly crouching down, and with both hands covering her shoulder she shrieked out, 'O Christ! it has seized me!'

"It was ascertained," added Mr. Swifte, "that no optical action from the outside could have produced any manifestation within, and hence the mystery has remained unsolved." *Notes and Queries* also reported how "one of the night sentries at the jewel house was alarmed by a figure like a bear issuing from underneath the jewel room door. He thrust at it with his bayonet which stuck in the door. He dropped in a fit and was carried senseless to the guard-room. . . . In another day or two the brave and steady soldier died."

In February 1933, a sentry at the Tower reported seeing the ghostly figure of a woman in white, floating towards him. A newspaper report stated: "Confronted by such an apparition, the sentry fled, making his way to the guardroom, greatly unnerved."

On February 12, 1957, a young Welsh Guardsman was on duty, and at 3 a.m. saw a "white shapeless form" forty feet up on the battlements of the Salt Tower. He called for a search party, who found nothing, although another guardsman later admitted to seeing a shapeless white apparition. The time and the date tallied exactly with the execution of Lady Jane Grey, four hundred and three years earlier.

Trance

An abnormal state, either spontaneous or induced, bearing some analogy to the ordinary sleep state, but differing from it in certain marked particulars.

The term is loosely applied to many varied pathological conditions e.g., hypnosis, ecstasy, catalepsy, somnambulism, certain forms of hysteria, and the mediumistic trance. Sometimes, as in catalepsy, there is a partial suspension of the vital functions; generally, there is insensibility to pain and to any stimulus applied to the sense-organs, while the main distinguishing feature of the trance is that the subject retains consciousness and gives evidence of intelligence, either his or her own normal intelligence or, as in cases of **possession** and impersonation, some foreign intelligence.

In hypnosis the subject, although indifferent to the application of sensory stimuli, has been known to exhibit a curious sensitiveness to such stimuli applied to the person of the hypnotist (see **Community of Sensation**).

In **ecstasy,** which is frequently allied with **hallucination,** the subject remains in rapt contemplation of some transcendental vision, deaf and blind to the outside world. It was formerly considered to indicate that the soul of the ecstatic was viewing some great event distant in time or place or some person or scene from the celestial sphere. Nowadays such a state is believed to be brought about by intense and sustained emotional concentration on some particular mental image, by means of which hallucination may be induced.

The mediumistic trance is recognized as having an affinity with hypnosis, for the hypnotic trance, frequently induced, may gradually become spontaneous, when it exhibits strong resemblances to the trance of the medium.

Some Spiritualists have objected to the term being generally applied in any case where there is no sign of spirit possession. The entranced medium (who seems able to produce this state at will) frequently displays an exaltation of memory (hypermnesia), of the special senses (hyperæsthesia), and even of the intellectual faculties.

Automatic writing and utterances are generally produced in the trance state, and often display knowledge of which the medium normally knows nothing, or which, according to some authorities, gives evidence of **telepathy.** Such were the trance utterances of the medium Mrs. L. E. **Piper,** whose automatic phenomena provided a wide field for research for many men of science both in Britain and on the Continent.

Naturally these phenomena, and those of all trance mediums, are referred by Spiritualists to the agency of disembodied intelligences—the spirits of the dead—acting through the medium's physical organism, as distinct from ancient ideas that trance personalities were all demonic possession. Moreover, the trance messages of Spiritualist mediums are asserted to come from the spirits of deceased persons and this assertion is often supported by a close representation of the voice, appearance, or known opinions of the deceased friend or relative whose spirit it claims to be.

Such trance representations supply a large part of the evidence on which the structure of Spiritualism rests. In cases of **fraud,** however, the information concerning the deceased thus reproduced, may have been obtained by normal means, or, in some genuine cases, telepathically from the minds of the sitters. While there is strong evidence for the Spiritualist view, there are also borderline cases when other explanations may be valid. Moreover, there are confusing cases in which there appears to be impersonation by other spirits than the claimed personality.

Subjective Aspects of Trance

The true nature of trance is still a controversial matter, but can be learned from subjective experiences.

The great medium D. D. **Home** testified before the Committee of the **London Dialectical Society** in 1869 as follows: "I feel for two or three minutes in a dreamy state, then I become quite dizzy, and then I lose all consciousness. When I awake I find my feet and limbs cold, and it is difficult to restore the circulation. When told of what has taken place during the trance it is quite unpleasant to me, and I ask those present not to tell me at once when I awake. I myself doubt what they tell me."

Lord **Adare,** speaking of Home's trance state, said: "The change which takes place in him is very striking; he becomes, as it were, a being of higher type. There is a union of sweetness, tenderness and earnestness in his voice and manner which is very attractive."

The Rev. W. Stainton **Moses** added these observations: "By degrees Mr. Home's hands and arms began to twitch and move involuntarily. I should say that he has been partly paralysed, drags one of his legs, moves with difficulty, stoops and can endure very little physical exertion. As he passed into the trance state he drew power from the circle by extending his arms to them and mesmerising himself. All these acts are involuntary. He gradually passed into the trance state, and rose from the table, erect and a different man from what he was. He walked firmly, dashed out his arms and legs with great power and passed round to Mr. Crookes. He mesmerised him, and appeared to draw power from him."

The medium William **Eglinton** said of his experiences: "I seemed to be no longer of this earth. A most ecstatic feeling came over me, and I presently passed into trance."

"I feel a cold shivering," stated Mrs. J. B. **Mellon,** "a sensation as of water running down my back, noise in my ears, and a feeling as if I were sinking down into the earth; then I lose consciousness."

"I feel," said Mrs. **Piper,** "as if something were passing over my brain, making it numb; a sensation similar to that experienced when I was etherised, only the unpleasant odour of the ether is absent. I feel a little cold, too, not very, just a little, as if a cold breeze passed over me, and people and objects become smaller until they finally disappear; then, I know nothing more until I wake up, when the first thing I am conscious of is bright, a very bright light, and then darkness, such darkness. My hands and arms begin to tingle just as one's foot tingles after it has been 'asleep,' and I see, as if from a great distance, objects and people in the room; but they are very small and very black."

It is interesting to note that when the Seeress of Prevorst (Frederica **Hauffe**) awoke from trance, she also said that the persons around her looked so thick and heavy that she could not imagine how they could move.

Objective Aspects of Trance

On awakening from trance, Mrs. Piper often pronounced names and fragments of sentences which appeared to have been the last impression on her brain. After that, she resumed the conversation at the point where it was broken off before she fell into trance.

These trances had three distinct stages—Subliminal I, in which the medium was partly conscious of her surroundings, but saw things distorted and grotesque; Subliminal II, in which she was possessed by spirits; and lost contact with the material world and Subliminal III, deep trance in which the loss of consciousness was complete, the body became anaesthetic and automatic writing commenced.

Describing the development in Mrs. Piper's trances, Sir Oliver **Lodge** wrote in his book *The Survival of Man* (1909): "In the old days the going into trance seemed rather a painful process, or at least a process involving muscular effort; there was some amount of contortion of the face and sometimes a slight tearing of the hair; and the same actions accompanied the return of consciousness. Now the trance seems nothing more than an exceptionally heavy sleep, entered into without effort—a sleep with the superficial appearance of that induced by chloroform; and the return to consciousness, though slow and for a time accompanied by confusion, is easy and natural . . . For half an hour or so after the trance had disappeared the medium continues slightly dazed and only partly herself . . . A record was also made of the remarks of Mrs. Piper during the period of awaking from trance . . . part of them nearly always consisted of expressions of admiration for the state of experience she was leaving, and of repulsion—almost disgust—at the commonplace terrestrial surroundings in which she found herself. Even a bright day was described as dingy or dark, and the sitter was stared at in an unrecognising way, and described as a full and ugly person, or sometimes as a negro."

It is significant to quote from among the mumbled remarks during her return to consciousness, "I came in on a cord, a silver cord." Before she became conscious she heard a snap, sometimes two. They were physiological experiences. She said: "sounds like wheels clicking together and then snaps." Similar observations have been made by individuals reporting **Out-of-the-Body** experiences.

Prof. William **James** found Mrs. Piper's lips and tongue insensible to pain while she was in trance. Dr. Richard **Hodgson** later confirmed this by placing a spoonful of salt in Mrs. Piper's mouth. He also applied strong ammonia to the nostrils.

Drastic experiments were also tried. Prof. James made a small incision in Mrs. Piper's left wrist. During trance the wound did not bleed and no notice was taken of the action. It bled freely afterwards and the medium bore the scar for her life.

In England, Prof. Lodge pushed a needle suddenly into her hand. At another time, Prof. Charles **Richet** inserted a feather up her nostril. Harsh experiments in 1909 resulted in a badly blistered swollen tongue which caused the medium inconvenience for several days, while another test resulted in numbness and partial paralysis of the right arm for some time afterwards.

Although these scientific experiments were of great importance, it is arguable that the experimenters overstepped the mark in causing inconvenience and pain to the medium.

The trance of the medium Eusapia **Palladino** was described by Prof. Cesar **Lombroso** thus: "At the beginning of the trance her voice is hoarse and all the secretions—sweat, tears, even the menstrual secretion are increased. Hyperaesthesia . . . is succeeded by anaesthesia. . . . Reflex movement of the pupils and tendons are lacking. . . . Respiratory movements . . . passing from 18 inspirations to 15 and 12 a minute, . . . heartbeats increase from 70 to 90 and even 120. The hands are seized with jerkings and tremors. The joints of the feet and the hands take on movements of flexure or extension, and every little while become rigid.

"The passing from this state to that of active somnambulism is marked by yawns, sobs, perspirations on the forehead, passing of insensible perspiration through the skin of the hands, and strange physiognomic expressions. Now she seems a prey to a kind of anger, expressed by imperious commands and sarcastic and critical phrases, and now to a state of voluptuous erotic-ecstasy. In the state of trance she first becomes pale, turning her eyes upward and her sight inward . . . exhibiting many of the gestures that are frequent in hysterical fits. . . . Toward the end of the trance when the more important phenomena occur, she falls into true convulsions and cries like a woman who is lying-in, or else falls into a profound sleep while from the aperture in the parietal bone in her head there exhales a warm fluid or vapour, sensible to the touch.

"After the seance Eusapia is overcome by morbid sensitiveness, hyperaesthesy, photophobia and often by hallucinations and delirium (during which she asks to be watched from harm) and by serious disturbances of the digestion, followed by vomiting if she has eaten before the seance, and finally by true paresis of the legs, on account of which it is necessary for her to be carried and to be undressed by others."

"These disturbances are much aggravated . . . if she is exposed to unexpected light . . . "

"My eyes ache a good deal after a seance," said Mrs. Mellon, "and generally my lower limbs are thin, sometimes very thin, and usually I feel pain in the left side."

F. W. H. **Myers** distinguished between three successive stages in trance. In the first stage, the subliminal (subconscious) self obtains control. In the next stage, the incarnate spirit, whether or not maintaining control of the whole body, makes excursions into or holds telepathic intercourse with the spiritual world. In the third stage, the body of the medium is controlled by another discarnate spirit.

The first stage is well illustrated by the case of the Rev. C. B. Sanders whose trance personality had always called itself by the name of "X Y Z," and claimed to represent the incarnate spirit of Mr. Sanders exercising his higher faculties. He spoke of the normal Mr. Sanders as his "casket," but showed no evidence of direct communication with discarnate spirits.

The nineteenth-century histologist Gaëtano Salvioli, investigating hypnosis, noticed for the first time that in trance the flow of blood to the brain is greater than in the waking hours, consequently there is a greater psychical activity and an increase in muscular excitability.

Professor Theodore **Flournoy** frequently found complete "allochiria," a confusion between the right and left side, with the medium Mlle. Hélène **Smith.** In trance she would consistently look for her pocket on the left side instead of on the right. If one of her fingers was pricked or pinched behind a screen, it was the corresponding finger on the other hand which was agitated. Allochiria is one of the stigmata of hysteria.

Prof. Lombroso called attention to the fact that Eusapia Palladino, who was usually left-handed in sittings, became right-handed in one seance and Prof. Enrico **Morselli** himself became left-handed. This confirmed Dr. Audenino's hypothesis of transitory left-handedness in the abnormal state, and the transference to the sitters of the anomalies of the medium. The left-handedness seemed to indicate the increased participation of the right lobe of the brain in mediumistic states.

Prof. Morselli measured the left-handedness of Eusapia Palladino in dynamometric figures. He found, after a seance, a diminution of six kilograms for the right and fourteen for the left hand. The spirits of Mrs. Piper always communicated on the left side. The trance, as a rule, began with hissing intakes of breath and ended with deep expirations.

There is a suggestion in this of the **Yoga** system of breathing *(Pranayama).* "Like the fakirs," wrote Morselli, "when they wish to enter into trance, Eusapia begins to slacken her rate of breathing." The seer Emanuel **Swedenborg** believed that his powers were connected with a system of respiration. He said that in communing with the spirits he hardly breathed for half an hour at a time.

The poet Gerald **Massey,** who published new insights into the history of the world, wrote of his mystical vision: "You know Swedenborg and Blake claimed a kind of inner breathing. I know that is possible. I have got at times to where I find there needs to be no further need for expiring, it is all inspiration, I consider that consciously or unconsciously we all draw life from the spirit-world, just as we shall when we pass into it."

Similar concepts of the origin of genius in states of higher consciousness as a psycho-physical aspect of **Kundalini** energy have been discussed in the books of Pandit **Gopi Krishna.** However, a clear distinction exists between the active **meditation** of higher consciousness and the passive trance of the medium.

"I have tried to simulate the deep and rapid breathing of Rudi in the trance state," wrote psychical researcher Harry Price in his book *Rudi Schneider* (1930), "This breathing has been likened to a steam engine, a tyre being pumped up, etc. Taking off my collar and tie and with my watch in my hand, I found that in six and a quarter minutes I was exhausted and could not continue. I have known Rudi to continue this hard breathing, interspersed with spasms and the usual clonic movements, *for seventy-five minutes without cessation.* And this while being held and in a most uncomfortable position, while, of course, I was quite free."

Trances do not always come at pleasure and occasionally appear when not desired. At Cambridge, England, at the request of F. W. H. Myers, Mrs.

Piper looked into a crystal before going to bed. She saw nothing but looked exhausted next morning and said that she thought that she had been entranced during the night. The next time when she went into a trance, her spirit **control** "Phinuit" said that he came and called but no one answered. Mrs. Piper's trances generally lasted about an hour. On one occasion, in Sir Oliver Lodge's experience, it only lasted for about one minute.

The trance, as a rule, is continuous. In the mediumship of Mrs. J. H. **Conant,** much discomfort was caused at an earlier stage by the medium's return to consciousness as soon as the control left. She had to be entranced again for the next communicator. Each change took about ten minutes. In the case of Rudi Schneider, the trance was similarly intermittent but the same entity, "Olga," remained in control.

To be roused from trance by a materialized spirit is exceptional. The spirit form "Katie King" was said to have roused the medium Florence **Cook** when the time of her farewell arrived and a tearful scene was witnessed between the two. The novelist Florence **Marryat,** who was present at this scene, described a similar experience with the medium Mary **Showers:** "[The spirit 'Peter'] proceeded to rouse Rosie by shaking her and calling her name, holding me by one hand as he did so. As Miss Showers yawned and woke up from her trance, the hand slipped from mine, and 'Peter' evaporated. When she sat up I said to her gently: 'I am here! Peter had brought me in and was sitting on the mattress by my side till just this moment.' 'Ha, ha!' laughed his voice close to my ear, 'and I'm still here, my dears, though you can't see me.' " (from *There is No Death,* 1891)

The medium F. W. **Monck** was once apparently awakened by the common consent of the materialized spirit and the sitters. However, controversy surrounds the mediumship of Florence Cook, Mary Showers, and Monck.

Usually the medium brings back no remembrance of what has passed in the trance. To all intents and purposes he or she is an entirely different being while in that state, with physiological functions totally differ from the normal ones. Florence Marryat wrote that the medium Bessie **Williams** ate like a sparrow, and only the simplest things. "Dewdrop" (her **guide**), on the other hand, liked indigestible food, and devoured it freely, yet the medium never felt any inconvenience from it.

About 1846, the limbs of Mary Jane, servant girl of Dr. Larkin, of Wrentham, Massachusetts, were under the spirit influence of a rough sailor, thrown out of joint in several directions in a moment and without pain. Dr. Larkin was often obliged to call in the aid of his professional brethren and two or three strong assistants to replace them. On one occasion the knees and wrists of the girl were thrown out of joint twice in a single day. These painful feats were always accompanied by loud laughter and hoarse profane jokes.

On the testimony of S. W. Turner, of Cleveland, the *Spiritual Telegraph* reported in December 1847, the peculiar adventure of a medium called William Hume who, in trance, and under the control of "Capt. Kidd," threw himself into the lake to recover a ring and was brought out of the water, still in trance, after swimming for fifteen to twenty minutes, without injury to his health.

Trance in Animal Magnetism and Hypnotism

The first operation on a subject in Mesmeric trance was performed in France in April 1829, by M. Cloquet on Mme. Plantin, a sixty-four-year-old woman who suffered from an ulcerated cancer in the right breast. The operation lasted 10-12 minutes. The pulse and breathing remained unchanged. The patient was not awakened until two days later. The case was reported to the Section of Surgery of the Academy.

In 1836, Dr. Hamard invited a member of the Academy, M. Oudet, to extract a tooth from a somnambulic patient. The operation was a success.

In England the first operation in Mesmeric trance took place in 1842, in Nottinghamshire, on James Wombell, whose leg was amputated above the knee. W. Topham, a London barrister, was the Mesmerist, and the operation was performed by Squire Ward, M.R.C.S.

James Esdaile's book *Mesmerism in India* (1846) contains a great number of similar records.

There is one instance on record in the mediumship of F. L. H. Willis, who later acquired a medical degree and became Professor of Materia Medica in New York, when not the patient, but the operator was in trance. Controlled by the spirit of "Dr. Mason," Willis successfully performed a difficult operation on a lady.

Apart from Swedenborg's case, the first conversation with spirits of the departed through the instrumentality of trance was recorded in May 1778, by the Societé Exegetique Philantropique, of Stockholm. The forty-year-old wife of the gardener, Lindquist, was controlled in trance by her own infant daughter and another young child of the town, who gave accounts both of their earth lives and their existence in the spirit world.

The somnambulic state in **Mesmerism** was the discovery of the Marquis Chastenet de Puységur. **Mesmer** himself was aware of something unknown in the "magnetic sleep" and warned against deepening it. The use of **animal magnetism** was primarily for healing power. The possibility of intercourse with spirits was largely avoided. It cropped up as early as 1878 in Tardy de Montravel's writings but he opposed it. Kaleph Ben-Nathan admitted it in 1793 but contended that those spirits with which the somnambule holds intercourse are spirits of an inferior order and the magnetists practice sorcery and divination.

Dr. Alexandre Bertrand recorded the exclamation of his young somnambule: "There are no spirits, they are stories, yet I see them, the proof is perfect." J. P. F. **Deleuze** conceded in 1818 that the phenomena of **clairvoyance** established the spirituality of the soul, but he did not consider spirit intercourse proven by the phenomena of somnambulic trance. In later years, however, under the effect of Dr. G. P.

Billot's experiments, he appeared to have changed his belief.

Billot's somnambules were mediums in the present-day sense. The spirits who possessed them proclaimed themselves to be their guardian angels and produced physical phenomena as well.

Alphonse **Cahagnet** recorded fully developed trance communications through the early medium Adèle **Maginot.** Previous to Cahagnet's appearance, an official acknowledgment of trance took place in 1831 when an investigating commission of the Royal Academy of Medicine reported on the phenomena of animal magnetism and found the phenomena genuine and the state of somnambulism, although rare, well authenticated.

In Germany the theory of spiritual intercourse in trance took a quicker hold on the imagination of magnetizers. Jung-Stilling (J. H. **Jung**) founded the school with the theory of the psychic body and its elements, based on the luminiferous ether. Fräulein Auguste **Müller,** of Carlsruhe, appears to have been the first somnambule whose spirit communications and other phenomena were carefully recorded, Fräulein Römer the second. She was the first planetary traveler, making claimed clairvoyant excursions to the moon. The most stirring account of intercourse with the spirit world was published in 1826 by Dr. Justinus Kerner. It was the story of the Seeress of Prevorst, Frau Frederica **Hauffe.**

Amongst primitive peoples, trance states have been common since ancient times, used by a **shaman** or medicine man for demonstrations of paranormal knowledge. Such shamans were forerunners of the modern Spiritualist mediums. (See also **Animal Magnetism; Hypnotism; Mesmerism; Shaman; Somnambulism; Trance Personalities**)

Recommended reading:

Cahagnet, L. A. *The Celestial Telegraph; or, Secrets of the Life to Come Revealed Through Magnetism*, 2 vols., London & New York, 1851; one vol. ed. Arno Press, 1976

Dingwall, E. J. *Abnormal Hypnotic Phenomena,* 4 vols., Churchill, London, 1967-68

Esdaile, James. *Natural and Mesmeric Clairvoyance; With the Practical Application of Mesmerism in Surgery and Medicine,* London, 1852; Arno Press, 1975

Fahnestock, W. B. *Statuvolism, or Artificial Somnambulism,* Chicago, 1871

Flournoy, Theodore. *From India to the Planet Mars,* Harper & Bros., 1900

Garrett, Eileen J. *My Life as a Search for the Meaning of Mediumship,* Oquaga, New York/Rider & Co., London, 1939; Arno Press, 1975

Goodman, Felicitas D., Jeanette H. Henney & Esther Pressel. *Trance, Healing and Hallucination; Three Field Studies in Religious Experience,* Wiley-Interscience, 1974

Gopi Krishna. *The Biological Basis of Religion and Genius,* Harper & Row, 1972

Inglis, Brian. *Trance; A Natural History of Altered States of Mind,* Grafton, London, 1989

Kerner, Justinus. *The Seeress of Prevorst,* London, 1845

Laski, Marghanita. *Ecstasy,* Cresset, London, 1961

Salter, W. H. *Trance Mediumship; An Introductory Study of Mrs. Piper and Mrs. Leonard,* Society for Psychical Research, London, 1962 [pamphlet]

Spiegel, H. & D. *Trance and Treatment; Clinical Users of Hypnosis,* Basis Books, New York, 1978

Sunderland, La Roy. *The Trance, and How Introduced,* Boston, 1860

Wavell, Stewart, Audrey Butt & Nina Epton. *Trances,* Allen & Unwin, London, 1966

Trance Personalities

Trance messages purporting to come from the medium's spirit **control** do not always reveal a very definite personality. The control often reflects the thoughts and opinions of the medium and the sitters, possesses little knowledge that they do not possess, and is frequently a colorless or artificial personality. Yet not infrequently a trance medium is controlled by a spirit of distinct or distinguished personality, whose education and culture are on a much higher plane than the medium's, and whose ideas and opinions are quite independent.

Such spirits are generally given distinguishing names. They often control the medium alternately with other controls. On the other hand, the medium has generally a monopoly of one or more of these spirits, though sometimes one control may be shared by a number of mediums.

Among those who may justly be regarded as the common property of dubious mediums are the spirits of certain great men—Virgil, Socrates, Shakespeare, Milton, Benjamin Franklin, Victor Hugo, Swedenborg, and so on. The messages delivered through their control seldom resemble anything they wrote or said during their lives. It would indeed be ludicrous to hold these great men responsible for the feeble outpourings delivered in their name.

Not all the mediums involved in such counterfeit personalities are frauds. Some are self-deluded. Othersers exhibit the strange faculty of the subconscious mind to weave fantasies like the characters and incidents of a novelist. Similar artificial personalities sometimes manifest in the claimed **reincarnation** experiences of subjects in hypnotic regression as in the famous "Bridey Murphy" case (see Morey **Bernstein**).

Some trance personalities assume pseudonyms, suggesting the possibility that the personality of everyday life, which is modified from year to year, may suffer radical change after death, losing the distinctive nature which the physical body, memories and emotions normally reinforce.

Some of the most well-known pseudonymous trance personalities were those of the Rev. W. Stainton **Moses**—"Imperator," "Rector," "Mentor," "Prudens," and others. What the real names of these spirit controls might be was a matter for speculation, since Moses only revealed the secret to a few of his most intimate friends.

"Imperator" and "Rector" were also among the controls of the medium Mrs. L. E. **Piper** in subsequent years and indeed much of her automatic discourse did not come directly from communicating spirits, but was dictated by them to "Rector." It was suggested, however, by Sir Oliver **Lodge** and other investigators, that the controls of Mrs. Piper were not identical with those of Stainton Moses (by whom were written through his hand the well-known book *Spirit Teachings,* 1894) but were merely masqueraders.

However, Mrs. Piper had several interesting trance personalities of her own, without borrowing from anybody. One of her earliest controls was "Sebastian Bach," but before long he gave place to a spirit calling himself "Dr. Phinuit," who held sway for a considerable time, then giving place in his turn to George Pelham—"G. P."

Pelham was a young author and journalist who died suddenly in 1892. Soon after his death he purportedly controlled Mrs. Piper, and indeed gave many striking proofs of his identity. He constantly referred with intimate knowledge to the affairs of Pelham, recognized his friends, and gave to each his due welcome. He never failed to recognize an acquaintance, or give a greeting to one whom he did not know. Many of Pelham's old friends did not hesitate to recognize in him that which he claimed to be.

Only on one occasion, when asked for the names of two persons who had been associated with him in a certain enterprise, the spirit "G.P." refused, saying that as there was present one who knew the names, his mentioning them would be referred to **telepathy**! Later, however, he gave the names—incorrectly.

When "G.P." ceased to communicate as the principal control of Mrs. Piper, his place was taken by "Rector" and "Imperator," as mentioned above.

Another well-known trance medium, Mrs. R. **Thompson,** had as her chief control "Nelly," a daughter of hers who had died in infancy; also a "Mrs. Cartwright," and others. These controls of Mrs. Thompson were said not to have shown any very individual characteristics, but to resemble Mrs. Thompson herself very strongly both in voice and manner of speech, although Mrs. A. W. **Verrall,** one of the sitters, stated that the impersonations gave an impression of separate identity to the sitter. Mrs. Thompson's early trance utterances were controlled by another band of spirits, with even less individuality than those mentioned.

Frequently mediums and investigators themselves, on reaching the discarnate plane, seem to become controls in their turn. The psychical researchers F. W. H. **Myers,** Edmund **Gurney,** Dr. Richard **Hodgson,** and Professor Henry **Sidgwick** purported to speak and write posthumously through many mediums, notably through Mrs. Piper and Mrs. Thompson, Mrs. Verrall and Mrs. Holland (Alice K. **Fleming**). Many of the statements made by these controls were correct, and some matters revealed which were apparently outside the scope of the medium's normal knowledge. At the same time several fatal discrepancies were found to exist between the controls and those they were supposed to represent.

Thus the script produced by Mrs. Holland contained grave warnings, purporting to come from Myers, against the medium Eusapia **Palladino** and her physical phenomena, whereas Myers was known to hold in his lifetime opinions favorable to the physical manifestations.

On the whole, such trance personalities show themselves decidedly colored by the personality of the medium. In cases where the latter was acquainted with the control, the trance personality was proportionately strong, whereas when there was no personal acquaintance it was often of a neutral tint, and sometimes bad guesses were made, as when Mrs. Holland represented the Gurney control as of a brusque and almost discourteous temperament.

But such instances must not be taken as impeaching the medium's good faith. Even where the trance personality is patently the product of the medium's own consciousness, there is no reason to assume that there is any intentional deception. In some of the most definite cases, the evidence for the operation of a discarnate intelligence is very good indeed, and has proved satisfactory to many prominent investigators.

It is not always wise to ridicule the patently artificial personality of a claimed spirit control. By suspending criticism, such a personality sometimes consolidates into a more acceptable personality, and temporary acceptance of a trance personality has frequently resulted in the disclosure of paranormally acquired information or remarkable phenomena.

From 1972-73, members of the Toronto Society for Psychical Research, Canada, deliberately created an artificial seance entity named "Philip," with history, characteristics and appearance worked out by the group. Soon the experimenters obtained raps from the seance table and communications from "Philip."

It seems that in many instances, a spirit control is merely a convention of personality. In other cases, however, convincing evidence of true personality survival has been established. (See also Morey **Bernstein; Control; Guide; Medium;** Rev. W. Stainton **Moses; Personality; "Philip"; Trance**)

Recommended reading:

Broad, C. D. *Personal Identity and Survival,* Society for Psychical Research, London, 1968 [pamphlet]

Carington, Whately. *The Foundations of Spiritualism,* Dutton, 1920

Ducasse, C. J. *A Critical Examination of the Belief in a Life After Death,* C. C. Thomas, Springfield, Illinois, 1961

Garrett, Eileen J. *My Life as a Search for the Meaning of Mediumship,* Oquaga, New York/Rider & Co., London, 1939

Hart, Hornell. *The Enigma of Survival; The Case For and Against an After Life,* C. C. Thomas, Springfield, Illinois, 1959

M. A. (Oxon) (pseud. of Rev. W. Stainton Moses). *Spirit Identity,* London, 1879 etc.

Myers, F. W. H. *Human Personality and Its Survival of Bodily Death,* 2 vols., Longmans, Green, London, 1903

Owen, Iris M. & Margaret Sparrow. *Conjuring Up Philip,* Harper & Row, 1976

Penelhum, Terence. *Survival and Disembodied Existence,* Humanities Press, New York, 1970

Richmond, Kenneth. *Evidence of Identity,* G. Bell, London, 1939

Salter, W. H. *Trance Mediumship; An Introductory Study of Mrs. Piper and Mrs. Leonard,* Society for Psychical Research, London, 1962 [pamphlet]

Transcendental Meditation

A popular technique first taught by **Maharishi Mahesh Yogi,** owing its initial success to endorsement by the Beatles and other showbiz personalities during the 1960s.

In the 1970s, scientists and psychologists were enlisted to evaluate "TM" under the heading "Science of Creative Intelligence." Since then, the method has received worldwide endorsement at every level of society, including support from politicians, scientists, doctors and members of the general public.

Essentially the technique is a mass media packaging of the ancient Hindu initiation of bestowing a **mantra** or sacred Sanskrit word or phrase for the pupil to meditate upon for a short period each day. The benefits claimed are relaxation, clearer and more powerful thought, lowered blood pressure, confidence and tranquility.

This universal success syndrome of TM obscures the simple fact that similar benefits may be obtained from an after-lunch snooze, or repetition of the words "Maytag," "Kodak" or "Coca-Cola," dynamizing the subconscious in much the same way as a well-made television commercial, which also carries a message of success and well-being. Any technique which prevents the mind from brooding over problems undoubtedly does release latent energies and a conviction of success and well-being, enhancing personal achievement.

This is not to decry the very real benefits of TM or the psychological advantages of association with other meditators in the same movement, but rather to place TM in a context of traditional **meditation** aims and results.

There is nothing essentially "transcendental" or "spiritual" about TM in itself, which indeed specifically emphasizes enjoyment and mundane achievement in the tradition of **New Thought** and Dale Carnegie techniques (the popular TM of their day). In this, TM parts company with the Hindu mysticism from which it has emerged, and indeed from the other great world religions which have emphasized the need for patient and continuing self-purification through spiritual disciplines, in order to give integrity to spiritual growth or eventual transcendental consciousness.

Common sense also dictates that the general run of individuals, with all their individual hangups, cannot expect a "simple technique" sold for "a single gift of money" to dynamize spiritual growth overnight, any more than the high hopes of psychedelic spiritual experience through drug-taking which preceded TM.

Traditional Hindu mysticism regards meditation as a later stage in a program of continuing spiritual discipline, and passive meditation is considered secondary to active meditation in quality and results. Moreover *mantra-diksha* or initiation is not normally given until the aspirant has proved his or her fitness to engage in meditation. Hinduism also reserves its highest transcendental experiences for those who have properly fulfilled their social and religious obligations.

However, there is no denying the everyday value of TM and its superiority to many other simple techniques of relaxation and well-being. Moreover its general ambience of Hinduism and gurus is an inspiration to many individuals brought up in the down-to-earth self-centered civilizations of the Western countries. It is perhaps unfortunate that the equally important traditions of Christian spiritual meditation have not been so widely popularized. (See also **Maharishi Mahesh Yogi; Kundalini; Meditation; Mantra; Yoga; Vedanta**)

Recommended reading:

Akins, W. R. & George Nurnberg. *How to Meditate Without Attending a TM Class,* Crown, 1976

Forem, Jack. *Transcendental Meditation,* Dutton, 1974

Hemingway, Patricia D. *Transcendental Meditation Primer,* McKay, 1975

Kanellakos, Demetri P. & Jerome S. Lukas. *Psychobiology of Transcendental Meditation: a Literature Review,* W. A. Benjamin, 1974

Maharishi Mahesh Yogi. *Meditations of Maharishi Mahesh Yogi,* Bantam paperback, 1973

Scott, R. D. *Transcendental Misconceptions,* Beta Books paperback, San Diego, 1978

Transfiguration

The metamorphic power of certain mediums to assume facial or bodily characteristics of deceased people for their representation. The phenomenon was well illustrated by the account of the Rev. Will. J. Erwood in *The National Spiritualist,* Chicago, of a seance with the medium Mrs. Bullock in 1931. In light, which showed every movement of the medium, he claimed to have seen more than fifty faces in an hour and a half.

He wrote: "It was as though the medium's face were of plastic material being rapidly molded from one form to another by some master worker in plastics. Oriental faces, Indians, calm, dignified, serious, spiritual, in short, almost every type of face was depicted during the most unusual seance. One of the most striking was the impersonation of a paralysed girl whom I had known in the States. The medium's entire body, as well as face, was twisted out of all semblance of its normal state, to depict the condition of this victim of paralysis."

H. Dennis **Bradley,** in his book *The Wisdom of the Gods* (1925), described an experience with the medium Mrs. Scales: "Gradually the whole of the expression of the medium's face changed completely. It was a transformation. Whilst the outline remained, the eyes and the expression became beautiful . . . At first is was only with very great difficulty that the first few words were articulated. It was as if they were produced with considerable effort. Within a little while, however, the power strengthened considerably, and the spirit of my sister was able to assume complete control. It was my sister. It was her spirit, using the organism of another physical body, and speaking to me in her own voice."

Dr. J. **Maxwell** vouched for the following case of transfiguration in sleep, narrated by one of his colleagues in the magistracy: "On January 1, 1903, my father began to feel the first attacks of the painful disease from which he died after six months of terrible suffering . . . I watched him as he slept, and was not long in noticing that his physiognomy gradually assumed an aspect which was not his own. I finally observed that his face bore a striking resemblance to that of my mother. It was as though the mask of her face was placed over his own. My father had had no eyebrows for a long time, and I noticed above his closed eyes the very marked black eyebrows which my mother had retained to the last. The eyelids, the nose, the mouth, were those of my mother . . . My father wore his moustache and a pointed, but rather short beard. This beard and moustache, which I saw, helped, contrary to what might have been expected, in forming the features of my mother. The appearance lasted for ten or twelve minutes; then it gradually disappeared, and my father resumed his habitual physiognomy. Five minutes later he awoke, and I immediately asked him if he had not been dreaming, especially about his wife. He answered in the negative."

The phenomenon was witnessed by a woman servant who came into the room while it lasted. She was told: "Jeanne, look at Monsieur sleeping!" She cried out, "Oh, how he resembles poor Madame. It is striking, it is quite extraordinary!"

In the experiences of Allen **Kardec,** founder of French **Spiritism,** there was an extraordinary case of a young girl of fifteen whose metamorphic power extended to the duplication of the stature, mass and weight of deceased persons, especially of her brother, as well. Of another metamorphic medium. Mme. Krooke, Allan Kardec recorded that she saw one evening her own face changed. She observed a thick black beard and by it her son-in-law recognized his dead father. A little later, her face changed into that of an old woman with white hair. She preserved her consciousness in the meantime, yet felt through her entire body a prickling like that of a galvanic battery. No such miracles are recorded in modern experience.

It is usually in **materialization** seances that transfiguration is witnessed. It is claimed to involve grave risks for the medium. During experiments at the **British College of Psychic Science** with the medium Ada **Besinnet** in 1921, light was flashed on a face which was illuminated by a spirit lamp. It was seen that the medium was leaning over the table and illuminated her own face with light held in her hand. That light quickly vanished, so did the white drapery which enveloped her head. She was in trance and complained of great pain in the solar plexus when awakened. For three days she was shaken with muscular contractions.

There are some past experiences on record of the entire disappearance of the medium during materialization. In such cases the entire bodily substance of the medium is believed to have been withdrawn for the purpose of building up phantom bodies. Such occurrences are also spoken of as transfigurations.

Col. H. S. **Olcott** and Dr. J. N. **Newbrough** experienced this with the medium Mrs. Elizabeth J. **Compton.** While phantoms were parading in front of the sitters before the **cabinet,** she vanished from the chair into which she was tied in such a way that the least effort to liberate herself would have given her away. Not only her body was missed, but the fastenings, threads, wax-ends, seals, nails as well. Yet something must have been left in the chair, for Col. Olcott was expressly forbidden to touch the chair when he was allowed to go into the cabinet.

Where was the medium? According to Col. Olcott and Dr. Newbrough, she must have been transfigured into the phantom bodies. Frail girls, six-foot Indian warriors, whose weight varied between 50 and 150 pounds, were seen to emerge from the cabinet. Many of the phantoms were recognized as departed relatives and divulged intimate knowledge of the lives of their relations. If they were seized, and they were sometimes, they resolved into Mrs. Compton, whom such an ordeal always rendered ill.

Alexander N. **Aksakof** had a similar experience with the medium Mme. **d'Esperance,** in 1890, at a seance in Gothenburg. While the phantom "Yolande" was outside the cabinet, he slipped his arm through the curtains and felt for the medium's chair. He found it empty. At the same time his hand was flung aside. At the very moment "Yolande" retired into the cabinet, the seance came to an abrupt end, the medium was discovered on her chair in her red dress ("Yolande" was in white) and asked for water.

Through **automatic writing,** Aksakof, who did not tell of his part in the sudden disturbance, was told by "Walter," Mme. d'Esperance's **control,** that if the contribution of the circle was insufficient there might not be enough left of the medium to be visible, that a clairvoyant may still see the body, but in reality there might not be much more in her place than her organs of sense. In such cases a simple touch may do the medium serious injury.

When Aksakof asked what would happen if in such a case he should pull the band of cloth which encircled the medium's waist, whether it would not cut her body in two, he was answered in the affirmative. Mme. d'Esperance summed up her only sensations in this sentence: "I felt as I were empty inside." For details of claimed partial dematerialization of Mme. d'Esperance, see A. Aksakof's book *A Case of Partial Dematerialization of the Body of a Medium* (Boston, 1898).

The whole question of transfiguration is a difficult one, and many psychical researchers regard it with skepticism. Reported cases have been rare and it is unsatisfactory to attempt to assess them long after the event. Only a few cases were cited in *The Facts of Psychic Science* by A. Campbell Holms (1925; 1969).

A good actor or actress should be able to represent a character by facial and postural expression and emotional identification. This does not prove that transfiguration does not occur, however, since it could be a similar mechanism which might be employed also by a spirit entity. The more substantial evidence for materialization suggests that the molding of features could take place through **ectoplasm,** as distinct from manipulation of the medium's muscles and postures. Such transformations might be related to the equally strange phenomenon of **elongation,** reported evidentially of the medium D. D. **Home.**

Another possibly connected phenomenon is the frequently reported transfiguration of saints. The countenance of St. Philip Neri at his devotions was seen to be "shining with a bright light." Eyewitnesses also testified that they saw St. Columba continually surrounded by a dazzling golden light.

These possibilities remain merely speculative, and until there is a substantial amount of present-day phenomena to examine critically, the subject must remain controversial. (See also **Ectoplasm; Materialization;** Queenie **Nixon**)

Transition

Spiritualist term for death, used to emphasize survival of personality after death. Another term sometimes used is "promotion."

Transmutation of the Body

The aim of spiritual **Alchemy**—to restore a human being to the primordial condition of grace, strength, perfection, beauty and physical immortality.

With this in view, dedicated alchemists over the ages labored to discover the secret of the **Elixir of Life,** which mystics believed would, literally, achieve this renewal of youth, and therefore immortality. Endless recipes for this medicine have been given, and some alchemists honestly believed they had attained it, but the great secret still remains hidden from human eyes. (See also **Alchemy**)

Recommended reading:

Atwood, Mary Anne. *Suggestive Inquiry Into the Hermetic Mystery,* London, 1850; new ed. Belfast, Ireland, 1918; Julian Press, 1960

Redgrove, H. Stanley. *Alchemy; Ancient and Modern,* London, 1911; University Books, 1969

Transportation

Alternative term for the claimed phenomenon of **Teleportation,** the paranormal movement of human bodies through closed doors and over a distance. (See **Teleportation**)

Transposition of the Senses

An extraordinary phenomenon, first reported by Tardy de Montravel. In his *Essai sur la Theorie du Somnambulisme Magnetique* (1785), he described how his somnambule could see with the pit of his stomach.

In 1808, in France, Dr. Pététin found the senses of taste, smell and hearing also wandering from the pit of the stomach to the tip of the fingers and of the toes (see his book, *Electricité Animale,* 1808). Since then many similar cases have been recorded, especially with hysterical subjects.

Prof. Cesar **Lombroso** carefully observed the phenomenon with C.S., a young girl, who, near the age of puberty, lost the power of vision with her eyes, but as a compensation she saw with the same degree of acuteness at the point of the nose and the left lobe of the ear. Her sense of smell was transposed under the chin and later to the back of the foot. (See also **Eyeless Sight;** Seeing with the **Stomach**)

Transvection

Term used to indicate the claimed flying through the air of witches, usually on a broomstick, but also on a distaff, a shovel, or an animal.

The term was originally used in a religious sense for the transports of saints, such as St. Joseph of Copertino, of whom some seventy aerial flights were claimed, but from the sixteenth century onwards the flight of witches, considered a diabolical travesty of saintly phenomena, was also described as transvection.

The flight of witches was usually preceded by rubbing with a magical flying ointment. However, if the witches heard the sound of church bells while flying to the Sabbat, they might be grounded.

It is possible that the special ointments used to assist transvection may have had a hallucinatory effect, giving the illusion of traveling through the air. Another theory is that many claims of transvection were actually **astral projection** or **out-of-the-body experiences.** (See also **Levitation; Out-of-the-Body; Teleportation; Witchcraft**)

Tree Ghosts

Indian tree spirits were described by W. Crooke in his book *Religion and Folklore of Northern India* (1926). "These tree ghosts are, it is needless to say, very numerous. Hence most local shrines are constructed under trees; and in one particular tree, the Bira, the jungle tribes of Mirzapur locate Bagheswar, the tiger godling, one of their most dreaded deities. In the Konkan, according to Mr. Campbell, the medium or Bhagat who becomes possessed is called *Jhad,* or 'tree,' apparently because he is a favourite dwelling-place for spirits.

"In the Dakkhin it is believed that the spirit of the pregnant woman of Churel lives in a tree, and the Abors and Padams of East Bengal believe that spirits in trees kidnap children. Many of these tree spirits appear in the folk-tales. Thus, Devadatta worshipped a tree which one day suddenly clave in two and a nymph appeared who introduced him inside the tree, where was a heavenly palace of jewels, in which, reclining on a couch, appeared Vidyatprabha, the maiden daughter of the king of the

Yakshas [supernatural beings]; in another story the mendicant hears inside a tree the Yaksha joking with his wife. So Daphne is turned into a tree to avoid the pursuit of her lover."

Tree of Life, The, and The Tree of the Knowledge of Good and Evil

Two of the trees said to have been planted by God in the Garden of Eden, which were believed by St. Ambrose to be of mystical significance. The former is understood to be the manifestation of God, and the latter of the worldly wisdom to which our human nature is too apt to incline.

Tremblers of the Cevennes

A Protestant caste of convulsionaries, who during the sixteenth century spread themselves from their center in the Cevennes over almost the whole of Germany.

They possessed many points of resemblance with cases of possession (see **Obsession** and **Possession**), and are said to have been insensible to thrusts and blows with pointed sticks and iron bars, as well as to the oppression of great weights. They had visions, communicated with good and evil spirits, and are said to have performed many miraculous cures similar to the apostolic miracles. They made use of very peculiar modes of treatment called *grandes secours* or *secours meurtriers*, which were authenticated by the reports of eyewitnesses and by judicial documents.

Although they were belabored by the strongest men with heavy pieces of wood and bars of iron weighing at least thirty pounds, they complained of no injury, but of experiencing a sensation of pleasure. They also were covered with boards, on which as many as twenty men stood without its being painful to them.

They even bore as many as a hundred blows with a twenty pounds weight, alternately applied to the breast and the stomach with such force that the room trembled, and they begged the blows might be laid on harder, as light ones only increased their sufferings. Indeed only those who laid on the heaviest and most strenuous blows were thanked by their sick. It seemed that it was only when the power of these blows had penetrated to the most vital parts that they experienced real relief.

Joseph Ennemoser, author of *The History of Magic* (2 vols., 1854), explained this insensibility to pain by stating that in his experience "spasmodic convulsions maintain themselves against outward attempts, and even the greatest violence, with almost superhuman strength, without injury to the patient, as has often been observed in young girls and women, where anyone might have almost been induced to believe in supernatural influence. The tension of the muscles increases in power with the insensibility of the power, so that no outward force is equal to it; and when it is attempted to check the paroxysm with force, it gains in intensity, and according to some observers not less psychical than physical. . . . I have observed the same manifestations in children, in Catholics, Protestants and Jews, without the least variation, on which account I consider it to be nothing more than an immense abnormal and inharmonic *lusus naturœ.*" (See also **Convulsionaries of St. Médard**)

Trench, (William) Brinsley Le Poer (1911-)

Distinguished British authority on **UFOs.** He is the 8th Earl of Clancarty and a member of the House of Lords, the upper chamber of the British Parliament, where he introduced a serious debate on UFOs January 18, 1979.

This was an historic occasion, the first on which this subject had been discussed by the British Parliament in the 700 years of its history.

Born September 18, 1911, Trench is the 5th son of the 5th Earl of Clancarty and of Mary Gwatkin. He was educated at Nautical College, Pangbourne. He is at present married to May (widow of Commander Frank M. Beasley).

His interest in UFOs extends over thirty years. After World War II, he noticed many reports of UFO sightings and began to collect press cuttings on the subject. Through a meeting with Desmond **Leslie** (co-author with George **Adamski** of the book *Flying Saucers Have Landed,* 1953), he was encouraged to attend a lecture on flying saucers at Battersea Polytechnic, London.

Eventually Trench, together with Derek Dempster (aviation correspondent of the British newspaper *Daily Express*) and other interested individuals founded a company named Flying Saucer Service Ltd. and commenced publication of a magazine *Flying Saucer Review.* The first number appeared in Spring 1955 with Derek Dempster as editor, followed by Trench in September 1956, then in September 1959 by Waveney Girvan, the original publisher of the book by Leslie and Adamski.

After the death of Girvan, the magazine was edited by Charles Bowen, and after twenty-five years of publication, this remains the first authoritative British publication on the subject of UFOs. It is now included in the House of Lords library.

In 1967, Trench founded Contact International, a worldwide UFO organization with members in thirty-seven different countries. His own books on UFOs (under his name of Brinsley Le Poer Trench) include: *The Sky People* (1960), *Men Among Mankind* (1962), *Forgotten Heritage* (1964), *The Flying Saucer Story* (1966), *Operation Earth* (1969), *The Eternal Subject* (1973), *Secret of the Ages; UFOs From Inside the Earth* (1974; 1977). His recreations are listed as Ufology, travel and walking.

Trent, A. G. (1789-1850)

Pseudonym of philologist and author Richard **Garnett,** assistant keeper of printed books at the British Museum Library, who used this mask for his writings on **astrology,** at a time in which his professional reputation might have suffered if it had been known that he was actively interested in such a borderline subject.

Trevelyan, Sir George (Lowthian) (1906-)

Fourth Baronet, born November 5, 1906, eldest son of the Rt. Hon. Sir C. P. Trevelyan, who was Minister of Education in Ramsay MacDonald's first Labour Government in Britain. Sir George grew up with a background of liberal politics and progressive thought.

He was educated at Sidcot School and at Trinity College, Cambridge, where he read history. He worked as an artist-craftsman with Peter Waals workshops, creating fine furniture, from 1930-31.

From 1932-36, he trained and worked in the F. M. Alexander re-education method, a famous psychophysical system. From 1936-41, he taught at Gordonstoun School and Abinger Hill School. During World War II, he was a Home Guard Training Captain and taught at No. 1 Army College, Newbattle Abbey, from 1945-47. On retirement for the Army, he became principal of Attingham Park, the Shropshire Adult College, where he did pioneering work in the teaching of spiritual knowledge as adult education.

On his retirement in 1971, he founded the **Wrekin Trust,** concerned with dissolving the barriers between science and religion. The Trust has held important conferences on science in relation to mysticism, with papers from such distinguished individuals as Prof. Glen W. Schaefer, Prof. Joscelyn Godwin, and Pir Vilayat Inayat Khan.

Books by Sir George Trevelyan include: *A Vision of the Aquarian Age* (1977), and *The Active Eye in Architecture* (1977).

Trévisan, Bernard of (1406-1490)

The life of this Italian alchemist was a curious and intensely pathetic one. Bent on discovering the **philosopher's stone,** he began at an early age to lavish huge sums of money on the pursuit, but again and again he was baffled, and it was only when old age was stealing upon him, and he had disbursed a veritable fortune, that his labors were crowned with some measure of success.

Bernard of Trévisan, Comte de la Marche, was born at Padua, a town whose inhabitants were famous for erudition throughout many centuries in the Middle Ages. His father was a doctor of medicine, so it is probable that Bernard received his initial training in science at home, and from the age of fourteen he began to devote himself seriously to alchemy, having been lured to the subject by reading the works of the famous Eastern philosophers **Gerber** and **Rhasis.**

Bernard's father was rich, and accordingly, whenever it was known that the young man wanted to experiment in gold seeking, he found himself surrounded by charlatans offering counsel. His very first experiments resulted in his spending upwards of three thousand crowns, the bulk of which sum went into the pockets of the youth's fraudulent advisers.

He was not discouraged, however, and, finding new enthusiasts, and at the same time augmenting his learning by a close study of the writings of Sacrobosco and Rupecissa, he proceeded to make a new series of attempts. But these also proved futile. Once more, the alchemist did no more than enrich his assistants, and in consequence he vowed that henceforth he would continue his researches single-handed.

Bernard now engaged in a long course of sedulous reading, while he also began to give much time to prayer, thinking by this means to gain his desired end. He started fresh experiments, expending on these some six thousand crowns. But again his devotion and extravagance went unrewarded. Year after year went by in this fashion, and eventually Bernard realized that he was past the prime of life, yet had achieved nothing whatsoever.

His bitter disappointment brought on illness, but scarcely was he restored to health before he heard that one Henry, a German priest, had succeeded in creating the philosopher's stone. Thereupon Bernard hastened to Germany, accompanied by various other alchemists. After some difficulty they made the acquaintance of the cleric in question, who told them he would disclose all if they would supply a certain sum of money to procure the necessary tools and materials. They paid as desired, yet having devoted much time to watching the German at work they found themselves no nearer the goal than before.

This last piece of quackery opened Bernard's eyes, and he proclaimed his decision to forsake hermetic philosophy altogether in the future—a decision which was warmly applauded by his relatives, for already his researches had cost a king's ransom. But it soon transpired that the would-be alchemist was quite incapable of clinging to his resolution, and, growing more ardent than ever, he visited Spain, Great Britain, Holland and France, trying in each of these countries to enlarge his stock of learning, and to make the acquaintance of others who were searching like himself.

Eventually he even penetrated to Egypt, Persia and Palestine, while subsequently he travelled in Greece, where he witnessed many alchemist researchers, yet all proved vain, and ultimately Bernard found himself impoverished, and was forced to sell his parental estates.

Being thus without so much as a home, he retired to the Island of Rhodes, intending to live there quietly for the rest of his days, but even here his old passion continued to govern him, and, chancing to make the acquaintance of a priest who knew something of science, the thwarted and ruined alchemist proposed that they should start fresh experiments together.

The cleric professed himself willing to give all the help in his power, so the pair borrowed a large sum of money to allow them to purchase the necessary paraphernalia, and it was here, then, in this secluded island, and while in a literally bankrupt condition, that Bernard made the wonderful discovery with which he is traditionally credited. Perhaps the tradition has little foundation in fact, yet at least the philosopher deserved some reward for his indomitable if foolhardy perseverance, and it is pathetic to recall that his death occurred soon after the day of his claimed triumph.

In contradistinction to many other alchemists, Bernard appears to have loved actual experiments much better than writing about them. It is probable, however, that he was at least partly responsible for an octavo volume published in 1643, *Le Bernard d'Alchmague, cum Bernard Treveso,* while he is commonly credited with another work titled *La Philosophic Naturelle des Metaux.* In this latter work he insists on the necessity of much meditation on the part of the scientist who would create the philosopher's stone, and this rather trite observation is followed by a voluminous alchemistic treatise, most of it sadly obscure, and suggesting that the author was no great expert.

Bernard is often confused with two other individuals—Bernardo Trevisano (1652-1720), a Venetian devoted to languages, mathematics, philosophy and painting, and Bernardinus Trivisanus (1506-1583), who studied arts and medicine at Padua and became professor of logic and medical theory. (See also **Alchemy**)

Triad Group

Nonprofit organization founded by author Whitley **Strieber** to catalog and study "visitor experiences"—claims of contacts with extraterrestrials or other creatures. Follow-up studies are planned, involving mental and physical tests with selected volunteers. The project follows from Strieber's own claimed experiences as detailed in his book *Communion* (1987). (See also Whitley **Strieber**)

Triad Society

An ancient esoteric society of China. The candidate scantily clothed, was brought into a dark room by two members, who led him to the president, before whom he knelt. He was given a living cock and a knife, and in this posture he took a complicated oath to assist his brethren in any emergency, even at the risk of his life. He then cut off the head of the cock, and mingled it with his own, the three assisting individuals adding some of their own blood.

After being warned that death would be his punishment should he divulge the secrets of the society, he was initiated into them, and entrusted with the signs of recognition which were in triads. For example, a member had to lift any object with three fingers only. This society, originally altruistic, later became political.

Various Triad societies were recently revived in Hong Kong to operate criminal extortion and protection rackets. Cinema protection was a speciality of these gangs, and usually involved Triad members being employed as ushers, ticket-sellers or sub-managers.

Financial operations involve magic numerals, symbolic of the particular Triad society. For example, protection money may be demanded in sums relating to the figure 8, which is the lower half of the Chinese character *Hung,* used by some Triad societies. The numeral 3 denotes Heaven, Earth and Man, which the word Triad originally used as a mystical symbol.

In the 1970s, the widespread operations of Triad racketeers in Hong Kong resulted in the publication of a police manual *Triad Societies of Hong Kong,* restricted to police personnel.

In 1976, the Triad societies spread their operations to Britain, where cities like Birmingham, Bristol, Liverpool, Portsmouth, Southampton, Manchester and London with large Chinese populations could be victimized. Triad protection rackets even operate in the West End cinemas and clubs of London, where vicious fights have been reported involving Chinese thugs with meat-cleavers.

The protection rate for a good class Chinese restaurant in London can be as high as £100 per week. A top muscle-man in the Shing Wo Triad is known as "426," a numerical symbol for "Red stick" or "enforcer." In some British cities, the protection racket is being partially reduced by closing down illegal gambling clubs where Triad members meet or convert their funds.

Triangles (Network)

Quarterly publication of the Lucis Trust, formed to propagate the teachings of Alice **Bailey** (1880-1949), former Theosophist who founded her own Arcane School.

Triangles is also a term applied to a linking of individuals who employ constructive thought daily in groups of three, invoking "the energies of light and goodwill," part of the program of **World Goodwill.** The bulletin *Triangles* is obtainable in ten languages, published by Lucis Trust, 866 United Nations Plaza, New York, N.Y. 10017. British address: Suite 54, 3 Whitehall Court, London, SWIA 2EF, England.

Trintzius, Rene (1898-1953)

Writer and unorthodox healer. Born July 29, 1898 at Rouen, France, he became a novelist and playwright, and wrote biographical studies of Rousseau, Charlotte Corday, Jacques Cazotte and John Law.

His books included: *L'Astrologie à la portée de tous* (Astrology for All), *Lisez dans vos mains* (Palmistry), *La Magie a-t-elle raison* (Is Magic on the Right Lines?), *Les Guérisons supranormales* (Supernormal Cures), *Les Pouvoirs inconnus de l'Homme* (Man's Unknown Powers), *La Voyance et ses supports* (Clairvoyance and Its Supports), *Au seuil du Monde invisible* (On the Threshold of the Invisible World). He died in 1953.

Triskaidekaphobia Illuminatus Society

Founded in 1984, to deal with the common superstition about the unluckiness of the number 13. Membership comprises individuals who believe the number 13 has the ability to affect the balance of world power and political structure through the Illuminati (persons who are or who claim to be unusually enlightened).

The Society seeks to isolate seemingly unconnected events caused by the numerical forces inherent in the number 13, correlate the meanings of these events, and develop solutions and strategies.

It promotes the organization of Illuminated task forces for the elimination of Triskaidekaphobia (fear of the number 13) from society. It plans to develop a think tank. It bestows an annual award for the single most significant contribution concerning the power of the number 13, maintains a collection of newspaper and magazine clippings and videotapes from television shows. Publications: *The 13th Illuminated Stratum* Newsletter, 2-5 per year; *Thirteen* (editorial report), irregular intervals; *Fear to Feel the Illuminated Network of 13 Concealed Phantoms* (book). Address: P.O. Box 25129, Washington, D.C. 20007.

Trithemius (Johann) (1462-1519)

Reputed alchemist and magician. The son of a German vine grower named Heidenberg, he received his Latinized name from Trittenheim, a village in the electorate of Trêves, where he was born. He might reasonably be included among those earnest and enthusiastic souls who persevered in the pursuit of knowledge under difficulties, for he lost his father when one year old, and his mother, marrying a second time, had no love for the offspring of her first marriage.

The young Johann was ill-fed, ill-clothed, and overworked. He toiled all day in the vineyards, and at night devoted himself to the acquisition of knowledge. He stole away from his miserable home, and read whatever books he could beg or borrow, by the light of the moon. As his mind expanded, he became aware of the vast stores of learning to which his circumstances denied him access. He became discontented with the few crumbs of knowledge he had picked up with such difficulty. Extorting his small share of the patrimony bequeathed by his father, he wandered away to Trêves, entered himself a student of its celebrated University, and assumed the name of Trithemius.

His progress was now as rapid as his aspirations and the keenness of his intellect. At the age of twenty, he had acquired the reputation of a scholar, a reputation which was of great advantage in the fifteenth century. He now desired to see once more the mother whom he still loved, even although she had not treated him well, and in the winter of 1482 he left the cloistered shade of Trêves on a solitary journey to Trittenheim.

It was a dark day, ending in a gloomy, fast snowing night, and the student, on arriving at Spanheim, found the roads impassable. He sought refuge in a neighboring Benedictine monastery. There the weather imprisoned him for several days. The imprisonment proved so much to his liking that he voluntarily took the monastic vows, and retired from the world.

In the course of two years, he was elected abbot, and devoting himself to the repair and improvement of the monastery, he gained the love and reverence of the brotherhood, whom he inspired with his own love of learning.

But after a rule of twenty-one years, the monks forgot all his benefits, and remembered only the severity of his discipline. They broke out in revolt, and elected another abbot. The deposed Trithemius quitted Spanheim, and wandered from place to place, until finally elected abbot of St. James of Wurzburg, where he died in 1519.

His fame as a magician and alchemist rests on very innocent foundations. He devised a species of shorthand called *steoganographia,* which the ignorant stigmatized as a Kabalistic and necromantic writing, concealing the most fearful secrets. He wrote a treatise on the subject, another upon the supposed administration of the world by its guardian angels, a revival of the good and evil geniuses of the ancients, which the astrologer William **Lilly** translated into English in 1647. He wrote a third book on **Geomancy,** or divination by means of lines and circles on the ground, a fourth upon Sorcery, and a fifth on **Alchemy.**

In his work on Sorcery, he made an early mention of the popular story of Dr. Faustus (see **Faust**), and recorded the torments he himself occasionally suffered from the malice of a spirit named Hudekin.

He was said to have gratified the Emperor Maximilian with a vision of his deceased wife, the beautiful Mary of Burgundy, and was reputed to have defrayed the expenses of his monastic establishment at Spanheim by resources which mastery of the **philosopher's stone** put at his disposal. His writings show him to have been an amiable and credulous enthusiast with a sincere and ardent passion for knowledge. (See also **Alchemy; Faust; Philosopher's Stone**)

Trivah

Among the Dayaks of Borneo, the *trivah,* or feast of the dead used to be celebrated after a death had taken place. A panel containing a representation of *Tempon-teloris* (ship of the dead) was generally set up at the *trivah,* and sacrifices of fowls offered to it. Until the *trivah* had been celebrated, the souls were unable to reach the golden shores. (See also **Book of the Dead; Egypt; Temponteloris**)

Trollope, Thomas Adolphus (1810-1892)

British novelist, author of works of travel, biography and history, frequent investigator of the phenomena of the great medium D. D. **Home.**

In 1855, Trollope took a firm stand against Sir David Brewster when the latter published a denial of having witnessed genuine psychic phenomena with Home which he had admitted at the seance.

Eight years later, in a letter to *The Athenaeum* (April 1863), Trollope testified to "having seen and felt physical facts, wholly and utterly inexplicable, as I believe, by any known and generally received physical laws. I unhesitatingly reject the theory which considers such facts to be produced by means familiar to the best professors of legerdemain."

The report of the Committee of the **London Dialectical Society** contained his written testimony on a remarkable **apport** of jonquil flowers, through the mediumship of Mrs. **Guppy,** in his own home at Florence, Italy, under test conditions.

Tromp, S(olco) W(alie) (1909-1983)

Geophysicist, director of the Bioclimatological Research Center, Leiden, Netherlands, and writer on parapsychological subjects. Born March 9, 1909 at Djarkarta, Indonesia, he studied at University of Leiden (Ph.D. geology, 1932). In 1934 he married Mieke de Blauw.

After military service from 1932-33, he was a field geologist for oil companies in Indonesia and Egypt from 1933-40, advisor on oil exploration to Turkish Government from 1940-43, director of economic warfare, Netherlands Army (Australia and Indonesia) from 1943-45, physiological research, Netherlands in 1946, professor of geology at Fuad University, Cairo from 1947-50, geological consultant to U.N. Technical Assistance Programe, Near East, Afghanistan, Central America from 1950-54, geological consultant to Government of Afghanistan from 1954-56, director of Bioclimatological Research Center from 1955 onwards, Secretary-general of International Society of Biometeorology, secretary of Netherlands Society of Medical Geography and Comparative Pathology.

In addition to his writings on geological subjects, Dr. Tromp specialized in the study of phenomena connected with **Dowsing** (water divining). His books include: *Psychical Physics* (1949), *Dowsing and Science* (1950), *Fundamental Principles of Psychical Physics* (1952). His articles in the *Dutch Journal of Parapsychology* included: 'First Report on Experiments Concerning the Influence of Variations in the Strength of the Magnetic Field on Muscular Contraction' (January 1947), 'The Problem of the Possible Influence of Dowsing Zones on the Health of Men' (November 1948).

He died March 17, 1983, in the Netherlands.

Tron, Giorgio (1884-1963)

Italian physician who studied parapsychology. Born September 12, 1884 in Turin, Italy, he studied at University of Pavia (M.D. 1910, teaching diploma in hygiene 1924).

He was staff doctor at Hospital for Infectious Diseases, Milan from 1915-26, hygiene officer at Milan from 1927-38, director of Istituto Sieroterapico Italiano, Naples from 1940-53, member of the Italian Medical Society, Società Italiana di Parapsicologia (secretary 1955-59).

In addition to his writings on medical subjects, Dr. Tron contributed articles to the *Bulletin of the Società Italiana di Parapsicologia.* He also wrote the chapter on Unorthodox Healing in the book *Studia Parapsychologica* (1956) and on physical mediumistic phenomena in *Nuovi Problemi di Metapsichica* (1953).

He died February 5, 1963 in Rome.

True Black Magic, Book of the

A **grimoire** (manual of occult magic) which is simply an adapted version of the famous **Key of Solomon the King.** (See also **Ceremonial Magic**)

True World Order

Movement started by Swami **Vishnudevananda,** disciple of the late Swami **Sivananda** of Rishikesh, India, and a world famous exponent of **Hatha Yoga.**

T.W.O. is dedicated to promoting world peace and understanding, good health and happiness through yoga harmony, involving vegetarian diet. For information: Sivananda Yoga Vedanta Center, 8th Avenue, Val Morin, Quebec, Canada.

Trumpet

A simple funnel-shaped device of cardboard aluminum or other lightweight material used at Spiritualist seances for the manifestation of **direct voice** communication from spirits. Jonathan **Koons,** the nineteenth-century American farmer medium, appears to have been the first to use it.

It is believed to serve as a condenser of psychic energy, and to increase the volume of the spirit voice. Weak or inexperienced spirits often have to make use of the trumpet. It is seldom necessary for a spirit **guide.** Some mediums wet the trumpet with water, in the belief that this facilitates the phenomena.

The trumpet is usually coated with a marking of luminous paint. At dark room seances, the trumpet is seen to be levitated when there is sufficient psychic force, and to move around the circle, conveying personal messages to individual sitters. Unfortunately the circumstances are conducive to fraud, and many instances of fraud have been exposed.

As a safeguard, psychical researchers have devised techniques and even apparatus to attempt to exclude the possibility of a medium employing ventriloquism in producing voices ostensibly from the trumpet. One method is to fill the medium's mouth with water, under control conditions. During the investigation of the controversial medium "Margery" (see Mina Stinson **Crandon**), Dr. Mark Richardson of Boston invented a "Voice Control Machine" (see **direct voice**).

However, attempts to validate or disprove the reality of direct voice communication at seances by such methods present many problems, and it is often more productive to assess the communications on their content rather than the method of manifestation. (See also **Direct Voice**)

The American direct voice medium Mrs. Elizabeth **Blake** used a double trumpet with a saucer-shaped extension at the small ends to be placed on the ear of the sitter and on her own.

An improved trumpet, called the "Shastaphone," was developed through a psychic communication in Australia, but does not appear to have been widely used.

Truth Journal

Publication of the **Center of Spiritual Awareness,** concerned with the personal relationship between the individual soul and God; also with esoteric and occult studies. Address: P.O. Box 7, Lakemount, Georgia 30552.

Truzzi, Marcello (1935-)

Contemporary sociologist and scholar of occultism, editor of *The Zetetic* (formerly *Explorations*), a Newsletter of Academic Research into Occultism.

He was born September 6, 1935, in Copenhagen, Denmark, educated at Florida State University (B.A., 1957), University of Florida (M.A., 1962), Cornell University (Ph.D., 1970). He was instructor in sociology, University of South Florida, Tampa, 1966-68; assistant professor of sociology, University of Michigan, Ann Arbor, 1968-71; associate professor of sociology, New College, Sarasota, Florida, 1971 onwards; visiting instructor in sociology, Cornell University, summers 1965, 1968, 1971. He served in the U.S. Army, 1958-60. His memberships include American Sociological Association, American Psychological Association, American Association for the Advancement of Science.

His publications include: *Sociology and Everyday Life* (1968), *Cauldron Cookery; An Authentic Guide for Coven Connoisseurs* (1969), (ed.) *Sociology; The Classic Statements* (1971), (with D. M. Petersen, ed.) *Criminal Life* (1972), (with P. K. Manning, ed.) *Youth and Sociology* (1972). He has contributed articles and reviews to various journals of psychology, sociology and folklore, and edited a special issue of *Journal of Popular Culture* (vol. 6, No. 3, 1972). He was associate editor of *American Sociologist,* 1968-70, editor of *Subterranean Sociology Newsletter,* 1967 onwards.

Tsitsith, The

An article of Jewish religious apparel, the "fringe" or tassels attached to the outer garment, endowed with talismanic properties. In modern times, the fringe has survived in the praying shawl named *talith* or in a garment worn on the chest.

A sentence in the *Talmud* runs thus: "Whoever has the tephillin bound to his head and arm, and the *tsitsith* thrown over his garments . . . is protected from sin." (See also **Tephillin**)

Tubby, Gertrude Ogden (1878- ?)

Teacher, author and psychic researcher. Born June 18, 1878 at Kingston on Hudson, New York, she studied at Smith College, Northampton, Massachusetts (B.S. 1902).

She was a photographic laboratory technician from 1897-98, chemistry laboratory assistant at Smith College from 1899-1900, research secretary from 1902-07, special research assistant to James H. **Hyslop** (president of the American Society for Psychic Research) from 1907-20, secretary, ASPR, associate editor of ASPR *Journal* from 1920-24.

As a result of working as an assistant to Dr. Hyslop, Miss Tubby investigated a wide range of psychic phenomena, including mediumship, telepathy, clairvoyance, psychokinesis, and survival.

After the death of Hyslop, Miss Tubby collected from various mediums communications apparently from him, some of which had reference to each other, although manifested independently. These messages are discussed in Miss Tubby's book *James H. Hyslop—X, His Book* (1929). She also published the book *Psychics and Mediums, A Handbook for Students* (1935; British ed. 1938), as well as various articles in the *Journal* and *Proceedings* of the American Society for Psychical Research.

Tulku

Term for a Tibetan entity recognized as such in a present incarnation. Tibetan Buddhism teaches that highly evolved individuals become spiritually liberated by abandoning the sense of ego or separate identity, but the spiritual forces comprising such an individual may still elect to be reborn for the benefit of other people, although ultimately they too are only illusory manifestations sustained by the sense of ego.

Traditional tests exist for the identification of **tulkus,** especially in the case of the Dalai Lama. Other contemporaries **tulkus** include **Chogyam Trungpa,** author of the book *Born in Tibet* (London, 1966) and **Tarthang Tulku,** popularly known by his disciples as "Rinpoche," an honorific meaning "precious master."

Tulpa

Tibetan term for a phantom form generated by mental concentration. In her book *With Mystics & Magicians in Tibet* (1931 etc.), Alexandra David-Neel described how she herself created a *tulpa* of a fat jolly monk, who became a recognizable member of her party on a journey. However, in the course of time this phantom took on an independent life of its own, changing its character to a sly malignancy. Mdme. David-Neel had great difficulty in dissolving this phantom, which, she claimed, took six months of intense concentration.

A *tulpa* may also be a double of the magician who creates it, employed for protective purposes by appearing instead of its creator.

A *tulpa* should be distinguished from a *tulku,* which is either the reincarnation of a saintly individual or the incarnation of a non-human entity, such as a god, demon, or fairy.

As a highly respected and reliable informant, Mdme. David-Neel's accounts of *tulpas* are of special interest, throwing light on the possible mechanism of **ghosts** and **apparitions** generally, as well as such phenomena as **fairies.** (See also **Tulku**)

Tumah

According to the **Kabala,** physical or moral uncleanness. The latter is divided into three main divisions—idolatry, murder, and immorality. Sin, states the same authority, not only rendered imperfect man himself, but also affected the whole of nature, even to the sphere of angels, and the Divinity.

In physical uncleanness, there is a coarser and a more subtle form. The latter causes a dimness in the soul which is most keenly felt by those who are nearest to sacred things. Organic things which come into contact with the human body are more liable to the *Tumah* than remoter things.

The human corpse is more unclean than that of the lower animals, because its more complex nature involves a more repulsive decay. (See also **Kabala**)

Tumo

The Tibetan mystical practice of generating bodily heat, so that a hermit may spend winter naked in a cave amidst snow and freezing temperatures at an altitude between 11,000 and 18,000 feet. Adepts have distinguished various types of *tumo:* exoteric, which arises spontaneously in the course of mystical raptures; esoteric, that keeps a hermit comfortable on a snowy hill; mystic, which experiences a paradisiac bliss.

According to Madame Alexandra David-Neel in her book *With Mystics and Magicians in Tibet* (1931 etc.), *tumo* "is also the subtle fire with which warms the generative fluid and drives the energy in it, till it runs all over the body along the subtle channels . . ." In this respect it is clearly related to the ancient Hindu teachings of the nature of *Kundalini* energy, which may be aroused in subtle physical channels, and which is also related to the energy of sexual activity, and which may produce either heat or cold in the body. (See also **Kundalini; Tibet**)

Tunisa

Burmese diviners. (See **Burma**)

Turin Shroud

The most sacred relic of Christendom, believed for centuries to be the shroud in which Jesus was wrapped after crucifixion.

The four evangelists of the New Testament recorded the existence of a linen cloth used at the burial of Christ. There is no record of it after that until about 570 A.D. when a pilgrim reported that it was kept in a monastery by the river Jordan. In 670 A.D. the French bishop Arculph, returning from a pilgrimage to Jerusalem, was shipwrecked on the coast of Scotland and traveled to a monastery on the island of Iona. Here he said he had seen the Shroud and been allowed to kiss it.

Subsequent references were made by the Venerable Bede, St. Willibald, St. John Damascene and the Emperor Baldwin. In 1284, Robert de Clari, chronicler of the Fourth Crusade, described the triumphant entry of Crusaders into Constantinople and mentioned the monastery of Lady St. Mary of the Blachernes, in which the Shroud was kept. Nothing is known of its subsequent history until it turned up in the church of Lirey, Troyes, France, during the fourteenth century.

Between 1353 and 1356, the Shroud was placed in a small wooden church at Lirey by Geoffrey de Charny, Lord of Lirey, but exhibition of the relic aroused opposition from Henry of Poitiers, Bishop of Troyes. Many years later, the Lord of Lirey's son (Geoffrey II) obtained permission to exhibit the Shroud in 1389, but Henry's successor as Bishop of Troyes, Pierre d'Arcis, objected most strenuously.

In a statement to the Avignon Pope Clement VII, he complained that the exhibition was not for devotion, but for monetary gain, and that the relic was a forgery, "a certain cloth cunningly painted, upon which by clever sleight of hand was depicted the twofold image of one man, that is to say the back and the front [the canons at Lirey] falsely declaring and pretending that this was the actual shroud in which our Saviour Jesus Christ was enfolded in the tomb." D'Arcis claimed that Henry of Poitiers, thirty years earlier, after "diligent inquiry and examination" had established that the Shroud had been "cunningly painted, the truth being attested by the artist . . . that it was a work of human skill and not miraculously wrought . . . " and that the first exhibition by Geoffrey's father had been prohibited.

Meanwhile, however, Geoffrey's widow had remarried Aymon of Geneva, who had ecclesiastical influence with Pope Clement, and the prohibition was bypassed, much to the anger of d'Arcis, hence his complaint in 1389.

Pope Clement resolved the matter by declaring that Geoffrey II could continue exhibiting the Shroud provided that it was always stated that it was only "a figure or representation" of Christ's cloth, and that d'Arcis must keep silence in the matter under pain of excommunication.

This affair has often been revived as "proof" that the Shroud was a forgery, but the accusations of d'Arcis were never proved, and the original campaign against the genuineness of the Shroud had started on the somewhat flimsy grounds that if such a cloth imprinted with an image of Jesus Christ had really existed, it would have been mentioned in the Gospels, and that the exhibition at Lirey was all part of a plot to hire persons for pretended miracles of healing. The statement that diligent inquiry had revealed a cunning artist remains unconvincing, since the artist was never named or punished, although this would have been real proof of fraud. There is no record of any examination of an artist, nor indictment of any persons for pretending miracles, and such hearsay claims only underline a typical example of ecclesiastical rivalry and politicking.

After the death of Geoffrey II, his widow Margaret claimed that the relic had only been loaned to Lirey by her grandfather, but she was eventually obliged to give it up.

In 1452, it passed into the keeping of the Duke of Savoy. In 1532 it was kept in the sacristy of Sainte Chappelle, France, where it was nearly destroyed in a fire, then taken to the monastery of St. Clair where it was patched by nuns. It was brought to the Saint Charles Borromeo in Turin, Italy in 1578, and has since remained the property of the ruling House of Savoy from which came the kings of Italy. It was exhibited annually until it was feared that frequent handling might damage it. By the end of the nineteenth century it was exhibited rarely on very special occasions.

The Shroud had vague markings indicating the outlines of a body, but these took on a special significance at the end of the nineteenth century. Modern interest in the shroud dates from 1898, when Secundo Pia obtained permission to photograph it for the first time, and discovered that his negative plate revealed a perfect image of a noble and majestic face with forehead wounds suggesting a crown of thorns, and a body with wounds in the hands and side with marks of scourging.

The supposition is that in some unknown way, emanations from the body laid in the Shroud reacted with the spices used for burial in such a way as to cause an image on the cloth, rather like a photographic negative. Although the shroud had been venerated for centuries, nobody had formerly realized that the markings might be more revealing than supposed. Pia's negative plate showed a *positive picture*, virtually a full-length photograph of the occupant of the Shroud.

The publication of Pia's negative caused great excitement, and led to a scientific investigation by Dr. Paul Vignon, Professor of Biology at the Institut Catholique in Paris. With his co-worker Dr. Yves Delage he presented his findings, favorable to the authenticity of the shroud, to the French Academy of Science. The collaboration was a strange one, since Delage was an agnostic and Vignon a Catholic. Since then, the shroud received increased attention and scholarship, and Vatican experts spent some years studying and verifying historical documents connected with it.

On September 6, 1936, Pope Pius XI made the following pronouncement: "These are the images of the Divine Redeemer. We might say they are the most beautiful, most moving and dearest we can imagine."

The name "**Sindonology**" has been given to studies of the Shroud, and in 1939 the first Sindonological Congress was held in Turin. The Centro Internazionale di Sindonologia was created, drawing upon the highest academic, scientific and ecclesiastical authorities.

In August 1978, the Holy Shroud was publicly exhibited again in the Cathedral of Turin, Italy. Because Turin has been a flashpoint for Red Brigade terrorism, special precautions were taken to protect the relic. In addition to extra police protection, the Shroud itself was housed in a special display case with bulletproof glass. Archbishop Anastasio Ballestrero of Turin insisted that the Shroud should not be the subject of any form of commercialism, and the cost of the new protective case was born by a Turin exposition fund launched in the U.S.

In October 1978, at the end of the exposition, a special Shroud Congress was held in Turin attended by scientists from around the world. Advanced techniques of image analysis were discussed, including infra-red photography, photomicrography, high contrast photography, X-ray fluorescence, radiographic examination and carbon dating.

Unfortunately much of the scientific analysis and discussion resulted in controversy and confusion. Many issues were hotly debated, such as whether the amount of iron oxide on the Shroud indicated genuine blood stains or artistic pigment. The main issue of dating the Shroud was delayed through reluctance of the authorities to permit destruction of a sample piece of the material for carbon dating. Many of the arguments and counter-arguments are complex, involving scientific methods and interpretations that are difficult for a layman to follow. For an excellent presentation of scientific views for and against the authenticity of the Shroud, see the book *The Image on the Shroud* by H. David Sox (1981).

A significant breakthrough in the study of the Shroud occurred in early 1987, when Pope John Paul II finally approved a plan to test fragments of the cloth in laboratories for radio-carbon content. Tests had been scheduled to begin in 1986, but had been halted at the last minute by the Bishop of Turin.

Three major laboratories—in Switzerland, the U.S., and Britain—were involved in these carbon-14 dating tests.

Three other institutions were involved in statistical analysis of the results of tests, which included scientific controls using pieces of linen from known sources, ancient and modern. These included fragments of medieval cloth, a specimen from ancient Egypt, as well as modern cloth. The scientists involved did not know which cloth they were being provided with for testing until the results were correlated by the British Museum Research Laboratory and evaluated at the Vatican in Rome.

Prof. Edward Hall, of the Research Laboratory for Archaeology and Art at Oxford University, Britain, was one of the scientists involved in testing, using an Accelerator Mass Spectrometer, generating a charge of two million volts. This massive new tool for radio carbon dating is said to have influenced the Vatican decision to go ahead with the tests on actual fragments of the Turin Shroud. Earlier apparatus would have required the destruction of a sample about the size of a pocket handkerchief, whereas the new machine required a sample of only about a quarter of an inch.

In a report by Pearson Phillips in *The Times,* London, (April 15, 1987), Prof. Hall was quoted as stating: "If we get a medieval dating then we shall know it is a forgery and we can relax and forget the whole business. Although there will still be a mystery about how anyone in medieval times could have produced such a complex and effective fraud." Prof. Hall took an agnostic viewpoint, stating: "My view of Christ as a historical individual is that he was obviously a powerful personality. I suppose it is possible that, in some way we do not currently fully understand, some kind of impression from him was transferred to the shroud. But if we produce a carbon date around the start of the first century AD, the fat will really be in the fire. As a scientist, I would then find it difficult to dismiss the Shroud's authenticity."

In the event, an official report on October 13, 1988, revealed that the three laboratories in Oxford, Zürich, and Arizona, had independently carbon dated the cloth fragments as medieval, and not from the time of Jesus Christ! There was close agreement on the possible dates, giving an estimated span of circa 1260-1390. For most skeptics, this established once and for all that the Shroud was a medieval forgery.

Die-hard believers in the authenticity of the Shroud either questioned the accuracy of the scientific evidence or propounded fantastic theories to account for the dating of the cloth, e.g. that the image was formed by a burst of divine radiant energy that somehow altered the texture of the cloth.

It has to be admitted that the close concurrence in dating of three independent scientific laboratories, with the best and most accurate apparatus, cannot be dismissed lightly. The normal margin of error in carbon dating is considerated as about 100 years either way. But it is unlikely that these tests can resolve the enigma of the Shroud.

Scientific tests of any kind sometimes overlook anomalies revealed by later researches. Controversies still rage over the merits of vitamin therapies or polyunsaturated fats diets. "Wonder drugs" are hailed, and quickly found to be wanting in the light of later tests. In the case of the dating of the Shroud, there is no reason to doubt the good faith and accuracy of reputable scientific laboratories, but it is well to remember that the centuries-old Shroud has been through many vicissitudes, and we are dealing with minute fragments of material.

In 1532, when the Shroud was kept in a silver casket at the church of Sainte Chappelle in Chambery, France, a fire broke out in the sacristy, melting drops of silver which fell on the Shroud, burning away through folds in the cloth. In 1534, the burns on the cloth were patched by nuns at the monastery of St. Clair. The Shroud has also suffered damp stains, and may have been washed or cleaned with oil at some time. Could the samples tested for carbon dating have been contaminated with threads or solutions from the later history of the Shroud?

Moreover carbon dating, accurate or misleading, cannot explain the extraordinary and awe-inspiring character of the image on the Shroud as disclosed by the camera negative of Secondo Pia in 1898. There are no apparent brush marks, and other theories of production of the marks, however ingenious, hardly do justice to the beauty and accuracy of the icon. Commonsense suggests that even a medieval forger of genius would be unlikely to have the prescience to produce a perfect and noble image *in negative.* What the pilgrims of that period in an out-of-the-way French district would surely have expected to see would have been some stylized rudimentary positive image, more like the icons in stained glass windows or the paintings in churches.

Dr. Robert Otlet, of the Atomic Energy Research Establishment at Harwell, had hoped that his famous laboratory would be included in the carbon dating tests, and later commented: "It is most unfortunate—entirely unnecessary when you put the amount of material to be taken in context. It will lead to a result which will be wide open to criticism and sadly will not be seen as definitive."

It is clear that the riddle of the Shroud has not been finally answered. True believers in its authenticity will ignore or question the carbon dating evidence, while hardened skeptics will continue to express their faith in the infallibility of modern science. (See also **Sindonology; Veronica**)

Recommended reading:

Barnes, Arthur Stapylton. *The Holy Shroud of Turin,* Burns Oates & Washbourne, London, 1934

Heller, John H. *Report on the Shroud of Turin,* Houghton Mifflin (paperback), 1983

Reban, John. *Inquest on Jesus Christ,* Leslie Frewin, London, 1967

Rinaldi, Peter M. *The Man in the Shroud,* Vantage Press, 1972; Futura paperback, London, 1974; retitled *It Is The Lord; A Study of the Shroud of Christ,* Warner paperback, 1973

Sox, H. David. *The Image on the Shroud; Is the Turin Shroud a Forgery?* Unwin paperback, London, 1981

Sox. H. David. *The Shroud Unmasked; Uncovering the Greatest Forgery of All Time,* Lamp Press, Basingstoke, U.K. (paperback), 1988

Vignon, Paul. *The Shroud of Christ,* Constable, London, 1902; University Books, 1970

Walsh, John. *The Shroud,* W. H. Allen, London, 1964

Wilson, Ian. *The Turin Shroud,* Gollancz, London, 1978

Wuenschel, Edward. *Self-Portrait of Christ,* Esopus, New York, 1954

Turner, Ann

Nineteenth-century English reputed witch. (See **England**)

Turner, M(alcolm) E(lijah) (1929-)

Biometrician who has experimented in the field of parapsychology. Born May 27, 1929 in Atlanta, Georgia, he studied at Duke University (B.A. 1952),

North Carolina State College (M.S. experimental statistics 1955, Ph.D. 1959). In 1948 he married Ann Clay Bowers.

He was a research assistant at Duke University from 1950-51, fellow of University of North Carolina from 1953-55, senior research associate (1955), assistant professor (1955-58) at University of Cincinnati, assistant statistician at North Carolina State College (1957-58), associate professor of Medical College of Virginia from 1958-63, professor at Emory University, Atlanta from 1963 onwards. He is a member of the Biometric Society, American Statistical Association, Institute of Mathematical Statistics, Mathematical Association of America, American Association for the Advancement of Science, Society for Industrial and Applied Mathematics.

In the field of parapsychology, Dr. Turner has experimented in model-building and statistical inference. He collaborated with Ann B. **Turner** and Elizabeth **McMahan** in experiments relating to the effects of time and distance of success of card-calling. He worked with Dr. Karlis **Osis** on experiments in ESP over distance and developed a statistical model for evaluation of the problem of ESP over spatial distances. With Dr. Osis he published 'Distance and ESP; A Transcontinental Experiment' (*Proceedings* of the American Society for Psychical Research, vol. 27, 1968); and with Dr. Osis & M. L. Carlson, 'ESP Over Distance; Research on the ESP Channel' (*Journal* of the ASPR, vol. 65, 1971).

Turquoise

A number of ancient beliefs surround this precious stone. J. B. **Van Helmont** stated: "Whoever wears a Turquoise, so that it, or its gold-setting touches the skin, may fall from any height; and the stone attracts to itself the whole force of the blow, so that it cracks, and the person is safe."

Medieval writers stated that the turquoise grew paler if its owner sickened, lost color entirely at his death, but recovered color when placed upon the finger of a new and healthy owner. It was believed to be a good amulet for preventing accidents to horsemen and to prevent them from becoming tired. Another belief was that the turquoise moved itself when any danger threatened its possessor.

The turquoise originally came from Persia, where it would sometimes be engraved with a motto or a verse from the *Koran*. The stone was also prized by North American Indian medicine men.

Turvey, Vincent Newton (1873-1912)

British seer of remarkable psychic gifts, who refused to be classified as a medium since he was never entranced or controlled, did not develop his gifts (which were born with him), did not function by becoming mentally passive but by mental activity, and instead of being controlled was able to control others, similarly to a spirit.

He saw phantoms as a child. One such experience was a vision of his father while singing in church as a choir boy. The father died at the same time three hundred miles away. At the age of ten Vincent lost his visionary faculty. When he left school he studied engineering.

In 1902, while engaged in his profession, his health broke down completely, and he suffered a serious accident. It was nothing short of a miracle that he remained alive. For many years, he lived practically alone in his garden, in a tent, and spent ten or twelve hours a day reading, writing or meditating on occult things.

The result is best described in his own words: "After forty thousand hours on one topic, I think I can claim to be, in a small way, a yogi. My illness and my meditation have produced, or awakened, my psychic gifts; and all the Yoga, Vedic and Gnostic teachings which I now read (and much more besides) seem to be familiar to me. I seem to have evolved them in my own mind, during meditation from a sort of 'memory.' In fact I often pitch a book away and say 'Why, I know all this,' and yet I had not read it before. Many Eastern forms come and argue with me, and, of course, I learn from them; but they do not come to teach me as a guru would. They come 'to help you to teach yourself in this present life.' In a word, I am 'Self-taught'; but I owe a great deal to Eastern forms, many of whom visit me and give tests of their identity by talking to me in their own languages; and I get the messages translated."

It is an open question whether the psychic gifts of his childhood would have returned to Vincent Turvey without his prolonged illness. He paid dearly for them. Yet mentally there was nothing abnormal about him. He was a quick-witted business man with a well-trained, disciplined mind.

The Bournemouth Society of Spiritualists, of which he was vice-president from 1908, gave demonstrations of clairvoyance at the end of their Sunday service. Turvey announced from the platform the presence of spirit visitors before the service was over, so that those who recognized them could stay for a closer communion.

Often these spirits came to him days before and impressed their appearance on his mind. One such visitant appeared on that side of his bed which was only a few inches from the wall so that the visitor was partly in the wall. "Sometimes," wrote Turvey, "they will come at dead of night and wake me up; at other times they will come when I am alone in the tent in my garden, or in my drawing room, or, what is still more obliging of them, they will look in while passing when I have earthly visitors with me who can bear witness that I described the visitants to them, before I went to the hall!"

His book *The Beginnings of Seership* (1911) is a record of remarkable experiences in long-distance **clairvoyance,** in **out-of-the-body** traveling, **predictions,** spirit seeing and the curious phase of clairvoyance which he termed **"phone-voyance."** A voucher was printed in the book in which four men testified to having inspected the original documents and controlled their faithful reproduction. The famous journalist and Spiritualist W. T. **Stead,** in his preface, declared "Mr. Turvey is a man of truth, that his testimony is trustworthy evidence as to what is within his own knowledge, and that the witnesses' letters which are held for the scrutiny of inquirers are the genuine epistles of credible witnesses."

Turvey's prophecies were numerous and entailed physical suffering as he experienced a **community of sensation** with the victims of the accident foreseen. Many proofs of his foresight were available, as it was his habit to write out his visions in sealed letters as the time of the occurrence and send them to the Spiritualist journal *Light* for future opening.

"The signed evidence which I possess," he wrote in his book, "shows that out of one hundred and sixty descriptions given in public one hundred and forty-four were recognized as correct, that out of 300 in private, 96 per cent were correct, and that of prophecies, 30 out of 37 were fulfilled."

His remarkable book was reprinted by University Books, 1969. (See also **Phone-Voyance**)

Tutankhamun Curse

The discovery of the tomb of Tutankhamun, the boy king of Egypt, on November 26, 1922, in the Valley of the Kings, was one of the greatest achievements of archaeology. After three thousand years, four burial chambers were uncovered, crammed with nearly five thousand priceless objects of gold, alabaster, lapis lazuli, and onyx, in addition to the mummy of the boy king with its splendid gold mask. These fabulous treasures have enriched understanding of the art and history of ancient Egypt.

Two men were responsible for this great discovery—Howard Carter, a British painter-archaeologist, and George E. S. M. Herbert, fifth Earl of Carnarvon. Only a few weeks after the excavation, Carnarvon died suddenly, and this event, together with the deaths of various other individuals associated with the Tutankhamun tomb, gave rise to stories of a "Curse of the Pharaohs." One writer has claimed that the curse was responsible for the lives of some three dozen scientists, archaeologists, and scholars.

The story of the excavation is certainly a strange one, even if it does not satisfactorily validate the popular legend of a deadly curse.

Who Was Tutankhamun?

It has often been claimed that Tutankhamun was a great king because his tomb contained such great treasures. Others have suggested that he was the pharaoh of *Exodus* and that it was his wife Ankhesenpa-Aten who found Moses in the bulrushes and brought him up. In fact, both claims are incorrect.

Tutankhamun reigned during the Eighteenth Dynasty of the New Kingdom, an important period of Egyptian history, but was a boy of nine years when he came to the throne and his reign lasted only nine years, from about 1334 to 1325 B.C. He was not king of Egypt during the Exodus described in the Bible.

His name was originally Tutankhaten ("perfect life of Aten"). He married Ankhesenpa-Aten when only a child. He wife was a daughter of the king Amenhotep IV (1372-1334 B.C.) who had earlier attempted to supplant the god Amun by the Aten, in the process changing his name to Akhenaten ("pleasing to the Aten"). At that time, the priests of Amun had more power than the ruler, so as Akhenaten he reinforced his rule and suppressed worship of Amun.

During the reign of Tutankhamun, the priesthoods dissolved by Akhenaten were reinstated and new images installed in temples. However, in giving pride of place to Amun, there was no attempt to destroy the worship of Aten, only a displacement of former status as principal or sole god. Many of the treasures from the tomb of Tutankhamun indicate tolerance toward former gods. One inscription on a golden throne calls Tutankhamun "image of Ra, beloved of the gods," and a cabinet inscription states "eldest son of Aten in heaven." The memory of Akhenaten is also preserved in such tomb objects as a box bearing the name of Akhenaten, and an artist palette that belonged to Akhenaten's eldest daughter Meritaten. Apart from such a broad-minded religious outlook, there were no particularly important aspects of the reign of Tutankhamun, and achievements of the period are probably due to his advisors.

Tutankhamun died suddenly before a grand burial tomb could be prepared, and it is believed that the tomb used was one hastily converted for royal use. Its importance lies in the magnificence of its contents—chariot bodies, state chairs, gilded couches, royal apparel, trinkets, cosmetics, statues, alabaster vessels, even food, and the golden mask of Tutankhamun himself.

The Excavators

Major credit for discovery of the tomb must be given to Howard Carter. Born May 9, 1873, in Swaffham, Norfolk, England, son of a watercolor painter, he too had skill in painting animals, village scenes, and landscapes. At the age of seventeen, he had his first contact with Egyptology when he was hired by Prof. Percy E. Newberry of the Egyptian Museum of Antiquities to work at the British Museum, London, to make finished drawings of Egyptian inscriptions. Carter later became assistant to Sir William Flinders Petrie, a world famous Egyptologist, traveling in Egypt and recording in watercolors the paintings and inscriptions in temples.

In 1899, at the age of twenty-five, Carter became Inspector of Monuments in Upper Egypt and Nubia, employed by the Antiquities Service, then administered by the French authorities. In 1904, Britain and France partitioned North Africa, the French assuming control of Morocco, and the British of Egypt. But French rights in archaeology continued, and authorization to excavate tombs required the discoverer to be accompanied by an inspector of antiquities and to share finds with the Service on behalf of the Egyptians.

While Carter was an Inspector of Monuments, he worked for several seasons with American millionaire

Theodore M. Davis in excavations in the Valley of the Kings. Carter was a conscientious, uncompromising man, whose total dedication to his work eventually brought opposition from the Egyptians, the French, and newspapermen. He lost his position as an inspector in 1903 through an unfortunate incident in a tomb at Saqqara where Flinders Petrie was working.

A group of drunken Frenchmen came to the camp, demanded a guided tour of one of the tombs, and attempted to enter the women's quarters. Petrie sent for Howard Carter, who came with a squad of Egyptian guards. There was a scuffle, during which one of the Frenchmen was knocked down by a guard. In subsequent proceedings, the French consul general demanded an apology, which Carter refused, stoutly maintaining that the guard was doing his duty and that it was the French who should apologize. The incident became a political issue, and as a result of national pride on the part of the French officials, Carter was unjustly dismissed.

For a time, Carter existed by selling watercolor paintings to tourists and also making paintings for Theodore Davis. In 1907, he was engaged to work for the amateur archaeologist Lord Carnarvon.

George Edward Stanhope Molyneux Herbert, born June 26, 1866, became fifth Earl of Carnarvon on the death of his father in 1890. His father, a noted statesman who served in the Cabinet of Disraeli, had also taken an interest in British archaeology. The son's interest in Egyptian archaeology stemmed from an automobile accident when he suffered severe injuries, including difficulties in breathing. He was advised by physicians to avoid the damp English winter, and duly spent a year in Egypt, where he first became attracted to archaeological excavation, although it was several years before he became actively involved.

The partnership with Howard Carter was a strange one. Carnarvon was an exacting but whimsical aristocrat who pursued archaeology as a kind of hobby, motivated primarily by his desire to own the most beautiful Egyptian antiquities. Carter was a hardworking, implacably dedicated archaeologist, obstinate, somewhat humorless, absolutely wrapped up in his work and secretly resenting Carnarvon's role as dilettante.

It was clearly his employer who Carter had in mind when he wrote in his book *The Tomb of Tutankh-Amen* in 1923: "Excavation is a sort of super-tourist amusement, carried out with the excavator's own money if he is rich enough, or with other people's money if he can persuade them to subscribe it. . . . It is the dilettante archaeologist, the man who rarely does any work with his own hands, but as often as not is absent when the actual discovery is made, who is largely responsible for this opinion. The serious excavator's life is frequently monotonous and . . . quite as hard-working as that of any other member of society."

Carnarvon was often impatient for quick results, while Carter was thorough and tenacious, studying every clue like an archaeological detective, and conducting exploratory digs with the precision of a military campaign. The joint explorations of Carnarvon and Carter began in the winter of 1907-08, with excavations in the Valley of Der al-Bahari in Western Thebes. In 1910-11, they discovered an unfinished temple of Hatshepsut and other remains. In 1911-12, new ground was broken with excavations of Xois near the Nile delta. It was thought by 1922 that there were no more royal tombs in the Valley of Kings, but Carter persisted, and with Carnarvon's backing, achieved his greatest triumph in December 1922 with the discovery of the tomb of Tutankhamun.

On November 6, Carter sent a telegram to Carnarvon in England: "AT LAST HAVE MADE WONDERFUL DISCOVERY IN VALLEY. A MAGNIFICENT TOMB WITH SEALS INTACT. RE-COVERED SAME FOR YOUR ARRIVAL. CONGRATULATIONS." Carnarvon hurried to Egypt and twenty days later, the entrance to the tomb was finally excavated and Howard Carter entered, accompanied by Lord Carnarvon, Lady Evelyn Herbert (Carnarvon's sister) and an assistant. By the flickering light of a candle, Carter peered into the chamber and saw what he later described as "strange animals, statues, and gold—everywhere the glint of gold." Carnarvon whispered "Can you see anything?" Carter replied: "Yes, wonderful things."

But this was only the Antechamber. Because of the uniqueness of the find, Carter sought additional expert assistance from the Egyptian Department of New York's Metropolitan Museum of Art, who arranged for members of their staff to collaborate on the lengthy work of systematic handling of the contents of the tomb. In particular, the Museum's photographer Harry Burton was responsible for thousands of beautiful photographs.

Meanwhile Carnarvon had made a press announcement of the discovery of the tomb of Tutankhamun on November 29. Considerable bad feeling was caused by selling exclusive rights to *The Times* of London, so that other papers had to depend upon syndicated reports. However, Carnarvon and Carter wished to avoid hours of repetitious interviews with competing reporters from the world press. Because completion of excavation took many months of exacting work, the attentions of the press as well as thousands of curious sightseers became a considerable nuisance.

On February 17, 1923, Carter and Carnarvon penetrated the main burial chamber of Tutankhamun and witnessed a wall of gold, the entrance to the burial shrine itself. It was a solemn moment, as Carter later described: "I think at the moment we did not even want to break the seal, for a feeling of intrusion had descended heavily upon us with the opening of the doors, heightened, probably, by the almost painful impressiveness of a linen pall, decorated with golden rosettes. . . . We felt that we were in the presence of the dead King and must do him reverence, and in imagination could see the doors of the successive shrine open one after the other till the innermost disclosed the King himself."

The complex work of exact description, classification, and removal of the shrine contents, including the mummy of the pharaoh himself, could not take place for another season. There were also difficult and acrimonious disputes between Carter and the Egyptian authorities, notably with the Frenchman Pierre Lacau, appointed head of the Antiquities Service in Cairo in 1917.

These disputes concerned the ownership of the antiquities in the Tutankhamun tomb, Carnarvon and Carter claiming rights to a proportion of them, Lacau maintaining that all the contents were the property of the Antiquities Service and the Cairo Museum. Lacau's stance reduced all the costly and skilled excavations of Carter, Carnarvon, and others to a labor of love for scientific interest only!

Another complication was caused by the infatuation of Lady Evelyn, Carnarvon's sister, with Howard Carter, which led to a furious row between the two men. In March 1933, Carnarvon and Evelyn left for Cairo so that Carnarvon could negotiate for a "proper division" of the tomb antiquities.

However, Carnarvon did not live to see the conclusion of the dispute or even the removal of the marvelous golden funerary mask of the Tutankhamun mummy. In April, he became seriously ill after a razor had nicked a mosquito bite. Infection set in, followed by pneumonia. He died on April 6. The newspapers printed a sensational story that he was a victim of the "Curse of the Pharaohs."

The Legend of the Curse of the Pharaohs

Curses were certainly known in ancient Egypt, usually invoking the wrath of the gods against those seeking to embezzle funds for guards, occasionally against thieves. Many tombs suffered from grave robbers over the centuries. An inscription of the Fifth Dynasty of the Old Kingdom, over five thousand years ago, read: "As for any people who shall take possession of this tomb as their mortuary property or shall do any evil thing to it, judgment shall be had with them by the great God."

In his book *The Curse of the Pharaohs* (1975), Philipp Vandenberg states that there were some twenty-two other mysterious deaths of individuals associated with the tomb. The American archaeologist Arthur Mace, who had assisted Carter to open the tomb, suffered from exhaustion after the death of Carnarvon and fell into a deep coma, dying in the same hotel as Carnarvon. George J. Gould, son of the financier, had visited the tomb and died the next day after a high fever ascribed to bubonic plague. Joel Wood, a British industrialist who visited the tomb, died of a high fever on the ship carrying him back to England. Archibald Douglas Reid, a radiologist who had worked on the Tutankhamun mummy, suffered from weakness, and died after returning to England.

Other fatalities associated with the tomb included Prof. Winlock, Prof. Foucraft, archaeologists Garry Daviés, Edward Harkness, and Douglas Derry. Carnarvon's wife, Lady Alimina, died in 1929, apparently from an insect bite, and Carter's secretary Richard Bethell died the same year with a circulatory collapse. When Bethell's father heard the news, he committed suicide, and his hearse ran over a boy on the way to the cemetery.

Vandenberg further claimed that Carter had found a clay tablet in the antechamber with an inscription that Prof. Alan Gardiner deciphered as "Death will slay with his wings whoever disturbs the peace of the pharaoh." However, such a tablet was never cataloged and there is no trace of it.

One newspaper reported that there was a hieroglyphic curse on the door of the inner shrine: "They who enter this sacred tomb shall swift be visited by wings of death," but this story is a fabrication. Similarly another report cited an inscription on the mud base of a candle which stated: "It is I who hinder the sand from choking the secret chamber. I am for the protection of the deceased and I will kill all those who cross this threshold," but the last phrase was another invention.

"The Curse of the Pharaohs" became a sensational newspaper topic for many years, and every death of an individual even distantly associated with the tomb long after the excavation was solemnly recorded as another victim of the curse.

Some of these claims were ludicrously remote. They included the friend of a tourist who had actually entered the burial chamber; the friend was knocked down by a Cairo taxicab. An associate curator of Egyptology at the British Museum in London died peacefully in his bed, while an Egyptologist in France died of old age—both were reported as curse victims. A workman in the British Museum was said to have died suddenly while labeling objects from the tomb—although none ever found their way to the British Museum. For some time after, such stories panicked collectors with Egyptian antiquities, who hurriedly donated their souvenirs to museums.

It is not possible that some deaths associated with visits to the tomb may have been the result of conscious or unconscious morbid fascination with the sinister story of the curse of the pharaohs. Many tourists at that time had been recommended to visit Egypt because of respiratory problems associated with damp climates. Carnarvon himself had suffered in this way, and was clearly overworked and worried at the climax of the tomb excavations. The archaeologist Arthur Mace had also suffered from pleurisy. The climate of Egypt was dry, but there were night chills, and fevers of one kind or another were common.

Lord Carnarvon's son was interviewed on NBC Television in New York on July 14, 1977, and questioned about the "curse" stated that he "neither believed it nor disbelieved it," but added that he would "not accept a million pounds to enter the tomb of Tutankhamun in the Valley of the Kings." A New York *Daily News* report claimed that the same evening, Lord Carnarvon was attending a dinner in an apartment high above Manhattan and looked out over the city and saw all the lights flicker and black out. After candles were lit, he said to his hosts: "It is again the curse of Tutankhamun."

But a curse of a different kind had hung over Howard Carter, the man whose dogged persistence and skill had first located the tomb of Tutankhamun. He utterly confuted the proponents of the curse of the pharaohs by living on for seventeen years after his great discovery, dying March 2, 1939, in his mid-sixties.

But his later years in Egypt were dogged by persistent and painful feuds with the Antiquities Service and the Egyptian authorities over ownership of the priceless contents of the tomb. After the death of Carnarvon, Carter was the focus of political and archaeological intrigues. He supported himself precariously on fees from a lecture tour in the U.S., during which Yale University conferred an honorary doctorate on him, and from his books on archaeology. He doggedly persisted with the completion of his excavation work on the tomb of Tutankhamun in the face of accusations of eccentricity and bad faith, and harassment by officials, tourists, and newspapermen.

It is ironic that long after Carter's early career as an archaeologist had been unjustly cut short by the political intrigues of the Antiquities Service, he should have his greatest archaeological triumph dogged by bitter and long drawn-out feuds with officials. He may not have been the most tactful or diplomatic of men, but his courage, expertise, skill, and sheer determination unearthed and preserved the greatest treasure house of ancient Egypt.

It has to be stressed that both Lord Carnarvon and Howard Carter had been overwhelmed by the beauty and significance of the Tutankhamun tomb and were reverent in their handling of object and the mummy itself. Carter was the major figure throughout the excavation, and the fact that he lived on for seventeen years afterwards surely confuted the story of some generalized curse on those who handled the sacred objects of the tomb. Moreover if some fatal destiny was really attached to handling pharaohnic tombs and mummies, the world's great museums would have been decimated of all curators and assistants.

For decades, the beautiful and priceless relics of Tutankhamun remained in the Cairo Museum, limited by space, and many objects were not even displayed. In June 1974, President Richard M. Nixon visited Egypt, where President Anwar Sadat suggested that an exhibition of the masterpieces of Tutankhamun in the U.S. could affirm the friendly accord and goodwill between the two nations.

Subsequently the fabulous *Treasures of Tutankhamun* exhibition was mounted in the U.S. in 1961-63, in Japan in 1965, in Paris in 1967, at the British Museum in London in 1972, and in the Soviet Union in 1974. The incomparable beauty and craftsmanship of these exhibitions and the light they shed upon ancient Egypt astonished and delighted thousands upon thousands of visitors.

The subject of "King Tut's Curse" has been raised from time to time, and still finds credulous believers, but the term is more familiarly used by travelers in the Middle East to describe the hazard of diarrhea, also known in Mexico as "Montezuma's Revenge." (See also **Egypt**)

Recommended reading

Budge, Sir. E. A. W. *Tutankhamen; Amenism, Atenism and Egyptian Monotheism,* M. Hopkinson & Co., London, 1923; Bell Publishing Co., 1979

Carter, Howard. *The Tomb of Tut-ankh-Amen,* 3 vols., Cassell, London, 1923-33

Gilber, Katherine S., with Joan K. Holt & Sara Hudson (ed.) *Treasures of Tutankhamun* [Catalog of an Exhibition between 1976 and 1979], Ballantine Books/Metropolitan Museum of Art, 1976

Herbert, G. E. S. M. (5th Earl of Carnarvon) & H. Carter. *Five Years' Explorations at Thebes, 1907-1911,* H. Frowde, London, 1912

Hoving, Thomas. *Tutankhamun; The Untold Story,* Simon & Schuster/Hamish Hamilton, London, 1978

Vandenberg, Philipp. *The Curse of the Pharaohs,* J. B. Lippincott, 1975 [English translation of *Der Fluch der Pharaonen,* Scherz Verlag, 1973]

Vandenberg, Philipp. *The Golden Pharaoh,* Macmillan/Hodder & Stoughton, London, 1980 [English translation of *Der Vergessene Pharao,* C. Bertelsmann Verlag, 1978]

Wynne, Barry. *Behind the Mask of Tutankhamun,* Taplinger, 1973

Tuttle, Hudson (1836-1910)

Famous American seer of the early days of Spiritualism. He was born October 4, 1836, in Berlin Heights, Ohio, and spent his early years in a wilderness on the southern shores of Lake Erie. His father's house was the headquarters for itinerant Unitarian preachers and the atmosphere was burdened with dogmatic disputations. As a result young Tuttle became at an early age skeptical of the entire Church scheme.

He attended his first Spiritualist seance at the home of a retired congregational minister who had heard of the **Rochester rappings** and called in a few friends of experiment. He fell into **trance** and wrote spirit messages automatically. Simultaneously with his **automatic writing, raps** developed and the table moved.

The seances were free. The communicators, in hours of seclusion, were his teachers. "It was my only source of knowledge," he wrote in his preface to his book *Arcana of Spiritualism* (1871 etc.), "for I had access to few books. I had attended school eleven months in all, six of which were at a district school, and five at a small academy."

In 1857, he married Emma Rood, writer, lecturer on education, and composer of songs.

The first article Tuttle published was on prayer in *The Spiritual Telegraph.* He often wrote and rewrote a script several times before the influence would declare the result satisfactory. He began writing a story founded on spirit life. It was entitled *Scenes in the Spirit World* (1855). In England it was published under the title *Life in Two Spheres* (1895). After completing it, he began a monumental scientific work, *Arcana of Nature.*

His impression was that Lamarck and Alexander von Humboldt were associated with other intelligences in its production. But he knew nothing of these great minds. He was only entering his eighteenth year. When the book was completed, his spirit guides declared it to be unsatisfactory and demanded the destruction of the script. Reluctantly he consigned the large bulk of manuscript to the flames and started again.

For two years, the remaining manuscript lay on his table and some correction or addition was made nearly every day. The engravings in both volumes were made by the same influences that wrote them. He claimed no merit for himself and said: "Mine has been the task of an amanuensis, writing that which has been given to me. I claim no honour, except honestly and faithfully attempting to perform my part of the task."

Arcana of Nature, 2 vols., published 1860-63, was certainly a remarkable book. It was quoted by F. C. L. Büchner in his own book *Force and Matter* (1864) to strengthen his materialistic position, while Charles Darwin in the *Descent of Man* quoted statements from Tuttle's later *Origin and Antiquity of Physical Man.* Both Büchner and Darwin were unaware that the book was produced by an ignorant farm boy. This ignorance vanished, of course, as the years passed by.

The spirit controls were good educators. But Hudson Tuttle never gave up his modest life as a farmer and breeder of horses at Berlin Heights, Ohio. In 1857, he married Emma D. Rood, who was a frequent contributor to the Spiritualist press.

The spirit influences did not come to Tuttle at all times. He said: "Sometimes I have prolific periods, and again, I go over a deserted country. For days, weeks, even months, I feel forsaken and alone. The very fountains of thought seem dried up. No incitement can compel me to write, or if I attempt to do so it is worthless, or worse, unreliable. It sometimes seems to me that I have never written anything of value, and I am sure I never can again. At the same time, when I study it, this experience is one of the most convincing tests that some superior intelligence comes into my life."

Of the many other books he produced, the following should be mentioned: *Origin and Antiquity of Physical Man* (1866), *The Arcana of Spiritualism* (c. 1867), *Career of the God—Idea in History* (1869), *Career of the Christ—Idea in History* (1869), *Career of Religious Ideas* (1869), *Ethics of Spiritualism* (1878), *Religion of Man and Ethics of Science* (1890), *Studies in Outlying Fields of Psychic Science* (1889), *Philosophy of Spirit and the Spirit World* (1896), *Mediumship and Its Laws* (1900), *Stories from Beyond the Borderland* (by Hudson and Emma Rood Tuttle, 1910).

He died December 15, 1910, at Berlin Heights, Ohio.

Tweedale, Mrs. Violet (1862-1936)

British novelist, granddaughter of author Robert **Chambers,** a convinced Spiritualist.

She attended seances with Lord Haldane, Arthur and James Balfour. W. E. Gladstone had sittings in her house. Most of her experiences came through the mediumship of Charles **Williams** and Cecil **Husk.**

She was a powerful witness in the famous trial when trance speaker Mrs. Meurig **Morris** sued the *Daily Mail* for libel in 1932. In addition to many poems and novels, she published the following books on psychic subjects: *Ghosts I Have Seen* (1920), *Phantoms of the Dawn* (1924); *Mellow Sheaves* (1927), *The Cosmic Christ* (1930).

She died December 10, 1936.

Tweedale, Rev. Charles L(akeman) (died 1944)

Prominent British writer on Spiritualism. He was educated at Durham University, England and became Vicar of Weston, Otley, Yorkshire.

He was a talented and versatile man—astronomer, musician and inventor. He published books on astronomy and discovered a comet.

He was also a close friend of psychic photographer William **Hope,** whom he defended against hostile criticism.

His books on Spiritualism included *Man's Survival After Death* (1909, translated into Italian, Norwegian, Dutch, Greek, Swedish and other languages), *News From the Next World* (1940), *The Vindication of William Hope* (n.d.), *Present Day Spirit Phenomena and the Churches* (n.d.).

He died June 29, 1944

Twigg, Ena (1914-)

Well-known modern British medium. Born in Kent, England, January 6, 1914, she was one of a psychic family in which parents and other children had sensitive ability. She played with spirit children at the age of seven, and at fourteen predicted the death of her father. Her psychic gifts disturbed her marriage to Harry Twigg.

After a serious illness, spirit visitors assured her that she would be restored to health, and when she was eventually healed she made a decision to devote her life to helping other people. She became a member of the **Marylebone Spiritualist Association** and in due course opened her own healing clinic.

She has a high reputation as a clairvoyant, healer and trance medium. Her autobiography (in collaboration with Ruth Hagy Brod) is titled *Ena Twigg; Medium* (1972).

Twins

It has long been believed that there is a special sympathy between identical twins, but modern research has shown that there are startling correspondences between temperaments, personality, lifestyles and even sensitivity to names. Some of these coincidences are so striking that it seems impossible to assign them to mere chance.

In 1979, the University of Minnesota began a study of identical twins, the first for over forty years, in which twins separated for years were investigated and subjected to medical and psychological tests. The results of nine identical twin studies, involving over 15,000 questions, demonstrated astonishing affinities between the subjects.

Unknown to each other, Jim Spring and Jim Lewis were raised in different Ohio towns. Both married and divorced women called Linda and chose a woman named Betty as the second wife. Each of the two Jims named their sons James Allan and had a favorite dog named Toy. Both twins had remarkable similarities in medical profiles, including identical blood pressure, sleep and heart-beat patterns. Both also suddenly put on 10 pounds extra weight at the same time in their lives. At the age of 18, both Jim twins had also suffered similar syndromes of intermittent migraine. Their drinking and smoking habits were also identical, and both chewed their fingernails.

Another pair of identical twins, Jack and Oscar, were raised apart with completely different backgrounds. Jack was brought up as an American Jew by his father after separation of the parents; the mother took Oscar back to Germany (where she was born) where he was raised as a Catholic, later joining the Nazi Youth party. In adult life, Jack ran a store in San Diego, while Oscar became a factory supervisor in Germany. But both men wear wire-rimmed eyeglasses and a mustache, and two-pocket shirts with epaulets. Both were absent-minded and had other matching idiosyncracies such as storing rubber bands on their wrists.

Bridget and Dorothy were two identical British twins who were raised apart soon after their birth, yet when they met each other in 1941, each wore two bracelets on one wrist, and a watch and bracelet on the other. Each sister also wore seven rings! Each twin had married and had a family of a boy and a girl each. The sons had been christened Richard Andrew and Andrew Richard, while the daughters were Karen Louise and Catherine Louise.

Many such identical twins share similar IQ and psychological profiles, as well as EEG tracings. It is not yet clear whether the astonishing coincidences derive from some kind of **Telepathy** or whether they indicate unusual manifestation of inheritance. In the latter eventuality, many existing concepts of heredity and free will may have to be revised substantially.

Recommended reading:

Watson, Peter. *Twins: An Investigation Into the Strange Coincidences in the Lives of Separated Twins*, Hutchinson, London, 1981

Twitchell, (John) Paul (c. 1908-1971)

Founder of the **ECKANKAR** spiritual movement, teaching the "ancient science of soul travel," a kind of **astral projection** to other planes.

Accounts of Twitchell's life are somewhat vague and legendary, but he appears to have been born on a Mississippi riverboat around 1908 and brought up by foster parents in China Point in southern America. His foster father was supposed to have learnt about soul travel from an Indian holy man Sudar Singh, originally from Allahabad, who Twitchell was also supposed to have met in Paris, France. It has been claimed that soul travel derived from a mysterious Tibetan master named "Rebazar Tarzs," who first appeared to Twitchell in 1944 while serving on a U.S. Navy vessel in the pacific.

After World War II, Twitchell became a freelance writer for pulp magazines. He visited India and upon returning to the U.S. began writing books about ECKANKAR, allegedly dictated by Rebazar Tarzs. Twitchell subsequently traveled through Europe, lecturing in London, Amsterdam, Copenhagen and Zürich. Eck study group centers were established throughout the world. In 1968, it was necessary to organize Eckankar as a corporation, known as Eck, Inc.

Twitchell composed his books at great speed, often working on two manuscripts simultaneously. He also read omnivorously, sometimes twenty books per day. His own books are a heady mixture of claimed personal experience of **out-of-the-body** travel, redigested occult facts and speculations in which traditional Hindu or Sikh religious terms are used side by side with arbitrary Eck terminology. In this respect, Eckankar is a kind of neo-Theosophy, complete with mysterious masters and an ancient book of wisdom.

According to David C. Lane in his publication *The Making of a Spiritual Movement* (2nd rev. ed., 1979), one of the prior influences which preceded Twitchell's launching of Eck was the teachings of Swami Premananda of the Self-Revelation Church of Absolute Monism, Washington D.C., which was associated with Paramhansa **Yogananda** of the **Self-Realization Fellowship.** Twitchell and his first wife Camille became members of the Self-Revelation Church and lived on the Temple grounds for more than five years. They left the Church in 1955 and in the same year applied for separation, being finally divorced in 1960.

From 1950 onwards, Twitchell appears to have joined **Scientology,** becoming a staff member of a group and attaining the title of "clear." Twitchell then became initiated by the Sikh movement Ruhani Satsang, headed by Kirpal Singh, a disciple of the **Radhasoami** Beas Master, Sawan Singh. This contact apparently lasted for several years until 1963, when Twitchell brought Gail Atkinson to be initiated. Gail became his second wife about 1964.

From 1963 onwards, the foundations of Eckankar began to emerge in various articles expounding the philosophy of "The Cliff Hanger," as Twitchell described himself and the movement. In the *Psychic Observer* (July 1964), he stated that Eckankar was based on Shabd-Yoga ". . . the Hindu locution for the cosmic sound current." Eckankar itself was officially founded October 22, 1965.

Given the background of Hindu and Sikh mysticism, it is easy to see how their special terms could have become part of the Eckankar synthesis. Twitchell had earlier identified "Eckankar" as a Hindu word meaning union with God. Much the same interpretation, allied with the mysticism of sound, is implied by "Eck Omkar." *Omkar* denotes the mystical Hindu trisyllable "AUM" which precedes the reading of Sanskrit prayers, and is associated with the sound vibration involved in the creation of the universe. "Eck" means "One."

There seems little doubt that Twitchell had certain psychic experiences and talents, and to the extent that his Eckankar system is a colorful restatement of some basic Hindu esoteric traditions, it is spiritually inspiring to popular readers who prefer a romantic presentation to the authentic tradition.

The overall message of Eckankar emphasizes admirable spiritual values, but its concept of "God-realization" falls short of traditional Vedantic teachings, although using some Vedantic terminology. The term "Sugmad" for Supreme God does not occur in Vedanta and the Eck pathway to God-realization is heterodox so far as Hinduism and Tibetan Buddhism are concerned.

Twitchell's mixture of Hindu metaphysical terms with Eck words can be confusing, and is very reminiscent of the Theosophy of Madame **Blavatsky** in which astral revelations ranked equally with traditional Hindu scripture and concepts. Indeed, Twitchell often referred to the *Shariyat-Ki-Sugmad* claimed as "an ancient scripture of Eckankar," which recalls Blavatsky's *Stanzas of Dzyan* as an unverifiable astral manuscript. Twitchell's *Eckankar Dictionary* (1973) is an essential companion when reading his books.

Towards the end of his life, Twitchell was quoted as believing himself to be under attack by individuals who disagreed with his doctrine and had attempted to injure him personally. He died in 1971.

His many publications included: *All About Eck* (c. 1968), *Eckankar, the Key to Secret Worlds* (1969), *The Flute of God* (c. 1969; 1972), *The Tiger's Fang* (1969), *Anitya, the Book of Contemplation* (c. 1969), *Dialogues with the Master* (c. 1970), *The Shariyat-Ki-Sugmad* (1970-71), *The Spiritual Notebook* (c. 1971), *The Far Country* (1971), *Herbs: the Magic Healers* (1971).

A biography, *In My Soul I Am Free* by Brad **Steiger** (1968), is vague on essential data but is based on firsthand interviews with Twitchell. The term "Sri" bestowed upon Twitchell and his successor Darwin Gross and later, Harold Klemp, is a Hindu honorific, traditionally used for gods, kings and learned men, but in present-day Indian usage a polite form for "Mr."

For an official summary of Eckankar, its beliefs and teachings, see *A Profile of Eckankar,* obtainable from Eckankar, P.O. Box 3100 Menlo Park, California 94025. For a critical history of Eckankar, see *The Making of a Spiritual Movement; The Untold Story of Paul Twitchell and Eckankar* by David Christopher Lane (1979), published by B. William Walsh Publication (Theses Division), Berkeley, California. (See also **Theosophical Society; Vedanta**)

Two Worlds, The (Newspaper)

Spiritualist weekly founded in 1888 in Manchester Britain, by Mrs. Emma Hardinge **Britten.** It was edited for some time by Ernest W. **Oaten.** Another weekly paper under the same title was started in London in 1858 and ran for a brief period.

In modern times, *Two Worlds* was edited for many years by veteran Spiritualist Maurice **Barbanell** (died 1981). It is currently published by the Headquarters Publishing Co. Ltd., 5 Alexandria Road, West Ealing, London W13 ONP, England.

Typtology

The science of communicating with spirits by means of rapping, various codes being arranged for the purpose. Thus the sitters may read the alphabet aloud, or slowly pass a pencil down a printed alphabet, the rappings indicating the correct letters which, on being joined together, form a message or an answer to some question propounded. One rap may be made to mean "yes," two "no," and so on.

It seems possible that there might be some relationship with the energies involved in the use of the **divining-rod** and pendulum in **dowsing.** (See also **Divining-Rod; Pendulums; Radiesthesia; Raps; Table-Turning**)

Tyromancy (or Tiromancy)

An old form of **divination** based on interpretations from cheese. Unfortunately, the method does not appear to have been recorded.

Tyrrell, G(eorge) N(ugent) M(erle) (1879-1952)

Mathematician, president of the **Society for Psychical Research,** London from 1945-46, member of Council from 1940-52, a prominent British parapsychologist. Born in 1879, he was educated at Haileybury School, Seafield Engineering College and London University (degrees in physics and mathematics). He was a pioneer in the study of wireless telegraphy, working under Guglielmo Marconi. He served in the British Army in World War I and was mentioned in dispatches.

He joined the Society for Psychical Research in 1908. After conducting a series of experiments in **telepathy** and **precognition** with Miss Gertrude Johnson, he devoted himself exclusively to psychical research.

He undertook further experiments with Miss Johnson in 1924, using quantitative methods, and invented mechanical devices to randomize selection and scoring. His apparatus was destroyed during an air raid in World War II, but he then studied theoretical and philosophical aspects of extrasensory perception as distinct from experimentation.

He published a number of articles on parapsychology, including (in *Proceedings* of the Society for Psychical Research): 'Individuality' (vol. 44, part 144, 1936), 'Further Research in Extrasensory Perception' (vol. 44, part 147, 1936-37), 'Presidential Address' (vol. 47, part 171, 1945). His books included: *Grades of Significance* (1930), *Science and Psychical Phenomena* (1938), *The Personality of Man* (1946), *Homo Faber* (1951).

He died October 29, 1952.

U

Übersinnliche Welt, Die (Journal)

German Spiritualist monthly, founded in 1893, changed into fortnightly in 1902, merging with *Psyche* under the title *Psyche und die Übersinnliche Welt.* No longer published.

Udumbara (Center)

Alternative name for **Minnesota Zen Meditation Center,** and also the title of their biannual periodical.

UFO (Unidentified Flying Object)

General term for a wide range of mysterious celestrial phenomena, including what are popularly known as **"Flying Saucers,"** i.e., mysterious aerial objects of a saucer-like shape.

For many centuries, the reported appearance of objects in the sky (fire-balls, comets, bright stars) has been taken as a portent of doom or a happy omen, but in addition to such natural celestial phenomena, there have also been many reports of disk or wheel-like objects in the sky from the time of Ezekiel onwards.

There was no systematic attempt to list and discuss such phenomena until the iconoclastic writer Charles **Fort** published *The Book of the Damned* (1919). (The "damned" were the data ignored or explained away by orthodox scientists). This book listed many instances of inexplicable objects seen in the sky or landing on earth or sea from 1779 onwards.

The book was little known at a popular level until reprinted with Fort's other remarkable works *New Lands, Lo!* and *Wild Talents* in one volume as *The Books of Charles Fort* (1941), when wider circulation stimulated many individuals to carry on the work of Fort in listing and studying such phenomena.

In addition, the increased aerial activity during World War II led to many observations by pilots and ground crews, who reported strange balls of light or disk-like shapes which followed them in their missions over Germany and Japan. These were known as "foo-fighters," derived from a pun in the comic strip "Smokey Stover" ("Where there's foo, there's a fire"). These objects were regarded as "mass hallucination" by the U.S. Eighth Army.

From 1946-48 there were many reports from Scandinavia of mysterious cigar-shaped objects in the sky. These became known as "ghost rockets." It is possible that the wartime V1 and V2 weapons from Germany may have stimulated other secret rocket experiments elsewhere.

The modern period of UFO sightings really began soon afterwards, when U.S. pilot Kenneth Arnold saw nine bright disk-shaped flying objects between the peaks of Mount Rainier and Mount Adams. Arnold had taken off from Chehalis, Washington on June 24, 1947 on a rescue mission to find a crashed plane in the Cascade Mountain area. In describing the strange objects to a reporter, Arnold said they flew in close formation at an estimated speed of 1,700 m.p.h. with a movement like "a saucer skipping over water." Newspapers coined the term "flying saucers," which has struck ever since, although official organizations investigating such phenomena prefer the term "unidentified flying objects."

Other sightings were reported and public interest in the phenomenon grew rapidly. The U.S. Air Force began to take a keen interest in UFO sightings, both to resolve public pressure and to discover whether foreign powers might be developing secret weapons. By the end of 1947, the Air Force had officially received 156 sightings of UFOs and on December 30, 1947 an official project code name "Sign" was set up "to collect, collate, evaluate and distribute to interested government agencies and contractors all information concerning sightings and phenomena in the atmosphere which can be construed to be of concern to the national security." This was the first of a number of official investigations into UFOs, most of which attempted to explain away the phenomena or damp down public concern.

Meanwhile, only a few months after the Arnold sighting, Arnold himself published several articles in *Fate* magazine describing other strange disks and lights, and in *Fate* (Summer 1948) his article 'Are Space Visitors Here?' helped to launch the popular mythology of flying saucers being spacecraft from other planets. This was reinforced by other writers, notably Donald Keyhoe, a retired Marine Corps major who had flown with Charles Lindberg. Keyhoe's book *The Flying Saucers Are Real* (Fawcett, 1950) suggested that the Air Force investigation project was set up to conceal from the public that the saucers were from another planet.

Gerald Heard, a reputable British author, published *The Riddle of the Flying Saucers; Is Another World Watching?* (London, 1950; U.S. 1951) which put forward the theory that the saucers came from the planet Mars and might be piloted by 'superbees' about two inches long with a higher intelligence than man.

In *Flying Saucers Have Landed* (1953), authors Desmond Leslie and George Adamski solemnly affirmed that Adamski had photographed flying saucers from the planet Venus and met a spaceman occupant from one saucer, who had left mysterious footprints in the Arizona desert. Desmond Leslie's section of the book was an uncritical compilation of ancient legends about flying chariots, Theosophical speculations and popular occult traditions. The twin elements of romantic occultism and claims to actual contact with beings from outer space stimulated a wave of new sightings and claimed contacts of a science-fiction character throughout the 1950s, often resulting in the formation of mystical cults in which the contactees were recipients of grave warnings or higher teachings of love and brotherhood from masters of wisdom in outer space.

Four other writers whose books helped to reinforce this pattern by their own claims to be contactees were Truman Betherun (*Aboard a Flying Saucer,* 1954), Daniel Fry (*White Sands Incident,* 1954), Orfeo Angelucci (*Secret of the Saucers,* 1955), Howard Menger (*From Outer Space to You,* 1959).

Other individuals claimed telepathic communication with outer space beings, or delivered lectures from them while in a state of trance, or produced tape recordings with alleged supernormally impressed messages from space intelligences.

A high proportion of such communications were depressingly banal and terrestrial in character, mostly complaining about the atom bomb and suggesting that peace is better than war. A further development of space-people mythology was the claim that they are already amongst us incognito, working for the good of mankind and universal brotherhood. So far, no positive evidence of their existence or beneficent influence has been produced.

Meanwhile many thousands of new sightings of UFOs over the last two decades produced great public pressure for further official investigation. A succession of U.S. Air Force projects and reports attempted to reduce public anxiety but only succeeded in arousing accusation of conspiracy to suppress evidence.

Typical of the somewhat paranoid wing of the conspiracy theories was the Men in Black mythology, originally launched by Gray Barker's book *They Knew Too Much About Flying Saucers* (1956). This related how Albert K. **Bender,** organizer of a flying saucer bureau, discovered important data on the origin of UFOs but was silenced in September 1953 by the visit of three mysterious men dressed in black. Men in Black were at first supposed to be government officials, but were later represented as malevolent beings, possibly supernatural in origin.

The occult and pseudo-occult branch of UFOlogy has tended to obscure the very genuine and complex mystery of UFOs which have been reported all over the world, and for which it is likely that no single explanation will suffice. Typical of space peoplecults is the **Aetherius Society,** founded around the trance addresses of George **King.**

A high proportion of sightings may relate to natural phenomena such as ball-lightning, air inversions, meteorites and tricks of lighting, as well as objects like kites, weather balloons, aircraft lights, etc. Some hoaxes have been exposed, including deliberately faked photographs. Other observations may lie within the realm of mass hysteria and hallucination. Some sightings may be connected with experimental aerial craft on the secret list, and it must be said that from the 1950s onwards there was research on Electrogravitics in various countries, concerned with disk-like anti-gravity devices, a subject on which little has so far appeared in print.

But in addition to many conventional explanations and possibilities, there is also a solid core of evidence for the reality of some UFO phenomena, and strong presumptive evidence that there are intelligently guided craft of a disk-like or cigar-shaped form. How far that is an entirely objective phenomenon still remains in doubt. It is interesting to note that from 1896-97, thousands of sightings of mysterious airships were reported in the U.S. at a time that the feasibility of heavier-than-air craft was still a theoretical matter.

Over the centuries, unusual appearance of one kind or another have taken on shapes and characteristics in relation to the conventions of their time. Where some people have seen nature-spirits, others have seen angels or fairies, or perhaps visitors from Mars and Venus. In the religious revivals that swept England and Wales in 1904, there were reports of supernatural luminous beings and fire-balls. The wildfire nineteenth-century growth of Spiritualism produced materializations of Red Indian guides and messages from other worlds. Is there some kind of shape-changing reality, taking different forms at different times?

One modern offshoot of the UFO experience is the proliferation of the **"Chariots of the Gods"** theme started by Erich von Däniken, suggesting that earth was colonized by spacemen in some remote prehistory.

A claim to UFO experience was the story of Barney and Betty (Eunice) Hill, who stopped their car in New Hampshire to take their dog for a walk, and noticed a bright light in the sky. They saw a huge flying saucer, but suffered a period of two hours amnesia. Under hypnosis they revealed that they were taken on board the spacecraft and examined by humanoids before being released. The story is told by John G. Fuller in *The Interrupted Journey* (1966).

Did it really happen? There have been many contactee experiences related by sincere individuals who do not appear to be telling lies, but who may have suffered some strange hallucination, perhaps encountered an area of experience outside the normal range of human sensory reality. This led to the concept of "missing time," to describe claimed abduction experiences by mysterious aliens, coupled withamnesia. Similar cases were researched by Budd Hopkins for his book *Missing Time* (1981), and later by horror story writer Whitley **Strieber** in his book *Communion* (1987).

Although scientists have often been reluctant to commit themselves to belief in UFOs and have usually found it convenient to ridicule or explain away the phenomena, a few individuals have taken an enlightened interest. Amongst these was J. Allen **Hynek,** professor of astronomy at Ohio State University and head of the McMillan Observatory, whose book *The UFO Experience: A Scientific Enquiry* (1972) criticized the Air Force treatment of UFO reports and details procedures for proper scientific study of the subject.

In addition to official U.S. Air Force reports on Projects Sign, Grudge and Bluebook, there have been a number of civilian organizations dealing with UFOs, including **Amalgamated Flying Saucers Clubs of America** (which believes that flying saucers are extraterrestrial in origin and studies contactee reports and space tapes), **Saucer and Unexplained Celestial Events Research Society** (uncommitted on origins of UFOs) and **National Investigations Committee on Aerial Phenomena** (which includes technical advisors, scientists, aviation experts, and gathers reliable information on all aspects of UFOs and related phenomena).

In 1973, while campaigning for the presidency of the United States, Governor Jimmy Carter of Georgia reported seeing a UFO. He promised that if elected he would ensure that there was no official secrecy on the subject of UFOs. In 1978, NASA rejected a White House suggestion to reopen government investigation into UFOs, claiming that it would be "wasteful and probably unproductive." However, NASA expressed willingness to analyze substantive material on UFOs that was "bona fide physical evidence from credible sources."

On January 18, 1979, the subject of Unidentified Flying Objects was debated for the first time in the House of Lords, the upper chamber of the British Parliament. This historic debate was introduced by the Earl of Clancarty (Brinsley Le Poer **Trench**), himself an enthusiastic researcher and author of various books about flying saucers. He opened by calling attention to the increasing number of sightings on a worldwide scale, and proceeded to give a review of the history of the subject and official organizations and attitudes to it. He stated: "Is it not time that Her Majesty's Government informed our people of what they know about UFOs? I think it is time our people were told the truth."

In the debate which followed, many distinguished people took part. Lord Clancarty was supported by the Earl of Kimberley, Liberal Party spokesman on aerospace, and Lord Gainford, who stated that, together with other witnesses, he had seen a UFO. The opposition was represented by two Conservative peers, Lord Tregfarne and Lord Hewlett while Lord Strabolgi replied for the Government. Lord Kings-Norton (former president of the Royal Institution) and Lord Halsbury (member of many scientific committees) were two distinguished scientists who spoke in the debate, which lasted for three hours.

Lord Clancarty proposed an inter-governmental study on UFOs, and several colleagues subsequently expressed a desire to join such a group. Accordingly, the House of Lords All Party Study Group on UFOs was formed and held its first meeting June 19, 1979.

The debate was reported in full in *Hansard,* the official record of British Parliament, but the demand for copies was so great that H. M. Stationery Office sold out. However, permission was granted to reprint and the full transcript was accordingly published, with annotations, as *The House of Lords UFO Debate* with prefaceby Lord Clancarty and Notes by John Mitchell (Open Head/Pentacle Books, London, U.K., 1979).

The literature of UFOs is vast, ranging from books to promoting occult cults to official Government reports. In between are hundreds of books and articles discussing sightings or indulging in special pleading. From this mass of literature a representative selection is listed below covering typical aspects of a vast and complex subject.

Two useful works are Lynn E. Catoe's monumental bibliography, *UFO's and Related Subjects,* reissued with a supplement by Kay Rodgers in 1978 by Gale Research Co., and the *UFO Encyclopedia* of Margaret Sachs (1980).

More recently, the comprehensive bibliography *UFOs and The Extraterrestrial Movement* by George M. Eberhart (2 vols., 1986) is an indispensible work. For skeptical views, see *UFOs and Outer Space Mysteries; A Symapthetic Skeptic's Report* by James Oberg (1982), and *UFOs; The Public Deceived* by Philip J. Klass (1983). A thoughtful and scientific view for and against the phenomena is presented in *UFO's; A Scientific Debate,* (ed.) Carl Sagall & Thorton Page (1974).

Public fascination with UFOs received a powerful stimulus through the Steven Spielberg movies "Close Encounters of the Third Kind" (1977) and the recent success "E.T." (Extraterrestrial), both stimulating a new wave of UFO movies and public interest in the theme. Sightings continue and new books are published by the paperback press, some of them thoughtful, others cashing in on a popular trend. Intelligent and responsible analyses of the UFO phenomenon rub shoulders with wild speculations and romantic myths. More than ever, it is essential for the serious investigator or the informed member of the public to be aware of the scope of earlier publications and materials in this controversial field.

Recommended reading:

Catoe, Lynn E. *UFOs and Related Subjects: An Annotated Bibliography,* U.S. Government Printing Office, 1969; reissued together with *Supplement* by Kay Rodgers, Gale Research Co., 1978

Condon, Edward U. *Scientific Study of Unidentified Flying Objects,* Bantam, 1969

Condon, Edward U. (ed. Daniel S. Gillmor). *Final Report of the Scientific Study of Unidentified Flying Objects,* Bantam, 1969

Eberhart, George M. *UFOs and the Extraterrestrial Contact Movement,* 2 vols., Scarecrow Press, 1986

Hoband, Ion & Julien Weverberg. *UFOs From Behind The Iron Curtain,* London, 1974; Corgi, 1975

Hopkins, Budd. *Missing Time; A Documented Study of the UFO Abductions,* R. Marek, New York, 1981; Ballantine paperback, 1981

Hynek, J. Allen. *The UFO Experience; A Scientific Inquiry;* Henry Regnery, Chicago/Abelard-Schuman, London, 1972; Ballantine, 1977

Jacobs, David M. *The UFO Controversy in America,* Indiana University Press, 1975; Signet 1976

Jung, Carl G. *Flying Saucers: A Modern Myth of Things Seen in theSkies,* Harcourt Brace, 1959; Signet, 1969

Keyhoe, Donald. *Flying Saucers: Top Secret,* G. P. Putnam, 1960

Klass, *UFOs; The Public Deceived,* Prometheus Books, 1983

Klass, Philip J. *UFO Abductions: A Dangerous Game,* Prometheus Books, 1983

Leslie, Desmond & George Adamski. *Flying Saucers Have Landed,* London, 1953

McDonald, James E. *Unidentified Flying Objects; Greatest Scientific Problem of Our Times,* National Investigations Committee on Aerial Phenomena, 1967

Oberg, James. *UFOs and Outer Space Mysteries; A Sympathetic Skeptic's Report,* Donning Co., Virginia, 1982

Reich, Wilhelm. *CORE (Space Ships, DOR and Drought),* vol. VI, Nos. 1-4, Orgone Institute Press, 1954

Ruppelt, Edward J. *The Report on Unidentified Flying Objects,* Doubleday, 1956; 1959. *Symposium on Unidentified Flying Objects: Hearing Before the Committee on Science and Astronautics, U.S. House of Representatives, Ninetieth Congress, Second Session, July 29, 1968, No. 7,* U.S. Government Printing Office, 1968

Sachs, Margaret. *The UFO Encyclopedia,* Putnam, 1980

Sagan, Carl & Thorton Page (eds.). *UFOs; A Scientific Debate,* W. W. Norton, 1974

Storey, Ronald D. (ed.) *The Encyclopedia of UFOs,* Dolphin Books (Doubleday), 1980

Spencer, John & Hilary Evans. *Phenomena. From Flying Saucers to UFOs-Forty Years of Facts & Research,* Futura, London, 1988

U.S. Air Force. Projects Grudge and Bluebook Reports 1-12, Washington, D.C., National Investigations Committee on Aerial Phenomena, 1968

Vallee, Jacques. *Messengers of Deception; UFO Contacts and Cults,* Bantam paperback, 1980

UFO Examiner, The (Journal)

Quarterly publication of Private UFO Investigations, a group concerned with UFO reports and international sightings. Address: Route 1, Hazelton, Iowa 50641.

UFO Information Network (UFOIN)

New name of former Page Research Library, publishing a *Newsletter.* This merged with *Ohio Sky Watcher* in 1979, and now appears as *UFO Ohio.*

UFOIN collects and collates information on UFOs and other Fortean phenomena. Address: UFOIN, Box 5012, Rome, Ohio 44085.

UFO Information Retrieval Center

Founded in 1966, to collect, analyze, publish, and disseminate information on reports of unidentified flying objects. The Center compiles statistics, conducts research programs, maintains library, on-line data base, children's and students' services, speakers bureau, and referrals. From time to time it publishes *Reference for Outstanding UFO Sighting Reports.* Address: 3131 W. Cochise Drive, No. 158, Phoenix, Arizona 85021.

UFO Investigator (Newsletter)

Monthly newsletter of **National Investigations Committee on Aerial Phenomena.** Address: 5012 Del Ray Avenue, Washington, D.C. 20014.

UFO Magazine New Bulletin

Quarterly publication reporting UFO sightings with critical analyses. Address: 3403 West 119th Street, Cleveland, Ohio 44111.

UFO Nachrichten (Journal)

Bimonthly publication concerned with Unidentified Flying Objects: German language. Address: Karl L. Veit, Deutsche UFO-Studiengesellschaft, Ventla-Verlag, Postfach 13185, 6200 Wiesbaden 13, West Germany (B.R.D.).

UFO Newsclipping Service

Monthly publication which reproduces U.S., Canadian and other newspaper reports of UFOs and other unexplained phenomena. Address: Route 1, Box 220, Plumerville, Arkansas 72127.

UFO Nyt (Journal)

Danish-language periodical (with English summary) dealing with Unidentified Flying Objects, published bimonthly. Address: Skandinavisk UFO Information, Postbox 6, DK-2920, Gentofte, Denmark.

UFO Quebec (Periodical)

Canadian quarterly publication concerned with Unidentified Flying Objects, edited by Claude McDuff, with articles in French. Address: BP 53, Dollard-des-Ormeaux, PQ Canada H9G 2H5.

UFO Reporter (Journal)

Bi-monthly publication reporting UFO sightings and related events: includes discussions and reviews. Published: P.O. Box 2656, La Mesa, California 92041.

UFO Research Newsletter

Monthly journal edited by Gordon I. R. Lore. Address: 3122 N. Beachwood Drive, Los Angeles, California 90068.

UFOCAT

Computerized files of reports of Unidentified Flying Objects and related material, compiled by David Saunders, University of Chicago, Illinois.

The files include over 50,000 entries, which may be retrieved under such headings as date, geographic location, special features. The files are available at minimum cost to serious researchers. The Center for UFO Studies has also published a statistical analysis of UFOCAT entries under the title *The UFO Phenomenon.* Inquiries concerning UFOCAT should be directed to the Center for UFO Studies, P.O. Box 1402, Evanston, Illinois 60204.

Uhland, Ludwig (1787-1862)

Famous German poet who figured posthumously in an interesting lawsuit in Berlin over ownership of a holograph parchment **apport** obtained in a seance with Fräulein Else Arnheim in 1920.

The medium, in trance, described the presence of Ludwig Uhland. Taking a few steps in the half-darkened room, suddenly there appeared in her hands, which were tightly clasped by a well-known German author, a piece of parchment, yellow with age, with two short verses scrawled upon it, signed: "Uhland, 1920."

The handwriting was pronounced identical with that of Uhland, the parchment was of his age, the verses were in genuine Uhland style. A **clairvoyant,** to whom Uhland's handwriting and the parchment were shown, declared upon touching both papers that they were written by the same hand but that a long interval elapsed between the writing of them.

The German author whose hand had encircled the medium's when the parchment appeared, claimed the paper. As the witnesses stated that it was thrust into the medium's hand, the court decided that the parchment belonged to the medium. (See also **Apports**)

Ullman, Montague (1916-)

Psychiatrist, parapsychologist, trustee of the American Society for Psychical Research. Born September 9, 1916 in New York, N.Y., he studied at City College of New York (B.S. 1935), New York University College of Medicine (M.S. 1938), New York Medical College (1948, graduate comprehensive course in psychoanalysis). In 1941 he married Janet Simon. He was an intern at Morrisania City Hospital from 1939-41, neurology residency, Montefiore Hospital, New York from 1941-42, psychiatry residency, New York State Psychiatric Institute from 1942-43, U.S. Army officer from 1943-45, member of the psychoanalytic faculty of New York Medical College from 1950-62, assistant clinical professor of pyschiatry, New York Medical College from 1956-62, assistant clinical professor of psychiatry at New York University College of Medicine from 1956-1962, thereafter director of psychiatry at Maimonides Hospital, New York, and associate professor of psychiatry at Downstate Medical Center, State University of New York.

He was president of the Society of Medical Psychoanalysts from 1956-58, charter fellow of the Academy of Psychoanalysis, fellow of the American Psychiatric Association, founding member of Medical Section of American Society for Psychical Research (president, 1971), president of the Parapsychological Association, 1966, member of Society of Medical Psychoanalysts, Society of Biological Psychiatry, Association for Research in Nervous and Mental Disease, member of council of American Association for the Advancement of Science.

Dr. Ullman has taken special interest in telepathy, and clinical investigation of telepathic dreams occurring during psychotherapy. In 1962 he established the **Dream Laboratory** at Maimonides Medical Center, New York, as part of the Department of Psychiatric Services, of which he was chairman. This Laboratory investigated the question of telepathy and dreams by means of the REM (Rapid Eye Movement) monitoring technique.

In addition his papers on psychiatric subjects, Dr. Ullman has published the following articles in the ASPR *Journal:* 'Communication' (April 1948), 'On the Occurrence of Telepathic Dreams' (April 1959). His books include: *Behavioral Changes in Patients Following Strokes* (1962), (joint editor with Roberto Cavanna) *Proceedings of an International Conference on Hypnosis, Drugs, Dreams and Psi: Psi and Altered States of Consciousness* (Parapsychology Foundation, 1968), *A Giant Step* (1969), (with Stanley **Krippner**) *Dream Studies and Telepathy: An Experimental Approach* (Parapsychology Foundation, 1970), (with S. Krippner & A. Vaughan) *Dream Telepathy* (1973), (with Nan Zimmerman) *Working with Dreams* (1979; 1980).

Umbanda

A contemporary Brazilian Spiritist cult involving drumming, candles, spirit possession and healing.

It was founded in 1920 when a young man named Zélio de Moraes was inspired by an Indian spirit. The name itself may be a corruption of Sanskrit. Umbanda was originally a kind of white magic, calling on the gods for good works and charity, but in later developments it has veered towards black magic. (See also **Spiritism**)

Recommended reading:

St. Clair, David. *Drum and Candle,* Doubleday/Bell/Macdonald, London, 1971

Underhill, Mrs. David

Leah, the eldest of the famous Fox sisters, who launched American Spiritualism, who became Mrs. Underhill by her third marriage. She published the book *The Missing Link in Modern Spiritualism* (1885; reprinted 1976). (See also **Fox Sisters**)

Understanding Cults and Spiritual Movements (Research Publication Series)

A tri-yearly research publication designed to analyze critically new religious groups and their leaders. Its aims are defined as follows: "With the continuing growth of new spiritual movements, it is imperative for both the scholar and the seeker to be able to discriminate between groups which are fraudulent and manipulative and those which are genuine and beneficial. The failure to do so has troublesome consequences: witness Jim Jones and Jonestown. What is necessary, therefore, in the examination of religion and its mystical claims—be they old and traditional like Roman Catholicism or new and emerging like Eckankar—is unbridled rational scrutiny. That is, the opportunity to fully investigate every facet about the particular spiritual movement: from the biography of its founder, the history of its organization, the value of its teachings, to the practical application of its techniques, etc.

"*Understanding Cults and Spiritual Movements* is . . . interested in promoting rational inquiries into the entire cult phenomenon. Editorially, it does not hold to any particular religious doctrine, nor does it have any church affiliation. Thus, in this way, it is an open system of study primarily concerned with documented appraisements which help in developing a keen sense of critical discrimination."

Edited by David Christopher **Lane,** it has already established a high standard of scholarly reporting and crucial investigation. Lane is regarded as a leading authority on the history of the Radhasoami spiritual movement which had its origins in Agra, India, in the mid-nineteenth century. Address: Del Mar Press, P.O. Box 2508, Del Mar, California 92508.

Understanding Magazine

Published ten times per year, edited by Daniel W. Fry, author of the book *White Sands Incident* (1954), in which he claimed contact with a **UFO.** *Understanding* promotes the universal spirituality said to relate to the message of visitors in UFOs. Address: Understanding, Inc., Star Route Box 588-F, Tonopah, Arizona 85354.

Underwood, Peter (1923-)

British writer on occultism and psychical investigation. He has also written on the cinema. He is a member of the Society of Psychical Research, Vice-president of the Unitarian Society for Psychical Studies, and former member of the Research Committee of the Psychic Research Organization.

He took part in the first official investigation into a haunting, conducted worldwide tests in telepathy and ESP and has compiled comprehensive files of hauntings in the British Isles. He has been President and Chairman of the **Ghost Club** for many years. He has broadcast and lectured extensively on psychic matters.

His books include: *A Gazetteer of British Ghosts* (1971), *Into the Occult* (1972), *Horror Man: The Life of Boris Karloff* (U.S. title *Karloff,* 1972) *Into the Occult* (1972), *A Gazetteer of Scottish and Irish Ghosts* (1973), *Haunted London* (1973), *A Host of Hauntings* (1973), (with Paul Tabori) *The Ghosts of Borley* (1973), *Life's A Drag: A Biography of Danny La Rue* (1974), *The Vampire's Bedside Companion* (1975), (with Leonard Wilder) *Lives to Remember: A Case-Book on Reincarnation* (1975), *Deeper Into the Occult* (1975), *Hauntings; New Light on the Greatest True Ghost Stories of the World* (1977), *Dictionary of the Supernatural* (1978; reissued as *Dictionary of the Occult of Supernatural, 1979), Ghosts of North-West England* (1978), *Ghosts of Wales* (1978), *A Ghost Hunter's Handbook* (1980), *The Complete Book of Dowsing & Divining* (1980), *No Common Task; The Autobiography of a Ghost Hunter* (1983), *Queen Victoria's Other World* (1987).

Unguents

General term for ointments used in anointing ceremonies in Christianity and also in *witchcraft.* There are many kinds of witchcraft unguents, each with its peculiar properties. It was believed that the devil compounded them in order to harm the human race.

One such unguent was composed of human fat, and said to be used by the witches to enable them to fly through the air to Sabbat.

Many old recipes exist for unguents to induce sleep or visions, and these were compounded from various strange ingredients. Some of them are described in *Des Science Occultes* by Eusèbe Salverte (1829). It is possible that some witch unguents contained hallucinatory drugs, which induced the illusion of flying through the air. (See also **Transvection; Witchcraft**)

Unification Church

Founded by the Rev. Sun Myung **Moon,** a South Korean engineer who leads a millionaire evangelistic cult based on his own interpretation of the Bible. The movement claims three million followers, spread over more than forty countries. Its funds derive from Moon's South Korean armaments factory, titanium plant and tea company, as well as the daily street sales of flowers, candies and peanuts by young devotees. The cult is known in Korea as the Tong-il Church.

Moon's unification principle places great stress on the sanctity of the family, and much of his success arises from the community settlements of followers, who study in an atmosphere of intense indoctrination. Moon is reported as saying to his followers "I am your brain." Anything or anyone that opposes the movement or the faith of the believer is considered an attack from the spirits of Satan.

Teenage converts whose parents object to their involvement are advised to break off relations with them, and in 1967 a release organization similar to **FREECOG** was formed in Korea, charging that the movement had brainwashed their children. However, young devotees, now generally known as "Moonies," are apparently happy, tidy and resolutely resistant to attempts to wean them away from their Church, and so far the "deprogramming" techniques resorted to by desperate parents have been aggressive and more brutal than any indoctrination.

In the process of helping to establish the kingdom of God on earth, which the Rev. Moon considers an imminent event, the movement had a right-wing political slant, and during the Watergate scandals in the 1970s, Moon crusaded in favor of Richard Nixon as a God-chosen president.

The Church has been widely criticized in many different countries. Two of its practices which have been specially condemned are "Love bombing" and "Heavenly deception." In "Love bombing," recruits are often overwhelmed by constant group affection—pats, handholding, smiles and affectionate contact, augmented by continuous activity, lack of sleep and mental bombardment. "Heavenly deception" is deceitful and misleading behavior, based on the Church's premise that the outside world is evil, and thus fair game for deception provided that it is for the benefit of the Unification Church.

The Rev. Myung Moon's books include: *Divine Principle* (1957), *Christianity in Crisis, New Future of Christianity,* the latter two paperbacks published by the Unification Church, New York.

Opponents of the Unification Church charge that it recruits under a large number of religious and cultural front organizations, such a International One World Crusade, Jewish Friendship League, Creative Community Project, Students for an Ethical Society, U.S. Youth Council, etc.

Recommended reading:

Conway, Flo & Jim Siegelman. *Snapping; America's Epidemic of Sudden Personality Change,* Lippincott, 1978; Delta paperback, 1979

Swatland, Susan & Anne. *Escape From the Moonies,* New English Library, London, 1982

Union Esperitista Cristiana de Filipinas, Inc.

A kind of trade union of the psychic surgeons in the Philippines. (See also **Psychic Surgery**)

Union Spirite Bordelaise (Journal)

Nineteenth-century Spiritist journal, published in Bordeaux, France, incorporating other journals. (See also **France; Spiritism**)

Union Spirite Française

French Spiritualist organization founded at 8 Rue Copernic, Paris, president Léon Chevreuil, vice-president Jean **Meyer,** official organ: *Le Bulletin de l'Union Spirite Francaise.* The organization was based at the same address as the *Maison des Spirities,* founded by Jean Meyer, and was active in the 1930s. (See also **France; Spiritualism**)

Unity-in-Diversity Council

An international coordinating body devoted to linking metaphysical and **New Age** groups. It was originally formed as the **International Cooperation Council,** coordinating cultural and religious organizations which, in their own ways, "foster the emergence of a new universal person and a civilization based on unity in diversity among all peoples. Formed to propagate the ideals and activities of such organizations during International Cooperation Year, it was voted into being in 1965 by the General Assembly of the United Nations. Unity-in-Diversity Council continues the work of publicizing the aims and ideas of humanitarian groups which bring together the methods and discoveries of modern science and the deeper insights of religion, philosophy, and the arts. Much of this synthesis is concerned with developing areas of awareness in human consciousness and unorthodox healing techniques.

In the early period, the Council took part in a New Age Institute, as a result of an educational conference held in 1974 in Los Angeles, directed toward public and private education. A World-View Exploration Seminar, formed in Spring 1969, grew out of the Fifth Annual International Cooperation festival, composed primarily of professional individuals from the fields of science, religion, art, education, and philosophy, meeting on the campus of the California State College at Los Angeles, to explore "the meaning of the new universal person and the world civilization."

In place of the magazine *The Cooperator,* the Unity-in-Diversity Council now issues the journal *Spectrum,* and also publishes the *Directory for a New World.* Address: 1010 S. Flower Street, Suite 500, Los Angeles, California 90015. (See also **International Cooperation Council**)

Univercoelum (Journal)

The organ which Andrew Jackson **Davis** started in December 1847, in New York, for "the establishment of a universal system of Truth, the Reform and Reorganization of Society." It ran for a year and a half and was absorbed in July, 1849, in W. M. Channing's *The Present Age.* (See also Andrew Jackson **Davis**)

Univercolian (Magazine)

Quarterly publication growing out of former *Pyramid Guide* Newsletter, concerned with earth mysteries, featuring articles on such subjects as Easter Island, Stonehenge, Atlantis, UFOs, and energy centers. Address. P.O. Box 292, Dalton, Massachusetts 01226.

Universal Balm

An elixir sought by alchemists, which was supposed to be a remedy for every malady, and would even bring the dead back to life. (See also **Alchemy; Elixir of Life**)

Universe Quarterly

Quarterly journal of the Vortex Institute, Inc. of Fairbanks, Alaska, concerned with spiritual life in Alaska, self-growth techniques and meditation. Address: 331 Fifth Avenue, Fairbanks, Alaska 99707.

Universities (Occult)

In many works on the occult sciences, allusions are made to schools and universities for the instruction of those who were drawn to them. Thus we are told that Salamanca abounded in such schools, that Jechiel, a Jewish rabbi of medieval France, kept such a seminary.

There is reason to believe that in past ages such institutions were by no means uncommon. The novelist Balzac alluded to one of them in the story *The Secret of Ruggier,* which he placed at the time of Catherine de Medici. He stated: "At this epoch the occult sciences were cultivated with an adour which put to shame the incredulous spirit of our century. . . . The universal protection accorded to these sciences by the ruling sovereigns of the times was quite remarkable." He went on to say that at the commencement of the sixteenth century, Ruggier was the member of a secret university for the study of the occult sciences, where astrologers, alchemists, and others, studied several branches of hidden knowledge, but he gave no details as to its locality, or as to the exact nature of its curriculum.

There is no doubt that during the Middle Ages many extramural lecturers taught **alchemy** and kindred subjects at great universities. Thus **Paracelsus** lectured on alchemy at the University of Basel, and he was preceded and followed there and elsewhere by many illustrious professors of that and other occult arts.

Louis Figuier in his book *L'alchimie et les alchimistes* (1854) (see **Alchemy**) alluded to a school in Paris frequented by alchemists, which he himself attended in the middle of the nineteenth century. The school—an ordinary chemical laboratory during the day—became in the evening a center of the most elaborate alchemical study, where Figuier met many alchemical students, visionary and practical, with one of whom he had a prolonged argument, cited in the entry on **"Alchemy."**

Many professors of the occult sciences in early and later times drew around them bands of students and assistants and formed distinct schools for the practice of occult magic and alchemy, principally the latter.

The College of Augurs in Rome and the Calmecac of Ancient Mexico are distinct examples of institutions for the study of at least one branch of occult science, and in this connection, the House of Wisdom of the Ismaelite sect at Cairo, Egypt, may be mentioned. It is likely that in ancient Egypt and Babylonia, institutions of the kind flourished more or less in secret.

Mme. **Blavatsky** insisted that a great "school" of illuminated occult adepts flourished in Tibet, but as nobody except herself and her immediate friends ever saw them, or had any dealings with them, and since all the evidence is against the existence of such a semi-divine brotherhood, her statements must be taken as being somewhat open to question.

There is, however, little reason to doubt that bodies of men who studied higher occultism did exist in various Asiatic centers, whatever the nature of their powers, supernormal or otherwise. Vague rumors have reached students of occultism from time to time of schools or colleges on the continent of Europe, the purpose of which was to train aspirants in the occult arts, but as definite information has seldom been forthcoming regarding these, they can only be merely alluded to here.

The "School for the Discovery of the Lost Secrets of Antiquity," which flourished in California, was founded by Katherine **Tingley** late in the nineteenth century, and was under Theosophical auspices. Numerous small bodies for the study of occultism existed in many cities in Europe and America, but these could hardly be dignified by the name of "schools," as they were for the most part private affairs, the occultism of which was of an extremely amateurish and dubious character.

The real modern equivalent of ancient occult universities is the secret order or society, such as the **Golden Dawn,** where occult and mystical subjects were taught to students, with grades of advancement. Many such orders, less illustrious than the Golden Dawn, are still in existence, in addition to the ubiquitous mail-order occult schools and the pop occult cults which are so marked a feature of modern life.

Occultism is also no stranger to conventional university courses. During the occult boom of the 1960s, various American universities included courses on magic, witchcraft and other occult history, Philip E. I. **Bonewits** attained fame in 1970 as the first accredited Bachelor of Arts with a major in Magic, awarded by the University of California.

University Books, Inc.

One of the most influential imprints in occult publishing from the 1950s onwards, founded by Felix **Morrow,** who played a major role in initiating the modern occult revival by reprinting rare and important scholarly works of occultism and mysticism which had long been unavailable.

In addition to sales to libraries, the books reached a large general public through the Mystic Arts Book Club. The occult revival has drawn heavily from these literary sources, and most of the books published by University Books during the 1950s and 1960s have been source material for occultists.

In 1966, the company was absorbed by Lyle Stuart, Inc., which continued occult publishing under the Citadel Press imprint. (See also Felix **Morrow**)

University of London Council for Psychical Investigation

A reorganization of the National Laboratory of Psychical Research which had been founded by psychical researcher Harry **Price** in 1926. The National Laboratory passed under the direction of the University of London Council on June 6, 1934. At that date the premises were still at the National Laboratory address of 13d Roland Gardens, South Kensington, London, S.W.7, but by the end of 1936 the great library formed by Harry Price was moved to University College, London.

Later the National Laboratory's seance room and laboratory equipment were transferred to the administrate offices of the University Council at 19

Berkeley Street, London, W.1, but practical experimentation ceased with the outbreak of World War II. After the death of Harry Price in 1948, the library was bequeathed to the University of London at Senate House, Male Street, London, W.C.1, where it is still available for research.

A Short-Title Catalogue of the library was issued as vol. 1, part 2 of the *Proceedings* of the National Laboratory of Psychical Research; a Supplement was issued as Bulletin 1 of the University of London Council for Psychical Investigation.

Other *Bulletins* issued by the University of London Council were: *Bulletin II, A Report on Two Experimental Fire-Walks; Bulletin III, Preliminary Studies of a Vaudeville Telepathist.* (See also **National Laboratory of Psychical Research;** Harry **Price; Proceedings of the National Laboratory of Psychical Research**)

University of the Trees

An experimental school community for world change through consciousness research and related spiritual development. The main thrust of teaching is directed towards self-discovery and creative individual change, and in addition to community life courses, teaching is also maintained through correspondence with students all over the world. Courses are wide-ranging including Art, Literature, Changing, Environmental Studies, Transpersonal Awareness, Alternative Energy Systems, Health and Yoga, Healing, History and Neurology of Consciousness, Philosophy, Mysticism, Radiational Physics and "Supersensonics" (radiesthesia, dowsing, pyramid research, psychotronics). The term "the Trees" denoted the nerve dendrites in the brain, and the "Tree of Life" of the nervous system that can combine with knowledge to enhance direct perception of truth from within the individual.

This university is authorized to grant degrees in consciousness research, but aims to provide students with methods of study that deepen their inner awareness rather than just accumulate additional mental data.

The community was founded in 1973 and grew out of the teachings of Christopher **Hills,** a **New Age** teacher, researcher and yogi who directs the work of the university. Associated with the university is a **Research Institute for Supersensonic Healing Energies.** Address: P.O. Box 644, 13151 Pine Street, Boulder Creek, California 95006.

Unknown, The (Magazine)

British monthly magazine "exploring strange phenomena." The first issue, published July 1985, includes discussions at a popular level of Spontaneous Combustion, Ley Lines, Wolf Children, Lost Civilizations, Sea Serpents, Alchemy, and the Fatima apparitions. Apparently no longer published.

Unknown World, The (Journal)

Occult and metaphysical journal edited by Arthur Edward **Waite** (1857-1942). It was devoted to "The Occult Sciences, Magic, Mystical Philosophy, Alchemy, Hermetic Archaeology, and the Hidden Problems of Science, Literature, Speculation and History." It appeared from 1895-96.

Unknown Worlds (Newsletter)

Bi-monthly newsletter reporting strange phenomena of a Fortean kind. Published by: World Investigators of Strange Phenomena, Route 2, Box 159, Vina, Alabama 35593.

Uphoff, Walter (1913-)

Professor of economics who has also written and lectured extensively in the field of parapsychology. Born February 28, 1913 in Sheboygan County, Wisconsin, he studied at University of Wisconsin (B.S. 1934, Ph.M. 1935).

He was since concerned with educational programs and farmer-labor relations, becoming manager in Oregon and Wisconsin of Fellowship Farm Co-Op from 1941-50; from 1951-53 he was research associate, Industrial Relations Center, University of Minnesota, Minneapolis; assistant professor 1953-61; associate professor of industrial relations and head of labor education 1961-63; professor of economics and director of labor education at University of Colorado, Boulder 1963-73; secretary of Wisconsin Association of Cooperatives 1948-52. In 1938 he married Mary Jo Weiler, who has co-authored some of his writings on parapsychology.

He is a member of the American Society for Psychical Research, Spiritual Frontiers Fellowship, ESP Research Associates Foundation (board member), Academy of Parapsychology & Medicine, Society for Psychical Research (London). Between 1958-59 he worked at University of Cologne on a Fulbright Senior research grant.

His publications include: *The Kohler Strike* (1935), *Kohler on Strike: Thirty Years of Conflict* (1966; 1967); (ed) *Prepaid Group Practice Health Plans* (1968), (contrib.) Harold Sherman: *You Can Communicate with the Unseen World* (1974), (with Mary Jo Uphoff) *New Psychic Frontiers; Your Key to New Worlds* (1975). He has contributed to the journal *Psychic Researcher,* and is co-author of a newspaper column "Beyond the Five Senses."

He founded the *New Frontiers Center Newsletter,* published: Fellowship Farm, RR 1, Oregon, Wisconsin 53575.

Upright Man, The

In the sixteenth century, the vagabonds and beggars of Britain were organized into unions with rules and grades. Of these grades, the order of the "Upright Man" seems to have some special significance and authority, and is believed by some authorities to have descended from the folk adherents of paganism, the "Old Religion" or **witchcraft.**

Ura

A Babylonian spirit. (See **Babylonia**)

Urantia

A nineteenth-century psychically inspired gospel expressed in *The Urantia Book* (1955). It explains that the true name of Earth is Urantia and that we are part of the universe of Nebadon, or the larger universe of Orvonton, whose central committee of Uversa dictated the work.

The book presents a heterodox view of human origins, including precursors of Adam and Eve, and a claimed more accurate version of the life and teaching of Jesus (said to have been really Michael of Nebadon, one of the myriad Sons of the Eternal Son). The miracles are given largely natural explanations, and the crucifixion was apparently not a blood atonement, original sin being said to be an error of the Bible. Much of the work, which includes remarkable statements of a pseudoscientific kind, reads like science fiction.

The book owes its publication to William S. Sadler (1875-1969), former Seventh-Day Adventist minister, who served as a surgeon in Adventist hospitals before leaving the movement. Although skeptical of psychic phenomena, he became involved with the Urantia writings which proceeded from an unnamed individual who "became a clearing house for the coming and going of alleged extraplanetary personalities." These channeled communications were first studied in the 1920s by a group of individuals named The Forum. The Urantia Brotherhood was formed in 1950 in Chicago, Illinois, and is now association with the continued publication and study of *The Urantia Book.*

For a critical and skeptical view of this work, see 'The Great Urantia Mystery' by Martin Gardner in *The Skeptical Inquirer* (vo. 14, No. 2, Winter 1990). For information on the Urantia Brotherhood and copies of the book, contact: Urantia Brotherhood, 533 Diversey Parkway, Chicago, Illinois 60614.

Urantia News (Newsletter)

Quarterly newsletter concerned with the **Urantia** Papers, a psychically inspired American scripture.

Now superseded by *Urantia Brotherhood Bulletin* and *Urantia,* published by The Urantian Brotherhood, 533 Diversey parkway, Chicago, Illinois 60614. (See also **Urantia**)

Urban, Hubert Josef (1904-)

Professor of neuropsychiatry who investigated areas of parapsychology. Born June 4, 1904 at Linz, Austria, he studied at University of Vienna (B.A. 1923, M.D. 1929), special studies in neurology, neurosurgery, neuro-anatomy and psychiatry in Venice, San Francisco, Paris, Stockholm, Breslau, Buenos Aires. In 1934 he married Mathilde Schoerg.

He was professor of neuropsychiatry at University of Innsbruck, Austria from 1938 onwards, visiting professor at University of Malaya, Singapore, University of St. John, Shanghai from 1948-49.

Dr. Urban took special interest in telepathy, clairvoyance and mediumship as related to psychiatry, and studied the question of extrasensory ability before and after shock treatment or narcoanalysis. Between 1948 and 1958, he made visits to India to conduct field work in psychiatry, and also investigated spontaneous psi phenomena. He published articles on connections between psi, psychiatry and medicine in such magazines as *Deutsche Medizinische Rundschau* and *Neue Wissenschaft.*

Urim and Thummim

A means of **divination** employed by the ancient Hebrews, and which it was believed consisted of a species of casting lots.

Their form and methods of use is uncertain, but from passages in the book of *Samuel,* it seems probable that (1) they were used to determine guilt and innocence, and (2) that this was done by means of categorical questions, to which the suspected person answered "Yes" or "No." They appear to have been the prerogative of the priesthood.

Urine

Urine has long been credited with magical and medicinal properties. It has been featured in witchcraft and black magic rituals. It has been mixed with wine, herbs or oils, used as an ointment or in pills, employed in **amulets, talismans** and charms, used in aphrodisiacs and fertility potions.

Medicinally, urine has unusual properties. It contains ammonia, which can neutralize acids, and is usually free from bacteria, thus having disinfectant properties. Women have drunk urine from their husbands to speed up childbirth, or have been given their own urine to relieve hysteria. Male urine contains androsterone, a male hormone, and it has long been believed that drinking one's urine improves health and virility.

Even in modern times, Moraji Desai, former prime minister of India, openly admitted to drinking a small quantity of his own urine each morning for health reasons.

U.S. Psychotronics Association

Founded in 1975 for persons interested in the study of psychotronics, "the science of mind-body-environment relationships, concerned with the interactions of matter, energy and consciousness," and psychic phenomena, free energy systems, **radionics,** and alternative health methodologies.

It provides a forum for the exchange of current research developments in psychotronics. It seeks to maintain high standards of ethical, humanitarian and scientific practices in the study and applications of psychotronics. It promotes standardization in investigation, testing, reporting, and evaluation of **psychotronics,** preserves the history of the field.

It also promotes continuing education and training of members, presents members' views to the government, the public and other organizations, bestows research awards, and makes available cassette recordings of conference lectures. Research programs include: Anti-Gravity, Agri-Radionics, Free Energy, Psychic Detectors, Psychic Instrumentation (hardware types), Radionics, Tens Units, Tesla Waves. Publication: quarterly *Newsletter.* Address: 2141 W. Agatite, Chicago, Illinois 60625.

U.S.S.R.

During the 1960s, it became evident that there was widespread modern interest in parapsychology in the U.S.S.R. after the ultra conservative science of the Stalin era. One of the pioneers in this psychic renaissance was Leonid L. **Vasiliev** (1891-1966), who helped to establish the first parapsychology laboratory in the Soviet Union, at Leningrad. His book *Mysterious Manifestations of the Human Psyche* (1959) was published in the U.S. under the title *Mysterious Phenomena of the Human Psyche* (University Books, 1965).

One possible stimulus for Soviet interest in ESP was the story leaked in the French press in 1959 that the U.S. Navy had experimented with telepathic communication between the atomic submarine *Nautilus* and a shore base. It was clear that ESP might have military significance.

Another surprising Soviet interest was disclosed in the readiness of the authorities to permit lectures and demonstrations by Hindu hatha yogis. This had nothing to do with pre-revolutionary bourgeois cults of mysticism, but rather indicated willingness to learn about the alleged paranormal physical feats claimed for **yoga.** It has to be remembered that Russians have always placed great importance on physical training and sport. In addition, any system of physical culture which promised unusual feats of endurance or control of automatic nervous functions might also have relevance to the physical stresses involved in space travel.

By 1966, the Soviet Union was financing over twenty centers for the scientific study of the paranormal, involving an annual budget of around 12 to 20 million rubles ($13 to $21 million). Soviet parapsychologists studied reports of such American psychics as Edgar **Cayce,** Jeane **Dixon,** and Ted **Serios,** as well as the parapsychological researches of J. B. **Rhine** and others.

Throughout the sixties, Soviet parapsychologists investigated the phenomena of their own sensitives in such fields as **Dowsings, Psychokinesis, Telepathy,** Psychic **Healing** and **Eyeless Sight.** The remarkable feats of such talented Soviet individuals as Nina **Kulagina** in PK and Rosa **Kuleshova** in Fingertip Vision (Eyeless Sight) became widely known and discussed outside the Soviet Union.

Perhaps because of such international publicity, Soviet authorities have from time to time suppressed information on parapsychological researches, whilst a backlash of dogmatic conservatism has sometimes ridiculed or impeded parapsychology studies. However, the essentially practical investigations into paranormal faculties by Soviet scientists hold promise that they may achieve a real breakthrough in such fields of study.

In his book *Psychic Warfare: Threat or Illusion,* (1983) Martin Ebon claimed that in the early 1970s, the KGB took over extensive parapsychological research to attempt to identify psi particles, to discover unknown communication channels in living cells for the transfer of information, and follow-up studies on such subjects as hypnosis at a distance. On a popular level, interest has grown in such areas as "thoughtography" and UFOs.

In the book *Psychic Discoveries Behind the Iron Curtain* (1970), Sheila Ostrander and Lynn Schroeder revealed the wide range of important Soviet research in parapsychology. Much of their book was based on firsthand interviews and observations during visits to the Soviet Union and other Communist countries. The book is a valuable source for information on individuals and organizations concerned in the Communist psychic renaissance. Some of these are reviewed briefly below.

Rosa Kuleshova, exponent of "fingertip vision" or Eyeless Sight suffered from over-exposure of her talent and for a time was accused of cheating before her strange abilities were reasserted. Meanwhile Abram Novemeisky at the Nizhnig Tagil Pedagogical Institute in the Urals experimented with graphic arts students; he claimed that one is six individuals could distinguish between two colors by fingertip vision.

Dr. Yakov Fishelev of the Sverdlovsk Pedagogical Institute confirmed such findings and also experimented with subjects at the Pyshma school for the blind, starting with fingertip color recognition and then developing the ability to distinguish shapes of letters.

Dr. S. N. Dobronravov of Sverdlovsk reported that he had found "skin sight" potential in 72% of children, mostly between the ages of 7 and 12.

At the Filatov Institute Laboratory of the Physiology of Vision, in Odessa, a strange experiment was conducted by Dr. Andrei Shevalev. His subject was Vania Dubrovich, an eight-year-old boy blind from early childhood, whose eyes and optical nerves had been removed. Dr. Shevalev attached a lens to Vania's forehead, and the boy learnt to distinguish degrees of light through the lens. This experiment may open up new possibilities of "skin glasses."

In the field of Psychokinesis, the unusual ability of Nina Kulagina to move small objects at a distance without contact was first discovered by Dr. L. L. Vasiliev, after Nina had demonstrated a talent for "skin vision." Dr. Vasiliev found that she could influence a compass needle by holding her hands over it. In further PK tests it was discovered that Nina could disturb or move objects at a distance. Film records have been made demonstrating such remarkable PK ability. Amongst other feats Nina has apparently changed the flow of sand in an hour-glass and made letters appear on photographic paper by mental force. In early reports, her identity was at first hidden by the pseudonym "Nelya Mikhailovna."

In March 1988, Nina won an astonishing libel action against the magazine *Man and Law,* published by the Soviet Justice Ministry. Two articles by Vyacheslav Strelkov published in the magazine described Nina as "a swindler and a crook." The Moscow Court ruled that Strelkov had no firm evidence on which to base his allegations, and the magazine was ordered to publish an apology to Nina. In a subsequent appeal to the Moscow City Court, the District Court's ruling was upheld "that the articles published by 'Man and Law' besmirch the honor and dignity of Nina Kulagina and that it must publish an apology."

In the freer atmosphere of public debate and expression of opinion arising from the Gorbachev policy of *glasnost,* public support and discussion of psychic matters has increased. Psychic healing has received much attention, and the healer Barbara Ivanova has treated many prominent officials. In recent times she has undertaken distant healing through telephone.

In the field of Dowsing and Radiesthesia, Soviet scientists like Prof. G. Bogomolov and Dr. Nikolai Sochevanov have assembled impressive data to validate the reality of such phenomena. New techniques and apparatus have been developed. Dowsers have now been used to locate damaged cables, water pipes, electrical lines, as well as underground minerals and water. One series of dowsing tests suggested that women dowsers have a higher ability than men. Dowsing and Radiesthetic work is now reported as the "Biophysical Effect."

Soviet experiments in telepathy are well advanced. Dr. L. L. Vasiliev studied spontaneous telepathy for nearly forty years and collected hundreds of circumstantial accounts. In 1967, Yuri Kamensky in Moscow successfully relayed a telepathic message to Karl Nikolaiev in Leningrad; the message was in kind of Morse code.

Other telepathy experiments involved the transmission of emotions, monitored by EEG records. A number of experiments were conducted to ascertain optimum conditions for telepathic transmission, involving a complex of touch, visualization and thought.

Sometimes a biological sympathy between sender and receiver (heart beat, brain wave and similar synchronism) was found to facilitate transmission. Even the influence of high-frequency electro-magnetic waves on telepathy has been studied, whilst the neurologist Vladimir Bekhterev has experimented with telepathy between human beings and animals.

One of the most remarkable developments in Soviet parapsychology is the technique of **Kirlian Photography,** developed by Semyon D. Kirlian and Valentina C. Kirlian, a method of photographing an aura in human beings and nature generally; this luminous aura has been found to vary in different conditions of health.

Although the Soviet Academy of Sciences declared in 1968 that the search for UFOs was "unscientific," it seems that reports of UFOs are still closely studied, and Soviet scientists are prepared to consider the possibility of extraterrestrial intelligences.

Over the past two or three decades, there have been many reports of UFO phenomena from the USSR, and on October 9, 1989, the Soviet News Agency *TASS* astonished the world by reporting claims that a UFO had landed on the evening of September 27, 1989, in a park at Voronezh, a city of 900,000 inhabitants some three hundred miles southeast of Moscow, and that the UFO occupants had walked about and been seen by many people. For a detailed report and evaluation of this remarkable story, see *Flying Saucer Review* (vol. 34, No. 4, 1898).

The essentially practical and scientific investigations of Soviet scientists into every major aspect of the paranormal is in sharp contrast to the more romantic interest of Western countries, where psychics demonstrate for entertainment. The down-to-earth Soviet approach into the how and why of the paranormal appears to be yielding remarkable results with clearly practical applications.

For an authoritative survey of Soviet researches in parapsychology and psychotronics, see the journal *Psi Research* edited by Larissa Vilenskaya, published quarterly by Washington Research Institute & Parapsychology Research Group, San Francisco, California. (See also **Russia**)

Recommended reading:

Ebon, Martin. *Psychic Discoveries by the Russians,* Parapsychology Foundation, 1963; Signet paperback, 1971

Ebon, Martin. *Psychic Warfare Threat or Illusion,* McGraw Hill, 1983

Hobana, Ion & J. Weverbergh. *Unidentified Flying Objects from Behind the Iron Curtain,* Souvenir Press, London, 1974; Corgi paperback, 1975; Bantam paperback, 1976

Ostrander, Sheila & Lynn Schroeder. *Psychic Discoveries Behind the Iron Curtain,* Prentice-Hall, 1970;Bantam paperback, 1971. (The same authors have also published a phonotape reel titled 'Parapsychology in Communist Countries,' Big Sur Recordings No. 647, 1972. This includes new material.)

V

Valentine, Basil (c. 1413)

This German adept in alchemical philosophy is commonly supposed to have been born at Mayence towards the close of the fourteenth century. As a young man he took holy orders, and entered the Abbey of St. Peter, at Erfurt, and eventually became its Prior, but otherwise very little is known concerning him, and even the date of his death is not known. Indeed, even his existence is believed to be mythical by some authorities, and in the absence of any definitive data on this individual, we have only popular belief and sparse reference on which to sketch his life.

He appears to have been a very modest person, for according to Olaus Borrichius, the author of *De Ortu et Progressu Chemiæ*, Valentine hid all the manuscripts of his writings inside one of the pillars of the Abbey Church, and they might have remained for an indefinite period, but for a thunderstorm, when they were discovered by a flash of lightning that dislodged them from their curious hiding-place. This reluctance for his work to be known may have been prompted by fear of the Inquisition discovering his researches in alchemy.

Valentine's works certainly mark him as a very shrewd man and a capable scientist. Unlike much other medieval literature, his treatises were not all in Latin, some of them being in high Dutch and others in German. Prominent among those in his own language is *The Triumphal Chariot of Antimony*, first published at Leipzig in 1624. In this work, Valentine extolled antimony as an excellent medicine, while the volume likewise embodies a lengthy metrical treatise on the **philosopher's stone,** the writer contending that whoever would discover and use this must do charitable deeds, mortify the flesh, and pray without ceasing. Among the alchemist's further writings, are *Apocalypsis Chymica, De Microcosmo degue Magno Mundi Mysterio et Medecina Hominis* and *Practica unà cum duodecim Clavibus et Appendice*. All these were originally published in Germany at the beginning of the seventeenth century, and various passages in them demonstrate that the author understood the distillation of brandy, and was acquainted with the method of obtaining chlorohydric acid from salt-water, while reverting to his faith in antimony, he has been credited with having been the first to extract this from sulphuret. (See also **Alchemy; Philosopher's Stone**)

Valiantine, George (c. 1874- ?)

Direct voice medium of Williamsport, New York. Much controversy surrounded his mediumship. He was a small manufacturer when at the age of forty-three, his mediumship was discovered by accident. At a hotel where he was staying he heard distinct **raps** on the door. No physical agency could be detected and he was deeply puzzled. A lady acquaintance who was familiar with Spiritualism later persuaded him to hold a seance with the table.

The result was surprising. His deceased brother-in-law, Bert Everett, claimed to be present and rapped out that the spirits for a long time had been trying to attract Valiantine's attention.

"Everett" instructed Valiantine to make a **cabinet.** One evening, the medium went into trance and "Bert Everett" appeared in a materialized form. But direct voice communications became the chief feature of the seances as Valiantine's organism appeared to lend itself with facility to this manifestation. "Bert Everett" found assistants in other controls: "Dr. Barnett," who often gave medical prescriptions, "Hawk Chief" and "Kokum," two Red Indians with booming voices and "Black Foot," another Indian, the last usually speaking in deep tones from the center of the floor.

In 1923 *The Scientific American* of New York offered a prize of $2,500 for the production of genuine physical phenomena. Valiantine was one of the mediums tested. He was designated as Mr. X. Dr. Gardner **Murphy** of the Columbia University and Kenneth Andrews of the *New York World* visited him at Wilkes-Barre for two preliminary sittings. Both of them were successful and they returned impressed. Thereupon Valiantine came to New York.

During his first two seances before the Committee of *The Scientific American,* eight distinct spirits manifested and spoke to the sitters. For the third seance, an electrical control apparatus had been secretly fixed to the medium's chair. It was meant to disclose to observers in another room whether the medium left his chair during the seance, under the cover of the darkness, to reach after the trumpet. The apparatus did not register the medium's full weight for fifteen seconds on one occasion and from 1-14 seconds on other occasions.

For this reason, although the voices admittedly came from high in the air and carried on prolonged conversation, the result, in the report published in the July 1923 issue of *The Scientific American,* was ruled out as evidence. Over the construction of the report, which conveyed the impression that Valiantine was actually caught in fraud, a controversy arose between psychical researcher J. Malcolm **Bird** and British author H. Dennis **Bradley,** who pointed out the weaknesses of the report and its important admissions which, however, were not sufficiently emphasized.

On several occasions, Bradley vigorously defended Valiantine. He met him at Arlena Towers, Ramsey, New York, in the home of Joseph de Wyckoff, a wealthy American financier who had been in close association with Valiantine for some years.

In November 1923, Wyckoff received long scripts from Valiantine which Valiantine said he had obtained in **direct writing** in his home. They were signed by "Everett" and "Dr. Barnett," and referred to a material project involving an expedition to Guiana. Wyckoff discovered by chance that Valiantine's handwriting showed striking resemblance to the spirit scripts and took them to a handwriting expert who pronounced them identical.

Wyckoff showed the report to Valiantine. He insisted that he did not do the writings. A test seance was arranged at his own house at Williamsport. Valiantine, at his request, was tied up. The seance was a failure. Wyckoff thereupon broke his relations with Valiantine.

Not long afterwards, Wyckoff went to Europe. He met Bradley, who convinced him, by showing indirect evidence which he obtained in sittings with the medium Mrs. Osborne **Leonard,** that his evaluation of the Valiantine communications was unjust. Thereupon Wyckoff cabled to Valiantine from Europe and invited him to come and join him. Valiantine arrived in February 1924, and gave seances almost daily for five weeks in Bradley's home.

In the presence of more than fifty prominent people, over one hundred different spirit voices manifested and carried on long conversations in Russian, German, Spanish and even in idiomatic Welsh, Mr. Caradoc Evans, the Welsh novelist, speaking with his father's spirit in Cardiganshire Welsh.

But the seeds of suspicion had been sown in Wyckoff's heart. He soon leveled a second charge against Valiantine. It grew out of a sitting in the St. Regis Hotel in New York on April 19, 1924. When the sitting was closed by the address of "Dr. Barnett," the trumpet had fallen sideways between Valiantine's legs, with the small end against the edge of the chair. As the medium was setting it upright, Wyckoff struck a match and scolded him for his action. Moreover, as J. Malcolm Bird pointed out in a letter to *Light,* "examination of the trumpet developed the facts that it was quite warm at the point where a human hand would naturally and conveniently grasp it, and that the mouthpiece was damp."

Bradley answered that this is exactly what would happen with independent voice phenomena. In his own seances, in which the luminous trumpet was seen sailing about the room, at the finish the inside was found moist, according to Bradley, for the simple reason that it is necessary for a spirit to materialize the vocal organs and breath in order to produce its voice.

In the following year, Valiantine paid another visit to England. In March 1925, he gave two test sittings before the Society for Psychical Research at Tavistock Square. Five words were spoken at the first, none at the second. They were considered blank.

Following this failure, Una, Lady Troubridge and Miss Radcliffe Hall of the Society, attended some sittings in Bradley's house. Later they were joined by Dr. Woolley, research officer of the Society. Eleven distinct and individual voices were heard. Dr. Woolley agreed that he heard them and could not account for them. He was also satisfied that the movement of the luminous trumpet in the air was supernormal. Shortly afterwards E. J. **Dingwall,** in company with Dr. Woolley, the other research officer of the Society, obtained voices in daylight inside Valiantine's trumpet.

In his report in the *Journal* of the Society for Psychical Research (vol. 26, pp. 70-71; vol. 27, p. 170; *Proceedings* vol. 36, pp. 52-53) Woolley wrote of these experiences and stated: "Both of us heard raps which seemed similar to those she [Lady Troubridge] has described, but as I wish only to deal in this account with evidential utterances I do not propose to consider them in further detail. Both of us also heard whispering sounds, apparently in the trumpet, at times when we were convinced that Mr. Valiantine's lips were entirely closed, and I was able also to distinguish the words 'Father Woolley,' but nothing further."

The Coming of Confucius

But the most important phase of Valiantine's mediumship was yet to come. Strange languages were heard in seances in New York, and it was decided to test their nature by inviting a scholar. Dr. Neville **Whymant,** an authority on Chinese history, philosophy and ancient literature, who happened to be in New York was requested by Judge and Mrs. Cannon to come to a seance. He was slightly amused, but accepted.

To quote from his notes: "Suddenly, out of the darkness was heard a weird, crackling, broken little sound, which at once carried my mind straight back to China. It was the sound of a flute, rather poorly played, such as can be heard in the streets of the Celestial Land but nowhere else. Then followed in a low, but very audible voice the words 'K'ung-fu T'Zu.' Few persons, except Chinese, could pronounce the name correctly as the sounds cannot be represented in English letters. The idea that it might be Confucius himself never occurred to me. I had imagined that it might be somebody desirous of discussing the life and philosophy of the great Chinese teacher."

When, however, correct personal information was given, Dr. Whymant decided to test the matter to the full. He said: "There is among your writings a passage written wrongly; should it not read thus?" At this point, Whymant began to quote as far as he knew, that is to say, to about the end of the first line. At once the words were taken out of his mouth, and the whole passage was recited in Chinese, exactly as it is recorded in the standard works of reference. After a pause of about fifteen seconds, the passage was again repeated, this time with certain alterations which gave it a new meaning. "Thus read," said the voice, "does not its meaning become plain?" Previous to the voice of "Confucius," Dr. Whymant heard a Sicilian chant and conversed with one of the controls, "Cristo d'Angelo," in Italian.

At the next seance at which Dr. Whymant was present, after having been absent through illness, "Confucius" again manifested and, omitting all ceremonious expressions, referred to Whymant's indisposition, saying "the weed of sickness was growing beside thy door." This metaphor was used in ancient Chinese literature but it is no longer current in the language. Nor was the dialect in which Confucius spoke any longer used in the Chinese Empire.

There are only about twelve Chinese sounds of which it can be definitely said that it was known how the Chinese of Confucius' time would have pronounced them. The voice which claimed to be that of Confucius used these archaic sounds correctly. Moreover, there were at that time only about six Chinese scholars in the world whose knowledge would have been equal to the one displayed by the direct voice. None of them was in America at the time.

In 1927, when Valiantine paid a third visit to England further tests of importance took place. Countess Ahlefeldt-Laurvig brought an ancient Chinese shell to a sitting in the apartment of Lord Charles Hope. At the top of the shell, circular folds ended in a small hollow mouthpiece. In China the shell was used as a horn and blown on occasions as a "call." The sitters tried it but could produce no sound whatever. Yet at one period during the sitting, from high up in the room, the shell horn was blown, and the peculiar notes were rendered in the correct Chinese fashion.

But the most important Chinese test tried was in making a phonograph record of the voice of "Confucius." The attempt was successful. The voice of "Confucius," who died in 479 B.C., was recorded in 1927 in London. It has curious flute-like tones, which rise and fall, and sometimes break into a peculiar sing-song tone. Dr. Whymant could only interpret a few sentences because the voice was faint and became blurred in the recording. But he recognized a number of the peculiar intonations. He could gather the meaning of the recorded speech by the tonal values. The voice was identical with the one he heard in America.

From H. Dennis Bradley's summary of this strange occurrence it is interesting to quote: "I have heard the K'ung-fu T'ze voice speaking on two or three occasions in archaic Chinese. I have also heard the same voice with its peculiar intonation, speaking to me personally in English. The voice has spoken slowly, but with quite beautiful cadences. It possessed an extraordinary dignity."

New Controversies

In his books *Towards the Stars* (1942) and *The Wisdom of the Gods* (1925), Bradley published many important accounts of sittings with Valiantine. On several occasions he heard Valiantine speak simultaneously with the voices. He listened to the voices of the controls of Valiantine in seances with other mediums and heard "Feda," the control of Mrs. Osborne Leonard, and "Cristo d'Angelo," who later associated himself with the Marquis **Centurione Scotto,** speak through Valiantine.

Including the 1927 period, Bradley conducted over a hundred experiments of which 95 percent were successful. This high percentage of success was undoubtedly partly due to the powerful direct voice mediumship which Bradley and his wife themselves developed after the first sittings with Valiantine in New York. But the physical manifestation was only part of the evidence.

"He is a man of instinctive good manners," wrote Bradley of Valiantine in his book . . . *And After* (1931), "but it is essential to state that he is semi-illiterate. He possesses no scholastic education whatever, beyond the ordinary simplicities; he is ill-versed in general conversation and ideas. I mention these facts because many of the communications which have been made in the direct voice under his mediumship have been brilliant in their expressions and culture."

On April 26, 1929, Valiantine arrived for the fourth time in England from America. He spent one day with Bradley and then left with Mr. and Mrs. Bradley for Berlin. The sittings were held in Frau von Dirksen's house. Bradley considered them comparatively poor in result. Some members of the Berlin Occult Society, for which the seances had been arranged, subsequently claimed imposture and supported their assertions by referring to Bradley's and Valiantine's refusal to permit strict control.

The charges were published five months afterwards by Dr. Kroner in the *Zeitschrift für Parapsychologie* in the winter of 1929. Dr. Kroner attended only three of the sittings. Two lady sitters made direct allegations of fraudulent movements on Valiantine's part. However, no definite proof of having caught Valiantine in fraud was brought forward.

In May 1929, Valiantine gave a series of seances at the house of the Marquis Centurione Scotto in Genoa. One of the sittings, held in the presence of psychical researcher Ernesto **Bozzano,** was rigorously controlled. Valiantine was fastened to his chair and an adhesive bandage secured over his mouth. The knots were sealed, the doors were locked.

The results were excellent. The enthusiasm, however, was soon marred by a charge by M. Rossi and the Marquis Centurione Scotto. Rossi claimed to have distinctly felt Valiantine in one of their sittings lean forward and speak into the trumpet. He also said that Mr. Castellani caught hold of Mrs. Bradley's hand which was touching the back of his (Castellani's) head. Both of them were furiously indignant and left immediately. Castellani later withdrew his allegation against Mrs. Bradley and Rossi also became wavering.

As Bradley pointed out there was a truly bizarre aspect in the situation: "The Marquis Centurione Scotto, Mr. Rossi and Madame Rossi, unknown before to me or to Valiantine, visit me in England in 1927. The Marquis, to his astonishment, speaks to his [dead] son in Italian. The Marquis and Mrs.

Rossi then develop voice mediumship entirely from, and because of, their meeting and initiation with Valiantine. Valiantine then, in 1929, visits them in Italy and is accused of being a fraud. The poet is right when he declares 'It is a mad world.' "

In 1931, Valiantine was again invited to England. This visit ended in a tragic note. Bradley asked him to devote six evenings to experiments for psychic imprint (molds). Striking previous successes were recorded in the book *The Wisdom of the Gods.* Since then, famous people whom Bradley knew had died and their original left and right hand imprints were in the possession of palmistry authority Noel **Jaquin.** Scientifically, therefore, the experiments held potential promise. The claimed spirits of Sir Arthur Conan **Doyle,** Lord Dewar and Sir Henry Segrave all apparently complied with Bradley's eager request, but the plastic substance used in the seances, unknown to Valiantine, was chemically prepared. A stain was found on Valiantine's elbow and expert examination disclosed that the spirit thumbprint of "Sir Arthur Conan Doyle" was exactly similar to the print of Valiantine's big toe on his right foot, a spirit thumbprint of "Lord Dewar" to that of Valiantine's left big toe, a spirit fingerprint of "Sir Henry Segrave" to the print of Valiantine's middle finger and another spirit impression to that of Valiantine's elbow.

Ex-Chief Detective Inspector Bell, the head of the fingerprint department at New Scotland Yard, declared that in a court-of-law the resemblance would be sufficient to hang a man charged with murder. According to Bradley, when Valiantine was confronted with this evidence, he broke down completely and sobbed. He would not, however, admit fraud. His only answer to questions was: "I cannot understand it."

Bradley believed that the rapid accumulation of money and fame as a professional medium did not have a beneficial effect upon Valiantine's character. He found that he had progressively changed, becoming a conceited and arrogant man. Yet "his reason for attempting these imprint frauds will remain incomprehensible. He received no money from me, and for him to imagine that in the presence of imprint experts he could commit palpable fraud and escape detection was a sign of sheer lunacy." (For other cases of imprints and molds, see **Plastics**)

Besides Valiantine, his controls were also compromised, as on the fatal night, just near the end of the sitting, "Bert Everett" spoke in his usual shrill tones, announcing the presence of "Segrave" and also that an imprint had been made which was excellent. Mr. X., with whom Valiantine stayed during the visit, obtained the fingerprint of "Walter Stinson," control of the American medium Margery (Mrs. **Crandon**). This print was identified by Noel Jacquin as identical with that of the middle finger of Valiantine's left hand.

After the exposure, Valiantine gave twelve seances to Dr. Vivian. The report stated that while two voices were speaking, Valiantine was simultaneously heard to draw the attention of the sitters to the two voices. Surgeon Admiral Nimmo had two sittings in daylight. The voice which he heard to come distinctly from within the trumpet gave intelligent and evidential communication. In the presence of a second doctor, the voices were heard again, speaking distinctly and intelligently. During the phenomena, the doctors kept Valiantine's face under acute observation but they did not discover any movement whatever on it.

The experiences of Dr. Whymant with the voice of "Confucius" came before the Society for Psychical Research in 1927. Dr. Whymant delivered a lecture, played the phonograph record of the voice and submitted his account of twelve seances. No action was taken. Thereupon the records were the subject of a book by Dr. Whymant, published in 1931 under the title *Psychic Adventures in New York.* In *Proceedings* of the Society for Psychical Research (vol. 40, pt. 125), the report of Lord Charles Hope on his sittings in 1927 concluded: "I was disappointed at the lack of evidence for survival which the voices had given me. I was left uncertain whether Valiantine was a genuine medium or not."

The case of Valiantine illustrates the problem of fraud in mediumistic phenomena. There can be no doubt of Valiantine's guilt in the faked fingerprints. Other accusations of cheating were less conclusive, but the extraordinary "Confucius" voice phenomena seems inexplicable on any basis of fraud. It is always easy to dismiss a medium as entirely fradulent on the basis of certain proved fraud, but when genuine phenomena are rare and elusive, it is tempting to any medium to augument them by occasional frauds, particular when the medium is vain, of weak character, or has been too highly praised.

Recommended reading:

Bradley, H. Dennis. *Towards the Stars,* T. Werner Laurie, London, 1924

Bradley, H. Dennis. *The Wisdom of the Gods,* T. Werner Laurie, London, 1925

Bradley, H. Dennis. . . . *And After,* T. Werner Laurie, London, 1931.

Whymant, Neville. *Psychic Adventures in New York,* Morley & Mitchell, London, 1931

Valkhoff, Marius (1905-)

Professor of Romance Studies who investigated areas of parapsychology. Born January 7, 1905 at Zwolle, Netherlands, he studied at University of Amsterdam (D.Litt. 1931). In 1935 he married Johanna-Wilhelmina Dumbar. He was lecturer in Rumanian in 1932, extraordinary professor of Romance philology and French from 1933-40, secretary of Faculty of Arts from 1940-45, Amsterdam University, Rector of Amsterdam University from 1949-50, head of Department of Romance Studies, professor of French at University of Witwatersrand, Johannesburg, South Africa from 1951-62, dean of Faculty of Arts 1963, member of the board of Witwatersrand University Press 1952, administrator of the Ernest Oppenheimer Institute of Portuguese Studies 1953.

He was chairman of South African Society for Psychical Research, member of Dutch Literary Academy, Afrikaanse Skrywerkskring, committee member of Johannesburg Alliance Française, Gewnootskap Nederland-Suid-Afrika; Chevalier of the French Legion of Honor, Commander of the Order of the Crown of Rumania. In addition to his writings on philology and literature, he published various articles on parapsychology in *Tijdschrift voor Parapsychologie* and in publications of the South African Society for Psychical Research. He experimented with psychokinesis and with drug-induced states related to extrasensory perception.

Vallee, Jacques F. (1939-)

French scientist who is also an authority on Unidentified Flying Objects. He was born September 24, 1939, in Pontoise, France, and received a B.S. in Mathematics from the Sorbonne in 1959, M.S. in Astrophysics, Lille University, 1961, Ph.D. in Computer Science, Northwestern University, 1967. In 1960, he married Janine Saley.

From 1961-62 he was a research scientist for the French Committee for Space Studies, Paris, later research engineer for the Thompson-Houston Co. in France, research associate at University of Texas and McDonald Observatory from 1962-63, Texas computer consultant on Mars Map Project from 1962-65, mathematical analyst for Northwestern University Technological Institute from 1963-1967. He organized a computer company in Northern California, and became a member of the editorial board of *Telecommunications Policy.*

In 1975, he spoke at a United Nations meeting to recommend setting up a department to research UFOs and related phenomena. Vallee was said to be the original of the character "Lacombe" in Steven Spielberg's popular movie "Close Encounters of the Third Kind."

In addition to many articles on scientific and UFO subjects Vallee has published science fiction novels in French language, and the following books: *Anatomy of a Phenomenon; Unidentified Objects in Space, A Scientific Appraisal* (1965), (with Janine Vallee) *Challenge to Science; The UFO Enigma* (1966), *Passport to Magonia* (1969), (with J. Allen Hyneck) *The Edge of Reality* (1975), *The Invisible College* (1975), *Messengers of Deception* (1979; 1980). This latter book speculates that UFOs operate independently of normal space-time physics and appear to be connected with a conditioning process affecting human imagery and behavior, and may be related to various modern cults. (See also **Close Encounters of the Third Kind; Flying Saucers; UFO**)

Vambéry, Arminius (1832-1913)

Hungarian traveler and scholar who probably communicated to author Bram **Stoker** the facts and legends concerning the real Prince Dracula (Vlad V) which supplied the inspiration for Stoker's famous occult thriller *Dracula.*

Stoker and Vambéry met at the Beefsteak Club room on April 30, 1890, after a performance of Henry Irving in the play *The Dead Heart,* and also two years later at Trinity College, Dublin, where Vambéry was presented with an honorary degree.

For biographical information, see *The Dervish of Windsor Castle* by Lory Adler & Richard Dalby (Bachman & Turner, London, 1979). (See also **Dracula;** Bram **Stoker; Vampire**)

Vampire

(Russian *Vampir,* South Russian *upuir,* probably from the root *pi,* to drin, with the prefix *va,* or *av.*) A dead person who returns in spirit form from the grave for the purpose of sucking the blood of living persons, or a living sorcerer who takes a special form for destructive purpose. *Webster's International Dictionary* defined a vampire as: "a blood-sucking ghost or reanimated body of a dead person; a soul or re-animated body of a dead person believed to come from the grave and wander about by night sucking the blood of persons asleep, causing their death."

The belief in vampires is an ancient one. It was found in ancient India, Babylonia, Greece, and for a time accepted by early Christians. The conception of the vampire was common among Slavonic peoples, and especially in the Balkan countries, and in Hungary, Bohemia, Moravia, and Silesia.

In these territories from 1730-35, there was a claimed epidemic of vampirism, but it was by no means confined to them. In Russia and the Ukraine it was believed that vampires were generally wizards or sorcerers, but in Bulgaria and Serbia it was thought that any corpse over which a cat or a dog jumped or over which a bird had flown was liable to become a vampire. In **Greece,** a vampire was known as a *broncolaia* or *bourkabakos,* which was identified with the Slavonic name for "**werwolf,**" *vlkodlak,* or *vukodlak.* The vampire, too, was often supposed to steal the heart of his victim and to roast it over a slow fire, thus causing interminable amorous longings.

Marks of Vampirism

Vampirism is said to be epidemic in character. Where one instance is discovered it is almost invariably followed by several others. This is accounted for by the circumstance that it is believed that the victim of a vampire pines away and dies and becomes in turn a vampire after death, and so duly infects others.

On the disinterment of a suspected vampire, various well-known signs are looked for by experienced persons. Thus, if several holes about the breadth of a man's finger are observed in the soil above the grave, the vampire character of its occupant may be suspected. On unearthing the corpse, it is usually found with wide-open eyes, ruddy and life-like complexion and lips and a general appearance of freshness, and showing no signs of corruption.

It may also be found that the hair and nails have grown as in life. On the throat, two small livid marks may be looked for. The coffin is also very often full of blood, the body has a swollen and gorged appearance, and the shroud is frequently half-devoured. The blood contained in the veins of the corpse is found, on examination, to be in a fluid condition as in life, and the limbs are pliant and flexible and have none of the rigidity of death.

Examples of Vampirism

Many well-authenticated cases of vampirism have been recorded. Charles Ferdinand de Schertz, in his work *Magia Posthuma,* printed at Olmutz in 1706 related several stories of apparitions of this sort, and detailed the mischief done by them.

One, among others, was of a herdsman of the village of Blow near the town of Kadam in Bohemia, who appeared for a considerable length of time, and visited several persons, who all died within eight days.

At last, the inhabitants of Blow dug up the herdsman's body, and fixed it in the ground with a stake driven through it. The man, even in this condition, laughed at the action of the people about him, and told them they were very obliging to furnish him with a stick with which to defend himself from the dogs.

The same night, he extricated himself from the stake, frightened several persons by appearing to them, and caused the deaths of many more individuals than before. He was then delivered into the hands of the hangman, who put him into a cart, in order to burn him outside the town. As they went along, the carcass shrieked in the most hideous manner, and threw about its arms and legs, as if it had been alive, and upon being again run through with a stake, it gave a loud cry, and a great quantity of fresh, florid blood issued from the wound.

At last, the body was burned to ashes, and this execution put a final stop to the specter appearing and infecting the village.

Augustine Calmet, in his *Dissertation on Vampires* appended to his *Dissertation upon the Apparitions of Angels, Demons, and Ghosts* (English translation, 1759), gave several well authenticated instances of vampirism as follows:

"It is now about fifteen years since a soldier, who was quartered in the house of a Haidamack peasant, upon the frontiers of Hungary, saw, as he was at the table with his landlord, a stranger come in and sit down by them. The master of the house and the rest of the company were strangely terrified, but the soldier knew not what to make of it. The next day the peasant died, and, upon the soldier's enquiring into the meaning of it, he was told that it was his landlord's father who had been dead and buried above ten years that came and sat down at table, and gave his son notice of his death.

"The soldier soon propagated the story through his regiment, and by this means it reached the general officers, who commissioned the count de Cabreras, a captain in Alandetti's regiment of foot, to make an exact enquiry into the fact. The count, attended by several officers, a surgeon, and a notary, came to the house, and took the deposition of all the family, who unanimously swore that the spectre was the landlord's father, and that all the soldier had said was strictly true. The same was also attested by all the inhabitants of the village.

"In consequence of this the body of the spectre was dug up, and found to be in the same state as if it has been but just dead, the blood like that of a living person. The court de Cabreras ordered its head to be cut off, and the corpse to be buried again. He then proceeded to take depositions against other spectres of the same sort, and particularly against a man who had been dead above thirty years, and had made his appearance there several times in his own house at meal-time. At his first visit he had fastened upon the neck of his own brother, and sucked his blood; at his second, he had treated one of his children in the same manner; and the third time, he fastened upon a servant of the family, and all three died upon the spot.

"Upon this evidence, the count gave orders that he should be dug up, and being found, like the first, with his blood in a fluid state, as if he had been alive, a great nail was drove through his temples, and he was buried again. The count ordered a third to be burnt, who had been dead above sixteen years, and was found guilty of murdering two of his own children by sucking their blood. The commissioner then made his report to the general officers, who sent a deputation to the emperor's court for further directions; and the emperor dispatched an order for a court, consisting of officers, lawyers, physicians, chirurgeons, and some divines, to go and enquire into the cause of these extraordinary events, upon the spot.

"The gentleman who acquainted me with all these particulars, had them from the count de Cabreras himself, at Fribourg in Brisgau, in the year 1730."

Other cases alluded to by Calmet are as follows:

"In the part of Hungary, known in Latin by the name of *Oppida Heidonum,* on the other side of the Tibiscus, vulgarly called the Teyss; that is, between that part of this river which waters the happy country of Tockay, and the frontiers of Transylvania, the people named *Heydukes* have a notion that there are dead persons, called by them *vampires,* which suck the blood of the living, so as to make them fall away visibly to skin and bones, while the carcasses themselves, like leeches, are filled with blood to such a degree that it comes out at all the apertures of their body. This notion has lately been confirmed by several facts, which I think we cannot doubt the truth of, considering the witnesses who attest them. Some of the most considerable of these facts I shall now relate. "About five years ago, an Heyduke, named Arnold Paul, an inhabitant of Medreiga, was killed by a cart full of hay that fell upon him. About thirty days after his death, four persons died suddenly, with all the symptoms usually attending those who are killed by *vampires.* It was then remembered that this Arnold Paul had frequently told a story of his having been tormented by a Turkish *vampire,* in the neighbourhood of Cassova, upon the borders of Turkish Servia (for the notion is that those who have been passive *vampires* in their life-time become active ones after death; or, in other words, that those who have had their blood sucked become suckers in their turn) but that he had been cured by eating some of the earth upon the *vampire's* grave, and by rubbing himself with his blood. This precaution, however, did not hinder him from being guilty himself after his death; for, upon digging up his corpse forty days after his burial, he was found to have all the marks of an arch-vampire. His body was fresh and ruddy, his hair, beard, and nails were grown, and his veins were full of fluid blood, which ran from all parts of his body upon the shroud that he was buried in. The *hadnagy,* or bailiff of the village, who was present at the digging up of the corpse, and was very expert in the whole business of vampirism, ordered a sharp stake to be drove quite through the body of the deceased, and to let it pass through his heart, which is attended with a hideous cry from the carcass, as if it had been alive. This ceremony being performed, they cut off the head, and burnt the body to ashes. After this, they proceeded in the same manner with the four other persons that died of vampirism, lest they also should be troublesome. But all these executions could not hinder this dreadful prodigy from appearing again last year, at the distance of five years from its first breaking out. In the space of three months, seventeen persons of different ages and sexes died of vampirism, some without any previous illness, and others after languishing two or three days. Among others, it was said, that a girl, named Stanoska, daughter of the Heyduke Jotuitzo, went to bed in perfect health, but awoke in the middle of the night, trembling, and crying out that the son of the Heyduke Millo, who died about nine weeks before, had almost strangled her while she was asleep. From that time she fell into a languishing state, and died at three days' end. Her evidence against Millo's son was looked upon as a proof of his being a *vampire,* and, upon digging up his body, he was found to be such. "At the consultation of the principal inhabitants of the place, attended by physicians and chirurgeons, it was considered how it was possible that the plague of vampirism should break out afresh, after the precautions that had been taken some years before: and, at last, it was found out that the original offender, Arnold Paul, had not only destroyed the four persons mentioned above, but had killed several beasts, which the late *vampires,* and particularly the son of Millo, had fed upon. Upon this foundation a resolution was taken to dig up all the persons that had died within a certain time. Out of forty were found seventeen, with all the evident tokens of vampirism; and they had all stakes drove through their hearts, their heads cut off, their bodies burnt, and their ashes thrown into the river.

"All these several enquiries and executions were carried on with all the forms of law, and attested by several officers who were in garrison in that country, by the chirurgeon-majors of the regiments, and by the principal inhabitants of the place. The original papers were all sent, in January last, to the Imperial council of war at Vienna, which had issued out a commission to several officers, to enquire into the truth of the fact."

Methods of Extirpation

The commonest methods of extirpation of vampires are—(a) beheading the suspected corpse, (b) taking out the heart, (c) impaling the corpse with a white-thorn stake (in Russia an aspen), and (d) burning it. Sometimes more than one or all of these precautions is taken.

Instances are on record where the graves of as many as thirty or forty persons have been disturbed during the course of an epidemic of vampirism and their occupants impaled or beheaded.

Persons who dread the visits or attacks of a vampire sleep with a wreath made of garlic round the neck, as that esculent is supposed to be especially obnoxious to the vampire.

When impaled, the vampire is usually said to emit a dreadful cry, but it has been pointed out that the gas from the intestines may be forced through the throat by the entry of the stake into the body, and that this may account for the sound.

The method of discovering a vampire's grave in Serbia was to place a virgin boy upon a coal-black stallion which had never served a mare and marking the spot which the horse refuses to pass. An officer quartered in Wallachia wrote to Calmet as follows, giving him an instance of this method:

"At the time when we were quartered at Temeswar in Wallachia, there died of this disorder two dragoons of the company in which I was cornet, and several more who had it would have died also, if the corporal of the company had not put a stop to it, by applying a remedy commonly made use of in that country. It is of a very singular kind, and, though infallibly to be depended on, I have never met with it in any Dispensatory.

"They pick out a boy, whom they judge to be too young to have lost his maidenhead, and mount him bare upon a coal-black stone-horse, which has never leaped a mare. This virgin-pair is led about the church-yard, and across all the graves, and wherever the animal stops, and refuses to go on, in spite of all the whipping they can give him, they conclude they have discovered a *vampire.* Upon opening the grave, they find a carcass as fleshy and fair as if the person were only in a slumber. The next step is to cut off his head with a spade, and there issues from the wound such a quantity of fresh and florid blood, that one would swear they had cut the throat of a man in full health and vigour. They then fill up the pit, and it may be depended on that the disorder will cease, and that all who were ill of it will gradually get strength, like people that recover slowly after a long illness. Accordingly this happened to our troopers, who were attacked with the distemper. I was at that time commanding officer of the troop, the captain and lieutenant being absent, and was extremely angry at the corporal for having made this experiment without me. It was with great difficulty that I prevailed with myself not to reward him with a good cudgel, a thing of which the officers of the emperor's service are usually very liberal. I would not, for the world, have been absent upon this occasion, but there was now no remedy."

A Bulgarian belief was that a wizard or sorcerer may entrap a vampire by placing in a bottle some food for which the vampire has a partiality, and on his entry in the shape of fluff or straw, sealing up the flask and throwing it into the fire.

Scientific Views of Vampirism

The British custom of piercing suicide's bodies with a stake would appear to be a survival of the belief in vampirism. Such demons were also to be seen in the Polynesian *tii,* the Malayan *hantu penyardin* (a dog-headed water-demon), and the *kephn* of the Karens, which, under the form of a wizard's head and stomach devoured human souls.

The anthropologist E. B. Tylor considered vampires to be "causes conceived in spiritual form to account for specific facts of wasting disease." The Russian folklorist Alexandr N. Afansyev regarded them as thunder-gods and spirits of the storm, who during winter slumber in their cloud-coffins, to rise again in spring and draw moisture from the clouds. But this theory will scarcely recommend itself to anyone with even a slight knowledge of mythological science.

Calmet's difficulty in accepting vampires was that he could not understand how a spirit could leave its grave and return thence with ponderable matter in the form of blood, leaving no traces showing that the surface of the earth above the grave had been stirred. But this view might be combated by the theory of the precipitation of matter.

In modern times, it is easy to understand how individuals in an unrecognized condition of cataleptic trance might have been prematurely buried alive and upon regaining consciousness have struggled to escape from their horrible plight. Their bodies would exhibit many of the signs associated with vampires.

It is now also generally known that some individuals suffer from a morbid fascination with human blood, and it would have been easy in the past to associate such unnatural appetite with vampirism. The infamous Countess Elizabeth Bathory of Transylvania (died 1614) was reputed to have murdered nearly 700 young women in the belief that their blood would keep her young.

No doubt the observed activities of the various types of vampire bats (*Desmodus Rufus, Didemus Yungi, Diphylla Caudata, Desmodus Rotunda*) in sucking blood from cattle and horses have helped to spread legends of vampires. The vampire bat drinks 20 ccs of blood per day, and has been known to attack human beings. It also spreads rabies, thus enhancing stories of a vampire plague.

However, in spite of commonsense explanations for a morbid and supernatural tradition of vampires, there remain some disturbing firsthand accounts in history which leave room for a suspicion of doubt, or perhaps for some psychic explanation.

Psychic Theories of Vampires

It is well known that some individuals have the ability to draw some kind of psychic energy from others. Every stage performer or public speaker is aware of the rapport which exists between performer and audience, and many have become expert at gaining confidence and power through some instinctive techniques of centralizing and transforming psychic or nervous energy. Talented but unscrupulous occultists have also perfected methods of sustaining the attention of victims and drawing their vital energies from them.

The common experience of **out-of-the-body** traveling or **astral projection** has sometimes been associated with visits to other individuals, as well as contacts with frightening **elementals** on the astral plane. Some occultists appear to have mastered techniques by which they can astrally project, and visit their victims while asleep and drain their vitality from them.

During the nineteenth century, the French Spiritualist Z. J. Pierart attempted to reconcile the theory of premature burial with astral projection by those who died after being buried alive: He wrote: "Poor dead cataleptics, buried as if really dead in cold and dry spots where morbid causes are incapable of effecting the destruction of their bodies, the astral spirit enveloping itself with a fluidic ethereal body, is prompted to quite the precincts of its tomb and to exercise on living bodies acts peculiar to physical life, especially that of nutrition, the result of which, by a mysterious link between soul and body which spiritualistic science will some day explain, is forwarded to the material body lying still within the tomb, and the latter is thus helped to perpetuate its vital existence."

Adolphe d'Assier, in his book *Posthumous Humanity* (1887), admitted that the body of the vampires may be dead but the spirit earthbound and obsessed with the idea that the physical body must be saved from dissolution. Consequently the dense astral body feeds on human victims and, by some mysterious process, conveys the blood into the tomb.

Both speculations furnish plausible, if not wholly satisfying, explanation of the attestation of numerous ancient chronicles that fresh blood was found in the exhumed and uncorrupted body of dead people suspected of vampirism.

Prevailing ideas of vampirism which may act as a strong suggestion or even obsession on the mind of the living and dead, may have some connection with other features of this strange traditional belief and it may well be that the mystery of vampirism has vague and elusive points of contact with psychic science.

Following the occult boom of the 1950s, Stoker's powerful but much neglected masterpiece *Dracula* was exhumed and examined by higher criticism, and found to be as full of vitality as during Stoker's own lifetime. Almost by psychic contagion, it has generated a plethora of horror movies, plays and other vampire thrillers.

In Britain, the Dracula Society with a general interest in Gothic themes, pioneered tourist expeditions to Transylvania, and in Stoker's Ireland, a Bram Stoker Society was founded to honor a much neglected Irishman. In the U.S., the most active organization is the Count Dracula Fan Club at Penthouse North, 29 Washington Square W., New York, N.Y. 10011, which promotes and encourages the study of vampirism and fantasy themes. (See also **Dracula; Dracula Society; Greece; Magia Posthuma; Monsters;** Bram **Stoker;** Arminius **Vambréy; Werwolf**)

Recommended reading:

Barber, Paul. *Vampires, Buried, and Death;* Folklore and Reality, Yale University Press, 1988

Burton, Sir Richard. *Vikram and the Vampire, or Tales of Hindu Devilry,* Tilston & Edwards, London, 1832

Calmet, Augustine. *Dissertations Upon the Apparitions of Angels, Demons, and Ghosts, and Concerning . . . Vampires,* London, 1759

Calmet, Augustine. *The Phantom World; or, The Philosophy of Spirits, Apparitions, &c.,* 2 vols., Richard Bentley, London, 1850

De Schertz, Charles F. *Magia Posthuma,* Olmutz, 1706

Dresser, Norine. *American Vampires; Fans, Victims & Practitioners,* W. W. Norton, N.Y. & London/Penguin, Canada, 1989

Ennemoser, Joseph. *The History of Magic,* 2 vols., Bohn, London, 1854; University Books, 1970

Glut, Donald F. *The Dracula Book,* Scarecrow Press, Metuchen, New Jersey, 1975

Harenburg, Johann C. *Von Vampyren,* 1739

Hartmann, Franz. *Premature Burial,* Swann Sonnenschein, London, 1896

Hertz, Wilhelm. *Der Werwolf,* Stuttgart, 1862

Mackenzie, Andrew. *Dracula Country,* Arthur Barker, London, 1977

McNally, Raymond T. *Dracula Was a Woman,* McGraw-Hill, 1983

McNally, Raymond T. & Radu Florescu. *In Search of Dracula; A True History of Dracula and Vampire Legends,* New York Graphic Society, 1972

Mannhardt, W. *Über Vampirismus* (see vol. 4 of *Zeitschrift für Deutsche Mythologie und Sittenkunde*), Göttingen, 1858

Masters, Anthony. *The Natural History of the Vampire,* Ruper Hart-Davis, London, 1972; Mayflower paperback, London, 1974

Ralston, W. R. S. *The Songs of the Russian People,* London, 1872

Ralston, W. R. S. *Russian Folk Tales,* Smith, Elder, 1873

Ranfft, Michael. *De Masticatione Mortuorum in Tumulis,* Leipzig, 1728

Rohr, Philip. *De Masticatione Mortuorum,* 1679

Ronay, Gabriel. *The Dracula Myth,* W. H. Auden, London, 1972; Pan paperback, London, 1975

Roth, Phyllis A. *Bram Stoker,* Twayne Publishers, Boston, 1982

Shepard, Leslie. *The Dracula Book of Great Vampire Stories,* Citadel, 1977; Jove/-BJ paperback, 1978

Summers, Montague. *The Vampire, His Kith and Kin,* Kegan, Paul, London, 1928; University Books, 1960

Summers, Montague. *The Vampire in Europe,* Kegan, Paul, London, 1929; University Books, 1962

Thompson, R. Campbell. *The Devils and Evil Spirits of Babylonia,* 2 vols., London, 1903-04

Underwood, Peter. *The Vampire's Bedside Companion; The Amazing World of Vampires in Fact and Fiction,* Leslie Frewin, London, 1972

Wright, Dudley. *The Book of Vampires,* 2nd enl. ed., London, 1924; Causeway Books, 1973

Zopfius, Johan Heinrich. *Dissertatio de Vampiris Seruiensibus,* Halle, 1733

Vampire (Journal)

Publication of a Special Interest Group of American MENSA Ltd. Address: Terry Cottrell, 5116 Mill Race Circle, Richmond, Virginia 23234.

Vampire Information Exchange

Clearinghouse for information on the subject of **vampires.** Issues a Newsletter six times per year. For information on Newsletter and membership, write to: Eric Held, Dir., P.O. Box 328, Brooklyn, New York 11229-0328.

Vampire Journal, The

Publication devoted to the subject of **vampires.** Address: Dracula & Company, Sharida Rizzuto, P.O. Box 994, Metrairie, Louisiana 70004.

Vampire Quarterly (Magazine)

Magazine devoted to the subject of **vampires.** Address: Susan M. Garrett, 142 Sunvalley Drive, Toms River, New Jersey 08753.

Vampire Studies Society

An American organization formed by Martin V. Riccardo to bring together individuals interested in vampires and associated mysteries. The Society published a *Journal of Vampirism* which includes articles, poems, fiction and reviews of books, movies and plays on vampire themes.

Apparently no longer active.

Van Bruhesen, Peter (died 1571)

A Dutch doctor and astrologer who died at Bruges. He published in that town in 1550 a *Grand and Perpetual Almanack* in which he scrupulously indicated by the tenets of judicial astrology the correct days for bathing, shaving, haircutting and so forth.

The work caused offense to a certain magistrate of Bruges who plied the tonsorial trade, with the result that there appeared against *Bruhesen's* volume another *Grand and Perpetual Almanack,* with the flippant subtitle *a scourge for empirics and charlatans.* This squib was published by a rival medico, François Rapaert, but Peter Haschaerts, a surgeon, and a protagonist of astrological science, warmly defended Bruhesen in his *Astrological Buckler.* (See also **Astrology**)

Van Busschbach, J(ohan) G(eorge) (1896-1974)

Dutch Inspector of Schools who was winner of the first McDougall Award for Distinguished Research in Parapsychology, for his work in investigating ESP between teachers and pupils in American schools (see *Journal of Parapsychology*, June 1956).

He was born July 3, 1896, in Amsterdam. He was a primary school teacher from 1916-21, teacher in psychology 1927-39, director of training school for teachers 1940-49, inspector of schools, Amsterdam, 1944-61. In 1921, he married M. L. de-Flines.

He was a charter member of the Parapsychological Association and Council member of the Parapsychologisch Onderzoek (Amsterdam Foundation for Parapsychological Studies) and member of the Netherlands Society for Psychical Research.

His papers included: in *Journal of Parapsychology:* 'An Investigation of Extrasensory Perception in School Children' (vol. 17, 1953), 'A Further Report on an Investigation of ESP in School Children' (vol. 19, 1955), 'An Investigation of ESP Between Teacher and Pupils in American Schools' (vol. 20, 1956).

Van de Castle, Robert L(eon) (1927-)

Clinical psychologist and parapsychologist. Born November 16, 1927 at Rochester, New York, he studied at Syracuse University (B.A. 1951), University of Missouri (M.A. 1953), University of North Carolina (Ph.D. 1959). In 1949 he married Doris J. Van Valkenburg.

He was a research assistant at Florida Southern College in 1954, research associate at Duke Parapsychology Laboratory from 1954-55, psychology instructor at Idaho State College from 1958-69, assistant professor of psychology at University of Denver from 1959 onwards. He went on to conduct dream research with Calvin Itall at the Institute of Dream Research in Miami, publishing a joint work *The Content Analysis of Dreams* (1966).

In 1967, he became director of the Sleep and Dream Laboratory at University of Virginia until 1975, remaining professor of clinical psychology in the Department of Psychiatry.

Since 1969, he has been a council member of the Parapsychological Association, president in 1970.

He was an outstanding subject for dream/ESP experiments at the Maimonides Medical Center. He is a charter member of the Parapsychological Association, member of the American Psychological Association, president of Colorado Psychological Association, U.S. Public Health fellowships.

Dr. Van de Castle studied personality correlates in extrasensory perception and psychokinesis, and conducted experiments relating psychological tests to extrasensory ability, on grants from the Parapsychology Foundation. His articles in the *Journal of Parapsychology* include: 'An Exploratory Study of Some Variables in Individual ESP Performance' (vol. 17, 1953), 'A Report on a Sentence Completion Form of Sheep-Goat Attitude Scale' (with R. R. **White,** vol. 19, 1955), (in *Journal* of the American Society for Psychical Research:) 'Differential Patterns of ESP Scoring as a Function of Differential Attitudes Towards ESP' (vol. 51, 1957), 'An Exploratory Study of Some Personality Correlates Associated with PK Performance' (vol. 52, 1958), (in the *International Journal of Parapsychology:*) 'A Review of ESP Tests Carried Out in the Classroom' (vol. 1, 1959), 'Development and Validation of a Perceptual Maturity Scale Using Figure Preferences' (*Journal of Consultative Psychology*, vol. 29, 1965), (with R. L. & K. R. Davis) 'The Relationship of Suggestibility to ESP Scoring Level' (*Journal of Parapsychology*, vol. 26, 1962), 'The Facilitation of ESP Through Hypnosis' (*American Journal of Clinical & Experimental Hypnosis*, vol. 12, 1969), 'Psi Abilities in Primitive Groups' (*Proceedings* of the Parapsychological Association, No. 7, 1970), 'An Investigation of Psi Abilities Among the Cuna Indians of Panama' (*Journal of Parapsychology*, vol. 38, June 1974).

He contributed the chapter 'Anthropology and Psychical Research' in *Psychic Exploration* by E. J. Mitchell et al., (1974), and the papers 'Parapsychology and Anthropology' and 'Sleep and Dreams' to *Handbook of Parapsychology*, ed. B. B. Wolman (1977).

Van Eeden, Frederik (1860-1932)

Dutch physician, author, and poet, who was also actively interested in psychiatry and psychical research, and was acquainted with F. W. H. **Myers.** Dr. van Eeden conducted important research with the non-professional British medium Rosina **Thompson.** Dr. van Eeden also made valuable contributions to the study of dreams, in particular "**lucid dreams,**" a term which he coined to denote dreams in which the sleeper is aware of dreaming, i.e., some degree of waking consciousness persists in the dream state, often a preliminary to **out-of-the-body** experiences. He appears to have had some OOB experience himself, since he described it in one of his novels (*The Bride of Dreams*, 1918). He also obtained cross-correspondences between his own dreams and the trance utterances of "Nelly," the control of Mrs. Thompson, while van Eeden was in Holland and Mrs. Thompson in England.

His paper 'A Study of Dreams' was published in *Proceedings* of the Society for Psychical Research (vol. 26, 1913).

Van Gelder, Dora (1904-)

Contemporary American psychic, born in Java, where she grew up on her father's sugar plantation. Here she saw and communed with **fairies** as a natural thing, being unaware that this was a special psychic faculty. At the age of eleven, she left Java for Australia, where she studied with an Anglican priest who also possessed unusual psychic abilities. At the age of twenty-two, she married an American and moved to the U.S., where she became president of a corporation concerned with teaching materials, while her husband became head of an educational foundation.

As Dora Van Gelder has never been a professional paid medium, she has not publicized her psychic abilities, but instead has worked unobtrusively with physicians on difficult cases for diagnostic and healing purposes. She has shown a natural ability to see the psychic energy patterns in human beings and their relationship to conditions of health and disease. She also has the unusual ability of being able to predict specific illness, sometimes as long as eighteen months in advance.

She has never lost her ability to commune with fairy life. When she was a young woman she wrote about her fairy experiences, and this early manuscript was recently revised and published as *The Real World of Fairies* (Quest paperback, Theosophical Publishing House, 1977).

She states that fairy life is still apparent, but becoming less evident in the growing pollution of cities and urban life. She has, however, seen fairies even in Central Park, New York. Her sensitive and unaffected record of her own experiences of fairy life and psychic perception is wholly convincing through its qualities of simplicity and gentle truthfulness, as distinct from the sensationalism of so many occultists and skeptics. (See also **Cottingley Fairies; Fairies**)

Van Helmont, Jean Baptiste (1577-1644)

Belgian physician, chemist and physiologist, whose researches were associated with occult theories. He was undoubtedly one of the pioneers of science by reason of his experimental researches, his acute judgment, his penetrating attitude of mind (leading him to say "Names do not trouble me, I contemplate the thing in itself as near as I can"), and his untiring search for the truth, not for personal aggrandizement or power, but in the service of progress and for the good of mankind.

He was born of a noble family in Brussels. Studying at Louvain, he early attained distinction in the science of mathematics, lecturing on physics at the age of seventeen. Before he was twenty-two, he had read Hippocrates and the Greek and Arabianauthors and become eminent in the doctrines of Aristotle and Galen and the practice of medicine according to Vopiscus and Plempius.

In the year 1599, he took his degree of doctor of medicine. After this, some years were spent in the practice of medicine, but meeting a follower of **Paracelsus,** he became interested in his theories of chemical medicine to such a degree that he retired to the castle of Vilvorde, near Brussels, to spend the rest of his life in the study of experimental chemistry on which he wrote various treatises, becoming famous throughout Europe for his scientific knowledge.

He revolutionized medicine as known in his day, turning aside from the theories of Galen and the Arabs, and created an epoch in the history of physiology, being the first to recognize the functions of the stomach and its relation to the other organs of the body.

His many and varied experiments led him to deal with aerial fluids, to which he gave the name of gas—carbonic acid gas being his discovery—and it is said that without him the chemistry of steel in all probability would have been unknown to science.

The writings of van Helmont contain many truths, foreshadowings of ideas and principles now accepted as indispensable commonplaces, although these almost of necessity were hidden under much of the incomprehensible beliefs and illusions prevalent in his time.

Alchemy, with its visions of the **Elixir of Life** and the **Philosopher's Stone** presented themselves to him as another field of experiment and research and although he never pretended to the art of making the transmuting powder, he testified his belief in the transmutation of metals, claiming to have seen the experiment performed many times.

Among other things he became a firm believer in Mineral and Human Magnetism, anticipating **Mesmer** in almost the very terms of the later exponent of the theory, and basing his argument on the well-known facts of the sympathy or antagonism spontaneously arising between individuals and the influence exerted by a firm will over a weak imagination.

In 1609, he retired to Vilvorde, near Brussels, and devoted himself to medical practice and chemical experiments. He declined to leave his retirement, although his fame brought him flattering invitations and offers from the Emperor and Elector Palatine. Almost unknown to his neighbors he attended anyone stricken by illness without accepting any fees for his services.

His published writings included: *De Magnetica Vulnerum naturali et Legitima Curatione* (1621), *De aquis Leondiensibus medicatis* (1624), *Opuscula Medica inaudita* (1641), *Febrium doctrina inaudita* (1642). Some of these were translated into Dutch, French and German. English translations of his tracts included: *A Ternary of Paradoxes; The Magnetick Cure of Wounds, The Nativity of Tartar in Wine, The Image of God in Man* (1650), and *Deliramenta Catarrhi: or the Incongruities, Impossibilities and Absurdities couched under the vulgar opinion of Defluxions* (1650).

He died December 30, 1644.

Van Peursen, C(ornelis) A(nthonie) (1920-)

Dutch professor of philosophy who has written on parapsychology. Born July 8, 1920 at Rotterdam, Netherlands, he studied at University of Leiden (Ph.D. 1948). In 1950 he married Jeanne Marguerite Ueltschi.

He was secretary of the Netherlands Committee for UNESCO from 1948-50, lecturer in philosophy at University of Utrecht from 1950-53, professor of philosophy at University of Groningen from 1953-60, professor of philosophy at University of Leiden from 1960 onwards. Dr. van Peursen's books include: *Riskante Philosophie* (Daring Philosophy, 1948), *Filosofische Orientatie* (Philosophical Orientation, 1958), *Leib, Seele, Geist; Einführung in Eine Phänomenologische Anthropologie* (Introduction to Phenomenological Anthropology, 1959; translated in English edition as *Body, Soul, Mind,* 1963). In addition to his many articles on philosophy, Dr. van Peursen also published 'Parapsychologie en Wijsgerige Bezinning' Parapsychology and Philosophical Reflection, *Tijdschrift voor Parapsychologie,* No. 1-3, 1959). He was also a member of the editorial board of a Dutch journal dealing with parapsychology.

Van Tassel, George W. (1910-1978)

Author of *I Rode in a Flying Saucer* (New Age Publishing Co., 1952) and organizer of **Giant Rock Space Convention,** held annually at Giant Rock Airport, near Yucca Valley, California. Van Tassel was proprietor of the airport and had some background of aeronautics.

He claimed to have visits from the inhabitants of flying saucers and to have contacted them telepathically. He often went into a trance in his circle of friends and communicated messages allegedly from **UFO** entities. Such communications were published in his journal *Proceedings of the College of Universal Wisdom.*

He constructed a round domed building called an "Integraton" at Giant Rock, based on instructions from his outer space contacts. The Integraton was designed to assist the development of antigravity and time travel. Van Tassel also published *Into this World and Out Again; a modern proof of the origin of humanity and its retrogression from the original creation of man. Verified by the Holy Bible. Revelations received through thought communication* (1956).

Van Tassel died February 9, 1978 after a sudden heart attack. The work of completing the Integraton was being continued by an associate designated as successor by Van Tassel in 1977 and later purchased by The Christology Church, P.O. Box 4648, San Diego, California 92104. The work of his **College of Universal Wisdom** was continued by Van Tassel's widow Doris, named as president. (See also **Giant Rock Space Convention; UFO**)

Vandermeulen Spirit Indicator

One of various devices invented from time to time to facilitate communication with spirits through mechanical means.

It consisted of two glass prisms, one plain, the other resinous fixed face-to-face on a board. Between them hung a very light triangle of wire. The prisms were connected to the positive and negative pole of a dry bell battery.

If the hanging triangle swung out and touched the positive wire, the circuit was closed and the bell rang. The spirits were expected to generate electricity in the prisms. If this was done, the hanging triangle which was wired to the negative pole would be repelled by the negative prism and attracted to the positive wire. The bell would ring, which was taken as an indication that a spirit desired to communicate, and the observers would rush to the **ouija board** to obtain the message.

The young inventor died in 1930 before his apparatus could be tested properly, but it was revived by M. Rutot, a Belgian professor, a member of the Royal Academy of Sciences. M. Rutot claimed that by means of the apparatus he had been able to contact the dead inventor. The apparatus was described in *Revue Métapsychique* (May-June, 1930, p. 256), and Rutot's own experiences were published in the *Bulletin due Conseil de Recherches Métapsychiques de Belgique* (July 1930). An English-language description of the apparatus, with detailed instructions for construction, was published by Robert J. Strong in his book *Spiritual Engineering* (1931).

For a detailed report of tests, with photographs, see the chapter 'Rutor's Triangles' in *Laboratory Investigations into Psychic Phenomena* by Hereward Carrington (n.d.). It was not possible to confirm the "instrumental communication with the dead" claimed by M. Rutot, but mechanical faults were not ruled out, and it was suggested that M. Rutot's claimed results may have been due to experimenters with mediumistic or telekinetic powers.

(See also **Electronic Voice Phenomenon; Ouija Board; Rutot's Spirit Indicator**)

Vanga

The unenrolled members of the Ndembo secret society of the Lower Congo. (See **Ndembo**)

Vardøgr

A psychic **double** or forerunner, which appears in advance to announce the arrival of an individual.

Sometimes it may manifest simply as familiar sounds associated with the individual concerned. Occasionally it may appear to the individual himself or herself, as in the celebrated experience of the great German poet **Goethe,** who met his double on the road to Drusenheim dressed in a garment which Goethe was to wear by accident eight years later on the same route.

Little has been published on the curious phenomenon of the vardøgr apart from an article in 1917 by Wiers Jensen, editor of the *Norwegian Journal of Psychical Research.* (See also **Double; Goethe**)

Varley, Cromwell Fleetwood (1828-1883)

Renowned consulting electrician of the Atlantic Telegraph Company and of the Electric and International Telegraph Company. He was born at Kentish Town, London, April 6, 1828, named after two of his ancestors, Oliver Cromwell and General Fleetwood. He was educated in South London, and went on to study telegraphy, joining the Electric and International Telegraph Company in 1846.

He was first attracted to Spiritualism in 1850.

He investigated the hypothesis that table rapping is the result of an electric force and demonstrated that this hypothesis was altogether unfounded.

In later years, he had many curious psychic experiences, discovered that he possessed Mesmeric healing power and effected cures on his wife. Mrs.

Varley had clairvoyant visions and spells of trance in which she foretold the exact course of her illness. After the birth of a son, Varley was one night aroused by three tremendous **raps.** He felt impelled to go into his wife's room, where he found the nurse intoxicated and Mrs. Varley rigid and in a cataleptic state.

He made the acquaintance of the famous medium Daniel Dunglas **Home.** Narrating his experiences before the committee of the **London Dialectical Society** in 1869, he concluded: "Still, I was too astonished to be able to feel satisfied. Fortunately, when I got home, a circumstance occurred which got rid of the element of doubt. While alone in the drawing room, thinking intently on what I had witnessed, there were raps. The next morning I received a letter from Mr. Home, in which he said 'When alone in your room last night you heard sounds. I am so pleased.' He stated the spirits had told him they followed me, and were enabled to produce sounds. I have the letter in my possession now, to show that imagination had nothing to do with the matter."

Of other personal occurrences Varley gave very impressive accounts. In the winter of 1864, at Beckenham Kent, he was woken up during the night by raps. Mrs. Varley was lying by his side in trance and he saw the transparent phantom of a man in military dress in the air. He asked him, through the voice of his wife, to deliver a message to his brother in Birmingham (see **Apparitions**).

Varley also had other curious experiences. In a dream state, he saw and heard the **double** of his sister-in-law. Next morning she confirmed everything by narrating her own dream experience. At another time, having accidentally chloroformed himself, he had vivid **out-of-the-body** experiences which were similarly confirmed by his wife. In 1860, at Halifax, his double, anxious to wake his physical self, made him dream of a bomb explosion and when the shock woke him he found the scene outside his window exactly corresponding to what his double saw (see **Double**).

In New York, he made the acquaintance of several mediums and made many experiments in the home of C. F. Livermore, the banker, with the famous medium Kate Fox (see **Fox Sisters**). His efforts to find out the laws that govern the physical phenomena of Spiritualism were fruitless. He began to suspect that powers other than electricity and magnetism were at work. On the basis of his varied experiences he was led to believe "that we are not our bodies; that when we die we exist just as much as before, and that under certain conditions we are able to hold communications with those on earth; but I also believe that many of the phenomena are often caused by the spirits of those whose bodies are present."

When Sir William **Crookes** started his famous investigation into the phenomena of Spiritualism, Varley assisted him in devising means of electric control. For his outspoken stand he was subject to abuse from the skeptical Dr. W. B. Carpenter who, in October 1871, in the *Quarterly Review,* assured readers that there were grave doubts of his scientific ability and that these misgivings of the learned world had kept Mr. Varley out of the Royal Society. At the time of this attack, Varley had been a fellow of the Royal Society for more than three months.

In addition to his important researches in Spiritualism, Varley was renowned for his important part in the successful laying of the first Atlantic cable.

He died at Bexley Heath, Kent, September 2, 1883.

Varma, Devendra P. (1923-)

Leading authority on the Gothic novel, author or editor of over two hundred books on the subject.

Dr. Varma was born in northeastern India, on the borders of the Himalayan Mountains. He has been a professor of English in Katmandu, Nepal, and also taught at the University of Damascus in Syria and in Cairo. For twenty-three years he has taught English at Dalhousie University in Halifax, Nova Scotia, specializing in the Gothic romance.

In 1977, he was awarded the Queen's Silver Jubilee Medal in Britian for his contributions to education and the arts. The distinguished critic Herbert Read commented: "Dr. Varma has made a permanent contribution to the history of English literature."

His published works include: *The History of the Gothic Novel in England* (1957; 1966), *The Evergreen Tree of Diabolical Knowledge* (1972). He edited the seven volumes of the "horrid novels" mentioned in Jane Austen's *Northanger Abbey,* Gothic Studies and Dissertations Series in 36 volumes, and three series of *Gothic Novels* reprinted by Arno Press (including *The Complete Works of Sheridan LeFanu) in 52 volumes.*

He has taken a particular interest in the study of vampires, and discussed the subject in his introduction to the three-volume reprint of *Varney the Vampire* by Thomas Prest, an early nineteenth-century shocker dealing with the **vampire** legend. In 1973, he traveled to Castle Dracula in Transylvania to investigate the background of Bram Stoker's famous novel *Dracula,* first published in 1897.

Varma has kept in close touch with such Hollywood directors of horror movies as Curtis Harrington, Frank Cunningham, Walter Doughty, and Forrest Ackermann, and has many friends among such actors as Christopher Lee and Vincent Price. Price once wrote to Varma: "You have done a great service to all lovers of the Gothic novel. I look to you as the foremost authority on the subject and hope I may have the privilege of working with you on a film or one of the many subjects you have rediscovered."

Vasiliev, Leonid Leonidovich (1891-1966)

Soviet physiologist and parapsychologist. Born in Russia, he graduated at Petersburg University in 1914. He was a teacher of biological sciences at Ufa, Bashkir from 1914-21, head of the Physiology Department, Bekhterev Brain Institute, Leningrad from 1921-38, professor of physiology at Leningrad University from 1943 onwards. He was Corresponding Member of the Academy of Medical Science of the Soviet Union.

In addition to his work in physiology, Prof. Vasiliev was a pioneer of parapsychology in the Soviet Union, and helped to establish the first parapsychology laboratory at Leingrad. He was author of the book *Mysterious Manifestations of the Human Psyche* (1959), issued in the U.S. under the title *Mysterious Phenomena of the Human Psyche* (University Books, 1965), and *Suggestion at Distance: Notes of a Psysiologist* (1962).

For other books describing Soviet work and attitudes to psychical phenomena, see also *Psychic Discoveries by the Russians* edited by Martin **Ebon** (Parapsychology Foundation, 1963; Signet paperback 1971) and *UFO's From Behind the Iron Curtain* by Ion Hobana & Julien Weverbergh (London, 1974; Corgi paperback 1975). (See also **U.S.S.R.**)

Vassago

According to the *Lemegeton* (Book of the Spirits), a famous grimoire attributed to Solomon the King, Vassago was one of the seventy-two spirits to be conjured up by magical evocation. Vassago is described as a Prince in the hierarchy of genii, favored by those who would know the unknown; he could tell of the future of past and present, or of anything lost or stolen.

As with other Princes among the spirits, Vassago could be conjured into a mystical triangle, but Kings and Emperors among the spirits could be conjured into a magical crystal (see also **Crystal Gazing**)

Vasse, Christiane M(aria) Piot (Mrs. Paul Vasse) (1922-)

Teacher who has written on parapsychology. Born December 8, 1922 in Salouel, France; B.A. 1941. She is a charter member of the Parapsychological Association.

She has experimented in extrasensory perception with children, and studied teacher-student relationships in these tests. She collaborated with her husband on experiments involving dice placement and also plant growth. She is co-author of various articles with her husband Dr. Paul M. **Vasse,** and translated into French the *Handbook of Tests in Parapsychology* by Betty Humphrey **Nicols.**

Vasse, Paul M(arie) (1910-)

Physician who experimented in areas of parapsychology. Born February 17, 1910 at Amiens, France, he studied at University of Paris (B.A. 1928, M.D. 1936). In 1947 he married Christiane M(aria) Piot.

He is a charter member of the Parapsychological Association, member of the Ordre des Medécins. In collaboration with his wife, Dr. Vasse conducted experiments in dice placement and in the growth of plants, and lectured on his results of the Institut Métapsychique. His articles on parapsychology (with his wife) include: 'Plant Growing Experiments' (*Revue Métapsychique,* April-June 1948), 'Comparison of Two Subjects in PK' (*Journal of Parapsychology,* December 1951), 'ESP Test with French First Grade School Children' (*Journal of Parapsychology,* Sept. 1958).

"Vates"

One of the spirit controls of the Rev. W. Stainton **Moses.** "Vates" was an assistant to the control "Imperator," said to have been the prophet Daniel. (See also **"Imperator"**; Rev. W. Stainton **Moses**)

Vaughan, Alan (1936-)

Author, editor, who has written widely on psychical and parapsychological topics. Born December 28, 1936, in Akron, Ohio, he studied at University of Akron (A.B. 1958), graduate study at Rutgers University, 1958-59, New School for Social Research, 1966-67, College of Psychic Studies, London, England, and University of Freiburg (both 1967-68). His first marriage was to Iris Collins in 1967, second, Diane Dudley in 1975.

In 1963, he was a researcher and cartoon editor for *National Enquirer,* New York; information specialist, International Nickel, New York City, 1964-65; science editor of college textbooks, American Book Co., New York City, 1965-67; science editor of college textbooks, Van Nostrand Reinhold Co., 1968-69. From 1969-72, he was Eastern editor of *Psychic* Magazine (since *New Realities*), co-editor 1973, articles editor 1973-75, editor 1976-77. From 1978 onwards he was president of New Ways of Consciousness Foundation, San Francisco; staff instructor at Psychic Integration Institute; faculty member at Sonoma State College 1973-74, and Institute for the Study of Consciousness, 1974-75; lecturer at seminars, conferences, and colleges. He was a member of board of directors at Central Premonitions Registry from 1968 onwards. He has appeared on national television and radio programs, including those of Merv Griffin, David Frost, and Phil Donohue, and programs in Canada, England, and Italy. He served in the U.S. Army from 1959-62. He has started a Los Angeles based computer software company called Mind Technology Systems. He is an associate member of the Parapsychological Association. He was awarded a grant from the Parapsychology Foundation, 1967-68, honorary doctorate from El Instituto de Ciencias Parapsicologias Hispano-Americano, 1977.

His publications include: *Patterns of Prophecy* (1973), (with Montague Ullman & Stanley Krippner) *Dream Telepathy* (1973), (with James Bolem) *Psychics* (1972), (contributor) Edgar D. Mitchell and other editors, *Psychic Exploration* (1974), *Incredible Coincidence; The Baffling World of Synchronicity* (1979), *The Edge of Tomorrow* (1982). He has contributed a great many articles and interviews to *Psychic* and *Parapsychology Review.*

He states: "The transition from a skeptical science textbook editor to a parapsychologist and practicing psychic was a painful one. I had to give up the cherished idea of traditional science to discover the more important underlying realities of consciousness and its psychic effects. The research leading to *Patterns of Prophecy* opened up my own prophetic talent, and enabled me to teach others how to develop their latent psi gifts. . . . Each of us has a unique consciousness and a unique task in life. We also have unique problems to solve. But only *our* consciousness has the answers to *our* problems. Your inner self has the wisdom of the universe locked up within it. By finding the key to unlock that wisdom, you will enrich your life."

Vaughan, Diana

A mythical figure in a famous nineteenth-century occult hoax initiated by "Leo **Taxil**," pseudonym of Gabriel **Jogand-Pagés,** an unscrupulous French journalist.

From 1885-86, "Taxil" published a sensational story that one branch of Freemasons were following a form of Devil-worship called Palladianism, of which the High Priestess was one Diana Vaughan, supposed to be the descendent of the seventeenth-century alchemist Thomas **Vaughan.**

These revelations synchronized with Roman Catholic opposition to Freemasonry and were profitable to "Taxil." Diana Vaughan was supposed to have repented to her Satanist background and embraced the Catholic Church. Her memoirs were read with satisfaction by the Pope himself.

Diana herself was announced as giving a Press Conference on Easter Monday, 1897. Instead, "Taxil" appeared and calmly revealed his hoax, stating that he was merely anxious to see how far he could dupe the Church!

News of this deception was badly received, for the plot had lasted three or four years, and "Taxil" had to be smuggled away under police protection.

In Britain, the hoax was exposed by occult scholar Arthur Edward **Waite** in his book *Devil Worship in France; or, The Question of Lucifer: A Record of Things Seen and Heard in the Secret Societies According to the Evidence of Initiates* (London, 1896). (See also **Devil Worship;** Gabriel **Jogand-Pagés**)

Vaughan, Thomas (1622-1666)

British alchemist and poet, who wrote under the pseudonym "Eugenius **Philalethes.**"

He was born April 17, 1622 at Newton, Breconshire, the younger twin brother of poet Henry Vaughan. He matriculated at Oxford, and entered Jesus College, Oxford University, becoming a fellow of his college. In 1640, at the age of eighteen, he received the living of St. Bridget's, Breconshire, and on February 18, 1642, too the B.A. degree. He was a royalist during the Civil War, and in 1658 was accused of "drunkeness, swearing, and incontinency, being no preacher," and deprived of the living of St. Bridget's. However, this may have been no more than high spirits. He became a devoted student of chemistry, following his researches both in Oxford and London, under the patronage of Sir Robert Murray.

He died February 27, 1665-66 at the rectory of Albury, Oxfordshire, allegedly from inhalation of fumes of mercury, upon which he was experimenting.

Vaughan was an ardent follower of Cornelius **Agrippa,** to whom, as he stated, "he acknowledged that, next to God, he owed all that he had." He claimed to be a philosopher of nature rather than a vulgar alchemist. In one of his manuscripts he recorded strange dreams of promonitions that he had experienced, and prayed for forgiveness of past errors, including former revels and drunkeness. Although he published a translation of a Rosicrucian work with a preface by himself, he explicitly stated that he was not a member of any such fraternity. Under the pseudonym of "Eugenius Philalethes," he published the following works: *Anthroposophia Theomagica,* with *Anima Magica* (London, 1650, Amsterdam 1704, in Germany, Leipzig, 1749), *Magia Adamica; or the Antiquities of Magic* (London, 1650, 1656; Amsterdam, 1704, in German), *Lumen de Lumine* (London, 1651, Hof, 1750, in German). *Aula Lucis; or the House of Light* (London, 1652), *Euphrates; or the Waters of the East* (London, 1655, 167; Stockholm & Hamburg, 1689, in German), *The Chymists Key to shut, and to open; or the True Doctrine of Corruption and Generation* (London, 1657). He contributed verses for Thomas Powell's *Elementa Opticæ* (1651), for the English translation of Cornelius Agrippa's *Three Books of Occult Philosophy* (1651), and William Cartwright's *Comedies* (1651). A collection of his Latin verses was included at the end of Henry Vaughan's *Thalia Rediviva* (1678).

Vaughan was falsely ientified with the mystical writer "Eirenæus Philalethes" through the "Diana Vaughan" writings of Leo **Taxil,** who also popularized a false legend of a pack between Satan and Thomas Vaughan. (See also Gabriel **Jogand-Pagés;** Eirenæus **Philalethes;** Eugenius **Philalethes;** Diana **Vaughan**)

Vaulderie

A term indicating connection with Satanic powers, so called from Robinet de Vaulx, a hermit, one of the first persons accused of the crime.

In 1453, the Prior of St. Germain-en-Laye, Guillaume de l'Allive, a doctor of theology, was accused of Vaulderie, and sentenced to perpetual imprisonment. Six years later there was burned at Lille a hermit named Alphonse, who preached heterodox doctrines. During the fifteenth century, many accusations of witchcraft were directed against those who followed the heretical sect of the Waldenses or Vaudois.

Such were the preludes of a persecution which, in the following year, the Vicar of the Inquisition, administrator of the Diocese of Arras, seconded by the Count d'Etampes, Governor of Artois, directed at first against loose women, but afterwards against citizens, magistrates, knights, and especially the wealthy.

The procedures against the accused had almost always for their basis some accusation of sorcery. Most of the unhappy creatures confessed to having attended the "Witch's Sabbat," and the strange revelations wrung from them by torture, gave some idea of the ceremonies which according to the popular tradition, were enacted in the lurid festivals presided over by Satan.

The following are some extracts from the judgment pronounced at Arras in 1460 upon five women, a painter, and a poet, nicknamed "an abbé of little sense," and aged about seventy, and several others, who all perished in the flames kindled by barbarous ignorance and fed by a cruel superstition:

"And the said Inquisition did say and declare, that those hereinunder named had been guilty of Vaulderie in manner following, that is to say:—'That when they wished to go to the said Vaulderie, they, with an ointment given to them by the devil, anointed a small wooden rod and their palms and their hands; then they put the wand between their legs, and soon they flew wherever they wished to go, over fair cities, woods and streams; and the devil carried them to the place where they should hold their assembly, and in this place they found others, and tables placed, loaded with wines and viands; and there they found a demon in the form of a goat, a dog, an ape, or sometimes a man; and they made their oblation and homage to the said demon, and adored him, and yielded up to him their souls, and all, or at least some portion of their bodies; then, with burning candles in their hands, they kissed the rear of the goat-devil. . . . [Here the Inquisitor becomes untranslatable].

" ' . . . And this homage done, they trod and trampled upon the Cross, and befouled it with their spittle, in contempt of Jesus Christ, and the Holy Trinity, then turned their backs towards heaven and the firmament in contempt of God. And after they had all eaten and drunk well, they had carnal intercourse all together, and even the devil assumed the guise of man and woman, and had intercourse with both sexes. And many other crimes, most filthy and detestable, they committed, as much against God as against nature, which the said Inquisitor did not dare to name, that innocent ears might not be told of such villainous enormites.' "

The eagerness displayed by the Inquisitor and his acolytes so excited the public indignation, that at the close of the year 1460 the judges did not dare any longer to condemn to death the unfortunate wretches accused. It was said that the persecution was only for the purpose of depriving them of their property. As in the case of many great wrongs, a reaction set in favor of justice.

Thirty years later, when the country of Artois had been reunited to the Crown, the Parliament of Paris declared, on May 20, 1491, that these trials were "abusive, void, and falsely made," and condemned the heirs of the duke of Burgundy and the principal judges to an amend of 500 Parisian livres, to be distributed to a reparation among the heirs of the victims. (See also **Sabbat; Witchcraft**)

Vay, Baroness Adelma (1840-1924)

Authoress, medium, pioneer of Spiritualism in Hungary. Her powers, inherited from her mother the Countess Teleki, later Duchess Solm, first blossomed in 1865.

She became clairvoyant, wrote, spoke and drew in trance, had the prophetic gift and performed many wonderful cures. In 1873, with her husband, she formed the Hungarian Spiritualist Association of which they became the first presidents. Her best known books are: *Spirit, Force and Matter* (1869), *Studies on the Spirit World* (1874), *From My Life* (1900), *Pictures from the Beyond* (1905).

Vedanta

The highest teaching of the *Vedas,* the ancient Sanskrit scriptures of India. There are four *Vedas:* the *Rig-Veda,* the *Yajur-Veda,* the *Sama-Veda* and the *Artharva-Veda.* These are regarded as divine revelation.

The word "Vedanta" means the end or highest point of the Vedic teaching, which is not simply a formal instruction but a revelatory experience of transcendental consciousness.

Hindu scriptures differ from the sacred writings of some other religions insofar as they go beyond faith in any particular deities (regarded as rather like legal fictions, useful only at certain stages in life) to awareness of an Absolute, beyond time, space and causality.

The *Vedas* were originally an oral tradition, later codified in scriptures called the *Upanishads* (meaning nearness to wisdom). There are some 108 *Upanishads,* and these are regarded as the conclusion of the *Vedas* and hence "Vedanta." Of the many *Upanishads,* some ten are regarded as the principle ones.

Recommended reading:

Nikhilananda, Swami (tansl.) *The Upanishads,* 4 vols., Phoenix House, London, 1951-59; Ramakrishna-Vivekananda Center, New York, 1959

Vedanta Societies

American Vedanta Societies stem from the visit to the U.S. by Swami **Vivekananda** in 1893, when he lectured on Hinduism at the World Parliament of Religions held in Chicago. The Swami founded the Vedanta Society of New York in 1896, followed by the Vedanta Society of San Francisco in 1900.

Swami Vivekananda became the foremost interpreter of Yoga and Hinduism in Western countries, basing his teachings on the inspiration of his master Sri **Ramakrishna.**

Vedanta comprises the supreme wisdom of the *Vedas,* the ancient Sanskrit scriptures of India, together with the *Upanishads* which derived from them. This wisdom is manifest as a revelatory experience after following spiritual disciplines (such as the various forms of **Yoga**) in conjunction with scripture study under the guidance of a qualified *guru* or teacher.

There are now some sixteen Vedanta Centers in the U.S. which form branches of the Ramakrishna Order of India. Addresses: Vedanta Society of Northern California, 2323 Vallejo Street, San Francisco, California 94123; Vedanta Society of Southern California, 1946 Vedanta Place, Hollywood, California 90068. There are also Vedanta Center/Ananda Ashrama communities providing spiritual retreats in both Massachusetts and Southern California. Addresses: Vedanta Center, 130 Beechwood Street, Cohasset, Massachusetts 02025; Ananda Ashrama, Box 8555, La Crescenta, California 91214.

Vehm-Gerichte

A secret tribunal which, during the Middle Ages, exercised a peculiar jurisdiction in Germany and especially in Westphalia.

Its origin is uncertain. The sessions were often held in secret, and the uninitiated were forbidden to attend them on pain of death. The most absurd stories have been circulated concerning them—that they met in underground chambers and so forth. These have been discounted by modern research. Far from dabbling in the occult, these courts frequently punished persons convicted of **witchcraft** and sorcery.

Veleda (c. 70 A.D.)

A prophetess among the ancient Germans, of whom the historian Tacitus stated: "She exercises a great authority, for women have been held here from the most ancient times to be prophetic, and, by excessive superstition, as divine. The fame of Veleda stood on the very highest elevation, for she foretold to the Germans a prosperous issue, but to the legions their destruction! Veleda dwelt upon a high tower, whence messengers were dispatched bearing her oracular counsels to those who sought them; but she herself was rarely seen, and none was allowed to approach her. Cercalis is said to have secretly begged her to let the Romans have better success in war. In the reign of the Emperor Vespasian she was honored as a goddess."

Veleda predicted the success of Claudius Civilis in the Batavian revolt against Rome (69-70 A.D.) and the fall of the Roman Empire.

Velikovsky, Immanuel (1895-1979)

Original thinker who formulated a controversial theory of the past history of the solar system, involving various cataclysmic disasters. In the most recent catastrophe, about the time of the prophet Moses in 1500 B.C., a comet from the planet Jupiter is supposed to have collided with Mars, formed the planet Venus, and shifted the orbit of the earth, displacing oceans and reversing the earth's poles.

Born June 10, 1895, at Vitebsk, Russia in 1895, Velikovsky attended the Medvednikov Gymnasium in Moscow, graduating with full honors. After a short period of study at Montpellier, France, he traveled in Palestine, then started pre-medical studies in natural science at Edinburgh, Scotland in 1914.

On the outbreak of World War I, he enrolled in the Free University in Moscow, studying law and ancient history. In 1915 he took up medical studies again at the University of Moscow, and received his medical diploma in 1921. He removed to Berlin, where together with Prof. Heinrich Loewe he founded and published *Scripta Universitatis,* a series of scholarly volumes contributed by Jewish scholars in various countries. Velikovsky became friendly with Albert Einstein, who edited the mathematical-physical volumes.

Velikovsky married violinist Elisheva Kramer, and moved to Palestine, where he practiced as a physician for fifteen years; they had two children. Velikovsky also acted as a psychoanalyst, and published some papers on psychology, to which he made important contributions.

He then spent some time in New York researching a study of Freud's own dreams and the relationship of Freud's thought to such figures as Oedipus, Akhnaton and Moses, but in the course of his researches, he became intrigued by the suggestion that there might have been a catastrophe at the time of the Exodus of the Israelites from Egypt.

A new book began to develop, under the title *Ages in Chaos,* followed by a further manuscript *Worlds in Collision.* The latter work was published first in 1950, and created a storm in the scientific world, when orthodox American scientists compelled the original publisher to drop the book.

This extraordinary campaign of suppression is fully documented in Alfred de Grazia's book *The Velikovsky Affair; the Warfare of Science and Scientism* (University Books, 1966). Diehard and intolerant scientists were later infuriated when various hypotheses of Velikovsky, originally sneered at as "unscientific" and inaccurate, were eventually proved correct. Velikovsky correctly predicted the existence of geomagnetic planetary fields, the negative electrical charge of the sun, the high temperature of Venus, the existence of hydrocarbon clouds surrounding Venus, and emission of radio sounds from Jupiter—all vindicated by space probes and other recent scientific developments.

Velikovsky's other publications include: *Ages in Chaos* (1952), *Earth in Upheaval* (1955), *Oedipus and Akhnaton; Myth and History* (1960), *Peoples of the Sea* (1977).

He died in 1979 in Princeton, New Jersey.

Veltis

An evil spirit who assaulted St. Margaret of Cortona (died 1297), but was overcome by her. On being asked by St. Margaret who he was and whence he came, he replied: "My name is Veltis, and I am one of those whom Solomon by virtue of his spells, confined in a copper cauldron at Babylon, but when the Babylonians, in the hope of finding treasure dug up the cauldron and opened it, we all made our escape. Since that time our efforts have been directed to the destruction of righteous persons, and I have long been striving to turn thee from the course thou hast embraced."

Verdelet

Said to be a demon of the second order, master of ceremonies at the infernal court. He was charged with the transport of witches to the **Sabbat.** He took the names of "Master Persil," "Sante-Buisson," and other names of a pleasant sound, so as to entice women into his snares.

Verdun, Michel (died 1521)

A self-confessed werwolf, burned at Besançon, France, in 1521 together with his accomplice Pierre Burgot. They had stated that they stripped naked and anointed themselves with a certain **unguent,** after which they changed shape and became werwolves, hunting and attacking children and adults.

Verdun was discovered after attacking a traveler who wounded the animal. Following the trail of the wounded creature, the traveler discovered Verdun, who had returned to human form, with his wife bathing the wound. (See also **Werwolf**)

Recommended reading:

Summers, Montague. *The Werewolf,* London, 1933; University Books, 1966

Vérité, La (Journal)

Nineteenth-century Spiritualist journal. Published in Lyons, France.

Verograph

One of various modern devices for experimenting with Aura-electronics or **Kirlian Photography.** It is small enough to be conveniently portable.

Veronica

A religious term for a cloth bearing the likeness of Jesus imprinted miraculously. The term was coined by St. Gregory of Tours (538-594 A.D.), deriving from the Greek *icon* (image) and Latin *vera* (true).

The apocryphal story of the veronica is that a woman of rank, living in the Via Dolorosa, broke through the procession bearing Jesus to the Cross when it stopped for Simon of Cyrene to assist in carrying the Cross. The woman, usually named as Seraphia (sometimes called Veronica) wiped the face of Jesus with a cloth, and the miraculous portrait became impressed from the blood and sweat. Other versions of the story claim that the woman simply handed the cloth to Jesus, who wiped his own face and returned the cloth.

A detailed and highly circumstantial version of the incident was given by Catherine Emmerich (see **Germany**) when in an ecstatic trance.

A claimed veronica was placed in a marble coffer on the altar of a chapel attached to St. Peter's church in Rome during the period of Sixtus V, but it was moved in 1440 and said to be deposited in the Vatican.

Another cloth with a similar miraculous portrait was presented by two Fathers to the seventh synod of Nice, A.D. 787. Such miraculous likenesses not made by people are also known as Acheropites.

In 1813, when a vault was opened in St. George's Chapel, Windsor, England, one of the coffins, believed to be that of Charles I, was opened, and a portrait found on the grave cloth which had wrapped the body. (See also **Turin Shroud**)

Verrall, Arthur Woollgar (1851-1912)

Classical scholar, husband of the psychical researcher Mrs. Margaret de Gaudrion **Verrall,** and father of researcher Mrs. W. H. **Salter.** After his death he was one of the purported communicators in the famous "**cross correspondence**" tests of the **Society for Psychical Research,** London, in which Mrs. Verrall and Mrs. Salter were responsible for automatic scripts.

Born February 5, 1851 in Brighton, England, he studied at Wellington College and Trinity College, Cambridge University, England (B.A. 1873, M.A. 1874). He lectured at Trinity College, Cambridge, where he became First King Edward VII Professor of English Literature in 1911. He died June 18, 1912.

Verrall, Margaret de Gaudrion Merrifield (Mrs. A. W. Verrall) (1859-1916)

Prominent British psychical researcher, Lecturer in Classics at Newnham College, wife of Dr. A. W. **Verrall,** the well-known classical scholar and the first occupant of the King Edward VII Chair of English.

She was born December 21, 1859, at Brighton, England, educated at Newnham College, Cambridge University. She married A. W. Verrall in 1882.

She joined the **Society for Psychical Research,** London, in 1889, wrote many important papers for the *Proceedings,* was elected to the Council in 1901, developed psychic powers herself and at the request of F. W. H. **Myers,** held sittings with the medium Mrs. **Piper** when she visited England.

In **automatic writing** Mrs. Verrall obtained in 1901 the first results after the death of Myers and produced afterwards hundreds of scripts which often contained matter of supernormal interest. In 1906, she published in the *Proceedings* an analysis of her scripts. This paper formed the starting point of a serious study in **cross correspondence.**

Sir Oliver **Lodge** paid the following tribute to Mrs. Verrall in his book *The Survival of Man* (1909): "The fame of Mrs. Piper has spread into all lands, and I should think the fame of Mrs. Verrall also. In these recent cases of automatism the Society has been singularly fortunate, for in the one we have a medium who has been under strict supervision and competent management for the greater part of her psychical life; and in the other we have one of the sanest and acutest of our own investigators, fortunately endowed with some power herself, some power of acting as translator or interpreter between the psychical and the physical worlds."

Mrs. Verrall's conclusions, after years of experiments and testing, were: "It cannot be denied that the 'communicator' of the Piper sittings and of my own scripts presents a consistent personality dramatically resembling that of the person he claims to be. I entirely acquiesce in this judgment. In fact I am one of those who, though they would like to see further and still stronger and more continued proofs are of the opinion that a good case has been made out, and that as the best working hypothesis at the present time it is legitimate to grant that lucid moments of intercourse with deceased persons may in the best cases supervene; amid a mass of supplementary material, quite natural under the circumstances, but mostly of a presumably subliminal and less evidential kind. The boundary between the two states—the known and the unknown—is still substantial, but it is wearing thin in places; and like excavators engaged in boring a tunnel from opposite ends, amid the roar of water and other noises we are beginning to hear now and again the strokes of the pickaxes of our comrades on the other side of the partition as on our side; there has been distinct cooperation between those on the material side and those on the immaterial side; and we are at liberty, not indeed to announce any definite conclusion, but to adopt as a working hypothesis the ancient doctrine of a possible intercourse of intelligence between the material and some other, perhaps ethereal order of existence.

She died July 2, 1916, at Cambridge. Mrs. Verrall's daughter Helen married W. H. **Salter,** another prominent psychical researcher.

Versailles Adventure

One of the most famous psychic experiences reported at the beginning of the twentieth century. In August 1901, two English ladies, Miss Moberly and Miss Jourdain took an afternoon walk in the Gardens of Versailles, France, and found themselves transported to the Trianon of 1789, complete with buildings and other people of the period.

They described their experience with much corroborative detail in their book *An Adventure* by C. A. E. Moberly & E. F. Jourdain, first published London, 1911. In the first edition their identity was concealed by the names "Miss Morison" and "Miss Lamont."

The book went into many editions and generated much controversy, coinciding with rising British interest in psychic phenomena through the work of the **Society for Psychical Research,** London. In spite of many subsequent attempts to discredit the writers, the adventure still stands as a unique experience.

For a valuable and sympathetic paper on the claimed experience, see 'Richard's Garden Revisited' (*Journal* of the Society for Psychical Research, vol. 41, No. 712, June 1962.

Recommended reading:

Flew, Antony G. N. *A New Approach to Psychical Research,* Watts, London, 1953

Gibbons, M. E. & A. O. *The Trianon Adventure,* Museum Press, London, 1958

Iremonger, Lucille. *The Ghosts of Versailles,* Faber & Faber, London, 1957

Mackenzie, Andrew. *The Unexplained: Some Strange Cases of Psychical Research,* A. Barker, London, 1953, Abelard, New York, 1968 [includes a critical appendix dealing with the Moberly-Jourdain case]

Moberly, C. A. E. & E. F. Jourdain. *An Adventure,* Faber & Faber, London, 1911, frequently reprinted

Olivier, Edith. *Four Victorian Ladies of Wiltshire,* Faber & Faber, London, 1945 [by a friend of Miss Moberly, disclosing that Anne Moberly had the faculty of second sight]

Parrott, Ian. *The Music of 'An Adventure,'* Regency Press (paperback), London, 1966

Sturge-Whiting, J. R. *The Mystery of Versailles; A Complete Solution,* Rider, London, 1938

Vervain

A sacred herb used to cleanse the table of Zeus before a feast in ancient Greece. It was also strewn on the altars of Jupiter in ancient Rome. Water containing vervain was also sprinkled in houses to cast out evil spirits.

Among the Druids particularly it was employed in connection with many forms of superstition. They gathered it at daybreak, before the sun had risen. Later sorcerers followed the same usage, and demonologists believed that in order to evoke demons it was necessary to be crowned with vervain.

During the Crusades it was believed that when the nails were driven into the hands of Christ, vervain sprang up on Calvary.

The old herbalists recommended vervain to ease childbirth, and for jaundice, dropsy, gout, worms, stomach complaints, wound healing, ulcers and piles. North American Indians used vervain to cure menstrual disorders among their women.

Vestigia (Organization)

Founded in 1976, with membership of scientists, engineers, technicians, and interested individuals, to investigate and conduct research into unexplained scientific phenomena. It trains members in investigative techniques, supplies speakers to universities and organizations.

The name of the group is the Latin word for "investigate," which, in itself, means footprint.

The group sponsors charitable program, maintains library and biographical archives, compiles statistics, offers computerized services. It has committees on Photography and Technical matters, and divisions on Aerial Phenomena, Biological matters, Earth Sciences, Parapsychology. Publication: annual Newsletter. Address: 56 Brookwood Road, Stanhope, New Jersey 07874. (See also **Fortean Society; International Fortean Organization; Society for the Investigation of the Unexplained**)

Vett, Carl Christian (1871-1956)

Danish agriculturalist and author, who played a leading part in organizing international cooperation and spread of information in the field of parapsychology. He was born September 25, 1871, at Aarhus, Denmark. He became a director of textile companies in Scandinavia. During World War I he was a diplomatic courier and cultural advisor to the Danish Ministry of Education on museum acquisitions. He was also a pioneer of biodynamic agricultural methods.

Mr. Vett was intensely interested in psychical research as a proper scientific study, and it was largely through his efforts that the First International Congress on Psychic Research was held in Copenhagen in 1921, with researchers from fifteen different countries. He became general secretary of a permanent committee for the organization of later international congresses of this kind, held at Warsaw (1923), Paris (1927), Athens (1930), Oslo (1935). A tribute was paid to his work at the First International Conference of Parapsychological Studies held in Utrecht, Netherlands in 1953. In his later years, Mr. Vett lectured and wrote articles in Mexico and the U.S. His reminiscences were published in his article 'Memoirs of Psychic Research' (*Tomorrow,* vol. 3, No. 4, Summer 1955).

He died February 1, 1956 in Rome, Italy.

Vibrations

Sound vibrations are believed to play a mysterious part in the production of psychic phenomena. In the form of lively conversation, singing or music they are always asked for by the invisible operators.

"We can walk on the vibrations made by your laughing," said "Walter," the control of "Margery" (Mrs. **Crandon**). "Walter" claimed to get more than half of the energy used in the production of the phenomena from phonograph vibrations but the only explanation he gave was that as they came off the machine they converted into another and more useful form of energy.

Music as the means to induce the trance state is found as far back as Biblical times. Elisha stated: "But now bring me a minstrel; and it came to pass when the minstrel played that the hand of the Lord came upon him."

It is said that the great tenor Caruso was able to shatter a crystal glass by singing a high note upon it. Soldiers have to break step when they cross a bridge.

There are many legends of the miraculous power of music, and in Indian religious philosophy, the world was said to have been created through subtle vibrations, paralleling the Biblical statement of creation "And God said . . . " Experiments have shown that music stimulates plant growth.

So far, there is no definite scientific evidence of music vibrations facilitating psychical phenomena, but it is possible that the effect is more likely through the emotional conditions which music stimulates, together with a relaxation of defensive aspects of consciousness. It is also a matter of common experience that different kinds of music excite emotions and the ideas associated with them, and it is a commonplace to speak of the vibrations being good or bad in different groups of people. (See also **Music; Rock Music**)

Victoria, Queen (1819-1901)

Queen of England, Scotland and Ireland, Empress of India, who presided over the great days of the British Empire. She was known to be sympathetic to Spiritualism, and to have held seances with Prince Albert and other individuals. She approved of the book *Our Life After Death* by medium Robert James **Lees,** and was said to have used Lees as a personal medium. Her belief in the possibility of communication between the spirit world and the living is illustrated by an entry in her journal commenting on the story that Princess Feodora, when at the point of death, had talked about a beloved child who had died earlier: "Surely at the approach of death the veil is raised and such pure spirits are allowed to see a glimpse of those dear ones waiting for them.

A short time before the death of Prince Albert, he had told the Queen: "We don't know in what state we shall meet again, but that we shall recognize each other and be together in eternity I am perfectly certain." After the death of Prince Albert, the Queen relied heavily on the companionship of her personal servant, the rough Highlander John **Brown,** and there were even rumors that he was her lover, and that he took part in Spiritualist seances with her. After his death in 1883, the Queen erected a statue to him at Balmoral.

Victoria's Prime Minister W. E. Gladstone was also sympathetic to psychical research, and was an early member of the Society for Psychical Research, London. He once summoned the famous palmist "**Cheiro**" to explain his theories, and also sat with the medium William **Eglinton.**

For an interesting study of the facts and speculations concerning Queen Victoria and the paranormal, see *Queen Victoria's Other World* by Peter Underwood (Harrap, London, 1986). (See also John **Brown**)

Vidya

In **Theosophy,** the knowledge by which man on the Path of Life can discern the true from the false and so direct his efforts correctly by means of the mental faculties which he has learnt to use. It is the antithesis of *Avidya* (ignorance). Both terms are borrowed from Hindu religious philosophy. (See also The **Path; Theosophy; Vedanta**)

Viedma

Russian name for a witch. (See **Slavs**)

Vila, The

Vili were nymphs who frequented the forests that clothe the bases of the Eastern Alps. According to popular belief, they could be seen traversing glades, mounted on stags, or driving from peak to peak on chariots of cloud.

Old Serbian ballads tell how Marko, the great hero of ancient Serbia, was joined in bond of brotherhood with a *Vila,* who showed to him the secrets of the future.

At that period, Serbia was a mighty nation, extending from the Alps to the Black Sea, from the Danube to the Adriatic, before her freedom was lost at the battle of Varna.

Vinchon, Jean (1884-   )

French neuropsychiatrist who published books in areas of parapsychology. Born June 21, 1884 in Department of the Somme, France, he took his M.D. in 1911 at Paris. In 1921 he married Jeanne Chabault.

He was medical director of the Neuropsychiatric Center of the French Army of the East from 1917-18, director of clinic of Paris Medical School, director of Army Neuropsychiatric Center, Paris Region from 1939-40, thereafter neuropsychiatrist at War Veterans Ministry, neuropsychiatric consultant at Hôpital de le Pitié. Member of Société Médico-Psychologique, former president of Société d'Histoire de la Médecine, former president of the Institut Métapsychique.

In addition to his books on medical and psychiatric subjects, Dr. Vinchon also published: (with Maurice Garçon) *Le Diable* (The Devil, 1928, English translation London, 1929), *Mesmer et son secret* (Mesmer and His Secret, 1936), *L'Art et la Folie* (Art and Insanity, 1950), *La Magie du dessin: Du griffonage automatique au dessin thérapeutique* (The Magic Drawing: From Automatic Scribbling to Therapeutic Drawing, 1959).

Vintras, Eugène (1807-1875)

A Normandy peasant of great devoutness, who in the year 1839 was nominated by a strange sect named the Saviours of Louis XVII, as a fitting successor to their prophet Thomas Martin who had just died.

The sect believed that the child of Louis XVII and Marie Antoinette did not die in prison and would be restored to the throne of France. The Saviours addressed a letter to the pretended Louis XVII and arranged that it should fall into the hands of Vintras. It abounded in good promises for the reign to come and in mystical expressions calculated to inflame the brain of a person of weak and excitable character such as Vintras. In a letter Vintras himself described the manner in which this communication reached him as follows:

"Towards nine o'clock I was occupied in writing, when there was a knock at the door of the room in which I sat, and supposing that it was a workman who came on business, I said rather brusquely, 'Come in.' Much to my astonishment, in place of the expected workman, I saw an old man in rags. I asked merely what he wanted. He answered with much tranquility, 'Don't disturb yourself, Pierre Michel.' Now, these names are never used in addressing me, for I am known everywhere as Eugène, and even in signing documents I do not make use of my first names. I was conscious of a certain emotion at the old man's answer, and this increased when he said: 'I am utterly tired, and wherever I appear they treat me with disdain, or as a thief.' The words alarmed me considerably, though they were spoken in a saddened and even a woeful tone. I arose and placed a ten sous piece in his hand, saying, 'I do not take you for that, my good man,' and while speaking I made him understand that I wished to see him out. He received it in silence but turned his back with a pained air. No sooner had he set foot on the last step than I shut the door and locked it. I did not hear him go down, so I called a workman and told him to come up to my room. Under some business pretext, I was wishing him to search with me all the possible places which might conceal my old man, whom I had not seen go out. The workman came accordingly. I left the room in his company, again locking my door. I hunted through all the nooks and corners, but saw nothing.

"I was about to enter the factory when I heard on a sudden the bell ringing for mass, and felt glad that, notwithstanding the disturbance, I could assist at the sacred ceremony. I ran back to my room to obtain a prayer book and, on the table where I had been writing, I found a letter addressed to Mme. de Generès in London; it was written and signed by M. Paul de Montfleury of Caen, and embodied a refutation of heresy, together with a profession of orthodox faith. The address notwithstanding, this letter was intended to place before the Duke of Normandy the most important truths of our holy Catholic, Apostolic and Roman religion. On the document was laid the ten sous piece which I had given to the old man."

Vintras immediately concluded that the bringer of the letter was a messenger from heaven, and became devoted to the cause of Louis XVII. He became a visionary. He had bloody sweats, he saw hearts painted with his own blood appear on hosts, accompanied by inscriptions in his own spelling.

Many believed him a prophet and followed him, among them several priests, who alleged that they partook of his occult vision. Doctors analysed the fluid which flowed from the hosts and certified it to be human blood. His enemies referred these miracles to the Devil. The followers of Vintras regarded him as a new Christ.

But one follower named Gozzoli, published scandalous accounts of his activities, alleging that horrible obscenities and sacrilegious masses took place in their private chapel at Tilly-sur-seules. The unspeakable abominations alluded to were contained in a pamphlet entitled *Le Prophète Vintras* (1851). The sect was formally condemned by the Pope, and Vintras constituted himself sovereign Pontiff.

He was arrested on a charge of exploiting his cult for money, was tried at Caen, and sentenced to five years' imprisonment. When freed in 1845, he went to England, and in London resumed the leadership of his cult, which flourished for some time afterwards. He later returned to France, settling in Lyons.

For a brief account of the sect the Saviours of Louis XVII, see *Studies in Mysticism* by A. E. Waite (1906). (see also **Stigmata**)

Vishnudevananda, Swami (1927-   )

Disciple of the late Swami **Sivananda,** a famous exponent of Hatha Yoga and founder-president of the Sivananda Yoga Vedanta Centers, with branches in Canada, the U.S. and Europe.

Born in Kerala, India, he became a school teacher at the age of 17, then later joined the Indian Army, serving for two years. By chance he read a pamphlet by Swami Sivananda which emphasized the importance of studying the Hindu scripture *Bhagavad-Gita.* He did so, and felt a strong impulse to visit the Sivananda Ashram.

In 1946, while on army leave, he went to Rishikesh and became a disciple of the Swami. He decided to leave his family and become a renunciate. He was initiated by the Swami and settled at the ashram, becoming a leading exponent of the science of **Hatha Yoga.**

At the suggestion of his guru, he undertook a tour of India, demonstrating Hatha Yogas *asanas* and training many hundreds of individuals.

In 1957, he undertook a world tour, spending two years traveling throughout the U.S. and eventually settling in Canada, where he founded a Sivananda Yoga Vendanta Center.

He became the first yoga instructor to obtain a pilot's license and flew a private "peace plane" decorated by artist Peter Max to such disturbed areas of the world as Northern Ireland, West Pakistan and the Suez Canal, dropping peace leaflets.

He established yoga centers in twenty-five communities, including a large yoga camp in Quebec, Canada and another in the Bahamas. He also founded True World Order, an organization dedicated to yoga harmony, health, peace and vegetarian diet.

Swami Vishnudevananda is author of *The Complete Illustrated Book of Yoga* (Julian Press, 1960).

The address of his Sivananda Yoga Ashram is: 8th Avenue, Val Morin, Quebec, Canada. There are branch centers in Los Angeles and San Francisco, California; Washington, D.C.; Fort Lauderdale, Orlando and Palm Beach, Florida; Chicago, Illinois; New York, N.Y.; Hamilton and Toronto, Ontario; Montreal.

Vision (Ocular and Inner)

Ocular vision is the perception of material objects in accordance with optical laws from a definite point in space. Difficult to classify are those rare cases when the sense of sight is transposed and the subject "sees" with his elbows, forehead, fingertips or stomach, since it is not clear what mechanism of vision is involved.

Inner vision is independent of space, objective existence and optical laws. The simplest type of inner vision is presented by memory images, waking dreams, and images of imagination. The latter type may attain such an intensity as to emerge spontaneously and reach the pitch of **hallucination.**

Hallucination is the widest extent of inner vision. **Dreams** represent the primary type. They are hallucinations of low intensity. Generally, hallucinations appear to conform to all factors of ocular vision—space, optical laws, objectivity. The images appear externalized in space.

Indeed, objectivity in some cases of hallucinations may be more than an appearance, as some believe that a camera may register an apparition when outwardly nothing is visible and the vision must have taken place internally (see **Psychic Photography**).

A still stronger proof of objectivity is furnished by cases of veridical visions in which the perception is afterwards found to be a true visual representation of incidents taking place at a distance.

On the other hand, no objectivity is discoverable in degenerative hallucinations, in the dogs and snakes of the drunkard, the scarlet fire of the epileptic, or the visions of the insane.

Inner vision may be developed empirically in **crystal gazing** and afford fruitful study for the determination of what elements are externalized from the subconscious mind of the scryer or of discarnate intelligences.

Another classification of visions is: spontaneous and induced. (See also **Apparitions; Crystal Gazing; Double; Dreams; Eyeless Sight; Hallucination; Psychic Photography;** Seeing with the **Stomach; Transposition of the Senses; Visions**)

Visions

Term derived from Latin *visus,* past participle of *videre,* to see, indicating the appearance to human beings of supernatural persons or scenes. Of great frequency in early and medieval times, and among primitive or semi-civilized races, visions seem to have decreased proportionately with the advance of learning and enlightenment. Thus, among the Greeks and Romans of the classic period, they were comparatively rare, although visions of demons or gods were occasionally seen. On the other hand, among Oriental races, the seeing of visions was a common occurrence, and these visions took more varied shapes.

In medieval Europe, visions were almost commonplaces, and directions were given by the Church to enable men to distinguish visions of divine origin from false delusions which were the work of the Devil.

Visions may be roughly divided into two classes—those which are spontaneous, and those which are induced. The great majority belong to the latter class.

Joseph Ennemoser, in his work *The History of Magic* (2 vols., 1854), enumerated the causes of such appearances thus: (1) Sensitive organism and delicate constitution, (2) Religious education and ascetic life (fasting, penance, etc.), (3) Narcotics—opium, wine, incense, narcotic salves (witchsalves), (4) Delirium, monomania, (5) Fear and expectation, preparatory words, songs, and prayers.

Among the visions induced by prayer and fasting, and the severe self-discipline of the religious ascetic, must be included many historical or traditional instances—the visions of St. Francis of Assisi, St. Anthony, St. Bernard Ignatius, St. Catherine of Siena, St. Hildegarde, Joan of Arc. It may be noted that the convent has often been the special haunt of religious visions, probably for the reasons above mentioned. But apparitions of the Virgin Mary continue to be reported in modern times, and the percipients are usually young peasant children without any background of severe spiritual disciplines (see **Apparitions; Garabandal; Medjugorge**).

But the most potent means for the inductions of visionary appearances are those originally made use of by Oriental people. Narcotics of all kinds—opium, hashish, and so on—have been indulged in, and certain physical means used for this express purpose. Thus some fakirs and yogis will gaze for hours at a time at one object, will remain for months in practically the same position, or will practice mortification of the body, so that they may fall at length into the visionary sleep (a species of catalepsy). Another ancient method of inducing visionary experience was staring into a crystal (see **Crystal Gazing**).

The narcotic salves with which some anoint themselves are said to be similar to the witch **unguents** used in the Middle Ages, which induced in the witch the **hallucination** that she was flying through the air on a goat or a broomstick.

Opium is also said to produce a sensation of flying, as well as visions of celestial delight. Alcoholic intoxication induces visions of insects and small animals, as does also nitrogen. The vapors rising from the ground in some places, or those to be found in certain caverns, are said to exercise an effect similar to that of narcotics.

The Indians of North America practiced similar external methods of inducing visions—solitude, fasting, and the use of salves or ointments. In some African, West Indian, and Arabic countries certain dances produced severe dizziness, helping them towards the desired visionary **ecstasy.** Rhythmic and repetitive music also assisted this process.

Spontaneous visions, although less common, are yet sufficiently numerous to merit attention here. The difficulty is, of course, to know just how far "fear and expectation" may have operated to induce the vision. In many cases, as in that of the seer Emanuel **Swedenborg,** the visions may have commenced as "visions of the night," hardly to be distinguished from dreams, and so from vision of an "internal" nature to clearly externalized **apparitions. Swedenborg** himself declared that when seeing visions of the latter class he used his senses exactly as when awake, dwelling with the spirits as a spirit, but able to return to his body when he pleased. An interesting case of spontaneous vision was that of Benvenuto **Cellini.** Visions are by no means confined to the sense of sight.

Taste, hearing, smelling, touch, may all be experienced in a vision. Joan of Arc, for instance, heard voices encouraging her to be the deliverer of her country. Examples may be drawn from the Bible, as the case of the child Samuel in the Temple, and instances could be multiplied from all ages and all times.

The visions of John Pordage (1607-1681) and the "Philadelphia Society," or, as they called themselves later, the "Angelic Brethren," in 1651 were noteworthy in this respect because they included the taste of "brimstone, salt, and soot." In the presence of the "Angelic Brethren," pictures were drawn on the windowpanes by invisible hands, and were seen to move about.

In spite of the name, the Philadelphia Society was a British organization, stemming from the mysticism of Jakob **Boehme.** Pordage published a work titled *Truth Appearing Through the Clouds of Undeserved Scandal* (1655).

Physiological explanations of visions have been offered from time to time. Plato said: "The eye is the organ of a fire which does not burn but gives a mild light. The rays proceeding from the eye meet those of the outward light. With the departure of the outward light the inner also becomes less active; all inward movements become calmer and less disturbed; and should any more prominent influences have remained they become in various points where they congregate, so many pictures of the fancy."

Democritus held that visions and dreams are passing shapes, ideal forms proceeding from other beings. Of death bed visions Plutarch said: "It is not probable that in death the soul gains new powers which it was not before possessed of when the heart was confined within the chains of the body; but it is much more probable that these powers were always in being, though dimmed and clogged by the body; and the soul is only then able to practise them when the corporeal bonds are loosened, and the drooping limbs and stagnating juices no longer oppress it."

The Spiritualist theory of visions can hardly be called a physiological one, save insofar as spirit is regarded as refined matter. An old theory of visionary ecstasy on these lines was that the soul left the body and proceeded to celestial spheres, where it remained in contemplation of divine scenes and persons.

In modern times, the idea of the soul as an entity distinct from the physical body has been studied under the name of "**Out of the Body Experience.**" Stemming from this concept is the modern study of "**Near Death Experience,**" in which individuals regarded as clinically dead have been revived, and have described visionary experiences (see **Death**).

Very similar to this was the doctrine of Swedenborg, whose spirit, he believed, could commune with discarnate spirits (the souls of the dead) as one of themselves. To this may be traced the doctrines of modern **Spiritualism,** which thus regarded visions as actual spirits or spirit scenes, visible to the ecstatic or entranced subject whose spirit was projected to discarnate planes.

The question whether or not visions are contagious has been much disputed. It has been said that such appearances may be transferred from one person to another by the laying on of hands. In the case of Scottish seers (see **Second Sight**), such a transference may take place even by accidental contact with the seer. The vision of the second person is, however, less distinct than that of the original seer.

The same idea prevailed with regard to the visions of "magnetized" patients in the days of **animal magnetism.** Insofar as these may be identified with the collective hallucinations of the hypnotic state, there is no definite scientific evidence to prove their existence.

Visions have by no means been confined to the ignorant or the superstitious. Many men of genius have been subject to visionary appearance. While Raphael was trying to paint the Madonna, she appeared to him in a vision. The famous composition known as the "Devil's Sonata" was said to have been dictated to Tartini by the Devil himself. **Goethe** also had visions. William **Blake**'s portraits of the Patriarchs were done from visionary beings which appeared to him in the night. There have been a number of such instances. (See also **Apparitions; Clairvoyance; Crystal Gazing; Death; Dreams; Garabandal; Hallucination; Medjugorge; Out of the Body** Travel; **Prediction; Vision**)

Recommended reading:

Barrett, Sir William. *Death Bed Visions,* Methuen, London, 1926

Besterman, Theodore. *Crystal-Gazing; A Study in the History, Distribution, Theory and Practice of Scrying,* William Rider, London, 1924; University Books, 1965

Fielding-Ould, Fielding. *The Wonders of the Saints in the Light of Spiritualism,* John M. Watkins, London, 1919

Halifax, Joan. *Shamanic Voices: A Survey of Visionary Narratives,* Dutton, 1979

Hall, Manly P. *Visions and Metaphysical Experiences,* Philosophical Research Society, Los Angeles, n.d. (paperback)

Huxley, Aldous. *The Doors of Perception,* Chatto & Windus, London, 1954; Harper & Row, 1970

Klonsky, Milton. *William Blake, The Seer and His Visions,* Crown Publishers, 1977

Lewis, David. *The Life of S. Teresa of Jesus,* London, 1970 etc.

Muldoon, Sylvan J. & Hereward Carrington. *The Projection of the Astral Body,* Rider & Co., London & New York, 1929 etc. (frequently reprinted)

Ring, Kenneth. *Life at Death; A Scientific Investigation of the Near-Death Experience,* William Morrow, 1980

Visions (Magazine)

Monthly publication containing articles on psychic phenomena, energy fields, unorthodox healing; includes book reviews. Published by: American National Institute for Psychical Research, 11222 La Cienega Boulevard, Inglewood, California 90304.

Visitants

Another term for spirit apparitions. (See **Apparitions**)

Vitality

Vitality is that force or principle possessed by living things. In the case of human beings, controversy has long raged between those who interpret vitality mechanistically as the energy derived from food and oxygen intake, and those who support theories of Vitalism, a doctrine that the origin and phenomena of life derive from a vital principle as distinct from a purely chemical or physical force.

The mechanistic view appears inadequate as a matter of everyday experience, since there are limits to the vitality obtainable from oxidation of food and air. At a certain point of eating and breathing one becomes tired, and it is impossible to regain vitality without rest and sleep.

Exactly what happens in the sleep state to enhance vitality is still not entirely clear. It does appear, however, that the human body is not simply an internal combustion machine, but rather an energy *transforming* machine. Contrary to the energy combustion view is the fact that fasting may often enhance vitality rather than deplete it.

The mind also has a profound effect on the vital condition of the body, as is clear from one's attitude to life, as well as the special phenomena of hypnosis and the profound effects which are possible through meditation techniques.

It would seem that subtle processes are involved in energy transformation of food and air, and the relationship of such transformation to the psychic life of human beings, their mental activities, states of consciousness, and sociological and spiritual aspirations.

Various great religions posit the existence of an individual soul, as an essential principle of a human being, influenced by the physical and mental life as well as by environment and food intake, but independent from the physical body and surviving it after death. Spiritualists and psychical researchers have offered evidence for such survival, much of it impressive, while materialists have argued that such apparent survival may be nothing more than mental artifacts. However, even this latter view also predicates mental life as capable of existing in a form as subtle as that of the claimed soul.

From a subjective point of view, the experience of **out-of-the-body** travel or **astral projection** has usually carried an overwhelming awareness of individuality as distinct from the body, which it apparently leaves, and for many individuals the experience has been one of deep religious conviction.

Sylvan **Muldoon,** a pioneer writer on the subject, has argued in the light of his out-of-the-body experiences that the sleep state is a condition of vitality transfer between a "soul body" and the physical body, drawing upon some subtle life force outside the body.

Such a view reads like a restatement of ancient Hindu concepts of *prana,* a subtle principle in the air and in food, which is transformed into *kundalini* energy in the body. A proportion of *kundalini* remains static in the body, but may become dynamic in sexual activity. It may also be diverted to subtle centers in the body through the spinal column by the practice of meditation in conjunction with the psycho-physical effects of purification of the mind and emotions, traditionally through self-purification and ethical living.

The *Kundalini* eventually ascends to a center in the head, resulting in higher consciousness, as experienced by saints and mystics in many different religious traditions. This is sometimes accompanied by side effects of a paranormal character, such as the miracles ascribed to saints, or the psychic faculties associated with mediums. But since the mediumistic condition is a passive one, it does not normally result in the profound spiritual experiences associated with mystics.

Ancient Hindu treatises on *prana* have described at length the atomic structure of matter and its connection with the subtle currents of *prana* operating in the universe generally as well as modified in the individual human being.

In modern times, Pandit **Gopi Krishna** of Srinagar, who experienced a traditional arousal of *kundalini* energy, resulting in higher consciousness, has described his experiences in several books on the subject.

He affirms that the application of *kundalini* energy in higher consciousness is not antithetical to its use in sexual activity, but stresses the need for balance in preserving the vital currents of the body. This involves care in diet, meditation and the living of an ethical and socially useful life.

The Pandit regards *kundalini* as an evolutionary force in human life which will lead human beings to higher goals of extended consciousness and ethical social life, instead of gross physical desires of greed, selfishness and hatred which divide peoples, engender wars and result in cultural degeneration. It also seems likely that the goal of higher consciousness, interfused with daily social life, might also result in the development of faculties at present classed as paranormal. (See also **Kundalini; Prana; Theosophy; Yoga**)

Recommended reading:

Carrington, Hereward. *Vitality, Fasting and Nutrition,* Rebman & Co., New York, 1908

Crookall, Robert. *During Sleep; The Possibility of "Co-Operation" Between the Living and the Dead,* University Books, 1974

Gopi Krishna. *The Biological Basis of Religion and Genius,* Harper & Row, 1972

Gopi Krishna. *The Secret of Yoga,* Harper & Row, 1972

Hollander, Bernard. *In Search of the Soul and the Mechanism of Thought, Emotion, and Conduct,* 2 vols., Kegan Paul, London/E. P. Dutton, 1920

LeShan, Lawrence L. *The Medium, The Mystic and The Physicist,* Viking/Turnstone Books, London, 1974

Muldoon, Sylvan J. & Hereward Carrington. *The Projection of the Astral Body,* Rider & Co., London & New York, 1920 etc. (frequently reprinted)

Rama Prasad. *The Science of Breath and the Philosophy of Tattvas . . . Nature's Finer Forces,* 3rd rev. ed., Theosophical Publishing Society, London, New York & Madras, 1897 etc.

Wheeler, L. Richmond. *Vitalism; Its History and Validity,* Witherby, London, 1939

Vivekananda, Swami (1863-1902)

Hindu monk who became the leading interpreter of Yoga and Hinduism in the West; founder of the Rama-krishna Mission. Born as Narendra Nath Dutt in Calcutta in a Bengali family, January 12, 1863, he was educated at a Christian College in Calcutta. Here he was much impressed by the analytic and scientific methods of Westerners. For a time, Narendra was influenced by the Brahmo Samaj movement, but its rationalistic spirit did not altogether satisfy him.

When eighteen years old, he first met his spiritual teacher Paramahamsa **Ramakrishna,** who was much impressed by the boy's beautiful singing. Within a couple of years, Narendra was won over by the deep spiritual realization of Sri Ramakrishna and became his follower.

He made a number of visits to Sri Ramakrishna at Dakshineswar, but after the death of his father was obliged to take charge of family affairs, and got a job in an attorney's office. Eventually he persuaded Sri Ramakrishna to use his spiritual powers to ensure that his mother and brothers would never lack food and clothing, then renounced his worldly life.

Sri Ramakrishna died in 1886 and Narendra adopted the name Vivekananda in 1893, when he sailed from Bombay May 31 to attend the Parliament of Religions held in Chicago in connection with the World's Fair.

In his opening address he caused tumultuous applause by commencing "Sisters and Brothers of America," and thereafter his clear simple trenchant style, his grasp of both Hindu and Christian beliefs, won over many audiences. His book on *Raja Yoga* attracted the attention and respect of such enlightened thinkers as William **James** and Leo Tolstoy. Vivekananda lectured throughout Chicago, Detroit, Boston and New York for two years, then visited England, where he also aroused great enthusiasm, before returning to Calcutta in 1897.

Back in India, he took up the cause of ordinary people with realism as well as spiritual insight, stating: "the great national sin is the neglect of the masses and that is one of the causes of our downfall. No amount of politics would be of any avail until the masses of India are once more well educated and well cared for."

Soon afterwards he established the Ramakrishna Mission for training young monks and preachers. In June 1899, he made a second journey to the West, but by now his strength was giving out. He spent some time in California, which was congenial to his health and his teachings, and in December 1900 returned to India, where he passed away July 4, 1902 in Behur Monastery.

Today there are Ramakrishna Vedanta Centers in a number of countries, and the books of Swami Vivekananda remain one of the best and clearest introductions to Hindu spiritual teachings and yoga.

These books are constantly reprinted, and include such popular works as *Jnana Yoga, Raja Yoga, Bhakti Yoga,* and *Karma Yoga.* His *Collected Works* cover eight volumes. The standard biography is by Swami Nikhilananda: *Swami Vivekananda; A Biography,* Adraita Ashram, Calcutta, India, 1975.

Vjestica

A Slav name for a witch. (See **Slavs**)

Voices (Paranormal)

Paranormal voices may be objective or subjective. The latter category is covered by **clairaudience.** The former is on the borderline of **apparitions,** as in the Biblical statement: "And he fell to the earth, and heard a voice saying unto him: Saul, Saul, why persecutest thou me? . . . And the men which journeyed with him stood speechless, hearing a voice, but seeing no man." *Acts,* ix, 4, 7.

According to Eusebius, a spirit voice was heard by the crowds at the martyrdom of Bishop Polycarp: "Be brave, Oh Polycarp." St. Francis, praying in a little ruined church, heard a voice from the painted wooden crucifix, before which he knelt: "Francis, seest thou not that my house is being destroyed? Go, therefore, and repair it for me."

Joan of Arc was started on her mission by voices. "A very bright cloud appeared to her and out of the cloud came a voice." The sentence of death was based on admission of her monitary voices. She heard them first at thirteen years of age. They came mainly when she was awake, but also roused her sometimes from sleep. They were not always intelligible. She believed in them implicitly. The predictions of the voices were mainly fulfilled: the siege of Orleans was raised, Charles VII was crowned at Rheims and Joan was wounded, all as foretold.

The preacher George Fox stated in his *Journal:* "When my troubles and torments were great, when all my hopes in men were gone so that I had nothing outwardly to help me, nor could I tell what to do, then, O then, I heard a voice which said: 'There is one, even Jesus Christ, that can speak to thy condition.' When I heard it my heart did leap for joy."

Dr. Edwin Ash, in his book *Faith and Suggestion* (1912) described the case of Dorothy Kerin, who after a long illness, on the point of death, suddenly heard a voice say "Dorothy." She woke up, saw the bed enveloped in light and a beautiful woman holding an Annunciation lily in her hand, saying "Dorothy, you are quite well," putting the stress on "quite." She became instantly well. For her own account, see Dorothy Kerin's book *The Living Touch* (1919).

There are various types of clairaudience. As a conscious subjective phenomenon, many writers, from Socrates onwards, have claimed that their works were dictated by an inner voice. In **automatic writing**, psychics and Spiritualist mediums are usually (but not invariably) unaware what is being written through their hands. Many Spiritualist mediums go into trance and apparently transmit messages from the spirits of the dead through their own vocal organs, sometimes with the tones and mannerisms of the deceased, but often only an approximation. **Inspirational speakers** or channelers sometimes also speak with the voices of spirit entities, sometimes, however, with their own vocal mannerisms, only the message being dictated by inner inspiration.

In the case of a clairvoyant, images of the deceased are perceived and described by the mediums, sometimes in conjunction with clairaudient messages. Both clairvoyance and clairaudience are classed as mental phenomena, involving **extrasensory perception.** In such cases, the voices may be paranormal in origin, but not in manifestation, and sometimes they may be more reasonably credited to unconscious mental activity.

Much controversy surrounds the phenomenon of "**direct voice**" in Spiritualist seances, where spirits are claimed to speak independently of the medium, either through a **trumpet** or through a "voice box" built up from **ectoplasm** drawn from the medium.

In recent times, in line with modern technological developments, a new type of paranormal vocal phenomenon has emerged—"**Raudive Voices,**" or "**Electronic Voice Phenomenon.**" It is claimed that messages, often individual words or phrases apparently from deceased individuals, have appeared paranormally on audio-tape recordings. In spite of much research, the evidence is, as yet, ambiguous, as some apparent successes might be due to some kind of mediumistic power on the part of the investigator, rather than to some susceptibility of audio-recording to communications from deceased individuals.

A variant phenomenon which has been reported anecdotally in modern times in the "Electronic Visual (or Video) Phenomenon," in which it is believed that paranormal images have appeared on video-tape recordings. Much research remains to be done before such claims can be validated. (See also **Automatic Writing; Channeling; Clairaudience; Clairvoyance; Direct Voice; Electronic Voice Phenomenon; Inspiration; Inspirational Speakers; Raudive Voices; SPIRICOM**)

Recommended reading:

Ellis, David. *The Mediumship of the Tape Recorder,* D. J. Ellis, Pulborough, U.K. (paperback), 1978

Lang, Andrew. *The Valet's Tragedy and Other Studies,* Longmans Green, London & New York, 1903 [includes detailed chapter on 'The Voices of Jeanne D'Arc']

Raudive, Konstantin. *Breakthrough: An Amazing Experiment in Electronic Communication with the Dead,* Colin Smythe, Gerrards Cross, U.K./Taplinger, New York, 1971; Lancer Books (paperback), 1973

Smith, Hester Travers. *Voices from the Void,* William Rider, London, 1919

Stokes, Doris. *Voices in My Ear,* Futura (paperback), 1981

Swaffer, Hannen. *Adventures with Inspiration,* Kennerly, Morely & Mitchell, London, 1929

Volguine, Alexandre (died 1976)

Prominent French astrologer. In 1937 he founded *Les Cahiers Astrologiques,* a forum of French astrological research, which he edited until his death in 1976. He wrote a number of works on astrology, some of which have now been published in English translation by ASI Publishers Inc. These include: *The Technique of Solar Returns, Lunar Astrology, The Ruler of the Nativity.*

Vollhardt, Maria (Frau Rudloff) (c. 1925)

Wife of an official in the Berlin Postal Ministry, a physical medium whom Dr. F. Schwab, author of *Teleplasma und Telekinese* (Berlin, 1923) made the subject of searching studies for two years. Maria Vollhardt produced **telekinesis** (movements of objects at a distance) **levitations, apports, ectoplasm** and **stigmata** phenomena of a baffling character.

In his book *My Psychic Adventures* (1924), the psychical researcher J. Malcolm **Bird** wrote of having seen a quantity of angry-looking pricks, some actually bleeding, appear in a rough square pattern on the medium's hand. The only suggestion he could make for normal duplication was a battery of three or four forks or a section of nutmeg grater.

The mystery of how such wounds were produced, deepened when the sitters declared that they had seen on Maria Vollhardt's hand a small object, the shape of a bird's beak, or claw. They put a pot full of farina on the table and asked for an imprint. They got it—in the shape of a chicken's foot.

Once the medium's hand was stigmatized across the hand of one of the sitters who was controlling her. At each puncture, the medium gave a sharp cry of pain. She stated that she felt as though an electric current had entered at the skin and passed through the body.

Dr. Schwab observed the phenomenon some fifty times outside the seance room in good light. When he made photographs with a stereoscopic camera he got a picture of a sort of claw of several branches, poised upon the perfectly controlled hand of the medium. He believed it was a materialized symbol of the medium's subconscious notion of oppression and torture.

In 1925, Maria Vollhardt figured in court proceedings. At a seance given to a number of scientists and doctors her arms, linked up in the orthodox manner, were found, on the lights being turned up, encircled by two massive rings. Prof. Albert Moll refused to believe in the penetration of **matter through matter** and later declared in a book that the medium must have had the rings concealed under her sleeves. The medium retorted with libel proceedings and offered to demonstrate her powers before the Bench. The offer came to nothing as Prof. Moll insisted that the demonstration should be done in daylight.

Prof. Paul Degner testified on behalf of Maria Vollhardt. The court found Prof. Moll guilty of calumny, but acquitted him as his statement was made "in defense of justified interests." The medium appealed against the acquittal and lost her case. Prof. Busch testified that the apports produced were fraudulently introduced by the medium while in a "semi-conscious condition."

Volometer

An instrument invented by Dr. Sydney Alrutz (1868-1925) of Uppsala University, Sweden, to measure will as a dynamic power. (See **Will**)

Von Däniken, Erich (1935-)

Swiss writer whose books on **Chariots of the Gods** and other ancient mysteries have launched a new school of popular and often uncritical literature of occult speculation about ancient history and religion.

Born in Zofingen, Switzerland April 14, 1935, he was brought up in a conservative Roman Catholic setting at St. Michel College in Fribourg. At an early age von Däniken was fascinated by "inconsistencies" between religious doctrine and the accounts of mysterious events in the Bible. After leaving school, he took various jobs in hotels, and this seasonal work left him with spare time which he spent in traveling and reading. He visited South America, Russia and Egypt, seeing at firsthand the monuments of the past.

In his reading, he was particularly impressed by the Biblical account of Ezekiel's fiery wheel, and by Sumerian accounts of the coming of the Sun God in the ancient epic of *Gilgamesh.* Von Däniken began to evolve a theory of sky-borne gods in vehicles resembling accounts of **flying saucers,** built around the religious legends and myths of ancient civilizations. With the advent of American and Soviet space travel, such theories became at least plausible.

In 1961, von Däniken started publishing articles about his theories and by 1966 had prepared a book *Erinnerungen an die Zukunft,* which was published in Germany and serialized in the Swiss newspaper *Die Weltwoche.*

This book was translated into English and published in the U.S. by Putnam under the title *Chariots of the Gods?* (1970). Von Däniken's introduction stated: "I claim that our forefathers received visits from the universe in remote past. Even though I do not know who these extraterrestrial intelligences were or from which planet they came, I nevertheless proclaim that these 'strangers' annihilated part of mankind existing at the time and produced a new, perhaps the first *homo sapiens.*"

As evidence, von Däniken cited accounts of cosmic battles in ancient legends and inscriptions suggestive of space travel. In later books—*Gods From Outer Space; Return to the Stars* (1971), *The Gold of the Gods* (1973), *In Search of Ancient Gods; My Pictorial Evidence for the Impossible* (1974)—he supported his theories by further legends, traveler's tales and photographs of ancient religious inscriptions.

Typical of his facile interpretations are claims that Mayan temple figures and inscriptions represent spacemen at the controls of their vehicles. Often such interpretations reveal a misunderstanding of ancient religious motifs and a false assumption that "ancient astronauts" would employ twentieth-century technology and design.

Moreover, Von Däniken himself has admitted to making false statements. In an interview on the PBS *Nova* science program on television in 1978, he confessed that he had not really explored an artifact-filled cave in South America as claimed in his book *The Gold of the Gods* (1973)! He admitted: "No that did not happen, but I think when somebody writes books in my style and in my sense, which are not scientific books, we call it in German 'Sachbucher.' It's a kind of popular book but it's not science fiction, though all the facts do exist but with other interpretations. Then an author is allowed to use effects. So some little things like this are not really important because they do not touch the facts . . . " This astonishing defense of falsehood in order to strengthen a romantic interpretation of facts necessarily casts doubt on Von Däniken's theories.

Side by side with such dubious material, von Däniken has popularized genuinely puzzling riddles of the past, such as the extraordinary ground markings at **Nazca,** Peru, claimed by von Däniken and others as a spaceport for ancient astronauts (see **Nazca "Spaceport"**)

For refutation of von Däniken's theories, see *Crash Go the Chariots* by Clifford Wilson (Lancer, 1973) and *The Space-Gods Revealed* by Ronald D. Story (Harper & Row, 1976; Barnes & Noble, 1978).

Von Däniken is not perturbed by adverse criticism from scholars and scientists. He believes that his unconventional interpretations of mythology and archaeology will be generally accepted in the course of time.

Although much of his writing resembles science-fiction themes, his controversial theories would have been welcomed by such arch-enemies of dogma and establishment judgment as the late Charles (Hoy) **Fort,** who was one of the first researchers to correlate such topics as unidentified flying objects and ancient artifacts. However, Fort would probably have deplored the growing cult of the orthodoxy of the unconventional which has developed as a result of von Däniken's books.

Voodoo

A group of superstitious beliefs and practices, including sorcery, serpent worship and sacrificial rites amongst West Indians and blacks. Voodoo or Vaudoux is said to derive from a Dahomey word *vodu,* meaning "gods," as a modification of African beliefs.

Today, the practice of Voodoo is officially banned in the U.S., but firmly entrenched in the island of Haiti, where it is virtually a national religion.

It is basically a form of **Spiritism,** in which gods and the spirits of the dead are invoked to take possession of the priests, protect worshipers and perform feats of divination and magic. As with African tribal religions from which Voodoo stems, illness and misfortune are considered due to the hostility of neighbors or spirits, and it is the task of the *houngan* or priest to discover the source of this hostility and neutralize it.

The diagnosis of illness or misfortune involves a mixture of folk medicine (operating on the body) and sympathetic magic (operating on the souls of victim and persecutor). Spells, magic powders and special rituals are employed by the *houngan.* These priests are trained by special rites in a complex initiation ceremony of rebirth and possession by one of many *loa* or gods (deriving from the traditional gods of African tribes).

Another Voodoo practitioner is the *tonton macoute* or itinerant magician, sometimes used by parents as a bogeyman who will take away children if they don't behave. Significantly the term was also applied to the sinister army of the late President Duvalier, some of whom were rumored to be **Zombies** (dead bodies revived by magic as soulless robots). It is now known that Zombies are created artificially by ruthless *hounyans* using toxic substances that affect the brain and cause paralysis.

Much of Voodoo is a nightmare world of spells, counterspells and distasteful rites, rather like the underworld of Western black magic practices, with major emphasis on power over others, fear and superstition.

However, for thousands of followers, Voodoo is a legitimate religion, in which mysterious entities and spirits of the dead are associated with the actions of the living. This integration of a rich mythology with everyday spiritist practices undoubtedly has a very real power. (See also **Africa; West Indian Islands; Zombies**)

Recommended reading:

Christesen, Barbara. *The Magic and Meaning of Voodoo,* Raintree, 1977

Courlander, H. & R. Basilien. *Religion & Politics on Haiti,* I.C.R., Washington, D.C., 1970

Davis, Wade. *The Serpent and the Rainbow,* Collins, London, 1986

Denning, Melita & Osborne Phillips. *Voodoun Fire; The Living Reality of Mystical Religion,* Llewellyn Publications, Minnesota, 1979

Deren, Maya. *Divine Horsemen; Voodoo Gods of Haiti,* Chelsea House Publishers, New York, 1970

Huxley, Francis, *The Invisibles; Voodoo Gods in Haiti,* McGraw, 1964; Chelsea House, 1970

Métraux, Alfred, *Voodoo in Haiti,* Oxford University Press, U.K., 1959; paperback, Schocken, 1972

Vril

A word invented by Edward Bulwer **Lytton,** famous novelist, politican and occultist, to describe a kind of psychic energy. It was featured in his book *The Coming Race* (1871), which told how Vril enabled a race to reach a high degree of civilization and develop a Utopian society without poverty, inequality, or war.

Lytton himself had some connections with occultism and received the magician Éliphas **Lévi** at his house. The idea of Vril was widely copied by occultists, and in prewar Germany there was a Vril Society founded in Berlin. (See also Bulwer **Lytton**)

W

Wafer (in Devil Worship)

The sacred Communion wafer is often used by devil worshipers for purposes of profanation (see **Devil worship**). It was alleged that in the house of the Irish notorious witch, Dame Alice **Kyteler,** a wafer of sacramental bread was found, bearing thereon the name of the Devil. (See also **Wales; Witchcraft**)

Wagner, Edward A. (1906-)

Prominent American astrologer. Born in Philadelphia, he worked as a reporter on the Cleveland Press. He was associated with famous escapologist Harry **Houdini** in exposing fraudulent Spiritualist mediums, but later became convinced that much of occultism and astrology was genuine.

He became connected with the publications section of a Rosicrucian group, then founded his own publishing company for books on **astrology.** He edited the *National Astrological Journal* and syndicated many articles on astrology. In 1945 he married Julia Coppa, who assisted him in publishing *Horoscope* and other astrological publications.

Waite, Arthur Edward (1857-1942)

A leading British scholar of occultism and mysticism. Born October 2, 1857 in Brooklyn, New York, he was brought to London, England by his family when only a baby. He was educated at Catholic schools. As a boy, he cherished an affection for "penny dreadfuls," the romantic popular pulp literature of the day, which fired his imagination. In later life, the thirst for juvenile adventures was superseded by a deeper desire for the quest of the soul, revealed in his poems and his books on mysticism.

He grew up amidst the first European renaissance of occultism which stretched from the end of the nineteenth century to the outbreak of World War I, and he numbered among his personal friends men like Arthur **Machen** and The Hon. Ralph **Shirley.** He also met W. B. **Yeats,** Madame **Blavatsky,** Annie **Besant,** Rudolf **Steiner,** Dr. Wynn **Westcott,** Algernon **Blackwood** and Aleister **Crowley.**

He was a regular contributor to Ralph Shirley's *Occult Review,* the finest journal of its kind, and for some twenty years edited anonymously the monthly "Review of Periodical Literature," which was one of its most perceptive features. During this period he acquired an unrivaled knowledge of every major current development in occultism all over the world.

He was also a respected Freemason and an authority on Masonic writings. He was responsible for first British publication of many important occult and mystical texts. He translated and publicized the writings of occultists Éliphas **Lévi** (Alphonse Louis Constant). In his own writings, his immense scholarship was sometimes shrouded by a portentous and obscure style, deriving from the occult tradition of reluctance to reveal openly the esoteric mysteries, but instead giving hints and symbolic explanations.

In 1888, he married Ada Lakeman, to whom he gave the mystical name "Lucasta," also the title of one of his volumes of poetry. His many publications include: *The Real History of the Rosicrucians* (1888, revised and expanded as *The Brotherhood of the Rosy Cross,* 1924; reprinted 1961), (edited) *Lives of Alchemystical Philosophers* (1888; reprinted as *Alchemists Through the Ages,* (1970), (ed.) *Songs and Poems of Fairyland* (1888), *A Handbook of Cartomancy, Fortune-Telling and Occult Divination* (1889, revised as *A Manual of Cartomancy,* (1909), *The Occult Sciences: a compendium of Transcendental Doctrine and Experiment* (1891, 1923), *Azoth: or, The Star in the East* (1893; 1973), (ed.) Éliphas Lévi's *Transcendental Magic* (1896, revised 1923; 1970), *The Book of Black Magic and of Pacts* (1898, revised as *The Book of Ceremonial Magic,* 1911; 1961; 1970), *Studies in Mysticism and Certain Aspects of the Secret Tradition* (1906), *The Hidden Church of the Holy Grail* (1909), *The Pictorial Key to the Tarot* (1911; 1960), *The Secret Tradition in Freemasonry* (2 vols., 1911; 1 vol. ed. 1937), *The Book of Destiny* (1912), *The Secret Doctrine in Israel; a Study of the Zohar* (1913), (transl. & ed.) Éliphas Lévi's *The History of Magic* (1913 etc.), *Lamps Of Western Mysticism; Essays on the Life of the Soul in God* (1923), *The Secret Tradition in Alchemy* (1926; 1970), *The Holy Kabbalah: A Study of the Secret Tradition in Israel* (1929), *The Holy Grail, Its Legends & Symbolism* (1933; reprinted as *The Holy Grail: the Galahad Quest in the Arthurian Literature,* 1961).

In addition he translated or edited alchemical treatises by Thomas Vaughan, Benedictus Figulus, Edward Kelly, Martin Ruland the Elder, Bonus of Ferrara and others. His separate works *The Book of Destiny* and *A Handbook of Cartomancy* were reissued in a two-volume set under the title *Complete Manual of Occult Divination* by University Books, 1972. For a useful bibliography including many minor works, see: *Arthur Edward Waite, Occult Scholar and Christian Mystic; a Chronological Bibliography* by Robert **Galbreath** (*Bulletin of Bibliography,* vol. 30, No. 2, April-June 1973) and Harold van Buren's *Arthur Ed-*

ward Waite; A Checklist of his writings (privately printed, Red Bank, N.J., 1932).

A comprehensive work *A. E. Waite; A Bibliography* by R. A. Gilbert was published by Aquarian Press, U.K. (1983). R. A. Gilbert also published an excellent biography: *A. E. Waite; Magician of Many Parts* (Crucible, Thorsons Publishing Group, Wellingborough, U.K., 1987). See also Waite's autobiography *Shadows of Life and Thought* (1938). Waite died May 19, 1942.

Waldenses

The name of a heterodox Christian sect which arose in the south of France about 1170. They were much the same in origin and ethics as the **Albigenses,** that is, their religious system rested upon that of Manicheism, which believed in dualism and severe asceticism. It undoubtedly arose from the desire of the bourgeois class to have changes made in the clerical discipline of the Roman Church.

Its adherents called themselves *cathari,* thus demonstrating the eastern origin of their system. There were two classes of *cathari: credentes* and *perfecti,* or neophytes and adepts, the *perfecti* only being admitted to the esoteric doctrines of the Waldensian Church.

Outwardly its aim and effort was rationalistic, but the inner doctrine partook more of the occult.

In 1170, Peter Waldo, a rich merchant of Lyons, sold his goods and gave them to the poor, and from him the sect was named. The earliest account of Waldensian beliefs is that of an enemy, Sacconi, an Inquisitor of the Holy Office, who wrote about the middle of the thirteenth century.

He divided the Waldensians into two classes, those of Lombardy, and those north of the Alps. The latter believed that any layman might consecrate the sacrament of the altar, and that the Roman Church was not the Church of Christ; while the Lombardian sect held that the Roman Church was the Scarlet Woman of the Apocalypse. They also believed that all men were priests.

As their opinions became more widespread, persecution became more severe, and the Waldensians later withdrew themselves altogether from the Church of Rome, and chose ministers for themselves by election.

Papal bulls were issued for their extermination, and a crusade was directed against them, but they survived these attacks, and as late as the time of Cromwell were protected by him against the Duke of Savoy and the French king. Their ministers were later subsidized by the government of Queen Anne, and this subsidy was carried on until the time of Napoleon, when he granted them an equivalent.

Afterwards they received much assistance from various Protestant countries of Europe, especially from England, and at the present time claim some several thousand communicants as an accepted Protestant sect.

During the Middle Ages, it was strongly held by the priesthood of the Roman Church that, like the Albigenses, the Waldensians had a diabolical element in their religion and from time to time they were classed with the various secret societies that sprang up in medieval Europe, such as the **Templars,** the **Rosicrucians.**

But although they possessed an esoteric doctrine of their own, there is no reason to believe that this was in any way magical, nor in any manner more "esoteric" than the inner doctrine of any other Christian sect. (See also **Albigenses; Cathari; Gnosticism**)

Walder, Phileas (c. 1890)

A Swiss Lutheran minister who became an occultist and Spiritualist, friend of French occultist Éliphas Lévi.

In the malicious anti-clerical hoax of Léo Taxil (Gabriel Jogand-Pagès), Walder and Miss Sophia Walder were represented as associates of Freemason Albert **Pike** in Satanist rites in Charleston, U.S.A. (see also **Devil Worship**)

In reality, Walder was an earnest Freemason and mystic. (See also Gabriel **Jogand-Pagès;** Albert **Pike**)

WALES

Magic and Witchcraft

Wales shares with other Celtic countries an ancient mythology and traditional lore, although much of this was suppressed with the spread of Christianity from the fifth century onwards, and a succession of conquests by Romans, Normans and English. Many of the enchanted stories of the King **Arthur** cycle are also found in Welsh tradition.

In the seventeenth century, Puritanism took a firm hold, and the Methodism of the eighteenth century did much to eradicate magical traditions, although the religious revivals of the nineteenth century had a wild, almost pagan fervor and were accompanied by strange paranormal phenomena.

One of the great sources of Welsh magical legends is the *Mabinogion,* dating from medieval times, containing stories for oral recitation by bards in the halls of the ancient princes of Wales. Typical motifs in these tales are supernatural birth, visits to the Other World, and magical shape-changing. Rhiannon, the wife of Pwyll, possessed marvelous birds which came from the Unseen World, and their singing held warriors spellbound for eighty years. In another story, Lvevelys helps his brother Lludd to eradicate three plagues which had devastated Britain—the Coranians, a strange race whose knowledge was infinite and who heard everything uttered, even the softest whisper; a horrifying shriek which penetrated every house on a May evening, caused by the battle between two dragons; and a great giant who carried off all the food from the king's palace.

A well known story is that of the birth of Taliesin, chief of the bards of the west. The hero Gwion Bach went to the Land Under Waves at the bottom of Lake Bala in North Wales. Here he found the giant Tegid the Bald and his wife Ceridwen, goddess of poetry and knowledge. Ceridwen owned an immense cauldron, in which she brewed a mixture of science and inspiration, with the aid of her books of magic. This great brew had to simmer for a year and a day, and she set the blind man Morda to keep the fire going and Gwion to stir the brew. It was to yield three magical drops.

Towards the end of the year, as Ceridwen was picking herbs and making incantations, three drops of the brew spurted out of the cauldron and fell upon the finger of Gwion Bach. With the sudden heat on his finger, he put it in his mouth to cool, whereupon the three drops instantly gave him knowledge and meaning of all things, and he became aware that he must guard against the cunning of Ceridwen, so he fled to his own land. Meanwhile the cauldron burst and the rest of the brew was a black poison, which overflowed into the waters, poisoning the horses of Gwyddno Garanhir.

Ceridwen seized a billet of wood and struck blind Morda on the head, but he declared that he was innocent and that it was the fault of Gwion Bach. So she ran in pursuit of Gwion. He saw her coming and changed himself into a hare. But she changed herself into a greyhound and turned him. So he ran towards a river and became a fish, but she in the form of an otter chased him under the water, so he had to turn himself into a bird. She became a hawk and gave him no rest in the sky. Just as she was going to swoop on him, he saw a heap of winnowed wheat on the floor of a barn, so he dropped among the wheat and turned himself into one of the grains. Then she turned herself into a black hen, scratched at the wheat and swallowed him.

Then she carried him for nine months, and was delivered of him, but could not kill him because of his beauty. So she wrapped him in a leather bag and cast him into the sea to the mercy of God. But he was carried into the weir of Gwyddno Garanhir and found by Prince Elphin, who had come to catch fish in his net. Elphin renamed him "Taliesin," which can mean "beautiful brow" or "great value."

Druids

Wales was also claimed as a center for the cult of the Druids (see **Celts**), who were mentioned around 200 B.C. They were said to practice human sacrifice, although it has also been claimed that the victims were criminals. They also employed methods of **divination.**

The Druids are thought to have come from ancient Gaul, where they were suppressed in the Roman Conquest as a rival source of power and prestige. The historian **Pliny** recorded their association with the mistletoe plant in their sacred rites.

He also mentioned a mysterious object used by the Druids, which he named the "serpent's egg." It was roughly the size and shape of a small apple, and it was said that a mass of hissing serpents threw this egg into the air. If it could be caught in a white cloak before touching the ground, it would convey magical powers to the possessor, such as floating against a river current, and achieving success in legal undertakings.

Witchcraft and Demonology

Sir Dafydd Llwyd, who lived in Cardiganshire in the reign of Charles II, had studied black magic at Oxford. He practiced as a physician and was famous for his wonderful cures, but his skill was due to a **familiar** spirit or demon, which he kept locked up in a book of spells.

One day he accidently left this **grimoire** behind, and sent his pageboy home to fetch it, commanding him on no account to open it. Like most lads, the boy could not resist being inquisitive, and turned over the leaves with their weird inscriptions.

Suddenly there came forth a huge demon who frowned and in a hoarse grumbling voice asked to be set to work. In spite of his terror, the boy had the wit to say: "Fetch me some stones out of the River Wye." In a few moments, stones and pebbles began hurtling through the air, when Sir Dafydd, aware that something was wrong, came hurrying back and conjured the spirit back into the book before any serious harm could take place.

As early as the twelfth century, priests in Wales were warned about letting the Host get into the hands of magicians and witches, who might secretly slip it out of their mouths and hide it in a handkerchief or glove. In 1582, the wife of Edward Jones was called upon to prove to the satisfaction of the Archdeacon of Lewes "that she did eat the Communion bread and put yt not in hir glove."

As late as the opening years of the eighteenth century, two old dames were said to have attended the morning service at Llanddewi Brefi Church to partake of Holy Communion, but instead of eating it like the other communicants, they kept it in their mouths and went out. Then they walked round the church nine times, and at the ninth circuit the Devil came out of the Church wall in the form of a frog, to whom they gave the Host from their mouths, and by doing this, sold themselves to Satan and became witches.

There are many stories about Dr. John Harries (1785-1839), a celebrated Welsh physician and seer of Cŵrt-y-Cadno, Carmarthenshire, who was said to possess a Great Book of Magic, which was kept locked to prevent any ignorant person from letting loose its powerful influences. Harries boasted of his knowledge of future and distant events, imparted to him by familiar spirits.

Belief in witchcraft persisted into the twentieth century in Wales, but it concerned "white witches," who cast useful spells and horoscopes, or averted evil events. In 1933, there was a wise man in Llangwrig, Montgomeryshire, who was famous throughout Wales for breaking the spells of witches. He kept his book of divination and an almanac in a rosewood casket.

In November 1936, a correspondent in *John O'London's Weekly* stated that "even now belief in witchcraft in the upper parts of the Wye Valley is not quite extinct." In the following month, another correspondent stated: "When we lived in a small village in Montgomeryshire some years ago we found a widespread belief in witchcraft among the farmers of the district." If the cattle became sick, farmers visited the wise man to find who had bewitched their beasts. If two farmers had a serious quarrel, one of them went to the wise man to obtain a charm to injure his neighbor.

Phenomena at Religious Revivals

Welsh preaching is celebrated for its fervor, and the traditional **Hwyl** or peroration of a sermon is said to have quite magical effects. During the nineteenth century, there were reports of mysterious **luminous phenomena** associated with revivalism, and such accounts were again current in 1904-05 during the inspired revival campaigns of Mrs. Mary Jones, of Egryn, Merionethshire.

Mrs. Jones was then a happily married peasant woman with a family, when in December 1904 she received beatific visions instructing her to undertaking the work of religious revival which had earlier been the mission of the preacher Evan Roberts in Glamorgan.

The first night's mission of Mrs. Jones was marked by the appearance of a mysterious star and various lights. She herself reported seeing "a circle of small stars, encompassing a cross of diamond stars, and on this cross at times the draped figure of the Saviour."

The strange luminous phenomena were witnessed by other individuals. A skeptical businessman was driving Mrs. Jones home one evening from a meeting, and prayed that he might be accorded a sign if Mrs. Jones was indeed a divinely ordained preacher. Immediately there appeared above the road, in front of the car, a misty star, in which, as the man gazed, was formed a luminous cross sparkling with diamonds, and upon this a draped figure with bowed head.

On another occasion, Mrs. Jones herself reported seeing the Devil, who first appeared in the figure of a man, but when she started singing revival hymns, suddenly stopped, turned upon her and became transformed into an enormous black dog. Mrs. Jones prayed for strength, and the dog rushed growling into a hillock.

The star and the light were seen by many people from the first day of Mrs. Jones' mission. The star seemed to rest above particular houses where converts later came to the meetings. It also followed Mrs. Jones on her journeys. On her journey to Criccieth, the lights were witnessed by the people with her. At Bryncrug, a few miles inland from Towyn, the gallery of the chapel was flooded during the service by the mysterious light. After the service, the light, in the form of a ball of fire casting its rays down to earth, was seen by a party of young quarrymen who, overtaking the light which had stopped, knelt down in the middle of the road and held a prayer meeting, bathed in the unearthly light.

Some of these lights and their movements were reminiscent of many modern accounts of unidentified flying objects (see **UFO**). (See also **Hwyl; Luminous Phenomena; Witchcraft**)

Recommended reading:

Charlton, I. W. *The Revival in Wales,* London, 1905/ pamphlet

Guest, Lady Charlotte (transl.). *The Mabinogion; from the Llyfr Coch o Hergest,* 3 vols., London, 1948 etc. (frequently reprinted)

Graves, Robert. *The White Goddess,* Faber & Faber, London, 1948

Jones, Edmund. *A Relation of Ghosts and Apparitions Which Commonly Appear in the Principality of Wales,* Bristol, U.K., 1767

Jones, T. Gwynn. *Welsh Folklore and Folk Customs,* Metheun, London, 1930

Morgan, J. V. *The Welsh Religious Revival,* 1904-5, Chapman & Hall, London, 1909

Walker, Kenneth Macfarlane (1882-1966)

Surgeon, author of books relating to parapsychology and mysticism. Born 1882 in London, England, he studied at Cambridge University, (M.A., M.B., Ch.B.), Royal College of Surgeons, International College of Surgeons, Royal Society of Medicine. In 1926 he married Eileen Marjorie Wilson; second marriage in 1944 to Mary Ginette.

He was a captain in the Royal Army Medical Corps from 1915-19 (mentioned in dispatches), consulting surgeon at London hospitals, medical secretary of the British Social Hygiene Council.

He published the articles 'The Finer Bodies of Man' (*Tomorrow,* Autumn 1953) and 'The Non-Mechanical Mind' (*Tomorrow,* Summer 1954). In addition to his books on medical subjects, his publications included: *Diagnosis of Man* (1942), *Meaning and Purpose* (1944), *I Talk of Dreams* (1946), *Venture with Ideas* (1951), *Only The Silent Hear* (1953), *So Great a Mystery* (1954), *A Study of Gurdjieff's Teachings* (1957), *Beyond the Five Senses* (1957), *Life's Long Journey* (1959), *The Unconscious Mind* (1961), *The Making of Man* (1963).

He died January 22, 1966.

Walker, Roland (1907-)

Professor of biology who has written on parapsychology. Born February 8, 1907 at Stellenbosch, South Africa, he studied at Oberlin College, Ohio (B.A. 1928, M.A. 1939) and Yale University (Ph.D. 1934). In 1942 he married Vivian Trombetta.

He was instructor in physiology at Oberlin from 1931-32, instructor in biology from 1934-42, assistant professor of biology from 1942-46, associate professor of biology from 1946-54, professor of biology from 1954 onwards, at Rennselaer Polytechnic Institute, Troy, N.Y. Memberships include: American Society of Zoologists, American Ornithologists Union, Wildlife Society, American Association for Advancement of Science, American Association of University Professors.

In addition to his many papers on medical and scientific subjects, he published the article 'Parapsychology and Dualism,' a philosophical critique of J. B. **Rhine**'s interpretations of ESP and PK (*Scientific Monthly,* July 1954).

Walker, Thane (c. 1890-)

Founder (with Phez Kahlil) of the **Prosperos,** a group stemming from the philosophy of G. I. **Gurd-**

jieff. Born in Nowaway County, Missouri, Walker was married twice. He claimed to have been one of America's first psychologists, and to have been imprisoned in a Nazi concentration camp after writing an article "I Saw Hitler Make Black Magic." He was a Marine Corp officer, and entertained American troops in Japan during the occupation in World War II.

As a former pupil of Gurdjieff, he has himself become a Gurdjieff style figure, teaching students through stories and disorienting activities and demands, but also drawing upon Freudian and Jungian psychology, and occult and astrological traditions.

The Prosperos group was founded in Florida in 1956, but the organization has since moved around the country, and now claims some 3,000 members in California.

A charismatic figure, Walker emphasized the importance of personal and verbal teaching in order to awaken students from the misleading reality of everyday sensory experience and limited personality to a wider reality. (See also G. I. **Gurdjieff**)

Walker, William (c. 1912)

British spirit photographer, a member of the **Crewe Circle** associated with William **Hope.** Walker produced the first psychic photographs with spirit "extras" in color. (See also **Psychic Photography**)

Wallace, Dr. Alfred Russel (1823-1913)

Famous British naturalist, co-discoverer with Charles Darwin of the principles of evolution. Wallace was a confirmed philosophical skeptic, a materialist so through that before he became acquainted with the facts of Spiritualism there was no place in his mind for the conception of spiritual existence or for any agencies in the universe other than matter and force. But the facts overcame him.

To quote his own words from his preface to his book *On Miracles and Modern Spiritualism* (1874): "They compelled me to accept them, as facts, long before I could accept the spiritual explanation of them: there was at that time 'no place in my fabric of thought into which it could be fitted.' (Argument of Dr. Carpenter). By slow degrees a place was made."

Wallace was led to believe (1) in the existence of a number of preterhuman intelligences of various grades, (2) that some of these intelligences, although usually invisible and intangible to us, can and do act on matter, and do influence our minds. It was by the latter doctrine that he accounted for some of the residual phenomena in his work *Contributions to the Theory of Natural Selection* (1870).

Wallace was born January 8, 1823, at Usk, Monmouthshire. After leaving school he worked as a land surveyor and architect. He began to take an interest in botany around 1840, and started a herbarium. In 1845, he was an English master at the Collegiate School, Leicester, where he met H. W. Bates, who influenced him to collect and study beetles.

In 1848, they commenced a joint naturalist expedition to the River Amazon. On the return journey, most of Wallace's collection was destroyed in a fire on the ship, but his book *A Narrative of Travels on the Amazon and Rio Negro* appeared in 1853. He next traveled in the Malay Archipelago, and his large insect collections passed to Oxford University and the British Museum.

In February 1858, during a severe attack of fever, he was thinking about Malthus' *Essay on Population* when, to quote his own words: "There suddenly flashed upon me the idea of the survival of the fittest." He drafted a theory which he posted to Charles Darwin a few days later. By an extraordinary coincidence, Wallace's paper was virtually an abstract of Darwin's own theory, written in 1842, which Wallace had never seen or heard of.

Wallace's earliest experiences relating to Spiritualism dated from 1844 when he was a schoolmaster in Leicester. Influenced by a lecture of Spencer Hall on **Mesmerism,** he tried similar experiments and attained surprising success. Later, during twelve years of tropical wanderings occupied in the study of natural history, he heard occasionally of "**table-turning**" and "spirit **rapping.**" He resolved to investigate them on his return.

His first opportunity came on July 22, 1865, in the house of a friend, a skeptic. After more than a dozen sittings he became satisfied that "there is an unknown power developed from the bodies of a number of persons placed in connection by sitting round a table with all their hands on it."

The next stage of his inquiry began in September 1865, and was devoted to the physical and mental phenomena of Mrs. Mary **Marshall.** In broad daylight, Wallace observed **levitation,** movement of objects without contact (**telekinesis**) and the alteration of weight. Although unknown to Mrs. Marshall, the place name Para, where Wallace's brother died, his name and that of the last friend who saw him, were spelled out. Messages came spelled backwards, **direct writing** on a privately marked paper was produced.

Impressed by these occurrences, Wallace investigated in his own home with the help of a lady with mediumistic talents. Remarkable phenomena were obtained and from November 1866 onwards, Wallace had the rare opportunity of watching the development of the powerful mediumship of Miss Nichols, later Mrs. **Guppy.** A heavy and stout woman, she was lifted noiselessly on the top of the table while sitting in her chair, with five or six persons close around her. Delicate musical sounds were heard without the presence of instruments. A German lady guest, a perfect stranger, sang several songs and the strains of music, as if coming from a fairy music-box, accompanied her throughout.

The most remarkable feats of Miss Nichols were **apports** of flowers and fruit. In mid-winter, after Miss Nichols sat for four hours in a small, warm, gas-lighted room in the Wallace home, a quantity of flowers appeared upon a bare table—anemones, tulips, chrysanthemums, Chinese primroses and several ferns. Wallace stated: "All were absolutely fresh as if just gathered from a conservatory. They were covered with a fine cold dew. Not a petal was crumpled or broken, not the most delicate point or pinnule of the ferns was out of place."

Wallace stated that the phenomenon was repeated afterwards hundreds of times. The flowers sometimes arrived in large quantities. They were often brought on request, fruits as well as flowers. A friend of Wallace asked for a sunflower, and one six feet high fell on the table, having a large mass of earth about its roots.

The distinguished naturalist formed one of the Committee of the **London Dialectical Society** in 1869 and witnessed, under test conditions, a great variety of telekinetic phenomena. When the possibility of **spirit photography** was for the first time demonstrated in England in the studio of Frederick A. **Hudson,** by the contribution of Mrs. Guppy's powers, Wallace was anxious to test this new phenomenon. Sitting with Mrs. Guppy, he obtained a communication by raps that his mother would try to appear on the plate of Hudson.

He sat three times, choosing his own position, and found a male figure with a short sword on the first photographic plate, and a female figure on the two other plates. Both of the latter represented an unmistakable likeness of his mother, that of the second plate differed in period and was unlike any photograph previously taken of her. Under a magnifying glass, this second picture disclosed a remarkable special feature of his mother's face.

In view of these experiences and the large amount of testimony in the literature of Spiritualism to similar occurrences, Alfred Russel Wallace declared that the phenomena of Spiritualism in their entirety did not require further confirmation. "They are proved, quite as well as any facts are proved in other sciences."

His later attitude was in accordance with this conviction. He never missed an opportunity to test genuine psychic phenomena. He made several attempts to convince the pillars of scientific skepticism and started by inviting Dr. W. B. Carpenter to attend some sittings in his own home. Carpenter came one evening. **Raps** were heard, and these were repeated, sometimes in different tones, and sounding, at request, in any part of the table.

Dr. Carpenter sat quite still, and made hardly any comment. He knew from the statements of his host that this was a mere trifle to what often occurred and never came again.

Exactly the same thing happened with Prof. Tyndall, another skeptic. T. H. Huxley, to whom, in 1866, Wallace sent his paper *The Scientific Aspect of the Supernatural,* which was later included in *On Miracles and Modern Spiritualism,* answered "I am neither shocked nor disposed to issue a commission of lunacy against you. It may be true, for anything that I know to the contrary, but really I cannot get up interest in the subject."

G. H. Lewes accepted an invitation to the Wallace home but never went.

Between 1870-80, Alfred Russell Wallace had many opportunities of witnessing interesting phenomena in the houses of various friends. Through a member of his own family, **automatic writing** was received in his own home, purporting to come from his deceased brother William, and containing many predictions which were later fulfilled.

In 1874, Wallace was asked by the *Fortnightly Review* to write an article on Spiritualism. It appeared under the title *A Defence of Modern Spiritualism* and formed part, with another paper which he read before the London Dialectical Society, of *On Miracles and Modern Spiritualism,* a book which was so much in demand that a third edition was issued in 1895, enlarged with two new chapters on the nature and purpot of **apparitions.** The book was first published in 1875 and the earlier editions did not include the author's further personal experiences in his seances with Miss Katie **Cook,** with the mediums **Haxby, Monck, Eglinton** and others.

Wallace defended Henry **Slade** and gave evidence of the genuineness of his phenomena at the trial in Bow Street Police Court, London, in 1876. In the same year, by his casting vote as president of the anthropological sub-committee of the British Association for the Advancement of Science he made possible the reading of Prof. W. F. **Barrett**'s paper on Spiritualism before this body.

When J. N. **Maskelyne** sued Archdeacon **Colley** for a thousand pounds challenge, it was largely on Alfred Russel Wallace's testimony on behalf of the powers of Monck that the stage magician lost his suit.

In the years 1886-87, during a lecture tour of America, Wallace stayed for some time in three centers of Spiritualism—Boston, Washington and San Francisco. He attended **materialization** seances with a medium named Mrs. Ross, and when it was rumored that she was caught in fraud he testified on her behalf in a letter to the *Banner of Light.*

In Washington, in the company of Prof. Elliot Coues, General Lippitt and Mr. D. Lyman, Wallace had remarkable experiences with the medium Pierre L. O. A. **Keeler,** and he sat in San Francisco at an outstanding **slate-writing** seance with Fred P. **Evans** in which writing was produced in five different colors and, on his impromptu suggestion, six crayon drawings were precipitated on six pieces of paper placed between a pair of slates, some of the drawings having personal relevance.

In later years, Dr. Alfred Russel Wallace did not encounter much Spiritualist phenomena but he remained true to his convictions up to the end of his busy life.

In 1910, he received the Order of Merit for his scientific researches. He died at Broadstone, Dorset, on November 7, 1913.

For biographical information, see his own work *My Life; An Autobiography* (2 vols., 1905)

Wallis, E. W. (1848-1914)

British trance medium, inspirational speaker, healer, lecturer and author. "Lightheart," the spirit of a South American Indian, claimed responsibility for his mediumistic development. "Standard Bearer," "Leader" and "Tom Joyce" were others of his well-known controls.

Assisted by his wife, also a notable psychic, Wallis did great propaganda work for many decades. He was instrumental in the starting of the journal *The Two Worlds* in Manchester, which he edited until 1899. In that year he came to London and became editor of *Light,* which position he held until his decease. He wrote *Spiritualism Explained* (1897), and, jointly with his wife, published *A Guide to Mediumship and Psychical Unfoldment* (1903), *Spirit-Guided* (n.d.) and *Spiritualism in the Bible* (1904). An independent volume of inspirational poems was published by Mrs. Wallis under the title *As They Come Through* (n.d.)

As a medium, Mrs. Wallis was never in deep trance. She could hear the words which were impressed on her mind but could not prevent herself from saying them.

Her mediumship began at the age of eighteen in 1872. A young Spanish Indian girl, "Veina Goree," was her first control. From 1875 onwards, she gave inspirational addresses at the Spiritual Institution founded by James **Burns.** While speaking there, Mrs. Wallis was suddenly controlled by "Morambo," a negro slave who passed over in South America. He produced physical phenomena and for many years, while Mrs. Wallis was associated with the **London Spiritualist Alliance,** and answered questions on Spiritualism in afternoon meetings.

"Walter"

The claimed spirit **control** of the medium "Margery" (Mrs. Mina Stinson **Crandon**). In his lifetime, Walter Stinson was a brother of the medium who lost his life in a railway accident in 1911 at the age of twenty-eight. He manifested at a seance for the first time during his sister's chance visit to a clairvoyant. "Walter" furnished proofs of personal identity, and, with the development of "Margery's" psychic powers, took charge of her sittings.

As a spirit communicator, he was amazingly active, had a keen sense of humor, showed no pretence of saintliness, and, on occasions, swore and cursed in justified indignation. He was highly intelligent, full of energy and curiosity. He never pretended to know whether he could accomplish something new, but was always ready to try and was gratified at his own achievements.

He gave the impression that he himself was learning about conditions while giving a demonstration. "I don't give a damn about convincing the public or anyone. You have no idea why I am here" he said once.

He often threatened the sitters: "When this is done I am going away, and I shan't come back. My crowd came here because we liked you people, and you kept us here working at this damned thing." However, he never kept this threat. The satisfaction which his increasing dexterity gave him in producing high grade psychic phenomena was enough to bind him to the "Margery" circle.

He introduced many new features into the experiments, provided most convincing **cross correspondences** and even gave his fingerprints (see **Plastics**). Unfortunately these fingerprints were later found to be those of another living individual, prompting accusations that the mediumship of "Margery" was partly or wholly fraudulent.

"Walter" was also manifested at Dr. Glen **Hamilton**'s circle at Winnipeg, being the chief control of the medium "Mary M." He proved his identity and was responsible for the best experimental results.

For an account of the controversial mediumship of "Margery" and her control "Walter," see *'Margery' the Medium* by J. Malcolm Bird (1925) and *Margery* by Thomas R. Tietze (1973). (See also Mina Stinson **Crandon;** Dr. T. Glen **Hamilton**)

Walter, W(illiam) Grey (1910-1977)

Physiologist with special interests in the study of such neurophysiological correlates of paranormal states as hypnosis, sleep, trance and hallucinations. Born February 19, 1910 in Kansas City, Missouri, he studied at Cambridge University, England (B.A. 1931, M.A. 1935, D.Sc. 1947) and University of Aix-Marseille (hon. Ph.D. 1949). In 1933 he married Monica Ratcliffe; second marriage in 1947 to Vivian Dovey; third marriage 1960 to Lorraine Donn.

He was director of the Physiological Department at Burden Neurological Institute, Bristol, England from 1939 onwards, founder of the EEG Society, Editor of *EEG Journal,* president of International Society for Cybernetics, member of the Physiological Society, International Federated Societies for EEG and Clinical Neurophysiology (president from 1953-57), member of International Brain Research Organization of UNESCO, 1959-60; consultant to British Aircraft Corporation.

His papers included: 'The Neurophysiological Aspects of Hallucination and Illusory Experience' (the 1960 Frederic W. H. Myers Memorial Lecture, *Proceedings* of the Society for Psychical Research, London), 'Where Vital Things Happen' (1959 Adolf Meyer Research Lecture, *American Journal of Psychiatry,* 1960). His famous book *The Living Brain* (1953) was translated into several foreign languages. His other publications included *The Curve of the Snowflake* (a science fiction novel, British title *Further Outlook,* 1956), *Observations on Man, His Frame, His Duty, and His Expectations* (1969), *Introduction to Microbiology* (1973). He was co-founder and co-editor of *Electroencephalography and Clinical Neurophysiology* in 1947.

He died May 6, 1977.

Walther, Gerda (1897-)

Psychical researcher and author. Born March 18, 1897 at Nordrach-Colonie, Baden, Germany, she studied at Ludwig Maximilians University, Munich, Germany (Ph.D. summa cum laude 1921). She was a member of Schutzverband Deutscher Schiftsteller.

She investigated many aspects of parapsychology in a number of countries from 1920 onwards. She lectured widely on aspects of psychic research.

In 1928, she became scientific secretary to Dr. A. von **Schrenck-Notzing,** famous German psychic researcher, and assisted his investigations of the mediums Willi and Rudi **Schneider.** During 1941 in Germany, her researches in parapsychology resulted in a short period of imprisonment under the Hitler regime.

She published a number of articles on psi phenomena in *Zeitschrift für Parapsychologie, Zeitschrift für Metapsychische Forschung, Neue Wissenshaft, Journal* of the American Society for Psychical Research, Psychic Science, Tomorrow. She edited the posthumously published books of Schrenck-Notzing: *Gesammelte Aufsätze zur Parapsychologie* (1929, revised as *Grundfragen der Parapsychologie,* 1962), *Die Entwicklung des Okkultismus zur Wissenchaftlichen Parapsychologie in Deutschland* (1932), *Die Phänomene des Mediums Rudi Schneider* (1931). She was author of *Zur Phänomenologie der Mystik* (1923, revised 1955).

Wandering Jew, The

A medieval German legend which has several forms. Through various writers, and differing in detail, the essential features of the narratives which have been handed down to us, are basically the same.

The legend is that as Christ was dragged on his way to Calvary, he passed the house of a Jew, and stopping there, sought to rest a little, being weary under the weight of his cross. The Jew, however, inspired with the adverse enthusiasm of the mob, drove Him on, and would not allow Him to rest there. Jesus, looking at him, said, "I shall stand and rest, but thou shalt go till the last day." Ever afterwards the Jew was compelled to wander over the earth, until this prophecy should be fulfilled.

The legend of the Wandering Jew is to be regarded as the epic of the Semite people in the Middle Ages. Unfortunately it has often become a vehicle for crude anti-Semitic propaganda and persecution.

In some parts of Germany, the Wandering Jew theme has been identified with the Wild Huntsman, whilst in several French districts that mythical character is regarded as the wind of the night. The blast in his horn, rushing through the valleys, creates a hollow booming sound not unlike a great bugle. From a literary point of view this legend was treated by Eugène Sue in his popular novel *Le Juif errant* (10 vols., 1844-45) and the British author George Croly in his novel *Salathiel; A Story of the Past, The Present and The Future* (1829).

Something of the same atmosphere also pervades the legend of the *Flying Dutchman.*

For a valuable survey of the Wandering Jew legend, see *Curious Myths of the Middle Ages* by S. Baring-Gould (1866-68; reprinted University Books, 1967).

Wang, Chung Yu (1880-1958)

Metallurgist, with interests in various aspects of parapsychology. Born 1880 in Hong Kong, he studied at Queens College and Peiyang University, graduate work at University of California and Columbia University (M.A. mining and geology). He married Ella Lang.

He was a member of the American Society for Psychical Research, and author of the article 'China's Unwanted Heritage' (*Tomorrow,* Autumn 1955). His book *Old Age, Afterlife and the Spirit, an Anthology of Great Thoughts* was published posthumously.

He died August 30, 1958 in New York, N.Y.

Wannein Nat

A Burmese evil spirit. (See **Burma**)

Warcollier, Rene (1881-1962)

Chemical engineer, author, parapsychologist. He was president of Institut Métapsychique International, Paris from 1951-62. Born April 8, 1881 at Ormonville-la-Rogue (Manche), France, he studied at Ecole Nationale Supérieure de Chimie, Paris (Ch.E. 1903). In 1910 he married Germaine Loinard.

He was treasurer of the Institut Métapsychique from 1929-38, editor of *Revue Métapsychique* from 1938-40. In addition to his work as a chemical engineer, he studied telepathy and collaborated with such experimenters as Cesar **de Vesme** and Eugene **Osty** on investigations of clairvoyance and related phenomena.

His articles on parapsychology included: (in *Revue Métapsychique*) 'La Télepathie Experimentale' (1926, 1927), 'Etude de dessins télépathiques de M. Vigneron au cours de vingt ans d'expérimentation' (1951- 1952), (in *Journal* of the American Society for Psychical Research) 'A Proposed Cancellation Test for Group Experiments' (vol. 43, 1949; also published *Revue Métapsychique,* 1950), (*Tomorrow*) 'Fifty Years of Telepathy' (Summer 1961). His books included: (with Edmond Duchatel) *Les Miracles de la Volonté* (Miracles of the Will, 1912, Italian transl. 1947), *Experimental Telepathy* (edited and abridged by Dr. Gardner **Murphy,** 1938; 1975), *Experiments in Telepathy* (1938; 1975), *La Métapsychique* (1940; 1946), *Mind to Mind* (transl. of *La Télépathie* 1938; 1948).

He died May 23, 1962 in Paris, France.

Ward, Arthur Henry (Sarsfield) (1883-1959)

Author who wrote under the pseudonym "Sax Rohmer," and created the celebrated fictional character Dr. Fu-Manchu and was also a student of the occult. Born of Irish Catholic parents in Birmingham, England, February 15, 1883, he had no formal schooling until the age of nine, when he attended a day school in London. When quite young he gave up attending mass and became an agnostic. His first job was as a bank clerk in London, after which he worked briefly as a newspaper reporter.

He started writing short stories at the age of twenty and used the pseudonym "Sax Rohmer" in 1912. He also wrote some successful songs for music hall comedians George Robey and Little Tich. In 1909 he married Rose Elizabeth Knox.

His famous character Fu-Manchu was based on reports of a Chinese master criminal operating a world-wide opium racket, and the atmosphere of Limehouse, London's Chinatown district, provided local color. The first Fu-Manchu book was published in 1913, but Rohmer did not immediately settle down to developing his character. Instead, he spent much time on his non-fiction study *The Romance of Sorcery,* first published London, 1914; E. P. Dutton, 1915.

The book brought a flattering letter from illusionist Harry **Houdini,** who became a friend.

Rohmer is said to have become a member of the occult society the **Golden Dawn** and may also have belonged to a Rosicrucian order. However, his occult interests were eventually overshadowed by the success of his Fu-Manchu books. In 1929, Paramount Pictures produced *The Mysterious Dr. Fu-Manchu,* starring Warner Oland and Jean Arthur.

Rohmer's book *The Romance of Sorcery* was reprinted by Causeway, 1973. Rohmer died June 1, 1959.

Warminster UFO News

Monthly publication of the British UFO Society, dealing with news and sightings in the Warminster district of Britain, where hundreds of local residents have reported **UFO** phenomena since the 1960s. Address: Preston House, Warminster, Wiltshire, England.

Warner, Abby (c. 1852)

An illiterate American orphan girl who was instrumental in arousing lively interest in Spiritualism in Ohio soon after the phenomenon of the **Rochester Rappings.** Mrs. Kellogg of Massillon, in whose house Abby performed domestic services, discovered that **raps** were produced in the girl's presence. Soon a **trance** state developed and the uneducated girl, who at eighteen could only read printed characters imperfectly, wrote perfectly with both hands at the same time on different subjects, while a third communication was spelt out by raps.

The reports of the seances began to be widely circulated. Dr. Abel Underhill took the girl into his family for medical treatment and wrote her history. The occurrences at St. Timothy's Church on Christmas Eve, 1851, put her in the limelight of the Press. Unusually powerful raps resounded in the Church in her presence and the attention of the whole assembly was attracted. The minister desired that "those knockings might cease." Instead they increased in vehemence.

Abby Warner was arrested on a charge of disturbing a religious meeting, and brought before a public tribunal. The trial commenced on December 27 and lasted for three days. As "not a single witness could be found who could swear that they perceived the slightest movement in the accused party; on the contrary, when closely examined, those who professed to have scrutinized the action of the spirit rapper narrowly were compelled to admit that they could not detect the least perceptible motion, even of her dress, at the times when the knocks were most numerous and emphatic" the defendant was discharged.

Following the acquittal, Dr. Underhill announced an investigation by a carefully selected committee, under stringent test conditions, of the medium's physical and mental phenomena. Four seances were held. The committee found the phenomena wholly unaccountable and genuine evidences of an occult and intelligent force outside the medium.

Warner, Lucien (Hynes) (1900-)

Psychologist, opinion analyst, who conducted surveys in parapsychology. Born September 9, 1900 at Irvington, New York, he studied at Oberlin College (B.A. 1922), Columbia University (Ph.D. 1927). In 1922 he married Helen Wentworth French; second marriage 1950 to Grace Williams York; third marriage 1957 to Harriet Eugenie Gaines.

He was instructor in literature at Yenching University, Peiping, China from 1922-23, psychological research at Columbia University from 1923-27, instructor in psychology at New York University from 1926-27, fellow, biological sciences, National Research Council, Washington, D.C. from 1928-30, research director of L'Oeil Qui Voit, Switzerland (working in genetics and methods of training guide dogs for the blind) from 1932-34.

He was a research fellow at Duke University from 1935-37, research director, vice-president of Opinion Research Corporation, Princeton, N.J. from 1938-41, special services of the Bureau of Intelligence, U.S. Office of War Information from 1942-43, associate director of research, *Life* magazine from 1944-48, professor of biology and psychology at Claremont Men's College and Graduate School, Claremont, California from 1948-60. He is a fellow of American Association for the Advancement of Science, New York Academy of Science, member of American Psychological Association, Society for Psychological Study of Social Issues, American Marketing Association.

His books include: *Animal Motivation* (1931), *Principles and Methods of Comparative Psychology* (1935). In 1938, 1952 and 1955 he conducted surveys among psychologists to ascertain attitudes to extrasensory perception. His reports were published in the *Journal of Parapsychology* (vol.2, 1938; vol.16, 1952, vol.19, 1955).

Wartime Occult Phenomena (World War I)

A surprising number of ideas regarding the supernatural crystallized around the circumstances of World War I. Perhaps the most striking of these was the alleged vision of **Angels of Mons.** The first notice regarding this was the story in the London

Evening News for September 14, 1915, by writer Arthur **Machen** describing a statement by an officer who was in the retreat from Mons. This officer saw a large body of horsemen who later vanished. Machen suggested that they were spirits of the English bowmen who had fought at Agincourt.

Although this story was simply fiction, it stimulated many corroborative reports of phantom armies. Men at the war front stated to interviewers that phantasms of the dead frequently appeared in the "No Man's Land" between German and British trenches.

In his book *On the Side of the Angels* (1915), Harold Begbie confirmed that a vision of angels was seen in the retreat from Mons and gives the narrative of a soldier, who states that an officer came up to him "in a state of great anxiety" and pointed out to him a "strange light which seemed to be quite distinctly outlined and was not a reflection of the moon, nor were there any clouds in the neighbourhood. The light became brighter and I could see quite distinctly three shapes, one in the centre having what looked like outspread wings. The other two were not so large, but were quite plainly distinct from the centre one. They appeared to have a long, loose-hanging garment of a golden tint and they were above the German line facing us. We stood watching them for about three-quarters of an hour."

All the men in the battalion who saw this with the exception of five were killed. Mr. Begbie went on to say that he was told by a nurse that a dying soldier spoke to her of the reluctance of the Germans to attack the British line, "because of the thousands of troops behind us." This man had heard German prisoners say so and fully believed in the phantasmal nature of those supporting hosts.

Ralph **Shirley** published a pamphlet titled *Prophecies and Omens of the Great War* (1914; 1915) dealing with various oracular utterances on the great struggle.

Stories were also current in the early period of the war regarding the appearance of saintly and protective figures resembling the patrons of the several allied countries. Thus the English were convinced that in certain engagements they had beheld the figure of Saint George mounted on a white charger and the French were equally sure that the figure in question was either Saint Denis or Joan of Arc. Wounded men in base hospitals asked for medallions or coins on which the likenesses of these saints were impressed, in order to verify the statements they made. (See also **Angels of Mons; Apparitions**)

Warts

Small skin lesions on face, fingers, or elbows, and sometimes on the genitals, caused by a virus, as distinct from **moles,** which are birthmarks. The general medical term for a wart is *verruca,* but warts on the genitals or around the anus are known as *condylomae* or venereal warts.

Warts often appear and disappear without any obvious cause, and this characteristic tended to reinforce belief in many old folk cures or wart-charming. In eastern Massachusetts, central New York, and parts of England, it used to be believed that warts could be removed by rubbing them with spittle. Other widespread superstitions were as follows:

To cure warts, wash the hands in the moon's rays focused in a dry metal basin, saying:

I wash my hands in this thy dish,
O man in the moon, do grant my wish
And come and take away this!

Water taken from a gravestone and rubbed on warts will cure them.

To strike warts with an undertaker's hammer will cure them.

To remove warts from the hand, watch for a funeral procession to pass, and as it goes by, say secretly: "I do sincerely hope that these warts will pass off my hands as that body decays in the ground."

If a person steals an egg and secretly buries it in the ground, his or her warts will disappear when the egg decays.

Pick up an old marrow bone, touch it to your warts, walk off, throwing it behind you, and don't look back.

If you take as many pins as you have warts and give them to someone else, your warts will be transferred to the other person.

Take as many pebbles as you have warts and touch each wart with a pebble, then wrap the stones in cloth or paper and throw them away in the roadway. Whoever picks up the parcel of pebbles will get your warts, and you will lose them.

Take a piece of string and tie as many knots in it as there are warts and lay the string under a stone. Whoever treads on the stone will be attached to the warts.

Such superstitions were often very ancient. **Pliny** (23-79 A.D.) recommended that warts should be touched with chick peas on the first day of the moon, and the peas wrapped in cloth and thrown away behind you. The pebbles charm was known to Marcellus of Bordeaux in the fourth century, cited in his book *De Mendicamentis.*

Apart from natural remission, it is possible that many wart cures worked through a process analagous to self-hypnosis. Other wart remedies were of a pseudo-medical nature, such as rubbing warts with milkweed, or the fluid from grasshoppers, or the fresh blood of mice. Modern medical remedies involve treating warts with a substance that dissolves the hard layer and cauterizes the remainder, which is then scraped off.

During the great witchcraft manias of the sixteenth and seventeenth centuries, warts and moles were considered "devil's marks" if they did not bleed when pricked. (See also **Moles,** [Birthmarks])

Wasserman, Gerhard Dietrich (1919-)

University lecturer in applied mathematics who has experimented in the field of parapsychology.

Born December 12, 1919 at Leipzig, Germany, he studied at Queen Mary College, University of London (B.Sc. hons. math. 1942, Ph.D. quantum mechanics 1946). In 1948 he married Bertha Edith Weiss.

He was an industrial research assistant from 1943-44, lecturer in mathematics at Mining and Technical College, Wigan, England from 1944-45, research assistant in theoretical physics at University of Bristol, England from 1947-48, lecturer in applied mathematics at King's College Newcastle-upon-Tyne, Durham University from 1948 onwards.

In the field of parapsychology he has taken special interest in the construction of theoretical models for psi phenomena. His article 'An Outline of a Field Theory of Organismic Form and Behavior' was published in a Ciba Foundation symposium on extrasensory perception. Dr. Wasserman has lectured on ESP at universities in Britain.

Wasson, R(obert) Gordon (1898-1986)

New York banker who launched a new science of "ethno-mycology", the claimed relationship of wild mushrooms (especially hallucinogenic varieties) to various human cultures throughout history.

Born September 22, 1898, at Great Falls, Montana, he studied at Columbia school of Journalism 1920 (B.Litt.). In 1926 he married Dr. Valentina Pavlovna Guercken, who has shared his researches in ethno-mycology. Mr. Wasson was an instructor in English at Columbia College from 1921-22, editorial writer and political correspondent, New Haven (Conn.) *Register* from 1922-24, associate editor *Current Opinion* from 1924-25, financial reporter for *New York Herald Tribune* from 1925-28; with Guaranty Co. of New York from 1928-34, Morgan Guaranty Trust Co., New York 1943. He served in the U.S. Army during World War I.

His books included: *Mushrooms Russia and History* (Pantheon, 1957), *Soma: Divine Mushrooms of Immortality* (The Hague, Mouton, 1968; Harcourt Brace, 1971), *The Hall Carbine Affair; An Essay in Historiography* (3rd ed., 1971), *Persephone's Quest; Entheogens and the Origin of Religions* (published posthumously, 1987).

Wasson and his wife conducted field researches in Mexico, studying at first hand the sacred mushroom ceremonies of the Mazatec Indians. Their record album *Mushroom Ceremony of the Mazatec Indians of Mexico* (Folkways Records, New York, 1957) was the first documented recording of its kind.

It was Wasson's researches which were unfortunately popularized and vulgarized in the psychedelic revolution which followed publication of Aldous Huxley's *The Doors of Perception* (1954) and *Heaven and Hell* (1956).

Wasson himself was also misled in identifying the "**Soma**" of ancient India with the *amanita muscaria* mushroom and suggesting that Hindu mysticism arose from intoxication of the priests by means of this mushroom, considered as the elixir of immortality! This fallacy was revived approvingly in the journal *ReVision* (vol.10, No.4, Spring 1988), together with the extraordinary suggestion that *amaita muscaria* was the forbidden fruit of the tree in the Garden of Eden in the Old Testament story. This recalls the extravagant speculations of John M. Allegro in his book *The Sacred Mushroom and the Cross* (1970) which suggested that the crucifixion story of Jesus was a myth, symbolic of the ecstasy of a drug cult.

For an effective rebuttal of the Soma theory, see the series of three articles by Gene Kieffer, 'ReVision Revisits the Sacred Mushroom,' 'More About ReVision and the Sacred Mushroom' and 'The Mushroom as the Mechanism of Evolution?' in *SFF Newsletter* (Spiritual Frontiers Fellowship, Aug.-Oct.1988). (See also John M. **Allegro; Drugs; Hallucinogens; Kundalini;** Timothy **Leary; Mushrooms; Soma**)

Waterfall Astrological Directory

Annual reference work for individuals involved in Astrology; edited by Tony Waterfall. Address: P.O. Box 35668, Station E, Vancouver, British Columbia, Canada V6M.

Watkins, Geoffrey (1896-1981)

Proprietor and later a director of **Watkins Book Shop,** the preeminent London center for publications on mysticism and occultism since 1894, when Watkins' father John M. Watkins founded the company at the instigation of Theosophist Madame **Blavatsky.**

The bookshop has long been a meeting place for leading personalities in such subjects as metaphysics, mystical and hermetic studies, oriental and comparative religion, parapsychology, astrology, and the occult. John Watkins was a close friend of Madame Blavatsky, founder of the Theosophical Society. C. G. **Jung,** Aldous **Huxley,** W. B. **Yeats,** and magician Aleister **Crowley** were all frequent visitors to the shop. Crowley was reputed to have caused all the thousands of books in the store to vanish and reappear by his occult powers, but, like some other legends about Crowley, this apocryphal story is highly suspect. One individual closely associated with the bookshop at that period stated that Crowley was last seen at the shop as a "pathetically decrepit person who came to flog the last copies of his *Book of Thoth.*"

The influence of Madame Blavatsky in promoting mysticism, hermetic studies, and comparative religion, as distinct from occultism as such, was reinforced by the large framed portrait of H.P.B. which hung on the wall of one of the bookshop rooms.

Geoffrey Watkins, who carried on his father's tradition in the bookshop, was born June 7, 1896. He attended a private school in Heidelberg, Germany. Known to close friends as "Wattie" or "Nigel," he was employed by British Intelligence in World War I & II. In World War I, his duties included interrogation of German officer prisoners of war. In World War II, he was concerned with the distribution of top secret documents to appropriate government departments.

One of his closest friends was Christmas **Humphreys,** G.C. (later Judge Humphreys), who was for many years president of the Buddhist Society and author of numerous books on Buddhism and Eastern philosophy. Humphreys acknowledged the valuable assistance of Geoffrey Watkins in a preface to his book **Concentration and Meditation** (1935).

Geoffrey Watkins took over the work of running the bookshop when his father suffered from blindness. Those who visited the bookshop during the period of Geoffrey Watkins came from all over the world, and remembered him as a kindly, courteous, and exceptionally helpful individual, more of a spiritual guide than a bookseller. He disliked the word "occultism" because of the perjorative usage it had acquired. His own special interest did not lie in magic and the paranormal, but in depth psychology and the spiritual wisdom of East and West. The most modest of men, he described himself as a student of the "perennial philosophy," a term popularized by Aldous Huxley in his book of that name.

Geoffrey Watkins was a lifelong scholar of esoteric wisdom, but did not insist on propagating any personal convictions, but rather assisting the development of individual customers in relation to their stage of development at the time. The wide range of mystical and occult works in the bookshop catered to the different needs and levels of awareness of his many customers. He advised them in relation to their own particular needs.

As Kathleen Raine stated in a sympathetic obituary in *Temonos* (No.2, 1982): "Geoffrey Watkins was far more than a bookseller; indeed he was perhaps the only bookseller who made a practice of advising customers (many of whom were, or became, his friends) against purchasing books which he thought unsuitable for their particular interests, or too valuable to be entrusted to ignorant hands. . . . As to his courtesy, he welcomed his customers as his guests, assuming that we were seekers for wisdom, and meeting each of us at the level of our learning (or our ignorance) as he was well able to do. He seemed always to have time to listen. When we left, he saw us to the door of his shop like a courteous host."

He had an encyclopedic knowledge of books, and was extremely well informed on all aspects of the groups, societies, and individuals active in the fields of mysticism and occultism. He gave valuable and wise information to many individuals who became famous in their own right. Kathleen Raine herself, who has since published many works of poetry, literary criticism and philosophy, acknowledged the valuable help given to her by Geoffrey Watkins in her special studies on Thomas Taylor the Platonist. Alan **Watts** also paid tribute in his autobiography *In My Own Way* (1972): "Nigel [Geoffrey Watkins] runs the most magical bookshop in the world, and is the most unobstrusively enlightened person I have ever known. . . . Nigel not only became my bibliographer on Buddhism, comparative religion, and mysticism, but also my most trusted adviser on the various gurus, pandits, and psychotherapists then flourishing in London. . . . In the Watkins bookshop one would expect at any moment, to come across a Mahatma or a high Lama visiting England on a secret mission to feel out academically accredited professors. Instead of giving lectures and holding seminars, he simply tells you what to read. . . . He never tries to convert anyone to a system. He is what the Japanese would call a *buji-nin;* a man without affectations, who has also compassion and clarity of mind."

With the passing of Geoffrey Watkins, many regular customers at the bookshop, whether famous or humble seekers after wisdom, felt that they had lost a true friend and wise guide. Meanwhile, the bookshop started by his father continues to flourish. (See also **Watkins Book Shop**)

Watkins Book Shop

Long established British bookshop specializing in occultism, mysticism, comparative religion, parapsychology, and related topics, founded by John M. Watkins in 1894. Watkins was a friend of Madame **Blavatsky** and other leading figures in the early period of occultism. The shop in Cecil Court, Charing Cross Road, London, was a meeting place for such famous and varied individuals as A. E. **Waite,** W. B. **Yeats** and Aleister **Crowley.** Watkins also published important texts in the fields of occultism and mysticism. After his death, the business was carried on by his son Geoffrey Watkins.

All through the prewar occult boom of the 1920s and 1930s and the more recent occult explosion of the 1960s, the Watkins Book Shop has been a central focus of occultism, with a strong emphasis on mysticism and Eastern religion.

After the death of Geoffrey Watkins, the company went through various changes of title, including Stuart & Watkins (associated with Stuart & Robinson), but retained its essential character, as familiar to British students of occultism and mysticism as the **Weiser Bookshop** in New York.

In April 1984, the company became firmly linked with the Weiser Bookshop through the formation of Watkins Books Ltd., with directors Donald Weiser and Henry Suzuki of Samuel Weiser, Inc., and Valerie Chris of Robert Chris Bookseller (also in Cecil Court). Formerly a general literary book shop, Robert Chris is now a leading supplier of books on Health and Alternative Medicine. (See also Geoffrey **Watkins; Weiser Bookshop**)

Watseka Wonder, The

One of the most remarkable cases of continued spirit control. The story as detailed in a pamphlet by Dr. E. W. Stevens (*The Watseka Wonder*) is briefly as follows.

In 1865, at the age of nineteen, a girl named Mary Roff died in Watseka in raving mania. Thirteen years later, another Watseka girl, Lurancy Vennum, almost a stranger to the Roff family, became similarly afflicted. Dr. Stevens diagnosed her case as an **obsession.** In the hypnotic state, Lurancy Vennum confirmed the diagnosis.

Dr. Stevens suggested that she should try to induce a good spirit to control her. She answered that several spirits were about who would be willing. "There is one who was called Mary Roff." The father of Mary Roff was present, and approved of the idea. So "Mary Roff" was asked to control Lurancy Vennum. She did so.

On February 1, 1878, she possessed Lurancy's body and remained in possession for sixteen weeks in an almost unbroken continuity. As soon as she appeared, she took over Lurancy's body and behaved like Mary Roff in her lifetime. She did not know Lurancy's parents, went "home," recognized every old object in the Roff house, the friends she knew and continued where she left off over thirteen years before. She exhibited paranormal faculties during this time, gave proofs of **clairvoyance,** made **predictions,** had **out-of-body** experiences in trance and described her astral journeys on her return to consciousness.

On May 21, 1878, she took leave in tears from her Roff parents and all of her friends, fell into trance and awoke as Lurancy Vennum again. The new Lurancy was mentally and physically reestablished, but seems to have been watched over for a time by "Mary Roff," who even came back occasionally in trance. Three and a half years later, Lurancy Vennum married and when her first baby came "Mary Roff" put her into trance to save her the pains of childbirth.

It should be added that "Mary Roff" never appeared to anyone at Watseka, except through the body of Lurancy. She never materialized independently.

The psychical researcher Dr. Richard Hodgson investigated the case on behalf of the **American Society for Psychical Research,** and concluded: "I have no doubt that the incidents occurred substantially as described in the narrative by Dr. Stevens, and in my view the only other interpretation of the case—besides the spiritistic—that seems at all plausible, is that which has been put forward as the alternative to the spiritistic theory to account for the trance communications of Mrs. Piper, and similar cases, viz., secondary personality with supernormal powers. It would be difficult to disprove this hypothesis in the case of the Watseka Wonder, owing to the comparative meagreness of the record and the probable abundance of 'suggestion' in the environment, and any conclusion that we may reach would probably be determined largely by our convictions concerning other cases. My personal opinion is that the 'Watseka Wonder' case belongs in the main manifestations to the spiritistic category."

The case was also verified in all its details by Col. J. Bundy, editor of the *Religio-Philosophical Journal* of Chicago, whom British psychical researcher F. W. H. **Myers** described as a "well-known, skilful and scrupulously honest investigator."

The case was cited in F. W. H. Myers' book *Human Personality and Its Survival of Bodily Death* (2 vols., 1903), and a detailed report reappeared in *The Spiritualist* (September & October 1878). An account of the case by Dr. E. W. Stevens, *The Watseka Wonder,* was published Chicago, 1879. The evidence obtained by Dr. Richard Hodgson was published in the *Religio-Philosophical Journal* (December 20, 1890).

For a skeptical modern reassessment of this famous case, see the article 'The Watseka Wonder; A Critical Re-evaluation' by Rodger J. Anderson (*Theta,* vol.8, No.4, 1980)

Watson, Lyall (1939-)

Zoologist and archaeologist whose book *Supernature* attempted to bridge the gap between science and the occult, between natural and supernatural phenomena.

Author Colin **Wilson,** himself an authority on the occult, described *Supernature* as "a book of considerable importance, perhaps the most significant book about the 'super-natural' to appear in the past decade."

Watson's wide scientific experience in such disciplines as zoology, biology and anthropology gave this book authority, and broadened the scope of occult investigation. His brilliant overview places the paranormal within the same context as the everyday miracles of biology, chemistry and physics which comprise the world of nature.

Watson was born April 12, 1939 in Johannesburg, South Africa, and educated at University of Witwatersrand (B.S. 1958), University of Natal (M.S. 1959), University of London, England (Ph.D. 1963). From 1964-65 he was director of the Zoological Gardens of Johannesburg, South Africa, from 1966-67 produced documentary films for the British Broadcasting Corporation, London, from 1968-72 was expedition leader and researcher in Antarctica, in Amazon River area, in Seychelles, and in Indonesia.

He has worked closely with Desmond Morris of the London Zoo, and in archaeology with American School of Oriental Research at sites in Jordan and Saudi Arabia, as well as anthropological work in Northern Nigeria. In 1967 he founded the life science consultancy Biologic of London. He was a contributor to Reader's Digest Services' "Living World of Animals" series in 1970.

His books include: *Omnivore* (*The Omnivorous Ape,* 1970), *Supernature* (1973), *The Romeo Error* (1974), *Gifts of Unknown Things* (1976), *Lifetide; The Biology of The Unconscious* (1979), *Sea Guide to Whales of the World; A Complete Guide to the World's Living Whales, Dophins & Porpoises* (1981).

Watts, Alan (Wilson) (1915-1973)

British-born American philosopher, scholar of Eastern religions, pioneer popularizer of Eastern philosophy in the U.S. Born January 6, 1915 in Chislehurst, Kent, England, he came to the U.S. in 1938, where he was naturalized in 1943. He was ordained as an Anglican priest in 1944, was religious counselor at Northwestern University, Evanston, Illinois 1944-50. He studied at Seabury-Western Theological Seminary, S.T.M., 1948, University of Vermont, D.D., 1958. At the American Academy of

Asian Studies, San Francisco, California, he was professor of comparative philosophy 1951-57, dean 1953-56.

He became well known as a writer and lecturer from 1956 onwards, traveling to universities throughout the U.S. He was married three times (two divorces), his third marriage being to Mary Jane Yates King in 1963.

He directed the "Eastern Wisdom and Modern Life" series on station KQED, San Francisco, 1959-60, and was a committee member of the World Congress of Faiths 1937-39, member of the American Oriental Society, Society for Comparative Philosophy (president). He was a Bollingen Foundation research fellow 1951-53, 1962-64; Harvard University research fellow 1962-64.

He left the Christian church "not because it doesn't practice what it preaches, but because it preaches," preferring an individual interpretation of philosophy based on Eastern religion.

He was associated with such charismatic figures as Timothy Leary, Richard **Alpert,** Jack Kerouac, Gary Snyder and Allen Ginsberg. He has been called "the brain and the Buddha of American Zen," and had a considerable influence on the American swing to Eastern religion and philosophy from the 1960s onwards.

His prolific literary output included the following books: *Outline of Zen Buddhism* (1933, reissued in revised and enlarged editions as *Zen Buddhism* and *Zen,* 1947, 1948), *The Spirit of Zen* (1963, 1958, 1960), *The Legacy of Asia and Western Man* (1937), *The Meaning of Happiness* (1940, 1953), *Behold the Spirit* (1947, 1971), *The Supreme Identity* (1950, 1972), *The Wisdom of Insecurity* (1951), *Myth and Ritual in Christianity* (1953, 1959), *The Way of Zen* (1957), *Nature, Man and Woman* (1958), *This Is It* (1960), *Psychotherapy, East and West* (1961), *The Joyous Cosmology* (1962), *The Two Hands of God: The Myths of Polarity* (1963), *Beyond Theology: The Art of Godmanship* (1964), *The Book on the Taboo Against Knowing Who You Are* (1966), *Does It Matter? Essays on Man's Relation to Materiality* (1971), *In My Own Way: An Autobiography, 1915-1945* (1972), *The Art of Contemplation* (1973).

He died November 16, 1973.

Wayland Smith

A famous character in German mythological romance, father of Weltich, whom he trained in the art of warfare and sent to the Court of Dietrich in Bern. To him he gave the sword Miming and told him of a **mermaid,** his ancestress, to whom he was to apply when in difficulty.

Wayland Smith is also referred to in the Sigfried story, being in company with another smith named Mimi, when Sigfried joins the smithy. His workmanship is praised in the Beowulf Saga and he is mentioned there and elsewhere as a maker of impregnable armor. He is the supernatural smith of the Teutonic peoples, and is comparable to the god Vulcan in Roman, and to Hephaistos in Greek mythology.

Weatherhead, Leslie (Dixon) (1893-1976)

British Methodist minister who took an interest in aspects of parapsychology. Born October 14, 1893 in London, he studied at University of Manchester (M.A. 1926), Richmond College, University of London (Ph.D. 1950), University of Puget Sound, Washington (D.Litt. 1954). In 1920 he married Evelyn Triggs.

He was a lieutenant in the Indian Army, political officer in the Middle East, chaplain to British troops in World War I, minister of English Church, Madras, India from 1918-22, minister at Oxford Road Methodist Church, Manchester from 1922-25, minister at Brunswick Methodist Church, Leeds from 1925-36, minister at City Temple, London from 1936 onwards. C.B.E. 1959, D.D. (hon.) universities of Edinburgh and California.

His many books included: *After Death* (1930), *Healing Through Prayer* (1947), *Psychology, Religion and Healing* (1951), *The Case for Reincarnation* (1958), *The Resurrection of Christ in the Light of Modern Science and Psychical Research* (1959), *The Manner of the Resurrection in the Light of Psychical Research* (1960), *Wounded Spirits* (1962), *The Christian Agnostic* (1965), *Time for God* (1967), *Daily Readings from the Works of Leslie D. Weatherhead* (1969).

He died January 5, 1976.

Webb, James (C. N.) (1946-1980)

Scottish author of important historical surveys of the occult. Born 1946 in Edinburgh, Scotland, he was educated at Harrow, and Trinity College, Cambridge University. He spent some years as a ghostwriter, television producer-trainer and schoolmaster, becoming a full-time writer from 1969 onwards.

He was Advisory Editor of *The Occult,* a series of thirty-three reprints chosen to illustrate the origins and development of modern occultism, and also *Perspectives in Psychical Research,* a series of 34 books, both programs for Arn Press, New York, 1976, and contributed to *Man, Myth and Magic* (Marshall Cavendish Corp., 1970), and *Encyclopedia of the Unexplained* (McGraw-Hill, 1974).

He made a special study of the complex historical and cultural background of Western occultism and documented its relationship to extremist political movements.

His scholarly in-depth surveys of the ideas and personalities preceding today's occult revival constitute an overview of the problem of the twentieth century as a battleground between reason and irrationalism. These books include: *The Occult Underground* (1974; British title *The Flight from Reason,* 1971), *The Occult Establishment* (1976), *The Harmonious Circle* (1980). He edited *The Quest Anthology* (1976), *The Subliminal Consciousness* (selections from writings by Frederic W. H. Myers, in *Proceedings* of the Society for Psychical Research, London, 1976), *The Mediums and the Conjurers* (anthology of writings by J. N. Maskelyne, G. Smith-Buck, George Sexton, 1976).

He started his writings with a somewhat skeptical viewpoint, but in the course of time experienced unusual visions and insights, unfortunately associated with hallucinations and a nervous breakdown.

He died May 8, 1980, in Scotland. For a sympathetic commentary on Webb's life, which includes a posthumous communication through a medium, see 'James Webb and the Occult' by Colin **Wilson** in *Light* (Summer, 1982). The same issue also includes 'A Precognitive Dream: James Webb' by Joyce Collin-Smith.

Wege—Zur Synthese von Natur und Mensch (Magazine)

Bimonthly German-language publication, including articles, programme of mystical/spiritual activities in Frankfurt area, lists of organizations, etc. Address: Aviva, Kobachstr. 12, D-6000 Frankfurt 50 FN, Germany.

Weiant, C(larence) W(olsey) (1897-)

Anthropologist and chiropractor with interests in parapsychology. Born November 30, 1987 at West Haverstraw, New York, he studied at School of General Studies, Columbia University (B.S. 1937), graduate work in 1937 at Instituto de Filosofia y Letras, Mexico City, Columbia University (Ph.D. 1943). In 1930 he married Marian Gargett Webber.

He was dean emeritus of the Chiropractic Institute of New York 1963, lecturer in Department of Sociology and Anthropology at Hunter College, New York from 1943-51, president of Peekskill Board of Education from 1961-62, fellow of the American Anthropological Association, American Association for the Advancement of Science, member of National Chiropractic Association, Society for American Archaeology, hon. member of Archaeological Society of Bolivia.

Dr. Weiant was interested in clairvoyance, mediumship, reincarnation and survival theories. He translated the book *Lo Sagrado entre los Primitivos y la Parapsicologia* (The Sacred Among Primitive Peoples, and Parapsychology) by Juan Rogers, and contributed to *Tomorrow* magazine. His paper on 'Parapsychology and Anthropology' was published in *Manas* (vol. 13, 1960).

Weinberger, Julius (1893-)

Radio engineer who wrote on parapsychology. Born July 22, 1893 in New York, N.Y. he studied at College of the City of New York (B.S. 1913). In 1943 he married Helen Wright Faddis.

He was manager in charge of research at Radio Corporation of America from 1916-28, manager of Research Department of RCA from 1928-30, engineer in charge of Acoustical Research, RCA from 1930-34, staff member of RCA Laboratories from 1934 until retirement in 1958. He was a volunteer associate in research on mental illness at the Northport (N.Y.) Veterans Hospital.

In addition to his articles on radio engineering, he also published: 'A Physicist Looks at Survival' (*Tomorrow,* Autumn, 1956), 'Some Findings of Experimental Psychical Research' (*Proceedings of the Seminar on Decline of Material,* Nov. 1956, 'A Physicist Looks at Spiritual Healing' (*Laymen's Movement Review,* vol. 1, No. 5, 1958, vol. 2, No. 1, 1959), 'On Apparatus Communication with Discarnate Persons' (*International Journal of Parapsychology,* vol. 3, No. 1, Winter 1961). He also contributed the chapter 'Is There a Non-Physical World?' to the book *Does Man Survive Death?* (1957).

Weingarten, Henry

Prominent American astrologer, executive secretary of the National Astrological Society and editor of *NASO Journal.* He has lectured extensively on astrology, and taught at the NASO School of Astrology in New York. He is author of *A Modern Introduction to Astrology* (1974) and *The Study of Astrology,* 3 vols. (1977), *Principles of Synastry* (1978).

Weiser Bookshop

Perhaps the most famous occult bookstore in the U.S., the New York equivalent of London's **Watkins Book Shop** or **Atlantis Bookshop,** patronized by occultists and students of the occult.

Samuel Weiser's earlier shop was at 117 Fourth Avenue, then a large rambling store at 845 Broadway with largely antiquarian stock and an occult section downstairs. His regular catalogs of new and old occult books issued through the 1950s have since become useful bibliographical records.

In the 1960s, the store moved to 740 Broadway, and was managed by Weiser's son Donald. The stock still included both new and old books, reflecting the contemporary range of occult interest, and there was a rare book section for some of the older hard-to-find titles. The store also carried notices and announcements of religious, mystical and occult societies.

After a long period at 740 Broadway, New York, this famous bookstore moved again, to 132 East 24 Street, New York, N.Y. 10010, at Park Avenue and Lexington.

In April 1984, Donald Weiser and Henry Suzuki of Samuel Weiser, Inc., became directors (with Valerie Chris, England) of the famous Watkins Book Shop in Cecil Court, Charing Cross Road, London. (See also **Watkins Book Shop;** Geoffrey **Watkins**)

Weisman, Kenneth E(arl) (1930-)

Schoolteacher who has been active in the field of parapsychology. Born November 16, 1930 in Chicago, Illinois, he studied at Bradley University, Peoria, Ill. (B.S. biology 1958). In 1955 he married Susan Merry Begeman.

He served in the U.S. Army from 1951-54, was instructor at Harrison School, Peoria from 1958 onwards. Member of board of directors of Peoria Academy of Science, Society for the Study of Evolution, American Entomological Society.

Mr. Weisman conducted experiments among school-children to correlate clairvoyant ability with class grades, sex, achievement-test ratings and teacher-attitude towards pupils.

W.E.L.

Initialism for *Welt-Eis-Lehre* (Cosmic Ice Theory), a cult built around the eccentric theories of Austrian engineer Hans **Hörbiger,** author of a vast pseudo-scientific work *Glazial-Kosmogonie* (1912) which had a great vogue in Nazi Germany. These theories involved a complex system of "cosmic ice" which generated stellar systems in which smaller planets become moons and are captured by larger planets. According to Hörbiger, earth's present moon is coated with ice 140 miles thick and is now moving towards earth with a spiral motion.

After Hörbiger's death, his theories were further developed by the British mythologist Hans Schindler Bellamy in his book *Moons, Myths, and Man* (1936). The W.E.L. cult combined such theories with Nazi political philosophy and rabid anti-Semitism. The paranoid character of W.E.L. is indicated by such statements as: "Our Nordic ancestors grew strong in ice and snow; belief in the World Ice is consequently the natural heritage of Nordic Man . . . Just as it needed a child of Austrian Culture—Hitler!—to put the Jewish politicians in their place, so it needed an Austrian to cleanse the world of Jewish science."

Wellman, Adele

Born in Brooklyn, New York. Has acted as executive secretary, **American Society for Psychical Research.**

Wendigo (or Windigo)

A weird cannibalistic creature of the forests, which features in the mythology of North American and Canadian Indians. Algonquin tribes believe that a hunter lost in the bush without food may become a wendigo, seeking other human beings in order to eat their flesh.

Ojibwa Indians use the term "windigo" to denote a ferocious ogre who will take away children if they do not behave properly.

A powerful horror story *The Wendigo* was written by novelist Algernon **Blackwood** (1869-1951), first published in *The Lost Valley & Other Stories*, London, 1910. It was probably drawn from legends encountered by the author during his own travels in the Canadian backwoods.

A recent book has assembled a great deal of information on the legendary Wendigo. This is: *Windigo; An Anthology of Facts and Fantastic Fiction* edited by John R. Colombo (University of Nebraska Press, 1982). Colombo states: "Windigo has been described as the phantom of hunger which stalks the forests of the north in search of lone Indians, halfbreeds, or white men to consume. It may take the form of a cannibalistic Indian who breathes flames. Or it may assume the guise of a supernatural spirit with a heart of ice that flies through the night skies in search of a victim to satisfy its craving for human flesh. Like the vampire, it feasts on flesh and blood. Like the werewolf, it shape-changes at will."

Colombo lists some thirty-seven variant forms of the word "Windigo" or "Wendigo" and states that the first appearance of the word in print appears to be in an account by the French traveler Bacqueville de la Potherie in 1722, when it appeared as "Onaouientagos." The word derives from the Algonkian Indian root *witiku* meaning "evil spirit" or "cannibal" and legends of the Wendigo are current among the Algonkian tribes in the Northwest Territories of Canada and the northern regions of Quebec, Ontario, Manitoba, Saskatchewan, and Alberta.

The Wendigo is said to inhabit a large territory bounded by the Atlantic Ocean in the east, the Arctic Ocean in the North, and the Rocky Mountains in the west.

According to Algonkian belief, a human being may "turn windigo" through an act of cannibalism, or being in the presence of the demon, or through the sorcery of a shaman. Such transformation has much in common with legends of the vampire and werwolf.

Colombo's book is significant for assembling both factual information and fictional accounts of the Wendigo, and included Algernon Blackwood's story *The Wendigo.* (See also **Dracula; Vampire; Werwolf**)

Wenzl, Aloys (1887-)

Professor emeritus, philosophy; was active in the field of parapsychology. Born January 25, 1887 in Munich, Germany, he studied at University of Munich (Ph.D. 1912). In 1928 he married Dorothea Reinlein.

He was a lecturer of philosophy and psychology at University of Munich from 1926-38, but discharged on ideological grounds during the Nazi regime. He became professor of philosophy at University of Munich from 1946 onwards. Member of Bayrische Akademie der Wissenschaften, Allgemeine Deutsche Gesellschaft für Philosphie, Deutsche Gesellschaft für Psychologie. Prof. Wenzl has taken an interest in clairvoyance and psychokinesis, and attended the International Conference on Philosophy and Parapsychology at St. Paul de Vence, France, held in 1954.

His books included: *Wissenschaft und Weltanschauung* (Science and World Outlook, 1936, 1949), *Philosophie als Weg von den Grenzen der Wissenschaft an die Grenzen der Religion* (Philosophy as a Road from the Frontiers of Science to the Frontiers of Religion, 1939, 1956), *Unsterblichkeit* (Immorality, 1951), *Theorie der Begabung* (Theory of Natural Gifts, 1934, 1957), *Philosophische Grenzfragen der Naturwissenchaften* (Philosophical Border Problems of the Natural Sciences, 1956).

Wereide, Thorstein (1882-)

Professor emeritus, physics, at University of Oslo, founder-member of Norwegian Society for Psychical Research in 1919, president of Norwegian Society for Psychical Research 1927 onwards. Born March 9,

1882 at Nordfjord, Norway, he studied at University of Oslo (B.A. 1910, Ph.D. 1914). In 1925 he married Sophie Bredsdorff.

He was physics professor at Medical College, University of Oslo from 1919 onwards. He was editor of *Psykisk Tidsskrift,* journal of the Norwegian SPR from 1926-39, president of International Congress of Psychical Research, Oslo in 1935, delegate to international psychical research congresses at Copenhagen (1920), Warsaw (1923), Paris (1927), Athens (1930). He also attended the International Conference on Parapsychological Studies at Utrecht in 1953, the International Conference on Spontaneous Phenomena at Cambridge, England 1955.

His investigations covered mediumship, materialization and multiple personality phenomena. He made a special study of the Norwegian medium Ingeborg Koeber, and the multiple personality of Hungarian Luisa Ignath. His articles included: 'Norway's Human Doubles' (*Tomorrow,* Winter 1955), 'Medium or Murderess' (*Tomorrow,* Winter 1957), 'The Physical Phenomena of Mediumship as Evidence of Survival' (1958). He also published the following books: *Mysteriesamfund* (Mystery Societies, under pseudonym of 'Scarabaeus,' (1948), *Menneskets Metafysikk* (The Metaphysics of Man, 1953), *Byggesamfund* (Building Societies, 1956).

Werwolf (or Werewolf)

A human being temporarily or permanently transformed into a wolf, from the Anglo-Saxon *wer,* a man, and *wulf,* a wolf. It is a phase of **Lycanthropy,** and in ancient and medieval times was of very frequent occurrence. It was, of course, in Europe where the wolf was one of the largest carnivorous animals, that the superstition gained currency, similar tales in other countries usually introducing bears, tigers, leopards or other animals.

The belief is probably a relic of early cannibalism. Communities of semi-civilized people would begin to shun those who devoured human flesh, who would be ostracized and classed as wild beasts. The idea that they had something in common with animals would grow, and the conception that they were able to transform themselves into veritable animals would be likely to arise.

There were two kinds of *werwolf,* voluntary and involuntary. The voluntary would be, as has been said, those persons who, because of their taste for human flesh, had withdrawn from association with their fellows.

These possessed a reputation for the magical power to transform themselves into the animal shape at will. This they effected by merely disrobing, by the taking off a girdle made of human skin, or putting on a similar belt of wolf-skin, obviously a substitute for an entire wolf-skin. There were also cases of donning the entire skin. In other instances, the body was rubbed with a magic ointment, or water was drunk out of a wolf's footprint. The brains of the animal were also eaten. Olaus Magnus (1490-1558) stated "that the *werwolves* of Livonia drained a cup of beer on initiation, and repeated certain magic words.

In order to throw off the wolf shape, the animal girdle was removed, or else the magician merely muttered a certain formula. In some instances, the transformation was supposed to be the work of Satan.

The superstition regarding werwolves seems to have been exceedingly prevalent in France during the sixteenth century, as is evidenced by numerous trials, in some of which it is clearly shown that murder and cannibalism took place. Self-hallucination may have accounted for some of these cases, the supposed werwolves fully admitting that they had transformed themselves and had slain numerous persons, but at the beginning of the seventeenth century, persons making such confessions were not credited. However, self-hallucination does not cover a number of cases where werwolves were seen by witnesses. In Teutonic and Slavonic countries, it was complained by men of learning that werwolves did more damage than the real criminals, and a regular "college" or institution for the practice of the art of animal transformation was attributed to them.

Involuntary werwolves were often persons transformed into an animal shape because of the commission of sin, and condemned to pass so many years in that form. Thus, certain saints metamorphosed sinners into wolves. In Armenia, it was thought that sinful women were condemned to pass seven years in the form of a wolf. To such a woman a demon appeared, bringing a wolf-skin. He commanded her to don it, from which moment she became a wolf with all the nature of a wild beast, devouring her own children and those of strangers, wandering forth at night, undeterred by locks, bolts, or bars, returning only in the morning to resume her human form.

French romance literature often mentions werwolves, and there are complete romances on the theme, such as The *Lais du Bisclavret* of Marie de France and the *Guillaume de Palerne* (known as *William and the Werwolf*) of the twelfth century. However, in such romances the werwolf was the innocent victim of magic, rather than a dangerous cannibal.

Many werwolves were innocent persons suffering through the witchcraft of others. To regain their true form it was necessary for them to kneel in one spot for a hundred years, to lose three drops of blood, to be hailed as a werwolf, to have the sign of the cross made on their bodies, to be addressed thrice by their baptismal names, or to be stuck thrice on the forehead with a knife.

According to Donat de Hautemer, quoted by Simon Goulart (1543-1628), "there are some lycanthropes who are so dominated by their melancholy humour that they really believe themselves to be transformed into wolves. This malady, according to the testimony of Aetius in his sixth book, chapter XI., and Paulus in his third book, chapter XVI., and other moderns, is a sort of melancholy, of a black and dismal nature. Those who are attacked by it leave their homes in the months of February, imitate wolves in almost every particular, and wander all night long among the cemeteries and sepulchres, so that one may observe a marvellous change in the mind and disposition, and, above all in the depraved imagination, of the lycanthrope. The memory, however, is still vigorous, as I have remarked in one of this lycanthropic melancholiacs whom we call *werwolves.* For one who was well acquainted with me was one day seized with his affliction, and on meeting him I withdrew a little, fearing that he might injure me. He, having glanced at me for a moment, passed on followed by a crowd of people. On his shoulder he carried the entire leg and thigh of a corpse. Having received careful medical treatment, he was cured of this malady. On meeting me on another occasion he asked me if I had not been afraid when he met me at such and such a place, which made me think that his memory was not hurt by the vehemence of his disease, though his imagination was so greatly damaged."

Guillaume de Brabant, in the narrative of Wier, repeated by Goulart, has written in his *History* that a certain man of sense and settled understanding was still so tormented by the evil spirit that at a particular season of the year he would think himself a ravening wolf, and would run here and there in the woods, caves and deserts, chasing little children. It was said that this man was often found running about in the deserts like a man out of his senses, and that at last by the grace of God he came to himself and was healed. There was also, as is related by Job Fincel in the second book *On Miracles* a villager near Paule in the year 1541, who believed himself to be a wolf, and assaulted several men in the fields, even killing some. Taken at last, though not without great difficulty, he stoutly affirmed that he was a wolf, and that the only way in which he differed from other wolves was that they wore their hairy coats on the outside, while he wore his between his skin and his flesh. Certain persons, more inhuman and wolfish than he, wished to test the truth of this story, and gashed his arms and legs severely. Then, learning their mistake, and the innocence of the melancholiac, they passed him over to the consideration of the surgeons, in whose hands he died some days after. Those afflicted with this disease are pale, with dark and haggard eyes, seeing only with difficulty; the tongue is dry, and the sufferer very thirsty. Pliny and others write that the brain of a bear excites such bestial imaginations. It is even said that one was given to a Spanish gentleman to eat in our times, which so disturbed his mind, that imagining himself to be transformed into a bear, he fled to the mountains and deserts.

"As for the lycanthropes, whose imagination was so damaged that by some Satanic efficacy they appeared wolves and not men to those who saw them running about and doing all manner of harm. Bodin maintains that the devil can change the shape of one body into that of another, in the great power that God gives him in this elementary world. He says, then, that there may be lycanthropes who have really been transformed into wolves, quoting various examples and histories to prove his contention. In short, after many disputes, he believes in Colt's form of lycanthropy. And as for the latter, there is represented at the end of this chapter the summary of his proposition, to wit, that men are sometimes transformed into beasts, retaining in that form the human reason; it may be that this comes about by the direct power of God, or it may be that he gives this power to Satan, who carries out his will, or rather his redoubtable judgments. And if we confess (he says) the truths of the sacred history in Daniel, concerning the transformation of Nebuchadnezzar, and the history of Lot's wife changed into motionless stone, the changing of men into an ox or a stone is certainly possible; and consequently the transformation to other animals as well."

Gaspar Peucer (1525-1602) stated, in speaking of lycanthropy: "As for me I had formerly regarded as ridiculous and fabulous the stories I had often heard concerning the transformation of men into wolves; but I have learnt from reliable sources, and from the testimony of trustworthy witnesses, that such things are not at all doubtful or incredible, since they tell of such transformations taking place twelve days after Christmas in Livonia and the adjacent countries; as they have been proved to be true by the confessions of those who have been imprisoned and tortured for such crimes.

"Here is the manner in which it is done. Immediately after Christmas day is past, a lame boy goes round the country calling these slaves of the devil, of which there are a great number, and enjoining them to follow him. If they procrastinate or go too slowly, there immediately appears a tall man with a whip whose thongs are made of iron chains, with which he urges them onwards, and sometimes lashes the poor wretches so cruelly, that the marks of the whip remain on their bodies till long afterwards, and cause them the greatest pain. As soon as they have set out on their road, they are all changed into wolves. . . .

"They travel in thousands, having for their conductor the bearer of the whip, after whom they march. When they reach the fields, they rush upon the cattle they find there, tearing and carrying away all they can, and doing much other damage; but they are not permitted to touch or wound persons. When they approach any rivers, their guide separates the waters with his whip, so that they seem to open up and leave a dry space by which to cross. At the end of twelve days the whole band scatters, and everyone returns to his home, having regained his own proper form. This transformation, they say, comes about in this wise. The victims fall suddenly on the ground as though they were taken with sudden illness, and remain motionless and extended like corpses, deprived of all feeling, for they neeither stir, nor move from one place to another, nor are in any wise transformed into wolves, thus resembling carrion, for although they are rolled or shaken, they give no sign of life."

Jean **Bodin** (1529-1596) related several cases of lycanthropy and of men changed into beasts, including the following:

"Pierre Mamot, in a little treatise he has written on sorcerers, says that he has observed this changing of men into wolves, he being in Savoy at the time. Henry of Cologne in his treatise *de Lamiis* regards the transformation as beyond doubt. And Ulrich in a little book dedicated to the emperor Sigismund, writes of the dispute before the emperor, and says that it was agreed, both on the ground of reason, and of the experience of innumerable examples, that such transformation was a fact; and he adds that he himself had seen a lycanthrope at Constance, who was accused, convicted, condemned, and finally executed after his confession. And several books published in Germany say that one of the greatest kings of Christendom, who is not long dead, and who had the reputation of being one of the greatest sorcerers in the world, often changed into a wolf.

"I remember that the attorney-general of the King, Bourdin, has narrated to me another which was sent to him from the Low Countries, with the whole trial signed by the judge and the clerks, of a wolf, which was struck by an arrow on the thigh, and afterwards found himself in bed, with the arrow (which he had torn out), on regaining his human shape, and the arrow was recognised by him who had fired it—the time and place testified by the confession of the person."

"Garnier, tried and condemned by the parliament of Dole, being in the shape of a *werwolf,* caught a girl of ten or twelve years in a vineyard of Chastenoy, a quarter of a league from Dole, and having slain her with his teeth and claw-like hands, he ate part of her flesh and carried the rest to his wife. A month later, in the same form, he took another girl, and would have eaten her also, had he not, as he himself confessed, been prevented by three persons who happened to be passing by; and a fortnight after he strangled a boy of ten in the vineyard of Gredisans, and ate his flesh; and in the form of a man and not of a wolf, he killed another boy of twelve or thirteen years in a wood of the village of Porouse with the intention of eating him, but was again prevented. He was condemned to be burnt, and the sentence was executed.

"At the parliament of Bezançon, the accused were Pierre Burgot and Michel Verdun, who confessed to having renounced God, and sworn to serve the devil. And Michel Verdun led Burgot to the bord du Chastel Charlon where everyone carried a candle of green wax which shone with a blue flame. There they danced and offered sacrifices to the devil. Then after being anointed they were turned into wolves, running with incredible swiftness, then they were changed again into men, and suddenly transformed back to wolves, when they enjoyed the society of female wolves as much as they had done that of their wives. They confessed also that Burgot had killed a boy of seven years with his wolf-claws and teeth, intending to eat him, but the peasants gave chase, and prevented him. Burgot and Verdun had eaten four girls between them; and they had caused people to die by the touch of a certain power.

"Job Fincel, in the eleventh book of his *Marvels* wrote that there was at Padua a lycanthrope who was caught and his wolf-claws cut, and at the same instant he found his arms and feet cut. That is given to strengthen the case against the sorcerers of Vernon (1556) who assembled themselves in an old and ruined chateau under the shape of an infinite number of cats. There happened to arrive there one evening four or five men, who decided to spend the night in the place. They were awakened by a multitude of cats, who assaulted them, killed one of their number, and wounded others. The men, however, succeeded in wounding several of the cats, who found on recovering their human shape that they were badly hurt. And incredible as it may seem, the trial was not proceeded with.

"But the five inquisitors who had experimented in these causes have left it in writing that there were three sorcerers in Strasbourg who, in the guise of three large cats, assaulted a labourer, and in defending himself he wounded and dispersed the cats, who found themselves, at the same moment, laid on sick-beds, in the form of women severely wounded. At the trial they accused him who had struck them, and he told the judges the hour and the place where he had been assaulted by the cats, and how he had wounded them."

Belief in transformation of human beings into predatory animals has persisted in relatively modern times in Africa, India, Java, Malaya and other countries. In Africa there were tiger men and even a leopard society of wizards.

Some cases of lycanthropy may have been a cover for a perverse appetite for drinking blood or eating human flesh, but it is also possible that there were cases of psychic transformations, in which the astral double of a lycanthrope was projected in the form of a beast, similar to other stories of witches and wizards attacking their victims in an astral form.

Another aspect of lycanthropy is that Romulus and Remus theme of abandoned children reared by wolves. One classic case of such "feral children," as they are termed, is that of the two wolf girls of Midnapore, India, who were rescued by the Rev. J. A. L. Singh in 1942. This case is discussed in detail by Charles Maclean in his book *The Wolf Children* (1978). (See also **Lycanthropy; Vampire**)

Recommended reading

Baring-Gould, Sabine. *The Book of Were-Wolves,* London, 1965; Causeway Books, New York, 1973

Dunn, Charles W. *The Foundling and the Werwolf; A Literary-Historical Study of Guillaume de Palerne,* University of Toronto Press, 1960

Gesell, Arnold. *Wolf-Child and Human Child,* Harper/Methuen, London, 1941

Hamel, Frank. *Human Animals,* London, 1915; University Books, 1969

Kaigh, Frederick. *Witchcraft & Magic of Africa,* Richard Lesley & Co., London, 1947

Maclean, Charles. *The Wolf Children,* Hill & Wang, 1978

O'Donnell, Elliott. *Werwolves,* London, 1912; revised edition, Wholesale Book Corporation, New York, 1972

Summers, Montague. *The Werewolf,* London, 1933; University Books, 1966

Woodward, Ian. *The Werewolf Delusion,* Paddington Press, London & New York, 1979

Weschcke, Carl L. (1930-)

Prominent American astrologer, occultist and publisher, owner-president of **Llewellyn Publications,** St. Paul, Minnesota (originally founded as Llewellyn Publishing Company by Welsh astrologer Llewellyn **George** in 1905).

Born September 10, 1930 in St. Paul Minnesota, Mr. Weschcke was educated at St. Paul Academy, Babson Institute of Wellesley Hills, Mass., University of Minnesota (Dept. of Philosophy).

He purchased Llewellyn Publishing Co. of Los Angeles, California in 1960 and moved the business to St. Paul, Minnesota. It is now one of the largest wholesale dealers in occult books and products in the U.S.

The Llewellyn enterprise also includes Gnostica, a large retail bookstore housed in a 12,000 square foot former mortuary in St. Paul. In addition to publishing a number of popular occult books, Llewellyn has also issued *Gnostica* magazine, *Astrology Now* magazine, the annual *Moon Sign Book* (established by Llewellyn George in 1905) and *Daily Planetary Guide.*

Mr. Weschcke was editor-in-chief of *Gnostica* magazine, and his own writings included articles on lunar astrology, gardening, Tantra and witchcraft.

He is a practicing witch and has chaired the Council of American Witches. In addition to many appearances on radio and television interview programs, he was responsible for a half-hour commercial television program on Halloween, and prepared a videotape on witchcraft for the University of Wisconsin.

He is vice-president of the Minnesota chapter of the American Civil Liberties Union, president of the Minnesota State chapter NAACP, member of the University Club of Saint Paul.

West, D(onald) J(ames) (1924-)

Psychiatrist. Research officer at **Society for Psychical Research** London, from 1947-50, president 1963-65. Born June 9, 1924 in Liverpool, England, he studied at Liverpool University (M.B., Ch.B. 1947, M.D. 1958), London University (D.P.M. 1952), Cambridge University, England (M.A. 1960).

He has been assistant director of research at Cambridge University, Institute of Criminology, honorary consultant psychiatrist, Cambridge; assistant editor of *International Journal of Social Psychiatry.*

Dr. West has played an important part in British laboratory experiments in extrasensory perception. He was joint winner in 1958 (with G. W. **Fisk**) of the William McDougall Award for Distinguished Research in Parapsychology, described in 'Psychokinetic Experiments with a Single Subject' (*Parapsychology Newsletter,* Nov.-Dec. 1957). He has contributed articles to the *Journal* and *Proceedings* of the Society for Psychical Research, London. His books include: *Psychical Research Today* (1956, 1962), *Homosexuality* (1954, 1960), *Eleven Lourdes Miracles* (1955, U.S. ed. 1958), *The Habitual Prisoner* (1963), *Murder Followed by Suicide* (1965), *The Young Offender* (1967), *Present Conduct and Future Delinquency* (1969), *Who Becomes Delinquent* (1973).

West Indian Islands

Magic and sorcery in the West Indian Islands is widespread among the black population, who possess special magical cults called *Obeah* and *Vaudoux,* variants of West African **fetishism.**

The root idea of Obeahism and Vaudoux is the worship and propitiation of the snake-god Obi—a West African word typifying the Spirit of Evil. Vaudoux or Voodoo is a form of Obeah practiced in Haiti, San Domingo, and the French West Indies. Its rites are accompanied by the sacrifice of fowls and goats, and in some cases in past history by the offering up of the "goat without horns"—the human sacrifice, usually a young girl or boy.

The lonely groves and mountain caves where the devotees of Vaudoux used to enjoy the orgies of a Walpurgis night seldom gave up their secrets. There were two sects of Vaudoux—the white and the red. The former, which only believed in the sacrifice of white fowls and goats, was tolerated by the laws of Haiti, and its rites were as commonly practiced as those of the Catholic Church. But even the red sect, which openly stood for human sacrifice, was seldom interfered with. The authorities did not dare to suppress it, for their own policemen and soldiers stood in awe of the "Papalio," and "Mamaloi"—the priests and priestess of the snake-god.

Former presidents of Haiti believed in Vaudoux. Hippolyte was even a "Papaloi" himself. He beat the black goatskin drum in the streets of the capital to call the faithful together to see him kill the *sen-sel* fowl. Another president, Geffard, tried to stamp out the cult. A terrible revenge was taken upon him. His young daughter Cora was shot dead as she knelt in prayer before the altar of a church in Port-au-Prince. A temple of the red sect in the Haitian capital near a triumphal arch was inscribed with the unctuous words, "Liberty—education—progress."

Under British rule Obeahism took forms less dangerous to the social order than in Haiti; but it was none the less a constant feature of life in Jamaica and the other West Indian Islands until independence. It was a bitter foe of religion, education and social advancement.

In olden days it worked by means of wholesale poisoning. A favorite method of the Obeahman, both in Jamaica and Haiti, was to mix the infinitesimal hairs of the bamboo in the food of persons who refused to submit to them. This method finally sets up malignant dysentery. If the afflicted one remained defiant, he died; if he made his peace with the Obeahman, and gave him a handsome present, the slow process of poisoning ceased, and he lived.

In all the crises and troubles of life it used to be common to approach the Obeahman. If one had to appear at the Police Court he paid the Obeahman to go there also and "fix the eye" of the magistrate so that he would be discharged.

Perhaps he had been turned out of his office of deacon in the Baptist Chapel by a white minister for immorality. In that case, the Obeahman would arrange for a choice collection of the most powerful spells—such as dried lizards, fowls' bones, and graveyard earth—to be placed in the minister's Bible for him to stare upon when he looked up the text of his sermon. Then, if the Obeah worked properly, the erring deacon would be received back to office.

Even men of education and official position were often tainted with Obeahism. They often made use of it for profit and to increase their power over the ignorant. A mulatto chairman of a Parochial Board—the Jamaican equivalent of a city Council—was sent to gaol for practicing Obeah about forty years ago.

A prominent member of the Kingston City Council was the leading Obeahman in the island—the pontiff of the cult. He was so clever that the police could never catch him, although he was supposed to make over £3,000 a year by his nefarious practices. Once some detectives raided his place, but he received timely warning and fled.

A writer to the press thus described a "red" Vaudoux ceremony: "I had seen the 'white' ritual several times in Port-au-Prince and elsewhere when at last I was permitted through the kindness of a mulatto general, to witness the 'red' rite. I was informed that only cocks and goats would be sacrificed, and that turned out to be the fact. The General conducted me to a small wood about three miles from the town of Jacmel. By the light of kerosene oil flares I saw about forty men and women gathered round a rude stone altar, on which, twined around a *cocomacacque* stick, was the sacred green snake. The 'Mamaloi,' a tall, evil-looking negress, was dressed in a scarlet robe, with a red turban on her head.

"She was dancing a sinuous dance before the altar, and droning an ancient West African chant, which the onlookers repeated. Rapidly she worked herself up to a frantic pitch of excitement, pausing now and then to take a drink from one of the rum bottles which passed freely from hand to hand. At last she picked up a glittering *machete* from the altar, and with her other hand seized a black cock held by a bystander. She whirled the bird round her head violently until the feathers were flying in all directions, and then severed the head from the body with one swift stroke. The tense and horrible excitement had kept the worshippers silent, but they burst into a savage yell when the priestess pressed the bleeding neck of the slaughtered fowl to her lips. Afterwards she dipped her finger in the blood and made the sign of the cross on her forehead and pressed it to the forehead of some of her disciples."

The Obeah man could always be recognized easily. He had an indescribably sinister appearance. He was unwashed, ragged, often half mad, usually diseased, and almost always had an ulcerated leg. This last, indeed, was said to be a badge of the tribe. Often he was a very old black who knew "slavery days" and more than half believed in his magical pretensions. But not all were of this disreputable type.

Even some of the white planters themselves did not hesitate to make use of Obeah, although, of course, they had no belief in it. The theft of growing crops was one of the greatest trials of their lives. Sometimes they adorned the trees round the edge of a "banana piece" or orange grove with miniature coffins, old bones, bottles of dirty water, and other Obeah objects; and then the workers did not dare to enter and steal. An interesting report published in a Jamaican journal during 1908 gave particulars of an Obeah case of possession or haunting as follows:

"The *cause célèbre* at Half-way Tree Court, Jamaica, recently, was the case of Rex v. Charles Donaldson for unlawfully practising Obeah. Robert Robinson, who stated that he was a labourer living at Trench Pen, in the parish of St. Andrew, stated that on Tuesday, the 8th ult., he was sitting down outside the May Pen cemetery on the Spanish Town Road. He was on his way from work, and had a white handkerchief tied around his head. He was feeling sick, and that led him to sit down. While there sitting the prisoner came to him. He did not know the man before, but he began by asking him what was the matter. Witness replied, 'I am well sick.' The prisoner said, 'No, you are not sick; you have two ghosts on you—one creole and one coolie.' Witness told the prisoner to go away and was left. He next saw prisoner on Wednesday 9th. He came to him at Bumper Hall, where he was working, and he said to him, 'Man, how you find me here?' " 'Oh,' replied the prisoner, 'if a man is in hell self I can find him; I come for you to give me the job?' Witness then inquired, 'What job?' and accused told him he wanted to 'take off the two ghosts.' He would do it for £25, and he 'killed' for any sum from £25 to £50. He had worked for all classes—white, black, coolie, Chinese, etc. Witness said he did not give him any 'good consent' at the time, but reported the matter after the accused left to Clark and Wright, two witnesses in the case. Clark told him he must not scare the man but go home. On Thursday, the 10th, the defendant came to him at his yard at French Pen. The accused told him he would come back to him to take off the ghost. He also told him to get a bottle of rum and 5s. He (witness) consented to the arrangement. The defendant began by taking off his jacket. He then opened his 'brief bag' and took out a piece of chalk. The accused then made three marks on the table and took out a phial and a white stone. The phial contained some stuff which appeared like quicksilver. He arrayed his paraphernalia on the table. They consisted of a large whisky bottle with some yellow stuff, a candle, a pack of cards, a looking-glass, three cigarette pictures, a pocket knife, etc. The accused also took out a whistle which he sounded, and then placed the cards on the table. He then asked for the 5s. which was given to him. He placed the coins on the cards around a lighted candle. The pint of rum which he (witness) had brought was on the table and prisoner poured some of it into a pan. He went outside and sprinkled the rum at the four corners of the house. Accused came back in and said, 'Papa! papa! your case is very bad! There are two ghosts outside. Thc creole is bad, but the coolie is rather worse. But if he is made out of hell I will catch him.' The prisoner then began to blow his whistle in a very funny way—a way in which he had never heard a whistle blown before. He also began to speak in an unknown tongue and to call up the ghosts.

"Mr. Lake—'Aren't there a lot of you people who believe that ghosts can harm and molest you?'

Witness—'No, I am not one.'

Mr. Lake—'Did you not tell him that a duppy [Jamaican ghost] struck you on your back and you heard voices calling you?'

Witness—'He told me so.' Continuing, witness said he had seen all sorts of ghosts at all different times and of different kinds also.

Mr. Lake—'Of all different sexes, man and woman?'

Witness—'Yes; any man who can see ghosts will know a man ghost from a woman ghost. Dem never walk straight.'"

Today, Voodoo cults remain a living reality in Haiti. Voodoo is apparently a more complex matter than indicated by earlier commentators, and appears to be a powerful religion with both beneficent and decadent aspects. According to a recent study, *Voudoun Fire; The Living Reality of Mystical Religion* by Melita Denning & Osborne Phillips (1979), Voodoo has its roots in ancient powerful gods and goddesses from Africa. In their book they include astonishing color photographs of claimed paranormal light patterns observed during power points in Voodoo ceremonies.

On the decadent side, debased forms of Voodoo undoubtedly continue, with crude and distasteful black magic style rites. The zombies or living dead, associated with Voodoo practitioners, appear to be a reality, and are discussed in a separate entry. (See also **Obeah; Voodoo; Zombies**)

Recommended reading

Bell, Henry H. *Obeah; Witchcraft in the West Indies,* London, 1889; Greenwood, 1978

Denning, Melita & Osborne Phillips. *Voudoun Fire; The Living Reality of Mystical Religion,* Llewellyn Publications, St. Paul, Minnesota, 1979

Deren, Maya. *Divine Horsemen; The Voodoo Gods of Haiti,* Chelsea House, New York, 1970

Emerick, Abraham J. *Obeah and Duppyism in Jamaica,* privately printed, Woodstock, 1915

Huxley, Francis. *The Invisibles,* Rupert Hart-Davis, London, 1966

Métraux, Alfred. *Voodoo in Haiti,* Andre Deutsch, London, 1959

Williams, Joseph J. *Voodoos and Obeahs; Phases of West Indian Witchcraft,* Dial Press, 1932

Westcar Papyrus

An Egyptian papyrus dating from the eighteenth century B.C., devoted chiefly to tales of magic and enchantment. The commencement and ending are missing yet enough of the subject matter has survived to enable us to form a fairly correct idea of the whole.

Prof. Alfred Wiedemann, in his book *Popular Literature of Ancient Egypt* (1902), described these tales of magic and enchantment from 1800 B.C. as follows: "The papyrus tells how Kheops—the king whom notices of Greek writers have made universally famous as the builder of the Great Pyramid of Gizeh—commands stories of magic to be told to him. The first of these, of which the conclusion only remains, is supposed to have occurred in the reign of King T'eser of the Third Dynasty. The next, which is complete, belongs to the reign of Nebka, a somewhat earlier king.

"In those days it came to the ears of a great nobleman that his faithless wife was in the habit of meeting her lover by the side of a lake. Being skilled in magic he modelled a crocodile in wax and ordered one of his servants to cast it into the water. It was immediately transformed into a real crocodile and devoured the lover. Seven days later the king was walking by the lake with his friend the nobleman, when at the command of the latter the crocodile came to the shore and laid its victim at their feet. The king shuddered at the sight of the monster but at the touch of its maker it became once more a mere figure of wax. Then the whole astonishing story was told to the king, who thereupon granted the crocodile permission to take away that which was its own. The creature plunged into the depths of the lake and disappeared with the adulterer, while the guilty wife was burnt to death and her ashes were scattered in the stream.

"A tale of enchantment follows, the scene of which is laid during the reign of King Sneferu, the predecessor of Kheops. The king was one day taking his pleasure on a lake in a boat rowed by twenty beautiful maidens, when one of the girls dropped a malachite ornament into the water. The king promised to give her another in its stead, but this did not content her, for she wanted her own jewel and no other. A magician was summoned who repeated a spell by the might of which he piled one half of the lake on the top of the other, so that the water, which at first was twelve ells deep in the middle of the lake, now stood twenty-four ells high. The jewel, found lying in the mud in the dry portion of the lake, was restored to its owner; and the magician having once more mumbled his spell the water returned to its former place.

"When Kheops had listened for some time with much interest to the accounts of the strange events that had transpired in the days of his predecessors, then stepped forward Prince Horduduf, who is really known to us from the song in the tomb-temple of King Antef as renowned for his wisdom. He told the king that all marvels were not things of the past but that even then there was living a magician named Deda, who was one hundred and ten years old, and consumed every day five hundred loaves, a side of beef, and a hundred jars of beer.

"Kheops was so much interested that he sent the prince to escort the magician to his presence. Deda obeyed the royal summons and performed his chief feat before the king. This consisted in decapitating a goose, a duck, and an ox, and charming the heads back again on to the bodies so that the creatures lived and breathed as before. Kheops fell into talk with the magician, who told him that the wife of a priest in Sakhebu was awaiting the birth of three sons, children of the god Ra, who should one day sit on the throne of Egypt. Deda sought to allay the king's natural distress at this information by prophesying that only after the reigns of his son and grandson should the power fall into the hands of the descendants of the Sun-god. But Kheops was not to be consoled; he inquired into the details of the story and announced that he would himself travel to Sakhebu, no doubt with the ultimate intention of finding an opportunity to put out of the way the pretenders to his throne.

"The scene of the sequel is laid in Sakhebu. The birth and infancy of the three children are described in detail, and all sorts of marvellous incidents are represented as influencing their fate. The gods cared for the safety of the little ones. A maid to whom the secret was known being enraged by a severe punishment inflicted upon her, threatened to betray all to Kheops. Her own brother beat her, and when she went down to the water she was carried off by a crocodile. Here the papyrus ceases, but it is possible to a certain extent to restore the conclusion. The names of the three children of Ra show that they stand for the first three kings of the Fifth Dynasty, the family that followed the house of Kheops. The papyrus must therefore have told how the boys escaped all the snares laid for their lives and in due time ascended the throne for which they were destined." (See also **Egypt**)

Recommended reading

Budge, E. A. W. *Egyptian Magic,* Kegan, Paul, London, 1899

Maspero, G. *Les contes populaires de l'Egypte ancienne,* Paris, 1881

Wiedemann, A. *Popular Literature in Ancient Egypt,* David Nutt, London, 1902.

Westcott, William Wynn (1848-1925)

Prominent British occultist, one of the founders of the Hermetic Order of the **Golden Dawn.** Born December 1848 at Leamington, Warwickshire, England, he lost both parents before the age of ten and was adopted by Richard Wescott Martyn, an uncle who was surgeon by profession. Wescott was educated at the Queen Elizabeth Grammar School at Kingston-upon-Thames, London and studied medicine at University College, London

He qualified as a physician in 1871 and became a partner in his uncle's practice in Somerset, joining a Masonic Lodge in Crewkerne. After 1879, he removed to Hendon, where he studied occultism for two years.

About 1880, he became a leading member of the **Societas Rosicruciana in Anglia** (Rosicrucian Society of England). A year later he was appointed Deputy Coroner and later Coroner for North-East London. He wrote a number of articles for the Medical Directory, but his occultism remained a closely guarded secret.

In 1887, he acquired an old manuscript written in cipher, said to have been bought from a bookstall in Farringdon Road, London. In the pages of the manuscript was a sheet of paper with the name and address of Fraulein **Sprengel,** a Rosicrucian adept living in Germany. Westcott deciphered the manuscript, which contained fragments of mystical rituals.

These rituals were expanded by Westcott's occultist friend S. L. Macgregor **Mathers,** also a member of the Societas Rosicruciana in Anglia. Westcott thereupon corresponded with Fraulein Sprengel, who authorized him to found an English branch of the German occult society Die Goldene Dämmerung, and so Westcott, Mathers and Dr. W. R. **Woodman** thereupon founded the Isis-Urania temple of the Hermetic Order of the Golden Dawn in 1888. Westcott's occult motto in the order was "Sapere Aude" (Dare to Be Wise).

This is the official story of the foundation of the famous Golden Dawn order, but there is strong reason to suppose that the manuscript may have been an invention of Westcott or his associates, and that Fraulein Sprengel never existed. Correspondence with the lady has been produced, but competent students of occultism have doubted its genuineness.

For all that, the G.D. attracted some of the most eminent talents of its day, including poet W. B. **Yeats,** until it eventually degenerated into undignified squabbles, expulsions, resignations and complex fragmentation.

Meanwhile Westcott had retired from the G.D. by 1897, possibly through pressure relating to his official status as a coroner. He continued to be a member of the Soc. Ros. in Anglia, and after the death of Dr. Woodman in 1891 became Supreme Magus.

He published a number of short books or pamphlets on occult and mystical subjects, including: *Numbers: Their Occult Power and Mystic Virtue* (1890), *The Science of Alchymy* (1893), *The Pymander of Hermes* (1894), *Somnium Scipionis* (1894), *Rosicrucians, Their History and Aims* (1894), *Aesch Mezareph, or Purifying Fire* (1894), *The Chaldean Oracles of Zoroaster* (1895), *Egyptian Magic* (1896), *Sepher Yetzirah, the Book of Formation* (1911).

In his later years, Westcott removed to Durban, South Africa, where he became vice-president of two *Theosophical Society* lodges.

He died June 30, 1925.

Recommended reading
Gilbert, R. A. (ed.) *The Magical Mason; Forgotten Hermetic Writings of William Wynn Westcott,* Aquarian Press, Wellingborough, U.K., 1983

Westlake, Aubrey T(homas) (1893-1985)

Prominent British authority on **radiesthesia,** alternative medical therapies, and holistic health. Born in Redhill, Surrey, he was educated at the Quaker Sidcot school, and trained in medicine at Birmingham and Cambridge Universities and St. Bartholomew's Hospital, London (B.A., M.B., B.Ch., M.R.C.S., L.R.C.P.). He entered general practice in Bermondsey, London, where he married Marjorie Harrod (3 sons; 2 daughters). In 1938, they moved to the family estate at Fordingbridge, Hampshire, where Dr. Westlake continued the private practice of medicine.

He also spent many years investigating a wide range of alternative studies beyond the purely physical parameters of orthodox medical science, such as the **Bach** flower remedies, medical **dowsing,** radiesthesia, **radionics,** the Odic Force of Baron von **Reichenbach,** the **orgone** energy of Dr. Wilhelm **Reich, Huna,** homeopathy, and anthroposophical medicine.

In 1956, he formed a study group with several associates, investigating the use of radiesthesia techniques in healing patients at a distance.

The wide range of his inquiries is demonstrated in his important paper 'Vis Medicatrix Naturae,' given at the Scientific and Technical Congress of Radionics and Radiesthesia, London, May 16, 1950. He published a number of important articles, and a major work *The Pattern of Health* (1961).

He was a founder member of the Soil Association, and an active member of the Medical Society for the Study of Radiesthesia, an Honorary Fellow of the Radionic Association, an Honorary Life Vice-President of the **British Society of Dowsers,** and President of the Psionic Medical Society.

He died at the age of 92 in Fordingbridge, on October 30, 1985.

Westwood, Horace (1884-1956)

Unitarian minister who wrote on parapsychology. Born August 17, 1884 at Wakefield, England, he was ordained minister of the Methodist Episcopal Church in 1906, joined the Unitarian Church in 1910, D.D. 1914, Lombard College. In 1904 he married Lucy Ann Wright; second marriage 1920 to Elizabeth Ann Farrow.

He was pastor at Sault Ste. Marie, Michigan from 1906-08, First Unitarian Church, Youngstown, Ohio from 1910-12, All Soul's Church, Winnipeg, Manitoba, Canada from 1912-19, pastor at First Church, Toledo, Ohio from 1919-27, mission preacher, Unitarian Laymen's League, minister at large, Unitarian Church from 1927-33, minister at First Unitarian Church, Berkeley, California from 1934-45.

He studied psychic research for a number of years, and described his personal attitudes in his book *There Is a Psychic World* (1949). His other books were: *This Do and Live* (1938), *Apostle of Darkness and Prophet of Light* (1939).

He died December 24, 1956.

Weyer, Johan (also known as **John Wier** or **Wierus**) (1515-1588)

Protestant physician who compiled an inventory of devils in 1568, in which he estimated that there was an army of 7,405,926 devils and demons, organized in 1,111 divisions of 6,666 each. During the Reformation, this total was raised by the Lutherans, who calculated that the true figure was 2,665,866,746,664 devils.

However, in his major work *De Praestigiis Daemonum et Incantationibus ac Veneficiis* (Basel, 1568), Weyer denounced witch hunters for extracting confessions under torture, pointing out that extreme hardships would force even the most innocent to confess themselves guilty.

For a summary of Weyer's comprehensive book, see H. C. Lea, *Materials Toward a History of Witchcraft* (arr. and ed. Arthur C. Howland, 3 vols., 1957), vol. 2. (See also **Demonology; Devil**)

Weza

Burmese sorcerers. (See **Burma**)

Wheatley, Dennis (Yates) (1897-1977)

British author of many fictional works on occult themes. Described by a British newspaper as "the greatest adventure-writer of our time," Wheatley was writing enthralling stories about black magic and witchcraft during the first occult revival of the 1930s.

Although essentially a popular writer with a prodigious output, many of his occult thrillers have retained their appeal over several decades and are constantly reprinted; some have been filmed, others translated into twenty-seven different languages. A versatile individual, Wheatley traveled in fifty-six countries, became proprietor of a wine merchant business, was a member of Churchill's War Cabinet Secret Planning Committee, and invented (with J. G. Links) the Crime Dossier Murder series of fictional stories in the form of complete dossiers, with clues and reports, in the manner of a police file. Born January 8, 1897 in London, England, he was educated at Dulwich College (1911) and privately in Germany. Upon the death of his father in 1926 he became sole owner of a wine company. He served in the British Army in World War I from 1914-19, becoming second lieutenant. After the war he became a director of various companies. His first marriage in 1923 was to Nancy Madelaine Leslie Robinson; second marriage 1931 to Joan Gwendoline Johnstone.

From 1940-41, Wheatley toured England as a member of Sir John Anderson's panel of voluntary speakers on National Service. In 1945 he was a wing commander serving on Sir Winston Churchill's staff, and worked for three years in offices of the War

Cabinet. He was awarded U.S. Bronze Star. He was a member of the Royal Society of Literature (fellow), Royal Society of Arts (fellow), Old Comrades Association (president 1960), St. James' Club, Paternoster Club. His hobbies included collecting books, Georgian furniture, Persian rugs, stamps and fine wines, as well as building (he estimated he had laid more than sixty thousand bricks in his Hampshire garden).

His books included: *The Forbidden Territory* (1933, filmed), *Such Power is Dangerous* (1933), *Old Rowley (a Private Life of Charles II)* (1933), *Black August* (1934), *The Fabulous Valley* (1934), *The Devil Rides Out* (1935, filmed), *The Eunuch of Stamboul* (1935, filmed), *They Found Atlantis* (1936), (with J. G. Links) *Murder off Miami* (1936), *Contraband* (1936), *The Secret War* (1937), (with Links) *Who Killed Robert Prentice?* (1937), *Red Eagle; A Life of Marshal Voroshilov* (1937), *Uncharted Seas* (1938, filmed as *The Lost Continent*), *The Malinsay Massacre* (1938), *The Golden Spaniard* (1938), *The Quest of Julian Day* (1939), (with Links) *Herewith the Clues!* (1939), *Sixty Days to Live* (1939), *Those Modern Musketeers* (1939), *Three Inquisitive People* (1940), *The Scarlet Impostor* (1940), *Faked Passports* (1940), *The Black Baroness* (1940), *Strange Conflict* (1941), *The Sword of Fate* (1941), *Total War* (1941), *V for Vengeance* (1942), *Mediterranean Nights* (1942), *Gunmen, Gallants and Ghosts* (1943), *The Man Who Missed the War* (1945), *Codeword Golden Fleece* (1946), *Come Into My Parlour* (1946), *The Launching of Roger Brook* (1947), *The Shadow of Tyburn Tree* (1948), *The Haunting of Toby Jugg* (1948, filmed), *The Rising Storm* (1949), *The Seven Ages of Justerini* (company history of Justerini & Brooks, 1949), *The Second Seal* (1950), *The Man Who Killed the King* (1951), *Star of Ill Omen* (1952), *To the Devil—a Daughter* (1953), *Curtain of Fear* (1953), *The Island Where Time Stands Still* (1954), *The Dark Secret of Josephine* (1955), *The Ka of Gifford Hillary* (1956), *The Prisoner in the Mask* (1957), *Traitor's Gate* (1958), *Stranger Than Fiction* (1959), *The Rape of Venice* (1959), *The Satanist* (1960), *Saturdays With Bricks* (1961), *Vendetta in Spain* (1961), *Mayhem in Greece* (1962), *The Sultan's Daughter* (1963), *Bill for the Use of a Body* (1964), *They Used Dark Forces* (1964), *Dangerous Inheritance* (1965), *The Wanton Princess* (1966), *Unholy Crusade* (1968), *Evil in a Mask* (1969), *Gateway to Hell* (1970), *The Devil and All His Works* (1971), *The Ravishing of Lady Mary Ware* (1971), *The Strange Story of Linda Lee* (1971).

Wheatley also edited the Dennis Wheatley Library of the Occult, a series of reprints of significant occult books by other writers.

He died November 12, 1977.

Wheatley, J(ames) M(elville) O(wen) (1924-)

Assistant professor of philosophy, active in the field of parapsychology. Born February 29, 1924 at Guelph, Ontario, Canada, he studied at University of New Brunswick (B.S. 1947, M.A. 1949) and University of Toronto (Ph.D. philosophy 1957). In 1943 he married Marguerite Gallant (later divorced).

He was research assistant in physiology at University of Toronto from 1945-50, sessional lecturer in philosophy at University of New Brunswick from 1951-52, Ford Intern, philosophy and biology at Brown University from 1954-55, visiting assistant professor in philosophy at University of Alabama from 1955-56, lecturer, assistant professor of philosophy at University of Toronto from 1956 onwards.

He is a member of the American Association of University Professors, American Philosophical Association, associate member of Parapsychological Association; Governor-General's Gold Medal 1947, Beaverbrook Overseas Scholarship, University of London from 1950-61, partial fellowship, Humanities Research Council of Canada, 1954.

Dr. Wheatley has taken special interest in the philosophy of parapsychology, the question of survival, quantitative research in extrasensory perception, psychokinesis and epistemological aspects of psi. He worked with Dr. Karlis **Osis** in an exploratory study among college students of clairvoyance scores in card reading. He has contributed to various journals, including *Analysis, Canadian Forum, Journal* of the American Society for Psychical Research, *International Journal of Parapsychology.*

Whistling

Various superstitions are connected with whistling. It has long been considered unlucky for women to whistle. It was unlucky for sailors to whistle aboard ship. This was of the nature of sympathetic magic, as it was thought that it might raise a wind. It was also considered unlucky for miners to whistle in a mine, since this might be followed by an explosion.

A more recent superstition is that whistling in a theater or in the dressing rooms may cause the play to fail.

White, Rhea A(melia) (1931-)

Prominent American parapsychologist. Born May 6, 1931 in Utica, New York, she studied at Pennsylvania State University (B.A. 1953). She was a research fellow at the Parapsychology Laboratory, Duke University from 1954-58, research assistant at Foundation for Integral Research, 1959, research and editorial associate at **American Society for Psychical Research** from 1959-62, research fellow at Menninger Foundation, 1963. She was a charter member, secretary (1958, 1962), council member 1958, 1960-63), director of information, 1965 onwards, of the Parapsychological Association; assistant reference librarian, East Meadow, N.Y., 1965 onwards; librarian for psychiatry department, Maimonides Hospital, 1965-67; member of the Society for Psychical Research, London; member of research committee, publications committee, chairman, library committee, American Society for Psychical Research.

She is also a member of the American Library Association, Special Libraries Association, American Association for the Advancement of Science, Association of Transpersonal Psychology, Analytical Psychology Club of New York.

She has taken special interest in telepathy, clairvoyance and precognition, and investigated teacher-pupil attitudes related to clairvoyance test results, the relationship between various forms of attention to ESP success or failure, claimed telepathy in animals, ESP and creativity, subliminal perception.

Her articles in *Journal of Parapsychology* include: (with R. L. Van de Castle) 'A Report on a Sentence Completion Form of Sheep-Goat Attitude Scale' (vol. 19, No. 3, 1955), (with Margaret Anderson) 'Teacher-Pupil Attitudes and Clairvoyance Test Results' (vol. 20, No. 3, 1956) and 'A Further Investigation of Teacher-Pupil Attitudes and Clairvoyance Test Results' (vol. 21, No. 2, 1957) 'ESP Score Level in Relation to Students' Attitudes Toward Teacher-Agents Acting Simultaneously' (vol. 22, No. 1, 1958), 'The Relationship Between Changes in Student Attitude and ESP Scoring' (vol. 22, No. 3, 1958), 'A Survey of Work on ESP and Teacher-Pupil Attitudes' (vol. 22, No. 4, 1958). Other articles include: 'Depth Perspectives and Experimental Parapsychology (*International Journal of Parapsychology,* vol. II, No. 2, 1960); (in ASPR *Journal*): (with Jean **Angstadt**) 'A Résumé of Research at the A.S.P.R. into Teacher-Pupil Attitudes and Clairvoyance Test Results, 1956-1960' (vol. 55, No. 4, 1961) and 'Student Preferences in a Two Classroom GESP Experiment with Two Student Agents Acting Simultaneously' (vol. 57, No. 1, 1963), (with Laura A. **Dale** and Gardner **Murphy**) 'A Selection of Cases from a Recent Survey of Spontaneous ESP Phenomena' (vol. 56, No. 1, 1962), (with Frederick C. **Dommeyer**) 'Psychical Research in Colleges and Universities, Part I (vol. 57, No. 1, 1963), 'Comparison of Old and New Methods of Response to Targets in ESP Experiments' (vol. 58, No. 21-56, 1964).

She has also published the following books: (with Gardner Murphy) *Challenge of Psychical Research: A Primer of Parapsychology* (1961), (with Laura A. Dale) *Parapsychology: Sources of Information* (1973), *Surveys in Parapsychology: Reviews of the Literature, with Updated Bibliographies* (1976), (ed.) *Surveys in Parapsychology* (1976), contributor to *Advances in Parapsychological Research,* vol. 1, edited by Stanley Krippner (1977), (with Michael Murphy) *Spiritual Underground in Sports* (1978), *Bibliography and Index of Parapsychological Periodicals in English, 1937-1977* (1979).

She is managing editor of *Parapsychological Research: A Biennial Review* and has contributed to numerous publications on parapsychology.

With the establishment in 1983 of the Parapsychology Sources of Information Center (Psi Center), she has now created one of the most valuable resources for parapsychologists. The Center has a computerized database of the periodical literature of parapsychology, and has entered thousands of items into *PsiLine,* which provides computer searches online covering dissertations, chapters from books, psi-related publications. This service uses the Textbank software, and can be contacted at the Center by calling (516) 271-1243 weekdays between 9 a.m. and 3 p.m. or by mail.

In addition, the Center publishes *Parapsychology Abstracts International,* providing brief summaries of periodical literature from English, Spanish, Dutch, Portúguêse, Italian, German, French, Polish, Japanese, and Russian researchers. Other important publications of the Center include bibliographies on specific paranormal topics, and reading lists for students from grades 4 to 12, or the general public, or specialists. The address of the Center is: 2 Plane Tree Lane, Dix Hills, New York 11746.

White, Stewart Edward (1873-1946)

Author who published a number of books on parapsychological subjects. Born March 12, 1873 at Grand Rapids, Michigan, he studied at University of Michigan (Ph.B. 1895, M.A. 1903). In 1904 he married Elizabeth Grant (died 1939). He was a Fellow of the Royal Geographic Society, member of the American Association for the Advancement of Science, American Society for Psychical Research.

He published many books, articles and short stories dealing with his experiences in mining and lumber camps, and on exploration. In 1937 he wrote *The Betty Book,* dealing with statements by his wife while in trance, claimed to originate from entities named "The Invisibles." White believed that these messages embodied a valuable philosophy and religious interpretation for daily life. The second "Betty" book was *Across the Unknown* (1939).

After the death of his wife, White received communications apparently from her through a medium, and these were published in his book *The Unobstructed Universe* (1940). These books brought a large correspondence from readers seeking advice and further information, as a result of which White published further books: *The Road I Know* (1942), *Anchors to Windward* (1943), *The Stars Are Still There* (1946). His books *With Folded Wings* (1947) and *The Job of Living* (1948) were published posthumously.

He died September 18, 1946 at Hillsborough, California.

White Eagle Lodge

British Spiritualist organization founded in 1936, arising from the mediumship of Mrs. Grace **Cooke** and the teachings of her Red Indian spirit guide White Eagle. These teachings present "a way of life which is gentle and in harmony with the laws of life," involving the belief that "God, the eternal spirit, is both Father and Mother, and that the Son—the Cosmic Christ—is also the light which shines in every human heart."

The Lodge teaches that there is a unity which runs through all forms of life, visible and invisible, including the fairy and angelic kingdom. White Eagle puts forward five Cosmic Laws: (1) Reincarnation; the soul may return to earth many times until it has mastered all the lessons it must learn; (2) Cause and Effect: this is the belief in the Law of Karma, i.e.; "as you sow, so you will reap"; (3) Opportunity: every experience in life is an opportunity for an individual to become more Godlike and everyone is placed in exactly the right conditions needed "to learn lessons and give service"; (4) Correspondence: the belief that "as above, so below." The microcosm is part of the macrocosm. We are cells of the cosmos, just as our bodies, in turn, are made up of cells, with the same laws applying at all levels; (5) Equilibrium and Balance: the law connected to karma, described as "the Law of Compensation." It claims that no action can continue indefinitely, but will travel just as far before a reaction pulls things back to normal. Human joy and sorrow follow this law, i.e., extremes of emotion will eventually cause a reaction which pulls the soul back to normal.

The physical body is considered the outer garment of the soul, which includes subtler bodies of emotions and thoughts, and the spirit which is the heart of the soul and is known as the "Christ Spirit" or real self. Spiritual healing involves concentrating Divine power on the soul of the sick person to dissolve the disharmony causing the sickness. In Absent Healing, six healers sit as a group, sending out "rays of Spiritual Light." In Lone Healing, thirty-six healers combine their meditative healing from their own homes. In Contact Healing, there is a laying on of hands at special Lodge services. The Lodge also propagates "spiritual communion," a pure form of meditation.

Membership of the Lodge is in three stages—ordinary membership, progressing to Outer Brother and eventually to Inner Brother. The Lodge publishes the bimonthly magazine *Stella Polaris* which includes White Eagle teachings, answers to readers' questions and general articles on healing and meditation. Address: White Eagle Lodge, New Lands, Rake, Liss, Hampsire GU33, 7HY, England, and 9 St. Mary Abbot's Place, Kensington, London, W8 6L5, England. There are also branches in Scotland, Bournemouth, Plymouth, Worthing, Reading, and at New Jersey in the U.S. (See also Grace **Cooke**)

"White Sands Incident"

Title of a book by Daniel Fry, published 1954, claiming that the author saw a flying saucer land at White Sands Proving Ground, New Mexico and took a trip in it.

Fry has importance in UFO history as being the first modern contactee claiming to take a trip. (See also **UFO**)

Whiteman, J(oseph) H(ilary) M(ichael) (1906-)

Writer on mysticism, religion, philosophy, mathematics and physics, music, and parapsychology. He was born November 2, 1906, educated at Highgate School, London, Gonville & Caius College, Cambridge, University of Cape Town (Ph.D. & M.Mus.). From 1939-41 he was junior lecturer in Pure Mathematics, lecturer in Applied Mathematics 1941-53, senior lecturer 1953-62, associate professor 1962-71, Emeritus associate professor from 1972 onwards, University of Cape Town; lecturer in Music, Rhodes University College, Grahamstown, 1944-45; council member South African Society of Music Teachers from 1947 onwards (three times president). He was recipient of the Valkhoff Medallion from the South African Society for Psychical Research for his contributions to parapsychology.

He published some 100 editorial or other articles on Music in the *South African Music Teacher* journal, and also contributed to various symposia on Music. He also contributed some 40 papers on parapsychology and related subjects to various publications. His books include: *The Mystical Life* (1961), *Philosophy of Space and Time* (1967), 'Old and New Evidence on the Meaning of Life' vol. 1, *An Introduction to Scientific Mysticism* (1986), 'The Mystical Way, and Habitualizing of Mystical States' in *Handbook of States of Consciousness,* ed. B. Wolman (1986).

Whittlesey, John R. B. (1927-)

Data processing analyst who experimented in areas of parapsychology. Born July 21, 1927 in Los Angeles, California, he studied at California Institute of Technology (B.S. physics 1948, M.S. astronomy 1950), graduate study in mathematical statistics at University of North Carolina from 1951-54, Graduate School of Religion, University of Southern California from 1960-61.

He was instrumentation analyst in U.S. Army Ordnance from 1954-56, graduate research mathematician in Department of Psychiatry, University of California at Los Angeles from 1957-59, assistant research analyst, behavioral sciences and electronic data processing at Department of Psychiatry, UCLA Medical Center from 1959 onwards, in charge of electronic Data Processing Laboratory, Brain Research Institute, UCLA Medical Center from 1962 onwards, National Institutes of Health special research fellow from 1963-64.

Mr. Whittlesey designed an experiment in the use of the chemical LSD and analyzed data in its relation to extrasensory perception, working with several psychiatrists. He also designed and built an electronic device for experimental testing of precognition, using non-verbal responses from subjects influenced by drugs.

He has also taken special interest in computer statistics and probability as related to ESP, and ESP in its relationship to religion and mystical experience. He is co-author of various papers on LSD experiences read before the American Psychiatric Association and the California State Psychological Association. His articles in the *Journal of Parapsychology* include: 'Further Comments on Causality' (vol. 17, September 1953), 'Some Comments Apropos of Pooling' (vol. 23, June 1959), 'Some Curious ESP Results in Terms of Variance' (vol. 24, September 1960).

Whole Again Research Guide

Comprehensive annual directory and resource guide (incorporating *Guide to Psi Periodicals*), concerned with alternative technologies and therapies,

New Age teachings, psychic studies, spiritual growth, **yoga, UFOs,** nature religions, environmental issues, minority rights, etc. The Guide covers magazines, newspapers, journals, newsletters, sourcebooks, directories, and bibliographies. First published 1982, edited by Tim Ryan and Rae Jappinen, with nearly thirty contributors, including Elizabeth M. Werner (of *Guide to Psi Periodicals* and other publications) and Elisabeth Kübler-Ross. This is the most detailed and comprehensive publication of its kind. Address: SourceNet, Capra Press, P.O. Box 6767, Santa Barbara, California 93160.

Whole Life Expo (Fair)

Annual world fair concerned with **New Age** subjects, featuring leading pioneers and spokespeople in the fields of health, fitness, education, social action, science, the environment, **yoga,** spiritual growth, and related topics. Address: Whole Life Expo, National Headquarters, 803 Fourth Street, Suite 7, San Rafael, California 94901.

Whole Life Times; Journal for Personal and Planetary Health

Journal with a wide range of subject matter, including holistic health, macrobiotics, ecology, spiritual growth, **yoga, gurus,** and **myticism.** It features a National Calendar of events and personalities, as well as directory information. Address: The Whole Life Company, Inc., 18 Shepard Street, Brighton, Massachusetts 02135.

Whymant, (A.) Neville (John) (1894- ?)

Author and editor who investigated the phenomena of the medium George **Valiantine.** Born September 4, 1894 at Rothwell, England, he studied at Oxford University, England (Ph.D., Litt. D.). In 1920 he married Agnes Louisa Mayor.

During the early 1920s, he was professor of Oriental literature and philosophy at the Universities of Tokyo and Peking. He was Far East editor of the *New International Encyclopedia* from 1926-27; editorial staff of the *Encyclopedia Britannica* from 1927-29; foreign correspondent for *The Times* newspaper from 1929-31; editor of *The Indian Nation,* Patna. He was advisor to the embassy of the Republic of China in London from 1947-50.

In addition to various books on China and the Chinese, he published *Psychical Research in China* (1925), dealing with sand painting and "ghost photographs," and *Psychic Adventures in New York* (1928). Dr. Whymant was present at seances with the medium George Valiantine, who produced messages in ancient Chinese languages. A report of the phenomena was published in *Journal* of the American Society for Psychical Research (April 1928).

WICA Newsletter

Published monthly by Witchcraft International Craft Association, edited by Dr. Leo Louis **Martello.** Address: Hero Press, Suite 1B, 153 West 80 Street, New York, N.Y. 10024.

Apparently no longer published at this address.

Wicca

Believed to be an old term for Witchcraft or "Wisecraft," dating from Anglo-Saxon times. The word *wiccan* as a plural for witch was used in the ninth and twelfth centuries. The word witch or "wise woman" was *wicce* with the masculine form as *wicca.*

These terms have been widely used in the present-day occult revival as modern synonyms for witches and witchcraft. (See also **Witchcraft**)

Wickland, Carl August (1861- ?)

Physician and psychiatrist who spent thirty years researching and experimenting in psychical aspects of mental abberrations. Born February 14, 1861 in Leiden, Sweden, he qualified as M.D. at Dunham Medical College, Chicago, Illinois, becoming a member of Chicago Medical Society, Illinois State Medical Society, American Association for the Advancement of Science; medical advisor, National Psychological Institute, Los Angeles.

He claimed that discarnate spirits caused some phases of mental illness in the living, and his book *Thirty Years Among the Dead* (1924) reported his experiences, using the services of his wife as medium. Their work in diagnosing and treating mental patients believed to be obsessed by spirit entities had much in common with that of Dr. Titus **Bull.** Mrs. Wickland died in March 1937. (See also Titus **Bull; Rescue Circles**)

Wiesinger, Alois (1885-1955)

Abbot of the Cistercian Order, who was active in the field of parapsychology. Born June 3, 1885 at Magdalenaberg, Upper Austria, he was ordained 1909, D.Th. 1912. He studied at the University of Innsbruck.

He was professor of philosophy from 1912-17, Abbot of Cistercian Monastery, Schlierbach from 1917-55. He took a great interest in such parapsychological phenomena as poltergeist and materialization.

In addition to his writings on Christianity, he was editor-publisher of the journal *Glaube und Erkenntnis* (Journal for Christian Parapsychology) and author of *Okkulte Phanomene im Lichte der Theologie* (Occult Phenomena from the Theological Point of View, 1948). He also published the article 'Wie Stellt Sich der Katholik zu den okkulten Erscheinungen?' (The Attitude of the Catholic Toward Occult Phenomena, *Neue Wissenschaft,* 1953).

He died January 3, 1955 at Schlierbach, Upper Austria. The German periodical *Die Vergorgene Welt* published a tribute to his lasting contributions as a parapsychologist.

Wilber, Ken

Contemporary American writer on mysticism and transpersonal consciousness. For several years, he was editor-in-chief of the Journal *ReVision,* prior to its acquisition by Heldref Publications.

Wilber has taken a special interest in the study of new religions movements in the light of transpersonal psychology, arguing for a non-reductionistic approach, rooted in a transcendental structuralism, taking into account the various stages of human evolution and culminating in God-Realization. Wilber has hailed the mystic Da Free **John** as a New Age Avatar.

His publications include: *The Spectrum of Consciousness* (1977), *No Boundary* (1981), *Up From Eden; A Transpersonal View of Human Evolution* (1981), *A Sociable God; A Brief Introduction to a Transcendental Sociology* (1983), *Eye to Eye; The Quest for the New Paradigm* (1983), (with Jack Engler & Daniel P. Brown) *Transformation of Consciousness; Conventional and Contemplative Perspectives on Development* (1986).

Wild-Women

A species of nature spirits believed in by German peasants in former times. They were described as follows by Thomas Keightley in his book *The Fairy Mythology* (1850): concerning them: "The Wilde Frauen or Wild-women of Germany bear a very strong resemblance to the Elle-maids of Scandinavia. Like them they are beautiful, have fine flowing hair, live within hills, and only appear singly or in the society of each other. They partake of the piety of character we find among the German Dwarfs.

"The celebrated Wunderberg, or Underberg, on the great moor near Salzburg, is the chief haunt of the Wild-women. The Wunderberg is said to be quite hollow, and supplied with stately palaces, churches, monasteries, gardens, and springs of gold and silver. Its inhabitants, besides the Wild-women, are little men, who have charge of the treasures it contains, and who at midnight repair to Salzburg to perform their devotions in the cathedral; giants, who used to come to the church of Grödich and exhort the people to lead a godly and pious life; and the great emperor Charles V., with golden crown and sceptre, attended by knights and lords. His grey beard has twice encompassed the table at which he sits, and when it has the third time grown round it, the end of the world and the appearance of the Antichrist will take place.

"The following is the only account we have of the Wild-women.

"The inhabitants of the village of Grödich and the peasantry of the neighbourhood assert that frequently, about the year 1753, the Wild-women used to come out of the Wunderberg to the boys and girls that were keeping the cattle near the hole within Glanegg, and give them bread to eat.

"The Wild-women used frequently to come to where the people were reaping. They came down eagerly in the morning, and in the evening, when the people left off work, they went back into the Wunderburg without partaking of the supper.

"It once happened near this hill, that a little boy was sitting on a horse which his father had tethered on the headland of the field. Then came the Wild-women out of the hill and wanted to take away the boy by force. But the father, who was well acquainted with the secrets of this hill, and what used to occur there, without any dread hasted up to the women and took the boy from them, with these words: 'What makes you presume to come so often out of the hill, and now to take away my child with you? What do you want to do with him?' The Wild-women answered: 'He will be better with us, and have better care taken of him than at home. We shall be very fond of the boy, and he will meet with no injury.' But the father would not let the boy out of his hands, and the Wild-women went away weeping bitterly.

"One time the Wild-women came out of the Wunderberg, near the place called the Kugelmill, which is prettily situated on the side of this hill, and took away a boy who was keeping cattle. This boy, whom every one knew, was seen about a year after by some wood-cutters, in a green dress, and sitting on a block of this hill. Next day they took his parents with them, intending to search the hill for him, but they all went about it to no purpose, for the boy never appeared any more." (See also **Fairies)**

Will

Many attempts have been made in the past to prove that the human will is a dynamic energy. The earliest experimental apparatus was constructed by M. E. Savary d'Odiardy. An investigation of the instrument by the Society for Psychical Research, London (*Proceedings,* vol.8, p. 249) disproved claims.

Another instrument was designed by Dr. Sydney Alrutz, of the University of Uppsala, Sweden. He called it a "**Volometer**" or "Will Board." It comprised a small board resting on knife-edged pegs. The longer and heavier end was supported by means of a string attached to a letter scale and held the board in horizontal position. In this position the scale registered a pressure of five ounces. If the short end was depressed, the long end rose and the letter scale showed a decrease of weight.

The task put before the subjects of Dr. Alrutz's experiments was to fix their attention on the long end and will its depression. In a number of cases, 40-100 grammes of pressure was thus obtained. Among those who made the experiments were many members of the Sixth Psychological Congress at Geneva in August, 1909.

Professor Theodore **Flournoy** wrote after his own test: "I was able to prove conclusively, after three trials, and under conditions precluding all possibility of fraud or illusion, that the will of these ladies, concentrated upon a certain material object, with a desire to produce a movement in it, ended by producing this movement as if by means of a fluid or an invisible force obeying their mental command."

These results seemed conclusive. One may wonder, however, whether some of the old Mesmerists would not have attributed the success to "mesmeric fluid" instead of the direct action of the will. Spiritualists might conclude that ectoplasmic emanation in an incipient stage was responsible for the result. The experiences with the medium Eusapia **Palladino** certainly bear out this possibility. She could move a stool by placing her hand above it and make it follow her over the floor. She could even transfer this power to somebody else by placing her hand over the shoulder. As long as her hand was kept there the stool obeyed a stranger as well.

Similar power was noticed by Dr. Ochorowitz in Mlle. Stanislawa **Tomczyk.** Eusapia Palladino used to say that she could move objects if her will was sufficiently "solid."

Other devices for testing a claimed human psychic force have often been too sensitive to heat or air current changes to permit definite conclusions, moreover they have not indicated the kind of powerful force effects demonstrated by Eusapia Palladino. (See also **Biometer of Baradac; De Tromelin Cylinder; Sthenometer; Magnetometer**)

Willett, Mrs.

(Pseudonym of medium Winifred Margaret Serocold **Coombe-Tennant**).

William Rufus (William II of England) (c.1056-1100)

Son of William the Conqueror, and tyrant of England in the eleventh century; a wicked and cruel prince. He was much disliked, particularly by priests and monks, whom he reduced to the extremest poverty.

One day when he was out hunting in the year 1100 (the forty-fourth year of his life, the thirtieth of his reign), he was killed by an arrow launched by an invisible hand. There is a legend that while Rufus was drawing his last breath, the Comte de Comonailles, who had been separated from the hunt, saw a shaggy black goat carrying off a mangled human form, pierced by an arrow.

The Comte cried aloud to the goat to halt, and asked who he was, and where he was going. The goat responded that he was the devil, and was carrying off William Rufus, to present him before the great tribunal, where he would be condemned for his tyranny and forced to accompany him (the devil) to his abode.

Williams, Bessie (c. 1894)

British clairvoyant, **trance** and healing medium, later known as Mrs. Fitzgerald and Mrs. Russell Davies. Her spirit **control** was "Dewdrop," claimed to be a Red Indian girl, who played all the tricks of a mischievous secondary personality on the medium, such as controlling her in an omnibus and talking Indian loudly until the passengers were frightened that they were traveling with a lunatic.

For a long time, Miss Williams assisted a well-known spiritualist healer called Dr. Mack as a medical diagnoser. She gave her services free. As,however, she took on all the symptoms of the illnesses diagnosed, her failing health compelled her, after a while, to give up this pursuit.

Enthusiastic accounts of her mediumship are contained in Florence **Marryat**'s books *There Is No Death* (1892) and *The Spirit World* (1894). Florence Marryat also edited the book *The Clairvoyance of Bessie Williams. Related by Herself* (1893).

W. T. Stead thought highly of the medium's powers, and included articles by her on the subject of haunted houses in his journal *Borderland.*

Williams, Charles (c. 1878)

British **materialization** medium, claiming the spirit **control** "John King," working from 1871 onwards, in partnership with fellow medium Frank **Herne.** They gave public seances at 61 Lamb's Conduit Street, in west central London. The first was held under the patronage of the medium Mrs. **Guppy.** The famous **transportation** of Mrs. Guppy occurred at one of these seances.

Williams often sat with the Rev. W. Stainton **Moses,** but the results were always very meager. Stainton Moses was in doubt about the genuineness of the mediumship of Williams, and asked his controls for information. They were reluctant to give it. Catherine Berry's book *Experiences in Spiritualism* (1876) and A. Smedley's *Some Reminiscences* (1900) contained enthusiastic accounts, but fraud was often suspected and at least in one case glaringly proved.

In Paris, at a seance on May 14, 1874, an attempt was made to seize "John King." He eluded the grasp and left a piece of drapery behind, the further history of which is not known. The medium was found in his seat. The search of his person revealed nothing suspicious.

In 1878, the Research Committee of the **British National Association of Spiritualists** constructed a **cabinet** with an automatic recording apparatus. An observer sat in another cabinet with a lighted lamp to make the readings. In a sitting with Williams, a spirit form appeared, sometimes ten or twelve feet from the cabinet. There appearances corresponded with fluctuations recorded by the self-registering apparatus. The maximum loss of weight amounted to 100 pounds. There was no weight in the cabinet which could have been fixed on the weighing platform.

The objection of researcher Frank **Podmore** that the medium need only have fastened the suspended cabinet to the floor by a gimlet or a piece of string could not explain the extreme variations in weight.

It was a few months after this experiment that in a Spiritualist circle in Amsterdam, Williams and his fellow medium, A. **Rita,** were exposed. " Charlie," a materialized spirit, was seized and found to be identical with Rita. Many handkerchiefs, a bottle of phosphorized oil, several yards of very dirty white muslin, a false black beard, with brown silk ribbon and other paraphernalia were found on the persons of the two mediums.

During a visit to Russia, Prof. Boutlerof and Alexander **Aksakof** had very convincing experiences.

In a note to Prof. Boutlerof's account in *Psychische Studien,* Aksakof added: "I can testify to having received the confirmation of the appearance of John King from Mr. Crookes in his own house, Mrs. Crookes' hand being on William's shoulder while while he was asleep behind the curtain; also that in the house of Mrs. MacDougall Gregory, the curtain behind which Williams was placed was in a niche almost hermetically sealed; and that John King appeared above the table, round which the company were assembled in front of the curtain."

Williams, Mrs. M. A. (c. 1894)

American **materialization** medium. Florence **Marryat** who sat with her in a public seance in New York without being introduced, described in her book *There is No Death* (1892) the appearance of her daughter Florence, exactly the same as she had seen her in Europe under the different mediumship of Florence **Cook,** Arthur **Colman,** Charles **Williams** and William **Eglinton.**

Another familiar apparition was "Joey," the spirit **control** of William Eglinton. Altogether forty different materializations were witnessed that evening.

In 1894, Mrs. Williams was the guest of the Duchess of Pomar in Paris. Paul Leymarie, the son of the editor of *La Revue Spirite,* slipped behind the curtain during the seance and grasped the spirit. On lights being brought, Mrs. Williams was found in flesh tights and the whole apparatus of her fraudulent spirit puppet-show was discovered in the cabinet.

Williamson, Cecil H.

Contemporary British occultist who claimed to conjure up spirits by ritual magic. An expert on witchcraft, he is proprietor of a museum of black magic and witchcraft known as the Witches' House, situated in the small Cornish village of Bocastle, England, near Tintagel.

The museum was originally based at Bourton-on-the-Water in the Cotswold countryside, but closed about 1966 and was removed to Cornwall.

Williamson was formerly an associate and friend of witchcraft revivalist Gerald B. **Gardner.** He was a graduate of Malvern College and spent some time as a tobacco planter in Rhodesia. During World War II he was in the British Intelligence Service. (See also **Museum of Magic and Witchcraft**)

Williamson, George Evans (1887-   )

Businessman active in South African parapsychology. Born January 14, 1887 at Malvern, England, he studied at Rugby School from 1900-05; M.A., LL.B. 1908, Cambridge University, England. In 1915 he married Lina Katherine Goddard; second marriage 1934 to Rita Sanders.

He was called to the bar in England in 1909, served in British Army from 1914-18, retiring as captain. He was in business in England from 1918-39, in South Africa thereafter. He was a founding member and president for some years of Cape Town Psychic Club and Library, and a Fellow of the College of Psychic Science, London.

Willington Mill

A famous British haunted house. The story of the Mill was reported in the *Journal* of the Society for Psychical Research, London (vol. 5 pp. 341, 348). It was owned by Mr. Proctor, who was quite used to the ghosts. The following extracts give some idea of the manifestations:

"When two of Mrs. Proctor's sisters were staying at the Mill on a visit their bed was suddenly violently shaken, the curtains hoisted up all round to their tester, and then as rapidly let down again, and this again in rapid succession. The curtains were taken off the next night, with the result that they both saw a female figure, of mysterious substance and of a greyish-blue hue, come out of the wall at the head of the bed and lean over them. They both saw it distinctly. They saw it come out of and go back again into the wall . . . Mrs. Davidson's sister-in-law had a curious experience on one occasion. One evening she was putting one of the bedrooms aright, and, looking towards the dressing table, saw what she supposed was a white towel lying on the ground. She went to pick it up, but imagine her surprise when she found that it rose up, and went behind the dressing table over the top, down on the floor across the room, disappearing under the door, and was heard to descend the stairs with a heavy step! The noise which it made in doing so was distinctly heard by Mr. Proctor and others in the house."

The old mill foreman saw a bald-headed luminous figure at a window. The body was as brilliant as a star, diffusing a radiance all round, then it turned a bluish tinge and gradually faded away from head downwards. One of the little girls living in the house said on one occasion: "There is a lady sitting on the bed in Mamma's bedroom. She has eyeholes but no eyes, and she looked so hard at me."

It was the opinion of Andrew Lang that the noises and apparitions at Willington Mill were a stimulus to the novelist Bulwer Lytton in writing his famous supernatural story *The Haunted and the Haunters.*

For a detailed report of the Willington Mill phenomena, see the book *The Haunted and the Haunters by Lord Lytton, With an Introduction; and an account of the Haunted House at Willington* by Harold Armitage, published by Simpkin, Marshall, London, 1925.

Willis, Dr. F. L. H. (c. 1880)

Professor of Materia Medica in a New York college, who was hounded out of Harvard University in 1857 because of his psychic faculties. He came from a respected family in Cambridge, Mass., and was a good speaker, and an improvisor of poetry. While studying for Divinity at Harvard, he was discovered to be a strong physical medium and as a result of charges brought against him by Professor Eustis, he was expelled from the University.

Dr. Willis produced **apports, direct writing,** direct **music,** was levitated, had gifts of healing and once, controlled by the spirit of "Dr. Mason," performed a difficult operation on a lady while he was in trance. This feat was achieved prior to his medical studies.

He was charged with simulating spiritual phenomena at Harvard, although the genuineness of the phenomena were attested by the famous author and reformer Thomas Wentworth Higginson.

Dr. Willis was known to Epes **Sargent,** author of *The Scientific Basis of Spiritualism* (1880), who published in this book extracts from a letter written by Dr. Willis in May 1879 regarding his materialization of spirit hands. Dr. Willis wrote: "It is twenty-three years ago that these materializations of hands occurred. . . . On one occasion a gentleman present drew a knife from his pocket with a long, keen blade, and taking no one into his counsel, watching his opportunity, pierced with a violent blow one of the psychic hands. The medium [Willis] uttered a shriek of pain. The sensation was precisely as if the knife had passed through his hand. The gentleman sprang to his feet exultant, thinking he had made a most triumphant exposé of trickery, and fully expected to find the medium's hand pierced and bleeding. To his utter chagrin and amazement there was no trace of a scratch even upon either hand of the medium; and yet to him the sensation was precisely as if the knife had passed through muscle and tendon, and the sensation of pain and soreness remained for hours . . . "

This account of early materialization of spirit hands, long before the days of Eusapia **Palladino** and other physical mediums, is of special interest for its claim that violence to pseudopodic **ectoplasm** reacts painfully upon the medium.

Dr. Willis described events in his life during a lecture at the Spiritual Institute in London, in 1869, published in *The Spiritual Magazine* (1870, p. 193) and in *Human Nature* (1869, p.573). For an account of his mediumship see *Modern American Spiritualism* by Emma Hardinge [Britten] (1870, pp. 173-185).

Willow Tree

There are many superstitions connected with the willow, ever since, according to the authorized version of the English Bible, the Israelites were said to have hung their harps on willow trees. The weeping willow was said to have drooped its branches ever since the time of the captivity of the Jews in Babylon, in sympathy with this circumstance.

The common willow was once popularly believed to be under the protection of the devil, and it was said that, if any were to cast a knot upon a young willow, and sit under it, and thereupon renounce his or her baptism, the devil would confer upon them supernatural power.

It was believed in Bulgaria that a fever would depart if you ran three times round a willow tree at sunset, crying "The fever shall take thee and the sun shall warm me."

Wilson, Cedric W(illiam) M(alcolm) (1925-)

Lecturer in pharmacology who has also written on parapsychology. Born November 23, 1925 in Edinburgh, Scotland, he studied at University of Edinburgh (B.Sc. 1947, M.C. Ch.B. 1949, Ph.D. 1954, M.D. 1958). In 1951 he married Joan M. Russell.

He had a distinguished medical career, and was lecturer in pharmacology and general therapeutics at University of Liverpool from 1955, member of the British Pharmacological Society, Physiological Society, Society for Psychical Research.

In addition to his articles on medical and pharmacological subjects, he has contributed to the *Journal of Parapsychology* and the *International Journal for Parapsychology.* Dr. Wilson also conducted experiments on the telepathic control of automatic responses and the influence of drugs on such responses.

Wilson, Colin (Henry) (1931-)

Perceptive British writer on occultism who attracted worldwide attention with his first book *The Outsider.* Born June 26, 1931 in Leicester, England, he was educated at the Gateway School, Leicester, and worked on a great variety of jobs before finding his true profession as a writer. In 1947 he was employed by a wool company, from 1947-48 was a laboratory assistant at a secondary technical school, from 1947-49 he was a tax collector, and after that a laborer, digging ditches, worker in a plastics factory, hospital porter, and office worker. He spent time in Germany and France, and while in Paris worked on *Merlin* and *Paris Review.* His first marriage was to Dorothy Betty Troop in 1951 (separated 1952), second marriage to Pamela Joy Stewart in 1960.

While preparing his first book *The Outsider* (1956), Wilson researched at public libraries, slept outdoors, and wrote in coffee houses. The book was an instant success, and the term "outsider" passed into common use to denote a type of brilliant misfit capable of surveying life in an original way.

As an outsider himself, Wilson's other writings have often displayed originality, and in recent years he has achieved the status of an authority on the occult for his many writings and reviews in this subject area.

His major study *The Occult* is a substantial work, full of valuable research and fresh viewpoints. It was first published by Hodder & Stoughton, London, and Random, New York, 1971, subsequently in paperback in 1973. Wilson was writer-in-residence at Hollins College, Virginia from 1966-67, but now lives in Cornwall, England. He was awarded a Ford Foundation Grant 1961, and is a member of Society of Authors, Dionysus Club (London), Gentleman's Club (Cornwall), Savage Club (London).

His non-fiction works include: *The Outsider* (1956), *Religion and the Rebel* (1957), *The Age of Defeat* (1959, U.S. title *The Stature of Man), The Strength of Dream* (1962), *Origins of the Sexual Impulse* (1962), (with Patricia Pitman) *An Encyclopedia of Murder* (1962), *Rasputin and the Fall of the Romanovs* (1964), *The Brandy of the Damned* (1964, U.S. title *Chords and Discords* 1966), *Beyond the Outsider* (1965), *Eagle and Earwig* (1965), *Introduction to the New Existentialism* (1966), *Voyage to a Beginning* (autobiography, 1966), *Bernard Shaw; A Reassessment* (1969), *Poetry and Mysticism* (1969), *Case Book of Murder* (1969), *The Philosopher's Stone* (1969), *The Occult* (1971), *New Pathways in Psychology* (1972), *Strange Powers* (1973), *Reich, Borges, Hesse* (1973), *The Craft of the Novel* (1975), *Mysterious Powers* (U.S. title *They Had Strange Powers,* (1975), *The Unexplained* (1975), *Enigmas and Mysteries* (1976), *The Geller Phenomena* (1976), (ed.) *Dark Dimensions; A Celebration of the Occult* (1978), *Mysteries; An Investigation into the Occult, The Paranormal, and the Supernatural* (1978), *Science Fiction as Existentialism* (1978), (with George Hay) *Necronomicon* (1978), (with John Grant) *Directory of Possibilities* (1981), *The Quest for Wilhelm Reich* (1981), *Poltergeist* (1981), *Anti-Sartre* (1981), *Access to luner Worlds* (1982), *The Criminal History of Mankind* (1981), (with Donald Seaman) *Modern Encyclopedia of Murder* (1983), *Psychic Detectives* (1983), *Jung; The Lord of the Underworld* (1984), *Afterlife* (1985), *Rudolf Steiner; The Man and His Work* (1985), *The Personality Surgeon* (1985), *Existential Essays* (1985), *The Essential Colin Wilson* (1985), (with Donald Seaman) *An Encyclopedia of Scandal* (1986), (with Christopher Evans, eds.) *Great Mysteries* (1986), *Beyond the Occult* (1988), *The Magician from Siberia* (1988).

His works of fiction include: *Ritual in the Dark* (1960), *Adrift in Soho* (1961), *The Violent World of Hugh Greene* (1963, British title *World of Violence*), *Man Without a Shadow: The Diary of an Existentialist* (1963), *The Sex Diary of Gerard Sorme* (1963), *Necessary Doubt* (1964), *The Glass Cage* (1966), *The Mind Parasites* (1966), *The Philosopher's Stone* (1969), *The Killer* (U.S. title *Lingard,* 1970), *The God of the Labyrinth* (U.S. title *The Hedonists,* 1971), *Strindberg; Playscript 31* (1970), *The Black Room* (1971), *The Schoolgirl Murder Case* (1974), *Return of the Lloigor* (1974), *The Space Vampires* (1975). He also published the following plays: "Viennese Interlude" (1960), "The Metal Flower" (1960), "The Death of God" (1966), "Pictures in a Bath of Acid" (1970).

Wilson, Graham (1940-)

New consciousness entrepreneur who organized the international annual **Mind-Body-Spirit Festivals.** Born in Yorkshire, England, he spent his preschool years on a farm. After World War II his family returned to London, where Wilson attended Wandsworth Grammar School, studying advanced level Zoology and Botany, and investigating the writers of Rudolph Steiner and other mystics in his spare time. He was also active in sports, and became London Youth Athletics champion for the the half-mile and cross country events at the age of 18. He played Rugby and soccer football as well as squash, and took a great interest in the "peak" experiences of athletes.

After a varied business career, Wilson teamed up with Terry Ellis in 1976 to hire an exhibition hall in London and present the first Festival for Mind and Body, drawing upon his own knowledge of mystical and spiritual philosophies and athletic experiences. He put all his own money into the venture which was presented in April 1977 in London. It was a success, and led to successive annual festivals in Britain and America.

In organizing these festivals, Wilson and his associates have provided a regular focal point for **New Age** and mystical activities, and he himself believes that "you can use the best of the commercial world to allow in a spiritual flow in such a way that the final product has quality and integrity."

Wilson, John C.

Pseudonym of Felix **Morrow,** pioneer publisher of occult and metaphysical books under the imprint of University Books, Inc.

Wilson, Percy (1893-)

Electronics and acoustics consultant who also wrote on psychical subjects. Born March 8, 1893 in Halofax, Yorkshire, England; M.A. 1918, Oxford. In 1919 he married Dorothy Jennett Kingston (died 1949); second marriage in 1952 to Elizabeth Muriel Smith (died 1961); third marriage in 1962 to Winifred Berry.

Mr. Wilson was head of Roads Department, Ministry of Transport, London from 1938-49, technical editor of *The Gramophone* magazine from 1924 onwards, chairman of Psychic Press, consultant in electronics and acoustics.

He was president of the **Spiritualists' National Union** from 1950-53, member of the Society for Psychical Research, London, vice-president of the College of Psychic Science, London. He was author of the books *Modern Gramophones* (1929) and *The Gramophone Handbook* (1957), and also published a number of articles on physical and trance mediumship, clairvoyance, clairaudience and healing in the periodicals *Two Worlds, Psychic News* and *Light.*

Wilson, Richard (1926-)

Physics professor who has been active in the field of parapsychology. Born April 29, 1926 in London, England, he studied at Oxford University (M.S., Ph.D., 1929) and Harvard University, Mass. (M.A. hon. 1957). In 1952 he married Andrée DesireAe DuMond.

He was research lecturer at Christ Church, Oxford from 1948-53, research associate at University of Rochester, New York from 1950-51, research associate at Stanford University, California from 1951-52, research associate at Oxford University from 1953-55, assistant professor (1955-57), associate professor (1957-61), professor (1961 onwards) at Harvard University.

He is a member of the American Physical Society, Physical Society (London), American Academy of Arts and Sciences, corresponding member of the

Society for Psychical Research, London, assistant editor of *Annals of Physics.* Dr. Wilson devised a random number selector for extrasensory perception, reporting on his experiments in 'A Random Number Selector' (*Proceedings,* American Society for Psychical Research, vol.48, 1946-49).

Winds (Paranormal)

Paranormal breezes, currents of air or cooling of temperature, are frequently reported seance room phenomena, as well as traditionally associated with the subjective effects of hauntings. We do not know the means by which the effects are brought about and it is an open speculation whether they serve a direct purpose or are only byproducts. In some cases, such effects are a subjective experience, but in others, the phenomenon is an objective and measurable reality.

Such thermic manifestations are a great convenience both for the sitters and the medium, who sometimes suffer excessively from perspiration. It is difficult to allot the part which the organism of the sitters and of the medium plays in the phenomenon. Sometimes the source is plainly the medium.

The spouting fountain of air of which psychical researcher Prof. C. **Lombroso** wrote in his account of seances with Eusapia **Palladino** issued from a depression on the medium's forehead. This depression was due to an accident in childhood. It is interesting to recall that the center of the forehead is one of the **chakras** or mystical centers in **Yoga** meditation.

Dr. Hereward **Carrington** noticed that after a good seance the breeze was strong, and after a poor one it was altogether lacking. Yet the breeze is not normally an after-seance effect. It usually precedes and heralds strong physical phenomena.

Mrs. Celestine **Sanders,** a New York medium, used to feel so unnaturally cold during her seances that she enveloped herself in many coverings and shawls to counteract the effect.

The chilly feeling with which apparitions are accompanied may, for all we know, be the result of a sudden drop in the temperature. All those who saw the apparition of a wooden cross in the Haunted B. House (see **Haunting**) felt unnaturally cold.

"Walter," the spirit **control** of the medium "Margery" (Mrs. Mina S. **Crandon**), said that the cold breezes and the drop in temperature was the result of some psychic emanation from the sitters' brains. This emanation might be more or less profuse and it might affect the thermometer before being actually used for the phenomena.

"Walter" found immense pleasure in using the thermometer as an indicator of the physical conditions confronting him. He said that he looked at it and if it was steady he used "Margery" alone, if it was going down, he used the sitters' brains as well. If he used "Margery" alone no cold breezes or drop in temperature was produced.

"Walter's" statement contains nothing new. A control of the famous medium D. D.**Home** said more than half a century earlier: "It is through your brains that the atmosphere we make use of is thrown off."

It is curious to note that at a still earlier age the phenomenon was a great puzzle to the seer Emanuel **Swedenborg.** He wrote in his *Spiritual Diary:* "A spirit is compared to the wind (*John* iii, 8); hence it is that spirits have come to me both now, and very frequently before, with wind, which I felt in the face; yea, it also moved the flame of the candle, and likewise papers; the wind was cold, and indeed most frequently when I raised my right arm, which I wondered at, the cause of which I do not yet know."

The same experience has been recorded with many physical mediums. Lord **Adare,** in a seance with D. D. Home, heard the sound of a great wind. "We also felt the wind strongly," he wrote "the moaning, rushing sound was the most weird thing I ever heard."

Sir William **Crookes** wrote in *Researches into the Phenomena of Spiritualism* (1874): "These movements, and indeed, I may say the same of every kind of phenomenon, are generally preceded by a peculiar cold air, sometimes amounting to a decided wind. I have had sheets of paper blown about by it, and a thermometer lowered several degrees. On some occasions I have not detected any actual movement of the air, but the cold has been so intense that I could only compare it to that felt when the hand has been within a few inches of frozen mercury."

In the experiments at the **Millesimo Castle** with the Marquis **Centurione Scotto,** the psychical researcher Ernesto **Bozzano** recorded: "On the evening of July 7, 1928, the heat was very oppressive... we happened to mention this disadvantage, and immediately blasts of unusually strong, icy air were felt by us all. . . . There was a continual change in the direction from which these air currents came; sometimes they descended from the ceiling, then we felt them in front of us, or at our side, or blowing from behind us; sometimes they were like small whirlwinds. It felt as though several electric fans were working in the centre, outside and above the circle."

In the next seance, the phenomenon was repeated and perfected: "Almost immediately we felt strong blasts of icy air which rapidly increased in force, giving one the impression of a powerful supernormal electric fan which periodically wafted its pleasant, cooling currents of air over the sitters . . . These currents were so strong that our hair waved in the wind, and men's coats, and the lace on the ladies' dresses were blown about."

Ernesto Bozzano added that not the slightest sound accompanied the production of this phenomenon. The breezes sometimes brought down the temperature of the seance room by as much as 20 degrees.

Prof. George **Henslow** described the sensations of the sitters of Dr. T. d'Aute **Hooper** of Birmingham, England, as of that of "an intensely cold dew or mist, as though a vapour of methylated spirit were floating about the room." While **apports** were being produced, "the sitters felt as if they were sitting up to their knees in cold water."

The psychihcal researcher Harry **Price** established a definite connection between the phenomenon of **telekinesis** and the drop in temperature. In his experiments with the medium **Stella C.** at the **National Laboratory of Psychical Research** he noticed a maximum drop of 20.5 degrees Fahrenheit. At the close of the seance the temperature was again normal. But often the drop in the temperature of the room was permanent. The medium's temperature was always higher at the end of the sitting, but she herself always complained of feeling cold. The rapidity of her pulse beats was always accompanied in the trance by a pronounced coldness in the extremities.

In the "Margery" seances, a maximum-and-minimum thermometer was employed to measure the temperature. In one case the initial temperature dropped from 68 to 42, a difference of 26 degrees. After the breezes had been blowing for a while "Margery" often complained of feeling as though cobwebs were on her face.

General experience as regards the nature of the cold breezes was curiously contradicted in an address of the British clairvoyant Robert King (*Light,* April 25, 1903). He stated that the peculiar cold air of the seance room is not a wind, "it does not move things. I have watched pieces of paper placed on the table when these cold airs have been playing around. If a wind of that intensity had been blowing, the paper would have been moved, so I rather incline to the opinion that this phenomenon is due to a difference in pressure caused by abstraction of etheric matter from the sitters." (See also **Emanations; Psychic Force**)

Recommended reading:

Hack, Gwendolyn Kelley. *Modern Psychic Mysteries,* Rider & Co. (1929).

Windsor Castle

One of the largest inhabited castles in the world. Windsor Castle, in Berkshire, England, is one of the royal residences and headquarters of the Order of the Garter.

The Castle is said to be the haunt of numerous specters. Queen Elizabeth, Henry VIII, Charles I, and some of the Georges have all been reputed to haunt the Castle, while Herne the Hunter is also said to roam in the twelve-acre Great Park.

In February 1897, Lieutenant Carr Glynn of the Grenadier Guards, was sitting in the library reading in the twilight when he heard a rustle of silken dress, and, looking up, saw the ghost of Queen Elizabeth I glide across the room. He buckled on his sword, and reported the matter. The story attracted the attention of the country for some weeks. Sir Richard Holmes and his assistants kept watch for many nights, but the ghost did not reappear.

On another occasion, a housemaid in St. John's Tower thought she saw a ghost, and was so frightened that she became ill, and had to be sent home.

In 1908, a sentry discharged five rounds of ball cartridge at a figure which he declared was a specter which appeared on the terrace.

A famous ghost is that of Sir George Villiers, father of the Duke of Buckingham in the reign of James I. Herne the Hunter, who is said to lead a wild hunt in the park, was immortalized in W. Harrison Ainsworth's novel *Windsor Castle* (1843).

Today, Windsor Castle is open daily except when used for royal visits. There are historic treasures in the state apartments, including period furniture, fittings, paintings and suits of armor. The Castle also houses Queen Mary's Dolls' House, which is a popular exhibit. (See also **Apparitions; Haunted Houses; Haunting**)

Wingfield, Kate (died 1927)

British non-commercial medium, the **"Miss A."** of whom psychical researcher F. W. H. **Myers** wrote enthusiastically in *Proceedings* of the Society for Psychical Research (vol. 8, pp. 498-516: vol. 9, pp. 73-92), and in his book *Human Personality and Its Survival of Bodily Death* (1903). Miss Wingfield was also the "Miss Rawson" of J. G. **Piddington's** report, in *Proceedings* of the S.P.R. (vol. 18), on **cross correspondence** with Mrs. Thompson.

The identity was revealed by Sir Lawrence J. Jones, President of the Society for 1928 in his presidential address in *Proceedings* (vol.38). He told the story of a series of sittings which he and his wife had with Kate Wingfield in the years 1900-01, when her **clairvoyance** and **automatic writing** developed into **trance** mediumship. He observed many physical phenomena, **raps,** table tilting, movement of objects (**telekinesis**) and **apports.** In one instance, three tiny unset turquoises were brought as **apports.**

But it was the trance speaking phase of Miss Wingfield's mediumship that convinced Sir Lawrence Jones of **survival.** Deceased relatives proved their identity and on several occasions her living daughter came through as a communicator (see **Control**).

Among the guides of the medium was an entity "Semirus," who claimed to have been a doctor in ancient Egypt. Once a sitter desired some information from him. "Semirus" did not come. Later in the day he came through in automatic writing and explained that he heard the call, but was unable to come as he assisted in a new operation at X. Hospital. The operation was successful.

On inquiry the story of the operation was found true. "Semirus" could report on patients at a great distance with incredible rapidity. Someone asked information about the health of his aunt. "Semirus" went away and came back to say that the aunt was dead. The sitter hurried away and to his relief found his aunt alive. But he suddenly realized that he had given, by mistake, the address of a neighbor's house. A day or two later, a funeral took place from there.

The sittings of Miss Wingfield primarily served the purpose of **rescue circles** in a milder sense. Many spirits were brought by the controls and the error of their ways was pointed out. The sittings of Miss Wingfield were abandoned in 1901, as the family objected that she should be known as a trance medium. The automatic teachings that came through her hand were published in two little books: *Guidance from Beyond* (1923) and *More Guidance from Beyond* (1925).

Wirdig's Magnetic Sympathy

This was the doctrine of magnetic attraction and repugnance formulated by Tenzel Wirdig, professor at Rostock, who published his *Tenzelius Wirdig, Nova medicina spirituum* in 1673.

Wirdig believed that everything in the universe possessed a soul, and that the earth itself was merely a larger animal. Between the souls of things in accordance with each other there was a "magnetic sympathy" and a perpetual antipathy between those of an uncongenial nature. To this sympathy and antipathy Wirdig gave the name of "magnetism."

He stated: "Out of this relationship of sympathy and antipathy arises a constant movement in the whole world, and in all its parts, and an uninterrupted communion between heaven and earth, which produces universal harmony. The stars whose emanations consist merely of fire and spirits, have an undeniable influence on earthly bodies; and their influence on man demonstrates itself by life, movement, and warmth, those things without which he cannot live. The influence of the stars is the strongest at birth. The newborn child inhales this influence, and on whose first breath frequently his whole constitution depends, nay, even his whole life." (See also **Animal Magnetism; Hypnotism; Mesmerism**)

Wisconsin Phalanx

A Spiritualist community founded by Warren **Chase** in 1844. Chase had settled in Southport, Wisconsin, in 1838, and with his wife and child, he lived there for a time in deepest poverty. At length, however, their circumstances brightened, and Chase attained to a position of civic honor in Southport. Meanwhile he had studied Mesmerism and socialism with the aid of a few periodicals such as La Roy **Sunderland**'s *Magnet* and the *New York Tribune,* and was filled with the idea of founding a community where his ideals of social order and harmony might be carried out.

With the aid of his friends such a community was formed, each member with a share of twenty-five dollars. The chosen settlement—near the town of Ripon—was christened "Ceresco," in honor of Ceres. For six years the Wisconsin Phalanx flourished, having as its leader and ruling spirit Warren Chase himself.

But at last dissensions arose, and in 1850 it was dissolved. When its affairs were wound up it was found that a considerable profit fell to the share of its members. In all, it was one of the most successful Spiritualist or socialist communities of the time. For information on the Wisconsin Phalanx, see *History of American Socialisms* by John Humphrey Noyes (1870; reissued by Dover Publications under title *Strange Cults & Utopius of 19th-Century America,* 1966). (See also **Apostolic Circle; Mountain Cove Community**)

Witch Balls

Decorative gloves made of glass or metal, used as ornaments and also to avert ill fortune or witchcraft. These appear to date from the eighteenth century. One variety specially favored by antique collectors and occultists is that manufactured in Nailsea, near Bristol, England. These balls are full of swirling colors.

Witchcraft

The term witchcraft derives from the Saxon *Wicca,* a contraction of *witega,* a wise person, prophet or sorcerer. The (name) "warlock" for a male witch was a later Scottish term. According to the fanatical religious authorities of past ages, witchcraft was the cult of persons who, by means of Satanic assistance or the aid of evil spirits or **familiars,** were enabled to practice black magic.

The difference between the sorcerer and the witch was that the former was believed to have sold his or her soul to Satan for complete dominion for a stated period, whereas the witch usually appeared as the devoted and often badly treated servant of the diabolic power, although mistress of a familiar, bound to the witch as a slave.

Witches were predominently female, and because of this, the centuries of religious persecution represented an unparalleled rationalization of male prejudice and cruelty to women, many of them old and defenseless.

Early civil law did not punish the "white magic" of healing disease and similar beneficial practices stemming from knowledge of the secrets of nature. However, by the year 900 A.D., the church authorities considered that such socially valuable practices as well as these for an evil purpose were both the result of a pact with the devil, to be punished by excommunication. At a later date, the punishment became more sadistic.

The original concept of witchcraft was perhaps brought into being by the mythic influence of conquered races. It closely resembles in ritual and practice the religion of pagan races, from which it probably sprang. The non-Aryan peoples of Europe who preceded the Aryan population, carried on the practice and traditions of their religions more or less in secret, which awoke in the Aryan mind the idea that such practices were of a "magical" character. This was probably exaggerated by the Aryan, to whom earlier gods would appear as "devils," and their religious ritual as sorcery.

This view has been opposed on the ground that the gap between, say, the extinction of the pre-Aryan religion known as Druidism and the first notices of witchcraft, is too great to bridge. But Druidism continued to exist long after it was officially extinct, and British witchcraft was its lineal successor.

The theory is further advanced that on the failure of the non-Aryan priesthood, novices would be adopted from the invading race for the purpose of carrying on the old religion. It seems that the circumstance that the greater number of the upholders of this ancient tradition were women, points to the likelihood of an early custom of the adoption or marriage of Aryan women by a non-Aryan people who would prefer to recruit their novices and devotees from women, distrusting the masculine section of an alien people to fall in with their religious ideas, and that the almost exclusive employment of women in the cult (in Britain, at least) originated in this practice.

The folklorist G. Laurence Gomme, in his book *Folklore as an Historical Science* (1908): "I am inclined to lay great stress upon the act of initiation. It emphasises the idea of a caste distinct from the general populace, and it postulates the existence of this caste anterior to the time when those who practice their supposed powers first come into notice. Carrying back this act of initiation age after age, as the dismal records of witchcraft enable us to do for some centuries, it is clear that the people from time to time thus introduced into the witch caste carried on the practices and assumed the functions of the caste even though they came to it as novices and strangers. We thus arrive at an artificial means of descent of a peculiar group of superstition, and it might be termed initiatory descent."

This concept, according to Gomme, was influenced in the Middle Ages by another:

"Traditional practices, traditional formulae, and traditional beliefs are no doubt the elements of witchcraft, but it was not the force of tradition which produced the miserable doings of the Middle Ages, and of the seventeenth century against witches. These were due to a psychological force, partly generated by the newly acquired power of the people to read the Bible for themselves, and so to apply the witch stories of the Jews to neighbours of their own who possessed powers or peculiarities which they could not understand, and partly generated by the carrying on of traditional practices by certain families or groups of persons who could only acquire knowledge of such practices by initiation or family teaching. Lawyers, magistrates, judges, nobles and monarchs are concerned with witchcraft. These are not minds that have been crushed by civilisation, but minds which have misunderstood it or misused it."

Through the ruthless pressure of dogmatic Christianity, which usurped the old pagan festivals and damned the followers of the old religions as evil sorcerers in league with the Devil, religious bigotry actually created the black magic witchcraft against which it fulminated. Many witches accepted and reveled in their role as representatives of the power of Satan against the repressions of the Christian Church. Side by side with this neurosis of declining paganism, the use of torture created delusions and false confessions.

The Sabbat

The medieval criminal records abound in descriptions of a ceremony at which the rites of the witch cult were periodically celebrated. This was the witches' Sabbat, regarded by the religious authorities as a parody of the Christian Sabbath.

The Sabbat was generally held in some wild and solitary spot, often in the midst of forests or on the heights of mountains, at a great distance from the residence of most of the visitors. The circumstance connected with it most difficult of proof was the method of transport from one place to another.

The witches themselves nearly all agreed in the statement that they took off their clothes and anointed their bodies with a special **unguent** or ointment. They then strode across a stick, or any similar article, and, muttering a charm, were carried through the air to the place of meeting in an incredible short space of time. Sometimes the stick was to be anointed as well as the witch. They generally left the house by the window or by the chimney, which perhaps suggests survival of the custom of an earth-dwelling people. Sometimes the witch went out by the door, and there found a demon in the shape of a goat, or at times of some other animal, who carried her away on his back, and brought her home again after the meeting was dissolved.

In the confessions extorted from them, usually under torture, the witches and sorcerers bore testimony to the truth of all these details, but those who judged them, and who wrote upon the subject, asserted that they had many other independent proofs in corroboration.

The witchcraft legalist Jean Bodin (1529—1596) stated that a man who lived at the little town of Loches, France, having observed that his wife frequently absented herself from the house in the night, became suspicious of her conduct, and at last by his threats obliged her to confess that she was a witch, and that she attended the Sabbats. To appease the anger of her husband, she agreed to gratify his curiosity by taking him with her to the next meeting, but she warned him on no account whatever to allow the name of God or of the Savior to cross his lips.

At the appointed time the couple stripped and anointed themselves, and, after uttering the necessary magical formula, they were suddenly transported to Bordeaux, at an immense distance from their own dwelling. The husband there found himself in the midst of a great assembly of both sexes in the same nude state as himself and his wife, and in one part he saw the devil in a hideous form.

In the first moment of his surprise, he inadvertently uttered the exclamation, "Mon Dieu! ou sommes-nous?" whereupon everyone suddenly disappeared from his view, leaving him cold and naked in the middle of the fields, where he wandered until morning, when the country-men coming to their daily occupations told him where he was and he made his way home in the best manner he could. But he lost no time in denouncing his wife, who was brought to her trial, confessed, and was burnt.

As the witches generally went from their beds at night to the meetings, leaving their husbands and family behind them, it may seem extraordinary that their absence was not more frequently perceived.

They had, however, a method of providing against this danger, by casting a drowsiness over those who might be witnesses, and by placing in their bed an image which, to all outward appearance, bore an exact resemblance to themselves, although in reality was nothing more than a besom or some other similar article.

But the belief was so inculcated that the witches did not always go in body to the Sabbat—that they were present only in spirit, whilst their body remained in bed. Some of the more rational writers on witchcraft taught that this was the only manner in which they were ever carried to the Sabbats, and various instances are deposed to where that was manifestly the case. This would be analogous with what is now called **out-of-the-body** traveling or **astral projection.**

A president, of the court named Touretta told Bodin that he had examined a witch, who was subsequently burnt in the Dauphine area, and who was carried to the Sabbat in this manner. Her master one night found her stretched on the floor before the fire in a state of insensibility and imagined her to be dead. In his attempt to arouse her, he first beat her body with great severity, and then applied fire to the more sensitive parts, and when this had no effect, he left her, in the belief that she had died suddenly.

His astonishment was great when in the morning he found her in her own bed, in an evident state of great suffering. When he asked what ailed her, her only answer was, "Ha! mon maîstre, tant m'avez batue!" When further pressed, however, she confessed that during the time her body lay in a state of insensibility, she had been herself to the witches' Sabbat, and upon this avowal she was committed to prison.

Bodin further stated that at Bordeaux, in 1571, an old woman, who was condemned to the fire for witchcraft, confessed that she was transported to the Sabbat in this manner. One of her judges, known personally to Bodin, pressed the woman during examination to show him how this was effected, and released her from the fetters for that purpose. She rubbed herself in different parts of the body with "a certain grease," and immediately became stiff and insensible and, to all appearance, dead. She remained in this state for about five hours, and then as quickly revived, and told her inquisitors a great number of extraordinary things, which showed that she must have been spiritually transported to far distant places.

The description of the Sabbat given by the witches differed only in slight particulars of detail, but it must be stressed that their examinations were all under torture. The Sabbat was, they claimed, an immense assemblage of witches and demons, sometimes from distant parts of the earth, at others only from the province or district in which it was held.

On arriving, the visitors performed their homage to the Devil with unseemly ceremonies, and presented their new converts. They then gave an account of all the mischief they had done since the last meeting. Those who had neglected to do evil, or who had so far overlooked themselves as to do good, were treated with disdain, or severely punished.

Several of the victims of the French courts in the latter part of the sixteenth century confessed that, having been unwilling or unable to fulfil the commands of the Devil when they appeared at the Sabbat, he had beaten them in the most cruel manner. He took one woman, who had refused to bewitch her neighbor's daughter, and threatened to drown her in the river.

Others were plagued in their bodies, or by destruction of their property. Some were punished for their irregular attendance at the Sabbat, and one or two, for slighter offenses, were condemned to walk home from the Sabbat instead of being carried through the air. Those, on the other hand, who had exerted most their mischievous propensities were highly honored at the Sabbat, and often rewarded with gifts of money.

After this examination was passed, the Devil distributed among his worshipers unguents, powders, and other articles for the perpetration of evil. A French witch, executed in 1580, confessed that some of her companions offered a sheep or a heifer, and another, executed the following year, stated that animals of a black color were most acceptable. A third, executed at Gerbeville in 1585, declared that no one was exempt from this offering, and that the poorer sort offered a hen or a chicken, and some even a lock of their hair, a little bird, or any trifle they could put their hands upon. Severe punishments followed the neglect of this ceremony. In many instances, according to the confessions of the witches, besides their direct worship of the Devil, they were obliged to show their abhorrence of the faith they had deserted by trampling on the cross, and blaspheming the saints, and by other profanations.

Before the termination of the meeting, the new witches received their familiars, or imps, who they generally addressed as their "little masters," although they were bound to attend at the bidding of the witches, and execute their desires. These received names, generally of a popular character, such as were given to cats, dogs and other pet animals and the similarity these names bear to each other in different countries is very remarkable.

After all these preliminary ceremonies had been transacted, a great banquet was laid out, and the whole company fell to eating and drinking and making merry. At times, every article of luxury was placed before them, and they feasted in the most sumptuous manner. Often, however, the meats served on the table were nothing but toads and rats, and other articles of a revolting nature. In general they had no salt, and seldom bread. But, even when best served, the money and the victuals furnished by the demons were of the most unsatisfactory character, a circumstance for which no rational explanation was given. The coin when brought forth by open daylight, was generally found to be nothing better than dried leaves or bits of dirt, and, however, greedily they may have eaten at the table, they commonly left the meeting in a state of exhaustion from hunger.

The tables were next removed, and feasting gave way to wild and uproarious dancing and revelry. The common carole or round dance of the Middle Ages appears to have been performed by the persons taking each other's hand in a circle, alternately a man and a woman. This, probably the ordinary dance among the peasantry, was the one generally practiced at the Sabbat of the witches, with this peculiarity, that their backs instead of their faces were turned inwards. The old writers endeavor to account for this, by supposing that it was designed to prevent them from seeing and recognizing each other. But this, it is clear, was not the only dance of the Sabbat. Perhaps more fashionable ones were introduced for witches in better conditions in society, and moralists of the succeeding age maliciously insinuated that many dances of a not very decorous character invented by the Devil himself to heat the imaginations of his victims, had subsequently been adopted in classes in society who did not frequent the Sabbat.

It may be observed, as a curious circumstance, that the modern waltz was first traced among the meetings of the witches and their imps! It was also confessed, in almost every case, that the dances at the Sabbats produced much greater fatigue than commonly arose from such exercises. Many of the witches declared that, on their return home, they were usually unable to rise from their bed for two to three days.

Their music, also, was by no means of an ordinary character. The songs were generally obscene, or vulgar, or ridiculous. Of instruments there was considerable variety, but all partaking of the burlesque character of the proceedings. "Some played the flute upon a stick or bone; another was seen striking a horse's skull for a lyre; there you saw them beating the drum on the trunk of an oak, with a stick; here, others were blowing trumpets with the branches." The louder the instrument, the greater satisfaction it gave, and the dancing became wilder and wilder, until it merged into as vast scene of confusion, and ended in scenes of debauchery minutely described in the old treatises on demonology. The witches separated in time to reach their homes before cock-crow.

It seems that the Devil had taken the place of the deities of the older and abandoned cults of the non-Aryans, whose sexual rites were attended by "initiated" or "adopted" neophytes of a race to the generality of which they were abominable, that witches often worked magic by means of familiars, whose shapes they were able to take, or by means of direct Satanic agency. But there were probably mythological elements in witchcraft as well.

What is not clear is the extent to which the confessions of witches were exaggerated or colored by the fanatically repressive religious authorities of the time. Both witches and persecuted clearly shared a common mania.

Powers of Witches

In the eyes of the populace, the powers of witches were numerous. The most peculiar of these were: The ability to blight by means of the **evil eye,** the sale of winds to sailors, power over animals, and the power of witches to transform themselves into animal shapes.

According to G. Laurence Gomme: "The most usual transformations are into cats and hares, and less frequently into red deer, and these have taken the place of wolves. Thus, cat-transformations are found in Yorkshire, hare-transformations in Devonshire, Yorkshire and Wales, and Scotland, deer-transformations in Cumberland, raven-transformations in Scotland, cattle-transformations in Ireland. Indeed the connection between witches and the lower animals is a very close one, and hardly anywhere in Europe does it occur that this connection is relegated to a subordinate place. Story after story, custom after custom is recorded as appertaining to witchcraft, and animal transformation appears always.

Witches were also believed to possess the power of making themselves invisible, by means of a magic ointment supplied to them by the devil, and of harming others by thrusting nails into a waxen image representing them.

Witchcraft Among Primitive Peoples

Witchcraft among primitive peoples is, of course, allied to the various cults of demonism in vogue all over the world. These are indicated in the various entries dealing with such races. The name witchcraft is merely a convenient label for such demon-cults, as is "witch-doctors" applied to those who "smell out" these practitioners of evil.

Evidence for Witchcraft

According to Frank **Podmore,** in his book *Modern Spiritualism* (1902), the evidence for witchcraft falls under four main headings: (a) the confessions of witches themselves, (b) the corroborative evidence of **lycanthropy, apparitions,** etc., (c) the witch-marks, (d) the evidence of the evil effects produced upon the supposed victims. Podmore stated:

"(a) The confessions, as is notorious, were for the most part extracted by torture, or by lying promises of release. In England, where torture was not countenanced by the law, the ingenuity of Matthew Hopkins and other professional witch-finders could generally devise some equally efficient substitute, such as gradual starvation, enforced sleeplessness, or the maintenance for hours of a constrained and painful posture. But apart from these extorted confessions, there is evidence that in some cases the accused persons were actually driven by the accumulation of testimony against them, by the pressure of public opinion, and the singular circumstances in which they were placed, to believe and confess that they were witches indeed. Some of the women in Salem who had pleaded guilty to witchcraft explained afterwards, when the persecution had died down and they were released, that they had been 'consternated and affrighted even out of their reason' to confess that of which they were innocent. And there were not a few persons who voluntarily confessed to the practice of witchcraft, nocturnal rides, compacts with the devil, and all the rest of it. . . .

The most striking instances of this voluntary confession are afforded by children. For even among the earlier writers on witchcraft the opinion was not uncommonly held that the nocturnal rides and banquets with the devil were merely delusions, though the guilt of the witch was not lessened thereby. And in the sixteenth century, at least in English-speaking countries this belief seems to have been generally held by believers in witchcraft and their opponents. Thus Gaule: "But the more prodigious or stupendous [of the things narrated by witches in their confessions] are affected merely by the devil; the witches all the while either in a rapt ecstasie, a charmed sleepe, or a melancholy dreame; and the witches imagination, phantasie, common sense, only deluded with what is now done, or pretended." Antoinette Boruignon, a schoolmistress in Lille, in 1639, observing her scholars eat "great pieces of bread and butter" at breakfast, pointed out to them that they could not have such good appetites if they had really fed on dainty meats at the devil's Sabbath the night before.

"(b) But if the witch's own account of her marvellous feats may be explained as, at best, the vague remembrance of a nightmare, it is hardly necessary to go beyond this explanation to account for the prodigies reported by others. In most cases there is no need to suppose even so much foundation for the marvels, since the evidence (e.g., for lycanthropy) is purely traditional. And when we get accounts at first hand, they are commonly concerned, not with such matters as levitation, or transformation of hares into old women, but merely with vague shapes seen in the dusk, or the unexplained appearance of a black dog. Even so the evidence comes almost exclusively from ignorant peasants, and is given years after the events. . . .

"(c) The evidence for 'witch-marks' does not greatly concern us. The insensible patches on which Matthew Hopkins and other witch-finders relied may well have been genuine in some cases. Such insensible areas are known to occur in hysterical subjects, and the production of insensibility by means of suggestion is a commonplace in modern times. The supposed witches' teats, which the imps sucked, appear to have been found almost exclusively, like the imps themselves, in the English-speaking countries. Any wart, boil, or swelling would probably form a sufficient warrant for the accusation; we read in Cotton Mather of a jury of women finding a preternatural teat upon a witch's body, which could not be discovered when a second search was made three or four hours later, and of a witch's mark upon the finger of a small child, which took the form of 'a deep red spot, about the bigness of a flea-bite.' And the witch-mark which brought conviction to the mind of Increase Mather in the case of George Burroughs was his ability to hold a heavy gun at arm's length, and to carry a barrel of cider from the canoe to the shore. . . .

"(d) Of most of the evidence based upon the injuries suffered by the witches' supposed victims, it is difficult to speak seriously. If a man's cow ran dry, if his horse stumbled, his cart stuck in a gate, his pigs or fowls sickened, if his child had a fit, his wife or himself an unaccustomed pain, it was evidence acceptable in a court of law against any old woman who might be supposed within the last twelve months—or twelve years—to have conceived some cause of offence against him and his. Follies of this kind are too well known to need repetition.

"But there is another feature of witchcraft, at any rate of the cases occurring in the sixteenth and seventeenth centuries in England and America, which is not so well recognised, and which has a more direct bearing upon our present inquiry—the predominant part played in the initial stages of witch persecution by malevolent or merely hysterical children and young women. . . . "

Symptoms of Bewitchment

Frank Podmore commented: "The symptoms of the alleged bewitchment were, in all these cases monotonously alike. The victims would fall into fits or convulsions, of a kind which the physicians called in were unable to diagnose or to cure. In these fits the children would commonly call out on the old woman who was the imaginary cause of their ailment; would profess, at times, to see her shape present in the room, and would even stab at it with a knife or other weapon. (In the most conclusive cases the record continues that the old woman, being straightway sought for, would be found attempting to conceal a corresponding wound on her person.) These fits, which sometimes lasted, with slight intermission, for weeks together would be increased in violence by the approach of the supposed witch; or, as Hutchinson notes [*An Historical Essay Concerning Witchcraft* by Francis Hutchinson, 1718], by the presence of sympathetic spectators. The fits, as was also commonly noted by contemporary chroniclers, would diminish or altogether cease when the witch was imprisoned or condemned; on the other hand, if the supposed witch were released the victim would continue to suffer horrible tortures, insomuch that at the Salem trials one old woman who had been acquitted by the jury was, because of the hideous outcry from the afflicted persons in court, straightway re-tried and condemned. The witch's touch would always provoke severe attacks, indeed, contact with the witch or the establishment of rapport between her and the victim by means of some garment worn by the latter, as in Mistress Faith Corbet's case [see *A Collection of Modern Relations . . . Concerning Witches and Witchcraft* by Lord Chief Justice Hale, 1693], was generally regarded as an essential pre-requisite of the enchantment. Once this rapport established the mere look of the witch, or the direction of her evil will would suffice. The afflicted in Salem were, as the Mathers testify, much tortured in court by the the malevolent glances of the poor wretches on trial; and two 'visionary' girls added greatly to the weight of the evidence by foretelling with singular accuracy, when such or such of the afflicted persons then present would feel the baneful influence, and howl for anguish. It should be added—though the evidence as we now understand the word, for the fact alleged is of course practically negligible—that it was commonly reported that the witch's victim could, although blindfolded, distinguish her tormentor by the touch alone from all other persons, and could even foresee her approach and discern her actions at a considerable distance.

"The effect of the convulsions and cataleptic attacks, which modern science would unhesitatingly dismiss as being simply the result of hysteria, was heightened in many cases by manifestations of a more material kind. It was a common feature for the victim to vomit pins, needles, wood, stubble, and other substances; or for thorns or needles to be found embedded in her flesh. In a case recorded by Glanvil an hysterical servant girl, Mary Longdon, in addition to the usual fits, vomiting of pins etc., was tormented by stones being continually flung at her, which stones when they fell to the ground straightway vanished. Her master bore witness in court to the falling of the stones and their miraculous disappearance. Moreover, the same Mary Longdon would frequently be transported by an invisible power to the top of the house, and there 'laid on a board betwixt two Sollar beams,' or would be put into a chest, or half suffocated between two featherbeds.

"Gross as these frauds appear to us, it is singular that for the most part they remained undetected, and even, it would seem, unsuspected, not merely by the ignorant peasants, for whose benefit the play was acted in the first instance, but in the larger theatre of a law court. But there are some notorious instances of confession or detection. Edmund Robinson, the boy on whose accusation the Lancashire witches were tried, subsequently confessed to imposture. Other youths were detected with blacklead in their mouths when foaming in sham epileptic fits, colouring their urine with ink, concealing crooked pins about their persons in order to vomit them later, scratching the bed posts with their toes, and surreptitiously eating to repletion during a pretended fast. But commonly the spectators were so convinced beforehand of the genuineness of such portents that they held it superfluous to examine the claims of any particular performance of this kind on their credence.

"It is difficult to know in such cases where self-deception ends and where malevolent trickery begins. Nor would the examination of these bygone outbreaks of hysteria trivial in themselves as terrible in their consequences—be of interest in the present connection, except for the fact that we find here the primitive form of those Poltergeist manifestations which gave the popular impetus in 1848 to the belief in Modern Spiritualism, and which are still appealed by those who maintain the genuineness of the physical manifestations of the séance room as instances of similar phenomena occurring spontaneously. (See also **Poltergeist**)

Differences Between British and Continental Witchcraft

The salient difference between British and Continental witchcraft systems seems to have been that whereas the former was an almost exclusively female system, the Continental one favored the inclusion in the ranks of sorcerers (as foreign witches were called) of the male element; this at least was the case in France and Germany, but there is evidence that in Hungary and the Slavonic countries, the female element was the more numerous.

In Ireland, women were also preeminent. This is probably to be accounted for by the circumstance noted earlier that the non-alien priesthoods in their decline became almost entirely dependent upon the offices of women. But the various forms of witchcraft are discussed in the various entries dealing with European countries.

Growth of Belief in Witchcraft

It is significant that in early times the supernatural side of witchcraft won little public credence. People believed in such things as magical poisoning and the raising of tempests by witches, but they refused to believe such superstitions as that the witch rode through the air or had communion in any way with diabolic agency.

As early as 800 A.D., an Irish synod pronounced the belief of flight through the air and vampirism, to be incompatible with Christian doctrine, and many early writers like Stephen of Hungary and Regino stated that flight by night and kindred practices were merely a delusion. Indeed those who held these beliefs were actively punished by penance.

In face of the later development of belief in witchcraft, this frank skepticism is almost amazing, and it is most strange that the tenth and eleventh centuries should have rejected superstitions embraced widely by the sixteenth and seventeenth.

From the thirteenth to the fifteenth centuries the conception of witchcraft and demonology was greatly furthered and assisted by the writings of scholars and the institution of the Inquisition to deal with the rise of unbelief. A vast amount of literature was circulated dealing with questions relating to magic and sorcery, and regarding the habits and customs of witches, magicians and practitioners in "black magic," and many hairs were split.

The Church gladly joined in this campaign against what it regarded as the forces of darkness, and indeed both accused and accusers seem to have lingered under the most dreadful delusions—delusions which were to cost society dear as a whole. The scholastic conception of demonology was that the witch was not a woman but a demon. Rationalism was at a discount and the ingenuity of medieval scholars disposed of all objections to the phenomena of witchcraft.

The deities of pagan times were cited as examples of sorcery, and erudition, especially in ecclesiastical circles, ran riot on the subject. There also arose a class of judges or inquisitors like Jean **Bodin** in France and Jakob **Sprenger** in Germany, who composed lengthy treatises upon the manner of discovering witches, of putting them to the test, and generally of presiding in witchcraft trials.

The cold-blooded cruelty of these textbooks on demonology can only be accounted for by the likelihood that their authors felt themselves justified in their composition through motives of fidelity to their church and religion.

The awful terror disseminated, especially among the intelligent, by the possibility of a charge of witchcraft being brought against them at any moment brought about an intolerable strain in everyday life. The intellectual might be arraigned at any time on a charge of witchcraft by any rascal who cared to make it. Position or learning were no safeguard against such a charge, and it is peculiar that the more thoughtful and serious section of the population should not have made some attempt to put a stop to the dreadful condition of affairs brought about by ignorance and superstition. Of course the principal reason against their being able to do so was the fact that the whole system was countenanced by the Church, in whose hands the entire procedure of trials for witchcraft lay.

Strangely enough even convents and monasteries were often the centers of demoniac possession. The conception of the **incubi** and **succubi** undoubtedly arose from the ascetic tortures of the monk and the nun. Wholesale trials, too, of wretched people who were alleged to attend Sabbatic orgies of the Devil on dreary heaths were detailed with an elaborateness which spread terror in the public mind.

The tortures inflicted on those unfortunates were generally of the most fiendish description, but they were supposed to be for the good of the souls of those who bore them. In France, the majority of these trials took place in the fifteenth century, whereas in England most of them were current in the seventeenth century. Details regarding these will be found in the entries on **France** and **England.**

The famous outburst of fanaticism in New England under Cotton Mather (see **America**) from 1691 to 1692 was by no means the last in an English-speaking country, for in 1712 a woman was convicted of witchcraft in England, and in Scotland the last trial and execution for sorcery took place in 1722.

In Spain, there were burnings by the Inquisition in 1781; in Germany as late as 1793, and in South America a woman was burned in Peru as recently as 1888.

The death of the belief in witchcraft was eventually brought about by a more sane spirit of criticism than had hitherto obtained. Even the dull wits of the Inquisitorial and other courts began to see that the wretched creatures upon whom they passed sentence either confessed because of the extremity of torture they had to suffer, or else were under hallucination regarding the nature of their connection with the satanic power.

Reginald Scot, in his book *Discovery of Witchcraft* (1584) proved that the belief on the part of the witch that she was a servant of the Devil was purely imaginary, and in consequence drew upon his work the wrath of the British monarch James I, who responded with some heat in his own book *Demonologie* (1597).

But Friedrich von Spee's *Cautio Criminalis* (1631) advanced considerations of still greater weight from the rationalistic point of view—considerations of such weight indeed that Jean Bodin, the archdemonologist, denounced him and demanded that he should be added to the long list of victims.

The Psychology of Witchcraft

Little doubt exists nowadays when the conditions of savage witchcraft have been closely examined and commented upon, that the witch and the sorcerer of the Middle Ages, like their analogues in early Africa, America, Asia and elsewhere, had a firmly-rooted belief in their own magical powers, and in their connection with unseen and often diabolic agencies.

It is a strange circumstance that in many instances the confessions wrung from two or more witches, when a number of them have been concerned in the same case, have tallied with one another in almost every detail.

This would imply that these women suffered from collective hallucination, and actually believed that they had seen the supernatural beings with whom they confessed fellowship, and had gone through the rites and acts for which they suffered. A period arrived in the medieval campaign against witchcraft when it was admitted that the whole system was one of hallucination, yet, said the demonologists, this was no palliation of the offence, for it was equally as evil to imagine such diabolic acts as actually to take part in them!

There is also evidence which would lead to the belief some witches possessed certain powers of **hypnotism** and **telepathy,** which would give real confidence in belief that they wielded magical terrors. Again the phenomena of Spiritualism and the large possibilities it has offered for fraud suggests that some kindred system might have been in use amongst the more shrewd or the leaders in these Sabbatic meetings, which would thoroughly convince the ignorant among the sisterhood of the existence in their midst of diabolic powers.

There is good reason to believe that trance, hysteria, drugs and salves were also common, but the great source of witch belief undoubtedly exists in **auto-suggestion,** fostered and fomented from ecclesiastical and scholastic sources, and by no means lessened by popular belief.

However, against the theory of hallucination is the case put forward by Margaret A. **Murray,** based on the suggestions of C. G. **Leland,** in his book *Aradia, or the Gospel of the Witches* (1899) and those of other modern writers. Dr. Murray inclined to the hypothesis that witchcraft was in reality the modern and degraded descendant of an ancient nature religion, the rites of which were actually carried out in deserted places and included child sacrifice and other barbarous customs.

In the Satanic presence at such gatherings, she saw the attendance of a priest of the cult. In brief, her case tended to prove the actual reality of the witch religion as against that of hallucination which, until recently, was the explanation accepted by students of the subject. Her remarks upon the familiar, too, go to show that a large body of proof exists for the belief that this conception also rested upon actual occurrences.

The writer Lewis **Spence** accepted the soundness of these views, but added the conviction that witchcraft religion was, in some manner, possessed of an equestrian connection, the precise nature of which remains obscure.

The broomstick appears to be the magical equivalent of a horse. Witches occasionally rode to the Sabbat on horseback, and one of the tests for a witch was to see if her eye held the reflection or likeness of a horse.

Spence thought it possible that the witch religion was the remnant of a prehistoric horse-totem cult. He also found good evidence for the existence of a witch cult similar to that of Europe in pre-Columbian Mexico, and even encountered a picture of a naked witch with peaked cap riding on a broomstick in the native Mexican painting known as the Codex Fejèrvàry-Mayer, which seems to show that the witch religion was in no sense limited to Europe, and was of most ancient origin.

The Modern Witchcraft Revival

Fragments of folklore belief in witchcraft rituals persisted into modern history in isolated parts of Britain, Europe and America, usually in the tradition of "white witches" and "hex" masters performing useful spells and supplying charms, rather than worshiping a Devil or causing mischief.

However, the occult boom of the 1950s stimulated a worldwide revival of witchcraft as a pagan nature religion, echoing the theories of Marguerite Murray, and later as actual Satanic cults of an anti-Christian nature.

The more innocent witchcraft as nature religion cults were largely inspired by the British writer Gerald B. **Gardner,** drawing upon the work of Margaret Murray to promulgate a witchcraft revival which fitted the anything-goes mood of the permissive society of postwar affluence.

It became fashionable for people to join covens and prance around in the nude, performing rituals with swords, cups, incense and candles, supported by a booming paperback industry of histories of occultism and witchcraft.

Unfortunately such frolics often became tame, and after being hotted up by kinky sex and drug abuse, white magic rapidly became black, and sinister cults sprang up with horrifying orgies and murders.

The case of Charles Manson, who claimed to be the Devil and do his work, is still fresh in the public memory. Secured decades after the occult boom, however, things have very much died down, and pop religious cults have taken the place of trendy witchcraft, often with equally tragic results as in the horrific story of the **Peoples Temple** cult of the Rev. Jim **Jones.**

The witchcraft of the Middle Ages arose from the theological problem of the place of evil in human affairs, as much as the fragments of paganism which lingered in peasant societies. Undoubtedly despotic religious authorities projected their own repressed sexual fantasies and guilt feelings onto their victims, sharing a common mania.

But much of the witchcraft and black magic of today is primarily a malady of an affluent and permissive society, pursuing a pleasure principle through sensationalism to cults of violence. In an age of condoned pornography, drug abuse and sexual license, it has flourished on dreams of power over others and over the forces of nature.

It is also, perhaps something of an escape from the harsh realities of world depression and the threat of atomic holocaust. Together with the mass psychopathology of dangerous new religious cults, it poses a challenge to the established religions for reappraisal of their role in modern society.

Not all modern witchcraft is necessarily decadent. Many discriminating modern white witches follow a revived pagan religion which is more concerned with the psychic and healing forces in nature known to ancient people before the advent of Christianity. At a time when much of Christianity itself has become secularized, fragmented, or has retreated into crude fundamentalism, the best of modern witchcraft is often a sincere desire to recapture reverence for the forces of nature and the great mysteries of life. In this, it surely has as much right to respect and coexistence with other religions as the Christianity which persecuted it so many centuries ago.

Witchcraft and the Phenomena of Psychical Research

As mentioned earlier, psychical researcher Frank **Podmore** attempted to trace the roots of Spiritualist phenomena (as distinct from its religious beliefs) in the witchcraft phenomena of former centuries. Edmund **Gurney,** another psychical researcher, drew similar parallels in order to emphasize a skeptical view of the claimed phenomena.

In the book *Phantasms of the Living* (1886), which he coauthored with F. W. H. Myers and Frank Podmore, he stated: ". . . on a careful search through about 260 books on the subject, and a large number of contemporary records of trial" that "there is a total absence of respectable evidence, and an almost total absence of any first hand evidence at all, for those phenomena of magic and witchcraft which cannot be accounted for as the results of diseased imagination, hysteria, hypnotism and occasionally, perhaps, of telepathy,"

However, since Gurney wrote these lines, many phenomena of Spiritualism attributed in his time by psychical researchers to diseased imagination have been found genuinely occurring, so that the absence of respectable evidence no longer militates against the possible reality of similar early manifestations.

Besides, Gurney neglected the importance of William Lecky's statement in his book *History of the Rise and Influence of Rationalism in Europe* (2 vols., 1865), according to which: "The wisest men in

Europe shared in the belief of these facts; the ablest defended it; the best were zealous foes of all who assailed it. For hundreds of years no man of any account rejected it. Lord Bacon could not divest himself of it. Shakespeare accepted it, as did the most enlightened of his contemporaries. Sir Thomas Browne declared that those who denied the existence of witchcraft were not only infidels, but also, by implication, atheists."

John Wesley wrote in his *Journal* under the date May 25, 1768: "It is true likewise that the English in general, and indeed most of the men of learning in Europe, have given up all accounts of witches and apparitions as mere old wives' fables. I am sorry for it, and I willingly take this opportunity of entering my solemn protest against this violent compliment, which so many that believe the Bible, pay to those who do not believe it. I owe them no such service."

Sir William Blackstone stated in the fourth book of his *Commentaries on the Laws of England* (4 vols., 1765-69 etc.): "To deny the possibility, nay, actual existence of witchcraft and sorcery, is at once flatly to contradict the revealed Word of God in various passages of both the Old and New Testament; and the thing itself is a truth to which every nation in the world hath borne testimony, either by examples seemingly well attested or by prohibitory laws, which, at least, suppose the possibility of commerce with evil spirits."

The evidence for witchcraft is fourfold: (1) Confessions of witches. In the majority of cases this was the result of torture or mental confusion and suggestion; (2) Evidence of lycanthropy, apparitions of the witch in animal shapes. All testimonies are of a vague, hazy nature; (3) Witch-marks; insensible patches on the body, witches' tears, warts, boils taken as such; (4) Evil effects produced on the witches. This category produced most of the evidence.

The witnesses were usually children who fell into fits and vomited nails and crooked pins. These fits sometimes lasted for weeks and increased at the approach of the witch. The children called out on seeing them, sometimes professed to see their shapes in the room, stabbed at them with a knife which was supposed to wound them in the flesh and the fits usually decreased or ceased when the witch was imprisoned or condemned. Imaginary harm caused by witches to cattle, such as the running dry of cows, resulted in many other depositions of serious consequence.

The phenomena are very similar to some mediumistic manifestations. **Levitation,** speaking in **tongues, trance** convulsions, phantasmal projections, stone throwing, **poltergeist** disturbances, marks of **stigmata** were considered sure signs of bewitchment. At the trial of Mary London, for witchcraft, at Cork in 1661, several witnesses declared that the accused young girl "was removed strangely, in the twinkling of an eye, out of the bed, sometimes into the bottom of a chest with linen, under all the linen, and the linen not at all disturbed, sometimes between the two beds she lay on, sometimes under a parcel of wool; and once she was laid on a small deal board, which lay on the top of the house between two sollar beams where it was necessary to rear up ladders to have her fetched down." Plenty of testimonies were also adduced to the phenomena of stone-throwing.

Fraud was seldom detected. But superstition and ignorance magnified every abnormal manifestation. Nevertheless, the nocturnal rides and feasts with the devil were mostly attributed to delusion. But such delusions were not considered circumstances of extenuation.

As late as 1849, the servant of Dr. Larkin, of Wrentham, Massachusetts, was convicted on a charge of necromancy and sentenced to sixty days' solitary confinement for the phenomena which occurred in her presence.

Some of the early manifestations of Spiritualist phenomena were declared to be the work of the Devil, and even in modern times, many dogmatic clergymen continue to denounce Spiritualism as diabolical. (See also **Church of Satan; Cults;** Gerald B. **Gardner; Hallucination; Lycanthropy; Malleus Maleficarum;** Margaret A. **Murray; Obsession & Possession; Out-of-the-Body; Poltergeist; Transvection; Witches' Cradle**)

Recommended reading:

Buckland, Raymond. *Buckland's Complete Book of Witchcraft,* Llewellyn Publications, 1986

De Vesme, Caesar. *A History of Experimental Spiritualism, 2 vols. (*vol.1 *Primitive Man;* vol. 2 *Peoples of Antiquity*), Rider & Co. London, 1931

Ewen, C. l'Estrange. *Witch Hunting and Witch Trials,* Kegan Paul, London, 1929

Farrar, Stewart. *What Witches Do; The Modern Coven Revealed,* Peter Davies, London/Coward, New York, 1973; Sphere paperback, 1973

Fritscher, John J. *Popular Witchcraft; Straight from the Witch's Mouth,* Bowling Green University Popular Press, 1972

Gardner, Gerald B. *Witchcraft Today,* Rider & Co., London, 1954

Glanvill, Joseph. *Saducismus Triumphatus,* London, 1681 etc.

Gomme, G. Laurence. *Folklore as an Historical Science,* London, 1908

Guazzo, Francesco Maria. *Compendium Maleficarum,* 1595; (ed. Montague Summers) John Rodker, London, 1929; University Books, 1974

Hopkins, Matthew. *The Discovery of Witches,* London, 1647; (ed. Montague Summers) Cayme Press, London, 1928

Irvine, Doreen. *From Witchcraft to Christ,* Corcordia paperback, London, 1973

LaVey, Anton Szandor. *The Satanic Bible,* Avon paperback, 1969

Lea, Henry Charles. *Materials Towards a History of Witchcraft,* 3 vols., Thomas Yoseloff, 1957

Leland, Charles G. *Aradia; or the Gospel of the Witches,* David Nutt, London, 1899; Samuel Weiser, 1974

Maple, Eric. *The Dark World of Witches,* London, 1962; Pegasus paperback, 1970; reprinted together with Maple's *The Domain of Devils* and *The Realm of Ghosts* in one vol., A. S. Barnes, n.d.

Mather, Cotton, *Wonders of the Invisible World,* Boston & London, 1693; Amherst Press paperback, Wisconsin, n.d.

Michelet, Jules. *The Sorceress; A Study in Middle Age Superstition,* Paris 1904; Imperial Press, London, 1905; reissued under title *Satanism and Witchcraft;* Wehman, 1939 etc. (frequently reprinted)

Murray, Margaret A. *The Witch-Cult in Western Europe,* Oxford University Press, 1921; Oxford paperback, 1963 etc.

Notestein, Wallace. *A History of Witchcraft in England from 1558 to 1718,* American Historical Association, 1911; Russell & Russell, 1965

Podmore, Frank. *Modern Spiritualism,* 2 vols., London/Scribner's, 1902; reprinted under title *Mediums of the 19th Century,* 2 vols., University Books, 1963

Remy, Nicolas. *Demonolatry,* 1595; (ed. Montague Summers) John Rodker, London, 1930; University Books, 1974

Robbins, Rossell Hope. *The Encyclopedia of Witchcraft and Demonology,* Crown Publishers/Spring Books, London, 1959 etc.

Sanders, Ed. *The Family; The Story of Charles Manson's Dune Buggy Attack Battalion,* E. P. Dutton, 1971; Avon paperback, 1972

Scot, Reginald. *Discoverie of Witcfhcfraft,* London, 1584; Dover paperback, 1974

Shepard, Leslie. *How to Protect Yourself Against Black Magic & Witchcraft,* Citadel, 1978

Sinclair, George. *Satan's Invisible World Discovered,* Edinburgh, Scotland, 1685 etc.; Thomas George Stevenson, 1871

Sprenger, J. & H. Kramer. *Malleus Maleficarum,* 1486 etc.; (transl. & ed. Montague Summers) John Rodker, London, 1928; Benjamin Blom, 1969

Summers, Montague. *The History of Witchcraft and Demonology.* Kegan Paul, London, 1926; University Books, 1926

Summers, Montague. *The Geography of Witchcraft,* Kegan Paul, London, 1927; University Books, 1958

Valiente, Doreen. *An ABC of Witchcraft Past & Present,* Robert Hale, London, 1973; St. Martin's Press, New York, 1974

Witchcraft Digest; Voice of the Old Religion

A supplement to *WICA Newsletter*, edited by Dr. Leo Louis **Martello,** published by Witchcraft International Craft Association, Hero Press, Suite 1B, 153 West 80 Street, New York, N.Y. 10024.

Witchcraft International Craft Association (WICA)

Organized, in conjunction with **Witches Anti-Defamation League,** by author Dr. Leo Louis Martello. WICA and WADL "exist to educate the public, counteract false accusations, take legal steps, obtain IRS recognition, paid legal holidays (such as Halloween) for members, fight distortion and discrimination, sponsor seminars across the country, hold regular festivals." These organizations represent people from all walks of life, world over, "who practice the pre-Judeo-Christian, Pagan religion as outlined in Dr. Martello's book *Witchcraft; The Old Religion.* They are not Satanists, do not believe in the devil, their main deities are Mother Goddess and Horned God, and they are nature worshipers."

In 1970, WICA, backed by American Civil Liberties Union, sued the New York Parks Department for discrimination when refused a permit for their "Witch-In," and won, the first such victory for Witches in the history of the world. Address: Hero Press, 153 W. 80 Street, Suite 1B, New York, New York 10024.

Witches Anti-Defamation League (WADL)

Organized by author Dr. Leo Louis Martello "to educate the public, counteract false accusations, take legal steps, obtain IRS recognition, paid legal holidays (such as Halloween) for members, fight distortions, hold regular festivals," In conjunction with Witchcraft International Craft Association, Dr. Martello claims that witches are descendants of the Pagan religions before Christianity, as outlined in his book *Witchcraft; The Old Religion.* Members of WADL and WICA are not Satanists, do not believe in the devil, their main deities being Mother Goddess and Horned God, nature worship. Address: Witches Anti-Defamation League, Hero Press, 153 W. 80 Street, Suite 1B, New York, N.Y. 10024.

Witches' Cradle

During the witchcraft persecutions in Europe, Inquisitors are said to have sometimes put an accused witch in a bag, which was strung up over the limb of a tree and set swinging. When witches learnt about this punishment they experimented with it themselves and found that the **Sensory Deprivation** or confusion of senses induced hallucinatory experiences.

A similar swinging motion has long been used by shamans and dervishes and is sometimes known as "dervish dangling." It involves being suspended by a rope tied round the waist.

A scientific development of this technique is the ASCID (Altered States of Consciousness Induction Device) devised by Robert **Masters** and Jean **Houston** of the **Foundation for Mind Research.** This technological age witches' cradle is a metal swing in which the subject stands upright while blindfolded and with ear baffles. The motion of the swing is a complex one, exaggerating the slightest movements of the occupant. Profoundly altered states of consciousness involving hallucinatory visions and sensations often take place within twenty minutes.

Witches Newsletter

Edited by Dr. Leo Louis Martello since 1970, published quarterly by Hero Press, Suite 1B, 153 West 80 Street, New York, N.Y. 10024. This publication supersedes *New Age Intellectual Newsletter.*

Wolf, The

Amongst the ancient Romans, the wolf was a fruitful source of augury, and there are many tales in which the wolf figured as a good or evil omen.

A wolf running to the right with his mouth full was a sign of great joy. If a wolf escaped unhurt after he had entered a Roman camp, it was regarded as a sign of the army's defeat, and the terrible result of the second Punic war was said to have been augured from the carrying off of the sword of a sentinel in the camp by a wolf.

Plutarch related the story of a wolf who ate the landmarks of a proposed new settlement at Libya and thus stopped its colonization, but later another wolf which had stolen a burnt sacrifice led his pursuers to a place where they afterwards settled in.

It is said that a wolf ran off with Hiero's slate when he was a schoolboy, and this was regarded as a sign of his future greatness.

The peasants of Sweden used to avoid speaking of a wolf by name but called him the "grey one" or "old grey"; they regarded the pronouncing of his name as unlucky.

The wolf featured in Roman mythology with the story of Romulus and Remus, and throughout history there have been stories of feral children—orphans reared by wolves. For a modern case, see Charles Maclean, *The Wolf Children* (1978). (See also **Lycanthropy; Werwolf**)

Wolfsohn, Alfred (died 1962)

German singing teacher who established a school of psychophysical vocal development in England during the 1940s and 50s, reviving legends of the occult power of sound.

During World War I he served in the trenches, and suffered a breakdown, haunted by the sound of a voice calling for help. When the Nazis came to power, he was deeply impressed by the evil power associated with the voice of Adolf Hitler, amplified over street corners and the great square at Nuremberg and moving people to destructive acts of folly, hatred, ambition and unspeakable cruelty.

Wolfsohn played a significant role in the life of artist Charlotte Salomon, and features in her posthumous autobiography *Leben oder Theater?* (1981). Wolfsohn had been engaged by Charlotte's stepmother, opera singer Paula Lindberg, and soon Wolfsohn deeply affected the life and art of Charlotte. Charlotte herself, a German Jew, was murdered in the infamous Auschwitz extermination camp by the Nazis, but her paintings and prose had been left with a doctor in France before she was arrested. Charlotte's book has been compared with the *Diary* of Anne Frank, and was the basis of the film *Charlotte* by Dutch director Frans Weisz.

Before he escaped from Germany to serve with the British forces, Wolfsohn had the idea that it must be possible for the voice to have power in a positive way. He also believed that ordinary men and women have potentialities seldom shown unless under stress, when they could achieve feats of physical endurance, run faster, see further, shout louder or bear pain in a way they had not believed possible. Wolfsohn became a kind of voice doctor, working to restore fine and beautiful tones to singers suffering through fear or overstrain, and also developing a kind of psychotherapy around the vocal possibilities of ordinary individuals.

In his studio in North West London, England, he experimented to prove that the conventional musical classifications of male and female voices from bass to soprano was an artificial division, and that any normal human male or female could develop the whole range in a single voice, and in the process discover heightened consciousness. Long before the debut of Peruvian singer Yma Sumac with electronically enhanced recording, Wolfsohn demonstrated a range of eight octaves in male and female voices, old or young. His pupils figured in the *Guinness Book of Records* after demonstrating phenomenal vocal range.

Wolfsohn's work has been described as a spontaneous revival of the yoga of sound vibration (see also Swami **Nadabrahmananda**). After his death, some members of his group carried on under the tuition of his pupil Roy Hart, and a movie film record was made of their remarkable *sprechstimme* performances. The group has tended to concentrate on a new application of extended vocal range in theater rather than in musical sound. Roy Hart also died soon afterwards, but his group have carried on his work.

The only extant record of the work of Wolfsohn's pupils is the Album *Vox Humana* (No. FPX.123) issued by Folkways Records, New York in 1956. Former pupils of Wolfsohn who adapted his techniques to theater under Roy Hart as the Roy Hart Theatre Group, are located at Chateau de Malerargues, Thoiras, Aduze 30140, France.

In recent years, the therapeutic aspect of Wolfsohn's work was been carried on by Derek Gale at The Gale Centre for Creative Therapy, Whitakers Way, Loughton, Essex, England. (See also Paranormal **Music; Nada;** Swami **Nadabrahmananda** Saraswati)

Wood, Miss C. E. (1854- ?)

British **materialization** medium. She was born in October, 1854. In 1873, at the age of eighteen she was employed, with Miss Annie Fairlamb, as the official medium by the Newcastle Spiritual Evidence Society. Miss Fairlamb was a year younger.

Both mediums apparently demonstrated strong **telekinesis.** Miss Wood showed the first signs of psychic power a year before at a meeting of the society where she was taken by her father, a mechanic. She stayed with the society for three years.

In 1874, partial **materializations** were obtained, followed by full-sized phantoms under conditions of which T. B. Barkas, a prominent Newcastle investigator, wrote in the *Medium and Daybreak* (May 4, 1877): "I have seen, through the mediumship of Miss Wood, in a private house, living forms walk from the curtained recess, which it was utterly impossible for her to simulate. I have seen children, women and men of various ages, walk forth under her mediumship. I have seen a materialised form and the medium at the same time. I have had through her mediumship a child-like form standing beside me for about half an hour together; the child has placed its arms around my neck and permitted me at the same time to place my arm around her neck, and has laid its cheek against mine, breathed upon my face, and, in fact, caressed me precisely as a child would do its parent or guardian. This was not in darkness but in light, and in the presence of professors and fellows of one of the leading universities in the kingdom. I have, under these conditions, and after having handled the psychic form, seen it gradually vanish or dematerialise and become invisible in the middle of the room."

Barkas also remarked that "she is subject to strange controls, which there is some difficulty in banishing." When in the same year at Blackburn the materialized form was seized and found to be the medium, Miss Wood protested "that she was an unconscious instrument temporarily in the hands of an evil power."

The protest deserved consideration in view of the series of sittings reported in the book *Some Reminiscences* by Alfred Smedley (1900). They took place a short time before the exposure. While the medium was enclosed in a wire cage her phantom "Bennie" left excellent paraffin wax molds of his foot. He dipped his foot before the sitters into the hot dish of paraffin and cold water, then put his left leg across his right knee, tapped the mold, dematerialized his leg and when the mold was free handed it to Mr. Adshead. In the same seance, another left leg mold was obtained from "Maggie," the deceased sister of Miss Wood. On measurement it was found to be one inch less in length and one and three quarter inches less in breadth than Miss Wood's foot.

In 1878, Prof. Henry **Sidgwick** engaged her for seances at Cambridge University and at the house of Arthur **Balfour.** F. W. H. **Myers** and Edmund **Gurney** were among the investigators. Dr. Alfred Russel **Wallace** wrote in his book in *My Life* (2 vols., 1905) that Myers showed him several books full of notes of these seances and described the test which they applied.

They tied the wrists of the medium securely with tape, leaving two long ends which they tacked down to the floor and then covered with sealing wax and sealed. The medium was lying on a mattress on the bare floor. The light was sufficient to see phantom figures of children and adults issuing from the cabinet. The tapes, knots and seals were found afterwards untampered with.

On the chance objection that the medium might provide herself with tape, tacks, wax and seal, they varied the color of the sealing wax and the pattern of the seal and also employed a hammock which, by means of pulleys, was put on a weighing machine. Nevertheless, the phenomena occurred as before. Myers had never published these experiences.

In 1882 Miss Wood was exposed in Peterborough by spirit grabbing. "Pocka," her Indian child **control,** was found to be the medium on her knees, partially undressed and covered with muslin which she attempted to conceal about her person.

Nevertheless this revelation of fraud cannot adequately explain descriptions like Morell Theobald's in his book *Spirit Workers in the Home Circle* (1887). "Pocka," a "vivacious coloured little sprite about three feet high" not only came out of the cabinet, but "went to my wife who was sitting 4 or 5 feet from the cabinet, took her hand, and as my wife leaned downwards she put her tiny arms round her neck and kissed her. Crossing over the room she took my hands, then my daughter's and afterwards my daughter-in-law's hands, fondled them a bit, and retired to the cabinet." (See also Mrs. J. B. **Mellon**)

Recommended reading:

Smedley, Alfred & T. P. Barkas. *Some Reminiscences of Alfred Smedley. . . . also an Account of Miss Wood's Mediumship*, "Light," London, 1900

Woodhull, Victoria Claflin (1838-1927)

American Spiritualist, social reformer, and feminist. Born September 23, 1838 in Homer, Licking County, Ohio, she traveled with a medicine show when only a child, giving demonstrations of fortune-telling and Spiritualist seances together with her younger sister Tennessee (1846-1923). Victoria married Dr. Canning Woodhull before she was sixteen, was divorced in 1864 and later remarried twice.

In 1868 the sisters removed to New York City where they met Cornelius Vanderbilt, who was interested in Spiritualism. Vanderbilt installed them in a stock-brokerage office as Woodhull, Claflin & Company, where the "Lady Brokers" made considerable profits. From this enterprise they founded the journal *Woodhull and Claflin's Weekly* in 1870. This publication advocated equal rights for women, free love and other feminist issues.

In 1871, Victoria Woodhull spoke on women's rights before the House Judiciary Committee and became a prominent leader in the cause of women's suffrage. In 1872 she was the first woman to be nominated for the presidency, sponsored by the Equal Rights Party. Although she did not expect to be elected, she and her sister publicized their cause and attracted much attention by attempting to vote.

The February 2, 1872 issue of their *Weekly* contained a sensational story alleging intimacy between Henry Ward Beecher and the wife of Theodore Tilton. This scandal was largely to discredit Beecher's sisters, who had attacked the *Weekly's* stand on free love. In the event, Beecher went on a trial for adultery, but was exonerated. Anthony Comstock instituted libel proceedings against Victoria and Tennessee, but they were acquitted. Another *Weekly* sensation was the first publication in America of the *Communist Manifesto.*

In 1877, the sisters removed to England, where they continued to publicize women's rights. Victoria married a wealthy London banker and became well known for charitable work. With her sister, she published *The Human Body the Temple of God* (1890) and on her own account *Stirpiculture, or the Scientific Propagation of the Human Race* (1888) and *Humanitarian Money* (1892). With her daughter Zula Maud Woodhull, Victoria published *Humanitarian* magazine from 1892-1910. Meanwhile Tennessee Claflin married Francis (later Baronet) Cook. Victoria died in England June 10, 1927.

Woodman, William Robert (1828-1891)

British physician who was a member of the **Societas Rosicruciana in Anglia** and one of the founders (with W. W. **Westcott** and S. L. M. **Mathers**) of the famous occult society the Hermetic Order of the **Golden Dawn.**

Woodman practiced medicine in the Stoke Newington area of north London, but removed to Exeter in 1871. After six years he moved back to London. He was a student of **Kabala,** Egyptian antiquities, **Gnosticism** and Platonism. In 1867 he became secretary of the Rosicrucian Society and in 1878 was Supreme Magus. His magical motto in the Golden Dawn was "Vincit Omnia Veritas" (Truth Rules All). (See also **Golden Dawn**)

Woodroffe, Sir John (1865-1936)

The preeminent Western scholar of **Tantra,** a group of religious and occult Hindu scriptures emphasizing the female energy known as **Kundalini** *Shakti.*

He was born December 15, 1865, eldest son of J. T. Woodroffe, Advocate General of Bengal, India. He was educated at Woburn Park School and Oxford University, England, where he took classes in jurisprudence and the B.C.L. examinations.

He was called to the Bar in 1889, and a year later was enrolled as an advocate of the Calcutta High Court. He became a Fellow of Calcutta University and was appointed Tagore Law Professor. In collaboration with Ameer Ali he published the widely used textbook *Civil Procedure in British India.*

In 1902 he became standing Counsel to the Government of India, and in 1904 was raised to the High Court Bench, where he served for a number of years before being appointed Chief Justice in 1915. Upon his retirement he became Reader in Indian Law to the University of Oxford. He died at Beausoleil (Alpes Maritimes) January 16, 1936 at the age of 70.

In addition to his official duties, he spent many years in translation of little-known Hindu scriptures and other studies in Hindu culture, using the pseudonym "Arthur Avalon." His publications include: *Hymns to the Goddess* (1913), *The Serpent Power* (1918), *The Garland of Letters; Studies in the Mantra Shastra* (1922), *The Great Liberation (Mahanirvana Tantra)* (1928). He also published several volumes of *Tantrik Texts.*

Woodruff, Joseph L(eroy) (1913-)

Associate professor of psychology active in the field of parapsychology. Born October 8, 1913 at Galesburg, Illinois, he studied at Tarkio College, Missouri (B.A. 1936), Duke University, Durham, N.C. (M.A. 1939), Ph.D. 1941). In 1949 he married Betty Burke.

He was vocational counselor at Rutgers University, New Brunswick, N.J. 1946, faculty member, associate professor of psychology at City College of New York from 1946 onwards. He was secretary-treasurer of Division of General Psychology, New York State Psychological Association; trustee from 1950 onwards, secretary of the board of trustees from 1959 onwards of American Society for Psychical Research; charter member of the Parapsychological Association, member of the American Psychological Association, Eastern Psychological Association.

For some years Dr. Woodruff conducted quantitative research in extrasensory perception, with particular reference to the relationship between certain subjective aspects of card-calling and success in calling. His articles on parapsychology include: (in *Journal of Parapsychology*) 'Size of Stimulus Symbols in Extrasensory Perception' (with J. G. **Pratt,** vol. 3, 1939), 'Effect of Incentives of ESP and Visual Perception' (with Gardner **Murphy,** vol. 7, 1943), 'ESP Tests Under Various Physiological Conditions' (vol. 7, 1943), (with J. G. Pratt) 'An Exploratory Investigation of PK Position Effects' (vol. 10, 1948), 'Some Basic Problems for Parapsychological Research' (vol. 12, 1948); (in *Journal* of the American Society for Psychical Research), (with L. A. **Dale**) 'The Psychokinetic Effect; Further ASPR Experiments' (vol. 41, 1947), 'Subject and Experimenter Attitudes in Relation to ESP Scoring' (with L. A. Dale, vol. 44, 1950), 'ESP Function and the Psychogalvanic Response' (with L. A. Dale, vol. 46, 1952).

Woodruff, Maurice (died 1973)

Famous clairvoyant whose U.S. television shows attracted record numbers of viewers. His syndicated column reached nearly fifty million circulation, and he received five thousand letters a week from individuals seeking advice.

His predictions were exceptionally accurate and were made under any conditions, without special atmosphere or restrictions. He successfully forecast the petering out of the Vietnam war, the death of President John F. Kennedy and many other important world events. He died from a heart attack in 1973 while in Singapore.

Worcester, Constance Rulison (1896-)

Daughter of Dr. Elwood Worcester. She was born July 25, 1896, at Bethlehem, Pennsylvania, educated at Bryn Mawr College, 1915-17; Radcliffe College, Cambridge, Mass. (B.A. 1921).

She worked with James H. **Hyslop** and Walter Franklin **Prince** on study of spontaneous parapsychological phenomena during the 1920s and 1930s, and later with Dr. Gardner **Murphy** and J. B. **Rhine.**

Worcester, Elwood (1862-1940)

Protestant Episcopal clergyman, founder of the Emmanuel movement which pioneered medicine and psychotherapy in conjunction with spiritual guidance for individuals with physical, mental or nervous problems. Through James H. **Hyslop** he became interested in psychical research, and served as president of the Boston Society for Psychic Research from 1925 until his death.

Born May 16, 1862 at Massillon, Ohio, he studied at Columbia College, New York (B.A. 1886), was a student at General Theological Seminary, New York in 1887, Leipzig University (Ph.D. 1889), was ordained 1891. In 1894 he married Blanche Stanley Rulison.

He was rector at St. Stephen's Church, Philadelphia from 1896-1904, rector at Emmanuel Church, Boston from 1904-1929. He received honorary degrees from Hobart College, University of Pennsylvania, Columbia University. His books included: *Religion and Medicine* (with Samuel McComb, 1908), *The Christian Religion as a Healing Power* (1909), *Allies of Religion* (1929), *Body, Mind and Spirit* (with S. McComb, 1931). He also published an autobiography *Life's Adventure* (1931).

He died July 19, 1940, at Kennebunkport, Maine.

World Congress of Faiths

Founded in 1936 by British explorer soldier and mystic Sir Francis **Younghusband** (1863-1942). The Congress is dedicated to the work of reconciliation between different world faiths and the removal of intolerance and exclusivism, to "... instill a spirit of fellowship among mankind through religion, and ... to revitalise all that is highest in man's spiritual being."

The Congress combines dissemination of genuine knowledge of the world religions with the buildingof friendly relationships between them. It encourages inter-religious understanding through personal contacts and frank dialogue and believes that all great religions have much to learn from each other.

It arranges lectures, debates, visits to religious centers, "All Faith Services" and annual conferences. Speakers from different faiths give talks at schools and colleges. The Congress headquarters is located at Younghusband House, 26 Norfolk Square, London, W2 1RU, England. There are also branches in Kent, Bath and Bristol. A quarterly journal *World Faiths* includes news of activities, book reviews and articles of religious interest.

World Goodwill

Organization founded in 1932 to propagate the teachings of former Theosophist Alice **Bailey** (1880-1949), who founded her own Arcane School. World Goodwill seeks to mobilize the constructive power of goodwill in dealing with problems throughout the world and is preparing for the second coming of Jesus Christ on earth.

The organization supports the work of the United Nations and provides advice and assistance to individuals and groups concerned with world service projects. One of its activities has been the formation of **Triangles,** a linkage of individuals who employ constructive thought in a daily meditation of groups of three, invoking "the energies of light and goodwill" in a "network of light."

The energies are visualized as circulating through three points of a triangle, connecting with other triangles. This network carries the Great Invocation or universal prayer forming "a channel for the downpouring of light and love into the body of humanity." The bulletin *Triangles* is obtainable in ten languages, published by World Goodwill.

Address of World Goodwill: 113 University Place, 11th floor, New York, N.Y. 10003.

World Union Journal

Journal of the World Union Community propagating the teachings of Sri **Aurobindo** and the ideal of human unity. Published bi-monthly by: World Union International, Pondicherry 2, India 605002.

Worlds, Planes, or Spheres (in Theosophy)

According to the teachings of **Theosophy,** deriving from esoteric Hinduism, these are seven in number and are as follows, the older Sanskrit names, which are now superseded, being given for reference: Divine, or *Adi;* Monadic or *Anutadaka*, Spiritual or *Nirvana*, Intuitional or *Buddhi*, Mental or *Manas*, Astral or *Kama*, and Physical or *Sthulu*. These worlds are not physically separate in the manner which planets appear to be, but interpenetrate each other, and they depend for their differences on the relative density of the matter which composes them, and the consequent difference in the rates at which the matter of each world vibrates.

Except for the physical world (the densest), our knowledge of them, so far as it extends, is dependent on **clairvoyance,** and the more exalted the vision of the clairvoyant, the higher the world to which his or her vision can pierce. Each world has its appropriate inhabitants, clothed in appropriate bodies, and possessing appropriate states of consciousness.

The two highest worlds, the Divine and the Monadic, are at present incapable of attainment by human powers, the remaining five are attainable in greater or lesser degree. The Monad for the purpose of gathering experience and for development, finds it necessary to pass downwards into the material sphere, and, when it has taken possession of the spiritual, intuitional, and higher Mental Worlds, it may be looked on as an ego or soul embodying will, intuition and intellect, continuing eternally the same entity, never altering except by reason of increasing development, and hence being immortal.

These Worlds, however, do not afford sufficient scope to the Monad and it presses still further down into matter, through the lower Mental, into the Astral and Physical Worlds. The bodies with which it is there clothed form its personality and this personality suffers death and is renewed at each fresh incarnation. At the death of the physical body, the ego has merely cast aside a garment and thereafter continues to live in the next higher world, the Astral.

At the death of the **Astral body** in turn, another garment is cast aside, the ego is clear of all appendages and as it was before its descent into denser matter, having returned to the Mental World, the Heaven World. The ego finds itself somewhat strange to this situation, owing to insufficient development, and it again descends into matter as before. This round is completed again and again, and each time the ego returns with a fresh store of experience and knowledge, which strengthens and perfects the mental body.

When at last this process is complete, this body in turn is cast aside and the ego is clothed with its causal body. Again it finds itself strange and the round of descents into matters again begins and continues till the causal body has been fully developed. The two remaining worlds are but imperfectly known but the intuitional, as its name indicates, is that where the ego's vision is quickened to see things as they really are, and in the Spiritual World the divine and the human become unified and the divine purpose is fulfilled. (See also **Evolution of Life; Logos; Monad; Reincarnation; Spheres; Theosophy; Theosophical Society)**

Worlds Beyond (Fund)

A special appeal fund of the **National Spiritualist Association of Churches**, to promote knowledge of **Spiritualism** on radio and television. Formerly titled "Satellite Seances," this fund states: "It is an opportunity to show to the world the true facts about 'life after death' and 'communication.' Even now, many outside organizations are stimulating their forces to counter-censor or attempt to head off these facts. . . . Those in spirit are anxious for us to open wide the door between the two worlds of life. All we have to do is present the facts in the true light . . . The time is now for unification of world Spiritualism. The time is now for Spiritualists to step forward confidently and face the 21st century. The time is now for Worlds Beyond. Once these programs are on the air they can attract the support they need to continue through direct appeals to viewers." Address: N.S.A.C. Special Fund, P.O. Box 128, Cassadaga, Florida 32706.

Worrall, Ambrose Alexander (1899-1972)

Administrator and charismatic healer. Born January 18, 1899 at Barrow-in-Furness, Lancashire, England, he studied mechanical engineering. In 1928 he married Olga Nathalie Ripich.

From 1924-64 he was employed by the Martin Company, Baltimore, Maryland, becoming administrator, department manager; vice-president Makari Research Laboratories, Englewood, N.J., 1966; director, Life Energies Research, New York, 1968; consultant for Martin Marietta Corp., 1964-68 and Westinghouse Electric Co., Aerospace Division, Baltimore, 1969.

He was a member of the **Churches Fellowship for Psychical Study,** England, **Association for Research and Enlightenment,** Virginia Beach, Va., **Spiritual Frontiers Fellowship,** Evanston, Illinois, Fellowship of the Healing Christ, Methodist Church, and Masons; member of the board of Springfield College, Springfield, Mass.

He contributed to the annual seminars on spiritual healing held by the Laymen's Movement, Wainwright House, Rye, New York. In addition to his own healing work his interests included clairvoyance, clairaudience, clairsentience, psychokinesis, psychometry and theories of survival.

He published several pamphlets on spiritual healing and related subjects, including: *Meditation and Contemplation, Essay on Prayer, The Gift of Healing, Supernormal Healing, Practical Religion Concerning Spiritual Gifts, Philosophy and Methodology of Healing, Silentium Altum, Basic Principles of Spiritual Healing.* He also contributed articles to *Science of Mind* magazine.

His books included: (with Olga **Worrall)** *The Gift of Healing; A Personal Story of Spiritual Therapy* (1965), (with Olga Worrall) *Miracle Healers* (1968), (with O. Worrall & Will Oursler) *Explore Your Psychic World* (1970). He lectured widely on ESP and spiritual healing at colleges, churches and other associations. (See also Olga Nathalie Ripich **Worrall)**

Worrall, Olga Nathalie Ripich (Mrs. Ambrose Worrall) (1906-1985)

Associate director of New Life Clinic, Mount Washington Methodist Church, Baltimore, Maryland. Born November 30, 1906 at Cleveland, Ohio. In 1928 she married Ambrose Alexander **Worrall.**

She was a member of the **Churches Fellowship for Psychical Studies,** England; **Association for Research and Enlightenment,** Evanston, Ill.; Fellowship of the Healing Christ, Methodist Church; Academy of Religion and Mental Health. She shared her husband's interests in parapsychological studies, and was author of the book *How to Start a Healing Service* (1957). She contributed articles to *Spiritual Frontiers Journal, Science of Mind, Fate* magazine.

Mrs. Worrall was co-author of the following books: (with husband Ambrose A. Worrall) *The Gift of Healing: A Personal Story of Spiritual Therapy* (1965), (with A. A. Worrall) *Miracle Healers* (1968), (with A. A. Worrall & Will Oursler) *Explore Your Psychic World* (1970).

In addition to her writings on spiritual healing, Mrs. Worrall was also a well-known healer. For a great many years she had been healing the sick through a psychic talent manifest at the age of eight years. In addition to human beings, she even healed cats, dogs, horses, chickens and plants.

Her special gift was of great interest to physicians, some of whom have been her patients. One physician who sought her aid was Dr. John Cerutti, who had suffered from severe back pain for many years. Dr. Cerutti's experience with the healer was so profound that his wife Edwina, originally a skeptic, was won over and eventually published a book about the healer: *Olga Worrall, Mystic with the Healing Hands* (Harper & Row).

Mrs. Worrall lectured to more than 1,000 doctors at Stanford University. In an article in the September 1973 issue of *Medical Economics,* senior editor John Carlova wrote: "scores of M.D.s have gone to Olga Worrall for treatment of their own ailments and scores more have unofficially referred 'hopeless' cases to the faith healer."

Mrs. Worrall stated: "Since I am gifted in psychic abilities such as clairvoyance, etc. and spiritual healing, I am interested in the scientific research approach into parapsychological demonstrations motivated by personal experiences, especially in the areas of proving immortality and spiritual healing."

She died January 9, 1985, in Baltimore, Maryland, where she had given her healing services at the New Life Clinic. (See also Ambrose A. **Worrall**)

Wortcunning

Anglo-Saxon term for knowledge of the medical and occult properties of plants. (See also **Cunning**)

Wraith

The apparition or "**double**" of a living person, generally supposed to be an omen of death. The wraith closely resembles its prototype in the flesh, even to details of dress. There are accounts of people seeing their own wraith and among those who were warned of approaching death in this way are said to be Queen Elizabeth I, the poet Percy Bysshe Shelley, and Catherine of Russia. The latter, seeing her "double" seated upon the throne, ordered her guards to fire upon it!

But wraiths of others may appear to one or more persons. Lord Balcarres of Scotland saw the wraith of his friend "Bonnie Dundee" at the moment when the latter fell at the Battle of Killiecrankie, while poet Ben Jonson saw his eldest son's double when the original was dying of the plague.

The belief in the wraith flourishes in Europe, and in different parts of Britain it goes under different names, such as "waff," "swarth," "task," "fye," etc. Variants of the wraiths are the Irish "**fetch**," and the Welsh "lledrith."

In Scotland it was formerly believed that the wraith of one about to die might be seen wrapped in a shroud. The higher the shroud reached, the nearer was the approach of death.

Something analogous to wraith-seeing comes within the scope of modern psychical science, and the **apparition** is explained in various ways, as a projection of the "astral body" (see **astral projection**), an emanation from the person of its living prototype, or perhaps on a telepathic basis.

A well-known case was that of the Birkbeck Ghost, where three children witnessed the apparition of their mother shortly before her death. This instance, reported in *Proceedings* of the Society for Psychical Research (vol. 1, 1882, pp. 121-122), is noteworthy because of the fact that Mrs. Birkbeck was conscious before she died of having spent the time with her children. (See also **Apparitions; Astral Projection; Double; Fetch;** J. W. **Goethe; Vardøgr**)

Wrekin Trust

British based organization "concerned with the spiritual nature of Man and the Universe. It is not affiliated to any particular doctrine or dogma, does not offer any one way to 'the truth' and helps people find the disciplines most suited to them. After more than twelve years of pioneering courses and conferences on the holistic world view and introductory approaches to various disciplines, the Trust is now offering in addition, a curriculum for ongoing spiritual training. The inspiration is derived from the medieval concept of the University, which was concerned to find and orchestrate methods and systems of knowledge leading to union with the One, as the term 'Universus,' turned to the One, reveals."

The Trust was founded by Sir George Trevelyan in 1971, and is especially concerned with dissolving the barriers between science and religion. The Trust has been honored to receive the Right Livelihood Award, known as the "Alternative Nobel Prize," given in Stockholm for "Work forming an essential contribution to making life more whole, healing the planet and uplifting humanity."

The Trust has organized important conferences on science and mysticism, with papers from such distinguished individuals as Prof. Glen W. Schaefer, Prof. Joscelyn Godwin and Pir Vilayat Inayat Khan.

Address: Wrekin Trust, Runnings Park, Croft Bank, West Malvern, Worcestershire WR14 4BP, England. (See also Sir George **Trevelyan**)

Wriedt, Mrs. Etta (c. 1859-1942)

Powerful American professional **direct voice** medium, who used to charge a nominal fee of one dollar for a successful seance. She never sat in a **cabinet,** did not pass into **trance,** and often joined in the conversation of the voices with the visitors.

Admiral Usborne Moore, author of *The Voices* (1913), heard three voices talking at once, one in each ear, and one through the **trumpet.** Mrs. Wriedt only spoke English, but the voices knew no linguistic limitation. Dutch, French, Spanish, Norwegian and Arabic were often heard.

The spirit **control** of Mrs. Wriedt was an entity called "Dr. John Sharp," who claimed that he was born in Glasgow, Scotland, in the eighteenth century, lived most of his life in the United States as an apothecary farmer and died in Evansville, Indiana. He took great care of the medium—often at the nervous or psychic expense of the sitters. Admiral Moore found the strain so great on his system while sitting with the medium in Detroit that he did not recover his normal health until six weeks after he landed in Europe.

Mrs. Wriedt paid five visits to England. She came the first time in 1911, at the age of 51, on the invitation of W. T. **Stead,** and held seances at **Julia's**

Bureau. In 1912 and 1913, the arrangements for her visits were made by Admiral Moore. In 1915 and 1919, she sat chiefly in Rothesay, Scotland.

Miss E. K. Harper, W. T. Stead's secretary, recorded nearly 200 sittings with Mrs. Wriedt. She often heard the **direct voice** in daylight. There were other features to the seance, such as luminous forms gliding about the room in the darkness. Sometimes dogs materialized and barked.

The spirit control "**John King**" claimed responsibility for the physical phenomena in England. Flowers were taken from vases and placed in the hands of sitters in the dark in different parts of the room, invisible fingers touched the sitters and rapped by the trumpet to urge a hesitating person to answer promptly when spoken to, luminous discs, like a full moon and quite as brilliant, were seen to move round inside the circle. The sitters were often sprinkled with drops of water, wafts of cool air were felt and heavy objects were displaced.

"W. T. Stead" frequently communicated and gave many particulars of his passing over. He said that he was struck on the head when the "Titanic" sank, and never felt the actual sensation of drowning.

Mrs. Wriedt could clairvoyantly read names "written up," as she put it, in the dark. When a name was recognized, the voice was immediately heard from the trumpet. Once a name met with no recognition. Suddenly "John King's" voice broke the silence: "You had better clear out, my friend, nobody knows you." Admiral Moore was greeted by the voice of "Grayfeather," the Indian control of the medium J. B. **Jonson,** of Detroit, who had never manifested before through Mrs. Wriedt.

The psychical researcher Sir William F. **Barrett** heard voices simultaneously with Mrs. Wriedt. "Prof. Henry Sidgwick" came through. Barrett stated: "Mrs. Wriedt doubtless had heard his name, but he died before she visited England, and I doubt if she, or many others who knew him by name, were aware that he stammered badly. So I asked the voice 'Are you all right now?' not referring to his stammering. Immediately the voice replied: 'You mean the impediment in my speech, but I do not stutter now' . . . I went to Mrs. Wriedt's seances in a somewhat sceptical spirit, but I came to the conclusion that she is a genuine and remarkable medium, and has given abundant proof to others besides myself that the voices and the contents of the messages given are wholly beyond the range of trickery or collusion."

Chedo Miyatovich, a Serbian diplomatist and member of several learned societies, sat with Mrs. Wriedt in the company of a Croatian lawyer friend, Mr. H. Hinkovitch, who had just arrived in London. Voices of deceased friends and relatives spoke to them in Serbian, Croatian and at a later seance in German when to which Frau Professor Margarette Selenka, of Germany was present.

An attempt to discredit Mrs. Wriedt's phenomena was made in Christiania in August 1912, by Professor Birkenhead and State Chemist L. Schmelck. They averred that the noises in the trumpet were caused by lycopodium, a mildly inflammable powder used by druggists to coat pills. The claim, however, was very flimsy, and other chemists held the report up to ridicule, moreover it became known that Prof. Birkenhead was extremely deaf and could not judge voices at all.

Mrs. Wriedt died in Detroit, Michigan, September 13, 1942.

Wyllie, Edward (1848-1911)

Spirit photographer, who was psychic from his childhood, which was spent in Calcutta. He served in New Zealand in the Maori war with rank of a captain and settled in California in 1886 as a photographer. Spots and lights threatened to ruin his business until a lady, who heard of **spirit photography,** examined his plates and suggested this explanation.

The Pasadena Society for Psychical Research investigated the case on November 27, 1900, in Los Angeles. Their report stated: "As a committee we have no theory, and testify only to that which we do know. Individually we differ as to probable causes, but unanimously agree concerning the palpable facts." The committee promised $25 to any Los Angeles photographer who by trick or skill could produce similar results under similar conditions.

The early scene of Wyllie's psychic photography was Sycamore Grove, near Los Angeles. He had to move from there as the psychic "extras" obtained were dissolute-looking men and women with bleared and maudlin faces. It was suggested as an explanation that about fifty years earlier the place was the scene of wild orgies. The authorities stamped them out but the evil influences apparently clung to the place.

Wyllie was accused by Mr. P. A. Jensen in *The Progressive Thinker* of producing his spirit faces by the superposition of a prepared negative. The basis of the charge was that such a suspicious negative was found in a house where Wyllie had been. But according to James Coates in *Photographing the Invisible* (1911), Jensen had not been able to produce a single case where the negative in question had been used.

Another charge was raised by a Dr. Woillard. He said that Wyllie, for a financial consideration, taught him how to take spirit pictures. The method was to hold in the hollow of his arched hand a photo prepared with luminous paint, and keep it over plates in the dark room previous to exposure. He said that he found two such miniatures prepared with India Ink and luminous paint and that Wyllie had confessed.

As well as being a spirit photographer, Wyllie was credited with powers of **psychometry.** He could obtain photographic "extras" through the influence pertaining to some objects. James Coates sent him in California a lock of his and his wife's hair. Two human heads were obtained on a photograph and one was recognized as Mrs. Coates's grandmother. It was as a result of this experiment that Wyllie was invited to England. Coates gave the following summary of his experiments:

"About 60 percent of the photographs taken exhibited psychic extras, and 25 percent of these were identified as those of departed persons. To all the subjects Mr. Wyllie was a complete stranger, and of the origins of the psychic extras or portraits he could have no knowledge; and except in the cases where flowers—roses and lilies—were produced there was a marked absence of symbolism in the photographs taken." (See also **Spirit Photography**)

X

Xavier, Francisco Candido (1910-   )

Famous Brazilian Spiritist medium (**Spiritism** is the Brazilian form of Spiritualism, stemming from the teachings of Allan **Kardec**). Known throughout Brazil as "Chico Xavier" (pronounced *Sheeko Shaveer*), he was born April 2, 1910 in the interior town of Pedro Leopoldo in the central state of Minas Gerais. He was one of a family of nine children. His mother died when he was only five, but Chico saw her materialize after her death, and during his period at primary school three years later, be became accustomed to hearing voices and sensing spirit presences.

He won an honorable mention for an essay contest with an entry which appeared to be dictated to him by a spirit form. On being challenged to produce another "spirit essay," he went straight to the blackboard and started writing a profound statement on the theme suggested, after which the teacher recommended him to stop talking about spirit voices and to pray on conventional Catholic lines.

While still at school, Chico worked in a textile plant, and on leaving school at the age of thirteen was a counter salesman before getting a minor post at an office of the Ministry of Agriculture, where he stayed from 1933 until retiring in 1961.

He became a practicing medium in 1927 soon after one of his sisters was cured of apparent possession through the efforts of a healing medium. The whole Xavier family became Spiritists, and the medium's wife Mrs. Carmen Perácio founded an evangelical Spiritist center, where Chico manifested an ability for automatic writing. At one of these sessions, Mrs. Perácio had a vision of a priestly spirit "Emmanuel," who became Chico's spirit guide thereafter. Chico's mediumship continued in the form of automatic writing from spirit dictation.

Although nearly blind in one eye through most of his life and with only a rudimentary primary education, Chico produced a prodigious output of books recognizably in the style of hundreds of deceased Brazilian and Portuguese authors whose own works he has never had the opportunity to study. He slept only four hours and was up at seven in the morning, typing manuscripts and dealing with correspondence involving some 200 letters a day.

In addition, he visited invalids in the district and undertook voluntary social work at his Pedro Leopoldo Spiritist Center at Uberaba. Hundreds of visitors came to this center for a personal message delivered by Chico in trance, with instructions on individual problems, whether spiritual or medical. Chico published about 130 books, of which over 3,000,000 copies have been sold in 415 editions. Some of these books have been translated into Spanish, French, Japanese and Esperanto.

Two books translated into English are: *Christian Agenda* (Regency Press, London, 1970) and *The World of the Spirit* (Philosophical Library, n.d.). Chico's book *Evolucão em dois mundos* (Evolution in Two Worlds, 1959) was written in collaboration with Dr. Waldo Vieira, living 250 miles away. The chapters were written alternately in uniform style and continuity, and the work occupied only forty days.

It contained advanced scientific concepts well beyond the understanding of Chico and there is no possible doubt that such information does not come from the medium's own subconscious. Incidentally, Brazilian Spiritists follow Allan Kardec in clearly distinguishing between *escrita automatica* (automatic writing involving the medium's own subconscious) and *psiografia* (involving a spirit entity).

In spite of the enormous popularity of his prodigious literary output, Chico never accepted payment for any of his books and even disclaimed personal credit by the phrase "dictated by the spirit of—" on the title-page.

He only left Brazil on two occasions. In 1965 and 1966 he made brief trips to Spiritualist centers abroad and a pilgrimage to the tomb of Allan Kardec in Paris, France. Chico appeared on Brazilian television programs, but remained a modest, sincere individual who devoted his psychic gift to the service of mankind. He was made an honorary citizen of São Paulo in 1973, and similarly honored by other cities and towns in Brazil, including Rio de Janeiro, Uberada, Campinas and São Bernardo.

In 1977, the Government of Brazil endorsed Chico's half century as a medium by issuing a postage stamp in his honor. This official recognition of Spiritism is unique to Brazil, which has also issued postage stamps honoring Allan Kardec and his teachings.

Xenoglossis

Speaking in tongues unknown to the medium or psychic. It is also a characteristic phenomenon of some religious revivalist movements (see **Pentecostalism**). According to certain classifications the term should cover writing in tongues and "**glossolalia**" should be employed for speaking them, but some researchers like Ernesto **Bozzano,** reserved the term for speaking nonexistent pseudo-languages. Professor Charles Richet used the term "xenoglossis" inclusively to cover the various aspects.

Speaking in an unknown language is perhaps a far more impressive phenomenon than writing in it. Subconscious visual memory may account for occasional reproduction of foreign sentences, but the explanation becomes more difficult if the problem of intonation is superadded, since it necessitates an auditive memory, the subconscious retention of fragments of strange languages actually heard somewhere sometime.

H. Freeborn in 'On Temporary Reminiscence of a Long Forgotten Language During Delirium' (*Journal* of the Society for Psychical Research, vol. 10, p. 279) quoted the case of an old lady who, seized with delirium in the course of pneumonia, began to speak an unknown tongue, Hindustani, which she had neither spoken nor heard since she was brought to England at the age of four years. This is, however, a rare instance which successfully explains the gift of tongues by normal mental resources. The case was not very strong, as the language was known at an early age and the story itself was not sufficiently authenticated.

Considering the frequency of the gift of languages with modern mediums, it should have been expected that if this explanation was correct, many other similar instances would have been discovered. Even then the complication which the **direct voice** phenomenon introduces would have to be grappled with. Few people go so far as to suggest that subconscious memory can be externalized in an auditive form. Besides there are cases in which the assumption that an archaic language of a remote country has been heard, spoken and intelligently registered on the medium's brain presents unsurmountable difficulties.

The paramount question, therefore, is what is the evidence for xenoglossis? Speaking historically, in medieval times speaking in foreign languages was one of the four principal signs of the presence of a demon. The belief was bound to have its subconscious effect. The Ursuline Nuns of **Loudon,** (according to their earliest historian in *La Véritable Histoire des Diables de Loudun, par un Témoin, â Poitiers,* 1634) spoke Latin, Greek, Turkish, Spanish and in a Red Indian tongue, and confessed to having been obsessed by the devil.

In later religious revivals, the outbreak was a sign of celestial inspiration. The recitals of the refugees from the Cevennes (reported in *Le Thèâtre Sacré des Cevennes,* by M. Misson, London, 1707) contained numerous accounts of the gift among unlettered Camisard adults and also of suckling babes who spoke French in the purest diction (see also **Tremblers of the Cevennes**).

The phenomenon was noticed among the **Convulsionairies of St. Medard** in 1730, and there are very interesting accounts of how the gift descended on the congregation of the Rev. Edward **Irving** in 1831. Robert Baxter, in his book *Narrative of Facts Characterising the Supernatural Manifestations in Members of Mr. Irving's Congregation* (London, 1833), gave a very interesting narrative of his own experiences: ". . . The power of the Spirit was so great upon me that I was obliged to call out, as in agony, for pardon and forgiveness and for strength to bear a faithful testimony. In these cryings I was, however, at the time conscious of a power of utterance carrying me beyond the natural expression of my feelings . . . for the space of more than ten minutes I was, as it were, paralysed under a shaking of my limbs, my knees rapping one against the other, and no expression except a sort of convulsive sigh. During this period I had no other consciousness than this bodily emotion, and an inexpressible constraint upon my mind, which although it left me composed and sensible of all I was doing, yet prevented my utterance and gave no distinct impression, beyond a desire to pray for the knowledge of the Lord's will. This increased so much that I was led to fall on my knees and cry in a loud voice 'Speak, Lord, for they servant hearest,' and this I repeated many times, until the same power of the Spirit which I had before felt, came upon me, and I was made to cry out with great vehemence, both of tone and action, that the coming of the Lord should be declared, and the messengers of the Lord should bear it forth upon the mountains and upon the hills, and tell it to the winds, that all the earth should hear it and tremble before the Lord."

The utterances often began in an unknown tongue and then passed into English. One witness described them thus: "The tongue invariably preceded, which at first I did not comprehend, because it burst forth with an astonishing and terrible crash, so suddenly and in such short sentences that I seldom recovered from the shock before the English commenced."

The phrases were mostly taken from the Scriptures and repeated again and again. The actual words of the tongues were not recorded. Baxter believed them to be a jargon of sounds. The fact, however, was that the possessed spoke with extraordinary fluency in those languages, too, with which they were but imperfectly acquainted. The utterances were grandiose both in manner and diction.

In a pamphlet *Drei Tage in Gros Almerode (Three Days in Great Almerode)* J. Busching, a theological student of Leipzig, described ten cases of xenoglossis at a religious revival in 1907 at Almerode, a small town in Hesse. The phenomena began with a hissing or peculiar gnashing sound. These sounds were caused by the subject, not wishing to disturb the order of service by interrupting a prayer already commenced, exerting himself to repress the inward impulse acting on his organs of speech. But the sounds had to come out, and the momentarily repressed glossolalies only burst forth with increased vigor.

The "interpretation of tongues" does not always occur even when it is prayed for. When it occurs the speakers may either see the translation written before them, or hear it inwardly, or perceive directly the meaning of the foreign words.

It is interesting to note that the psychical researcher F. W. H. **Myers** did not believe in the phenomenon. He said that he only knew of a few instances when a few words, fragments of a language, came through the medium—some Italian and Hawaiian words in Mrs. Piper's utterances and a few Kaffir and Chinese words through Miss Browne. "We have no modern case, no case later than the half-mythical Miracles of the Cevennes, where such utterance has proved to be other than gibberish."

Apparently Myers ruled out or was unaware of many interesting early cases, among them the testimony of Judge J. W. **Edmonds.** His daughter, Miss Laura Edmonds, was the first medium in modern Spiritualism with the gift of tongues. Foreign sitters could converse through her with spirits in their native language, even if it was a country as remote as Greece or Poland.

Judge Edmonds wrote in a letter dated October 27, 1857: "One evening when some 12 or 15 persons were in my parlor, Mr. E. D. Green, an artist of this city, was shown in, accompanied by a gentleman whom he introduced as Mr. Evangelides, of Greece. He spoke broken English, but Greek fluently. Ere long, a spirit spoke to him through Laura, in English, and said so many things to him that he identified him as a friend who had died at his house a few years before but of whom none of us had ever heard. Occasionally, through Laura, the spirit would speak a word or a sentence in Greek, until Mr. E. inquired if he could be understood if he spoke in Greek. The residue of the conversation, for more than an hour, was, on his part, entirely in Greek, and on hers sometimes in Greek and sometimes in English. At times Laura would not understand what was the idea conveyed, either by her or him. At other times she would understand him, though he spoke in Greek, and herself when uttering Greek words. . . .

"One day my daughter and niece came into my library and began a conversation with me in Spanish, one speaking a part of a sentence and the other the residue. They were influenced, as I found, by a spirit of a person whom I had known when in Central America, and reference was made to many things which had occurred to me there, of which I knew they were as ignorant as they were of Spanish. . . . Laura has spoken to me in Indian, in the Chippewa and Menomonie tongues. I knew the language, because I had been two years in the Indian country."

According to the book *Modern American Spiritualism* by Emma Hardinge [Britten] (1870), in addition to Miss Edmonds, the gift was demonstrated at an early period by Miss Jenny Keyes who sang in trance in Italian and Spanish, and by Mrs. Shepherd, Mrs. Gilbert Sweet, Miss Inman, Mrs. Tucker, Miss Susan Hoyt, A. D. **Ruggles** and several others whose names she was not permitted to make public. They frequently spoke in Spanish, Danish, Italian, Hebrew, Greek, Malay, Chinese and Indian.

In 1859, nineteen people testified in the *Banner of Light* to thirty-four cases of persons who occasionally spoke or wrote in tongues. Prof. J. J. **Mapes** and Governor N. P. **Tallmadge** bore witness to numerous instances in which uneducated mediums conversed with poor strangers in the streets in various foreign languages.

In 1869, a Mr. Lowenthal testified in England before the Committee of the **London Dialectical Society:** "I am frequently made to speak the language of another nation. I believe it to be an Indian language. My mouth utters sounds that I do not understand and which have no meaning to me. I think it is the language of some North American tribe. It is a soliloquy, and I get an impression on the brain, an idea that it means so and so. A voice articulate but not audible conveys a meaning to me. I have been among the Indians a great deal, and it sounds to me like their language."

Archdeacon Thomas **Colley** wrote of having heard the "Mahedi," a materialized Egyptian in the mediumship of Dr. **Monck** (who knew no English) speak in that language under the control of Monck's regular guide, "Samuel." This appears to be the only instance on record where a claimed materialized individual is used as an automatic instrument by another spirit.

The Italian medium Alfredo **Pansini,** who, with his brother Paolo, was the subject of remarkable bodily transportation (see **teleportation**) by mediumistic power, spoke in a sort of hypnotic trance at the age of seven, in French, Latin and Greek, and recited in a wonderful manner several cantos of the *Divina Commedia.* On one occasion he spoke successively in twelve different voices.

Dr. F. **van Eeden** recorded in *Proceedings* of the Society for Psychical Research (vol. 17, 1901, pp. 59, 75) a Dutch conversation with a deceased friend through the medium Mrs. Thompson: "During a few minutes . . . I felt absolutely as if I were speaking to my friend myself. I spoke Dutch and got immediate and correct answers. The expression of satisfaction and gratification in face and gesture, when we seem to understand one another was too vivid to be acted. Quite unexpected Dutch words were pronounced, details were given which were far from my mind, some of which, as that about my father's uncle in a former sitting, I had never known, and found to be true only on inquiry afterwards."

Many eminent German orientalists testified that when the stigmatic subject Thérèse **Neumann** relived the Passion of Christ, she spoke in ancient Aramaic. The weakness of the case is that the phrases which she used exist in print with translations in modern languages. But if this were not so, the authenticity of language could not be proved anyway.

The New York *Evening Post* reported on November 10, 1930, the case of a little four-year-old girl at Warsaw. Although the parents of Marie Skotnicki only spoke Polish, she developed the extraordinary habit of talking to herself in a foreign tongue which no one about her could understand, but which was later established to be pure Gaelic. It is interesting to add that her great-grandfather came from the Island of Lewis in the Scottish Hebrides.

In *The Two Worlds* (March 31, 1933), Dr. F. H. Wood wrote of the medium Rosemary and "Lady Nona," her ancient Egyptian **control:** "The fact is now established beyond disproof that over 140 Egyptian word-phrases which were in common use when the great Temple of Luxor in Egypt was built, have been spoken fluently through an English girl who normally knows nothing about the ancient tongue." Howard Hulme of Brighton, Sussex, the translator of the Egyptian phrases, after a preliminary test by post which resulted in an unexpected but correct Egyptian answer, had also heard "Lady Nona" speak. After an amazing dialogue in the dead tongue of the pyramid builders, "Nona cleared up many points of pronunciation, gave her own earth name and explained the full meaning of some of her previous language tests."

For a modern review of the background and literature of the Rosemary case, see the article 'The Rosemary Case of Alleged Egyptian Xenoglossy' by William H. Kautz (*Theta*, vol. 10, No. 2, Summer 1982). Dr. Kautz also announced an important computer-based project at the Research Center for Applied Intuition (of which he is founder director), involving the preparation of a translation and lexicon of the Rosemary Egyptian language text, to be studied in conjunction with all relevant publications relating to Egyptian language of the 18th Dynasty, and a reconstitution of vocal Egyptian of the same period. The lexicon will be compared with written Egyptian language and also with the reconstitution of the spoken form.

There is apparently no special difficulty of speaking in a foreign tongue through **direct voice** mediumship. If the explanation of the spirit communicators is to be accepted, that an artificial larynx is built up out of **ectoplasm** in space, outside the medium's body, the brain and vocal organs of the medium seem almost entirely ruled out. Almost, because there are indications that the ectoplasmic matter for this artificial larynx is drawn from the oral cavity and may not be always adaptable to unusual inflections. The spirit control "John King," in direct voice, spoke English. Through the medium Eusapia **Palladino,** he could only speak Italian.

But there is very little ground for generalization. The strangeness of inflection did not prevent the direct voices of the medium Mrs. Etta **Wriedt** from speaking in many unknown tongues, and no stranger inflection could be imagined than the archaic Chinese which the voice of "Confucius" used in speaking through the medium George **Valiantine** to Dr. Neville **Whymant,** the renowned Oriental scholar. Whymant heard fourteen languages spoken in twelve seances, and the strangest of all was the speech which came to him in fluent classical Chinese: "Greetings, O son of learning, and reader of strange books," and gave a complete new reading of poems and of the Analects of Confucius, over which learned scholars have differed for centuries. Dr. Whymant's book *Psychic Adventures in New York* (1931) is the most convincing record of the gift of tongues in the present age.

Spirit Languages—The Primeval Tongue

The gift is not restricted to languages known to the sitters or known at all. Possibly such unknown tongues are pure gibberish or attempts at a subconscious creation of a new language.

Professor William **James** communicated 'A Case of Psychic Automatiom . . . ' (*Proceedings* of Society for Psychical Research vol. 12, 1896), dealing with the experiences of Mr. Albert Le Baron (pseudonym), an American journalist in a Spiritualist camp. He spoke automatically in an unknown tongue, fragments of which were written down by himself, others spoken into a phonograph in the presence of Professor James and Dr. Richard **Hodgson.** The following is a specimen: *Te rumete tau. Ilee lete leele luto scele. Impe re scele lee luto. Onko keere scete tere lute. Ombo te scele to bere te kure. Sinte lute sinte Kuru. Orumo imbo impe rute scelete. Singe, singe, singe eru. Imba, Imba, Imba.*

The translation was furnished by the medium himself: "The old word! I love the old word of the heavens! The love of the heavens is emperor. The love of the darkness is slavery. The heavens are wise, the heavens are true, the heavens are sure. The love of the earth is past. The King now rules in the heavens."

Governor N. P. **Tallmadge** reported seeing a lady translating the Old Testament into hieroglyphics, which were said to be the original language in which it was written. There is, of course, no justification for the lady's belief, but her activity is an interesting example of subconscious creativity.

Some spirit languages were allegedly so condensed that (as psychical researcher Frank **Podmore** quoted) the phrase "Ki-e-lou-cou-ze-ta" required no less than forty-five words to furnish an adequate translation in English.

The primeval language and the claimed "Martian" languages (see Hélène **Smith**) present the most interesting problems. The primeval language or nature language was described as the inner language of the soul, the universal tongue of men before the Fall, of which Hebrew is a corrupted form. In origin it is the language of the angels of which the seer Emanuel **Swedenborg** wrote in his book *The True Christian Religion* as follows:

"There is a universal language, proper to all angels and spirits, which has nothing in common with any language spoken in the world. Every man, after death, uses this language, for it is implanted in every one from creation; and therefore throughout the whole spiritual world all can understand one another. I have frequently heard this language and, having compared it with languages in the world, have found that it has not the slightest resemblance to any of them; it differs from them in this fundamental respect, that every letter of every word has a particular meaning."

Further, in his book *Heaven and Hell* Swedenborg stated:

"Writing in the inmost heaven consists of various inflected and circumflected forms and the inflections and circumflections are according to the form of heaven. By these the angels express the arcana of their wisdom, many of which cannot be uttered by words; and, what is wonderful, the angels are skilled in such writing without being taught, for it is implanted in them like their speech . . . and therefore this writing is heavenly writing, which is not taught, but inherent, because all extensions of the thoughts and affections of the angels, and thus all communication of their intelligence and wisdom, proceeds according to the form of heaven, and hence their writing also flows into that form. I have been told that the most ancient people on this earth wrote in the same manner before the invention of letters, and that it was transferred into the letters of the Hebrew language which in ancient times were all inflected. Not one of them had the square form in use at this day; and hence it is that the very dots, iotas and minutest parts of the word contain heavenly arcana and things Divine."

The first record of the existence of such a language seems to be in the experiments of Dr. John Dee (1527-1608). The next, apart from Swedenborg, was in the visions of the Seeress of Prevorst (see Frau Frederica **Hauffe**), confirmed by another somnambule of Heinrich Werner a few years later, cited in his book *Die Schutzgeister, oder Merkwürdige Blicke zweier Seherinnen in die Geisterwelt* (Stuttgart, 1839).

In Dr. Dee's notes, the invocation of the spirits was given in the "primeval language." It was accompanied by a word for word translation. The properties of this ancient tongue claimed as that which Adam employed and the angels speak, are singular. To quote: "Every letter signifieth the member of the substance whereof is speaketh: every word signifieth the quiddity of the substance . . . signifying substantially the thing that is spoken of in the centre of his Creator, whereby even as the mind of man moveth at an ordered speech, and is easily persuaded in things that are true, so are the creatures of God stirred up in themselves, when they hear the words wherewithal they were nursed and brought forth . . . the creatures of God understand you not. You are not of their Cities: you are become enemies, because you are separated from Him that governeth the City, by ignorance. . . . Men in his Creation, being made innocent was also authorised and made partaker of the Power and Spirit of God, whereby he did know all things under his Creation, and spoke of them properly, naming them as they were."

In plain language, this apparently means that the original speech bore an organic relation to the outer world, that each name expressed the properties of the thing spoken of and that the utterances of that name had a compelling power over that creature. This has analogues in the mystical traditions of the Hebrew **shemhamphorash,** the secret name of God, and the mystical traditions connected with Hindu mantras.

In his book *The Seeress of Prevorst* (1845), Justinus Kerner wrote: "In her sleep-waking state, Mrs. H. frequently spoke in a language unknown to us, which seemed to bear some resemblance to the Eastern tongues. She said that this language was the one which Jacob spoke, and that it was natural to her and to all men. It was very sonorous, and as she was perfectly consistent in her use of it, those who were much about her gradually grew to understand it. She said, by it only could she fully express her innermost feelings; and that, when she had to express these in German, she was obliged first to translate them from this language. It was not from her head, but from her epigastric region that it proceeded. She knew nothing of it when she was awake. The names of things in this language, she told us, expressed their properties and quality. Philologists discovered in it a resemblance to the Coptic Arabic and Hebrew: for example, the word 'Elschaddai,' which she often used for God, signifies, in Hebrew, the self-sufficient, or all-powerful. The word 'dalmachan' appears to be Arabic, and 'Bianachli' signifies in Hebrew: I am sighing, or in sighs.

"Here follow a few of the words of this inner language, and their interpretations: 'Handacadi,' physician: 'alentana,' lady; 'chlann,' glass; 'schmado,' moon; 'nohin,' no; 'mochiane,' nightingale; 'bianna fina,' many coloured flowers; 'moy', how; 'toi,' what; 'optini poga,' thou must sleep; 'mo li arato,' I rest, etc.

"The written characters of this language were always connected with numbers. She said that words with numbers had a much deeper and more comprehensive signification than without. She often said, in her sleep-waking state, that the ghosts spoke this language; for although spirits could read the thoughts, the soul, to which this language belonged, took it with it when it went above; because the soul formed an ethereal body for the spirit."

Some pages further, Kerner stated:

"With respect to the inner language, the Seherin [Seeress] said, that one word of it frequently expressed more than whole lines of ordinary language; and that, after death, in one single symbol or character of it, man would read his whole life. It is constantly observed that persons in a sleep-walking state, and those who are deep in the inner-life, find it impossible to express what they feel in ordinary language. Another somnambule used often to say to me, when she could not express herself 'Can no one speak to me in the language of nature?'

"The Seherin observed by Mayers said, that to man, in the magnetic state, all nature was disclosed, spiritual and material; but that there were certain things which could not be well expressed in words, and thus arose apparent inconsistencies and errors. In the archives of animal magnetism, an example is given of this peculiar speech; the resemblance of which to the eastern languages doubtless arises from its being a remnant of the early language of mankind. Thus, sleep-walkers cannot easily recall the names of persons and things, and they cast away all conventionalities of speech. Mayers' Seherin says, that as the eyes and ears of man are deteriorated by the fall, so he has lost in a great degree the language of his sensations; but it still exists in us, and would be found, more or less, if sought for. Every sensation or perception has its proper figure or sign and this we can no longer express.

"In order to describe these perceptions, Mrs. H. constructed figures which she called 'her sun sphere,' 'her life sphere' and so forth."

"Many instances proved how perfect her memory for this inner language was. On bringing her the lithograph of what she had written a year before, she objected that there was a dot too much over one of the signs; and on referring to the copy which I had by me, I found she was right. She had no copy herself."

Heinrich Werner in his book *Die Schutzgeister oder Merkwürdige Blicke Zweier Seherinen in die Geisterwelt,* (Stuttgart, 1839) gave a dissertation on the inner language, traces of which he found in the babbling of children, and stated that in rare states of exaltation the inner spirit can recover the lost vocabulary. However the confirmation of Werner's somnambule of the revelations of the Seeress of Prevorst has no evidential value, since it cannot be supposed that she was unacquainted with Werner's very popular book.

With the advent of modern Spiritualism, the idea of the primeval tongue faded out. Nor did spirit languages hold out for long. Mrs. Newton **Crosland** was one of the last of its recorders in Britain. In her book *Light in the Valley* (1857) she wrote:

"Three years ago a young lady, a medium whom I shall designate The Rose was taught by spirits, directly communicating with her, three spirit languages; that is to say, she was taught the meaning of certain characters and inflections, which are quite distinct, so far as I have been able to ascertain, from any known languages ancient or modern. . . . Introduced last autumn to another medium, a young lady whom we have been instructed to call Comfort, The Rose discovered that her new acquaintance wrote by spirit power the first-taught of these mystic languages. . . . Subsequently five other mediums, all personally known to me, have developed as writers of the first spirit language; and one of them, an author of repute and M.A. of the University of Oxford, has also on two or three occasions written in the second of the spirit languages, the characters of which seem mainly composed of dots."

The universal language of Swedenborg, if we are to trust the revelations of Mrs. Crosland, developed dialects. Unfortunately the sample of spirit writing in *Light in the Valley* is the plainest scribble and no evidence whatever was introduced to show how the identity, if any, was established among the strange ornaments of spiral and shell forms, with dots and scroll-like ciphers which adorned the spirit drawing illustrations.

The Language of the Red Planet

Of the Martian language, the first revelation and translation was given by Mlle. Hélène **Smith.** The exhaustive analysis of Professor Theodore **Flournoy,** however, clearly proved that the originator of this language modeled it after French, and that this marvel of subconscious activity could not be ascribed to extra-terrene sources. The following samples give a fair idea of this French-Martian:

men mess Astané cé ames é vi itech li
Ami grand Astané je viens à toi toujours par

tés alizé neümi assilé kà inaniné
cet élément mysterieux immense qui enveloppe

êzi atèv ni lé tazié é vi med iées éziné
mon être et me lance à toi ptoutres mes

rabris ni tibras man amès di ouradé ké
pensées et besoins Ami viens te souvenir qu
e

Matêmi uzénir cheé kida ni ké chée brizi pi déz anir évaï diviné tès luné.

Matêmi attendra ta faveur et que ta sagesse lui répondra. Sois heureux ce jour.

(Friend, great Astané, I come to Thee always by this element, mysterious, immense, which envelops my being and launches me to thee by all my thoughts and desires. Friend, come Thou to remember that Matêmi will await thy favour, and that thy wishes will answer them. Be happy to-day.)

sazeni kiché nipunêze dodé né pit léziré bèz neura évaï dastrée firêzi zé bodri né dorimé zi pastri tubré né tuxé.

Sazeni pourquoi craindre? Ceci est sans souffrance ni danger sois paisible; certainement le os est sain le sang seul est malade.

(Sazeni, why fear? This is without suffering or danger, be peaceful; certainly the flesh is well, the blood alone is ill.)

Another Martian language was produced, a few years later, by the medium Mrs. **Smead** in America. It was illustrated by the following words and sentences: Zentin (cold), zentinen (very cold), dirnstze (north temperate zone), dirnstzerin (south temperate zone), emerincenren (equator), mimtenirimte (continent); ti inin amarivim (the boy walks); mare (man), maren (men, kare (woman), karen (women), ti maren arivie warire ti marenensis aru ti Artez feu ti timeviol (the men went with the subjects of the chief ruler to the temple); moken irin trinen minin aru ti maren inine tine (flowers bloom there, many of the great men plant them).

In the third Martian language, that of Dr. Mansfield Robinson, Oom ga wa na wa, was supposed to mean God is all in all. In 1928, it was sent as a message to Mars by Dr. Robinson in radio signals. He listened in vain for a reply.

To Hélène Smith, the original producer of a Martian tongue, we also owe linguistic records of an Ultra-Martian, an Uranian and a Lunarian romance. According to Prof. Fournoy they were efforts of her subconscious to overcome the deficiencies of the Martian achievement and defy an earthly explanation. The following trilingual fragment illustrates the Ultra-Martian language:

Ultra-Martian: Bak sanak top
Martian: Sirima nêbé viniâ-ti-mis-métiche
French: Rameau vert nom de un homme

anok sik Etip vané sanim
ivré toué viniâ-ti-misé-bigâ azâni maprinié
sacré dans nom de un enfant malentré

batam icem tanak vanem sébim
imizi kramâ ziné viniâ-ti-mis-zaki datrinié
sous panier bleu nom de un aninal caché

mazak tatak sakam
tuzé vâmé gâmié
malade triste pleure

The Uranian tongue was a very musical one. But no translation was given while Prof. Flournoy had an opportunity of investigation. The following is a sample:

pa lalato lito nalito bo. . . . té zototi zolota matito yoto . . . mé linoti to toda pé fâ mâ . . . nana tatazô ma oto dô. . . .

The points stand for stops in the clairaudient reception of the words.

Of the Lunarian language, no sample came into Prof. Flournoy's possession. All these interstellar languages were accompanied by alphabetical scripts except the Uranian, the writing of which was ideographic, its curious hieroglyphs expressing words and not letters.

Writing in Tongues

To return from interstellar space, writing in tongues is a comparatively frequent phenomenon; it is unnecessary to over-emphasize it.

According to Dr. Hodgson, "the chief difficulty, apparently, in getting another language written by the hand is that strange words tend to be written phonetically unless they are thought out slowly letter by letter.

The medium William **Eglinton** produced messages in a seance with the statesman Gladstone in Spanish, French and Greek in direct writing. He did not know Spanish and Greek. An apparition at a seance with Mme. **d'Esperance,** calling herself "Nepenthes," wrote in classic Greek in Prof. L.'s notebook: "I am Nepenthes, thy friend. When thy soul is oppressed by overmuch pain, call on me, Nepenthes, and I will speedily come to assuage thy trouble."

In the experience of Prof. Charles Richet, Mrs. X. (Mrs. Laura Finch) a young woman of thirty, "wrote long sentences in Greek, with some errors, that clearly show mental vision of one or more Greek books. After much research . . . I was able to discover the book from which Mrs. X. had drawn most of the long Greek sentences that she had written in my presence. The book is not to be found in Paris except in the National Library—the Greco-French and Franco-Greek dictionary by Byzantios and Coromelas. As it is a dictionary of modern Greek, it is not in use in any school."

Prof. Richet further stated that Mrs. X. wrote some twenty lines of Greek with about eight percent of small errors, that she was looking into space as if she were copying from the text of a language unknown to her of which she saw the characters without knowing their meaning, that Mme. X. knew no Greek at all and could not understand the sentences that appeared before her mental vision.

Several other examples of the gift are to be found in Florizel von Reuter's two books: *Psychic Experiences of a Musician* (1928) and *The Consoling Angel* (1930). The Chinese **cross correspondences** of "Margery" (Mrs. M. S. **Crandon**) furnish especially striking instances.

Dr. George B. Cutten, former president of Colgate University, published a comprehensive book on *Speaking with Tongues* (1927). Another valuable monograph on the subject is Ernesto Bozzano's *Polyglot Mediumship* (1932). (See also **Glossolalia; Pentecostalism; Tongues**)

Recommended reading:

Bozzano, Ernesto. *Polyglot Mediumship (Xenoglossy)*, Rider & Co., London, 1932

Cutten, George B. *Speaking With Tongues: Historically and Psychologically Considered*, Yale University Press, 1927

Dalton, Robert Chandler. *Tongues Like As of Fire*, Gospel Publishing House, Springfield, Missouri, 1945

Kelsey, Morton T. *Tongue Speaking; An Experiment in Spiritual Experience*, Waymark paperback (Doubleday), 1968

Lombard, Emile. *De la Glossolalie chez les Premiers Chrétiens et des Phénomènes Similaires*, Bridel, Lausanne, 1910

Lovekin, Arthur Adams. *Glossolalia; A Critical Study of Alleged Origins, the New Testament and the Early Church*, (unpublished master's thesis), Graduate School of Theology, University of the South, Sewanee, Tennessee, 1962

Martin, Ira Jay. *Glossolalia in the Apostolic Church*, Berea College Press, Kentucky, 1960

Wood, F. H. *After Thirty Centuries*, Rider, London, 1935

Wood, F. H. *This Egyptian Miracle*, Rider, London, 1940; revised ed. J. M. Watkins, London, 1955

Xibalba

The Hades of the Kiche (or Quiché) Indians of Central America. (See **Mexico and Central America**)

Xylomancy

Divination by means of wood, practiced particularly in Slavonia. It was the art of reading omens from the position of small pieces of dry wood found in one's path.

Presages of future events were also drawn from the arrangement of logs in the fireplace, and from the manner in which they burned. It is perhaps a survival of this mode of divination when people say, when a burning log is disturbed, that "they are going to have a visitor."

Y

Yadachi

A Mongolian weather changer. (See **Siberia**)

Yadageri

The science of inducing rain and snow by means of enchantment. (See **Siberia**)

Yaksha (or Jak)

A kind of Hindu supernatural being, usually inoffensive, but sometimes troublesome. Yakshas seem to have been somewhat analogous with the fairies of other countries.

According to W. Crooke, author of *Religion and Folklore of Northern India* (1926): "The *Jak* is the modern representative of the *Yaksha,* who in better times was the attendant of Kuvera, the god of wealth, in which duty he was assisted by the Guhyaka. The character of the *Yaksha* is not very certain. He was called Punay-janas, 'the good people,' but he sometimes appears as an imp of evil. In the folktales, it must be admitted, the *Yakshas* have an equivocal reputation. In one story the female, or *Yakshini,* bewilders travellers at night, makes horns grow on their foreheads, and finally devours them; in another the *Yakshas* have, like the *Churel,* feet turned the wrong way and squinting eyes, in a third they separate the hero from the heroine because he failed to make due offerings to them on his wedding day. On the other hand, in a fourth tale the Yakshini is described as possessed of heavenly beauty; she appears again when a sacrifice is made in a cemetery to get her into the hero's power, as a heavenly maiden beautifully adorned, seated in a chariot of gold surrounded by lovely girls; and lastly, a Brahman meets some Buddhist ascetics, performs the *Uposhana* vow, and would have become a god, had it not been that a wicked man compelled him by force to take food in the evening, and so he was reborn as a *Guhyaka.*

"In the modern folk-lore of Kashmir, the *Yaksha* has turned into the *Yech* or *Yach,* a humorous, though powerful, sprite in the shape of a civet cat of a dark colour, with a white cap on his head. This small cap is one of the marks of the Irish fairies, and the *Incubones* of Italy wear caps, 'the symbols of their hidden, secret natures.' The feet of the *Yech* are so small as to be almost invisible, and it squeaks in a feline way. It can assume any shape, and if its white cap can be secured, it becomes the servant of the possessor, and the white cap makes him invisible.

"In the *Vishnu Purana* we read that Vishnu created the *Yakshas* as beings emaciate with hunger, of hideous aspect, and with big beards, and that from their habit of crying for food they were so named. By the Buddhists they were regarded as benignant spirits. One of them acts as sort of chorus in the *Meghaduta* or 'Cloud of Messenger' of Kalidasa. Yet we read of the *Yaka Alawaka,* who, according to the Buddhist legend, used to live in a Banyan tree, and slay any one who approached it; while in Ceylon they are represented as demons whom Buddha destroyed. In later Hinduism they are generally of fair repute, and one of them was appointed by Indra to be the attendant of the Jaina Saint Mahavira." (See also **Fairies**)

Yantra

Hindu mystical diagram, often inscribed on copper. Divine energy is invoked into the *yantra* by special prayers. The *yantra* is clearly a precursor of the magic diagrams of Western occultists, although in India it was used in a religious rather than an occult context. (See also **Magical Diagrams**)

Yarker, John (1833-1913)

British Freemason and occultist, active in Manchester, England. He was initiated as a Mason at the age of 21 in the Lodge of Integrity, No. 189, Manchester, October 25, 1854, becoming Master of this Lodge in 1857. He became the first Worshipful Master of the Fidelity Lodge of Mark Masters, No. 31. At the age of 23, he was installed a Knight Templar in the Jerusalem Conclave on July 11, 1856. There followed various Masonic honors, and in 1864 he was appointed Masonic Grand Constable of England. He also traveled extensively, visiting America, the West Indies, and Cuba. At a time of Masonic renaissance, he revived many rites, and promoted a number of rites on his own, probably more for vanity than profit. These included the Rites of Sat B'Hai, Swedenborg, Mizraim, and the Ancient and Primitive Rite. The latter was later associated with occultists Theodor **Reuss** and Aleister **Crowley.**

Yarker was thus associated with the fringe Masonic secret orders which preceded the establishment of the **O.T.O.** and **Golden Dawn.** The O.T.O. originated in a charter from Yarker to the German occultists Joshua Klein, Franz **Hartmann,** and Theodore **Reuss,** licensing them to set up in Berlin a Grand Lodge of the Masonic rite of Mizraim and Memphis. By 1904, occultist Karl Kellner was also involved. The August Order of Light, developed by Maurice Portman was passed to Yarker circa 1890, who amalgamated it with rituals from his Sat B'Hai Rite, later passing to the **Societas Rosicruciana in Anglia.**

Yarker published a number of Masonic works, and also an abridged translation of Alphonse **Cahagnet's** *Magie Magnétique* under the title *Magnetic Magic* (1898). His most well-known work was *The Arcane Schools; A Review of Their Origin and Antiquity; with a General History of Freemasonry* (1909). He also edited a periodical *The Kneph* (1881-95), concerned with Masonic matters.

He died on March 30, 1913.

Yasodhara Ashram

Spiritual retreat and study center founded in 1962 by German-born woman Swami Sivananda **Radha** in Canada, a disciple of the late Swami **Sivananda** Saraswati of Rishikesh, Himalayas, India.

The Yasodhara Ashram is situated in beautiful surroundings of lake, forests and mountains, and includes residential buildings, a guest lodge, prayer room, print shop, bookstore, office, recording studio, and a Temple of All Faiths.

In addition to the ashram residents, facilities are offered for temporary residents to follow teaching programs in courses and workshops dealing with Eastern spiritual teachings and Western techniques for self-development. A Yoga Teachers Course is also organized. The ashram publishes a journal *Ascent* three times a year, and issues tape and disc recordings concerned with Meditation, Mantras and Kundalini Yoga. Address: Yasodhara Ashram, Kootenay Bay, British Columbia, Canada VOP 1XO.

Yauhahu

A spirit supposed to cause diseases amongst Indians of British Guiana. (See **America**)

Yeats, W(illiam) B(utler) (1865-1939)

Famous Irish poet, playwright and mystic. He was born at Sandymount, near Dublin, Ireland, on June 13, 1865. His father John Yeats was a talented portrait painter, whose works included a fine likeness of J. M. Synge. William's brother Jack Butler Yeats was also an artist, and his sisters Elizabeth and Lily assisted in the establishment of the Dun Emer (later Cuala) Press.

Much of William's childhood was spent in London, where he attended the Godolphin School, Hammersmith, but he also spent time in Dublin and County Sligo, in Western Ireland. At the age of fifteen, he attended Erasmus Smith School, Dublin, then studied art for three years, turning to literature at the age of twenty-one. His first book, a little play titled *Mosada* was published in 1886. It was followed by two books of poems, *The Wanderings of Oisin* (1889) and *The Wind Among the Reeds* (1899). In 1888, he had edited a collection titled *Fairy and Folk Tales of the Irish Peasantry,* which included some of his fairy verse. He became one of the leading figures in the Irish literary renaissance.

In London he was a founder of the Rhymers' Club and friend of Ernest Rhys, Ernest Dowson, Lionel Johnson, William Morris, W. E. Henley, and Arthur Symons. In Ireland, he was associated with J. M. Synge, "AE" (George W. **Russell**), Douglas Hyde, George Moore and Lady Gregory. He helped to establish the Irish Literary Theatre in 1899 (later the Abbey Theatre). His poems and plays have become world famous. He was a member of the Irish Senate from 1922-28, and received the Nobel Prize for Literature, 1923.

The occult and mystical side of his life and work received less publicity than his splendid literary work, yet he believed that his poetry owed much to his occult studies. In 1892, he wrote: "If I had not made magic my constant study I could not have written a single word of my Blake book, nor would *The Countess Kathleen* have ever come to exist. The mystical life is the centre of all that I do and all that I think and all that I write."

His interest in the writings of Theosophists led to the formation of the **Hermetic Society,** Dublin, and he presiding over its first meeting on June 16, 1885. While in London at the end of 1888, he joined the Esoteric Section of the **Theosophical Society.** In 1890, he joined the famous occult society the **Golden Dawn,** taking the magical motto "Demon Est Deus Inversus" (DEDI) and continued to be associated with the G.D. over some thirty years. In April 1900, he clashed with occultist Aleister **Crowley,** also a G.D. member, in a leadership crises.

Yeats' book *Ideas of Good and Evil* (1903) contains studies of the mystic element in Blake and Shelley and another essay is titled 'The Body of the Father Christian Rosencrux.'. Another essay titled 'Magic' commences: "I believe in the practice and philosophy of what we have agreed to call magic, and what I must call the evocation of spirits, though I do not know what they are, in the power of creating magic illusions, in the visions of truth in the depths of the minds when the eyes are closed.

After his declaration, he related how once an acquaintance of his, gathering together a small party in a darkened room, held a mace over "a tablet of many coloured squares," at the time repeating "a form of words," and straightway Yeats found that his "imagination began to move itself and to bring before me vivid images . . . "

It was S. L. MacGregor **Mathers** of the Golden Dawn, stated Yeats, "who convinced me that images well up before the mind's eye from a deeper source than conscious or subconscious memory."

In a lecture on 'Psychic Phenomena' before the Dublin Society for Psychical Research (reported in the Dublin *Daily Express,* November 1913), he spoke of most amazing experiences during his investigation, which lasted for many years, and declared that so far as he was concerned, the controversy about the meaning of psychic phenomena was closed. But he was not "converted," in the true sense of the word, since he was a born believer, and he had never seriously doubted the existence of the soul or of God.

Lecturing on 'Ghosts and Dreams' before the **London Spiritualist Alliance** in April, 1914, he gave another clear account of his beliefs and experiences. In his book *Per Amica Silentia Lunae* (1918), he spoke as a poet and mystic in dealing with some of the deeper issues of Spiritualism.

In 1917, he had married Georgia Hyde Lees and discovered that his wife was a medium and capable of automatic writing.

In 1934, Yeats wrote a one-act play "The Words Upon the Window-Pane." built around a Spiritualist seance at which the spirit of Jonathan Swift communicated.

He showed considerable courage in making known some of his occult beliefs, although he did not publicize his Golden Dawn connections.

His mystical inclinations which he had been stimulated by the Hindu religious philosophy of the **Theosophical Society,** which had also attracted fellow poet "AE," continued to develop. When in his sixties, he became friendly with the Hindu monk Shri **Purohit Swami,** and wrote introductions to the Swami's autobiography *An Indian Monk* (Macmillan, London, 1932) and his translation of the book by the Swami's guru titled *The Holy Mountain* (Faber, London, 1934). In 1935, the Swami published a translation of the *Bhagaved-Gita* under the title *The Geeta; The Gospel of the Lord Shri Krishna* (Faber, London), which he dedicated "To my friend William Butler Yeats" on the poet's seventieth birthday. In the same year, the Swami also published a translation of the *Mandukya Upanishad,* for which Yeats provided a perceptive introduction. He had planned to travel to India to assist the Swami in translating the ten principal Upanishads, but eventually the work was completed by the two friends at Majorca in 1936.

Yeats died January 28, 1939 in the town of Roquebrune, overlooking Monaco, and was buried in the cemetery there until nine years later, when his remains were transferred to the churchyard of Drumcliffe, near Sligo. (See also **Golden Dawn;** Shri **Purohit Swami;** George W. **Russell**)

Yeats-Brown, Francis (Charles Clayton) (1886-1944)

British soldier, author and early popularizer of Yoga in Western countries. Born at Genoa, Italy, August 15, 1886, he was a son of the British Consul-General in Genoa. He was educated at Harrow-on-the-Hill, and Sandhurst, England. He was second lieutenant in King's Royal Rifle Corps at Bareilly, India in 1906, posted to 17th Cavalry, Indian Army in 1907, adjutant in 1931, served in France with 5th Lancers and in Mesopotamia with the Royal Flying Corps (D.F.C.). He was imprisoned in Turkey in November 1915 but escaped in 1918. He retired on pension in 1925. From 1926-28 he was editor of the British journal *The Spectator.* In 1938 he married Olga Phillips.

He published several books, the most famous of which was *Bengal Lancer* (1930), based on his nineteen years in India and his intense interest in **Yoga.** The book became a best-seller and was translated into Italian, Spanish, German, Danish, Norwegian, Swedish and Roumanian. It attracted worldwide interest in the subject of Yoga. A film version of the book under the title "Lives of a Bengal Lancer" was produced in 1935, directed by Henry Hathaway, starring Gary Cooper, Franchot Tone and Richard Cromwell.

Yeats-Brown also published *Yoga Explained* (1937), but in spite of his great interest in Yoga philosophy he remained a Christian throughout his life. His other books included: *Caught by the Turks* (1919), *Golden Horn* (1932), *Escape: A Book of Escapes of All Kinds* (1933), *Dogs of War* (1934), *Lancer at Large* (1937), *European Jungle* (1939), *Indian Pageant* (1942), *Martial India* (1945).

During the 1930s, Yeats-Brown was a news correspondent in Germany, and expressed admiration for Hitler, whom he compared with Gandhi and T. E. Lawrence. It seems likely that this unfortunate judgment stemmed from Yeats-Brown's enthusiasm for German physical fitness and military precision, and that he never really understood the real implications of Nazi philosophy and ambitions.

From 1943-44 Yeats-Brown re-entered the British Army, touring the India and Burma war fronts.

He died in London, December 19, 1944.

Yerger, Eloise Barrangon (Mrs. Roy Yerger) (1915-)

American writer who also conducted parapsychology experiments to investigate teacher-pupil attitudes and clairvoyance test results among students in fifth, sixth and seventh grade levels. Born January 16, 1915 at Northampton, Mass. she studied at Smith College (B.A.). In 1935 she married Roy Yerger.

She was a public relations director in New York (1956-1960), freelance writer from 1935 onwards, member of Authors Guild, Parapsychological Association, American Society for Psychical Research.

Yes! Bookshop

Founded in 1972 by Cris Popenhoe at 1035 31st Street, N.W., Washington, D.C. 20007. The bookshop covers every aspect of spiritual development and positive occult teachings, stemming from Ms. Popenhoe's conviction that social and political change necessitates individual transformation.

She has published an excellent annotated bibliography: *Books for Inner Development* (1976), reissued in revised format as *Inner Development; the Yes! Bookshop Guide,* 1979. This covers a wide range of subjects in a comprehensive and judicious manner, and must be regarded as a classic bibliography of its kind.

Yeti

Also known as the "Abominable Snowman," the mysterious humanoid creature reported from the Himalayan snowline.

The Soviet Ministry of Culture established a group of "cryptzoologists" to locate the Yeti, according to a report from *Tass,* the Soviet Press Agency, January 9, 1988. The agency stated that nearly one hundred sightings had been collated by Zhanna Kofman, Moscow. (See **Cryptozoology; Monsters; Yowie**)

Yezidis

A religious sect of Kurdistan in the region of Mosul, who are known as devil worshipers. Amongst themselves they are called Dasni, but other Kurds give them the name Yezidi, which is thought to derive from the Persian *Yazdan,* meaning "God."

Their religion seems to be a mixture of Mazdaism, Islam and Christianity, and their theology resembles that of the Gnostic and Albigensian heresies. The world is regarded as the creation of Lucifer, the fallen angel, as an agent of the supreme God, and Lucifer is propitiated by worship in the symbolic form of the peacock. This avoids mentioning the devil by name and thus averts evil.

The Yezidees consider Christ as an angel in human form, and Mohammed as a prophet with Abraham and others. They practice baptism and circumcision. Their sacred texts were translated by F. Nau, *Recueil de textes et de documents sur les Yézidis* (1918). Other books describing the Yezidis and their beliefs are: *The Cult of the Peacock Angel* by R. H. Empson (1928), *Adventures in Arabia among the Bedouins Druses Whirling Derivishes & Yezidee Devil-worshipers* by W. B. Seabrook (1928), *Peacock Angel* by E. S. Drower (1941). (See also **Albigenses; Devil Worship**).

Yin and Yang

According to ancient Chinese philosophy, the dual principles of nature. *Yin* signifies earth, passive, negative, female, yielding, weak, or dark; *Yang* signifies heaven, active, positive, male, strong, or light. These principles are manifest throughout nature and in the human body. They relate to mental, physical, and spiritual structure, and are affected by food, drink, action, and inaction. The balance of *ying* and *yang* in the individual, in nature and the cosmos is symbolized by a circle separated by an "S" shape, one half of the circle dark and the other light. This has something in common with the ancient Greek al-chemical symbol of a serpent or dragon eating its tail, known as **Ouroboros.**

The *Yin-Yang* symbol represents unity and duality, a universal dual monism. It is also inherent in the ancient Chinese system of divination of the *I Ching* (Book of Changes). It is basic to the teachings of Taoism, as embodied in the classic work *Tao-te-Ching* (Book of the Right Way) of the philosopher Lao Tzu.

In modern times, the *yin* and *yang* principles are a vital part of the revived system of diet known as macrobiotics, where health and mental and spiritual balance are developed by the correct proportions of *yin* and *yang* foods, properly prepared. (See also **China; I Ching; Ouroboros; Tao; Taoism**)

Y-Kim (or I Ching), Book of

A Chinese mystical book attributed to the Emperor Fo-Hi, and ascribed to the year 3468 B.C. It consists of ten chapters, and was stated by Éliphas Lévi in his *History of Magic* to be a complement and an appendix to the Kabalistic *Zohar,* the record of the utterances of Rabbi Simeon Ben Jochai. The *Zohar,* stated Lévi, explains universal equilibrium, and the *Y-Kim* is the hieroglyphic and ciphered demonstration thereof.

The key to the *Y-Kim* is the pentacle known as the Trigrams of Fo-Hi. In the *Vay-Ky* of Leon-Tao-Yuen, composed in the Som dynasty (about eleventh century) it was recounted that the Emperor Fo-Hi was one day seated on the banks of a river, deep in meditation, when to him there appeared an animal having the parts of both a horse and a dragon.

Its back was covered with scales, on each of which shone the mystic Trigrammic symbol. The animal initiated the just and righteous Fo-Hi into universal science. Numbering its scales, he combined the Trigrams in such a manner that there arose in his mind a synthesis of sciences compared and united with one another through the harmonies of nature. From this synthesis sprang the tables of the *Y-Kim.*

According to Éliphas Lévi, the numbers of Fo-Hi are identical with those of the **Kabala,** and his pentacle is similar to that of Solomon. His tables are in correspondence with the subject matter of the *Sephir Yesirah* and the *Zohar.* The whole is a commentary upon the Absolute which is concealed from the profane, concluded Lévi, but as he had little real acquaintance with the subject, these analogies must be taken as of small value.

Since Lévi's time, much scholarship has been expended on the symbolism and mystical significance of this important work under its more generally expressed title of *I Ching.* (See also **I Ching**)

Yoga

General term for various spiritual disciplines in Hindu mysticism. The word "yoga" implies "yoking" (as with oxen to the ox-cart) and is used to express the linking of man with divine reality. This union is a transcendental experience beyond the plane of words and ideas, and has to be achieved by release from the limiting fields of physical, emotional, mental and intellectual experience. This requires purification at all levels, and according to Hindu belief might take many lifetimes, but sincere exertions in one birth should bear fruit in the next.

The most generally accepted yoga system is that of the sage Patanjali (c. 200 B.C.) which taught that in order to experience true reality one must transcend the body and mind. In his *Yoga Sutras* he outlined the following special stages: *yama* and *niyama* (ethical restraints and moral observations), *asna* (physical postures), *pranayama* (breathing exercises), *pratyahara* (sense withdrawal), *dharana* (concentration), *dhyana* (meditation), culminating in various degrees of *samadhi* (superconsciousness).

In Patanjali's system, *asana* or physical posture was chiefly directed to the achievement of a firm cross-legged sitting position for meditation. Other yoga authorities, however, have elaborated the stages of Patanjali yoga to meet the requirements of different temperaments, so that they may be harmonized. A number of specialized yogas were developed, notably the following:

Hatha Yoga

The science of physical exercises (this is the yoga most familiar to Westerners). Mind, body and spirit are linked, and in hatha yoga the purification of the body is also intended to enhance mental and spiritual development, balance and harmony. Good health is an essential preliminary to the strenuous disciplines of yoga.

Hatha yoga consists of a number of *asanas* which develop flexibility in associated muscle groups throughout the body, and affect favorably the tone of veins and arteries. They are also believed to improve the function of the ductless glands through persistent gentle pressure.

These *asans* differ from Western gymnastics in featuring static postures instead of active movements. There are theoretically some 8,400,000 *asanas,* of which 84 are said to be the best and 32 the most useful for good health. These are named after creatures, e.g., cow, peacock, locust, cobra, lion, etc.

An *asana* is considered to be mastered when the yogi can maintain the position without strain for three hours. *Asanas* are supplemented by special symbolic gestures and positions called *mudras.*

Various cleansing techniques of the nasal passages, throat, stomach and bowels are practiced in conjunction with asanas, as well as *pranayama* breathing exercises designed to arouse **Kundalini** or vital energy.

Karma Yoga or Kriya Yoga

The science of *karmas* or actions. All actions have inescapable consequences, some producing immediate results, others delayed results, and some bearing fruit in future lives. Emphasis is placed on altruistic actions which purify the individual soul and release it from petty desires. In Karma Yoga, actions are spiritualized by dedicating them to selfless service and divine will.

Bhakti Yoga

The path of love and devotion. An emotional temperament can transform emotions so that they are absorbed in spiritual service instead of being attached to physical or sensory gratification. Love can be centered on a familiar form of God or a great saint, or on some great task in life.

Mantra Yoga

The science of sound vibration and prayer, of hermetic utterance. According to Hindu mystical belief, the world evolved from the essence of sound, through the diversity and intricacy of vibration and utterance.

One of the most sacred *mantras* is the three-syllabled OM or **AUM,** origin of the Universe, comparable with the Hebrew Shemhamphorash and the creative Word of God in the Gospel of St. John. The reading of Hindu scriptures is prefixed and ended by the sacred sound AUM.

Jnana of Sankya Yoga

The path of knowledge, science and wisdom. This begins with the fine distinctions that may be evolved by careful observation, study and experiment, combining knowledge with the ability to reflect, meditate and develop intuition.

Rajah Yoga

The path of spiritual science, particularly suitable for those of a more abstract or metaphysical temperament. This combines religious study with refinement of all levels of the individual, culminating in transcendental awareness. Rajah Yoga is thus the summation of all other yogas. Ancient textbooks of Hatha Yoga emphasize that it should only be practiced in conjunction with Rajah Yoga.

No single pathway of yoga is regarded as an alternative to the others, but simply as a means of purifying and harmonizing individual temperaments. A very intellectual individual might profitably concentrate on Bhakti Yoga or Karma Yoga; an emotional temperament might benefit from Jnana Yoga and Hatha Yoga. The practice of Hatha Yoga without proper actions, devotion and ethical codes might be harmful or result simply in circus gymnastics without spiritual development. Ultimately all the yogas are interdependent.

Amongst other paths of Yoga are **Tantric Yoga** (associated with arousal of sexual energy and its conversion into Kundalini,) KUNDALINI YOGA (emphasizing Hatha Yoga and Mantra Yoga techniques to arouse Kundalini), ASPARSHA YOGA (reintegration through non-touching, avoiding all forms of contact with others), JAPA YOGA (a branch of Mantra Yoga with emphasis on repetition of prayers and sacred syllables), LAYA YOGA (absorption in meditation, merging mind and breath in the divine) ATMA YOGA (concentration upon the *Atma* or divine self of all).

Only the Hindu passion for classification and elaboration makes these different yogas appear to be distinct entities. They are all interrelated and are implicit in the basic system of Patanjali.

Many Western followers of Yoga falsify the total method and aim by simply practicing the physical exercises of Hatha Yoga, believing that in itself this will make them superior individuals. It might make them good gymnasts, or in certain temperaments may even have a harmful effect by arousing special sensitivities that are not harmonized in the personality.

Hence the value of the traditional warning that one should seek a properly qualified *guru* who can guide the individual. Unfortunately in modern times the yoga scene is full of self-appointed *gurus* who have not eradicated the pride and ambition which the *yama* and *niyama* preliminaries of Patanjali are designed to purify. For a deeper knowledge of yoga than contemporary popularizations, a study of the Hindu scriptures *Bhagavad-Gita* and the *Yoga-Sutras* of Patanjali is strongly recommended . (See also **Asanas; Hatha Yoga; Kundalini; Vedanta**)

Recommended reading:

Bhagavadgita of The Song Divine, Gita Press, Gorakhpur, India, 1943 etc. (frequently reprinted)

Bhagavad Gita (transl. S. Radhakrishnan), Allen & Unwin, London, 1948

The Bhagavad-Gita; The Song of God, (transl. Christopher Isherwood & Swami Prabhavananda), London/Marcel Rodd Co., Hollywood, California, 1944.

Bernard, Theos. *Hatha Yoga*, Rider & Co., London, 1950; Weiser paperback, 1970

Danielou, Alain. *Yoga; The Method of Re-Integration*, Christopher Johnson, London, 1949; University Books, 1956

Dvivedi, M. N. (transl.). *The Yoga-Sutras of Patanjali*, Theosophical Publishing House, 1890 etc.

Gopi Krishna. *The Secret of Yoga*, Harper & Row, 1972

Gopi Krishna. *The Awakening of Kundalini*, Dutton paperback, 1975

Majumdar, S. M. *Introduction to Yoga Principles and Practices*, University Books, 1964

Vishnudevananda, Swami. *The Complete Illustrated Book of Yoga*, Bell Publishing Co., 1960; Pocket Books, 1971

Wood, Ernest. *Yoga*, London, 1959; Penguin paperback, 1962

(See also; Long-Play Record Album *The Sounds of Yoga-Vedanta; Documentary of Life in an Indian Ashram*, with booklet of notes on Yoga. Folkways Records, New York, Album FR. 8970)

Yoga Journal

Bi-monthly journal of California Yoga Teachers Association, dealing with various aspects of yoga, nutrition and health; includes book reviews. Lists annually an international directory of Yoga teachers and centers. Address: 2054 University Avenue, Suite 604, San Francisco, California 94704.

Yoga Life (Magazine)

Illustrated magazine with articles on Yoga, meditation and relaxation; includes information on branch activities of the Sivananda Yoga Vedanta Center. Published three times a year by: Sivananda Yoga Vendanta Center, 8th Avenue, Val Morin, Quebec, Canada VOT 2RO.

Yoga-Mimamsa Journal

Indian journal devoted to the serious study of Hatha Yoga and Pranayama, with papers describing medical and scientific researches as well as popular aspects. Edited by Swami **Kuvalayananda,** a noted authority on Yoga. The Journal commenced publication in 1935 and describes researches carried out at the Kaivalyadhama S.M.Y.M. Samiti, India. Address: Yoga-Mimamsa Office, Lonavla (C.R.), India.

Yoga Research Foundation, Inc.

Founder-president Swami **Jyotir Maya Nanda,** vice-president Swami Lalitananda (formerly Miss Leonora Rego), disciples of the late Swami **Sivananda** of Rishikesh, India.

The Foundation (formerly the International Yoga Society) publishes books, audio cassettes, and study courses on Yoga and Hindu Philosophy and a monthly magazine *International Yoga Guide.* Swami Jyotir Maya Nanda is an authority on the little-known Hindu scripture *Yoga-Vasishtha Maharamayana,* had lectured widely and taken part in radio and television programs.

The Foundation is an international organization, dedicated to "elevating the consciousness, alleviating suffering and enriching the lives of all humanity" through Integral Yoga (a system integrating the four major yogas: Raja Yoga, Bhakti Yoga, Karma Yoga, Jnana Yoga), providing "a basis for upgrading the cultural growth of humanity while bringing about a worldwide level of social and religious harmony." Regular classes are conducted, teaching yoga, Vedanta, and Indian philosophy. Address: 6111 S.W. 74th Avenue, Miami, Florida 33143.

Yoga Society of San Francisco

Organization offering classes in yoga, meditation, and massage therapy, and teacher training courses. Address: 2872 Folsom Street, San Francisco, California 94110.

Yoga Today (Magazine)

Comprehensive and lavishly produced monthly magazine dealing with all aspects of **Yoga** as seen from a British and European viewpoint. Typical articles cover interviews with major yogis, sidelights on yoga teaching and practitioners, health and diet, traditional yoga treatises. Special features include book reviews and worldwide news cover. Address: Yoga Today Ltd., 21 Caburn Crescent, Lewes, East Sussex, BN7 INR, England.

Yogananda, Paramahansa (1893-1952)

Well-known and respected yogi, one of the early Hindu masters to visit and teach in Western countries. Born Mukunda Lal Ghosh in the Calcutta area, he manifested psychic powers as a child. As a young man he was fascinated by the holy men of India and visited many of them. He was eventually initiated by Swami Yukteswar in the spiritual line of Swami Babaji, a Himalayan master.

Yogananda came to the U.S. in 1920 and taught yoga deriving basically from the classic text and *Yoga Sutras of Patanjali*, and also developed his own variety of *kriya yoga*, involving withdrawal of life-energy from outward affairs to inner spiritual centers (basically a form of **Kundalini** Yoga).

Yogananda laid great emphasis on reconciliation with Christian teachings and established "Churches of All Religions." His **Self-Realization Fellowship** was founded in 1920 and now has forty-four centers in the U.S. with branches abroad. The honorific "Paramahansa" is a Sanskrit term for the highest type of master (literally "greatest swan").

Yogananda passed into *mahasamadhi* (great sleep of death) in 1952, but his body is said to have remained free from decay for twenty years afterwards. (See also **Self-Realization Fellowship**)

"Yolande"

The spirit of a young Arabian girl of fifteen, materialized through the mediumship of Madame **d'Esperance** (1885-1919). Yolande appeared to manifest as an independent entity and was photographed, like the equally famous "Katie **King**" of the medium Florence **Cook.**

'You' and E. S. P (Newsletter)

Monthly newsletter issued by the Temple of the Inner Flame, headed by Carol Ann Liaros, concerned with such psychic activities as Fingertip Vision (**Eyeless Sight**) and alternative medical treatments; includes information on psychic fairs. Address: 3329 Niagara Falls Boulevard, North Tonawanda, N.Y. 14120

Younghusband, Sir Francis (Edward) (1863-1942)

British explorer, soldier, author and mystic. Born at Murree, India, May 31, 1863, he was educated at Clifton and Sandhurst, England. He joined the British army in 1882.

From 1886-87 he traveled across central Asia from Peking to Yarkand and on to India, crossing the Karakoram Range by the Muztagh Pass. He discovered the Aghil Mountains and showed that the Great Karakoram was the water divide between India and Turkistan. On later explorations beyond the Karakoram he was able to trace the river Shaksgam to its junction with the Yarkand, and explored the Pamirs. During his period in the 1st Dragoon Guards, Younghusband held the rank of Captain.

In 1890 he transferred to the Indian political department and served in northwest frontier stations, visiting South Africa in 1896. He was a special correspondent the *The Times* newspaper, London, in the Chitral Expedition in 1895, political agent in Haraoti and Tonk in 1898, Resident at Indore, Central India 1902-03, British Commissioner to Tibet 1902-04, Resident at Kashmir 1906-09.

While in Tibet, he led the British mission to Lhasa, culminating in the Anglo-Tibetan Treaty of September 7, 1904. For this he was honored by the decoration of Knight Commander of the Indian Empire. He was one of the first modern British explorers to investigate the almost legendary territory of Tibet and enter the mysterious city of Lhasa, long fabled by Theosophists and others as the center of mysterious adepts and Masters.

He found no secret occult forces. However, his life in Tibet and India led to sympathetic consideration of Eastern religions and recognition of the spiritual center of their mysticism.

In 1905 he returned to England, where he became Rede lecturer at Cambridge University, before traveling to Kashmir as Resident. He was honored as Knight Commander of the Star of India in 1917. After his retirement in 1919, he became chairman of the Royal Geographical Society, who had awarded him their gold medal in 1891. He also formed and was chairman of the Mount Everest Committee. His other honors included LL.D. (Hon.) Edinburgh, D.Sc. (Hon.) Cambridge, LL.D. (Hon.) Bristol.

Younghusband typified the best of the old-style British patriots of the British Empire period. He was an excellent and courageous soldier and explorer, yet deeply sympathetic to the aspirations and spiritual ideals of other peoples. He recognized the need for self-government in India. His book *Modern Mystics* (1935; reissued University Books, 1970) expressed his sympathy with the mysticism of different faiths and his belief in an underlying spiritual unity. In 1936 he founded the **World Congress of Faiths.** Other books expressing his ideals are *Life in the Stars* (1928) and *The Living Universe* (1933). His other publications included: *Heart of a Continent* (1896), *South Africa of Today* (1898), *Kashmir* (1909), *India and Tibet* (1910), *Within* (1912), *The Heart of Nature* (1921), *The Gleam* (1923), *Wonders of the Himalaya* (1924), *But in Our Lives* (1926), *The Epic of Mount Everest* (1926), *The Light of Experience* (1927), *The Coming Country* (1928), *Dawn in India* (1930), *World Fellowship of Faiths* (1935), *Everest: the Challenge* (1936), *The World Congress of Faith* (1938). He died July 31, 1942. For biographical information see: *Francis Younghusband: Explorer and Mystic* by George F. Seaver (London, 1952) and *Man of the Spirit: Sir Francis Younghusband* by Herbert L. Samuel (London, 1953).

He died at Lytchett Minster, near Poole, Britain, on July 31, 1942.

Your Astrology (Journal)

Quarterly journal which includes monthly and daily guide for all signs, with articles on Astrology for lay readers. Published by: Charlton Publications, Inc., Charlton Building, Derby, Conn. 06418.

Yowie

Australian equivalent of the **Yeti** or "Abominable Snowman." A recent account of a yowie sighting was reported in the British *Sunday Express* in September 1979, when Leo and Patricia George were picnicking in the Blue Mountains, west of Sydney, and saw the mutilated carcass of a kangeroo. A large shaggy creature "at least ten feet tall" shambled away.

The name "yowie" comes from aborigine folklore and means "great hairy man." Naturalist Rex Gilroy has studied accounts of the creature and found over 3,000 yowie sightings in the eastern mountain areas of Australia. (See also **Cryptozoology; Monsters; Yeti**)

"Yram" (1884-1917)

Pseudonym of Dr. Marcel Louis Forhan, pioneer French experimenter and writer on **Astral Projection (Out-of-the-Body** traveling).

His book *Practical Astral Projection* (English translation of *Le Medecine de l'Ame*) was first published London, n.d. (1935), reprinted Weiser circa 1966.

Forhan was born November 17, 1884 at Corbell, France. About 1911 he became a member of the **Theosophical Society** and investigated psychic phenomena and hypnotism.

About this time he had his first experience of Astral Projection, and developed awareness of higher worlds. It is claimed that he was able to travel astrally from China (where he lived for some years) to France, where he had friends and relatives. His experience of invisible worlds is related in his book *L'Evolution dans les mondes supérieures.*

He died in China October 1, 1917.

Z

Zabulon

Name of a demon said to have possessed a lay sister of Loudon, France in 1633. (See Nuns of **Loudon**)

Zacaire, Denis (1510- ?)

This French alchemist is chiefly remembered by his book, *Opuscule Tres-Excellent de la Philosophie naturelle des Metaux* (published 1567). This includes a Preface written by Zacaire in his lifetime, giving some account of his life, yet he fails to state the precise date at which he was born. However, he appears to have been born in 1510, in Guienne, and his parents were comfortably off, if not actually rich.

As a young man he studied at Bordeaux under an alchemist and subsequently at Toulouse, intending to become a lawyer. He soon became more interested in alchemy than in legal affairs, and in 1535, on his father's death, came into possession of some money. He thereupon decided to try and multiply it by artificial means. Associating himself with an abbé who was considered a great adept in gold-making, Denis had soon disposed of the bulk of his patrimony, but far from the charlatan's futile experiments disillusioning him, they served rather to encourage him to further endeavors.

In 1539, he went to Paris, where he made the acquaintance of many renowned alchemists. From one of them, so he declares, he learned the precious secret, and thereupon he hastened to the court of Antoine d'Albert the King of Navarre, grandfather of Henri IV, offering to make gold if the requisite materials were supplied.

The king was deeply interested, and promised a reward of no less than four thousand crowns in the event of the researches proving fruitful, but unfortunately Zacaire's vaunted skill failed him in the hour of need, and he retired discomfited to Toulouse. Here he became friendly with a certain priest, who advised him strongly to renounce his quest, and study natural science instead, so Denis went off to Paris once more, intending to act in accordance with his counsel. But after a little while, he was deep in the study of alchemy again, making experiments, studying closely the writings of Raymond **Lully** and Arnaldus de **Villanova.**

According to his own account, on Easter day in the year 1550, he succeeded in converting a large quantity of quicksilver into gold. Then, some time after this alleged triumph, he left France to travel in Switzerland, and lived for a while at Lausanne. Later on he wandered to Germany, and there he died. It is probable that his closing years were spent in dire poverty, but this is not recorded definitely, nor has the exact date of the alchemist's death ever been ascertained.

There is a story that he married before setting out to travel through Germany, but on reaching Cologne, he was murdered in his sleep by his servant, who escaped with his wife and his store of transmuting powder. The story of Zacaire's life was told in verse by De Delle, court poet of emperor Rudolph II (1552-1622), who took a great interest in alchemy, chemistry, and astrology.

Zacaire's *Opuscule* was published originally at Antwerp and repeatedly reprinted. It won the honor of being translated into Latin, while even in modern times it was sought keenly by French philosophers with a taste for the curious. See also the article by T. L. Davis; "The Autobiography of Denis Zacaire; An Account of an Alchemist's Life in the Sixteenth Century" (*Isis*, vol. 8, No. 2, 1926). (See also **Alchemy**)

Zacornu

A tree in the Mohamedan hell, which has for fruit the heads of devils.

Zadkiel

(1) One of the angels in the Jewish rabbinical legend of the celestial hierarchies. He is the ruler of Jupiter, and through him pass grace, goodness, mercy, piety, and munificence, and he bestows clemency, benevolence and justice on all.

(2) Pseudonym of Richard James Morrison (1795-1874), one of the most celebrated British astrologers of the nineteenth century. He was a friend of Robert Cross Smith ("Raphael") who published *Raphael's Astronomical Ephemeris,* and himself published *Zadkiel's Almanac,* which had a large circulation. Morrison calculated horoscopes for the Prince Consort and the Princess Royal which were gratefully accepted, but Queen Victoria later expressed concern about predictions for the Prince Consort, possibly because they were so accurate as to cause some disquiet.

Zaebos

Said to be Grand Count of the infernal regions. He appears in the shape of a handsome soldier mounted on a crocodile. His head is adorned with a ducal coronet. He is of a gentle disposition.

Zagam

Said to be Grand king and president of the infernal regions. He appears under the form of a bull with the wings of a griffin. He changes water into wine, blood into oil, the fool into a wise man, lead into silver, and copper into gold. Thirty legions obey him.

Zahuris (or Zahories)

French people who had traveled in Spain frequently had curious tales to tell concerning the *Zahuris*—people who were so keen-sighted that they could see streams of water and veins of metal hidden in the earth, and could indicate the whereabouts of buried treasure and the bodies of murdered persons.

Explanations were offered on natural lines. It was said that these men knew where water was to be found by the vapors arising at such spots, and that they were able to trace mines of gold and silver and copper by the particular herbs growing in their neighborhood. But to the Spaniards, such explanations were unsatisfactory, they persisted in believing that the *Zahuris* were gifted with supernatural faculties, that they were *en rapport* with demons, and that, if they wished, they could, without any physical aid, read thoughts and discover secrets which were as a sealed book to the grosser senses of ordinary mortals. The *Zahuris* were said to have red eyes, and in order to be a *Zahuri* it was necessary to have been born on a Good Friday. (See also **Dowsing: Water-Divining**)

Zain, C. C. (1882-1951)

Pseudonym of Elbert Benjamine (1882-1951), astrologer and occultist. He was born December 12, 1882, in Iowa who founded the Church of Light in Los Angeles in 1932. It is supposedly based on Zain's psychic and occult studies which culminated in contact with a mysterious arcane order called The Brotherhood of Light, deriving from an Egyptian priesthood circa 2440 B.C., surviving as "The Religion of the Stars."

Zain died November 18, 1951, and was succeeded by Edward Doane as president of the church.

Zain's system of occult instructions occupies twenty-two books. The Church of Light has fifty degrees of initiation, of which the highest is the Soul Degree, requiring demonstration of states of higher consciousness. Religious services are held at the Church.

The Church published the *Church of Light Quarterly,* which includes articles on the Teachings of Zain, horoscopes, and a list of the Church's 57 centers throughout the world.

Zancig, Julius (1857-1929) and Mrs.

Famous Danish thought-reading couple, whose demonstrations at the London Alhambra in Britain caused much excitement, newspaper and scientific controversy. Mrs. Zancig could correctly name any article, number or word at which her husband cast a glance. The *Daily Mail* arranged a series of tests in their offices on November 30, 1906, and published the conclusion that the performance was the result of true **telepathy.** The *Daily Chronicle* differed, and considered a clever code system sufficient explanation. The questions and answers were registered by a phonograph record. Nothing was discovered.

The psychical researcher W. W. **Baggally** conducted some experiments. He concluded that although the alleged transmission of thought might possibly depend on a code or codes which he was unable to unravel, yet the performance was of such a nature that it was worthy of serious scientific examination.

The **Society for Psychical Research,** London, investigated on January 18, 1907. The result was not published. However, it appeared sufficiently favorable for some of the members present to subsequently form an official committee to carry on further tests. The report stated: "While we are of opinion that the records of experiments in telepathy made by the S.P.R. and others raise a presumption for the existence of such a faculty at least strong enough to entitle it to serious scientific attention, the most hopeful results hitherto obtained have not been in any way comparable as regards accuracy and precision with those produced by Mr. and Madame Zancig . . . Those who have only witnessed the public theatre performances, clever and perplexing as these are, will not appreciate how hard it is to offer any plausible explanation of their *modus operandi.*"

The Zancigs claimed telepathy as an explanation, and Mrs. Zancig had well-developed clairvoyant faculties. At the **British College of Psychic Science,** London, she passed successfully book-reading tests.

In his book *Rudi Schneider* (1930), the psychical researcher Harry **Price** took a different view: "The Zancigs' performance took years of study to perfect, and several hours practice daily were needed to keep the performers in good form. I have the Zancigs' codes in my library and know the hard work that both Mr. Julius Zancig and his wife put into their 'act,' a matter which I have discussed with Mr. Zancig himself."

Will Goldston, in his book *Sensational Tales of Mystery Men* (1929) spoke from the inside knowledge of a magician: "The pair worked on a very complicated and intricate code. There was never any question of thought transference in the act. By framing his question in a certain manner Julius was able to convey to his wife exactly what sort of object or design had been handed to him. Long and continual practice had brought their scheme as near perfection as is humanly possible. On several occasions confederates were placed in the audience and at such times the effects seemed nothing short of miraculous. All their various tests were cunningly faked and their methods were so thorough that detection was an absolute impossibility to the layman."

"Zanoni"

Title of an occult novel by Bulwer **Lytton.** (See Occult English **Fiction**)

Zapan

According to demonologist Johan **Weyer,** one of the Kings of Hell.

Zazen

Term used in **Zen** Buddhism to indicate the sitting position for meditation, which usually takes place in the *Zen-do* or meditation hall in Zen monasteries. The meditation position is known as *Dhyanasana,* usually resembling the "Lotus" position of **Hatha Yoga** known as *padmasana,* although there are simpler variations of this position for those unable to maintain a full "lotus" position. (See also **Hatha Yoga; Zen**)

ZCLA Journal

Periodical concerned with past and present writings of Zen Masters on the subject of Zen Buddhism. Some of the contents include material not previously translated into Western languages. Published three times a year by: Zen Center of Los Angeles, 923 South Normandie Avenue, Los Angeles, California 90006. (See also **Zen**)

Zedekias (c. 9th century A.D.)

Said to have been a Jewish physician of the ninth century who was in great favor with the Emperor Charles the Bald. Zedekias had a reputation as a Kabalist and wizard, and was said to have eaten a whole load of hay, together with the driver and horses, in the presence of the Emperor's court. On another occasion he is said to have flown around in the air. This sounds like mass hypnotism or the invention of a fabulist.

Zedekias was mentioned by the Abbe N. de Montfaucon de Villars in his strange book *Comte de Gabalis* (1670). According to de Villars, Zedekias was anxious to show the world that elementary spirits really existed, and advised the sylphs to show themselves in the air to everyone: "These beings were seen in the Air in human form, sometimes in battle array marching in good order, halting under arms, or encamped beneath magnificent tents. Sometimes on wonderfully constructed aerial ships, whose flying squadrons roved at the will of the Zephyrs. What happened? . . . The people straightway believed that sorcerers had taken possession of the Air for the purpose of raising tempests and bringing hail upon their crops . . . The Emperors believed it as well; and this ridiculous chimera went so far that the wise Charlemagne, and after him Louis the Débonnaire, imposed grievous penalties upon all these supposed Tyrants of the Air. You may see an account of this in the first chapter of the Capitularies of these two Emperors." (See also **Comte de Gabalis: Elementary Spirits; France**)

Zeernebooch

A dark god, monarch of the empire of the dead among the ancient Germans.

Zeitschrift für Metapsychische Forschung

Monthly psychical research magazine, established in 1930, published in connection with the Institute für Metapsychische Forschung, by Professor Dr. Christop Schroeder, in Berlin, Germany.

No longer published.

Zeitschrift für Parapsichologie

A monthly German periodical of psychical research, originally founded by Alexander **Aksakof** in 1874 under the title *Psychische Studien*; new title assumed in 1925.

Ceased publication in 1934.

Zeitschrift für Parapsychologie und Grenzgebiete der Psychologie (Journal)

Journal of Parapsychology and Border Areas of Psychology, published by the **Institut für Grenzgebiete der Psychologie und Psychohygiene** (Institute for Border Areas of Psychology and Mental Hygiene), P.O. Box 5204, D-7800 Freiburg im Br., West Germany. Many articles in the journal contain summaries in the English language.

Zen (or Ch'an)

The only traditional form of instant enlightenment in Oriental religions. However, it normally demands a long preliminary period of monastic life and spiritual discipline culminating in the somewhat surrealist techniques which give instant *satori* or enlightenment.

Zen is a special branch of the Mahayanna Buddhist school dating from 520 A.D. when Bodhi-Dharma came to China with a mission later codified in the four maxims: "a special transmission outside the scriptures; no dependence upon words and letters; direct pointing at the soul of man; seeing into one's nature; and the attainment of Buddhahood."

Zen depends very much upon sudden or startling paradoxes, embodied in such *koans* or mystical riddles as "Emptyhanded I come, carrying a spade." Modern interest in Zen often misunderstands the nature of such riddles, where the verbal factor is merely a trigger to intensify stress in the pupil, and as a result many Westerners tend to treat Zen as a kind of intellectual exercise.

In practice, however, such paradoxes were the culmination of a more formal monastic training emphasizing traditional spiritual values. The disciple would be fully extended on all levels of his nature—physically, in the everyday hard work of the monastery; mentally, in the assimilation of spiritual teaching; emotionally, in the sudden clash of unconventional techniques of Zen.

The *koans* merely accentuated an intolerable pressure at all levels, culminating in the sudden flash of enlightenment by transcendence on a higher, spiritual plane. (See also **ZCLA Journal; Zazen; Zen Studies Society**)

Recommended reading:

Humphreys, Christmas. *Zen Buddhism,* Heinemann, London, 1949; Macmillan, 1967

Suzuki, D. T. *Manual of Zen Buddhism,* Grove Press, 1960

Suzuki, D. T. (ed. William Barrett). *Zen Buddhism; Selected Writings of D. T. Suzuki,* Doubleday/Anchor paperback, 1956.

Zen Studies Society

American organization for the study of traditional **Zen** meditation in the U.S. There is an International Dai Bosantsu Zendo, open to lay people for full-time Zen practice with daily meditation, study work and community life. The leader is the Roshi (Abbot) Eido Tai Shimano. The Society publishes a quarterly newsletter and the writings of Zen teachers. Address: Dai Bosatsu Zendo, Kongo-Ji, H.C.R. #1, P.O. Box 80, H.C.R. #1, Lewbeach, N.Y. 12753.

Zen Writings (Journal)

Quarterly periodical in book format which publishes English translations of important Zen texts and commentaries. Address: Zen Center of Los Angeles, 923 South Normandie Avenue, Los Angeles, California 90006. (See also **Zen**)

Zener Cards

A pack of twenty-five cards bearing simple symbols in groups of five of a kind: star, circle, square, cross and waves, used by parapsychologists in testing extrasensory faculty under laboratory conditions. The use of the Zener card pack dates from the work of Dr. J. B. **Rhine** in the Department of Psychology at Duke University, North Carolina from 1927 onwards, first reported in Rhine's monograph *Extrasensory Perception,* published 1934 by the Boston Society for Psychic Research.

Prior to the work of Dr. Rhine, ordinary playing cards had been used in testing telepathy, notably by Mrs. A. W. **Verrall** between 1890 and 1895 (reported in *Proceedings* of the Society for Psychical Research vol. ii, part 28, 1895; 'Analysis of Mrs. Verrall's Card Experiments' by C. P. Sanger). Later significant tests were carried out in Britain by Miss Ina Jephson and other members of the Society for Psychical Research from 1924 onwards (reported in *Proceedings* of the SPR, vol. 38, pp. 223-271, 'Evidence for Clairvoyance in Card-Guessing' and vol. 39, pp. 375-414, 'Report on a Series of Experiments in Clairvoyance [conducted at a distance]').

The Zener card pack was devised by Dr. Karl Zener of the psychology faculty at Duke University, as a means of avoiding preferences for individual playing cards during tests, and in order to facilitate evaluation of test scores. (See also **Parapsychology;** J. B. **Rhine**)

Zepar

Said to be the Grand duke of the infernal empire, possibly identical with Vepar, or Separ. Nevertheless, under the name of Zepar he had the form of a warrior. He cast men into the evil passions. Twenty-eight legions obeyed him.

Zeroid

Term used by some Ufologists to denote creatures or animals which may exist and live in space. As yet, no positive evidence exists for their reality, but they might be life forms intermediate between organic and inorganic, perhaps feeding on sunlight, or on the pre-organic molecules found in space.

The *Weekly World News,* for October 1, 1985, reported that "a herd of space animals, the size and shape of the Goodyear blimp, grazed for three hours on cattle pastures near the remote Argentine ranching settlement of Villa Iruya."

Zetetic Journal

Formerly titled **Explorations.** Founded in 1972 as a newsletter of academic research into Occultism. The title was changed after vol. 2 to avoid confusion with the Explorations Institute in Berkeley, California.

"Zetetic" derives from the Greek philosophical school of Pyrrho (365-275 B.C.) and indicates extreme skepticism. *Zetetic Journal* circulated to serious academics researching occultism or to organizations and individuals in the field. It contained critical notes and news of current events and personalities in occultism, a who's who in occult research and valuable lists of books and articles in the fields of occultism and parapsychology.

After vol. 2, No. 2 (Fall/Winter 1977), the title of the *Zetetic Journal* was again changed to *The Skeptical Inquirer.*

At the same time, Dr. Marcello Truzzi who had founded *Explorations* and the *Zetetic Journal,* disassociated himself from *The Skeptical Inquirer* on policy grounds, and announced publication of *Zetetic Scholar* as an independent scientific review of claims of anomalies and the paranormal. Vol. 1, No. 1 was issued in 1978, published from the Department of Sociology, Eastern Michigan University, Ypsilanti, Michigan 48197.

There are, therefore, two independent journals examining the paranormal in a zetetic spirit—*The Skeptical Inquirer* (published by the Committee for the Scientific Investigation of Claims of the Paranormal) and *Zetetic Scholar* (published by Dr. Marcello Truzzi and associates). (See also **Committee for the Scientific Investigation of Claims of the Paranormal:** Marcello **Truzzi; Zetetic Scholar**)

Zetetic Scholar (Journal)

In 1978, following policy disagreements with the Committee for the Scientific Investigation of Claims of the Paranormal, Dr. Marcello **Truzzi** who had been editor of the Committee's journal *Zetetic,* resigned from the Committee and launched a new independent journal titled *Zetetic Scholar.*

At the same time, the Committee's journal changed its title to *The Skeptical Inquirer* as from vol. II, No. 2 (Spring/Summer 1978) onwards.

Thus there are now two independent journals examining claims of the paranormal in a skeptical spirit. The new editors of *The Skeptical Inquirer* included Kendrick Frazier, with an editorial board of Martin Gardner, Ray Hyman, Philip J. Klass, Paul Kurtz, James Randi and Dennis Rawlins. The address is: P.O. Box 229, New York 14215-0229.

The *Zetetic Scholar,* edited by Dr. Truzzi, is a substantial publication which conducts in-depth surveys of subjects and permits a wide range of opinion and discussion. It has an exceptionally high standard, is well documented and has valuable bibliographical reference. Address: Zetetic Scholar, Department of Sociology, Eastern Michigan University, Ypsilanti, Michigan 48197. (See also **Committee for the Scientific Investigation of Claims of the Paranormal;** Marcello **Truzzi; Zetetic Journal**)

Ziazaa

A mysterious fabled black and white stone. It was said to render its possessor litigious, and cause terrible visions.

Zierold, Maria Reyes

A Mexican sensitive who was the subject of experiments by Dr. Gustav **Pagenstecher** (1855-1942) from about 1919 onwards. Mrs. Zierold was a housewife whom Dr. Pagenstecher treated for insomnia by means of hypnosis. To Dr. Pagenstecher's surprise, Mrs. Zierold manifested psychometric ability while in hypnotic trance.

A medical committee in Mexico City also examined Mrs. Zierold's abilities and reported that the phenomena seemed genuinely paranormal.

Dr. Pagenstecher reported the facts to the American Society for Psychical Research in an article 'A Notable Psychometrist' (ASPR *Journal* vol. 14, 1920). In 1921 Dr. Walter Franklin **Prince,** then principal research officer of the ASPR, visited Mexico to observe Pagenstecher's experiments and to conduct his own.

Prince endorsed the phenomena of Mrs. Zierold, which he reported in his article 'Psychometric Experiments with Maria Reyes de Z.' (ASPR *Journal* vol. 16, Jan., 1922) and a more detailed article under the same title in ASPR *Proceedings* (vol. 15, 1921).

Dr. Pagenstecher contributed a further article to ASPR *Proceedings:* 'Past Events Seership' (vol. 16, Jan. 1922) and published a book *Die Geheimnisse der Psychometrie oder Hellsehen in die Vergangenheit* (Secrets of Psychometry or Clairvoyance into the Past, 1928). The case of Mrs. Zierold was also discussed in a chapter on mediumship in the book *The Personality of Man: New Facts and Their Significance* (Penguin, U.K. 1947) by G. N. M. **Tyrrell.** (See also Gustav **Pagenstecher**)

Ziito (c. 14th century)

One of the most remarkable magicians of whom history has left any record. He was a sorcerer at the court of King Wenceslaus of Bohemia (afterwards Emperor of Germany) towards the end of the fourteenth century.

Among his more famous exploits was one chronicled by Janus Dubravius, Bishop of Olmutz, in his *Historiae Regni Boiemiae* (History of Bohemia, 1552 etc.). On the occasion of the marriage of Wenceslaus with Sophia, daughter of the elector Palatine of Bavaria, the elector, knowing his son-in-law's liking for juggling and magical exhibitions, brought a number of morris dancers, jugglers and other entertainers. When they came forward to give their exhibition Ziito remained unobtrusively among the spectators. He was not entirely unnoticed, however, for his remarkable appearance drew the attention of those about him. His oddest feature was his mouth, which actually stretched from ear to ear.

After watching the magicians for some time in silence, Ziito appeared to become exasperated at the halting way in which the tricks were carried through, and going up to the principal magician, he taunted him with incompetency. The rival professor hotly defended his performance, and a discussion ensued which was ended at last by Ziito swallowing his opponent, just as he stood, leaving only his shoes, which he said were dirty and unfit for consumption!

After this extraordinary feat, he retired for a little while to a closet, from which he shortly emerged, leading the rival magician by the hand. He then gave a performance of his own which put the former exhibition entirely in the shade. He changed himself into many different shapes, taking the form of first one person and then another, none of whom bore any resemblance either to himself or to each other.

In a car drawn by barn-door fowls, he kept pace with the King's carriage. When the guests were assembled at dinner, he played a multitude of elfish tricks on them, to their amusement or annoyance, as the case might be.

Indeed, he was at all times an exceedingly mischievous creature, as is shown by another story told of him. Pretending to be in want of money, and apparently casting about anxiously for the means of obtaining some, he at length took a handful of corn, and made it look like thirty fat hogs. These he took to Michael, a rich but very mean dealer. The latter purchased them after some haggling, but was warned not to let them drink at the river. But the warning was disregarded, the hogs drank and were turned into grains of corn.

The enraged dealer went in search of Ziito, whom he found at last in a vintner's shop. In vain Michael shouted and stamped, the magician took no notice, but seemed to be in a fit of abstraction. Eventually the dealer, beside himself, seized Ziito's foot and pulled it as hard as he could. To his dismay, the foot and leg came right off, while Ziito screamed lustily, and hauled Michael before the judge, where the two presented their complaints. What the decision was, history does not relate, but it is unlikely that the ingenious Ziito came off worse.

Zikr

A Sufi term meaning "remembrance," indicating the constant awareness of Divine consciousness in humanity. In sufi groups, Zikr takes the form of a specific ritual to bring individuals into a higher state of consciousness. This involves circular movements of the group similar to those practiced by dervishes. (See also **Dervishes; Sufism**)

Zizaa

A fabulous precious stone, said to produce marvelous dreams for those who looked at it before sleeping. Illustrated in *Hortus Sanitatis* by Johannis de Cuba, Strassburg, c. 1483.

Zizis

The name which modern Jews give to their phylacteries.

Zlokobinca

Slavonic name for a witch, meaning "evil dealer." (See **Slavs**)

Zoaphite

According to the seventeenth-century traveler Jan Struys, a zoaphite was a species of cucumber which fed on neighboring plants. Its fruit had the form of a lamb, with the head, feet, and tail of that animal distinctly apparent, whence it is called, in the language of the country, *Canaret,* or *Conarer,* signifying a lamb. Struys described this Triffid-like plant in his book *Drie aanmerkelijke en seer rampspoedige* (1676), translated as *The Voiages and travels of Jan Struys* (1684).

Its skin was covered with a white down as delicate as silk. The ancient Tartars thought a great deal of it and most of them kept it carefully in their houses, where Jan Struys says he saw it several times.

It grew on a stalk about three feet in height, to which it was attached by a sort of tendril. On this tendril it could move about, and turn and bend towards the herbs on which it fed, and without which it soon dried up and withered. Wolves loved it, and devoured it with avidity, because it tasted like the flesh of lamb. The author added that he had been assured that it had bones, flesh, and blood, whence it was known in its native country as Zoaphite, or animal plant.

Zoist, The (Journal)

The journal of medical Mesmerists in Britain during the nineteenth century. It was under the directions of Dr. John Elliotson and was published from 1843-56. The popular side of Mesmerism was represented by *The Phreno-Magnet,* another periodical started at the same time and edited by Spencer T. Hall. *The Zoist* flourished from 1843-1856.

"Zolar"

Pseudonym of successful astrologer Bruce **King.**

Zöllner, Johann C. F. (1834-1882)

Professor of physics and astronomy at the University of Leipzig, a profound scientist who, by his work *The Nature of the Comets,* also attracted the attention of the philosophic world in view of the many original ideas he advanced.

His investigation of the phenomena of the medium Dr. Henry **Slade** and his subsequent book *Transcendental Physics* (1880) rendered his name famous in the annals of psychical research and subjected him to persecution, contempt and ridicule from the scientific fraternity.

His experiments began in December 1877. He was assisted by William Edward Weber, Professor of Physics, W. Scheibner, Professor of Mathematics, and Gustave Theodore Fechner, Professor of Physics, who, to quote Zöllner's words, became "perfectly convinced of the reality of the observed facts, altogether excluding imposture or prestidigitation." Prof. Fichte, of Stuttgart, and Prof. Ulrici, of Halle, also endorsed the experiments which were further supported by an affidavit of Bellachine, the conjurer at the court of Berlin.

The evidential value of the investigation was somewhat weakened by Zöllner's insistence on the theory of fourth dimension as an explanation. Of the theory itself, the astronomer G. V. Schiaparelli wrote in a letter to Camille **Flammarion:** "it is the most ingenious and probable that can be imagined. According to this theory, mediumistic phenomena would lose their mystic or mystifying character and would pass into the domain of ordinary physics and physiology. They would lead to a very considerable extension of the sciences, an extension such that their author would deserve to be placed side by side with Galileo and Newton. Unfortunately, these experiments of Zöllner were made with a medium of poor reputation."

Prof. Zöllner, after his sittings with Slade, had further interesting experiences with Mme. **d'Esperance.** In March, 1880, Baron von Hoffmann engaged the medium William **Eglinton** to give twenty-five sittings to Zöllner. He was very satisfied with the result and intended to write another book on his experiences. He died before he could do it.

The report of the skeptical **Seybert Commission** quoted testimonies from Professors Scheibner, Fechner and some others that Zöllner, at the time of his experiments, was of unsound mind. As he filled his chair up to moment of his sudden death, this charge cannot be seriously supported. Baron **Hellenbach** wrote in his book *Birth and Death as a Change of Form of Perception* (1886) that Zöllner "was in his last days deeply wounded and embittered by the treatment of his colleagues, whose assaults he took too much to heart. Zöllner, however, was in perfect possession of his intellect till his last breath."

When the report of the Seybert Commission was made public, anti-Spiritualists, like Joseph McCabe, seized upon the Zöllner part putting him down as "elderly and purblind." Dr. Isaac **Funk,** the New York publisher and psychical investigator, wrote to Leipzig and received from Dr. Karl Bücher, the Rector Magnificus of the University of Leipzig, a letter, dated November 7, 1903, that "information received from Zöllner's colleagues states that during his entire studies at the university here, until his death, he was of sound mind; moreover, in the best of health. The cause of his death was a hemorrhage of the brain on the morning of April 26, 1882, while he was at breakfast with his mother, and from which he died shortly after."

Transcendental Physics was translated into English by C. C. Massey and published in 1880, second edition 1882. (See also **Matter Passing Through Matter**)

Zombies

In Haitian **Voodoo** superstition, a zombie is a dead body revived by magic to act as a soulless robot. The *houngans* or voodoo priests are said to dig up corpses and reanimate them by magical rituals. Another way of creating a zombie is to feed the victim a preparation which stupefies the soul, leaving the body a living corpse.

The cure for a zombie is said to be giving it salt water to drink. Special burial techniques are sometimes used to prevent the corpse being used as a zombie. The corpse may be buried face downwards and its mouth filled with earth; sometimes the lips are sewn together, presumably to prevent the soul leaving by the mouth. A somewhat naive custom is to strew handfuls of sesame seed on the grave, so that the spirit of the deceased will always be occupied in counting the seeds.

Zombies provide cheap labor and are beaten harshly to keep them cowed. They are thus indistinguishable from mentally retarded individuals, and it is probably that many stories of zombies have arisen from the traditional rough treatment of mentally defective individuals. However, there are various firsthand accounts of zombies in relatively modern times. Author Alfred Métraux stated that six months after the death of a friend he saw that friend as a zombie at the house of a *houngan.*

In recent years, stories of zombies spread throughout Western countries through Hollywood horror films about the walking dead.

A rational explanation for zombies was the suggestion that certain powerful drugs might be capable of influencing certain centers in the brain concerned with conscious control.

This theory was recently validated by an expedition to Haiti which was the subject of a remarkable B.B.C. television program presented by John Tusa in 1984. In interviews with *houngans,* the secret of creating zombies was disclosed. A poisonous substance from the puffer fish (*Diodon hystrix*) is carefully prepared by the *houngan* and administered to the victim, who thereafter appears dead and is buried. He is exhumed by the *houngan* and used as a zombie. The poison stupefies certain conscious brain centers.

The poison was analyzed by Leon Roizy, Professor of Neurobiology at Columbia University, and identified as tetrodotoxin, found in the puffer fish which is the exquisitely dangerous gourmet dish of Japanese Fugu, requiring skillful preparation by experienced chefs in order to avoid poisoning the diner.

When eaten sliced raw (*sashimi*), the flesh is relatively safe, but amongst eaters of the partly cooked dish known as *chiri,* which includes toxic cooked livers, there are over a hundred deaths annually.

In 1982, Wade Davis, a Harvard ethnobotanist, visited Haiti to investigate the creation of zombies, and succeeded in penetrating the secret societies and understanding and documenting the voodoo culture, including the use of secret poisons. His experiences are related in his book *The Serpent and the Rainbow* (1985), which was later the basis for a movie of the same title. (See also **Voodoo; West Indian Islands**)

Zoomancy

A system of **divination** based on the appearances and behavior of animals.

Zorab, George A(vetoom) M(arterus) (1898-)

Author and parapsychologist. Born January 11, 1898 at Surabaya, Java. In 1924, he married Amalia Lorch. He experimented in parapsychology from 1932 onwards, studying spontaneous paranormal phenomena and quantitative experiments in extrasensory perception with psychotics.

He was chairman of the International Committee for the Study of Spontaneous Paranormal Phenomena, The Hague, was a secretary for the First International Conference on Parapsychological Studies in Utrecht, Netherlands in 1953, and took part in the Conference on Spontaneous Paranormal Phenomena at Cambridge, England in 1955, and the International Conference on Psychology and Parapsychology at Royaumont, France in 1956.

He was corresponding member of the Society for Psychical Research, London, and the Societa Parapsicologia Italiana, Rome; honorary member of the College of Psychic Science, London, honorary secretary of the Netherlands Society for Psychical Research from 1945-57, former director of the Parapsychology Foundation's European Research Center at St. Paul de Vence, France; European review editor of the *Indian Journal of Parapsychology.*

He contributed many articles to *Tijdschrift voor Parapsychologie, Journal* of the SPR, *Parapsicologia, Journal of Parapsychology, Tomorrow* including 'A Case for Survival' (*Journal* of Society for Psychical Research, vol. 31, 1946, 'ESP Experiments with Psychotics' (*Journal* of S.P.R., vol. 39, 1957), 'A Further Comparative Analysis of Some Poltergeist Phenomena Cases from Continental Europe' (*Journal* of American Society for Psychical Research, vol. 58, 1964).

He was co-editor (with Dr. P. A. Dietz & Dr. K. H. E. de Jong) of *Parapsychologische Woordentolk* (A parapsychological dictionary, 1956), and compiled the *Bibliography of Parapsychology* (published Parapsychology Foundation, 1957). His books included: *De Jacht op het Spiritistisch Bewijs* (In Quest of Proof for Survival, 1940), *De Opstandingsverhalen in het Licht de Parapsychologie* (The Resurrection Narratives in the Light of Parapsychology, 1949), *Wichelroede en Aardstralen* (The Divining Rod and Earthrays, 1950), *Magnetiseurs en Wondergenezers* (Magnetism and Miracle Healers, 1952), *Proscopie, Het Raadsel der Toekomst* (Precognition, the Riddle of the Future, 1953), *Wonderen der Parapsychologie* (Wonders of Parapsychology, 1954), *Parapsychologie* (Parapsychology, 1958), *D. D. Home, il Medium* (Milan, 1976).

Zos Kia Cultus

The magical system developed by occult artist Austin Osman **Spare,** involving a complete symbolism of form, sound, desire and will, deriving from sexual energy. The word "Zos" was not only Spare's magical name but also a symbol of the body as a whole, which could project desires and modify the world of matter.

For details of Spare's system against the background of other occult systems, see *The Magical Revival* by Kenneth Grant, Frederick Muller, London, 1972 (Chapter 11).

Zschokke, (Johannes) Heinrich (Daniel) (1771-1848)

German-Swiss writer, actor and pastor, born at Magdeburg, March 22, 1771, educated at Frankfurt-on-Oder, studying theology, philosophy and jurisprudence. He encountered difficulties with authorities on account of his pronounced political opinions, but eventually concentrated on writing plays and Gothic romances, influenced by Sir Walter Scott.

His romance *Abaeillino, der grosse Bandit* was produced in 1794 and had an enormous success, being dramatized the following year. It was adapted by the English writer Matthew Gregory Lewis as *The Bravo of Venice* in 1804 and greatly influenced themes in Gothic romance.

Zschokke died at Aarau June 27, 1848.

Zuccarini, Amedee (c. 1907)

Italian non-professional medium of Bologna, a state employee who exhibited extraordinary phenomena of **levitation** which were studied in great detail by Dr. L. Patrizi, Professor of Physiology at the University of Modena and Professor Creste Murani, of the Milan Polytechnic. (*Annales des Sciences Psychiques,* vol. 17, pp. 528-549). For an English-language account, see *Annals of Psychical Science* (vol. 6, No. 34, 1907, pp. 303-306).

Flashlight photographs showed him up in the air without support. Zuccarini had two trance personalities, a deceased brother, and a doctor who had died in 1600. (See also **Levitation**)

Zügun, Eleonore (1914-)

A Romanian peasant girl, born in 1914 at Talpa, Romania, the subject of strange *poltergeist* persecution and phenomena of **stigmata.**

Her phenomena filled the superstitious Romanian peasants with dread. When they appeared, about 1925, the peasants attributed them to Dracu, the devil, which idea the girl accepted. She was incarcerated in an asylum. The Countess Wassilko-Serecki and her friends heard of the strange case, rescued the girl and took her to Vienna. The Countess published an article, 'Observations on Eleonore Zügun,' in the Sept.-Oct. issue of the *Journal* of the American Society for Psychical Research and a book *Der Spuk von Talpa* (München, 1926).

The British psychical researcher Harry **Price** was the next to report on Zügun ('Some Account of the Poltergeist Phenomena of Eleonore Zügun,' *Journal* of the A.S.P.R., August 1926) on the basis of his experiences in May 1926, in Vienna. He found the phenomena genuine.

On Price's invitation, the Countess and her protegee came to London for an investigation at the **National Laboratory of Psychical Research.** The case was reported in the N.L.P.R. *Proceedings* (vol. 1, part 1, January 1927) and widely discussed in the Press.

Capt. Seton-Karr, F.R.G.S., testified on October 19, 1926: "I was present on October 5, when the so-called stigmatic markings appeared on the face, arms and forehead of Eleonore Zügun under conditions which absolutely precluded the possibility of Eleonore producing them by scratching or other normal means. The marks were photographed in my presence."

The report of the National Laboratory of Psychical Research after describing various telekinetic and **apport** phenomena, concluded on the stigmata as follows: "There is not the slightest doubt that our careful experiments, made under ideal scientific conditions, have proved that:

"(a) Stigmatic markings appeared spontaneously in various parts of Eleonore's body;

"(b) That Eleonore was not consciously responsible for the production of the marks.

"(c) That under scientific test conditions movements of small objects without physical contact undoubtedly took place. The experimenters, unless they are bereft of all human perceptions, cannot possibly come to any other conclusions. . . .

"What has happened to Eleonore is apparently this: During her early childhood when the so-called 'poltergeist' phenomena became first apparent, the simple peasants threatened her so often with *Dracu* (the Devil) and what he would do to her that her subconscious mind became obsessed with the idea of whippings, bitings, etc., which the ignorant peasants said would be her lot at the hands—or teeth—of *Dracu.* Remove the *Dracu* complex and the girl would probably be troubled no further with stigmatic markings.

"If we have discovered the cause of the 'stigmata' I am afraid we cannot lay claim to having unraveled the mystery of the telekinetic movements of the coins, etc. We have merely proved that they happen."

Towards the end of her fourteenth year, at the approach of the menses, Eleonore Zügun completely lost her psychic powers. (See also **Apport; Dermography; Stigmata Telekinesis**)

Zwaan Rays

Energy field demonstrated by N. Zwaan, Dutch delegate to the International Spiritualist Federation Congress in London, 1948, supposed to be capable of stimulating the psychic senses into activity.

Subsequently the Spirit Electronic Communication Society was founded in Manchester, England, on September 10, 1949, and apparatus shown which was claimed to improve the Zwaan effect. An account of the work of the Society was published in the pamphlet *Electronic Communication for the Spiritual Emancipation of the People* by Mark Dyne (The Spirit Electronic Communication Society, Manchester, U.K., Revised edition, 1954). (See also **Ashkir-Jobson Trianion**)

Notes on Indexes

Indexing has been guided by user needs; thus, the indexes are organized into two sets: General Index and Topical Indexes.

The General Index includes all key material cited in Volumes 1 and 2. Cross references for related topics appear under appropriate entry citations. The page number on which each entry appears is also provided. For added convenience in locating entries related to a selected special topic, the General Index also includes bold-type subheadings, covering:

- Alchemy
- Astrology
- Fairies
- Fortean Phenomena
- Parapsychology
- Psychical Research
- Spiritualism
- UFO (Unidentified Flying Object)
- Witchcraft
- Yoga

The Topical Indexes are divided into the nine categories listed below. Specific entries relating to these topics are cited along with appropriate page references.

- Animals, Birds, Insects
- Demons
- Gems
- Geographical (Places of Phenomena)
- Gods
- Paranormal Phenomena (with 52 subheadings)
- Periodicals
- Plants & Flowers
- Societies & Organizations

Types of Paranormal Phenomena listed are those generally studied by psychical researchers and parapsychologists. Definitions of such phenomena are included under each subheading. The types of phenomena listed should not be considered rigid, however, since much phenomena overlap, such as Healing and Psychic Surgery, or Ouija Board and Planchette. Types of phenomena not listed under the Paranormal Phenomena subheadings will be found in the General Index.

The Periodicals section represents a conspectus of publications concerned with occult, psychical, or parapsychological topics, although some non-occult publications have been indexed when they have relevance to historical aspects of the paranormal. In addition some lesser-known foreign periodicals have been indexed.

Well-known cults and movements, in addition to groups specifically concerned with psychical or parapsychological studies, are indexed under Societies and Organizations.

Notes on Indexes

General Index

A

General Index

B

C

D

E

General Index

F

G

H

I

J

K

L

M

N

O

Q

R

S

T

U

V

W

X

Y

Z

Topical Indexes

(A) ANIMALS, BIRDS, INSECTS

(A) ANIMALS, BIRDS, INSECTS *continued*

(A) ANIMALS, BIRDS, INSECTS *continued*

(B) DEMONS

(B) DEMONS *continued*

(C) GEMS *continued*

(D) GEOGRAPHICAL (Places of Phenomena)

(Although most paranormal phenomena are not confined to one geographical locale, some phenomena have been specifically associated with a particular place, or are characteristic of that place.)

(D) GEOGRAPHICAL *continued*

(D) GEOGRAPHICAL *continued*

(D) GEOGRAPHICAL *continued*

(E) GODS

(E) GODS *continued*

(E) GODS *continued*

(F) PARANORMAL PHENOMENA

(1) Animal Magnetism (*See also* **Mesmerism)**

An early concept of vital force in living creatures, associated with psychic faculties and healing, **56**

(F) PARANORMAL PHENOMENA *continued*

(2) Animals, Psychic

Animals apparently demonstrating psychic ability, **56**

(3) Apparitions (*includes* **Ghosts & Phantoms**)

Paranormal appearances suggesting the real existence of someone distant or deceased. The perception is usually visual or aural and spontaneous, **64**

(F) PARANORMAL PHENOMENA *continued*

(F) PARANORMAL PHENOMENA *continued*

(F) PARANORMAL PHENOMENA *continued*

(11) Crop Circles

(12) Cross-Correspondence

Concordant automatism to eliminate the hypothesis of telepathic communication, **355**

(13) Crystal Gazing (*or* **Scrying)**

Ancient form of clairvoyant divination using a crystal ball or other bright object as a focus, **362**

(14) Direct Voice

Paranormal voice communication in space without visible source, sometimes using a trumpet, **426**

(F) PARANORMAL PHENOMENA *continued*

(19) Eyeless Sight

(F) PARANORMAL PHENOMENA *continued*

(F) PARANORMAL PHENOMENA *continued*

(24) Hypnotism

Abnormal trance condition induced by an operator or self-induced, **799**

(F) PARANORMAL PHENOMENA *continued*

(F) PARANORMAL PHENOMENA *continued*

(F) PARANORMAL PHENOMENA *continued*

(F) PARANORMAL PHENOMENA *continued*

(28) Mesmerism

Early phase of hypnotism associated with theories of Animal Magnetism and psychic phenomena, **1086**

(29) Metal Bending

Paranormal deformation or breaking of metal by visual concentration, hand movements without contact, or light stroking, **1089**

(30) Multiple Personality

Secondary or multiple personalities alternating with an individual's normal personality.

(31) Ouija Board (*See also* Planchette)

Device which indicates letters or phrases when under the hand of a medium, conveying paranormal messages. **1231**

(F) PARANORMAL PHENOMENA *continued*

(32) Out-of-the-Body Experience (Astral Projection)
Consciousness outside the physical body.

(33) Pendulum Divination (*See also* **Dowsing**)
Form of divination involving the indications of a small suspended object with pendulum movements.

(34) Planchette (*See also* **Ouija Board**)
Device containing a pencil which writes paranormally when under the hand of medium, without conscious control, **1295**

(35) Poltergeist
Noisy spirits causing psychic disturbances, **1305**

(F) PARANORMAL PHENOMENA *continued*

(36) Possession & Exorcism

Displacement of normal personality by an alien or malicious entity, usually banished by religious ritual.

(37) Precognition (*includes* **Premonition & Prediction)**

Paranormal awareness of impending events, **1320**

(38) Psi

Modern term indicating psychic faculty or phenomena, **1345**

(F) PARANORMAL PHENOMENA *continued*

(F) PARANORMAL PHENOMENA *continued*

(42) Psychometry *or* **Object-Reading**

Clairvoyant faculty stimulated by holding an object, **1365**

(43) Raps

Percussive sounds without visible, known or normal physical agency, **1392**

(F) PARANORMAL PHENOMENA *continued*

(44) Shell-hearing (*See also* **Clairaudience**)

Category of clairaudience involving holding a shell or similar object to the ear.

(45) Slate-writing

Category of paranormal writing, when messages from disembodied entities appear on a slate, **1529.**

(46) Somnambulism

Trance condition associated with sleep-walking or psychic faculty, **1550**

(47) Spirit Communication

Messages from disembodied entities through a medium or mediumistic device.

(F) PARANORMAL PHENOMENA *continued*

(48) Stigmata

Skin markings (such as simulacra of the wounds of Christ) appearing on emotionally charged sensitives or hysterical persons, **1616**

(49) Table-tipping (Table-turning)

Purposive movements of a table when the hands of a group of sitters are laid on it; the table appears to communicate messages from disembodied entities through movements or raps related to the alphabet.

(50) Telekinesis

Early term for paranormal movement of objects at a distance without physical contact, **1667**

(See also **Psychokinesis**)

(51) Telepathy (Thought-Transference)

Paranormal thought transmission between individuals, independent of recognized sensory channels, **1667**

(F) PARANORMAL PHENOMENA *continued*

(52) Teleportation (or **Transportation**)
Paranormal movement of individuals through space and intervening materials; a combination of levitation and apport, **1675**

For additional types of phenomena not listed above, see separate entries (and associated cross-references) for the following subjects:

(G) PERIODICALS

(G) PERIODICALS *continued*

(G) PERIODICALS *continued*

(G) PERIODICALS *continued*

(G) PERIODICALS *continued*

(G) PERIODICALS *continued*

(H) PLANTS & FLOWERS

(H) PLANTS & FLOWERS *continued*

(I) SOCIETIES & ORGANIZATIONS

(Includes Specialized Groups)

(I) SOCIETIES & ORGANIZATIONS *cont'd*

(I) SOCIETIES & ORGANIZATIONS *cont'd*

(I) SOCIETIES & ORGANIZATIONS *cont'd*

(I) SOCIETIES & ORGANIZATIONS *cont'd*

(I) SOCIETIES & ORGANIZATIONS *cont'd*

(I) SOCIETIES & ORGANIZATIONS *cont'd*